CHILTON®

CHRYSLER
SERVICE MANUAL
2008 EDITION
VOLUME II

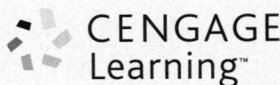

CENGAGE Learning™

Australia • Brazil • Japan • Korea • Mexico • Singapore • Spain • United Kingdom • United States

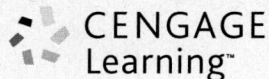

CENGAGE Learning™

CHILTON®
Chrysler Service Manual
2008 Edition
Volume II

Vice President,
Technology Professional Business Unit:
Gregory L. Clayton

Publisher,
Technology Professional Business Unit:
David Koontz

Director of Marketing:
Beth A. Lutz

Production Director:
Patty Stephan

Editorial Assistant:
Jason Yager

Production Manager:
Andrew Crouth

Marketing Specialist:
Jennifer Stall

Marketing Assistant:
Rachael Conover

Publishing Coordinator:
Paula Baillie

Sr. Content Project Manager:
Elizabeth C. Hough

Managing Editor:
Terry L. Blomquist

Editors:
Nick D'Andrea
Eugene F. Hannon Jr.
Will Kesseler
David G. Olson
Christine Sheeky
Jon Wallace

Graphical Designer:
Melinda Possinger

For more information contact:
Cengage Learning
Executive Woods
5 Maxwell Drive, PO Box 8007,
Clifton Park, NY 12065-8007
Visit us at **www.chiltonsonline.com**
For more learning solutions, visit **www.cengage.com**
For permission to use material from
the text or product, contact us by
Tel. (800) 730-2214
Fax (800) 730-2215
ww v.cengage.com/permissions

Cengage Learning products are represented in Canada by Nelson Education, Ltd.

ISBN 10: 1-4283-2207-8
ISSN 13: 978-14283-2207-3
ISSN: 1939-621X

NOTICE TO THE READER

Publisher does not warrant or guarantee any of the products described herein or perform any independent analysis in connection with any of the product information contained herein. Publisher does not assume, and expressly disclaims, any obligation to obtain and include information other than that provided to it by the manufacturer.

The reader is expressly warned to consider and adopt all safety precautions that might be indicated by the activities herein and to avoid all potential hazards. By following the instructions contained herein, the reader willingly assumes all risks in connection with such instructions.

The publisher makes no representation or warranties of any kind, including but not limited to, the warranties of fitness for particular purpose or merchantability, nor are any such representations implied with respect to the material set forth herein, and the publisher takes no responsibility with respect to such material. The publisher shall not be liable for any special, consequential, or exemplary damages resulting, in whole or part, from the readers' use of, or reliance upon, this material.

Printed in the United States of America
1 2 3 4 5 xx12 11 10 09 08 07

Table of Contents

Sections

Model Index

USING THIS INFORMATION

Organization

To find where a particular model section or procedure is located, look in the Table of Contents. Main topics are listed with the page number on which they may be found. Following the main topics is an alphabetical listing of all of the procedures within the section and their page numbers.

Manufacturer and Model Coverage

This product covers 2005–2008 Chrysler models that are produced in sufficient quantities to warrant coverage, and which have technical content available from the vehicle manufacturers before our publication date. Although this information is as complete as possible at the time of publication, some manufacturers may make changes which cannot be included here. While striving for total accuracy, the publisher cannot assume responsibility for any errors, changes, or omissions that may occur in the compilation of this data.

Part Numbers & Special Tools

Part numbers and special tools are recommended by the publisher and vehicle manufacturer to perform specific jobs. Before substituting any part or tool for the one recommended, you must be completely satisfied that neither your personal safety, nor the performance of the vehicle will be endangered.

ACKNOWLEDGEMENT

The publisher would like to express appreciation to Chrysler LLC for its assistance in producing this publication. No further reproduction or distribution of the material in this manual is allowed without the expressed written permission of Chrysler LLC and the publisher.

PRECAUTIONS

Before servicing any vehicle, please be sure to read all of the following precautions, which deal with personal safety, prevention of component damage, and important points to take into consideration when servicing a motor vehicle:

- Always wear safety glasses or goggles when drilling, cutting, grinding or prying.
- Steel-toed work shoes should be worn when working with heavy parts. Pockets should not be used for carrying tools. A slip or fall can drive a screwdriver into your body.
- Work surfaces, including tools and the floor should be kept clean of grease, oil or other slippery material.
- When working around moving parts, don't wear loose clothing. Long hair should be tied back under a hat or cap, or in a hair net.
- Always use tools only for the purpose for which they were designed. Never pry with a screwdriver.
- Keep a fire extinguisher and first aid kit handy.
- Always properly support the vehicle with approved stands or lift.
- Always have adequate ventilation when working with chemicals or hazardous material.
- Carbon monoxide is colorless, odorless and dangerous. If it is necessary to operate the engine with vehicle in a closed area such as a garage, always use an exhaust collector to vent the exhaust gases outside the closed area.
- When draining coolant, keep in mind that small children and some pets are attracted by ethylene glycol antifreeze, and are quite likely to drink any left in an open container, or in puddles on the ground. This will prove fatal in sufficient quantity. Always drain the coolant into a sealable container.
- To avoid personal injury, do not remove the coolant pressure relief cap while the engine is operating or hot. The cooling system is under pressure; steam and hot liquid can come out forcefully when the cap is loosened slightly. Failure to follow these instructions may result in personal injury. The coolant must be recovered in a suitable, clean container for reuse. If the coolant is contaminated it must be recycled or disposed of correctly.
- When carrying out maintenance on the starting system be aware that heavy gauge leads are connected directly to the battery. Make sure the protective caps are in place when maintenance is completed. Failure to follow these instructions may result in personal injury.
- Do not remove any part of the engine emission control system. Operating the engine without the engine emission control system will reduce fuel economy and engine ventilation. This will weaken engine performance and shorten engine life. It is also a violation of Federal law.
- Due to environmental concerns, when the air conditioning system is drained, the refrigerant must be collected using refrigerant recovery/recycling equipment. Federal law requires that refrigerant be recovered into appropriate recovery equipment and the process be conducted by qualified technicians who have been certified by an approved organization, such as MACS, ASI, etc. Use of a recovery machine dedicated to the appropriate refrigerant is necessary to reduce the possibility of oil and refrigerant incompatibility concerns. Refer to the instructions provided by the equipment manufacturer when removing refrigerant from or charging the air conditioning system.
- Always disconnect the battery ground when working on or around the electrical system.
- Batteries contain sulfuric acid. Avoid contact with skin, eyes, or clothing. Also, shield your eyes when working near batteries to protect against possible splashing of the acid solution. In case of acid contact with skin or eyes, flush immediately with water for a minimum of 15 minutes and get prompt medical attention. If acid is swallowed, call a physician immediately. Failure to follow these instructions may result in personal injury.
- Batteries normally produce explosive gases. Therefore, do not allow flames, sparks or lighted substances to come near the battery. When charging or working near a battery, always shield your face and protect your eyes. Always provide ventilation. Failure to follow these instructions may result in personal injury.
- When lifting a battery, excessive pressure on the end walls could cause acid to spew through the vent caps, resulting in personal injury, damage to the vehicle or battery. Lift with a battery carrier or with your hands on opposite corners. Failure to follow these instructions may result in personal injury.
- Observe all applicable safety precautions when working around fuel. Whenever

servicing the fuel system, always work in a well-ventilated area. Do not allow fuel spray or vapors to come in contact with a spark, open flame, or excessive heat (a hot drop light, for example). Keep a dry chemical fire extinguisher near the work area. Always keep fuel in a container specifically designed for fuel storage; also, always properly seal fuel containers to avoid the possibility of fire or explosion. Do not smoke or carry lighted tobacco or open flame of any type when working on or near any fuel-related components.

• Fuel injection systems often remain pressurized, even after the engine has been turned OFF. The fuel system pressure must be relieved before disconnecting any fuel lines. Failure to do so may result in fire and/or personal injury.

• The evaporative emissions system contains fuel vapor and condensed fuel vapor. Although not present in large quantities, it still presents the danger of explosion or fire. Disconnect the battery ground cable from the battery to minimize the possibility of an electrical spark occurring, possibly causing a fire or explosion if fuel vapor or liquid fuel is present in the area. Failure to follow these instructions can result in personal injury.

• The EPA warns that prolonged contact with used engine oil may cause a number of skin disorders, including cancer! You should make every effort to minimize your exposure to used engine oil. Protective gloves should be worn when changing oil. Wash your hands and any other exposed skin areas as soon as possible after exposure to used engine oil. Soap and water, or waterless hand cleaner should be used.

• Some vehicles are equipped with an air bag system, often referred to as a Supplemental Restraint System (SRS) or Supplemental Inflatable Restraint (SIR) system. The system must be disabled before performing service on or around system components, steering column, instrument panel components, wiring and sensors. Failure to follow safety and disabling procedures could result in accidental air bag deployment, possible personal injury and unnecessary system repairs.

• Always wear safety goggles when working with, or around, the air bag system. When carrying a non-deployed air bag, be sure the bag and trim cover are pointed away from your body. When placing a non-deployed air bag on a work surface, always face the bag and trim cover upward, away from the surface. This will reduce the motion of the module if it is accidentally deployed.

• Electronic modules are sensitive to electrical charges. The ABS module can be damaged if exposed to these charges.

• Brake pads and shoes may contain asbestos, which has been determined to be a cancer-causing agent. Never clean brake surfaces with compressed air. Avoid inhaling brake dust. Clean all brake surfaces with a commercially available brake cleaning fluid.

• When replacing brake pads, shoes, discs or drums, replace them as complete axle sets.

• When servicing drum brakes, disassemble and assemble one side at a time, leaving the remaining side intact for reference.

• Brake fluid often contains polyglycol ethers and polyglycols. Avoid contact with the eyes and wash your hands thoroughly after handling brake fluid. If you do get brake fluid in your eyes, flush your eyes with clean, running water for 15 minutes. If eye irritation persists, or if you have taken brake fluid internally, immediately seek medical assistance.

• Clean, high quality brake fluid from a sealed container is essential to the safe and proper operation of the brake system. You should always buy the correct type of brake fluid for your vehicle. If the brake fluid becomes contaminated, completely flush the system with new fluid. Never reuse any brake fluid. Any brake fluid that is removed from the system should be discarded. Also, do not allow any brake fluid to come in contact with a painted or plastic surface; it will damage the paint.

• Never operate the engine without the proper amount and type of engine oil; doing so will result in severe engine damage.

• Timing belt maintenance is extremely important! Many models utilize an interference-type, non-freewheeling engine. If the timing belt breaks, the valves in the cylinder head may strike the pistons, causing potentially serious (also time-consuming and expensive) engine damage.

• Disconnecting the negative battery cable on some vehicles may interfere with the functions of the on-board computer system (s) and may require the computer to undergo a relearning process once the negative battery cable is reconnected.

• Steering and suspension fasteners are critical parts because they affect performance of vital components and systems and their failure can result in major service expense. They must be replaced with the same grade or part number or an equivalent part if replacement is necessary. Do not use a replacement part of lesser quality or substitute design. Torque values must be used as specified during reassembly to ensure proper retention of these parts.

JEEP

Grand Cherokee

9

SPECIFICATIONS AND MAINTENANCE CHARTS

ENGINE AND VEHICLE IDENTIFICATION

Engine						
Code	Liters (cc)	Cu. In.	Cyl.	Fuel Sys.	Engine Type	Eng. Mfg.
K	3.7 (3701)	226	6	MFI	SOHC	Chrysler
N	4.7 (4701)	287	8	MFI	SOHC	Chrysler
P	4.7 (4701)	287	8	FFV	SOHC	Chrysler
2	5.7 (5653)	345	8	MFI	OHV	Chrysler

Model Year	
Code	Year
5	2005
6	2006
7	2007

SOHC: Single overhead camshaft

OHV: Overhead Valve

MFI: Multi-port Fuel Injection

FFV: Flex Fuel Vehicle

22043_CHER_C0001

GENERAL ENGINE SPECIFICATIONS

Year	Model	Engine Displ. Liters	Engine VIN	Net Horsepower @ rpm	Net Torque @ rpm (ft. lbs.)	Bore x Stroke (in.)	Com-pression Ratio	Oil Pressure @ rpm
2005	Grand Cherokee	3.7	K	210@5200	225@4200	3.66x3.40	9.1:1	25-110@3000
		4.7	N	235@4800	295@3200	3.66x3.40	9.0:1	25-110@3000
		5.7	2	335@5200	370@4200	3.91x3.58	9.6:1	25-110@3000
2006	Grand Cherokee	3.7	K	210@5200	225@4200	3.66x3.40	9.1:1	25-110@3000
		4.7	N	235@4800	295@3200	3.66x3.40	9.0:1	25-110@3000
		5.7	2	335@5200	370@4200	3.91x3.58	9.6:1	25-110@3000
2007	Grand Cherokee	3.7	K	210@5200	225@4200	3.66x3.40	9.1:1	25-110@3000
		4.7	N	235@4800	295@3200	3.66x3.40	9.0:1	25-110@3000
		4.7	P	235@4800	295@3200	3.66x3.40	9.0:1	25-110@3000
		5.7	2	335@5200	370@4200	3.91x3.58	9.6:1	25-110@3000

22043_CHER_C0002

GASOLINE ENGINE TUNE-UP SPECIFICATIONS

Year	Engine Displacement Liters	Engine VIN	Spark Plug Gap (in.)	Ignition Timing (deg.)	Fuel Pump (psi)	Idle Speed (rpm)	Valve Clearance	
							Intake	Exhaust
2005	3.7	K	0.042	①	44-54	②	HYD	HYD
	4.7	N	0.040	①	47-51	②	HYD	HYD
	5.7	2	0.045	①	49.0-49.4	②	HYD	HYD
2006	3.7	K	0.042	①	44-54	②	HYD	HYD
	4.7	N	0.040	①	47-51	②	HYD	HYD
	5.7	2	0.045	①	49.0-49.4	②	HYD	HYD
2007	3.7	K	0.042	①	44-54	②	HYD	HYD
	4.7	N	0.040	①	47-51	②	HYD	HYD
	4.7	P	0.040	①	47-51	②	HYD	HYD
	5.7	2	0.045	①	49.0-49.4	②	HYD	HYD

NOTE: The Vehicle Emission Control Information (VECI) label often reflects specification changes made during production. The label figures must be used if they differ from those in this chart.

HYD: Hydraulic

① Ignition timing is controlled by the PCM and is not adjustable.

② Idle speed is controlled by the PCM and is not adjustable

22043_CHER_C0003

CAPACITIES

Year	Model	Engine Displ. Liters	Engine VIN	Engine Oil with Filter (qts.)	Transmission (pts.)	Transfer Case (pts.)	Drive Axle Front (pts.)	Drive Axle Rear (pts.)	Fuel Tank (gal.)	Cooling System (qts.)
2005	Grand Cherokee	3.7	K	5.0	①	②	3.6	③	20.0	9.0
		4.7	N	6.0	①	②	3.6	③	20.0	14.5
		5.7	2	7.0	①	②	3.6	③	20.0	14.5
2006	Grand Cherokee	3.7	K	5.0	①	②	3.6	③	20.0	9.0
		4.7	N	6.0	①	②	3.6	③	20.0	14.5
		5.7	2	7.0	①	②	3.6	③	20.0	14.5
2007	Grand Cherokee	3.7	K	5.0	①	②	3.6	③	20.0	9.0
		4.7	N	6.0	①	②	3.6	③	20.0	14.5
		4.7	P	6.0	①	②	3.6	③	20.0	14.5
		5.7	2	7.0	①	②	3.6	③	20.0	14.5

NOTE: All capacities are approximate. Add fluid gradually and check to be sure a proper fluid level is obtained.

① 545RFE Fluid drain/filter service, 2wd: 11 pts.; 4wd: 13 pts.; Overhaul: 28 pts.

② NV140/146: 1.4 pts.; NV245: 3.8 pts.

③ The following values include 0.25 pt. of friction modifier for LSD axles.
C213R axle: 4.4 pts.
C213RE axle: 4.7 pts.

22043_CHER_C0004

FLUID SPECIFICATIONS

Year	Model	Engine Displacement Liters	Engine ID/VIN	Engine Oil	Auto. Trans.	Drive Axle	Power Steering Fluid	Brake Master Cylinder
2005	Grand Cherokee	3.7	K	5W-30	Mopar ATF+4	①	Mopar ATF+4	DOT-3
		4.7	N	5W-30	Mopar ATF+4	①	Mopar ATF+4	DOT-3
		5.7	2	5W-20	Mopar ATF+4	①	Mopar ATF+4	DOT-3
2006	Grand Cherokee	3.7	K	5W-30	Mopar ATF+4	①	Mopar ATF+4	DOT-3
		4.7	N	5W-30	Mopar ATF+4	①	Mopar ATF+4	DOT-3
		5.7	2	5W-20	Mopar ATF+4	①	Mopar ATF+4	DOT-3
2007	Grand Cherokee	3.7	K	5W-20	Mopar ATF+4	①	Mopar ATF+4	DOT-3
		4.7	N	5W-20	Mopar ATF+4	①	Mopar ATF+4	DOT-3
		4.7	P	5W-20	Mopar ATF+4	①	Mopar ATF+4	DOT-3
		5.7	2	5W-20	Mopar ATF+4	①	Mopar ATF+4	DOT-3

DOT: Department Of Transpotation

NA: Not Applicable

① Mopar Synthetic Gear Lube 75W-140

22043_CHER_C0005

VALVE SPECIFICATIONS

Year	Engine Displ. Liters	Engine VIN	Seat Angle (deg.)	Face Angle (deg.)	Spring Test Pressure (lbs. @ in.)	Spring Installed Height (in.)	Stem-to-Guide Clearance (in.)		Stem Diameter (in.)	
							Intake	Exhaust	Intake	Exhaust
2005	3.7	K	44.5-45	45-45.5	221-242@ 1.107	1.619	0.0008-0.0028	0.0019-0.0039	0.2729-0.2739	0.2717-0.2728
	4.7	N	44.5-45	45-45.5	176.7-193.3 @1.1670	1.601	0.0008-0.0028	0.0019-0.0039	0.2729-0.2739	0.2717-0.2728
	5.7	2	44.5-45	45-45.5	95@1.81	1.81	0.0008-0.0025	0.0019-0.0037	0.3120-0.3130	0.3110-0.3120
2006	3.7	K	44.5-45	45-45.5	221-242@ 1.107	1.619	0.0008-0.0028	0.0019-0.0039	0.2729-0.2739	0.2717-0.2728
	4.7	N	44.5-45	45-45.5	176.7-193.3 @1.1670	1.601	0.0008-0.0028	0.0019-0.0039	0.2729-0.2739	0.2717-0.2728
	5.7	2	44.5-45	45-45.5	95@1.81	1.81	0.0008-0.0025	0.0019-0.0037	0.3120-0.3130	0.3110-0.3120
2007	3.7	K	44.5-45	45-45.5	221-242@ 1.107	1.619	0.0008-0.0028	0.0019-0.0039	0.2729-0.2739	0.2717-0.2728
	4.7	N	44.5-45	45-45.5	176.7-193.3 @1.1670	1.601	0.0008-0.0028	0.0019-0.0039	0.2729-0.2739	0.2717-0.2728
	4.7	P	44.5-45	45-45.5	176.7-193.3 @1.1670	1.601	0.0008-0.0028	0.0019-0.0039	0.2729-0.2739	0.2717-0.2728
	5.7	2	44.5-45	45-45.5	95@1.81	1.81	0.0008-0.0025	0.0019-0.0037	0.3120-0.3130	0.3110-0.3120

22043_CHER_C0006

CAMSHAFT AND BEARING SPECIFICATIONS CHART

All measurements are given in inches.

Year	Engine Displacement Liters	Engine VIN	Journal Diameter	Brg. Oil Clearance	Shaft End-play	Runout	Journal Bore	Lobe Lift Intake	Lobe Lift Exhaust
2005	3.7	K	1.0227-1.0235	0.0010-0.0026	0.0030-0.0079	NA	NA	NA	NA
	4.7	N	1.0227-1.0235	0.0010-0.0026	0.0030-0.0079	NA	NA	NA	NA
	5.7	2	①	②	0.0031-0.0114	NA	NA	0.2830	0.2830
2006	3.7	K	1.0227-1.0235	0.0010-0.0026	0.0030-0.0079	NA	NA	NA	NA
	4.7	N	1.0227-1.0235	0.0010-0.0026	0.0030-0.0079	NA	NA	NA	NA
	5.7	2	①	②	0.0031-0.0114	NA	NA	0.2830	0.2830
2007	3.7	K	1.0227-1.0235	0.0010-0.0026	0.0030-0.0079	NA	NA	NA	NA
	4.7	N	1.0227-1.0235	0.0010-0.0026	0.0030-0.0079	NA	NA	NA	NA
	4.7	P	1.0227-1.0235	0.0010-0.0026	0.0039-0.0079	NA	NA	NA	NA
	5.7	2	①	②	0.0031-0.0114	NA	NA	0.2830	0.2830

NA: Not Available

① No. 1: 2.29 in.
No. 2: 2.27 in.
No. 3: 2.26 in.
No. 4: 2.24 in.
No. 5: 1.72 in.

② No. 1: 0.0015-0.0030 in.
No. 2: 0.0019-0.0035 in.
No. 3: 0.0015-0.0030 in.
No. 4: 0.0019-0.0035 in.
No. 5: 0.0015-0.0030 in.
No. 5: 0.0031-0.0114 in.

22043_CHER_C0007

CRANKSHAFT AND CONNECTING ROD SPECIFICATIONS

All measurements are given in inches.

Year	Engine Displ. Liters	Engine VIN	Crankshaft Main Brg. Journal Dia.	Crankshaft Main Brg. Oil Clearance	Crankshaft Shaft End-play	Thrust on No.	Connecting Rod Journal Diameter	Connecting Rod Oil Clearance	Connecting Rod Side Clearance
2005	3.7	K	2.4996-2.5005	0.0020-0.0034	0.0021-0.0112	2	2.2794-2.2797	0.0004-0.0019	0.0040-0.0138
	4.7	N	2.4996-2.5005	0.0008-0.0021	0.0021-0.0112	2	2.0076-2.0082	0.0006-0.0022	0.0040-0.0138
	5.7	2	2.5585-2.5595	0.0009-0.0020	0.0020-0.0110	3	2.1250-2.1260	0.0007-0.0023	0.0030-0.0137
2006	3.7	K	2.4996-2.5005	0.0020-0.0034	0.0021-0.0112	2	2.2794-2.2797	0.0004-0.0019	0.0040-0.0138
	4.7	N	2.4996-2.5005	0.0008-0.0021	0.0021-0.0112	2	2.0076-2.0082	0.0006-0.0022	0.0040-0.0138
	5.7	2	2.5585-2.5595	0.0009-0.0020	0.0020-0.0110	3	2.1250-2.1260	0.0007-0.0023	0.0030-0.0137
2007	3.7	K	2.4996-2.5005	0.0020-0.0034	0.0021-0.0112	2	2.2794-2.2797	0.0004-0.0019	0.0040-0.0138
	4.7	N	2.4996-2.5005	0.0008-0.0021	0.0021-0.0112	2	2.0076-2.0082	0.0006-0.0022	0.0040-0.0138
	4.7	P	2.4996-2.5005	0.0008-0.0021	0.0021-0.0112	2	2.0076-2.0082	0.0006-0.0022	0.0040-0.0138
	5.7	2	2.5585-2.5595	0.0009-0.0020	0.0020-0.0110	3	2.1250-2.1260	0.0007-0.0023	0.0030-0.0137

22043_CHER_C0008

PISTON AND RING SPECIFICATIONS

All measurements are given in inches.

Year	Engine Displ. Liters	Engine VIN	Piston Clearance	Ring Gap Top Comp.	Ring Gap Bottom Comp.	Ring Gap Oil Control	Ring Side Clearance Top Comp.	Ring Side Clearance Bottom Comp.	Ring Side Clearance Oil Control
2005	3.7	K	0.0014	0.0146-0.0249	0.0146-0.0249	0.0100-0.0300	0.0020-0.0037	0.0016-0.0031	0.0007-0.0091
	4.7	N	0.0014	0.0146-0.0249	0.0146-0.0249	0.0099-0.0300	0.0020-0.0037	0.0016-0.0031	0.0175-0.0185
	5.7	2	0.0008-0.0019	0.0090-0.0149	0.0137-0.0236	0.0059-0.0259	0.0007-0.0026	0.0007-0.0022	0.0007-0.0091
2006	3.7	K	0.0014	0.0146-0.0249	0.0146-0.0249	0.0100-0.0300	0.0020-0.0037	0.0016-0.0031	0.0007-0.0091
	4.7	N	0.0014	0.0146-0.0249	0.0146-0.0249	0.0099-0.0300	0.0020-0.0037	0.0016-0.0031	0.0175-0.0185
	5.7	2	0.0008-0.0019	0.0090-0.0149	0.0137-0.0236	0.0059-0.0259	0.0007-0.0026	0.0007-0.0022	0.0007-0.0091
2007	3.7	K	0.0014	0.0146-0.0249	0.0146-0.0249	0.0100-0.0300	0.0020-0.0037	0.0016-0.0031	0.0007-0.0091
	4.7	N	0.0014	0.0146-0.0249	0.0146-0.0249	0.0099-0.0300	0.0020-0.0037	0.0016-0.0031	0.0175-0.0185
	4.7	P	0.0014	0.0146-0.0249	0.0146-0.0249	0.0099-0.0300	0.0020-0.0037	0.0016-0.0031	0.0175-0.0185
	5.7	2	0.0008-0.0019	0.0090-0.0149	0.0137-0.0236	0.0059-0.0259	0.0007-0.0026	0.0007-0.0022	0.0007-0.0091

22043_CHER_C0009

TORQUE SPECIFICATIONS

All readings in ft. lbs.

Year	Engine Displ. Liters	Engine VIN	Cylinder Head Bolts	Main Bearing Bolts	Rod Bearing Bolts	Crankshaft Damper Bolts	Flexplate Bolts	Manifold Intake	Manifold Exhaust	Spark Plugs	Oil Pan Drain Plug
2005	3.7	K	①	②	③	130	70	④	18	20	25
	4.7	N	①	⑤	③	130	45	④	18	20	25
	5.7	2	⑥	⑦	⑧	90	70	④	18	13	25
2006	3.7	K	①	②	③	130	70	④	18	20	25
	4.7	N	①	⑤	③	130	45	④	18	20	25
	5.7	2	⑥	⑦	⑧	90	70	④	18	13	25
2007	3.7	K	①	②	③	130	70	④	18	20	25
	4.7	N	①	⑤	③	130	45	④	18	20	25
	4.7	P	①	⑤	③	130	45	④	18	20	25
	5.7	2	⑥	⑦	⑧	90	70	④	18	13	25

① See text

② See the illustration

Step 1: Hand tighten bolts 1D, 1G and 1F until bedplate contacts the block

Step 2: tighten bolts 1A-1J to 40 ft. lbs.

Step 3: Tighten bolts 1-8 to 60 inch lbs.

Step 4: Tighten bolts 1-8 an additional 90 degrees

Step 5: Tighten bolts A-E to 20 ft. lbs.

③ 20 ft. lbs. plus 90 degrees

④ 105 inch lbs.

⑤ Bed plate bolt sequence. Refer to illustration

Step 1: Bolts A-L to 40 ft. lbs.

Step 2: Bolts 1-10 25 inch lbs.

Step 3: Bolts 1-10 plus 90 degrees

Step 4: Bolts A1-A6 20 ft. lbs.

⑥ M8

Step 1: 15 ft. lbs.

Step 2: 25 ft. lbs.

M12

Step 1: 25 ft. lbs.

Step 2: 40 ft. lbs.

Step 3: plus 90 degree turn

⑦ See the illustration

Step 1: Bolts 1-10 to 20 ft. lbs.

Step 2: bolts 1-10 an additional 90 degrees

Step 3: Bolts (cross bolts) A-J to 21 ft. lbs.

⑧ 15 ft. lbs. Plus 90 degrees

22043_CHER_C0010

WHEEL ALIGNMENT

Year	Model		Caster Range (+/-Deg.)	Caster Preferred Setting (Deg.)	Camber Range (+/-Deg.)	Camber Preferred Setting (Deg.)	Toe-in (deg.)
2005	Grand Cherokee	F	0.50	+4.00	0.50	-0.25	0.25+/-0.25
		R	—	—	0.25	-0.25	0.25+/-0.25
2006	Grand Cherokee	F	0.50	+4.00	0.50	-0.25	0.25+/-0.25
		R	—	—	0.25	-0.25	0.25+/-0.25
2007	Grand Cherokee	F	0.50	+4.00	0.50	-0.25	0.25+/-0.25
		R	—	—	0.25	-0.25	0.25+/-0.25

22043_CHER_C0011

TIRE, WHEEL AND BALL JOINT SPECIFICATIONS

Year	Model	OEM Tires Standard	OEM Tires Optional	Tire Pressures (psi) Front	Tire Pressures (psi) Rear	Wheel Size	Ball Joint Inspection	Lug Nut Torque (ft. lbs.)
2005	Grand Cherokee	P235/65R17	P245/65R17	①	①	①	②	85-115
2006	Grand Cherokee	P235/65R17	P245/65R17	①	①	①	②	85-115
2007	Grand Cherokee	P235/65R17	P245/65R17	①	①	①	②	85-115

OEM: Original Equipment Manufacturer

STD: Standard

OPT: Optional

① See placard on vehicle

② Replace if any measurable movement is found.

22043_CHER_C0012

BRAKE SPECIFICATIONS

All measurements in inches unless noted

			Brake Disc			Brake Drum			Minimum Lining Thickness		Caliper Mounting Bolts
Year	Model		Original Thickness	Minimum Thickness	Maximum Run-out	Original Inside Diameter	Max. Wear Limit	Maximum Machine Diameter	Front	Rear	(ft. lbs.)
2005	Grand Cherokee	F	NA	1.122	0.0008	—	—	—	0.030	—	53
		R	NA	0.492	0.0008	—	—	—	—	0.030	26
2006	Grand Cherokee	F	NA	1.122	0.0008	—	—	—	0.030	—	53
		R	NA	0.492	0.0008	—	—	—	—	0.030	26
2007	Grand Cherokee	F	NA	1.122	0.0008	—	—	—	0.030	—	53
		R	NA	0.492	0.0008	—	—	—	—	0.030	26

F - Front

R - Rear

22043_CHER_C0013

SCHEDULED MAINTENANCE INTERVALS
GRAND CHEROKEE

TO BE SERVICED	TYPE OF SERVICE	VEHICLE MILEAGE INTERVAL (x1000)												
		3	6	9	12	15	18	21	24	27	30	33	36	39
Engine oil & filter	R	✓	✓	✓	✓	✓	✓	✓	✓	✓	✓	✓	✓	✓
Tires	Rotate		✓		✓		✓		✓		✓		✓	
Brake hoses & linings	S/I				✓				✓				✓	
Lubricate steering and suspension ball joints	C/L		✓		✓		✓		✓		✓		✓	
Brake caliper pins	C/L				✓				✓				✓	
Air filter	I/R		✓		✓		✓		✓		✓		✓	
Spark plugs	R										✓			
Drive axle lubricant	R				✓				✓				✓	
Transfer case fluid	R										✓			
PCV valve	I/R										✓			
Accessory drive belt	S/I	Every 60,000 miles												
Spark plug cables (5.7L)	I/R	Every 60,000 miles												
Automatic trans. fluid and filter (4.7L and 5.7L)	R	Every 60,000 miles												
Engine coolant	R	Every 60,000 miles												

R: Replace   S/I: Service or Inspect   C/L: Clean and lubricate   I/R: Inspect and rerplace if necessary

The above schedule is to be used if you drive under any of the following conditions:

Driving in temperatures under 32 degrees F

Stop and go traffic

Extensive engine idling

Driving in dusty conditions

Frequent trips under 10 miles

More than 50 % of your driving is in hot weather (90 deg. F) above 50 miles per hour

Trailer towing

Taxi, police or delivery service

Off-road driving

If none of these conditions is met, double the maintenance intervals

22043_CHER_C0014

PRECAUTIONS

Before servicing any vehicle, please be sure to read all of the following precautions, which deal with personal safety, prevention of component damage, and important points to take into consideration when servicing a motor vehicle:

- Never open, service or drain the radiator or cooling system when the engine is hot; serious burns can occur from the steam and hot coolant.
- Observe all applicable safety precautions when working around fuel. Whenever servicing the fuel system, always work in a well-ventilated area. Do not allow fuel spray or vapors to come in contact with a spark, open flame, or excessive heat (a hot drop light, for example). Keep a dry chemical fire extinguisher near the work area. Always keep fuel in a container specifically designed for fuel storage; also, always properly seal fuel containers to avoid the possibility of fire or explosion. Refer to the additional fuel system precautions later in this section.
- Fuel injection systems often remain pressurized, even after the engine has been turned **OFF**. The fuel system pressure must be relieved before disconnecting any fuel lines. Failure to do so may result in fire and/or personal injury.
- Brake fluid often contains polyglycol ethers and polyglycols. Avoid contact with the eyes and wash your hands thoroughly after handling brake fluid. If you do get brake fluid in your eyes, flush your eyes with clean, running water for 15 minutes. If eye irritation persists, or if you have taken brake fluid internally, IMMEDIATELY seek medical assistance.
- The EPA warns that prolonged contact with used engine oil may cause a number of skin disorders, including cancer. You should make every effort to minimize your exposure to used engine oil. Protective gloves should be worn when changing oil. Wash your hands and any other exposed skin areas as soon as possible after exposure to used engine oil. Soap and water, or waterless hand cleaner should be used.
- All new vehicles are now equipped with an air bag system, often referred to as a Supplemental Restraint System (SRS) or Supplemental Inflatable Restraint (SIR) system. The system must be disabled before performing service on or around system components, steering column, instrument panel components, wiring and sensors. Failure to follow safety and disabling procedures could result in accidental air bag deployment, possible personal injury and unnecessary system repairs.
- Always wear safety goggles when working with, or around, the air bag system. When carrying a non-deployed air bag, be sure the bag and trim cover are pointed away from your body. When placing a non-deployed air bag on a work surface, always face the bag and trim cover upward, away from the surface. This will reduce the motion of the module if it is accidentally deployed. Refer to the additional air bag system precautions later in this section.
- Clean, high quality brake fluid from a sealed container is essential to the safe and proper operation of the brake system. You should always buy the correct type of brake fluid for your vehicle. If the brake fluid becomes contaminated, completely flush the system with new fluid. Never reuse any brake fluid. Any brake fluid that is removed from the system should be discarded. Also, do not allow any brake fluid to come in contact with a painted surface; it will damage the paint.
- Never operate the engine without the proper amount and type of engine oil; doing so WILL result in severe engine damage.
- Timing belt maintenance is extremely important. Many models utilize an interference-type, non-freewheeling engine. If the timing belt breaks, the valves in the cylinder head may strike the pistons, causing potentially serious (also time-consuming and expensive) engine damage. Refer to the maintenance interval charts for the recommended replacement interval for the timing belt, and to the timing belt section for belt replacement and inspection.
- Disconnecting the negative battery cable on some vehicles may interfere with the functions of the on-board computer system(s) and may require the computer to undergo a relearning process once the negative battery cable is reconnected.
- When servicing drum brakes, only disassemble and assemble one side at a time, leaving the remaining side intact for reference.
- Only an MVAC-trained, EPA-certified automotive technician should service the air conditioning system or its components.

BRAKES — ANTI-LOCK BRAKE SYSTEM (ABS)

GENERAL INFORMATION

PRECAUTIONS

- Certain components within the ABS system are not intended to be serviced or repaired individually.
- Do not use rubber hoses or other parts not specifically specified for and ABS system. When using repair kits, replace all parts included in the kit. Partial or incorrect repair may lead to functional problems and require the replacement of components.
- Lubricate rubber parts with clean, fresh brake fluid to ease assembly. Do not use shop air to clean parts; damage to rubber components may result.
- Use only DOT 3 brake fluid from an unopened container.
- If any hydraulic component or line is removed or replaced, it may be necessary to bleed the entire system.
- A clean repair area is essential. Always clean the reservoir and cap thoroughly before removing the cap. The slightest amount of dirt in the fluid may plug an orifice and impair the system function. Perform repairs after components have been thoroughly cleaned; use only denatured alcohol to clean components. Do not allow ABS components to come into contact with any substance containing mineral oil; this includes used shop rags.
- The Anti-Lock control unit is a microprocessor similar to other computer units in the vehicle. Ensure that the ignition switch is **OFF** before removing or installing controller harnesses. Avoid static electricity discharge at or near the controller.
- If any arc welding is to be done on the vehicle, the control unit should be unplugged before welding operations begin.

SPEED SENSORS

REMOVAL & INSTALLATION

Front

See Figure 1.

1. Raise and support the vehicle.
2. Remove the tire and wheel assembly.
3. Remove the caliper adapter bolts. Support the caliper and adapter assembly.

✲✲ WARNING

Do not let the assembly hang by the hose.

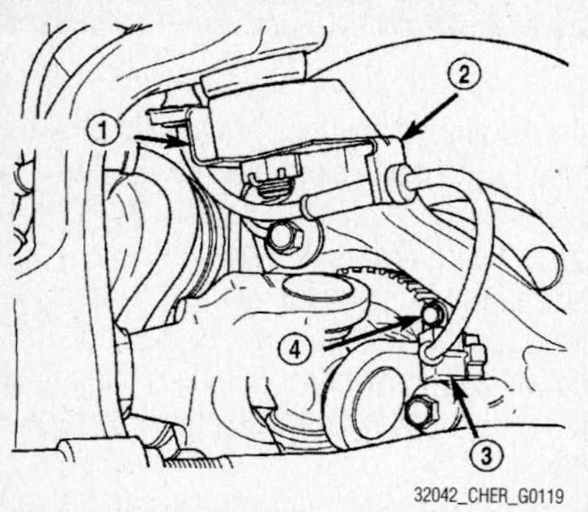

Fig. 1 Front wheel speed sensor for the Grand Cherokee

4. Remove the disc brake rotor.
5. Remove the front wheel sensor mounting nut to the hub.
6. Remove the wheel speed sensor from the hub.
7. Disconnect the wire sensor routing clips.
8. Disconnect the wheel speed sensor wire connector.
9. Remove the sensor and wire.

To install:

10. Reconnect the wheel speed sensor wire connector.
11. Reroute and connect the wheel speed sensor wire to the routing clips.
12. Install the wheel speed sensor into the hub and the install the mounting nut and tighten the nut to 106–124 inch lbs. (12–14 Nm).
13. Check the sensor wire routing. Be sure the wire is clear of all chassis components and is not twisted or kinked at any spot.
14. Install the disc brake rotor.
15. Install the caliper adapter over the rotor.
16. Install the caliper adapter bolts and tighten to 66–85 ft. lbs. (90–115 Nm).
17. Install the tire and wheel assembly.
18. Remove the support and lower vehicle.

Rear

See Figure 2.

1. Raise and support the vehicle.
2. Remove the wheel speed sensor mounting bolt from the rear support plate.
3. Remove the wheel speed sensor the support plate.
4. Disconnect the wheel speed sensor electrical connector.

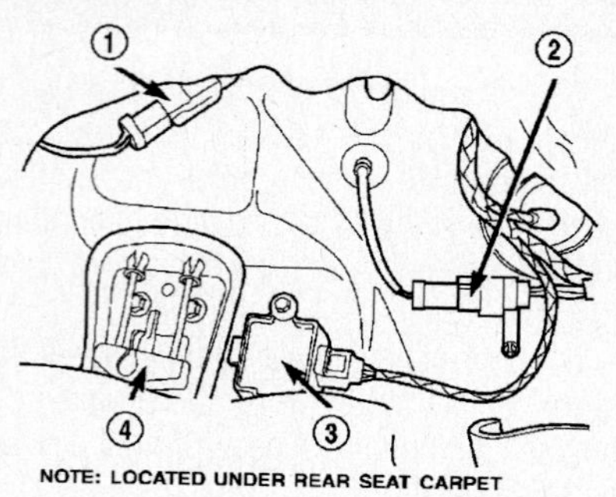

Fig. 2 The wire at the harness connectors for the rear wheel speed sensor on the Grand Cherokee

To install:

5. Insert the wheel speed sensor through the support plate.
6. Tighten the wheel speed sensor bolt to 106–124 inch lbs. (12–14 Nm).
7. Secure the wheel speed sensor wire to the routing clips. Verify that the sensor wire is secure and clear of the rotating components.
8. Reconnect the wheel speed sensor electrical connector.
9. Lower the vehicle.

BRAKES

BLEEDING THE BRAKE SYSTEM

BLEEDING PROCEDURE

BLEEDING PROCEDURE

➡Add only fresh, clean brake fluid from a sealed container when bleeding the brakes. If pressure bleeding equipment is used, the front brake metering valve will have to be held open to bleed the front brakes. The valve stem is located in the forward end or top of the combination valve. The stem must either be pressed inward or held outward slightly. Follow equipment manufacturer's instructions carefully when using pressure equipment. Do not exceed the maker's pressure recommendations. Generally, a tank pressure of 15—20 psi is sufficient. Do not pressure bleed without the proper master cylinder adapter.

When any part of the hydraulic system has been disconnected for repair or replacement, air may get into the lines and cause spongy pedal action (because air can be compressed and brake fluid cannot). To correct this condition, it is necessary to bleed the hydraulic system so to be sure all air is purged.

Bleeding must start where the lines were disconnected. If lines were disconnected at the master cylinder, for example, bleeding must be done at that point before proceeding downstream.

When bleeding the brake system, bleed one brake bleeder point at a time. Failure to do so may result in more air being drawn into the lines.

If the existing system fluid seems dirty or if the vehicle has covered considerable mileage, it is recommended that the system be completely purged and refilled with fresh, clean fluid. The best way to start is to siphon the old fluid out of the master cylinder reservoir and fill it completely with fresh fluid.

Brake fluid tends to darken over time. This does not necessarily indicate contamination. Examine fluid closely for foreign matter.

The primary and secondary hydraulic brake systems are separate and are bled independently. During the bleeding operation, do not allow the reservoir to run dry. Keep the master cylinder reservoir filled with brake fluid. Never use brake fluid that has been drained from the hydraulic system, no matter how clean it seems.

1. Clean all dirt from around the master cylinder fill cap, remove the cap and fill the master cylinder with brake fluid until the level is within ¼ in. (6mm) of the top edge of the reservoir.
2. Clean the bleeder screws at all 4 wheels. The bleeder screws are located on the back of the brake calipers.
3. Bleeder screws should be protected with rubber caps. If they are missing, the orifice may easily become clogged with road dirt. If the screw refuses to bleed when loosened, remove it and blow clear. Aftermarket caps are readily available.

Manual Bleeding

See Figures 3 through 5.

Manual bleeding requires two people and a degree of patience and cooperation. Bleeding should be performed in this order: (1) Right rear, (2) Left rear, (3) Right front, (4) Left front.

1. Follow the preparatory steps, above.
2. Attach a length of rubber hose over the bleeder screw and place the other end of the hose in a glass jar, submerged in brake fluid.
3. Have your assistant press down on the brake pedal, then open the bleeder screw ½–¾ turn.

4. The brake pedal will go to the floor.
5. Close the bleeder screw—preferably before the pedal reaches the floor. Tell your assistant to allow the brake pedal to return slowly.
6. Repeat these steps to purge all air from the system.
7. When bubbles cease to appear at the end of the bleeder hose, close the bleeder screw and remove the hose. Check that the pedal is firm or at least more firm than it was when you started. If not, continue the procedure.
8. Check the master cylinder fluid level and add fluid accordingly. Do this after bleeding each wheel.
9. Repeat the bleeding operation at the remaining three wheels, ending with the one closet to the master cylinder.
10. Fill the master cylinder reservoir to the proper level.

➡If there is excessive air in the system, it is possible that the stroke of the brake pedal will be insufficient to purge the lines. In this case a pressure bleeder or vacuum bleeder is the easiest solution.

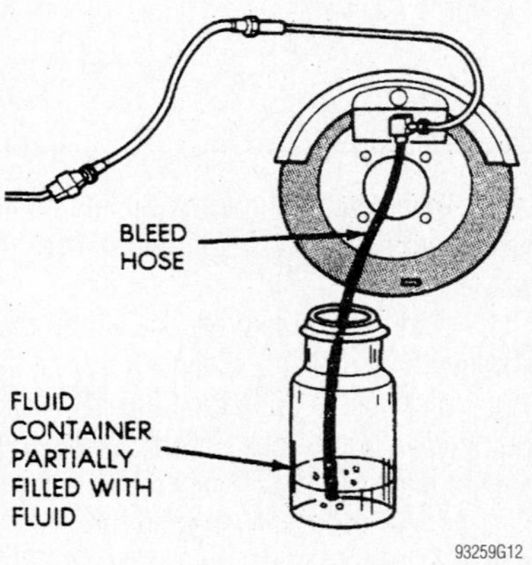

Fig. 3 Proper setup for manual bleeding procedure

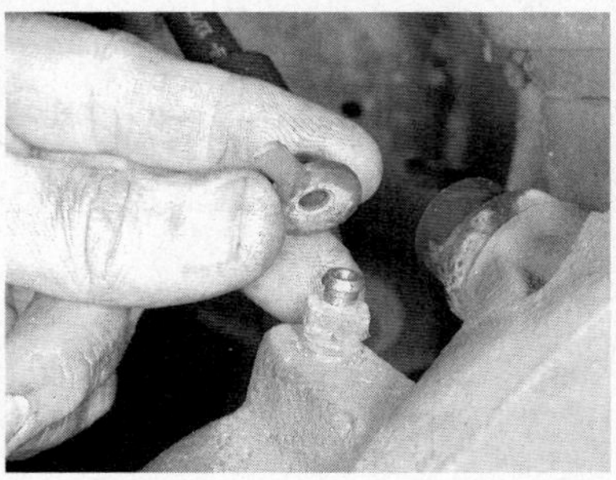

Fig. 4 Bleed screw caps are a must to keep the bleed screw passages clear

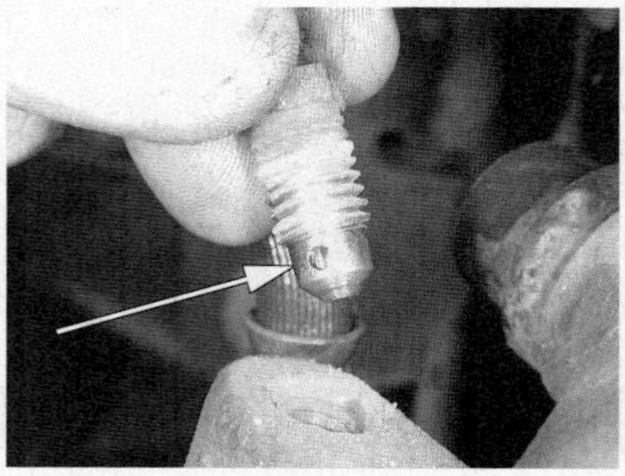

Fig. 5 Lack of cap may cause bleeder screw passages to become clogged

Vacuum Bleeding

See Figure 6.

Vacuum bleeding can be carried out by one person. Since a good vacuum bleeder will normally move more fluid than a brake pedal stroke, this procedure is preferred. These tools are inexpensive and readily available at auto parts outlets. Bleeding should be performed in this order: (1) Right rear, (2) Left rear, (3) Right front, (4) Left front.

1. Follow the preparatory steps, above.
2. Attach the vacuum bleeder according to the manufacturer's recommendations.
3. Pump up the unit until maximum vacuum is reached. Loosen the bleeder screw slightly until bubbles and fluid issue forth. Close the screw before the vacuum is equalized.

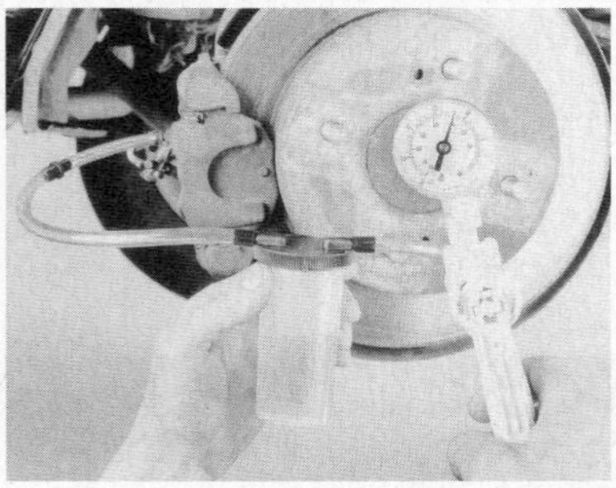

Fig. 6 There are tools, such as this Mighty-Vac, available to assist in vacuum bleeding of the brake system

4. Repeat the procedure until fluid without bubbles issues from the bleeder screw.
5. Keep a close check on master cylinder fluid level during this procedure as vacuum bleeders move considerable amounts of fluid.

MASTER CYLINDER BLEEDING

See Figure 7.

✲✲ CAUTION

When clamping the master cylinder in a vise, only clamp the master cylinder by its mounting flange. Do not clamp the master cylinder piston rod, reservoir, seal or body.

1. Clamp the master cylinder in a vise.
2. Attach special tools for bleeding master cylinder in the following fashion:
3. Thread one adapter in each outlet port. Tighten the adapters to 145 inch lbs. (17 Nm). Next, thread a bleeder tube into each adapter. Flex the bleeder tubes and place the open ends into the mouth of the fluid reservoir as far down as possible.

➡Make sure open ends of bleeder tubes stay below surface of brake fluid once reservoir is filled to proper level.

4. Fill brake fluid reservoir with brake fluid meeting DOT 3 specifications. Make sure fluid level is above tips of bleeder tubes in reservoir to ensure no air is ingested during bleeding.
5. Using a wooden dowel as a pushrod, slowly depress the master cylinder pistons, then release pressure, allowing the pistons to return to the released position.
6. Repeat several times until all air bubbles are expelled. Make sure the fluid level stays above the tips of the bleeder tubes in the reservoir while bleeding.
7. Remove the bleeder tubes from the master cylinder outlet ports, then plug the outlet ports and install the fill cap on the reservoir.
8. Install the master cylinder on vehicle then follow the brake bleeding procedure.

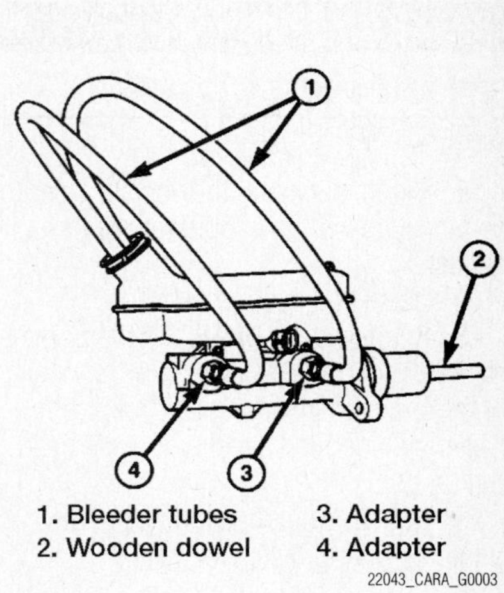

Fig. 7 Setup the master cylinder as shown to bleed it

BLEEDING THE ABS SYSTEM

ABS system bleeding requires conventional bleeding methods plus use of the DRB scan tool. The procedure involves performing a base brake bleeding, followed by use of the scan tool to cycle and bleed the HCU pump and solenoids. A second base brake bleeding procedure is then required to remove any air remaining in the system.

1. Perform base brake bleeding.
2. Connect scan tool to the Data Link Connector (DLC).
3. Select ANTI-LOCK BRAKES, followed by MISCELLANEOUS, then ABS BRAKES. Follow the instructions displayed. When scan tool displays TEST COMPLETE, disconnect scan tool and proceed.
4. Perform base brake bleeding a second time.
5. Top off master cylinder fluid level and verify proper brake operation before moving vehicle.

BRAKES

FRONT DISC BRAKES

⁂ CAUTION

Dust and dirt accumulating on brake parts during normal use may contain asbestos fibers from production or aftermarket brake linings. Breathing excessive concentrations of asbestos fibers can cause serious bodily harm. Exercise care when servicing brake parts. Do not sand or grind brake lining unless equipment used is designed to contain the dust residue. Do not clean brake parts with compressed air or by dry brushing. Cleaning should be done by dampening the brake components with a fine mist of water, then wiping the brake components clean with a dampened cloth. Dispose of cloth and all residue containing asbestos fibers in an impermeable container with the appropriate label. Follow practices prescribed by the Occupational Safety and Health Administration (OSHA) and the Environmental Protection Agency (EPA) for the handling, processing, and disposing of dust or debris that may contain asbestos fibers.

BRAKE CALIPER

REMOVAL & INSTALLATION

See Figure 8.

1. Before servicing the vehicle, refer to the precautions in the beginning of this manual.
2. Raise and support vehicle.
3. Remove front wheel and tire assembly.
4. Drain small amount of fluid from master cylinder brake reservoir with clean suction gun.
5. Bottom caliper pistons into the caliper by prying the caliper over.
6. Remove brake hose banjo bolt and gasket washers. Discard gasket washers.
7. Remove the caliper slide bolts.
8. Remove the caliper from the adapter.

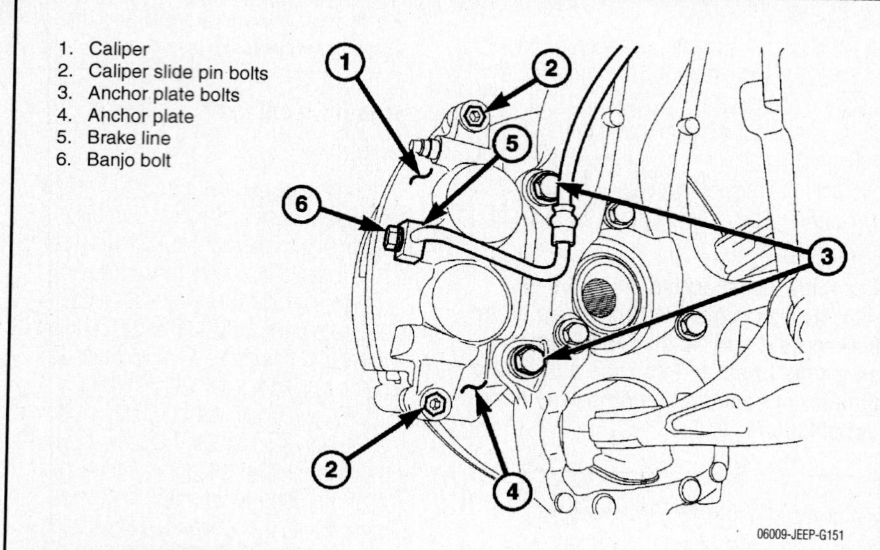

Fig. 8 Front caliper mounting

To install:

9. Install the caliper on the adapter.
10. Caliper slide pins should be free from debris and lightly lubricated.
11. Install the caliper slide pin bolts and tighten to 53 ft. lbs. (72 Nm).
12. Gently lift one end of the slide pin boot to equalize air pressure, then release the boot and verify that the boot is fully covering the slide pin.

⁂ WARNING

Verify brake hose is not twisted or kinked before tightening banjo bolt.

13. Install brake hose to caliper with new copper washers and tighten banjo bolt to 23 ft. lbs. (31 Nm).
14. Fill and bleed brake system.
15. Install wheel and tire assemblies.
16. Remove supports and lower vehicle.
17. Verify brake fluid level.

DISC BRAKE PADS

REMOVAL & INSTALLATION

See Figure 9.

1. Before servicing the vehicle, refer to the precautions in the beginning of this manual.
2. Drain ⅔ of the brake fluid from the front reservoir. Use the bleeder screw at the front outlet port to drain the fluid. If equipped with anti-lock brakes, relieve the system pressure.
3. Raise and safely support the vehicle.
4. Remove the wheels.

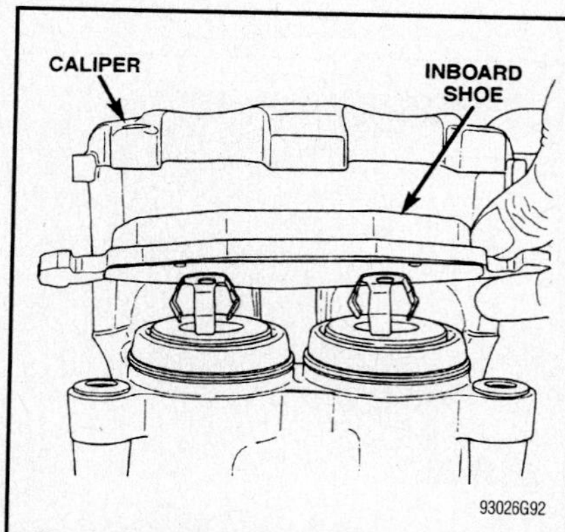

Fig. 9 Installing the inward brake pad on the front caliper pistons—Grand Cherokee

5. Insert a small prybar through the caliper opening and pry the caliper (using the outboard brake pad) to bottom the pistons in the caliper bore.

➡**This will back the brake pads off of the rotor surface to facilitate the removal and installation of the caliper assembly.**

6. Pry the caliper support spring out of the caliper.
7. Remove both caliper slide pin bushing caps and slide pins.
8. Lift the caliper from the anchor.
9. Using a piece of mechanic's wire, support the caliper so there is not tension on the brake hose.
10. Remove the brake pads from the caliper.

To install:

11. Position the brake pads onto the caliper.
12. Position the caliper into place on the anchor.
13. Coat the caliper slide pins with silicone grease and torque them to 21–30 ft. lbs. (29–41 Nm). Install the slide pin bushing caps.
14. Install the caliper support spring in the top of the caliper under the anchor; then, install the other end into the lower caliper hole.

➡**Hold the spring in the caliper hole with your thumb while prying the spring end out and under the anchor.**

15. Fill the master cylinder with fluid and bleed the brake system.
16. Before driving the vehicle, pump the brakes several times to seat the pads.
17. Install the wheels.

BRAKES — REAR DISC BRAKES

CAUTION

Dust and dirt accumulating on brake parts during normal use may contain asbestos fibers from production or aftermarket brake linings. Breathing excessive concentrations of asbestos fibers can cause serious bodily harm. Exercise care when servicing brake parts. Do not sand or grind brake lining unless equipment used is designed to contain the dust residue. Do not clean brake parts with compressed air or by dry brushing. Cleaning should be done by dampening the brake components with a fine mist of water, then wiping the brake components clean with a dampened cloth. Dispose of cloth and all residue containing asbestos fibers in an impermeable container with the appropriate label. Follow practices prescribed by the Occupational Safety and Health Administration (OSHA) and the Environmental Protection Agency (EPA) for the handling, processing, and disposing of dust or debris that may contain asbestos fibers.

BRAKE CALIPER

REMOVAL & INSTALLATION

See Figures 10 and 11.

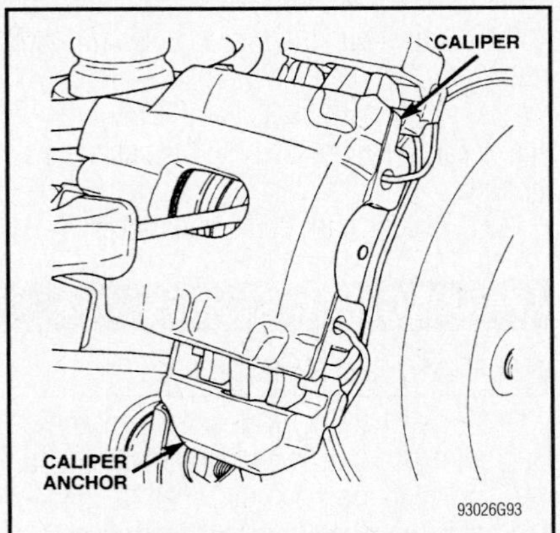

Fig. 10 Bottoming the piston in the rear caliper

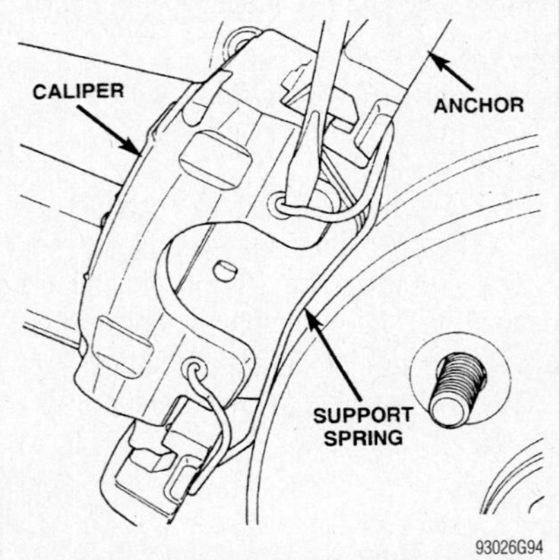

Fig. 11 View of the support springs on the rear caliper

1. Before servicing the vehicle, refer to the precautions in the beginning of this manual.
2. Drain ⅔ of the brake fluid from the front reservoir. Use the bleeder screw at the front outlet port to drain the fluid. If equipped with anti-lock brakes, relieve the system pressure.
3. Raise and safely support the vehicle.
4. Remove the wheels.
5. Insert a small prybar through the caliper opening and pry the caliper (using the outboard brake pad) to bottom the piston in the caliper bore.

➡**This will back the brake pads off of the rotor surface to facilitate the removal and installation of the caliper assembly.**

6. Remove the brake hose-to-caliper bolt, hose and washers.
7. Pry the caliper support spring out of the caliper.
8. Remove both caliper slide pin bushing caps and slide pins.
9. Lift the caliper from the anchor.

To install:

10. Position the caliper into place on the anchor.
11. Coat the caliper slide pins with silicone grease and torque them to 26 ft. lbs. (35 Nm). Install the slide pin bushing caps.
12. Install the caliper support spring in the top of the caliper under the anchor; then, install the other end into the lower caliper hole.

➡**Hold the spring in the caliper hole with your thumb while prying the spring end out and under the anchor.**

13. Using new gasket washers, install the brake line and torque the fitting bolt to 23 ft. lbs. (31 Nm).
14. Fill the master cylinder with fluid and bleed the brake system.
15. Before driving the vehicle, pump the brakes several times to seat the pads.
16. Install the wheels.

DISC BRAKE PADS

REMOVAL & INSTALLATION

1. Before servicing the vehicle, refer to the precautions in the beginning of this manual.
2. Drain ⅔ of the brake fluid from the front reservoir. Use the bleeder screw at the front outlet port to drain the fluid. If equipped with anti-lock brakes, relieve the system pressure.
3. Raise and safely support the vehicle.
4. Remove the wheels.

5. Insert a small prybar through the caliper opening and pry the caliper (using the outboard brake pad) to bottom the piston in the caliper bore.

➡This will back the brake pads off of the rotor surface to facilitate the removal and installation of the caliper assembly.

6. Pry the caliper support spring out of the caliper.
7. Remove both caliper slide pin bushing caps and slide pins.
8. Lift the caliper from the anchor.
9. Using a piece of mechanics wire, support the caliper so there is not tension on the brake hose.
10. Remove the brake pads from the caliper.

To install:

11. Position the brake pads onto the caliper.
12. Position the caliper into place on the anchor.
13. Coat the caliper slide pins with silicone grease and torque them to 21–30 ft. lbs. (29–41 Nm). Install the slide pin bushing caps.
14. Install the caliper support spring in the top of the caliper under the anchor; then, install the other end into the lower caliper hole.

➡Hold the spring in the caliper hole with your thumb while prying the spring end out and under the anchor.

15. Fill the master cylinder with fluid and bleed the brake system.
16. Before driving the vehicle, pump the brakes several times to seat the pads.
17. Install the wheels.

PARKING BRAKE

PARKING BRAKE CABLES

ADJUSTMENT

Adjustment can be made with a standard brake gauge or with adjusting tool. Adjustment is performed with the complete brake assembly installed on the backing plate.

1. Be sure parking brake lever is fully released.
2. Raise vehicle so rear wheels can be rotated freely.
3. Remove plug from each access hole in brake support plates.
4. Loosen parking brake cable adjustment nut until there is slack in front cable.
5. Insert adjusting tool through support plate access hole and engage tool in teeth of adjusting screw star wheel.
6. Rotate adjuster screw star wheel (move tool handle upward) until slight drag can be felt when wheel is rotated.
7. Push and hold adjuster lever away from star wheel with thin screwdriver.
8. Back off adjuster screw star wheel until brake drag is eliminated.
9. Repeat adjustment at opposite wheel. Be sure adjustment is equal at both wheels.
10. Install support plate access hole plugs.
11. Adjust parking brake cable and lower vehicle.
12. Apply park brake hand lever and make sure park brakes hold the vehicle stationary.
13. Release park brake hand lever.

PARKING BRAKE SHOES

REMOVAL & INSTALLATION

Rear disc parking brakes are dual shoe, internal expanding units with an automatic self adjusting mechanism. When the parking brake pedal is depressed the brake cable pulls the brake shoes outward against the brake drum. When the brake pedal is released the return springs attached to the brake shoes pull the shoes back to their original position.

1. Raise and support the vehicle.
2. Remove the tire and wheel assembly.
3. Remove the disc brake caliper.
4. Remove the disc brake rotor.
5. Disengage the park brake cable from behind the rotor assembly to allow easier disassembly of the park brake shoes.
6. Disassemble the rear park brake shoes.

To install:

7. Reassemble the rear park brake shoes.
8. Install park brake cable to the lever behind support plate.
9. Adjust the rear brake shoes:
   a. Measure the drum diameter with the gauge and lock it into position.
   b. Turn the gauge around and check the shoe diameter diagonally across at the top of one shoe and bottom of the opposite shoe (widest point). The gauge should be a light drag fit over the shoes.
   c. If the gauge is not a light drag fit over the shoes, turn the star wheel by hand to move the shoes in or out so that the correct clearance can be achieved.
10. Install the disc brake rotor.
11. Install the disc brake caliper.
12. Install the wheel.
13. Lower the vehicle.

➡On a new vehicle or after parking brake lining replacement, it is recommended that the parking brake system be conditioned prior to use. This is done by making one stop from 25 mph on dry pavement or concrete using light to moderate force on the parking brake foot pedal.

GENERAL INFORMATION

** CAUTION

These vehicles are equipped with an air bag system. The system must be disarmed before performing service on, or around, system components, the steering column, instrument panel components, wiring and sensors. Failure to follow the safety precautions and the disarming procedure could result in accidental air bag deployment, possible injury and unnecessary system repairs.

SERVICE PRECAUTIONS

Disconnect and isolate the battery negative cable before beginning any airbag system component diagnosis, testing, removal, or installation procedures. Allow system capacitor to discharge for two minutes before beginning any component service. This will disable the airbag system. Failure to disable the airbag system may result in accidental airbag deployment, personal injury, or death.

Do not place an intact undeployed airbag face down on a solid surface. The airbag will propel into the air if accidentally deployed and may result in personal injury or death.

When carrying or handling an undeployed airbag, the trim side (face) of the airbag should be pointing towards the body to minimize possibility of injury if accidental deployment occurs. Failure to do this may result in personal injury or death.

Replace airbag system components with OEM replacement parts. Substitute parts may appear interchangeable, but internal differences may result in inferior occupant protection. Failure to do so may result in occupant personal injury or death.

Wear safety glasses, rubber gloves, and long sleeved clothing when cleaning powder residue from vehicle after an airbag deployment. Powder residue emitted from a deployed airbag can cause skin irritation. Flush affected area with cool water if irritation is experienced. If nasal or throat irritation is experienced, exit the vehicle for fresh air until the irritation ceases. If irritation continues, see a physician.

Do not use a replacement airbag that is not in the original packaging. This may result in improper deployment, personal injury, or death.

The factory installed fasteners, screws and bolts used to fasten airbag components have a special coating and are specifically designed for the airbag system. Do not use substitute fasteners. Use only original equipment fasteners listed in the parts catalog when fastener replacement is required.

During, and following, any child restraint anchor service, due to impact event or vehicle repair, carefully inspect all mounting hardware, tether straps, and anchors for proper installation, operation, or damage. If a child restraint anchor is found damaged in any way, the anchor must be replaced. Failure to do this may result in personal injury or death.

Deployed and non-deployed airbags may or may not have live pyrotechnic material within the airbag inflator.

Do not dispose of driver/passenger/curtain airbags or seat belt tensioners unless you are sure of complete deployment. Refer to the Hazardous Substance Control System for proper disposal.

Dispose of deployed airbags and tensioners consistent with state, provincial, local, and federal regulations.

After any airbag component testing or service, do not connect the battery negative cable. Personal injury or death may result if the system test is not performed first.

If the vehicle is equipped with the Occupant Classification System (OCS), do not connect the battery negative cable before performing the OCS Verification Test using the scan tool and the appropriate diagnostic information. Personal injury or death may result if the system test is not performed properly.

Never replace both the Occupant Restraint Controller (ORC) and the Occupant Classification Module (OCM) at the same time. If both require replacement, replace one, then perform the Airbag System test before replacing the other.

Both the ORC and the OCM store Occupant Classification System (OCS) calibration data, which they transfer to one another when one of them is replaced. If both are replaced at the same time, an irreversible fault will be set in both modules and the OCS may malfunction and cause personal injury or death.

If equipped with OCS, the Seat Weight Sensor is a sensitive, calibrated unit and must be handled carefully. Do not drop or handle roughly. If dropped or damaged, replace with another sensor. Failure to do so may result in occupant injury or death.

If equipped with OCS, the front passenger seat must be handled carefully as well. When removing the seat, be careful when setting on floor not to drop. If dropped, the sensor may be inoperative, could result in occupant injury, or possibly death.

If equipped with OCS, when the passenger front seat is on the floor, no one should sit in the front passenger seat. This uneven force may damage the sensing ability of the seat weight sensors. If sat on and damaged, the sensor may be inoperative, could result in occupant injury, or possibly death.

DISARMING THE SYSTEM

Disconnect and isolate the negative battery cable. Wait 2 minutes for the system capacitor to discharge before performing any service.

ARMING

To arm the system, connect the negative battery cable.

CLOCKSPRING CENTERING

Disconnect and isolate the battery negative cable before beginning any airbag system component diagnosis, testing, removal, or installation procedures. Allow system capacitor to discharge for two minutes before beginning any component service. This will disable the airbag system. Failure to disable the airbag system may result in accidental airbag deployment, personal injury, or death.

The clockspring is mounted on the steering column behind the steering wheel. Its purpose is to maintain a continuous electrical circuit between the wiring harness and the driver's side air bag module. This assembly consists of a flat, ribbon-like electrically conductive tape that winds and unwinds with the steering wheel rotation.

Service replacement clocksprings are shipped pre-centered and with a molded plastic locking pin that snaps into a receptacle on the rotor and is engaged between two tabs on the upper surface of the rotor case. The locking pin secures the centered clockspring rotor to the clockspring case during shipment, but the locking pin must be removed from the clockspring after it is installed on the steering column. This locking pin should not be removed until the clockspring has been installed on the steering column. If the locking pin is removed before the clockspring is installed on a steering column, the clockspring centering procedure must be performed.

➡The clockspring cannot be repaired. If the clockspring is faulty, damaged, or if the driver airbag has been deployed, the clockspring must be replaced.

➡Before starting this procedure, be certain to turn the steering wheel until the front wheels are in the straight-ahead position.

1. Place the front wheels in the straight-ahead position.
2. Remove the clockspring from the steering column.
3. Rotate the clockspring rotor counter–clockwise to the end of its travel. Do not apply excessive torque.
4. From the end of the counter–clockwise travel, rotate the rotor about three turns clockwise.
5. The clockspring is now centered. Turn the rotor slightly clockwise or counterclockwise as necessary so that the clockspring airbag pigtail wires and connector receptacles are at the top and the holes for the clockspring locking pin are in alignment.
6. The front wheels should still be in the straight-ahead position. Reinstall the clockspring onto the steering column.

DRIVETRAIN

AUTOMATIC TRANSMISSION ASSEMBLY

REMOVAL & INSTALLATION

545RFE

➡The transmission and torque converter must be removed as an assembly to avoid component damage. The converter drive plate, converter hub O-ring, or oil seal can be damaged if the converter is left attached to the drive plate during removal. Be sure to remove the transmission and converter as an assembly.

1. Before servicing the vehicle, refer to the precautions in the beginning of this manual.
2. Disconnect the negative battery cable.
3. Raise and support the vehicle.
4. Mark propeller shaft and axle yokes for assembly alignment.
5. Remove the rear propeller shaft
6. Remove the front propeller shaft.
7. Remove the engine to transmission collar.
8. Remove the exhaust support bracket from the rear of the transmission.
9. Disconnect and lower or remove any necessary exhaust components.
10. Remove the starter motor.
11. Rotate crankshaft in clockwise direction until converter bolts are accessible. Then remove bolts one at a time. Rotate crankshaft with socket wrench on dampener bolt.
12. Disconnect wires from solenoid and pressure switch assembly, input and output speed sensors, and line pressure sensor.
13. Disconnect gearshift cable from transmission manual valve lever.
14. Disconnect transfer case shift cable from the transfer case shift lever.
15. Remove the clip securing the transfer case shift cable into the cable support bracket.
16. Disconnect transmission fluid cooler lines at transmission fittings and clips.
17. Disconnect the transmission vent hose from the transmission.
18. Support rear of engine with safety stand or jack.
19. Raise transmission slightly with service jack to relieve load on crossmember and supports.
20. Remove bolts securing rear support and cushion to transmission and crossmember.
21. Remove bolts attaching crossmember to frame and remove crossmember.
22. Remove transfer case.
23. Remove all remaining converter housing bolts.
24. Carefully work transmission and torque converter assembly rearward off engine block dowels.
25. Hold torque converter in place during transmission removal.
26. Lower transmission and remove assembly from under the vehicle.
27. To remove torque converter, carefully slide torque converter out of the transmission.

To install:

28. Check torque converter hub and hub drive flats for sharp edges burrs, scratches, or nicks. Polish the hub and flats with 320/400 grit paper and crocus cloth if necessary. Verify that the converter hub O-ring is properly installed and is free of any debris. The hub must be smooth to avoid damaging pump seal at installation.
29. If a replacement transmission is being installed, transfer any components necessary, such as the manual shift lever and shift cable bracket, from the original transmission onto the replacement transmission.
30. Lubricate oil pump seal lip with transmission fluid.
31. Align converter and oil pump.
32. Carefully insert converter in oil pump. Then rotate converter back and forth until fully seated in pump gears.
33. Check converter seating with steel scale and straightedge. Surface of converter lugs should be at least 13mm (½ in.) to rear of straightedge when converter is fully seated.
34. Temporarily secure converter with C-clamp.
35. Position transmission on jack and secure it with chains.
36. Check condition of converter drive plate. Replace the plate if cracked, distorted or damaged.

➡Be sure transmission dowel pins are seated in engine block and protrude far enough to hold transmission in alignment.

37. Apply a light coating of Mopar® High Temp Grease to the torque converter hub pocket in the rear pocket of the engine's crankshaft.
38. Raise transmission and align the torque converter with the drive plate and the transmission converter housing with the engine block.
39. Move transmission forward. Then raise, lower, or tilt transmission to align the converter housing with the engine block dowels.
40. Carefully work transmission forward and over engine block dowels until converter hub is seated in crankshaft. Verify that no wires, or the transmission vent hose, have become trapped between the engine block and the transmission.
41. Install two bolts to attach the transmission to the engine.
42. Install remaining torque converter housing to engine bolts. Tighten to 50 ft. lbs. (68 Nm).
43. Install rear transmission crossmember. Tighten crossmember to frame bolts to 50 ft. lbs. (68 Nm).
44. Install rear support to transmission. Tighten bolts to 35 ft. lbs. (47 Nm).
45. Lower transmission onto crossmember and install bolts attaching transmission mount to crossmember. Tighten clevis

bracket to crossmember bolts to 35 ft. lbs. (47 Nm). Tighten the clevis bracket to rear support bolt to 50 ft. lbs. (68 Nm).

46. Install both the left and right side oil pan to transmission bolts, 5.7L only. Torque the bolts to 39 ft. lbs. (57 Nm).

47. Remove engine support fixture.

48. Install new plastic retainer grommet on any shift cable that was disconnected. Grommets should not be reused. Use pry tool to remove rod from grommet and cut away old grommet. Use pliers to snap new grommet into cable and to snap grommet onto lever.

49. Connect gearshift cable to transmission.

50. Connect wires to solenoid and pressure switch assembly connector, input and output speed sensors, and line pressure sensor. Be sure transmission harnesses are properly routed.

➡It is essential that correct length bolts be used to attach the converter to the drive plate. Bolts that are too long will damage the clutch surface inside the converter.

51. Install all torque converter-to-drive plate bolts by hand.

52. Verify that the torque converter is pulled flush to the drive plate. Tighten bolts to 270 inch lbs. (31 Nm).

53. Install starter motor and cooler line bracket.

54. Connect cooler lines to transmission.

55. Install transmission fill tube.

56. Install exhaust components.

57. Install transfer case. Tighten transfer case nuts to 26 ft. lbs. (35 Nm).

58. Install the transfer case shift cable to the cable support bracket and the transfer case shift lever.

59. Install the structural dust cover onto the transmission and the engine.

60. Align and connect propeller shaft(s).

61. Adjust gearshift cable if necessary.

62. Lower vehicle.

63. Fill transmission with Mopar® ATF +4, Automatic Transmission fluid.

NAG1

See Figure 12.

➡If the transmission is being reconditioned (clutch/seal replacement) or replaced, it is necessary to perform the TCM Adaptation Procedure using the scan tool.

1. Before servicing the vehicle, refer to the precautions in the beginning of this manual.

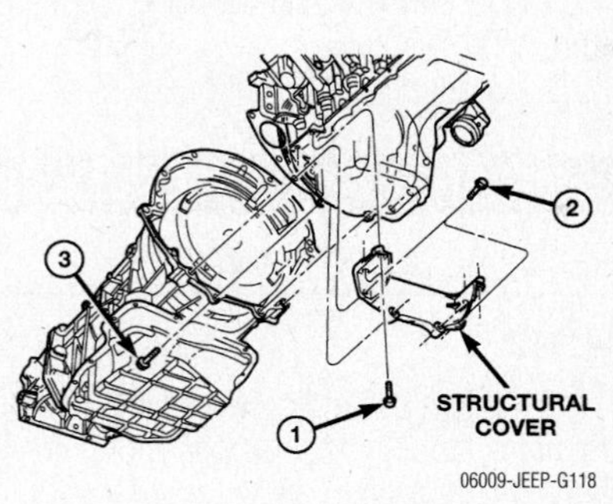

Fig. 12 Structural cover—NAG1 transmission

2. Disconnect the negative battery cable.

3. Raise and support the vehicle.

4. Remove the drive shafts.

5. Remove the bolts holding the starter motor to the transmission.

6. Remove the starter from the transmission starter pocket and safely relocate.

7. Remove the bolts holding the structural cover to the transmission and engine.

8. Remove the structural cover from the vehicle.

9. Rotate crankshaft in clockwise direction until converter bolts are accessible. Then remove bolts one at a time. Rotate crankshaft with socket wrench on dampener bolt.

10. Disconnect the gearshift cable from the transmission manual valve lever.

11. Remove the shift cable from the gearshift cable bracket.

12. Disconnect 13-pin plug connector. Turn bayonet lock of guide bushing counterclockwise.

13. Remove the 13-pin connector from the transmission.

14. Disconnect transmission fluid cooler lines at transmission.

15. Disconnect the transmission vent hose from the transmission.

16. Remove the bolts holding the transmission fill tube to the transmission.

17. Support rear of engine with safety stand or jack.

18. Raise transmission slightly with service jack to relieve load on crossmember and supports.

19. Remove bolts securing rear support and cushion to transmission crossmember.

20. Remove bolts attaching crossmember to frame and remove crossmember.

21. Remove all remaining bolts holding the engine to the transmission. Note the location of any wiring harness clips.

22. Carefully work transmission and torque converter assembly rearward off engine block dowels.

23. Hold torque converter in place during transmission removal.

24. Lower transmission and remove assembly from under the vehicle.

25. To remove torque converter, carefully slide torque converter out of the transmission.

To install:

26. Check torque converter hub and hub drive flats for sharp edges burrs, scratches, or nicks. Polish the hub and flats with 320/400 grit paper and crocus cloth if necessary. The hub must be smooth to avoid damaging pump seal at installation.

27. If a replacement transmission is being installed, transfer any components necessary, such as the manual shift lever and shift cable bracket, from the original transmission onto the replacement transmission.

28. Lubricate oil pump seal lip with transmission fluid.

29. Place torque converter in position on transmission.

WARNING

Do not damage oil pump seal or converter hub while inserting torque converter into the front of the transmission.

30. Align torque converter to oil pump seal opening.

31. Insert torque converter hub into oil pump.

32. While pushing torque converter inward, rotate converter until converter is fully seated in the oil pump gears.

33. Check converter seating with a scale and straightedge. Surface of converter lugs should be at least 19mm (¾ in.) to rear of straightedge when converter is fully seated.

34. If necessary, temporarily secure converter with C-clamp attached to the converter housing.

35. Check condition of converter drive plate. Replace the plate if cracked, distorted or damaged. Also be sure transmission dowel pins are seated in engine block and protrude far enough to hold transmission in alignment.

36. Apply a light coating of Mopar® High Temp Grease to the torque converter hub pocket in the rear pocket of the engine's crankshaft.

37. Raise transmission and align the torque converter with the drive plate and the transmission converter housing with the engine block.

38. Move transmission forward. Then raise, lower, or tilt transmission to align the

converter housing with the engine block dowels.

39. Carefully work transmission forward and over engine block dowels until converter hub is seated in crankshaft. Verify that no wires, or the transmission vent hose, have become trapped between the engine block and the transmission.

40. Install two bolts to attach the transmission to the engine.

41. Install remaining torque converter housing to engine bolts. Tighten to 29 ft. lbs.(36 Nm).

42. Install rear transmission crossmember. Tighten crossmember to frame bolts to 50 ft. lbs. (68 Nm).

43. Install rear support to transmission. Tighten bolts to 35 ft. lbs. (47 Nm).

44. Lower transmission onto crossmember and install bolts attaching transmission mount to crossmember. Tighten clevis bracket to crossmember bolts to 35 ft. lbs. (47 Nm). Tighten the clevis bracket to rear support bolt to 50 ft. lbs. (68 Nm).

45. Remove engine support fixture.

46. Install the engine to transmission structural cover.

47. Connect gearshift cable to the gearshift cable bracket and transmission.

48. Check O-ring on plug connector, and replace if necessary.

49. Install the plug connector into the guide bushing. Turn bayonet lock of guide bushing clockwise to connect plug connector.

WARNING

It is essential that correct length bolts be used to attach the converter to the drive plate. Bolts that are too long will damage the clutch surface inside the converter.

50. Install all torque converter-to-drive plate bolts by hand.

51. Verify that the torque converter is pulled flush to the drive plate. Tighten bolts to 30 ft. lbs. (42 Nm).

52. Install starter motor.

53. Install transmission fill tube.

54. Connect cooler lines to transmission.

55. Install exhaust components.

56. Install transfer case, if necessary. Tighten transfer case nuts to 26 ft. lbs. (35 Nm).

57. Align and connect drive shafts.

58. Adjust gearshift cable if necessary.

59. Lower vehicle.

60. Connect negative battery cable.

61. Fill transmission with the appropriate fluid.

62. Verify proper operation.

TRANSFER CASE ASSEMBLY

REMOVAL & INSTALLATION

NV140

1. Before servicing the vehicle, refer to the precautions in the beginning of this manual.

2. Raise vehicle.

3. Remove transfer case drain plug and drain the transfer case lubricant.

➡Do not allow drive shafts to hang at attached end. Damage to joint can result.

4. Remove the front and rear propeller shafts.

5. Support transmission with jack stand.

6. Remove rear crossmember and skid plate, if equipped.

7. Disconnect transfer case vent hose.

8. Support transfer case with transmission jack and secure with chains.

9. Remove nuts attaching transfer case to transmission.

10. Pull transfer case and jack rearward to disengage transfer case.

11. Remove transfer case from under vehicle.

To install:

12. Mount transfer case on a transmission jack.

13. Secure transfer case to jack with chains.

14. Position transfer case under vehicle.

15. Align transfer case and transmission shafts and install transfer case onto the transmission.

16. Install and tighten transfer case attaching nuts to 26 ft. lbs. (35 Nm).

17. Connect front and rear drive shafts. Torque the front driveshaft-to-transfer case bolts to 24 ft. lbs. (32 Nm). Torque the rear driveshaft-to-transfer case bolts to 80 ft. lbs. (108 Nm).

18. Fill transfer case with correct fluid. Check transmission fluid level. Correct as necessary.

19. Install the transfer case fill plug. Tighten the plug to 15–25 ft. lbs. (20–34 Nm).

20. Install rear crossmember and skid plate, if equipped. Tighten crossmember bolts to 30 ft. lbs. (41 Nm).

21. Remove transmission jack and support stand.

22. Lower vehicle and verify transfer case shift operation.

NV245

1. Before servicing the vehicle, refer to the precautions in the beginning of this manual.

2. Shift transfer case into NEUTRAL.

3. Raise vehicle.

4. Remove transfer case drain plug and drain transfer case lubricant.

5. Support transmission with jack stand.

6. Remove rear crossmember and skid plate, if equipped.

7. Disconnect front propeller shaft from transfer case at companion flange. Remove rear propeller shaft from vehicle.

➡Do not allow drive shafts to hang at attached end. Damage to joint can result.

8. Disconnect the transfer case shift motor and mode sensor connector.

9. Disconnect transfer case vent hose.

10. Support transfer case with transmission jack.

11. Secure transfer case to jack with chains.

12. Remove nuts attaching transfer case to transmission.

13. Pull transfer case and jack rearward to disengage transfer case.

14. Remove transfer case from under vehicle.

To install:

15. Mount transfer case on a transmission jack.

16. Secure transfer case to jack with chains.

17. Position transfer case under vehicle.

18. Align transfer case and transmission shafts and install transfer case onto transmission.

19. Install and tighten transfer case attaching nuts to 26 ft. lbs. (35 Nm).

20. Connect the transfer case vent hose to the transfer case.

21. Install rear crossmember and skid plate, if equipped.

22. Remove transmission jack and support stand.

23. Connect front and rear drive shafts. Torque the front driveshaft-to-transfer case bolts to 24 ft. lbs. (32 Nm). Torque the rear driveshaft-to-transfer case bolts to 80 ft. lbs. (108 Nm).

24. Fill transfer case with correct fluid. Check transmission fluid level. Correct as necessary.

25. Install the transfer case fill plug. Tighten the plug to 15–25 ft. lbs. (20–34 Nm).
26. Connect the shift motor and mode sensor wiring connector.
27. Lower vehicle and verify transfer case shift operation.

FRONT DRIVESHAFT

REMOVAL & INSTALLATION

1. Before servicing the vehicle, refer to the precautions in the beginning of this manual.
2. Mark propeller shaft and pinion flange for installation reference.
3. Remove front propeller shaft.

To install:

4. Install propeller shaft with reference marks aligned.
5. Using new bolts, tighten them to 24 ft. lbs. (32 Nm).

FRONT HALFSHAFT

REMOVAL & INSTALLATION

1. Before servicing the vehicle, refer to the precautions in the beginning of this manual.
2. With vehicle in neutral, position vehicle on hoist.
3. Remove half shaft hub/bearing nut.
4. Remove wheel speed sensor from hub/bearing.
5. Remove brake calipers bolts and remove calipers from caliper adapters.
6. Remove lower stabilizer link bolt from control arm.
7. Remove outer tie rod end nuts and separate tie rods from knuckles with the proper tool.
8. Remove upper ball joint nuts and separate ball joints from knuckles with the proper tool.
9. Remove shock clevis bolt and nut from lower control arm.
10. Lean the knuckle out and push half shaft out of the hub/bearing.
11. Pry half shafts from axle/axle tube with pry bar.

To install:

12. Install half shaft on the axle and through the hub/bearing. Verify halfshaft has engaged.
13. Install shock clevis on lower control arm and tighten nut to 60 ft. lbs. (81 Nm).
14. Install upper control arm on knuckle. Torque to 55 ft. lbs. (75 Nm).
15. Install tie rod end on knuckle. Torque to 70 ft. lbs. (95 Nm).
16. Install stabilizer link on lower control arm. Torque to 85 ft. lbs. (115 Nm).
17. Install caliper on caliper adapter.
18. Install wheel speed sensor on the hub/bearing.
19. Install half shaft hub/bearing nut and tighten to 100 ft. lbs. (135 Nm).

CV-JOINTS OVERHAUL

Outer Joint

➡CV joint is serviced with the shaft, the boot can be serviced separately

1. Remove inner CV boot and joint.
2. Cut outer CV boot clamps.
3. Cut boot off CV housing and shaft.

To install:

4. Clean the CV joint then apply new grease to the joint.
5. Slide the new boot on to the shaft and on the CV housing.
6. Install boot clamps in original locations.
7. Install inner CV joint and boot.

Inner Joint

1. Clamp shaft in a vise (with soft jaws) and support C/V joint.
2. Remove clamps with a cut-off wheel or grinder.
3. Slide boot down the shaft.
4. Remove lubricant from housing to expose the C/V snap ring and remove snap ring.
5. Remove bearings from the cage.
6. Rotate cage 30 degrees and slide cage off the inner race and down the shaft.
7. Remove spread inner race snap ring and remove race from the shaft.
8. Remove boot from the shaft and discard.
9. Clean and inspect housing , cage , bearings , housing snap-ring , inner race snap-ring and inner race for wear or damage.

To install:

10. Apply a coat of grease supplied with the joint/boot to the C/V joint components before assembling them.
11. Place new clamps on the new boot and slide boot down the shaft.
12. Slide cage onto the shaft with the small diameter end towards the boot.
13. Install the inner race onto the shaft. Pull on the race to verify snap ring has engaged.
14. Align cage with the inner race and slide over the race.
15. Turn the cage 30 degrees to align the cage windows with the race.
16. Apply grease to the inner race and bearings and install the bearings.
17. Apply grease to the housing bore then install the bearing assembly into the housing.
18. Install the housing snap ring and verify it is seated in the groove.
19. Fill the housing and boot with the remaining grease.
20. Slide the boot onto the C/V housing into it's original position. Ensure boot is not twisted and remove any excess air.
21. Secure both boot clamps with Clamp Installer C-4975A. Place tool on clamp bridge and tighten tool until the jaws of the tool are closed.

FRONT PINION SEAL

REMOVAL & INSTALLATION

1. Before servicing the vehicle, refer to the precautions in the beginning of this manual.
2. Raise and support the vehicle.
3. Remove skid plate, if equipped.
4. Remove both half shafts.
5. Mark the propeller shaft and pinion companion flange for installation reference.
6. Remove the front propeller shaft.
7. Rotate the pinion gear three or four times and verify pinion rotates smoothly.
8. Record pinion rotating torque with an inch pound torque wrench, for installation reference.
9. Position Holder C-3281, or equivalent, against the companion flange and install a four bolts and washers into the threaded holes and tighten the bolts.
10. Remove the pinion nut.
11. Remove the companion flange with Remover C-452, or equivalent.
12. Remove pinion seal with a pry tool or a slide hammer mounted screw.

To install:

13. Apply a light coating of gear lubricant on the lip of pinion seal.
14. Install seal with Installer C-3972-A and Handle C-4171, or equivalent,
15. Install the companion flange onto the pinion with Installer 9616, or equivalent.
16. Position holder against the companion flange and install four bolts and washers into the threaded holes. Tighten the bolt and washer so that the holder is held to the flange.
17. Install a new pinion nut onto the pinion shaft and tighten the pinion nut in stages.

➡Never loosen pinion nut to decrease pinion bearing rotating torque and never exceed specified preload torque. If preload torque or rotating torque is exceeded a new collapsible spacer must be installed.

18. Record the pinion rotating torque using a torque wrench. The rotating torque should be equal to the reading recorded during removal plus an additional 0.56 Nm (5 inch lbs.).
19. If the rotating torque is low, tighten the pinion nut in 6.8 Nm (5 ft. lbs.) increments until the proper rotating torque is achieved.

➡If the maximum tightening torque is reached prior to reaching the required rotating torque, the collapsible spacer may have been damaged. Replace the collapsible spacer.

20. Install propeller shaft with reference marks aligned.
21. Add gear lubricant to differential housing if necessary.
22. Install half shafts.

REAR AXLE HOUSING

REMOVAL & INSTALLATION

1. Raise and support vehicle.
2. Remove fill hole plug from the differential housing cover.
3. Remove differential housing cover and drain fluid.
4. Remove axle shafts.
5. Note the reference letters stamped on the bearing caps and housing machined sealing surface.
6. Loosen the differential bearing cap bolts.
7. Position Spreader W-129-B with Adapter Kit 6987B on differential locating holes. Install hold down clamps and tighten the turnbuckle finger-tight.
8. Install a Pilot Stud C-3288-B at the left side of the differential housing. Attach Dial Indicator C-3339 to pilot stud. Load the indicator plunger against the opposite side of the housing and zero the indicator.

⁂ CAUTION

Never spread the housing over 0.25mm (0.010 in). If housing is over-spread, it could distorted and damaged the housing.

9. Spread housing enough to remove the differential case from the housing. Measure the distance with the dial indicator.
10. Remove the dial indicator.
11. While holding the differential case in position, remove the differential bearing cap bolts and caps.
12. Remove differential from the housing and tag differential bearing cups to indicate location.
13. Remove spreader from housing.
14. Clean the housing cavity with flushing oil, light engine oil or lint free cloth.

➡ Do not use water, steam, kerosene or gasoline for cleaning.

To install:

⁂ CAUTION

The weight of the vehicle must be supported by the springs before suspension arms and track bar fasteners are tightened. If springs are not at their normal ride position, vehicle ride height and handling could be affected.

15. Raise axle with lift and align coil springs.
16. Install lower suspension arms in axle brackets. Install nuts and bolts, do not tighten bolts at this time.
17. Install upper suspension arm on rear axle ball joint.
18. Install rear axle ball joint nut and tighten to 90 ft. lbs. (122 Nm).
19. Install track bar and attachment bolts, do not tighten bolts at this time.
20. Install shock absorbers and tighten nuts to 44 ft. lbs. (60 Nm).
21. Install stabilizer bar links and tighten nuts to 27 ft. lbs. (36 Nm).
22. Install wheel speed sensors.
23. Connect parking brake cable to brackets and lever.
24. Install brake rotors and calipers.
25. Install the brake hose to the axle junction block.
26. Install axle vent hose.
27. Align propeller shaft and pinion yoke reference marks. Install U-joint straps and nuts tighten to 14 ft. lbs. (19 Nm).
28. Install the wheels and tires.
29. Add gear lubricant, if necessary.
30. Remove support and lower the vehicle.
31. Tighten lower suspension arm bolts to 130 ft. lbs. (177 Nm).
32. Tighten track bar bolts to 74 ft. lbs. (100 Nm).

REAR AXLE SHAFT, BEARING & SEAL

REMOVAL & INSTALLATION

See Figure 13.

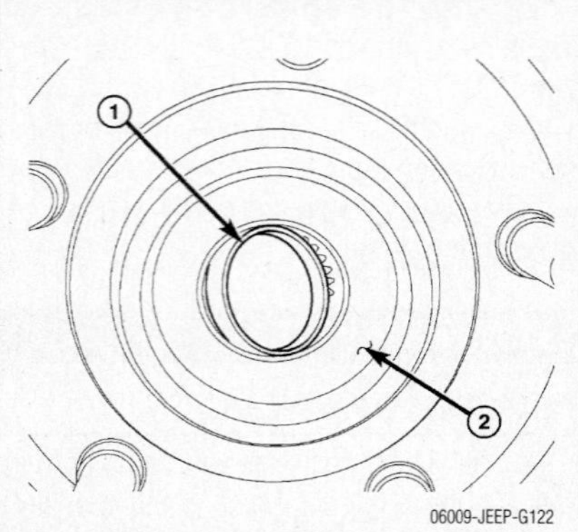

Fig. 13 Tap axle end plug loose from the axle flange

1. Before servicing the vehicle, refer to the precautions in the beginning of this manual.
2. With vehicle in neutral, position on hoist.
3. Remove calipers and rotors.
4. Tap axle end plug loose from the axle flange with a hammer and punch. Pull plug out of axle flange.
5. Remove speed sensors from axle tube flange.
6. Remove axle flange nuts from axle.
7. Pull axle shaft and backing plate out of axle tube until axle bearing is exposed.
8. Remove O-ring from the axle bearing.
9. Slide axle shaft from axle tube and backing plate.
10. Tap axle shaft out of the bearing and axle flange through the plug hole with a hammer and brass drift.

To install:

11. Tap axle shaft into through axle bearing into axle flange.
12. Install axle shaft into axle tube and backing plate with new O-ring on axle.
13. Slip O-ring through backing plate, then push axle through backing plate until bearing is exposed.
14. Install O-ring axle bearing.
15. Push axle into axle tube.
16. Install axle flange nuts and tighten to 88 ft. lbs. (119 Nm).
17. Install speed sensors in axle tube flange.
18. Coat new axle flange plug with Mopar® Stud and Bearing Mount Adhesive, or equivalent, and install plug.
19. Install calipers and rotors.

REAR DRIVESHAFT

REMOVAL & INSTALLATION

1. Before servicing the vehicle, refer to the precautions in the beginning of this manual.

2. Mark propeller shaft and pinion flange for installation reference.
3. Remove the front propeller shaft.

To install:

4. Install the propeller shaft with reference marks aligned.
5. Using new bolts, tighten them to 80 ft. lbs. (108 Nm).

REAR PINION SEAL

REMOVAL & INSTALLATION

1. Before servicing the vehicle, refer to the precautions in the beginning of this manual.
2. Raise and support the vehicle.
3. Mark the universal joint, companion flange and pinion shaft for installation reference.
4. Remove companion flange bolts and secure the shaft in an upright position to prevent damage to the rear universal joint.
5. Remove the wheel and tire assemblies.
6. Remove brake calipers and rotors to prevent any drag.
7. Rotate companion flange three or four times and verify flange rotates smoothly.
8. Measure rotating torque of the pinion with an inch pound torque wrench and record the reading for installation reference.
9. Install bolts into two of the threaded holes in the companion flange 180° apart.
10. Position Holder C–3281, or equivalent, against the companion flange and install a bolt and washer into one of the remaining threaded holes. Tighten the bolts so the Holder 6719, or equivalent, is held to the flange.
11. Remove the pinion nut and washer.
12. Remove companion flange with Remover C-452, or equivalent.
13. Remove pinion seal with a pry tool or slide hammer mounted screw.

To install:

➡The outer perimeter of the seal is pre-coated with a special sealant.

14. Apply a light coating of gear lubricant on the lip of pinion seal.
15. Install new pinion seal with Installer C-3972A and Handle C-4171, or equivalent.
16. Install companion flange on the end of the shaft with the reference marks aligned.
17. Install bolts into two of the threaded holes in the companion flange 180° apart.
18. Position the holder against the companion flange and install a bolt and washer into one of the remaining threaded holes. Tighten the bolts so the holder is held to the flange.
19. Install companion flange on pinion shaft.
20. Install the pinion washer and a new pinion nut. The convex side of the washer must face outward.

➡Do not exceed the minimum tightening torque when installing the companion flange retaining nut at this point. Damage to collapsible spacer or bearings may result.

21. Hold companion flange with and tighten the pinion nut to 210 ft. lbs (285 Nm). Rotate pinion several revolutions to ensure the bearing rollers are seated.
22. Rotate pinion with an inch pound torque wrench. Rotating torque should be equal to the reading recorded during removal plus an additional 5 inch lbs. (0.56 Nm).

➡Never loosen pinion nut to decrease pinion bearing rotating torque and never exceed specified preload torque. If rotating torque is exceeded, a new collapsible spacer must be installed.

23. If rotating torque is low tighten pinion nut in 5 ft. lbs. (6.8 Nm) increments until proper rotating.

➡The bearing rotating torque should be constant during a complete revolution of the pinion. If the rotating torque varies, this indicates a binding condition.

24. Install propeller shaft with the installation reference marks aligned.
25. Install the brake components.
26. Check the differential housing lubricant level.
27. Install wheel and tire assemblies and lower the vehicle.

ENGINE COOLING

ENGINE FAN

REMOVAL & INSTALLATION

Except 5.7L Engines

1. Disconnect the negative battery cable.
2. Access the cooling fan.
3. Label and disconnect the cooling fan electrical harness.

➡It may be necessary to loosen the mounting bolts for the air conditioning condenser to the body

4. Remove the fasteners that mount the cooling fan to the air conditioning condenser or radiator.
5. Lift the cooling fan out of the vehicle.

To install:

6. Insert the cooling fan into the vehicle.
7. Mount the cooling fan to the air conditioning condenser or radiator.
8. Connect the cooling fan electrical harness.
9. If removed, install any shrouding or grills.
10. Connect the negative battery cable.

5.7L Engines

1. Disconnect the negative battery cable.
2. Raise and safely support the vehicle.
3. Drain the cooling system.

➡The hydraulic fan drive is driven by the power steering pump. When removing lines or hoses from fan drive assembly use a drain pan to catch any power steering fluid that may exit the fan drive or the lines and hoses.

4. Disconnect two high pressure lines at hydraulic fan drive. Remove and discard o-rings from line fittings.
5. Disconnect low pressure return hose at hydraulic fan drive.

➡The lower mounting bolts can only be accessed from under vehicle.

6. Remove two lower mounting bolts from the shroud.
7. Lower the vehicle.
8. Unplug the electrical connector for the fan control solenoid.
9. Disconnect the radiator upper hose at the radiator and position out of the way.
10. Disconnect the power steering gear outlet hose and fluid return hose at the cooler.
11. Remove two upper mounting bolts from the shroud.
12. Remove the shroud and fan drive from vehicle.

13. Installation is the reverse of removal. Lubricate the O-rings on the fittings with power steering fluid then connect inlet and outlet high pressure lines to fan drive. Tighten inlet line to 36 ft. lbs. (49 Nm) and tighten the outlet line to 22 ft. lbs. (29 Nm). Refill the power steering fluid reservoir and bleed the air from the steering system.

RADIATOR

REMOVAL & INSTALLATION

1. Disconnect the negative battery cable at battery.
2. Drain coolant from radiator.
3. Remove the front grill.
4. Remove two radiator mounting bolts.
5. Disconnect both transmission cooler lines from radiator.
6. Disconnect electrical connector for the fan control solenoid.
7. Disconnect the power steering cooler line from cooler and filter.
8. Disconnect the radiator upper and lower hoses.
9. Disconnect the overflow hose from radiator.
10. Remove the air inlet duct at the grill.
11. The lower part of radiator is equipped with two alignment dowel pins. They are located on the bottom of radiator tank and fit into rubber grommets. These rubber grommets are pressed into the radiator lower crossmember.

**** WARNING**

The air conditioning system (if equipped) is under a constant pressure even with the engine off.

12. Remove the cooling fan assembly.
13. Gently lift up and remove radiator from vehicle. Be careful not to scrape the radiator fins against any other component. Also be careful not to disturb the air conditioning condenser (if equipped).

To install:

**** CAUTION**

Before installing the radiator or A/C condenser, be sure the radiator-to-body and radiator-to-A/C condenser rubber air seals are properly fastened to their original positions. These are used at the top, bottom and sides of the radiator and A/C condenser. To prevent overheating, these seals must be installed to their original positions.

14. Equipped with air conditioning: Gently lower the radiator and fan shroud into the vehicle. Guide the two radiator alignment dowels through the holes in the rubber air seals first and then through the A/C support brackets. Continue to guide the alignment dowels into the rubber grommets located in lower radiator crossmember. The holes in the L-shaped brackets (located on bottom of A/C condenser) must be positioned between bottom of rubber air seals and top of rubber grommets.
15. Connect the radiator upper and lower hoses and hose clamps to radiator.

**** CAUTION**

The tangs on the hose clamps must be positioned straight down.

16. Install coolant reserve/overflow tank hose at radiator.
17. Connect both transmission cooler lines at the radiator.
18. Install both radiator mounting bolts.
19. Install air inlet duct at grill.
20. Attach electric connector for hydraulic fan control solenoid.
21. Install the grill.
22. Install the cooling fan assembly.
23. Connect the power steering filter hoses to the filter. Install new hose clamps.
24. Rotate the fan blades (by hand) and check for interference at fan shroud.
25. Refill cooling system.
26. Refill the power steering reservoir and bleed air from system.
27. Connect battery cable at battery.
28. Start and warm engine. Check for leaks.

THERMOSTAT

REMOVAL & INSTALLATION

3.7L and 4.7L Engines

**** WARNING**

Do not loosen radiator drain cock with system hot and pressurized. Serious burns from coolant can occur.

➡Do not waste reusable coolant. If solution is clean, drain coolant into a clean container for reuse. If thermostat is being replaced, be sure that replacement is specified thermostat for vehicle model and engine type.

1. Disconnect negative battery cable at battery.
2. Drain cooling system.
3. Raise vehicle on hoist.
4. Remove splash shield.
5. Remove lower radiator hose clamp and lower radiator hose at thermostat housing.
6. Remove thermostat housing mounting bolts, thermostat housing and thermostat.

To install:

7. Clean mating areas of timing chain cover and thermostat housing.
8. Install thermostat (spring side down) into recessed machined groove on timing chain cover.
9. Position thermostat housing on timing chain cover.
10. Install two housing-to-timing chain cover bolts. Tighten bolts to 115 inch lbs. (13 Nm).

**** CAUTION**

Housing must be tightened evenly and thermostat must be centered into recessed groove in timing chain cover. If not, it may result in a cracked housing, damaged timing chain cover threads or coolant leaks.

11. Install lower radiator hose on thermostat housing.
12. Install splash shield.
13. Lower vehicle.
14. Fill cooling system.
15. Connect negative battery cable to battery.
16. Start and warm the engine. Check for leaks.

5.7L Engine

**** WARNING**

Do not loosen radiator drain cock with system hot and pressurized. Serious burns from coolant can occur.

➡Do not waste reusable coolant. If solution is clean, drain coolant into a clean container for reuse. If thermostat is being replaced, be sure that replacement is specified thermostat for vehicle model and engine type.

1. Disconnect the negative battery cable.
2. Drain the cooling system.
3. Remove the radiator hose clamp and radiator hose at the thermostat housing.
4. Remove the thermostat housing mounting bolts , thermostat housing and thermostat.

To install:

5. Position the thermostat and housing on the front cover.

6. Install thermostat housing bolts. Tighten the bolts to 112 inch lbs. (13 Nm).
7. Install the radiator hose onto the thermostat housing.
8. Fill the cooling system.
9. Connect negative battery cable.
10. Start and warm the engine. Check for leaks.

WATER PUMP

REMOVAL & INSTALLATION

3.7L Engine

See Figure 14.

1. Before servicing the vehicle, refer to the precautions in the beginning of this manual.
2. Drain the cooling system.
3. Remove or disconnect the following:
   - Negative battery cable
   - Fan and clutch assembly from the pump
   - Fan shroud and fan assembly. If you're reusing the fan clutch, keep it upright to avoid silicone fluid loss!
   - Lower hose
   - Water pump (8 bolts)
4. Installation is the reverse of removal. Tighten the bolts, in sequence, to 40 ft. lbs. (54 Nm).

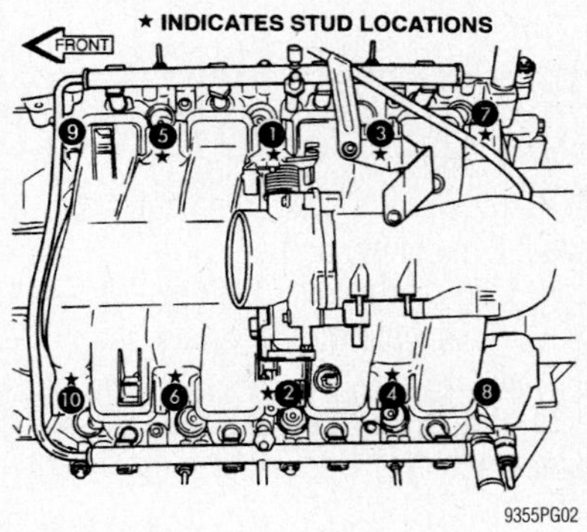

Fig. 14 Water pump tightening sequence—3.7L engine

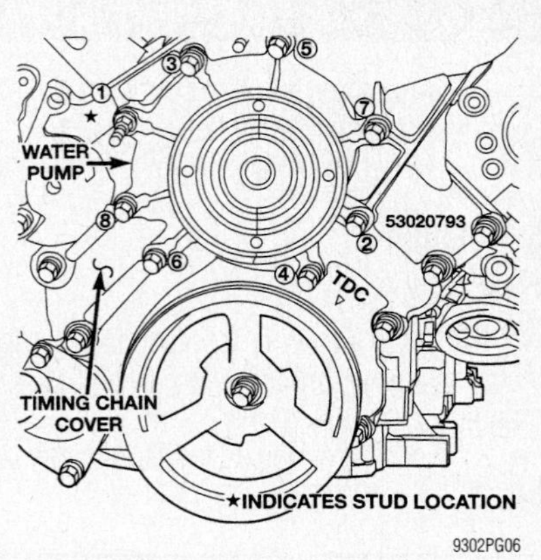

Fig. 15 Water pump torque sequence—4.7L engine

4.7L Engine

See Figure 15.

1. Before servicing the vehicle, refer to the precautions in the beginning of this manual.
2. Drain the cooling system.
3. Remove or disconnect the following:
   - Negative battery cable
   - Fan and clutch assembly from the pump
   - Fan shroud and fan assembly. If you're reusing the fan clutch, keep it upright to avoid silicone fluid loss!
   - Drive belt
   - Lower radiator hose from the water pump
   - Water pump
4. Clean the mating surfaces of all gasket material.

To install:

5. Install or connect the following:
   - Water pump using a new gasket. Torque the bolts to 40 ft. lbs. (54 Nm).
   - Lower radiator hose
   - Drive belt
   - Negative battery cable
6. Fill and bleed the cooling system.
7. Start the engine, check for leaks and repair if necessary.

5.7L Engine

1. Before servicing the vehicle, refer to the precautions in the beginning of this manual.
2. Disconnect negative battery cable.
3. Drain coolant.
4. Remove serpentine belt.
5. Remove fan clutch assembly.
6. Remove coolant fill bottle.
7. Disconnect washer bottle wiring and hose.
8. Remove fan shroud assembly.
9. Remove A/C compressor and generator brace.
10. Remove idler pulleys.
11. Remove belt tensioner assembly.
12. Remove upper and lower radiator hoses.
13. Remove heater hoses.
14. Remove water pump mounting bolts and remove pump.

To install:

15. Install water pump and mounting bolts. Tighten mounting bolts to 18 ft. lbs. (24 Nm).
16. Install heater hoses.
17. Install upper and lower radiator hoses.
18. Install belt tensioner assembly.
19. Install idler pulleys.
20. Install A/C compressor and alternator brace. Tighten bolt and nuts to 21 ft. lbs. (28 Nm).
21. Install fan shroud assembly.
22. Connect washer bottle wiring and hose.
23. Install coolant fill bottle.
24. Install fan clutch assembly.
25. Install serpentine belt.
26. Connect negative battery cable.
27. Fill coolant.
28. Pressure test coolant system.

ALTERNATOR

REMOVAL & INSTALLATION

Except 5.7L Engine

See Figure 16.

1. Before servicing the vehicle, refer to the precautions in the beginning of this manual.
2. Remove or disconnect the following:
   - Negative battery cable
   - Accessory drive belt
   - Alternator harness connectors
   - Alternator
   - Mounting bolts and alternator

➡The 3.7L and 4.7L engines have 1 vertical and 2 horizontal bolts.

To install:

3. Before servicing the vehicle, refer to the precautions in the beginning of this manual.
4. Install the alternator and tighten the bolts to the following specifications:
   - 3.7L engine: Tighten the horizontal bolts to 42 ft. lbs. (57 Nm), then the vertical bolt to 29 ft. lbs. (40 Nm)
   - 4.7L engine: Vertical bolt and long horizontal bolt to 41 ft. lbs. (56 Nm), short horizontal bolt to 55 ft. lbs. (74 Nm)
5. Install or connect the following:
   - Alternator harness connectors
   - Accessory drive belt
   - Negative battery cable

5.7L Engine

See Figure 17.

1. Before servicing the vehicle, refer to the precautions in the beginning of this manual.
2. Disconnect negative battery cable at battery.
3. Remove generator drive belt.
4. Unsnap plastic insulator cap from B+ output terminal.
5. Remove B+ terminal mounting nut at rear of generator. Disconnect terminal from generator.
6. Disconnect field wire connector at rear of generator by pushing on connector tab.
7. Remove 2 generator mounting bolts.
8. Remove generator from vehicle.

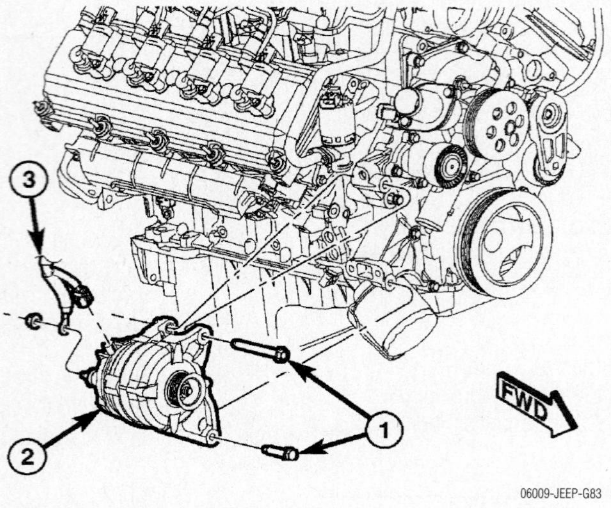

Fig. 17 Alternator mounting—5.7L engine

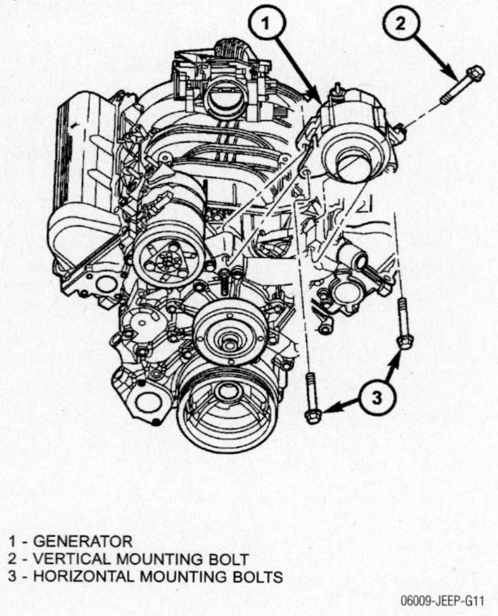

Fig. 16 3.7L engine alternator mounting

To install:

9. Position generator to engine and install 2 mounting bolts.
10. Tighten bolts to 30 ft. lbs. (41 Nm).
11. Snap field wire connector into rear of generator.
12. Install B+ terminal eyelet to generator output stud. Tighten mounting nut.

WARNING

Never force a belt over a pulley rim using a screwdriver. The synthetic fiber of the belt can be damaged.

➡When installing a serpentine accessory drive belt, the belt MUST be routed correctly. The water pump may be rotating in the wrong direction if the belt is installed incorrectly, causing the engine to overheat.

13. Install generator drive belt.
14. Install negative battery cable to battery.

FIRING ORDER

See Figures 18 through 20.

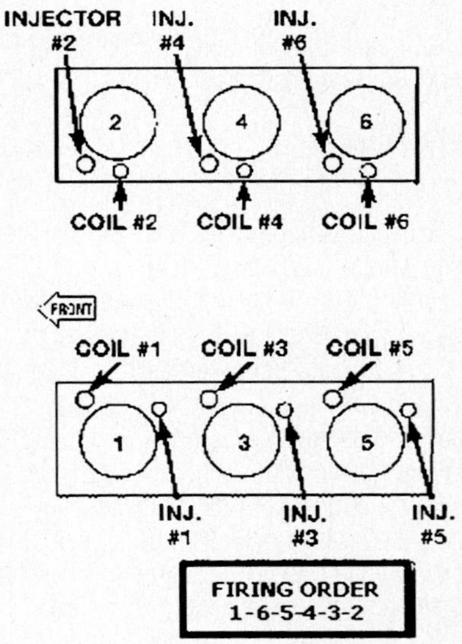

32050_DAKO_G0025

Fig. 18 3.7L engine
Firing order: 1-6-5-4-3-2
Distributorless ignition

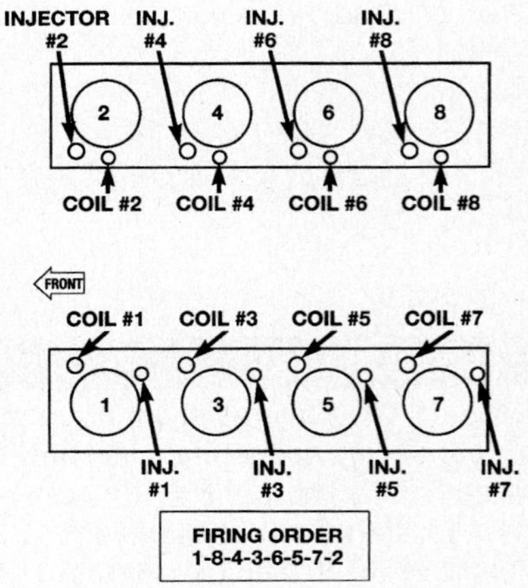

67189-DAKO-G50

Fig. 19 4.7L engine
Firing order: 1-8-4-3-6-5-7-2
Distributorless ignition

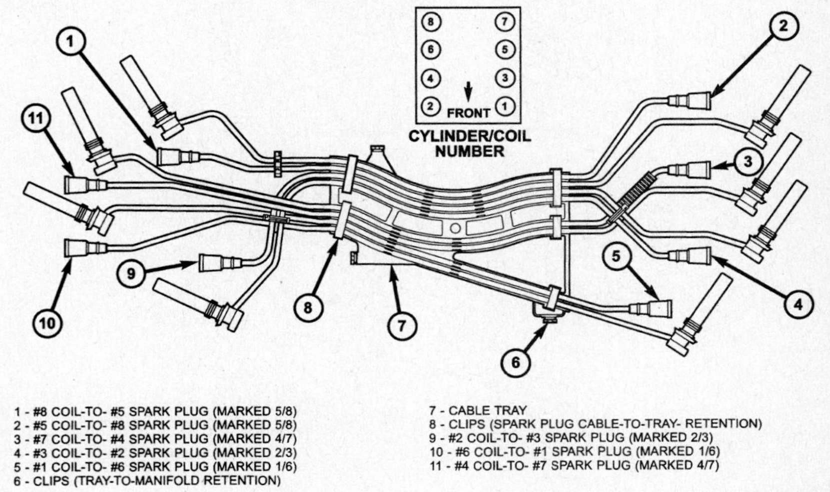

67189-DURA-G05

Fig. 20 5.7L Engine
Firing order: 1–8–4–3–6–5–7–2
Distributorless ignition

IGNITION COIL

REMOVAL & INSTALLATION

3.7L and 4.7L Engines

See Figures 21 and 22.

1. Certain coils may require removal of the throttle body air intake tube or intake box for access.
2. Disconnect the negative battery cable.
3. Detach the electrical connector from the coil by pushing downward on the release lock on top of the connector and pulling the connector from the coil.
4. Clean the area at the base of each coil with compressed air.
5. Remove the coil mounting nut(s). Pull the coil up with a slight twisting action and remove it from the vehicle.
6. Installation is the reverse of removal. Smear the coil O–ring with silicone grease.

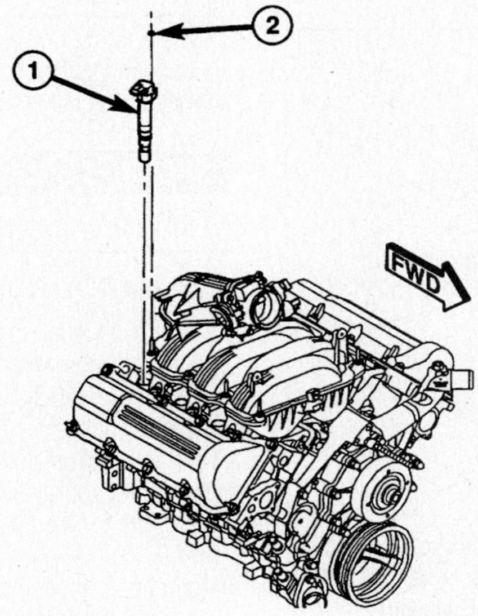

32050_DAKO_G0008

Fig. 21 3.7L V6 Coil Location (1) Ignition Coil (2) Coil Mounting Nut

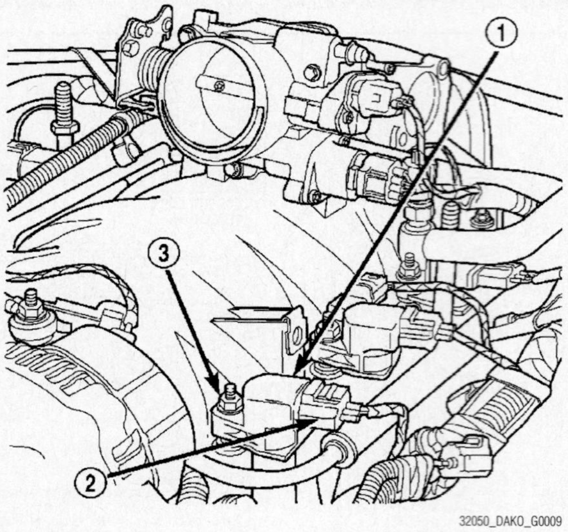

Fig. 22 4.7L V8 Coil Location (1) Ignition Coil (2) Coil Electrical Connector (3) Coil Mounting Stud/Nut

Tighten the mounting nut to 70 inch lbs. (8 Nm). Connect the wiring.

5.7L Engines

See Figure 23.

1. Certain coils may require removal of the throttle body air intake tube or intake box for access.
2. Disconnect the negative battery cable.
3. Unlock connector by first releasing slide lock and pressing on lock release while pulling connector from coil.
4. Remove secondary high—voltage wire with a twisting motion.
5. Loosen coil mounting bolts; the mounting bolts are retained by the coil body.
6. Pull the coil up with a slight twisting action.
7. Installation is the reverse of removal. Smear the coil O–ring with silicone grease. Tighten the mounting nut to 9 ft. lbs. (12 Nm). Connect the wiring.

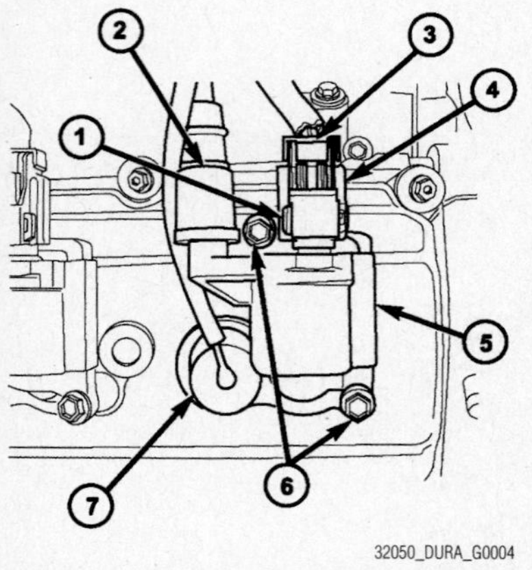

Fig. 23 5.7L Coil location on valve cover. (1) Slide lock (2) Secondary wire (3) Lock release (4) Coil electrical connector (5) Ignition coil (6) Mounting bolts (7) Secondary wire

➡To prevent ignition crossfire, spark plug cables MUST be placed in cable tray (routing loom) into their original position.

IGNITION TIMING

ADJUSTMENT

The ignition timing is controlled by the Powertrain Control Module (PCM). No adjustment is necessary or possible.

SPARK PLUGS

REMOVAL & INSTALLATION

3.7L and 4.7L Engines

Each individual spark plug is located under each ignition coil. Each individual ignition coil must be removed to gain access to each spark plug. Refer to Ignition Coil Removal/Installation. Prior to removing a spark plug, spray compressed air around base of the ignition coil at cylinder head. This will help prevent foreign material from entering combustion chamber.

1. Remove spark plug from cylinder head using a quality socket with a rubber or foam insert.
2. Inspect spark plug condition.

To install:

3. Start the spark plug into the cylinder head by hand to avoid cross threading.
4. Before installing coil(s), check condition of coil O–ring and replace as necessary. To aid in coil installation, apply silicone to coil O–ring.
5. Tighten spark plugs to 20 ft. lbs. (27 Nm) torque.
6. Install ignition coil(s). Refer to Ignition Coil Removal/Installation.

5.7L Engines

See Figure 24.

Sixteen spark plugs (2 per cylinder) are used with 5.7L V8 engines.

Eight of the 16 spark plugs are located under an ignition coil; the other 8 are not. If the spark plug being removed is under a coil, the coil must be removed to gain access to the spark plug. Refer to Ignition Coil Removal/Installation.

Before removing or disconnecting any spark plug cables, note their original position. Remove cables one at a time. To prevent ignition crossfire, spark plug cables **MUST** be placed in cable tray (routing loom) into their original position. Refer to Spark Plug Cable Removal for proper routing.

Before installing spark plug cables to either the spark plugs or coils, apply dielectric grease to inside of boots.

1. Remove necessary air filter tubing at throttle body.
2. Prior to removing an ignition coil (if necessary), spray compressed air around the coil base at cylinder head cover.
3. Prior to removing a spark plug, spray compressed air into cylinder head opening. This will help prevent foreign material from entering combustion chamber.
4. Remove spark plug from cylinder head using a quality socket with a rubber or foam insert.
5. Inspect spark plug condition.

To install:

⁂ WARNING

The 5.7L V8 is equipped with torque critical design spark plugs. Do not exceed 15 ft. lbs. (20 Nm) torque during installation. Special care should be taken when installing spark plugs into the cylinder head spark plug wells; be sure the plugs do not drop into the plug wells as electrodes can be damaged.

6. Start the spark plug into cylinder head by hand to avoid cross threading aluminum

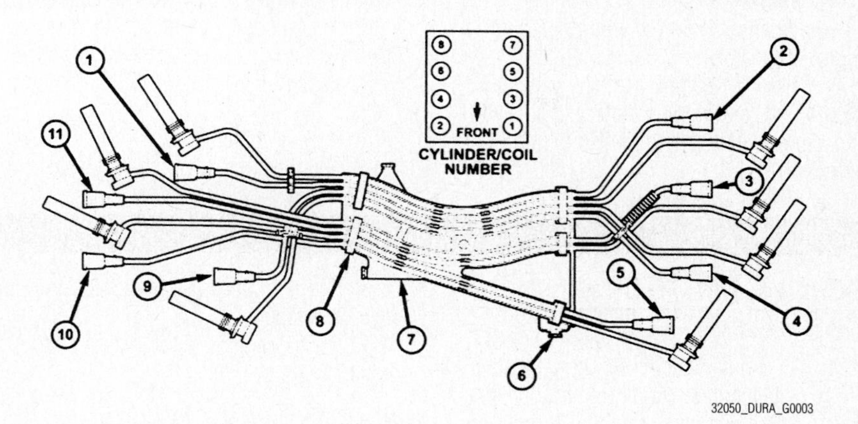

Fig. 24 Spark Plug Cable Routing—5.7L engine

threads. To aid in installation, attach an old spark plug boot or a piece of rubber hose to spark plug.

7. Before installing spark plug cables to either the spark plugs or coils, apply dielectric grease to inside of boots.

8. To prevent ignition crossfire, spark plug cables **MUST** be placed in cable tray (routing loom) into their original position.

9. Spark plug cables on the 5.7L engine are paired on cylinders 1 & 6, 2 & 3, 4 & 7 and 5 & 8. Before removing or disconnecting any spark plug cables, **note their original position** and remove cables one at a time. To prevent ignition crossfire, spark plug cables **MUST** be placed in cable tray (routing loom) into their original position. The cable retention clips must also be securely locked.

10. Install ignition coil(s) to necessary spark plugs. Refer to Ignition Coil Installation.

11. Install spark plug cables to remaining spark plugs. Remember to apply dielectric grease to inside of boots.

12. Tighten spark plugs.

ENGINE ELECTRICAL

STARTING SYSTEM

STARTER

REMOVAL & INSTALLATION

3.7L and 4.7L Engines

See Figure 25.

1. Disconnect and isolate negative battery cable.
2. Raise and support vehicle.
3. Note: If equipped with 4WD and certain transmissions, a support bracket is used between front axle and side of transmission. Remove 2 support bracket bolts at transmission. Pry support bracket slightly to gain access to lower starter mounting bolt.
4. Remove two bolts if equipped with an automatic transmission.
5. Move starter motor towards front of vehicle far enough for nose of starter pinion housing to clear housing. Always support starter motor during this process, do not let starter motor hang from wire harness.
6. Tilt nose downwards and lower starter motor far enough to access and remove nut that secures battery positive cable wire harness connector eyelet to solenoid battery terminal stud. Do not let starter motor hang from wire harness.
7. Remove battery positive cable wire harness connector eyelet from solenoid battery terminal stud.
8. Disconnect battery positive cable wire harness connector from solenoid terminal connector receptacle.
9. Remove starter motor.

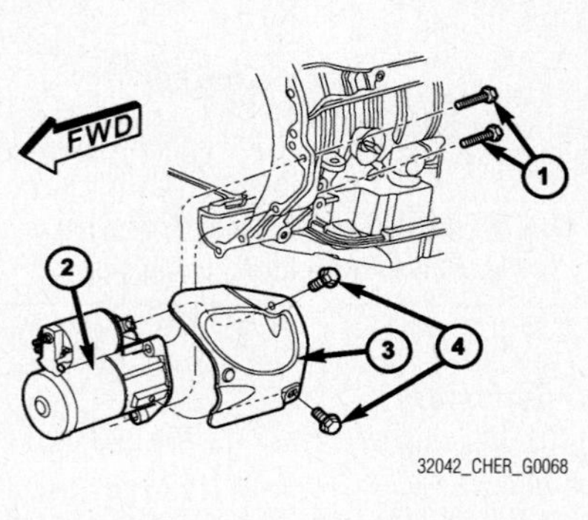

Fig. 25 Starter mounting—3.7L and 4.7L engines

To install:

10. Connect solenoid wire to starter motor (snaps on).
11. Position battery cable to solenoid stud. Install and tighten battery cable eyelet nut. Do not allow starter motor to hang from wire harness.
12. Position starter motor to transmission.
13. If equipped with automatic transmission, slide cooler tube bracket into position.
14. Install and tighten both bolts.
15. Lower vehicle.
16. Connect negative battery cable.

5.7L Engine

See Figure 26.

1. Disconnect and isolate negative battery cable.
2. Raise and support vehicle.
3. Note: If equipped with 4WD and certain transmissions, a support bracket is used between front axle and side of transmission. Remove 2 support bracket bolts at transmission. Pry support bracket slightly to gain access to lower starter mounting bolt.
4. Remove two mounting bolts.
5. Move starter motor towards front of vehicle far enough for nose of starter pinion housing to clear housing. Always support starter motor during this process, do not let starter motor hang from wire harness.
6. Tilt nose downwards and lower starter motor far enough to access and remove nut that secures battery positive cable wire harness connector eyelet to solenoid battery terminal stud. Do not let starter motor hang from wire harness.

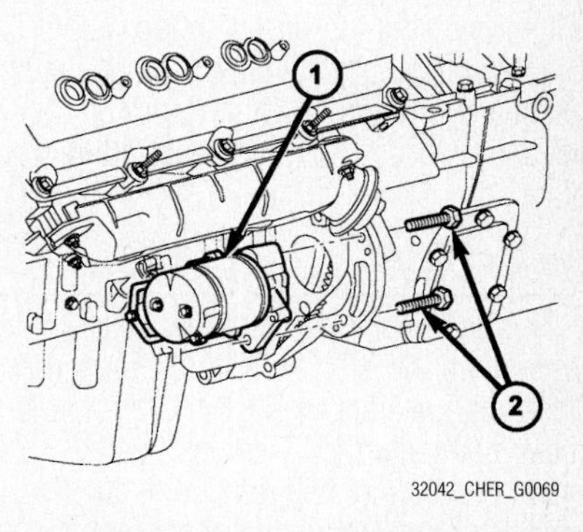

Fig. 26 The 5.7L engine starter mounting point

7. Remove battery positive cable wire harness connector eyelet from solenoid battery terminal stud.

8. Disconnect battery positive cable wire harness connector from solenoid terminal connector receptacle.

9. Remove starter motor.

To install:

10. Connect solenoid wire to starter motor (snaps on).

11. Position battery cable to solenoid stud. Install and tighten battery cable eyelet nut. Do not allow starter motor to hang from wire harness.

12. Position starter motor to engine.

13. If equipped with automatic transmission, slide cooler tube bracket into position.

14. Install and tighten both mounting bolts.

15. Lower vehicle.

16. Connect negative battery cable.

ENGINE MECHANICAL

➡Disconnecting the negative battery cable may interfere with the functions of the on board computer systems and may require the computer to undergo a relearning process, once the negative battery cable is reconnected.

ACCESSORY DRIVE BELTS

ACCESSORY BELT ROUTING

See Figure 27.

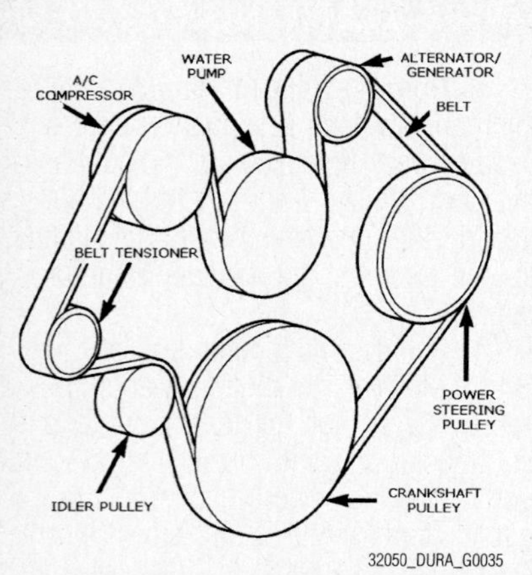

Fig. 27 Belt routing—3.7L, 4.7L and 5.7L engines

INSPECTION

Inspect the drive belt for signs of glazing or cracking. A glazed belt will be perfectly smooth from slippage, while a good belt will have a slight texture of fabric visible. Cracks will usually start at the inner edge of the belt and run outward. All worn or damaged drive belts should be replaced immediately.

ADJUSTMENT

It is not necessary to adjust belt tension on the 3.7L, 4.7L or 5.7L engines. These engines are equipped with an automatic belt tensioner. The tensioner maintains correct belt tension at all times; consequently, do not attempt to use a belt tension gauge on these engines.

REMOVAL & INSTALLATION

See Figure 28.

1. Disconnect negative battery cable.

2. Rotate belt tensioner until it contacts its stop. Remove belt, then slowly rotate the tensioner into the freearm position.

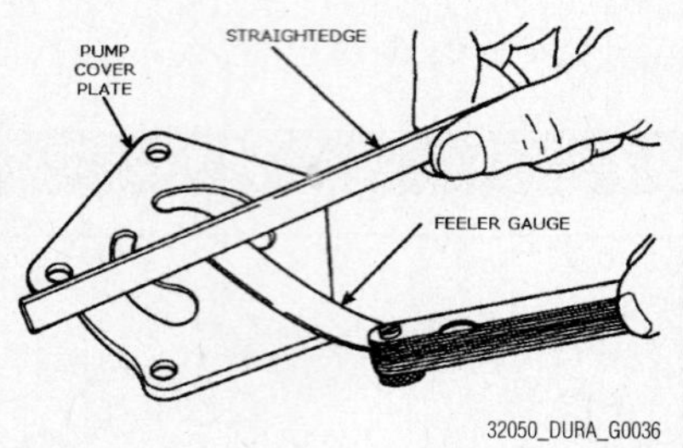

Fig. 28 Belt tensioner. Note dimension "A" when working with 4.7L engines

To install:

3. Install new belt. Route the belt around all pulleys except the idler pulley.

4. Rotate the tensioner arm until it contacts its stop position.

5. Route the belt around the idler and slowly let the tensioner rotate into the belt. Make sure the belt is seated onto all pulleys.

6. With the drive belt installed, inspect the belt wear indicator. On 4.7L Engines only, the gap between the tang and the housing stop (measurement A) must not exceed 0.94 inches (24 mm). If the measurement exceeds this specification replace the serpentine accessory drive belt.

CAMSHAFT AND VALVE LIFTERS

INSPECTION

1. Inspect the camshaft bearing journals for wear or damage.

2. Inspect the cylinder head and check oil return holes.

3. Check the tooth surface of the distributor drive gear teeth of the right camshaft for wear or damage.

4. Check both camshaft surfaces for wear or damage.

5. Check camshaft lobe height and replace if out of limit.

REMOVAL & INSTALLATION

3.7L and 4.7L Engines

See Figures 29 through 32.

1. Before servicing the vehicle, refer to the precautions in the beginning of this manual.

2. Remove or disconnect the following:
   - Negative battery cable
   - Valve covers
   - Rocker arms
   - Hydraulic lash adjusters

➡Keep all valvetrain components in order for assembly.

3. Set the engine at Top Dead Center (TDC) of the compression stroke for the No. 1 cylinder.

4. Install Timing Chain Wedge 8350 to retain the chain tensioners.

5. Matchmark the timing chains to the camshaft sprockets.

6. Install Camshaft Holding Tool 6958 and Adapter Pins 8346 to the left camshaft sprocket.

7. Remove or disconnect the following:
   - Right camshaft timing sprocket and target wheel
   - Left camshaft sprocket
   - Camshaft bearing caps, by reversing the tightening sequence
   - Camshafts

To install:

8. Install or connect the following:
   - Camshafts. Tighten the bearing cap bolts in ½ turn increments, in sequence, to 100 inch lbs. (11 Nm).
   - Target wheel to the right camshaft
   - Camshaft timing sprockets and chains, by aligning the matchmarks

9. Remove the tensioner wedges and tighten the camshaft sprocket bolts to 90 ft. lbs. (122 Nm).

10. Install or connect the following:
   - Hydraulic lash adjusters in their original locations

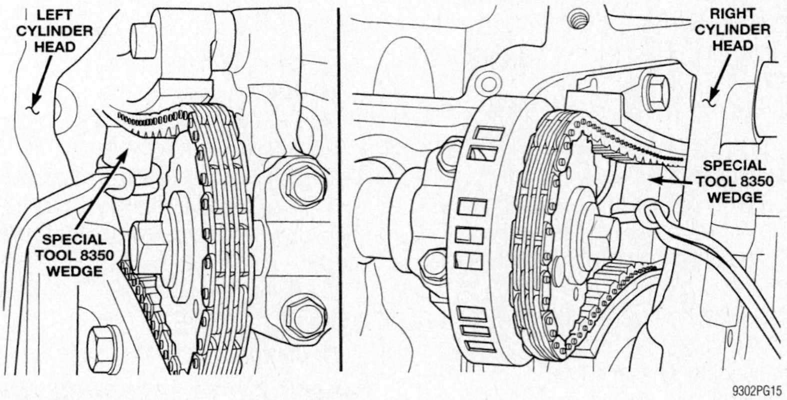

Fig. 29 Chain Tensioner Retaining Wedges—4.7L engine

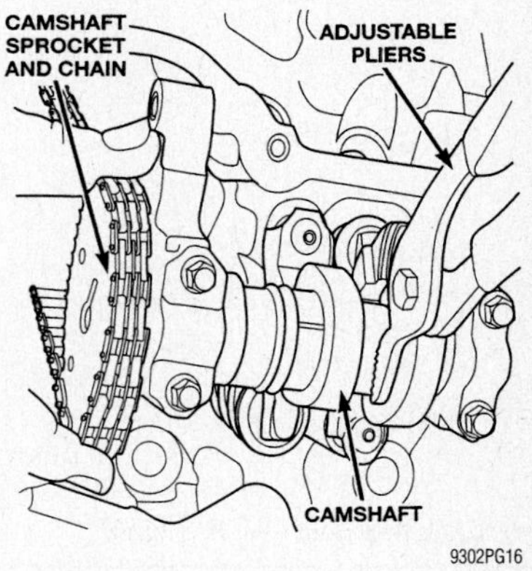

Fig. 32 Turn the camshaft with pliers, if needed, to align the dowel in the sprocket—4.7L engine

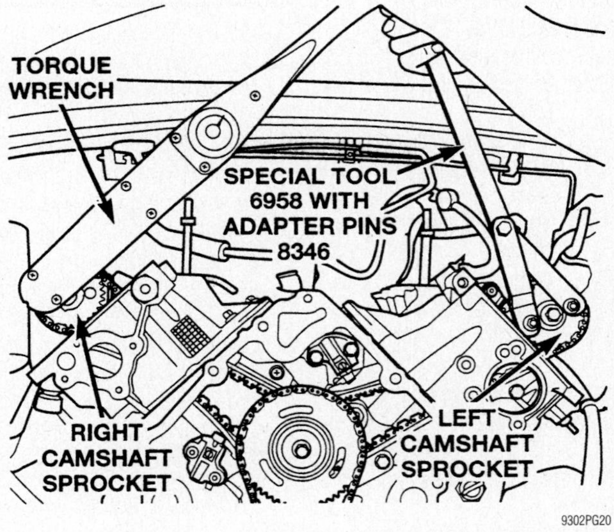

Fig. 30 Hold the left camshaft sprocket with a spanner wrench while removing or installing the camshaft sprocket bolts—3.7L and 4.7L engine

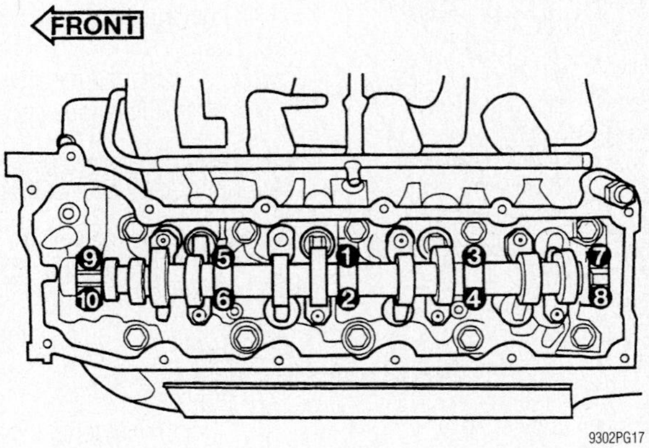

Fig. 31 Camshaft bearing cap bolt tightening sequence—3.7L and 4.7L engines

- Rocker arms in their original locations
- Valve covers
- Negative battery cable

5.7L Engine

See Figure 33.

1. Before servicing the vehicle, refer to the precautions in the beginning of this manual.
2. Drain the cooling system.
3. Recover the A/C refrigerant, if equipped with air conditioning.
4. Set the crankshaft to Top Dead Center (TDC) of the compression stroke for the No. 1 cylinder.
5. Remove or disconnect the following:
   - Negative battery cable
   - Camshaft rear cam bearing core plug
   - Air cleaner
   - Accessory drive belt
   - Alternator
   - A/C compressor
   - Radiator
   - Intake manifold
   - Valve covers
   - Cylinder heads
   - Oil pan
   - Front cover
   - Oil pickup tube
   - Oil pump
   - Timing chain and sprockets
   - Camshaft thrust plate
   - Hydraulic lifters
   - Camshaft

To install:

6. Install or connect the following:
   - Camshaft
   - Camshaft thrust plate. Tighten the bolts to 21 ft. lbs. (28 Nm).

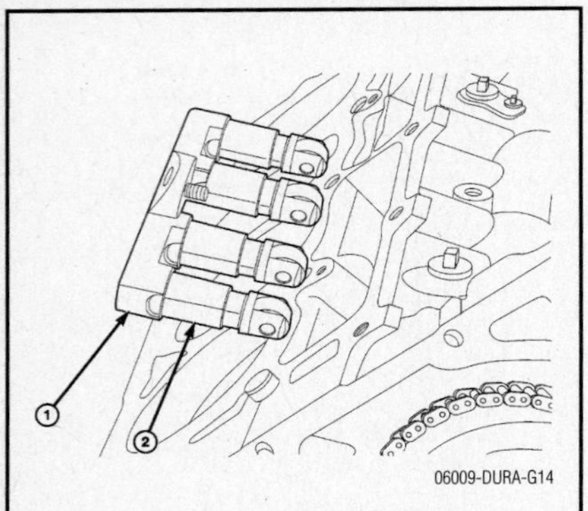

Fig. 33 Lifter group—5.7L engine

- Timing chain and sprockets
- Oil pump
- Oil pickup tube

➡**Lifters must be replaced in their original positions.**

- Hydraulic lifters
- Cylinder heads
- Pushrods
- Rocker arms
- Front cover
- Oil pan
- Valve covers
- Intake manifold
- A/C compressor
- Alternator
- Accessory drive belt
- Radiator
- Air cleaner
- Camshaft rear cam bearing core plug
- Negative battery cable

7. Fill the cooling system.
8. Recharge the A/C system, if equipped.
9. Start the engine and check for leaks.

CRANKSHAFT FRONT SEAL

REMOVAL & INSTALLATION

3.7L and 4.7L Engines

See Figure 34.

1. Disconnect the negative battery cable.
2. Drain the cooling system.
3. Remove the accessory drive belt.
4. Remove the A/C compressor mounting bolts and set the compressor aside.

➡**It is not necessary to disconnect the A/C lines from the compressor.**

5. Remove the upper radiator hose.
6. Disconnect the engine fan electrical connector, located inside the radiator shroud.
7. Remove the engine fan.
8. Remove the camshaft damper bolt.
9. Using Special Tool 8513 Insert and 1026 three-jaw puller, remove the crankshaft damper.
10. Remove the seal using Special Tool 8511.

To install:

11. Using Special Tools 8348 and 8512, install the crankshaft front seal.
12. Install the crankshaft damper as follows:
    a. Align the crankshaft damper slot with the key in the crankshaft. Slide the damper onto the crankshaft.
    b. Assemble Special Tool 8512-A. The nut is threaded onto the threaded rod first. Then the roller bearing is placed onto the threaded rod (The hardened bearing surface of the bearing MUST face the nut). Then the hardened washer slides onto the threaded rod. Once assembled coat the threaded rod's threads with Mopar® Nickel Anti-Seize or equivalent.
    c. Using Special Tool 8512-A, press the damper onto the crankshaft.
13. Install the crankshaft damper bolt and tighten to 130 ft. lbs. (175 Nm).
14. Install the engine fan.
15. Install the upper radiator hose.
16. Install the A/C compressor and tighten the mounting bolts to 40 ft. lbs. (54 Nm).
17. Install the accessory drive belt.
18. Refill the cooling system to the correct level.
19. Connect the negative battery cable.
20. Start the engine and check for leaks.

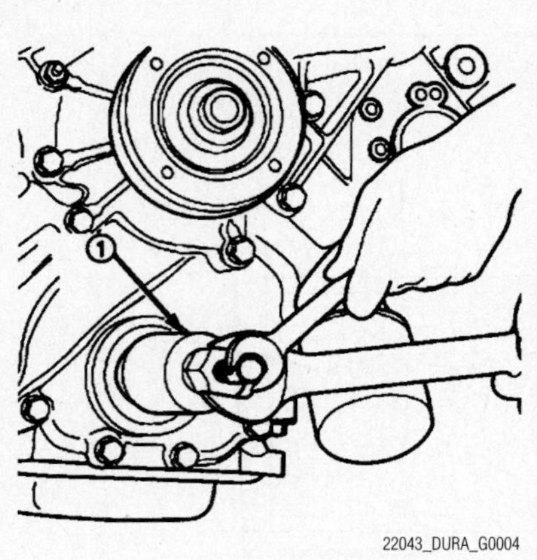

Fig. 34 A special tool is required to remove and install the seal without removing the front timing cover

5.7L Engines

1. Disconnect the negative battery cable.
2. Drain the cooling system.
3. Remove the accessory drive belt.
4. Remove the upper radiator hose.
5. Remove the engine fan.
6. Remove the crankshaft damper bolt.
7. Using Special Tool 8513 Insert and 1026 three-jaw puller, remove the crankshaft damper.
8. Using Special Tool 9071, remove the crankshaft front seal.

To install:

⁂ WARNING

The front crankshaft seal must be installed dry, without any lubricant applied to the sealing lip or outer edge.

9. Using Special Tools 9072 and 8512-A, install the crankshaft front seal.
10. Install the crankshaft damper as follows:
    a. Align the crankshaft damper slot with the key in the crankshaft. Slide the damper onto the crankshaft.
    b. Assemble Special Tool 8512-A. The nut is threaded onto the threaded rod first. Then the roller bearing is placed onto the threaded rod (The hardened bearing surface of the bearing MUST face the nut). Then the hardened washer slides onto the threaded rod. Once assembled coat the threaded rod's threads with Mopar® Nickel Anti-Seize or equivalent.
    c. Using Special Tool 8512-A, press the damper onto the crankshaft.
11. Install the crankshaft damper bolt and tighten to 129 ft. lbs. (176 Nm).
12. Install the engine fan.
13. Install the upper radiator hose.
14. Install the accessory drive belt.
15. Refill the cooling system to the correct level.
16. Connect the negative battery cable.
17. Start the engine and check for leaks.

CYLINDER HEAD

REMOVAL & INSTALLATION

3.7L Engine

Left Side

See Figures 35 through 38.

1. Before servicing the vehicle, refer to the precautions in the beginning of this manual.

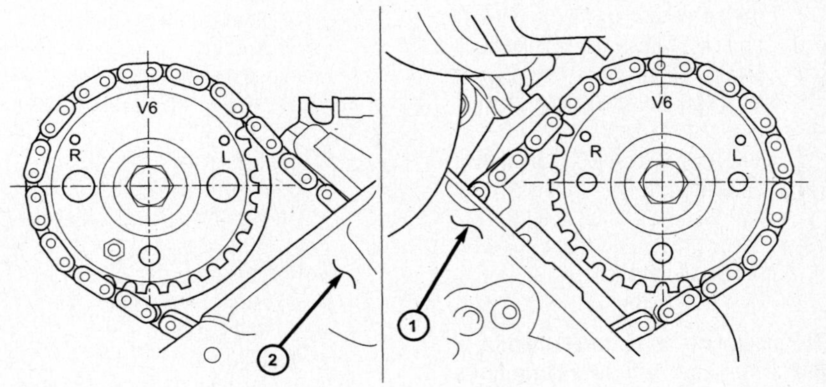

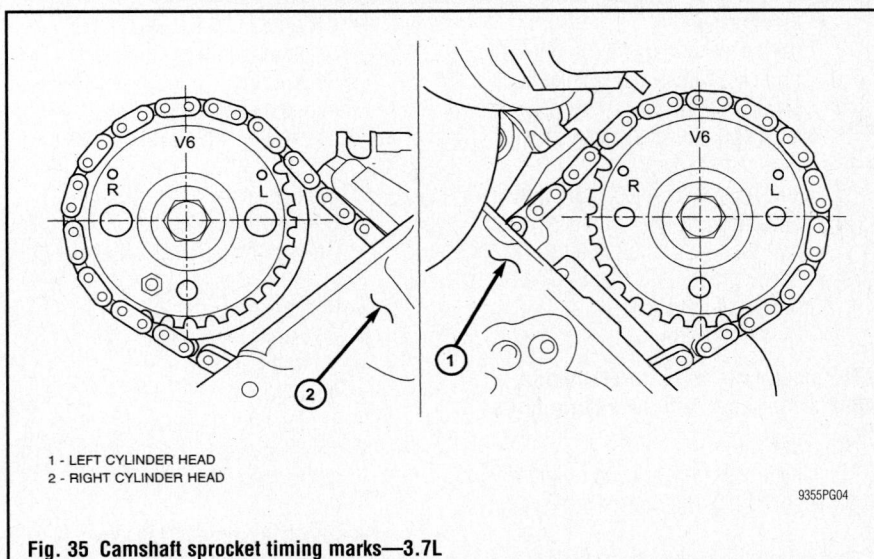

1 - LEFT CYLINDER HEAD
2 - RIGHT CYLINDER HEAD

9355PG04

Fig. 35 Camshaft sprocket timing marks—3.7L

2. Drain the cooling system.
3. Properly relieve the fuel system pressure.
4. Remove or disconnect the following:
   - Negative battery cable
   - Exhaust Y-pipe
   - Intake manifold
   - Cylinder head cover
   - Engine cooling fan and shroud
   - Accessory drive belt
   - Power steering pump
5. Rotate the crankshaft so that the crankshaft timing mark aligns with the Top Dead Center (TDC) mark on the front cover, and the **V6** marks on the camshaft sprockets are at 12 o'clock as shown.
   - Crankshaft damper
   - Front cover

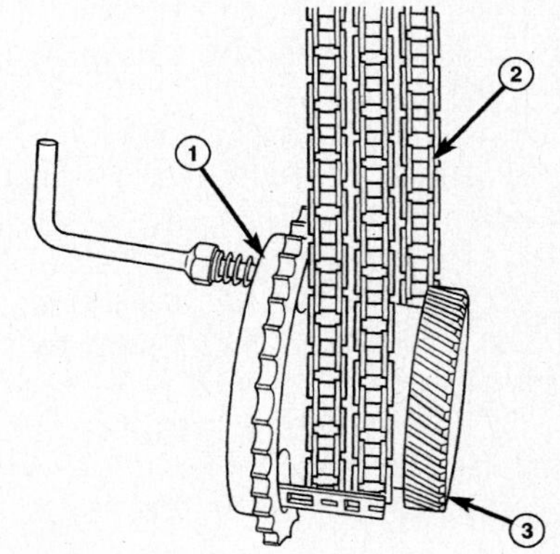

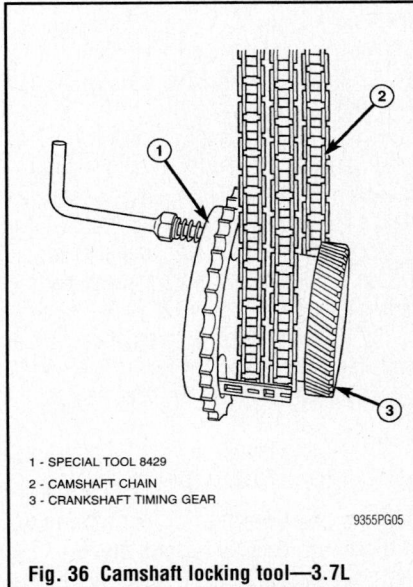

1 - SPECIAL TOOL 8429
2 - CAMSHAFT CHAIN
3 - CRANKSHAFT TIMING GEAR

9355PG05

Fig. 36 Camshaft locking tool—3.7L

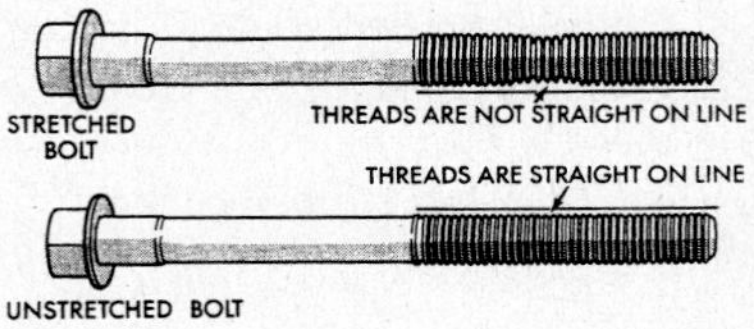

9302PG10

Fig. 37 Examine the head bolts for signs of stretching—3.7L engine

6. Lock the secondary timing chain to the idler sprocket with Timing Chain Locking tool 8429.
7. Matchmark the secondary timing chain one link on each side of the V6 mark to the camshaft sprocket.
   - Left secondary timing chain tensioner
   - Cylinder head access plug
   - Secondary timing chain guide
   - Camshaft sprocket
   - Cylinder head

➡**The cylinder head is retained by twelve bolts. Four of the bolts are smaller and are at the front of the head.**

To install:

8. Check the cylinder head bolts for signs of stretching and replace as necessary.
9. Lubricate the threads of the 11mm bolts with clean engine oil.
10. Coat the threads of the 8mm bolts with Mopar® Lock and Seal Adhesive, or equivalent.

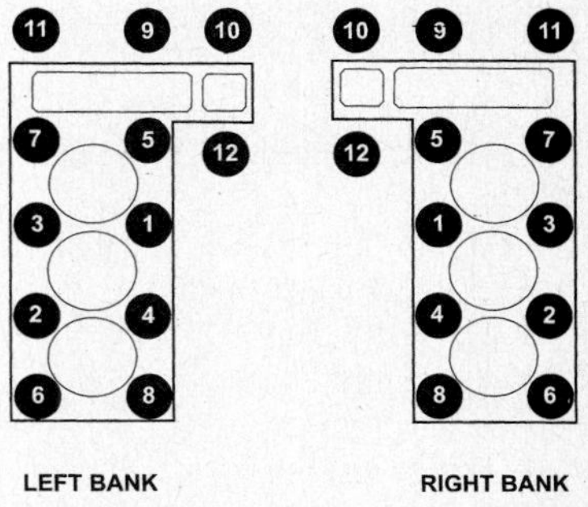

9355PG03

Fig. 38 Cylinder head bolt torque sequence—3.7L

11. Install the cylinder heads. Use new gaskets and tighten the bolts, in sequence, as follows:
    a. Step 1: Bolts 1–8 to 20 ft. lbs. (27 Nm)
    b. Step 2: Bolts 1–10 verify torque without loosening
    c. Step 3: Bolts 9–12 to 10 ft. lbs. (14 Nm)
    d. Step 4: Bolts 1–8 plus ¼ (90 degree) turn
    e. Step 5: Bolts 1–8 plus ¼ (90 degree) turn again
    f. Step 6: Bolts 9–12 to 19 ft. lbs. (26 Nm)
12. Install or connect the following:
    - Camshaft sprocket. Align the secondary chain matchmarks and tighten the bolt to 90 ft. lbs. (122 Nm).
    - Secondary timing chain guide
    - Cylinder head access plug
    - Secondary timing chain tensioner. Refer to the timing chain procedure in this section.
13. Remove the Timing Chain Locking tool.
14. Install or connect the following:
    - Front cover
    - Crankshaft damper. Torque the bolt to 130 ft. lbs. (175 Nm).
    - Power steering pump
    - Accessory drive belt
    - Engine cooling fan and shroud
    - Cover
    - Intake manifold
    - Exhaust Y-pipe
    - Negative battery cable
15. Fill and bleed the cooling system.
16. Start the engine, check for leaks and repair if necessary.

Right Side

See Figures 39 and 40.

1. Before servicing the vehicle, refer to the precautions in the beginning of this manual.
2. Drain the cooling system.
3. Properly relieve the fuel system pressure.
4. Remove or disconnect the following:
   - Negative battery cable
   - Exhaust Y-pipe
   - Intake manifold
   - Valve cover
   - Engine cooling fan and shroud
   - Accessory drive belt
   - Oil fill housing
   - Power steering pump
5. Rotate the crankshaft so that the crankshaft timing mark aligns with the Top Dead Center (TDC) mark on the front cover, and the **V6** marks on the camshaft sprockets are at 12 o'clock as shown.
6. Remove or disconnect the following:
   - Crankshaft damper
   - Front cover
7. Lock the secondary timing chains to the idler sprocket with Timing Chain Locking tool 8429.
8. Matchmark the secondary timing chains to the camshaft sprockets.
9. Remove or disconnect the following:
   - Secondary timing chain tensioners
   - Cylinder head access plugs
   - Secondary timing chain guides
   - Camshaft sprockets
   - Cylinder heads

➡Each cylinder head is retained by eight 11mm bolts and four 8mm bolts.

To install:

10. Check the cylinder head bolts for signs of stretching and replace as necessary.
11. Lubricate the threads of the 11mm bolts with clean engine oil.
12. Coat the threads of the 8mm bolts with Mopar® Lock and Seal Adhesive, or equivalent.
13. Install the cylinder heads. Use new gaskets and tighten the bolts, in sequence, as follows:
    a. Step 1: Bolts 1–8 to 20 ft. lbs. (27 Nm)
    b. Step 2: Bolts 1–10 verify torque without loosening
    c. Step 3: Bolts 9–12 to 10 ft. lbs. (14 Nm)
    d. Step 4: Bolts 1–8 plus ¼ (90 degree) turn
    e. Step 5: Bolts 9–12 to 19 ft. lbs. (26 Nm)
14. Install or connect the following:
    - Camshaft sprockets. Align the secondary chain matchmarks and tighten the bolts to 90 ft. lbs. (122 Nm).
    - Secondary timing chain guides
    - Cylinder head access plugs
    - Secondary timing chain tensioners. Refer to the timing chain procedure in this section.
15. Remove the Timing Chain Locking tool.
16. Install or connect the following:
    - Front cover
    - Crankshaft damper. Torque the bolt to 130 ft. lbs. (175 Nm).
    - Rocker arms
    - Power steering pump
    - Oil fill housing
    - Accessory drive belt
    - Engine cooling fan and shroud
    - Valve covers
    - Intake manifold
    - Exhaust Y-pipe
    - Negative battery cable
17. Fill and bleed the cooling system.
18. Start the engine, check for leaks and repair if necessary.

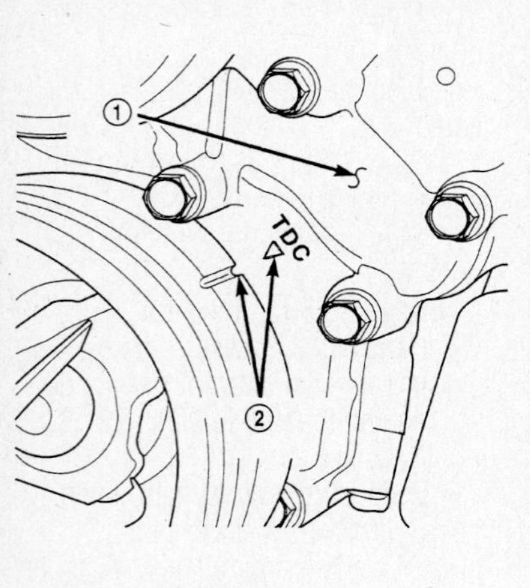

1 – TIMING CHAIN COVER
2 – CRANKSHAFT TIMING MARKS

9308PG04

Fig. 39 Crankshaft timing marks—3.7L engine

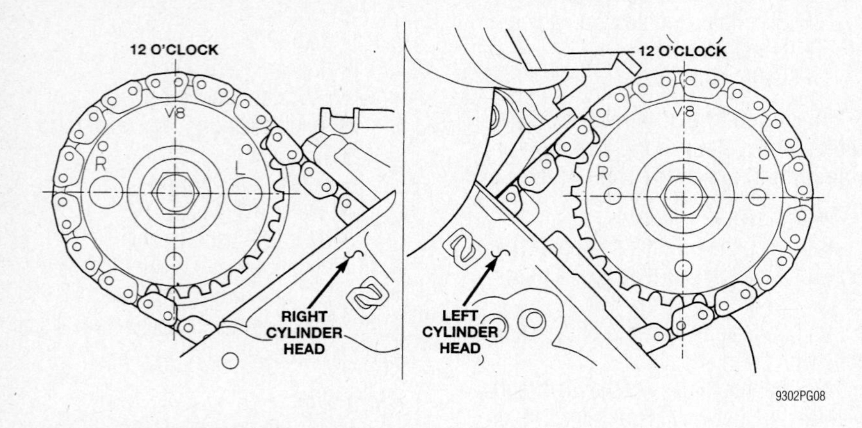

9302PG08

Fig. 40 Camshaft positioning—3.7L engine

4.7L Engine

Left Side

See Figure 41.

1. Before servicing the vehicle, refer to the precautions in the beginning of this manual.
2. Drain the cooling system.
3. Remove or disconnect the following:
   - Negative battery cable
   - Exhaust pipe
   - Intake manifold
   - Cylinder head cover
   - Fan shroud and fan
   - Accessory drive belt
   - Power steering pump
4. Rotate the crankshaft until the damper mark is aligned with the TDC mark. Verify that the V8 mark on the camshaft sprocket is at the 12 o'clock position.
5. Remove or disconnect the following:
   - Vibration damper
   - Timing chain cover
6. Lock the secondary timing chains to the idler sprocket with tool 8515, or equivalent.
7. Mark the secondary timing chain, on link on either side of the V8 mark on the cam sprocket.
8. Remove the left side secondary chain tensioner.
9. Remove the cylinder head access plug.
10. Remove the chain guide.
11. Remove the camshaft sprocket.

➡There are 4 smaller bolts at the front of the head. Don't overlook these.

12. Remove the head bolts and head.

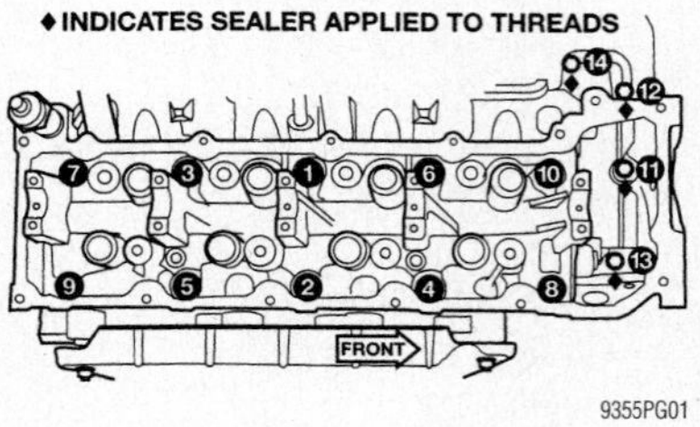

Fig. 41 Cylinder head tightening sequence—4.7L

⁂ WARNING

Don't lay the head on its sealing surface. Due to the design of the head gasket, any distortion to the head sealing surface will result in leaks.

13. Installation is the reverse of removal. Observe the following:
   - Check the head bolts. If any necking is observed, replace the bolt.
   - The 4 small bolts must be coated with sealer.
   - The head bolts are tightened in the following sequence:

Step 1: Bolts 1-10 to 15 ft. lbs. (20 Nm)
Step 2: Bolts 1-10 to 35 ft. lbs. (47 Nm)
Step 3: Bolts 11-14 to 18 ft. lbs. (25 Nm)
Step 4: Bolts 1-10 90 degrees
Step 5: Bolts 11-14 to 22 ft. lbs.

Right Side

1. Before servicing the vehicle, refer to the precautions in the beginning of this manual.
2. Drain the cooling system.
3. Remove or disconnect the following:
   - Negative battery cable
   - Exhaust pipe
   - Intake manifold
   - Cylinder head cover
   - Fan shroud and fan
   - Oil filler housing
   - Accessory drive belt
4. Rotate the crankshaft until the damper mark is aligned with the TDC mark. Verify that the V8 mark on the camshaft sprocket is at the 12 o'clock position.
5. Remove or disconnect the following:
   - Vibration damper
   - Timing chain cover
6. Lock the secondary timing chains to the idler sprocket with tool 8515, or equivalent.
7. Mark the secondary timing chain, on link on either side of the V8 mark on the cam sprocket.
8. Remove the left side secondary chain tensioner.
9. Remove the cylinder head access plug.
10. Remove the chain guide.
11. Remove the camshaft sprocket.

⁂ WARNING

Do not pry on the target wheel for any reason!

➡There are 4 smaller bolts at the front of the head. Don't overlook these.

12. Remove the head bolts and head.

⁂ WARNING

Do not lay the head on its sealing surface. Due to the design of the head gasket, any distortion to the head sealing surface will result in leaks.

13. Installation is the reverse of removal. Observe the following:
   - Check the head bolts. If any necking is observed, replace the bolt.
   - The 4 small bolts must be coated with sealer.
   - The head bolts are tightened in the following sequence:

Step 1: Bolts 1-10 to 15 ft. lbs. (20 Nm)
Step 2: Bolts 1-10 to 35 ft. lbs. (47 Nm)
Step 3: Bolts 11-14 to 18 ft. lbs. (25 Nm)
Step 4: Bolts 1-10 90 degrees
Step 5: Bolts 11-14 to 22 ft. lbs.

5.7L Engine

See Figures 42 and 43.

1. Before servicing the vehicle, refer to the precautions in the beginning of this manual.
2. Drain the cooling system.
3. Properly relieve the fuel system pressure.
4. Remove or disconnect the following:
   - Negative battery cable
   - Air cleaner resonator and ducts
   - Alternator
   - Closed crankcase ventilation system
   - EVAP control system
   - Heater hoses
   - Cylinder head covers
   - Intake manifold
   - Rocker arms and pushrods
   - Cylinder heads

To install:

➡The head gaskets are not interchangeable. They are marked "L" and "R".

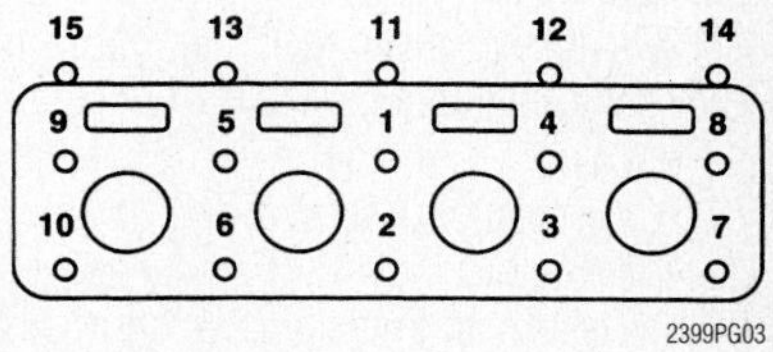

Fig. 42 Cylinder head torque sequence—5.7L engine

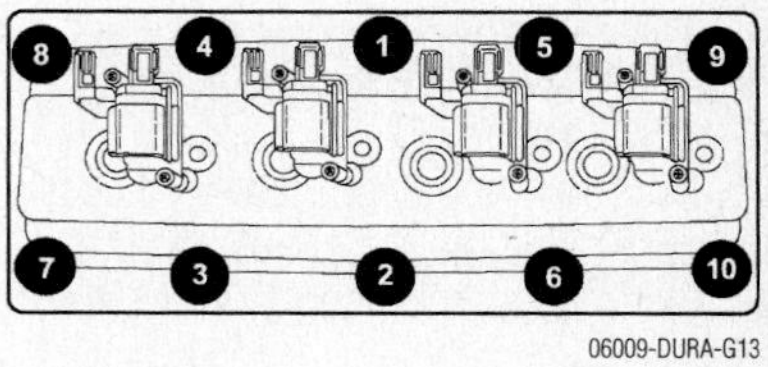

Fig. 43 Cylinder head cover torque sequence—5.7L engine

5. Install the cylinder heads. Use new gaskets and tighten the bolts, in sequence, as follows:
   a. Step 1: 12 mm bolts–25 ft. lbs. (34 Nm); 8mm bolts–15 ft. lbs. (20 Nm)
   b. Step 2: 12mm bolts–40 ft. lbs. (54 Nm); 8mm bolts retorque–15 ft. lbs. (20 Nm)
   c. Step 3: 12mm bolts–plus 90 degrees; 8mm bolts–25 ft. lbs. (34 Nm)
6. Install or connect the following:
   - Rocker arms and pushrods
   - Intake manifold
   - Heater hoses
   - Alternator
   - Cylinder head covers. Torque the studs and bolts to 70 inch lbs.
   - Air cleaner resonator and ducts
   - Negative battery cable

ENGINE ASSEMBLY

REMOVAL & INSTALLATION

3.7L Engine

See Figure 44.

1. Before servicing the vehicle, refer to the precautions in the beginning of this manual.

2. Properly relieve the fuel system pressure.
3. Drain the cooling system.
4. Drain the engine oil.
5. Remove or disconnect the following:
- Negative battery cable
- Hood
- Air cleaner assembly
- Radiator
- Electric and mechanical fan assemblies
- A/C compressor, if equipped, and secure it out of the way with the lines attached. DO NOT DISCHARGE!
- Power steering pump, with the lines attached
- Alternator
- Coolant bottle
- Heater hoses
- Accelerator and speed control cables
- Lower and upper radiator hoses
- Engine ground straps
- Intake Air Temperature (IAT) sensor
- Fuel injection wiring connectors
- Throttle Position (TP) sensor
- Idle Air Control (IAC) motor
- Oil pressure sender connector
- Engine Coolant Temperature (ECT) sensor
- Manifold Absolute Pressure (MAP) sensor
- Camshaft position sensor
- Ignition coil wiring connector
- Crankshaft Position (CKP) sensor
- Coil pack
- Fuel rail
- PCV hose
- Vacuum hoses from the intake manifold
- Knock sensor connectors
- Oil dipstick tube
- Intake manifold
- Heated Oxygen (HO_2S) sensor connector
- Block heater connector
- Front drive shaft at the differential
- Starter
- Structural cover
- With a manual transmission, remove the transmission
- Torque converter bolts and matchmark the converter
- Automatic transmission-to-engine bolts
- Exhaust front pipes
- Left and right engine mounts

6. Place a support stand under the transmission.
7. Install an engine lift plate
8. Lift the engine out of the vehicle.

To install:

9. If equipped with a manual transmission, install the transmission
10. Lower the engine and install the mounts. Don't tighten the bolts yet.
11. If equipped with an automatic transmission, perform the following steps:
   a. Align the torque converter housing to the engine.
   b. Torque the bolts to 30 ft. lbs. (41 Nm).
   - Install the torque converter to flexplate bolts. Torque the bolts to 50 ft. lbs. (68 Nm).
12. Install or connect the following:
- Torque the through bolts to 45 ft. lbs. (61 Nm).
- Engine ground strap
- Starter motor
- CKP sensor
- Block heater cable
- Structural cover.

✱✱ WARNING

The structural cover must be held tightly against the engine and bell housing during tightening. The torque for all bolts is 40 ft. lbs. (54 Nm); the bolts must be tightened in the order shown.

- Exhaust pipes. New flange clamps MUST be used!
- HO_2S sensor connectors
- KS sensors
- Intake Manifold
- Dipstick tube
- Vacuum hoses to the intake manifold
- PCV and breather hoses
- Fuel rail
- Ignition coil
- IAT sensor
- Fuel injector connectors
- TP sensor
- IAC motor

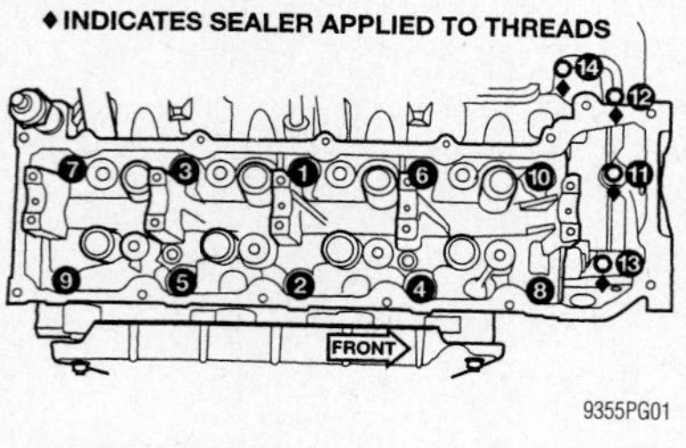

Fig. 44 Tighten the structural cover bolts in this order—3.7L

- Oil pressure sender
- ECT sensor electrical connector
- MAP sensor
- CMP sensor
- Radiator hoses
- Cruise control cable, if equipped
- Throttle cable
- Heater hoses
- Coolant bottle
- Power steering pump
- Alternator
- A/C compressor
- Radiator
- Fan assemblies
- Air cleaner assembly
- Negative battery cable

13. Fill and bleed the power steering system.
14. Fill the engine with clean oil.
15. Start the engine and check for leaks, repair if necessary.

4.7L Engine

See Figures 45 and 46.

1. Before servicing the vehicle, refer to the precautions in the beginning of this manual.
2. Drain the cooling system.
3. Drain the engine oil.
4. Drain the power steering system.
5. Properly relieve the fuel system pressure.
6. Recover the A/C refrigerant.
7. Remove or disconnect the following:
- Negative battery cable
- Front fascia
- Exhaust crossover pipe
- Engine ground straps
- Crankshaft Position (CKP) sensor
- Structural collar
- Starter
- Left and right inner fender liners
- Headlamp mounting module
- Air intake resonator
- Accelerator cable
- Cruise control cable
- Crankcase breather tubes
- Accessory drive belt
- A/C compressor
- Cooling fan assemblies
- Radiator hoses
- Transmission oil cooler lines
- Radiator
- A/C condenser
- Alternator
- Heater hoses
- Throttle Position (TP) sensor connector
- Intake Air Temperature (IAT) sensor connector
- Fuel injector harness connectors

- Engine Coolant Temperature (ECT) sensor connector
- Idle Air Control (IAC) valve connector
- Manifold Absolute Pressure (MAP) sensor connector
- Ignition coils
- Fuel line
- Power steering pump
- Oil fill tube
- Oil dipstick tube
- Heated Oxygen (HO_2S) sensor connectors
- Engine oil filter
- Exhaust crossover pipe
- Structural cover
- Rubber splash shield
- Starter motor
- Crankshaft Position (CKP) sensor connector
- Camshaft Position (CMP) sensor connector
- Torque converter
- Engine ground straps
- Left and right motor mounts
- Transmission flange bolts

8. Install Engine Lifting Fixture 8347 as shown.
9. Place a support stand under the transmission.
10. Lift the engine out of the vehicle.

To install:

11. Lower the engine in to the vehicle and position to the transmission.
12. Remove the engine lifting fixture.
13. Install or connect the following:
    - Transmission flange bolts. Tighten the bolts to 50 ft. lbs. (68 Nm).
    - Left and right motor mounts. Tighten the bolts to 45 ft. lbs. (61 Nm).
    - Engine ground straps
    - Torque converter. Tighten the bolts to 23 ft. lbs. (31 Nm).
    - CMP sensor connector
    - CKP sensor connector
    - Starter motor
    - Rubber splash shield
14. Install the structural cover as follows:
    a. Install all the bolts finger-tight.
    b. Hold the cover tightly against the transmission and the engine.
    c. Tighten the bolts in sequence to 40 ft. lbs. (54 Nm).
15. Install or connect the following:
    - Exhaust crossover pipe
    - Engine oil filter
    - HO_2S sensor connectors
    - Oil dipstick tube
    - Oil fill tube
    - Power steering pump
    - Fuel line
    - Ignition coils
    - MAP sensor connector
    - IAC valve connector
    - ECT sensor connector
    - Fuel injector harness connectors
    - IAT sensor connector
    - TP sensor connector
    - Heater hoses
    - Alternator
    - A/C condenser
    - Radiator
    - Transmission oil cooler lines
    - Radiator hoses
    - Cooling fan assemblies
    - A/C compressor
    - Accessory drive belt
    - Crankcase breather tubes
    - Cruise control cable
    - Accelerator cable
    - Air intake resonator
    - Headlamp mounting module
    - Left and right inner fender liners
    - Front fascia
    - Negative battery cable
16. Fill and bleed the cooling system.
17. Fill and bleed the power steering system.
    - Fill the engine with clean oil.
18. Recharge the A/C system.
19. Start the engine, check for leaks and repair if necessary.

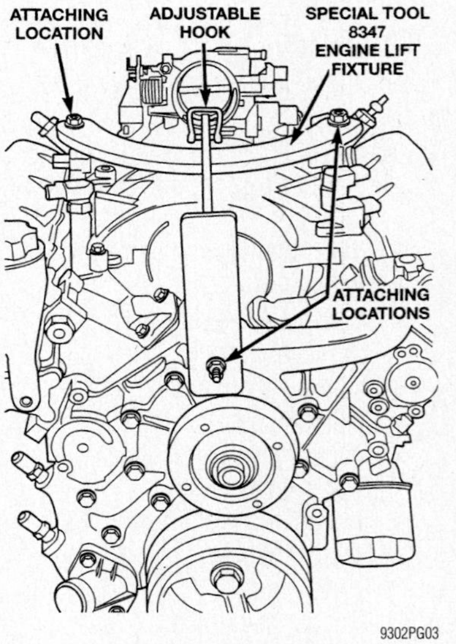

Fig. 45 Engine Lifting Fixture—4.7L engine

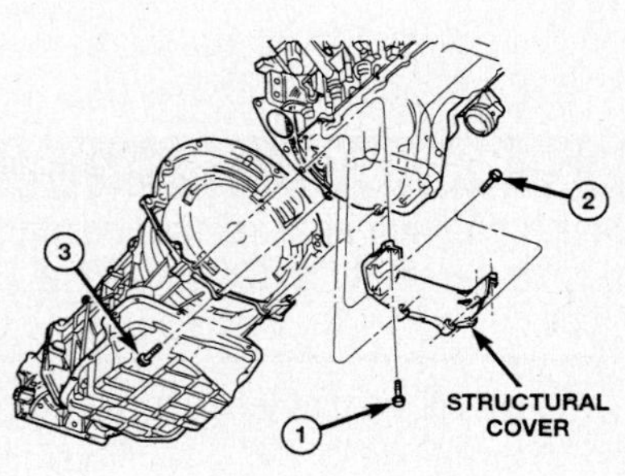

SEQUENCE	ITEM	TORQUE
1	BOLT (Qty 4)	54 N·m (40 ft. lbs.)
2	BOLT (Qty 2)	54 N·m (40 ft. lbs.)
3	BOLT (Qty 2)	54 N·m (40 ft. lbs.)

9308PG02

Fig. 46 Structural cover torque sequence—4.7L engine

5.7L Engine

1. Remove the strut tower support.
2. Remove the engine cover.
3. Perform the Fuel System Pressure Release procedure.
4. Disconnect the battery negative cable.
5. Remove the air cleaner resonator and duct work as an assembly.
6. Drain cooling system.
7. Remove the accessory drive belt.
8. Remove radiator fan shroud.
9. Remove the A/C compressor with the lines attached. Secure compressor out of the way.
10. Remove generator assembly.
11. Remove the intake manifold and IAFM as an assembly.
12. Remove the ground wires from the rear of each cylinder head.
13. Disconnect the heater hoses.

➡It is not necessary to disconnect P/S hoses from pump, for P/S pump removal.

14. Remove the power steering pump and set aside.
15. Disconnect the fuel supply line.
16. Raise and support the vehicle on a hoist and drain the engine oil.
17. Remove engine front mount to frame bolts and nuts.
18. Disconnect the transmission oil cooler lines from their retainers at the oil pan bolts.
19. Disconnect exhaust pipe at manifolds.
20. Disconnect the starter wires. Remove starter motor.
21. Remove the structural dust cover.
22. Remove drive plate to converter bolts.

23. Remove the oil pan to transmission bolts.
24. Remove transmission bell housing to engine block bolts.
25. Lower the vehicle.
26. Install engine lift fixture, special tool no. 8984 and 8984—UPD.
27. Separate engine from transmission, remove engine from vehicle, and install engine assembly on a repair stand.

To install:

28. Install engine lift fixture Special tool no. 8984 and 8984—UPD.
29. Position the engine in the engine compartment.
30. Lower engine into compartment and align engine with transmission.
31. Mate engine and transmission and install two transmission to engine block mounting bolts finger tight.
32. Lower engine assembly until the engine mounts rests in frame perches.
33. Install remaining transmission to engine block mounting bolts and the oil pan to transmission bolts and tighten.
34. Install and tighten engine mount to frame bolts and nuts.
35. Install drive plate to torque converter bolts.
36. Install the structural dust cover.
37. Install the starter and connect the starter wires.
38. Install exhaust pipe to manifold.
39. Lower the vehicle.
40. Remove engine lift fixture, special tool no. 8984 and 8984—UPD.
41. Connect the fuel supply line.
42. Reinstall the power steering pump.
43. Connect the heater hoses.
44. Reconnect the ground wires to the rear of each cylinder head.
45. Install the intake manifold.
46. Install the generator, and wire connections.
47. Install a/c compressor.
48. Install the accessory drive belt.
49. Install the radiator fan shroud.
50. Connect the radiator lower hose.
51. Connect the transmission oil cooler lines to the radiator.
52. Connect the radiator upper hose.
53. Install the air cleaner resonator and duct work.
54. Add engine oil to crankcase.
55. Fill cooling system.
56. Install the engine cover.
57. Install the strut tower support.
58. Connect battery negative cable.
59. Start engine and inspect for leaks.
60. Road test vehicle.

EXHAUST MANIFOLD

REMOVAL & INSTALLATION

3.7L Engines

Right Side

1. Before servicing the vehicle, refer to the precautions in the beginning of this manual.
2. Disconnect the negative cable from the battery.
3. Raise and support the vehicle.
4. Remove the bolts and nuts attaching the exhaust pipe to the engine exhaust manifold.
5. Lower the vehicle.
6. Remove the exhaust heat shield.
7. Remove bolts, nuts and washers attaching manifold to cylinder head.
8. Remove manifold and gasket from the cylinder head.

To install:

⁂ WARNING

If the studs came out with the nuts when removing the engine exhaust manifold, install new studs. Apply sealer on the coarse thread ends. Water leaks may develop at the studs if this precaution is not taken.

9. Position the engine exhaust manifold and gasket on the two studs located on the cylinder head. Install conical washers and nuts on these studs.
10. Install remaining conical washers. Starting at the center arm and working outward, tighten the bolts and nuts to 18 ft. lbs. (25 Nm).
11. Install the exhaust heat shields.
12. Raise and support the vehicle.

⁂ WARNING

Over tightening heat shield fasteners, may cause shield to distort and/or crack.

13. Assemble exhaust pipe to manifold and secure with bolts, nuts and retainers. Tighten the bolts and nuts to 25 ft. lbs. (34 Nm).

Left Side

1. Before servicing the vehicle, refer to the precautions in the beginning of this manual.
2. Disconnect the negative cable from the battery.
3. Raise and support the vehicle.
4. Remove the bolts and nuts attaching the exhaust pipe to the engine exhaust manifold.
5. Lower the vehicle.
6. Remove the exhaust heat shields.
7. Remove bolts, nuts and washers attaching manifold to cylinder head.
8. Remove manifold and gasket from the cylinder head.

To install:

⁂ WARNING

If the studs came out with the nuts when removing the engine exhaust manifold, install new studs. Apply sealer on the coarse thread ends. Water leaks may develop at the studs if this precaution is not taken.

9. Position the engine exhaust manifold and gasket on the two studs located on the cylinder head. Install conical washers and nuts on these studs.
10. Install remaining conical washers. Starting at the center arm and working outward, tighten the bolts and nuts to 18 ft. lbs. (25 Nm).
11. Install the exhaust heat shields.
12. Raise and support the vehicle.

⁂ WARNING

Over tightening heat shield fasteners, may cause shield to distort and/or crack.

13. Assemble exhaust pipe to manifold and secure with bolts, nuts and retainers. Tighten the bolts and nuts to 25 ft. lbs. (34 Nm).

4.7L Engine

1. Before servicing the vehicle, refer to the precautions in the beginning of this manual.
2. Drain the cooling system.
3. Remove or disconnect the following:
   - Battery
   - Power distribution center
   - Battery tray
   - Windshield washer fluid bottle
   - Air cleaner assembly
   - Accessory drive belt
   - A/C compressor
   - A/C accumulator bracket
   - Heater hoses
   - Exhaust manifold heat shields
   - Exhaust Y-pipe
   - Starter motor
   - Exhaust manifolds

To install:

4. Install or connect the following:

- Exhaust manifolds, using new gaskets. Torque the bolts to 18 ft. lbs. (25 Nm), starting with the inner bolts and work out to the ends.
- Starter motor
- Exhaust Y-pipe
- Exhaust manifold heat shields
- Heater hoses
- A/C accumulator bracket
- A/C compressor
- Accessory drive belt
- Air cleaner assembly
- Windshield washer fluid bottle
- Battery tray
- Power distribution center
- Battery

5. Fill and bleed the cooling system.
6. Start the engine, check for leaks and repair if necessary.

5.7L Engine

See Figures 47 and 48.

1. Before servicing the vehicle, refer to the precautions in the beginning of this manual.
2. Disconnect negative battery cable.
3. Raise vehicle.
4. Remove exhaust pipe to manifold bolts.
5. Remove engine mount to frame fasteners.
6. Using suitable jack, raise engine enough to remove manifolds.

➡Do not damage engine harness while raising the engine.

7. Remove the engine mount.
8. Remove heat shield.
9. Remove manifold bolts using sequence provided.
10. Remove manifold and gasket.

To install:

11. Inspect manifold for cracks.
12. Inspect mating surfaces of manifold for flatness with a straightedge. Gasket surfaces must be flat within 0.2mm per 300mm (0.008 inch per foot).
13. Install manifold gasket and manifold.
14. Install manifold bolts and tighten to 25 ft. lbs. (34 Nm).
15. Install heat shield and tighten nuts to 70 inch lbs (8 Nm).
16. Install front engine mount. Torque to 70 ft. lbs. (95 Nm).
17. Lower engine.

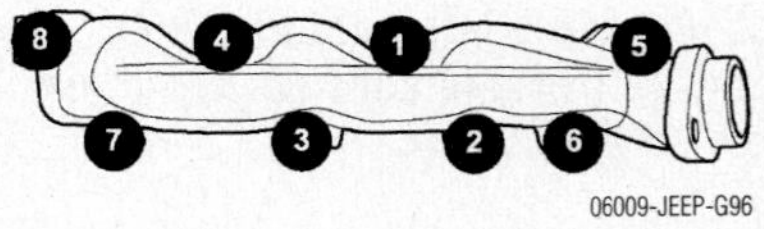

Fig. 47 Left side exhaust manifold—5.7L engine

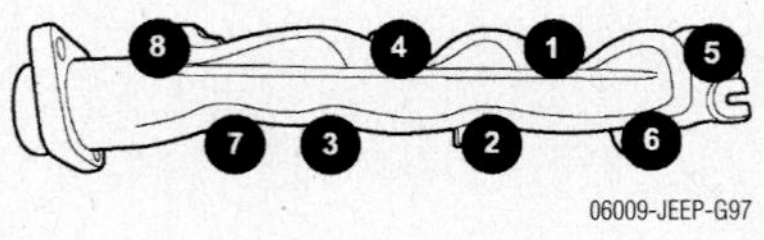

Fig. 48 Right side exhaust manifold—5.7L engine

⁂ WARNING

Do not damage engine harness while lowering the engine.

18. Install and tighten right and left side engine mount to frame fasteners. Torque to 70 ft. lbs. (95 Nm).
19. Install exhaust flange to pipe bolts.
20. Lower vehicle.
21. Connect negative battery cable.

INTAKE MANIFOLD

REMOVAL & INSTALLATION

3.7L and 4.7L Engine

See Figure 49.

1. Before servicing the vehicle, refer to the precautions in the beginning of this manual.
2. Drain the cooling system.
3. Remove or disconnect the following:
   - Negative battery cable
   - Air cleaner assembly
   - Accelerator cable
   - Cruise control cable
   - Manifold Absolute Pressure (MAP) sensor connector
   - Intake Air Temperature (IAT) sensor connector
   - Throttle Position (TP) sensor connector
   - Idle Air Control (IAC) valve connector
   - Engine Coolant Temperature (ECT) sensor
   - Positive Crankcase Ventilation (PCV) valve and hose
   - Canister purge vacuum line
   - Brake booster vacuum line
   - Cruise control servo hose
   - Accessory drive belt
   - Alternator
   - A/C compressor
   - Engine ground straps
   - Ignition coil towers
   - Oil dipstick tube
   - Fuel line
   - Fuel supply manifold
   - Throttle body and mounting bracket
   - Cowl seal
   - Right engine lifting stud
   - Intake manifold. Remove the fasteners in reverse of the tightening sequence.

To install:

4. Install or connect the following:
   - Intake manifold using new gaskets. Tighten the bolts, in sequence, to 105 inch lbs. (12 Nm).
   - Right engine lifting stud
   - Cowl seal
   - Throttle body and mounting bracket
   - Fuel supply manifold
   - Fuel line
   - Oil dipstick tube
   - Ignition coil towers
   - Engine ground straps
   - A/C compressor
   - Alternator
   - Accessory drive belt
   - Cruise control servo hose
   - Brake booster vacuum line
   - Canister purge vacuum line
   - PCV valve and hose
   - ECT sensor
   - IAC valve connector
   - TP sensor connector
   - IAT sensor connector
   - MAP sensor connector
   - Cruise control cable

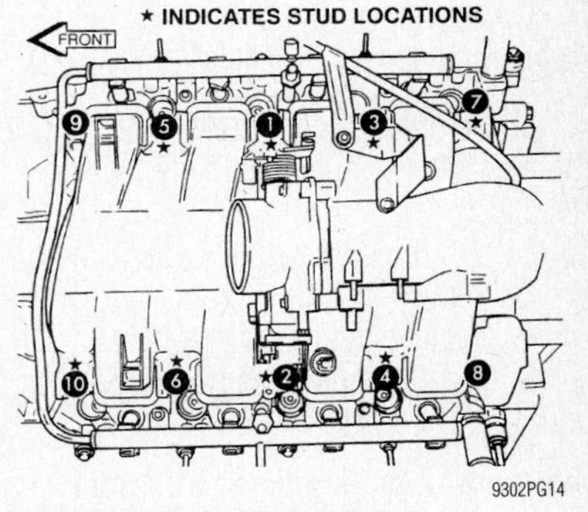

Fig. 49 Intake manifold torque sequence—3.7L and 4.7L engine

- Accelerator cable
- Air cleaner assembly
- Negative battery cable

5. Fill the cooling system.
6. Start the engine and check for leaks.

5.7L Engine

1. Before servicing the vehicle, refer to the precautions in the beginning of this manual.
2. Drain the cooling system.
3. Relieve the fuel system pressure.
4. Remove or disconnect the following:
   - Negative battery cable
   - Air cleaner assembly
   - Accessory drive belt
   - MAP connector
   - IAT connector
   - TPS connector
   - CTS connector
   - Brake booster hose
   - PCV hose
   - Alternator
   - A/C compressor
   - Intake manifold bolts, in a criss-cross pattern, from the outside to the center
   - Intake manifold/IAFM

To install:

5. Position new intake manifold seals.
6. Install the intake manifold. Tighten the bolts in sequence from the center outwards, to 105 inch lbs. (12 Nm).
7. Install or connect the following:
   - Electrical connectors
   - Alternator
   - A/C compressor
   - Brake booster hose
   - PCV hose
   - Accessory drive belt
   - Negative battery cable
   - Air cleaner assembly

OIL PAN

REMOVAL & INSTALLATION

3.7L Engine

See Figure 50.

1. Before servicing the vehicle, refer to the precautions in the beginning of this manual.
2. Disconnect negative battery cable.
3. Remove the radiator fan.
4. Remove the intake manifold.
5. Install engine lifting Tool 8534, or equivalent.

➡Do not raise engine at this time.

6. Remove the structural cover using sequence shown.

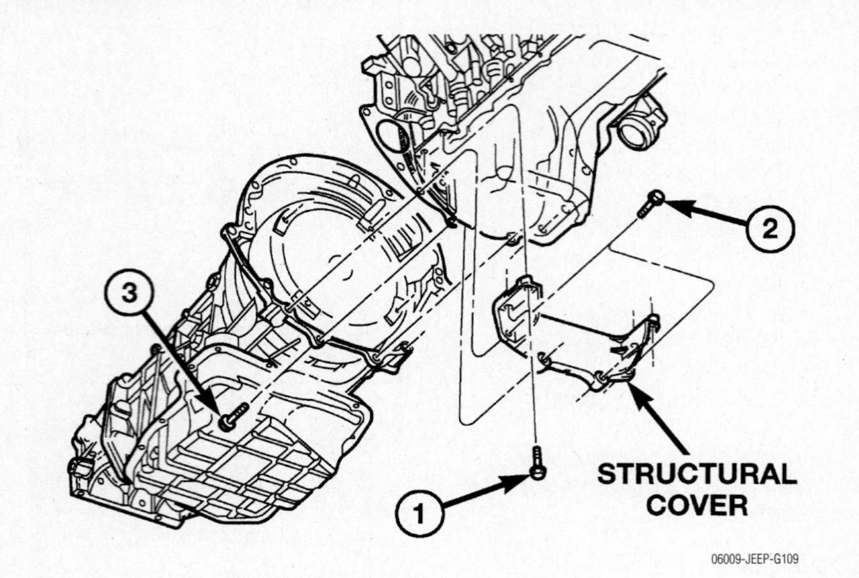

Fig. 50 Structural cover removal and installation sequence—3.7L and 4.7L engines

7. Remove both left and right side engine mount through bolts.
8. Raise engine to provide clearance to remove oil pan.
9. Drain engine oil and remove oil filter.

➡Do not pry on oil pan or oil pan gasket. Gasket is mounted to engine and does not come out with oil pan.

10. Remove the oil pan mounting bolts and oil pan.
11. Unbolt oil pump pickup tube and remove tube and oil pan gasket from engine.

To install:

12. Clean the oil pan gasket mating surface of the bedplate and oil pan.
13. Inspect integrated oil pan gasket, and replace as necessary.
14. Position the integrated oil pan gasket/windage tray assembly.
15. Install the oil pickup tube
16. If removed, install stud at position No. 9.
17. Install the mounting bolt and nuts. Tighten nuts to 20 ft. lbs. (28 Nm).
18. Position the oil pan and install the mounting bolts. Tighten the mounting bolts to 15 Nm (11 ft. lbs.) in the sequence shown.
19. Install structural dust cover
20. Lower the engine into mounts.
21. Remove the lifting tool.
22. Install both the left and right side engine mount through bolts. Tighten the nuts to 50 ft. lbs. (68 Nm).
23. Install the intake manifold.
24. Fill engine oil.
25. Reconnect the negative battery cable.
26. Start engine and check for leaks.

4.7L Engine

1. Before servicing the vehicle, refer to the precautions in the beginning of this manual.
2. Disconnect the negative battery cable.
3. Install engine support fixture special tool 8534, or equivalent.

➡Do not raise engine at this time.

4. Loosen both left and right side engine mount through bolts. Do not remove bolts.
5. Remove the structural dust cover.
6. Drain engine oil.

WARNING

Only raise the engine enough to provide clearance for oil pan removal. Check for proper clearance at fan shroud to fan and cowl to intake manifold.

7. Raise engine using special tool 8534 to provide clearance to remove oil pan.

➡Do not pry on oil pan or oil pan gasket. Gasket is integral to engine windage tray and does not come out with oil pan.

8. Remove the oil pan mounting bolts and oil pan.
9. Unbolt oil pump pickup tube and remove tube.
10. Inspect the integral windage tray and gasket and replace as needed.

To install:

11. Clean the oil pan gasket mating surface of the bedplate and oil pan.
12. Position the oil pan gasket and pickup tube with new O-ring. Install the mounting bolt and nuts. Tighten bolt and nuts to 20 ft. lbs. (28 Nm).
13. Position the oil pan and install the mounting bolts. Tighten the mounting bolts to 15 Nm (11 ft. lbs.) in the sequence shown.
14. Lower the engine into mounts using special tool 8534.
15. Install both the left and right side engine mount through bolts. Tighten the nuts to 50 ft. lbs. (68 Nm).
16. Remove special tool 8534.
17. Install structural dust cover.
18. Fill engine oil.
19. Reconnect the negative battery cable.
20. Start engine and check for leaks.

5.7L Engine

See Figures 51 and 52.

1. Before servicing the vehicle, refer to the precautions in the beginning of this manual.
2. Disconnect the negative battery cable.
3. Remove the engine cover.
4. Remove the intake manifold.
5. Raise vehicle.
6. Remove both left and right side engine mount to frame bolts.
7. Drain engine oil and remove the oil filter.
8. Remove the engine oil dipstick and tube from the oil pan.
9. Lower the vehicle.
10. Install engine support fixture special tool 8534, or equivalent.

➡Do not use the third leg.

11. Raise engine using special tool 8534 to provide clearance to remove oil pan.
12. Raise the vehicle.
13. Remove the front axle.
14. Remove the structural dust cover.

➡Do not pry on oil pan or oil pan gasket. Gasket is integral to engine windage tray and does not come out with oil pan.

➡The horizontal M10 fasteners are 5mm longer in length, and must be reinstalled in original locations.

15. Remove the M10 fasteners (vertical and horizontal) from the rear of the oil pan to the transmission and engine.
16. Remove the oil pan mounting bolts using the sequence provided, and oil pan.

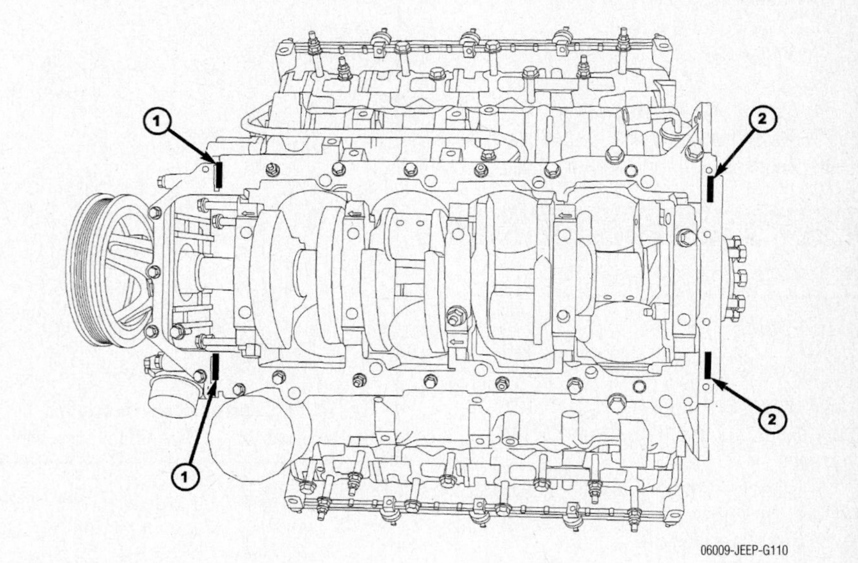

Fig. 51 Mopar® Engine RTV, or equivalent, must be applied to the 4 T-joints—5.7L engine

➡When the oil pan is removed, a new oil pan gasket/windage tray assembly must be installed. The old gasket cannot be reused.

17. Discard the integral windage tray and gasket and replace.

To install:

18. Clean the oil pan gasket mating surface of the block and oil pan.

➡Mopar® Engine RTV, or equivalent, must be applied to the 4 T-joints, (area where front cover, rear retainer, block, and oil pan gasket meet). The bead of RTV should cover the bottom of the gasket. This area is approximately 4.5mm x 25mm in each of the 4 T-joint locations.

19. Apply Mopar® T Engine RTV at the 4 T- joints.

➡When the oil pan is removed, a new oil pan gasket/windage tray assembly must be installed. The old gasket cannot be reused.

20. Install a new oil pan gasket/windage tray assembly.
21. If removed, reinstall the oil pump pickup tube with new O-ring. Tighten tube to pump fasteners to 250 inch lbs. (28 Nm).

➡The horizontal M10 fasteners are 5mm longer in length, and must be reinstalled in original locations.

➡The horizontal M10 fasteners are 5mm longer in length, and must be reinstalled in original locations.

22. Align the rear of the oil pan with the rear face of the engine block, and install the M10 and M6 oil pan fasteners finger tight. Using the following torque sequence, torque the M6 mounting bolts to 44 inch lbs. (5 Nm).
23. Using the following torque sequence, torque the M10 oil pan fasteners to 39 ft. lbs. (54 Nm).
24. Using the following torque sequence, torque the M6 oil pan fasteners to 106 inch lbs. (12 Nm).
25. Install both the left and right side oil pan to transmission bolts. Torque the bolts to 39 ft. lbs. (54 Nm).
26. Lower the engine into mounts.
27. Install both the left and right side engine mount bolts and nuts. Torque the studs and nuts to 39 ft. lbs. (54 Nm).
28. Install the engine oil dipstick and tube.
29. Remove special tool 8534.

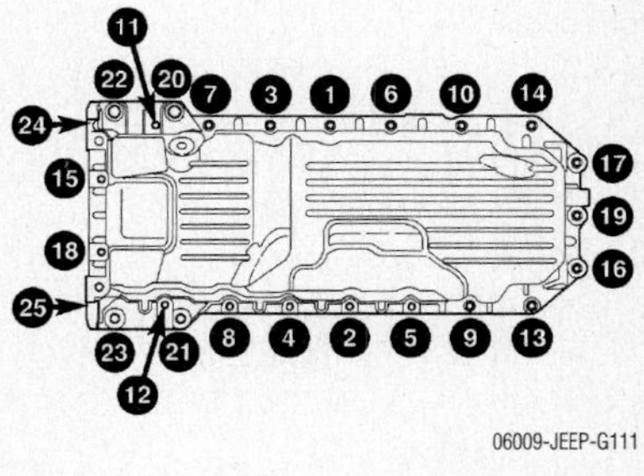

Fig. 52 Oil pan bolt torque sequence—5.7L engine

30. Install the intake manifold.
31. Install the front axle.
32. Install the engine cover.
33. Fill engine oil.
34. Install oil filter, if removed.
35. Reconnect the negative battery cable.
36. Start engine and check for leaks.

OIL PUMP

REMOVAL & INSTALLATION

3.7L Engine

See Figure 53.

1. Before servicing the vehicle, refer to the precautions in the beginning of this manual.
2. Remove or disconnect the following:
   - Oil Pan
   - Timing chain cover
   - Timing chains and tensioners
   - Oil pump
3. Installation is the reverse of removal. Torque the pump bolts, in sequence, to 21 ft. lbs. (28 Nm),

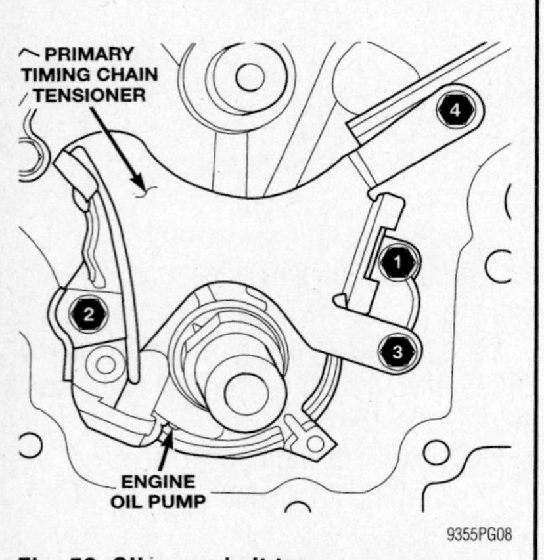

Fig. 53 Oil pump bolt torque sequence—3.7L

4.7L Engine

See Figure 54.

1. Before servicing the vehicle, refer to the precautions in the beginning of this manual.
2. Drain the engine oil.
3. Remove or disconnect the following:
   - Valve covers
   - Front cover
   - Timing chains and sprockets
   - Oil pan and pickup tube
   - Oil pump and primary timing chain tensioner

To install:

4. Install or connect the following:

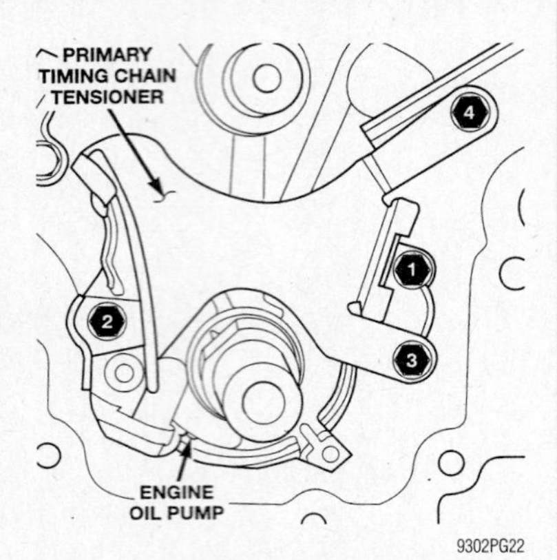

Fig. 54 Oil pump and chain tensioner torque sequence—4.7L engine

   - Oil pump and primary timing chain tensioner. Torque the bolts in sequence to 21 ft. lbs. (28 Nm).
   - Oil pan and pickup tube
   - Timing chains and sprockets
   - Front cover
   - Valve covers
5. Fill the engine with clean oil.
6. Start the engine, check for leaks and repair if necessary.

5.7L Engine

1. Before servicing the vehicle, refer to the precautions in the beginning of this manual.
2. Remove the oil pan and pick-up tube.
3. Remove the timing chain cover.
4. Remove the four bolts, and the oil pump.

***** WARNING**

Oil pump pressure relief valve and spring should not be removed from the oil pump. If these components are disassembled and or removed from the pump the entire oil pump assembly must be replaced.

5. Remove the pump cover.
6. Clean all parts thoroughly. Mating surface of the oil pump housing should be smooth. If the pump cover is scratched or grooved the oil pump assembly should be replaced.
7. Slide outer rotor into the body of the oil pump. Press the outer rotor to one side of the oil pump body and measure clearance between the outer rotor and the body. If the measurement is 0.235mm (0.009 in.) or more the oil pump assembly must be replaced.
8. Install the inner rotor in the into the oil pump body. Measure the clearance between the inner and outer rotors. If the clearance between the rotors is 0.150mm (0.006 in.) or more the oil pump assembly must be replaced.
9. Place a straightedge across the body of the oil pump (between the bolt holes), if a feeler gauge of 0.095mm (0.0038 in.) or greater can be inserted between the straightedge and the rotors, the pump must be replaced.
10. Reinstall the pump cover. Torque fasteners to 132 inch lbs. (15 Nm).

➡The 5.7 Oil pump is released as an assembly. There are no DaimlerChrysler part numbers for sub-assembly components. In the event the oil pump is not functioning or out of specification it must be replaced as an assembly.

To install:

11. Position the oil pump onto the crankshaft and install the 4 oil pump retaining bolts.
12. Tighten the oil pump retaining bolts to 250 inch lbs. (28 Nm).
13. Install the timing chain cover.
14. Install the pick-up tube and oil pan.

INSPECTION

3.7L and 4.7L Engine

See Figures 55 through 60.

***** WARNING**

Oil pump pressure relief valve and spring should not be removed from the oil pump. If these components are disassembled and or removed from the pump the entire oil pump assembly must be replaced.

1. Clean all parts thoroughly. Mating surface of the oil pump housing should be smooth. If the pump cover is scratched or grooved the oil pump assembly should be replaced.
2. Lay a straight edge across the pump cover surface. If a 0.025 mm (0.001 in.) feeler gauge can be inserted between the cover and the straight edge the oil pump assembly should be replaced.
3. Measure the thickness of the outer rotor. If the outer rotor thickness measures at 12.005 mm (0.472 in.) or less the oil pump assembly must be replaced.
4. Measure the diameter of the outer rotor. If the outer rotor diameter measures at 85.925 mm (3.382 in.) or less the oil pump assembly must be replaced.
5. Measure the thickness of the inner

rotor. If the inner rotor thickness measures at 12.005 mm (0.472 in.) or less then the oil pump assembly must be replaced.

6. Slide outer rotor into the body of the oil pump. Press the outer rotor to one side of the oil pump body and measure clearance between the outer rotor and the body. If the measurement is 0.235mm (0.009 in.) or more the oil pump assembly must be replaced.

7. Install the inner rotor in the into the oil pump body. Measure the clearance between the inner and outer rotors. If the clearance between the rotors is.150 mm (0.006 in.) or more the oil pump assembly must be replaced.

8. Place a straight edge across the body of the oil pump (between the bolt holes); if a feeler gauge of.095 mm (0.0038 in.) or greater can be inserted between the straightedge and the rotors, the pump must be replaced.

➡The 3.7L/4.7L oil pump is released as an assembly; there are no sub-assembly components. In the event the oil pump is not functioning or out of specification it must be replaced as an assembly.

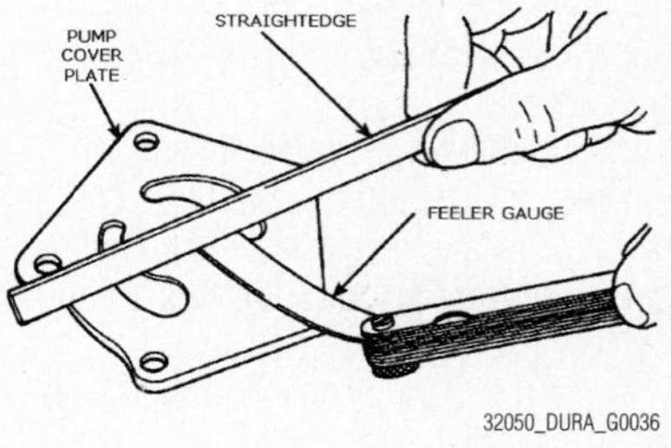

Fig. 55 Checking oil pump cover plate

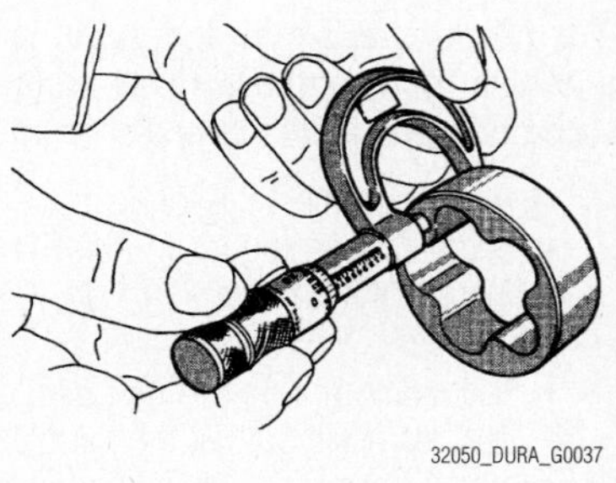

Fig. 56 Measuring outer rotor thickness

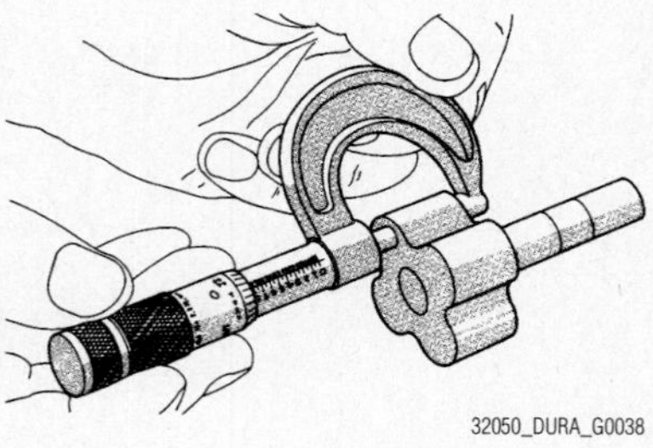

Fig. 57 Measuring inner rotor thickness

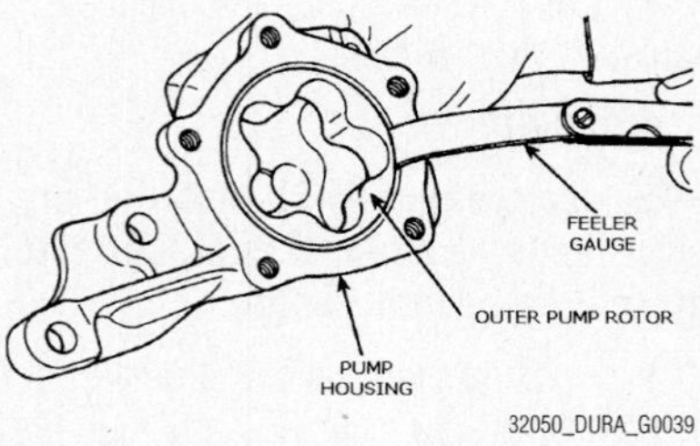

Fig. 58 Measuring clearance between pump housing and outer rotor

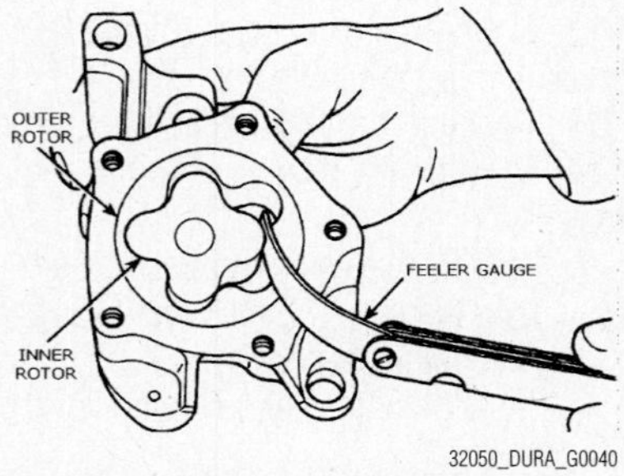

Fig. 59 Measuring clearance between inner and outer rotor

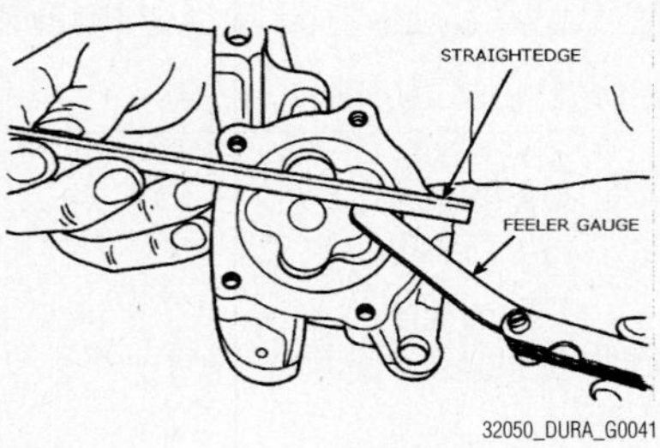

Fig. 60 Measuring clearance between rotors and pump body cover

5.7L Engine

1. Remove the pump cover.
2. Clean all parts thoroughly. Mating surface of the oil pump housing should be smooth. If the pump cover is scratched or grooved the oil pump assembly should be replaced.
3. Slide outer rotor into the body of the oil pump. Press the outer rotor to one side of the oil pump body and measure clearance between the outer rotor and the body. If the measurement is 0.235mm (0.009 in.) or more the oil pump assembly must be replaced.
4. Install the inner rotor in the into the oil pump body. Measure the clearance between the inner and outer rotors. If the clearance between the rotors is 0.150 mm (0.006 in.) or more the oil pump assembly must be replaced.
5. Place a straight edge across the body of the oil pump (between the bolt holes); if a feeler gauge of 0.095 mm (0.0038 in.) or greater can be inserted between the straightedge and the rotors, the pump must be replaced.
6. Reinstall the pump cover. Torque fasteners to 132 inch lbs. (15 Nm).

➡The 5.7 oil pump is released as an assembly. There are no DaimlerChrysler part numbers for Sub-Assembly components. In the event the oil pump is not functioning or out of specification it must be replaced as an assembly.

PISTON AND RING

POSITIONING

See Figures 61 and 62.

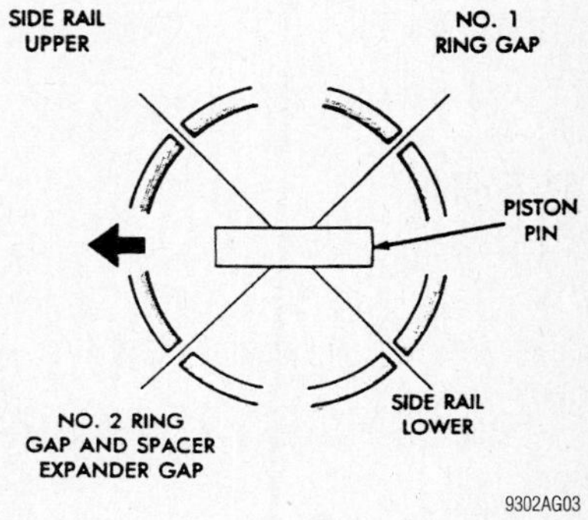

Fig. 61 Piston ring end-gap spacing. Position raised "F" on piston toward front of engine—3.7L and 4.7L engine

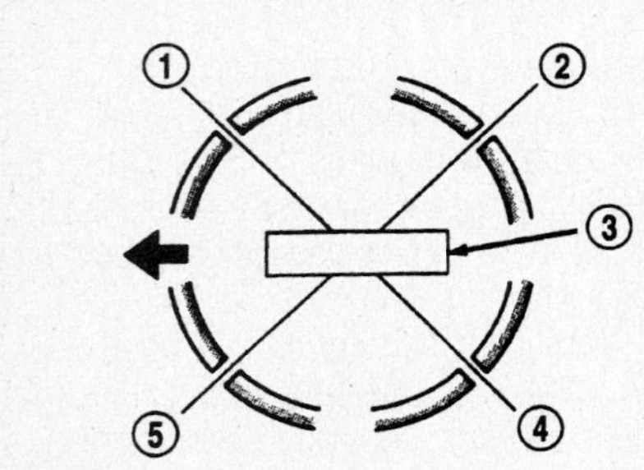

Fig. 62 Piston ring end-gap spacing—5.7L engines

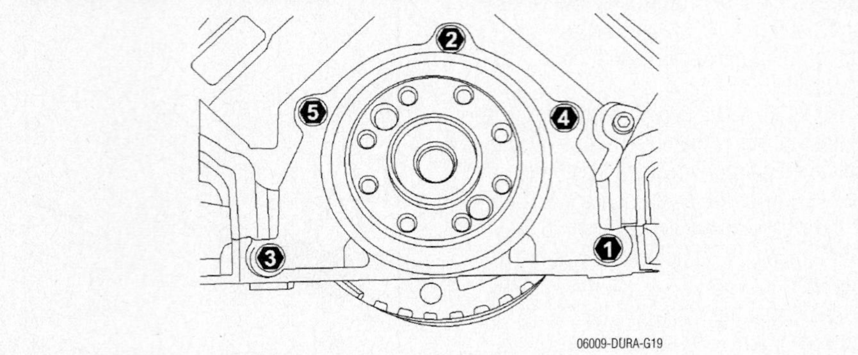

Fig. 63 Rear seal retainer torque sequence—5.7L engine

REAR MAIN SEAL

REMOVAL & INSTALLATION

3.7L and 4.7L Engines

1. Before servicing the vehicle, refer to the precautions in the beginning of this manual.
2. Remove or disconnect the following:
   - Transmission
   - Flexplate
3. Thread Oil Seal Remover 8506 into the rear main seal as far as possible and remove the rear main seal.

To install:

4. Install or connect the following:
   - Seal Guide 8349-2 onto the crankshaft
   - Rear main seal on the seal guide
   - Rear main seal, using the Crankshaft Rear Oil Seal Installer 8349 and Driver Handle C-4171; tap it into place until the installer is flush with the cylinder block
   - Flexplate. Tighten the bolts to 45 ft. lbs. (60 Nm) for 4.7L; 70 ft. lbs. (95 Nm) for the 3.7L engine.
   - Transmission
5. Start the engine and check for leaks.

5.7L Engine

See Figure 63.

1. Before servicing the vehicle, refer to the precautions in the beginning of this manual.
2. Disconnect negative cable from battery.
3. Remove the transmission.
4. Remove the flexplate.
5. Remove the oil pan.
6. Remove the rear oil seal retainer mounting bolts.
7. Carefully remove the retainer from the engine block.
8. Using a seal puller, remove the crankshaft rear oil seal.

To install:

➡The rear seal must be installed dry for proper operation. Do not lubricate the seal lip or outer edge.

9. Position the plastic seal guide onto the crankshaft rear face. Then position the crankshaft rear oil seal onto the guide.
10. Using a seal driver and hammer, tap the seal into place. Continue to tap on the driver handle until the seal installer seats against the cylinder block crankshaft bore.
11. Thoroughly clean all gasket residue from the engine block.
12. Use extreme care and clean all gasket residue from the retainer.
13. Position the gasket onto the retainer.
14. Position the retainer onto the engine block.
15. Install the retainer mounting bolts. Tighten the bolts to 132 inch lbs. (15 Nm).
16. Install the oil pan.
17. Install the flexplate. Tighten to 70 ft. lbs. (95 Nm).
18. Install the transmission.
19. Check and verify engine oil level.
20. Start engine and check for leaks.

TIMING CHAIN, SPROCKETS, FRONT COVER AND SEAL

REMOVAL & INSTALLATION

3.7L Engines

See Figures 64 through 73.

1. Before servicing the vehicle, refer to the precautions in the beginning of this manual.
2. Drain the cooling system.
3. Remove or disconnect the following:
   - Negative battery cable
   - Valve covers
   - Radiator fan
4. Rotate the crankshaft so that the crankshaft timing mark aligns with the Top Dead Center (TDC) mark on the front cover, and the**V6** marks on the camshaft sprockets are at 12 o'clock.
   - Power steering pump
   - Access plugs from the cylinder heads
   - Oil fill housing
   - Crankshaft damper
5. Compress the primary timing chain tensioner and install a lockpin.
6. Remove the secondary timing chain tensioners.
7. Hold the left camshaft with adjustable pliers and remove the sprocket and chain. Rotate the **left** camshaft 15 degrees **clockwise** to the neutral position.
8. Hold the right camshaft with adjustable pliers and remove the camshaft sprocket. Rotate the **right** camshaft 45 degrees **counterclockwise** to the neutral position.
9. Remove the primary timing chain and sprockets.

To install:

10. Use a small prytool to hold the ratchet pawl and compress the secondary timing chain tensioners in a vise and install locking pins.

➡The black bolts fasten the guide to the engine block and the silver bolts fasten the guide to the cylinder head.

11. Install or connect the following:
    - Secondary timing chain guides. Tighten the bolts to 21 ft. lbs. (28 Nm).
    - Secondary timing chains to the idler sprocket so that the double plated links on each chain are visible through the slots in the primary idler sprocket

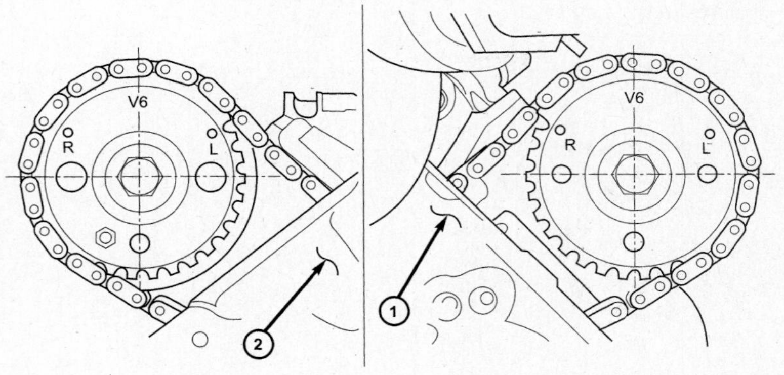

1 - LEFT CYLINDER HEAD
2 - RIGHT CYLINDER HEAD

9355PG09

Fig. 64 Camshaft sprocket timing marks—3.7L engine

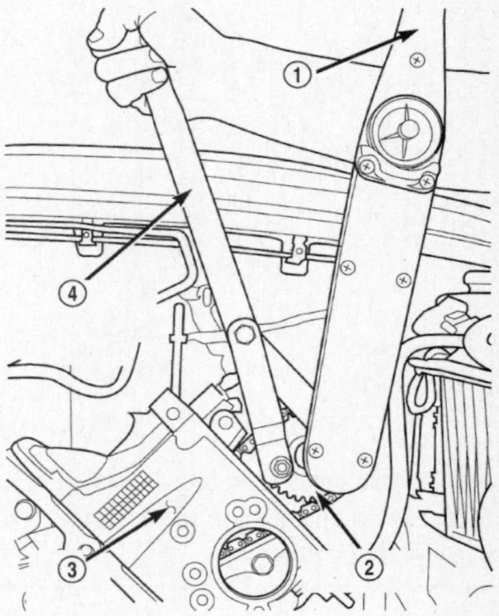

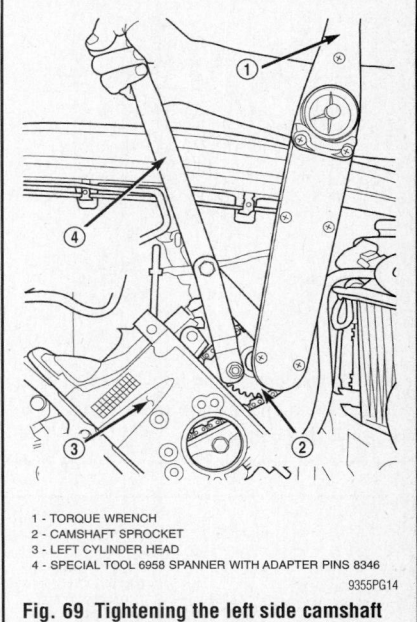

1 - TORQUE WRENCH
2 - CAMSHAFT SPROCKET
3 - LEFT CYLINDER HEAD
4 - SPECIAL TOOL 6958 SPANNER WITH ADAPTER PINS 8346

9355PG14

Fig. 69 Tightening the left side camshaft sprocket—3.7L engine

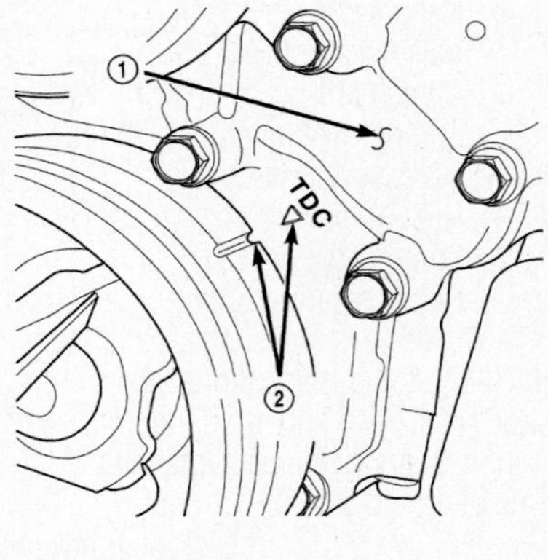

1 - TIMING CHAIN COVER
2 - CRANKSHAFT TIMING MARKS

9355PG10

Fig. 65 Crankshaft timing marks—3.7L engine

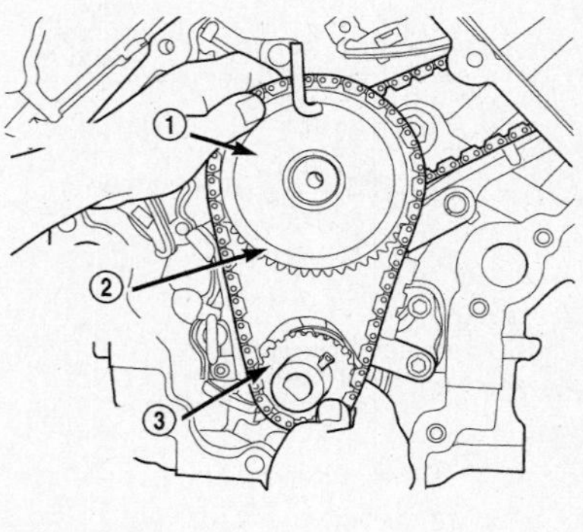

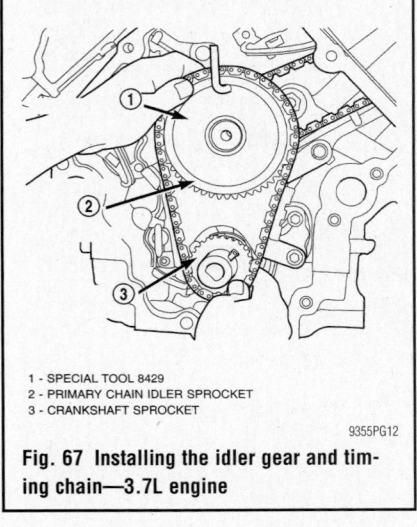

1 - SPECIAL TOOL 8429
2 - PRIMARY CHAIN IDLER SPROCKET
3 - CRANKSHAFT SPROCKET

9355PG12

Fig. 67 Installing the idler gear and timing chain—3.7L engine

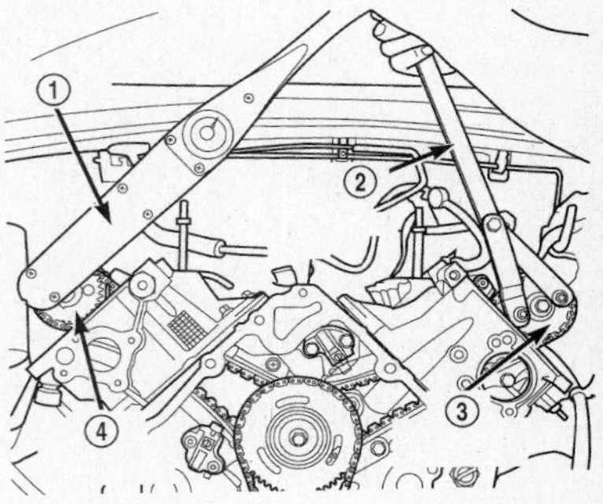

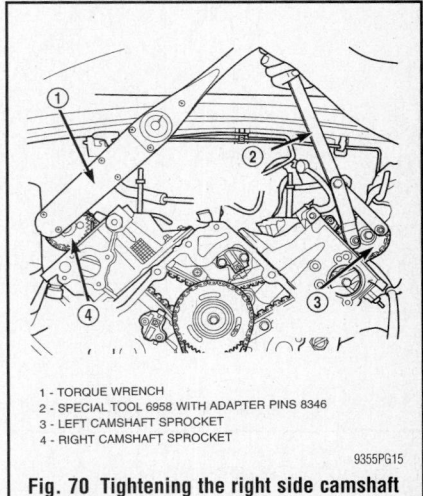

1 - TORQUE WRENCH
2 - SPECIAL TOOL 6958 WITH ADAPTER PINS 8346
3 - LEFT CAMSHAFT SPROCKET
4 - RIGHT CAMSHAFT SPROCKET

9355PG15

Fig. 70 Tightening the right side camshaft sprocket—3.7L engine

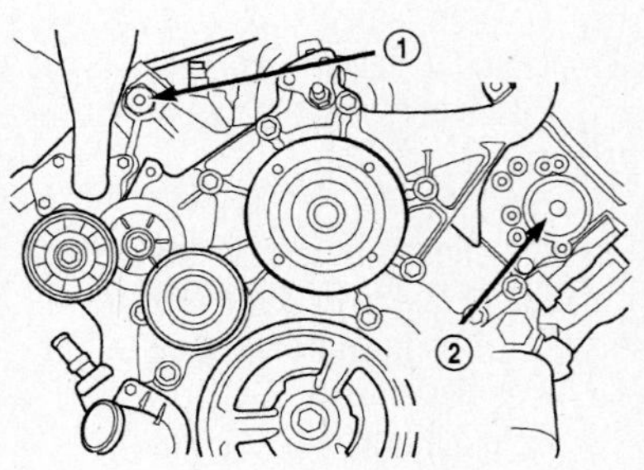

1 - RIGHT CYLINDER HEAD ACCESS PLUG
2 - LEFT CYLINDER HEAD ACCESS PLUG

9355PG11

Fig. 66 Cylinder head access plugs—3.7L engine

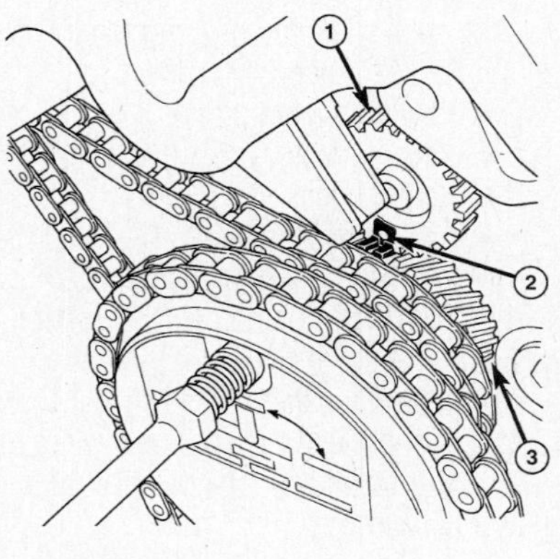

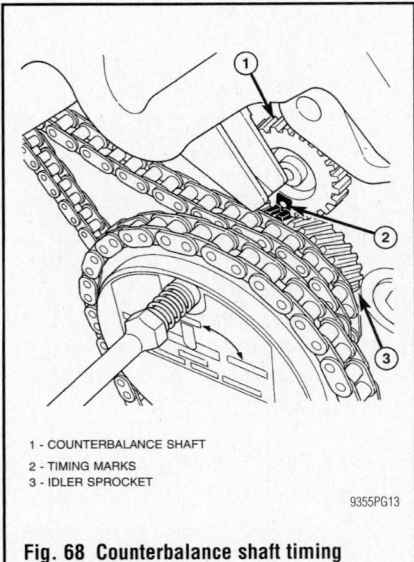

1 - COUNTERBALANCE SHAFT
2 - TIMING MARKS
3 - IDLER SPROCKET

9355PG13

Fig. 68 Counterbalance shaft timing marks—3.7L engine

12. Lock the secondary timing chains to the idler sprocket with Timing Chain Locking tool as shown.

13. Align the primary chain double plated links with the idler sprocket timing mark and the single plated link with the crankshaft sprocket timing mark.

14. Install the primary chain and sprockets. Tighten the idler sprocket bolt to 25 ft. lbs. (34 Nm).

15. Align the secondary chain single plated links with the timing marks on the secondary sprockets. Align the dot at the **L** mark on the left sprocket with the plated link on the left chain and the dot at the **R** mark on the right sprocket with the plated link on the right chain.

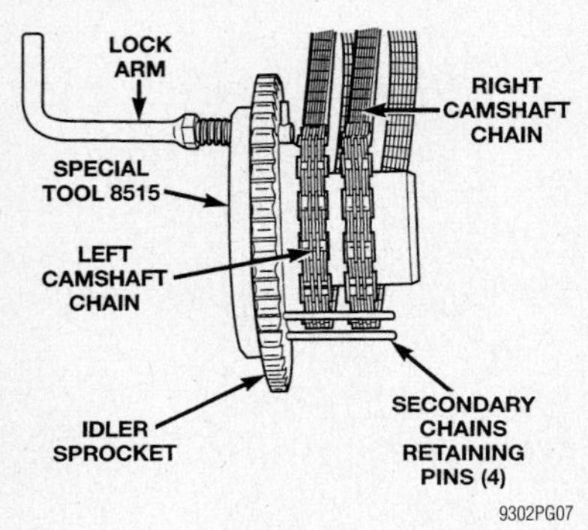

Fig. 71 Use the Timing Chain Locking tool to lock the timing chains on the idler gear—3.7L engine

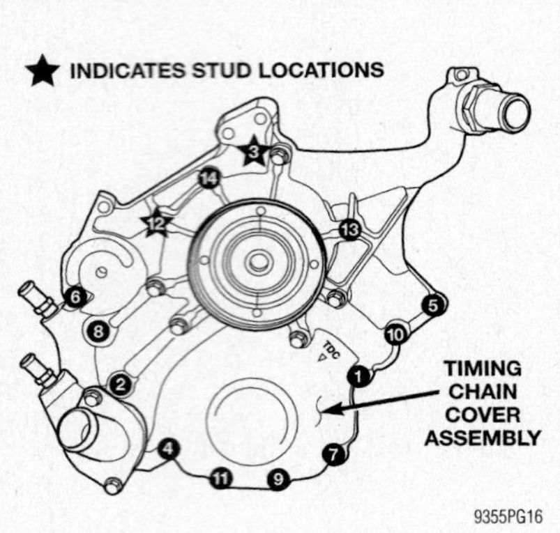

Fig. 73 Timing cover bolt torque sequence—3.7L engine

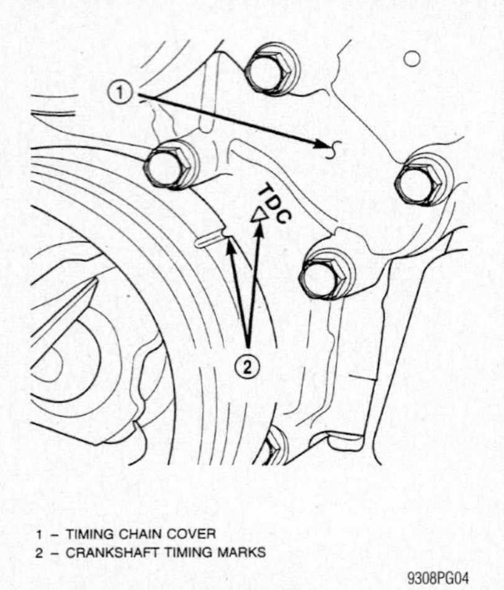

Fig. 74 Crankshaft timing marks—4.7L engine

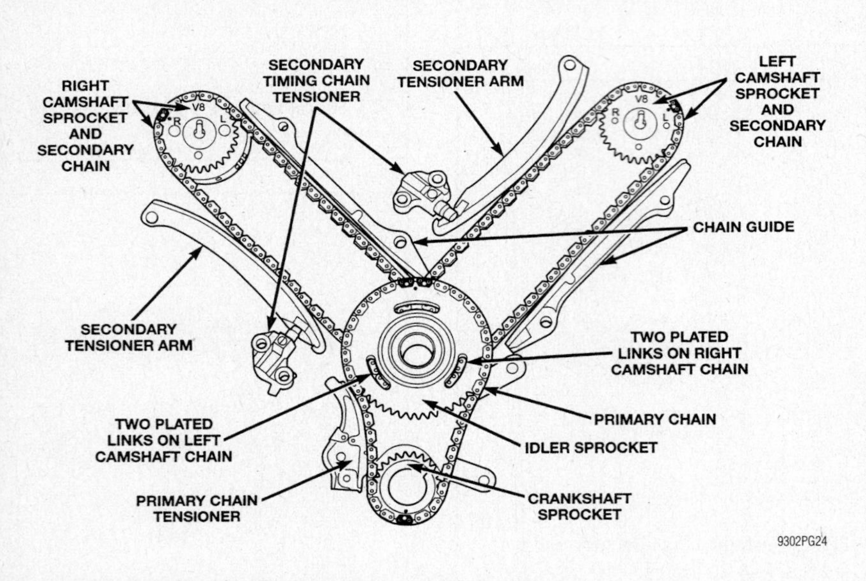

Fig. 72 Timing chain system and alignment marks—3.7L engine

16. Rotate the camshafts back from the neutral position and install the camshaft sprockets.
17. Remove the secondary chain locking tool.
18. Remove the primary and secondary timing chain tensioner locking pins.
19. Hold the camshaft sprockets with a spanner wrench and tighten the retaining bolts to 90 ft. lbs. (122 Nm).
20. Install or connect the following:
    - Front cover. Tighten the bolts, in sequence, to 40 ft. lbs. (54 Nm).
    - Front crankshaft seal
    - Cylinder head access plugs
    - A/C compressor
    - Alternator
    - Accessory drive belt tensioner. Tighten the bolt to 40 ft. lbs. (54 Nm).
    - Oil fill housing
    - Crankshaft damper. Tighten the bolt to 130 ft. lbs. (175 Nm).
    - Power steering pump
    - Lower radiator hose
    - Heater hoses
    - Accessory drive belt
    - Engine cooling fan and shroud
    - Camshaft Position (CMP) sensor
    - Valve covers
    - Negative battery cable
21. Fill and bleed the cooling system.
22. Start the engine, check for leaks and repair if necessary.

4.7L Engine

See Figures 71 and 74 through 79.

1. Before servicing the vehicle, refer to the precautions in the beginning of this manual.
2. Drain the cooling system.
3. Remove or disconnect the following:
    - Negative battery cable
    - Valve covers
    - Camshaft Position (CMP) sensor
    - Engine cooling fan and shroud
    - Accessory drive belt
    - Heater hoses
    - Lower radiator hose
    - Power steering pump
4. Rotate the crankshaft so that the crankshaft timing mark aligns with the Top Dead Center (TDC) mark on the front cover, and the **V8** marks on the camshaft sprockets are at 12 o'clock.
5. Remove or disconnect the following:
    - Crankshaft damper
    - Oil fill housing
    - Accessory drive belt tensioner
    - Alternator
    - A/C compressor
    - Front cover
    - Front crankshaft seal
    - Cylinder head access plugs
    - Secondary timing chain guides
6. Compress the primary timing chain tensioner and install a lockpin.
7. Remove the secondary timing chain tensioners.
8. Hold the left camshaft with adjustable pliers and remove the sprocket and chain. Rotate the **left** camshaft 15 degrees **clockwise** to the neutral position.
9. Hold the right camshaft with adjustable pliers and remove the camshaft sprocket. Rotate the **right** camshaft 45 degrees **counterclockwise** to the neutral position.
10. Remove the primary timing chain and sprockets.

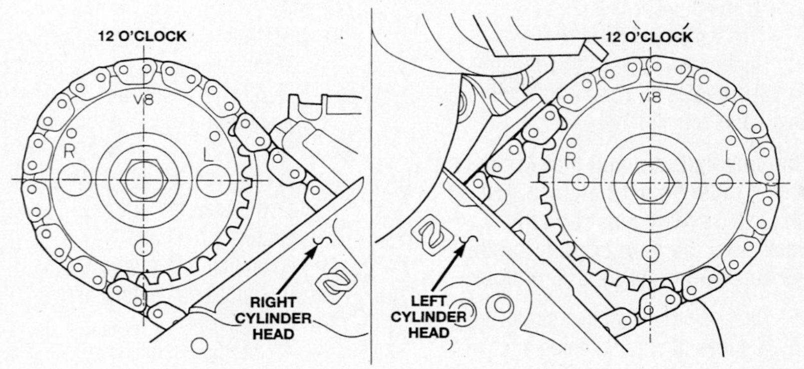

Fig. 75 Camshaft positioning—4.7L engine

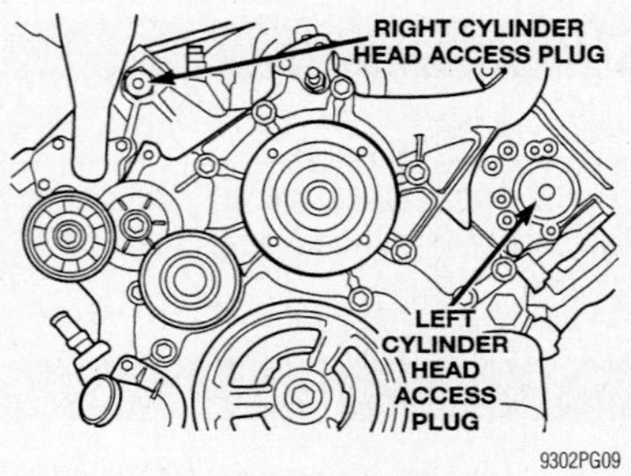

Fig. 76 Cylinder head access plug locations—4.7L engine

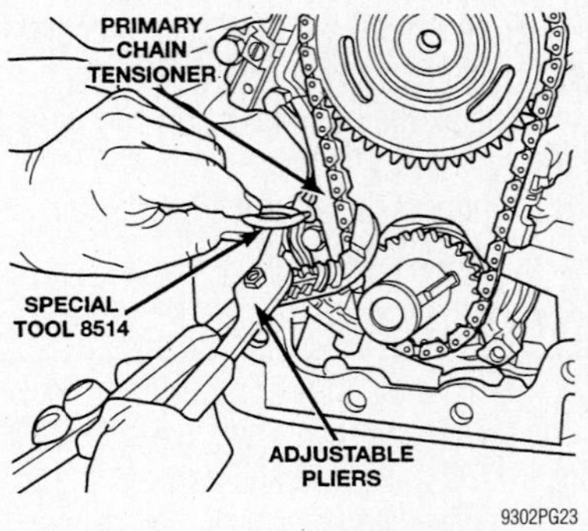

Fig. 77 Compress and lock the primary chain tensioner—4.7L engine

To install:

11. Use a small prytool to hold the ratchet pawl and compress the secondary timing chain tensioners in a vise and install locking pins.

➡The black bolts fasten the guide to the engine block and the silver bolts fasten the guide to the cylinder head.

12. Install or connect the following:
   - Secondary timing chain guides.

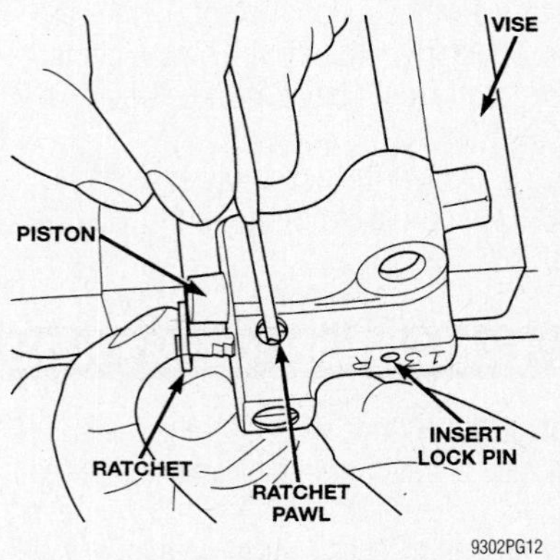

Fig. 78 Secondary timing chain tensioner preparation—4.7L engine

   Tighten the bolts to 21 ft. lbs. (28 Nm).
   - Secondary timing chains to the idler sprocket so that the double plated links on each chain are visible through the slots in the primary idler sprocket

13. Lock the secondary timing chains to the idler sprocket with Timing Chain Locking tool 8515 as shown.
14. Align the primary chain double plated links with the idler sprocket timing mark and the single plated link with the crankshaft sprocket timing mark.
15. Install the primary chain and sprockets. Tighten the idler sprocket bolt to 25 ft. lbs. (34 Nm).
16. Align the secondary chain single plated links with the timing marks on the secondary sprockets. Align the dot at the **L** mark on the left sprocket with the plated link on the left chain and the dot at the **R** mark on the right sprocket with the plated link on the right chain.
17. Rotate the camshafts back from the

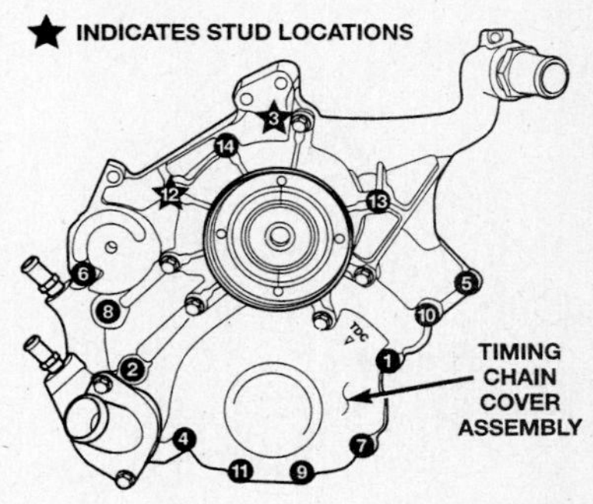

Fig. 79 Timing chain cover bolt torque sequence—4.7L engine

neutral position and install the camshaft sprockets.

18. Remove the secondary chain locking tool.
19. Remove the primary and secondary timing chain tensioner locking pins.
20. Hold the camshaft sprockets with a spanner wrench and tighten the retaining bolts to 90 ft. lbs. (122 Nm).
21. Install or connect the following:
   - Front cover. Tighten the bolts, in sequence, to 40 ft. lbs. (54 Nm).
   - Front crankshaft seal
   - Cylinder head access plugs
   - A/C compressor
   - Alternator
   - Accessory drive belt tensioner. Tighten the bolt to 40 ft. lbs. (54 Nm).
   - Oil fill housing
   - Crankshaft damper. Tighten the bolt to 130 ft. lbs. (175 Nm).
   - Power steering pump
   - Lower radiator hose
   - Heater hoses
   - Accessory drive belt
   - Engine cooling fan and shroud
   - Camshaft Position (CMP) sensor
   - Valve covers
   - Negative battery cable
22. Fill the cooling system.
23. Start the engine and check for leaks.

5.7L Engine

See Figure 80.

1. Before servicing the vehicle, refer to the precautions in the beginning of this manual.
2. Drain the cooling system.
3. Remove or disconnect the following:
   - Negative battery cable
   - Drive belt
   - Radiator fan
   - Coolant and washer bottles
   - Fan shroud

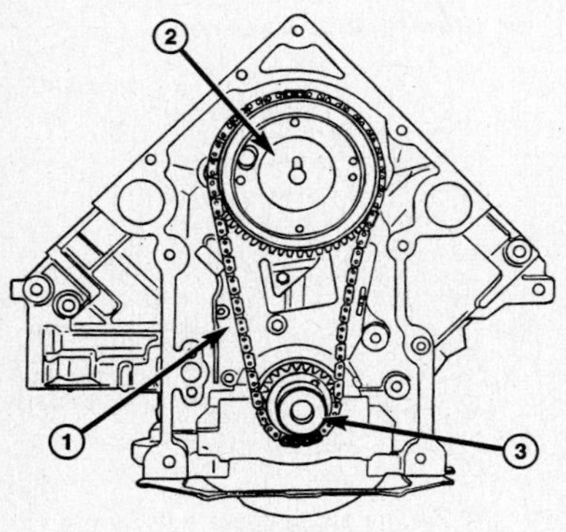

Fig. 80 Timing mark alignment—5.7L engine

- A/C compressor
- Alternator
- Radiator and heater hoses
- Tensioner and idler pulleys
- Crankshaft damper
- Power steering pump
- Oil pan and pickup tube
- Timing cover
- Re-install the damper

4. Rotate the crankshaft so that the camshaft sprocket and crankshaft sprocket timing marks are aligned.

➡**The camshaft pin and slot in the cam sprocket must be a 12 o'clock, the crankshaft keyway must be at 2 o'clock, and the dots or paint on the crank sprocket must be at 6 o'clock.**

5. Pin back the tensioner shoe.
6. Remove the timing chain and sprockets.

To install:

7. With the timing marks aligned, wrap the chain around the sprockets. The chain must be installed with the single plated link aligned with the dot or paint on the cam sprocket. The dot or paint on the crank sprocket should be aligned between the 2 plated links.
8. Install the assembly and torque the cam sprocket bolt to 90 ft. lbs. (122 Nm).
9. Unpin the tensioner and verify the alignment.
10. Install or connect the following:
    - Timing cover. Torque all fasteners to 21 ft. lbs. (28 Nm). Torque the large lifting lug to 40 ft. lbs. (55 Nm)
    - Oil pan and pickup tube
    - Power steering pump
    - Crankshaft damper
    - Tensioner and idler pulleys
    - Radiator and heater hoses
    - Alternator
    - A/C compressor
    - Fan shroud
    - Coolant and washer bottles
    - Radiator fan
    - Drive belt
    - Negative battery cable

VALVE LASH

ADJUSTMENT

These engines use hydraulic lifters. No maintenance or periodic adjustment is required.

ENGINE PERFORMANCE & EMISSION CONTROL

CAMSHAFT POSITION (CMP) SENSOR

LOCATION

See Figure 81.

The Camshaft Position (CMP) sensor is bolted to the right-front side of the right cylinder head on 3.7L and 4.7L engines. On 5.7L engines, it is located below the alternator on the timing chain cover.

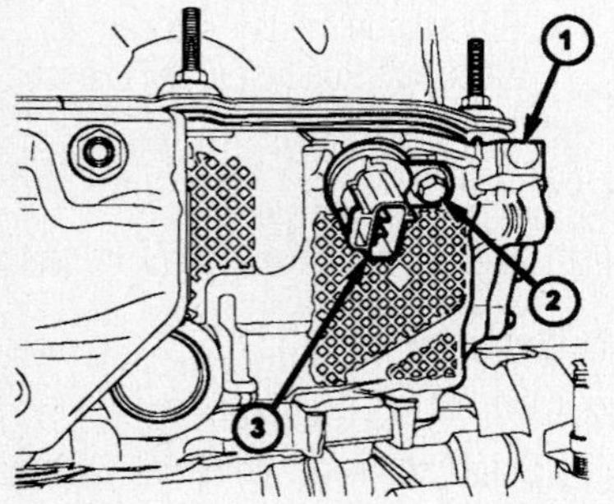

Fig. 81 CMP sensor mounting on 3.7L and 4.7L engines

OPERATION

The Camshaft Position Sensor (CMP) sensor contains a hall effect device referred to as a sync signal generator. A rotating target wheel (tone wheel) for the CMP is located at the front of the camshaft for the right cylinder head. This sync signal generator detects notches located on a tone wheel. As the tone wheel rotates, the notches pass through the sync signal generator. The signal from the CMP sensor is used in conjunction with the Crankshaft Position Sensor (CKP) to differentiate between fuel injection and spark events. It is also used to synchronize the fuel injectors with their respective cylinders.

When the leading edge of the target wheel notch enters the tip of the CMP, the interruption of magnetic field causes the voltage to switch high, resulting in a sync signal of approximately 5 volts. When the trailing edge of the target wheel notch leaves the tip of the CMP, the change of the magnetic field causes the sync signal voltage to switch to 0 volts.

REMOVAL & INSTALLATION

1. Raise and safely support the vehicle.
2. Disconnect the CMP electrical connector.
3. Remove the CMP sensor mounting bolts.
4. Carefully twist the sensor from the cylinder.

To install:

5. Check the condition of the sensor O-ring.
6. Clean out the machined hole in the cylinder head.
7. Apply a small amount of clean engine oil to the sensor O-ring.
8. Install the CMP sensor into the cylinder head with a slight rocking and twisting action.
9. Install the mounting bolt and tighten to 106 inch lbs. (12 Nm).
10. Connect the electrical connector.
11. Lower the vehicle.

TESTING

1. Using a diagnostic scan tool, check for the presence of any Diagnostic Trouble Codes (DTCs). Record and address these codes as necessary.
2. Turn the ignition **OFF** and disconnect the Camshaft Position (CMP) Sensor harness connector.

➡**If any of the test results fall outside of the specification, stop and repair the affected component.**

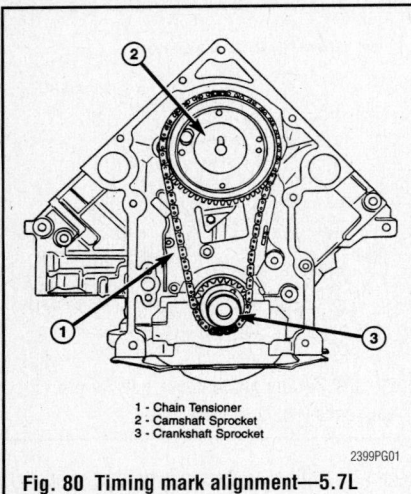

3. With the Ignition on, and engine not running, measure the voltage on the (F856) 5-volt Supply circuit in the CMP Sensor harness connector. Is the voltage between 4.5 and 5.2 volts?
4. If it is, measure the voltage on the (K44) CMP Signal circuit in the CMP Sensor harness connector. The

voltage should be between 4.5 and 5.0 volts.

5. If it is, turn the ignition off and disconnect the C2 ECM harness connector.

⁂ CAUTION

Do not probe the ECM harness connectors. Probing the ECM harness connectors will damage the ECM terminals resulting in poor terminal to pin connection. Install Miller Special Tool #8815 to perform diagnosis.

6. Measure the resistance of the (K900) Sensor ground circuit from the CMP Sensor harness connector to the appropriate terminal of special tool #8815. If the resistance is below 5.0 ohms, proceed to the next step, otherwise repair the open ground in the K900 sensor.

7. Measure the resistance between the (K44) CMP Signal circuit and the (F856) 5-volt Supply circuit in the CMP Sensor harness connector. If the resistance is below 5.0 ohms, repair the short between the (K44) CMP Signal circuit and the (F856) 5-volt Supply circuit.

➡Inspect the Camshaft sprocket for damage per the Service Information. If a problem is found repair as necessary.

CRANKSHAFT POSITION (CKP) SENSOR

LOCATION

See Figure 82.

The Crankshaft Position (CKP) sensor is mounted into the right rear side of the cylinder block.

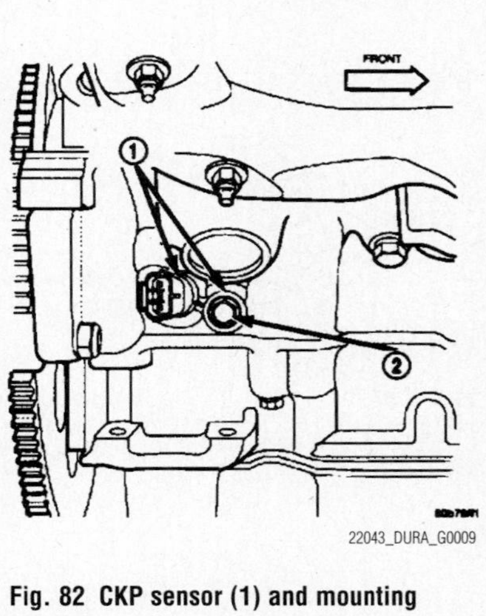

Fig. 82 CKP sensor (1) and mounting bolt (2)

OPERATION

The sensor generates pulses that are the input sent to the Electronic Control Module (ECM). The ECM interprets the sensor input to determine the crankshaft position and engine speed.

The sensor is a hall effect device combined with an internal magnet. It is also sensitive to steel within a certain distance from it. A tonewheel is bolted to the engine crankshaft. The tonewheel has notches that cause a pulse to be generated when they pass under the sensor.

REMOVAL & INSTALLATION

1. Raise and safely support the vehicle.
2. Disconnect the sensor electrical connector.
3. Remove the Crankshaft Position (CKP) sensor mounting bolt.
4. Carefully twist the CKP sensor from the cylinder block.

To install:

5. Check the condition of the O-ring.
6. Clean out the machined hole in the engine block.
7. Apply a small amount of clean engine oil to the sensor O-ring.
8. Install the CKP sensor into the engine block with a slight rocking and twisting action.
9. Install the mounting bolt and tighten to 21 ft. lbs. (28 Nm).
10. Connect the electrical connector.
11. Lower the vehicle.

TESTING

1. Using a diagnostic scan tool, check for the presence of any Diagnostic Trouble Codes (DTCs). Record and address these codes as necessary.
2. Turn the ignition off. Disconnect the Crankshaft Position (CKP) Sensor harness connector.

➡If the test results fall outside of the specification, stop and repair the affected component.

3. With the Ignition on, and engine not running, measure the voltage on the (F855) 5-volt Supply circuit in the CKP Sensor harness connector. Voltage should be between 4.5 and 5.2 volts.
4. If it is, measure the voltage on the (K24) CKP Signal circuit in the CKP Sensor harness connector. The sensor voltage should be approximately 5.0 volts (plus or minus.1 volt) with the connector disconnected.
5. If it is, turn the ignition off and disconnect the C2 ECM harness connector.

⁂ CAUTION

Do not probe the ECM harness connectors. Probing the ECM harness connectors will damage the ECM terminals resulting in poor terminal to pin connection. Install Miller Special Tool #8815 to perform diagnosis.

6. Measure the resistance of the (K900) Sensor ground circuit from the CKP Sensor harness connector to the appropriate terminal of special tool no. 8815. Resistance should be below 5.0 ohms.
7. If it is, measure the resistance between the (K24) CKP Signal circuit and the (F855) 5-volt Supply circuit in the CKP Sensor harness connector. If the resistance below 5.0 ohms, repair the short between the (K24) CKP Signal circuit and the (F855) 5-volt Supply circuit.
8. If not, replace the crankshaft position sensor.

ELECTRONIC CONTROL MODULE (ECM)

LOCATION

The Electronic Control Module (ECM) is attached to the inner fender located in the engine compartment

OPERATION

The Electronic Control Module (ECM) receives input signals from various switches and sensors. Based on these inputs, the ECM regulates various engine and vehicle operations through different system components. These components are referred to as Electronic Control Module (ECM) Outputs. The sensors and switches that provide inputs to the ECM are considered Electronic Control Module (ECM) Inputs.

The ECM adjusts ignition timing based upon inputs it receives from sensors that react to: engine rpm, manifold absolute pressure, engine coolant temperature, throttle position, transmission gear selection (automatic transmission), vehicle speed and the brake switch.

The ECM adjusts idle speed based on inputs it receives from sensors that react to: throttle position, vehicle speed, transmission gear selection, engine coolant temperature and from inputs it receives from the air conditioning clutch switch and brake switch.

Based on inputs that it receives, the ECM adjusts ignition coil dwell. The ECM also adjusts the generator charge rate through control of the generator field and provides speed control operation.

REMOVAL & INSTALLATION

⁂ WARNING

The use of a diagnostic scan tool is required the Electronic Control Module (ECM) is being in order to reprogram the new ECM.

1. Disconnect the negative battery cable.
2. Unplug the 38-way connectors from the ECM.

➡A locating pin is used in place of one of the mounting bolts.

3. Pry the clip from the locating pin.
4. Remove the two remaining mounting bolts.
5. Remove the ECM from the vehicle.

To install:

6. Position the ECM to the body and install the two mounting bolts.

➡Position the ground strap in place before tightening the mounting bolts.

7. Install the clip to the locating pin.
8. Tighten the mounting bolts to 35 inch lbs. (4 Nm).
9. Carefully plug in the 38-way connectors to the ECM.
10. Connect the negative battery cable.
11. Use a diagnostic scan tool to reprogram the ECM with the VIN and original mileage if ECM has been replaced.

TESTING

1. Start the engine and allow it to reach normal operating temperature. Using a diagnostic scan tool, check for the presence of any Diagnostic Trouble Codes (DTCs). Record and address these codes as necessary.
2. Refer to any Technical Service Bulletins (TSBs) that may apply.
3. Review the scan tool Freeze Frame information. If possible, try to duplicate the conditions under which the DTC set.
4. With the engine running at normal operating temperature, monitor the scan tool parameters related to the DTC while wiggling the wire harness. Look for parameter values to change and/or a DTC to set. Turn the ignition off.
5. Visually inspect the related wire harness. Disconnect all the related harness connectors. Look for any chafed, pierced, pinched, partially broken wires and broken, bent, pushed out, or corroded terminals. Perform a voltage drop test on the related circuits between the suspected inoperative component and the ECM.

⁂ CAUTION

Do not probe the ECM harness connectors. Probing the ECM harness connectors will damage the ECM terminals resulting in poor terminal to pin connection. Install Miller Special Tool #8815 to perform diagnosis.

6. Inspect and clean all ECM, engine, and chassis grounds that are related to the most current DTC.
7. If numerous trouble codes were set, use a wire schematic and look for any common ground or supply circuits.
8. For any Relay DTCs, actuate the Relay with the scan tool and wiggle the related wire harness to try to interrupt the actuation.
9. For intermittent Evaporative Emission trouble codes perform a visual and physical inspection of the related parts including hoses and the Fuel Filler cap.
10. Use the scan tool to perform a System Test if one applies to failing component. A co-pilot, data recorder, and/or lab scope should be used to help diagnose intermittent conditions.

ENGINE COOLANT TEMPERATURE (ECT) SENSOR

LOCATION

3.7 and 4.7L Engines

The Engine Coolant Temperature (ECT) sensor is installed into a water jacket at the front of the intake manifold.

5.7L Engine

See Figure 83.

The Engine Coolant Temperature (ECT) sensor is located under the air conditioning compressor. It is installed into a water jack at the front of the cylinder block.

OPERATION

The sensor provides an input to the Electronic Control Module (ECM). As coolant temperature varies, the sensor resistance changes, resulting in a different input voltage to the ECM. When the engine is cold, the ECM will demand slightly richer air-fuel mixtures and higher idle speeds until normal operating temperatures are reached.

The engine coolant sensor input also determines operation of the low and high speed cooling fans.

REMOVAL & INSTALLATION

3.7 and 4.7L Engines

1. Drain the cooling system.
2. Disconnect the sensor electrical connector.
3. Remove the Engine Coolant Temperature (ECT) sensor.

To install:

4. Apply thread sealant to the sensor threads.
5. Install the ECT sensor into the engine block and tighten the mounting bolt to 8 ft. lbs. (11 Nm).
6. Connect the electrical connector.
7. Refill the cooling system to the correct level.

5.7L Engine

1. Drain the cooling system.
2. Remove the accessory drive belt.

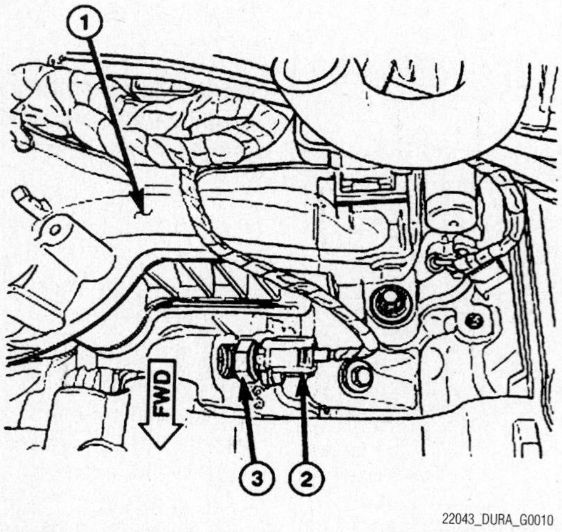

Fig. 83 ECT sensor mounting used on 5.7L engines

3. Carefully unbolt the A/C compressor. Temporarily support the compressor to access the Engine Coolant Temperature (ECT) sensor.

➡It is not necessary to disconnect the A/C lines from the compressor.

4. Disconnect the sensor electrical connector.
5. Remove the ECT sensor from the engine block.

To install:

6. Apply thread sealant to the sensor threads.
7. Install the sensor into the engine block and tighten the mounting bolt to 8 ft. lbs. (11 Nm).
8. Connect the electrical connector.
9. Position the A/C compressor into place and tighten the mounting bolts.
10. Install the accessory drive belt.
11. Refill the cooling system to the correct level.

TESTING

1. Turn the ignition **OFF**. If possible, allow the vehicle to sit with the ignition off for more than 8 hours in an environment where the temperature is consistent and above 20°F (-7°C).
2. Test drive the vehicle. The vehicle must exceed 30 mph (48 km/h) during the test drive. Do not cycle the ignition off when the test drive is completed.
3. With a scan tool, select View DTCs.
4. Turn the ignition off. Allow the vehicle to sit with the ignition off in an environment where the temperature is consistent and above 20°F (-7°C) until the engine coolant temperature is equal to ambient temperature. Turn the ignition on. With a scan tool, compare the AAT, ECT, and IAT sensor values.
5. If the ECT sensor value is not within 18°F (10°C) of the other two sensor values , perform the following:
6. Refer to any Technical Service Bulletins (TSBs) that may apply.
7. Review the scan tool Freeze Frame information. If possible, try to duplicate the conditions under which the DTC set.
8. With the engine running at normal operating temperature, monitor the scan tool parameters related to the DTC while wiggling the wire harness. Look for parameter values to change and/or a DTC to set. Turn the ignition off.
9. Visually inspect the related wire harness. Disconnect all the related harness connectors. Look for any chafed, pierced, pinched, partially broken wires and broken, bent, pushed out, or corroded terminals. Perform a voltage drop test on the related circuits between the suspected inoperative component and the ECM.

⁂ CAUTION

Do not probe the ECM harness connectors. Probing the ECM harness connectors will damage the ECM terminals resulting in poor terminal to pin connection. Install Miller Special Tool no. 8815 to perform diagnosis.

10. Inspect and clean all ECM, engine, and chassis grounds that are related to the most current DTC.
11. If numerous trouble codes were set, use a wire schematic and look for any common ground or supply circuits.
12. For any Relay DTCs, actuate the Relay with the scan tool and wiggle the related wire harness to try to interrupt the actuation.
13. For intermittent Evaporative Emission trouble codes perform a visual and physical inspection of the related parts including hoses and the Fuel Filler cap.
14. Use the scan tool to perform a System Test if one applies to failing component. A co-pilot, data recorder, and/or lab scope should be used to help diagnose intermittent conditions.

HEATED OXYGEN (HO2S) SENSOR

LOCATION

See Figure 84.

If equipped with a Federal Emission Package, two sensors are used: upstream (referred to as 1/1) and downstream (referred to as 1/2). With this emission package, the upstream sensor (1/1) is located just before the main catalytic converter. The downstream sensor (1/2) is located just after the main catalytic converter.

If equipped with a California Emission Package, 4 sensors are used: 2 upstream (referred to as 1/1 and 2/1) and 2 downstream (referred to as 1/2 and 2/2). With this emission package, the right upstream sensor (2/1) is located in the right exhaust downpipe just before the mini-catalytic converter. The left upstream sensor (1/1) is located in the left exhaust downpipe just before the mini-catalytic converter. The right downstream sensor (2/2) is located in the right exhaust downpipe just after the mini-catalytic converter, and before the main catalytic converter. The left downstream sensor (1/2) is located in the left exhaust downpipe just after the mini-catalytic converter, and before the main catalytic converter.

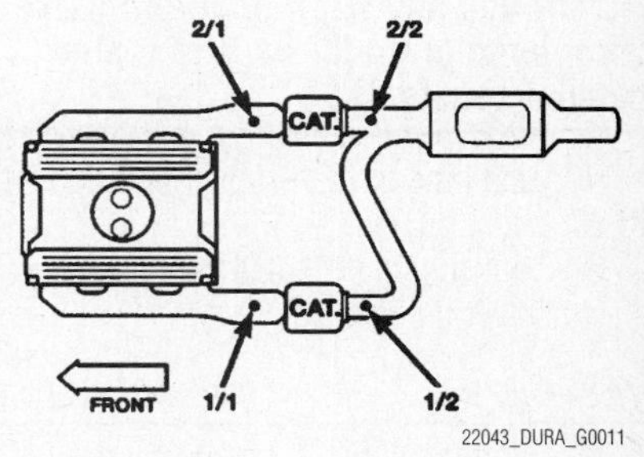

Fig. 84 Oxygen sensor mounting points

OPERATION

An O2 sensor is a galvanic battery that provides the ECM with a voltage signal (0-1 volt) inversely proportional to the amount of oxygen in the exhaust. In other words, if the oxygen content is low, the voltage output is high; if the oxygen content is high the output voltage is low. The ECM uses this information to adjust injector pulse-width to achieve the 14.7to1 air/fuel ratio necessary for proper engine operation and to control emissions.

The O2 sensor must have a source of oxygen from outside of the exhaust stream for comparison. Current O2 sensors receive their fresh oxygen (outside air) supply through the O2 sensor case housing.

Four wires (circuits) are used on each O2 sensor: a 12volt feed circuit for the sensor heating element; a ground circuit for the heater element; a low-noise sensor return circuit to the ECM, and an input circuit from the sensor back to the ECM to detect sensor operation.

REMOVAL & INSTALLATION

1. Raise and safely support the vehicle.
2. Disconnect the wire connector from oxygen sensor.

⁂ WARNING

When disconnecting sensor electrical connector, do not pull directly on wire going into sensor.

3. Remove the sensor with an oxygen sensor removal and installation tool.
4. Clean threads in exhaust pipe using appropriate tap.

To install:

➡Threads of new oxygen sensors are factory coated with anti-seize compound.

✻✻ WARNING

Do not add any additional anti-seize compound to the threads of a new oxygen sensor.

5. Install the oxygen sensor and tighten to 22 ft. lbs. (30 Nm).
6. Connect the electrical connector.
7. Lower the vehicle.

TESTING

1. Start the engine and allow it to idle for at least 60 seconds. Using a diagnostic scan tool, check for the presence of any Diagnostic Trouble Codes (DTCs). Record and address these codes as necessary.
2. Turn the ignition off, allow the sensor to cool down to room temperature disconnect the oxygen sensor wiring harness. Measure the resistance across the sensor heater control terminal and ground terminal. If resistance is not between 2 and 30 ohms, replace the sensor.
3. Refer to any Technical Service Bulletins (TSBs) that may apply.
4. Review the scan tool Freeze Frame information. If possible, try to duplicate the conditions under which the DTC set.
5. With the engine running at normal operating temperature, monitor the scan tool parameters related to the DTC while wiggling the wire harness. Look for parameter values to change and/or a DTC to set. Turn the ignition off.
6. Visually inspect the related wire harness. Disconnect all the related harness connectors. Look for any chafed, pierced, pinched, partially broken wires and broken, bent, pushed out, or corroded terminals. Perform a voltage drop test on the related circuits between the suspected inoperative component and the PCM.

✻✻ CAUTION

Do not probe the PCM harness connectors. Probing the PCM harness connectors will damage the PCM terminals resulting in poor terminal to pin connection. Install Miller Special Tool no. 8815 to perform diagnosis.

7. Inspect and clean all PCM, engine, and chassis grounds that are related to the most current DTC.
8. If numerous trouble codes were set, use a wire schematic and look for any common ground or supply circuits.
9. For any Relay DTCs, actuate the Relay with the scan tool and wiggle the related wire harness to try to interrupt the actuation.
10. For intermittent Evaporative Emission trouble codes perform a visual and physical inspection of the related parts including hoses and the Fuel Filler cap.
11. Use the scan tool to perform a System Test if one applies to failing component. A co-pilot, data recorder, and/or lab scope should be used to help diagnose intermittent conditions.

INTAKE AIR TEMPERATURE (IAT) SENSOR

LOCATION

The Intake Air Temperature (IAT) sensor is installed in the air inlet tube.

OPERATION

The IAT sensor is a two-wire Negative Thermal Coefficient (NTC) sensor. Meaning, as inlet air temperatures increase, resistance (voltage) in the sensor decreases. As temperature decreases, resistance (voltage) in the sensor increases.

The IAT sensor provides an input voltage to the Electronic Control Module (ECM) indicating the density of the air entering the intake manifold based upon intake manifold temperature. At key-on, a 5volt power circuit is supplied to the sensor from the ECM. The sensor is grounded at the ECM through a low-noise, sensor-return circuit.

REMOVAL & INSTALLATION

See Figure 85.

1. Disconnect the electrical connector form the Intake Air Temperature (IAT) sensor.
2. Clean any dirt from the air inlet tube at the sensor base.
3. Gently lift the small plastic release tab and rotate the sensor about ¼ turn counterclockwise to remove.

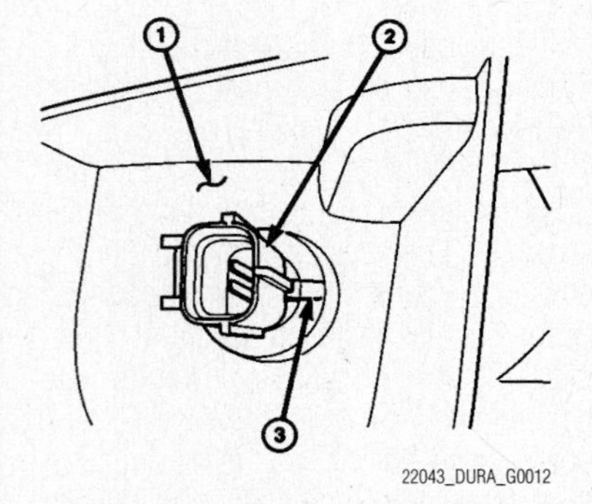

Fig. 85 The IAT sensor (2) is located in the air inlet (1). Lift the tab (3) to remove it

To install:

4. Check the condition of the sensor O-ring.
5. Clean the sensor mounting hole.
6. Position the sensor into the intake air tube and rotate clockwise until the release tab clicks into place.
7. Install the electrical connector.

TESTING

1. Turn the ignition off. If possible, allow the vehicle to sit with the ignition off for more than 8 hours in an environment where the temperature is consistent and above 20°F (-7°C).
2. Test drive the vehicle. The vehicle must exceed 30 mph (48 km/h) during the test drive. Do not cycle the ignition off when the test drive is completed.
3. With a scan tool, select View DTCs.
4. If a DTC is not active, perform the following:
5. Refer to any Technical Service Bulletins (TSBs) that may apply.
6. Review the scan tool Freeze Frame information. If possible, try to duplicate the conditions under which the DTC set.
7. With the engine running at normal operating temperature, monitor the scan tool parameters related to the DTC while wiggling the wire harness. Look for parameter values to change and/or a DTC to set. Turn the ignition off.
8. Visually inspect the related wire harness. Disconnect all the related harness connectors. Look for any chafed, pierced, pinched, partially broken wires and broken, bent, pushed out, or corroded terminals. Perform a voltage drop test on the related circuits between the suspected inoperative component and the ECM.

✻✻ CAUTION

Do not probe the ECM harness connectors. Probing the ECM harness connectors will damage the ECM terminals resulting in poor terminal to pin connection. Install Miller Special Tool no. 8815 to perform diagnosis.

9. Inspect and clean all ECM, engine, and chassis grounds that are related to the most current DTC.
10. If numerous trouble codes were set, use a wire schematic and look for any common ground or supply circuits.
11. For any Relay DTCs, actuate the Relay with the scan tool and wiggle the related wire harness to try to interrupt the actuation.
12. For intermittent Evaporative Emission trouble codes perform a visual and

physical inspection of the related parts including hoses and the Fuel Filler cap.

13. Use the scan tool to perform a System Test if one applies to failing component. A co-pilot, data recorder, and/or lab scope should be used to help diagnose intermittent conditions.

KNOCK SENSOR (KS)

LOCATION

3.7L and 4.7L Engines

Two Knock Sensors (KS) are bolted into the engine block under the intake manifold.

5.7L Engine

Two Knock Sensors (KS) are bolted into each side of the engine block under the exhaust manifolds.

OPERATION

Two knock sensors are used; one for each cylinder bank. When the knock sensor detects a knock in one of the cylinders on the corresponding bank, it sends an input signal to the Electronic Control Module (ECM). In response, the ECM retards ignition timing for all cylinders by a scheduled amount.

Knock sensors contain a piezoelectric material which constantly vibrates and sends an input voltage (signal) to the ECM while the engine operates. As the intensity of the crystal's vibration increases, the knock sensor output voltage also increases.

REMOVAL & INSTALLATION

3.7L and 4.7L Engines

1. Disconnect the knock sensor dual pigtail harness from engine wiring harness. This connection is made near rear of engine.
2. Remove the intake manifold
3. Remove the Knock Sensor (KS) mounting bolts.
4. Remove the sensors from engine.

To install:

5. Thoroughly clean the KS mounting holes.
6. Install the sensors into the engine block. Tighten the mounting bolts to 15 ft. lbs. (20 Nm).
7. Install the intake manifold.
8. Connect the KS wiring harness to the engine wiring harness at the rear of the engine.

5.7L Engine

1. Raise and safely support the vehicle.
2. Disconnect the Knock Sensor (KS) electrical connector.
3. Remove the KS mounting bolt.
4. Remove the sensor from the engine.

To install:

5. Thoroughly clean the KS mounting holes.
6. Install the sensors into the engine block. Tighten the mounting bolts to 15 ft. lbs. (20 Nm).
7. Connect the KS electrical connectors.
8. Lower the vehicle.

TESTING

1. Start the engine and allow it to reach normal operating temperature. Using a diagnostic scan tool, check for the presence of any Diagnostic Trouble Codes (DTCs). Record and address these codes as necessary.
2. Refer to any Technical Service Bulletins (TSBs) that may apply.
3. Review the scan tool Freeze Frame information. If possible, try to duplicate the conditions under which the DTC set.
4. With the engine running at normal operating temperature, monitor the scan tool parameters related to the DTC while wiggling the wire harness. Look for parameter values to change and/or a DTC to set. Turn the ignition off.
5. Visually inspect the related wire harness. Disconnect all the related harness connectors. Look for any chafed, pierced, pinched, partially broken wires and broken, bent, pushed out, or corroded terminals. Perform a voltage drop test on the related circuits between the suspected inoperative component and the ECM.

⁂ CAUTION

Do not probe the ECM harness connectors. Probing the ECM harness connectors will damage the ECM terminals resulting in poor terminal to pin connection. Install Miller Special Tool no. 8815 to perform diagnosis.

6. Inspect and clean all ECM, engine, and chassis grounds that are related to the most current DTC.
7. If numerous trouble codes were set, use a wire schematic and look for any common ground or supply circuits.
8. For any Relay DTCs, actuate the Relay with the scan tool and wiggle the related wire harness to try to interrupt the actuation.
9. For intermittent Evaporative Emission trouble codes perform a visual and physical inspection of the related parts including hoses and the Fuel Filler cap.
10. Use the scan tool to perform a System Test if one applies to failing component. A co-pilot, data recorder, and/or lab scope should be used to help diagnose intermittent conditions.

MANIFOLD ABSOLUTE PRESSURE (MAP) SENSOR

LOCATION

3.7L and 4.7L Engines

The Manifold Absolute Pressure (MAP) sensor is mounted to the front of the intake manifold with two bolts.

5.7L Engine

The Manifold Absolute Pressure (MAP) sensor is mounted to the back of the intake manifold by a quarter turn fastener.

OPERATION

The MAP sensor is used as an input to the Electronic Control Module (ECM). It contains a silicon based sensing unit to provide data on the manifold vacuum that draws the air/fuel mixture into the combustion chamber. The ECM requires this information to determine injector pulse width and spark advance. When manifold absolute pressure (MAP) equals Barometric pressure, the pulse width will be at maximum.

A 5-volt reference is supplied from the ECM and returns a voltage signal to the ECM that reflects manifold pressure. The zero pressure reading is 0.5V and full scale is 4.5V. For a pressure swing of 015 psi, the voltage changes 4.0V. To operate the sensor, it is supplied a regulated 4.8 to 5.1 volts. Ground is provided through the low-noise, sensor return circuit at the ECM.

The MAP sensor input is the number one contributor to fuel injector pulse width. The most important function of the MAP sensor is to determine barometric pressure. The ECM needs to know if the vehicle is at sea level or at a higher altitude, because the air density changes with altitude. It will also help to correct for varying barometric pressure. Barometric pressure and altitude have a direct inverse correlation; as altitude goes up, barometric goes down. At key-on, the ECM powers up and looks at MAP voltage, and based upon the voltage it sees, it knows the current barometric pressure (relative to altitude). Once the engine starts, the ECM looks at the voltage again, continuously every 12 milliseconds, and compares the current voltage to what it was at key-on. The difference between current voltage and what it was at Key On is the manifold vacuum.

During key-on (engine not running) the sensor reads (updates) barometric pressure. A normal range can be obtained by monitoring a known good sensor.

As the altitude increases, the air becomes thinner (less oxygen). If a vehicle is started and driven to a very different altitude than where it was at key-on, the barometric pressure needs to be updated. Any time the ECM sees Wide Open Throttle (WOT), based upon Throttle Position Sensor (TPS) angle and RPM, it will update barometric pressure in the MAP memory cell. With periodic updates, the ECM can make its calculations more effectively.

REMOVAL & INSTALLATION

3.7L and 4.7L Engines

See Figure 86.

1. Disconnect the sensor electrical connector.
2. Clean the area around the Manifold Absolute Pressure (MAP) sensor.
3. Remove the two mounting screws.
4. Remove the MAP sensor from the intake manifold.

To install:

5. Inspect the condition of the sensor O-ring and replace if necessary.
6. Position the MAP sensor into the manifold and install the two mounting screws.
7. Connect the electrical connector.

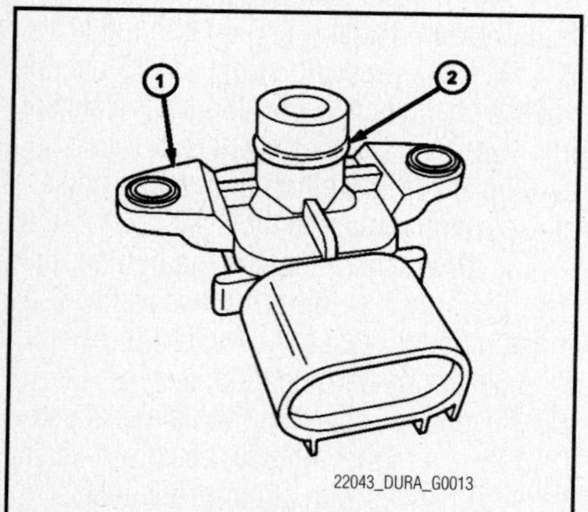

Fig. 86 MAP sensor (1) and o-ring (2)

5.7L Engine

1. Disconnect the electrical connector at the Manifold Absolute Pressure (MAP) sensor by sliding the release lock out. Then press down on the lock tab.
2. Rotate the MAP sensor ¼ turn counter-clockwise to remove.

To install:

3. Inspect the condition of the sensor O-ring and replace if necessary.
4. Position the MAP sensor into the intake manifold and rotate ¼ turn clockwise.
5. Connect the electrical connector to the MAP sensor until it clicks into place.

TESTING

1. Start the engine and allow it to reach normal operating temperature. Using a diagnostic scan tool, check for the presence of any Diagnostic Trouble Codes (DTCs). Record and address these codes as necessary.
2. Refer to any Technical Service Bulletins (TSBs) that may apply.
3. Review the scan tool Freeze Frame information. If possible, try to duplicate the conditions under which the DTC set.
4. With the engine running at normal operating temperature, monitor the scan tool parameters related to the DTC while wiggling the wire harness. Look for parameter values to change and/or a DTC to set. Turn the ignition off.
5. Visually inspect the related wire harness. Disconnect all the related harness connectors. Look for any chafed, pierced, pinched, partially broken wires and broken, bent, pushed out, or corroded terminals. Perform a voltage drop test on the related circuits between the suspected inoperative component and the ECM.

CAUTION

Do not probe the ECM harness connectors. Probing the ECM harness connectors will damage the ECM terminals resulting in poor terminal to pin connection. Install Miller Special Tool no. 8815 to perform diagnosis.

6. Inspect and clean all ECM, engine, and chassis grounds that are related to the most current DTC.
7. If numerous trouble codes were set, use a wire schematic and look for any common ground or supply circuits.
8. For any Relay DTCs, actuate the Relay with the scan tool and wiggle the related wire harness to try to interrupt the actuation.
9. For intermittent Evaporative Emission trouble codes perform a visual and physical inspection of the related parts including hoses and the Fuel Filler cap.
10. Use the scan tool to perform a System Test if one applies to failing component. A co-pilot, data recorder, and/or lab scope should be used to help diagnose intermittent conditions.

THROTTLE POSITION SENSOR (TPS)

LOCATION

3.7L and 4.7L Engines

The Throttle Position Sensor (TPS) is mounted on the throttle body and connected to the throttle blade shaft.

5.7L Engine

The 5.7L engine does not use a separate Throttle Position Sensor (TPS) on the throttle body. If it is determined, that the TPS signal is bad, the throttle body assembly must be replaced.

OPERATION

The Throttle Position Sensor (TPS) is a 3-wire variable resistor that provides the Electronic Control Module (ECM) with an input signal (voltage) that represents the throttle blade position of the throttle body. The sensor is connected to the throttle blade shaft. As the position of the throttle blade changes, the resistance (output voltage) of the TPS changes.

The ECM supplies approximately 5 volts to the TPS. The TPS output voltage (input signal to the ECM) represents the throttle blade position. The ECM receives an input signal voltage from the TPS. This will vary in an approximate range of from.26 volts at minimum throttle opening (idle), to 4.49 volts at wide-open throttle. Along with inputs from other sensors, the ECM uses the TPS input to determine current engine operating conditions. In response to engine operating conditions, the ECM will adjust fuel injector pulse width and ignition timing.

REMOVAL & INSTALLATION

1. Remove the air intake tube.
2. Disconnect the Throttle Position Sensor (TPS) electrical connector.
3. Remove the TPS mounting screws.
4. Remove the TPS.

To install:

➡The throttle shaft end of throttle body slides into a socket in TPS. The TPS must be installed so that it can be rotated a few degrees. If sensor will not rotate, install the sensor with throttle shaft on other side of socket tangs. The TPS will be under slight tension when rotated.

5. Install the TPS and tighten the mounting screws to 60 inch lbs. (7 Nm).
6. Connect the TPS electrical connector.

7. Manually operate the throttle by hand to check for any TPS binding before starting the engine.
8. Install the air intake tube.

TESTING

1. Start the engine and allow it to reach normal operating temperature. Using a diagnostic scan tool, check for the presence of any Diagnostic Trouble Codes (DTCs). Record and address these codes as necessary.
2. Refer to any Technical Service Bulletins (TSBs) that may apply.
3. Review the scan tool Freeze Frame information. If possible, try to duplicate the conditions under which the DTC set.
4. With the engine running at normal operating temperature, monitor the scan tool parameters related to the DTC while wiggling the wire harness. Look for parameter values to change and/or a DTC to set. Turn the ignition off.
5. Visually inspect the related wire harness. Disconnect all the related harness connectors. Look for any chafed, pierced, pinched, partially broken wires and broken, bent, pushed out, or corroded terminals. Perform a voltage drop test on the related circuits between the suspected inoperative component and the ECM.

CAUTION

Do not probe the ECM harness connectors. Probing the ECM harness connectors will damage the ECM terminals resulting in poor terminal to pin connection. Install Miller Special Tool no. 8815 to perform diagnosis.

6. Inspect and clean all ECM, engine, and chassis grounds that are related to the most current DTC.
7. If numerous trouble codes were set, use a wire schematic and look for any common ground or supply circuits.
8. For any Relay DTCs, actuate the Relay with the scan tool and wiggle the related wire harness to try to interrupt the actuation.
9. For intermittent Evaporative Emission trouble codes perform a visual and physical inspection of the related parts including hoses and the Fuel Filler cap.
10. Use the scan tool to perform a System Test if one applies to failing component. A co-pilot, data recorder, and/or lab scope should be used to help diagnose intermittent conditions.

VEHICLE SPEED SENSOR (VSS)

LOCATION

The Vehicle Speed Sensor (VSS) is located on the left side of the transmission case.

OPERATION

The Vehicle Speed Sensor generates an AC signal as its coil is excited by rotation of the rear planetary carrier lugs. The Transmission Control Module (TCM) interprets this information as output shaft RPM.

REMOVAL & INSTALLATION

1. Raise and safely support the vehicle.
2. Place a suitable catch pan under the transmission for any fluid.
3. Remove the wiring connector from the output speed sensor.
4. Remove the mounting bolt and remove the speed sensor from the transmission case.

To install:

5. Install the speed sensor into the transmission case and tighten the bolt to 105 inch lbs. (12 Nm).
6. Install the wiring connector to the speed sensor.
7. Verify the proper transmission fluid level and refill as necessary.
8. Lower the vehicle.

TESTING

1. Start the engine and allow it to reach normal operating temperature. Using a diagnostic scan tool, check for the presence of any Diagnostic Trouble Codes (DTCs). Record and address these codes as necessary.
2. Refer to any Technical Service Bulletins (TSBs) that may apply.
3. Review the scan tool Freeze Frame information. If possible, try to duplicate the conditions under which the DTC set.
4. With the engine running at normal operating temperature, monitor the scan tool parameters related to the DTC while wiggling the wire harness. Look for parameter values to change and/or a DTC to set. Turn the ignition off.
5. Visually inspect the related wire harness. Disconnect all the related harness connectors. Look for any chafed, pierced, pinched, partially broken wires and broken, bent, pushed out, or corroded terminals. Perform a voltage drop test on the related circuits between the suspected inoperative component and the ECM.

CAUTION

Do not probe the ECM harness connectors. Probing the PCM harness connectors will damage the PCM terminals resulting in poor terminal to pin connection. Install Miller Special Tool no. 8815 to perform diagnosis.

6. Inspect and clean all ECM, engine, and chassis grounds that are related to the most current DTC.
7. If numerous trouble codes were set, use a wire schematic and look for any common ground or supply circuits.
8. For any Relay DTCs, actuate the Relay with the scan tool and wiggle the related wire harness to try to interrupt the actuation.
9. For intermittent Evaporative Emission trouble codes perform a visual and physical inspection of the related parts including hoses and the Fuel Filler cap.
10. Use the scan tool to perform a System Test if one applies to failing component. A co-pilot, data recorder, and/or lab scope should be used to help diagnose intermittent conditions.

FUEL SYSTEM SERVICE PRECAUTIONS

Safety is the most important factor when performing not only fuel system maintenance but any type of maintenance. Failure to conduct maintenance and repairs in a safe manner may result in serious personal injury or death. Maintenance and testing of the vehicle's fuel system components can be accomplished safely and effectively by adhering to the following rules and guidelines.

- To avoid the possibility of fire and personal injury, always disconnect the negative battery cable unless the repair or test procedure requires that battery voltage be applied.
- Always relieve the fuel system pressure prior to disconnecting any fuel system component (injector, fuel rail, pressure regulator, etc.), fitting or fuel line connection. Exercise extreme caution whenever relieving fuel system pressure to avoid exposing skin, face and eyes to fuel spray. Please be advised that fuel under pressure may penetrate the skin or any part of the body that it contacts.
- Always place a shop towel or cloth around the fitting or connection prior to loosening to absorb any excess fuel due to spillage. Ensure that all fuel spillage (should it occur) is quickly removed from engine surfaces. Ensure that all fuel soaked cloths or towels are deposited into a suitable waste container.
- Always keep a dry chemical (Class B) fire extinguisher near the work area.
- Do not allow fuel spray or fuel vapors to come into contact with a spark or open flame.
- Always use a back-up wrench when loosening and tightening fuel line connection fittings. This will prevent unnecessary stress and torsion to fuel line piping.
- Always replace worn fuel fitting O-rings with new Do not substitute fuel hose or equivalent where fuel pipe is installed.

Before servicing the vehicle, make sure to also refer to the precautions in the beginning of this section as well.

RELIEVING FUEL SYSTEM PRESSURE

1. Before servicing the vehicle, refer to the precautions in the beginning of this manual.
2. Disconnect the negative battery cable.
3. Remove the fuel tank filler cap to release any fuel tank pressure.
4. Remove the fuel pump relay from the PDC.
5. Start and run the engine until it stops.
6. Unplug the connector from any injector and connect a jumper wire from either injector terminal to the positive battery terminal. Connect another jumper wire to the other terminal and momentarily touch the other end to the negative battery terminal.

**** WARNING**

Just touch the jumper to the battery. Powering the injector for more than a few seconds will permanently damage it.

7. Place a rag below the quick-disconnect coupling at the fuel rail and disconnect it.

FUEL FILTER

REMOVAL & INSTALLATION

A separate fuel filter is not used. The fuel filter is built into the fuel pump module.

FUEL INJECTORS

REMOVAL & INSTALLATION

3.7L and 5.7L Engines

1. Remove fuel rail.
2. Disconnect clip(s) that retain fuel injector(s) to fuel rail.

To install:

3. Install fuel injector(s) into fuel rail assembly and install retaining clip(s).
4. If same injector(s) is being reinstalled, install new O-ring(s).
5. Apply a small amount of clean engine oil to each injector O-ring. This will aid in installation.
6. Install fuel rail.
7. Start engine and check for fuel leaks.

4.7L Engine

1. Before servicing the vehicle, refer to the precautions in the beginning of this manual.
2. Relieve fuel system pressure.
3. Remove or disconnect the following:
   - Negative battery cable
   - Air intake assembly
   - Alternator wiring connectors
   - Fuel line
   - Throttle body vacuum lines and electrical connectors
   - Fuel injector connectors
   - Manifold Absolute Pressure (MAP) sensor connector
   - Intake Air Temperature (IAT) sensor connector
   - Ignition coils
   - Fuel supply manifold with injectors attached
   - Fuel injectors

To install:

4. Install or connect the following:
   - Fuel injectors, using new O-rings
   - Fuel supply manifold with injectors attached. Tighten the bolts to 20 ft. lbs. (27 Nm).
   - Ignition coils
   - IAT sensor connector
   - MAP sensor connector
   - Fuel injector connectors
   - Throttle body vacuum lines and electrical connectors
   - Fuel line
   - Alternator wiring connectors
   - Air intake assembly
   - Negative battery cable
5. Start the engine and check for leaks.

FUEL PUMP

REMOVAL & INSTALLATION

See Figure 87.

1. Before servicing the vehicle, refer to the precautions in the beginning of this manual.

**** CAUTION**

The fuel system is under a constant pressure (even with the engine off). Before servicing the fuel pump module, the fuel system pressure must be released.

2. Drain the tank.
3. Release fuel system pressure.
4. Raise vehicle.
5. Thoroughly clean area around fuel fill fitting and rubber fuel fill hose at rear of fuel tank.
6. Loosen clamp at tank fitting and disconnect rubber fuel fill hose at fuel tank fitting. Using an approved gas holding tank, drain fuel tank through this fitting.
7. Loosen clamp and disconnect rubber fill hose at tank fitting.
8. At rear of tank, disconnect fuel pump module electrical jumper connector from body connector.
9. At rear of tank, disconnect EVAP lines and from lines and.

10. At front of tank, disconnect fuel and EVAP lines and from lines and.
11. Support tank with a hydraulic jack.
12. Remove bolts and at right side of fuel tank.
13. Remove bolts at left side of fuel tank.
14. Lower tank for removal.
15. Note rotational position of module before attempting removal. An indexing arrow is located on top of module for this purpose.
16. Position Special Tool 9340, or equivalent, into notches on outside edge of lockring.
17. Install ½ inch drive breaker bar to tool 9340.
18. Rotate breaker bar counter-clockwise to remove lockring.
19. Remove lockring. The module will spring up slightly when lockring is removed.
20. Remove module from fuel tank. Be careful not to bend float arm while removing.

To install:

➡Whenever the fuel pump module is serviced, the rubber seal (gasket) must be replaced.

21. Using a new seal (gasket), position fuel pump module into opening in fuel tank.
22. Position lockring over top of fuel pump module.
23. Rotate module until embossed alignment arrow points to center alignment mark. This step must be performed to prevent float from contacting side of fuel tank. Also be sure fuel fitting on top of pump module is pointed to driver's side of vehicle.
24. Install Special Tool 9340 to lockring.
25. Install ½ drive breaker into Special Tool 9340.
26. Tighten lockring (clockwise) until all seven notches have engaged.
27. Position fuel tank to hydraulic jack.
28. Raise tank until positioned to body.
29. Install and tighten bolts to 50 ft. lbs. (68 Nm).
30. Remove hydraulic jack.
31. Connect EVAP, ORVR, fuel and NVLD lines at front and rear of tank.
32. Connect fuel pump module electrical jumper connector to body connector.
33. Connect rubber fill hose to tank fitting and tighten clamp.
34. Lower vehicle.
35. Fill fuel tank with fuel.
36. Start engine and check for fuel leaks near top of module.

FUEL TANK

REMOVAL & INSTALLATION

See Figure 88.

1. Before servicing the vehicle, refer to the precautions in the beginning of this manual.
2. Release the fuel system pressure.
3. Raise and safely support the vehicle.
4. Drain the fuel tank
5. Loosen the clamp and disconnect the rubber fill hose at tank fitting.
6. At the rear of the tank, unplug the fuel pump module electrical jumper connector from the body connector.
7. At the rear of the tank, disconnect the EVAP lines.
8. At the front of the tank, disconnect fuel and EVAP lines.
9. Support the tank with a hydraulic jack.
10. Remove the bolts at the right side of the fuel tank.
11. Remove the bolts at the left side of the fuel tank.
12. Lower the tank for removal.
13. Installation is the reverse of removal. Tighten the strap bolts to 50 ft. lbs. (68 Nm).

IDLE SPEED

ADJUSTMENT

Idle speed/mixture is maintained by the Electronic Control Module (ECM). No adjustment is necessary or possible.

THROTTLE BODY

REMOVAL & INSTALLATION

3.7L Engine

A (factory adjusted) set screw is used to mechanically limit the position of the throttle body throttle plate. Never attempt to adjust the engine idle speed using this screw. All idle speed functions are controlled by the Power train Control Module (PCM).

1. Remove air cleaner tube at throttle body.
2. Disconnect throttle body electrical connectors at IAC motor and TPS.
3. Remove all control cables from throttle body (lever) arm.
4. Disconnect necessary vacuum lines at throttle body.
5. Remove three throttle body mounting bolts.
6. Remove throttle body from intake manifold.
7. Check condition of old throttle body-to-intake manifold O-ring.

To install:

8. Check condition of throttle body-to-intake manifold O-ring. Replace as necessary.
9. Clean mating surfaces of throttle body and intake manifold.

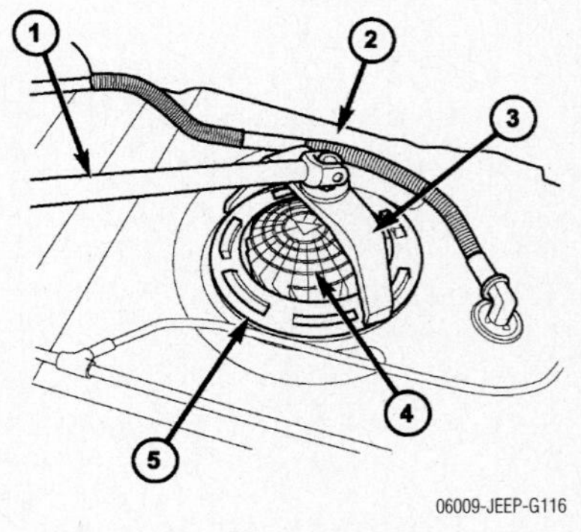

Fig. 87 Installing the fuel module (1) breaker bar, (2) tank, (3) tool 9340, (4) module, (5) locking ring

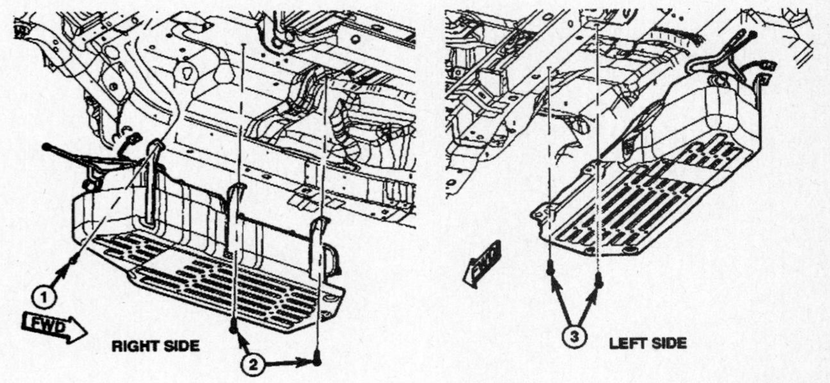

Fig. 88 Exploded view of the fuel tank mounting bolt locations

10. Install throttle body-to-intake manifold O-ring.
11. Install throttle body to intake manifold.
12. Install 3 mounting bolts. Tighten bolts to 105 inch lbs. (12 Nm).
13. Install control cables.
14. Install electrical connectors.
15. Install necessary vacuum lines.
16. Install air plenum.

4.7L Engine

See Figure 89.

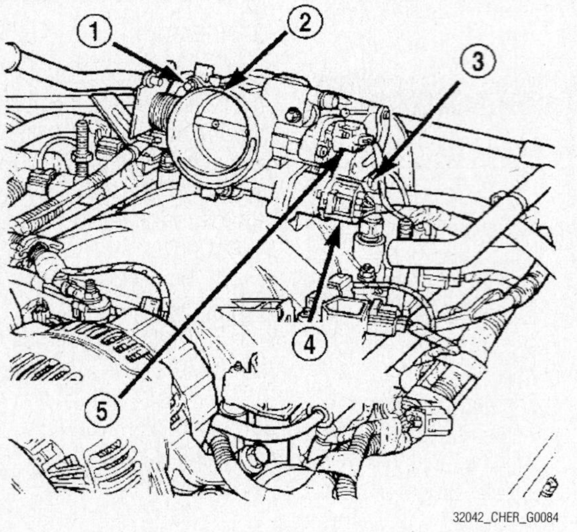

Fig. 89 Throttle body, sensors and electrical connectors for the 4.7L engine

1. Remove the air duct and air resonator box at throttle body.
2. Disconnect throttle body electrical connectors at IAC motor and TPS.
3. Remove vacuum line at throttle body.
4. Remove all control cables from throttle body (lever) arm.
5. Remove three throttle body mounting bolts.
6. Remove throttle body from intake manifold.

To install:

7. Clean throttle body-to-intake manifold O-ring.
8. Clean mating surfaces of throttle body and intake manifold.
9. Install throttle body to intake manifold by positioning throttle body to manifold alignment pins.
10. Install three mounting bolts. Tighten bolts to 105 in. lbs. (12 Nm).
11. Install control cables.
12. Install vacuum line to throttle body.
13. Install electrical connectors.
14. Install air duct/air box at throttle body.

5.7L Engine

✻✻ CAUTION

Do not use spray (carburetor) cleaners on any part of the throttle body. Do not apply silicone lubricants to any part of the throttle body.

1. Remove air duct and air resonator box at throttle body.
2. Disconnect electrical connector at throttle body.
3. Remove four throttle body mounting bolts.
4. Remove throttle body from intake manifold.
5. Check condition of throttle body O-ring.

To install:

✻✻ CAUTION

Do not use spray (carburetor) cleaners on any part of the throttle body. Do not apply silicone lubricants to any part of the throttle body.

6. Clean and check condition of throttle body-to-intake manifold O-ring.
7. Clean mating surfaces of throttle body and intake manifold.
8. Install throttle body to intake manifold by positioning throttle body to manifold alignment pins.
9. Install 4 mounting bolts.
10. Install electrical connector.
11. Install air plenum.
12. A Scan Tool may be used to learn electrical parameters.
13. If the previous step is not performed, a Diagnostic Trouble Code (DTC) will be set.
14. If necessary, use a scan tool to erase any Diagnostic Trouble Codes (DTCs) from PCM.

HEATING & AIR CONDITIONING SYSTEM

BLOWER MOTOR

REMOVAL & INSTALLATION

See Figure 90.

1. Disconnect and isolate the negative battery cable.
2. Remove the instrument panel silencer from the passenger side of the instrument panel.
3. Remove the glove box from the instrument panel.
4. Disconnect the blower motor wire harness connector from the blower motor power module or resistor , depending on how equipped.
5. Remove the three screws that secure the blower motor to the HVAC housing.
6. Remove the blower motor from the HVAC housing.

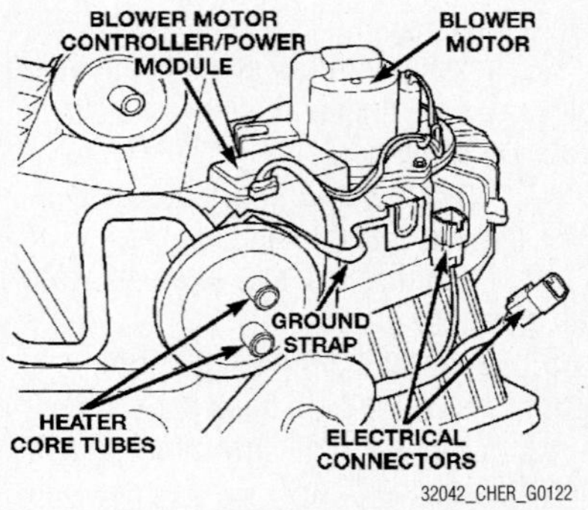

Fig. 90 View of the blower motor (housing removed) on the Grand Cherokee

To install:

7. Position the blower motor into the HVAC housing.
8. Install the three screws that secure the blower motor to the HVAC housing. Tighten the screws to 20 inch lbs. (2.2 Nm).
9. Connect the wire harness connector to the blower motor power module or resistor, depending on how equipped.
10. Install the glove box into the instrument panel.
11. Install the instrument panel silencer onto the passenger side of the instrument panel.
12. Reconnect the negative battery cable.

HEATER CORE

REMOVAL & INSTALLATION

See Figure 91.

1. Before servicing the vehicle, refer to the precautions in the beginning of this manual.

✲✲ CAUTION

On vehicles equipped with airbags, disable the airbag system before attempting any steering wheel, steering column, or instrument panel component diagnosis or service. Disconnect and isolate the negative battery (ground) cable, then wait two minutes for the airbag system capacitor to discharge before performing further diagnosis or service. This is the only sure way to disable the airbag system. Failure to take the proper precautions could result in accidental airbag deployment and possible personal injury or death.

2. Drain the engine cooling system.
3. If required, disconnect the heater hoses from the heater core tubes in the engine compartment.
4. Remove the bolts and remove the driver's side hush panel.
5. Using a trim stick, separate the upper clips and rotate the cover down and release the lower hinges at the bottom and remove the opening cover.

✲✲ CAUTION

Before servicing the steering Column the airbag system must be disarmed. Failure to do so may result in accidental deployment of the airbag and possible personal injury.

6. Remove the three bolts in the lower shroud.

➡Use care not to break off the tangs on the shrouds.

7. Then unsnap the lower shroud from the upper shroud.
8. Disconnect the steering column electrical connectors.
9. Remove the pinch bolt.
10. Remove the column support bolts.
11. Remove the column cross bolt and slide the column downward off the bracket and remove the steering column.
12. Remove the nuts attaching the instrument panel to the pedal support bracket.
13. Using a trim stick, remove the ignition cylinder bezel.
14. Remove the screws and remove the ignition cylinder
15. Disconnect the electrical connector.
16. Using a trim stick, remove the left side cover.
17. Remove the left side door sill trim.
18. Remove the driver's side cowl trim panel.
19. Disconnect the electrical connectors.
20. Disconnect the electrical connectors.
21. Remove the bolts and disconnect the ground wires within the steering column opening to the left of the steering column.
22. Disconnect the white adjustable pedal electrical connector.
23. Remove the bolts and remove the left a-pillar trim.
24. Remove the two left side bolts and one screw at the a-pillar support.
25. Using a trim stick, remove the shifter bezel ring.
26. Using a trim stick, remove the shifter bezel.
27. Remove the center console back cover and disconnect the electrical connector.
28. Remove the screws and remove the console.
29. Disconnect the electrical connectors under the console.
30. Open the glove box and push the stop tabs down to drop the glove box out of the instrument panel.
31. Rotate the box down and release the door hinges at the bottom and remove the glove box.
32. Remove the passenger side hush panel.
33. Remove the right side door sill trim.
34. Remove the nut, separate the right cowl trim panel and remove.
35. Remove the right side end cap.
36. Disconnect the electrical connectors.
37. Remove the bolts and remove the right a-pillar trim panel.
38. Remove the two right side bolts and one screw at the a-pillar support.
39. Using a trim stick, remove the defroster grills.
40. Remove the two fence line nuts.
41. Using a trim stick, remove the radio bezel.
42. Using a trim stick, remove the center bezel and disconnect the electrical connectors.
43. Remove the nut from the HVAC support stud behind the center bezel.
44. Remove the screw to the HVAC from under the glove box opening.
45. Remove the HVAC bracket bolt from the glove box opening.

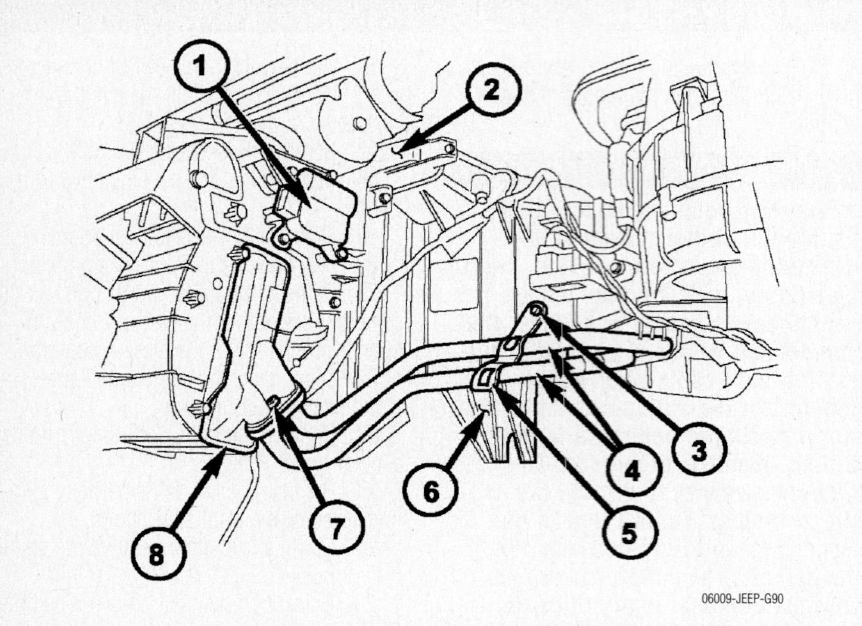

Fig. 91 Heater core plumbing and related parts: (1) blend door actuator, (2) HVAC air distribution housing, (3) heater core tube screw, (4) heater core tubes, (5) retaining bracket, (6) HVAC housing, (7) core tube bolt, (8) heater core

46. Remove the left and right center support brackets.
47. Remove the center floor duct.
48. Remove the radio.
49. Remove the two HVAC bolts from the radio opening.
50. Remove the instrument panel assembly.
51. Remove the five screws that secure the heater core and tube cover to the HVAC housing.
52. Remove the heater core and tube cover from the HVAC housing.
53. If equipped with dual zone heating-A/C, remove the blend door actuator from the passenger side of the HVAC air distribution housing.
54. Remove the screw that secure the heater core tubes and retaining bracket to the HVAC housing.

➡Take proper precautions to protect the carpeting from engine coolant. Have absorbent toweling readily available to clean up any spills.

55. Remove the bolt that secures the heater tubes to the heater core.
56. Disconnect the heater core tubes from the heater core and remove and discard the O-ring seals.
57. Install plugs in, or tape over the opened heater core ports.
58. Carefully pull the heater core out of the HVAC air distribution housing.
59. If required, remove the heater core tubes from the vehicle.

To install:

60. Carefully install the heater core into the passenger's side of the HVAC air distribution housing.
61. Remove the tape or plugs from the heater core ports.
62. If removed, position the heater core tubes into the vehicle.
63. Lubricate new rubber O-ring seals with clean engine coolant and install them onto the heater core tubes. Use only the specified O-ring as they are made of a special material for the engine cooling system.
64. Connect the heater core tubes to the heater core.
65. Install the bolt that secures the heater core tubes to the heater core. Tighten the bolt securely.
66. Install the screw that secures the heater core tube retaining bracket to the HVAC housing. Tighten the screw to 20 inch lbs. (2.2 Nm).
67. If equipped with dual zone heating-A/C, install the blend door actuator onto the passenger side of the HVAC air distribution housing.
68. Install the heater core and tube cover onto the HVAC housing.
69. Install the five screws that secure the heater core and tube cover to the HVAC housing. Tighten the screws to 20 inch lbs. (2.2 Nm).
70. Before proceeding with installation of the instrument panel assembly, remove the load clips from each a-pillar and install onto the sides of the panel using the screw.
71. Place the instrument panel into the vehicle and position onto the a-pillars using the load clips.
72. Install the two bolts on the right side and tighten the bolts to 95 inch lbs. (11 Nm).
73. Install the two fence line nuts.
74. Guide the peddle support studs on the driver's side, into the slots in the instrument panel reinforcement.
75. Position the center stack brackets in front of the duct work.
76. Rotate the instrument panel back and guide the HVAC stud.
77. Continue to rotate the instrument panel back and guide the tube brackets located in the radio opening, into the HVAC.
78. Install the screw at the bottom of the column opening next to the center stack up from the bottom attaching the HVAC.
79. Install the bolt at the HVAC blower motor housing.
80. Install the screw at the bottom of the glove box opening to the blower motor housing support
81. Snap the lower glove box hinges over the pivots and rotate up.
82. Push the stop tabs down and close the glove box.
83. Connect the right side wiring.
84. Install the right hush panel trim.
85. Install the right cowl trim and position the door seal back.
86. Position the right side door sill trim and seat fully.
87. Install the right a-pillar trim, the bolts and position the door seal back.
88. Install the two bolts on the left side and tighten to 95 inch lbs. (11 Nm).
89. Position the right side end cap and seat fully.
90. Install the two nuts on the studs above the column tighten the nuts to 105 inch lbs. (12 Nm).
91. Connect the two left bulk connectors.
92. Connect the two fuse block connectors.
93. Connect the white connector to adjustable brake pedal.
94. Install the grounds within the steering column opening and install the bolts.
95. Install the left cowl trim panel and install the nut
96. Install the left door sill.
97. Install the column cross bolt and tighten to 105 inch lbs. (12 Nm).
98. Position the steering column shaft into the slip joint.

99. Lift the column into position and install the bolts.

100. Tighten the bolts to 105 inch lbs. (12 Nm).

101. Slide the coupler onto the column shaft and install a new coupler bolt. Tighten the coupler bolt to 36 ft. lbs. (49 Nm).

102. Connect the shifter cable and electrical connectors to the ignition.

103. Install the ignition cylinder and install the screws.

104. Position the ignition bezel and seat fully.

105. Connect the electrical connector for the multifunction switch

106. Install the upper shroud on the column.

107. Install the lower shroud to the column.

108. Snap the two halves back into place.

109. Install the three mounting bolts to secure the shroud in place.

110. Snap the steering column opening cover lower hinges onto the pins and roll cover up.

111. Seat the upper retaining clips fully.

112. Install the hush panel.

113. Connect the column electrical connectors.

114. Install the column covers.

115. Install the left a-pillar trim, the bolts and position the door seal back.

116. Position the left side end cap and seat fully.

117. Install the center support nut onto the stud.

118. Install the two HVAC bolts within the radio opening.

119. Install the radio.

120. Install the radio bezel.

121. Install the left and right center support brackets and nuts and tighten to 105 inch lbs. (12 Nm).

122. Position the center wire harness and connect the electrical connectors.

123. Install the center bezel.

124. Position the defroster vents and seat fully.

125. Connect the center harness electrical connectors (ground, module, shifter, brake lever).

126. Install the center floor duct.

127. Position the console into the vehicle and install the screws.

128. Connect the electrical connector and install the rear cover onto the console.

129. Position the shifter bezel and seat fully.

130. Position the shifter bezel trim ring and seat fully.

131. If disconnected, connect the heater hoses to the heater core tubes in the engine compartment.

132. Connect the negative battery cable.

133. If the heater core is being replaced, flush the cooling system.

134.Refill the engine cooling system.

STEERING

POWER STEERING GEAR

REMOVAL & INSTALLATION

See Figures 92 through 100.

1. Before servicing the vehicle, refer to the precautions in the beginning of this manual.
2. Place the front wheels in the straight ahead position with the steering wheel centered and locked with a steering wheel lock.
3. Drain or siphon the power steering system.
4. Remove the column coupler shaft bolt and remove the shaft from the gear.
5. Remove the oil drip tray.
6. Remove the pressure line at the gear.

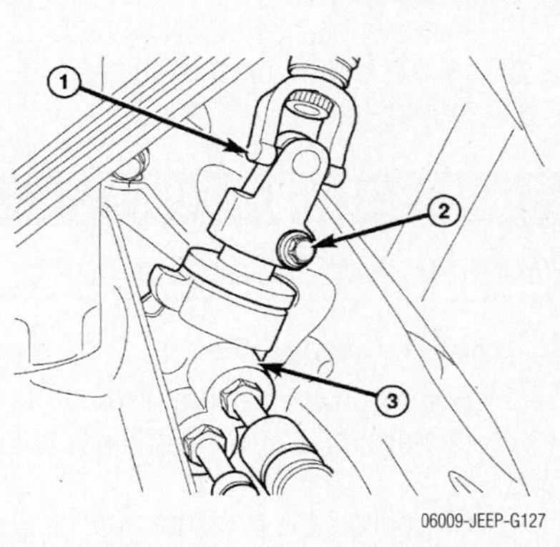

Fig. 92 Remove the column (1) coupler shaft bolt (2) and remove the shaft from the gear (3)

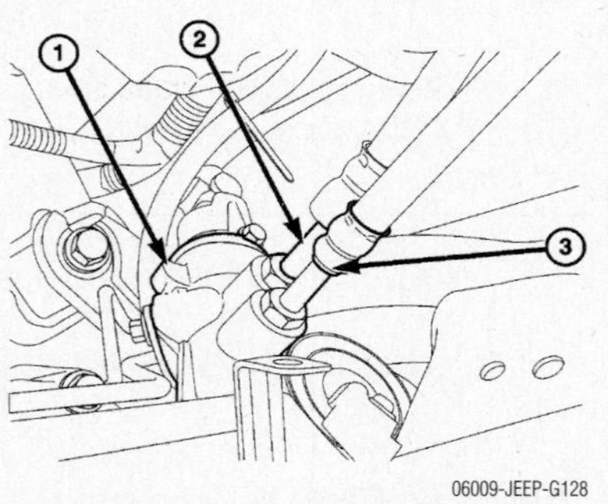

Fig. 93 Remove the pressure line (1) and return line (2) at the gear (3)

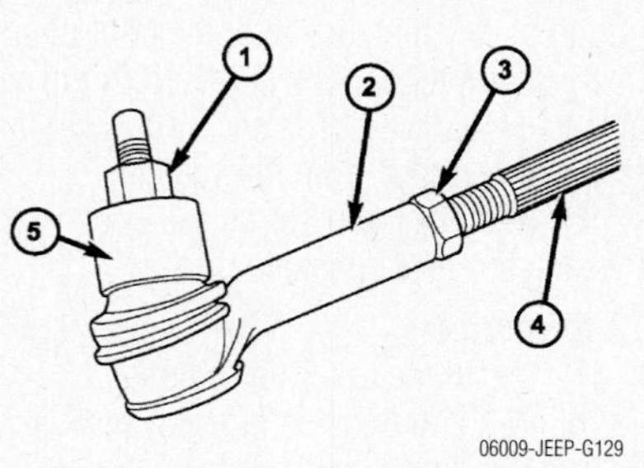

Fig. 94 Tie rod end. (1) ball stud nut, (2) tie rod end, (3) jam nut, (4) tie rod, (5) ball joint

7. Remove the return line at the gear.
8. Raise and support the vehicle.
9. Remove the front tires.
10. Loosen the tie rod end jam nuts.

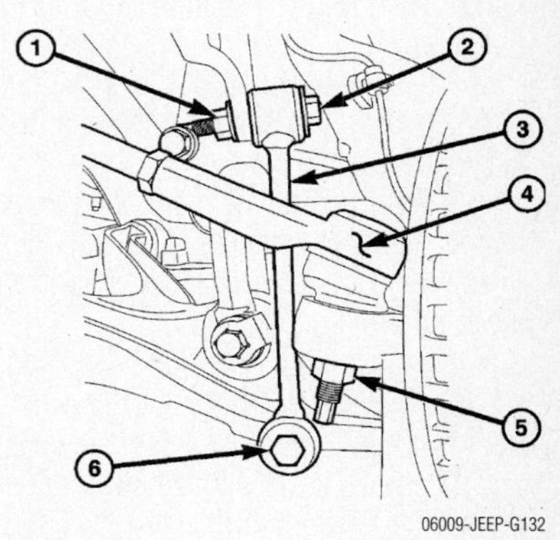

Fig. 95 Stabilizer link upper attaching nut (1), upper attaching bolt (2), stabilizer link (3), tie rod end (4), tie rod ball stud nut (5), lower link attaching bolt (6)

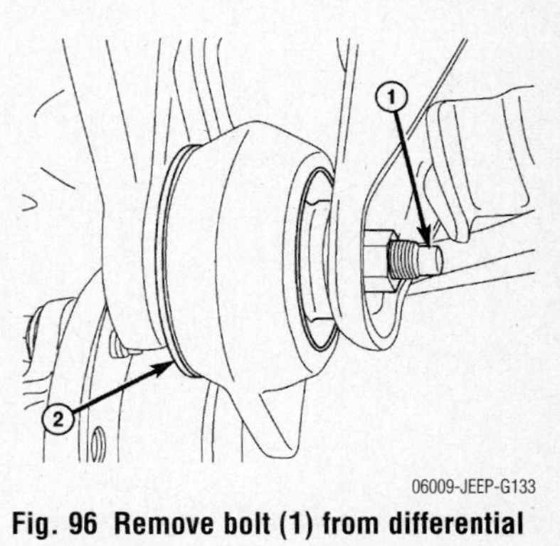

Fig. 96 Remove bolt (1) from differential bushing (2)

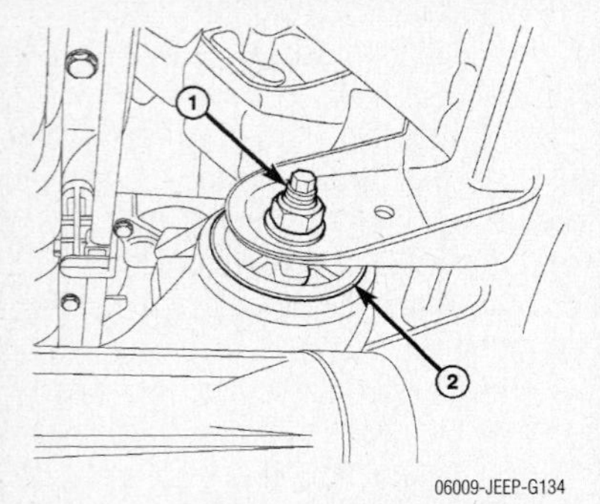

Fig. 97 Remove bolt (1) from axle tube bushing (2)

11. Remove the outer tie rod end nut and separate the tie rod from the knuckle using the proper tool.
12. Remove the front splash shield.
13. With 4-wheel drive:
   a. With vehicle in neutral, position vehicle on hoist.
   b. Remove skid plate.
   c. Remove differential housing drain plug and drain fluid.
   d. Mark front driveshaft and pinion flange. Remove driveshaft from pinion flange.
   e. Remove halfshaft hub/bearing nuts.
   f. Remove wheel speed sensors from hub/bearings.
   g. Remove brake calipers bolts and remove calipers from caliper adapters.
   h. Remove stabilizer links bolts from lower control arms.
   i. Remove upper ball joint nuts and separate ball joints from knuckles with Remover 8677, or equivalent.
   j. Remove lower shock clevis nuts bolts from lower control arm.
   k. Lean the knuckles out and push half shafts out of the hub/bearings.
   l. Pry half shafts off the axles.
   m. Remove differential vent hose.
   n. Support axle with a lift/jack.

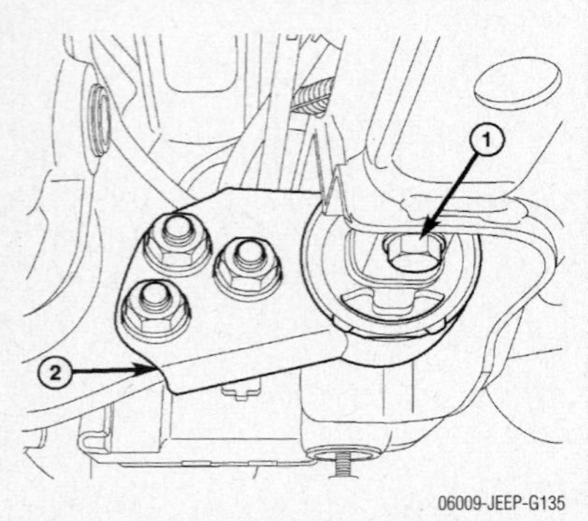

Fig. 98 Remove bolts (1) from differential cover bracket (2) bushing

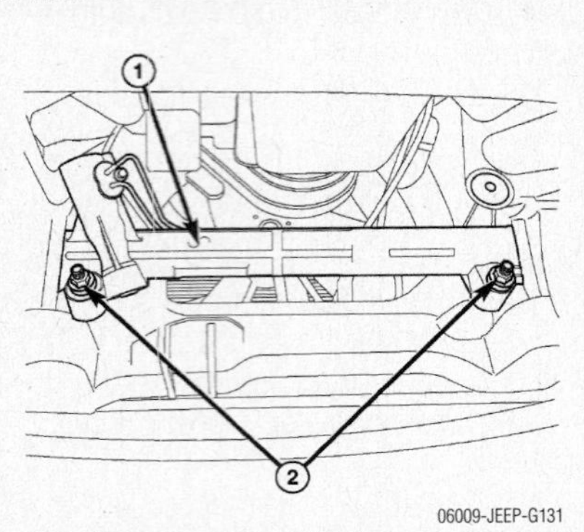

Fig. 99 Steering gear mounting bolts (1)

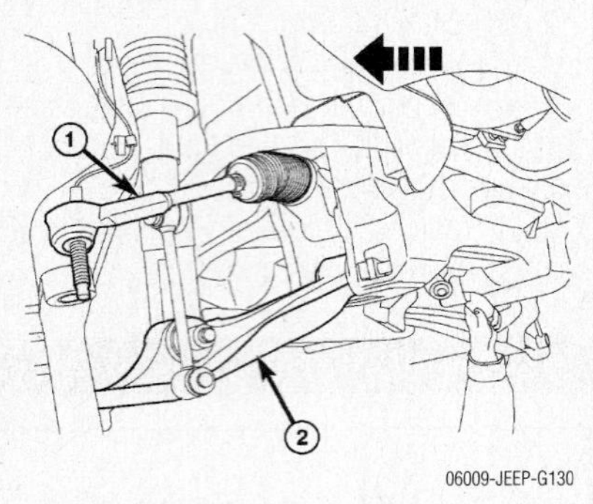

Fig. 100 Move the gear (1) to the full right position to allow clearance over the control arm

   o. Remove bolt from differential bushing.
   p. Remove bolt from axle tube bushing.
   q. Remove bolts from differential cover bracket bushing.
   r. Lower axle and from vehicle.
14. Remove the two steering gear mounting bolts.
15. Move the gear to the full right position to allow clearance over the control arm then lower the gear down, then turn the gear to the full left position then to allow clearance then remove from the vehicle.
16. Remove the outer tie rod ends from the steering gear (if needed).

To install:

17. Install the outer tie rod ends.
18. Position the steering gear back into the vehicle the same way it was removed.
19. Install the steering gear mounting bolts. Tighten to 160 ft. lbs. (217 Nm).
20. Install the front splash shield.
21. Install the outer tie rod ends jam nuts loosely.
22. Install the outer tie rod ends to the knuckle and tighten the tie rod end nut to 70 ft. lbs. (95 Nm).
23. Install the pressure and return hoses to the steering gear and tighten to 21 ft. lbs. (28 Nm).
24. Install the oil filter drip tray.
25. Install the column coupler shaft into the lower coupling and install a new bolt. Tighten to 36 ft. lbs. (49 Nm).
26. With 4-wheel drive:
   a. Raise axle to vehicle.
   b. Install differential cover axle bracket bushing bolts and tighten bolts to 35 ft. lbs. (47 Nm)
   c. Install axle tube bushing bolt and nut. Tighten nut to 70 ft. lbs. (95 Nm).
   d. Install differential bushing bolt and nut. Tighten nut to 70 ft. lbs. (95 Nm).
   e. Install differential vent hose.
   f. Install half shaft into axle and knuckles. Verify axles are engaged in the axle.
   g. Install clevis bolt and nut on lower control arms and tighten to specification.
   h. Install upper control arms on knuckles and tighten ball joint nuts to specifications.
   i. Install tie rod ends and nuts on knuckles and tighten to specifications.
   j. Install stabilizer bar links and bolts on lower control arms and tighten to specifications.
   k. Install brake calipers on knuckles.
   l. Install wheel speed sensor on hub/bearing.
   m. Install halfshaft hub nuts and tighten to 100 ft. lbs. (136 Nm).
   n. Install drive shaft on pinion flange with reference marks aligned.
   o. Install drain plug and tighten to 44 ft. lbs. (60 Nm).
   p. Fill differential housing and install fill plug. Tighten plug to 44 ft. lbs. (60 Nm).
   q. Install skid plate.
27. Install the wheel and tire assembly.
28. Remove the support and lower the vehicle.
29. Remove the steering wheel lock.
30. Fill the power steering pump.
31. Set the toe.

POWER STEERING PUMP

REMOVAL & INSTALLATION

3.7L and 4.7L Engines

1. Siphon power steering reservoir.
2. Remove the cooler return hose at the reservoir.
3. Disconnect the pressure hose nut at the pump.
4. Remove the pressure hose at the pump.

5. Remove serpentine drive belt.
6. Remove 3 pump mounting bolts.
7. Remove pulley from pump if necessary.

To install:

8. Install pulley on pump if removed.
9. Install 3 pump mounting bolts and tighten to 20 ft. lbs. (27 Nm).
10. Install the drive belt.
11. Install the pressure hose on the pump and tighten the nut to 21 ft. lbs. (28 Nm).
12. Install the cooler return hose at the reservoir.
13. Add power steering fluid.

5.7L Engine

1. Siphon power steering reservoir.
2. Remove the air intake tube.
3. Remove the drive belt.
4. Disconnect the supply hose at the pump.
5. Disconnect the pressure line at the pump.
6. Remove the three pump mounting bolts.

To install:

7. Install pulley on pump if removed.
8. Install 3 pump mounting bolts and tighten to 20 ft. lbs. (27 Nm).
9. Install the pressure hose on the pump and tighten the nut to 21 ft. lbs. (28 Nm).
10. Reconnect the supply hose at the pump.
11. Install the drive belt.
12. Install the air intake tube.
13. Fill the system with power steering fluid.
14. Bleed the hydraulic fan system using a scan tool.

BLEEDING

WARNING

The fluid level should be checked with the engine off to prevent injury from any moving components.

WARNING

Use Mopar® Power Steering Fluid or equivalent. Do not use automatic transmission fluid and do not overfill.

1. Wipe filler cap clean, then check the fluid level. The dipstick should indicate COLD when the fluid is at normal ambient temperature.
2. Fill the pump fluid reservoir to the proper level and let the fluid settle for at least two minutes.
3. Start the engine and let run for a few seconds then turn engine off.
4. Add fluid if necessary. Repeat the above procedure until the fluid level remains constant after running the engine.
5. Raise the front wheels off the ground.
6. Slowly turn the steering wheel right and left, lightly contacting the wheel stops at least 20 times.
7. Check the fluid level add if necessary.
8. Lower the vehicle, start the engine and turn the steering wheel slowly from lock to lock.
9. Stop the engine and check the fluid level and refill as required.

CAUTION

Do not run a vehicle with foamy fluid for an extended period. This may cause pump damage.

10. If the fluid is extremely foamy or milky looking, allow the vehicle to stand a few minutes and repeat the procedure.

SUSPENSION

FRONT SUSPENSION

COIL SPRING

REMOVAL & INSTALLATION

See Figures 101 and 102.

1. Before servicing the vehicle, refer to the precautions in the beginning of this manual.
2. Remove the strut.
3. Install the strut assembly in the Branick 7200T spring removal/installation tool or equivalent.

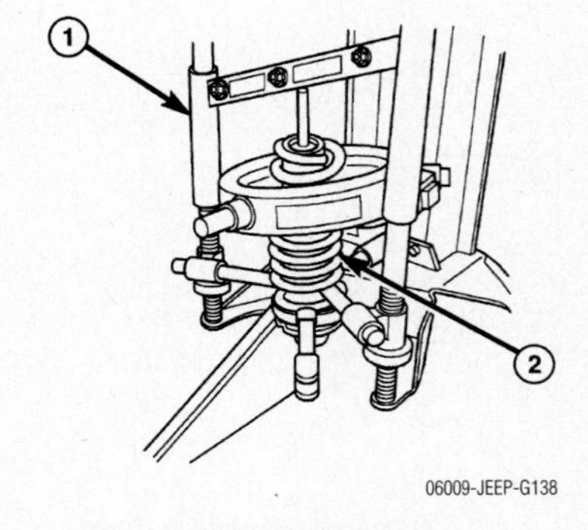

Fig. 101 Strut installed in a spring compressor—2005 Grand Cherokee

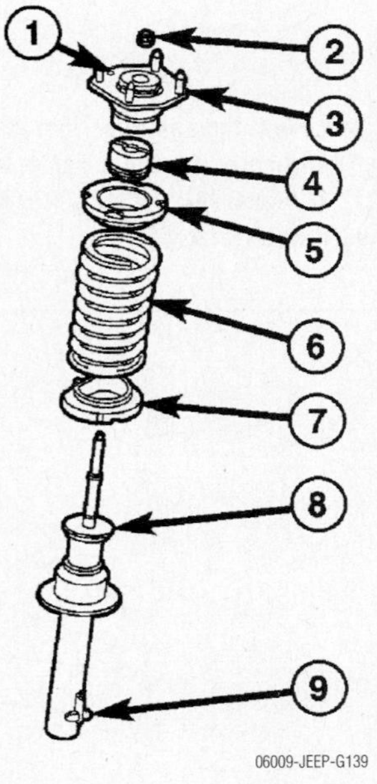

Fig. 102 Strut components. (1) nub hole, (2) upper nut, (3) strut plate, (4) jounce bumper, (5) upper isolator, (6) spring, (7) lower isolator, (8) strut, (9) bracket—2005 Grand Cherokee

4. Compress the spring.
5. Remove the upper strut nut.

➡**The nub in the upper strut mount must be 180° from the centerline of the lower bracket on the strut for proper installation.**

6. Remove the strut.
7. Remove the strut upper mounting plate.
8. Remove and inspect the upper and lower spring isolators.

To install:

9. Compress the spring.
10. Install the lower isolator.
11. Position the strut into the coil spring. Make sure the jounce bumper is on the strut rod.
12. Install the upper isolator.

➡**For proper orientation the nub hole in the upper strut plate must be 180° in a centerline from the bracket at the bottom of the strut.**

13. Install the upper strut mounting plate.
14. Install the strut upper mounting nut. Tighten to 25 ft. lbs. (39 Nm).
15. Decompress the spring.

16. Remove the strut assembly from the spring compressor tool.
17. Install the strut assembly.

LOWER BALL JOINT

REMOVAL & INSTALLATION

See Figures 103 through 106.

1. Before servicing the vehicle, refer to the precautions in the beginning of this manual.
2. Remove the tire and wheel assembly.
3. Remove the brake caliper and rotor.
4. Disconnect the tie rod from the steering knuckle using special tool C-3894-A.
5. Separate the upper ball joint from the knuckle using special tool 8677.
6. Separate the lower ball joint from the steering knuckle using special tool 8677.
7. Remove the steering knuckle.
8. Move the halfshaft to the side and support the halfshaft out of the way (4X4 only).
9. Chisel out the ball joint stakes.

➡Extreme pressure lubrication must be used on the threaded portions of the tool. This will increase the longevity of the tool and insure proper operation during the removal and installation process.

10. Press the ball joint from the lower control arm.

To install:

➡Extreme pressure lubrication must be used on the threaded portions of the tool. This will increase the longevity of the tool and insure proper operation during the removal and installation process.

11. Install the ball joint into the control arm.
12. Stake the ball joint flange in four evenly spaced places around the ball joint flange, using a chisel and hammer.
13. Remove the support for the halfshaft and install into position (4X4 only).
14. Install the steering knuckle.
15. Install the tie rod end into the steering knuckle.
16. Install and tighten the halfshaft nut to 185 ft. lbs. (251 Nm) (if equipped).
17. Install the brake caliper and rotor.
18. Install the tire and wheel assembly.
19. Check the vehicle ride height
20. Perform a wheel alignment.

LOWER CONTROL ARM

REMOVAL & INSTALLATION

See Figure 107.

1. Before servicing the vehicle, refer to the precautions in the beginning of this manual.
2. Raise and support the vehicle.
3. Remove the tire and wheel assembly.
4. Remove the steering knuckle.
5. Remove the shock clevis bracket from the lower control arm.
6. Remove the nut and bolt from the front of the lower control arm.
7. Remove the rear bolts and flag nuts from the lower control arm.
8. Remove the lower control arm from the vehicle.

To install:

9. Position the lower suspension arm into the frame rail bracket.
10. Install the rear bolts for the lower control arm to the frame, Tighten to 142 Nm (105 ft lbs).

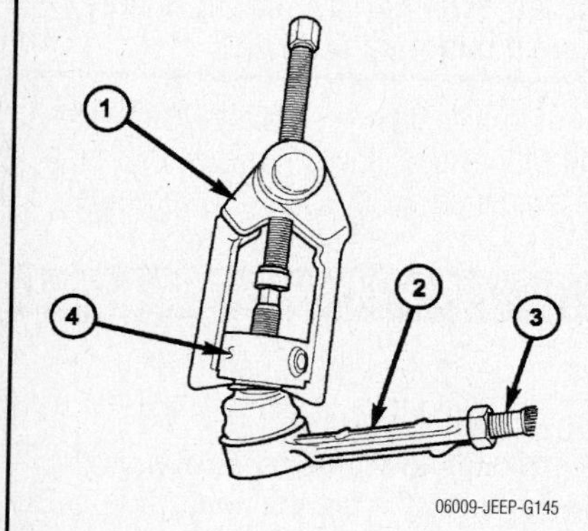

Fig. 103 Disconnect the tie rod (1) from the steering knuckle using special tool C-3894-A (2)

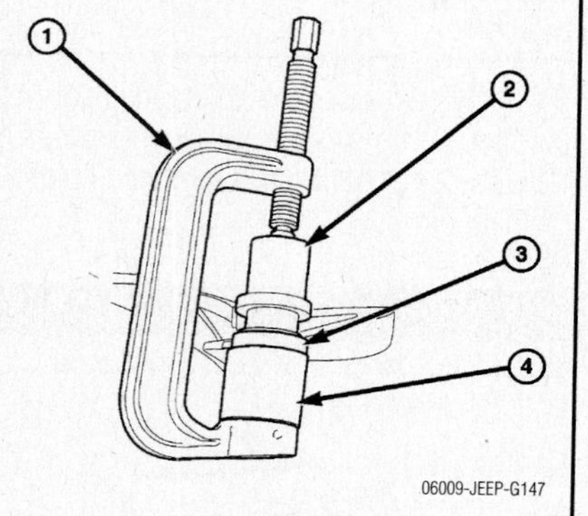

Fig. 105 Press the ball joint from the lower control arm (1) using special tools C-4212-F (Press) (2), C-4212-3 (Driver) (3) and 9654-3 (Receiver) (4)

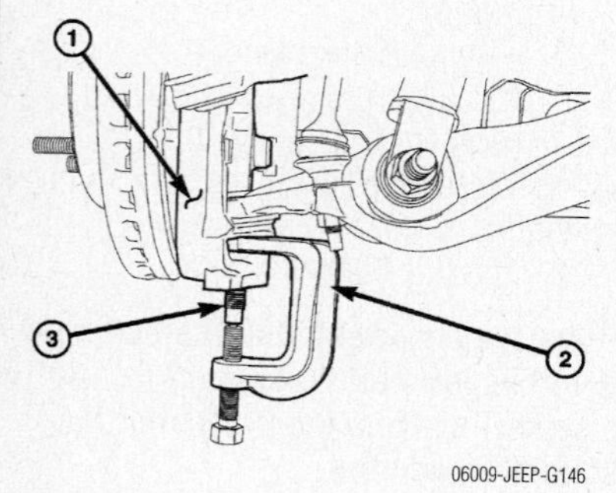

Fig. 104 Separate the lower ball joint (1) from the steering knuckle (2) using special tool 8677 (3)

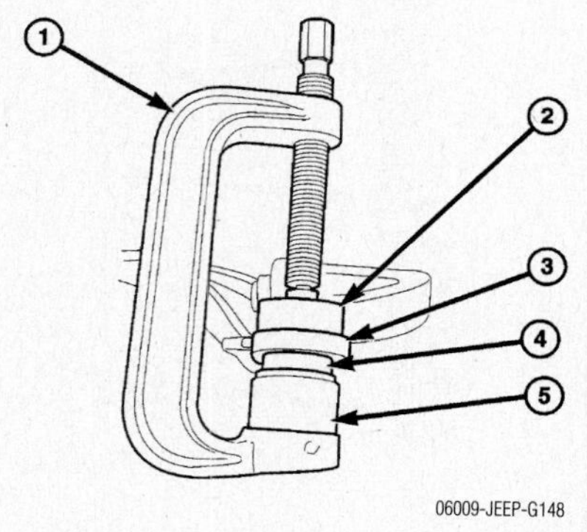

Fig. 106 Install the ball joint (1) into the control arm (2) and press in using special tools C-4212-F (press) (3), 9654-1 (Driver) (4) and 9654-2 (Receiver) (5)

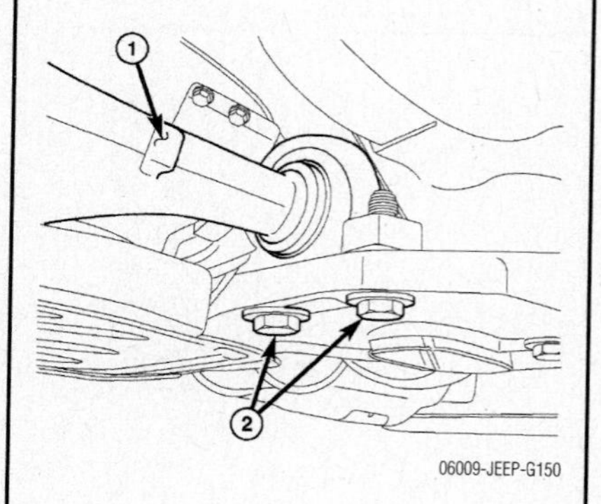

Fig. 107 Lower control arm (1) mounting bolts (2)

11. Install the nut and bolt for the front of the lower control arm Tighten to 169 Nm (125 ft lbs).
12. Install the lower clevis bolt at the lower control arm and tighten to 65 ft. lbs. (88 Nm).
13. Install the steering knuckle and tighten the nut to 55 ft. lbs. (75 Nm).
14. Install the tire and wheel assembly.
15. Lower the vehicle.
16. Perform wheel alignment.

CONTROL ARM BUSHING REPLACEMENT

The lower control arm bushings are serviced with the control arms as complete assemblies.

SHOCK ABSORBER

REMOVAL & INSTALLATION

Left Side

1. Remove the air box cover and air intake hose.
2. Remove the 3 PDC bracket nuts.
3. Move the PDC off to the side to access the four upper shock mount nuts.
4. Remove the four upper shock mount nuts.
5. Raise and support the vehicle.
6. Remove the tire.
7. Remove the two brake caliper adapter bolts.
8. Support the brake caliper adapter and caliper. Do not allow the caliper to hang by the brake hose.
9. Remove the disc brake rotor.
10. Remove the upper ball joint nut.
11. Separate the upper ball joint from the knuckle using special tool 8677.
12. Remove the lower clevis bolt at the lower control arm.
13. Remove the lower stabilizer bolt at the lower control arm.
14. Remove the shock from the vehicle.
15. Remove the spring if necessary.

To install:

16. Install the clevis bracket to the shock and tighten to 90 ft. lbs. (122 Nm).
17. Install the shock assembly to the vehicle.
18. Install the four upper shock nuts, Tighten to 70 ft. lbs. (95 Nm).
19. Install the 3 PDC bracket nuts.
20. Raise the vehicle up.
21. Install the lower stabilizer bolt at the lower control arm and tighten to 85 ft. lbs. (115 Nm).
22. Install the lower clevis bolt at the lower control arm and tighten to 125 ft. lbs. (169 Nm).
23. Install the upper ball joint into the knuckle and tighten the nut to 55 ft. lbs. (75 Nm).
24. Install the disc brake rotor.
25. Install the caliper adapter mounting bolts to 130 ft. lbs. (176 Nm).
26. Install the tire and wheel assembly.
27. Lower the vehicle.

Right Side

See Figures 108 and 109.

1. Remove the air box cover and air intake hose.
2. Disconnect the cruise control servo electrical connector.
3. Remove the coolant reservoir mounting bolt and move the coolant reservoir off to the side.
4. Remove the four upper shock mounting nuts.
5. Raise and support the vehicle.
6. Remove the tire.
7. Remove the two brake caliper adapter bolts.
8. Support the brake caliper adapter and caliper. Do not allow the caliper to hang by the brake hose.
9. Remove the disc brake rotor.
10. Remove the upper ball joint nut.
11. Separate the upper ball joint from the knuckle using special tool 8677.
12. Remove the lower clevis bolt at the lower control arm.
13. Remove the lower stabilizer bolt at the lower control arm.
14. Remove the shock from the vehicle.
15. Remove the spring if necessary.

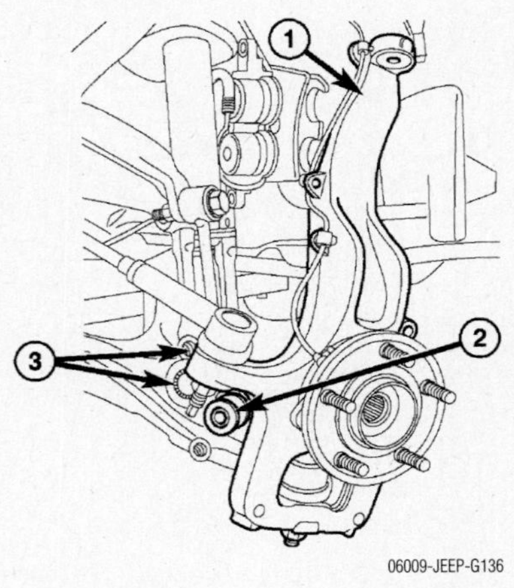

Fig. 108 Knuckle (1), Lower clevis bolt (2), Lower stabilizer bolt (3)

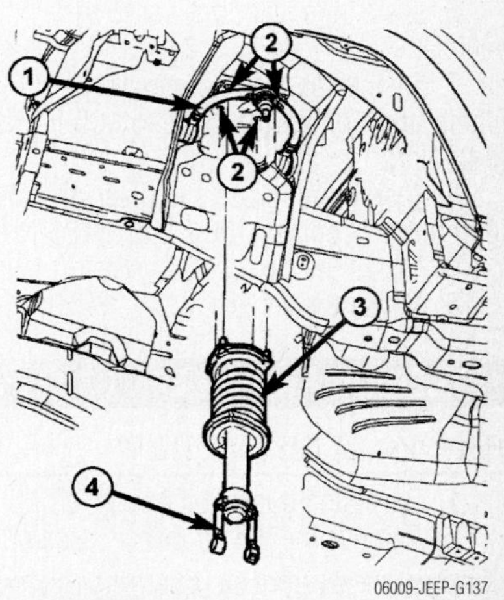

Fig. 109 Shock absorber and related components: (1) upper control arm, (2) upper strut mounting holes, (3) strut, (4) strut clevis

To install:

16. Install the clevis bracket to the shock and tighten to 90 ft. lbs. (122 Nm).
17. Install the shock assembly to the vehicle.
18. Install the four upper shock nuts, Tighten to 70 ft. lbs. (95 Nm).
19. Install the coolant reservoir bolt.
20. Reconnect the cruise control servo wiring connector.
21. Install the air box cover and air intake hose.
22. Raise the vehicle up.
23. Install the lower stabilizer bolt at the lower control arm.
24. Install the lower clevis bolt at the lower control arm and tighten to 125 ft. lbs. (169 Nm).
25. Install the upper ball joint into the knuckle and tighten the nut to 55 ft. lbs. (75 Nm).
26. Install the disc brake rotor.
27. Install the caliper adapter mounting bolts to 130 ft. lbs. (176 Nm).
28. Install the tire and wheel assembly.
29. Lower the vehicle.

STABILIZER BAR

REMOVAL & INSTALLATION

1. Raise and support the vehicle.
2. Remove the front splash shield.
3. Remove the stabilizer bar link upper nut and bolt.
4. Remove the two stabilizer bushing clamp bolts.
5. Remove the stabilizer bar.

To install:

6. Install the stabilizer bar to the vehicle.
7. Install the stabilizer bushing clamp and tighten the bolts to 105 ft. lbs. (142 Nm).
8. Install the upper stabilizer link and ighten nut & bolt to 100 ft. lbs. (135 Nm).
9. Install the front splash shield.
10. Lower the vehicle.

STEERING KNUCKLE

REMOVAL & INSTALLATION

1. Raise and support the vehicle.
2. Remove the tire and wheel assembly.

⁂ CAUTION

Never allow the disc brake caliper to hang from the brake hose. Damage to the brake hose will result. Provide a suitable support to hang the caliper securely.

3. Remove the brake caliper.
4. Remove the caliper adapter
5. Remove the O-ring and discard then remove disc brake rotor
6. Remove the wheel speed sensor.
7. Remove the axle shaft nut (if equipped with four wheel drive).
8. Remove the hub/bearing.
9. Remove the outer tie rod end retaining nut.
10. Separate the outer tie rod end from the steering knuckle using special tool 8677.
11. Remove the lower ball joint nut.
12. Separate the lower ball joint from the knuckle using tool C-4150A.
13. Remove the upper ball joint nut.
14. Separate the upper ball joint from the knuckle using tool 8677.
15. Remove the knuckle from the vehicle.

To install:

16. Install the knuckle to the vehicle.
17. Install the lower ball joint into the knuckle.
18. Install the lower ball joint nut. Tighten the nut to 60 ft. lbs. (81 Nm).
19. Install the upper ball joint into the knuckle
20. Install the upper ball joint nut. Tighten the nut to 60 ft. lbs. (81 Nm).
21. Install the outer tie rod end to the steering knuckle.
22. Install the hub/bearing. Tighten to 100 ft. lbs. (136 Nm).
23. If equipped with four wheel drive, install the axle shaft nut. Tighten the nut to 96 ft. lbs. (135 Nm).
24. Install the wheel speed sensor.
25. Install the disc brake rotor.
26. Install the caliper adapter.
27. Install the tire and wheel assembly.
28. Perform wheel alignment

UPPER BALL JOINT

REMOVAL & INSTALLATION

See Figures 110 through 112.

1. Before servicing the vehicle, refer to the precautions in the beginning of this manual.
2. Raise vehicle and support the axle.
3. Remove the tire and wheel.
4. Remove the upper ball joint retaining nut.
5. Separate the upper ball joint from the knuckle using special tool 8677.
6. Remove the wheel speed sensor wire from the upper control arm.
7. Move the knuckle out of the way to allow ball joint removal tool access.

➡Extreme pressure lubrication must be used on the threaded portions of the tool. This will increase the longevity of the tool and insure proper operation during the removal and installation process.

8. Press the ball joint from the upper control arm using special tools C-4212-F and 9652.

To install:

➡Extreme pressure lubrication must be used on the threaded portions of the tool. This will increase the longevity of the tool and insure proper operation during the removal and installation process.

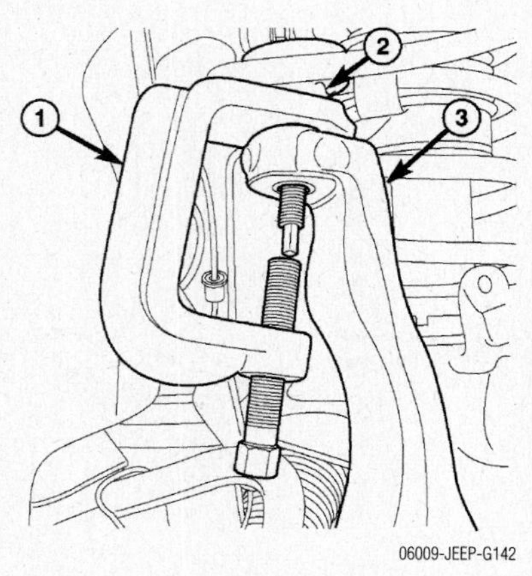

Fig. 110 Separate the upper ball joint from the knuckle using special tool 8677

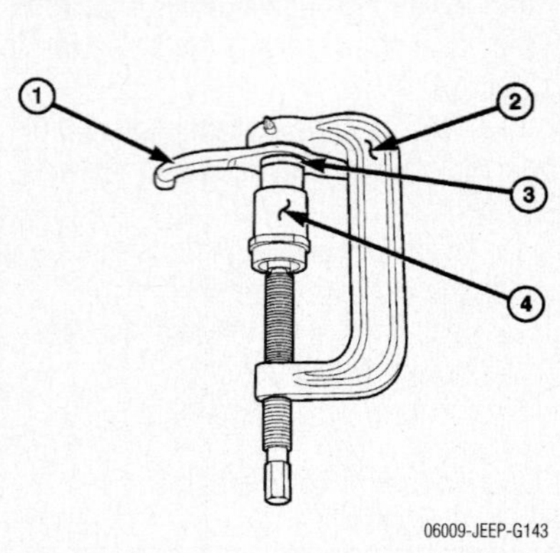

Fig. 111 Press the ball joint from the upper control arm (1) using special tools C-4212-F (press) (2) and 9652 (Driver) (3)

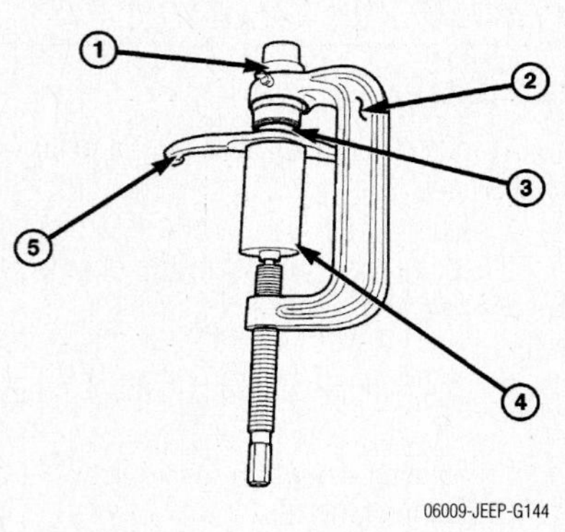

Fig. 112 Install the ball joint (1) into the upper control arm (2) and press in using special tools C-4212-F (press) (3), 9652 (Driver) (4) and 8975-2 (Receiver) (5)

9. Install the ball joint into the upper control arm.
10. Install the upper ball joint into the knuckle.
11. Install the upper ball joint retaining nut and tighten to 55 ft. lbs. (75 Nm).
12. Install the wheel speed sensor wire to the upper control arm.
13. Install the tire and wheel.
14. Remove the supports and lower the vehicle.
15. Perform a wheel alignment.

UPPER CONTROL ARM

REMOVAL & INSTALLATION

See Figure 113.

1. Before servicing the vehicle, refer to the precautions in the beginning of this manual.
2. Raise vehicle and support the axle.
3. Remove the tire and wheel.

4. Remove the inner fender well.
5. Remove the upper ball joint retaining nut.
6. Separate the upper ball joint from the knuckle using special tool 8677.
7. Remove the wheel speed sensor wire from the upper control arm.
8. Remove the nut and bolt securing the upper control arm to the body.
9. Remove the upper control arm from the vehicle.

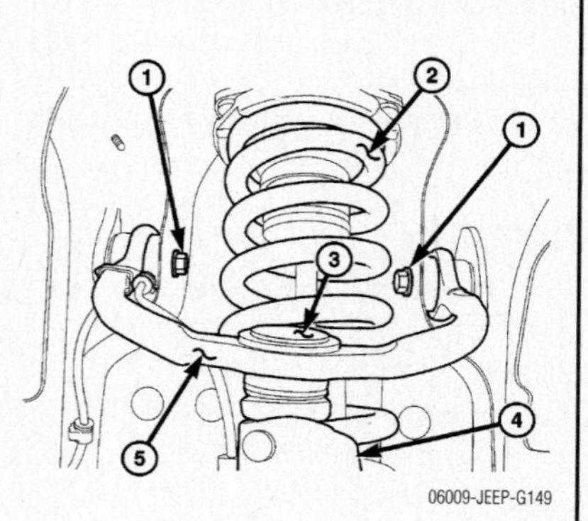

Fig. 113 Upper control arm mounting. (1) control arm bolts, (2) spring, (3) ball joint, (4) knuckle, (5) upper control arm

To install:

10. Install the upper control arm to the vehicle.
11. Install the nut and bolt securing the upper control arm to the body.
12. Install the wheel speed sensor wire to the upper control arm.
13. Install the upper ball joint into the knuckle.
14. Install the upper ball joint retaining nut and tighten the nut to 60 ft. lbs. (81 Nm).
15. Install the inner fender well.
16. Install the tire and wheel.
17. Remove the supports and lower the vehicle.
18. Perform a wheel alignment.

CONTROL ARM BUSHING REPLACEMENT

The upper control arm bushings are serviced with the control arms as complete assemblies, with the exception of the front upper axle bushing, which may be replaced after removing the upper control arm.

WHEEL BEARINGS

REMOVAL & INSTALLATION

1. Raise and support the vehicle.
2. Remove the wheel and tire assembly. Support the caliper, Do not let the caliper hang by the hose.
3. Remove the disc brake caliper.
4. Remove the brake caliper adapter
5. Remove and discard the O-ring and then remove the disc brake rotor.
6. Remove the wheel speed sensor nut.
7. Remove the wheel speed sensor.
8. Remove the 3 hub bearing mounting bolts from the back of the steering knuckle. Remove hub bearing from the steering knuckle.

To install:

9. Install the hub bearing to the knuckle.
10. Install the hub bearing to knuckle and the 3 bolts then tighten to 100 ft. lbs. (136 Nm) for Grand Cherokee.
11. Install the wheel speed sensor.
12. Install the wheel speed sensor nut.
13. Install the brake rotor
14. Install the brake caliper adapter.
15. Install the caliper.
16. Install the wheel and tire assembly.
17. Remove the support and lower the vehicle.

ADJUSTMENT

These models utilize a hub/bearing assembly which is not adjustable.

SUSPENSION

REAR SUSPENSION

COIL SPRING

REMOVAL & INSTALLATION

See Figures 114 and 115.

1. Before servicing the vehicle, refer to the precautions in the beginning of this manual.
2. Raise and support the vehicle. Position a hydraulic jack under the axle to support the axle.
3. Remove the wheel and tire assemblies.
4. Remove the lower shock bolt from the axle bracket.
5. Remove the stabilizer bar link from the body rail.
6. Lower the hydraulic jack and tilt the axle and remove the coil spring.
7. Remove and inspect the spring isolators.

To install:

8. Install the upper isolator.
9. Install the lower isolator.
10. Pull down on the axle and position the coil spring in the lower isolator.
11. Raise the axle with the hydraulic jack.

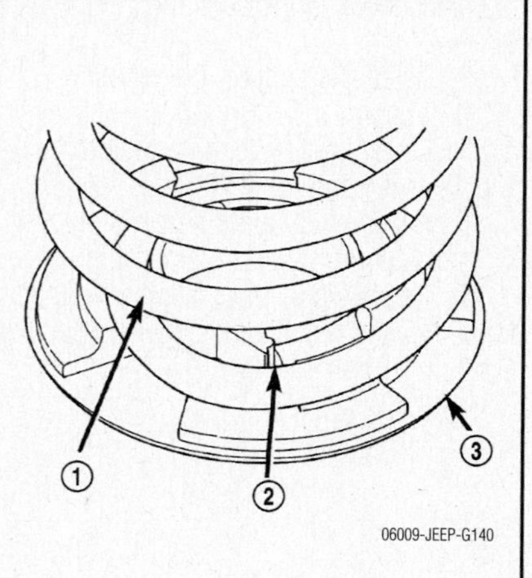

Fig. 114 Proper rear spring positioning

12. Install the shock absorber to the axle bracket and tighten to 85 ft. lbs. (115 Nm).
13. Install the stabilizer bar link to the body rail, tighten to 75 ft. lbs. (102 Nm).
14. Install the wheel and tire assemblies.
15. Remove the supports and lower the vehicle.

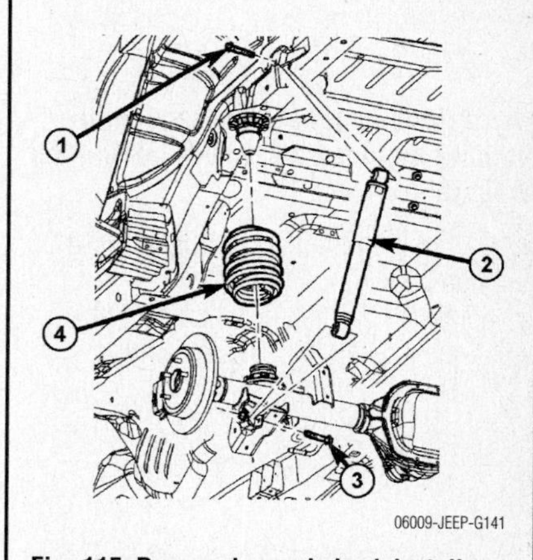

Fig. 115 Rear spring and shock installation (1) upper shock bolt, (2) shock, (3) lower shock bolt, (4) spring

LOWER CONTROL ARM

REMOVAL & INSTALLATION

Left Side

1. Before servicing the vehicle, refer to the precautions in the beginning of this manual.

2. Raise the vehicle and support the rear axle.
3. Remove the fuel tank.
4. Remove the lower suspension arm nut and bolt from the axle bracket.
5. Remove the nut and bolt from the frame rail and remove the lower suspension arm.

➡All torques should be done with vehicle on the ground with full vehicle weight.

To install:

6. Position the lower suspension arm in the frame rail.
7. Install the frame rail bracket bolt and nut. Tighten to130 ft. lbs.(176 Nm).
8. Position the lower suspension arm in the axle bracket.
9. Install the axle bracket bolt and nut. Tighten to 155 ft. lbs. (210 Nm).
10. Install the fuel tank.
11. Remove the supports and lower the vehicle.

Right Side

1. Before servicing the vehicle, refer to the precautions in the beginning of this manual.
2. Raise the vehicle and support the rear axle.
3. Remove the lower suspension arm nut and bolt from the axle bracket.
4. Remove the nut and bolt from the frame rail and remove the lower suspension arm.

To install:

➡All torques should be done with vehicle on the ground with full vehicle weight.

5. Position the lower suspension arm in the frame rail.
6. Install the frame rail bracket bolt and nut tighten to to130 ft. lbs.(176 Nm).
7. Position the lower suspension arm in the axle bracket.
8. Install the axle bracket bolt and nut. Tighten to 155 ft. lbs. (210 Nm).
9. Remove the supports and lower the vehicle.

SHOCK ABSORBERS

REMOVAL & INSTALLATION

1. Before servicing the vehicle, refer to the precautions in the beginning of this manual.
2. Remove or disconnect the following:
   - Upper locknut and washer from the frame bracket stud
   - Lower bolt, nut and washers from the axle shaft tube bracket
   - Shock absorber

To install:

3. Place the shock absorber upper end in position and tighten the fasteners to 70 ft. lbs. (95 Nm).
4. Place the shock absorber lower end in position and tighten the fasteners to 85 ft. lbs. (115 Nm).

UPPER CONTROL ARM

REMOVAL & INSTALLATION

Left Side

1. Before servicing the vehicle, refer to the precautions in the beginning of this manual.
2. Raise and support the vehicle.
3. Support the rear axle.
4. Lower the fuel tank in order to gain access to the bolt.
5. Remove the upper suspension arm nut and bolt from the axle bracket.
6. Remove the nut and bolt from the frame rail and remove the upper suspension arm.

To install:

➡All torques should be done with vehicle on the ground with full vehicle weight.

7. Position the upper suspension arm in the frame rail bracket.
8. Install the mounting bolt and nut tighten to 95 ft. lbs. (129 Nm).
9. Position the upper suspension arm in the axle bracket.
10. Install the mounting bolt and nut tighten to 100 ft. lbs. (136 Nm).
11. Raise the fuel tank back into place and secure.
12. Remove the supports and lower the vehicle.

Right Side

1. Before servicing the vehicle, refer to the precautions in the beginning of this manual.
2. Raise and support the vehicle.
3. Support the rear axle.
4. Remove the upper suspension arm nut and bolt from the axle bracket.
5. Remove the nut and bolt from the frame rail and remove the upper suspension arm.

To install:

➡All torques should be done with vehicle on the ground with full vehicle weight.

6. Position the upper suspension arm in the frame rail bracket.
7. Install the mounting bolt and nut tighten to 95 ft. lbs. (129 Nm).
8. Position the upper suspension arm in the axle bracket.
9. Install the mounting bolt and nut tighten to 100 ft. lbs. (136 Nm).
10. Remove the supports and lower the vehicle.

JEEP

10

Liberty • Wrangler

SPECIFICATIONS AND MAINTENANCE CHARTS

ENGINE AND VEHICLE IDENTIFICATION

	Engine					
Code	Liters (cc)	Cu. In.	Cyl.	Fuel Sys.	Engine Type	Eng. Mfg.
1	2.4 (2429)	148	4	MFI	DOHC	Chrysler
5	2.8 (2776)	169	4	Turbo Diesel	DOHC	VM Motori
K	3.7 (3701)	226	6	MFI	SOHC	Chrysler
1	3.8 (3778)	231	6	MFI	OHV	Chrysler
S	4.0 (3966)	242	6	MFI	OHV	Chrysler

Model Year	
Code	Year
5	2005
6	2006
7	2007

MFI: Multi-port Fuel Injection

OHV: Over Head Valve

SOHC: Single Overhead Camshaft

DOHC: Dual Overhead Camshafts

22043_LIBE_C0001

GENERAL ENGINE SPECIFICATIONS

Year	Model	Engine Displ. Liters	Engine VIN	Net Horsepower @ rpm	Net Torque @ rpm (ft. lbs.)	Bore x Stroke (in.)	Comp. Ratio	Oil Pressure @ rpm
2005	Wrangler	2.4	1	150@5200	165@4000	3.44x3.98	9.5:1	25-80@3000
		4.0	S	181@4600	222@2800	3.88x3.44	8.8:1	37@1600
	Liberty	2.4	1	150@5200	165@4000	3.44x3.98	9.5:1	25-80@3000
		2.8	5	163@3800	295@1800	3.70x3.94	17.5:1	29@3800
		3.7	K	210@5200	225@4200	3.66x3.40	9.1:1	25-110@3000
2006	Wrangler	2.4	1	150@5200	165@4000	3.44x3.98	9.5:1	25-80@3000
		4.0	S	181@4600	222@2800	3.88x3.44	8.8:1	37@1600
	Liberty	2.8	5	163@3800	295@1800	3.70x3.94	17.5:1	29@3800
		3.7	K	210@5200	225@4200	3.66x3.40	9.1:1	25-110@3000
2007	Wrangler	3.8	1	202@5200	237@4000	3.78x3.43	9.6:1	30-80@3000
	Liberty	3.7	K	210@5200	225@4200	3.66x3.40	9.1:1	25-110@3000

22043_LIBE_C0002

GASOLINE ENGINE TUNE-UP SPECIFICATIONS

Year	Engine Displ. Liters	Engine VIN	Spark Plug Gap (in.)	Ignition Timing (deg.)	Fuel Pump (psi)	Idle Speed (rpm)	Valve Clearance	
							Intake	Exhaust
2005	2.4	1	0.050	①	②	①	HYD	HYD
	3.7	K	0.042	①	②	①	HYD	HYD
	4.0	S	0.040	①	56-60	①	HYD	HYD
2006	2.4	1	0.050	①	②	①	HYD	HYD
	3.7	K	0.042	①	②	①	HYD	HYD
	4.0	S	0.040	①	56-60	①	HYD	HYD
2007	3.7	K	0.042	①	②	①	HYD	HYD
	3.8	1	0.048	①	56-60	①	HYD	HYD

Note: The information on the Vehicle Emission Control label must be used, if different from the figures in this chart.

HYD: Hydraulic

① Ignition timing and idle speed are controlled by the PCM. No adjustment is necessary.

② Liberty:

If equipped with JTEC PCM (3 connectors): 44-54

If equipped with NGC PCM (4 connectors): 53-63

Wrangler: 56-60

22043_LIBE_C0003

DIESEL ENGINE TUNE-UP SPECIFICATIONS

Year	Engine Displacement Liters	Engine VIN	Valve Clearance Intake (in.)	Valve Clearance Exhaust (in.)	Intake Valve Opens (deg.)	Injection Pump Setting (deg.)	Injection Nozzle Pressure psi (new)	Idle Speed (rpm)	Cranking Compression Pressure (psi)
2005	2.8	5	HYD.	HYD.	15.6 A	①	23,000 max.	NA	②
2006	2.8	5	HYD.	HYD.	15.6 A	①	23,000 max.	NA	②

NOTE: The Vehicle Emission Control Information (VECI) label figures must be used if they differ from those in this chart

NA: Information not available

A: After TDC

① PCM controlled

② Maximum difference among cylinders: 72.5 psi

22043_LIBE_C0004

CAPACITIES

Year	Model	Engine Displ. Liters	Engine VIN	Engine Oil with Filter	Transmission (pts.) Man.	Transmission (pts.) Auto.	Transfer Case (pts.)	Drive Axle Front (pts.)	Drive Axle Rear (pts.)	Fuel Tank (gal.)	Cooling System (qts.)
2005	Wrangler	2.4	1	4.0	3.17	17.5	①	②	③	19.0	9.0
		4.0	S	6.0	3.17	17.5	①	②	③	19.0	10.5
	Liberty	2.4	1	5.0	4.8	—	④	2.6	4.4	19.5	10.1
		2.8	5	6.4	3.17	⑤	⑥	2.6	4.4	19.5	11.8
		3.7	K	5.0	4.8	⑤	④	2.6	4.4	19.5	14.0
2006	Wrangler	2.4	1	4.0	3.17	17.5	①	②	③	19.0	9.0
		4.0	S	6.0	3.17	17.5	①	②	③	19.0	10.5
	Liberty	3.7	K	5.0	4.8	⑤	④	2.6	4.4	19.5	14.0
		2.8	5	6.4	3.17	⑤	⑥	2.6	4.4	19.5	11.8
2007	Wrangler	3.8	1	6.0	3.17	⑦	①	⑧	⑨	⑩	13
	Liberty	3.7	K	5.0	4.8	⑤	④	2.6	4.4	19.5	14.0

NOTE: All capacities are approximate. Add fluid gradually and check to be sure a proper fluid level is obtained.
For rear axles, when equipped with Trac Lok, add 4 oz. of limited slip additive.
Capacities for automatic trnasmissions is for complete drain/fill or overhaul.

① NV231: 2.2 pts.
NV241: 4.2 pts.

② Model 30: 2.5 pts.
Model 44: 4.0 pts.

③ Model 35: 3.5 pts.
Model 44: 4.0 pts.

④ NV231: 2.95 pts.
NV241: 3.4 pts.

⑤ 45RFE: 28.0
42RLE: 17.6

⑥ NV231: 2.95
NV241 GEN II: 4.2
NV242: 3.4

⑦ 45RFE/545RFE:14.8-16.9
42RLE: 17.6

⑧ Model 30: 2.1 pts.
Model 44: 2.7 pts.

⑨ Model 35: 3.8 pts.
Model 44: 4.75 pts.

⑩ 2 door: 18.6
4 door: 23.0

22043_LIBE_C0005

FLUID SPECIFICATIONS

Year	Model	Engine Displacement Liters	Engine ID/VIN	Engine Oil	Auto. Trans.	Drive Axle	Power Steering Fluid	Brake Master Cylinder
2005	Wrangler	2.4	1	5W-30	Mopar ATF+4	①	Mopar ATF+4	DOT-3
		4.0	S	5W-30	Mopar ATF+4	①	Mopar ATF+4	DOT-3
	Liberty	2.4	1	5W-30	Mopar ATF+4	①	Mopar ATF+4	DOT-3
		2.8	5	0W-40	Mopar ATF+4	①	Mopar ATF+4	DOT-3
		3.7	K	5W-30	Mopar ATF+4	①	Mopar ATF+4	DOT-3
2006	Wrangler	2.4	1	5W-30	Mopar ATF+4	①	Mopar ATF+4	DOT-3
		4.0	S	5W-30	Mopar ATF+4	①	Mopar ATF+4	DOT-3
	Liberty	2.8	5	0W-40	Mopar ATF+4	①	Mopar ATF+4	DOT-3
		3.7	K	5W-30	Mopar ATF+4	①	Mopar ATF+4	DOT-3
2007	Wrangler	3.8	1	5W-20	Mopar ATF+4	①	Mopar ATF+4	DOT-3
	Liberty	3.7	K	5W-20	Mopar ATF+4	①	Mopar ATF+4	DOT-3

DOT: Department Of Transpotation

NA: Not Applicable

① Except Liberty front axle: Mopar Synthetic Gear Lube 75W-140

Liberty front axle: Mopar 80W-90

22043_LIBE_C0006

VALVE SPECIFICATIONS

Year	Engine Displ. Liters	Engine VIN	Seat Angle (deg.)	Face Angle (deg.)	Spring Test Pressure (lbs. @ in.)	Spring Installed Height (in.)	Stem-to-Guide Clearance (in.) Intake	Stem-to-Guide Clearance (in.) Exhaust	Stem Diameter (in.) Intake	Stem Diameter (in.) Exhaust
2005	2.4	1	44.5-45	44.5-45	136@1.172	1.496	0.0018-0.0025	0.0029-0.0037	0.2337-0.2344	0.2326-0.2333
	2.8	5	NA	45.45-55.55	401@1.496	1.496	0.0012-0.0023	0.0012-0.0023	0.2343-0.2350	0.2334-0.2343
	3.7	K	44.5-45	45-45.5	221-242@1.107	1.619	0.0008-0.0028	0.0019-0.0039	0.2729-0.2739	0.2717-0.2728
	4.0	S	44.5	46.5	202-218@1.216	1.640	0.0010-0.0030	0.0010-0.0030	0.3110-0.3120	0.3110-0.3120
2006	2.4	1	44.5-45	44.5-45	136@1.172	1.496	0.0018-0.0025	0.0029-0.0037	0.2337-0.2344	0.2326-0.2333
	2.8	5	NA	45.45-55.55	401@1.496	1.496	0.0012-0.0023	0.0012-0.0023	0.2343-0.2350	0.2334-0.2343
	3.7	K	44.5-45	45-45.5	221-242@1.107	1.619	0.0008-0.0028	0.0019-0.0039	0.2729-0.2739	0.2717-0.2728
	4.0	S	44.5	46.5	202-218@1.216	1.640	0.0010-0.0030	0.0010-0.0030	0.3110-0.3120	0.3110-0.3120
2007	3.7	K	44.5-45	45-45.5	221-242@1.107	1.619	0.0008-0.0028	0.0019-0.0039	0.2729-0.2739	0.2717-0.2728
	3.8	1	45-45.5	45-45.5	①	1.61-1.68	0.0010-0.0025	0.0020-0.0037	0.2718-0.2725	0.2718-0.2725

NA: Information not available

① Type A Valve Closed: 84.9-95.6 lbs. @ 1.65 in.

Type A Valve Open: 194.2-215.8 @ 1.65 in

Type B Valve Open: 197.9-216.3 @ 122 in.

Type B Valve Closed: 84.4-95.2 @ 1.65 in.

22043_LIBE_C0007

CAMSHAFT AND BEARING SPECIFICATIONS CHART

All measurements are given in inches.

Year	Engine Displacement Liters	Engine VIN	Journal Diameter	Brg. Oil Clearance	Shaft End-play	Runout	Journal Bore	Lobe Lift	
								Intake	Exhaust
2005	2.4	1	1.022-1.0230	0.009-0.0025	0.0019-0.0066	NA	NA	NA	NA
	2.8	5	1.179-1.180	0.009-0.0025	0.001-0.003	NA	NA	NA	NA
	3.7	K	1.0227-1.0235	0.0010-0.0026	0.0030-0.0079	NA	NA	NA	NA
	4.0	S	①	NA	NA	0.001	NA	0.4075	0.4145
2006	2.4	1	1.022-1.0230	0.009-0.0025	0.0019-0.0066	NA	NA	NA	NA
	2.8	5	1.179-1.180	0.009-0.0025	0.001-0.003	NA	NA	NA	NA
	3.7	K	1.0227-1.0235	0.0010-0.0026	0.0030-0.0079	NA	NA	NA	NA
	4.0	S	①	NA	NA	0.001	NA	0.4075	0.4145
2007	3.7	K	1.0227-1.0235	0.0010-0.0026	0.0030-0.0079	NA	NA	NA	NA
	3.8	L	②	0.0010-0.0040	0.0010-0.0020	NA	NA	NA	NA

NA: Not Available

① No. 1: 2.029-2.030 in.
No. 2: 2.019-2.020 in.
No. 3: 2.009-2.010 in.
No. 4: 1.999-2.000 in.

② No 1: 1.997-1.999
No 2: 1.9809-1.9829
No 3: 1.9659-1.9679
No 4: 1.9499-1.9520

22043_LIBE_C0008

CRANKSHAFT AND CONNECTING ROD SPECIFICATIONS

All measurements are given in inches.

Year	Engine Displ. Liters	Engine VIN	Crankshaft				Connecting Rod		
			Main Brg. Journal Dia.	Main Brg. Oil Clearance	Shaft End-play	Thrust on No.	Journal Diameter	Oil Clearance	Side Clearance
2005	2.4	1	2.3620-2.3625	0.0007-0.0024	0.0035-0.0094	NA	1.9680-1.9685	0.0009-0.0027	0.0050-0.0150
	2.8	5	①	②	0.0031-0.0110	3	2.1236-2.1242	0.0008-0.0029	NA
	3.7	K	2.4996-2.5005	0.0020-0.0034	0.0021-0.0112	2	2.2794-2.2797	0.0004-0.0019	0.0040-0.0138
	4.0	S	③	0.0010-0.0025	0.0015-0.0065	2	2.0934-2.0955	0.0015-0.0020	0.0100-0.0190
2006	2.4	1	2.3620-2.3625	0.0007-0.0024	0.0035-0.0094	NA	1.9680-1.9685	0.0009-0.0027	0.0050-0.0150
	2.8	5	①	②	0.0031-0.0110	3	2.1236-2.1242	0.0008-0.0029	NA
	3.7	K	2.4996-2.5005	0.0020-0.0034	0.0021-0.0112	2	2.2794-2.2797	0.0004-0.0019	0.0040-0.0138
	4.0	S	③	0.0010-0.0025	0.0015-0.0065	2	2.0934-2.0955	0.0015-0.0020	0.0100-0.0190
2007	3.7	K	2.4996-2.5005	0.0020-0.0034	0.0021-0.0112	2	2.2794-2.2797	0.0004-0.0019	0.0040-0.0138
	3.8	1	2.5194-2.5202	0.0005-0.0022	0.0036-0.0095	2	2.2827-2.2837	0.017-0.020	0.005-0.0130

NA: Information not available

① No.1: 2.4797-2.4805
No. 2: 2.4805-2.4811
No. 3: 3.5425-3.5433

② No.1: 0.0010 max.
No.2: 0.0002-0.0003
No. 3: 0.0010-0.0030

③ No 7: 2.4980-2.4995
Others: 2.4996-2.5001

22043_LIBE_C0009

PISTON AND RING SPECIFICATIONS

All measurements are given in inches.

Year	Engine Displ. Liters	Engine VIN	Piston Clearance	Ring Gap Top Compression	Ring Gap Bottom Compression	Ring Gap Oil Control	Ring Side Clearance Top Compression	Ring Side Clearance Bottom Compression	Ring Side Clearance Oil Control
2005	2.4	1	0.0009-0.0022	0.0098-0.0200	0.0090-0.0180	0.0098-0.0250	0.0011-0.0031	0.0011-0.0031	0.0004-0.0070
	2.8	5	0.0003-0.0008	0.0012-0.0018	0.0012-0.0019	0.0009-0.0019	0.0031-0.0054	0.0028-0.0043	0.0016-0.0031
	3.7	K	0.0014	0.0146-0.0249	0.0146-0.0249	0.0100-0.0300	0.0020-0.0037	0.0016-0.0031	0.0007-0.0091
	4.0	S	0.0008-0.0015	0.0090-0.0240	0.0190-0.0380	0.0100-0.0600	0.0017-0.0033	0.0017-0.0033	0.0024-0.0083
2006	2.4	1	0.0009-0.0022	0.0098-0.0200	0.0090-0.0180	0.0098-0.0250	0.0011-0.0031	0.0011-0.0031	0.0004-0.0070
	2.8	5	0.0003-0.0008	0.0012-0.0018	0.0012-0.0019	0.0009-0.0019	0.0031-0.0054	0.0028-0.0043	0.0016-0.0031
	3.7	K	0.0014	0.0146-0.0249	0.0146-0.0249	0.0100-0.0300	0.0020-0.0037	0.0016-0.0031	0.0007-0.0091
	4.0	S	0.0008-0.0015	0.0090-0.0240	0.0190-0.0380	0.0100-0.0600	0.0017-0.0033	0.0017-0.0033	0.0024-0.0083
2007	3.7	K	0.0014	0.0146-0.0249	0.0146-0.0249	0.0100-0.0300	0.0020-0.0037	0.0016-0.0031	0.0007-0.0091
	3.8	1	0.0002-0.0015	0.007-0.0150	0.011-0.0220	0.009-0.0300	0.0012-0.0027	0.0016-0.0033	0.0015-0.0078

22043_LIBE_C0010

TORQUE SPECIFICATIONS

All readings in ft. lbs.

Year	Engine Displ. Liters	Engine VIN	Cylinder Head Bolts	Main Bearing Bolts	Rod Bearing Bolts	Crankshaft Damper Bolts	Flywheel Bolts	Manifold Intake	Manifold Exhaust	Spark Plugs	Oil Pan Drain Plug
2005	2.4	1	①	②	③	100	④	21	17	13	20
	2.8	5	⑤	⑥	⑦	203	32	18	26	—	NA
	3.7	K	⑧	⑨	③	130	70	9	18	20	25
	4.0	S	⑩	80	33	80	105	⑪	⑪	22	25
2006	2.4	1	①	②	③	100	④	21	17	13	20
	2.8	5	⑤	⑥	⑦	203	32	18	26	—	NA
	3.7	K	⑧	⑨	③	130	70	9	18	20	25
	4.0	S	⑩	80	33	80	105	⑪	⑪	22	25
2007	3.7	K	⑧	⑨	③	130	70	9	18	20	25
	3.8	1	⑫	⑬	⑭	40	65	⑮	17	20	20

NA: Information not available

① Step 1: 25 ft. lbs.
Step 2: 50 ft. lbs.
Step 3: 50 ft. lbs.
Step 4: Plus 1/4 turn

② Refer to illustration.
Step 1: Hold crankshaft forward w/ a wood wedge
Step 2: Bolts 1-10 30 ft. lbs.
Step 3: Remove wedge
Step 4: Bolts 1-10 30 ft. lbs.
Step 5: Bolts 1-10: Plus 90 degree turn
Step 6: Install bedplate
Step 7: Bolts 11-20: 20 ft. lbs.

③ 20 ft. lbs. + 90 degrees

④ Flexplate: 70 ft. lbs.
Flywheel: 60 ft. lbs.

⑤ Refer to the procedure.
Step 1: 22 ft. lbs., in sequence
Step 2: Plus 75 degrees, in sequence
Step 3: Lateral bolts an additional 75 degrees, in sequence
Step 4: All bolts an additional 75 degrees, in sequence

⑥ Main bearing supports: 32 ft. lbs.

⑦ Step 1: 88 inch lbs.
Step 2: 22 ft. lbs.
Step 3: Plus 60 degrees
Step 4: 65 ft. lbs.

⑧ Step 1: Bolts 1-8 to 20 ft. lbs.
Step 2: Bolts 1-10, verify torque
Step 3: Bolts 9-12 to 10 ft. lbs.
Step 4: Bolts 1-8, plus 90 degrees
Step 5: Bolts 9-12 to 19 ft. lbs.

⑨ Bed plate bolt sequence. Refer to illustration
Step 1: Hand tighten bolts 1D,1G, 1F until bedplate contacts block.
Step 2: Tighten bolts 1A - 1J to 40 ft. lbs.
Step 3: Tighten bolts 1 - 8 to 5 ft. lbs.
Step 4: Turn bolts 1 - 8 an additional 90 degrees
Step 5: Tighten bolts A - E to 20 ft. lbs.

⑩ Step 1: 22 ft. lbs.
Step 2: 45 ft. lbs.
Step 3: Bolts 1-10 to 110 ft. lbs.
Step 4: Bolt 11 to 100 ft. lbs.
Step 5: Bolts 12-14 to 110 ft. lbs.

⑪ Bolts 1-5 and 8-11: 24 ft. lbs.
Bolts 6-7: 23 ft. lbs.

⑫ Step 1: 45 ft. lbs.
Step 2: 65 ft. lbs.
Step 3: 65 ft. lbs.
Step 4: Plus 90 degrees

⑬ Step 1: 30 ft. lbs.
Step 2: Plus 90 degrees

⑭ Step 1: 40 ft. lbs.
Step 2: Plus 90 degrees

⑮ Lower manifold: Step 1: 10 inch lbs.
Step 2: 200 inch lbs.
Step 3: 200 inch lbs.
Upper manifold: 105 inch lbs.

22043_LIBE_C0011

WHEEL ALIGNMENT

Year	Model		Caster Range (+/-Deg.)	Caster Preferred Setting (Deg.)	Camber Range (+/-Deg.)	Camber Preferred Setting (Deg.)	Toe-in (deg.)
2005	Wrangler	F	1.00	+7.00	0.63	-0.25	0.15+/-0.07
		R	—	—	0.25	-0.25	0.25+/-0.25
	Liberty	F	0.50	+3.9	0.375	-0.375	0.20+/-0.125
		R	—	—	0.375	-0.25	0.25+/-0.41
2006	Wrangler	F	1.00	+7.00	0.63	-0.25	0.15+/-0.07
		R	—	—	0.25	-0.25	0.25+/-0.25
	Liberty	F	0.50	+3.9	0.375	-0.375	0.20+/-0.125
		R	—	—	0.375	-0.25	0.25+/-0.41
2007	Wrangler	F	0.50	+4.2	0.37	-0.25	0.20+/-0.03
		R	—	—	0.50	-0.25	0.25+/-0.5
	Liberty	F	0.50	+3.9	0.375	-0.375	0.20+/-0.125
		R	—	—	0.375	-0.25	0.25+/-0.41

22043_LIBE_C0012

TIRE, WHEEL AND BALL JOINT SPECIFICATIONS

Year	Model	OEM Tires Standard	OEM Tires Optional	Tire Pressures (psi) Front	Tire Pressures (psi) Rear	Wheel Size	Ball Joint Inspection	Lug Nut Torque (ft. lbs.)
2005	Wrangler SE	P215/75R15	P225/75R15	①	①	std: 6 opt.: 7	②	85-115
	Wrangler Sport	P215/75R15	P225/75R15 30x9.5R15LT	①	①	6JJ/7JJ 8JJ	②	85-115
	Wrangler X	P215/75R15	P225/75R15	①	①	7	②	85-115
	Wrangler Rubicon	LT245/75R16	none	①	①	8	②	85-115
	Liberty	P215/75R16	P225/75R15 P235/70R16 P235/65R17	①	①	①	②	85-115
2006	Wrangler SE	P215/75R15	P225/75R15	①	①	std: 6 opt.: 7	②	85-115
	Wrangler Sport	P215/75R15	P225/75R15 30x9.5R15LT	①	①	6JJ/7JJ 8JJ	②	85-115
	Wrangler X	P215/75R15	P225/75R15	①	①	7	②	85-115
	Wrangler Rubicon	LT245/75R16	none	①	①	8	②	85-115
	Liberty	P215/75R16	P225/75R15 P235/70R16 P235/65R17	①	①	①	②	85-115
2007	Wrangler Sahara	255/75R17	none	①	①	①	②	92-132
	Wrangler X	225/75R16	none	①	①	①	②	92-132
	Wrangler Rubicon	255/75R17	none	①	①	①	②	92-132
	Liberty	P215/75R16	P225/75R15 P235/70R16 P235/65R17	①	①	①	②	85-115

OEM: Original Equipment Manufacturer

STD: Standard

OPT: Optional

① See placard on vehicle

② Replace if any measurable movement is found.

22043_LIBE_C0013

BRAKE SPECIFICATIONS

All measurements in inches unless noted

Year	Model		Brake Disc: Original Thickness	Brake Disc: Minimum Thickness	Brake Disc: Maximum Run-out	Brake Drum: Original Inside Diameter	Brake Drum: Max. Wear Limit	Brake Drum: Maximum Machine Diameter	Minimum Lining Thickness: Front	Minimum Lining Thickness: Rear	Caliper Mounting Bolts (ft. lbs.)
2005	Wrangler	F	0.940	0.837	0.005	—	—	—	0.030	—	11
		R	0.472	0.4330	0.004	9.00	—	9.06	—	①	18
	Liberty	F	1.102	1.0236	0.004	—	—	—	NA	NA	11
		R	0.472	0.4331	0.004	—	—	—	NA	NA	18
2006	Wrangler	F	0.940	0.837	0.005	—	—	—	0.030	—	11
		R	0.472	0.4330	0.004	9.00	—	9.06	—	①	18
	Liberty	F	1.102	1.0236	0.004	—	—	—	NA	NA	11
		R	0.472	0.4331	0.004	—	—	—	NA	NA	18
2007	Wrangler	F	0.940	0.837	0.005	—	—	—	0.030	—	26
		R	0.472	0.4330	0.004	—	—	—	—	NA	26
	Liberty	F	1.102	1.0236	0.004	—	—	—	NA	NA	11
		R	0.472	0.4331	0.004	—	—	—	NA	NA	18

F- Front

R - Rear

① Riveted brake shoes: 0.030 in.
Bonded brake shoes: 0.060 in.

22043_LIBE_C0014

SCHEDULED MAINTENANCE INTERVALS
Liberty with Gasoline Engines

TO BE SERVICED	TYPE OF SERVICE	VEHICLE MILEAGE INTERVAL (x1000): 3	6	9	12	15	18	21	24	27	30	33	36	39
Engine oil & filter	R	✓	✓	✓	✓	✓	✓	✓	✓	✓	✓	✓	✓	✓
Tires	Rotate		✓		✓		✓		✓		✓		✓	
Brake hoses & linings	I				✓				✓				✓	
Drive axle fluid	R				✓				✓				✓	
Air filter	I/R					✓					✓			
Spark plugs	R										✓			
Transfer case fluid level	I										✓			
PCV valve	I/R										✓			
Transfer case fluid	R	Drain, flush and refill every 60,000 miles												
Accessory drive belt	I/R	Every 45,000 miles												
Engine coolant	R	Every 60,000 miles												
Automatic trans. Fluid & filter	R	Every 60,000 miles												
Timing belt (2.4L)	R	Replace every 90,000 miles												
Ignition cables (2.4L)	R	Every 60,000 miles												

R: Replace S/I: Service or Inspect I/R: Inspect and replace as necessary

The above schedule is to be used if you drive under any of the following conditions:

Driving in temperatures under 32 degrees F
Stop and go traffic
Extensive engine idling
Driving in dusty conditions
Frequent trips under 10 miles
More than 50 % of your driving is in hot weather (90 deg. F) above 50 miles per hour
Trailer towing
Taxi, police or delivery service
Off-road driving

If none of these conditions are met, double the maintenance intervals

22043_LIBE_C0015

SCHEDULED MAINTENANCE INTERVALS
Liberty with 2.8L Diesel Engine

TO BE SERVICED	TYPE OF SERVICE	VEHICLE MILEAGE INTERVAL (x1000)												
		6.25	12.5	18.75	25	31.25	37.5	43.75	50	56.25	62.5	68.75	75	81.25
Engine oil & filter	R	✓	✓	✓	✓	✓	✓	✓	✓	✓	✓	✓	✓	✓
Brake linings	I		✓		✓		✓		✓		✓		✓	
Fuel/water separator	R				✓				✓				✓	
Air filter	I/R	✓	✓	✓	✓	✓	✓	✓	✓	✓	✓	✓	✓	✓
Air filter	R		✓		✓		✓		✓		✓		✓	
Drive axle fluid	R		✓		✓		✓		✓		✓		✓	
Automatic trans. fluid & filter	R										✓			
Transfer case fluid	R										✓			
Accessory drive belt	R						✓						✓	
Engine coolant	R	Every 100,000 miles												
Timing belt and idler pulleys	R	Every 100,000 miles												
Timing belt tensioner	R	Every 100,000 miles												

R: Replace S/I: Service or Inspect I/R: Inspect and replace as necessary

The above schedule is to be used if you drive under any of the following conditions:

Driving in temperatures under 32 degrees F
Stop and go traffic
Extensive engine idling
Driving in dusty conditions
Frequent trips under 10 miles
More than 50 % of your driving is in hot weather (90 deg. F) above 50 miles per hour
Trailer towing
Taxi, police or delivery service
Off-road driving

If none of these conditions is met, double the maintenance intervals

22043_LIBE_C0016

SCHEDULED MAINTENANCE INTERVALS
Wrangler

TO BE SERVICED	TYPE OF SERVICE	VEHICLE MILEAGE INTERVAL (x1000)												
		3	6	9	12	15	18	21	24	27	30	33	36	39
Engine oil & filter	R	✓	✓	✓	✓	✓	✓	✓	✓	✓	✓	✓	✓	✓
Tires	Rotate		✓		✓		✓		✓		✓		✓	
Brake hoses & linings	S/I				✓				✓				✓	
Drive axle fluid	R				✓				✓				✓	
Engine coolant level, hoses & clamps	S/I	✓	✓	✓	✓	✓	✓	✓	✓	✓	✓	✓	✓	✓
Outer tie rod ends	L	✓	✓	✓	✓	✓	✓	✓	✓	✓	✓	✓	✓	✓
Ball joints	L		✓		✓		✓		✓		✓		✓	
Air filter	I/R					✓					✓			
Spark plugs	R										✓			
Transfer case fluid level	I										✓			
PCV valve	I/R										✓			
Transfer case fluid	R	Every 60,000 miles												
Automatic trans. Fluid & filter	R	Every 60,000 miles												
Accessory drive belt	I/R	Every 45,000 miles												
Timing belt (2.4L)	R	Every 90,000 miles												
Engine coolant	R	Every 60,000 miles												
Ignition cables (2.4L)	I/R	Every 60,000 miles												

R: Replace S/I: Service or Inspect I/R: Inspect and replace if necessary L: Lubricate

The above schedule is to be used if you drive under any of the following conditions:

Driving in temperatures under 32 degrees F

Stop and go traffic

Extensive engine idling

Driving in dusty conditions

Frequent trips under 10 miles

More than 50 % of your driving is in hot weather (90 deg. F) above 50 miles per hour

Trailer towing

Taxi, police or delivery service

Off-road driving

If none of these conditions is met, double the maintenance intervals

22043_LIBE_C0017

PRECAUTIONS

Before servicing any vehicle, please be sure to read all of the following precautions, which deal with personal safety, prevention of component damage, and important points to take into consideration when servicing a motor vehicle:

- Never open, service or drain the radiator or cooling system when the engine is hot; serious burns can occur from the steam and hot coolant.
- Observe all applicable safety precautions when working around fuel. Whenever servicing the fuel system, always work in a well-ventilated area. Do not allow fuel spray or vapors to come in contact with a spark, open flame, or excessive heat (a hot drop light, for example). Keep a dry chemical fire extinguisher near the work area. Always keep fuel in a container specifically designed for fuel storage; also, always properly seal fuel containers to avoid the possibility of fire or explosion. Refer to the additional fuel system precautions later in this section.
- Fuel injection systems often remain pressurized, even after the engine has been turned **OFF**. The fuel system pressure must be relieved before disconnecting any fuel lines. Failure to do so may result in fire and/or personal injury.
- Brake fluid often contains polyglycol ethers and polyglycols. Avoid contact with the eyes and wash your hands thoroughly after handling brake fluid. If you do get brake fluid in your eyes, flush your eyes with clean, running water for 15 minutes. If eye irritation persists, or if you have taken brake fluid internally, IMMEDIATELY seek medical assistance.
- The EPA warns that prolonged contact with used engine oil may cause a number of skin disorders, including cancer. You should make every effort to minimize your exposure to used engine oil. Protective gloves should be worn when changing oil. Wash your hands and any other exposed skin areas as soon as possible after exposure to used engine oil. Soap and water, or waterless hand cleaner should be used.
- All new vehicles are now equipped with an air bag system, often referred to as a Supplemental Restraint System (SRS) or Supplemental Inflatable Restraint (SIR) system. The system must be disabled before performing service on or around system components, steering column, instrument panel components, wiring and sensors. Failure to follow safety and disabling procedures could result in accidental air bag deployment, possible personal injury and unnecessary system repairs.
- Always wear safety goggles when working with, or around, the air bag system. When carrying a non-deployed air bag, be sure the bag and trim cover are pointed away from your body. When placing a non-deployed air bag on a work surface, always face the bag and trim cover upward, away from the surface. This will reduce the motion of the module if it is accidentally deployed. Refer to the additional air bag system precautions later in this section.
- Clean, high quality brake fluid from a sealed container is essential to the safe and proper operation of the brake system. You should always buy the correct type of brake fluid for your vehicle. If the brake fluid becomes contaminated, completely flush the system with new fluid. Never reuse any brake fluid. Any brake fluid that is removed from the system should be discarded. Also, do not allow any brake fluid to come in contact with a painted surface; it will damage the paint.
- Never operate the engine without the proper amount and type of engine oil; doing so WILL result in severe engine damage.
- Timing belt maintenance is extremely important. Many models utilize an interference-type, non-freewheeling engine. If the timing belt breaks, the valves in the cylinder head may strike the pistons, causing potentially serious (also time-consuming and expensive) engine damage. Refer to the maintenance interval charts for the recommended replacement interval for the timing belt, and to the timing belt section for belt replacement and inspection.
- Disconnecting the negative battery cable on some vehicles may interfere with the functions of the on-board computer system(s) and may require the computer to undergo a relearning process once the negative battery cable is reconnected.
- When servicing drum brakes, only disassemble and assemble one side at a time, leaving the remaining side intact for reference.
- Only an MVAC-trained, EPA-certified automotive technician should service the air conditioning system or its components.

BRAKES — ANTI-LOCK BRAKE SYSTEM (ABS)

GENERAL INFORMATION

PRECAUTIONS

- Certain components within the ABS system are not intended to be serviced or repaired individually.
- Do not use rubber hoses or other parts not specifically specified for and ABS system. When using repair kits, replace all parts included in the kit. Partial or incorrect repair may lead to functional problems and require the replacement of components.
- Lubricate rubber parts with clean, fresh brake fluid to ease assembly. Do not use shop air to clean parts; damage to rubber components may result.
- Use only DOT 3 brake fluid from an unopened container.
- If any hydraulic component or line is removed or replaced, it may be necessary to bleed the entire system.
- A clean repair area is essential. Always clean the reservoir and cap thoroughly before removing the cap. The slightest amount of dirt in the fluid may plug an orifice and impair the system function. Perform repairs after components have been thoroughly cleaned; use only denatured alcohol to clean components. Do not allow ABS components to come into contact with any substance containing mineral oil; this includes used shop rags.
- The Anti-Lock control unit is a microprocessor similar to other computer units in the vehicle. Ensure that the ignition switch is **OFF** before removing or installing controller harnesses. Avoid static electricity discharge at or near the controller.
- If any arc welding is to be done on the vehicle, the control unit should be unplugged before welding operations begin.

SPEED SENSORS

REMOVAL & INSTALLATION

2005–06 Wrangler

Front

1. Raise vehicle and turn wheel outward to access the sensor.
2. Disconnect sensor wire connector at harness plug.
3. Remove sensor wire from mounting retainers.
4. Clean sensor and surrounding area with shop towel before removal.

5. Remove bolt attaching sensor to steering knuckle and remove sensor

To install:

6. If original sensor will be installed, wipe all traces of old spacer material off sensor pickup face Use a dry shop towel for this purpose.

7. Apply Mopar®Lock N' Seal or Loctite t 242 on bolt that secures sensor in steering knuckle. Use new sensor bolt if original bolt is worn or damaged.

8. Position sensor on steering knuckle. Seat sensor locating tab in hole in knuckle and install sensor attaching bolt finger tight.

9. Tighten sensor attaching bolt to 34–50 inch lbs. (4–6 Nm).

10. If original sensor has been installed, check sensor air gap. Air gap should be 0.40 to 0.0157 to 0.051 inches (1.3 mm). If gap is incorrect, sensor is either loose, or damaged.

11. Route sensor wire and install into mounting retainers.

12. Connect sensor wire to harness

Rear

1. Disconnect sensors at rear harness connectors.

2. Remove wheel and tire assembly.

3. Remove brake drum.

4. Remove clips securing sensor wires to brake lines, rear axle and, brake hose.

5. Unseat sensor wire support plate grommet.

6. Remove bolt attaching sensor to bracket and remove sensor

To install:

7. If original sensor is being installed, remove any remaining pieces of cardboard spacer from sensor pickup face. Use dry shop towel only to remove old spacer material.

8. Insert sensor wire through support plate hole Then seat sensor grommet in support plate.

9. Apply Mopar®Lock N' Seal or Loctite t 242 to original sensor bolt. Use new bolt if original is worn or damaged.

10. Install sensor bolt finger tight only at this time.

11. If original rear sensor was installed, adjust sensor air gap to 0.011–0.059 in. (0.28–1.5 mm). Use feeler gauge to measure air gap. Tighten sensor bolt to 106–124 inch lbs. (12–14 Nm).

12. If new sensor was installed, push cardboard spacer on sensor face against tone ring . Then tighten sensor bolt to 106–124 inch lbs. (12–14 Nm). Correct air gap will be established as tone ring rotates and peels spacer off sensor face.

13. Secure the rear sensor wires to the retainer clips. Verify that wire is clear of rotating components.

14. Connect sensor wire to harness connector.

15. Install brake drum and wheel and tire assembly.

16. Lower vehicle.

17. Connect sensor wire to harness connector.

Liberty

Front

1. Disconnect the front wheel speed sensor wire connector that is located on the inboard side of the respective wheel house.

2. Raise and support the vehicle.

3. Remove the tire and wheel assembly.

4. Remove the caliper adapter.

⁂ CAUTION

Never allow the disc brake caliper to hang from the brake hose. Damage to the brake hose with result. Provide a suitable support to hang the caliper securely.

5. Remove the disc brake rotor.

6. Remove the wheel speed sensor mounting bolt to the hub .

7. Remove the wheel speed sensor wire from the hub/bearing .

8. Remove the wheel speed sensor wire hold down from the knuckle .

9. Remove the wheel speed sensor wire thru the wheel well.

10. Remove the wheel speed sensor from the vehicle.

To install:

11. Install the wheel speed sensor to the vehicle.

12. Install the wheel speed sensor wire thru the wheel well.

13. Install the wheel speed sensor wire to the hub/bearing.

14. Install the wheel speed sensor wire hold down to the knuckle.

15. Install the wheel speed sensor mounting bolt to the hub. Tighten the mounting bolt to 120 inch lbs. (13.5 Nm).

16. Install the disc brake rotor.

17. Install the disc brake caliper adapter.

18. Install the tire and wheel assembly.

19. Reconnect the front wheel speed sensor wire connector to the inboard side of the wheel house being worked on.

Rear

1. Raise vehicle on hoist.

2. Disconnect the sensor wire harness.

3. Remove mounting stud from the sensor.

4. Remove sensor.

To install:

5. Connect harness to sensor. Be sure seal is securely in place between sensor and wiring connector.

6. Install O-ring on sensor (if removed).

7. Insert sensor in differential housing.

8. Install the sensor mounting stud and tighten to 80 inch lbs. (9 Nm).

9. Install the sensor electrical connector.

10. Lower vehicle.

BLEEDING PROCEDURE

BLEEDING PROCEDURE

➡Add only fresh, clean brake fluid from a sealed container when bleeding the brakes. If pressure bleeding equipment is used, the front brake metering valve will have to be held open to bleed the front brakes. The valve stem is located in the forward end or top of the combination valve. The stem must either be pressed inward or held outward slightly. Follow equipment manufacturer's instructions carefully when using pressure equipment. Do not exceed the maker's pressure recommendations. Generally, a tank pressure of 15—20 psi is sufficient. Do not pressure bleed without the proper master cylinder adapter.

When any part of the hydraulic system has been disconnected for repair or replacement, air may get into the lines and cause spongy pedal action (because air can be compressed and brake fluid cannot). To correct this condition, it is necessary to bleed the hydraulic system so to be sure all air is purged.

Bleeding must start where the lines were disconnected. If lines were disconnected at the master cylinder, for example, bleeding must be done at that point before proceeding downstream.

When bleeding the brake system, bleed one brake bleeder point at a time. Failure to do so may result in more air being drawn into the lines.

If the existing system fluid seems dirty or if the vehicle has covered considerable mileage, it is recommended that the system be completely purged and refilled with fresh, clean fluid. The best way to start is to siphon the old fluid out of the master cylinder reservoir and fill it completely with fresh fluid.

Brake fluid tends to darken over time. This does not necessarily indicate contamination. Examine fluid closely for foreign matter.

The primary and secondary hydraulic brake systems are separate and are bled independently. During the bleeding operation, do not allow the reservoir to run dry. Keep the master cylinder reservoir filled with brake fluid. Never use brake fluid that has been drained from the hydraulic system, no matter how clean it seems.

1. Clean all dirt from around the master cylinder fill cap, remove the cap and fill the master cylinder with brake fluid until the level is within ¼ in. (6mm) of the top edge of the reservoir.
2. Clean the bleeder screws at all 4 wheels. The bleeder screws are located on the back of the brake calipers.
3. Bleeder screws should be protected with rubber caps. If they are missing, the orifice may easily become clogged with road dirt. If the screw refuses to bleed when loosened, remove it and blow clear. Aftermarket caps are readily available.

Manual Bleeding

See Figures 1 through 3.

Manual bleeding requires two people and a degree of patience and cooperation. Bleeding should be performed in this order: (1) Right rear, (2) Left rear, (3) Right front, (4) Left front.

1. Follow the preparatory steps, above.
2. Attach a length of rubber hose over the bleeder screw and place the other end of the hose in a glass jar, submerged in brake fluid.
3. Have your assistant press down on the brake pedal, then open the bleeder screw ½–¾ turn.
4. The brake pedal will go to the floor.
5. Close the bleeder screw—preferably before the pedal reaches the floor. Tell your assistant to allow the brake pedal to return slowly.
6. Repeat these steps to purge all air from the system.
7. When bubbles cease to appear at the end of the bleeder hose, close the bleeder screw and remove the hose. Check that the pedal is firm or at least more firm than it was when you started. If not, continue the procedure.
8. Check the master cylinder fluid level and add fluid accordingly. Do this after bleeding each wheel.
9. Repeat the bleeding operation at the remaining three wheels, ending with the one closet to the master cylinder.
10. Fill the master cylinder reservoir to the proper level.

➡If there is excessive air in the system, it is possible that the stroke of the brake pedal will be insufficient to purge the lines. In this case a pressure bleeder or vacuum bleeder is the easiest solution.

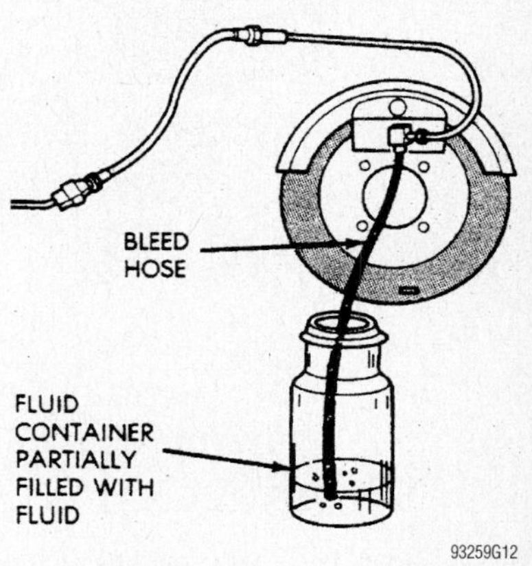

Fig. 1 Proper setup for manual bleeding procedure

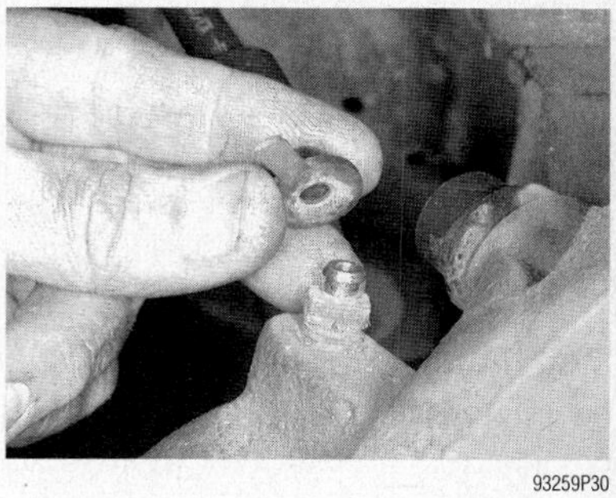

Fig. 2 Bleed screw caps are a must to keep the bleed screw passages clear

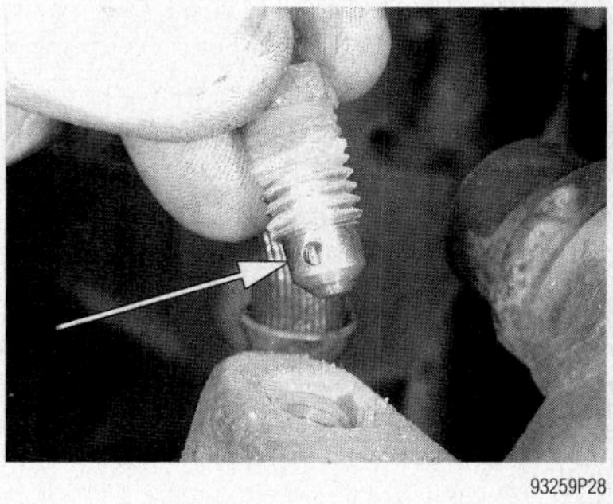

Fig. 3 Lack of cap may cause bleeder screw passages to become clogged

Vacuum Bleeding

See Figure 4.

Vacuum bleeding can be carried out by one person. Since a good vacuum bleeder will normally move more fluid than a brake pedal stroke, this procedure is preferred. These tools are inexpensive and readily available at auto parts outlets. Bleeding should be performed in this

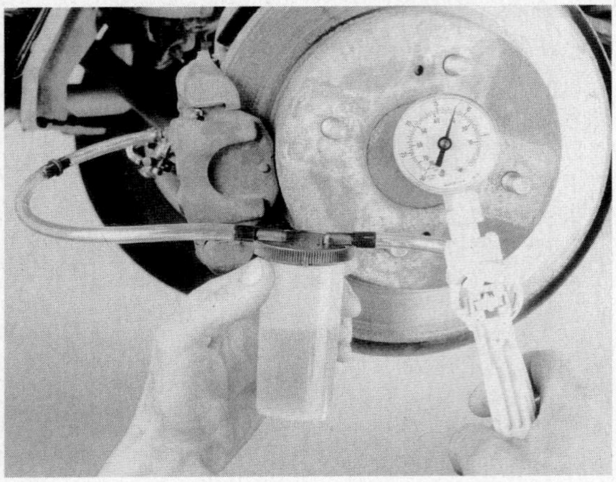

TCCA9P08

Fig. 4 There are tools, such as this Mighty-Vac, available to assist in vacuum bleeding of the brake system

order: (1) Right rear, (2) Left rear, (3) Right front, (4) Left front.

1. Follow the preparatory steps, above.
2. Attach the vacuum bleeder according to the manufacturer's recommendations.
3. Pump up the unit until maximum vacuum is reached. Loosen the bleeder screw slightly until bubbles and fluid issue forth. Close the screw before the vacuum is equalized.
4. Repeat the procedure until fluid without bubbles issues from the bleeder screw.
5. Keep a close check on master cylinder fluid level during this procedure as vacuum bleeders move considerable amounts of fluid.

MASTER CYLINDER BLEEDING

See Figure 5.

⁂ CAUTION

When clamping the master cylinder in a vise, only clamp the master cylinder by its mounting flange. Do not clamp the master cylinder piston rod, reservoir, seal or body.

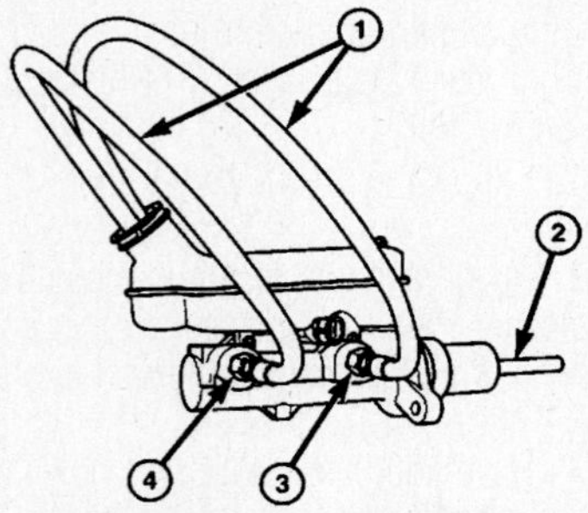

1. Bleeder tubes
2. Wooden dowel
3. Adapter
4. Adapter

22043_CARA_G0003

Fig. 5 Setup the master cylinder as shown to bleed it

1. Clamp the master cylinder in a vise.
2. Attach special tools for bleeding master cylinder in the following fashion:
3. Thread one adapter in each outlet port. Tighten the adapters to 145 inch lbs. (17 Nm). Next, thread a bleeder tube into each adapter. Flex the bleeder tubes and place the open ends into the mouth of the fluid reservoir as far down as possible.

➡Make sure open ends of bleeder tubes stay below surface of brake fluid once reservoir is filled to proper level.

4. Fill brake fluid reservoir with brake fluid meeting DOT 3 specifications. Make sure fluid level is above tips of bleeder tubes in reservoir to ensure no air is ingested during bleeding.
5. Using a wooden dowel as a pushrod, slowly depress the master cylinder pistons, then release pressure, allowing the pistons to return to the released position.
6. Repeat several times until all air bubbles are expelled. Make sure the fluid level stays above the tips of the bleeder tubes in the reservoir while bleeding.
7. Remove the bleeder tubes from the master cylinder outlet ports, then plug the outlet ports and install the fill cap on the reservoir.
8. Install the master cylinder on vehicle then follow the brake bleeding procedure.

BLEEDING THE ABS SYSTEM

ABS system bleeding requires conventional bleeding methods plus use of the DRB scan tool. The procedure involves performing a base brake bleeding, followed by use of the scan tool to cycle and bleed the HCU pump and solenoids. A second base brake bleeding procedure is then required to remove any air remaining in the system.

1. Perform base brake bleeding.
2. Connect scan tool to the Data Link Connector (DLC).
3. Select ANTI-LOCK BRAKES, followed by MISCELLANEOUS, then ABS BRAKES. Follow the instructions displayed. When scan tool displays TEST COMPLETE, disconnect scan tool and proceed.
4. Perform base brake bleeding a second time.
5. Top off master cylinder fluid level and verify proper brake operation before moving vehicle.

CAUTION

Dust and dirt accumulating on brake parts during normal use may contain asbestos fibers from production or aftermarket brake linings. Breathing excessive concentrations of asbestos fibers can cause serious bodily harm. Exercise care when servicing brake parts. Do not sand or grind brake lining unless equipment used is designed to contain the dust residue. Do not clean brake parts with compressed air or by dry brushing. Cleaning should be done by dampening the brake components with a fine mist of water, then wiping the brake components clean with a dampened cloth. Dispose of cloth and all residue containing asbestos fibers in an impermeable container with the appropriate label. Follow practices prescribed by the Occupational Safety and Health Administration (OSHA) and the Environmental Protection Agency (EPA) for the handling, processing, and disposing of dust or debris that may contain asbestos fibers.

BRAKE CALIPER

REMOVAL & INSTALLATION

2005–06 Wrangler

See Figures 6 and 7.

1. Before servicing the vehicle, refer to the precautions in the beginning of this section.
2. Drain ⅔ of the brake fluid from the front reservoir. Use the bleeder screw at the front outlet port to drain the fluid. If equipped with anti-lock brakes, relieve the system pressure.
3. Raise and safely support the vehicle.
4. Remove the wheels.
5. Place a C-clamp on the caliper so the solid end contacts the back of the caliper and screw end contacts the metal part of the outboard brake pad.
6. Tighten the clamp until the caliper moves far enough to force the piston to the bottom of the piston bore. This will back the brake pads off of the rotor surface to facilitate the removal and installation of the caliper assembly.
7. Remove the C-clamp.
8. Remove both of the mounting bolts and lift the caliper off the rotor.

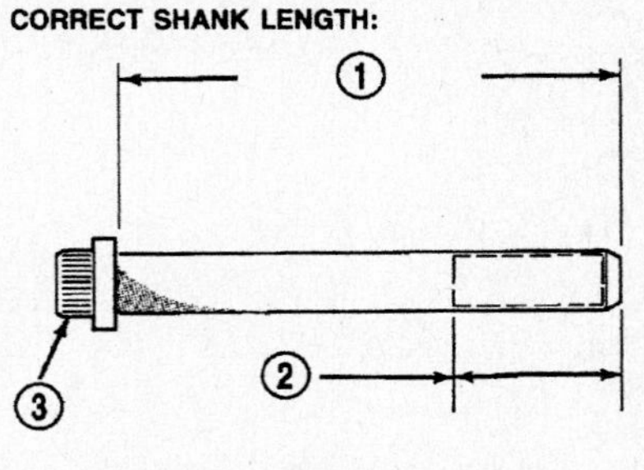

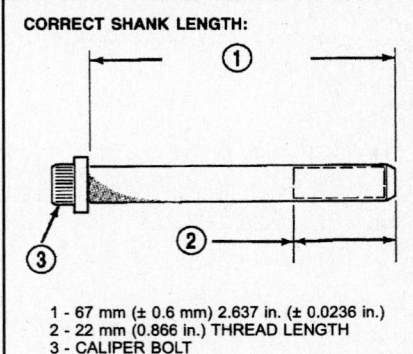

1 - 67 mm (± 0.6 mm) 2.637 in. (± 0.0236 in.)
2 - 22 mm (0.866 in.) THREAD LENGTH
3 - CALIPER BOLT

06009-JEEP-G197

Fig. 6 Caliper lubrication points—Wrangler

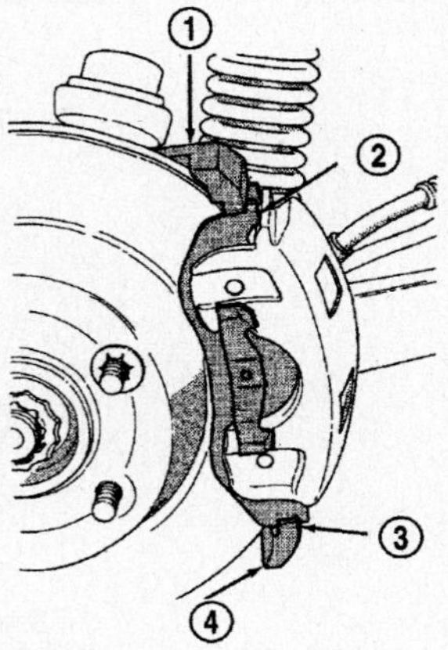

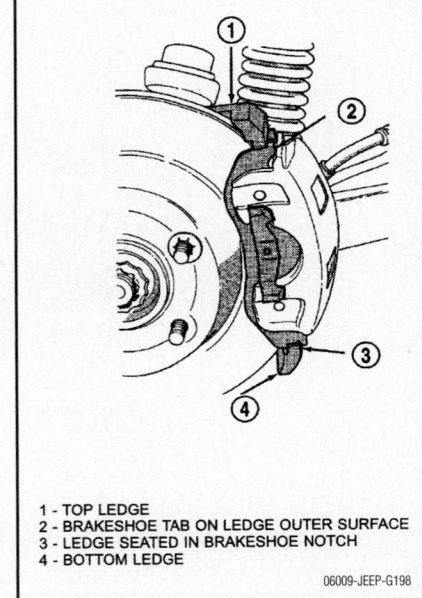

1 - TOP LEDGE
2 - BRAKESHOE TAB ON LEDGE OUTER SURFACE
3 - LEDGE SEATED IN BRAKESHOE NOTCH
4 - BOTTOM LEDGE

06009-JEEP-G198

Fig. 7 Caliper installation—Wrangler

9. If the caliper is being removed, it is necessary to disconnect the brake fluid hose. Clean the brake fluid hose-to-caliper connection thoroughly. Remove the hose-to-caliper bolt. Cap or tape the open ends to keep dirt out. Discard the copper gaskets.

To install:

WARNING

If new caliper bolts are being installed, or if the original reason for repair was a drag/pull condition, check caliper bolt length before proceeding. Bolts must not have a shank length greater than 2.66 inches (67.6 mm).

10. Connect the brake line to the caliper with new sealing washers and fitting bolt. Hand-tighten the fitting bolt.
11. Position the caliper into place over the rotor.
12. Coat the caliper mounting bolt with silicone grease and torque them to 11 ft. lbs. (15 Nm).
13. Position the brake line clear of all chassis components, untwisted and free of kinks. Torque the fitting bolt to 23 ft. lbs. (31 Nm).
14. Install the wheels.
15. Fill the master cylinder with fluid and bleed the brake system.
16. Before driving the vehicle, pump the brakes several times to seat the pads.

Liberty

See Figure 8.

1. Before servicing the vehicle, refer to the precautions in the beginning of this section.
2. Drain⅔ of the brake fluid from the front reservoir. Use the bleeder screw at the front outlet port to drain the fluid. If equipped with anti-lock brakes, relieve the system pressure.
3. Raise and safely support the vehicle.
4. Remove the wheels.
5. Remove both of the mounting bolts and lift the caliper off the rotor.
6. If the caliper is being removed, it is necessary to disconnect the brake fluid hose. Clean the brake fluid hose-to-caliper connection thoroughly. Remove the hose-to-caliper bolt. Cap or tape the open ends to keep dirt out. Discard the copper gaskets.

To install:

7. Connect the brake line to the caliper with new sealing washers and fitting bolt. Hand-tighten the fitting bolt.
8. Position the caliper into place over the rotor.
9. Coat the caliper mounting bolts with silicone grease and torque them to 11 ft. lbs. (15 Nm).
10. Position the brake line clear of all chassis components, untwisted and free of kinks. Use new copper washers. Torque the fitting bolt to 23 ft. lbs. (31 Nm).
11. Install the wheels.
12. Fill the master cylinder with fluid and bleed the brake system.
13. Before driving the vehicle, pump the brakes several times to seat the pads.

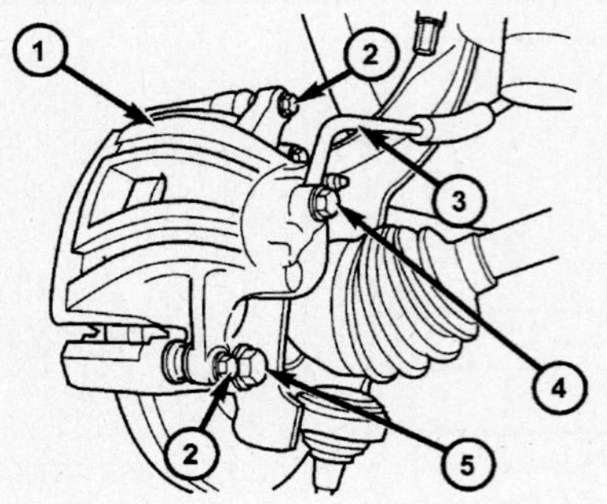

Fig. 8 Front caliper—Liberty

12. Install wheel and tire assembly.
13. Remove support and lower vehicle.
14. Pump brake pedal until caliper pistons and brake shoes are seated.
15. Top off brake fluid level if necessary.

Liberty

See Figure 11.

1. Before servicing the vehicle, refer to the precautions in the beginning of this section.
2. Drain⅔ of the brake fluid from the front reservoir. Use the bleeder screw at the front outlet port to drain the fluid. If equipped with anti-lock brakes, relieve the system pressure.
3. Raise and safely support the vehicle.
4. Remove the wheels.

DISC BRAKE PADS

REMOVAL & INSTALLATION

2005–06 Wrangler

See Figures 9 and 10.

1. Before servicing the vehicle, refer to the precautions in the beginning of this section.
2. Raise and support vehicle.
3. Remove wheel and tire assembly.
4. Remove caliper.
5. Pressing one end of outboard shoe inward to disengage shoe lug. Then rotate shoe upward until retainer spring clears caliper. Press opposite end of shoe inward to disengage shoe lug and rotate shoe up and out of caliper.
6. Grasp ends of inboard shoe and tilt shoe outward to release springs from caliper piston and remove shoe from caliper.

➡If original brake shoes will be used, keep them in sets left and right. They are not interchangeable.

7. Secure caliper to nearby suspension part with wire. Do not allow brake hose to support caliper weight.
8. Wipe caliper off with shop rags or towels.

To install:

9. Install inboard shoe in caliper and verify shoe retaining is fully seated into the piston.
10. Start one end of outboard shoe in caliper and rotate shoe downward into place. Verify shoe locating lugs and shoe spring are seated.
11. Install caliper.

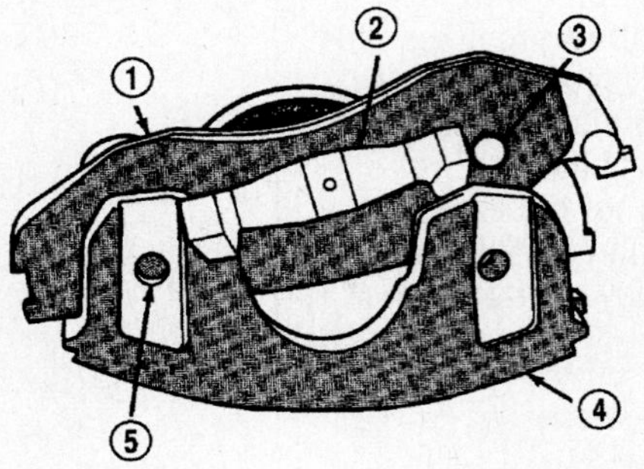

Fig. 9 Outboard front brake pad removal/installation—Wrangler

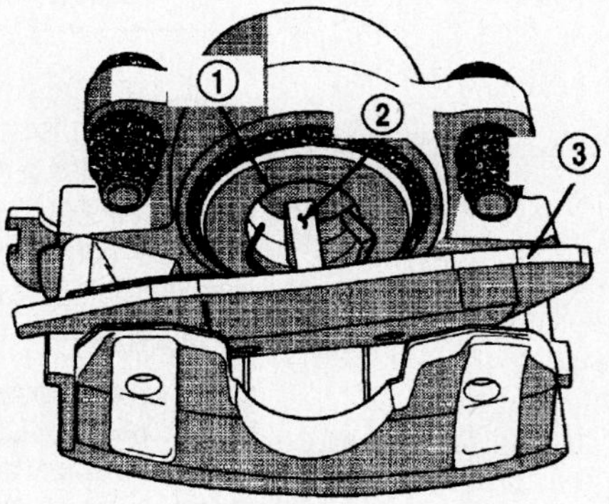

Fig. 10 Inboard front brake pad removal/installation—Wrangler

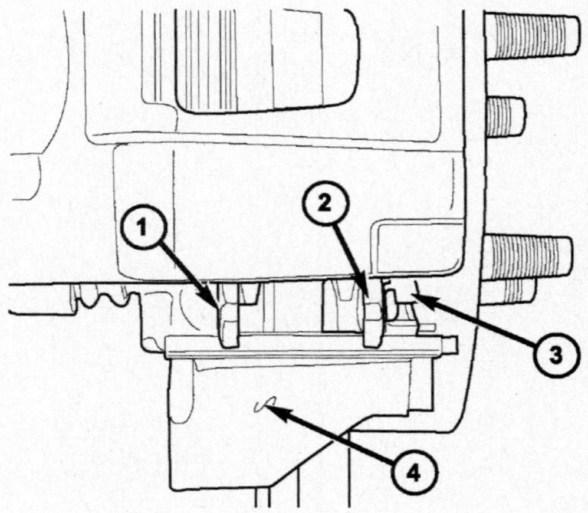

Fig. 11 Front brake pad anti-rattle clip installation—Liberty

5. Remove both caliper slide pin bushing caps and slide pins.
6. Lift the caliper from the anchor.
7. Using a piece of mechanic's wire, support the caliper so there is not tension on the brake hose.
8. Remove the brake pads from the caliper.

To install:

9. Position the brake pads onto the caliper.
10. Position the caliper into place on the anchor.
11. Coat the caliper slide pins with silicone grease and torque them to 11 ft. lbs. (15 Nm). Install the slide pin bushing caps.

➡Hold the spring in the caliper hole with your thumb while prying the spring end out and under the anchor.

12. Fill the master cylinder with fluid and bleed the brake system.
13. Before driving the vehicle, pump the brakes several times to seat the pads.
14. Install the wheels.

BRAKES — REAR DISC BRAKES

⁂ CAUTION

Dust and dirt accumulating on brake parts during normal use may contain asbestos fibers from production or aftermarket brake linings. Breathing excessive concentrations of asbestos fibers can cause serious bodily harm. Exercise care when servicing brake parts. Do not sand or grind brake lining unless equipment used is designed to contain the dust residue. Do not clean brake parts with compressed air or by dry brushing. Cleaning should be done by dampening the brake components with a fine mist of water, then wiping the brake components clean with a dampened cloth. Dispose of cloth and all residue containing asbestos fibers in an impermeable container with the appropriate label. Follow practices prescribed by the Occupational Safety and Health Administration (OSHA) and the Environmental Protection Agency (EPA) for the handling, processing, and disposing of dust or debris that may contain asbestos fibers.

BRAKE CALIPER

REMOVAL & INSTALLATION

2005–06 Wrangler

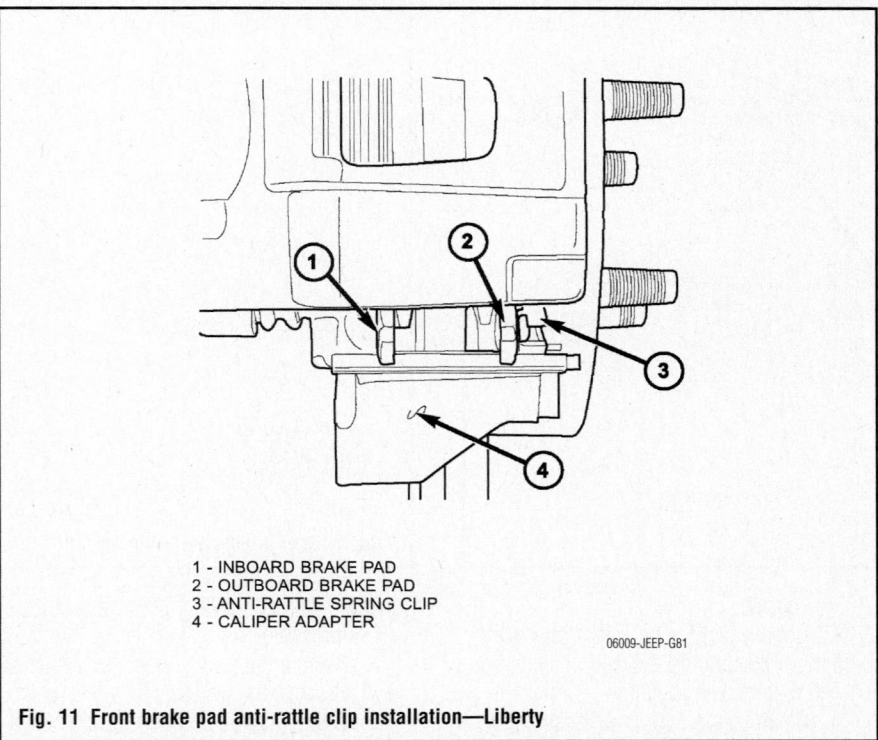

1. Before servicing the vehicle, refer to the precautions in the beginning of this section.
2. Drain ⅔ of the brake fluid from the front reservoir. If equipped with anti-lock brakes, relieve the system pressure.
3. Raise and safely support the vehicle.
4. Remove the wheels.
5. Insert a small prybar through the caliper opening and pry the caliper (using the outboard brake pad) to bottom the piston in the caliper bore.

➡This will back the brake pads off of the rotor surface to facilitate the removal and installation of the caliper assembly.

6. Remove the brake hose-to-caliper bolt, hose and washers.
7. Remove both caliper slide pin bushing caps and slide pins.
8. Lift the caliper from the anchor.

To install:

9. Position the caliper into place on the anchor.
10. Coat the caliper slide pins with silicone grease and torque them to 11 ft. lbs. (15 Nm). Install the slide pin bushing caps.
11. Using new gasket washers, install the brake line and torque the fitting bolt to 23 ft. lbs. (31 Nm).
12. Fill the master cylinder with fluid and bleed the brake system.
13. Before driving the vehicle, pump the brakes several times to seat the pads.
14. Install the wheels.

Liberty

See Figure 12.

1. Before servicing the vehicle, refer to the precautions in the beginning of this section.
2. Drain ⅔ of the brake fluid from the front reservoir. If equipped with anti-lock brakes, relieve the system pressure.
3. Raise and safely support the vehicle.
4. Remove the wheels.
5. Remove the brake hose-to-caliper bolt, hose and washers.
6. Remove both caliper slide pin bushing caps and slide pins.
7. Lift the caliper from the anchor.

To install:

8. Position the caliper into place on the anchor.

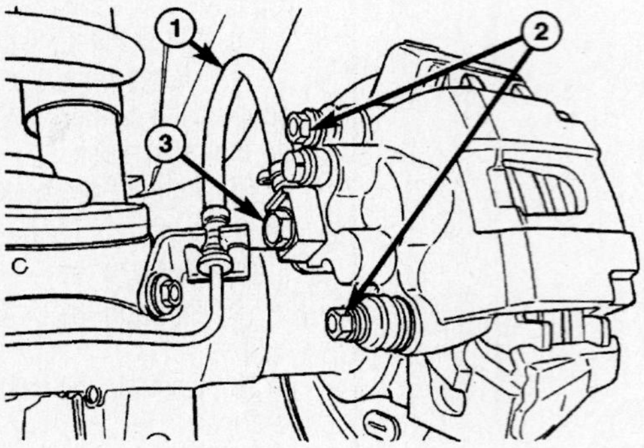

Fig. 12 Rear brake caliper—Liberty

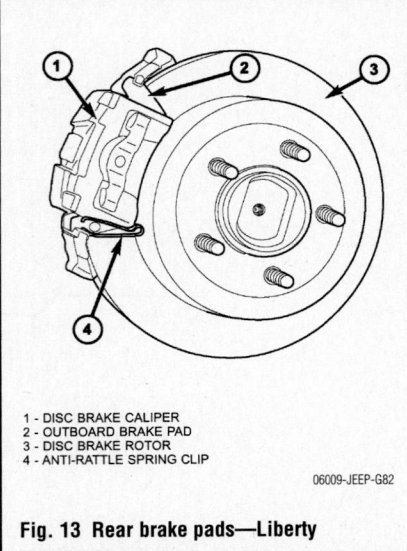

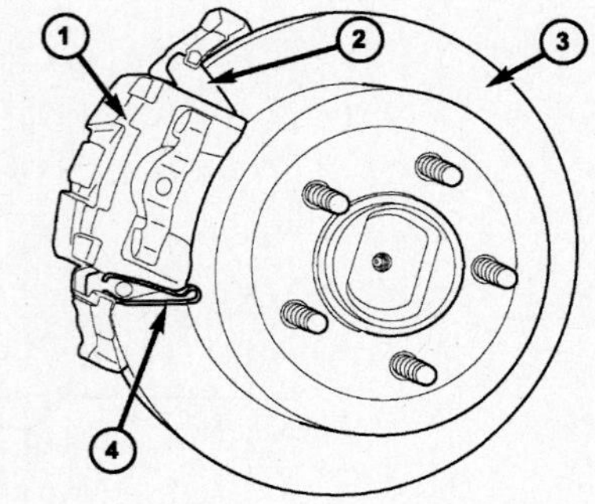

Fig. 13 Rear brake pads—Liberty

9. Coat the caliper slide pins with silicone grease and torque them to 18 ft. lbs. Install the slide pin bushing caps.
10. Using new gasket washers, install the brake line and torque the fitting bolt to 23 ft. lbs. (31 Nm).
11. Fill the master cylinder with fluid and bleed the brake system.
12. Before driving the vehicle, pump the brakes several times to seat the pads.
13. Install the wheels.

DISC BRAKE PADS

REMOVAL & INSTALLATION

2005–06 Wrangler

1. Before servicing the vehicle, refer to the precautions in the beginning of this section.
2. Raise and support vehicle.
3. Remove the wheel and tire assemblies.
4. Compress the caliper.
5. Remove the caliper.
6. Remove the caliper by tilting the top up and off the caliper adapter.

➡Do not allow brake hose to support caliper assembly.

7. Support and hang the caliper.
8. Remove the inboard brake pad from the caliper adapter.
9. Remove the outboard brake pad from the caliper adapter.

To install:

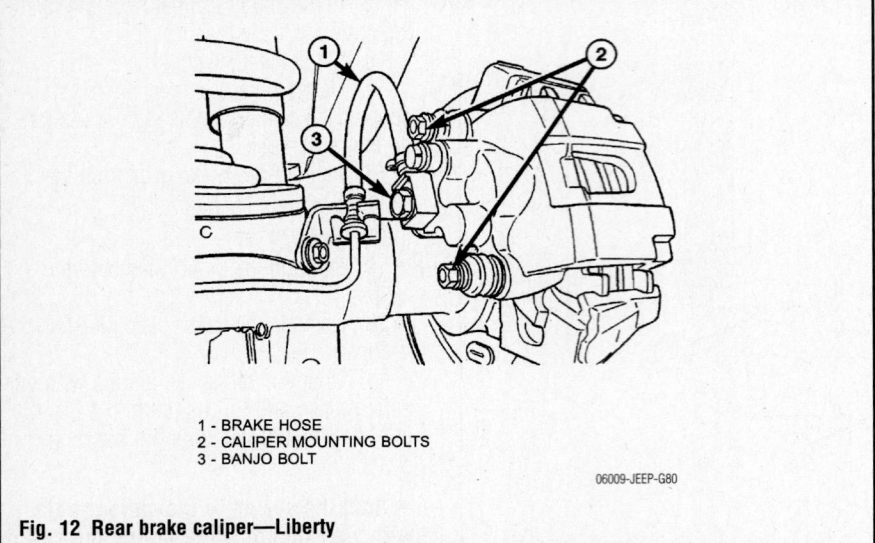

10. Bottom pistons in caliper bore with C-clamp. Place an old brake shoe between a C-clamp and caliper piston.
11. Clean caliper mounting adapter and anti-rattle springs.
12. Lubricate anti-rattle springs with Mopar®brake grease, or equivalent.
13. Install anti-rattle springs.

➡Anti-rattle springs are not interchangeable.

14. Install inboard brake pad in adapter.
15. Install outboard brake pad in adapter.
16. Tilt the top of the caliper over rotor and under adapter. Then push the bottom of the caliper down onto the adapter.
17. Install caliper.
18. Install wheel and tire assemblies and lower vehicle.
19. Apply brakes several times to seat caliper pistons and brake shoes and obtain firm pedal.
20. Top off master cylinder fluid level.

Liberty

See Figure 13.

1. Before servicing the vehicle, refer to the precautions in the beginning of this section.
2. Drain⅔ of the brake fluid from the front reservoir. Use the bleeder screw at the front outlet port to drain the fluid. If equipped with anti-lock brakes, relieve the system pressure.
3. Raise and safely support the vehicle.
4. Remove the wheels.
5. Pry the caliper support spring out of the caliper.
6. Remove both caliper slide pin bushing caps and slide pins.
7. Lift the caliper from the anchor.
8. Using a piece of mechanics wire, support the caliper so there is not tension on the brake hose.
9. Remove the brake pads from the caliper.

To install:

10. Position the brake pads onto the caliper.
11. Position the caliper into place on the anchor.
12. Coat the caliper slide pins with silicone grease and torque them to 18 ft. lbs. (25 Nm). Install the slide pin bushing caps.
13. Install the caliper support spring in the top of the caliper under the anchor; then, install the other end into the lower caliper hole.

➡Hold the spring in the caliper hole with your thumb while prying the spring end out and under the anchor.

14. Fill the master cylinder with fluid and bleed the brake system.
15. Before driving the vehicle, pump the brakes several times to seat the pads.
16. Install the wheels.

✲✲ CAUTION

Dust and dirt accumulating on brake parts during normal use may contain asbestos fibers from production or aftermarket brake linings. Breathing excessive concentrations of asbestos fibers can cause serious bodily harm. Exercise care when servicing brake parts. Do not sand or grind brake lining unless equipment used is designed to contain the dust residue. Do not clean brake parts with compressed air or by dry brushing. Cleaning should be done by dampening the brake components with a fine mist of water, then wiping the brake components clean with a dampened cloth. Dispose of cloth and all residue containing asbestos fibers in an impermeable container with the appropriate label. Follow practices prescribed by the Occupational Safety and Health Administration (OSHA) and the Environmental Protection Agency (EPA) for the handling, processing, and disposing of dust or debris that may contain asbestos fibers.

BRAKE DRUM

REMOVAL & INSTALLATION

2005–06 Wrangler

1. Before servicing the vehicle, refer to the precautions in the beginning of this section.
2. Raise and safely support the vehicle.
3. Remove the wheel.
4. Remove the spring nuts (if installed) from the lug bolts and remove the drum from the vehicle.

To install:

5. Ensure the contacting surfaces are clean and flat. Install the drum on the hub.
6. Adjust the brake shoes, if necessary.
7. Install the spring nuts on the lug bolts.
8. Install the wheel.

BRAKE SHOES

REMOVAL & INSTALLATION

2005–06 Wrangler

See Figure 14.

1. Before servicing the vehicle, refer to the precautions in the beginning of this section.
2. Raise and safely support the vehicle.
3. Remove the wheel and brake drum.
4. Remove the U-clip and washer securing the adjuster cable to the parking brake lever.
5. Remove the primary and secondary return springs from the anchor pin.
6. Remove the hold-down springs, retainers and pins.
7. Install spring clamps on the wheel cylinders to hold the pistons in place.
8. Remove the adjuster lever, adjuster screw and spring.
9. Remove the adjuster cable and cable guide.
10. Remove the brake shoes and parking brake strut.
11. Disconnect the cable from the parking brake lever and remove the lever.

To install:

12. Clean the support plate with brake cleaner.
13. Apply multi-purpose grease to the brake shoe contact surfaces on the backing plate.
14. Lubricate the adjuster screw threads.
15. Attach the parking brake lever to the secondary brake shoe. Use a new washer and U-clip.
16. Remove the wheel cylinder clamps.
17. Attach the parking brake cable to the lever.
18. Install the brake shoes on the support plate. Secure the shoes with new hold-down springs, pins and retainers.
19. Install the parking brake strut and spring.
20. Install the guide plate and adjuster cable to the anchor pin.
21. Install the return springs.
22. Install the adjuster cable guide on the secondary shoe.
23. Install the adjuster screw, spring and lever. Connect to the adjuster cable.
24. Adjust the shoes to the drum. Install the drum.
25. Install the wheel/tire assemblies and lower the vehicle.
26. Verify a firm brake pedal before moving the vehicle

ADJUSTMENT

1. Be sure parking brake lever is fully released.
2. Raise vehicle so rear wheels can be rotated freely.
3. Remove plug from each access hole in brake support plates.

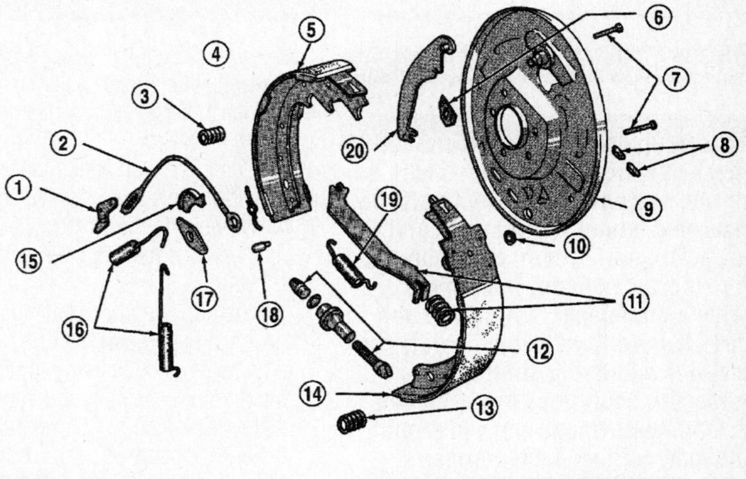

1 - ADJUSTER LEVER
2 - ADJUSTER CABLE
3 - HOLDDOWN SPRING AND RETAINERS
4 - ADJUSTER LEVER SPRING
5 - TRAILING SHOE
6 - CYLINDER-TO-SUPPORT SEAL
7 - HOLDDOWN PINS
8 - ACCESS PLUGS
9 - SUPPORT PLATE
10 - CABLE HOLE PLUG
11 - PARK BRAKE STRUT AND SPRING
12 - ADJUSTER SCREW ASSEMBLY
13 - HOLDDOWN SPRING AND RETAINERS
14 - LEADING SHOE
15 - CABLE GUIDE
16 - SHOE RETURN SPRINGS
17 - SHOE GUIDE PLATE
18 - PIN
19 - SHOE SPRING
20 - PARK BRAKE LEVER

06009-JEEP-G201

Fig. 14 Drum brake components, right side shown—Wrangler

4. Loosen parking brake cable adjustment nut until there is slack in front cable.
5. Insert adjusting tool through support plate access hole and engage tool in teeth of adjusting screw star wheel .
6. Rotate adjuster screw star wheel (move tool handle upward) until slight drag can be felt when wheel is rotated.
7. Push and hold adjuster lever away from star wheel with thin screwdriver.
8. Back off adjuster screw star wheel until brake drag is eliminated.
9. Repeat adjustment at opposite wheel. Be sure adjustment is equal at both wheels.
10. Install support plate access hole plugs.
11. Adjust parking brake cable and lower vehicle.
12. Apply park brake hand lever and make sure park brakes hold the vehicle stationary.
13. Release park brake hand lever.

BRAKES — PARKING BRAKE

PARKING BRAKE CABLES

ADJUSTMENT

No adjustment is needed as the parking brake cables are self–adjusting. If the cables have been replaced, follow the parking shoe replacement procedure to set the shoes correctly.

PARKING BRAKE SHOES

REMOVAL & INSTALLATION

With Rear Drum Brakes

The rear drum brake shoes serve as the parking brakes. Refer to the procedures under Rear Drum Brakes for service.

With Rear Disc Brakes

Rear disc parking brakes are dual shoe, internal expanding units with an automatic self adjusting mechanism. When the parking brake pedal is depressed the brake cable pulls the brake shoes outward against the brake drum. When the brake pedal is released the return springs attached to the brake shoes pull the shoes back to their original position.

1. Raise and support the vehicle.
2. Remove the tire and wheel assembly.
3. Remove the disc brake caliper.
4. Remove the disc brake rotor.
5. Disengage the park brake cable from behind the rotor assembly to allow easier disassembly of the park brake shoes.
6. Disassemble the rear park brake shoes.

To install:

7. Reassemble the rear park brake shoes.
8. Install park brake cable to the lever behind support plate.
9. Adjust the rear brake shoes:
   a. Measure the drum diameter with the gauge and lock it into position.
   b. Turn the gauge around and check the shoe diameter diagonally across at the top of one shoe and bottom of the opposite shoe (widest point). The gauge should be a light drag fit over the shoes.
   c. If the gauge is not a light drag fit over the shoes, turn the star wheel by hand to move the shoes in or out so that the correct clearance can be achieved.
10. Install the disc brake rotor.
11. Install the disc brake caliper.
12. Install the wheel.
13. Lower the vehicle.

➡On a new vehicle or after parking brake lining replacement, it is recommended that the parking brake system be conditioned prior to use. This is done by making one stop from 25 mph on dry pavement or concrete using light to moderate force on the parking brake foot pedal.

CHASSIS ELECTRICAL — AIR BAG (SUPPLEMENTAL RESTRAINT SYSTEM)

GENERAL INFORMATION

⁂ CAUTION

These vehicles are equipped with an air bag system. The system must be disarmed before performing service on, or around, system components, the steering column, instrument panel components, wiring and sensors. Failure to follow the safety precautions and the disarming procedure could result in accidental air bag deployment, possible injury and unnecessary system repairs.

SERVICE PRECAUTIONS

Disconnect and isolate the battery negative cable before beginning any airbag system component diagnosis, testing, removal, or installation procedures. Allow system capacitor to discharge for two minutes before beginning any component service. This will disable the airbag system. Failure to disable the airbag system may result in accidental airbag deployment, personal injury, or death.

Do not place an intact undeployed airbag face down on a solid surface. The airbag will propel into the air if accidentally deployed and may result in personal injury or death.

When carrying or handling an undeployed airbag, the trim side (face) of the airbag should be pointing towards the body to minimize possibility of injury if accidental deployment occurs. Failure to do this may result in personal injury or death.

Replace airbag system components with OEM replacement parts. Substitute parts may appear interchangeable, but internal differences may result in inferior occupant protection. Failure to do so may result in occupant personal injury or death.

Wear safety glasses, rubber gloves, and long sleeved clothing when cleaning powder residue from vehicle after an airbag deployment. Powder residue emitted from a deployed airbag can cause skin irritation. Flush affected area with cool water if irritation is experienced. If nasal or throat irritation is experienced, exit the vehicle for fresh air until the irritation ceases. If irritation continues, see a physician.

Do not use a replacement airbag that is not in the original packaging. This may result in improper deployment, personal injury, or death.

The factory installed fasteners, screws and bolts used to fasten airbag components have a special coating and are specifically designed for the airbag system. Do not use substitute fasteners. Use only original equipment fasteners listed in the parts catalog when fastener replacement is required.

During, and following, any child restraint anchor service, due to impact event or vehicle repair, carefully inspect all mounting hardware, tether straps, and anchors for proper installation, operation, or damage. If a child restraint anchor is found damaged in any way, the anchor must be replaced. Failure to do this may result in personal injury or death.

Deployed and non-deployed airbags may or may not have live pyrotechnic material within the airbag inflator.

Do not dispose of driver/passenger/curtain airbags or seat belt tensioners unless you are sure of complete deployment. Refer to the Hazardous Substance Control System for proper disposal.

Dispose of deployed airbags and tensioners consistent with state, provincial, local, and federal regulations.

After any airbag component testing or service, do not connect the battery negative cable. Personal injury or death may result if the system test is not performed first.

If the vehicle is equipped with the Occupant Classification System (OCS), do not connect the battery negative cable before performing the OCS Verification Test using the scan tool and the appropriate diagnostic information. Personal injury or death may result if the system test is not performed properly.

Never replace both the Occupant Restraint Controller (ORC) and the Occupant Classification Module (OCM) at the same time. If both require replacement, replace one, then perform the Airbag System test before replacing the other.

Both the ORC and the OCM store Occupant Classification System (OCS) calibration data, which they transfer to one another when one of them is replaced. If both are replaced at the same time, an irreversible fault will be set in both modules and the OCS may malfunction and cause personal injury or death.

If equipped with OCS, the Seat Weight Sensor is a sensitive, calibrated unit and must be handled carefully. Do not drop or handle roughly. If dropped or damaged, replace with another sensor. Failure to do so may result in occupant injury or death.

If equipped with OCS, the front passenger seat must be handled carefully as well. When removing the seat, be careful when setting on floor not to drop. If dropped, the sensor may be inoperative, could result in occupant injury, or possibly death.

If equipped with OCS, when the passenger front seat is on the floor, no one should sit in the front passenger seat. This uneven force may damage the sensing ability of the seat weight sensors. If sat on and damaged, the sensor may be inoperative, could result in occupant injury, or possibly death.

DISARMING THE SYSTEM

Disconnect and isolate the negative battery cable. Wait 2 minutes for the system capacitor to discharge before performing any service.

ARMING

To arm the system, connect the negative battery cable.

CLOCKSPRING CENTERING

Disconnect and isolate the battery negative cable before beginning any airbag system component diagnosis, testing, removal, or installation procedures. Allow system capacitor to discharge for two minutes before beginning any component service. This will disable the airbag system. Failure to disable the airbag system may result in accidental airbag deployment, personal injury, or death.

The clockspring is mounted on the steering column behind the steering wheel. Its purpose is to maintain a continuous electrical circuit between the wiring harness and the driver's side air bag module. This assembly consists of a flat, ribbon-like electrically conductive tape that winds and unwinds with the steering wheel rotation.

Service replacement clocksprings are shipped pre-centered and with a molded plastic locking pin that snaps into a receptacle on the rotor and is engaged between two tabs on the upper surface of the rotor case. The locking pin secures the centered clockspring rotor to the clockspring case during shipment, but the locking pin must be removed from the clockspring after it is installed on the steering column. This locking pin should not be removed until the clockspring has been installed on the steering column. If the locking pin is removed before the clockspring is installed on a steering column, the clockspring centering procedure must be performed.

➡The clockspring cannot be repaired. If the clockspring is faulty, damaged, or if the driver airbag has been deployed, the clockspring must be replaced.

➡Before starting this procedure, be certain to turn the steering wheel until the front wheels are in the straight-ahead position.

1. Place the front wheels in the straight-ahead position.
2. Remove the clockspring from the steering column.
3. Rotate the clockspring rotor clockwise to the end of its travel. Do not apply excessive torque.
4. From the end of the clockwise travel, rotate the rotor about two and one-half turns counterclockwise.
5. The engagement dowel and yellow rubber boot should end up at the bottom, and the arrows on the clockspring rotor and case should be in alignment. The clockspring is now centered.
6. The front wheels should still be in the straight-ahead position. Reinstall the clockspring onto the steering column.

DRIVETRAIN

AUTOMATIC TRANSMISSION ASSEMBLY

REMOVAL & INSTALLATION

2005–06 Wrangler

1. Before servicing the vehicle, refer to the precautions in the beginning of this section.
2. Disconnect battery negative cable.
3. Raise and support vehicle.
4. Disconnect and lower or remove necessary exhaust components.
5. Remove engine-to-transmission bending braces or engine collar.
6. Remove starter motor.
7. On 4.0L engine equipped vehicles, disconnect and remove crankshaft position sensor. Retain sensor attaching bolt.

➡The crankshaft position sensor can be damaged during transmission removal (or installation) if the sensor is left in place. To avoid damage, remove the sensor before removing the transmission.

8. If transmission is being removed for overhaul, remove transmission oil pan, drain fluid and reinstall pan.
9. Remove torque converter access cover.
10. Rotate crankshaft in clockwise direction until converter bolts are accessible. Then remove bolts one at a time. Rotate crankshaft with socket wrench on dampener bolt.
11. Mark propeller shaft and axle yokes for assembly alignment. Then disconnect and remove propeller shafts.
12. Disconnect wires from the input and output speed sensors.
13. Disconnect wires from the transmission range sensor and the solenoid/pressure switch assembly.
14. Disconnect gearshift cable from transmission manual valve lever.
15. Disconnect shift rod from transfer case shift lever or remove shift lever from transfer case.
16. Support rear of engine with safety stand or jack.
17. Raise transmission slightly with service jack to relieve load on skid plate and transmission support.
18. Remove bolts securing rear support and cushion to transmission and skid plate. Raise transmission slightly, slide exhaust hanger arm from bracket and remove rear support.
19. Remove bolts attaching skid plate to frame and remove skid plate.
20. Disconnect transfer case vent hose.
21. Remove transfer case.
22. Remove fill tube bracket bolts and pull tube out of transmission. Retain fill tube seal. Remove the bolt attaching transfer case vent tube to converter housing.
23. Disconnect fluid cooler lines at transmission.
24. Remove all converter housing bolts.
25. Carefully work transmission and torque converter assembly rearward off engine block dowels.
26. Hold torque converter in place during transmission removal.
27. Lower transmission and remove assembly from under the vehicle.
28. To remove torque converter, carefully slide torque converter out of the transmission.

To install:

29. Check torque converter hub and hub drive notches for sharp edges burrs, scratches, or nicks. Polish the hub and notches with 320/400 grit paper and crocus cloth if necessary. The hub must be smooth to avoid damaging pump seal at installation.
30. Lubricate converter drive hub and oil pump seal lip with transmission fluid.
31. Align converter and oil pump.
32. Carefully insert converter in oil pump. Then rotate converter back and forth until fully seated in pump gears.
33. Check converter seating with steel scale and straightedge. Surface of converter lugs should be ½ in. to rear of straightedge when converter is fully seated.
34. Temporarily secure converter with C-clamp.
35. Lightly grease crankshaft flange hole.
36. Position transmission on jack and secure it with safety chains.
37. Check condition of converter driveplate. Replace the plate if cracked, distorted or damaged.

➡Be sure transmission dowel pins are seated in engine block and protrude far enough to hold transmission in alignment.

38. Raise transmission and align converter with drive plate and converter housing with engine block.
39. Move transmission forward. Then raise, lower or tilt transmission to align converter housing with engine block dowels.
40. Carefully work transmission forward and over engine block dowels until converter hub is seated in crankshaft.
41. Install and tighten bolts that attach transmission converter housing to engine block to 40 ft. lbs. (54 Nm).

➡Be sure the converter housing is fully seated on the engine block dowels before tightening any bolts.

42. Install torque converter attaching bolts. Tighten bolts to 65 ft. lbs. (88 Nm).
43. On 4.0L engine equipped vehicles, install the crankshaft position sensor.
44. Install transmission fill tube and seal. Install new fill tube seal in transmission before installation.
45. Connect transmission cooler lines to transmission.
46. Install transfer case onto transmission.
47. Install skid plate. Torque to 33 ft. lbs. (45 Nm). Attach transmission rear support to skid plate. Torque to 26 ft. lbs. (33 Nm).
48. Remove engine support fixture.
49. Remove transmission jack.
50. Connect input and output speed sensor wires.
51. Connect wires to the transmission range sensor and the solenoid/pressure switch assembly.
52. Install converter housing access cover.
53. Install exhaust pipes and support brackets, if removed.
54. Install starter motor and cooler line bracket.
55. Install new plastic retainer grommet on any shift linkage rod or lever that was disconnected. Grommets should not be reused. Use pry tool to remove rod from grommet and cut away old grommet. Use pliers to snap new grommet into lever and to snap rod into grommet at assembly.
56. Connect gearshift cable.
57. Connect transfer case shift linkage.
58. Adjust gearshift linkage, if necessary.
59. Align and connect propeller shaft(s).
60. Fill transfer case to bottom edge of fill plug hole.
61. Lower vehicle and connect battery negative cable.
62. Fill transmission to correct level with Mopar® ATF +4.

Liberty

See Figures 15 through 17.

1. Before servicing the vehicle, refer to the precautions in the beginning of this section.

2. Disconnect the negative battery cable.
3. Raise and support the vehicle.
4. Remove any necessary skid plates.
5. Mark propeller shaft and axle companion flanges for assembly alignment.
6. Remove the rear propeller shaft.
7. Remove the front propeller shaft, if necessary.
8. Disconnect wires from the input and output speed sensors.
9. Disconnect wires from the transmission range sensor and the solenoid/pressure switch assembly.
10. Remove the bolts holding the exhaust crossover pipe to the pre-catalytic converter pipe flanges.
11. Remove the bolts holding the exhaust crossover pipe to the catalytic converter flange.
12. Disconnect gearshift cable from transmission manual valve lever.
13. Disengage the shift cable from the cable support bracket.
14. Remove the starter motor.
15. Remove the engine to transmission collar.
16. Rotate crankshaft in clockwise direction until converter bolts are accessible. Then remove bolts one at a time. Rotate crankshaft with socket wrench on dampener bolt.
17. Disconnect the transmission vent hose from the transmission.
18. Remove transfer case.
19. Support rear of engine with safety stand or jack.
20. Raise transmission slightly with service jack to relieve load on crossmember and supports.
21. Remove bolts securing rear support and cushion to transmission and crossmember.
22. Remove bolts attaching crossmember to frame and remove crossmember.
23. Disconnect transmission fluid cooler lines at transmission fittings and clips.
24. Remove all remaining converter housing bolts.
25. Carefully work transmission and torque converter assembly rearward off engine block dowels.
26. Hold torque converter in place during transmission removal.
27. Lower transmission and remove assembly from under the vehicle.
28. To remove torque converter, carefully slide torque converter out of the transmission.

To install:

29. Check torque converter hub and hub drive flats for sharp edges burrs, scratches, or

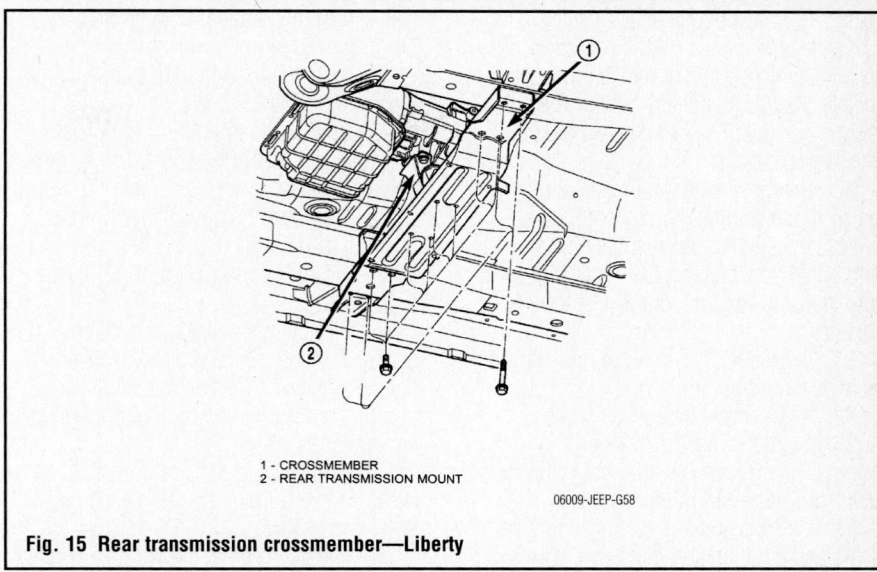

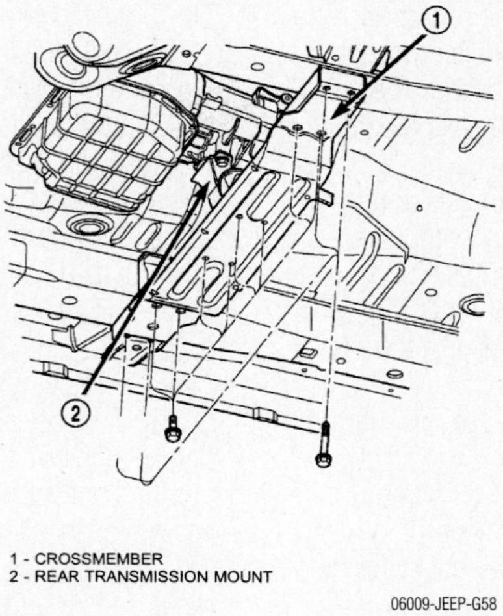

Fig. 15 Rear transmission crossmember—Liberty

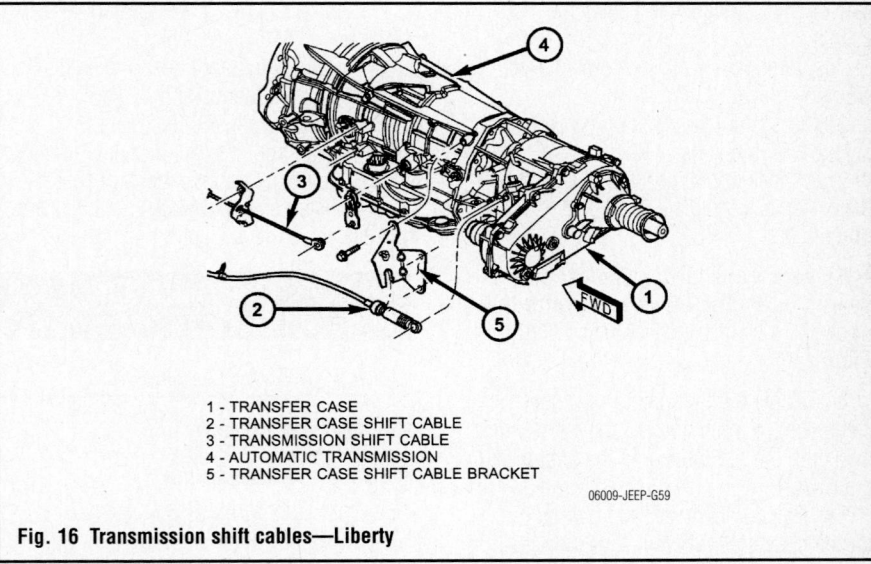

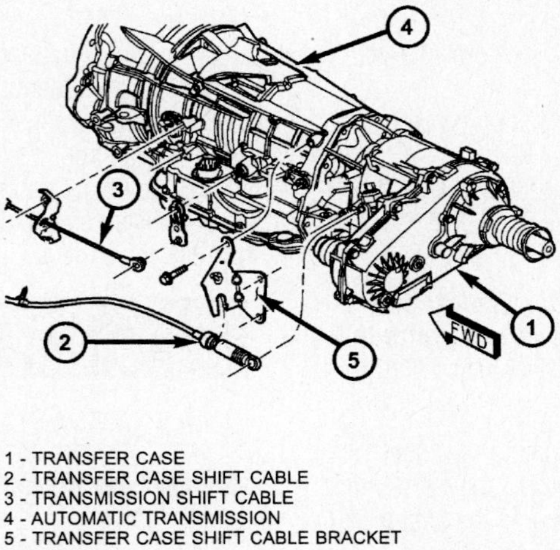

Fig. 16 Transmission shift cables—Liberty

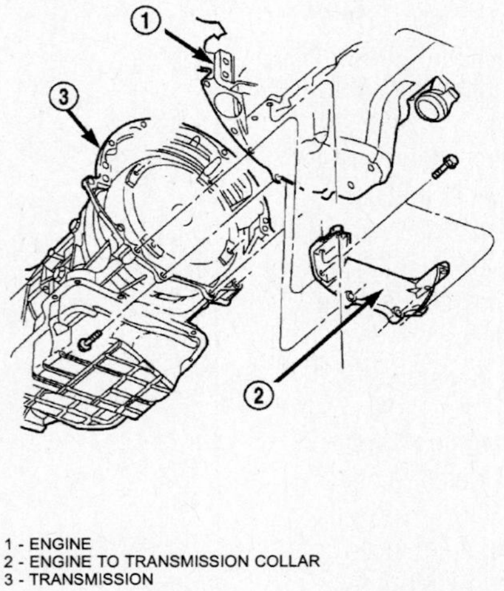

Fig. 17 Transmission collar—Liberty

nicks. Polish the hub and flats with 320/400 grit paper and crocus cloth if necessary. Verify that the converter hub O-ring is properly installed and is free of any debris. The hub must be smooth to avoid damaging pump seal at installation.

30. If a replacement transmission is being installed, transfer any components necessary, such as the manual shift lever and shift cable bracket, from the original transmission onto the replacement transmission.

31. Lubricate oil pump seal lip with transmission fluid.

32. Align converter and oil pump.

33. Carefully insert converter in oil pump. Then rotate converter back and forth until fully seated in pump gears.

34. Check converter seating with steel scale and straightedge. Surface of converter lugs should be at least 13mm (½ in.) to rear of straightedge when converter is fully seated.

35. Temporarily secure converter with C-clamp.

36. Position transmission on jack and secure it with chains.

37. Check condition of converter driveplate. Replace the plate if cracked, distorted or damaged.

➡Be sure transmission dowel pins are seated in engine block and protrude far enough to hold transmission in alignment.

38. Apply a light coating of Mopar® High Temp Grease to the torque converter hub pocket in the rear pocket of the engine's crankshaft.

39. Raise transmission and align the torque converter with the drive plate and transmission converter housing with the engine block.

40. Move transmission forward. Then raise, lower or tilt transmission to align the converter housing with engine block dowels.

41. Carefully work transmission forward and over engine block dowels until converter hub is seated in crankshaft. Verify that no wires, or the transmission vent hose, have become trapped between the engine block and the transmission.

42. Install two bolts to attach the transmission to the engine.

43. Install remaining torque converter housing to engine bolts. Tighten to 50 ft. lbs. (68 Nm).

44. Install transfer case, if equipped. Tighten transfer case nuts to 26 ft. lbs. (35 Nm).

45. Install rear transmission crossmember. Tighten crossmember to frame bolts to 50 ft. lbs. (68 Nm).

46. Install rear support to transmission. Tighten bolts to 35 ft. lbs. (47 Nm).

47. Lower transmission onto crossmember and install bolts attaching transmission mount to crossmember. Tighten clevis bracket to crossmember bolts to 35 ft. lbs. (47 Nm). Tighten the clevis bracket to rear support bolt to 50 ft. lbs. (68 Nm).

48. Remove engine support fixture.

49. Connect gearshift cable to support bracket and transmission manual lever.

50. Connect input and output speed sensor wires.

51. Connect wires to the transmission range sensor and the solenoid/pressure switch assembly.

52. Install torque converter-to-driveplate bolts. Tighten bolts to 65 inch lbs. (88 Nm).

53. Install starter motor and cooler line bracket.

54. Connect cooler lines to transmission.

55. Install transmission fill tube.

56. Install exhaust components.

57. Align and connect propeller shaft(s).

58. Adjust gearshift cable if necessary.

59. Install any skid plates removed previously.

MANUAL TRANSMISSION ASSEMBLY

REMOVAL & INSTALLATION

2005–06 Wrangler

NSG370 Transmission

See Figures 18 through 22.

1. Before servicing the vehicle, refer to the precautions in the beginning of this section.

2. Disconnect negative battery cable.

3. With vehicle in neutral, position vehicle on hoist.

4. Remove drain plug and drain fluid.

5. Mark installation reference marks on driveshafts and remove shafts.

6. Remove transfer case shift linkage, wiring connector, and vent hose, if equipped.

7. Remove transfer case, if equipped.

8. Support transmission with jack.

9. Remove transmission mount and crossmember.

10. Remove catalyst assembly.

11. Remove clutch slave cylinder nuts and remove cylinder.

12. Remove backup lamp switch wiring connector.

13. Remove shift lever tower bolts and remove shift lever tower.

14. Remove starter bolts and remove starter.

15. Remove transmission bolt and remove transmission.

To install:

16. Install transmission on engine.

17. On 2.4L engine tighten bolts to 55 ft. lbs. (75 Nm). Install lower dust shield and tighten bolts to 25 ft. lbs. (34 Nm).

18. On 4.0L engine tighten bolts to 27 ft. lbs. (37 Nm). Install side and lower dust shield and tighten bolts to 43 ft. lbs. (58 Nm).

19. Clean shift tower and mating surface then apply Mopar® Gasket Maker, or equivalent, to shift tower.

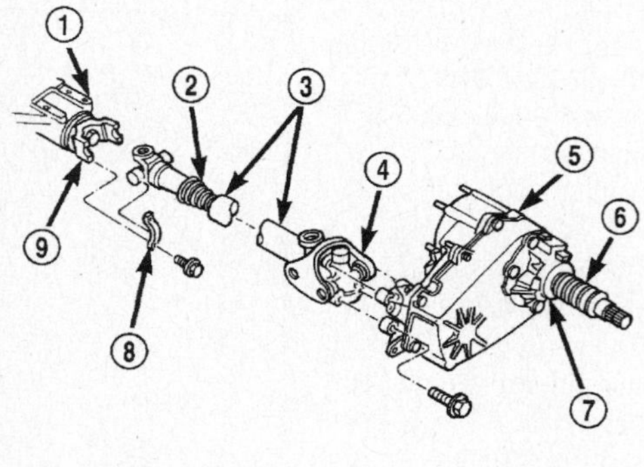

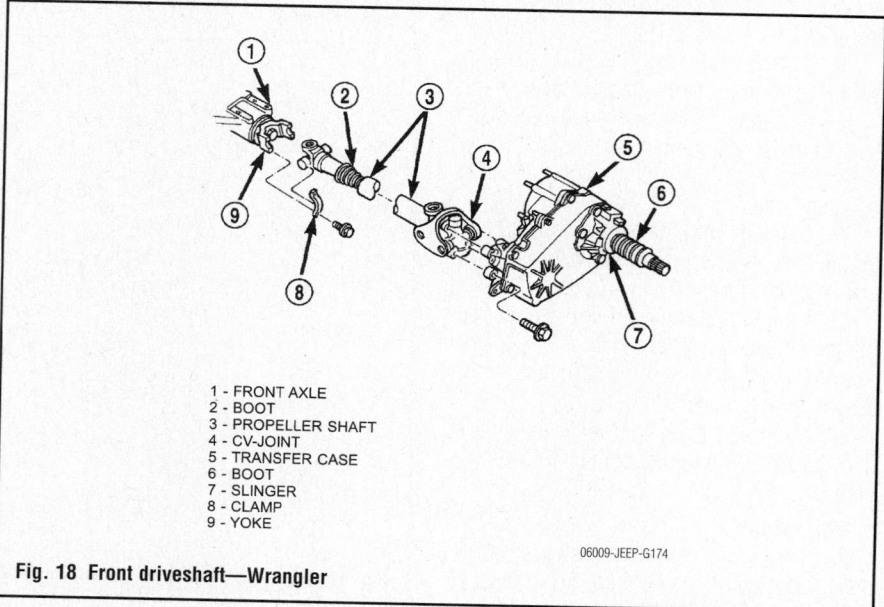

1 - FRONT AXLE
2 - BOOT
3 - PROPELLER SHAFT
4 - CV-JOINT
5 - TRANSFER CASE
6 - BOOT
7 - SLINGER
8 - CLAMP
9 - YOKE

06009-JEEP-G174

Fig. 18 Front driveshaft—Wrangler

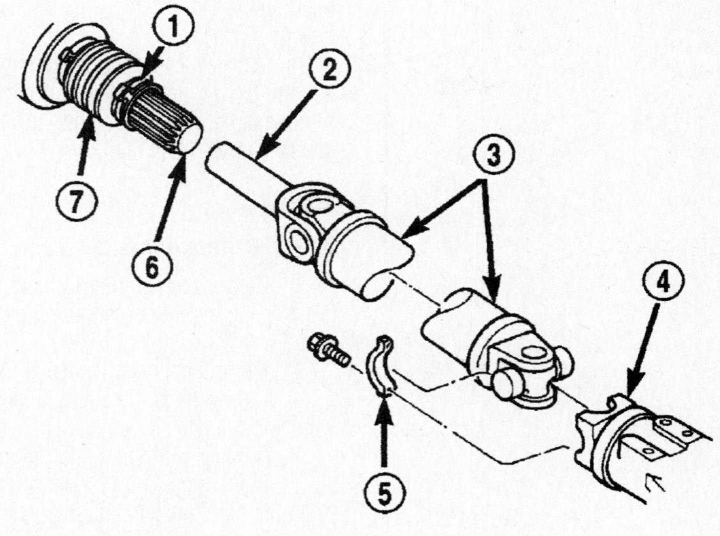

Fig. 19 Rear driveshaft—Wrangler, except Rubicon

20. Install shift tower and tighten bolts to 7 ft. lbs. (10 Nm).
21. Install backup lamp wiring connector.
22. Install clutch slave cylinder and mounting nuts.
23. Install catalyst assembly on 2.4L engine.
24. Install transmission cross member and tighten bolts to 35 ft. lbs. (47 Nm). Install transmission mount bolts and tighten to 35 ft. lbs. (47 Nm).
25. Install transfer case, if equipped.
26. Install transfer case shift linkage.
27. Install transfer case wiring connector and vent hose.
28. Install driveshafts with reference marks aligned. Torque as follows:
   - Front driveshaft to axle: 14 ft. lbs. (19 Nm)
   - Front driveshaft to transfer case: 20 ft. lbs. (27 Nm)
   - Rear driveshaft to axle: 14 ft. lbs. (19 Nm)
   - Rear driveshaft to transfer case (Rubicon): 85 ft. lbs. (115 Nm)
29. Remove fill plug and fill transmission with lubricant.
30. Locate narrow adapter plate opening towards the rear of the engine and top of the transmission bell housing from the driver's side of the engine compartment.

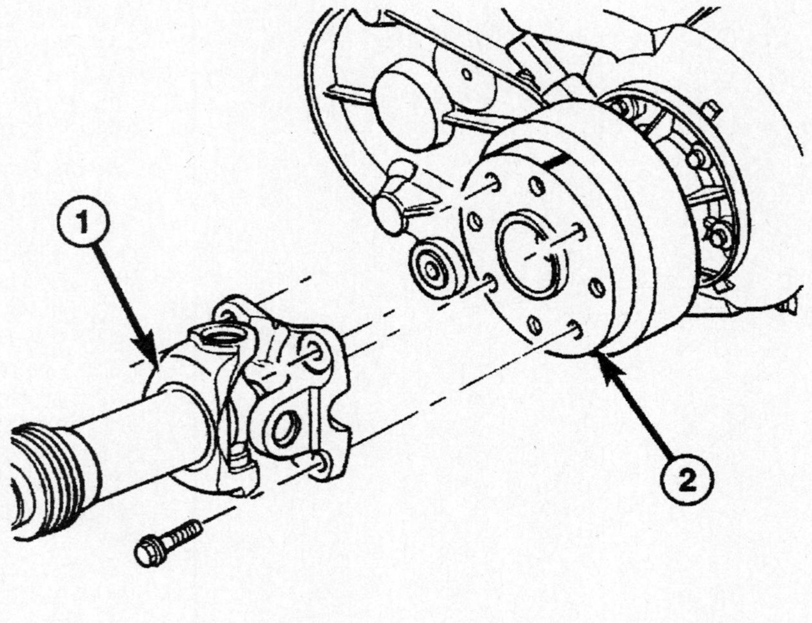

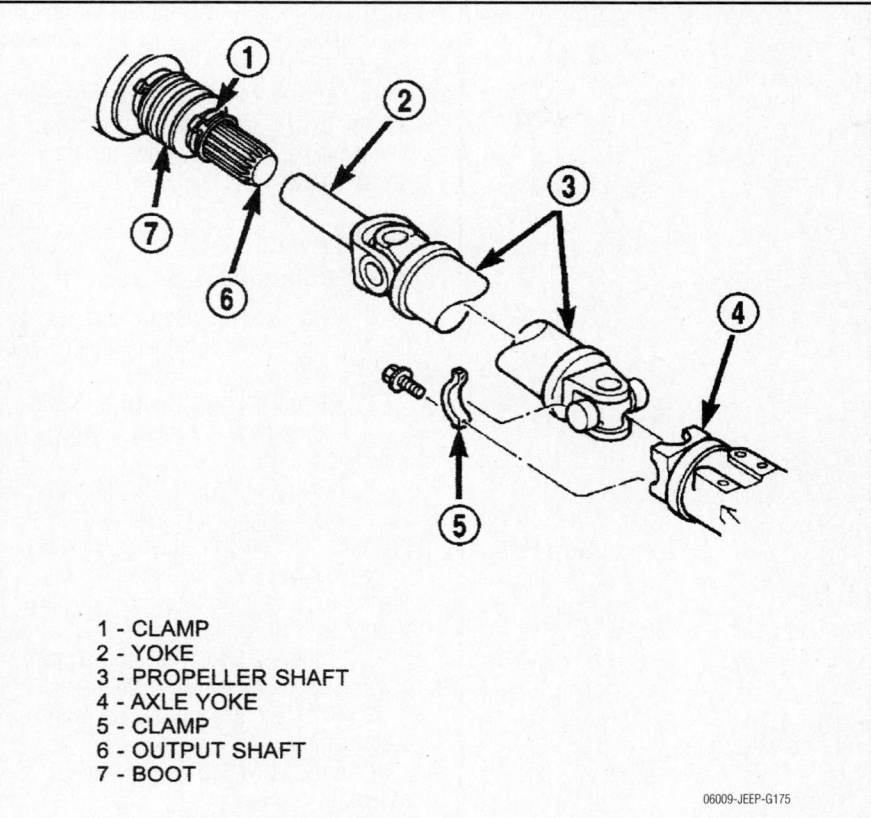

Fig. 20 Rear driveshaft—Rubicon

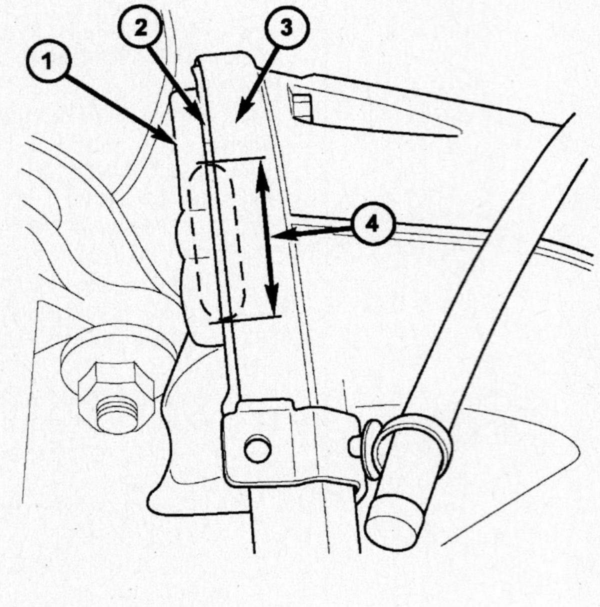

Fig. 21 Adapter opening detail—Wrangler

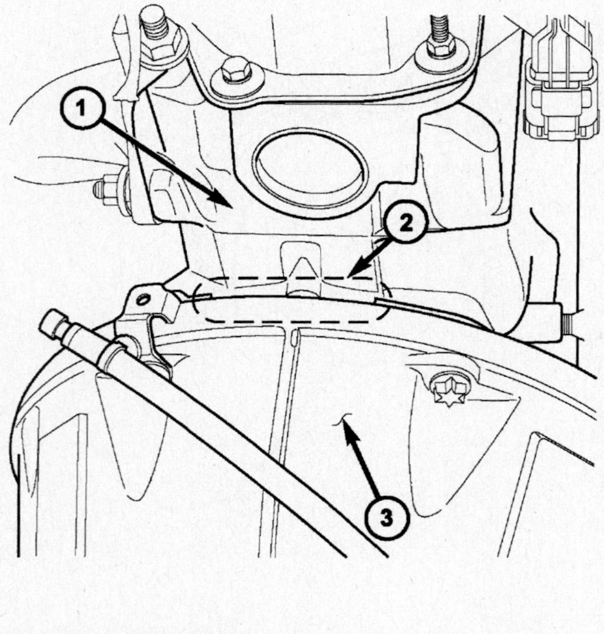

Fig. 22 Location of adapter opening—Wrangler

31. Thoroughly clean around the adapter opening with throttle body cleaner and allow cleaner to dry.
32. With your finger, apply a sufficient amount of RTV over the spacer opening. Verify that the adapter opening is completely sealed off by the RTV.

Liberty

NSG370 Transmission

1. Before servicing the vehicle, refer to the precautions in the beginning of this section.
2. Disconnect negative battery cable.
3. With vehicle in neutral, position vehicle on hoist.
4. Remove drain plug and drain fluid.
5. Mark installation reference marks on propeller shaft/shafts and remove shafts.
6. Remove transfer case shift cable bracket nuts, cable, wiring connector, and vent hose, if equipped.
7. Remove transfer case, if equipped.
8. Support transmission with jack.
9. Remove transmission mount and crossmember.
10. On 2.4L engine remove catalyst assembly.
11. Remove clutch slave cylinder nuts and remove cylinder.
12. Remove backup lamp switch wiring connector.
13. Remove shift lever tower bolts and remove shift lever housing.
14. Remove starter bolts and remove starter.
15. Remove transmission bolt and remove transmission.

To install:

16. Install transmission on engine.
17. On 3.7L engine tighten bolts to 30 ft. lbs. (41 Nm). Tighten bolts to 50 ft. lbs. (67 Nm). Tighten bolts to 40 ft. lbs. (54 Nm).
18. On 2.4L engine tighten bolts to 55 ft. lbs. (75 Nm). Install lower dust shield and tighten bolts to 25 ft. lbs. (34 Nm).
19. On 2.8L diesel engine tighten bolts to 30 ft. lbs. (41 Nm). Tighten bolts to 50 ft. lbs. (67 Nm). Tighten bolts to 40 ft. lbs. (54 Nm).
20. Clean shift tower and mating surface then apply Mopar® Gasket Maker to shift tower.
21. Install shift tower and tighten bolts to 7 ft. lbs. (10 Nm).
22. Install back-up lamp wiring connector.
23. Install clutch slave cylinder and mounting nuts.
24. Install catalyst assembly on 2.4L engine.

25. Install transmission crossmember and tighten bolts to 35 ft. lbs. (47 Nm). Install transmission mount bolts and tighten to 35 ft. lbs. (47 Nm).

26. Install transfer case, if equipped.

27. Install transfer case shift cable on 2.4L. Install transfer case shift linkage on 3.7L.

28. Install transfer case wiring connector and vent hose.

29. Install propeller shaft/shafts with reference marks aligned.

30. Remove fill plug and fill transmission with lubricant.

CLUTCH

REMOVAL & INSTALLATION

2005–06 Wrangler

1. Before servicing the vehicle, refer to the precautions in the beginning of this section.
2. Remove or disconnect the following:
   - Negative battery cable
   - Transfer case, if equipped
   - Transmission
   - Pressure plate. Loosen the bolts evenly in ½ turn steps.
   - Clutch disc

To install:

3. Install or connect the following:
   - Clutch disc and pressure plate. Tighten the pressure plate bolts evenly in ½ turns to 23 ft. lbs. (31 Nm) for 2.4L engines; 37 ft. lbs. (50 Nm) for 4.0L engines.
   - Transmission
   - Transfer case, if equipped
   - Negative battery cable

Liberty

Gasoline Engines

1. Before servicing the vehicle, refer to the precautions in the beginning of this section.

2. Remove the transmission.

3. Mark position of pressure plate on flywheel with paint or a scriber for assembly reference, if clutch is not being replaced.

4. Loosen pressure plate bolts evenly and in rotation to relieve spring tension and avoid warping the plate.

5. Remove pressure plate bolts and pressure plate and disc.

To install:

6. Lightly scuff sand flywheel face with 180 grit emery cloth, then clean with a wax and grease remover.

7. Lubricate pilot bearing with Mopar®high temperature bearing grease or equivalent.

8. Check runout and operation of a new clutch disc.

➡Disc must slide freely on transmission input shaft splines.

9. With the disc on the input shaft, check face runout with dial indicator. Check runout at disc hub ¼ inches (6 mm.) from outer edge of facing. Obtain another clutch disc if runout exceed 0.020 in.(0.5 mm).

10. Position clutch disc on flywheel with side marked flywheel against the flywheel.

➡If not marked, the flat side of disc hub goes towards the flywheel on the 3.7L engine and towards the transmission on 2.4L engine.

11. Insert clutch alignment tool through the clutch disc and into the pilot bearing.

12. Position clutch pressure plate over disc and on the flywheel.

13. Install pressure plate bolts finger tight.

⁂ WARNING

Use only the factory bolts to mount the pressure plate. The bolts must be the correct size. If bolts are too short, there isn't enough thread engagement, if too long bolts interfere with the Dual Mass Flywheel.

14. Tighten pressure plate bolts evenly and in rotation a few threads at a time.

⁂ WARNING

The bolts must be tightened evenly and to specified torque. Failure to follow these instructions will distort the pressure plate.

15. Tighten pressure plate bolts to 23 ft. lbs. (31 Nm) on 2.4L engines and 37ft. lbs. (50 Nm) on 3.7L engines.

16. Apply light coat of Mopar®high temperature bearing grease or equivalent to clutch disc hub and splines of transmission input shaft.

➡Do not over lubricate shaft splines. This will result in grease contamination of disc.

17. Install the transmission.

2.8L Diesel Engine

1. Before servicing the vehicle, refer to the precautions in the beginning of this section.

2. Remove transmission.

3. Mark position of pressure plate on flywheel with paint or a scriber for assembly reference, if clutch is not being replaced.

4. Loosen pressure plate bolts evenly and in rotation to relieve spring tension and avoid warping the plate.

5. Remove pressure plate bolts and pressure plate and disc.

To install:

6. Lightly scuff sand flywheel face with 180 grit emery cloth, then clean with a wax and grease remover.

7. Lubricate pilot bearing with Mopar®high temperature bearing grease or equivalent.

8. Check runout and operation of the new clutch disc.

➡Disc must slide freely on transmission input shaft splines.

9. With the disc on the input shaft, check face runout with dial indicator. Check runout at disc hub ¼ inches (6 mm.) from outer edge of facing. Obtain another clutch disc if runout exceed 0.020 in.(0.5 mm).

10. Position clutch disc on flywheel with side marked flywheel side against the flywheel. If not marked, the flat side of disc hub goes towards the flywheel.

11. Insert clutch alignment tool through the clutch disc and into the pilot bearing.

12. Position clutch pressure plate over disc and on the flywheel.

13. Install pressure plate bolts finger tight.

14. Tighten pressure plate bolts evenly and in rotation a few threads at a time.

⁂ WARNING

The bolts must be tightened evenly and to specified torque. Failure to follow these instructions will distort the pressure plate.

15. Tighten pressure plate bolts to 40 ft. lbs. (54 Nm).

16. Apply light coat of Mopar® high temperature bearing grease, or equivalent, to clutch disc hub and splines of transmission input shaft.

➡Do not over lubricate shaft splines. Failure to follow these instructions will result in contamination of disc.

17. Install the transmission.

BLEEDING

➡The clutch master cylinder, slave cylinder and fluid line are serviced only as an assembly. Bleeding is not possible.

TRANSFER CASE ASSEMBLY

REMOVAL & INSTALLATION

2005–06 Wrangler

NV231

1. Before servicing the vehicle, refer to the precautions in the beginning of this section.
2. Shift transfer case into NEUTRAL.
3. Raise vehicle.
4. Drain transfer case lubricant.
5. Mark front and rear propeller shaft yokes for alignment reference.
6. Support transmission with jack stand.
7. Remove rear crossmember, or skid plate.
8. Disconnect front/rear propeller shafts at transfer case.
9. Disconnect vehicle speed sensor wires.
10. Disconnect transfer case linkage rod from range lever.
11. Disconnect transfer case vent hose and indicator switch harness, if necessary.
12. Support transfer case with transmission jack.
13. Secure transfer case to jack with chains.
14. Remove nuts attaching transfer case to transmission.
15. Pull transfer case and jack rearward to disengage transfer case.
16. Remove transfer case from under vehicle.

To install:

17. Mount transfer case on a transmission jack.
18. Secure transfer case to jack with chains.
19. Position transfer case under vehicle.
20. Align transfer case and transmission shafts and install transfer case on transmission.
21. Install and tighten transfer case attaching nuts to 26 ft. lbs. (35 Nm) torque.
22. Connect vehicle speed sensor wires, and vent hose.
23. Connect indicator switch harness to transfer case switch, if necessary. Secure wire harness to clips on transfer case.
24. Align and connect propeller shafts.
25. Fill transfer case with correct fluid. Check transmission fluid level. Correct as necessary.
26. Install rear crossmember, or skid plate. Tighten crossmember bolts to 30 ft. lbs. (41 Nm).
27. Remove transmission jack and support stand.
28. Connect shift rod to transfer case range lever.
29. Adjust transfer case shift linkage.
30. Lower vehicle and verify transfer case shift operation.

NV242

1. Before servicing the vehicle, refer to the precautions in the beginning of this section.
2. Raise and support vehicle.
3. Remove skid plate, if equipped.
4. Position drain oil container under transfer case.
5. Remove transfer case drain plug and drain lubricant into container.
6. Disconnect vent hose and vacuum harness at transfer case switch.
7. Disconnect shift rod from grommet in transfer case shift lever, or from floor shift arm whichever provides easy access. Use pliers to press rod out of lever grommet.
8. Support transmission with jack stand.
9. Remove rear crossmember.
10. Mark front and rear propeller shafts for assembly reference.
11. Remove front and rear propeller shafts.
12. Support transfer case with suitable jack. Secure transfer case to jack with safety chains.
13. Remove nuts attaching transfer case to transmission.
14. Move transfer case assembly rearward until free of transmission output shaft.
15. Lower jack and move transfer case from under vehicle.

To install:

16. Align and seat transfer case on transmission. Be sure transfer case input gear splines are aligned with transmission output shaft. Align splines by rotating transfer case rear output shaft yoke if necessary.

➡Do not install any transfer case attaching nuts until the transfer case is completely seated against the transmission.

17. Install and tighten transfer case attaching nuts. Tighten nuts to 20–30 ft. lbs. (30–41 Nm).
18. Install rear crossmember.
19. Remove jack stand from under transmission.
20. Align and connect propeller shafts.
21. Connect vacuum harness and vent hose.
22. Connect shift rod to transfer case lever or floor shift arm. Use pliers to press rod back into lever grommet.
23. Adjust shift linkage, if necessary.
24. Fill transfer case with recommended transmission fluid and install fill plug.
25. Install skid plate, if equipped.
26. Lower vehicle

NV241

1. Before servicing the vehicle, refer to the precautions in the beginning of this section.
2. Raise and support vehicle.
3. Remove skid plate, if equipped.
4. Position drain oil container under transfer case.
5. Remove transfer case drain plug and drain lubricant into container.
6. Disconnect vent hose and vacuum harness at transfer case switch.
7. Disconnect shift rod from grommet in transfer case shift lever, or from floor shift arm whichever provides easy access. Use channel lock style pliers to press rod out of lever grommet.
8. Support transmission with jackstand.
9. Remove rear crossmember.
10. Mark front and rear propeller shafts for assembly reference.
11. Remove front and rear propeller shafts.
12. Support transfer case with suitable jack. Secure transfer case to jack with safety chains.
13. Remove nuts attaching transfer case to transmission.
14. Move transfer case assembly rearward until free of transmission output shaft.
15. Lower jack and move transfer case from under vehicle.

To install:

16. Align and seat transfer case on transmission. Be sure transfer case input gear splines are aligned with transmission output shaft. Align splines by rotating transfer case rear output shaft yoke if necessary. Do not install any transfer case attaching nuts until the transfer case is completely seated against the transmission.
17. Install and tighten transfer case attaching nuts. Tighten nuts to 20–30 ft. lbs. (30–41 Nm).
18. Install rear crossmember.
19. Remove jackstand from under transmission.
20. Align and connect propeller shafts. Torque as follows:
    - Front driveshaft to axle: 14 ft. lbs. (19 Nm)
    - Front driveshaft to transfer case: 20 ft. lbs. (27 Nm)

- Rear driveshaft to axle: 14 ft. lbs. (19 Nm)
- Rear driveshaft to transfer case (Rubicon): 85 ft. lbs. (115 Nm)

21. Connect vacuum harness and vent hose.
22. Connect shift rod to transfer case lever or floor shift arm. Use channel lock style pliers to press rod back into lever grommet.
23. Adjust shift linkage, if necessary.
24. Fill transfer case with recommended transmission fluid and install fill plug.
25. Install skid plate, if equipped.
26. Lower vehicle.

Liberty

NV231

See Figure 23.

1. Before servicing the vehicle, refer to the precautions in the beginning of this section.
2. Shift transfer case into NEUTRAL.
3. Raise the vehicle.
4. Remove skid plate.
5. Drain transfer case lubricant.
6. Mark front and rear propeller shaft yokes for alignment reference.
7. Disconnect front/rear propeller shafts at transfer case.
8. Disconnect transfer case position sensor connector.
9. Disconnect transfer case shift cable at the range lever.
10. Disconnect the transfer case shift cable from the shift cable bracket.
11. Disconnect transfer case vent hose.
12. Support transfer case with transmission jack.
13. Secure transfer case to jack with chains.
14. Remove the nuts attaching transfer case to transmission.
15. Pull transfer case and jack rearward to disengage transfer case.
16. Remove transfer case from under vehicle.

To install:

17. Mount transfer case on a transmission jack.
18. Secure transfer case to jack with chains.
19. Position transfer case under vehicle.
20. Align transfer case and transmission shafts and install transfer case on transmission.
21. Install and tighten transfer case attaching nuts to 26 ft. lbs. (35 Nm) torque.
22. Connect vent hose.

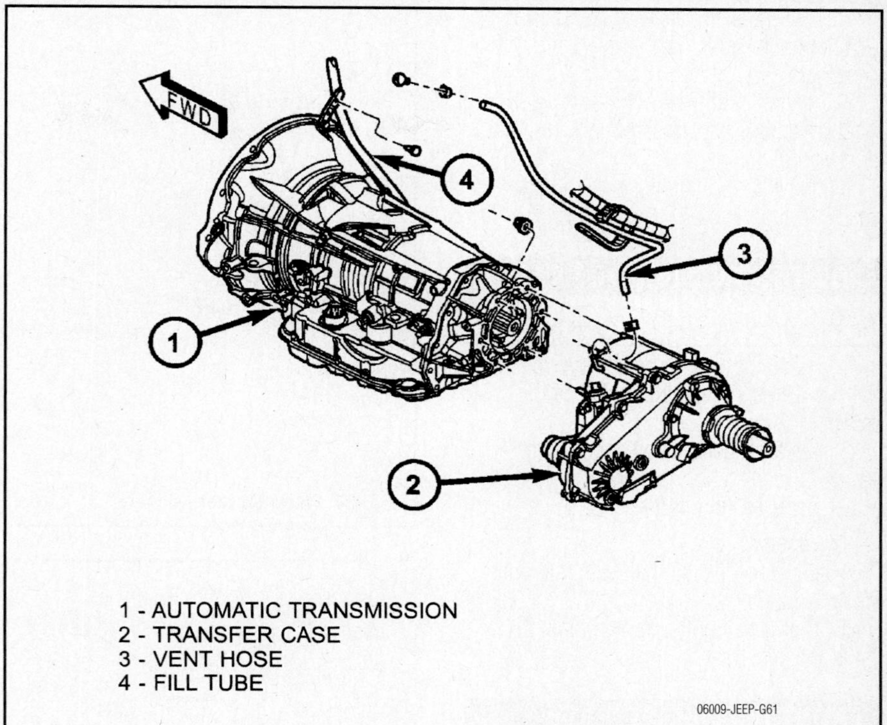

Fig. 23 Typical transfer case mounting—Liberty

23. Connect transfer case position sensor connector to sensor.
24. Align and connect propeller shafts. Torque the rear companion flange nuts to 85 ft. lbs. (115 Nm), the front companion flange nuts to 22 ft. lbs. (30 Nm).
25. Fill transfer case with correct fluid. Check transmission fluid level. Correct as necessary.
26. Install skid plate.
27. Remove transmission jack and support stand.
28. Connect shift cable to transfer case range lever.
29. Lower vehicle and verify transfer case shift operation.

NV241 GENII

1. Before servicing the vehicle, refer to the precautions in the beginning of this section.
2. Shift transfer case into NEUTRAL.
3. Raise vehicle.
4. Remove skid plate.
5. Drain transfer case lubricant.
6. Mark front and rear propeller shaft yokes for alignment reference.
7. Remove the front/rear propeller shafts at transfer case.
8. Disconnect transfer case position sensor connector from the position sensor.
9. Disconnect transfer case shift cable at the range lever.
10. Disconnect the transfer case shift cable from the shift cable bracket.
11. Disconnect transfer case vent hose.
12. Support transfer case with transmission jack.
13. Secure transfer case to jack with chains.
14. Remove nuts attaching transfer case to transmission.
15. Pull transfer case and jack rearward to disengage transfer case.
16. Remove transfer case from under vehicle.

To install:

17. Mount transfer case on a transmission jack.
18. Secure transfer case to jack with chains.
19. Position transfer case under vehicle.
20. Align transfer case and transmission shafts and install transfer case on transmission.
21. Install and tighten transfer case attaching nuts to 26 ft. lbs. (35 Nm) torque.
22. Connect vent hose.
23. Connect transfer case position sensor connector to sensor.
24. Align and connect propeller shafts. Torque the rear companion flange nuts to 85 ft. lbs. (115 Nm), the front companion flange nuts to 22 ft. lbs. (30 Nm).
25. Connect shift cable to transfer case range lever.

26. Fill transfer case with correct fluid. Check transmission fluid level. Correct as necessary.
27. Install skid plate.
28. Remove transmission jack and support stand.
29. Lower vehicle and verify transfer case shift operation.

FRONT DRIVESHAFT

REMOVAL & INSTALLATION

1. Before servicing the vehicle, refer to the precautions in the beginning of this manual.
2. Mark propeller shaft and pinion flange for installation reference.
3. Remove front propeller shaft.

To install:

4. Install propeller shaft with reference marks aligned.
5. Using new bolts, tighten them to 24 ft. lbs. (32 Nm).

FRONT HALFSHAFT

REMOVAL & INSTALLATION

Liberty

See Figures 24 and 25.

1. Before servicing the vehicle, refer to the precautions in the beginning of this section.
2. Remove or disconnect the following:
   - Wheel
   - Hub nut
   - Stabilizer link
   - Lower clevis bolt
   - Ball joint from the lower arm
3. Pull on the hub and push the halfshaft from the knuckle

➡The right side has a splined axle shaft that will stay in the axle.

To install:

4. Apply a light coating of wheel bearing grease on the splines of the inner joint, and in the hub bearing bore.
5. Install or connect the following:
   - Halfshaft on the axle shaft splines

➡Push firmly enough to engage the snapring. Pull on it to verify engagement.

   - Halfshaft into the knuckle
   - Lower ball joint and pinch bolt
   - Lower clevis bolt
   - Stabilizer link
   - Hub nut. Torque to 100 ft. lbs. (136 Nm).
   - Wheel

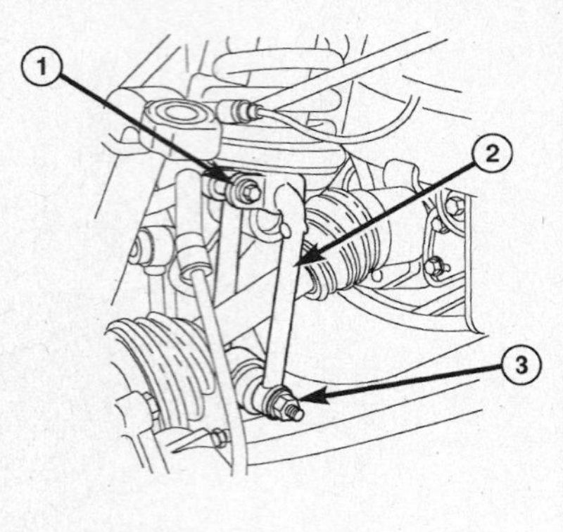

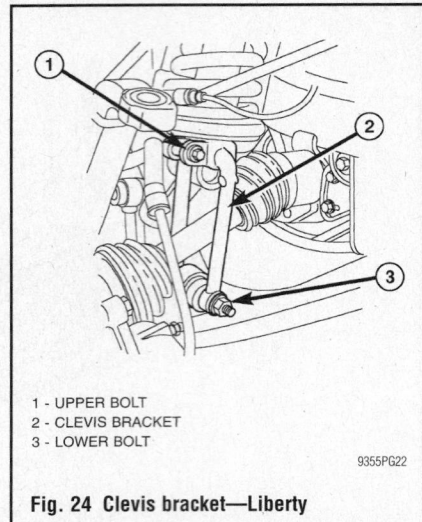

Fig. 24 Clevis bracket—Liberty

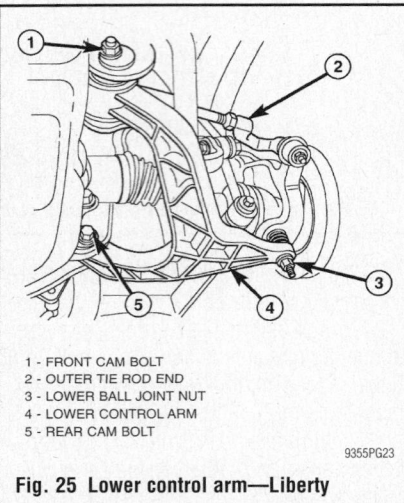

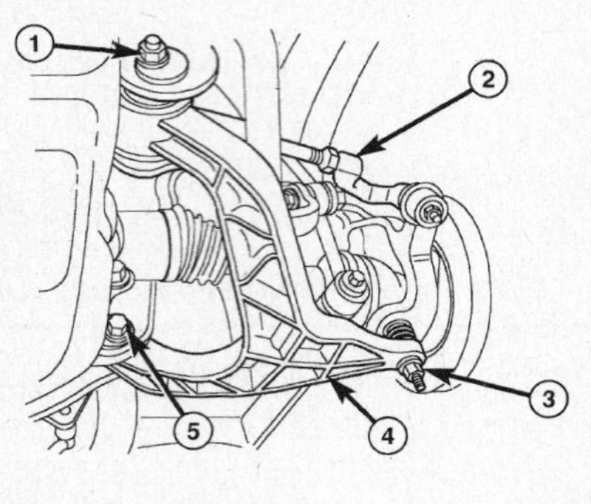

Fig. 25 Lower control arm—Liberty

CV-JOINTS OVERHAUL

Liberty

Outer CV Joint

See Figure 26.

1. Place shaft in vise with soft jaws and support C/V joint.

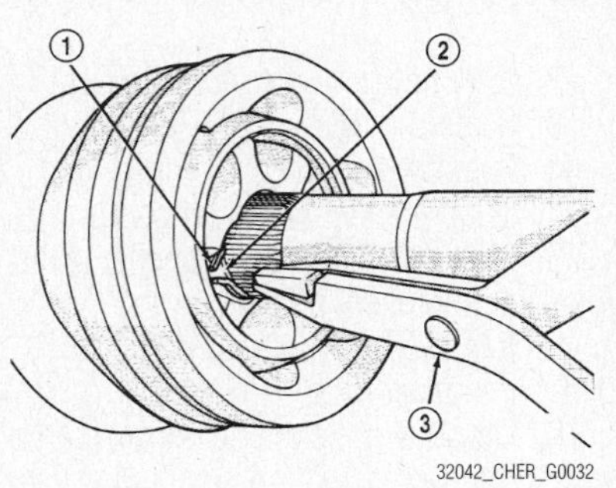

Fig. 26 Outer CV boot for the Liberty

⁂ CAUTION

Do not damage C/V housing or half shaft.

2. Remove clamps with a cut-off wheel or grinder .
3. Slide the boot down the shaft.
4. Remove lubricant to expose the C/V joint snap ring.
5. Spread snap ring and slide the joint off the shaft .
6. Slide boot off the shaft and discard old boot.
7. Mark alignment marks on the inner race/ hub (2), bearing cage and housing with dabs of paint .
8. Clamp C/V joint in a vertical position in a soft jawed vise.
9. Press down one side of the bearing cage to gain access to the ball at the opposite side.

➡If joint is tight, use a hammer and brass drift to loosen the bearing hub. Do not contact the bearing cage with the drift.

10. Remove ball from the bearing cage .
11. Repeat step above until all six balls are removed from the bearing cage.
12. Lift cage and inner race upward and out from the housing .
13. Turn inner race 90° in the cage and rotate the inner race/hub out of the cage .

To install:

14. Apply a light coat of grease to the C/V joint components before assembling them.
15. Align inner race, cage and housing according to the alignment reference marks.
16. Insert inner race into the cage and rotate race into the cage.
17. Rotate inner race/hub in the cage.
18. Insert cage into the housing.
19. Rotate cage 90° into the housing.
20. Apply lubricant included with replacement boot/joint to the ball races. Spread lubricant equally between all the races.
21. Tilt inner race/hub and cage and install the balls .
22. Place new clamps onto new boot and slide boot onto the shaft to it's original position.
23. Apply the rest of lubricant to the C/V joint and boot.
24. Push the joint onto the shaft until the snap ring seats in the groove . Pull on the joint to verify the span ring has engaged.
25. Position boot on the joint in it's original position. Ensure boot is not twisted and remove any excess air.

26. Secure both boot clamps with Clamp Installer C-4975A. Place tool on clamp bridge and tighten tool until the jaws of the tool are closed.

Inner CV Joint

See Figure 27.

1. Clamp shaft in a vise (with soft jaws) and support C/V joint.
2. Remove clamps with a cut-off wheel or grinder.
3. Slide boot down the shaft.
4. Remove lubricant from housing to expose the C/V snap ring and remove snap ring.
5. Remove bearings from the cage.
6. Rotate cage 30° and slide cage off the inner race and down the shaft.
7. Remove spread inner race snap ring and remove race from the shaft.
8. Remove boot from the shaft and discard.
9. Clean and inspect housing, cage, bearings, housing snap-ring, inner race snap-ring and inner race for wear or damage.

To install:

10. Apply a coat of grease supplied with the joint/ boot to the C/V joint components before assembling them.
11. Place new clamps on the new boot and slide boot down the shaft.
12. Slide cage onto the shaft with the small diameter end towards the boot.
13. Install the inner race onto the shaft. Pull on the race to verify snap ring has engaged.
14. Align cage with the inner race and slide over the race.
15. Turn the cage 30° to align the cage windows with the race.
16. Apply grease to the inner race and bearings and install the bearings.
17. Apply grease to the housing bore then install the bearing assembly into the housing.

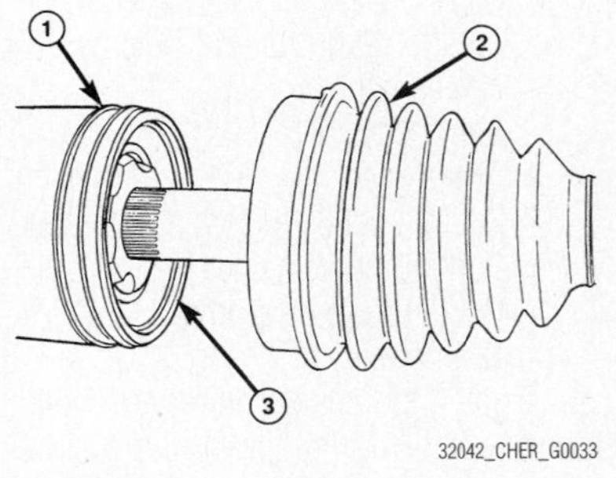

Fig. 27 Inner CV boot for the Liberty

18. Install the housing snap ring and verify it is seated in the groove.
19. Fill the housing and boot with the remaining grease.
20. Slide the boot onto the C/V housing into it's original position. Ensure boot is not twisted and remove any excess air.
21. Secure both boot clamps with Clamp Installer C-4975A. Place tool on clamp bridge and tighten tool until the jaws of the tool are closed.

FRONT PINION SEAL

REMOVAL & INSTALLATION

Wrangler

181FBI Front Axle

See Figures 28 and 29.

1. Before servicing the vehicle, refer to the precautions in the beginning of this section.
2. With vehicle in neutral, position vehicle on hoist.
3. Remove brake rotors and calipers.
4. Remove propeller shaft from the yoke.
5. Rotate pinion gear three or four times.
6. Record rotating torque of the pinion gear with an inch pound torque wrench, for installation reference.
7. Hold pinion yoke with Wrench 6958 and remove pinion nut and washer, or equivalent.
8. Remove pinion yoke with Remover C-452 and Wrench C-3281, or equivalent.
9. Remove seal with a pry tool or a slide hammer mounted screw.

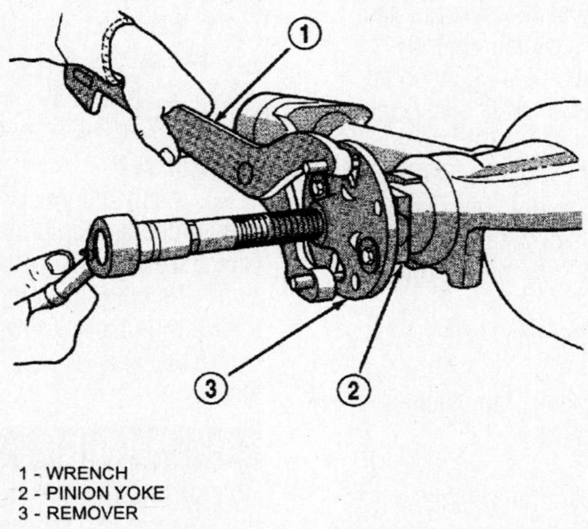

Fig. 28 Pinion yoke remover—181FBI axle

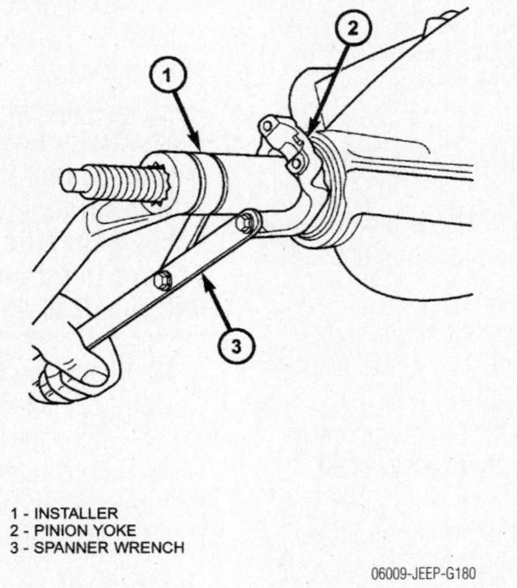

Fig. 29 Pinion yoke installer—181FBI axle

To install:

10. Apply a light coating of gear lubricant on the lip of pinion seal. Install seal with an appropriate installer.

11. Install yoke on pinion gear with Installer W-162-D, Cup 8109 and Holder 6958, or equivalent.

⁂ WARNING

Do not exceed the minimum tightening torque when installing the pinion yoke retaining nut at this point. Failure to heed caution may result in damage

12. Install pinion washer and a new nut on the pinion gear shaft.

➡Tighten nut only enough to remove the shaft end play.

13. Tighten pinion nut to 160 ft. lbs. (217 Nm).

14. Rotate pinion shaft using an inch pound torque wrench. Rotating torque should be equal to the reading recorded during removal, plus an additional 5 inch lbs. (0.56 Nm).

15. If rotating torque is low, use Spanner 6958, or equivalent, to hold the pinion yoke and tighten pinion shaft nut in 60 inch lbs. (6.8 Nm) increments until proper rotating torque is achieved.

16. Install propeller shaft with reference marks aligned.

17. Install brake rotors and calipers.

261FBI Front Axle

1. Before servicing the vehicle, refer to the precautions in the beginning of this section.

2. Mark the propeller shaft and pinion yoke for installation reference.

3. Remove propeller shaft from the yoke.

4. Rotate pinion gear three or four times and verify it rotates smoothly.

5. Remove pinion yoke nut and washer with Remover C-452 and Flange Wrench C-3281, or equivalent.

6. Remove pinion shaft seal with a pry tool or slide hammer mounted screw.

To install:

7. Apply a light coating of gear lubricant on the lip of pinion seal. Install seal with an appropriate installer.

8. Install yoke on the pinion gear with Installer W-162-D and Spanner Wrench 6958, or equivalent.

9. Install a new nut on the pinion gear and tighten the nut to 160–0 ft. lbs. (217–271 Nm).

10. Installation propeller shaft with reference marks aligned.

11. Check and add gear lubricant to axle if necessary.

Liberty

1. Before servicing the vehicle, refer to the precautions in the beginning of this section.

2. With vehicle in neutral, position vehicle on hoist.

3. Remove brake calipers and rotors.

4. Remove propeller shaft.

5. Rotate pinion gear a minimum of ten times and verify the pinion rotates smoothly.

6. Record torque to rotate the pinion gear with an inch pound torque wrench.

7. Using a short piece of pipe and Spanner Wrench 6958 to hold the pinion companion flange and remove the pinion nut.

8. Remove pinion companion flange with Remover C-452 and Spanner Wrench 6958, or equivalent.

9. Pry pinion seal out with a seal pick.

To install:

10. Apply a light coating of gear lubricant on the lip of pinion seal. Install seal with a seal driver.

11. Install pinion companion flange on the pinion gear with Installer W-162-D, Cup 8109 and Wrench 6958, or equivalent.

⁂ WARNING

Do not exceed the minimum tightening torque 160 ft. lbs. (216 Nm) while installing pinion nut at this point. Failure to follow these instructions will result in damage.

12. Install a new nut on the pinion gear. Tighten the nut only enough to remove the shaft end play.

⁂ WARNING

Never loosen pinion nut to decrease pinion rotating torque and never exceed specified preload torque. Failure to follow these instructions will result in damage.

13. Rotate pinion a minimum of ten time and verify pinion rotates smoothly. Rotate the pinion shaft with an inch pound torque wrench. Rotating torque should be equal to the reading recorded during removal plus 5 inch lbs. (0.56 Nm).

14. If rotating torque is low, use Spanner Wrench 6958 to hold the pinion companion flange and tighten the pinion nut in 60 inch lbs. (6.8 Nm) increments until proper rotating torque is achieved.

⁂ WARNING

If maximum tightening torque is reached prior to reaching the required rotating torque, the collapsible spacer may have been damaged. Failure to follow these instructions will result in damage.

15. Install propeller shaft.

16. Fill differential with gear lubricant.

REAR AXLE HOUSING

REMOVAL & INSTALLATION

1. Before servicing the vehicle, refer to the precautions in the beginning of this section.

2. Remove or disconnect the following:
   - Rear wheels
   - Brake rotors or drums
   - Parking brake cables
   - Wheel speed sensors, if equipped
   - Brake hose
   - Vent hose
   - Driveshaft
   - Stabilizer bar links
   - Shock absorbers
   - Track bar
   - Upper and lower control arms
   - Coil springs
   - Axle housing

To install:

➡The weight of the vehicle must be supported by the springs when the control arm and track bar fasteners are tightened.

3. Install or connect the following:
   - Axle housing and coil springs to the vehicle
   - Upper and lower control arms
   - Track bar
   - Shock absorbers
   - Stabilizer bar links. Tighten the nuts to 40 ft. lbs. (54 Nm).
   - Driveshaft
   - Vent hose
   - Brake hose
   - Wheel speed sensors, if equipped
   - Parking brake cables
   - Brake rotors or drums
   - Rear wheels

4. Tighten the upper control arm bolts to 55 ft. lbs. (75 Nm), the lower control arm bolts to 130 ft. lbs. (177 Nm) and the track bar bolts to 74 ft. lbs. (100 Nm).

REAR AXLE SHAFT, BEARING & SEAL

REMOVAL & INSTALLATION

C-Clip Type Rear Axle Shaft

2005–06 Wrangler

See Figures 30 and 31.

1. Before servicing the vehicle, refer to the precautions in the beginning of this section.
2. Remove or disconnect the following:
   - Negative battery cable
   - Rear wheel
   - Brake drum
   - Differential cover
   - Differential gear shaft retainer
   - Differential gear shaft
   - C-clip
   - Axle shaft
   - Axle seal
   - Axle bearing

To install:

3. Install or connect the following:
   - Axle bearing
   - Axle seal
   - Axle shaft
   - C-clip
   - Differential gear shaft. Use Loctite® and tighten the retainer to 14 ft. lbs. (19 Nm).
   - Differential cover. Tighten the bolts to 30 ft. lbs. (41 Nm).
   - Brake drum
   - Rear wheel
4. Fill the axle assembly with gear oil and check for leaks.

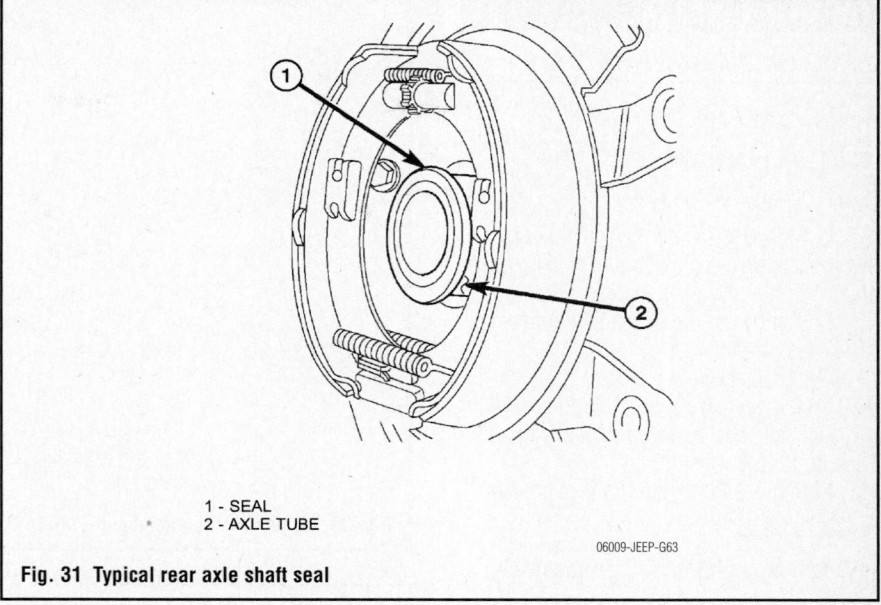

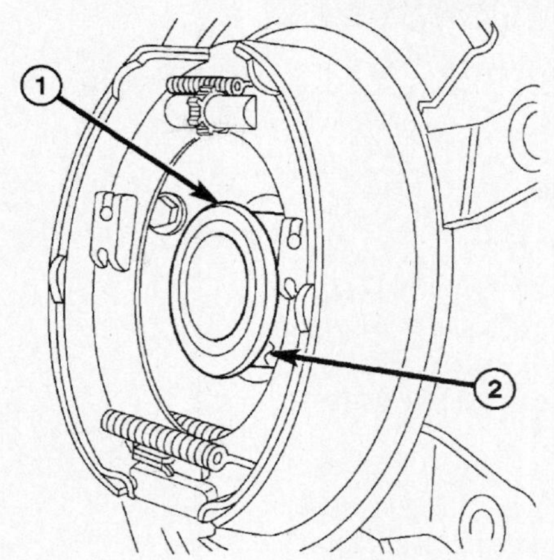

Fig. 31 Typical rear axle shaft seal

Liberty

1. Before servicing the vehicle, refer to the precautions in the beginning of this section.
2. With vehicle in neutral, position vehicle on hoist.
3. Remove differential housing cover and drain lubricant.
4. Rotate differential case so pinion mate shaft lock screw is accessible. Remove lock screw and pinion mate shaft from differential case.
5. Push axle shaft inward and remove axle shaft C-lock from the axle shaft.
6. Remove axle shaft from side gear and axle tube.
7. Remove axle shaft seal from axle tube with a seal pick.

To install:

8. Remove any old sealer/burrs from axle tube.
9. Coat new seal lip with axle lubricant and install seal with a seal driver.
10. Lubricate bearing bore and seal lip with gear lubricant.
11. Install axle shaft through seal, bearing and engage into side gear splines.
12. Install C-lock in axle shaft end, then push axle shaft outward to seat C-lock in side gear.
13. Install pinion mate shaft into differential case and through thrust washers and differential pinions.
14. Align hole in shaft with hole in the differential case and install lock screw with Loctite on the threads. Tighten lock screw to 8 ft. lbs. (11 Nm).
15. Install the differential cover.
16. Install rear brake components.

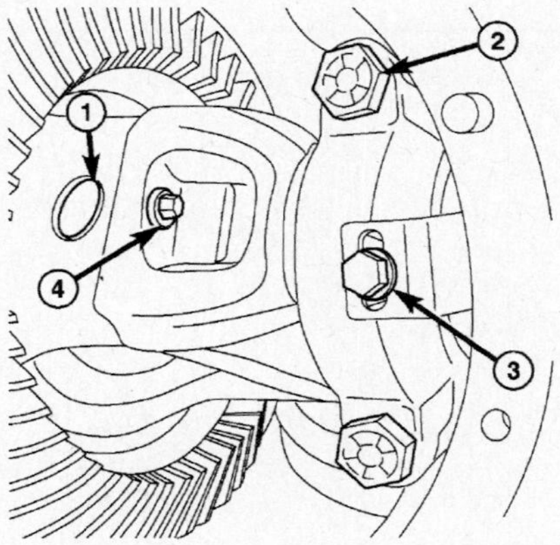

Fig. 30 Typical rear axle shaft lock screw

REAR DRIVESHAFT

REMOVAL & INSTALLATION

1. Before servicing the vehicle, refer to the precautions in the beginning of this manual.
2. Mark propeller shaft and pinion flange for installation reference.
3. Remove the front propeller shaft.

To install:

4. Install the propeller shaft with reference marks aligned.
5. Using new bolts, tighten them to 80 ft. lbs. (108 Nm).

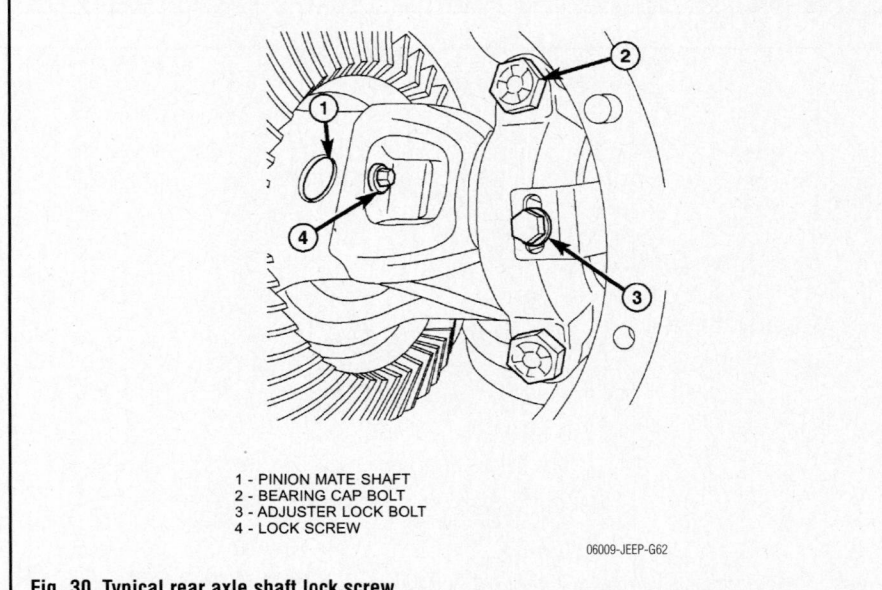

REAR PINION SEAL

REMOVAL & INSTALLATION

C-Clip Type Axle

2005–06 Wrangler

See Figures 32 through 35.

1. Before servicing the vehicle, refer to the precautions in the beginning of this section.
2. Remove or disconnect the following:
   - Wheels
   - Brake drums
   - Driveshaft
3. Check the bearing preload with an inch lb. torque wrench.
4. Remove the pinion flange and seal.

To install:

➡Use a new pinion nut for assembly.

5. Install the new pinion seal and flange. Tighten the nut to 200 ft. lbs. (271 Nm).
6. Check the bearing preload. The bearing preload should be equal to the reading taken earlier, plus 5 inch lbs.
7. If the preload torque is low, tighten the pinion nut in 5 inch lb. increments until the torque value is reached. Do not exceed 350 ft. lbs. (474 Nm) pinion nut torque.
8. If the pinion bearing preload torque cannot be attained at maximum pinion nut torque, replace the collapsible spacer.
9. Install or connect the following:
   - Driveshaft
   - Brake drums
   - Wheels
10. Fill the axle assembly with gear oil and check for leaks.

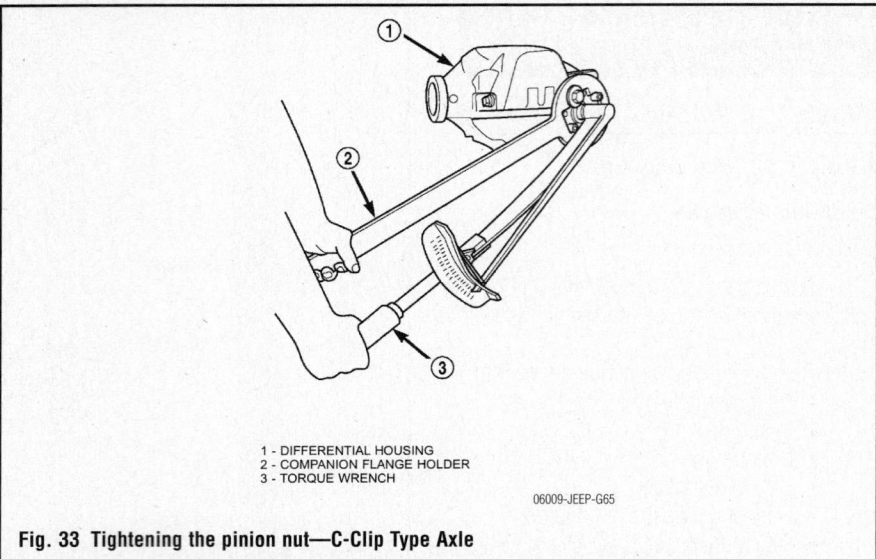

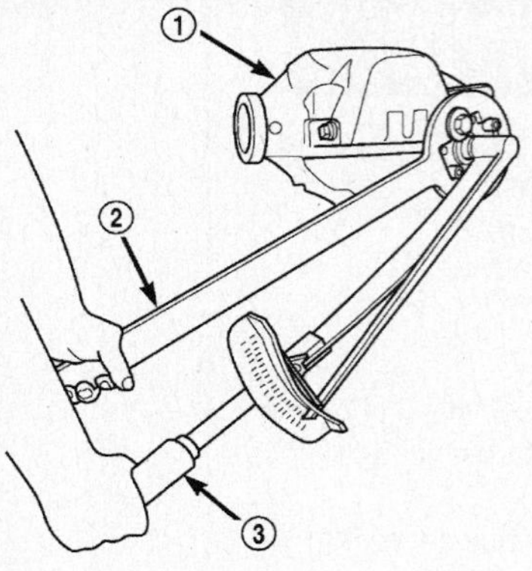

Fig. 33 Tightening the pinion nut—C-Clip Type Axle

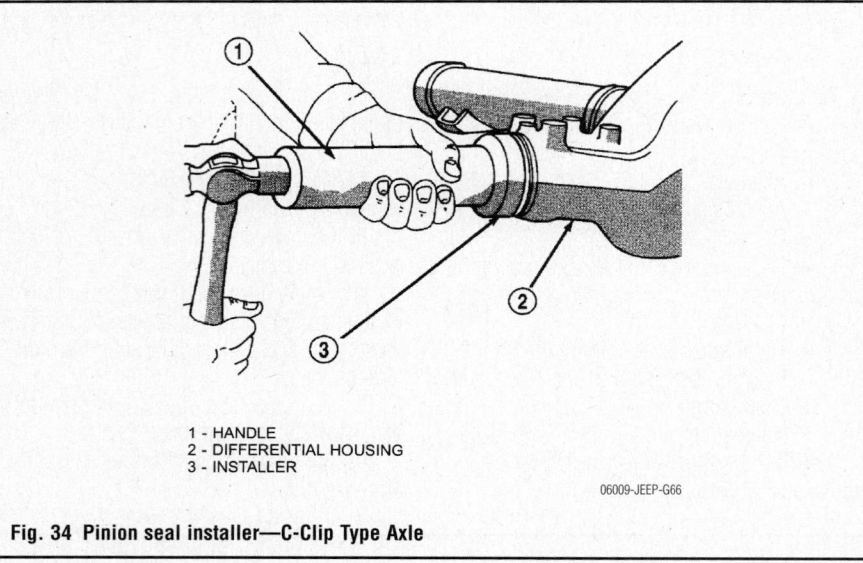

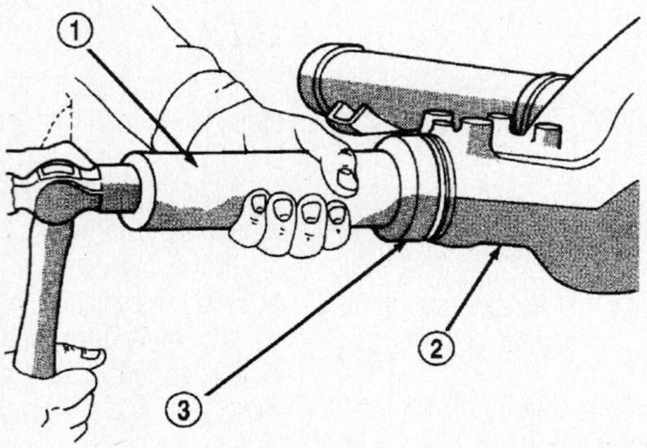

Fig. 34 Pinion seal installer—C-Clip Type Axle

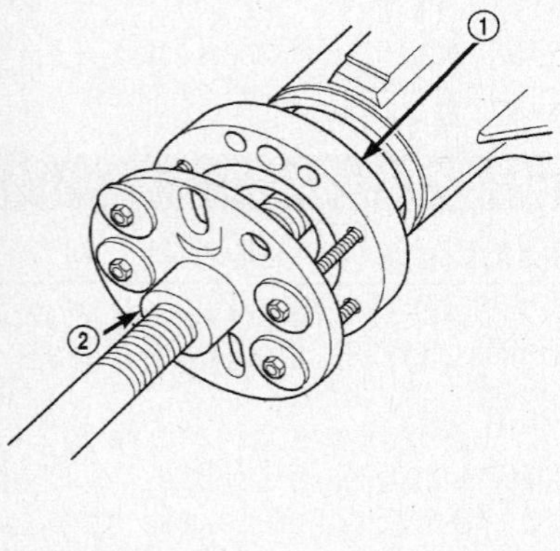

Fig. 32 Companion shaft puller—C-Clip Type Axle C-Clip Type Axle

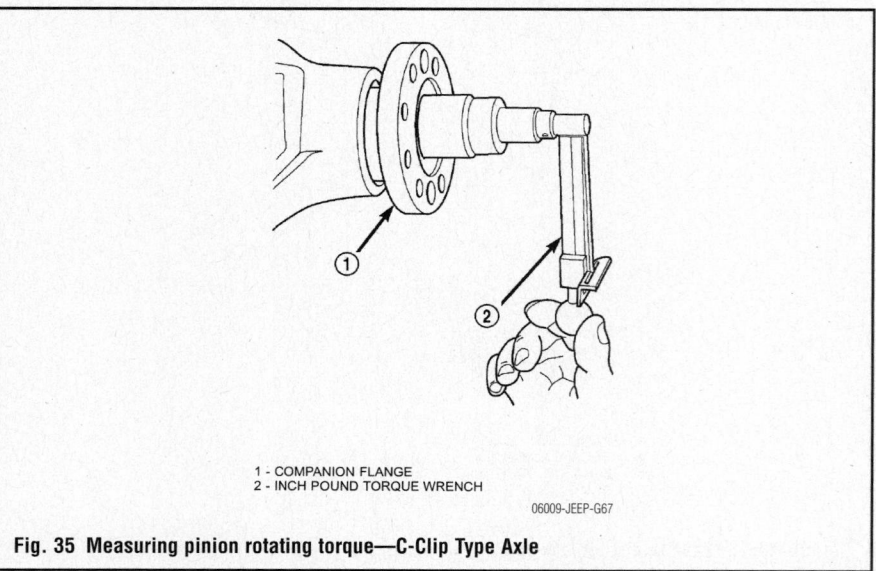

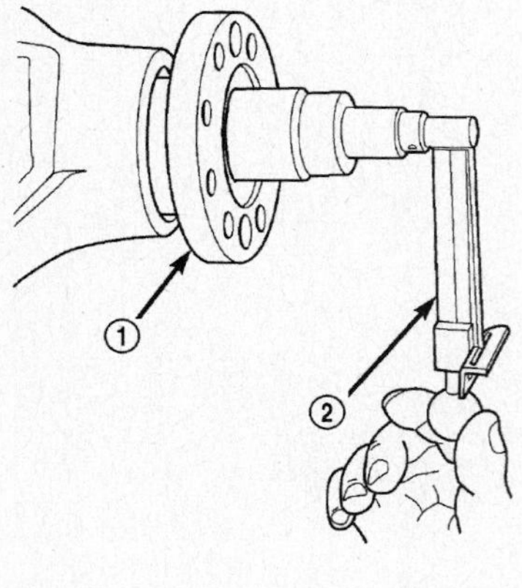

Fig. 35 Measuring pinion rotating torque—C-Clip Type Axle

Liberty

1. Before servicing the vehicle, refer to the precautions in the beginning of this section.
2. With vehicle in neutral, position vehicle on hoist.
3. Mark a reference line across the axle companion flange and propeller shaft flange yoke.
4. Remove companion flange bolts and remove propeller shaft.
5. Remove wheel and tire assemblies.
6. Remove brake calipers and rotors to prevent any drag.
7. Rotate companion flange three or four times and verify flange rotates smoothly.
8. Measure rotating torque of the pinion with a inch pound torque wrench and record reading for installation reference.
9. Install bolts into two of the threaded holes in the companion flange 180° apart.
10. Position Holder 6719, or equivalent, against the companion flange and install a bolt and washer into one of the remaining threaded holes. Tighten the bolts so the Holder 6719 is held to the flange.
11. Remove the pinion nut and washer.
12. Remove companion flange with Remover C-452, or equivalent.
13. Remove pinion seal with a seal pick.

To install

14. Apply a light coating of gear lubricant on the lip of pinion seal.
15. Install new pinion seal with Installer C-4076-B and Handle C-4735, or equivalent.
16. Install companion flange on the end of the shaft with the reference marks aligned.
17. Install bolts into two of the threaded holes in the companion flange 180° apart.
18. Position Holder 6719 against the companion flange and install a bolt and washer into one of the remaining threaded holes. Tighten the bolts so Holder 6719 is held to the flange.
19. Install companion flange on pinion shaft with Installer C-3718 and Holder 6719.
20. Install the pinion washer and a new pinion nut. The convex side of the washer must face outward.

➡Do not exceed the minimum tightening torque when installing the companion flange retaining nut at this point. Failure to heed caution may result in damage.

21. Hold companion flange with Holder 6719 and with a torque wrench tighten pinion nut to 210 ft. lbs. (285 Nm). Rotate pinion several revolutions to ensure the bearing rollers are seated.
22. Rotate pinion with an inch pound torque wrench. Rotating torque should be equal to the reading recorded during removal plus an additional 5 inch lbs. (0.56 Nm).

WARNING

Never loosen pinion nut to decrease pinion bearing rotating torque and never exceed specified preload torque. Failure to follow these instructions will result in damage.

23. If rotating torque is low use Holder 6719 to hold the companion flange and tighten pinion nut in 60 inch lbs. (6.8 Nm) increments until proper rotating torque is achieved.

➡The seal replacement is unacceptable if final pinion nut torque is less than 210 ft. lbs. (285 Nm). The bearing rotating torque should be constant during a complete revolution of the pinion. If the rotating torque varies, this indicates a binding condition.

24. Install propeller shaft with installation reference marks aligned.
25. Tighten companion flange bolts to 85 ft. lbs. (115 Nm).
26. Install rear brake components.

ENGINE COOLING

ENGINE FAN

REMOVAL & INSTALLATION

2.4L Engine

See Figure 36.

1. Remove the coolant recovery bottle and position out of the way.
2. Remove and position the power steering reservoir out of the way.
3. Disconnect the electrical connector.
4. Remove the mounting screws.
5. Remove the cooling fan assembly.

To install:

6. Position the cooling fan assembly.
7. Install four mounting screws. Tighten to 50 inch lbs. (5.5 Nm).
8. Connect the electrical connector.
9. Install the power steering reservoir.
10. Install the coolant recovery bottle.

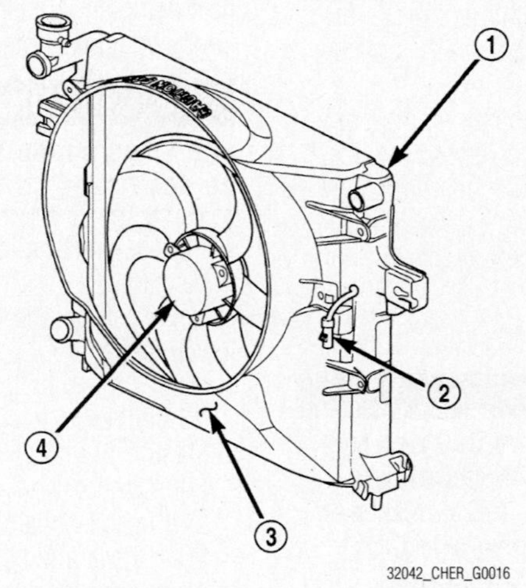

Fig. 36 The radiator fan for the 2.4L engine

3.7L Engine

➡If the fan blade is bent, warped, cracked or damaged in any way, it must be replaced only with a replacement fan blade. Do not attempt to repair a damaged fan blade.

➡For 3.7L Heavy Duty/Max Cool/Trailer Tow cooling package, the viscous fan cannot be removed separate from the shroud. Both fan and shroud must be removed together.

1. Disconnect battery negative cable.
2. Using special tool 6958 wrench and 8346 adapters, remove the viscous fan from the water pump .
3. Gently lay fan into shroud.

4. Disconnect the electrical connector for the electric fan, then disconnect connector from shroud.

5. Remove the two fan shroud mounting bolts connecting the fan shroud to the radiator.

6. Remove the shroud and fan from the vehicle.

To install:

➡For 3.7L Heavy Duty/Max Cool/Trailer Tow cooling package, the viscous fan cannot be installed separate from the shroud. Both fan and shroud must be installed together.

7. Gently lay viscous fan into shroud.

8. Install fan shroud assembly into the vehicle. Tighten fan shroud to radiator bolts to 50 inch lbs. (5.5 Nm).

9. Using special tool 6958 wrench and 8346 adapters, install the viscous fan on the water pump.

10. Connect fan motor wire connector to harness connector, and attach connector to shroud.

11. Connect battery negative cable.

12. Start engine and check fan operation.

4.0L Engine

1. Remove the thermal viscous fan drive/fan blade assembly.

2. Remove the four fan retaining bolts.

3. Separate the fan blade from the thermal viscous fan drive

To install:

4. Position the fan blade on the thermal viscous fan drive.

5. Install four mounting bolts. Tighten to 210 inch lbs. (23 Nm).

6. Install the thermal viscous fan drive.

RADIATOR

REMOVAL & INSTALLATION

2005–06 Wrangler

See Figure 37.

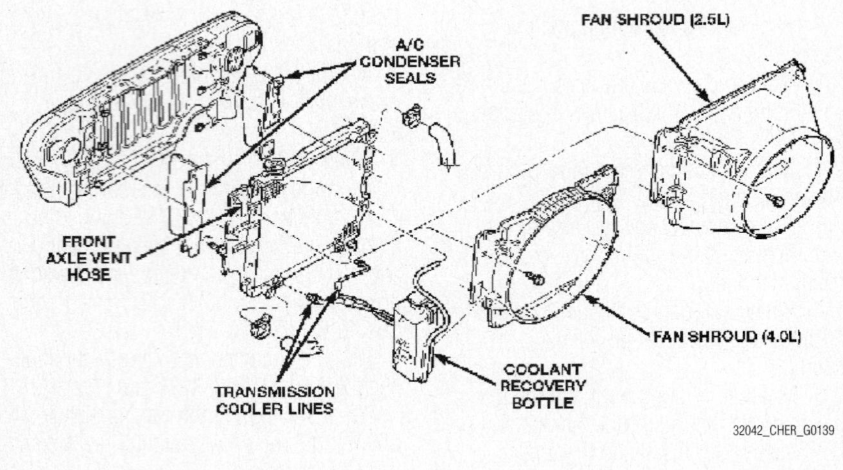

Fig. 37 Exploded view of the radiator mounting location for the 4.0L engine

1. Disconnect negative battery cable at battery.

2. Remove the radiator cap.

3. Remove the condenser lower seal from the lower core support .

4. Drain cooling system drain coolant into a clean container for reuse.

5. Remove radiator upper and lower hose clamps Remove radiator hoses.

6. Disconnect coolant reserve/overflow tank hose from radiator.

7. 2.4L ONLY - Remove the electric cooling fan.

8. 4.0L ONLY - Remove the reservoir tank and power steering reservoir and position out of the way.

9. 4.0L ONLY - Remove the four fan shroud mounting bolts. Position the fan shroud back over the fan blades.

10. If equipped, disconnect and plug automatic transmission fluid cooler lines.

11. Remove six radiator mounting bolts. Position the front axle vent hose to the side.

12. The lower part of radiator is equipped with two alignment dowel pins . They are located on the bottom of radiator tank and fit into rubber grommets. These rubber grommets are pressed into the radiator lower crossmember.

13. Lift radiator straight up and out of vehicle taking care not to damage radiator fins.

14. When removing radiator, note position of the rubber seals located on the top and bottom of radiator (on certain models only) . To prevent possible overheating, these seals must be installed to their original positions.

To install:

⁂ CAUTION

Before installing the radiator or A/C condenser, be sure the radiator-to-body and radiator-to- A/C condenser rubber air seals are properly fastened to their original positions. These are used at the top, bottom and sides of the radiator and A/C condenser. To prevent overheating, these seals must be installed to their original positions.

15. Guide the two radiator alignment dowels into the rubber grommets located in lower radiator cross member. Install and tighten the six mounting bolts to 72 inch lbs. (8 Nm) torque.

16. Close radiator drain cock.

17. 2.4L ONLY - Install the electric cooling fan.

18. Position fan shroud and power steering reservoir tank (if equipped). Install and tighten four mounting bolts to 72 inch lbs. (8 Nm) torque.

19. If equipped, remove plugs and connect automatic transmission fluid cooler lines and constant tension clamps.

⁂ CAUTION

The tangs on the hose clamps must be positioned straight down.

20. Connect radiator hoses and install hose clamps.

21. Position and install the condenser lower seal.

22. Connect battery negative cable.

23. Fill cooling system with correct coolant.

24. Connect coolant recovery bottle hose.

25. Install radiator cap.

26. Check and adjust automatic transmission fluid level (if equipped).

27. Start engine and check for leaks.

Liberty

2.4L Engine

See Figure 38.

1. Disconnect the negative battery cable at battery.
2. Drain coolant from radiator.
3. Remove the front grill.
4. Remove the cooling fan from the engine, if equipped.
5. Remove the two radiator mounting bolts.
6. Disconnect the connector for the electric fan.
7. Disconnect the power steering cooler line from cooler.
8. Disconnect the radiator upper and lower hoses.
9. Disconnect the overflow hose from radiator.
10. The lower part of radiator is equipped with two alignment dowel pins . They are located on the bottom of radiator tank and fit into rubber grommets. These rubber grommets are pressed into the radiator lower cross member.

✱✱ WARNING

The air conditioning system (if equipped) is under a constant pressure even with the engine off.

➡The radiator and radiator cooling fan can be removed as an assembly. It is not necessary to remove the cooling fan before removing or installing the radiator.

11. Gently lift up and remove radiator from vehicle. Be careful not to scrape the radiator fins against any other component. Also be careful not to disturb the air conditioning condenser (if equipped).

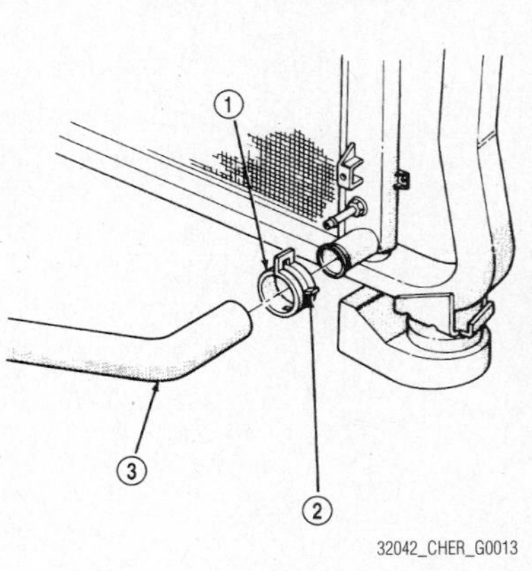

Fig. 38 Radiator hose clamp location on the 2.4L engine

To install:

12. Gently lower the radiator and fan shroud into the vehicle. Guide the two radiator alignment dowels into the rubber grommets located in lower radiator cross member.
13. Connect the radiator upper and lower hoses and hose clamps to radiator.

✱✱ CAUTION

The tangs on the hose clamps must be positioned straight down.

14. Install coolant reserve/overflow tank hose at radiator.
15. Install both radiator mounting bolts.
16. Reconnect the electric cooling fan.
17. Install the grill.
18. Reinstall the cooling fan to the engine.
19. Rotate the fan blades (by hand) and check for interference at fan shroud.
20. Refill cooling system.
21. Connect battery cable at battery.
22. Start and warm engine. Check for leaks.

3.7L Engines and 2.8L Diesel Engines

1. Disconnect the negative battery cable at battery.
2. Drain coolant from radiator.
3. Remove the front grill.
4. Remove the cooling fan from the engine, if equipped.
5. Remove the two radiator mounting bolts.
6. Disconnect the connector for the electric fan.
7. Disconnect the power steering cooler line from cooler.
8. Disconnect the radiator upper and lower hoses.
9. Disconnect the overflow hose from radiator.
10. The lower part of radiator is equipped with two alignment dowel pins. They are located on the bottom of radiator tank and fit into rubber grommets. These rubber grommets are pressed into the radiator lower cross member.

✱✱ WARNING

The air conditioning system (if equipped) is under a constant pressure even with the engine off.

➡The radiator and radiator cooling fan can be removed as an assembly. It is not necessary to remove the cooling fan before removing or installing the radiator.

11. Gently lift up and remove radiator from vehicle. Be careful not to scrape the radiator fins against any other component. Also be careful not to disturb the air conditioning condenser (if equipped).

To install:

12. Gently lower the radiator and fan shroud into the vehicle. Guide the two radiator alignment dowels into the rubber grommets located in lower radiator crossmember.
13. Connect the radiator upper and lower hoses and hose clamps to radiator.

✱✱ CAUTION

The tangs on the hose clamps must be positioned straight down.

14. Install coolant reserve/overflow tank hose at radiator.
15. Install both radiator mounting bolts.
16. Reconnect the electric cooling fan.
17. Install the grill.
18. Reinstall the cooling fan to the engine.
19. Rotate the fan blades (by hand) and check for interference at fan shroud.
20. Refill cooling system.
21. Connect battery cable at battery.
22. Start and warm engine. Check for leaks.

THERMOSTAT

REMOVAL & INSTALLATION

✱✱ WARNING

Do not loosen radiator drain cock with system hot and pressurized. Serious burns from coolant can occur.

➡Do not waste reusable coolant. If solution is clean, drain coolant into a clean container for reuse. If thermostat is being replaced, be sure that replacement is specified thermostat for vehicle model and engine type.

2005–06 Wrangler

See Figure 39.

1. Drain cooling system below thermostat housing level.
2. Disconnect engine coolant temperature sensor.
3. Disconnect heater supply hose.
4. Remove housing attaching bolts.
5. Remove housing, gasket and thermostat.

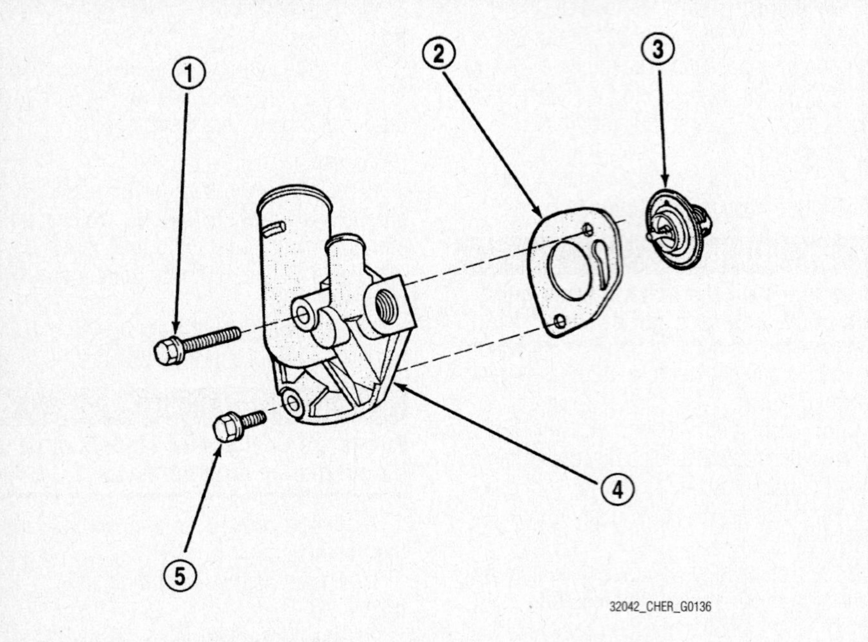

Fig. 39 The removal of the thermostat (3) from its housing (4) on the 4.0L engine

To install:

6. Install the replacement thermostat so that the pellet, which is encircled by a coil spring, faces the engine. All thermostats are marked on the outer flange to indicate the proper installed position.

7. Observe the recess groove in the engine cylinder head .

8. Position thermostat into this groove with arrow and air bleed hole on outer flange pointing up.

9. Install replacement gasket and thermostat housing

CAUTION

Tightening the thermostat housing unevenly or with the thermostat out of its recess may result in a cracked housing.

10. Tighten the housing bolts to 15 ft. lbs. (20 Nm) torque.

11. Install hoses to thermostat housing.

12. Install electrical connector to coolant temperature sensor.

13. Be sure that the radiator draincock is tightly closed. Fill the cooling system.

14. Start and warm the engine. Check for leaks.

Liberty

2.4L Engine

See Figure 40.

1. Drain cooling system below thermostat housing level.

2. Disconnect engine coolant temperature sensor.

3. Disconnect heater supply hose.

4. Remove housing attaching bolts .

5. Remove housing, gasket and thermostat .

To install:

6. Clean all gasket sealing surfaces.

7. Place a new gasket (dipped in clean water) on the coolant outlet connector surface. Position thermostat with air bleed at 12 o'clock position in thermostat housing.

8. Position the coolant outlet connector and gasket over the thermostat, making sure thermostat is seated in the thermostat housing .

9. Position outlet connector to thermostat housing and install bolts. Tighten bolts to 20 ft. lbs. (28 Nm).

10. Install radiator hose to coolant outlet housing.

11. Connect engine coolant temperature sensor.

12. Fill cooling system.

2.8L Diesel Engine

➡ The thermostat is not serviced separately. The thermostat and housing must be replaced as an assembly.

1. Disconnect negative battery cable.
2. Remove engine cover.
3. Partially drain cooling system.
4. Disconnect upper radiator hose and bypass hoses at thermostat housing.
5. Remove thermostat housing retaining bolts, support bracket and housing from cylinder head, discard gasket .

To install:

6. Clean old gasket material from cylinder head and thermostat housing.

7. Install thermostat housing with gasket and support bracket to cylinder head. Torque bolts to 20 ft. lbs. (27.5 Nm).

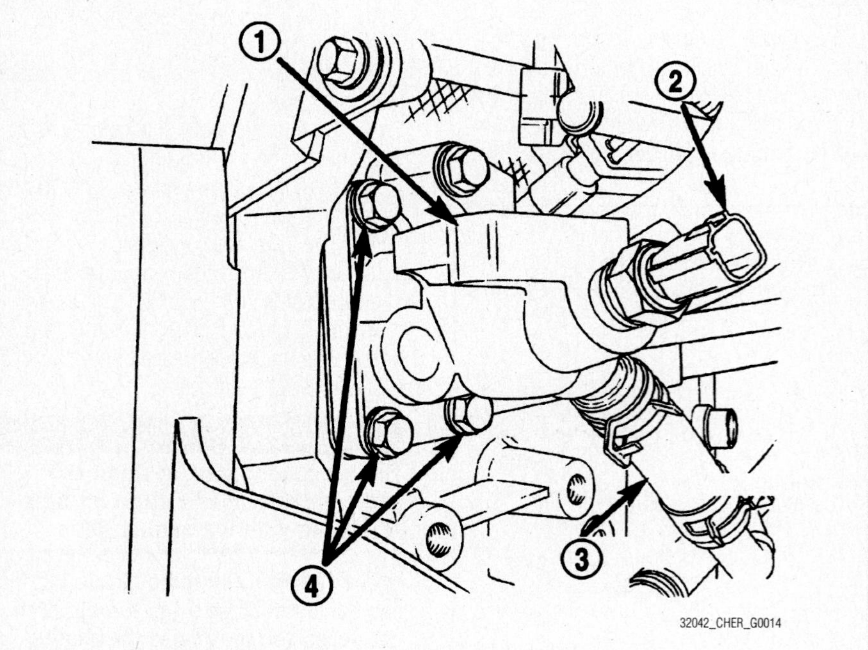

Fig. 40 The removal of the thermostat from its housing

8. Connect coolant bypass hose and upper radiator hose to thermostat housing.
9. Refill cooling system.
10. Install engine cover.
11. Connect negative battery cable.

3.7L Engine

See Figure 41.

1. Disconnect negative battery cable at battery.
2. Drain cooling system.
3. Raise vehicle on hoist.
4. Remove splash shield.
5. Remove lower radiator hose clamp and lower radiator hose at thermostat housing.
6. Remove thermostat housing mounting bolts, thermostat housing and thermostat.

To install:

7. Clean mating areas of timing chain cover and thermostat housing.
8. Install thermostat (spring side down) into recessed machined groove on housing assembly. Make sure rubber seal locating tab is positioned in the corresponding notch in the housing.
9. Position thermostat housing on timing chain cover.
10. Install two housing-to-timing chain cover bolts. Tighten bolts to 105 inch lbs. (12 Nm) torque.
11. Install lower radiator hose on thermostat housing.
12. Install splash shield.
13. Lower vehicle.
14. Fill cooling system.
15. Connect negative battery cable to battery.
16. Start and warm the engine. Check for leaks.

WATER PUMP

REMOVAL & INSTALLATION

2.4L Engine

Liberty

See Figures 42 and 43.

1. Before servicing the vehicle, refer to the precautions in the beginning of this section.
2. Disconnect negative cable from battery.
3. Raise vehicle on a hoist.
4. Remove the accessory drive belts.
5. Remove the belt tensioner.
6. Drain the cooling system.
7. Remove the generator.
8. Remove the power steering pump.
9. Remove the A/C compressor.
10. Remove the accessory drive bracket.
11. Remove the timing belt.
12. Remove timing belt idler pulley.
13. Hold camshaft sprocket with Special tool C-4687 and adapter C-4687-1, or equivalent, while removing bolt. Remove both cam sprockets.
14. Remove the timing belt rear cover.
15. Remove water pump to engine attaching screws.
16. Replace water pump body assembly if it has any of these defects:
    a. Cracks or damage on the body.

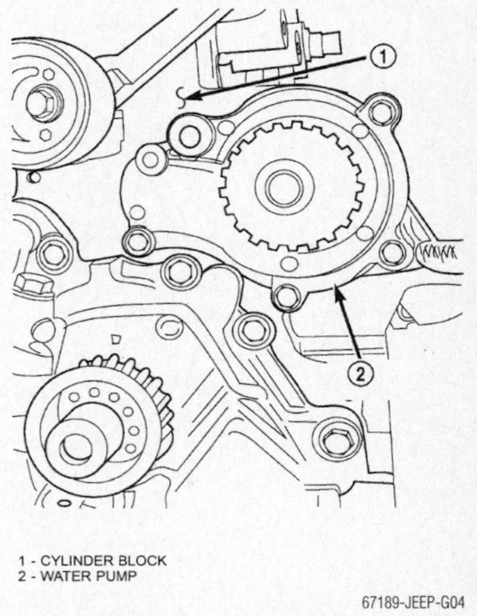

Fig. 42 Water pump mounting—2.4L engines

    b. Coolant leaks from the shaft seal, evident by wet coolant traces on the pump body.
    c. Loose or rough turning bearing.
    d. Impeller rubs either the pump body or the engine block.
    e. Impeller loose or damaged.
    f. Sprocket or sprocket flange loose or damaged.

To install:

17. Install new O-ring gasket in water pump body O-ring locating groove.

➡Make sure O-ring is properly seated in water pump groove before tightening screws. An improperly located O-ring may be damaged and cause a coolant leak.

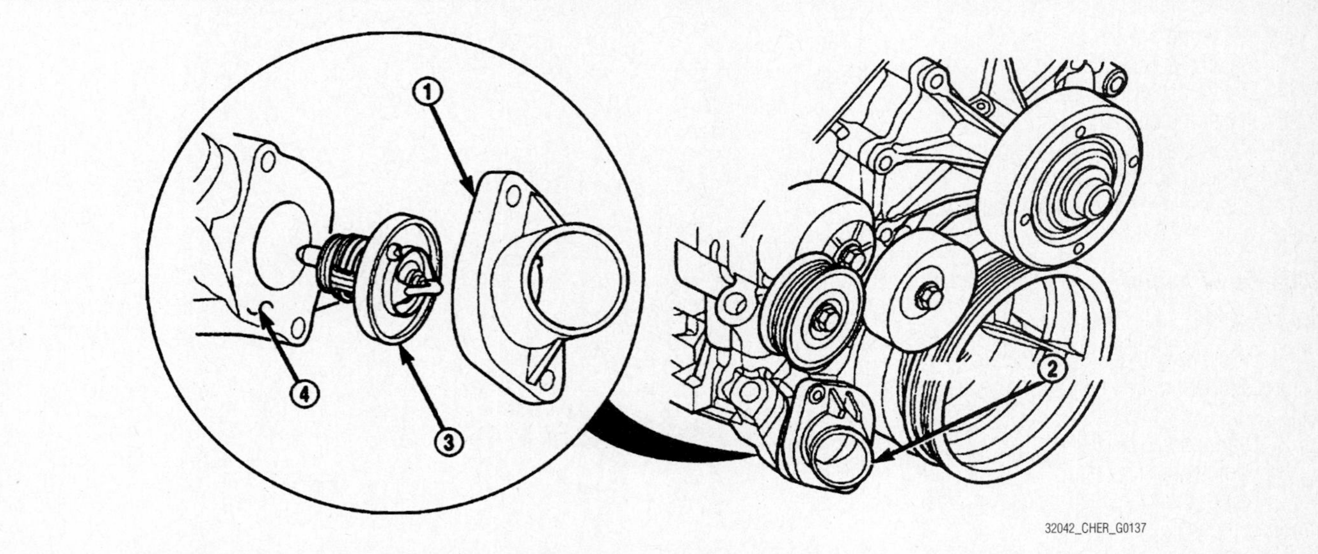

Fig. 41 The location of the thermostat (3) and its housing on the 3.7L engine

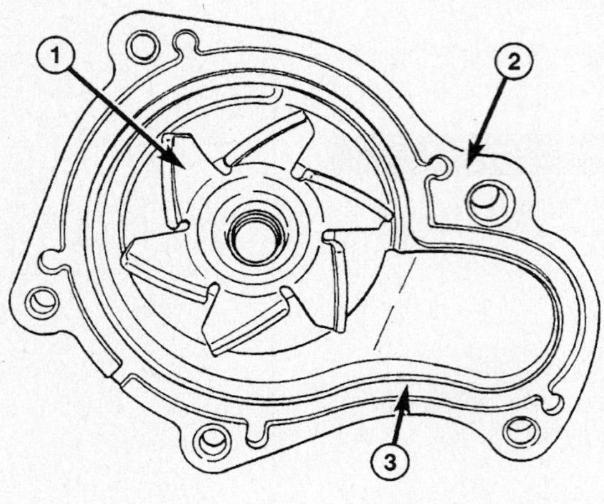

Fig. 43 Water pump body—2.4L engines

18. Assemble pump body to block and tighten screws to 105 inch lbs. (12 Nm). Pressurize cooling system to 15 psi (103.4 Kpa) with pressure tester and check water pump shaft seal and O-ring for leaks.
19. Rotate pump by hand to check for freedom of movement.
20. Install the timing belt rear cover.
21. Install camshaft sprockets and target ring. Torque bolts to 75 ft. lbs. (101 Nm) while holding camshaft sprocket.
22. Install timing belt idler pulley and torque mounting bolt to 45 ft. lbs. (61 Nm).
23. Install the timing belt.
24. Install the accessory drive mounting bracket.
25. Install the power steering pump.
26. Install the generator.
27. Install the A/C compressor.
28. Install the belt tensioner.
29. Install the accessory drive belts.
30. Fill the cooling system.
31. Lower vehicle and connect battery cable.

2005–06 Wrangler

See Figure 44.

1. Before servicing the vehicle, refer to the precautions in the beginning of this section.
2. Drain cooling system.
3. Remove timing belt.
4. Remove camshaft sprockets and rear timing belt cover.
5. Remove screws attaching water pump to engine. Remove pump.

To install:

6. Apply Mopar® Dielectric Grease, or equivalent, to new O-ring before installation.
7. Install O-ring gasket in water pump body groove.

⁂ WARNING

Make sure O-ring gasket is properly seated in water pump groove before tightening screws. An improperly located O-ring may cause damage to the O-ring, resulting in a coolant leak.

8. Assemble pump body to block and tighten screws to 105 inch lbs. (12 Nm).
9. Rotate pump by hand to check for freedom of movement.
10. Fill cooling system. Pressurize cooling system to 15 psi (103 Kpa) with pressure tester and check water pump shaft seal and O-ring for leaks.
11. Install rear timing belt cover and camshaft sprockets.
12. Install timing belt.

2.8L Diesel Engine

1. Disconnect negative battery cable.
2. Drain cooling system.
3. Remove timing belt inner and outer covers.
4. Remove water pump retaining bolts and pump .

To install:

5. Clean mating surfaces of water pump housing and engine block as necessary.
6. Place new O-ring in groove in water pump housing. Install water pump and retaining bolts. Torque bolts to 24.4 Nm.
7. Install both inner and outer timing belt covers.
8. Refill cooling system.
9. Connect negative battery cable.

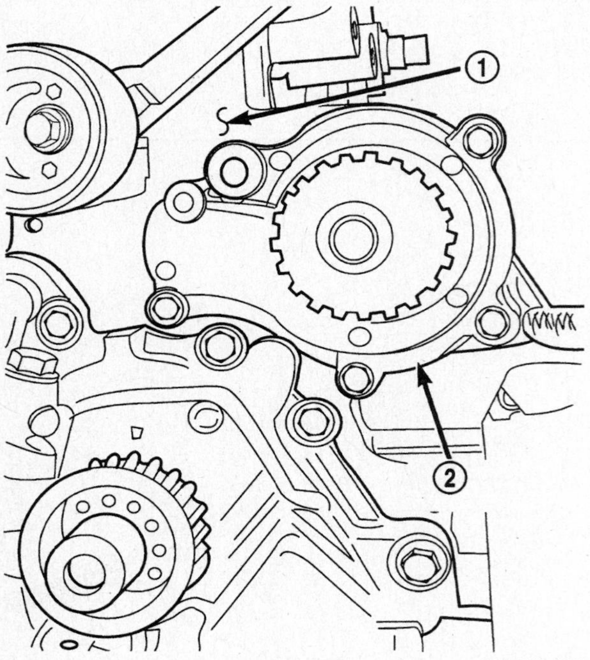

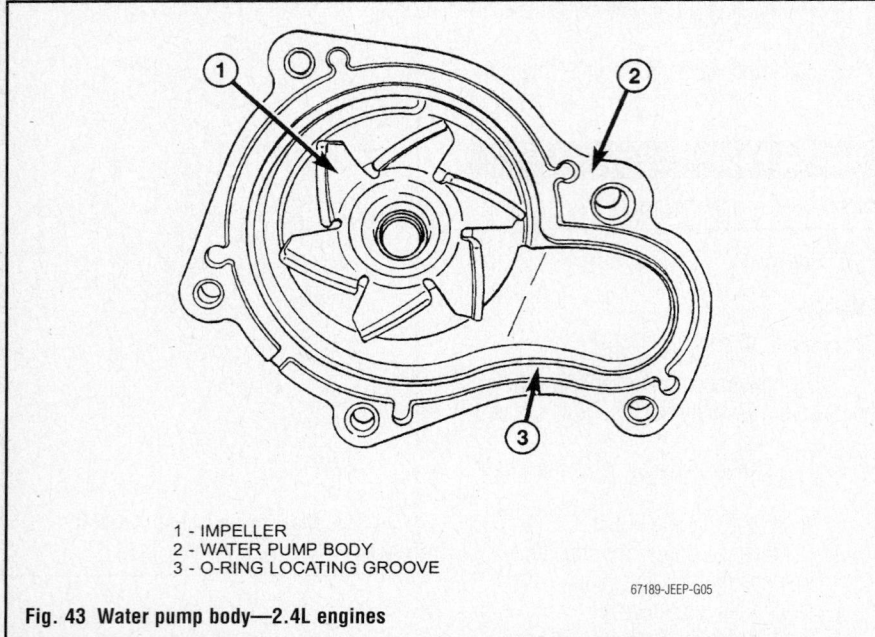

Fig. 44 Water pump mounting on Wrangler with 2.4L engine

3.7L Engine

See Figure 45.

1. Before servicing the vehicle, refer to the precautions in the beginning of this section.
2. Drain the cooling system.
3. Remove or disconnect the following:
   - Negative battery cable
   - Fan and clutch assembly from the pump
   - Fan shroud and fan assembly. If you're reusing the fan clutch, keep it upright to avoid silicone fluid loss!
   - Lower hose
   - Water pump (8 bolts)
4. Installation is the reverse of removal. Tighten the bolts, in sequence, to 40 ft. lbs. (54 Nm).

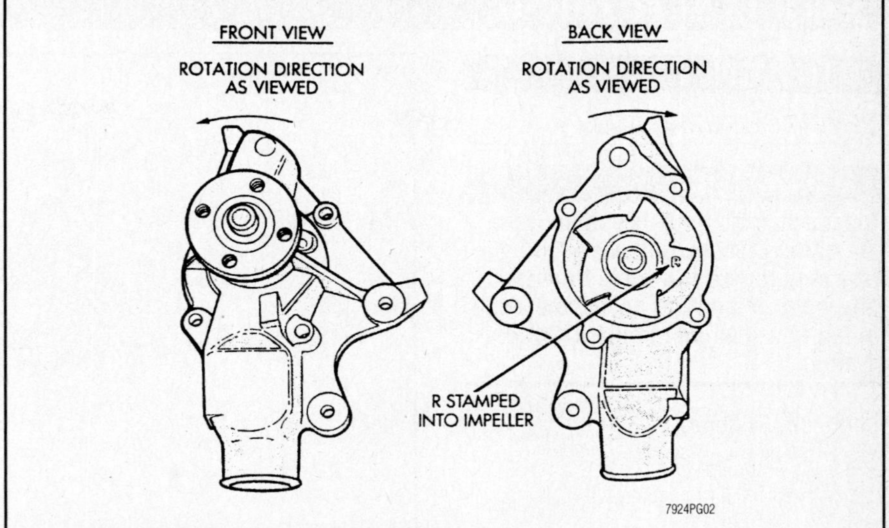

Fig. 46 Reverse rotation water pump—4.0L engines

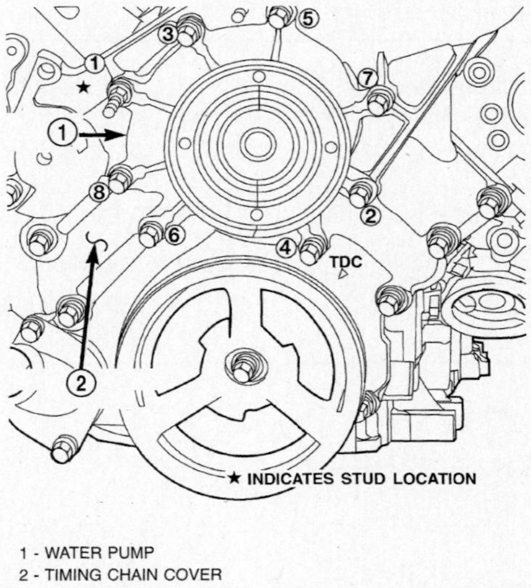

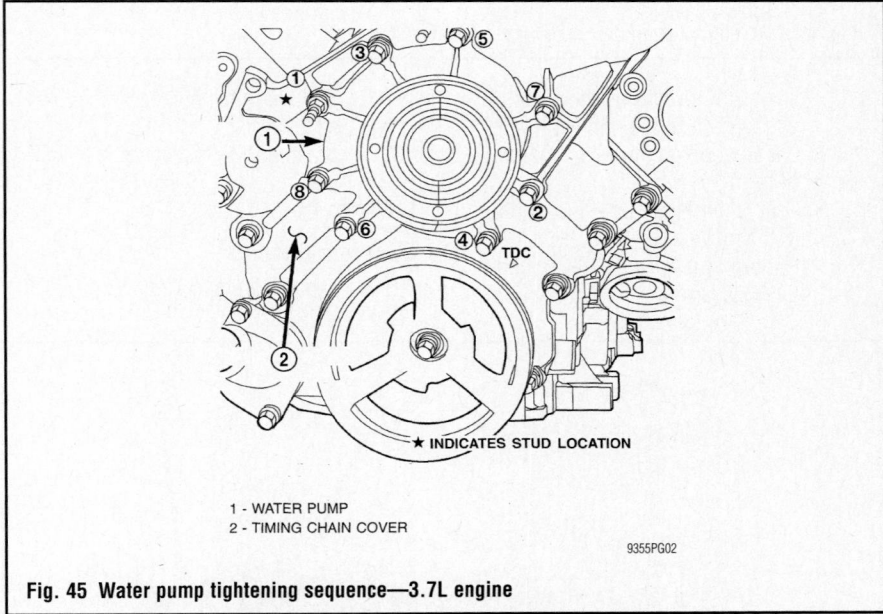

Fig. 45 Water pump tightening sequence—3.7L engine

4.0L Engines

See Figure 46.

➡The 4.0L engines covered use a reverse rotation water pump. The letter R is stamped on the impeller to identify. Engines from previous years may be equipped with forward rotation water pumps. Installation of the wrong water pump will cause engine over heating.

1. Before servicing the vehicle, refer to the precautions in the beginning of this section.
2. Drain the cooling system.
3. Remove or disconnect the following:
   - Negative battery cable
   - Electric cooling fan connector
   - Accessory drive belt
   - Engine cooling fan and pulley

➡Some 4.0L engines are equipped with a fan clutch that threads directly on to the water pump shaft. This fan clutch is equipped with right-hand threads.

➡Do not store the fan clutch assembly horizontally, silicone may leak into the bearing grease and cause contamination.

   - Water pump pulley
   - Power steering pump
   - Lower radiator hose from the water pump
   - Heater hose
   - Water pump and discard the gasket

➡One of the water pump bolts is longer than the others. Note the location for reassembly.

To install:

4. Clean the mating surfaces of all gasket material.
5. Install or connect the following:
   - Water pump using a new gasket. Torque the bolts to 17 ft. lbs. (23 Nm).
   - Heater hose
   - Lower radiator hose
   - Water pump pulley. Torque the bolts to 20 ft. lbs. (27 Nm).
   - Power steering pump
   - Engine cooling fan and shroud. Torque the bolts to 31 inch lbs. (3 Nm).
   - Accessory drive belt
   - Electric cooling fan connector
   - Negative battery cable
6. Fill and bleed the cooling system.
7. Start the engine, check for leaks and repair if necessary.

ALTERNATOR

REMOVAL & INSTALLATION

WARNING

Disconnect the negative cable from the battery before removing the battery output wire (B+ wire) from the alternator. Failure to do so can result in injury or damage to the electrical system.

2005–06 Wrangler

See Figures 47 and 48.

1. Disconnect negative battery cable at battery.
2. Remove alternator drive belt.
3. Remove alternator pivot and mounting bolts/nut and position generator for access to wire connectors.
4. If equipped, unsnap plastic cover from B+ terminal.
5. Remove B+ cable output terminal mounting nut at rear of generator, or Disconnect terminal from alternator.
6. Disconnect field wire connector at rear of alternator by pushing on connector tab.
7. Remove generator from vehicle

To install:

8. Position generator to engine and snap field wire connector into rear of alternator.
9. Install B+ terminal to alternator mounting stud. Tighten mounting nut.
10. If equipped, snap plastic cover to B+ terminal.
11. Install alternator mounting fasteners and tighten

CAUTION

Never force a belt over a pulley rim using a screwdriver. The synthetic fiber of the belt can be damaged

CAUTION

When installing a serpentine accessory drive belt, the belt MUST be routed correctly. The water pump will be rotating in the wrong direction if the belt is installed incorrectly, causing the engine to overheat.

12. Install generator drive belt.
13. Tighten alternator hardware as follows:
    - Generator upper mounting bolt–All engines–41 ft. lbs. (55 Nm)
    - Generator lower mounting bolt–All engines–41 ft. lbs. (55 Nm)
    - Battery terminal nut–75 inch lbs. (8.5 Nm)
    - Ground terminal nut–75 inch lbs. (8.5 Nm)
    - Harness hold-down nut–75 inch lbs. (8.5 Nm)
    - Field terminal nuts–25 inch lbs. (2.8 Nm)
14. Install negative battery cable to battery.

Liberty

Gasoline Engines

See Figures 49 through 51.

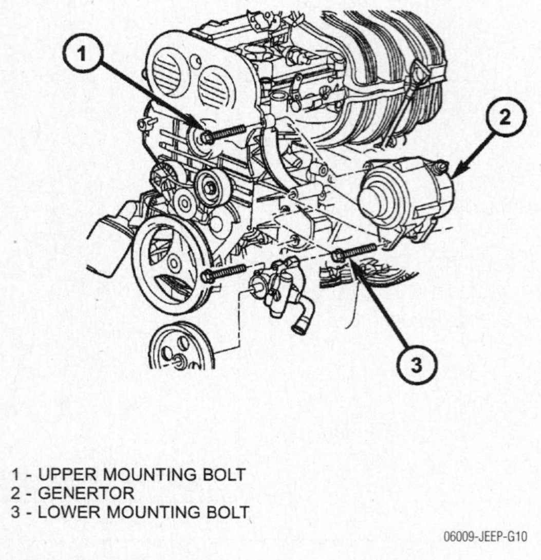

Fig. 47 2.4L engine alternator mounting

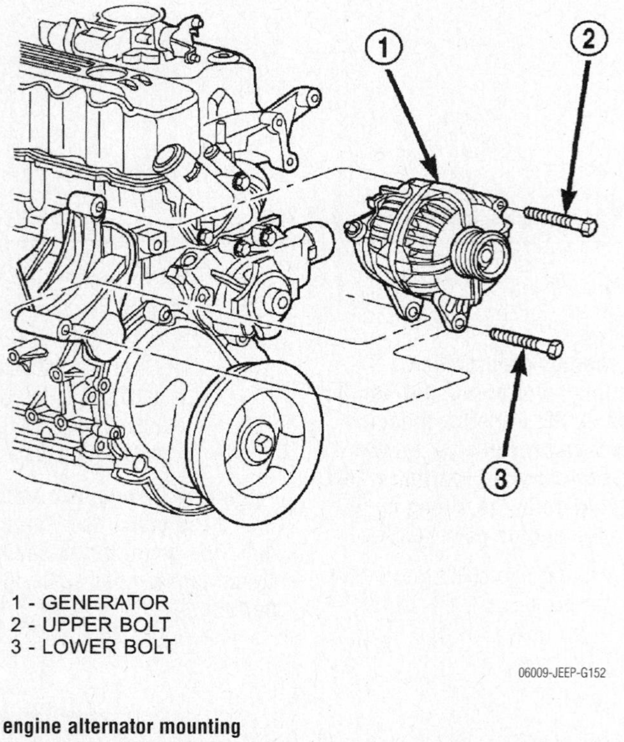

Fig. 48 4.0L engine alternator mounting

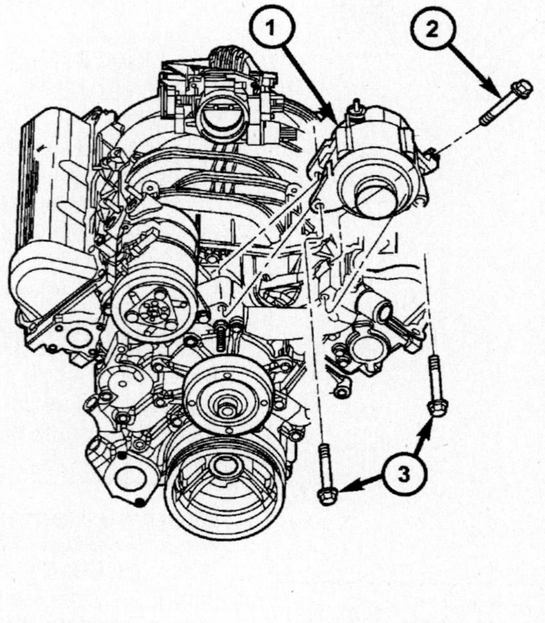

Fig. 49 3.7L engine alternator mounting

⁂ CAUTION

Disconnect negative cable from the battery before removing battery output wire from the alternator. Failure to do so can result in injury.

1. Disconnect and isolate negative battery cable at battery.

⁂ CAUTION

Never force a belt over a pulley rim using a screwdriver. The synthetic fiber of the belt can be damaged.

⁂ CAUTION

When installing a serpentine accessory drive belt, the belt MUST be routed correctly. The water pump will be rotating in the wrong direction if the belt is installed incorrectly, causing the engine to overheat. Refer to belt routing label in engine compartment.

2. Remove alternator drive belt.
3. Unsnap plastic protective cover from B+ mounting stud.
4. Remove B+ terminal mounting nut at top of alternator.
5. Disconnect field wire electrical connector at rear of alternator by pushing on connector tab.
6. 2.4L Engine: Remove 2 generator mounting bolts.
7. 3.7L Engine: Remove 1 vertical generator mounting bolt and 2 horizontal mounting bolts.
8. Remove alternator from vehicle.

To install:

9. 2.4L Engine: Position alternator to engine and install 2 mounting bolts.
10. 3.7L Engine: Position alternator to engine and install 3 mounting bolts. Tighten 2 horizontal mounting bolts to specified torque. Tighten 1 vertical mounting bolt to specified torque.
11. Snap field wire connector into rear of generator.
12. Install B+ terminal and nut to alternator mounting stud.
13. Snap plastic protective cover to B+ terminal.

⁂ CAUTION

Never force a belt over a pulley rim using a screwdriver. The synthetic fiber of the belt can be damaged.

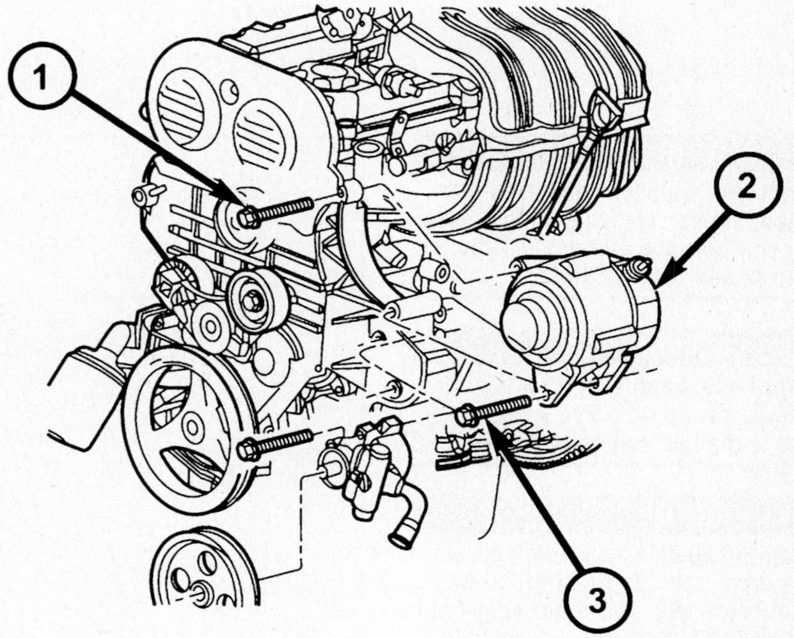

Fig. 50 The generator (2) for the 2.4L engine

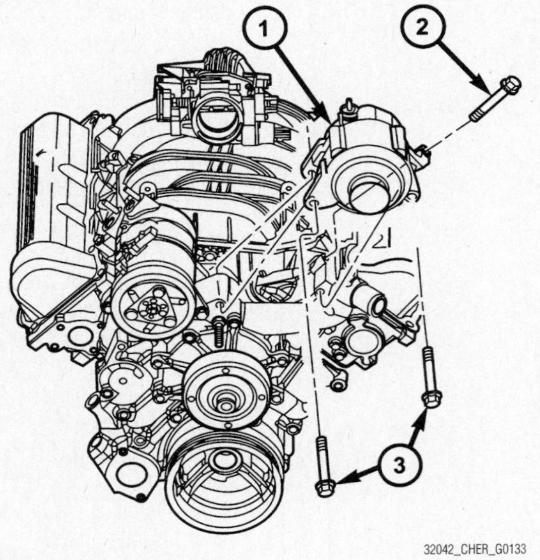

Fig. 51 The generator (1) for the 3.7L engine

⁂ CAUTION

When installing a serpentine accessory drive belt, the belt MUST be routed correctly. The water pump will be rotating in the wrong direction if the belt is installed incorrectly, causing the engine to overheat. Refer to belt routing label in engine compartment.

14. Install drive belt.
15. Install negative battery cable to battery.

Diesel Engine

See Figure 52.

⁂ CAUTION

Disconnect negative cable from the battery before removing battery output wire from the alternator. Failure to do so can result in injury.

⁂ CAUTION

Never force a belt over a pulley rim using a screwdriver. The synthetic fiber of the belt can be damaged.

⁂ CAUTION

When installing a serpentine accessory drive belt, the belt MUST be routed correctly. The water pump will be rotating in the wrong direction if the belt is installed incorrectly, causing the engine to overheat. Refer to belt routing label in engine compartment.

1. Disconnect and isolate negative battery cable.
2. Remove engine oil fill cap and engine oil dipstick.
3. Remove plastic decorative engine cover. Cover snaps onto engine.
4. Remove generator drive belt.
5. Remove protective plastic cover from B+ stud at top of generator.
6. Remove nut securing battery output cable to B+ terminal at top of generator.
7. Unplug field terminal connector at rear of generator.
8. Loosen support bracket bolts and nut.
9. Remove 2 alternator mounting bolts.
10. Remove alternator from vehicle.

To install:

11. Position alternator to engine.
12. Install alternator mounting bolts/nuts.
13. Connect field terminal connector at rear of alternator.
14. Install battery output cable and nut to B+ terminal at top of alternator.
15. Install protective plastic cover to B+ stud at top of generator.

⁂ CAUTION

Never force a belt over a pulley rim using a screwdriver. The synthetic fiber of the belt can be damaged.

⁂ CAUTION

When installing a serpentine accessory drive belt, the belt MUST be routed correctly. The water pump will be rotating in the wrong direction if the belt is installed incorrectly, causing the engine to overheat. Refer to belt routing label in engine compartment.

16. Install alternator drive belt.
17. Install engine oil fill cap and engine oil dipstick.
18. Install plastic decorative engine cover. Cover snaps onto engine.
19. Connect negative battery cable.
20. Check charging system for proper operation.

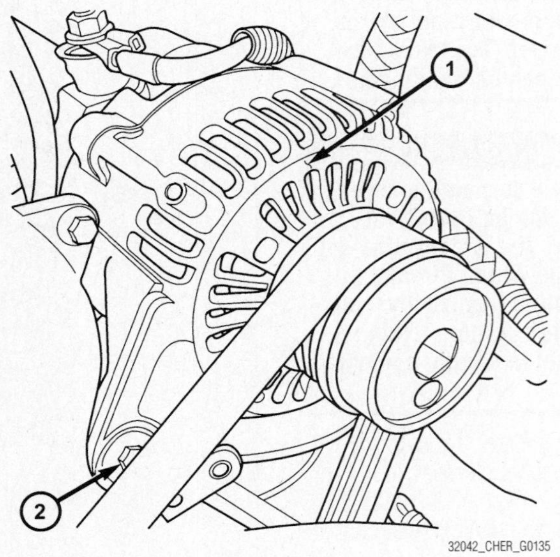

Fig. 52 Alternator mounting—Liberty with diesel engine

FIRING ORDER

See Figures 53 through 55.

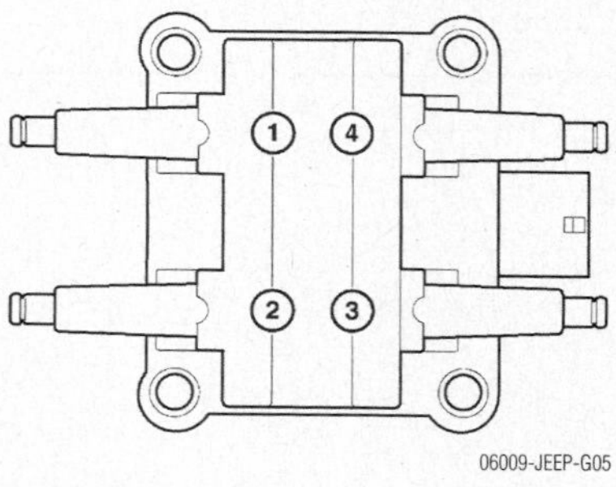

Fig. 53 2.4L Engine
Firing order: 1–3–4–2
Distributorless ignition system

Fig. 54 3.7L Engine
Firing order: 1–6–5–4–3–2
Distributorless ignition system

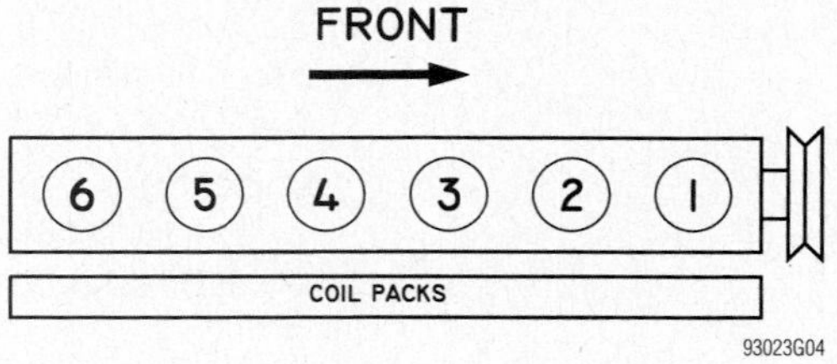

Fig. 55 4.0L Engine
Firing order: 1–5–3–6–2–4
Distributorless ignition system

IGNITION COIL

REMOVAL & INSTALLATION

2005–06 Wrangler

2.4L Engine

1. Disconnect electrical connector at rear of coil.
2. Remove all secondary cables from coil.
3. Remove 4 coil mounting bolts .
4. Remove coil from vehicle

To install:

5. Position coil to engine.
6. Install 4 mounting bolts.
7. Install secondary cables.
8. Install electrical connector at rear of coil.
9. Install air cleaner tube and housing.

4.0L Engine

See Figure 56.

A one-piece coil rail assembly containing three individual coils is used on the 4.0L engine. The coil rail must be replaced as one assembly. The bottom of the coil is equipped with 6 individual rubber boots to seal the 6 spark plugs to the coil. Inside each rubber boot is a spring. The spring is used for an electrical contact between the coil and the top of the spark plug. These rubber boots and springs are a permanent part of the coil and are not serviced separately.

1. Disconnect negative battery cable at battery.
2. The coil is bolted directly to the cylinder head.
3. Remove 4 coil mounting bolts .
4. Carefully pry up coil assembly from spark plugs. Do this by prying alternately at each end of coil until rubber boots have disengaged from all spark plugs. If boots will not release from spark plugs, use a commercially available spark plug boot removal tool. Twist and loosen a few boots from a few spark plugs to help remove coil.
5. After coil has cleared spark plugs, position coil for access to primary electrical connector. Disconnect connector from coil by pushing slide tab outwards to right side of vehicle . After slide tab has been positioned outwards, push in on secondary release lock on side of connector and pull connector from coil.
6. Remove coil from vehicle.

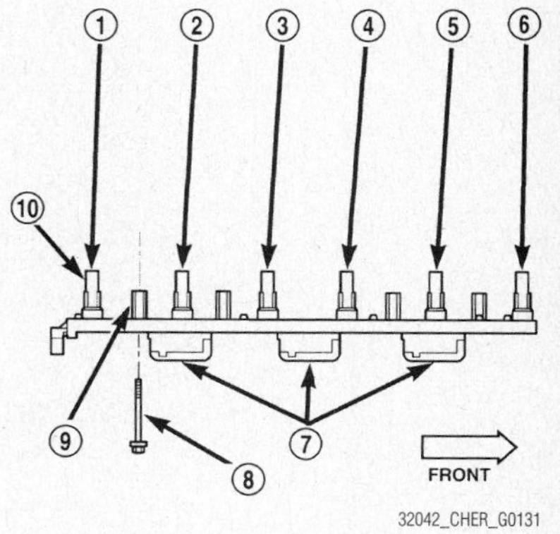

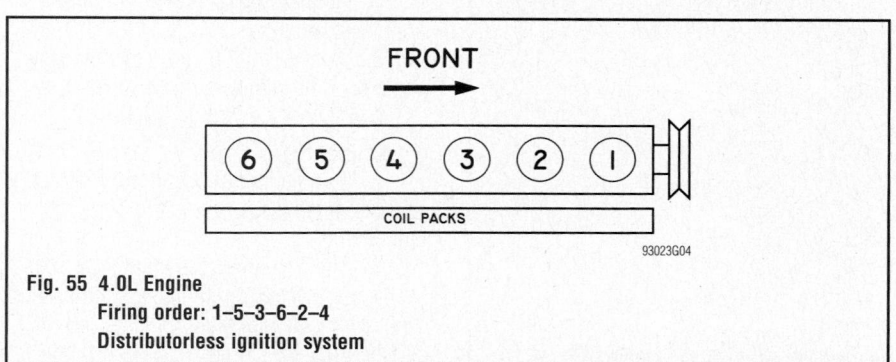

Fig. 56 The removal and installation of the ignition coil on the 4.0L engine

To install:

7. Connect engine harness connector to coil by snapping into position. Move slide tab towards engine for a positive lock.
8. Position ignition coil rubber boots to all spark plugs. Push down on coil assembly until bolt bases have contacted cylinder head.
9. Install 4 coil mounting bolts. Loosely tighten 4 bolts just enough to allow bolt bases to contact cylinder head. Do a final tightening of each bolt in steps down to 250 inch lbs. (29 Nm) torque. Do not apply full torque to any bolt first.
10. Connect negative battery cable to battery.

Liberty

2.4L Engine

See Figure 57.

1. Disconnect electrical connector at rear of coil.
2. Remove all secondary cables from coil.
3. Remove 4 coil mounting bolts .
4. Remove coil from vehicle.

To install:

5. Position coil to engine.
6. Install 4 mounting bolts.
7. Install secondary cables.
8. Install electrical connector at rear of coil.
9. Install air cleaner tube and housing.

3.7L Engine

See Figure 58.

An individual ignition coil is used for each spark plug . The coil fits into machined holes in the cylinder head. A mounting stud/nut secures each coil to the top of the intake manifold . The bottom of the coil is equipped with a rubber boot to seal the spark plug to the coil. Inside each rubber boot is a spring. The spring is used for a mechanical contact between the coil and the top of the spark plug. These rubber boots and springs are a permanent part of the coil and are not serviced separately. An O-ring is used to seal the coil at the opening into the cylinder head.

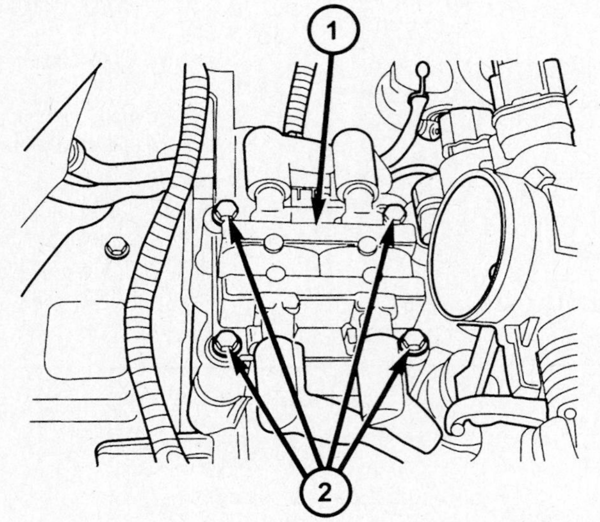

Fig. 58 3.7L ignition coil mounting bolts (2) for the Liberty

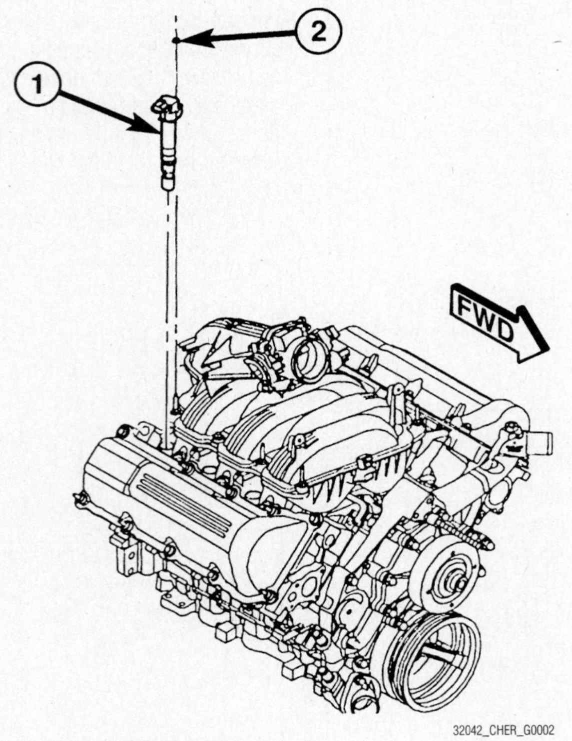

Fig. 57 Removal and installation of the 2.4L engine ignition coil (1) on the Liberty

1. Depending on which coil is being removed, the throttle body air intake tube or intake box may need to be removed to gain access to coil.
2. Disconnect electrical connector from coil by pushing downward on release lock on top of connector and pull connector from coil.
3. Clean area at base of coil with compressed air before removal.
4. Remove coil mounting nut from mounting stud.
5. Carefully pull up coil from cylinder head opening with a slight twisting action.
6. Remove coil from vehicle.

To install:

7. Using compressed air, blow out any dirt or contaminants from around top of spark plug.
8. Check condition of coil O-ring and replace as necessary. To aid in coil installation, apply silicone to coil O-ring.
9. Position ignition coil into cylinder

head opening and push onto spark plug. Do this while guiding coil base over mounting stud.

10. Install coil mounting stud nut.
11. Connect electrical connector to coil by snapping into position.
12. If necessary, install throttle body air tube or box.

IGNITION TIMING

ADJUSTMENT

Ignition timing is controlled by the Powertrain Control Module (PCM). No adjustment is possible.

SPARK PLUGS

REMOVAL & INSTALLATION

2.4L Engine

➡If spark plug for no. 2 or no. 3 cylinder is being removed, throttle body must be removed.

1. Remove air cleaner tube and housing.
2. Twist secondary cable at cylinder head to break loose at spark plug. Remove cable from plug.
3. Prior to removing spark plug, spray compressed air into cylinder head opening. This will help prevent foreign material from entering combustion chamber.
4. Remove spark plug from cylinder head using a quality socket with a rubber or foam insert.
5. Inspect spark plug condition.

To install:

⁂ CAUTION

Spark plug tightening on the 2.4L is torque critical. The plugs are equipped with tapered seats. Do not exceed 15 ft. lbs. (20 Nm) torque.

6. Special care should be taken when installing spark plugs into the cylinder head spark plug wells. Be sure the plugs do not drop into the plug wells as electrodes can be damaged.
7. Always tighten spark plugs to the specified torque. Over tightening can cause distortion resulting in a change in the spark plug gap or a cracked porcelain insulator.
8. Start the spark plug into the cylinder head by hand to avoid cross threading.
9. Tighten spark plugs.
10. Install throttle body.
11. Install air cleaner tube and housing.

3.7L Engine

➡ Each individual spark plug is located under each ignition coil. Each individual ignition coil must be removed to gain access to each spark plug

1. Prior to removing ignition coil, spray compressed air around coil base at cylinder head.
2. Prior to removing spark plug, spray compressed air into cylinder head opening. This will help prevent foreign material from entering combustion chamber.
3. Remove spark plug from cylinder head using a quality socket with a rubber or foam insert. Also check condition of ignition coil O-ring and replace as necessary.
4. Inspect spark plug condition.

To install:

➡Special care should be taken when installing spark plugs into the cylinder head spark plug wells. Be sure the plugs do not drop into the plug wells as electrodes can be damaged.

➡Always tighten spark plugs to the specified torque. Over tightening can cause distortion resulting in a change in the spark plug gap or a cracked porcelain insulator.

5. Start the spark plug into the cylinder head by hand to avoid cross threading.
6. Tighten spark plugs.
7. Before installing coil(s), check condition of coil O-ring and replace as necessary. To aid in coil installation, apply silicone to coil O-ring.
8. Install ignition coil(s).

4.0L Engine

➡On the 4.0L 6-cylinder engine the spark plugs are located below the coil rail assembly.

1. Prior to removing the spark plug, spray compressed air around the spark plug hole and the area around the spark plug. This will help prevent foreign material from entering the combustion chamber.
2. Remove the spark plug using a quality socket with a rubber or foam insert.
3. Inspect the spark plug condition.

To install:

4. Always tighten spark plugs to the specified torque. Over tightening can cause distortion. This may result in a change in the spark plug gap, or a cracked porcelain insulator.
5. When replacing the spark plug and ignition coil cables, route the cables correctly and secure them in the appropriate retainers. Failure to route the cables properly can cause the radio to reproduce ignition noise. It could cause cross ignition of the spark plugs, or short circuit the cables to ground.
6. Start the spark plug into the cylinder head by hand to avoid cross threading.
7. Tighten the spark plugs to 26–30 ft. lbs. (35–41 Nm) torque.
8. Install coil rail.

STARTER

REMOVAL & INSTALLATION

2005–06 Wrangler

2.4L Engine

See Figure 59.

1. Disconnect and isolate negative battery cable.
2. Raise and support vehicle.
3. While supporting starter motor, remove two bolts securing starter motor to transmission .
4. Lower starter motor far enough to access and remove nut securing battery cable to starter solenoid B(+) terminal stud . Always support starter motor during this process. Do not let starter motor hang from wire harness.
5. Remove battery cable at starter.
6. Disconnect solenoid terminal wire harness connector from starter solenoid.
7. Remove starter motor.

To install:

8. Connect solenoid terminal wire harness connector to starter solenoid. Always support starter motor during this process. Do not let starter motor hang from wire harness.
9. Install battery cable eyelet onto starter solenoid stud.
10. Position starter motor to transmission. Install and tighten 2 bolts.
11. Lower vehicle.
12. Connect negative battery cable.

4.0L Engine

See Figures 60 and 61.

1. Disconnect and isolate negative battery cable.
2. Raise and support vehicle.
3. 4.0L With Manual Transmission: Remove lower bolt (forward facing) securing starter motor to transmission housing .
4. 4.0L With Manual Transmission: While supporting starter motor, remove upper bolt (rearward facing) securing starter motor to transmission housing.
5. 4.0L With 42 RLE Automatic Transmission: Remove 2 starter mounting bolts.
6. Lower starter motor from front of transmission housing far enough to access and remove nut securing battery to starter solenoid. Always support starter motor during this process. Do not let starter motor hang from wire harness.
7. Remove battery cable at starter solenoid.
8. Disconnect solenoid terminal wire harness connector from starter solenoid.
9. Remove starter motor from transmission housing.

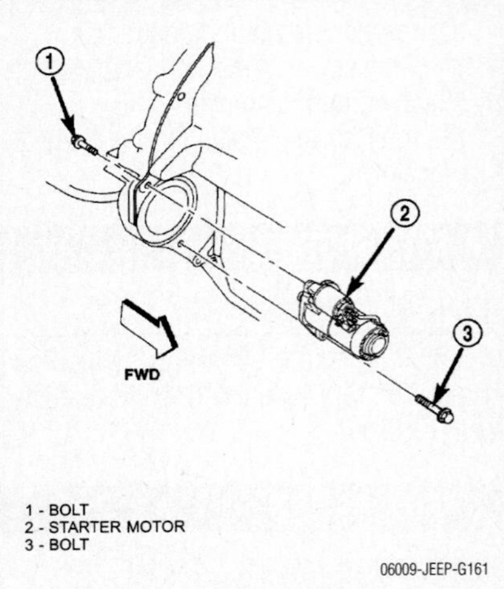

Fig. 60 Starter mounting—4.0L engine w/manual transmission

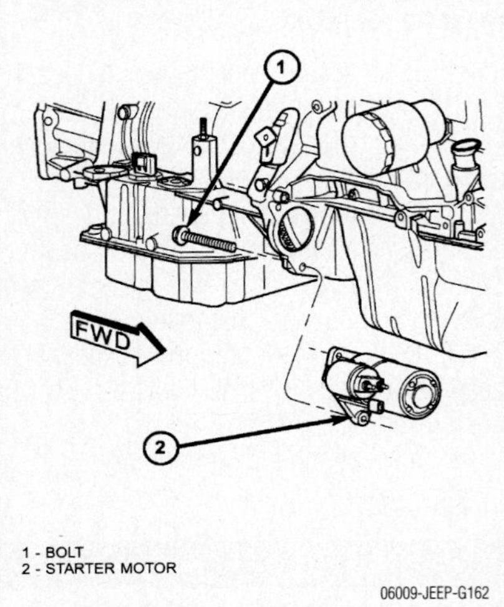

Fig. 61 Starter mounting—4.0L engine w/42RLE automatic transmission

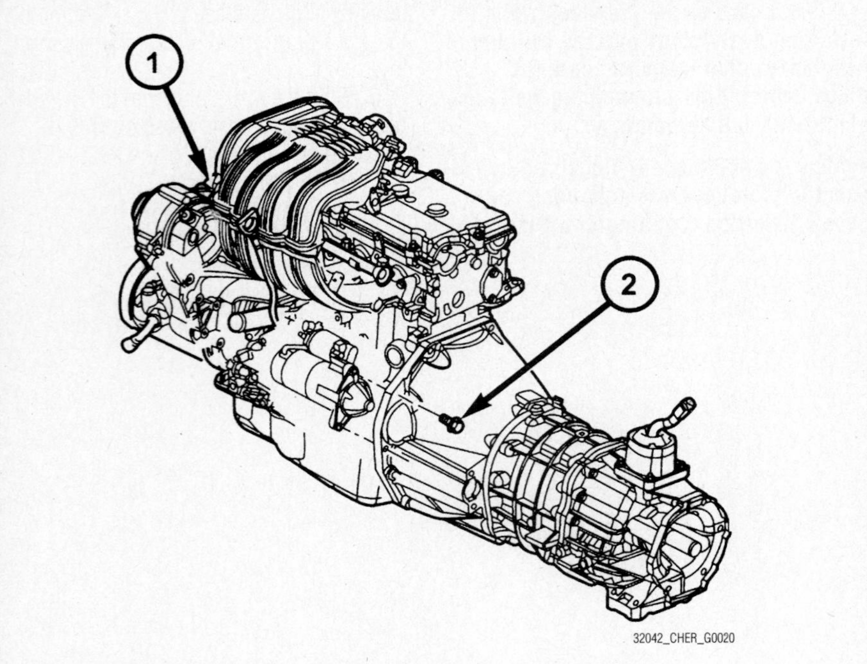

Fig. 59 Starter position for the 2.4L engine

To install:

10. Connect solenoid terminal wire harness connector to starter solenoid. Always support starter motor during this process. Do not let starter motor hang from wire harness.
11. Install battery cable eyelet onto starter solenoid stud.
12. Position starter motor to transmission housing Loosely install two mounting bolts.
13. Tighten upper (rearward facing) mounting bolt to 35 ft. lbs. (47.5 Nm).
14. Tighten lower (forward facing) mounting bolt to 30 ft. lbs. (40.7 Nm).
15. Lower vehicle.
16. Connect negative battery cable.

Liberty

2.4L Engine

1. Disconnect and isolate negative battery cable.
2. Raise and support vehicle.
3. Remove solenoid wire from solenoid terminal.
4. Remove battery cable from stud on starter solenoid .
5. Remove 2 starter mounting bolts and remove starter from vehicle.

To install:

6. Position starter into bell housing and install 2 bolts.
7. Install battery cable and nut to stud on starter solenoid.
8. Install solenoid wire connector to solenoid terminal.
9. Lower vehicle.
10. Connect negative battery cable.

2.8L Engine

1. Disconnect and isolate negative battery cable.
2. Raise and support vehicle.
3. Disconnect solenoid wire connector from solenoid terminal
4. Remove battery cable from stud on starter solenoid.
5. Remove 3 starter mounting bolts.
6. Remove starter from transmission bellhousing.

To install:

7. Position starter motor to transmission housing.
8. Connect battery cable solenoid terminal wire harness connector to connector receptacle on starter solenoid. Always support starter motor during this process. Do not let starter motor hang from wire harness.
9. Install battery cable eyelet terminal onto solenoid B(+) terminal stud.
10. Install nut securing battery cable eyelet terminal to starter solenoid B(+) terminal stud.
11. Refer to torque specifications.
12. Position starter motor and install 3 bolts. Tighten 3 bolts in this sequence: top bolt, bottom bolt, middle bolt. Refer to torque specifications.
13. Lower vehicle.
14. Connect negative battery cable.

3.7L Engine

See Figure 62.

1. Disconnect and isolate negative battery cable.
2. Raise and support vehicle.
3. Remove 2 flange bolts securing left exhaust downpipe to crossover pipe. Lower pipe slightly to allow front propeller shaft removal.
4. Remove front propeller shaft.
5. Remove 2 starter heat shield bolts at side of starter.
6. Remove starter heat shield nut at front of starter.
7. Remove starter heat shield.
8. Remove solenoid wire from solenoid terminal.
9. Remove battery cable from stud on starter solenoid.
10. Remove 2 starter mounting bolts.
11. Position front of starter to face rear of vehicle.

Rotate starter until solenoid position is located below starter.

12. Remove starter from vehicle by passing it between exhaust pipe and transmission bell housing.

To install:

13. Position front of starter towards rear of vehicle with solenoid position rotated until it is located below starter. Install starter by passing it between exhaust pipe and transmission bell housing.
14. Position starter into bell housing and install 2 bolts.
15. Install battery cable and nut to stud on starter solenoid.
16. Install solenoid wire connector to solenoid terminal.
17. Position starter heat shield and install nut at front of starter.
18. Install 2 starter heat shield bolts at side of starter.
19. Install front propeller shaft.
20. Install 2 flange bolts securing left exhaust down-pipe to crossover pipe.
21. Lower vehicle.
22. Connect negative battery cable.

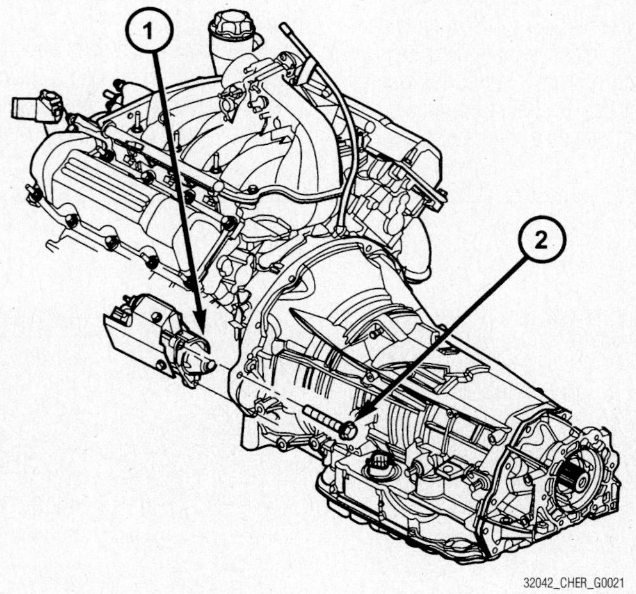

Fig. 62 The starter position for the 3.7L engine

ENGINE MECHANICAL

➡Disconnecting the negative battery cable may interfere with the functions of the on board computer systems and may require the computer to undergo a relearning process, once the negative battery cable is reconnected.

ACCESSORY DRIVE BELTS

ACCESSORY BELT ROUTING

See Figures 63 through 65.

INSPECTION

See Figure 66.

Although many manufacturers recommend that the drive belt(s) be inspected every 30,000 miles (48,000 km) or more, it is really a good idea to check them at least once a year, or at every major fluid change. Whichever interval you choose, the belts should be checked for wear or damage. Obviously, a damaged drive belt can cause problems should it give way while the vehicle is in operation. But, improper length belts (too short or long), as well as excessively worn belts, can also cause problems. Loose accessory drive belts can lead to poor engine cooling and diminished output from the alternator, air conditioning compressor or power steering pump. A belt that is too tight places a severe strain on the driven unit and can wear out bearings quickly.

Serpentine drive belts should be inspected for rib chunking (pieces of the ribs breaking off), severe glazing, frayed cords or other visible damage. Any belt which is missing sections of 2 or more adjacent ribs which are ½ inches. (13mm) or longer must be replaced. You might want to note that serpentine belts do tend to form small cracks across the backing. If the only wear you find is in the form of one or more cracks are across the backing and NOT parallel to the ribs, the belt is still good and does not need to be replaced.

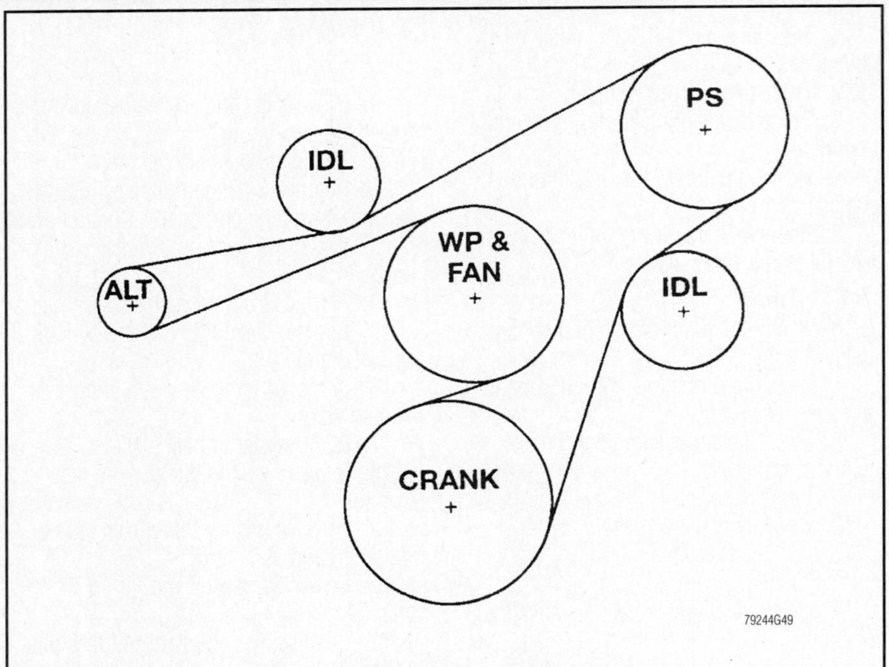

Fig. 64 Accessory serpentine belt routing—2.4L and 4.0L engines

Fig. 63 Often the underhood label will display the serpentine drive belt routing

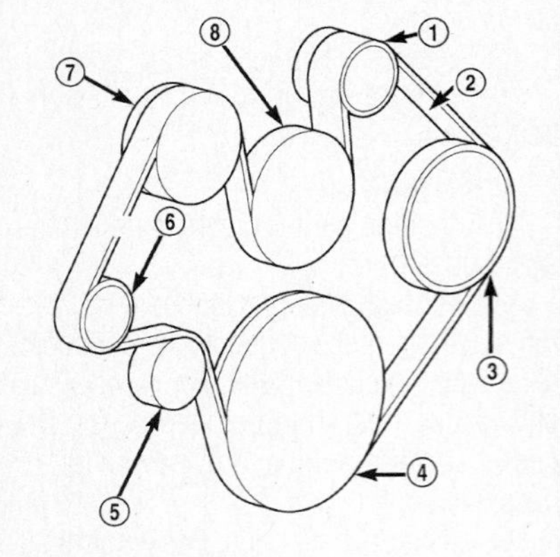

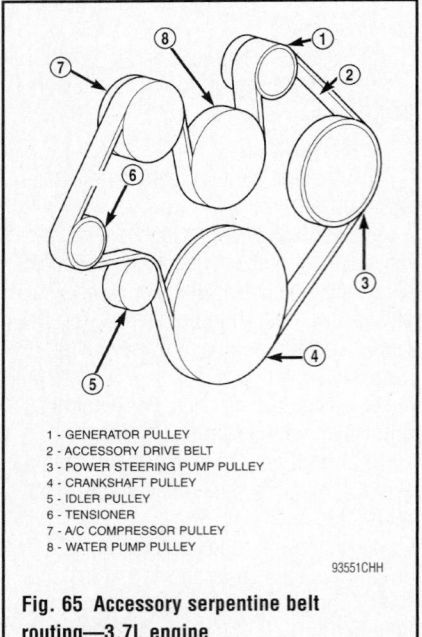

1 - GENERATOR PULLEY
2 - ACCESSORY DRIVE BELT
3 - POWER STEERING PUMP PULLEY
4 - CRANKSHAFT PULLEY
5 - IDLER PULLEY
6 - TENSIONER
7 - A/C COMPRESSOR PULLEY
8 - WATER PUMP PULLEY

93551CHH

Fig. 65 Accessory serpentine belt routing—3.7L engine

ADJUSTMENT

See Figure 66.

Periodic drive belt tensioning is not necessary, because an automatic spring-loaded tensioner is used with these belts to maintain proper adjustment at all times. The tensioner is also useful as a wear indicator. When the belt is properly installed, the arrow on the tensioner housing must point within the acceptable range lines on the tensioner's face. If the arrow falls outside the range, either an improper belt has been installed or the belt is worn beyond its useful life span. In either case, a new belt must be installed immediately to assure proper engine operation and to prevent possible accessory damage.

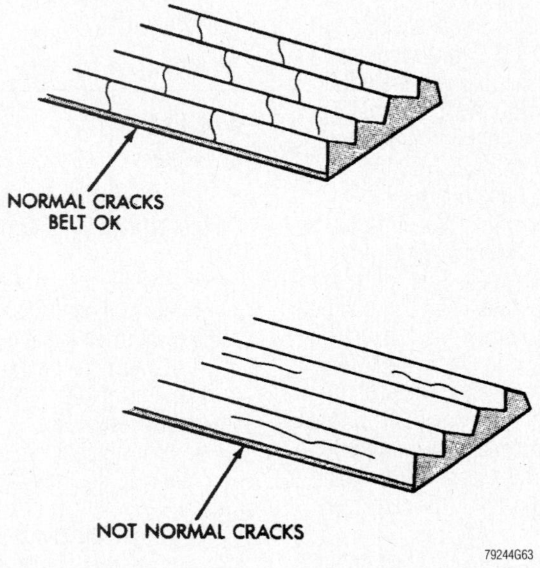

Fig. 66 Typical wear patterns for a serpentine drive belt

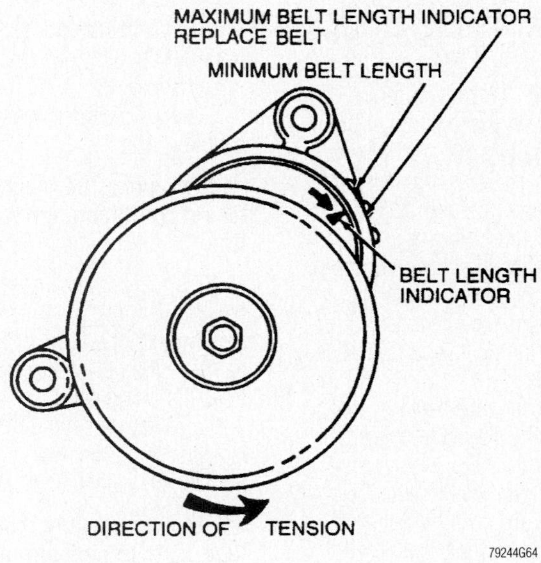

Fig. 67 Typical drive belt automatic tensioner wear indicator

REMOVAL & INSTALLATION

2.4L Engine

➡The belt routing schematics are published from the latest information available at the time of publication. If anything differs between these schematics and the Belt Routing Label, use the schematics on Belt Routing Label. This label is located in the engine compartment.

⁂ CAUTION

Do not let tensioner arm snap back to the free arm position, as severe damage may occur to the tensioner.

➡Belt tension is not adjustable. Belt adjustment is maintained by an automatic (spring load) belt tensioner

1. Disconnect negative battery cable from battery.
2. Rotate belt tensioner until it contacts its stop. Remove belt, then slowly rotate the tensioner into the free-arm position.

To install:

3. Check condition of all pulleys.

⁂ CAUTION

When installing the serpentine accessory drive belt, the belt MUST be routed correctly. If not, the engine may overheat due to the water pump rotating in the wrong direction.

4. Install new belt. Route the belt around all pulleys except the idler pulley. Rotate the tensioner arm until it contacts its stop position. Route the belt around the idler and slowly let the tensioner rotate into the belt. Make sure the belt is seated onto all pulleys.
5. With the drive belt installed, inspect the belt wear indicator. On 2.4L Engines the gap between the tang and the housing stop (measurement A) must not exceed 24 mm (.94 inches).

2.8L Diesel Engine

1. Disconnect negative battery cable.
2. Rotate belt tensioner until it contacts its stop. Remove belt, then slowly rotate the tensioner into the free arm position.

To install:

3. Check condition of all pulleys.

⁂ CAUTION

When installing the serpentine accessory drive belt, the belt MUST be routed correctly. If not, the engine may overheat due to the water pump rotating in the wrong direction.

4. Install new belt. Route the belt around all pulleys except the idler pulley. Rotate the

tensioner arm until it contacts its stop position. Route the belt around the idler and slowly let the tensioner rotate into the belt. Make sure the belt is seated onto all pulleys.

3.7L Engine

1. Disconnect negative battery cable from battery.
2. Rotate belt tensioner until it contacts its stop. Remove belt, then slowly rotate the tensioner into the free arm position.

To install:

3. Check condition of all pulleys.

✱✱ CAUTION

When installing the serpentine accessory drive belt, the belt MUST be routed correctly. If not, the engine may overheat due to the water pump rotating in the wrong direction.

4. Install new belt . Route the belt around all pulleys except the idler pulley. Rotate the tensioner arm until it contacts its stop position. Route the belt around the idler and slowly let the tensioner rotate into the belt. Make sure the belt is seated onto all pulleys.
5. With the drive belt installed, inspect the belt wear indicator. On 3.7L engines the gap between the tang and the housing stop (measurement A) must not exceed 24 mm (.94 inches).

4.0L Engine

Because serpentine belts use a spring loaded tensioner for adjustment, belt replacement tends to be somewhat easier than it used to be on engines where accessories were pivoted and bolted in place for tension adjustment. Basically, all belt replacement involves is to pivot the tensioner to loosen the belt, then slide the belt off of the pulleys. The two most important points are to pay CLOSE attention to the proper belt routing (since serpentine belts tend to be "snaked" all different ways through the pulleys) and to make sure the V-ribs are properly seated in all the pulleys.

Although belt routing diagrams have been included in this section, the first places you should check for proper belt routing are the labels in your engine compartment. These should include a belt routing diagram which may reflect changes made during a production run.

1. Disconnect the negative battery cable for safety. This will help assure that no one mistakenly cranks the engine over with your hands between the pulleys, and that the cooling fan cannot activate while servicing the belt(s).

➡Take a good look at the installed belt and make a note of the routing. Before removing the belt, make sure the routing matches that of the belt routing label or one of the diagrams in this book. If for some reason a diagram does not match (you may not have the original engine or it may have been modified), carefully note the changes on a piece of paper.

2. For tensioners equipped with a ½ in. (13mm) square hole, insert the drive end of a large breaker bar into the hole. Use the breaker bar to pivot the tensioner away from the drive belt. For tensioners not equipped with this hole, use the proper-sized socket and breaker bar (or a large handled wrench) on the tensioner idler pulley center bolt to pivot the tensioner away from the belt. This will loosen the belt sufficiently that it can be pulled off of one or more of the pulleys. It is usually easiest to carefully pull the belt out from underneath the tensioner pulley itself.
3. Once the belt is off one of the pulleys, gently pivot the tensioner back into position. DO NOT allow the tensioner to snap back, as this could damage the tensioner's internal parts.
4. Now finish removing the belt from the other pulleys and remove it from the engine.

To install:

5. While referring to the proper routing diagram (which you identified earlier), begin to route the belt over the pulleys, leaving whichever pulley you first released it from for last.
6. Once the belt is mostly in place, carefully pivot the tensioner and position the belt over the final pulley. As you begin to allow the tensioner back into contact with the belt, run your hand around the pulleys and make sure the belt is properly seated in the ribs. If not, release the tension and seat the belt.
7. Once the belt is installed, take another look at all the pulleys to double check your installation.
8. Connect the negative battery cable, then start and run the engine to check belt operation.
9. When the engine has reached normal operating temperature, turn the ignition **OFF** and check that the belt tensioner arrow is within the proper adjustment range.

CAMSHAFT AND VALVE LIFTERS

INSPECTION

1. Inspect the camshaft bearing journals for wear or damage.
2. Inspect the cylinder head and check oil return holes.
3. Check the tooth surface of the distributor drive gear teeth of the right camshaft for wear or damage.
4. Check both camshaft surfaces for wear or damage.
5. Check camshaft lobe height and replace if out of limit.

REMOVAL & INSTALLATION

2.4L Engine

See Figures 68 through 70.

1. Before servicing the vehicle, refer to the precautions in the beginning of this section.
2. Remove the cylinder head cover.
3. Remove the camshaft position sensor and camshaft target magnet.
4. Remove the timing belt.
5. Remove the camshaft sprockets and timing belt rear cover.
6. Bearing caps are identified for location. Remove the outside bearing caps first.
7. Loosen the camshaft bearing cap attaching fasteners in the sequence shown, one camshaft at a time.

➡Camshafts are not interchangeable. The intake cam number 6 thrust bearing face spacing is wider.

8. Identify the camshafts before removing from the head. The camshafts are not interchangeable.
9. Remove the camshafts from the cylinder head.

➡If removing the rocker arms, identify for reinstallation in the original position.

10. Inspect the camshaft bearing journals for damage and binding. If the journals are binding, check the cylinder head for damage. Also the check cylinder head oil holes for clogging.
11. Check the cam lobe and bearing surfaces for abnormal wear and damage. Replace the camshaft if defective.

➡If the camshaft is replaced due to lobe wear or damage, always replace the rocker arms.

12. Measure the lobe actual wear

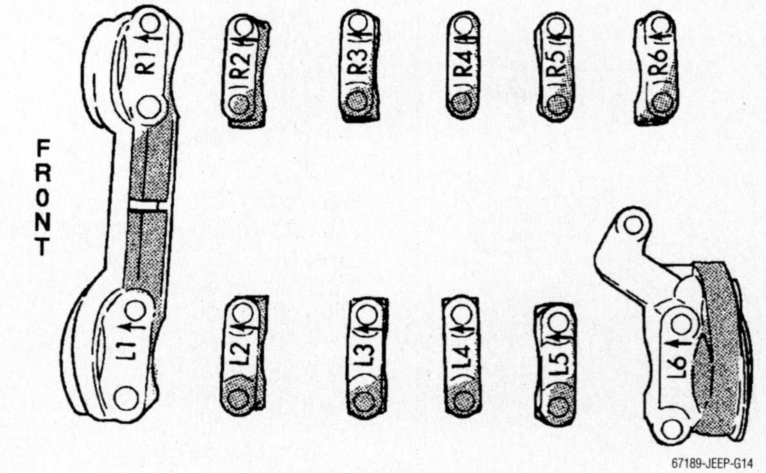

Fig. 68 Camshaft bearing cap identification—2.4L engines

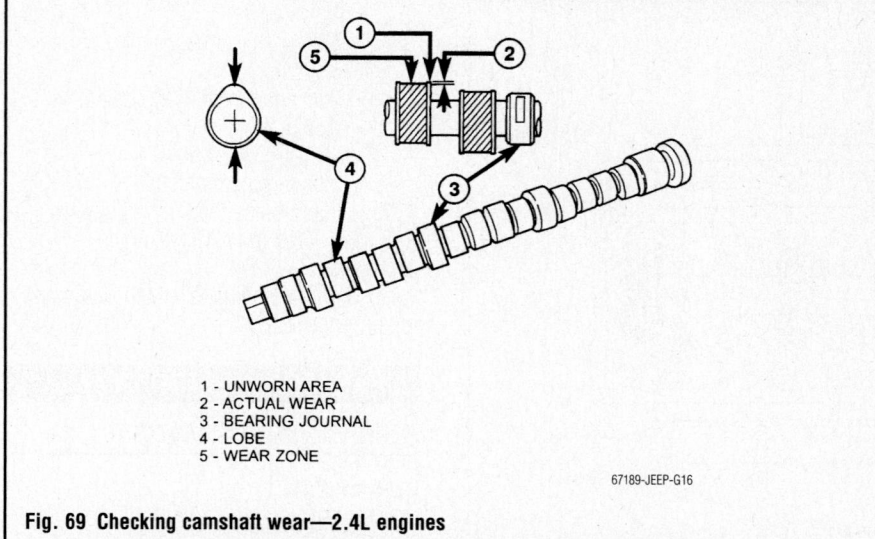

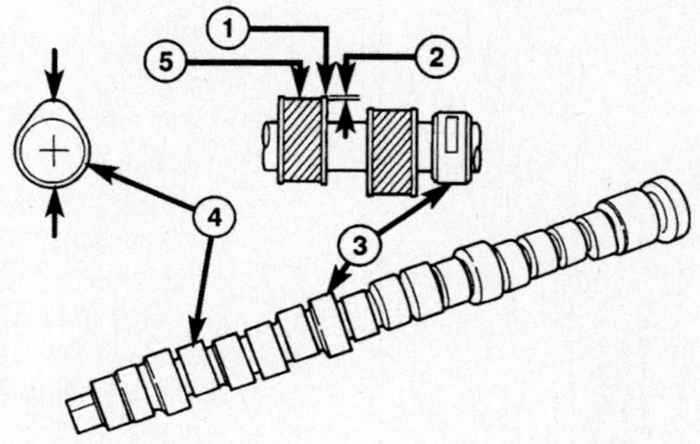

Fig. 69 Checking camshaft wear—2.4L engines

(unworn area minus wear zone = actual wear) and replace the camshaft if out of limit. Standard value is 0.001 inches (0.0254 mm), wear limit is 0.010 inches (0.254 mm).

To install:

➡Ensure that NONE of the pistons are at top dead center when installing the camshafts.

13. Lubricate all camshaft bearing journals, rocker arms and camshaft lobes.
14. Install all rocker arms in original positions, if reused.
15. Position the camshafts on cylinder head bearing journals. Install the right and left camshaft bearing caps No. 2—5 and right No. 6. Tighten M6 fasteners to 105 inch lbs. (12 Nm) in the sequence shown.
16. Apply Mopar® Gasket Maker, or equivalent, to the No. 1 and No. 6 bearing caps. Install the bearing caps and tighten the M8 fasteners to 250 inch lbs. (28 Nm).
17. Install the camshaft oil seals.
18. Install the camshaft target magnet and camshaft position sensor.
19. Install the cylinder head cover.
20. Install the timing belt rear cover and camshaft sprocket.
21. Install the timing belt.

3.7L Engine

See Figures 71 and 72.

1. Before servicing the vehicle, refer to the precautions in the beginning of this section.
2. Remove or disconnect the following:
   - Negative battery cable
   - Cylinder head covers
   - Rocker arms
   - Hydraulic lash adjusters

➡Keep all valvetrain components in order for assembly.

3. Set the engine at Top Dead Center (TDC) of the compression stroke for the No. 1 cylinder.
4. Install Timing Chain Wedge 8379 to retain the chain tensioners.
5. Matchmark the timing chains to the camshaft sprockets.
6. Install Camshaft Holding Tool 8428 to the left camshaft sprocket.
7. Remove or disconnect the following:
   - Right camshaft timing sprocket and target wheel
   - Left camshaft sprocket
   - Camshaft bearing caps, by reversing the tightening sequence
   - Camshafts

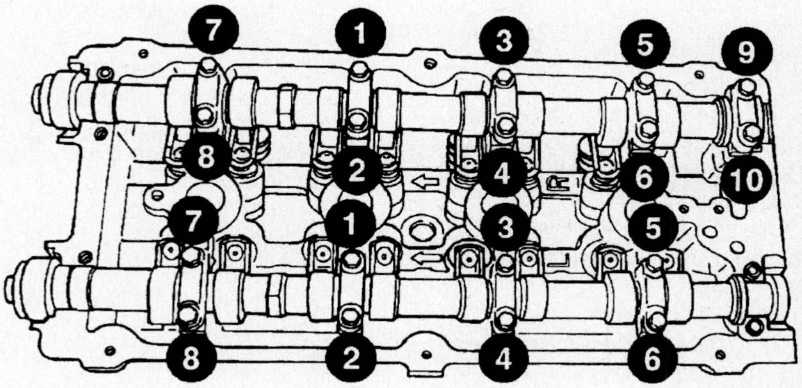

Fig. 70 Camshaft bearing cap torque sequence—2.4L engines

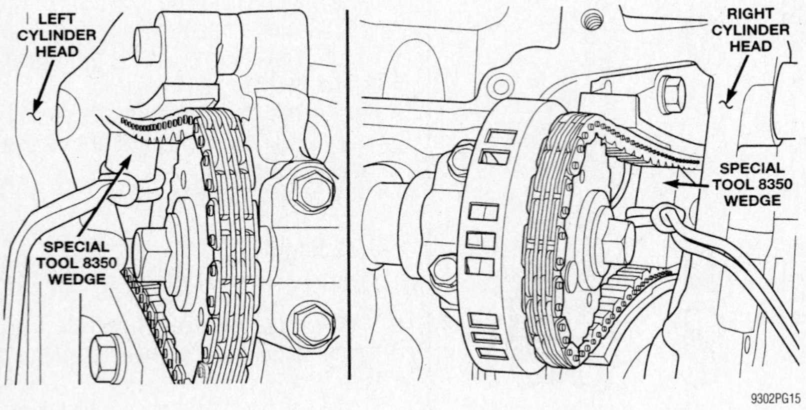

Fig. 71 Chain Tensioner Retaining Wedges—3.7L Engine

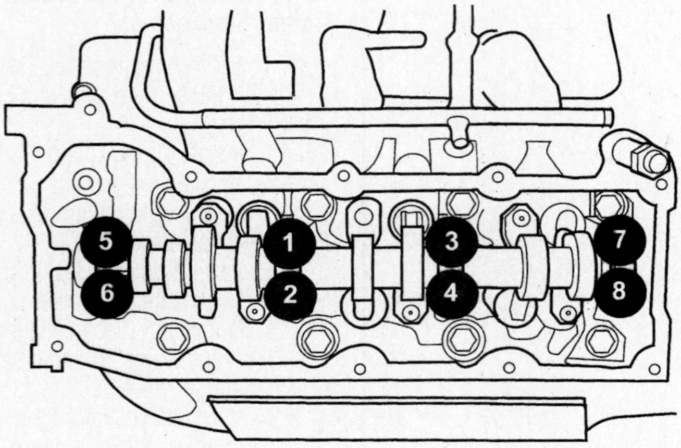

Fig. 72 Camshaft bearing cap bolt tightening sequence—3.7L

To install:

8. Install or connect the following:
   - Camshafts. Torque the bearing cap bolts in ½ turn increments, in sequence, to 100 inch lbs. (11 Nm).
   - Target wheel to the right camshaft
   - Camshaft timing sprockets and chains, by aligning the matchmarks
9. Remove the tensioner wedges and tighten the camshaft sprocket bolts to 90 ft. lbs. (122 Nm).
10. Install or connect the following:
    - Hydraulic lash adjusters in their original locations
    - Rocker arms in their original locations
    - Cylinder head covers
    - Negative battery cable

4.0L Engine

1. Before servicing the vehicle, refer to the precautions in the beginning of this section.
2. Drain the cooling system.
3. Recover the A/C refrigerant, if equipped with air conditioning.
4. Remove or disconnect the following:
   - Negative battery cable
   - Grille, if necessary
   - Radiator
   - A/C condenser, if equipped
   - Distributor or camshaft sensor housing
   - Valve cover

➡Keep all valvetrain components in order for assembly.

   - Rocker arms and pushrods
   - Cylinder head
   - Hydraulic valve tappets
   - Accessory drive belt
   - Crankshaft damper
   - Front cover
   - Timing chain and gears
   - Thrust plate
   - Camshaft

To install:

5. Lubricate the camshaft with clean engine oil.
6. Install or connect the following:
   - Camshaft
   - Thrust plate. Torque the bolts to 18 ft. lbs. (24 Nm).
   - Timing chain and gears
   - Front cover
   - Crankshaft damper
   - Accessory drive belt
   - Hydraulic valve tappets
   - Cylinder head
   - Rocker arms and pushrods
   - Valve cover
   - Distributor or camshaft sensor housing
   - A/C condenser, if equipped
   - Radiator
   - Grille, if removed
   - Negative battery cable
7. Fill and bleed the cooling system.
8. Recharge the A/C system, if equipped.
9. Start the engine, check for leaks and repair if necessary.

CRANKSHAFT FRONT SEAL

REMOVAL & INSTALLATION

2.4L Engine

See Figures 73 through 77.

1. Before servicing the vehicle, refer to the precautions in the beginning of this section.

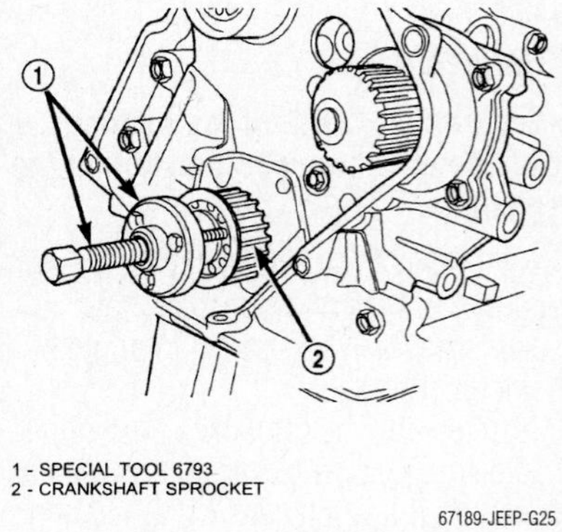

Fig. 73 Crankshaft sprocket removal—2.4L engines

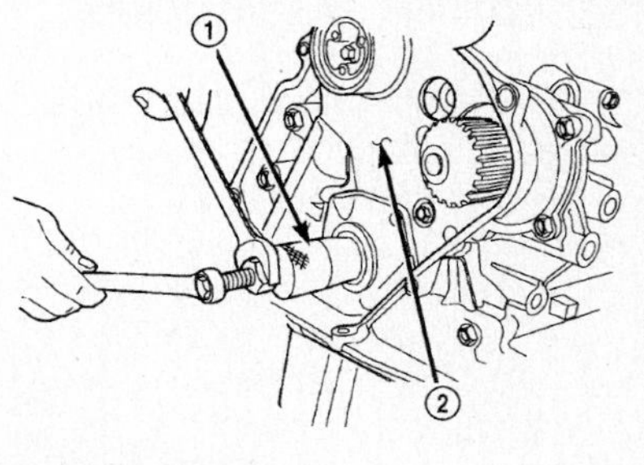

1 - SPECIAL TOOL 6771
2 - REAR TIMING BELT COVER

67189-JEEP-G26

Fig. 74 Front crankshaft seal removal—2.4L engines

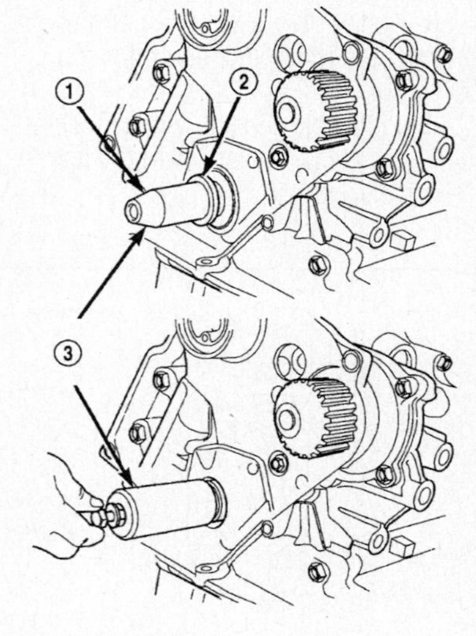

1 - PROTECTOR
2 - SEAL
3 - SPECIAL TOOL 6780

67189-JEEP-G28

Fig. 75 Front crankshaft seal installation—2.4L engines

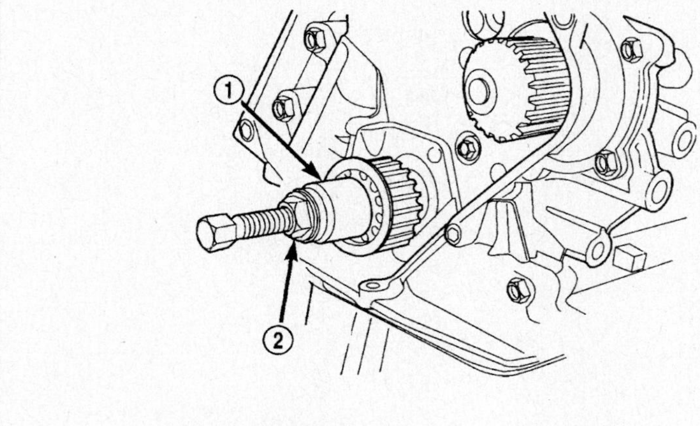

1 - SPECIAL TOOL 6792
2 - TIGHTEN NUT TO INSTALL

67189-JEEP-G27

Fig. 76 Crankshaft sprocket installation—2.4L engines

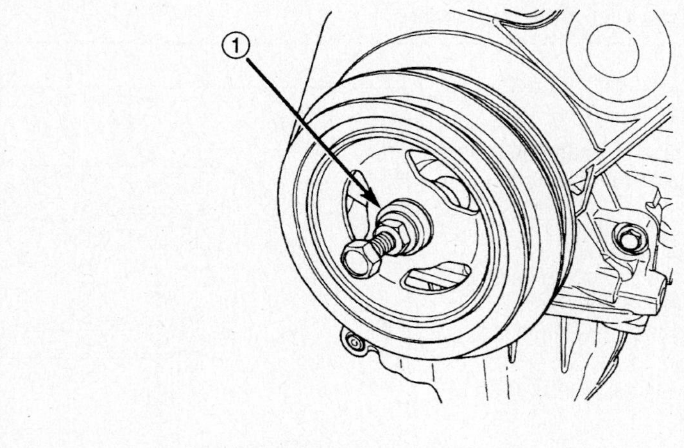

1 - SPECIAL TOOL 6792

67189-JEEP-G29

Fig. 77 Crankshaft damper installation—2.4L engines

2. Remove the crankshaft vibration damper.
3. Remove timing belt.
4. Remove crankshaft sprocket using Special Tool 6793 and insert C-4685-C2, or equivalent.

➡Do not nick shaft seal surface or seal bore.

5. Using Tool 6771, or equivalent, remove front crankshaft oil seal. Be careful not to damage the seal surface of cover.

To install:

6. Install new seal by using Special Tool 6780, or equivalent.
7. Place seal into opening with seal spring towards the inside of engine. Install seal until flush with cover.
8. Install crankshaft sprocket using Special Tool 6792, or equivalent.
9. Install timing belt.
10. Install crankshaft vibration damper.

CYLINDER HEAD

REMOVAL & INSTALLATION

2.4L Engine

See Figures 78 through 81.

1. Before servicing the vehicle, refer to the precautions in the beginning of this section.
2. Perform fuel system pressure release procedure before attempting any repairs.
3. Disconnect the battery negative cable.
4. Drain the cooling system.
5. Remove air filter housing and inlet tube.
6. Remove the intake manifold.
7. Remove the heater tube support bracket from the cylinder head.
8. Disconnect the radiator upper and heater supply hoses from the water outlet connections.
9. Remove the accessory drive belts.
10. Raise the vehicle and remove the exhaust pipe from the manifold.
11. Remove the power steering pump and set aside. Do not disconnect lines.
12. Remove the accessory drive bracket.
13. Remove the ignition coil and wires from the engine.
14. Disconnect the cam sensor and fuel injector wiring connectors.
15. Remove the timing belt and camshaft sprockets.
16. Remove the timing belt idler pulley and rear timing belt cover.

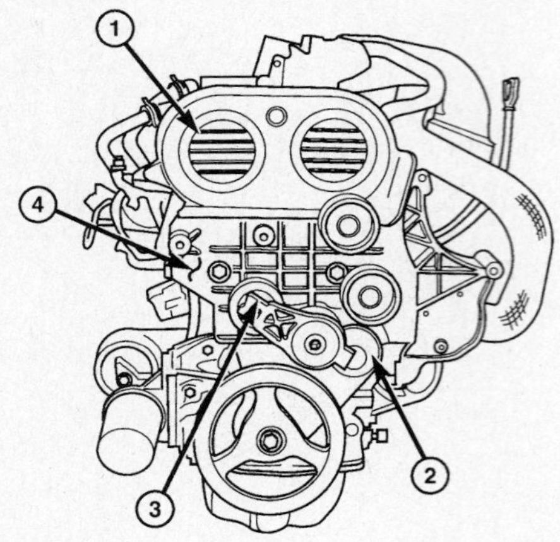

1- UPPER TIMING BELT COVER
2- LOWER TIMING BELT COVER
3- BELT TENSIONER
4- ACCESSORY DRIVE BRACKET

67189-JEEP-G06

Fig. 78 Accessory drive belt bracket—2.4L engines

17. Remove the cylinder head cover.
18. Remove camshafts.

➡Identify the rocker arm positions to ensure correct installation in original position, if reused.

19. Remove the rocker arms.
20. Remove the cylinder head bolts in reverse of the tightening sequence.
21. Remove the cylinder head from the engine block.
22. Inspect and clean the cylinder head.

To install:

➡The cylinder head bolts should be examined before reuse. If the threads are necked down, the bolts must be replaced.

23. Before installing the bolts, the threads should be coated with engine oil.
24. Position the cylinder head gasket on the engine block.

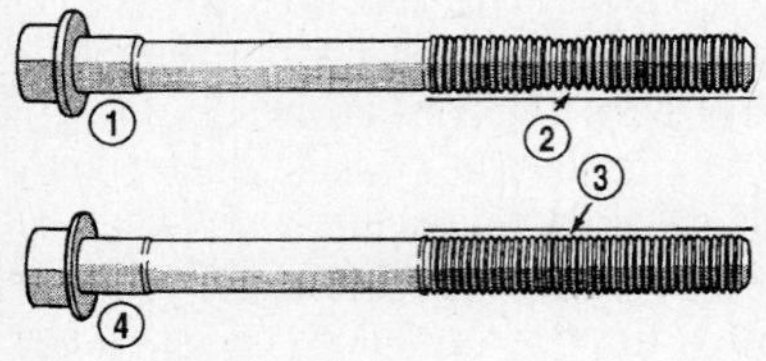

1 - STRETCHED BOLT
2 - THREADS ARE NOT STRAIGHT ON LINE
3 - THREADS ARE STRAIGHT ON LINE
4 - UNSTRETCHED BOLT

67189-JEEP-G07

Fig. 79 Checking the head bolts for stretching—2.4L engines

25. Install the cylinder head on the engine block.
26. Tighten the cylinder head bolts in the sequence shown. Tighten in 4 steps:
    - First: 25 ft. lbs. (34 Nm)
    - Second: 50 ft. lbs. (68 Nm)
    - Third: 50 ft. lbs. (68 Nm)
    - Fourth: an additional ¼ turn
27. Install the rocker arms.
28. Install the camshafts.
29. Install the cylinder head cover.
30. Install the timing belt rear cover and timing belt idler pulley.
31. Install the timing belt and camshaft sprockets.
32. Connect the cam sensor and fuel injectors wiring connectors.
33. Install the ignition coil and wires. Connect the ignition coil wiring connector.
34. Install the accessory drive bracket.
35. Install the power steering pump to the cylinder head.

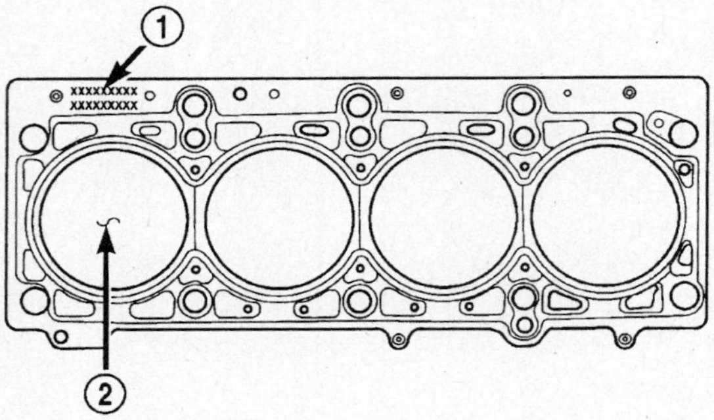

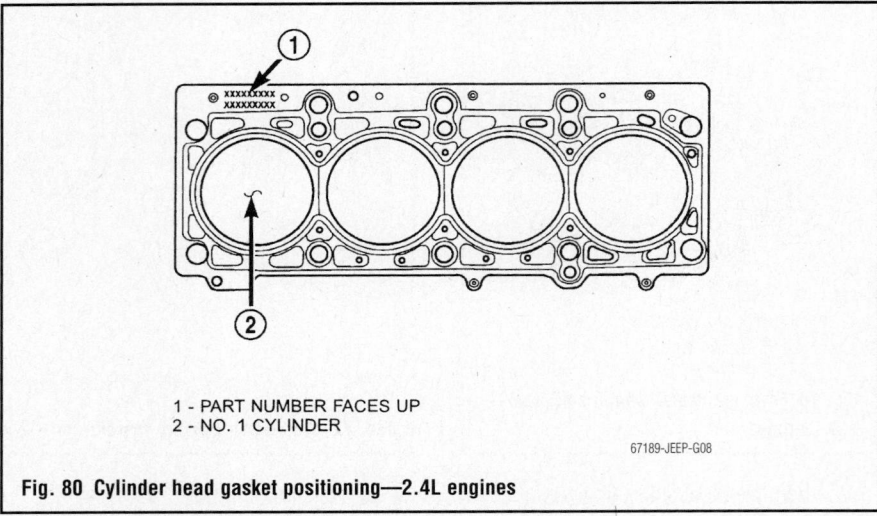

1 - PART NUMBER FACES UP
2 - NO. 1 CYLINDER

67189-JEEP-G08

Fig. 80 Cylinder head gasket positioning—2.4L engines

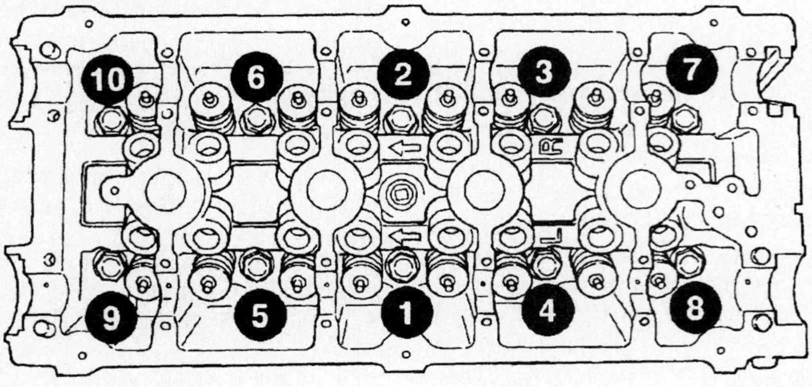

67189-JEEP-G09

Fig. 81 Cylinder head tightening sequence—2.4L engines

36. Raise the vehicle and install the exhaust pipe to the manifold.
37. Install the accessory drive belts.
38. Install the heater tube support bracket to the cylinder head.
39. Install the intake manifold.
40. Connect all vacuum lines, electrical wiring, ground straps and fuel line.
41. Fill the cooling system.
42. Connect the battery negative cable.

2.8L Diesel Engine

See Figure 82.

1. Disconnect negative battery cable.
2. Remove engine cover and bracket.
3. Drain cooling system.
4. Evacuate A/C.
5. Remove radiator core support.
6. Remove cooling fan and fan drive viscous clutch assembly.
7. Remove accessory drive belt.
8. Remove accessory drive belt tensioner and both idler pulleys, Idler pulley bolts are L.H. thread.
9. Remove power steering pump pulley.
10. Remove front engine lift bracket.
11. Remove cooling fan support.
12. Remove generator and support bracketing.
13. Remove viscous heater.
14. Rotate the engine to 90 degrees ATDC, or the 3 o-clock position at the crankshaft hub.
15. Remove vibration damper.
16. Disconnect main engine wiring harness connectors from right inner wheel housing.
17. Disconnect main engine wiring harness ancillary components and set harness aside.
18. Remove air cleaner housing.
19. Remove exhaust manifold heat shield.
20. Remove turbocharger heat shield retaining bolt and position shield aside .
21. Remove turbocharger oil supply line from turbocharger.
22. Raise and support vehicle.
23. Disconnect exhaust stabilizer bracket at lower exhaust manifold.
24. Disconnect exhaust system bracket at transmission cross member.
25. Lower the vehicle and remove the exhaust manifold retaining nuts.
26. Slide the exhaust manifold and turbocharger off of exhaust manifold studs .
27. Remove coolant hoses at thermostat housing.
28. Disconnect fuel return hose from fuel injectors and set aside.
29. Remove fuel injector pressure lines.
30. Disconnect fuel pump high pressure line at fuel rail.
31. Disconnect oil level indicator tube from intake manifold.
32. Disconnect brake booster line bracket from intake manifold and position aside.
33. Remove fuel injectors.

**** CAUTION**

Before removing the cylinder head cover/ intake manifold or timing belt the crankshaft hub must placed at 90° ATDC or the 3 O'clock position. Failure to do so could result in valve and/or piston damage during reassembly.

34. Remove timing belt outer cover.
35. Remove timing belt.
36. Using VM.1085, remove both camshaft gears.
37. Remove timing belt inner cover.
38. Remove cylinder head cover/intake manifold.
39. Remove rocker arm and lifter assemblies from cylinder head. Be sure to keep in same order as removed.
40. Remove cylinder head cover/intake manifold gasket from cylinder head.
41. Disconnect glow plug and engine coolant temperature electrical connectors.
42. Remove turbocharger outlet to charge air cooler hose.
43. Remove cylinder head bolts.
44. Remove cylinder head assembly from engine block.

To install:

**** CAUTION**

Piston protrusion must be measured to determine cylinder head gasket thickness if one or more cylinder liners have been replaced.

➡If cylinder liner(s) have not been removed, the same thickness head gasket that was removed can be used.

45. Clean and inspect gasket mating surfaces.
46. Position correct head gasket on engine block.
47. Place cylinder head on engine block.

**** CAUTION**

New cylinder head bolts must be used. Do not lubricate new cylinder head bolts. They already are coated with an anti scuff treatment.

48. Tighten cylinder head bolts following procedure below.
49. Cylinder Head Bolt Torquing Procedure
   a. Tighten all cylinder head bolts to 22 ft. lbs. (30 Nm) starting from the center bolts, following the cylinder head scheme and the following sequence: 3-2-1-10-9-8-7-6-5-4-11-12-13-14-15-16-17-18.
   b. Without loosening any bolts, starting from the center bolts, tighten each bolt an additional 75° in the following sequence: 10-9-8-7-6-5-4-3-2-1.
   c. Tighten the lateral cylinder head bolts an additional 50° in the following sequence: 11-12-13-14-15- 16-17-18.
   d. Finally tighten all bolts an additional 75° in the following sequence: 10-9-8-7-6-5-4-3-2-1-11-12-13-14-15-16-17-18.
50. Slide exhaust manifold and turbocharger on exhaust manifold studs .
51. Install exhaust manifold retaining nuts. Tighten the nuts to. 27 ft. lbs. (36 Nm) in a cross sequence beginning in the middle and working outward, then perform the tightening sequence to the exhaust manifold nuts again.
52. Install exhaust manifold heat shield. Torque bolts to 217 inch lbs. (24.5 Nm).
53. Install turbocharger outlet to charge air cooler pipe.
54. Install upper radiator hose.
55. Connect glow plug and coolant temperature sensor electrical connectors.
56. Install new cylinder head cover/intake manifold gasket.
57. Install rocker arm and lifter assemblies. Be sure to put rocker arm and lifter assemblies in same location as removed.

**** CAUTION**

Care must be taken not to knock the rocker arms off of the valves when installing the cylinder head cover/intake manifold.

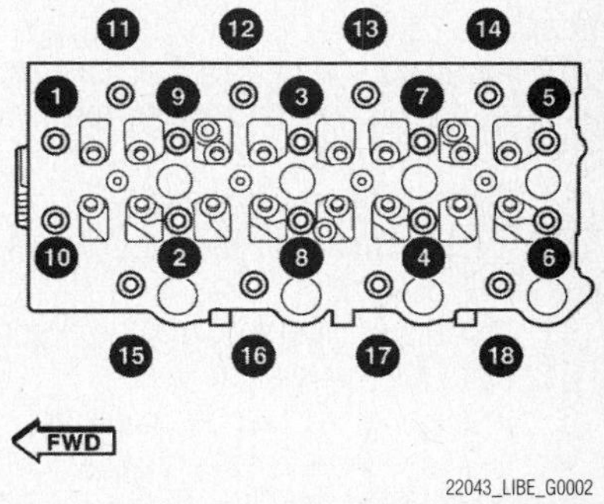

Fig. 82 2.8L cylinder head bolt tightening sequence

58. Install cylinder head cover/intake manifold.
59. Install timing belt inner cover.

➡**Make sure the crankshaft is rotated to the 90 ° ATCD, or the 3 O'clock position.**

60. Install both camshaft gears and tighten bolts finger tight.
61. Install timing belt.
62. Using VM.1085, torque cam gear retaining bolts to 108 Nm.
63. Install timing belt outer cover.
64. Remove both camshaft locking pins at this time.
65. Install fuel injectors.
66. Install brake booster line bracket to intake manifold.
67. Install oil level indicator tube to intake manifold.
68. Connect fuel pump high pressure line to fuel rail.
69. Install fuel injector pressure lines.
70. Connect fuel return hose to fuel injectors.
71. Connect engine coolant hoses to thermostat housing.
72. Raise vehicle.
73. Reconnect exhaust system bracket at transmission cross member.
74. Connect exhaust stabilizer bracket to lower exhaust manifold .
75. Install turbocharger oil supply line to turbocharger.
76. Lower vehicle.
77. Install turbocharger heat shield.
78. Install exhaust manifold heat shield.
79. Install air cleaner housing.
80. Install main engine wiring harness and connect all ancillary electrical components.
81. Install viscous heater.
82. Install vibration damper.
83. Install generator.
84. Install cooling fan support.
85. Install front engine lift bracket.
86. Install power steering pump pulley.
87. Install accessory drive belt tensioner and both idler pulleys. Idler pulley retaining bolts are L.H. Thread.
88. Install accessory drive belt.
89. Install cooling fan and fan drive viscous clutch assembly.
90. Install upper radiator core support.
91. Refill cooling system.
92. Install engine cover and bracket.
93. Connect negative battery cable.
94. Start engine and allow to warm. Turn engine off and inspect for leaks.

3.7L Engine

See Figures 83 through 86.

Left Side

1. Before servicing the vehicle, refer to the precautions in the beginning of this section.
2. Drain the cooling system.
3. Properly relieve the fuel system pressure.
4. Remove or disconnect the following:
   - Negative battery cable
   - Exhaust Y-pipe
   - Intake manifold
   - Cylinder head cover
   - Engine cooling fan and shroud
   - Accessory drive belt
   - Power steering pump
5. Rotate the crankshaft so that the crankshaft timing mark aligns with the Top Dead Center (TDC) mark on the front cover, and the **V6** marks on the camshaft sprockets are at 12 o'clock as shown.
   - Crankshaft damper
   - Front cover
6. Lock the secondary timing chain to the idler sprocket with Timing Chain Locking tool 8429.
7. Matchmark the secondary timing chain one link on each side of the V6 mark to the camshaft sprocket.
   - Left secondary timing chain tensioner
   - Cylinder head access plug
   - Secondary timing chain guide
   - Camshaft sprocket
   - Cylinder head

➡**The cylinder head is retained by twelve bolts. Four of the bolts are**

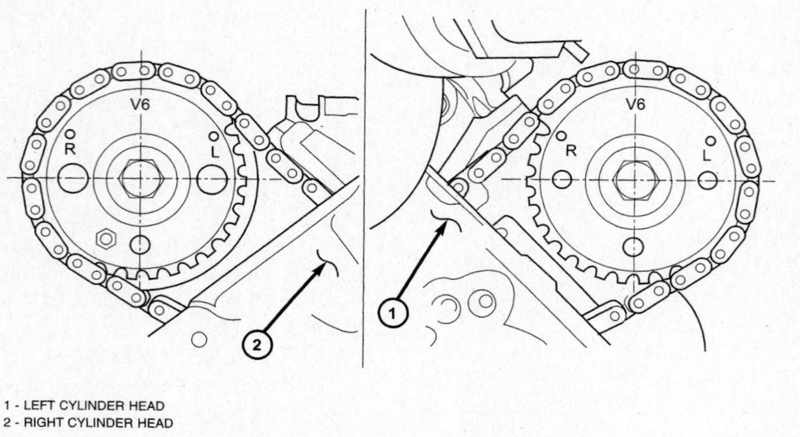

Fig. 83 Camshaft sprocket timing marks—3.7L

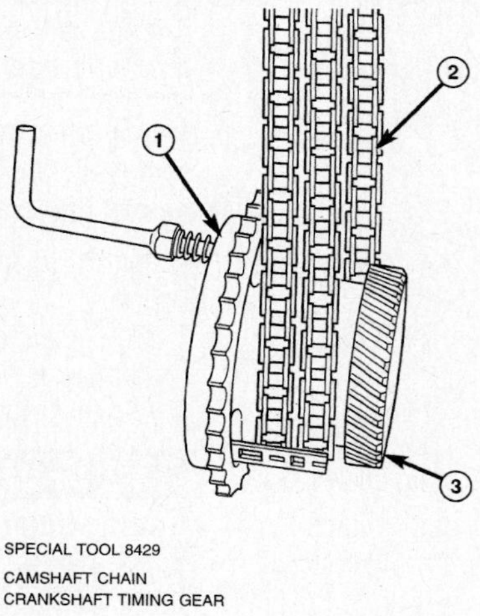

Fig. 84 Camshaft locking tool—3.7L

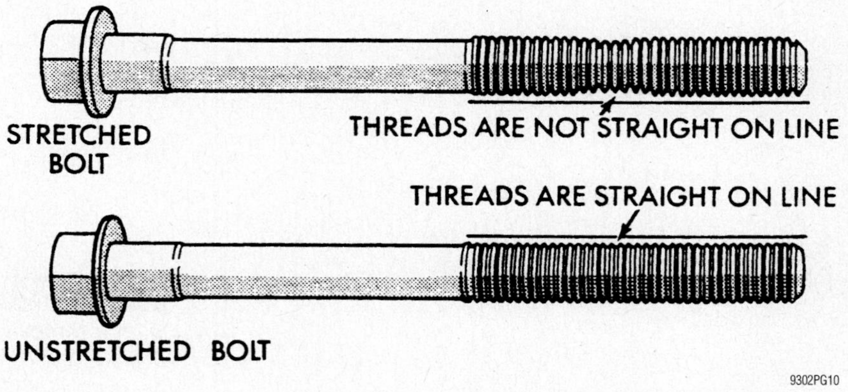

Fig. 85 Examine the head bolts for signs of stretching—3.7L engine

smaller and are at the front of the head.

To install:

8. Check the cylinder head bolts for signs of stretching and replace as necessary.
9. Lubricate the threads of the 11mm bolts with clean engine oil.
10. Coat the threads of the 8mm bolts with Mopar® Lock and Seal Adhesive.
11. Install the cylinder heads. Use new gaskets and tighten the bolts, in sequence, as follows:
    a. Step 1: Bolts 1–8 to 20 ft. lbs. (27 Nm)
    b. Step 2: Bolts 1–10 verify torque without loosening
    c. Step 3: Bolts 9–12 to 10 ft. lbs. (14 Nm)
    d. Step 4: Bolts 1–8 plus ¼ (90°) turn
    e. Step 5: Bolts 9–12 to 19 ft. lbs. (26 Nm)
12. Install or connect the following:
    - Camshaft sprocket. Align the secondary chain matchmarks and tighten the bolt to 90 ft. lbs. (122 Nm).
    - Secondary timing chain guide
    - Cylinder head access plug
    - Secondary timing chain tensioner.
13. Remove the Timing Chain Locking tool.
14. Install or connect the following:
    - Front cover
    - Crankshaft damper. Torque the bolt to 130 ft. lbs. (175 Nm).
    - Power steering pump
    - Accessory drive belt
    - Engine cooling fan and shroud
    - Cover
    - Intake manifold
    - Exhaust Y-pipe

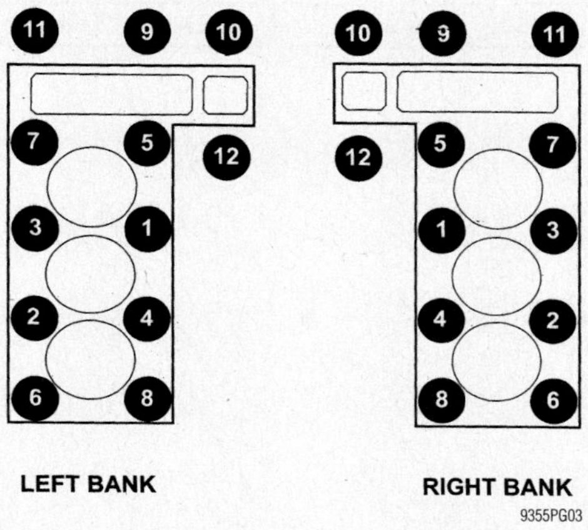

Fig. 86 Cylinder head bolt torque sequence—3.7L engine

- Negative battery cable

15. Fill and bleed the cooling system.
16. Start the engine, check for leaks and repair if necessary.

Right Side

See Figures 87 and 88.

1. Before servicing the vehicle, refer to the precautions in the beginning of this section.
2. Drain the cooling system.
3. Properly relieve the fuel system pressure.
4. Remove or disconnect the following:
    - Negative battery cable
    - Exhaust Y-pipe
    - Intake manifold
    - Valve cover
    - Engine cooling fan and shroud
    - Accessory drive belt
    - Oil fill housing
    - Power steering pump
5. Rotate the crankshaft so that the crankshaft timing mark aligns with the Top Dead Center (TDC) mark on the front cover, and the **V6** marks on the camshaft sprockets are at 12 o'clock as shown.
6. Remove or disconnect the following:
    - Crankshaft damper
    - Front cover
7. Lock the secondary timing chains to the idler sprocket with Timing Chain Locking tool 8429.
8. Matchmark the secondary timing chains to the camshaft sprockets.
9. Remove or disconnect the following:
    - Secondary timing chain tensioners
    - Cylinder head access plugs
    - Secondary timing chain guides
    - Camshaft sprockets
    - Cylinder heads

➡Each cylinder head is retained by 8 11mm bolts and four 8mm bolts.

To install:

10. Check the cylinder head bolts for signs of stretching and replace as necessary.

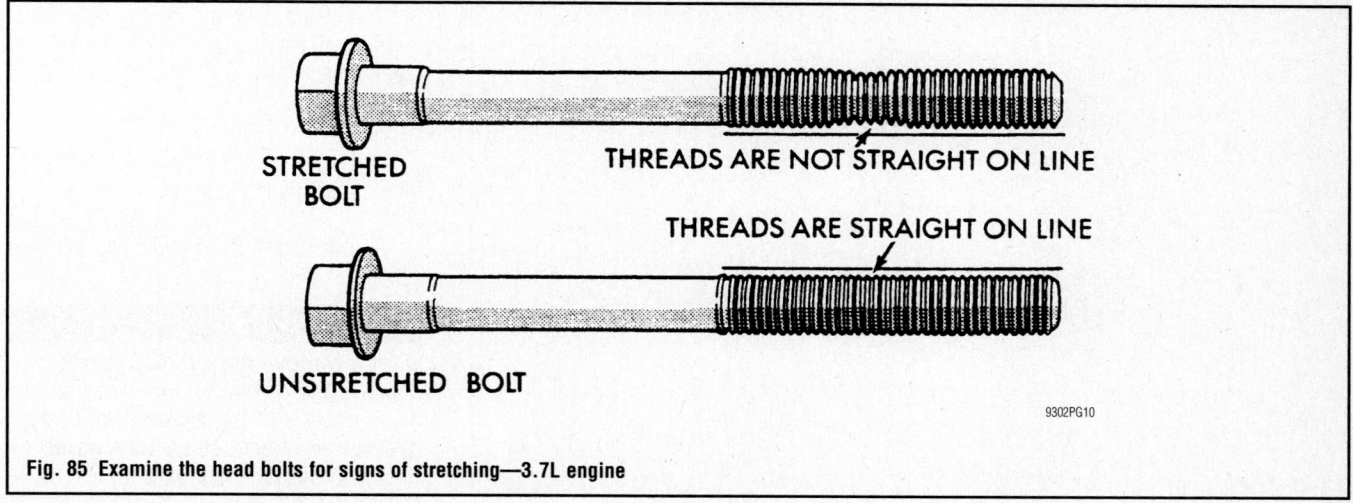

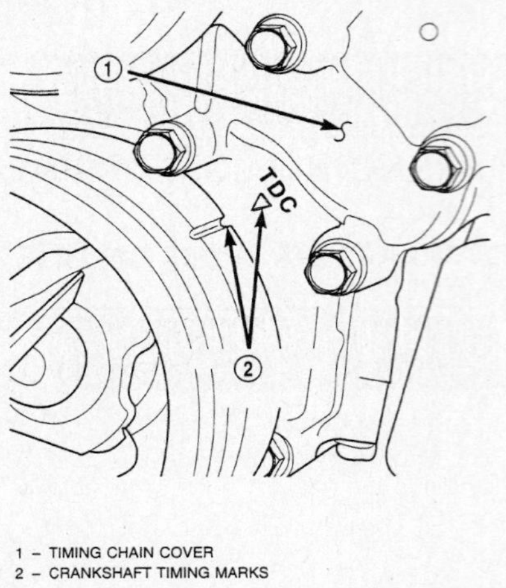

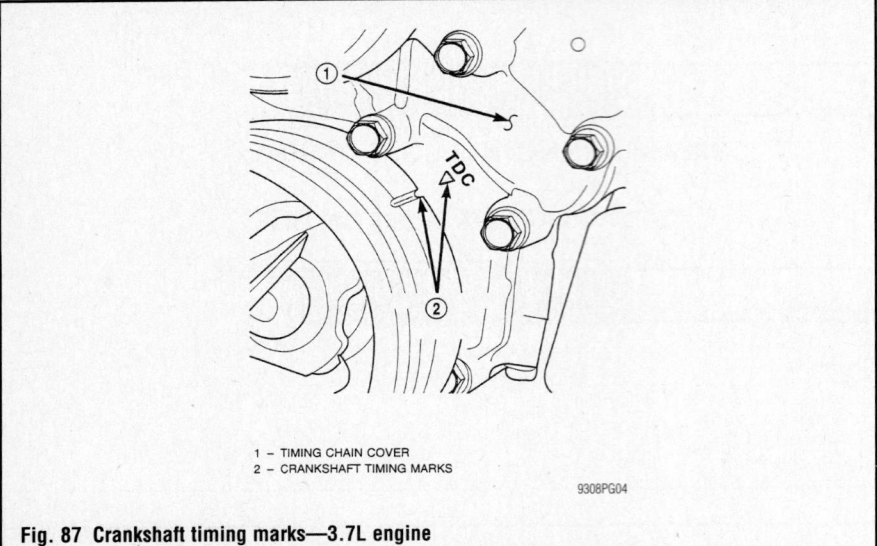

Fig. 87 Crankshaft timing marks—3.7L engine

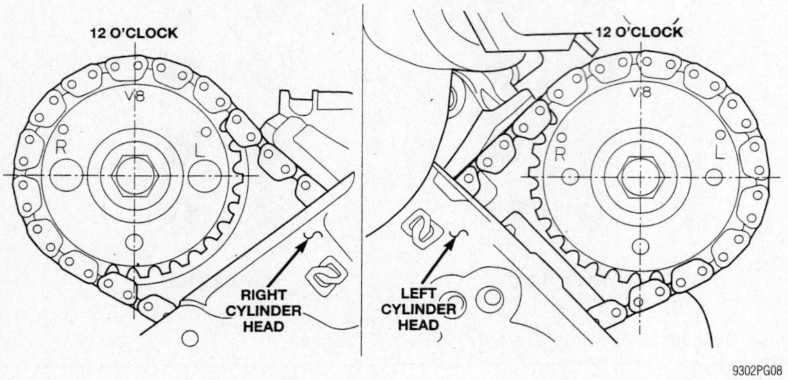

Fig. 88 Camshaft positioning—3.7L engine

11. Lubricate the threads of the 11mm bolts with clean engine oil.
12. Coat the threads of the 8mm bolts with Mopar® Lock and Seal Adhesive.
13. Install the cylinder heads. Use new gaskets and tighten the bolts, in sequence, as follows:
   a. Step 1: Bolts 1–8 to 20 ft. lbs. (27 Nm)
   b. Step 2: Bolts 1–10 verify torque without loosening
   c. Step 3: Bolts 9–12 to 10 ft. lbs. (14 Nm)
   d. Step 4: Bolts 1–8 plus ¼ (90°) turn
   e. Step 5: Bolts 9–12 to 19 ft. lbs. (26 Nm)
14. Install or connect the following:
   - Camshaft sprockets. Align the secondary chain matchmarks and tighten the bolts to 90 ft. lbs. (122 Nm).
   - Secondary timing chain guides
   - Cylinder head access plugs
   - Secondary timing chain tensioners.
15. Remove the Timing Chain Locking tool.
16. Install or connect the following:
   - Front cover
   - Crankshaft damper. Torque the bolt to 130 ft. lbs. (175 Nm).
   - Rocker arms
   - Power steering pump
   - Oil fill housing
   - Accessory drive belt
   - Engine cooling fan and shroud
   - Valve covers
   - Intake manifold
   - Exhaust Y-pipe
   - Negative battery cable
17. Fill and bleed the cooling system.
18. Start the engine, check for leaks and repair if necessary.

4.0L Engine

1. Before servicing the vehicle, refer to the precautions in the beginning of this section.
2. Disconnect the battery negative cable.

CAUTION

Do not remove the cylinder block drain plugs or loosen the radiator drain cock with the system hot and pressurized because serious burns from the coolant can occur.

3. Drain the coolant and disconnect the hoses at the engine thermostat housing and the water pump inlet. DO NOT waste reusable coolant. If the solution is clean and is being drained only to service the engine or cooling system, drain the coolant into a clean container for reuse.
4. Remove the air cleaner assembly.
5. Remove the cylinder head cover.
6. Remove the capscrews, bridge and pivot assemblies and rocker arms.
7. Remove the push rods. Retain the pushrods, bridges, pivots and rocker arms in the same order as removed.
8. Remove the accessory drive belt.
9. Remove the A/C compressor mounting bolts and secure the compressor to the side.
10. Remove the power steering pump and bracket from the intake manifold and water pump. Set the pump and bracket aside. DO NOT disconnect the hoses.
11. Perform the Fuel System Pressure Release procedure.
12. Disconnect the fuel supply line at the fuel rail.
13. Remove the intake and exhaust manifolds from the engine cylinder head.
14. Disconnect the coil rail electrical connectors and remove the coil rail.
15. Remove spark plugs.
16. Disconnect the temperature sending unit wire connector.
17. Remove the engine cylinder head bolts.

➡Bolt No.14 cannot be removed until the head is moved forward. Pull bolt No.14 out as far as it will go and then suspend the bolt in this position (tape around the bolt).

18. Remove the engine cylinder head and gasket.
19. If this was the first time the bolts

were removed, put a paint dab on the top of the bolt. If the bolts have a paint dab on the top of the bolt or it isn't known if they were used before, discard the bolts.

20. Stuff clean lint free shop towels into the cylinder bores.

To install:

The engine cylinder head gasket may be a composition gasket. This gasket is to be installed DRY. Do not use a gasket sealing compound on the gasket. If the engine cylinder head is to be replaced and the original valves used, measure the valve stem diameter. Only standard size valves can be used with a service replacement engine cylinder head unless the replacement head valve stem guide bores are reamed to accommodate oversize valve stems. Remove all carbon buildup and reface the valves.

21. Remove the shop towels from the cylinder bores. Coat the bores with clean engine oil.

22. Position the engine cylinder head gasket (with the numbers facing up) using the alignment dowels in the cylinder block, to position the gasket.

WARNING

Engine cylinder head bolts should be reused only once. Replace the head bolts if they were used before or if they have a paint dab on the top of the bolt.

23. With bolt No.14 held in place (tape around bolt), install the engine cylinder head over the same dowels used to locate the gasket. Remove the tape from bolt No.14.

24. Coat the threads of stud bolt No.11 with Loctite® 592 sealant, or equivalent.

25. Tighten the engine cylinder head bolts in sequence according to the following procedure.

WARNING

During the final tightening sequence, bolt No.11 will be tightened to a lower torque than the rest of the bolts. DO NOT overtighten bolt No.11.

- Bolts 1 through 14 to 22 ft. lbs. (30 Nm).
- Bolts 1 through 14 to 45 ft. lbs. (61 Nm).
- Check all bolts to verify they are set to 45 ft. lbs. (61 Nm).
- Bolts 1 through 10 to 110 ft. lbs. (149 Nm).
- Bolt 11 to 100 ft. lbs. (135 Nm).
- Bolts 12 through 14 to 110 ft. lbs. (149 Nm).
- Check all bolts in sequence to verify the correct torque.
- If not already done, clean and mark each bolt with a dab of paint after tightening. Should you encounter bolts which were painted in an earlier service operation, replace them.

26. Install the spark plugs.

27. Connect the temperature sending unit wire connector.

28. Install the ignition coil rail and coil rail electrical connectors.

29. Install the intake and exhaust manifolds.

30. Install the fuel line and the vacuum advance hose.

31. Attach the power steering pump and bracket.

32. Install the push rods, rocker arms, pivots and bridges in the order they were removed.

33. Install the engine cylinder head cover.

34. Attach the air conditioner compressor mounting bracket to the engine cylinder head and block. Tighten the bolts to 30 ft. lbs. (40 Nm) torque.

35. Attach the air conditioning compressor to the bracket. Tighten the bolts to 20 ft. lbs. (27 Nm) torque.

WARNING

The serpentine drive belt must be routed correctly. Incorrect routing can cause the water pump to turn in the opposite direction causing the engine to overheat.

36. Install the serpentine drive belt.

37. Install the air cleaner and ducting.

38. Connect the hoses to the engine thermostat housing and fill the cooling system to the specified level.

39. The automatic transmission throttle linkage and cable must be adjusted after completing the engine cylinder head installation.

40. Install the temperature sending unit and connect the wire connector.

41. Position the A/C compressor into the engine compartment.

42. Install the bolts and nut that secure the A/C compressor to the engine. Tighten the bolts and nut fastening the compressor to the cylinder block to 35–50 ft. lbs. (45–65 Nm). Tighten the bolts fastening the rear brace to the compressor and cylinder block to 30–40 ft. lbs. (40–55 Nm).

43. Connect negative cable to battery.

CAUTION

Use extreme caution when the engine is operating. Do not stand in direct line with the fan. Do not put hands near the pulleys, belts or fan. Do not wear loose clothing.

44. Operate the engine with the radiator cap off. Inspect for leaks and continue operating the engine until the engine thermostat opens. Add coolant, if required.

ENGINE ASSEMBLY

REMOVAL & INSTALLATION

2005–06 Wrangler

1. Before servicing the vehicle, refer to the precautions in the beginning of this section.
2. Properly relieve the fuel system pressure.
3. Drain the cooling system.
4. Drain the engine oil.
5. Evacuate the A/C system.
6. Drain the power steering fluid, if equipped.
7. Remove or disconnect the following:
   - Negative battery cable
   - Air cleaner assembly
   - Upper radiator hose
   - Accessory drive belt and fan drive assembly
   - Transmission cooler lines, if equipped
   - Lower radiator hose
   - Radiator and fan shroud
   - Starter electrical connectors
   - Alternator wiring connectors
   - A/C compressor, if equipped
   - Ignition coil wiring connector
   - Oil pressure sender connector
   - Wiring harness ground at the dipstick tube
   - Heater hoses from the thermostat housing
   - Water pump inlet tube
   - Closed Crankcase Ventilation (CCV) hoses from the cylinder head and intake manifold
   - Accelerator, transmission line pressure and speed control cables, if equipped
   - Engine ground strap
   - Power steering pressure switch, if equipped
   - Engine Coolant Temperature (ECT) sensor
   - Fuel injection wiring connectors
   - Intake Air Temperature (IAT) sensor
   - Idle Air Control (IAC) motor

- Throttle Position (TP) sensor
- Manifold Absolute Pressure (MAP) sensor
- Crankshaft Position (CKP) sensor
- Heated Oxygen (HO_2S) sensor connector
- Vacuum hoses from the intake manifold
- Fuel line and bracket
- Power steering hoses from the steering gear, if equipped
- Oil filter
- Starter
- Engine support through bolts
- Exhaust front pipe
- Flywheel cover
- Torque converter, if equipped with automatic transmission
- Transmission flange bolts
- Left and right motor mounts
- Engine shock damper bracket

8. Place a support stand under the transmission.
9. Lift the engine out of the vehicle.

To install:

10. If equipped with a manual transmission, perform the following steps:
   a. Insert the transmission shaft into the clutch spline.
   b. Align the flywheel housing to the engine.
   c. Install the flywheel housing bolts. Torque the bolts to 28 ft. lbs. (38 Nm).
11. If equipped with an automatic transmission, perform the following steps:
   a. Align the torque converter housing to the engine.
   b. Torque the bolts to 28 ft. lbs. (38 Nm).
   - Install the torque converter to flexplate bolts. Torque the bolts to 50 ft. lbs. (68 Nm).
12. Install or connect the following:
   - Engine onto the engine brackets. When properly aligned, torque the through bolts to 60 ft. lbs. (81 Nm).
   - Inspection cover. Torque the bolts to 138 inch lbs. (16 Nm).
   - Exhaust pipe. Torque the bolts to 23 ft. lbs. (31 Nm).
   - Starter motor. Tighten the bolts to 33 ft. lbs. (45 Nm).
   - Oil filter
   - Power steering hoses
   - Fuel supply line to the fuel rail
   - Fuel supply rail to the intake manifold
   - Vacuum hoses to the intake manifold
   - Power steering pressure switch electrical connector
   - ECT sensor electrical connector
   - Fuel injector connectors
   - IAT sensor
   - IAC motor
   - TP sensor
   - MAP sensor
   - CKP sensor
   - HO_2S sensor connector
   - Engine ground strap
   - Heater hoses and water pump inlet tube
   - Cruise control cable, if equipped
   - Throttle cable
   - Fan shroud and radiator. Torque the bolts to 75 inch lbs. (8 Nm).
   - Transmission cooler lines, if equipped. Torque the bolts to 10 ft. lbs. (15 Nm).
   - Fan drive assembly. Torque the bolts to 20 ft. lbs. (27 Nm).
   - Drive belt
   - Radiator hoses
   - Ignition coil
   - Distributor
   - A/C compressor
   - A/C high pressure switch
   - Alternator
   - Oil pressure sender
   - Harness ground at the oil dipstick tube bracket
   - A/C hoses
   - Air cleaner assembly
   - Negative battery cable
13. Fill and bleed the power steering system.
14. Fill the engine with clean oil.
15. Fill and bleed the cooling system.
16. Recharge the A/C system.
17. Start the engine and check for leaks, repair if necessary.

Liberty

2.4L Engine

See Figures 89 through 91.

1. Disconnect the battery negative cable.
2. Remove hood. Mark hood hinge location for reinstallation.
3. Remove air cleaner assembly.
4. Remove radiator core support bracket.
5. Remove fan shroud with electric fan assembly.
6. Remove drive belt.

➡It is not necessary to discharge the A/C system to remove the engine.

7. Remove A/C compressor and secure away from engine with lines attached.
8. Remove generator and secure away from engine.

➡Do not remove the phenolic pulley from the P/S pump. It is not required for P/S pump removal.

9. Remove power steering pump with lines attached and secure away from engine.
10. Drain cooling system.
11. Remove coolant bottle.
12. Disconnect the heater hoses from the engine.
13. Disconnect heater hoses from heater core and remove hose assembly.
14. Disconnect throttle and speed control cables.
15. Remove upper radiator hose from engine.
16. Remove lower radiator hose from engine.
17. Disconnect the engine to body ground straps at the left side of cowl.
18. Disconnect the engine wiring harness at the following points:
   - Intake air temperature (IAT) sensor
   - Fuel Injectors
   - Throttle Position (TPS) Switch
   - Idle Air Control (IAC) Motor
   - Engine Oil Pressure Switch
   - Engine Coolant Temperature (ECT) Sensor
   - Manifold Absolute Pressure MAP) Sensor
   - Camshaft Position (CMP) Sensor
   - Coil Over Plugs
   - Crankshaft Position Sensor
19. Remove coil over plugs.
20. Release fuel rail pressure.
21. Remove fuel rail and secure away from engine.
22. Remove the PCV hose.
23. Remove the breather hoses.
24. Remove the vacuum hose for the power brake booster.
25. Disconnect knock sensors.
26. Secure the left and right engine wiring harnesses away from engine.
27. Raise vehicle.
28. Disconnect oxygen sensor wiring.
29. Disconnect crankshaft position sensor.
30. Disconnect the engine block heater power cable, if equipped.
31. Disconnect the front driveshaft at the front differential and secure out of way.
32. Remove the starter.
33. Remove the ground straps from the engine
34. Disconnect the exhaust pipes at the manifold.
35. Remove the structural cover, if equipped.
36. Remove torque converter bolts, and mark location for reassembly.

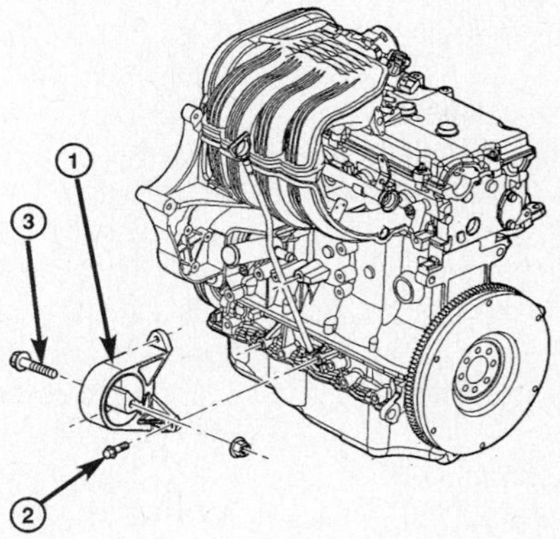

Fig. 89 Left side engine mount—2.4L engines

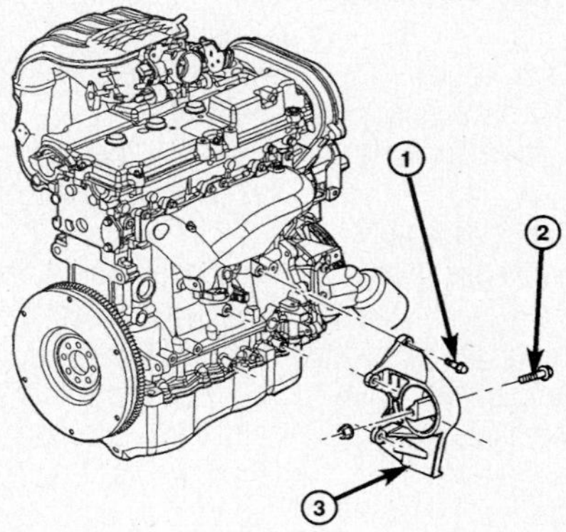

Fig. 90 Right side engine mount—2.4L engines

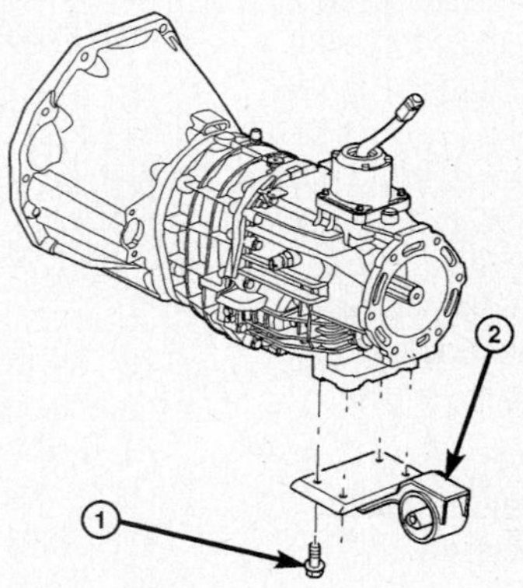

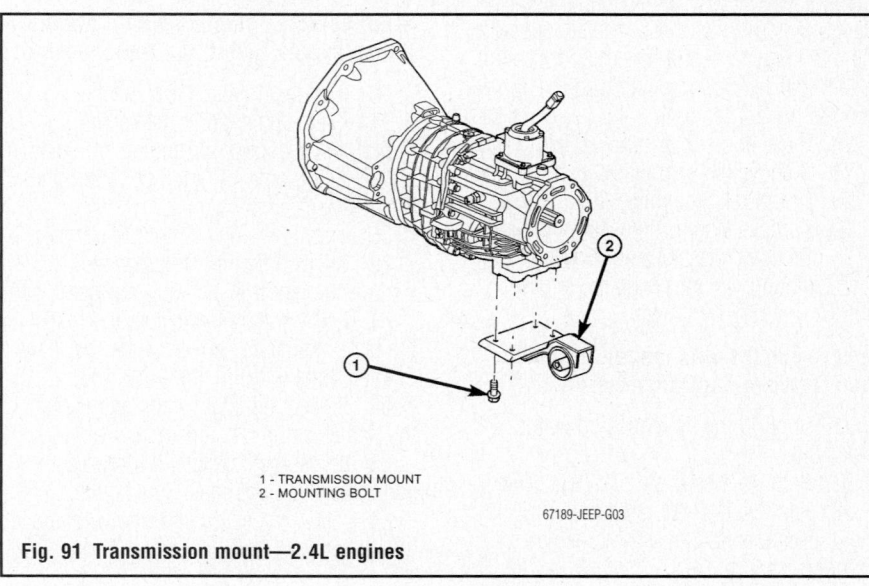

Fig. 91 Transmission mount—2.4L engines

37. Remove transmission bellhousing to engine bolts.
38. Loosen left and right engine mount thru bolts.

➡It is not necessary to completely remove engine mount thru bolts, for engine removal.

39. Lower the vehicle.
40. Support the transmission with a suitable jack.
41. Connect a suitable engine hoist to the engine.

⁂ WARNING

The engine with a manual transmission, can be removed without removing the manual transmission. Use caution when attempting this procedure as the clearance is tight.

42. Remove engine from vehicle.

To install:

43. Position the engine in the vehicle.
44. Install both left and right side engine mounts into the frame mounts.
45. Raise the vehicle.
46. Install the transmission bellhousing to engine mounting bolts. Tighten the bolts to 30 ft. lbs. (41 Nm).
47. Tighten the engine mount thru bolts.
48. Install the torque converter bolts.
49. Connect the ground straps on the left and right side of the engine.
50. Install the starter.
51. Connect the crankshaft position sensor.
52. Install the engine block heater power cable, if equipped.

⁂ WARNING

The structural collar requires a specific torque sequence. Failure to follow this sequence may cause severe damage to the collar.

53. Install the structural collar.

Perform the following steps for installing structural collar.

a. Step 1: Position collar between transmission and oil pan. Install collar to transmission bolts, hand start only.
b. Step 2: Install collar to oil pan bolts, hand snug only.
c. Step 3: Tighten collar to transmission bolts.
d. Step 4: Tighten collar to oil pan bolts.

54. Install the exhaust pipe.
55. Connect the oxygen sensors.
56. Lower vehicle.
57. Connect the knock sensors.

58. Connect the engine to body ground straps.
59. Install the power brake booster vacuum hose.
60. Install the breather hoses.
61. Install the PCV hose.
62. Install the fuel rail.
63. Install the coil over plugs.
64. Reconnect the engine wiring harness at the following points:
- Intake Air Temperature (IAT) sensor
- Fuel Injectors
- Throttle Position (TPS) Switch
- Idle Air Control (IAC) Motor
- Engine Oil Pressure Switch
- Engine Coolant Temperature (ECT) Sensor
- Manifold Absolute Pressure (MAP) Sensor
- Camshaft Position (CMP) Sensor
- Coil Over Plugs
- Crankshaft Position Sensor

65. Connect lower radiator hose.
66. Connect upper radiator hose.
67. Connect throttle and speed control cables.
68. Install the heater hose assembly.
69. Install coolant recovery bottle.
70. Install the power steering pump.
71. Install the generator.
72. Install the A/C compressor.
73. Install the drive belt.
74. Install the fan shroud with the electric fan assembly.
75. Install the radiator core support bracket.
76. Install the air cleaner assembly.
77. Refill the engine cooling system.
78. Install the hood.
79. Check and fill engine oil.
80. Connect the battery negative cable.
81. Start the engine and check for leaks.

2.8L Diesel Engine

1. Disconnect negative battery cable.
2. Drain cooling system.
3. Remove engine cover.
4. Remove engine cover mounting bracket retaining bolts and remove the bracket from the top of the engine.
5. Remove air cleaner assembly from the engine bay.
6. Recover refrigerant from A/C system.
7. Disconnect high side refrigerant line from the upper radiator support bracket.
8. Remove upper radiator support bracket retaining bolts and remove the support bracket.
9. Remove front grille and head lamp panel.
10. Remove high side refrigerant line retaining nut and remove the line from the condenser assembly. Position the line out of the way.
11. Remove low side refrigerant line retaining nut and remove line from the condenser assembly. Position the line out of the way.
12. Remove high side refrigerant line from A/C compressor and remove high side line.
13. Remove cooling fan and fan drive viscous clutch assembly .
14. Remove fan shroud retaining bolts and remove fan assembly and shroud together.
15. Disconnect charge air cooler outlet hose from charge air cooler .
16. Remove the charge air inlet hose from the charge air cooler .
17. Disconnect engine coolant hoses from engine assembly.
18. Disconnect coolant reservoir hoses and remove reservoir.
19. Remove power steering cooler retaining bolts and unclip air deflectors from both sides of the radiator (cooling module) assembly.
20. Remove cooling module assembly .
21. Remove accessory drive belt from the engine.
22. Accessing bolts through the pump pulley, remove power steering pump retaining bolts and position pump aside with lines still attached.
23. Disconnect heater core inlet and outlet hoses from the heater core .
24. Remove generator from engine. This will provide access to the wires beneath it.
25. Trace engine wiring and disconnect electrical connectors and tie straps one at a time until all wiring is disconnected from the engine assembly. When all the engine electrical harness is disconnected, separate the main engine wiring harness connectors at the right rear inner fender well then position the harness aside.
26. Raise and support the vehicle.
27. Remove the skid plate .
28. Disconnect the oil sending unit.
29. Remove starter motor from engine.
30. Remove chassis ground wire above starter mounting location on the engine block.

➡For vehicles with manual transmission, remove the transmission.

31. Support the transmission with a jackstand.
32. Remove the flexplate access cover.
33. Remove the flexplate fasteners.
34. Remove transmission cross member fasteners.
35. Lower the transmission.
36. Remove the upper transmission to engine fasteners.
37. Raise the transmission.
38. Install the transmission cross member fasteners.
39. Remove the transmission jack.
40. Remove exhaust inlet pipe retaining bolts and disconnect exhaust pipe from turbocharger .
41. Remove transmission to engine retaining bolts.
42. Separate transmission cooler line(s) from retainer.
43. Remove both right and left side engine mount retaining nut.
44. Lower vehicle.
45. Remove left side engine mount retaining nut.
46. Remove exhaust manifold rear heat shield.
47. Disconnect the fuel supply and return lines.
48. Remove crankshaft sensor heat shield.
49. Disconnect crankshaft position sensor, located on the right rear of the engine .
50. Remove the oil separator from the cylinder head cover/intake manifold .
51. Connect a suitable lifting device to engine assembly.
52. Place a floor jack under the transmission to support the transmission.
53. With engine and transmission supported by a lifting device separate the engine from the transmission.
54. Lift the engine assembly out of the engine bay.

To install:

55. Install engine assembly and align with the transmission .

➡For vehicle equipped with a manual transmission, Install the transmission.

56. Remove engine lifting devise.
57. Raise and support the vehicle.
58. Install accessible engine to transmission housing bolts. Tighten bolts to 50 ft. lbs. (68 Nm).
59. Install the engine mount fasteners.
60. Support the transmission and remove the rear transmission crossmember.
61. Lower the transmission and install the upper transmission to engine fasteners. Tighten bolts to 50 ft. lbs. (68 Nm).
62. Raise the transmission and install the transmission crossmember.
63. Install the flexplate to torque converter fasteners and install the shield.
64. Install the engine ground wire above the starter.

65. Install the starter.
66. Connect the transmission cooler lines to the oil pan retainers.
67. Connect the exhaust.
68. Lower the vehicle.
69. Install the oil separator.
70. Connect the crankshaft sensor and install the heat shield.
71. Connect the heater hose inlet and out let hoses.
72. Install the power steering pump.
73. Install the generator.
74. Connect the fuel lines.
75. Position and connect the main engine wiring harness.
76. Install the accessory drive belt.
77. Install the cooling module .
78. Connect the power steering cooler and fasten the air deflectors.
79. Install the coolant reservoir .
80. Connect the engine coolant hoses.
81. Connect the charge air inlet hose .
82. Connect the charge air outlet hose .
83. Install the cooling fan assembly and shroud.
84. Install high side refrigerant line.
85. Install the low side refrigerant line.
86. Install the front grille and head lamp panel.
87. Install the upper radiator support bracket.
88. Install the air cleaner assembly.
89. Install the engine cover bracket and engine cover.
90. Evacuate and recharge A/C.
91. Fill cooling system.
92. Fill crankcase with the correct viscosity oil, to the proper level.
93. Start engine, allow to warm, turn engine off and inspect for leaks.

3.7L Engine

See Figure 92.

1. Before servicing the vehicle, refer to the precautions in the beginning of this section.
2. Properly relieve the fuel system pressure.
3. Drain the cooling system.
4. Drain the engine oil.
5. Remove or disconnect the following:
   - Negative battery cable
   - Hood
   - Air cleaner assembly
   - Radiator
   - Electric and mechanical fan assemblies
   - A/C compressor, if equipped, and secure it out of the way with the lines attached. DO NOT DISCHARGE!
   - Power steering pump, with the lines attached
   - Alternator
   - Coolant bottle
   - Heater hoses
   - Accelerator and speed control cables
   - Lower and upper radiator hoses
   - Engine ground straps
   - Intake Air Temperature (IAT) sensor
   - Fuel injection wiring connectors
   - Throttle Position (TP) sensor
   - Idle Air Control (IAC) motor
   - Oil pressure sender connector
   - Engine Coolant Temperature (ECT) sensor
   - Manifold Absolute Pressure (MAP) sensor
   - Camshaft position sensor
   - Ignition coil wiring connector
   - Crankshaft Position (CKP) sensor
   - Coil pack
   - Fuel rail
   - PCV hose
   - Vacuum hoses from the intake manifold
   - Knock sensor connectors
   - Oil dipstick tube
   - Intake manifold
   - Heated Oxygen (HO_2S) sensor connector
   - Block heater connector
   - Front driveshaft at the differential
   - Starter
   - Structural cover
   - With a manual transmission, remove the transmission
   - Torque converter bolts and matchmark the converter
   - Automatic transmission-to-engine bolts
   - Exhaust front pipes
   - Left and right engine mounts
6. Place a support stand under the transmission.
7. Install an engine lift plate
8. Lift the engine out of the vehicle.

To install:

9. If equipped with a manual transmission, install the transmission.
10. Lower the engine and install the mounts. Don't tighten the bolts yet.
11. If equipped with an automatic transmission, perform the following steps:
    a. Align the torque converter housing to the engine.
    b. Torque the bolts to 30 ft. lbs. (41 Nm).
    - Install the torque converter to flexplate bolts. Torque the bolts to 50 ft. lbs. (68 Nm).
12. Install or connect the following:
    - Torque the through bolts to 45 ft. lbs. (61 Nm).
    - Engine ground strap
    - Starter motor
    - CKP sensor
    - Block heater cable
    - Structural cover.

WARNING

The structural cover must be held tightly against the engine and bellhousing during tightening. The torque for all bolts is 40 ft. lbs. (54 Nm); the bolts must be tightened in the order shown.

- Exhaust pipes. New flange clamps MUST be used!
- HO_2S sensor connectors
- KS sensors
- Intake Manifold
- Dipstick tube
- Vacuum hoses to the intake manifold
- PCV and breather hoses
- Fuel rail
- Ignition coil
- IAT sensor
- Fuel injector connectors
- TP sensor
- IAC motor
- Oil pressure sender
- ECT sensor electrical connector
- MAP sensor
- CMP sensor
- Radiator hoses
- Cruise control cable, if equipped
- Throttle cable
- Heater hoses
- Coolant bottle
- Power steering pump

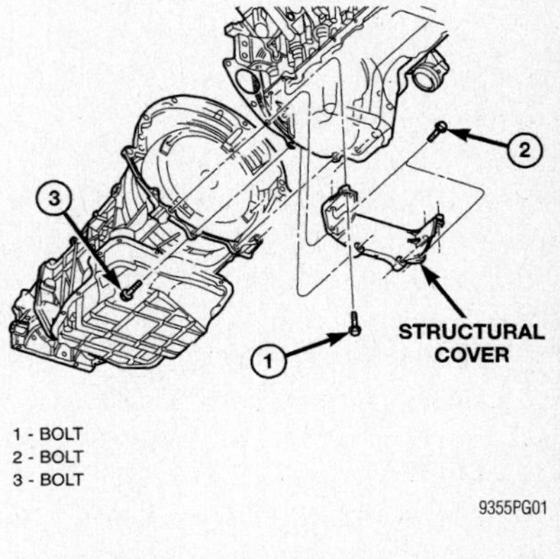

Fig. 92 Tighten the structural cover bolts in this order—3.7L engine

- Alternator
- A/C compressor
- Radiator
- Fan assemblies
- Air cleaner assembly
- Negative battery cable

13. Fill and bleed the power steering system.
14. Fill the engine with clean oil.
15. Start the engine and check for leaks, repair if necessary.

EXHAUST MANIFOLD

REMOVAL & INSTALLATION

2.4L Engine

1. Before servicing the vehicle, refer to the precautions in the beginning of this section.
2. Raise the vehicle and disconnect the exhaust pipe from the exhaust manifold.
3. Lower the vehicle.
4. Disconnect the upstream oxygen sensor connector at the rear of the exhaust manifold.
5. Remove the air cleaner bracket.
6. Remove the heat shield.
7. Remove the bolts attaching the manifold to the cylinder head.
8. Remove the exhaust manifold.
9. Inspect the manifold.
10. Discard the gasket (if equipped) and clean all surfaces of the manifold and cylinder head.
11. Inspect the manifold gasket surfaces for flatness with a straight edge. Surface must be flat within 0.15 mm per 300 mm (0.006 in. per foot) of manifold length.
12. Inspect the manifolds for cracks or distortion. Replace the manifold as necessary.

To install:

13. Clean the manifold mating surfaces.
14. Install the exhaust manifold with a new gasket. Tighten the attaching nuts to 175 inch lbs. (20 Nm).
15. Attach the exhaust pipe to the exhaust manifold and tighten the fasteners to 27 ft. lbs. (37 Nm).
16. Install and connect the oxygen sensor.
17. Install the heat shield.
18. Install the air cleaner bracket.

2.8L Engine

Refer to the Turbocharger procedure. The turbocharger and exhaust manifold is removed as an assembly.

3.7L Engines

1. Before servicing the vehicle, refer to the precautions in the beginning of this section.
2. Remove or disconnect the following:
   - Negative battery cable
   - Exhaust manifold heat shields
   - Exhaust Gas Recirculation (EGR) tube
   - Exhaust Y-pipe
   - Exhaust manifolds

To install:

➡If the exhaust manifold studs came out with the nuts when removing the exhaust manifolds, replace them with new studs.

3. Install or connect the following:
   - Exhaust manifolds. Torque the fasteners to 20 ft. lbs. (27 Nm), starting with the center nuts and work out to the ends.
   - Exhaust Y-pipe
   - EGR tube
   - Exhaust manifold heat shields
   - Negative battery cable
4. Start the engine, check for leaks and repair if necessary.

4.0L Engine

Refer to the Intake Manifold procedure. The intake and exhaust manifold is removed as an assembly.

INTAKE MANIFOLD

REMOVAL & INSTALLATION

2.4L Engine with 2-Piece Aluminum Manifold

See Figure 93.

Upper

See Figure 94.

The intake manifold is a two piece aluminum casting that attaches to the cylinder head with fasteners.

1. Before servicing the vehicle, refer to the precautions in the beginning of this section.
2. Disconnect the negative cable from the battery.
3. Disconnect the connector from the inlet air temperature sensor.
4. Disconnect the air intake tube at the throttle body and remove the upper air cleaner housing.
5. Disconnect the connector from the Throttle Position Sensor (TPS).
6. Disconnect the connector from the Idle Air Control (IAC) motor.
7. Disconnect the connector from the Manifold Absolute Pressure (MAP) sensor.
8. Remove the vacuum lines for the purge solenoid and the Positive Crankcase Ventilation (PCV) valve at the intake manifold.
9. Remove the vacuum lines for the power brake booster, LDP, Exhaust-Gas Recirculation (EGR) transducer, and speed control vacuum reservoir (if equipped) at the upper intake manifold fittings.
10. Disconnect the throttle, speed control (if equipped), and transaxle control (if equipped) and cables from the throttle lever and bracket.
11. Perform the fuel system pressure release procedure before attempting any repairs.
12. Disconnect the fuel line.
13. Disconnect the coolant temperature sensor.

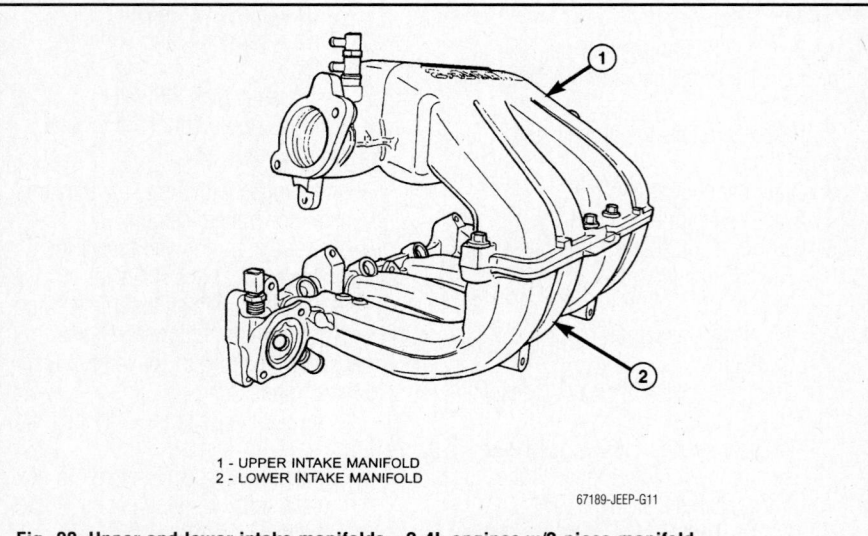

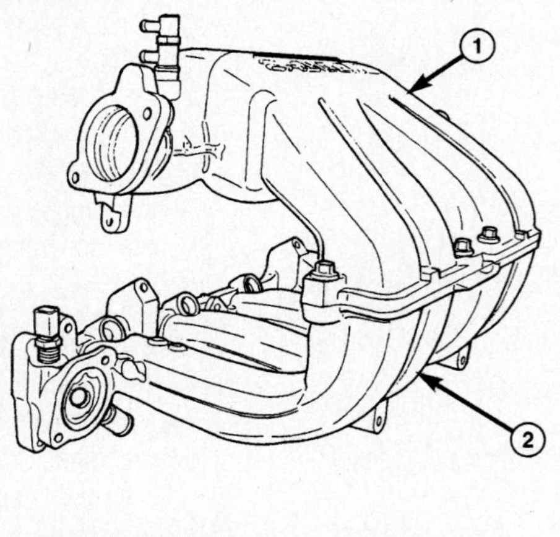

Fig. 93 Upper and lower intake manifolds—2.4L engines w/2-piece manifold

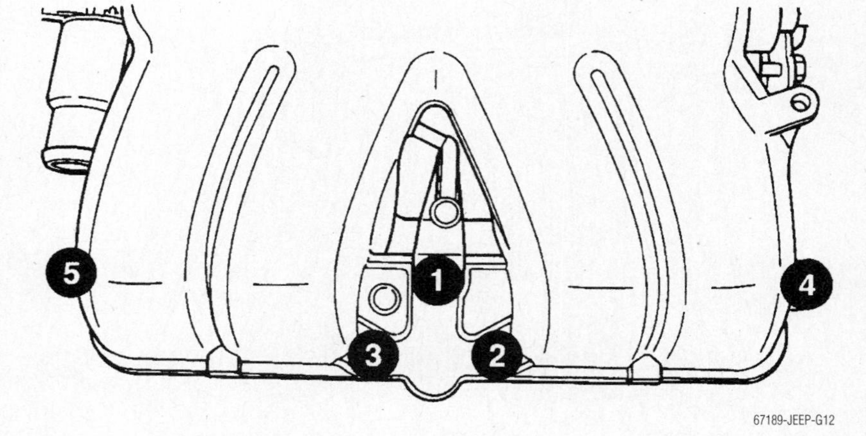

Fig. 94 Upper intake manifold torque sequence—2.4L engines w/2-piece manifold

➡Cover the intake manifold openings to prevent foreign material from entering the engine.

14. Inspect the manifold injector wire harness connector.
15. Disconnect the fuel injector harness.
16. Remove the intake manifold to cylinder head fasteners.
17. Remove the manifold from engine.

To install:

18. Clean the manifold sealing surfaces.
19. Apply a 1.5 mm (0.060 in.) bead Mopar® Gasket Maker, or equivalent, to the perimeter of the lower intake manifold runner openings.
20. Install the upper intake manifold and tighten the fasteners to 250 inch lbs. (28 Nm) in the sequence shown in. Repeat this procedures until all fasteners are at the specified torque.
21. Install the engine oil dipstick.
22. Install the upper bolt in the intake manifold to front support bracket.
23. Install the EGR tube.
24. Install the throttle cables in the bracket.
25. Connect the throttle, speed control, (if equipped), cables to the throttle lever.
26. Connect the vacuum lines for the power brake booster, LDP, EGR transducer, and speed control vacuum reservoir (if equipped) at the upper intake manifold fittings.
27. Connect the vacuum lines for the purge solenoid and PCV valve.
28. Connect the electrical connectors for the MAP sensor, Throttle Position Sensor (TPS), and Idle Air Control (IAC) motor.
29. Install the air cleaner upper housing and air intake tube to throttle body.
30. Connect the inlet air temperature sensor connector.
31. Connect the negative cable to the battery.

Lower

See Figure 95.

1. Before servicing the vehicle, refer to the precautions in the beginning of this section.
2. Disconnect the negative cable from the battery.
3. Disconnect the connector from the inlet air temperature sensor.
4. Disconnect the air intake tube at the throttle body and remove the upper air cleaner housing.
5. Disconnect the connector from the Throttle Position Sensor (TPS).
6. Disconnect the connector from the Idle Air Control (IAC) motor.
7. Disconnect the connector from the MAP sensor.
8. Remove the vacuum lines for the purge solenoid and PCV valve at the intake manifold.
9. Remove the vacuum lines for the power brake booster, LDP, EGR transducer, and speed control vacuum reservoir (if equipped) at the intake manifold fittings.
10. Disconnect the throttle, speed control (if equipped), and transaxle control (if equipped) and cables from the throttle lever and bracket.
11. Perform the fuel system pressure release procedure before attempting any repairs.
12. Disconnect the fuel line.
13. Disconnect the coolant temperature sensor/fuel injector wire harness connector.
14. Disconnect the fuel injector harness.
15. Remove the intake manifold to cylinder head fasteners.
16. Remove the manifold from engine.

➡Cover the intake manifold openings to prevent foreign material from entering engine.

17. Inspect the manifold.
18. Check the manifold surfaces for flatness with straight edge. Surface must be flat within 0.006 inches per foot (0.15 mm per 300 mm) of manifold length.
19. Inspect the manifold for cracks or distortion. Replace the manifold if necessary.

To install:

If the following items were removed, install and torque to specifications:

- Fuel rail bolts: 200 inch lbs. (22 Nm)
- Coolant outlet connector bolts: 250 inch lbs. (28 Nm).
- Coolant temperature sensor: 60 inch lbs. (7 Nm)

20. Position a new gasket on the cylinder head and install the lower manifold.
21. Install and tighten the intake manifold fasteners to 250 inch lbs. (28 Nm) in the sequence shown in. Repeat the procedure until all bolts are at the specified torque.
22. Install the lower intake manifold support bracket bolts. Torque the bolts to the intake to 250 inch lbs. (28 Nm). Torque the bolts to the engine block to 40 ft. lbs. (54 Nm).
23. Connect the fuel line.
24. Connect the coolant temperature sensor/fuel injector wiring harness electrical connector.
25. Install the radiator upper and heater supply hoses.
26. Install the upper intake manifold.
27. Fill the cooling system.

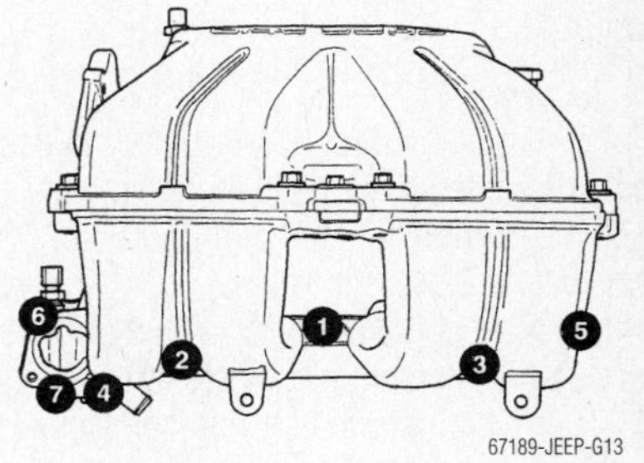

Fig. 95 Lower intake manifold torque sequence—2.4L engines w/2-piece manifold

2.4L Engine with 1-Piece Composite Manifold

See Figure 96.

The intake manifold is a one piece composite module that attaches to the cylinder head with fasteners.

1. Before servicing the vehicle, refer to the precautions in the beginning of this section.
2. Disconnect negative cable from battery.
3. Disconnect connector from inlet air temperature sensor.
4. Disconnect air intake tube at throttle body and remove upper air cleaner housing.
5. Disconnect connector from Throttle Position Sensor (TPS).
6. Disconnect the connector from the Throttle Position Sensor (TPS).
7. Disconnect the connector from the Idle Air Control (IAC) motor.
8. Disconnect the connector from the Manifold Absolute Pressure (MAP) sensor.
9. Remove the vacuum lines for the purge solenoid and the Positive Crankcase Ventilation (PCV) valve at the intake manifold.
10. Remove the vacuum lines for the power brake booster, LDP, Exhaust Gas Recirculation (EGR) transducer, and speed control vacuum reservoir (if equipped) at the upper intake manifold fittings.
11. Disconnect throttle, speed control (if equipped), and transaxle control (if equipped) and cables from throttle lever and bracket.
12. Perform fuel system pressure release procedure before attempting any repairs.
13. Disconnect fuel line.
14. Disconnect coolant temperature sensor/fuel injector wire harness connector.
15. Disconnect fuel injector harness.
16. Remove intake manifold to cylinder head fasteners.
17. Remove the manifold from engine.

➡Cover intake manifold openings to prevent foreign material from entering engine.

To install:

18. Check manifold surfaces for flatness with straightedge. Surface must be flat within 0.15 mm per 300 mm (0.006 in. per foot) of manifold length.
19. Inspect manifold for cracks or distortion. Replace manifold if necessary.
20. Clean manifold sealing surfaces.
21. Install new manifold to cylinder head seals.
22. Install manifold to head.
23. Install and tighten intake manifold fasteners to 250 inch lbs. (28 Nm) in the sequence shown. Repeat procedure until all bolts are at specified torque.

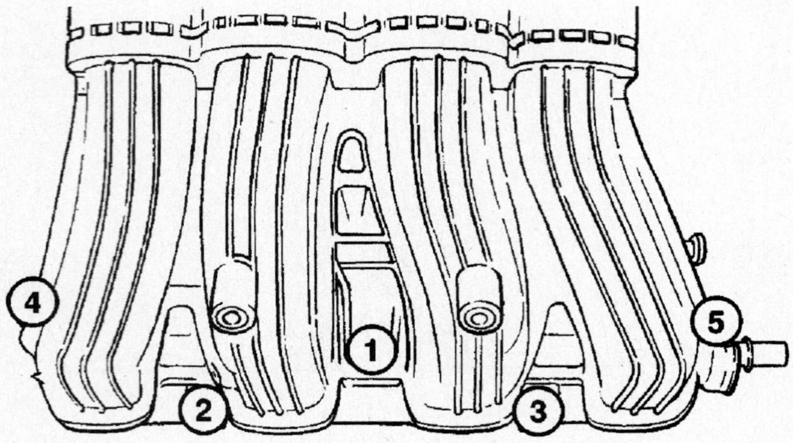

Fig. 96 Intake manifold torque sequence—2.4L engines w/1-piece composite manifold

24. Install throttle cables in bracket.
25. Connect throttle, speed control, (if equipped), cables to throttle lever.
26. Connect vacuum lines for power brake booster, LDP, EGR transducer, and speed control vacuum reservoir (if equipped) at upper intake manifold fittings.
27. Connect vacuum lines for purge solenoid and PCV valve.
28. Connect electrical connectors for MAP sensor, Throttle Position Sensor (TPS), and Idle Air Control (IAC) motor.
29. Connect the fuel line.
30. Connect coolant temperature sensor/fuel injector wiring harness electrical connector.
31. Install the air cleaner housing and air intake tube to throttle body.
32. Connect inlet air temperature sensor connector.
33. Connect negative cable to battery.

2.8L Diesel Engine

See Figure 97.

1. Disconnect negative battery cable.
2. Remove engine cover and bracket.
3. Drain cooling system.
4. Evacuate A/C.
5. Remove radiator core support.
6. Remove cooling fan and fan drive viscous clutch assembly.
7. Remove accessory drive belt.
8. Remove accessory drive belt tensioner and both idler pulleys, Idler pulley bolts are L.H. thread.
9. Remove power steering pump pulley.
10. Remove front engine lift bracket.
11. Remove cooling fan support.
12. Remove generator and support bracketing.
13. Remove viscous heater.
14. Rotate the engine to 90 ° ATDC, or the 3 o-clock position at the crankshaft hub.
15. Remove vibration damper.
16. Disconnect main engine wiring harness connectors from right inner wheel housing.
17. Disconnect main engine wiring harness ancillary components and set harness aside.
18. Remove air cleaner housing.
19. Remove exhaust manifold heat shield.
20. Remove turbocharger heat shield retaining bolt and position shield aside .
21. Remove turbocharger oil supply line from turbocharger.
22. Raise and support vehicle.
23. Disconnect exhaust stabilizer bracket at lower exhaust manifold .
24. Disconnect exhaust system bracket at transmission cross member.
25. Lower the vehicle and remove the exhaust manifold retaining nuts.
26. Slide the exhaust manifold and turbocharger off of exhaust manifold studs .
27. Remove coolant hoses at thermostat housing.
28. Disconnect fuel return hose from fuel injectors and set aside.
29. Remove fuel injector pressure lines.
30. Disconnect fuel pump high pressure line at fuel rail.

31. Disconnect oil level indicator tube from intake manifold.
32. Disconnect brake booster line bracket from intake manifold and position aside.
33. Remove fuel injectors.

⁂ CAUTION

Before removing the cylinder head cover/ intake manifold or timing belt the crankshaft hub must placed at 90° ATDC or the 3 O'clock position. Failure to do so could result in valve and/or piston damage during reassembly.

34. Remove timing belt outer cover.
35. Remove timing belt.
36. Using VM.1085, remove both camshaft gears.
37. Remove timing belt inner cover.
38. Remove cylinder head cover/intake manifold.

To install:

39. Slide exhaust manifold and turbocharger on exhaust manifold studs .
40. Install exhaust manifold retaining nuts. Tighten the nuts to 27 ft. lbs. (36 Nm) in a cross sequence beginning in the middle and working outward, then perform the tightening sequence to the exhaust manifold nuts again.
41. Install exhaust manifold heat shield. Torque bolts to 217 inch lbs. (24.5 Nm).
42. Install turbocharger outlet to charge air cooler pipe.
43. Install upper radiator hose.
44. Install new cylinder head cover/intake manifold gasket.
45. Install cylinder head cover/intake manifold. Tighten the bolts as follows:
    a. Alternate between bolts 11 and 16 to seat cylinder head cover/intake manifold on cylinder head. Tighten the bolts to 62 inch lbs. (7 Nm).
    b. Tighten all cylinder head cover/intake manifold retaining bolts to 18 ft. lbs. (25 Nm) in numerical order starting with 1 and ending with 16.
46. Install timing belt inner cover.

➡Make sure the crankshaft is rotated to the 90° ATCD, or the 3 O'clock position.

47. Install both camshaft gears and tighten bolts finger tight.
48. Install timing belt.
49. Using VM.1085, torque cam gear retaining bolts to 108 Nm.
50. Install timing belt outer cover.

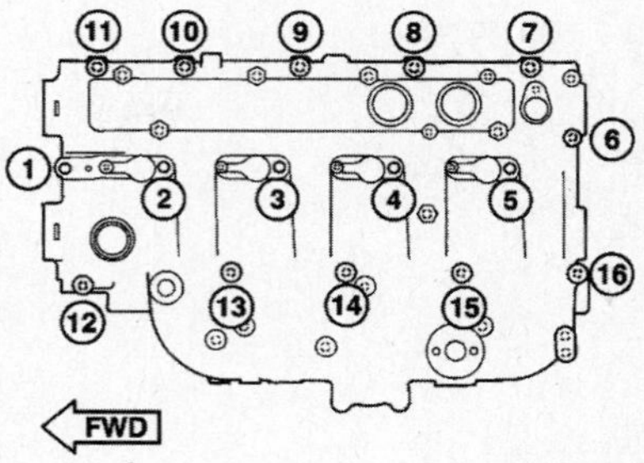

Fig. 97 2.8L engine cover bolt tightening sequence

51. Remove both camshaft locking pins at this time.
52. Install fuel injectors.
53. Install brake booster line bracket to intake manifold.
54. Install oil level indicator tube to intake manifold.
55. Connect fuel pump high pressure line to fuel rail.
56. Install fuel injector pressure lines.
57. Connect fuel return hose to fuel injectors.
58. Connect engine coolant hoses to thermostat housing.
59. Raise vehicle.
60. Reconnect exhaust system bracket at transmission cross member.
61. Connect exhaust stabilizer bracket to lower exhaust manifold .
62. Install turbocharger oil supply line to turbocharger.
63. Lower vehicle.
64. Install turbocharger heat shield.
65. Install exhaust manifold heat shield.
66. Install air cleaner housing.
67. Install main engine wiring harness and connect all ancillary electrical components.
68. Install viscous heater.
69. Install vibration damper.
70. Install generator.
71. Install cooling fan support.
72. Install front engine lift bracket.
73. Install power steering pump pulley.
74. Install accessory drive belt tensioner and both idler pulleys. Idler pulley retaining bolts are L.H. Thread.
75. Install accessory drive belt.
76. Install cooling fan and fan drive viscous clutch assembly.
77. Install upper radiator core support.
78. Refill cooling system.
79. Install engine cover and bracket.
80. Connect negative battery cable.
81. Start engine and allow to warm. Turn engine off and inspect for leaks.

3.7L Engine

See Figure 98.

1. Before servicing the vehicle, refer to the precautions in the beginning of this section.
2. Drain the cooling system.
3. Properly relieve the fuel system pressure.
4. Remove or disconnect the following:
    - Negative battery cable
    - Air cleaner assembly
    - Accelerator cable
    - Cruise control cable
    - Manifold Absolute Pressure (MAP) sensor connector
    - Intake Air Temperature (IAT) sensor connector
    - Throttle Position (TP) sensor connector
    - Idle Air Control (IAC) valve connector
    - Engine Coolant Temperature (ECT) sensor
    - Positive Crankcase Ventilation (PCV) valve and hose
    - Canister purge vacuum line
    - Brake booster vacuum line
    - Cruise control servo hose
    - Accessory drive belt
    - Alternator
    - A/C compressor
    - Engine ground straps
    - Ignition coil towers
    - Oil dipstick tube
    - Fuel line
    - Fuel supply manifold
    - Throttle body and mounting bracket
    - Cowl seal
    - Right engine lifting stud
    - Intake manifold. Remove the fasteners in reverse of the tightening sequence.

To install:

5. Install or connect the following:
    - Intake manifold using new gaskets. Torque the bolts, in sequence, to 105 inch lbs. (12 Nm).
    - Right engine lifting stud
    - Cowl seal
    - Throttle body and mounting bracket
    - Fuel supply manifold
    - Fuel line
    - Oil dipstick tube
    - Ignition coil towers
    - Engine ground straps
    - A/C compressor
    - Alternator
    - Accessory drive belt
    - Cruise control servo hose
    - Brake booster vacuum line
    - Canister purge vacuum line

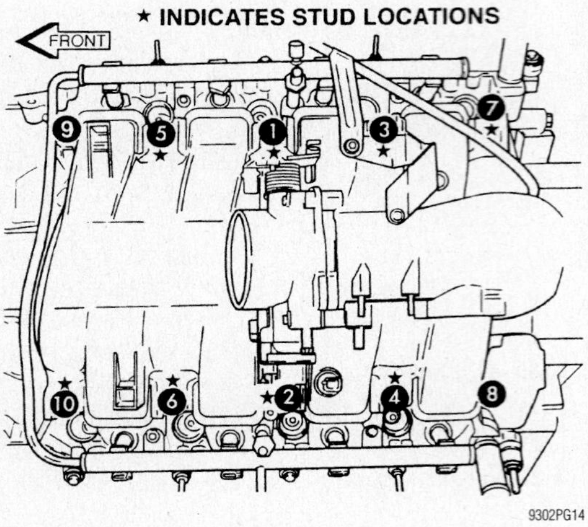

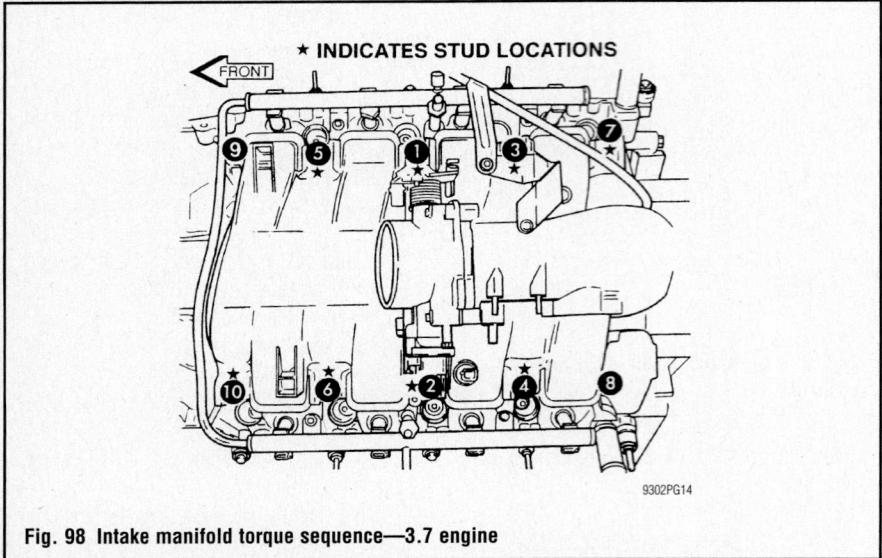

Fig. 98 Intake manifold torque sequence—3.7 engine

- PCV valve and hose
- ECT sensor
- IAC valve connector
- TP sensor connector
- IAT sensor connector
- MAP sensor connector
- Cruise control cable
- Accelerator cable
- Air cleaner assembly
- Negative battery cable

6. Fill and bleed the cooling system.
7. Start the engine, check for leaks and repair if necessary.

4.0L Engine

See Figure 99.

➡The intake and exhaust manifold is removed as an assembly.

1. Before servicing the vehicle, refer to the precautions in the beginning of this section.
2. Disconnect the battery negative cable.
3. Remove air cleaner inlet hose from the resonator assembly.
4. Remove the air cleaner assembly.
5. Remove the throttle cable, vehicle speed control cable (if equipped) and the transmission line pressure cable.
6. Disconnect the following electrical connections and secure their harness out of the way:
   - Throttle Position Sensor
   - Idle Air Control Motor
   - Coolant Temperature Sensor (at thermostat housing)
   - Intake Air Temperature Sensor
   - Oxygen Sensor
   - Crank Position Sensor
   - Six Fuel Injector Connectors
   - Manifold Absolute Pressure (MAP) Sensor.
7. Disconnect HVAC, and Brake Booster vacuum supply hoses at the intake manifold.
8. Perform the fuel pressure release procedure.
9. Disconnect and remove the fuel system supply line from the fuel rail assembly.
10. Remove the accessory drive belt.
11. Remove the power steering pump from the intake manifold and set aside.
12. Raise the vehicle.
13. Disconnect the exhaust pipes from the engine exhaust manifolds.
14. Lower the vehicle.
15. Remove the intake manifold and exhaust manifold bolts and manifolds.

To install:

➡If the manifold is being replaced, ensure all the fittings, etc. are transferred to the replacement manifold.

16. Install a new engine exhaust/intake manifold gasket over the alignment dowels on the cylinder head.
17. Position the engine exhaust manifolds to the cylinder head. Install fastener Number 3 and finger tighten at this time.
18. Install intake manifold on the cylinder head dowels.
19. Install washers and fasteners 1, 2, 4, 5, 8, 9, 10 and 11.
20. Install washers and fasteners 6 and 7.
21. Tighten the fasteners in sequence and to the specified torque.
    - Fasteners 1 through 5: 24 ft. lbs. (33 Nm).
    - Fasteners 6 and 7: Tighten to 23 ft. lbs. (31 Nm).
    - Fasteners 8 through 11: 24 ft. lbs. (33 Nm).
22. Install the power steering pump to the intake manifold.
23. Install the accessory drive belt.
24. Install the fuel system supply line to the fuel rail assembly.
25. Connect all electrical connections on the intake manifold.
26. Connect the vacuum hoses previously removed.
27. Install throttle cable, vehicle speed control cable (if equipped).
28. Install the transmission line pressure cable (if equipped).
29. Install air cleaner assembly.
30. Connect air inlet hose to the resonator assembly.

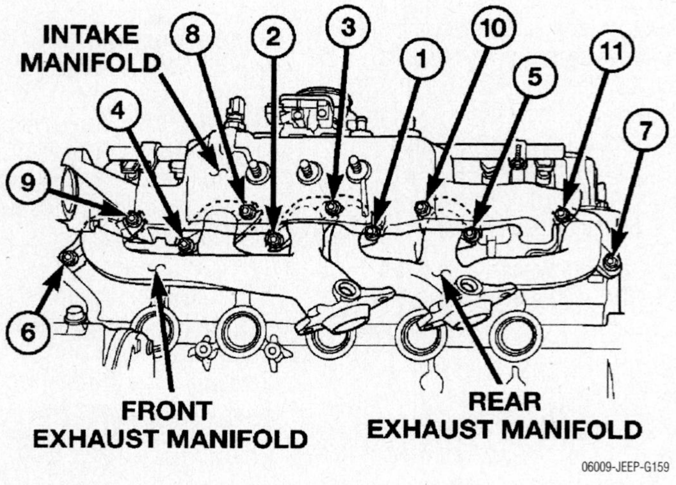

Fig. 99 Manifold torque sequence—4.0L engine

31. Raise the vehicle.
32. Connect the exhaust pipes to the engine exhaust manifolds. Tighten the bolts to 23 ft. lbs. (31 Nm)
33. Lower the vehicle.
34. Connect the battery negative cable.
35. Start the engine and check for leaks.

OIL PAN

REMOVAL & INSTALLATION

2.4L Engine

See Figure 100.

1. Before servicing the vehicle, refer to the precautions in the beginning of this section.
2. Remove air cleaner assembly.
3. Raise the vehicle on a hoist and drain the engine oil.
4. Loosen the engine mount through bolts.
5. Disconnect the exhaust pipe at the manifold.
6. Remove the structural collar, if equipped.
7. Remove the front axle mounting bolts, and lower the axle as far possible, if equipped.
8. Position Special Tool 8534, or equivalent, on the fender lip and align the slots in the brackets with the fender mounting holes.
9. Secure the brackets to the fender using four M6 X 1.0 X 25 mm flanged cap screws.
10. Tighten the thumbscrews to secure the sleeves to the support tube.
11. Secure the support tube in an upright position.
12. Assemble the flat washer, thrust bearing, hook and T handle.
13. Using the M10 X 1.5 X 40 mm capscrew supplied with the support fixture, secure the chain to the front cover and the hook.
14. Support the engine as needed.
15. Remove the oil pan attaching bolts.
16. Remove the oil pan.
17. Clean the oil pan and all gasket surfaces.

To install:

18. Install the oil pan gasket to the block.
19. Apply a 3mm (1⁄8 inch) bead of Mopar® Engine RTV, or equivalent, at the oil pump to engine block parting line.
20. Install the pan and tighten the screws to 105 inch lbs. (12 Nm).
21. Lower the engine, and remove Special Tool 8534.

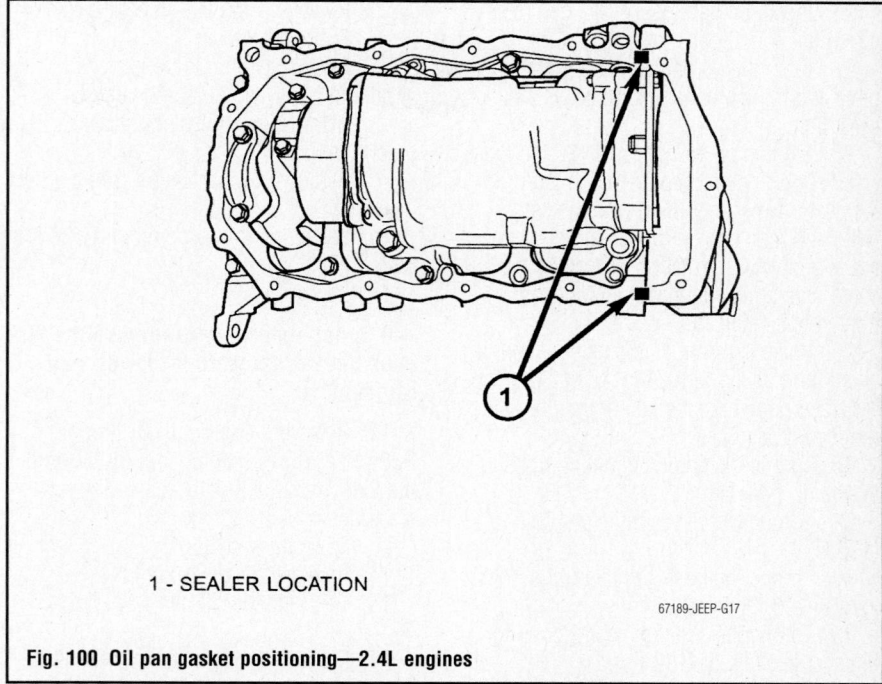

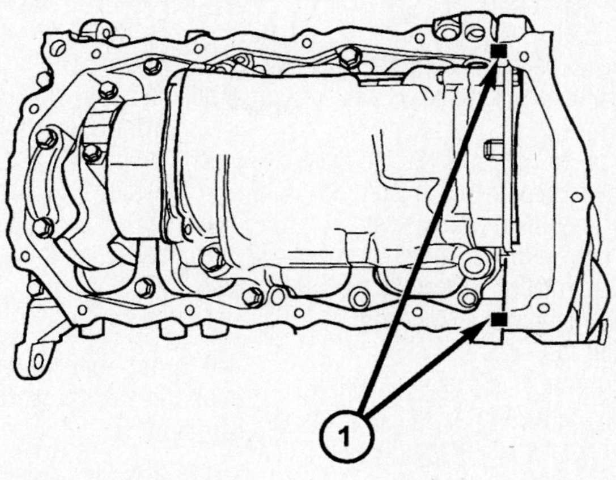

Fig. 100 Oil pan gasket positioning—2.4L engines

22. Tighten the engine mount through bolts.
23. Raise the front axle into position, and reinstall the front axle mounting bolts, if equipped.
24. Reconnect the exhaust pipe to the manifold.
25. Install the structural collar, if equipped.
26. Lower the vehicle.
27. Fill the engine crankcase with the proper oil to the correct level.
28. Reinstall the air cleaner assembly.

2.8L Engine

RWD Models

1. Disconnect negative battery cable.
2. Remove engine cover.

➡When installing engine support fixture, care must be taken not to damage the hood ajar switch mounted to the right inner fender.

3. Install engine support fixture, special tool no. 8534.
4. Raise vehicle on hoist.
5. Remove both front wheel and tire assemblies.
6. Remove front skid plate (if equipped).
7. Drain engine oil.
8. Disconnect the front drive shaft from the front drive axle.
9. Loosen both engine mount through bolts.
10. Lower vehicle.
11. Raise engine using support fixture, special tool no. 8534, until the viscous fan almost touches the fan shroud.
12. Raise vehicle on hoist.
13. Support the front cradle assembly with a suitable lifting devise.
14. Mark the front cradle to under body position to assure proper alignment during assembly.
15. Remove both inner rail cradle alignment bolts in the front wheel housing.
16. Loosen both power steering gear retaining bolts, leave the retaining nuts on the bolts.
17. Loosen power steering lines from cradle.
18. Remove both lower front strut bolts.
19. Loosen both front cradle mounting bolts.
20. Loosen both rear cradle mounting bolts.
21. Disconnect the oil sending unit harness connector.
22. Remove all oil pan retaining bolts, separate the oil level indicator tube from the pan and lower oil pan.
23. Lower front cradle using the suitable lifting devise until enough clearance is obtained to remove the oil pan.

To install:

24. Clean oil pan and sealing surfaces. Inspect oil pan and engine block.
25. Install a new oil filter on the oil pan.

➡If installing a new oil pan, exchange the oil sending unit and install a new oil filter.

26. Install oil pan, gasket, oil pan retaining bolts, hand tight.
27. Push the oil pan against adapter plate and tighten transmission to oil pan bolts first.
28. Tighten oil pan bolts to 130 inch lbs. (14.7 Nm), tighten oil pan nuts to 217 inch lbs. (24.5 Nm), beginning with the center bolts and then tighten the remaining fasteners in a clockwise rotation. Retighten the center two bolts again after all bolts are tighten to specification.
29. Raise the front cradle using a suitable lifting devise and align the cradle with the underbody marks made during the removal procedure.
30. Torque the cradle mounting bolts to 90 lbs. ft. (122 Nm).
31. Torque the cleves bolts to 100 ft. lbs. (136 Nm).
32. Torque the inner rail mounting bolts to 35 lbs. ft. (47 Nm).
33. Torque the steering gear mounting bolts to 120 lbs. ft. (162 Nm).
34. Remove the cradle support devise and lower the vehicle.
35. Lower the engine using support fixture, special tool no. 8534, until the engine mount through bolts are seated in the cradle.
36. Raise the vehicle.
37. Torque engine mount through bolts to 65 lbs. ft. (88 Nm).
38. Connect the oil sending unit harness connector.
39. Install front axle skid plate (if equipped).
40. Install both front wheel and tire assemblies and tighten to 85–115 lbs. ft. (115–155 Nm).

➡When removing engine support fixture, care must be taken not to damage the hood ajar switch mounted to the right inner fender well (if equipped).

41. Lower the vehicle and remove the engine support fixture.
42. Refill engine to proper level with the correct viscosity engine oil.
43. Connect negative battery cable.
44. Start engine and inspect for leaks.
45. Install engine cover.
46. Perform complete front wheel alignment.

4WD Models

1. Disconnect Battery.
2. Install Engine Support Fixture, special Tool 8534.
3. Raise and support vehicle.
4. Remove front wheel and tire assemblies.
5. Remove skid plate (if equipped).
6. Drain engine oil.
7. Remove engine to transmission structural cover, (if equipped).
8. Remove transmission oil cooler line bracket.
9. Remove the front axle assembly from the vehicle.
10. Loosen both engine mount through bolts.
11. Lower the vehicle.

➡It is not necessary to remove the viscous fan , or fan shroud, for oil pan removal.

12. Raise the engine using Engine Support Fixture, special Tool 8534, until the viscous fan almost touches the fan shroud.
13. Raise the vehicle.
14. Remove the oil pan bolts.
15. Separate the oil pan from the engine.
16. Remove the nuts and bolt holding the oil pump pick-up tube, and windage tray in place.

➡It will be necessary to move the oil pan from side to side to gain access to these fasteners.

17. Drop the oil pump pick-up tube into the oil pan, and remove the oil pan, pick-up tube, and the windage tray, as an assembly, from the front of the vehicle.

To install:

18. Inspect oil pan gasket for defects, and replace if necessary.
19. Clean the oil pan and block gasket mating surfaces.
20. Drop the oil pump pick-up tube into the oil pan, and install the oil pan, pick-up tube, and the windage tray, as an assembly, from the front of the vehicle.
21. Install the windage tray, then the oil pump pick-up tube, and the nuts and bolt holding the oil pump pick-up tube, in place.

➡It will be necessary to move the oil pan from side to side to gain access to these fasteners.

22. Torque the pick-up tube fasteners.
23. Install the oil pan.
24. Install and torque the oil pan bolts.
25. Install the engine to transmission structural cover, (if equipped).
26. Lower the vehicle.
27. Lower the engine using Engine Support Fixture, special Tool no. 8534.
28. Remove the Engine Support Fixture, special Tool no. 8534.
29. Raise the vehicle.
30. Tighten both engine mount through bolts.
31. Install the transmission oil cooler line bracket.
32. Install the front axle assembly to the vehicle.
33. Install the skid plate (if equipped).
34. Install the front wheel and tire assemblies.
35. Lower the vehicle.
36. Refill engine oil.
37. Reconnect battery.
38. Start engine, and check for leaks.

3.7L Engine

1. Before servicing the vehicle, refer to the precautions in the beginning of this section.
2. Disconnect the negative battery cable.
3. Install engine support fixture special tool 8534, or equivalent.

➡Do not raise engine at this time.

4. Loosen both left and right side engine mount through bolts. Do not remove bolts.
5. Remove the structural dust cover.
6. Drain engine oil.

⁂ WARNING

Only raise the engine enough to provide clearance for oil pan removal. Check for proper clearance at fan shroud to fan and cowl to intake manifold.

7. Raise engine using special tool 8534 to provide clearance to remove oil pan.

➡Do not pry on oil pan or oil pan gasket. Gasket is integral to engine windage tray and does not come out with oil pan.

8. Remove the oil pan mounting bolts and oil pan.
9. Unbolt oil pump pickup tube and remove tube.
10. Inspect the integral windage tray and gasket and replace as needed.

To install:

11. Clean the oil pan gasket mating surface of the bedplate and oil pan.
12. Position the oil pan gasket and pickup tube with new O-ring. Install the mounting bolt and nuts. Tighten bolt and nuts to 20 ft. lbs. (28 Nm).
13. Position the oil pan and install the mounting bolts. Tighten the mounting bolts to 11 ft. lbs. (15 Nm) in the sequence shown.

14. Lower the engine into mounts using special tool 8534.

15. Install both the left and right side engine mount through bolts. Tighten the nuts to 50 ft. lbs. (68 Nm).

16. Remove special tool 8534.

17. Install structural dust cover.

18. Fill engine oil.

19. Reconnect the negative battery cable.

20. Start engine and check for leaks.

4.0L Engine

See Figures 101 through 103.

1. Disconnect negative cable from battery.

2. Raise the vehicle.

3. Remove the oil pan drain plug and drain the engine oil.

4. Disconnect the exhaust pipe at the exhaust manifold.

5. Disconnect the exhaust hanger at the catalytic converter and lower the pipe.

6. Remove the starter motor.

7. Remove the engine flywheel and transmission torque converter housing access cover.

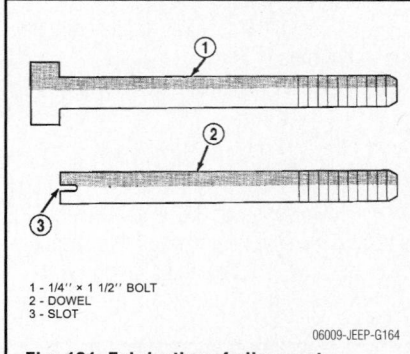

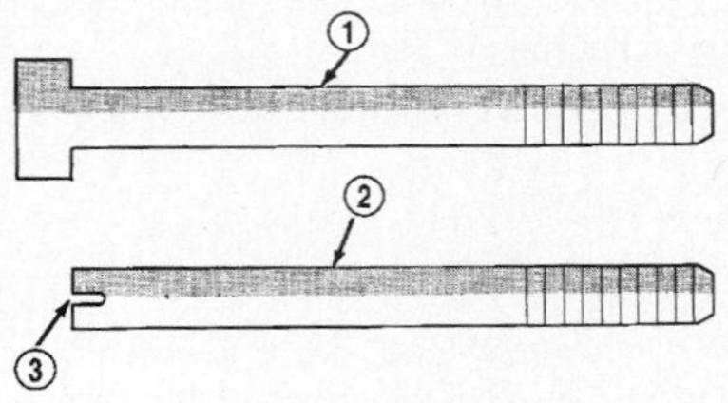

Fig. 101 Fabrication of alignment dowels—4.0L engine

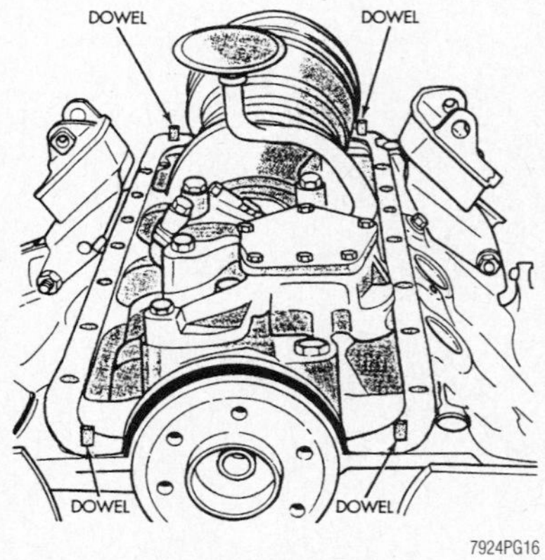

Fig. 102 Oil pan alignment dowel placement—4.0L engines

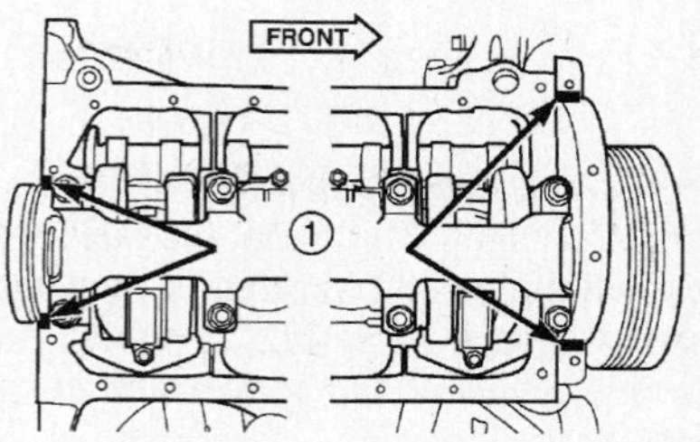

Fig. 103 RTV sealer application points—4.0L engine

8. If equipped with an oil level sensor, disconnect the sensor.

9. Position a jack stand directly under the engine vibration damper.

10. Place a piece of wood (2 x 2) between the jack stand and the engine vibration damper.

11. Remove the engine mount through bolts.

12. Using the jack stand, raise the engine until adequate clearance is obtained to remove the oil pan.

13. Remove the oil pan bolts. Carefully slide the oil pan and gasket to the rear. If equipped with an oil level sensor, take care not to damage the sensor.

To install:

14. Fabricate 4 alignment dowels from 1½ in. x ¼ in. bolts. Cut the heads off the bolts and cut a slot into the top of the dowel to allow installation/removal with a screwdriver.

15. Install or connect the following:
- Dowels
- RTV sealer at the points shown
- Oil pan, using a new gasket. Torque the ¼ inch bolts to 85 inch lbs. (9.5 Nm) and the 5⁄16 inch bolts to 11 ft. lbs. (15 Nm).

16. Replace the alignment dowels with ¼ inch bolts and torque them to 85 inch lbs. (9.5 Nm).

17. Install or connect the following:
- Left and right motor mounts
- Oil level sensor connector, if equipped
- Bell housing access cover
- Starter motor
- Exhaust front pipe
- Negative battery cable

18. Fill the engine with clean oil.

19. Start the engine, check for leaks and repair if necessary.

OIL PUMP

REMOVAL & INSTALLATION

2.4L Engine

See Figures 104 through 108.

1. Before servicing the vehicle, refer to the precautions in the beginning of this section.

2. Disconnect the negative cable from battery.

3. Remove the timing belt.

4. Remove the timing belt rear cover.

5. Remove the oil pan.

6. Remove the crankshaft sprocket using Special Tools 6793 and C-4685-C2, or equivalent.

7. Remove the crankshaft key.

8. Remove the oil pick-up tube.

9. Remove the oil pump and front crankshaft seal.

To install:

10. Make sure all surfaces are clean and free of oil and dirt.

11. Apply Mopar® Gasket Maker, or equivalent, to the oil pump as shown. Install

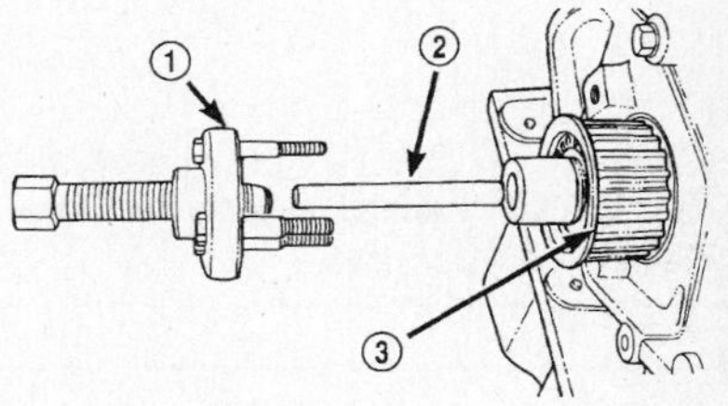

Fig. 104 Crankshaft sprocket removal—2.4L engines

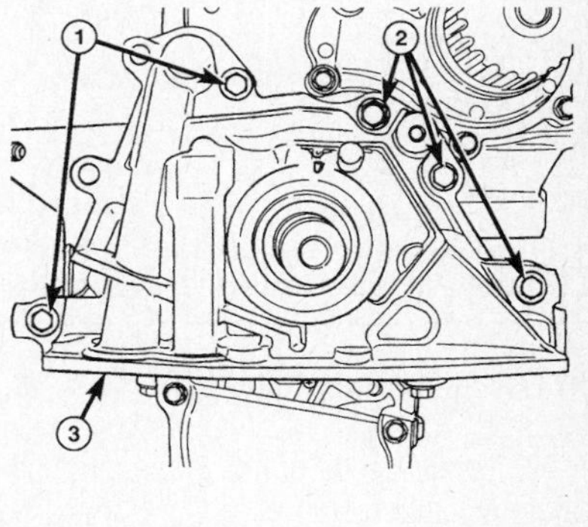

Fig. 105 Oil pump—2.4L engines

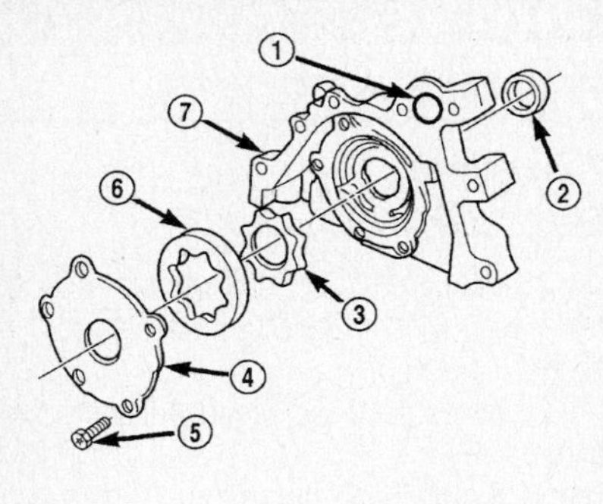

Fig. 106 Oil pump parts—2.4L engines

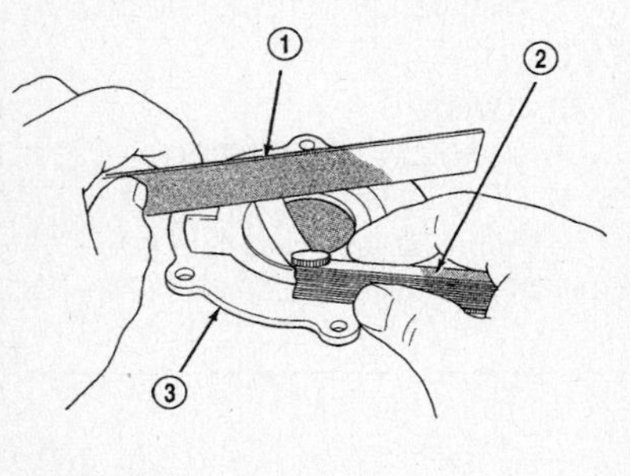

Fig. 107 Checking the oil pump body for flatness—2.4L engines

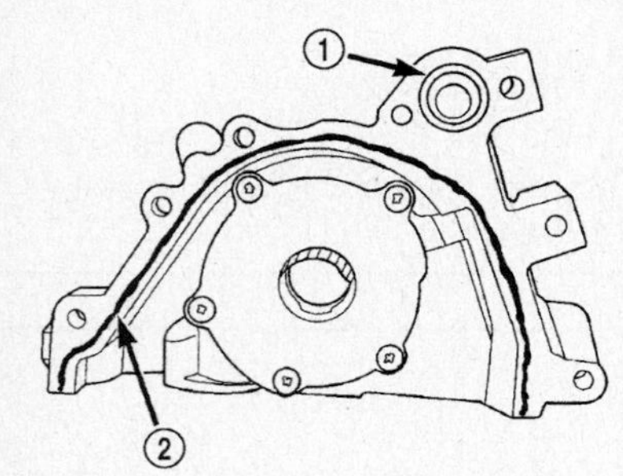

Fig. 108 Oil pump sealing—2.4L engines

the O-ring into the oil pump body discharge passage.

12. Prime the oil pump with engine oil before installation.

13. Align the oil pump rotor flats with the flats on the crankshaft. Install the oil pump to the block.

➡To align, the front crankshaft seal MUST be out of the pump, or damage may result.

14. Install a new front crankshaft seal.
15. Install the crankshaft key.

➡The crankshaft sprocket is set to a predetermined depth from the factory for correct timing belt tracking. If removed, use of Special Tool 6792, or equivalent, is required to set the sprocket to original installation depth. An incorrectly installed sprocket will result in timing belt and engine damage.

16. Install the crankshaft sprocket using Special Tool 6792.
17. Install the oil pump pick-up tube.
18. Install the oil pan.
19. Install the timing belt rear cover.
20. Install the timing belt.

2.8L Diesel Engine

See Figure 109.

1. Disconnect negative battery cable.
2. Remove cooling fan and fan drive viscous clutch assembly.
3. Remove accessory drive belt.
4. Remove cooling fan support.
5. Remove vibration damper.
6. Remove the power steering pump pulley.
7. Remove timing belt outer cover.

➡The crankshaft must be rotated to 90° ATDC and special tool VM.1089 installed.

8. Remove timing belt.
9. Remove timing belt inner cover.
10. Remove front engine cover.
11. Remove crankshaft sprocket.
12. Remove oil pump retaining bolts and remove pump from engine block.

To install:

13. Lubricate oil pump rotor with engine oil.
14. Install oil pump in bore in engine block.
15. Install oil pump retaining bolts. Torque bolts to 96 inch lbs. (10.8 Nm.).
16. Install crankshaft sprocket. Torque bolts to inch lbs. (10.8 Nm.).
17. Install front engine cover and seal.
18. Install timing belt inner cover.
19. Install the lower timing belt gear and hand tighten fastener.
20. Connect special tool no. 6958 to the lower timing gear using the vibration damper bolts and tighten the timing gear fastener to 203 ft. lbs. (275 Nm).
21. Remove special tool no. 6958.
22. Install timing belt.
23. Install timing belt outer cover.
24. Install vibration damper.
25. Install power steering pump pulley.
26. Install cooling fan support.
27. Install accessory drive belt.
28. Install cooling fan and fan drive viscous clutch assembly.
29. Remove the crankshaft and camshaft alignment pins.
30. Connect negative battery cable.

3.7L Engine

See Figure 110.

1. Before servicing the vehicle, refer to the precautions in the beginning of this section.
2. Remove or disconnect the following:
   - Oil Pan

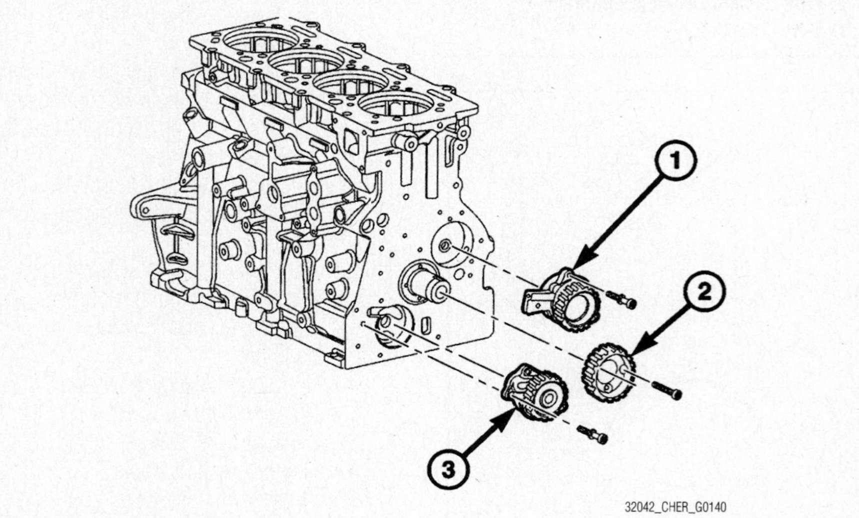

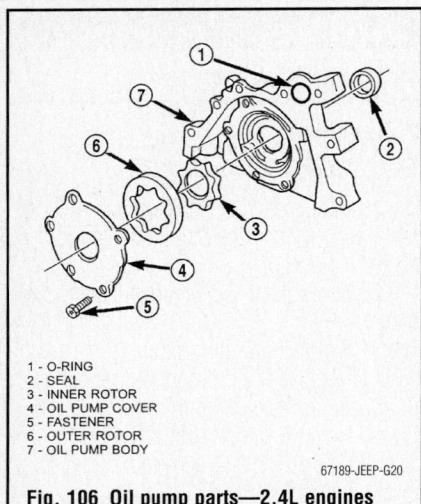

Fig. 109 The oil pump location for the 2.8L diesel engine

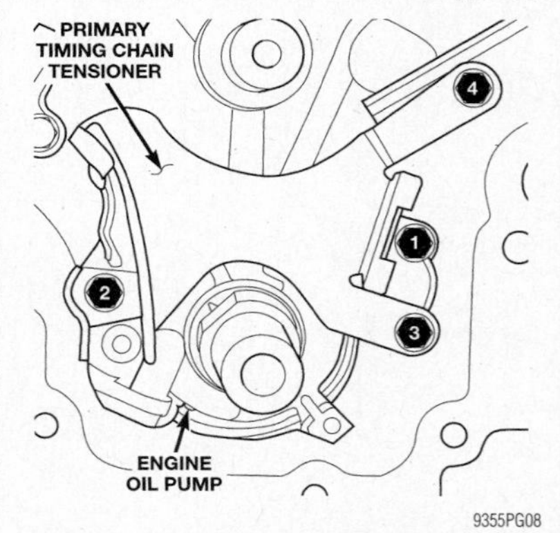

Fig. 110 Oil pump bolt torque sequence—3.7L engine

- Timing chain cover
- Timing chains and tensioners
- Oil pump

3. Installation is the reverse of removal. Torque the pump bolts, in sequence, to 21 ft. lbs. (28 Nm),

4.0L Engines

See Figure 111.

⁂ WARNING

Before servicing the vehicle, refer to the precautions in the beginning of this section.

➡A gear-type oil pump is mounted at the underside of the cylinder block opposite the No.4 main bearing. The pump incorporates a nonadjustable pressure relief valve to limit maximum pressure to 75 psi (517 kPa) In the relief position, the valve permits oil to bypass through a passage in the pump body to the inlet side of the pump. Oil pump removal or replacement will not affect the distributor timing because the distributor drive gear remains in mesh with the camshaft gear.

1. Drain the engine oil.
2. Remove or disconnect the following:
   - Negative battery cable
   - Oil pan
   - Oil pump and pickup tube

➡If the oil pump is not to be serviced, do not disturb the position of the oil inlet tube and strainer assembly in the pump body. If the tube is moved within the pump body, a replacement tube and strainer assembly must be installed to assure an airtight seal.

To install:

3. Install or connect the following:

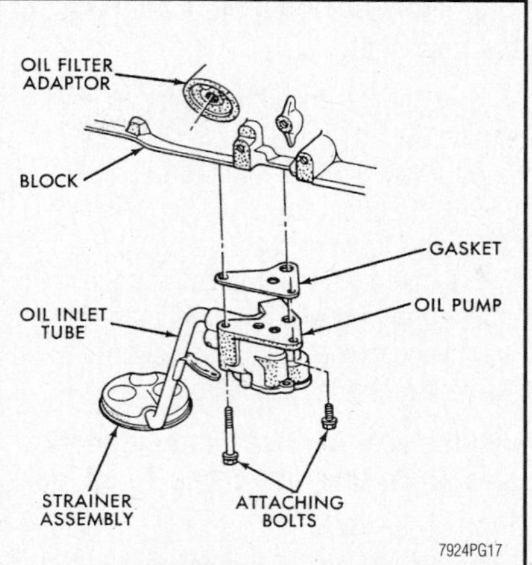

Fig. 111 Exploded view of the oil pump assembly—4.0L engine

- Oil pump. Torque the mounting bolts to 17 ft. lbs. (23 Nm).
- Oil pan
- Negative battery cable

4. Fill the engine with the proper type and quantity of oil.
5. Start the engine, check for leaks and repair if necessary.

INSPECTION

The oil pump is replaced as an assembly; there are no subassembly components. In the event the oil pump is not functioning it must be replaced as an assembly.

PISTON AND RING

POSITIONING

See Figures 112 through 115.

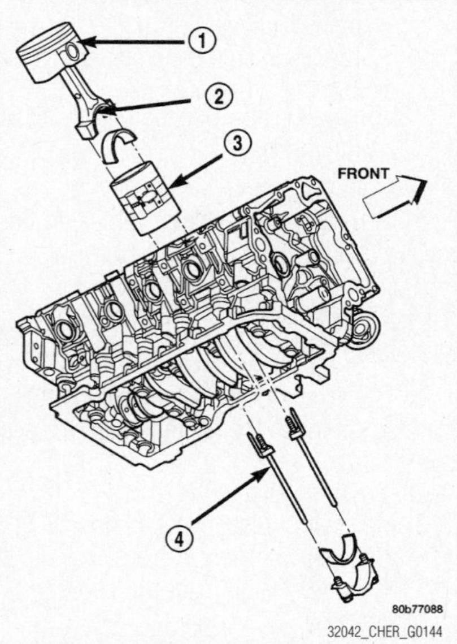

Fig. 112 Piston to engine position—3.7L engine

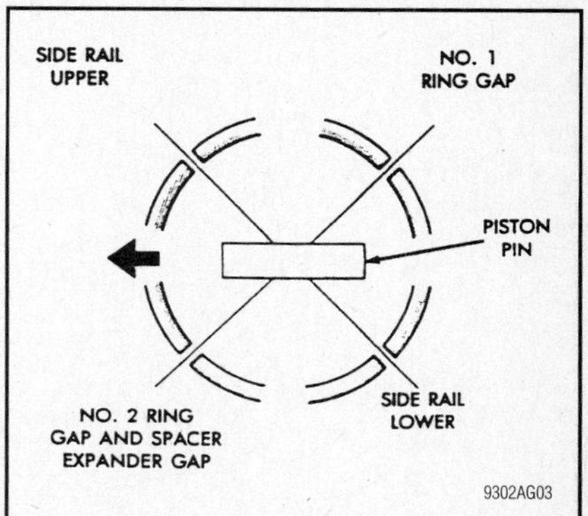

Fig. 113 Piston ring end-gap spacing. Position raised "F" on piston towards front of engine—3.7L engine

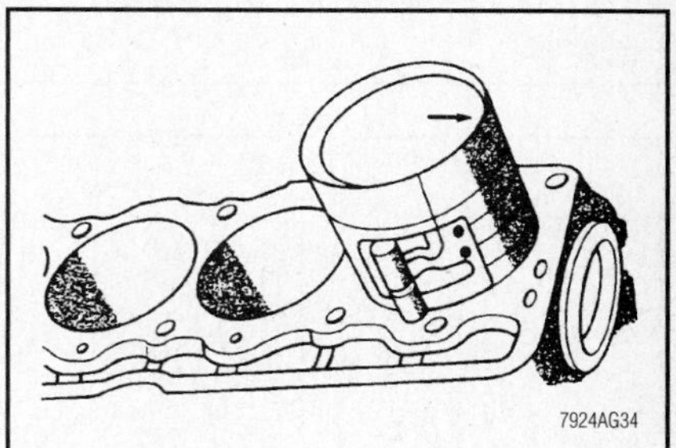

Fig. 114 Piston to engine positioning—4.0L engine

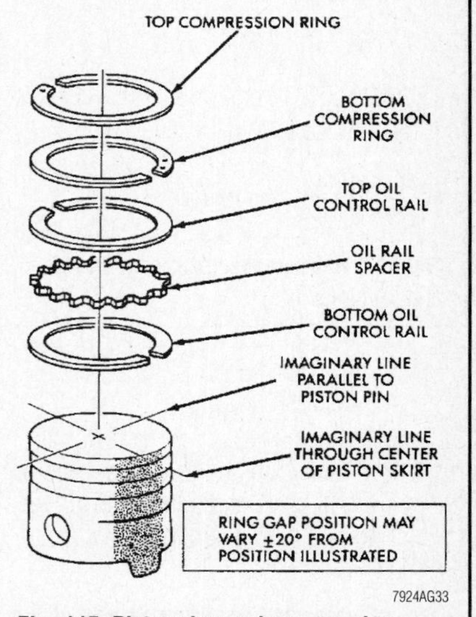

Fig. 115 Piston ring end-gap spacing—4.0L engine

REAR MAIN SEAL

REMOVAL & INSTALLATION

2.4L Engine

See Figures 116 and 117.

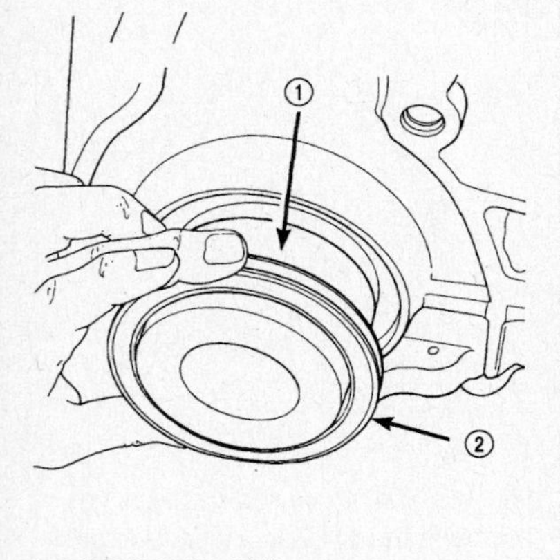

1 - SPECIAL TOOL 6926-1 PILOT
2 - SEAL

67189-JEEP-G23

Fig. 116 Rear crankshaft seal—2.4L engines

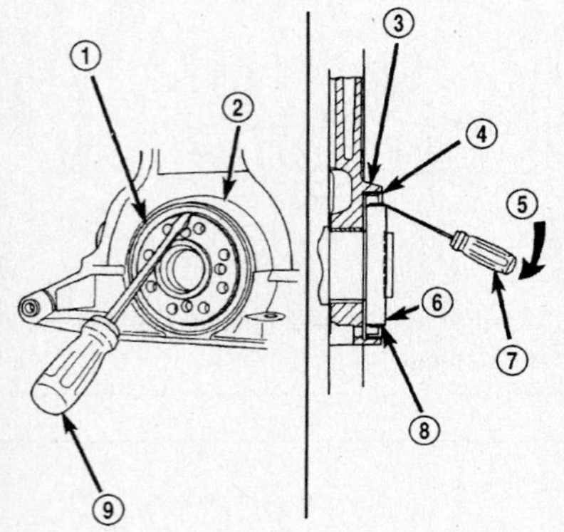

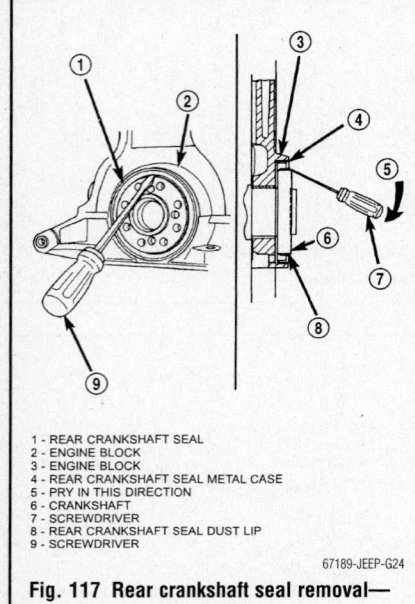

1 - REAR CRANKSHAFT SEAL
2 - ENGINE BLOCK
3 - ENGINE BLOCK
4 - REAR CRANKSHAFT SEAL METAL CASE
5 - PRY IN THIS DIRECTION
6 - CRANKSHAFT
7 - SCREWDRIVER
8 - REAR CRANKSHAFT SEAL DUST LIP
9 - SCREWDRIVER

67189-JEEP-G24

Fig. 117 Rear crankshaft seal removal—2.4L engines

1. Remove the transmission.
2. Remove the flexplate.
3. Insert a 3⁄16 flat bladed screwdriver between the dust lip and the metal case of the crankshaft seal. Angle the screwdriver through the dust lip against metal case of the seal. Pry out seal.

➡Do not permit the screwdriver blade to contact the crankshaft seal surface. Contact of the screwdriver blade against the crankshaft edge (chamfer) is permitted.

To install:

➡If burrs or scratches are present on the crankshaft edge (chamfer), cleanup with 400 grit sand paper to prevent seal damage during the installation of the new seal.

4. Lubricate the crankshaft flange with engine oil.
5. Place Special Tool 6926-1 Seal Guide, or equivalent, on the crankshaft.
6. Position the seal over the guide tool. The guide tool should remain on the crankshaft during installation of the seal. Ensure that the lip of the seal is facing towards the crankcase during installation.

➡If the seal is driven into the block past flush, this may cause an oil leak.

7. Drive the seal into the block using Special Tool 6926-2 and handle C-4171, or equivalent, until the tool bottoms out against the block.
8. Install the flexplate. Apply Mopar® Lock & Seal Adhesive to the bolt threads and tighten the bolts to 70 ft. lbs. (95 Nm).
9. Install the transmission.

3.7L Engine

1. Before servicing the vehicle, refer to the precautions in the beginning of this section.
2. Remove or disconnect the following:
   - Transmission
   - Flexplate
3. Thread Oil Seal Remover 8506 into the rear main seal as far as possible and remove the rear main seal.

To install:

4. Install or connect the following:
   - Seal Guide 8349-2 onto the crankshaft
   - Rear main seal on the seal guide
   - Rear main seal, using the Crankshaft Rear Oil Seal Installer 8349 and Driver Handle C-4171; tap it into place until the installer is flush with the cylinder block
   - Flexplate. Torque the bolts to 45 ft. lbs. (60 Nm).
   - Transmission
5. Start the engine, check for leaks and repair if necessary.

4.0L Engine

See Figure 118.

1. Before servicing the vehicle, refer to the precautions in the beginning of this section.
2. Drain the engine oil.
3. Remove or disconnect the following:
   - Negative battery cable
   - Transmission inspection cover
   - Oil pan
   - Main bearing cap brace
   - No. 7 main bearing cap

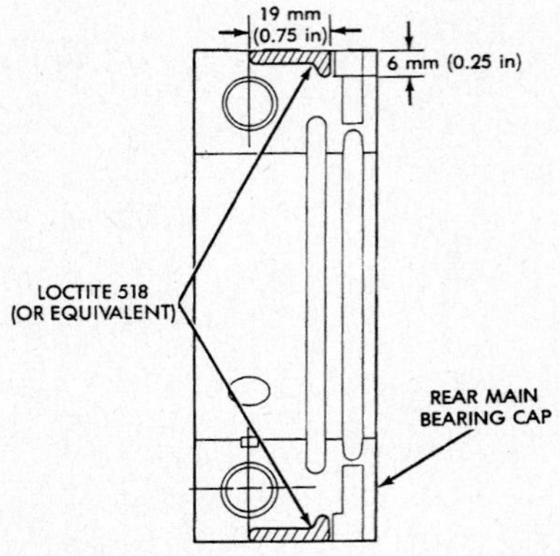

Fig. 118 Sealant application locations—4.0L engine

4. Loosen the other main bearing cap bolts for clearance and remove the rear main seal halves.

To install:

5. Install or connect the following:
   - New upper seal half to the cylinder block
   - New lower seal half to the bearing cap after applying sealant to the bearing cap
   - No. 7 main bearing cap. Torque **all** main bearing cap bolts to 80 ft. lbs. (108 Nm).
   - Main bearing cap brace. Tighten the nuts to 35 ft. lbs. (47 Nm).
   - Oil pan
   - Transmission inspection cover
   - Negative battery cable
6. Fill the engine with clean oil.
7. Start the engine, check for leaks and repair if necessary.

TIMING BELT, FRONT COVER AND SEAL

REMOVAL & INSTALLATION

2.4L Engines

See Figures 119 through 126.

1. Remove the air cleaner upper cover, housing, and clean air tube.
2. Raise the vehicle on hoist.
3. Remove the accessory drive belts.
4. Remove the crankshaft vibration damper.
5. Remove the air conditioner/generator belt tensioner and pulley assembly.
6. Remove the timing belt lower front cover bolts and remove cover.
7. Lower the vehicle.
8. Remove the bolts attaching timing belt upper front cover and remove cover.

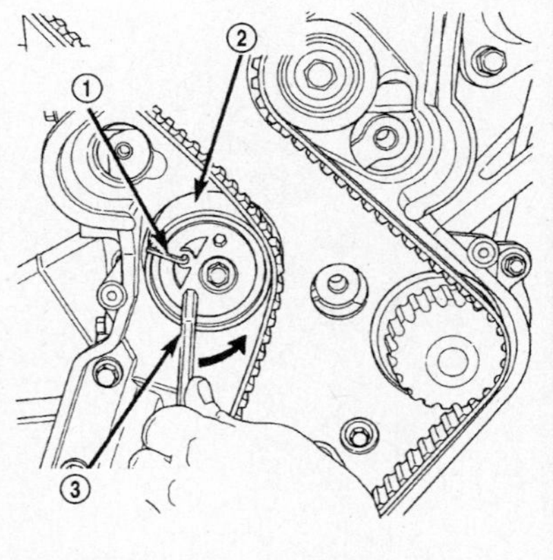

1 - 1/8 OR 3mm ALLEN WRENCH
2 - BELT TENSIONER
3 - 6mm ALLEN WRENCH

67189-JEEP-G30

Fig. 119 Locking the tensioner—2.4L engines

➡When aligning the crankshaft and camshaft timing marks always rotate engine by the crankshaft. Camshaft should not be rotated after the timing belt is removed. Damage to the valve components may occur. Always align the timing marks before removing the timing belt.

9. Before removal of the timing belt, rotate the crankshaft until the TDC mark on the oil pump housing aligns with the TDC mark on the crankshaft sprocket (trailing edge of the sprocket tooth).

➡The crankshaft sprocket TDC mark is located on the trailing edge of the sprocket tooth. Failure to align the trailing edge of sprocket tooth to TDC mark on oil pump housing will cause the camshaft timing marks to be misaligned.

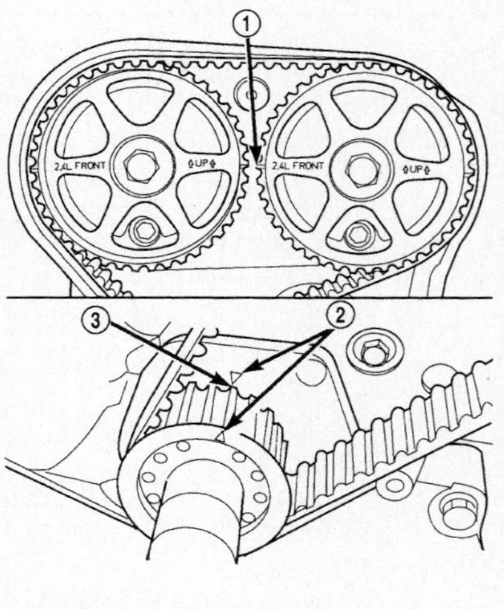

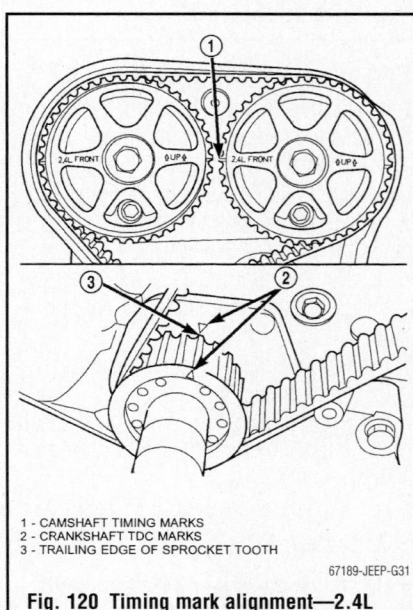

1 - CAMSHAFT TIMING MARKS
2 - CRANKSHAFT TDC MARKS
3 - TRAILING EDGE OF SPROCKET TOOTH

67189-JEEP-G31

Fig. 120 Timing mark alignment—2.4L engines

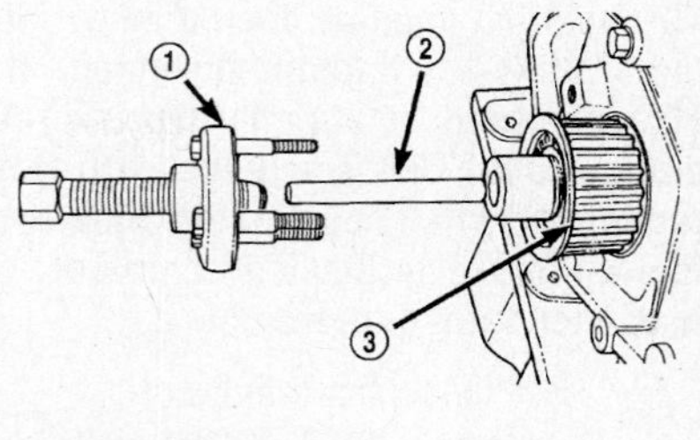

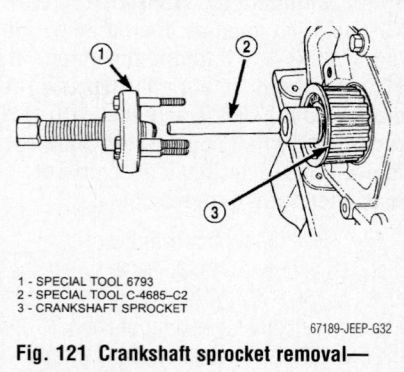

1 - SPECIAL TOOL 6793
2 - SPECIAL TOOL C-4685-C2
3 - CRANKSHAFT SPROCKET

67189-JEEP-G32

Fig. 121 Crankshaft sprocket removal—2.4L engines

10. Install 6 mm Allen wrench into belt tensioner. Before rotating the tensioner, insert the long end of a 1/8 inch or 3 mm Allen wrench into the pin hole on the front of the tensioner. While rotating the tensioner counterclockwise, push in lightly on the 1/8 inch or 3 mm Allen wrench, until it slides into the locking hole.

11. Remove timing belt.

12. Remove crankshaft sprocket using Special Tools 6793 and insert C-4685-C2, or equivalent.

To install:

➡The crankshaft sprocket is set to a predetermined depth from the factory for correct timing belt tracking. If removed, use of Special Tool 6792 is required to set the sprocket to original installation depth. An incorrectly installed sprocket will result in timing belt and engine damage.

13. Install crankshaft sprocket using Special Tool 6792, or equivalent.

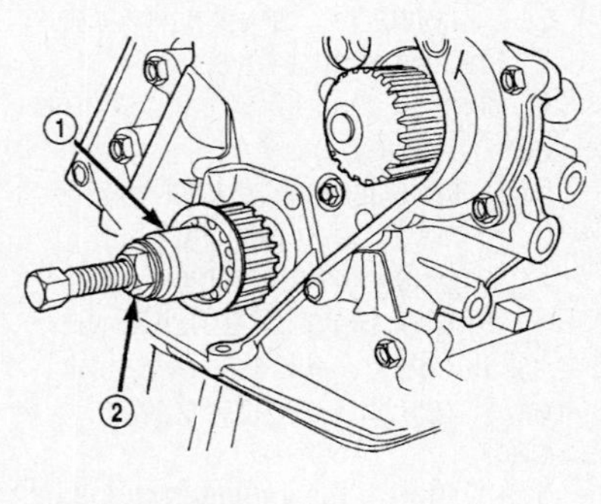

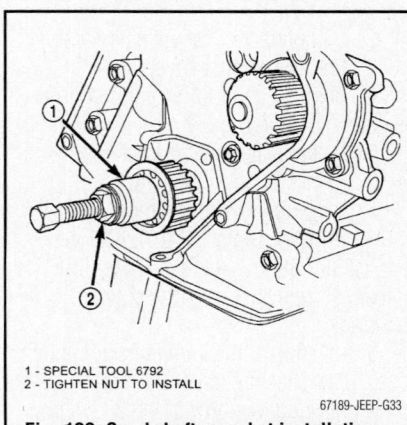

1 - SPECIAL TOOL 6792
2 - TIGHTEN NUT TO INSTALL

67189-JEEP-G33

Fig. 122 Crankshaft sprocket installation—2.4L engines

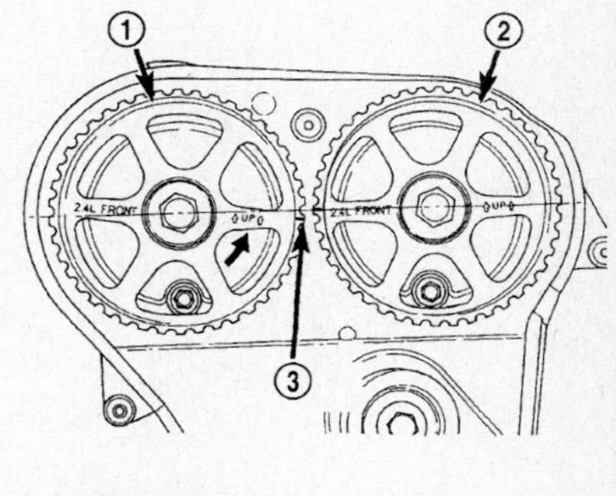

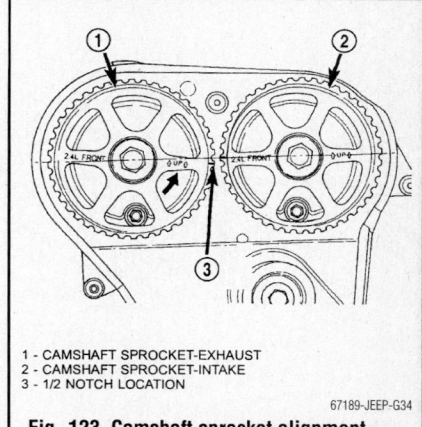

1 - CAMSHAFT SPROCKET-EXHAUST
2 - CAMSHAFT SPROCKET-INTAKE
3 - 1/2 NOTCH LOCATION

67189-JEEP-G34

Fig. 123 Camshaft sprocket alignment—2.4L engines

14. Set crankshaft sprocket to TDC by aligning the sprocket with the arrow on the oil pump housing.

15. Set camshafts timing marks so that the exhaust camshaft sprocket is a 1/2 notch below the intake camshaft sprocket.

CAUTION

Ensure that the arrows on both camshaft sprockets are facing up.

16. Install timing belt. Starting at the crankshaft, go around the water pump sprocket, idler pulley, camshaft sprockets and then around the tensioner.

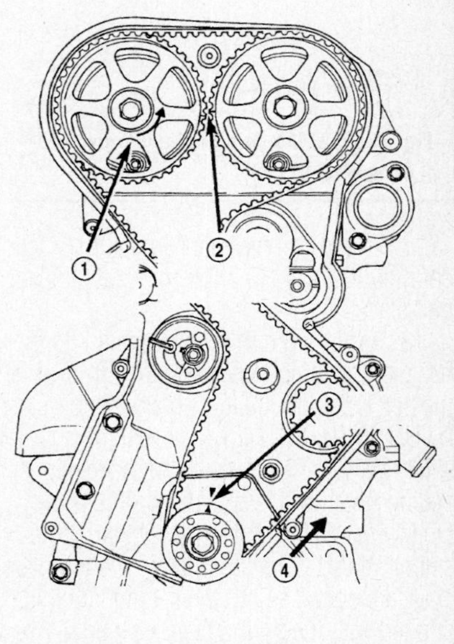

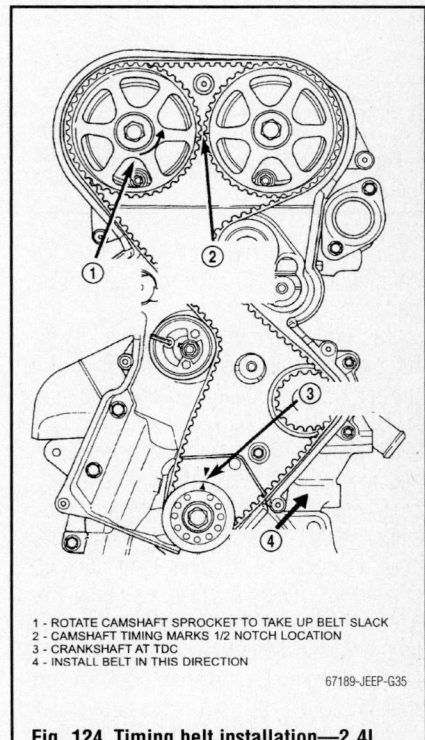

1 - ROTATE CAMSHAFT SPROCKET TO TAKE UP BELT SLACK
2 - CAMSHAFT TIMING MARKS 1/2 NOTCH LOCATION
3 - CRANKSHAFT AT TDC
4 - INSTALL BELT IN THIS DIRECTION

67189-JEEP-G35

Fig. 124 Timing belt installation—2.4L engines

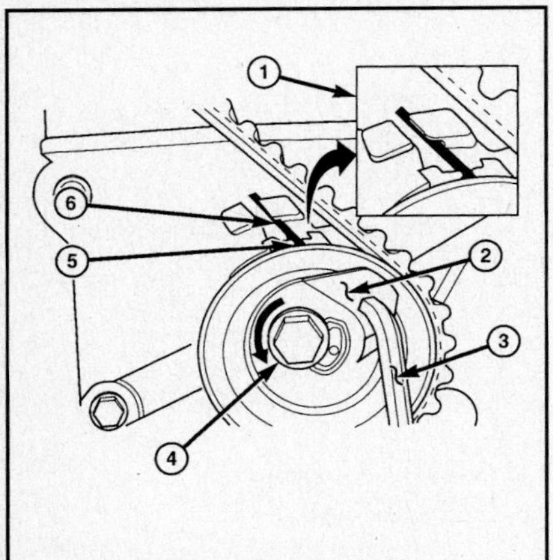

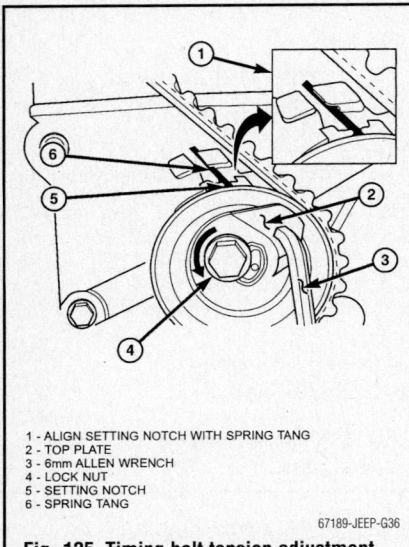

1 - ALIGN SETTING NOTCH WITH SPRING TANG
2 - TOP PLATE
3 - 6mm ALLEN WRENCH
4 - LOCK NUT
5 - SETTING NOTCH
6 - SPRING TANG

67189-JEEP-G36

Fig. 125 Timing belt tension adjustment—2.4L engines

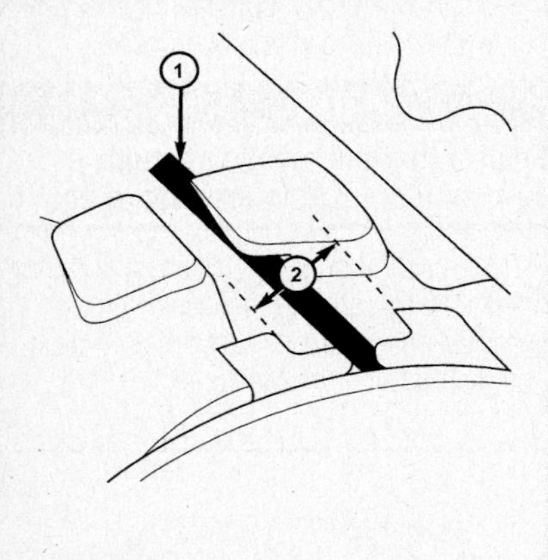

1 - SPRING TANG
2 - TOLERANCE WINDOW

67189-JEEP-G37

Fig. 126 Timing belt tension verification—2.4L engines

17. Move the exhaust camshaft sprocket counterclockwise to align marks and take up belt slack.

18. Insert a 6 mm Allen wrench into the hexagon opening located on the top plate of the belt tensioner pulley. Rotate the top plate COUNTERCLOCKWISE. The tensioner pulley will move against the belt and the tensioner setting notch will eventually start to move clockwise. Watching the movement of the setting notch, continue rotating the top plate counterclockwise until the setting notch is aligned with the spring tang. Using the Allen wrench to prevent the top plate from moving, torque the tensioner lock nut to 22 ft. lbs. (30 Nm). Setting notch and spring tang should remain aligned after lock nut is torqued.

19. Remove Allen wrench and torque wrench.

➡Repositioning the crankshaft to the TDC position must be done only during the CLOCKWISE rotation movement. If TDC is missed, rotate a further two revolutions until TDC is achieved. DO NOT rotate crankshaft counterclockwise as this will make verification of proper tensioner setting impossible.

20. Once the timing belt has been installed and tensioner adjusted, rotate the crankshaft CLOCKWISE two complete revolutions manually for seating of the belt, until the crankshaft is repositioned at the TDC position. Verify that the camshaft and crankshaft timing marks are in proper position.

21. Check if the spring tang is within the tolerance window. If the spring tang is within the tolerance window, the installation process is complete and nothing further is required. If the spring tang is not within the tolerance window, repeat Steps 5 through 7.

22. Install timing belt front covers and bolts.

23. Install air conditioning/generator belt tensioner and pulley.

24. Install crankshaft vibration damper.

25. Install accessory drive belts.

26. Install drive belt splash shield.

27. Install air cleaner housing, upper cover, and clean air tube.

2.8L Engine

See Figures 127 through 131.

1. Before servicing the vehicle, refer to the precautions in the beginning of this section.

⁂ WARNING

Before removing the timing belt, the engine must be placed at 90° after TDC. Failure to do so may result in valve and/or piston damage during assembly.

2. Disconnect negative battery cable.

3. Remove engine cover.

4. Remove cooling fan and fan drive viscous clutch assembly.

5. Remove accessory drive belt.

6. Remove cooling fan support.

7. Remove vibration damper.

8. Bring piston no. 1 to TDC, turn crankshaft until the witness line on the crankshaft hub is at the 12 o'clock position.

9. Looking at the engine from the belt side, rotate the crankshaft 90° clockwise so the witness mark is now at the 3 o'clock position.

10. Remove the alternator.

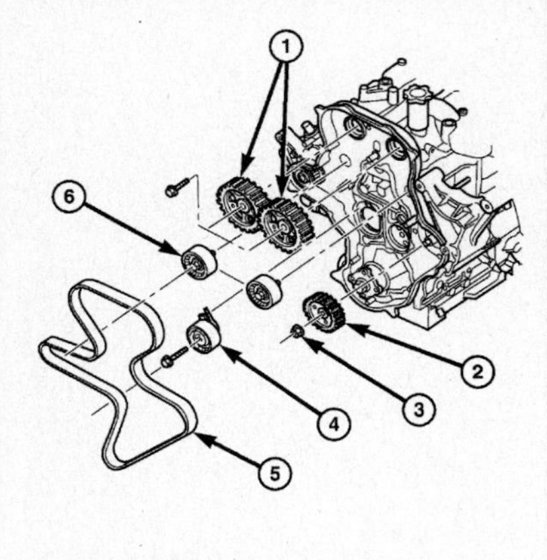

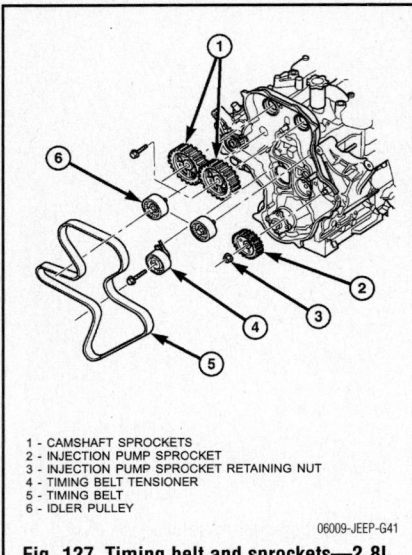

1 - CAMSHAFT SPROCKETS
2 - INJECTION PUMP SPROCKET
3 - INJECTION PUMP SPROCKET RETAINING NUT
4 - TIMING BELT TENSIONER
5 - TIMING BELT
6 - IDLER PULLEY

06009-JEEP-G41

Fig. 127 Timing belt and sprockets—2.8L diesel engine

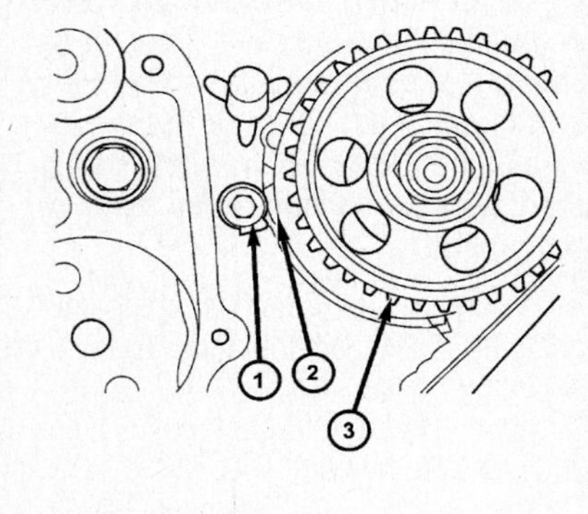

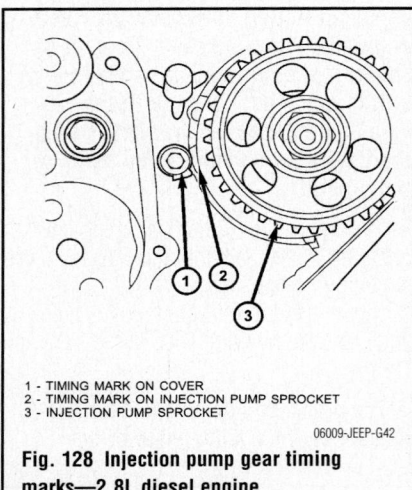

1 - TIMING MARK ON COVER
2 - TIMING MARK ON INJECTION PUMP SPROCKET
3 - INJECTION PUMP SPROCKET

06009-JEEP-G42

Fig. 128 Injection pump gear timing marks—2.8L diesel engine

11. Remove the intake and exhaust camshaft plugs from the camshaft cover, to introduce the camshaft timing pins VM.1052 Intake, and VM.1053 Exhaust (if the engine is timed correctly, the pins can be installed flush with the intake manifold/cylinder head cover).

12. Remove timing belt outer cover.

13. Loosen timing belt tensioner and remove timing belt.

14. Remove the intake and exhaust camshaft alignment pins.

15. Loosen camshaft gears using special tool VM 1085 to retain the gears when loosening the bolts.

16. Remove special tool VM 1085.

To install:

➡There are marks on both camshaft gears. These ARE NOT alignment marks and should be disregarded.

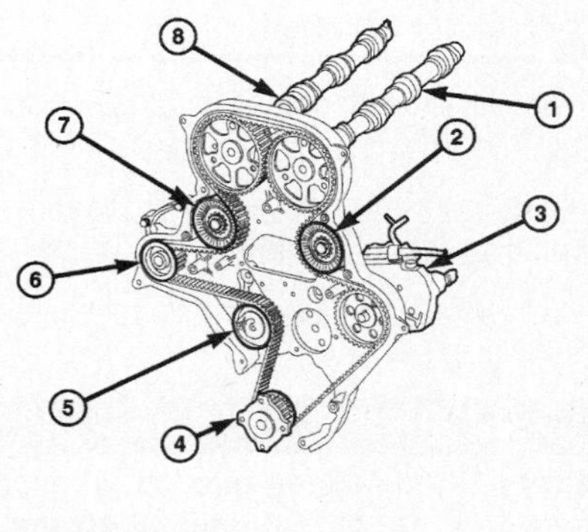

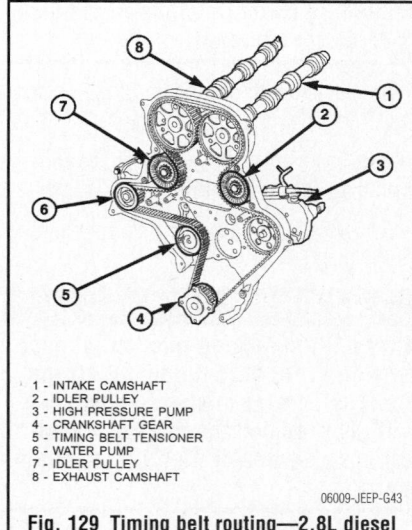

1 - INTAKE CAMSHAFT
2 - IDLER PULLEY
3 - HIGH PRESSURE PUMP
4 - CRANKSHAFT GEAR
5 - TIMING BELT TENSIONER
6 - WATER PUMP
7 - IDLER PULLEY
8 - EXHAUST CAMSHAFT

06009-JEEP-G43

Fig. 129 Timing belt routing—2.8L diesel engine

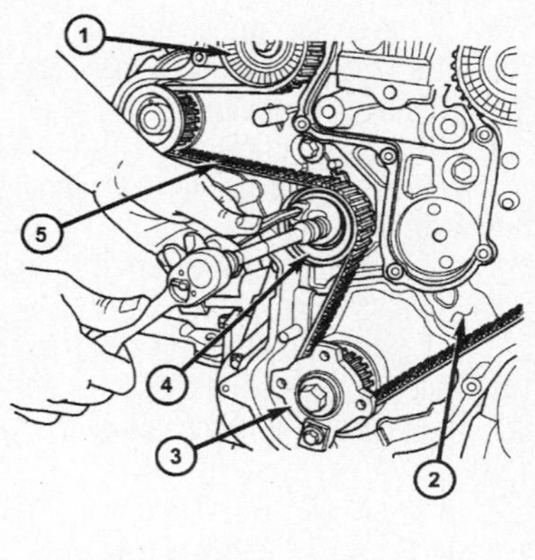

1 - TIMING BELT IDLER PULLEY
2 - ENGINE FRONT COVER
3 - CRANKSHAFT HUB
4 - TIMING BELT TENSIONER
5 - TIMING BELT

06009-JEEP-G44

Fig. 130 Timing belt tensioner adjustment—2.8L diesel engine

17. With both camshaft alignment pins still installed and the engine rotated at 90° after TDC, verify that the camshaft gears are loose.
18. Align the timing mark on the high pressure injection pump gear with the timing mark on the inner cover.

➡DO NOT remove the timing belt from the package until it's ready to be installed. DO NOT expose timing belt to oil, grease or water contamination. DO NOT crimp belt at a sharp angle. DO NOT clean belt, pulleys or tensioner with solvent. Check that pulleys and bearings are not seized or damage before installing belt.

19. Install timing belt on crankshaft hub.
20. Route the belt around high pressure

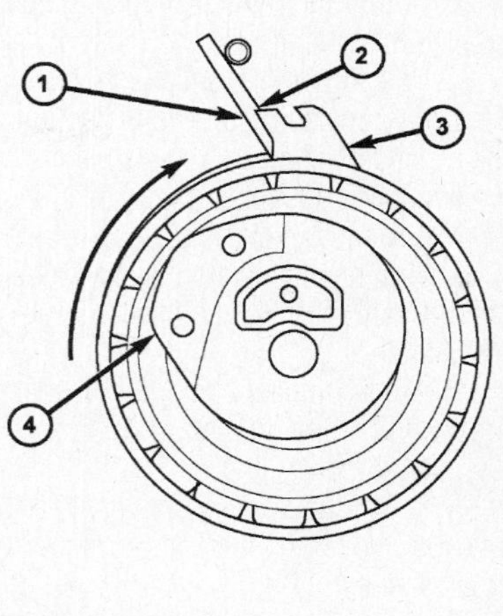

1 - TENSIONER SPRING
2 - 1MM ALIGNMENT POINTER OVERLAP
3 - TENSIONER ALIGNMENT POINTER
4 - TENSIONER ASSEMBLY

06009-JEEP-G45

Fig. 131 Timing belt tensioner adjustment—2.8L diesel engine

injection pump, idler pulley, intake camshaft gear, exhaust camshaft gear, idler pulley, and water pump gear.

21. Adjust the timing belt tensioner (turn it clockwise) using special tool VM.9660, lining up the center notch with the aluminum cover dowel pin. Tighten the retaining bolt to 20 ft. lbs. (28 Nm).
22. Install special tool VM.1085 between camshaft gears and tighten thumb screws to engage and retain the camshaft gears.
23. Tighten the camshaft gear bolts to 80 ft. lbs. (108 Nm) while holding the gears with special tool VM 1085.
24. Remove camshaft gear locking tool.
25. Remove intake and exhaust alignment pins.

⁂ WARNING

If intake manifold/cylinder head cover was removed wait 30 minutes before rotating crankshaft.

26. Rotate the engine clockwise 2 revolutions (looking at engine from the belt side).
27. With the crankshaft hub witness mark aligned to 90° ATDC, or the 3 o'clock position, check that the intake and exhaust camshaft alignment pins (VM 1052 and VM 1053) can be installed into the camshaft alignment access holes.
28. Install timing belt outer cover.

⁂ WARNING

If the camshaft alignment pins can not be installed at this time, repeat the procedure from the beginning.

29. Install the camshaft access plugs.
30. Install vibration damper.
31. Install the alternator.
32. Install cooling fan support.
33. Install accessory drive belt.
34. Install cooling fan and fan drive viscous clutch assembly.
35. Install engine cover.
36. Connect negative battery cable.

TIMING CHAIN, SPROCKETS, FRONT COVER AND SEAL

REMOVAL & INSTALLATION

3.7L Engine

1. Disconnect negative cable from battery.
2. Drain cooling system.
3. Remove right and left cylinder head covers.
4. Remove radiator fan shroud.
5. Rotate engine until timing mark on crankshaft damper aligns with TDC mark on timing chain cover

   and the camshaft sprocket "V6" marks are at the 12 o'clock position (no. 1 TDC exhaust stroke).
6. Remove power steering pump.
7. Remove access plug from left and right cylinder heads for access to chain guide fasteners .
8. Remove the oil fill housing to gain access to the right side tensioner arm fastener.
9. Remove crankshaft damper and timing chain cover.
10. Collapse and pin primary chain tensioner.

⁂ CAUTION

Plate behind left secondary chain tensioner could fall into oil pan. Therefore, cover pan opening.

11. Remove secondary chain tensioners.
12. Remove camshaft position sensor .

⁂ CAUTION

Care should be taken not to damage camshaft target wheel. Do not hold target wheel while loosening or tightening camshaft sprocket. Do not place the target wheel near a magnetic source of any kind. A damaged or magnetized target wheel could cause a vehicle no start condition.

CAUTION

Do not forcefully rotate the camshafts or crankshaft independently of each other. Damaging intake valve to piston contact will occur. Ensure negative battery cable is disconnected to guard against accidental starter engagement.

13. Remove left and right camshaft sprocket bolts.
14. While holding the left camshaft steel tube with Special Tool 8428 Camshaft Wrench, remove the left camshaft sprocket. Slowly rotate the camshaft approximately 5° clockwise to a neutral position.
15. While holding the right camshaft steel tube with Special Tool 8428 Camshaft Wrench, remove the right camshaft sprocket.
16. Remove idler sprocket assembly bolt.
17. Slide the idler sprocket assembly and crank sprocket forward simultaneously to remove the primary and secondary chains.
18. Remove both pivoting tensioner arms and chain guides.
19. Remove primary chain tensioner.

To install:

20. Using a vise, lightly compress the secondary chain tensioner piston until the piston step is flush with the tensioner body. Using a pin or suitable tool, release ratchet pawl by pulling pawl back against spring force through access hole on side of tensioner.
21. While continuing to hold pawl back, Push ratchet device to approximately 2 mm from the tensioner body. Install Special Tool 8514 lock pin into hole on front of tensioner. Slowly open vise to transfer piston spring force to lock pin.
22. Position primary chain tensioner over oil pump and insert bolts into lower two holes on tensioner bracket. Tighten bolts to 250 inch lbs. (28 Nm).
23. Install right side chain tensioner arm. Install Torx® bolt. Tighten Torx® bolt to 250 inch lbs. (28 Nm).

CAUTION

The silver bolts retain the guides to the cylinder heads and the black bolts retain the guides to the engine block.

24. Install the left side chain guide. Tighten the bolts to 250 inch lbs. (28 Nm).
25. Install left side chain tensioner arm, and Torx® bolt. Tighten Torx® bolt to 250 inch lbs. (28 Nm).
26. Install the right side chain guide. Tighten the bolts to 250 inch lbs. (28 Nm).
27. Install both secondary chains onto the idler sprocket. Align two plated links on the secondary chains to be visible through the two lower openings on the idler sprocket (4 o'clock and 8 o'clock). Once the secondary timing chains are installed, position special tool 8429 to hold chains in place for installation.
28. Align primary chain double plated links with the timing mark at 12 o'clock on the idler sprocket.
29. Align the primary chain single plated link with the timing mark at 6 o'clock on the crankshaft sprocket.
30. Lubricate idler shaft and bushings with clean engine oil.

➡The idler sprocket must be timed to the counterbalance shaft drive gear before the idler sprocket is fully seated.

31. Install all chains, crankshaft sprocket, and idler sprocket as an assembly. After guiding both secondary chains through the block and cylinder head openings, affix chains with a elastic strap or equivalent. This will maintain tension on chains to aid in installation. Align the timing mark on the idler sprocket gear to the timing mark on the counterbalance shaft drive gear, then seat idler sprocket fully . Before installing idler sprocket bolt, lubricate washer with oil, and tighten idler sprocket assembly retaining bolt to 25 ft. lbs. (34 Nm).

➡It will be necessary to slightly rotate camshafts for sprocket installation.

32. Align left camshaft sprocket "L" dot to plated link on chain.
33. Align right camshaft sprocket "R" dot to plated link on chain.

CAUTION

Remove excess oil from the camshaft sprocket bolt. Failure to do so can result in over torque of bolt resulting in bolt failure.

34. Remove Special Tool 8429, then attach both sprockets to camshafts. Remove excess oil from bolts, then Install sprocket bolts, but do not tighten at this time.
35. Verify that all plated links are aligned with the marks on all sprockets and the "V6" marks on camshaft sprockets are at the 12 o'clock position.

CAUTION

Ensure the plate between the left secondary chain tensioner and block is correctly installed.

36. Install both secondary chain tensioners. Tighten bolts to 250 inch lbs. (28 Nm).

➡Left and right secondary chain tensioners are not common.

37. Remove all locking pins from tensioners.

CAUTION

After pulling locking pins out of each tensioner, DO NOT manually extend the tensioner(s) ratchet. Doing so will over tension the chains, resulting in noise and/or high timing chain loads.

38. Using Special Tool 6958, Spanner with Adapter Pins 8346, tighten left and right . camshaft sprocket bolts to 90 ft. lbs. (122 Nm).
39. Rotate engine two full revolutions. Verify timing marks are at the follow locations:
    a. Primary chain idler sprocket dot is at 12 o'clock
    b. Primary chain crankshaft sprocket dot is at 6 o'clock
    c. Secondary chain camshaft sprockets "V6" marks are at 12 o'clock
    d. Counter balancer shaft drive gear dot is aligned to the idler sprocket gear dot.
40. Lubricate all three chains with engine oil.
41. After installing all chains, it is recommended that the idler gear end play be checked. The end play must be within mm 0.004–0.010 inches (0.10–0.25). If not within specification, the idler gear must be replaced.
42. Install timing chain cover and crankshaft damper.
43. Install cylinder head covers.

➡Before installing threaded plug in right cylinder head, the plug must be coated with sealant to prevent leaks.

44. Coat the large threaded access plug with Mopar® Thread Sealant with Teflon, then install into the right cylinder head and tighten to 60 ft. lbs. (81 Nm).
45. Install the oil fill housing.
46. Install access plug in left cylinder head.
47. Install power steering pump.
48. Fill cooling system.
49. Connect negative cable to battery.

4.0L Engine

1. Disconnect negative cable from battery.
2. Remove the fan and shroud.

3. Remove the serpentine drive belt.
4. Remove the crankshaft vibration damper.
5. Remove the timing case cover.
6. Rotate crankshaft until the "0" timing mark is closest to and on the center line with camshaft sprocket timing mark.
7. Remove the oil slinger from the crankshaft.
8. Remove the camshaft sprocket bolt and washer.
9. Remove the crankshaft sprocket, camshaft sprocket and timing chain as an assembly.
10. Installation of the timing chain with the timing marks on the crankshaft and camshaft sprockets properly aligned ensures correct valve timing. A worn or stretched timing chain will adversely affect valve timing. If the timing chain deflects more than 12.7 mm (½ inch) replace it.

To install:

➡Assemble the timing chain, crankshaft sprocket and camshaft sprocket with the timing marks aligned.

11. Apply Mopar® Silicone Rubber Adhesive Sealant to the keyway in the crankshaft and insert the key. With the key in the keyway on the crankshaft, install the assembly on the crankshaft and camshaft.
12. Install the camshaft sprocket bolt and washer. Tighten the bolt to 50 ft. lbs. (68 Nm) torque.
13. To verify correct installation of the timing chain, rotate the crankshaft 2 revolutions. The camshaft and crankshaft sprocket timing mark should align.
14. Install the crankshaft oil slinger.
15. Replace the oil seal in the timing case cover.
16. Install the timing case cover and gasket.
17. With the key installed in the crankshaft keyway, install the vibration damper.
18. Install the serpentine drive belt.
19. Install the fan, hub assembly and shroud.
20. Connect negative cable to battery.

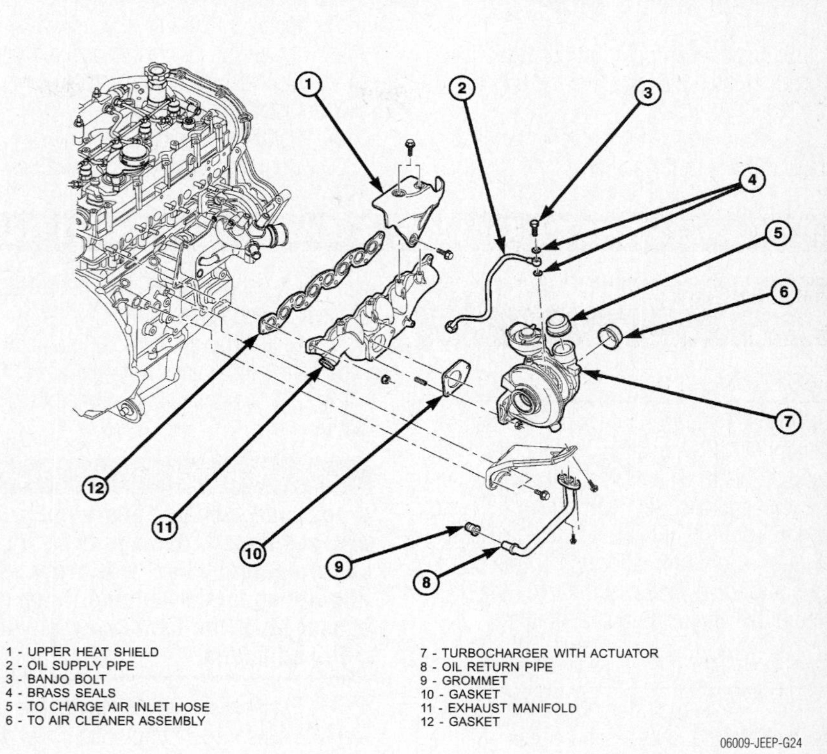

Fig. 132 Turbocharger and oil lines—2.8L diesel engine

TURBOCHARGER

REMOVAL & INSTALLATION

2.8L Diesel Engine

See Figure 132.

➡The turbocharger and exhaust manifold is removed as an assembly.

1. Before servicing the vehicle, refer to the precautions in the beginning of this section.
2. Disconnect negative battery cable.
3. Remove engine cover.
4. Disconnect the inlet air pressure sensors wiring harness connectors, disconnect the air outlet duct from the turbocharger, and remove air cleaner assembly.
5. Remove charge air cooler outlet hose from turbocharger.
6. Drain cooling system.
7. Remove coolant reservoir.
8. Disconnect the turbocharger actuator vacuum hose and position aside.
9. Remove turbocharger upper heat shield.
10. Raise and support the vehicle.
11. Remove the lower splash shield.
12. Disconnect the front exhaust pipe from the turbocharger.
13. Remove the turbocharger support bracket.
14. Disconnect turbocharger oil return line at turbocharger.
15. Lower the vehicle.
16. Remove the turbocharger oil supply line.
17. Remove turbocharger and exhaust manifold retaining nuts. If necessary, separate turbocharger from exhaust manifold.

To install:

18. Install a new exhaust manifold gasket and position the exhaust manifold into place. Hand tighten fasteners.

➡After tightening the exhaust manifold to specification using a diagonal-cross pattern, retrace the pattern checking the correct torque value again.

19. Tighten the exhaust manifold to cylinder head fasteners in a diagonal-cross pattern to 26 ft. lbs. (36 Nm).
20. Connect turbocharger to exhaust manifold with new gasket. Torque retaining nuts to 24 ft. lbs. (32 Nm).
21. Connect oil supply line at turbocharger. Torque banjo fitting to 18 ft. lbs. (24 Nm).
22. Raise and support the vehicle.
23. Connect the oil return pipe to the turbocharger with new gasket and tighten the fasteners to 95 inch lbs. (10 Nm).
24. Install the turbocharger support bracket and tighten fasteners to 18 ft. lbs. (24 Nm).
25. Connect the front exhaust pipe to the turbocharger.

26. Install the lower skid plate.
27. Lower the vehicle.
28. Install the upper turbocharger heat shield. Tighten the fasteners to 18 ft. lbs. (24 Nm).
29. Connect the turbocharger actuator vacuum hose to the actuator.
30. Install the coolant reservoir.
31. Install the charge air outlet hose
32. Install the air cleaner assembly and connect the electrical connectors.
33. Install engine cover.
34. Refill cooling system.
35. Connect negative battery cable.

VALVE LASH

ADJUSTMENT

These engines are equipped with hydraulic valve lifters. No valve clearance adjustments are necessary.

ENGINE PERFORMANCE & EMISSION CONTROL

CAMSHAFT POSITION (CMP) SENSOR

LOCATION

On 2.4L engines, the Camshaft Position Sensor (CMP) is located on the side of the cylinder head, on the exhaust camshaft side. On 3.7L engines, the CMP sensor is located on the front/top of the right cylinder head. On 4.0L engines, it is located on top of the oil pump drive shaft assembly (on the right side of the engine, near the oil filter).

OPERATION

The CMP sensor contains a hall effect device referred to as a sync signal generator. The CMP sensor target wheel is equipped with a cutout (notch) around 180° of the wheel. The CMP detects this cutout every 180 ° of camshaft gear rotation. Its signal is used in conjunction with the Crankshaft Position Sensor (CKP) to differentiate between fuel injection and spark events. It is also used to synchronize the fuel injectors with their respective cylinders.

When the leading edge of the target wheel cutout enters the tip of the CMP, the interruption of magnetic field causes the voltage to switch high, resulting in a sync signal of approximately 5 volts. When the trailing edge of the target wheel cutout leaves the tip of the CMP, the change of magnetic field causes the sync signal voltage to switch low to 0 volts.

REMOVAL & INSTALLATION

2.4L Engine

See Figure 133.

1. Disconnect electrical connector at CMP sensor.
2. Remove 2 sensor mounting bolts.
3. Remove sensor from cylinder head by sliding towards rear of engine.

To install:

4. Remove plastic, upper timing belt cover (timing gear cover) by removing 3 bolts. Before attempting to remove cover, remove electrical connector from Engine Coolant Temperature (ECT) sensor. This will prevent damage to sensor.
5. Rotate (bump over) engine until camshaft timing gear and target wheel (tone wheel) are positioned and aligned to face of sensor.

⁂ WARNING

If gear and tone wheel are not properly positioned, damage to both sensor and target wheel will occur when attempting to start engine. Face of sensor MUST be behind target wheel while adjusting.

6. Position sensor to cylinder head and install 2 sensor mounting bolts finger tight.
7. Set air gap between rear of target wheel and face of sensor to .030. This can best be accomplished using an L-shaped, wire-type spark plug gapping gauge. A piece of .030 brass shim stock may also be used.
8. Gently push sensor forward until it contacts gapping gauge. Do not push hard on sensor. Tighten 2 sensor mounting bolts.

⁂ WARNING

After tightening sensor mounting bolts, recheck air gap and adjust as necessary. Retorque bolts.

9. Install upper timing belt cover and 3 bolts.
10. Connect electrical connector to ECT sensor.

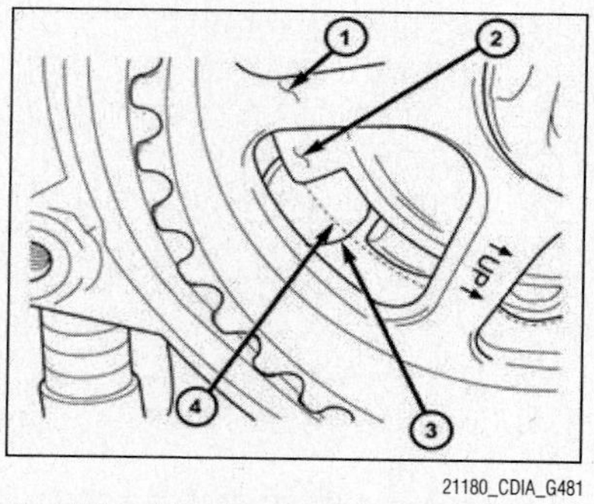

21180_CDIA_G481

Fig. 133 CMP sensor and mounting on 2.4L engines

11. Connect electrical connector to CMP sensor.

3.7L Engine

See Figure 134.

1. Disconnect electrical connector at CMP sensor.
2. Remove sensor mounting bolt.
3. Carefully remove sensor from cylinder head in a rocking and twisting action. Twisting sensor eases removal.

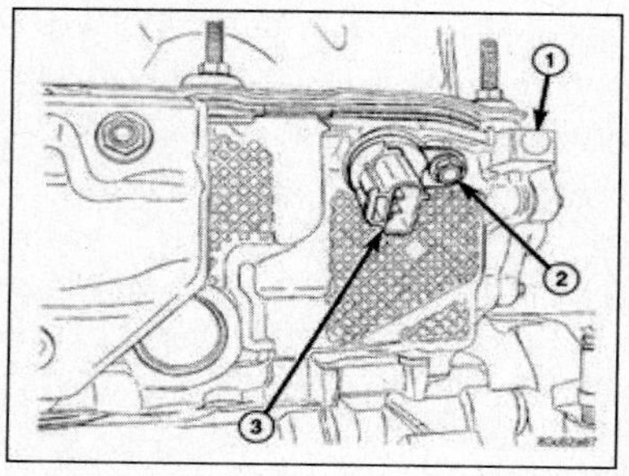

21180_CDIA_G484

Fig. 134 Showing the CMP sensor (3) and mounting bolt (2) on the right front cylinder head (1) on the 3.7L engine

To install:

4. Check condition of sensor O-ring.
5. Clean out machined hole in cylinder head.
6. Apply a small amount of engine oil to sensor O-ring.
7. Install sensor into cylinder head with a slight rocking and twisting action.

⁂ WARNING

Before tightening sensor mounting bolt, be sure sensor is completely flush to cylinder head. If sensor is not flush, damage to sensor mounting tang may result.

8. Install mounting bolt and tighten.
9. Connect electrical connector to sensor.

4.0L Engine

See Figure 135.

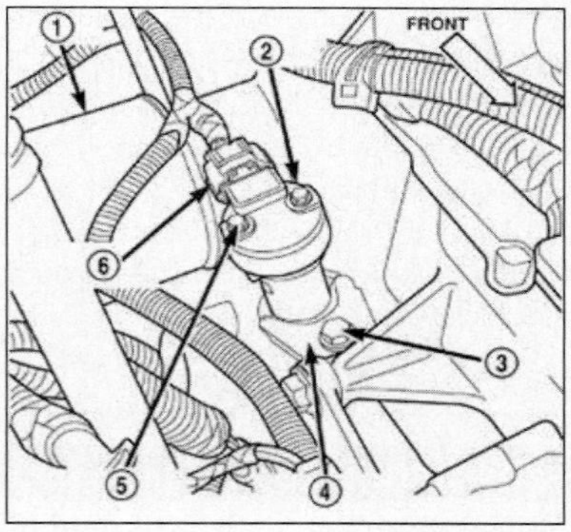

21180_CDIA_G486

Fig. 135 Identifying the location of the CMP sensor (2) and related components on the 4.0L engine: oil filter (1); clamp bolt (3); hold-down clamp (4); mounting bolts (5); electrical connector (6)

1. Disconnect electrical connector at CMP sensor.
2. Remove 2 sensor mounting bolts.
3. Remove sensor from oil pump drive.

To install:

4. Install sensor to oil pump drive.
5. Install 2 sensor mounting bolts and tighten to 15 inch lbs. (2 Nm).
6. Connect electrical connector to CMP sensor.

TESTING

1. Inspect the CMP sensor for correct installation. Remove the CMP sensor from the engine and inspect the sensor O–ring for damage. If the sensor is loose, incorrectly installed, or damaged, replace the CMP sensor.
2. Engage the CMP sensor harness connector to the CMP sensor.
3. Connect the scan tool to the diagnostic connector.
4. With the ignition **ON**, engine off observe the CMP Active counter parameter on the scan tool.
5. Pass a flat steel object across the tip of the sensor repeatedly. The CMP Active counter parameter should increment with each pass of the steel object.
6. If the parameter does not increment, replace the CMP sensor.

CRANKSHAFT POSITION (CKP) SENSOR

LOCATION

On 2.4L engines, the Crankshaft Position (CKP) sensor is mounted to the right front side of the cylinder block. On 3.7L engines, is mounted into the right rear side of the cylinder block. On 4.0L engines, it is mounted to the transmission bellhousing on the left rear side of the engine.

OPERATION

The sensor is a Hall effect device combined with an internal magnet. It is sensitive to steel within a certain distance. A tone wheel (target wheel) is a part of the engine crankshaft. This tone wheel has sets of notches at its outer edge. The notches cause a pulse to be generated when they pass under the sensor. The pulses are the input to the PCM.

REMOVAL & INSTALLATION

2.4L Engine

See Figure 136.

1. Disconnect sensor electrical connector.
2. Remove sensor bolt.
3. Carefully twist sensor from cylinder block.
4. Check condition of sensor O-ring.

To install:

5. Clean out machined hole in engine block.
6. Apply a small amount of engine oil to sensor O-ring.
7. Install sensor into engine block with a slight rocking action. Do not twist sensor into position as damage to O-ring may result.

WARNING

Before tightening sensor mounting bolt, be sure sensor is completely flush to cylinder block. If sensor is not flush, damage to sensor mounting tang may result.

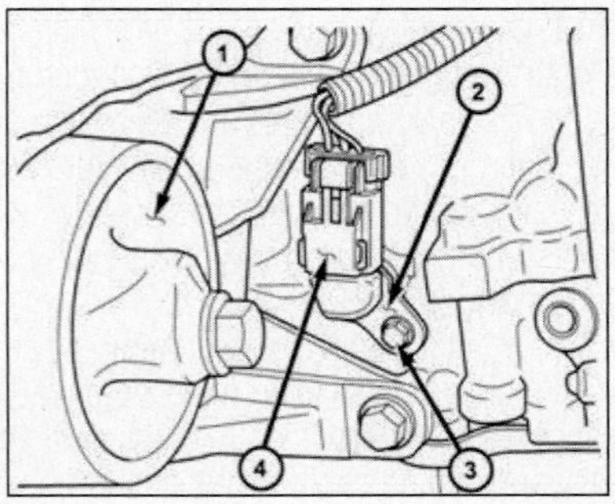

21180_CDIA_G492

Fig. 136 Identifying the RF engine mount (1), CKP sensor (2), mounting bolt (3), and electrical connector (4) on 2.4L engines

8. Install mounting bolt and tighten to 21 ft. lbs. (28 Nm).
9. Connect electrical connector to sensor.

3.7L Engine

See Figure 137.

1. Raise vehicle.
2. Disconnect sensor electrical connector.
3. Remove sensor mounting bolt.
4. Carefully remove sensor from cylinder block in a rocking and twisting action.
5. Check condition of sensor O-ring.

To install:

6. Clean out machined hole in engine block.
7. Apply a small amount of engine oil to sensor O-ring.
8. Install sensor into engine block with a slight rocking and twisting action.

WARNING

Before tightening sensor mounting bolt, be sure sensor is completely flush to cylinder block. If sensor is not flush, damage to sensor mounting tang may result.

9. Install mounting bolt and tighten to 21 ft. lbs. (28 Nm).
10. Connect electrical connector to sensor.

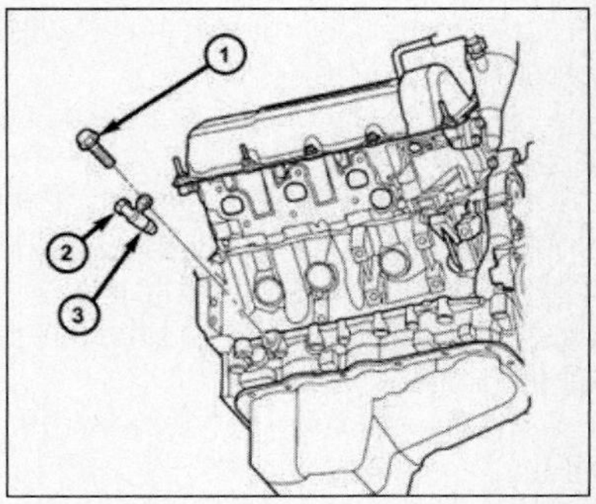

21180_CDIA_G493

Fig. 137 Mounting bolt (1) CKP sensor (2) O-ring (3) on the 3.7L engine

4.0L Engine

See Figure 138.

1. Disconnect sensor pigtail harness (3way connector) from main engine wiring harness.
2. Remove sensor mounting bolt.
3. Remove wire shield and sensor.

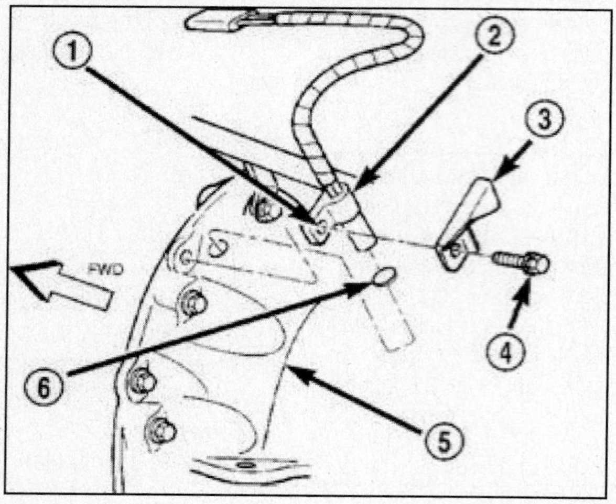

Fig. 138 Showing the Crankshaft Position (CKP) sensor (2) and related components slotted hole (1), wire shield (3), mounting bolt (4), transmission housing (5), and paper spacer (6) for installation reference

➡New replacement sensors will be equipped with a paper spacer glued to bottom of sensor. If installing (returning) a used sensor to vehicle, a new paper spacer must be installed to bottom of sensor. This spacer will be ground off the first time engine is started. If spacer is not used, sensor will be broken the first time engine is started.

4. On new sensors, be sure paper spacer is installed to bottom of sensor. If not, obtain spacer PN05252229. On used sensors, clean bottom of sensor and install spacer PN05252229.
5. Install sensor into transmission bell-housing hole.
6. Position sensor wire shield to sensor.
7. Push sensor against flywheel/drive plate. With sensor pushed against flywheel/drive plate, tighten mounting bolt to 7 Nm (60 inch lbs.) torque.
8. Route sensor wiring harness into wire shield.
9. Connect sensor pigtail harness electrical connector to main wiring harness.

TESTING

1. Inspect the CKP sensor for correct installation. Remove the CKP sensor from the engine and inspect the sensor O–ring for damage. If the sensor is loose, incorrectly installed, or damaged, replace the CKP sensor.
2. Engage the CKP sensor harness connector to the CKP sensor.
3. Connect the scan tool to the diagnostic connector.
4. With the ignition **ON**, engine off observe the CKP Active counter parameter on the scan tool.
5. Pass a flat steel object across the tip of the sensor repeatedly. The CKP Active counter parameter should increment with each pass of the steel object.
6. If the parameter does not increment, replace the CKP sensor.

ELECTRONIC CONTROL MODULE (ECM)

LOCATION

The Electronic Control Module (ECM) is attached to the inner fender located in the engine compartment

OPERATION

The Electronic Control Module (ECM) receives input signals from various switches and sensors. Based on these inputs, the ECM regulates various engine and vehicle operations through different system components. These components are referred to as Electronic Control Module (ECM) Outputs. The sensors and switches that provide inputs to the ECM are considered Electronic Control Module (ECM) Inputs.

The ECM adjusts ignition timing based upon inputs it receives from sensors that react to: engine rpm, manifold absolute pressure, engine coolant temperature, throttle position, transmission gear selection (automatic transmission), vehicle speed and the brake switch.

The ECM adjusts idle speed based on inputs it receives from sensors that react to: throttle position, vehicle speed, transmission gear selection, engine coolant temperature and from inputs it receives from the air conditioning clutch switch and brake switch.

Based on inputs that it receives, the ECM adjusts ignition coil dwell. The ECM also adjusts the generator charge rate through control of the generator field and provides speed control operation.

REMOVAL & INSTALLATION

⁂ WARNING

The use of a diagnostic scan tool is required the Electronic Control Module (ECM) is being in order to reprogram the new ECM.

1. Disconnect the negative battery cable.
2. Unplug the 38-way connectors from the ECM.

➡A locating pin is used in place of one of the mounting bolts.

3. Pry the clip from the locating pin.
4. Remove the two remaining mounting bolts.
5. Remove the ECM from the vehicle.

To install:

6. Position the ECM to the body and install the two mounting bolts.

➡Position the ground strap in place before tightening the mounting bolts.

7. Install the clip to the locating pin.
8. Tighten the mounting bolts to 35 inch lbs. (4 Nm).
9. Carefully plug in the 38-way connectors to the ECM.
10. Connect the negative battery cable.
11. Use a diagnostic scan tool to reprogram the ECM with the VIN and original mileage if ECM has been replaced.

TESTING

1. Start the engine and allow it to reach normal operating temperature. Using a diagnostic scan tool, check for the presence of any Diagnostic Trouble Codes (DTCs). Record and address these codes as necessary.
2. Refer to any Technical Service Bulletins (TSBs) that may apply.
3. Review the scan tool Freeze Frame information. If possible, try to duplicate the conditions under which the DTC set.
4. With the engine running at normal operating temperature, monitor the scan tool parameters related to the DTC while wiggling the wire harness. Look for parameter values to change and/or a DTC to set. Turn the ignition off.

5. Visually inspect the related wire harness. Disconnect all the related harness connectors. Look for any chafed, pierced, pinched, partially broken wires and broken, bent, pushed out, or corroded terminals. Perform a voltage drop test on the related circuits between the suspected inoperative component and the ECM.

CAUTION

Do not probe the ECM harness connectors. Probing the ECM harness connectors will damage the ECM terminals resulting in poor terminal to pin connection. Install Miller Special Tool no. 8815 to perform diagnosis.

6. Inspect and clean all ECM, engine, and chassis grounds that are related to the most current DTC.
7. If numerous trouble codes were set, use a wire schematic and look for any common ground or supply circuits.
8. For any Relay DTCs, actuate the Relay with the scan tool and wiggle the related wire harness to try to interrupt the actuation.
9. For intermittent Evaporative Emission trouble codes perform a visual and physical inspection of the related parts including hoses and the Fuel Filler cap.
10. Use the scan tool to perform a System Test if one applies to failing component. A co-pilot, data recorder, and/or lab scope should be used to help diagnose intermittent conditions.

ENGINE COOLANT TEMPERATURE (ECT) SENSOR

LOCATION

The Engine Coolant Temperature (ECT) sensor is installed into a water jacket at the front of the intake manifold.

OPERATION

The sensor provides an input to the Electronic Control Module (ECM). As coolant temperature varies, the sensor resistance changes, resulting in a different input voltage to the ECM. When the engine is cold, the ECM will demand slightly richer air-fuel mixtures and higher idle speeds until normal operating temperatures are reached.

The engine coolant sensor input also determines operation of the low and high speed cooling fans.

REMOVAL & INSTALLATION

1. Drain the cooling system.
2. Disconnect the sensor electrical connector.
3. Remove the Engine Coolant Temperature (ECT) sensor.

To install:

4. Apply thread sealant to the sensor threads.
5. Install the ECT sensor into the engine block and tighten the mounting bolt to 8 ft. lbs. (11 Nm).
6. Connect the electrical connector.
7. Refill the cooling system to the correct level.

TESTING

1. Turn the ignition **OFF**. If possible, allow the vehicle to sit with the ignition off for more than 8 hours in an environment where the temperature is consistent and above 20°F (-7°C).
2. Test drive the vehicle. The vehicle must exceed 30 mph (48 km/h) during the test drive. Do not cycle the ignition off when the test drive is completed.
3. With a scan tool, select View DTCs.
4. Turn the ignition off. Allow the vehicle to sit with the ignition off in an environment where the temperature is consistent and above 20°F (-7°C) until the engine coolant temperature is equal to ambient temperature. Turn the ignition on. With a scan tool, compare the Ambient Air Temperature (AAT) sensor, ECT, and Intake Air Temperature (IAT) sensor values.
5. If the ECT sensor value is not within 18°F (10°C) of the other two sensor values, perform the following:
6. Refer to any Technical Service Bulletins (TSBs) that may apply.
7. Review the scan tool Freeze Frame information. If possible, try to duplicate the conditions under which the DTC set.
8. With the engine running at normal operating temperature, monitor the scan tool parameters related to the DTC while wiggling the wire harness. Look for parameter values to change and/or a DTC to set. Turn the ignition off.
9. Visually inspect the related wire harness. Disconnect all the related harness connectors. Look for any chafed, pierced, pinched, partially broken wires and broken, bent, pushed out, or corroded terminals.

Perform a voltage drop test on the related circuits between the suspected inoperative component and the ECM.

CAUTION

Do not probe the ECM harness connectors. Probing the ECM harness connectors will damage the ECM terminals resulting in poor terminal to pin connection. Install Miller Special Tool no. 8815 to perform diagnosis.

10. Inspect and clean all ECM, engine, and chassis grounds that are related to the most current DTC.
11. If numerous trouble codes were set, use a wire schematic and look for any common ground or supply circuits.
12. For any Relay DTCs, actuate the Relay with the scan tool and wiggle the related wire harness to try to interrupt the actuation.
13. For intermittent Evaporative Emission trouble codes perform a visual and physical inspection of the related parts including hoses and the Fuel Filler cap.
14. Use the scan tool to perform a System Test if one applies to failing component. A co-pilot, data recorder, and/or lab scope should be used to help diagnose intermittent conditions.

HEATED OXYGEN (HO2S) SENSOR

LOCATION

See Figure 139.

If equipped with a Federal Emission Package, two sensors are used: upstream (referred to as 1/1) and downstream (referred to as 1/2). With this emission package, the upstream sensor (1/1) is located just before the main catalytic converter. The downstream sensor (1/2) is located just after the main catalytic converter.

If equipped with a California Emission Package, 4 sensors are used: 2 upstream (referred to as 1/1 and 2/1) and 2 downstream (referred to as 1/2 and 2/2). With this emission package, the right upstream sensor (2/1) is located in the right exhaust downpipe just before the mini-catalytic converter. The left upstream sensor (1/1) is located in the left exhaust downpipe just before the mini-catalytic converter. The right downstream sensor (2/2) is located in the right exhaust downpipe just after the mini-catalytic converter, and before the main catalytic converter. The left downstream sensor (1/2) is located in the left exhaust downpipe just after the mini-catalytic converter, and before the main catalytic converter.

OPERATION

An O2 sensor is a galvanic battery that provides the ECM with a voltage signal (0-1

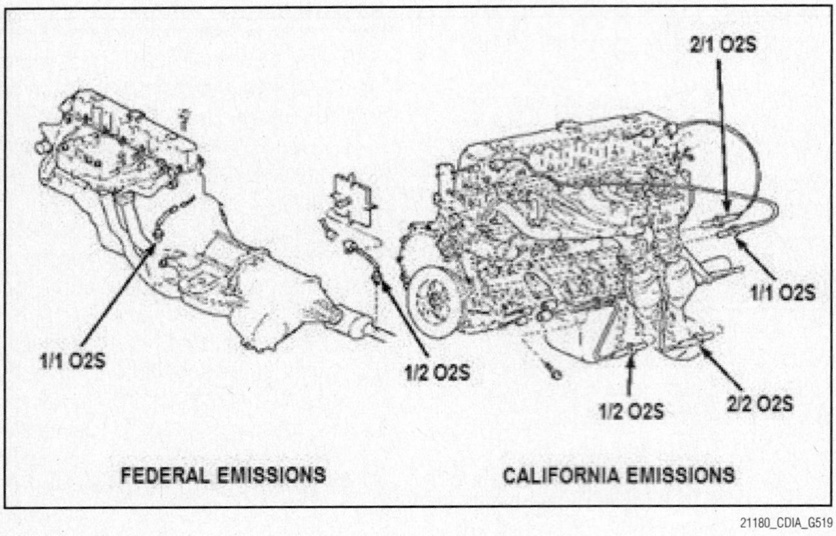

Fig. 139 HO2S sensor locations on 4.0L engines

volt) inversely proportional to the amount of oxygen in the exhaust. In other words, if the oxygen content is low, the voltage output is high; if the oxygen content is high the output voltage is low. The ECM uses this information to adjust injector pulse-width to achieve the 14.7to1 air/fuel ratio necessary for proper engine operation and to control emissions.

The O2 sensor must have a source of oxygen from outside of the exhaust stream for comparison. Current O2 sensors receive their fresh oxygen (outside air) supply through the O2 sensor case housing.

Four wires (circuits) are used on each O2 sensor: a 12volt feed circuit for the sensor heating element; a ground circuit for the heater element; a low-noise sensor return circuit to the ECM, and an input circuit from the sensor back to the ECM to detect sensor operation.

REMOVAL & INSTALLATION

1. Raise and safely support the vehicle.
2. Disconnect the wire connector from oxygen sensor.

⁂ WARNING

When disconnecting sensor electrical connector, do not pull directly on wire going into sensor.

3. Remove the sensor with an oxygen sensor removal and installation tool.
4. Clean threads in exhaust pipe using appropriate tap.

To install:

➡Threads of new oxygen sensors are factory coated with anti-seize compound.

⁂ WARNING

Do not add any additional anti-seize compound to the threads of a new oxygen sensor.

5. Install the oxygen sensor and tighten to 22 ft. lbs. (30 Nm).
6. Connect the electrical connector.
7. Lower the vehicle.

TESTING

1. Start the engine and allow it to idle for at least 60 seconds. Using a diagnostic scan tool, check for the presence of any Diagnostic Trouble Codes (DTCs). Record and address these codes as necessary.
2. Turn the ignition off, allow the sensor to cool down to room temperature disconnect the oxygen sensor wiring harness. Measure the resistance across the sensor heater control terminal and ground terminal. If resistance is not between 2 and 30 ohms, replace the sensor.
3. Refer to any Technical Service Bulletins (TSBs) that may apply.
4. Review the scan tool Freeze Frame information. If possible, try to duplicate the conditions under which the DTC set.
5. With the engine running at normal operating temperature, monitor the scan tool parameters related to the DTC while wiggling the wire harness. Look for parameter values to change and/or a DTC to set. Turn the ignition off.
6. Visually inspect the related wire harness. Disconnect all the related harness connectors. Look for any chafed, pierced, pinched, partially broken wires and broken, bent, pushed out, or corroded terminals. Perform a voltage drop test on the related circuits between the suspected inoperative component and the PCM.

⁂ CAUTION

Do not probe the PCM harness connectors. Probing the PCM harness connectors will damage the PCM terminals resulting in poor terminal to pin connection. Install Miller Special Tool no. 8815 to perform diagnosis.

7. Inspect and clean all PCM, engine, and chassis grounds that are related to the most current DTC.
8. If numerous trouble codes were set, use a wire schematic and look for any common ground or supply circuits.
9. For any Relay DTCs, actuate the Relay with the scan tool and wiggle the related wire harness to try to interrupt the actuation.
10. For intermittent Evaporative Emission trouble codes perform a visual and physical inspection of the related parts including hoses and the Fuel Filler cap.
11. Use the scan tool to perform a System Test if one applies to failing component. A co-pilot, data recorder, and/or lab scope should be used to help diagnose intermittent conditions.

INTAKE AIR TEMPERATURE (IAT) SENSOR

LOCATION

The Intake Air Temperature (IAT) sensor is installed in the intake manifold with the sensor element extending into the air stream.

OPERATION

The IAT sensor is a two-wire Negative Thermal Coefficient (NTC) sensor. Meaning, as intake manifold temperature increases, resistance (voltage) in the sensor decreases. As temperature decreases, resistance (voltage) in the sensor increases.

The IAT sensor provides an input voltage to the Powertrain Control Module (PCM) indicating the density of the air entering the intake manifold based upon intake manifold temperature. At key-on, a 5volt power circuit is supplied to the sensor from the PCM.

The sensor is grounded at the PCM through a low-noise, sensor-return circuit.

The PCM uses this input to calculate injector pulse-width and adjustment of spark timing (to help prevent spark knock with high intake manifold air-charge temperatures)

REMOVAL & INSTALLATION

3.7L Engine

See Figure 140.

1. Disconnect electrical connector from IAT sensor. Clean dirt from intake manifold at sensor base.
2. Gently lift on small plastic release tab or and rotate sensor about 1/4 turn counterclockwise. Check condition of sensor O-ring.

To install:

3. Clean the sensor mounting hole in the intake manifold.
4. Position the sensor into intake manifold and rotate clockwise until past release tab.
5. Install electrical connector.

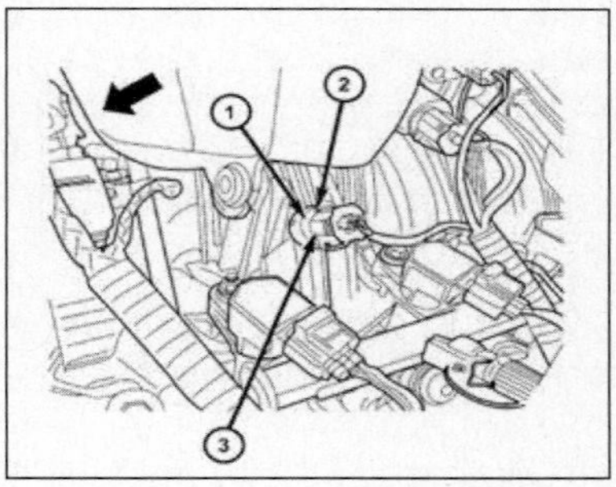

Fig. 140 IAT sensor (1), release tab (2), and electrical connector (3) on 3.7L engines

4.0L Engine

1. Disconnect electrical connector from sensor.
2. Remove sensor from intake manifold.

To install:

3. Install sensor into intake manifold. Tighten sensor to 20 ft. lbs. (28 Nm).
4. Connect electrical connector to sensor.

TESTING

1. Turn the ignition off. If possible, allow the vehicle to sit with the ignition off for more than 8 hours in an environment where the temperature is consistent and above 20°F (-7°C).
2. Test drive the vehicle. The vehicle must exceed 30 mph (48 km/h) during the test drive. Do not cycle the ignition off when the test drive is completed.
3. With a scan tool, select View DTCs.
4. If a DTC is not active, perform the following:
5. Refer to any Technical Service Bulletins (TSBs) that may apply.
6. Review the scan tool Freeze Frame information. If possible, try to duplicate the conditions under which the DTC set.
7. With the engine running at normal operating temperature, monitor the scan tool parameters related to the DTC while wiggling the wire harness. Look for parameter values to change and/or a DTC to set. Turn the ignition off.
8. Visually inspect the related wire harness. Disconnect all the related harness connectors. Look for any chafed, pierced, pinched, partially broken wires and broken, bent, pushed out, or corroded terminals. Perform a voltage drop test on the related circuits between the suspected inoperative component and the ECM.

**** CAUTION**

Do not probe the ECM harness connectors. Probing the ECM harness connectors will damage the ECM terminals resulting in poor terminal to pin connection. Install Miller Special Tool no. 8815 to perform diagnosis.

9. Inspect and clean all ECM, engine, and chassis grounds that are related to the most current DTC.
10. If numerous trouble codes were set, use a wire schematic and look for any common ground or supply circuits.
11. For any Relay DTCs, actuate the Relay with the scan tool and wiggle the related wire harness to try to interrupt the actuation.
12. For intermittent Evaporative Emission trouble codes perform a visual and physical inspection of the related parts including hoses and the Fuel Filler cap.
13. Use the scan tool to perform a System Test if one applies to failing component. A co-pilot, data recorder, and/or lab scope should be used to help diagnose intermittent conditions.

KNOCK SENSOR (KS)

LOCATION

The Knock Sensors (KS) are bolted into the cylinder block under the intake manifold. The sensors are used only with the 3.7L engine.

OPERATION

Two knock sensors are used on the 3.7L V-6 engine; one for each cylinder bank. When the knock sensor detects a knock in one of the cylinders on the corresponding bank, it sends an input signal to the Powertrain Control Module (PCM). In response, the PCM retards ignition timing for all cylinders by a scheduled amount.

Knock sensors contain a piezoelectric material, which constantly vibrates and sends an input voltage (signal) to the PCM while the engine operates. As the intensity of the crystals vibration increases, the knock sensor output voltage also increases.

The voltage signal produced by the knock sensor increases with the amplitude of vibration. The PCM receives the knock sensor voltage signal as an input. If the signal rises above a predetermined level, the PCM will store that value in memory and retard ignition timing to reduce engine knock. If the knock sensor voltage exceeds a preset value, the PCM retards ignition timing for all cylinders. It is not a selective cylinder retard.

The PCM ignores knock sensor input during engine idle conditions. Once the engine speed exceeds a specified value, knock retard is allowed.

Knock retard uses its own short-term and long-term memory program. Long-term memory stores previous detonation information in its battery-backed RAM. The maximum authority that long term memory has over timing retard can be calibrated. Short-term memory is allowed to retard timing up to a preset amount under all operating conditions (as long as rpm is above the minimum rpm) except at Wide Open Throttle (WOT). The PCM, using short-term memory, can respond quickly to retard timing when engine knock is detected. Short-term memory is lost any time the ignition key is turned OFF.

➡Over or under tightening the sensor mounting bolts will affect knock sensor performance, possibly causing improper spark control. Always use the specified torque when installing the knock sensors.

REMOVAL & INSTALLATION

See Figure 141.

➡The left sensor is identified by an identification tag (LEFT). It is also identified by a larger bolt head. The Powertrain Control Module (PCM) must have and know the correct sensor left/right positions. Do not mix the sensor locations.

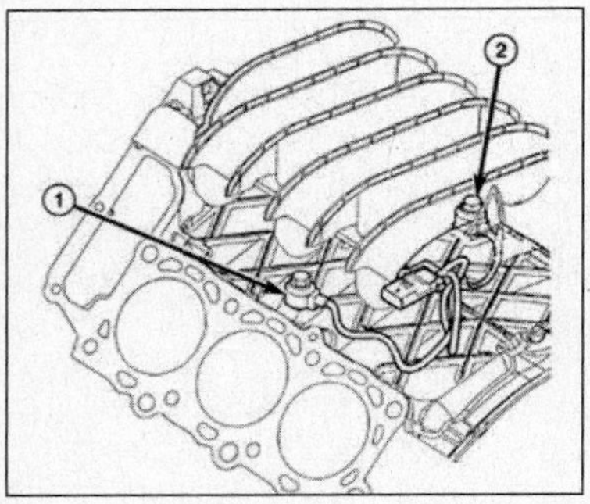

Fig. 141 Knock sensor locations (1) and mounting bolts (2)—3.7L engine

1. Disconnect knock sensor dual pigtail harness from engine wiring harness. This connection is made near rear of left valve cover.
2. Remove intake manifold.
3. Remove sensor mounting bolts. Remove sensors from engine.

➡Note the foam strip on bolt threads. This foam is used only to retain the bolts to sensors for plant assembly. It is not used as a sealant. Do not apply any adhesive, sealant or thread locking compound to these bolts.

To install:

WARNING

Over or under tightening the sensor mounting bolts will affect knock sensor performance, possibly causing improper spark control. Always use the specified torque when installing the knock sensors. The torque for the knock sensor bolt is relatively light for an 8mm bolt.

4. Thoroughly clean knock sensor mounting holes.
5. Install sensors into cylinder block.
6. Install and tighten mounting bolts to 15 ft. lbs. (20 Nm).
7. Install intake manifold.
8. Connect knock sensor wiring harness to engine harness at rear of intake manifold.

TESTING

1. Start the engine and allow it to reach normal operating temperature. Using a diagnostic scan tool, check for the presence of any Diagnostic Trouble Codes (DTCs). Record and address these codes as necessary.
2. Refer to any Technical Service Bulletins (TSBs) that may apply.
3. Review the scan tool Freeze Frame information. If possible, try to duplicate the conditions under which the DTC set.
4. With the engine running at normal operating temperature, monitor the scan tool parameters related to the DTC while wiggling the wire harness. Look for parameter values to change and/or a DTC to set. Turn the ignition off.
5. Visually inspect the related wire harness. Disconnect all the related harness connectors. Look for any chafed, pierced, pinched, partially broken wires and broken, bent, pushed out, or corroded terminals. Perform a voltage drop test on the related circuits between the suspected inoperative component and the ECM.

CAUTION

Do not probe the ECM harness connectors. Probing the ECM harness connectors will damage the ECM terminals resulting in poor terminal to pin connection. Install Miller Special Tool no. 8815 to perform diagnosis.

6. Inspect and clean all ECM, engine, and chassis grounds that are related to the most current DTC.
7. If numerous trouble codes were set, use a wire schematic and look for any common ground or supply circuits.
8. For any Relay DTCs, actuate the Relay with the scan tool and wiggle the related wire harness to try to interrupt the actuation.
9. For intermittent Evaporative Emission trouble codes perform a visual and physical inspection of the related parts including hoses and the Fuel Filler cap.
10. Use the scan tool to perform a System Test if one applies to failing component. A co-pilot, data recorder, and/or lab scope should be used to help diagnose intermittent conditions.

MANIFOLD ABSOLUTE PRESSURE (MAP) SENSOR

LOCATION

On 3.7L engines, the Manifold Absolute Pressure (MAP) sensor is located on the front of the intake manifold. On 4.0L engines, the sensor is located on the engine throttle body.

OPERATION

The MAP sensor is used as an input to the Powertrain Control Module (PCM). It contains a silicon based sensing unit to provide data on the manifold vacuum that draws the air/fuel mixture into the combustion chamber. The PCM requires this information to determine injector pulse width and spark advance. When manifold absolute pressure equals Barometric pressure, the pulse width will be at maximum.

A 5-volt reference is supplied from the PCM and returns a voltage signal to the PCM that reflects manifold pressure. The zero pressure reading is 0.5V and full scale is 4.5V. For a pressure swing of 015 psi, the voltage changes 4.0V. To operate the sensor, it is supplied a regulated 4.8 to 5.1 volts. Ground is provided through the low-noise, sensor return circuit at the PCM.

The MAP sensor input is the number one contributor to fuel injector pulse width. The most important function of the MAP sensor is to determine barometric pressure. The PCM needs to know if the vehicle is at sea level or at a higher altitude, because the air density changes with altitude. It will also help to correct for varying barometric pressure. Barometric pressure and altitude have a direct inverse correlation; as altitude goes up, barometric goes down. At key-on, the PCM powers up and looks at MAP voltage, and based upon the voltage it sees, it knows the current barometric pressure (relative to altitude). Once the engine starts, the PCM looks at the voltage again, continuously every 12 milliseconds, and compares the current voltage to what it was at key-on. The difference between current voltage and what it was at Key On is the manifold vacuum.

During key-on (engine not running) the sensor reads (updates) barometric pressure. A normal range can be obtained by monitoring a known good sensor.

As the altitude increases, the air becomes thinner (less oxygen). If a vehicle is started and driven to a very different altitude than where it was at key-on, the barometric pressure needs to be updated. Any time the PCM sees Wide Open Throttle (WOT), based upon Throttle Position Sensor (TPS) angle and RPM, it will update barometric pressure in the MAP memory cell. With periodic updates, the PCM can make its calculations more effectively. The PCM uses the MAP sensor input to aid in calculating the following:

- Manifold pressure
- Barometric pressure
- Engine load
- Injector pulse-width
- Spark-advance programs
- Shift-point strategies (certain automatic transmissions only)
- Idle speed
- Decel fuel shutoff

The MAP sensor signal is provided from a single piezo-resistive element located in the center of a diaphragm. The element and diaphragm are both made of silicone. As manifold pressure changes, the diaphragm moves causing the element to deflect, which stresses the silicone. When silicone is exposed to stress, its resistance changes. As manifold vacuum increases, the MAP sensor input voltage decreases proportionally. The sensor also contains electronics that condition the signal and provide temperature compensation.

The PCM recognizes a decrease in manifold pressure by monitoring a decrease in voltage from the reading stored in the barometric pressure memory cell. The MAP sensor is a linear sensor; meaning as pressure changes, voltage changes proportionately. The range of voltage output from the sensor is usually between 4.6 volts at sea level to as low as 0.3 volts at 26 in. of Hg. Barometric pressure is the pressure exerted by the atmosphere upon an object. At sea level on a standard day, no storm, barometric pressure is approximately 29.92 in Hg. For every 100 feet of altitude, barometric pressure drops .10 in. Hg. If a storm goes through it can change barometric pressure from what should be present for that altitude. You should know what the average pressure and corresponding barometric pressure is for your area.

REMOVAL & INSTALLATION

3.7L Engine

See Figure 142.

1. Disconnect electrical connector at sensor.
2. Clean area around MAP sensor.
3. Remove 2 sensor mounting screws.
4. Remove MAP sensor from intake manifold.

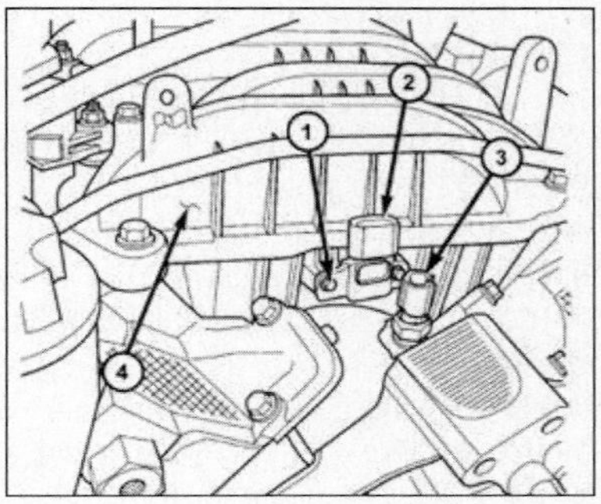

Fig. 142 Indicating the location of the MAP sensor mounting screws: MAP sensor screws (1), MAP sensor (2), ECT sensor (3), and intake manifold (4)

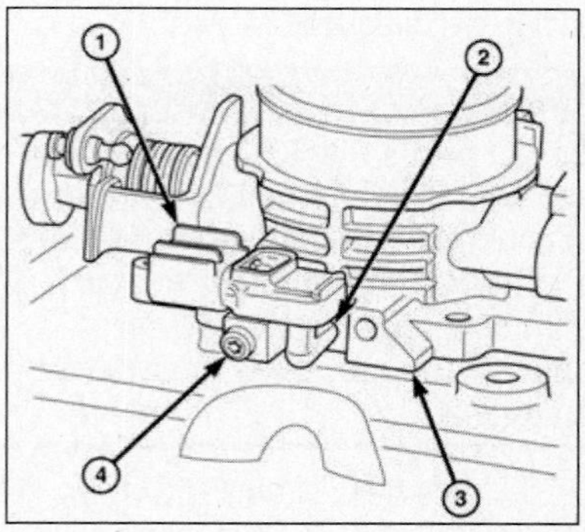

Fig. 143 Identifying the MAP sensor (2), rubber fitting (2), throttle body (3) and mounting screw (4) on 4.0L engines

To install:

5. Check condition of sensor O-ring.
6. Clean MAP sensor mounting hole at intake manifold.
7. Check MAP sensor O-ring seal for cuts or tears.
8. Position sensor into manifold.
9. Install MAP sensor mounting bolts (screws). Tighten screws to 25 inch lbs. (3 Nm).
10. Connect electrical connector.

4.0L Engine

See Figure 143.

1. Remove air cleaner duct and air resonator box at throttle body.
2. Remove MAP sensor mounting bolt (screw).
3. While removing MAP sensor, slide the rubber L-shaped fitting from the throttle body.
4. Remove rubber L-shaped fitting from MAP sensor.

To install:

5. Install rubber L-shaped fitting to MAP sensor.
6. Position sensor to throttle body while guiding rubber fitting over throttle body vacuum nipple.
7. Install MAP sensor mounting bolt (screw). Tighten screw to 25 inch lbs. (3 Nm).
8. Install air cleaner duct/air box.

TESTING

1. Start the engine and allow it to reach normal operating temperature. Using a diagnostic scan tool, check for the presence of any Diagnostic Trouble Codes (DTCs). Record and address these codes as necessary.
2. Refer to any Technical Service Bulletins (TSBs) that may apply.
3. Review the scan tool Freeze Frame information. If possible, try to duplicate the conditions under which the DTC set.
4. With the engine running at normal operating temperature, monitor the scan tool parameters related to the DTC while wiggling the wire harness. Look for parameter values to change and/or a DTC to set. Turn the ignition off.
5. Visually inspect the related wire harness. Disconnect all the related harness connectors. Look for any chafed, pierced, pinched, partially broken wires and broken, bent, pushed out, or corroded terminals. Perform a voltage drop test on the related circuits between the suspected inoperative component and the ECM.

**** CAUTION**

Do not probe the ECM harness connectors. Probing the ECM harness connectors will damage the ECM terminals resulting in poor terminal to pin connection. Install Miller Special Tool no. 8815 to perform diagnosis.

6. Inspect and clean all ECM, engine, and chassis grounds that are related to the most current DTC.
7. If numerous trouble codes were set, use a wire schematic and look for any common ground or supply circuits.
8. For any Relay DTCs, actuate the Relay with the scan tool and wiggle the related wire harness to try to interrupt the actuation.
9. For intermittent Evaporative Emission trouble codes perform a visual and physical inspection of the related parts including hoses and the Fuel Filler cap.
10. Use the scan tool to perform a System Test if one applies to failing component. A co-pilot, data recorder, and/or lab scope should be used to help diagnose intermittent conditions.

THROTTLE POSITION SENSOR (TPS)

LOCATION

The Throttle Position Sensor (TPS) is mounted on the throttle body and is connected to the throttle blade.

OPERATION

The TPS is a 3 wire variable resistor that provides the Powertrain Control Module (PCM) with an input signal (voltage) that represents the throttle blade position of the throttle body. The sensor is connected to the throttle blade shaft. As the position of the throttle blade changes, the resistance (output voltage) of the TPS changes.

The PCM supplies approximately 5 volts to the TPS. The TPS output voltage (input signal to the PCM) represents the throttle blade position. The PCM receives an input signal voltage from the TPS. This will vary in an approximate range of from .26 volts at minimum throttle opening (idle), to 4.49 volts at wide-open throttle. Along with inputs from other sensors, the PCM uses the TPS input to determine current engine operating conditions. In response to engine operating conditions, the PCM will adjust fuel injector pulse width and ignition timing.

REMOVAL & INSTALLATION

1. Disconnect TPS electrical connector.
2. Remove TPS mounting screws.
3. Remove TPS.

To install:

4. The throttle shaft end of throttle body slides into a socket in the TPS. The TPS must be installed so that it can be rotated a few degrees. (If sensor will not rotate, install sensor with throttle shaft on other side of socket tangs). The TPS will be under slight tension when rotated.
5. Install TPS and retaining screws.
6. Tighten screws to 60 inch lbs. (7 Nm).
7. Connect TPS electrical connector to TPS.
8. Manually operate throttle (by hand) to check for any TPS binding before starting engine.

TESTING

1. Start the engine and allow it to reach normal operating temperature. Using a diagnostic scan tool, check for the presence of any Diagnostic Trouble Codes (DTCs). Record and address these codes as necessary.
2. Refer to any Technical Service Bulletins (TSBs) that may apply.
3. Review the scan tool Freeze Frame information. If possible, try to duplicate the conditions under which the DTC set.
4. With the engine running at normal operating temperature, monitor the scan tool parameters related to the DTC while wiggling the wire harness. Look for parameter values to change and/or a DTC to set. Turn the ignition off.
5. Visually inspect the related wire harness. Disconnect all the related harness connectors. Look for any chafed, pierced, pinched, partially broken wires and broken, bent, pushed out, or corroded terminals. Perform a voltage drop test on the related circuits between the suspected inoperative component and the ECM.

CAUTION

Do not probe the ECM harness connectors. Probing the ECM harness connectors will damage the ECM terminals resulting in poor terminal to pin connection. Install Miller Special Tool no. 8815 to perform diagnosis.

6. Inspect and clean all ECM, engine, and chassis grounds that are related to the most current DTC.
7. If numerous trouble codes were set, use a wire schematic and look for any common ground or supply circuits.
8. For any Relay DTCs, actuate the Relay with the scan tool and wiggle the related wire harness to try to interrupt the actuation.
9. For intermittent Evaporative Emission trouble codes perform a visual and physical inspection of the related parts including hoses and the Fuel Filler cap.
10. Use the scan tool to perform a System Test if one applies to failing component. A co-pilot, data recorder, and/or lab scope should be used to help diagnose intermittent conditions.

VEHICLE SPEED SENSOR (VSS)

LOCATION

The Vehicle Speed Sensor (VSS) is located on the left side of the transmission case.

OPERATION

The VSS generates an AC signal as its coil is excited by rotation of the rear planetary carrier lugs. The Transmission Control Module (TCM) interprets this information as output shaft RPM.

REMOVAL & INSTALLATION

1. Raise and safely support the vehicle.
2. Place a suitable catch pan under the transmission for any fluid.
3. Remove the wiring connector from the output speed sensor.
4. Remove the mounting bolt and remove the speed sensor from the transmission case.

To install:

5. Install the speed sensor into the transmission case and tighten the bolt to 105 inch lbs. (12 Nm).
6. Install the wiring connector to the speed sensor.
7. Verify the proper transmission fluid level and refill as necessary.
8. Lower the vehicle.

TESTING

1. Start the engine and allow it to reach normal operating temperature. Using a diagnostic scan tool, check for the presence of any Diagnostic Trouble Codes (DTCs). Record and address these codes as necessary.
2. Refer to any Technical Service Bulletins (TSBs) that may apply.
3. Review the scan tool Freeze Frame information. If possible, try to duplicate the conditions under which the DTC set.
4. With the engine running at normal operating temperature, monitor the scan tool parameters related to the DTC while wiggling the wire harness. Look for parameter values to change and/or a DTC to set. Turn the ignition off.
5. Visually inspect the related wire harness. Disconnect all the related harness connectors. Look for any chafed, pierced, pinched, partially broken wires and broken, bent, pushed out, or corroded terminals. Perform a voltage drop test on the related circuits between the suspected inoperative component and the ECM.

CAUTION

Do not probe the ECM harness connectors. Probing the PCM harness connectors will damage the PCM terminals resulting in poor terminal to pin connection. Install Miller Special Tool no. 8815 to perform diagnosis.

6. Inspect and clean all ECM, engine, and chassis grounds that are related to the most current DTC.
7. If numerous trouble codes were set, use a wire schematic and look for any common ground or supply circuits.
8. For any Relay DTCs, actuate the Relay with the scan tool and wiggle the related wire harness to try to interrupt the actuation.
9. For intermittent Evaporative Emission trouble codes perform a visual and physical inspection of the related parts including hoses and the Fuel Filler cap.
10. Use the scan tool to perform a System Test if one applies to failing component. A co-pilot, data recorder, and/or lab scope should be used to help diagnose intermittent conditions.

FUEL SYSTEM SERVICE PRECAUTIONS

Safety is the most important factor when performing not only fuel system maintenance but any type of maintenance. Failure to conduct maintenance and repairs in a safe manner may result in serious personal injury or death. Maintenance and testing of the vehicle's fuel system components can be accomplished safely and effectively by adhering to the following rules and guidelines.

- To avoid the possibility of fire and personal injury, always disconnect the negative battery cable unless the repair or test procedure requires that battery voltage be applied.
- Always relieve the fuel system pressure prior to disconnecting any fuel system component (injector, fuel rail, pressure regulator, etc.), fitting or fuel line connection. Exercise extreme caution whenever relieving fuel system pressure to avoid exposing skin, face and eyes to fuel spray. Please be advised that fuel under pressure may penetrate the skin or any part of the body that it contacts.
- Always place a shop towel or cloth around the fitting or connection prior to loosening to absorb any excess fuel due to spillage. Ensure that all fuel spillage (should it occur) is quickly removed from engine surfaces. Ensure that all fuel soaked cloths or towels are deposited into a suitable waste container.
- Always keep a dry chemical (Class B) fire extinguisher near the work area.
- Do not allow fuel spray or fuel vapors to come into contact with a spark or open flame.
- Always use a back-up wrench when loosening and tightening fuel line connection fittings. This will prevent unnecessary stress and torsion to fuel line piping.
- Always replace worn fuel fitting O-rings with new Do not substitute fuel hose or equivalent where fuel pipe is installed.

Before servicing the vehicle, make sure to also refer to the precautions in the beginning of this section as well.

RELIEVING FUEL SYSTEM PRESSURE

1. Before servicing the vehicle, refer to the precautions in the beginning of this section.
2. Disconnect the negative battery cable.
3. Remove the fuel tank filler cap to release any fuel tank pressure.
4. Remove the fuel pump relay from the PDC.
5. Start and run the engine until it stops.
6. Unplug the connector from any injector and connect a jumper wire from either injector terminal to the positive battery terminal. Connect another jumper wire to the other terminal and momentarily touch the other end to the negative battery terminal.

⁂ WARNING

Just touch the jumper to the battery. Powering the injector for more than a few seconds will permanently damage it.

7. Place a rag below the quick-disconnect coupling at the fuel rail and disconnect it.

FUEL FILTER

REMOVAL & INSTALLATION

2005–06 Wrangler

The combination Fuel Filter/Fuel Pressure Regulator is located on the fuel pump module. The fuel pump module is located on top of fuel tank.

1. Before servicing the vehicle, refer to the precautions in the beginning of this section.
2. Remove fuel tank.
3. Clean area around filter/regulator.
4. Disconnect fuel line at filter/regulator.
5. Remove retainer clamp from top of filter/regulator. Clamp snaps to tabs on pump module. Discard old clamp.
6. Pry filter/regulator from top of pump module with 2 screwdrivers. Unit is snapped into module.
7. Discard gasket below filter/regulator.

To install:

8. Clean recessed area in pump module where filter/regulator is to be installed.
9. Obtain new filter/regulator (two new O-rings should already be installed).
10. Apply a small amount of clean engine oil to O-rings. Do not install O-rings separately into fuel pump module. They will be damaged when installing filter/regulator.
11. Install new gasket to top of fuel pump module.
12. Press new filter/regulator into pump module until it snaps into position (a positive click must be heard or felt).
13. Install the module.
14. Install fuel tank.

Liberty

See Figures 144 through 146.

1. Before servicing the vehicle, refer to the precautions in the beginning of this section.

The fuel filter is attached to the front of the fuel tank.

2. Before servicing the vehicle, refer to the precautions in the beginning of this section.
3. Relieve the fuel system pressure.

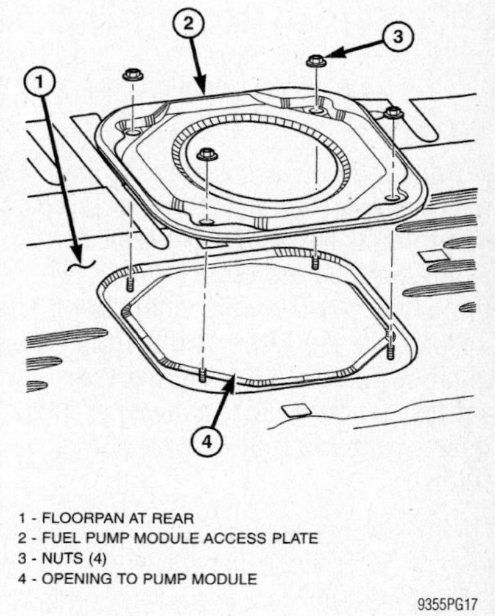

Fig. 144 Access plate—Liberty

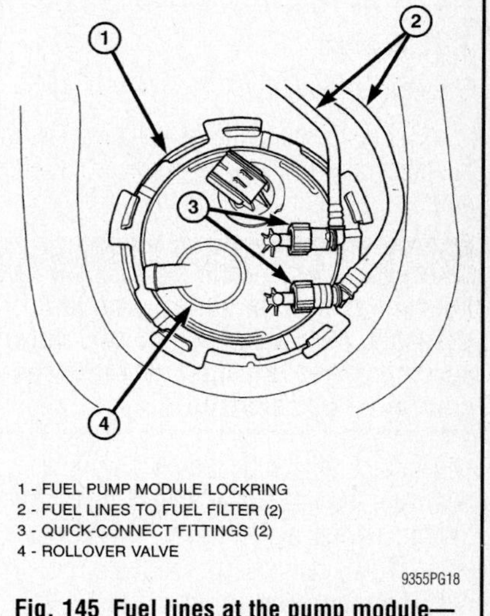

Fig. 145 Fuel lines at the pump module—Liberty

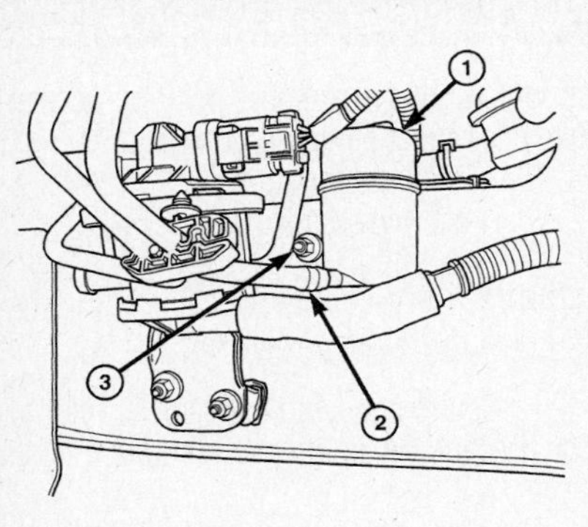

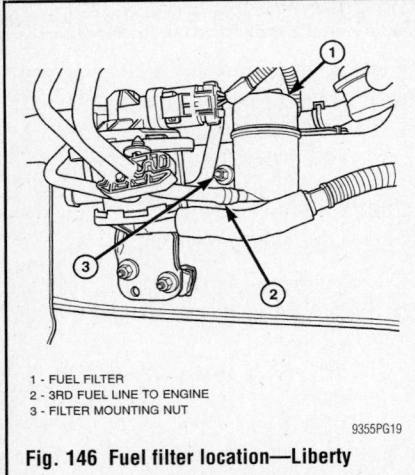

1 - FUEL FILTER
2 - 3RD FUEL LINE TO ENGINE
3 - FILTER MOUNTING NUT

9355PG19

Fig. 146 Fuel filter location—Liberty

4. Remove or disconnect the following:
   - Negative battery cable
   - 2 rear cargo hold-down clamps by drilling the rivets
   - 4 fuel pump module access plate nuts

➡Once the nuts are removed, the plate must be removed by applying a heat gun to melt the adhesive. Take care to avoid bending the plate. Once removed, you can disconnect the 2 top hoses from the filter. The bottom hose must be removed from under the vehicle. The disconnect point on this hose is about a foot in front of the filter.

   - Ground strap
   - Mounting nut and filter.
5. Installation is the reverse of removal.

FUEL INJECTORS

REMOVAL & INSTALLATION

2.4L Engine

See Figures 147 and 148.

1. Before servicing the vehicle, refer to the precautions in the beginning of this section.

⁂ CAUTION

the fuel system is under constant pressure even with engine off. Before servicing fuel rail, fuel system pressure must be released.

The fuel rail can be removed without removing the intake manifold if the following procedures are followed.

2. Remove fuel tank filler tube cap.
3. Perform Fuel System Pressure Release Procedure.

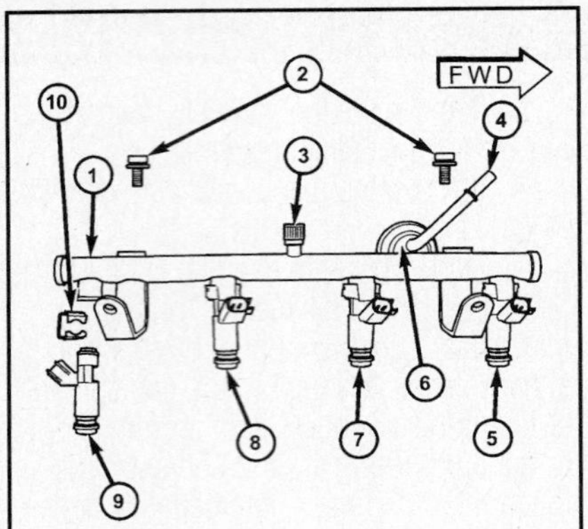

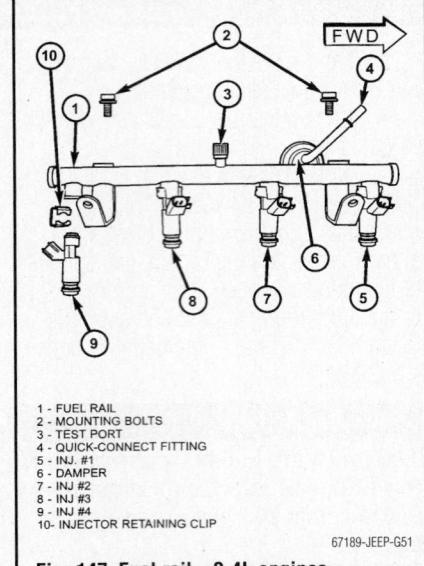

1 - FUEL RAIL
2 - MOUNTING BOLTS
3 - TEST PORT
4 - QUICK-CONNECT FITTING
5 - INJ. #1
6 - DAMPER
7 - INJ #2
8 - INJ #3
9 - INJ #4
10- INJECTOR RETAINING CLIP

67189-JEEP-G51

Fig. 147 Fuel rail—2.4L engines

4. Remove negative battery cable at battery.
5. Remove air duct at throttle body.
6. Disconnect fuel line latch clip and fuel line at fuel rail. A special tool will be necessary for fuel line disconnection.
7. Remove necessary vacuum lines at throttle body.
8. Drain engine coolant and remove thermostat and thermostat housing.
9. Remove PCV hose and valve at valve cover.
10. Remove 3 upper intake manifold mounting bolts, but only loosen 2 lower bolts about 2 turns.
11. Disconnect 2 main engine harness connectors at rear of intake manifold.

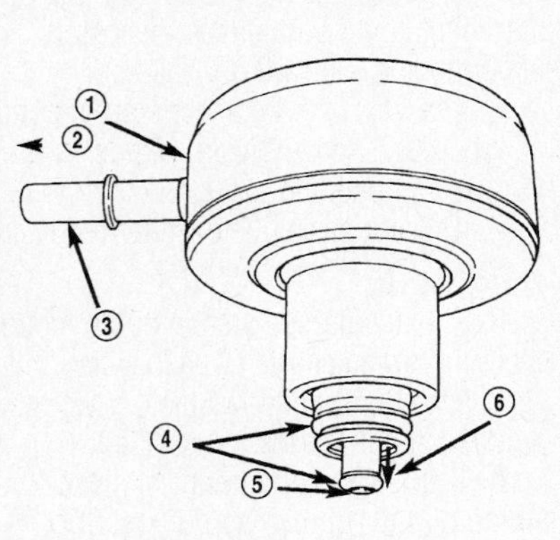

1 - FUEL FILTER/FUEL PRESSURE REGULATOR
2 - TO FUEL INJECTORS
3 - FUEL SUPPLY TUBE
4 - O-RINGS
5 - FUEL INLET FROM PUMP
6 - FUEL RETURN TO TANK

67189-JEEP-G53

Fig. 148 Fuel pressure regulator—2.4L engines

12. Disconnect 2 injection wiring harness clips at harness mounting bracket.
13. Disconnect electrical connectors at all 4 fuel injectors. Push red colored slider away from injector. While pushing slider, depress tab and remove connector from injector. The factory fuel injection wiring harness is numerically tagged (INJ 1, INJ 2, etc.) for injector position identification. If harness is not tagged, note wiring location before removal.
14. Remove 2 injection rail mounting bolts.
15. Gently rock and pull fuel rail until fuel injectors just start to clear machined holes in intake manifold.
16. Remove fuel rail (with injectors attached) from intake manifold. Remove the injector clips, then remove the injectors from the rail.

To install:

17. Clean out fuel injector machined bores in intake manifold.
18. Apply a small amount of engine oil to each fuel injector O-ring. This will help in fuel rail installation.
19. Position fuel rail/fuel injector assembly to machined injector openings in intake manifold.
20. Guide each injector into cylinder head. Be careful not to tear injector O-rings.
21. Push fuel rail down until fuel injectors have bottomed on shoulders.
22. Install 2 fuel rail mounting bolts and tighten to 250 inch lbs. (28 Nm).
23. Connect electrical connectors at all fuel injectors. Push connector onto injector and then push and lock red colored slider. Verify connector is locked to injector by lightly tugging on connector.
24. Snap 2 injection wiring harness clips into brackets.
25. Connect 2 main engine harness connectors at rear of intake manifold.
26. Tighten 5 intake manifold mounting bolts.
27. Install PCV valve and hose.
28. Install thermostat and radiator hose. Fill with coolant.
29. Connect necessary vacuum lines to throttle body.
30. Connect fuel line latch clip and fuel line to fuel rail.
31. Install air duct to throttle body.
32. Connect battery cable to battery.
33. Start engine and check for leaks.

3.7L Engine

See Figure 149.

1. Before servicing the vehicle, refer to the precautions in the beginning of this section.

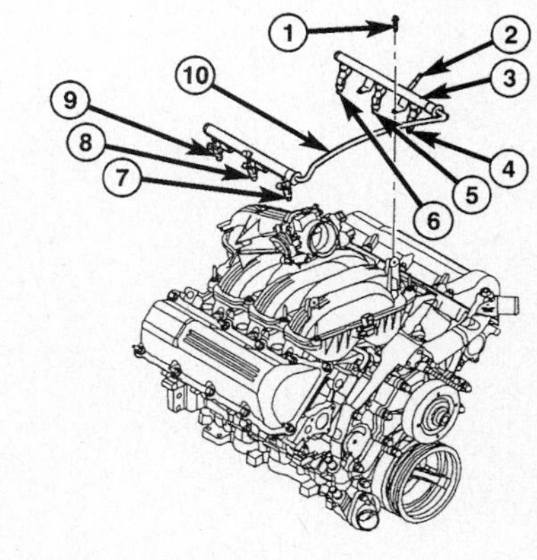

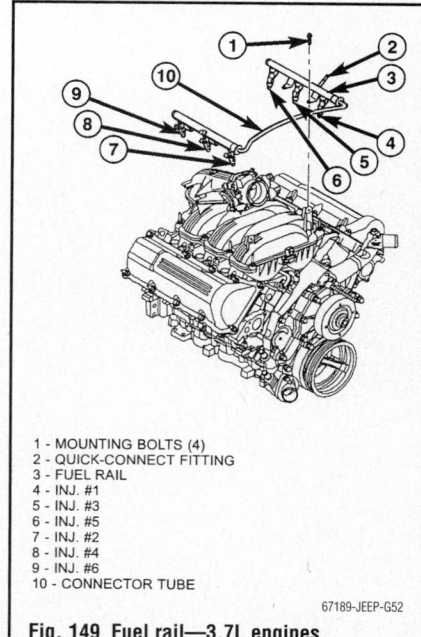

1 - MOUNTING BOLTS (4)
2 - QUICK-CONNECT FITTING
3 - FUEL RAIL
4 - INJ. #1
5 - INJ. #3
6 - INJ. #5
7 - INJ. #2
8 - INJ. #4
9 - INJ. #6
10 - CONNECTOR TUBE

67189-JEEP-G52

Fig. 149 Fuel rail—3.7L engines

CAUTION

the fuel system is under constant pressure even with engine off. Before servicing fuel rail, fuel system pressure must be released.

➡The left and right fuel rails are replaced as an assembly. Do not attempt to separate rail halves at connector tube. Due to design of tube, it does not use any clamps. Never attempt to install a clamping device of any kind to tube. When removing fuel rail assembly for any reason, be careful not to bend or kink tube.

2. Remove fuel tank filler tube cap.
3. Perform Fuel System Pressure Release Procedure.
4. Remove negative battery cable at battery.
5. Remove air duct at throttle body air box.
6. Remove air box at throttle body.
7. Disconnect fuel line latch clip and fuel line at fuel rail. A special tool will be necessary for fuel line disconnection.
8. Remove necessary vacuum lines at throttle body.
9. Disconnect electrical connectors at all 6 fuel injectors. Push red colored slider away from injector. While pushing slider, depress tab and remove connector from injector. The factory fuel injection wiring harness is numerically tagged (INJ 1, INJ 2, etc.) for injector position identification. If harness is not tagged, note wiring location before removal.
10. Disconnect electrical connectors at throttle body sensors.
11. Remove 6 ignition coils.
12. Remove 4 fuel rail mounting bolts.
13. Gently rock and pull left side of fuel rail until fuel injectors just start to clear machined holes in cylinder head. Gently rock and pull right side of rail until injectors just start to clear cylinder head holes. Repeat this procedure (left/right) until all injectors have cleared cylinder head holes.
14. Remove fuel rail (with injectors attached) from engine. Remove the injector clips, then remove the injectors from the rail.

To install:

15. Clean out fuel injector machined bores in intake manifold.
16. Apply a small amount of engine oil to each fuel injector O-ring. This will help in fuel rail installation.
17. Position fuel rail/fuel injector assembly to machined injector openings in cylinder head.
18. Guide each injector into cylinder head. Be careful not to tear injector O-rings.
19. Push right side of fuel rail down until fuel injectors have bottomed on cylinder head shoulder. Push left fuel rail down until injectors have bottomed on cylinder head shoulder.
20. Install 4 fuel rail mounting bolts and tighten to 100 inch lbs. (11 Nm).
21. Install 6 ignition coils.
22. Connect electrical connectors to throttle body.
23. Connect electrical connectors at all fuel injectors. Push connector onto injector and then push and lock red colored slider. Verify connector is locked to injector by lightly tugging on connector.
24. Connect necessary vacuum lines to throttle body.
25. Connect fuel line latch clip and fuel line to fuel rail.
26. Install air box to throttle body.
27. Install air duct to air box.
28. Connect battery cable to battery.
29. Start engine and check for leaks.

4.0L Engines

See Figure 150.

1. Before servicing the vehicle, refer to the precautions in the beginning of this section.

CAUTION

The fuel system is under constant fuel pressure even with engine off.

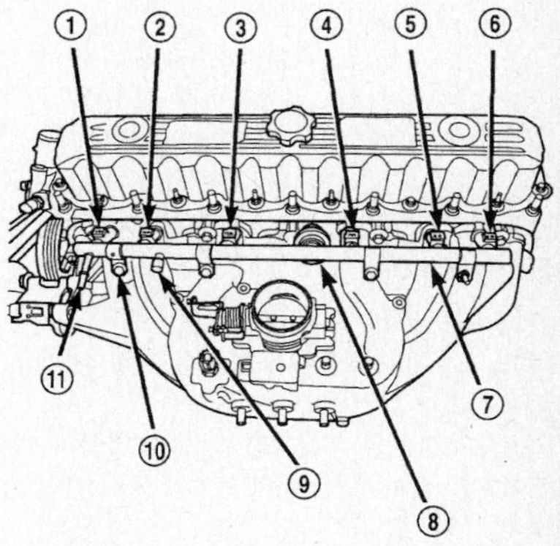

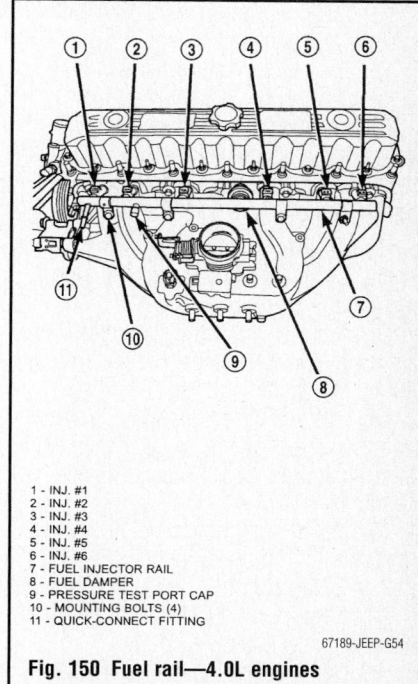

1 - INJ. #1
2 - INJ. #2
3 - INJ. #3
4 - INJ. #4
5 - INJ. #5
6 - INJ. #6
7 - FUEL INJECTOR RAIL
8 - FUEL DAMPER
9 - PRESSURE TEST PORT CAP
10 - MOUNTING BOLTS (4)
11 - QUICK-CONNECT FITTING

67189-JEEP-G54

Fig. 150 Fuel rail—4.0L engines

This pressure must be released before servicing fuel rail.

➡The fuel damper is not serviced separately

2. Remove fuel tank filler tube cap.
3. Perform Fuel System Pressure Release Procedure.
4. Disconnect negative battery cable from battery.
5. Remove air tube at top of throttle body.

➡Some engine/vehicles may require removal of air cleaner ducts at throttle body.

6. Disconnect electrical connectors at all 6 fuel injectors. Push red colored slider away from injector. While pushing slider, depress tab and remove connector from injector. The factory fuel injection wiring harness is numerically tagged (INJ 1, INJ 2, etc.) for injector position identification. If harness is not tagged, note wiring location before removal.
7. Disconnect fuel supply line latch clip and fuel line at fuel rail.
8. Disconnect throttle cable at throttle body.
9. Disconnect speed control cable at throttle body (if equipped).
10. Disconnect automatic transmission cable at throttle body (if equipped).
11. Remove cable routing bracket at intake manifold.
12. If equipped, remove wiring harnesses at injection rail studs by removing nuts.

13. Clean dirt/debris from each fuel injector at intake manifold.

14. Remove fuel rail mounting nuts/bolts.

15. Remove fuel rail by gently rocking until all the fuel injectors are out of intake manifold. Remove the injector clips, then remove the injectors from the rail.

To install:

16. Clean each injector bore at intake manifold.

17. Apply a small amount of clean engine oil to each injector O-ring. This will aid in installation.

18. Position tips of all fuel injectors into the corresponding injector bore in intake manifold. Seat injectors into manifold.

19. Install and tighten fuel rail mounting bolts to 100 +/-25 inch lbs. (11 +/-3 Nm) torque.

20. If equipped, connect wiring harnesses to injection rail studs.

21. Connect electrical connectors at all fuel injectors. Push connector onto injector and then push and lock red colored slider. Verify connector is locked to injector by lightly tugging on connector.

22. Connect fuel line and fuel line latch clip to fuel rail.

23. Install protective cap to pressure test port fitting (if equipped).

24. Install cable routing bracket to intake manifold.

25. Connect throttle cable at throttle body.

26. Connect speed control cable at throttle body (if equipped).

27. Connect automatic transmission cable at throttle body (if equipped).

28. Install air tube (or duct) at top of throttle body.

29. Install fuel tank cap.

30. Connect negative battery cable to battery.

31. Start engine and check for fuel leaks.

FUEL PUMP

REMOVAL & INSTALLATION

2005–06 Wrangler

See Figure 151.

⁂ CAUTION

The fuel system is under a constant pressure (even with the engine off). Before servicing the fuel pump module, the fuel system pressure must be released.

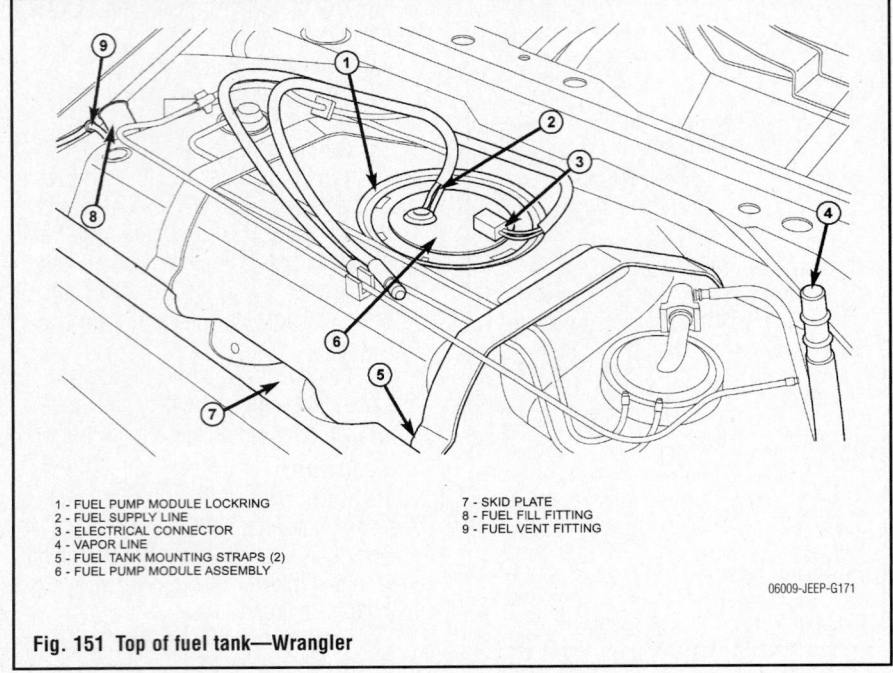

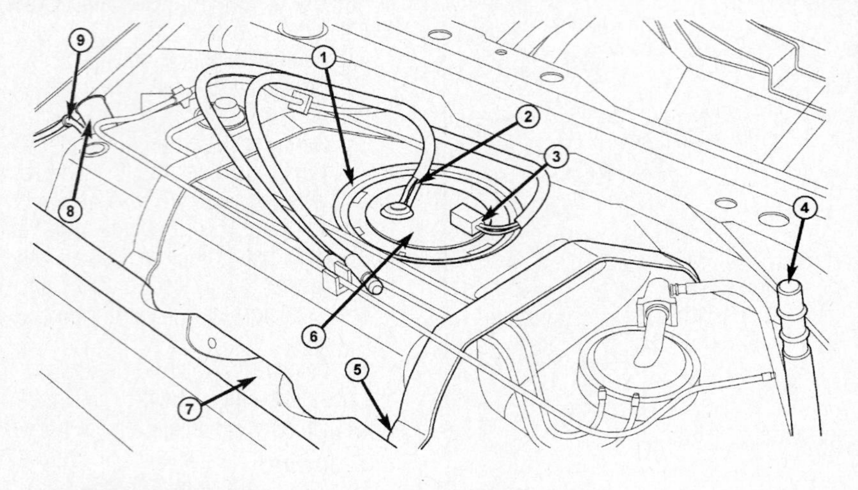

Fig. 151 Top of fuel tank—Wrangler

1. Before servicing the vehicle, refer to the precautions in the beginning of this section.

2. Remove the fuel tank.

➡Note rotational position of module before attempting removal. An indexing arrow is located on top of module for this purpose.

3. Position Special Tool 9340 into notches on outside edge of lockring.

4. Install ½ inch drive breaker bar to tool 9340.

5. Rotate breaker bar counter-clockwise to remove lockring.

6. Remove lockring. The module will spring up slightly when lockring is removed.

7. Remove module from fuel tank. Be careful not to bend float arm while removing.

To install:

8. Using a new seal (gasket), position fuel pump module into opening in fuel tank.

9. Position lockring over top of fuel pump module.

10. Rotate module until embossed alignment arrow points to center alignment mark. This step must be performed to prevent float from contacting side of fuel tank. Also be sure fuel fitting on top of pump module is pointed to front of vehicle.

11. Install Special Tool 9340 to lockring.

12. Install ½ inch drive breaker into Special Tool 9340.

13. Tighten lockring (clockwise) until all seven notches have engaged.

14. Install the fuel tank. Start vehicle and inspect for leaks.

Liberty

See Figures 152 and 153.

The fuel filter is attached to the front of the fuel tank.

1. Before servicing the vehicle, refer to the precautions in the beginning of this section.

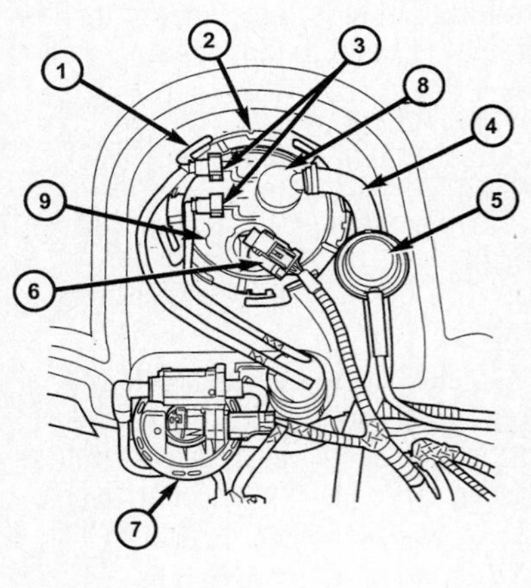

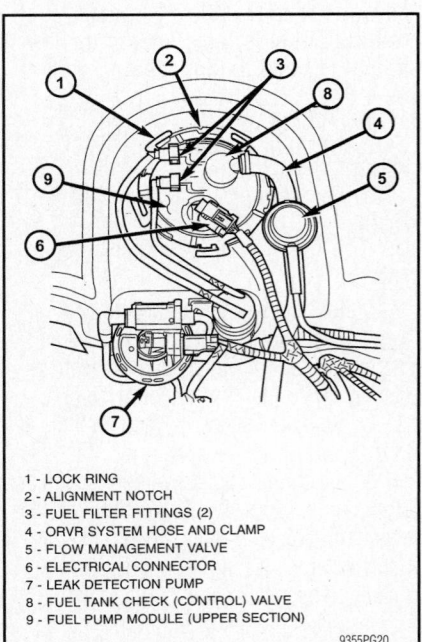

Fig. 152 Top view of the fuel pump module—Liberty

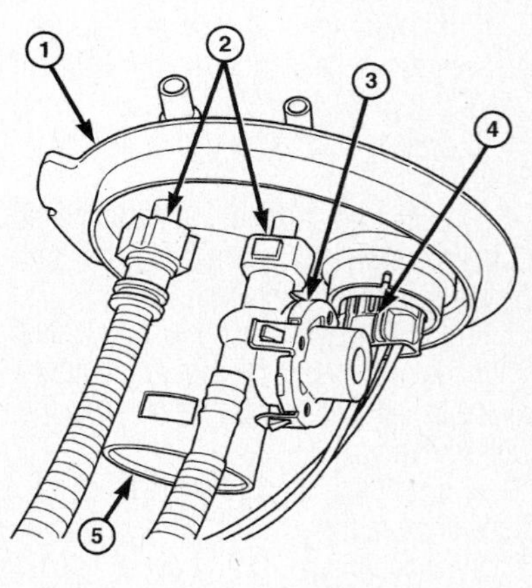

1 - UPPER SECTION OF PUMP MODULE
2 - QUICK-CONNECT FITTINGS
3 - FUEL PRESSURE REGULATOR
4 - 4-WIRE ELECTRICAL CONNECTOR
5 - FUEL TANK CHECK (CONTROL) VALVE

9355PG21

Fig. 153 Fuel pressure regulator—Liberty

2. Relieve the fuel system pressure.
3. Remove or disconnect the following:
   - Negative battery cable
   - 2 rear cargo hold-down clamps by drilling the rivets
   - 4 fuel pump module access plate nuts

➡Once the nuts are removed, the plate must be removed by applying a heat gun to melt the adhesive. Take care to avoid bending the plate.

   - Fuel lines at the module
   - Electrical connector by first sliding the red tab, then pushing the gray tab
   - ORVR hose
   - Module lockring
   - Module from the tank

✱✱ WARNING

Lift the module out slowly and carefully until you can secure the rubber gasket. If you're not careful, the gasket will fall into the tank.

   - Electrical connector from the upper module section
   - Fuel pressure regulator
   - Fuel return line
   - Upper module section
4. Drain the tank through the module opening.
5. Remove or disconnect the following:
   - Lower module section by pushing gently on the release tab while sliding the lock tab upward
6. Installation is the reverse of removal.

FUEL TANK

REMOVAL & INSTALLATION

2005–06 Wrangler

See Figures 154 through 157.

✱✱ CAUTION

The fuel system is under a constant pressure (even with the engine off). Before servicing the fuel pump module, the fuel system pressure must be released.

This vehicle is equipped with an On-Board Refueling Vapor Recovery (ORVR) system. Because of this, the fuel tank may be drained the conventional way through the filler cap opening. On this model, the fuel tank is mounted to the vehicle skid plate.

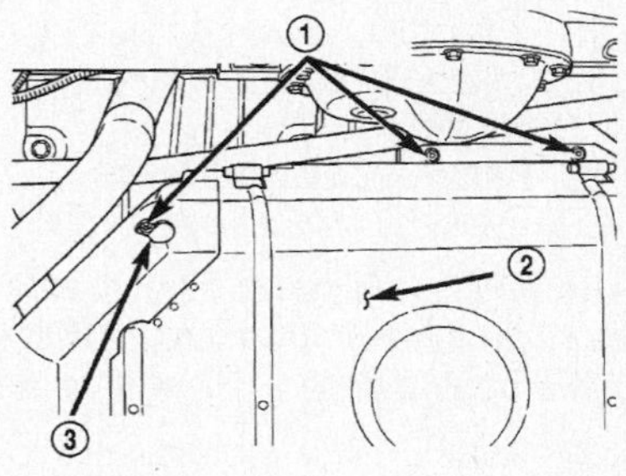

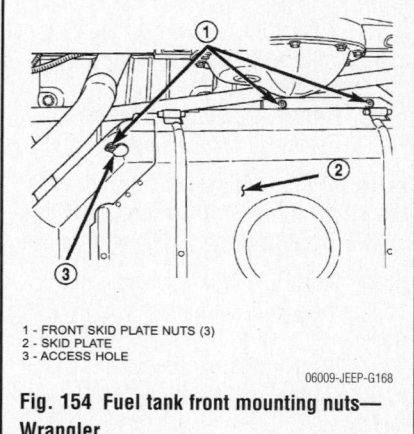

1 - FRONT SKID PLATE NUTS (3)
2 - SKID PLATE
3 - ACCESS HOLE

06009-JEEP-G168

Fig. 154 Fuel tank front mounting nuts—Wrangler

The skid plate is mounted to vehicle body. The tank and skid plate are removed as one assembly.

1. Before servicing the vehicle, refer to the precautions in the beginning of this section.
2. Remove fuel filler cap.
3. Perform the fuel system pressure release procedure as described elsewhere in this group.
4. Disconnect negative battery cable.
5. Using an approved portable gasoline siphon/storage tank, drain fuel from tank through filler cap opening.
6. Remove 8 screws retaining plastic fuel filler bezel to body. Remove plastic fuel filler bezel.
7. To prevent contaminants from entering tank, temporarily install fuel cap to fill hoses.
8. Remove right/rear tire/wheel.
9. Remove wheelhouse liner at right/rear wheel.
10. Remove vertical support bracket to gain access to ORVR vapor line.
11. A vapor line connects the fuel tank to the EVAP canister and NVLD pump. This connection is made near the right/rear corner of the fuel tank. Carefully disconnect this vapor line. Be very careful not to bend or kink the vapor lines. If vapor lines leak, a Diagnostic Trouble Code (DTC) will be set.
12. Cut plastic tie wrap securing rear axle vent hose to fuel fill hose.
13. Disconnect fuel tank electrical connector at left/front of fuel tank.
14. Disconnect 2 vapor lines at left/front of fuel tank.

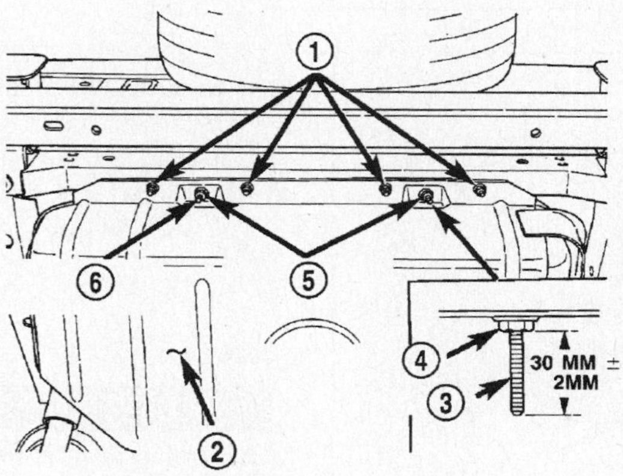

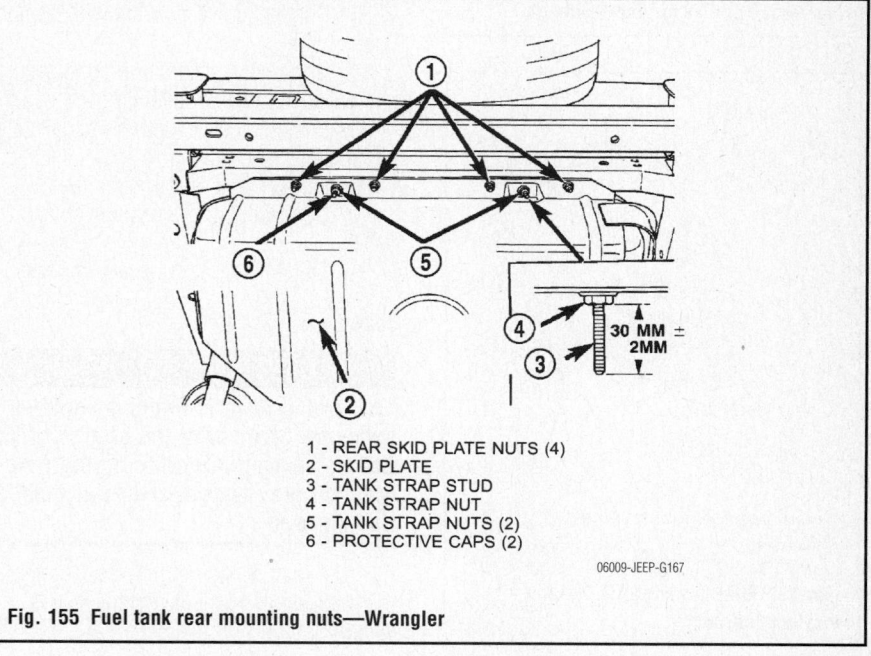

1 - REAR SKID PLATE NUTS (4)
2 - SKID PLATE
3 - TANK STRAP STUD
4 - TANK STRAP NUT
5 - TANK STRAP NUTS (2)
6 - PROTECTIVE CAPS (2)

06009-JEEP-G167

Fig. 155 Fuel tank rear mounting nuts—Wrangler

15. Disconnect quick-connect fitting from fuel supply line at front of fuel tank.

16. The fuel tank and skid plate are removed as an assembly. Centrally position a transmission jack (or equivalent lifting device) under skid plate/fuel tank assembly. Secure tank assembly to jack.

17. Remove three skid plate-to-body nuts at front of tank. Remove one of the nuts through access hole on skid plate.

18. Remove four skid plate-to-body nuts at rear of tank. Do not loosen tank strap nuts.

19. Lower the tank assembly.

20. Disconnect fuel filler hose at tank. Before disconnecting, mark and note the hose rotational position in relation to tank fitting.

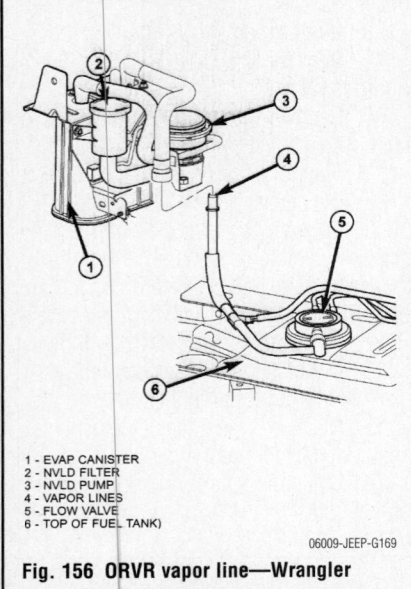

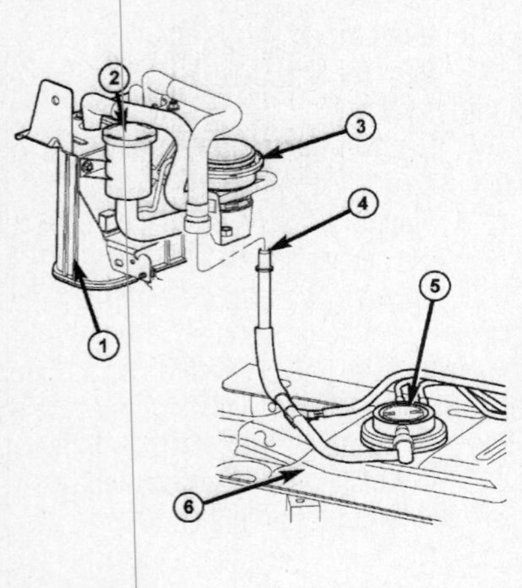

Fig. 156 ORVR vapor line—Wrangler

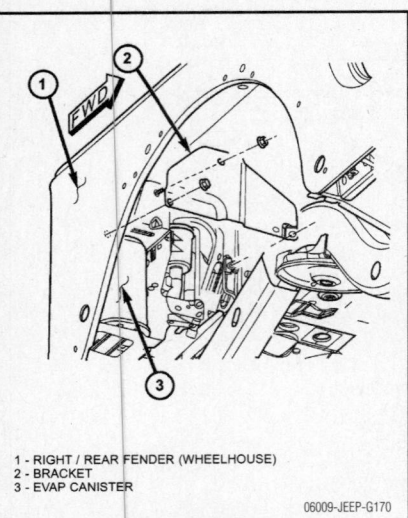

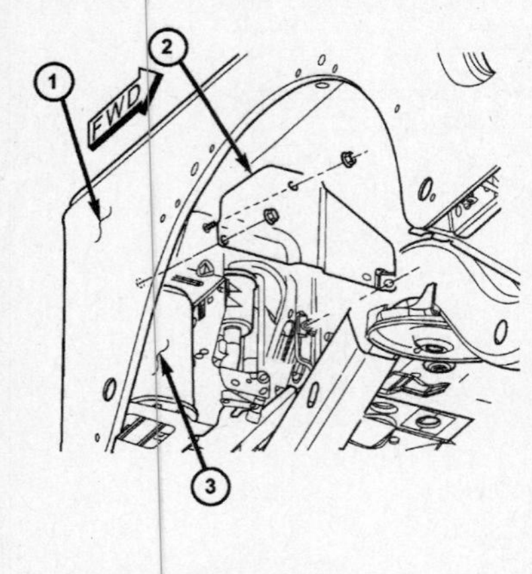

Fig. 157 EVAP canister/NVLD pump location—Wrangler

21. To separate tank from skid plate, remove two protective caps at tank strap studs and remove tank strap nuts.

22. Remove both straps and remove tank from skid plate.

To install:

23. Place fuel tank into skid plate. Wrap straps around tank with strap studs inserted through holes in skid plate. Tighten strap nuts to attain 30 mm (+/-2 mm) between bottom of nut to end of strap stud. Do not over tighten nuts.

24. Install two protective caps to tank strap studs.

25. Connect fuel fill hose at tank. Tighten hose clamp.

26. Raise skid plate/fuel tank assembly into position on body while carefully guiding plastic vapor lines and fill hose.

27. Install four skid plate mounting nuts at rear of tank. Tighten to 141 inch lbs. (16 Nm) torque.

28. Install three skid plate mounting nuts at front of tank. Tighten to 141 inch lbs. (16 Nm)torque.

29. Remove tank jacking device.

30. Carefully connect the vapor line.

➡Be very careful not to bend or kink the vapor lines. If lines leak, a Diagnostic Trouble Code (DTC) will be set.

31. Install EVAP canister bracket.

32. Install wheelhouse liner at right/rear wheel.

33. Install right/rear tire/wheel.

34. Connect electrical connector at of fuel tank.

35. Connect vapor line at left/front of fuel tank.

36. Connect quick-connect fitting to fuel supply fitting.

37. Use a new plastic tie wrap to secure rear axle vent hose to fuel fill hose.

38. Position fuel fill bezel to body. Install eight screws and tighten.

39. Fill fuel tank. Install filler cap.

40. Connect negative battery cable to battery.

41. Start vehicle and inspect for leaks.

Liberty

CAUTION

The fuel system is under a constant pressure (even with the engine off). Before servicing the fuel pump module, the fuel system pressure must be released.

1. Before servicing the vehicle, refer to the precautions in the beginning of this section.

2. Remove the fuel filler cap.

3. Perform the fuel system pressure release procedure as described elsewhere in this group.

4. Disconnect the negative battery cable.

5. Using an approved portable gasoline siphon/storage tank, drain fuel from tank through filler cap opening.

6. If equipped, remove fuel tank skid plate and tow hooks. Certain equipment packages will also require removal of the trailer hitch.

7. Label and disconnect fuel line fittings at the tank

8. Disconnect fuel fill hose at left side of tank.

9. Disconnect fuel pump module electrical connector jumper. This is located near front of fuel tank.

10. Support tank with a hydraulic jack.

11. Remove the four fuel tank mounting bolts from tank straps (2 at front of tank; 2 at rear of tank), and remove both tank support straps.

12. Carefully lower tank a few inches.

13. Continue lowering tank while guiding remaining hoses and lines through plastic isolator sleeve.

14. Installation is the reverse of removal. Tighten the strap mounting bolts to 45 ft. lbs. (61 Nm).

IDLE SPEED

ADJUSTMENT

Idle speed is controlled by the Powertrain Control Module (PCM). No adjustment is possible.

THROTTLE BODY

REMOVAL & INSTALLATION

2.4L and 3.7L Engines

See Figures 158 and 159.

A (factory adjusted) set screw is used to mechanically limit the position of the throttle body throttle plate. Never attempt to adjust the engine idle speed using this screw. All idle speed functions are controlled by the Powertrain Control Module (PCM).

1. Remove air cleaner tube at throttle body.

2. Disconnect throttle body electrical connectors at IAC motor and TPS.

3. Remove all control cables from throttle body (lever) arm.

4. Disconnect necessary vacuum lines at throttle body.

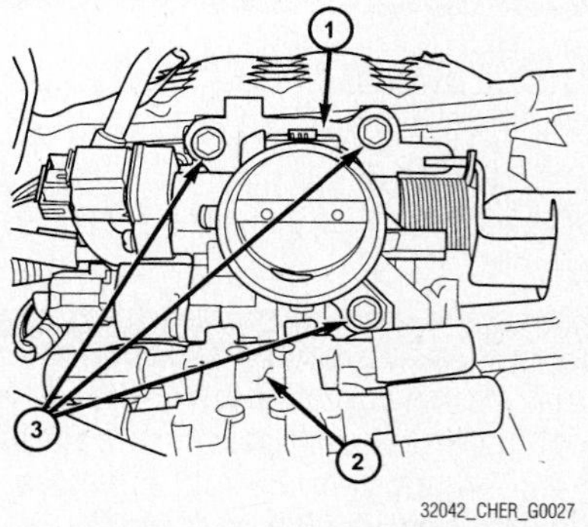

Fig. 158 Throttle body mount bolts on the 2.4L engine

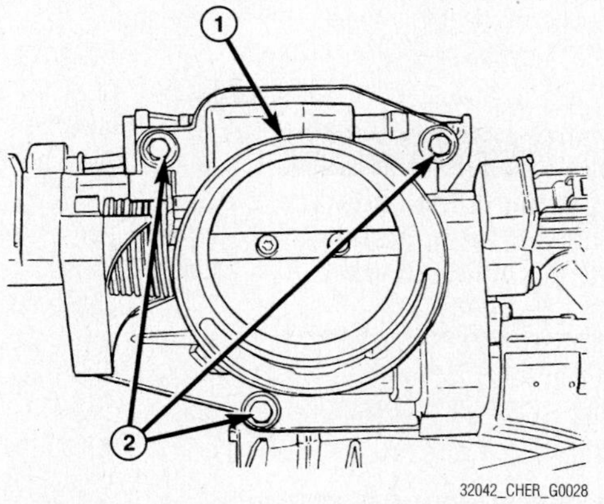

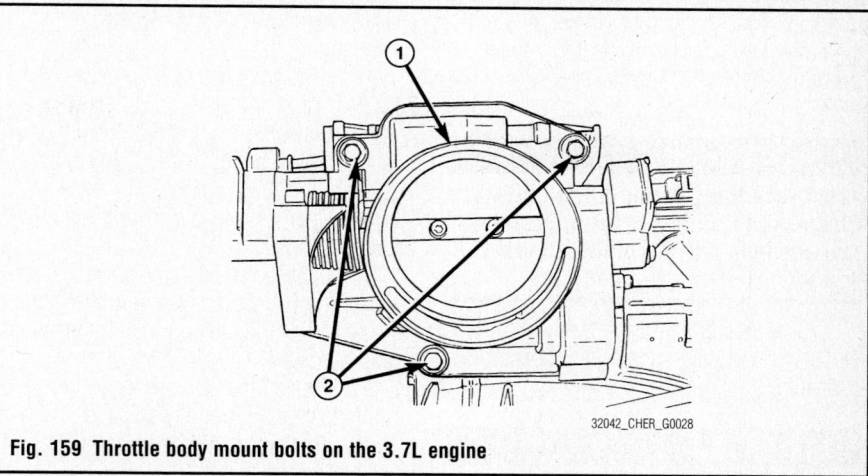

Fig. 159 Throttle body mount bolts on the 3.7L engine

5. Remove three throttle body mounting bolts.
6. Remove throttle body from intake manifold.
7. Check condition of old throttle body-to-intake manifold O-ring.

To install:

8. Check condition of throttle body-to-intake manifold O-ring. Replace as necessary.
9. Clean mating surfaces of throttle body and intake manifold.
10. Install throttle body-to-intake manifold O-ring.
11. Install throttle body to intake manifold.
12. Install 3 mounting bolts. Tighten bolts to 105 inch lbs. (12 Nm) torque.
13. Install control cables.
14. Install electrical connectors.
15. Install necessary vacuum lines.
16. Install air plenum.

4.0L Engine

A (factory adjusted) set screw is used to mechanically limit the position of the throttle body throttle plate. Never attempt to adjust the engine idle speed using this screw. All idle speed functions are controlled by the Powertrain Control Module (PCM).

1. Remove air cleaner tube at throttle body.
2. Disconnect throttle body electrical connectors.
3. Remove all control cables from throttle body (lever) arm.
4. Remove four throttle body mounting bolts.
5. Remove throttle body from intake manifold.
6. Discard old throttle body-to-intake manifold gasket

To install:

7. Clean mating surfaces of throttle body and intake manifold.
8. Install new throttle body-to-intake manifold gasket.
9. Install throttle body to intake manifold.
10. Install four mounting bolts. Tighten bolts to 100 inch lbs. (11 Nm) torque.
11. Install control cables.
12. Install electrical connectors.
13. Install air cleaner at throttle body

FUEL — DIESEL FUEL INJECTION SYSTEM

FUEL SYSTEM SERVICE PRECAUTIONS

Safety is the most important factor when performing not only fuel system maintenance but any type of maintenance. Failure to conduct maintenance and repairs in a safe manner may result in serious personal injury or death. Maintenance and testing of the vehicle's fuel system components can be accomplished safely and effectively by adhering to the following rules and guidelines.

- To avoid the possibility of fire and personal injury, always disconnect the negative battery cable unless the repair or test procedure requires that battery voltage be applied.
- Always relieve the fuel system pressure prior to disconnecting any fuel system component (injector, fuel rail, pressure regulator, etc.), fitting or fuel line connection. Exercise extreme caution whenever relieving fuel system pressure to avoid exposing skin, face and eyes to fuel spray. Please be advised that fuel under pressure may penetrate the skin or any part of the body that it contacts.
- Always place a shop towel or cloth around the fitting or connection prior to loosening to absorb any excess fuel due to spillage. Ensure that all fuel spillage (should it occur) is quickly removed from engine surfaces. Ensure that all fuel soaked cloths or towels are deposited into a suitable waste container.
- Always keep a dry chemical (Class B) fire extinguisher near the work area.
- Do not allow fuel spray or fuel vapors to come into contact with a spark or open flame.
- Always use a back-up wrench when loosening and tightening fuel line connection fittings. This will prevent unnecessary stress and torsion to fuel line piping.
- Always replace worn fuel fitting O-rings with new. Do not substitute fuel hose or equivalent where fuel pipe is installed.

Before servicing the vehicle, make sure to also refer to the precautions in the beginning of this section as well.

RELIEVING FUEL SYSTEM PRESSURE

1. Before servicing the vehicle, refer to the precautions in the beginning of this section.
2. Disconnect the negative battery cable.
3. Remove the fuel tank filler cap to release any fuel tank pressure.
4. Remove the fuel pump relay from the PDC.
5. Start and run the engine until it stops.
6. Unplug the connector from any injector and connect a jumper wire from either injector terminal to the positive battery

terminal. Connect another jumper wire to the other terminal and momentarily touch the other end to the negative battery terminal.

WARNING

Just touch the jumper to the battery. Powering the injector for more than a few seconds will permanently damage it.

7. Place a rag below the quick-disconnect coupling at the fuel rail and disconnect it.

FUEL FILTER

REMOVAL & INSTALLATION

1. Before servicing the vehicle, refer to the precautions in the beginning of this section.
2. Disconnect the negative battery cable.
3. Disconnect the Water In Fuel (WIF) sensor wiring harness connector.
4. Drain the fuel filter/water separator.
5. Unscrew the filter assembly from the head assembly by rotating the housing counterclockwise.
6. Separate the WIF sensor and seal from the housing by rotating counterclockwise

To install:

7. Lubricate the fuel filter seal with clean diesel fuel.
8. Install the WIF sensor hand tight .
9. Screw filter assembly onto the fuel filter/water separator head. Tighten filter to 159 in. lbs. (18 Nm).
10. Connect the WIF wiring harness connector.
11. Prime the fuel system.
12. Start the engine and allow to warm.
13. Turn engine off and inspect for leaks.

DRAINING WATER FROM THE SYSTEM

1. Before servicing the vehicle, refer to the precautions in the beginning of this section.

WARNING

Store fuel in approved and properly marked containers. Wear safety goggles and adequate protective clothing when servicing fuel system.

2. Disconnect the negative battery cable.
3. Disconnect the Water In Fuel (WIF) wiring harness connector located under the fuel filter.
4. Connect a drain hose to the WIF sensor.
5. Place the other end of the drain hose in a approved and properly marked container.
6. Open the bleed screw on top of the fuel filter housing.
7. Loosen the WIF sensor on the bottom of the fuel filter to begin draining.
8. Allow the filter to drain into the container until fuel is visible.
9. Tighten the WIF sensor, remove the drain hose and clean any spillage.
10. Tighten the bleeder screw on top of the fuel filter housing.
11. Connect the WIF wiring harness connector.
12. Connect the negative battery cable.

FUEL SYSTEM PURGING

BLEEDING

WARNING

Cranking the engine for an extended period with out a fuel supply may result in damage to the high pressure fuel pump. DO NOT force the plunger when priming the fuel system. Damage to the plunger or fuel filter/water separate will result.

The fuel system must be primed if the fuel system has been serviced. This is done using the fuel primer button located at the top of the fuel filter/water separator.

1. Depress the fuel primer 20 consecutive times then open the bleeder screw on top of the housing to dispel trapped air.
2. Close the bleeder screw and continue the step above until the primer button becomes slightly harder to depress.
3. Turn the ignition to **START** and crank the engine a maximum of ten seconds.

➡If the engine does not start with in ten seconds, repeat the priming procedure. The engine will typically start within ten seconds; the engine may idle, idle rough, or stall, purging any trapped air from the lines and filter.

4. Tighten bleeder screw until just snug.

INJECTION TIMING

ADJUSTMENT

The injection timing is not adjustable. If incorrect valve timing is suspected refer to the Timing Belt procedure.

INJECTION LINES

REMOVAL & INSTALLATION

See Figure 160.

1. Before servicing the vehicle, refer to the precautions in the beginning of this section.

CAUTION

High pressure lines deliver diesel fuel under extreme pressure from the injection pump to the fuel injectors. This may be as high as 23,200 psi.(1600 bar). Use extreme caution when inspecting for high pressure fuel leaks. Fuel under this amount of pressure can penetrate skin causing personal injury or death. Inspect for high pressure fuel leaks with a sheet of cardboard. Wear safety goggles and adequate protective clothing when servicing fuel system.

2. Disconnect negative battery cable.
3. Remove engine cover and bracket assembly.
4. Disconnect fuel pressure sensor electrical connector.

➡If fuel rail is being replaced it is necessary to replace the fuel rail solenoid.

5. Disconnect the fuel rail solenoid electrical connector.
6. Disconnect fuel rail return line at fuel rail.
7. Disconnect fuel high pressure line from injection pump to fuel rail at fuel rail.
8. Disconnect fuel high pressure line from fuel rail to fuel injector at fuel rail.
9. Remove fuel rail retaining bolts and remove rail from cylinder head cover/intake manifold

To install:

➡The fuel rail solenoid must be replaced upon removal. When replacing fuel lines or solenoid it is necessary to counterhold and correctly torque the fitting. Refer to the proper procedure.

10. Replace the fuel rail solenoid.
11. Install the fuel pressure sensor.
12. Install fuel rail on cylinder head cover/intake manifold. Torque retaining bolts to 27 Nm.
13. Connect injector high pressure fuel lines at fuel rail.
14. Connect fuel rail high pressure fuel line at fuel rail.
15. Connect fuel rail fuel return line at fuel rail.

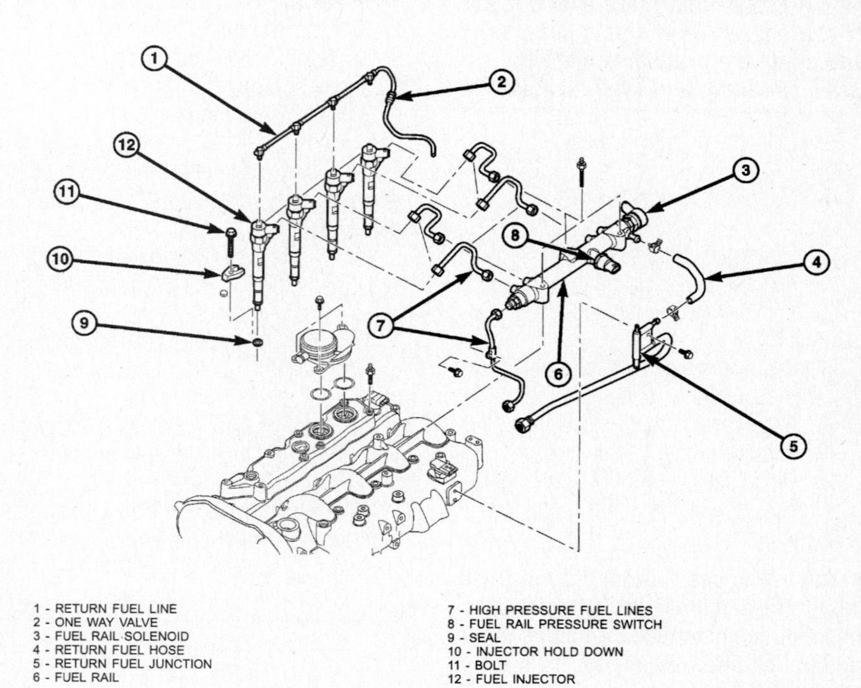

Fig. 160 Diesel fuel system components

16. Connect fuel pressure sensor electrical connector.
17. Install engine cover and bracket assembly.
18. Connect negative battery cable.

INJECTORS

REMOVAL & INSTALLATION

1. Before servicing the vehicle, refer to the precautions in the beginning of this section.

⁂ CAUTION

High pressure lines deliver diesel fuel under extreme pressure from the injection pump to the fuel injectors. This may be as high as 23,200 psi.(1600 bar). Use extreme caution when inspecting for high pressure fuel leaks. Fuel under this amount of pressure can penetrate skin causing personal injury or death. Inspect for high pressure fuel leaks with a sheet of cardboard. Wear safety goggles and adequate protective clothing when servicing fuel system.

2. Disconnect negative battery cable.
3. Remove engine cover.
4. Disconnect injector electrical connector.

⁂ WARNING

Repeated mounting of the retaining ring is not permitted.

5. Remove fuel return line from injector.
6. Remove fuel injector high pressure line.
7. Remove fuel injector retainer and retaining bolt.

➡DO NOT use a wire brush to clean the fuel injector or nozzle. Possible restriction of the injector needle may result.

8. Remove fuel injector from cylinder head.

➡If the fuel injectors will not come out of the cylinder head, assemble and install injector extractor special tool VM 9075A on to injector and cylinder head.

To install:

➡Be sure a new copper washer/seal is installed on end of injector before installing in cylinder head. Apply anti-seize compound to injector body.

9. Install fuel injector in cylinder head with new seal and O-ring.
10. Install fuel injector retainer and bolt. Torque bolt to 32 Nm.
11. Install fuel injector high pressure line.
12. Install fuel return line to injector.
13. Connect fuel injector electrical connector.
14. Install engine cover and bracket assembly.
15. Connect negative battery cable.
16. Start the engine, allow to warm, turn off the ignition, inspect for leaks.

FUEL SUPPLY PUMP

REMOVAL & INSTALLATION

1. Disconnect negative battery cable.
2. Remove engine cover and bracket.
3. Evacuate A/C system.
4. Remove accessory drive belt.
5. Remove cooling fan and fan shroud.
6. Remove charge air cooler outlet hose to intake manifold.
7. Remove fan support assembly.
8. Remove timing belt outer cover.
9. Using special tool VM.1055, remove high pressure injection pump sprocket retaining nut .

➡The use of special tool VM.1067 will allow you to remove the high pressure injection pump without removing the timing belt from the engine. This will allow you to remove and install the high pressure injection pump without altering injection pump timing.

10. Install feet from VM.1067 in injection pump sprocket as shown .
11. Install inner flange of special tool VM.1067 on injection pump sprocket as shown . Secure flange to feet in injection pump sprocket with Allen bolts supplied with tool.
12. Screw the high pressure injection pump sprocket holding plate assembly into flange of VM.1067 Using left hand threaded bolt supplied, secure holding plate assembly to timing belt inner cover.
13. Disconnect A/C lines at compressor.
14. Remove charge air inlet hose.
15. Remove the EGR airflow control valve from the intake manifold.
16. Remove high pressure injection pump to fuel rail high pressure line.
17. Disconnect high pressure injection pump quantity control valve electrical connector.
18. Disconnect fuel supply and return lines at high pressure injection pump.
19. Remove alternator to intake manifold bracket.

⁂ CAUTION

Care must be taken not to bend the brake vacuum tube when removing high pressure pump.

20. Remove high pressure injection pump retaining nuts and remove pump .

To install:

21. Loosen bolt in center of injection pump holding plate and slide high pressure injection pump through the accessory bracket into the injection pump sprocket.
22. Install high pressure injection pump retaining nuts . Torque nuts to 20 ft. lbs. (27.5 Nm).
23. Unscrew injection pump holding plate (part of VM.1067) from inner timing belt cover and remove.
24. Install high pressure injection pump sprocket retaining nut to hold sprocket in place.
25. Remove flange and feet (both part of VM.1067) from high pressure injection pump sprocket .
26. Using special tool VM.1055 , torque high pressure injection pump sprocket retaining nut to 65 ft. lbs. (88.3 Nm).
27. Connect fuel quantity control valve electrical connector.
28. Connect fuel supply and return lines at high pressure injection pump.
29. Install the EGR airflow control valve.
30. Install outer timing belt cover.
31. Install fan support assembly.
32. Install accessory drive belt.
33. Install cooling fan and shroud assembly.
34. Install charge air cooler outlet hose.
35. Install engine cover and bracket.
36. Connect negative battery cable.
37. Evacuate and recharge A/C system.

INJECTION PUMP

REMOVAL & INSTALLATION

See Figures 161 through 166.

1. Before servicing the vehicle, refer to the precautions in the beginning of this section.

⁂ CAUTION

High pressure lines deliver diesel fuel under extreme pressure from the injection pump to the fuel injectors. This may be as high as 23,200 psi.(1600 bar). Use extreme caution when inspecting for high pressure fuel leaks. Fuel under this amount of pressure can penetrate skin causing personal injury or death. Inspect for high pressure fuel leaks with a sheet of cardboard. Wear safety goggles and adequate protective clothing when servicing fuel system.

2. Disconnect negative battery cable.
3. Remove engine cover and bracket.
4. Evacuate A/C system.
5. Remove accessory drive belt.
6. Remove cooling fan and fan shroud.
7. Remove charge air cooler outlet hose to intake manifold.
8. Remove fan support assembly.
9. Remove timing belt outer cover.
10. Using special tool VM.1055, remove high pressure injection pump sprocket retaining nut.

➡The use of special tool VM.1067 will allow you to remove the high pressure injection pump without removing the timing belt from the engine. This will allow you to remove and install the high pressure injection pump without altering injection pump timing.

11. Install feet from VM.1067 in injection pump sprocket as shown.
12. Install inner flange of special tool VM.1067 on injection pump sprocket as shown. Secure flange to feet in injection pump sprocket with Allen bolts supplied with tool.
13. Screw the high pressure injection pump sprocket holding plate assembly into flange of VM.1067. Using left hand threaded bolt supplied, secure holding plate assembly to timing belt inner cover.
14. Disconnect A/C lines at compressor.
15. Remove charge air inlet hose.
16. Remove the EGR airflow control valve from the intake manifold.
17. Remove high pressure injection pump to fuel rail high pressure line.
18. Disconnect high pressure injection pump quantity control valve electrical connector.
19. Disconnect fuel supply and return lines at high pressure injection pump.
20. Remove alternator to intake manifold bracket.

⁂ WARNING

Care must be taken not to bend the brake vacuum tube when removing high pressure pump.

21. Remove high pressure injection pump retaining nuts and remove pump.

To install:

22. Loosen bolt in center of injection pump holding plate and slide high pressure injection pump through the accessory bracket into the injection pump sprocket.
23. Install high pressure injection pump retaining nuts. Torque nuts to 20 ft. lbs. (27 Nm).
24. Unscrew injection pump holding plate (part of VM.1067) from inner timing belt cover and remove.
25. Install high pressure injection pump sprocket retaining nut to hold sprocket in place.
26. Remove flange and feet (both part of VM.1067) from high pressure injection pump sprocket.
27. Using special tool VM.1055, torque high pressure injection pump sprocket retaining nut to 65 ft. lbs. (88 Nm).

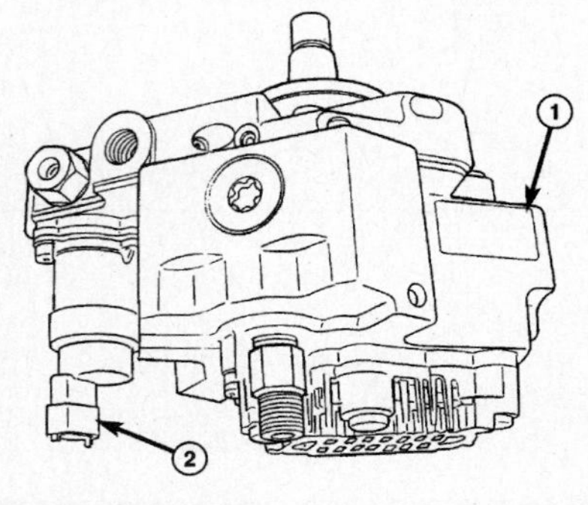

Fig. 161 Fuel injection pump—2.8L diesel

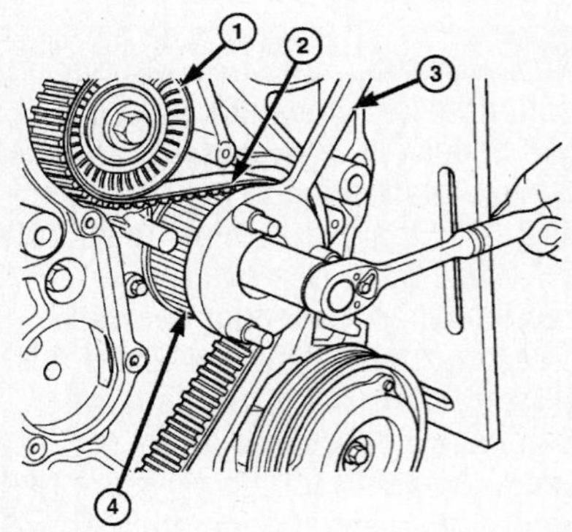

Fig. 162 Injection pump sprocket retaining nut removal—2.8L diesel

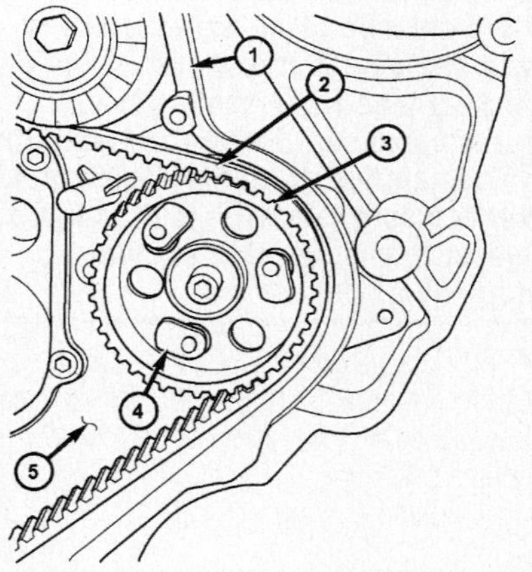

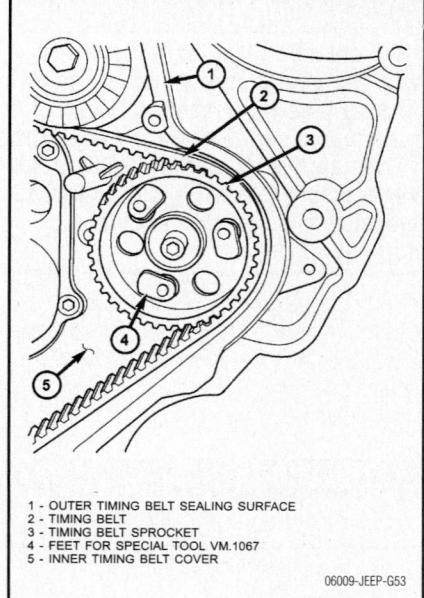

1 - OUTER TIMING BELT SEALING SURFACE
2 - TIMING BELT
3 - TIMING BELT SPROCKET
4 - FEET FOR SPECIAL TOOL VM.1067
5 - INNER TIMING BELT COVER

06009-JEEP-G53

Fig. 163 Special tool feet installation—2.8L diesel

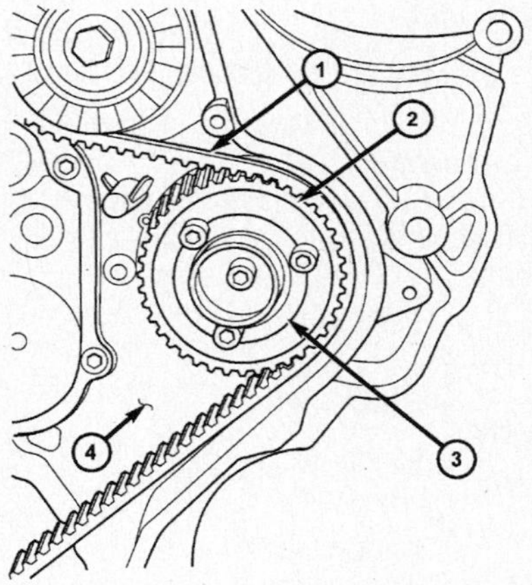

1 - TIMING BELT
2 - INJECTION PUMP SPROCKET
3 - FLANGE OF VM.1067
4 - INNER TIMING BELT COVER

06009-JEEP-G54

Fig. 164 Special tool installation—2.8L diesel

28. Connect fuel quantity control valve electrical connector.
29. Connect fuel supply and return lines at high pressure injection pump.
30. Install the EGR airflow control valve.
31. Install outer timing belt cover.
32. Install fan support assembly.
33. Install accessory drive belt.
34. Install cooling fan and shroud assembly.
35. Install charge air cooler outlet hose.

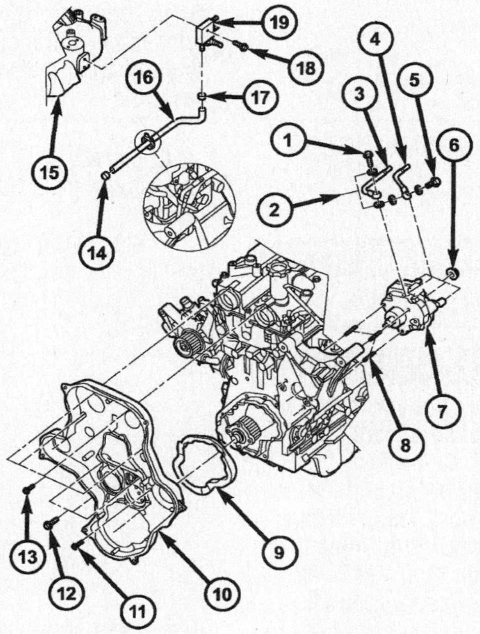

1 - BANJO FITTING
2 - BRASS WASHERS
3 - FUEL INLET LINE
4 - FUEL OUTLET LINE
5 - BANJO FITTING
6 - INJECTION PUMP RETAINING NUT
7 - INJECTION PUMP
8 - MOUNTING STUDS
9 - INNER TIMING COVER SEAL
10 - INNER TIMING COVER
11 - RETAINING BOLT
12 - RETAINING BOLT
13 - RETAINING BOLT
14 - HOSE CLAMP
15 - CYLINDER HEAD COVER/INTAKE MANIFOLD
16 - FUEL RETURN LINE TO INJECTION PUMP
17 - HOSE CLAMP
18 - FUEL RETURN JUNCTION BLOCK RETAINING BOLT
19 - FUEL RETURN JUNCTION BLOCK

06009-JEEP-G55

Fig. 165 Injection pump removal—2.8L diesel

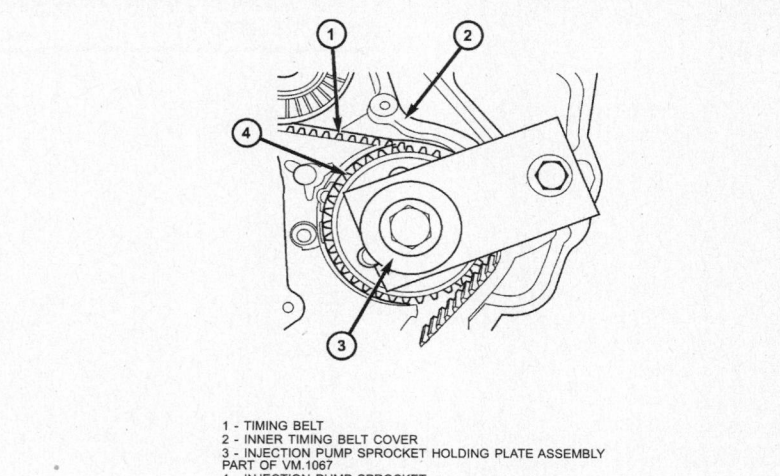

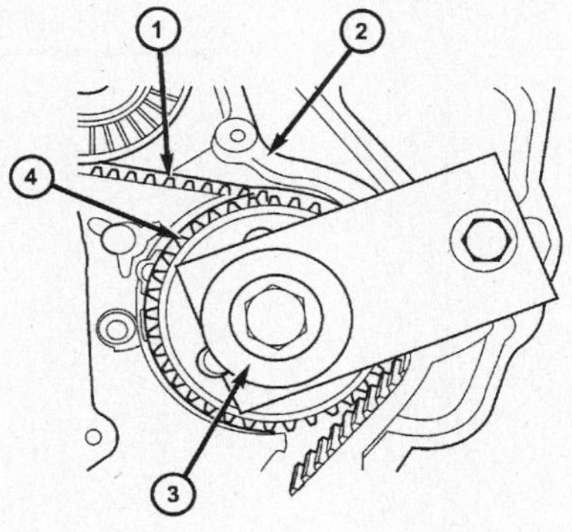

1 - TIMING BELT
2 - INNER TIMING BELT COVER
3 - INJECTION PUMP SPROCKET HOLDING PLATE ASSEMBLY PART OF VM.1067
4 - INJECTION PUMP SPROCKET

06009-JEEP-G56

Fig. 166 Injection pump gear removal—2.8L diesel

36. Install engine cover and bracket.
37. Connect negative battery cable.
38. Evacuate and recharge A/C system.

INJECTION TIMING

The injection timing is not adjustable. If incorrect valve timing is suspected refer to the Timing Belt procedure.

FUEL PRESSURE REGULATOR

REMOVAL & INSTALLATION

**** CAUTION**

High pressure lines deliver diesel fuel under extreme pressure from the injection pump to the fuel injectors. This may be as high as 23,200 psi.(1600 bar). Use extreme caution when inspecting for high pressure fuel leaks. Fuel under this amount of pressure can penetrate skin causing personal injury or death. Inspect for high pressure fuel leaks with a sheet of cardboard. Wear safety goggles and adequate protective clothing when servicing fuel system.

**** WARNING**

No sparks, open flames or smoking. Risk of poisoning from inhaling and swallowing fuel. Risk of injury to eyes and skin from contact with fuel. Pour fuels only into suitable and appropriately marked containers. Wear protective clothing.

1. Disconnect negative battery cable.
2. Remove fuel rail
3. Clamp fuel rail securely in vise with protective jaws.

**** CAUTION**

Once removed, the solenoid must always be replaced. Counterhold and unscrew the fuel pressure solenoid.

To install:

4. Position the fuel rail into a soft jawed vise.
5. Screw the fuel pressure solenoid to the fuel rail until hand tight.
6. Tighten the fuel rail solenoid as follows :
   - Tighten the nut to 44 ft. lbs. (60 Nm).
   - Loosen the nut 90°.
   - Retighten the nut to 59 ft. lbs. (80 Nm).
   - Install fuel rail
7. Connect negative battery cable.
8. Start engine, allow to warm, turn engine off and inspect for leaks.

OIL PRESSURE REGULATOR

REMOVAL & INSTALLATION

1. Remove engine oil pan.
2. Using special tool VM.1054, remove oil pressure relief valve from engine block.

To install:

3. Thoroughly clean all components and relief valve pocket in cylinder block.
4. Lubricate all oil pressure relief valve components with engine oil.
5. Install oil pressure relief valve plunger, spring, and cap.

**** WARNING**

DO NOT strike the oil pressure valve cap with a hammer.

**** CAUTION**

Care must be taken not to interfere with the engine front cover or the oil pick up tube when seating the oil relief valve cap. Failure to install the valve cap flush with the engine block surface correctly will result in low oil pressure and possible engine damage.

6. Using a driver with a flat surface, carefully tap the oil pressure relief valve cap into place until the cap seats flush with engine block .
7. Install oil pan.

GLOW PLUGS

REMOVAL & INSTALLATION

1. Disconnect negative battery cable.
2. Remove generator.
3. Disconnect glow plug electrical connectors.

➡The intake manifold inlet tube must be removed to remove the cylinder 3 glow plug.

4. Remove glow plugs from cylinder head.

To install:

5. Install glow plugs all the way into cylinder head, hand tight, until the thread stops.
6. Tighten glow plugs to 110 inch lbs. (12.5 Nm).
7. Connect glow plug electrical connectors.
8. Install intake manifold air inlet tube.
9. Install generator.
10. Connect negative battery cable.

HEATING & AIR CONDITIONING SYSTEM

BLOWER MOTOR

REMOVAL & INSTALLATION

⁂ CAUTION

Disable the airbag system before attempting any steering wheel, steering column, or instrument panel component diagnosis or service. Failure to take the proper precautions could result in accidental airbag deployment and possible personal injury or death.

➡The blower motor is located on the passenger side of the vehicle under the instrument panel. The blower motor can be removed without having to remove the instrument panel or the HVAC housing.

1. Disconnect and isolate the negative battery cable.
2. Disconnect the wire harness connector from the blower motor.
3. Release the locking tab that secures the blower motor to the HVAC housing and rotate blower motor counterclockwise.
4. Rotate and tilt the blower motor as needed for clearance to remove the blower motor and wheel from the HVAC housing.

To install:

➡Failure to install the blower motor assembly correctly could result in an air leak or the blower motor assembly becoming completely disengaged from the HVAC housing.

5. Align and install the blower motor into the HVAC housing.
6. Rotate the blower motor until all of the locking tabs have secured the blower motor assembly to the HVAC housing.
7. Connect the wire harness connector to the blower motor.
8. Reconnect the battery negative cable.
9. Test the blower motor for proper installation by turning the blower motor speed to its fastest position and checking around the outer edges of the blower assembly for air leaks. If any air leaks are found, remove and reinstall the blower motor.

HEATER CORE

REMOVAL & INSTALLATION

2005–06 Wrangler

See Figures 167 through 169.

1. Before servicing the vehicle, refer to the precautions in the beginning of this section.
2. Disconnect and remove the negative battery.

⁂ CAUTION

After disconnecting the negative battery cable, wait 2 minutes for the driver's/passenger's air bag system capacitor to discharge before attempting to do any work around the steering column or instrument.

3. Drain the cooling system into a clean container for reuse.
4. Remove the instrument panel by performing the following procedure:
   a. Turn the steering wheel in the straight-ahead position.
   b. Remove the knee blocker from the instrument panel.
   c. Remove the steering column; do not remove the air bag module, the steering wheel or switches from the steering column.
   d. From under the driver's side of the instrument panel, disconnect the following items:
      - Instrument panel wiring harness connector from the 100-way wiring harness connector at the left side of the inner panel.
      - Side window demister hose at the heater/air conditioning housing demister/defroster duct on the driver's side.
   e. Remove the glove box.
   f. Reaching through the glove box opening, disconnect the following items:
      - Two halves of the heater/air conditioning system vacuum harness connector.
      - Instrument panel wiring harness connector from the heater/air conditioning system wiring harness connector.
      - Instrument panel wiring harness connector from the passenger's side air bag module wiring harness connector.
      - Side window demister hose at the heater/air conditioning housing demister/defroster duct (passenger's side).
      - Two halves of the radio antenna coaxial cable connector.
      - Two instrument panel wiring harness connectors from the passenger air bag ON/OFF switch wiring harness connector.
      - Passenger's side air bag ON/OFF switch wiring harness from the retainer clip on the plenum bracket that supports the heater/air conditioning housing just inboard of the fuse block module.
      - Two lower passenger's side air bag module bracket-to-dash panel nuts.
   g. Remove the upper cover from the instrument panel.
   h. Remove the 3 instrument panel-to-door hinge pillar screws.
   i. Remove the 4 upper instrument panel-to-dash nuts.
   j. Using an assistant, remove the instrument panel from the vehicle.
5. If equipped with air conditioning, discharge and recover the air conditioning system refrigerant.
6. Disconnect the refrigerant lines from the evaporator. Plug the refrigerant openings to prevent evaporation.
7. Disconnect the heater hoses from the heater core tubes.
8. Disconnect the heater/air conditioning system vacuum supply line connector from the T-fitting near the heater core tubes.
9. In the engine compartment, remove the 5 heater/air conditioning housing-to-chassis nuts. If necessary, loosen the battery hold-downs and reposition the battery for access.
10. Remove the cowl plenum drain tube from the heater/air conditioning housing stud; it's located behind the cylinder head on the cowl.
11. From the bottom of the heater/air conditioning housing, remove the floor duct.
12. On the passenger side, remove the heater/air conditioning housing-to-plenum bracket screw.
13. Pull the heater/air conditioning housing down far enough to clear the defrost/demist and fresh air ducts, then, rearward far enough to clear the mounting studs and the evaporator drain tube to clear the dash panel holes.
14. Remove the heater/air conditioning housing assembly from the vehicle.
15. Remove the heater/air conditioning housing upper case.
16. Lift the heater core from the lower half of the heater/air conditioning housing.

To install:

17. Assemble the heater core into the lower half of the heater/air conditioning housing.

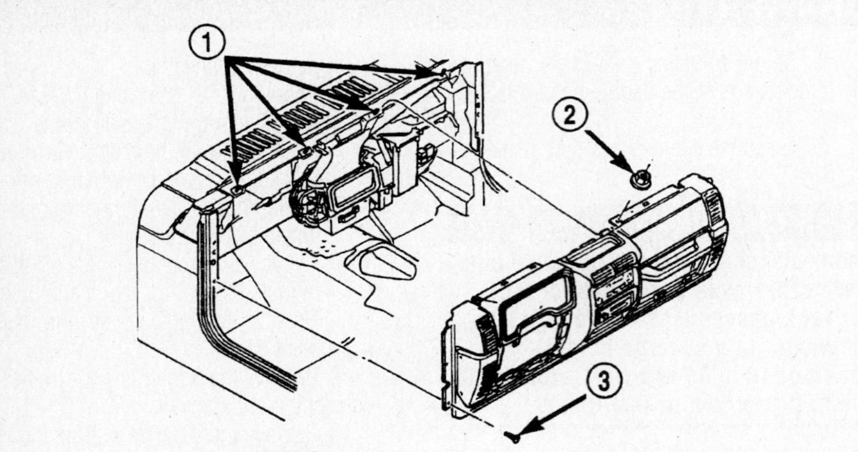

Fig. 167 View of the instrument panel and fasteners—Wrangler

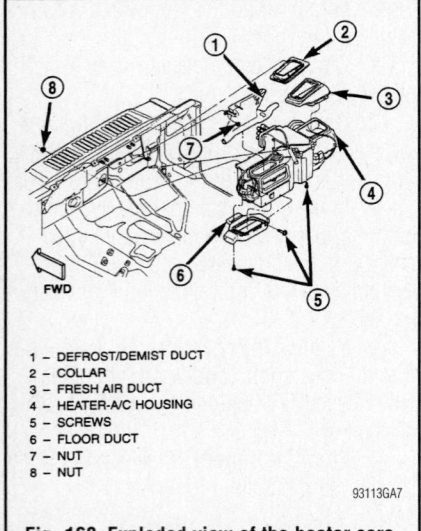

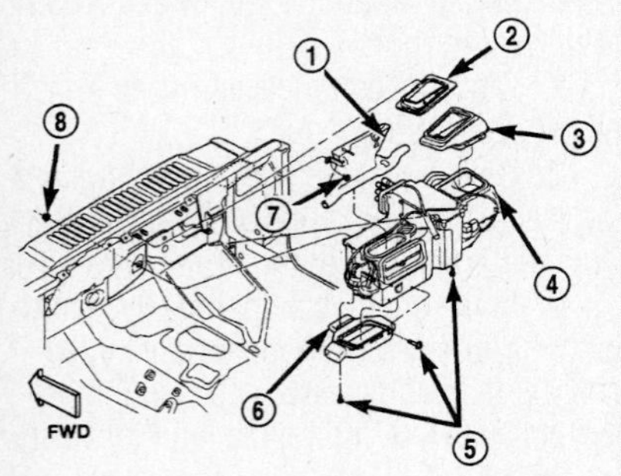

Fig. 168 Exploded view of the heater core assembly—Wrangler

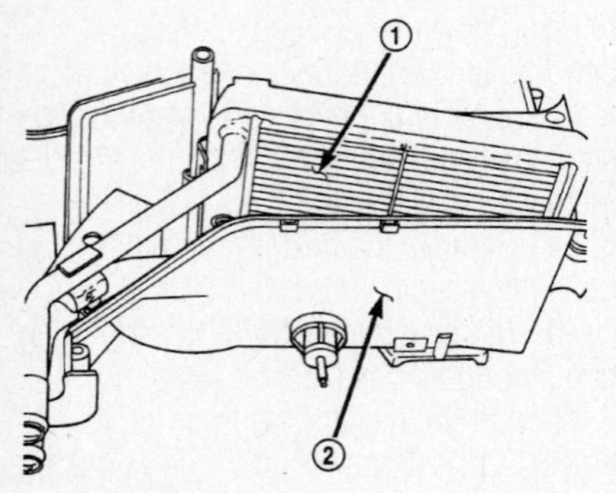

Fig. 169 View of the heater core—Wrangler

18. Install the heater/air conditioning housing upper case.
19. Install the heater/air conditioning housing assembly to the vehicle.
20. On the passenger's side, install the heater/air conditioning housing-to-plenum bracket screw.
21. At the bottom of the heater/air conditioning housing, install the floor duct.
22. Install the cowl plenum drain tube to the heater/air conditioning housing stud; it's located behind the cylinder head on the cowl.
23. In the engine compartment, install the 5 heater/air conditioning housing-to-chassis nuts.
24. Connect the heater/air conditioning system vacuum supply line connector to the T-fitting near the heater core tubes.
25. Connect the heater hoses to the heater core tubes.
26. Connect the refrigerant lines to the evaporator.
27. If equipped with air conditioning, evacuate and charge the air conditioning system refrigerant.
28. Install the instrument panel by performing the following procedure:
    a. Using an assistant, install the instrument panel to the vehicle.
    b. Install the 4 upper instrument panel-to-dash nuts.
    c. Install the 3 instrument panel-to-door hinge pillar screws.
    d. Install the upper cover to the instrument panel.
    e. Reaching through the glove box opening, connect the following items:
        - Two lower passenger's side air bag module bracket-to-dash panel nuts.
        - Passenger's side air bag ON/OFF switch wiring harness to the retainer clip on the plenum bracket that supports the heater/air conditioning housing just inboard of the fuse block module.
        - Two instrument panel wiring harness connectors to the passenger air bag ON/OFF switch wiring harness connector.
        - Two halves of the radio antenna coaxial cable connector.
        - Side window demister hose at the heater/air conditioning housing demister/defroster duct (passenger's side).
        - Instrument panel wiring harness connector to the passenger's side air bag module wiring harness connector.
        - Instrument panel wiring harness connector to the heater/air conditioning system wiring harness connector.
        - Two halves of the heater/air conditioning system vacuum harness connector.
    f. Install the glove box.
    g. Under the driver's side of the instrument panel, connect the following items:
        - Side window demister hose at the heater/air conditioning housing demister/defroster duct on the driver's side.
        - Instrument panel wiring harness connector to the 100-way wiring harness connector at the left side of the inner panel.
    h. Install the steering column.
    i. Install the knee blocker to the instrument panel.
29. Connect and remove the negative battery.
30. Refill the cooling system.
31. Run the engine to normal operating temperatures; then, check the climate control operation and check for leaks.

Liberty

See Figure 170.

1. Before servicing the vehicle, refer to the precautions in the beginning of this section.
2. Disconnect and remove the negative battery.

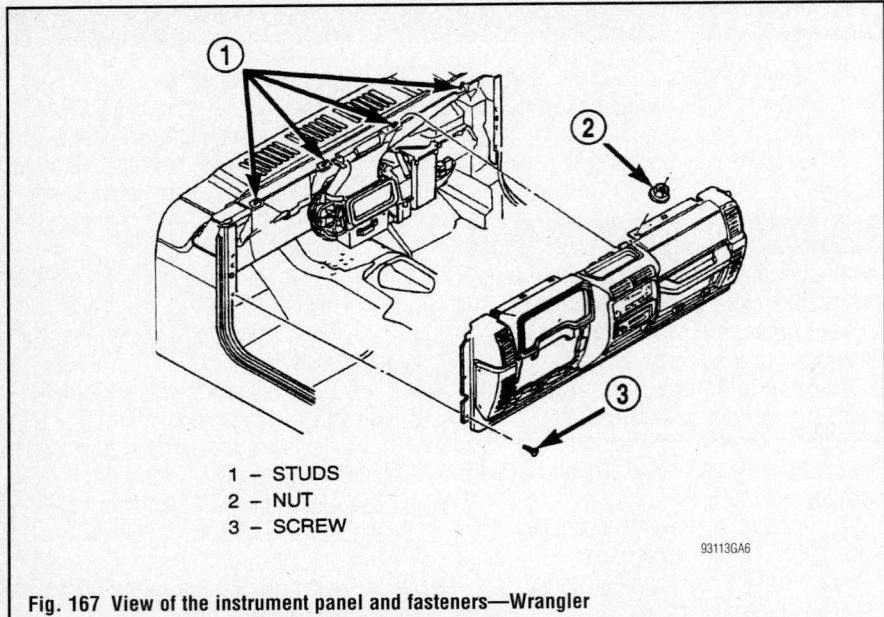

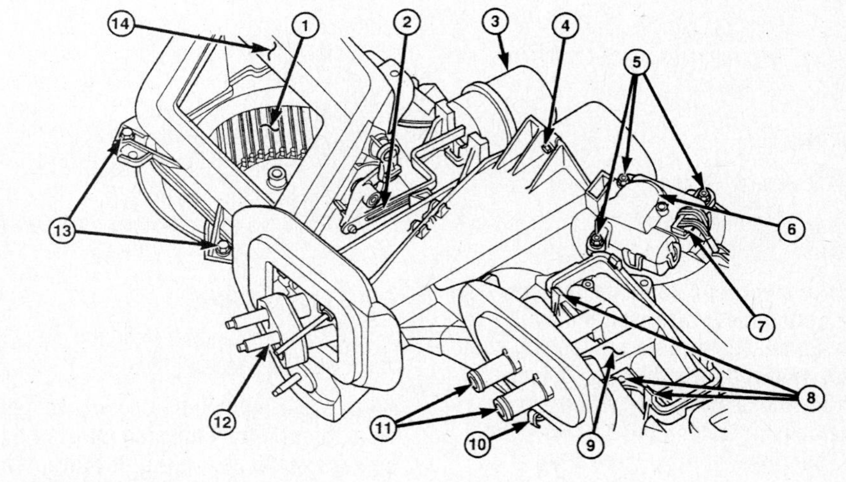

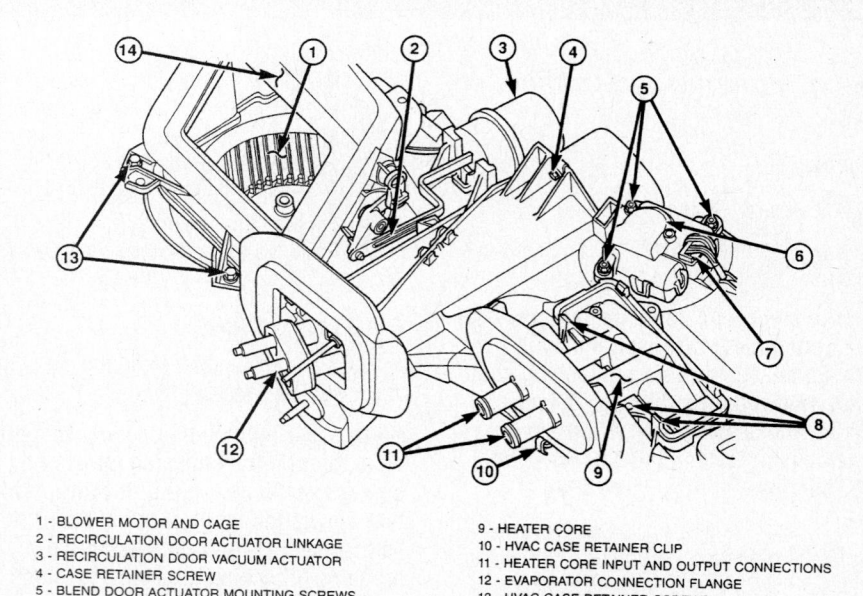

1 - BLOWER MOTOR AND CAGE
2 - RECIRCULATION DOOR ACTUATOR LINKAGE
3 - RECIRCULATION DOOR VACUUM ACTUATOR
4 - CASE RETAINER SCREW
5 - BLEND DOOR ACTUATOR MOUNTING SCREWS
6 - ELECTRIC BLEND DOOR ACTUATOR
7 - ELECTRICAL CONNECTOR FOR BLEND DOOR ACTUATOR
8 - HEATER CORE RETAINER TABS (4) AND SCREWS (2)
9 - HEATER CORE
10 - HVAC CASE RETAINER CLIP
11 - HEATER CORE INPUT AND OUTPUT CONNECTIONS
12 - EVAPORATOR CONNECTION FLANGE
13 - HVAC CASE RETAINER SCREWS
14 - HVAC HOUSING

9355PG99

Fig. 170 HVAC case components—Liberty

⁂ CAUTION

After disconnecting the negative battery cable, wait 2 minutes for the driver's/passenger's air bag system capacitor to discharge before attempting to do any work around the steering column or instrument.

3. Drain the cooling system into a clean container for reuse.
4. Remove the instrument panel by performing the following procedure:
   a. Turn the steering wheel in the straight-ahead position.
   b. Remove the A-pillar trim from both sides of the vehicle.
   c. Remove the top cover from the instrument panel.
   d. Remove the speakers.
   e. Remove the floor console.
   f. Remove the radio.
   g. Remove the center support bracket.
   h. Remove the trim panels from both sides of the inner cowl.
   i. Remove the fuse cover from the junction box.
   j. Remove the instrument panel cluster bezel.
   k. Remove the steering column opening cover from the instrument panel.
   l. Remove the steering column bracket from the instrument panel column support bracket.
   m. Remove the lower steering column shroud cover-to-multifunction switch screw; then, unsnap both halves of the shroud cover from the steering column.
   n. Disconnect the instrument panel wiring harness connectors from the following steering column components:
      - Both lower clockspring connector receptacles
      - Left multifunction switch receptacle
      - Right multifunction switch receptacle
      - Both ignition switch receptacles
      - Shifter interlock solenoid receptacle
      - Sentry Key Immobilizer Module (SKIM) receptacle, if equipped
   o. Turn the ignition switch to **ON** position; then, release and remove the shifter interlock cable connector from the ignition lock housing receptacle.
   p. Turn the ignition switch to **OFF** position; this will prevent the steering wheel from turning and the loss of the clockspring centering following steering column removal.
   q. Remove the 4 steering column-to-instrument panel steering column bracket nuts.
   r. Remove the steering column from the instrument panel.
5. Remove the driver's side cowl trim cover.
6. Disconnect the green and light blue wire harness bulk connectors at the junction block.
7. Disconnect the electrical connector at the inner side of the pedal support bracket.
8. Remove the 2 bolts from the front and the 2 from the side of the pedal support bracket.
9. Remove the glove box.
10. Remove the 2 HVAC mounting bolts behind the center trim.
11. Remove the passenger trim bezel.
12. Remove the HVAC mount bolt above the glove box.
13. Remove the HVAC bolt at the lower outside glove box opening.
14. Remove the passenger trim cover, disconnect the blower resistor, remove the rolldown brackets at the right cowl side panel.
15. Disconnect the vacuum check valve and the vacuum reservoir.
16. Disconnect the blower connectors.
17. Remove the 4 top bolts connecting the instrument panel to the cowl.
18. Roll the instrument panel rearward and disconnect the wiring.
19. Remove the panel.
20. Discharge and recover the air conditioning system refrigerant.
21. Disconnect the air conditioning system lines at the evaporator. Plug the openings to prevent contamination.
22. Disconnect the heater hoses from the heater core. Plug the openings to prevent coolant loss.
23. If equipped with a manual temperature control system, unplug the heater/air conditioning system vacuum supply line connector from the T-fitting located near the heater core tubes.
24. Remove all remaining fasteners and connections and remove the HVAC unit.
25. Disconnect all remaining hoses and wires.
26. Remove the blower motor.
27. Pop out the grommet on the vacuum supply line and slide hole.
28. Remove the foam gasket from around the heater core tubes.
29. Pry off the 4 snap clips that hold the halves of the unit together and separate the unit halves.
30. Installation is the reverse of removal.
31. Refill the cooling system.
32. Connect the negative battery.
33. Evacuate, charge and leak test the system.
34. Run the engine to normal operating temperatures. Check the climate control operation and check for leaks.

STEERING

POWER STEERING GEAR

REMOVAL & INSTALLATION

2005–06 Wrangler

See Figure 171.

➡The steering column on vehicles with an automatic transmission may not be equipped with an internal locking shaft that allows the ignition key cylinder to be locked with the key. Alternative methods of locking the steering wheel for service will have to be used.

1. Place the front wheels in the straight ahead position with the steering wheel centered and locked.
2. Siphon out as much power steering fluid as possible.
3. Remove the bumper shield.
4. Remove power steering hoses/tubes from steering gear.
5. Remove the column coupler shaft from the gear.
6. Remove pitman arm from gear.
7. Remove the steering gear retaining bolts and remove the gear

To install:

8. Install steering gear on the frame rail and tighten bolts to 70 ft. lbs. (95 Nm).
9. Align and install the pitman arm and tighten nut to 185 ft. lbs. (251 Nm).
10. Align the column coupler shaft to steering gear Install a new coupler pinch bolt and tighten to 36 ft. lbs. (49 Nm).
11. Install power steering hoses/tubes to steering gear and tighten to 21 ft. lbs. (28 Nm).

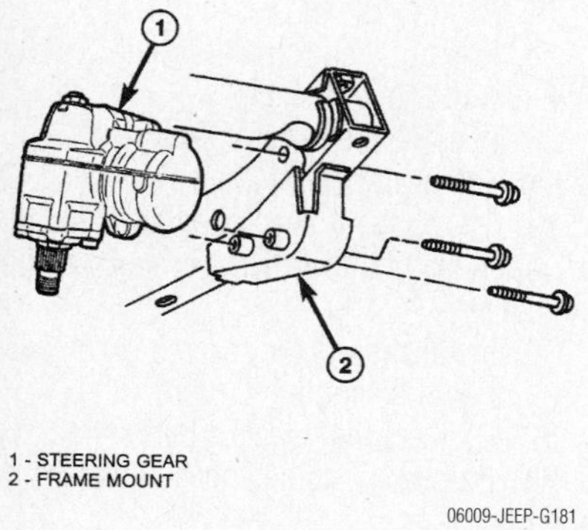

Fig. 171 Steering gear mounting—Wrangler

12. Install the bumper shield.
13. Fill power steering system to proper level.

Liberty

4WD Except Diesel

1. Siphon the power steering fluid from the power steering reservoir.

➡The steering column on vehicles with an automatic transmission may not be equipped with an internal locking shaft that allows the ignition key cylinder to be locked with the key. Alternative methods of locking the steering wheel for service will have to be used.

2. Lock the steering wheel to prevent spinning of the clockspring.
3. Raise and support the vehicle.
4. Remove the skid plate from under the front end to gain access to the gear.
5. Remove the front tire and wheel assemblies.

➡Mark the alignment adjusting cams for easier installation.

6. Remove the lower control arms.
7. Remove the front axle.
8. Remove the tie rod end nuts.
9. Separate tie rod ends from the knuckles with Puller C-3894-A.
10. Remove the intermediate shaft lower coupler pinch bolt and slide the coupler off the gear.
11. Remove power steering pressure hose bracket.
12. Remove the power steering lines from the gear .
13. Remove the mounting bolts from the gear to the front cradle.
14. Remove the steering gear from the vehicle.

To install:

15. Transfer the tie rod ends to the new steering gear (if needed).
16. Install the steering gear to the vehicle.
17. Install the gear mounting bolts.
18. to the front cradle. Tighten the gear mounting bolts to 120 ft. lbs. (162 Nm).
19. Install the power steering lines to the gear.
20. Install the power steering pressure hose bracket.
21. Install the lower coupler bolt and slide the coupler on to the gear.
22. Install the tie rod end to the knuckle and tighten the nuts.
23. Install the front axle.
24. Install the lower control arms.
25. Install the tire and wheel assembly.
26. Install the skid plate.
27. Lower the vehicle.
28. Unlock the steering wheel.
29. Fill the power steering fluid.
30. Reset the toe and center the steering wheel.

RWD Except Diesel

1. Siphon the power steering fluid from the power steering reservoir.

➡The steering column on vehicles with an automatic transmission may not be equipped with an internal locking shaft that allows the ignition key cylinder to be locked with the key. Alternative methods of locking the steering wheel for service will have to be used.

2. Lock the steering wheel to prevent spinning of the clockspring.
3. Raise and support the vehicle.
4. Remove the skid plate from under the front end to gain access to the gear.
5. Remove the tire and wheel assembly.

➡Mark the alignment adjusting cams and tie rod end jam nuts on the steering gear for easier installation.

6. Remove the tie rod end nuts.
7. Separate tie rod ends from the knuckles with Puller C-3894-A.
8. Remove the lower intermediate shaft coupler pinch bolt and slide the coupler off the gear.
9. Remove power steering pressure hose bracket.
10. Remove the power steering lines from the gear.
11. Remove the mounting bolts from the gear to the front cradle.
12. Remove the steering gear from the vehicle.

To install:

13. Transfer the outer tie rod ends to the new steering gear (if needed).
14. Install the steering gear to the vehicle.
15. Install the gear mounting bolts to the front cradle. Tighten the gear mounting bolts to 120 ft. lbs. (162 Nm).
16. Install the power steering lines to the gear.
17. Install the power steering pressure hose bracket .
18. Install the lower coupler pinch bolt and slide the coupler on to the gear .

19. Install the tie rod end to the knuckle and tighten the nuts.
20. Install the tire and wheel assembly.
21. Install the skid plate.
22. Lower the vehicle.
23. Unlock the steering wheel.
24. Fill the power steering fluid.
25. Reset the toe and center the steering wheel.

Diesel Engines

1. Siphon the power steering fluid from the power steering reservoir.

➡The steering column on vehicles with an automatic transmission may not be equipped with an internal locking shaft that allows the ignition key cylinder to be locked with the key. Alternative methods of locking the steering wheel for service will have to be used.

2. Lock the steering wheel to prevent spinning of the clockspring.
3. Raise and support the vehicle.
4. Remove the skid plate from under the front end to gain access to the gear
5. Remove the tire and wheel assembly.

➡Mark the alignment adjusting cams for easier installation.

6. Remove the lower control arms.
7. Remove the front axle.
8. Remove the tie rod end nuts.
9. Separate tie rod ends from the knuckles with Puller C-3894-A.
10. Remove the lower coupler pinch bolt and slide the coupler off the gear.
11. Remove power steering pressure hose bracket.
12. Remove the power steering lines from the gear.
13. Remove the mounting bolts from the gear to the front cradle .
14. Remove the steering gear from the vehicle.

To install:

15. Transfer the tie rod ends to the new steering gear (if needed).
16. Install the steering gear to the vehicle.
17. Install the gear mounting bolts to the front cradle. Tighten the gear mounting bolts to 120 ft. lbs. (162 Nm)
18. Install the power steering lines to the gear.
19. Install the power steering pressure hose bracket .
20. Install the lower coupler pinch bolt and slide the coupler on to the gear .
21. Install the tie rod end to the knuckle and tighten the nuts.
22. Install the front axle.
23. Install the lower control arms.
24. Install the tire and wheel assembly.
25. Install the skid plate.
26. Lower the vehicle.
27. Unlock the steering wheel.
28. Fill the power steering fluid.
29. Align the front end.

POWER STEERING PUMP

REMOVAL & INSTALLATION

2005–06 Wrangler

2.4L Engine

1. Remove serpentine drive belt.
2. Remove pressure and return hoses from pump and drain the pump.
3. Remove 3 pump mounting bolts through pulley access holes.
4. Loosen the 3 pump bracket bolts.
5. Tilt pump downward and remove from engine.
6. Remove pulley from pump

To install:

7. Install pulley on pump.
8. Install pump on the engine mounting bracket.
9. Tighten pump bracket bolts to 35 ft. lbs. (47 Nm).
10. Install 3 pump mounting bolts and tighten to 20 ft. lbs. (27 Nm).
11. Install the pressure line on the pump and tighten to 21 ft. lbs. (28 Nm).
12. Install return hoses on pump.
13. Install drive belt.
14. Add power steering fluid.

4.0L Engine

1. Remove serpentine drive belt.
2. Remove pressure and return hoses from pump and drain the pump.
3. Loosen the pump bracket bolt at the engine block.
4. Remove 3 pump mounting bolts through pulley access holes.
5. Tilt pump downward and remove from engine.
6. Remove pulley from pump

To install:

7. Install pulley on pump.
8. Install pump on the engine mounting bracket.
9. Install 3 pump mounting bolts and tighten to 20 ft. lbs. (27 Nm).
10. Tighten pump bracket bolt to 42 ft. lbs. (57 Nm).
11. Install the pressure line on the pump and tighten to 21 ft. lbs. (28 Nm).
12. Install return hoses on pump.
13. Install drive belt.
14. Add power steering fluid

Liberty

2.4L Engine

See Figure 172.

⁂ CAUTION

On vehicles equipped with the 2.4L, do not reuse the old power steering pump pulley it is not intended for reuse. A new pulley must be installed if removed.

1. Siphon out as much power steering fluid as possible.
2. Remove the serpentine drive belt.
3. Remove the power steering high pressure hose at the pump using care not to remove the flow control valve.
4. Remove the return hose at the pump.
5. Remove the two nuts securing the wire loom behind the pump bracket.
6. Remove the three bolts securing the pump to the bracket thru the holes in the pulley.
7. Remove the pump from the vehicle.

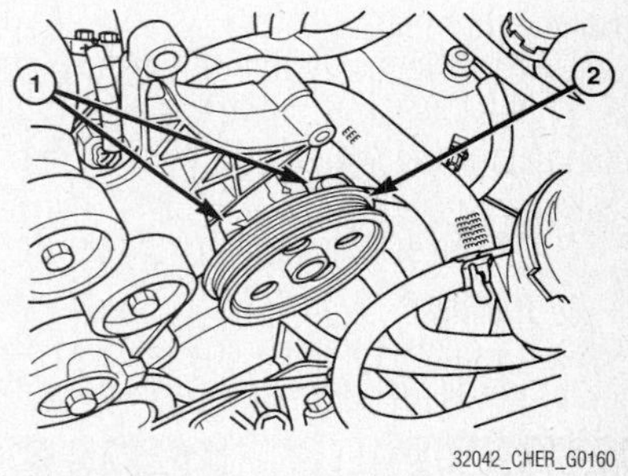

Fig. 172 The power steering pump for the 2.4L engine

To install:

8. Install the pump to the vehicle.
9. Install the three bolts securing the pump to the engine. Tighten the bolts to 35 ft. lbs. (47 Nm).
10. Install the two nuts securing the wire loom to the pump bracket.
11. Install the power steering pressure and supply hoses.
12. Install the serpentine belt
13. Refill the power steering fluid and check for leaks.

2.8L Diesel Engine

1. Siphon out as much power steering fluid as possible.
2. Remove the engine cooling fan.

3. Remove the fan shroud
4. Remove the serpentine drive belt.
5. Remove the three bolts securing the pulley to the pump.
6. Remove the power steering hoses.
7. Remove the three bolts securing the pump to the bracket.
8. Remove the pump from the vehicle.

To install:

9. Install the pump to the vehicle.
10. Install the three bolts securing the pump to the bracket.
11. Install the power steering hoses.
12. Install the three bolts securing the pulley to the pump.
13. Install the serpentine belt.
14. Install the fan shroud
15. Install the engine cooling fan.
16. Refill the power steering fluid and bleed the system

3.7L Engine

See Figure 173.

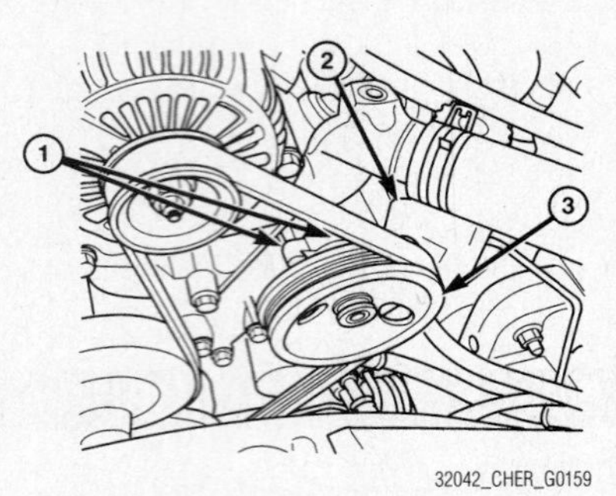

Fig. 173 The power steering pump for the 3.7L engine

1. Siphon out as much power steering fluid as possible.
2. Remove the radiator cross member.
3. Remove the engine cooling fan.
4. Remove the fan shroud
5. Remove the serpentine drive belt.
6. Remove the power steering high pressure hose at the pump.
7. Remove the return hose at the pump.
8. Remove the three bolts securing the pump to the bracket thru the holes in the pulley.
9. Remove the pump from the vehicle.

To install:

10. Install the pump to the vehicle.
11. Install the three bolts securing the pump to the engine. Tighten the bolts to 35 ft. lbs. (47 Nm).
12. Install the power steering hoses.
13. Install the serpentine belt.
14. Install the fan shroud
15. Install the engine cooling fan.
16. Install the radiator crossmember.
17. Refill the power steering fluid and check for leaks.

BLEEDING

CAUTION

The fluid level should be checked with engine OFF to prevent injury from moving components.

WARNING

MOPAR® ATF+4 is to be used in the power steering system. No other power steering or automatic transmission fluid is to be used in the system. Damage may result to the power steering pump and system if any other fluid is used. Do not overfill.

1. Wipe filler cap clean, then check the fluid level. The dipstick should indicate COLD when the fluid is at normal temperature (before engine has been operated).
2. Turn steering wheel all the way to the left
3. Fill the pump fluid reservoir to the proper level and let the fluid settle for at least two (2) minutes.
4. Raise the front wheels off the ground.
5. Slowly turn the steering wheel lock-to-lock 20 times with the engine **OFF** while checking the fluid level.

➡Vehicles with long return lines or oil coolers turn wheel 40 times.

6. Start the engine. With the engine idling maintain the fluid level.
7. Lower the front wheels and let the engine idle for two minutes.
8. Turn the steering wheel in both direction and verify power assist and quiet operation of the pump.
9. If the fluid is extremely foamy or milky looking, allow the vehicle to stand a few minutes and repeat the procedure.

WARNING

Do not run a vehicle with foamy fluid for an extended period. This may cause pump damage.

SUSPENSION

FRONT SUSPENSION

COIL SPRING

REMOVAL & INSTALLATION

2005–06 Wrangler

See Figures 174 through 176.

1. Before servicing the vehicle, refer to the precautions in the beginning of this section.
2. Raise and support the vehicle.
3. Remove the wheel and tire assemblies.
4. Position a hydraulic jack under the axle to support it.
5. Remove the front shocks at the lower mountings.
6. Remove the Anti-lock Brake System (ABS) wire mounting brackets at the axle, if equipped.

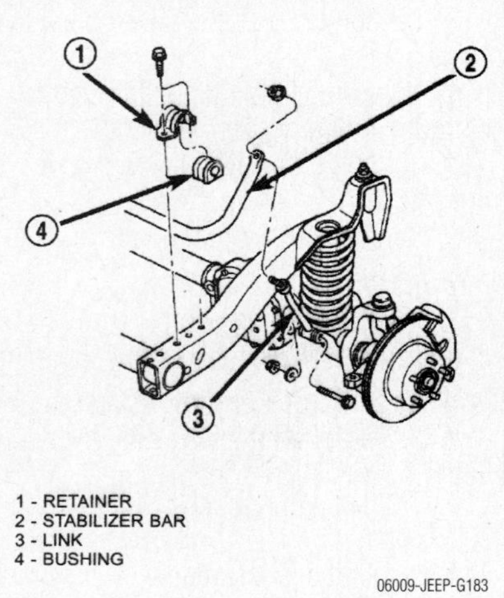

Fig. 174 Stabilizer bar—Wrangler

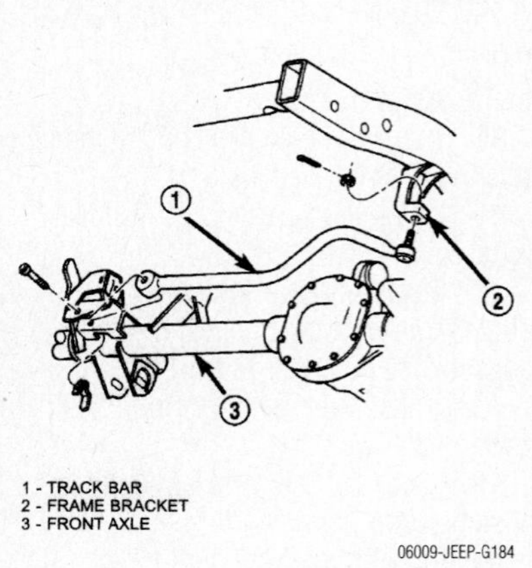

Fig. 175 Track bar—Wrangler

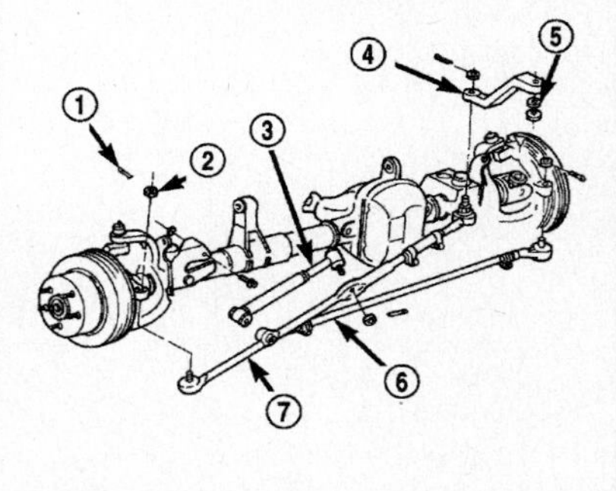

Fig. 176 Steering linkage—Wrangler

7. Remove lower suspension arms mounting nuts and bolts from the frame.
8. Remove the track bar from the axle bracket.
9. Remove the right side of the drag link from the right side knuckle.
10. Lower the axle until the spring is free from the upper mount.

➡Rotation of the spring and prying down slightly on the axle will aid in removal.

11. Remove the coil spring retainer clip and remove the spring.
12. Remove the upper spring isolator, if needed.
13. Pull jounce bumper out of mount, if needed.

To install:

14. Install jounce bumper into mount.
15. Install the spring isolator.

➡Rotation of the spring and prying down slightly on the axle will aid in installation.

16. Position the coil spring on the axle pad. It may be necessary to rotate the spring while installing.
17. Install the spring retainer clip and bolt. Tighten bolt to 16 ft. lbs. (21 Nm).
18. Raise the axle into position until the spring seats in the upper mount.
19. Install the shock at the axle.
20. Install the ABS wire mounting brackets at the axle, if equipped.
21. Install the track bar to the axle bracket. Torque to 40 ft. lbs. (47 Nm).
22. Install the lower suspension arms to the frame. Install mounting bolts and nuts finger tight.
23. Install the drag link to the right side knuckle. Torque to 35 ft. lbs. (47 Nm). Use new cotter pins.
24. Remove the hydraulic jack from under the axle
25. Install the wheel and tire assemblies.
26. Remove the supports and lower the vehicle.
27. Tighten the lower suspension arms nuts to 85 ft. lbs. (115 Nm) at normal ride height with the vehicle weight.

Liberty

See Figure 177.

1. Raise and support the vehicle.
2. Remove the tire and wheel assembly.
3. Remove the shock.
4. Secure the shock assembly into a Pentastar Service Equipment W-7200 Spring compressor.
5. Compress the spring.
6. Remove the shock mount nut.
7. Remove the shock from the spring compressor.
8. Transfer the necessary parts to the type of repair being done (Insulator, Spring, shock and mount).

To install:

9. Install the shock to the spring and spring compressor, After the transfer of the necessary parts to the type of repair being done (Insulator, Spring, shock and mount).
10. Install the shock mounting nut. Tighten the bolt to 30 ft. lbs. (41 Nm).
11. Loosen the compressed spring.
12. Remove the shock assembly from the spring compressor.
13. Install the shock to the vehicle.
14. Install the tire and wheel assembly.
15. Remove the support and lower the vehicle.
16. Installation is the reverse of removal. Torque the nut to 30 ft. lbs. (41 Nm).

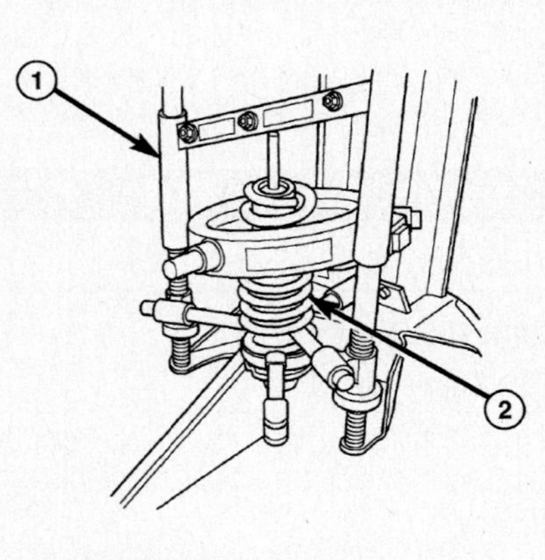

Fig. 177 Front coil spring removal—Liberty

CONTROL LINKS

REMOVAL & INSTALLATION

Track Bar

The track bar is used on Wrangler models.

1. Raise and support the vehicle.
2. Remove the cotter pin and nut from the ball stud end at the frame rail bracket .
3. Use a universal puller tool to separate the track bar ball stud from the frame rail bracket.
4. Remove the bolt and flag nut from the axle bracket .
5. Remove the track bar

To install:

6. Install the track bar at axle tube bracket. Loosely install the retaining bolt and flag nut.
7. It may be necessary to pry the axle assembly over to install the track bar at the frame rail. Install track bar at the frame rail bracket. Install the retaining nut on the stud.
8. Tighten the ball stud nut to 60 ft. lbs. (81 Nm) and install a new cotter pin.
9. Remove the supports and lower the vehicle.
10. Tighten the bolt at the axle bracket to 40 ft. lbs. (47 Nm).
11. Check alignment if a new track bar was installed.

LOWER BALL JOINT

REMOVAL & INSTALLATION

2005–06 Wrangler

See Figure 178.

1. Before servicing the vehicle, refer to the precautions in the beginning of this section.
2. Remove hub/bearing and axle shaft.
3. Disconnect the tie-rod or drag link from the steering knuckle arm.
4. Remove the cotter pins from the upper and lower ball studs.
5. Remove the upper and lower ball stud nuts.
6. Using special tool C-4150A separate the ball joints from the steering knuckle. Remove knuckle from ball studs.

To install:

7. Position the steering knuckle on the ball studs.
8. Install and tighten the bottom retaining nut to 80 ft. lbs. (109 Nm) torque. Install new cotter pin.
9. Install and tighten the top retaining nut to 75 ft. lbs. (101 Nm) torque. Install new cotter pin.

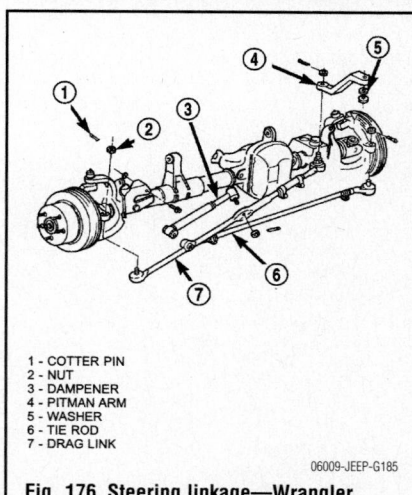

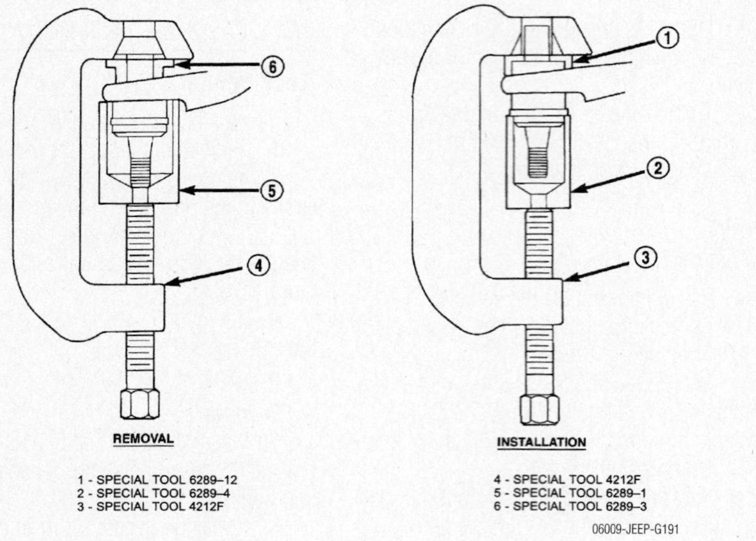

Fig. 178 Lower ball joint removal/installation—Wrangler

10. Install the hub bearing and axle shaft.
11. Connect the tie-rod or drag link end to the steering knuckle arm. Torque to 35 ft. lbs. (47 Nm).

Liberty

See Figures 179 and 180.

1. Before servicing the vehicle, refer to the precautions in the beginning of this section.
2. Remove or disconnect the following:
   - Front wheel
   - Lower clevis bracket bolt from the control arm
   - Stabilizer link at the control arm
   - Lower ball joint nut
   - Control arm from lower ball joint with tool C4150A, or equivalent

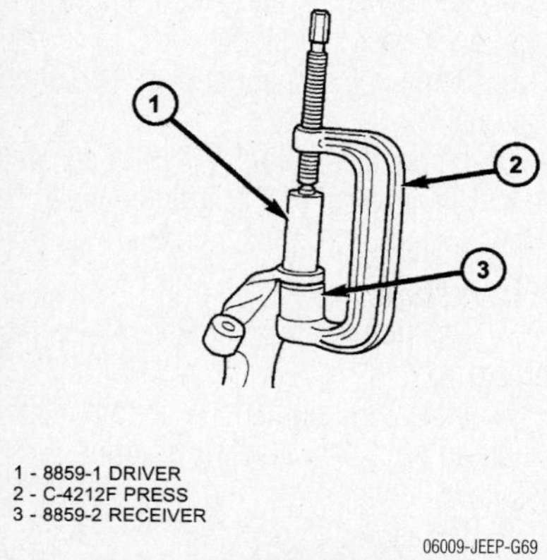

Fig. 179 Front lower ball joint removal—Liberty

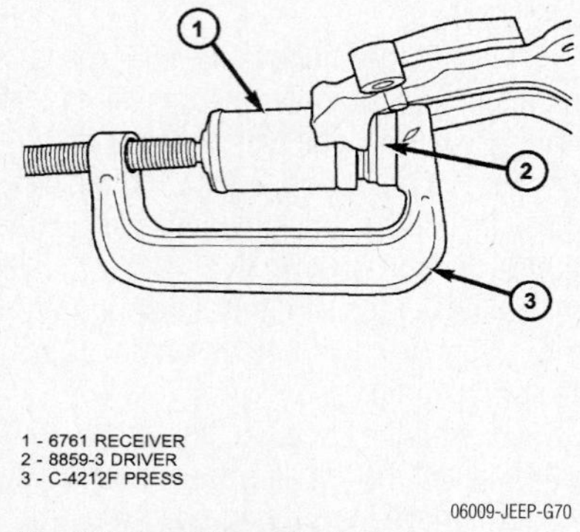

Fig. 180 Front lower ball joint installation—Liberty

3. Installation is the reverse of removal. Torque the ball joint nut to 60 ft. lbs. (81 Nm); the stabilizer link bolt to 100 ft. lbs. (136 Nm); the lower clevis bracket bolt to 110 ft. lbs. (150 Nm).

LOWER CONTROL ARM

REMOVAL & INSTALLATION

2005–06 Wrangler

See Figure 181.

1. Before servicing the vehicle, refer to the precautions in the beginning of this section.
2. Raise and support the vehicle.
3. If equipped with ABS brakes remove sensor wire from the inboard side of the arm.
4. If the vehicle is equipped with a cam bolt service package paint or scribe

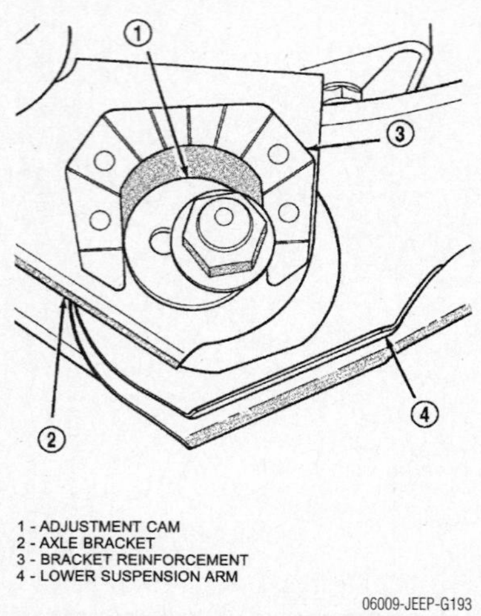

Fig. 181 Cam bolt service package—Wrangler

alignment marks on the cam adjusters and suspension arm for installation reference.

5. Remove the lower suspension arm nut and bolt from the axle.
6. Remove the nut and bolt/cam bolt from the frame rail bracket and remove the lower suspension arm.

To install:

7. Position the lower suspension arm in the axle bracket and frame rail bracket.

➡Small holes in the side of the arm face inboard.

8. Install the rear bolt and nut finger tighten.
9. Install bolt/cam bolt and new nut finger tighten in the axle and align the reference marks.
10. If equipped with ABS brakes install sensor wire to the inboard side of the arm with new clips.
11. Lower the vehicle.
12. Tighten axle bracket nut to 130 ft. lbs. (176 Nm).
13. Tighten frame bracket nut to 130 ft. lbs. (176 Nm).

Liberty

See Figure 182.

1. Before servicing the vehicle, refer to the precautions in the beginning of this section.
2. Remove or disconnect the following:
   - Front wheel
   - Lower clevis bracket bolt from the control arm
   - Stabilizer link at the control arm
   - Lower ball joint nut
   - Control arm from lower ball joint with tool C4150A

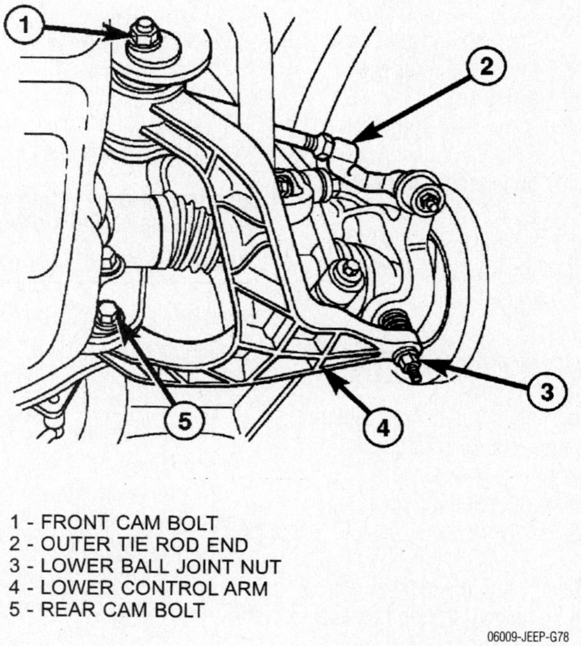

Fig. 182 Front lower control arm—Liberty

➡Matchmark the front and rear control arm pivot bolts.

- Front pivot bolt
- Rear pivot bolt
- Control arm

To install:

3. Install or connect the following:
   - Lower control arm
   - Rear pivot bolt
   - Front pivot bolt
   - Ball joint nut. Torque the ball joint nut to 60 ft. lbs. (81 Nm)
4. Align the matchmarks and tighten the pivot bolts to 125 ft. lbs. (170 Nm).
5. The remainder of the installation is the reverse of removal. Torque the stabilizer link bolt to 100 ft. lbs. (136 Nm); the lower clevis bracket bolt to 110 ft. lbs. (150 Nm).

CONTROL ARM BUSHING REPLACEMENT

The lower control arm bushings are serviced with the control arms as complete assemblies.

SHOCK ABSORBER

REMOVAL & INSTALLATION

2005–06 Wrangler

See Figure 183.

1. Before servicing the vehicle, refer to the precautions in the beginning of this section.
2. Remove or disconnect the following:
   - Upper nut, washer and grommet from the upper stud
   - Lower fasteners
   - Shock absorber

To install:

3. Install or connect the following:
   - Shock absorber. Torque the lower fasteners to 19 ft. lbs. (28 Nm).
   - Upper grommet, washer, and nut to the stud. Torque it to 16 ft. lbs. (23 Nm).

STABILIZER BAR

REMOVAL & INSTALLATION

2005–06 Wrangler

See Figure 184.

1. Remove upper link nuts and separate the links from the stabilizer bar with Remover MB-991113.
2. Remove front bumper valence.
3. Remove stabilizer retainer bolts and remove retainers.
4. Remove stabilizer bar.
5. Remove lower link nuts and bolts and remove links

To install:

6. Center stabilizer bar on top of the frame rails and install retainers and bolts. Tighten bolts to 45 ft. lbs. (61 Nm).
7. Position links on axle brackets and into the stabilizer bar. Install lower link bolts and nuts and tighten to 75 ft. lbs. (102 Nm).
8. Install upper link nuts and tighten to 45 ft. lbs. (61 Nm).
9. Install bumper valence.

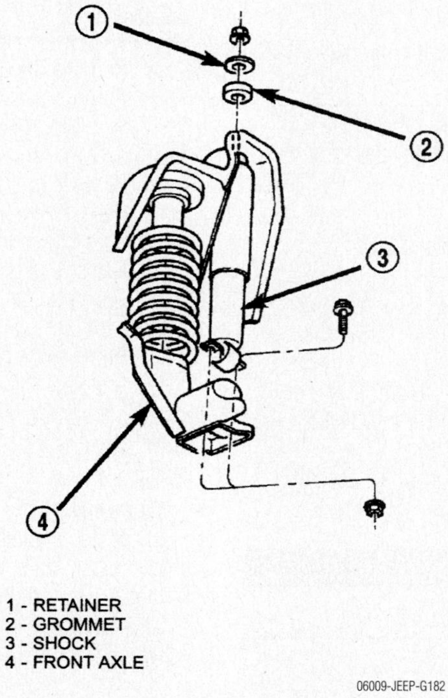

Fig. 183 Coil spring and shock absorber—Wrangler

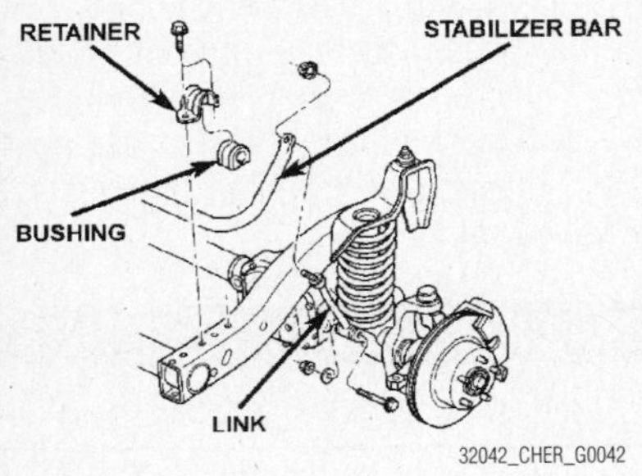

Fig. 184 Front stabilizer bar for the Wrangler

Liberty

See Figure 185.

1. Raise and support the vehicle.
2. Remove the tire and wheel assembly.
3. Remove the upper stabilizer link bolts at the stabilizer bar.
4. Remove the stabilizer bar bushing clamps from the frame .

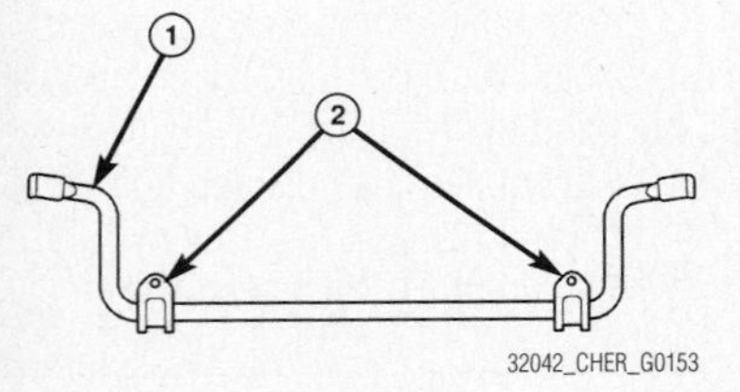

Fig. 185 Front stabilizer bar for the Liberty

5. Remove the stabilizer bar from the vehicle.

To install:

6. Install the stabilizer bar to the vehicle.
7. Install the stabilizer bar bushing clamps. Tighten the nuts to 110 ft. lbs. (149 Nm).
8. Install the upper stabilizer link bolts and washer at the stabilizer bar. Tighten the bolt to 100 ft. lbs. (136 Nm).
9. Install the tire and wheel assembly.
10. Lower the vehicle.

STEERING KNUCKLE

REMOVAL & INSTALLATION

2005–06 Wrangler

Ball stud service procedures below require removal of the hub bearing and axle shaft. Removal and installation of upper and lower ball studs require the use of Tool Kit 6289.

1. Remove hub bearing and axle shaft.
2. Disconnect the tie-rod or drag link from the steering knuckle arm.
3. Remove the cotter pins from the upper and lower ball studs.
4. Remove the upper and lower ball stud nuts.
5. Using special tool C-4150A separate the ball joints from the steering knuckle. Remove knuckle from ball studs

To install:

6. Position the steering knuckle on the ball studs.
7. Install and tighten the bottom retaining nut to 80 ft. lbs. (109 Nm) torque. Install new cotter pin.
8. Install and tighten the top retaining nut to 75 ft. lbs. (101 Nm) torque. Install new cotter pin.
9. Install the hub bearing and axle shaft.
10. Connect the tie-rod or drag link end to the steering knuckle arm

Liberty

1. Raise and support the vehicle.
2. Remove the tire and wheel assembly.
3. Remove the caliper adapter.

**** CAUTION**

Never allow the disc brake caliper to hang from the brake hose. Damage to the brake hose will result. Provide a suitable support to hang the caliper securely.

4. Remove the disc brake rotor.
5. Remove the wheel speed sensor.
6. Remove the axle shaft nut. (if equipped with four wheel drive).
7. Remove the hub/bearing.
8. Separate the outer tie rod end from the steering knuckle.
9. Remove the lower ball joint nut.
10. Separate the lower ball joint from the suspension arm using tool C-4150A.
11. Remove the upper ball joint nut.
12. Separate the upper ball joint from the knuckle using tool C-4150A.
13. Remove the knuckle from the vehicle.

To install:

14. Install the knuckle to the vehicle.
15. Install the upper ball joint nut. Tighten the nut to 60 ft. lbs. (81 Nm).
16. Install the lower ball joint nut. Tighten the nut to 60 ft. lbs. (81 Nm).
17. Install the outer tie rod end to the steering knuckle.
18. Install the hub/bearing.
19. Install the axle shaft nut. Tighten the nut to 96 ft. lbs. (135 Nm).
20. Install the wheel speed sensor.
21. Install the disc brake rotor.
22. Install the caliper adapter.
23. Install the tire and wheel assembly.
24. Perform the set toe procedure.

STRUT & SPRING ASSEMBLY

REMOVAL & INSTALLATION

Liberty

See Figures 186 and 187.

Left

1. Disconnect the battery.
2. Remove the battery.
3. Unclip the power center and move it to the side out of the way.
4. Remove the battery tray.
5. Disconnect the battery temperature sensor from the battery tray.
6. Remove the four upper shock mounting nuts.
7. Raise and support the vehicle.
8. Remove the left tire and wheel assembly.
9. Remove the lower bolt at the lower control securing the clevis bracket.
10. Remove the stabilizer link.
11. Remove the lower ball joint nut.
12. Separate the lower ball joint from the lower control arm using tool C-4150A.
13. Rotate the lower control arm downward to allow access.
14. Remove the clevis bracket at the shock.
15. Remove the shock assembly from the vehicle.
16. Remove the spring from the shock (if needed).

To install:

17. Install the spring to the shock (if removed).
18. Install the shock assembly to the vehicle.
19. Install the four upper shock mounting nuts. Tighten the nuts to 80 ft. lbs. (108 Nm).
20. Install the clevis bracket at the shock. Tighten the bolt to 65 ft. lbs. (88 Nm).
21. Raise the lower control into place and reconnect the lower ball joint nut. Tighten the nut to 60 ft. lbs. (81 Nm).
22. Install the clevis bracket at the lower control arm. Tighten the bolt to 110 ft. lbs. (150 Nm).
23. Install the lower stabilizer link at the lower control arm. Tighten the bolt to 100 ft. lbs. (136 Nm).
24. Install the left tire and wheel assembly.

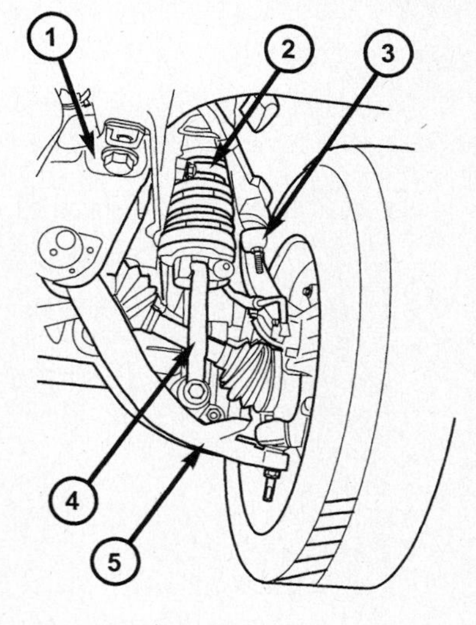

Fig. 186 Strut and clevis assembly—Liberty

25. Lower the vehicle.
26. Reconnect the battery temperature sensor.
27. Install the battery tray.
28. Install the battery.
29. Reconnect the battery cables.

Right

1. Remove the air box.
2. Remove the two cruise control servo mounting nuts.
3. Remove the upper shock mounting nuts.
4. Raise and support the vehicle.
5. Remove the right side tire assembly.
6. Remove the lower bolt at the lower control securing the clevis bracket.
7. Remove the stabilizer link.
8. Remove the lower ball joint nut.
9. Separate the lower ball joint from the lower control arm using tool C-4150A.
10. Rotate the lower control arm downward to allow access.
11. Remove the clevis bracket at the shock.
12. Remove the shock assembly from the vehicle.
13. Remove the spring from the shock (if needed).

To install:

14. Install the spring to the shock (if removed).
15. Install the shock assembly to the vehicle.

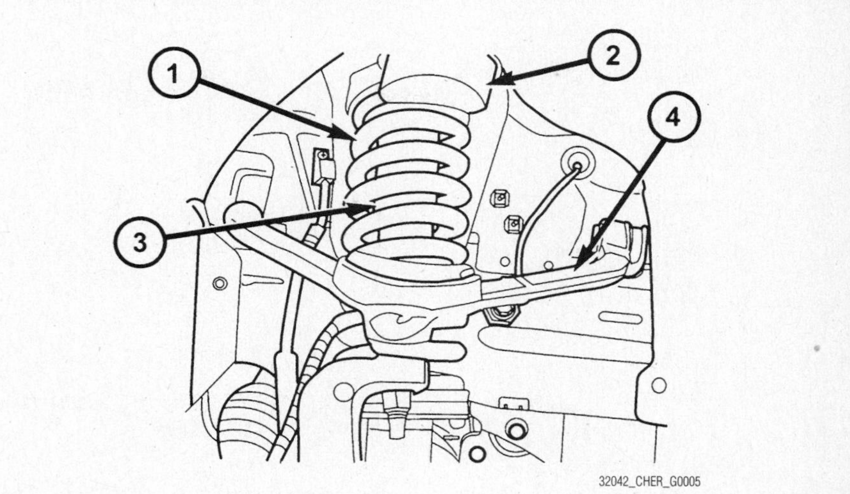

Fig. 187 Front shock absorber assembly for the Liberty

16. Install the four upper shock mounting nuts. Tighten the nuts to 80 ft. lbs. (108 Nm).
17. Install the clevis bracket at the shock. Tighten the bolt to 65 ft. lbs. (88 Nm).
18. Raise the lower control into place and reconnect the lower ball joint nut. Tighten the nut to 60 ft. lbs. (81 Nm).
19. Install the clevis bracket at the lower control arm. Tighten the bolt to 110 ft. lbs. (150 Nm).
20. Install the lower stabilizer link at the lower control arm. Tighten the bolt to 100 ft. lbs. (136 Nm).
21. Install the right tire and wheel assembly.
22. Lower the vehicle.
23. Install the cruise control servo mounting nuts.
24. Install the airbox.

UPPER BALL JOINT

REMOVAL & INSTALLATION

2005–06 Wrangler

See Figures 188 and 189.

1. Before servicing the vehicle, refer to the precautions in the beginning of this section.
2. Remove hub/bearing and axle shaft.
3. Disconnect the tie-rod or drag link from the steering knuckle arm.
4. Remove the cotter pins from the upper and lower ball studs.

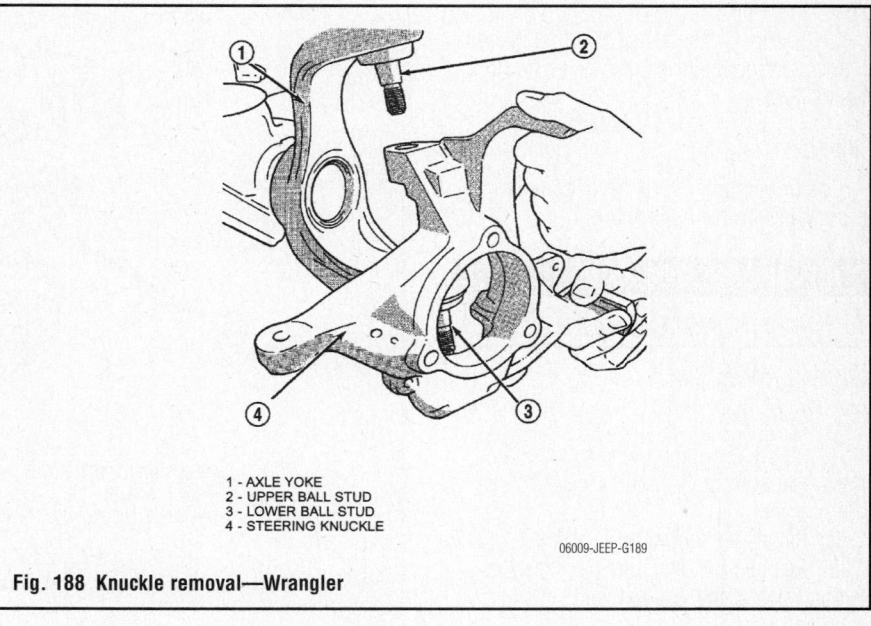

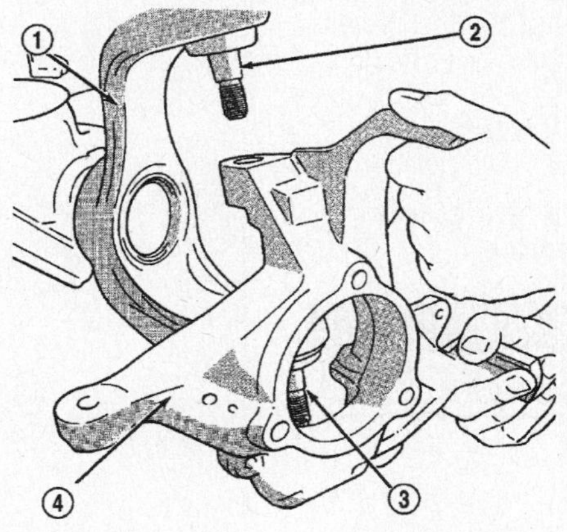

Fig. 188 Knuckle removal—Wrangler

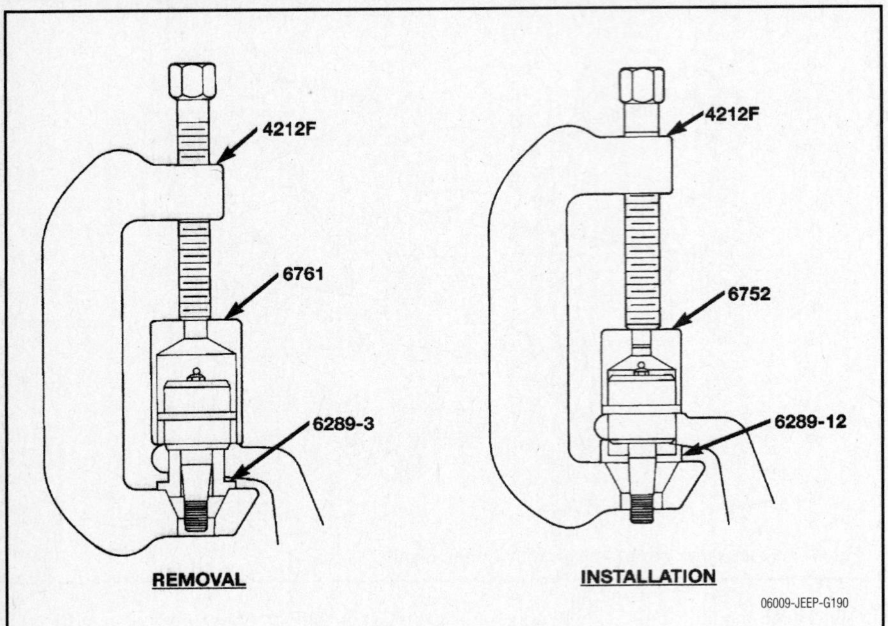

Fig. 189 Upper ball joint removal/installation—Wrangler

5. Remove the upper and lower ball stud nuts.
6. Using special tool C-4150A separate the ball joints from the steering knuckle. Remove knuckle from ball studs.

To install:

7. Position the steering knuckle on the ball studs.
8. Install and tighten the bottom retaining nut to 80 ft. lbs. (109 Nm) torque. Install new cotter pin.
9. Install and tighten the top retaining nut to 75 ft. lbs. (101 Nm) torque. Install new cotter pin.
10. Install the hub bearing and axle shaft.
11. Connect the tie-rod or drag link end to the steering knuckle arm. Torque to 35 ft. lbs. (47 Nm).

Liberty

The upper ball joint is serviced as an assembly with the control arm.

UPPER CONTROL ARM

REMOVAL & INSTALLATION

2005–06 Wrangler

See Figure 190.

1. Before servicing the vehicle, refer to the precautions in the beginning of this section.
2. Raise and support the vehicle.
3. Remove the upper suspension arm nut and bolt at the axle bracket.
4. Remove the nut and bolt at the frame rail and remove the upper suspension arm.

To install:

5. Position the upper suspension arm at the axle and frame rail.
6. Install the bolts and finger tighten the nuts.
7. Remove the supports and lower the vehicle.
8. Tighten the nut at the axle and frame brackets to 60 ft. lbs. (81 Nm).

Liberty

Right

1. Before servicing the vehicle, refer to the precautions at the beginning of this section.
2. Remove or disconnect the following:
   - Wheel
   - Upper ball joint nut
   - Upper Ball joint from the knuckle
   - Air box
   - Cruise control servo mounting nuts
   - Upper arm rear bolt
   - Upper arm front bolt
   - Upper arm
3. Installation is the reverse of removal. Observe the following torques:
   - Front and rear bolts: 90 ft. lbs. (122 Nm)
   - Ball joint stud nut: 60 ft. lbs. (81 Nm)

Left

See Figures 191 and 192

1. Before servicing the vehicle, refer to the precautions at the beginning of this section.
2. Remove or disconnect the following:
   - Wheel
   - Ball joint nut
   - Ball joint from the knuckle
   - Battery
   - Power center
   - Battery tray
   - Battery temperature sensor
   - Control arm rear bolt, by using

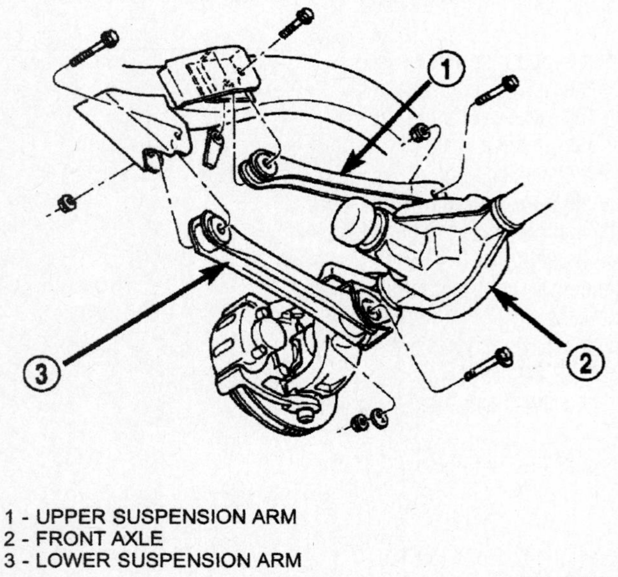

Fig. 190 Upper and lower front control arms—Wrangler

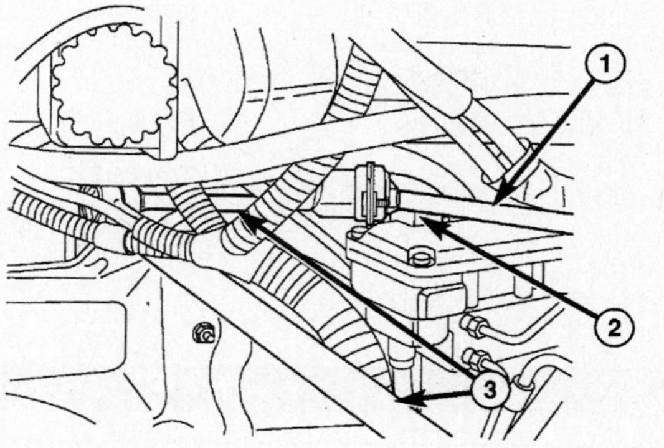

Fig. 191 Accessing the front left side upper control arm rear bolt—Liberty

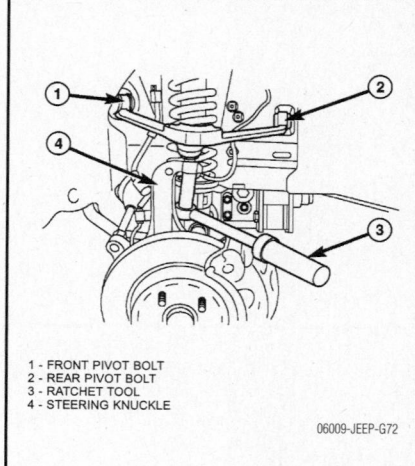

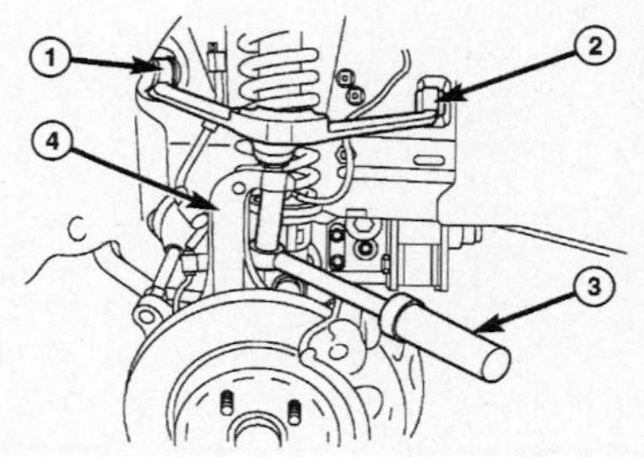

Fig. 192 Front left side upper control arm removal—Liberty

a ratchet and extension under the steering shaft, positioned by the power steering reservoir

- Control arm front bolt
- Control arm

3. Installation is the reverse of removal. Observe the following torques:

- Front and rear bolts: 90 ft. lbs. (122 Nm)
- Ball joint stud nut: 60 ft. lbs. (81 Nm)

CONTROL ARM BUSHING REPLACEMENT

The upper control arm bushings are serviced with the control arms as complete assemblies, with the exception of the front upper axle bushing, which may be replaced after removing the upper control arm.

WHEEL BEARINGS

REMOVAL & INSTALLATION

2005–06 Wrangler

See Figure 193.

1. Before servicing the vehicle, refer to the precautions in the beginning of this section.
2. Raise and support the vehicle.
3. Remove the wheel and tire assembly.
4. Remove the brake caliper, rotor and ABS wheel speed sensor.
5. Remove the cotter pin, nut retainer and axle hub nut.
6. Remove the hub bearing mounting bolts from the back of the steering knuckle. Remove hub bearing from the steering knuckle and off the axle shaft.

To install:

7. Install the hub bearing and brake dust shield to the knuckle.
8. Install the hub bearing to knuckle bolts and tighten to 75 ft. lbs. (102 Nm).
9. Install the hub washer and nut. Tighten the hub nut to 175 ft. lbs. (237 Nm). Install the nut retainer and a new cotter pin.
10. Install the brake rotor, caliper and ABS wheel speed sensor.
11. Install the wheel and tire assembly.
12. Remove support and lower the vehicle.

Liberty

1. Before servicing the vehicle, refer to the precautions in the beginning of this section.
2. Raise and support the vehicle.
3. Remove the tire and wheel assembly.
4. Remove the caliper adapter.

⁂ WARNING

Never allow the disc brake caliper to hang from the brake hose. Damage to the brake hose will result. Provide a suitable support to hang the caliper securely.

5. Remove the disc brake rotor.
6. Remove the wheel speed sensor.

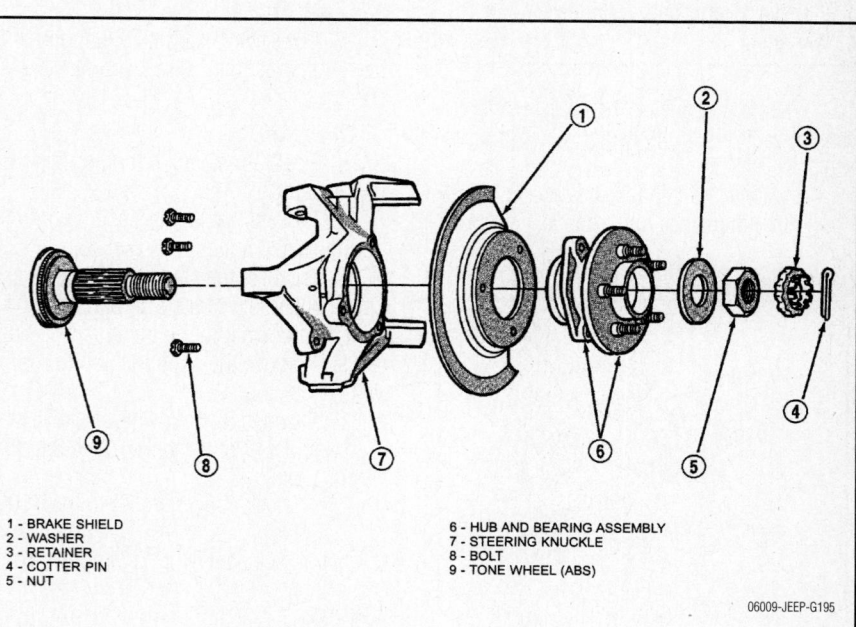

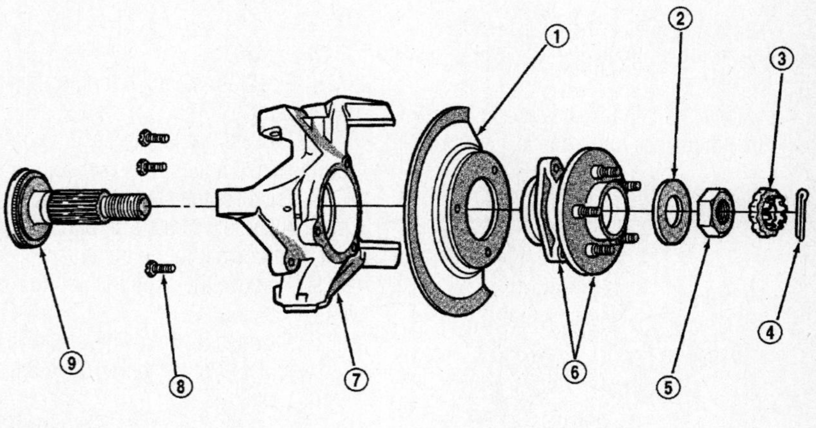

Fig. 193 Hub/bearing and knuckle—Wrangler

7. Remove the bracket securing the wheel speed sensor wire.
8. Remove the axle shaft nut, if equipped with four wheel drive.
9. Remove the three mounting bolts for the hub/bearing assembly.
10. Remove the hub/bearing.

To install:

11. Install the hub/bearing assembly to the vehicle.
12. Install the three mounting bolts for the hub/bearing. Tighten the bolt to 96 ft. lbs. (130 Nm).
13. Install the axle shaft nut. Tighten the nut to 100 ft. lbs. (135 Nm), if equipped with four wheel drive.
14. Install the bracket to the wheel speed sensor wire.
15. Install the wheel speed sensor to the hub. Tighten the bolt to 10 ft. lbs. (13.5 Nm).
16. Install the disc brake rotor.
17. Install the disc brake caliper adapter. Tighten the nut to 100 ft. lbs. (135 Nm).
18. Install the tire and wheel assembly.

ADJUSTMENT

The front wheel bearings are not adjustable.

SUSPENSION — REAR SUSPENSION

COIL SPRING

REMOVAL & INSTALLATION

2005–06 Wrangler

See Figures 194 through 196.

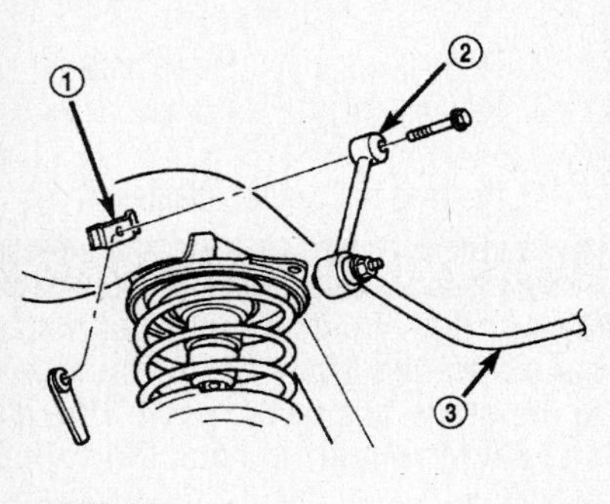

Fig. 194 Rear stabilizer bar link—Wrangler

1. Before servicing the vehicle, refer to the precautions in the beginning of this section.
2. Raise and support the vehicle. Position a hydraulic jack under the axle to support it.

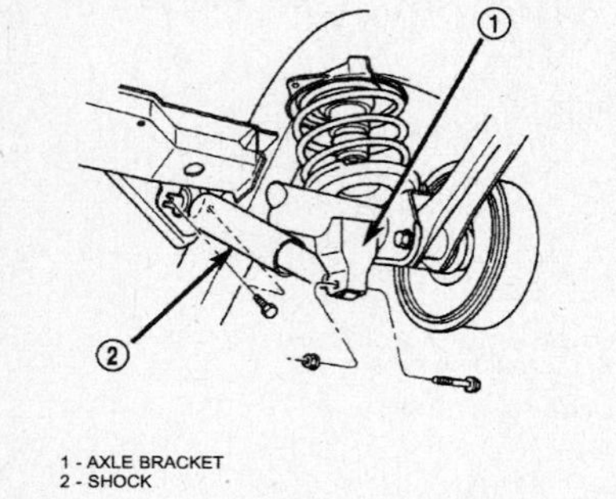

Fig. 195 Rear spring and shock absorber—Wrangler

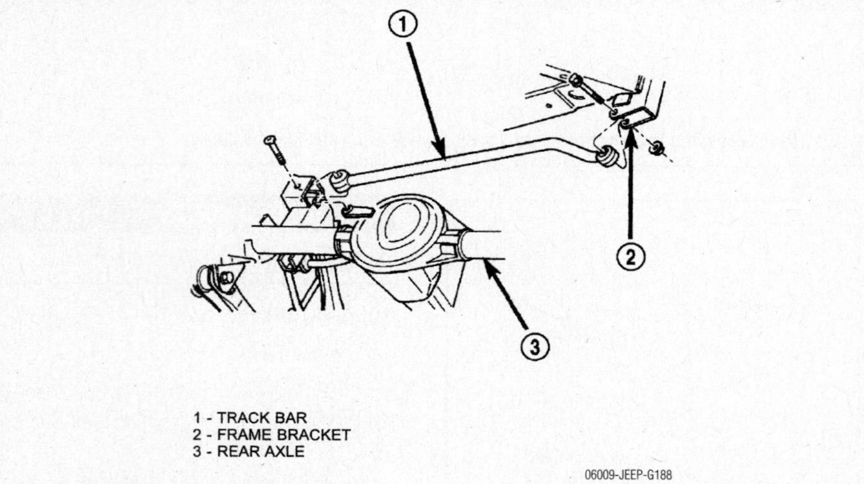

Fig. 196 Rear track bar—Wrangler

3. Disconnect the stabilizer bar links and shock absorbers from the axle brackets.
4. Disconnect the track bar from the frame rail bracket.
5. Lower the axle until the spring is free from the upper mount seat and remove the spring.

To install:

6. Position the coil spring on the axle pad isolator.
7. Raise the axle into position until the spring seats on the upper isolator.
8. Connect the stabilizer bar links and shock absorbers to the axle bracket. Connect the track bar to the frame rail bracket.
9. Remove the supports and lower the vehicle.
10. Observe the following torques:
    - Stabilizer bar links: 40 ft. lbs. (54 Nm)
    - Shock absorbers: 74 ft. lbs. (100 Nm)
    - Track bar: 74 ft. lbs. (100 Nm)

Liberty

See Figure 197.

1. Before servicing the vehicle, refer to the precautions in the beginning of this section.
2. Raise and support the vehicle. Position a hydraulic jack under the axle to support the axle.
3. Remove the shock absorber lower bolt from the axle bracket.
4. Lower the hydraulic jack and tilt the axle and remove the coil spring.
5. Remove and inspect the upper and lower spring isolators.

To install:

6. Install the upper isolator.
7. Install the lower isolator.
8. Pull down on the axle and position the coil spring in the lower isolator.

CAUTION

Ensure the spring is positioned on the lower isolator.

9. Raise the axle with the hydraulic jack.
10. Install the shock absorber to the axle bracket and tighten to 85 ft. lbs. (115 Nm).
11. Remove the supports and lower the vehicle.

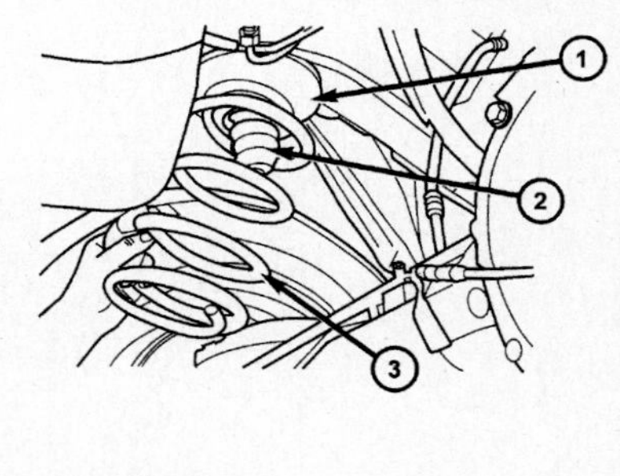

Fig. 197 Rear coil spring—Liberty

12. Tighten the stabilizer bar links to 73 ft. lbs. (99 Nm).

LOWER CONTROL ARM

REMOVAL & INSTALLATION

See Figures 198 and 199.

1. Before servicing the vehicle, refer to the precautions in the beginning of this section.
2. Support the axle with a jackstand.

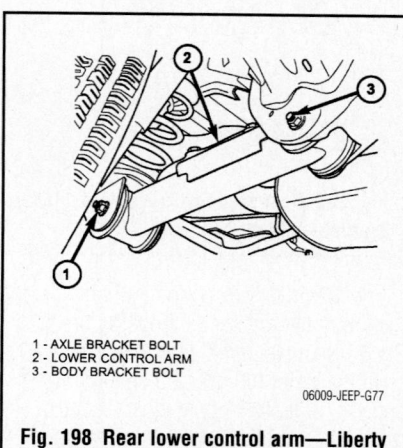

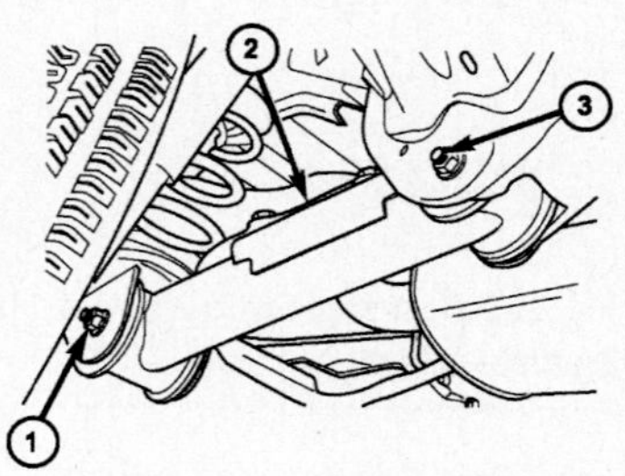

Fig. 198 Rear lower control arm—Liberty

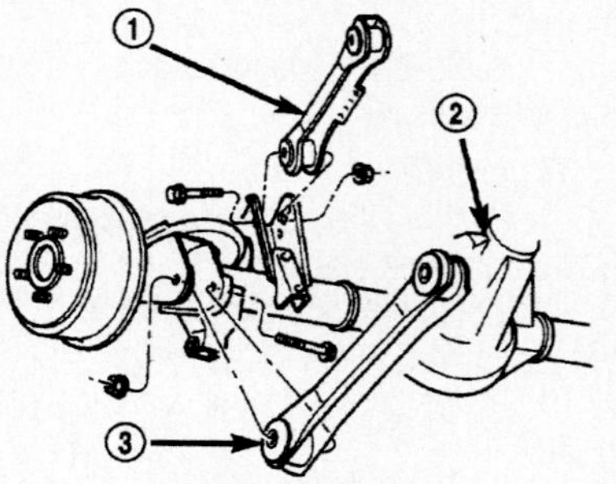

Fig. 199 Rear upper and lower control arms—Wrangler

3. On the Liberty, disconnect the stabilizer bar from the arm.
4. Unbolt and remove the lower control arm.

➡On the Liberty's right arm, it will be necessary to pry the exhaust pipe slightly to get to the frame rail-to-arm bolt.

To install:

➡The weight of the vehicle must be supported by the springs before tightening the control arm fasteners.

5. Install the lower control arm.
6. Tighten the lower control arm fasteners to the following specifications:
   - Wrangler: Both fasteners to 150 ft. lbs. (203 Nm)
   - Liberty: Both fasteners to 120 ft. lbs. (163 Nm)

SHOCK ABSORBERS

REMOVAL & INSTALLATION

2005–06 Wrangler

See Figure 200.

1. Raise and support the vehicle and the axle.
2. Remove the upper mounting bolts .
3. Remove the lower nut and bolt from the axle bracket. Remove the shock absorber

To install:

4. Install the shock absorber on the upper frame rail and install mounting bolts.
5. Tighten the upper bolts to 23 ft. lbs. (31 Nm).
6. Install lower bolt and nut finger tight.
7. Remove the supports and lower the vehicle.
8. Tighten the lower nut to 74 ft. lbs. (100 Nm)

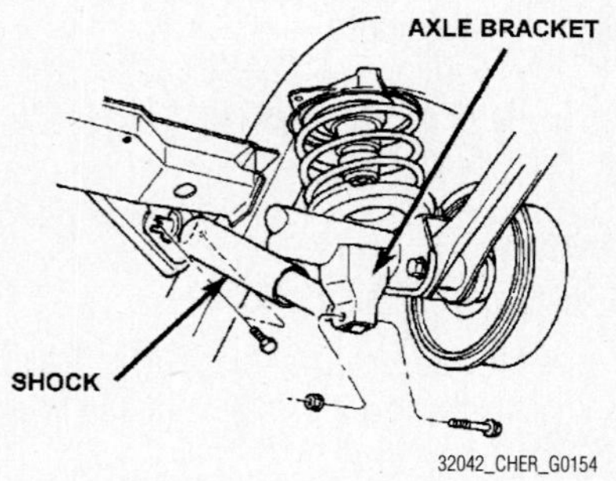

Fig. 200 Shock absorber assembly for the Wrangler

Liberty

See Figure 201.

1. Raise and support the vehicle. Position a hydraulic jack under the axle to support the axle.

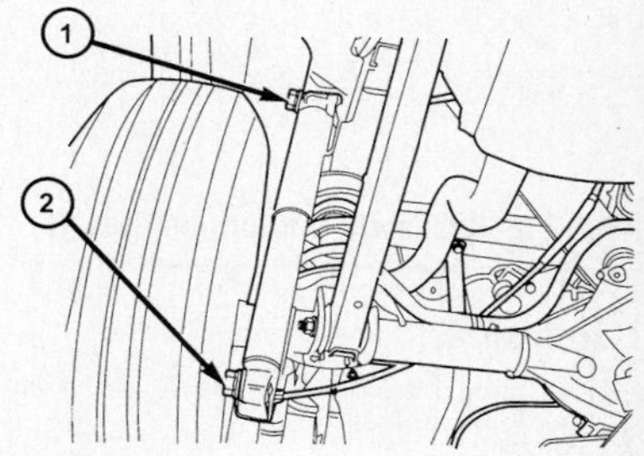

Fig. 201 Rear shock absorber assembly for the Liberty

✲✲ CAUTION

Do not allow the axle to hang from the upper suspension arm ball joint.

2. Remove the upper nut and bolt from the frame bracket.
3. Remove the lower nut and bolt from the axle bracket. Remove the shock absorber.

To install:

4. Install the shock absorber in the frame bracket and install the bolt and nut.
5. Install the shock absorber in the axle bracket and install the bolt and nut.
6. Remove the supports and lower the vehicle.
7. Tighten the upper mounting nuts to 80 ft. lbs. (108 Nm). Tighten the lower mounting nuts to 85 ft. lbs. (115 Nm).

STABILIZER BAR

REMOVAL & INSTALLATION

2005–06 Wrangler

See Figure 202.

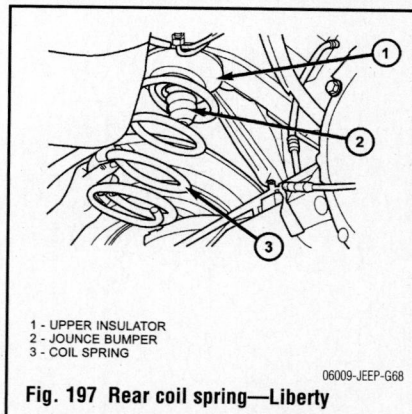

1. Raise and support the vehicle.
2. Remove the stabilizer bar link bolts from the frame mounts .
3. Remove the link bolts from the stabilizer bar.
4. Remove the stabilizer bar retainer bolts and retainers from the axle mounts and remove the bar

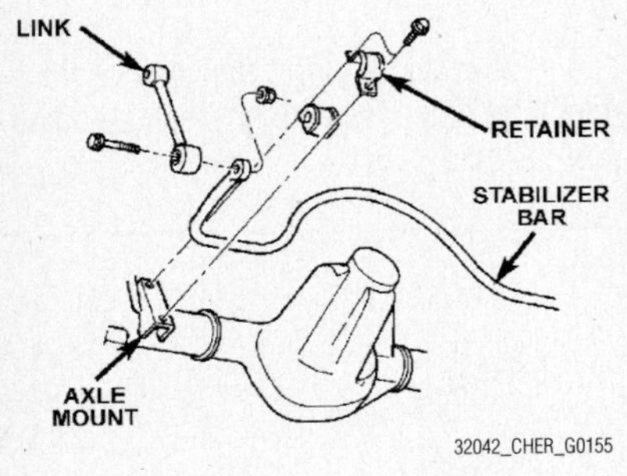

Fig. 202 Rear sway bar for the Wrangler

To install:

5. Install the stabilizer bar on the axle mounts and install the retainers and bolts

➡Ensure the bar is centered with equal spacing on both sides and is positioned above the differential housing .

6. Tighten the retainer bolts to 40 ft. lbs. (54 Nm).
7. Install the links onto the stabilizer bar and frame mounts. Install the bolts and nuts finger tight.
8. Remove support and lower vehicle.
9. Tighten the link nuts/bolts to 40 ft. lbs. (54 Nm)

Liberty

See Figure 203.

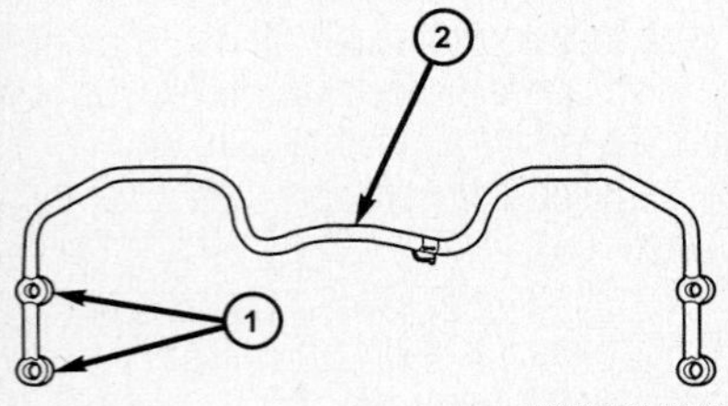

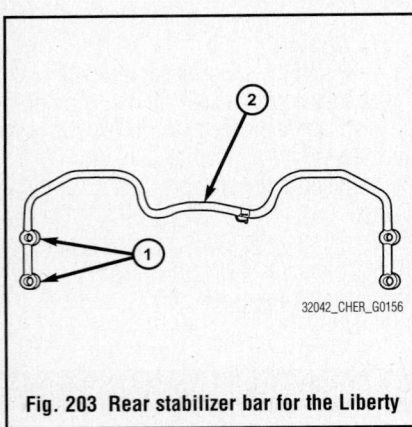

Fig. 203 Rear stabilizer bar for the Liberty

1. Raise and support the vehicle.
2. Remove the stabilizer bar bolts from the lower suspension arm.
3. Remove the stabilizer bar.

To install:

4. Position the stabilizer bar over the axle and install the bolts to the lower suspension arm. Ensure the bar is centered with equal spacing on both sides. Tighten the bolts to 73 ft. lbs. (99 Nm).
5. Remove support and lower the vehicle.

TRACK BAR

REMOVAL & INSTALLATION

2005–06 Wrangler

1. Raise and support the vehicle.
2. Remove the bolt and nut from the frame rail bracket.
3. Remove the bolt from the axle bracket and remove the track bar

To install:

4. Install the track bar in the axle bracket and install the bolt loosely.
5. Install the track bar in the frame rail bracket and loosely install the bolt and nut

➡It may be necessary to pry the axle assembly over to install the track bar.

6. Remove supports and lower the vehicle.
7. Tighten the track bar nut/bolt at both ends to 74 ft. lbs. (100 Nm)

UPPER CONTROL ARM

REMOVAL & INSTALLATION

2005–06 Wrangler

1. Before servicing the vehicle, refer to the precautions in the beginning of this section.
2. Support the axle with a jackstand.
3. Remove or disconnect the following:
   - Parking brake cable and bracket
   - Wheel speed sensor wiring bracket, if equipped
   - Upper control arm

To install:

➡The weight of the vehicle must be supported by the springs before tightening the control arm fasteners.

4. Install or connect the following:
   - Upper control arm
   - Wheel speed sensor wiring bracket, if equipped
   - Parking brake cable and bracket
5. Torque the control arm fasteners to 55 ft. lbs. (75 Nm).

Liberty

See Figures 204 and 205.

1. Before servicing the vehicle, refer to the precautions in the beginning of this section.
2. Raise and support the vehicle.
3. Support the rear axle with a hydraulic jack.

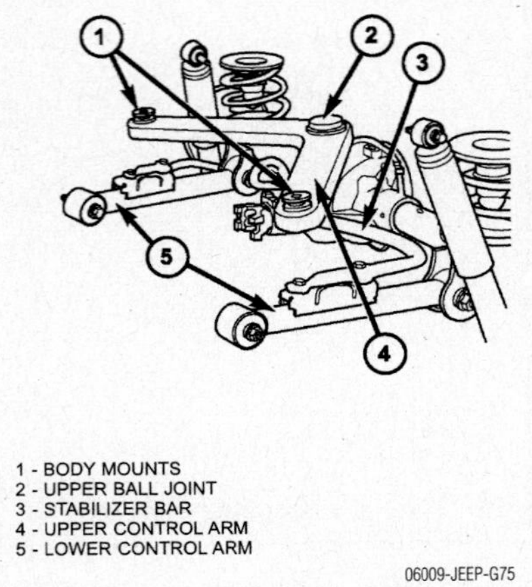

Fig. 204 Rear suspension upper control arm—Liberty

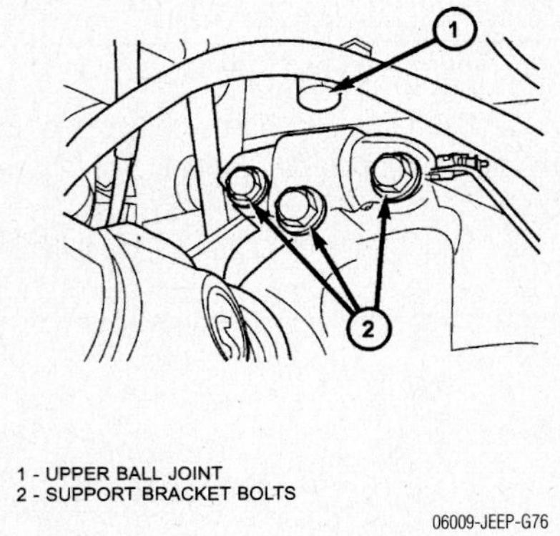

Fig. 205 Rear suspension upper ball joint bracket—Liberty

4. Remove the ball joint pinch bolt from the top of the differential housing bracket.
5. Remove partial nuts from the heat shield in order to lower the shield down enough to get the proper clearance to remove the right side bolt from the body.
6. Remove the upper suspension arm mounting bolts from the body and remove the arm.
7. Remove the support bracket mounting bolts if needed.

To install:

8. Position the upper suspension arm in the frame rail brackets.
9. Install the mounting bolts and tighten to 74 ft. lbs. (100 Nm).
10. Retighten the heat shield back into place.
11. Pull the arm down on the differential housing bracket and install the pinch bolt and nut. Tighten the nut to 70 ft. lbs. (95 Nm).
12. Remove the supports and lower the vehicle.

CHRYSLER

Pacifica

11

SPECIFICATIONS AND MAINTENANCE CHARTS

ENGINE AND VEHICLE IDENTIFICATION

Engine						
Code ①	Liters (cc)	Cu. In.	Cyl.	Fuel Sys.	Engine Type	Eng. Mfg.
4	3.5 (3518)	215	V6	MFI	SOHC	Chrysler
L	3.8 (3785)	231	V6	SMFI	OHV	Chrysler
X	4.0 (3966)	244	V6	SMFI	SOHV	Chrysler

Model Year	
Code ②	Year
5	2005
6	2006
7	2007
8	2008

MFI: Multi-point Fuel Injection

SMFI: Sequential Multi-port Fuel Injection

SOHC: Single Overhead Camshaft

① 8th position of the Vehicle Identification Number (VIN)

② 10th position of VIN

22043_PACI_C0001

GENERAL ENGINE SPECIFICATIONS

All measurements are given in inches.

Year	Model	Engine Displacement Liters (VIN)	Net Horsepower @ rpm	Net Torque @ rpm (ft. lbs.)	Bore x Stroke (in.)	Com-pression Ratio	Oil Pressure @ rpm
2005	Pacifica	3.5 (4)	250@6400	255@3950	3.78x3.18	10:01	45-105@3000
		3.8 (L)	210@5000	240@4000	3.79x3.42	9.6:1	30-80@3000
2006	Pacifica	3.5 (4)	250@6400	255@3950	3.78x3.18	10:01	45-105@3000
		3.8 (L)	210@5000	240@4000	3.79x3.42	9.6:1	30-80@3000
2007	Pacifica	3.8 (L)	210@5000	240@4000	3.79x3.42	9.6:1	30-80@3000
		4.0 (X)	253@6000	262@4100	3.78x3.58	10.2:1	45-105@3000
2008	Pacifica	3.8 (L)	210@5000	240@4000	3.79x3.42	9.6:1	30-80@3000
		4.0 (X)	253@6000	262@4100	3.78x3.58	10.2:1	45-105@3000

22043_PACI_C0002

ENGINE TUNE-UP SPECIFICATIONS

Year	Engine Displacement Liters (VIN)	Spark Plug Gap (in.)	Ignition Timing (deg.)	Fuel Pump (psi)	Idle Speed (rpm)	Valve Clearance	
						Intake	Exhaust
2005	3.5 (4)	0.048-0.053	①	58	②	HYD	HYD
	3.8 (L)	0.048-0.053	①	58	②	HYD	HYD
2006	3.5 (4)	0.048-0.053	①	58	②	HYD	HYD
	3.8 (L)	0.048-0.053	①	58	②	HYD	HYD
2007	3.8 (L)	0.048-0.053	①	58	②	HYD	HYD
	4.0 (X)	0.048-0.053	①	58	②	HYD	HYD
2008	3.8 (L)	0.048-0.053	①	58	②	HYD	HYD
	4.0 (X)	0.048-0.053	①	58	②	HYD	HYD

NOTE: The Vehicle Emission Control Information label often reflects specification changes made during production.

The label figures must be used if they differ from those in this chart.

HYD: Hydraulic

① Ignition timing is regulated by the Powertrain Control Module (PCM), and cannot be adjusted

② Idle speed is controled by the Powertrain Control Module (PCM), and cannot be adjusted

22043_PACI_C0003

CAPACITIES

Year	Model	Engine Displacement Liters (VIN)	Engine Oil with Filter (qts.)	Auto. Transmission (pts.) ①	Transfer Case (pts.)	Front Drive Axle (pts.)	Fuel Tank (gal.)	Cooling System (qts.)
2005	Pacifica	3.5 (4)	5.5	19.8	1.22	2.0	23.0	10.5
	Pacifica	3.8 (L)	5.0	19.8	1.22	2.0	23.0	10.5
2006	Pacifica	3.5 (4)	5.5	19.8	1.22	2.0	23.0	10.5
	Pacifica	3.8 (L)	5.0	19.8	1.22	2.0	23.0	10.5
2007	Pacifica	3.8 (L)	5.0	18.0	1.22	1.48	23.0	11.8
	Pacifica	4.0 (X)	5.5	18.0	1.22	1.48	23.0	10.7
2008	Pacifica	3.8 (L)	5.0	18.0	1.22	1.48	23.0	11.8
	Pacifica	4.0 (X)	5.5	18.0	1.22	1.48	23.0	10.7

NOTE: All capacities are approximate. Add fluid gradually and ensure a proper fluid level is obtained.

① 2005 and 2006 Overhaul fill capacity with torque converter empty

Estimated service fill: 8 pts.

22043_PACI_C0004

FLUID SPECIFICATIONS

Year	Model	Engine Displacement Liters (cc)	Engine ID/VIN	Engine Oil	Auto. Trans.	Drive Axle	Power Steering Fluid	Brake Master Cylinder
2005	Pacifica	3.5 (3518)	4	①	②	③	②	DOT 3
		3.8 (3785)	L	①	②	③	②	DOT 3
2006	Pacifica	3.5 (3518)	4	①	②	①	②	DOT 3
		3.8 (3785)	L	①	②	③	②	DOT 3
2007	Pacifica	3.8 (3785)	L	①	②	④	②	DOT 3
		4.0 (3966)	X	①	②	④	②	DOT 3
2008	Pacifica	3.8 (3785)	L	5W-20	②	④	②	DOT 3
		4.0 (3966)	X	10W-30	②	④	②	DOT 3

DOT: Department Of Transpotation

22043_csfr_c0014

① See owners manual

② Mopar ATF+4 fluid

③ AWD power transfer unit: 75W-90 gear and axle lubricant
AWD rear driveline module fluid: 75W-90 gear and axle lubricant

④ AWD power transfer unit: 75W-90 gear and axle lubricant
AWD rear driveline module differential carrier: 75W-90 gear and axle lubricant. Overrunning clutch housing does not require lubricant.

22043_PACI_C0014

VALVE SPECIFICATIONS

Year	Engine Displacement Liters (VIN)	Seat Angle (deg.)	Face Angle (deg.)	Spring Test Pressure (lbs. @ in.)	Spring Installed Height (in.)	Stem-to-Guide Clearance (in.)		Stem Diameter (in.)	
						Intake	Exhaust	Intake	Exhaust
2005	3.5 (4)	45-45.5	44.5-45	①	1.496	0.0009-0.0026	0.0020-0.0037	0.2730-0.2737	0.2719-0.2726
	3.8 (L)	45-45.5	45-45.5	②	1.61-1.68	0.0010-0.0025	0.0020-0.0037	0.2718-0.2725	0.2718-0.2725
2006	3.5 (4)	45-45.5	44.5-45	①	1.496	0.0009-0.0026	0.0020-0.0037	0.2730-0.2737	0.2719-0.2726
	3.8 (L)	45-45.5	45-45.5	②	1.61-1.68	0.0010-0.0025	0.0020-0.0037	0.2718-0.2725	0.2718-0.2725
2007	3.8 (L)	45-45.5	45-45.5	②	1.61-1.68	0.0010-0.0025	0.0020-0.0037	0.2718-0.2725	0.2718-0.2725
	4.0 (X)	45-45.5	44.5-45	NA	③	0.0009-0.0026	0.0020-0.0037	0.2730-0.2737	0.2719-0.2726
2008	3.8 (L)	45-45.5	45-45.5	②	1.61-1.68	0.0010-0.0025	0.0020-0.0037	0.2718-0.2725	0.2718-0.2725
	4.0 (X)	45-45.5	44.5-45	NA	③	0.0009-0.0026	0.0020-0.0037	0.2730-0.2737	0.2719-0.2726

NA: Not Available

① Intake: 69.5-80.5 lbs.@1.496 in. valve closed
Intake: 188.0-204.0 lbs.@1.1594 in. valve opened
Exhaust: 71-79 lbs.@1.4961 in. valve closed
Exhaust: 130-144 lbs.@1.239 in. valve opened

② Type A Valve Closed: 84.9-95.6 lbs. @ 1.65 in.
Type A Valve Open: 194.2-215.8 @ 1.65 in
Type B Valve Open: 197.9-216.3 @ 122 in.
Type B Valve Closed: 84.4-95.2 @ 1.65 in.

③ 1.496, spring seat to bottom retainer

22043_PACI_C0005

CAMSHAFT SPECIFICATIONS

All measurements are given in inches.

Year	Engine Displ. Liters	Engine VIN	Journal Diameter	Diametrical Clearance	Shaft End-play	Runout	Lobe Height Intake	Lobe Height Exhaust
2005	3.5	4	1.6905-1.6913	0.003-0.0047	0.0010-0.0140	NA	NA	NA
	3.8	L	①	0.0010-0.0040	0.0010-0.0020	NA	NA	NA
2006	3.5	4	1.6905-1.6913	0.003-0.0047	0.0010-0.0140	NA	NA	NA
	3.8	L	①	0.0010-0.0040	0.0010-0.0020	NA	NA	NA
2007	3.8	L	①	0.0010-0.0040	0.0010-0.0020	NA	NA	NA
	4.0	X	1.6905-1.6913	0.003-0.0047	0.0020-0.0200	NA	NA	NA
2008	3.8	L	①	0.0010-0.0040	0.0010-0.0020	NA	NA	NA
	4.0	X	1.6905-1.6913	0.003-0.0047	0.0020-0.0200	NA	NA	NA

NA: Information not available

① No 1: 1.997-1.999
No 2: 1.9809-1.9829
No 3: 1.9659-1.9679
No 4: 1.9499-1.9520

22043_PACI_C0013

CRANKSHAFT AND CONNECTING ROD SPECIFICATIONS

All measurements are given in inches.

Year	Engine Displacement Liters (VIN)	Crankshaft Main Brg. Journal Dia.	Crankshaft Main Brg. Oil Clearance	Crankshaft Shaft End-play	Crankshaft Thrust on No.	Connecting Rod Journal Diameter	Connecting Rod Oil Clearance	Connecting Rod Side Clearance
2005	3.5 (4)	2.5190-2.5200	0.0004-0.0022	0.0040-0.0120	2	2.2830-2.2840	0.0008-0.0034	0.0050-0.0150
	3.8 (L)	2.5194-2.5202	0.0005-0.0022	0.0036-0.0095	2	2.2827-2.2837	0.017-0.020	0.005-0.0130
2006	3.8 (L)	2.5194-2.5202	0.0005-0.0022	0.0036-0.0095	2	2.2827-2.2837	0.017-0.020	0.005-0.0130
	3.8 (L)	2.5194-2.5202	0.0005-0.0022	0.0036-0.0095	2	2.2827-2.2837	0.017-0.020	0.005-0.0130
2007	3.8 (L)	2.5194-2.5202	0.0005-0.0022	0.0036-0.0095	2	2.2827-2.2837	0.017-0.020	0.005-0.0130
	4.0 (X)	2.7170-2.7160	0.0013-0.0024	0.0020-0.0100	2	2.2828-2.2835	0.0009-0.0021	NA
2008	3.5 (4)	2.5190-2.5200	0.0004-0.0022	0.0040-0.0120	2	2.2830-2.2840	0.0008-0.0034	0.0050-0.0150
	4.0 (X)	2.7170-2.7160	0.0013-0.0024	0.0020-0.0100	2	2.2828-2.2835	0.0009-0.0021	NA

NA: Not Available

22043_PACI_C0006

PISTON AND RING SPECIFICATIONS

All measurements are given in inches.

Year	Engine Displacement Liters (VIN)	Piston Clearance	Ring Gap Top Compression	Ring Gap Bottom Compression	Ring Gap Oil Control	Ring Side Clearance Top Compression	Ring Side Clearance Bottom Compression	Ring Side Clearance Oil Control
2005	3.5 (4)	0.0003-0.0018	0.008-0.014	0.0091-0.0197	0.010-0.030	0.0016-0.0031	0.0016-0.0031	0.0015-0.0073
	3.8 (L)	0.0002-0.0015	0.007-0.0150	0.011-0.0220	0.009-0.0300	0.0012-0.0027	0.0016-0.0033	0.0015-0.0078
2006	3.5 (4)	0.0003-0.0018	0.008-0.014	0.0091-0.0197	0.010-0.030	0.0016-0.0031	0.0016-0.0031	0.0015-0.0073
	3.8 (L)	0.0002-0.0015	0.007-0.0150	0.011-0.0220	0.009-0.0300	0.0012-0.0027	0.0016-0.0033	0.0015-0.0078
2007	3.8 (L)	0.0002-0.0015	0.007-0.0150	0.011-0.0220	0.009-0.0300	0.0012-0.0027	0.0016-0.0033	0.0015-0.0078
	4.0 (X)	0.0020-0.0006	0.008-0.014	0.0078-0.0157	0.010-0.030	0.0016-0.0031	0.0016-0.0031	0.0015-0.0073
2008	3.8 (L)	0.0002-0.0015	0.007-0.0150	0.011-0.0220	0.009-0.0300	0.0012-0.0027	0.0016-0.0033	0.0015-0.0078
	4.0 (X)	0.0020-0.0006	0.008-0.014	0.0078-0.0157	0.010-0.030	0.0016-0.0031	0.0016-0.0031	0.0015-0.0073

22043_PACI_C0007

TORQUE SPECIFICATIONS

All readings in ft. lbs.

Year	Engine Displacement Liters (VIN)	Cylinder Head Bolts	Main Bearing Bolts	Rod Bearing Bolts	Crankshaft Damper Bolts	Flywheel Bolts	Manifold Intake	Manifold Exhaust	Spark Plugs	Oil Pan Drain Plug
2005	3.5 (4)	①	②	③	70	70	④	⑤	20	20
	3.8 (L)	⑥	⑦	⑧	40	65	⑨	⑩	20	20
2006	3.5 (4)	①	②	③	70	70	④	⑤	20	20
	3.8 (L)	⑥	⑦	⑧	40	65	⑨	⑩	20	20
2007	3.8 (L)	⑥	⑦	⑧	40	65	⑨	⑩	20	20
	4.0 (X)	⑥	NA	⑪	70	70	⑫	⑬	20	20
2008	3.8 (L)	⑥	⑦	⑧	40	65	⑨	⑩	20	20
	4.0 (X)	⑥	NA	⑪	70	70	⑫	⑬	20	20

NA: Not Available

① Step 1: 45 ft. lbs.
Step 2: 65 ft. lbs.
Step 3: 65 ft. lbs.
Step 4: Plus 1/4 turn
Final torque should be over 90 ft. lbs.

② Main cap inside bolts: 15 ft. lbs. plus 1/4 turn
Main cap outside bolts: 20 ft. lbs. plus 1/4 turn
Main cap tie bolts: 250 inch lbs.

③ Step 1: 20 ft. lbs.
Step 2: Plus 1/4 turn

④ Upper 105 inch lbs.
Lower 250 inch lbs.

⑤ 200 inch lbs.

⑥ Step 1: 45 ft. lbs.
Step 2: 65 ft. lbs.
Step 3: 65 ft. lbs.
Step 4: Plus 90 degrees

⑦ Step 1: 30 ft. lbs.
Step 2: Plus 90 degrees

⑧ Step 1: 40 ft. lbs.
Step 2: Plus 90 degrees

⑨ Lower manifold: Step 1: 10 inch lbs.
Step 2: 200 inch lbs.
Step 3: 200 inch lbs.
Upper manifold: 105 inch lbs.

⑩ Refer to procedure for torque sequence and specs

⑪ Step 1: 20 ft. lbs.
Step 2: Plus 90 degrees

⑫ Lower 250 inch lbs.
Upper 105 inch lbs.

⑬ 250 inch lbs.

22043_PACI_C0008

WHEEL ALIGNMENT

Year	Model		Caster Range (+/-Deg.)	Caster Preferred Setting (Deg.)	Camber Range (+/-Deg.)	Camber Preferred Setting (Deg.)	Toe-in (in.)
2005	Pacifica	F	+4.00 to + 5.00	+ 4.50	-0.60 to +0.20	-0.20	0.10 +/- 0.20
		R	—	—	-0.90 to +0.10	-0.40	0.10 +/- 0.30
2006	Pacifica	F	+4.00 to + 5.00	+ 4.50	-0.60 to +0.20	-0.20	0.10 +/- 0.20
		R	—	—	-0.90 to +0.10	-0.40	0.10 +/- 0.30
2007	Pacifica	F	+4.00 to + 5.00	+ 4.50	-0.60 to +0.20	-0.20	0.10 +/- 0.20
		R	—	—	-0.90 to +0.10	-0.40	0.10 +/- 0.30
2008	Pacifica	F	+4.00 to + 5.00	+ 4.50	-0.60 to +0.20	-0.20	0.10 +/- 0.20
		R	—	—	-0.90 to +0.10	-0.40	0.10 +/- 0.30

22043_PACI_C0009

TIRE, WHEEL AND BALL JOINT SPECIFICATIONS

Year	Model	OEM Tires Standard	OEM Tires Optional	Tire Pressures (psi) Front	Tire Pressures (psi) Rear	Wheel Size	Ball Joint Inspection	Lug Nuts (ft. lbs.)
2005	Pacifica	P235/65/R17	None	①	①	7-JJ	②	100
2006	Pacifica	P235/65/R17	None	①	①	7-JJ	②	100
2007	Pacifica	P235/65/R17	None	①	①	7-JJ	②	100
2008	Pacifica	P235/65/R17	None	①	①	7-JJ	②	100

OEM: Original Equipment Manufacturer

PSI: Pounds Per Square Inch

① Refer to driver's door opening (pillar B) or rear surface of the driver's door for specification.

② Do not lift vehicle. Grasp the grease fitting and attempt to move or rotate. Replace if any movement is found.

22043_PACI_C0010

BRAKE SPECIFICATIONS

All measurements in inches unless noted

Year	Model		Brake Disc Original Thickness	Brake Disc Minimum Thickness	Brake Disc Maximum Runout	Brake Drum Diameter Original Inside Diameter	Brake Drum Diameter Max. Wear Limit	Brake Drum Diameter Maximum Machine Diameter	Minimum Lining Thickness	Brake Caliper Mounting Bolts (ft. lbs.)
2005	Pacifica	F	1.107	1.040	0.0014	—	—	—	0.250	32
		R	0.556	0.492	0.0055	—	—	—	0.280	17
2006	Pacifica	F	1.107	1.040	0.0014	—	—	—	0.250	32
		R	0.556	0.492	0.0055	—	—	—	0.280	17
2007	Pacifica	F	1.107	1.040	0.0014	—	—	—	0.250	32
		R	0.556	0.492	0.0055	—	—	—	0.280	17
2008	Pacifica	F	1.107	1.040	0.0014	—	—	—	0.250	32
		R	0.556	0.492	0.0055	—	—	—	0.280	17

F: Front

R: Rear

22043_PACI_C0011

SCHEDULED MAINTENANCE INTERVALS
Chrysler—Pacifica

TO BE SERVICED	TYPE OF SERVICE	VEHICLE MILEAGE INTERVAL (x1000)												
		7.5	15	22.5	30	37.5	45	52.5	60	67.5	75	82.5	90	97.5
Engine oil & filter	R	✓	✓	✓	✓	✓	✓	✓	✓	✓	✓	✓	✓	✓
Exhaust system	S/I	✓	✓	✓	✓	✓	✓	✓	✓	✓	✓	✓	✓	✓
Brake hoses	S/I	✓	✓	✓	✓	✓	✓	✓	✓	✓	✓	✓	✓	✓
CV joints & front suspension components	S/I	✓	✓	✓	✓	✓	✓	✓	✓	✓	✓	✓	✓	✓
Rotate tires	S/I	✓	✓	✓	✓	✓	✓	✓	✓	✓	✓	✓	✓	✓
Coolant level, hoses & clamps	S/I	✓	✓	✓	✓	✓	✓	✓	✓	✓	✓	✓	✓	✓
Accessory drive belts	S/I		✓		✓		✓		✓		✓		✓	
Brake linings	S/I		✓	✓				✓	✓				✓	
Spark plugs	R				✓				✓				✓	
Air filter element	R				✓				✓				✓	
Lubricate steering linkage & tie rod ends	S/I				✓				✓				✓	
Engine coolant	R						✓				✓			
PCV valve	S/I								✓				✓	
Ignition cables	R								✓					
Camshaft timing belt	R								✓					

R: Replace S/I: Service or Inspect

FREQUENT OPERATION MAINTENANCE (SEVERE SERVICE)

If a vehicle is operated under any of the following conditions it is considered severe service:

- Extremely dusty areas

- 50% or more of the vehicle operation is in 32°C (90°F) or higher temperatures, or constant operation in temperatures below 0°C (32°F)

Prolonged idling (vehicle operation in stop and go traffic)

- Frequent short running periods (engine does not warm to normal operating temperatures)

- Police, taxi, delivery usage or trailer towing usage

CV joints & front suspension components: check every 3000 miles

Oil & oil filter change: change every 3000 miles

Rotate tires: every 3000 miles

Brake linings: check every 9000 miles

Air filter element: change every 15,000 miles

Automatic transaxle fluid: change every 15,000 miles

Differential fluid: change every 15,000 miles

Tie rod ends & steering linkage: lubricate every 15,000 miles

PCV valve: check every 30,000 miles

22043_PACI_C0012

PRECAUTIONS

Before servicing any vehicle, please be sure to read all of the following precautions, which deal with personal safety, prevention of component damage, and important points to take into consideration when servicing a motor vehicle:

- Never open, service or drain the radiator or cooling system when the engine is hot; serious burns can occur from the steam and hot coolant.
- Observe all applicable safety precautions when working around fuel. Whenever servicing the fuel system, always work in a well-ventilated area. Do not allow fuel spray or vapors to come in contact with a spark, open flame, or excessive heat (a hot drop light, for example). Keep a dry chemical fire extinguisher near the work area. Always keep fuel in a container specifically designed for fuel storage; also, always properly seal fuel containers to avoid the possibility of fire or explosion. Refer to the additional fuel system precautions later in this section.
- Fuel injection systems often remain pressurized, even after the engine has been turned **OFF**. The fuel system pressure must be relieved before disconnecting any fuel lines. Failure to do so may result in fire and/or personal injury.
- Brake fluid often contains polyglycol ethers and polyglycols. Avoid contact with the eyes and wash your hands thoroughly after handling brake fluid. If you do get brake fluid in your eyes, flush your eyes with clean, running water for 15 minutes. If eye irritation persists, or if you have taken brake fluid internally, IMMEDIATELY seek medical assistance.
- The EPA warns that prolonged contact with used engine oil may cause a number of skin disorders, including cancer. You should make every effort to minimize your exposure to used engine oil. Protective gloves should be worn when changing oil. Wash your hands and any other exposed skin areas as soon as possible after exposure to used engine oil. Soap and water, or waterless hand cleaner should be used.
- All new vehicles are now equipped with an air bag system, often referred to as a Supplemental Restraint System (SRS) or Supplemental Inflatable Restraint (SIR) system. The system must be disabled before performing service on or around system components, steering column, instrument panel components, wiring and sensors. Failure to follow safety and disabling procedures could result in accidental air bag deployment, possible personal injury and unnecessary system repairs.
- Always wear safety goggles when working with, or around, the air bag system. When carrying a non-deployed air bag, be sure the bag and trim cover are pointed away from your body. When placing a non-deployed air bag on a work surface, always face the bag and trim cover upward, away from the surface. This will reduce the motion of the module if it is accidentally deployed. Refer to the additional air bag system precautions later in this section.
- Clean, high quality brake fluid from a sealed container is essential to the safe and proper operation of the brake system. You should always buy the correct type of brake fluid for your vehicle. If the brake fluid becomes contaminated, completely flush the system with new fluid. Never reuse any brake fluid. Any brake fluid that is removed from the system should be discarded. Also, do not allow any brake fluid to come in contact with a painted surface; it will damage the paint.
- Never operate the engine without the proper amount and type of engine oil; doing so WILL result in severe engine damage.
- Timing belt maintenance is extremely important. Many models utilize an interference-type, non-freewheeling engine. If the timing belt breaks, the valves in the cylinder head may strike the pistons, causing potentially serious (also time-consuming and expensive) engine damage. Refer to the maintenance interval charts for the recommended replacement interval for the timing belt, and to the timing belt section for belt replacement and inspection.
- Disconnecting the negative battery cable on some vehicles may interfere with the functions of the on-board computer system(s) and may require the computer to undergo a relearning process once the negative battery cable is reconnected.
- When servicing drum brakes, only disassemble and assemble one side at a time, leaving the remaining side intact for reference.
- Only an MVAC-trained, EPA-certified automotive technician should service the air conditioning system or its components.

BRAKES

ANTI-LOCK BRAKE SYSTEM (ABS)

GENERAL INFORMATION

PRECAUTIONS

- Certain components within the ABS system are not intended to be serviced or repaired individually.
- Do not use rubber hoses or other parts not specifically specified for and ABS system. When using repair kits, replace all parts included in the kit. Partial or incorrect repair may lead to functional problems and require the replacement of components.
- Lubricate rubber parts with clean, fresh brake fluid to ease assembly. Do not use shop air to clean parts; damage to rubber components may result.
- Use only DOT 3 brake fluid from an unopened container.
- If any hydraulic component or line is removed or replaced, it may be necessary to bleed the entire system.
- A clean repair area is essential. Always clean the reservoir and cap thoroughly before removing the cap. The slightest amount of dirt in the fluid may plug an orifice and impair the system function. Perform repairs after components have been thoroughly cleaned; use only denatured alcohol to clean components. Do not allow ABS components to come into contact with any substance containing mineral oil; this includes used shop rags.
- The Anti-Lock control unit is a microprocessor similar to other computer units in the vehicle. Ensure that the ignition switch is **OFF** before removing or installing controller harnesses. Avoid static electricity discharge at or near the controller.
- If any arc welding is to be done on the vehicle, the control unit should be unplugged before welding operations begin.

SPEED SENSORS

REMOVAL & INSTALLATION

Front

See Figures 1 and 2.

1. Access and remove front brake rotor.
2. Disconnect vehicle wiring harness from wheel speed sensor connector.
3. Unclip wheel speed sensor connector from frame rail outer reinforcement, then open routing clip on reinforcement and remove cable.
4. Remove screw fastening wheel speed sensor routing bracket to strut assembly.

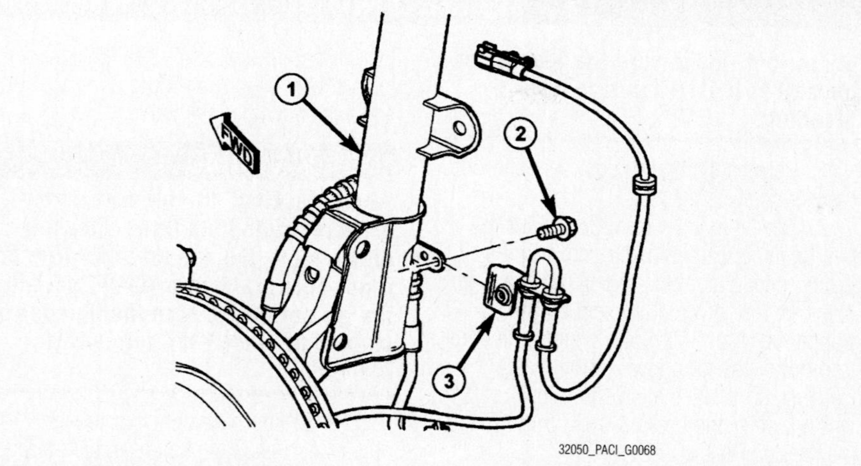

Fig. 1 The wheel speed sensor routing bracket (3) is mounted to the strut (1) with a screw (2)

5. Open routing clip at knuckle and remove wheel speed sensor cable.

⁂ WARNING

Before removal, clean the area around sensor head to help prevent contaminants from entering bearing when sensor head is removed.

6. Remove screw fastening speed sensor head to hub and bearing.
7. Remove wheel speed sensor from hub and bearing.

To install:

8. Apply bearing grease (supplied with part) to sensor head shaft and O-ring.

⁂ WARNING

Make sure that the sensor mounting surface on bearing is clean before sensor installation.

9. Push sensor head into mounting hole in hub and bearing and align mounting screw hole.
10. Install NEW mounting screw. Tighten mounting screw to 15 ft. lbs. (20 Nm).
11. Place wheel speed sensor cable grommet into routing clip at knuckle and close clip.
12. Attach wheel speed sensor routing bracket to strut assembly.
13. Tighten screw to 115 inch lbs. (13 Nm).
14. Clip wheel speed sensor connector and routing clip to frame rail outer reinforcement.
15. Connect vehicle wiring harness to wheel speed sensor connector.
16. Install brake rotor as well as all components necessary to access it.
17. Verify that wheel speed sensor cable is properly routed and not coming into contact with rotor or other moving parts.
18. Road test vehicle to ensure proper operation of the base brakes and ABS.

Rear

See Figure 3.

1. Access and remove rear hub and bearing from vehicle.

⁂ WARNING

Prior to removal, clean area around sensor head to help prevent contaminants from entering bearing when sensor head is removed.

2. Remove screw fastening speed sensor head to hub and bearing.
3. Remove wheel speed sensor from hub and bearing.

To install:

4. Apply bearing grease (supplied with part) to sensor head shaft and O-ring.

⁂ WARNING

Make sure that sensor mounting surface on bearing is clean before sensor installation.

5. Push sensor head into mounting hole in hub and bearing and align mounting screw hole.
6. Install NEW mounting screw. Tighten mounting screw to 15 ft. lbs. (20 Nm).
7. Install hub and bearing with wheel speed sensor as well as all components necessary to access it.
8. Road test vehicle to ensure proper operation of the base brakes and ABS.

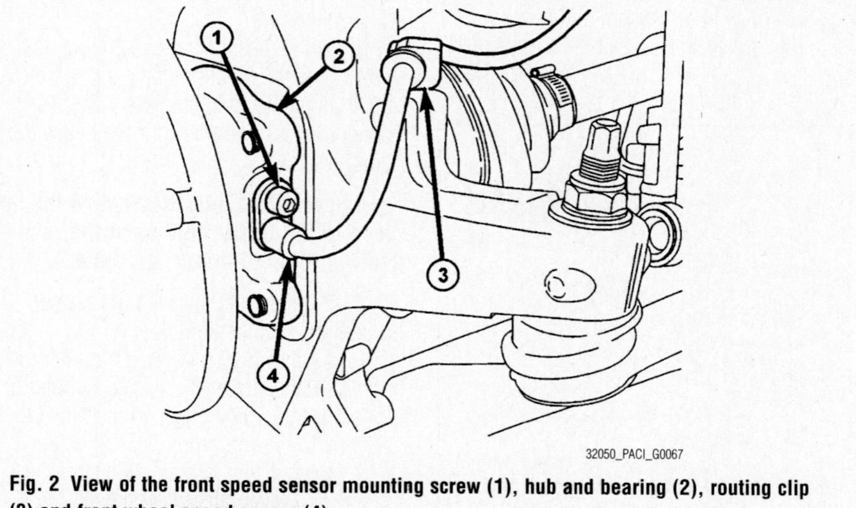

Fig. 2 View of the front speed sensor mounting screw (1), hub and bearing (2), routing clip (3) and front wheel speed sensor (4)

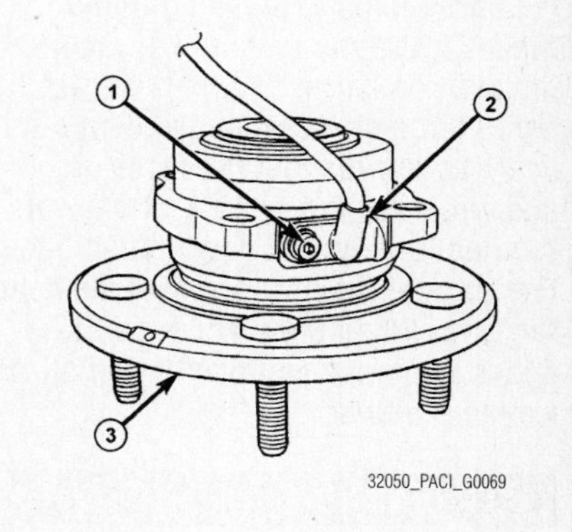

Fig. 3 Remove the retaining screw (1), the remove the rear wheel speed sensor (2) from the hub and bearing (3)

BLEEDING PROCEDURE

BLEEDING PROCEDURE

➡This bleeding procedure is only for the vehicle's base brakes hydraulic system. For bleeding the antilock brakes hydraulic system, refer to the ABS section.

WARNING

Before removing the master cylinder cover, thoroughly clean the cover and master cylinder fluid reservoir to prevent dirt and other foreign matter from dropping into the master cylinder fluid reservoir.

The following wheel sequence should be used when bleeding the brake hydraulic system. The use of this wheel sequence will ensure adequate removal of all trapped air from the brake hydraulic system.

- Left Rear Wheel
- Right Front Wheel
- Right Rear Wheel
- Left Front Wheel

➡When bleeding the brake system, some air may be trapped in the brake lines or valves far upstream, as much as ten feet from the bleeder screw. Therefore, it is essential to have a fast flow of a large volume of brake fluid when bleeding the brakes to ensure all the air gets out.

The brakes may be manually bled or pressure bled. Refer to the appropriate following procedure.

Manual Bleeding Procedure

➡Correct manual bleeding of the brakes hydraulic system will require the aid of a helper. Pump the brake pedal three or four times and hold it down before the bleeder screw is opened. Push the brake pedal toward the floor and hold it down. Then open the left rear bleeder screw at least one full turn. When the bleeder screw opens the brake pedal will drop all the way to the floor.

WARNING

"Just cracking" the bleeder screw often restricts fluid flow, allowing only a slow, weak fluid discharge of fluid. This practice will NOT get all the air out. Make sure the bleeder is opened at least 1 full turn when bleeding.

1. Release the brake pedal only after the bleeder screw is closed.
2. Repeat steps 1 through 3, four or five times, at each bleeder screw in the proper sequence. This should pass a sufficient amount of fluid to expel all the trapped air from the brake system. Be sure to monitor the fluid level in the master cylinder, so it stays at a proper level so air will not enter the brake system through the master cylinder.
3. Check pedal travel. If pedal travel is excessive or has not been improved, enough fluid has not passed through the system to expel all the trapped air. Continue to bleed system as necessary.
4. Test drive vehicle to be sure brakes are operating correctly and that pedal is solid.

Pressure Bleeding Procedure

See Figure 4.

WARNING

Use bleeder tank Special Tool C-3496-B or equivalent with Adapter, Special Tool 6921, to pressurize the hydraulic system for bleeding.

1. Follow pressure bleeder manufacturer's instructions for use of pressure bleeding equipment.
2. Install the Adapter Master Cylinder Pressure Bleed Cap, Special Tool 6921 on the fluid reservoir of the master cylinder. Attach the fluid hose from the pressure bleeder to the fitting on Special Tool 6921.
3. Attach a clear plastic hose to the bleeder screw at one wheel and feed the hose into a clear jar containing fresh brake fluid.

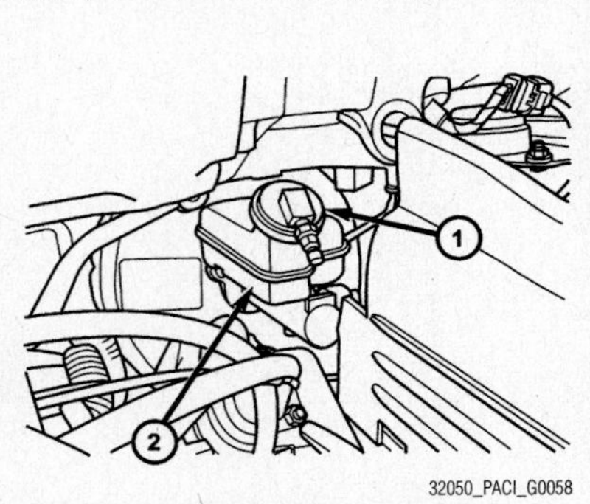

Fig. 4 Special tool (1) installed on the master cylinder (2) for pressure bleeding

4. Open the left rear wheel bleeder screw at least one full turn or more to obtain an adequate flow of brake fluid.

WARNING

"Just cracking" the bleeder screw often restricts fluid flow, allowing only a slow, weak fluid discharge of fluid. This practice will NOT get all the air out. Make sure the bleeder is opened at least 1 full turn when bleeding.

5. After approximately four to eight ounces of brake fluid has been bled through the hydraulic system, and an air-free flow is maintained in the hose and jar, a good bleed of the hydraulic system has been obtained.
6. Repeat the procedure at all the other remaining bleeder screws.
7. Check pedal travel. If pedal travel is excessive or has not been improved, enough fluid has not passed through the system to expel all the trapped air. Be sure to monitor the fluid level in the pressure bleeder, so it stays at a proper level so air will not enter the brake system through the master cylinder.
8. Test drive vehicle to be sure brakes are operating correctly and that pedal is solid.

MASTER CYLINDER BLEEDING

1. Clamp the master cylinder in a vise.

➡ Only clamp the master cylinder by its mounting flange. Do not clamp the piston rod, reservoir, seal or body.

2. Thread the bleeder tube, tool 8358-1 or equivalent into each master cylinder outlet port.
3. Tighten each tube to 120 inch lbs.
4. Flex the bleeder tubes and put the open ends into the fluid reservoir, as far down as possible to keep them below the fluid level.

➡Be sure the tubes stay below the surface of the brake fluid once the reservoir is filled to the proper level.

5. Fill the reservoir with the proper grade and type brake fluid.
6. Use a wooden dowel as a push rod and slowly depress the master cylinder pistons. Release the pressure and allow the pistons to return to their normal detent.
7. Repeat several times. Be sure the brake fluid level remains constant.
8. Remove the bleeder tool from the

master cylinder. Plug the outlet ports. Install the fill cap.

9. Remove the master cylinder from the vise. Install the master cylinder.

BLEEDING THE ABS SYSTEM

The base brake's hydraulic system must be bled anytime air enters the hydraulic system. The ABS though, particularly the ICU (HCU), should only need to be bled when the HCU is replaced or removed from the vehicle. The ABS must always be bled anytime it is suspected that the HCU has ingested air. Under most circumstances that require the bleeding of the brakes hydraulic system, only the base brake hydraulic system needs to be bled.

When bleeding the ABS system, the following bleeding sequence must be followed to insure complete and adequate bleeding.

1. Make sure all hydraulic fluid lines are installed and properly torqued.
2. Connect a suitable scan tool to the Data Link Connector. The connector is located under the lower steering column cover to the left of the steering column.
3. Using the scan tool, check to make sure the CAB (MK25) or ABM (Mk25e) does not have any fault codes stored. If it does, clear them using the scan tool.

**** CAUTION**

When bleeding the brake system wear safety glasses. A clear bleed tube must be attached to the bleeder screws and submerged in a clear container filled part way with clean brake fluid. Direct the flow of brake fluid away from yourself and the painted surfaces of the vehicle. Brake fluid at high pressure may come out of the bleeder screws when opened.

4. Bleed the base brake system.
5. Using the scan tool, select ANTILOCK BRAKES, followed by MISCELLANEOUS, then BLEED BRAKES. Follow the instructions displayed. When the scan tool displays TEST COMPLETED, disconnect the scan tool and proceed.
6. Bleed the base brake system a second time. Check brake fluid level in the reservoir periodically to prevent emptying, causing air to enter the hydraulic system.
7. Fill the master cylinder reservoir to the full level.
8. Test drive the vehicle to be sure the brakes are operating correctly and that the brake pedal does not feel spongy.

BRAKES

FRONT DISC BRAKES

**** CAUTION**

Dust and dirt accumulating on brake parts during normal use may contain asbestos fibers from production or aftermarket brake linings. Breathing excessive concentrations of asbestos fibers can cause serious bodily harm. Exercise care when servicing brake parts. Do not sand or grind brake lining unless equipment used is designed to contain the dust residue. Do not clean brake parts with compressed air or by dry brushing. Cleaning should be done by dampening the brake components with a fine mist of water, then wiping the brake components clean with a dampened cloth. Dispose of cloth and all residue containing asbestos fibers in an impermeable container with the appropriate label. Follow practices prescribed by the Occupational Safety and Health Administration (OSHA) and the Environmental Protection Agency (EPA) for the handling, processing, and disposing of dust or debris that may contain asbestos fibers.

BRAKE CALIPER

REMOVAL & INSTALLATION

See Figures 5 through 7.

➡Using a brake pedal holding tool, depress the brake pedal past its first inch of travel and hold it in this position. This will isolate the master cylinder from the hydraulic brake system and will not allow brake fluid to drain out of the reservoir while the brake lines are open.

1. Before servicing the vehicle, refer to the precautions in the beginning of this section.
2. Remove or disconnect the following:
   - Negative battery cable
   - Front wheels
   - Banjo bolt retaining the brake hose to the caliper. Be sure to plug the end of the brake hose or cover it with a plastic bag to prevent contamination from entering the hydraulic system.

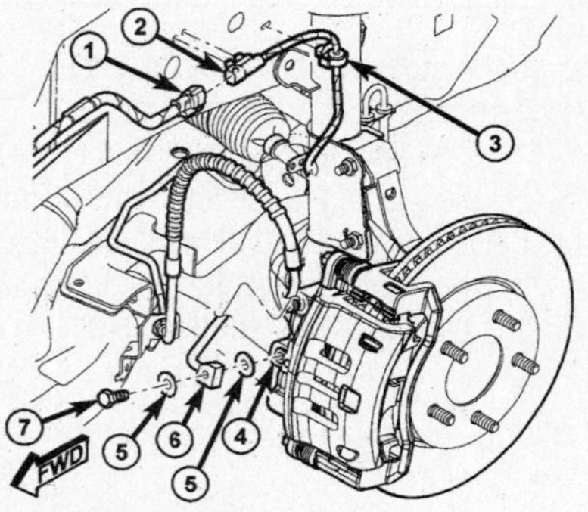

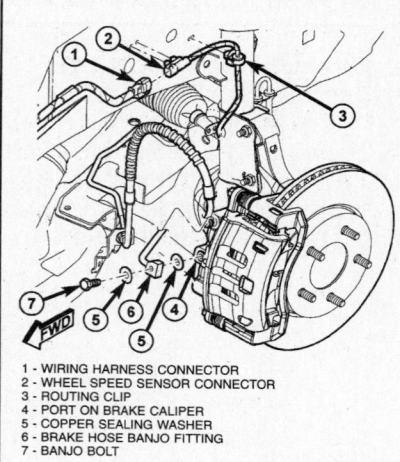

1 - WIRING HARNESS CONNECTOR
2 - WHEEL SPEED SENSOR CONNECTOR
3 - ROUTING CLIP
4 - PORT ON BRAKE CALIPER
5 - COPPER SEALING WASHER
6 - BRAKE HOSE BANJO FITTING
7 - BANJO BOLT

23990G57

Fig. 5 Exploded view of the banjo bolt and related components

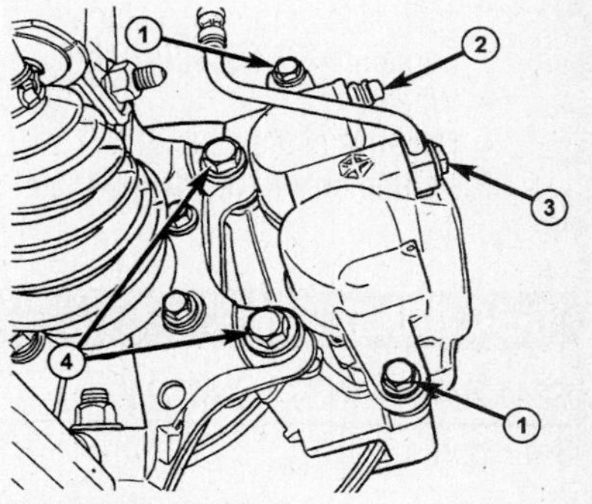

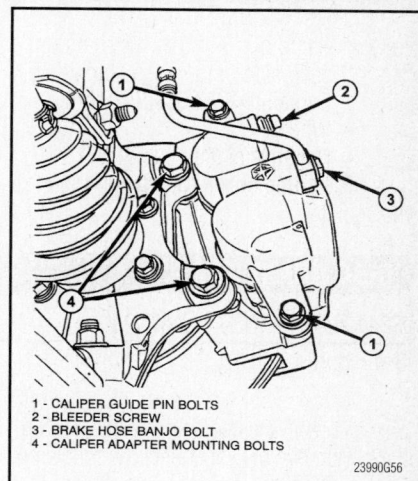

1 - CALIPER GUIDE PIN BOLTS
2 - BLEEDER SCREW
3 - BRAKE HOSE BANJO BOLT
4 - CALIPER ADAPTER MOUNTING BOLTS

23990G56

Fig. 6 Exploded view of the caliper and adapter mounting

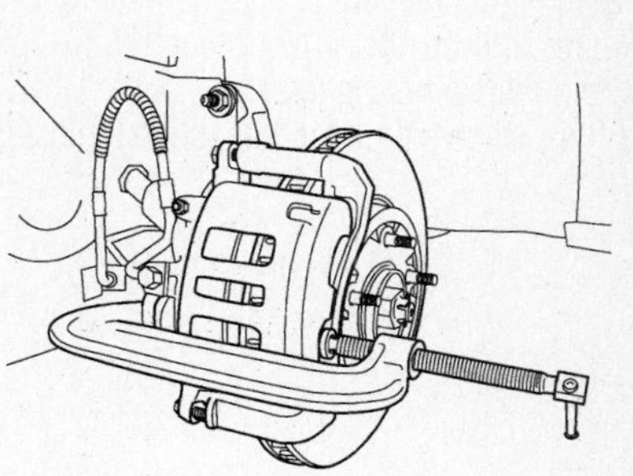

23990G55

Fig. 7 Place a C-clamp over the caliper as illustrated

3. Place a C-clamp over the caliper as illustrated, place a screw drive head against the outboard pad and hook against the rear of the caliper. Slowly tighten the screw drive and retract the caliper pistons into their bores and breaking the outboard brake pad from the caliper fingers.

4. Once the pad is free, slide the caliper in on the guides to provide clearance between the rotor and inboard pad.

5. Place an appropriate prytool through the center opening in the top of the caliper behind the inboard pad between the pistons using care not to contact the piston boots. Pry the pad to free it from the pistons.

6. Remove the two caliper guide pin bolts and caliper.

To install:

7. Completely compress the caliper pistons

8. Install or connect the following:

- Caliper and align the guide pin bolt holes with the guide pins. Install the pin bolts and tighten to 32 ft. lbs. (43 Nm).
- Banjo bolt with new washers on each side of the hose fitting and tighten to 35 ft. lbs. (47 Nm)
- Wheels
- Negative battery cable

9. Bleed the brake system and road test the vehicle.

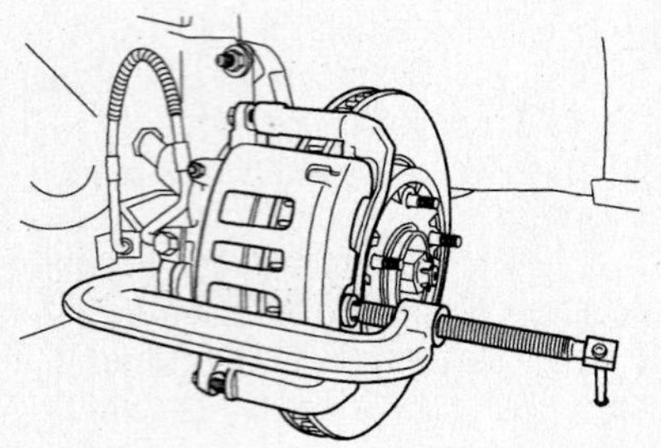

Fig. 8 Place a C-clamp over the caliper as illustrated

DISC BRAKE PADS

REMOVAL & INSTALLATION

See Figures 8 and 9.

1. Before servicing the vehicle, refer to the precautions in the beginning of this section.

2. Remove or disconnect the following:

- Negative battery cable
- Front wheels

3. Place a C-clamp over the caliper as illustrated, place a screw drive head against the outboard pad and hook against the rear of the caliper. Slowly tighten the screw drive and retract the caliper pistons into their bores and breaking the outboard brake pad from the caliper fingers.

4. Once the pad is free, slide the caliper in on the guides to provide clearance between the rotor and inboard pad.

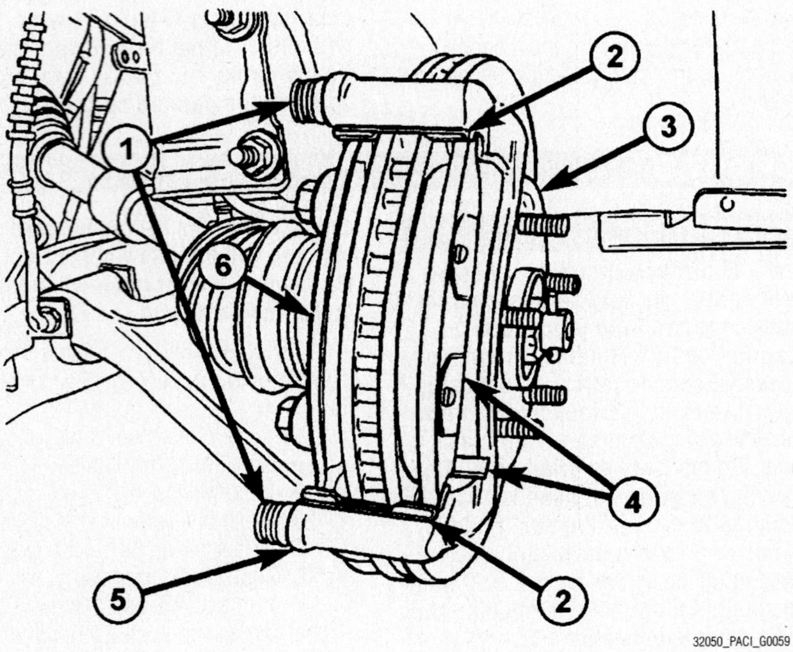

Fig. 9 View of the caliper guide pins and boots (1), anti-rattle clips (2), brake rotor (3), outboard pad (4), caliper adapter (5) and inboard pad (6)

5. Place an appropriate prytool through the center opening in the top of the caliper behind the inboard pad between the pistons using care not to contact the piston boots. Pry the pad to free it from the pistons.

6. Remove the two caliper guide pin bolts and position the caliper aside. Remove the brake pads.

To install:

7. Completely compress the caliper pistons

8. Install or connect the following:

- Brake pads with anti-rattle clips onto the adapter
- Caliper and align the guide pin bolt holes with the guide pins. Install the pin bolts and tighten to 32 ft. lbs. (43 Nm).
- Banjo bolt with new washers on each side of the hose fitting and tighten to 35 ft. lbs. (47 Nm)
- Wheels
- Negative battery cable

9. Check and adjust the brake system fluid level and road test the vehicle.

⁂ CAUTION

Dust and dirt accumulating on brake parts during normal use may contain asbestos fibers from production or aftermarket brake linings. Breathing excessive concentrations of asbestos fibers can cause serious bodily harm. Exercise care when servicing brake parts. Do not sand or grind brake lining unless equipment used is designed to contain the dust residue. Do not clean brake parts with compressed air or by dry brushing. Cleaning should be done by dampening the brake components with a fine mist of water, then wiping the brake components clean with a dampened cloth. Dispose of cloth and all residue containing asbestos fibers in an impermeable container with the appropriate label. Follow practices prescribed by the Occupational Safety and Health Administration (OSHA) and the Environmental Protection Agency (EPA) for the handling, processing, and disposing of dust or debris that may contain asbestos fibers.

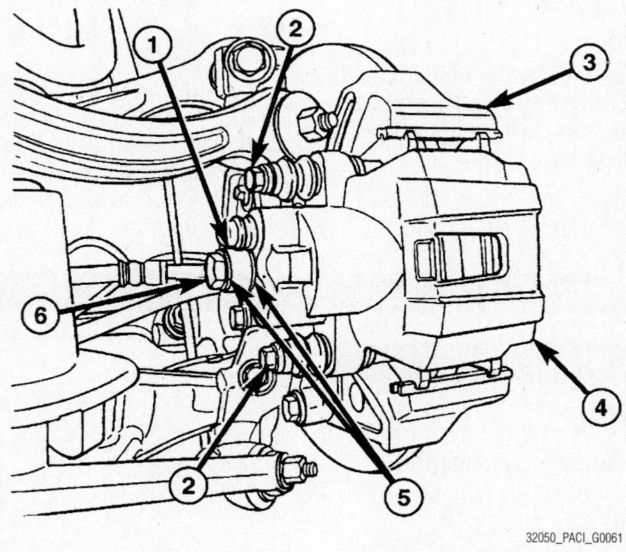

Fig. 10 Brake hose banjo fitting (1), caliper guide pin bolt (2), caliper adapter (3), caliper (4), copper seal washers (5) and banjo bolt (6)

BRAKE CALIPER

REMOVAL & INSTALLATION

See Figure 10.

➡Using a brake pedal holding tool, depress the brake pedal past its first inch of travel and hold it in this position. This will isolate the master cylinder from the hydraulic brake system and will not allow brake fluid to drain out of the reservoir while the brake lines are open.

1. Before servicing the vehicle, refer to the precautions in the beginning of this section.
2. Remove or disconnect the following:
   - Negative battery cable
   - Rear wheels
   - Banjo bolt retaining the brake hose to the caliper. Be sure to plug the end of the brake hose or cover it with a plastic bag to prevent contamination from entering the hydraulic system.
   - Caliper guide pin bolts
   - Caliper assembly from the brake adapter by rotating the bottom of the caliper away from the rotor, then lift the caliper with the pads away from the adapter abutment
   - Brake pads by pushing (outboard) or pulling (inboard) from the caliper fingers and piston

To install:

3. Completely compress the caliper piston.
4. Install or connect the following:
   - Inboard pad clip against the piston cavity and press the pad until the clip is seated making sure the pad backing plate is flush against the piston

➡The outboard pads are side oriented, make sure the spring clip is installed so it is positioned downwards when the caliper is installed.

   - Outboard pad making sure the locating pins are positioned against the ramps. Slide the pad onto the caliper and ensure the locating pins are squarely seated into the holes on the caliper and the pad is flush against the caliper fingers.
5. Make sure the abutment shims are in place on both slide abutments.
6. Retract the caliper guide pins to clear the caliper adapter bosses.
   - Brake caliper. Staring with the upper end, position the caliper and shoes over the rotor and align the outboard pad upper edge with the caliper slide abutment. Rotate the lower end of the caliper into position
   - Caliper guide pin bolts and tighten to 200 inch lbs. (23 Nm)
   - Banjo bolt with new washers on each side of the hose fitting and tighten to 35 ft. lbs. (47 Nm)
   - Wheels
   - Negative battery cable
7. Bleed the brake system and road test the vehicle.

DISC BRAKE PADS

REMOVAL & INSTALLATION

1. Before servicing the vehicle, refer to the precautions in the beginning of this section.
2. Remove or disconnect the following:
   - Negative battery cable
   - Rear wheels
   - Caliper guide pin bolts
   - Caliper assembly from the brake adapter by rotating the bottom of the caliper away from the rotor, then lift the caliper with the pads away from the adapter abutment
   - Brake pads by pushing (outboard) or pulling (inboard) from the caliper fingers and piston

To install:

3. Completely compress the caliper piston
4. Install or connect the following:

- Inboard pad clip against the piston cavity and press the pad until the clip is seated making sure the pad backing plate is flush against the piston

➡The outboard pads are side oriented. Make sure the spring clip is installed so it is positioned downwards when the caliper is installed.

- Outboard pad making sure the locating pins are positioned against the ramps. Slide the pad onto the caliper and ensure the locating pins are squarely seated into the holes on the caliper and the pad is flush against the caliper fingers.

5. Make sure the abutment shims are in place on both slide abutments.
6. Retract the caliper guide pins to clear the caliper adapter bosses.

- Brake caliper. Staring with the upper end, position the caliper and shoes over the rotor and align the outboard pad upper edge with the caliper slide abutment. Rotate the lower end of the caliper into position
- Caliper guide pin bolts and tighten to 200 inch lbs. (23 Nm)
- Wheels
- Negative battery cable

7. Check and adjust the brake system fluid level and road test the vehicle.

PARKING BRAKE CABLES

ADJUSTMENT

Automatic Adjuster Locking Out

See Figures 11 through 13.

1. Place an assistant inside passenger compartment with pin (pin punch or drill bit) to be used in Step 5.
2. Place parking brake lever in "released" position.
3. Raise and support vehicle.
4. Grasp exposed section of parking brake cable at cable connector (front-to-right rear cable) and pull outward on front cable. Pull on cable until it stops and hold it in this position.
5. Have assistant inside passenger compartment insert pin punch (locking pin or drill bit) into hole in lever and foot pedal, past tang on adjuster mechanism, and through hole in backing plate of lever. Hold pin in place. This pin will lock automatic adjuster spring out once the person under the vehicle releases grasp on cables and will allow safe removal of cables and lever as necessary.

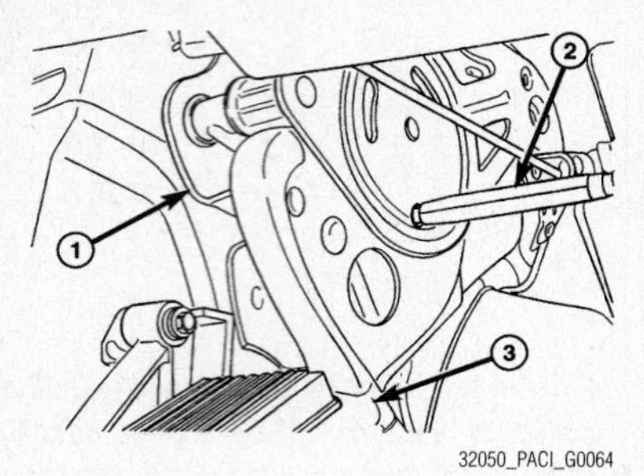

Fig. 12 Have assistant inside passenger compartment insert pin punch (2) into hole in lever (1) and foot pedal (3)

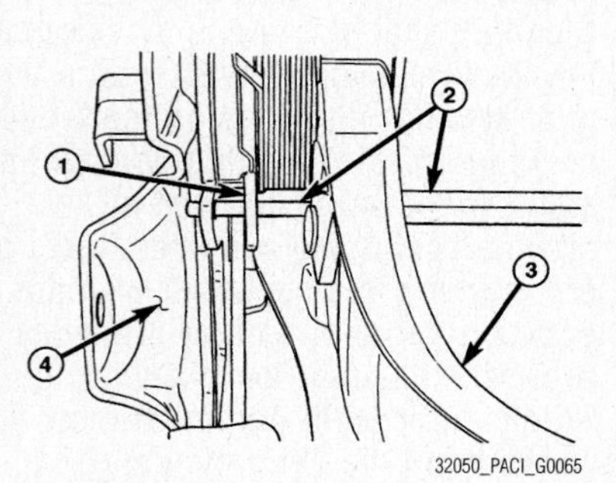

Fig. 13 View of the tang (1), pin punch (2), foot pedal (3) and backing plate (4)

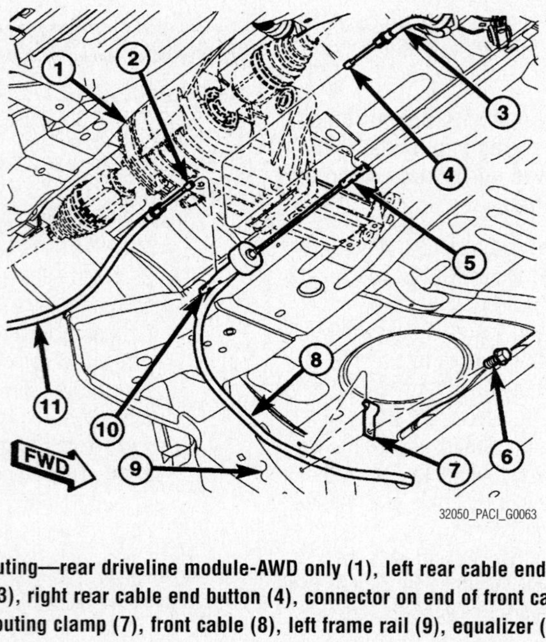

Fig. 11 Cable routing—rear driveline module-AWD only (1), left rear cable end button (2), right rear cable (3), right rear cable end button (4), connector on end of front cable (5), screw (6), front cable routing clamp (7), front cable (8), left frame rail (9), equalizer (10) and left rear cable (11)

⁂ CAUTION

Do not release the automatic adjuster lockout device unless the parking brake cables and equalizer are connected. Keep hands out of automatic adjuster sector and pawl area. Failure to observe caution in handling this mechanism could lead to serious injury.

6. Release grasp on cable underneath vehicle.
7. Lower vehicle and remove assistant from passenger compartment.

Automatic Adjuster Unlocking

See Figure 12.

1. Assure that all cables are connected properly.

⁂ CAUTION

Do not release the automatic adjuster lockout device unless the parking brake cables and equalizer are connected. Keep hands out of automatic adjuster sector and pawl area. Failure to observe caution in handling

this mechanism could lead to serious injury.

2. Keeping hands clear of automatic adjuster sector and pawl area, firmly grasp pin punch (drill bit, or locking pin if a new lever has been installed) installed in lever mechanism, then quickly remove it from parking brake lever mechanism. This action allows parking brake lever mechanism to automatically take up any slack.
3. Cycle parking brake lever once to position parking brake cables, then return lever its released position.
4. Raise vehicle far enough for rear wheels to clear floor.
5. Check rear wheels of vehicle. They should rotate freely without dragging with lever in released position.
6. Lower vehicle.

PARKING BRAKE SHOES

REMOVAL & INSTALLATION

See Figure 14.

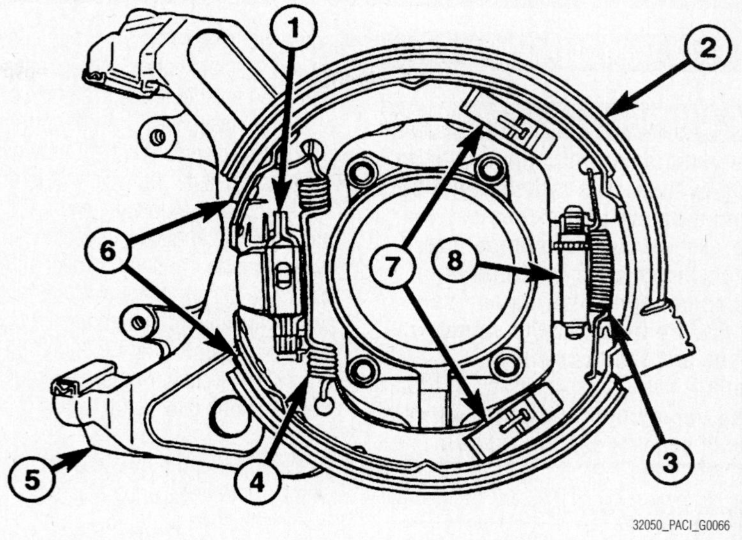

Fig. 14 View of the actuator (1), support (2), adjuster spring (3), return spring (4), caliper adapter (5), shoes (6), hold-down clips and pins (7) and adjuster (8)

➡The following procedure may be used to remove shoes on either side of the vehicle.

1. Lock out automatic adjuster in parking brake lever.
2. Raise and support vehicle.
3. Access and remove rear hub and bearing.
4. Remove parking brake cable bolt at knuckle.
5. Completely back off parking brake shoe adjustment.
6. Remove parking brake shoe adjuster spring.
7. Remove shoe adjuster.
8. Remove upper brake shoe hold-down clip and pin.
9. Remove lower brake shoe hold-down clip and pin.
10. Remove upper and lower shoes with return spring from shoe actuator.
11. Remove return spring from shoes.

To install:

➡The following procedure may be used to install shoes on either side of the vehicle.

12. Install return spring between upper and lower shoes.

➡Before installing shoes on actuator, make sure actuator hooked to rear cable is positioned with word "UP" facing outward.

13. Install upper and lower shoes with return spring on shoe actuator located on parking brake cable.
14. Install lower brake shoe hold-down pin through rear of support and lower shoe, then install hold-down clip.
15. Install upper brake shoe hold-down pin through rear of support and upper shoe, then install hold-down clip.
16. Install shoe adjuster. Place end of adjuster with star wheel upward.
17. Install parking brake shoe adjuster spring.
18. Install bolt securing parking brake cable to knuckle and tighten bolt to 21 ft. lbs. (28 Nm).
19. Using Brake Shoe Gauge, Special Tool C-3919, or equivalent, measure inside diameter of parking brake drum portion of rotor.
20. Place Gauge over parking brake shoes at widest point.
21. Using adjuster star wheel, adjust parking brake shoes until linings on both park brake shoes just touch jaws on gauge. This will give a good preliminary adjustment of parking brake shoes, before a final adjustment is made at end of this procedure.
22. Install hub and bearing with wheel speed sensor as well as all components necessary to access it.
23. Lower vehicle.
24. Unlock automatic adjuster in parking brake lever.
25. Perform final adjustment of parking brake shoes.

ADJUSTMENT

1. Place parking brake lever in "full released" position.
2. Raise and support vehicle.
3. Remove plug in parking brake shoe support to access adjuster star-wheel.
4. Through the access hole, rotate the adjuster star wheel in the following direction to expand the shoes outward against the drum:
   a. Left brake – Rotate star-wheel toward rear of vehicle.
   b. Right brake – Rotate star-wheel toward front of vehicle.
5. Using an appropriate tool, turn adjuster star wheel until wheel will not rotate (dead lock).
6. Back off adjuster six detents (teeth).
7. Rotate wheel, checking for light drag. If drag is too heavy, continue to back off adjuster one detent at a time until light drag is present. Do not back off star-wheel more than 17 detents from wheel lock.
8. Install access plug.
9. Adjust opposite wheel parking brake shoes using same method.
10. Lower vehicle.
11. Apply and release parking brake lever once to ensure proper operation of parking brakes.

GENERAL INFORMATION

CAUTION

These vehicles are equipped with an air bag system. The system must be disarmed before performing service on, or around, system components, the steering column, instrument panel components, wiring and sensors. Failure to follow the safety precautions and the disarming procedure could result in accidental air bag deployment, possible injury and unnecessary system repairs.

SERVICE PRECAUTIONS

Disconnect and isolate the battery negative cable before beginning any airbag system component diagnosis, testing, removal, or installation procedures. Allow system capacitor to discharge for two minutes before beginning any component service. This will disable the airbag system. Failure to disable the airbag system may result in accidental airbag deployment, personal injury, or death.

Do not place an intact undeployed airbag face down on a solid surface. The airbag will propel into the air if accidentally deployed and may result in personal injury or death.

When carrying or handling an undeployed airbag, the trim side (face) of the airbag should be pointing towards the body to minimize possibility of injury if accidental deployment occurs. Failure to do this may result in personal injury or death.

Replace airbag system components with OEM replacement parts. Substitute parts may appear interchangeable, but internal differences may result in inferior occupant protection. Failure to do so may result in occupant personal injury or death.

Wear safety glasses, rubber gloves, and long sleeved clothing when cleaning powder residue from vehicle after an airbag deployment. Powder residue emitted from a deployed airbag can cause skin irritation. Flush affected area with cool water if irritation is experienced. If nasal or throat irritation is experienced, exit the vehicle for fresh air until the irritation ceases. If irritation continues, see a physician.

Do not use a replacement airbag that is not in the original packaging. This may result in improper deployment, personal injury, or death.

The factory installed fasteners, screws and bolts used to fasten airbag components have a special coating and are specifically designed for the airbag system. Do not use substitute fasteners. Use only original equipment fasteners listed in the parts catalog when fastener replacement is required.

During, and following, any child restraint anchor service, due to impact event or vehicle repair, carefully inspect all mounting hardware, tether straps, and anchors for proper installation, operation, or damage. If a child restraint anchor is found damaged in any way, the anchor must be replaced. Failure to do this may result in personal injury or death.

Deployed and non-deployed airbags may or may not have live pyrotechnic material within the airbag inflator.

Do not dispose of driver/passenger/curtain airbags or seat belt tensioners unless you are sure of complete deployment. Refer to the Hazardous Substance Control System for proper disposal.

Dispose of deployed airbags and tensioners consistent with state, provincial, local, and federal regulations.

After any airbag component testing or service, do not connect the battery negative cable. Personal injury or death may result if the system test is not performed first.

If the vehicle is equipped with the Occupant Classification System (OCS), do not connect the battery negative cable before performing the OCS Verification Test using the scan tool and the appropriate diagnostic information. Personal injury or death may result if the system test is not performed properly.

Never replace both the Occupant Restraint Controller (ORC) and the Occupant Classification Module (OCM) at the same time. If both require replacement, replace one, then perform the Airbag System test before replacing the other.

Both the ORC and the OCM store Occupant Classification System (OCS) calibration data, which they transfer to one another when one of them is replaced. If both are replaced at the same time, an irreversible fault will be set in both modules and the OCS may malfunction and cause personal injury or death.

If equipped with OCS, the Seat Weight Sensor is a sensitive, calibrated unit and must be handled carefully. Do not drop or handle roughly. If dropped or damaged, replace with another sensor. Failure to do so may result in occupant injury or death.

If equipped with OCS, the front passenger seat must be handled carefully as well. When removing the seat, be careful when setting on floor not to drop. If dropped, the sensor may be inoperative, could result in occupant injury, or possibly death.

If equipped with OCS, when the passenger front seat is on the floor, no one should sit in the front passenger seat. This uneven force may damage the sensing ability of the seat weight sensors. If sat on and damaged, the sensor may be inoperative, could result in occupant injury, or possibly death.

DISARMING THE SYSTEM

CAUTION

The Air Bag system must be disarmed before repair and/or removal of any component in its immediate area including the air bag itself. Failure to do so may cause accidental deployment of the air bag, resulting in unnecessary system repairs and/or personal injury.

1. Disconnect the negative battery cable and isolate the cable using an appropriate insulator (wrap with quality electrical tape).
2. Allow the system capacitor to discharge for 2 minutes before starting any repair on any air bag system or related components. This will disable the air bag system.

CAUTION

Always wear safety goggles when working with or around the air bag system. When carrying a live air bag, be sure the bag and trim cover are pointed away from the body. In the unlikely event of an accidental deployment, the bag will, then deploy with minimal chance of injury. When placing a live air bag on a bench or other surface, always face the bag and trim cover up, away from the surface. This will reduce the motion of the module if it is accidentally deployed.

ARMING THE SYSTEM

1. To arm the Air Bag system, remove the electrical tape from the negative battery cable, then connect the negative battery cable to the battery.

Perform Supplemental Restraint System (SRS) verification test. Reconnect the battery. The supplemental restraint system will self-initialize.

SUPPLEMENTAL RESTRAINT SYSTEM (SRS) VERIFICATION TEST

The following procedure requires using a scan tool to verify proper Supplemental Restraint System (SRS) operation following the service or replacement of any SRS component.

1. Be sure that the negative battery cable is disconnected and isolated.
2. Connect the scan tool to the Data Link Connector (DLC).
3. Exit the vehicle but maintain contact with the scan tool.
4. Turn the ignition switch to the ON position.
5. Be sure no one is in the vehicle.
6. Connect the negative battery cable.
7. Using the scan tool, read and record any active (current) Diagnostic Trouble Code (DTC) data.
8. Use the scan tool to read and record any stored (historical) Diagnostic Trouble Code (DTC) data.
9. If any DTC's are found, refer to the appropriate diagnostic data.
10. Use the scan tool to erase any stored DTC data.
11. Turn the ignition switch to the OFF position. Wait 15 seconds, and then turn the ignition switch to the ON position.
12. Observe the airbag warning indicator in the instrument cluster for proper operation.
13. If a fault is detected, it must be corrected.

CLOCKSPRING CENTERING

The clockspring is designed to wind and unwind when the steering wheel is rotated, but is only designed to rotate the same number of turns (about five complete rotations) as the steering wheel can be turned from stop to stop. Centering the clockspring indexes the clockspring tape to other steering components so that it can operate within its designed travel limits. The rotor of a centered clockspring can be rotated two and one-half turns in either direction from the centered position, without damaging the clockspring tape. However, if the clockspring is removed for service or if the steering column is disconnected from the steering gear, the clockspring tape can change position relative to the other steering components. The clockspring must then be re-centered following completion of such service or the clockspring tape may be damaged.

➡Before starting this procedure, be certain to turn the steering wheel until the front wheels are in the straight-ahead position.

1. Place the front wheels in the straight-ahead position.
2. Remove the clockspring from the steering column.
3. Hold the clockspring case in one hand so that it is oriented as it would be when it is installed on the steering column.
4. Use your other hand to rotate the clockspring rotor clockwise to the end of its travel. Do not apply excessive torque.
5. From the end of the clockwise travel, rotate the rotor about two and one-half turns counterclockwise, until the arrows on the clockspring rotor label and the clockspring case are aligned. The uppermost pin on the lower surface of the clockspring rotor should now be aligned with the oblong pin.
6. The clockspring is now centered. Secure the clockspring rotor to the clockspring case to maintain clockspring centering until it is reinstalled on the steering column.
   a. The front wheels should still be in the straight-ahead position.
7. Reinstall the clockspring onto the steering column.

DRIVETRAIN

AUTOMATIC TRANSAXLE ASSEMBLY

REMOVAL & INSTALLATION

See Figures 15 through 20.

1. Before servicing the vehicle, refer to the precautions in the beginning of this section.
2. Remove or disconnect the following:
   - Battery cables
   - Battery and tray
   - Gearshift cable from the manual valve lever
   - Oil cooler off of hose fitting connection.
3. Use a suitable cutting tool, cut the oil cooler hoses off flush at the fittings. A service splice kit will be required during installation. Cap the hoses.
   - Ground cable from the transaxle case
   - Input and output speed sensor connections
   - Crankshaft Position Sensor (CKP)
   - Transaxle range sensor and solenoid/pressure switch connections
   - Transaxle harness from retainers and position aside
   - Coolant bypass tube-to-engine and transaxle retainers
   - Front brake lines from the Hydraulic Control Unit (HCU) and position aside
   - Intermediate shaft extension from the steering gear using tool 6831A to remove the roll pin and then slide the shaft extension off the gear
4. Install a powertrain support fixture such as 8534B and adapter kit 8534-12.
   - Oil dipstick tube-to-cylinder head bolt
5. Install lift support bracket 8534-8 and use the dipstick tube bolt to secure it.
6. Remove the Coolant Temperature Sensor (CTS) at the thermostat housing. Remove the engine harness-to-cylinder head bolt and position the harness aside.
7. Install lift support bracket 8534-7 and bolt.
8. Assemble mounting bracket/sleeve assemblies 8534-2 to support tube 8534-1 and install on the vehicle allowing the brackets to rest on the inner fender ledges.
9. Assemble cross bar 8534-3, clamp 8534-5 and support leg 8534-4 to support tube allowing the support leg to rest on the radiator upper support.
10. Tighten the cross bar-to-support tube clamp 8534-5 as well as mounting bracket/sleeve 8534-3.
11. Install lift bracket assemblies as shown in the accompanying illustration.

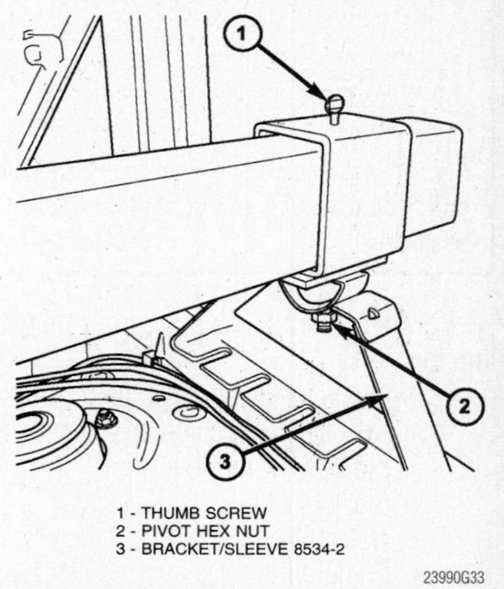

Fig. 15 Assemble the torque thumb screw and pivot nut bracket assembly as shown

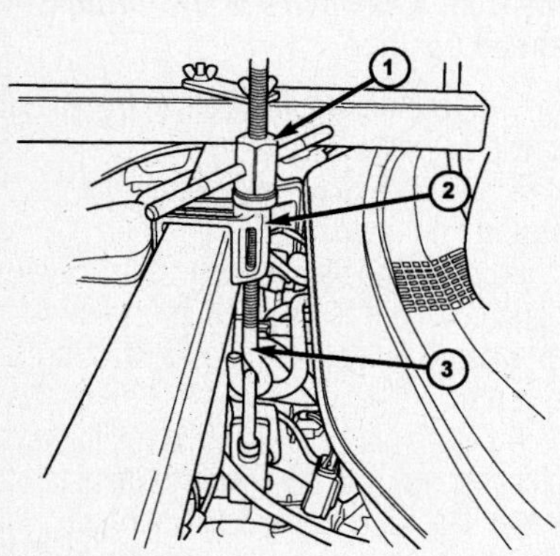

Fig. 16 Assemble the T–handle, bracket and hook assembly at the rear lift bracket as illustrated

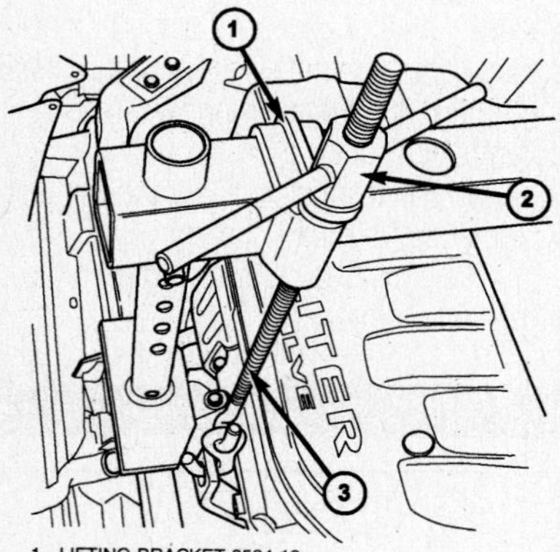

Fig. 17 Assemble the T–handle, bracket and hook assembly at the front lift bracket as shown

12. Raise the vehicle and remove the front wheels.
13. Remove or disconnect the following:
    - ABS sensor connector and sensor brackets from the struts
    - Sway bar links from struts
    - Halfshafts
    - Engine front and rear mount-to-cradle nuts
    - Brake lines and brackets from the frame rails
    - Power steering hydraulic line from the bracket at the cradle located on the passenger side
    - Power steering oil cooler from the cradle
    - Power steering pressure and return lines from the steering gear and cap the lines

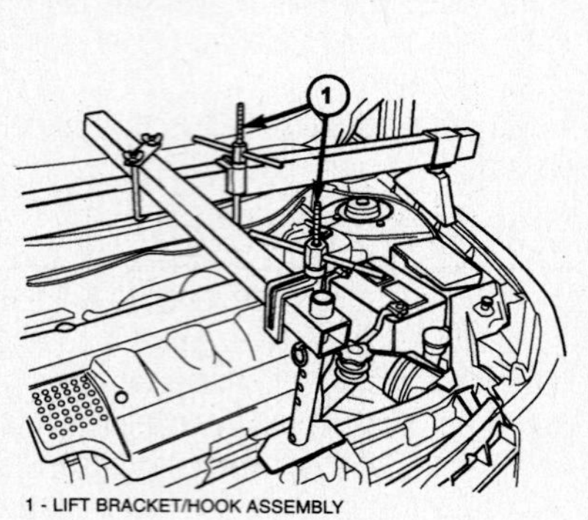

Fig. 18 The engine support system slack is taken up by using the T–handles

    - Transmission-to-cradle torque strut
14. Position drive line support table 8874 into position and lower the vehicle until the cradle and fixture engage as shown in the accompanying illustration.
15. Scribe alignment marks to reference cradle-to-body alignment to help during installation, then remove the four cradle-to-body bolts.
16. Slowly raise the vehicle and separate the cradle from the vehicle. Check the overhead fixture is secure on the fenders and radiator support.
17. Have an assistant guide the brake and power steering lines through as they remain attached.
18. Remove or disconnect the following:
    - Engine front mount/bracket
    - Starter motor
19. On All Wheel Drive (AWD) models remove or disconnect the following:

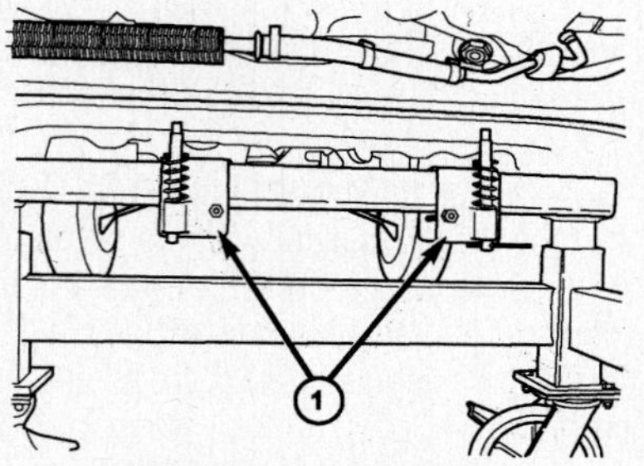

Fig. 19 Position drive line support table 8874 into position and lower the vehicle until the cradle and fixture engage

    - Propeller shaft
    - Power Transfer Unit (PTU) rear mount bracket
    - Oil pan-to-transaxle collar
    - Heat shield
    - PTU-to-transaxle upper bolts
    - PTU-to-bracket lower bolts
    - PTU
20. Remove or disconnect the following:
    - Torque converter dust shield
    - Four torque converter-to-flexplate bolts. Upon removing the bolts a tight tolerance (slotted) bolt will be found. Mark this location on the converter and flexplate to use as a reference during assembly.
    - Four transaxle upper bellhousing bolts
21. Use the overhead fixture to lower the engine/transaxle assembly. and secure the transmission to a suitable jack.
22. Remove the two transaxle-to-engine lower bolts and remove the transaxle.

To install:

23. Install or connect the following:
    - Transaxle
    - Two transaxle-to-engine lower bolts and tighten to 70 ft. lbs. (95 Nm)
24. Remove the transmission jack.
    - Four transaxle upper bellhousing bolts and tighten to 70 ft. lbs. (95 Nm)

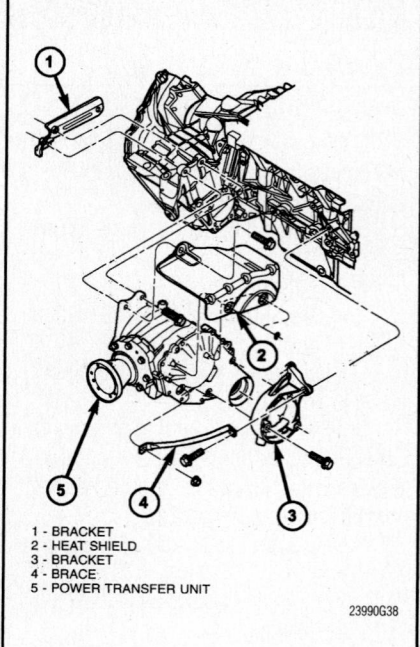

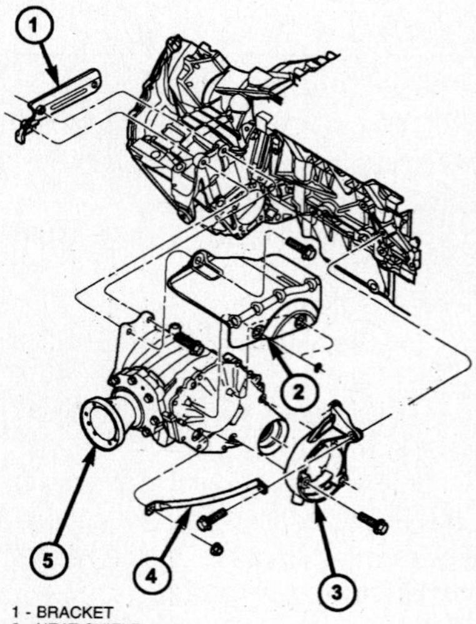

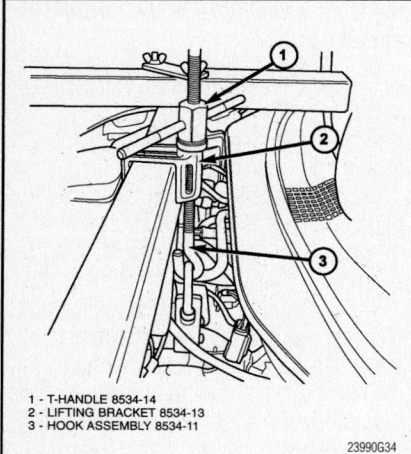

Fig. 20 Exploded view of the Power Transfer Unit mounting and related components

- Four torque converter-to-flexplate bolts and tighten to 65 ft. lbs. (88 Nm)
- Torque converter dust shield

25. Loosely install the engine-to-transaxle collar.
26. On AWD models install or connect the following:
    - PTU lower bracket and PTU
    - PTU-to-bracket lower bolts and tighten to 21 ft. lbs. (28 Nm)
    - PTU-to-transaxle upper bolts and tighten to 40 ft. lbs. (54 Nm)
    - PTU rear mount bracket and tighten the bolts to 40 ft. lbs. (54 Nm)
    - Heat shield
    - Propeller shaft
27. Install or connect the following:
    - Starter motor
    - Engine front mount/bracket and tighten the bolts to 50 ft. lbs. (67 Nm)
28. Align the scribe alignment marks made to reference cradle-to-body alignment during removal, then install the four cradle-to-body bolts and tighten to 120 ft. lbs. (162 Nm).
29. Route the brake and power steering lines.
30. Remove the overhead support fixture.
31. Install or connect the following:
    - Engine front and rear mount-to-cradle nuts and tighten to 40 ft. lbs. (54 Nm)
    - Steering shaft-to-gear coupler using tool 6831A
    - Power steering pressure and return lines to the steering gear and tighten the fittings to 23 ft. lbs. (31 Nm)
    - Power steering oil cooler and hose routing clip to the cradle
    - Transmission-to-cradle torque strut and tighten to 40 ft. lbs. (54 Nm)
    - Halfshafts
    - Sway bar links to the struts and tighten the nuts to 65 ft. lbs. (88 Nm)
    - ABS sensor brackets and electrical connectors
    - Both wheels
    - Front brake lines to the HCU
    - Coolant bypass tube fasteners
    - Solenoid/pressure switch and tighten the screw to 35 inch lbs. (4 Nm)
    - Transaxle range sensor connection
    - Input and output speed sensor connections
    - Transaxle harness using the retainers
    - CKP sensor
    - Transaxle oil cooler splice kit using the kit instructions
    - Gearshift cable to the manual valve lever
    - Battery tray, battery and cables
32. Bleed the brakes.
33. Add power steering fluid.
34. Check and fill the transmission fluid to the proper level.
35. If equipped with AWD, remove the PTU fill plug, check the fluid level. The PTU should have 2.1 pints of 75W-90 gear and axle lubricant. After checking the fluid lever, install the fill plug and tighten to 26 ft. lbs. (35 Nm).
36. Check and adjust the wheel alignment.

TRANSFER CASE ASSEMBLY

REMOVAL & INSTALLATION

If equipped with AWD the vehicle will use a Power Transfer Unit assembly (PTU).

2005–06 Models

1. Disconnect the negative battery cable.
2. Raise and support the vehicle safely.
3. Remove the right halfshaft assembly.
4. Remove the engine cradle crossmember.
5. Remove the driveshaft.
6. Remove the PTU rear mount bracket.
7. Remove the oil pan to transaxle collar.
8. Remove the heat shield. Remove the bracket and brace.
9. Remove the PTU to transaxle upper bolts.
10. Remove the PTU to bracket lower bolts.
11. Carefully remove the assembly from the vehicle.

To install:

12. Installation is the reverse of the removal procedure.
13. Install the PTU lower bracket.
14. Install the PTU to transaxle upper bolts. Tighten to 40 ft. lbs.
15. Install the PTU in position. Tighten the two lower PTU to bracket bolts to 21 ft. lbs.
16. Install the brace and bracket.
17. Install the heat shield.
18. Install the PTU rear mount bracket. Tighten the six bolts to 40 ft. lbs.
19. Install the driveshaft.
20. Install the right halfshaft assembly.
21. Install the engine cradle crossmember.
22. Check and adjust the PTU fluid level. The unit holds 1.7 pints of 75W-90 gear and axle lubricant.

2007–08 Models

1. Disconnect the negative battery cable.
2. Raise and support the vehicle safely.
3. Remove the right halfshaft assembly.
4. Remove the exhaust system.
5. Remove the engine cradle crossmember.
6. Remove the driveshaft.
7. Remove the PTU rear mount bracket.
8. Remove the heat shield. Remove the bracket and brace.
9. Remove the PTU to transaxle upper bolts.
10. Remove the PTU to bracket lower bolts.
11. Carefully remove the assembly from the vehicle.

To install:

12. Installation is the reverse of the removal procedure.
13. Loosen the PTU to transaxle bracket, if not already done.
14. Install a new O-ring onto the PTU. Apply RTV sealant, part number 05010884AA to the O-ring.

➡The sequence below should always be followed when installing the PTU.

15. Install the PTU in position. Tighten the two PTU to transaxle adapter bolts to 30 ft. lbs.
16. Install the heat shield.
17. Install the two PTU to transaxle upper bolts. Tighten to 40 ft. lb.
18. Install the three PTU to transaxle lower bolts. Tighten to 75 ft. lbs.
19. Install the PTU rear mount bracket. Tighten to 40 ft. lbs.
20. Install the driveshaft.
21. Install the right halfshaft assembly.
22. Install the engine cradle crossmember.
23. Install the exhaust system.
24. Check and adjust the PTU fluid level. The unit holds 1.7 pints of 75W-90 gear and axle lubricant.

FRONT HALFSHAFT

REMOVAL & INSTALLATION

See Figures 21 and 22.

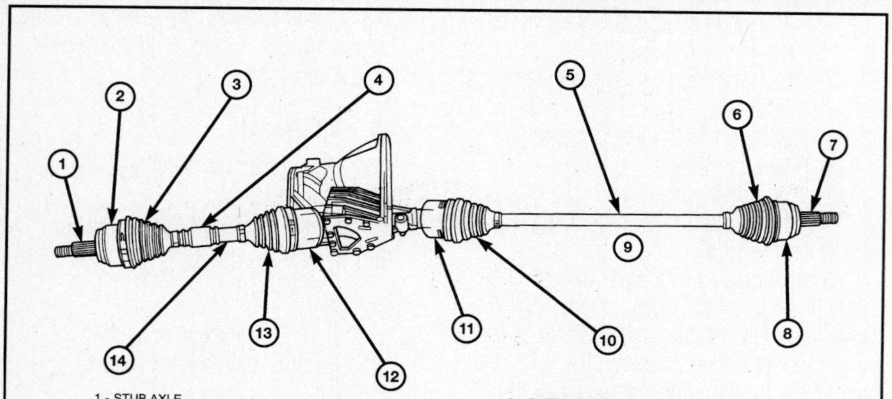

Fig. 21 Exploded view of the front halfshaft and related components—typical

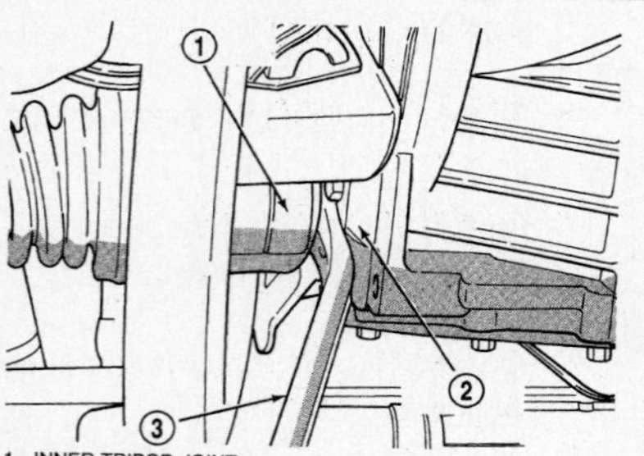

Fig. 22 Use a prybar to disengage the halfshaft from the transaxle

2005–06 Models

1. Before servicing the vehicle, refer to the precautions in the beginning of this section.
2. Disconnect the negative battery cable.
3. Raise and support the vehicle safely.
4. Remove the cotter pin and nut lock retainer.
5. Remove the wave washer from the end of the halfshaft.
6. Remove the tire and wheel assembly.
7. Loosen and remove the halfshaft nut.

➡Apply the vehicle's brakes to keep the hub from turning in order to remove the nut.

8. Remove the two disc brake caliper adapter to steering knuckle attaching bolts.
9. Remove the caliper assembly. Properly support the caliper as not to cause damage to the brake line hose.
10. Remove the brake rotor.
11. Remove the steering knuckle to strut retaining bolts from the steering knuckle.
12. Pull the steering knuckle from the strut clevis bracket.

➡Care must be taken not to separate the inner CV joint during this operation. Do not allow the halfshaft to hang by the inner CV joint after removing the outer CV joint from the hub and bearing assembly in the steering knuckle. The end of the halfshaft must be supported.

13. Pull the steering knuckle assembly and down and away from the outer CV joint of the halfshaft assembly while pulling the joint out of the hub bearing.
14. Support the outer end of the halfshaft. Insert a prybar between the inner tripod joint and the transaxle case. Pry against the inner tripod joint until the snapring is disengaged from the transaxle side gear.
15. Hold the inner tripod joint and interconnecting shaft of the halfshaft.
16. Remove the inner tripod joint from the transaxle by pulling it straight out of the transaxle side gear and transaxle oil seal.

➡When removing the tripod joint, do not let the spline or snapring drag across the sealing lip of the transaxle to tripod joint oil seal.

To install:

17. Install the Tri-pot joint side of the halfshaft by performing the following procedure:
    a. Replace the inner Tri-pot joint retaining circlip and O-ring seal on the transaxle stub shaft. These components are not reusable and must be replaced whenever the halfshaft is removed.
    b. Apply an even coat of grease on the splines of the inner Tri-pot joint, where the O-ring seats against the Tri-pot joint.
    c. Grasp the inner joint in 1 hand and interconnecting shaft in the other. Align the inner Tri-pot joint spline with the stub shaft spline on the transaxle. Use a rocking motion with the inner Tri-pot joint to get it past the circlip on the transaxle stub shaft.
    d. Continue pushing the Tri-pot joint onto transaxle stub shaft until it stops moving. The O-ring on the stub shaft should not be visible when the inner Tri-pot joint is fully installed. Check that the inner Tri-pot joint is locked in position by grasping the inner joint and pulling. If locked in position, the joint will not move on the stub shaft.
18. Install the outer CV-joint into the hub and bearing assembly.

⁂ WARNING

The steering knuckle-to-strut assembly bolts are serrated and must not be turned during installation. Also if the vehicle is equipped with eccentric strut assembly bolts, the eccentric bolt must be installed in the bottom (slotted) hole on the strut bracket.

19. Install or connect the following:
    - Steering knuckle in the bracket of the damper assembly
    - Strut damper-to-steering knuckle bolts and tighten to 65 ft. lbs. (88 Nm) plus an additional ¼ turn
    - Rotor, caliper. Tighten the caliper adapter bolts to 125 ft. lbs. (169 Nm)
    - Washer and bearing-to-stub axle bolt and hand-tighten.
    - Wheels
20. Apply the brakes and tighten the bearing-to-stub axle bolt to 180 ft. lbs. (244 Nm) and install the cotter pin.
21. Road test the vehicle to check for noise or vibration.

2007–08 Models

1. Before servicing the vehicle, refer to the precautions in the beginning of this section.
2. Disconnect the negative battery cable.
3. Raise and support the vehicle safely.
4. Remove the cotter pin and nut lock retainer.
5. Remove the wave washer from the end of the halfshaft.
6. Remove the tire and wheel assembly.
7. Loosen and remove the halfshaft nut.

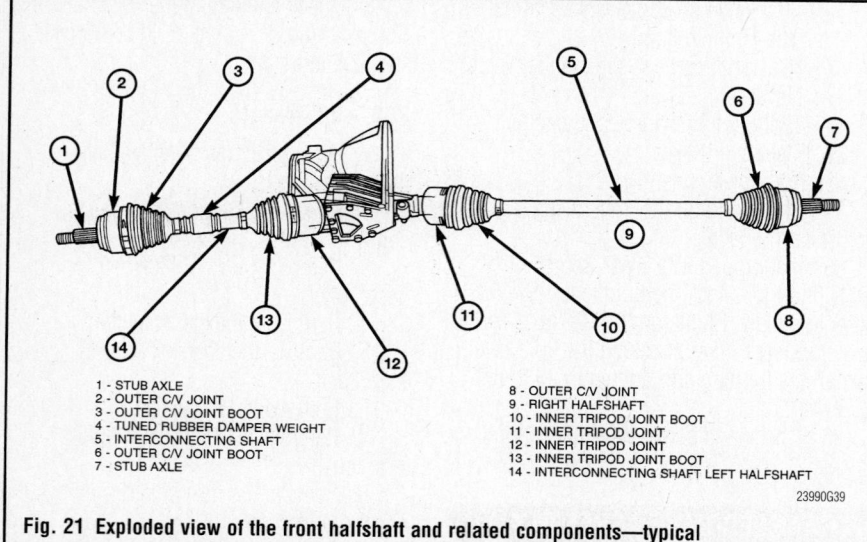

➡Apply the vehicle's brakes to keep the hub from turning in order to remove the nut.

8. Remove the two disc brake caliper adapter to steering knuckle attaching bolts.
9. Remove the caliper assembly. Properly support the caliper as not to cause damage to the brake line hose.
10. Remove the brake rotor.
11. Remove the steering knuckle to strut retaining bolts from the steering knuckle.
12. Pull the steering knuckle from the strut clevis bracket.

➡Care must be taken not to separate the inner CV joint during this operation. Do not allow the halfshaft to hang by the inner CV joint after removing the outer CV joint from the hub and bearing assembly in the steering knuckle. The end of the halfshaft must be supported.

13. Pull the steering knuckle assembly and down and away from the outer CV joint of the halfshaft assembly while pulling the joint out of the hub bearing.
14. Support the outer end of the halfshaft. Insert a prybar between the inner tripod joint and the transaxle case. Pry against the inner tripod joint until the snapring is disengaged from the transaxle side gear.
15. Pull the steering knuckle from the strut clevis bracket.
16. Pull the steering knuckle assembly down and away from the outer CV joint of the halfshaft assembly while pulling the joint out of the intermediate shaft.
17. Remove the bolts at the heat shield and remove the heat shield, if equipped.
18. Remove the three bolts holding the midshaft bearing to the block.
19. Remove the intermediate shaft.

To install:

➡A rubber coated washer should be used on the outer CV joint stem during assembly.

20. Installation is the reverse of the removal procedure.

⁂ WARNING

The steering knuckle-to-strut assembly bolts are serrated and must not be turned during installation. Also if the vehicle is equipped with eccentric strut assembly bolts, the eccentric bolt must be installed in the bottom (slotted) hole on the strut bracket.

21. Road test the vehicle to check for noise or vibration.

CV-JOINTS OVERHAUL

2005–06 Models

Inner (Tri-Pot) Joint

See Figures 23 through 25.

1. Before servicing the vehicle, refer to the precautions in the beginning of this section.
2. Disconnect the negative battery cable.
3. Remove the halfshaft and retaining clamps.
4. Slide the boot down the shaft away from the tri-pot housing.

➡When separating the spider joint from the tri-pot joint housing, hold the rollers in place on the trunnions to prevent the rollers and needle bearings from falling away.

5. Carefully, slide the shaft/spider assembly from the tri-pot housing.
6. Remove the spider assembly-to-shaft snapring; then, slide the spider assembly off the shaft.

⁂ WARNING

If necessary, tap the spider assembly off the shaft using a brass drift; be careful not to hit the outer bearings.

7. Slide the boot off the shaft.
8. Thoroughly, inspect all parts for signs of excessive wear; if necessary, replace the halfshaft.

➡Component parts are not serviceable and must be replaced as an assembly.

To install:

9. Slide the inner tri-pot boot clamp and boot onto the shaft; then, position the boot so that only the thinnest (sight) groove is visible on the shaft.

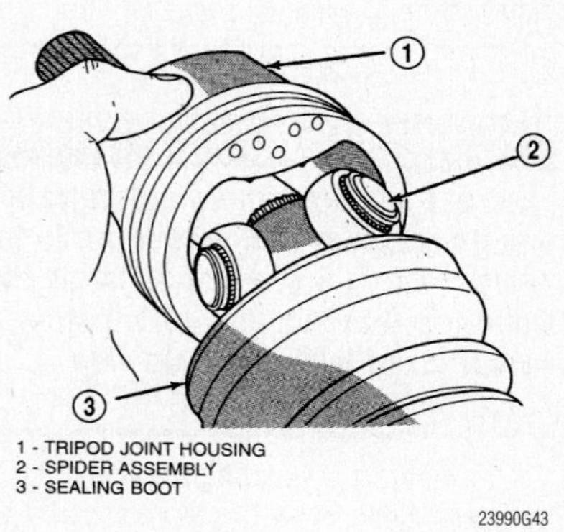

Fig. 23 Slide the boot down the shaft away from the tri-pot housing

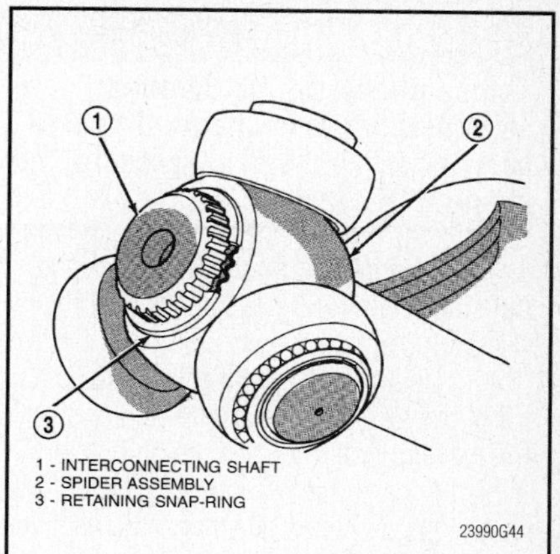

Fig. 24 Remove the spider assembly-to-shaft snapring; then, slide the spider assembly off the shaft

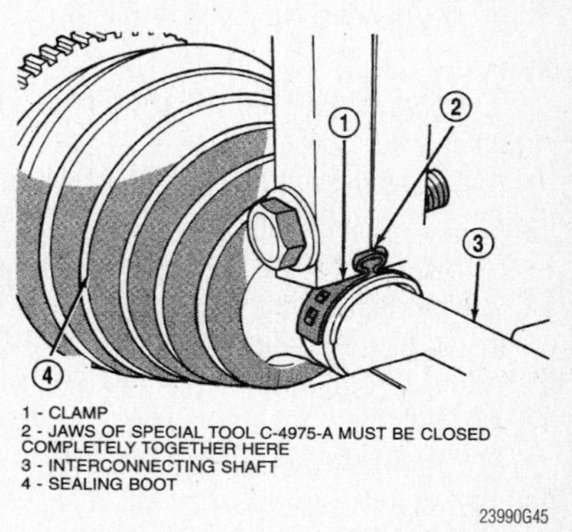

Fig. 25 Securing the halfshaft boot clamp

10. Install the spider assembly onto the shaft just far enough so that the snapring can be installed.

⁂ WARNING

If necessary, tap the spider assembly onto the shaft using a brass drift; be careful not to hit the outer bearings.

11. Install the snapring onto the shaft; make sure that the snapring is fully seated in the groove.
12. If installing a new boot, distribute ½ of the grease in the service package inside the tri-pot housing and the other ½ inside the boot.
13. Carefully, slide the spider assembly and shaft into the tri-pot housing.
14. Position the inner boot clamp evenly on the sealing boot.
15. Using the Crimper tool C-4975, place the tool over the clamp bridge, tighten the tool nut until the jaws are completely closed (face-to-face).

⁂ WARNING

The seal must not be dimpled, stretched or out of shape. If necessary, equalize the seal pressure and shape it by hand.

16. Position the boot onto the tri-pot housing retaining groove and install the retaining clamp evenly on the boot.

17. Using the Crimper tool C-4975, place the tool over the clamp bridge, tighten the tool nut until the jaws are completely closed (face-to-face).

18. Install the halfshaft into the vehicle.

Outer CV Joint

See Figures 26 and 27.

1. Before servicing the vehicle, refer to the precautions in the beginning of this section.
2. Disconnect the negative battery cable.
3. Remove the halfshaft and the retaining clamps.
4. Slide the boot down the shaft away from the CV-joint housing.
5. Remove the grease to expose the CV-joint-to-shaft retaining ring.
6. Spread the snapring ears apart and slide the CV-joint assembly off of the shaft.
7. Slide the boot off the shaft.
8. Thoroughly, clean and inspect all parts for signs of excessive wear; if necessary, replace the halfshaft.

➡Component parts are not serviceable and must be replaced as an assembly.

To install:

9. Slide the outer CV-joint boot clamp and boot onto the shaft; then, position the boot so that only the thinnest (sight) groove is visible on the shaft.
10. Slide the outer CV-joint assembly on the shaft, spread the snapring ears, position the CV-joint and verify that the snapring is fully seated in the shaft groove.
11. If installing a new boot, distribute ½ of the grease in the service package into the CV-joint housing and the other ½ inside the boot.
12. Position the outer boot clamp evenly on the sealing boot.
13. Using the Crimper tool C-4975, place the tool over the clamp bridge, tighten the tool nut until the jaws are completely closed (face-to-face).

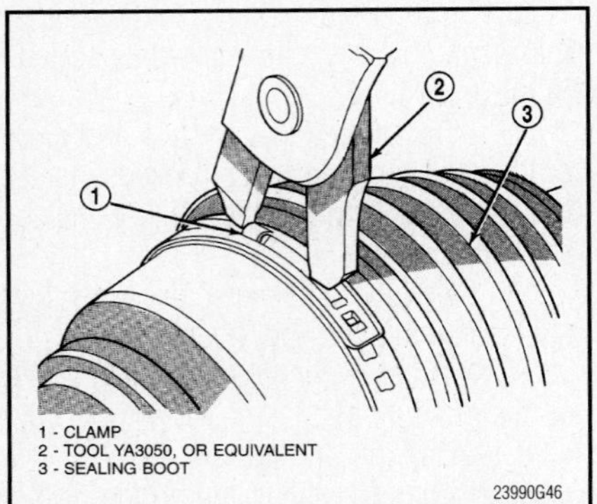

Fig. 26 The latch type boot clamp is tightened as illustrated. . . . .

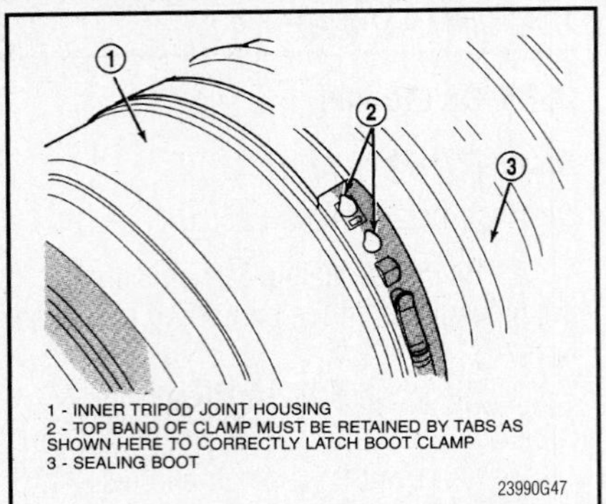

Fig. 27 . . . . and should look like this when properly installed

⁂ WARNING

The seal must not be dimpled, stretched or out of shape. If necessary, equalize the seal pressure and shape it by hand.

14. Position the boot onto the CV-joint housing retaining groove and install the retaining clamp evenly on the boot.
15. Using the Crimper tool C-4975, place the tool over the clamp bridge, tighten the tool nut until the jaws are completely closed (face-to-face).
16. Install the halfshaft into the vehicle.

REAR HALFSHAFT

REMOVAL & INSTALLATION

See Figures 28 and 29.

⁂ WARNING

The rear suspension and drivetrain design requires this procedure to be performed on a drive on hoist as the front and rear suspension must be compressed to the vehicle ride height.

1. Before servicing the vehicle, refer to the precautions in the beginning of this section.
2. Remove or disconnect the following:
   - Negative battery cable
   - Wheel cover cap
   - Cotter pin, locknut and washer
   - Exhaust system center hanger at the propeller shaft center bearing
   - Exhaust system at the rear hanger and lower at least 10 inches (254mm) before securing with wire
3. Mark the propeller shaft and rear driveline module flanges for reference during installation.
   - 3 propeller shaft-to-driveline module bolts. Do not disconnect the shaft from the module as it will be disconnected upon lowering the module.
4. Support the driveline module with a transmission jack.
5. Using a suitable prytool, partially dislodge the halfshaft from the differential.
6. Install seal protector tool 9099 to protect the seal during disassembly.
7. Remove the 3 driveline-to-crossmember bolts.
8. Lower the driveline module enough to remove the shaft from the differential, making sure tool 9099 engages the seal.

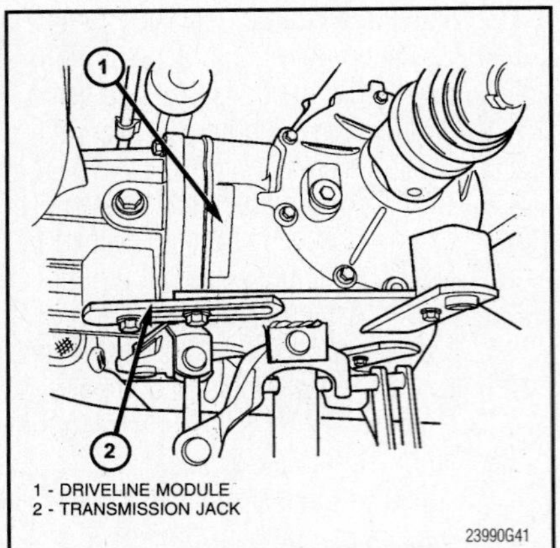

Fig. 28 Support the driveline module using a transmission jack

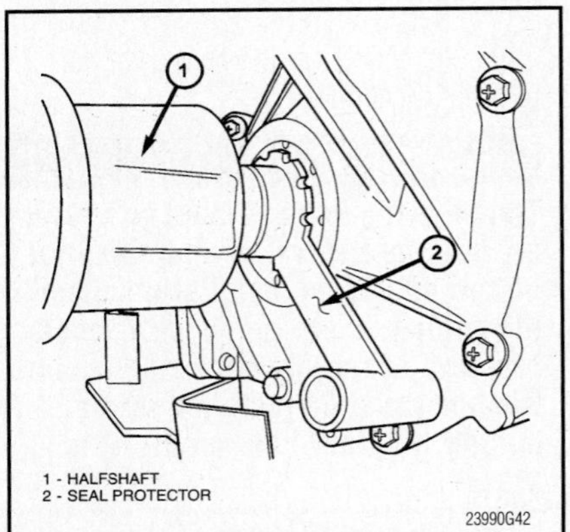

Fig. 29 Use seal protector tool 9099 to protect against seal damage

9. Disconnect the propeller shaft from the differential and secure it to the exhaust system.
10. Remove the halfshaft from the bearing assembly.

To install:

11. Remove the halfshaft from the bearing assembly. Install the hub nut and washer and hand tighten.
12. Attach the shaft to the differential, using tool 9099.
13. Connect the propeller shaft to the module flange. Install but do not tighten the 3 bolts.
14. Position the module and tighten the module-to-cradle bolts to 75 ft. lbs. (102 Nm).
15. Tighten the propeller shaft-to-module bolts to 40 ft. lbs. (54 Nm).
16. Tighten the halfshaft nut.
17. Install or connect the following:
- Washer, nut and new cotter pin
- Wheel cover cap
- Negative battery cable

18. Check and adjust the differential fluid.
19. Road test the vehicle to check for noise or vibration.

CV-JOINT OVERHAUL

2005–06 Models

Inner (Tri-Pot) Joint

See Figures 30 through 32.

1. Before servicing the vehicle, refer to the precautions in the beginning of this section.
2. Disconnect the negative battery cable.
3. Remove the halfshaft and retaining clamps.
4. Slide the boot down the shaft away from the tri-pot housing.

➡When separating the spider joint from the tri-pot joint housing, hold the rollers in place on the trunnions to prevent the rollers and needle bearings from falling away.

5. Carefully, slide the shaft/spider assembly from the tri-pot housing.
6. Remove the spider assembly-to-shaft snapring; then, slide the spider assembly off the shaft.

⁂ WARNING

If necessary, tap the spider assembly off the shaft using a brass drift; be careful not to hit the outer bearings.

7. Slide the boot off the shaft.

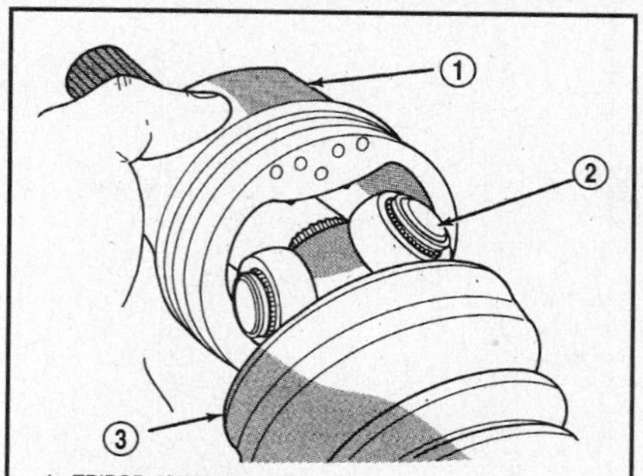

Fig. 30 Slide the boot down the shaft away from the tri-pot housing

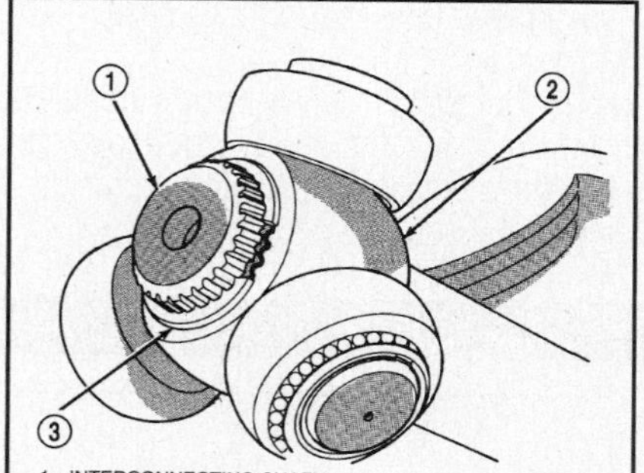

Fig. 31 Remove the spider assembly-to-shaft snapring; then, slide the spider assembly off the shaft

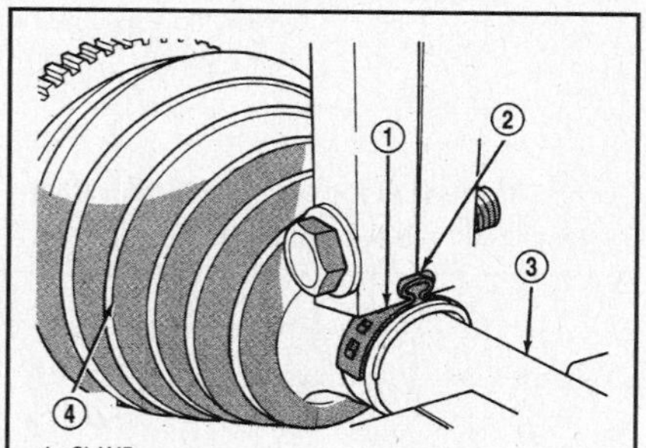

Fig. 32 Securing the halfshaft boot clamp

8. Thoroughly, inspect all parts for signs of excessive wear; if necessary, replace the halfshaft.

➡Component parts are not serviceable and must be replaced as an assembly.

To install:

9. Slide the inner tri-pot boot clamp and boot onto the shaft; then, position the boot so that only the thinnest (sight) groove is visible on the shaft.
10. Install the spider assembly onto the shaft just far enough so that the snapring can be installed.

⁂ WARNING

If necessary, tap the spider assembly onto the shaft using a brass drift; be careful not to hit the outer bearings.

11. Install the snapring onto the shaft; make sure that the snapring is fully seated in the groove.
12. If installing a new boot, distribute ½ of the grease in the service package inside the tri-pot housing and the other ½ inside the boot.
13. Carefully, slide the spider assembly and shaft into the tri-pot housing.
14. Position the inner boot clamp evenly on the sealing boot.
15. Using the Crimper tool C-4975, place the tool over the clamp bridge, tighten the tool nut until the jaws are completely closed (face-to-face).

⁂ WARNING

The seal must not be dimpled, stretched or out of shape. If necessary, equalize the seal pressure and shape it by hand.

16. Position the boot onto the tri-pot housing retaining groove and install the retaining clamp evenly on the boot.
17. Using the Crimper tool C-4975, place the tool over the clamp bridge, tighten the tool nut until the jaws are completely closed (face-to-face).
18. Install the halfshaft into the vehicle.

Outer CV Joint

See Figures 33 and 34.

1. Before servicing the vehicle, refer to the precautions in the beginning of this section.
2. Disconnect the negative battery cable.
3. Remove the halfshaft and the retaining clamps.
4. Slide the boot down the shaft away from the CV-joint housing.
5. Remove the grease to expose the CV-joint-to-shaft retaining ring.
6. Spread the snapring ears apart and slide the CV-joint assembly off of the shaft.
7. Slide the boot off the shaft.
8. Thoroughly, clean and inspect all parts for signs of excessive wear; if necessary, replace the halfshaft.

➡Component parts are not serviceable and must be replaced as an assembly.

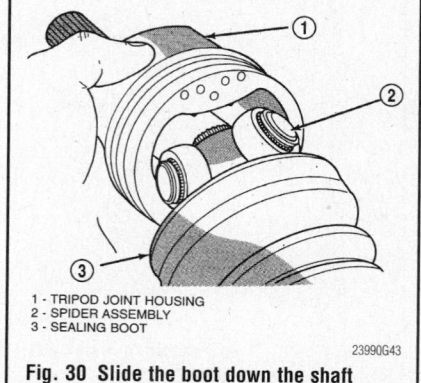

Fig. 33 The latch type boot clamp is tightened as illustrated. . . . .

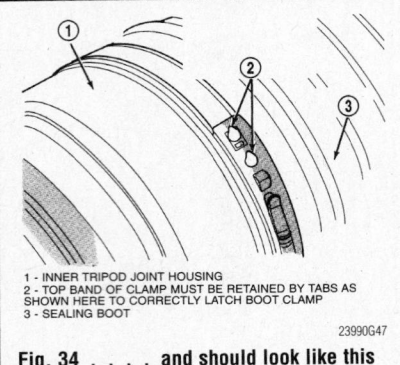

To install:

9. Slide the outer CV-joint boot clamp and boot onto the shaft; then, position the boot so that only the thinnest (sight) groove is visible on the shaft.

10. Slide the outer CV-joint assembly on the shaft, spread the snapring ears, position the CV-joint and verify that the snapring is fully seated in the shaft groove.

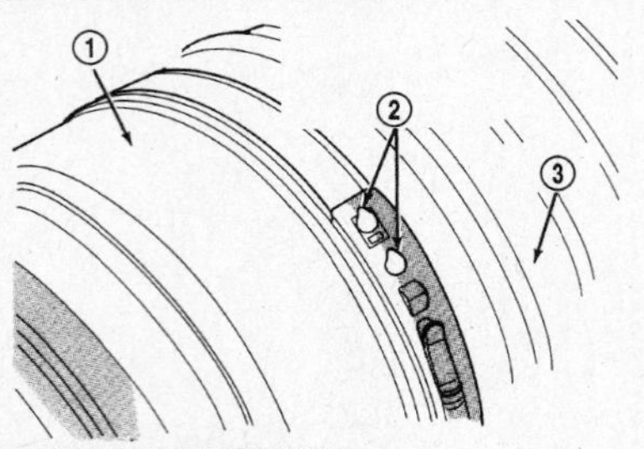

Fig. 34 . . . . and should look like this when properly installed

11. If installing a new boot, distribute ½ of the grease in the service package into the CV-joint housing and the other ½ inside the boot.

12. Position the outer boot clamp evenly on the sealing boot.

13. Using the Crimper tool C-4975, place the tool over the clamp bridge, tighten the tool nut until the jaws are completely closed (face-to-face).

WARNING

The seal must not be dimpled, stretched or out of shape. If necessary, equalize the seal pressure and shape it by hand.

14. Position the boot onto the CV-joint housing retaining groove and install the retaining clamp evenly on the boot.

15. Using the Crimper tool C-4975, place the tool over the clamp bridge, tighten the tool nut until the jaws are completely closed (face-to-face).

16. Install the halfshaft into the vehicle.

ENGINE COOLING

ENGINE FAN

REMOVAL & INSTALLATION

See Figures 35 and 36.

There are no repairs to be made to the fan or shroud assembly. If the fan is warped, cracked, or otherwise damaged, it must be replaced as an assembly.

1. Remove the front fascia, as follows:
   a. Release hood latch and open hood.
   b. Remove the headlamp assemblies, as necessary.
   c. Hoist vehicle and support with safety stands, as necessary.
   d. Remove the four screws attaching bottom of fascia/air dam to radiator closure panel.

➡The whole front splash shield does not need to be removed.

   e. Remove three screws attaching front fascia to front splash shield on each side.
   f. Remove the screw attaching fascia to the front fenders on each side.
   g. Disconnect fog lamp wire connectors, if necessary.
   h. Lower vehicle.
   i. Remove push pins attaching the upper appearance panel to upper crossmember.
   j. Remove screw attaching the upper grille support to the headlamp mounting panel at each side of the grille.
   k. Remove bumper fascia from vehicle.
   l. Place fascia on a clean surface.

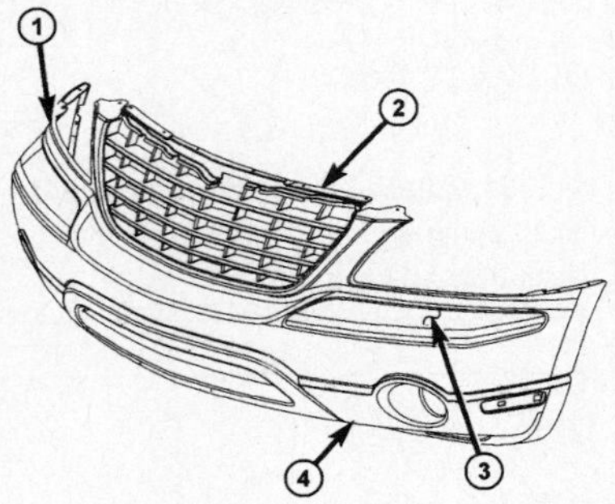

Fig. 35 View of the upper and lower front fascia and related components—typical

   m. Remove spring clips attaching upper and lower fascia together.
   n. Using a trim stick release locking tabs and separate the upper and lower fascia.
   o. Remove the bright chrome molding from the upper fascia. Using a trim stick, starting at the outer edge of the fascia release the locking tabs. Grip the molding and pull outward from the fascia while releasing the locking tabs.
   p. Remove molding from fascia.
   q. Remove grille from fascia.

2. Disconnect the radiator fan electrical connectors.

3. Remove radiator fan(s) retaining screw.

4. Remove the radiator fan(s) by lifting upward to release from mounts.

To install:

5. Install the radiator fan(s) into mounts and attaching clips on the radiator.

6. Install radiator fan(s) attaching screws and tighten to 45 inch lbs (5 Nm).

7. Connect the radiator fan(s) electrical connectors.

8. Install the front fascia, as follows:
   a. Place bright chrome molding in position on the upper fascia.
   b. Using hand presser press bright chrome molding locking tabs in the full lock position.
   c. Position upper and lower fascia on a clean surface so that locking tabs align with the slots.
   d. Press the fascia together to lock locking tabs into position.
   e. Install new spring clips attaching upper and lower fascia together. The spring clips are not reusable.
   f. Place bumper fascia into position on vehicle.
   g. Install grille to fascia.
   h. Install screw attaching the upper grille support to the headlamp mounting panel at each side of the grille.
   i. Install push pins attaching the upper appearance panel to upper crossmember.
   j. Raise vehicle and support with safety stands, as necessary.
   k. Connect fog lamp wire connectors, if necessary.
   l. Position and align fascia slotted cut out into fender push fastener.

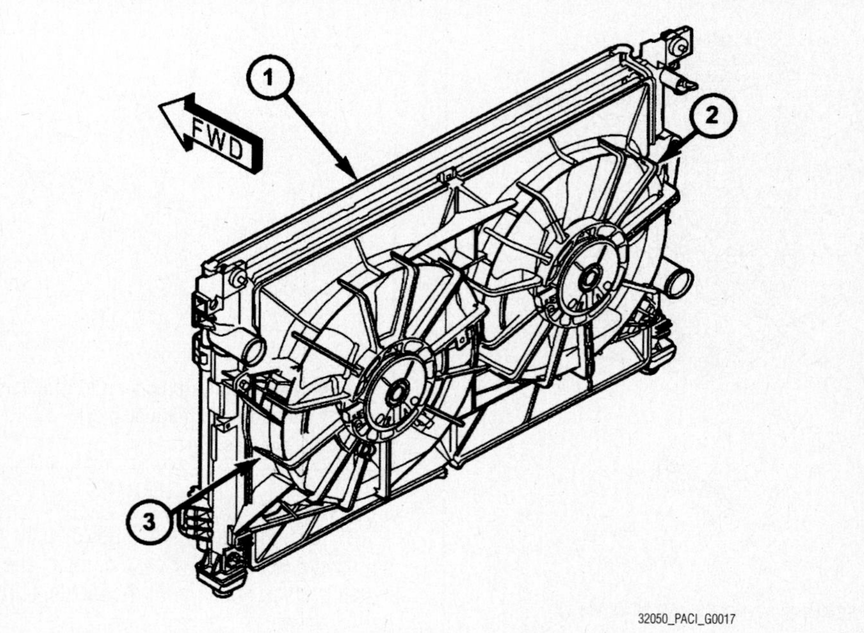

Fig. 36 Exploded view of the radiator (1), left fan (2) and right fan (3)

m. Install screw attaching fascia to the front fenders on each side.

n. Install front wheelhouse splash shields fasteners as necessary.

o. Install front wheels.

p. Install the four screws attaching bottom of fascia/air dam to radiator closure panel.

q. Lower vehicle.

r. Install the headlamp assemblies, as necessary.

s. Close hood.

t. Install the upper radiator mounts to the crossmember bolts, if removed. Tighten to 70 inch lbs. (8 Nm).

RADIATOR

REMOVAL & INSTALLATION

See Figures 37 and 38.

1. Disconnect negative cable from battery.
2. Properly discharge the A/C system.
3. Remove the front fascia, as follows:

a. Release hood latch and open hood.

b. Remove the headlamp assemblies, as necessary.

c. Hoist vehicle and support with safety stands, as necessary.

d. Remove the four screws attaching bottom of fascia/air dam to radiator closure panel.

➡The whole front splash shield does not need to be removed.

e. Remove three screws attaching front fascia to front splash shield on each side.

f. Remove the screw attaching fascia to the front fenders on each side .

g. Disconnect fog lamp wire connectors, if necessary.

h. Lower vehicle.

i. Remove push pins attaching the upper appearance panel to upper crossmember.

j. Remove screw attaching the upper grille support to the headlamp mounting panel at each side of the grille.

k. Remove bumper fascia from vehicle.

l. Place fascia on a clean surface.

m. Remove spring clips attaching upper and lower fascia together.

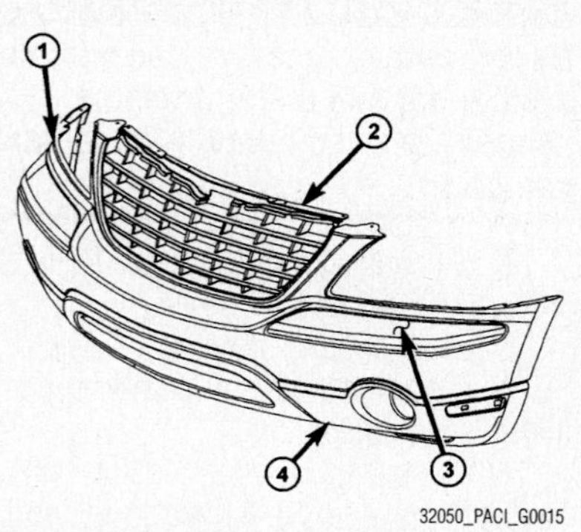

Fig. 37 View of the upper and lower front fascia and related components—typical

n. Using a trim stick release locking tabs and separate the upper and lower fascia.

o. Remove the bright chrome molding from the upper fascia. Using a trim stick, starting at the outer edge of the fascia release the locking tabs. Grip the molding and pull outward from the fascia while releasing the locking tabs.

p. Remove molding from fascia.

q. Remove grille from fascia.

⁂ CAUTION

Do not remove the cylinder block plug or the radiator draincock with the system hot and under pressure because serious burns from coolant can occur.

4. Drain the cooling system.
5. Disconnect the radiator fan electrical connectors.
6. Disconnect coolant reserve/recovery hose.
7. Remove A/C lines.
8. Remove the auxiliary transmission cooler hoses.
9. Remove the pushpins and the upper radiator seal.
10. Remove the pushpins and the LH and RH radiator seal.
11. Remove the A/C condenser side brackets to radiator attaching screws. Separate the condenser from the radiator by lifting upward to disengage from lower mounts. Allow the condenser to rest in front of radiator.
12. Remove the upper and lower radiator hoses.
13. Radiator can now be lifted free from engine compartment. Care should be taken not to damage radiator cooling fins or water tubes during removal.
14. Remove the auxiliary transmission from the radiator module.
15. Remove the cooling fan assembly from the radiator module.

To install:

16. Install A/C condenser, (if removed).
17. Install radiator fan assemble, if removed.
18. Install auxiliary transmission cooler, if removed.
19. Slide radiator down into position. Seat the radiator with the rubber isolators into the mounting holes provided, with a 10 lb. force.
20. Install mounting screws.
21. Connect the cooling fan electrical connector.

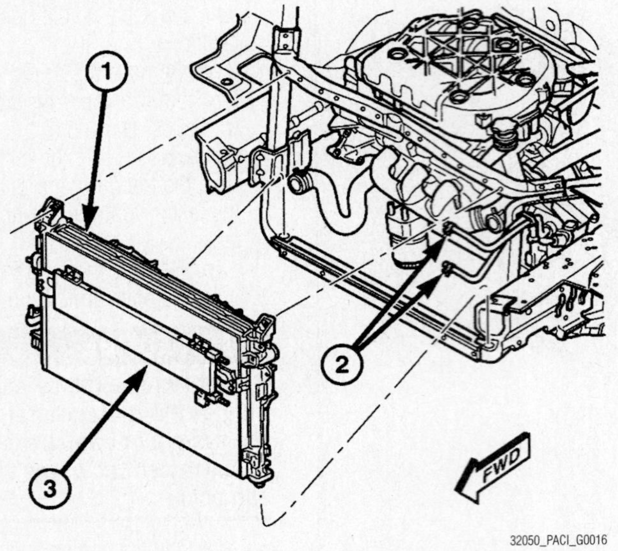

Fig. 38 Exploded view of the radiator module (1), auxiliary transaxle cooler hoses (2) and cooler (3)

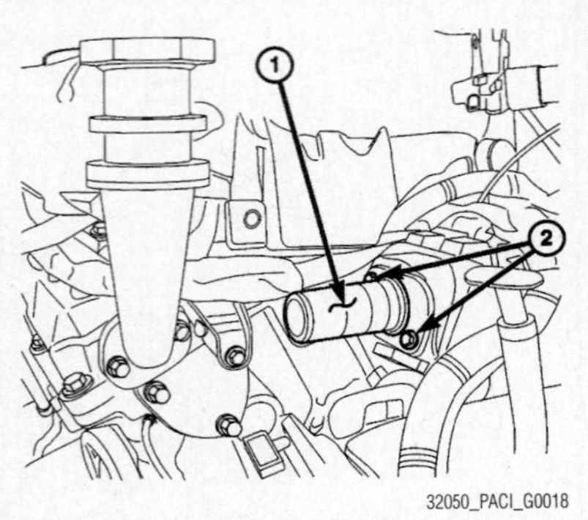

Fig. 39 View of the coolant outlet connector (1) and thermostat housing (2)—3.5L and 4.0L engines

22. Install the radiator upper and lower hoses.
23. In the LH and RH radiator seals.
24. Install the upper radiator seal.
25. Install the auxiliary transmission cooler hoses.
26. Connect the coolant reserve/recovery hose.
27. Install the front fascia, as follows:
   a. Place bright chrome molding in position on the upper fascia.
   b. Using hand presser press bright chrome molding locking tabs in the full lock position.
   c. Position upper and lower fascia on a clean surface so that locking tabs align with the slots.
   d. Press the fascia together to lock locking tabs into position.
   e. Install new spring clips attaching upper and lower fascia together. The spring clips are not reusable.
   f. Place bumper fascia into position on vehicle.
   g. Install grille to fascia.
   h. Install screw attaching the upper grille support to the headlamp mounting panel at each side of the grille.
   i. Install push pins attaching the upper appearance panel to upper cross-member.
   j. Raise vehicle and support with safety stands, as necessary.
   k. Connect fog lamp wire connectors, if necessary.
   l. Position and align fascia slotted cut out into fender push fastener.
   m. Install screw attaching fascia to the front fenders on each side.
   n. Install front wheelhouse splash shields fasteners as necessary.
   o. Install front wheels.
   p. Install the four screws attaching bottom of fascia/air dam to radiator closure panel.
   q. Lower vehicle.
   r. Install the headlamp assemblies, as necessary.
   s. Close hood.
28. Fill the cooling system.
29. Connect negative cable to battery.

THERMOSTAT

REMOVAL & INSTALLATION

3.5L and 4.0L Engines

See Figure 39.

⁂ CAUTION

Never remove pressure cap with the system hot and under pressure because serious burns from coolant can occur.

1. Disconnect negative cable from remote jumper terminal.
2. Drain cooling system.
3. Disconnect radiator upper hose from thermostat housing.
4. Remove thermostat housing bolts.
5. Remove housing, thermostat, and gasket.
6. Clean gasket sealing surfaces.

To install:

7. Install thermostat and gasket into thermostat housing. For ease of installation, install bolts in housing for thermostat and gasket retention.
8. Install thermostat and housing to the intake manifold. Tighten the bolts to 105 inch lbs. (12 Nm).
9. Connect radiator hoses and install hose clamp.
10. Refill cooling system.
11. Connect negative cable to remote jumper terminal.

3.8L Engine

See Figures 40 through 42.

1. Drain cooling system down below the thermostat level.
2. Remove radiator upper hose from coolant outlet connector.
3. Remove coolant outlet connector bolts and connector.
4. Remove thermostat from outlet connector.
5. Discard gasket and clean both gasket sealing surfaces.

To install:

6. To ensure proper seating of replacement thermostat, carefully remove the bulged metal from the wall of the outlet connector recess that was created during the staking procedure that held the OEM thermostat in place. It is not necessary to restake the replacement thermostat into the connector.
7. Position thermostat to coolant outlet connector. Align the two locating notches on thermostat to the connector. This position will ensure proper location of the thermostat air bleed.
8. Position a new gasket over the thermostat and connector making sure thermostat is in proper position and in the recess provided.

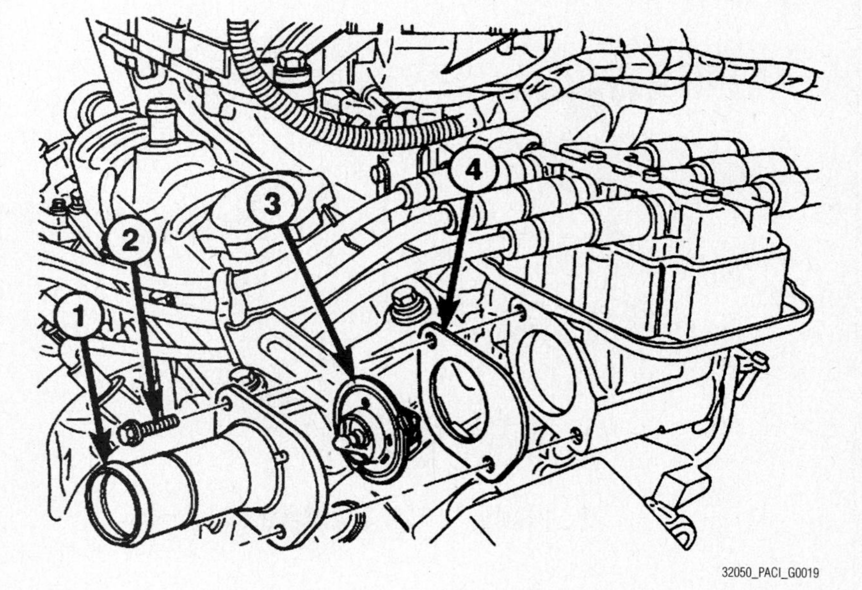

Fig. 40 View of the coolant outlet connector (1), bolt (2), thermostat (3) and gasket (4)—3.8L engine

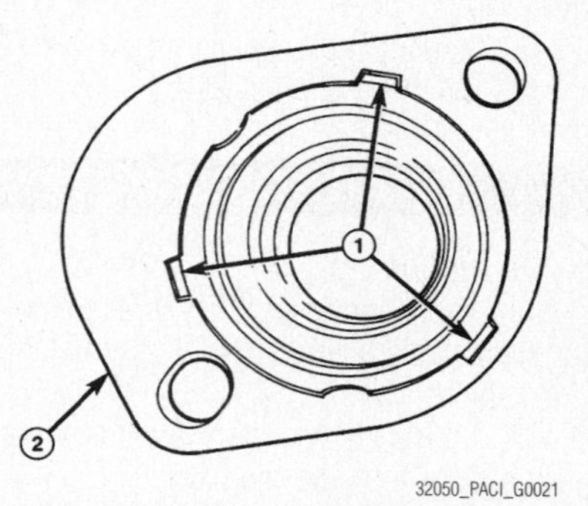

Fig. 41 View of the stake (1) and outlet connector (2)—3.8L engine

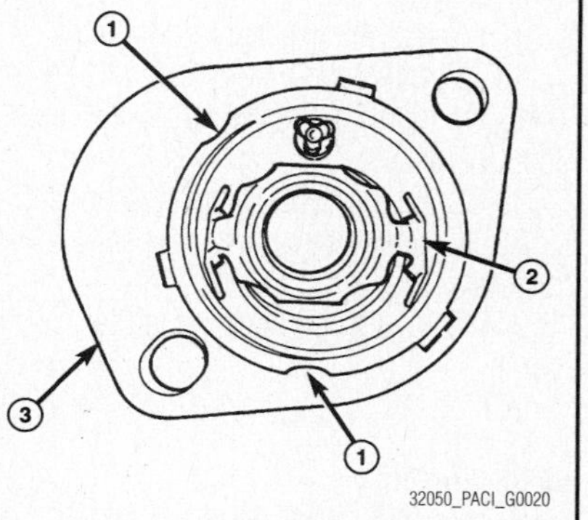

Fig. 42 Position thermostat to coolant outlet connector. Align the two locating notches (1) on thermostat (2) to the connector (3). This position will ensure proper location of the thermostat air bleed

9. Install thermostat and connector assembly to the intake manifold. Tighten bolts to 21 ft. lbs. (28 Nm).
10. Install the radiator upper hose to coolant outlet connector.
11. Refill the cooling system to the proper level.

WATER PUMP

REMOVAL & INSTALLATION

3.5L and 4.0L Engines

See Figure 43.

The water pump has a die cast aluminum body and a stamped steel impeller. It bolts directly to the chain case cover using an O-ring for sealing. It is driven by the back side of the serpentine belt.

It is normal for a small amount of coolant to drip from the weep hole located on the water pump body (small black spot). If this condition exists, DO NOT replace the water pump. Only replace the water pump if a heavy deposit or steady flow of brown/green coolant is visible on the water pump body from the weep hole, which would indicate shaft seal failure. Before replacing the water pump, be sure to perform a thorough inspection. A defective pump will not be able to circulate heated coolant through the long heater hose.

1. Before servicing the vehicle, refer to the precautions in the beginning of this section.
2. Drain the cooling system.

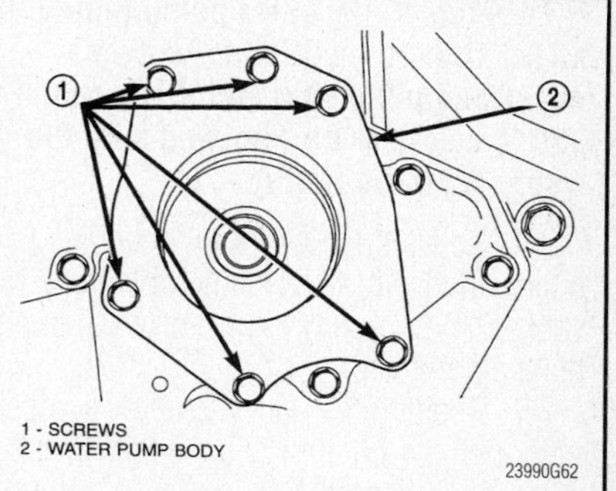

Fig. 43 Location of the water pump mounting bolts—3.5L and 4.0L engines

✲✲ WARNING

Do not use pliers to open the plastic drain.

3. Remove or disconnect the following:
   - Negative battery cable
   - Coolant recovery cap and open the thermostat bleed valve
   - Timing belt

➡It is good practice to turn the crankshaft until the No. 1 cylinder is at Top Dead Center (TDC) of its compression stroke (firing position).

   - Water pump mounting bolts and pump. Discard the O-ring seal.
4. Clean the gasket sealing surfaces, being careful not to scratch the aluminum surfaces.

To install:

5. Install or connect the following:
   - New O-ring and coat with dielectric grease prior to installation
   - Water pump with a new O-ring. Torque the water pump-to-engine bolts to 105 inch lbs. (12 Nm).

✲✲ WARNING

Rotate the pump and check for freedom of movement.

   - Timing belt
6. Fill the cooling system.
7. Reconnect the negative battery cable. Start the engine and allow it to reach normal operating temperatures.
8. Check the cooling system for leaks and correct coolant level.

3.8L Engine

See Figure 44.

1. Drain the cooling system.
2. Remove the accessory drive belt shield.
3. Remove the accessory drive belt.
4. Remove the water pump pulley bolts.

➡To remove the water pump pulley, it MUST first be positioned between water pump housing and drive hub. The pulley can then be removed with the water pump assembly.

5. Rotate the pulley until openings in pulley align with water pump drive hub spokes. Move pulley inward between pump housing and hub.
6. Position the pulley to allow access to water pump mounting bolts. Remove water pump mounting bolts.
7. Remove the water pump with the pulley loosely positioned between hub and the pump body.
8. Remove and discard the seal.
9. Clean the seal groove and sealing surfaces on pump and timing chain case cover. Take care not to scratch or gouge sealing surfaces.

To install:

➡The water pump pulley MUST be positioned loosely between the pump housing and drive hub BEFORE water pump installation.

10. Position the water pump pulley loosely between pump housing and drive hub.

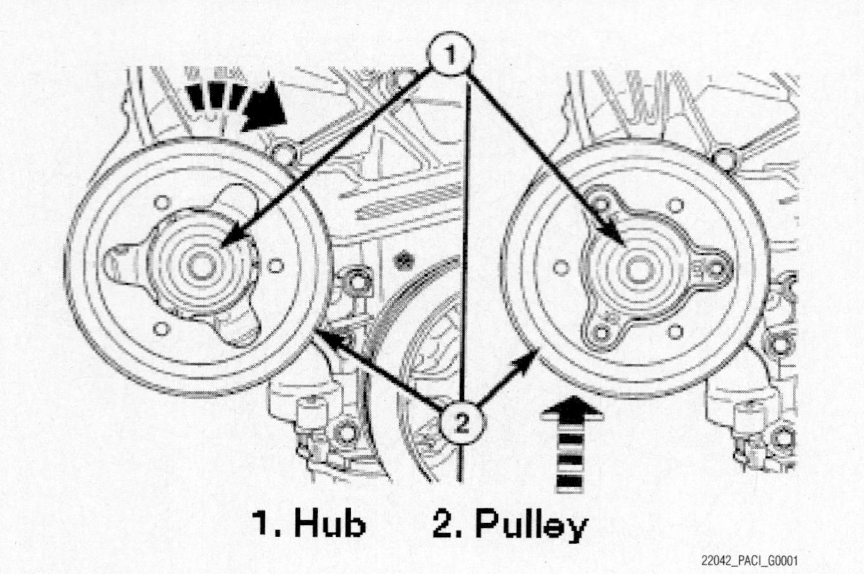

Fig. 44 Water pump pulley alignment—3.8L engine

11. Install the water pump and pulley to the timing chain case cover. Tighten water pump bolts to 105 inch lbs. (12 Nm).
12. Position the pulley on water pump hub. Install bolts and tighten to 21 ft. lbs. (28 Nm).
13. Rotate the pump by hand to check for freedom of movement.
14. Install the accessory drive belt.
15. Install the drive belt shield.
16. Fill the cooling system.

ENGINE ELECTRICAL

CHARGING SYSTEM

ALTERNATOR

REMOVAL & INSTALLATION

3.5L Engine

1. Before servicing the vehicle, refer to the precautions in the beginning of this section.
2. Remove or disconnect the following:
   - Negative battery cable
   - Engine cover
   - Drive belt
   - Alternator B+ terminal nut and wire
   - Alternator field circuit wiring by pushing the red locking tab
   - Upper mounting bracket
   - Lower mounting bolts and the alternator

To install:

3. Install or connect the following:
   - Alternator and lower mounting bolts, tighten to 40 ft. lbs. (54 Nm)
   - Upper mounting bracket and tighten the bolts 20 ft. lbs. (28 Nm)
   - Alternator field circuit wiring making sure to engage the red locking tab
   - Alternator B+ terminal nut and wire, tighten the nut to 110 inch lbs. (12 Nm)
   - Drive belt
   - Engine cover
   - Negative battery cable

3.8L Engine

1. Before servicing the vehicle, refer to the precautions in the beginning of this section.
2. Disconnect the negative battery cable.
3. Remove the air cleaner assembly.
4. Disconnect the alternator electrical connectors.
5. Remove the cover from the battery cable at the rear of the alternator.
6. Disconnect the positive battery cable from rear of the alternator.
7. Remove the accessory drive belt.
8. Remove the three mounting bolts for the power Steering assembly and set the assembly aside.
9. Remove the idler pulley/lower mounting bolt.
10. Remove the alternator rear mounting bolt.
11. Remove the alternator upper mounting bolt.
12. Remove the alternator and idler pulley.

To install:

13. Attach the idler pulley to alternator and install the alternator/idler assembly in the vehicle.
14. Loosely install the alternator upper, rear and lower mounting bolts.
15. Tighten all mounting bolts to 40 ft. lbs. (54 Nm).
16. Install the power steering pump assembly and tighten the bolts to 200 inch lbs. (23 Nm).
17. Install the accessory drive belt.
18. Connect the battery cable to the alternator and tighten the nut to 110 inch lbs. (12 Nm).
19. Snap the cable cover into position.
20. Connect the alternator electrical connectors
21. Connect the negative battery cable.
22. Install the air cleaner assembly.

4.0L Engine

1. Before servicing the vehicle, refer to the precautions in the beginning of this section.
2. Remove or disconnect the following:
   - Negative battery cable

- Drive belt
- Alternator B+ terminal nut and wire
- Alternator field circuit wiring by pushing the locking tab
- Mounting bolts and the alternator

To install:

3. Installation is the reverse of the removal procedure.
4. Tighten the mounting bolts to 40 ft. lbs.
5. Tighten the mounting nut stud to 115 inch lbs.

➡When installing the drive belt be sure it is routed correctly. The water pump will rotate in the wrong direction, causing overheating, if the belt is installed wrong. Never force the belt over the pulley rim as the synthetic fiber of the belt can be damaged.

ENGINE ELECTRICAL

IGNITION SYSTEM

FIRING ORDER

See Figures 45 and 46.

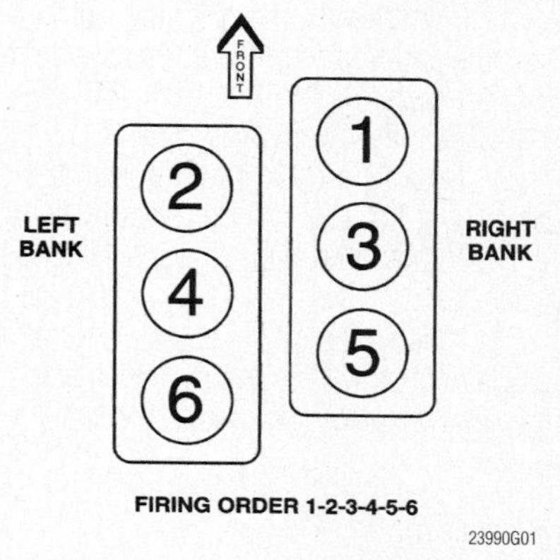

Fig. 45 3.5L VIN 4 and 4.0L VIN X Engines Firing Order: 1–2–3–4–5–6 Distributorless ignition system

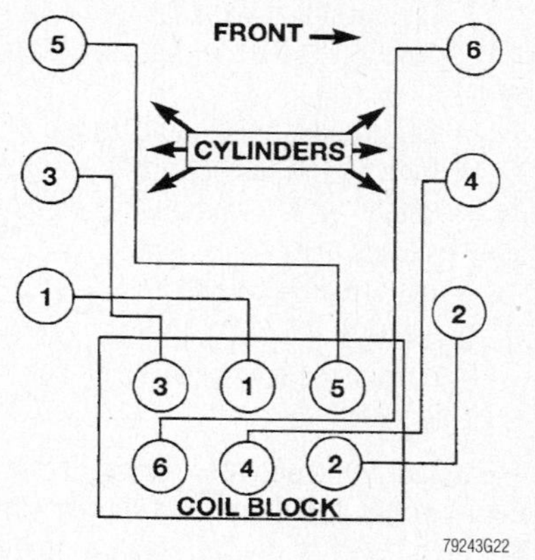

Fig. 46 3.8L VIN L Engine Firing order: 1–2–3–4–5–6 Distributorless ignition system

IGNITION COIL

REMOVAL & INSTALLATION

3.5L Engine

Front

See Figure 47.

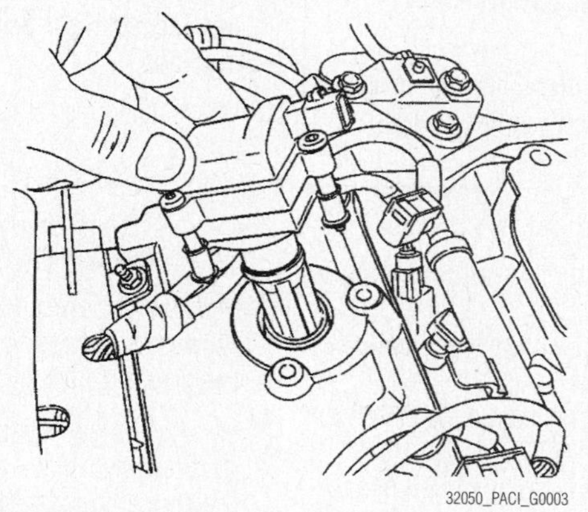

Fig. 47 Removing the ignition coils—3.5L engine

1. Before servicing the vehicle, refer to the precautions in the beginning of this section.
2. Remove the electrical connector from the ignition coil.
3. Disconnect the negative battery cable.
4. Remove the upper intake manifold.

➡Prior to removing the ignition coils, spray compressed air around the coil area and spark plug.

5. It is necessary to loosen the screws by alternating back and forth. Do not lose the spacers under the coil when loosening the screws.
6. Remove the ignition coil.

To install:

7. Install the ignition coil.
8. Hand-tighten coil screws and tighten to 60 inch lbs. (6.7 Nm).
9. Install and lock the electrical connector to the ignition coil.
10. Install the upper intake manifold.
11. Connect the negative battery cable.

Rear

See Figure 47.

1. Before servicing the vehicle, refer to the precautions in the beginning of this section.
2. Disconnect the negative battery cable.
3. Remove the electrical connector from the ignition coil.

➡Prior to removing the ignition coils, spray compressed air around the coil area and spark plug.

4. It is necessary to loosen the screws by alternating back and forth. Do not lose the spacers under the coil when loosening the screws.
5. Remove the ignition coil.

To install:

6. Install the ignition coil.
7. Hand tighten coil screws and tighten to 60 inch lbs. (6.7 Nm).
8. Install and lock the electrical connector to the ignition coil.
9. Connect the negative battery cable.

3.8L Engine

See Figure 49.

1. Before servicing the vehicle, refer to the precautions in the beginning of this section.
2. Disconnect the negative battery cable.
3. Unlock and disconnect the electrical connector from ignition coil.
4. Grasping the spark plug cable, twist the assembly 1/2 turn and pull the cable from the ignition coil.
5. Remove the nuts from the mounting studs.
6. Pull coil assembly straight up and off of mounting studs.

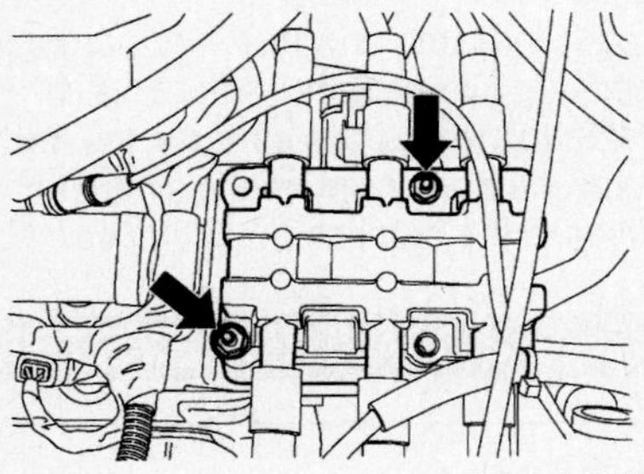

Fig. 49 Unlock and disconnect the electrical connector from the ignition coil—3.8L engine

To install:

7. Install ignition coil over mounting studs.
8. Connect and lock the electrical connector to ignition coil.
9. Install mounting nuts and tighten to 105 inch lbs. (11.5 Nm).
10. Install ignition cables to coil assembly.
11. Connect the negative battery cable.

4.0L Engine

1. Before servicing the vehicle, refer to the precautions in the beginning of this section.
2. Disconnect the negative battery cable.
3. Remove the intake manifold.
4. Disconnect the electrical connector from the coil.
5. Remove the mounting bolt.
6. Remove the coil assembly by turning the assembly 1/2 turn and pulling straight up in a steady motion.

To install:

7. Installation is the reverse of the removal procedure.
8. Tighten the coil retaining bolt to 71 inch lbs.

IGNITION TIMING

ADJUSTMENT

This vehicle utilize a Distributorless Ignition System (DIS). It is a fixed ignition timing system, which means that basic ignition timing cannot be adjusted. All spark advance is permanently set by the Powertrain Control Module (PCM).

SPARK PLUGS

REMOVAL & INSTALLATION

3.5L Engine

➡Always remove the ignition coil assembly by grasping at the spark plug boot, turning the assembly 1/2 turn and pulling straight back in a steady motion.

1. Disconnect the negative battery cable.
2. If removing the front spark plugs, remove the intake manifold.
3. Remove the ignition coil.

➡Prior to removing the ignition coils, spray compressed air around the coil area and spark plug.

4. It is necessary to loosen the screws by alternating back and forth. Do not lose the spacers under the coil when loosening the screws.
5. Remove spark plug(s).

To install:

➡To avoid cross threading, start the spark plug into the cylinder head by hand.

6. Install the spark plugs and tighten to 13 ft. lbs. (17 Nm).
7. Install ignition coil assembly onto spark plug.
8. Hand-tighten the coil screws to 60 inch lbs. (6.7 Nm).
9. Connect and lock the electrical connector.
10. If removed, install the intake manifold.
11. Connect the negative battery cable.

3.8L Engine

✱✱ WARNING

When replacing the spark plugs and spark plug cables, route the cables correctly and secure them in the appropriate retainers. Failure to route the cables properly can cause the radio to reproduce ignition noise, cross ignition of the spark plugs or short circuit the cables to ground.

➡Always remove cables by grasping at the boot, rotating the boot ½ turn, and pulling straight back in a steady motion.

1. Prior to removing the spark plug, spray compressed air around the spark plug hole and the area around the spark plug.
2. Remove the spark plug using a quality socket with a foam insert.
3. Inspect the spark plug condition.

To install:

4. Coat threads of spark plug with a suitable anti-seize lubricant. Be sure not to get anti-seize ANYWHERE BUT ON THE THREADS OF THE SPARK PLUG.
5. To avoid cross threading, start the spark plug into the cylinder head by hand.
6. Tighten the spark plugs to 13 ft. lbs. (17.5 Nm).
7. Install spark plug cables over spark plugs. A click will be heard and felt when the cable properly attaches to the spark plug.

4.0L Engine

1. Before servicing the vehicle, refer to the precautions in the beginning of this section.
2. Disconnect the negative battery cable.
3. Remove the intake manifold.
4. Disconnect the electrical connector from the coil.
5. Remove the mounting bolt.
6. Remove the coil assembly by turning the assembly 1/2 turn and pulling straight up in a steady motion.
7. Remove the spark plug.

To install:

8. Installation is the reverse of the removal procedure.

➡Do not over apply anti-seize compound, only use enough to lightly coat the plug threads. Install each plug by hand, then torque to specification.

9. Tighten the spark plug to 20 ft. lbs. (27 Nm).
10. Tighten the coil retaining bolt to 71 inch lbs. (8 Nm).

STARTER

REMOVAL & INSTALLATION

3.5L Engine

1. Before servicing the vehicle, refer to the precautions in the beginning of this section.
2. Disconnect the negative battery cable.
3. Remove or disconnect the following:
   - Upper radiator crossmember
   - Radiator fan module
   - Wiring harness clip from the front mount
   - Coolant line clamp bolt
   - Upper nut from the front mount
   - Upper starter mounting bolt
   - Middle starter bolt
   - Lower front mount nut
   - Lower bracket-to-transmission bolt
   - Lower bracket-to-engine block bolt
4. Move the front mount and bracket out of the way.
   - Positive battery cable from the starter
   - Solenoid connector from the starter
   - Lower starter bolt and the starter.

To install:

5. Install or connect the following:
   - Starter and lower bolt. Tighten to 35 ft. lbs. (47 Nm)
   - Solenoid connector to the starter
   - Positive battery cable to the starter
6. Move the front mount and bracket into position.
   - Middle starter bolt. Tighten to 35 ft. lbs. (47 Nm)
   - Lower bracket-to-engine block bolt. Tighten to 50 ft. lbs. (67 Nm)
   - Lower bracket-to-transmission bolt. Tighten to 50 ft. lbs. (67 Nm)
   - Lower front mount nut. Tighten to 75 ft. lbs. (101 Nm)
   - Upper starter mounting bolt. Tighten to 35 ft. lbs. (47 Nm)
   - Upper nut to the front mount
   - Coolant line clamp bolt
   - Wiring harness clip from the front mount
   - Radiator fan module
   - Upper radiator crossmember
   - Negative battery cable

3.8L Engine

1. Before servicing the vehicle, refer to the precautions in the beginning of this section.
2. Disconnect the negative battery cable.
3. Remove and relocate the speed control servo.
4. Unlock the electrical connector and disconnect the vacuum hose from servo.

(4)Unlock and disconnect the electrical connectors from the cooling module.

5. Disconnect the wiring clips from cooling module.
6. Remove the retaining clip from the top of the cooling module.
7. Remove the two fasteners and remove fan module from the vehicle.
8. Remove the bolt from the oil cooler line bracket in the front motor mount.
9. Remove the battery positive cable from the starter.
10. Remove the lower, middle and upper starter bolt.
11. Place a piece of cardboard in front of the radiator core, to keep from damaging the radiator.
12. Remove the starter, and disconnect the solenoid wire from the starter.
13. Remove the starter.

To install:

14. Place a piece of cardboard in front of the radiator core, to keep from damaging the radiator.
15. Place the starter on the lower crossmember and connect the starter solenoid connector.
16. Install the dust shield on the nose of the starter, make sure of proper orientation.
17. Loosely install the starter mounting bolts.
18. Tighten the mounting bolts to 35 ft. lbs. (47 Nm).
19. Install the remaining components in the reverse order of removal.

4.0L Engine

See Figure 50.

1. Before servicing the vehicle, refer to the precautions in the beginning of this section.
2. Disconnect the negative battery cable.
3. Install engine support tool 8534-12, or equivalent.
4. Remove the left exhaust manifold.
5. Disconnect the starter electrical connectors.
6. Remove the transaxle to starter retaining bolt.
7. Support the engine/transaxle assembly using a suitable jack.
8. Remove the two front transaxle mount to starter mounting bolts.
9. Remove the starter from its mounting.

➡Rotate the starter to allow removal from the vehicle.

To install:

10. Installation is the reverse of the removal procedure.
11. Tighten the two front transaxle mount to starter mounting bolts to 40 ft. lbs.
12. Tighten the transaxle to starter mounting bolt to 35.5 ft. lbs.

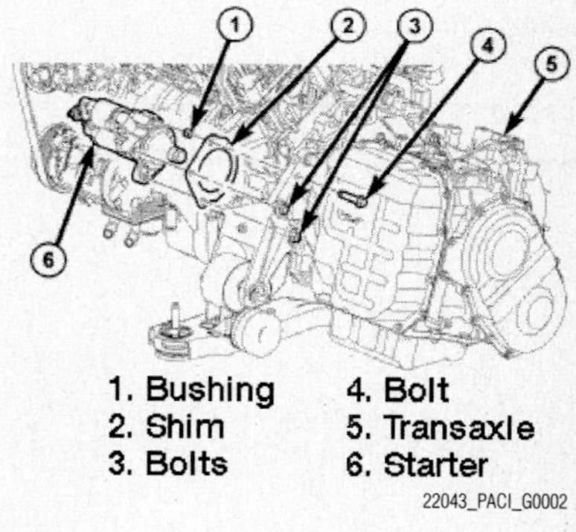

Fig. 50 Starter and related components—4.0L engine

ENGINE MECHANICAL

➡Disconnecting the negative battery cable may interfere with the functions of the on board computer systems and may require the computer to undergo a relearning process, once the negative battery cable is reconnected.

ACCESSORY DRIVE BELTS

ACCESSORY BELT ROUTING

See Figures 51 through 53.

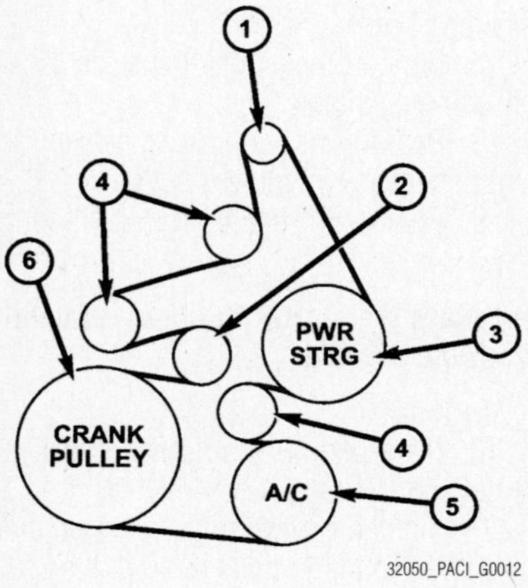

Fig. 51 Accessory drive belt routing: Alternator (1), Automatic Tensioner (2), P/S Pump (3), Idler Pulley (4), A/C Compressor (5), Crankshaft Pulley (6)—3.5L engine

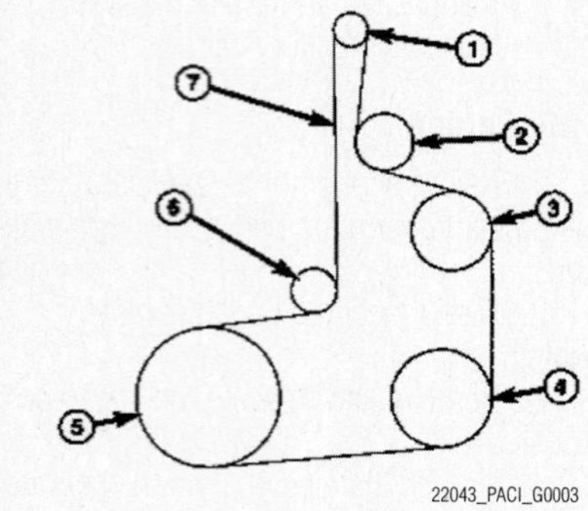

Fig. 53 Accessory drive belt routing: Alternator (1), Idler pulley (2), P/S Pump (3), A/C Compressor pulley (4), Crankshaft pulley (5), Accessory Drive Belt tensioner (6), Accessory Drive Belt (7)—4.0L engine

INSPECTION

See Figure 54.

Belt replacement under any or all of the following conditions is required:

- Excessive wear
- Frayed cords
- Severe glazing

Poly-V Belt system may develop minor cracks across the ribbed side (due to reverse bending). These minor cracks are considered normal and acceptable. Parallel cracks are not acceptable and require belt replacement.

➡Do not use any type of belt dressing or restorer on Poly-V Belts.

ADJUSTMENT

The tension of the drive belts on these vehicles is maintained by automatic tensioners. No adjustments are necessary.

REMOVAL & INSTALLATION

See Figures 55 and 56.

1. Before servicing the vehicle, refer to the precautions in the beginning of this section.
2. Raise and safely support the vehicle.
3. Remove the drive belt shield.

⁂ CAUTION

Never allow drive belt tensioner to snap back, as damage to tensioner and/or personal injury could result.

4. Position a wrench on the belt tensioner lug.
5. Release belt tension by rotating the tensioner counterclockwise.
6. Remove the drive belt.
7. Carefully return tensioner to its relaxed position.

To install:

8. Route and position the drive belt onto all pulleys, except for the crankshaft.
9. Rotate belt tensioner counterclockwise until belt can be installed onto the crankshaft pulley. Slowly release belt tensioner.
10. Verify belt is properly routed and engaged on all pulleys.
11. Install drive belt shield and lower vehicle.

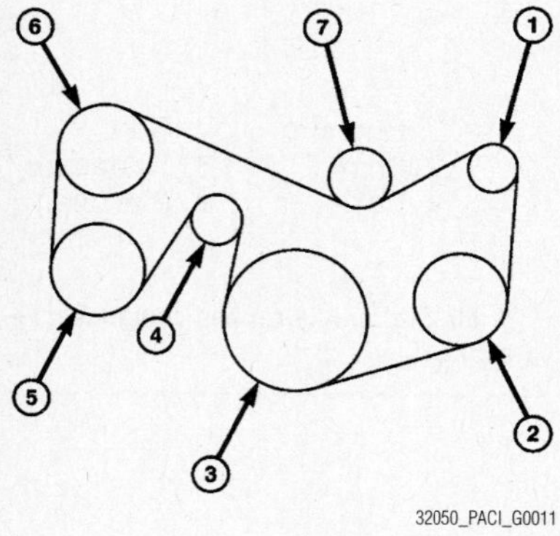

Fig. 52 Accessory V-belt routing: Alternator pulley (1), A/C Compressor pulley (2), Crankshaft pulley (3), Tensioner pulley (4), Water Pump pulley (5), P/S Pump pulley (6), Idler pulley (7)—3.8L engine

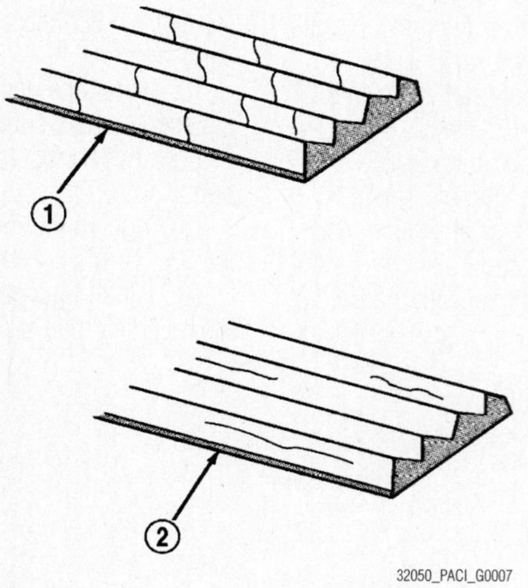

Fig. 54 View of belt with normal cracks – belt OK (1) and abnormal cracks – belt requires replacement (2)

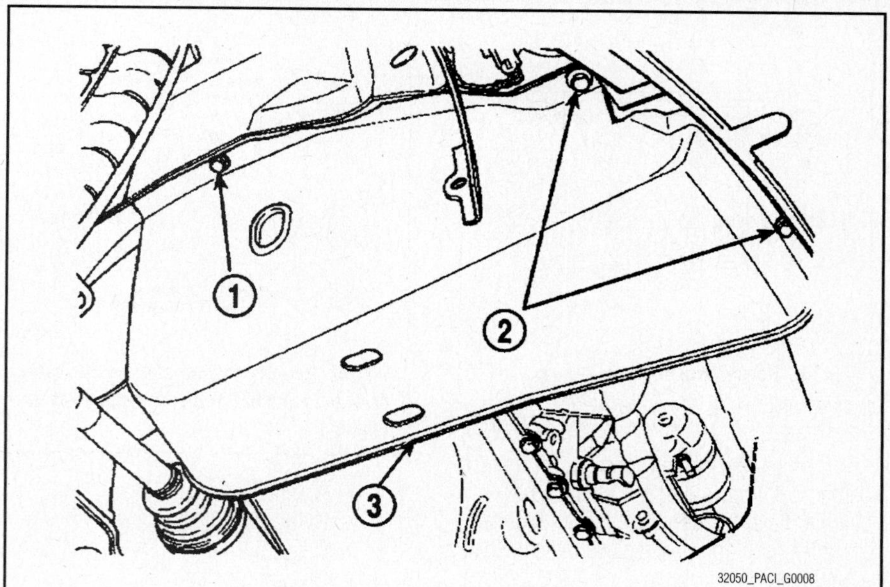

Fig. 55 Remove the attaching screws (1 & 2) and remove the splash shield (3)—3.5L and 4.0L engines

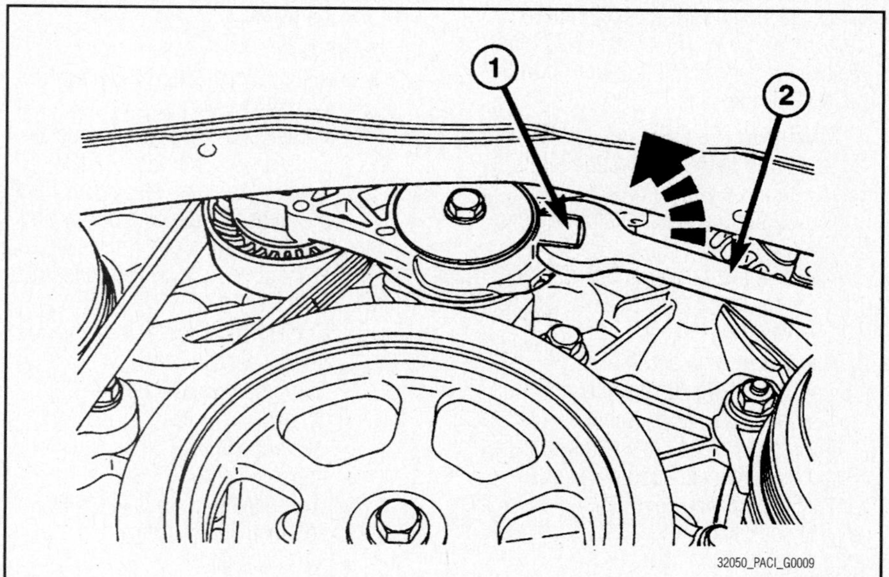

Fig. 56 Position a wrench (2) on the belt tensioner lug (1), then release belt tension by rotating the tensioner counterclockwise—3.5L and 4.0L engines

CAMSHAFT AND VALVE LIFTERS

INSPECTION

3.5L and 4.0L Engines

See Figure 57.

1. Inspect camshaft bearing journals for damage and binding. If journals are binding, check the cylinder head for damage. Also check cylinder head oil holes for clogging.

2. Check the cam lobe and bearing surfaces for abnormal wear and damage. Replace camshaft if defective.

➡If the camshaft is replaced due to lobe wear or damage, always replace the rocker arms.

3. Measure the lobe actual wear and replace camshaft if out of limit. Standard value is 0.001 in. (0.0254mm), wear limit is 0.010 in. (0.254mm).

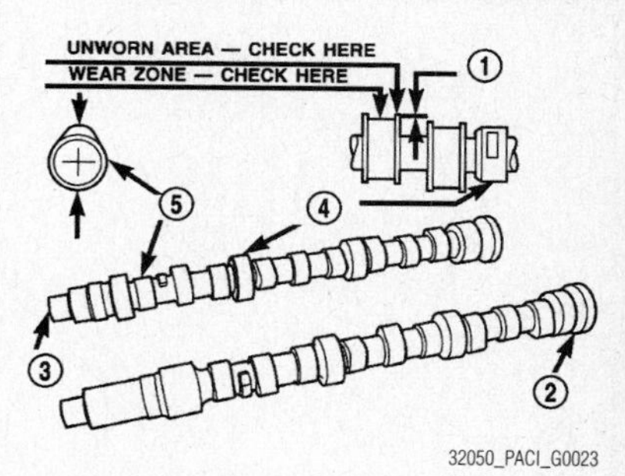

Fig. 57 Measure the lobe actual wear (1), left camshaft (2), right camshaft (3), bearing journal (4) and camshaft lobe (5)—3.5L engine

3.8L Engine

See Figure 58.

1. Check the cam lobes and bearing surfaces for abnormal wear and damage. Replace camshaft as required.

➡If camshaft is replaced due to lobe wear or damage, always replace the lifters.

2. Measure the lobe actual wear (unworn area - wear zone = actual wear) and replace camshaft if out of limit. Standard value is 0.001 in. (0.0254mm), wear limit is 0.010 in. (0.254mm).

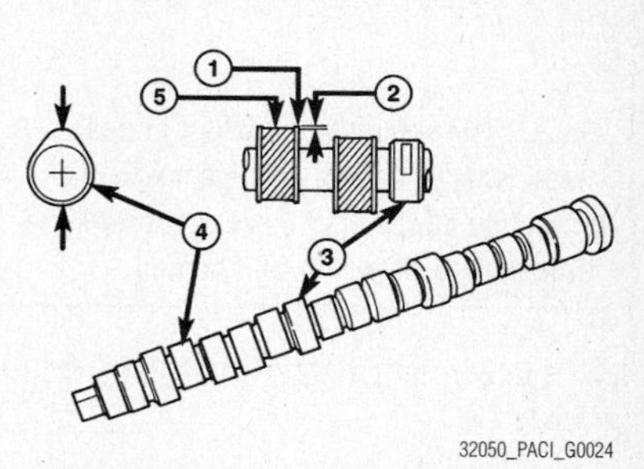

Fig. 58 Camshaft unworn area (1), actual wear (2), bearing journal (3), lobe (4) and wear zone (5)—3.8L engine

REMOVAL & INSTALLATION

3.5L and 4.0L Engines

See Figures 59 through 61.

1. Before servicing the vehicle, refer to the precautions in the beginning of this section.

Camshafts are serviced from the rear of the cylinder head. Although the engine does not need to be removed for camshaft service, the cylinder head must be removed from the vehicle. Note too, that the camshaft sprockets have a D-shaped hole that allows

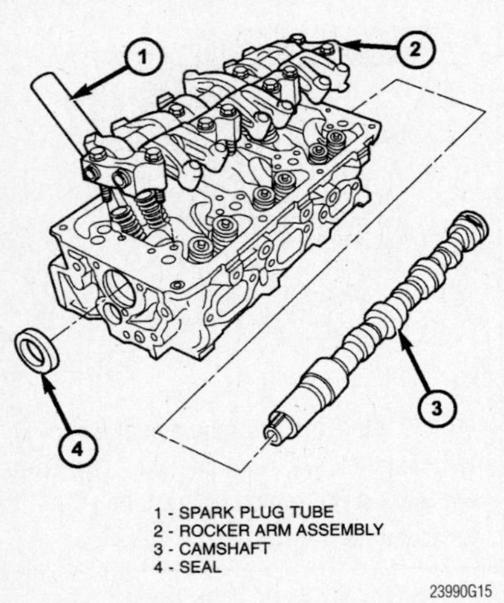

Fig. 59 Exploded view of the camshaft assembly—3.5L and 4.0L engines

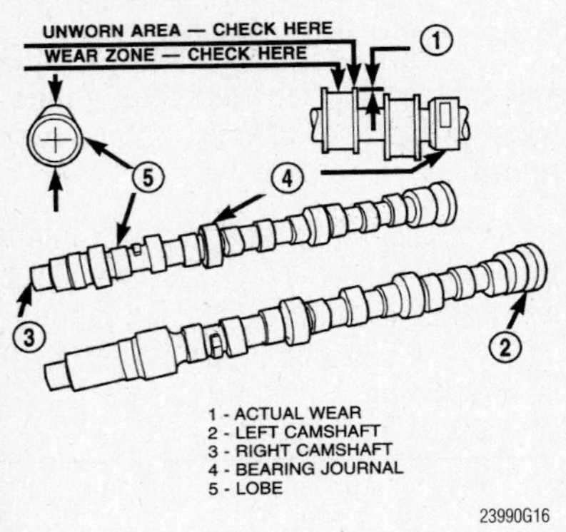

Fig. 60 Measure the camshaft to ensure it meets specifications, if the camshaft is worn beyond the specifications it must be replaced—3.5L and 4.0L engines

it to rotate several degrees in each direction on its shaft.

2. Properly relieve the fuel system pressure.
3. Drain the cooling system.
4. Remove or disconnect the following:
   - Cylinder head bolts and cylinder head

➡Mark the rocker arm assembly to note component locations before disassembly.

5. Remove the rocker arm and shaft assemblies.
6. Remove the rear camshaft cover and O-ring.

⁂ WARNING

Carefully, remove the camshaft from the rear of the head taking care not to nick or scratch the journals.

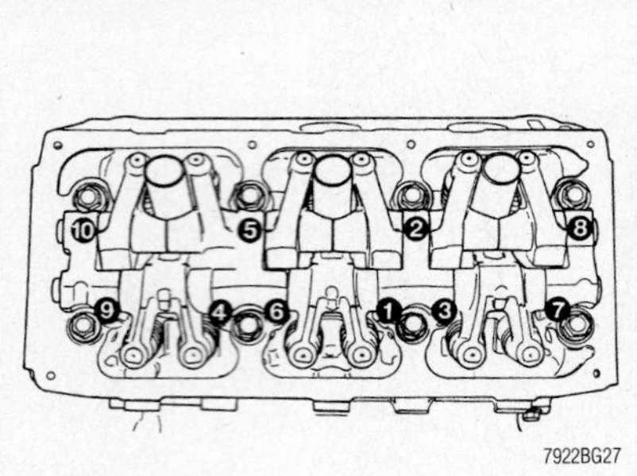

Fig. 61 Rocker arm/shaft tightening sequence—3.5L and 4.0L engines

7. Inspect camshaft journals for wear or damage. If wear is present, inspect the cylinder head for damage. Inspect the head oil holes for clogging. Replace the camshaft as required.
8. Measure the height of the cam using a micrometer. Measure in 2 places: the unworn area and in the wear zone. Subtract the figures to get cam wear. The standard specification is 0.001 in. (0.0254mm) with the wear limit being 0.010 in. (0.254mm). Replace the camshaft if it is worn beyond this specification.

To install:

9. Lubricate the camshaft journals and lobes with clean engine oil.
10. Install or connect the following:
    - Camshaft
    - Camshaft cover and O-ring and torque the bolts to 21 ft. lbs. (28 Nm)
    - Rocker arm assemblies
    - Cylinder head assembly
    - Negative battery cable
11. Fill and bleed the cooling system. An oil and filter change is recommended.
12. Start the vehicle, check for leaks and repair if necessary.

3.8L Engine

See Figure 62.

➡Keep all valvetrain components in order for assembly.

1. Before servicing the vehicle, refer to the precautions in the beginning of this section.
2. Remove the engine from the vehicle and mount it on a stand.
3. Remove or disconnect the following:
   - Valve covers
   - Rocker arm and shaft assemblies
   - Pushrods
   - Intake manifold
   - Cylinder heads
   - Yoke retainer

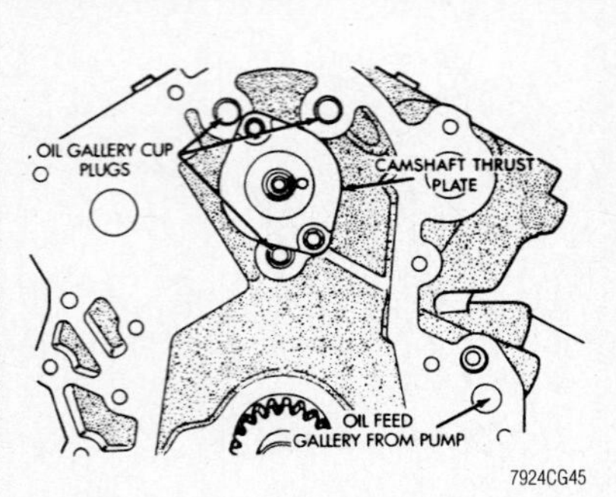

Fig. 62 Remove the thrust plate and withdraw the camshaft from the engine—3.8L engine

   - Aligning yokes
   - Hydraulic lifters
   - Oil pan
   - Oil pump pickup tube
   - Crankshaft pulley
   - Front cover
   - Timing chain and sprockets
   - Camshaft thrust plate
   - Camshaft

To install:

4. Install or connect the following:
   - Camshaft
   - Camshaft thrust plate. Torque the bolts to 105 inch lbs. (12 Nm).
   - Timing chain and sprockets. Torque the camshaft sprocket bolt to 40 ft. lbs. (54 Nm).
   - Front cover. Torque the bolts to 20 ft. lbs. (27 Nm).
   - Crankshaft pulley. Torque the bolt to 40 ft. lbs. (54 Nm).
   - Oil pump pickup tube
   - Oil pan
   - Hydraulic lifters
   - Aligning yokes
   - Yoke retainer. Torque the bolts to 105 inch lbs. (12 Nm).
   - Cylinder heads
   - Intake manifold
   - Pushrods
   - Rocker arm and shaft assemblies
   - Valve covers
5. Install the engine to the vehicle.

CRANKSHAFT FRONT SEAL

REMOVAL & INSTALLATION

3.5L and 4.0L Engines

See Figures 63 and 64.

Note that the timing belt must be removed from the vehicle to perform this service. Use care to be sure all valve timing marks are carefully aligned both before

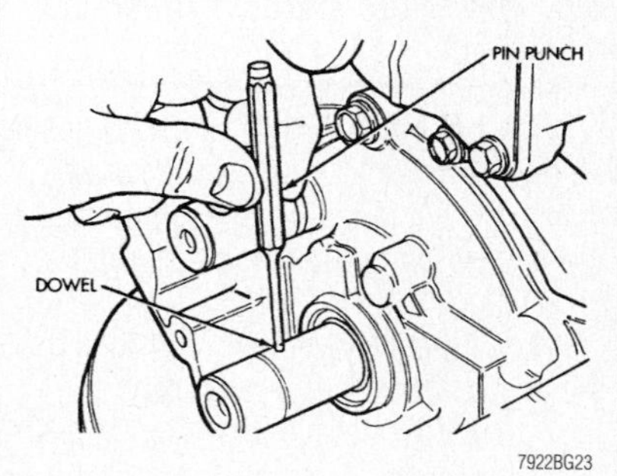

Fig. 63 Removing the timing belt sprocket dowel pin from the crankshaft—3.5L and 4.0L engines

removing the belt and after belt installation and all service has been completed. It may be good practice to set the engine to Top Dead Center (TDC) No. 1 cylinder compression stroke (firing position) and aligning all timing marks before removing the timing belt. This serves as a reference for all work that follows.

1. Before servicing the vehicle, refer to the precautions at the beginning of this section.
2. Properly relieve the fuel system pressure.
3. Drain the cooling system.
4. Remove or disconnect the following:
   - Negative battery cable
   - Radiator and cooling fan module assembly
   - Accessory drive belts
   - Crankshaft damper bolt
   - Timing belt front cover

➡The sealer on the timing belt front cover may be reusable and should not be removed. Use silicone rubber adhesive sealant to replace any missing sealer.

   - Timing belt and tensioner
   - Crankshaft timing belt sprocket
5. Locate the small dowel pin in the crankshaft. With a small punch, carefully tap out the dowel from the end of the crankshaft.
6. Remove the crankshaft seal using tool 6341A, taking care not to nick the shaft seal surface or seal bore during removal.

To install:

7. Inspect the crankshaft seal lip surface for varnish and dirt. Polish the area using 400 grit sandpaper to remove varnish as necessary.
8. Install or connect the following:
   - Crankshaft seal using seal installer tool 6342
   - Rear lower timing belt cover

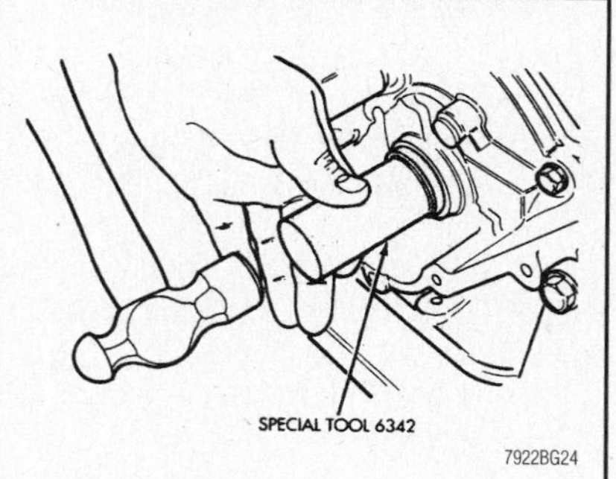

Fig. 64 Installing the crankshaft oil seal—3.5L and 4.0L engines

   - Dowel into the crankshaft so that it protrudes 0.047 in. (1.2mm)
   - Timing belt sprocket at the crankshaft using tool C-4685C1, thrust bearing, washer and 12mm bolt or an equivalent setup to pull the sprocket onto crankshaft. Do not hammer on the sprocket.
9. Verify that all valve timing marks are aligned.
   - Timing belt and tensioner using the recommended procedure
10. Rotate the crankshaft 2 complete turns and recheck the timing marks on the camshafts and crankshaft. The marks must align with their respective locations. If the marks do not align, repeat the timing belt installation procedure. When correct valve timing has been verified, install the timing belt covers.
   - Crankshaft damper. Hold the crankshaft damper, using tool L-3281, and torque the bolt to 85 ft. lbs. (115 Nm).
   - Accessory drive belts and adjust to the proper tension
   - Radiator and cooling fan assemblies
   - Negative battery cable
11. Fill and bleed the cooling system.
12. Start the vehicle, check for leaks and repair if necessary.

3.8L Engine

See Figures 65 and 66.

1. Before servicing the vehicle, refer to the precautions in the beginning of this section.
2. Remove or disconnect the following:
   - Negative battery cable
   - Right wheel and splash shield
   - Accessory drive belts
   - Crankshaft pulley
3. Place tool 6341A on the crankshaft nose and screw the tool into the seal until it is engaged being careful not to damage the crankshaft seal surface cover.

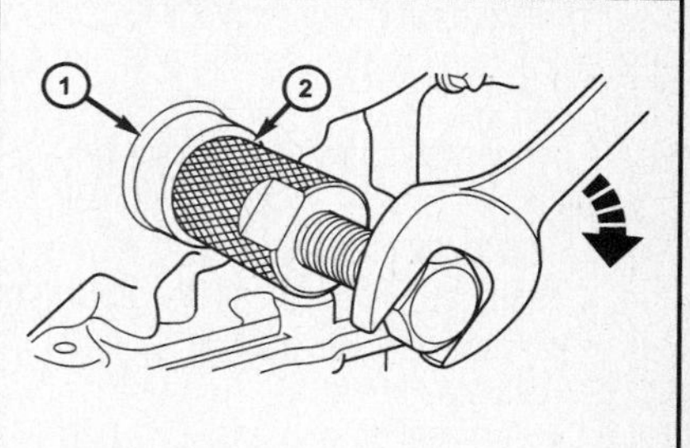

Fig. 65 Removing the front seal using tool 6341A—3.8L engine

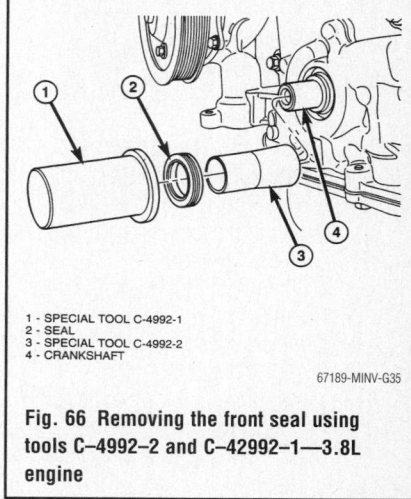

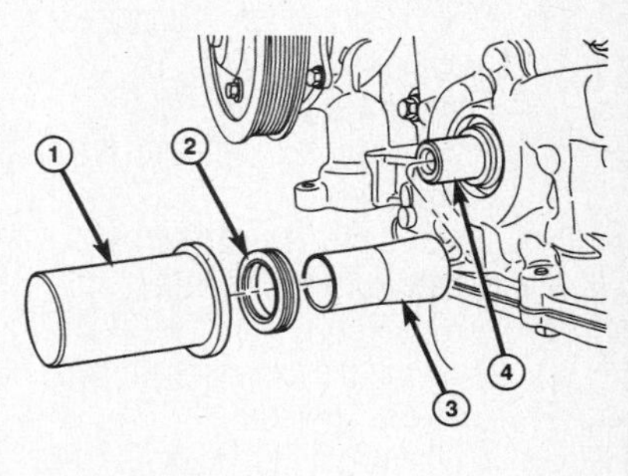

Fig. 66 Removing the front seal using tools C–4992–2 and C–42992–1—3.8L engine

4. Turn the forcing screw on the tool to remove the seal.

To install:

5. Position guide C–4992–2 on the crankshaft nose.
6. Position a new seal over the guide with the seal spring facing the engine cover.
7. Install the seal using tool C–42992–1 until the seal is flush with the cover and remove the tools.
8. Install or connect the following:
   - Crankshaft pulley and tighten the bolt to 40 ft. lbs. (54 Nm)
   - Accessory drive belts
   - Right wheel and splash shield
   - Negative battery cable

CYLINDER HEAD

REMOVAL & INSTALLATION

3.5L and 4.0L Engines

Right Side

See Figure 67.

1. Before servicing the vehicle, refer to the precautions in the beginning of this section.

2. Properly relieve the fuel system pressure.

3. Drain the cooling system.

4. Remove or disconnect the following:

- Negative battery cable
- Engine cover
- Air cleaner assembly
- Fuel line from the rail
- Upper intake manifold
- Lower intake manifold
- Right front wheel
- Right inner splash shield
- Drive belt
- Crankshaft damper using the proper puller
- Lower drive belt idler pulley
- Power steering bolts and set the pump aside
- Lower timing belt cover bolts
- Catalytic converter nuts
- Oxygen (O_2S) sensor electrical wiring at the exhaust manifold and catalytic converter
- Muffler-to-tail pipe union
- Catalytic converter
- Exhaust cross over pipe lower bolts
- Right exhaust manifold
- Upper drive belt idler pulley
- Belt tensioner

5. Support the engine with jackstands and wood blocks.

- Upper engine mount
- Power steering reservoir bolts and set aside
- All remaining outer timing belt cover bolts

6. Rotate the engine until it is at Top Dead center (TDC).

➡Mark the timing belt running direction for installation. Align the camshaft sprockets with the marks on the rear covers.

- Timing belt tensioner and reset the tensioner

7. Pre-load the timing belt tensioner as follows:

a. Place tensioner in a vise the same way it is mounted on the engine.

b. Slowly compress the plunger into the tensioner body.

c. Once the plunger is compressed, install a pin through the body and plunger to retain it in place until the tensioner is installed.

- Timing belt
- Right vale cover
- Exhaust Gas Recirculation (EGR) and tube assembly
- Right cylinder head cover
- Right rocker arm assembly
- Right rear camshaft thrust plate
- Holding the camshaft gear, unfasten the right cam gear retaining bolt

8. Push the camshaft about 3.5 inches out of the back of the cylinder head and remove the cam gear.

- Inner timing cover-to-cylinder head bolts

➡On the 4.0L engine, due to clearance restrictions the front four cylinder head bolts must be loosened, raised and supported with a rubber band before the head can be removed.

- Cylinder head bolts in the reverse of tightening sequence. Refer to the cylinder head bolt tightening sequence illustration.
- Cylinder head and gasket.

To install:

9. Thoroughly clean and dry the mating surfaces of the head and block.

⁂ WARNING

When cleaning the cylinder head and block mating surfaces, do not use a metal scraper because the soft aluminum surfaces could be cut or damaged. Instead, use a scraper made of wood or plastic.

10. Check the cylinder head for cracks, damage or engine coolant leakage. Check the head for flatness. End-to-end, the head should be within 0.002 in. (0.051mm) normally with 0.008 in. (0.203mm) the maximum allowed out of true. The resurface limit is 0.008 in. (0.203mm) maximum, the combined total dimension of stock removal from the cylinder head, if any, and block top surface.

11. Place a new head gasket on the cylinder block locating dowels, being sure the gasket is on the correct side.

12. Inspect the cylinder head bolts for necking (stretching) by holding a straightedge against the threads of each bolt. If all of the threads are not contacting the scale, the bolt should be replaced.

⁂ WARNING

Due to the cylinder head bolt torque method used, it is imperative that the threads of the bolts be inspected for necking prior to installation. If the threads are necked down, the bolt should be replaced. Failure to do so may result in parts failure or damage. New bolts are always recommended.

13. Install the cylinder head into position on the engine block and over the dowels. Install the cylinder head bolts, lubricating the threads with clean engine oil prior to installation.

14. Torque the cylinder head bolts using the proper sequence as follows:

a. Step 1: torque in sequence to 45 ft. lbs. (61 Nm).

b. Step 2: torque in sequence to 65 ft. lbs. (88 Nm).

c. Step 3: torque in sequence to 65 ft. lbs. (88 Nm).

d. Step 4: torque in sequence an additional ¼ turn by using a torque angle meter.

➡Inspect the bolt torque after tightening. The torque should be over 90 ft. lbs. (122 Nm). If not, replace the cylinder head bolt.

15. Install or connect the following:

- Inner timing cover-to-cylinder head bolts and tighten to 40 ft. lbs. (54 Nm)
- Cam gear, holding the camshaft gear, fasten the right cam gear retaining bolt to 75 ft. lbs. (102 Nm) plus an additional ¼ turn
- Rear camshaft thrust plate

16. Rotate the camshaft gear until it is properly aligned and check the left camshaft gear and crankshaft timing alignment marks.

- Timing belt
- Timing belt outer cover
- Power steering reservoir
- Crankshaft damper
- Upper engine mount
- Belt tensioner
- Upper drive belt idler pulley
- Right exhaust manifold
- Exhaust cross over pipe

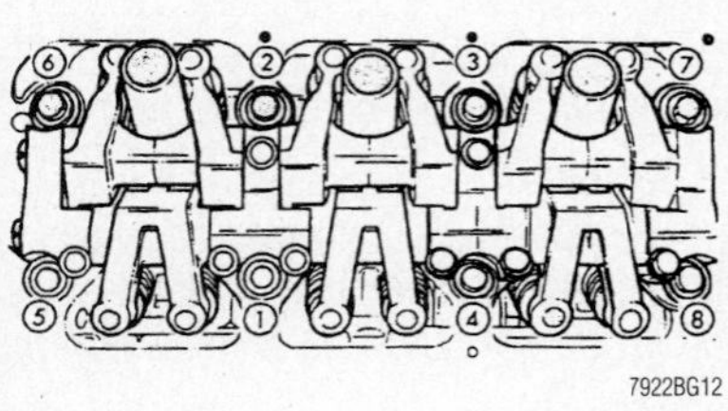

Fig. 67 Cylinder head bolt tightening sequence—3.5L and 4.0L engines

- Catalytic converter
- Muffler-to-tail pipe union
- O_2S sensor electrical wiring at the exhaust manifold and catalytic converter
- Right rocker arm assembly
- Right cylinder head cover
- EGR and tube assembly
- Lower drive belt idler pulley
- Right vale cover
- Lower intake manifold and fuel rail
- Upper intake manifold
- Fuel line to the rail
- Power steering pump
- Drive belt
- Air cleaner assembly
- Engine cover
- Right inner splash shield
- Right front wheel
- Negative battery cable

Left Side

See Figure 67.

1. Before servicing the vehicle, refer to the precautions in the beginning of this section.
2. Properly relieve the fuel system pressure.
3. Drain the cooling system.
4. Remove or disconnect the following:
   - Negative battery cable
   - Engine cover
   - Air cleaner assembly
   - Radiator close out panel
   - Radiator core support and fan assembly
   - Fuel line from the rail
   - Upper intake manifold
   - Lower intake manifold
   - Crankshaft damper
   - Upper engine mount
   - Upper drive belt idler pulley
   - Belt tensioner
   - Left exhaust manifold
   - Exhaust cross over pipe
   - Outer timing belt cover
5. Rotate the engine until it is at Top Dead center (TDC).

➡Mark the timing belt running direction for installation. Align the camshaft sprockets with the marks on the rear covers.

- Timing belt tensioner and reset the tensioner

6. Pre-load the timing belt tensioner as follows:
   a. Place tensioner in a vise the same way it is mounted on the engine.
   b. Slowly compress the plunger into the tensioner body.
   c. Once the plunger is compressed, install a pin through the body and plunger to retain it in place until the tensioner is installed.
   - Timing belt
   - Left cylinder head cover
   - Left rocker arm assembly
   - Left rear camshaft thrust plate
   - Holding the camshaft gear, unfasten the right cam gear retaining bolt
7. Push the camshaft about 3.5 inches out of the back of the cylinder head and remove the cam gear.
   - Front timing belt housing-to-cylinder head bolts
   - Cylinder head bolts in the reverse of tightening sequence. Refer to the cylinder head bolt tightening sequence illustration.
   - Cylinder head and gasket

To install:

8. Thoroughly clean and dry the mating surfaces of the head and block.

⁂ WARNING

When cleaning the cylinder head and block mating surfaces, do not use a metal scraper because the soft aluminum surfaces could be cut or damaged. Instead, use a scraper made of wood or plastic.

9. Check the cylinder head for cracks, damage or engine coolant leakage. Check the head for flatness. End-to-end, the head should be within 0.002 in. (0.051mm) normally with 0.008 in. (0.203mm) the maximum allowed out of true. The resurface limit is 0.008 in. (0.203mm) maximum, the combined total dimension of stock removal from the cylinder head, if any, and block top surface.
10. Place a new head gasket on the cylinder block locating dowels, being sure the gasket is on the correct side.
11. Inspect the cylinder head bolts for necking (stretching) by holding a straightedge against the threads of each bolt. If all of the threads are not contacting the scale, the bolt should be replaced.

⁂ WARNING

Due to the cylinder head bolt torque method used, it is imperative that the threads of the bolts be inspected for necking prior to installation. If the threads are necked down, the bolt should be replaced. Failure to do so may result in parts failure or damage. New bolts are always recommended.

12. Install the cylinder head into position on the engine block and over the dowels. Install the cylinder head bolts, lubricating the threads with clean engine oil prior to installation.
13. Torque the cylinder head bolts using the proper sequence as follows:
   a. Step 1: torque in sequence to 45 ft. lbs. (61 Nm).
   b. Step 2: torque in sequence to 65 ft. lbs. (88 Nm).
   c. Step 3: torque in sequence to 65 ft. lbs. (88 Nm).
   d. Step 4: torque in sequence an additional ¼ turn by using a torque angle meter.

➡Inspect the bolt torque after tightening. The torque should be over 90 ft. lbs. (122 Nm). If not, replace the cylinder head bolt.

14. Install or connect the following:
   - Inner timing cover-to-cylinder head bolts and tighten to 40 ft. lbs. (54 Nm)
   - Cam gear, holding the camshaft gear, fasten the right cam gear retaining bolt to 75 ft. lbs. (102 Nm) plus an additional ¼ turn
   - Rear camshaft thrust plate
15. Rotate the camshaft gear until it is properly aligned and check the left camshaft gear and crankshaft timing alignment marks.
   - Timing belt
   - Timing belt front cover
   - Crankshaft damper
   - Upper engine mount
   - Belt tensioner
   - Upper drive belt idler pulley
   - Left exhaust manifold
   - Exhaust cross over pipe
   - Left rocker arm assembly
   - Left cylinder head cover
   - Lower drive belt idler pulley
   - Lower intake manifold and fuel rail
   - Upper intake manifold
   - Fuel line to the rail
   - Radiator core support and fan assembly
   - Radiator close out panel
   - Drive belt
   - Air cleaner assembly
   - Engine cover
   - Negative battery cable

3.8L Engine

See Figure 68.

1. Before servicing the vehicle, refer to the precautions in the beginning of this section.

2. Drain the cooling system.
3. Relieve the fuel system pressure.
4. Remove or disconnect the following:
   - Negative battery cable
   - Upper and lower intake manifolds

CAUTION

The intake manifold gaskets are made of a very thin metal and can cause injury if not properly handled.

   - Valve covers.
   - Spark plugs
   - Dipstick tube
   - Exhaust manifolds

➡Keep all valvetrain components in order for assembly

   - Rocker arm and shaft assemblies
   - Cylinder head bolts, heads and gaskets
5. Clean all gasket mating surfaces.

To install:

6. Examine the cylinder head bolts and replace any that have stretched.
7. Install the cylinder head with a new gasket. The left bank gasket has an L on it and is located at the front of the engine. The right gasket has an R stamped on it and is located at the rear of the engine. Tighten the bolts in sequence, as follows:
   a. Step 1: Tighten bolts 1–8 to 45 ft. lbs. (61 Nm).
   b. Step 2: Tighten bolts 1–8 to 65 ft. lbs. (88 Nm).
   c. Step 3: Tighten bolts 1–8 to 65 ft. lbs. (88 Nm).
   d. Step 4: Bolts 1–8 plus 90 degrees.
8. Check that the torque on bolts 1–8 has exceeded 90 ft. lbs. (122 Nm). If not, replace the bolt.
9. Install or connect the following:
   - Pushrods
   - Rocker arm and shaft assemblies
   - Valve covers
   - Exhaust manifolds

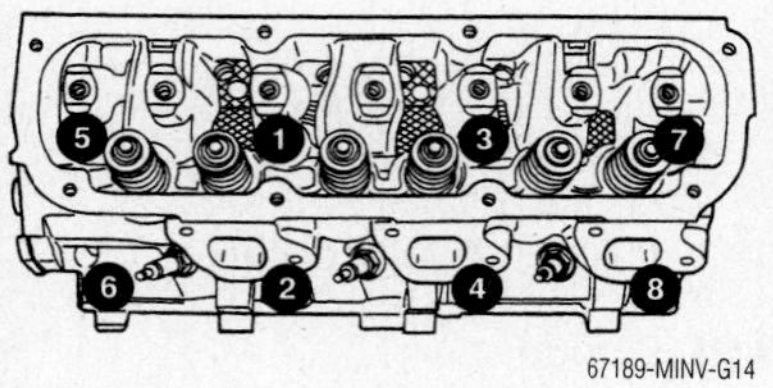

Fig. 68 Cylinder head torque sequence—3.8L engine

   - Dipstick tube with a new O–ring
   - Spark plugs
   - Intake manifolds
   - Negative battery cable
10. Fill the cooling system.
11. Start the engine and check for leaks.

ENGINE ASSEMBLY

REMOVAL & INSTALLATION

3.5L and 4.0L Engines

See Figures 69 through 73.

1. Before servicing the vehicle, refer to the precautions in the beginning of this section.
2. Drain the engine oil.
3. Drain the engine coolant.
4. Properly relieve the fuel system pressure.
5. Remove or disconnect the following:
   - Negative battery cable
   - Hood, as necessary
   - Cruise control servo
   - Radiator closure panel
   - Radiator core support
   - Upper radiator hose
   - Cooling fan
   - Air cleaner assembly
6. Recover the A/C system refrigerant using approved recycling equipment.
   - Throttle and cruise control cable from the throttle body

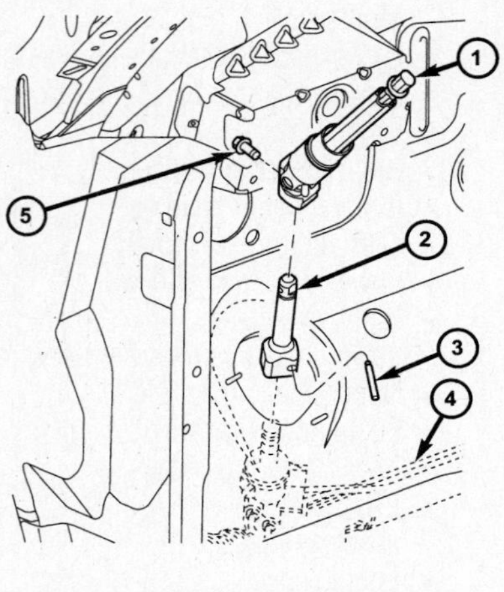

Fig. 70 Lower steering column coupling assembly—3.5L and 4.0L engines

   - Cruise control and power brake booster vacuum hoses from the engine
   - Transmission wiring harness from the solenoid pack, input and output sensors and the range sensor connectors
   - Engine wiring harness grounds from the inner frame rail

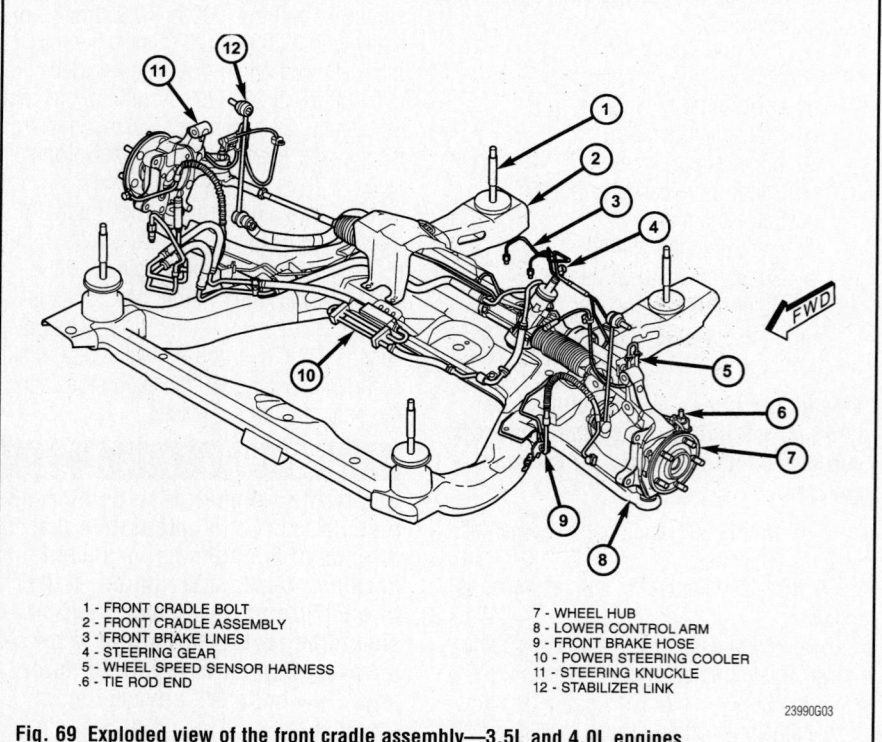

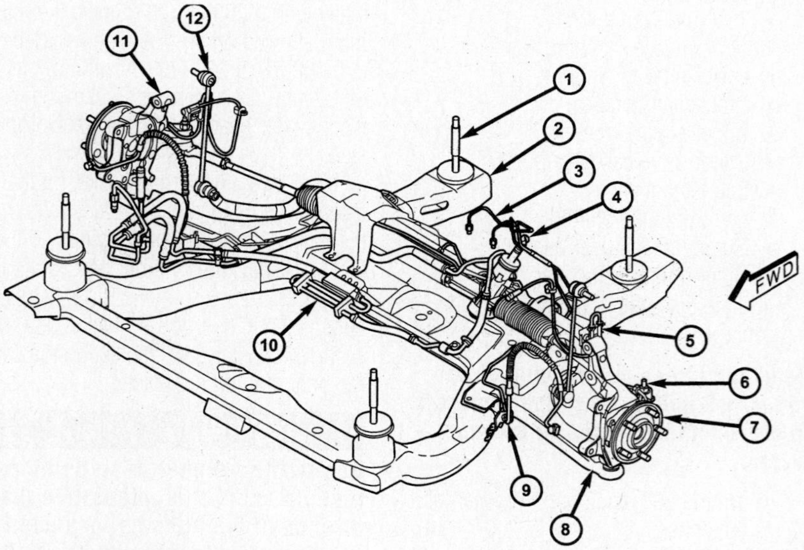

Fig. 69 Exploded view of the front cradle assembly—3.5L and 4.0L engines

- Transmission shift cable
- Transmission cooler lines
- Engine block heater connector, if equipped
- Coolant reservoir houses from the thermostat housing
- Heater hoses from the heater core
- Upper radiator hoses from the thermostat housing
- Brake lines from the Hydraulic Control Unit (HCU)
- A/C suction discharge hoses from the compressor and plug the openings
- Lower radiator hose from the engine outlet
- A/C clutch connection
- Oil pressure sender and alternator connections
- Fuel supply line from the fuel rail
- Ignition harness connection at the intake manifold
- Front wheel
- Left inner fender well
- Engine harness from the Powertrain Control Module (PCM)
- Left wheel speed sensor and retainer
- Left sway bar link from the strut
- Left drive axle nut
- Both left front steering knuckle pinch bolts
- Left steering knuckle from the strut and support the knuckle
- Negative battery cable from the transmission
- Left fascia screws
- Right inner fender well
- Right fascia screws
- Right wheel speed sensor and retainer
- Right sway bar link from the strut
- Right drive axle nut
- Both right front steering knuckle pinch bolts
- Right steering knuckle from the strut and support the knuckle
- Fascia driving lamps, if equipped
- Front fascia
- Starter connectors and harness retainers
- Oxygen (O_2S) sensor electrical wiring at the exhaust manifold and catalytic converter
- Exhaust from the manifold
- Driveshaft after marking the position at the front and rear of the shaft. This will help with installation and retain driveshaft balance.
- Engine-to-transmission plate
- Transmission inspection plate
- Flex plate-to-torque converter bolt

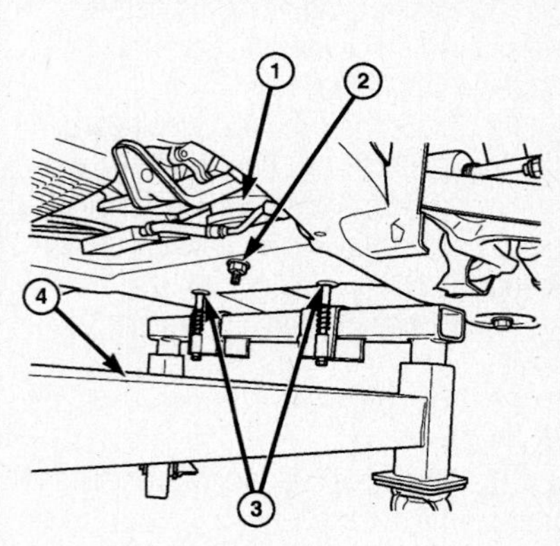

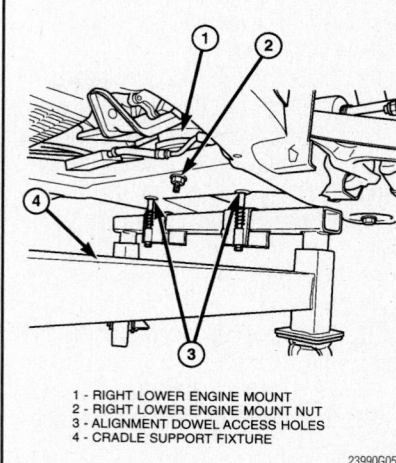

Fig. 71 Rear cradle support fixture mounting—3.5L and 4.0L engines

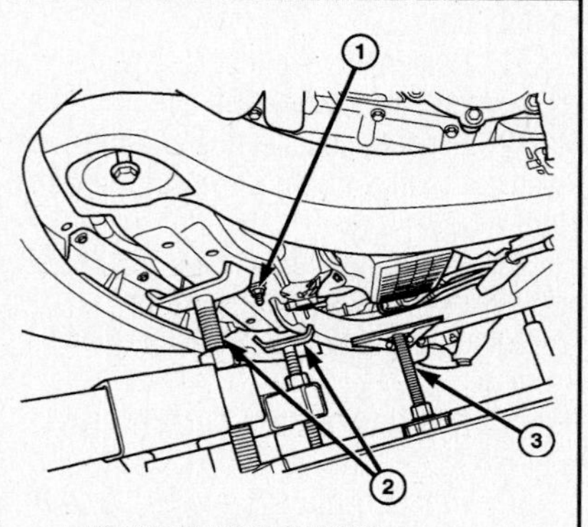

Fig. 72 Adjust the cradle support fixture to fit flush with the cradle—3.5L and 4.0L engines

WARNING

Secure the steering wheel to prevent it rotating which may cause damage to the steering column clock spring.

7. Remove or disconnect the following:
   - Lower steering column coupling pin using tool 6831-A and separate the union
   - Both lower engine mount bolts
8. Matchmark using paint the front cradle-to-body location and position the engine cradle support under the vehicle.
9. Remove or disconnect the following:
10. Lower the vehicle until it is just above the cradle.
11. Align the cradle support dowels with cradle access holes and adjust the engine support fixture to fit flush with the oil pan and adjust the cradle support fixture support to fit flush with the cradle.
12. Carefully lower the vehicle onto the cradle.
13. Remove the upper engine mount.
14. Very **carefully** remove the front and rear cradle mounting bolts and raise the vehicle to separate the engine/transmission and cradle from the vehicle.
15. Connect lifting brackets to the engine, separate the Power Transfer Unit (PTU), if equipped.
16. Separate the engine from transmission using the lift brackets.

To install:

17. Installation is the reverse of removal, please note the following important specifications.
18. Remove or disconnect the following:
    - Cradle supporting bolts: 120 ft. lbs. (163 Nm)
    - Upper engine mount bolt to timing cover to 40 ft. lbs. (54 Nm) and the bolt to right rail to 50 ft. lbs. (68 Nm)
    - Drive axle-to-steering knuckle nut to 180 ft. lbs. (244 Nm)
    - Steering knuckle-to-strut bolts to 180 ft. lbs. (244 Nm)
    - Front speed sensor support bracket bolts to 105 inch lbs. (12 Nm)
    - Brake line support bracket bolts to 105 inch lbs. (12 Nm)
    - Flex plate-to-torque converter bolts to 55 ft. lbs. (75 Nm)
    - Engine-to-transmission support collar bolts to 40 ft. lbs. (54 Nm)

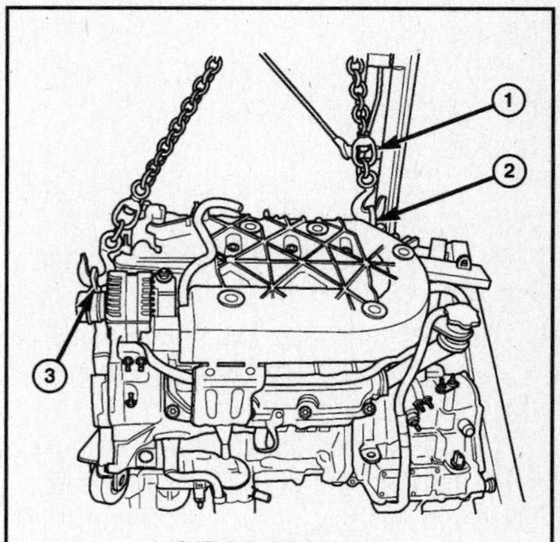

Fig. 73 Use suitable lift brackets and a hoist assembly to separate the engine from the transaxle—3.5L and 4.0L engines

19. Fill the cooling system to the proper level.
20. Fill the engine with clean oil.
21. Bleed the brakes.
22. Recharge the A/C system
23. Check wheel alignment.
24. Start the vehicle, check for leaks and repair if necessary.

3.8L Engine

See Figures 74 through 77.

1. Before servicing the vehicle, refer to the precautions in the beginning of this section.
2. Drain the cooling system.
3. Drain the engine oil.
4. Relieve the fuel system pressure.
5. Recover the A/C refrigerant.
6. Secure the steering wheel in the straight ahead position.
7. Disconnect the CCV hose from the left cylinder head cover.
8. Remove the air cleaner cover and housing.
9. Disconnect the throttle and cruise control cables from the throttle body, separate the cables from the bracket and set to one side.
10. Disconnect the cruise control and power brake booster vacuum hoses and set aside.
11. Disconnect the upper radiator hose from the thermostat housing and the lower radiator hose from the radiator.
12. Disconnect the heater hoses and coolant reservoir hose from the intake manifold.
13. Disconnect the transmission controller and transmission sensor wire harness connectors.
14. Disconnect the brake controller wire harness connector.
15. Disconnect the transmission shift cable and remove the cable from the bracket.
16. Disconnect the transmission lines using tool 8875.
17. Disconnect the alternator electrical connectors.
18. Disconnect the fuel line from fuel rail
19. Disconnect the EVAP hose from the throttle body.
20. Disconnect the Throttle Position (TP), Idle Air Control (IAC) motor, Heated Oxygen (HO02s), Camshaft Position (CMP), Manifold Absolute Pressure (MAP) sensors and the two engine wiring harness connectors. Remove the harness from the cover studs and set aside.
21. Disconnect the purge solenoid harness connector.
22. Remove engine wiring harness retainer from the left cylinder head cover and the oil dipstick tube.
23. Disconnect the A/C electrical connector, and both A/C lines from the compressor. Cover and seal all openings of hoses and compressor to avoid contamination.
24. Disconnect the oil pressure sending unit.
25. Disconnect the coolant hose at the engine oil cooler.
26. Raise and support the vehicle and remove the front wheels.
27. Remove the front fascia.
28. Disconnect the starter wiring and push pin.
29. Remove the flex plate inspection cover.
30. Rotate the engine at the crankshaft pulley bolt and remove the torque converter bolts.
31. Disconnect the rear O02s sensor and remove the exhaust system.
32. Separate the steering column intermediate shaft from the steering gear using tool # 6831-A.
33. Disconnect the Knock (KS) sensor wiring harness connector and remove the Crankshaft Position (CKP) sensor.
34. Disconnect the in block heater, if equipped.
35. Disconnect the left wheel speed sensor and sensor harness push pin from the body, and set the harness aside.

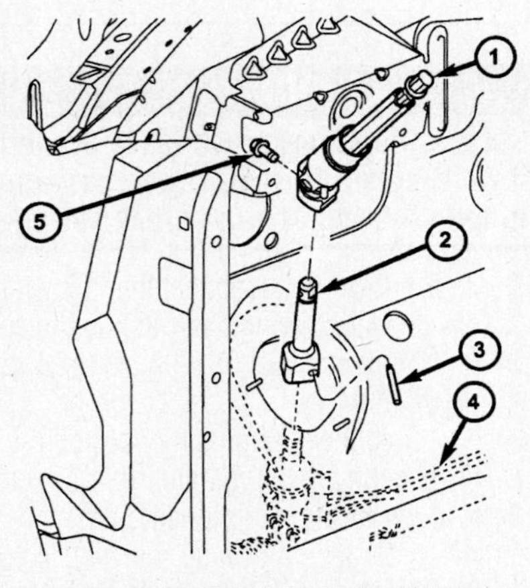

Fig. 74 Exploded view of the steering column coupling—3.8L engine

36. Disconnect the left upper stabilizer link.
37. Disconnect the left strut to steering knuckle bolts and separate the union.
38. Disconnect the right wheel speed sensor and sensor harness push pin from the body, and set the harness aside.
39. Disconnect the right upper stabilizer link.
40. Disconnect the right strut to steering knuckle bolts and separate the union.
41. Disconnect the engine harness ground at the transmission.
42. Disconnect the rear transmission mount from the body.
43. Set up and adjust the cradle support fixture arms and dowels, refer to the accompanying illustrations for cradle support set up. Paint mark the cradle to body location at all four cradle bolt positions.

CAUTION

Do not apply the total vehicle weight on the cradle support fixture.

44. Lower the front cradle onto the table and remove all four front cradle mount bolts.

➡Use a brake pedal prop rod and depress the brake pedal to prevent excessive brake fluid loss when the brake system is open.

45. Disconnect both front brake lines at the brake controller and route aside.
46. Disconnect the right front engine mount.
47. Remove the left powertrain torque strut to frame bracket bolt.

CAUTION

While slowly separating the body from the cradle assembly, constant checks must be performed to assure proper positioning and that no damage occurs during separation.

48. Carefully raise the vehicle off of the engine and cradle assembly.
49. Connect an engine lift bracket, using tool # 8534-8 to the left cylinder head and tool # 8534-7 to the right cylinder head.
50. Separate the engine and transmission from the cradle using the lift brackets.
51. Separate the transmission from the engine.

To install:

52. Installation is the reverse of removal, keep in mind the following important steps and torque values.

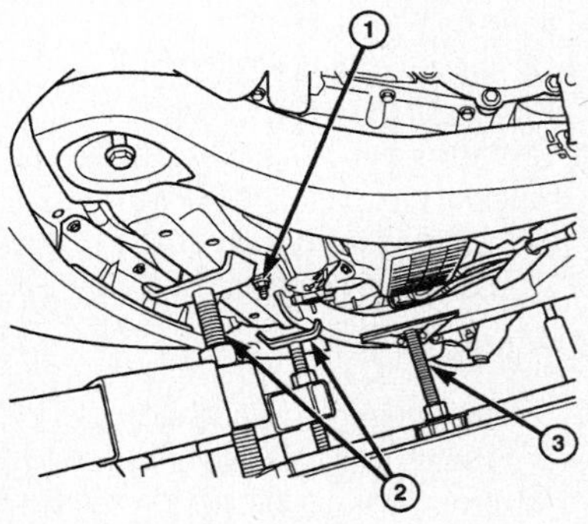

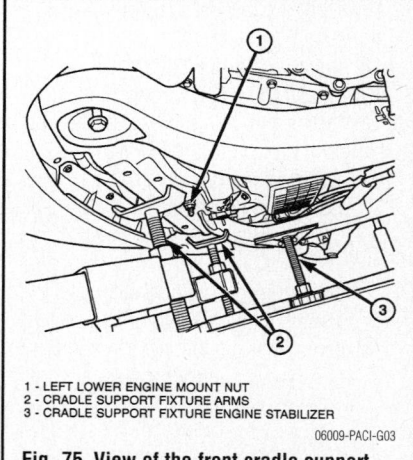

1 - LEFT LOWER ENGINE MOUNT NUT
2 - CRADLE SUPPORT FIXTURE ARMS
3 - CRADLE SUPPORT FIXTURE ENGINE STABILIZER

06009-PACI-G03

Fig. 75 View of the front cradle support positioning—3.8L engine

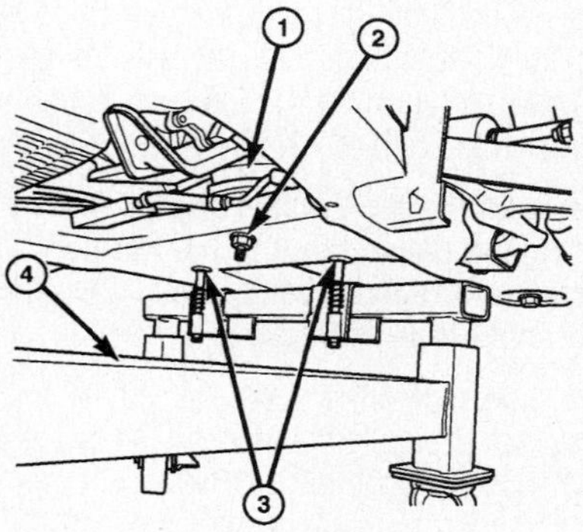

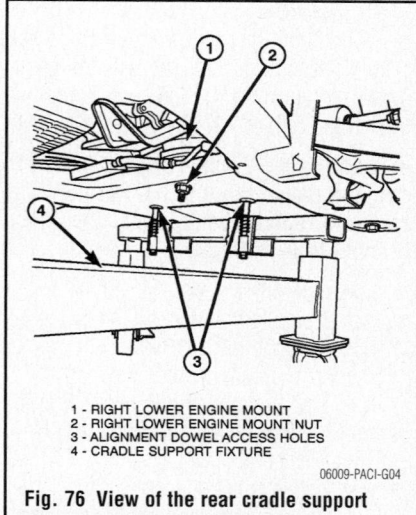

1 - RIGHT LOWER ENGINE MOUNT
2 - RIGHT LOWER ENGINE MOUNT NUT
3 - ALIGNMENT DOWEL ACCESS HOLES
4 - CRADLE SUPPORT FIXTURE

06009-PACI-G04

Fig. 76 View of the rear cradle support positioning—3.8L engine

CAUTION

While slowly lowering the body to the cradle assembly, constantly check to assure proper positioning and no damage occurs to other components until union is made.

53. Tighten the cradle supporting bolts to 120 ft. lbs. (163 Nm).
54. Install the right engine mount. tighten the bolts to the timing cover to 40 ft. lbs. 54 Nm) and the bolts to the right rail to 50 ft. lbs. (68 Nm).
55. Tighten the rear transmission torque strut bolts to 40 ft. lbs. (54 Nm).
56. Tighten the left front strut to steering knuckle bolts to 60 ft. lbs. (81 Nm) and then tighten an additional 90 degrees.
57. Tighten the left stabilizer link to 65 ft. lbs. (88 Nm).

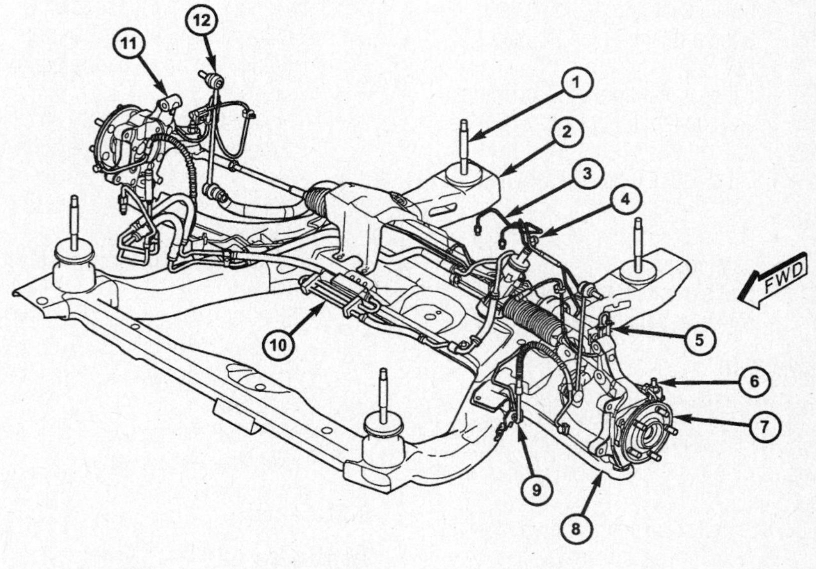

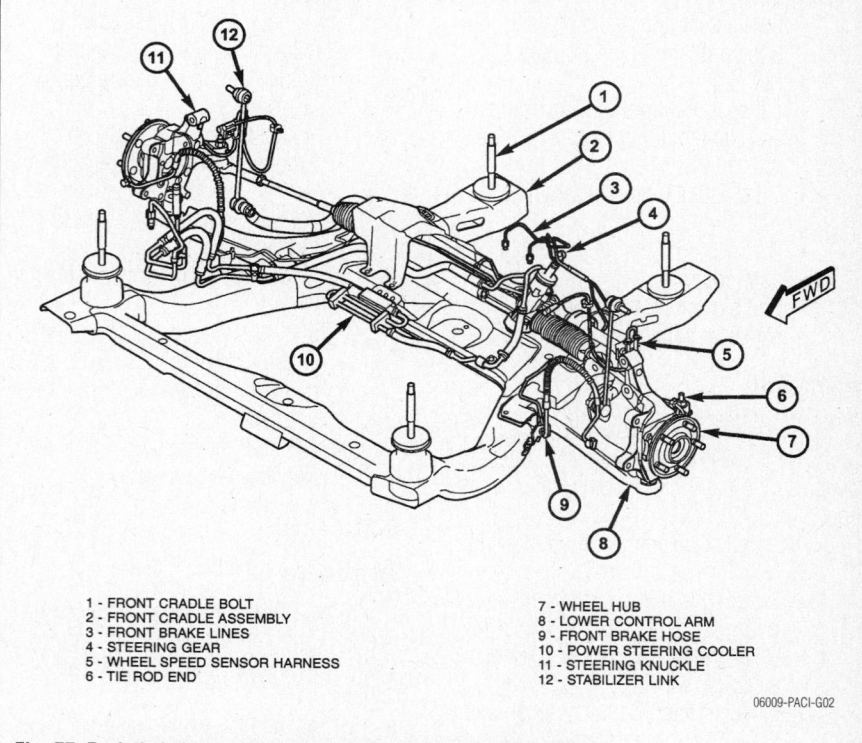

1 - FRONT CRADLE BOLT
2 - FRONT CRADLE ASSEMBLY
3 - FRONT BRAKE LINES
4 - STEERING GEAR
5 - WHEEL SPEED SENSOR HARNESS
6 - TIE ROD END
7 - WHEEL HUB
8 - LOWER CONTROL ARM
9 - FRONT BRAKE HOSE
10 - POWER STEERING COOLER
11 - STEERING KNUCKLE
12 - STABILIZER LINK

06009-PACI-G02

Fig. 77 Exploded view of the front cradle assembly—3.8L engine

58. Tighten the right front strut to steering knuckle bolts to 60 ft. lbs. (81 Nm) and then tighten an additional 90 degrees.
59. Tighten the right stabilizer link. Tighten to 65 ft. lbs. (88 Nm).
60. Tighten the torque converter bolts to 65 ft. lbs. (88 Nm).
61. Fill the cooling system.
62. Fill the engine with clean oil.
63. Recharge the A/C system.
64. Start the engine and check for leaks.

EXHAUST MANIFOLD

REMOVAL & INSTALLATION

3.5L Engine

Left Side

See Figure 78.

1. Before servicing the vehicle, refer to the precautions in the beginning of this section.
2. Remove or disconnect the following:
   - Negative battery cable
   - Radiator close out panel
   - Radiator core support and cooling fan assembly
   - Oil dipstick tube bolt and move the tube aside
   - Exhaust manifold crossover pipe bolts
   - Exhaust manifold bolts and manifold
3. Inspect the manifold for damage or cracks. Check for distortion against a straight-edge or thickness gauge. Replace manifold if required.
4. Remove all traces of the old manifold gasket and clean both gasket mating surfaces.

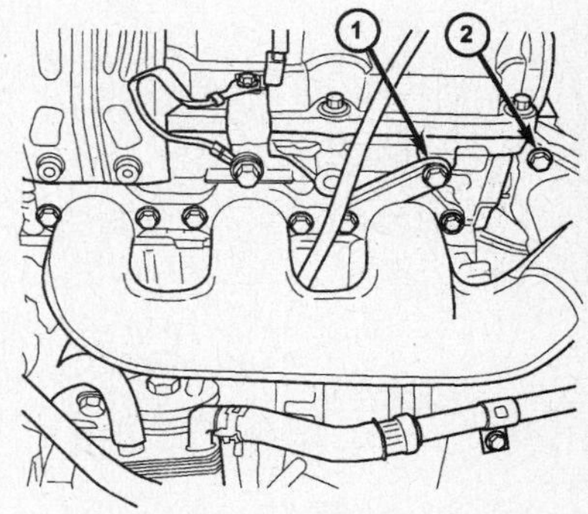

1 - OIL LEVEL INDICATOR TUBE RETAINING BOLT
2 - EXHAUST CROSS OVER PIPE UNION

23990G13

Fig. 78 The oil dipstick tube and exhaust crossover pipe bolts must be removed prior to removing the manifold—3.5L engine

To install:

- Exhaust manifold and gasket, tighten the bolts to 200 inch lbs. (23 Nm)
- Exhaust manifold crossover pipe and tighten the bolts to 275 inch lbs. (31 Nm)
- Oil dipstick tube and secure the bolt
- Radiator cooling fan assembly and core support
- Radiator close out panel
- Negative battery cable

Right Side

See Figure 79.

1. Before servicing the vehicle, refer to the precautions in the beginning of this section.
2. Remove or disconnect the following:
   - Negative battery cable
   - Exhaust manifold crossover pipe bolts
   - Downstream Oxygen (O_2S) sensor electrical wiring
   - Exhaust manifold flange bolts and the hangers from the pipe assembly
   - Exhaust system from the vehicle
   - Exhaust Gas Recirculation (EGR) tube support bracket bolt
   - Lower manifold bolts
   - Manifold and gasket
   - O_2S from the manifold
3. Inspect the manifold for damage or cracks. Check for distortion against a straight-edge or thickness gauge. Replace manifold if required.
4. Remove all traces of the old manifold gasket and clean both gasket mating surfaces.

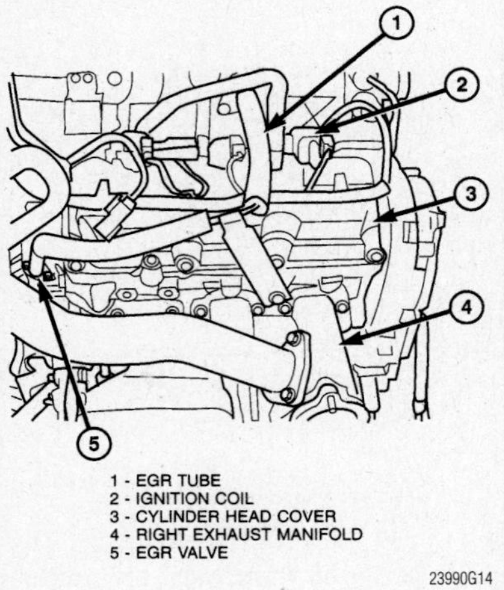

Fig. 79 Exhaust Gas Recirculation (EGR) valve and tube assembly—3.5L engine

To install:

5. Install or connect the following:
   - Exhaust manifold and gasket, tighten the bolts to 200 inch lbs. (23 Nm)
   - Exhaust system to the vehicle
   - Exhaust manifold flange bolts and the hangers to the pipe assembly. tighten the flange bolts to 22 ft. lbs. (30 Nm).
   - Downstream O_2S sensor electrical wiring
   - EGR tube support bracket bolt
   - Exhaust manifold crossover pipe bolts and tighten to 275 inch lbs. (31 Nm)
   - O_2S to the manifold
   - Negative battery cable

3.8L Engine

Right Side

1. Disconnect the negative battery cable.
2. Raise and safely support the vehicle.
3. Separate the exhaust pipe at the exhaust manifold.
4. Remove the bolts attaching the crossover pipe to exhaust manifold.
5. Remove the air cleaner housing.
6. Disconnect the Throttle Position (TP), Idle Air Control (IAC) sensor connectors and the purge vacuum hose from the throttle body.
7. Disconnect the upstream Oxygen (O_2S) sensor connector.
8. Disconnect the spark plug wires from the plugs.
9. Remove bolts attaching the exhaust manifold to the cylinder head and remove the manifold.
10. Discard gasket, if equipped and clean all mating surfaces.
11. Position the exhaust manifold on the cylinder head and install the bolts to the center runner (cyl # 3), and temporarily tighten to 25 inch lbs. (2.8 Nm).

➡Examine the crossover pipe bolts for damage caused due to heat or corrosion and replace using new OEM bolts if found to be defective.

12. Install a new gasket, attach the crossover pipe to the manifold and tighten the bolts to 30 ft. lbs. (41 Nm).
13. Install or connect the following:
    - Remaining manifold bolts. Torque the fasteners to 17 ft. lbs. (23 Nm).
14. Install and connect the upstream O_2S sensor.
15. Connect the spark plug.
16. Connect the IAC, TPS and the EVAP hose to the throttle body.
17. Install the air cleaner housing.
18. Attach the catalytic converter pipe to exhaust manifold using a new gasket and tighten bolts to 27 ft. lbs. (37 Nm).
19. Connect the negative battery cable.
20. Start the engine and check for leaks.

Left Side

1. Before servicing the vehicle, refer to the precautions in the beginning of this section.
2. Remove or disconnect the following:
   - Negative battery cable
   - Crossover pipe
   - Spark plug wires
   - Heat shield
   - Exhaust manifold bolt
   - Exhaust manifold and gasket

To install:

3. Position the exhaust manifold on the cylinder head and install the bolts to the center runner (cyl # 4), and temporarily tighten to 25 inch lbs. (2.8 Nm).

➡Examine the crossover pipe bolts for damage caused due to heat or corrosion and replace using new OEM bolts if found to be defective.

4. Install a new gasket, attach the crossover pipe to the manifold and tighten the bolts to 30 ft. lbs. (41 Nm).
5. Install or connect the following:
   - Remaining manifold bolts. Torque the fasteners to 17 ft. lbs. (23 Nm).
   - Heat shield
   - Negative battery cable
6. Start the engine and check for leaks.

4.0L Engine

Left Side

1. Before servicing the vehicle, refer to the precautions in the beginning of this section.
2. Disconnect the negative battery cable.
3. Remove the radiator close out panel.
4. Remove the radiator core support.
5. Remove the radiator cooling fan assembly.
6. Loosen the oil level indicator tube retaining bolt and position the assembly out of the way.
7. Disconnect both oxygen sensor electrical connectors.
8. Remove the three upper heat shield retainers and remove the upper heat shield.
9. Remove the lower exhaust manifold crossover pipe retaining bolts.
10. Remove the exhaust manifold retaining bolts.

11. Remove the exhaust manifold from the vehicle.

To install:

12. Installation is the reverse of the removal procedure.
13. Install the retaining bolts. Tighten them to 200 inch lbs, starting at the center and working outward.
14. Tighten the crossover pipe retaining bolts to 275 inch lbs.

Right Side

1. Before servicing the vehicle, refer to the precautions in the beginning of this section.
2. Disconnect the negative battery cable.
3. Raise and support the vehicle safely.
4. Disconnect both oxygen sensor electrical connectors.
5. Remove the rear heat shield retainers and remove the heat shield.
6. Remove the exhaust manifold inlet flange retaining fasteners. Disconnect the exhaust system hangers from the pipe assembly.
7. Remove the exhaust manifold retaining bolts.
8. Remove the exhaust manifold from the vehicle.

To install:

9. Installation is the reverse of the removal procedure.
10. Replace any damaged studs, as required. Tighten the studs to 20 inch lbs.
11. Install the retaining bolts. Tighten them to 200 inch lbs, starting at the center and working outward.
12. Tighten the exhaust system hangers to 22 ft. lbs.
13. Tighten the heat shield retaining bolts to 105 inch lbs.
14. Tighten the crossover pipe retaining bolts to 250 inch lbs.

INTAKE MANIFOLD

REMOVAL & INSTALLATION

3.5L and 4.0L Engines

Upper

See Figures 80 and 81.

1. Before servicing the vehicle, refer to the precautions in the beginning of this section.
2. Properly relieve the fuel system pressure.
3. Drain the cooling system.
4. Remove or disconnect the following:
   - Negative battery cable
   - Air cleaner assembly
   - Engine cover from the top of the intake manifold
   - ECT harness connector, as required
   - Accelerator and the speed control cable from the throttle lever
   - Two cable bracket bolts and position the bracket aside
   - Oil dipstick tube-to-upper intake bolt
5. Disconnect the following electrical connections:
   - Manifold Tuning Valve (MTV)
   - Sort Runner (SR) valve
   - Exhaust Gas Recirculation (EGR) valve
   - Throttle Position (TP) sensor
   - Idle Air Control (IAC) motor
   - Intake Air Temperature (IAT) sensor
   - Manifold Absolute Pressure (MAP) sensor
6. Remove or disconnect the following:
   - Alternator support bracket
   - EGR tube
7. Disconnect the following vacuum lines:
   - Positive Crankcase Ventilation (PCV) valve
   - Evaporative Emissions (EVAP) solenoid
   - Brake booster
   - Front and rear manifold support brackets
   - Intake plenum mounting bolts
8. Remove the intake manifold plenum from the intake manifold.

➡Discard the old gasket. Cover the intake manifold openings with tape to keep debris from entering the engine.

To install:

9. Install or connect the following:
   - Intake manifold plenum with a new gasket in place. Torque the mounting bolts, working from the center outward, to 105 inch lbs. (12 Nm)

➡Do not overtighten bolts when working with light alloys.

   - Oil dipstick tube-to-upper intake bolt
   - EGR tube
10. Connect the following vacuum lines:
    - PCV valve
    - EVAP solenoid
    - Brake booster
11. Install or connect the following:
    - Alternator support bracket
12. Connect the following electrical connections:
    - MTV valve
    - Sort Runner (SR) valve
    - EGR valve
    - TP sensor
    - IAC motor
    - IAT sensor
    - MAP sensor
13. Install or connect the following:
    - Cable bracket and bolts
    - Accelerator and the speed control cable to the throttle lever
    - Air cleaner assembly
    - ECT harness connector, as required
    - Engine cover
    - Negative battery cable
14. Fill and bleed the cooling system.
15. Change the engine oil and filter.

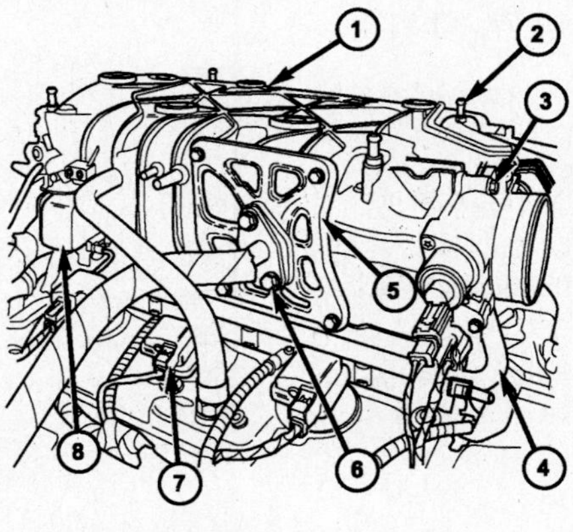

1 - UPPER INTAKE MANIFOLD
2 - ENGINE COVER MOUNTING STUD
3 - THROTTLE BODY
4 - FUEL RAIL
5 - UPPER INTAKE MANIFOLD RETAINING BRACKET
6 - EGR TUBE
7 - IGNITION COIL ASSEMBLY
8 - MANIFOLD TUNER VALVE ACTUATOR

23990G09

Fig. 80 Upper intake manifold and related components—3.5L and 4.0L engines

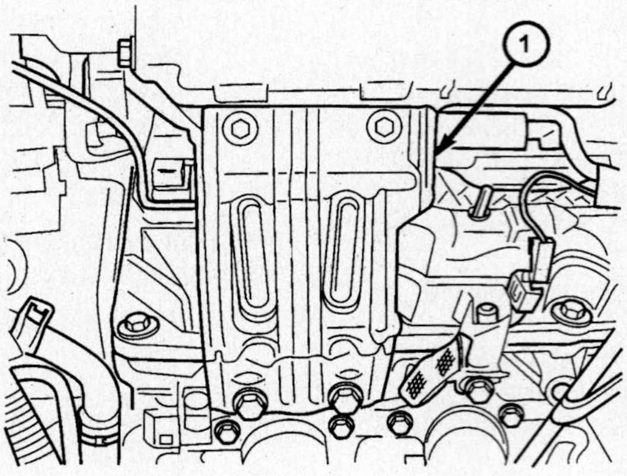

Fig. 81 Upper intake manifold support bracket–left shown, right similar—3.5L and 4.0L engines

3. Install or connect the following:
   - Intake manifold gasket, then the lower manifold. Torque the bolts in the proper sequence to specification
   - Fuel rail bolts and rail with the injectors as an assembly
   - Fuel supply hose to the rail
   - Heater hose to the intake manifold
   - Coolant container hose to the thermostat housing
   - Exhaust crossover bolt
   - Fuel injector and CTS sensor electrical connections
   - Power steering reservoir
   - Upper intake manifold
   - Upper radiator hose from the thermostat housing
4. Fill the cooling system and check for leaks.

16. Start the engine, check for fuel and coolant leaks and verify correct engine operation.

Lower

See Figures 82 and 83.

1. Before servicing the vehicle, refer to the precautions in the beginning of this section.
2. Remove or disconnect the following:
   - Upper radiator hose from the thermostat housing
   - Upper intake manifold
   - Power steering reservoir and position aside
   - Fuel injector and Coolant temperature (CTS) sensor electrical connections
   - Exhaust crossover bolt
   - Heater hose from the intake manifold
   - Coolant container hose at the thermostat housing
   - Fuel supply hose from the rail
   - Fuel rail bolts and rail with the injectors as an assembly
   - Lower intake manifold bolts and manifold

➡Clean all gasket mating surfaces and inspect for distortion with a good straightedge.

To install:

➡Verify that all intake manifold and cylinder head sealing surfaces are clean.

➡Be sure that the extruded holes in the gasket are installed in the recessed holes in the cylinder head

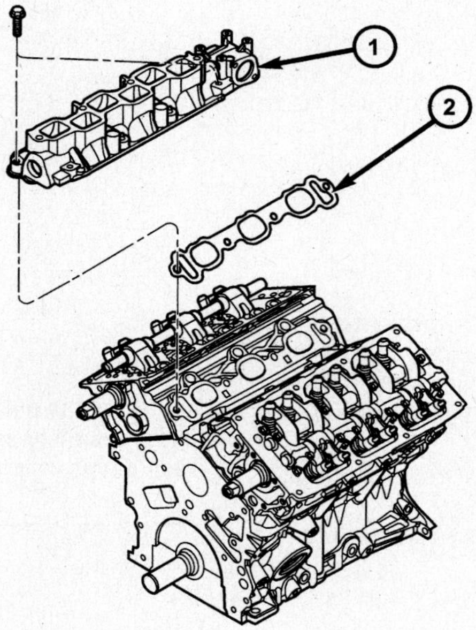

Fig. 82 Lower intake manifold and gasket—3.5L and 4.0L engines

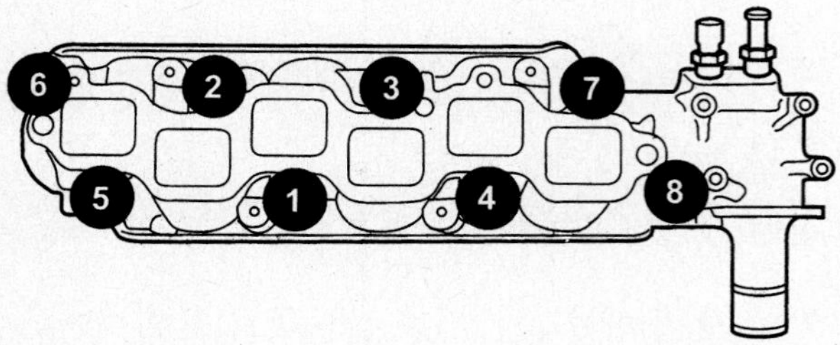

Fig. 83 Lower intake manifold tightening sequence—3.5L and 4.0L engines

3.8L Engine

See Figures 84 through 86.

1. Before servicing the vehicle, refer to the precautions in the beginning of this section.
2. Drain the cooling system.
3. Relieve the fuel system pressure.
4. Remove or disconnect the following:
   - Negative battery cable
   - Idle Air Temperature (IAT) sensor connector
   - Air cleaner and tube
   - Accelerator cable
   - Cruise control cable
   - EVAP hose from the throttle body
   - Exhaust Gas Recirculation (EGR) tube
   - Idle Air Control (IAC) motor and Throttle Position (TP) sensor connectors
   - Manifold Absolute Pressure (MAP) sensor connector
   - Positive Crankcase Ventilation (PCV) hose
   - Brake booster and cruise control hoses
   - Upper intake manifold bolts and manifold
   - Fuel line
   - Heater supply hose and Engine Coolant temperature (ECT) sensor
   - Fuel injector harness connectors
   - Fuel supply manifold with the injectors as an assembly
   - Upper radiator hose
   - Lower intake manifold bolts and manifold
   - Intake manifold seal retainer screws and the gasket

CAUTION

The intake manifold gasket is made of thin metal, handle with care to avoid injury.

5. Clean all gasket mating surfaces.

To install:

6. Install a ¼ inch bead of gasket maker onto each of the 4 manifold-to-cylinder head gasket corners.
7. Install the lower intake manifold gasket and tighten the seal retainer screws to 105 inch lbs. (12 Nm)
8. Install the lower intake manifold and tighten the bolts in sequence, as follows:
   a. Step 1: 10 inch lbs. (1 Nm).
   b. Step 2: 17 ft. lbs. (22 Nm).
   c. Step 3: 17 ft. lbs. (22 Nm).
9. Install or connect the following:
   - Fuel supply manifold and injectors as an assembly

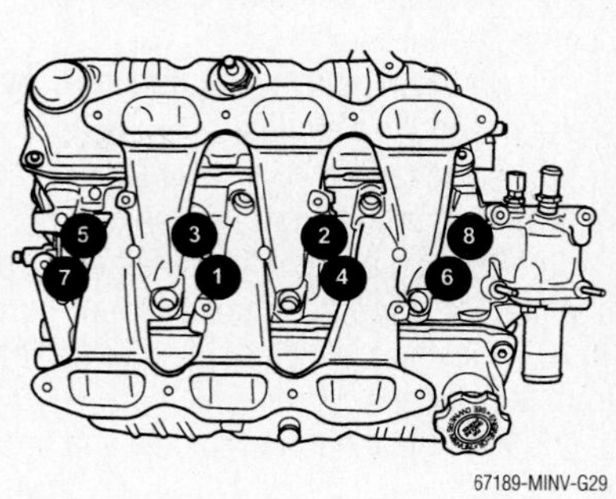

Fig. 84 Lower intake manifold torque sequence—3.8L engine

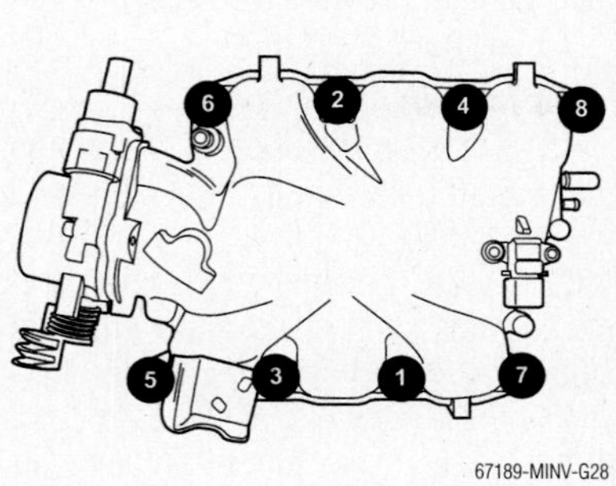

Fig. 85 Upper intake manifold torque sequence—3.8L engine

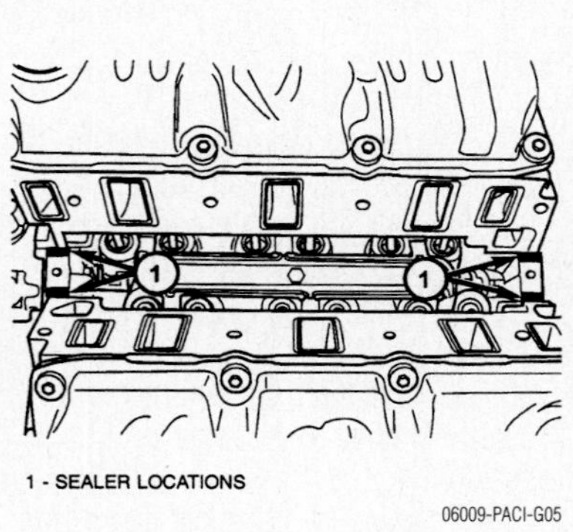

Fig. 86 Install a ¼ inch bead of gasket maker onto each of the 4 manifold-to-cylinder head gasket corners—3.8L engine

   - Fuel injector harness connectors
   - ECT sensor connector
   - Heater supply hose
   - Radiator hose
   - Fuel line
10. Place a new gasket in the channel and press lightly in place.
   - Upper intake manifold. Apply Mopar®thread and lock adhesive (medium strength) to each upper intake manifold bolt. Tighten the bolts to 105 inch lbs. (12 Nm) in the sequence illustrated.
   - MAP sensor connector
   - Brake booster and cruise control hoses

➡The special screws used to retain the EGR tube must be tightened slowly with hand tools only to avoid stripping the threads.

   - EGR tube
   - Cruise control cable
   - Accelerator cable
   - EVAP hose
   - IAC and TP sensor connectors
   - Air cleaner and tube
   - IAT connector
   - PCV hose
   - Negative battery cable
11. Fill the cooling system.
12. Start the engine, check for leaks and repair if necessary.

OIL PAN

REMOVAL & INSTALLATION

3.5L Engine

See Figures 87 and 88.

1. Before servicing the vehicle, refer to the precautions in the beginning of this section.
2. Drain the engine oil and remove the oil filter.
3. Remove or disconnect the following:
   - Negative battery cable
   - Radiator close out panel
   - Radiator core support
   - Radiator fans
   - Top and bottom A/C compressor bolts. It is not necessary to evacuate the system. Reposition the compressor.
   - A/C compressor bracket
   - Structural collar from the rear of the oil pan and transmission housing

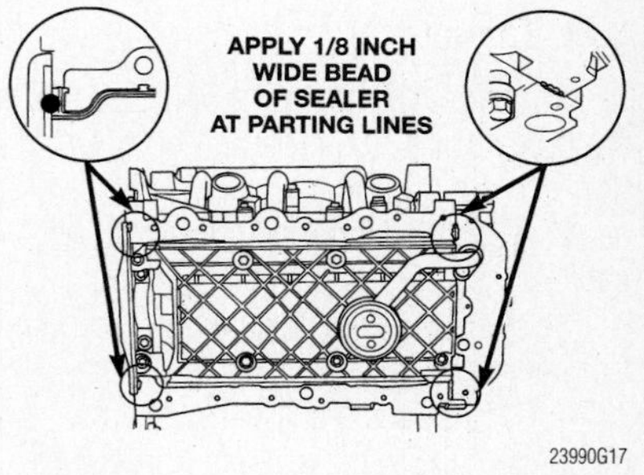

Fig. 87 To ensure a proper seal, apply sealer as shown—3.5L and 4.0L engines

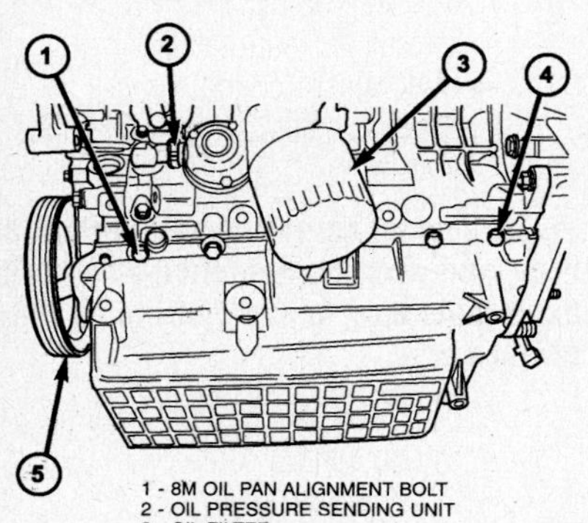

Fig. 88 Location of the oil pan alignment bolts—3.5L and 4.0L engines

- Inspection shield from between transmission and oil pan
- Dipstick and housing
- Oil pan mounting bolts, oil pan and gasket

4. Clean the oil pan and all gasket surfaces.

To install:

5. Apply a 1/8 in. (3mm) bead of sealer at the parting line of the oil pump body and the rear seal retainer.
6. Install or connect the following:
   - Oil pan and torque the M8 nuts/bolts to 21 ft. lbs. (28 Nm) and the M6 nuts/bolts to 105 inch lbs. (12 Nm)
   - Dipstick and housing
   - Inspection shield from between transmission and oil pan
   - Structural collar to the rear of the oil pan and transmission housing
   - A/C compressor bracket and tighten the bolts to 40 ft. lbs. (54 Nm)
   - Top and bottom A/C compressor bolts to 250 inch lbs. (28 Nm)
   - Radiator fans
   - Radiator core support
   - Radiator close out panel
   - Negative battery cable

3.8L Engine

1. Before servicing the vehicle, refer to the precautions in the beginning of this section.
2. Disconnect the negative battery cable.
3. Remove and relocate the speed control servo.
4. Unlock the electrical connector and disconnect the vacuum hose from servo.
5. Unlock and disconnect the electrical connectors from the cooling module.
6. Disconnect the wiring clips from cooling module.
7. Remove the retaining clip from the top of the cooling module.
8. Remove the two fasteners and remove fan module from the vehicle.
9. Remove the bolt from the oil cooler line bracket in the front motor mount.
10. Remove the battery positive cable from the starter.
11. Remove the lower, middle and upper starter bolt.
12. Place a piece of cardboard in front of the radiator core, to keep from damaging the radiator.
13. Remove the starter, and disconnect the solenoid wire from the starter.
14. Remove the starter.

To install:

15. Place a piece of cardboard in front of the radiator core, to keep from damaging the radiator.
16. Place the starter on the lower crossmember and connect the starter solenoid connector.
17. Install the dust shield on the nose of the starter, make sure of proper orientation.
18. Loosely install the starter mounting bolts.
19. Tighten the mounting bolts to 35 ft. lbs. (47 Nm).
20. Install the remaining components in the reverse order of removal.
21. Drain the engine oil.
22. Disconnect the negative battery cable.
23. Remove the dipstick tube.
24. Remove the right engine mount heat shield.
25. Disconnect the in block heater, if equipped.
26. Remove the right engine mount structural bracket at the engine and transaxle.
27. Remove the flex plate inspection cover.
28. Remove oil pan bolts, oil pan and gasket.

To install:

29. Clean the sealing surfaces and apply a 1/8 inch bead of sealer at the parting line of the chain case cover and the rear seal retainer.
30. Position a new pan gasket on the oil pan. Install oil pan and tighten the fasteners to 105 inch lbs. (12 Nm).
31. Install the flex plate cover.
32. Install the right engine mount bracket.
33. Connect the in block heater, if equipped.
34. Install the right engine mount heat.
35. Install the dipstick tube.
36. Fill the crankcase to the correct level.
37. Start the engine, check for leaks and repair if necessary.

4.0L Engine

See Figures 87 and 88.

➡On some vehicles it may be necessary to remove the compressor mounting bolts and position the unit aside. If the unit cannot be positioned to the side it will have to be removed from the vehicle.

1. Before servicing the vehicle, refer to the precautions in the beginning of this section.
2. Disconnect the negative battery cable.
3. Remove the radiator close out panel.
4. Remove the radiator core support.
5. Remove the radiator fan.
6. Remove the engine oil level indicator.
7. Raise and support the vehicle safely.
8. Drain the engine oil and remove the oil filter.
9. If equipped, remove the oil cooler mounting stud and position the cooler aside.
10. Remove the oil pan retaining bolts and remove the oil pan from its mounting.

To install:

11. Apply a 1/8 in. (3mm) bead of sealer at the parting line of the oil pump body and the rear seal retainer.
12. Install the oil pan gasket to the oil pan.
13. Install the pan while aligning the oil level indicator tube. Attach the fasteners, finger tight.
14. Tighten the M8 pan alignment (rear) bolt to 250 inch lbs. Tighten the pan alignment (front) bolt to 250 inch lbs.
15. Tighten the M8 bolts and nuts to 250 inch lbs.
16. Tighten the M6 bolts to 105 inch lbs.
17. Continue the installation in the reverse order of the removal procedure.
18. Be sure to fill the engine with the correct type engine oil.
19. Start the engine and check for leaks, correct as required.

OIL PUMP

REMOVAL & INSTALLATION

3.5L Engine

See Figures 89 and 90.

The timing belt must be removed to access the oil pump located behind the crankshaft drive sprocket. It is good practice to turn the crankshaft to Top Dead Center (TDC) No. 1 cylinder compression stroke (firing position) before starting disassembly. This should align all timing marks and be a good point of reference for all work to follow.

1. Before servicing the vehicle, refer to the precautions in the beginning of this section.
2. Drain the engine oil.
3. Drain the cooling system.
4. Remove or disconnect the following:
   - Negative battery cable
   - Timing belt
   - Crankshaft sprocket using tool L-4407-A
   - Oil pan
   - Oil pump pickup tube
   - Oil pump-to-engine screws and pump
   - Oil pump rotors
5. Wash all parts in solvent and inspect carefully for damage or wear.

To install:

6. Clean all parts well. There should be no traces of old gasket/sealer on any components.
7. Assemble the oil pump with new parts as required.
8. Install the oil pump cover. Torque the fasteners to 108 inch lbs. (12 Nm).
9. Prime the oil pump prior to installation by filling the rotor cavity with clean engine oil.
10. Install the oil pump and tighten the oil pump-to-engine screws to 250 inch lbs. (28 Nm)
11. Install or connect the following:
    - Oil pump pickup tube using a new O–ring
    - Oil pan
    - Crankshaft sprocket using tool C-4685C1, thrust bearing, washer and 12mm bolt to draw the sprocket onto the crankshaft
    - Timing belt
    - Negative battery cable
12. Fill and bleed the cooling system.
13. Fill the engine with the correct amount of clean SAE 5W-30 or SAE 10W-30 engine oil only. Do not mix the two grades of oil.
14. Start the engine, check for leaks and proper oil pressure.

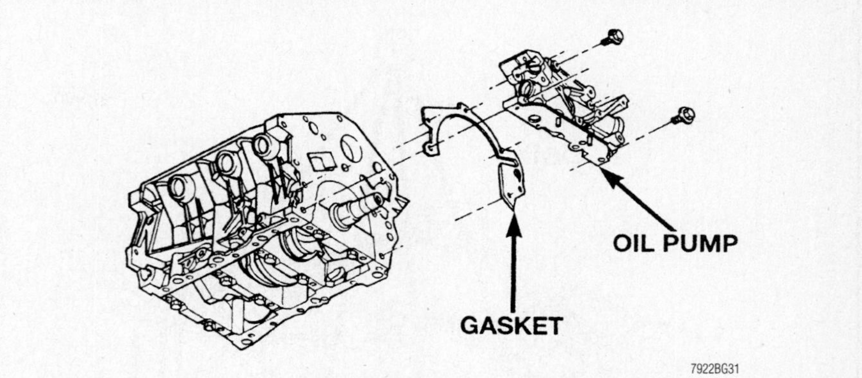

Fig. 90 Prime the oil pump before installation, because a dry pump will wear prematurely and cause low oil pressure—3.5L engine

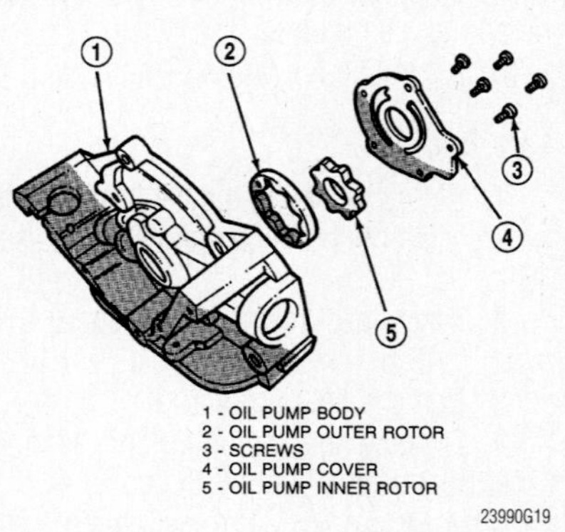

Fig. 89 Exploded view of the oil pump assembly—3.5L engine

3.8L Engine

See Figure 91.

1. Before servicing the vehicle, refer to the precautions in the beginning of this section.
2. Drain the cooling system.
3. Drain the engine oil.
4. Remove or disconnect the following:
   - Negative battery cable
   - Oil pan
   - Timing chain cover
   - Oil pump from the case cover

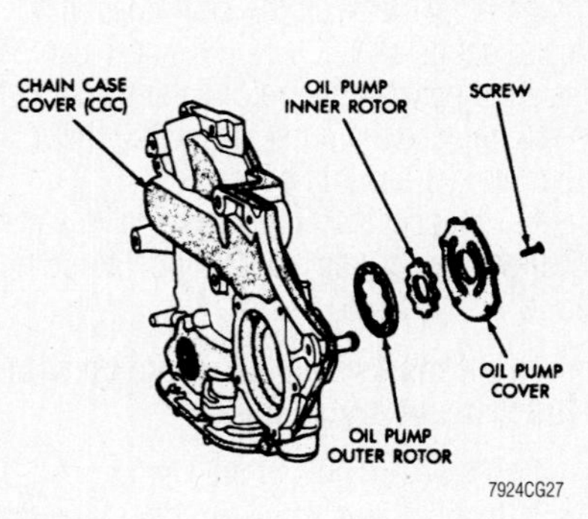

Fig. 91 Exploded view of the oil pump assembly—3.8L engine

To install:

5. Install or connect the following:
   - Oil pump to the front cover. Torque the cover screws to 105 inch lbs. (12 Nm).
   - Front cover. Torque the bolts to 20 ft. lbs. 927 Nm).
   - Oil pan
   - Negative battery cable
6. Fill the engine with clean oil.
7. Fill the cooling system.
8. Start the engine, check for leaks and repair if necessary.

4.0L Engine

See Figure 92.

The timing belt must be removed to access the oil pump located behind the crankshaft drive sprocket. It is good practice to turn the crankshaft to Top Dead Center (TDC) No. 1 cylinder compression stroke (firing position) before starting disassembly. This should align all timing marks and be a good point of reference for all work to follow.

1. Before servicing the vehicle, refer to the precautions in the beginning of this section.
2. Disconnect the negative battery cable. Drain the engine oil.
3. Drain the cooling system.
4. Raise and support the vehicle safely.
5. Drain the engine oil.
6. Remove or disconnect the following:
   - Timing belt
   - Crankshaft sprocket
   - Oil pan
   - Oil pump pickup tube
   - Oil pump-to-engine screws and pump

To install:

➡Thoroughly clean all bolt threads and threaded area in the engine, removing all oil residue, before assembly.

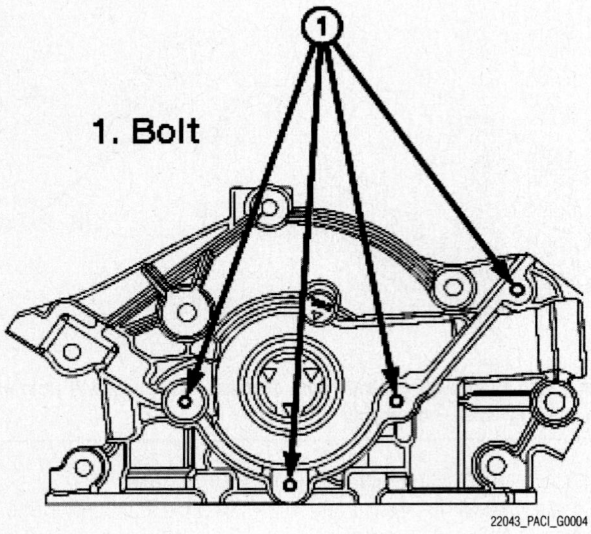

Fig. 92 Oil pump bolt locations—4.0L engine

7. Prime the oil pump prior to installation.
8. Install the oil pump and gasket carefully over the crankshaft and position the pump onto the engine block.

➡Do not apply the thread sealant to the underside of the bolt head.

9. Apply thread sealant to the oil pump cover bolts. The sealant must be applied from the tip to about 10mm of the thread length.
10. Tighten the pump cover bolts to 105 inch lbs.
11. Tighten the pump to block bolts to 250 inch lbs.
12. Install a new O-ring on the oil pickup tube. Install the pickup tube.
13. Continue the installation in the reverse order of the removal procedure.
14. Fill the cooling system with the proper grade and type coolant.
15. Fill the engine with the proper grade and type engine oil.
16. Start the engine and check for leaks, correct as required.

INSPECTION

3.5L Engine

1. Before servicing the vehicle, refer to the precautions in the beginning of this section.
2. Disconnect the negative battery cable.
3. Remove the oil pump.
4. Disassemble the oil pump. Clean all parts. Replace the pump if the cover is scratched or grooved. The mating surface of the pump housing should be smooth.
5. Lay a straightedge across the pump cover surface. If a 0.001 inch feeler gauge can be inserted between the cover and the straightedge, the cover should be replaced.
6. Measure the thickness and diameter of the outer rotor. If the outer rotor thickness is 0.563 inch or less or if the diameter is 3.141 inch or less, replace the outer rotor.
7. If the inner rotor measures 0.563 inch or less, replace the inner rotor.
8. Slide the outer rotor into the body. Press one side with your fingers and measure the clearance between the rotor and the body. If the measurement is 0.015 inch or more, replace the body.
9. Install the inner rotor into the body. If the clearance between the inner and outer rotors is 0.008 inch or more, replace both rotors.
10. Place a straightedge across the face of the body, between the bolt holes. If a feeler gauge of 0.003 inch or more can be inserted between the rotors and the straightedge, replace the pump assembly ONLY if the rotors are within spec.
11. Inspect the oil pressure relief valve plunger for scoring and free operation in its bore.

➡Small marks may be removed with 400 grit wet/dry sandpaper.

12. The spring has a free length of 1.95 inch. It should test between 23–25 lbs when compressed to 1 11/32 inch. Replace the spring, as required.
13. Assemble the pump.

3.8L Engine

1. Before servicing the vehicle, refer to the precautions in the beginning of this section.
2. Disconnect the negative battery cable.
3. Remove the oil pump.
4. Disassemble the oil pump. Clean all parts. Replace the pump if the cover is scratched or grooved. The mating surface of the pump housing should be smooth.
5. Lay a straightedge across the pump cover surface. If a 0.001 inch feeler gauge can be inserted between the cover and the straightedge, the cover should be replaced.
6. Measure the thickness and diameter of the outer rotor. If the outer rotor thickness is 0.301 inch or less or if the diameter is 3.148 inch or less, replace the outer rotor.
7. If the inner rotor measures 0.301 inch or less, replace the inner rotor.
8. Install the outer rotor into the chain case cover. Press one side with your fingers and measure the clearance between the rotor and the body. If the measurement is 0.015 inch or more, replace the chain case cover, only if the rotor is out of specification.
9. Install the inner rotor into the chain case cover. If the clearance between the inner and outer rotors is 0.008 inch or more, replace both rotors.
10. Place a straightedge across the face of the chain case cover, between the bolt holes. If a feeler gauge of 0.004 inch or more can be inserted between the rotors and the straightedge, replace the pump assembly ONLY if the rotors are within spec.
11. Inspect the oil pressure relief valve plunger for scoring and free operation in its bore.

➡Small marks may be removed with 400 grit wet/dry sandpaper.

12. The spring has a free length of 1.95 inch. It should test between 19.5–20.5 lbs when compressed to 1 11/32 inch. Replace the spring, as required.
13. Assemble the pump.

4.0L Engine

1. Before servicing the vehicle, refer to the precautions in the beginning of this section.
2. Disconnect the negative battery cable.
3. Remove the oil pump.
4. Disassemble the oil pump. Clean all parts. Replace the pump if the cover is scratched or grooved. The mating surface of the pump housing should be smooth.
5. Lay a straightedge across the pump

cover surface. If a 0.001 inch feeler gauge can be inserted between the cover and the straightedge, the cover should be replaced.

6. Measure the thickness and diameter of the outer rotor. If the outer rotor thickness is 0.563 inch or less or if the diameter is 3.141 inch or less, replace the outer rotor.

7. If the inner rotor measures 0.563 inch or less, replace the inner rotor.

8. Slide the outer rotor into the body. Press one side with your fingers and measure the clearance between the rotor and the body. If the measurement is 0.015 inch or more, replace the body.

9. Install the inner rotor into the body. If the clearance between the inner and outer rotors is 0.008 inch or more, replace both rotors.

10. Place a straightedge across the face of the body, between the bolt holes. If a feeler gauge of 0.003 inch or more can be inserted between the rotors and the straightedge, replace the pump assembly ONLY if the rotors are within spec.

11. Inspect the oil pressure relief valve plunger for scoring and free operation in its bore.

➡Small marks may be removed with 400 grit wet/dry sandpaper.

12. The spring has a free length of 1.95 inch. It should test between 23–25 lbs when compressed to 1 11/32 inch. Replace the spring, as required.

13. Assemble the pump.

PISTON AND RING

POSITIONING

See Figures 93 through 96.

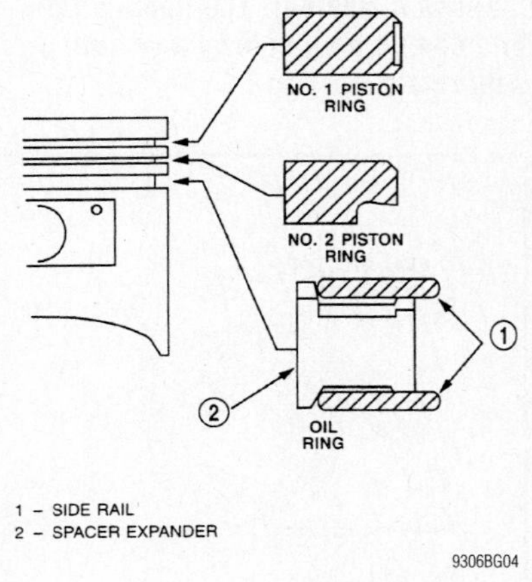

Fig. 93 Cross-sectional view of the piston rings—3.5L and 4.0L engines

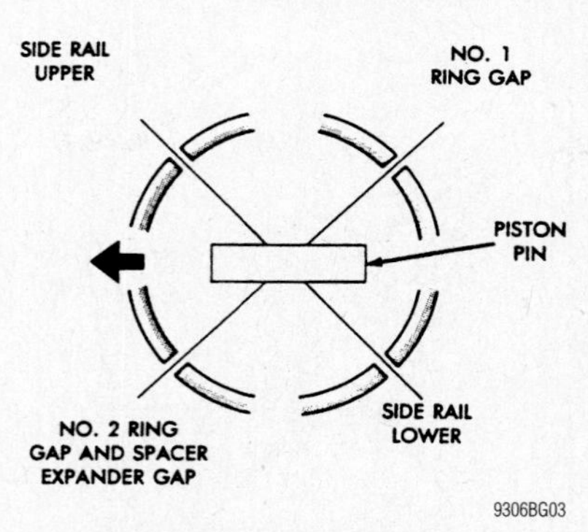

Fig. 94 Piston ring gap positions

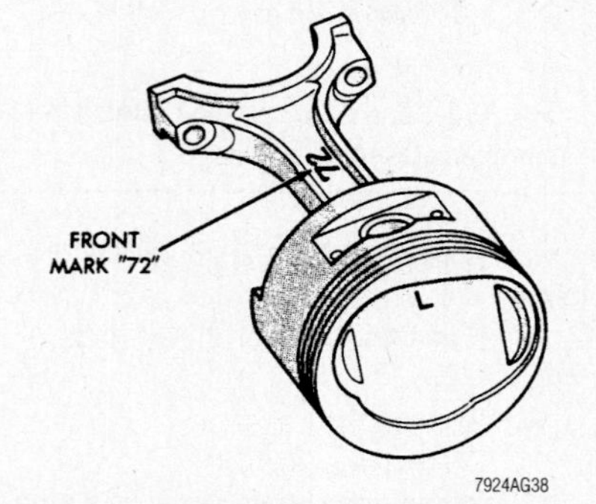

Fig. 95 Piston and connecting rod front mark locations—3.8L engine

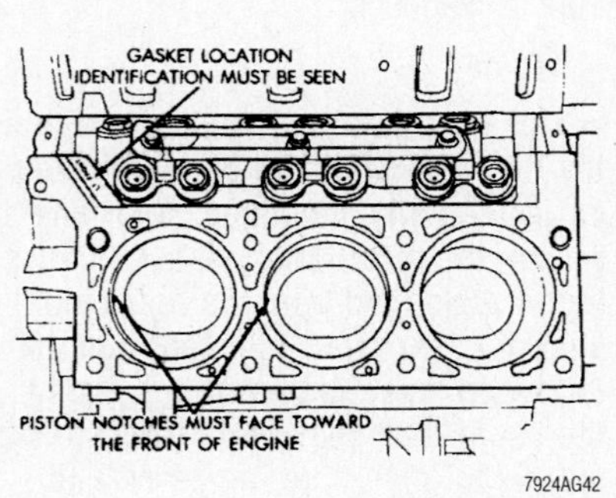

Fig. 96 Piston-to-engine positioning mark locations—3.8L engine

REAR MAIN SEAL

REMOVAL & INSTALLATION

3.5L Engine

See Figures 97 and 98.

1. Before servicing the vehicle, refer to the precautions in the beginning of this section.

2. Drain the transaxle fluid.

3. Remove the negative battery cable.

4. Remove the transaxle, inspection cover and flywheel/flexplate.

5. Using a small prytool, carefully pry out the rear oil seal. Be careful not to nick or damage the crankshaft flange seal surface or the retainer bore.

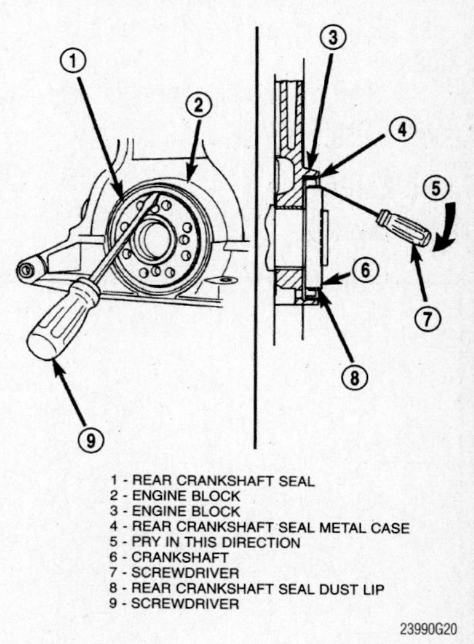

Fig. 97 Use a suitable prytool to remove the rear oil seal as shown—3.5L engine

To install:

6. Place the Seal Pilot tool 6926-1 on the crankshaft.

7. Apply a light coating of engine oil to the entire circumference of the oil seal lip.

8. Place the seal over tool 6926-1 and use installer 6926-2 and handle C-4171 to drive the seal into place until it is flush with the housing surface.

9. Install the flexplate/flywheel and transaxle.

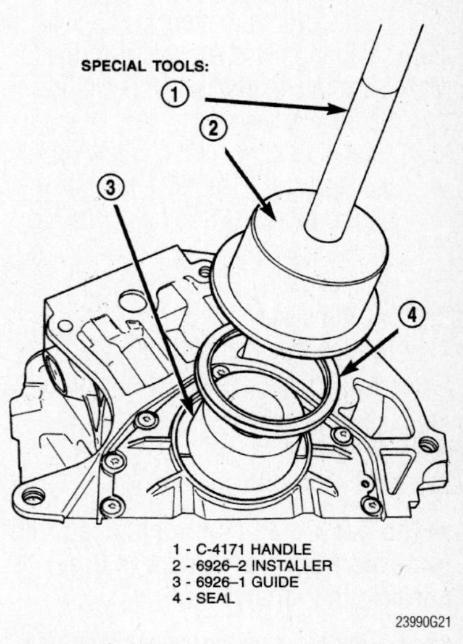

Fig. 98 Installing the rear main oil seal—3.5L engine

10. Connect the negative battery cable.
11. Fill the transaxle with the proper fluid.
12. Start the vehicle, check for leaks and repair if necessary.

3.8L Engine

See Figure 99.

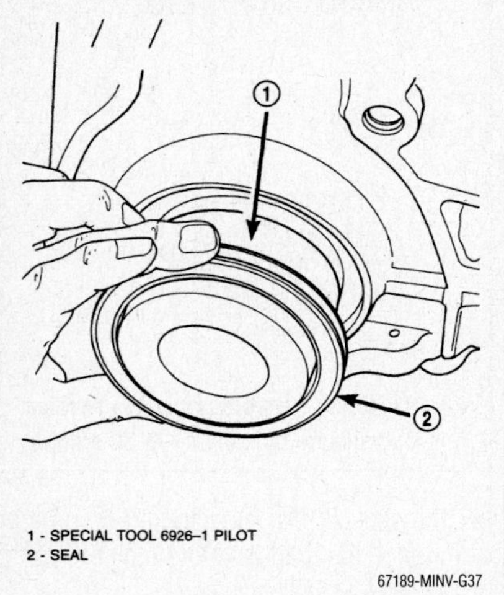

Fig. 99 Install the rear main seal flush with the cylinder block surface—3.8L engine

1. Before servicing the vehicle, refer to the precautions at the beginning of this section.
2. Remove or disconnect the following:
   - Negative battery cable
   - Transaxle
   - Flexplate
   - Rear main seal

To install:

3. Place seal guide tool 6926–1 on the crankshaft and place the seal over the tool. Make sure the lip of the seal is facing towards the crankcase.
4. Install or connect the following:
   - Rear main seal flush with the cylinder block surface using the tools illustrated.
   - Flexplate
   - Transaxle
   - Negative battery cable
5. Run the engine and check for leaks.

4.0L Engine

See Figures 100 through 103.

➡The engine oil pan may have to be removed from the vehicle in order to perform this operation.

1. Before servicing the vehicle, refer to the precautions in the beginning of this section.

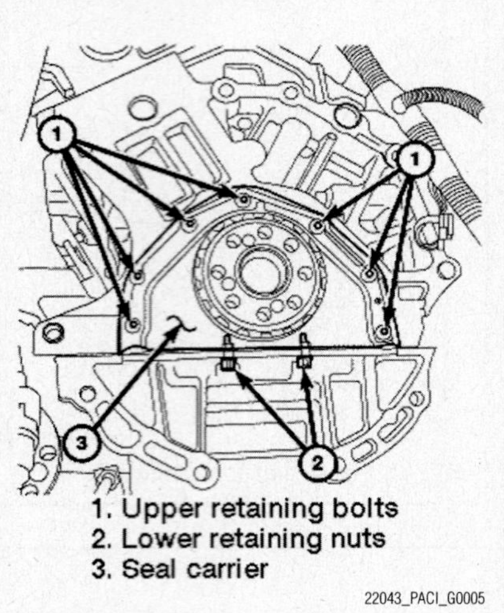

Fig. 100 Rear main seal and related components—4.0L engine

2. Remove the negative battery cable.
3. Raise and support the vehicle safely.
4. Remove the transaxle.
5. Remove the flexplate.
6. Remove the seven upper retaining bolts.
7. Remove the two lower retaining nuts.
8. Remove the rear mail seal carrier from its mounting.

To install:

➡This installation procedure assumes that the seal protector is not missing or accidentally dislodged. If for any reason the installation sleeve is missing or dislodged from the rear crankshaft oil seal prior to installation the following must be performed. Using the chamfered seal guide from special tool 6926, insert the tampered end into the transaxle side of the rear crankshaft oil seal assembly and push the seal guide through the seal assembly. This will ensure that the seal lip is positioned toward the engine when the seal assembly is installed.

9. Clean the sealant residue from the engine block and the oil pan.

➡The seal retainer gasket is bonded to the retainer and must be replaced as an assembly.

➡If a burr or scratch is present on the crankshaft edge (chamfer), clean the surface using 400 grit sand paper to prevent seal damage during installation. Be sure that the rear crankshaft oil seal surface is clean and free of any abrasive material.

➡The rear crankshaft oil seal and retainer are an assembly. Do not separate the seal protector from the rear crankshaft oil seal before installation on the engine. Damage to the seal lip will occur if the seal protector is removed and installed prior to installation on the engine.

10. Carefully position the oil seal retainer assembly and the seal protector on the crankshaft and push firmly into place on the engine block.

➡During the above step the seal protector will be pushed from the rear oil seal assembly as a result of installing the rear oil seal.

11. Hand tighten the rear oil seal fasteners.
12. Attach special tool 8225 to the pan rail using the oil pan fasteners.

➡The special tool is used to assist with the fit of the flush mount rear main seal retainer. The notch on the tool should be located away from the seal retainer.

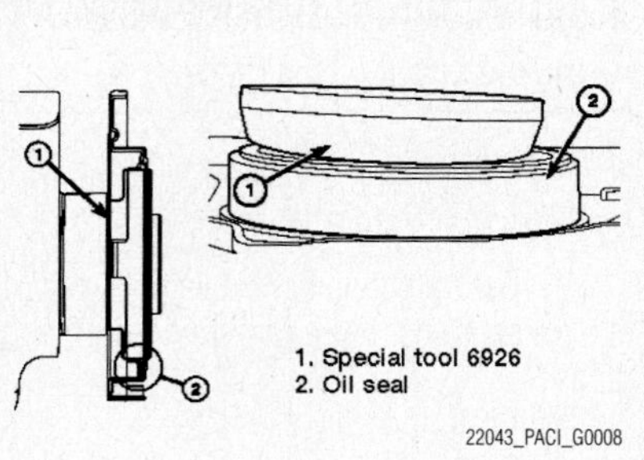

Fig. 101 Special tool 6926 installation—4.0L engine

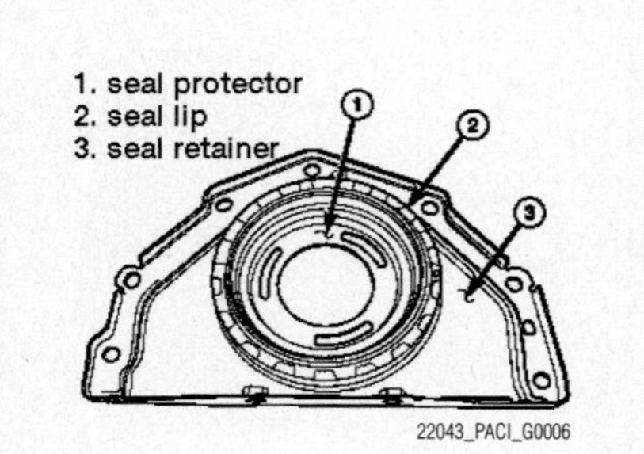

Fig. 102 Rear main seal positioning—4.0L engine

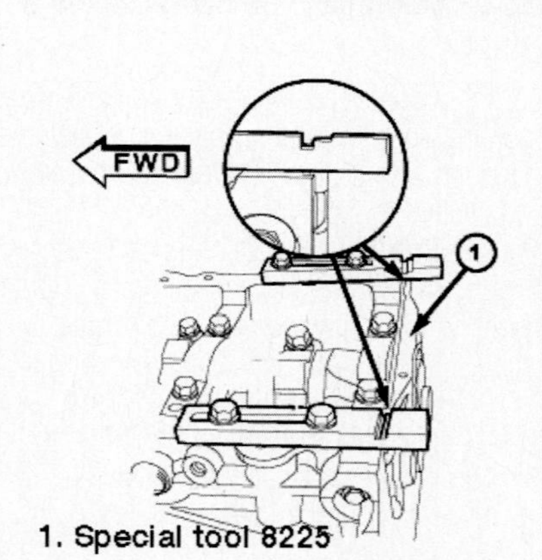

Fig. 103 Special tool 8225 installation—4.0L engine

13. While applying pressure to the seal retainer against the special tool, tighten the seal retainer screws to 105 inch lbs.

14. Remove the special tool. Be sure that the seal flange is flush with the block oil pan surface.

15. Continue the installation in the reverse order of the removal procedure.

TIMING BELT COVER, BELT AND SPROCKETS

REMOVAL & INSTALLATION

3.5L and 4.0L Engines

See Figures 104 and 105.

1. Before servicing the vehicle, refer to the precautions in the beginning of this section.

Use care when servicing a timing belt. Valve timing is absolutely critical to engine performance. If the valve timing marks on all drive sprockets are not properly aligned, engine damage will result. If only the belt and tensioner are being serviced, do not loosen the camshaft drive sprockets unless they are to be replaced. The sprockets have oversized openings and can be rotated several degrees in each direction on their shafts. This means the sprockets must be re-timed, requiring some special tools.

⁂ CAUTION

Fuel injection systems remain under pressure, even after the engine has been turned off. The fuel system pressure must be relieved before disconnecting any fuel lines. Failure to do so may result in fire and/or personal injury.

2. Loosen the valve train rocker assemblies before servicing the timing components.

3. Release the fuel system pressure using the recommended procedure.

4. Remove or disconnect the following:
   - Negative battery cable
   - Cylinder head covers
   - Accessory drive belts
   - Drive belt tensioner
   - Power steering pump bolts and position the pump aside
   - Crankshaft damper with a quality puller tool gripping the inside of the pulley
   - Lower front timing belt cover retainers

5. Support the engine with a floor jack.
   - Air cleaner assembly
   - Front engine mount
   - Fuel supply line from the rail
   - Upper timing belt cover bolts and the cover

6. If the timing belt is to be reused, mark the timing belt with the running direction for installation.

⁂ WARNING

Always align the timing marks always use the crankshaft to rotate the engine. Failure to do this will result in severe engine damage.

7. Rotate the engine clockwise until the crankshaft mark aligns with the Top Dead Center (TDC) mark on the oil pump housing and the camshaft sprocket timing marks align with the marks on the rear cover.

8. Remove the timing belt tensioner and the belt.

9. Pre-load the timing belt tensioner as follows:

   a. Place tensioner in a vise the same way it is mounted on the engine.

   b. Slowly compress the plunger into the tensioner body.

   c. Once the plunger is compressed, install a pin through the body and plunger to retain it in place until the tensioner is installed.

To install:

⁂ WARNING

If the camshafts have moved from the timing marks always rotate them towards the direction nearest to the timing marks. Never turn the camshafts a full turn or sever engine damage will occur.

10. Align the crankshaft sprocket with the TDC mark on the oil pump.

11. Align the camshaft sprockets timing marks with the mark on the rear cover.

12. Install the belt starting at the crankshaft sprocket going in a counterclockwise direction. Install the belt around the last sprocket always maintaining tension on the belt as it is positioned around the tensioner pulley.

➡If the camshaft gears have been removed it is only necessary to have the camshaft gear retaining bolts installed to a snug torque at this time.

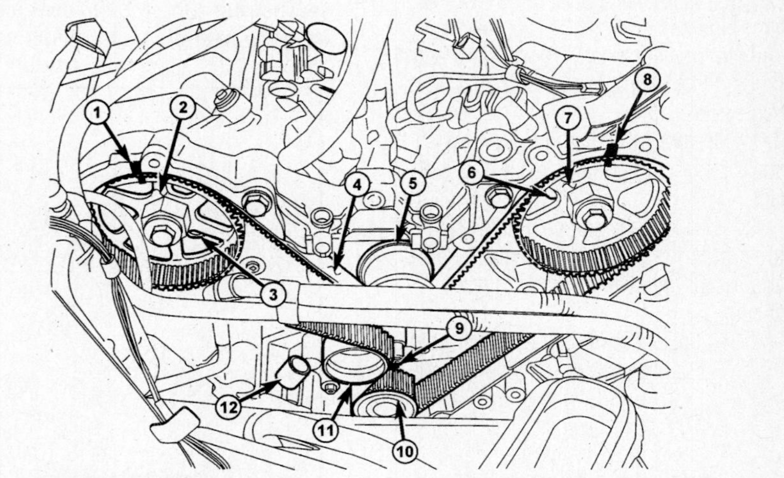

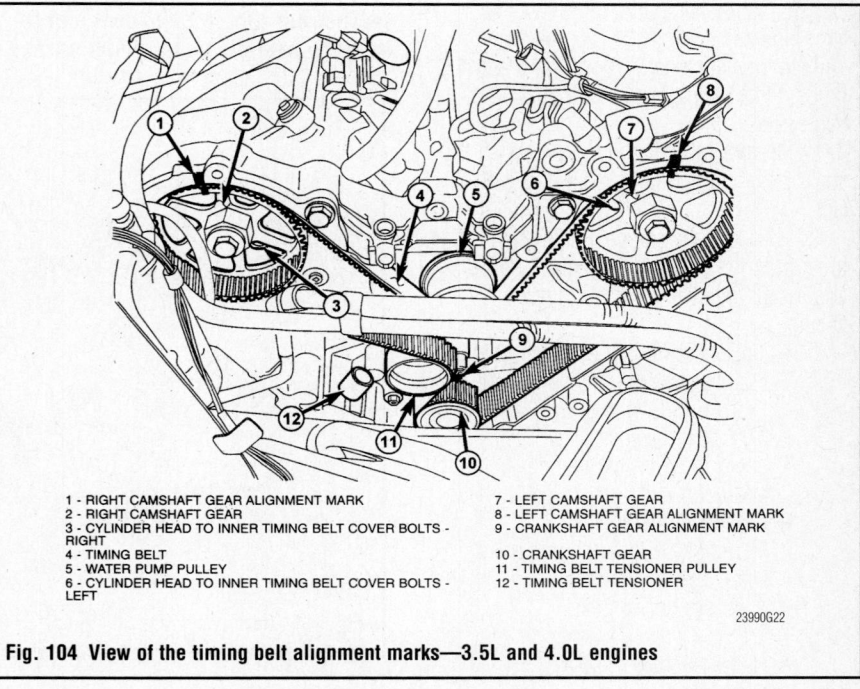

1 - RIGHT CAMSHAFT GEAR ALIGNMENT MARK
2 - RIGHT CAMSHAFT GEAR
3 - CYLINDER HEAD TO INNER TIMING BELT COVER BOLTS - RIGHT
4 - TIMING BELT
5 - WATER PUMP PULLEY
6 - CYLINDER HEAD TO INNER TIMING BELT COVER BOLTS - LEFT
7 - LEFT CAMSHAFT GEAR
8 - LEFT CAMSHAFT GEAR ALIGNMENT MARK
9 - CRANKSHAFT GEAR ALIGNMENT MARK
10 - CRANKSHAFT GEAR
11 - TIMING BELT TENSIONER PULLEY
12 - TIMING BELT TENSIONER

23990G22

Fig. 104 View of the timing belt alignment marks—3.5L and 4.0L engines

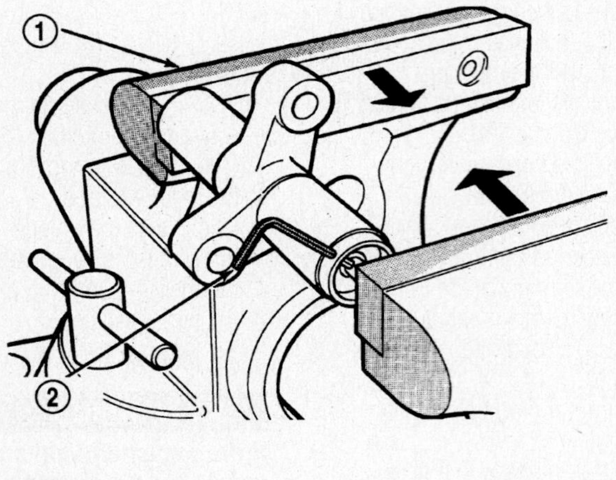

Fig. 105 Pre-load the timing belt tensioner—3.5L and 4.0L engines

13. Holding the tensioner pulley against the belt, install the tensioner into the housing and tighten to 250 inch lbs. (28 Nm) making sure all the alignment marks remain aligned. Pull the pin from the tensioner and allow the tensioner to extend to the pulley bracket.
14. Rotate the crankshaft sprocket 2 full turns and check the timing marks on the cam and crank shafts. Make sure the marks are aligned, if not repeat the procedure.
15. If the camshafts were removed using a dial indicator, position the number 1 piston at TDC.
16. Hold the camshaft sprocket hex with a 36mm wrench and tighten the right camshaft sprocket bolt to 75 ft. lbs. (102 Nm) plus an additional 90 degree turn. Tighten the left camshaft sprocket bolt to 85 ft. lbs. (115 Nm) plus an additional 90 degree turn.
17. Remove the dial indicator. Install the spark plug and tighten to 20 ft. lbs. (28 Nm).
18. Remove the camshaft alignment tools from the back of the cylinder heads and install the cam covers with new O-rings.

- Upper timing belt cover and bolts
- Fuel supply line to the rail
- Front engine mount
- Air cleaner assembly
- Lower front timing belt cover retainers
- Crankshaft damper
- Power steering pump and bolts
- Drive belt tensioner
- Accessory drive belts
- Cylinder head covers
- Negative battery cable

TIMING BELT REAR COVER

REMOVAL & INSTALLATION

3.5L Engine

See Figure 106.

1. Properly relieve the fuel system pressure.
2. Disconnect the negative battery cable.
3. Remove timing belt.
4. Remove camshaft sprockets.
5. Remove rear timing belt cover bolts.
6. Remove the rear cover.

To install:

➡The rear timing belt cover has O-rings to seal the water pump passages to cylinder block. Do not reuse the O-rings.

7. Clean rear timing belt cover O-ring sealing surfaces and grooves. Lubricate new O-rings with Mopar® Dielectric Grease or equivalent to facilitate assembly.
8. Position NEW O-rings on cover.
9. Install rear timing belt cover. Tighten bolts to the following specified torque:
   - M10 bolts: 40 ft. lbs. (54 Nm)
   - M8 bolts: 20 ft. lbs. (28 Nm)
   - M6 bolts: 105 inch lbs. (12 Nm)
10. Install camshaft sprockets.
11. Install timing belt.

TIMING CHAIN, SPROCKETS, FRONT COVER AND SEAL

REMOVAL & INSTALLATION

3.8L Engine

See Figures 107 and 108.

1. Before servicing the vehicle, refer to the precautions in the beginning of this section.
2. Disconnect the negative battery cable.
3. Properly relieve the fuel system pressure.
4. Evacuate air conditioning system.
5. Drain and recycle the engine coolant.
6. Remove the air cleaner.
7. Loosen the water pump pulley bolts.
8. Remove the accessory drive belt and belt tensioner.
9. Remove the power steering pump and set the pump aside.
10. Remove the alternator.
11. Disconnect the air conditioning com-

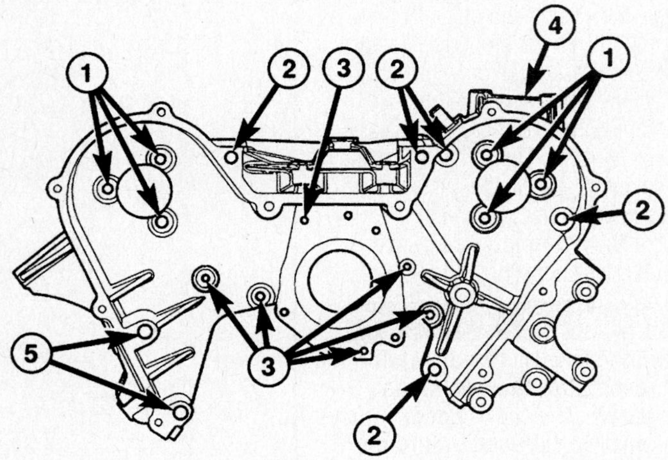

Fig. 106 View of the rear timing belt cover (4) and fasteners: M8 (1), M10 (2), M6 (3) and M10 stud/nut (5)—3.5L and 4.0L engines

pressor clutch electrical connector and suction discharge hoses.

12. Remove the dipstick tube.
13. Drain the engine oil.
14. Remove right wheel and inner splash shield.
15. Remove the oil pan.
16. Disconnect the lower radiator hose and the oil cooler hose at the coolant cross over pipe.
17. Separate the power steering lines from the A/C bracket and bracket at the cradle.
18. Separate the air conditioning compressor from the engine and set aside.
19. Remove the crankshaft damper using tool # 8454 and insert # 8450.
20. Remove the coolant cross over pipe fasteners and pipe.
21. Remove the accessible lower timing cover fasteners through the wheel well.
22. Remove Camshaft Position (CMP) sensor from the timing chain cover.
23. Remove the water pump.
24. Support the engine with a floor jack and remove the upper engine mount assembly.
25. Remove the timing chain cover fasteners and cover.
26. Clean the timing cover mating surfaces.
27. Rotate the engine so that the timing marks are aligned.
28. Remove or disconnect the following:
    - Camshaft sprocket attaching bolt
    - Timing chain and camshaft sprocket
    - Crankshaft sprocket with special tools 8539, 5048–6 and 5048–1

To install:

29. Rotate the engine so the timing arrow is at the 12 o'clock position.
30. Lubricate the chain and sprockets with clean oil.
31. Hold the camshaft sprocket and chain and place the chain around the sprocket aligning the plated link with the dot on the sprocket. Position the timing arrow at the 6 o'clock position.
32. Place the chain around the crankshaft sprocket with the plated link lined up with the dot on the sprocket and install the camshaft sprocket.
33. Use a straight edge to check the timing alignment marks.
34. Align the timing chain colored links with the dots on the timing sprockets.
35. Tighten the camshaft sprocket bolt to 40 ft. lbs. (54 Nm).

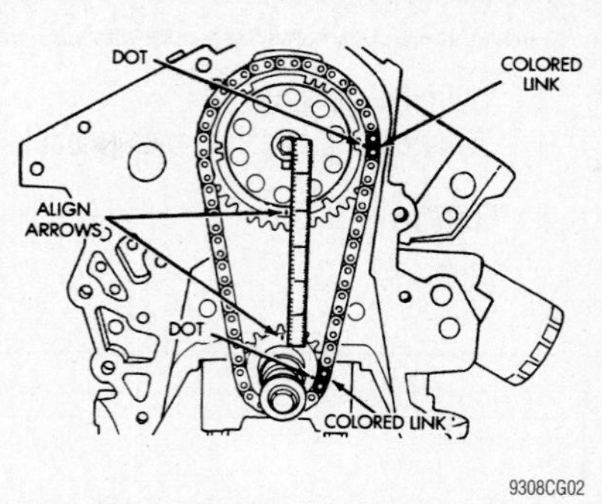

Fig. 107 Timing mark alignment—3.8L engine

36. Rotate the crankshaft 2 revolutions and verify the proper timing chain alignment, if not remove the components and reinstall as described above.

➡Do not use sealer on cover gasket

37. Position a new gasket on the timing cover. Adhere the new gasket to the chain case cover, making sure that the lower edge of the gasket is 0.020 inch (0.5 mm) beyond the lower edge of the cover.
38. Rotate the crankshaft so that the oil pump drive flats are in the vertical position.
39. Position the oil pump inner rotor so the mating flats are in the same position as the crankshaft drive flats.

CAUTION

Make sure the oil pump is engaged on the crankshaft correctly or severe damage may result.

40. Install the timing cover.
41. Install the timing chain cover bolts. Tighten the M8 bolts to 20 ft. lbs. (27 Nm) and the M10 bolts to 40 ft. lbs. (54 Nm).
42. Install the crankshaft front oil seal.
43. Install the crankshaft damper.
44. Install the coolant cross over pipe.
45. Install the A/C compressor.
46. Position and install the power steering line hold downs at the cradle and A/C bracket.
47. Connect the coolant hoses to the coolant crossover pipe.
48. Install the inner fender splash shield.
49. Install oil pump pick-up tube with a new O-ring. Tighten the bolt to 250 inch lbs. (28 Nm).
50. Install the oil pan.
51. Install the water pump and pulley.
52. Install the CMP sensor.
53. Connect the A/C electrical connector and the suction, discharge hoses.
54. Install the dipstick tube.
55. Install the alternator.
56. Install the power steering pump.
57. Install the idler pulley and drive belt.
58. Install the upper engine.
59. Fill the crankcase with engine oil to the proper level.
60. Fill the cooling system.
61. Evacuate and recharge the A/C system.
62. Check and refill all fluid levels.
63. Connect the negative battery cable.

VALVE LASH

ADJUSTMENT

These engines use hydraulic roller lifters to take up the free-play in the valve train system, therefore no lash adjustments are necessary.

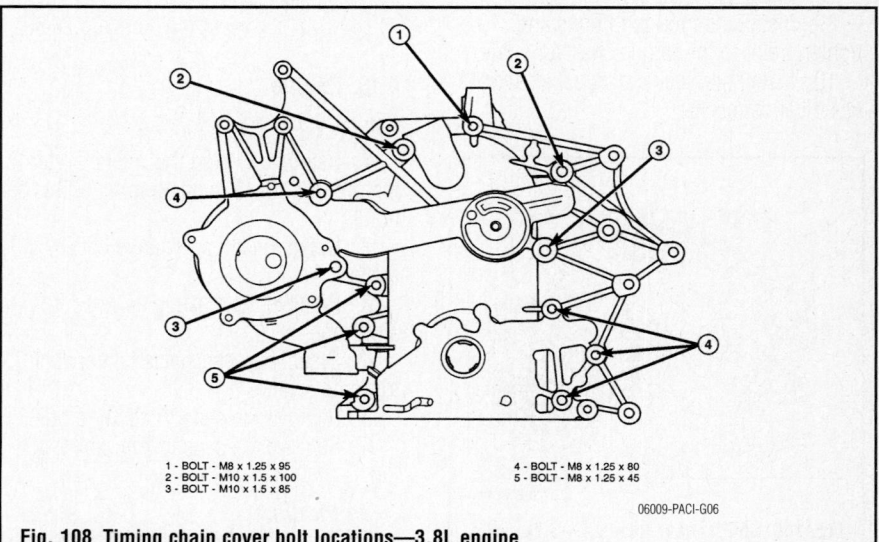

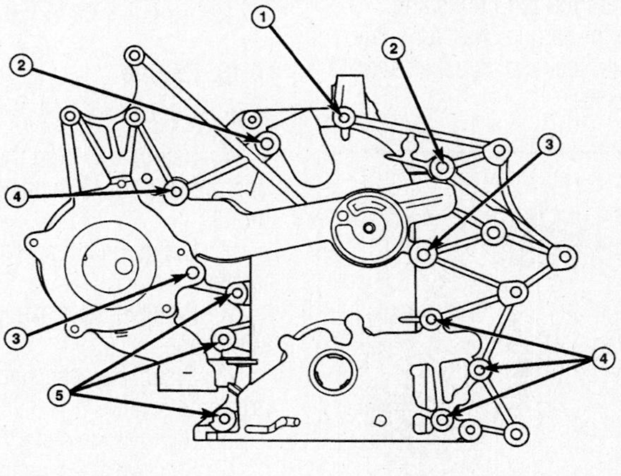

Fig. 108 Timing chain cover bolt locations—3.8L engine

ENGINE PERFORMANCE & EMISSION CONTROL

CAMSHAFT POSITION (CMP) SENSOR

LOCATION

This sensor is located in the engine compartment, on the engine next to the alternator.

OPERATION

The Camshaft Position (CMP) sensor contains a Hall-effect device that provides cylinder identification to the Powertrain Control Module (PCM). The sensor generates pulses as groups of notches on the camshaft sprocket pass underneath it. The PCM keeps track of crankshaft rotation and identifies each cylinder by the pulses generated by the notches on the camshaft sprocket.

REMOVAL & INSTALLATION

3.5L Engine

See Figure 109.

1. Before servicing the vehicle, refer to the precautions in the beginning of this section.
2. Disconnect the negative battery cable.
3. Remove air cleaner box.
4. Unlock the camshaft sensor electrical connector.
5. Disconnect the electrical connectors to the camshaft sensor.
6. Remove the mounting bolts.
7. Remove camshaft sensor.

To install:

8. Install camshaft sensor.
9. Install the mounting bolts and tighten, refer to the torque chart for value.
10. Install and lock the camshaft sensor electrical connector.

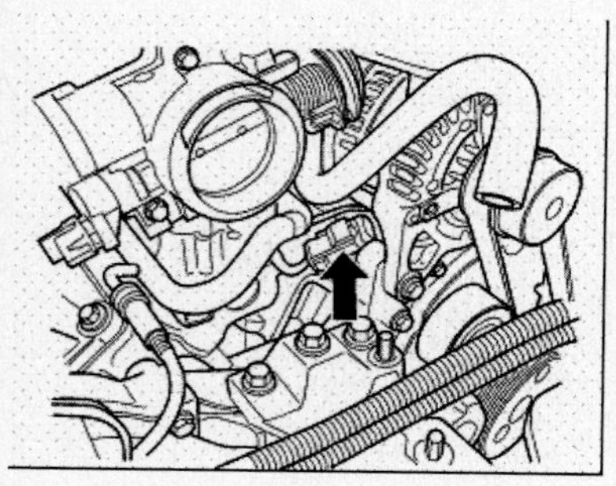

21180_CDIA_G293

Fig. 109 CMP sensor location—3.5L engine

11. Install air cleaner box.
12. Connect the negative battery cable.

3.8L Engine

See Figure 110.

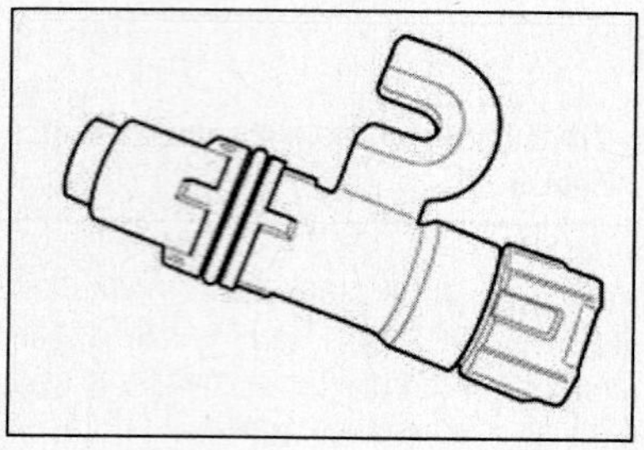

21180_CDIA_G295

Fig. 110 CMP sensor location—3.8L engine

1. Before servicing the vehicle, refer to the precautions in the beginning of this section.
2. Disconnect the negative battery cable.
3. Unlock the camshaft sensor electrical connector.
4. Disconnect the electrical connectors to the camshaft sensor.
5. Loosen the mounting bolts.
6. Remove camshaft sensor.

To install:

7. Install camshaft position sensor.
8. Tighten the mounting bolt to Nm 12 (106 inch lbs.).
9. Install and lock the camshaft sensor electrical connector.
10. Connect the negative battery cable.

4.0L Engine

See Figure 111.

1. Before servicing the vehicle, refer to the precautions in the beginning of this section.
2. Disconnect the negative battery cable.
3. Remove the makeup air hose from the air cleaner.
4. Disconnect the electrical connector from the sensor.
5. Remove the sensor retaining bolt.
6. Remove the sensor from its mounting.

To install:

7. Installation is the reverse of the removal procedure.

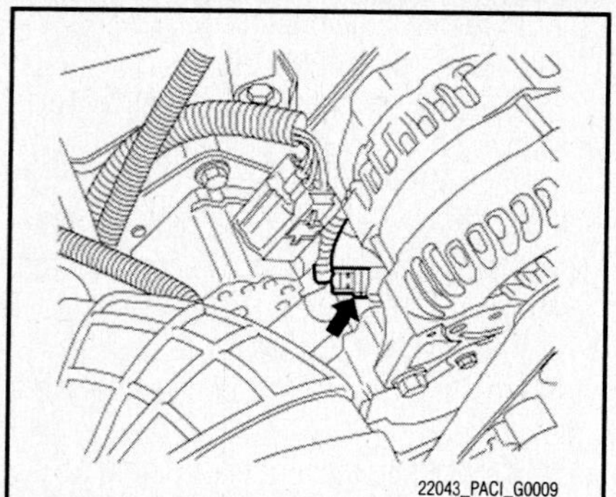

22043_PACI_G0009

Fig. 111 CMP sensor location—4.0L engine

8. Tighten the mounting bolt to 106 inch lbs.

CRANKSHAFT POSITION (CKP) SENSOR

LOCATION

The Crankshaft Position (CKP) sensor is located on the driver side of the vehicle, above the differential housing. The bottom of the sensor sits above the drive plate.

OPERATION

This sensor generates pulses that are signals sent to the PCM. The PCM interprets these signals to determine the crankshaft position. The PCM uses this data along with other inputs to determine injector sequence and ignition timing.

REMOVAL & INSTALLATION

2005–06 Models

See Figures 112 and 113.

1. Before servicing the vehicle, refer to the precautions in the beginning of this section.
2. Disconnect the negative and positive battery cable.
3. Remove the battery.
4. Unlock and disconnect electrical connector from crankshaft position sensor.

To install:

5. Install sensor and push sensor down until contact is made with the transmission case. While holding the sensor in this position, install and tighten the retaining bolt to 12 Nm (105 inch lbs.) torque.
6. Connect electrical connector and lock to crankshaft position sensor.
7. Install the battery and connect the positive cable, then the negative battery cable.

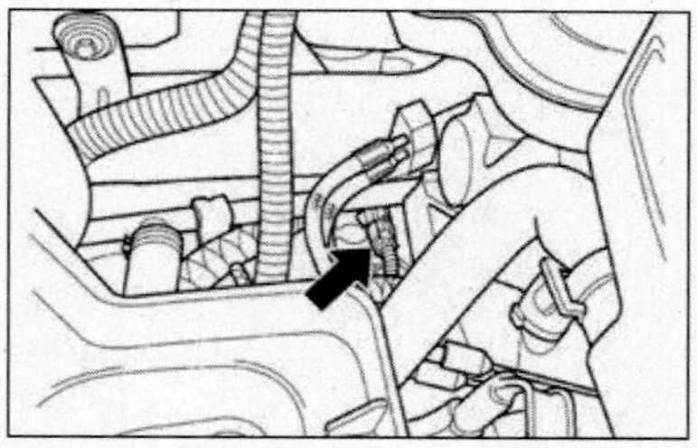
21180_CDIA_G297

Fig. 112 CKP sensor location—3.5L engine

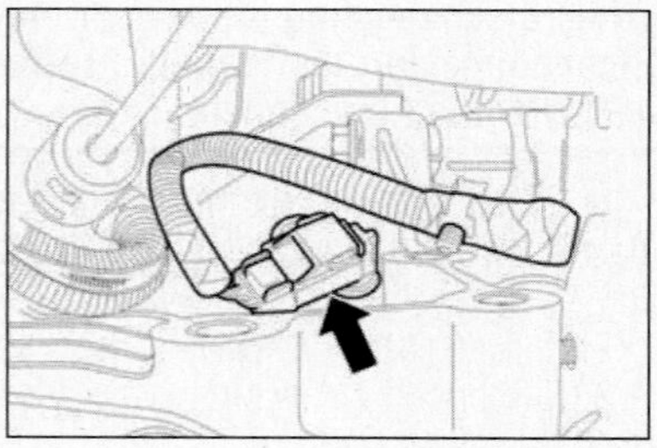
21180_CDIA_G298

Fig. 113 CKP sensor location—3.8L engine (2005–2006)

2007–08 Models

See Figures 114 and 115.

1. Before servicing the vehicle, refer to the precautions in the beginning of this section.

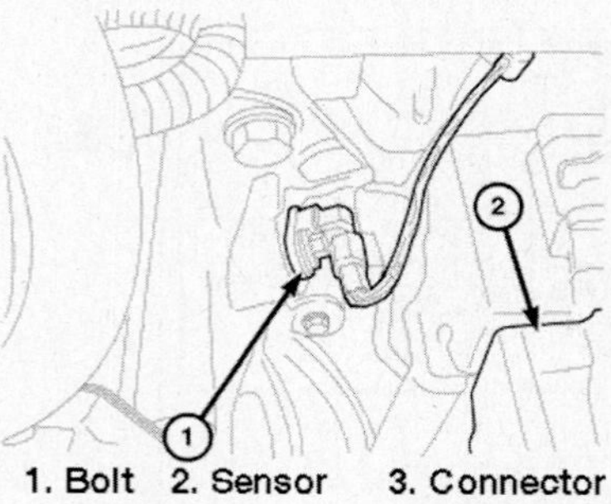

22043_PACI_G0010

Fig. 115 CKP sensor location—4.0L engine

2. Disconnect the negative and positive battery cable.
3. Disconnect the electrical connector from the sensor.
4. Remove the sensor retaining bolt.
5. Remove the sensor from its mounting.

To install:

6. Installation is the reverse of the removal procedure.
7. Tighten the mounting bolt to 106 inch lbs.

TESTING

2005–06 Models

1. Before servicing the vehicle, refer to the precautions in the beginning of this section.
2. Visually inspect the related wire harness. Look for any chafed, pierced, pinched, or partially broken wires.

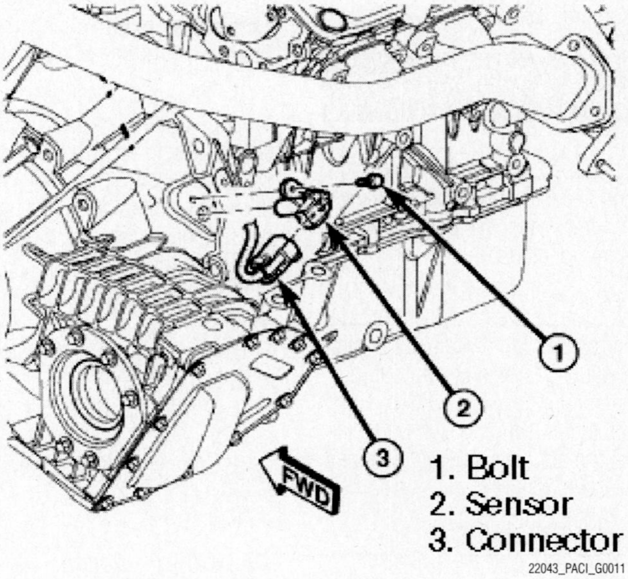

22043_PACI_G0011

Fig. 114 CKP sensor location—3.8L engine (2007–2008)

3. Visually inspect the related wire harness connectors. Look for broken, bent, pushed out, or corroded terminals.
4. Ensure the Crankshaft Position Sensor and the Camshaft Position Sensor are properly installed and the mounting bolt(s) tight.
5. Remove the Camshaft Position Sensor and inspect the Tone Wheel/Pulse Ring for damage, foreign material, or excessive movement.
6. If no problems were evident, start the engine.
7. Gently tap on the Cam Position Sensor and wiggle the Sensor.
8. Inspect the Sensor harness connector, PCM harness connector, Sensor connector, and PCM connector for loose, bent, corroded, or pushed out pins or terminals.
9. Inspect the related wire harness and the splices in the CMP circuits.
10. Repair any wiring and/or connector concerns, or replace the Camshaft Position Sensor.
11. With the proper lab scope probe and the Miller special tool #6801, backprobe the CKP Signal circuit at the CKP harness connector.
12. Start the engine. Observe the lab scope screen. Are there any irregular or missing signals?
13. If so, determine the cause and repair or replace the item, or refer to any TSBs that may apply.

ENGINE COOLANT TEMPERATURE (ECT) SENSOR

LOCATION

See Figures 116 and 117.

This sensor threads into a coolant passage on lower intake manifold near the thermostat. New sensors have sealant applied to the threads.

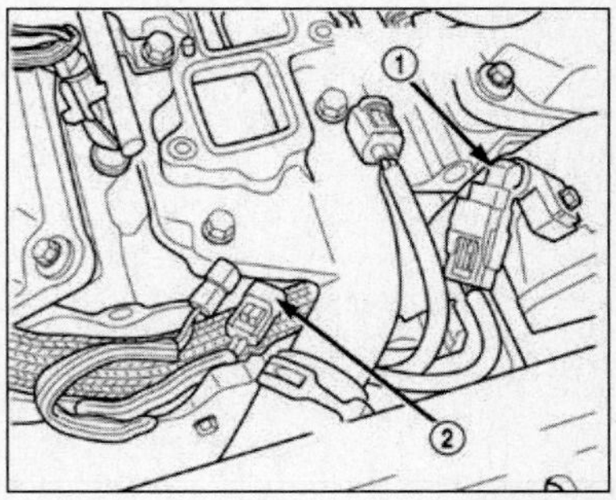

21180_CDIA_G300

Fig. 116 ECT sensor (2) and CMP sensor (1) location—3.5L and 4.0L engines

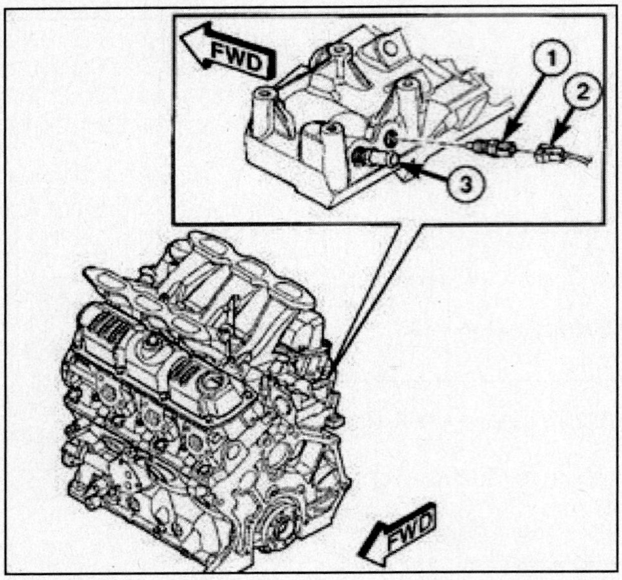

21180_CDIA_G301

Fig. 117 ECT sensor (1) with connector (2) and heater supply fitting (3) location—3.8L engine

OPERATION

This sensor provides coolant temperature data the PCM. When the engine is cold the PCM will demand slightly richer air/fuel mixtures and higher idle speeds until normal operating temperature is reached. This sensor also determines the operation of the radiator fan.

REMOVAL & INSTALLATION

3.5L and 4.0L Engines

1. Before servicing the vehicle, refer to the precautions in the beginning of this section.
2. Drain cooling system below engine coolant temperature sensor level.
3. Disconnect negative cable from remote jumper terminal.
4. With the engine cold, disconnect coolant sensor electrical connector and remove the sensor.

To install:

5. Install engine coolant temperature sensor. Tighten sensor to 7 Nm (60 inch lbs.).
6. Connect electrical connector to sensor.
7. Fill cooling system.

3.8L Engine

1. Before servicing the vehicle, refer to the precautions in the beginning of this section.
2. Drain cooling system below engine coolant temperature sensor level.
3. Remove power steering reservoir and relocate. Do not disconnect hoses.
4. Remove ignition coil and bracket.
5. Disconnect coolant sensor electrical connector. Remove coolant sensor.

To install:

6. Install engine coolant temperature sensor. Tighten sensor to 7 Nm (60 inch lbs.).
7. Connect electrical connector to sensor.
8. Install ignition coil bracket.
9. Install ignition coil.
10. Install power steering reservoir.
11. Fill cooling system.

HEATED OXYGEN (HO2S) SENSOR

LOCATION

The oxygen sensors are attached to and protrude into the exhaust system. This vehicle uses four sensors.

OPERATION

The sensor senses the oxygen concentration in the exhaust gas then converts it into a voltage and sends it on to the PCM. The PCM controls fuel injection based on the signal so that the air fuel ratio is maintained at the theoretical ration.

REMOVAL & INSTALLATION

3.5L Engine

See Figure 118.

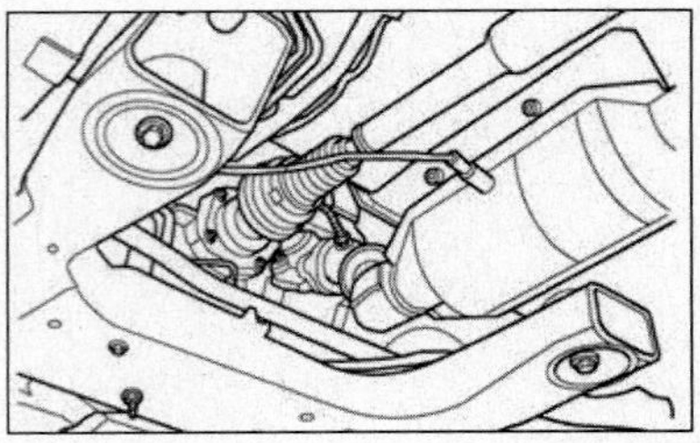

21180_CDIA_G310

Fig. 118 HO2S sensor location—3.5L engine

CAUTION

When disconnecting the sensor electrical connector, do not pull directly on wire going into sensor.

1. Before servicing the vehicle, refer to the precautions in the beginning of this section.
2. Disconnect the negative battery cable.
3. Disconnect the heated oxygen sensor electrical connector.
4. Use a socket such as a crowfoot wrench to remove oxygen sensor.

To install:

➡When replacing an HO2S Sensor, the PCM RAM memory must be cleared, either by disconnecting the PCM C-1 connector or momentarily disconnecting the battery negative terminal. The NGC learns the characteristics of each HO2S heater element and these old values should be cleared when installing a new HO2S sensor. The customer may experience driveability issues if this is not performed.

5. After removing the sensor, the threads must be cleaned with an 18 mm X 1.5 + 6E tap. If reusing the original sensor, coat the sensor threads with an anti-seize compound such as Loctite 771–64 or equivalent. New sensors have compound on the threads and do not require an additional coating. Tighten the sensor to 28 Nm (20 ft. lbs.) torque.
6. Connect the heated oxygen sensor electrical connector.
7. Install the wiring clip to the heat shield.
8. Connect the negative battery cable.

3.8L Engine

Downstream Sensor

See Figure 119.

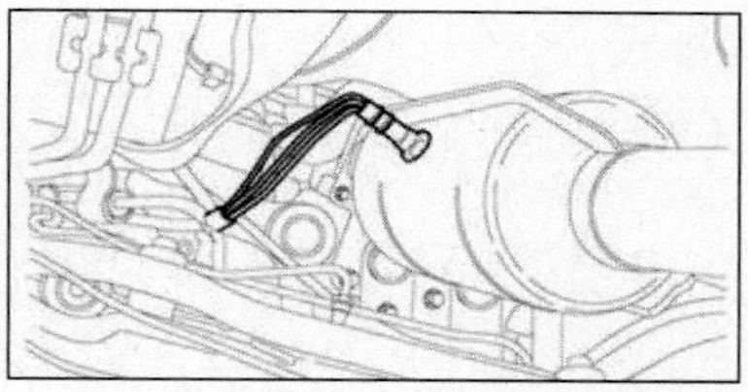

Fig. 119 Downstrean sensor location—3.8L engine

⁂ CAUTION

When disconnecting the sensor electrical connector, do not pull directly on wire going into sensor.

1. Before servicing the vehicle, refer to the precautions in the beginning of this section.
2. Disconnect negative battery cable.
3. Raise and support vehicle.
4. Disconnect the electrical connector.
5. Use a socket such as a crowfoot wrench to remove oxygen sensor.

To install:

➡When replacing an HO2S Sensor, the PCM RAM memory must be cleared, either by disconnecting the PCM C-1 connector or momentarily disconnecting the battery negative terminal. The NGC learns the characteristics of each HO2S heater element and these old values should be cleared when installing a new HO2S sensor. The customer may experience driveability issues if this is not performed.

6. After removing the sensor, the threads must be cleaned with an 18 mm X 1.5 + 6E tap. If reusing the original sensor, coat the sensor threads with an anti-seize compound such as Loctite 771–64 or equivalent. New sensors have compound on the threads and do not require an additional coating. Tighten the sensor to 28 Nm (20 ft. lbs.) torque.
7. Connect the heated oxygen sensor electrical connector.
8. Connect the negative battery cable.

Upstream Sensor

See Figure 120.

⁂ CAUTION

When disconnecting the sensor electrical connector, do not pull directly on wire going into sensor.

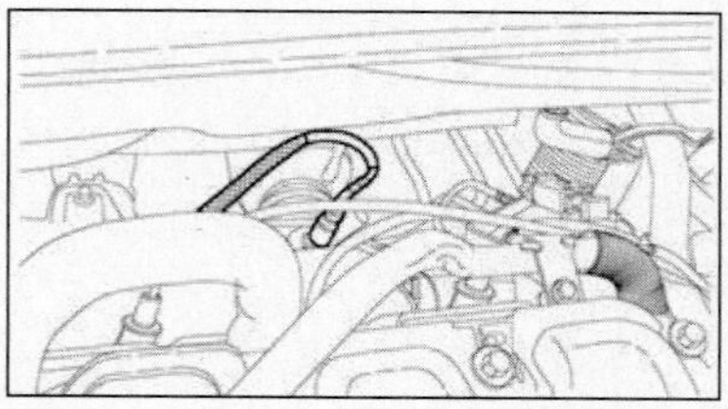

Fig. 120 Upstream sensor location—3.8L engine

1. Before servicing the vehicle, refer to the precautions in the beginning of this section.
2. Disconnect negative battery cable.
3. Disconnect the upper HO2S sensor connector.
4. Use a socket such as a crowfoot wrench to remove oxygen sensor.

To install:

➡When replacing an HO2S Sensor, the PCM RAM memory must be cleared, either by disconnecting the PCM C-1 connector or momentarily disconnecting the battery negative terminal. The NGC learns the characteristics of each HO2S heater element and these old values should be cleared when installing a new HO2S sensor. The customer may experience driveability issues if this is not performed.

5. After removing the sensor, the threads must be cleaned with an 18 mm X 1.5 + 6E tap. If reusing the original sensor, coat the sensor threads with an anti-seize compound such as Loctite 771–64 or equivalent. New sensors have compound on the threads and do not require an additional coating. Tighten the sensor to 28 Nm (20 ft. lbs.) torque.
6. Connect the heated oxygen sensor electrical connector.
7. Connect the negative battery cable.

4.0L Engine

See Figures 121 and 122.

1. Before servicing the vehicle, refer to the precautions in the beginning of this section.
2. Disconnect negative battery cable.
3. Raise and support the vehicle safely.
4. Disconnect the wiring harness retaining clips, if equipped.
5. Disconnect the electrical connector from the sensor.
6. Remove the sensor from its mounting.

To install:

➡Threads on a new oxygen sensor are factory coated with anti-seize compound, to aid in removal. Do not add any additional anti-seize compounds to the threads of a new sensor.

7. Installation is the reverse of the removal procedure.
8. Tighten the sensor to 30 ft. lbs.

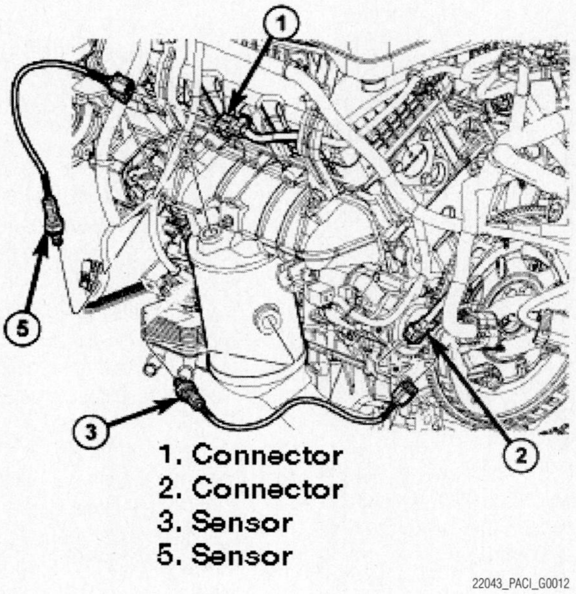

Fig. 121 HO2S sensor location (side one)—4.0L engine

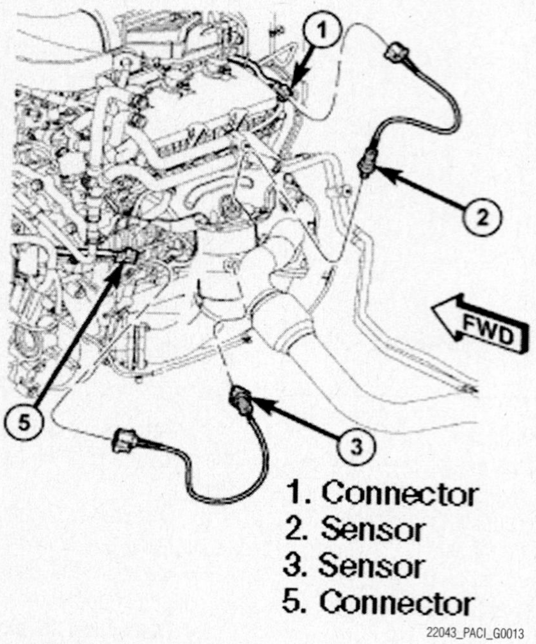

Fig. 122 HO2S sensor location (side two)—4.0L engine

TESTING

2005–06 Models

➡Allow the HO2S Sensor to cool down before conducting the test. The HO2S Sensor voltage should stabilize at 5.0 volts. Raising the hood may help in reducing under hood temps quicker.

1. Before servicing the vehicle, refer to the precautions in the beginning of this section.
2. Turn the ignition on, engine not running. With the scan tool, actuate the HO2S Heater Test.
3. With the scan tool, monitor HO2S Sensor voltage for at least 2 minutes. Does the HO2S Sensor voltage stay above 4.5 volts? If so, sensor is normal.
4. If voltage does not stay above 4.5v as indicated, check wiring and connectors. Check HO2S sensor for contamination.
5. If wiring from the HO2S sensor is damaged, DO NOT repair it; replace the HO2S sensor.
6. Turn the ignition off. Allow the HO2S sensor to cool down to room temperature.
7. Disconnect the HO2S Sensor harness connector.
8. Measure the resistance across the HO2S Sensor Heater element component side. Resistance for either HO2S Sensor should be 2.1-2.7 ohms.
9. If the HO2S Sensor is not within range, turn the ignition off.
10. Disconnect the HO2S Sensor harness connector. Turn the ignition to ON; engine not running.
11. With the proper scan tool, actuate the HO2S Heater Test.
12. Using a 12-volt test light connected to ground, probe the HO2S Heater Control circuit in the HO2S Sensor harness connector.
13. If the test light illuminates brightly and flashes on and off, replace the HO2S Sensor.
14. Confirm the repair with the appropriate Verification Test.
15. Turn the ignition off.
16. Disconnect the HO2S Sensor harness connector.
17. Disconnect the PCM harness connector.
18. Measure the resistance between ground and the HO2S Heater Control circuit in the HO2S Sensor harness connector.
19. Is the resistance below 5.0 ohms? If yes, repair the short to ground in the HO2S Sensor Heater Control circuit. If resistance is okay, go to step 20.
20. Confirm the repair.
21. If resistance was okay when measured in step 17, check the PCM harness connector terminals for corrosion, damage, or terminal push out. Repair as necessary.
22. If the resistance is still not within specified range, replace and program the Powertrain Control Module in accordance with the service information.
23. Confirm the repair.

INTAKE AIR TEMPERATURE (IAT) SENSOR

OPERATION

This sensor detects the intake air temperature. According to the intake air temperature reading the PCM will control the necessary amount of fuel injection.

REMOVAL & INSTALLATION

See Figures 123 and 124.

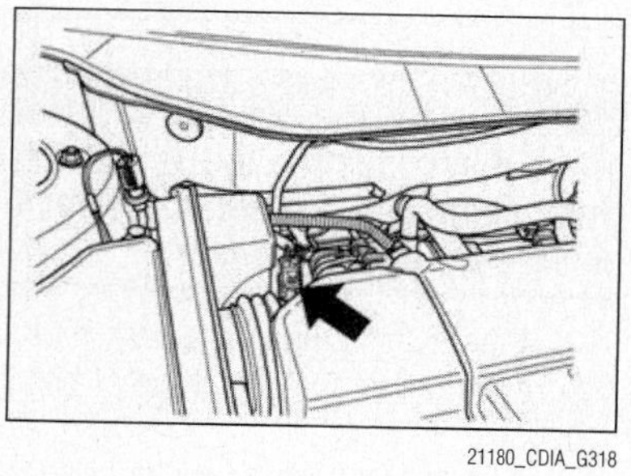

Fig. 123 IAT sensor location—3.5L and 3.8L engines

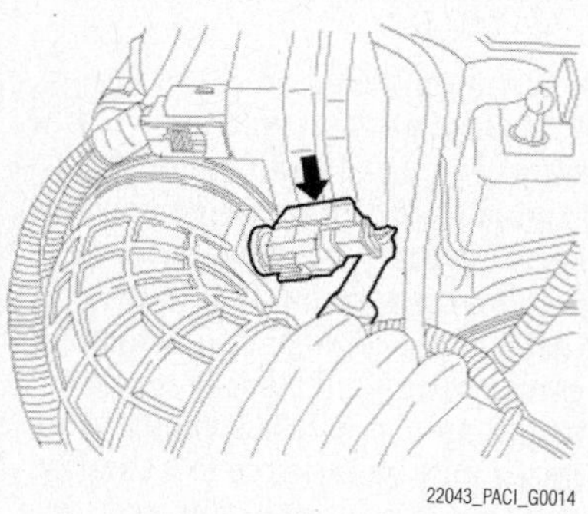

Fig. 124 IAT sensor location—4.0L engine

1. Before servicing the vehicle, refer to the precautions in the beginning of this section.
2. Disconnect the negative battery cable.
3. Unlock and disconnect the electrical connector.
4. Remove sensor from hose.

To install:

5. Install sensor into inlet hose.
6. Connect and lock the electrical connector.
7. Connect the negative battery cable.

KNOCK SENSOR (KS)

LOCATION

On the 3.5L and 4.0L engines this sensor is located below the intake manifold in the engine valley. On the 3.8L engine this sensor is located on the engine block near the oil pan.

OPERATION

When the knock sensor detects a knock in one of the cylinders, it sends an input signal to the PCM. In response, the PCM retards ignition timing for all cylinders by a scheduled amount. Knock sensors contain a piezoelectric material, which constantly vibrates and sends an input voltage (signal) to the PCM while the engine operates. As the intensity of the crystals vibration increases, the knock sensor output voltage also increases.

The voltage signal produced by the knock sensor increases with the amplitude of vibration. The PCM receives as an input the knock sensor voltage signal. If the signal rises above a predetermined level, the PCM will store that value in memory and retard ignition timing to reduce engine knock. If the knock sensor voltage exceeds a preset value, the PCM retards ignition timing for all cylinders. It is not a selective cylinder retard.

The PCM ignores knock sensor input during engine idle conditions. Once the engine speed exceeds a specified value, knock retard is allowed. Knock retard uses its own long-term and short-term memory program.

Long-term memory stores previous detonation information in its battery-backed RAM. The maximum authority that long term memory has over timing retard can be calibrated. Short-term memory is allowed to retard timing up to a preset amount under all operating conditions (as long as rpm is above the minimum rpm) except WOT. The PCM, using short-term memory, can respond quickly to retard timing when engine knock is detected. Short-term memory is lost any time the ignition key is turned off.

REMOVAL & INSTALLATION

3.5L and 4.0L Engines

See Figures 125 through 127.

➡Improper tightening affects sensor performance, possibly causing improper spark control.

1. Before servicing the vehicle, refer to the precautions in the beginning of this section.
2. Disconnect the negative battery cable.
3. Remove the upper intake manifold.
4. Disconnect the electrical connector.
5. Remove the knock sensor.

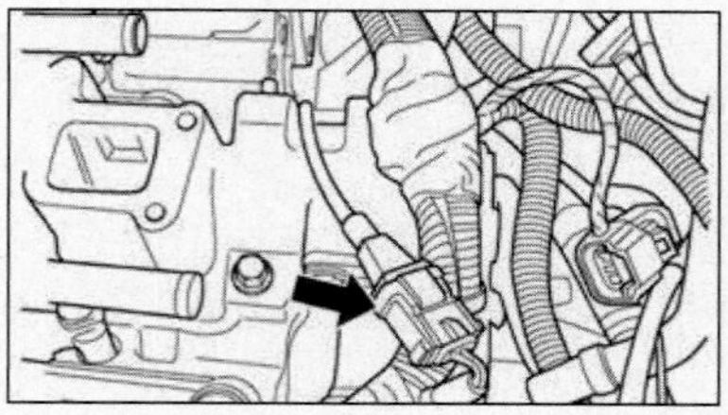

Fig. 125 Knock sensor connector location—3.5L engine

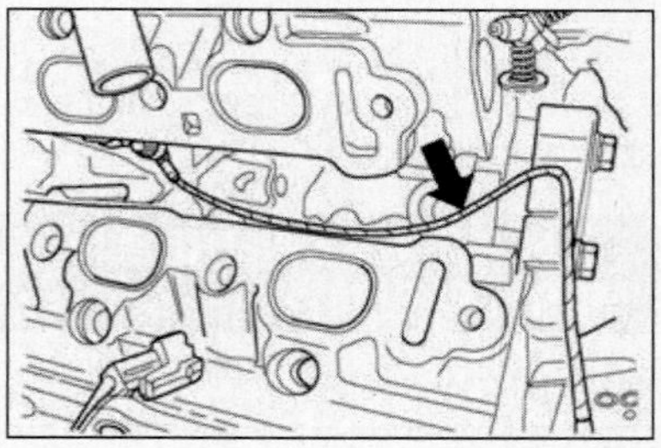

Fig. 126 Observe proper wire routing—3.5L engine

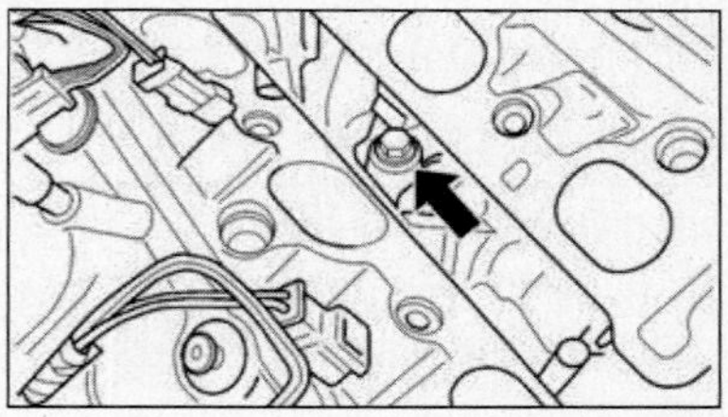

Fig. 127 Knock sensor location—3.5L and 4.0L engines

To install:

6. Install knock sensor. Tighten knock sensor to 20 Nm (15 ft. lbs.) torque.
7. Route the knock sensor wire in the proper location.
8. Install the upper intake manifold.
9. Connect the electrical connector.
10. Connect the negative battery cable.

3.8L Engine

See Figure 128.

1. Before servicing the vehicle, refer to the precautions in the beginning of this section.

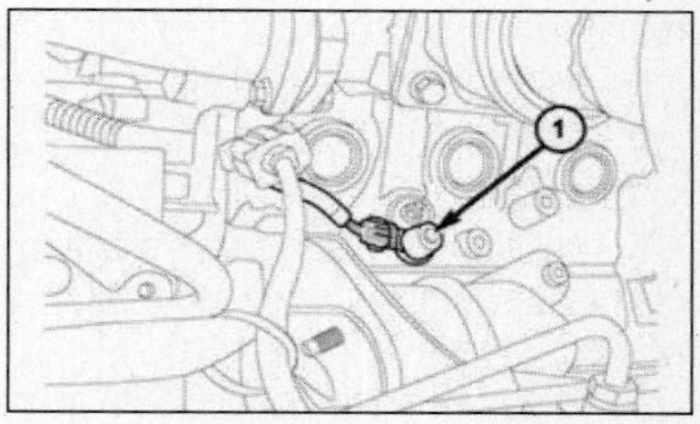

Fig. 128 Knock sensor (1) location—3.8L engine

2. Disconnect the negative battery cable.
3. Raise vehicle and support.
4. Remove the sensor cover, if equipped.
5. Disconnect the electrical connector.
6. Remove mounting bolt and sensor.

To install:

7. Install knock sensor. Tighten knock sensor to 20 Nm (15 ft. lbs.) torque.
8. Route the knock sensor wire in the proper location.
9. Connect the electrical connector.
10. Install the sensor cover, if equipped.
11. Lower vehicle.
12. Connect the negative battery cable.

MANIFOLD ABSOLUTE PRESSURE (MAP) SENSOR

OPERATION

This sensor monitors the pressure in the intake manifold.

REMOVAL & INSTALLATION

3.5L Engine

See Figure 129.

1. Before servicing the vehicle, refer to the precautions in the beginning of this section.

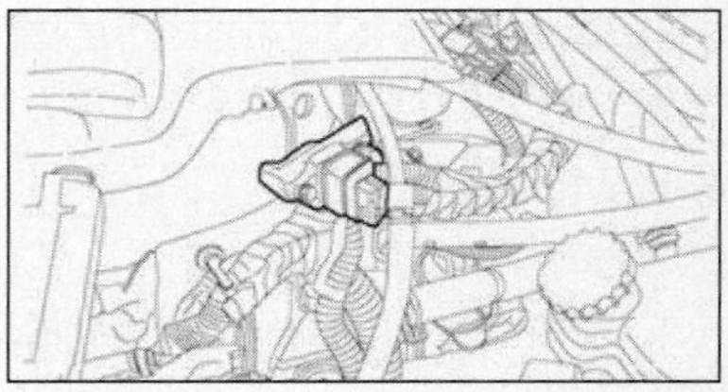

Fig. 129 MAP sensor location—3.5L engine

2. Remove the negative battery cable.
3. Disconnect the electrical connector from the MAP sensor.
4. Remove bolt from sensor.
5. Remove sensor.

To install:

6. Position the sensor onto intake manifold plenum. Tighten screws to 4.5 Nm (40 inch lbs.) torque.
7. Attach electrical connector to sensor.
8. Install the negative battery cable.

3.8L Engine

See Figure 130.

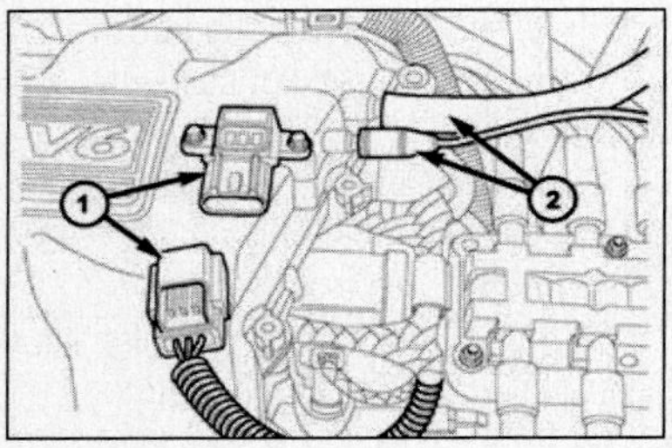

21180_CDIA_G325

Fig. 130 MAP sensor location—3.8L engine

1. Before servicing the vehicle, refer to the precautions in the beginning of this section.
2. Remove the negative battery cable.
3. Disconnect the electrical connector from the MAP sensor.
4. Remove bolt from sensor.
5. Remove sensor.

To install:

➡When servicing components, always reassemble components with new O-rings and seals where applicable. If assembly of component is difficult, a light coat of engine oil may be applied to the O-Rings only to aid assembly.

6. Install MAP sensor.
7. Install and tighten screws.
8. Connect and lock electrical connector.
9. Connect negative battery cable.

4.0L Engine

See Figure 131.

1. Before servicing the vehicle, refer to the precautions in the beginning of this section.
2. Remove the negative battery cable.
3. Disconnect the electrical connector from the sensor.

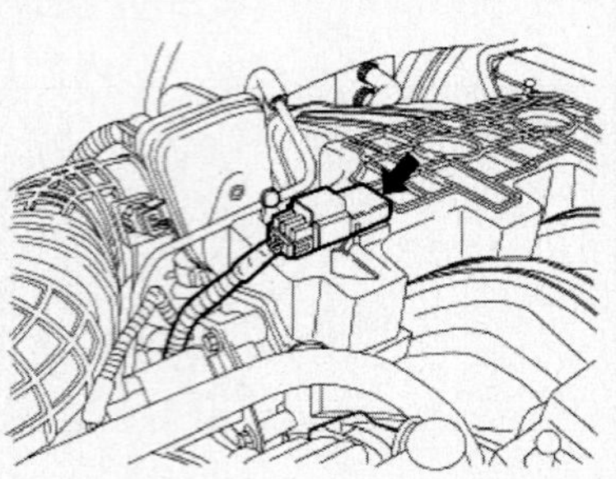

22043_PACI_G0015

Fig. 131 MAP sensor location—4.0L engine

4. Rotate the sensor and lift upward to remove it from its mounting.

To install:

5. Installation is the reverse of the removal procedure.

POWERTRAIN CONTROL MODULE (ECM)

OPERATION

The Powertrain Control Module (PCM) is a digital computer containing a microprocessor. The PCM receives input signals from various switches and sensors referred to as Powertrain Control Module Inputs. Based on these inputs, the PCM adjusts various engine and vehicle operations through devices referred to as Powertrain Control Module Outputs.

REMOVAL & INSTALLATION

See Figures 132 and 133.

1. Before servicing the vehicle, refer to the precautions in the beginning of this section.
2. Disconnect the negative battery cable.
3. Raise vehicle and support.
4. Remove the left front wheel.

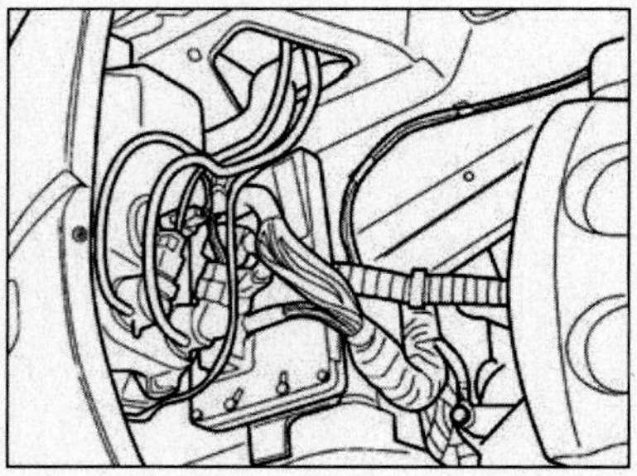

21180_CDIA_G331

Fig. 132 PCM location

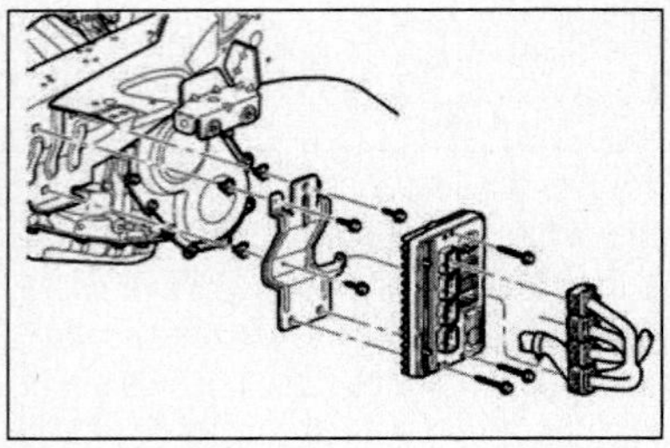

21180_CDIA_G332

Fig. 133 Removing/installing PCM

5. Remove the left front splash shield.
6. Unlock and remove the 4 connectors.
7. Remove the 3 mounting screws.
8. Remove the PCM.

To install:

9. Install the PCM.
10. Install the 3 mounting screws.
11. Tighten screws.
12. Install and lock the 4 electrical connectors.
13. Install the left front splash shield.
14. Install the left front wheel.
15. Lower the vehicle. Connect the negative battery cable.

THROTTLE POSITION SENSOR (TPS)

REMOVAL & INSTALLATION

3.5L Engine

See Figure 134.

1. Before servicing the vehicle, refer to the precautions in the beginning of this section.
2. Disconnect the negative battery cable.
3. Disconnect the TPS electrical connector.
4. Remove the TPS mounting screws and remove the TPS.

To install:

➡The throttle shaft end of the throttle body slides into a socket in the TPS. The socket has two tabs inside it. The throttle shaft rests against the tabs. When indexed correctly, the TPS can rotate clockwise a few degrees to line up the mounting screw holes with the screw holes in the throttle body. The TPS has slight tension when rotated into position. If it is difficult to rotate the TPS into position, install the sensor with the throttle shaft on the other side of the tabs in the socket.

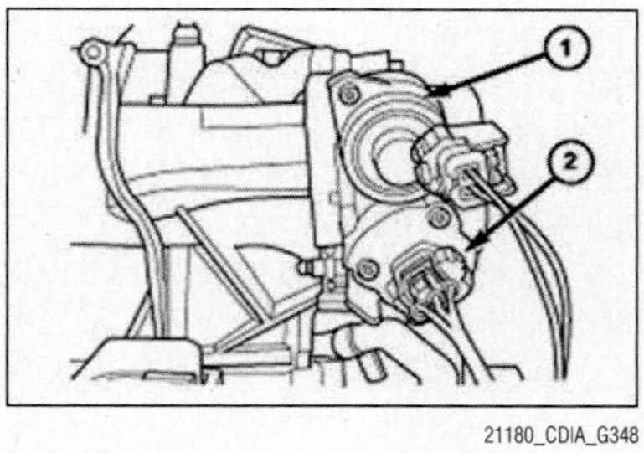

Fig. 134 TPS sensor (2) and IAC motor (1) location—3.5L engine

5. Tighten TPS sensor mounting screws to 5.1 Nm (45 inch lbs.) torque.
6. The throttle plate should be closed. If the throttle plate is open, install the sensor on the other side of the tabs in the socket.
7. Attach electrical connector to the TPS sensor.
8. Connect the negative battery cable.

3.8L Engine

See Figure 135.

1. Before servicing the vehicle, refer to the precautions in the beginning of this section.
2. Disconnect negative battery cable.
3. Disconnect the TPS electrical connector.
4. Remove the TPS mounting screws.
5. Remove the TPS.

To install:

➡The throttle shaft end of the throttle body slides into a socket in the TPS. The socket has two tabs inside it. The throttle shaft rests against the tabs. When indexed correctly, the TPS can rotate clockwise a few degrees to line up the mounting screw holes with the screw holes in the throttle body. The TPS has slight tension when rotated into position. If it is difficult to rotate the TPS into position, install the sensor with the throttle shaft on the other side of the tabs in the socket.

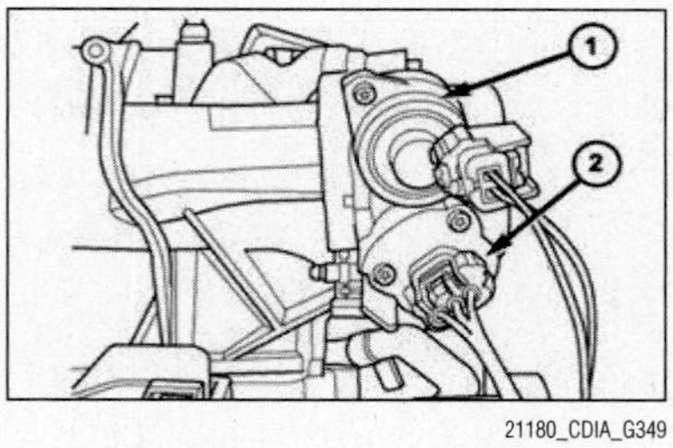

Fig. 135 TPS sensor (2) and IAC motor (1) location—3.8L engine

6. Tighten TPS sensor mounting screws to 5.1 Nm (45 inch lbs.) torque.
7. The throttle plate should be closed. If the throttle plate is open, install the sensor on the other side of the tabs in the socket.
8. Attach electrical connector to the TPS sensor.
9. Connect the negative battery cable.

VEHICLE SPEED SENSOR (VSS)

OPERATION

The vehicle speed signal is taken from the Output Speed Sensor. The PCM converts this signal into a pulse per mile signal and sends the vehicle speed message across the communication bus to the BCM. The BCM sends this signal to the Instrument Cluster to display vehicle speed to the driver. The vehicle speed signal pulse is roughly 8000 pulses per mile.

REMOVAL & INSTALLATION

See Figure 136.

1. Before servicing the vehicle, refer to the precautions in the beginning of this section.
2. Disconnect battery negative cable.
3. Raise vehicle on hoist.
4. Disconnect output speed sensor connector.
5. Unscrew and remove output speed sensor.
6. Inspect speed sensor O-ring and replace if necessary.

To install:

7. Verify O-ring is installed into position.
8. Install and tighten output speed sensor to 27 Nm (20 ft. lbs.).
9. Connect speed sensor connector.
10. Connect battery negative cable.

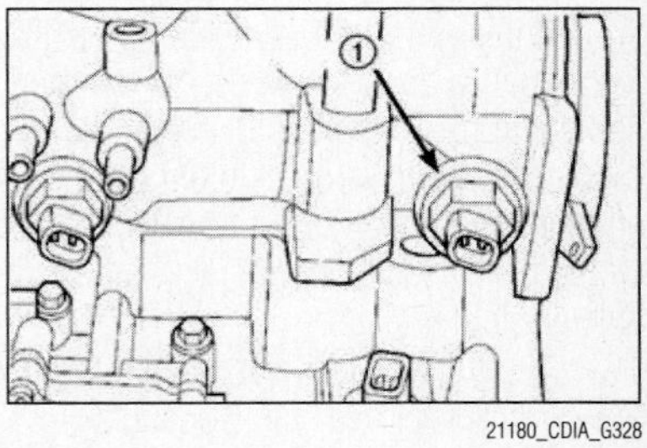

Fig. 136 VSS sensor location

FUEL SYSTEM SERVICE PRECAUTIONS

Safety is the most important factor when performing not only fuel system maintenance but any type of maintenance. Failure to conduct maintenance and repairs in a safe manner may result in serious personal injury or death. Maintenance and testing of the vehicle's fuel system components can be accomplished safely and effectively by adhering to the following rules and guidelines.

- To avoid the possibility of fire and personal injury, always disconnect the negative battery cable unless the repair or test procedure requires that battery voltage be applied.
- Always relieve the fuel system pressure prior to disconnecting any fuel system component (injector, fuel rail, pressure regulator, etc.), fitting or fuel line connection. Exercise extreme caution whenever relieving fuel system pressure to avoid exposing skin, face and eyes to fuel spray. Please be advised that fuel under pressure may penetrate the skin or any part of the body that it contacts.
- Always place a shop towel or cloth around the fitting or connection prior to loosening to absorb any excess fuel due to spillage. Ensure that all fuel spillage (should it occur) is quickly removed from engine surfaces. Ensure that all fuel soaked cloths or towels are deposited into a suitable waste container.
- Always keep a dry chemical (Class B) fire extinguisher near the work area.
- Do not allow fuel spray or fuel vapors to come into contact with a spark or open flame.
- Always use a back-up wrench when loosening and tightening fuel line connection fittings. This will prevent unnecessary stress and torsion to fuel line piping.
- Always replace worn fuel fitting O-rings with new Do not substitute fuel hose or equivalent where fuel pipe is installed.

Before servicing the vehicle, make sure to also refer to the precautions in the beginning of this section as well.

RELIEVING FUEL SYSTEM PRESSURE

1. Before servicing the vehicle, refer to the precautions in the beginning of this section.
2. At the Power Distribution Center (PDC), remove the Fuel Pump Relay.
3. Operate the engine until the engine stalls; then, continue restarting the engine until it will no longer run.
4. Turn the ignition switch **OFF**.
5. Place a rag or towel below the fuel line quick connect fitting at the fuel rail.
6. Disconnect the quick connect fitting at the fuel rail.
7. At the Power Distribution Center (PDC), install the fuel pump relay.

➡After servicing the fuel system one or more Diagnostic Trouble Codes (DTC's) may be stored in the Powertrain Control Module (PCM) memory. A DRB scan tool must by used to clear the DTC's.

FUEL FILTER

REMOVAL & INSTALLATION

The fuel filter is only replaceable as part of the fuel pump module.

FUEL INJECTORS

REMOVAL & INSTALLATION

3.5L Engine

See Figures 137 and 138.

1. Before servicing the vehicle, refer to the precautions in the beginning of this section.
2. Relieve the fuel system pressure.
3. Remove or disconnect the following:
   - Negative battery cable
   - Intake manifold plenum and cover opening with a clean cloth
4. Tag the injectors to match them with their correct cylinder during installation.
5. Place a shop rag under the fuel rail's quick-connect fitting; then, squeeze the quick-connect fitting's retainer tabs together and pull the fitting assembly off of the fuel tube nipple.
   - Fuel injector electrical connectors
   - Fuel rail-to-engine bolts and fuel rail
   - Fuel injector-to-fuel rail retainer clips
   - Fuel injectors

To install:

6. Lubricate the injector O-rings with clean engine oil.
7. Install or connect the following:
   - Fuel injector and secure with retaining clips
   - Fuel rail onto cylinder head and press rail into place. Make sure that the injectors are fully seated.

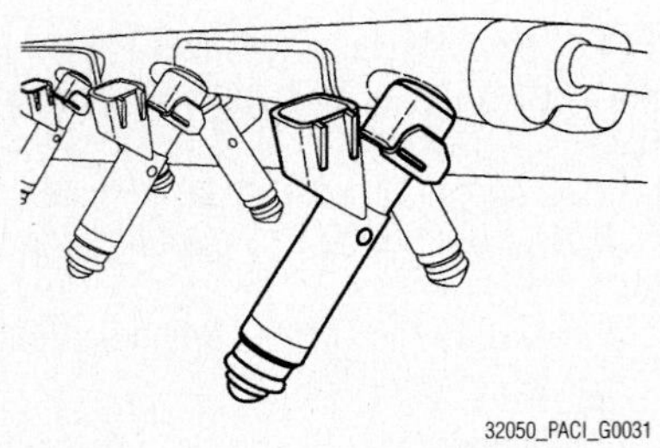

32050_PACI_G0031

Fig. 138 Installed view of the fuel injectors—3.5L engine

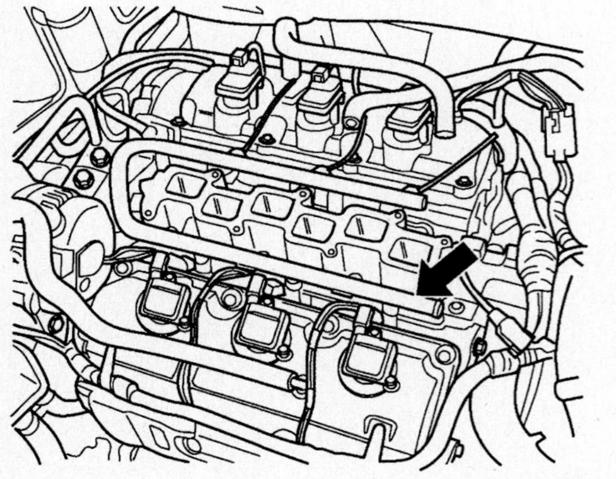

32050_PACI_G0030

Fig. 137 Fuel rail mounting—3.5L engine

- Fuel rail-to-cylinder head bolts and torque bolts to 250 inch lbs. (28 Nm)
- Fuel injector electrical connectors
- Intake plenum

8. Lubricate the quick-connect fitting's O-rings with clean engine oil; then, push the connector together until the retainer seats and a click is heard.
9. Connect the negative battery cable.

3.8L Engine

See Figure 139.

1. Before servicing the vehicle, refer to the precautions in the beginning of this section.
2. Relieve the fuel system pressure.
3. Remove the air cleaner housing and inlet hose.
4. Remove the engine cover.
5. Disconnect the Throttle Position (TP) sensor connector.
6. Disconnect the Idle Air Control (IAC) valve connector.
7. Disconnect the purge line.
8. Disconnect the throttle and cruise control cables, if equipped.
9. Disconnect the Manifold Absolute Pressure (MAP) sensor connector.
10. Disconnect the vacuum lines.
11. Remove the Exhaust Gas Recirculation (EGR) tube.
12. Remove the upper intake manifold.
13. Disconnect the injector electrical connectors.
14. If the injector connectors are not tagged with their cylinder number, tag them to identify the correct cylinder.
15. Remove the 4 mounting bolts from the fuel rail.
16. Disconnect the fuel supply line from the fuel rail.
17. Lift fuel rail straight up off of cylinder head.
18. Remove the retaining clips from fuel injectors at the fuel rail.
19. Remove the fuel injector from fuel rail.

To install:

20. Inspect and replace any damaged fuel injector O-rings.
21. Lightly lubricate the fuel injector O-rings with a couple drops of clean engine oil.
22. Install retaining clips on fuel.
23. Install the fuel injector locator flange on fuel rail.
24. Push the injectors into the fuel injector rail until the clips are in the correct position.
25. Position the fuel rail over the cylinder heads, and push the rail into place. Tighten the fuel rail mounting bolts to 250 inch lbs. (28 Nm).

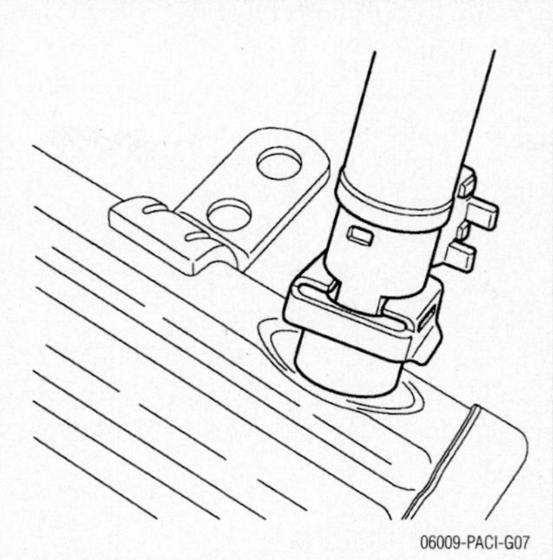

Fig. 139 Proper positioning of the fuel injector in the fuel rail—3.8L engine

26. Connect the electrical connectors to the fuel injectors.
27. Connect the fuel supply tube quick connect fitting to the fuel rail.
28. Install the upper intake manifold.
29. Connect and electrical connection for the MAP sensor.
30. Connect the vacuum lines.
31. Connect the electrical connectors to the TPS and IAC.
32. Connect the purge line.
33. Install all remaining components.
34. Connect the negative cable to battery.

4.0L Engine

1. Before servicing the vehicle, refer to the precautions in the beginning of this section.
2. Relieve the fuel system pressure.
3. Disconnect the negative battery cable.
4. Remove the air cleaner hose from the throttle body.
5. Use a fuel release tool and disconnect the quick connect fuel line from the fuel rail.
6. Remove the upper intake manifold.

➡Mark the fuel injector electrical harness connectors with the correct corresponding cylinder numbers.

7. Disconnect the fuel injector electrical connectors.
8. Remove the fuel rail mounting bolts from the fuel rail.
9. Lift the fuel rail straight up off of the cylinder heads.
10. Remove the retaining clips from the fuel injectors at the fuel rail.

➡When replacing individual injectors, each injector must be installed in it's original position. Mark each injector to identify the correct cylinder.

11. Remove the injectors from the fuel rail.

To install:

12. Installation is the reverse of the removal procedure.
13. Inspect and replace any damaged fuel injector O-rings.
14. Lightly lubricate the fuel injector O-rings with a couple drops of clean engine oil.
15. Tighten the fuel rail retaining bolts to 20 ft. lbs.

✱✱ CAUTION

Make sure that the fuel line quick connector is connected properly. Failure to connect the line properly may result in a fuel leak at the rail assembly. Fuel leaked on to a hot engine may ignite resulting to damage to the vehicle.

16. Use a scan tool to pressurize the fuel system.
17. Start the engine and check for leaks, correct as required.

FUEL PUMP

REMOVAL & INSTALLATION

2005–06 Models

1. Before servicing the vehicle, refer to the precautions in the beginning of this section.
2. Properly relieve the fuel system pressure.
3. Disconnect the negative battery cable.
4. Drain the fuel tank.
5. Disconnect the exhaust system between the catalytic converter and the muffler.
6. Support the exhaust system with jack stands.
7. Remove muffler hanger rubber grommets and the center exhaust hanger rubber grommets.
8. Remove the rear portion of the exhaust system.
9. Disconnect the fuel tank electrical connector.
10. Disconnect the fuel line and EVAP line.
11. Disconnect the vapor recirculation tube.
12. Mark the driveshaft rear connection

and disconnect the driveshaft rear connection.

13. Remove the driveshaft support/bearing.

14. Support the driveshaft with a jack.

15. Remove the left rear tire and splash shield.

16. Remove the fuel filler tube from the rubber hose at fuel tank.

17. Support the fuel tank with a transmission jack.

18. Remove the 2 fuel tank straps and lower fuel tank.

19. Drain any remaining fuel from the tank and remove the tank.

20. Clean around the fuel pump module lockring prior to removal.

21. Disconnect the vapor line and electrical connector.

22. Remove the fuel pump module lockring using a brass punch to remove the ¼ turn lockring.

23. Remove fuel pump module top.

24. Disconnect electrical connector.

25. Disconnect the wire connector to the passenger side level sensor before removing the reservoir from the tank.

26. Remove the return line from pump module. Use a suitable tool to pry the tab back and tip the hose to one side. Pry the tab on other side back to release the hose.

⁂ CAUTION

Care should be taken to not crack/break the locking tabs or supply line fitting.

27. Remove the fuel line from the top of the pump module. Use a small screwdriver to pry the tab back and tip hose to one side. Pry the tab on the other side back to release the hose.

28. Tip fuel pump module on its side to remove the fuel from the reservoir.

29. Remove the fuel pump module.

To install:

30. Install the fuel pump module into the fuel tank.

31. Connect the siphon and fuel lines to fuel pump module.

32. Connect the fuel pump electrical connector to the bottom of the module top.

33. Connect the wire connector to the passenger side level sensor.

34. Install the fuel pump module top to the module.

35. Install the fuel pump module gasket and lockring. Use a brass punch to install the ¼ turn lockring.

36. Connect the vapor line and electrical connector.

37. Support the fuel tank with a transmission jack.

38. Raise fuel tank and install in the vehicle.

39. Install the 2 fuel tank straps.

40. Install the remaining components in the reverse order of removal.

41. Connect the negative battery cable.

42. Fill the fuel tank and use the DRBIII® scan tool to pressurize the fuel system. Check for leaks.

2007–08 Models

1. Before servicing the vehicle, refer to the precautions in the beginning of this section.

2. Remove the fuel cap.

3. Properly relieve the fuel system pressure.

4. Disconnect the negative battery cable.

5. Drain the fuel tank.

6. Remove the exhaust system, from the resonator back.

7. If equipped with AWD mark the driveshaft rear connection and remove it (driveshaft).

8. Disconnect the fuel pump electrical connector from the chassis connector.

9. Disconnect the vapor canister line at the right front of the fuel tank.

10. Disconnect the fuel supply line. Disconnect the EVAP vapor line.

11. Disconnect the fuel vapor recirculation line at the right rear of the fuel tank.

12. Loosen the clamp and remove the fuel fill hose from the fuel tank.

➡Properly support the fuel tank, with a transmission/transaxle jack or equivalent. Use retaining straps to secure the fuel tank to the jack. Failure to properly support and secure the tank during removal may cause fuel to spill or the tank to fall from the jack.

13. Remove the fuel tank retaining strap bolts and straps.

14. Lower the tank.

15. Disconnect and remove all necessary lines and hoses from the tank.

16. Remove the tank from the vehicle.

➡Clean the area around the fuel pump, prior to removal. Failure to clean this area may cause dirt to get into the fuel system causing damage to the fuel system and/or engine.

17. Disconnect all lines and electrical connections.

18. Remove the fuel pump module lockring using a brass punch to remove the ¼ turn lockring.

19. Remove the module lock ring. Remove the module top.

20. Drain the fuel from the tank using approved siphoning equipment.

➡The wire connector to the passenger side level sensor needs to be disconnected before removing the reservoir from the tank.

21. Remove the return line from the pump, using a suitable tool.

22. Remove the fuel line from the top of the pump.

23. Tip the pump module on its side to remove fuel from the reservoir.

24. Remove the fuel pump module.

To install:

25. Installation is the reverse of the removal procedure.

➡The fuel pump module top and bottom need to be correctly installed in order for the fuel level to be on the correct side of the fuel tank. If installed incorrectly, the fuel level arm will not be in the correct position inside the fuel tank and cause inaccurate fuel level readings.

➡Make sure that all fuel line hoses are connected properly. Failure to connect fuel lines properly may result in a fuel leak.

26. Fill the fuel tank and use the DRBIII® scan tool to pressurize the fuel system.

27. Start the engine and check for leaks. Correct as required.

FUEL TANK

REMOVAL & INSTALLATION

2005–06 Models

1. Before servicing the vehicle, refer to the precautions in the beginning of this section.

2. Properly relieve the fuel system pressure.

3. Disconnect the negative battery cable.

4. Drain the fuel tank.

5. Disconnect the exhaust system between the catalytic converter and the muffler.

6. Support the exhaust system with jack stands.

7. Remove muffler hanger rubber grommets and the center exhaust hanger rubber grommets.

8. Remove the rear portion of the exhaust system.

9. Disconnect the fuel tank electrical connector.
10. Disconnect the fuel line and EVAP line.
11. Disconnect the vapor recirculation tube.
12. Mark the driveshaft rear connection and disconnect the driveshaft rear connection.
13. Remove the driveshaft support/ bearing.
14. Support the driveshaft with a jack.
15. Remove the left rear tire and splash shield.
16. Remove the fuel filler tube from the rubber hose at fuel tank.
17. Support the fuel tank with a transmission jack.
18. Remove the 2 fuel tank straps and lower fuel tank.
19. Drain any remaining fuel from the tank and remove the tank.

To install:

20. Installation is the reverse of the removal procedure.

➡Make sure that all fuel line hoses are connected properly. Failure to connect fuel lines properly may result in a fuel leak.

21. Fill the fuel tank and use the DRBIII® scan tool to pressurize the fuel system.
22. Start the engine and check for leaks, correct as required.

2007–08 Models

See Figure 140.

1. Before servicing the vehicle, refer to the precautions in the beginning of this section.
2. Remove the fuel cap.
3. Properly relieve the fuel system pressure.
4. Disconnect the negative battery cable.
5. Drain the fuel tank.
6. Remove the exhaust system, from the resonator back.
7. If equipped with AWD mark the driveshaft rear connection and remove it (driveshaft).
8. Disconnect the fuel pump electrical connector from the chassis connector.
9. Disconnect the vapor canister line at the right front of the fuel tank.
10. Disconnect the fuel supply line. Disconnect the EVAP vapor line.
11. Disconnect the fuel vapor recirculation line at the right rear of the fuel tank.
12. Loosen the clamp and remove the fuel fill hose from the fuel tank.

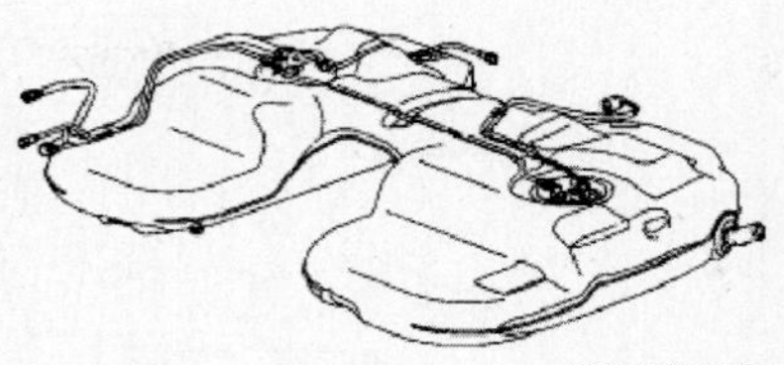

22043_PACI_G0016

Fig. 140 Fuel tank and related components—2007–08 models

➡Properly support the fuel tank, with a transmission/transaxle jack or equivalent. Use retaining straps to secure the fuel tank to the jack. Failure to properly support and secure the tank during removal may cause fuel to spill or the tank to fall from the jack.

13. Remove the fuel tank retaining strap bolts and straps.
14. Lower the tank.
15. Disconnect and remove all necessary lines and hoses from the tank.
16. Remove the tank from the vehicle.

To install:

17. Installation is the reverse of the removal procedure.
18. Tighten the tank retaining strap bolts to 40 ft. lbs.

➡Make sure that all fuel line hoses are connected properly. Failure to connect fuel lines properly may result in a fuel leak.

19. Fill the fuel tank.
20. Use the DRBIII® scan tool to pressurize the fuel system.
21. Start the engine and check for leaks, correct as required.

IDLE SPEED

ADJUSTMENT

Idle speed is maintained by the Powertrain Control Module (PCM). No adjustment is necessary or possible.

THROTTLE BODY

REMOVAL & INSTALLATION

3.5L Engine

See Figures 141 and 142.

1. Before servicing the vehicle, refer to the precautions in the beginning of this section.

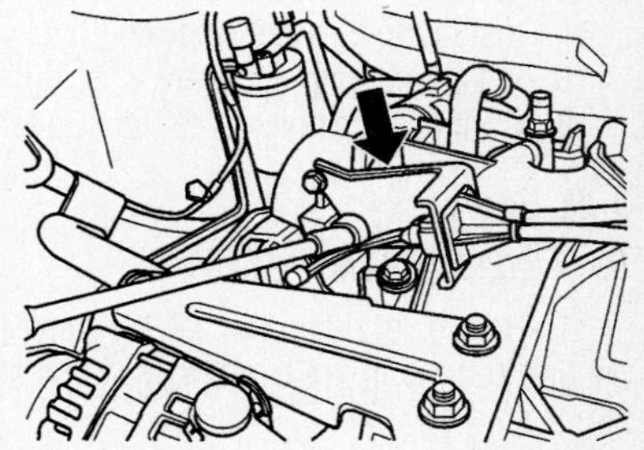

32050_PACI_G0026

Fig. 141 Remove the throttle cable bracket—3.5L engine

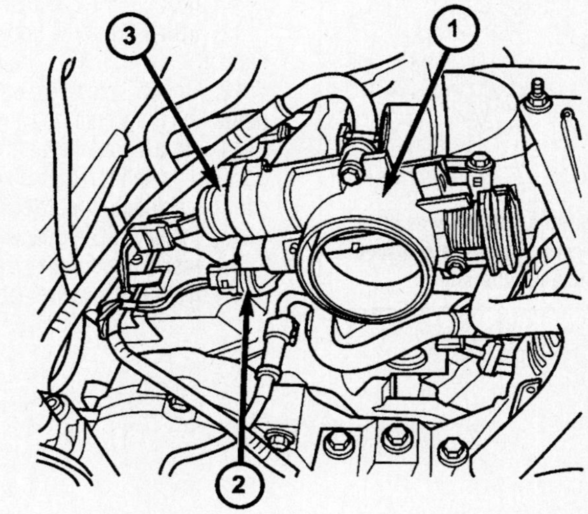

32050_PACI_G0027

Fig. 142 Disconnect the TPS (2) and IAC motor (2) connectors from the throttle body

2. Disconnect negative cable from battery
3. Remove the engine cover.
4. Remove the air cleaner box.
5. Hold throttle lever in wide open position. Remove throttle cable and speed control cables from throttle arm.
6. Remove throttle cable bracket.
7. Disconnect electrical connectors from throttle body.
8. Remove 3 throttle body bolts.
9. Remove throttle body.
10. Clean mating surfaces. Inspect and replace throttle body gasket if necessary.

To install:

11. Install throttle body gasket.
12. Install throttle body.
13. Install 3 throttle body bolts and tighten.
14. Connect electrical connectors to throttle body.
15. Install throttle cable bracket.
16. Hold throttle lever in wide open position. Install throttle cable and speed control cables to throttle arm.
17. Install the air cleaner box.
18. Install the engine cover.
19. Connect negative cable from battery.

3.8L Engine

See Figures 143 and 144.

1. Before servicing the vehicle, refer to the precautions in the beginning of this section.

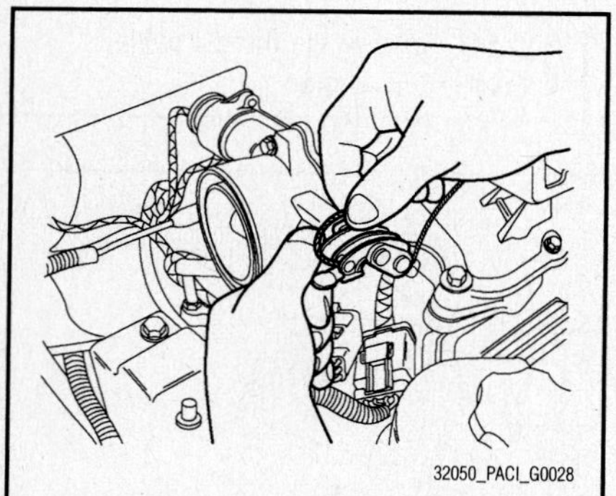

Fig. 143 Hold throttle lever in wide open position. Remove throttle cable and speed control cables from throttle arm

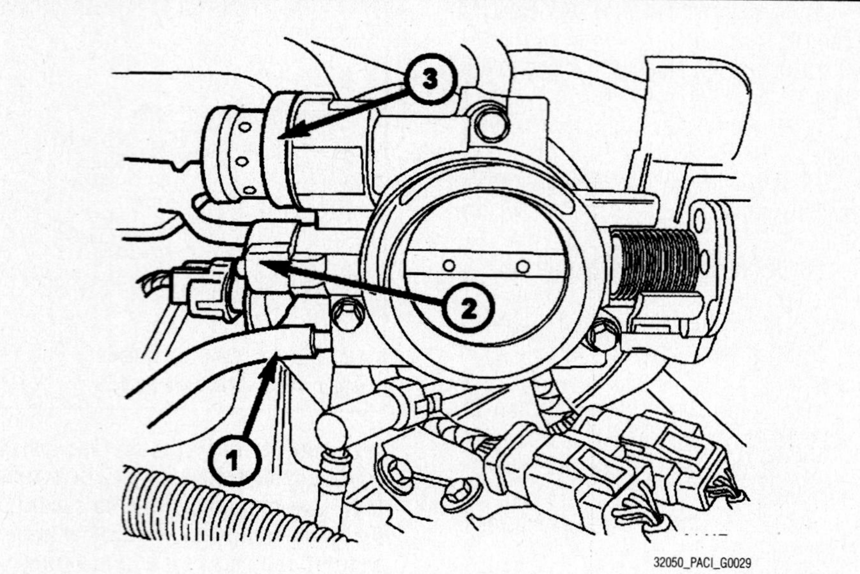

Fig. 144 Disconnect the purge line (1), TPS (2) and IAC motor (3) electrical connectors from the throttle body—3.8L engine

2. Disconnect negative cable from battery
3. Remove the air cleaner box.
4. Remove throttle and speed control cables.
5. Hold throttle lever in wide open position. Remove throttle cable and speed control cables from throttle arm.
6. Disconnect electrical connectors and purge line from throttle body.
7. Remove 3 throttle body bolts.
8. Remove throttle body.
9. Clean mating surfaces. Inspect and replace throttle body gasket if necessary.

To install:

10. Install throttle body gasket.
11. Install throttle body.
12. Install 3 throttle body bolts and tighten.
13. Connect electrical connectors and purge line to throttle body.
14. Hold throttle lever in wide open position. Install throttle cable and speed control cables to throttle arm.
15. Install the air cleaner box.
16. Install the engine cover.
17. Connect negative cable from battery.

4.0L Engine

1. Before servicing the vehicle, refer to the precautions in the beginning of this section.
2. Disconnect negative cable from battery
3. Remove the engine cover.
4. Remove the air cleaner box.
5. Disconnect the electrical connectors from the assembly.
6. Remove the throttle body retaining bolts. Remove the throttle body from its mounting.
7. Remove the seal.

To install:

8. Installation is the reverse of the removal procedure.
9. Inspect and replace the gasket, as required.

➡The retaining bolts must be tightened in a criss-cross pattern.

10. Tighten the retaining bolts to 50 inch lbs, in a criss-cross pattern.
11. Use the DRBIII® scan tool and perform the ETC RELEARN function.

BLOWER MOTOR

REMOVAL & INSTALLATION

Front

See Figures 145 and 146.

CAUTION

This vehicle is equipped with airbags, disable the airbag system before attempting any steering wheel, steering column, or instrument panel component diagnosis or service. Disconnect and isolate the battery negative (ground) cable, then wait two minutes for the airbag system capacitor to discharge before performing further diagnosis or service. This is the only sure way to disable the airbag system. Failure to take the proper precautions could result in an accidental airbag deployment and possible personal injury or death.

➡**The blower motor is located on the passenger side of the vehicle under the instrument panel. The blower motor can be removed from the vehicle without having to remove the HVAC housing.**

1. Disconnect and isolate the negative battery cable.
2. Remove the passenger side cowl trim panel, as follows:
   a. Remove instrument panel side cover.
   b. Remove front door sill scuff plate.
   c. Remove A-pillar cowl side trim panel from vehicle by disengaging hidden clips.
3. Position the carpet to access the front upper screw that secures the air inlet housing.
4. Remove the recirculation door actuator, as follows:
   a. Pull the carpet on the passenger side front floor away from the dash panel far enough to access the recirculation door actuator.
   b. Disconnect the HVAC wire harness connector from the recirculation door actuator.
   c. Remove the two screws that secure the recirculation door actuator to the air inlet housing and remove the actuator.
5. Disconnect the blower motor wire lead connector from the blower motor resistor or power module, depending on application.

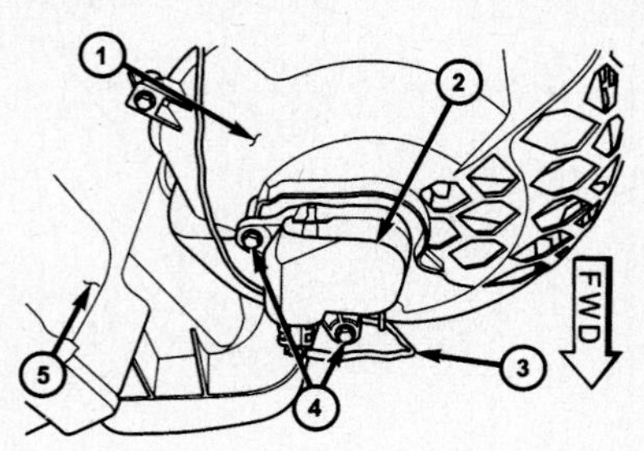

Fig. 145 View of the air inlet housing (1), recirculation door actuator (2), HVAC wire harness (2), screws (4) and lower HVAC housing (5)

6. Remove the one screw (from the top) that secures the lower air inlet housing to the upper air inlet housing.
7. Remove the four screws (from the bottom) that secure the lower air inlet housing to the upper air inlet housing and the lower HVAC housing.
8. Push the rubber grommet through the opening in the lower air inlet housing.
9. Route the blower motor wire lead through the opening in the lower air inlet housing and remove the lower air inlet housing from the vehicle.
10. Position the recirculation-air door as necessary to access and remove the three screws that secure the blower motor to the lower half of the HVAC housing.
11. Gently flex the recirculation-air door downward to gain access to remove the blower motor from the HVAC housing.

➡**To aid in installation, note the position of the blower motor mounting tabs prior to removal.**

12. Remove the blower motor from the HVAC housing by rotating and tilting the blower motor as necessary.

To install:

13. Gently flex the recirculation-air door downward to gain access to install the blower motor into the HVAC housing.
14. Position the blower motor to the HVAC housing and tilt and rotate the blower motor as necessary to install it into the HVAC housing.
15. Align the blower motor mounting tabs to the locations noted during removal and install the three screws that secure the blower motor to the HVAC housing. Tighten the screws to 17 inch lbs. (2 Nm).
16. Route the blower motor wire lead through the opening in the lower air inlet housing and seat the rubber grommet.
17. Position the recirculation door pivot shaft into the lower air inlet housing and install the inlet housing.
18. Install the four screws (from the bottom) that secure the lower air inlet housing to the upper air inlet housing and the lower HVAC housing. Tighten the screws to 17 inch lbs. (2 Nm).
19. Install the one screw (from the top) that secures the lower air inlet housing to the upper air inlet housing. Tighten the screw to 17 inch lbs. (2 Nm).
20. Connect the blower motor wire lead connector to the blower motor resistor or power module, depending on application.
21. Install the recirculation door actuator.
22. Reposition the carpet.
23. Install the passenger side cowl trim panel.
24. Reconnect the negative battery cable.
25. Perform the heater-A/C control calibration procedure, as follows:

➡**The A/C-heater control module must be recalibrated each time an actuator motor or the A/C-heater control is replaced. If the vehicle is so equipped, the calibration procedure also includes rear HVAC positions for each actuator motor.**

   d. Turn the ignition switch to the **ON** position.
   e. If equipped with the Manual Temperature Control (MTC) system, press and hold the Power and Recirculation buttons for at least five seconds. If equipped with the automatic temperature control (ATC) system, simultaneously

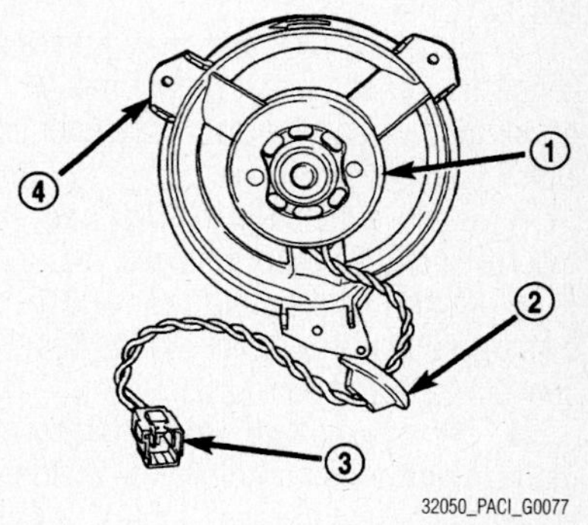

Fig. 146 View of the blower motor (1), rubber grommet (2), blower motor connector (3) and mounting tabs (4)

press and hold the Power and Recirculation buttons on the A/C-heater control for at least five seconds. The MTC A/C-heater control Power button light emitting diode (LED) and Recirculation button LED, or the ATC A/C-heater control Delay and Recirculation graphics will begin to flash when the calibration procedure has begun.

f. The calibration procedure should take less than two minutes to complete for the manual A/C-heater control, and less than twenty seconds for the ATC A/C-heater control. When the LEDs or graphics stop flashing, the calibration procedure is complete.

g. If the LEDs or graphics continue to flash beyond the two minute (manual) or twenty second (ATC) calibration time, it indicates that the A/C-heater control has detected a failure and a Diagnostic Trouble Code (DTC) has been set. The LEDs or graphics will continue to flash even after the ignition switch is cycled Off and On, until a successful calibration is completed or until the vehicle has been driven about 8 miles (13 km).

Rear

See Figures 147 and 148.

➡The rear blower motor and blower wheels are serviced only as a balanced unit. If either component is faulty or damaged, the entire blower motor and wheel assembly must be replaced.

1. Remove the front center floor console cover:
   a. Remove attaching screw(s) from the left and/or right console closeout panels.
   b. Remove center console closeout panel.
2. Disconnect and isolate the negative battery cable.
3. Disconnect the body wire harness connectors from the rear blower motor power module and the rear mode door actuator.
4. Remove the body wire harness bracket from the console support bracket.
5. Remove the eight screws and the two console support brackets from the floor console base and duct assembly
6. Remove the four screws that secure the rear blower motor housing to the floor console base and duct assembly.
7. Remove the rear blower motor housing and place it on a bench.
8. Disconnect the rear blower motor wire harness connector from the power module.

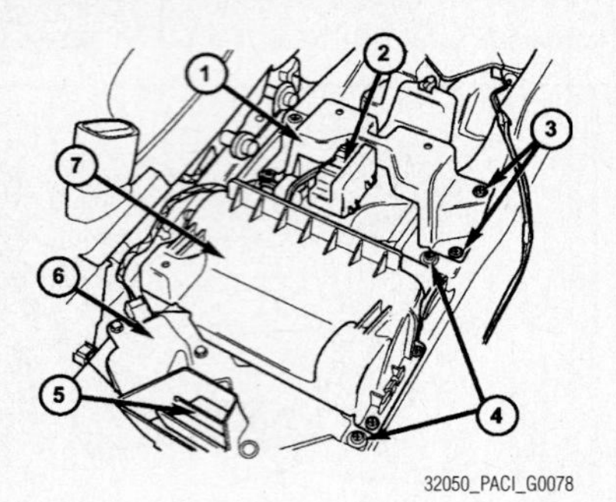

Fig. 147 View of the front support bracket (1), power module (2), screws (3 & 4), rear blower motor housing (5), rear mode door actuator (6), rear support bracket (7)

9. Remove the eleven retaining clips and three screws that secure the housing together.
10. Carefully separate the two halves of the housing.
11. Remove the blower motor wire harness and grommet from the housing and remove the blower motor.

To install:

12. Position the rear blower motor into the housing and install the blower motor wire harness and grommet.
13. Assemble the two halves of the rear blower motor housing and install the eleven retaining clips and three screws. Tighten the screws to 17 inch lbs. (2 Nm).
14. Connect the rear blower motor wire harness connector to the rear blower motor power module.
15. Position the rear blower motor housing into the floor console.
16. Install the four screws that secure the rear blower motor housing to the floor console base. Tighten the screws to 17 inch lbs. (2 Nm).

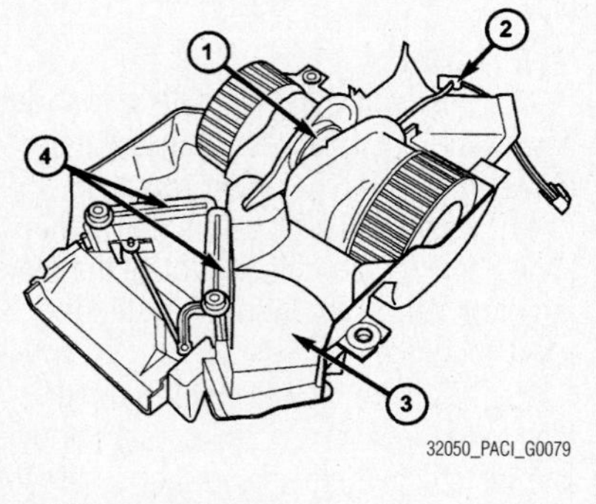

Fig. 148 Rear blower motor (1), wire harness grommet (2), rear blower motor housing (3), center console mode doors (4)

17. Position the two console support brackets onto the floor console base.
18. Install the eight screws that secure the support brackets to the floor console base. Tighten the screws to 17 inch lbs. (2 Nm).
19. Install the body wire harness bracket onto the console rear support bracket.
20. Connect the body wire harness connectors to the rear blower motor power module and the rear mode door actuator.
21. Reconnect the negative battery cable.
22. Install the front center floor console.
23. Perform the heater-A/C control calibration procedure, as follows:

➡The A/C-heater control module must be recalibrated each time an actuator motor or the A/C-heater control is replaced. If the vehicle is so equipped, the calibration procedure also includes rear HVAC positions for each actuator motor.

c. Turn the ignition switch to the **ON** position.

d. If equipped with the Manual Temperature Control (MTC) system, press and hold the Power and Recirculation buttons for at least five seconds. If equipped with the automatic temperature control (ATC) system, simultaneously press and hold the Power and Recirculation buttons on the A/C-heater control for at least five seconds. The MTC A/C-heater control Power button light emitting diode (LED) and Recirculation button LED, or the ATC A/C-heater control Delay and Recirculation graphics will begin to flash when the calibration procedure has begun.

e. The calibration procedure should take less than two minutes to complete for the manual A/C-heater control, and less than twenty seconds for the ATC A/C-heater control. When the LEDs or graphics stop flashing, the calibration procedure is complete.

f. If the LEDs or graphics continue to flash beyond the two minute (manual) or twenty second (ATC) calibration time, it indicates that the A/C-heater control has detected a failure and a Diagnostic Trouble Code (DTC) has been set. The LEDs or graphics will continue to flash even after the ignition switch is cycled Off and On, until a successful calibration is completed or until the vehicle has been driven about 8 miles (13 km).

HEATER CORE

REMOVAL & INSTALLATION

2005–06 Models

See Figure 149.

1. Before servicing the vehicle, refer to the precautions in the beginning of this section.
2. Disable the airbag system, by disconnecting the negative battery cable. Tape the end of the cable to avoid it grounding and wait 2 minutes for the system capacitor to discharge before performing any service.

➡If the vehicle is adjustable pedals, these must be removed prior to heater core removal.

3. Drain the cooling system.

⁂ WARNING

Do not use pliers to open the plastic drain.

4. Remove or disconnect the following:
   - Negative battery cable if not already done to disable the air bag system
   - Silencer boot fasteners located around the base of the lower steering shaft from the dash panel so it can be moved aside
   - Brake lamp switch from the bracket
   - Power brake booster push rod from the pin on the brake pedal arm
5. Place plastic below the heater core inside the vehicle to protect against spills.
6. Remove or disconnect the following:
   - Screw that secures the heater core to tube sealing plate to the supply and return ports
   - Heater core tubes by pushing simultaneously towards the dash panel and disengaging the fittings and cap the tube fittings and heater core ports
   - Two screws that retain the heater core mounting plate to the distribution housing

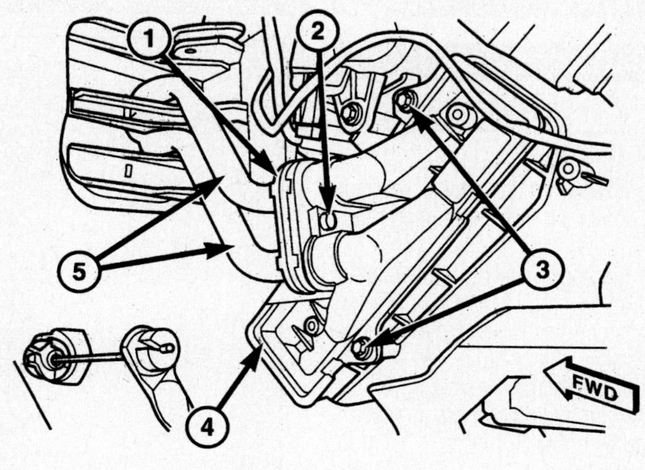

Fig. 149 Heater core mounting and related components—2005–06 models

7. Push the brake pedal downward and at the same time pull the accelerator pedal up to create enough clearance to remove the heater core.

To install:

8. Push the brake pedal downward and at the same time pull the accelerator pedal up to create enough clearance to install the heater core.
   - Two screws that retain the heater core mounting plate to the distribution housing and tighten to 17 inch lbs. (2 Nm)
9. Remove the plugs from the heater core tubes and if using the same heater core the core as well. Position the heater core tubes and sealer plate as a unit beneath the instrument panel.
10. Position both heater core tubes and the sealing plate at the same time to the heater core supply and return ports.
11. The tubes have a slot that must be indexed to a location tab within each of the core ports. Adjust the tube position so that the sealing plate fits flush against the supply and return ports which will ensure the tubes are correctly indexed.
12. Install or connect the following:
    - Screw that retains the heater core tube sealing plate to the supply and return ports and tighten to 27 inch lbs. (3 Nm)
    - Silencer under the driver side end if the instrument panel
    - Heater hoses to the tubes
    - Power brake booster push rod to the pin on the brake pedal arm
    - Brake lamp switch
    - Silencer boot and secure the
    - Negative battery cable
13. Fill the cooling system and operate for two thermostat cycles to assure elimination of air in the cooling system.

POWER STEERING GEAR

REMOVAL & INSTALLATION

See Figures 150 and 151.

1. Before servicing the vehicle, refer to the precautions in the beginning of this section.
2. Turn the front wheels to the straight-ahead position.
3. Remove or disconnect the following:
   - Negative battery cable
   - Cap from the power steering fluid reservoir and siphon out as much fluid as possible
   - Front wheels
4. If transferring tie rod ends to a new gear, loosen the jam nuts.
   - Nut attaching tie rod end to the knuckle on both sides
   - Tie rod ends from the knuckle using tool C-3894-A
5. Remove the roll pin fastening intermediate shaft extension-to-power steering gear shaft as follows:
   a. Insert removal tool 631A through the roll pin attaching the intermediate shaft extension to the steering gear.
   b. Thread the knurled nut all the way onto the remover.
   c. Hold the remove head steady and turn the hex nut to pull the pin from the shafts and remove the tool.
6. Remove or disconnect the following:
   - Intermediate shaft extension off the gear shaft
   - Tube nut attaching return hose to the gear
   - Return hose from the gear port
   - Two gear mounting bolts
7. Carefully remove the gear. Tip the gear forward at the top, then slide the gear out the left side of the wheel opening. Use care not to cut the tie rod boots on the shields as the gear is being removed.

➡On vehicles equipped with the 4.0L engine, remove the mounting screws securing the heat shield in front of the steering gear. Remove the right stabilizer bar cushion retainer mounting bolts. Remove the right stabilizer bar cushion retainer (with the heat shield).

8. If necessary, remove the tie rod ends counting how many turns it takes as this will aid during installation.

To install:

9. If removed, install the tie rod ends.
10. Install or connect the following:

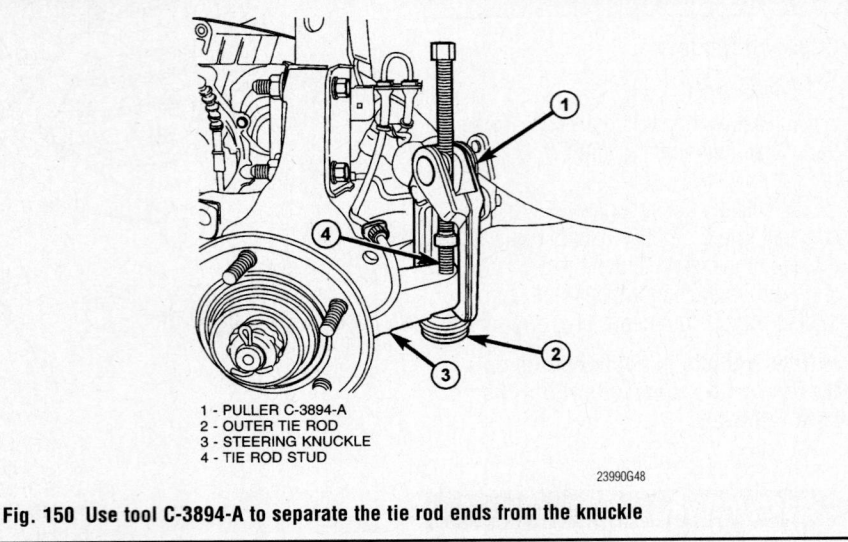

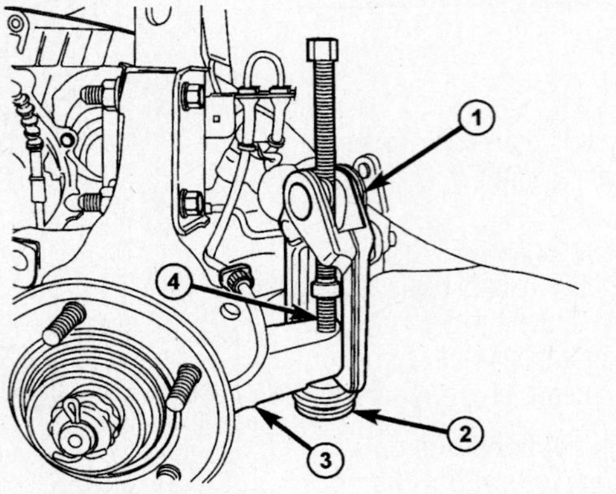

Fig. 150 Use tool C-3894-A to separate the tie rod ends from the knuckle

   - Gear through the left wheel well being careful of the tie rod end shields

➡The drivers side gear mounting bolt is longer than the passenger side bolt.

   - Gear bolts after centering the gear over the mounting bosses over the holes in the cradle and tighten to 120 ft. lbs. (163 Nm)
   - On 4.0L engine, install heat shield and right stabilizer bar cushion. Tighten cushion retainer bolts to 40 ft. lbs.

11. Wipe the power steering hoses on the gear, the connections with a lint free cloth and replace the O-rings coated with clean power steering fluid.

➡On 3.8L engine, when installing the hoses to the steering gear, it is important to position the hose tubes within 18mm of one another to avoid incorrect routing issues due to engine movement during driving maneuvers.

   - Pressure and return hoses to the gear and tighten the tube nut to 23 ft. lbs. (31 Nm)

12. Find the gear's center of travel and match the splines inside the intermediate shaft extension with those on the gear shaft, then slide the extension onto the shaft.

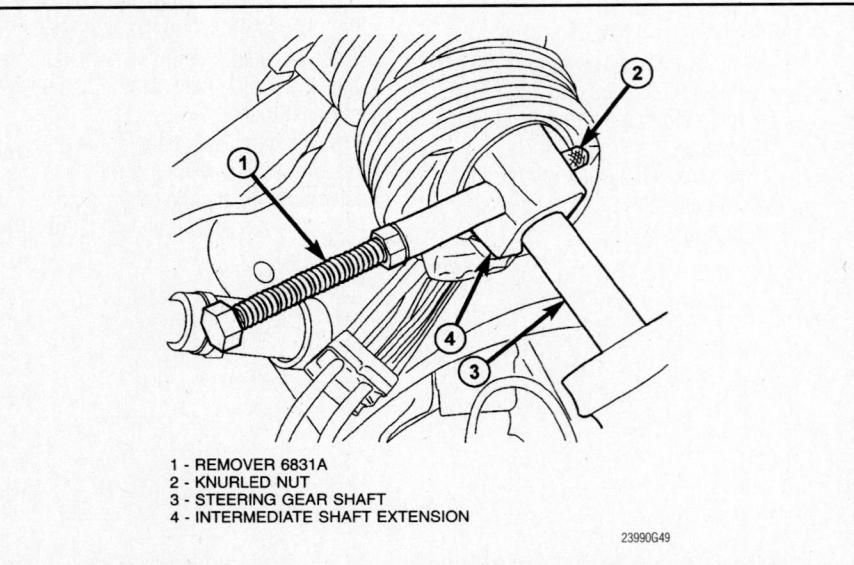

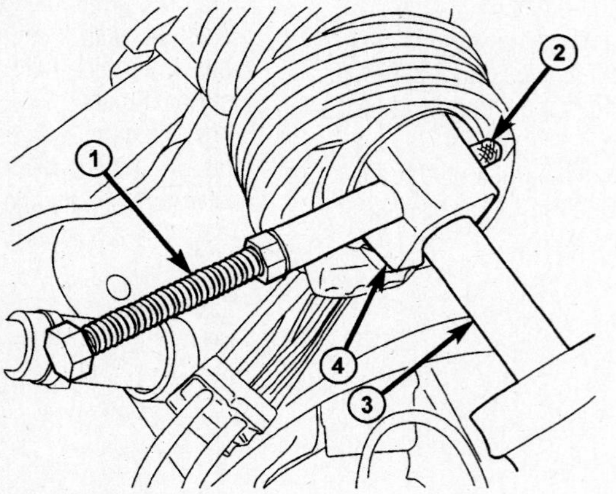

Fig. 151 Insert removal tool 631A through the roll pin attaching the intermediate shaft extension to the steering gear

13. Install the roll pin as follows:
   a. Position installer 6381-A onto the extension and gear shaft.
   b. Slide the roll pin onto the remover shaft.
   c. Thread the knurled nut all the way onto the end of the installer.
   d. While holding the install head, turn the hex nut to pull the pin into the shafts. Once the pin is centered in the intermediate shaft extension, remove the tool.
14. Install or connect the following:
   - Shaft cover over the top of the gear
   - Outer tie rod ends to the knuckle using new nuts and tighten to 35 ft. lbs. (47 Nm), then an additional 180 degree (½) turn
   - Snug the jam nuts. Do not tighten to specification at this time.
   - Wheels
   - Negative battery cable
15. Fill and bleed the power steering system.
16. Perform a wheel alignment and tighten the tie rod jam nuts to 55 ft. lbs. (75 Nm).

POWER STEERING PUMP

REMOVAL & INSTALLATION

3.5L Engine

See Figures 152 and 153.

1. Before servicing the vehicle, refer to the precautions in the beginning of this section.
2. Disconnect and isolate the negative battery cable.
3. Remove cap from power steering fluid reservoir.
4. Using a siphon pump, remove as much power steering fluid as possible from power steering fluid reservoir.
5. Remove engine appearance cover.
6. Remove upper radiator closure panel, as follows
   a. Remove four push pins attaching radiator closure panel to radiator crossmember.
   b. Remove one bolt on each side attaching to radiator crossmember.
   c. Remove six screws attaching radiator closure to the upper grille.
   d. Remove radiator closure panel from vehicle.
7. Remove power steering fluid reservoir, as follows:
   a. Remove clamp attaching return hose to power steering fluid reservoir. Remove hose from reservoir.
   b. Remove clamp attaching supply hose to power steering fluid reservoir. Remove hose from reservoir.
   c. Remove two upper mounting bolts securing reservoir in place.
   d. Loosen, but do not remove, lower mounting bolt securing reservoir in place.
   e. Slide reservoir upward, off lower mounting bolt.
8. Remove clamp, then remove fluid supply hose from pump.
9. Disconnect pressure hose from pump.
10. Remove generator wiring harness routing clip from pump.
11. Raise and safely support the vehicle.
12. Remove right front tire and wheel assembly.
13. Remove drive belt splash shield.
14. Remove nut, then hose tube routing clamp at A/C compressor mounted bracket.
15. Remove nuts mounting front and rear motor mounts to engine cradle (one nut each mount).
16. Remove accessory drive belt.
17. Carefully lower the vehicle.
18. Remove air cleaner housing, as follows:
   a. Disconnect the Intake Air Temperature (IAT) sensor wiring harness connector.
   b. Remove the air inlet hose at the throttle body.
   c. Disconnect the air circulation hose at the element housing.
   d. Remove the housing retaining bolt.
   e. Pull housing up and off of the locating pin.
   f. Remove element housing from vehicle.
19. Remove two bolts fastening right motor mount to frame rail.
20. Move pressure and return hoses away from pump toward cooling module as far as possible without bending lines.
21. Place floor jack with an appropriate sized block of wood on it below engine oil pan.

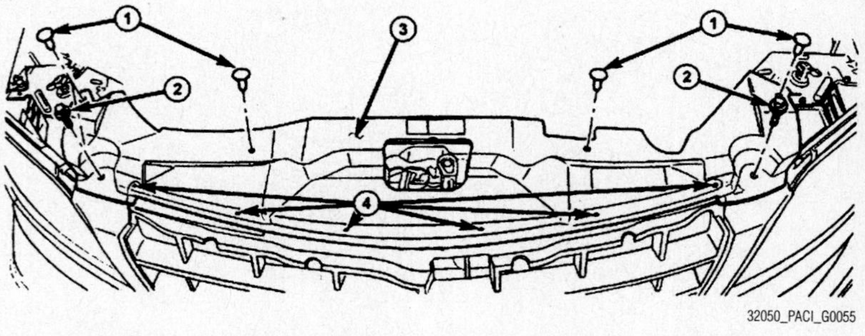

Fig. 152 To remove the radiator closure panel (3), remove the push pins (1), bolts (2) and attaching screws (4)—3.5L engine

WARNING

When lifting engine, DO NOT raise engine more than necessary or damage to driveline half shaft (and possibly other components) will occur.

22. Carefully raise accessory drive end of engine with floor jack approximately 2 inches (or just enough to access pump mounting bolts).
23. Remove three pump mounting bolts through pulley.
24. Remove pump (with pulley) from engine compartment.

To install:

25. Install power steering pump back in engine compartment using reverse order of its removal.
26. Install power steering pump on its mounting bracket.
27. Install three power steering pump mounting bolts through pulley. Tighten pump mounting bolts to 17 ft. lbs. (23 Nm).
28. Lower floor jack allowing engine to return to normal position. Remove jack.
29. Install two bolts fastening right motor mount to frame rail. Tighten bolts to 50 ft. lbs. (68 Nm).
30. Reposition pressure and return hoses to their original locations at pump.

➡Before installing power steering pressure hose on power steering pump, replace O-ring on end of power steering pressure hose. Lubricate O-ring using clean power steering fluid.

31. Install pressure hose into pump fitting. Thread pressure hose tube nut into pump and tighten to 23 ft. lbs. (31 Nm).
32. Raise vehicle.
33. Install nuts mounting front and rear motor mounts to engine cradle (one nut

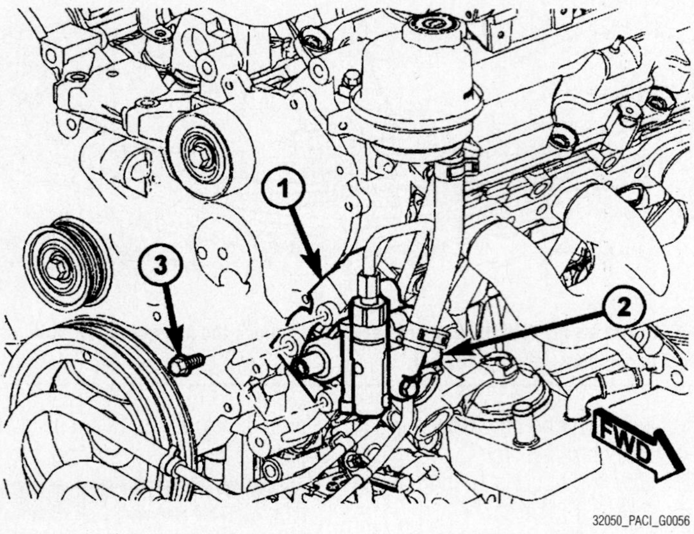

Fig. 153 Pump mounting bracket on engine (1), power steering pump (2) and mounting bolts (3))—3.5L engine

each mount). Tighten nuts to 75 ft. lbs. (102 Nm).

34. Install accessory drive belt.

35. Place pressure and return hoses on A/C compressor mounted bracket and install routing clamp and nut. Tighten the nut to 105 inch lbs. (12 Nm).

36. Install drive belt splash shield.

37. Install tire and wheel assembly. Tighten the lug nuts to 100 ft. lbs. (135 Nm).

38. Lower vehicle.

39. Install air cleaner housing, as follows:

a. Install housing into vehicle and the locating pin.

b. Install housing retaining bolt.

c. Connect the air inlet hose to the throttle body and tighten clamp.

d. Connect the air circulation hose to housing.

e. Connect the IAT sensor wiring harness connector.

40. Install generator wiring harness routing clip into pump.

41. Slide fluid supply hose onto pump fitting and install clamp securing it in place.

42. Install power steering fluid reservoir, as follows:

a. Slide fluid reservoir over lower mounting bolt and into place on engine.

b. Install two upper mounting bolts securing reservoir in place.

c. Tighten all three reservoir mounting bolts to 105 inch lbs. (12 Nm).

d. Install supply hose onto reservoir. Slide hose clamp into position on fluid reservoir and attach it. Be sure hose clamp in installed past bead on fluid reservoir fitting.

e. Install return hose onto reservoir. Slide hose clamp into position on fluid reservoir and attach it. Be sure hose clamp in installed past bead on fluid reservoir fitting.

43. Install upper radiator closure panel, as follows:

a. Place radiator closure panel into position.

b. Install one bolt on each side attaching to radiator crossmember.

c. Install four push pins attaching radiator closure panel to radiator crossmember.

d. Install six screws attaching radiator closure to the upper grille.

44. Install engine appearance cover.

45. Connect negative (-) battery cable on negative battery post.

46. Fill and bleed power steering system.

47. Inspect for leaks.

3.8L Engine

See Figure 154.

1. Before servicing the vehicle, refer to the precautions in the beginning of this section.

2. Disconnect and isolate the negative battery cable.

3. Remove cap from power steering fluid reservoir.

4. Using a siphon pump, remove as much power steering fluid as possible from power steering fluid reservoir.

5. Remove air cleaner housing, as follows:

a. Disconnect the Intake Air Temperature (IAT) sensor wiring harness connector.

b. Remove the air inlet hose at the throttle body.

c. Disconnect the air circulation hose at the element housing.

d. Remove the housing retaining bolt.

e. Pull housing up and off of the locating pin.

f. Remove element housing from vehicle.

6. Remove accessory drive belt.

7. Remove clamp, then remove return hose at reservoir.

8. Unthread tube nut and remove pressure hose at pump.

9. Remove three pump mounting bolts through pulley.

10. Remove pump (with pulley and reservoir) from engine compartment.

To install:

11. Position power steering pump on engine.

12. Install three power steering pump mounting bolts through pulley. Tighten pump mounting bolts to 16 ft. lbs. (23 Nm).

➡Before installing power steering pressure hose on power steering pump, replace O-ring on end of power steering pressure hose. Lubricate the O-ring using clean power steering fluid.

13. Install pressure hose into pump fitting.

14. Thread pressure hose tube nut into pump and tighten to 23 ft. lbs. (31 Nm).

15. Slide return hose onto reservoir fitting and install clamp securing it in place.

16. Install accessory drive belt.

17. Install air cleaner housing, as follows:

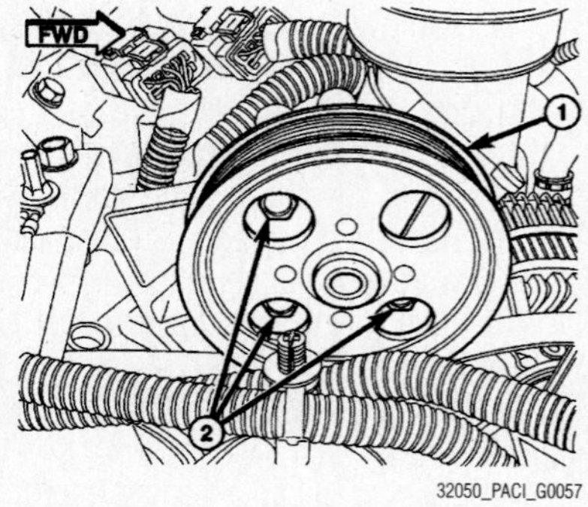

Fig. 154 Remove the power steering pump mounting bolts (2) through the openings in the pulley (1))—3.8L engine

a. Install housing into vehicle and the locating pin.

b. Install housing retaining bolt.

c. Connect the air inlet hose to the throttle body and tighten clamp.

d. Connect the air circulation hose to housing.

e. Connect the IAT sensor wiring harness connector.

18. Connect the negative battery cable.

19. Fill and bleed power steering system.

20. Check the power steering pump for leaks.

4.0L Engine

See Figure 155.

1. Before servicing the vehicle, refer to the precautions in the beginning of this section.
2. Disconnect and isolate the negative battery cable.
3. Drain the power steering fluid.
4. Remove the power steering reservoir.
5. Remove the pressure hose from the pump.
6. Raise and support the vehicle safely.
7. Remove the nuts retaining the front and rear motor mounts to the engine cradle.
8. Lower the vehicle.
9. Remove the air cleaner housing.
10. Remove the accessory drive belt.
11. Remove the two bolts retaining the upper motor mount to the frame rail.
12. Position a floor jack, with the proper size wooden block on the jack lifting surface, below the oil pan.

➡When lifting the engine, do not raise the engine more than necessary or damage to the driveline halfshaft, fuel tubes from the frame rail to the engine and possibly other components will occur.

13. Carefully raise the accessory drive end of the engine with a floor jack about one inch, measured between the right motor mount and the frame rail.
14. Remove the three pump mounting bolts, through the pump pulley.
15. Remove the A/C wiring harness routing clip from the rear of the pump.
16. Remove the pump with the pulley and the supply hose from the engine.

To install:

17. Installation is the reverse of the removal procedure.
18. Before installing the power steering pressure hose on the pump, replace the O-ring. Lubricate the new O-ring with clean power steering fluid.

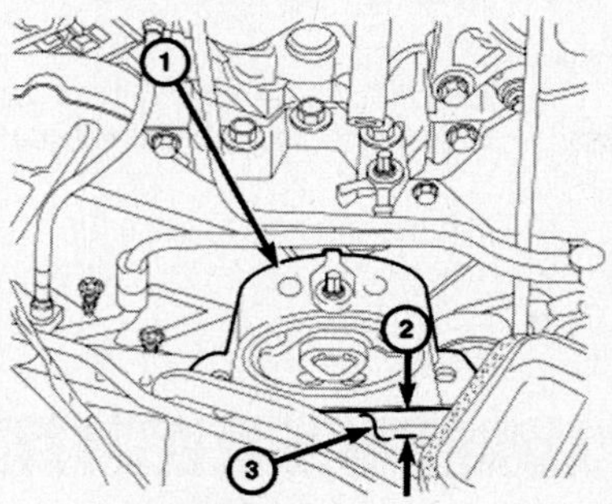

Fig. 155 Jack positioning and measurement location—4.0L engine

19. Be sure to fill the system with the proper grade and type power steering fluid.
20. Start the engine and check for leaks.
21. Bleed the power steering system.

BLEEDING

2005–06 Models

⁂ CAUTION

The fluid level should be checked and adjusted with engine off to prevent injury from moving engine components.

⁂ WARNING

Use only Mopar® ATF+4 Automatic Transmission Fluid (MS-9602) in power steering system. Use of other Mopar® power steering fluids (MS5931 and MS9933) should be avoided to ensure peak performance of the power steering system under all operating conditions. Do not overfill.

1. Read the fluid level through the side of the power steering fluid reservoir. The fluid level should be within "FILL RANGE" when the fluid is at a temperature of approximately 70–80°F (21–27°C).
2. Before servicing the vehicle, refer to the precautions in the beginning of this section.
3. Wipe the filler cap and area clean, then remove the cap.
4. Fill the fluid reservoir to the proper level and let the fluid settle for at least two (2) minutes.
5. Start the engine and let run for a few seconds, then turn the engine off.
6. Add fluid if necessary. Repeat the above steps until the fluid level remains constant after running the engine.
7. Raise the front wheels off the ground.
8. Start the engine.
9. Slowly turn the steering wheel right and left, lightly contacting the wheel stops.
10. Add fluid if necessary.
11. Lower the vehicle, then turn the steering wheel slowly from lock-to-lock.
12. Stop the engine. Check the fluid level and refill as required.
13. If the fluid is extremely foamy, allow the vehicle to stabilize a few minutes, then repeat the above procedure.

2007–08 Models

⁂ CAUTION

The fluid level should be checked and adjusted with engine off to prevent injury from moving engine components.

⁂ WARNING

Use only Mopar® ATF+4 Automatic Transmission Fluid (MS-9602) in power steering system. Use of other Mopar® power steering fluids (MS5931 and MS9933) should be avoided to ensure peak performance of the power steering system under all operating conditions. Do not overfill.

➡If the air is not purged from the system correctly, pump failure could result.

1. Before servicing the vehicle, refer to the precautions in the beginning of this section.
2. Check the fluid level. As measured on the side of the reservoir the level should indicate between "MAX" and "MIN" when the fluid is at normal ambient temperature. Adjust the fluid level as required.

➡Be sure that the vacuum tool is clean and free of any fluids.

3. Tightly insert the power steering cap adapter onto the end of the vacuum pump reservoir, special tool 9688 or equivalent.

➡Failure to use a vacuum pump reservoir may allow fluid to be sucked into the hand vacuum pump.

4. Assemble the vacuum pump, special tool C-4207 or equivalent, along with the reservoir and cap adapter.

⁂ CAUTION

Do not run the engine while vacuum is applied to the power steering system. Damage to the pump can occur.

➡When performing the following steps be sure the vacuum level is maintained during the entire time period.

5. Using the pump, apply 68–85 kPa (20–25 in. Hg) of vacuum to the system for a minimum of three minutes.
6. Slowly release the vacuum and remove the special tools.
7. Adjust the fluid level, as required.
8. Repeat the above procedure, until the fluid level no longer drops when vacuum is applied.
9. Start the engine and cycle the steering wheel from lock to lock, three times.

➡Do not hold the steering wheel at the stops.

10. Stop the engine and check for leaks at all connections.
11. Check for signs of air in the reservoir, correct as required.
12. Check the fluid level, correct as required.

FRONT SUSPENSION

LOWER BALL JOINT

REMOVAL & INSTALLATION

➡The lower ball joints on these vehicles are not serviced separately. The lower ball joints operate with no free-play. If defective, the entire lower control arm must be replaced.

LOWER CONTROL ARM

REMOVAL & INSTALLATION

See Figures 156 through 159.

1. Before servicing the vehicle, refer to the precautions in the beginning of this section.
2. Remove or disconnect the following:
   - Negative battery cable
   - Front wheels
   - Hub and bearing-to-stub axle cotter pin and retainer nut
   - Front caliper assembly from steering knuckle
   - Front brake rotor from the hub
   - Wheel Speed Sensor (WSS) harness connector and unclip the connector and retaining clip from the frame rail
   - Screw attaching the WSS routing bracket to the strut, open the routing clip at the knuckle and remove the cable
3. Push in the outer end of the halfshaft to disengage the splines from the hub splines.
   - Tie rod end nut from the steering knuckle by holding the tie rod while loosening the nut, then use tool C-3894-A to separate the tie rod from the knuckle
   - Steering knuckle-to-strut bolts
   - Steering knuckle from the strut bracket
4. Tip the knuckle outward at the top and remove the halfshaft from the hub and suspend the halfshaft using wire.
   - Ball joint nut using an impact gun, then reinstall the nut until the top of the nut is even with the stud. This will prevent the stud from distorting while performing the next step.
5. Place removal tool C-4150A over the ball joint and stud and tighten the tool to release the stud. It may help to rotate the knuckle around so the inside of the knuckle faces outwards, then remove the tool.
   - Knuckle
   - Bolts attaching the lower control arm to the engine cradle and the control arm

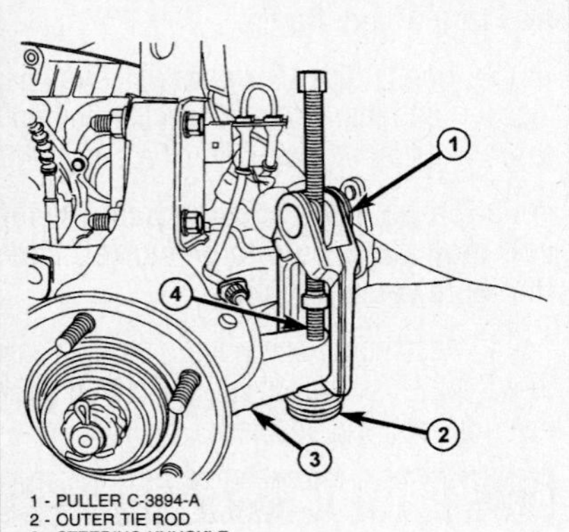

Fig. 156 Use tool C-3894-A to separate the tie rod ends from the knuckle

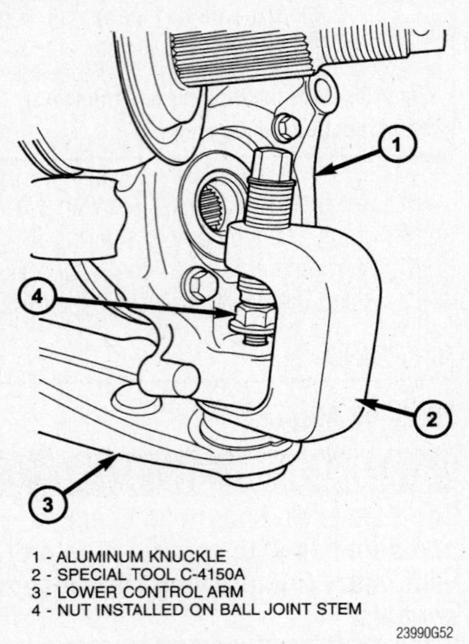

Fig. 157 Place removal tool C-4150A over the ball joint and stud and tighten the tool to release the stud. It may help to rotate the knuckle around so the inside of the knuckle faces outwards

To install:

➡When installing the lower control arm-to-cradle rear mounting bolts, make sure the flag on the left control arm nut are positioned upwards (above the control arm) and the right control arm nut are positioned downwards (below the control arm).

6. Install or connect the following:
   - New lower control arm and the control arm to cradle bolts from the rear as illustrated and hand tighten
7. Clean the ball joint stud and knuckle contact surfaces of grease and dirt to avoid damage.
   - Steering knuckle on the ball stud
   - New knuckle to ball joint nut, then tighten the nut while holding the stud with a hex wrench and

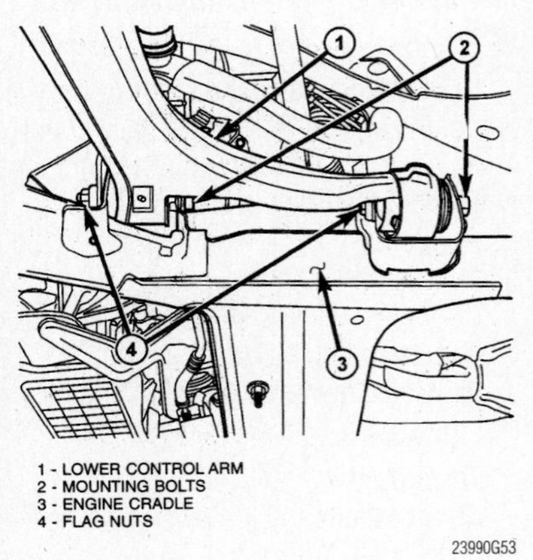

Fig. 158 Exploded view of the lower control arm mounting, note the orientation of the bolts for installation purposes

tighten to 60 ft. lbs. (81 Nm) plus an additional 90 degrees (1/4) turn

- Halfshaft into the hub assembly

WARNING

The steering knuckle-to-strut assembly bolts are serrated and must not be turned during installation.. Also if the vehicle is equipped with eccentric strut assembly bolts, the eccentric bolt must be installed in the bottom (slotted) hole on the strut bract.

➡The strut-to-steering are installed differently on each side. The left hand side bolts are installed from the vehicle rear to front and the right side bolts are installed from the vehicle front to rear.

8. Position the steering knuckle neck into the strut assembly. Install the strut assembly-to-steering knuckle bolts. Install the nuts onto the attaching bolts and torque to 60 ft. lbs. (81 Nm), then tighten an additional 1/4 or 90 degrees turn.
9. Clean the tie rod end and knuckle contact areas to prevent damage.
10. Install or connect the following:
   - Tie rod end to the knuckle and hand tighten the nut. While using a socket to hold the stud, tighten the nut to 35 ft. lbs. (47 Nm) plus an additional 180 degree (1/2 turn).
   - WSS sensor clip, cable, routing clip and attach the connection
   - Rotor and caliper
11. Have an assistant apply the brakes, install the washer, and hub nut. Tighten the nut to 180 ft. lbs. (244 Nm).
   - Spring washer, new hub nut and cotter pin
   - Wheels
   - Tighten the lower arm frame bolts to 120 ft. lbs. (163 Nm)

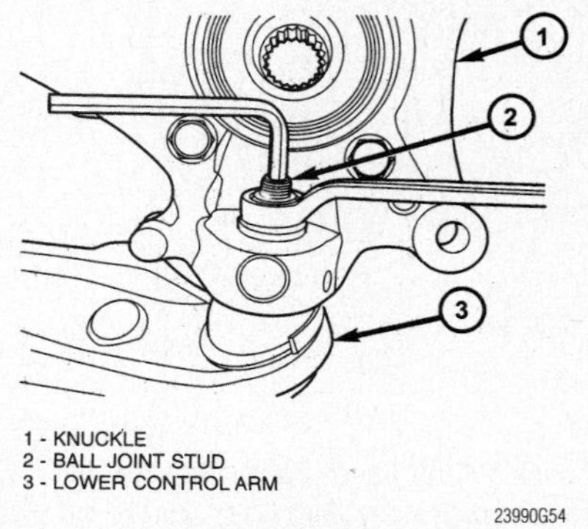

Fig. 159 Tightening the ball joint nut

12. Check and adjust the brake fluid and brakes.
13. Align the vehicle.

CONTROL ARM BUSHING REPLACEMENT

The control arm bushings are an integral part of the assembly. If worn or damaged, the control arm assembly must be replaced.

MACPHERSON STRUT

REMOVAL & INSTALLATION

See Figure 160.

1. Before servicing the vehicle, refer to the precautions in the beginning of this section.

➡Service of the coil spring requires the use of a coil spring compressor tool. It is required that 5 coils be captured within the jaws of the compressor tool.

➡Do not support the vehicle by placing supports under the suspension arms. The suspension arms must hang freely.

2. Remove or disconnect the following:
   - Negative battery cable
   - Front wheel(s)
   - Speed sensor wiring harness mounting bracket from the strut, if equipped with Antilock Brake System (ABS)

➡When removing the nut from the stud of the stabilizer bar link, do not allow the stud to rotate in the socket by holding with an open ended wrench.

   - Strut-to-steering knuckle bolts and nuts
   - Stabilizer bar attaching link at the strut assembly

WARNING

The steering knuckle-to-strut assembly bolts are serrated and must not be turned during installation.

3. If removing the left strut assembly, unfasten the nuts attaching the coolant recovery bottle and position the bottle and hoses aside.
4. Remove the 3 strut assembly upper mount-to-shock tower mounting nuts and washers. Remove the strut from the vehicle.
5. Disassemble the strut by performing the following procedure:
   a. Securely mount the strut assembly into a vise. Using paint, mark the strut unit, lower spring isolator, spring and upper strut mount for indexing of the parts at assembly.
   b. Position the spring compressor tool onto the strut. Compress the coil spring until all load is off the upper strut mount assembly.
   c. Install Strut Rod Socket tool 6864 on the strut shaft nut and a 10mm socket on the end of the strut shaft to prevent it from turning. Remove the strut shaft nut.
   d. Remove the upper mount assembly, jounce bumper and seat bearing and dust shield as an assembly.
   e. Remove the coil spring and compressor as an assembly from the strut. Remove the lower spring isolator from the strut assembly lower spring seat.
   f. Inspect all components for abnormal wear, oil leakage or failure. Replace parts as required.

To install:

6. Assemble the strut by performing the following procedure:
   a. Inspect the strut assembly for signs of leakage. Actual leakage will be a stream of fluid running down the side and dripping off the lower end of the strut. A slight amount of seepage between the strut rod and strut shaft seal is not unusual and does not affect performance of the strut assembly.
   b. Install the lower spring isolator on the strut unit. Install the compressed coil spring onto the strut assembly aligning the paint marks made during removal.
   c. Install the strut bearing into the bearing seat. The bearing must be installed into the seat with the notches on the bearings facing down.
   d. Lower the seat bearing and dust shield onto the strut and spring assembly. Align the paint marks made during removal.
   e. Install the jounce bumper and upper mount on the strut shaft, aligning the paint marks.
   f. Install the strut mount-to-shaft retainer nut. Inspect all alignment marks made during removal and align as required. While holding the strut shaft from turning with a 10mm socket, torque the strut shaft nut to 85 ft. lbs. (115 Nm).
   g. Equally loosen the spring compressor tool until all tension is released. Remove the spring compressor tool.
7. Install the front strut into the strut tower. Torque the 3 upper nuts to 250 inch lbs. (28 Nm).
8. If installing the left strut assembly, position the coolant recovery bottle and hoses. Fasten the bottle retainers.

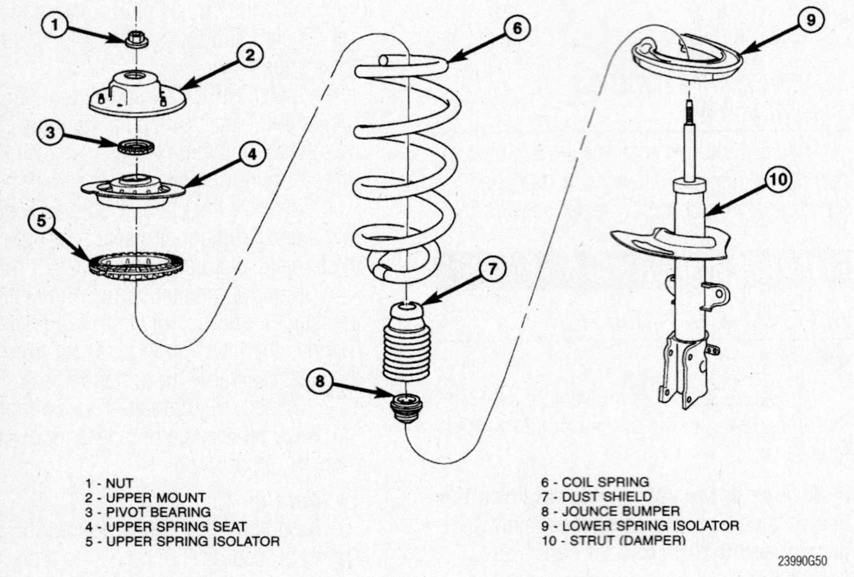

Fig. 160 Exploded view of the front strut assembly

WARNING

The steering knuckle-to-strut assembly bolts are serrated and must not be turned during installation.. Also if the vehicle is equipped with eccentric strut assembly bolts, the eccentric bolt must be installed in the bottom (slotted) hole on the strut bract.

➡The strut-to-steering are installed differently on each side. The left hand side bolts are installed from the vehicle rear to front and the right side bolts are installed from the vehicle front to rear.

9. Position the steering knuckle neck into the strut assembly. Install the strut assembly-to-steering knuckle bolts. Install the nuts onto the attaching bolts and torque to 60 ft. lbs. (81 Nm), then tighten an additional 1/4 or 90 degrees turn.

➡When installing the nut to the stud of the stabilizer bar link, do not allow the stud to rotate in the socket by holding with an open ended wrench.

10. Install or connect the following:
    - Stabilizer bar attaching link to the strut assembly, hand thread the nut then tighten to 65 ft. lbs. (88 Nm) using an open ended wrench on the machine surfaced to prevent from turning.
    - Speed sensor wiring harness mounting bracket to the strut and tighten the retainers to 115 inch lbs. (13 Nm)
    - Front wheel(s)
    - Negative battery cable
11. Align the vehicle.

STABILIZER BAR

REMOVAL & INSTALLATION

See Figures 161 through 163.

1. Before servicing the vehicle, refer to the precautions in the beginning of this section.
2. Raise and support vehicle.
3. Remove both front wheel and tire assemblies.
4. Remove nut attaching outer tie rod to steering knuckle by holding rod end stud stationary while loosening and removing nut with a wrench.
5. Remove tie rod end from steering knuckle using Remover, Special Tool C-3894-A.

WARNING

When removing nut from stud of stabilizer bar link, do not allow stud to rotate in it's socket. Hold stud from rotating by placing an open-end wrench on flat machined into stud.

6. Remove stabilizer bar links from each end of stabilizer bar. To do so, place an open-end wrench on flat machined into link's mounting stud, then remove nut while holding wrench in place. Push each stud out of hole in stabilizer bar.
7. If equipped with the 4.0L engine, remove the heat shield.
8. Remove stabilizer bar cushion retainers as follows:
    a. Loosen front bolts at each retainer (Do not remove). An open-end wrench works best, but a socket may be used if correct length extension is used.

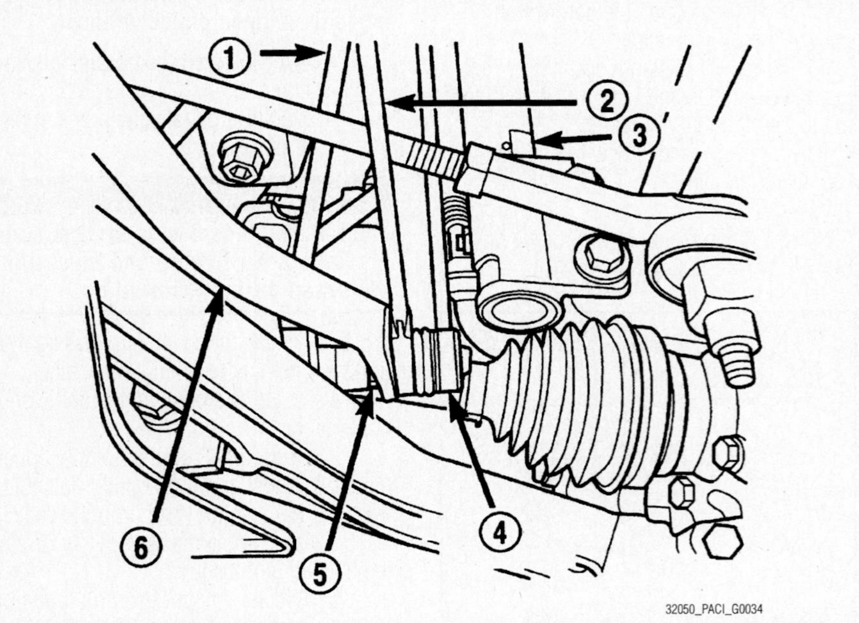

Fig. 161 To remove the links (4) from each end of the stabilizer bar (6), place an open-end wrench (2) on flat machined into link's mounting stud, then use a ratchet (1) to remove nut (5) while holding wrench in place. Push each stud out of hole in stabilizer bar.

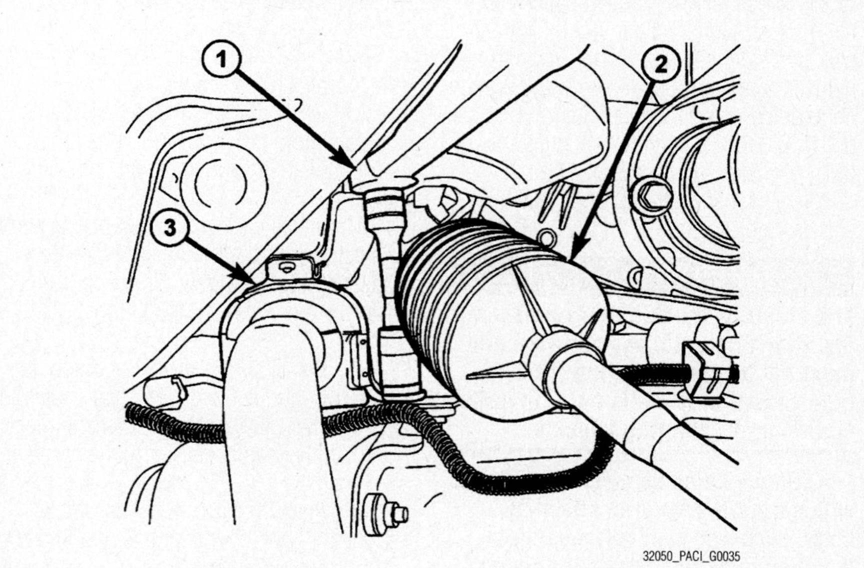

Fig. 162 View of the ratchet/torque wrench with extension and socket (1), power steering gear boot (2) and cushion retainer (3)

b. Remove rear bolts at each retainer.

c. Slide stabilizer toward rear of vehicle.

d. Remove both retainers and cushions from bar.

9. Remove stabilizer bar out through right wheel opening by carefully rotating bar up-and-down, and back-and-forth as necessary.

To install:

➡When installing stabilizer bar, make sure it installed so that bar curves upward at ends to meet stabilizer links.

10. Insert stabilizer bar over cradle through right front wheel opening in reverse direction it was removed in. Ensure bar gets routed in front of brake tubes on cradle.

➡When installing cushion retainers, make sure shielded retainer is installed on right side with shield pointing forward.

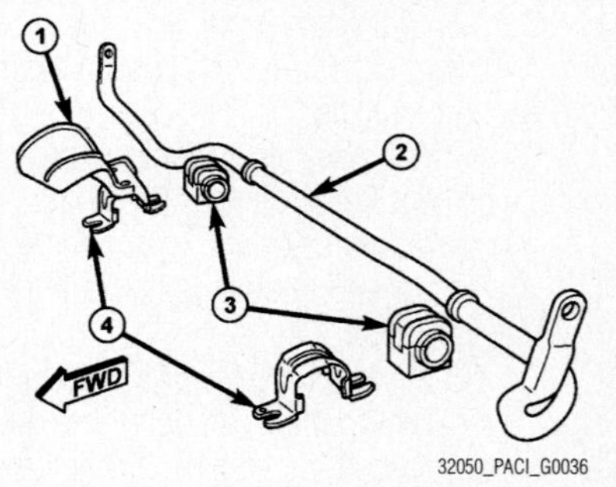

Fig. 163 Exploded view of the stabilizer bar (2), shield mounted to right retainer (1), cushions (3) and retainers (4)

➡If equipped with the 4.0L engine, when installing the cushion retainers be sure that the shielded retainer is installed on the right side with the shield pointing forward.

11. Install cushions on stabilizer bar utilizing slits in cushions. Install each cushion so its slit faces forward and flat side is positioned toward cradle once installed.

12. Install retainers on cushions. Make sure retainer with shield is placed over right cushion with shield facing forward.

13. Slide stabilizer bar forward engaging slotted holes on retainers with retainer mounting bolts in cradle.

14. Install rear retainer mounting bolts. Tighten all four retainer mounting bolts to 40 ft. lbs. (54 Nm).

➡Once retainer bolts are tightened, make sure heat shields are not bent or mis-positioned.

15. On 4.0L engine, install the heat shield. Tighten the retaining screws to 35 inch lbs.

16. Install each stabilizer bar link mounting stud through hole in each end of stabilizer bar.

WARNING

When installing nut on mounting stud of stabilizer bar link, do not allow stud to rotate in it's socket. Hold stud stationary by placing an open-end wrench on flat machined into stud.

17. Hand-thread nut on end of each stabilizer bar link studs. Then hold studs from turning by placing an open-end wrench on flat machined into each link's mounting stud, then tighten each nut. Tighten each nut to 65 ft. lbs. (88 Nm).

18. Install outer tie rods to steering knuckles. Start NEW nut onto stud of each outer tie rod. Start nut onto tie rod stud. While holding stud stationary using a socket, tighten nut using a wrench. Using a crowfoot wrench on a torque wrench, tighten nut to 35 ft. lbs. (47 Nm). Then, tighten nut an additional ½ (180°) turn after that torque is met.

19. Install tire and wheel assembly. Tighten wheel mounting nuts to 100 ft. lbs. (135 Nm) torque.

20. Lower vehicle.

STEERING KNUCKLE

REMOVAL & INSTALLATION

1. Before servicing the vehicle, refer to the precautions in the beginning of this section.
2. Raise and support vehicle.
3. Remove wheel and tire assembly.
4. Remove cotter pin, nut lock and spring washer from end of halfshaft stub shaft and hub nut.
5. With aid of a helper applying brakes to keep front hub from turning, remove hub nut.
6. Access and remove front brake rotor.
7. Disconnect vehicle wiring harness from wheel speed sensor connector.
8. Unclip wheel speed sensor connector and routing clip from frame rail outer reinforcement.
9. Remove screw fastening wheel speed sensor routing bracket to strut assembly.
10. Open routing clip at knuckle and remove wheel speed sensor cable.
11. Push in on end of halfshaft stub shaft, pushing its splines out of hub splines.
12. Remove nut attaching outer tie rod to steering knuckle by holding outer tie rod stud stationary while loosening and removing nut with a wrench.
13. Remove tie rod from steering knuckle using Remover, Special Tool C-3894-A.
14. Remove two bolts attaching strut clevis to steering knuckle.
15. Tip knuckle outward at top and remove halfshaft stub shaft from hub and

bearing. Suspend driveshaft straight outward using a bungee cord or wire. Do not allow driveshaft to hang by inner joint.

16. Remove ball joint nut using a power impact wrench. Because tapered stud is held sufficiently in knuckle at this time, it is not necessary to hold stud stationary to remove nut.

17. Reinstall ball joint nut until top of nut is even with top of ball joint stud. This action will keep stud from distorting while stud is released from knuckle in following step.

WARNING

Do not remove ball joint stud from steering knuckle using a hammer. Damage to Aluminum knuckle, ball joint or control arm will result.

➡Lubricate Remover, Special Tool C-4150A, screw-drive threads before use to ease use and promote tool longevity.

18. Place Remover, Special Tool C-4150A, over ball joint stud and nut as shown. Release ball joint stud from steering knuckle by tightening tool screw-drive. To ease remover installation and use, it may help to rotate knuckle around so inside of knuckle faces outward.

19. Remove tool and nut from top of ball joint stud.

20. Remove steering knuckle from vehicle.

21. If hub and bearing needs to be transferred, remove four bolts attaching hub and bearing to knuckle, then remove hub and bearing.

To install:

22. If hub and bearing needs to be installed in knuckle, place hub and bearing squarely into center hole of knuckle with wheel speed sensor positioned toward trailing end of knuckle. Align threaded mounting holes of hub and bearing with mounting holes in steering knuckle, then install four mounting bolts. Progressively tighten mounting bolts in a crisscross pattern. Tighten mounting bolts to 45 ft. lbs. (65 Nm).

WARNING

Before installing knuckle on ball joint stud, wipe ball joint stud and knuckle contact area free of any grease or debris, otherwise damage to knuckle can occur. Use a clean shop cloth with Mopar® Brake Parts Cleaner applied to it for proper cleaning. Do not spray stud directly.

23. Place knuckle on ball joint stud.

24. Install a NEW steering knuckle to ball joint stud nut. Tighten nut by holding ball joint stud with hex wrench while turning nut with a wrench. Using a crowfoot wrench on a torque wrench, tighten nut to 60 ft. lbs. (81 Nm). Then, tighten nut an additional ¼ (90°) turn after that torque is met.

25. Slide halfshaft stub shaft into hub and bearing assembly.

WARNING

The steering knuckle to strut assembly attaching bolts are serrated and must not be turned during installation. Install nuts while holding bolts stationary in steering knuckle.

➡If vehicle being serviced is equipped with eccentric cam strut attaching bolts, eccentric cam bolt must be installed in bottom (slotted) hole on strut clevis bracket.

➡The strut clevis-to-steering knuckle bolts are installed differently on each side. Left hand side bolts are to be installed from vehicle rear to front. Right side bolts are to be installed from vehicle front to rear.

26. Align steering knuckle in clevis bracket of strut. Install strut clevis-to-steering knuckle attaching bolts. Install nuts on ends of bolts and tighten to 60 ft. lbs. (81 Nm). Then, tighten nuts an additional ¼ (90°) turn after that torque is met.

WARNING

Before installing tie rod stud in knuckle steering arm, wipe stud and knuckle contact area free of any grease or debris, otherwise damage to knuckle can occur. Use a clean shop cloth with Mopar® Brake Parts Cleaner applied to it for proper cleaning. Do not spray stud directly.

27. Install outer tie rod stud into knuckle steering arm from bottom. Start nut onto tie rod stud. While holding stud stationary using a socket, tighten nut using a wrench. Using a crowfoot wrench on a torque wrench, tighten nut to 35 ft. lbs. (47 Nm). Then, tighten nut an additional ½ (180°) turn after that torque is met.

28. Place wheel speed sensor cable grommet in clip at knuckle. Close clip.

29. Attach wheel speed sensor routing bracket to strut assembly. Tighten screw to 115 inch lbs. (13 Nm).

30. Clip wheel speed sensor connector and routing clip to frame rail outer reinforcement.

31. Connect vehicle wiring harness to wheel speed sensor connector.

32. Install brake rotor, then install disc brake caliper and adapter assembly.

33. Verify that wheel speed sensor is not routed improperly allowing cable to come in contact with brake rotor or other moving parts.

34. Install washer and hub nut on end of halfshaft stub shaft. With aid of a helper applying brakes to keep front hub from turning, tighten hub nut to 180 ft. lbs. (244 Nm).

35. Install spring washer and hub nut lock over hub nut and stub shaft. Install a NEW cotter pin securing nut lock in place and tightly wrap cotter pin prongs around nut lock.

36. Install tire and wheel assembly. Tighten wheel mounting nuts to a torque of 100 ft. lbs. (135 Nm).

37. Lower vehicle.

38. Pump brake pedal several times to ensure vehicle has a firm brake pedal before moving vehicle.

39. Check and adjust brake fluid level as necessary.

40. Perform wheel alignment.

STRUT & SPRING ASSEMBLY

REMOVAL & INSTALLATION

Refer to the front strut removal and installation procedure.

WHEEL BEARINGS

REMOVAL & INSTALLATION

See Figures 164 and 165.

1. Before servicing the vehicle, refer to the precautions in the beginning of this section.
2. Remove or disconnect the following:
   - Negative battery cable
   - Front wheels
   - Hub and bearing-to-stub axle cotter pin and retainer nut
   - Front caliper assembly from steering knuckle
   - Front brake rotor from the hub
   - Wheel Speed Sensor (WSS) harness connector and unclip the connector and retaining clip from the frame rail
   - Screw attaching the WSS routing bracket to the strut, open the routing clip at the knuckle and remove the cable
3. Push in the outer end of the halfshaft to disengage the splines from the hub splines.

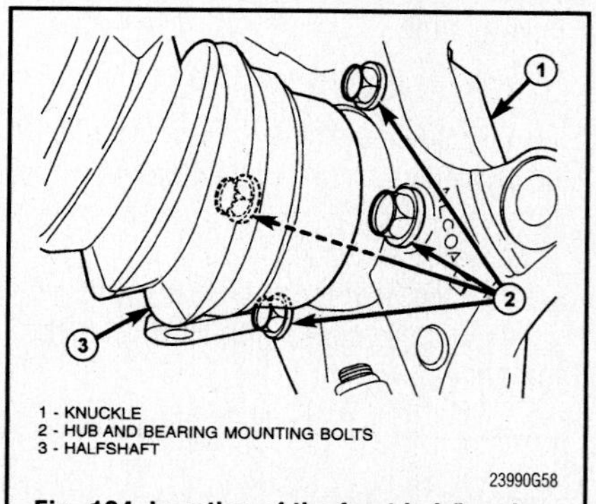

Fig. 164 Location of the front hub/bearing mounting bolts

- Four hub/bearing bolts from the rear of the knuckle
- Hub/bearing with the WSS

To install:

4. Clean all mating and mounting surfaces prior to installation to prevent damage.

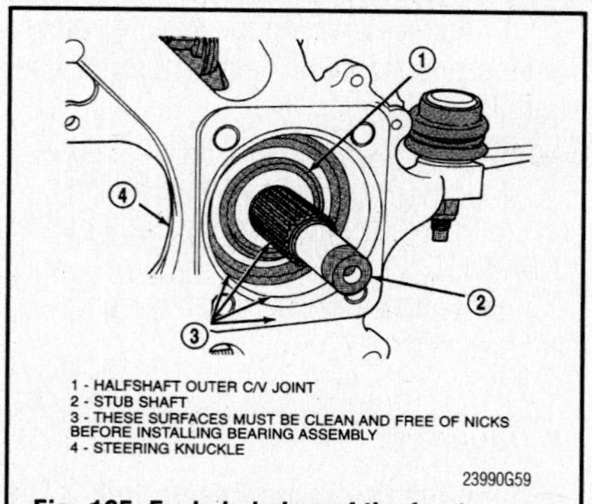

Fig. 165 Exploded view of the front hub/bearing assembly

5. Install or connect the following:
   - Hub/bearing onto the halfshaft stub shaft and into the knuckle until it is squarely seated on the face of the knuckle.
   - Four hub/bearing bolts and using a crisscross pattern tighten progressively and equally to 45 ft. lbs. (65 Nm)
   - WSS sensor clip, cable, routing clip and attach the connection
   - Rotor and caliper
6. Have an assistant apply the brakes, install the washer, and hub nut. Tighten the nut to 180 ft. lbs. (244 Nm).
   - Spring washer , new hub nut and cotter pin
   - Wheels
7. Check and adjust the brake fluid and brakes.
8. Align the vehicle.

ADJUSTMENT

This vehicle is equipped with permanently sealed front wheel bearings. There is no periodic lubrication or maintenance recommended for these units.

SUSPENSION

REAR SUSPENSION

COIL SPRING

REMOVAL & INSTALLATION

Refer to the rear shock removal and installation procedure.

LINKS

REMOVAL & INSTALLATION

Camber Link

See Figures 166 and 167.

1. Before servicing the vehicle, refer to the precautions in the beginning of this section.

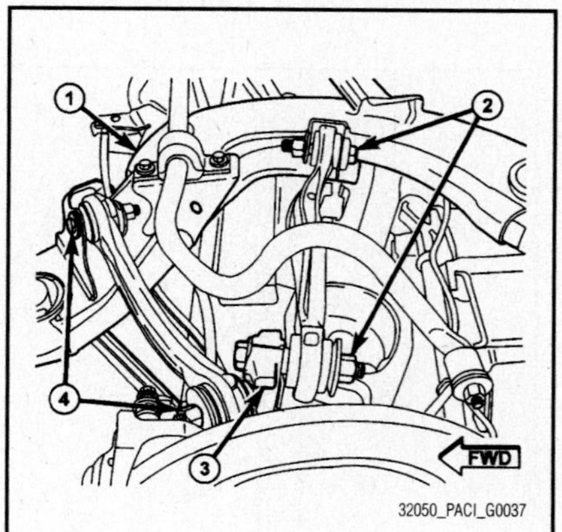

Fig. 166 View of the rear suspension crossmember (1), camber link mounting bolts (2), knuckle (3) and tension link mounting bolts (4)

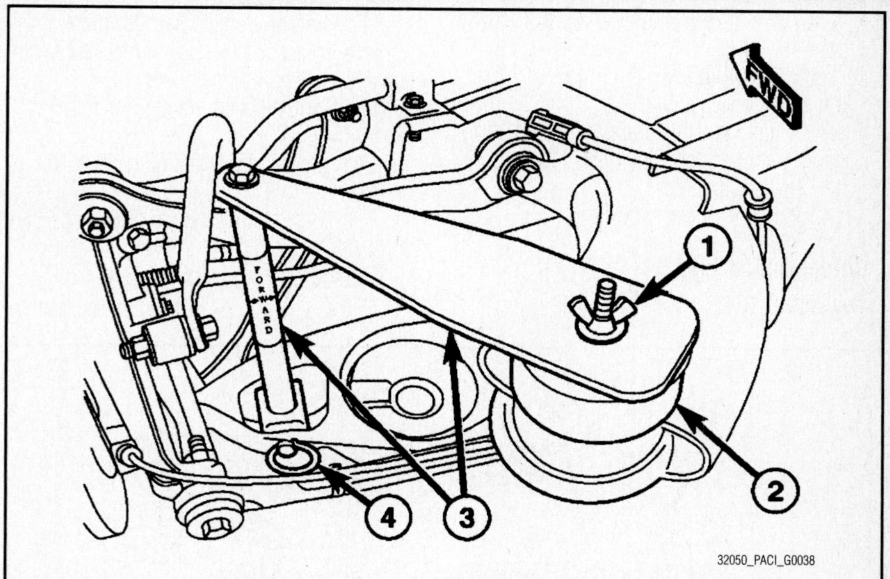

Fig. 167 Curb height gauge mounted in place—Wing nut and bolt (1), Receiver 9031-3 (2), Gauge 9094 (3), and Pin (4)

2. Raise and support vehicle.
3. Access and remove rear shock absorber.

➡Repair-side of crossmember must be lowered from body approximately three inches in order to properly access link mounting bolts at crossmember. Do not lower crossmember any further than necessary.

4. Remove nut and bolt mounting link to knuckle.
5. Remove nut and bolt mounting link to crossmember.
6. Remove link.

To install:

When installing link, ensure the following to avoid mis-installation:

- Heavier, thicker end goes toward crossmember
- Fore-or-aft bow faces forward (curves around coil spring)
- Up-or-down bow faces downward

7. Place link in bracket on crossmember.

Install bolt and nut as shown in the accompanying figure. Do not tighten bolt at this time.

8. Install bolt and nut mounting link to knuckle as shown in the accompanying figure. Do not tighten bolt at this time.

9. Set repair-side of rear suspension to curb height using following tools:

a. Place Receiver, Special Tool 9031-3, cup-side-down over top of crossmember rear mount bushing.

b. Place Curb Height Gage, Special Tool 9094, into shock absorber pocket in spring link and opposite end of tool over Receiver, Special Tool 9031-3.

c. Install bolt through crossmember rear mount bushing, Receiver, Special Tool 9031-3, and Curb Height Gage, Special Tool 9094. Install wing nut, hand tightening it tools in place.

d. Move spring link up or down as necessary aligning shock mounting bolt hole with Curb Height Gage hole, then insert pin through both.

10. Tighten camber link mounting bolts as follows:

a. Bolt at crossmember: 50 ft. lbs. (68 Nm)

b. Bolt at knuckle: 70 ft. lbs. (95 Nm)

11. Remove special tools.

12. Install rear shock absorber and components removed to access it.

13. Lower vehicle.

14. Perform wheel alignment.

Compression Link

See Figure 168.

1. Before servicing the vehicle, refer to the precautions in the beginning of this section.
2. Raise and support vehicle.
3. Remove tire and wheel assembly.
4. Remove bolt and nut mounting link at knuckle.
5. Remove bolt and nut mounting link at crossmember.
6. Remove link.

To install:

➡Although the compression link is different end-to-end, there is no top and bottom.

7. Position link and install bolt and nut mounting link at crossmember. Do not tighten bolt at this time.
8. Install bolt and nut mounting link at knuckle. Do not tighten bolt at this time.
9. Install tire and wheel assembly. Tighten the lug nuts to 100 ft. lbs. (135 Nm).
10. Lower vehicle.
11. Position vehicle on alignment rack/drive-on hoist. Raise vehicle as necessary to access link fasteners.
12. Tighten compression link fasteners as follows:

a. Bolt at crossmember: 50 ft. lbs. (68 Nm)

b. Bolt at knuckle: 60 ft. lbs. (81 Nm)

13. Perform wheel alignment.

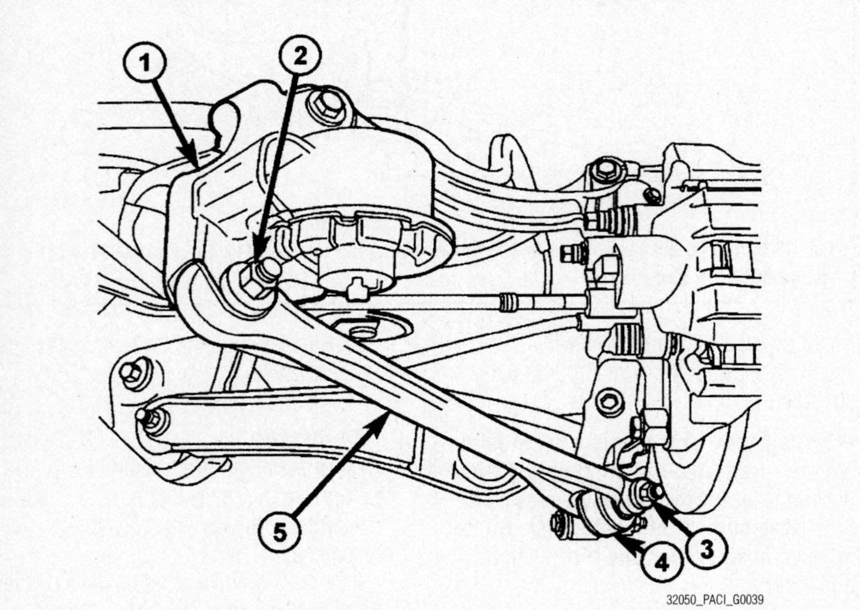

Fig. 168 View of the rear suspension crossmember (1), mounting bolts and nuts (2 & 3), knuckle (4) and compression link (5)

Spring Link

See Figures 169 through 173

1. Before servicing the vehicle, refer to the precautions in the beginning of this section.
2. Raise and support vehicle.
3. Access and remove rear spring.
4. Remove spring link-to-knuckle nut and bolt.

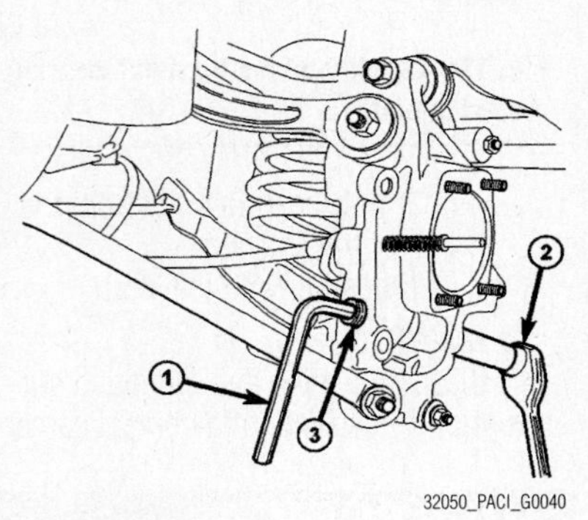

Fig. 169 Use a hex wrench (1) on the bolt head (3) with a ratchet and socket on the nut (2) to remove the spring link-to-knuckle bolt and nut

⁂ WARNING

It is important to use Guide, Special Tool 9050A-2, when tapping sleeve to help keep Tap, Special Tool 9050A-1, straight during use or damage to Tap may occur.

5. Place Guide 9050A-2 against sleeve in knuckle as shown.

6. Insert Tap 9050A-1, on an appropriate handle, through Guide and into sleeve. Cut threads approximately halfway through bush-

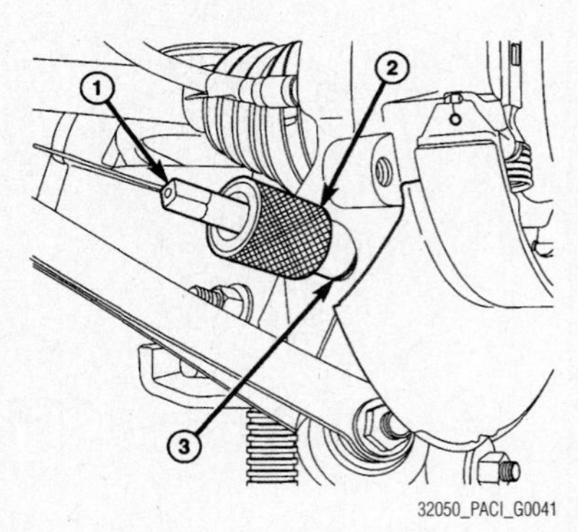

Fig. 170 Place Guide 9050A-2 (2) against sleeve in knuckle. Insert Tap 9050A-1 (1), on an appropriate handle, through Guide and into sleeve (3)

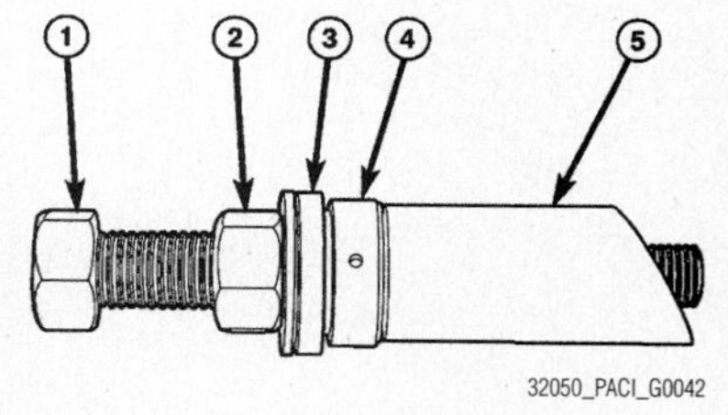

Fig. 171 Assembled Remover 9050A—bolt 9050A-3 (1), Nut (2), Spherical Washer (3), Thrust Bushing (4) and Sleeve 9050A-5 (5)

ing (or about six complete threads). It is important to back Tap out often and clean out burrs that can build up inside Guide. Keep Tap well lubricated to avoid damaging it.

➡Prior to using Remover, Special Tool 9050A, lubricate Bolt threads to provide ease of use and promote tool longevity.

7. Assemble Remover 9050A as shown.

➡When installing thrust bearing on Remover, be sure to place hardened side toward nut.

8. Remove sleeve retaining spring link ball joint in knuckle as follows:
   a. Hand thread assembled Remover 9050A into tapped knuckle sleeve until it stops.
   b. Rotate Nut down, matching Sleeve 9050A-5 angled end with angled face of knuckle.
   c. Continue to rotate Nut until knuckle sleeve is removed from knuckle. Discard knuckle sleeve; replace it with new upon installation.
9. Remove bolt and nut fastening spring link to crossmember.
10. Remove spring link.

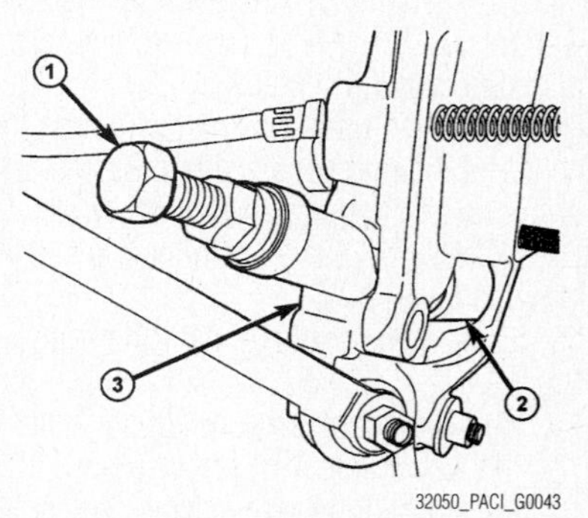

Fig. 172 Remover 9050A (1) positioned for sleeve removal

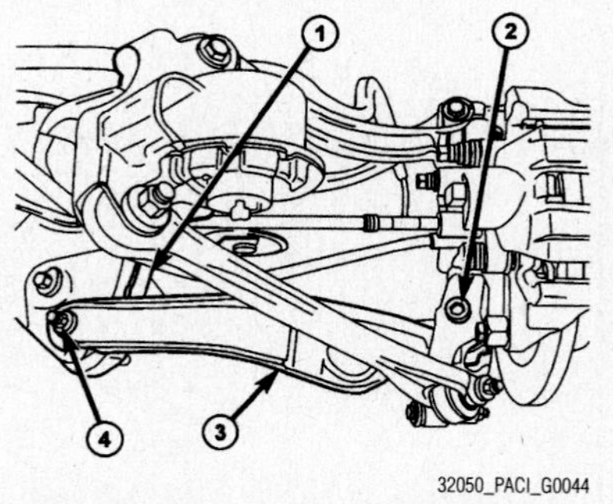

Fig. 173 Exploded view of the crossmember (1), mounting bolt and nut (2), spring link (3) and mounting bolt and nut (4)

To install:

11. Guide ball joint end of spring link into mounting pocket of knuckle, then swing opposite end up to bushing in crossmember and install bolt and nut fastening spring link to crossmember. Do not tighten bolt at this time.

➡Prior to using Special Tool 9050A, lubricate Bolt threads to provide ease of use and promote tool longevity.

12. Place new knuckle sleeve onto Installer Bolt, Special Tool 9050-4, and slide it up to bolt's head.
13. Install NEW sleeve in knuckle as follows:
14. Slide Installer Bolt 9050A-4 (with sleeve) through knuckle and spring link ball joint starting from knuckle forward end.
15. Install thrust bearing and nut on end of bolt. When installing thrust bearing on Installer Bolt, be sure to place hardened side toward nut.
16. While holding Bolt head stationary, rotate Nut (using hand tools) installing sleeve in knuckle. Install sleeve until Nut can no longer be turned. Do not overtighten Nut.
17. Remove tool.
18. Install spring link-to-knuckle bolt and nut as shown. While holding bolt head stationary, tighten nut to 95 ft. lbs. (129 Nm).
19. Install rear spring as well as all components necessary to access it.
20. Lower vehicle.
21. Position vehicle on alignment rack/drive-on hoist. Raise vehicle as necessary to access mounting bolt.
22. Tighten spring link bolt at crossmember to 80 ft. lbs. (108 Nm).
23. Perform wheel alignment.

Tension Link

See Figures 174 and 175.

1. Before servicing the vehicle, refer to the precautions in the beginning of this section.
2. Raise and support vehicle. Access and remove rear shock absorber.

➡Repair-side of crossmember must be lowered from body approximately three inches in order to properly access link mounting bolts at crossmember.

3. Remove nut and bolt mounting link to knuckle.
4. Remove nut and bolt mounting link to crossmember.
5. Remove link.

To install:

➡When installing link, although the link is the same end-to-end, ensure that the center bow faces downward.

6. Place link in bracket on crossmember. Install bolt and nut as shown in the accompanying figure. Do not tighten bolt at this time.
7. Install bolt and nut mounting link to knuckle as shown in the accompanying figure. Do not tighten bolt at this time.
8. Set repair-side of rear suspension to curb height using following tools:
   a. Place Receiver, Special Tool 9031-3, cup-side-down over top of crossmember rear mount bushing.
   b. Place Curb Height Gage, Special Tool 9094, into shock absorber pocket in spring link and opposite end of tool over Receiver, Special Tool 9031-3.
   c. Install bolt through crossmember rear mount bushing, Receiver, Special Tool 9031-3, and Curb Height Gage, Special Tool 9094. Install wing nut, hand tightening it tools in place.
   d. Move spring link up or down as necessary aligning shock mounting bolt hole with Curb Height Gage hole, then insert pin through both.

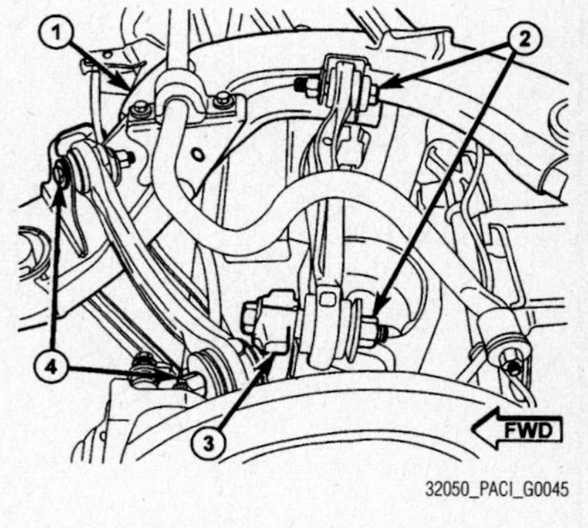

Fig. 174 View of the rear suspension crossmember (1), camber link mounting bolts (2), knuckle (3) and tension link mounting bolts (4)

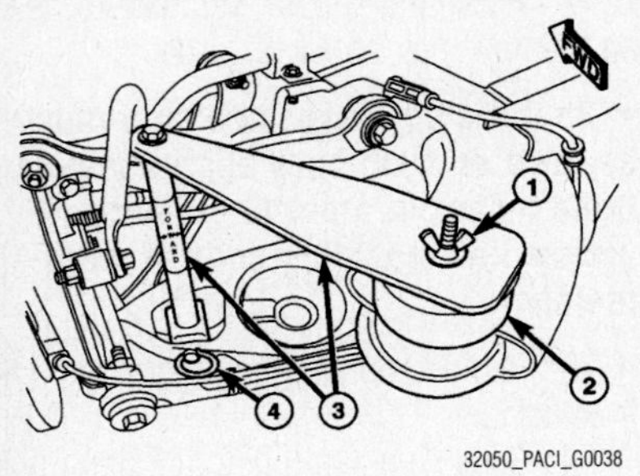

Fig. 175 Curb height gauge mounted in place—Wing nut and bolt (1), Receiver 9031-3 (2), Gauge 9094 (3), and Pin (4)

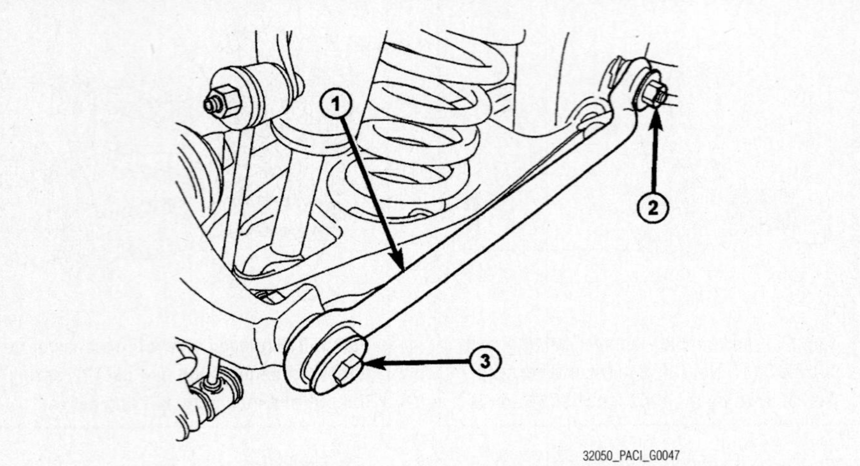

Fig. 177 View of the toe link (1), mounting nut and crossmember (2) and mounting bolt at knuckle (3)

9. Tighten tension link mounting bolts as follows:
   a. Bolt at crossmember: 50 ft. lbs. (68 Nm)
   b. Bolt at knuckle: 88 ft. lbs. (119 Nm)
10. Remove special tools.
11. Install rear shock absorber and components removed to access it.
12. Lower vehicle.
13. Perform wheel alignment.

Toe Link

See Figures 176 and 177.

1. Before servicing the vehicle, refer to the precautions in the beginning of this section.
2. Raise and support vehicle.
3. Remove tire and wheel assembly.
4. If removing the right side link, move rear exhaust out of way as necessary to access toe link mounting nut at crossmember.
5. Unclip wheel speed sensor cable from toe link.
6. While holding toe adjustment cam bolt from rotating. remove nut securing toe link at crossmember.
7. Remove bolt and nut at knuckle.
8. Remove link.

To install:

➡Make sure cam washer is installed on end of cam bolt before installing toe link on cam bolt. Slide offset end of toe link over cam bolt at crossmember.

9. Install bolt and nut securing link to knuckle. Do not tighten bolt at this time.
10. While holding toe adjustment cam bolt from rotating (cam facing upward). Install nut securing toe link at crossmember. Do not tighten nut at this time.
11. Clip wheel speed sensor cable along top of toe link at flats machined into link.
12. If removed, install rear exhaust as necessary.
13. Install tire and wheel assembly. Torque the lug nuts to 100 ft. lbs. (135 Nm).
14. Lower vehicle.
15. Position vehicle on alignment rack/drive-on hoist. Raise vehicle as necessary to access mounting bolts.
16. Tighten toe link fasteners as follows:
   a. Nut at crossmember: 127 ft. lbs. (172 Nm). This nut may be tightened after rear wheel alignment toe is set.
   b. Bolt at knuckle: 80 ft. lbs. (108 Nm).
17. Perform wheel alignment.

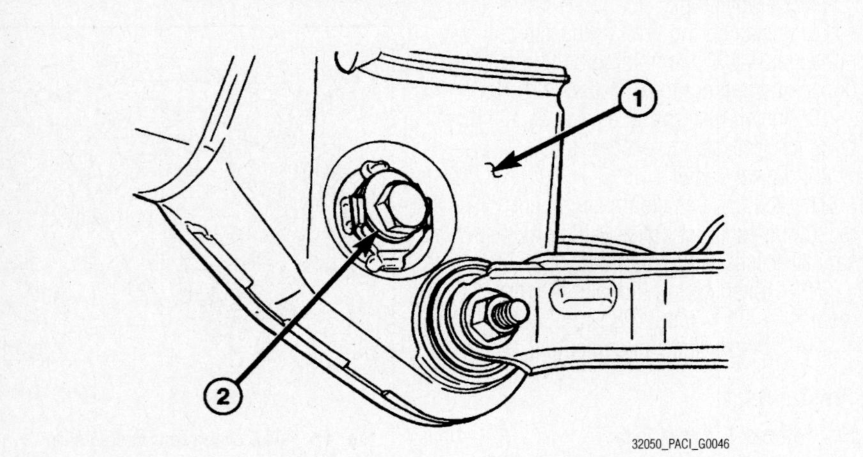

Fig. 176 While holding toe adjustment cam bolt (1) from rotating, remove nut securing toe link at crossmember (2)

SHOCK ABSORBER

REMOVAL & INSTALLATION

See Figure 178.

1. Before servicing the vehicle, refer to the precautions in the beginning of this section.
2. Remove or disconnect the following:
   - Rear wheel
3. Position jack stands under the forward end of the engine cradle to support and stabilizer the vehicle.
4. Place a transmission jack under the center of the rear suspension crossmember on models not equipped with All Wheel Drive (AWD) or rear driveline module, if equipped with AWD.
5. Remove or disconnect the following:
   - Two shock absorber upper bolts
   - Lower shock absorber bolts
   - Front and rear crossmember bolts
6. Lower the jack slowly enough so to allow the top of the shock absorber to clear

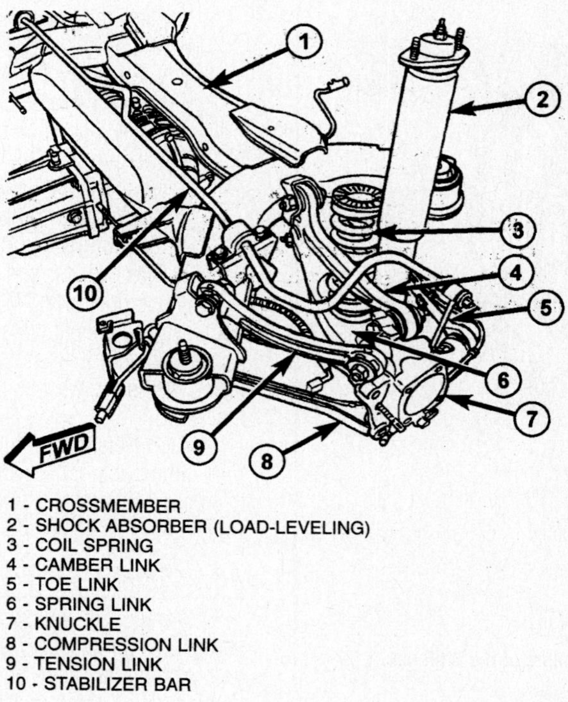

Fig. 178 Exploded view of the rear suspension components

the body flange and remove the shock absorber by tipping it outwards and lifting the lower end out of the pocket in the spring link.

7. Remove the coil spring and isolator lower end first, if necessary. Never lower the jack any more than necessary for removal and installation.

To install:

8. Install or connect the following:
   - Coil spring isolator on top of the sprint, then the spring top end first. Match the lower end coil against the abutment in the spring link.
   - Shock absorber by setting the lower end into the pocket in the spring link, then tipping the top inwards. Hand start the upper mounting bolts

9. Raise the jack slowly guiding the spring and lower end of the shock absorber into position. Once the bolt holes are aligned, stop jacking. Install and hand tighten the bolts.

10. Raise the jack until the two crossmember bolts can be installed and tighten to 120 ft. lbs. (163 Nm).

11. Tighten the upper shock absorber bolts to 45 ft. lbs. (61 Nm) and remove the jack.

12. Install the wheels, position the vehicle on an alignment rack and raise the vehicle enough to access the lower shock absorber bolts. Tighten the bolts to 75 ft. lbs. (102 Nm).

13. Have the rear wheel toe set to specifications.

WHEEL BEARINGS

REMOVAL & INSTALLATION

See Figures 179 and 180.

1. Before servicing the vehicle, refer to the precautions in the beginning of this section.

2. Remove or disconnect the following:
   - Rear wheel

3. If equipped with All Wheel Drive (AWD), remove the cotter pin, nut and spring washer. Have someone apply the brake pedal and remove the hub nut.
   - Brake caliper and rotor
   - Wheel Speed Sensor (WSS) connector from the spare tire mounting support
   - Two sensor cable routing clips along the toe link
   - Sensor cable from the bracket on the brake support
   - Loosen but do not remove the hub/bearing retaining bolts. Once loosened, push the bolts against the rear of the hub to keep the brake support in place when the hub is removed.
   - Hub and thread the WSS cable through the hole in the brake support plate as you remove the hub

To install:

4. Install or connect the following:
   - Hub/bearing bolts through the rear of the knuckle and parking brake support just enough to hold the support in place
   - Hub/bearing first feeding the WSS cable through the hole in the brake support. At the same time, slide the hub/bearing onto the halfshaft, if equipped with AWD. Place the hub/bearing through the brake support onto the knuckle and align the

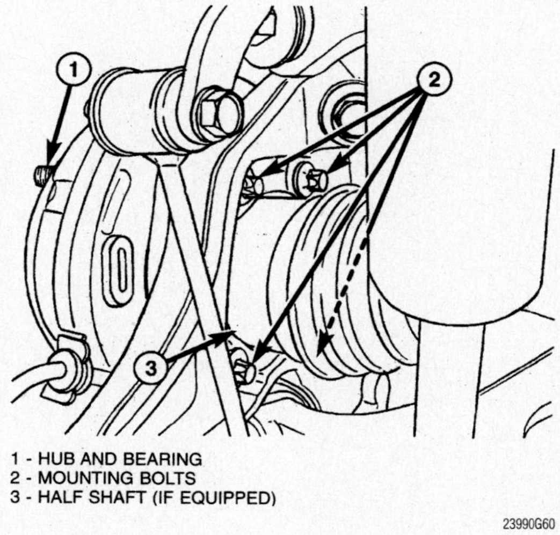

Fig. 179 Location of the rear hub/bearing mounting bolts

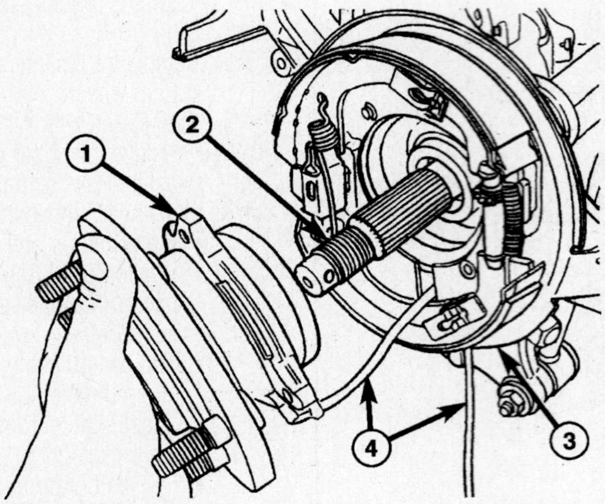

Fig. 180 When removing/installing the rear hub/bearing assembly, thread the WSS cable through the hole in the brake support plate

bolt mounting holes with bolts and place the WSS head at the bottom.

- Four hub/bearing bolts and tighten to 60 ft. lbs. (81 Nm)
- Sensor cable onto the bracket on the brake support and route the cable
- Two sensor cable routing clips along the toe link
- WSS connector to the spare tire mounting support
- Brake caliper and rotor

5. If equipped with AWD, install the hub nut, have someone apply the brake and tighten the nut to 180 ft. lbs. (244 Nm). Install the spring washer, nut lock and cotter pin.

- Wheels

6. Pump the brake pedal several times to ensure proper operation and road test the vehicle.

ADJUSTMENT

This vehicle is equipped with permanently sealed rear wheel bearings. There is no periodic lubrication or maintenance recommended for these units.

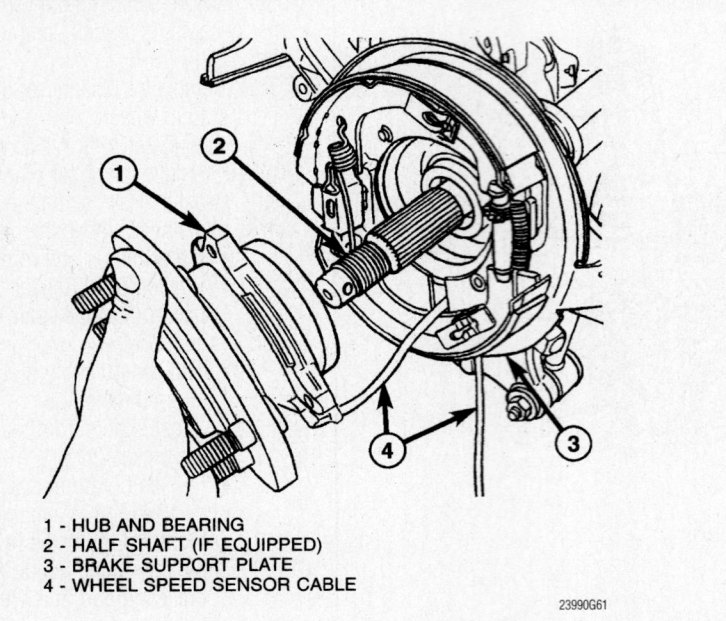

CHRYSLER

12

PT Cruiser

SPECIFICATIONS AND MAINTENANCE CHARTS

ENGINE AND VEHICLE IDENTIFICATION

Engine							Model Year	
Code ①	Liters (cc)	Cu. In.	Cyl.	Fuel Sys.	Engine Type	Eng. Mfg.	Code ②	Year
B	2.4 (2429)	148	L4	SMFI	DOHC	Chrysler	5	2005
							6	2006
							7	2007

DOHC: Double Overhead Camshaft

SMFI: Sequential Multi-port Fuel Injection

① 8th position of VIN

② 10th position of VIN

22043_PTCR_C0001

GENERAL ENGINE SPECIFICATIONS

Year	Model	Engine Displacement Liters	Net Horsepower @ rpm	Net Torque @ rpm (ft. lbs.)	Bore x Stroke (in.)	Com-pression Ratio	Oil Pressure @ rpm
2005	PT Cruiser	2.4	150@5200	164@4000	3.44x3.98	9.4:1	25-80@3000
2006	PT Cruiser	2.4	150@5200	164@4000	3.44x3.98	9.4:1	25-80@3000
2007	PT Cruiser	2.4	150@5200	164@4000	3.44x3.98	9.4:1	25-80@3000

22043_PTCR_C0002

ENGINE TUNE-UP SPECIFICATIONS

Year	Engine Displacement Liters	Spark Plug Gap (in.)	Ignition Timing (deg.)	Fuel Pump (psi)	Idle Speed (rpm)	Valve Clearance	
						In.	Ex.
2005	2.4	0.048-0.053	①	49	②	HYD	HYD
2006	2.4	0.048-0.053	①	49	②	HYD	HYD
2007	2.4	0.048-0.053	①	49	②	HYD	HYD

NOTE: The Vehicle Emission Control Information label often reflects specification changes made during production.

The label figures must be used if they differ from those in this chart.

HYD: Hydraulic

① Ignition timing is regulated by the Powertrain Control Module (PCM), and cannot be adjusted.

② Idle speed is controled by the Powertrain Control Module (PCM), and cannot be adjusted.

22043_PTCR_C0003

CAPACITIES

Year	Model	Engine Displacement Liters	Engine ID/VIN	Engine Oil with Filter (qts.)	Transmission (pts.)		Fuel Tank (gal.)	Cooling System (qts.)
					5-Spd	Auto.		
2005	PT Cruiser	2.4	B	5.0	5.0-5.6	8.0	15.0	6.5
2006	PT Cruiser	2.4	B	5.0	5.0-5.6	8.0	15.0	6.5
2007	PT Cruiser	2.4	B	5.0	5.0-5.6	8.0	15.0	6.5

NOTE: All capacities are approximate. Add fluid gradually and ensure a proper fluid level is obtained.

22043_PTCR_C0004

FLUID SPECIFICATIONS

Year	Model	Engine Displacement Liters	Engine ID/VIN	Engine Oil	Auto. Trans.	Manual Trans.	Power Steering Fluid	Brake Master Cylinder
2005	PT Cruiser	2.4	B	5W-30	①	①	②	③
2006	PT Cruiser	2.4	B	5W-30	①	①	②	③
2007	PT Cruiser	2.4	B	5W-30	①	①	②	③

DOT: Department Of Transportation

① Mopar® ATF+4 Automatic Transmission Fluid or equivalent.

② Mopar® Power Steering Fluid+4, Mopar® ATF+4 Automatic Transmission Fluid or equivalent.

③ Mopar® DOT 3, SAE J1703 should be used. If DOT 3, SAE J1703 brake fluid is not available, then DOT 4 is acceptable. Use only recommended brake fluids.

22043_PTCR_C0005

VALVE SPECIFICATIONS

Year	Engine Displacement Liters	Seat Angle (deg.)	Face Angle (deg.)	Spring Test Pressure (lbs. @ in.)	Spring Installed Height (in.)	Stem-to-Guide Clearance (in.)		Stem Diameter (in.)	
						Intake	Exhaust	Intake	Exhaust
2005	2.4	45	44.5-45.0	129-143@ 1.17	1.50	0.0018-0.0025	0.0029-0.0037	0.2340	0.2330
2006	2.4	45	44.5-45.0	129-143@ 1.17	1.50	0.0018-0.0025	0.0029-0.0037	0.2340	0.2330
2007	2.4	45	44.5-45.0	129-143@ 1.17	1.50	0.0018-0.0025	0.0029-0.0037	0.2340	0.2330

22043_PTCR_C0006

CAMSHAFT AND BEARING SPECIFICATIONS CHART

All measurements are given in inches.

Year	Engine Displ. Liters	Engine ID/VIN	Journal Dia.	Brg. Oil Clearance	Shaft End-play	Runout	Journal Bore	Lobe Height	
								Intake	Exhaust
2005	2.4	B	1.0220-1.0230	0.0009-0.0025	0.0019-0.0066	NA	NA	0.3240	0.2590
2006	2.4	B	1.0220-1.0230	0.0009-0.0025	0.0019-0.0066	NA	NA	0.3240	0.2590
2007	2.4	B	1.0220-1.0230	0.0009-0.0025	0.0019-0.0066	NA	NA	0.3240	0.2590

NA: Not Available

22043_PTCR_C0007

CRANKSHAFT AND CONNECTING ROD SPECIFICATIONS

All measurements are given in inches.

Year	Engine Displacement Liters	Crankshaft				Connecting Rod		
		Main Brg. Journal Dia.	Main Brg. Oil Clearance	Shaft End-play	Thrust on No.	Journal Diameter	Oil Clearance	Side Clearance
2005	2.4	2.3610-2.3625	0.0007-0.0023	0.0035-0.0094	2	1.9670-1.9685	0.0009-0.0027	0.0051-0.0150
2006	2.4	2.3610-2.3625	0.0007-0.0023	0.0035-0.0094	2	1.9670-1.9685	0.0009-0.0027	0.0051-0.0150
2007	2.4	2.3610-2.3625	0.0007-0.0023	0.0035-0.0094	2	1.9670-1.9685	0.0009-0.0027	0.0051-0.0150

22043_PTCR_C0008

PISTON AND RING SPECIFICATIONS

All measurements are given in inches.

Year	Engine Displacement Liters	Piston Clearance	Ring Gap			Ring Side Clearance		
			Top Compression	Bottom Compression	Oil Control	Top Compression	Bottom Compression	Oil Control
2005	2.4	0.0009-0.0022	0.0098-0.0200	0.0090-0.0180	0.0098-0.0250	0.0011-0.0031	0.0011-0.0031	0.0004-0.0070
2006	2.4	0.0009-0.0022	0.0098-0.0200	0.0090-0.0180	0.0098-0.0250	0.0011-0.0031	0.0011-0.0031	0.0004-0.0070
2007	2.4	0.0009-0.0022	0.0098-0.0200	0.0090-0.0180	0.0098-0.0250	0.0011-0.0031	0.0011-0.0031	0.0004-0.0070

22043_PTCR_C0009

TORQUE SPECIFICATIONS

All readings in ft. lbs.

Year	Engine Displacement Liters	Cylinder Head Bolts	Main Bearing Bolts	Rod Bearing Bolts	Crankshaft Damper Bolts	Flywheel Bolts	Manifold Intake	Manifold Exhaust	Spark Plugs	Oil Pan Drain Plug
2005	2.4	①	②	③	100	70	④	17	20	20
2006	2.4	①	②	③	100	70	④	17	20	20
2007	2.4	①	②	③	100	70	④	17	20	20

① Step 1: 25 ft. lbs.
Step 2: 50 ft. lbs.
Step 3: 50 ft. lbs.
Step 4: Plus 1/4 turn

② M8 bolts: 20 ft. lbs.
M11 bolts: 30 ft. lbs. plus 1/4 turn

③ Step 1: 20 ft. lbs.
Step 2: Plus 1/4 turn

④ Lower manifold: non turbo models 105 inch lbs.
Lower manifold: turbo models 250 inch lbs.
Upper manifold: non turbo models 105 inch lbs.
Upper manifold: turbo models 250 inch lbs.

22043_PTCR_C0010

WHEEL ALIGNMENT SPECIFICATIONS

Year	Model		Caster Range (+/-Deg.)	Caster Preferred Setting (Deg.)	Camber Range (+/-Deg.)	Camber Preferred Setting (Deg.)	Toe-in (in.)
2005	PT Cruiser	F	+1.00	+2.45	+0.40	0.00	0.00 + 0.40
		R	—	—	+0.40	+0.20	+0.00 + 0.40
2006	PT Cruiser	F	+1.00	+2.45	+0.40	0.00	0.00 + 0.40
		R	—	—	+0.40	+0.20	+0.00 + 0.40
2007	PT Cruiser	F	+1.00	+2.45	+0.40	0.00	0.00 + 0.40
		R	—	—	+0.40	+0.20	+0.00 + 0.40

F: Front
R: Rear

22043_PTCR_C0011

TIRE, WHEEL AND BALL JOINT SPECIFICATIONS

Year	Model	OEM Tires Standard	OEM Tires Optional	Tire Pressures (psi) Front	Tire Pressures (psi) Rear	Wheel Size	Ball Joint Inspection	Lug Nuts
2005	PT Cruiser	P205/55R16	None	①	①	5.5-J	②	100
2006	PT Cruiser	P205/55R16	None	①	①	5.5-J	②	100
2007	PT Cruiser	P205/55R16	None	①	①	5.5-J	②	100

OEM: Original Equipment Manufacturer

PSI: Pounds Per Square Inch

① See placard on vehicle

② Replace if any measurable movement is found

22043_PTCR_C0012

BRAKE SPECIFICATIONS

All measurements in inches unless noted

Year	Model		Brake Disc Original Thickness	Brake Disc Minimum Thickness	Brake Disc Maximum Run-out	Brake Drum Diameter Original Inside Diameter	Brake Drum Diameter Max. Wear Limit	Brake Drum Diameter Maximum Machine Diameter	Min. Lining Thick-ness	Caliper Guide Pin Bolts (ft. lbs.)
2005	PT Cruiser	F	0.902-0.909	0.803	0.005	—	—	—	0.313	26
		R	0.344-0.364	0.285	0.005	8.63-8.65	NA	NA	①	16
2006	PT Cruiser	F	0.902-0.909	0.803	0.005	—	—	—	0.313	26
		R	0.344-0.364	0.285	0.005	8.63-8.65	NA	NA	①	16
2007	PT Cruiser	F	0.902-0.909	0.803	0.005	—	—	—	0.313	26
		R	0.344-0.364	0.285	0.005	8.63-8.65	NA	NA	①	16

NA: Not Available

F: Front

R: Rear

① Rear Disc: 0.350 in.

Rear Bonded Shoes: 0.062 in.

Rear Riveted Shoes: 0.031 in.

22043_PTCR_C0013

SCHEDULED MAINTENANCE INTERVALS
Chrysler—PT Cruiser

TO BE SERVICED	TYPE OF SERVICE	VEHICLE MILEAGE INTERVAL (x1000)												
		7.5	15	22.5	30	37.5	45	52.5	60	67.5	75	82.5	90	97.5
Engine oil & filter	R	✓	✓	✓	✓	✓	✓	✓	✓	✓	✓	✓	✓	✓
Brake hoses	S/I	✓	✓	✓	✓	✓	✓	✓	✓	✓	✓	✓	✓	✓
Coolant level, hoses & clamps	S/I	✓	✓	✓	✓	✓	✓	✓	✓	✓	✓	✓	✓	✓
CV joints & front suspension components	S/I	✓	✓	✓	✓	✓	✓	✓	✓	✓	✓	✓	✓	✓
Exhaust system	S/I	✓	✓	✓	✓	✓	✓	✓	✓	✓	✓	✓	✓	✓
Manual transaxle oil	S/I	✓	✓	✓	✓	✓	✓	✓	✓	✓	✓	✓	✓	✓
Rotate tires	S/I	✓	✓	✓	✓	✓	✓	✓	✓	✓	✓	✓	✓	✓
Accessory drive belts	S/I		✓		✓		✓		✓		✓		✓	
Brake linings	S/I			✓			✓			✓			✓	
Air filter element	R				✓				✓				✓	
Spark plugs	R				✓				✓				✓	
Lubricate ball joints	S/I				✓				✓				✓	
Engine coolant ①	R													
PCV valve	S/I								✓				✓	
Ignition cables	R								✓					
Camshaft timing belt ②	R													

R: Replace S/I: Service or Inspect

① Engine coolant: flush and replace at 100,000 miles.

② Camshaft timing belt: replace at 120,000 miles.

FREQUENT OPERATION MAINTENANCE (SEVERE SERVICE)

If a vehicle is operated under any of the following conditions it is considered severe service:

- Extremely dusty areas.

- 50% or more of the vehicle operation is in 32°C (90°F) or higher temperatures, or constant operation in temperatures below 0°C (32°F).

- Prolonged idling (vehicle operation in stop and go traffic).

- Frequent short running periods (engine does not warm to normal operating temperatures).

- Police, taxi, delivery usage or trailer towing usage.

Oil & oil filter change: change every 3000 miles.

Rotate tires every 6000 miles.

Brake linings: inspect every 12,000 miles.

Air filter element: service or inspect every 15,000 miles.

Automatic transaxle: change fluid & adjust bands every 15,000 miles.

Manual transaxle fluid: replace every 15,000 miles.

Engine coolant: replace at 36,000 miles and every 30,000 miles thereafter.

22043_PTCR_C0014

PRECAUTIONS

Before servicing any vehicle, please be sure to read all of the following precautions, which deal with personal safety, prevention of component damage, and important points to take into consideration when servicing a motor vehicle:

- Never open, service or drain the radiator or cooling system when the engine is hot; serious burns can occur from the steam and hot coolant.
- Observe all applicable safety precautions when working around fuel. Whenever servicing the fuel system, always work in a well-ventilated area. Do not allow fuel spray or vapors to come in contact with a spark, open flame, or excessive heat (a hot drop light, for example). Keep a dry chemical fire extinguisher near the work area. Always keep fuel in a container specifically designed for fuel storage; also, always properly seal fuel containers to avoid the possibility of fire or explosion. Refer to the additional fuel system precautions later in this section.
- Fuel injection systems often remain pressurized, even after the engine has been turned **OFF**. The fuel system pressure must be relieved before disconnecting any fuel lines. Failure to do so may result in fire and/or personal injury.
- Brake fluid often contains polyglycol ethers and polyglycols. Avoid contact with the eyes and wash your hands thoroughly after handling brake fluid. If you do get brake fluid in your eyes, flush your eyes with clean, running water for 15 minutes. If eye irritation persists, or if you have taken brake fluid internally, IMMEDIATELY seek medical assistance.
- The EPA warns that prolonged contact with used engine oil may cause a number of skin disorders, including cancer. You should make every effort to minimize your exposure to used engine oil. Protective gloves should be worn when changing oil. Wash your hands and any other exposed skin areas as soon as possible after exposure to used engine oil. Soap and water, or waterless hand cleaner should be used.
- All new vehicles are now equipped with an air bag system, often referred to as a Supplemental Restraint System (SRS) or Supplemental Inflatable Restraint (SIR) system. The system must be disabled before performing service on or around system components, steering column, instrument panel components, wiring and sensors. Failure to follow safety and disabling procedures could result in accidental air bag deployment, possible personal injury and unnecessary system repairs.
- Always wear safety goggles when working with, or around, the air bag system. When carrying a non-deployed air bag, be sure the bag and trim cover are pointed away from your body. When placing a non-deployed air bag on a work surface, always face the bag and trim cover upward, away from the surface. This will reduce the motion of the module if it is accidentally deployed. Refer to the additional air bag system precautions later in this section.
- Clean, high quality brake fluid from a sealed container is essential to the safe and proper operation of the brake system. You should always buy the correct type of brake fluid for your vehicle. If the brake fluid becomes contaminated, completely flush the system with new fluid. Never reuse any brake fluid. Any brake fluid that is removed from the system should be discarded. Also, do not allow any brake fluid to come in contact with a painted surface; it will damage the paint.
- Never operate the engine without the proper amount and type of engine oil; doing so WILL result in severe engine damage.
- Timing belt maintenance is extremely important. Many models utilize an interference-type, non-freewheeling engine. If the timing belt breaks, the valves in the cylinder head may strike the pistons, causing potentially serious (also time-consuming and expensive) engine damage. Refer to the maintenance interval charts for the recommended replacement interval for the timing belt, and to the timing belt section for belt replacement and inspection.
- Disconnecting the negative battery cable on some vehicles may interfere with the functions of the on-board computer system(s) and may require the computer to undergo a relearning process once the negative battery cable is reconnected.
- When servicing drum brakes, only disassemble and assemble one side at a time, leaving the remaining side intact for reference.
- Only an MVAC-trained, EPA-certified automotive technician should service the air conditioning system or its components.

BRAKES

ANTI-LOCK BRAKE SYSTEM (ABS)

GENERAL INFORMATION

PRECAUTIONS

- Certain components within the ABS system are not intended to be serviced or repaired individually.
- Do not use rubber hoses or other parts not specifically specified for and ABS system. When using repair kits, replace all parts included in the kit. Partial or incorrect repair may lead to functional problems and require the replacement of components.
- Lubricate rubber parts with clean, fresh brake fluid to ease assembly. Do not use shop air to clean parts; damage to rubber components may result.
- Use only DOT 3 brake fluid from an unopened container.
- If any hydraulic component or line is removed or replaced, it may be necessary to bleed the entire system.
- A clean repair area is essential. Always clean the reservoir and cap thoroughly before removing the cap. The slightest amount of dirt in the fluid may plug an orifice and impair the system function. Perform repairs after components have been thoroughly cleaned; use only denatured alcohol to clean components. Do not allow ABS components to come into contact with any substance containing mineral oil; this includes used shop rags.
- The Anti-Lock control unit is a microprocessor similar to other computer units in the vehicle. Ensure that the ignition switch is **OFF** before removing or installing controller harnesses. Avoid static electricity discharge at or near the controller.
- If any arc welding is to be done on the vehicle, the control unit should be unplugged before welding operations begin.

SPEED SENSORS

REMOVAL & INSTALLATION

Front

See Figures 1 and 2.

1. Raise the vehicle.
2. Disconnect the wheel speed sensor cable connector from the wiring harness on the inside of the frame rail above the front suspension crossmember. The connector has a locking tab which that must be pulled

back before the connector release tang can be depressed, releasing the connection.

3. If the sensor being removed is a left front, unclip the speed sensor cable from the brake tube on the inside of and under the frame rail.

4. Remove the speed sensor cable grommet from the retaining bracket attached to the brake hose on the outside of the frame rail.

5. Remove the bolt mounting the wheel speed sensor head to the steering knuckle.

⁂ CAUTION

When removing a wheel speed sensor from the knuckle, do not use pliers on the sensor head. This may damage the sensor head. If the sensor has seized, use a hammer and a punch to tap the edge of the sensor head ear, rocking the sensor side-to-side until free.

6. Carefully, remove the sensor head and heat shield from the steering knuckle.

7. Remove the screw securing the wheel speed sensor to the rear of the strut. Remove the wheel speed sensor.

To install:

⁂ CAUTION

Failure to install speed sensor cables properly may result in contact with moving parts or an over extension of cables causing an open circuit. Be sure that cables are installed, routed, and clipped properly.

8. Attach the wheel speed sensor to the strut using the mounting screw.

9. Install the wheel speed sensor head

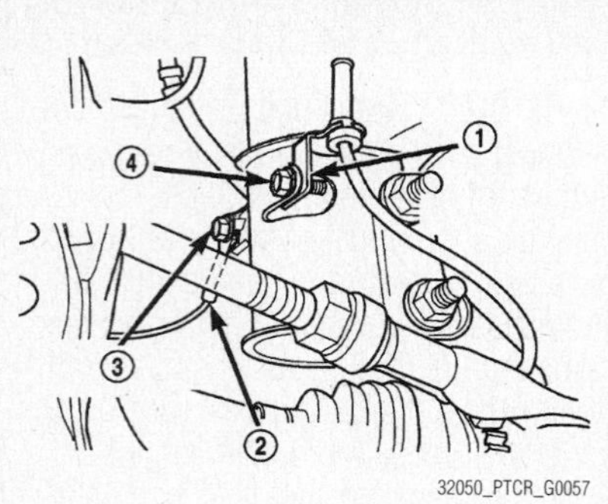

Fig. 2 Wheel speed sensor shown at strut

in the steering knuckle. Install the mounting bolt. Tighten the mounting bolt to a torque of 105 inch lbs. (12 Nm).

10. From the sensor bracket on the strut, loop the sensor cable upward, then downward at the outside of the frame rail. Install the speed sensor cable grommet onto the retaining bracket attached to the brake hose on the outside of the frame rail.

11. Loop the wheel speed sensor cable around the bottom of the frame rail and connect it to the wiring harness connector on the inside of the frame rail. Remember to push in the locking tab on the connector.

12. If the sensor being installed is the left front, clip the speed sensor cable to the brake tube on the inside of and under the frame rail.

13. Install the tire and wheel assembly. Progressively tighten wheel mounting nuts to 100 ft. lbs. (135 Nm).

14. Lower the vehicle.

15. Road test the vehicle to ensure proper operation of the base brakes and ABS.

Rear

See Figures 3 and 4.

1. Raise the vehicle.

2. Remove the tire and wheel assembly from the vehicle.

3. Disconnect the wheel speed sensor cable connector from the vehicle wiring harness.

4. Remove the clip attaching wheel speed sensor cable connector to the vehicle's body.

5. Disconnect the wheel speed sensor cable routing clips running along the brake tube, brake hose and axle trailing arm.

⁂ CAUTION

When removing a wheel speed sensor from the rear disc brake adapter, do not use pliers on the sensor head. This may damage the sensor head. If the sensor has seized, use a hammer and a punch to tap the edge of the sensor head ear, rocking the sensor side-to-side until free.

6. Remove the bolt attaching the wheel speed sensor to the rear disc brake adapter or drum brake support plate, then carefully remove the sensor head from the rear disc brake adapter and vehicle.

To install:

⁂ CAUTION

Failure to install speed sensor cables properly may result in contact with moving parts or an over extension of cables causing an open circuit. Be sure that cables are installed, routed, and clipped properly.

7. Install the wheel speed sensor head into the disc brake adapter or drum brake support plate.

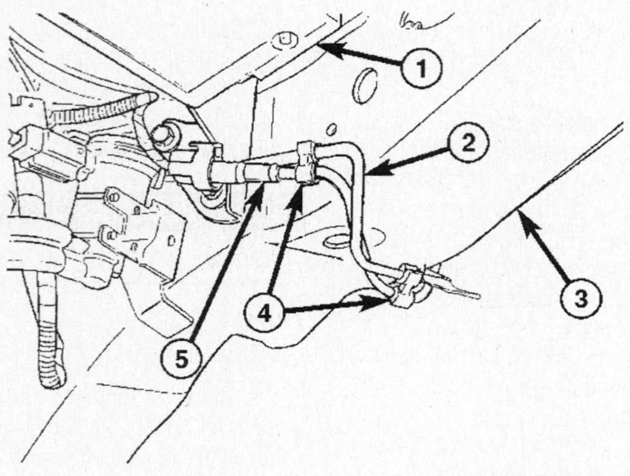

Fig. 1 Wheel sensor cable routing path—left shown

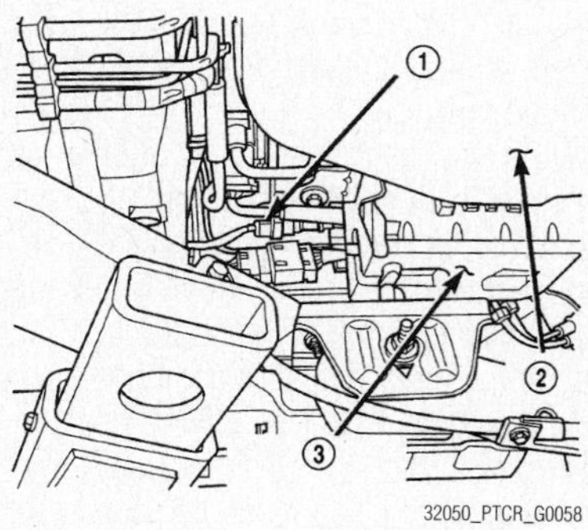

Fig. 3 Rear wheel speed sensor connection point

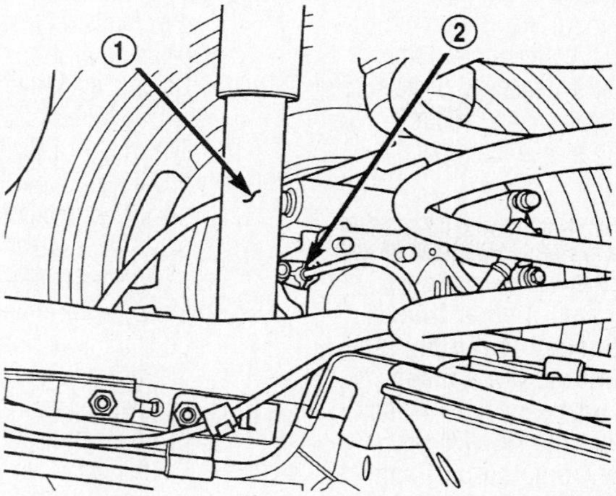

Fig. 4 Rear wheel speed sensor

8. Install the wheel speed sensor mounting bolt. Tighten the mounting bolt to a torque of 105 inch lbs. (12 Nm).

9. Install wheel speed sensor cable into the routing clips on the brake tube, brake hose and axle trailing arm.

10. Connect the wheel speed sensor cable connector into vehicle wiring harness. Install the clip attaching the wheel speed sensor cable connector to vehicle's body.

11. Install the tire and wheel assembly on vehicle. Progressively tighten wheel mounting nuts to 100 ft. lbs. (135 Nm).

12. Lower the vehicle.

13. Road test the vehicle to ensure proper operation of the base brakes and ABS.

BRAKES — BLEEDING THE BRAKE SYSTEM

BLEEDING PROCEDURE

BLEEDING PROCEDURE

⁂ WARNING

Before removing the master cylinder cap, wipe it clean to prevent dirt and other foreign matter from dropping into the master cylinder reservoir.

⁂ WARNING

Use only MOPAR® brake fluid, or equivalent, from a fresh, tightly sealed container. Brake fluid must conform to DOT 3 specifications.

Do not pump the brake pedal at any time while having a bleeder screw open during the bleeding process. This will only increase the amount of air in the system and make additional bleeding necessary.

Do not allow the master cylinder reservoir to run out of brake fluid while bleeding the system. An empty reservoir will allow additional air into the brake system. Check the fluid level frequently and add fluid as needed.

The following wheel circuit sequence for bleeding the brake hydraulic system should be used to ensure adequate removal of all trapped air from the hydraulic system.

- Left rear wheel
- Right front wheel
- Right rear wheel
- Left front wheel

1. Before servicing the vehicle, refer to the Precautions Section.

2. Attach a clear plastic hose to the bleeder screw and feed the hose into a clear jar containing enough fresh brake fluid to submerge the end of the hose.

3. Have a helper pump the brake pedal three or four times and hold it in the down position.

4. With the pedal in the down position, open the bleeder screw at least one full turn.

5. Once the brake pedal has dropped, close the bleeder screw. After the bleeder screw is closed, release the brake pedal.

6. Repeat the above steps until all trapped air is removed from that wheel circuit (usually four or five times).

7. Bleed the remaining wheel circuits in the same manner until all air is removed from the brake system. Monitor the fluid level in the master cylinder reservoir to make sure it does not go dry.

8. Check and adjust brake fluid level to the FULL mark.

9. Check the brake pedal travel. If pedal travel is excessive or has not been improved, some air may still be trapped in the system. Re-bleed the brakes as necessary.

10. Test drive the vehicle to verify the brakes are operating properly and pedal feel is correct.

MASTER CYLINDER BLEEDING

1. Before servicing the vehicle, refer to the Precautions Section.

2. Clamp the master cylinder in a vise with soft-jaw caps.

3. Attach the special tools for bleeding the master cylinder in the following fashion:

a. Thread Special Tool 8822-2 Bleeder Tube Adapters into the primary and secondary outlet ports of the master cylinder. Tighten the Adapters to 150 inch lbs. (17 Nm).

b. Thread Special Tool 8358-1 Bleeder Tube into each Adapter. Tighten tube nuts to 150 inch lbs. (17 Nm).

c. Flex each Bleeder Tube and place the open ends into the neck of the master cylinder reservoir. Position the open ends of the tubes into the reservoir so their outlets are below the surface of the brake fluid in the reservoir when filled.

➡Make sure the ends of the Bleeder Tubes stay below the surface of the brake fluid in the reservoir at all times during the bleeding procedure.

4. Fill the brake fluid reservoir with fresh MOPAR® Brake Fluid (DOT 3), or equivalent.

5. Using an appropriately sized wooden dowel as a pushrod, slowly press the pistons inward discharging brake fluid through the Bleeder Tubes, then release the pressure, allowing the pistons to return to the released position. Repeat this several times until all air bubbles are expelled from the master cylinder bore and Bleeder Tubes.

6. Remove the Bleeder Tubes and Adapters from the master cylinder and plug the master cylinder outlet ports.

7. Install the fill cap on the reservoir.

8. Remove the master cylinder from the vise.

9. Install the master cylinder on the vehicle.

BLEEDING THE ABS SYSTEM

➡The base brake's hydraulic system must be bled anytime air enters the hydraulic system. The ABS though, particularly the ICU (HCU), should only need to be bled when the HCU is replaced or removed from the vehicle. The ABS must always be bled anytime it is suspected that the HCU has ingested air. Under most circumstances that require the bleeding of the brake hydraulic system, only the base brake hydraulic system needs to be bled.

When bleeding the ABS system, the following bleeding sequence must be followed to insure complete and adequate bleeding.

- Make sure all hydraulic fluid lines are installed and properly torqued.
- Connect the DRBIII® scan tool to the Data Link Connector. The connector is located under the lower steering column cover to the left of the steering column.
- Using the DRBIII®, check to make sure the CAB does not have any fault codes stored. If it does, clear them using the DRBIII®.

⁂ WARNING

When bleeding the brake system, wear safety glasses. A clear bleed tube must be attached to the bleeder screws and submerged in a clear container filled part way with clean brake fluid. Direct the flow of the brake fluid away from yourself and the painted surfaces of the vehicle. Brake fluid at high pressure may come out of the bleeder screws when opened.

- Bleed the base brake system using the standard pressure or manual bleeding procedure.
- Using the DRBIII®, select ANTILOCK BRAKES, followed by MISCELLANEOUS, then BLEED BRAKES. Follow the instructions displayed. When the scan tool displays TEST COMPLETED, disconnect the scan tool and proceed.
- Bleed the base brake system a second time. Check brake fluid level in the reservoir periodically to prevent emptying, causing air to enter the hydraulic system.
- Fill the master cylinder reservoir to the full level.
- Test drive the vehicle to be sure the brakes are operating correctly and that the brake pedal does not feel spongy.

BRAKES

FRONT DISC BRAKES

⁂ CAUTION

Dust and dirt accumulating on brake parts during normal use may contain asbestos fibers from production or aftermarket brake linings. Breathing excessive concentrations of asbestos fibers can cause serious bodily harm. Exercise care when servicing brake parts. Do not sand or grind brake lining unless equipment used is designed to contain the dust residue. Do not clean brake parts with compressed air or by dry brushing. Cleaning should be done by dampening the brake components with a fine mist of water, then wiping the brake components clean with a dampened cloth. Dispose of cloth and all residue containing asbestos fibers in an impermeable container with the appropriate label. Follow practices prescribed by the Occupational Safety and Health Administration (OSHA) and the Environmental Protection Agency (EPA) for the handling, processing, and disposing of dust or debris that may contain asbestos fibers.

BRAKE CALIPER

REMOVAL & INSTALLATION

See Figure 5.

1. Before servicing the vehicle, refer to the precautions in the beginning of this section.
2. Isolate the master cylinder as follows:
   a. Use a brake pedal holding tool and depress the brake pedal past its first one inch of travel and hold it in this position. (This will keep brake fluid from draining from the master cylinder).
3. Remove or disconnect the following:
   - Front wheels
   - 2 caliper guide pin bolts
   - Brake hose from the caliper
   - Caliper from the steering spindle

To install:

4. Install or connect the following:
   - Brake hose to the caliper and torque to 210 inch lbs. (24 Nm)
   - Caliper to the steering spindle
   - Caliper guide pin bolts and torque to 26 ft. lbs. (35 Nm)
5. Properly bleed the brake system.
   - Front wheels and lower the vehicle.
6. Pump the brake pedal to seat the front brake pads before moving the vehicle.
7. Road test the vehicle and check for proper operation.

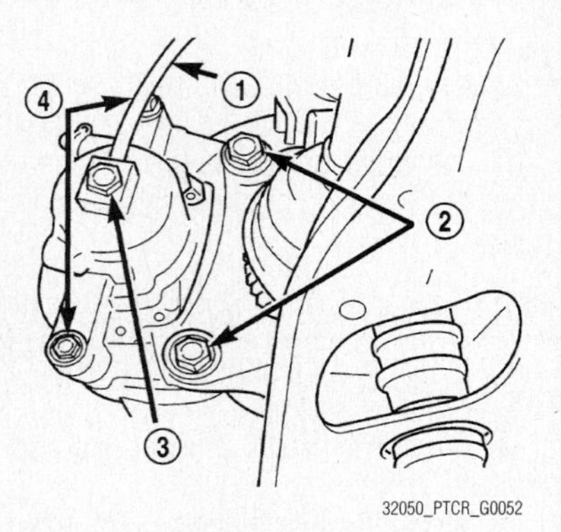

Fig. 5 Front brake caliper mounting point

DISC BRAKE PADS

REMOVAL & INSTALLATION

See Figure 6.

1. Before servicing the vehicle, refer to the precautions in the beginning of this section.
2. Remove or disconnect the following:
   - Front wheels
   - 2 caliper to steering knuckle guide pin bolts
   - Caliper away from the steering knuckle by first rotating the free end of the caliper away from the steering knuckle. Then, slide the opposite end of the caliper out from under the machined end of the steering knuckle.
3. Support the caliper from the upper control arm to prevent the weight of the caliper from being supported by the brake flex hose that will damage the hose.
   - Brake pads from the caliper
   - Outboard brake pad by prying the pad retaining clip over the raised area on the caliper. Then, slide the pad down and off the caliper
   - Inboard brake pad by pulling it away from the piston until the retaining clip is free from the cavity in the piston.
   - Rotor, if necessary, by pulling it

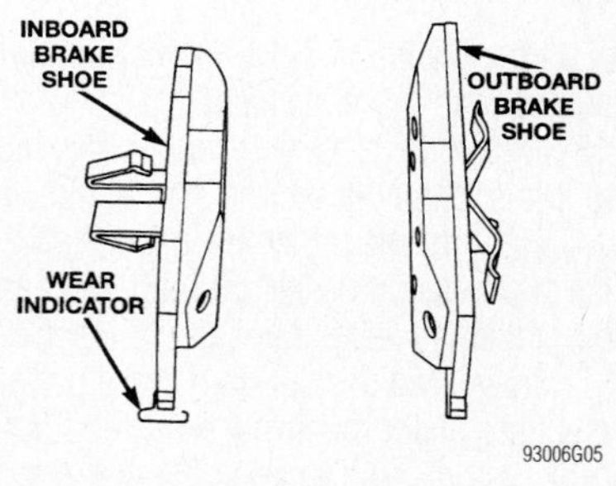

Fig. 6 Disc brake pad identification

straight off the wheel mounting studs

To install:

4. Clean all parts well. Inspect the caliper for piston seal leaks (brake fluid in and around the boot area and inboard lining) and for any ruptures of the piston dust boot. If the boot is damaged or fluid leak is visible, disassemble the caliper and install a new seal and boot (and piston, if scored).
5. Inspect the caliper pin bushings. Replace if damaged, dry or brittle.
6. Completely compress the piston into the caliper using a large C-clamp or other suitable tool.
7. Lubricate the area on the steering knuckle where the caliper slides with high temperature grease.
8. Install or connect the following:
   - Rotor if removed
   - Brake pads into the caliper. Note that the inboard and outboard pads are different. Make sure the inboard brake shoe assembly is positioned squarely against the face of the caliper piston.

➡Be sure to remove the noise suppression gasket paper cover if the pads come so equipped.

   - Caliper and brake shoe assemblies over the rotor by hooking the lower end of the caliper over the steering knuckle. Then, rotate the caliper into position at the top of the steering knuckle. Make sure the caliper guide pin bolts, bushings and sleeves are clear of the steering knuckle bosses.
   - Caliper guide pin bolts and torque to 26 ft. lbs. (35 Nm) on the front caliper or 192 inch lbs. (22 Nm) on the rear caliper
   - Wheels and torque the mounting bolts to 100 ft. lbs. (135 Nm)
9. Pump the brake pedal until the brake pads are seated and a firm pedal is achieved before attempting to move the vehicle.
10. Road test the vehicle for proper operation.

BRAKES — REAR DISC BRAKES

⁂ CAUTION

Dust and dirt accumulating on brake parts during normal use may contain asbestos fibers from production or aftermarket brake linings. Breathing excessive concentrations of asbestos fibers can cause serious bodily harm. Exercise care when servicing brake parts. Do not sand or grind brake lining unless equipment used is designed to contain the dust residue. Do not clean brake parts with compressed air or by dry brushing. Cleaning should be done by dampening the brake components with a fine mist of water, then wiping the brake components clean with a dampened cloth. Dispose of cloth and all residue containing asbestos fibers in an impermeable container with the appropriate label. Follow practices prescribed by the Occupational Safety and Health Administration (OSHA) and the Environmental Protection Agency (EPA) for the handling, processing, and disposing of dust or debris that may contain asbestos fibers.

BRAKE CALIPER

REMOVAL & INSTALLATION

See Figure 7.

1. Before servicing the vehicle, refer to the precautions in the beginning of this section.
2. Isolate the master cylinder as follows:
   a. Use a brake pedal holding tool and depress the brake pedal past its first one inch of travel and hold it in this position. (This will keep brake fluid from draining from the master cylinder).
3. Remove or disconnect the following:
   - Front wheels
   - 2 caliper guide pin bolts
   - Brake hose from the caliper
   - Caliper from the steering spindle

To install:

4. Install or connect the following:
   - Brake hose to the caliper and torque to 210 inch lbs. (24 Nm)
   - Caliper to the steering spindle
   - Caliper guide pin bolts and torque to 192 inch lbs. (22 Nm)
5. Properly bleed the brake system.
   - Front wheels and lower the vehicle.
6. Pump the brake pedal to seat the front brake pads before moving the vehicle.
7. Road test the vehicle and check for proper operation.

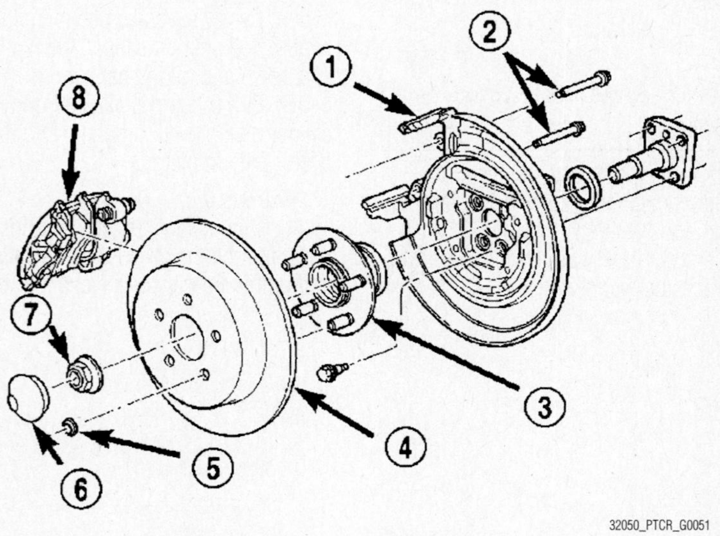

Fig. 7 Rear brake caliper assembly (8) and related components

DISC BRAKE PADS

REMOVAL & INSTALLATION

See Figures 8 through 10.

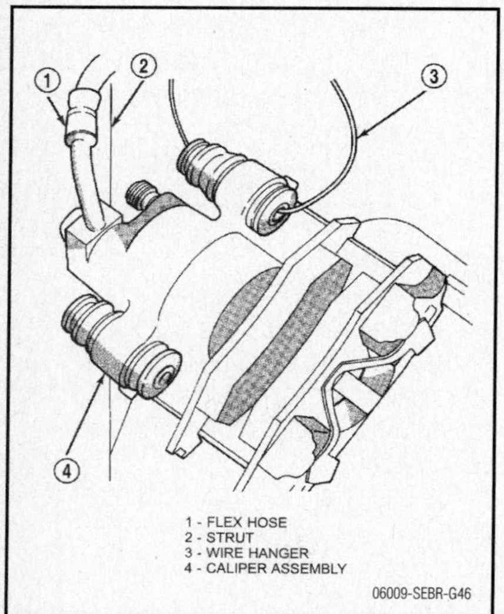

Fig. 8 Hanging the rear caliper

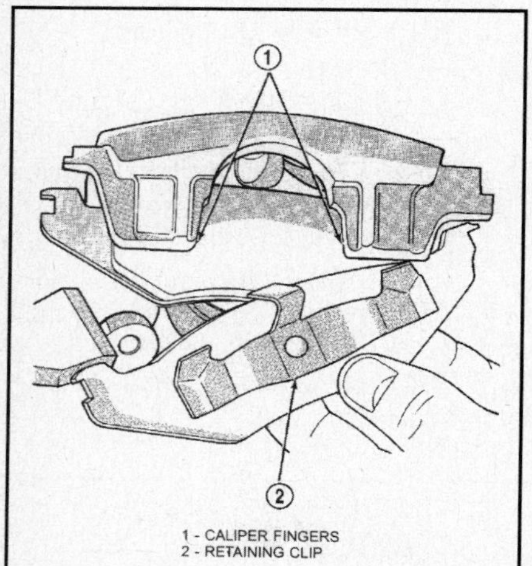

Fig. 9 Removing outboard brake pad—rear brakes

1. Before servicing the vehicle, refer to the Precautions Section.
2. Remove about half of the brake fluid from the master cylinder.

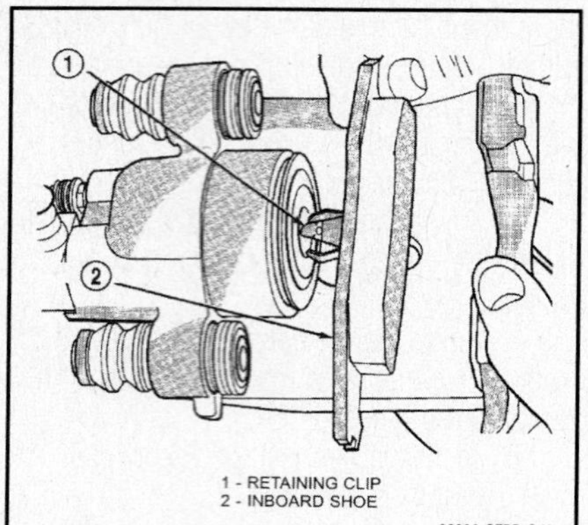

Fig. 10 Removing inboard brake pad—rear brakes

3. Raise the vehicle.
4. Remove the rear wheels and tires from vehicle.
5. Remove the 2 guide pin bolts mounting the caliper to the adapter.
6. Remove the caliper from adapter and rotor by first rotating the top of the caliper away from adapter, and then lifting the caliper off the lower machined abutment on adapter.

**** WARNING**

Supporting weight of caliper by the flexible brake fluid hose can damage the hose.

7. Support caliper from rear strut.
8. Remove the rear rotor from hub/bearing. Then inspect drum-in-hat parking brake shoes and parking brake braking surface on rotor for any signs of excessive wear or damage. Replace parking brake shoes if required.
9. Remove the outboard brake pad from caliper by prying brake pad retaining clip over raised area on caliper. Then slide brake pad down and off the caliper.
10. Pull inboard brake pad away from caliper piston, until retaining clip is free from cavity in piston.

To install:

11. Completely retract the caliper piston back into the piston bore of the caliper. This is required for caliper installation when new brake pad assemblies are installed on caliper.
12. Lubricate both adapter abutments with a liberal amount of MOPAR® Multipurpose Lubricant, or equivalent.
13. Install the rear rotor on hub making sure it is squarely seated on face of hub.
14. Remove the protective paper from noise suppression gasket on both inner and outer brake pad assemblies (if equipped).
15. Install the new inboard brake pad into caliper piston by firmly pressing it into bore of piston using thumbs. Be sure inboard brake pad is positioned squarely against face of piston.
16. Slide new outboard brake pad onto the caliper. Be sure retaining clip is squarely seated in the depressed areas on the caliper.

**** WARNING**

Use care when installing caliper assembly onto adapter, so the guide pin bushings and sleeves do not get damaged by the mounting bosses on adapter.

17. Carefully lower caliper and brake pads over rotor reversing the required removal procedure. Make sure that caliper guide pin bolts, bushings and sleeves are clear of the adapter bosses.

**** WARNING**

Extreme caution should be taken not to cross thread the caliper guide pin bolts when they are installed.

18. Install the caliper guide pin bolts into adapter. Tighten the guide pin bolts to 16 ft. lbs. (22 Nm).
19. Install the wheels and tires.
20. Tighten the wheel mounting stud nuts in proper sequence until all nuts are torqued to half specification. Then repeat the tightening sequence to the full specified torque of: 100 ft. lbs. (135 Nm).
21. Lower vehicle.
22. Pump the brake pedal several times. This will set the pads to the brake rotor.
23. Check and adjust brake fluid level as necessary.

BRAKE DRUM

REMOVAL & INSTALLATION

See Figure 11.

1. Before servicing the vehicle, refer to the precautions in the beginning of this section.
2. Remove or disconnect the following:
   - Rear wheels
   - Rubber plug from the top of the brake support plate (backing plate)
3. Insert a small prying tool through the adjuster access hole and engage the teeth on the adjuster wheel.
4. Rotate the adjuster wheel so it is moved toward the front of the vehicle. This will back off the adjustment of the rear brake shoes. Continue moving the adjuster wheel toward the front of the vehicle until it stops moving.
   - Rear brake drum from the hub assembly

To install:

5. Inspect the brake drums for cracks or signs of overheating. Measure the drum runout and diameter. If not to specification, resurface the drum. Runout should not exceed 0.006 inch (0.152mm). The diameter variation (oval shape) of the drum braking surface must not exceed either 0.0025 inch (0.0635mm) in 30° or 0.0035 inch (0.089mm) in 360°. All brake drums are marked with the maximum allowable brake drum diameter on the face of the drum.
6. Install or connect the following:
   - Rear brake drum onto the hub assembly
   - Wheels and properly adjust the brakes
7. Road test vehicle to check brake operation.

BRAKE SHOES

REMOVAL & INSTALLATION

See Figure 12.

1. Before servicing the vehicle, refer to the precautions in the beginning of this section.
2. Remove or disconnect the following:
   - Rear wheels
   - Drums
   - Automatic adjuster spring and lever
   - Hold-down clips and pins
3. Rotate the automatic adjuster starwheel enough so both shoes move out far enough to be free of the wheel cylinder boots.
   - Parking brake cable from the actuating lever
   - Lower shoe-to-shoe spring
   - Shoes from the backing plate, holding them together by the upper shoe-to-shoe spring

To install:

4. Thoroughly clean and dry the backing plate. To prepare the backing plate, lubricate the bosses, anchor pin and parking brake actuating lever pivot surface lightly with lithium based grease.
5. Remove, clean and dry all brake components. Lubricate the starwheel shaft threads with anti-seize lubricant and transfer all parts to their proper locations on the new shoes.
6. Install or connect the following:
   - Lower spring
   - Parking brake cable
   - Automatic adjuster lever and spring
7. Adjust the starwheel.
8. Remove any grease from the linings and install the drum.
   - Wheels and properly adjust the brakes
9. Check for proper brake system operation.

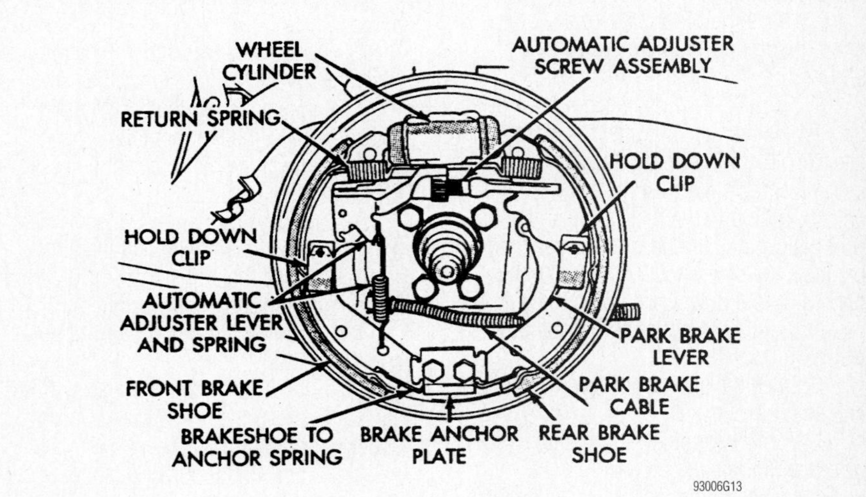

Fig. 12 Kelsey Hayes rear brake assembly (left side shown)

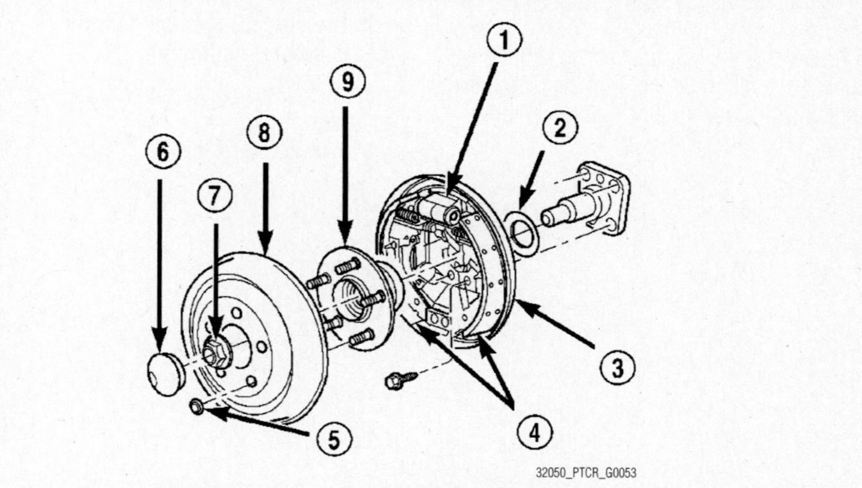

Fig. 11 Rear brake drum assembly (8) and related components

PARKING BRAKE CABLES

ADJUSTMENT

1. Verify the parking brake lever is in the fully released position.
2. Raise the vehicle.

➡**Perform the following steps on each rear drum brake assembly.**

3. Remove the tire and wheel assembly from the vehicle.
4. Remove the brake drum.
5. Using a brake shoe gauge, Special Tool C-3919 or equivalent, measure the inside diameter of the brake drum. Tighten the gauge set-screw at this measurement.
6. Place the other side of the brake shoe gauge on the brake shoes as shown.
7. Adjust the shoe diameter to the setting on the gauge. To adjust the shoe diameter, turn the adjuster-screw star-wheel using a screwdriver inserted through the adjusting hole in the rear of the shoe support plate. Once the tip of the screwdriver contacts the star-wheel teeth, move the handle of tool downward using the support plate as a pivot to adjust the shoes outward.
8. Once the shoe diameter is set, reinstall the brake drum.
9. Turn the drum. A slight drag should be felt while rotating the drum.
10. Install the tire and wheel assembly. Tighten the wheel mounting nuts to a torque of 100 ft. lbs. (135 Nm).
11. After adjusting both rear drum brakes, lower the vehicle.
12. Apply and release the parking brake lever one time after the adjustment process is completed so the parking brakes can readjust themselves to the new brake shoe adjustment.
13. Road test vehicle stopping in both forward and reverse directions. Automatic-adjuster will continue to adjust brakes as necessary during road test.

PARKING BRAKE SHOES

REMOVAL & INSTALLATION

See Figure 13.

1. Raise the vehicle.
2. Remove the rear tire and wheel assembly.
3. Remove the rear disc brake caliper assembly from the brake rotor and store it out of the way.
4. Remove rear brake rotor.
5. Remove the dust cap from the rear hub and bearing.
6. Remove the rear hub and bearing assembly retaining nut and washer.
7. Remove the rear hub and bearing assembly from the rear spindle.
8. Remove the rear brake shoe assembly hold-down clip.
9. Turn the brake shoe adjuster wheel until the adjuster is at shortest length.
10. Remove the adjuster assembly from the parking brake shoe assemblies.
11. Remove the lower shoe-to-shoe spring.
12. Pull the rear brake shoe away from anchor. Remove the rear brake shoe and upper return spring.
13. Remove the front brake shoe hold-down clip. Remove the front brake shoe assembly.

To install:

14. Install the front brake shoe and secure it in place with a hold-down clip.
15. Install the rear brake shoe and the upper shoe return spring. Pull the rear brake shoe over the anchor block until it is properly located on the adapter.

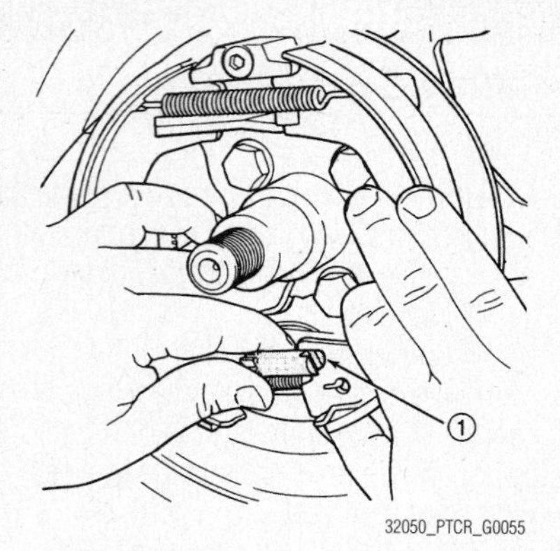

Fig. 13 Parking brake shoes assembly

16. Install the lower shoe-to-shoe return spring.
17. Install the brake shoe adjuster assembly with the star wheel towards the rear.
18. Install the rear brake shoe hold down clip.
19. Adjust the parking brake shoes to a diameter of 6.75 inches (171mm).
20. Install the rear hub and bearing assembly on spindle.
21. Install a new hub and bearing assembly retaining nut. Tighten the retaining nut to a torque of 160 ft. lbs. (217 Nm).
22. Install the hub and bearing dust cap.
23. Install the rear brake rotor.
24. Install rear disc brake caliper.
25. Install the tire and wheel assembly. Tighten the wheel mounting nuts to a torque of 100 ft. lbs. (135 Nm).

➡**Do the preceding steps to both wheels before continuing.**

26. Adjust the parking brake shoes as necessary.
27. Lower the vehicle.

GENERAL INFORMATION

✱✱ CAUTION

These vehicles are equipped with an air bag system. The system must be disarmed before performing service on, or around, system components, the steering column, instrument panel components, wiring and sensors. Failure to follow the safety precautions and the disarming procedure could result in accidental air bag deployment, possible injury and unnecessary system repairs.

SERVICE PRECAUTIONS

Disconnect and isolate the battery negative cable before beginning any airbag system component diagnosis, testing, removal, or installation procedures. Allow system capacitor to discharge for two minutes before beginning any component service. This will disable the airbag system. Failure to disable the airbag system may result in accidental airbag deployment, personal injury, or death.

Do not place an intact undeployed airbag face down on a solid surface. The airbag will propel into the air if accidentally deployed and may result in personal injury or death.

When carrying or handling an undeployed airbag, the trim side (face) of the airbag should be pointing towards the body to minimize possibility of injury if accidental deployment occurs. Failure to do this may result in personal injury or death.

Replace airbag system components with OEM replacement parts. Substitute parts may appear interchangeable, but internal differences may result in inferior occupant protection. Failure to do so may result in occupant personal injury or death.

Wear safety glasses, rubber gloves, and long sleeved clothing when cleaning powder residue from vehicle after an airbag deployment. Powder residue emitted from a deployed airbag can cause skin irritation. Flush affected area with cool water if irritation is experienced. If nasal or throat irritation is experienced, exit the vehicle for fresh air until the irritation ceases. If irritation continues, see a physician.

Do not use a replacement airbag that is not in the original packaging. This may result in improper deployment, personal injury, or death.

The factory installed fasteners, screws and bolts used to fasten airbag components have a special coating and are specifically designed for the airbag system. Do not use substitute fasteners. Use only original equipment fasteners listed in the parts catalog when fastener replacement is required.

During, and following, any child restraint anchor service, due to impact event or vehicle repair, carefully inspect all mounting hardware, tether straps, and anchors for proper installation, operation, or damage. If a child restraint anchor is found damaged in any way, the anchor must be replaced. Failure to do this may result in personal injury or death.

Deployed and non-deployed airbags may or may not have live pyrotechnic material within the airbag inflator.

Do not dispose of driver/passenger/curtain airbags or seat belt tensioners unless you are sure of complete deployment. Refer to the Hazardous Substance Control System for proper disposal.

Dispose of deployed airbags and tensioners consistent with state, provincial, local, and federal regulations.

After any airbag component testing or service, do not connect the battery negative cable. Personal injury or death may result if the system test is not performed first.

If the vehicle is equipped with the Occupant Classification System (OCS), do not connect the battery negative cable before performing the OCS Verification Test using the scan tool and the appropriate diagnostic information. Personal injury or death may result if the system test is not performed properly.

Never replace both the Occupant Restraint Controller (ORC) and the Occupant Classification Module (OCM) at the same time. If both require replacement, replace one, then perform the Airbag System test before replacing the other.

Both the ORC and the OCM store Occupant Classification System (OCS) calibration data, which they transfer to one another when one of them is replaced. If both are replaced at the same time, an irreversible fault will be set in both modules and the OCS may malfunction and cause personal injury or death.

If equipped with OCS, the Seat Weight Sensor is a sensitive, calibrated unit and must be handled carefully. Do not drop or handle roughly. If dropped or damaged, replace with another sensor. Failure to do so may result in occupant injury or death.

If equipped with OCS, the front passenger seat must be handled carefully as well. When removing the seat, be careful when setting on floor not to drop. If dropped, the sensor may be inoperative, could result in occupant injury, or possibly death.

If equipped with OCS, when the passenger front seat is on the floor, no one should sit in the front passenger seat. This uneven force may damage the sensing ability of the seat weight sensors. If sat on and damaged, the sensor may be inoperative, could result in occupant injury, or possibly death.

DISARMING THE SYSTEM

Disconnect and isolate the negative battery cable. Wait 2 minutes to allow the system capacitor to fully discharge before servicing the vehicle.

ARMING THE SYSTEM

Reconnect the negative battery cable.

CLOCKSPRING CENTERING

➡If the rotating tape within the clock spring is not positioned properly with the steering wheel and the front wheels, the clock spring may fail during use. The following procedure MUST BE USED to center the clock spring if:

- The clock spring is not known to be properly positioned.
- The front wheels were moved.
- The steering wheel was moved from the half turn (180 degrees) to the right (clockwise) position.

1. Open hood.
2. Disconnect and isolate the battery negative cable. Allow system capacitor to discharge for two minutes before beginning.
3. Remove clock spring.
4. Rotate the clock spring rotor in the CLOCKWISE DIRECTION to the end of travel. Do not apply excessive torque.
5. From the end of travel, rotate the rotor three full turns in the counterclockwise direction. The horn wire and the squib wire should end up at the bottom. If not, rotate the rotor counter clockwise until the wires are properly oriented, but not more than half turn (180 degrees). Engage clock spring locking mechanism.
6. Install the clock spring.

✱✱ WARNING

Do not yet connect battery negative cable.

7. Close hood.
8. Verify vehicle and system operation.

DRIVETRAIN

AUTOMATIC TRANSAXLE ASSEMBLY

REMOVAL & INSTALLATION

40/41TE Transaxle

See Figure 14.

1. Before servicing the vehicle, refer to the precautions in the beginning of this section.
2. Drain the transaxle fluid.
3. Remove or disconnect the following:
   - Battery cables
   - Air cleaner assembly
   - Battery and tray
   - Upper starter-to-transaxle bell housing bolt
   - Transaxle dipstick and tube
   - Gearshift cable end from the transaxle shift lever
   - Gearshift cable bracket bolt from the transaxle
   - Transaxle oil cooler lines. Plug the lines to prevent contamination.
   - Input and output speed sensor electrical connectors
   - Transaxle range sensor connector
   - Solenoid/pressure switch assembly connector
   - Both front wheels
   - Left front splash shield
   - Both halfshafts
   - Power steering hose from the structural collar
   - Left and right side engine-to-transaxle lateral brace and structural collar
   - Starter motor electrical connectors
   - Starter
   - Gearshift cable bracket
   - Driveplate-to-torque converter bolts and support the powertrain assembly
   - Transaxle upper mount to bracket bolts and lower the powertrain assembly
   - Transaxle

To install:

4. Install or connect the following:
   - Transaxle and torque the bolts to 80 ft. lbs. (105 Nm) while supporting the transaxle with a jack
   - Mount-to-transaxle bracket. Torque the bolts to 50 ft. lbs. (68 Nm) and remove the jack.
   - Driveplate-to-torque converter bolts and torque the bolts to 65 ft. lbs. (88 Nm)
   - Starter and hand tighten the bolts
   - Dipstick tube and secure the bracket to the transaxle. Torque the upper starter bolt to 40 ft. lbs. (54 Nm).
   - Cable bracket to the bell housing and torque the bolt to 45 ft. lbs. (61 Nm)
   - Starter lower bolt and torque the bolt to 40 ft. lbs. (54 Nm)
   - Starter electrical connections
   - Bell housing dust cover
   - Lower dust shield screws and torque the bell housing cover bolts to 108 inch lbs. (12 Nm)
   - Right side lateral bending brace and torque the bolts to 60 ft. lbs. (81 Nm)
   - Both halfshafts
   - Left side splash shield and both wheels
   - Cooler lines to the transaxle and secure with constant tension clamps
   - Solenoid/pressure switch assembly
   - Transmission range sensor connector
   - Input/output sensor connectors
   - Gearshift cable to the bracket and connect it to the manual valve lever
   - Battery tray and battery
   - Air cleaner assembly
   - VSS wiring
   - Battery cables
5. Fill the transaxle fluid to the proper level.
6. Be sure the vehicle's back-up lights and speedometer are working properly.

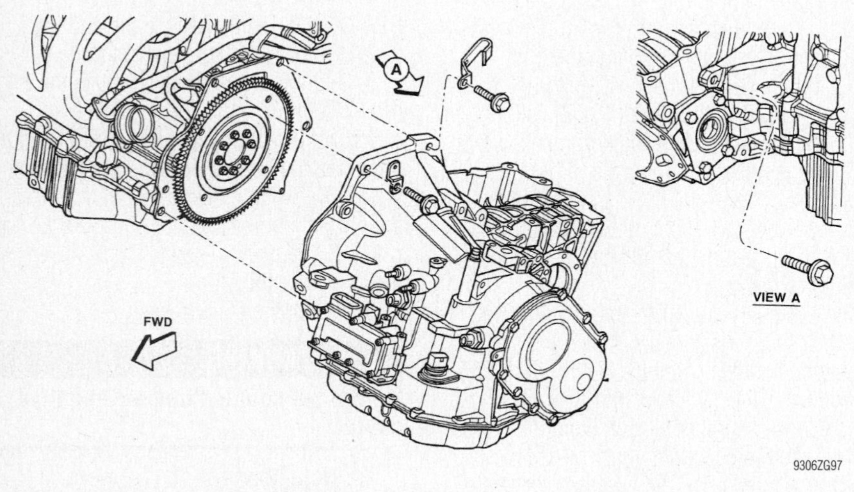

Fig. 14 Exploded view of automatic transaxle removal

MANUAL TRANSAXLE ASSEMBLY

REMOVAL & INSTALLATION

T350 Transaxle

See Figure 15.

1. Drain the transaxle fluid.
2. Remove or disconnect the following:
   - Battery cables
   - Battery and tray
   - Air cleaner
   - Back-up lamp switch wiring from the transaxle
   - Shift selector and crossover cable and move them out of the way
   - Vehicle Speed Sensor (VSS) wire
   - Clutch master cylinder hydraulic tube from the slave cylinder
   - Both halfshafts
   - Bell housing dust cover
   - Power steering hose from the structural collar
   - Left side engine-to-transaxle lateral bending brace and structural collar
   - Right side engine-to-transaxle lateral bending brace
   - Starter
   - Driveplate-to-clutch module bolts and support the engine at the oil pan
   - Transaxle upper mount bolts and lower the powertrain assembly onto the support
   - Transaxle-to-engine mounting bolts
   - Transaxle

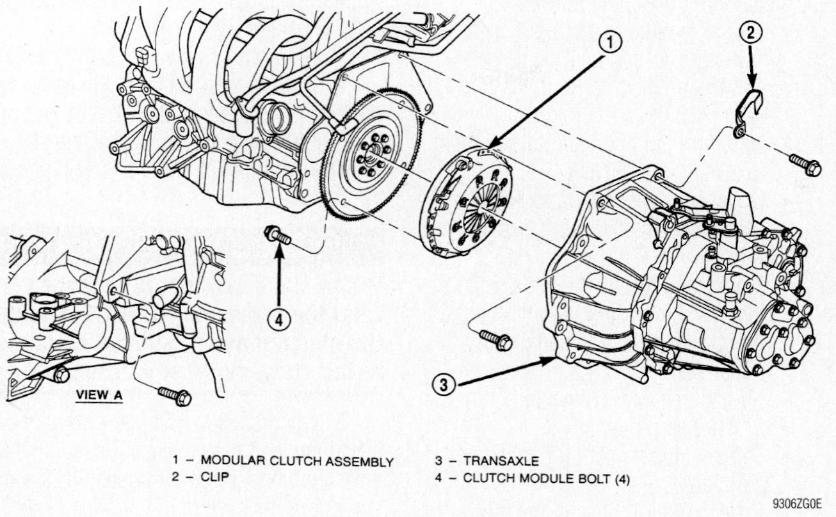

Fig. 15 Remove the clutch module from the transaxle assembly

- Clutch module from the input shaft
- Slave cylinder
- Upper transaxle mount

To install:

3. Install or connect the following:
   - Clutch module to the transaxle input shaft and place the transaxle into position
   - Transaxle-to-engine mounting bolts and torque them to 80 ft. lbs. (108 Nm)
   - Upper transaxle mount and torque the bolts to 45 ft. lbs. (62 Nm)
   - Driveplate-to-clutch module bolts and torque to 65 ft. lbs. (88 Nm)
   - Starter
   - Starter electrical connectors
   - Bell housing dust cover
   - Left side engine-to-transaxle bending brace and structural brace. Torque the bolts to 60 ft. lbs. (81 Nm).
   - Right lateral bending brace and torque the bolts to 60 ft. lbs. (81 Nm)
   - Power steering hose to the structural collar
   - Both halfshafts
   - Clutch master cylinder tube to the slave cylinder
   - VSS electrical connector
   - Shift crossover and selector cables to the shift lever
   - Cables to the bracket and install a new retainer clip
   - Back-up lamp switch connector
   - Battery tray
   - Battery and cables
   - Air cleaner assembly

4. Fill the transaxle fluid to the proper level.

5. Be sure the vehicle's back-up lights and speedometer are functioning properly.

6. Start the vehicle and check for leaks, repair if necessary.

G288 Transaxle

1. Before servicing the vehicle, refer to the precautions in the beginning of this section.
2. Drain the transaxle fluid.
3. Remove or disconnect the following:
   - Negative battery cable
   - Air cleaner
   - Power Distribution Center (PDC) from the bracket
   - Air cleaner/PDC mounting bracket
   - Gearshift cable from the shift mechanism
   - Gearshift cable bracket
   - Back-up lamp switch wiring from the transaxle
   - Vehicle Speed Sensor (VSS) wire
   - Clutch master cylinder hydraulic tube from the slave cylinder
   - Upper transaxle bell housing bolts
   - Transaxle drain plug, drain the fluid and reinstall the plug
   - Both halfshafts
   - Intermediate shaft/bearing bolts and the shaft assembly
   - 2 intercooler connector pipe-to-oil pan bolts and position aside
   - Oil pan-to-bell housing bolts
4. Place a screw jack with a piece of wood on top onto the oil pan.
   - 2 transaxle upper mount-to-bracket bolts and lower the engine onto the wood and screw jack
   - Transaxle upper mount bracket
   - Attach a transaxle jack to the transaxle
   - Starter lower bolt and ground cable
   - 4 modular clutch drive-to-drive plate bolts. While removing the bolts one tolerance (slotted) drive plate hole will be seen. When this bolt is removed, mark the drive plate and clutch assembly alignment to aid during reinstallation for proper alignment
   - Remaining transaxle-to-engine bolts
   - Transaxle

To install:

5. Install or connect the following:
   - Transaxle into position
   - Accessible transaxle-to-engine mounting bolts and torque them to 80 ft. lbs. (108 Nm)
   - 4 modular clutch-to-drive plate bolts, align the drive plate and clutch assembly marks made during removal, start with the slotted hole first and tighten the bolts to 65 ft. lbs. (88 Nm)
   - Upper mount bracket
   - Raise the transaxle using the jack until the mount bracket is aligned and install the bolts
   - Starter motor bolt and ground cable
   - Lower bell housing bolt
   - 2 intercooler connector pipe-to-oil pan bolts
   - Remove the drain plug and fill the transaxle with the correct type and amount of fluid. Install the plug and tighten to 35 ft. lbs. (47 Nm).
   - Intermediate/bearing assembly and tighten the bolts
   - Both halfshafts
   - Clutch master cylinder tube to the slave cylinder
   - VSS electrical connector
   - Gearshift cable bracket and tighten the bolts
   - Gearshift crossover and selector cables and secure using new clips
   - Back-up lamp switch connector
   - PDC/air cleaner bracket
   - PDC
   - Air cleaner assembly
   - negative battery cable
6. Be sure the vehicle's back-up lights and speedometer are functioning properly.
7. Start the vehicle and check for leaks, repair if necessary.

CLUTCH

REMOVAL & INSTALLATION

See Figure 16.

1. Before servicing the vehicle, refer to the precautions in the beginning of this section.
2. Remove or disconnect the following:
   - Negative battery cable
   - Air cleaner assembly
   - Battery and tray
   - Back-up lamp electrical connector
   - Shift cable-to-bracket clips
   - Shift lever and crossover cable from the levers. Move the cables out of the way.
   - Vehicle Speed Sensor (VSS) electrical connector
   - Clutch master cylinder tube from the slave cylinder using a clutch hydraulic quick connect Tool 6638A
   - Both halfshafts
   - Power steering hose from the structural collar
   - Left side lateral bending brace and structural collar
   - Bell housing dust cover
   - Right side lateral bending brace
   - Starter
   - Driveplate-to-clutch module bolts and support the engine at the oil pan
   - Transaxle upper mount bolts and lower the engine/transaxle assembly
   - Modular clutch from the input shaft

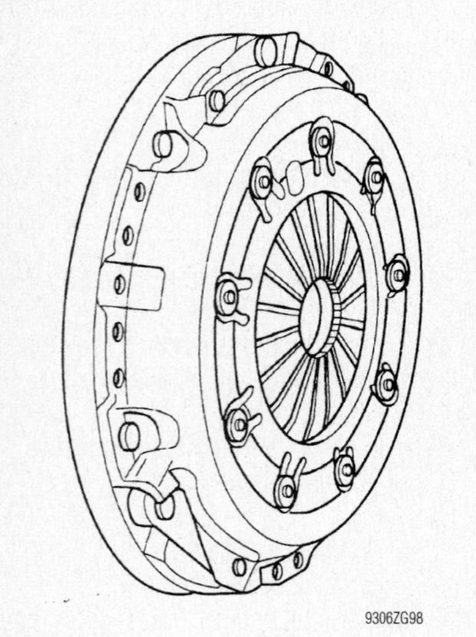

Fig. 16 Exploded View of the modular clutch assembly

To install:

3. Install or connect the following:
   - Clutch module to the input shaft
   - Transaxle-to-engine mount bolts and torque them to 80 ft. lbs. (108 Nm)
   - Upper mount bolts and torque them to 65 ft. lbs. (88 Nm)
   - Driveplate-to-clutch module bolts and torque them to 65 ft. lbs. (88 Nm)
   - Starter and torque the bolts to 40 ft. lbs. (54 Nm). Make certain that the ground cable is fastened to the upper bolt.
   - Starter electrical connectors
   - Bell housing dust cover
   - Left side lateral bending brace and structural collar
   - Power steering hose to the structural collar
   - Right side lateral bending brace and torque the bolts to 60 ft. lbs. (81 Nm)
   - Both halfshafts
   - Clutch master cylinder tube to the slave cylinder
   - VSS electrical connector
   - Back-up lamp switch electrical connector
   - Air cleaner assembly
   - Battery and tray
   - Battery cables
4. Fill the transmission to the proper level.
5. Road test the vehicle and check for proper clutch operation.
6. Check the fluid level and adjust if needed.

BLEEDING

See Figure 17.

➡It is necessary to bleed the clutch hydraulic release system if the system has lost an excessive amount of fluid and has allowed air into the circuit. Air in the system typically results in a spongy pedal feel, and/or improper clutch release. If air cannot be removed from the system using this procedure, it is necessary to replace both the clutch master cylinder and slave cylinder assemblies.

Except Turbocharged Models

1. From driver's seat, actuate clutch pedal 60–100 times. Verify clutch operation/pedal feel. If pedal still feels spongy, or clutch does not fully disengage, excessive air is still trapped within the system. Perform the following procedure:
2. Verify fluid level in clutch master cylinder reservoir. Top off with DOT 3 brake fluid as necessary.
3. Raise and safely support the vehicle.
4. Remove clutch slave cylinder assembly from the transaxle case, but do not disconnect from the system. Allow the slave cylinder hang, making it the lowest part of the system.

**** CAUTION**

While slave cylinder is detached from the transaxle, DO NOT actuate the clutch master cylinder. Damage to the slave cylinder will result.

5. Depress slave cylinder pushrod until it bottoms and then release. Repeat this at least ten times, forcing trapped air upwards and out of the system.
6. Re-install slave cylinder into position. Torque slave cylinder to case bolt to 168 inch lbs. (19 Nm).
7. Carefully lower the vehicle.
8. Check and adjust clutch master cylinder fluid level. Actuate clutch pedal thirty (30) times. Verify clutch operation/pedal feel. If pedal still feels spongy, or clutch does not fully disengage, air is still trapped within the system. Repeat Step 3 through Step 7 until air is purged. If several attempts at purging air from the system are unsuccessful, replace both the clutch master cylinder and slave cylinder assemblies.
9. Raise and safely support the vehicle.
10. Carefully lower the vehicle.
11. Top off clutch master cylinder fluid level with DOT 3 brake fluid as necessary.

Turbocharged Models

➡Due to the angle and design of the turbo hydraulic system components, gravity and pedal bleeding are less effective and less efficient than the reverse fluid injection method (reverse bleeding). Reverse bleeding is recommended for this system, and requires the use of commercially available injection bleeding equipment.

Recommended Procedure (Reverse Bleeding)

1. Remove reservoir cap and inspect fluid level. Top off with DOT 3 Brake Fluid. Actuate clutch pedal briskly at least 50 times. Verify release system function. Repeat. If release system is still inoperative, continue with procedure.
2. Remove reservoir from bracket and empty into collection container.
3. Raise and safely support the vehicle.

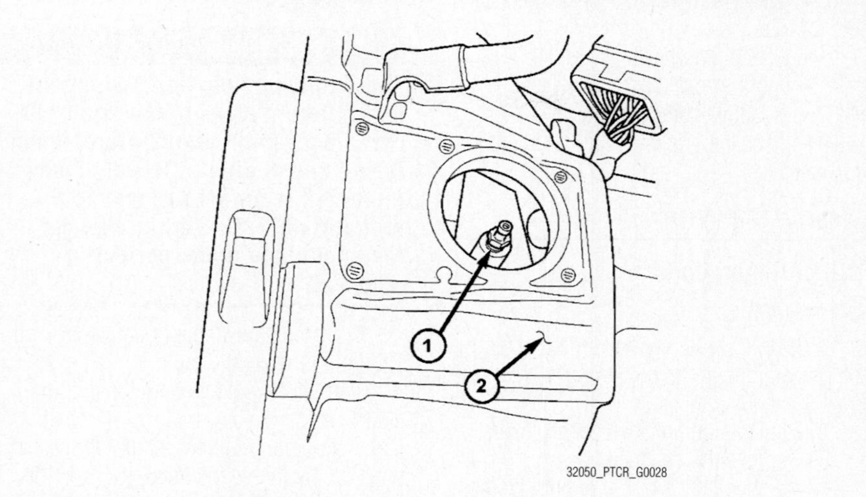

Fig. 17 Location of the bleed screw (1) for the 2.4L engine

4. Remove clutch bell housing access cap to expose system bleed screw.

⁂ CAUTION

Use care not to allow fluid to drain into clutch bell housing. Excessive fluid will be agitated and sprayed around inside the clutch bell housing by the rotating flywheel, contaminating the flywheel, disc, and pressure plate, resulting in poor clutch engagement.

5. Using suitable socket/wrench, loosen bleed screw.
6. Quickly attach hand operated bleed apparatus to bleed screw. Use care not to over-fill reservoir and spill fluid into engine compartment.
7. Operate bleed gun sufficiently to expel air upward through circuit and out of master cylinder reservoir. Fill and empty reservoir three times.
8. Remove bleed apparatus and tighten bleed screw to 62 inch lbs. (7 Nm). Do not over-tighten.
9. Carefully lower the vehicle.
10. Top off reservoir with fluid, then return the cap.
11. Verify system operation. Actuate clutch pedal 50 times. If necessary, repeat procedure until road test confirms that shift issues no longer exist.

Alternate Procedure (Pedal Bleeding)

1. Remove reservoir cap and inspect fluid level. Top off with DOT 3 Brake Fluid. Actuate clutch pedal briskly at least 50 times. Verify release system function. Repeat. If release system is still inoperative, continue with procedure.
2. Raise and safely support the vehicle.
3. Remove clutch bell housing access cap to expose system bleed screw.

⁂ WARNING

Use care not to allow fluid to drain into clutch bell housing. Excessive fluid will be agitated and sprayed around inside the clutch bell housing by the rotating flywheel, contaminating the flywheel, disc, and pressure plate, resulting in poor clutch engagement.

4. Using suitable socket/wrench, loosen bleed screw. Immediately install rubber hose to bleed screw to prevent fluid from entering clutch bell housing. Tighten bleed screw gently with suitable wrench.
5. Lower vehicle.
6. Have helper actuate clutch pedal to floor.
7. Place collection container at end of hose to capture expelled fluid.
8. Using suitable wrench, break bleeder screw loose and tighten to 62 inch lbs. (7 Nm). Do not over-tighten.
9. Have helper release pedal, returning it to at–rest position, and then actuate pedal to floor.
10. Break bleeder screw loose and tighten to 62 inch lbs. (7 Nm). Do not over-tighten.
11. Repeat procedure as necessary, keeping master cylinder reservoir full during the process, until air bubbles are no longer visible in collection container.
12. When air bubbles are no longer visible, actuate clutch pedal briskly at least 50 times.
13. Verify release system function and top off fluid as necessary.

FRONT HALFSHAFT

REMOVAL & INSTALLATION

See Figure 18.

1. Before servicing the vehicle, refer to the precautions in the beginning of this section.
2. Place the transaxle in the **P** position, for automatic and neutral for manual.
3. Remove or disconnect the following:
   - Negative battery cable
   - Front wheel
   - Cotter pin, locknut and spring washer from the end of the outer Constant Velocity (CV) joint stub axle
   - Driveshaft to hub and bearing nut
   - Front wheel speed sensor, if equipped
   - Steering knuckle from the ball joint
   - Driveshaft from the steering knuckle and support the outer end of the driveshaft

⁂ WARNING

Be careful when separating the ball joint stud from the steering knuckle, so the ball joint seal does not get damaged.

⁂ WARNING

Be careful when separating the inner CV-joint during this operation. Do not let the driveshaft hang by the inner CV-joint, the driveshaft must be supported.

➡Inner Tri-Pot joint removal is easier by applying outward pressure on the joint while hitting the punch with a hammer.

4. Inner Tri-Pot joints from the transmission side gears using a punch to dislodge the inner Tri-Pot joint retaining ring from the transmission side gear. If removing the right side inner Tri-Pot joint, position the punch against the inner Tri-Pot joint. Hit the punch sharply with a hammer to dislodge the right inner joint from the side gear. If removing the left side inner Tri-Pot joint, position the punch in the groove of the inner Tri-Pot joint. Hit the punch sharply with a hammer to dislodge the left inner Tri-Pot joint from the side gear.
5. Hold the inner Tri-Pot joint and interconnecting shaft of the driveshaft assembly. Remove the inner Tri-Pot joint from the transaxle by pulling it straight out of the transaxle side gear and transmission oil seal. When removing the Tri-Pot joint,

do not let the spline or snapring drag across the sealing lip of the transaxle-to-Tri-Pot joint oil seal.

WARNING

The driveshaft, when installed, acts as a bolt which secures the front hub and bearing assembly. If the vehicle is to be supported or moved on its wheels with a driveshaft removed, install a proper-sized bolt and nut through the front hub. Tighten the bolt and nut to 135 ft. lbs. (183 Nm). This will ensure that the hub bearing cannot loosen.

To install:

6. Thoroughly clean the spline and oil seal sealing surface on the Tri-Pot joint. Lightly lubricate the oil seal sealing surface on the Tri-Pot joint with fresh, clean transmission fluid.
7. Holding the driveshaft assembly by the Tri-Pot joint and interconnecting shaft, install the Tri-Pot joint into the transaxle side gear as far as possible by hand
8. Align the Tri-Pot joint with the transmission side gears, grasp the driveshaft interconnecting shaft and push the Tri-Pot joint into the transaxle side gear until fully seated. Be sure the snapring is fully engaged with the side gear by trying to remove the Tri-Pot joint from the transaxle by hand. If the snapring is fully seated with the side gear, the Tri-Pot joint will not be removable by hand.
9. Install or connect the following:
   - Driveshaft back into the front hub
   - Steering knuckle into the ball joint stud
   - New steering knuckle-to-ball joint stud bolt and nut. Torque the nut and bolt to 70 ft. lbs. (95 Nm).
   - Washer and hub nut to the stub axle and torque the nut to 180 ft. lbs. (244 Nm)
   - Spring washer, locknut and cotter pin
   - VSS, if equipped
   - Front wheel
   - Negative battery cable
10. Check the transaxle fluid and adjust if needed.

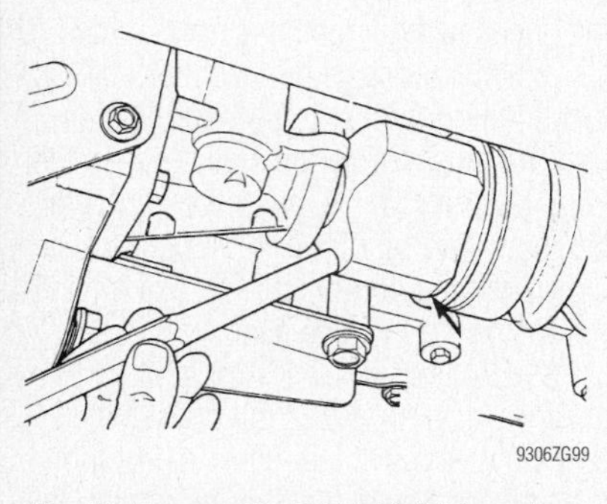

Fig. 18 Remove the Tri-Pot joint from the transaxle

CV-JOINTS OVERHAUL

Tri-Pot (Inner) Joint

See Figure 19.

1. Before servicing the vehicle, refer to the precautions in the beginning of this section.
2. Remove the negative battery cable.
3. Remove the halfshaft.
4. Remove the tri-pot joint boot clamps and slide the boot down the shaft.

WARNING

When removing the spider joint, hold the rollers in place on the trunnions to keep the rollers and needle bearings in place.

5. Slide the interconnecting shaft and spider assembly from the tri-pot housing.
6. Remove the snapring from the shaft.
7. Remove the spider assembly.

➡If necessary, tap the spider assembly from the shaft with a brass drift.

WARNING

When removing the spider assembly, do not hit the outer bearings.

8. Remove the boot by sliding it off the shaft.

WARNING

If any parts show excessive wear, replace the halfshaft assembly; the component parts are not serviceable.

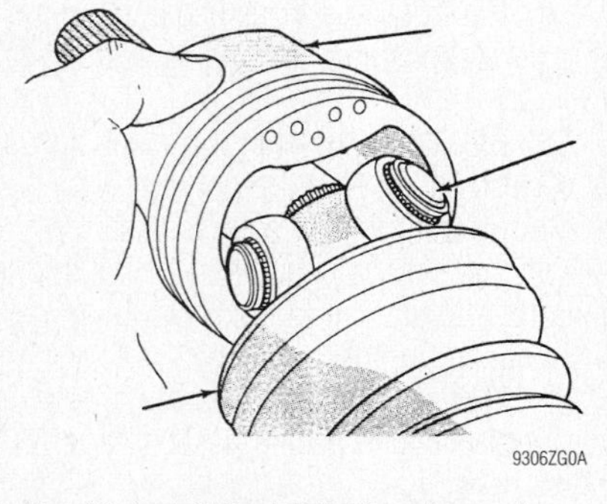

Fig. 19 Install the Tri-Pot housing on to the spider assembly

To install:

WARNING

The Tri-pot sealing boots are made of 2 different types of material, silicon rubber (high temperature) which is soft and pliable or Hytrel plastic (standard temperature) which is stiff and rigid. Be sure to replace the boot made of the correct material.

9. Install a new small boot clamp and slide it on the shaft.
10. Install the boot and slide it on the shaft.
11. Position the boot so that the raised bead on the inside the boot seal is in the shaft groove.
12. Install the spider assembly, face the chamfered side toward the shaft.
13. Install the snapring making sure it is fully seated in the groove.
14. Install the spider/shaft assembly into the tri-pot housing.
15. Install a new inner boot clamp and position it evenly on the sealing boot.
16. Using a trim stick, adjust the boot length to 115mm (Hytrel plastic) or 115mm (silicone rubber).
17. If installing a high profile boot clamp, perform the following procedure:
   a. Using the Crimper Tool C-4975-A, place the tool over the clamp bridge, tighten the tool nut until the jaws are completely closed (face-to-face).

WARNING

The seal must not be dimpled, stretched or out of shape. If necessary, equalize the seal pressure and shape it by hand.

   b. Position the boot onto the tri-pot housing retaining groove and install the retaining clamp evenly on the boot.
   c. Using the Crimper Tool C-4975-A, place the tool over the clamp bridge, tighten the tool nut until the jaws are completely closed (face-to-face).
18. If installing a low profile latching type boot clamp, position Snap-On® Clamp Locking Tool YA3050 prongs in the clamp holes and squeeze the tool until the upper clamp band is latched behind the 2 tabs on the lower clamp band.
19. Install the halfshaft.
20. Connect the negative battery cable.

Outer Joint

See Figure 20.

1. Before servicing the vehicle, refer to the precautions in the beginning of this section.
2. Remove the halfshaft.
3. Remove the clamps from the CV-joint boot and discard.
4. Remove the boot from the CV-joint housing and slide it down the interconnecting shaft.
5. Remove the outer CV-joint from the interconnecting shaft by sharply hitting it with a soft-faced hammer to drive it off the shaft.
6. Remove the circlip from the shaft.
7. Remove the CV-joint by sliding it off the shaft.

⁂ WARNING

If any parts show excessive wear, replace the halfshaft assembly; the component parts are not serviceable.

To install:

8. Install a new small boot clamp and slide it onto the shaft.
9. Install the boot and slide it onto the shaft.
10. Install the circlip.
11. Position the boot so that the raised bead on the inside the boot seal is in the shaft groove.
12. Install the halfshaft hub nut onto the joint threaded shaft so it is flush with the end.
13. Align the shaft splines and tap it onto the shaft with a soft-faced hammer so it locks on the circlip.
14. Distribute ½ of the grease in the service package inside the joint housing and the other ½ inside the boot.
15. Install a new small boot clamp and position it evenly on the sealing boot.

⁂ CAUTION

Clamp the boot to the shaft using the Crimper Tool C-4975-A, place the tool over the clamp bridge, tighten the tool nut until the jaws are completely closed (face-to-face).

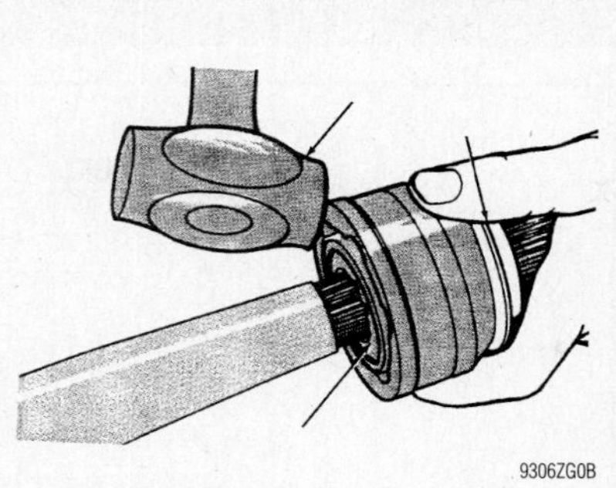

Fig. 20 Remove the outer C/V joint from the interconnecting shaft

⁂ WARNING

The seal must not be dimpled, stretched or out of shape. If necessary, equalize the seal pressure and shape it by hand.

16. Position the boot onto the retaining groove and install the retaining clamp evenly on the boot.
17. Clamp the boot to the outer CV-joint housing using the Crimper Tool C-4975-A, place the tool over the clamp bridge, tighten the tool nut until the jaws are completely closed (face-to-face).
18. Install the halfshaft.

REAR AXLE SHAFT, BEARING & SEAL

REMOVAL & INSTALLATION

The PT Cruiser is equipped with a sealed hub and bearing assemblies. The hub and bearing assembly is non-serviceable. If the assembly is damaged, the complete unit must be replaced.

1. Before servicing the vehicle, refer to the precautions in the beginning of this section.
2. Remove or disconnect the following:
   - Wheel
   - Rear brake drum, if equipped
   - Caliper (suspend on a wire) and the rotor, if equipped with rear disc brakes

⁂ WARNING

DO NOT allow the caliper to hang by the brake hose.

   - Dust cap from the rear hub/bearing
   - Hub/bearing assembly-to-knuckle/spindle nut

➡Discard the hub nut and replace with a new one during installation.

   - Hub/bearing from the spindle by pulling it off the end of the spindle by hand

To install:

⁂ WARNING

The hub/bearing nut must be tightened to, but NOT over, the specified torque value. The proper specification is crucial to the life of the hub bearing.

3. Position the hub/bearing assembly on the rear spindle/knuckle. Install a NEW hub nut and tighten to 160 ft. lbs. (217 Nm).
4. Install or connect the following:
   - Dust cap and seat it using a soft face hammer to carefully tap it into place
   - Brake drum, if equipped
   - Rotor, if equipped
   - Caliper and 2 guide pin bolts, if equipped with disc brakes. Torque the bolts to 16 ft. lbs. (22 Nm).

ENGINE COOLING

ENGINE FAN

REMOVAL & INSTALLATION

See Figure 21.

➡The fan motor, fan, and the shroud are serviced as an assembly.

⁂ CAUTION

Do not open the radiator draincock with the system hot and under pressure, because serious burns from coolant can occur.

1. Disconnect negative cable from battery.
2. Remove battery and battery tray.
3. Drain cooling system below upper radiator hose level.
4. Remove grille.
5. Remove upper radiator closure panel and center brace.
6. Disconnect upper radiator hose from radiator.
7. For turbocharger equipped vehicles: Remove radiator inlet neck.
8. Hoist vehicle.
9. Disconnect radiator fan electrical connector.
10. Remove the two lower and left side radiator fan screws and.
11. Lower vehicle and remove the remaining radiator fan attaching screws.

⁂ WARNING

Care should be taken not to damage the radiator cooling fins and tubes during fan removal.

12. Remove radiator fan by lifting up from the engine compartment.

To install:

13. Install the radiator fan into position on the radiator.
14. Hand-start all radiator fan fasteners.
15. Tighten all radiator fan retaining screws to 55 inch lbs. (6 Nm).
16. Connect the radiator fan electrical connector.
17. Carefully lower the vehicle.
18. For turbocharger equipped vehicles: Inspect radiator inlet neck O-ring. Replace if necessary. Install radiator inlet neck. Torque fasteners to 55 inch lbs. (6 Nm).
19. Connect the upper radiator hose to radiator. Align hose and position clamp so it will not interfere with the engine or the hood.

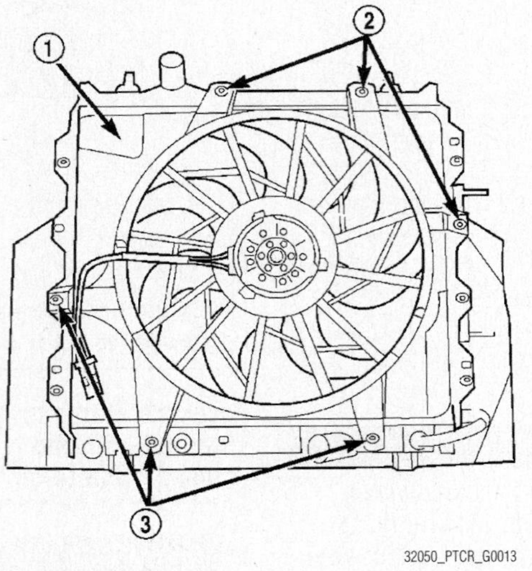

Fig. 21 Radiator fan mounting points

20. Install upper radiator closure panel and center brace.
21. Install grille.
22. Install battery tray and battery.
23. Connect cables to battery.
24. Fill cooling system.

RADIATOR

REMOVAL & INSTALLATION

See Figure 22.

⁂ CAUTION

Do not open the radiator draincock with the system hot and under pressure, because serious burns from coolant can occur.

➡It is not necessary to discharge the air conditioning system to remove the radiator.

1. Drain the cooling system.
2. Remove the radiator fan.
3. Turbocharger Equipped Vehicles: Disconnect and cap the power steering hoses.
4. Disconnect lower radiator hose.
5. Non-Turbo Vehicles with Automatic Transmission: Remove two fasteners attaching transmission oil cooler to radiator.
6. Non-Turbo Vehicles: Dislodge lower radiator air seal from side radiator air seals.
7. Remove the fasteners attaching A/C condenser to radiator. Reposition A/C condenser.
8. Turbocharger Equipped Vehicles: Remove fasteners attaching charge air cooler to radiator.
9. Remove the radiator assembly by lifting it up from the engine compartment. Care should be taken not to damage the cooling fins and tubes during removal.
10. Non-Turbo Vehicles: Remove the lower air seal from radiator.

To install:

11. Non-Turbo Vehicles: Install the lower air seal to radiator.

➡Turbocharger Equipped Vehicles: When lowering radiator, make sure lower radiator pins engage properly through charge air cooler locating tabs.

12. Position radiator into mounting position.
13. Position A/C condenser against radiator. Hand start fasteners.
14. Turbocharger Equipped Vehicles: Install fasteners attaching charge air cooler to radiator. Torque fasteners to 70 inch lbs. (8 Nm).
15. Install radiator fan/shroud assembly. Hand start fasteners.
16. Torque all condenser fasteners to 70 inch lbs. (8 Nm).
17. Torque all radiator fan fasteners to 55 inch lbs. (6 Nm).
18. Non-Turbo Vehicles with Automatic Transmission: Install fasteners attaching transmission oil cooler to radiator. Torque fasteners to 70 inch lbs. (8 Nm).
19. Raise and safely support the vehicle.
20. Non-Turbo Vehicles: Connect the lower air seal to the side air seals.
21. Connect lower radiator hose. Align the hose and position the clamp so it will not interfere with engine components.

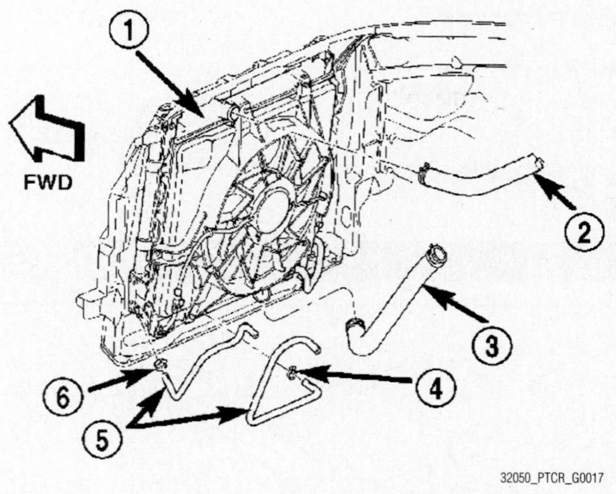

Fig. 22 The location of the radiator hoses (2, 3)

22. Connect the radiator fan electrical connector.
23. Turbocharger Equipped Vehicles: Connect the power steering hoses.
24. Close radiator draincock.
25. Carefully lower the vehicle.
26. Turbocharger equipped vehicles: Inspect radiator inlet neck O-ring. Replace if necessary. Install radiator inlet neck. Torque fasteners to 55 inch lbs. (6 Nm).
27. Connect upper radiator hose. Align the hose and position the clamp to prevent interference with the engine or hood.
28. Install upper radiator closure panel and center brace.
29. Install the grille.
30. Install the battery tray and battery.
31. Connect the positive battery cable. Connect negative battery cable.
32. Install air cleaner housing assembly.
33. Fill the cooling system with coolant.
34. Operate engine until it reaches normal operating temperature. Check cooling system for correct fluid level.
35. Turbocharger Equipped Vehicles: Check power steering fluid level. Fill as needed.

THERMOSTAT

REMOVAL & INSTALLATION

See Figure 23.

1. Disconnect negative battery cable.
2. Drain the cooling system below thermostat housing level.
3. Remove thermostat.
4. Disconnect engine coolant temperature sensor.
5. Disconnect heater supply hose.
6. Turbocharger equipped vehicles:
    - Recover the refrigerant from the refrigerant system.
    - Disconnect A/C suction line from A/C compressor.
7. Remove housing attaching bolts.
8. Remove housing and gasket.

To install:

9. Clean all gasket sealing surfaces.
10. Install gasket and housing. Tighten bolts to 20 ft. lbs. (28 Nm).
11. Turbocharger equipped vehicles:
    - Connect A/C suction line to A/C compressor.
    - Evacuate the refrigerant system.
    - Charge the refrigerant system.
12. Connect heater supply hose.
13. Connect engine coolant temperature sensor.
14. Install thermostat.

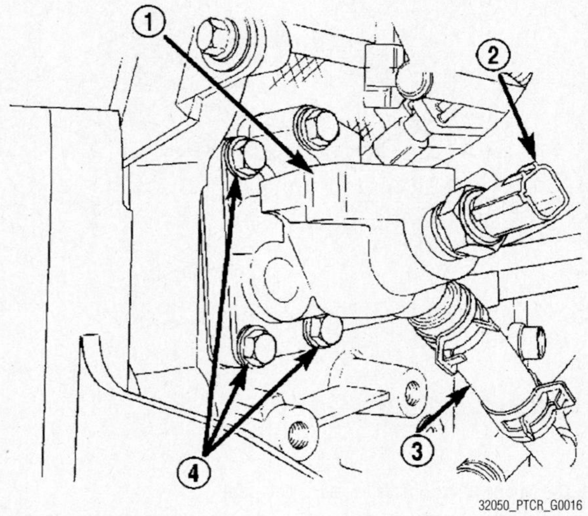

Fig. 23 Thermostat location

15. Fill cooling system.
16. Connect negative battery cable.

WATER PUMP

REMOVAL & INSTALLATION

See Figure 24.

1. Before servicing the vehicle, refer to the precautions in the beginning of this section.
2. Drain the cooling system.
3. Remove or disconnect the following:
    - Negative battery cable
    - Timing belt
    - Camshaft sprockets
    - Rear timing belt cover
    - Water pump and discard the O-ring

To install:

➡Apply dielectric grease to the new O-ring before installation.

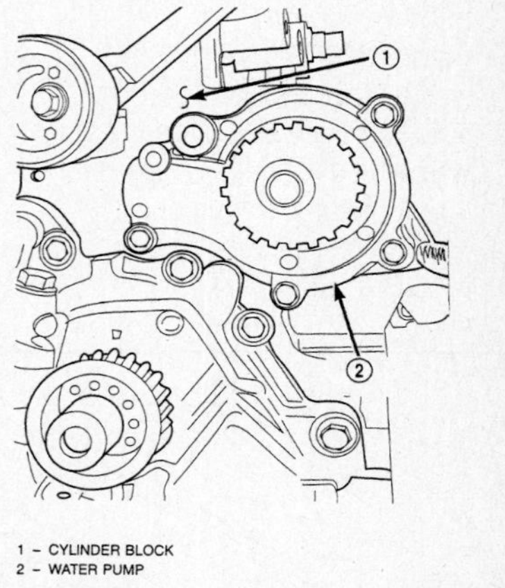

Fig. 24 Exploded view of the water pump

4. Install or connect the following:
   - New O-ring in the water pump groove

WARNING

Before proceeding, be sure the O-ring gasket is properly seated in the water pump groove before tightening the screws. An improperly installed O-ring could cause a coolant leak.

   - Water pump and torque the bolts to 105 inch lbs. (12 Nm)

➡Rotate the pump by hand to check for freedom of movement.

   - Rear timing belt cover
   - Camshaft sprockets
   - Timing belt
   - Negative battery cable
5. Fill the cooling system.
6. Start the vehicle and check for leaks, repair if necessary.

ENGINE ELECTRICAL

CHARGING SYSTEM

ALTERNATOR

REMOVAL & INSTALLATION

See Figures 25 and 26.

Remove or disconnect the following:

- Negative battery cable
- Air cleaner lid
- Inlet Air Temperature (IAT) sensor and make-up hose
- Upper alternator adjustment lock nut, loosen only
- Right front wheel
- Splash shield
- Support bracket
- Lower pivot bolt, loosen only
- Drive belt T-bolt, loosen only
- Alternator wiring connectors
- Alternator belt
- Axle retaining nut

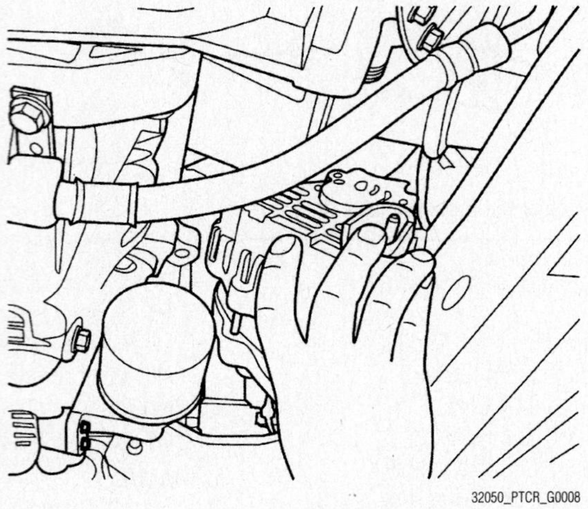

Fig. 26 The removal and installation of the alternator

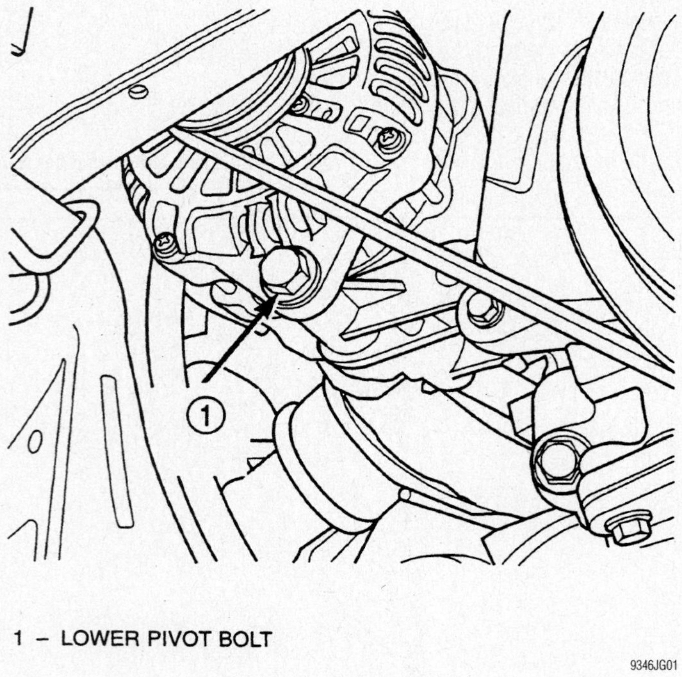

Fig. 25 Remove the lower pivot bolt from the alternator

- Lower control arm from the steering knuckle
- Axle shaft
- Lower mounting bolt from the upper adjustment bracket
- Alternator

To install:

Install or connect the following:

- Alternator
- Alternator drive belt
- Axle shaft
- Lower control arm to the steering knuckle
- Lower ball joint nut and torque the nut to 70 ft. lbs. (95 Nm)
- Axle retaining nut and torque the nut to 120 ft. lbs. (163 Nm)
- Support bracket
- Alternator electrical connectors and torque the B+ terminal nut to 100 inch lbs. (11 Nm)
- Splash shield and right front wheel
- Right front wheel
- Upper pivot nut and torque to 40 ft. lbs. (54 Nm)
- Negative battery cable
- Air cleaner lid, IAT sensor and make up hose

FIRING ORDER

See Figure 27.

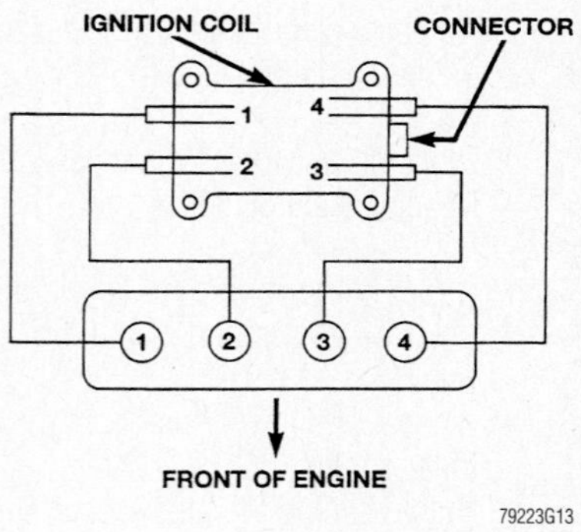

**Fig. 27 2.4L Engine
Firing order: 1–3–4–2
Distributorless Ignition System**

IGNITION COIL

REMOVAL & INSTALLATION

See Figure 28.

1. Remove the negative battery cable.
2. Disconnect electrical connector from coil pack.
3. Remove coil pack mounting nuts.
4. Remove coil pack.

To install:

5. Install coil pack on valve cover. Tighten the bolts to 105 ±20 inch lbs. (11.8 Nm)
6. Transfer spark plug cables to new coil pack. The coil pack towers are numbered with the cylinder identification. Be sure the ignition cables snap onto the towers.
7. Install the negative battery cable.

IGNITION TIMING

ADJUSTMENT

The ignition timing is controlled by the Powertrain Control Module (PCM). No adjustment is necessary or possible.

SPARK PLUGS

REMOVAL & INSTALLATION

**** WARNING**

Failure to route the cables properly could cause the radio to reproduce ignition noise, cross ignition of the spark plugs or short circuit the cables to ground.

➡ Remove cables from coil first before removing spark plug insulator. Special care should be used when installing spark plugs in the 2.4L cylinder head spark plug wells. Be sure the plugs do not drop into the wells, damage to the electrodes can occur. Always tighten spark plugs to the specified torque. Over tightening can cause distortion resulting in a change in the spark plug gap. Over tightening can also damage the cylinder head.

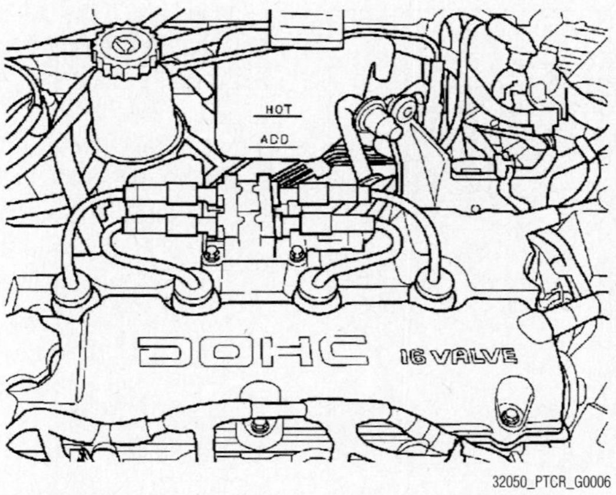

Fig. 28 The electronic ignition coil pack attaches directly to the valve cover

1. Remove the air cleaner lid, disconnect the inlet air sensor and makeup air hose.
2. Disconnect the negative battery cable.
3. Remove the upper intake manifold, refer to the Engine section for more information.
4. Disconnect the cable from the ignition coil first.
5. Always remove the spark plug cable by grasping the top of the spark plug insulator, rotate the boot 90° and pulling straight up in a steady motion.
6. Remove the spark plug using a quality socket with a rubber or foam insert.
7. Inspect the spark plug condition.

To install:

8. To avoid cross threading, start the spark plug into the cylinder head by hand.

**** WARNING**

The tapered seat plugs for this application are torque-critical! It is imperative that 11–15 ft. lbs. (16–20 Nm) is NOT exceeded.

9. Tighten spark plugs to 11–15 ft. lbs. (16–20 Nm).
10. Install spark plug insulators over spark plugs. Ensure the top of the spark plug insulator covers the upper end of the spark plug tube.
11. Install spark plug cable to coil.
12. Install the upper intake manifold, refer to the Engine section for more information
13. Connect the negative battery cable.
14. Install the air cleaner lid and connect the inlet air temperature sensor and makeup hose.

STARTER

REMOVAL & INSTALLATION

2.4L Non-Turbo Engine

See Figures 29 through 31.

1. Before servicing the vehicle, refer to the precautions in the beginning of this section.
2. Remove or disconnect the following:
   - Negative battery cable
   - Air cleaner box cover
   - Engine structural collar
   - Starter electrical connectors
   - Starter

To install:

3. Install the starter and torque the bolts to 40 ft. lbs. (54 Nm). Attach the starter electrical connectors.
4. Install the engine structural collar on models with an automatic transaxle as follows, refer to the illustration for bolt locations:
   a. Place the collar in position and hand tighten the collar to transaxle bolt.
   b. Position the power steering hose support bracket and install the collar to oil pan bolt.
   c. Place the bending strut in place and hand start the bolt.
   d. Install the bolt through the strut and collar and hand tighten.
   e. Place the power steering hose support bracket in position and install and hand tighten the remaining bolts.
   f. Tighten the collar-to-transmission bolts to 75 ft. lbs. (101 Nm).
   g. Install the bolts through the strut and into the block.
   h. Tighten the remaining bolts to 45 ft. lbs. (61 Nm).

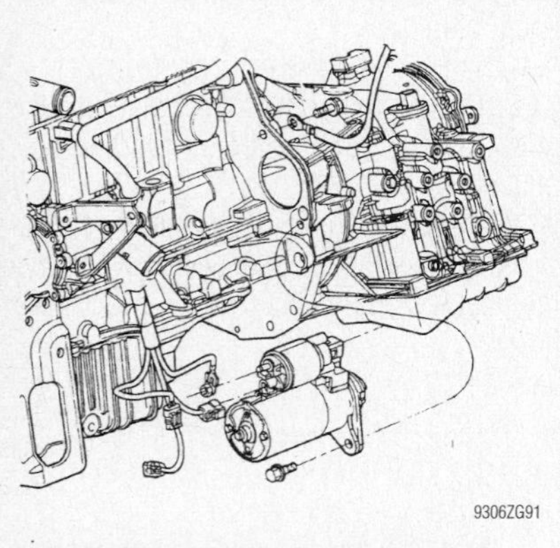

Fig. 29 Removal of the starter motor mounting

5. Install the engine structural collar on models with a manual transaxle as follows, refer to the illustration for bolt locations:
   a. Place the collar in position and hand tighten the collar to transaxle bolt.
   b. Position the power steering hose support bracket and install the collar to oil pan bolt.
   c. Position the clutch slave cylinder into position and hand start the bolts.
   d. Tighten bolts (1) to 75 ft. lbs. (101 Nm).
   e. Tighten bolts (2 and 5) to 45 ft. lbs. (61 Nm).

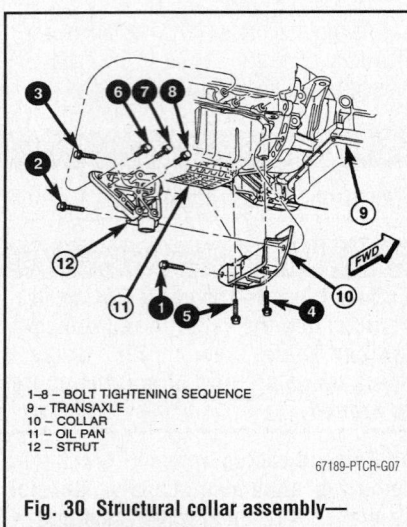

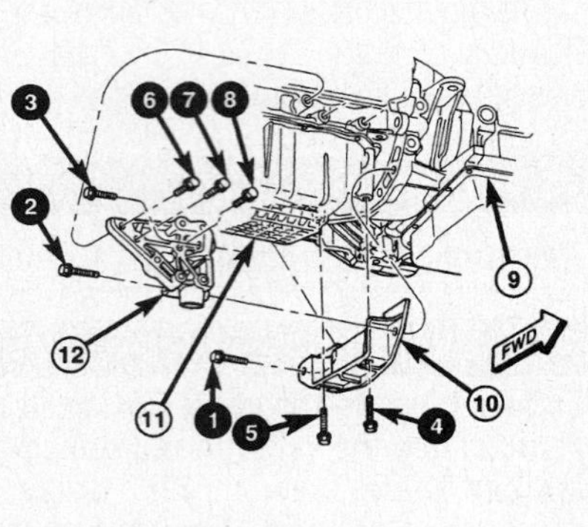

Fig. 30 Structural collar assembly—automatic transaxle

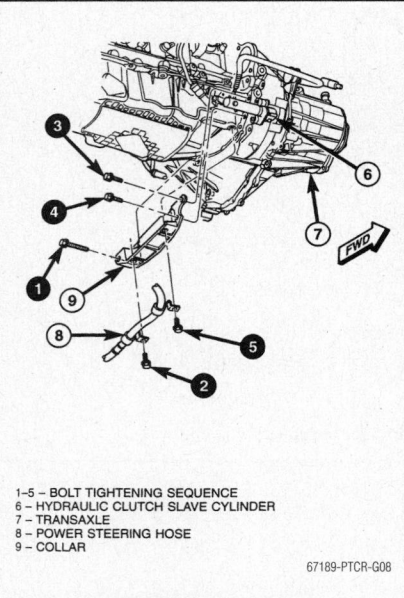

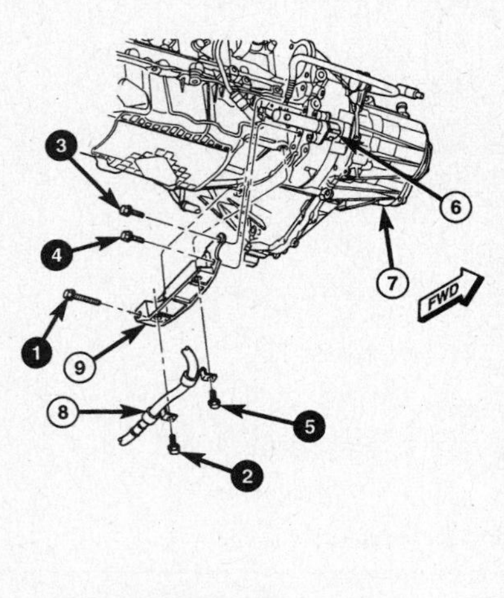

Fig. 31 Structural collar assembly—manual transaxle

   f. Tighten bolts (3 and 4) to 20 ft. lbs. (28 Nm).
6. Install the air cleaner box cover and connect the negative battery cable.

2.4L Turbo Engine

See Figure 32.

1. Before servicing the vehicle, refer to the precautions in the beginning of this section.
2. Remove or disconnect the following:
   - Negative battery cable
   - Air cleaner box cover
   - Upper starter bolt by pushing the inner cooler up and out of the way
   - Inner cooler lower hose from the inner cooler
   - Nuts retaining the inner cooler tube
   - Studs retaining the power steering lines
   - Position the power steering lines aside
   - Engine structural collar
   - Starter electrical connectors
   - Starter

To install:

3. Install the starter and torque the bolts to 40 ft. lbs. (54 Nm). Attach the starter electrical connectors.
4. Install the engine structural collar on models with an automatic transaxle as follows; refer to the illustration for bolt locations:
   a. Place the collar in position and hand tighten the collar to transaxle bolt.
   b. Position the power steering hose support bracket and install the collar to oil pan bolt.
   c. Place the bending strut in place and hand start the bolt.
   d. Install the bolt through the strut and collar and hand tighten.
   e. Place the power steering hose support bracket in position and install and hand tighten the remaining bolts.
   f. Tighten the collar-to-transmission bolts to 75 ft. lbs. (101 Nm).
   g. Install the bolts through the strut and into the block.
   h. Tighten the remaining bolts to 45 ft. lbs. (61 Nm).
5. Install the engine structural collar on models with a manual transaxle as follows, refer to the illustration for bolt locations:
   a. Place the collar in position and hand tighten the collar to transaxle bolt.
   b. Position the power steering hose

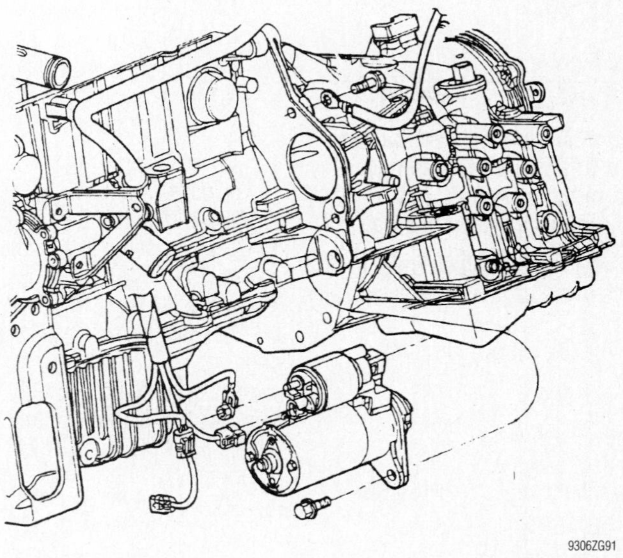

Fig. 32 Removal of the starter motor mounting

support bracket and install the collar to oil pan bolt.

c. Position the clutch slave cylinder into position and hand start the bolts.

d. Tighten bolts (1) to 75 ft. lbs. (101 Nm).

e. Tighten bolts (2 and 5) to 45 ft. lbs. (61 Nm).

f. Tighten bolts (3 and 4) to 20 ft. lbs. (28 Nm).

6. Install or connect the following:
   - Power steering lines aside
   - Studs retaining the power steering lines and tighten to 45 ft. lbs. (61 Nm)
   - Nuts retaining the inner cooler tube
   - Inner cooler lower hose to the inner cooler
   - Upper starter bolt by pushing the inner cooler up and out of the way. Tighten to 40 ft. lbs. (54 Nm).
   - Air cleaner box cover
   - Negative battery cable

ENGINE MECHANICAL

➡Disconnecting the negative battery cable may interfere with the functions of the on board computer systems and may require the computer to undergo a relearning process, once the negative battery cable is reconnected.

ACCESSORY DRIVE BELTS

ACCESSORY BELT ROUTING

See Figure 33.

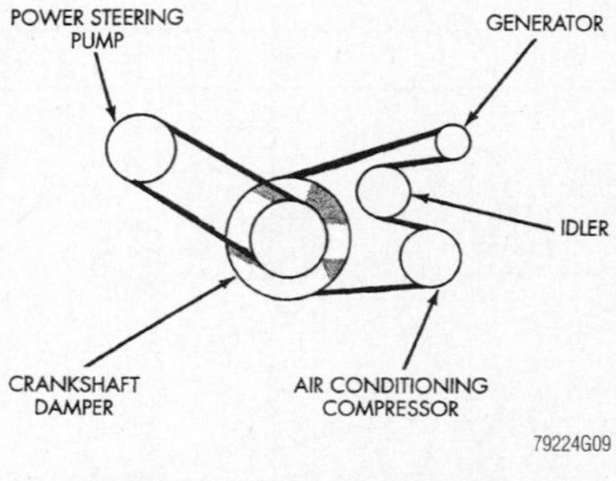

Fig. 33 Accessory drive belt routing—2.4L engine

INSPECTION

Inspect the drive belt for signs of glazing or cracking. A glazed belt will be perfectly smooth from slippage, while a good belt will have a slight texture of fabric visible. Cracks will usually start at the inner edge of the belt and run outward. All worn or damaged drive belts should be replaced immediately.

ADJUSTMENT

Power Steering and Air Conditioning Compressor Belt

The power steering and air conditioning belt is automatically adjusted with a spring tensioner.

Alternator Belt

The alternator belt must be adjusted manually for proper tension.

1. Check belt tension using Special Tool 8371—Belt Tension Gauge Adapter, and the DRBIII® using the following procedures:

⁂ CAUTION

Do not check belt tension with the engine running.

2. Connect 8371 to the DRBIII® following the instructions provided in tool kit.
3. Place end of microphone probe approximately 1 in. (2.54cm) from belt at one of the belt center span locations.
4. Pluck the belt a minimum of 3 times. (Use your finger or other suitable object).
5. The frequency of the belt in hertz (Hz) will display on DRBIII® screen.
6. Adjust belt to obtain proper frequency (tension). Refer to the belt tension chart for specifications.
7. Tighten pivot bolt to 40 ft. lbs. (54 Nm) and locking nut to 40 ft. lbs. (54 Nm).
8. Install power steering pump/air conditioning compressor drive belt.

REMOVAL & INSTALLATION

Power Steering and Air Conditioning Compressor Belt

1. Remove belt splash shield.
2. Using a wrench, rotate belt tensioner clockwise until belt can be removed from power steering pump pulley. Gently, release spring tension on tensioner.
3. Remove belt.

To install:

➡When installing drive belt onto pulleys, make sure that belt is properly routed and all V-grooves make proper contact with pulley grooves.

4. Install belt over all pulleys except for the power steering pump pulley.
5. Using a wrench, rotate belt tensioner clockwise until belt can be installed onto power steering pump pulley. Release spring tension onto belt.
6. After belt is installed, inspect belt length indicator marks. The indicator mark should be within the minimum belt length and maximum belt length marks. On a new belt, the indicator mark should align approximately with the nominal belt length mark.
7. Install belt splash shield.

Alternator Belt

1. Remove power steering pump/air conditioning compressor drive belt.
2. Loosen the pivot bolt, then the locking nut, and adjusting bolt.
3. Remove the alternator belt.

To install:

➡When installing drive belt onto pulleys, make sure that belt is properly routed and all V-grooves make proper contact with pulley grooves.

4. Install belt and/or adjust belt tension by tightening adjusting bolt. Adjust belt to specification shown in Belt Tension Chart.
5. Check belt tension using Special Tool 8371—Belt Tension Gauge Adapter, and the DRBIII® using the following procedures:

⁂ CAUTION

Do not check belt tension with the engine running.

6. Connect 8371 to the DRBIII® following the instructions provided in tool kit.
7. Place end of microphone probe approximately 1 in. (2.54cm) from belt at one of the belt center span locations.
8. Pluck the belt a minimum of 3 times. (Use your finger or other suitable object).
9. The frequency of the belt in hertz (Hz) will display on DRBIII® screen.
10. Adjust belt to obtain proper frequency (tension). Refer to the belt tension chart for specifications.
11. Tighten pivot bolt to 40 ft. lbs. (54 Nm) and locking nut to 40 ft. lbs. (54 Nm).
12. Install power steering pump/air conditioning compressor drive belt.

CAMSHAFT AND VALVE LIFTERS

INSPECTION

1. Inspect camshaft bearing journals for damage and binding. If journals are binding, check the cylinder head for damage. Also check cylinder head oil holes for clogging.
2. Check the cam lobe and bearing surfaces for abnormal wear and damage. Replace camshaft if defective.

➡If camshaft is replaced due to lobe wear or damage, always replace the rocker arms.

3. Measure the lobe actual wear (unworn area - wear zone = actual wear) and replace camshaft if out of limit. Standard value is 0.001 inches (0.0254mm), wear limit is 0.010 inches (0.254mm).

REMOVAL & INSTALLATION

See Figures 34 and 35.

➡After all components are installed on the engine, a DRB® scam tool is necessary to perform the camshaft and crankshaft timing relearn procedure.

1. Before servicing the vehicle, refer to the precautions in the beginning of this section.
2. Relieve the fuel system pressure.
3. Remove or disconnect the following:
   - Negative battery cable
   - Cylinder head cover
   - Camshaft Position (CMP) sensor and target magnet
   - Timing belt
   - Camshaft sprocket
   - Rear timing belt cover
   - Loosen the camshaft bearing caps in sequence from the rear of the cylinder head
   - Camshafts

To install:

Make certain that the pistons are **NOT** at Top Dead Center (TDC) before installing the camshafts.

4. Install the camshafts and cam followers, lubricate the bearing journals thoroughly.
5. Install the left and right camshaft bearing caps, No's 2–5 and right side No. 6. Torque these fasteners to 105 inch lbs. (12 Nm). Apply MOPAR® gasket maker to No. 1 and left side No. 6. Torque these fasteners

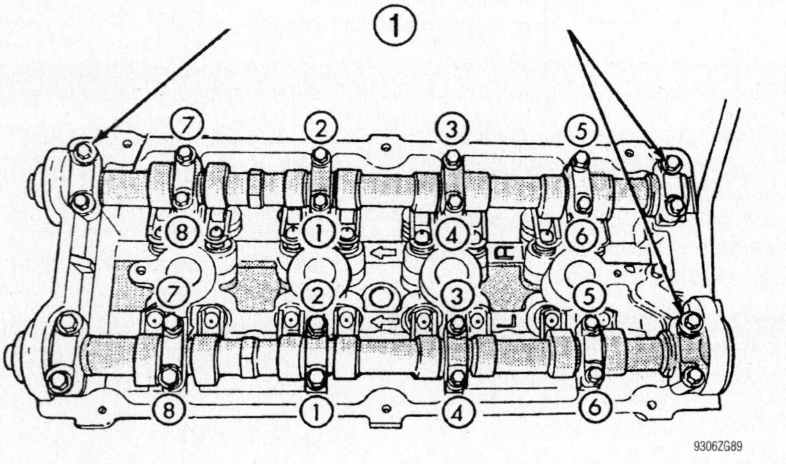

Fig. 34 Remove the camshaft bearing caps in sequence

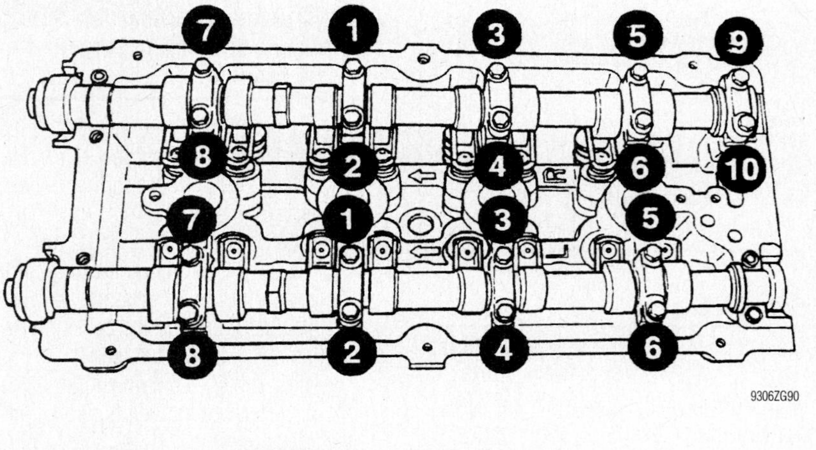

Fig. 35 Camshaft bearing cap tightening sequence

to 18 ft. lbs. (24 Nm) on 2002 models or 250 ft. lbs. (28 Nm) on 2003–06 models.

6. Install or connect the following:
   - Camshaft seals
   - Rear timing belt cover
   - Camshaft sprockets and torque the bolt to 85 ft. lbs. (115 Nm)
   - Timing belt
   - Target magnet
   - CMP sensor and torque the screws to 85 inch lbs. (9.6 Nm)
   - Cylinder head cover
   - Negative battery cable

➡An oil and filter change are recommended.

7. Use a DRB® scam tool to perform the camshaft and crankshaft timing relearn procedure, as follows:
   a. Connect the scan tool to the DLC (located under the instrument panel, near the steering column).
   b. Turn the ignition switch **ON** and access the "miscellaneous" screen.
   c. Select the "re-learn cam/crank" option, then follow the instructions on the scan tool screen.
8. Start the engine and check for leaks. Run the engine with the radiator cap off so as the engine warms and the thermostat opens, coolant can be added to the radiator. Test drive vehicle to check for proper operation.

CRANKSHAFT FRONT SEAL

REMOVAL & INSTALLATION

See Figures 36 and 37.

1. Before servicing the vehicle, refer to the precautions in the beginning of this section.
2. Remove or disconnect the following:
   - Negative battery cable
   - Crankshaft damper bolt
   - Crankshaft damper, using Puller Tool 1026 and Insert Tool 6827-A
   - Timing belt
   - Crankshaft sprocket, using Tool 6793 and Insert Tool C-4685-C2
   - Crankshaft oil seal, using a Seal Puller Tool 6771

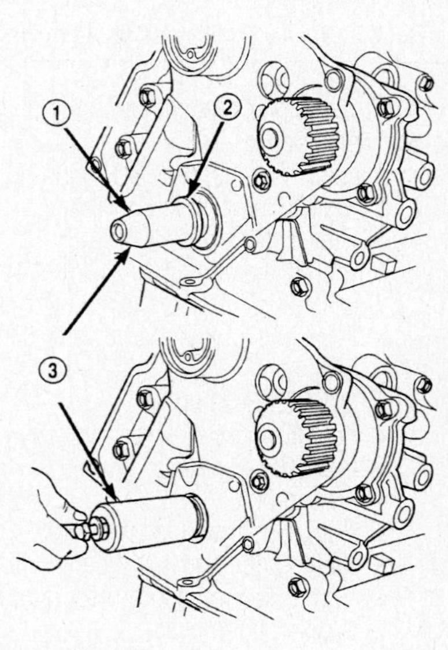

Fig. 37 Installing a new seal using Seal Installer 6780–1; proceed with caution if using substitute tools

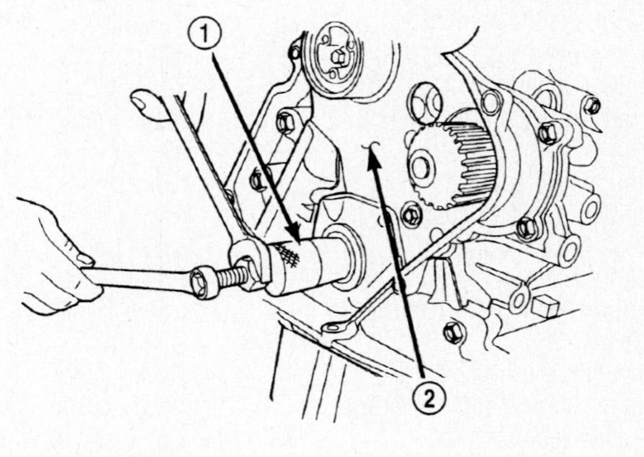

Fig. 36 Removing the front crankshaft oil seal

➡Be careful not to damage the seal surface of the cover.

To install:

3. Install or connect the following:
   - New front crankshaft oil seal with the seal spring facing the engine, using Crankshaft Installer Tool 6780
   - Crankshaft sprocket with special T 6792

➡Make sure the word FRONT on the crankshaft sprocket is facing outward.

   - Timing belt
   - Crankshaft damper using thrust bearing washer and bolt from Installer Tool 6792. Torque the damper bolt to 105 ft. lbs. (142 Nm).
   - Negative battery cable
4. Start the vehicle and check for leaks, repair if necessary.

CYLINDER HEAD

REMOVAL & INSTALLATION

See Figures 38 and 39.

➡After all components are installed on the engine, a DRB® scam tool is necessary to perform the camshaft and crankshaft timing relearn procedure.

1. Before servicing the vehicle, refer to the precautions in the beginning of this section.
2. Properly relieve the fuel system pressure.
3. Drain the cooling system.
4. Remove or disconnect the following:
   - Negative battery cable
   - Air cleaner inlet duct and air cleaner
   - Inlet Air Temperature (IAT) sensor and make-up air hose
   - Upper intake manifold
   - Dipstick tube fastener
   - Lower intake manifold support bracket on turbo models
   - Fuel supply line from the fuel rail
   - Heater tube support bracket
   - Upper radiator hose
   - Heater supply hoses
   - Accessory drive belt
   - Exhaust pipe from the manifold
5. On turbo models perform the following:
   a. Remove the turbocharger heat shields.
   b. Remove the elbow support bracket.
   c. Remove the turbocharger support bracket.

d. Remove the oil return, oil supply, coolant return and coolant supply hoses.

6. Remove or disconnect the following:
- Power steering pump, move it aside. DO NOT disconnect the fluid lines.
- Ignition coil pack wiring connector
- Ignition coil pack and bracket
- Cam sensor electrical connector
- Timing belt
- Timing belt idler pulley
- Camshaft sprocket
- Power steering pump reservoir and bracket, if necessary on Non-Turbo models
- Cylinder head cover
- Camshaft and cam followers
- Cylinder head bolts, working from the center outward
- Cylinder head

➡The cylinder head bolts must be inspected before they can be reused. If the threads of bolts are stretched, they must be replaced. Check for thread stretching by holding a scale or other straightedge against the threads. If all the threads do not contact the scale, the bolts must be replaced.

⁂ WARNING

Use only a plastic scraper to clean the mating surfaces. NEVER use metal, as this may gouge the surfaces and cause leaks.

7. Cover the combustion chambers, then use a plastic scraper to thoroughly and carefully clean the engine block and cylinder head mating surfaces.

To install:

8. Install the cylinder head with a new gasket. Make certain that the part number on the new gasket is facing up.

9. Lubricate the cylinder head bolt threads with clean engine oil.

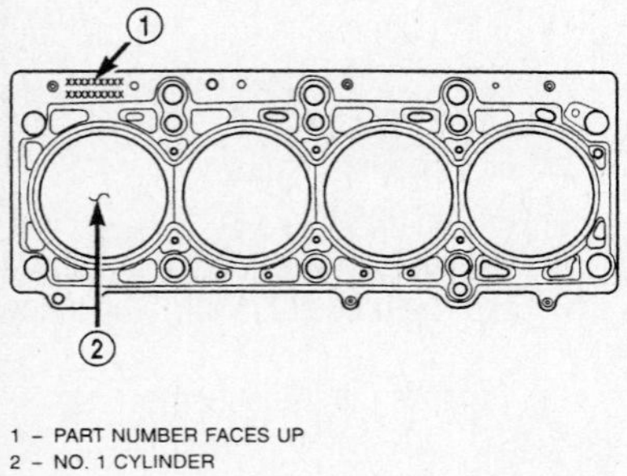

Fig. 38 Install the new gasket with the part number facing upward

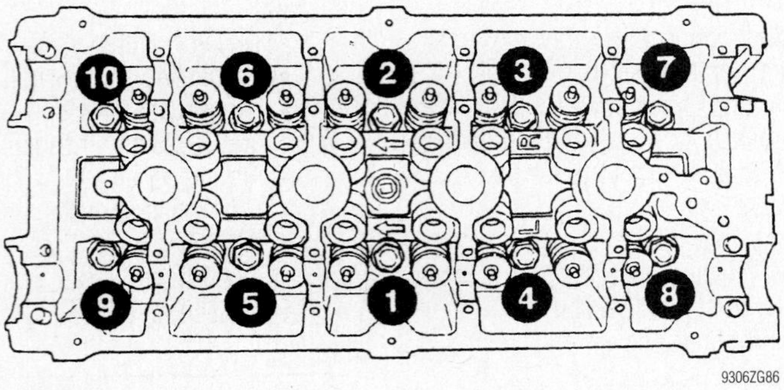

Fig. 39 Cylinder head bolt torque sequence

10. Torque the cylinder head bolts, in the following sequence:
   a. Step 1: 25 ft. lbs. (34 Nm).
   b. Step 2: 50 ft. lbs. (68 Nm).
   c. Step 3: 50 ft. lbs. (68 Nm).
   d. Step 4: An additional 1/4 turn.

11. Install or connect the following:
- Camshaft and cam follower assemblies
- Cylinder head cover
- Rear timing belt cover and pulley
- Camshaft sprockets
- Timing belt
- Cam sensor wiring connector
- Ignition coil and spark plug wires
- Power steering pump reservoir and bracket, if removed

12. On turbo models perform the following:
   a. Install the oil return, oil supply, coolant return and coolant supply hoses.
   b. Install the elbow support bracket.
   c. Install the turbocharger heat shields.
   d. Install the turbocharger support bracket.

13. Install or connect the following:
- Exhaust pipe to the manifold
- Accessory drive belts
- Lower intake manifold
- Upper radiator and heater supply hose
- Heater support bracket
- Lower intake manifold support bracket on turbo models
- Dipstick tube fastener
- Power brake vacuum hose to the intake manifold
- Fuel supply line to the fuel rail
- Vacuum lines and electrical wiring
- Upper intake manifold
- Air cleaner inlet duct and air cleaner
- IAT sensor and make up hose
- Negative battery cable

14. Fill the cooling system.

15. Turn the ignition switch **ON**, and access the "Miscellaneous" screen.

16. Select the "re-learn cam/crank" option, then follow the instructions on the scan tool screen.

ENGINE ASSEMBLY

REMOVAL & INSTALLATION

See Figures 40 and 41.

➡After all components are installed on the engine, a DRB® scam tool is necessary to perform the camshaft and crankshaft timing relearn procedure.

1. Before servicing the vehicle, refer to the precautions in the beginning of this section.
2. Properly recover the air conditioning system refrigerant.
3. Properly relieve the fuel system pressure.
4. Drain the cooling system.
5. Drain the engine oil.
6. Remove or disconnect the following:
- Battery and battery tray
- Throttle and cruise control cables
- Powertrain Control Module (PCM) wiring harness
- Positive cable from the Power Distribution Center (PDC) and ground wire
- Ground wire from the body to the engine
- Brake booster vacuum hose
- Proportional purge hoses from the intake manifold
- Coolant recovery hose
- Heater hoses
- Upper radiator support crossmember
- Upper and lower radiator hoses
- A/C line from the condenser
- A/C lines from the junction at the upper torque strut
- Cooler lines, if equipped
- Fan cooling module assembly

- Transmission shift linkage and electrical connectors
- Clutch hydraulic lines, if equipped
- Power steering hoses from the radiator on turbo models
- Radiator fan, radiator and condenser on 2003–06 models
- Both front wheels and the right inner splash shield
- Halfshafts
- Accessory drive belts
- Alternator and support brackets
- Charge air cooler hoses on turbo models
- Downstream Oxygen Sensor (O_2S)
- Exhaust system from the manifold
- Power steering pressure hose on Non-Turbo models
- Power steering hoses from the steering gear on turbo models
- Lower engine torque strut, if equipped
- Upper and lower heat shields, elbow support bracket, turbocharger support bract and elbow if equipped with a turbocharger
- Structural collar
- Torque converter bolts
- A/C compressor
- Power steering return line
- Power steering pump

7. Raise the vehicle enough to allow an engine dolly and cradle to be placed under the engine.

8. Loosen the engine support posts in order to allow movement for positioning onto the engine locating holes and flange on the engine bedplate. Lower the vehicle and position the cradle until the engine is resting on the support posts. Tighten the mounts to the cradle frame. This will keep the support posts from moving when removing or installing the engine and transaxle.

9. Install safety straps around the engine to the cradle; tighten the straps and lock them into position.

10. Raise the vehicle enough to see if the straps are tight enough to hold the cradle assembly to the engine.

11. Lower the vehicle so the weight of the engine and transaxle ONLY is on the cradle.

12. Remove the engine and transaxle mount through-bolts.

13. Raise the vehicle slowly, it might be necessary to move the engine/transaxle assembly with the cradle to allow removal around the body flanges.

To install:

14. Install or connect the following:
- Engine/transaxle assembly by lowering the vehicle over the assembly

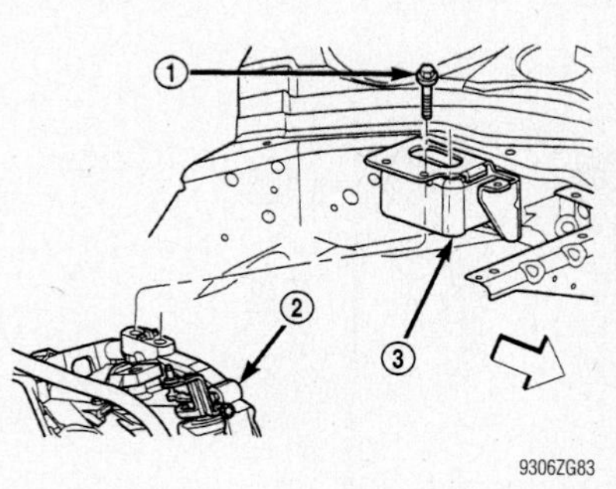

Fig. 40 Left engine mount (3) location and bolt (1) identification

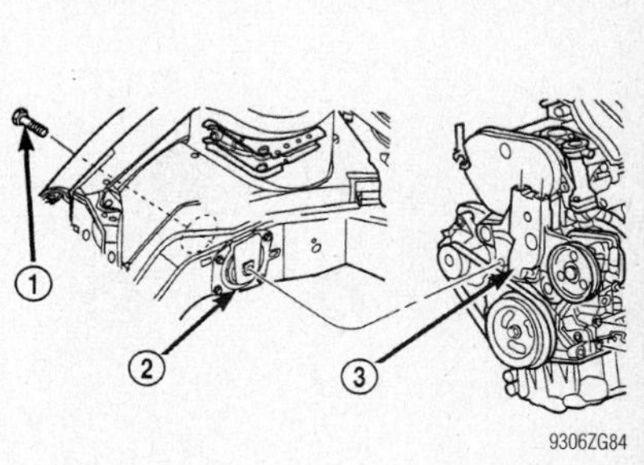

Fig. 41 Exploded view of the right mount through bolt (1)

- Engine and transaxle mounts and torque the bolts to 87 ft. lbs. (118 Nm)
- Upper torque strut

15. Remove the support fixtures.
- Alternator and support brackets
- Halfshafts

16. Install the structural collar and torque the bolts, in 3 steps, using the following procedure:

a. Step 1: Collar-to-oil pan bolts to 30 inch lbs. (3 Nm).

b. Step 2: Collar-to-transmission bolts to 80 ft. lbs. (108 Nm).

c. Step 3: Collar-to-oil pan bolts to 40 ft. lbs. (54 Nm).

17. Install or connect the following:
- Upper and lower heat shields, elbow support bracket, turbocharger support bract and elbow if equipped with a turbocharger
- Lower engine torque strut and torque the through bolts to 87 ft. lbs. (118 Nm)
- Exhaust pipe to the manifold
- Downstream O_2S connector
- Charge air cooler hoses on turbocharged models
- Power steering pressure hose to the steering gear
- A/C compressor
- Power steering pump
- Drive belts
- Right inner splash shield and both front wheels
- Power steering return hose
- Clutch hydraulic line, electrical connectors and shift linkage, if equipped
- Shift linkage and cooler lines, if equipped
- Fuel lines
- Heater hoses
- Engine wiring harness and ground strap
- Lower and upper radiator hoses
- Fan module assembly
- Throttle and speed control cables
- PDC, positive battery cable and ground strap
- PCM
- Battery and battery tray
- Battery cables

18. Perform the camshaft and crankshaft synchronization procedure.

19. Fill the engine with clean oil.

20. Fill the cooling system.

21. Recharge the A/C system.

22. After all components are installed, perform the camshaft and crankshaft timing relearn procedure as follows:

a. Connect a DRB or equivalent, scan tool to the DLC (located under the instrument panel, near the steering column).

b. Turn the ignition switch **ON**, and access the "miscellaneous" screen.

c. Select "re-learn cam/crank" option and follow the directions on the scan tool screen.

23. Start the vehicle and check for leaks, repair if necessary.

EXHAUST MANIFOLD

REMOVAL & INSTALLATION

Non-Turbo Models

See Figure 42.

1. Before servicing the vehicle, refer to the precautions in the beginning of this section.

2. Remove or disconnect the following:
- Negative battery cable
- Air cleaner assembly and bracket
- Throttle and speed control cables
- Manifold Absolute Pressure (MAP) sensor electrical connector
- Power steering reservoir, move it aside. DO NOT disconnect the fluid lines.
- Coolant recovery bottle
- Exhaust manifold upper heat shield

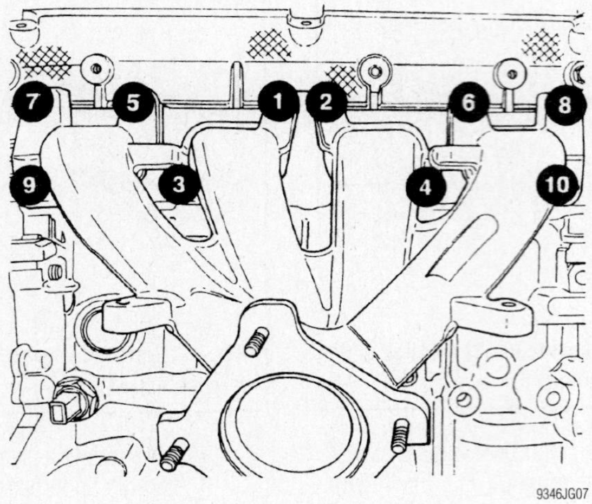

Fig. 42 Torque the exhaust manifold bolts in sequence

- Exhaust pipe from the manifold
- Engine wiring heat shield
- Manifold support bracket
- Lower exhaust manifold heat shield
- Upstream Heated Oxygen Sensor (HO_2S) connector
- Exhaust manifold and discard the gasket

3. Thoroughly clean the mating surfaces.

To install:

4. Install or connect the following:
   - New gasket
   - Exhaust manifold and torque the bolts, in sequence, to 17 ft. lbs. (23 Nm)
   - Alternator bracket bolt, if loosened
   - Exhaust manifold heat shields and torque the bolts to 105 inch lbs. (12 Nm)
   - Exhaust manifold support bracket
   - Engine wiring heat shield
   - Upstream HO_2 sensor wiring connector
   - Exhaust pipe to the manifold and torque the bolts to 21 ft. lbs. (28 Nm)
   - Coolant recovery bottle
   - Power steering pump reservoir
   - MAP sensor connector
   - Throttle and speed control cables
   - Air cleaner bracket and assembly
   - Negative battery cable
5. Start the vehicle and check for leaks, repair if necessary.

Turbo Models

The exhaust manifold on turbocharged models is removed as an assembly with the turbocharger.

INTAKE MANIFOLD

REMOVAL & INSTALLATION

Upper

Non-Turbo Models

See Figures 43 and 44.

1. Before servicing the vehicle, refer to the precautions in the beginning of this section.
2. Properly relieve the fuel system pressure.
3. Remove or disconnect the following:
   - Negative battery cable
   - Inlet Air Temperature (IAT) sensor and air hose
   - Engine cover
   - Throttle and cruise control cables from the throttle lever bracket

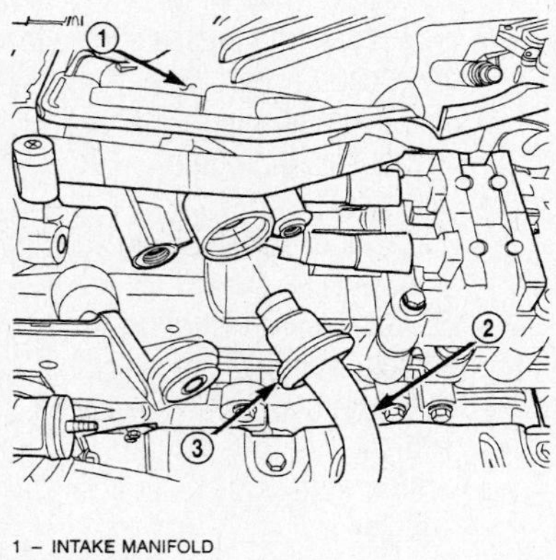

1 – INTAKE MANIFOLD
2 – EGR TUBE
3 – SEAL

9346JG05

Fig. 43 Remove the EGR tube from the upper intake manifold

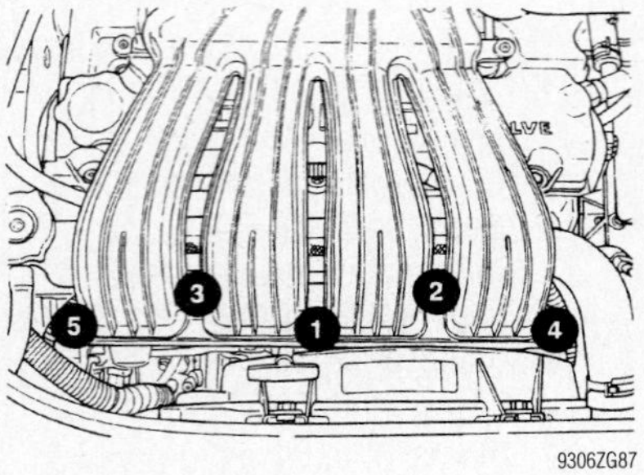

Fig. 44 Upper intake manifold bolt torque sequence—Non-Turbo models

   - Manifold Absolute Pressure (MAP) sensor
   - Idle Air Control (IAC) motor electrical connector
   - Throttle Position (TPS) sensor wiring connector
   - Proportional purge hoses
   - Brake booster vacuum hose
   - Positive Crankcase Ventilation (PCV) hose from the intake manifold
   - Throttle body support bracket bolt
   - Exhaust Gas Recirculation (EGR) tube from the upper intake manifold
   - Upper intake manifold
4. Clean the mating surfaces.

To install:

5. Install or connect the following:
   - New gaskets and seals
   - Intake manifold on the EGR tube then on the lower intake manifold. Torque the bolts, in sequence, to 20 ft. lbs. (28 Nm) on 2002 models or 105 inch lbs. (12 Nm) on 2003–06 models.
   - Throttle body support bracket and torque the bolt to 28 ft. lbs. (20 Nm)
   - EGR retainer plate and torque the smaller bolt to 95 inch lbs. (11 Nm) and the large bolt to 28 ft. lbs. (21 Nm)
   - PCV hose to the intake manifold
   - MAP sensor electrical connector
   - Proportional purge hoses
   - Brake booster hose
   - IAC motor and TPS connectors
   - Throttle and speed control cables
   - Air cleaner assembly
   - Engine cover
   - IAT sensor
   - Negative battery cable

Turbo Models

See Figure 45.

➡The engines in these vehicles are equipped with either an aluminum or plastic manifold.

1. Before servicing the vehicle, refer to the precautions in the beginning of this section.
2. Properly relieve the fuel system pressure.
3. Remove or disconnect the following:
   - Negative battery cable
   - Inlet Air Temperature (IAT) sensor
   - Manifold Absolute Pressure (MAP) sensor
   - Throttle inlet pressure hose
   - Charge air cooler hose from the throttle body
   - Idle Air Control (IAC) motor electrical connector
   - Throttle control shield
   - Throttle and cruise control cables from the throttle lever bracket
   - Throttle cable bracket
   - Brake booster vacuum hose
   - Positive Crankcase Ventilation (PCV) hose from the intake manifold
   - Purge solenoid hose from the throttle body
   - Upper intake manifold support bracket and manifold

➡Cover the lower intake manifold to avoid dirt and other objects from entering.

4. Clean the mating surfaces.

To install:

5. Remove the cover from the lower intake manifold.
6. Install or connect the following:
   - New gasket
   - Intake manifold on the lower intake manifold. If equipped with an aluminum manifold, torque the bolts in sequence to 250 inch lbs. (28 Nm). If equipped with a plastic manifold, torque the bolts in sequence to 105 inch lbs. (12 Nm).
   - Upper intake manifold support bracket Torque the retainers to 250 inch lbs. (28 Nm).
   - Purge solenoid hose to the throttle body
   - Brake booster vacuum hose
   - PCV hose
   - Throttle cable bracket and tighten the screws to 105 inch lbs. (12 Nm)
   - Throttle and cruise control cables to the throttle lever bracket
   - Throttle control shield
   - IAC motor electrical connector
   - MAP sensor
   - Charge air cooler hose to the throttle body
   - IAT sensor
   - Throttle inlet pressure hose
   - Negative battery cable

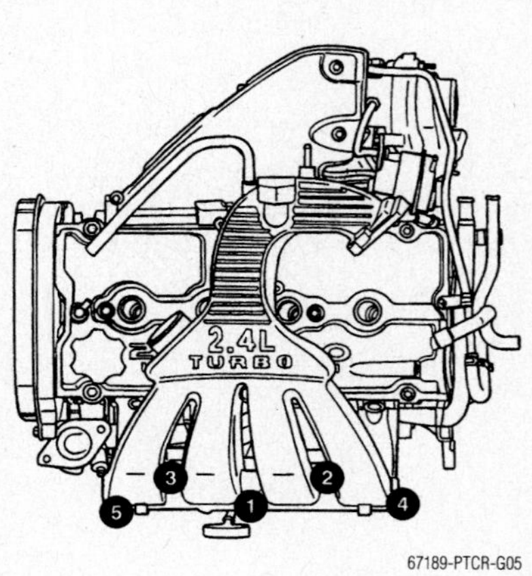

Fig. 45 Upper intake manifold bolt torque sequence—turbo models

Lower

See Figures 46 and 47.

➡The engines in these vehicles are equipped with either an aluminum or plastic manifold.

1. Before servicing the vehicle, refer to the precautions in the beginning of this section.
2. Properly relieve the fuel system pressure.
3. Drain the coolant system.
4. Remove or disconnect the following:
   - Negative battery cable
   - Inlet Air Temperature (IAT) sensor and make-up hose
   - Air cleaner
   - Upper intake manifold
   - Upper radiator hose and coolant outlet connector
   - Fuel supply line quick-connect from the fuel rail
   - Fuel injector wiring harness
   - Oil dipstick tube from the lower intake manifold
   - Intake manifold and discard the gaskets and seals
5. Thoroughly clean the gasket mating surfaces.

To install:

6. Install or connect the following:
   - New seals on Non-Turbo models
   - Intake manifold and torque the bolts in sequence to 105 inch lbs. (12 Nm) on Non-Turbo models
   - New gaskets on turbo models
   - Intake manifold. If equipped with an aluminum manifold, torque the bolts in sequence to 250 inch lbs. (28 Nm). If equipped with a plastic manifold, torque the bolts in sequence to 150 inch lbs. (12 Nm) on turbo models.
   - Lower intake manifold support bracket retainers on turbocharged models to 40 ft. lbs. (54 Nm)
   - Fuel injector wiring harness
   - Fuel supply line quick-connect to the fuel tube assembly
   - Oil dipstick tube to the lower intake manifold

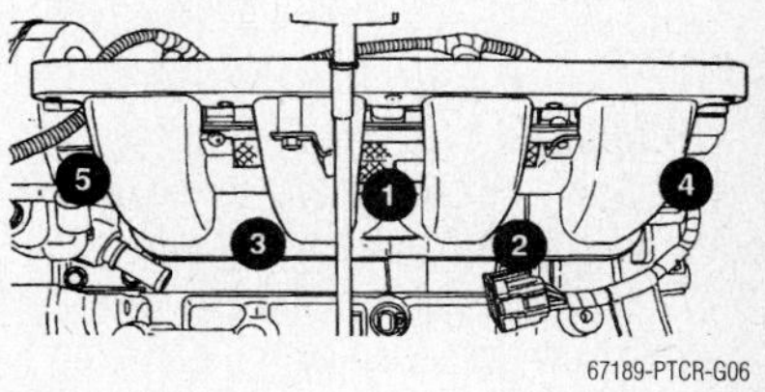

Fig. 47 Lower intake manifold bolt torque sequence

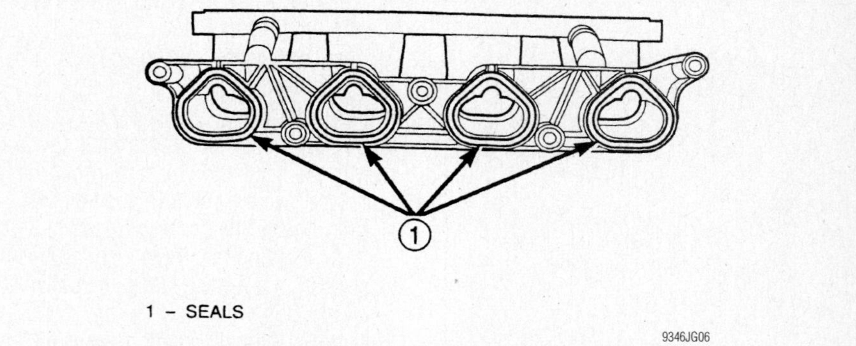

Fig. 46 Install new seals on the lower intake manifold-Non-Turbo models

- Upper radiator hose
- Upper intake manifold
- IAT sensor
- Air cleaner assembly
- Negative battery cable

7. Fill the coolant system.
8. Pressurize the fuel system.
9. Start the vehicle and check for leaks, repair if necessary.

OIL PAN

REMOVAL & INSTALLATION

See Figures 48 and 49.

1. Before servicing the vehicle, refer to the precautions in the beginning of this section.
2. Drain the engine oil and remove the oil filter.
3. Support the powertrain assembly.
4. Remove or disconnect the following:
   - Negative battery cable
   - Right inner splash shield
   - Turbocharger-to-charge air cooler hose assembly, if equipped
   - Oil cooler connector bolt, if equipped with a turbocharger. Do not disconnect the coolant lines from the oil cooler and reposition the cooler.
   - Engine structural collar
   - Lower torque strut
   - Oil filter adapter
   - Oil pan and gasket
5. Thoroughly clean all gasket mating surfaces.

To install:

6. Apply silicone sealer to the oil pump-to-engine block parting line.
7. Install or connect the following:
   - New gasket on the oil pan
   - Oil pan and torque the bolts to 105 inch lbs. (12 Nm)
   - Oil filter and adapter and torque the screws to 105 inch lbs. (12 Nm)

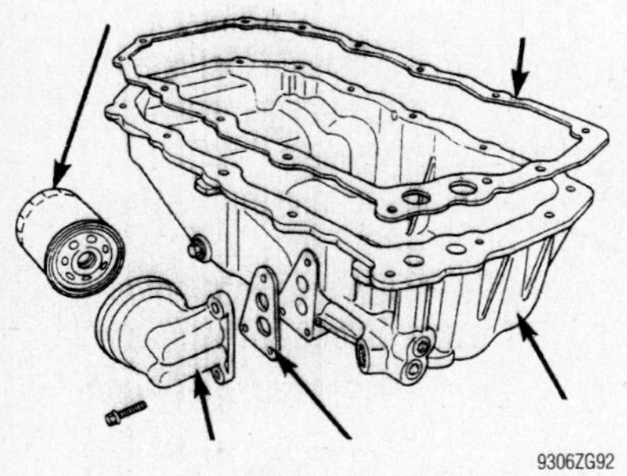

Fig. 48 Remove the oil filter adapter

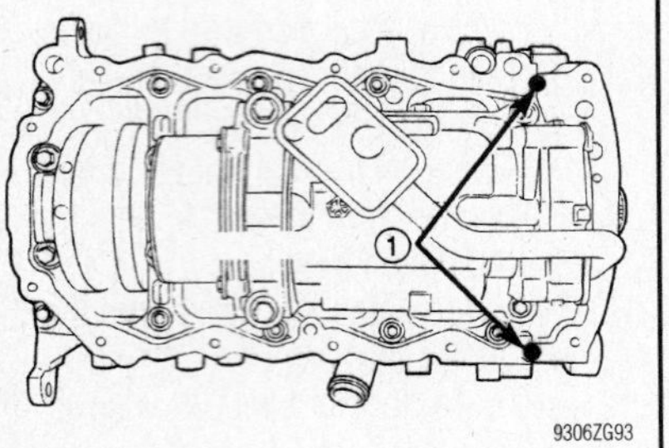

Fig. 49 Silicone sealer application locations

8. If equipped with a turbocharger, replace the oil cooler seal. Lubricate the seal with and place the oil cooler-to-oil filter adapter in position making sure to align the notch on the tab. Install the oil cooler connector bolt and tighten to 41 ft. lbs. (55 Nm).

WARNING

Follow the proper tightening sequence for the structural collar or damage to the collar or oil pan may occur.

9. Install the engine structural collar on models with an automatic transaxle as follows, refer to the illustration for bolt locations:
   a. Place the collar in position and hand tighten the collar to transaxle bolt.
   b. Position the power steering hose support bracket and install the collar to oil pan bolt.
   c. Place the bending strut in place and hand start the bolt.
   d. Install the bolt through the strut and collar and hand tighten.
   e. Place the power steering hose support bracket in position and install and hand tighten the remaining bolts.
   f. Tighten the collar-to-transmission bolts to 75 ft. lbs. (101 Nm).
   g. Install the bolts through the strut and into the block.
   h. Tighten the remaining bolts to 45 ft. lbs. (61 Nm).
10. Install the engine structural collar on models with a manual transaxle as follows, refer to the illustration for bolt locations:
   a. Place the collar in position and hand tighten the collar to transaxle bolt.
   b. Position the power steering hose support bracket and install the collar to oil pan bolt.
   c. Position the clutch slave cylinder into position and hand start the bolts.
   d. Tighten bolts (1) to 75 ft. lbs. (101 Nm).
   e. Tighten bolts (2 and 5) to 45 ft. lbs. (61 Nm).
   f. Tighten bolts (3 and 4) to 20 ft. lbs. (28 Nm).
11. Install or connect the following:
   - Lower torque strut
   - Turbocharger-to-charge air cooler hose assembly, if equipped
   - Right inner splash shield
   - Negative battery cable
12. Fill the engine with clean oil and a new filter.
13. Start the vehicle and check for leaks, repair if necessary.

OIL PUMP

REMOVAL & INSTALLATION

See Figures 50 and 51.

1. Before servicing the vehicle, refer to the precautions in the beginning of this section.
2. Drain the engine oil.
3. Remove or disconnect the following:
   - Negative battery cable
   - Timing belt and rear cover
   - Oil pan
   - Crankshaft sprocket, using Tool 6793 and Insert Tool C-4685-C2
   - Crankshaft key
   - Oil pickup tube
   - Oil pump

To install:

4. Wash all parts in a solvent; then, inspect carefully for damage or wear, as follows:
   a. Inspect the mating surface of the oil pump should be smooth. Replace the pump cover, if scratched or grooved.

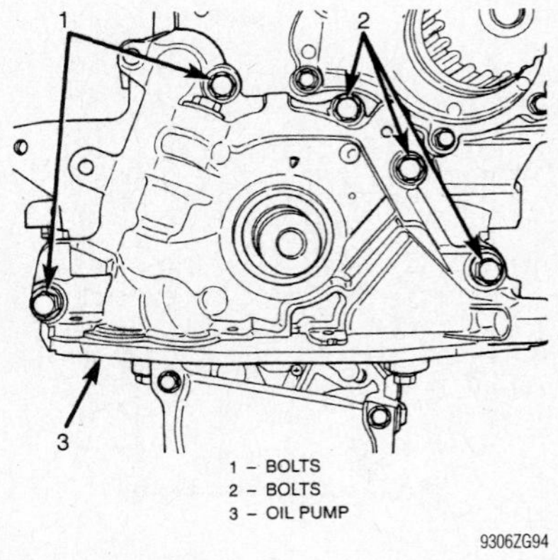

Fig. 50 Exploded view of the oil pump mounting bolts

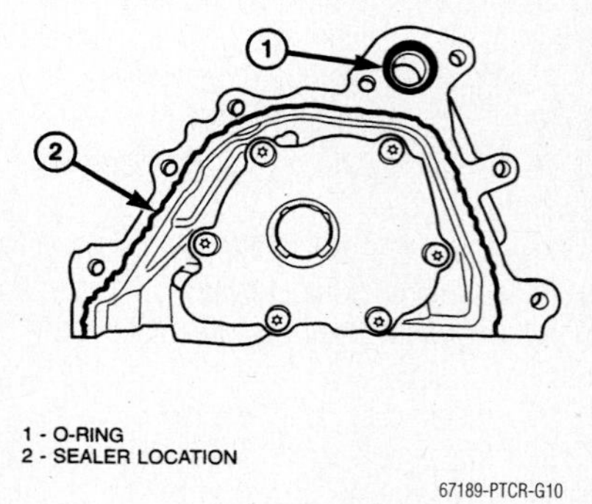

Fig. 51 Apply a small amount of gasket maker to the pump body cover mounting surface

b. Apply MOPAR® gasket maker to the oil pump.

c. Install the O-ring into the oil pump body discharge passage.

5. Prime the oil pump before installation by filling the rotor cavity with engine oil.

6. Install or connect the following:

- Oil pump, align the rotor flats with the crankshaft flats and torque the bolts to 21 ft. lbs. (28 Nm).

⁂ WARNING

The front crankshaft seal MUST be out of the pump to align or damage may result.

- New front crankshaft seal, using Seal Driver Tool 6780
- Crankshaft key
- Crankshaft sprocket, using a Crankshaft Sprocket Installer Tool 6792
- Oil pump pickup tube
- Oil pan
- Rear timing belt cover
- Timing belt
- Negative battery cable

7. Fill the engine with clean oil.

8. Start the engine and check for leaks; repair if necessary.

INSPECTION

1. Inspect the mating surface of the oil pump. Surface should be smooth. Replace pump cover if scratched or grooved.

2. Lay a straightedge across the pump cover surface. If a 0.001 inches (0.025mm) feeler gauge can be inserted between cover and straight edge, cover should be replaced.

3. Measure thickness and diameter of outer rotor. If outer rotor thickness measures 0.421 inches (10.699mm) or less, or if the diameter is 3.383 inches (85.924mm) or less, replace outer rotor.

4. If inner rotor measures 0.421 inches (10.699mm) or less replace inner rotor.

PISTON AND RING

POSITIONING

See Figures 52 and 53.

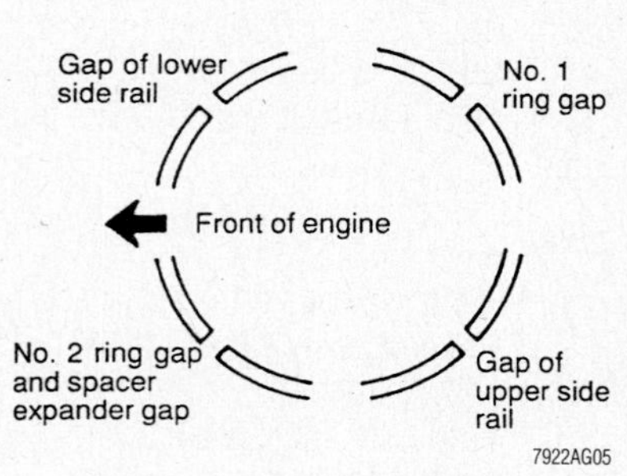

Fig. 52 Piston ring end-gap spacing—2.4L engine

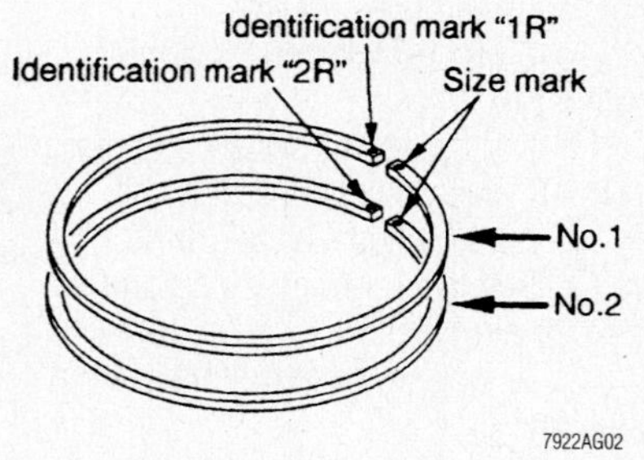

Fig. 53 Common Chrysler piston ring identification mark locations

REAR MAIN SEAL

REMOVAL & INSTALLATION

See Figures 54 and 55.

1. Before servicing the vehicle, refer to the precautions in the beginning of this section.

2. Remove or disconnect the following:

- Transmission
- Flexplate/flywheel
- Rear main seal

3. Insert a seal remover between the dust lip and the metal case of the crankshaft seal. Angle the tool through the dust lip against the metal case of the seal. Pry out the seal.

⁂ WARNING

DO NOT let the pry tool contact the crankshaft seal surface. Contact of the tool blade against the crankshaft edge (chamfer) is permitted.

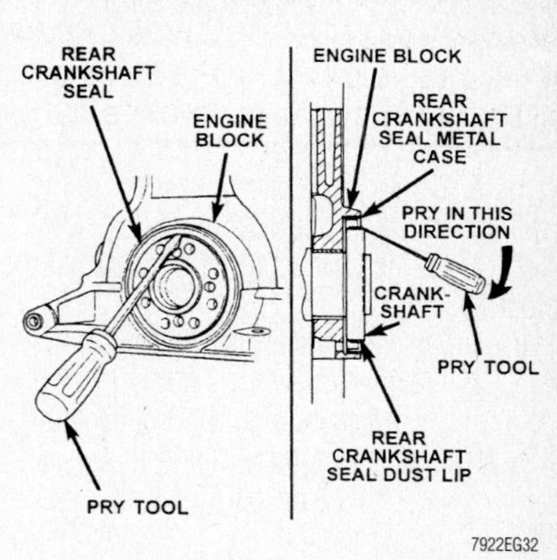

Fig. 54 When prying the seal out, be sure to use the pry tool at the proper angle

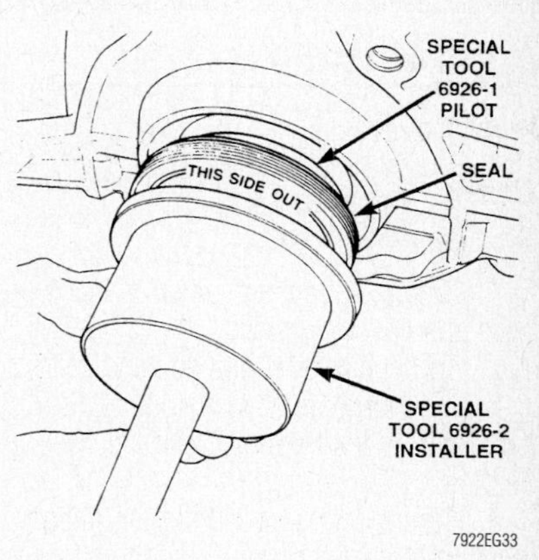

Fig. 55 Place a proper size pilot tool with a magnetic base on the crankshaft

To install:

⁂ WARNING

If the crankshaft edge (chamfer) has any burrs or scratches on the, clean it up with 400 grit sand paper to prevent seal damage during installation of the new seal.

➡No lubrication is necessary when installing the seal.

4. Place Crankcase Seal Pilot Tool 6926-1 on the crankshaft; this is a pilot tool with a magnetic base

5. Position the seal over the pilot Tool; be sure the words THIS SIDE OUT on the seal can be read.

➡The pilot tool should stay on the crankshaft during installation of the seal. Be sure the seal lip faces the crankcase during installation.

⁂ WARNING

If the seal is driven in the block past flush, this may cause an oil leak.

6. Drive the seal into the block, using Crankshaft Seal Tool 6926-2 and handle C-4171, until the tool bottoms out against the block.
7. Install or connect the following:
   - Flexplate/flywheel. Apply Lock & Seal Adhesive to the bolt treads and torque the bolts in a star pattern, to 70 ft. lbs. (95 Nm).
   - Transmission
   - Negative battery cable
8. Start the vehicle and check for leaks, repair if necessary.

TIMING CHAIN, SPROCKETS, FRONT COVER AND SEAL

REMOVAL & INSTALLATION

Front Cover

Upper

See Figure 56.

1. Remove upper torque strut attaching bolts and set strut aside.
2. Turbocharger equipped vehicles:
3. Discharge and evacuate the A/C system. Refer to the Heating & Air Conditioning Section.
4. Disconnect air conditioning lines at junction block near upper timing belt cover.
5. Remove upper timing belt cover fasteners and remove cover.

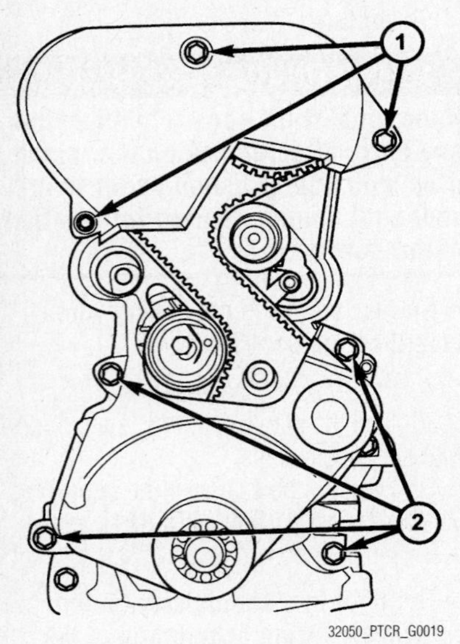

Fig. 56 Front timing belt covers and bolts (1, 2)

To install:

6. Install timing belt cover and tighten fasteners to 50 inch lbs. (6 Nm).
7. Install upper torque strut.
8. Turbocharger equipped vehicles:
   - Connect air conditioning lines at junction block near upper timing belt cover.
   - Recharge the A/C as outlined in the Heating & Air Conditioning Section.
9. Perform torque strut adjustment procedure.

Lower

1. Disconnect negative battery cable.
2. Raise and safely support the vehicle. Remove right front wheel.
3. Remove the right splash shield.
4. Remove accessory drive belts.
5. Remove crankshaft damper.
6. Remove the lower torque strut.
7. Disconnect exhaust system from manifold.
8. Disconnect A/C pressure switch at rear of compressor housing.
9. Lower vehicle and support engine with a jack.
10. Discharge A/C system and disconnect A/C lines at coupling block.
11. Remove upper torque strut.
12. Remove screw attaching ground strap to strut bracket.
13. Remove torque strut bracket from strut tower.
14. Remove upper radiator closure panel.
15. Remove power steering pump and bracket. Set pump aside. Do not disconnect lines from pump.
16. With engine properly supported, remove right engine mount through bolt.
17. Raise engine with jack until engine support bracket bolts are accessible.
18. Remove engine support bracket.
19. Remove timing belt cover fasteners and remove cover.

To install:

20. Install lower timing belt cover and tighten fasteners to 50 inch lbs. (6 Nm).
21. Install right engine support bracket. Ensure the power steering pump is properly located in mounting location on bracket. Tighten mount bracket bolts to 45 ft. lbs. (61 Nm).
22. Lower engine into mounting position and install right engine mount through bolt. Tighten bolt to 87 ft. lbs. (118 Nm).
23. Install power steering pump and bracket.
24. Install upper radiator closure panel.
25. Install torque strut bracket to strut tower.
26. Connect ground strap to bracket.
27. Install upper torque strut.
28. Connect A/C lines and charge A/C system.
29. Raise and safely support the vehicle.
30. Connect exhaust system to manifold.
31. Connect A/C pressure switch connector.
32. Install crankshaft damper.
33. Install accessory drive belts.
34. Install lower torque strut.
35. Perform torque strut adjustment procedure.
36. Install right splash shield.
37. Install right front wheel.
38. Connect negative cable to battery.

Timing Belt

See Figures 57 through 59.

1. Before servicing the vehicle, refer to the precautions in the beginning of this section.
2. Remove the A/C refrigerant using approved equipment. Refer to the Heating & Air Conditioning Section.
3. Remove or disconnect the following to remove the upper timing cover:
   - Negative battery cable
   - Upper torque strut bolts and set the strut aside
   - A/C lines at the junction block near the upper timing belt cover, if equipped with a turbocharger
   - Upper cover bolts and the cover
4. Remove or disconnect the following to remove the lower timing cover:
   - Right front wheel and inner splash shield
   - Accessory drive belts
   - Crankshaft damper
   - Lower torque strut
   - Exhaust system from the manifold
   - A/C compressor switch
   - Upper torque strut and bracket
   - Upper radiator support crossmember
   - Power steering pump and bracket without disconnecting the lines
   - Right engine mount through bolt after supporting the engine
   - Engine support bracket
   - Lower cover bolts and the cover
5. Rotate the crankshaft until the Top Dead Center (TDC) mark on the oil pump housing aligns with the TDC mark on the crankshaft sprocket.
6. Loosen the belt tensioner lock bolt.
7. Install a 6mm Allen wrench into the tensioner. Rotate the tensioner counter-

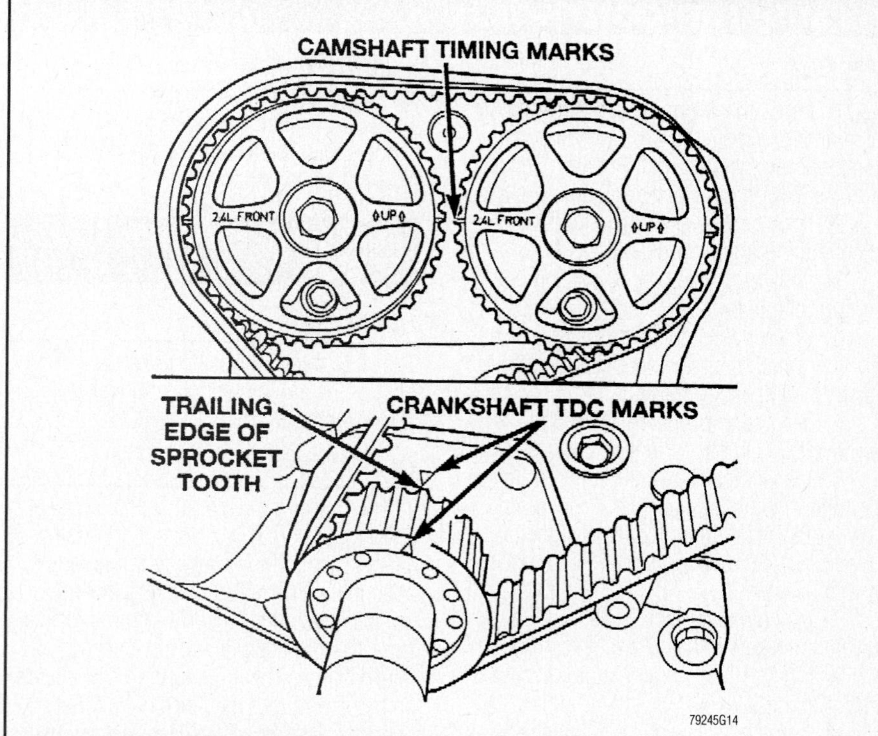

Fig. 57 Camshaft and crankshaft alignment marks—2.4L engine

clockwise while pushing on the wrench until it slides into the locking hole.

8. Remove the timing belt.

To install:

9. Set the crankshaft sprocket at TDC by aligning the sprocket with the arrow on the oil pump housing.

10. Set the camshafts timing marks so that the exhaust camshaft sprocket is a ½ notch below the intake camshaft sprocket.

11. Install the timing belt by starting at the crankshaft. Go around the water pump sprocket, idler pulley, camshaft sprockets and the tensioner.

12. Move the exhaust camshaft sprocket counterclockwise to align the marks and to remove any slack.

13. Insert a 6mm Allen wrench into the tensioner opening on the top plate of the tensioner pulley. Rotate the top plate counterclockwise. The pulley will move against the belt and the tensioner setting notch will start to move clockwise. Continue to move the top plate counterclockwise until the setting notch is aligned with the spring tang. Using the Allen wrench, to prevent the top plate from moving, tighten the tensioner lock bolt to 220 inch lbs. (25 Nm). Make sure the setting notch and spring tang are still aligned after the lock nut is tighten. If not repeat the procedure.

14. Remove the wrench from the belt tensioner.

➡When repositioning the crankshaft to the TDC position, this must be done during the clockwise rotation movement. If the TDC is missed, rotate a further two full turns until TDC is reached. Do not rotate the crankshaft counterclockwise as this will result in improper tensioner settings.

15. Rotate the crankshaft two full revolutions and verify that the TDC marks are properly aligned.

16. Check the spring tang is within the tolerance window, if not repeat the previous two steps.

17. Install or connect the following:
   - Lower timing belt cover and torque the bolts to 50 inch lbs. (6 Nm).
   - Upper timing belt cover and torque the bolts to 50 inch lbs. (6 Nm).
   - A/C lines at the junction block near the upper timing belt cover, if equipped with a turbocharger
   - Right engine support bracket and reposition the power steering pump. Torque the bracket bolts to 45 ft. lbs. (61 Nm).
   - Right engine mount through bolt and torque it to 87 ft. lbs. (118 Nm)
   - Upper radiator support crossmember
   - Torque strut bracket
   - Upper torque strut
   - A/C lines and pressure switch
   - Exhaust system to the manifold
   - Crankshaft damper
   - Accessory drive belts
   - Lower torque strut
   - Right splash shield and wheel
   - Negative battery cable

18. Recharge the A/C system.

19. Perform the camshaft/crankshaft synchronization procedure.

VALVE LASH

ADJUSTMENT

The engine in this vehicle does not require periodic valve lash adjustment.

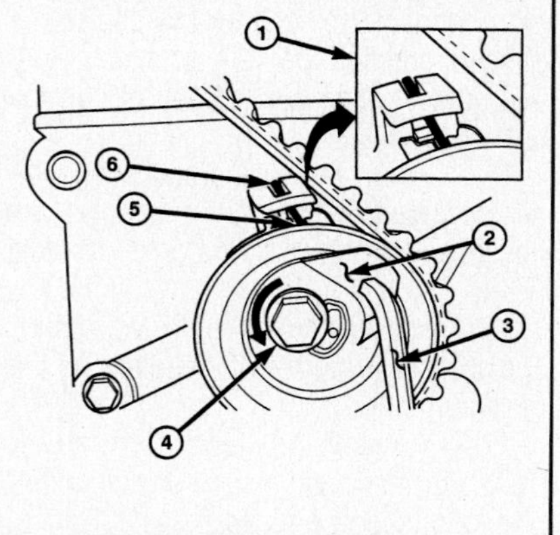

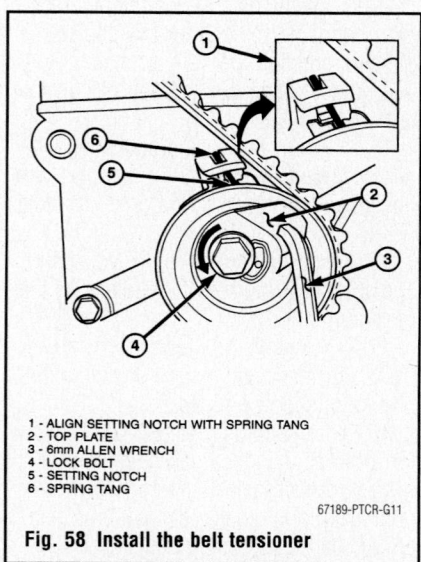

1 - ALIGN SETTING NOTCH WITH SPRING TANG
2 - TOP PLATE
3 - 6mm ALLEN WRENCH
4 - LOCK BOLT
5 - SETTING NOTCH
6 - SPRING TANG

67189-PTCR-G11

Fig. 58 Install the belt tensioner

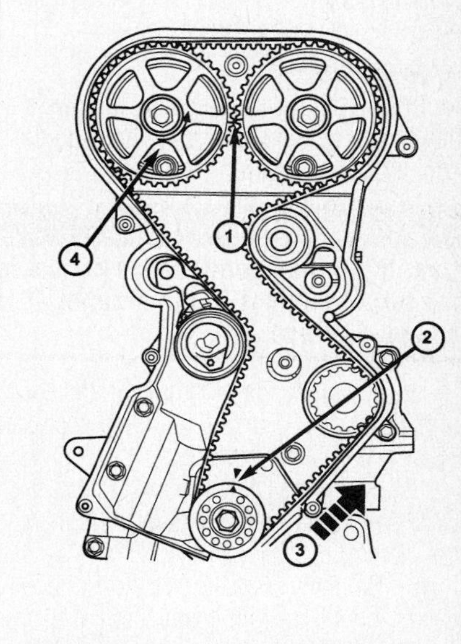

1 - CAMSHAFT TIMING MARKS 1/2 NOTCH LOCATION
2 - CRANKSHAFT AT TDC
3 - INSTALL BELT IN THIS DIRECTION
4 - ROTATE CAMSHAFT SPROCKET TO TAKE UP BELT SLACK

67189-PTCR-G12

Fig. 59 Proper timing belt routing

ENGINE PERFORMANCE & EMISSION CONTROL

CAMSHAFT POSITION (CMP) SENSOR

OPERATION

The Powertrain Control Module (PCM) sends approximately 5 volts to the Hall-effect sensor. This voltage is required to operate the Hall-effect chip and the electronics inside the sensor. The input to the PCM occurs on a 5 volt output reference circuit. A ground for the sensor is provided through the sensor return circuit. The PCM identifies camshaft position by registering the change from 5 to 0 volts, as signaled from the camshaft position sensor.

The PCM determines fuel injection synchronization and cylinder identification from inputs provided by the camshaft position sensor and crankshaft position sensor. From the two inputs, the PCM determines crankshaft position.

REMOVAL & INSTALLATION

1. Before servicing the vehicle, refer to the Precautions Section.
2. Remove the air cleaner lid, disconnect the inlet air temperature sensor and makeup air hose.
3. Remove the negative battery cable.
4. Disconnect electrical connector from the Camshaft Position (CMP).
5. Remove CMP mounting screws.
6. Remove CMP sensor.
7. Loosen screw attaching target magnet to the rear of camshaft.

To install:

The target magnet has locating dowels that fit into machined locating holes in the end of the camshaft.

WARNING

Over tightening could cause cracks in the target magnet. If the magnet cracks, replace it.

8. Install the target magnet in the end of the camshaft. Tighten mounting screw to 35 inch lbs. (4 Nm) torque.
9. Install the CMP sensor. Tighten the CMP sensor mounting screws to 80 inch lbs. (9 Nm) torque.
10. Carefully attach the electrical connector to CMP sensor. Installation at an angle may damage the sensor pins.
11. Install the negative battery cable.
12. Install the air cleaner lid, connect the inlet air temperature sensor and makeup air hose.

TESTING

1. Using the wiring diagram/schematic as a guide, inspect the wiring and connectors between the Camshaft Position Sensor and the Powertrain Control Module (PCM).
2. Look for any chafed, pierced, pinched, or partially broken wires.
3. Look for broken, bent, pushed out, or corroded terminals.
4. Inspect the Camshaft Position Sensor for conditions such as loose mounting screws, damage, or cracks.
5. If no other problems are found, remove the Camshaft Position Sensor.
6. Inspect the Camshaft Position Sensor and mounting area for any condition that would result in an incorrect signal, such as damage, foreign material, or excessive movement.
7. Using a diagnostic scan tool, check for the presence of any Diagnostic Trouble Codes (DTC's). Record and address these codes as necessary.
8. If no codes are present, review the scan tool environmental data. If possible, try to duplicate the conditions under which the DTC set.
9. If applicable, actuate the component with the scan tool.
10. Monitor the scan tool data relative to this circuit and wiggle test the wiring and connectors.
11. Look for the data to change, the actuation to be interrupted, or for the DTC to reset during the wiggle test.
12. Refer to any Technical Service Bulletins (TSB's) that may apply.
13. Turn the ignition off.
14. Visually inspect the related wire harness. Disconnect all the related harness connectors. Look for any chafed, pierced, pinched, partially broken wires and broken, bent, pushed out, or corroded terminals.
15. Perform a voltage drop test on the related circuits between the suspected component and the Powertrain Control Module (PCM).
16. Inspect and clean all PCM, engine, and chassis grounds that are related to the most current DTC.
17. If numerous trouble codes were set, use a schematic and inspect any common ground or supply circuits.
18. For intermittent Misfire DTC's check for restrictions in the Intake and Exhaust system, proper installation of Sensors, vacuum leaks, and binding components that are run by the accessory drive belt.
19. Use the scan tool to perform a System Test if one applies to the component.
20. A co-pilot, data recorder, and/or lab scope should be used to help diagnose intermittent conditions.

CRANKSHAFT POSITION (CKP) SENSOR

LOCATION

The Crankshaft Position Sensor is in the front of the engine block just under the starter motor.

OPERATION

The Powertrain Control Module (PCM) sends approximately 5 volts to the Hall-effect sensor. This voltage is required to operate the Hall-effect chip and the electronics inside the sensor. A ground for the sensor is provided through the sensor return circuit. The input to the PCM occurs on a 5 volt output reference circuit that operates as follows: The Hall-effect sensor contains a powerful magnet. As the magnetic field passes over the dense portion of the counterweight, the 5-volt signal is pulled to ground (0.3 volts) through a transistor in the sensor. When the magnetic field passes over the notches in the crankshaft counterweight, the magnetic field turns off the transistor in the sensor, causing the PCM to register the 5-volt signal. The PCM identifies crankshaft position by registering the change from 5 to 0 volts, as signaled from the Crankshaft Position sensor.

REMOVAL & INSTALLATION

1. Before servicing the vehicle, refer to the Precautions Section.
2. Disconnect the negative battery cable.
3. Raise and support the vehicle.
4. Remove the structural collar.
5. Unlock and disconnect the electrical connector to the Crankshaft Position (CKP) sensor.
6. Remove the CKP sensor bolt.
7. Remove the CKP.

To install:

8. Lubricate the CKP sensor O-ring with clean engine oil.
9. Install the CKP sensor using a twisting motion. Make sure the sensor is fully seated.

WARNING

Do not drive the sensor into the bore with the mounting bolt.

10. Tighten the mounting bolt to 80 inch lbs. (9 Nm).
11. Connect the electrical connector to the CKP sensor.
12. Install the structural collar.
13. Lower the vehicle.
14. Connect the negative battery cable.

TESTING

1. Using a diagnostic scan tool, check for the presence of any Diagnostic Trouble Codes (DTC's). Record and address these codes as necessary.
2. If no codes are present, review the scan tool environmental data. If possible, try to duplicate the conditions under which the DTC set.
3. If applicable, actuate the component with the scan tool.
4. Monitor the scan tool data relative to this circuit and wiggle test the wiring and connectors.
5. Look for the data to change, the actuation to be interrupted, or for the DTC to reset during the wiggle test.
6. Refer to any Technical Service Bulletins (TSB's) that may apply.
7. Turn the ignition off.
8. Visually inspect the related wire harness. Disconnect all the related harness connectors. Look for any chafed, pierced, pinched, partially broken wires and broken, bent, pushed out, or corroded terminals.
9. Perform a voltage drop test on the related circuits between the suspected component and the Powertrain Control Module (PCM).
10. Inspect and clean all PCM, engine, and chassis grounds that are related to the most current DTC.
11. If numerous trouble codes were set, use a schematic and inspect any common ground or supply circuits.
12. For intermittent Misfire DTC's check for restrictions in the Intake and Exhaust system, proper installation of Sensors, vacuum leaks, and binding components that are run by the accessory drive belt.
13. Use the scan tool to perform a System Test if one applies to the component.
14. A co-pilot, data recorder, and/or lab scope should be used to help diagnose intermittent conditions.

ELECTRONIC CONTROL MODULE (ECM)

LOCATION

The Powertrain Control Module (PCM), used in this vehicle, is located on the driver's side engine compartment and is forward of the shock suspension mounting where it is fastened to the inner fender.

OPERATION

The powertrain has electronic controls to reduce exhaust emissions while maintaining excellent drivability and fuel economy. The Powertrain Control Module (PCM)—used in this vehicle, is the control center of this system. The PCM monitors numerous engine and vehicle functions. The PCM constantly looks at the information from various sensors and other inputs, and controls the systems that affect vehicle performance and emissions. The PCM also performs the diagnostic tests on various parts of the system. The PCM can recognize operational problems and alert the driver via the Malfunction Indicator Lamp (MIL). When the PCM detects a malfunction, the PCM stores a Diagnostic Trouble Code (DTC). The problem area is identified by the particular DTC that is set. The control module supplies a buffered voltage to various sensors and switches. Review the components and wiring diagrams in order to determine which systems are controlled by the PCM. The following are some of the functions that the PCM controls:

- The engine fueling
- The Ignition Control (IC)
- The Knock Sensor (KS) system
- The Evaporative Emissions (EVAP) system
- The Secondary Air Injection (AIR) system (if equipped)
- The Exhaust Gas Recirculation (EGR) system
- The automatic transmission functions
- The alternator
- The A/C clutch control
- The cooling fan control

REMOVAL & INSTALLATION

The Electronic Control Module (ECM) or the Powertrain Control Module (PCM) engine control strategy prevents reduced idle speeds until after the engine operates for 200 miles (320 km). This vehicle utilizes a PCM. If the PCM is replaced after 200 miles (320 km) of usage, update the mileage and Vehicle Identification Number (VIN) in the new PCM. Use the scan tool to change the mileage and VIN in the PCM. If this step is not done, a Diagnostic Trouble Code (DTC) may be set and SKIM must be done or car will not start if it is a SKIM equipped car. With a SKIM car, you must do a secret key transfer also. Refer to the appropriate Powertrain Diagnostic Manual and the scan tool.

**** WARNING**

To avoid possible voltage spike damage to the PCM, the ignition key must be off, and the negative battery cable must be disconnected before unplugging the PCM connectors.

➡Take note of any radio presets before disconnecting the negative battery cable.

1. Before servicing the vehicle, refer to the Precautions Section.
2. Disconnect the negative battery cable and isolate the cable from making a connection unintentionally.

**** WARNING**

If the negative battery cable is not disconnected properly, there is the possibility of damaging the PCM by contacting the positive battery cable at the Power Distribution Center (PDC).

3. Remove the 2 nuts holding the PCM and Bracket.
4. Unlock and disconnect the electrical connectors at the PCM.
5. Remove the 3 fasteners holding the PCM to the bracket.

To install:

Use the scan tool to reprogram the new PCM with the original Vehicle Identification Number (VIN) and the vehicle's actual mileage. If this step is not done, a Diagnostic Trouble Code (DTC) may be set.

6. Install the PCM to the bracket.
7. Install the PCM and bracket to the vehicle and connect the electrical connectors and lock connectors.
8. Install the 2 nuts and tighten.
9. Connect the negative battery cable and reprogram the radio and clock.
10. Using a scan tool, program the mileage and VIN into the PCM. Refer to the scan tool and the appropriate Powertrain Diagnostic Manual.

TESTING

The Powertrain Control Module (PCM), used in this vehicle, is programmed with test routines that test the operation of the various systems the PCM controls. Some tests monitor internal PCM functions. Many tests are run continuously. Other tests run only under specific conditions, referred to as conditions for running the DTC. When the vehicle is operating within the conditions for running a particular test, the PCM monitors certain parameters and determines if the values are within an expected range. The parameters and values considered outside the range of normal operation are listed as conditions for setting the DTC. When the conditions for setting the DTC occur, the PCM executes the action taken when the DTC Sets. Some DTC's alert the driver via the Malfunction Indicator Lamp (MIL) or a message. Other DTC's do not trigger a driver warning, but are stored in memory. The PCM also saves data and input parameters when most DTC's are set. This data is stored in the freeze frame and/or failure records.

The DTC's are categorized by type. The DTC type is determined by the MIL operation and the manner in which the fault data is stored when a particular DTC fails. In some cases there may be exceptions to this structure. Therefore, when diagnosing the system it is important to read the action taken when the DTC sets and the conditions for clearing the DTC.

Many intermittent open or shorted circuits come and go with harness and connector movement caused by vibration, engine torque, bumps, and rough pavement.

1. Test the wiring harness and connectors by performing the following:
   - Move the related PCM connectors and wiring while monitoring the appropriate scan tool data
   - With the engine running, move the related connectors and wiring while monitoring engine operation
   - If harness or connector movement affects the data displayed, the component and system operation, or the engine operation, inspect and repair the harness or connections as necessary
2. Test the electrical connections and/or wiring by performing the following:
   - Inspect for incorrect mating of the connector halves, or terminals not fully seated in the connector body, backed-out
   - Inspect for improperly formed or damaged terminals. Test for incorrect terminal tension
   - Inspect for poor terminal to wire connections including terminals crimped over insulation. This requires removing the terminal from the connector body
   - Inspect for corrosion or water intrusion. Pierced or damaged insulation can allow moisture to enter the wiring. The conductor can corrode inside the insulation with little visible evidence. Look for swollen and stiff sections of wire in the suspect circuits
   - Inspect for wires that are broken inside the insulation

ENGINE COOLANT TEMPERATURE (ECT) SENSOR

OPERATION

The Engine Coolant Temperature (ECT) sensor provides an input to the Powertrain Control Module (PCM). As temperature increases, resistance of the sensor decreases. As coolant temperature varies, the ECT sensor resistance changes resulting in a different voltage value at the PCM ECT sensor signal circuit. The ECT sensor provides input for various PCM operations. The PCM uses the input to control air-fuel mixture, timing, and radiator fan on/off times.

TESTING

1. Using the wiring diagram/schematic as a guide, inspect the wiring and connectors between the Engine Coolant Temperature sensor(s) and the Powertrain Control Module (PCM).
2. Look for any chafed, pierced, pinched, or partially broken wires.
3. Look for broken, bent, pushed out or corroded terminals.
4. Turn the ignition on.
5. Monitor the scan tool data relative to the sensor(s) and wiggle test the wiring and connectors.
6. Look for the data to change or for a DTC to set during the wiggle test.
7. Check the engine coolant level and the condition of the engine coolant.
8. With the scan tool, read the Engine Coolant Temperature Sensor value for each sensor. If the engine was allowed to cool completely, the value should be approximately equal to the ambient temperature.
9. Monitor each sensor value on the scan tool and the actual coolant temperature with a thermometer.
10. Using a diagnostic scan tool, check for the presence of any Diagnostic Trouble Codes (DTC's). Record and address these codes as necessary.
11. If no codes are present, review the scan tool environmental data. If possible, try to duplicate the conditions under which the DTC set.
12. If applicable, actuate the component with the scan tool.
13. Monitor the scan tool data relative to this circuit and wiggle test the wiring and connectors.
14. Look for the data to change, the actuation to be interrupted, or for the DTC to reset during the wiggle test.
15. Refer to any Technical Service Bulletins (TSB's) that may apply.
16. Turn the ignition off.
17. Visually inspect the related wire harness. Disconnect all the related harness connectors. Look for any chafed, pierced, pinched, partially broken wires and broken, bent, pushed out, or corroded terminals.
18. Perform a voltage drop test on the related circuits between the suspected component and the Powertrain Control Module (PCM).
19. Inspect and clean all PCM, engine, and chassis grounds that are related to the most current DTC.
20. If numerous trouble codes were set, use a schematic and inspect any common ground or supply circuits.
21. For intermittent Misfire DTC's check for restrictions in the Intake and Exhaust system, proper installation of Sensors, vacuum leaks, and binding components that are run by the accessory drive belt.
22. Use the scan tool to perform a System Test if one applies to the component.
23. A co-pilot, data recorder, and/or lab scope should be used to help diagnose intermittent conditions.

HEATED OXYGEN (HO2S) SENSOR

OPERATION

As vehicles accumulate mileage, the catalytic converter deteriorates. The deterioration results in a less efficient catalyst. To monitor catalytic converter deterioration, the fuel injection system uses two heated oxygen sensors. One sensor is upstream of the catalytic converter, one is downstream of the converter. The Powertrain Control Module (PCM) compares the reading from the sensors to calculate the catalytic converter oxygen storage capacity and converter efficiency. Also, the PCM uses the upstream heated oxygen sensor input when adjusting injector pulse width.

When the catalytic converter efficiency drops below emission standards, the PCM stores a diagnostic trouble code and illuminates the Malfunction Indicator Lamp (MIL).

The Heated Oxygen Sensors (HO2S) produce a constant 2.5 volts on NGC (4 cylinder) vehicles, depending upon the oxygen content of the exhaust gas. When a large amount of oxygen is present (caused by a lean air/fuel mixture, can be caused by misfire and exhaust leaks), the sensors produce a low voltage. When there is a lesser amount of oxygen present (caused by a rich air/fuel mixture, which can be caused by internal engine problems) it produces a higher voltage. By monitoring the oxygen content and converting it to electrical voltage, the sensors act as a rich-lean switch.

The oxygen sensors are equipped with a heating element that keeps the sensors at proper operating temperature during all operating modes. Maintaining correct sensor temperature at all times allows the system to enter into closed loop operation sooner. Also, it allows the system to remain in closed loop operation during periods of extended idle.

In Closed Loop operation the PCM monitors the HO2S input (along with other inputs) and adjusts the injector pulse width accordingly. During Open Loop operation the PCM ignores the HO2S input. The PCM adjusts injector pulse width based on preprogrammed (fixed) values and inputs from other sensors.

The NGC Controller has a common ground for the heater in the HO2S. 12 volts is supplied to the heater in the HO2S by the NGC controller. Both the upstream and downstream HO2S for NGC are Pulse Width Modulation (PWM). NOTE: When replacing an HO2S, the PCM RAM memory must be cleared, either by disconnecting the PCM C-1 connector or momentarily disconnecting the Battery negative terminal. The NGC learns the characteristics of each HO2S heater element and these old values should be cleared when installing a new HO2S. You may experience driveability issues if this is not performed.

TESTING

1. Using a diagnostic scan tool, check for the presence of any Diagnostic Trouble Codes (DTC's). Record and address these codes as necessary.
2. If no codes are present, review the scan tool environmental data. If possible, try to duplicate the conditions under which the DTC set.
3. If applicable, actuate the component with the scan tool.
4. Monitor the scan tool data relative to this circuit and wiggle test the wiring and connectors.
5. Look for the data to change, the actuation to be interrupted, or for the DTC to reset during the wiggle test.
6. Refer to any Technical Service Bulletins (TSB's) that may apply.
7. Turn the ignition off.
8. Visually inspect the related wire harness. Disconnect all the related harness connectors. Look for any chafed, pierced, pinched, partially broken wires and broken, bent, pushed out, or corroded terminals.
9. Perform a voltage drop test on the related circuits between the suspected component and the Powertrain Control Module (PCM).
10. Inspect and clean all PCM, engine, and chassis grounds that are related to the most current DTC.
11. If numerous trouble codes were set, use a schematic and inspect any common ground or supply circuits.
12. For intermittent Misfire DTC's check for restrictions in the Intake and Exhaust system, proper installation of Sensors, vacuum leaks, and binding components that are run by the accessory drive belt.
13. Use the scan tool to perform a System Test if one applies to the component.
14. A co-pilot, data recorder, and/or lab scope should be used to help diagnose intermittent conditions.

INTAKE AIR TEMPERATURE (IAT) SENSOR

OPERATION

The Intake Air Temperature (IAT) sensor is a negative coefficient sensor that provides information to the Powertrain Control Module (PCM) regarding the temperature of the air entering the intake manifold.

TESTING

1. Turn the ignition off. If possible, allow the vehicle to sit with the ignition off for more than 8 hours in an environment where the temperature is consistent and above 20°F (-7°C).
2. Test drive the vehicle. The vehicle must exceed 30 mph (48 km/h) during the test drive. Do not cycle the ignition off when the test drive is completed.
3. With a scan tool, select View DTC's.
4. If a DTC is not active, perform the following:
5. Refer to any Technical Service Bulletins (TSB's) that may apply.
6. Review the scan tool Freeze Frame information. If possible, try to duplicate the conditions under which the DTC set.
7. With the engine running at normal operating temperature, monitor the scan tool parameters related to the DTC while wiggling the wire harness. Look for parameter values to change and/or a DTC to set. Turn the ignition off.
8. Visually inspect the related wire harness. Disconnect all the related harness connectors. Look for any chafed, pierced, pinched, partially broken wires and broken, bent, pushed out, or corroded terminals. Perform a voltage drop test on the related circuits between the suspected inoperative component and the PCM.

**** CAUTION**

Do not probe the PCM harness connectors. Probing the PCM harness connectors will damage the PCM terminals resulting in poor terminal to pin connection. Install Miller Special Tool #8815 to perform diagnosis.

9. Inspect and clean all PCM, engine, and chassis grounds that are related to the most current DTC.
10. If numerous trouble codes were set, use a wire schematic and look for any common ground or supply circuits.
11. For any Relay DTC's, actuate the Relay with the scan tool and wiggle the related wire harness to try to interrupt the actuation.
12. For intermittent Evaporative Emission trouble codes perform a visual and physical inspection of the related parts including hoses and the Fuel Filler cap.
13. Use the scan tool to perform a System Test if one applies to failing component. A co-pilot, data recorder, and/or lab scope should be used to help diagnose intermittent conditions.

KNOCK SENSOR (KS)

LOCATION

The knock sensor threads into the side of the cylinder block in front of the starter.

OPERATION

When the Knock Sensor (KS) detects a knock in one of the cylinders, it sends an input signal to the Powertrain Control Module (PCM). In response, the PCM retards ignition timing for all cylinders by a scheduled amount.

Knock sensors contain a piezoelectric material which constantly vibrates and sends an input voltage (signal) to the PCM while the engine operates. As the intensity of the crystal's vibration increases, the knock sensor output voltage also increases.

The voltage signal produced by the knock sensor increases with the amplitude of vibration. The PCM receives as an input the knock sensor voltage signal. If the signal rises above a predetermined level, the PCM will store that value in memory and retard ignition timing to reduce engine knock. If the knock sensor voltage exceeds a preset value, the PCM retards ignition timing for all cylinders. It is not a selective cylinder retard.

The PCM ignores knock sensor input

during engine idle conditions. Once the engine speed exceeds a specified value, ignition timing retard is allowed.

REMOVAL & INSTALLATION

1. Before servicing the vehicle, refer to the Precautions Section.
2. Disconnect the electrical connector from the Knock Sensor (KS).
3. Use a crow foot socket to remove the KS.

To install:

WARNING

Over or under tightening the KS effects KS performance, possibly causing improper spark control.

4. Install KS. Tighten KS to 88 inch lbs. (10 Nm) torque.
5. Attach electrical connector to knock sensor.

TESTING

1. Using the wiring diagram/schematic as a guide, inspect the wiring and connectors between the Knock Sensor (KS) and the Powertrain Control Module (PCM).
2. Look for any chafed, pierced, pinched, or partially broken wires.
3. Look for broken, bent, pushed out or corroded terminals.
4. Monitor the scan tool data relative to this circuit and wiggle test the wiring and connectors.
5. Look for the data to change or for the DTC to reset during the wiggle test.
6. Refer to any Technical Service Bulletins that may apply.
7. Review the scan tool Freeze Frame information. If possible, try to duplicate the conditions under which the DTC set.
8. With the engine running at normal operating temperature, monitor the scan tool parameters related to the DTC while wiggling the wire harness. Look for parameter values to change and/or a DTC to set. Turn the ignition off.
9. Visually inspect the related wire harness. Disconnect all the related harness connectors. Look for any chafed, pierced, pinched, partially broken wires and broken, bent, pushed out, or corroded terminals. Perform a voltage drop test on the related circuits between the suspected inoperative component and the PCM.

CAUTION

Do not probe the PCM harness connectors. Probing the PCM harness connectors will damage the PCM terminals resulting in poor terminal to pin connection. Install Miller Special Tool #8815 to perform diagnosis.

10. Inspect and clean all PCM, engine, and chassis grounds that are related to the most current DTC.
11. If numerous trouble codes were set, use a wire schematic and look for any common ground or supply circuits.
12. For any Relay DTC's, actuate the Relay with the scan tool and wiggle the related wire harness to try to interrupt the actuation.
13. For intermittent Evaporative Emission trouble codes perform a visual and physical inspection of the related parts including hoses and the Fuel Filler cap.
14. Use the scan tool to perform a System Test if one applies to failing component. A co-pilot, data recorder, and/or lab scope should be used to help diagnose intermittent conditions.

MANIFOLD ABSOLUTE PRESSURE (MAP) SENSOR

OPERATION

The Manifold Absolute Pressure (MAP) sensor serves as a Powertrain Control Module (PCM) input, using a silicon-based sensing unit, to provide data on the manifold vacuum that draws the air/fuel mixture into the combustion chamber. The PCM requires this information to determine injector pulse width and spark advance. When MAP equals Barometric pressure, the pulse width will be at maximum.

Also, like the camshaft and crankshaft sensors, a 5-volt reference is supplied from the PCM and returns a voltage signal to the PCM that reflects manifold pressure. The zero pressure reading is 0.5 volt and full scale is 4.5 volts. For a pressure swing of 0–15 psi, the voltage changes 4.0 volts. The sensor is supplied a regulated 4.8–5.1 volts to operate the sensor. Like the camshaft and crankshaft sensors, ground is provided through the sensor return circuit.

REMOVAL & INSTALLATION

1. Before servicing the vehicle, refer to the Precautions Section.
2. Disconnect the negative battery cable.
3. Disconnect the electrical connector from Manifold Absolute Pressure (MAP) sensor.
4. Remove 2 screws holding the MAP sensor to the intake manifold.

To install:

5. Install the MAP sensor. Install and tighten the 2 screws.
6. Connect the electrical connector to the MAP sensor.
7. Connect the negative battery cable.

TESTING

1. Turn the ignition off.
2. Using the wiring diagram/schematic as a guide, inspect the wiring and connectors between the Manifold Absolute Pressure (MAP) Sensor and the PCM.
3. Look for any chafed, pierced, pinched, or partially broken wires.
4. Look for broken, bent, pushed out, or corroded terminals.
5. Turn the ignition on.
6. Monitor the scan tool data relative to the sensor and wiggle test the wiring and connectors.
7. Look for the data to change or for a DTC to set during the wiggle test. If necessary, check each sensor circuit for high resistance or a shorted condition.
8. With a scan tool, read the Barometric Pressure. The Barometric Pressure should be approximately equal to the actual barometric pressure. If necessary, compare the Barometric Pressure value of the tested vehicle to the value of a known good vehicle of a similar make and model.
9. Connect a vacuum gauge to a manifold vacuum source and start the engine.
10. With the scan tool, read the MAP Sensor vacuum. The scan tool reading for MAP vacuum should be within 1 inch of the vacuum gauge reading.
11. With the scan tool, monitor the MAP Sensor signal voltage. With the engine idling in neutral or park, snap the throttle. The MAP Sensor signal voltage should change from below 2.0 volts at idle to above 3.5 volts at wide open throttle.

MASS AIR FLOW (MAF) SENSOR

OPERATION

The Mass Air Flow (MAF) sensor is an air flow meter that measures the amount of air entering the engine. The Electronic Control Module (ECM) uses the MAF sensor signal to provide the correct fuel delivery for all engine speeds and loads. A small quantity of air entering the engine indicates a deceleration or idle condition. A large quantity of air entering the engine indicates an acceleration or high load condition. The MAF sensor has the following circuits:

- An ignition 1 voltage circuit
- A ground circuit
- A MAF sensor signal circuit

- An IAT sensor signal circuit
- A low reference circuit

The ECM applies 5 volts to the MAF sensor on the MAF sensor signal circuit. The sensor uses the voltage to produce a frequency based on the inlet air flow through the sensor bore. The frequency varies in a range of near 1,700 Hertz at idle to near 9,500 Hertz at maximum engine load.

REMOVAL & INSTALLATION

1. Before servicing the vehicle, refer to the Precautions Section.
2. Disconnect negative battery cable.
3. Remove the air pump assembly.
4. Remove the 2 bracket mounting bolts.
5. Remove the bracket assembly.
6. Disconnect the electrical connector to Mass Air Flow (MAF) sensor.
7. Twist the MAF sideways and remove from bracket.
8. Remove the rubber mounting.

To install:

9. Install the rubber mounting to MAF sensor.
10. Twist the MAF sideways and install to bracket.
11. Connect the electrical connector to the MAF sensor.
12. Install the bracket assembly.
13. Install the 2 bracket mounting bolts.
14. Install the air pump assembly.
15. Connect negative battery cable.

TESTING

1. Verify the integrity of the air induction system by inspecting for the following conditions:
   - Damaged components
   - Loose or improper installation
   - An air flow restriction
   - Any vacuum leak
   - Water intrusion
2. With the engine running, observe the scan tool Mass Air Flow (MAF) sensor parameter. The reading should be between 1,700–3,200 Hz depending on the Engine Coolant Temperature (ECT).
3. Verify that any electrical aftermarket devices are properly connected and grounded.
4. Inspect the harness of the MAF sensor to verify that it is not routed too close to the following components:
   - Any aftermarket accessories
   - The secondary ignition wires or coils
   - Any solenoids
   - Any relays
   - Any motors
5. A low minimum air rate through the sensor bore at idle or during deceleration may cause a DTC to set. Inspect for the following conditions:
   - Any deposits on the throttle plate or in the throttle bore
   - Any vacuum leak downstream of the MAF sensor
6. Inspect for any contamination or debris on the sensing elements of the MAF sensor.
7. Inspect the air induction system for any water intrusion. Any water that reaches the MAF sensor will skew the sensor and may cause a DTC to set.
8. A Wide Open Throttle (WOT) acceleration from a stop should cause the MAF sensor parameter on the scan tool to increase rapidly. This increase should be from 3–10 g/s at idle to 150 g/s or more at the time of the 1 to 2 shift of the transmission. If the increase is not observed, inspect for a restriction in the induction system or the exhaust system.
9. Inspect for a skewed or stuck Engine Coolant Temperature (ECT) sensor.
10. Test for a high resistance of 15 ohms or more on the ignition 1 voltage circuit. This may cause a DTC to set. A high resistance may also cause a drivability concern before a DTC sets.

The Barometric Pressure (BARO) sensor that is used in order to calculate the predicted mass air flow value is initially based on the Manifold Absolute Pressure (MAP) sensor at key ON. When the engine is running, the BARO value is continually updated near WOT. A skewed MAP sensor will cause the calculated mass air flow value to be inaccurate and may result in a no start condition. The value shown for the MAP sensor parameter varies with the altitude. With the ignition ON and the engine OFF, 101 kPa is the approximate value near sea level. This value will decrease by approximately 3 kPa for every 1,000 feet (305 meters) of altitude.

THROTTLE POSITION SENSOR (TPS)

OPERATION

The Throttle Position Sensor (TPS) and throttle actuating DC motor are integral to the throttle body. The throttle body is a non-serviceable item; replace the throttle body as an assembly.

The throttle blade will not close completely when engine is shut down. This engine off blade position is for start up. The electric throttle body will adjust the throttle blade for idle control as the idle air control valve adjusted idle speed previously on cable actuated throttle bodies. The electric throttle body will also adjust the throttle blade for normal driving operation. The throttle blade will move to the engine off blade position if throttle body codes are set to provide air for limp-in mode.

TESTING

1. Using the wiring diagram/schematic as a guide, inspect the wiring and connectors between the Throttle Body and the Powertrain Control Module (PCM).
2. Look for any chafed, pierced, pinched, or partially broken wires.
3. Look for broken, bent, pushed out or corroded terminals.
4. Inspect the Throttle Body for any condition that would result in an incorrect signal, such as damage or contamination.
5. Inspect and clean all PCM, engine, and chassis grounds that are related to the most current DTC.
6. If numerous trouble codes were set, use a wire schematic and look for any common ground or supply circuits.
7. For any Relay DTC's, actuate the Relay with the scan tool and wiggle the related wire harness to try to interrupt the actuation.
8. Use the scan tool to perform a System Test if one applies to failing component. A co-pilot, data recorder, and/or lab scope should be used to help diagnose intermittent conditions.

VEHICLE SPEED SENSOR (VSS)

LOCATION

The Vehicle Speed Sensor (VSS) is mounted into the transaxle assembly.

OPERATION

The Vehicle Speed Sensor (VSS) is a Hall Effect sensor mounted to the transaxle. The sensor is triggered by the ring gear teeth passing below it. The VSS pulse signal to the speedometer/odometer is monitored by the PCM speed control circuitry to determine the vehicle speed and to maintain speed control set speed.

REMOVAL & INSTALLATION

1. Before servicing the vehicle, refer to the Precautions Section.
2. Raise and support the vehicle on a hoist.

3. Disconnect the Vehicle Speed Sensor (VSS) connector.

WARNING

Clean the area around the VSS before removing in order to prevent dirt from entering the transaxle during the VSS removal.

4. Remove the VSS retaining bolt.
5. Remove the VSS from transaxle.

WARNING

Carefully remove the VSS so that the sensor drive gear does not fall into the transaxle. Should the sensor drive gear fall into the transaxle during sensor removal, the drive gear must be reattached to the sensor.

6. Remove VSS drive gear from speed sensor.

To install:

7. Install the pinion gear to the VSS.
8. Using a NEW O-ring, install the VSS to the transaxle.
9. Install the retaining bolt and torque to 62 inch lbs. (7 Nm).
10. Connect VSS electrical connector.
11. Lower the vehicle and road test it in order to verify the proper speedometer operation.

FUEL — GASOLINE FUEL INJECTION SYSTEM

FUEL SYSTEM SERVICE PRECAUTIONS

Safety is the most important factor when performing not only fuel system maintenance but any type of maintenance. Failure to conduct maintenance and repairs in a safe manner may result in serious personal injury or death. Maintenance and testing of the vehicle's fuel system components can be accomplished safely and effectively by adhering to the following rules and guidelines.

- To avoid the possibility of fire and personal injury, always disconnect the negative battery cable unless the repair or test procedure requires that battery voltage be applied.
- Always relieve the fuel system pressure prior to disconnecting any fuel system component (injector, fuel rail, pressure regulator, etc.), fitting or fuel line connection. Exercise extreme caution whenever relieving fuel system pressure to avoid exposing skin, face and eyes to fuel spray. Please be advised that fuel under pressure may penetrate the skin or any part of the body that it contacts.
- Always place a shop towel or cloth around the fitting or connection prior to loosening to absorb any excess fuel due to spillage. Ensure that all fuel spillage (should it occur) is quickly removed from engine surfaces. Ensure that all fuel soaked cloths or towels are deposited into a suitable waste container.
- Always keep a dry chemical (Class B) fire extinguisher near the work area.
- Do not allow fuel spray or fuel vapors to come into contact with a spark or open flame.
- Always use a back-up wrench when loosening and tightening fuel line connection fittings. This will prevent unnecessary stress and torsion to fuel line piping.
- Always replace worn fuel fitting O-rings with new Do not substitute fuel hose or equivalent where fuel pipe is installed.

Before servicing the vehicle, make sure to also refer to the precautions in the beginning of this section as well.

RELIEVING FUEL SYSTEM PRESSURE

CAUTION

Relieve the fuel system pressure before servicing any components of the fuel system. Service vehicles in well ventilated areas and avoid ignition sources. NEVER smoke while servicing the vehicle!

1. Before servicing the vehicle, refer to the precautions in the beginning of this section.
2. Remove the negative battery cable.
3. Remove the fuel pump relay from the Power Distribution Center (PDC).
4. Start and run the engine until it stalls.
5. Turn the ignition key to the OFF position.

FUEL FILTER

REMOVAL & INSTALLATION

The fuel filter is part of the fuel pump module located in the fuel tank. It is serviced as part of the fuel pump module.

FUEL INJECTORS

REMOVAL & INSTALLATION

Non-Turbo Models

See Figure 60.

1. Before servicing the vehicle, refer to the precautions in the beginning of this section.
2. Release the fuel system pressure.
3. Remove or disconnect the following:

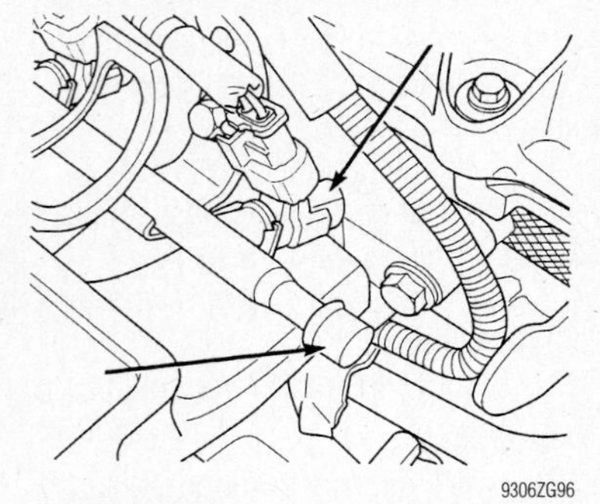

Fig. 60 Remove the fuel rail and injectors as an assembly

- Negative battery cable
- Remove the air cleaner lid
- Inlet Air Temperature (IAT) sensor and the make-up hose
- Engine cover or throttle control shield, if equipped
- Fuel supply tube from fuel rail
- Intake manifold
- Fuel injector electrical connectors
- Fuel rail with the fuel injectors
- Fuel injector(s) and discard the O-rings

To install:

➡Lubricate the O-rings with clean engine oil.

4. Install or connect the following:
   - Fuel injector(s) to the fuel rail using new O-rings
   - Fuel injector nozzles into the intake manifold and torque the fuel rail bolts to 8 ft. lbs. (12 Nm)
   - Fuel injector electrical connectors
   - Fuel supply tube to fuel rail
   - Intake manifold
   - Engine cover or throttle control shield, if equipped
   - IAT sensor and make-up hose
   - Air cleaner lid
   - Negative battery cable
5. Start the vehicle and check for leaks, repair if necessary.

Turbo Models

1. Before servicing the vehicle, refer to the precautions in the beginning of this section.
2. Release the fuel system pressure.
3. Drain the cooling system.
4. Remove or disconnect the following:
   - Negative battery cable
   - Throttle body inlet hose from the throttle body
   - Purge hose from the throttle body
   - Electrical connections from the throttle body
   - Throttle control shield
   - Accelerator and cruise control cable from the throttle body
   - Manifold Absolute Pressure (MAP) sensor connector
   - Vacuum lines from the rear of the intake manifold
   - 5 bolts from the front and 2 bolts from the rear of the intake manifold
   - Intake manifold and cover the lower manifold to avoid contamination
   - Upper radiator hose up and out of the way
   - 2 small hoses from the thermostat housing
   - 2 bolts from the thermostat housing and rotate the assembly up and out of the way
   - Fuel lines from the rail
   - Fuel injector electrical connectors and wire from the rail
   - Fuel rail with the fuel injectors
   - Fuel injector(s) and discard the O-rings

To install:

➡Lubricate the O-rings with clean engine oil.

5. Install or connect the following:
   - Fuel injector(s) to the fuel rail using new O-rings
   - Fuel injector nozzles into the intake manifold and torque the fuel rail bolts to 170 inch lbs. (19 Nm)
   - Fuel injector electrical connectors and wiring to the fuel rail
   - Fuel line to fuel rail
   - Rotate the thermostat assembly into position and tighten the 2 bolts
   - 2 small hoses to the thermostat housing
   - Upper radiator hose
   - Intake manifold
   - 5 bolts front and 2 rear bolts on the intake manifold
   - Vacuum lines to the rear of the intake manifold
   - MAP sensor connector
   - Accelerator and cruise control cable to the throttle body
   - Throttle control shield
   - Electrical connections to the throttle body
   - Purge hose to the throttle body
   - Throttle body inlet hose to the throttle body
   - Negative battery cable
6. Fill the cooling system.
7. Start the vehicle and check for leaks, repair if necessary.

FUEL PUMP

REMOVAL & INSTALLATION

See Figure 61.

The fuel pump is integral with the pump module, which also contains the fuel reservoir, level sensor, inlet strainer and fuel pressure regulator. The inlet strainer, fuel pressure regulator and level sensor are the only serviceable items. If the fuel pump requires service, replace the entire fuel pump module.

1. Before servicing the vehicle, refer to the precautions in the beginning of this section.
2. Properly relieve the fuel system pressure.
3. Remove or disconnect the following:
   - Negative battery cable
   - Air cleaner lid
   - Inlet Air Temperature (IAT) sensor and make up air hose
   - Fuel tank
   - Fuel pump module and seal from the tank
   - Locknut to release the fuel pump module, using a Ring Spanner Tool No. 6856
   - Fuel filter from the fuel pump module
   - Fuel pump and seal from the fuel tank

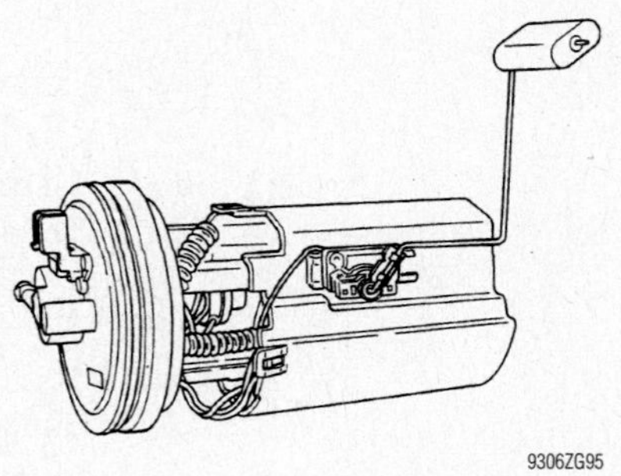

Fig. 61 Exploded view of the fuel pump module

To install:

4. Install or connect the following:
   - Fuel filter to the fuel pump module
   - Fuel filter lines to the fuel pump module
   - Fuel pump module in the tank
   - Locknut while holding the fuel pump in position. Using Tool 6856, torque the nut to 56 ft. lbs. (75 Nm).
   - Fuel tank
   - IAT sensor and make-up hose
   - Air cleaner lid
   - Negative battery cable
5. Fill the fuel tank.
6. Start the vehicle and check for leaks, repair if necessary.

FUEL TANK

REMOVAL & INSTALLATION

⁂ CAUTION

Release fuel system pressure before servicing fuel system components. Service vehicles in well ventilated areas and avoid ignition sources. Never smoke while servicing the vehicle. This may result in personal injury or death.

1. Before servicing the vehicle, refer to the Precautions Section.
2. Release fuel system pressure. Refer to Relieving Fuel System Pressure.
3. Remove the air cleaner lid, disconnect the inlet air temperature sensor and makeup air hose.
4. Remove the negative battery cable.
5. Remove fuel cap slowly to release tank pressure.
6. Raise and support the vehicle.
7. With vehicle on a hoist, drain fuel from tank.

⁂ CAUTION

There may be fuel in the fill tube. Remove hose carefully to reduce fuel splash.

8. Disconnect fuel tank from rubber fill hose.

➡wrap shop towels around hoses to catch any gasoline spillage.

9. Remove bolts from the fuel tank straps.
10. Disconnect fuel line, in the front of the fuel tank. This is a quick connect fitting.
11. Lower fuel tank and remove the EVAP line and recirculation line.
12. Remove vacuum line from LDP.

13. Unlock the electrical connector and disconnect the electrical connector.
14. Remove hoses from EVAP canister.
15. Remove fuel tank from vehicle.

To install:

16. Position fuel tank on transmission jack.
17. Raise fuel tank into position.
18. Connect vacuum line to LDP.
19. Install EVAP line and recirculation line.
20. Connect electrical connector and lock the connector.
21. Connect the fuel line.
22. Connect fuel fill tube to tank inlet. Tighten hose clamp to 35 inch lbs. (4 Nm) torque.
23. Position fuel tank straps. Tighten fuel tank strap bolts to 17 ft. lbs. (23 Nm) torque.
24. Remove transmission jack. Ensure straps are not twisted or bent.
25. Lower vehicle.
26. Fill fuel tank, install filler cap.
27. Install the negative battery cable.
28. Install the air cleaner lid, connect the inlet air temperature sensor and makeup air hose.
29. Use the scan tool ASD Fuel System Test to pressurize the fuel system. Check for leaks.

IDLE SPEED

ADJUSTMENT

The Powertrain Control Module (PCM) adjusts engine idle speed through the idle air control valve to compensate for engine load, coolant temperature, or barometric pressure changes. No adjustment is necessary or possible.

THROTTLE BODY

REMOVAL & INSTALLATION

Non-Turbo Models

See Figure 62.

1. Remove the air cleaner lid, disconnect the inlet air temperature sensor and makeup air hose.
2. Remove the negative battery cable.
3. Remove the engine cover or throttle control shield if equipped.
4. Remove throttle cable from the throttle body cam.
5. Lift the retaining tabs on the cable and slide cable out of bracket.
6. If equipped with speed control, remove speed control cable from throttle lever by sliding clasp out hole used for throttle cable.
7. Remove EVAP purge hose from nipple on throttle body.
8. Remove the electrical connectors from the throttle position sensor and idle air control motor.
9. Remove 2 screws holding cable mounting bracket and support bracket.
10. Remove throttle body mounting bolts.
11. Lift throttle body straight up and away to remove the throttle body.

To install:

12. Attach electrical connectors to idle air control motor and throttle position sensor.
13. Make sure that the throttle body gasket is in place in the manifold.
14. Position throttle body on intake and install mounting bolts. Do Not tighten bolts at this time.
15. Install throttle cable bracket. Do Not tighten bolts at this time.
16. Tighten throttle body bolts to 85–125 inch lbs. (10–14 Nm).
17. Tighten throttle cable bracket bolts to 85–125 inch lbs. (10–14 Nm).
18. Install EVAP purge hose to throttle body nipple.
19. Install cable housing(s) retainer tabs into bracket.
20. Install throttle body cables by rotating the throttle cam forward to the wide open position.
21. Install throttle control shield.
22. Install the negative battery cable.
23. Install the air cleaner lid, connect the inlet air temperature sensor and makeup air hose.

Turbo Models

See Figure 63.

1. Disconnect the negative battery cable.
2. Unlock and disconnect the electrical connector for the inlet air temperature sensor.
3. Unlock and disconnect the electrical connectors from the idle air control motor and throttle position sensor.
4. Remove the throttle control shield.
5. Remove the throttle cable from the throttle body cam.
6. If equipped with speed control, remove speed control cable from the throttle cam by sliding clasp out hole used for throttle cable.
7. Remove the 2 screws for the throttle cable bracket.
8. Remove bracket.
9. Disconnect the throttle body inlet hose and remove from throttle body.
10. Disconnect the purge hose from the throttle body.
11. Remove the 3 bolts from the throttle body.
12. Remove the throttle body.
13. Clean and replace gasket.

To install:

14. Discard old gasket and clean intake manifold surface.
15. Install the throttle body.
16. Install the 3 bolts to the throttle body and tighten to 85–125 inch lbs. (10–14 Nm).
17. Connect the purge hose to the throttle body.
18. Connect the throttle body inlet hose to the throttle body and tighten clamp.
19. Install bracket.

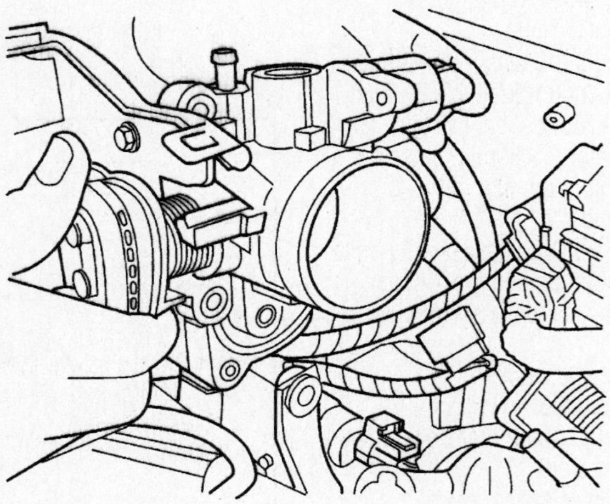

Fig. 62 Installation of the throttle body—2.4L non-turbo engine

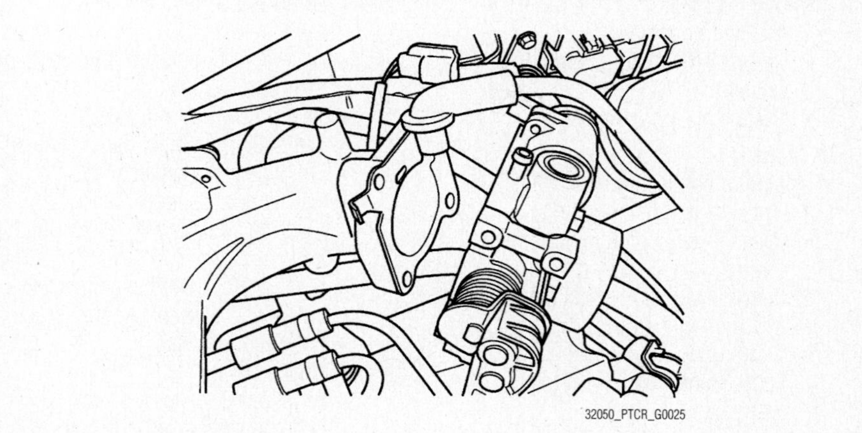

Fig. 63 Installation of the throttle body—2.4L turbo engine

20. Install the 2 screws for the throttle cable bracket and tighten to 85–125 inch lbs. (10–14 Nm).

21. If equipped with speed control, install speed control cable to the throttle cam by sliding clasp in the hole used for throttle cable.

22. Install the throttle cable to the throttle body cam.

23. Install the throttle control shield.

24. Connect and lock the electrical connectors from the idle air control motor and throttle position sensor.

25. Connect and lock the electrical connector for the inlet air temperature sensor.

26. Connect the negative battery cable.

HEATING & AIR CONDITIONING SYSTEM

BLOWER MOTOR

REMOVAL & INSTALLATION

See Figures 64 and 65.

The blower motor is located on the bottom right side of the HVAC housing. The blower motor can be removed from the vehicle without having to remove the HVAC housing.

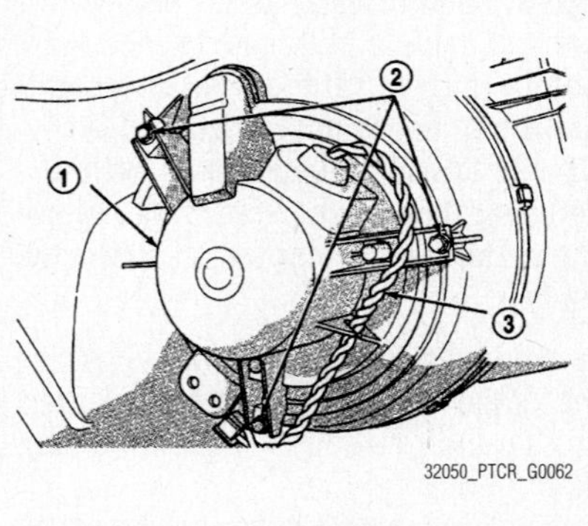

Fig. 64 Blower motor location (1)

With A/C

1. Disconnect and isolate the battery negative cable.

2. Remove the passenger side door sill scuff plate.

3. Pull back the carpet to access the blower motor.

4. Disconnect the blower motor wire harness connector.

5. Remove the screws that secure the blower motor to the HVAC housing.

6. Remove the blower motor from the HVAC housing.

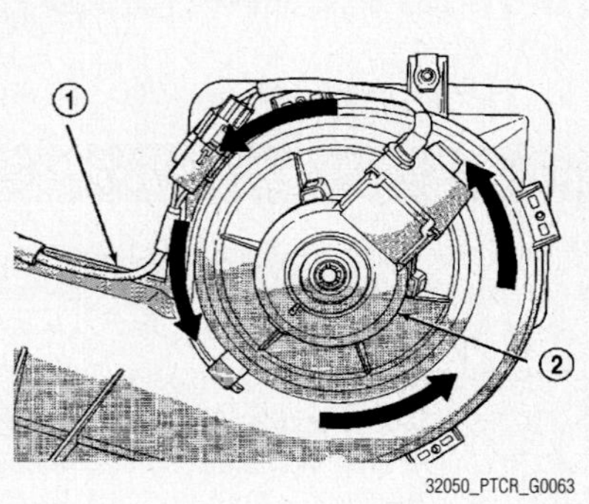

Fig. 65 Blower motor (2) removal—with or without air conditioning

To install:

7. Position the blower motor into the HVAC housing.

8. Install the blower motor retaining screws. Tighten the screws to 20 inch lbs. (2.3 Nm).

9. Connect the blower motor wire harness connector.

10. Reposition the carpet.

11. Install the door sill scuff plate.

12. Reconnect the negative battery cable.

Without A/C

1. Disconnect and isolate the battery negative cable.

2. Disconnect the blower motor wire harness connector.

3. Grasp the blower motor while pulling down on the locking tab. Turn the blower motor approximately 1/8 turn counterclockwise.

4. Remove the blower motor from the HVAC housing.

To install:

5. Position the blower motor into the housing.

6. Rotate the blower motor clockwise until the tab snaps into the locked position, approximately 1/8 turn.

7. Connect the blower motor wire harness connector.

8. Reconnect the negative battery cable.

HEATER CORE

REMOVAL & INSTALLATION

1. Before servicing the vehicle, refer to the precautions in the beginning of this section.

2. Remove the A/C refrigerant by using approved equipment.

3. Drain the cooling system.

4. Disconnect the negative battery cable.

5. Remove the instrument panel by removing or disconnecting the following:

- Left and right **A** pillar trim moldings using a trim stick
- Front power window switch
- Center bezel retaining screw
- Heating, Ventilation and Air Conditioning (HVAC) control knobs
- Center bezel using a trim stick
- Top cover retaining screws and pull it rearward to remove
- HVAC control unit from the instrument panel
- Retaining screws from the upper and lower steering column shrouds
- Left lower instrument panel bezel
- Steering column wire connectors
- Steering column

- Brake pedal support bracket
- Left side instrument panel end cap from the wiring connectors
- Rear power window switch from the console and pull the parking handle all the way up
- Auxiliary power outlet wire connector
- Center console
- Glove box assembly
- Right side instrument panel end cap
- 5 right side instrument panel wire connectors
- Instrument panel from the vehicle, with the help of an assistant

6. Remove or disconnect the following:
   - Heater hoses from the heater core
   - Reposition the vehicle speed control servo, if equipped
   - Suction and liquid lines from the evaporator
   - Drain tube
   - A/C vacuum harness connector
   - Defroster duct from the heater—A/C unit housing
   - Heater—A/C unit housing from the vehicle
   - Heater core from the housing

To install:

7. Install or connect the following:
   - Heater core to the housing
   - Heater—A/C unit housing to the vehicle
   - Defroster duct to the housing
   - A/C vacuum harness
   - Drain tube
   - Suction and liquid lines to the evaporator
   - Reposition the vehicle speed control servo, if equipped
   - Heater hoses to the heater core
8. Install the instrument panel by installing or connecting the following:
   - Instrument panel
   - Right side instrument panel wire connectors
   - Right side instrument panel end cap
   - Glove box assembly
   - Center console
   - Auxiliary power outlet wire connector
   - Rear power window switch
   - Left side instrument panel end cap
   - Left side wire connectors
   - Brake pedal support bracket
   - Steering column with a new pinch bolt
   - Steering column wire connectors
   - Left lower instrument panel bezel
   - HVAC control unit
   - Center bezel
   - Front power window switch
   - Left and right **A** pillar trim moldings
   - Negative battery cable
9. Fill the cooling system.
10. Recharge the A/C system.
11. Start the vehicle and verify proper system operations.
12. Road test the vehicle and check for any rattles, repair if necessary.

STEERING

POWER STEERING GEAR

REMOVAL & INSTALLATION

See Figures 66 through 69.

1. Place the steering wheel in the straight ahead position. Using a steering wheel holder, lock the steering wheel in place to keep it from rotating. This keeps the clockspring in the proper orientation.
2. Remove the silencer pad below the knee blocker panel below the steering column.
3. Fold down and remove the knee blocker.
4. Remove the steering column coupling retainer pin, back off the pinch bolt nut, and remove the steering column coupling pinch bolt (the pinch bolt nut is caged to the coupling and is not removable). Separate the upper and lower steering column couplings.
5. Raise the vehicle.
6. Remove both front tire and wheel assemblies from the vehicle.
7. Remove nuts attaching both outer tie rods to the steering knuckles. Remove each nut by holding the tie rod stud stationary while loosening and removing the nut with a crowfoot wrench (or open-end wrench).
8. Remove the outer tie rods from the steering knuckles using Remover, Special Tool MB991113.
9. Remove the tie rod heat shields.
10. On vehicles equipped with a power steering fluid pressure switch, release the locking tab on the wiring harness connector for the power steering fluid pressure switch, then remove the wiring harness connector from the power steering fluid pressure switch.
11. Back out the tube nut securing the power steering fluid pressure hose to the gear.
12. Disconnect the cooler or return hose at the power steering gear outlet port fitting.
13. On vehicles equipped with crossmember mounted power steering fluid coolers:
    - Remove the cooler tube from the right routing clip.
    - Remove the two screws securing the cooler to the front suspension crossmember.
14. Allow the cooler to hang out of the way.
15. Remove the pencil strut from the right front corner of the crossmember and body of the vehicle. Remove the washer behind the strut from the torque strut bolt.
16. Remove the screws fastening the front fascia to the reinforcement as necessary in order to access the drive belt splash shield forward fastener screw.
17. Remove the drive belt splash shield fasteners. Remove the shield.
18. Remove the bolt mounting the engine torque strut to the right forward corner of the front suspension crossmember.

➡Before removing the front suspension crossmember from the vehicle, the location of the crossmember must be scribed on the body of the vehicle. Do this so the crossmember can be relocated, upon reinstallation, against the body of vehicle in the same location as before removal. If the front suspension crossmember is not reinstalled in exactly the same location as before removal, the preset front wheel alignment settings (caster and camber) will be lost.

19. Using an awl, scribe a line marking the location of where the front suspension crossmember is mounted against the body of the vehicle.
20. Position a transmission jack under the center of the front suspension crossmember and raise it to support the bottom of the crossmember.
21. Loosen all six bolts attaching the front suspension crossmember to the frame rails of vehicle. Do not completely remove the two mounting bolts going through the lower control arm rear isolator bushings. They are designed to disengage from the body threads yet stay within the lower control arm rear isolator bushing. Back the two bolts out just enough to disengage the threaded tapping plates in the body of the vehicle. Completely remove the other four bolts.
22. Lower the front suspension cross-

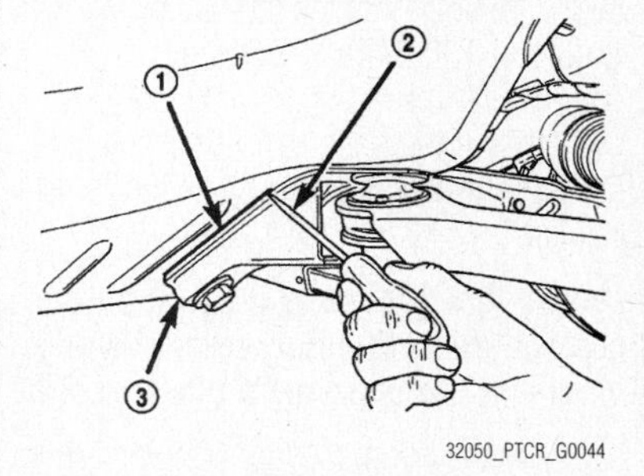

Fig. 66 Marking the location of the crossmember as it is mounted against the body of the vehicle

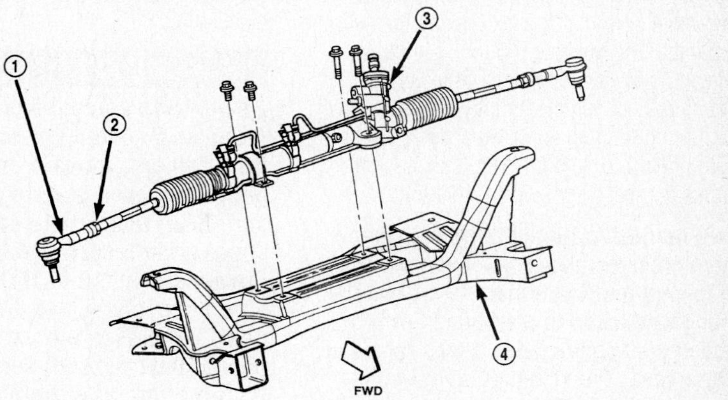

1 - OUTER TIE ROD
2 - JAM NUT
3 - STEERING GEAR
4 - FRONT SUSPENSION CROSSMEMBER

9306EG42

Fig. 68 View of the power steering gear and crossmember

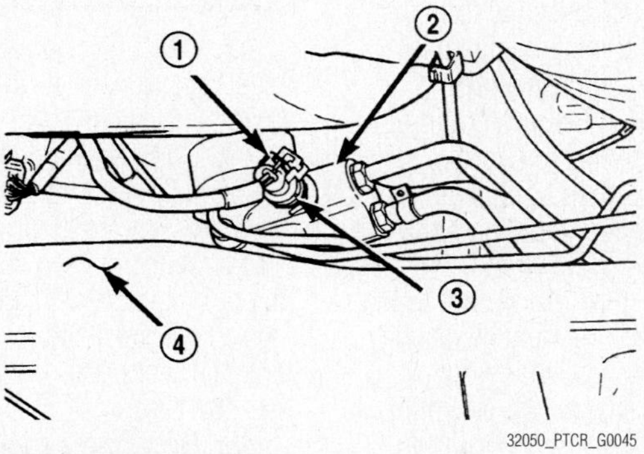

Fig. 69 Power steering pressure switch (3)

member using the transmission jack enough to allow the power steering gear to be removed from the rear of the crossmember. When lowering front suspension crossmember, do not let crossmember hang from lower control arms. The weight should be supported by the transmission jack.

23. Remove the roll pin securing the steering column lower coupling to the power steering gear pinion shaft using a roll pin punch. Push the steering column lower coupling up and off of the power steering gear pinion shaft.

24. Release the pinion shaft dash cover seal from the tabs cast into the power steering gear housing and remove the seal from the power steering gear.

25. Loosen and remove the four bolts attaching the power steering gear to the front suspension crossmember . Remove the power steering gear from the front suspension crossmember.

To install:

26. Install the steering gear on the front suspension crossmember. Install the four power steering gear mounting bolts. Tighten the mounting bolts to a torque of 45 ft. lbs. (61 Nm).

27. Install the pinion shaft dash cover seal over the power steering pinion shaft and onto the power steering gear housing. Align the holes on each side of the seal with the tabs cast into the power steering gear housing.

28. With the steering column lower coupling pushed partway up through its hole in the dash panel, match the flat on the inside of the steering column lower coupling to the flat on the power steering gear pinion shaft and slide the coupling onto the top of the pinion shaft. Align the roll pin hole in the coupling with the groove in the pinion shaft and install the roll pin through the coupling until it is centered.

29. Center the power steering gear rack in its travel.

30. Using the transmission jack, raise the front suspension crossmember and power steering gear until the crossmember contacts its mounting spot against the body and frame rails of the vehicle. As the crossmember is raised, carefully guide the steering column lower coupling up through its hole in the dash panel.

31. Start the two crossmember mounting bolts through the lower control arm rear

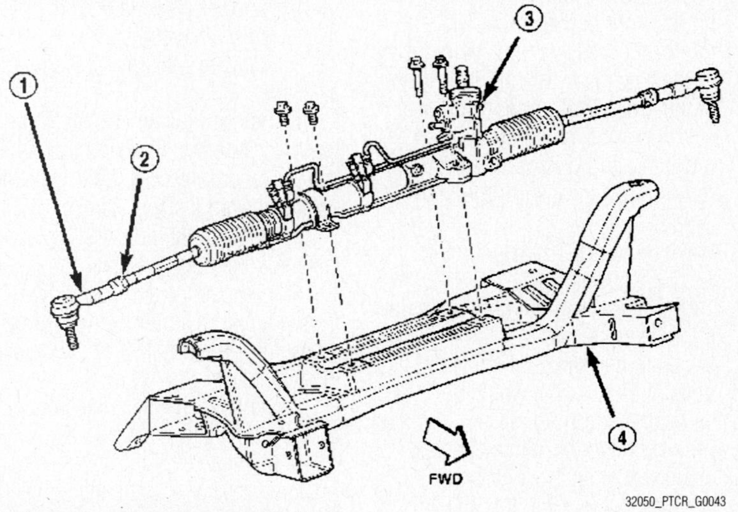

Fig. 67 The power steering gear assembly

isolator bushings into the tapping plates mounted in the body. Next, install the two front and the two rear mounting bolts attaching front suspension crossmember to frame rails of vehicle. Lightly tighten all six mounting bolts to approximately 20 inch lbs. (2 Nm) to hold the front suspension crossmember in position at this time.

➡When reinstalling the front suspension crossmember back in the vehicle, it is very important that the crossmember be attached to the body in exactly the same spot as when it was removed. Otherwise, the vehicle's wheel alignment settings (caster and camber) will be lost.

32. Using a soft face hammer, tap the front suspension crossmember back-and-forth or side-to-side until it is aligned with the previously scribed positioning marks on the body of the vehicle. Once the front suspension crossmember is correctly positioned, tighten the two crossmember mounting bolts through the lower control arm rear isolator bushings to a torque of 185 ft. lbs. (250 Nm), then tighten the four remaining crossmember mounting bolts to a torque of 113 ft. lbs. (153 Nm).
33. Fasten the engine torque strut to the right forward corner of the front suspension crossmember using its mounting bolt.
34. Install the washer on the end of the stud extending from the torque strut bolt.
35. Install the pencil strut to the right front corner of the crossmember and body of the vehicle). Tighten the pencil strut nuts to a torque of 38 ft. lbs. (52 Nm).
36. Install the drive belt splash shield and fasteners.
37. Install the screws fastening the front fascia to the reinforcement.
38. Using a lint free towel, wipe clean the open power steering hose ends and the power steering gear ports. Replace the pressure hose used O-ring with new. Lubricate the O-ring with power steering fluid.
39. On vehicles equipped with crossmember mounted power steering fluid coolers:
    - Place the cooler in mounting position and snap the cooler tube going to the gear into the right routing clip on the front of the gear. Close the routing clip.
    - Install the two screws securing the cooler to the front suspension crossmember.
40. Tighten the screws to a torque of 90 inch lbs. (10 Nm).
41. Slide the cooler or return hose onto the steel gear outlet port fitting. Secure the clamp on the hose past the bead on the steel fitting.

⁂ CAUTION

On vehicles equipped with crossmember mounted power steering fluid coolers, forward of the steering gear, the power steering fluid pressure hose routes between the front suspension crossmember and the driveshaft. When tightening the pressure hose tube nut to the steering gear, the pressure hose must be positioned (clocked) such that its final routing (after tightened to 23 ft. lbs. (31 Nm) offers 4-10 mm clearance to the front suspension crossmember (measured at the pressure hose steel-to-rubber coupling). There should be a clocking donut on the hose to preset this distance.

42. Attach the power steering fluid pressure hose to its port on the power steering gear.
43. On turbocharged vehicles, install routing clip up from gear outlet tube onto fluid pressure hose tube.
44. While making sure the pressure hose is not in contact with any vehicle components (see preceding caution), tighten the pressure hose tube nut at the gear to 23 ft. lbs. (31 Nm).
45. On vehicles equipped with a power steering fluid pressure switch, reconnect the wiring harness connector at the power steering fluid pressure switch. Be sure the locking tab on the wiring harness connector is securely latched.
46. Perform the following to each outer tie rod:
    - Place the tie rod heat shield on the knuckle's steering arm, aligning the hole in the shield with the hole in the knuckle and the tangs on the outside of the shield with the outside configuration of the steering arm. The shield should now be facing outboard, away from the power steering gear and tie rod.
    - Attach the outer tie rod end to its steering knuckle.
    - Start the attaching nut onto the stud of the outer tie rod.
    - While holding the stud of the tie rod stationary with a wrench, tighten the attaching nut.
    - Using a crowfoot wrench attached to a torque wrench, tighten the attaching nut to 40 ft. lbs. (54 Nm).
47. Install the tire and wheel assemblies back on vehicle. Tighten the wheel mounting nuts to 100 ft. lbs. (135 Nm).
48. Lower the vehicle to ground level.
49. Install the dash-to-lower coupling seal in place over the lower coupling's plastic collar.

➡Verify that grease is present on the lip of the dash-to-coupling seal where it contacts the coupling's plastic collar.

50. Inside the passenger compartment, reconnect the steering column lower coupling to the steering column upper coupling. Install the coupling pinch bolt and tighten the pinch bolt nut to a torque of 250 inch lbs. (28 Nm). Install the pinch bolt retainer pin.
51. Remove the steering wheel holder.
52. While looking under the instrument panel at the lower coupling, rotate the steering wheel back-and-forth to verify that the lower coupling does not squeak against the dash-to-coupling seal.
53. Install the knee blocker.
54. Install the silencer pad below the knee blocker panel below the steering column.
55. Perform the Power Steering Pump Initial Operation service procedure to properly fill and bleed the power steering system.
56. Check for fluid leaks.
57. Adjust the front toe setting on the vehicle.

POWER STEERING PUMP

REMOVAL & INSTALLATION

Non-Turbo Models

See Figures 70 and 71.

1. Siphon as much fluid as possible from the power steering fluid reservoir.
2. Raise the vehicle.
3. Remove the right front tire and wheel assembly.
4. Remove the screws fastening the front fascia to the reinforcement as necessary in order to access the drive belt splash shield forward fastener screw.
5. Remove the drive belt splash shield fasteners. Remove the shield.
6. Remove the accessory drive belt from the A/C compressor and power steering pump. Refer to the Cooling section for the procedure.
7. Remove the electrical connectors from the A/C compressor.
8. Remove the four bolts fastening the A/C compressor to the engine, then move the compressor toward the center of the

vehicle, allowing the compressor to settle in place.

9. Remove the pressure hose from the pump in the following fashion:

10. Place a crowfoot wrench on a long extension onto the pressure hose tube nut at the pump.

11. Place a shop towel between the crowfoot and the pump pulley to avoid slipping and possibly damaging the pulley.

12. Unthread the tube nut from the pump.

13. Lower the vehicle.

14. Remove the grille from the front of the vehicle.

15. Remove the hood-opening weatherstrip from across the radiator closure panel.

16. Remove the ambient temperature sensor from the radiator closure panel.

17. Remove the fasteners securing the upper radiator closure panel in place, then remove the panel.

18. Lift the cooling module out of its lower mounts and carefully move it toward the left side of the vehicle. It will move only a limited amount with the hoses still connected. Do not force it.

➡For additional room, the right side bolts securing the lower radiator closure panel in front of the cooling module can be removed.

19. Using a bungee cord, tie the cooling module forward as shown. Be sure to attach the cord in a location that will not damage the vehicle. Do not over tighten the bungee cord. It just needs to hold the module forward.

20. Remove the clamp securing the supply hose to the power steering pump supply fitting, then remove the hose from the supply fitting.

21. Remove the three bolts securing the pump in place.

22. Remove the 2 bolts securing the stamped steel support bracket to the engine block.

23. Remove the bracket.

24. Ease the cooling module forward, don't force it, and remove the power steering pump and pulley where shown.

To install:

25. Using a lint free towel, wipe clean the open power steering pressure hose end and the power steering pump port. Replace any used O-rings with new. Lubricate the O-ring with clean power steering fluid.

26. Ease the cooling module forward, don't force it, and install the power steering pump and pulley into its mounting area in the same fashion it was removed.

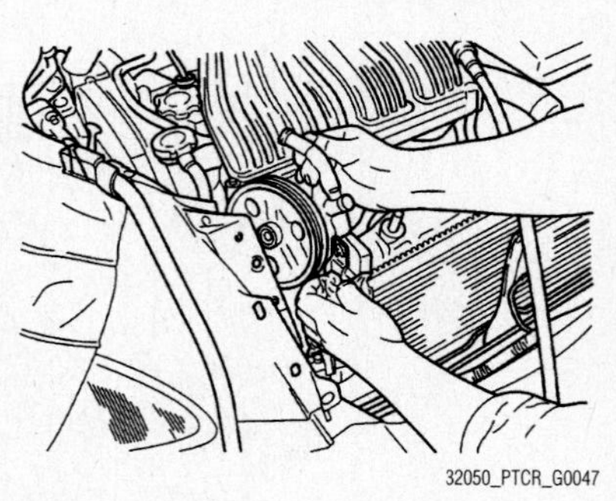

Fig. 70 Power steering pump removal—non-turbocharged models

27. Place the pump in mounting position with the stamped steel support bracket behind it. Install the three bolts through the bracket and pump, into the threaded engine cover. Do not tighten the bolts at this time.

28. Install the two bolts fastening the bracket to the engine block. Tighten the two bolts to a torque of 40 ft. lbs. (54 Nm).

29. Tighten the three pump mounting bolts previously installed to a torque of 250 inch lbs. (28 Nm).

30. Push the fluid supply hose onto the pump supply fitting. Expand the hose clamp and slide it over the hose and pump supply fitting. Secure the clamp once it is past the bead formed into the fluid reservoir fitting.

⁂ CAUTION

Make sure the supply hose is routed above the engine timing chain cover. The power steering fluid supply hose must remain clear of any unfriendly surface that can cause possible damage to it.

31. Raise the vehicle.

32. Thread the fluid pressure hose tube nut into the pump.

33. Using a crowfoot wrench on a long extension with a torque wrench, tighten the pressure hose tube nut at the power steering pump to a torque of 23 ft. lbs. (31 Nm).

34. Install the four bolts fastening the A/C compressor to the engine. Tighten the mounting bolts to a torque of 250 inch lbs. (28 Nm).

35. Install the A/C compressor electrical connectors.

36. Install the A/C drive belt. Refer to the Cooling section for the procedure.

37. Install the drive belt splash shield and fasteners.

38. Install the screws fastening the front fascia to the reinforcement.

39. Install the right front tire and wheel assembly. Install and tighten the wheel mounting nuts to a torque of 100 ft. lbs. (135 Nm).

40. Lower the vehicle.

41. Remove the bungee cord and move the cooling module back into is lower mounts.

42. If previously removed, install the right side bolts securing the lower radiator closure panel in front of the cooling module.

43. Install the radiator closure panel and fasten it in place.

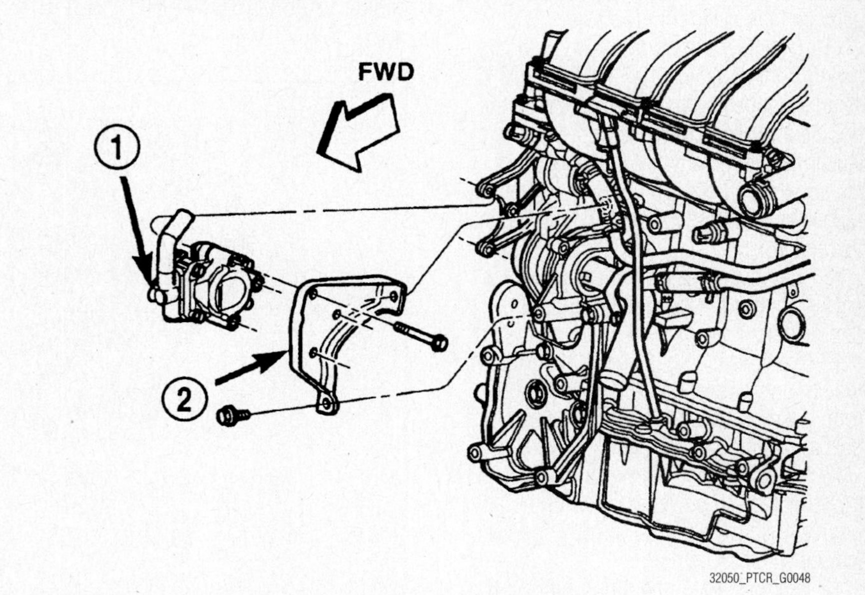

Fig. 71 Power steering pump (1) mounting non turbocharged models

44. Install the ambient temperature sensor on the radiator closure panel.
45. Install the hood-opening weatherstrip across the radiator closure panel.
46. Install the grille on the front of the vehicle.
47. Perform the Power Steering Pump Initial Operation service procedure to properly fill and bleed the power steering system.
48. Check for leaks.

Turbo Models

See Figures 72 and 73.

1. Siphon as much fluid as possible from power steering fluid reservoir.
2. Raise and safely support the vehicle.
3. Drain engine coolant.
4. Remove right front tire and wheel assembly.
5. Disconnect radiator fan wiring connector.
6. Remove two lower fan mounting screws.
7. Remove accessory drive belt splash shield.
8. Remove accessory drive belt.
9. Carefully lower the vehicle.
10. Remove grille from front of vehicle.
11. Remove hood-opening weather-strip from across radiator closure panel.
12. Remove ambient temperature sensors from radiator closure panel.
13. Remove fasteners securing upper radiator closure panel in place, then remove the panel and lay it out of way.
14. Remove 2 screws fastening upper radiator hose inlet neck to radiator, then separate inlet neck from radiator.
15. Carefully tip top of cooling module toward front of vehicle. DO NOT FORCE IT. Using a bungee cord or equivalent, tie the module forward in this position. Be sure to attach the cord in a location that will not damage the vehicle. Do not over tighten the bungee cord. It just needs to hold the module forward.
16. Remove remaining four screws fastening radiator fan to cooling module. Remove fan.
17. Remove clamp securing fluid return hose to pump reservoir, then remove hose from reservoir fitting. Cap off hose end and reservoir fitting.
18. Back out tube nut securing fluid pressure hose to power steering pump and remove hose from pump. Cap off hose end and pump pressure port.
19. Remove three mounting bolts securing power steering pump in place.
20. Remove 2 bolts securing stamped steel support bracket to engine block. Remove bracket.
21. Remove power steering pump with pulley and reservoir attached.

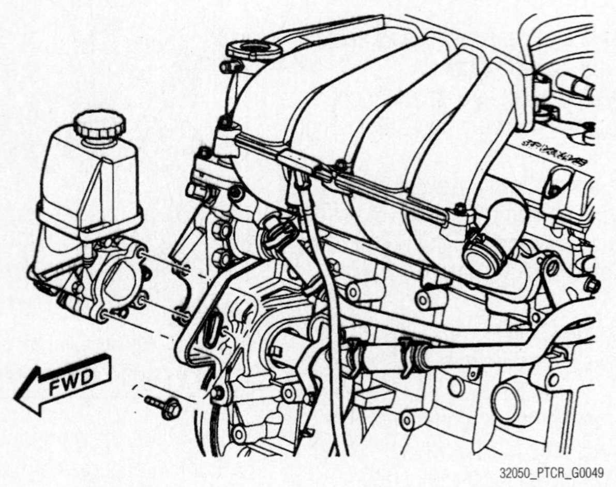

Fig. 72 Power steering pump mounting location—turbocharged models

To install:

22. Using a lint free towel, wipe clean open power steering pressure hose end and power steering pump pressure port. Replace any used O-rings with new. Lubricate O-ring with clean power steering fluid.
23. Install power steering pump with pulley and reservoir into its mounting area in same fashion it was removed.
24. Place pump in mounting position with stamped steel support bracket behind it. Install three pump mounting bolts through bracket and pump, into threaded engine cover. DO NOT TIGHTEN BOLTS AT THIS TIME.
25. Install two bolts fastening support bracket to engine block. Tighten two bolts to 40 ft. lbs. (54 Nm)
26. Tighten three pump mounting bolts previously installed to 250 inch lbs. (28 Nm)
27. Thread pressure hose tube nut into pump pressure fitting. Tighten tube nut to 23 ft. lbs. (31 Nm).
28. Install fluid return hose onto power steering fluid reservoir return fitting. Expand hose clamp and slide it over hose and pump return fitting. Secure clamp once it is past bead formed into fluid reservoir fitting.
29. Position radiator fan and install two upper and two side mounting screws. DO NOT TIGHTEN SCREWS AT THIS TIME. Tighten screws to 55 inch lbs. (6 Nm).
30. Position cooling module back into its lower mounts.

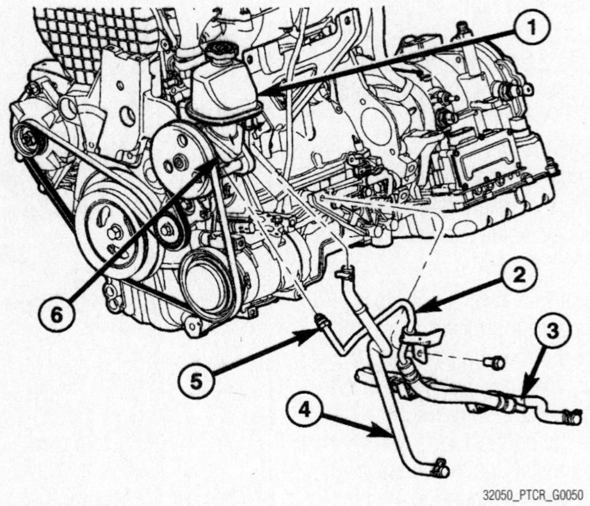

Fig. 73 Power steering pump hose connection locations—turbocharged models

31. Clean and inspect or replace upper radiator hose inlet neck O-ring, then install inlet neck to radiator. Install 2 mounting screws.
32. Install radiator closure panel and fasten it in place.
33. Install ambient temperature sensors on radiator closure panel.
34. Install hood-opening weather-strip across radiator closure panel.
35. Install grille on front of vehicle.
36. Raise and safely support the vehicle.
37. Install accessory drive belt.
38. Install accessory drive belt splash shield.
39. Install two remaining lower fan mounting screws. Tighten screws to 55 inch lbs. (6 Nm).
40. Connect radiator fan wiring connector.
41. Install right front tire and wheel assembly. Install and tighten wheel mounting nuts to 100 ft. lbs. (135 Nm).
42. Carefully lower the vehicle.
43. Tighten two upper and two side radiator fan mounting screws to 55 inch lbs. (6 Nm).
44. Fill cooling system.
45. Perform Power Steering Pump Initial Operation procedure to properly fill and bleed power steering system.
46. Check for leaks.

BLEEDING

WARNING

The fluid level should be check and adjusted with the engine off to prevent injury from moving the engine components.

CAUTION

Use only MOPAR® ATF+4 Automatic Transmission Fluid (MS-9602) in the power steering system. Do not overfill.

1. Fill the power steering fluid reservoir to the proper level, then let the fluid settle for at least two minutes.
2. Start the engine and let run for a few seconds, then turn the engine off.
3. Add fluid if necessary. Repeat the above procedure until the fluid level remains constant after running the engine.
4. Raise the front wheels off the ground.
5. Start the engine. Slowly turn the steering wheel right and left, lightly contacting the wheel stops.
6. Add power steering fluid if necessary.
7. Lower the vehicle and turn the steering wheel slowly from lock to lock.
8. Stop the engine. Check the fluid level and refill as required.
9. If the fluid is extremely foamy, allow the vehicle to stand a few minutes and repeat the above procedure.

SUSPENSION

FRONT SUSPENSION

COIL SPRING

REMOVAL & INSTALLATION

See Figure 74.

1. Before servicing the vehicle, refer to the precautions in the beginning of this section.
2. Remove the wheel.
3. Remove the strut assembly and place it in a Strut Spring Compressor Tool W-7200.
4. Set the lower hooks then the upper hooks. Position the clevis bracket straight outward away from the compressor tool
5. Install a clamp on the lower end of the coil spring to secure the strut when the nut is removed.

➡Do not remove the strut shaft nut until the coil spring is compressed. The coil spring is under pressure and must be compressed before the shaft nut is removed.

6. Compress the coil spring until all tension is removed from the upper mount.
7. Install a Strut Nut Socket Tool 6864 once the spring is compressed.
8. Install a socket on the hex end of the strut shaft and remove the nut.
9. Remove or disconnect the following:
   - Upper mount from the strut shaft
   - Upper spring seat, bearing and upper isolator as an assembly
   - Dust shield and jounce bumper
   - Clamp from the bottom of the coil spring
   - Strut through the bottom of the coil
   - Release the tension from the coil spring by backing off the compressor drive completely
   - Coil spring
10. Inspect the coil spring for any signs of damage.

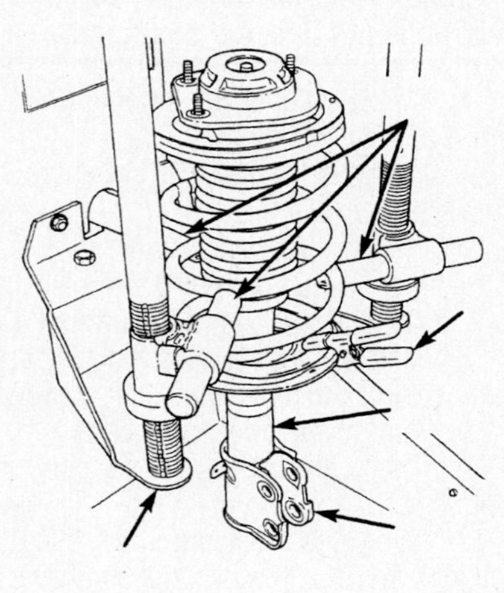

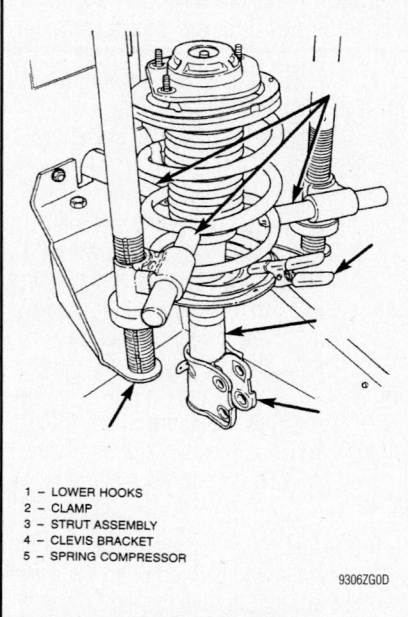

1 – LOWER HOOKS
2 – CLAMP
3 – STRUT ASSEMBLY
4 – CLEVIS BRACKET
5 – SPRING COMPRESSOR

9306ZG0D

Fig. 74 Coil spring mounted in the coil spring compressor tool

To install:

11. Install or connect the following:
   - Coil spring in the compressor. Rotate the spring so that the end of the top coil is directly in the front.
   - Slowly compress the coil until enough room is available to install the strut
   - Lower spring isolator on the lower spring seat
   - Strut through the bottom of the of coil spring until the lower spring seat contacts the lower end of the coil spring. Rotate the strut until the clevis bracket is positioned straight outward away from the compressor.
   - Clamp on the lower end of the coil spring and strut
   - Jounce bumper on the strut shaft with the smaller end pointing downward
   - Dust shield until the bottom of the shield snaps on to the retainer
   - Upper spring isolator
   - Upper spring seat and bearing on top of the coil spring. Position the notch formed into the edge of the upper seat straight out away from the compressor.
   - Strut upper mount over the strut shaft and onto the top of the upper spring seat and bearing. Position the mount so that the third mounting

stud is inward toward the compressor.
- Retaining nut on the strut shaft, loosely

12. Install the strut nut socket on the strut shaft retaining nut. Install a socket on the hex end of the shaft. Secure the strut shaft and torque the nut to 55 ft. lbs. (75 Nm).
13. Slowly release the tension from the coil spring by backing off the compressor completely.
14. Remove the clamp from the bottom of the coil spring and strut. Push back the spring compressor upper and lower hooks and remove the strut from the compressor.
15. Install the strut assembly to the vehicle.

CONTROL LINKS

REMOVAL & INSTALLATION

1. Before servicing the vehicle, refer to the Precautions Section.
2. Raise and support the vehicle.
3. On both sides of the vehicle, remove the control links (stabilizer bar links) assembly.
   - Remove each link by holding the upper retainer/nut with a wrench.
   - Turn the link bolt to remove the control link(s) from the vehicle.

To install:

4. Clean the threads of both control link bolts, then apply MOPAR® Lock And Seal, or equivalent, to the threads.
5. On each side of the vehicle, install the control link assemblies. Start each control link bolt with a bushing from the bottom, through the stabilizer bar, inner link bushing, lower control arm, and into the upper retainer/nut and bushing. Do not fully tighten the link assemblies at this time.
6. Lower the vehicle.

➡It may be necessary to put the vehicle on a platform hoist or alignment rack to gain access to the stabilizer bar mounting bolts with the vehicle at curb height.

7. Tighten each control link by holding the upper retainer/nut with a wrench while turning the link bolt. Tighten each link bolt to 21 ft. lbs. (29 Nm).

LOWER BALL JOINT

REMOVAL & INSTALLATION

See Figures 75 through 78.

The front suspension ball joints operate with no free-play. The ball joints are replaceable ONLY as an assembly. Do not attempt any type of repair on the ball joint assembly. The ball joint is a press fit into the lower control arm with the joint stud retained in the steering knuckle by the clamp bolt. To check the ball joint, with the weight of the vehicle resting on the road wheels, grasp the grease fitting and without using any tools, attempt to move the grease fitting. If the ball joint is worn the grease fitting will move easily. If movement is noted, replacement of the ball joint is recommended.

1. Before servicing the vehicle, refer to the precautions in the beginning of this section.
2. Remove the wheel.
3. Remove the stabilizer bar-to-lower control arm links.
4. Loosen, but do not remove the bolts holding the stabilizer bar retainers to the crossmember. Then, rotate the stabilizer bar and attaching links away from the lower control arms.

⁂ WARNING

Pulling the steering knuckle outward after releasing the ball joint can separate the inner CV-joint.

5. Remove the steering knuckle-to-ball joint stud's pinch bolt and nut.
6. Remove the ball joint from the steering knuckle using a pry bar.

⁂ WARNING

Be careful when separating the ball joint stud from the knuckle, so the seal does not become damaged.

7. If removing the right lower control arm, perform the following steps:
   a. Remove the drive belt splash shield.
   b. Remove the pencil strut from the right front corner of the crossmember
   c. Remove the engine torque strut.
8. Remove the pivot bolts attaching the lower control arm to the front crossmember.
9. Remove the lower control arm.
10. Remove the ball joint using a pry tool.
11. Using a hydraulic press, press the ball joint from the lower control arm using Receiver tool 6908-2 and Adapter Tool 6804.

To install:

12. Reinstall the ball joint into the lower control arm with the notch in the ball joint stud facing the front lower control arm bushing.
13. Using a hydraulic press, press the ball joint into the lower control arm using Receiver Tool 6758 and Adapter tool 6804.
14. Install the ball joint boot seal using a driver tool such as a large socket or suitable sized piece of pipe.

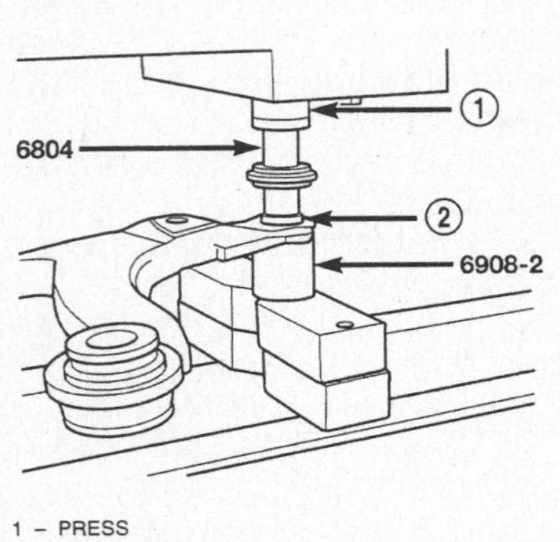

Fig. 75 Removing the ball joint from the control arm

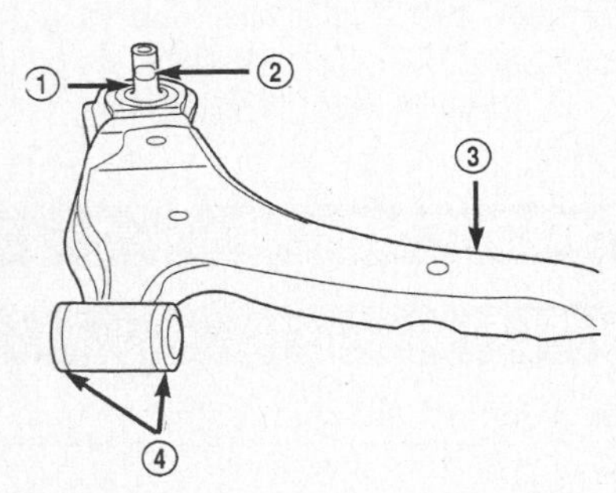

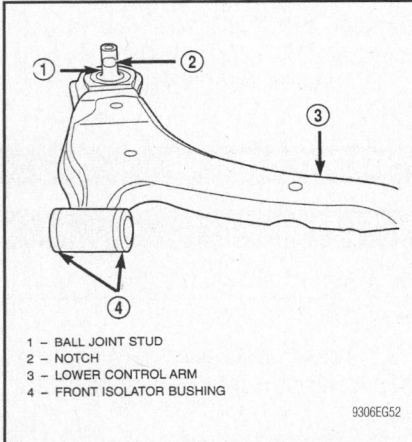

Fig. 76 Aligning the ball joint stud notch to the control arm

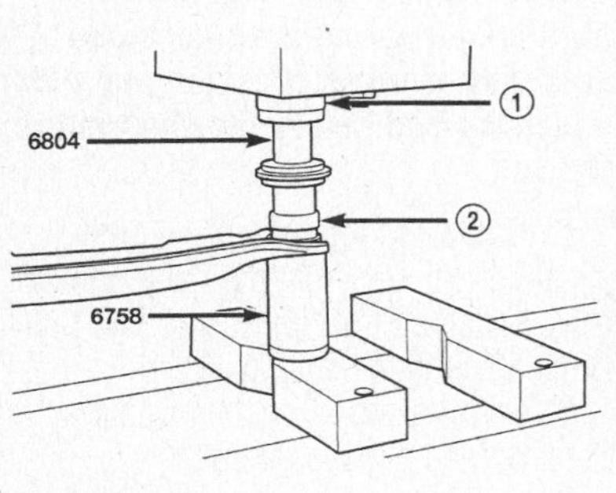

Fig. 77 Installing the ball joint to the control arm

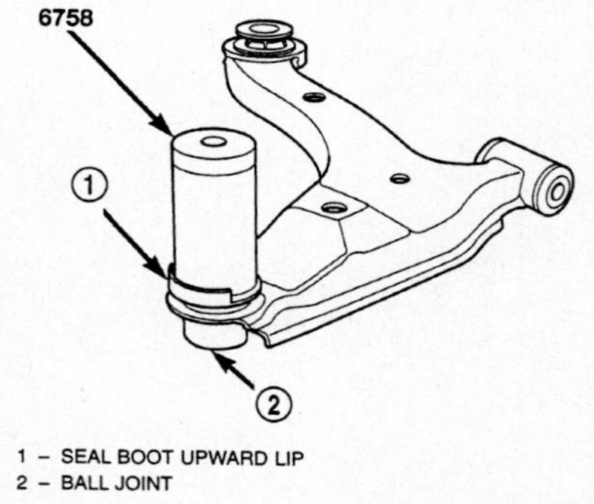

Fig. 78 Installing the ball joint boot seal

✲✲ WARNING

Do not use a shop press that was used to install the ball joint, for the press exerts too much force.

15. Install the lower control arm into the front crossmember.

16. Install the rear lower control arm-to-crossmember and frame rail bolt.

➡DO NOT tighten the rear bolt at this time.

17. Install the front lower control arm-to-crossmember nut and bolt.

18. Torque the lower control arm to rear pivot bolt to 185 ft. lbs. (250 Nm) and the front pivot bolt 120 ft. lbs. (163 Nm).

19. Install the ball joint stud into the steering knuckle. Torque the steering knuckle-to-ball joint stud pinch bolt/nut to 70 ft. lbs. (95 Nm).

20. If the right side lower control arm has been service, install the following:

21. Install the engine torque strut.

22. Install the pencil strut to the right front corner of the crossmember and torque the nuts to 43 ft. lbs. (58 Nm).

23. Install the drive belt splash shield.

24. Install the front fascia-to-reinforcement screws.

25. Install the stabilizer bar-to-lower control arm link assemblies and bushings.

26. Rotate the stabilizer bar into position, installing the stabilizer bar links into the lower control arms.

27. Install the top stabilizer bar link bushings and nuts. DO NOT tighten the link yet.

28. Install the wheel.

29. Lower the vehicle so the suspension is supporting the total weight of the vehicle.

30. Torque the stabilizer bar-to-lower control arm links to 21 ft. lbs. (28 Nm).

31. Torque the stabilizer bar bushing retainer-to-crossmember bolts to 21 ft. lbs. (28 Nm).

32. Check and/or adjust the toe, as necessary.

LOWER CONTROL ARM

REMOVAL & INSTALLATION

See Figure 79.

1. Raise the vehicle.

2. Remove the front tire and wheel assembly.

3. Remove both stabilizer bar links from the vehicle. Remove each link by holding the upper retainer/nut with a wrench and turning the link bolt.

4. Rotate the forward ends of the stabilizer bar downward. It may be necessary to loosen the stabilizer bar cushion retainer bolts a little to ease any turning resistance.

5. Remove the nut and pinch bolt clamping the ball joint stud to the steering knuckle.

✲✲ CAUTION

After removing the steering knuckle from the ball joint stud, do not pull outward on the knuckle. Pulling the steering knuckle outward at this point can separate the inner C/V joint on the driveshaft.

➡Use caution when separating the ball joint stud from the steering knuckle, so the ball joint seal does not get cut.

6. Separate the ball joint stud from the steering knuckle by prying down on lower control arm and up against the ball joint boss on the steering knuckle.

7. If the right lower control arm is being serviced, perform the following:

- Remove the screws fastening the front fascia to the reinforcement as necessary in order to access the drive belt splash shield forward fastener screw.
- Remove the drive belt splash shield fasteners. Remove the shield.
- Remove the pencil strut from the right front corner of the crossmember and body of the vehicle. Remove the washer behind the strut from the torque strut bolt.
- Remove the bolts mounting the engine torque strut in place, then remove the engine torque strut from the vehicle.

8. Remove the front pivot bolt attaching the lower control arm to the front suspension crossmember. Remove the rear pivot bolt attaching the lower control arm to the front suspension crossmember and frame rail. Remove the lower control arm from the crossmember.

To install:

9. Position the lower control arm into the crossmember. Install, but do not fully tighten, the rear pivot bolt attaching the lower control arm to the front suspension crossmember and frame rail. Install, but do not fully tighten, the front pivot bolt attaching the lower control arm to the front suspension crossmember.

10. With no weight on the lower control arm, tighten the lower control arm rear pivot (and suspension crossmember) bolt to a torque of 185 ft. lbs. (250 Nm), then tighten the lower control arm front pivot bolt to a torque of 125 ft. lbs. (170 Nm).

11. Install the ball joint stud into the steering knuckle aligning the bolt hole in the knuckle boss with the notch formed in the side of the ball joint stud.

12. If the right lower control arm has been serviced, perform the following:

- Install the engine torque strut). To properly align and tighten the torque strut.
- Install the washer on the end of the stud extending from the torque strut bolt.
- Install the pencil strut to the right front corner of the crossmember and body of the vehicle. Tighten the pencil strut nuts to a torque of 43 ft. lbs. (58 Nm).
- Install the drive belt splash shield and fasteners.
- Install the screws fastening the front fascia to the reinforcement.

13. Install a new ball joint stud pinch bolt and nut. Tighten the nut to a torque of 70 ft. lbs. (95 Nm).

14. Rotate the forward ends of the stabilizer bar into mounting position.

15. Clean the threads of the stabilizer bar

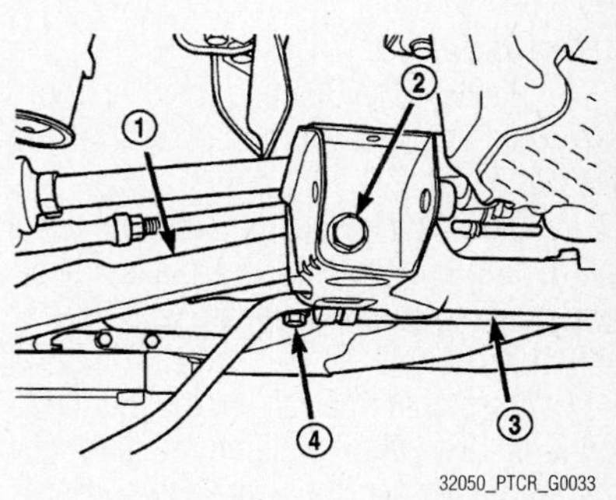

Fig. 79 Lower control arm mounting bolts and location

link bolts, then apply MOPAR® Lock And Seal or equivalent to the threads.

16. Install both stabilizer bar links back on vehicle. Start each stabilizer bar link bolt with bushing from the bottom, through the stabilizer bar, inner link bushings, lower control arm, and into the upper retainer/nut and bushing. Do not fully tighten the link assemblies at this time.

17. Lower the vehicle to ground level.

➡It may be necessary to put the vehicle on a platform hoist or alignment rack to gain access to the stabilizer bar mounting bolts with the vehicle at curb height.

18. Tighten each stabilizer bar link by holding the upper retainer/nut with a wrench and turning the link bolt. Tighten each link bolt to a torque of 250 inch lbs. (28 Nm)).

19. If previously loosened, tighten the stabilizer bar cushion retainer bolts to a torque of 250 inch lbs. (28 Nm).

CONTROL ARM BUSHING REPLACEMENT

Front Isolator Bushing

See Figures 80 and 81.

1. Before servicing the vehicle, refer to the precautions in the beginning of this section.

2. Remove the lower control arm assembly

3. Install the Bushing Remover Tool 6602-5 and Bushing Receiver Tool MB-990799 on Special Tool C-4212-F.

4. Position the lower control arm on the assembled removal tools.

➡Be sure the Bushing Receiver Tool MB-990799 is square on the lower control arm and Bushing Remover Tool 6602-5 is positioned correctly on the isolator bushing.

5. Tighten Special Tool C-4212-F to press the bushing from the lower control arm.

To assemble:

6. Position the Bushing Installer Tool 6876 onto the screw portion of Special Tool C-4212-F.

7. Start the new bushing into the lower control arm hole machined surface side by hand, making sure it is square with its mounting hole.

8. Assemble Special Tools 6758, 6876 and C-4212-F; then, position the lower control arm on the assembly, making sure that the tools are aligned.

9. Tighten Special Tool C-4212-F to

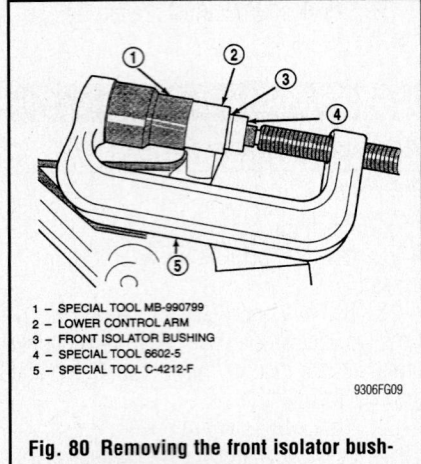

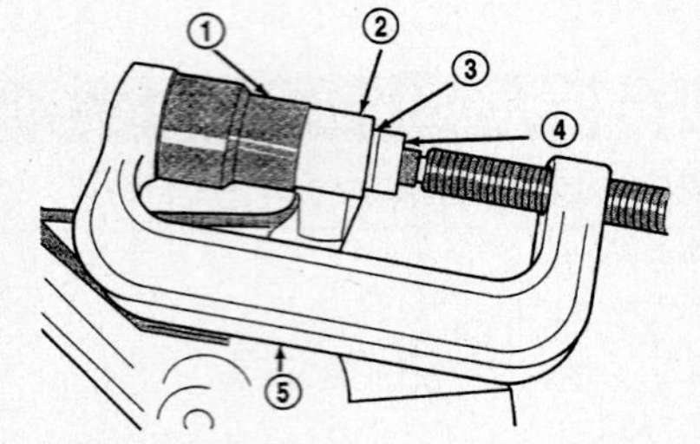

Fig. 80 Removing the front isolator bushing from the lower control arm

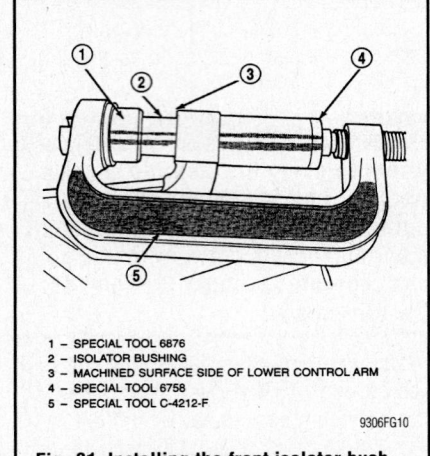

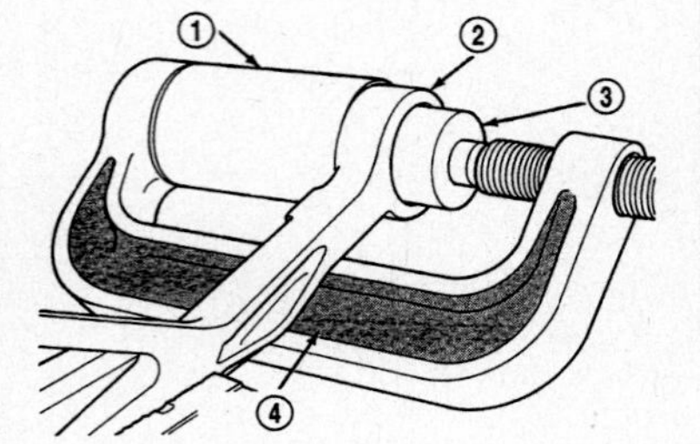

Fig. 82 Removing the rear isolator bushing from the lower control arm

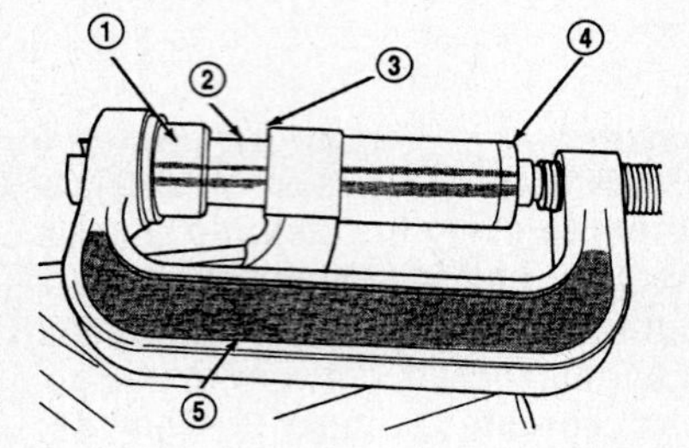

Fig. 81 Installing the front isolator bushing to the lower control arm

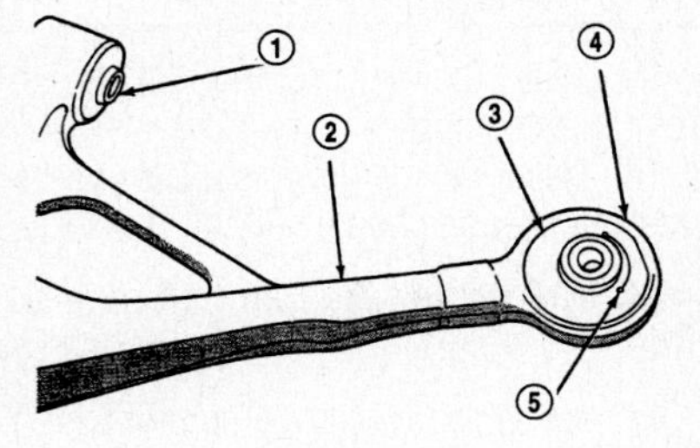

Fig. 83 Positioning the rear isolator bushing to the lower control arm

press the bushing into the lower control arm until it is flush on the machined surface.

10. Install the lower control arm assembly.

Rear Isolator Bushing

See Figures 82 through 84.

1. Before servicing the vehicle, refer to the precautions in the beginning of this section.

2. Remove the lower control arm assembly

3. Install the Bushing Remover Tool 6756 and Bushing Receiver Tool C-4366-2 on Special Tool C-4212-F.

4. Position the lower control arm on the assembled removal tools.

➡Be sure the Bushing Receiver Tool C-4366-2 is square on the lower control arm and Bushing Remover Tool 6756 is positioned correctly on the isolator bushing.

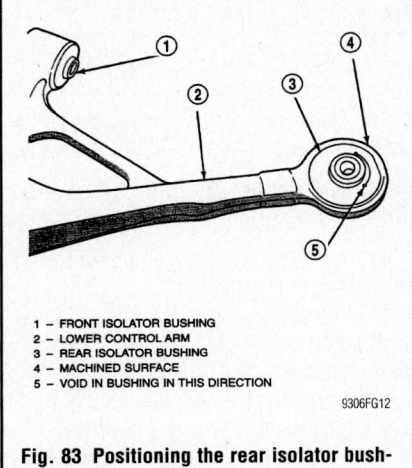

5. Tighten Special Tool C-4212-F to press the bushing from the lower control arm.

To assemble:

6. Position the Bushing Installer Tool 6760 onto the screw portion of special Tool C-4212-F.

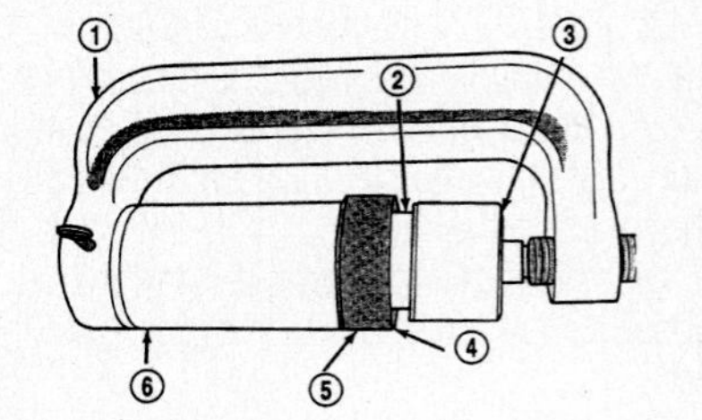

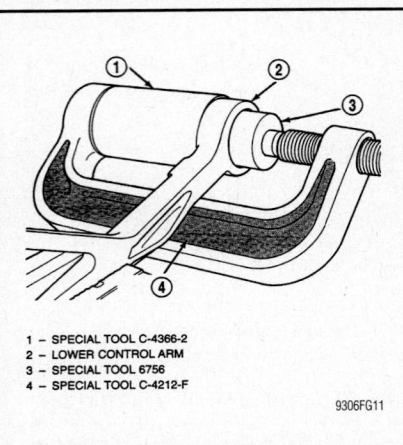

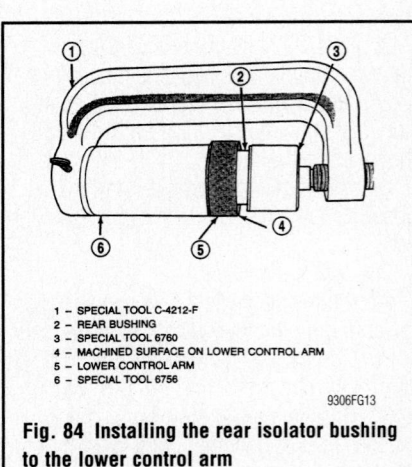

Fig. 84 Installing the rear isolator bushing to the lower control arm

7. Start the new bushing into the lower control arm hole's machined surface side by hand, making sure it is square with its mounting hole with the void in the rubber portion facing away from the ball joint.

8. Assemble Special Tools 6760 and 6756; then, position the lower control arm on the assembly, making sure that the tools are aligned.

9. Tighten Special Tool C-4212-F to press the bushing into the lower control arm until it is flush on the machined surface.

10. Install the lower control arm assembly.

Clevis Bushing

See Figures 85 and 86.

1. Before servicing the vehicle, refer to the precautions in the beginning of this section.
2. Remove the lower control arm assembly
3. Install the Bushing Remover Tool 6877 and Bushing Receiver Tool 6876 on Special Tool C-4212-F.
4. Position the lower control arm on the assembled removal tools.

➡Be sure the Bushing Receiver Tool 6876 is square on the lower control arm and Bushing Remover Tool 6877 is positioned correctly on the clevis bushing.

5. Tighten Special Tool C-4212-F to press the bushing from the lower control arm.

To assemble:

6. Position the Bushing Installer Tool 6877 onto the screw portion of special Tool C-4212-F.
7. Start the new bushing into the lower control arm hole's machined surface side by hand, making sure it is square with its mounting hole with the void in the rubber portion facing away from the ball joint.
8. Assemble special Tools 6876 and 6877; then, position the lower control arm on the assembly, making sure that the tools are aligned.
9. Tighten special Tool C-4212-F to press the bushing into the lower control arm until it is flush on the machined surface.
10. Install the lower control arm assembly.

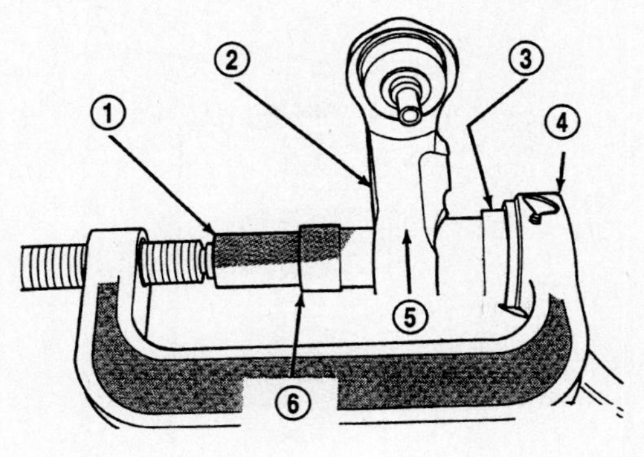

Fig. 86 Installing the clevis bushing to the lower control arm

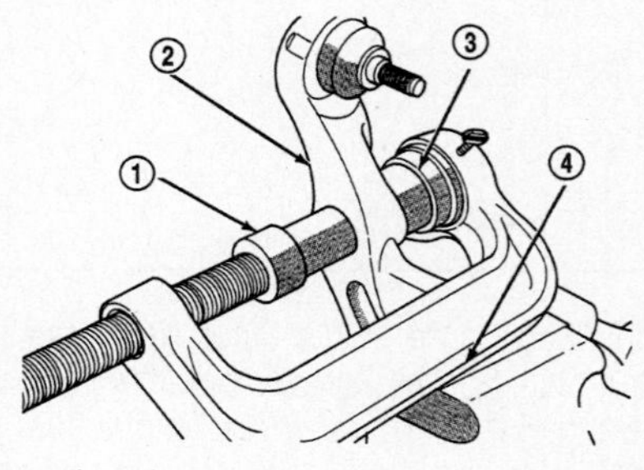

Fig. 85 Removing the clevis bushing from the lower control arm

MACPHERSON STRUT

REMOVAL & INSTALLATION

See Figure 87.

1. Before servicing the vehicle, refer to the precautions in the beginning of this section.
2. Install or connect the following:
   - Negative battery cable
   - Front wheels
   - Mark each one right or left, as applicable, if both struts are being removed
   - Ground strap from the rear of the strut
   - Anti-lock Brake System (ABS) wheel speed sensor from the strut, if equipped

⁂ WARNING

The steering knuckle-to-strut assembly attaching bolts are serrated and must not be turned during removal.

   - Steering knuckle nuts while holding the bolts stationary
   - 3 upper strut mount-to-strut tower nuts
   - Strut assembly

To install:

3. Install or connect the following:
   - Strut assembly into the strut tower by aligning the 3 upper strut mount studs with the shock tower holes. Torque the 3 upper strut mount nut/washer assemblies to 25 ft. lbs. (34 Nm).

⁂ WARNING

The steering knuckle-to-strut assembly attaching bolts are serrated and must not be turned during installation.

   - Steering knuckle nuts while holding the bolts stationary
   - Steering knuckle arm and position it into the strut assembly by aligning the strut assembly-to-steering knuckle holes
   - Both strut-to-steering knuckle bolts. On 2002–04 models, torque both bolts to 40 ft. lbs. (53 Nm), plus an additional 90 degrees after the specified torque is met. On 2005–06 models, torque both bolts to 120 ft. lbs. (163 Nm).

➡The bolts should be installed with the nuts facing the front of the vehicle.

   - ABS wheel sensor to the rear of the strut and torque the screw to 120 inch lbs. (13 Nm)

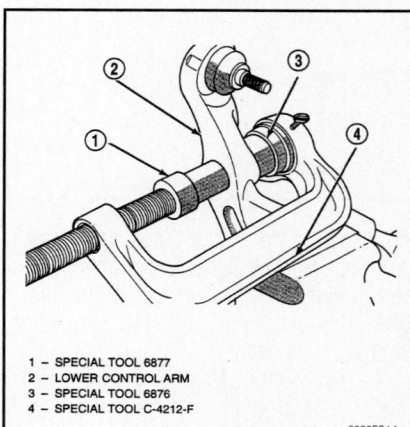

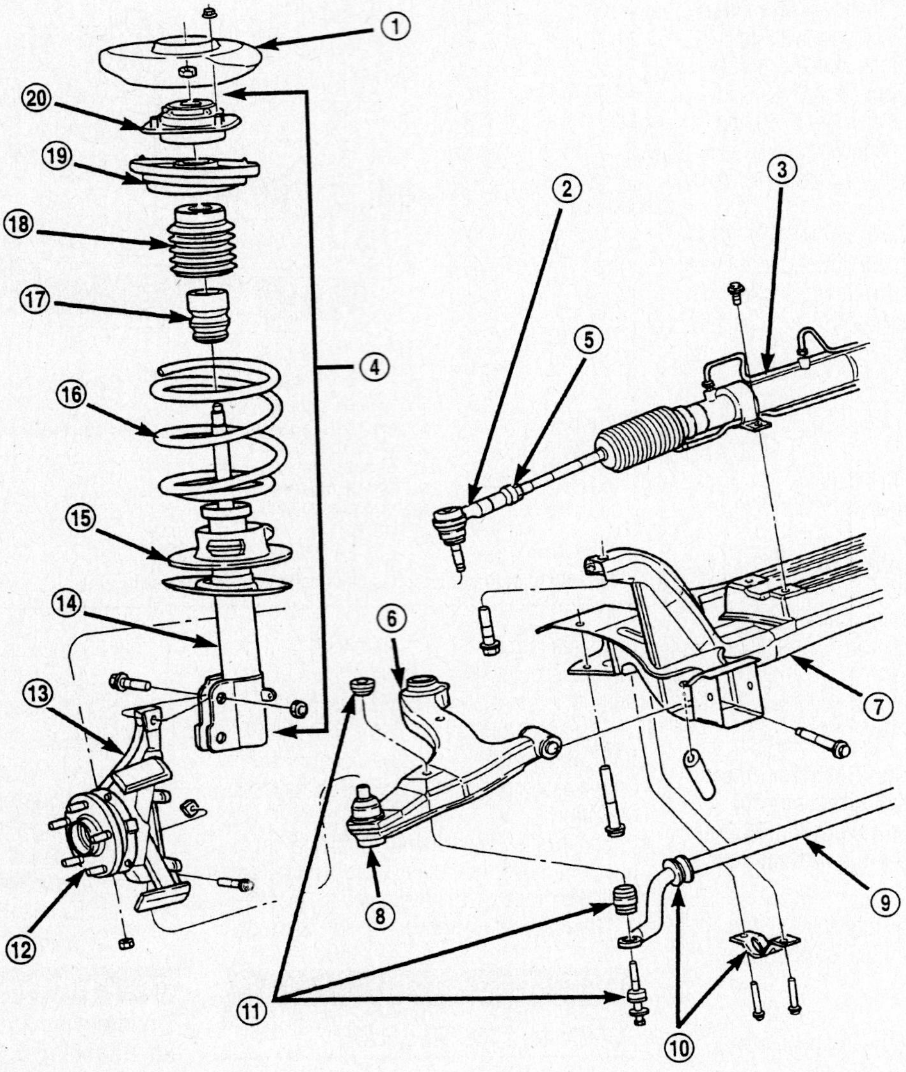

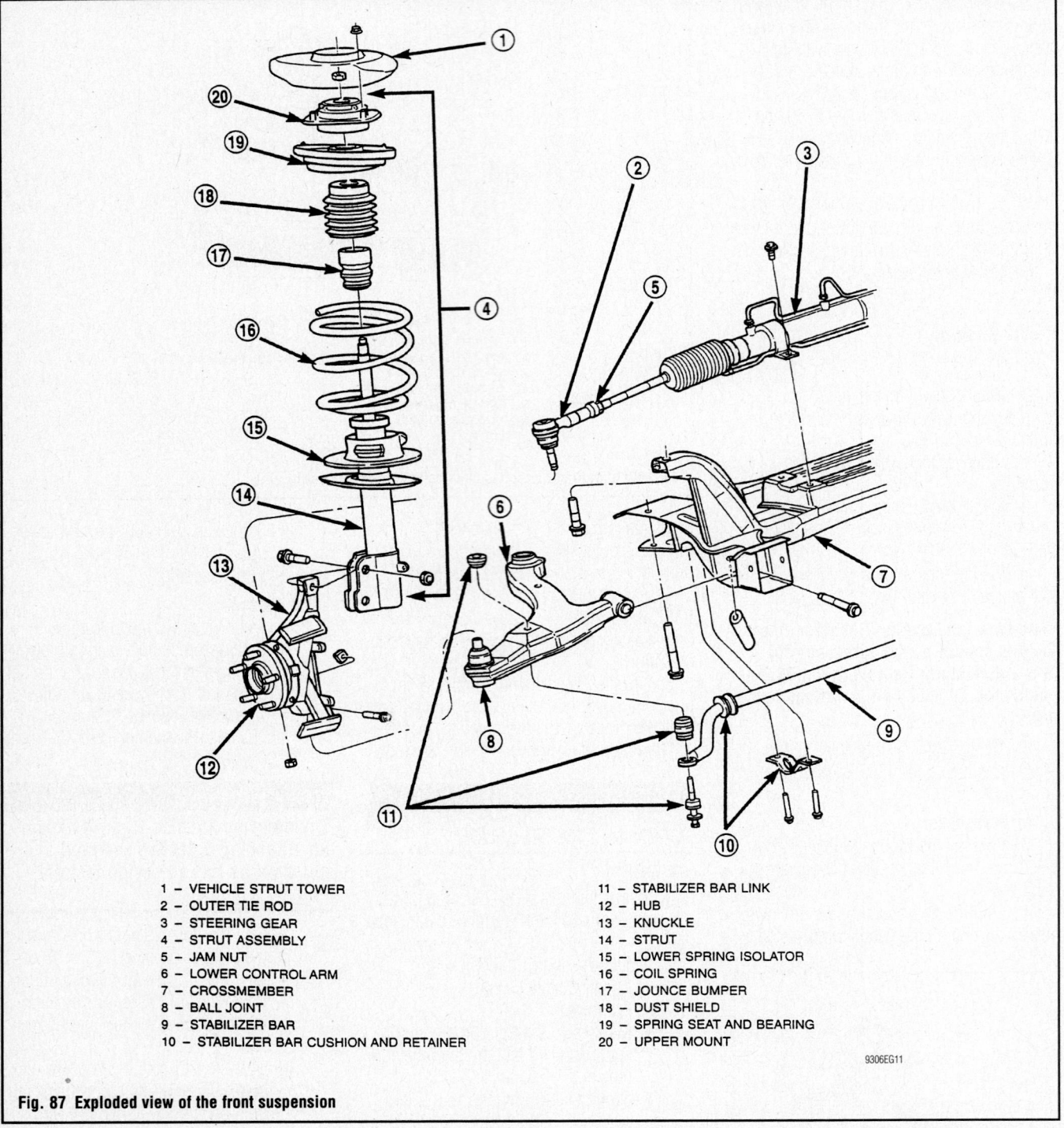

1 – VEHICLE STRUT TOWER
2 – OUTER TIE ROD
3 – STEERING GEAR
4 – STRUT ASSEMBLY
5 – JAM NUT
6 – LOWER CONTROL ARM
7 – CROSSMEMBER
8 – BALL JOINT
9 – STABILIZER BAR
10 – STABILIZER BAR CUSHION AND RETAINER
11 – STABILIZER BAR LINK
12 – HUB
13 – KNUCKLE
14 – STRUT
15 – LOWER SPRING ISOLATOR
16 – COIL SPRING
17 – JOUNCE BUMPER
18 – DUST SHIELD
19 – SPRING SEAT AND BEARING
20 – UPPER MOUNT

9306EG11

Fig. 87 Exploded view of the front suspension

- Ground strap to the rear of the strut and torque the screw to 120 inch lbs. (13 Nm)
- Front wheel
- Negative battery cable

OVERHAUL

See Figures 88 and 89.

1. Position the strut assembly in the strut coil spring compressor following the manufacturer's instructions and set the lower and upper hooks of the compressor on the coil spring. Position the strut clevis bracket straight outward, away from the compressor.

2. Compress the coil spring until all coil spring tension is removed from the upper mount and bearing.

3. Once the spring is sufficiently compressed, install Strut Nut Wrench, Special Tool 9362, on the strut rod nut. Next, install Strut Shaft Socket, Special Tool 9894, on the end of the strut rod. While holding the strut rod from turning, remove the nut using the strut nut wrench.

4. Remove the clamp (if installed) from the bottom of the coil spring and remove the strut (damper) out through the bottom of the coil spring. The dust shield and jounce bumper will come out with the strut.

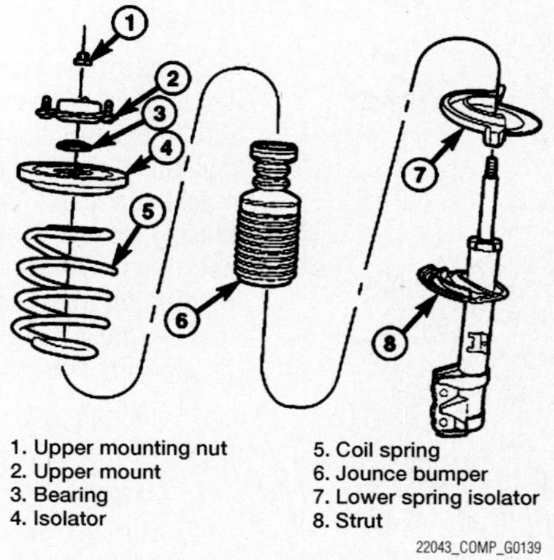

Fig. 88 Strut assembly components—Upper mounting nut (1), Upper mount (2), Bearing (3), Isolator (4), Coil spring (5), Jounce bumper (6), Lower spring isolator (7), Strut (8).

5. Remove the lower spring isolator from the strut seat.

6. Slide the dust shield and jounce bumper from the strut rod.

7. Remove the upper mount and bearing from the top of the upper spring seat and isolator.

8. Remove the upper spring seat and isolator from the top of the coil spring.

9. Release the tension from the coil spring by backing off the compressor drive completely. Push back the compressor hooks and remove the coil spring.

To assemble:

10. Place the coil spring in the spring compressor following the manufacturer's instructions. Before compressing the spring, rotate the spring so the end of the bottom coil is at approximately the 9 o'clock position as viewed from above (or to where the spring was when removed from the compressor). This action will allow the strut (damper) clevis bracket to be positioned outward, away from the compressor once installed.

11. Slowly compress the coil spring until enough room is available for strut assembly reassembly.

12. Install the upper spring seat and isolator on top of the coil spring.

13. Install the bearing and upper mount on top of the upper spring seat and isolator.

14. Install the lower spring isolator on the spring seat on the strut.

15. Slide the dust shield and jounce bumper onto the strut rod.

16. Install the strut up through the bottom of the coil spring and upper spring seat, mount, and bearing until the lower spring seat contacts the lower end of the coil spring. Rotate the strut as necessary until the end of the bottom coil comes in contact with the stop built into the lower spring isolator.

17. While holding the strut in position, install the nut on the end of the strut rod.

18. Install Special Tool 9632 Strut Nut Wrench on the strut rod nut. Next, install Special Tool 9894 Strut Shaft Socket on the end of the strut rod. While holding the strut rod from turning, tighten the strut rod nut to 44 ft. lbs. (60 Nm) using a torque wrench on the end of Special Tool 9362.

19. Slowly release the tension from the coil spring by backing off the compressor drive completely. As the tension is relieved, make sure the upper mount and bearing align properly. Verify the upper mount does not bind when rotated.

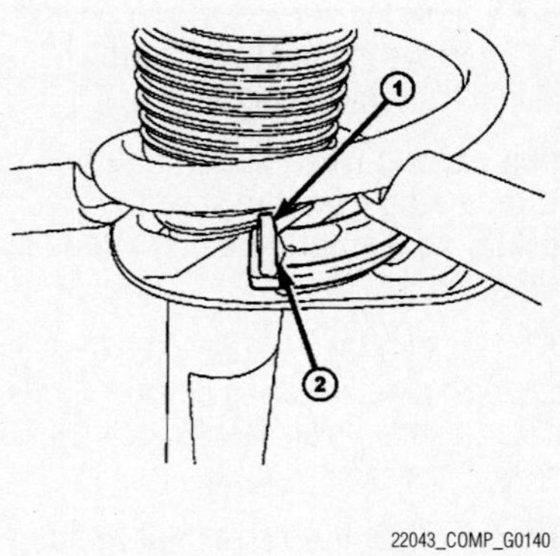

Fig. 89 Rotate the strut until the end of the bottom coil (2) comes in contact with the stop (1).

20. Remove the strut assembly from the spring compressor.

21. Install the strut assembly on the vehicle

STABILIZER BAR

REMOVAL & INSTALLATION

See Figure 90.

1. Raise the vehicle.

2. Remove both stabilizer bar links from the vehicle. Remove each link by holding the upper retainer/nut with a wrench and turning the link bolt.

3. Remove the stabilizer bar cushion retainer bolts and retainers, and remove the stabilizer bar with cushions attached from the vehicle.

4. To remove the cushions from the stabilizer bar, peel back each cushion at the slit and roll it off the bar.

To install:

➡Before stabilizer bar installation, inspect the cushions and links for excessive wear, cracks, damage and distortion. Replace any pieces failing inspection.

5. If removed, install the stabilizer bar cushions on the stabilizer bar utilizing the slit in each cushion. Position the cushions at each end of the bar's straight beam, just before it begins to curve.

➡Before installing the stabilizer bar, make sure the bar is not upside-down. The stabilizer bar must be installed with the curve on the outboard ends of the bar facing downward to clear the control arms once fully installed.

6. First, place the stabilizer bar in position on the front suspension crossmember. The slits in each cushion must point toward the front of the vehicle and sit directly on top of the raised beads formed into the stamping on the crossmember. Next, install the cushion retainers, matching the raised beads formed into the cushion retainers to the grooves formed into the cushions. Install the cushion retainer bolts, but do not completely tighten them at this time.

7. Clean the threads of the stabilizer bar link bolts, then apply MOPAR® Lock And Seal or equivalent to the threads.

8. Install both stabilizer bar links back on vehicle. Start each stabilizer bar link bolt with bushing from the bottom, through the stabilizer bar, inner link bushings, lower control arm, and into the upper retainer/nut and bushing. Do not fully tighten the link assemblies at this time.

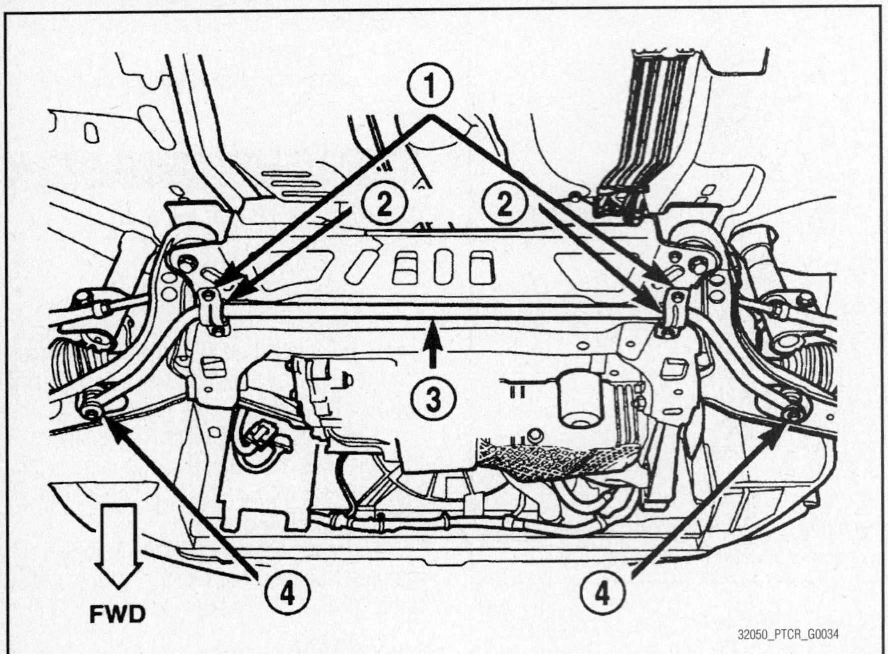

Fig. 90 Typical view of a stabilizer bar (3)

9. Lower the vehicle.

➡**It may be necessary to put the vehicle on a platform hoist or alignment rack to gain access to the stabilizer bar mounting bolts with the vehicle at curb height.**

10. Tighten each stabilizer bar link by holding the upper retainer/nut with a wrench and turning the link bolt. Tighten each link bolt to a torque of 250 inch lbs. (28 Nm).
11. Tighten the stabilizer bar cushion retainer bolts to a torque of 250 inch lbs. (28 Nm).

STEERING KNUCKLE

REMOVAL & INSTALLATION

See Figure 91.

1. Apply the brakes and hold in place.
2. Raise the vehicle.
3. Remove the front tire and wheel assembly.
4. Remove the cotter pin, lock nut and spring washer from the hub nut.
5. While the brakes are applied, loosen and remove the hub nut on the end of the driveshaft.
6. Release the brakes.
7. Remove the front disc brake caliper and adapter as an assembly, and the brake rotor from the steering knuckle.
8. Remove the nut attaching the outer tie rod to the steering knuckle. To do this, hold the tie rod end stud with a wrench while loosening and removing the nut with a standard wrench or crowfoot wrench.
9. Remove the tie rod end from the steering knuckle using Remover, Special Tool MB991113.
10. Remove the tie rod heat shield.
11. Remove the nut and pinch bolt clamping the ball joint stud to the steering knuckle.

⁂ CAUTION

The strut assembly-to-steering knuckle attaching bolts are serrated and must not be turned during removal. Hold the bolts stationary in the steering knuckles while removing the nuts, then tap the bolts out using a pin punch.

12. Remove the two bolts attaching the strut to the steering knuckle.

➡**Use caution when separating the ball joint stud from the steering knuckle, so the ball joint seal does not get cut.**

13. Separate the ball joint stud from the steering knuckle by prying down on lower control arm and up against the ball joint boss on the steering knuckle.

➡**Do not allow the driveshaft to hang by the inner C/V joint; it must be supported to keep the joint from separating during this operation.**

14. Pull the steering knuckle off the driveshaft outer C/V joint splines and remove the steering knuckle.

➡**The cartridge type front wheel bearing used on this vehicle is not transferable to the replacement steering knuckle. If the replacement steering knuckle does not come with a wheel bearing, a new bearing must be installed in the steering knuckle. Installation of the new wheel bearing and hub must be done before installing the steering knuckle on the vehicle.**

15. If the wheel bearing and hub need removal. Do not reuse the wheel bearing.

To install:

16. Slide the hub of the steering knuckle onto the splines on the driveshaft C/V joint.
17. Install the steering knuckle onto the ball joint stud aligning the bolt hole in the knuckle boss with the notch formed in the side of the ball joint stud.
18. Install a new ball joint stud pinch bolt and nut. Tighten the nut to a torque of 70 ft. lbs. (95 Nm).

⁂ CAUTION

The strut assembly-to-steering knuckle attaching bolts are serrated and must not be turned during installation. Install the nuts while holding the bolts stationary in the steering knuckle.

19. Position the lower end of the strut assembly in line with the upper end of the steering knuckle and align the mounting holes . Install the two attaching bolts. The bolts should be installed with so that the nuts face towards the front of the vehicle once installed. Install the nuts. Holding the bolts in place tighten the nuts to a torque of 40 ft. lbs. (53 Nm) plus an additional 90° turn after the specified torque is met.

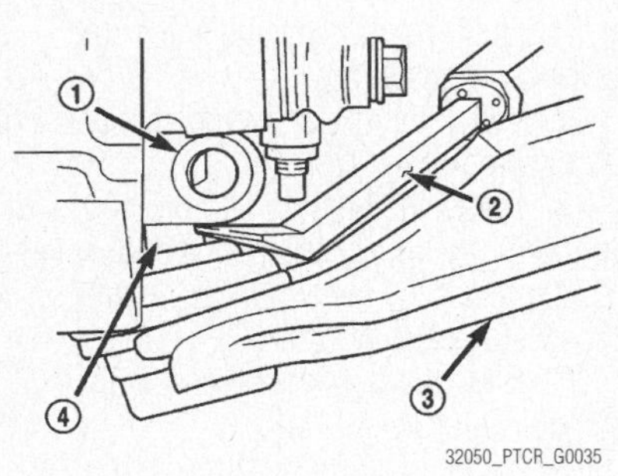

Fig. 91 The separation of the ball joint and the knuckle

20. Place the tie rod heat shield on the steering knuckle arm so that the shield is positioned straight away from the steering gear and tie rod end once installed. Align the hole in the shield with the hole in the steering knuckle arm. Install the outer tie rod ball stud into the hole in the steering knuckle arm. Start the tie rod attaching nut onto the stud. Hold the tie rod end stud with a wrench while tightening the nut with a standard wrench or crowfoot wrench. To fully tighten the nut to specifications, use a crowfoot wrench on a torque wrench to turn the nut, and a wrench on the stud.

21. Tighten the nut to a torque of 40 ft. lbs. (55 Nm). Install the brake rotor, disc brake caliper and adapter.

22. Clean all foreign matter from the threads of the driveshaft outer C/V joint. Install the hub nut in the end of the driveshaft and snug it.

23. Have a helper apply the brakes. With vehicle brakes applied to keep brake rotor and hub from turning, tighten the hub nut to a torque of 180 ft. lbs. (244 Nm).

24. Install the spring washer, lock nut and cotter pin on the hub nut. Wrap the cotter pin ends tightly around the lock nut.

25. Install the tire and wheel assembly. Install the wheel mounting nuts and tighten them to a torque of 100 ft. lbs. (135 Nm).

26. Lower the vehicle.

27. Set the front toe on the vehicle to required specification.

WHEEL BEARINGS

REMOVAL & INSTALLATION

See Figures 92 through 94.

1. Before servicing the vehicle, refer to the precautions in the beginning of this section.

2. Remove the steering knuckle and hub and bearing assembly.

3. Remove the wheel lug stud from the hub flange, using a C-clamp and Adapter Tool 4150A.

4. Rotate the hub to align the removed lug stud with the notch in the bearing retainer plate.

5. Rotate the hub so the stud hole is facing away from the brake caliper's lower rail on the steering knuckle.

6. Install ½ of a Bearing Splitter Tool 1130, between the hub and the bearing retainer plate. The threaded hole in this ½ is to be aligned with the caliper rail on the steering knuckle.

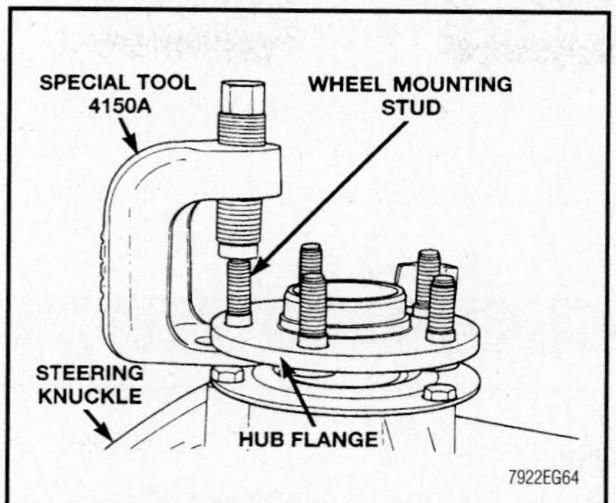

Fig. 92 Use a proper C-clamp and adapter tool to press out one of the lug studs

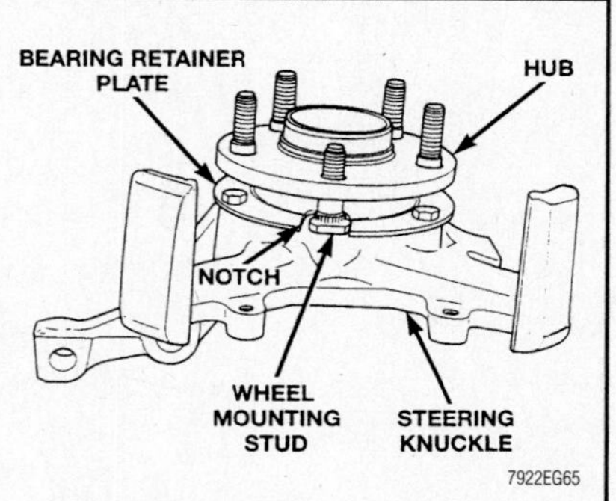

Fig. 93 Rotate the hub in order to remove the lug stud

7. Install the remaining pieces of the bearing splitter on the steering knuckle. Hand-tighten the nuts to hold the splitter in place on the knuckle.

8. When the bearing splitter is installed, be sure the 3 bolts attaching the bearing retainer plate to the knuckle are contacting the bearing splitter. The bearing retainer plate should not support the knuckle or contact the splitter.

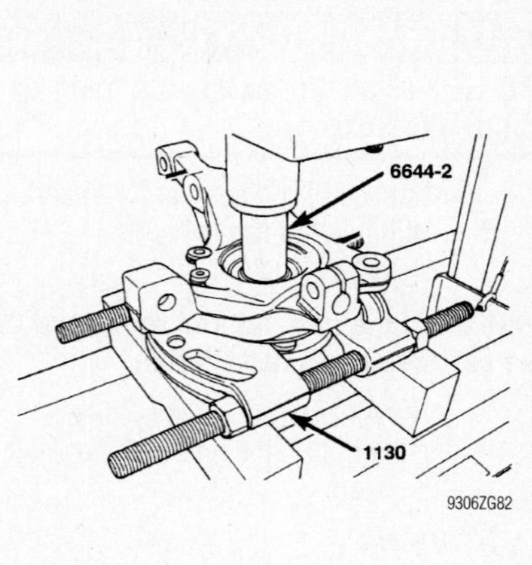

Fig. 94 Properly support the steering knuckle for hub and bearing removal

9. Place the steering knuckle in a hydraulic press, supported by the bearing splitter.

10. Position a driver on the small end of the hub. Using the press, remove the hub from the wheel bearing. The outer bearing race will come out of the wheel bearing when the hub is pressed out of the bearing.

11. Remove the bearing splitter tool from the knuckle.

12. Remove the 3 bolts mounting the bearing retainer plate to the steering knuckle.

13. Place the knuckle in a press supported by the press block. The blocks must not obstruct the bore in the steering knuckle so the wheel bearing can be pressed out of the knuckle. Place a driver on the outer race of the wheel bearing, then press the bearing out of the knuckle.

14. Install the bearing splitter on the hub. The splitter is to be installed on the hub so it is between the flange of the hub and the bearing race on the hub. Place the hub, bearing race and splitter in a press. Use a driver to press the hub out of the bearing race.

To install:

15. Use clean, dry cloth to wipe and grease or dirt from the bore of the steering knuckle.

16. Install a new wheel bearing into the bore of the steering knuckle. Be sure the bearing is placed squarely into the bore. Place the knuckle in a press with a Receiver Tool, C-4698-2 supporting the steering knuckle. Place a driver tool on the outer race of the wheel bearing. Press the wheel bearing into the steering knuckle until it is fully bottomed in the bore of the steering knuckle.

➡Only the original or original equipment replacement bolts should be used to mounting the bearing retainer to the knuckle. If a bolt requires replacement when installing the bearing retainer plate, be sure to get the proper type of replacement.

17. Install the bearing retainer plate on the steering knuckle. Install the 3 bearing retainer mounting bolts. Tighten the bolts to 21 ft. lbs. (28 Nm).

18. Install the wheel lug stud into the hub flange.

19. Place the hub with the lug stud installed, in a press supported by an Adapter Tool C-4698-1 and press the wheel lug stud into the hub flange until it is fully seated against the back side on the hub flange.

20. Place the steering knuckle with the

wheel bearing installed, in a press with special Receiver Tool MB-990799 supporting the inner race of the wheel bearing. Place the hub in the wheel bearing, making sure it is square with the bearing. Press the hub into the wheel bearing until it is fully bottomed in the wheel bearing.

21. Install the steering knuckle and the wheel.

22. Check and/or adjust the front alignment.

ADJUSTMENT

The PT Cruiser is equipped with a sealed hub and bearing assemblies. The hub and bearing assembly is non-serviceable. If the assembly is damaged, the complete unit must be replaced.

SUSPENSION

REAR SUSPENSION

COIL SPRING

REMOVAL & INSTALLATION

See Figure 95.

1. Before servicing the vehicle, refer to the precautions in the beginning of this section.
2. Remove or disconnect the following:
   - Both rear wheels
   - Watts link bell crank from the center of the axle
   - Sway bar cushion retainers
   - Sway bar from the rear axle and place a jack under the rear axle
   - Shock absorber and lower the jack
   - Coil springs and rubber isolators

To install:

3. Install or connect the following:
   - Rubber isolator on each end of the coil spring and wrap the finger around the coil
   - Coil springs on top of the axle spring perches and make certain that the upper coils end near the outboard sides of the vehicle and not at 180 degrees of that location
   - Coil springs into the spring mounting brackets
   - Washer and nut on the lower mounting bolts and torque the bolts to 65 ft. lbs. (88 Nm) on 2002–04 models or 65 ft. lbs. (88 Nm) on 2005–06 models.
   - Lower end of the sway bar retainers in the slots at the back of the axle
   - Mounting bolt through the cushion retainer and torque to 40 ft. lbs. (54 Nm) on 2002–04 models or 45 ft. lbs. (61 Nm) on 2005–06 models
   - Watts link bell crank to the center of the axle and torque the bolts to 90 ft. lbs. (122 Nm) on 2002–04 models or 110 ft. lbs. (149 Nm) on 2005–06 models
   - Rear wheels

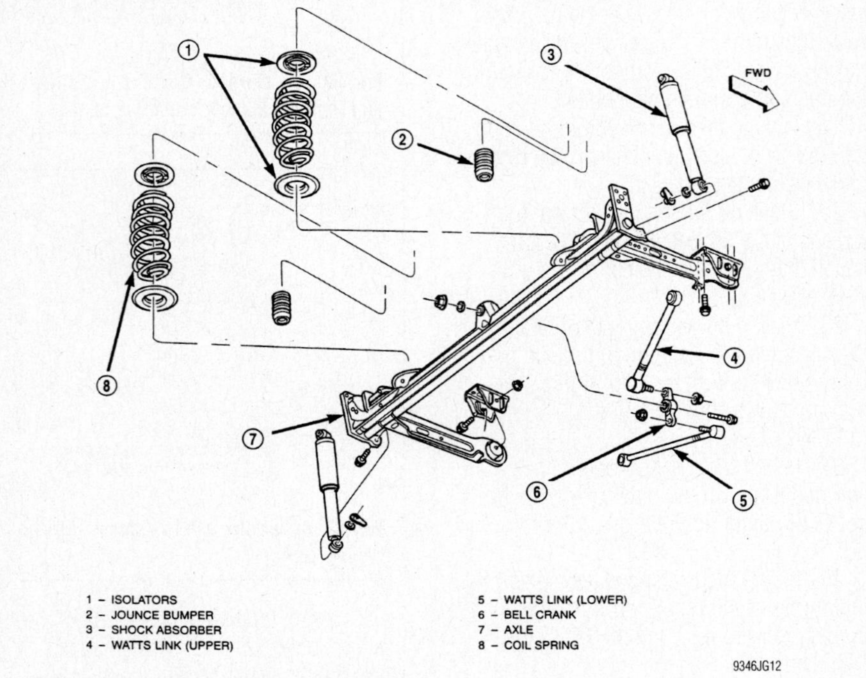

Fig. 95 Exploded view of the rear suspension

WHEEL BEARINGS

REMOVAL & INSTALLATION

1. Before servicing the vehicle, refer to the precautions in the beginning of this section.
2. Remove or disconnect the following:
   - Wheel
   - Rear brake drum, if equipped
   - Caliper (suspend on a wire) and the rotor, if equipped with rear disc brakes

⁂ WARNING

DO NOT allow the caliper to hang by the brake hose.

   - Dust cap from the rear hub/bearing
   - Hub/bearing assembly-to-knuckle/spindle nut

➡Discard the hub nut and replace with a new one during installation.

   - Hub/bearing from the spindle by pulling it off the end of the spindle by hand

To install:

⁂ WARNING

The hub/bearing nut must be tightened to, but NOT over, its specified torque value. The proper specification is crucial to the life of the hub bearing.

3. Position the hub/bearing assembly on the rear spindle/knuckle. Install a NEW hub nut and tighten to 160 ft. lbs. (217 Nm)
4. Install or connect the following:
   - Dust cap and seat it using a soft face hammer to carefully tap it into place
   - Brake drum, if equipped
   - Rotor, if equipped
   - Caliper and 2 guide pin bolts, if equipped with disc brakes. Torque the bolts to 16 ft. lbs. (22 Nm).

ADJUSTMENT

The PT Cruiser is equipped with a sealed hub and bearing assemblies. The hub and bearing assembly is non-serviceable. If the assembly is damaged, the complete unit must be replaced.

DODGE

Ram Trucks

13

SPECIFICATIONS AND MAINTENANCE CHARTS

ENGINE AND VEHICLE IDENTIFICATION

Engine						
Code ①	Liters (cc)	Cu. In.	Cyl.	Fuel Sys.	Engine Type	Eng. Mfg.
K	3.7 (3701)	226	6	MPI	SOHC	Chrysler
N	4.7 (4701)	287	8	MPI	SOHC	Chrysler
P	4.7 (4701)	287	8	Flex Fuel	SOHC	Chrysler
D	5.7 (5653)	345	8	SMPI	OHV	Chrysler
2	5.7 (5653)	345	8	MDS	OHV	Chrysler
C	5.9 (5882)	359	6	DSL-24V Turbo	OHV	Cummins
A	6.7 (6702)	409	6	DSL-24V Turbo	OHV	Cummins

Model Year	
Code ②	Year
5	2005
6	2006
7	2007
8	2008

OHV: Overhead Valve
DSL-24V: Diesel with 24-valve cylinder head
SMFI: Sequential Multi-port Fuel Injection

① 8th position of VIN

② 10th position of VIN

22043_RPUP_C0001

GENERAL ENGINE SPECIFICATIONS

Year	Model	Engine Displacement Liters	Engine Series (ID/VIN)	Net Horsepower @ rpm	Net Torque @ rpm (ft. lbs.)	Bore x Stroke (in.)	Com-pression Ratio	Oil Pressure @ rpm
2005	Ram Truck 1500	3.7	K	211@5200	236@4000	3.66x3.40	9.6:1	25-110@3000
		4.7	N	235@4800	295@3200	3.66x3.40	9.0:1	35-105@3000
		4.7	P	235@4800	295@3200	3.66x3.40	9.0:1	35-105@3000
		5.7	D	345@5400	375@4200	3.91x3.58	9.6:1	25-110@3000
		5.9	C	325@2900	600@1400	4.02x4.72	17.2:1	30@2500
	Ram Truck 2500	4.7	N	235@4800	295@3200	3.66x3.40	9.0:1	35-105@3000
		4.7	P	235@4800	295@3200	3.66x3.40	9.0:1	35-105@3000
		5.7	D	345@5400	375@4200	3.91x3.58	9.6:1	25-110@3000
		5.9	C	325@2900	600@1400	4.02x4.72	17.2:1	30@2500
	Ram Truck 3500	4.7	N	235@4800	295@3200	3.66x3.40	9.0:1	35-105@3000
		4.7	P	235@4800	295@3200	3.66x3.40	9.0:1	35-105@3000
		5.7	D	345@5400	375@4200	3.91x3.58	9.6:1	25-110@3000
		5.9	C	325@2900	600@1400	4.02x4.72	17.2:1	30@2500
2006	Ram Truck 1500	3.7	K	211@5200	236@4000	3.66x3.40	9.6:1	25-110@3000
		4.7	N	235@4800	295@3200	3.66x3.40	9.0:1	35-105@3000
		4.7	P	235@4800	295@3200	3.66x3.40	9.0:1	35-105@3000
		5.7	D	345@5400	375@4200	3.91x3.58	9.6:1	25-110@3000
		5.7	2	345@5400	375@4200	3.91x3.58	9.6:1	25-110@3000
		5.9	C	325@2900	600@1400	4.02x4.72	17.2:1	30@2500
	Ram Truck 2500	4.7	N	235@4800	295@3200	3.66x3.40	9.0:1	35-105@3000
		4.7	P	235@4800	295@3200	3.66x3.40	9.0:1	35-105@3000
		5.7	D	345@5400	375@4200	3.91x3.58	9.6:1	25-110@3000
		5.7	2	345@5400	375@4200	3.91x3.58	9.6:1	25-110@3000
		5.9	C	325@2900	600@1400	4.02x4.72	17.2:1	30@2500
	Ram Truck 3500	4.7	N	235@4800	295@3200	3.66x3.40	9.0:1	35-105@3000
		4.7	P	235@4800	295@3200	3.66x3.40	9.0:1	35-105@3000
		5.7	D	345@5400	375@4200	3.91x3.58	9.6:1	25-110@3000
		5.7	2	345@5400	375@4200	3.91x3.58	9.6:1	25-110@3000
		5.9	C	325@2900	600@1400	4.02x4.72	17.2:1	30@2500
2007	Ram Truck 1500	3.7	K	211@5200	236@4000	3.66x3.40	9.6:1	25-110@3000
		4.7	N	235@4800	295@3200	3.66x3.40	9.0:1	35-105@3000
		4.7	P	235@4800	295@3200	3.66x3.40	9.0:1	35-105@3000
		5.7	D	345@5400	375@4200	3.91x3.58	9.6:1	25-110@3000
		5.7	2	345@5400	375@4200	3.91x3.58	9.6:1	25-110@3000
		5.9	C	325@2900	600@1400	4.02x4.72	17.2:1	30@2500
		6.7	A	350@3013	650@1400	4.21x4.88	17.2:1	30@2500
	Ram Truck 2500	5.7	D	345@5400	375@4200	3.91x3.58	9.6:1	25-110@3000
		5.7	2	345@5400	375@4200	3.91x3.58	9.6:1	25-110@3000
		5.9	C	325@2900	600@1400	4.02x4.72	17.2:1	30@2500
		6.7	A	350@3013	650@1400	4.21x4.88	17.2:1	30@2500
	Ram Truck 3500	5.7	D	345@5400	375@4200	3.91x3.58	9.6:1	25-110@3000
		5.9	C	325@2900	600@1400	4.02x4.72	17.2:1	30@2500
		6.7	A	350@3013	650@1400	4.21x4.88	17.2:1	30@2500

22043_RPUP_C0002

GENERAL ENGINE SPECIFICATIONS

Year	Model	Engine Displacement Liters	Engine Series (ID/VIN)	Net Horsepower @ rpm	Net Torque @ rpm (ft. lbs.)	Bore x Stroke (in.)	Com-pression Ratio	Oil Pressure @ rpm
2008	Ram Truck 1500	3.7	K	211@5200	236@4000	3.66x3.40	9.6:1	25-110@3000
		4.7	N	235@4800	295@3200	3.66x3.40	9.0:1	35-105@3000
		5.7	D	345@5400	375@4200	3.91x3.58	9.6:1	25-110@3000
		5.7	2	345@5400	375@4200	3.91x3.58	9.6:1	25-110@3000
		5.9	C	325@2900	600@1400	4.02x4.72	17.2:1	30@2500
		6.7	A	350@3013	650@1400	4.21x4.88	17.2:1	30@2500
	Ram Truck 2500	4.7	N	235@4800	295@3200	3.66x3.40	9.0:1	35-105@3000
		5.7	D	345@5400	375@4200	3.91x3.58	9.6:1	25-110@3000
		5.7	2	345@5400	375@4200	3.91x3.58	9.6:1	25-110@3000
		5.9	C	325@2900	600@1400	4.02x4.72	17.2:1	30@2500
		6.7	A	350@3013	650@1400	4.21x4.88	17.2:1	30@2500
	Ram Truck 3500	5.7	D	345@5400	375@4200	3.91x3.58	9.6:1	25-110@3000
		5.9	C	325@2900	600@1400	4.02x4.72	17.2:1	30@2500
		6.7	A	350@3013	650@1400	4.21x4.88	17.2:1	30@2500

22043_RPUP_C0003

GASOLINE ENGINE TUNE-UP SPECIFICATIONS

Year	Engine Displacement Liters	Engine ID/VIN	Spark Plug Gap (in.)	Ignition Timing (deg.)	Fuel Pump (psi)	Idle Speed (rpm)	Valve Clearance	
							Intake	Exhaust
2005	3.7	K	0.042	①	NA	②	HYD	HYD
	4.7	N	0.040	①	NA	②	HYD	HYD
	4.7	P	0.040	①	NA	②	HYD	HYD
	5.7	D	0.045	①	NA	②	HYD	HYD
2006	3.7	K	0.042	①	NA	②	HYD	HYD
	4.7	N	0.040	①	NA	②	HYD	HYD
	4.7	P	0.040	①	NA	②	HYD	HYD
	5.7	D	0.045	①	NA	②	HYD	HYD
	5.7	2	0.045	①	NA	②	HYD	HYD
2007	3.7	K	0.042	①	NA	②	HYD	HYD
	4.7	N	0.040	①	NA	②	HYD	HYD
	4.7	P	0.040	①	NA	②	HYD	HYD
	5.7	D	0.045	①	NA	②	HYD	HYD
	5.7	2	0.045	①	NA	②	HYD	HYD
2008	3.7	K	0.042	①	NA	②	HYD	HYD
	4.7	N	0.040	①	NA	②	HYD	HYD
	5.7	D	0.045	①	NA	②	HYD	HYD
	5.7	2	0.045	①	NA	②	HYD	HYD

NOTE: The Vehicle Emission Control Information (VECI) label often reflects specification changes made during production.
The label figures must be used if they differ from those in this chart.

HYD: Hydraulic

① Ignition timing is controlled by the PCM and is not adjustable.

② Idle speed is controlled by the PCM and is not adjustable

22043_RPUP_C0004

DIESEL ENGINE TUNE-UP SPECIFICATIONS

Year	Engine Displacement Liters	Engine ID/VIN	Valve Clearance Intake (in.)	Valve Clearance Exhaust (in.)	Intake Valve Opens (deg.)	Injection Pump Setting (deg.)	Injection Nozzle Pressure (psi) New	Injection Nozzle Pressure (psi) Used	Idle Speed (rpm)	Cranking Compression Pressure (psi)
2005	5.9	C	0.006-0.015	0.021-0.034	NA	①	4250-4750	NA	②	350 ③
2006	5.9	C	0.006-0.015	0.021-0.034	NA	①	4250-4750	NA	②	350 ③
2007	5.9	C	0.006-0.015	0.021-0.034	NA	①	4250-4750	NA	②	350 ③
	6.7	A	0.006-0.015	0.021-0.034	NA	①	4250-4750	NA	②	350 ③
2008	5.9	C	0.006-0.015	0.021-0.034	NA	①	4250-4750	NA	②	350 ③
	6.7	A	0.006-0.015	0.021-0.034	NA	①	4250-4750	NA	②	350 ③

NOTE: The Vehicle Emission Control Information (VECI) label often reflects specification changes made during production.
The label figures must be used if they differ from those in this chart

NA: Not Available

① Federal models with manual transmissions: 13.5 degrees BTDC
Except Federal models with manual transmissions: 14.0 degrees BTDC

② Automatic transmission: 750-800 rpm
Manual transmission: 780 rpm

③ Minimum reading

22043_RPUP_C0005

CAPACITIES

Year	Model	Engine Displacement Liters	Engine ID/VIN	Engine Oil with Filter (qts.)	Transmission (pts.) Manual	Transmission (pts.) Auto. ①	Transfer Case (pts.)	Drive Axle Front (pts.)	Drive Axle Rear (pts.)	Fuel Tank (gal.)	Cooling System (qts.)
2005	Ram Truck 1500	3.7	K	5.0	②	③	④	⑤	⑥	⑦	16.2
		4.7	N	6.0	②	③	④	⑤	⑥	⑦	16.2
		4.7	P	6.0	②	③	④	⑤	⑥	⑦	16.2
		5.7	D	7.0	②	③	④	⑤	⑥	⑦	16.2
	Ram Truck 2500	5.7	D	7.0	②	③	④	⑤	⑥	⑦	16.2
		5.9	C	12.0	②	③	④	⑤	⑥	⑦	29.5
	Ram Truck 3500	5.7	D	7.0	②	③	④	⑤	⑥	⑦	16.2
		5.9	C	12.0	②	③	④	⑤	⑥	⑦	29.5
2006	Ram Truck 1500	3.7	K	5.0	②	③	④	⑤	⑥	⑦	16.2
		4.7	N	6.0	②	③	④	⑤	⑥	⑦	16.2
		4.7	P	6.0	②	③	④	⑤	⑥	⑦	16.2
		5.7	D	7.0	②	③	④	⑤	⑥	⑦	16.2
	Ram Truck 2500	5.7	D	7.0	②	③	④	⑤	⑥	⑦	16.2
		5.9	C	12.0	②	③	④	⑤	⑥	⑦	29.5
	Ram Truck 3500	5.7	D	7.0	②	③	④	⑤	⑥	⑦	16.2
		5.9	C	12.0	②	③	④	⑤	⑥	⑦	29.5
2007	Ram Truck 1500	3.7	K	5.0	②	③	④	⑤	⑥	⑦	16.2
		4.7	N	6.0	②	③	④	⑤	⑥	⑦	16.2
		4.7	P	6.0	②	③	④	⑤	⑥	⑦	16.2
		5.7	D	7.0	②	③	④	⑤	⑥	⑦	16.2
	Ram Truck 2500	5.7	D	7.0	②	③	④	⑤	⑥	⑦	16.2
		5.9	C	12.0	②	③	④	⑤	⑥	⑦	29.5
		6.7	A	12.0	②	③	④	⑤	⑥	⑦	23.0
	Ram Truck 3500	5.7	D	7.0	②	③	④	⑤	⑥	⑦	16.2
		5.9	C	12.0	②	③	④	⑤	⑥	⑦	29.5
		6.7	A	12.0	②	③	④	⑤	⑥	⑦	23.0

22043_RPUP_C0006

CAPACITIES

Year	Model	Engine Displacement Liters	Engine ID/VIN	Oil with Filter (qts.)	Engine Transmission (pts.) Manual	Engine Transmission (pts.) Auto. ①	Transfer Case (pts.)	Drive Axle Front (pts.)	Drive Axle Rear (pts.)	Fuel Tank (gal.)	Cooling System (qts.)
2008	Ram Truck 1500	3.7	K	5.0	②	③	④	⑤	⑥	⑦	16.2
		4.7	N	6.0	②	③	④	⑤	⑥	⑦	16.2
		4.7	P	6.0	②	③	④	⑤	⑥	⑦	16.2
		5.7	D	7.0	②	③	④	⑤	⑥	⑦	16.2
	Ram Truck 2500	5.7	D	7.0	②	③	④	⑤	⑥	⑦	16.2
		5.9	C	12.0	②	③	④	⑤	⑥	⑦	29.5
		6.7	A	12.0	②	③	④	⑤	⑥	⑦	23.0
	Ram Truck 3500	5.7	D	7.0	②	③	④	⑤	⑥	⑦	16.2
		5.9	C	12.0	②	③	④	⑤	⑥	⑦	29.5
		6.7	A	12.0	②	③	④	⑤	⑥	⑦	23.0

NOTE: All capacities are approximate. Add fluid gradually and check to be sure a proper fluid level is obtained.

① For fluid drain and filter replacement only.

② Getrag 238: 4.6 pts.
G56: 12.0 pts. Diesel Engines
G56: 10.0 pts. 5.7 Engines
NV4500: 8.0 pts.
NV5600: 9.5 pts.

③ 48RE: 8.0 pts.
42RLE: 8.0 pts
45RFE/545RFE:
4x2: 11.0 pts.
4x4: 13.0 pts.
68RFE:
4x2: 11.0 pts.
4x4: 13.0 pts.
AS68RC: 14.4 pts

④ NV241 GEN II: 3.4 pts.
NV243: 3.4 pts.
NV 271: 4.0 pts.
NV 246: 4.0 pts.
NV 273: 4.0 pts.

⑤ C205F: 3.5 pts.
9.25AA: 4.75 pts.
9.25AA EL: 4.30 pts.

⑥ 9.25: 4.9 pts. W/Trac-Lok + 4 oz. Additive
10.5AA: 4.75 pts.
11.5AA: 7.65 pts.
248RBI: (DANA 60) 2.9 pts W/Trac-Lock + 50oz Additive

⑦ 1500 Short bed: 26.0
2500/3500 Short bed: 34.0
Long bed: 35.0

22043_RPUP_C0007

FLUID SPECIFICATIONS

Year	Model	Engine Displacement Liters (cc)	Engine ID/VIN	Engine Oil	Manual Trans. ①	Auto. Trans. ②	Drive Axle ③	Power Steering Fluid	Brake Master Cylinder	Engine Coolant
2005	Ram 1500	3.7 (3701)	K	5W-30	ATF+4	ATF+4	75W-90 ④	ATF+4	DOT 3	Mopar® (HOA
	2500/3500	4.7 (4701)	N	5W-30	ATF+4	ATF+4	75W-90 ④	ATF+4	DOT 3	Mopar® (HOA
		4.7 (4701)	P	5W-30	ATF+4	ATF+4	75W-90 ④	ATF+4	DOT 3	Mopar® (HOA
		5.7 (5653)	D	5W-30	ATF+4	ATF+4	75W-90 ④	ATF+4	DOT 3	Mopar® (HOA
		5.9 (5882)	C	15W-40 ⑤	ATF+4	ATF+4	75W-90 ④	ATF+4	DOT 3	Mopar® (HOA
2006	Ram 1500	3.7 (3701)	K	5W-30	ATF+4	ATF+4	75W-90 ④	ATF+4	DOT 3	Mopar® (HOA
	2500/3500	4.7 (4701)	N P	5W-30	ATF+4	ATF+4	75W-90 ④	ATF+4	DOT 3	Mopar® (HOA
		5.7 (5653)	D	5W-30	ATF+4	ATF+4	75W-90 ④	ATF+4	DOT 3	Mopar® (HOA
		5.7 (5653)	2	5W-30	ATF+4	ATF+4	75W-90 ④	ATF+4	DOT 3	Mopar® (HOA
		5.9 (5882)	C	15W-40 ⑤	ATF+4	ATF+4	75W-90 ④	ATF+4	DOT 3	Mopar® (HOA
2007	Ram 1500	3.7 (3701)	K	5W-30	ATF+4	ATF+4	75W-90 ④	ATF+4	DOT 3	Mopar® (HOA
	2500/3500	4.7 (4701)	N P	5W-30	ATF+4	ATF+4	75W-90 ④	ATF+4	DOT 3	Mopar® (HOA
		5.7 (5653)	D	5W-30	ATF+4	ATF+4	75W-90 ④	ATF+4	DOT 3	Mopar® (HOA
		5.7 (5653)	2	5W-30	ATF+4	ATF+4	75W-90 ④	ATF+4	DOT 3	Mopar® (HOA
		5.9 (5882)	C	15W-40 ⑤	ATF+4	ATF+4	75W-90 ④	ATF+4	DOT 3	Mopar® (HOA
		6.7 (6702)	A	15W-40 ⑤	ATF+4	ATF+4	75W-90 ④	ATF+4	DOT 3	Mopar® (HOA
2008	Ram 1500	3.7 (3701)	K	5W-30	ATF+4	ATF+4	75W-90 ④	ATF+4	DOT 3	Mopar® (HOA
	2500/3500	4.7 (4701)	N	5W-30	ATF+4	ATF+4	75W-90 ④	ATF+4	DOT 3	Mopar® (HOA
		5.7 (5653)	D	5W-30	ATF+4	ATF+4	75W-90 ④	ATF+4	DOT 3	Mopar® (HOA
		5.7 (5653)	2	5W-30	ATF+4	ATF+4	75W-90 ④	ATF+4	DOT 3	Mopar® (HOA
		5.9 (5882)	C	15W-40 ⑤	ATF+4	ATF+4	75W-90 ④	ATF+4	DOT 3	Mopar® (HOA
		6.7 (6702)	A	15W-40 ⑤	ATF+4	ATF+4	75W-90 ④	ATF+4	DOT 3	Mopar® (HOA

NOTE: Check the engines oil cap or owners manual for specific engine oil grade variations.

DOT: Department Of Transpotation

① NV4500 and T-56 transmissions: 75W-85 Synthetic

② (6 Speed) AS86RC: Mopar® AS86RC Transmission fluid

③ Ram 1500 Models rear axle: Synthetic 75W-140 plus 4oz limited slip additive

④ Synthetic is recommended

⑤ Oils of the 5W-40 grade are preferred when temperatures consistently fall below -15 degrees

22043_RPUP_C0008

VALVE SPECIFICATIONS

Year	Engine Displacement Liters	Engine ID/VIN	Seat Angle (deg.)	Face Angle (deg.)	Spring Test Pressure (lbs. @ in.)	Spring Installed Height (in.)	Stem-to-Guide Clearance (in.) Intake	Stem-to-Guide Clearance (in.) Exhaust	Stem Diameter (in.) Intake	Stem Diameter (in.) Exhaust
2005	3.7	K	44.5-45	45-45.5	213-233@ 1.107	1.579	0.0008-0.0028	0.0019-0.0039	0.2729-0.2739	0.2717-0.2728
	4.7	N	44.5-45	45-45.5	174.4-195.5 @1.137	1.579	0.0008-0.0028	0.0019-0.0039	0.2729-0.2739	0.2717-0.2728
	4.7	P	44.5-45	45-45.5	174.4-195.5 @1.137	1.579	0.0008-0.0028	0.0019-0.0039	0.2729-0.2739	0.2717-0.2728
	5.7	D	44.5-45	45-45.5	242@1.322	1.810	0.0008-0.0025	0.0019-0.0037	0.3120-0.3130	0.3110-0.3120
	5.9	C	①	①	76.4@1.39	1.390	0.002	0.002	0.274-0.276	0.274-0.276
2006	3.7	K	44.5-45	45-45.5	213-233@ 1.107	1.579	0.0008-0.0028	0.0019-0.0039	0.2729-0.2739	0.2717-0.2728
	4.7	N	44.5-45	45-45.5	174.4-195.5 @1.137	1.579	0.0008-0.0028	0.0019-0.0039	0.2729-0.2739	0.2717-0.2728
	4.7	P	44.5-45	45-45.5	174.4-195.5 @1.137	1.579	0.0008-0.0028	0.0019-0.0039	0.2729-0.2739	0.2717-0.2728
	5.7	D	44.5-45	45-45.5	242@1.322	1.810	0.0008-0.0025	0.0019-0.0037	0.3120-0.3130	0.3110-0.3120
	5.7	2	44.5-45	45-45.5	242@1.322	1.810	0.0008-0.0025	0.0019-0.0037	0.3120-0.3130	0.3110-0.3120
	5.9	C	①	①	76.4@1.39	1.390	0.002	0.002	0.274-0.276	0.274-0.276
2007	3.7	K	44.5-45	45-45.5	213-233@ 1.107	1.579	0.0008-0.0028	0.0019-0.0039	0.2729-0.2739	0.2717-0.2728
	4.7	N	44.5-45	45-45.5	174.4-195.5 @1.137	1.579	0.0008-0.0028	0.0019-0.0039	0.2729-0.2739	0.2717-0.2728
	4.7	P	44.5-45	45-45.5	174.4-195.5 @1.137	1.579	0.0008-0.0028	0.0019-0.0039	0.2729-0.2739	0.2717-0.2728
	5.7	D	44.5-45	45-45.5	242@1.322	1.810	0.0008-0.0025	0.0019-0.0037	0.3120-0.3130	0.3110-0.3120
	5.7	2	44.5-45	45-45.5	242@1.322	1.810	0.0008-0.0025	0.0019-0.0037	0.3120-0.3130	0.3110-0.3120
	5.9	C	①	①	76.4@1.39	1.390	0.002	0.002	0.274-0.276	0.274-0.276
	6.7	A	①	①	76.4@1.39	1.390	0.002	0.002	0.274-0.276	0.274-0.276
2008	3.7	K	44.5-45	45-45.5	213-233@ 1.107	1.579	0.0008-0.0028	0.0019-0.0039	0.2729-0.2739	0.2717-0.2728
	4.7	N	44.5-45	45-45.5	174.4-195.5 @1.137	1.579	0.0008-0.0028	0.0019-0.0039	0.2729-0.2739	0.2717-0.2728
	5.7	D	44.5-45	45-45.5	242@1.322	1.810	0.0008-0.0025	0.0019-0.0037	0.3120-0.3130	0.3110-0.3120
	5.7	2	44.5-45	45-45.5	242@1.322	1.810	0.0008-0.0025	0.0019-0.0037	0.3120-0.3130	0.3110-0.3120
	5.9	C	①	①	76.4@1.39	1.390	0.002	0.002	0.274-0.276	0.274-0.276
	6.7	A	①	①	76.4@1.39	1.390	0.002	0.002	0.274-0.276	0.274-0.276

① Intake: 30 degrees
Exhaust: 45 degrees

22043_RPUP_C0009

CAMSHAFT AND BEARING SPECIFICATIONS CHART

All measurements are given in inches.

Year	Engine Displ. Liters	Engine ID/VIN	Journal Dia.	Brg. Oil Clearance	Shaft End-play	Runout	Journal Bore	Lobe Height Intake	Lobe Height Exhaust
2005	3.7	K	1.0227-1.0235	0.001-0.0026	0.003-0.0079	NA	1.0245-1.0252	NA	NA
	4.7	N	1.0227-1.0235	0.001-0.0026	0.003-0.0079	NA	1.0245-1.0252	NA	NA
	4.7	P	1.0227-1.0235	0.001-0.0026	0.003-0.0079	NA	1.0245-1.0252	NA	NA
	5.7	D	①	②	0.0031-0.0114	NA	NA	NA	NA
	5.9	C	③	NA	NA	NA	NA	1.857-1.8840	1.797-1.8230
2006	3.7	K	1.0227-1.0235	0.001-0.0026	0.003-0.0079	NA	1.0245-1.0252	NA	NA
	4.7	N	1.0227-1.0235	0.001-0.0026	0.003-0.0079	NA	1.0245-1.0252	NA	NA
	4.7	P	1.0227-1.0235	0.001-0.0026	0.003-0.0079	NA	1.0245-1.0252	NA	NA
	5.7	D	①	②	0.0031-0.0114	NA	NA	NA	NA
	5.7	2	①	②	0.0031-0.0114	NA	NA	NA	NA
	5.9	C	③	NA	NA	NA	NA	1.857-1.8840	1.797-1.8230
2007	3.7	K	1.0227-1.0235	0.001-0.0026	0.003-0.0079	NA	1.0245-1.0252	NA	NA
	4.7	N	1.0227-1.0235	0.001-0.0026	0.003-0.0079	NA	1.0245-1.0252	NA	NA
	4.7	P	1.0227-1.0235	0.001-0.0026	0.003-0.0079	NA	1.0245-1.0252	NA	NA
	5.7	D	①	②	0.0031-0.0114	NA	NA	NA	NA
	5.7	2	①	②	0.0031-0.0114	NA	NA	NA	NA
	5.9	C	③	NA	NA	NA	NA	1.857-1.8840	1.797-1.8230
	6.7	A	③	NA	NA	NA	NA	1.857-1.8840	1.797-1.8230

22043_RPUP_C0010

CAMSHAFT AND BEARING SPECIFICATIONS CHART

All measurements are given in inches.

Year	Engine Displ. Liters	Engine ID/VIN	Journal Dia.	Brg. Oil Clearance	Shaft End-play	Runout	Journal Bore	Lobe Height	
								Intake	Exhaust
2008	3.7	K	1.0227-1.0235	0.001-0.0026	0.003-0.0079	NA	1.0245-1.0252	NA	NA
	4.7	N	1.0227-1.0235	0.001-0.0026	0.003-0.0079	NA	1.0245-1.0252	NA	NA
	5.7	D	①	②	0.0031-0.0114	NA	NA	NA	NA
	5.7	2	①	②	0.0031-0.0114	NA	NA	NA	NA
	5.9	C	③	NA	NA	NA	NA	1.857-1.8840	1.797-1.8230
	6.7	A	③	NA	NA	NA	NA	1.857-1.8840	1.797-1.8230

NA: Not Available

① No.1: 2.29
No.2: 2.27
No.3: 2.26
No.4: 2.24
No.5: 1.72

② No.1, 3, 5: (0.0015-.003)
No.2, 4: (0.0019-.0035)

③ No.1 and 7: (2.127-2.128)
No.2 through 6: (2.1245-2.1265)

22043_RPUP_C0011

CRANKSHAFT AND CONNECTING ROD SPECIFICATIONS

All measurements are given in inches.

Year	Engine Displacement Liters	Engine ID/VIN	Crankshaft Main Brg. Journal Dia.	Crankshaft Main Brg. Oil Clearance	Crankshaft Shaft End-play	Crankshaft Thrust on No.	Connecting Rod Journal Diameter	Connecting Rod Oil Clearance	Connecting Rod Side Clearance
2005	3.7	K	2.4996-2.5005	0.0020-0.0034	0.0021-0.0112	2	2.2794-2.2797	0.0004-0.0022	0.0040-0.0138
	4.7	N	2.4996-2.5005	0.0008-0.0021	0.0021-0.0112	3	2.0076-2.0082	0.0006-0.0022	0.0040-0.0138
	4.7	P	2.4996-2.5005	0.0008-0.0021	0.0021-0.0112	3	2.0076-2.0082	0.0006-0.0022	0.0040-0.0138
	5.7	D	2.5585-2.5595	0.0009-0.0020	0.0020-0.0110	3	2.1250-2.1260	0.0007-0.0023	0.0030-0.0137
	5.9	C	3.2662-3.2682	0.0037-0.0057	0.0040-0.0017	6	2.7190-2.7200	0.0035	0.0040-0.0130
2006	3.7	K	2.4996-2.5005	0.0020-0.0034	0.0021-0.0112	2	2.2794-2.2797	0.0004-0.0022	0.0040-0.0138
	4.7	N	2.4996-2.5005	0.0008-0.0021	0.0021-0.0112	3	2.0076-2.0082	0.0006-0.0022	0.0040-0.0138
	4.7	P	2.4996-2.5005	0.0008-0.0021	0.0021-0.0112	3	2.0076-2.0082	0.0006-0.0022	0.0040-0.0138
	5.7	D	2.5585-2.5595	0.0009-0.0020	0.0020-0.0110	3	2.1250-2.1260	0.0007-0.0023	0.0030-0.0137
	5.7	2	2.5585-2.5595	0.0009-0.0020	0.0020-0.0110	3	2.1250-2.1260	0.0007-0.0023	0.0030-0.0137
	5.9	C	3.2662-3.2682	0.0037-0.0057	0.0040-0.0017	6	2.7190-2.7200	0.0035	0.0040-0.0130
2007	3.7	K	2.4996-2.5005	0.0020-0.0034	0.0021-0.0112	2	2.2794-2.2797	0.0004-0.0022	0.0040-0.0138
	4.7	N	2.4996-2.5005	0.0008-0.0021	0.0021-0.0112	3	2.0076-2.0082	0.0006-0.0022	0.0040-0.0138
	4.7	P	2.4996-2.5005	0.0008-0.0021	0.0021-0.0112	3	2.0076-2.0082	0.0006-0.0022	0.0040-0.0138
	5.7	D	2.5585-2.5595	0.0009-0.0020	0.0020-0.0110	3	2.1250-2.1260	0.0007-0.0023	0.0030-0.0137
	5.7	2	2.5585-2.5595	0.0009-0.0020	0.0020-0.0110	3	2.1250-2.1260	0.0007-0.0023	0.0030-0.0137
	5.9	C	3.2662-3.2682	0.0037-0.0057	0.0040-0.0017	6	2.7190-2.7200	0.0035	0.0040-0.0130
	6.7	A	3.2662-3.2682	0.001-0.0020	0.0040-0.0017	6	2.7190-2.7200	0.0035	0.0040-0.0130
2008	3.7	K	2.4996-2.5005	0.0020-0.0034	0.0021-0.0112	2	2.2794-2.2797	0.0004-0.0022	0.0040-0.0138
	4.7	N	2.4996-2.5005	0.0008-0.0021	0.0021-0.0112	3	2.0076-2.0082	0.0006-0.0022	0.0040-0.0138
	5.7	D	2.5585-2.5595	0.0009-0.0020	0.0020-0.0110	3	2.1250-2.1260	0.0007-0.0023	0.0030-0.0137
	5.7	2	2.5585-2.5595	0.0009-0.0020	0.0020-0.0110	3	2.1250-2.1260	0.0007-0.0023	0.0030-0.0137
	5.9	C	3.2662-3.2682	0.0037-0.0057	0.0040-0.0017	6	2.7190-2.7200	0.0035	0.0040-0.0130
	6.7	A	3.2662-3.2682	0.001-0.0020	0.0040-0.0017	6	2.7190-2.7200	0.0035	0.0040-0.0130

22043_RPUP_C0012

PISTON AND RING SPECIFICATIONS

All measurements are given in inches.

Year	Engine Displacement Liters	Engine ID/VIN	Piston Clearance	Ring Gap Top Compression	Ring Gap Bottom Compression	Ring Gap Oil Control	Ring Side Clearance Top Compression	Ring Side Clearance Bottom Compression	Ring Side Clearance Oil Control
2005	3.7	K	0.0014	0.0079-0.0142	0.0146-0.0249	0.0099-0.0300	0.0020-0.0037	0.0016-0.0031	0.0007-0.0091
	4.7	N	0.0008-0.0019	0.0079-0.0142	0.0146-0.0249	0.0100-0.0300	0.0020-0.0037	0.0016-0.0032	0.0007-0.0091
	5.7	D	0.0008-0.0019	0.0090-0.0149	0.0137-0.0236	0.0059-0.0259	0.0007-0.0026	0.0007-0.0022	0.0007-0.0091
	5.9	C	NA	0.0100-0.0140	0.0330-0.0450	0.0100-0.0210	NA	0.0018-0.0037	0.0016-0.0033
2006	3.7	K	0.0014	0.0079-0.0142	0.0146-0.0249	0.0099-0.0300	0.0020-0.0037	0.0016-0.0031	0.0007-0.0091
	4.7	N	0.0008-0.0019	0.0079-0.0142	0.0146-0.0249	0.0100-0.0300	0.0020-0.0037	0.0016-0.0032	0.0007-0.0091
	4.7	P	0.0008-0.0019	0.0079-0.0142	0.0146-0.0249	0.0100-0.0300	0.0020-0.0037	0.0016-0.0032	0.0007-0.0091
	5.7	D	0.0008-0.0019	0.0090-0.0149	0.0137-0.0236	0.0059-0.0259	0.0007-0.0026	0.0007-0.0022	0.0007-0.0091
	5.7	2	0.0008-0.0019	0.0090-0.0149	0.0137-0.0236	0.0059-0.0259	0.0007-0.0026	0.0007-0.0022	0.0007-0.0091
	5.9	C	NA	0.0100-0.0140	0.0330-0.0450	0.0100-0.0210	NA	0.0018-0.0037	0.0016-0.0033
2007	3.7	K	0.0014	0.0079-0.0142	0.0146-0.0249	0.0099-0.0300	0.0020-0.0037	0.0016-0.0031	0.0007-0.0091
	4.7	N	0.0008-0.0019	0.0079-0.0142	0.0146-0.0249	0.0100-0.0300	0.0020-0.0037	0.0016-0.0032	0.0007-0.0091
	4.7	P	0.0008-0.0019	0.0079-0.0142	0.0146-0.0249	0.0100-0.0300	0.0020-0.0037	0.0016-0.0032	0.0007-0.0091
	5.7	D	0.0008-0.0019	0.0090-0.0149	0.0137-0.0236	0.0059-0.0259	0.0007-0.0026	0.0007-0.0022	0.0007-0.0091
	5.7	2	0.0008-0.0019	0.0090-0.0149	0.0137-0.0236	0.0059-0.0259	0.0007-0.0026	0.0007-0.0022	0.0007-0.0091
	5.9	C	NA	0.0100-0.0140	0.0330-0.0450	0.0100-0.0210	NA	0.0018-0.0037	0.0016-0.0033
	6.7	A	NA	0.0120-0.0180	0.0320-0.0470	0.0100-0.0230	NA	0.0016-0.0033	0.0016-0.0033
2008	3.7	K	0.0014	0.0079-0.0142	0.0146-0.0249	0.0099-0.0300	0.0020-0.0037	0.0016-0.0043	0.0007-0.0091
	4.7	N	0.0008-0.0019	0.0079-0.0142	0.0146-0.0249	0.0100-0.0300	0.0020-0.0037	0.0016-0.0032	0.0007-0.0091
	4.7	P	0.0008-0.0019	0.0079-0.0142	0.0146-0.0249	0.0100-0.0300	0.0020-0.0037	0.0016-0.0032	0.0007-0.0091
	5.7	D	0.0008-0.0019	0.0090-0.0149	0.0137-0.0236	0.0059-0.0259	0.0007-0.0026	0.0007-0.0022	0.0007-0.0091
	5.7	2	0.0008-0.0019	0.0090-0.0149	0.0137-0.0236	0.0059-0.0259	0.0007-0.0026	0.0007-0.0022	0.0007-0.0091
	5.9	C	NA	0.0100-0.0140	0.0330-0.0450	0.0100-0.0210	NA	0.0018-0.0037	0.0016-0.0033
	6.7	A	NA	0.0120-0.0180	0.0320-0.0470	0.0100-0.0230	NA	0.0016-0.0033	0.0016-0.0033

NA - Not available

22043_RPUP_C0013

TORQUE SPECIFICATIONS

All readings in ft. lbs.

Year	Engine Displacement Liters	Engine ID/VIN	Cylinder Head Bolts	Main Bearing Bolts	Rod Bearing Bolts	Crankshaft Damper Bolts	Flywheel Bolts	Manifold Intake	Manifold Exhaust	Spark Plugs	Oil Pan Drain Plug
2005	3.7	K	①	②	③	130	45	12	18	20	④
	4.7	N	①	⑤	③	130	45	12	18	20	④
	4.7	P	①	⑤	③	130	45	12	18	20	④
	5.7	D	⑥	⑦	⑧	130	55	105	18	13	④
	5.9	C	⑨	⑩	⑪	92	101	18	32	—	④
2006	3.7	K	①	②	③	130	45	12	18	20	④
	4.7	N	①	⑤	③	130	45	12	18	20	④
	4.7	P	①	⑤	③	130	45	12	18	20	④
	5.7	D	⑥	⑦	⑧	130	55	105	18	13	④
	5.7	2	⑥	⑦	⑧	130	55	105	18	13	④
	5.9	C	⑨	⑩	⑪	92	101	18	32	—	④
2007	3.7	K	①	②	③	130	45	12	18	20	④
	4.7	N	①	⑤	③	130	45	12	18	20	④
	4.7	P	①	⑤	③	130	45	12	18	20	④
	5.7	D	⑥	⑦	⑧	130	55	105	18	13	④
	5.7	2	⑥	⑦	⑧	130	55	105	18	13	④
	5.9	C	⑨	⑩	⑪	92	101	18	32	—	④
	6.7	A	⑨	⑩	⑪	⑫	101	18	32	—	④
2008	3.7	K	①	②	③	130	45	12	18	20	④
	4.7	N	①	⑤	③	130	45	12	18	20	④
	5.7	D	⑥	⑦	⑧	130	55	105	18	13	④
	5.7	2	⑥	⑦	⑧	130	55	105	18	13	④
	5.9	C	⑨	⑩	⑪	92	101	18	32	—	④
	6.7	A	⑨	⑩	⑪	⑫	101	18	32	—	④

① Step 1: 1-8 to 20 ft. lbs.
Step 2: Repeat step 1: and tighten bolts 9-12 to 10 ft. lbs.
Step 3: Tighten bolts 1-8 plus 90 degrees
Step 4: Repeat step 3: and tighten bolts 9-12 to 19 ft. lbs.

② Bed plate: see procedure

③ 20 ft. lbs. plus 90 degrees

④ Gas engines: 25 ft. lbs.
Diesel engines: 37 ft. lbs.

⑤ Step 1: Bolts 1-10 to 25 inch lbs.
Step 2: Bolts 1-10 plus 90 degrees
Step 3: Bolts A-K to 40 ft. lbs.
Step 4: Bolts A1-A5 to 20 ft. lbs.

⑥ M8
Step 1: 15 ft. lbs.
Step 2: 25 ft. lbs.
M12
Step 1: 25 ft. lbs.
Step 2: 40 ft. lbs.
Step 3: plus 90 degree turn

⑦ M12 bolts: 12 ft. lbs. plus 90 degrees
M8 bolts: 13 ft. lbs.

⑧ 15 ft. lbs. plus 90 degrees

⑨ Step 1: 52 ft. lbs.
Step 2: Back off 360 degrees
Step 3: 77 ft. lbs.
Step 4: Recheck 77 ft. lbs.
Step 5: Plus 90 degrees

⑩ Note: Used bolt procedure as follows:
Step 1: 37 ft. lbs.
Step 2: 59 ft. lbs.
Step 3: Plus 90 degrees
Note: New bolt Procedure as follows:
Step 1: 89 ft. lbs.
Step 2: Loosen completely
Step 3: 44 ft. lbs.
Step 4: 63 ft. lbs.
Step 5: Plus 120 degrees

⑪ Step 1: 22 ft. lbs.
Step 2: 44 ft. lbs.
Step 3: Plus 60 degrees

⑫ Step 1: 30 ft. lbs.
Step 2: Plus 60 degrees

22043_RPUP_C0014

WHEEL ALIGNMENT

				Caster		Camber		
Year	Model	GVW	Wheel Base (in.)	Range (+/-Deg.)	Preferred Setting (Deg.)	Range (+/-Deg.)	Preferred Setting (Deg.)	Toe-in (in.)
2005	1500 2wd	—	120.5	0.75	+4.0	0.50	0	0.10+/-0.10
	1500 2wd	—	140.5	0.75	+4.2	0.50	0	0.10+/-0.10
	1500 2wd	—	160.5	0.75	+4.4	0.50	0	0.10+/-0.10
	1500 4wd	—	120.5	0.75	+4.2	0.50	0	0.10+/-0.10
	1500 4wd	—	140.5	0.75	+4.4	0.50	0	0.10+/-0.10
	1500 4wd	—	160.5	0.75	+4.6	0.50	0	0.10+/-0.10
	2500 & 3500 2wd	—	140.5	0.75	+4.0	0.50	0	0.10+/-0.05
	2500 & 3500 2wd	—	160.5	0.75	+4.3	0.50	0	0.10+/-0.05
	2500 & 3500 4wd	—	140.5	0.75	+4.5	0.5	+0.25	0.10+/-0.05
	2500 & 3500 4wd	—	160.5	0.75	+4.7	0.5	+0.25	0.10+/-0.05
2006	1500 2wd	—	120.5	0.75	+3.35	0.50	0.10	0.10+/-0.10
	1500 2wd	—	140.5	0.75	+3.35	0.50	0.10	0.10+/-0.10
	1500 2wd	—	160.5	0.75	+3.35	0.50	0.10	0.10+/-0.10
	1500 4wd	—	120.5	0.75	+3.35	0.50	0.10	0.10+/-0.10
	1500 4wd	—	140.5	0.75	+3.35	0.50	0.10	0.10+/-0.10
	1500 4wd	—	160.5	0.75	+3.35	0.50	0.10	0.10+/-0.10
	2500 & 3500 2wd	—	140.5	0.75	+4.0	0.50	0	0.10+/-0.05
	2500 & 3500 2wd	—	160.5	0.75	+4.0	0.50	0	0.10+/-0.05
	2500 & 3500 4wd	—	140.5	0.75	+4.5	0.50	+0.25	0.10+/-0.05
	2500 & 3500 4wd	—	160.5	0.75	+4.7	0.50	+0.25	0.10+/-0.05
2007	1500 2wd	—	120.5	0.75	+3.35	0.50	0.10	0.10+/-0.10
	1500 2wd	—	140.5	0.75	+3.35	0.50	0.10	0.10+/-0.10
	1500 2wd	—	160.5	0.75	+3.35	0.50	0.10	0.10+/-0.10
	1500 4wd	—	120.5	0.75	+3.35	0.50	0.10	0.10+/-0.10
	1500 4wd	—	140.5	0.75	+3.35	0.50	0.10	0.10+/-0.10
	1500 4wd	—	160.5	0.75	+3.35	0.50	0.10	0.10+/-0.10
	2500 & 3500 2wd	—	140.5	0.75	+4.0	0.50	0	0.10+/-0.05
	2500 & 3500 2wd	—	160.5	0.75	+4.0	0.50	0	0.10+/-0.05
	2500 & 3500 4wd	—	140.5	0.75	+4.5	0.50	+0.25	0.10+/-0.05
	2500 & 3500 4wd	—	160.5	0.75	+4.7	0.50	+0.25	0.10+/-0.05
2008	1500 2wd	—	120.5	0.50	+3.50①	0.50	0.10	0.10+/-0.10
	1500 2wd	—	140.5	0.50	+3.50①	0.50	0.10	0.10+/-0.10
	1500 2wd	—	160.5	0.50	+3.50①	0.50	0.10	0.10+/-0.10
	1500 4wd	—	120.5	0.50	+3.50①	0.50	0.10	0.10+/-0.10
	1500 4wd	—	140.5	0.50	+3.50①	0.50	0.10	0.10+/-0.10
	1500 4wd	—	160.5	0.50	+3.50①	0.50	0.10	0.10+/-0.10
	2500 & 3500 2wd	—	140.5	0.75	+4.0	0.50	0	0.10+/-0.05
	2500 & 3500 2wd	—	160.5	0.75	+4.0	0.50	0	0.10+/-0.05
	2500 & 3500 4wd	—	140.5	0.50	+4.5	0.50	+0.25	0.10+/-0.05
	2500 & 3500 4wd	—	160.5	0.50	+4.5	0.50	+0.25	0.10+/-0.05

① Right side 3.90 +/- 0.50

22043_RPUP_C0015

TIRE, WHEEL AND BALL JOINT SPECIFICATIONS

Year	Model	OEM Tires		Tire Pressures (psi)		Wheel	Wheel Lug
		Standard	Optional	Front	Rear	Size	Nut Torque
2005	1500 Laramie	P265/70R17	None	①	①	8	135
	1500 ST/SLT	P245/70R17	P265/70R17	①	①	8	135
	2500 ST	LT245/70R17	None	①	①	7.5	135
	2500 SLT/Laramie	LT265/70R17	None	①	①	8	135
	3500 Laramie	LT265/70R17	None	①	①	8	145
	3500 Laramie (DRW)	LT235/80R17	LT265/70R17	①	①	6	145
2006	1500 Laramie	P265/70R17	None	①	①	8	135
	1500 ST/SLT	P245/70R17	P265/70R17	①	①	8	135
	2500 ST	LT245/70R17	None	①	①	7.5	135
	2500 SLT/Laramie/Sport	LT265/70R17	None	①	①	8	135
	3500 Laramie/SLT/ST	LT265/70R17	LT235/80R17	①	①	8	145
	3500 Laramie/Sport (DRW)	LT235/80R17	LT265/70R17	①	①	6	145
2007	1500 Laramie	P265/70R17	None	①	①	8	135
	1500 ST/SLT	P245/70R17	P265/70R17	①	①	8	135
	2500 ST	LT245/70R17	None	①	①	7.5-8	155
	2500 SLT/Laramie/Sport	LT265/70R17	None	①	①	8	155
	3500 Laramie/SLT/ST	LT265/70R17	LT235/80R17	①	①	8	155
	3500 Laramie/Sport (DRW)	LT235/80R17	LT265/70R17	①	①	6	155
2008	1500 Laramie	P265/70R17	None	①	①	8	135
	1500 ST/SLT	P245/70R17	P265/70R17	①	①	8	135
	2500 ST	LT245/70R17	None	①	①	7.5-8	155
	2500 SLT/Laramie/Sport	LT265/70R17	None	①	①	8	155
	3500 Laramie/SLT/ST	LT265/70R17	LT235/80R17	①	①	8	155
	3500 Laramie/Sport (DRW)	LT235/80R17	LT265/70R17	①	①	6	155

OEM: Original Equipment Manufacturer

PSI: Pounds Per Square Inch

STD: Standard

OPT: Optional

① See sticker on drivers door

22043_RPUP_C0016

BRAKE SPECIFICATIONS

All measurements in inches unless noted

			Brake Disc			Brake Drum			Minimum Lining Thickness		Brake Caliper	
Year	Model		Original Thickness	Minimum Thickness	Maximum Run-out	Original Inside Diameter	Max. Wear Limit	Max. Machine Diameter	Front	Rear	Bracket Bolts (ft. lbs.)	Mounting Bolts (ft. lbs.)
2005	Ram Pick-up LD	F	NA	1.039	0.002	—	—	—	①	①	130	24
	1500	R	NA	.803	0.002	—	—	—	①	①	50	22
	Ram Pick-up HD	F	NA	1.33	0.005	—	—	—	①	①	250	24
	2500/3500	R	NA	1.117	0.005	—	—	—	①	①	150	22
2006	Ram Pick-up LD	F	NA	1.039	0.002	—	—	—	①	①	130	24
	1500	R	NA	.803	0.002	—	—	—	①	①	50	22
	Ram Pick-up HD	F	NA	1.33	0.005	—	—	—	①	①	250	24
	2500/3500	R	NA	1.117	0.005	—	—	—	①	①	150	22
2007	Ram Pick-up LD	F	NA	1.039	0.002	—	—	—	①	①	130	24
	1500	R	NA	.803	0.002	—	—	—	①	①	50	22
	Ram Pick-up HD	F	NA	1.33	0.005	—	—	—	①	①	250	24
	2500/3500	R	NA	1.117	0.005	—	—	—	①	①	150	22
2008	Ram Pick-up LD	F	NA	1.039	0.002	—	—	—	①	①	130	24
	1500	R	NA	.803	0.002	—	—	—	①	①	50	22
	Ram Pick-up HD	F	NA	1.33	0.005	—	—	—	①	①	250	24
	2500/3500	R	NA	1.117	0.005	—	—	—	①	①	150	22

NA: Not Available

① Riveted brake pads: 0.0625 in.
Bonded brake pads: 0.1875 in.

22043_RPUP_C0017

SCHEDULED MAINTENANCE INTERVALS

2005-08 LD RAM PICKUP

TO BE SERVICED	TYPE OF SERVICE	VEHICLE MILEAGE INTERVAL (x1000)														
		7.5	15	22.5	30	37.5	45	52.5	60	67.5	75	82.5	90	97.5	100	105
Engine oil & filter	R	✓	✓	✓	✓	✓	✓	✓	✓	✓	✓	✓	✓	✓		✓
Engine coolant & hoses	I	✓	✓	✓	✓	✓	✓	✓	✓	✓	✓	✓	✓	✓		✓
Brake hoses	I	✓	✓	✓	✓	✓	✓	✓	✓	✓	✓	✓	✓	✓		✓
Steering linkage	L	✓	✓	✓	✓	✓	✓	✓	✓	✓	✓	✓	✓	✓		✓
Manual trans. fluid level	I	✓	✓	✓	✓	✓	✓	✓	✓	✓	✓	✓	✓	✓		✓
Exhaust system	I	✓	✓	✓	✓	✓	✓	✓	✓	✓	✓	✓	✓	✓		✓
Brake linings	I			✓			✓			✓			✓			
Front wheel bearings (2wd)	S/I			✓			✓			✓			✓			
Ball joints	L			✓			✓			✓			✓			
Air cleaner element	R				✓				✓				✓			
Spark plugs	R				✓				✓				✓			
Transfer case fluid	R					✓					✓					
Rear drum brakes	Adj	✓	✓	✓	✓	✓	✓	✓	✓	✓	✓	✓	✓	✓		✓
Tires	Rotate	✓	✓	✓	✓	✓	✓	✓	✓	✓	✓	✓	✓	✓		✓
Engine coolant ①	R							✓								✓
Spark plug wires	R								✓							
PCV valve	S/I								✓							
Drive belt tensioner	S/I										✓					
Automatic trans. fluid	R														✓	
Automatic trans. bands	Adj														✓	

R: Replace S/I: Service or Inspect Adj: Adjust L: Lubricate

① Replace every 36 months, regardless of mileage.

FREQUENT OPERATION MAINTENANCE (SEVERE SERVICE)

If a vehicle is operated under any of the following conditions it is considered severe service:

- Extremely dusty areas.

- 50% or more of the vehicle operation is in 32°C (90°F) or higher temperatures, or constant operation in temperatures below 0°C (32°F).

- Prolonged idling (vehicle operation in stop and go traffic.

- Frequent short running periods (engine does not warm to normal operating temperatures).

- Police, taxi, delivery usage or trailer towing usage.

Oil & oil filter change: change every 3000 miles.

Air filter/air pump air filter: change every 24,000 miles.

Engine coolant level, hoses & clamps: check every 6,000 miles.

Exhaust system: check every 6000 miles.

Drive belts: check every 18,000 miles; replace every 24,000 miles.

Crankcase inlet air filter (6 & 8 cyl.): clean every 24,000 miles.

Oxygen sensor: replace every 82,500 miles.

Automatic transmission fluid, filter & bands: change & adjust every 12,000 miles.

Steering linkage: lubricate every 6000 miles.

Rear axle fluid: change every 12,000 miles.

22043_RPUP_C0018

SCHEDULED MAINTENANCE INTERVALS

2005-08 Medium Duty

TO BE SERVICED	TYPE OF SERVICE	VEHICLE MILEAGE INTERVAL (x1000)														
		6	12	18	24	30	36	42	48	54	60	66	72	78	84	90
Engine oil and filter	R	✓	✓	✓	✓	✓	✓	✓	✓	✓	✓	✓	✓	✓	✓	✓
Brake linings	I			✓			✓			✓			✓			✓
Front wheel bearings (2wd)	S/I			✓			✓			✓			✓			✓
Auto trans fluid and filter	R				✓				✓				✓			
Auto trans bands	Adj				✓				✓				✓			
Air cleaner element	R					✓					✓					✓
Spark plugs	R					✓					✓					✓
Exhaust system	I	✓	✓	✓	✓	✓	✓	✓	✓	✓	✓	✓	✓	✓	✓	✓
Brake hoses	I	✓	✓	✓	✓	✓	✓	✓	✓	✓	✓	✓	✓	✓	✓	✓
Rear drum brakes	Adj	✓	✓	✓	✓	✓	✓	✓	✓	✓	✓	✓	✓	✓	✓	✓
Tires	Rotate	✓	✓	✓	✓	✓	✓	✓	✓	✓	✓	✓	✓	✓	✓	✓
Steering linkage	L	✓	✓	✓	✓	✓	✓	✓	✓	✓	✓	✓	✓	✓	✓	✓
Transfer case fluid	R						✓						✓			
Engine coolant ①	R						✓						✓			
Spark plug wires	R										✓					

R: Replace S/I: Service or Inspect Adj: Adjust L: Lubricate

① Replace every 36 months, regardless of mileage.

FREQUENT OPERATION MAINTENANCE (SEVERE SERVICE)

If a vehicle is operated under any of the following conditions it is considered severe service:

- Extremely dusty areas.

- 50% or more of the vehicle operation is in 32°C (90°F) or higher temperatures, or constant operation in temperatures below 0°C (32°F).

- Prolonged idling (vehicle operation in stop and go traffic.

- Frequent short running periods (engine does not warm to normal operating temperatures).

- Police, taxi, delivery usage or trailer towing usage.

Oil & oil filter change: change every 3000 miles.

Air filter/air pump air filter: change every 24,000 miles.

Engine coolant level, hoses & clamps: check every 6,000 miles.

Exhaust system: check every 6000 miles.

Drive belts: check every 18,000 miles; replace every 24,000 miles.

Crankcase inlet air filter (6 & 8 cyl.): clean every 24,000 miles.

Oxygen sensor: replace every 82,500 miles.

Automatic transmission fluid, filter & bands: change & adjust every 12,000 miles.

Steering linkage: lubricate every 6000 miles.

Rear axle fluid: change every 12,000 miles.

22043_RPUP_C0019

SCHEDULED MAINTENANCE INTERVALS

2005-08 Heavy Duty

TO BE SERVICED	TYPE OF SERVICE	VEHICLE MILEAGE INTERVAL (x1000)														
		6	12	18	24	30	36	42	48	54	60	66	72	78	82.5	84
Engine oil and filter	R	✓	✓	✓	✓	✓	✓	✓	✓	✓	✓	✓	✓	✓		✓
Air cleaner element (8.0L)	R		✓				✓				✓					✓
Brake linings	I			✓			✓			✓			✓			
Front wheel bearings (4wd)	S/I			✓			✓			✓			✓			
Air cleaner element (5.9L)	R				✓				✓				✓			
Air pump filter	R				✓				✓				✓			
Crankcase inlet air filter (5.9L)	C/L				✓				✓				✓			
Auto trans fluid & filter	R				✓				✓				✓			
Auto trans bands	Adj				✓				✓				✓			
Front wheel bearings (2wd)	S/I				✓				✓				✓			
Spark plugs	R					✓					✓					
Transfer case fluid	R						✓						✓			
Exhaust system	I	✓	✓	✓	✓	✓	✓	✓	✓	✓	✓	✓	✓	✓		✓
Brake hoses	I	✓	✓	✓	✓	✓	✓	✓	✓	✓	✓	✓	✓	✓		✓
Tires	Rotate	✓	✓	✓	✓	✓	✓	✓	✓	✓	✓	✓	✓	✓		✓
Steering linkage	L	✓	✓	✓	✓	✓	✓	✓	✓	✓	✓	✓	✓	✓		✓
Engine coolant ①	R						✓						✓			
Spark plug wires	R										✓					
PCV valve (5.9L)	R										✓					
Distributor cap & rotor (5.9L)	R										✓					
Oxygen sensor (5.9L)	R														✓	

R: Replace S/I: Service or Inspect Adj: Adjust C/L: Clean & lubricate

① Replace every 36 months, regardless of mileage.

FREQUENT OPERATION MAINTENANCE (SEVERE SERVICE)

If a vehicle is operated under any of the following conditions it is considered severe service:

- Extremely dusty areas.

- 50% or more of the vehicle operation is in 32°C (90°F) or higher temperatures, or constant operation in temperatures below 0°C (32°F).

- Prolonged idling (vehicle operation in stop and go traffic.

- Frequent short running periods (engine does not warm to normal operating temperatures).

- Police, taxi, delivery usage or trailer towing usage.

Oil & oil filter change: change every 3000 miles.

Air filter/air pump air filter: change every 24,000 miles.

Engine coolant level, hoses & clamps: check every 6,000 miles.

Exhaust system: check every 6000 miles.

Drive belts: check every 18,000 miles; replace every 24,000 miles.

Crankcase inlet air filter (6 & 8 cyl.): clean every 24,000 miles.

Oxygen sensor: replace every 82,500 miles.

Automatic transmission fluid, filter & bands: change & adjust every 12,000 miles.

Steering linkage: lubricate every 6000 miles.

Rear axle fluid: change every 12,000 miles.

22043_RPUP_C0020

SCHEDULED MAINTENANCE INTERVALS
2005-08 Turbo Diesel

		VEHICLE MILEAGE INTERVAL (x1000)													
TO BE SERVICED	TYPE OF SERVICE	7.5	15	22.5	30	37.5	45	52.5	60	67.5	75	82.5	90	97.5	100
Engine oil & filter	R		✓		✓		✓		✓		✓		✓		
Crankcase breather canister	D	✓	✓	✓	✓	✓	✓	✓	✓	✓	✓	✓	✓	✓	
Water pump weep hole	I		✓		✓		✓		✓		✓		✓		
Fuel filter	R		✓		✓		✓		✓		✓		✓		
Fuel sensor	C		✓		✓		✓		✓		✓		✓		
Drive belts	I			✓			✓			✓			✓		
Brake linings	I			✓			✓			✓			✓		
Fan hub	I				✓				✓				✓		
Damper	I				✓				✓				✓		
Accessory drive belt	S/I			✓			✓			✓			✓		
Transfer case fluid	I				✓				✓				✓		
Auto trans & filter	R														✓
Auto trans bands	Adj				✓				✓				✓		
Front wheel bearings (2WD)	S/I				✓				✓				✓		
Engine coolant ①	R				✓				✓				✓		
Exhaust system	I	✓	✓	✓	✓	✓	✓	✓	✓	✓	✓	✓	✓	✓	
Steering linkage	L	✓	✓	✓	✓	✓	✓	✓	✓	✓	✓	✓	✓	✓	
Rear drum brakes	Adj	✓	✓	✓	✓	✓	✓	✓	✓	✓	✓	✓	✓	✓	
Tires	Rotate	✓	✓	✓	✓	✓	✓	✓	✓	✓	✓	✓	✓	✓	

R: Replace S/I: Service or Inspect D: Drain C: Clean Adj: Adjust

① Replace every 36 months, regardless of mileage

FREQUENT OPERATION MAINTENANCE (SEVERE SERVICE)

If a vehicle is operated under any of the following conditions it is considered severe service:

- Extremely dusty areas.

- 50% or more of the vehicle operation is in 32°C (90°F) or higher temperatures, or constant operation in temperatures below 0°C (32°F).

- Prolonged idling (vehicle operation in stop and go traffic.

- Frequent short running periods (engine does not warm to normal operating temperatures).

- Police, taxi, delivery usage or trailer towing usage.

Oil & oil filter change: change every 7500 miles.

Air filter/air pump air filter: change every 24,000 miles.

Engine coolant level, hoses & clamps: check every 6,000 miles.

Brake linings: check every 15,000 miles

Exhaust system: inspect every 6000 miles.

Drive belts: check every 18,000 miles; replace every 24,000 miles.

Crankcase inlet air filter (6 & 8 cyl.): clean every 24,000 miles.

Oxygen sensor: replace every 82,500 miles.

Automatic transmission fluid, filter & bands: change & adjust every 30,000 miles.

Manual transmission fluid: change every 75,000 miles

Steering linkage: lubricate every 6000 miles.

Rear axle fluid: change every 15,000 miles.

Valve lash: adjust every 150,000 miles.

22043_RPUP_C0021

PRECAUTIONS

Before servicing any vehicle, please be sure to read all of the following precautions, which deal with personal safety, prevention of component damage, and important points to take into consideration when servicing a motor vehicle:

- Never open, service or drain the radiator or cooling system when the engine is hot; serious burns can occur from the steam and hot coolant.
- Observe all applicable safety precautions when working around fuel. Whenever servicing the fuel system, always work in a well-ventilated area. Do not allow fuel spray or vapors to come in contact with a spark, open flame, or excessive heat (a hot drop light, for example). Keep a dry chemical fire extinguisher near the work area. Always keep fuel in a container specifically designed for fuel storage; also, always properly seal fuel containers to avoid the possibility of fire or explosion. Refer to the additional fuel system precautions later in this section.
- Fuel injection systems often remain pressurized, even after the engine has been turned **OFF**. The fuel system pressure must be relieved before disconnecting any fuel lines. Failure to do so may result in fire and/or personal injury.
- Brake fluid often contains polyglycol ethers and polyglycols. Avoid contact with the eyes and wash your hands thoroughly after handling brake fluid. If you do get brake fluid in your eyes, flush your eyes with clean, running water for 15 minutes. If eye irritation persists, or if you have taken brake fluid internally, IMMEDIATELY seek medical assistance.
- The EPA warns that prolonged contact with used engine oil may cause a number of skin disorders, including cancer. You should make every effort to minimize your exposure to used engine oil. Protective gloves should be worn when changing oil. Wash your hands and any other exposed skin areas as soon as possible after exposure to used engine oil. Soap and water, or waterless hand cleaner should be used.
- All new vehicles are now equipped with an air bag system, often referred to as a Supplemental Restraint System (SRS) or Supplemental Inflatable Restraint (SIR) system. The system must be disabled before performing service on or around system components, steering column, instrument panel components, wiring and sensors. Failure to follow safety and disabling procedures could result in accidental air bag deployment, possible personal injury and unnecessary system repairs.
- Always wear safety goggles when working with, or around, the air bag system. When carrying a non-deployed air bag, be sure the bag and trim cover are pointed away from your body. When placing a non-deployed air bag on a work surface, always face the bag and trim cover upward, away from the surface. This will reduce the motion of the module if it is accidentally deployed. Refer to the additional air bag system precautions later in this section.
- Clean, high quality brake fluid from a sealed container is essential to the safe and proper operation of the brake system. You should always buy the correct type of brake fluid for your vehicle. If the brake fluid becomes contaminated, completely flush the system with new fluid. Never reuse any brake fluid. Any brake fluid that is removed from the system should be discarded. Also, do not allow any brake fluid to come in contact with a painted surface; it will damage the paint.
- Never operate the engine without the proper amount and type of engine oil; doing so WILL result in severe engine damage.
- Timing belt maintenance is extremely important. Many models utilize an interference-type, non-freewheeling engine. If the timing belt breaks, the valves in the cylinder head may strike the pistons, causing potentially serious (also time-consuming and expensive) engine damage. Refer to the maintenance interval charts for the recommended replacement interval for the timing belt, and to the timing belt section for belt replacement and inspection.
- Disconnecting the negative battery cable on some vehicles may interfere with the functions of the on-board computer system(s) and may require the computer to undergo a relearning process once the negative battery cable is reconnected.
- When servicing drum brakes, only disassemble and assemble one side at a time, leaving the remaining side intact for reference.
- Only an MVAC-trained, EPA-certified automotive technician should service the air conditioning system or its components.

BRAKES

ANTI-LOCK BRAKE SYSTEM (ABS)

GENERAL INFORMATION

PRECAUTIONS

- Certain components within the ABS system are not intended to be serviced or repaired individually.
- Do not use rubber hoses or other parts not specifically specified for and ABS system. When using repair kits, replace all parts included in the kit. Partial or incorrect repair may lead to functional problems and require the replacement of components.
- Lubricate rubber parts with clean, fresh brake fluid to ease assembly. Do not use shop air to clean parts; damage to rubber components may result.
- Use only DOT 3 brake fluid from an unopened container.
- If any hydraulic component or line is removed or replaced, it may be necessary to bleed the entire system.
- A clean repair area is essential. Always clean the reservoir and cap thoroughly before removing the cap. The slightest amount of dirt in the fluid may plug an orifice and impair the system function. Perform repairs after components have been thoroughly cleaned; use only denatured alcohol to clean components. Do not allow ABS components to come into contact with any substance containing mineral oil; this includes used shop rags.
- The Anti-Lock control unit is a microprocessor similar to other computer units in the vehicle. Ensure that the ignition switch is **OFF** before removing or installing controller harnesses. Avoid static electricity discharge at or near the controller.
- If any arc welding is to be done on the vehicle, the control unit should be unplugged before welding operations begin.

SPEED SENSORS

REMOVAL & INSTALLATION

Front Wheel Speed Sensor

2WD Vehicles

1. Before servicing the vehicle, refer to the Precautions Section.
2. Raise and support the vehicle.
3. Remove the sensor bolt from the steering knuckle/hub and remove the sensor.
4. Disconnect the ABS wheel speed sensor wire and detach the wire from securing clips.

To install:

5. Tighten the sensor bolt to 17 ft. lbs. (23 Nm).

➡Use the original or replacement sensor bolt only. The bolt is special and must not be substituted.

6. The remainder of the procedure is the reverse of removal.

4WD Vehicles

See Figure 1.

1. Before servicing the vehicle, refer to the Precautions Section.
2. Raise and support the vehicle.
3. Remove the wheel.
4. Remove the brake caliper.
5. On 8—stud wheels, remove the rotor hub bearing assembly and separate the rotor from the hub bearing.
6. On other wheels, remove the rotor.
7. Remove the sensor attaching bolts.
8. Disconnect the wire and remove the sensor from the vehicle.

To install:

9. Tighten the bolts to 13 ft. lbs. (18 Nm).

➡Use the original or replacement sensor bolts only. The bolts are special and must not be substituted.

10. The remainder of the procedure is the reverse of removal.

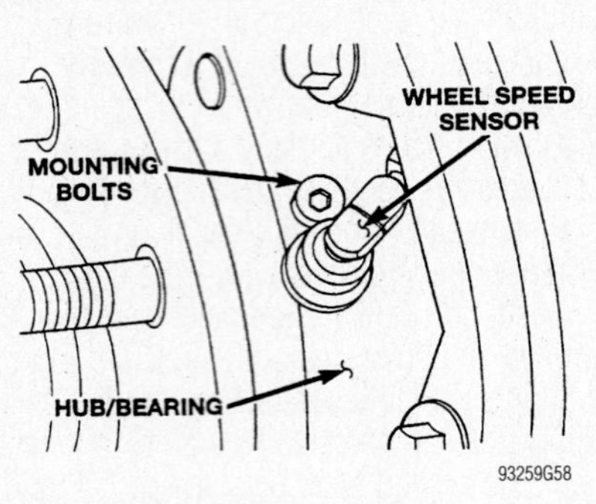

Fig. 1 Front wheel speed sensor installation—4WD

Rear Wheel Sensor

1. Before servicing the vehicle, refer to the Precautions Section.
2. Raise the vehicle.
3. Remove the brake line mounting nut, if fitted, and remove the brake line from the sensor stud.
4. Remove the mounting stud from the sensor and shield.
5. Remove the sensor and shield from the differential housing.
6. Disconnect the wire and remove the sensor.

To install:

7. Connect harness to sensor. Be sure the seal is securely in place between the sensor and wiring connector.
8. Install O—ring on sensor if removed.
9. Install the sensor on differential housing, sensor shield, mounting stud. Tighten to 18 ft. lbs. (24 Nm).
10. Install the brake line on the sensor stud and install the nut.

➡Use the original or replacement sensor bolt only. The bolt is special and must not be substituted.

11. Lower the vehicle.

BRAKES — BLEEDING THE BRAKE SYSTEM

BLEEDING PROCEDURE

BLEEDING PROCEDURE

Manual Bleeding

➡This procedure covers bleeding of the base brakes only. On vehicles equipped with ABS, refer to the bleeding procedure located under the ABS portion of this section.

➡Use Mopar® brake fluid, or an equivalent quality fluid meeting SAE J1703-F and DOT 3 standards only. Use fresh, clean fluid from a sealed container at all times.

1. Remove reservoir filler caps and fill reservoir.
2. If calipers were overhauled, open all caliper bleed screws. Then close each bleed screw as fluid starts to drip from it. Top off master cylinder reservoir once more before proceeding.
3. Attach one end of bleed hose to bleed screw and insert opposite end in glass container (2) partially filled with brake fluid. Be sure end of bleed hose is immersed in fluid.

➡Bleed procedure should be in this order: (1) Right rear (2) Left rear (3) Right front (4) Left front.

4. Open up bleeder, then have a helper press down the brake pedal. Once the pedal is down close the bleeder. Repeat bleeding until fluid stream is clear and free of bubbles. Then move to the next wheel.
5. Before moving the vehicle verify the pedal is firm and not mushy.
6. Top off the brake fluid and install the reservoir cap.

Pressure Bleeding

➡This procedure covers bleeding of the base brakes only. On vehicles equipped with ABS, refer to the bleeding procedure located under the ABS portion of this section.

➡Use Mopar® brake fluid, or an equivalent quality fluid meeting SAE J1703-F and DOT 3 standards only. Use fresh, clean fluid from a sealed container at all times.

1. Follow the manufacturers instructions carefully when using pressure equipment. Do not exceed the tank manufacturers pressure recommendations. Generally, a tank pressure of 15-20 psi is sufficient for bleeding.
2. Fill the bleeder tank with recommended fluid and purge air from the tank lines before bleeding.
3. Do not pressure bleed without a proper master cylinder adapter. The wrong adapter can lead to leakage, or drawing air back into the system.

BRAKE LINE BLEEDING

1. Remove reservoir filler caps and fill reservoir.
2. If calipers were overhauled, open all caliper bleed screws. Then close each bleed screw as fluid starts to drip from it. Top off master cylinder reservoir once more before proceeding.
3. Attach one end of bleed hose (1) to bleed screw and insert opposite end in glass container (2) partially filled with brake fluid. Be sure end of bleed hose is immersed in fluid.

➡ Bleed procedure should be in this order (1) Right rear (2) Left rear (3) Right front (4) Left front.

4. Open up bleeder, then have a helper press down the brake pedal. Once the brake pedal is down close the bleeder. Repeat bleeding until fluid stream is clear and free of bubbles. Then move to the next wheel
5. Before moving the vehicle verify the pedal is firm and not mushy.
6. Top off the brake fluid and install the reservoir cap.

BLEEDING THE ABS SYSTEM

ABS system bleeding requires conventional bleeding methods plus use of the DRB scan tool. The procedure involves performing a base brake bleeding, followed by use of the scan tool to cycle and bleed the HCU pump and solenoids. A second base brake bleeding procedure is then required to remove any air remaining in the system.

1. Perform base brake bleeding. Refer to the appropriate section.
2. Connect the scan tool to the data link connector beneath the dashboard.
3. Select **Antilock Brake** followed by **Miscellaneous**, then **ABS Brake**. Follow the instructions displayed until the unit displays "Test Complete", then disconnect the scan tool and proceed.
4. Perform a base brake bleeding a second time.
5. Top off master cylinder fluid level and verify proper brake operation before moving vehicle.

FRONT DISC BRAKES

**** CAUTION**

Dust and dirt accumulating on brake parts during normal use may contain asbestos fibers from production or aftermarket brake linings. Breathing excessive concentrations of asbestos fibers can cause serious bodily harm. Exercise care when servicing brake parts. Do not sand or grind brake lining unless equipment used is designed to contain the dust residue. Do not clean brake parts with compressed air or by dry brushing. Cleaning should be done by dampening the brake components with a fine mist of water, then wiping the brake components clean with a dampened cloth. Dispose of cloth and all residue containing asbestos fibers in an impermeable container with the appropriate label. Follow practices prescribed by the Occupational Safety and Health Administration (OSHA) and the Environmental Protection Agency (EPA) for the handling, processing, and disposing of dust or debris that may contain asbestos fibers.

BRAKE CALIPER

REMOVAL & INSTALLATION

See Figures 2 and 3.

**** CAUTION**

Dust and dirt accumulating on brake parts during normal use may contain asbestos fibers from production or aftermarket brake linings. Breathing excessive concentrations of asbestos fibers can cause serious bodily harm. Exercise care when servicing brake parts. Do not sand or grind brake lining unless equipment used is designed to contain the dust residue. Do not clean brake parts with compressed air or by dry brushing. Cleaning should be done by dampening the brake components with a fine mist of water, then wiping the brake components clean with a dampened cloth. Dispose of cloth and all residue containing asbestos fibers in an impermeable container with the appropriate label. Follow practices prescribed by the Occupational Safety and Health Administration (OSHA) and the Environmental Protection Agency (EPA) for the handling, processing, and disposing of dust or debris that may contain asbestos fibers.

1. Raise and support the front end on jackstands.
2. Remove the wheels.
3. Press the caliper piston back into the bore with a suitable prytool. Use a large C-clamp to drive the piston into the bore of additional force is required.
4. Remove the caliper mounting bolts with a 3/8 in. hex wrench or socket.
5. Loosen the bolt that secures the front brake hose fitting bolt in the caliper.
6. Rotate the caliper rearward off the rotor and out from its mount.

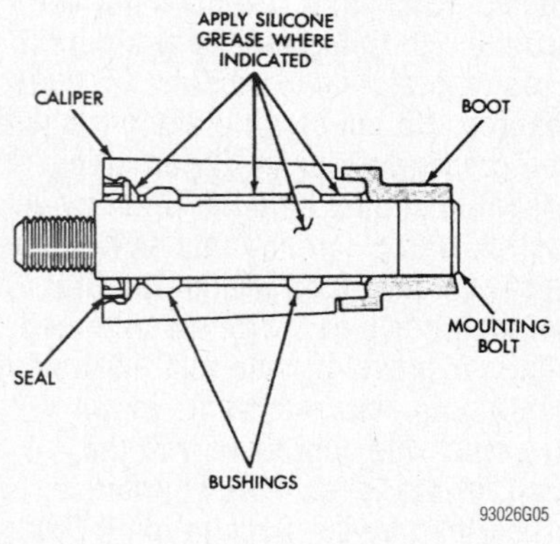

Fig. 2 Mounting bolt lubrication points—Ram Pick-Up 75mm caliper

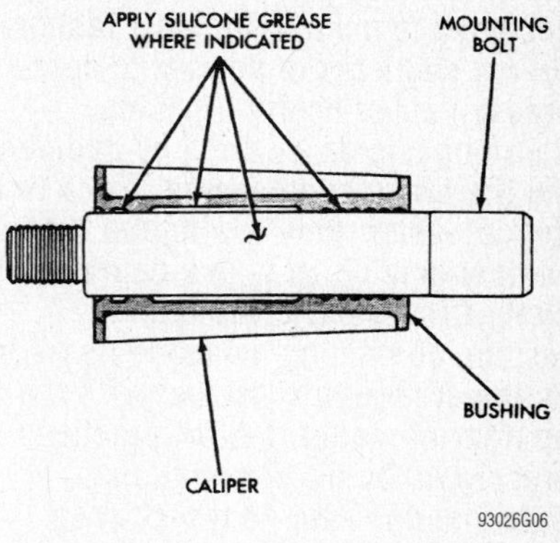

Fig. 3 Mounting bolt lubrication points—Ram Pick-Up 80 or 86mm caliper

7. Remove the front brake hose fitting bolt completely, then remove the caliper with the pads installed as an assembly. Take care not to drip fluid onto the pad surfaces.
8. Cover the open end of the front brake hose fitting to prevent dirt entry.

To install:

9. Clean the caliper and steering knuckle sliding surfaces with a wire brush. Then, apply a coat of Mopar® multi-mileage grease or equivalent.
10. Lubricate the caliper mounting bolts, collars, bushings and bores with Dow 111® or GE 661® silicone grease or equivalent.
11. Install the caliper over the rotor and seat it in its original position until flush.
12. Install the mounting bolts by hand, then tighten them to 24 ft. lbs. (32 Nm).
13. Attach the brake hose, using new washers, and torque the bolt to 20 ft. lbs. (27 Nm).
14. Install the wheels.
15. Lower the vehicle.
16. Pump the brakes several times to seat the pads.

DISC BRAKE PADS

REMOVAL & INSTALLATION

⁂ CAUTION

Dust and dirt accumulating on brake parts during normal use may contain asbestos fibers from production or aftermarket brake linings. Breathing excessive concentrations of asbestos fibers can cause serious bodily harm. Exercise care when servicing brake parts. Do not sand or grind brake lining unless equipment used is designed to contain the dust residue. Do not clean brake parts with compressed air or by dry brushing. Cleaning should be done by dampening the brake components with a fine mist of water, then wiping the brake components clean with a dampened cloth. Dispose of cloth and all residue containing asbestos fibers in an impermeable container with the appropriate label. Follow practices prescribed by the Occupational Safety and Health Administration (OSHA) and the Environmental Protection Agency (EPA) for the handling, processing, and disposing of dust or debris that may contain asbestos fibers.

1. Raise and support the front end on jackstands.
2. Remove the wheels.
3. Press the caliper piston back into the bore with a suitable prytool. Use a large C-clamp to drive the piston into the bore of additional force is required.
4. Remove the caliper mounting bolts with a 3/8 in. hex wrench or socket.
5. Rotate the caliper rearward off the rotor and out from its mount.
6. Set the caliper on a crate or sturdy box, then remove the inboard and outboard brake pads. The inboard pad has a spring clip that holds it in the caliper. Tilt this pad out at the top to unseat the clip. The outboard pad has a retaining spring that secures it in the caliper. Unseat 1 spring end and rotate the pad out of the caliper.
7. Secure the caliper to a chassis or suspension component with a sturdy wire. Do not let it hang from the hose.

To install:

8. Clean the caliper and steering knuckle sliding surfaces with a wire brush. Then, apply a coat of Mopar® multi-mileage grease or equivalent.

➡If there is minor rust or corrosion on the pins, first polish them with a crocus cloth. If they are severely rusted, replace them.

9. Lubricate the caliper mounting bolts, collars, bushings and bores with Dow 111® or GE 661® silicone grease or equivalent.
10. Install the inboard pad and its spring clip.
11. Install the outboard brake pad.
12. Install the caliper over the rotor and seat it until flush in its original position.
13. Install the mounting bolts by hand, then tighten them to 24 ft. lbs. (33 Nm).
14. Install the wheels.
15. Lower the vehicle.
16. Pump the brakes several times to seat the pads.

⁂ CAUTION

Dust and dirt accumulating on brake parts during normal use may contain asbestos fibers from production or aftermarket brake linings. Breathing excessive concentrations of asbestos fibers can cause serious bodily harm. Exercise care when servicing brake parts. Do not sand or grind brake lining unless equipment used is designed to contain the dust residue. Do not clean brake parts with compressed air or by dry brushing. Cleaning should be done by dampening the brake components with a fine mist of water, then wiping the brake components clean with a dampened cloth. Dispose of cloth and all residue containing asbestos fibers in an impermeable container with the appropriate label. Follow practices prescribed by the Occupational Safety and Health Administration (OSHA) and the Environmental Protection Agency (EPA) for the handling, processing, and disposing of dust or debris that may contain asbestos fibers.

BRAKE CALIPER

REMOVAL & INSTALLATION

See Figure 4.

⁂ CAUTION

Dust and dirt accumulating on brake parts during normal use may contain asbestos fibers from production or aftermarket brake linings. Breathing excessive concentrations of asbestos fibers can cause serious bodily harm. Exercise care when servicing brake parts. Do not sand or grind brake lining unless equipment used is designed to contain the dust residue. Do not clean brake parts with compressed air or by dry brushing. Cleaning should be done by dampening the brake components with a fine mist of water, then wiping the brake components clean with a dampened cloth. Dispose of cloth and all residue containing asbestos fibers in an impermeable container with the appropriate label. Follow practices prescribed by the Occupational Safety and Health Administration (OSHA) and the Environmental Protection Agency (EPA) for the handling, processing, and disposing of dust or debris that may contain asbestos fibers.

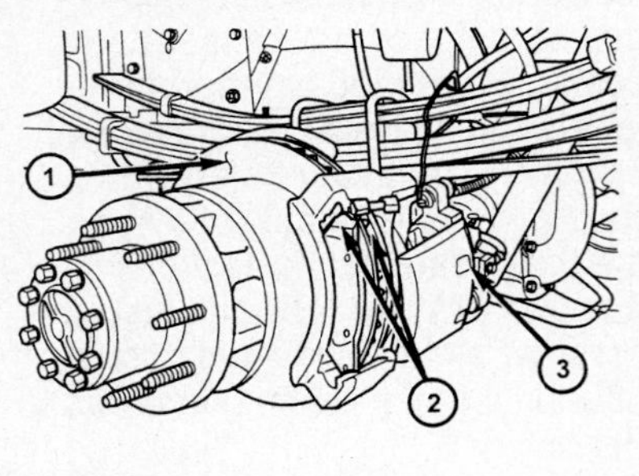

Fig. 4 Rear brake caliper

1. Before servicing the vehicle, refer to the Precautions Section.
2. Compress the piston.
3. Remove or disconnect the following:
   - Caliper pin bolts
   - Banjo bolt
   - Caliper
4. Installation is the reverse of removal. Use new copper washers, tighten the pin bolts to 11 ft. lbs. (15 Nm) and the banjo bolt to 23 ft. lbs. (32 Nm).

DISC BRAKE PADS

REMOVAL & INSTALLATION

See Figure 5.

⁂ CAUTION

Dust and dirt accumulating on brake parts during normal use may contain asbestos fibers from production or aftermarket brake linings. Breathing excessive concentrations of asbestos fibers can cause serious bodily harm. Exercise care when servicing brake parts. Do not sand or grind brake lining unless equipment used is designed to contain the dust residue. Do not clean brake parts with compressed air or by dry brushing. Cleaning should be done by dampening the brake components with a fine mist of water, then wiping the brake components clean with a dampened cloth. Dispose of cloth and all residue containing asbestos fibers in an impermeable container with the appropriate label. Follow practices prescribed by the Occupational Safety and Health Administration (OSHA) and the Environmental Protection Agency (EPA) for the handling, processing, and disposing of dust or debris that may contain asbestos fibers.

1. Before servicing the vehicle, refer to the Precautions Section.

⁂ WARNING

Never allow the disc brake caliper to hang from the brake hose. Damage to the brake hose will result. Provide a suitable support to hang the caliper securely.

2. Install prop rod on the brake pedal to keep pressure on the brake system, Holding pedal in this position will isolate master cylinder from hydraulic brake system and will not allow brake fluid to drain out of brake fluid reservoir while brake lines are open. This will allow you to bleed out the area of repair instead of the entire system.
3. Raise and support vehicle.
4. Remove the wheel and tire assembly.
5. Compress the caliper.
6. Remove caliper slide bolts.
7. Remove the caliper and then tilt the top up and off the caliper adapter.
8. Remove inboard and outboard brake pads from the caliper adapter.
9. Remove the top and bottom anti-rattle spring from the caliper adapter.

To install:

10. Clean caliper mounting adapter and anti-rattle springs.
11. Lubricate anti-rattle springs with Mopar® brake grease.

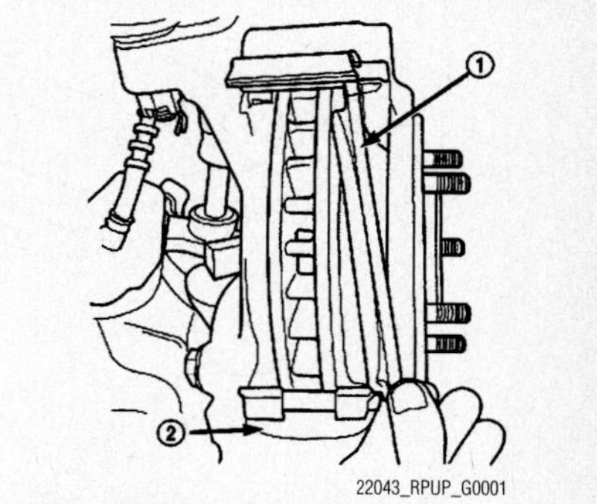

Fig. 5 Rear brake pad (1) caliper adapter (2)

12. Install new top and bottom anti-rattle spring
13. Install outboard and inboard brake pads in adapter.
14. Tilt the bottom of the caliper over rotor and under adapter. Then push the top of the caliper down onto the adapter.
15. Coat the caliper mounting slide pin bolts with silicone grease. Then install and tighten the bolts to 22 ft. lbs. (30 Nm).
16. Install the wheel and tire assemblies and lower vehicle.
17. Apply brakes several times to seat caliper pistons and brake shoes and obtain firm pedal.
18. Top off master cylinder fluid level.

BRAKES

PARKING BRAKE

PARKING BRAKE CABLES

ADJUSTMENT

➡Tensioner adjustment is only necessary when the tensioner, or a cable has been replaced or disconnected for service. When adjustment is necessary, perform adjustment only as described in the following procedure. This is necessary to avoid faulty park brake operation.

1. Raise the vehicle.
2. Back off the cable tensioner adjusting nut to create slack in the cables.
3. Remove the rear wheel/tire assemblies. Then remove the brake rotors.
4. Verify the brakes are in good condition and operating properly.
5. Verify the park brake cables operate freely and are not binding, or seized.
6. Check the rear brake shoe adjustment with standard brake gauge.
7. Install the rotors and verify that the rotors rotate freely without drag.
8. Install the wheel and tire assemblies.
9. Lower the vehicle enough for access to the park brake foot pedal. Then fully apply the park brakes.

➡Leave park brakes applied until adjustment is complete.

10. Raise the vehicle again.
11. Mark the tensioner rod ¼ inch. (6.35 mm) from edge of the tensioner.
12. Tighten the adjusting nut on the tensioner rod until the mark is no longer visible.

➡Do not loosen, or tighten the tensioner adjusting nut for any reason after completing adjustment.

13. Lower the vehicle until the rear wheels are (15–20 cm) 6–8 inch. off the shop floor.
14. Release the park brake foot pedal and verify that rear wheels rotate freely without drag. Then lower the vehicle.

PARKING BRAKE SHOES

REMOVAL & INSTALLATION

See Figures 6 through 9.

1. Raise and support the vehicle.
2. Remove the tire and wheel assembly.
3. Remove the disc brake caliper and rotor, as outlined in this section.
4. Lockout the parking brake cable.
5. Disengage the park brake cable from behind the rotor assembly to allow easier disassembly of the park brake shoes.
6. Disassemble the rear park brake shoes.

To install:

7. Reassemble the rear park brake shoes.
8. Release the parking brake cable.
9. Adjust the rear park brake shoes.
10. Install the disc brake rotor and caliper.
11. Install the tire and wheel assembly.
12. Lower the vehicle.

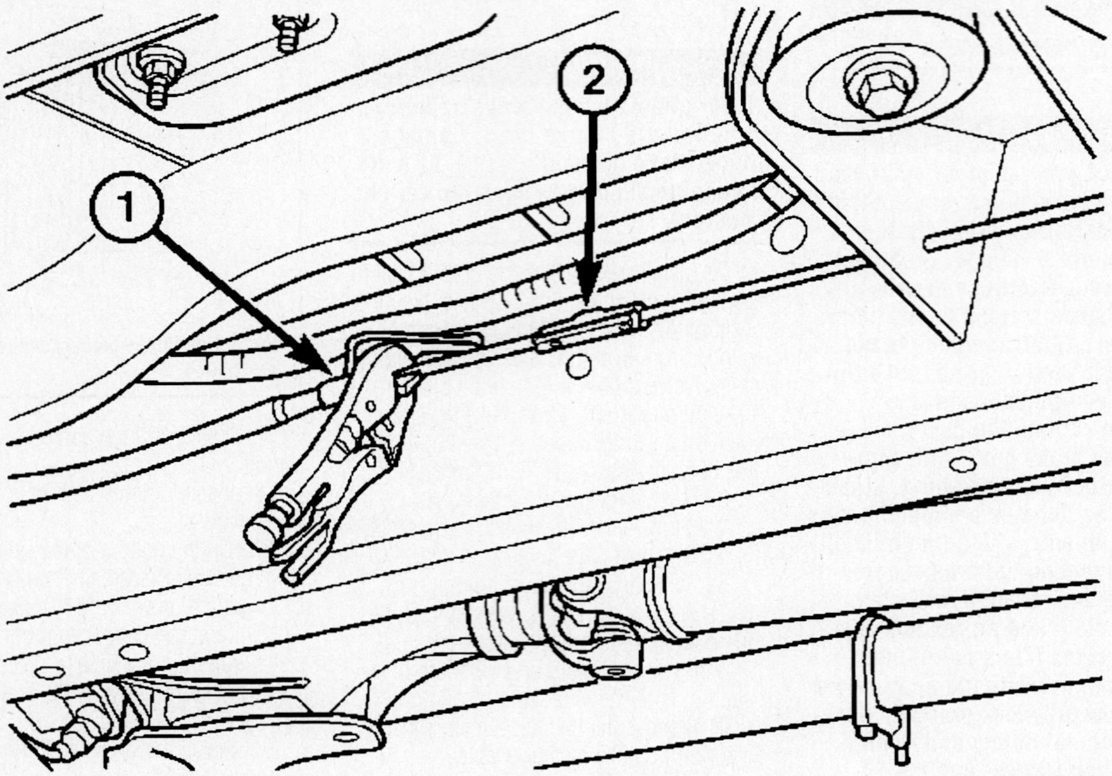

Fig. 6 Use a pair of locking pliers (1) to lock out the parking brake cable (2)

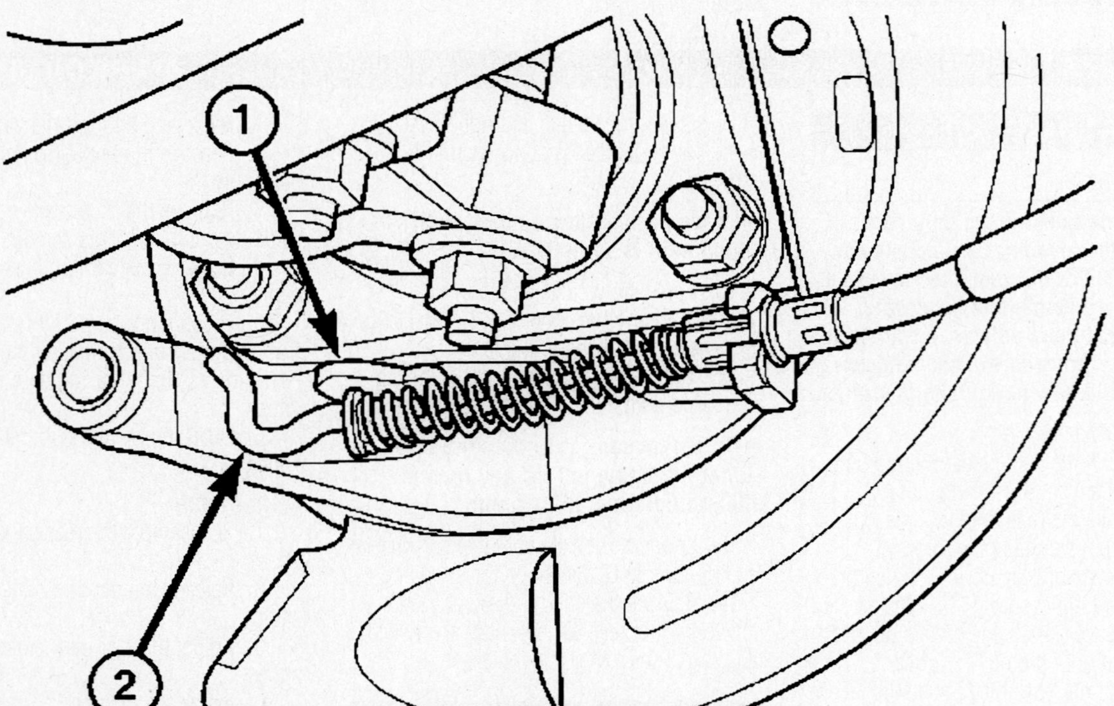

Fig. 7 View of the lever (1) and parking brake cable end (2)

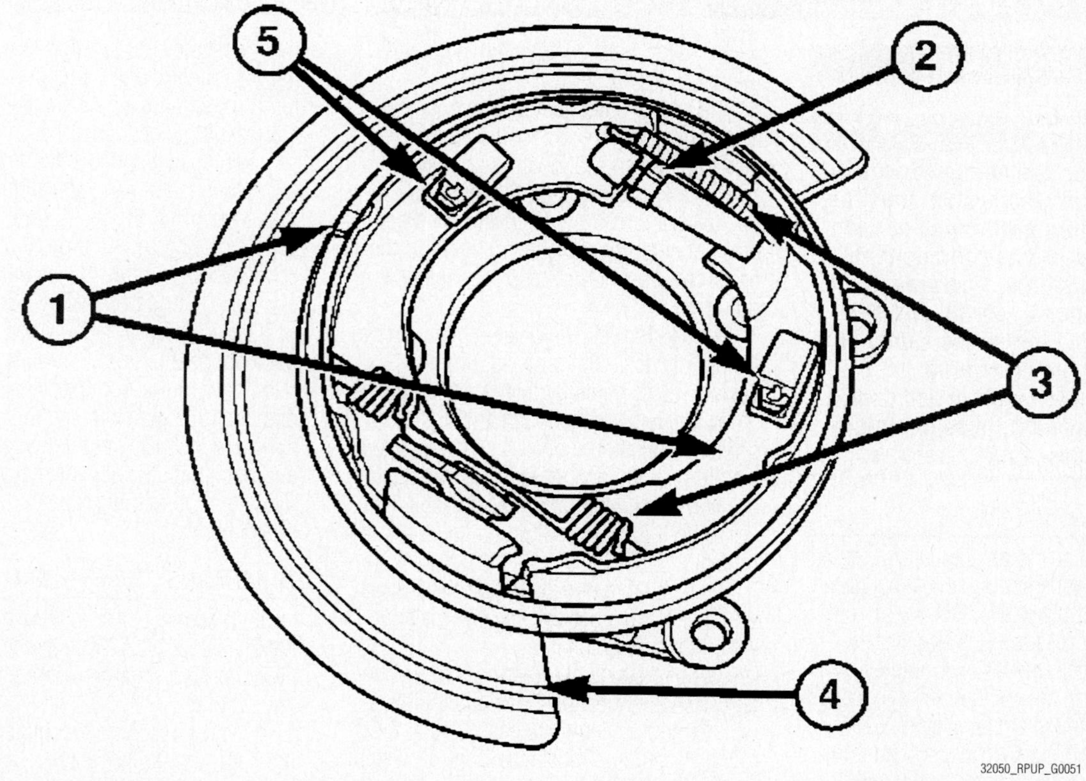

Fig. 8 View of the parking brake shoes (1), adjuster (2), return springs (3), splash shield (4) and hold-downs (5)

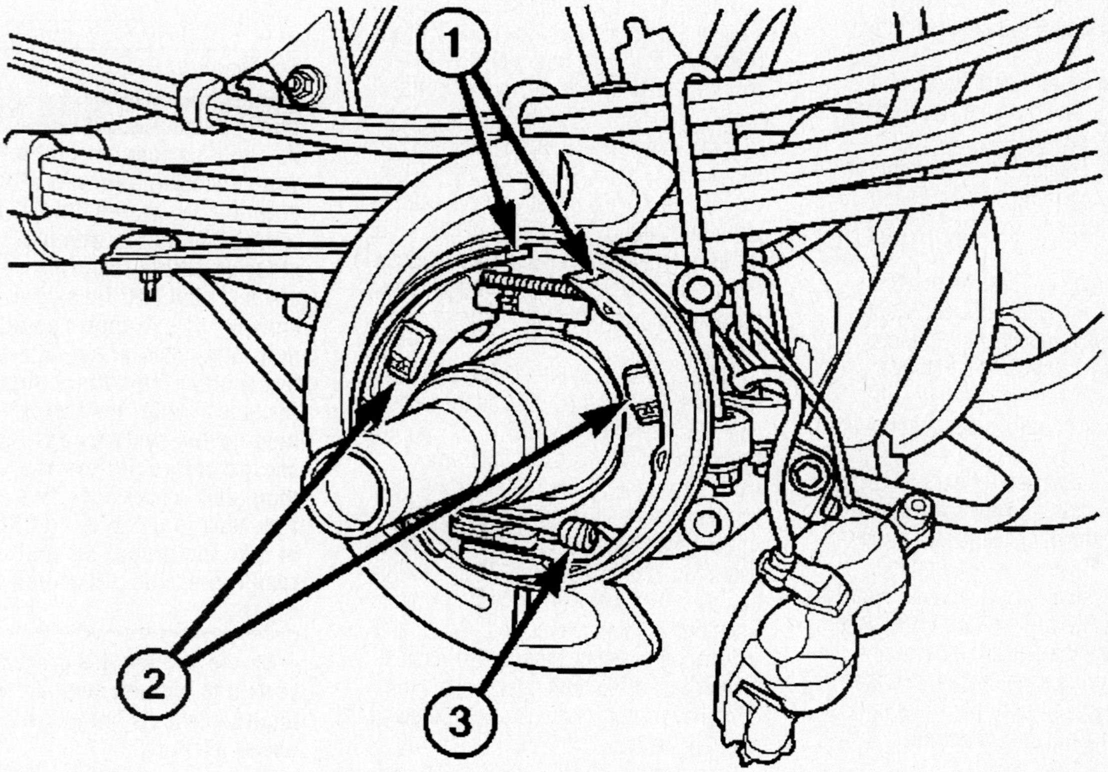

Fig. 9 View of the assembled parking brake shoes (1), hold-downs (2) and return springs (3)

GENERAL INFORMATION

CAUTION

These vehicles are equipped with an air bag system. The system must be disarmed before performing service on, or around, system components, the steering column, instrument panel components, wiring and sensors. Failure to follow the safety precautions and the disarming procedure could result in accidental air bag deployment, possible injury and unnecessary system repairs.

SERVICE PRECAUTIONS

Disconnect and isolate the battery negative cable before beginning any airbag system component diagnosis, testing, removal, or installation procedures. Allow system capacitor to discharge for two minutes before beginning any component service. This will disable the airbag system. Failure to disable the airbag system may result in accidental airbag deployment, personal injury, or death.

Do not place an intact undeployed airbag face down on a solid surface. The airbag will propel into the air if accidentally deployed and may result in personal injury or death.

When carrying or handling an undeployed airbag, the trim side (face) of the airbag should be pointing towards the body to minimize possibility of injury if accidental deployment occurs. Failure to do this may result in personal injury or death.

Replace airbag system components with OEM replacement parts. Substitute parts may appear interchangeable, but internal differences may result in inferior occupant protection. Failure to do so may result in occupant personal injury or death.

Wear safety glasses, rubber gloves, and long sleeved clothing when cleaning powder residue from vehicle after an airbag deployment. Powder residue emitted from a deployed airbag can cause skin irritation. Flush affected area with cool water if irritation is experienced. If nasal or throat irritation is experienced, exit the vehicle for fresh air until the irritation ceases. If irritation continues, see a physician.

Do not use a replacement airbag that is not in the original packaging. This may result in improper deployment, personal injury, or death.

The factory installed fasteners, screws and bolts used to fasten airbag components have a special coating and are specifically designed for the airbag system. Do not use substitute fasteners. Use only original equipment fasteners listed in the parts catalog when fastener replacement is required.

During, and following, any child restraint anchor service, due to impact event or vehicle repair, carefully inspect all mounting hardware, tether straps, and anchors for proper installation, operation, or damage. If a child restraint anchor is found damaged in any way, the anchor must be replaced. Failure to do this may result in personal injury or death.

Deployed and non-deployed airbags may or may not have live pyrotechnic material within the airbag inflator.

Do not dispose of driver/passenger/curtain airbags or seat belt tensioners unless you are sure of complete deployment. Refer to the Hazardous Substance Control System for proper disposal.

Dispose of deployed airbags and tensioners consistent with state, provincial, local, and federal regulations.

After any airbag component testing or service, do not connect the battery negative cable. Personal injury or death may result if the system test is not performed first.

If the vehicle is equipped with the Occupant Classification System (OCS), do not connect the battery negative cable before performing the OCS Verification Test using the scan tool and the appropriate diagnostic information. Personal injury or death may result if the system test is not performed properly.

Never replace both the Occupant Restraint Controller (ORC) and the Occupant Classification Module (OCM) at the same time. If both require replacement, replace one, then perform the Airbag System test before replacing the other.

Both the ORC and the OCM store Occupant Classification System (OCS) calibration data, which they transfer to one another when one of them is replaced. If both are replaced at the same time, an irreversible fault will be set in both modules and the OCS may malfunction and cause personal injury or death.

If equipped with OCS, the Seat Weight Sensor is a sensitive, calibrated unit and must be handled carefully. Do not drop or handle roughly. If dropped or damaged, replace with another sensor. Failure to do so may result in occupant injury or death.

If equipped with OCS, the front passenger seat must be handled carefully as well. When removing the seat, be careful when setting on floor not to drop. If dropped, the sensor may be inoperative, could result in occupant injury, or possibly death.

If equipped with OCS, when the passenger front seat is on the floor, no one should sit in the front passenger seat. This uneven force may damage the sensing ability of the seat weight sensors. If sat on and damaged, the sensor may be inoperative, could result in occupant injury, or possibly death.

DISARMING THE SYSTEM

1. Disconnect and isolate the negative battery cable. Wait 2 minutes for the system capacitor to discharge before performing any service.
2. When repairs are completed, connect the negative battery cable.

ARMING THE SYSTEM

To arm the Supplemental Restraint System (SRS), connect the negative battery cable.

CLOCKSPRING CENTERING

See Figure 10.

WARNING

To avoid serious or fatal injury on vehicles equipped with airbags, disable the Supplemental Restraint System (SRS) before attempting any steering wheel, steering column, airbag, seat belt tensioner, impact sensor, or instrument panel component diagnosis or service. Disconnect and isolate the battery negative (ground) cable, then wait two minutes for the system capacitor to discharge before performing further diagnosis or service. This is the only sure way to disable the SRS. Failure to take the proper precautions could result in accidental airbag deployment.

➡**Before starting this procedure, be certain to turn the steering wheel until the front wheels are in the straight-ahead position.**

1. Place the front wheels in the straight-ahead position.

2. Remove the clockspring from the steering column.

3. Rotate the clockspring rotor (7) clockwise to the end of its travel. Do not apply excessive torque.

4. From the end of the clockwise travel, rotate the rotor about two and one-half turns counterclockwise. The engagement dowel (5) should end up at the bottom, and the airbag pigtail wires (1) and connector receptacles (3) should be at the top. Turn the rotor slightly clockwise or counterclockwise as necessary so that the slots for the clockspring locking pin (2) are in alignment.

5. The clockspring is now centered. Secure the clockspring rotor to the clockspring case to maintain clockspring centering until it is reinstalled on the steering column.

6. The front wheels should still be in the straight-ahead position. Reinstall the clockspring onto the steering column.

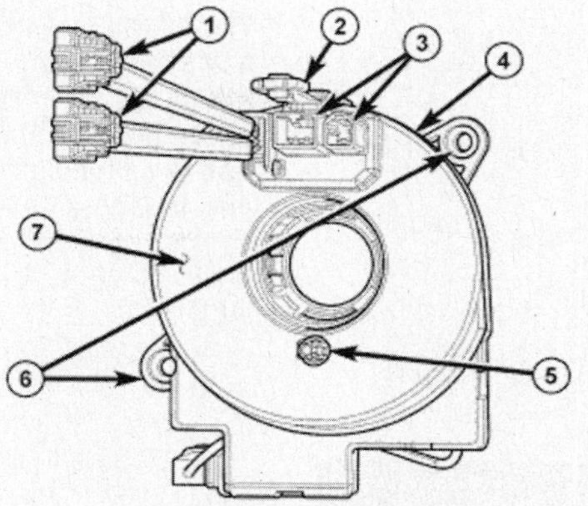

Fig. 10 Clockspring assembly

DRIVETRAIN

AUTOMATIC TRANSMISSION ASSEMBLY

REMOVAL & INSTALLATION

1. Before servicing the vehicle, refer to the Precautions Section.
2. Remove or disconnect the following:
   - Negative battery cable
   - Rear driveshaft
   - Crankshaft Position (CKP) sensor
   - Exhaust front pipe
   - Transmission braces and skid plates, if equipped
   - Starter motor
   - Transmission oil cooler lines
   - Torque converter access cover
   - Torque converter
   - Transmission oil dipstick tube
   - Vehicle Speed (VSS) sensor connector
   - Park/Neutral switch connector
   - Shift cable
   - Throttle valve cable, for vehicles with diesel engines remove Transmission Throttle Valve Actuator (TTVA).
   - Transmission mount and crossmember. Support the transmission.
   - Front driveshaft and transfer case, if equipped
   - Transmission flange bolts
   - Transmission

To install:

3. Install or connect the following:
   - Transmission. Tighten the flange bolts to 65 ft. lbs. (87 Nm).
   - Front driveshaft and transfer case, if equipped
   - Transmission mount and crossmember
   - Throttle valve cable
   - Shift cable
   - Park/Neutral switch connector
   - VSS sensor connector
   - Transmission oil dipstick tube
   - Torque converter. Tighten the bolts to 23 ft. lbs. (31 Nm) for 10.75 inch converters and to 35 ft. lbs. (47 Nm) for 12.2 inch converters.
   - Torque converter access cover
   - Transmission oil cooler lines
   - Starter motor
   - Transmission braces, if equipped. Tighten the bolts to 30 ft. lbs. (41 Nm).
   - Exhaust front pipe
   - CKP sensor
   - Rear driveshaft
   - Negative battery cable
4. Refill the transmission with MOPAR® ATF+4. For AS68RC transmissions use MOPAR® AS68RC Automatic Transmission Fluid only.

MANUAL TRANSMISSION ASSEMBLY

REMOVAL & INSTALLATION

1. Before servicing the vehicle, refer to the Precautions Section.
2. Remove or disconnect the following:
   - Negative battery cable
   - Shift lever and tower assembly
   - Crankshaft Position (CKP) sensor
   - Skidplate, if equipped
   - Rear driveshaft
   - Front driveshaft, if equipped
   - Transfer case shift linkage, if equipped
   - Transmission mount and crossmember. Support the transmission.
   - Exhaust front pipe
   - Clutch slave cylinder
   - Starter motor
   - Vehicle Speed (VSS) sensor connector
   - Reverse light switch connector
   - Transmission flange bolts
   - Transmission

To install:

3. Install or connect the following:
   - Transmission. Tighten the flange bolts to 40–45 ft. lbs. (54–61 Nm).
   - Reverse light switch connector
   - Vehicle Speed (VSS) sensor connector
   - Starter motor

- Clutch slave cylinder
- Exhaust front pipe
- Transmission mount and cross-member. Tighten the fasteners to 50 ft. lbs. (68 Nm).
- Transfer case shift linkage, if equipped
- Front driveshaft, if equipped
- Rear driveshaft
- Skidplate, if equipped
- CKP sensor
- Shift lever and tower assembly
- Negative battery cable

CLUTCH

REMOVAL & INSTALLATION

See Figure 11.

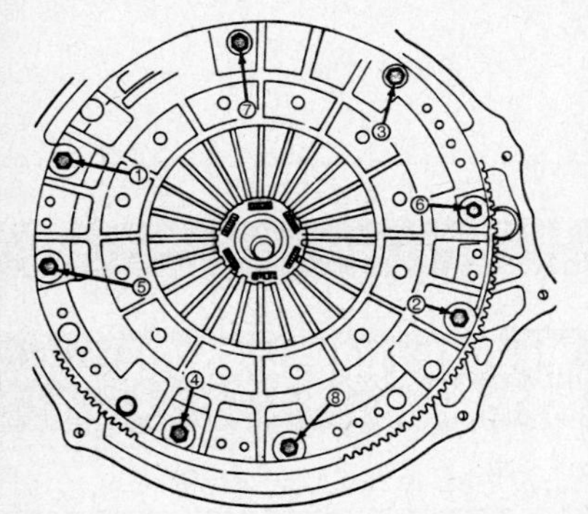

7924DG83

Fig. 11 Pressure plate torque sequence

1. Before servicing the vehicle, refer to the Precautions Section.
2. Remove or disconnect the following:
   - Negative battery cable
   - Transfer case, if equipped
   - Transmission
   - Pressure plate. Loosen the bolts evenly in ½ turn steps.
   - Clutch disc

To install:

3. Install or connect the following:
   - Clutch disc and pressure plate. Tighten the pressure plate bolts evenly in ½ turns to 21 ft. lbs. (28 Nm) for 2001; 37 ft. lbs. (50 Nm) for 2002–04 V6 and V8, or 23 ft. lbs. (30 Nm).
   - Transmission
   - Transfer case, if equipped
   - Negative battery cable

MASTER & SLAVE CYLINDER

REMOVAL & INSTALLATION

See Figures 12 and 13.

✲✲ WARNING

The hydraulic linkage has a quick disconnect at the slave cylinder. This fitting should never be disconnected or tampered with. Once the hydraulic line is connected to the slave cylinder, it should never be disconnected.

1. Before servicing the vehicle, refer to the Precautions Section.
2. Raise and support vehicle.
3. Remove nuts attaching slave cylinder to studs on clutch housing .
4. Remove heat shield over hydraulic line.
5. Remove slave cylinder from clutch housing.
6. Remove the plastic clip securing the hydraulic line to the dash panel from the lower dash panel flange.
7. Remove the plastic clip securing hydraulic line to the dash panel from the upper dash panel stud.
8. Lower the vehicle.
9. Disconnect clutch pedal interlock switch connector.
10. Remove clutch master cylinder rod pin.
11. Verify that cap on clutch master cylinder reservoir is tight. This will avoid spillage during removal.
12. Remove clutch master cylinder nuts holding cylinder to the dash panel.
13. Remove clutch cylinders, reservoir and connecting lines from vehicle.

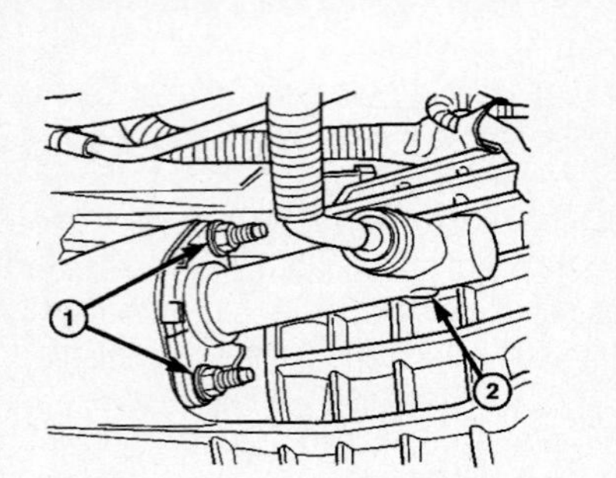

22043_RPUP_G0004

Fig. 13 Clutch Slave cylinder and retaining nuts

To install:

14. Position cylinders and connecting line in vehicle engine compartment. Position the clutch hydraulic line against the dash panel and behind all engine hoses and wiring.
15. Apply a light coating of grease to the inside diameter of the master cylinder push rod eye.
16. Install clutch master cylinder on dash panel and tighten clutch master cylinder nuts to 21 ft. lbs. (28 Nm).
17. Install clutch master cylinder push rod pin.
18. Connect clutch pedal position interlock switch connector.
19. Install the plastic clip securing hydraulic line to the dash panel into the lower dash panel flange.

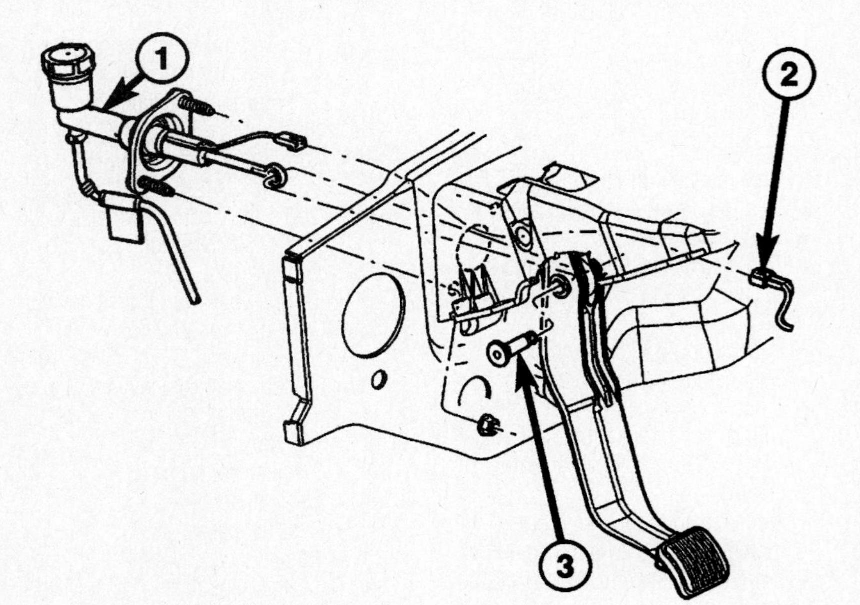

22043_RPUP_G0003

Fig. 12 Clutch master cylinder (1) and related parts

20. Install the plastic clip securing hydraulic line to the dash panel onto the upper dash panel stud.
21. Raise the vehicle.
22. Install slave cylinder and verify cylinder rod is properly seated in release lever.
23. Install and tighten slave cylinder nuts to 17 ft. lbs. (23 Nm).
24. If new clutch linkage is being installed, connect the clutch hydraulic line to the clutch slave cylinder.
25. Install heat shield over hydraulic line.
26. Operate the linkage several times to verify proper operation.

RELEASE BEARING

REMOVAL & INSTALLATION

1. Before servicing the vehicle, refer to the Precautions Section.
2. Remove transmission and transfer case, if equipped.
3. Remove spring clip.
4. Disconnect release bearing from release fork and remove bearing.
5. Inspect the bearing slide surface on the transmission front bearing retainer. Replace retainer if slide surface is scored, worn, or cracked.
6. Inspect the release lever and pivot stud. Be sure stud is secure and in good condition. Be sure fork is not distorted or worn. Replace fork spring clips if bent or damaged.

To install:

7. Lubricate input shaft splines, bearing retainer slide surface, lever pivot ball stud, and release lever pivot surface with Mopar® high temperature bearing grease.
8. Install the release fork and release bearing. Be sure fork and bearing are properly secured by spring clips. Also be sure that the release fork is installed properly. The rear side of the release lever has one end with a raised area. This raised area goes toward the slave cylinder side of the transmission.
9. Install clutch housing, if removed.
10. Install transmission and transfer case.
11. Check clutch master cylinder fluid level.

BLEEDING

Standard Procedure

To determine if the master cylinder assembly requires bleeding or if the complete system requires bleeding:

1. Uncouple the clutch master cylinder line from the clutch slave cylinder with quick Disconnect Tool 6638.
2. Slowly depress the clutch pedal.

⁂ WARNING

Do not apply too much force as this will cause the uncoupled male coupling to blow out.

3. If the pedal feels hard in a relatively short distance, air is present in the clutch slave cylinder.
4. If the pedal feels spongy air is present in the master cylinder assembly.

Linkage Bleed

1. Remove the reservoir cap taking care not to damage the diaphragm. If fluid level is not up to the step in the reservoir add D.O.T. 4 brake fluid.

⁂ WARNING

Use only D.O.T. 4 compatible brake fluid. Substitutes will cause system malfunction.

2. Slowly depressing the clutch pedal while opening the clutch slave cylinder bleed screw.
3. Holding down the clutch pedal and tighten bleed screw to 11–14 ft. lbs. (15–20 Nm).
4. Repeat Step 2 and Step 3 two times then check fluid level in reservoir.
5. Pump clutch pedal rapidly a minimum of 10 times. If clutch pedal still feels spongy, repeat Step 2 through Step 5.

Master Cylinder Bleed

1. Remove the reservoir cap taking care not to damage the diaphragm. If the fluid level is not up to the step in the reservoir, add D.O.T. 4 brake fluid.

⁂ WARNING

Use only D.O.T. 4 compatible brake fluid. Other than D.O.T 4 will cause system malfunction.

2. Open the male quick connect coupling by depressing the poppet in the coupling while depress the clutch pedal to the floor.
3. Close the quick connect coupling by releasing the poppet while holding the clutch pedal to the floor.
4. Release the pedal.
5. Repeat Step 3 through Step 5 two more times and check fluid level.
6. Couple the system back together. Then pump clutch pedal rapidly a minimum of 10 times.
7. If clutch pedal still feels spongy repeat Step 3 through Step 7.

TRANSFER CASE ASSEMBLY

REMOVAL & INSTALLATION

See Figure 14.

1. Before servicing the vehicle, refer to the Precautions Section.
2. Shift the transfer case into **2WD**.
3. Mark front and rear propeller shafts for alignment reference.
4. Support the transmission with jack stand.
5. Remove the transfer case skid plate, if equipped.
6. Disconnect front and rear propeller shafts at transfer case.
7. Disconnect transfer case shift motor and mode sensor wire connectors.
8. Disconnect transfer case vent hose.
9. Support transfer case with transmission jack.
10. Secure transfer case to jack with chains.
11. Remove nuts attaching the transfer case to transmission.
12. Pull transfer case and jack rearward to disengage transfer case.
13. Remove transfer case from under vehicle.

To install:

14. Mount transfer case on a transmission jack.
15. Secure transfer case to jack with chains.
16. Position transfer case under vehicle.
17. Align transfer case and transmission shafts and install transfer case onto the transmission.
18. Install and tighten transfer case attaching nuts to 23 ft. lbs. (31 Nm).
19. Connect the vent hose.
20. Connect the shift motor and mode sensor wiring connectors. Secure wire harness to clips on transfer case.
21. Align and connect the propeller shafts.
22. Fill transfer case with correct fluid as listed below:
23. Recommended lubricant for the NV241 GENII, NV271, NV243, NV244 GENII, and NV273 transfer cases is MOPAR® ATF +4, Automatic Transmission Fluid.
24. Recommended lubricant for the NV246 transfer case is MOPAR®NVG 246 Automatic Transmission Fluid or equivalent.
25. Install skid plate, if equipped.
26. Remove transmission jack and support stand.

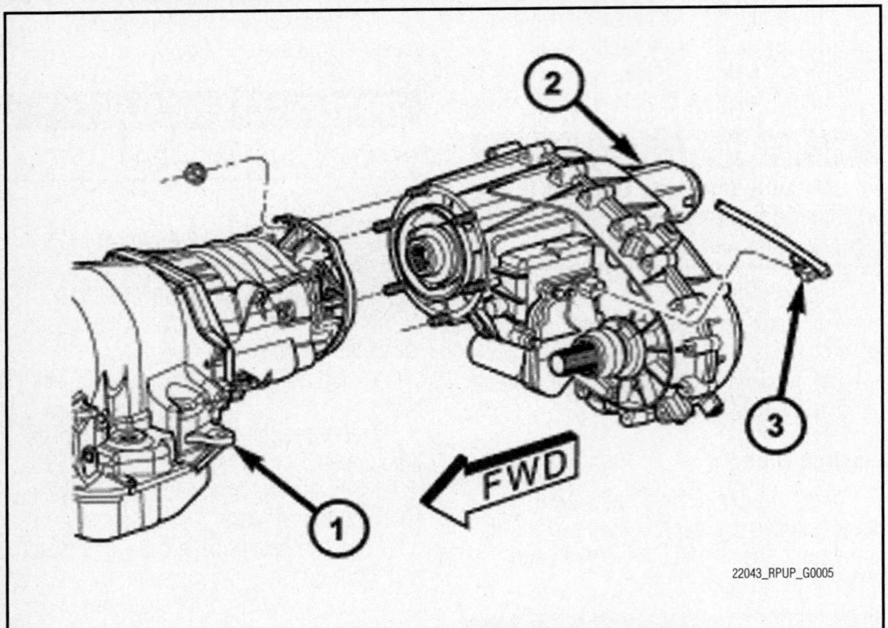

Fig. 14 Transfer case (2) removal from transmission (1) wire connectors (3)

27. Lower vehicle and verify transfer case shift operation.

FRONT DRIVESHAFT

REMOVAL & INSTALLATION

Light Duty

1. Before servicing the vehicle, refer to the Precautions Section.
2. With vehicle in neutral, position vehicle on hoist.
3. Remove exhaust crossover pipe.
4. Mark a line across the axle companion flange, propeller shaft, flange yoke and transfer case for installation reference.
5. Remove axle/transfer case companion flange bolts. Remove dust boot clamp from the C/V joint end of the shaft if equipped.
6. Remove the propeller shaft.

To install:

7. Install propeller shaft with all reference marks aligned.
8. Install with dust boot clamp at transfer case end.
9. Install new axle companion flange bolts and tighten to 85 ft. lbs. (115 Nm).

➡Companion flange bolts incorporate a Loctite® patch, new bolts should be used. If bolts are not available, clean bolts and apply Loctite® 242 to the threads.

10. Install skid plate, if equipped.

Heavy Duty

See Figure 15.

1. Before servicing the vehicle, refer to the Precautions Section.
2. With vehicle in neutral, position vehicle on hoist.
3. Remove exhaust crossover pipe.
4. Mark a line across axle/transfer case companion flange and propeller shaft flange yokes for installation reference.
5. Remove axle/transfer case companion flange bolts.
6. Remove the propeller shaft.

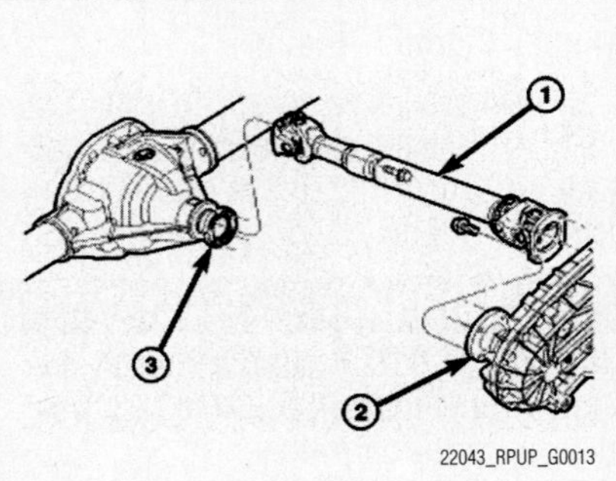

Fig. 15 Propeller shaft (1) axle Flange (2) transfer case flange

To install:

7. Install propeller shaft with all reference marks aligned.
8. Install transfer case companion flange (2) bolts and tighten to 65 ft. lbs. (88 Nm).
9. Install new axle companion flange (3) bolts and tighten to 21 ft. lbs. (28 Nm).

➡Companion flange bolts incorporate a Loctite® patch, new bolts should be used. If bolts are not available, clean the bolts and apply Loctite® 242 to the threads.

10. Install skid plate, if equipped.

FRONT HALFSHAFT

REMOVAL & INSTALLATION

See Figure 16.

1. Before servicing the vehicle, refer to the Precautions Section.
2. Remove or disconnect the following:
   - Skid plate, if equipped
   - Front wheel
   - Hub nut
   - Brake caliper and rotor
3. Unload the suspension with a jack.
4. Remove or disconnect the following:
5. Lower shock absorber bolt
6. Upper ball joint
7. Pry the inner joint out of the differential and remove the axle halfshaft.

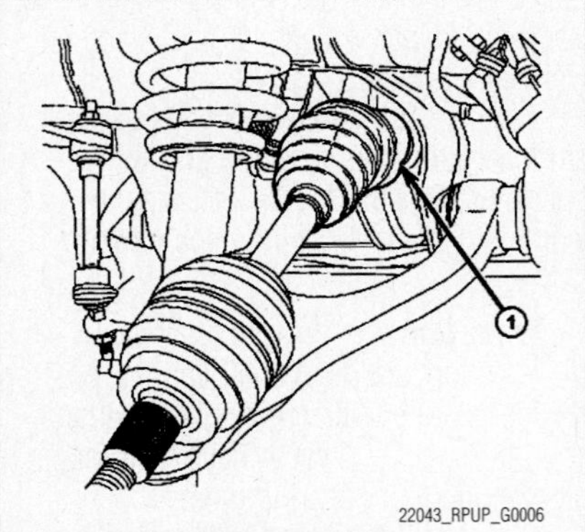

Fig. 16 Halfshaft removal

To install:

8. Install the axle halfshaft so that the snapring is felt to seat in the joint housing groove.
9. Install or connect the following:
   - Ball joint
   - Shock absorber
   - Brake caliper and rotor
   - Hub nut. Tighten the nut to 185 ft. lbs. (251 Nm).
   - Front wheel
   - Skid plate, if equipped

CV-JOINTS OVERHAUL

Outer CV-Joint

See Figure 17.

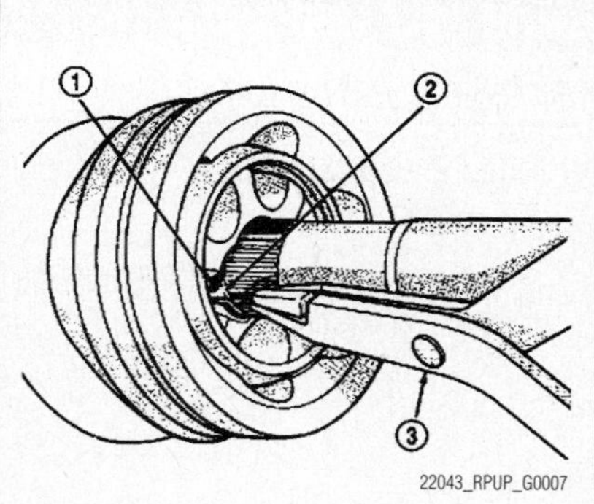

Fig. 17 CV-joint snap ring removal

1. Before servicing the vehicle, refer to the Precautions Section.
2. Remove or disconnect the following:
   - Axle halfshaft from the vehicle
   - CV-joint boot and clamps
   - Snapring
   - CV-joint

To install:

3. Install or connect the following:
   - CV-joint
   - Snapring
   - CV-joint boot and clamps
4. Fill the joint housing and boot with grease and tighten the boot clamps.
5. Install the axle halfshaft.

Inner Tripod Joint

See Figure 18.

1. Before servicing the vehicle, refer to the Precautions Section.
2. Remove or disconnect the following:
   - Axle halfshaft from the vehicle
   - Inner tripod joint boot clamps
   - Tripod joint housing
   - Snapring
   - Circlip
   - Tripod joint

To install:

➡Use new snaprings, clips, and boot clamps for assembly.

3. Install or connect the following:
   - Tripod joint
   - Circlip
   - Snapring
   - Tripod joint housing
4. Fill the tripod joint housing and boot with grease and tighten the boot clamps.
5. Install the axle halfshaft.

FRONT PINION SEAL

REMOVAL & INSTALLATION

9 1/4 AA

See Figure 19.

1. Before servicing the vehicle, refer to the Precautions Section.
2. Mark propeller shaft and pinion flange for installation reference.
3. Remove the propeller shaft.
4. Remove the hub bearings and axle shafts.
5. Rotate pinion gear three or four times.
6. Record pinion torque to rotate with an inch pound torque wrench for installation reference.
7. Hold pinion flange with flange wrench 8979 and remove pinion flange nut and washer.
8. Mark a line across the pinion shaft and flange for installation reference.
9. Remove pinion flange with pinion flange puller 8992.
10. Remove pinion seal with a seal puller.

To install:

11. Install new pinion seal with Installer 8882 and Handle C-4171.
12. Install flange on the pinion shaft with the reference marks aligned.
13. Lightly tap pinion flange onto the pinion, until a few threads are showing.
14. Install flange washer and new pinion nut.
15. Hold flange with flange wrench 8979 and tighten pinion nut until pinion end play is taken up.
16. Rotate pinion flange several times to seat bearings.
17. Measure pinion torque to rotate with an inch pound torque wrench. Pinion torque to rotate should be equal to recorded reading plus an additional 3–5 inch. lbs. (0.40–0.57 Nm).
18. If torque to rotating is low, tighten the pinion nut in 5 ft. lbs. (6.8 Nm) increments until pinion torque to rotate is achieved.
19. Rotate pinion several times then verify pinion torque to rotate again.
20. Install the axle shafts and hub bearings.
21. Install propeller shaft with reference marks aligned.

C205FD

See Figure 20.

1. Before servicing the vehicle, refer to the Precautions Section.
2. With axle in **2WD** remove front propeller shaft and left half shaft.
3. Rotate pinion gear three or four times and verify pinion rotates smoothly.
4. Record pinion torque to rotate with an inch pound torque wrench, for installation reference.
5. Position Holder 6719 against the companion flange and install a four bolts and washers into the threaded holes and tighten the bolts.
6. Remove pinion nut.
7. Mark a line across the pinion shaft and flange for installation reference.
8. Remove the companion flange with Remover C—452.

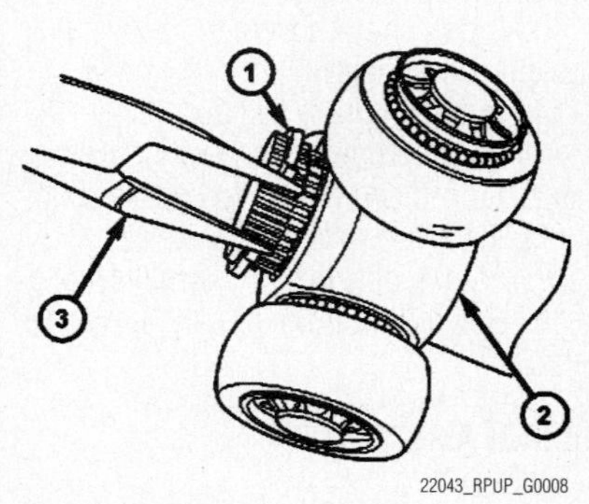

Fig. 18 Tripod snap ring removal

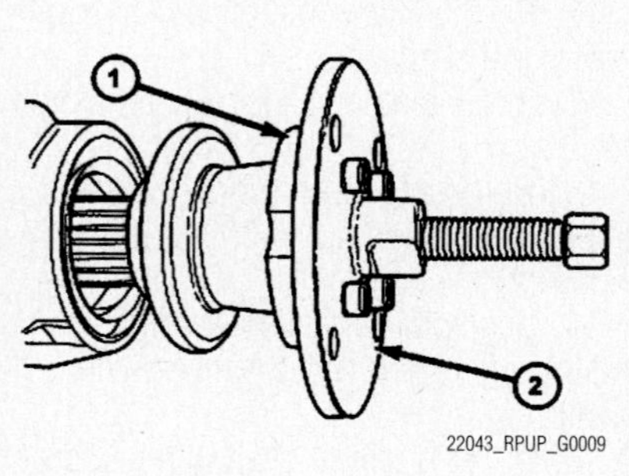

Fig. 19 Pinion flange removal with tool 8992

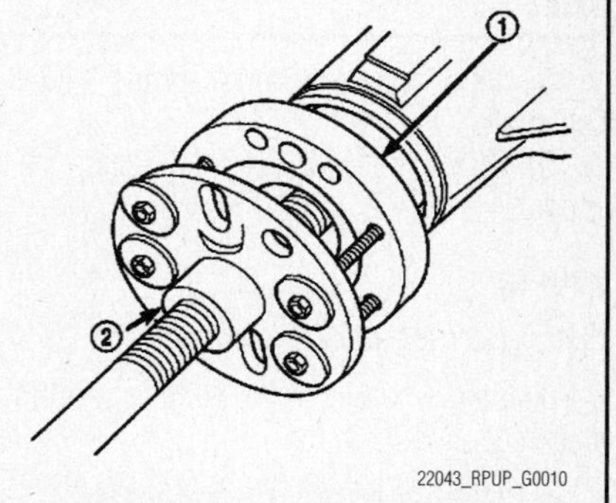

Fig. 20 Pinion flange (1) removal with C—452 (2)

9. Remove pinion seal with a seal puller.

To install:

10. Apply a light coating of gear lubricant on the lip of pinion seal
11. Install seal with Installer 8695 and Handle C-4171.
12. Install flange on the pinion shaft with the reference marks aligned.
13. Install companion flange onto the pinion with Installer C-3718 and Holder 6719A.
14. Position holder against the companion flange and install four bolts and washers into the threaded holes. Tighten the bolt and washer so that the holder is held to the flange.
15. Install a new pinion nut onto the pinion shaft and tighten the pinion nut until there is zero bearing end-play

✲✲ WARNING

Do not exceed 200 ft. lbs. (271 Nm) the minimum tightening torque when installing the companion flange at this point. Never loosen pinion nut to decrease pinion bearing rotating torque and never exceed specified preload torque. Failure to follow these instructions will damage the axle.

16. Measure pinion Torque To Rotate with an inch pound torque wrench. Pinion Torque To Rotate should be equal to recorded reading plus an additional 5 inch. lbs. (0.56 Nm).
17. If rotating torque is low, tighten the pinion nut in 5 ft. lbs. (6.8 Nm) increments until pinion Torque To Rotate is achieved.

✲✲ WARNING

If maximum tightening torque 350 ft. lbs. (475 Nm) is reached prior to reaching the required rotating torque, the collapsible spacer may have been damaged. Failure to follow these instructions will damage the axle.

18. Install the propeller shaft and the left half shaft.
19. Check the fluid level and add as needed.

275FBI

See Figures 21 and 22.

1. Before servicing the vehicle, refer to the Precautions Section.
2. With the vehicle in neutral, position vehicle on hoist.
3. Remove the propeller shaft.

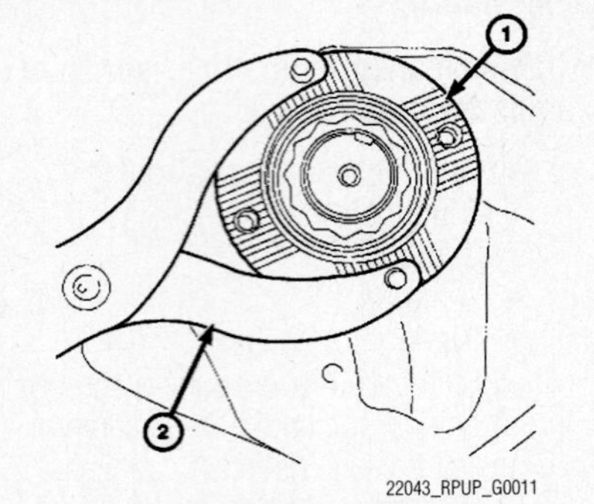

Fig. 21 Pinion flange (1) with Holder C — 3281 (2)

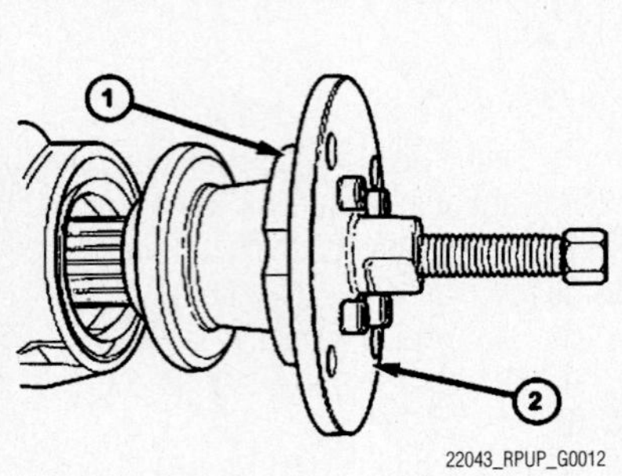

Fig. 22 Pinion flange (1) pinion flange puller 8992 (2)

4. Bend the pinion flange nut collar lock out of the pinion shaft keyway.
5. Hold the pinion flange with Holder C-3281 and remove pinion flange nut.
6. Mark a line across the pinion shaft and flange for installation reference.
7. Remove pinion flange with pinion flange puller 8992.
8. Remove pinion seal with a seal puller.

To install:

9. Install new pinion seal with installer 10069.
10. Apply a light coat of Teflon thread sealant, to pinion flange splines.
11. Position flange on pinion shaft with reference marks aligned.
12. Install pinion flange and new pinion nut.
13. Hold flange with Holder C-3281 and tighten pinion nut to 369 ft. lbs. (500 Nm)
14. Bend pinion flange nut collar into pinion keyway with a hammer and punch.
15. Install propeller shaft with reference marks aligned.
16. Check the fluid level and add as needed.

REAR AXLE HOUSING

REMOVAL & INSTALLATION

All Axles Except 302RBI

See Figure 23.

1. Before servicing the vehicle, refer to the Precautions Section.
2. With vehicle in neutral, position vehicle on hoist.
3. Position a lift under axle and secure lift to the axle.
4. Remove all brake components.
5. Mark propeller shaft and companion flange for installation alignment reference.
6. Remove the propeller shaft.
7. Remove the axle vent hose.
8. Remove shock absorbers from axle.
9. Remove the U-bolts from the axle.
10. Remove the axle from the vehicle.

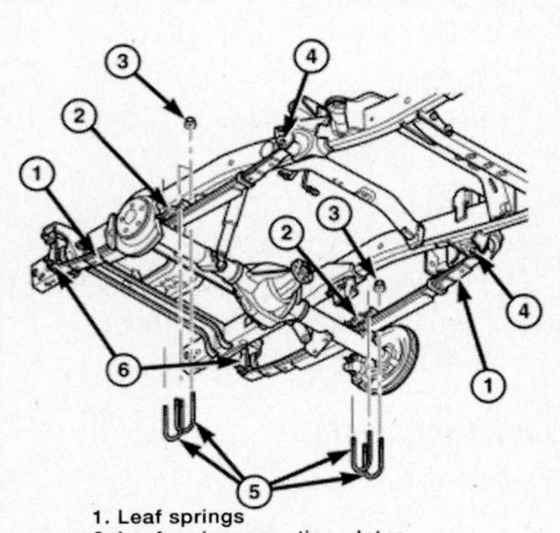

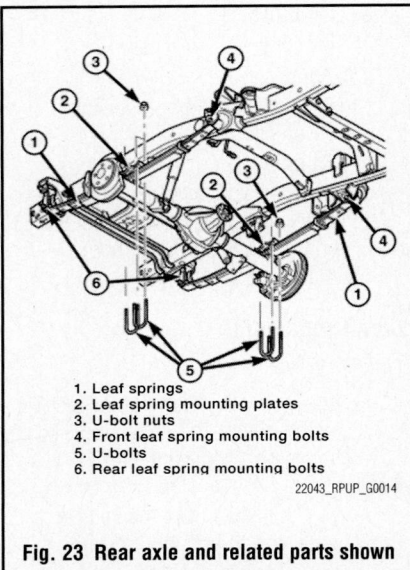

1. Leaf springs
2. Leaf spring mounting plates
3. U-bolt nuts
4. Front leaf spring mounting bolts
5. U-bolts
6. Rear leaf spring mounting bolts

22043_RPUP_G0014

Fig. 23 Rear axle and related parts shown

To install:

11. Raise axle with lift and align to the leaf spring centering bolts.
12. Install axle U-bolts and tighten to 110 ft. lbs. (149 Nm).
13. Install shock absorbers to axle and tighten to specification.
14. Install all brake components.
15. Install propeller shaft with reference marks aligned and tighten to specification.
16. Install the axle vent hose.
17. Fill the differential to specifications.
18. Remove lift from axle and lower the vehicle.

302RBI Axle

1. Before servicing the vehicle, refer to the Precautions Section.

2. With vehicle in neutral, position vehicle on hoist.
3. Position a lift under axle and secure lift to the axle.
4. Mark propeller shaft and companion flange for installation alignment reference.
5. Remove the propeller shaft from pinion flange.
6. Remove axle vent hose axle housing.
7. Remove wiring harness from the brake sensor.
8. Remove brake calipers, rotors, brake lines and park cables from axle housing.
9. Remove shock absorbers and stabilizer bar from the axle.
10. Remove U-bolts nuts from the axle.
11. Remove U-bolts and lower the axle from the vehicle.

To install:

12. Raise axle with lift and align to the leaf spring centering bolts.
13. Install axle U-bolts and tighten nuts to 336 ft. lbs. (455 Nm).
14. Install shock absorbers to axle and tighten nuts to 118 ft. lbs. (160 Nm).
15. Install stabilizer bar to axle and tighten nuts to 48 ft. lbs. (65 Nm).
16. Install rotors, brake calipers, brake lines and park cables to the axle housing.
17. Install the wiring harness to brake sensor.
18. Install the axle vent hose to axle housing.

REAR AXLE SHAFT, BEARING & SEAL

REMOVAL & INSTALLATION

C-Clip Type

See Figures 24 and 25.

1. Before servicing the vehicle, refer to the Precautions Section.
2. Remove or disconnect the following:

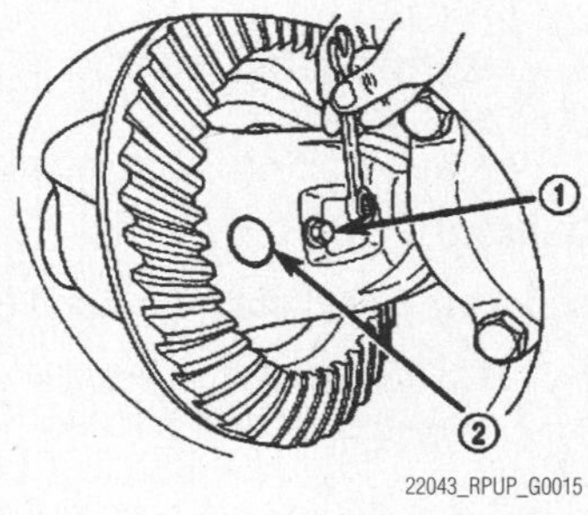

22043_RPUP_G0015

Fig. 24 Differential gear shaft retainer (1) pinion gear shaft (2)

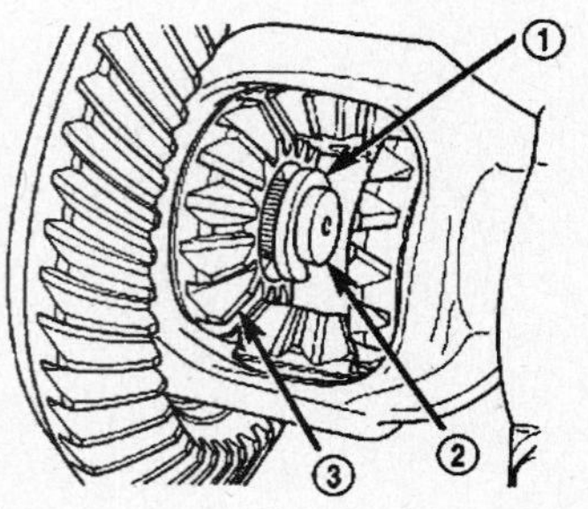

22043_RPUP_G0016

Fig. 25 Remove C-lock (1) from axle shaft (2)

- Rear wheel
- Brake drum
- Differential cover
- Differential gear shaft retainer
- Differential gear shaft
- C-clip
- Axle shaft
- Axle seal
- Axle bearing

To install:

3. Install or connect the following:
   - Axle bearing
   - Axle seal
   - Axle shaft
   - C-clip
   - Differential gear shaft. Use Loctite® and tighten the retainer to 14 ft. lbs. (19 Nm).
   - Differential cover. Tighten the bolts to 30 ft. lbs. (41 Nm).
   - Brake drum
   - Rear wheel
4. Fill the axle assembly with gear oil and check for leaks.

Non C-Clip Type

See Figures 26 through 31.

1. Before servicing the vehicle, refer to the Precautions Section.
2. Remove axle bolts from axle flange.
3. Remove the axle shaft from axle.
4. With Socket 10051 remove hub nut with integrated lock washer from hub spindle.
5. Slide the hub/rotor with bearings off hub spindle with the use of Guide tool 10064.
6. Remove outer bearing from hub.
7. Remove the hub seal from the back of the hub with seal puller.
8. Remove the inner bearing from hub.
9. Remove the outer and inner bearing race from hub with a hammer and brass drift.

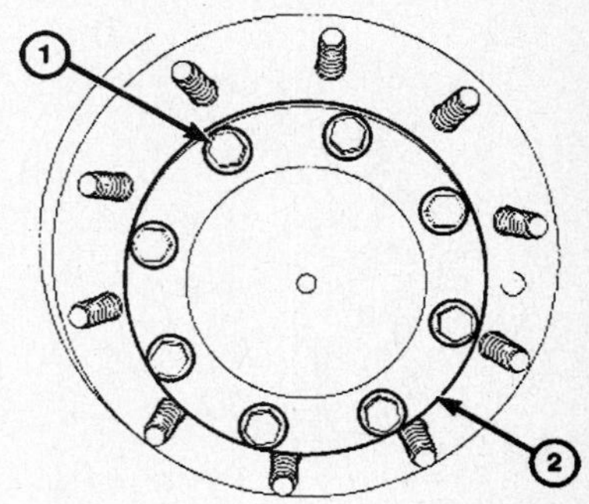

22043_RPUP_G0017

Fig. 26 Axle bolts (1) axle flange (2)

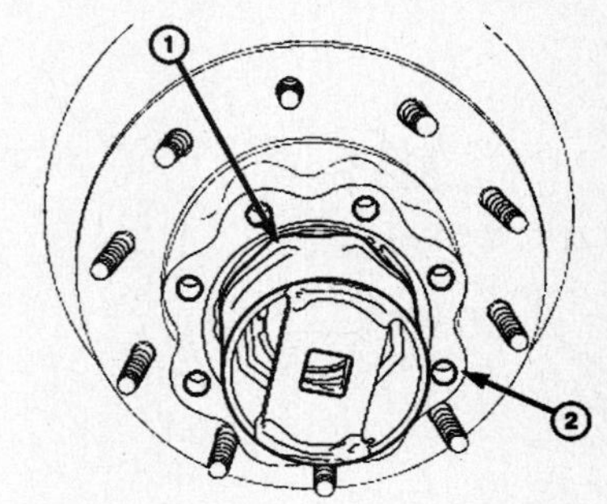

22043_RPUP_G0018

Fig. 27 Hub nut removal shown with socket 10051

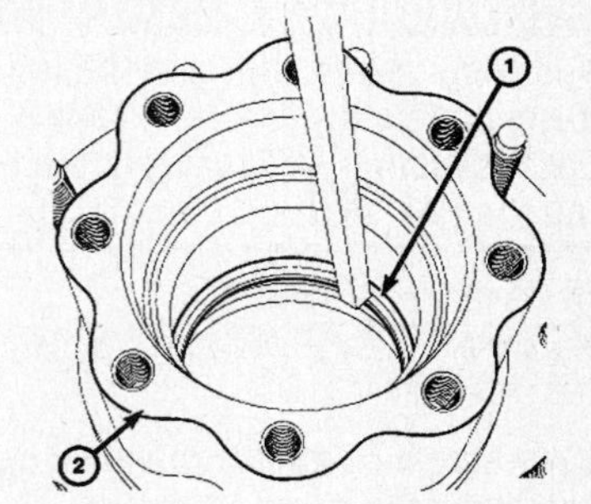

22043_RPUP_G0019

Fig. 28 Inner bearing race (1) removal shown from hub (2)

To install:

10. Install inner and outer hub bearing race, with seal and race driver kit.
11. Lubricate and install the inner hub bearing into hub.
12. Install the hub seal with seal installer kit.
13. Lubricate and install the outer hub bearing into hub.
14. Install the hub and rotor Guide 10064 into the axle spindle.
15. Carefully install the hub and rotor over Guide 10064 onto the axle spindle.

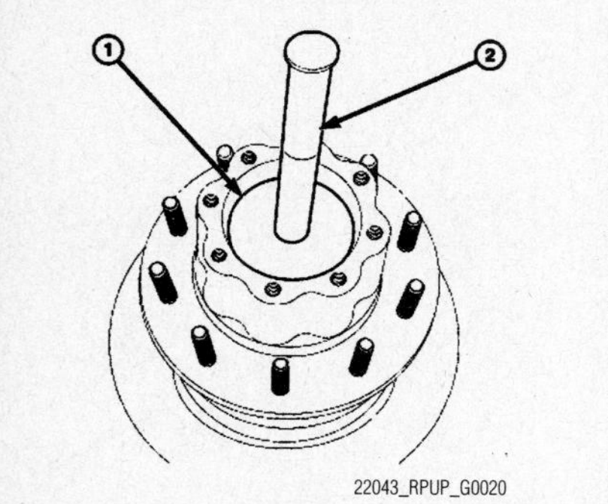

Fig. 29 Outer hub bearing race installation shown with special tools

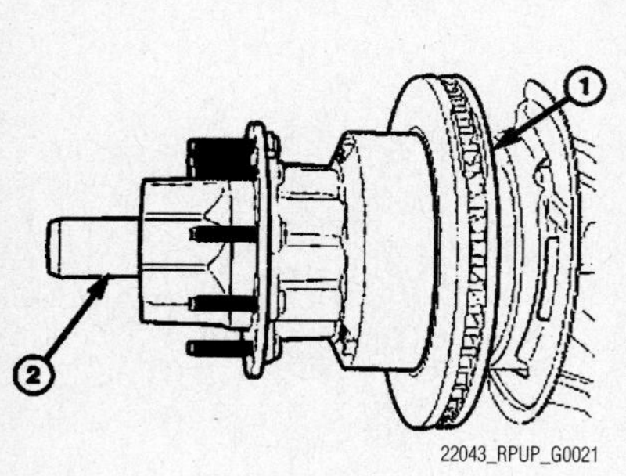

Fig. 30 Hub and rotor installation with guide tool 10064 installed

WARNING

Never support hub with just the inner bearing and seal. Failure to follow these instruction will result in damaging the hub seal.

16. Remove the guide tool.
17. Install the hub bearing nut with integrated lock washer.

➡Integrated lock washer tab must be aligned with the spindle keyway.

18. Tighten the hub nut with Socket 10051 to 70 ft. lbs. (95 Nm) while rotating the hub. Then back off nut 90 degrees and retighten nut to 30 ft. lbs. (41 Nm). This will set hub to zero end-play.
19. Install a new O-ring on axle flange.
20. Install the axle shaft.
21. Install axle bolts through axle flange and tighten to 98 ft. lbs. (133 Nm).
22. Remove fill plug, from right side of carrier.
23. With the axle level, fill carrier with lubricant to the bottom of the fill plug hole.
24. Install fill plug and tighten to 50 ft. lbs. (68 Nm).

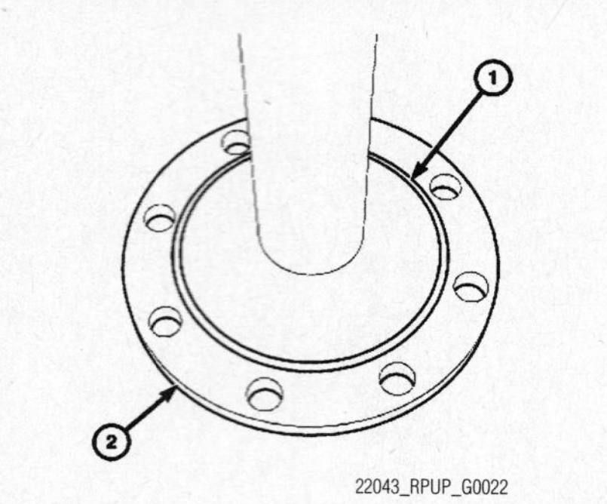

Fig. 31 O-ring (1) and Axle flange (2) shown

WARNING

Wheel hub cavities must be filled with lubricate before using axle. Failure to follow these instructions will result in hub bearing damage.

25. Wheel hub cavities oil fill instruction are as follows:
26. Raise right end of axle six inches. Hold in this position for one minute to fill left hub with lubricate.
27. Lower the axle.
28. Raise left end of axle six inches. Hold in this position for one minute to fill right hub with lubricate.
29. Lower the axle.
30. Remove fill plug, from right side of carrier.
31. With axle level, fill carrier with lubricant to the bottom of the fill plug hole.

➡Axle will require approximately 40 oz. (1.18 L) of additional lubricant.

32. Install fill plug and tighten to 50 ft. lbs. (68 Nm).

REAR DRIVESHAFT

REMOVAL & INSTALLATION

1. Before servicing the vehicle, refer to the Precautions Section.
2. With vehicle in neutral, position vehicle on hoist.
3. Mark propeller shaft pinion flange and propeller shaft flange with installation reference marks.
4. If equipped with manual transmission, mark manual transmission flange and propeller shaft flange for installation reference.
5. If equipped with a center bearing mark an outline of the center bearing on the center bearing bracket for installation reference. Then support propeller shaft and remove mounting bolts.
6. Remove pinion flange bolts from propeller shaft.
7. Slide propeller shaft back off automatic transmission/transfer case output shaft, then mark propeller shaft and transmission/transfer case output shaft for installation reference.
8. If equipped with manual transmission remove flange bolts.
9. Remove propeller shaft the from vehicle.

WARNING

Failure to follow these instructions may result in a driveline vibration.

To install:

10. Slide slip yoke onto automatic transmission/transfer case output shaft with reference marks aligned.
11. If equipped with manual transmission, align transmission flange and propeller shaft reference marks. Install new flange bolts and tighten to 85 ft. lbs. (115 Nm)
12. If two piece propeller shaft, align center bearing with reference marks on center bearing bracket and tighten bolts to 40 ft. lbs. (54 Nm).
13. Align reference marks on propeller shaft and pinion flange. Install new companion flange bolts and tighten to 85 ft. lbs. (115 Nm).

WARNING

Failure to follow these instructions may result in a driveline vibration.

REAR PINION SEAL

REMOVAL & INSTALLATION

C-Clip Type

1. Before servicing the vehicle, refer to the Precautions Section.
2. Remove or disconnect the following:
   - Wheels
   - Brake rotors
   - Driveshaft
3. Check the bearing preload with an inch lb. torque wrench.
4. Remove the pinion flange and seal.

To install:

➡Use a new pinion nut for assembly.

5. Install the new pinion seal and flange. Tighten the nut to 210 ft. lbs. (285 Nm).
6. Check the bearing preload. The bearing preload should be equal to the reading taken earlier, plus 5 inch lbs.

7. If the preload torque is low, tighten the pinion nut in 5 inch lb. increments until the torque value is reached. Do not exceed 350 ft. lbs. (474 Nm) pinion nut torque.

8. If the pinion bearing preload torque cannot be attained at maximum pinion nut torque, replace the collapsible spacer.

9. Install or connect the following:
- Driveshaft
- Brake rotors
- Wheels

10. Fill the axle assembly with gear oil and check for leaks.

Non C-Clip Type

1. Before servicing the vehicle, refer to the Precautions Section.

2. Remove or disconnect the following:
- Wheels
- Brake rotors or drums
- Driveshaft

3. Check the bearing preload with an inch lb. torque wrench.

4. Remove the pinion flange and seal.

To install:

➡Use a new pinion nut for assembly.

5. Install the new pinion seal, flange and new pinion nut.

6. Check the bearing preload. The bearing preload should be equal to the reading taken earlier, plus 5 inch lbs.

7. If the preload torque is low, tighten the pinion nut in 5 inch lb. increments until the torque value is reached. Do not exceed 260 ft. lbs. (353 Nm) pinion nut torque.

➡For 302RBI axles the pinion nut should be tightened to 689 ft. lbs. (937 Nm) with a torque multiplier (and torque wrench.

8. If the pinion bearing preload torque can not be attained at maximum pinion nut torque, remove one or more pinion preload shims.

9. Install or connect the following:
- Driveshaft
- Brake rotors or drums
- Wheels

10. Fill the axle assembly with gear oil and check for leaks.

ENGINE COOLING

ENGINE FAN

REMOVAL & INSTALLATION

3.7L, 4.7L & 5.7L Engines

See Figure 32.

⁂ WARNING

If the viscous fan drive is replaced because of mechanical damage, the cooling fan blades should also be inspected. Inspect for fatigue cracks, loose blades, or loose rivets that could have resulted from excessive vibration. Replace fan blade assembly if any of these conditions are found. Also inspect water pump bearing and shaft assembly for any related damage due to a viscous fan drive malfunction.

1. Before servicing the vehicle, refer to the Precautions Section.

2. Disconnect negative battery cable from battery.

3. Remove coolant reserve/overflow container from fan shroud and lay aside. **Do Not** disconnect the hoses or drain coolant from the container.

4. The thermal viscous fan drive/fan blade assembly is attached (threaded) to the water pump hub shaft . Remove the fan blade/viscous fan drive assembly from the water pump by turning the mounting nut counterclockwise as viewed from the front. Threads on the viscous fan drive are **RIGHT-HAND** A 36 MM fan wrench should be used to prevent pulley from rotating.

➡Do Not unbolt the fan blade assembly from viscous fan drive at this time.

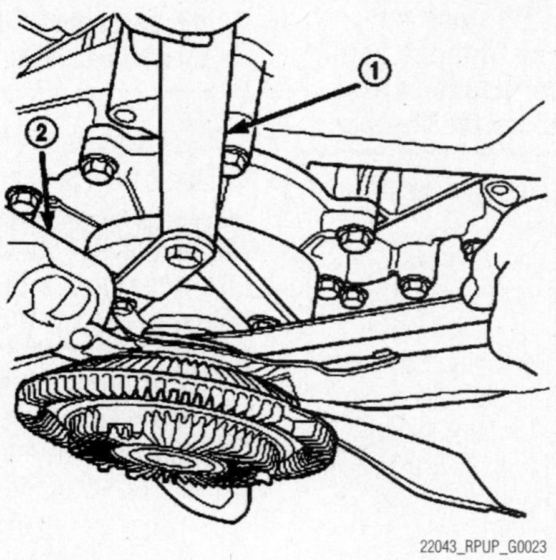

Fig. 32 Viscous fan drive assembly removal

5. Remove the fan shroud-to-radiator mounting bolts.

6. Pull the lower shroud mounts out of the radiator tank clips.

7. Remove the fan shroud and fan blade/viscous fan drive assembly as a complete unit from vehicle.

8. After removing the fan blade/viscous fan drive assembly, **do not** place the viscous fan drive in a horizontal position. If stored horizontally, silicone fluid in the viscous fan drive could drain into its bearing assembly and contaminate lubricant.

⁂ WARNING

Do not remove water pump pulley-to-water pump bolts. This pulley is under spring tension

9. Remove four bolts securing fan blade assembly to viscous fan drive .

⁂ WARNING

Some engines equipped with serpentine drive belts have reverse rotating fans and viscous fan drives. They are marked with the word REVERSE to designate their usage. Installation of the wrong fan or viscous fan drive can result in engine overheating.

To install:

➡Viscous Fan Drive Fluid Pump Out Requirement: After installing a new viscous fan drive, bring the engine speed up to approximately 2000 rpm and hold for approximately two minutes. This will ensure proper fluid distribution within the drive.

10. Install fan blade assembly to the viscous fan drive. Tighten the bolts to 18 ft. lbs. (24 Nm).

11. Position the fan shroud and the fan blade/viscous fan drive assembly to the vehicle as a complete unit.
12. Install the fan shroud.
13. Install the fan blade/viscous fan drive assembly to the water pump shaft . Tighten mounting nut to 37 ft. lbs. (50 Nm).
14. Install the coolant reserve/overflow container to the fan shroud.
15. Connect the negative battery cable.

5.9L & 2007–08 6.7L Engines

See Figures 33 and 34.

WARNING

If the electronically controlled viscous fan drive is replaced because of mechanical damage, the cooling fan blades should also be inspected. Inspect for fatigue cracks, or chipped blades that could have resulted from excessive vibration. Replace fan blade assembly if any of these conditions are found. Also inspect wiring harness and connectors for damage.

1. Before servicing the vehicle, refer to the Precautions Section.
2. Disconnect the battery negative cables.
3. Remove fan shroud-to-engine bracket nuts.
4. Detach the electronically controlled viscous fan electrical connector from the lower fan shroud bracket if equipped.
5. Remove wiring bracket -to-lower fan shroud bracket mounting bolt.

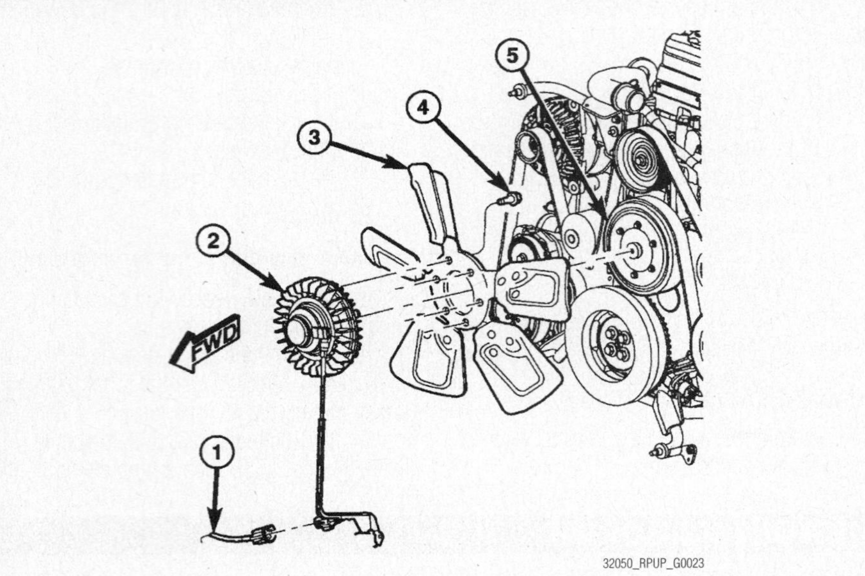

Fig. 34 Exploded view of the electrical connector (1), viscous fan drive (2), fan blade (3), bolts (4) and radiator fan pulley (5)—5.9L and 6.7L diesel engines

6. Remove the fan drive wire harness support from fan shroud.

CAUTION

Do not remove the fan pulley bolts. This pulley is under spring tension.

7. The electronically controlled viscous fan drive/fan blade assembly is attached (threaded) to the fan pulley shaft. Remove the fan blade/fan drive assembly from fan pulley by turning the mounting nut counter-clockwise (as viewed from front). Threads on the viscous fan drive are RIGHT-HAND. A 36mm Fan Wrench can be used. Place a bar or screwdriver between the fan pulley bolts to prevent pulley from rotating.

➡It may be necessary to loosen the top two fan shroud brackets. Removal of the engine mounted fan shroud brackets is not necessary unless removing or installing the engine.

8. Collapse fan shroud toward front of vehicle and remove fan drive/fan blade and fan shroud as an assembly.

WARNING

The electronically controlled viscous fan drive is vibration and impact sensitive, especially at the electrical connectors. Do not drop the unit.

9. Remove the six fan blade-to-viscous fan drive mounting bolts.
10. Inspect the fan for cracked, chipped or damaged fan blades.

To install:

➡Viscous Fan Drive Fluid Pump Out Requirement: After installing a new viscous fan drive, bring the engine speed up to approximately 2000 rpm and hold for approximately two minutes. This will ensure proper fluid distribution within the drive.

11. Install fan blade assembly to electrically controlled viscous fan drive. Tighten mounting bolts to 18 ft. lbs. (24 Nm).

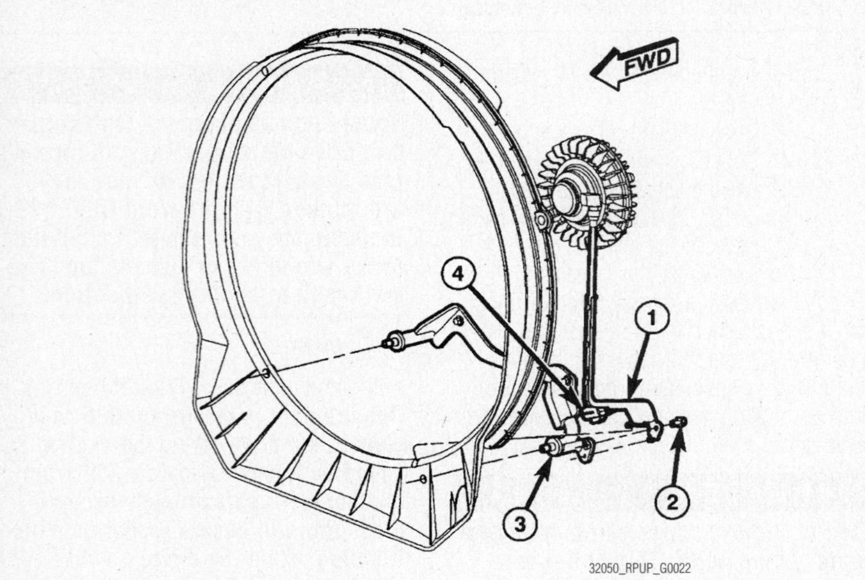

Fig. 33 View of the fan wiring bracket (1), bracket mounting bolts (2), shroud mounting bracket (3), viscous fan connector (4)—5.9L and 6.7L diesel engines

12. Loosen both upper engine mounted fan shroud brackets.

13. Make sure lower engine mounted fan shroud bracket bolts are tightened to 18 ft. lbs. (24 Nm).

14. Position fan/fan drive assembly inside fan shroud and lower into position.

15. Install the viscous fan drive assembly onto fan pulley hub shaft . Tighten mounting nut to 85 ft. lbs. (115 Nm).

16. Install the fan drive wire harness support to fan shroud.

17. Install viscous fan wiring bracket onto lower fan shroud bracket. Tighten nut to 18 ft. lbs. (24 Nm).

18. Install fan shroud onto fan shroud brackets.

19. Connect the fan drive wire harness.

20. Install fan shroud to upper engine fan shroud brackets. Tighten nut finger-tight.

21. Tighten upper engine fan shroud bracket bolts to 18 ft. lbs. (24 Nm).

22. Tighten four fan shroud bracket nuts to 18 ft. lbs. (24 Nm).

23. Make sure of fan tip clearance all the way around inside of fan shroud.

24. Connect the battery negative cables.

RADIATOR

REMOVAL & INSTALLATION

3.7L, 4.7L & 5.7L Engines

1. Before servicing the vehicle, refer to the Precautions Section.

2. Disconnect the negative battery cable.

⁂ CAUTION

Do not remove the cylinder block drain plugs or loosen the radiator draincock with the system hot and under pressure. Serious burns from the coolant can occur.

3. Drain the cooling system.

⁂ WARNING

Constant tension hose clamps are used on most cooling system hoses. When removing or installing, use only tools designed for servicing this type of clamp. Always wear safety glasses when servicing constant tension clamps. A number or letter is stamped into the tongue of constant tension clamps. If replacement is necessary, use only an original equipment clamp with a matching number or letter and the correct width.

4. Remove the hose clamps and hoses from radiator.

5. Remove the coolant reserve/overflow tank hose from the radiator filler neck.

6. Remove the coolant reserve/overflow tank from the fan shroud (pull straight up). The tank slips into slots on the fan shroud.

7. Unclip the power steering hoses from the fan shroud.

8. Disconnect the electrical connectors at the windshield washer reservoir tank and remove the tank.

9. Remove the fan shroud mounting bolts and pull up and out of the radiator tank clips. Position the shroud rearward over the fan blades towards engine.

10. Disconnect the transmission cooler lines from the transmission cooler, then plug the transmission lines and cooler to prevent leakage.

11. Disconnect the power steering lines from the power steering cooler, then plug the power steering lines and cooler to prevent leakage.

12. Remove the two radiator upper mounting bolts.

13. Lift the radiator straight up and out of the engine compartment. Take care not to damage cooling fins or tubes on the radiator and oil coolers when removing.

➡The radiator is equipped with one alignment dowel on the bottom of the outlet tank and one retaining bracket on the front side of the inlet tank. Both features have rubber insulators attached to them that must be present. The alignment dowel fits into a hole at the bottom of the front end sheet metal vertical support post and the support bracket rests on top of the lower radiator closure tube.

To install:

14. Position the fan shroud over the fan blades rearward towards engine.

15. Install the rubber insulators to the lower radiator mounting features (alignment dowel and support bracket at the lower part of the radiator).

16. Lower the radiator into position while guiding the alignment dowel into the vertical post bracket.

17. Position and seat the lower radiator support bracket onto the lower radiator closure tube.

18. Install the upper radiator mounting bolts. Tighten bolts to 90 inch lbs. (10 Nm).

19. Connect the lower radiator hose and install the clamp in the proper position.

20. Connect the power steering hoses to the power steering oil cooler and install the clamps.

21. Connect the transmission oil cooler lines to the transmission oil cooler and install the secondary latches.

22. Position the fan shroud into the mounting clips on the radiator tanks and secure with bolts. Tighten the bolts to 75 inch lbs. (8.5 Nm).

23. Secure the power steering hoses into the clip on the lower fan shroud.

24. Install the windshield washer reservoir tank and connect the hose and electrical connector.

25. Install coolant reserve/overflow container hose(s) to radiator filler neck and secure properly with clamps.

26. Install coolant reserve/overflow container or degas container to fan shroud and tighten the bolts to 75 inch lbs. (8.5 Nm).

27. Connect upper radiator hose and install clamp.

28. Install the battery negative cable.

29. Fill the cooling system with coolant.

30. Operate the engine until it reaches normal operating temperature. Check cooling system fluid levels.

5.9L & 2007–08 6.7L Engines

See Figure 35.

1. Before servicing the vehicle, refer to the Precautions Section.

2. Disconnect both battery negative cables.

3. Drain the cooling system.

4. Disconnect ambient air temperature sensor electrical connector and mass airflow sensor electrical connector (If equipped).

5. Remove air box and turbocharger inlet tube.

6. Remove coolant tank hose, washer bottle hose and the positive battery cable from the fastening clips located on top of the radiator.

7. Remove hose clamps and hoses from radiator.

8. Remove fan shroud mounting nuts from mounting brackets.

9. Pull shroud toward front of vehicle to clear mounting brackets

10. Turn shroud slightly and push toward engine to gain clearance for radiator.

To install:

11. Install rubber insulators to alignment dowels at lower part of radiator.

12. Lower the radiator into position while guiding the two alignment dowels into lower radiator support.

➡Different alignment holes are provided in the lower radiator support for each engine application.

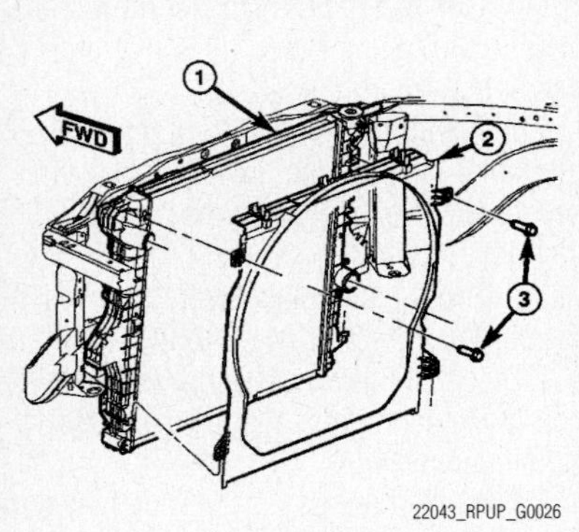

Fig. 35 Radiator (1), fan shroud (2) and bolts (3)

13. Install two upper radiator mounting bolts. Tighten bolts to 105 in. lbs. (12 Nm).
14. If equipped, connect transmission cooler lines to transmission cooler. Inspect quick connect fittings for debris and install until an audible **click** is heard. Tug on lines to verify connection.
15. Position power steering cooler on the radiator and tighten nuts to 90 inch lbs. (10 Nm).
16. Position fan shroud on brackets.
17. Install fan shroud mounting nut. Tighten nut to 18 ft. lbs. (24 Nm).
18. Install the coolant recovery container.
19. Position coolant recovery tank hose, washer bottle hose and the positive battery cable into the clips located on the top of the radiator.
20. Install the air box and turbocharger inlet hose. Tighten clamps to 35 inch lbs. (4 Nm).
21. Connect mass airflow sensor electrical connector and ambient air temp sensor electrical connector (if equipped).
22. Position the heater controls to the **Full Heat** position.
23. Fill the cooling system with coolant.
24. Operate engine until it reaches normal temperature. Check cooling system and automatic transmission (if equipped) fluid levels.

THERMOSTAT

REMOVAL & INSTALLATION

3.7L & 4.7L Engines

See Figure 36.

**** CAUTION**

Do not loosen the radiator draincock with the cooling system hot and pressurized. Serious burns from the coolant can occur.

Do not waste reusable coolant. If the solution is clean, drain the coolant into a clean container for reuse.

If the thermostat is being replaced, be sure that the replacement is the specified thermostat for the vehicle model and engine type.

1. Before servicing the vehicle, refer to the Precautions Section.
2. Disconnect the negative battery cable.
3. Drain the cooling system.
4. Raise and support the vehicle.
5. Remove the splash shield.
6. Remove the lower radiator hose clamp and the lower radiator hose at the thermostat housing.
7. Remove the thermostat housing mounting bolts, thermostat housing and thermostat.

To install:

8. Clean the mating areas of the timing chain cover and the thermostat housing.
9. Install the thermostat (spring side down) into the recessed machined groove on the timing chain cover.
10. Position the thermostat housing on the timing chain cover.
11. Install the housing-to-timing chain cover bolts. Tighten the bolts to 112 inch lbs. (13 Nm).

**** WARNING**

The housing must be tightened evenly and the thermostat must be centered into the recessed groove in the timing chain cover. If not, it may result in a cracked housing, damaged timing chain cover threads or coolant leaks.

12. Install the lower radiator hose on the thermostat housing.
13. Install the splash shield.
14. Lower the vehicle.
15. Fill the cooling system.
16. Connect negative battery cable.
17. Start and warm the engine. Check for leaks.

5.7L Engine

See Figure 37.

**** CAUTION**

Do not loosen the radiator draincock with the cooling system hot and pressurized. serious burns from the coolant can occur.

Do not waste reusable coolant. If the solution is clean, drain the coolant into a clean container for reuse.

If the thermostat is being replaced, be sure that the replacement is the specified thermostat for the vehicle model and engine type.

1. Before servicing the vehicle, refer to the Precautions Section.
2. Disconnect the negative battery cable.

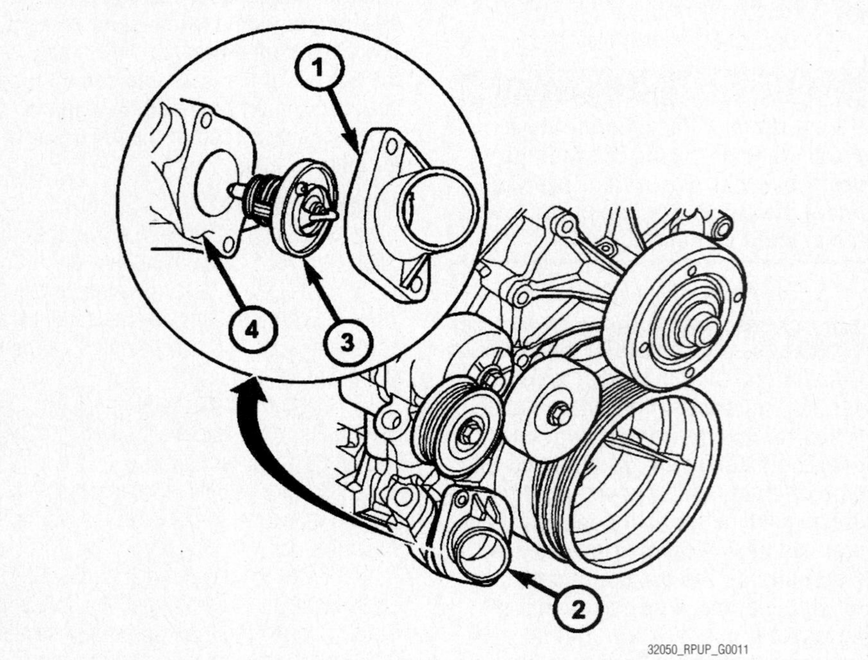

Fig. 36 Location of the thermostat (2), thermostat housing (1), thermostat & gasket (3) and timing chain cover (4)—3.7L & 4.7L engines

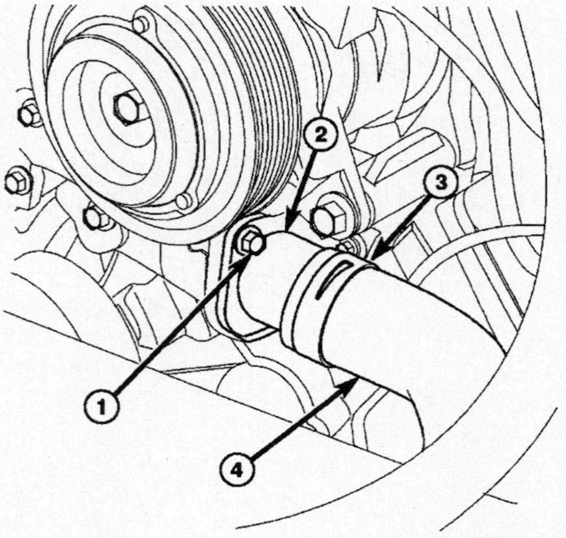

Fig. 37 View of the retaining bolt (1), thermostat housing (2), clamp (3) and radiator hose (4)—5.7L engine

3. Drain the cooling system
4. Remove the radiator hose clamp and radiator hose at the thermostat housing.
5. Remove the thermostat housing mounting bolts, thermostat housing and thermostat .

To install:

6. Position the thermostat and housing on the front cover.
7. Install the thermostat housing bolts. Tighten the bolts to 112 inch lbs. (13 Nm).
8. Install the radiator hose onto the thermostat housing.
9. Fill the cooling system.
10. Connect negative battery cable.
11. Start and warm the engine. Check for leaks.

5.9L Engine

See Figure 38.

1. Before servicing the vehicle, refer to the Precautions Section.
2. Disconnect the battery negative cables.
3. Drain cooling system until coolant level is below thermostat
4. Remove radiator hose clamp and hose from thermostat housing.
5. Remove the three water thermostat housing bolts and remove thermostat housing.
6. Clean the mating surfaces of thermostat housing and clean the thermostat seat groove at the top of the thermostat housing.

➡The thermostat for 5.9L engine and the 6.7L are different and are not interchangeable. Use caution when replacing the thermostat to ensure the proper part number is reinstalled.

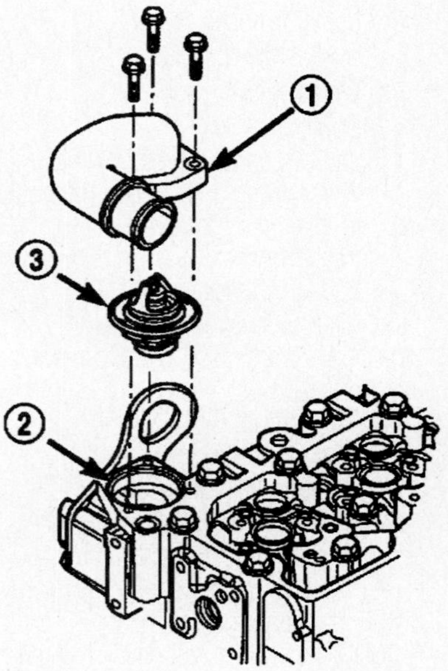

Fig. 38 5.9L Engine thermostat, housing, and bolts

7. Inspect the thermostat seal for cuts or nicks. Replace if damaged.
8. Install the thermostat into the groove in the top of the cylinder head
9. Install the thermostat housing and bolts. Tighten the bolts to 89 in. lbs. (10 Nm).
10. Install the radiator upper hose and clamp.
11. Fill the cooling system.
12. Connect the battery negative cables.
13. Start the engine and check for coolant leaks. Run engine to check for proper thermostat operation.

2007–08 6.7L Engine

See Figure 39.

1. Before servicing the vehicle, refer to the Precautions Section.
2. Disconnect the battery negative cables.
3. Remove vent plug near EGR cooler.
4. Drain cooling system until coolant level is below the thermostat.
5. Disconnect exhaust gas pressure sensor electrical connector.
6. Remove exhaust pressure tube from thermostat housing.
7. Remove EGR cooler cross over tube.
8. Remove radiator hose clamp and hose from thermostat housing.
9. Remove heat shield.
10. Remove the three water outlet-to-cylinder head bolts and remove the water outlet connector.
11. Clean the mating surfaces of the thermostat housing and clean the thermostat seat groove at the top of the thermostat housing.

To install:

12. Inspect the thermostat seal for cuts or nicks. Replace if damaged.
13. Install the thermostat into the groove in the top of the cylinder head.

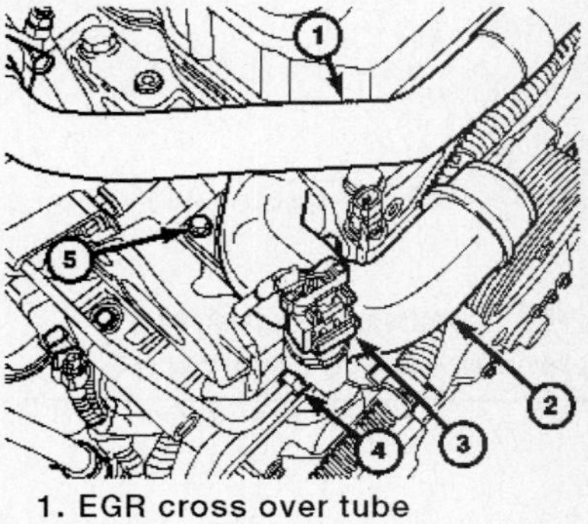

1. EGR cross over tube
2. Thermostat housing
3. Exhaust pressure sensor electrical connector
4. Exhaust pressure tube fitting
5. Thermostat housing bolts

22043_RPUP_G0025

Fig. 39 6.7L Engine thermostat housing and related parts

14. Install the thermostat housing and bolts. Tighten the bolts to 89 inch lbs. (10 Nm).
15. Install heat shield. Tighten bolts to 79 in. lbs. (9 Nm).
16. Install exhaust pressure tube. Tighten to 88 inch lbs. (10 Nm).
17. Connect exhaust pressure sensor electrical connector.
18. Install EGR cross over tube.
19. Install the P-clip and bolt. Tighten to 70 inch lbs. (8 Nm).
20. Install the radiator upper hose and clamp.
21. Fill the cooling system with coolant.
22. Connect the battery negative cables.
23. Start the engine and check for coolant leaks. Run engine to check for proper thermostat operation.

WATER PUMP

REMOVAL & INSTALLATION

3.7L and 4.7L Engines

See Figure 40.

1. Before servicing the vehicle, refer to the Precautions Section.
2. Drain the cooling system.
3. Remove or disconnect the following:
   - Negative battery cable

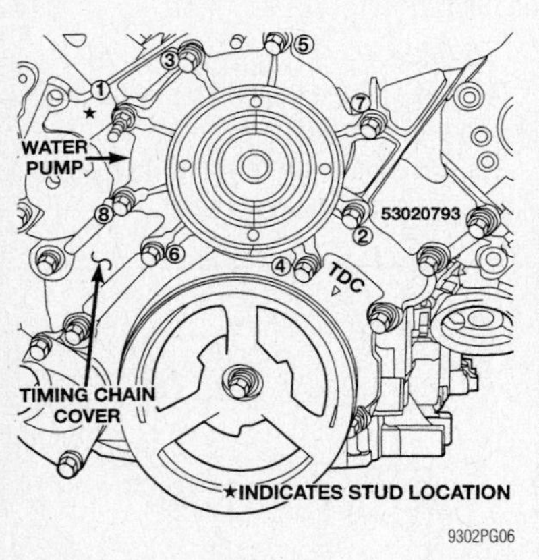

Fig. 40 Water pump tightening sequence—3.7L and 4.7L engines

   - Fan and clutch assembly from the pump
   - Fan shroud and fan assembly. If you're reusing the fan clutch, keep it upright to avoid silicone fluid loss!
   - Lower hose
   - 8 water pump bolts
4. Installation is the reverse of removal. Tighten the bolts, in sequence, to 40 ft. lbs. (54 Nm).

5.7L Engines

1. Before servicing the vehicle, refer to the Precautions Section.
2. Drain the cooling system.
3. Remove or disconnect the following:
   - Negative battery cable
   - Accessory drive belt
   - Engine cooling fan
   - Coolant recovery bottle
   - Washer bottle
   - Fan shroud
   - A/C compressor and alternator brace
   - Idler pulleys
   - Belt tensioner
   - Radiator hoses
   - Heater hoses
   - Water pump

To install:

4. Install or connect the following:
   - Water pump and tighten the bolts to 18 ft. lbs. (24 Nm)
   - Heater hoses
   - Radiator hoses
   - Idler pulleys
   - A/C compressor and alternator brace
   - Fan shroud
   - Washer bottle
   - Coolant recovery bottle
   - Accessory drive belt
   - Negative battery cable
   - Negative battery cable
5. Fill the cooling system.
6. Start the engine and check for leaks.

5.9L & 6.7L Engines

See Figure 41.

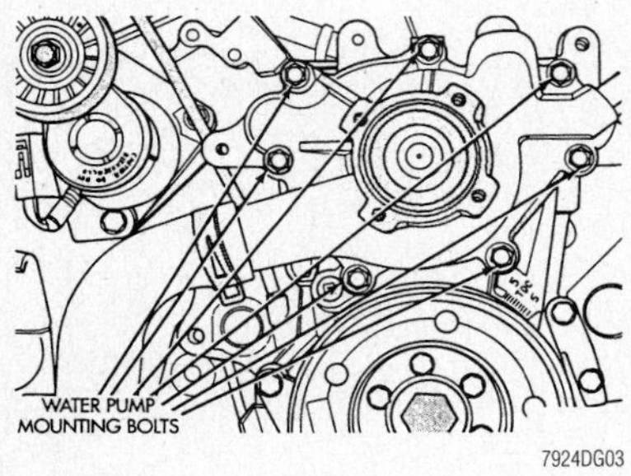

Fig. 41 Water pump mounting bolt locations—3.9L, 5.2L and 5.9L engines, 8.0L engine is similar

1. Before servicing the vehicle, refer to the Precautions Section.
2. Drain the cooling system.
3. Remove or disconnect the following:
   - Negative battery cable
   - Engine cooling fan and shroud

➡Do not store the fan clutch assembly horizontally, silicone may leak into the bearing grease and cause contamination.

   - Accessory drive belt
   - Water pump pulley
   - Lower radiator hose
   - Heater hose and tube
   - Bypass hose
   - Water pump

To install:

4. Install or connect the following:
   - Water pump, using a new gasket. Tighten the bolts to 30 ft. lbs. (40 Nm).
   - Bypass hose
   - Heater hose and tube. Use a new O-ring seal.
   - Lower radiator hose
   - Water pump pulley. Tighten the bolts to 20 ft. lbs. (27 Nm).
   - Accessory drive belt
   - Engine cooling fan and shroud
   - Negative battery cable
5. Fill the cooling system.
6. Start the engine and check for leaks.

ALTERNATOR

REMOVAL & INSTALLATION

3.7L, 4.7L and 5.7L Engines

1. Before servicing the vehicle, refer to the Precautions Section.
2. Remove or disconnect the following:
   - Negative battery cable
   - Accessory drive belt
   - Alternator harness connectors
   - Support bracket nuts and bolt
   - Mounting bolts and alternator

➡**The 3.7L and 4.7L engine has 1 vertical and 2 horizontal bolts.**

To install:

3. Before servicing the vehicle, refer to the Precautions Section.
4. Install the alternator and tighten the bolts to the following specifications:
   - 3.7L engine: Tighten the horizontal bolts to 42 ft. lbs. (57 Nm), then the vertical bolt to 29 ft. lbs. (40 Nm).
   - 4.7L engine: Vertical bolt and long horizontal bolt to 41 ft. lbs. (56 Nm), short horizontal bolt to 55 ft. lbs. (74 Nm).
   - 5.7L engine: Tighten bolts to 30 ft. lbs. (41 Nm). Position support bracket to front of generator and install bolt and nuts. Tighten bolt/nuts to 30 ft. lbs. (41 Nm).
5. Install or connect the following:
   - Alternator harness connectors. Tighten B+ terminal eyelet mounting nut to 8.8 ft. lbs. (12 Nm).
   - Accessory drive belt
   - Negative battery cable

5.9L & 2007–08 6.7L Engines

⁂ CAUTION

Disconnect both negative battery cables from both batteries before removing battery output wire (b+ wire) from alternator. Failure to do so can result in injury or damage to electrical system.

1. Before servicing the vehicle, refer to the Precautions Section.
2. Disconnect both negative battery cables at both batteries.
3. Remove the alternator drive belt.
4. Remove the upper mounting bracket bolt.
5. Remove the lower mounting bracket bolt and nut.
6. Remove the alternator from engine.
7. Unsnap the plastic insulator cap from B+ output terminal.
8. Remove the B+ terminal mounting nut at rear of generator. Disconnect terminal from alternator.
9. Disconnect field wire connector at rear of alternator by pushing on connector tab.

To install:

10. Position alternator to upper and lower mounting brackets and install upper bolt and lower bolt / nut.
11. Tighten all bolts/nut to 30 ft. lbs. (41 Nm).
12. Firmly snap the field wire connector into rear of alternator.
13. Install the B+ terminal eyelet to generator output stud. Tighten mounting nut.

⁂ WARNING

When installing a serpentine accessory drive belt, the belt MUST be routed correctly. The water pump may be rotating in the wrong direction if the belt is installed incorrectly, causing the engine to overheat.

14. Install the alternator drive belt.
15. Install both negative battery cables to both batteries.

TESTING

➡**Before testing, make sure all connections and mounting bolts are clean and tight. Many charging system problems are related to loose and corroded terminals or bad grounds. Don't overlook the engine ground connection to the body. On some vehicles, it is beneficial to add an additional ground between the engine and the chassis. This may solve many intermittent problems.**

➡**Alternators must be replaced if defective in any way. No internal service is possible.**

Voltage Drop Test

➡**Before proceeding, make sure the battery is in good condition and fully charged.**

Perform a voltage drop test of the positive side of the circuit as follows:

1. Start the engine and allow it to reach normal operating temperature.
2. Turn the headlamps, heater blower motor and interior lights ON.
3. Bring the engine to about 2,500 rpm and hold it there.
4. Connect the **negative** voltmeter lead directly to the battery **positive** terminal.
5. Touch the **positive** voltmeter lead directly to the alternator **B+** output stud, not the nut. The meter should read no higher than about 0.5 volts. If it does, there is higher than normal resistance between the positive side of the battery and the B+ output at the alternator.
6. Move the positive meter lead to the nut and see if the voltage reading drops substantially. If it does, there is resistance between the stud and the nut. The theory is to keep moving closer to the battery terminal, one connection at a time, in order to find the area of high resistance (bad connection).

Perform a voltage drop test of the negative side of the circuit as follows:

7. Start the engine and allow it to reach normal operating temperature.
8. Turn the headlamps, heater blower motor and interior lights ON.
9. Bring the engine to about 2,500 rpm and hold it there.
10. Connect the **negative** voltmeter lead directly to the **negative** battery terminal.
11. Touch the **positive** voltmeter lead directly to the alternator case or ground connection. The meter should read no higher than about 0.3 volts. If it does, there is higher than normal resistance between the battery ground terminal and the alternator ground.
12. Move the positive meter lead to the alternator mounting bracket. If the voltage reading drops substantially, you know that there is a bad electrical connection between the alternator and mounting bracket. The theory is to keep moving closer to the battery terminal, one connection at a time, in order to find the area of high resistance (bad connection).

Alternator Isolation Test

On some models, it is possible to isolate the alternator from the regulator by grounding the field terminal. Grounding the field terminal removes the EVR from the circuit and forces full alternator output. This may help determine whether the problem is the alternator or EVR.

➡Most alternators have two field terminals, one positive and one negative. With the engine running, the positive terminal will have battery voltage present and the negative terminal will have 3–5 volts less. Use a voltmeter to identify the negative terminal before carrying out the following test.

⁂ WARNING

Do not let the voltage get higher than 18 volts. Damage to electrical circuits may occur.

1. Connect a voltmeter across the battery terminals so the voltage can be monitored.
2. Start the engine and let it reach normal operating temperature.
3. Connect a jumper lead to a good ground.
4. Locate the field terminal (negative) on the back of the alternator.
5. Momentarily connect the grounded jumper to the field terminal. If the alternator is okay, the voltage will climb rapidly. Disconnect the jumper before the output reaches 18 volts. If the voltage does not rise, replace the alternator. If the voltage rises, the regulator circuits are bad.

ENGINE ELECTRICAL

IGNITION SYSTEM

FIRING ORDER

See Figures 42 and 43.

3.7L Engine firing order 1–6–5–4–3–2

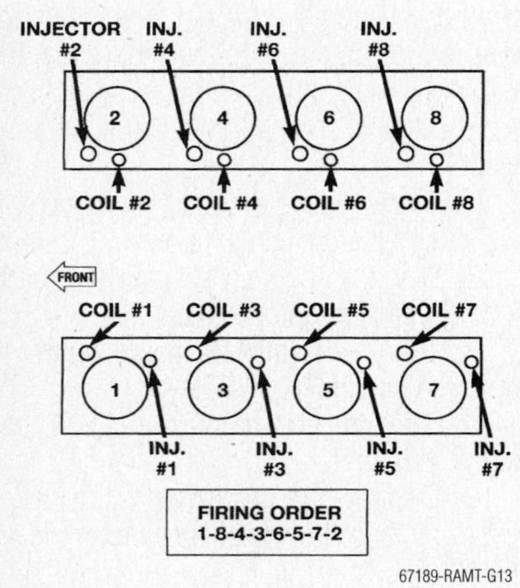

Fig. 42 4.7L engine firing order Distributorless ignition

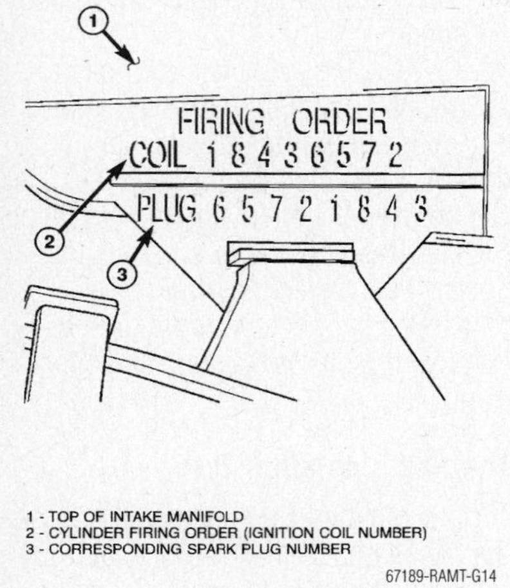

Fig. 43 5.7L engine firing order Distributorless ignition

IGNITION COIL

REMOVAL & INSTALLATION

3.7L Engine

See Figure 44.

An individual ignition coil is used for each spark plug. The coil fits into machined holes in the cylinder head. A mounting stud/nut secures each coil to the top of the intake manifold. The bottom of the coil is equipped with a rubber boot to seal the spark plug to the coil. Inside each rubber boot is a spring. The spring is used for a mechanical contact between the coil and the top of the spark plug. These rubber boots and springs are a permanent part of the coil and are not serviced separately. An O-ring is used to seal the coil at the opening into the cylinder head.

➡Depending on which of the coils are being removed, the throttle body air intake tube or intake box, may need to be removed to gain access to the coil.

1. Disconnect electrical connector from coil by pushing downward on release lock on top of connector and pull connector from coil.
2. Clean the area at base of coil with compressed air before removal.
3. Remove coil mounting nut from mounting stud.
4. Carefully pull up coil from cylinder head opening with a slight twisting action.
5. Remove coil from vehicle.

To install:

6. Using compressed air, blow out any dirt or contaminants from around top of spark plug.
7. Check condition of coil O-ring and replace as necessary. To aid in coil installation, apply silicone to coil O-ring.
8. Position ignition coil into cylinder head opening and push onto spark plug. Do this while guiding coil base over mounting stud.
9. Install coil mounting stud nut and tighten to 80 inch lbs. (7 Nm)
10. Connect the electrical connector to coil by snapping into position.
11. If necessary, install throttle body air tube.

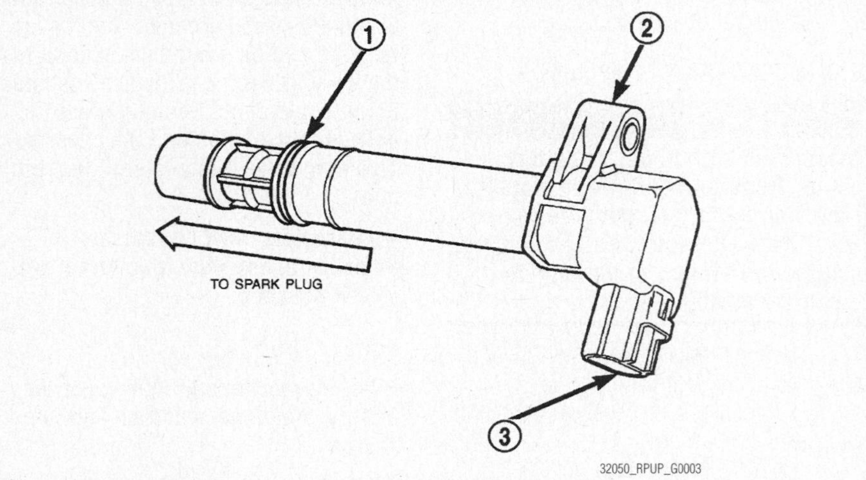

Fig. 44 View of the ignition coil (2), O-ring (1) and electrical connector (3)—3.7L engine

4.7L Engine

See Figure 45.

An individual ignition coil is used for each spark plug. The coil fits into machined holes in the cylinder head. A mounting stud/nut secures each coil to the top of the intake manifold. The bottom of the coil is equipped with a rubber boot to seal the spark plug to the coil. Inside each rubber boot is a spring. The spring is used for a mechanical contact between the coil and the top of the spark plug. These rubber boots and springs are a permanent part of the coil and are not serviced separately. An O-ring is used to seal the coil at the opening into the cylinder head.

➡Depending on which of the coils are being removed, the throttle body air intake tube or intake box, may need to be removed to gain access to the coil.

1. Disconnect electrical connector from coil by pushing downward on release lock on top of connector and pull connector from coil.
2. Clean the area at base of coil with compressed air before removal.
3. Remove coil mounting nut from mounting stud.
4. Carefully pull up coil from cylinder head opening with a slight twisting action.
5. Remove the coil from vehicle.

To install:

6. Using compressed air, blow out any dirt or contaminants from around top of spark plug.
7. Check condition of coil O-ring and replace as necessary. To aid in coil installation, apply silicone to coil O-ring.
8. Position ignition coil into cylinder head opening and push onto spark plug. Do this while guiding coil base over mounting stud.
9. Install coil mounting stud nut and tighten to 80 inch lbs. (7 Nm).
10. Connect the electrical connector to coil by snapping into position.
11. If necessary, install throttle body air tube.

2005–06 5.7L (SMPI) Engine

See Figure 46.

Before removing or disconnecting any spark plug cables, note their original position. Remove cables one-at-a-time. To prevent ignition crossfire, spark plug cables MUST be placed in cable tray (routing loom) into their original position.

An individual ignition coil is used at each cylinder. The coil mounts to the top of the valve cover with 2 bolts. The bottom of the coil is equipped with a rubber boot to seal the spark plug to the coil. Inside each rubber boot is a spring. The spring is used for a mechanical contact between the coil and the top of the spark plug.

➡Depending on which of the coils are being removed, the throttle body air intake tube or intake box, may need to be removed to gain access to the coil.

1. Unlock the electrical connector by moving slide lock first (1). Press on release lock (3) while pulling electrical connector from coil.
2. Disconnect secondary high—voltage cable (2) from coil with a twisting action.
3. Clean the area at base of coil with compressed air before removal.
4. Remove the two mounting bolts (6) (note that mounting bolts are retained to the coil).
5. Carefully pull up coil from cylinder head opening with a slight twisting action.
6. Remove coil from vehicle.

➡Before installing spark plug cables to either the spark plugs or coils, or before installing a coil to a spark plug, apply dielectric grease to inside of boots.

To install:

7. Using compressed air, blow out any dirt or contaminants from around top of spark plug.
8. Before installing spark plug cables to either the spark plugs or coils, or before installing a coil to a spark plug, apply dielectric grease to inside of boots.
9. Position ignition coil into cylinder head opening and push onto spark plug. Twist coil into position.
10. Install 2 coil mounting bolts and torque to 9 ft. lbs. (12 Nm).

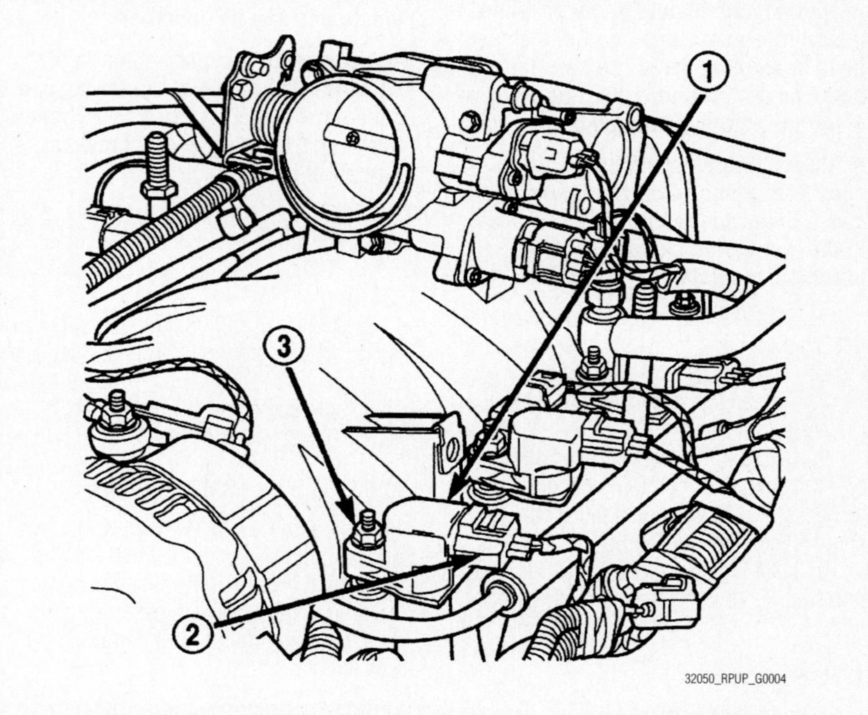

Fig. 45 Location of the ignition coil (1), electrical connector (2) and coil mounting stud/nut (3)—4.7L engine

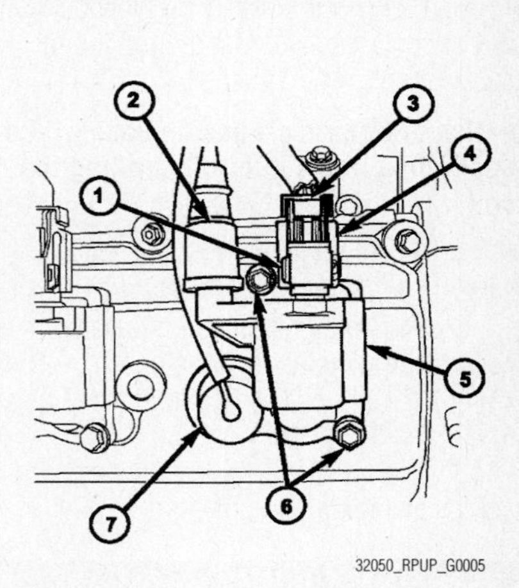

Fig. 46 View of the slide lock (1), spark plug cable (2), release lock/tab (3), electrical connector (4), ignition coil

11. Connect the electrical connector to coil by snapping into position.

12. Install cable to coil. To prevent ignition crossfire, spark plug cables MUST be placed in cable tray (routing loom) into their original position.

13. If necessary, install throttle body air tube.

2006–08 5.7L (MDS) Engine

See Figure 47.

1. Disconnect the electrical connector from coil.
2. Clean area at the base of the coil with compressed air before removal.
3. Remove two mounting bolts (note that mounting bolts are retained to coil).
4. Carefully pull up coil from valve cover.
5. Remove coil from vehicle.

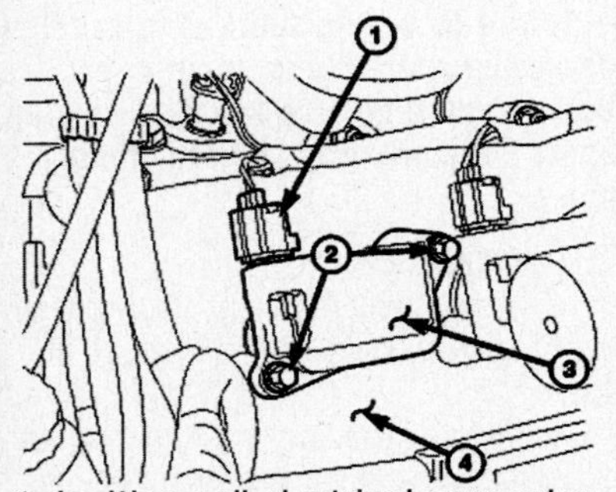

1. Ignition coil electrical connector
2. Mounting bolts
3. Ignition coil
4. Valve cover

22043_RPUP_G0027

Fig. 47 Ignition coil 5.7L (MDS) Engine

To install:

6. Using compressed air, blow out any dirt or contaminants from around top of spark plug.

➡Use dielectric grease on each of the spark plug boots before installing the coil.

7. Position ignition coil into valve cover and push onto spark plugs.
8. Position ignition coil into valve cover and push onto spark plugs.
9. Install 2 coil mounting bolts. Tighten to 62 inch lbs. (7 Nm).
10. Connect the electrical connector to coil by snapping into position.

IGNITION TIMING

ADJUSTMENT

The ignition timing is controlled by the Powertrain Control Module (PCM). No adjustment is necessary or possible.

SPARK PLUGS

REMOVAL & INSTALLATION

3.7L Engine

Each individual spark plug is located under each ignition coil. Each individual ignition coil must be removed to gain access to each spark plug. Refer to the Ignition Coil Removal & Installation procedure in this section.

1. Before servicing the vehicle, refer to the Precautions Section.
2. Remove necessary air filter tubing at throttle body.
3. Prior to removing ignition coil, spray compressed air around coil base at cylinder head.
4. Prior to removing spark plug, spray compressed air into cylinder head opening. This will help prevent foreign material from entering combustion chamber.
5. Remove spark plug from cylinder head using a quality socket with a rubber or foam insert. Also check condition of ignition coil O-ring and replace as necessary.
6. Inspect the condition of the spark plugs.

To install:

➡Special care should be taken when installing spark plugs into the cylinder head spark plug wells. Be sure the plugs do not drop into the plug wells as electrodes can be damaged.

➡Always tighten spark plugs to the specified torque. Over tightening can cause distortion resulting in a change in the spark plug gap or a cracked porcelain insulator.

7. Start the spark plug into the cylinder head by hand to avoid cross-threading.
8. Tighten the spark plugs to 20 ft. lbs. (27 Nm).
9. Before installing ignition coil(s), check condition of coil O-ring and replace as necessary. To aid in coil installation, apply silicone to coil O-ring.
10. Install ignition coil(s). Refer to Ignition Coil Removal/Installation in this section.

4.7L Engine

Each individual spark plug is located under each ignition coil. Each individual ignition coil must be removed to gain access to each spark plug. Refer to Ignition Coil Removal/Installation.

1. Before servicing the vehicle, refer to the Precautions Section.
2. Remove necessary air filter tubing at throttle body.
3. Prior to removing ignition coil, spray compressed air around coil base at cylinder head.
4. Prior to removing spark plug, spray compressed air into cylinder head opening. This will help prevent foreign material from entering combustion chamber.
5. Remove spark plug from cylinder head using a quality socket with a rubber or foam insert. Also check condition of ignition coil O-ring and replace as necessary.
6. Inspect the condition of the spark plugs.

To install:

✲✲ WARNING

The 4.7L V8 engine is equipped with copper core ground electrode spark plugs. They must be replaced with the same type/number spark plug as the original. If another spark plug is substituted, pre-ignition will result.

➡Special care should be taken when installing spark plugs into the cylinder head spark plug wells. Be sure the plugs do not drop into the plug wells as electrodes can be damaged.

➡Always tighten spark plugs to the specified torque. Over tightening can cause distortion resulting in a change in the spark plug gap or a cracked porcelain insulator.

7. Start the spark plug into the cylinder head by hand to avoid cross-threading.
8. Tighten the spark plugs to 20 ft. lbs. (27 Nm).
9. Before installing ignition coil(s), check condition of coil O-ring and replace as necessary. To aid in coil installation, apply silicone to coil O-ring.
10. Install ignition coil(s).

2005–06 5.7L (SMPI) Engine

Eight of the 16 spark plugs are located under an ignition coil; the other 8 are not. If spark plug being removed is under coil, coil must be removed to gain access to spark plug. Refer to Ignition Coil Removal/Installation.

➡Before removing or disconnecting any spark plug cables, note their original position. Remove cables one-at-a-

time. To prevent ignition crossfire, spark plug cables MUST be placed in cable tray (routing loom) into their original position. Refer to Spark Plug Cable Removal for a graphic.

➡Before installing spark plug cables to either the spark plugs or coils, apply dielectric grease to inside of boots.

1. Before servicing the vehicle, refer to the Precautions Section.
2. Remove necessary air filter tubing at throttle body.
3. Prior to removing ignition coil (if coil removal is necessary), spray compressed air around coil base at cylinder head cover.
4. Prior to removing spark plug, spray compressed air into cylinder head opening. This will help prevent foreign material from entering combustion chamber.
5. Inspect the condition of the spark plugs.

To install:

➡Special care should be taken when installing spark plugs into the cylinder head spark plug wells. Be sure the plugs do not drop into the plug wells as electrodes can be damaged.

6. Start the spark plug into cylinder head by hand to avoid cross-threading aluminum threads. To aid in installation, attach a piece of rubber hose, or an old spark plug boot to spark plug.

✻✻ WARNING

The 5.7L V8 is equipped with torque critical design spark plugs. Do not exceed 15 ft. lbs. (20 Nm) torque.

7. Tighten the spark plugs to 11–15 ft. lbs. (15–21 Nm).
8. Before installing spark plug cables to either the spark plugs or coils, apply dielectric grease to inside of boots.
9. To prevent ignition crossfire, spark plug cables MUST be placed in cable tray (routing loom) into their original position.
10. Install ignition coil(s) to necessary spark plugs. Refer to Ignition Coil Installation.
11. Install spark plug cables to remaining spark plugs. Remember to apply dielectric grease to inside of boots.

2006–08 5.7L (MDS) Engine

➡Each individual spark plug is located under each ignition coil. Each individual ignition coil must be removed to gain access to each spark plug.

1. Before servicing the vehicle, refer to the Precautions Section.
2. Remove necessary air filter tubing at throttle body.
3. Prior to removing the ignition coil, spray compressed air around coil base at cylinder head.
4. Prior to removing spark plug, spray compressed air into cylinder head opening. This will help prevent foreign material from entering combustion chamber.
5. Remove spark plug from cylinder head using a quality socket with a rubber or foam insert. Also check condition of ignition coil O-ring and replace as necessary.
6. Inspect spark plug condition.

To install:

➡Special care should be taken when installing spark plugs into the cylinder head spark plug wells. Be sure the plugs do not drop into the plug wells as electrodes can be damaged.

✻✻ WARNING

Always tighten spark plugs to the specified torque. Over tightening can cause distortion resulting in a change in the spark plug gap or a cracked porcelain insulator.

7. Start the spark plug into the cylinder head by hand to avoid cross threading.
8. The 5.7L is equipped with torque critical design spark plugs. Do not exceed 15 ft. lbs. Tighten spark plugs to 13 ft. lbs. (18 Nm).
9. Before installing ignition coils, check condition of coil O-ring and replace as necessary. To aid in coil installation, apply silicone to coil O-ring.
10. Install ignition coils.

ENGINE ELECTRICAL — STARTING SYSTEM

STARTER

REMOVAL & INSTALLATION

3.7L and 4.7L Engines

1. Before servicing the vehicle, refer to the Precautions Section.
2. Remove or disconnect the following:
   - Negative battery cable

➡If equipped with 4WD and certain transmissions, a support bracket is used between front axle and side of transmission. Remove 2 support bracket bolts at transmission. Pry support bracket slightly to gain access to lower starter mounting bolt.

   - Starter mounting bolts

➡On the 3.7L engine, the left side exhaust pipe and front driveshaft must be disconnected.

   - Starter solenoid harness connections
   - Starter

To install:

3. Connect the starter solenoid wiring connectors.
4. Install the starter and torque the bolts to 40 ft. lbs. (54 Nm).
5. On the 3.7L engine, the left side exhaust pipe and front driveshaft
6. Install the negative battery cable and check for proper operation.

5.7L Engines

1. Before servicing the vehicle, refer to the Precautions Section.
2. Remove or disconnect the following:
   - Negative battery cable

➡Depending on drivetrain configuration, a support bracket may be used.

   - Starter mounting bolts
   - Starter solenoid harness connections
   - Starter

To install:

3. Connect the starter solenoid wiring connectors.
4. Install the starter and torque the bolts to 50 ft. lbs. (68 Nm).
5. Install the negative battery cable and check for proper operation.

5.9L Diesel Engine

See Figure 48.

1. Disconnect and isolate both negative battery cables at both batteries.
2. Raise and support vehicle.
3. Remove 3 starter mounting bolts .
4. Move starter motor towards front of vehicle far enough for nose of starter pinion housing to clear housing. Always support starter motor during this process. Do not let starter motor hang from wire harness.
5. Tilt nose downward and lower starter

motor far enough to access and remove nuts securing starter wiring harness to starter . Do not let starter motor hang from wire harness.

➡Note: Certain diesel engines use an aluminum spacer . Note position and orientation of spacer before removal.

6. Remove the starter motor from the engine.

To install:

7. If equipped, position and hold aluminum spacer to rear of starter while positioning starter to engine.
8. Connect solenoid wire to starter motor. Tighten nut to 4.4 ft. lbs. (6 Nm).
9. Position the battery cable to starter stud. Install and tighten battery cable nut to 10.3 ft. lbs. (14 Nm).

➡Do not allow starter motor to hang from wire harness.

10. Position the starter motor to transmission.
11. If equipped with automatic transmission, slide cooler tube bracket into position.

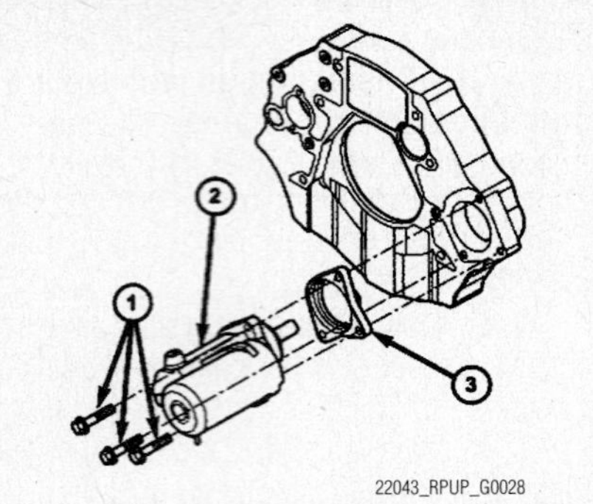

Fig. 48 Starter mounting bolts (1), starter motor (2), and spacer plate (3)

12. Install and tighten 3 starter mounting bolts to 32 ft. lbs. (43 Nm).
13. Lower the vehicle.
14. Connect both negative battery cables to both batteries.

6.7L Diesel Engine

1. Disconnect and isolate both negative battery cables at both batteries.
2. Raise and support vehicle.
3. Disconnect the solenoid electrical connector.
4. Remove the battery cable mounting nut.
5. Remove the battery cable from stud.
6. Remove three starter mounting bolts.
7. Remove the starter motor from engine.

To install:

8. Connect solenoid wire to starter motor. Tighten nut to 4.4 ft. lbs. (6 Nm).
9. Position the battery cable to starter stud. Install and tighten battery cable nut to 10.3 ft. lbs. (14 Nm).

➡Do not allow starter motor to hang from wire harness.

10. Position the starter motor to transmission.
11. Install and tighten 3 starter mounting bolts to 32 ft. lbs. (43 Nm).
12. Lower the vehicle.
13. Connect both negative battery cables to both batteries.

ENGINE MECHANICAL

➡Disconnecting the negative battery cable may interfere with the functions of the on board computer systems and may require the computer to undergo a relearning process, once the negative battery cable is reconnected.

ACCESSORY DRIVE BELTS

ACCESSORY BELT ROUTING

See Figures 49 through 52.

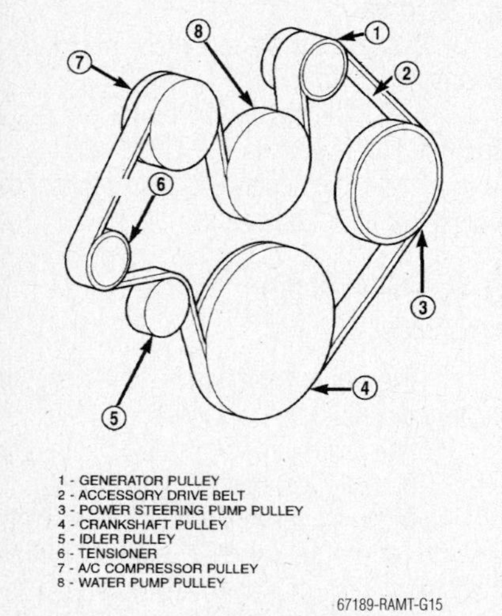

Fig. 49 Accessory serpentine belt routing—3.7L and 4.7L gasoline engines

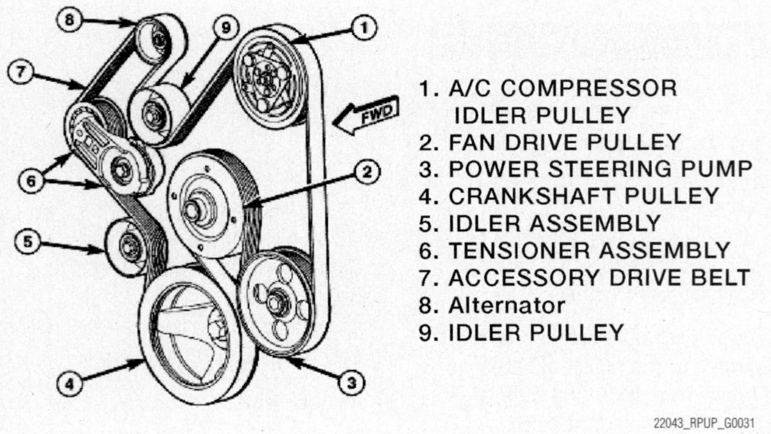

Fig. 50 Accessory serpentine belt routing—5.7L gasoline engines

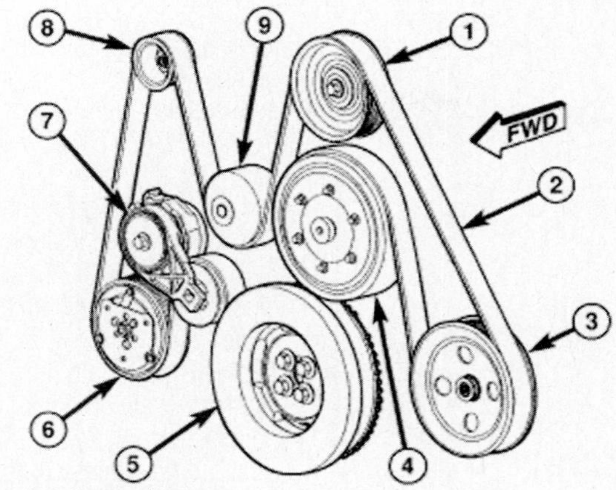

1. Idler pulley
2. Drive belt
3. Power steering pump pulley
4. Radiator fan pulley
5. Crankshaft pulley
6. A/C compressor pulley
7. Automatic belt tensioner
8. Alternator pulley
9. Water pump pulley

22043_RPUP_G0029

Fig. 51 Accessory serpentine belt routing—5.9L and 6.7L diesel engines with A/C

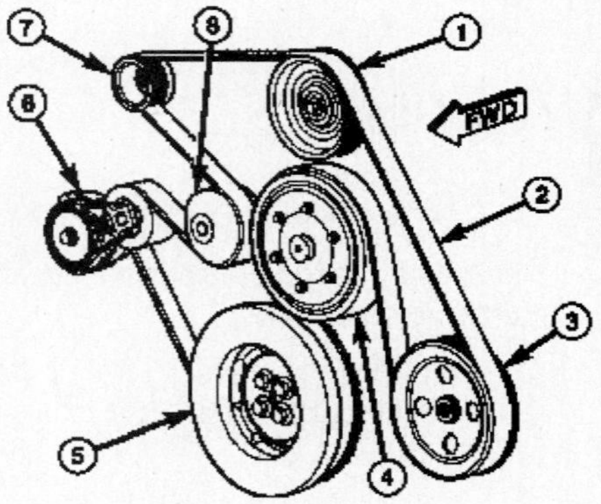

1. Idler pulley
2. Drive belt
3. Power steering pump pulley
4. Radiator fan pulley
5. Crankshaft pulley
6. Automatic belt tensioner
7. Alternator pulley

22043_RPUP_G0030

Fig. 52 Accessory serpentine belt routing—5.9L and 6.7L diesel engines without A/C

INSPECTION

Inspect the drive belt for signs of glazing or cracking. A glazed belt will be perfectly smooth from slippage, while a good belt will have a slight texture of fabric visible. Cracks will usually start at the inner edge of the belt and run outward. All worn or damaged drive belts should be replaced immediately.

ADJUSTMENT

Belt tension is not adjustable. Belt adjustment is maintained by an automatic (spring load) belt tensioner.

REMOVAL & INSTALLATION

3.7L & 4.7L Engines

See Figures 53 and 54.

WARNING

Do not let tensioner arm snap back to the free arm position, sever damage may occur to the tensioner.

Belt tension is not adjustable. Belt adjustment is maintained by an automatic (spring load) belt tensioner.

1. Disconnect negative battery cable from battery.
2. Rotate belt tensioner until it contacts its stop. Remove belt, then slowly rotate the tensioner into the free arm position..
3. Check condition of all pulleys.

WARNING

When installing the serpentine accessory drive belt, the belt MUST be routed correctly. If not, the engine may overheat due to the water pump rotating in the wrong direction.

To install:

4. Install new belt. Route the belt around all pulleys except the idler pulley. Rotate the tensioner arm until it contacts its stop position. Route the belt around the idler and slowly let the tensioner rotate into the belt. Make sure the belt is seated onto all pulleys.
5. With the drive belt installed, inspect the belt wear indicator. On 4.7L Engines only, the gap between the tang and the housing stop (measurement A) must not exceed 24 mm (.94 inches). If the measurement exceeds this specification replace the serpentine accessory drive belt.

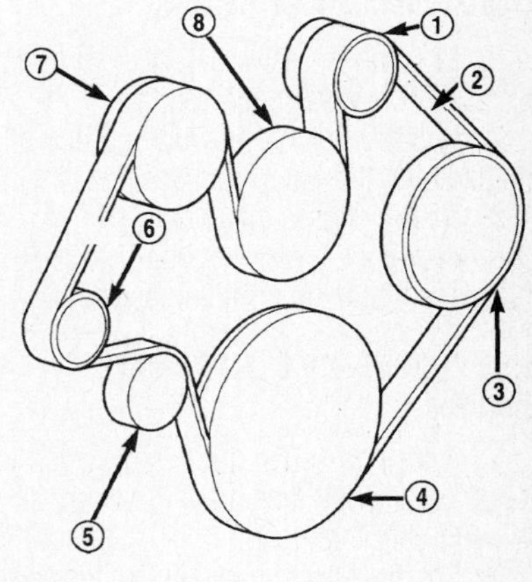

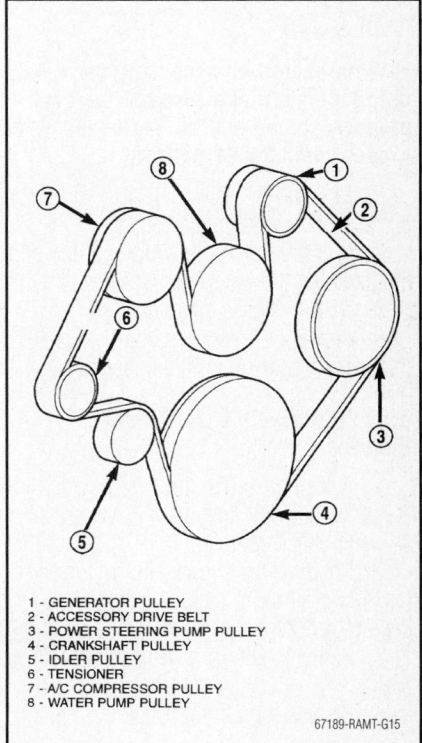

1 - GENERATOR PULLEY
2 - ACCESSORY DRIVE BELT
3 - POWER STEERING PUMP PULLEY
4 - CRANKSHAFT PULLEY
5 - IDLER PULLEY
6 - TENSIONER
7 - A/C COMPRESSOR PULLEY
8 - WATER PUMP PULLEY

67189-RAMT-G15

Fig. 53 Accessory serpentine belt routing—3.7L and 4.7L gasoline engines

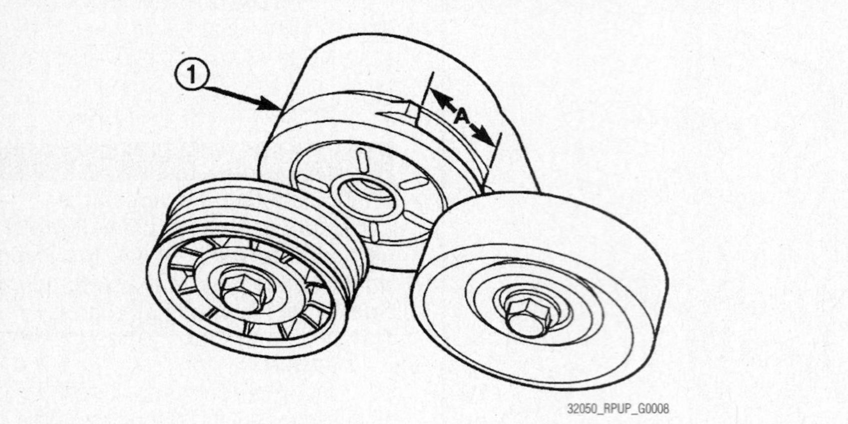

Fig. 54 With the drive belt installed, inspect the belt wear indicator. On 4.7L engines, the gap between the tang and the housing stop (measurement A) must not exceed 0.94 in. (24mm)

5.7L Engines

1. Remove the air intake tube between intake manifold and air filter assembly.
2. Insert a suitable square drive ratchet into the square hole on belt tensioner arm.
3. Release the belt tension by rotating the tensioner **clockwise**. Rotate belt tensioner until belt can be removed from pulleys.
4. Remove the drive belt.
5. Gently release tensioner.

To install:

➡When installing accessory drive belt onto pulleys, make sure that belt is properly routed and all V-grooves make proper contact with pulleys.

6. Position the drive belt over all pulleys except for the water pump pulley.
7. Rotate tensioner **clockwise** and slip the belt over the water pump pulley.
8. Gently release tensioner.
9. Install the air intake tube between intake manifold and air filter assembly.

5.9L & 2007–08 6.7L Diesel Engines

1. A ½ inch square hole is provided in the automatic belt tensioner. Attach a suitable tool into this hole.
2. Rotate tensioner assembly clockwise (as viewed from front) until tension has been relieved from belt.
3. Remove belt from water pump pulley first
4. Remove belt from vehicle.

To install:

WARNING

When installing the accessory drive belt, the belt must be routed correctly. If not, engine may overheat due to water pump rotating in wrong direction.

5. Position drive belt over all pulleys except water pump pulley.
6. Attach a suitable tool to the accessory drive belt tensioner.
7. Rotate the accessory drive belt tensioner clockwise. Place belt over water pump pulley. Let tensioner rotate back into place. Remove tool. Be sure belt is properly seated on all pulleys.

CAMSHAFT AND VALVE LIFTERS

INSPECTION

See Figure 55.

Inspect the valve lobes and bearing journals for cracks, pitting, scoring, or generally excessive wear.

Measure the bearing journals and lobes. Replace any camshaft that exceeds the allowable limits.

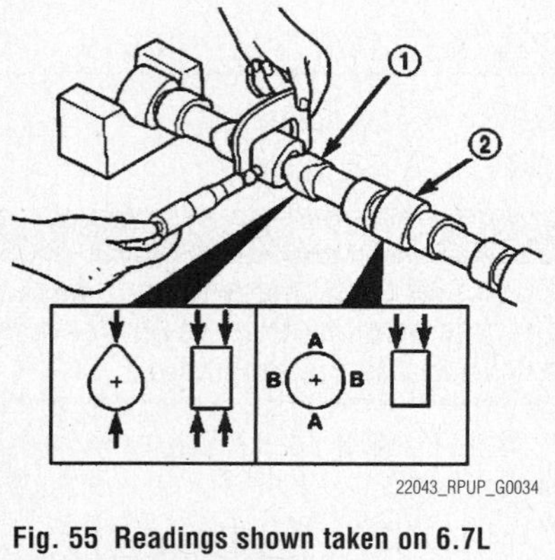

Fig. 55 Readings shown taken on 6.7L diesel engine camshaft

Before disassembling any part of the engine to correct lifter noise, check the oil pressure. If the vehicle has no oil pressure gauge, install a reliable gauge at the pressure sending-unit. The pressure should be between 30–70 psi (207–552 kPa) at 3,000 RPM.

Check the oil level after the engine reaches normal operating temperature. Allow 5 minutes to stabilize oil level, check dipstick. The oil level in the pan should never be above the FULL mark or below the ADD OIL mark on dipstick. Either of these two conditions could be responsible for noisy lifters.

1. To determine source of lifter noise, crank over engine with cylinder head covers removed.
2. Feel each valve spring or rocker arm to detect noisy lifter. The noisy lifter will cause the affected spring and/or rocker arm to vibrate or feel rough in operation.
3. Replace affected lifter as needed.

REMOVAL & INSTALLATION

3.7L and 4.7L Engines

See Figures 56 through 60.

1. Before servicing the vehicle, refer to the Precautions Section.
2. Remove or disconnect the following:
   - Negative battery cable
   - Cylinder head covers
   - Rocker arms
   - Hydraulic lash adjusters

➡Keep all valvetrain components in order for assembly.

3. Set the engine at Top Dead Center (TDC) of the compression stroke for the No. 1 cylinder.
4. Install Timing Chain Wedge (8350 4.7L; 8379 3.7L) to retain the chain tensioners.
5. Matchmark the timing chains to the camshaft sprockets.
6. Install Camshaft Holding Tool (6958 and Adapter Pins 8346 4.7L; 8428 3.7L) to the left camshaft sprocket.
7. On 3.7L engines, use tool 8428 and rotate the camshaft 5 degrees clockwise to eliminate valve load.
8. On 4.7L engines, use adjustable pliers to rotate the left camshaft 15 degrees clockwise to eliminate valve load. Use adjustable pliers to rotate the right camshaft 45 degrees counterclockwise to eliminate valve load.
9. Remove or disconnect the following:
   - Right camshaft timing sprocket and target wheel

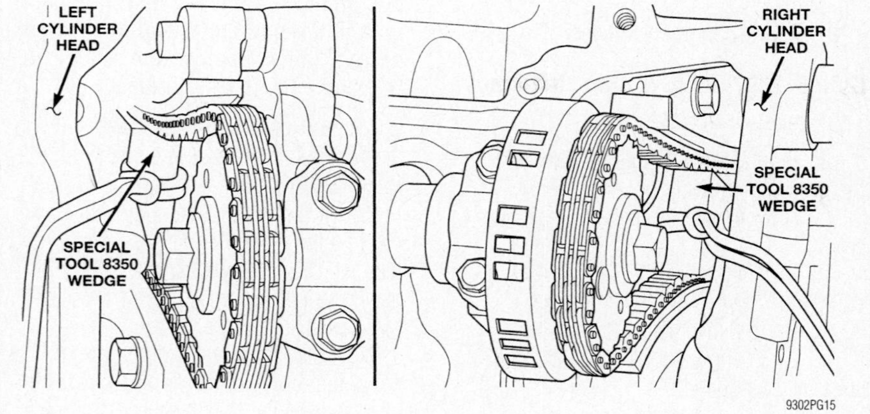

Fig. 56 Chain Tensioner Retaining Wedges—3.7L and 4.7L engines

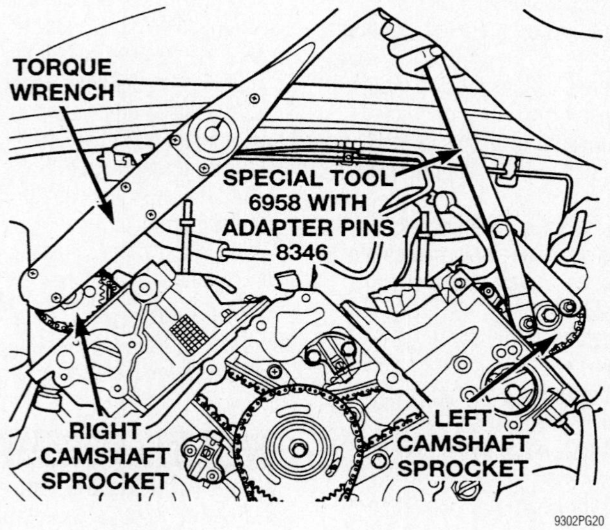

Fig. 57 Hold the left camshaft sprocket with a spanner wrench while removing or installing the camshaft sprocket bolts—4.7L engine

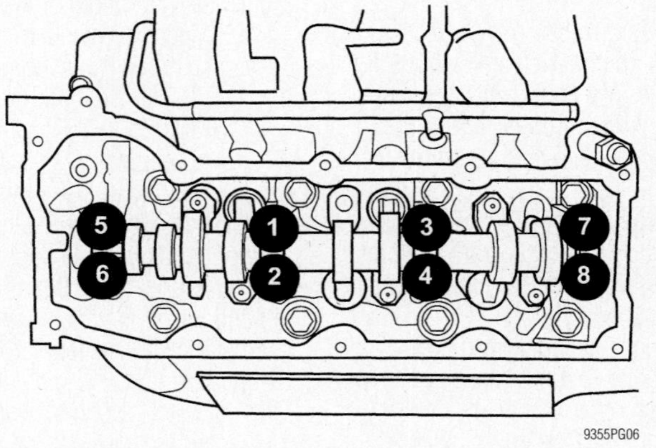

Fig. 58 Camshaft bearing cap bolt tightening sequence—3.7L

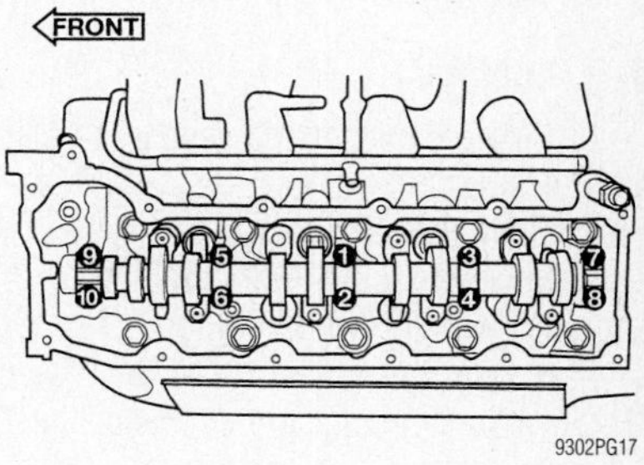

Fig. 59 Camshaft bearing cap bolt tightening sequence—4.7L engine

- Left camshaft sprocket
- Camshaft bearing caps, by reversing the tightening sequence
- Camshafts

To install:

10. Install or connect the following:
    - Camshafts. Torque the bearing cap bolts in ½ turn increments, in sequence, to 100 inch lbs. (11 Nm).
    - Target wheel to the right camshaft
    - Camshaft timing sprockets and chains, by aligning the matchmarks
11. Remove the tensioner wedges and tighten the camshaft sprocket bolts to 90 ft. lbs. (122 Nm).
12. Install or connect the following:
    - Hydraulic lash adjusters in their original locations

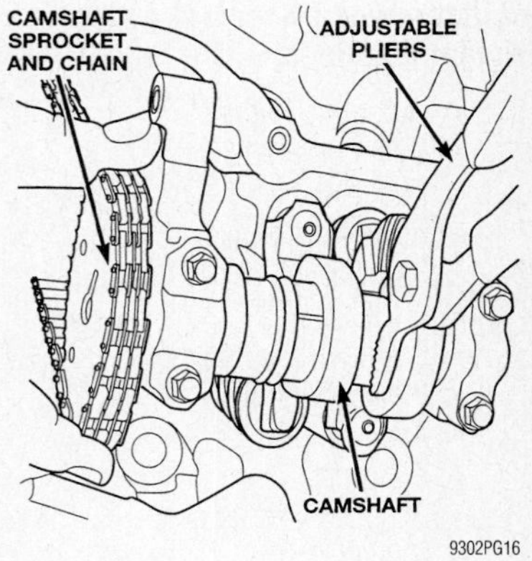

Fig. 60 Turn the camshaft with pliers, if needed, to align the dowel in the sprocket—4.7L engine

- Rocker arms in their original locations
- Cylinder head covers
- Negative battery cable

5.7L Engines

1. Before servicing the vehicle, refer to the Precautions Section.
2. Drain the cooling system.
3. Recover the A/C refrigerant, if equipped with air conditioning.
4. Set the crankshaft to Top Dead Center (TDC) of the compression stroke for the No. 1 cylinder.
5. Remove or disconnect the following:
    - Negative battery cable
    - Camshaft rear cam bearing core plug
    - Air cleaner
    - Accessory drive belt
    - Alternator
    - A/C compressor
    - Radiator
    - Intake manifold
    - Cylinder head covers
    - Cylinder heads
    - Oil pan
    - Front cover
    - Oil pickup tube
    - Oil pump
    - Timing chain and sprockets
    - Camshaft thrust plate
    - Hydraulic lifters
    - Camshaft

To install:

6. Install or connect the following:
    - Camshaft
    - Camshaft thrust plate. Tighten the bolts to 21 ft. lbs. (28 Nm).
    - Timing chain and sprockets
    - Oil pump
    - Oil pickup tube

➡Lifters must be replaced in their original positions.

- Hydraulic lifters
- Cylinder heads
- Pushrods
- Rocker arms
- Front cover
- Oil pan
- Cylinder head covers
- Intake manifold
- A/C compressor
- Alternator
- Accessory drive belt
- Radiator
- Air cleaner
- Camshaft rear cam bearing core plug
- Negative battery cable

7. Fill the cooling system.
8. Recharge the A/C system, if equipped.
9. Start the engine and check for leaks.

5.9L & 2007–08 6.7L Diesel Engines

See Figures 61 and 62.

1. Before servicing the vehicle, refer to the Precautions Section.
2. Disconnect both battery negative cables.
3. Recover A/C refrigerant (if A/C equipped)
4. Raise the vehicle.
5. Drain engine coolant into container suitable for re-use.
6. Lower the vehicle.
7. Remove the upper radiator hose.
8. Remove the viscous fan/drive/shroud assembly.
9. Disconnect the coolant recovery bottle hose from the radiator filler neck.
10. Disconnect lower radiator hose from radiator outlet.
11. For automatic Transmission models, disconnect transmission oil cooler lines from front of radiator using Special Tool 6931 (unless equipped with finger-release disconnect).
12. Remove radiator mounting screws and lift radiator out of engine compartment.
13. Remove the upper radiator support panel.
14. If A/C equipped, disconnect A/C condenser refrigerant lines.
15. Disconnect charge air cooler piping from the cooler inlet and outlet.
16. Remove the two charge air cooler mounting bolts.
17. Remove the charge air cooler (and A/C condenser if equipped) from vehicle.
18. Remove the accessory drive belt.
19. Remove the accessory drive belt tensioner.
20. Remove the fan support/hub assembly.
21. Remove crankshaft damper.
22. Remove the gear cover-to-housing bolts and gently pry the cover away from the housing, taking care not to mar the sealing surfaces. Remove dust seal with cover.
23. Using Special Tool 7471-B Crankshaft Barring Tool, rotate the crankshaft to align the timing marks on the crankshaft and the camshaft gears.
24. Remove the cylinder head cover
25. Remove the rocker arms, cross heads, and push rods. Mark each component so they can be installed in their original positions.

➡The number 5 cylinder intake and the number 6 cylinder intake and exhaust pushrods are removed by lifting them up and through the provided cowl panel access holes. Remove the rubber plugs to expose these relief holes.

26. Raise the tappets as follows, using the wooden dowel rods provided with the Miller Tool Kit 8502.
27. Insert the slotted end of the dowel rod into the tappet. The dowel rods for the rear two cylinders will have to be cut for cowl panel clearance. Press firmly to ensure that it is seated in the tappet.
28. Raise the dowel rod to bring the tappet to the top of its travel, and wrap a rubber band around the dowel rods to prevent the tappets from dropping into the crankcase.
29. Repeat this procedure for the remaining cylinders.
30. Verify that the camshaft timing marks are aligned with the crankshaft mark.
31. Remove the bolts from the thrust plate.
32. Remove engine mount through bolts.
33. Install engine support fixture special tool number 8534, and steel bracket/wing nut special tool number 8534 A.
34. Raise engine enough to allow camshaft removal.
35. Remove the camshaft, gear and thrust plate.

To install:

36. Lubricate the camshaft bushing and bores with fresh engine oil or suitable equivalent

⁂ WARNING

When installing the camshaft, DO NOT push it in farther than it will go with the thrust washer in place.

37. Install the camshaft and thrust plate. Align the timing marks.
38. Install the thrust plate bolts and tighten to 18 ft. lbs. (24 Nm).
39. Measure camshaft back lash and end clearance. Specifications are as follows:
    - Backlash: 0.003–0.010 inch (0.075–0.250 mm)
    - Clearance: 0.001–0.020 inch (0.025–0.500 mm)
40. Remove the wooden dowel rods and rubber bands from the tappets.
41. Lubricate the push rods with engine oil and install in their original location. Verify that they are seated in the tappets.
42. Lubricate the valve tips with engine oil and install the crossheads in their original locations.
43. Lubricate the crossheads and push

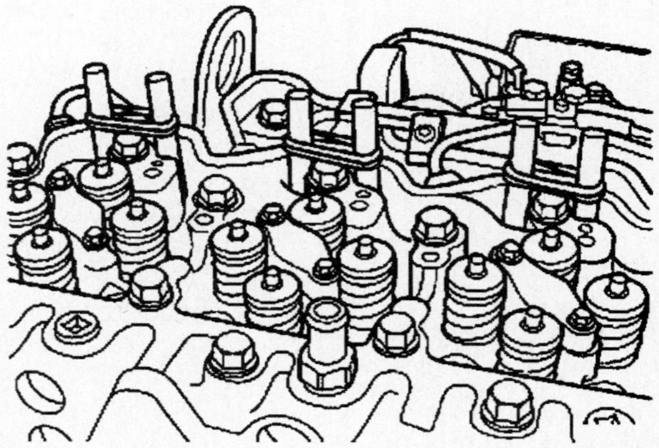

Fig. 61 Tappets secured using the wooden dowel rods provided with the Miller Tool Kit 8502.

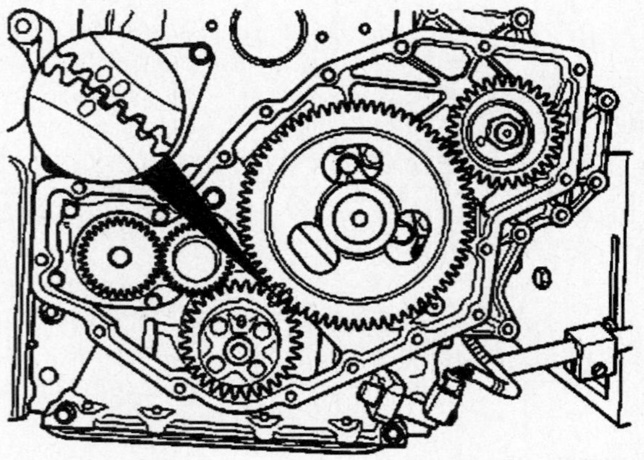

Fig. 62 Camshaft and crankshaft alignment marks

rod sockets with engine oil and install the rocker arms and pedestals in their original locations. Tighten bolts to 27 ft. lbs. (36 Nm).

44. Verify valve lash adjustment. Specifications are as follows:
    - Intake: 0.006 inch–0.015 inch (0.152 mm–0.381 mm)
    - Exhaust: 0.021 inch–0.034 inch (0.533 mm–0.863 mm)

➡If measured valve lash falls within these specifications, no adjustment/ reset is necessary. Engine operation within these ranges has no adverse affect on performance, emissions, fuel economy or level of engine noise

45. Install the cylinder head cover.
46. Install gear housing cover
47. Install front crankshaft dust seal.
48. Install the crankshaft damper.
49. Install the fan support/hub assembly.
50. Install the power steering pump.
51. Install the accessory drive belt tensioner. Tighten the bolts to 32 ft. lbs. (43 Nm).
52. Install the accessory drive belt
53. Install the charge air cooler (with a/c condenser and auxiliary transmission oil cooler, if equipped) and tighten the mounting bolts to 17 inch lbs. (2 Nm).
54. Connect charge air cooler inlet and outlet pipes. Tighten clamps to 95 in. lbs. (11 Nm)
55. Install the radiator upper support panel.
56. Close radiator petcock and lower the radiator into the engine compartment. Tighten the mounting bolts to 95 inch lbs. (11 Nm).
57. Raise the vehicle.
58. Connect radiator lower hose and install clamp.
59. Connect the transmission auxiliary oil cooler lines (if equipped).
60. Lower the vehicle.
61. Install the fan drive/shroud assembly.
62. Install the coolant recovery and windshield washer fluid reservoirs to the fan shroud.
63. Connect the coolant recovery hose to the radiator filler neck.
64. Add engine coolant.
65. Charge the A/C system with refrigerant (if A/C equipped).
66. Connect the battery negative cables.
67. Start engine and check for engine oil and coolant leaks.

CRANKSHAFT FRONT SEAL

REMOVAL & INSTALLATION

3.7L & 4.7L Engine

See Figures 63 and 64.

1. Before servicing the vehicle, refer to the Precautions Section.
2. Disconnect negative cable from battery.
3. Remove the accessory drive belt.
4. Remove the A/C compressor mounting fasteners and set compressor aside.
5. Drain the cooling system.
6. Remove the upper radiator hose.
7. Disconnect electrical connector for fan mounted inside radiator shroud.
8. Remove the radiator shroud attaching fasteners.

➡Transmission cooler line snaps into shroud lower right hand corner.

9. Remove radiator cooling fan and shroud.
10. Remove the crankshaft damper bolt.
11. Remove the damper using crankshaft insert 8513 and 1026 three jaw puller.
12. Using crankshaft front seal remover 8511, remove crankshaft front seal.

To install:

⁂ WARNING

To prevent severe damage to the crankshaft, damper or special tool 8512, thoroughly clean the damper bore and the crankshaft nose before installing Damper.

13. Using special tool 8348 and 8512, install crankshaft front seal.
14. Install the vibration damper. Tighten the bolt to 130 ft. lbs. (175 Nm).
15. Install the radiator cooling fan and shroud.
16. Install the upper radiator hose.
17. Install A/C compressor and tighten fasteners to 40 ft. lbs. (54 Nm).

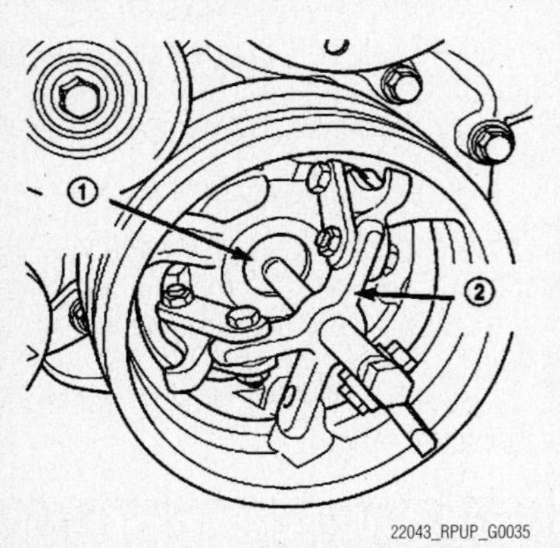

Fig. 63 Damper removal using crankshaft insert 8513 (1) and 1026 three jaw puller (2).

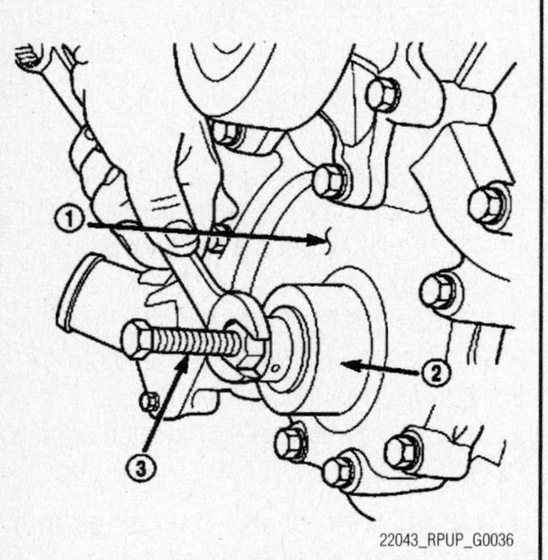

Fig. 64 Using special tools 8348 and 8512 (2,3), install crankshaft front seal.

18. Install the accessory drive belt.
19. Refill the cooling system.
20. Connect negative cable to battery.

5.7L Engine

See Figures 65 and 66.

1. Before servicing the vehicle, refer to the Precautions Section.
2. Disconnect negative cable from battery.
3. Remove the accessory drive belt.
4. Drain the cooling system.
5. Remove the upper radiator hose.
6. Remove the radiator shroud attaching fasteners.
7. Remove the radiator cooling fan and shroud.
8. Remove the crankshaft damper bolt.
9. Remove the damper using crankshaft insert 8513A and three jaw puller 1023.
10. Using crankshaft front seal remover 9071, remove crankshaft front seal.

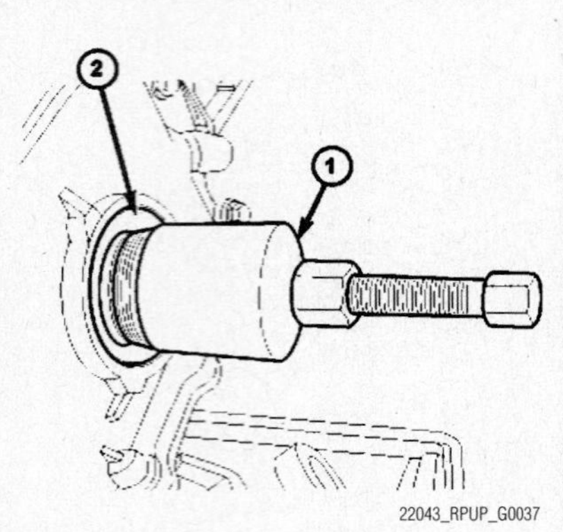

Fig. 65 Using Crankshaft Front Seal Remover 9071 (1), to remove crankshaft front seal (2).

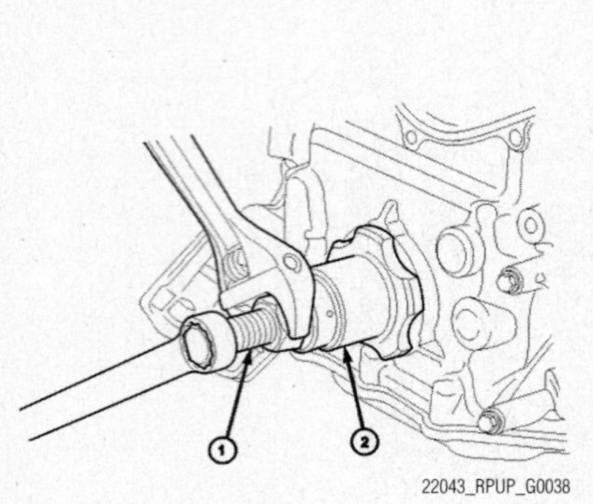

Fig. 66 Using crankshaft front oil seal installer 9072 (2) and damper installer 8512A (1), to install crankshaft front seal.

To install:

⁂ WARNING

The front crankshaft seal must be installed dry. Do not apply lubricant to sealing lip or to outer edge.

11. Using crankshaft front oil seal installer 9072 and damper installer 8512A, install crankshaft front seal.

⁂ WARNING

To prevent severe damage to the Crankshaft or Damper, thoroughly clean the damper bore and the crankshaft nose before installing Damper.

12. Install the vibration damper. Tighten bolt to 129 ft. lbs. (176 Nm).
13. Install radiator cooling fan and shroud.
14. Install the upper radiator hose.
15. Install the accessory drive belt refer
16. Refill the cooling system.
17. Connect negative cable to battery.

5.9L & 6.7L Engines

See Figure 67.

1. Disconnect both battery negative cables.
2. Raise the vehicle on hoist.
3. Partially drain the engine coolant.
4. Lower the vehicle.
5. Remove the radiator upper hose.
6. Disconnect the coolant recovery bottle hose from the radiator filler neck.
7. Disconnect windshield washer pump supply hose and electrical connections and lift washer bottle off of fan shroud.
8. Remove viscous fan/drive assembly.
9. Remove the cooling fan shroud and fan assembly from the vehicle.
10. Remove the accessory drive belt.
11. Remove the cooling fan support/hub from the front of the engine.
12. Raise the vehicle on hoist.
13. Remove the crankshaft damper and speed indicator ring.
14. Remove power steering pump.
15. Remove the accessory drive belt tensioner.
16. Remove the gear cover-to-housing bolts and gently pry the cover away from the housing, taking care not to mar the gasket surfaces. Remove crank seal dust shield with cover.
17. Support the cover on a flat work surface with wooden blocks, and using a suitable punch and hammer, drive the old seal out of the cover from the back side of the cover to the front side.

To install:

⁂ WARNING

The seal lip and the sealing surface on the crankshaft must be free of all oil residue, to prevent leaks. The crankshaft and seal surface must be completely dry when the seal is installed.

18. Clean cover and housing gasket mating surfaces. Use a suitable scraper and be careful not to damage the gear housing surface. Remove any old sealer from the oil seal bore. Thoroughly clean the front seal area of the crankshaft. Do not sand this surface. The seal lip and the sealing surface on the crankshaft must be free from all oil residue to prevent seal leaks.
19. Inspect the gear housing and cover for cracks and replace if necessary. Carefully straighten any bends or imperfections in the gear cover with a ball-peen hammer

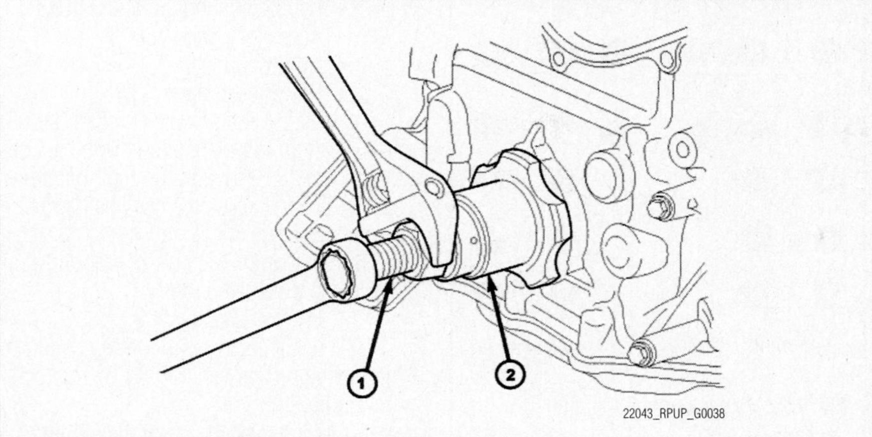

Fig. 67 Diesel engine front seal removal shown

on a flat surface. Inspect the crankshaft front journal for any grooves or nicks that would affect the integrity of the new seal.

20. Apply a bead of Mopar® Stud & Bearing Mount to the outside diameter of the seal. Do not lubricate the inside diameter of the new seal.
21. With the cover supported by wood blocks, install the seal into the rear of the cover using crankshaft seal installer special tool 8281 and driver handle C-4171. Strike the driver handle until the installation tool bottoms out on the inside of the cover.
22. Install the plastic seal pilot (provided with seal kit) into the crankshaft seal.
23. Apply a bead of Mopar® silicone rubber adhesive sealant or equivalent to the gear housing cover sealing surface.
24. Install the cover to the gear housing, aligning the seal pilot with the nose of the crankshaft.

➡Failure to follow the cover installation procedure can result in misalignment of the crankshaft seal to the crankshaft, causing an oil leak.

25. Install the cover bolts and hand snug 2 cap screws at the 3 o'clock and 9 o'clock position, to keep the cover from moving when the first cap screw is tightened. Tighten to 18 ft. lbs. (24 Nm). Remove pilot tool.
26. Install dust shield over nose of crankshaft.
27. Install the crankshaft damper and speed indicator ring. Tighten the bolts to 30 ft. lbs. (40 Nm). Then rotate an additional 60 degrees. Use the engine barring tool to keep the engine from rotating during tightening operation.
28. Install the fan support/hub assembly and tighten the bolts to 24 ft. lbs. (32 Nm).
29. Install power steering pump.
30. Install the accessory drive belt tensioner. Tighten the bolt to 32 ft. lbs. (43 Nm).
31. Install the cooling fan
32. Install the accessory drive belt.
33. Refill the cooling system.
34. Connect the battery negative cables.
35. Start engine and check for oil leaks.

CYLINDER HEAD

REMOVAL & INSTALLATION

3.7L Engine

Left Side

See Figures 68 through 71.

1. Before servicing the vehicle, refer to the Precautions Section.
2. Drain the cooling system.
3. Properly relieve the fuel system pressure.
4. Remove or disconnect the following:
   - Negative battery cable
   - Exhaust Y-pipe
   - Intake manifold
   - Brake booster and master cylinder
   - Cylinder head cover
   - Engine cooling fan and shroud
   - Accessory drive belt
   - Power steering pump
5. Rotate the crankshaft so that the crankshaft timing mark aligns with the Top Dead Center (TDC) mark on the front cover, and the **V6** marks on the camshaft sprockets are at 12 o'clock as shown.
   - Crankshaft damper
   - Front cover
6. Lock the secondary timing chain to the idler sprocket with Timing Chain Locking tool 8429.
7. Matchmark the secondary timing chain one link on each side of the V6 mark to the camshaft sprocket.
   - Left secondary timing chain tensioner
   - Cylinder head access plug
   - Secondary timing chain guide
   - Camshaft sprocket
   - Cylinder head

➡The cylinder head is retained by twelve bolts. Four of the bolts are smaller and are at the front of the head.

To install:

8. Check the cylinder head bolts for signs of stretching and replace as necessary.
9. Lubricate the threads of the 11mm bolts with clean engine oil.

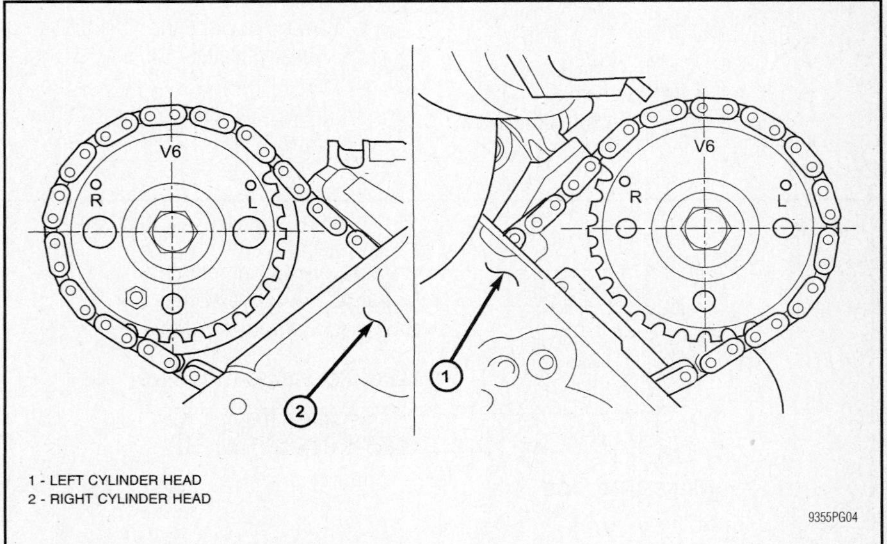

Fig. 68 Camshaft sprocket timing marks—3.7L

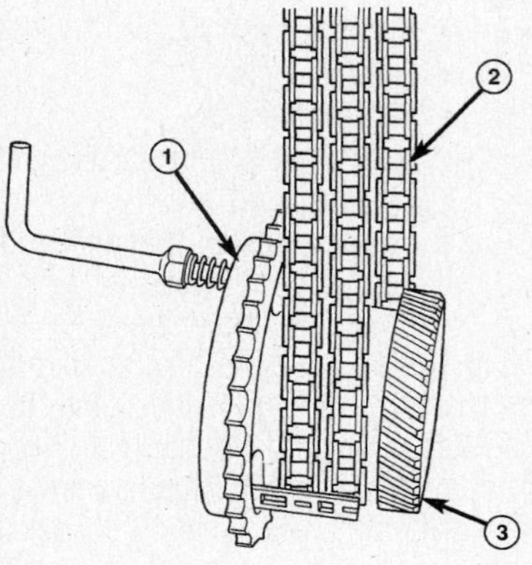

Fig. 69 Camshaft locking tool—3.7L

10. Coat the threads of the 8mm bolts with Mopar® Lock and Seal Adhesive.
11. Install the cylinder heads. Use new gaskets and tighten the bolts, in sequence, as follows:
  a. Step 1: Bolts 1–8 to 20 ft. lbs. (27 Nm)
  b. Step 2: Bolts 1–10 verify torque without loosening
  c. Step 3: Bolts 9–12 to 10 ft. lbs. (14 Nm)
  d. Step 4: Bolts 1–8 plus ¼ (90 degree) turn
  e. Step 5: Bolts 9–12 to 19 ft. lbs. (26 Nm)
12. Install or connect the following:
  - Camshaft sprocket. Align the secondary chain matchmarks and tighten the bolt to 90 ft. lbs. (122 Nm).
  - Secondary timing chain guide
  - Cylinder head access plug
  - Secondary timing chain tensioner. Refer to the timing chain procedure in this section.

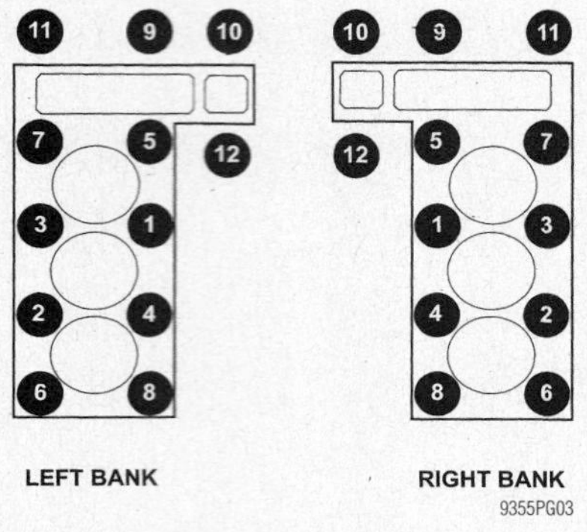

Fig. 71 Cylinder head bolt torque sequence—3.7L

13. Remove the Timing Chain Locking tool.
14. Install or connect the following:
  - Front cover
  - Crankshaft damper. Torque the bolt to 130 ft. lbs. (175 Nm).
  - Power steering pump
  - Accessory drive belt
  - Engine cooling fan and shroud
  - Cover
  - Intake manifold
  - Exhaust Y-pipe
  - Negative battery cable
15. Fill and bleed the cooling system.
16. Start the engine, check for leaks and repair if necessary.

Right Side

See Figures 72 and 73.

1. Before servicing the vehicle, refer to the Precautions Section.
2. Drain the cooling system.
3. Properly relieve the fuel system pressure.
4. Remove or disconnect the following:
  - Negative battery cable
  - Exhaust Y-pipe
  - Intake manifold
  - Valve cover
  - Engine cooling fan and shroud
  - Accessory drive belt
  - Oil fill housing
  - Power steering pump
5. Rotate the crankshaft so that the crankshaft timing mark aligns with the Top Dead Center (TDC) mark on the front cover, and the **V6** marks on the camshaft sprockets are at 12 o'clock as shown.
6. Remove or disconnect the following:
  - Crankshaft damper
  - Front cover
7. Lock the secondary timing chains to the idler sprocket with Timing Chain Locking tool 8429.
8. Matchmark the secondary timing chains to the camshaft sprockets.
9. Remove or disconnect the following:
  - Secondary timing chain tensioners
  - Cylinder head access plugs
  - Secondary timing chain guides
  - Camshaft sprockets
  - Cylinder heads

➡Each cylinder head is retained by 8 11mm bolts and four 8mm bolts.

To install:

10. Check the cylinder head bolts for signs of stretching and replace as necessary.
11. Lubricate the threads of the 11mm bolts with clean engine oil.
12. Coat the threads of the 8mm bolts with Mopar® Lock and Seal Adhesive.
13. Install the cylinder heads. Use new gaskets and tighten the bolts, in sequence, as follows:
  a. Step 1: Bolts 1–8 to 20 ft. lbs. (27 Nm)

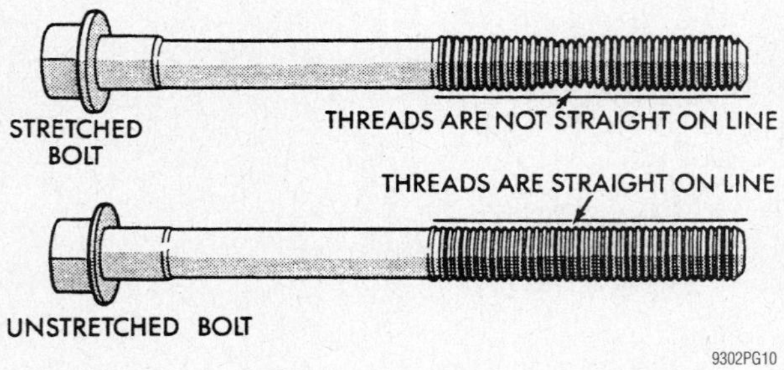

Fig. 70 Examine the head bolts for signs of stretching—3.7L engine

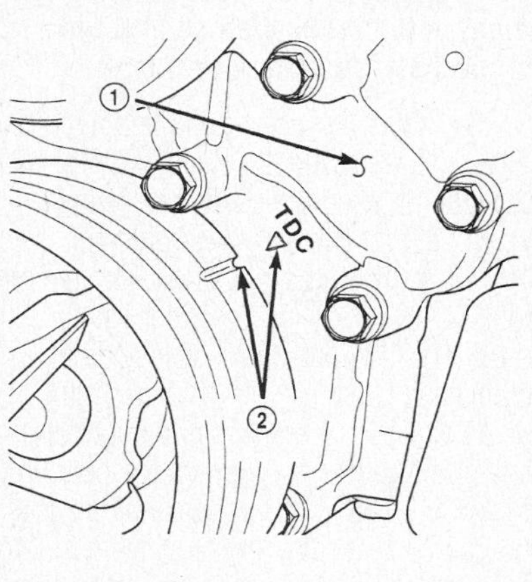

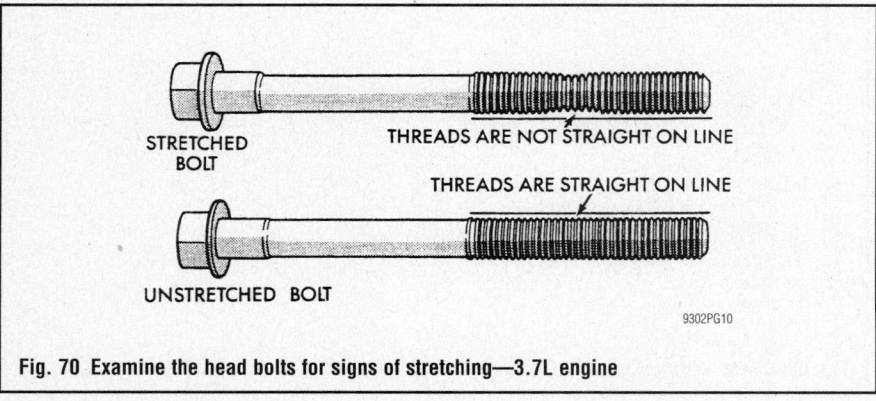

Fig. 72 Crankshaft timing marks—3.7L and 4.7L engines

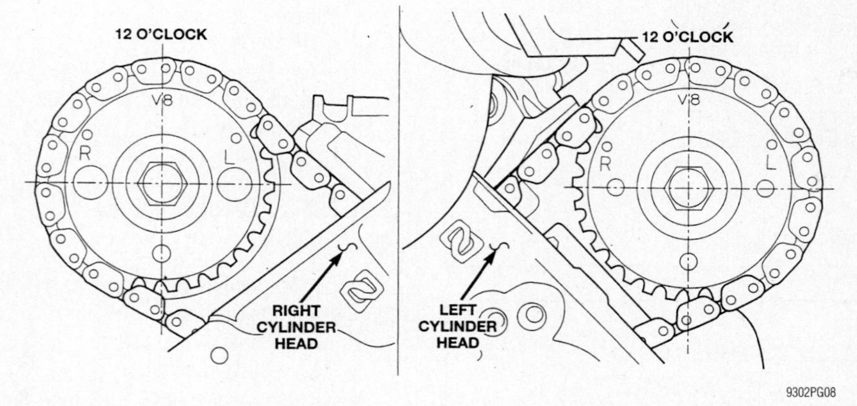

Fig. 73 Camshaft positioning—3.7L and 4.7L engines

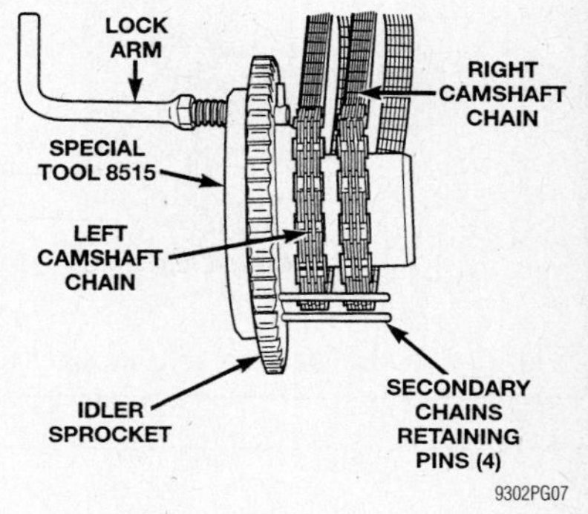

Fig. 75 Use the special tool to lock the timing chains on the idler gear—4.7L engine

b. Step 2: Bolts 1–10 verify torque without loosening

c. Step 3: Bolts 9–12 to 10 ft. lbs. (14 Nm)

d. Step 4: Bolts 1–8 plus ¼ (90 degree) turn

e. Step 5: Bolts 9–12 to 19 ft. lbs. (26 Nm)

14. Install or connect the following:
    - Camshaft sprockets. Align the secondary chain matchmarks and tighten the bolts to 90 ft. lbs. (122 Nm).
    - Secondary timing chain guides
    - Cylinder head access plugs
    - Secondary timing chain tensioners. Refer to the timing chain procedure in this section.
15. Remove the Timing Chain Locking tool.
16. Install or connect the following:
    - Front cover
    - Crankshaft damper. Torque the bolt to 130 ft. lbs. (175 Nm).
    - Rocker arms
    - Power steering pump
    - Oil fill housing
    - Accessory drive belt
    - Engine cooling fan and shroud
    - Valve covers
    - Intake manifold
    - Exhaust Y-pipe
    - Negative battery cable
17. Fill and bleed the cooling system.
18. Start the engine, check for leaks and repair if necessary.

4.7L Engine

See Figures 72 through 77.

1. Before servicing the vehicle, refer to the Precautions Section.
2. Drain the cooling system.
3. Properly relieve the fuel system pressure.
4. Remove or disconnect the following:
    - Negative battery cable
    - Exhaust Y-pipe
    - Intake manifold
    - Valve covers
    - Engine cooling fan and shroud
    - Accessory drive belt
    - Oil fill housing
    - Power steering pump
    - Rocker arms
5. Rotate the crankshaft so that the crankshaft timing mark aligns with the Top Dead Center (TDC) mark on the front cover, and the **V8** marks on the camshaft sprockets are at 12 o'clock as shown.
6. Remove or disconnect the following:
    - Crankshaft damper
    - Front cover
7. Lock the secondary timing chains to the idler sprocket with Timing Chain Locking tool 8515.
8. Matchmark the secondary timing chains to the camshaft sprockets.

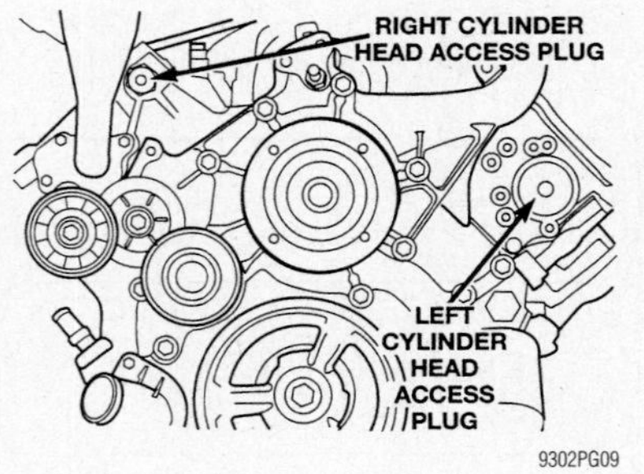

Fig. 74 Cylinder head access plug locations—4.7L engine

9. Remove or disconnect the following:
    - Secondary timing chain tensioners
    - Cylinder head access plugs
    - Secondary timing chain guides
    - Camshaft sprockets
    - Cylinder heads

➡Each cylinder head is retained by ten 11mm bolts and four 8mm bolts.

To install:

10. Check the cylinder head bolts for signs of stretching and replace as necessary.
11. Lubricate the threads of the 11mm bolts with clean engine oil.
12. Coat the threads of the 8mm bolts with Mopar® Lock and Seal Adhesive.
13. Install the cylinder heads. Use new gaskets and tighten the bolts, in sequence, as follows:

a. Step 1: Bolts 1–10 to 15 ft. lbs. (20 Nm)

b. Step 2: Bolts 1–10 to 35 ft. lbs. (47 Nm)

c. Step 3: Bolts 11–14 to 18 ft. lbs. (25 Nm)

d. Step 4: Bolts 1–10 plus ¼ (90 degree) turn

e. Step 5: Bolts 11–14 to 22 ft. lbs. (30 Nm)

14. Install or connect the following:
    - Camshaft sprockets. Align the secondary chain matchmarks and tighten the bolts to 90 ft. lbs. (122 Nm).
    - Secondary timing chain guides
    - Cylinder head access plugs
    - Secondary timing chain tensioners. Refer to the timing chain procedure in this section.
15. Remove the Timing Chain Locking tool 8515.

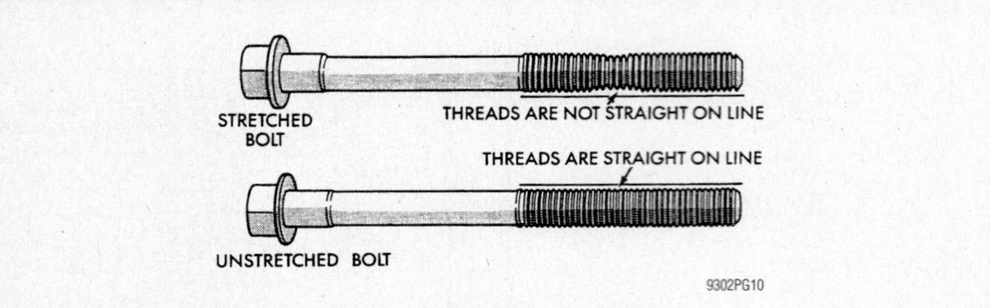

Fig. 76 Examine the head bolts for signs of stretching—4.7L engine

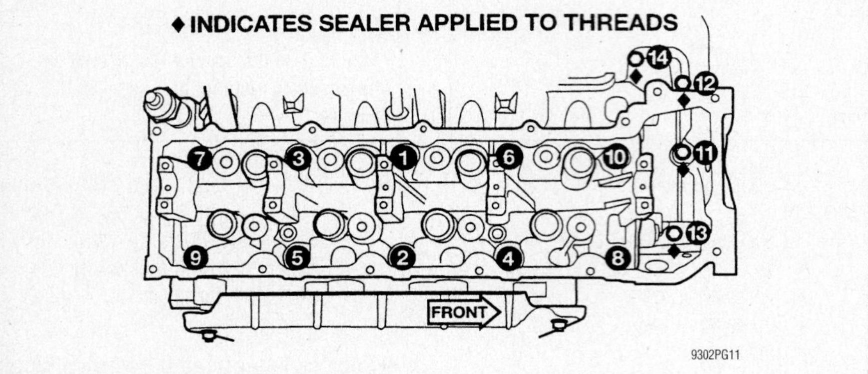

Fig. 77 Cylinder head torque sequence—4.7L engine

16. Install or connect the following:
   - Front cover
   - Crankshaft damper. Torque the bolt to 130 ft. lbs. (175 Nm).
   - Rocker arms
   - Power steering pump
   - Oil fill housing
   - Accessory drive belt
   - Engine cooling fan and shroud
   - Valve covers
   - Intake manifold
   - Exhaust Y-pipe
   - Negative battery cable
17. Fill and bleed the cooling system.
18. Start the engine, check for leaks and repair if necessary.

5.7L Engine

See Figure 78.

1. Before servicing the vehicle, refer to the Precautions Section.
2. Drain the cooling system.
3. Properly relieve the fuel system pressure.
4. Remove or disconnect the following:
   - Negative battery cable
   - Air cleaner resonator and ducts
   - Alternator
   - Closed crankcase ventilation system
   - EVAP control system
   - Heater hoses
   - Cylinder head covers
   - Intake manifold
   - Rocker arms and pushrods
   - Cylinder heads

To install:

➡The head gaskets are not interchangeable. They are marked “L” and “R”.

5. Install the cylinder heads. Use new gaskets and tighten the bolts, in sequence, as follows:
   a. Step 1: 12 mm bolts–25 ft. lbs. (34 Nm); 8mm bolts–15 ft. lbs. (20 Nm)
   b. Step 2: 12mm bolts–40 ft. lbs. (54 Nm); 8mm bolts retorque–15 ft. lbs. (20 Nm)
   c. Step 3: 12mm bolts–plus 90 degrees; 8mm bolts–25 ft. lbs. (34 Nm)
6. Install or connect the following:

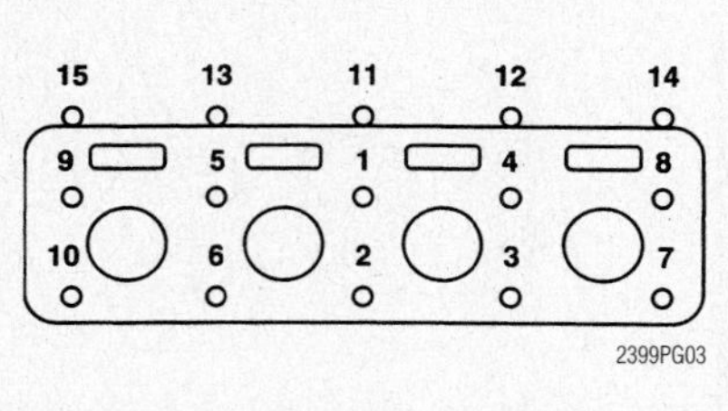

Fig. 78 Cylinder head torque sequence—5.7L engine

   - Rocker arms and pushrods
   - Intake manifold
   - Heater hoses
   - Alternator
   - Cylinder head covers. Torque the studs and bolts to 70 inch lbs.
   - Air cleaner resonator and ducts
   - Negative battery cable

5.9L & 6.7L Diesel Engines

See Figure 79.

1. Before servicing the vehicle, refer to the Precautions Section.
2. Drain the cooling system.
3. Drain the engine oil.
4. Remove or disconnect the following:
   - Negative battery cables
   - Radiator hoses
   - Heater hoses
   - Drive belt
   - Turbocharger
   - Exhaust Gas Recirculation (EGR) tube
   - Exhaust manifold
   - Accelerator pedal position sensor
   - Fuel lines and injector nozzles
   - Valve cover

➡Keep all valvetrain components in order for assembly.

   - Rocker levers and pedestal assemblies
   - Pushrods
   - Fuel filter and water separator assembly

➡If the cylinder head is hot, gradually loosen the cylinder head bolts using the TIGHTENING sequence. If the engine is cold, then the loosening sequence for the head bolts is not important.

➡The cylinder head bolts are different sizes. Note their locations for assembly.

   - Cylinder head bolts
   - Cylinder head

To install:

➡Check the cylinder head bolt length. If length exceeds 5.2 inches (132.1 mm), the bolt must be replaced.

5. Install or connect the following:
   - Cylinder head
   - Pushrods
   - Rocker levers and pedestal assemblies
6. Install the cylinder head bolts and tighten them in sequence as follows:
   a. Step 1: 52 ft. lbs. (70 Nm).
   b. Step 2: Back off 360 degrees in sequence.

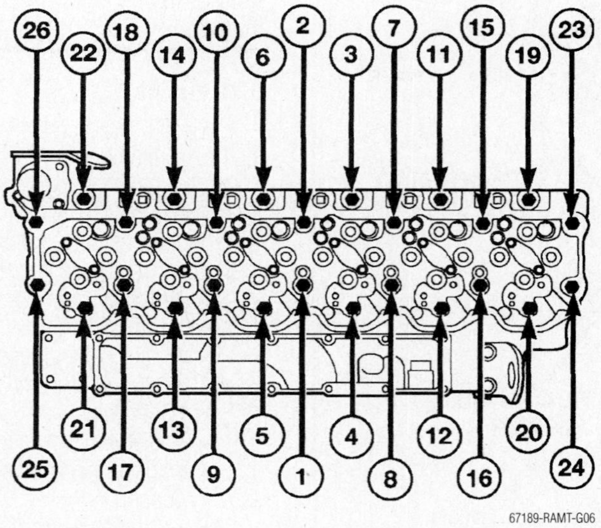

Fig. 79 Cylinder head torque sequence—5.9L diesel engine

c. Step 3: Tighten to 77 ft. lbs. (105 Nm).

d. Step 4: Recheck all bolts to 77 ft. lbs. (105 Nm).

e. Tighten all bolts an additional 90 degrees.

7. Install or connect the following:
   - Fuel filter and water separator assembly
   - Valve cover
   - Fuel lines and injector nozzles
   - Accelerator pedal position sensor
   - Exhaust manifold
   - EGR tube
   - Turbocharger
   - Drive belt
   - Heater hoses
   - Radiator hoses
   - Negative battery cables
8. Fill the crankcase to the correct level.
9. Fill the cooling system.
10. Start the engine and check for leaks.

ENGINE ASSEMBLY

REMOVAL & INSTALLATION

3.7L Engine

See Figure 80.

1. Before servicing the vehicle, refer to the Precautions Section.
2. Properly relieve the fuel system pressure.
3. Drain the cooling system.
4. Drain the engine oil.
5. Remove or disconnect the following:
   - Negative battery cable
   - Hood
   - Air cleaner assembly
   - Radiator
   - Electric and mechanical fan assemblies
   - Without discharging, remove the A/C compressor, if equipped, and secure it out of the way with the lines attached.
   - Power steering pump, with the lines attached
   - Alternator
   - Coolant bottle
   - Heater hoses
   - Accelerator and speed control cables
   - Lower and upper radiator hoses
   - Engine ground straps
   - Intake Air Temperature (IAT) sensor
   - Fuel injection wiring connectors
   - Throttle Position (TP) sensor
   - Idle Air Control (IAC) motor
   - Oil pressure sender connector
   - Engine Coolant Temperature (ECT) sensor
   - Manifold Absolute Pressure (MAP) sensor
   - Camshaft position sensor
   - Ignition coil wiring connector
   - Crankshaft Position (CKP) sensor
   - Coil pack
   - Fuel rail
   - PCV hose
   - Vacuum hoses from the intake manifold
   - Knock sensor connectors
   - Oil dipstick tube
   - Intake manifold
   - Heated Oxygen (HO_2S) sensor connector
   - Block heater connector
   - Front driveshaft at the differential
   - Starter
   - Structural cover
   - With a manual transmission, remove the transmission
   - Torque converter bolts and matchmark the converter
   - Automatic transmission-to-engine bolts
   - Exhaust front pipes
   - Left and right engine mounts
6. Place a support stand under the transmission.
7. Install an engine lift plate
8. Lift the engine out of the vehicle.

To install:

9. If equipped with a manual transmission, install the transmission
10. Lower the engine and install the mounts. Don't tighten the bolts yet.
11. If equipped with an automatic transmission, perform the following steps:

a. Align the torque converter housing to the engine.

b. Torque the bolts to 30 ft. lbs. (41 Nm).

12. Install or connect the following:
   - Install the torque converter to flexplate bolts. Torque the bolts to 50 ft. lbs. (68 Nm)
   - Torque the through bolts to 45 ft. lbs. (61 Nm)
   - Engine ground strap
   - Starter motor
   - CKP sensor
   - Block heater cable
   - Structural cover

WARNING

The structural cover must be held tightly against the engine and bellhousing during tightening. The torque for all bolts is 40 ft. lbs. (54 Nm); the bolts must be tightened in the order shown.

   - Exhaust pipes. New flange clamps MUST be used!
   - HO_2S sensor connectors
   - KS sensors
   - Intake Manifold
   - Dipstick tube
   - Vacuum hoses to the intake manifold
   - PCV and breather hoses
   - Fuel rail
   - Ignition coil
   - IAT sensor
   - Fuel injector connectors
   - TP sensor

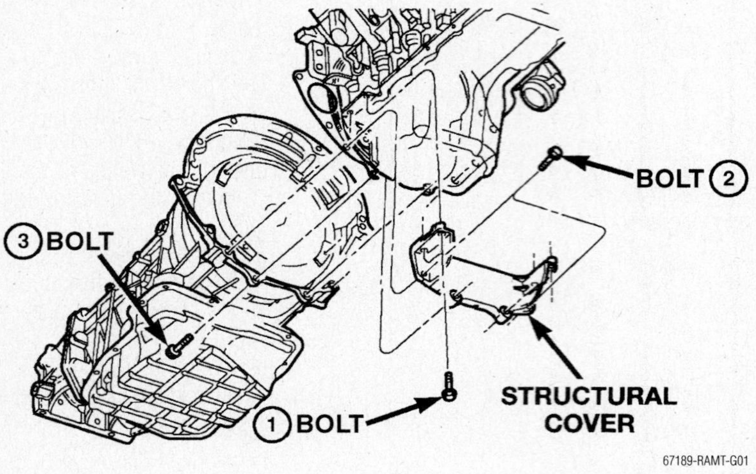

Fig. 80 Tighten the structural cover bolts in this order—3.7L, 4.7L and 5.7L engines

- IAC motor
- Oil pressure sender
- ECT sensor electrical connector
- MAP sensor
- CMP sensor
- Radiator hoses
- Cruise control cable, if equipped
- Throttle cable
- Heater hoses
- Coolant bottle
- Power steering pump
- Alternator
- A/C compressor
- Radiator
- Fan assemblies
- Air cleaner assembly
- Negative battery cable

13. Fill and bleed the power steering system.
14. Fill the engine with clean oil.
15. Start the engine and check for leaks, repair if necessary.

4.7L Engine

1. Before servicing the vehicle, refer to the Precautions Section.
2. Drain the cooling system and engine oil.
3. Remove or disconnect the following:
   - Negative battery cable
   - Battery and tray
   - Exhaust crossover pipe
   - On 4wd, the axle vent tube
   - Left and right engine mount through bolts
   - On 4wd, the left and right engine mount bracket locknuts
   - Ground straps
   - CKP sensor
   - On 4wd, the axle isolator bracket
   - Structural cover
   - Starter
   - Torque converter bolts
   - Transmission-to-engine bolts
   - Engine block heater
   - Resonator and air inlet
   - Throttle and speed control cables
   - Crankcase breathers
   - A/C compressor
   - Shroud and fan assemblies
   - Transmission cooler lines
   - Radiator hoses
   - Radiator
   - Alternator
   - Heater hoses
   - Engine harness
   - Vacuum lines
   - Fuel system pressure
   - Fuel line at the rail
   - Power steering pump
4. Install lifting eyes and take up the weight of the engine with a crane.
5. Support the transmission with a jack.
6. Remove the engine.
7. To install
8. Installation is the reverse of removal. Observe the following:
   - Left and right engine mount through bolts: 2wd 70 ft. lbs. (95 Nm); 4wd 75 ft. lbs. (102 Nm)
   - On 4wd, the bracket locknuts: 30 ft. lbs. (41 Nm)
   - Transmission-to-engine bolts: 30 ft. lbs. (41 Nm)

⁂ WARNING

The structural cover must be held tightly against the engine and bell-housing during tightening. The torque for all bolts is 40 ft. lbs. (54 Nm); the bolts must be tightened in the order shown.

5.7L Engine

1. Before servicing the vehicle, refer to the Precautions Section.
2. Drain the cooling system.
3. Drain the engine oil.
4. Relieve the fuel system pressure.
5. Remove or disconnect the following:
   - Negative battery cable
   - Hood
   - Air cleaner and resonator
   - Accessory drive belt
   - Engine fan
   - Radiator
   - Upper crossmember and top core support
   - A/C compressor, if equipped
   - Alternator
   - Intake manifold and IAFM as an assembly
   - Heater hoses
   - Power steering pump
   - Fuel line
   - Engine front mount thru-bolt nuts
   - Transmission oil cooler lines, if equipped
   - Exhaust pipes at the manifolds
   - Starter motor
   - Structural dust cover and transmission inspection cover
   - Torque converter-to-flexplate bolts
   - Transmission flange bolts. Support the transmission.
   - Engine

To install:

⁂ WARNING

The structural cover must be held tightly against the engine and bell-housing during tightening. The torque for all bolts is 40 ft. lbs. (54 Nm); the bolts must be tightened in the order shown.

6. Install or connect the following:
   - Engine. Tighten the engine mount thru-bolt finger-tight.
   - Transmission flange bolts. Tighten the bolts to 40–45 ft. lbs. (54–61 Nm). Then, tighten the mount bolt nuts to 70 ft. lbs. (95 Nm)
   - Transmission oil cooler lines, if equipped
   - Torque converter, if equipped. Tighten the bolts to 23 ft. lbs. (31 Nm).
   - Structural dust cover and transmission inspection cover

- Starter motor
- Fuel line
- Power steering pump
- Heater hoses
- Intake manifold and IAFM as an assembly
- Alternator
- A/C compressor, if equipped
- Upper crossmember and top core support
- Radiator
- Engine fan
- Accessory drive belt
- Air cleaner and resonator
- Hood
- Negative battery cable

7. Fill the crankcase to the correct level.
8. Fill the cooling system.
9. Start the engine and check for leaks.

5.9L & 6.7L Engines

1. Disconnect both battery negative cables.
2. Disconnect engine grid heater harness at grid heater relays.
3. Disconnect the electrical connections from rear of alternator.
4. Recover the A/C refrigerant.
5. Raise the vehicle on a hoist.
6. Drain engine coolant.
7. Remove engine oil drain plug and drain engine oil. Reinstall drain plug.
8. Lower the vehicle.
9. Remove fan and fan drive.
10. Remove fan shroud mounting bracket and shroud.
11. Remove the radiator upper hose.
12. Disconnect the coolant recovery bottle hose from the radiator fill neck.
13. Disconnect heater core supply and return hoses from the cylinder head fitting and coolant pipe.
14. Raise the vehicle on a hoist.
15. Remove transmission and transfer case (if equipped).
16. Disconnect exhaust pipe from turbocharger extension pipe.
17. Disconnect engine harness to vehicle harness connectors.
18. Remove the starter motor.
19. Remove the flywheel/flexplate.
20. Remove the transmission adapter. (If equipped).
21. Disconnect A/C suction/discharge hose from the rear of the A/C compressor.
22. Lower the vehicle.
23. Disconnect lower radiator hose from radiator outlet.
24. For automatic transmission models, disconnect transmission oil cooler lines from in front of radiator using special tool 6931
25. Remove the radiator.
26. If A/C equipped, disconnect A/C condenser refrigerant lines.
27. Disconnect charge air cooler piping.
28. Remove charge air cooler mounting bolts.
29. Remove charge air cooler from vehicle.
30. Remove the A/C condenser.
31. Remove damper and speed indicator ring from front of engine.
32. Remove the lower fan shroud bracket from engine.
33. Remove upper fan shroud brackets from engine
34. Disconnect engine block heater connector
35. Disconnect A/C compressor and pressure sensor electrical connectors.
36. Remove the passenger battery ground cable from the engine block. Remove the driver side battery ground cable from the engine block.
37. Remove power steering pump from engine by removing 3 bolts.
38. Disconnect the ECM power connector.
39. Disconnect the ECM ground wire from the hydroform screw.
40. Disconnect the fuel supply and return hoses.
41. Remove the cylinder head cover.
42. Disconnect the wire harnesses from the injectors.
43. Remove the cylinder head cover carrier gasket

➡Extreme care should be used to keep dirt/debris from entering the fuel lines. Plastic caps should be used on the ends of the fuel lines.

44. Loosen number 6 fuel line shield bolts and rotate shield out of the way.
45. Remove cylinder number 5 and number 6 high pressure fuel lines.
46. Remove the rear engine lift bracket.
47. Remove cylinder number 4, number 5, and number 6 intake and exhaust rocker arms, pedestals, and push tubes. (Note the original location for reassembly).
48. Remove the fuel connector tube nut and fuel connector tube. Remove cylinder number 5 and number 6 fuel injector.
49. Remove rocker housing.
50. Remove two cylinder head bolts and install tool number 9009. Tighten bolts to 77 ft. lbs. (105 Nm).
51. Loosen but do not remove engine mount through bolts and nuts.
52. Disconnect hood support struts and position hood out of the way.
53. Attach a chain with two hooks to the engine lift brackets.
54. While keeping engine level, lift straight up out of the mounts.
55. Rotate nose of the engine upward and pull out of the chassis.

To install:

56. Remove cylinder head bolts. Install special tool 9009. Tighten bolts to 77 ft. lbs. (105 Nm).
57. Lower engine into the engine compartment and install the engine mount through bolts and nuts.
58. Tighten the mount through bolts and nuts to 65 ft. lbs. (88 Nm).
59. Remove the engine lifting device tool 9009.
60. Check cylinder head cap screw length and install into cylinder head.
61. Tighten in 4 steps as follows:
    - Step 1: Tighten to 52 ft. lbs. (70 Nm)
    - Step 2: Back off 360 degrees
    - Step 3: Tighten to 77 ft. lbs. (105 Nm)
    - Step 4: Rotate 90 degrees
62. Install rocker housing. Torque to 18 ft. lbs. (24 Nm).
63. Replace injector o-ring and sealing washer on injectors number 5 and number 6.
64. Install injectors and tighten using the following steps:
    - Install injector hold-down cap screws and torque to 44 in. lbs. (5 Nm).
    - Loosen injector hold-down cap screws
    - Install HPC connector tube and nut. Tighten nut to 11 ft. lbs. (15 Nm).
    - Tighten the injector hold-down cap screws to 89 in. lbs. (10 Nm).
    - Tighten the HPC connector tube nut to 37 ft. lbs. (50 Nm).
65. Install rear engine lift bracket. Tighten to 57 ft. lbs. (77 Nm).
66. Install number 5 and number 6 high pressure fuel lines.
67. Tighten fuel line fittings to 22 ft. lbs. (30 Nm). Tighten brace cap screw and nut to 18 ft. lbs. (24 Nm).
68. Install push tubes, rocker arms, and pedestals for cylinders number 4, number 5, and number 6. Tighten the mounting bolts to 27 ft. lbs. (36 Nm).
69. Reset valve lash on cylinders number 4, number 5, and number 6. Tighten adjusting nuts to 18 ft. lbs. (24 Nm)
70. Install the injector wiring/gasket.
71. Install cylinder head cover carrier gasket

72. Connect the injector harness nuts to injectors. Tighten to 11 in. lbs (1.25 Nm).
73. Connect the injector wiring harness connectors to injector connections on cylinder head cover carrier gasket.
74. Install cylinder head cover
75. Connect breather tube and lube oil drain tube to cylinder head cover
76. Connect fuel supply and return hoses.
77. Connect ECM ground to hydroform screw. Connect ECM power connector.
78. Install the power steering pump.
79. Install the damper and speed indicator ring. Tighten to 30 ft. lbs. (40 Nm) plus 60 degrees.
80. Install the lower fan shroud bracket. Tighten to 18 ft. lbs. (24 Nm).
81. Install upper fan shroud brackets, but do not tighten fasteners at this time.
82. Connect the engine block heater connection.
83. Connect the A/C compressor and pressure sensor connectors
84. Install the charge air cooler. Install and tighten the charge air cooler mounting bolts to 17 in. lbs. (2 Nm).
85. Connect the charge air cooler tubes. Tighten all clamps to 72 in. lbs. (8 Nm).
86. Install the a/c condenser.
87. Connect the a/c refrigerant lines to the a/c condenser.
88. Install the radiator upper support panel.
89. Install the radiator.
90. Connect the transmission quick-connect oil cooler lines.
91. Raise the vehicle.
92. Connect A/C compressor suction/discharge hose (if equipped).
93. Install the radiator lower hose and clamps.
94. Install the battery negative cables to the engine block on the driver and passenger side.
95. Install the transmission adapter with a new camshaft rectangular ring seal. Tighten to 57 ft. lbs. (77 Nm).
96. Install the flywheel and adapter or flexplate. Tighten to 101 ft. lbs. (137 Nm).

➡If the engine is equipped with a flexplate or crankshaft adapter, a new clamp ring must be used. If the engine has a flywheel with washers, the washers can be reused.

97. Install the starter motor and tighten to 32 ft. lbs. (43 Nm).
98. Connect engine to vehicle harness connectors.
99. Install transmission and transfer case (if equipped).
100. Connect the exhaust pipe to the turbocharger elbow.
101. Connect the transmission auxiliary oil cooler lines (if equipped).
102. Lower the vehicle.
103. Connect the heater core supply and return hoses.
104. Fill the crankcase to the correct level.
105. Fill the cooling system.
106. Vacuum and recharge the A/C system (if equipped).
107. Start the engine and check for leaks.

EXHAUST MANIFOLD

REMOVAL & INSTALLATION

3.7L and 4.7L Engines

See Figure 81.

1. Before servicing the vehicle, refer to the Precautions Section.
2. Drain the cooling system.
3. Remove or disconnect the following:
   - Battery
   - Power distribution center
   - Battery tray
   - Windshield washer fluid bottle
   - Air cleaner assembly
   - Accessory drive belt
   - A/C compressor
   - A/C accumulator bracket
   - Heater hoses
   - Exhaust manifold heat shields
   - Exhaust Y-pipe
   - Starter motor
   - Exhaust manifolds

To install:

4. Install or connect the following:
   - Exhaust manifolds, using new gaskets. Tighten the bolts to 18 ft. lbs. (25 Nm), starting with the inner bolts and work out to the ends.
   - Starter motor
   - Exhaust Y-pipe
   - Exhaust manifold heat shields
   - Heater hoses
   - A/C accumulator bracket
   - A/C compressor
   - Accessory drive belt
   - Air cleaner assembly
   - Windshield washer fluid bottle
   - Battery tray
   - Power distribution center
   - Battery
5. Fill the cooling system.
6. Start the engine and check for leaks.

5.7L Engines

See Figures 82 and 83.

1. Before servicing the vehicle, refer to the Precautions Section.
2. Disconnect negative battery cable.
3. Raise the vehicle.
4. Remove exhaust pipe to manifold bolts.
5. Lower the vehicle.
6. Install engine support fixture special tool number 8534.

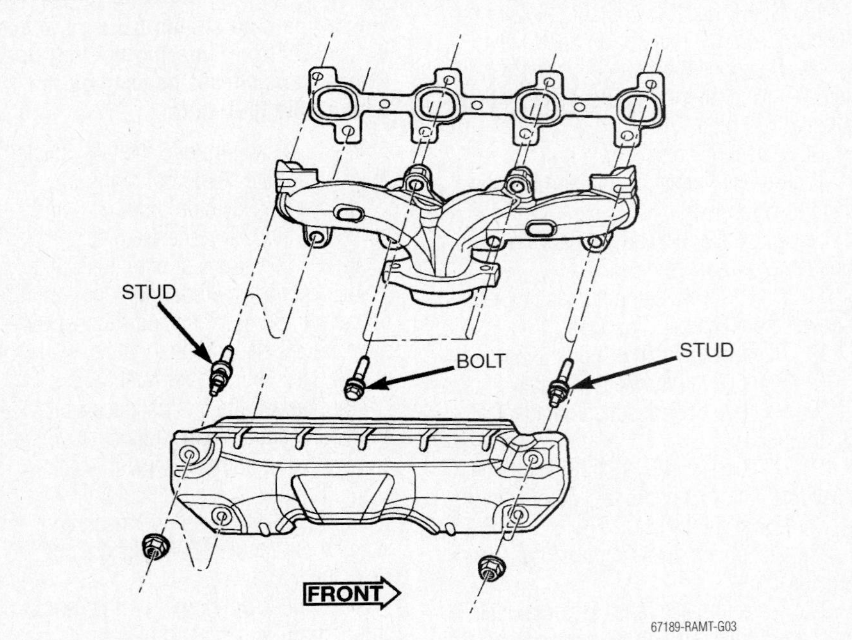

Fig. 81 Right side exhaust manifold—4.7L engine, left side and 3.7L engine similar

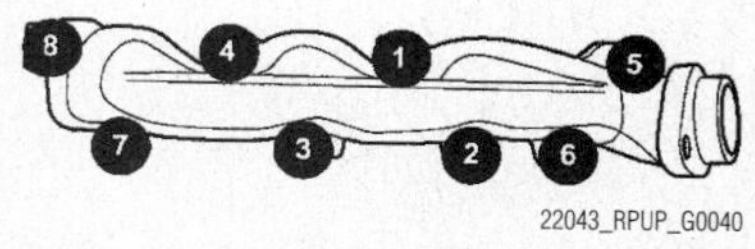

Fig. 82 Left exhaust manifold tighten sequence—5.7L engine

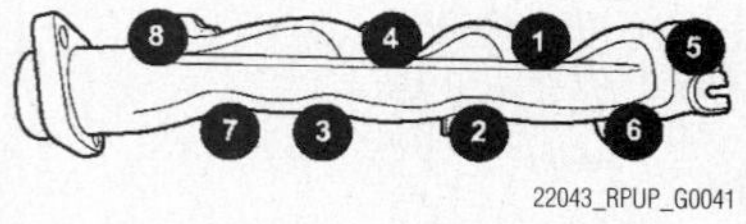

Fig. 83 Right exhaust manifold tighten sequence—5.7L engine

7. Raise the engine enough to remove manifolds.

⁂ WARNING

Do not damage the engine harness while raising the engine.

8. Remove heat shield.
9. Remove manifold bolts using sequence provided.
10. Remove the manifold and gasket.

To install:

11. Install manifold gasket and manifold.
12. Install manifold bolts and tighten using sequence provided to 18 ft. lbs. (25 Nm).
13. Install heat shield and tighten nuts to 11 ft. lbs. (15 Nm).
14. Lower the engine.

⁂ WARNING

Do not damage the engine harness while lowering the engine.

15. Remove engine support fixture from engine.
16. Raise the vehicle.
17. Tighten right and left side engine mount through bolts.
18. Install exhaust flange to pipe bolts.
19. Lower the vehicle.
20. Connect negative battery cable.

5.9L Engine

See Figure 84.

1. Before servicing the vehicle, refer to the Precautions Section.
2. Remove or disconnect the following:
    - Negative battery cables
    - Turbocharger
    - Exhaust Gas Recirculation (EGR) tube

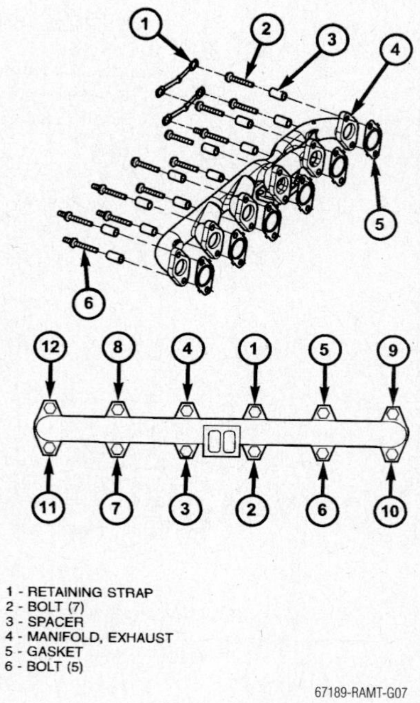

Fig. 84 Exhaust manifold torque sequence—5.9L diesel engine

    - Cab heater supply and return lines
    - Exhaust manifold

To install:

➡Use anti-seize compound on the exhaust manifold bolts.

3. Install or connect the following:
    - Exhaust manifold. Tighten the bolts in sequence to 32 ft. lbs. (43 Nm).
    - Cab heater supply and return lines
    - EGR tube. Tighten the bolts to 18 ft. lbs. (24 Nm).
    - Turbocharger
    - Negative battery cables
4. Start the engine and check for leaks.

6.7L Engine

See Figure 85.

1. Disconnect the battery negative cables.
2. Drain the coolant.
3. Raise the vehicle on hoist.
4. Remove the EGR cooler.
5. Remove the air filter housing.
6. Remove the air filter inlet hose from the turbo inlet.
7. Remove the delta P line bracket cap screw nuts and remove the delta P line from the exhaust manifold and thermostat housing.
8. Remove the heat shield and noise panel (if equipped) from the exhaust manifold.
9. Remove the four turbo to exhaust manifold nuts (15 mm).
10. Remove the two rear exhaust manifold cap screw lock plates.
11. Remove the Cab Heater tubing/bracket from the exhaust manifold stud (15 mm).
12. Remove the exhaust manifold.

To install:

13. Clean the exhaust manifold gasket surfaces.
14. Clean the cylinder head exhaust port gasket surfaces.
15. Clean the turbo mounting flange on the exhaust manifold.
16. Clean the turbo mounting flange on the turbocharger.
17. Install the exhaust manifold to turbocharger gasket and cap screws.
18. Install the exhaust manifold gasket.

➡The five exhaust manifold cap screws with studs are used at the number 1 and number 2 cylinder locations for the heat shield mounting and one on the rear lower corner of the manifold for the cabin heater tube bracket.

19. Install the exhaust manifold spacers and cap screws.
20. Starting from the center and moving in a pattern outward, torque the exhaust manifold bolts to 32 ft. lbs. (43 Nm).
21. Install the exhaust manifold cap screw lock plates.
22. Install the exhaust manifold heat shields/noise panels. Torque the mounting nuts to 18 ft. lbs. (24 Nm).
23. Torque the turbocharger mounting nuts to 32 ft. lbs. (43 Nm).
24. Attach the mounting tabs and start the delta-P tube to exhaust manifold and thermostat cap screws.
25. Torque the delta-P tube 15 mm nut to 18 ft. lbs. (24 Nm).

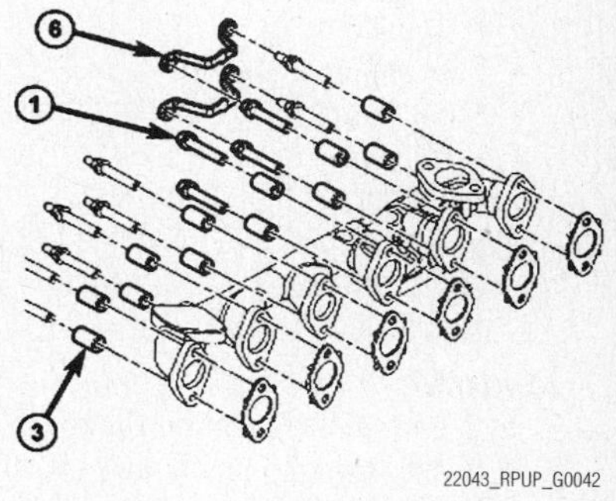

Fig. 85 Exhaust manifold and related parts 6.7L diesel engine

26. Torque the delta-P tube 6 mm nut to 89 in. lbs. (10 Nm).
27. Torque the delta-P flare nuts to 89 ft. lbs. (10 Nm).
28. Install the EGR cooler.
29. Install the air filter housing.
30. Fill the coolant.
31. Connect the battery negative cables.
32. Start the engine to check for leaks.

INTAKE MANIFOLD

REMOVAL & INSTALLATION

3.7L and 4.7L Engines

See Figure 86.

1. Before servicing the vehicle, refer to the Precautions Section.
2. Drain the cooling system.
3. Properly relieve the fuel system pressure.
4. Remove or disconnect the following:
   - Negative battery cable
   - Air cleaner assembly
   - Accelerator cable
   - Cruise control cable
   - Manifold Absolute Pressure (MAP) sensor connector
   - Intake Air Temperature (IAT) sensor connector
   - Throttle Position (TP) sensor connector
   - Idle Air Control (IAC) valve connector
   - Engine Coolant Temperature (ECT) sensor
   - Positive Crankcase Ventilation (PCV) valve and hose
   - Canister purge vacuum line
   - Brake booster vacuum line
   - Cruise control servo hose
   - Accessory drive belt
   - Alternator
   - A/C compressor
   - Engine ground straps
   - Ignition coil towers
   - Oil dipstick tube
   - Fuel line
   - Fuel supply manifold
   - Throttle body and mounting bracket
   - Cowl seal
   - Right engine lifting stud
   - Intake manifold. Remove the fasteners in reverse of the tightening sequence.

To install:

5. Install or connect the following:
   - Intake manifold using new gaskets. Torque the bolts, in sequence, to 105 inch lbs. (12 Nm).
   - Right engine lifting stud
   - Cowl seal
   - Throttle body and mounting bracket
   - Fuel supply manifold
   - Fuel line
   - Oil dipstick tube
   - Ignition coil towers
   - Engine ground straps
   - A/C compressor
   - Alternator
   - Accessory drive belt
   - Cruise control servo hose
   - Brake booster vacuum line
   - Canister purge vacuum line
   - PCV valve and hose
   - ECT sensor
   - IAC valve connector
   - TP sensor connector
   - IAT sensor connector
   - MAP sensor connector
   - Cruise control cable
   - Accelerator cable
   - Air cleaner assembly
   - Negative battery cable
6. Fill and bleed the cooling system.
7. Start the engine, check for leaks and repair if necessary.

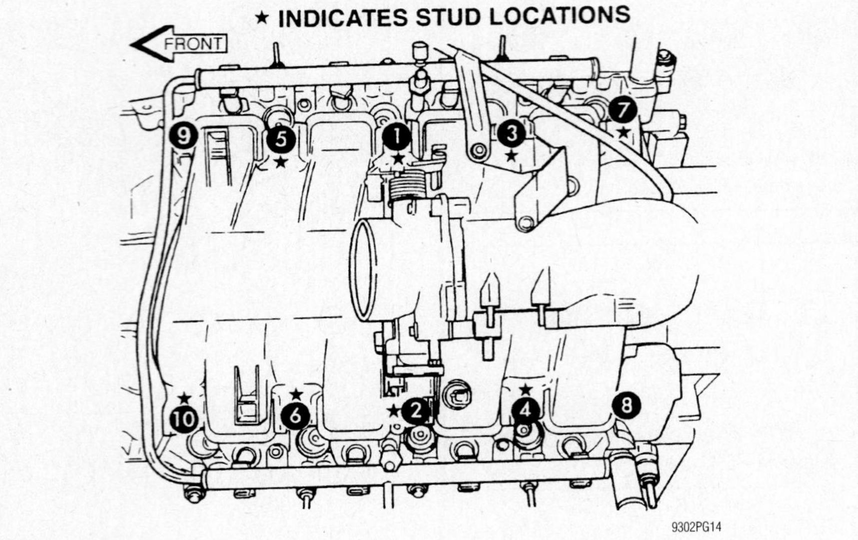

Fig. 86 Intake manifold torque sequence—4.7L engines, 3.7L similar

5.7L Engines

1. Before servicing the vehicle, refer to the Precautions Section.
2. Drain the cooling system.
3. Relieve the fuel system pressure.
4. Remove or disconnect the following:
   - Negative battery cable
   - Air cleaner assembly
   - Accessory drive belt
   - MAP connector
   - IAT connector
   - TPS connector
   - CTS connector
   - Brake booster hose
   - PCV hose
   - Alternator
   - A/C compressor
   - Intake manifold bolts, in a criss-cross pattern, from the outside to the center
   - Intake manifold/IAFM

To install:

5. Position new intake manifold seals.
6. Install the intake manifold. Tighten the bolts in sequence from the center outwards, to 105 inch lbs. (12 Nm).
7. Install or connect the following:
   - Electrical connectors
   - Alternator
   - A/C compressor
   - Brake booster hose
   - PCV hose
   - Accessory drive belt
   - Negative battery cable
   - Air cleaner assembly

5.9L Engines

See Figure 87.

1. Before servicing the vehicle, refer to the Precautions Section.
2. Remove or disconnect the following:
   - Negative battery cables
   - Intercooler outlet duct
   - Dipstick tube
   - Engine appearance cover
   - Air inlet housing
   - Exhaust Gas Recirculation (EGR) tube
   - Fuel line assembly

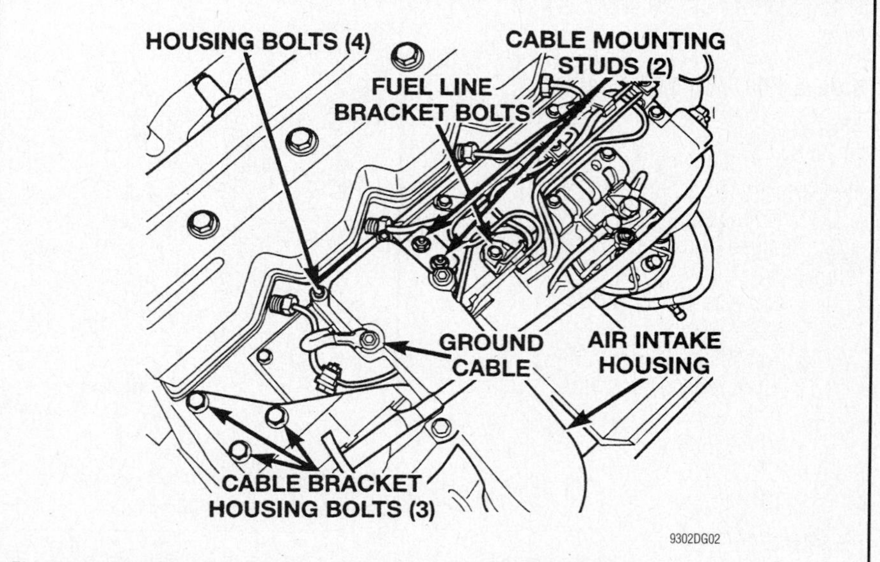

Fig. 87 Intake air heater electrical connections—5.9L diesel engine

- Air intake heater harness connectors
- Charge air temperature sensor connector
- Accelerator pedal position sensor bracket
- Intake manifold cover

To install:

➡Use liquid Teflon® sealer on the intake manifold cover bolts.

3. Install or connect the following:
   - Intake manifold cover. Tighten the bolts to 18 ft. lbs. (24 Nm).
   - Accelerator pedal position sensor bracket. Tighten the bracket to 32 ft. lbs. (43 Nm).
   - Charge air temperature sensor connector
   - Air intake heater harness connectors. Tighten the nuts to 10 ft. lbs. (14 Nm).
   - Fuel line assembly
   - Exhaust Gas Recirculation (EGR) tube
   - Air inlet housing. Tighten the bolts to 18 ft. lbs. (24 Nm).
   - Engine appearance cover
   - Dipstick tube
   - Intercooler outlet duct
   - Negative battery cables
4. Start the engine and check for leaks.

2007–08 6.7L Diesel engines

1. Before servicing the vehicle, refer to the Precautions Section.
2. Disconnect the batteries.
3. Disconnect the EGR air Transfer tube temperature sensor.
4. Disconnect the EGR Valve Actuator Connector.
5. Disconnect the Engine Oil level tube at the Air Inlet bracket
6. Loosen and remove both v-band clamps at each end of the Air Transfer tube
7. Remove the P-clip mounting cap screw
8. Remove the Air Transfer tube.
9. Loosen and remove six Air Inlet mounting cap screws.
10. Remove the air inlet.
11. Remove the injector fuel lines.
12. Disconnect the Fuel Rail Pressure sensor at the rear of the fuel rail manifold.
13. Remove the High Pressure fuel line from the dump/overflow valve.
14. Remove the fuel rail.
15. Remove the grid heater wiring connector.
16. Disconnect the TMAP sensor.
17. Remove the intake manifold cap screws.
18. Remove the intake manifold.

To install:

19. Clean the Intake Manifold and Cylinder Head Gasket area.
20. Install a new intake manifold gasket.
21. Position the intake manifold and Install the intake manifold cap screws finger tight.
22. Position the fuel rail and install the fuel rail manifold cap screws finger tight.
23. Tighten the intake manifold cap screws to 18 ft. lbs. (24 Nm).
24. Connect the fuel rail pressure sensor.
25. Connect the intake manifold grid heater. Torque the cap screw to 89 in. lbs. (10 Nm).
26. Install the fuel lines.
27. Tighten the fuel rail mounting cap screws to 18 ft. lbs. (24 Nm).
28. Clean the Air Inlet gasket area.
29. Clean the Intake Manifold to air inlet area.
30. Install the new Air Intake connection gasket.
31. Install the air intake connection to the intake manifold.
32. Tighten the intake manifold to 18 ft. lbs. (24 Nm).
33. Install the Oil Level Gauge tube and torque to 18 ft. lbs. (24 Nm).
34. Clean the gasket area of the Air Transfer Tube (both ends).
35. Clean the EGR cooler and EGR control valve gasket area.
36. Using new gaskets, install the Air Transfer Tube.
37. Install the V-band clamps.
38. Install the P-clip to the bracket. Torque the mounting cap screw to 18 ft. lbs. (24 Nm).
39. Tighten the V-band clamps to 89 lbs. in. (10 Nm).
40. Connect the EGR Valve Actuator connector.
41. Connect the EGR Gas Temperature connector.
42. Connect the batteries.
43. Start the engine and check for leaks.

OIL PAN

REMOVAL & INSTALLATION

3.7L, 4.7L and 5.7L Engines

See Figures 88 through 90.

1. Before servicing the vehicle, refer to the Precautions Section.
2. Drain the engine oil.
3. Attach an engine crane.
4. Loosen, but don't remove, the left and right mount through-bolts.
5. Remove or disconnect the following:
   - Negative battery cable
   - Structural cover
   - Front crossmember
6. Raise the engine just enough for clearance.
7. Remove or disconnect the following:

➡Don't pry on the pan. The gasket is integral with the windage tray, and doesn't come out with the pan.

- Pan bolts and studs
- Pan

➡The double ended studs must be installed in their original locations.

To install:

8. Install or connect the following:
   - Oil pan gasket
   - Oil pan. Tighten the bolts, in sequence, to 105 inch lbs. (12 Nm).
   - Front crossmember
   - Structural cover
   - Negative battery cable
9. Fill the crankcase to the proper level with engine oil.

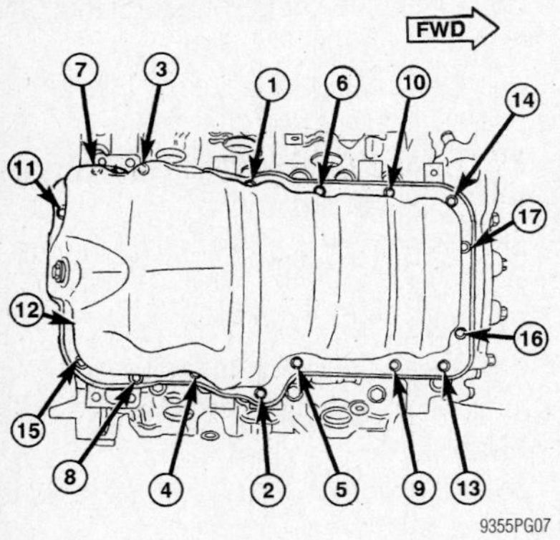

Fig. 88 Oil pan bolt torque sequence—3.7L engine

10. Start the engine and check for leaks.

5.9L & 2007–08 6.7L Engines

See Figure 91.

1. Before servicing the vehicle, refer to the Precautions Section.
2. Drain the engine oil.
3. Remove or disconnect the following:
   - Negative battery cables
   - Starter motor
   - Transmission
   - Flywheel and transmission adapter plate.
   - Oil pan bolts
   - Oil pump suction tube
   - Oil pan

To install:

4. Install or connect the following:
   - Oil pan
   - Oil pump suction tube. Tighten the bolts to 18 ft. lbs. (24 Nm).
   - Oil pan bolts. Tighten the bolts to 18 ft. lbs. (24 Nm).
   - Flywheel and transmission adapter plate.

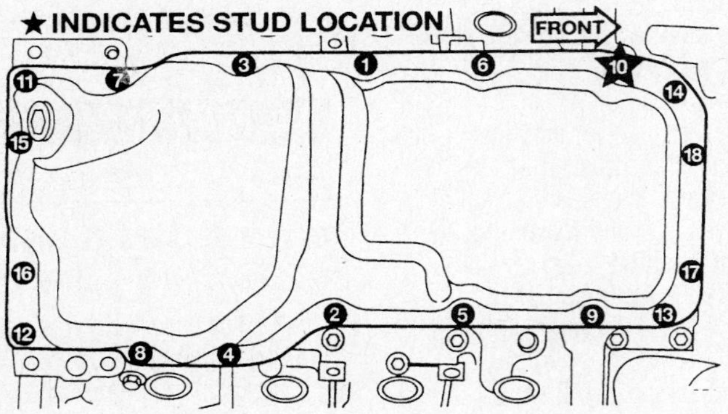

Fig. 89 Oil pan mounting bolt tightening sequence—4.7L engine

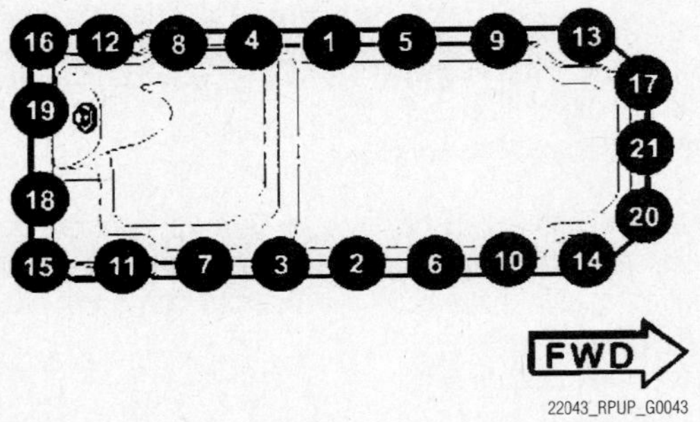

Fig. 90 Oil pan mounting bolt tightening sequence—5.7L engine

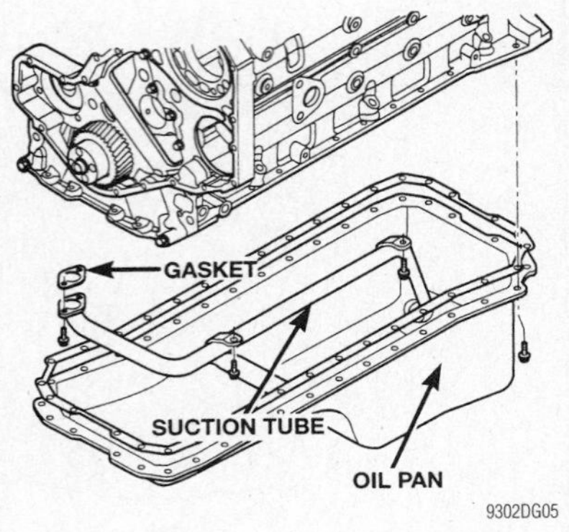

Fig. 91 Exploded view of the oil pan mounting—diesel engines

   - Transmission
   - Starter motor
5. Fill the crankcase to the correct level.

OIL PUMP

REMOVAL & INSTALLATION

3.7L Engine

1. Before servicing the vehicle, refer to the Precautions Section.
2. Remove or disconnect the following:
   - Oil Pan
   - Timing chain cover
   - Timing chains and tensioners
   - Oil pump
3. Installation is the reverse of removal. Torque the pump bolts, in sequence, to 21 ft. lbs. (28 Nm),

4.7L Engine

See Figure 92.

1. Before servicing the vehicle, refer to the Precautions Section.
2. Drain the engine oil.
3. Remove or disconnect the following:
   - Negative battery cable
   - Oil pan
   - Oil pump pick-up tube
   - Timing chains and tensioners
   - Oil pump

To install:

4. Install or connect the following:
   - Oil pump. Tighten the bolts to 21 ft. lbs. (28 Nm).
   - Timing chains and tensioners
   - Oil pump pick-up tube
   - Oil pan
   - Negative battery cable
5. Fill the crankcase to the correct level.
6. Start the engine and check for leaks.

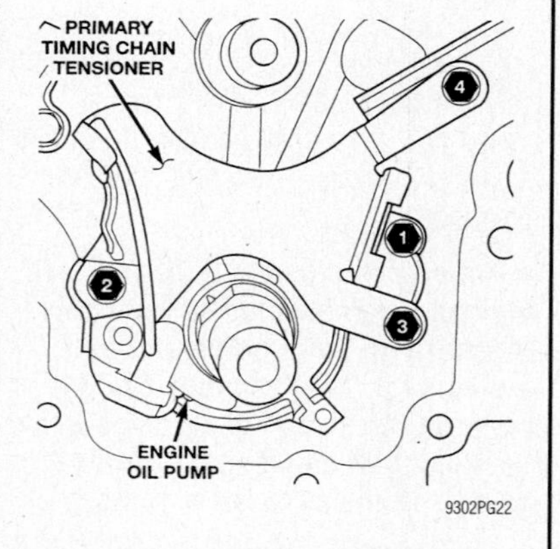

Fig. 92 Oil pump and chain tensioner torque sequence—3.7L and 4.7L engines

5.7L Engine

1. Before servicing the vehicle, refer to the Precautions Section.
2. Drain the engine oil.
3. Remove or disconnect the following:
   - Negative battery cable
   - Oil pan
   - Oil pump pick-up tube
   - Timing chains and tensioners
   - Oil pump

To install:

4. Install or connect the following:
   - Oil pump. Tighten the bolts to 21 ft. lbs. (28 Nm).
   - Timing chains and tensioners
   - Oil pump pick-up tube
   - Oil pan
   - Negative battery cable
5. Fill the crankcase to the correct level.
6. Start the engine and check for leaks.

5.9L & 2007–08 6.7L Engines

See Figure 93.

1. Before servicing the vehicle, refer to the Precautions Section.
2. Drain the cooling system.
3. Remove or disconnect the following:
   - Negative battery cables
   - Accessory drive belt
   - Cooling fan and shroud
   - Radiator
   - Oil fill tube and adapter
   - Crankshaft pulley
   - Front cover
   - Oil pump

To install:

➡When the pump is correctly installed, the flange on the pump does not touch the block; the back plate on the pump seats against the bottom of the bore.

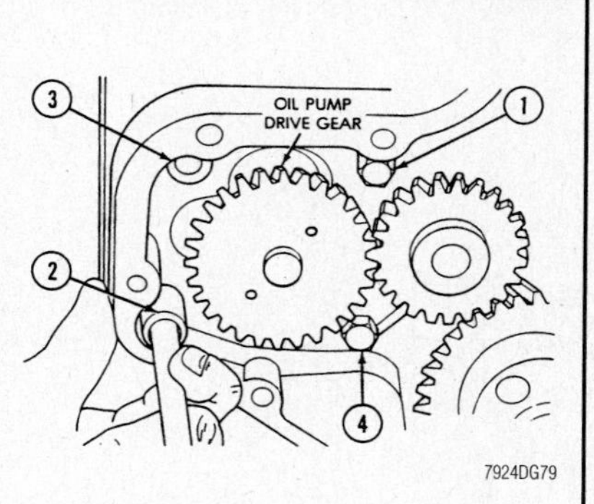

Fig. 93 Oil pump torque sequence—5.9L diesel engine

4. Install the oil pump. Tighten the bolts in sequence as follows:
   a. Step 1: 71 inch lbs. (8 Nm).
   b. Step 2: 18 ft. lbs. (24 Nm).
5. Install or connect the following:
   - Front cover
   - Crankshaft pulley
   - Oil fill tube and adapter
   - Radiator
   - Cooling fan and shroud
   - Accessory drive belt
   - Negative battery cables

INSPECTION

See Figures 94 through 99.

⁂ WARNING

Oil pump pressure relief valve and spring should not be removed from the oil pump. If these components are disassembled and or removed from the pump the entire oil pump assembly must be replaced.

⁂ WARNING

Oil pump pressure relief valve and spring should not be removed from the oil pump. If these components are disassembled and or removed from the pump the entire oil pump assembly must be replaced.

1. Clean all parts thoroughly. Mating surface of the oil pump housing should be smooth. If the pump cover is scratched or grooved the oil pump assembly should be replaced.
2. Lay a straight edge across the pump cover surface. If a 0.001 in. (0.025mm) feeler gauge can be inserted between the cover and the straight edge the oil pump assembly should be replaced.
3. Measure the thickness of the outer rotor. If the outer rotor thickness measures at 0.472 in. (12.005mm) or less the oil pump assembly must be replaced.

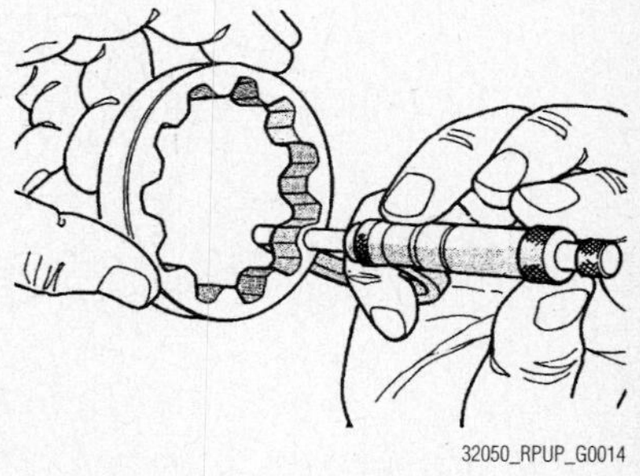

Fig. 95 Measure the thickness of the outer rotor. If the outer rotor thickness measures at 0.472 in. (12.005mm) or less the oil pump assembly must be replaced

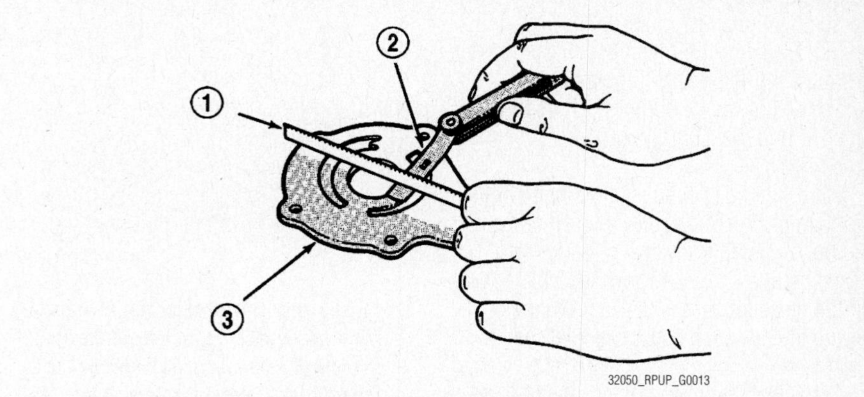

Fig. 94 Lay a straight edge (1) across the pump cover surface (3). If a 0.025 mm (0.001 in.) feeler gauge (2) can be inserted between the cover and the straight edge the oil pump assembly should be replaced

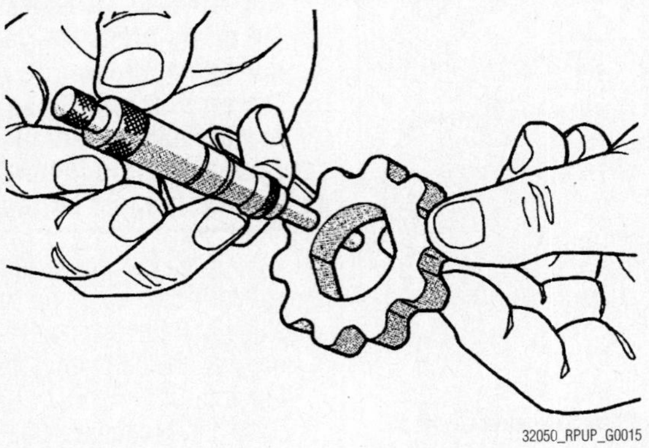

Fig. 96 Measure the diameter of the outer rotor. If the outer rotor diameter measures at 3.382 in. (85.925mm) or less the oil pump assembly must be replaced

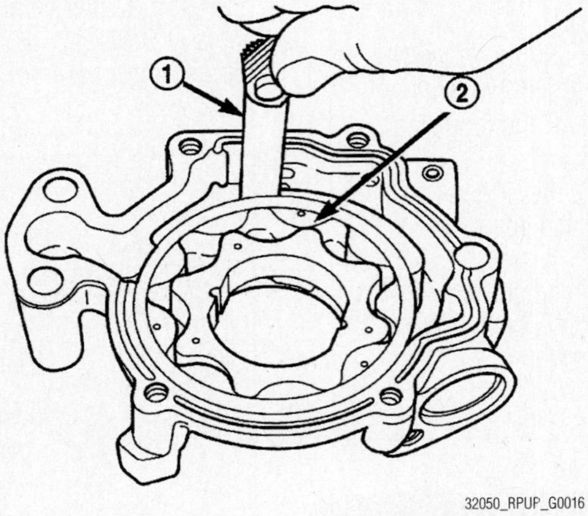

Fig. 97 Slide outer rotor (2) into the body of the oil pump. Press the outer rotor to one side of the oil pump body and use a feeler gauge (1) to measure clearance between the outer rotor and the body. If the measurement is 0.235mm (0.009 in.) or more the oil pump assembly must be replaced

4. Measure the diameter of the outer rotor. If the outer rotor diameter measures at 3.382 in. (85.925mm) or less the oil pump assembly must be replaced.
5. Measure the thickness of the inner rotor. If the inner rotor thickness measures at 0.472 (12.005mm) or less then the oil pump assembly must be replaced.
6. Slide outer rotor into the body of the oil pump. Press the outer rotor to one side of the oil pump body and measure clearance between the outer rotor and the body. If the measurement is 0.009 (0.235mm) or more the oil pump assembly must be replaced.
7. Install the inner rotor in the into the oil pump body. Measure the clearance between the inner and outer rotors. If the clearance between the rotors is 0.006 in. (0.150mm) or more the oil pump assembly must be replaced.
8. Place a straight edge across the body of the oil pump (between the bolt holes), if a feeler gauge of 0.0038 (0.095mm) or greater can be inserted between the straight-edge and the rotors, the pump must be replaced.

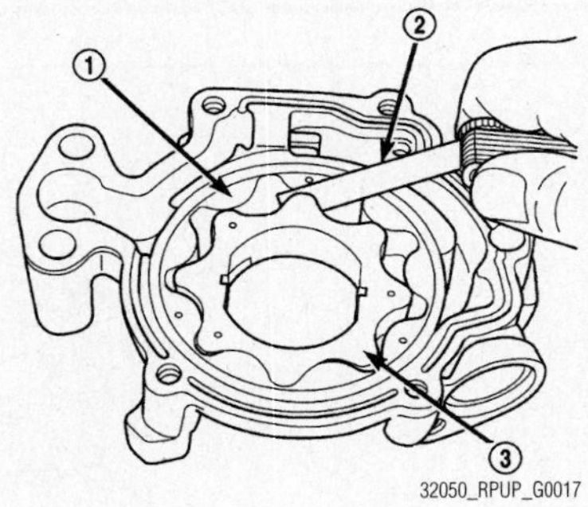

Fig. 98 Install the inner rotor in the into the oil pump body. Use a feeler gauge (2) to measure the clearance between the inner (3) and outer (1) rotors. If the clearance between the rotors is 0.006 in. (0.150mm) or more the oil pump assembly must be replaced.

➡The oil pump on the 3.7L and 4.7L engines is released as an assembly. There are no DaimlerChrysler part numbers for Sub-Assembly components. In the event the oil pump is not functioning or out of specification it must be replaced as an assembly.

PISTON AND RING

POSITIONING

See Figures 100 through 104.

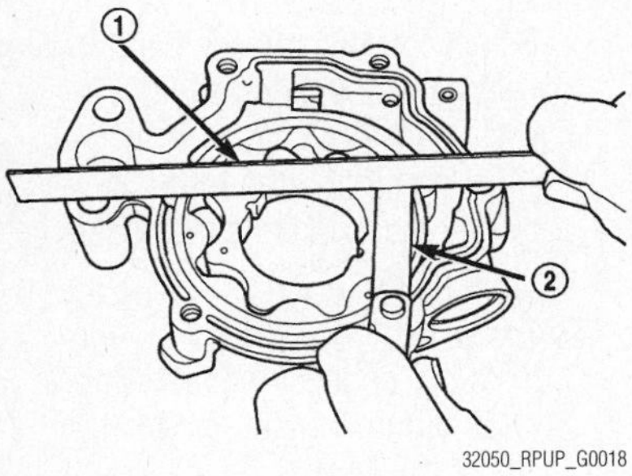

Fig. 99 Place a straight edge (1) across the body of the oil pump (between the bolt holes), if a feeler gauge (2) of 0.0038 (0.095mm) or greater can be inserted between the straightedge and the rotors, the pump must be replaced

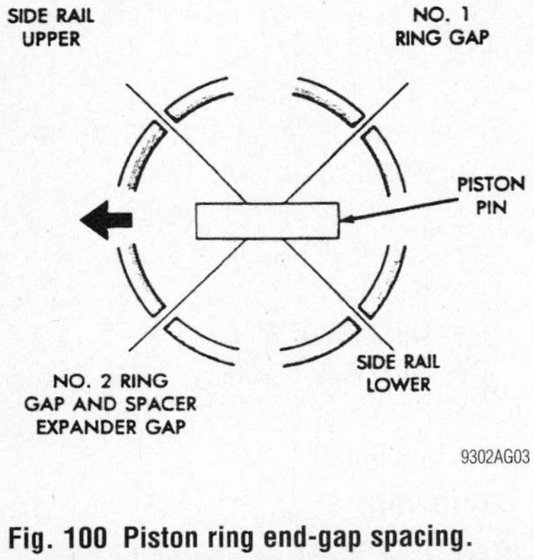

Fig. 100 Piston ring end-gap spacing. Position raised "F" on piston toward front of engine—3.7L and 4.7L engines

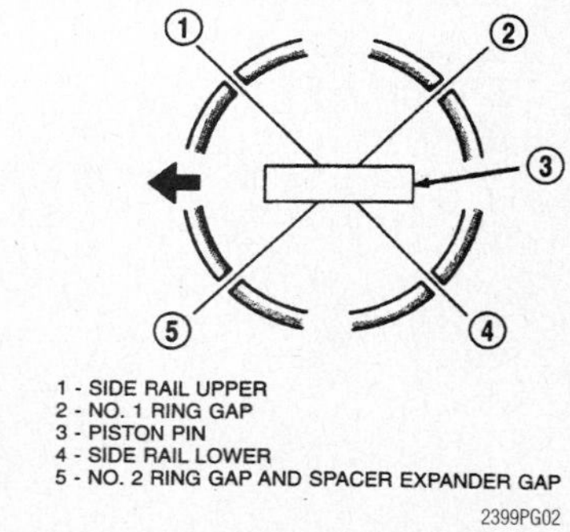

Fig. 101 Piston ring end-gap spacing—5.7L engines

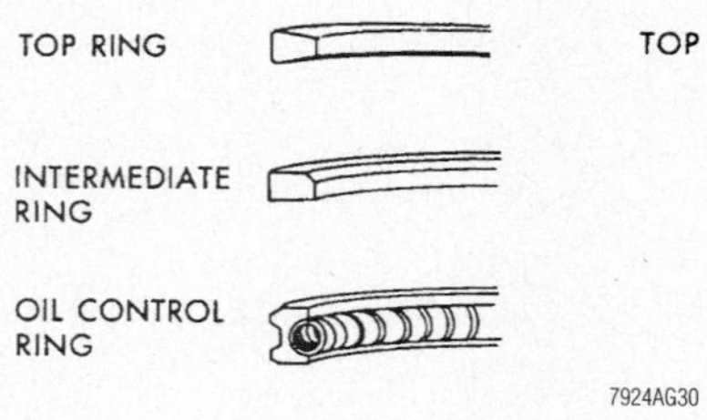

Fig. 102 Pin ring identification—5.9L and 6.7L diesel engines

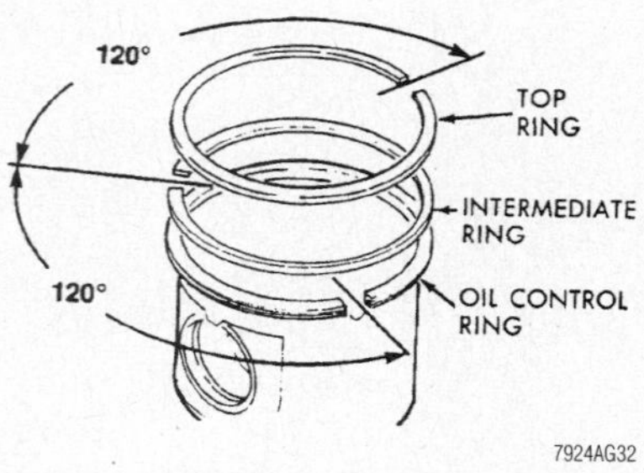

Fig. 103 Piston ring end gap spacing—5.9L and 6.7L diesel engines

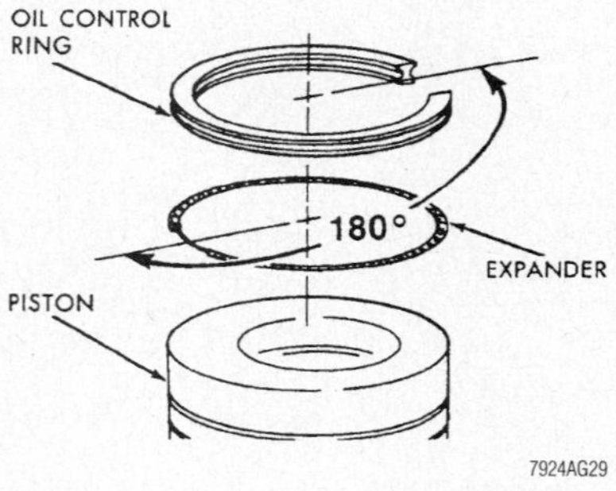

Fig. 104 Oil control ring-to-spacer end gap spacing—5.9L and 6.7L diesel engines

REAR MAIN SEAL

REMOVAL & INSTALLATION

3.7L, 4.7L and 5.7L Engines

See Figure 105.

1. Before servicing the vehicle, refer to the Precautions Section.
2. Remove or disconnect the following:
   - Transmission
   - Flexplate
3. Thread Oil Seal Remover 8506 into the rear main seal as far as possible and remove the rear main seal.

To install:

4. Install or connect the following:
   - Seal Guide 8349-2 onto the crankshaft
   - Rear main seal on the seal guide
   - Rear main seal, using the Crankshaft Rear Oil Seal Installer 8349 and Driver Handle C-4171; tap it into place until the installer is flush with the cylinder block
   - Flexplate. Torque the bolts in the sequence shown to 45 ft. lbs. (60 Nm) on auto trans., or 70 ft. lbs. (95 Nm) for man. trans.
   - Transmission
5. Start the engine, check for leaks and repair if necessary.

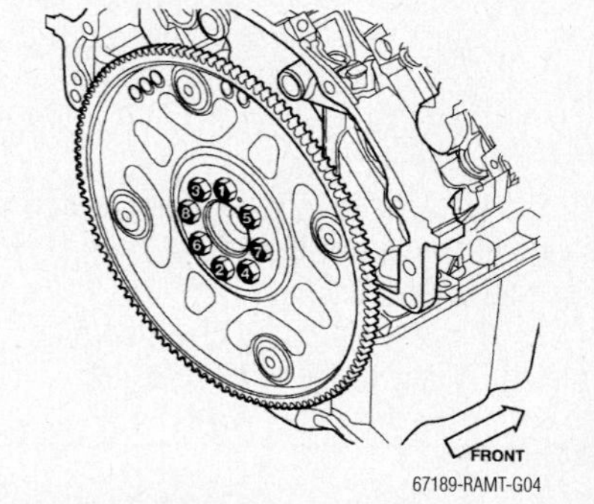

Fig. 105 Flexplate bolt tightening sequence—3.7L, 4.7L and 5.7L engines

5.9L & 2007–08 6.7L Diesel engines

See Figures 106 and 107.

1. Before servicing the vehicle, refer to the Precautions Section.
2. Remove or disconnect the following:
   - Negative battery cables
   - Transmission
   - Clutch and pressure plate, if equipped
   - Flywheel
   - Rear main seal

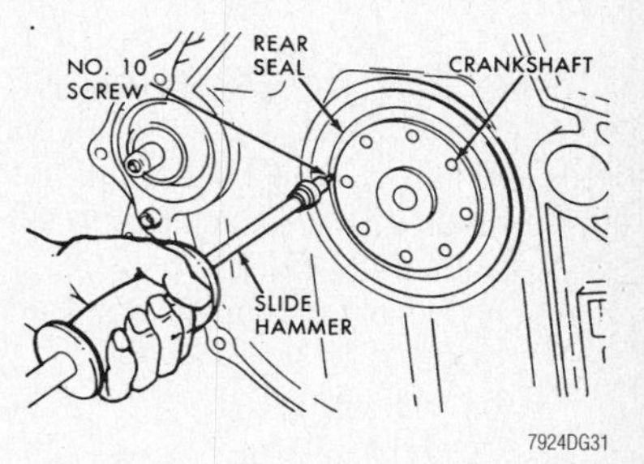

Fig. 106 Removing the rear seal with a sheet metal screw and slide hammer—5.9L and 6.7L diesel engines

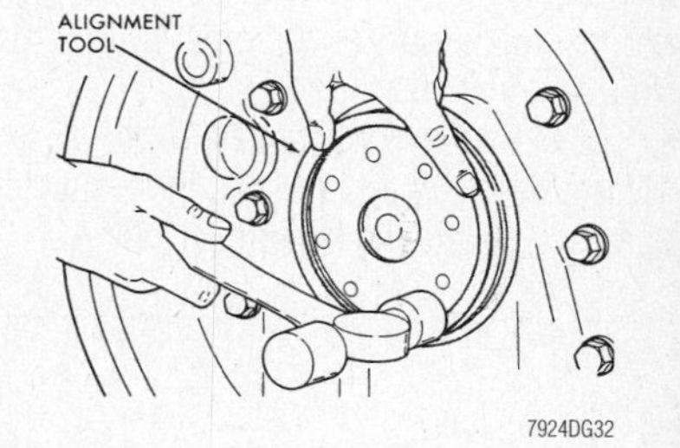

Fig. 107 Place the alignment tool on the seal and tap the seal into place—5.9L and 6.7L diesel engines

To install:

3. Install or connect the following:
   - Rear main seal. Use the alignment tool supplied with the seal kit.
   - Flywheel. Tighten the bolts to 101 ft. lbs. (137 Nm).
   - Clutch and pressure plate, if equipped
   - Transmission
   - Negative battery cables
4. Start the engine and check for leaks.

TIMING CHAIN, SPROCKETS, FRONT COVER AND SEAL

REMOVAL & INSTALLATION

3.7L and 4.7L Engines

See Figures 108 through 122.

1. Before servicing the vehicle, refer to the Precautions Section.
2. Drain the cooling system.
3. Remove or disconnect the following:
   - Negative battery cable
   - Valve covers
   - Radiator fan
   - Heater hoses
   - Alternator
   - Air conditioning compressor

- Power steering pump
- Front cover

4. Rotate the crankshaft so that the crankshaft timing mark aligns with the Top Dead Center (TDC) mark on the front cover, and the **V8 or V6** marks on the camshaft sprockets are at 12 o'clock.
   - Access plugs from the cylinder heads
   - Oil fill housing
   - Crankshaft damper
5. Compress the primary timing chain tensioner and install a lock pin.
6. Remove the secondary timing chain tensioners.
7. Hold the left camshaft with adjustable pliers and remove the sprocket and chain. Rotate the **left** camshaft 15 degrees **clockwise** to the neutral position.
8. Hold the right camshaft with adjustable pliers and remove the camshaft sprocket. Rotate the **right** camshaft 45 degrees **counterclockwise** to the neutral position.
9. Remove the primary timing chain and sprockets.

To install:

10. Use a small prytool to hold the ratchet pawl and compress the secondary timing chain tensioners in a vise and install locking pins.

➡The black bolts fasten the guide to the engine block and the silver bolts fasten the guide to the cylinder head.

11. Install or connect the following:
    - Secondary timing chain guides. Tighten the bolts to 21 ft. lbs. (28 Nm).
    - Secondary timing chains to the idler sprocket so that the double plated links on each chain are visible through the slots in the primary idler sprocket
12. Lock the secondary timing chains to the idler sprocket with Timing Chain Locking tool as shown.
13. Align the primary chain double plated links with the idler sprocket

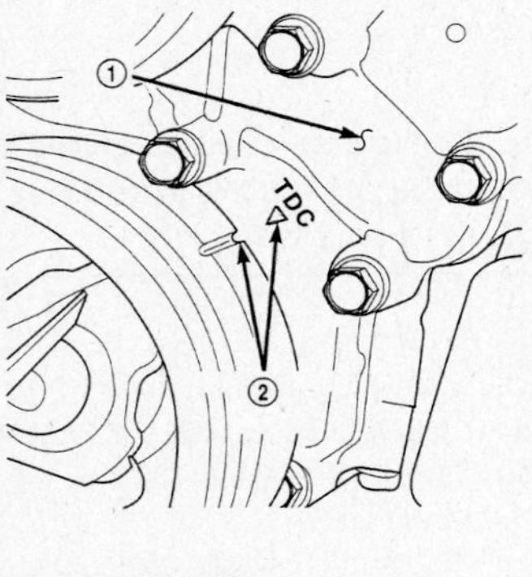

Fig. 108 Crankshaft timing marks—3.7L and 4.7L engines

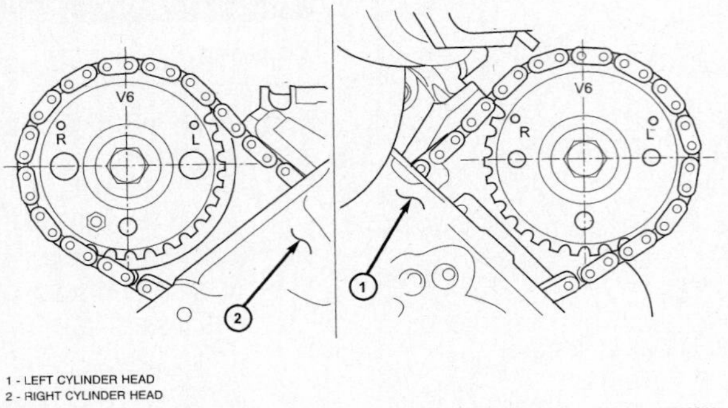

Fig. 110 Camshaft sprocket timing marks—3.7L

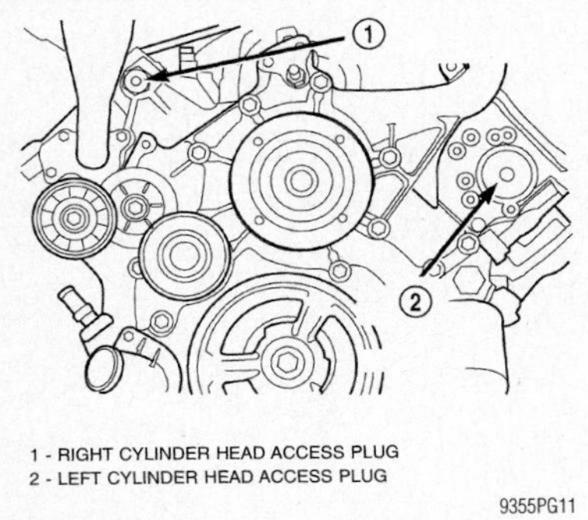

Fig. 111 Cylinder head access plugs—3.7L

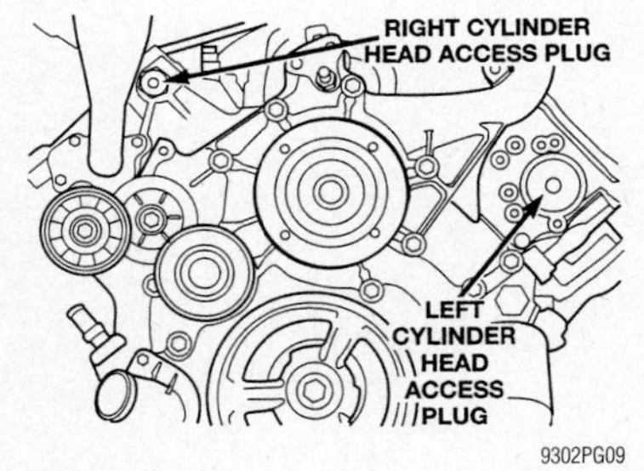

Fig. 112 Cylinder head access plug locations—4.7L engine

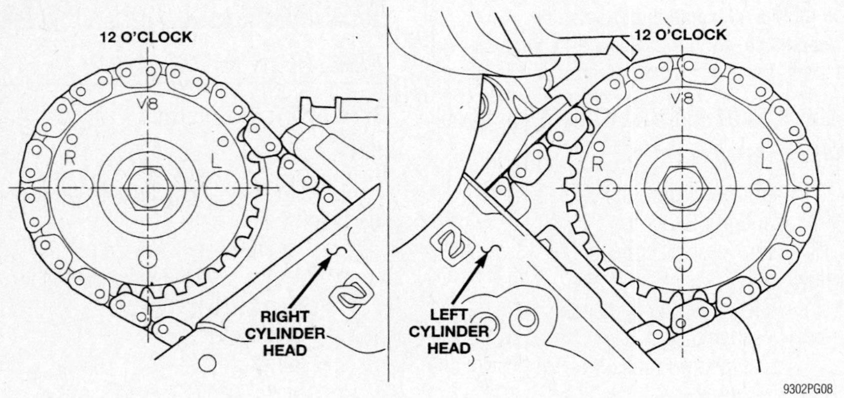

Fig. 109 Camshaft positioning—4.7L engine

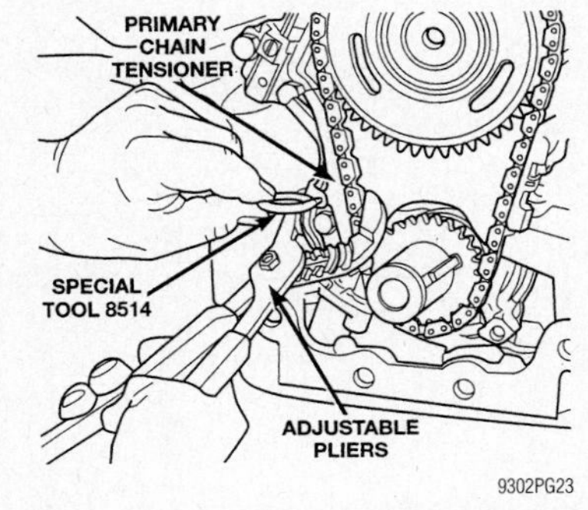

Fig. 113 Compress and lock the primary chain tensioner—4.7L engine

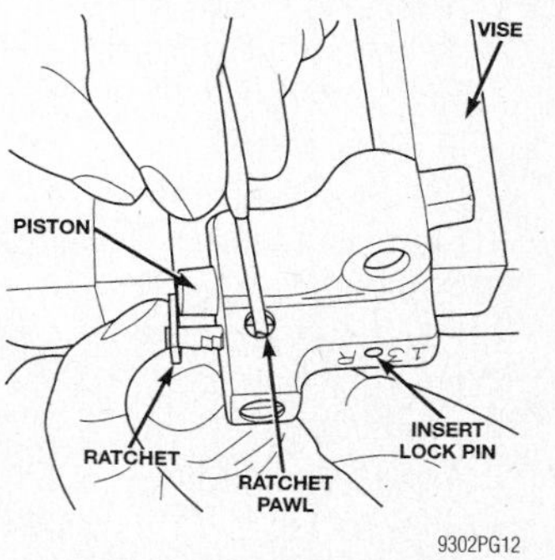

Fig. 114 Secondary timing chain tensioner preparation—3.7L and 4.7L engines

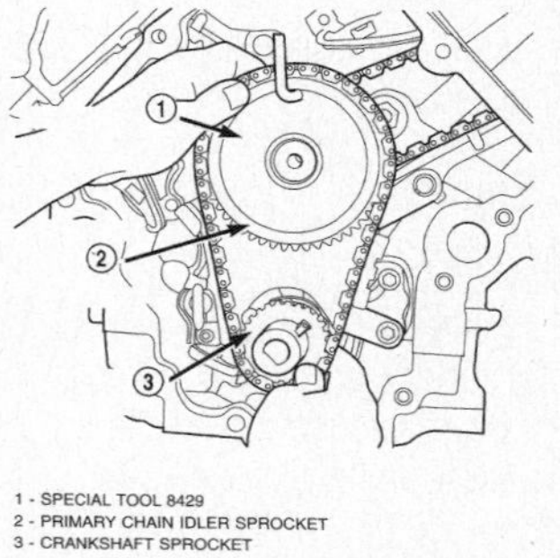

Fig. 115 Installing the idler gear and timing chains—3.7L and 4.7L engines

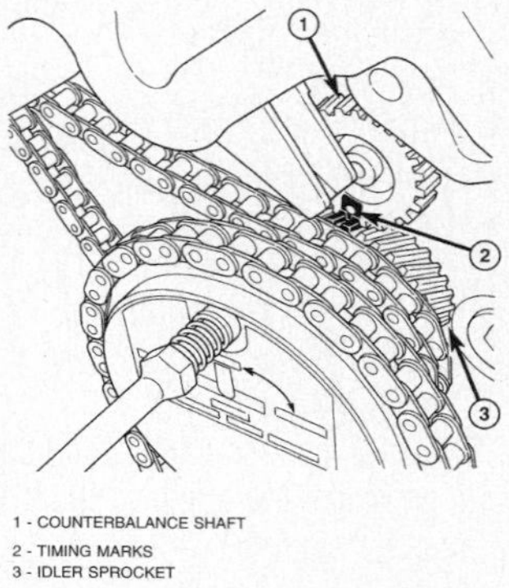

Fig. 116 Counterbalance shaft timing marks—3.7L

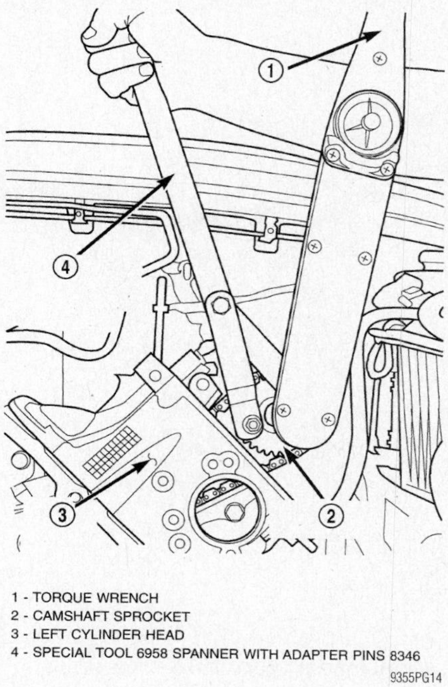

Fig. 117 Tightening the left side camshaft sprocket—3.7L and 4.7L engines

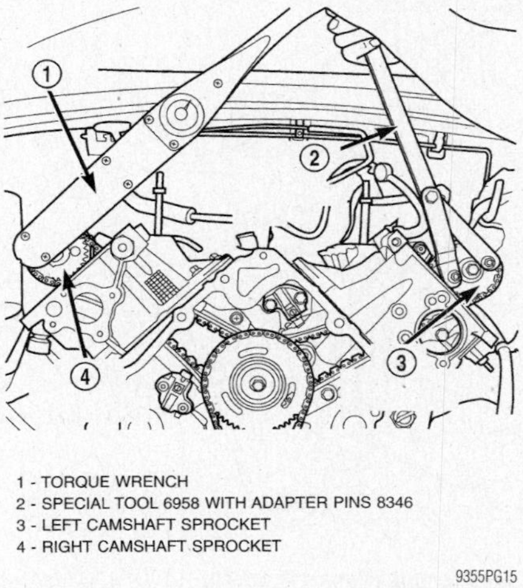

Fig. 118 Tightening the right side camshaft sprocket—3.7L and 4.7L engines

timing mark and the single plated link with the crankshaft sprocket timing mark.

14. Install the primary chain and sprockets. Tighten the idler sprocket bolt to 25 ft. lbs. (34 Nm).

15. Align the secondary chain single plated links with the timing marks on the secondary sprockets. Align the dot at the **L** mark on the left sprocket with the plated link on the left chain and the dot at the **R** mark on the right sprocket with the plated link on the right chain.

16. Rotate the camshafts back from the

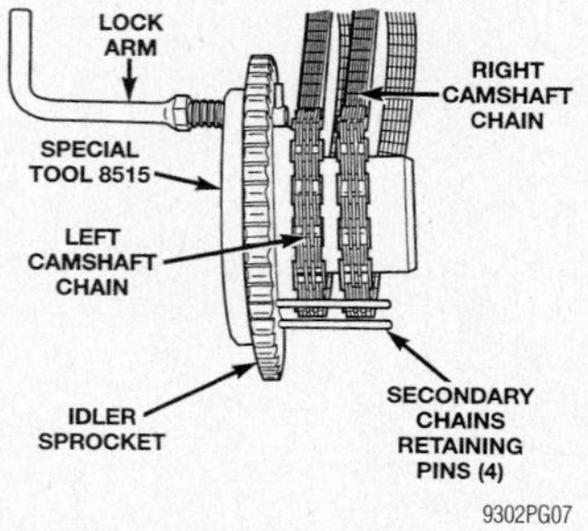

Fig. 119 Use the Timing Chain Locking tool to lock the timing chains on the idler gear—4.7L engine

neutral position and install the camshaft sprockets.

17. Remove the secondary chain locking tool.

18. Remove the primary and secondary timing chain tensioner locking pins.

19. Hold the camshaft sprockets with a spanner wrench and tighten the retaining bolts to 90 ft. lbs. (122 Nm).

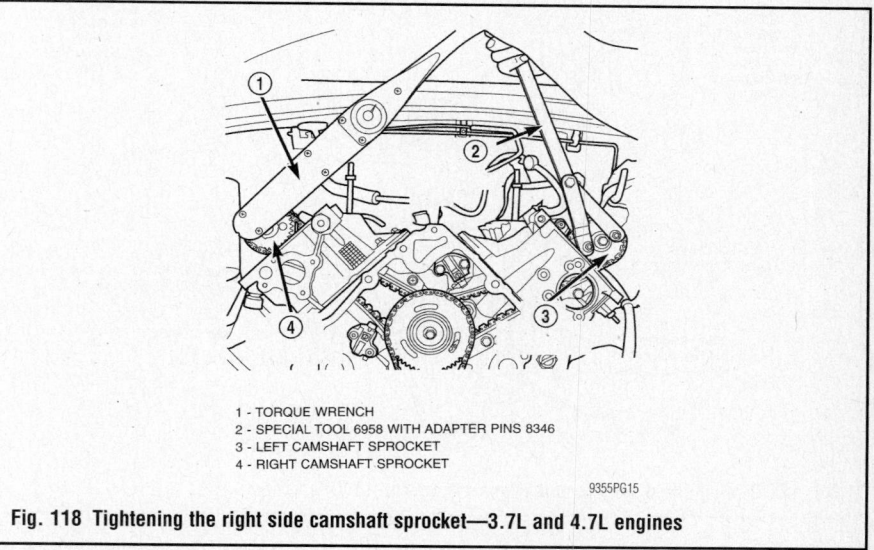

20. Install or connect the following:
- Front cover. Tighten the bolts, in sequence, to 40 ft. lbs. (54 Nm).
- Front crankshaft seal
- Cylinder head access plugs
- A/C compressor

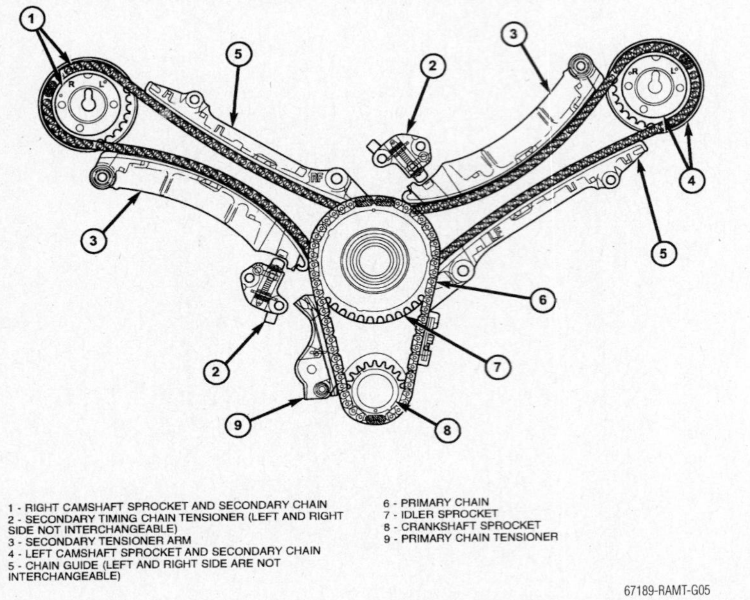

Fig. 120 Timing chain system and alignment marks—3.7L engine

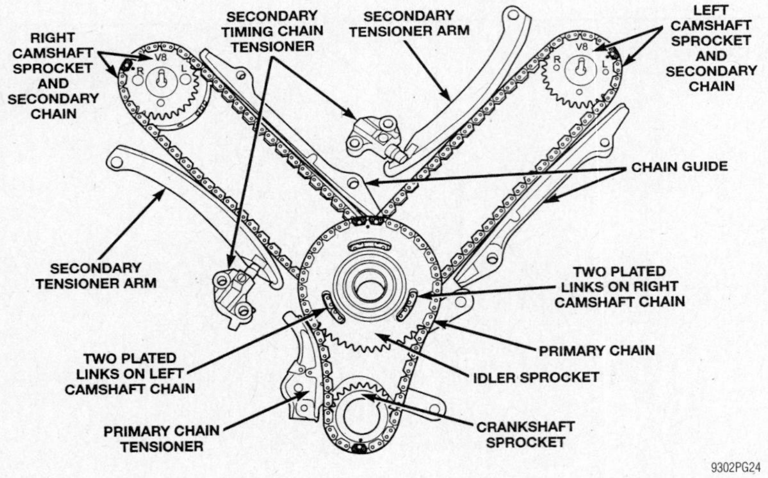

Fig. 121 Timing chain system and alignment marks—4.7L engine

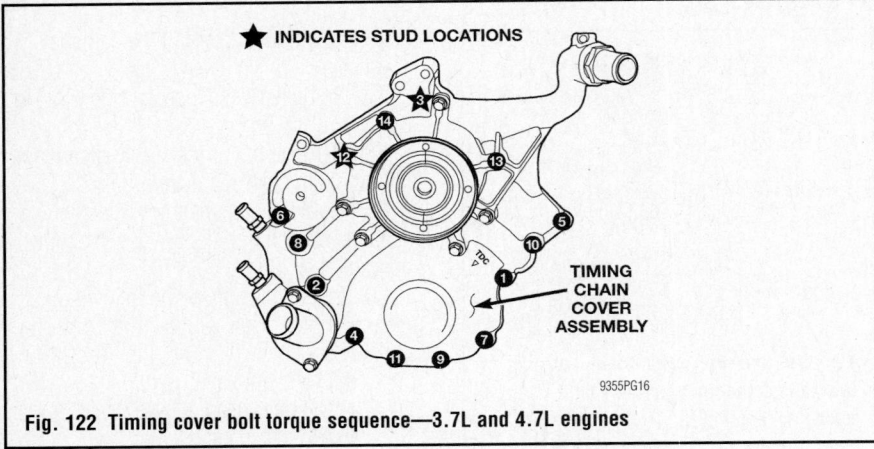

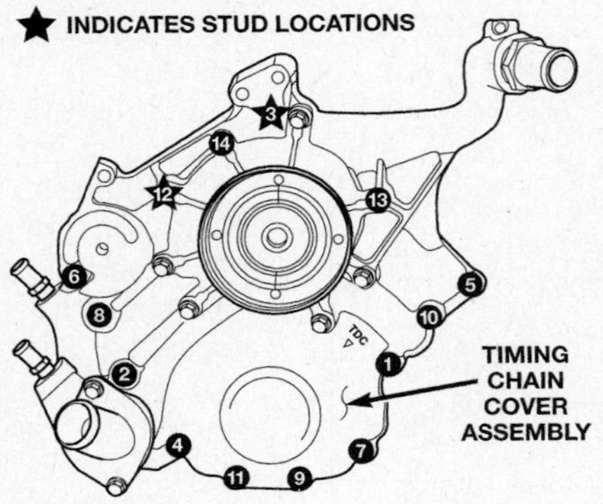

Fig. 122 Timing cover bolt torque sequence—3.7L and 4.7L engines

- Alternator
- Accessory drive belt tensioner. Tighten the bolt to 40 ft. lbs. (54 Nm).
- Oil fill housing
- Crankshaft damper. Tighten the bolt to 130 ft. lbs. (175 Nm).
- Power steering pump
- Lower radiator hose
- Heater hoses
- Accessory drive belt
- Engine cooling fan and shroud
- Camshaft Position (CMP) sensor
- Valve covers
- Negative battery cable

21. Fill and bleed the cooling system.
22. Start the engine, check for leaks and repair if necessary.

5.7L Engines

See Figure 123.

1. Before servicing the vehicle, refer to the Precautions Section.
2. Drain the cooling system.
3. Remove or disconnect the following:
   - Negative battery cable
   - Drive belt
   - Radiator and cooling fan
   - Coolant and washer bottles
   - Fan shroud
   - A/C compressor
   - Alternator
   - Radiator and heater hoses
   - Tensioner and idler pulleys
   - Crankshaft damper
   - Power steering pump
   - Oil pan and pickup tube
   - Timing cover
   - Re-install the damper
4. Rotate the crankshaft so that the camshaft sprocket and crankshaft sprocket timing marks are aligned.

➡The camshaft pin and slot in the cam sprocket must be a 12 o'clock, the crankshaft keyway must be at 2 o'clock, and the dots or paint on the crank sprocket must be at 6 o'clock.

5. Pin back the tensioner shoe.
6. Remove the timing chain and sprockets.

To install:

7. With the timing marks aligned, wrap the chain around the sprockets. The chain must be installed with the single plated link aligned with the dot or paint on the cam sprocket. The dot or paint on the crank sprocket should be aligned between the 2 plated links.

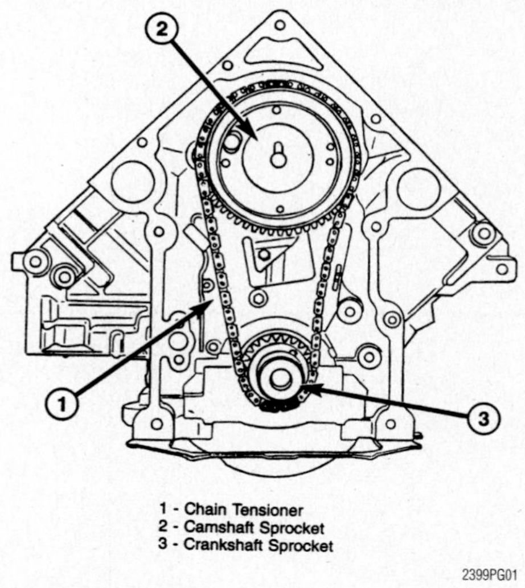

Fig. 123 Timing mark alignment—5.7L engine

8. Install the assembly and torque the cam sprocket bolt to 90 ft. lbs. (122 Nm).
9. Unpin the tensioner and verify the alignment.
10. Install or connect the following:
    - Timing cover. Torque all fasteners to 21 ft. lbs. (28 Nm). Torque the large lifting lug to 40 ft. lbs. (55 Nm).
    - Oil pan and pickup tube
    - Power steering pump
    - Crankshaft damper
    - Tensioner and idler pulleys
    - Radiator and heater hoses
    - Alternator
    - A/C compressor
    - Fan shroud
    - Coolant and washer bottles
    - Radiator fan
    - Drive belt
    - Negative battery cable

5.9L & 2007–08 6.7L engines

Front Cover and Seal

1. Before servicing the vehicle, refer to the Precautions Section.
2. Remove or disconnect the following:
    - Negative battery cables
    - Accessory drive belt
    - Cooling fan and shroud
    - Accessory drive belt tensioner
    - Oil fill tube and adapter
    - Crankshaft pulley
    - Front cover
    - Front crankshaft seal

To install:

3. Install or connect the following:
    - Front crankshaft seal
    - Front cover. Tighten the bolts to 18 ft. lbs. (24 Nm).
    - Crankshaft pulley
    - Oil fill tube and adapter. Tighten the bolts to 32 ft. lbs. (43 Nm).
    - Accessory drive belt tensioner. Tighten the bolts to 32 ft. lbs. (43 Nm).
    - Cooling fan and shroud
    - Accessory drive belt. Tighten the crankshaft pulley bolts to 92 ft. lbs. (125 Nm).
    - Negative battery cables
4. Start the engine and check for leaks.

Timing Gears

See Figures 124 and 125.

1. Before servicing the vehicle, refer to the Precautions Section.
2. Remove or disconnect the following:
    - Negative battery cables
    - Accessory drive belt
    - Cooling fan and shroud
    - Belt tensioner
    - Oil fill tube and adapter
    - Crankshaft pulley
    - Front cover
    - Camshaft
3. Press the camshaft out of the timing gear.

To install:

4. Install the camshaft key.
5. Heat the timing gear in an oven to 350°F (177°C) for 45 minutes.

➡The camshaft gear will be permanently distorted if overheated. Do not exceed 350°F (177°C).

6. Install the timing gear to the camshaft with the timing marks facing out and the gear seated on the camshaft shoulder.
7. Install or connect the following:
    - Camshaft with the timing marks aligned
    - Front cover. Tighten the bolts to 18 ft. lbs. (24 Nm).
    - Crankshaft pulley. Tighten the bolt to 92 ft. lbs. (125 Nm).
    - Oil fill tube and adapter. Tighten the mounting bolts to 32 ft. lbs. (43 Nm).
    - Belt tensioner. Tighten the mounting bolts to 32 ft. lbs. (43 Nm).
    - Cooling fan and shroud

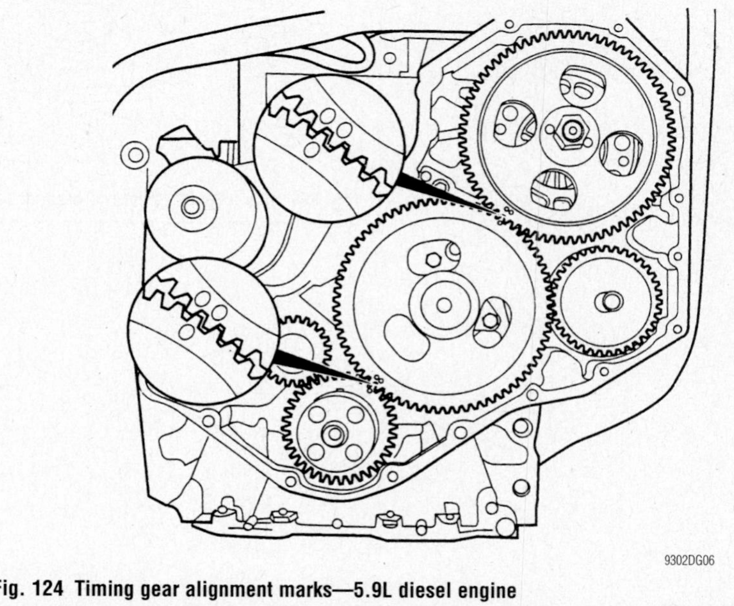

Fig. 124 Timing gear alignment marks—5.9L diesel engine

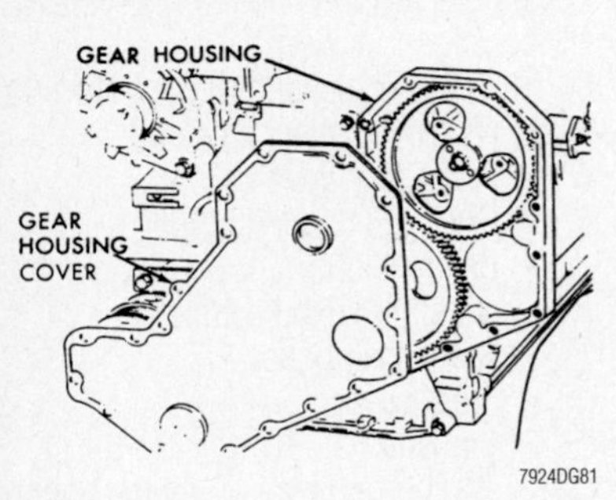

Fig. 125 Remove the gear cover to replace the timing gears—5.9L diesel engine

- Accessory drive belt
- Negative battery cables

VALVE LASH

ADJUSTMENT

3.7L, 4.7L, & 5.7L Engines

All gasoline engines covered in this section use hydraulic lifters. No maintenance or periodic adjustment is required.

5.9L & 2007-08 6.7L Diesel engines

See Figures 126 and 127.

1. Before servicing the vehicle, refer to the Precautions Section.
2. Remove or disconnect the following:
   - Negative battery cables
   - Valve cover
   - Fuel pump gear access cover
3. Position the gear as shown and measure the clearance of the indicated valves. No adjustment is necessary if the lash falls within the following specifications:
   a. Intake—0.006–0.015 inch (0.152–0.381mm).
   b. Exhaust—0.015–0.030 inch (0.381–0.762mm).
4. Install or connect the following:
Fuel pump access cover
   - Valve cover
   - Negative battery cables

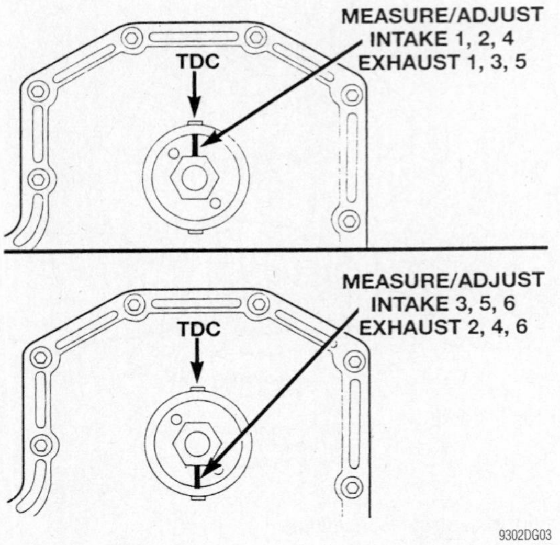

Fig. 126 Adjust the specified valves when the mark on the pump gear is in either of the 2 positions—diesel engines

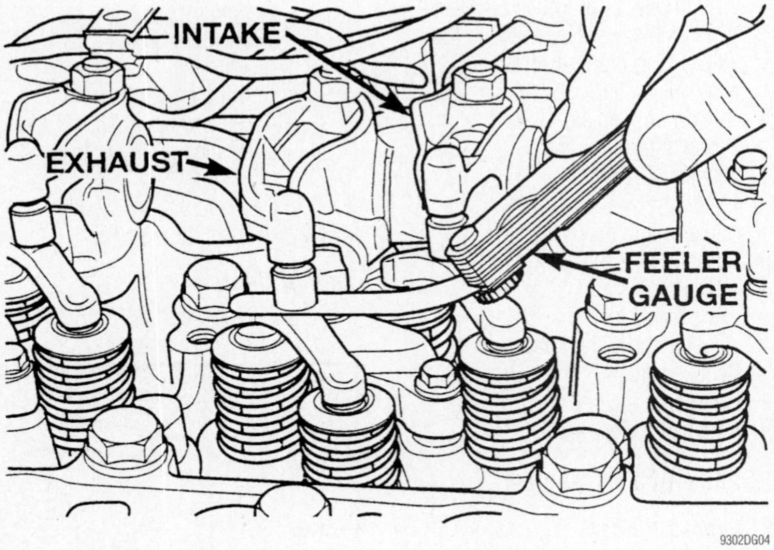

Fig. 127 Use a feeler gauge to measure the valve lash—diesel engine

ENGINE PERFORMANCE & EMISSION CONTROL

COMPONENT LOCATIONS

See Figures 128 through 131.

CAMSHAFT POSITION (CMP) SENSOR

LOCATION

3.7L & 4.7L Engines

See Figure 132.

The Camshaft Position Sensor (CMP) is bolted to the right-front side of the right cylinder head.

5.7L Engine

See Figure 133.

The Camshaft Position Sensor (CMP) is located below the generator on the timing chain /case cover on the right/front side of engine.

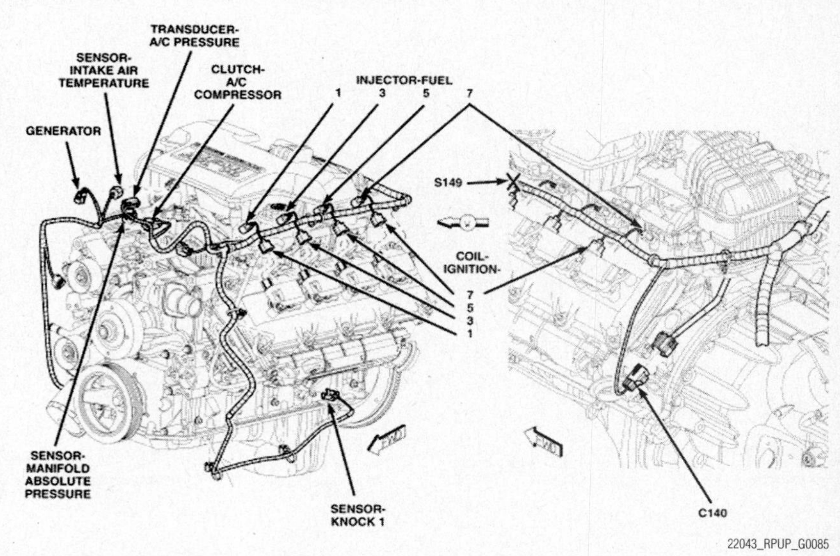

Fig. 128 Left side of engine view 3.7L–4.7L engines

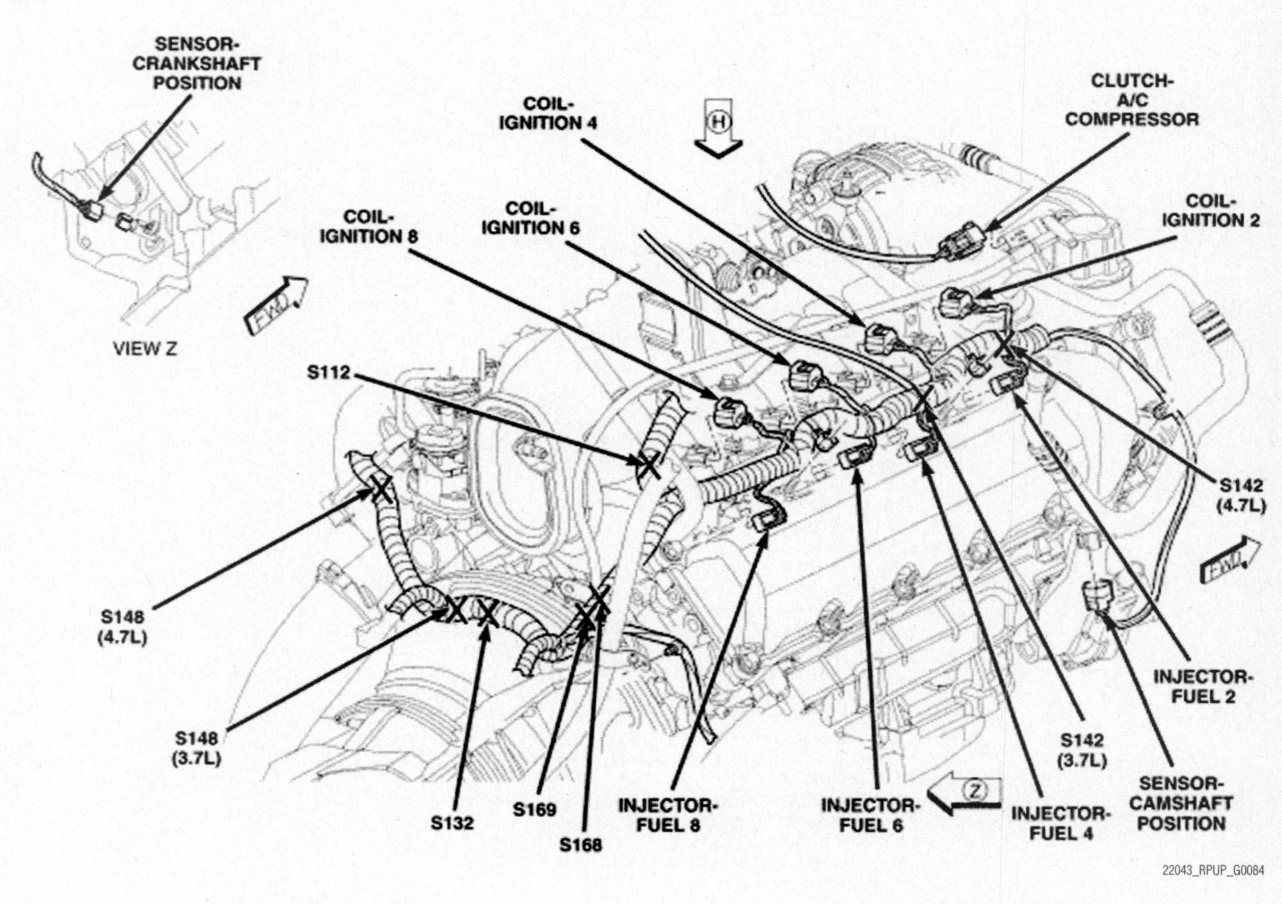

Fig. 129 Right top of engine view 3.7L–4.7L engines

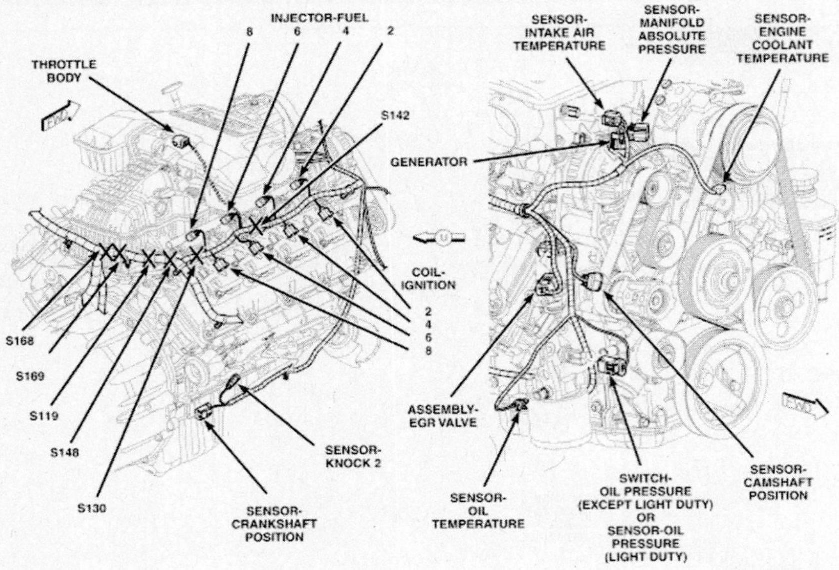

Fig. 130 Right rear engine view 5.7L engine

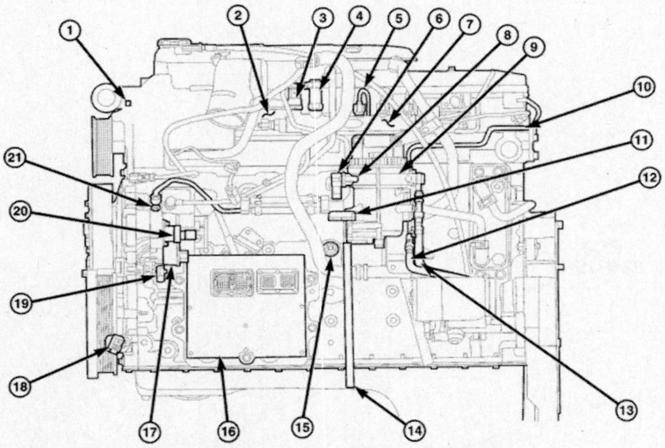

1. ENGINE COOLANT TEMPERATURE (ECT) SENSOR
2. INTAKE MANIFOLD AIR HEATER/ELEMENTS
3. FUEL PRESSURE SENSOR
4. FUEL PRESSURE LIMITING VALVE
5. HIGH-PRESSURE FUEL LINES
6. FUEL HEATER
7. HIGH-PRESSURE FUEL RAIL
8. FUEL HEATER TEMPERATURE SENSOR (THERMOSTAT)
9. FUEL FILTER/WATER SEPARATOR
10. FUEL DRAIN MANIFOLD (CYLINDER HEAD FUEL RETURN LINE)
11. DRAIN VALVE
12. FUEL RETURN LINE CONNECTION (TO FUEL TANK)
13. FUEL SUPPLY LINE (LOW-PRESSURE, TO ENGINE)
14. FUEL DRAIN TUBE
15. OIL PRESSURE SWITCH
16. ENGINE CONTROL MODULE (ECM)
17. FUEL INJECTION PUMP
18. CRANKSHAFT POSITION (ENGINE SPEED) SENSOR
19. CAMSHAFT POSITION SENSOR (CMP)
20. FUEL CONTROL ACTUATOR (FCA)
21. CASCADE OVERFLOW VALVE
22. SCREENED BANJO BOLT

22043_RPUP_G0081

Fig. 131 5.9L–6.7L Engine compartment view

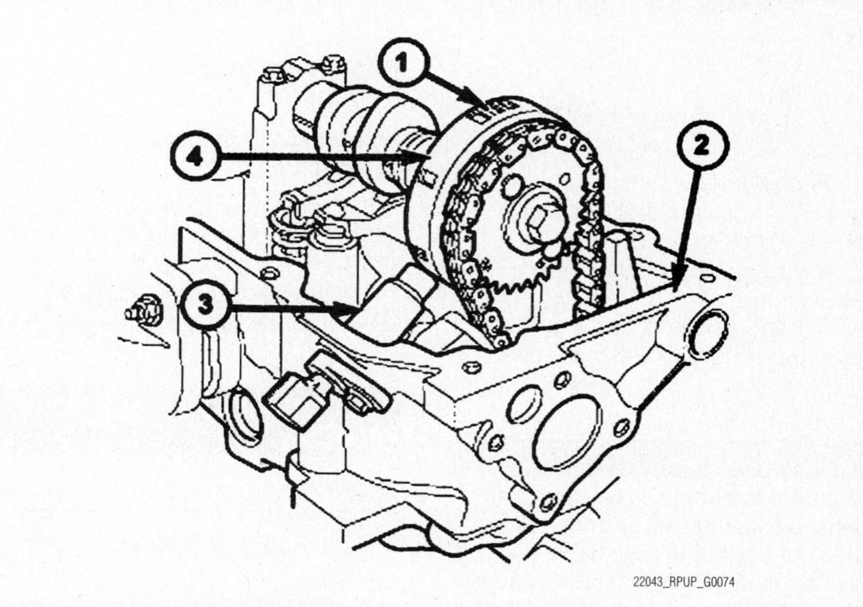

Fig. 132 Camshaft position sensor (3) location—3.7L–4.7L engines

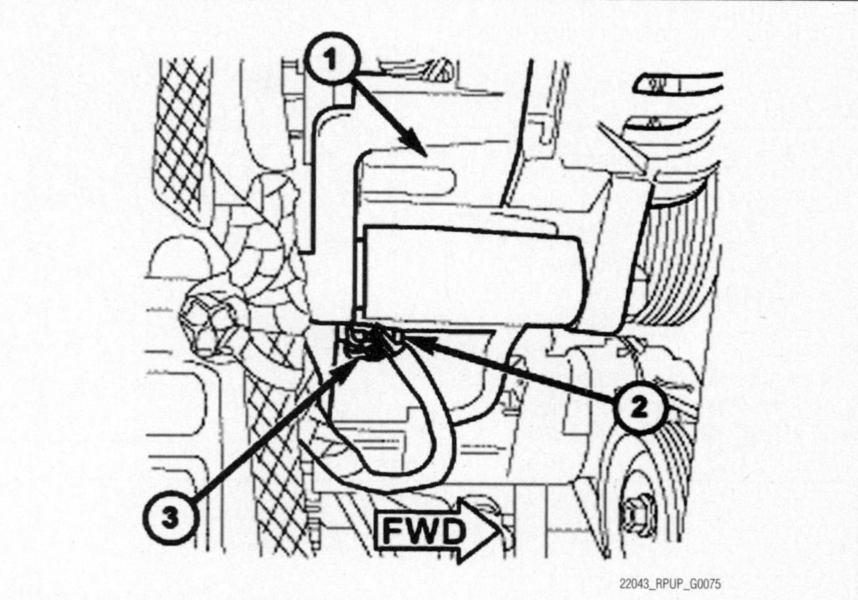

Fig. 133 Camshaft position sensor (3) location—5.7L engine

5.9L & 6.7L Diesel Engines

The Camshaft Position Sensor (CMP) on the diesel engine is located below the fuel injection pump. It is bolted to the back of the timing gear cover.

OPERATION

3.7L & 4.7L Engines

The Camshaft Position (CMP) sensor on the 3.7L and 4.7L engines contain a hall effect device referred to as a sync signal generator. A rotating target wheel (tonewheel) for the CMP is located at the front of the camshaft for the right cylinder head. This sync signal generator detects notches located on a tonewheel. As the tonewheel rotates, the notches pass through the sync signal generator. The signal from the CMP sensor is used in conjunction with the Crankshaft Position Sensor (CKP) to differentiate between fuel injection and spark events. It is also used to synchronize the fuel injectors with their respective cylinders.

When the leading edge of the tonewheel notch enters the tip of the CMP, the interruption of magnetic field causes the voltage to switch high, resulting in a sync signal of approximately 5 volts

When the trailing edge of the tonewheel notch leaves the tip of the CMP, the change of the magnetic field causes the sync signal voltage to switch low to 0 volts.

5.7L Engine

The CMP sensor is used in conjunction with the crankshaft position sensor to differentiate between fuel injection and spark events. It is also used to synchronize the fuel injectors with their respective cylinders. The sensor generates electrical pulses. These pulses (signals) are sent to the Powertrain Control Module (PCM). The PCM will then determine crankshaft position from both the camshaft position sensor and crankshaft position sensor.

The tonewheel is located at the front of the camshaft. As the tonewheel rotates, notches pass through the sync signal generator.

When the cam gear is rotating, the sensor will detect the notches. Input voltage from the sensor to the PCM will then switch from a low (approximately 0.3 volts) to a high (approximately 5 volts). When the sensor detects a notch has passed, the input voltage switches back low to approximately 0.3 volts.

5.9L & 6.7L Diesel Engines

The Camshaft Position Sensor (CMP) contains a hall effect device. A rotating target wheel (tonewheel) for the CMP is located on the front timing gear. This hall effect device detects notches located on the tonewheel. As the tonewheel rotates, the notches pass the tip of the CMP.

When the leading edge of the tonewheel notch passes the tip of the CMP, the following occurs: The interruption of magnetic field causes the voltage to switch high resulting in a signal of approximately 5 volts.

When the trailing edge of the tonewheel notch passes the tip of the CMP, the following occurs: The change of the magnetic field causes the signal voltage to switch low to 0 volts.

The CMP provides a signal to the Engine Control Module (ECM) at all times when the engine is running. The ECM uses the CMP information primarily on engine start-up. Once the engine is running, the ECM uses the CMP as a backup sensor for engine speed. The Crankshaft Position Sensor (CKP) is the primary engine speed indicator for the engine after the engine is running.

REMOVAL & INSTALLATION

3.7L & 4.7L Engines

1. Disconnect the electrical connector at Camshaft Position (CMP) sensor.
2. Remove the CMP sensor mounting bolt.
3. Carefully twist sensor from cylinder head.
4. Check condition of sensor O-ring.

To install:

5. Clean out the machined hole in the cylinder head.
6. Apply a small amount of engine oil to sensor O-ring.
7. Install the CMP sensor into cylinder head with a slight rocking and twisting action.

⁎⁎ WARNING

Before tightening sensor mounting bolt, be sure sensor is completely flush to cylinder head. If sensor is not flush, damage to sensor mounting tang may result.

8. Install mounting bolt and tighten to 106 in. lbs. (12 Nm).
9. Connect the electrical connector to sensor.

5.7L Engine

1. Disconnect the electrical connector at Camshaft Position (CMP) sensor.
2. Remove the CMP sensor mounting bolt.
3. Carefully twist CMP sensor from timing gear/chain cover.
4. Check condition of sensor O-ring.

To install:

5. Clean out machined hole in timing gear/chain cover.
6. Install the CMP sensor into timing gear/chain cover with a slight rocking action. Do not twist sensor into position as damage to O-ring may result.

⁎⁎ WARNING

Before tightening sensor mounting bolt, be sure sensor is completely flush to timing gear/chain cover. If sensor is not flush, damage to sensor mounting tang may result.

7. Install the CMP mounting bolt and tighten to 106 in. lbs. (12 Nm).
8. Connect the electrical connector to the CMP sensor.

5.9L & 6.7L Diesel Engines

1. Disconnect the electrical connector at the Camshaft Position (CMP) sensor.
2. Remove the CMP sensor mounting bolt.
3. Carefully twist sensor from timing gear cover.
4. Check condition of the CMP sensor o-ring.

To install:

5. Clean out machined hole in back of timing gear cover.
6. Apply a small amount of engine oil to sensor o-ring.
7. Install the CMP sensor into timing gear cover with a slight rocking action. Do not twist sensor into position as damage to o-ring may result.

⁎⁎ WARNING

Before tightening sensor mounting bolt, be sure sensor is completely flush to back of timing chain cover. If sensor is not flush, damage to sensor mounting tang may result.

8. Install mounting bolt and tighten to 106 inch. lbs. (12 Nm).
9. Connect the electrical connector to the CMP sensor.

TESTING

3.7L, 4.7L & 5.7L Engines

See Figure 134.

1. Disconnect the CMP Sensor connector.
2. Ignition on, engine not running.
3. Measure the voltage on the (F856) 5-volt Supply circuit in the CMP harness connector.
4. If the voltage is not between 4.5–5.2 volts. Repair the open or short to ground in the (F856) 5-volt Supply circuit.

5.9L & 6.7L Diesel Engines

1. Turn the ignition off.
2. Disconnect the cam sensor harness connector.

➡Check connectors and clean or repair as necessary.

3. Measure the resistance between the (F855) 5-volt supply circuit and the (K44) signal circuit of the sensor.
4. If the resistance is not between 900–1100 ohms, replace the camshaft sensor.

CRANKSHAFT POSITION (CKP) SENSOR

LOCATION

3.7L, 4.7L & 5.7L Engines

See Figure 135.

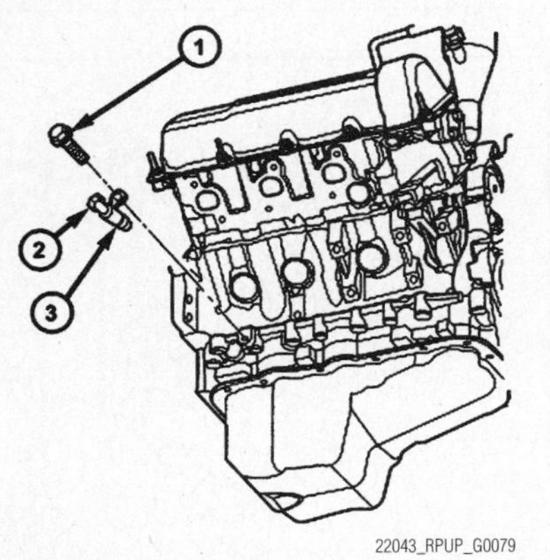

Fig. 135 Crankshaft position sensor location

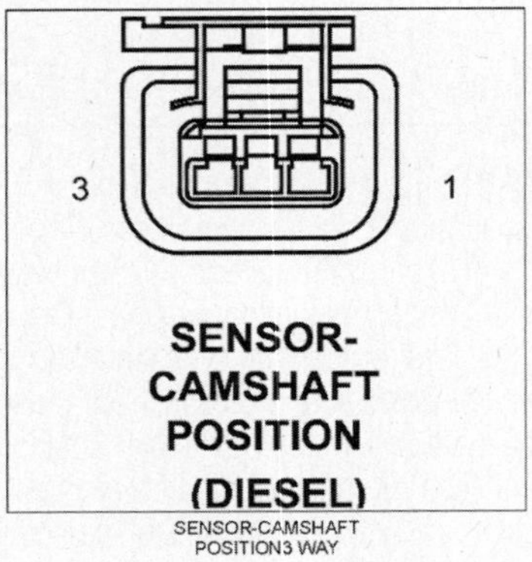

Fig. 134 Camshaft Position (CMP) sensor electrical connector 3.7L–4.7L–5.7L engines

The Crankshaft Position (CKP) sensor is mounted into the right rear side of the cylinder block. It is positioned and bolted into a machined hole.

5.9L & 6.7L Diesel Engines

See Figure 136.

The Crankshaft Position Sensor (CKP) on the diesel engine is attached at the front / left side of the engine next to the engine harmonic balancer (crankshaft damper).

crankshaft . This tonewheel has sets of notches at its outer edge.

The notches cause a pulse to be generated when they pass under the sensor. The pulses are the input to the PCM.

5.9L & 6.7L Engines

The Crankshaft Position Sensor (CKP) is the primary engine speed indicator for the engine after the engine is running.

The CKP contains a hall effect device.

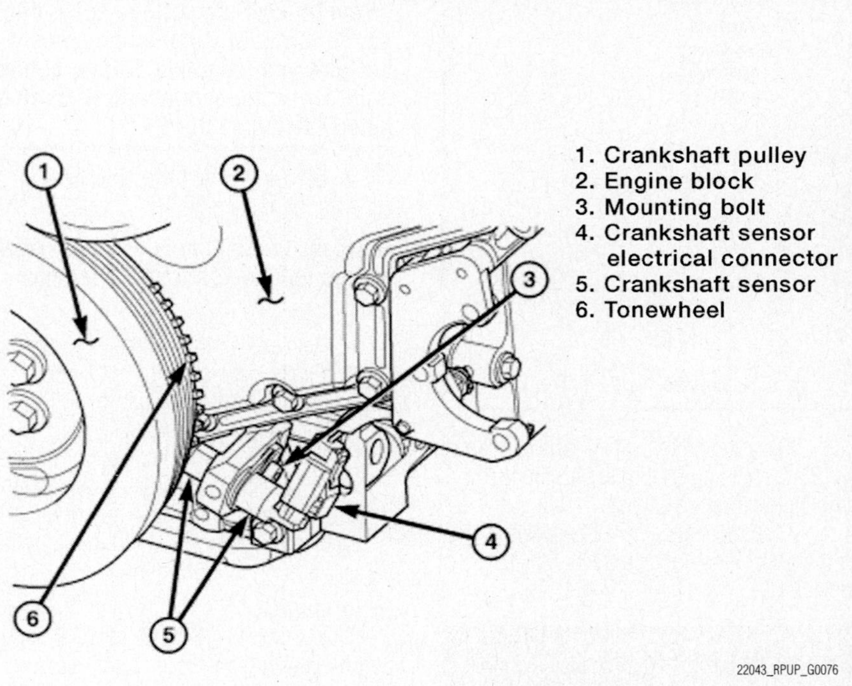

Fig. 136 Crankshaft Position Sensor (CKP) location

OPERATION

3.7L, 4.7L & 5.7LEngines

Engine speed and crankshaft position are provided through the CKP (Crankshaft Position) sensor. The sensor generates pulses that are the input sent to the Powertrain Control Module (PCM). The PCM interprets the sensor input to determine the crankshaft position. The PCM then uses this position, along with other inputs, to determine injector sequence and ignition timing.

The sensor is a hall effect device combined with an internal magnet. It is also sensitive to steel within a certain distance from it.

A tonewheel is bolted to the engine

A rotating, notched target wheel (tonewheel) for the CKP is located behind the engine harmonic balancer. This hall effect device detects notches located on the tonewheel. As the tonewheel rotates, the notches pass the tip of the CKP.

When the leading edge of the tonewheel notch passes the tip of the CKP, the following occurs: The interruption of magnetic field causes the voltage to switch high resulting in a signal of approximately 5 volts.

When the trailing edge of the tonewheel notch passes the tip of the CKP, the following occurs: The change of the magnetic field causes the signal voltage to switch low to 0 volts.

REMOVAL & INSTALLATION

3.7L, 4.7L & 5.7L Engines

1. Raise the vehicle.
2. Disconnect the Crankshaft Position Sensor (CKP) electrical connector.
3. Remove the CKP sensor mounting bolt.
4. Carefully twist sensor from cylinder block.
5. Check condition of sensor O-ring.

To install:

6. Clean out the machined hole in the engine block.
7. Apply a small amount of engine oil to sensor O-ring.
8. Install the CKP sensor into engine block with a slight rocking and twisting action.

**** WARNING**

Before tightening sensor mounting bolt, be sure sensor is completely flush to cylinder block. If sensor is not flush, damage to sensor mounting tang may result.

9. Install mounting bolt and tighten to 21 ft. lbs. (28 Nm).
10. Connect the electrical connector to the CKP sensor.
11. Lower the vehicle.

5.9L & 6.7L Engines

1. Raise and support vehicle
2. Disconnect the electrical connector at the Crankshaft Position Sensor (CKP).
3. Remove the CKP sensor mounting bolt.
4. Remove the CKP sensor.

To install:

5. Position and install CKP sensor to the engine.
6. Install CKP sensor mounting bolt and tighten to 80 in. lbs. (9 Nm).
7. Install the electrical connector to the CKP sensor.

TESTING

3.7L, 4.7L & 5.7L Engines

See Figure 137.

1. Turn the ignition off.
2. Disconnect the CKP Sensor harness connector.
3. Ignition on, engine not running.
4. Measure the voltage on the (F855) 5-volt Supply circuit in the CKP Sensor harness connector.
5. If the voltage is not between 4.5–5.2 volts. Repair the open or short to ground in the (F856) 5-volt Supply circuit.

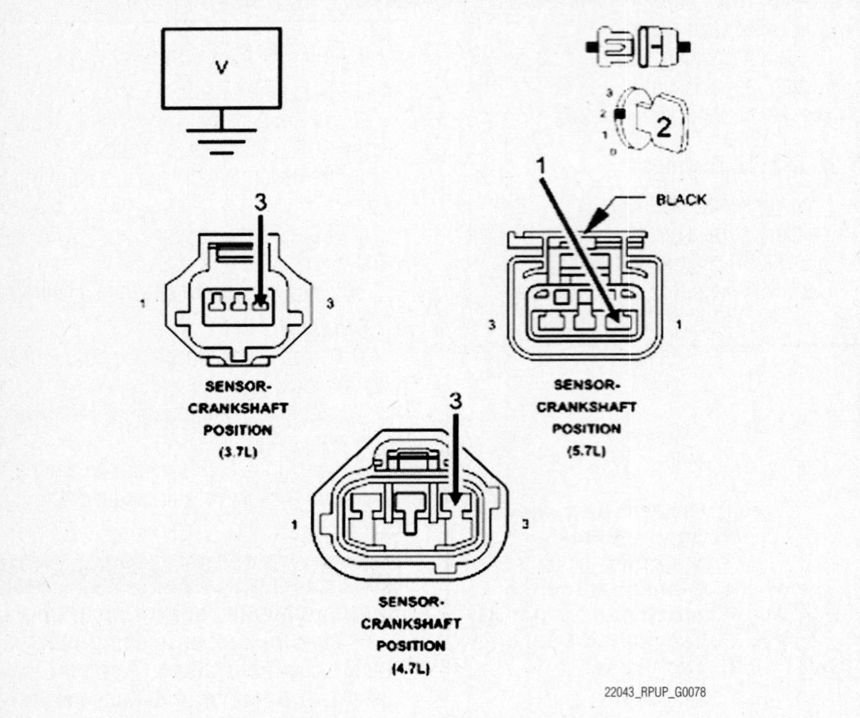

Fig. 137 Crankshaft sensor electrical connector 3.7L–4.7L–5.7L engines

5.9L & 6.7L Engines

See Figure 138.

1. Disconnect the CKP sensor harness connector.
2. Check connectors and clean or repair as necessary.

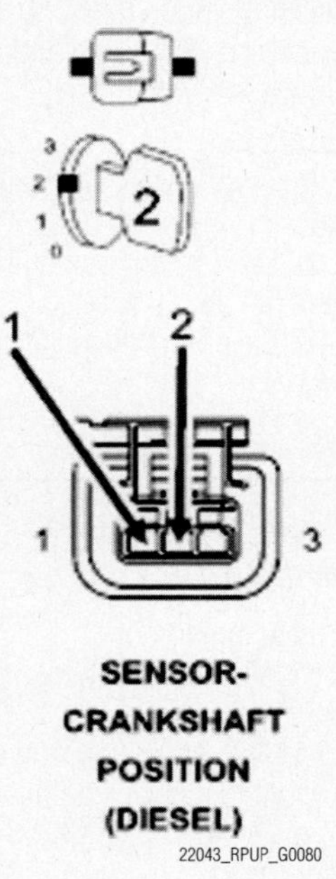

Fig. 138 Crankshaft position sensor electrical connector

3. Measure the resistance between the (K824) 5-volt supply circuit and the (K24) signal circuit of the sensor.
4. If the resistance is not between 900–1100 ohms, replace the crankshaft sensor.

ELECTRONIC CONTROL MODULE (ECM)

LOCATION

5.9L & 6.7L Engines

The Engine Control Module (ECM) for the 5.9L & 6.7L diesel engines are bolted to the left side of the engine below the intake manifold.

OPERATION

5.9L & 6.7L Engines

The main function of the Engine Control Module (ECM) is to electrically control the fuel system. The ECM also controls certain transmission and other functions previously controlled by the Powertrain Control Module (PCM).

The ECM can adapt its programming to meet changing operating conditions.

The ECM receives input signals from various switches and sensors. Based on these inputs, the ECM regulates various engine and vehicle operations through different system components. These components are referred to as ECM outputs. The sensors and switches that provide inputs to the ECM are considered ECM inputs.

REMOVAL & INSTALLATION

5.9L & 6.7L Engines

1. Record any Diagnostic Trouble Codes (DTC's) found in the Engine Control Module (ECM).

WARNING

To avoid possible voltage spike damage to the ECM, ignition key must be off, and both negative battery cables must be disconnected before unplugging ECM connectors.

2. Disconnect both negative battery cables at both batteries.

➡Access to the ECM is easier by working through the left front wheel opening.

3. Remove left front wheel.
4. Remove plastic left front fender splash shield. Refer to Slash Shield Front Wheel Hose in Body section.
5. Remove electrical connector bolts at ECM. As each bolt is being removed, very carefully remove connectors from the ECM.
6. Remove three ECM mounting bolts (6) and remove ECM from engine.

To install:

7. Position ECM (5) to the ECM support bracket and install mounting bolts. Tighten bolts to 18 ft. lbs. (24 Nm).
8. Check pins in electrical connectors for corrosion, damage or dirt intrusion. Also check all pins for being bent. Repair as necessary. Damaged, dirty, bent or corroded pins could result in poor conductivity, causing intermittent electrical issues or DTC's.
9. Clean pins in electrical connectors with an electrical contact cleaner.
10. Install the connectors to ECM. Tighten connector bolts to 27 in. lbs. (3 Nm).
11. Install the splash shield.
12. Install left front wheel.
13. Connect both negative battery cables.
14. Use a diagnostic scan tool to erase any (DTC's) from ECM.

TESTING

5.9L & 6.7L Engines

1. Turn the ignition off.
2. Disconnect the ECM harness connectors.

3. Using a 12-volt test light connected to 12-volts, check each of the ECM ground circuits in ECM harness connector.

4. If the test light illuminates for each cavity ECM Ground circuits are okay, if not repair open circuit.

5. Turn the ignition on to check fused ignition switch output.

6. Using a 12-volt test light connected to ground, check the fused ignition switch output circuit in ECM harness connector.

7. If the test light illuminates the fused ignition switch output circuit is okay, if not repair open circuit.

8. Turn the ignition off.

9. Using a 12-volt test light connected to ground, check each fused B+ circuit in the ECM harness connector.

10. If the test light illuminates brightly for each circuit, fused B+ circuit is okay. If not repair fused B+ circuit. The power and ground test is complete. Suspect faulty ECM

ENGINE COOLANT TEMPERATURE (ECT) SENSOR

LOCATION

3.7L & 4.7L Engines

See Figure 139.

The Engine Coolant Temperature (ECT) sensor is located in the intake manifold toward the front of the engine.

5.7L Engine

See Figure 140.

The Engine Coolant Temperature (ECT) sensor is located directly under the A/C compressor in the engine block. The A/C compressor must be unbolted to gain access to ECT sensor.

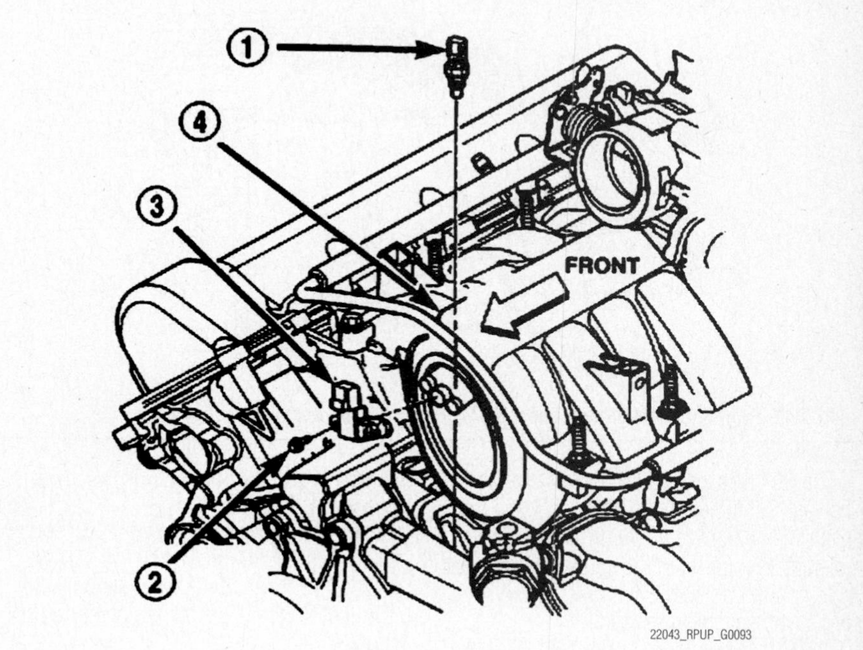

Fig. 140 The Engine Coolant Temperature (ECT) sensor (1) location 5.7L—engine

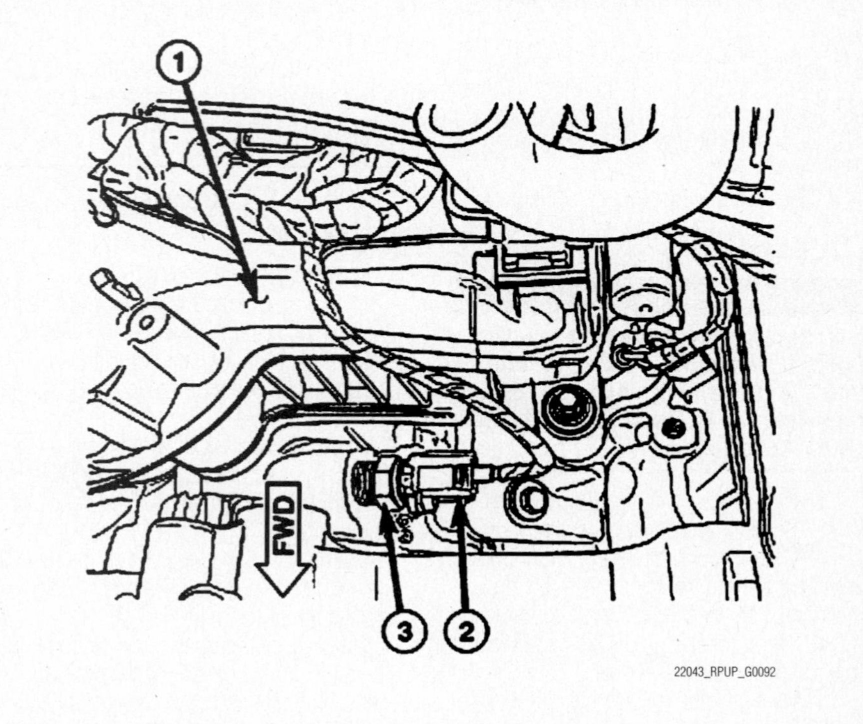

Fig. 139 Engine Coolant Temperature (ECT) sensor (3) location—4.7L shown; 3.7L similar

5.9L & 6.7L Engines

See Figures 141 and 142.

The Engine Coolant Temperature (ECT) sensor is located in the cylinder head toward the front of the engine.

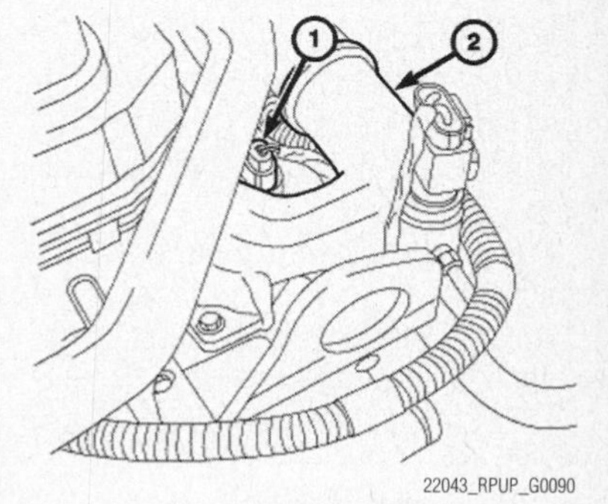

Fig. 141 Engine Coolant Temperature (ECT) sensor (1) location 5.9L—engine

OPERATION

The Engine Coolant Temperature (ECT) sensor is used to sense engine coolant temperature. The sensor protrudes into an engine water jacket.

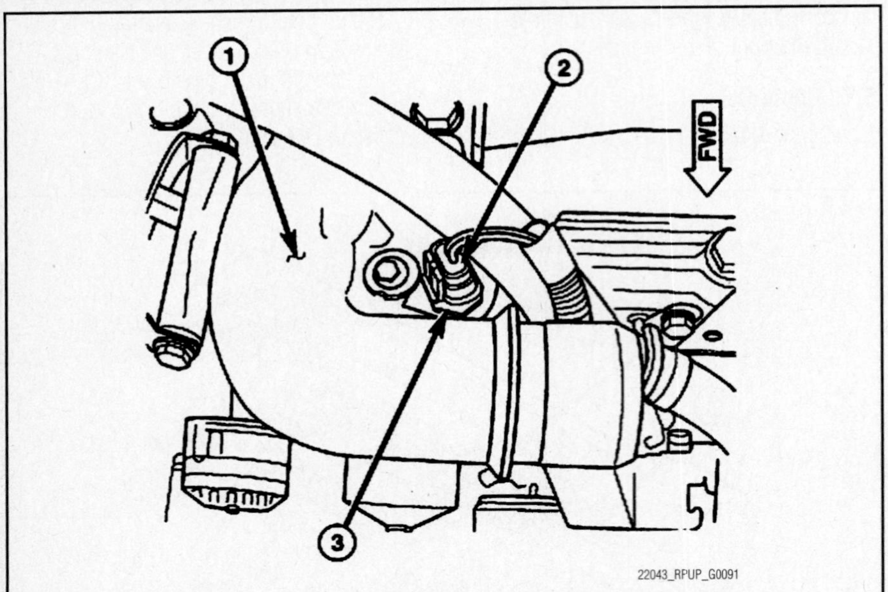

Fig. 142 Engine Coolant Temperature (ECT) sensor (3) location 6.7L—engine

The ECT sensor is a two-wire Negative Thermal Coefficient (NTC) sensor. Meaning, as engine coolant temperature increases, resistance (voltage) in the sensor decreases. As temperature decreases, resistance (voltage) in the sensor increases.

The PCM uses inputs from the ECT sensor for the following calculations:

- For engine coolant temperature gauge operation through CAN Bus communications
- Injector pulse-width
- Spark-advance curves
- ASD relay shut-down times
- Idle Air Control (IAC) motor key-on steps
- Pulse-width prime-shot during cranking
- O2 sensor closed loop times
- Purge solenoid on/off times
- Cooling fan control
- Temperature gauge operation
- A/C cutoff at high coolant temperatures
- EGR solenoid on/off times (if equipped)
- Leak Detection Pump operation (if equipped)
- Radiator fan relay on/off times (if equipped)
- Target idle speed

REMOVAL & INSTALLATION

3.7L & 4.7L Engines

⁂ CAUTION

Hot, pressurized coolant can cause injury by scalding. Cooling system must be partially drained before removing the coolant temperature sensor.

1. Partially drain the cooling system.
2. Disconnect the electrical connector from the Engine Coolant Temperature (ECT) sensor.
3. Remove the sensor from the intake manifold.

To install:

4. Apply thread sealant to ETC sensor threads.
5. Install the ETC sensor to engine.
6. Tighten the ETC sensor to 8 ft. lbs. (11 Nm).
7. Connect the electrical connector to ETC sensor.
8. Replace any lost engine coolant.

5.7L Engine

⁂ CAUTION

Hot, pressurized coolant can cause injury by scalding. Cooling system must be partially drained before removing the Engine Coolant Temperature (ECT) sensor.

1. Partially drain the cooling system.
2. Remove accessory drive belt
3. Carefully unbolt the air conditioning compressor from front of engine. Do not disconnect any A/C hoses from compressor.
4. Temporarily support the compressor to gain access to ECT sensor.
5. Disconnect the electrical connector from sensor.
6. Remove the ECT sensor from the cylinder block.

To install:

7. Apply thread sealant to ETC sensor threads.
8. Install the ETC sensor into engine.
9. Tighten the sensor to 8 ft. lbs. (11 Nm).
10. Connect the electrical connector to ETC sensor.
11. Install air conditioning compressor onto the front of engine
12. Install the accessory drive belt.
13. Replace any lost engine coolant.

5.9L & 6.7L Engines

⁂ CAUTION

Hot, pressurized coolant can cause injury by scalding. Cooling system must be partially drained before removing the Engine Coolant Temperature (ECT) sensor.

1. Partially drain the cooling system
2. Remove heat shield (if equipped).
3. Disconnect the electrical connector from the ETC sensor.
4. Remove the ETC sensor from the cylinder head.

To install:

5. Install the ECT sensor to the engine.
6. Tighten the ECT sensor to 13 ft. lbs (18 Nm).
7. Connect the electrical connector to the ETC sensor.
8. Install heat shield (if equipped).
9. Replace any lost engine coolant

TESTING

3.7L, 4.7L & 5.7L Engines

See Figure 143.

1. Turn the ignition off.
2. Disconnect the Engine Coolant Temperature (ECT) sensor harness connector.
3. Ignition on, engine not running.
4. Install a scan tool, read the ECT voltage.
5. Connect a jumper wire between the (K2) ECT signal circuit and the (K900) sensor ground circuit in the ECT harness connector.
6. The sensor voltage should be approximately 0.0 volts (plus or minus .1 volt) with the jumper wire in place.
7. Verify that there is good pin to terminal contact in the sensor and Powertrain Control Module (PCM) connectors. Replace the ECT Sensor if no problems were found with the connectors.

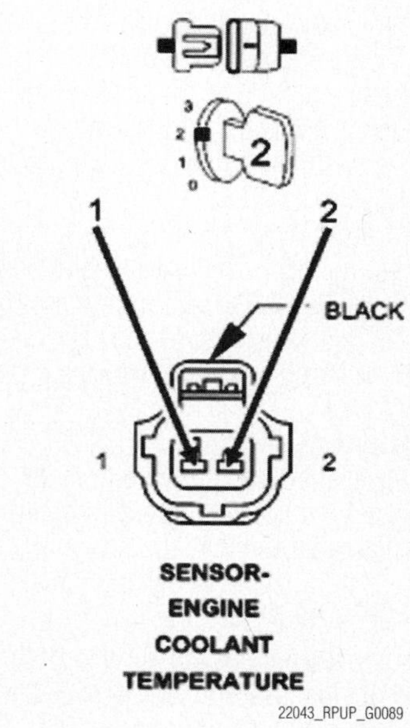

Fig. 143 Engine Coolant Temperature (ECT) sensor electrical Connector

5.9L & 6.7L Engines

1. Disconnect the coolant temperature sensor harness connector.
2. Check connectors clean or repair as necessary.
3. Measure the resistance of the coolant temperature sensor.
4. If the resistance is not between 300–90k ohms replace the coolant temperature sensor.

HEATED OXYGEN (HO2S) SENSOR

LOCATION

3.7L, 4.7L & 5.7L Engines

See Figures 144 and 145.

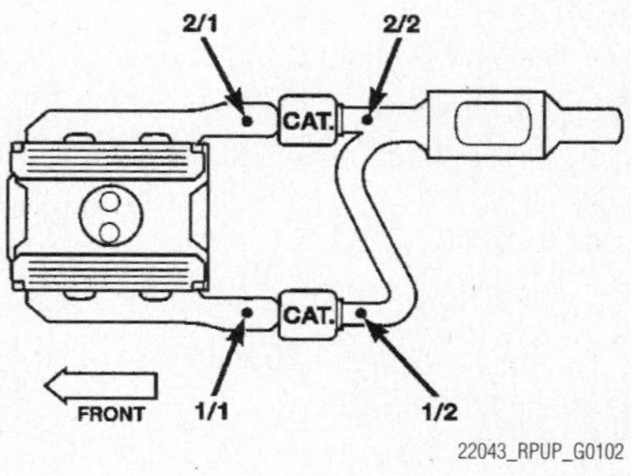

Fig. 144 Heated Oxygen (HO2S) Sensor location (Federal Emissions)

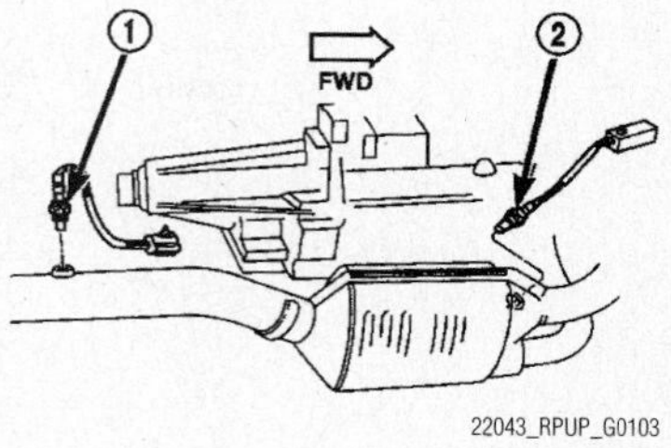

Fig. 145 Heated Oxygen (HO2S) Sensor location (California Emissions)

OPERATION

The HO2S detects the presence of oxygen in the exhaust and produces a variable voltage according to the amount of oxygen detected. A high concentration of oxygen (lean air/fuel ratio) in the exhaust produces a voltage signal less than 0.4 volt. A low concentration of oxygen (rich air/fuel ratio) produces a voltage signal greater than 0.6 volt. The HO2S provides feedback to the PCM indicating air/fuel ratio in order to achieve a near stoichiometric air/fuel ratio of 14.7:1during closed loop engine operation. The HO2S generates a voltage between 0.0 and 1.1 volts.

Embedded with the sensing element is the HO2S heater. The heating element heats the sensor to a temperature of 800°C (1,472°F). At approximately 300°C (572°F) the engine can enter closed loop operation. The PCM turns the heater on by providing the ground when the correct conditions occur. The heater allows the engine to enter closed loop operation sooner.

REMOVAL & INSTALLATION

3.7L, 4.7L & 5.7L Engines

CAUTION

The exhaust manifold, exhaust pipes and catalytic converter become very hot during the engine operation. Allow engine to cool before removing oxygen sensor.

1. Raise and support vehicle.
2. Disconnect wire connector from O2S sensor.

WARNING

When disconnecting sensor electrical connector, do not pull directly on wire going into sensor.

3. Remove the HO2S sensor with an oxygen sensor removal and installation tool.
4. Clean threads in exhaust pipe using appropriate tap.

To install:

➡Threads of new oxygen sensors are factory coated with anti-seize compound to aid in removal. DO NOT add any additional anti-seize compound to threads of a new oxygen sensor.

5. Install the HO2S sensor. Tighten to 30 ft. lbs. (41Nm).
6. Connect the HO2S sensor wire connector.
7. Lower the vehicle.

TESTING

3.7L, 4.7L & 5.7L Engines

See Figure 146.

This procedure checks the heater circuit of the HO2S.

1. Warm up the engine until operating temperature is reached.
2. Turn the ignition off.
3. Wait a minimum of 8 minutes to allow the O2 Sensor to cool down before continuing the test. Allow the O2 Sensor voltage to stabilize between 4.6–5.0 volts.

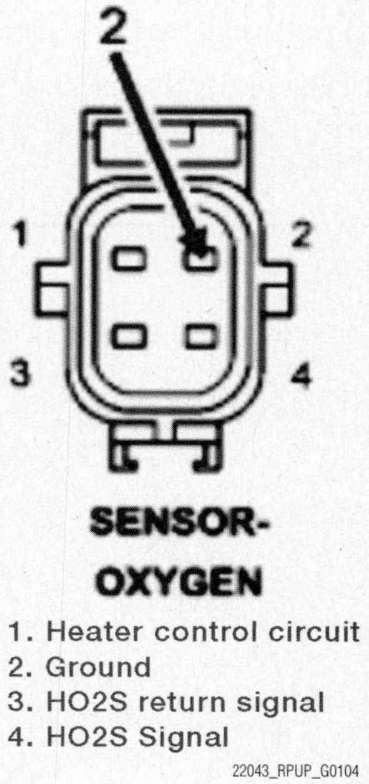

Fig. 146 Typical HO2S sensor harness connector

4. With the ignition on, engine not running.
5. Install a scan tool, actuate the HO2S heater test.
6. With the scan tool, monitor O2 Sensor voltage for at least 2 minutes.
7. If the voltage stays above 4.5 volts, turn the ignition off. (If not problem maybe intermittent).
8. Allow the O2 sensor to cool down to room temperature.
9. Disconnect the HO2S sensor harness connector.
10. Measure the resistance of the O2 heater element, between the HO2S heater control terminal and the O2 heater ground terminal in the HO2S sensor connector.
11. HO2S heater element resistance values should be measured at 21.1°C (70°F). The resistance value will vary with different temperature values.
12. The resistance of the HO2S sensor heater element should be between 2.0–30.0 ohms.
13. If the resistance is not as stated replace the HO2S sensor.

INTAKE AIR TEMPERATURE (IAT) SENSOR

LOCATION

3.7L & 4.7L Engines

See Figures 147 and 148.

The Intake Air Temperature (IAT) sensor is installed into the air intake tube near the throttle body.

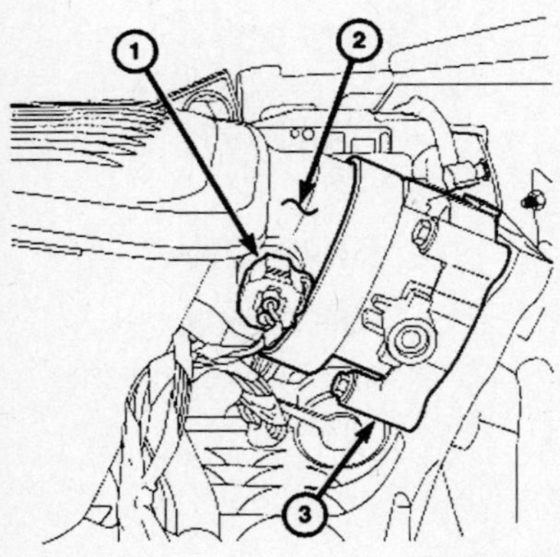

22043_RPUP_G0097

Fig. 147 Intake Air Temperature (IAT) sensor (1) location 3.7L engine

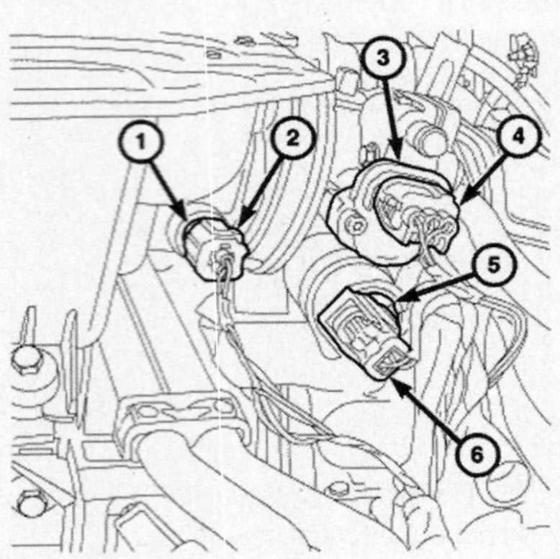

1. IAT sensor
2. IAT sensor electrical connector
3. TPS sensor
4. TPS sensor electrical connector
5. IAC sensor
6. IAC sensor electrical connector

22043_RPUP_G0098

Fig. 148 Intake Air Temperature (IAT) sensor location 4.7L engine

5.7L Engine

See Figure 149.

The intake manifold air temperature (IAT) sensor is installed into the front of the intake manifold air box plenum .

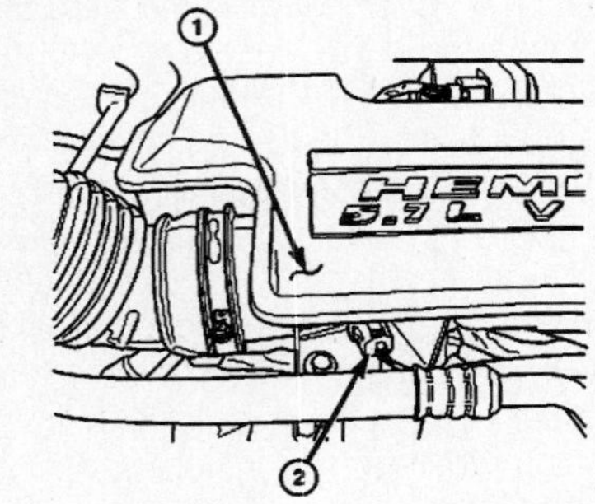

22043_RPUP_G0099

Fig. 149 Intake Air Temperature (IAT) sensor (2) location 5.7L engine

5.9L Diesel Engine

The combination, dual function Intake Manifold Air Temperature Sensor/MAP Sensor is installed into the top of the intake manifold.

6.7L Diesel Engine

The combination, dual function Intake Manifold Air Temperature Sensor/MAP (IAT/MAP) sensor is installed into the intake air connection manifold, below, and to the rear of the EGR valve.

OPERATION

3.7L, 4.7L & 5.7L Engines

The Intake Air Temperature (IAT) Sensor provides an input voltage to the Powertrain Control Module (PCM) indicating the density of the air entering the intake manifold based upon intake manifold temperature. At key-on, a 5-volt power circuit is supplied to the sensor from the PCM. The sensor is grounded at the PCM through a low-noise, sensor-return circuit. The resistance values of the IAT sensor are the same as for the Engine Coolant Temperature (ECT) sensor.

The PCM uses this input to calculate the following:

- Injector pulse-width
- Adjustment of spark timing (to help prevent spark knock with high intake manifold air-charge temperatures).

5.9L & 6.7L Engines

The combination, dual function Intake Manifold Air Temperature Sensor/MAP Sensor is installed into the top of the intake manifold with the sensor element extending into the air stream.

The IAT portion of the sensor provides an input voltage to the Engine Control Module (ECM) indicating intake manifold air temperature. The MAP portion of the sensor provides an input voltage to the ECM indicating turbocharger boost pressure.

REMOVAL & INSTALLATION

3.7L, 4.7L & 5.7L Engines

1. Before servicing the vehicle, refer to the Precautions Section.
2. Disconnect the electrical connector from IAT sensor.
3. Clean any dirt from intake tube at the sensor base.
4. Gently lift on small plastic release tab and rotate sensor about ¼ turn counterclockwise for removal.
5. Check the condition of IAT sensor O-ring.

To install:

6. Clean sensor mounting hole in air intake tube.
7. Position sensor into air intake tube and rotate clockwise until past release tab.
8. Install the electrical connector.

5.9L Engine

See Figure 150.

1. Before servicing the vehicle, refer to the Precautions Section.
2. Clean the area around the sensor.
3. Disconnect the electrical connector from IAT/MAP sensor.
4. Remove two T—15 Torx headed screws.

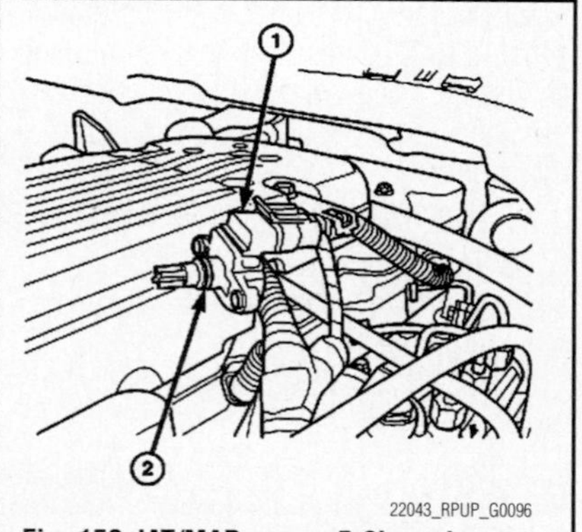

Fig. 150 IAT/MAP sensor 5.9L engine

5. Remove the sensor from the intake manifold.

6. Check condition of sensor O-ring.

To install:

7. Lubricate the sensor o-ring and sensor hole in the intake manifold cover with clean engine oil.

8. Clean sensor mounting area at intake manifold.

9. Position the sensor into intake manifold.

10. Install and tighten 2 sensor mounting screws to 1 Nm 9 in. lbs. (1 Nm).

11. Connect the electrical connector to the sensor.

6.7L Engine

1. Before servicing the vehicle, refer to the Precautions Section.

2. Clean the area around sensor.

3. Disconnect the electrical connector from IAT/MAP sensor.

4. Remove the mounting screw.

5. Remove the IAT/MAP sensor from manifold.

6. Check condition of sensor O-ring.

To install:

7. Clean sensor mounting area at intake manifold.

8. Lubricate the sensor O-ring and sensor mounting hole in intake manifold with clean engine oil.

9. Position the sensor into the intake manifold.

10. Install and tighten sensor mounting screw to 1 Nm 9 in. lbs. (1 Nm).

11. Connect the electrical connector to sensor.

TESTING

3.7L, 4.7L & 5.7L Engines

See Figure 151.

1. Turn the ignition off.

2. Disconnect the Intake Air Temperature (IAT) Sensor harness connector. Turn the ignition on.

3. Install a scan tool, read the IAT sensor voltage.

4. The sensor voltage should be approximately 5.0 volts (plus or minus .1 volt) with the connector disconnected. If not repair the open in the (K21) IAT Signal circuit.

5. If the voltage reading was okay connect a jumper wire between the (K21) IAT Signal circuit and the (K900) Sensor ground circuit in the IAT Sensor harness connector.

6. With the scan tool, read the IAT voltage.

7. The sensor voltage should be approximately 0.0 volts (plus or minus .1 volt) with the jumper wire in place. If the readings are as stated, verify that there is good pin to terminal contact in the sensor and Powertrain Control Module (PCM) connectors. Replace the IAT sensor if no problems were found with the connectors.

5.9L & 6.7L Engines

1. Remove the temperature sensor and reconnect the wiring to the sensor.

2. Turn on the ignition switch, engine off.

3. With the scan tool in sensors, monitor the Intake Air Temperature (IAT).

4. While heating the sensor with an external heat source (DO NOT USE OPEN FLAME).

5. The reading from the sensor should increase at least -15° C (5° F) on the scan tool.

6. If not replace the intake air temperature sensor.

KNOCK SENSOR (KS)

LOCATION

3.7L &4.7L Engines

See Figure 152.

The two knock sensors are bolted into the cylinder block under the intake manifold. The

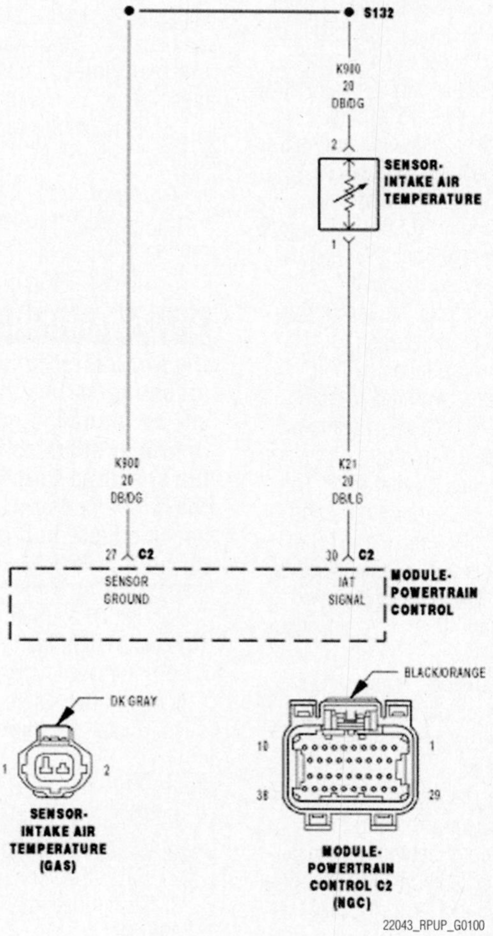

Fig. 151 Intake Air Temperature (IAT) Sensor, PCM harness connectors and wiring diagram

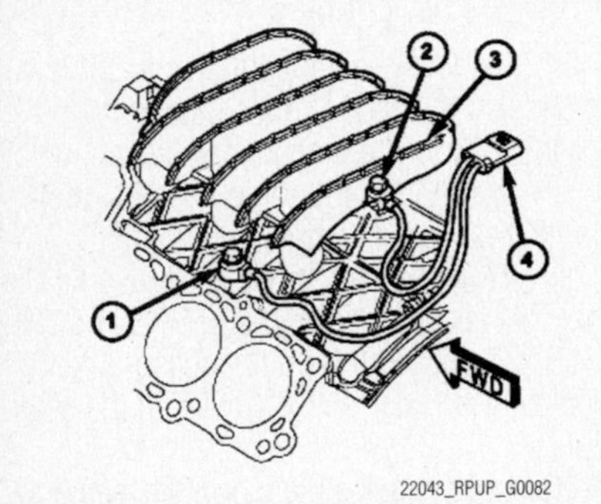

Fig. 152 Knock sensor location (1, 2) view 4.7L engine shown 3.7L similar

two sensors share a common wiring harness using one electrical connector. Because of this, they must be replaced as a pair.

5.7L Engine

Two knock sensors are bolted into each side of the cylinder block (outside) under the exhaust manifold.

OPERATION

Two knock sensors are used; one for each cylinder bank. When the knock sensor detects a knock in one of the cylinders on the corresponding bank, it sends an input signal to the Powertrain Control Module (PCM). In response, the PCM retards ignition timing for all cylinders by a scheduled amount.

Knock sensors contain a piezoelectric material which constantly vibrates and sends an input voltage (signal) to the PCM while the engine operates. As the intensity of the crystal's vibration increases, the knock sensor output voltage also increases.

The voltage signal produced by the knock sensor increases with the amplitude of vibration. The PCM receives the knock sensor voltage signal as an input. If the signal rises above a predetermined level, the PCM will store that value in memory and retard ignition timing to reduce engine knock. If the knock sensor voltage exceeds a preset value, the PCM retards ignition timing for all cylinders. It is not a selective cylinder retard.

The PCM ignores knock sensor input during engine idle conditions. Once the engine speed exceeds a specified value, knock retard is allowed.

Knock retard uses its own short term and long term memory program. Long term memory stores previous detonation information in its battery-backed RAM. The maximum authority that long term memory has over timing retard can be calibrated.

Short term memory is allowed to retard timing up to a preset amount under all operating conditions (as long as rpm is above the minimum rpm) except at Wide Open Throttle (WOT). The PCM, using short term memory, can respond quickly to retard timing when engine knock is detected. Short term memory is lost any time the ignition key is turned off.

REMOVAL & INSTALLATION

3.7L & 4.7L Engines

➡The left sensor is identified by an identification tag (LEFT) (2). It is also identified by a larger bolt head. The Powertrain Control Module (PCM) must have and know the correct sensor left/right positions. Do not mix the sensor locations.

1. Before servicing the vehicle, refer to the Precautions Section.
2. Remove the intake manifold.
3. Disconnect knock sensor dual pigtail harness from engine wiring harness. This connection is made near rear of engine.
4. Remove both sensor mounting bolts. Note foam strip on bolt threads. This foam is used only to retain the bolts to sensors for plant assembly. It is not used as a sealant. Do not apply any adhesive, sealant or thread locking compound to these bolts.
5. Remove the knock sensors from the engine.

To install:

6. Thoroughly clean the knock sensor mounting holes.
7. Install the sensors into cylinder block.

⁂ WARNING

Over or under tightening the sensor mounting bolts will affect knock sensor performance, possibly causing improper spark control. Always use the specified torque when installing the knock sensors. The torque for the knock sensor bolt is relatively light for an 8 mm bolt.

8. Install and tighten mounting bolts. Tighten to 15 ft. lbs. (20 Nm).
9. Connect knock sensor wiring harness to engine harness at rear of intake manifold.
10. Install the intake manifold.

5.7L Engine

1. Before servicing the vehicle, refer to the Precautions Section.
2. Raise the vehicle.
3. Disconnect the knock sensor electrical connector.
4. Remove knock sensor mounting bolt. Note foam strip on bolt threads. This foam is used only to retain the bolts to sensors for plant assembly. It is not used as a sealant. Do not apply any adhesive, sealant or thread locking compound to these bolts.
5. Remove knock sensor from the engine.

To install:

6. Thoroughly clean the knock sensor mounting hole.
7. Install knock sensor into the cylinder block.

⁂ WARNING

Over or under tightening the sensor mounting bolts will affect knock sensor performance, possibly causing improper spark control. Always use the specified torque when installing the knock sensors. The torque for the knock sensor bolt is relatively light for an 8 mm bolt.

8. Install and tighten mounting bolt. Tighten to 15 ft. lbs. (20 Nm).

TESTING

3.7L, 4.7L & 5.7L Engines

See Figure 153.

1. Start the engine and allow it to reach normal operating temperature.
2. With the scan tool, select view DTCs.

➡It may be necessary to test drive the vehicle within the DTC monitoring conditions in order for this DTC to reset.

3. If the DTC is Active or Pending at this time. Turn the ignition off.
4. Disconnect the Knock Sensor (KS) harness connector.
5. Disconnect the C2 PCM harness connector.
6. Ignition on, engine not running.
7. Measure the voltage on the (K42) KS number (1) signal circuit in the KS harness connector.
8. If there is any voltage present repair the short to voltage in the (K42) KS number (1) signal circuit.
9. If voltage was not present measure the resistance of the (K42) KS number (1) signal circuit from the KS harness connector to the appropriate terminal of pin out box tool 8815.
10. The resistance reading should be below 5.0 ohms.
11. If reading is not as stated repair the open in the (K42) KS number (1) signal circuit.

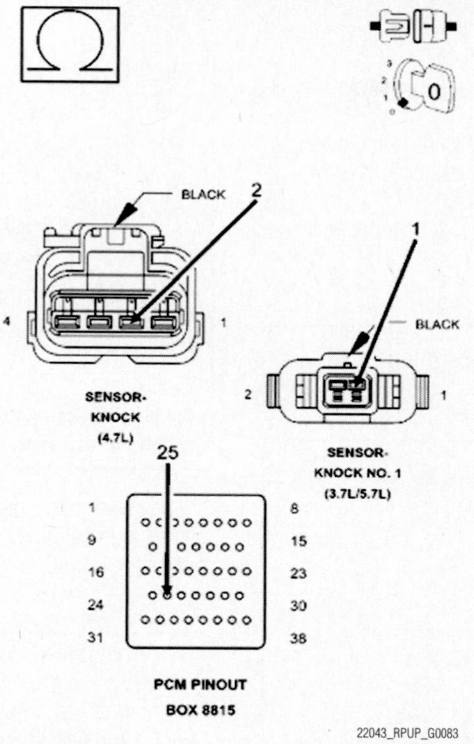

Fig. 153 Knock Sensor (KS) electrical connector views 3.7L–4.7L–5.7L engines

⁂ WARNING

Do not probe the PCM harness connectors. Probing the PCM harness connectors will damage the PCM terminals resulting in poor terminal to pin connection. Install pin out box tool 8815 to perform diagnosis.

MANIFOLD ABSOLUTE PRESSURE (MAP) SENSOR

LOCATION

3.7L & 4.7L Engines

See Figure 154.

The Manifold Absolute Pressure (MAP) sensor is mounted into the front of the intake manifold.

5.7L Engine

See Figure 155.

The Manifold Absolute Pressure (MAP) sensor is mounted to the front of the intake manifold air plenum box.

OPERATION

The MAP sensor is used as an input to the Powertrain Control Module (PCM). It contains a silicon based sensing unit to provide data on the manifold vacuum that draws the air/fuel mixture into the combustion chamber. The PCM requires this information to determine injector pulse width and spark advance. When Manifold Absolute Pressure (MAP) equals Barometric pressure, the pulse width will be at maximum.

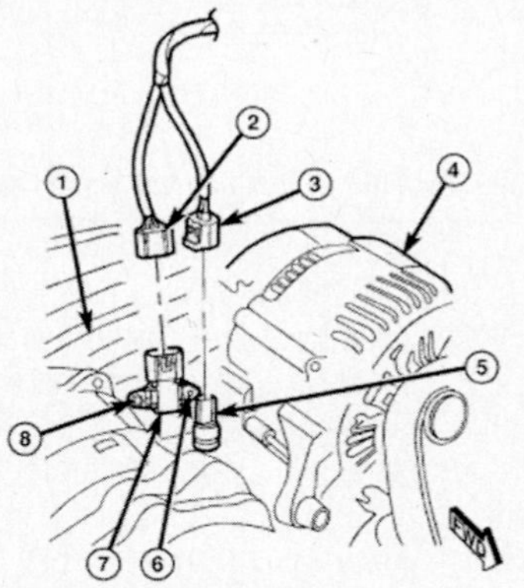

1. Upper intake manifold
2. MAP sensor electrical connector
3. ECT sensor electrical connector
4. Alternator
5. ECT sensor
6. Locating pin
7. MAP sensor
8. Mounting bolt

22043_RPUP_G0094

Fig. 154 Manifold Absolute Pressure (MAP) sensor location— 3.7L & 4.7L engines

A 5 volt reference is supplied from the PCM and returns a voltage signal to the PCM that reflects manifold pressure. The zero pressure reading is 0.5V and full scale is 4.5V. For a pressure swing of 0-15 psi, the voltage changes 4.0V. To operate the sensor, it is supplied a regulated 4.8 to 5.1 volts. Ground is provided through the low-noise, sensor return circuit at the PCM.

The MAP sensor input is the number one contributor to fuel injector pulse width. The most important function of the MAP sensor is to determine barometric pressure. The PCM needs to know if the vehicle is at sea level or at a higher altitude, because the air density changes with altitude. It will also help to correct for varying barometric pressure. Barometric pressure and altitude have a direct inverse correlation; as altitude goes up, barometric goes down. At key-on, the PCM powers up and looks at MAP voltage, and based upon the voltage it sees, it knows the current barometric pressure (relative to altitude). Once the engine starts, the PCM looks at the voltage again, continuously every 12 milliseconds, and compares the current voltage to what it was at key-on. The difference between current voltage and what it was at key-on, is manifold vacuum.

As the altitude increases, the air becomes thinner (less oxygen). If a vehicle is started and driven to a very different altitude than where it was at key-on, the barometric pressure needs to be updated. Any time the PCM sees Wide Open Throttle (WOT), based upon Throttle Position Sensor (TPS) angle and RPM, it will update barometric pressure in the MAP memory cell. With periodic updates, the PCM can make its calculations more effectively.

The MAP sensor signal is provided from a single piezoresistive element located in the center of a diaphragm. The element and diaphragm are both made of silicone. As manifold pressure changes, the diaphragm moves causing the element to deflect, which stresses the silicone. When silicone is exposed to

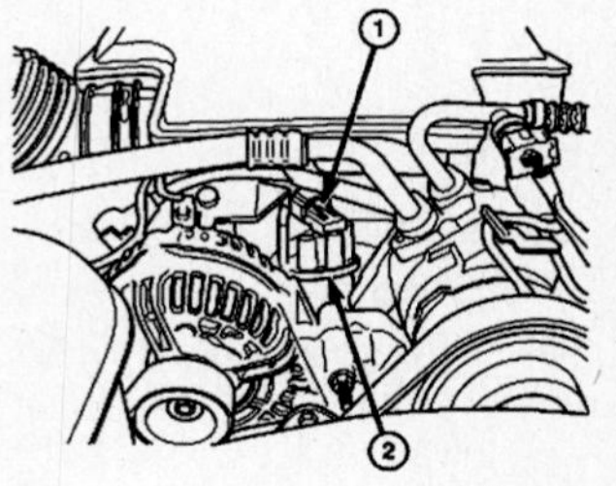

Fig. 155 Manifold Absolute Pressure (MAP) sensor (2) and connector (1) location 5.7L engine

stress, its resistance changes. As manifold vacuum increases, the MAP sensor input voltage decreases proportionally. The sensor also contains electronics that condition the signal and provide temperature compensation.

The PCM recognizes a decrease in manifold pressure by monitoring a decrease in voltage from the reading stored in the barometric pressure memory cell. The MAP sensor is a linear sensor; meaning as pressure changes, voltage changes proportionately. The range of voltage output from the sensor is usually between 4.6 volts at sea level to as low as 0.3 volts at 26 in. of Hg. Barometric pressure is the pressure exerted by the atmosphere upon an object. At sea level on a standard day, no storm, barometric pressure is approximately 29.92 in Hg. For every 100 feet of altitude, barometric pressure drops 0.10 in. Hg. If a storm goes through, it can change barometric pressure from what should be present for that altitude. You should know what the average pressure and corresponding barometric pressure is for your area.

REMOVAL & INSTALLATION

3.7L & 4.7L Engines

1. Before servicing the vehicle, refer to the Precautions Section.
2. Disconnect the electrical connector at the Manifold Absolute Pressure (MAP) sensor.
3. Clean the area around MAP sensor.
4. Remove one sensor mounting screw.
5. Remove MAP sensor from intake manifold by slipping it from locating pin.
6. Check condition of the sensor o-ring.

To install:

7. Clean the MAP sensor mounting hole at intake manifold.
8. Check the MAP sensor o-ring seal for cuts or tears.
9. Position MAP sensor into manifold by sliding the sensor over locating pin.
10. Install the mounting bolt. Tighten to 25 in. lbs. (3 Nm).
11. Connect the MAP sensor electrical connector.

5.7L Engine

1. Before servicing the vehicle, refer to the Precautions Section.
2. Disconnect electrical connector at Manifold Absolute Pressure (MAP) sensor by sliding release lock out. Press down on lock tab for removal.
3. Rotate the sensor a ¼ turn counterclockwise for removal.
4. Check the condition of sensor O-ring.

To install:

5. Clean the MAP sensor mounting hole at intake manifold.
6. Check the MAP sensor O-ring seal for cuts or tears.
7. Position the MAP sensor into manifold.
8. Rotate the MAP sensor a ¼ turn clockwise for installation.
9. Connect the MAP sensor electrical connector.

TESTING

3.7L, 4.7L & 5.7L Engines

See Figure 156.

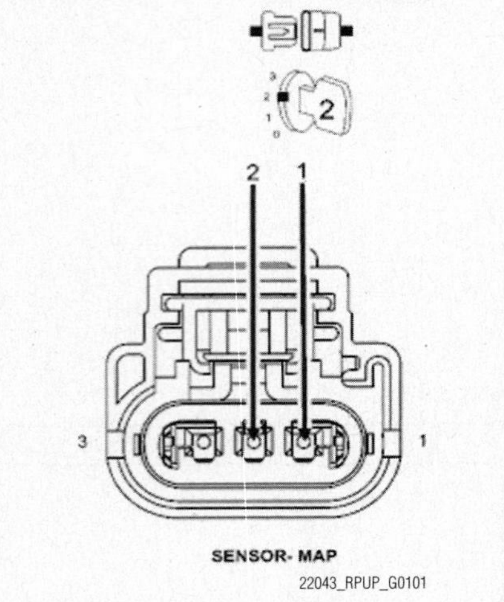

Fig. 156 MAP sensor harness connector

1. Turn the ignition off.
2. Disconnect the MAP sensor harness connector. Connect a jumper wire between the (K1) MAP signal circuit and the (K900) sensor ground circuit in the sensor harness connector.
3. Ignition on, engine not running.
4. Install a scan tool, monitor the MAP sensor voltage.
5. The sensor voltage should be approximately 0.0 volts (plus or minus .1 volt) with the jumper wire in place.
6. If the scan tool displays the voltage as described above suspect faulty MAP sensor.
7. Verify that there is good pin to terminal contact in the sensor and powertrain Control Module connectors. Replace the MAP sensor if no problems were found with the connectors.

POWERTRAIN CONTROL MODULE (PCM)

LOCATION

See Figure 157.

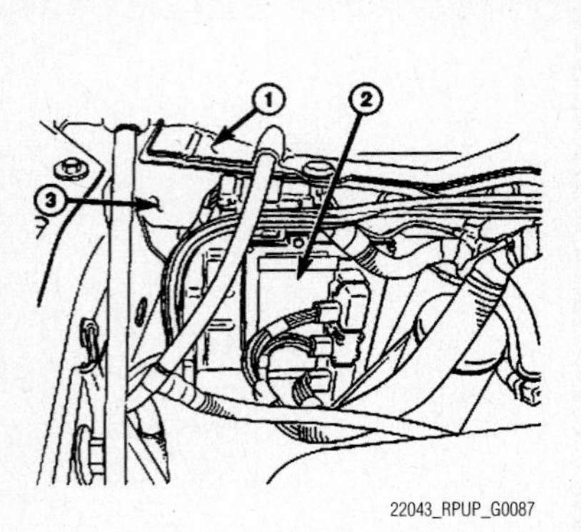

Fig. 157 Powertrain Control Module (PCM) location view

The Powertrain Control Module (PCM) is located in the engine compartment attached to the dash panel.

OPERATION

The Powertrain Control Module (PCM) operates the fuel system. The PCM is a pre-programmed, triple microprocessor digital computer. It regulates ignition timing, air-fuel ratio, emission control devices, charging system, certain transmission features, speed control, air conditioning compressor clutch engagement and idle speed. The PCM can adapt its programming to meet changing operating conditions

The PCM receives input signals from various switches and sensors. Based on these inputs, the PCM regulates various engine and vehicle operations through different system components. These components are referred to as Powertrain Control Module (PCM) Outputs. The sensors and switches that provide inputs to the PCM are considered Powertrain Control Module (PCM) Inputs.

The PCM adjusts ignition timing based upon inputs it receives from sensors that react to: engine rpm, manifold absolute pressure, engine coolant temperature, throttle position, transmission gear selection (automatic transmission), vehicle speed, power steering pump pressure, and the brake switch.

The PCM adjusts idle speed based on inputs it receives from sensors that react to: throttle position, vehicle speed, transmission gear selection, engine coolant temperature and from inputs it receives from the air conditioning clutch switch and brake switch.

Based on inputs that it receives, the PCM adjusts ignition coil dwell. The PCM also adjusts the generator charge rate through control of the generator field and provides speed control operation.

REMOVAL & INSTALLATION

See Figure 158.

⁂ WARNING

To avoid possible voltage spike damage to the Powertrain Control Module (PCM), ignition key must be off, and negative battery cable must be disconnected before unplugging PCM connectors.

➡Certain ABS systems rely on having the Powertrain Control Module (PCM) broadcast the Vehicle Identification Number (VIN) over the bus network. To prevent problems of DTCs and other items related to the VIN broadcast, it is recommend that you disconnect the ABS CAB controller temporarily when replacing the PCM. Once the PCM is replaced, write the VIN to the PCM using a scan tool. This is done from the engine main menu. Arrow over to the second page to Miscellaneous. Select (check VIN) from the choices. Make sure it has the correct VIN entered before continuing. When the VIN is complete, turn off the ignition key and reconnect the ABS module connector. This will prevent the setting of DTCs and other items associated with the lack of a VIN detected when you turn the key ON after replacing the PCM.

1. Before servicing the vehicle, refer to the Precautions Section.
2. Disconnect negative battery cable at battery.
3. Remove cover over electrical connectors. Cover snaps onto PCM.
4. Carefully unplug the three 32 way connectors (four 38-way connectors if equipped with NGC) from PCM.
5. Remove three PCM mounting bolts and remove PCM from vehicle.

To install:

6. Install PCM and 3 mounting bolts to vehicle.
7. Tighten bolts. Refer to torque specifications.
8. Check pin connectors in the PCM and the three 32-way connectors (four 38-way connectors if equipped with NGC) for corrosion or damage. Also, the pin heights in connectors should all be same. Repair as necessary before installing connectors.
9. Install three 32-way connectors (four 38-way connectors if equipped with NGC).
10. Install cover over electrical connectors. Cover snaps onto PCM.
11. Install negative battery cable.
12. The 5.7L V8 engine is equipped with a fully electronic accelerator pedal position sensor. If equipped with a 5.7L, also perform the following 3 steps:
    a. Connect negative battery cable to battery.
    b. Turn ignition switch ON, but do not crank engine.
    c. Leave ignition switch ON for a minimum of 10 seconds. This will allow PCM to learn electrical parameters.
    d. The scan tool may also be used to learn electrical parameters. Go to the Miscellaneous menu, and then select ETC Learn.
13. If the previous step is not performed, a Diagnostic Trouble Code (DTC) will be set.
14. If necessary, use a scan tool to erase any Diagnostic Trouble Codes (DTC's) from PCM. Also use the scan tool to reprogram new PCM with vehicles original Vehicle Identification Number (VIN) and original vehicle mileage.

TESTING

See Figure 159.

Service of the Powertrain Control Module (PCM) should consist of either replacement of the PCM or programming. If the diagnostic procedures call for the PCM to be replaced, the replacement PCM should be checked to ensure that the correct part is being used. If the correct part is being used, remove the faulty PCM and install the new service PCM.

1. Check for possible causes before replacement of PCM as follows:
    - (A918) Fused B (+) circuit open or shorted
    - (Z130) (Z131) ground circuit open
    - (F1) (F202) Fused ignition switch output circuit open or shorted
    - (D65) Can C Bus (+) circuit open
    - (D64) Can C Bus (-) circuit open

THROTTLE POSITION SENSOR (TPS)

LOCATION

2005–07 3.7L & 4.7L Engine

The 3-wire Throttle Position Sensor (TPS) is mounted on the throttle body and is connected to the throttle blade shaft.

5.7L Engine

The 5.7L V8 engine does not use a separate TPS on the throttle body. The throttle body on the 5.7L engine is an electrically controlled unit. A mechanical cable is not used to connect the throttle body to the accelerator pedal. The Accelerator Pedal Position Sensor (APPS) along with inputs from other sensors sets the throttle blade to pre-determined positions.

OPERATION

The 3-wire Throttle Position Sensor (TPS) provides the Powertrain Control Module (PCM) with an input signal (voltage) that represents the throttle blade position of the throttle body. The sensor is

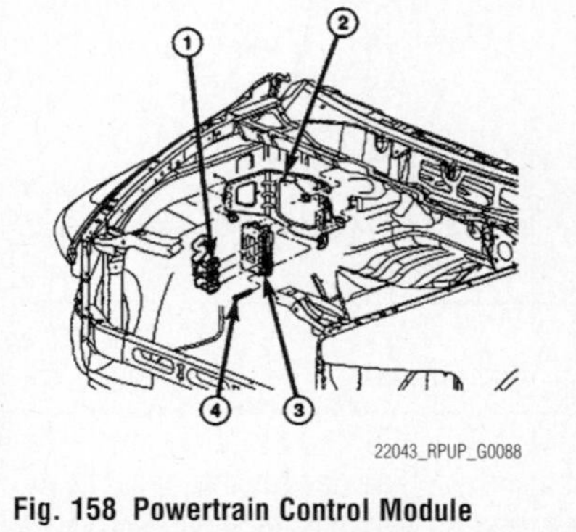

Fig. 158 Powertrain Control Module (PCM) electrical connectors (1), bracket (2), PCM (3), Mounting bolts (4)

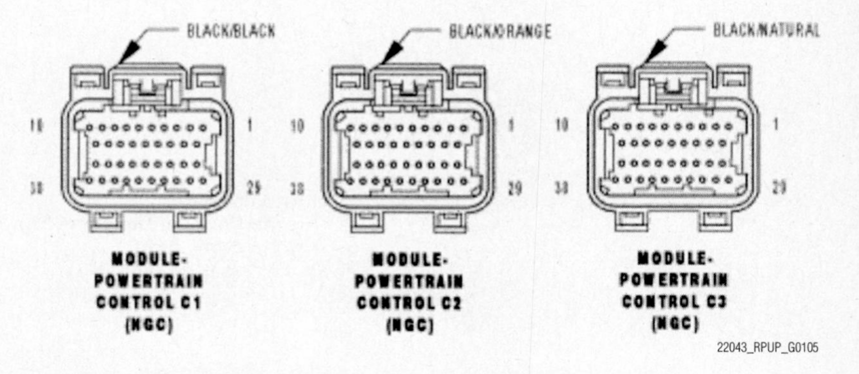

Fig. 159 Powertrain Control Module (PCM) harness connectors

connected to the throttle blade shaft. As the position of the throttle blade changes, the output voltage of the TPS changes.

The PCM supplies approximately 5 volts to the TPS. The TPS output voltage (input signal to the PCM) represents the throttle blade position. The PCM receives an input signal voltage from the TPS. This will vary in an approximate range of from .26 volts at minimum throttle opening (idle), to 4.49 volts at wide open throttle. Along with inputs from other sensors, the PCM uses the TPS input to determine current engine operating conditions. In response to engine operating conditions, the PCM will adjust fuel injector pulse width and ignition timing.

REMOVAL & INSTALLATION

2005–07 3.7L & 4.7L Engines

See Figure 160.

1. Before servicing the vehicle, refer to the Precautions Section.
2. Remove air resonator tube at throttle body.
3. Disconnect the Throttle Position Sensor (TPS) electrical connector.
4. Remove 2 TPS mounting screws.
5. Remove the TPS.

To install:

6. The throttle shaft end of throttle body slides into a socket in TPS. The TPS must be installed so that it can be rotated a few degrees. (If sensor will not rotate, install sensor with throttle shaft on other side of socket tangs). The TPS will be under slight tension when rotated.
7. Install the TPS and retaining screws.
8. Tighten screws to 60 inch lbs. (7 Nm).
9. Connect the TPS electrical connector to TPS.
10. Manually operate the throttle (by hand) to check for any TPS binding before starting engine.
11. Install air cleaner tube to throttle body.

TESTING

2005–07 3.7L & 4.7L Engines

See Figure 161.

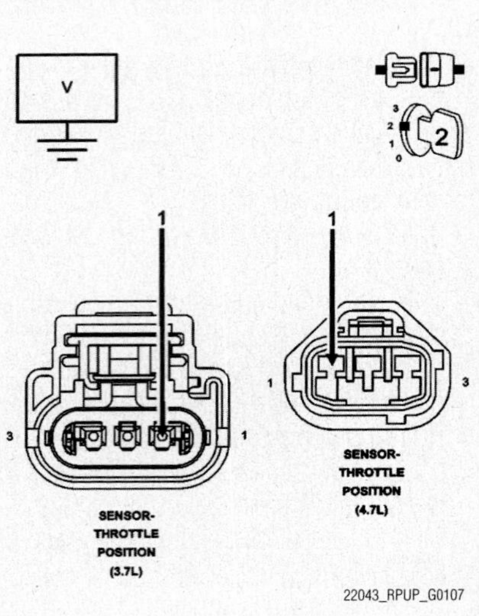

Fig. 161 Throttle Position Sensor (TPS) harness connectors 3.7L–4.7L engines

Voltage Supply Circuit Test

1. Turn the ignition off.
2. Disconnect the TP Sensor harness connector.
3. Ignition on, engine not running.
4. Measure the voltage on the (F855) 5-volt Supply circuit in the TP Sensor harness connector.
5. If the voltage is not between 4.5–5.2, repair the (F855) 5-volt Supply circuit.

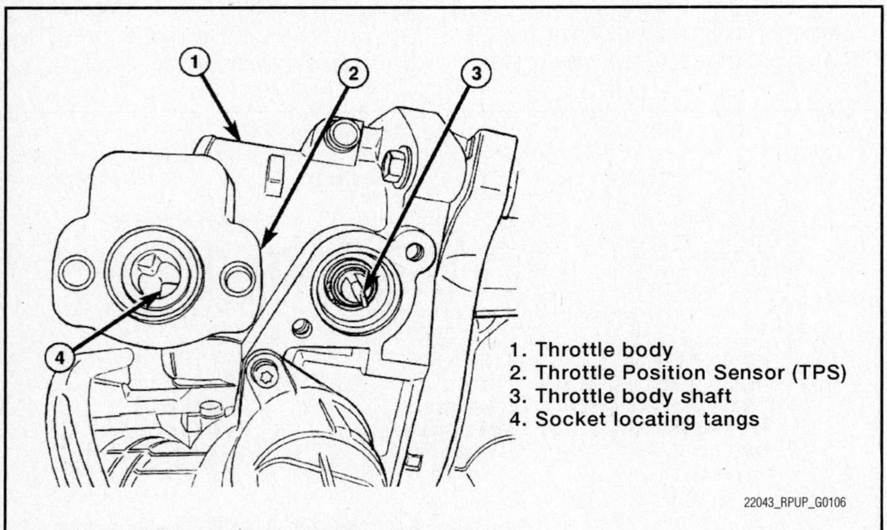

Fig. 160 Throttle Position Sensor (TPS) and related parts

Sensor Test

1. Visually check the connector, making sure it is attached properly and that all of the terminals are straight, tight and free of corrosion.
2. Connect the DVOM between the center terminal and sensor ground.
3. With the ignition key to the **ON** position and the engine off, check the output voltage at the center terminal wire of the connector.
4. Check the output voltage at idle and at Wide Open Throttle (WOT).
5. The TPS output voltage should be about 0.38–1.20 volts. At WOT, the output voltage should be about 3.1–4.4 volts.
6. The output voltage should gradually increase as the throttle plate moves slowly from idle to WOT.
7. If the voltage is not as stated, replace the TPS.

VEHICLE SPEED SENSOR (VSS)/(OSS)

LOCATION

See Figure 162.

The VSS/OSS is mounted in the left side of the transmission case.

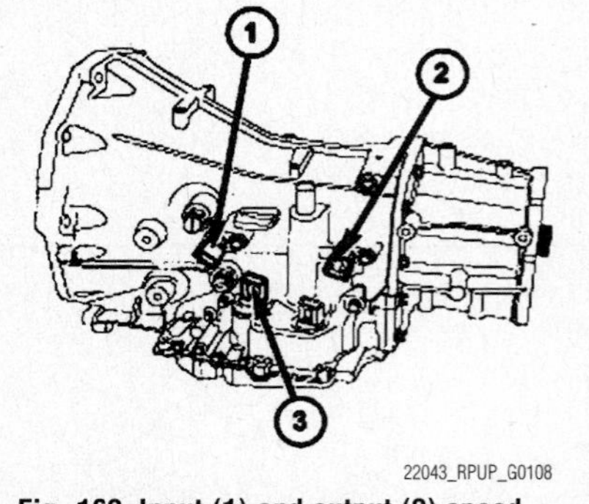

Fig. 162 Input (1) and output (2) speed sensor location

OPERATION

The Output Speed Sensor is a two—wire magnetic pickup devices that generate AC signals as rotation occurs. The Output Speed Sensor generates an AC signal in a similar fashion, though its coil is excited by rotation of the rear planetary carrier lugs. The TCM interprets this information as output shaft rpm.

REMOVAL & INSTALLATION

1. Before servicing the vehicle, refer to the Precautions Section.
2. Raise the vehicle.
3. Place a suitable fluid catch pan under the transmission.
4. Remove the wiring connector from the output speed sensor.

➡The speed sensor bolt has a sealing patch applied from the factory. Be sure to reuse the same bolt.

5. Remove the bolt holding the output speed sensor to the transmission case.
6. Remove the output speed sensor (2) from the transmission case.

To install:

7. Install the output speed sensor (2) into the transmission case.

➡Before installing the speed sensor bolt, it will be necessary to replenish the sealing patch on the bolt using MOPAR® Lock & Seal Adhesive.

8. Install the bolt to hold the output speed sensor into the transmission case. Tighten the bolt to 80 inch lbs. (9 Nm).
9. Install the wiring connector onto the output speed sensor.
10. Verify the transmission fluid level. Add fluid as necessary.
11. Lower the vehicle.

TESTING

1. Start the engine in park.
2. Raise the drive wheels off of the ground.

✻✻ CAUTION

Properly support the vehicle. Be sure to keep hands and feet clear of rotating wheels. Firmly apply the brakes and place the transmission selector in drive.

3. Release the brakes and allow the drive wheels to spin freely.
4. With the scan tool, read the output rpm.
5. Is the Output rpm below 100.
6. Turn the ignition off to the lock position.
7. Remove the Ignition Switch Feed fuse from the TIPM.

➡Removal of the Ignition Switch Feed fuse from the TIPM will prevent the vehicle from being started in gear.

✻✻ CAUTION

The Ignition Switch Feed fuse must be removed from the TIPM. Failure to do so can result in personal injury or death.

8. Install the Transmission Simulator, Miller tool number 8333 and the Electronic Transmission Adapter kit.
9. Ignition on, engine not running
10. With the Transmission Simulator, set the "Input/Output Speed" switch to "ON" and the rotary switch to the "3000/1250" position.
11. With the scan tool, read the Input and Output rpm.
12. If the input rpm reads 3000 and the output rpm reads 1250 (within 50 rpm). Replace the Output Speed Sensor (OSS)

FUEL — GASOLINE FUEL INJECTION SYSTEM

FUEL SYSTEM SERVICE PRECAUTIONS

Safety is the most important factor when performing not only fuel system maintenance but any type of maintenance. Failure to conduct maintenance and repairs in a safe manner may result in serious personal injury or death. Maintenance and testing of the vehicle's fuel system components can be accomplished safely and effectively by adhering to the following rules and guidelines.

- To avoid the possibility of fire and personal injury, always disconnect the negative battery cable unless the repair or test procedure requires that battery voltage be applied.
- Always relieve the fuel system pressure prior to disconnecting any fuel system component (injector, fuel rail, pressure regulator, etc.), fitting or fuel line connection. Exercise extreme caution whenever relieving fuel system pressure to avoid exposing skin, face and eyes to fuel spray. Please be advised that fuel under pressure may penetrate the skin or any part of the body that it contacts.
- Always place a shop towel or cloth around the fitting or connection prior to loosening to absorb any excess fuel due to spillage. Ensure that all fuel spillage (should it occur) is quickly removed from engine surfaces. Ensure that all fuel soaked cloths or towels are deposited into a suitable waste container.
- Always keep a dry chemical (Class B) fire extinguisher near the work area.
- Do not allow fuel spray or fuel vapors to come into contact with a spark or open flame.
- Always use a back-up wrench when loosening and tightening fuel line connection fittings. This will prevent unnecessary stress and torsion to fuel line piping.
- Always replace worn fuel fitting O-rings with new Do not substitute fuel hose or equivalent where fuel pipe is installed.

Before servicing the vehicle, make sure to also refer to the precautions in the beginning of this section as well.

RELIEVING FUEL SYSTEM PRESSURE

2005 Models

1. Before servicing the vehicle, refer to the Precautions Section.
2. Disconnect the negative battery cable.
3. Remove the fuel tank filler cap to release any fuel tank pressure.
4. Remove the fuel pump relay from the PDC.
5. Start and run the engine until it stops.
6. Unplug the connector from any injector and connect a jumper wire from either injector terminal to the positive battery terminal. Connect another jumper wire to the other terminal and momentarily touch the other end to the negative battery terminal.

✻✻ WARNING

Just touch the jumper to the battery. Powering the injector for more than a few seconds will permanently damage it.

7. Place a rag below the quick-disconnect coupling at the fuel rail and disconnect it.

2006–08 Models

See Figures 163 and 164.

1. Before servicing the vehicle, refer to the Precautions Section.

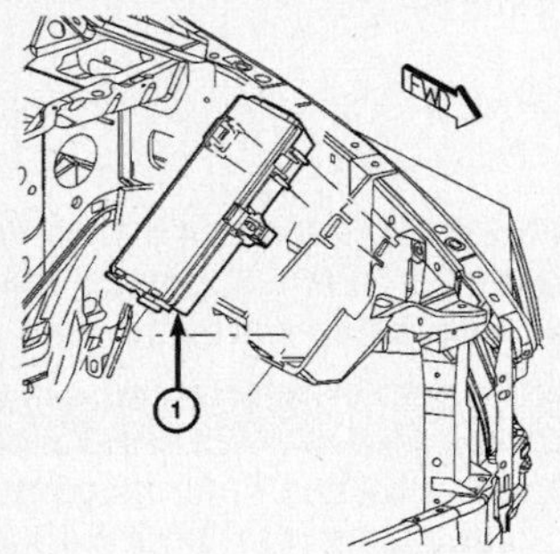

Fig. 163 Totally Integrated Power Module (TIPM) location (1)

➡Use following procedure if the fuel injector rail is, or is not equipped with a fuel pressure test port. A separate fuel pump relay is no longer used. A circuit within the Totally Integrated Power Module (TIPM) is used to control the electric fuel pump located within the fuel pump module. The TIPM is located in the engine compartment in front of the battery.

2. Remove fuel fill cap.
3. On bottom of vehicle, disconnect fuel pump module electrical connector. This can be accomplished at either of the two connectors.
4. Start and run engine until it stalls.
5. Attempt restarting engine until it will no longer run.
6. Turn the ignition key to **OFF** position.
7. Place a rag or towel below fuel line quick-connect fitting at fuel rail.
8. Disconnect quick-connect fitting at fuel rail. Refer to Quick-Connect Fittings.
9. Reconnect fuel pump module electrical connector on bottom of vehicle.
10. One or more Diagnostic Trouble Codes (DTC's) may have been stored in PCM memory due to disconnecting fuel pump module circuit. A diagnostic scan tool must be used to erase a DTC.

FUEL FILTER

REMOVAL & INSTALLATION

The fuel pump inlet filter (strainer) is located on the bottom of the fuel pump module. The fuel pump module is located inside of fuel tank. No external filter is used.

FUEL INJECTORS

REMOVAL & INSTALLATION

3.7L, 4.7L and 5.7L Engines

See Figure 165.

1. Before servicing the vehicle, refer to the Precautions Section.
2. Relieve fuel system pressure.
3. Remove fuel rail.
4. Disconnect clip(s) that retain fuel injector(s) to fuel rail.

To install:

5. Install fuel injector(s) into fuel rail assembly and install retaining clip(s).
6. If same injector(s) is being reinstalled, install new O-ring(s).
7. Apply a small amount of clean engine oil to each injector O-ring. This will aid in installation.
8. Install fuel rail.
9. Start engine and check for fuel leaks.

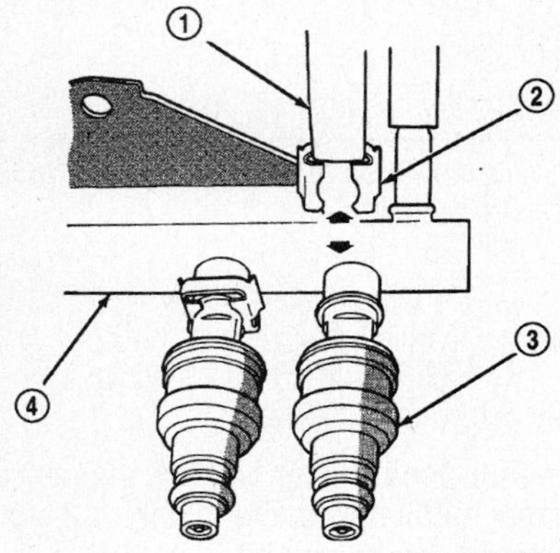

Fig. 165 Typical injector removal—pliers (1), injector clip (2), fuel injector (3) and fuel rail (4)

FUEL PUMP

REMOVAL & INSTALLATION

See Figure 166.

⁂ CAUTION

The fuel system may be under a constant pressure (even with the engine off). Before servicing the fuel pump module, the fuel system pressure must be released.

1. Before servicing the vehicle, refer to the Precautions Section.
2. Drain and remove fuel tank. Refer to Fuel Tank Removal/Installation.
3. Note the rotational position of module before attempting removal. An indexing arrow is located on top of module for this purpose.
4. Position special tool 9340 into notches on outside edge of lockring.
5. Install the ½ inch drive breaker bar to tool 9340.
6. Rotate breaker bar counter-clockwise to remove lockring.

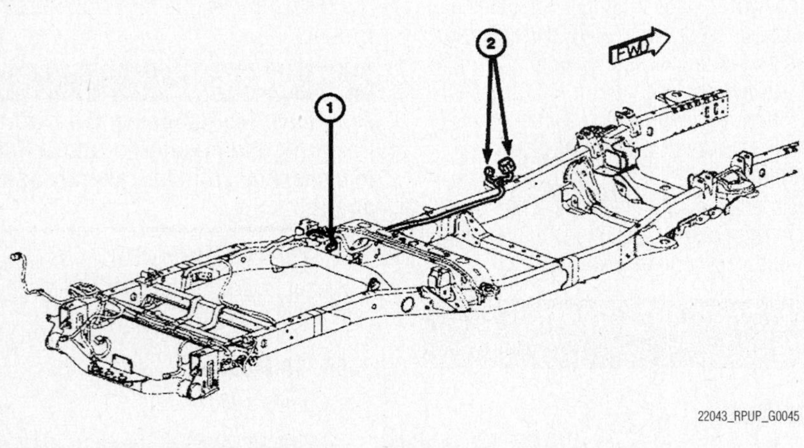

Fig. 164 Fuel pump module electrical connector views (1) and (2)

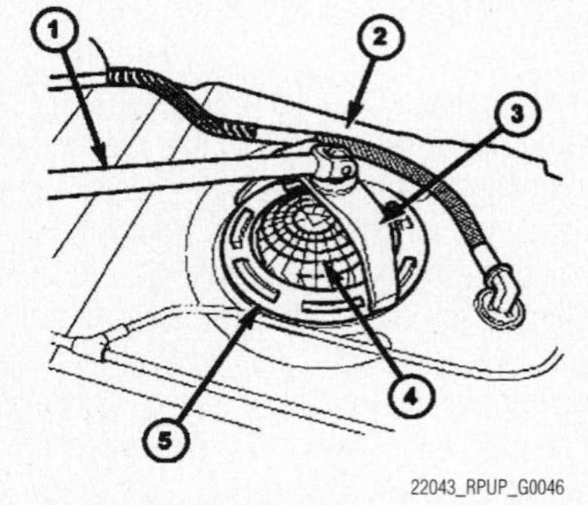

Fig. 166 Special tool 9340 shown in removal of lockring

7. Remove the lockring. The module will spring up slightly when lockring is removed.

8. Remove the module from fuel tank. Be careful not to bend float arm while removing.

To install:

9. Using a new seal (gasket), position the fuel pump module into opening in fuel tank.

10. Position the lockring over top of fuel pump module.

11. Rotate module until embossed alignment arrow points to center alignment mark.

12. This step must be performed to prevent float from contacting side of fuel tank. Also be sure fuel fitting on top of pump module is pointed to drivers side of vehicle.

13. Install the special tool 9340 to lockring.

14. Install ½ inch drive breaker into Special Tool 9340.

15. Tighten the lockring (clockwise) until all seven notches have engaged.

16. Install the fuel tank.

FUEL TANK

REMOVAL & INSTALLATION

See Figure 167.

1. Before servicing the vehicle, refer to the Precautions Section.
2. Drain fuel tank.
3. Support tank with a hydraulic jack.
4. Remove two fuel tank strap nuts and remove both tank support straps.
5. Carefully lower tank a few inches and disconnect fuel pump module electrical connector at top of tank. To disconnect electrical connector: Push upward on red colored tab to unlock. Push on black colored tab while removing connector.
6. Disconnect fuel supply and return lines at fuel tank module.
7. Continue to lower the fuel tank for removal.
8. If fuel tank is to be replaced, remove fuel tank module from tank.
9. If fuel tank is to be replaced, install fuel tank module into tank.
10. Position fuel tank (1) to hydraulic jack
11. Raise tank until positioned near body.
12. Connect fuel tank module electrical connector at top of tank.
13. Connect fuel supply and return lines to tank module.
14. Continue raising tank until positioned snug to body.

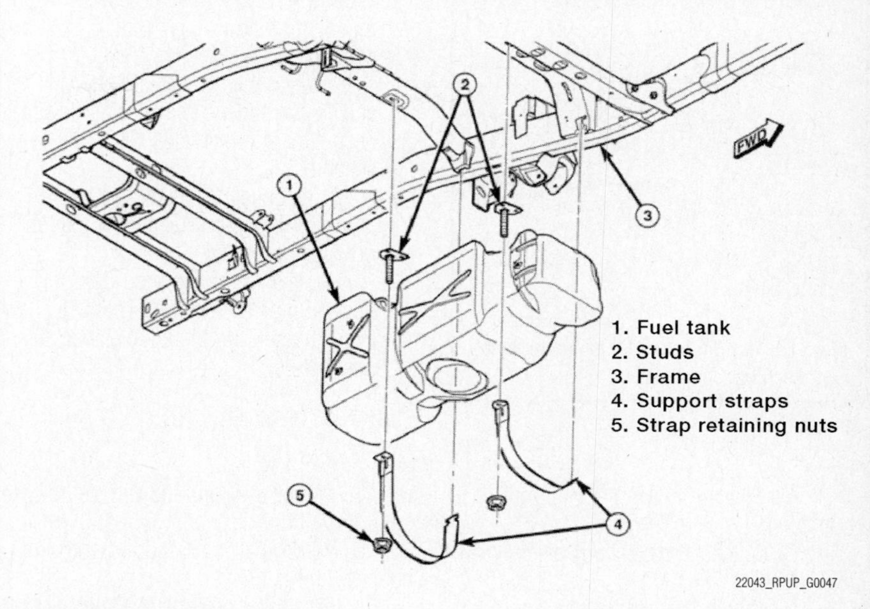

Fig. 167 Fuel tank, and related parts

15. Install and position both tank support straps. Install 2 fuel tank strap nuts and tighten to 30 ft. lbs. (41 Nm). Tighten rear strap nut first.
16. Remove the hydraulic jack.
17. Connect rubber fill hose to fuel fill tube and tighten clamp.
18. Install tire / wheel (if necessary).
19. Lower the vehicle.
20. Fill fuel tank with fuel.
21. Start engine and check for fuel leaks near top of module.

IDLE SPEED

ADJUSTMENT

Idle speed is maintained by the Powertrain Control Module (PCM). No adjustment is necessary or possible.

THROTTLE BODY

REMOVAL & INSTALLATION

2005–06 3.7L Engine

A (factory adjusted) set screw is used to mechanically limit the position of the throttle body throttle plate. Never attempt to adjust the engine idle speed using this screw. All idle speed functions are controlled by the Powertrain Control Module (PCM).

1. Remove air cleaner tube at throttle body.
2. Disconnect throttle body electrical connectors at Idle Air Control (IAC) motor and Throttle Position Sensor (TPS).
3. Remove all control cables from throttle body (lever) arm.
4. Disconnect necessary vacuum lines at throttle body.
5. Remove 3 throttle body mounting bolts.
6. Remove throttle body from intake manifold.
7. Check condition of old throttle body-to-intake manifold O-ring. Replace as necessary.

To install:

8. Clean mating surfaces of throttle body and intake manifold.
9. Install throttle body-to-intake manifold O-ring.
10. Install throttle body to intake manifold.
11. Install three mounting bolts. Tighten bolts to 105 inch lbs. (12 Nm).
12. Install control cables.
13. Install electrical connectors.
14. Install necessary vacuum lines.
15. Install air plenum.

2007–08 3.7L Engine

See Figure 168.

➡A (factory adjusted) set screw is used to mechanically limit the position of the throttle body throttle plate. Never attempt to adjust the engine idle speed using this screw. All idle speed functions are controlled by the Powertrain Control Module (PCM).

1. Before servicing the vehicle, refer to the Precautions Section.

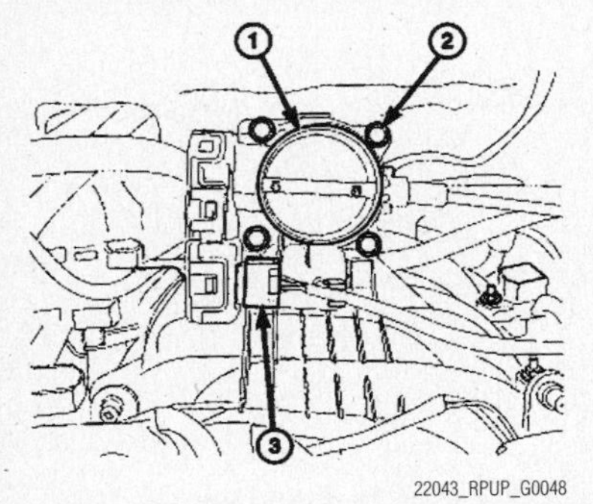

Fig. 168 Throttle body (1), mounting bolts (2), electrical connector (3)

2. Disconnect and isolate negative battery cable at battery.
3. Remove air intake tube at throttle body flange (1).
4. Disconnect throttle body electrical connector (3).
5. Disconnect necessary vacuum lines at throttle body.
6. Remove four throttle body mounting bolts (2).
7. Remove throttle body from intake manifold.
8. Check condition of old throttle body-to-intake manifold o-ring.

To install:

9. Check condition of throttle body-to-intake manifold O-ring. Replace as necessary.
10. Clean mating surfaces of throttle body and intake manifold.
11. Install O-ring between throttle body and intake manifold.
12. Position throttle body to intake manifold.
13. Install all throttle body mounting bolts finger tight.

WARNING

The throttle body mounting bolts must be torqued to specifications. DO NOT OVER TIGHTEN MOUNTING BOLTS. Over tightening can cause damage to the throttle body, throttle plate, gaskets, bolts and/or the intake manifold. Proper torque of the mounting bolts is critical to normal operation.

14. Tighten mounting bolts in a mandatory criss-cross pattern sequence to 65 in. lbs. (7.5 Nm).
15. Install the electrical connector (3).
16. Install all necessary vacuum lines.
17. Install air cleaner duct at throttle body
18. Connect negative battery cable.
19. If the throttle body has been changed, the following procedure must be performed:
    a. Disconnect negative battery cable from battery. Leave cable disconnected for approximately 90 seconds.
    b. Reconnect cable to battery.
    c. Turn ignition switch **ON**, but do not crank engine.
    d. Leave ignition switch **ON** for a minimum of 10 seconds. This will allow PCM to learn throttle body electrical parameters.

2005–07 4.7L Engine

See Figure 169.

1. Before servicing the vehicle, refer to the Precautions Section.
2. Remove air duct and air resonator box at throttle body.
3. Disconnect throttle body electrical connectors at Idle Air Control (IAC) motor and Throttle Position Sensor (TPS).
4. Remove vacuum line at throttle body.
5. Remove all control cables from throttle body (lever) arm.
6. Remove three throttle body mounting bolts.
7. Remove the throttle body from the intake manifold.
8. Clean throttle body-to-intake manifold O-ring.
9. Clean mating surfaces of throttle body and intake manifold.

To install:

10. Install throttle body to intake manifold by positioning throttle body to manifold alignment pins.
11. Install three mounting bolts and tighten to 105 inch lbs. (12 Nm).
12. Install control cables.
13. Connect the vacuum line to throttle body.
14. Attach the electrical connectors.
15. Install air plenum.

2008 4.7L Engine

See Figure 170.

WARNING

Never have the ignition key in the ON position when/if checking the throttle body shaft for a binding condition. This may set DTC's.

1. Before servicing the vehicle, refer to the Precautions Section.
2. Disconnect and isolate negative battery cable at battery.
3. Remove air duct and air resonator box at throttle body.
4. Disconnect throttle body electrical connector.
5. Disconnect all necessary vacuum lines at throttle body.
6. Remove four throttle body mounting bolts.
7. Remove throttle body from intake manifold.
8. Check condition of old throttle body-to-intake manifold o-ring.

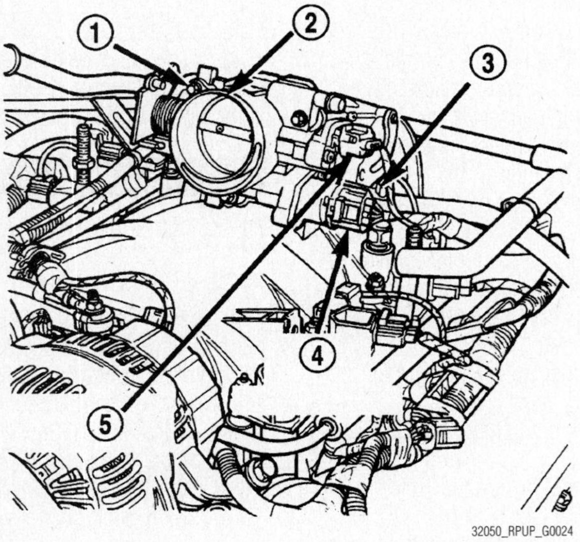

Fig. 169 Exploded view of the throttle body bolts (1), throttle body (2), IAT sensor connector (3), IAC motor connector (4), TPS connector (5)—4.7L Engine

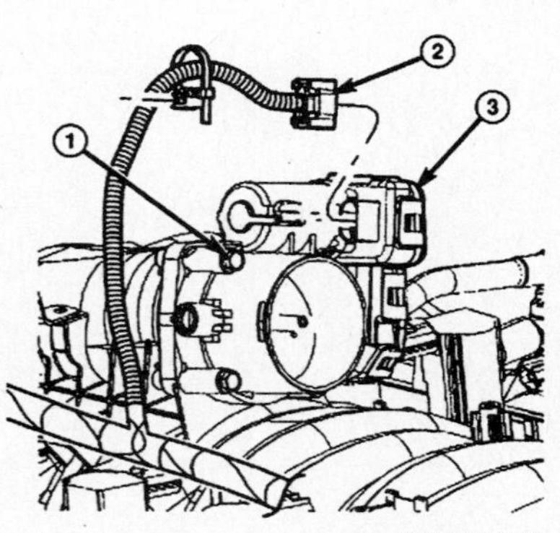

Fig. 170 Electronic Throttle Control (ETC) connector

9. Check condition of throttle body-to-intake manifold O-ring. Replace as necessary.
10. Clean mating surfaces of throttle body and intake manifold.
11. Install throttle body-to-intake manifold O-ring.
12. Install all throttle body mounting bolts finger tight.

⁂ WARNING

The throttle body mounting bolts must be torqued to specifications. DO NOT OVER TIGHTEN MOUNTING BOLTS. Over tightening can cause damage to the throttle body, throttle plate, gaskets, bolts and/or the intake manifold. Proper torque of the mounting bolts is critical to normal operation.

13. Tighten mounting bolts in a mandatory criss-cross pattern sequence to 65 in. lbs. (7.5 Nm).
14. Install the electrical connector (2).
15. Install all necessary vacuum lines.
16. Install air cleaner duct and plenum at throttle body.
17. Connect negative battery cable.
18. If the throttle body has been changed, the following procedure must be performed:
    a. Disconnect negative battery cable from battery. Leave cable disconnected for approximately 90 seconds.
    b. Reconnect cable to battery.
    c. Turn ignition switch **ON**, but do not crank engine.
    d. Leave ignition switch **ON** for a minimum of 10 seconds. This will allow PCM to learn throttle body electrical parameters.

2005–08 5.7L Engine

⁂ WARNING

Do not use spray (carb) cleaners on any part of the throttle body. Do not apply silicone lubricants to any part of the throttle body.

1. Before servicing the vehicle, refer to the Precautions Section.
2. Remove air duct and air resonator box at throttle body.
3. Disconnect electrical connector from the throttle body.
4. Remove 4 throttle body mounting bolts.
5. Remove throttle body from intake manifold.
6. Check condition of throttle body O-ring.
7. If the throttle body has been changed, the following procedure must be performed:
    a. Disconnect negative battery cable from battery. Leave cable disconnected for approximately 90 seconds.
    b. Reconnect cable to battery.
    c. Turn ignition switch **ON**, but do not crank engine.
    d. Leave ignition switch **ON** for a minimum of 10 seconds. This will allow PCM to learn throttle body electrical parameters.

To install:

8. Clean and check condition of throttle body-to-intake manifold O-ring.
9. Clean mating surfaces of throttle body and intake manifold.
10. Install the throttle body to the intake manifold by positioning the throttle body to the manifold alignment pins.
11. Install 4 mounting bolts and tighten to 105 inch lbs. (12 Nm).
12. Attach the electrical connector.
13. Install the air plenum.
14. If the throttle body has been changed, the following procedure must be performed:
    a. Disconnect negative battery cable from battery. Leave cable disconnected for approximately 90 seconds.
    b. Reconnect cable to battery.
    c. Turn ignition switch **ON**, but do not crank engine.
    d. Leave ignition switch **ON** for a minimum of 10 seconds. This will allow PCM to learn throttle body electrical parameters.

FUEL — DIESEL FUEL INJECTION SYSTEM

FUEL SYSTEM SERVICE PRECAUTIONS

Safety is the most important factor when performing not only fuel system maintenance but any type of maintenance. Failure to conduct maintenance and repairs in a safe manner may result in serious personal injury or death. Maintenance and testing of the vehicle's fuel system components can be accomplished safely and effectively by adhering to the following rules and guidelines.

- To avoid the possibility of fire and personal injury, always disconnect the negative battery cable unless the repair or test procedure requires that battery voltage be applied.
- Always relieve the fuel system pressure prior to disconnecting any fuel system component (injector, fuel rail, pressure regulator, etc.), fitting or fuel line connection. Exercise extreme caution whenever relieving fuel system pressure to avoid exposing skin, face and eyes to fuel spray. Please be advised that fuel under pressure may penetrate the skin or any part of the body that it contacts.
- Always place a shop towel or cloth around the fitting or connection prior to loosening to absorb any excess fuel due to spillage. Ensure that all fuel spillage (should it occur) is quickly removed from engine surfaces. Ensure that all fuel soaked cloths or towels are deposited into a suitable waste container.
- Always keep a dry chemical (Class B) fire extinguisher near the work area.
- Do not allow fuel spray or fuel vapors to come into contact with a spark or open flame.
- Always use a back-up wrench when loosening and tightening fuel line connection fittings. This will prevent unnecessary stress and torsion to fuel line piping.
- Always replace worn fuel fitting O-rings with new. Do not substitute fuel hose or equivalent where fuel pipe is installed.

Before servicing the vehicle, make sure to also refer to the precautions in the beginning of this section as well.

FUEL FILTER

REMOVAL & INSTALLATION

See Figure 171.

1. Remove left front tire/wheel.
2. Remove left front wheel splash shield.

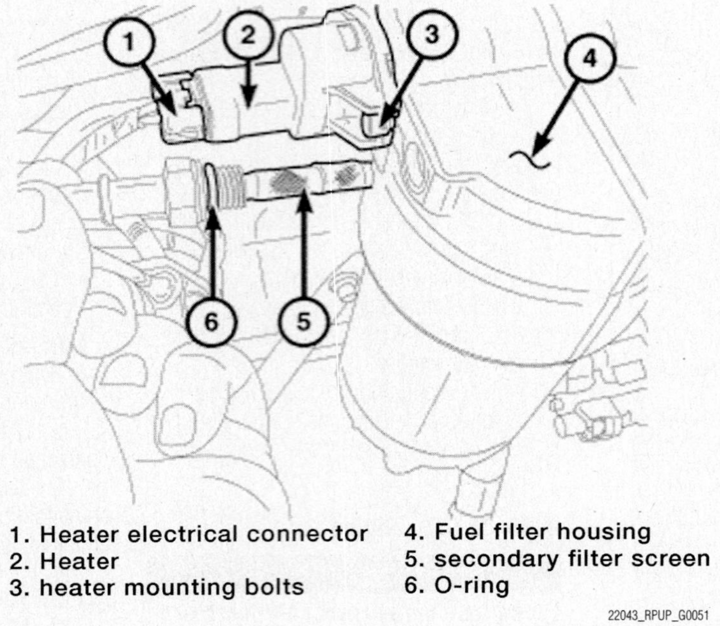

Fig. 171 Fuel filter housing and related parts 5.9L–6.7L diesel engines

3. Clean all debris from around filter canister and canister head.
4. Disconnect the Water In Fuel (WIF) sensor electrical connector.
5. Open the drain valve two complete revolutions. Drain approximately 1 cup of fuel into a waste canister.

➡Dispose of fuel according to environmental regulations.

6. Remove drain hose from drain valve.
7. Use an oil filter type wrench to loosen filter. Continue removing filter by hand.
8. After fuel filter removal, also check and clean secondary filter screen. Press button on quick-connect fitting. Disconnect fitting from fitting. Unscrew the fitting from canister head to expose screen.
9. Clean screen and check the condition of O-ring.

To install:

10. Reverse removal procedure for installation.

DRAINING WATER FROM THE SYSTEM

See Figure 172.

1. Before servicing the vehicle, refer to the Precautions Section.
2. A drain hose is located at the bottom of drain valve. Place drain pan under drain hose.
3. With engine not running, rotate drain valve approximately two revolutions to open it. Leave open until all water and contaminants have been removed and clean fuel exits. Hand tighten drain valve after tightening.
4. After draining operation, close and tighten drain valve.

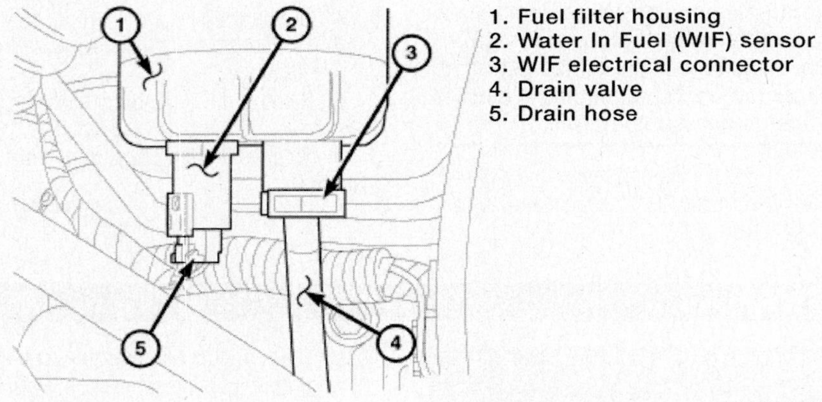

Fig. 172 Bottom view of fuel filter housing 5.9L–6.7L diesel engines

FUEL SYSTEM AIR

BLEEDING/PRIMING

Bleeding

See Figures 173 and 174.

1. Loosen the low pressure bleed bolt.
2. Operate the rubber push-button primer on the fuel transfer pump. Do this until the fuel exiting the bleed screw is free of air. If the primer button feels as if it is not pumping, rotate (crank) the engine approximately 90°, then continue pumping as described.
3. Tighten the low pressure bleed screw to 72 inch lbs. (8 Nm).

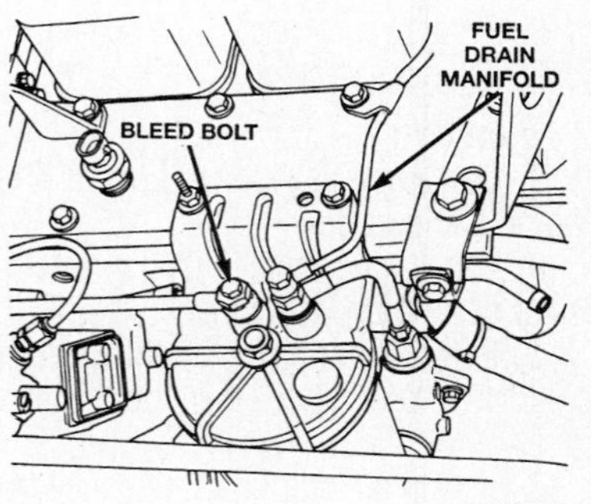

Fig. 173 Location of the low pressure bleed bolt—5.9L diesel engine

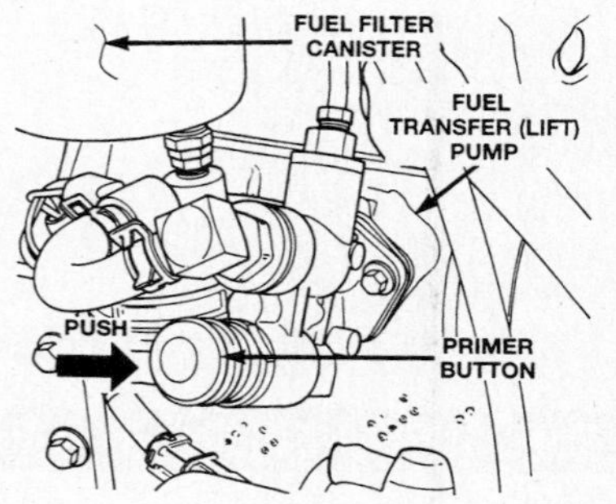

Fig. 174 Operate the push-button primer on the fuel transfer pump until the escaping fuel is free of air

Fuel System Priming

A certain amount of air becomes trapped in the fuel system when fuel system components on the supply and/or high-pressure side are serviced or replaced. Fuel system priming is accomplished using the electric fuel transfer (lift) pump.

1. Servicing or replacing fuel system components will not require fuel system priming.
2. The fuel transfer (lift) pump is self-priming: When the key is first turned on (without cranking engine), the pump operates for approximately 1 to 2 second and then shuts off. The pump will also operate for up to 25 seconds after the starter is quickly engaged, and then disengaged without allowing the engine to start. The pump shuts off immediately if the key is on and the engine stops running.
3. Turn the key to CRANK position and quickly release key to ON position before engine starts. This will operate fuel transfer pump for approximately 25 seconds.
4. Crank the engine. If the engine does not start after 25 seconds, turn the key OFF. Repeat previous step until engine starts.
5. Fuel system priming is now completed.
6. Attempt to the start engine. If engine will not start, proceed to following steps. When engine does start, it may run erratically and be noisy for a few minutes. This is a normal condition.

※※ WARNING

Do not engage the starter motor for more than 30 seconds at a time. Allow two minutes between cranking intervals.

7. Perform previous fuel priming procedure steps using fuel transfer pump. Be sure fuel is present at fuel tank.
8. Crank the engine for 30 seconds at a time to allow fuel system to prime.

※※ CAUTION

The fuel injection pump supplies extremely high fuel pressure to each individual injector through the high-pressure lines. Fuel under this amount of pressure can penetrate the skin and cause personal injury. Wear safety goggles and adequate protective clothing. Do not loosen fuel fittings while engine is running.

※※ CAUTION

Engine may start while cranking starter motor.

INJECTION LINES

REMOVAL & INSTALLATION

5.9L & 2007–08 6.7L Diesel Engines

※※ WARNING

Cleanliness cannot be overemphasized when handling or replacing diesel fuel system components. This especially includes the fuel injectors, high-pressure fuel lines and fuel injection pump. Very tight tolerances are used with these parts. Dirt contamination could cause rapid part wear and possible plugging of fuel injector nozzle tip holes. This in turn could lead to possible engine misfire. Always wash/clean any fuel system component thoroughly before disassembly and then air dry. Cap or cover any open part after disassembly. Before assembly, examine each part for dirt, grease or other contaminants and clean if necessary. When installing new parts, lubricate them with clean engine oil or clean diesel fuel only.

1. Disconnect both negative battery cables from both batteries. Cover and isolate ends of cables.
2. Thoroughly clean fuel lines at both ends.
3. If removing fuel line at either #1 or #2 cylinder, the intake manifold air heater elements must first be removed from top of intake manifold.
4. If removing fuel line at #6 cylinder, a bracket is located above fuel line connection at cylinder head. Two bolts secure this bracket to rear of cylinder head. The upper bolt hole is slotted. Loosen (but do not remove) these 2 bracket bolts. Tilt bracket down to gain access to #6 fuel line connection.
5. Remove engine lift bracket (if necessary).
6. Remove necessary insulated fuel line support clamps and bracket bolts at intake manifold. DO NOT remove insulators from fuel lines.
7. Place shop towels around fuel lines at fuel rail and injectors. If possible, do not allow fuel to drip down side of engine.

※※ WARNING

When loosening or tightening high-pressure lines attached to a separate fitting , use a back-up wrench on fitting. Do not allow fitting to rotate. Damage to both fuel line and fitting will result.

8. Carefully remove each fuel line from engine. Note position of each while removing. Do not bend lines while removing.

To install:

➡All high-pressure fuel lines are of the same length and inside diameter. Correct high-pressure fuel line usage and installation is critical to smooth engine operation.

※※ WARNING

Anytime a high-pressure line is removed from the engine, its fuel connector nut at the cylinder head must first be retorqued.

9. Tighten fuel lines at high pressure injector connector to 37 ft. lbs. (50 Nm).
10. Position fuel line support clamp(s) to fuel line(s). Install clamp nuts/bolts and tighten finger-tight.

11. Position the proper fuel line to the proper injector on engine. Tighten fittings hand tight at both ends of line.

12. Tighten fuel lines at fuel rail to 27 ft. lbs. (37 Nm).

13. Tighten clamp/support nuts and bolts.

14. Install engine lifting bracket and bolt. Tighten to 56 ft. lbs. 77 (Nm).

15. If fuel line at either Number 1 or Number 2 cylinder has been replaced, install intake manifold air heater elements to top of intake manifold.

16. If fuel line at Number 6 cylinder has been replaced, tilt metal bracket upward and tighten 2 bolts at rear of cylinder head to 32 Ft. lbs. (43 Nm).

17. Install remaining fuel line support clamps and bracket bolts at intake manifold.

18. Connect both negative battery cables to both batteries.

19. Prime the fuel system. Refer to Fuel System Priming.

20. Check lines/fittings for leaks.

INJECTORS

REMOVAL & INSTALLATION

5.9L & 2007–08 6.7L Diesel Engines

See Figures 175 through 177.

1. Before servicing the vehicle, refer to the Precautions Section.
2. Remove or disconnect the following:
   - Negative battery cables
   - Valve cover
   - Fuel line connector
   - Connector retainer nut
3. Use high pressure tool 9015 and remove high pressure connectors.

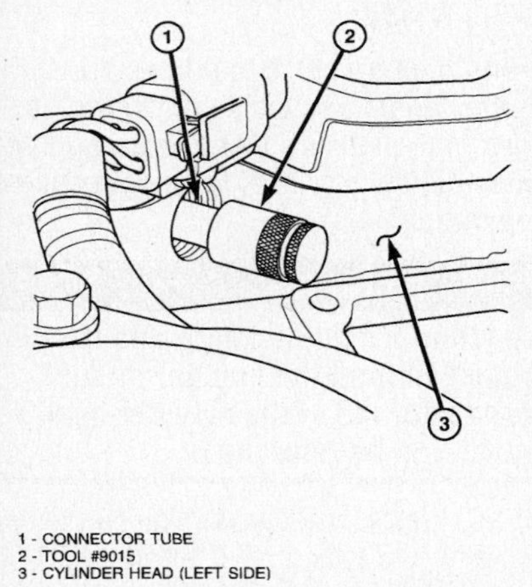

Fig. 175 Using tool 9015 to remove high pressure connectors

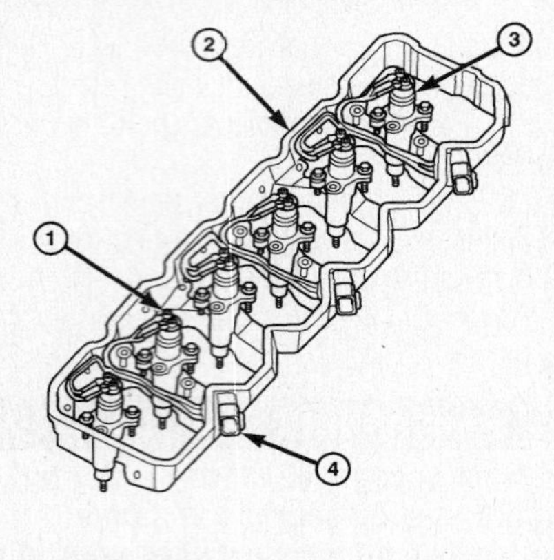

Fig. 176 Fuel injector mounting

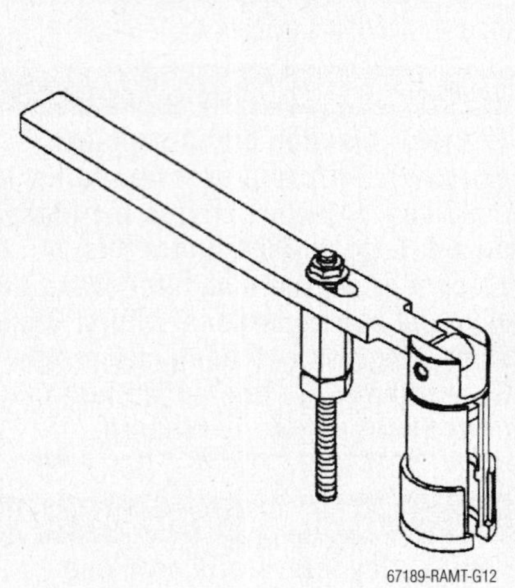

Fig. 177 Fuel injector removal tool 9010

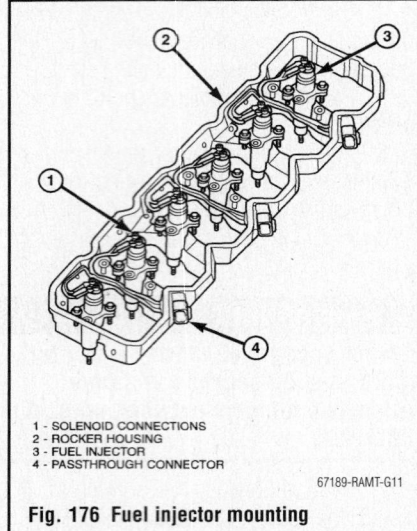

4. Remove the necessary exhaust rocker arms.
5. Disconnect the injector solenoid wire nuts from top of injectors.
6. Remove injector hold-down clamp bolts.
7. Remove the fuel injector using tool 9010 as follows:
   a. Remove rocker housing bolt.
   b. Install lower half of mounting stud to center of rocker housing bridge.
   c. Install upper half of mounting stud to lower half.
   d. Place tool handle to mounting stud and install nut loosely.
   e. Place lower part of clamshells to sides of injector.
   f. Place upper part of clamshells onto tool handle head.
   g. Slide retainer sleeve over pivoting handle.
   h. Depress handle downward to force injector up and out of cylinder head.
8. Remove and discard the sealing washer from the injector.

To install:

9. Use a new sealing washer and O-ring on the injector.
10. Install the injector with the male connector port facing intake manifold.
11. Fuel injector clamp. Tighten the bolt to 44 INCH lbs. (5 Nm), then loosen the bolts.
12. Install the high pressure connector and tighten the nut to 11 ft. lbs. (15 Nm).
13. Alternately tighten the injector hold down bolts to 89 INCH lbs. (10 Nm).
14. Retighten the high pressure retaining nut to 37 ft. lbs. (50 Nm).
15. Install solenoid wires and nuts. Tighten nuts to 11 INCH lbs. (1.25 Nm).
16. Install or connect the following:
    - Exhaust rocker arms
    - Check valve lash
    - Fuel line connector
    - Valve cover
    - Negative battery cables
17. Bleed the fuel system.
18. Start the engine and check for leaks.

FUEL SUPPLY PUMP

REMOVAL & INSTALLATION

5.9L & 2007–08 6.7L Diesel Engines

See Figure 178.

1. Before servicing the vehicle, refer to the Precautions Section.
2. Drain and remove fuel tank. Refer to Fuel Tank Removal/Installation.
3. Note the rotational position of module before attempting removal. An indexing arrow is located on top of module for this purpose.
4. Position special tool 9340 into notches on outside edge of lockring.

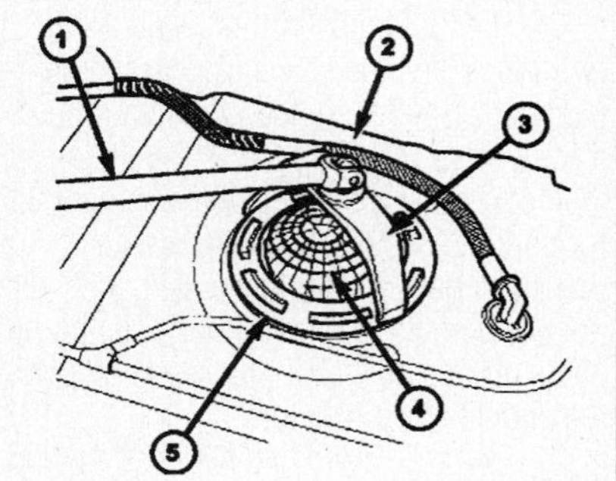

Fig. 178 Special tool 9340 shown in removal of lockring

5. Install the ½ inch drive breaker bar to tool 9340.

6. Rotate breaker bar counter-clockwise to remove lockring.

7. Remove the lockring. The module will spring up slightly when lockring is removed.

8. Remove the module from fuel tank. Be careful not to bend float arm while removing.

To install:

9. Using a new seal (gasket), position the fuel pump module into opening in fuel tank.

10. Position the lockring over top of fuel pump module.

11. Rotate module until embossed alignment arrow points to center alignment mark.

12. This step must be performed to prevent float from contacting side of fuel tank. Also be sure fuel fitting on top of pump module is pointed to drivers side of vehicle.

13. Install the special tool 9340 to lockring.

14. Install ½ inch drive breaker into Special Tool 9340.

15. Tighten the lockring (clockwise) until all seven notches have engaged.

16. Install the fuel tank.

INJECTION PUMP

REMOVAL & INSTALLATION

5.9L & 2007–08 6.7L Diesel Engines

See Figure 179.

1. Before servicing the vehicle, refer to the Precautions Section.

2. Remove or disconnect the following:
   - Negative battery cables
   - Intake air tube
   - Drive belt
   - Pump wiring harness
   - Injection pump supply line
   - Fuel lines
   - Drive gear access cover
   - Drive gear mounting nut

3. Using a gear puller, remove the drive gear and leave it hanging within the timing gear cover.

4. Remove 3 pump mounting nuts and remove the pump.

To install:

5. Install a new O-ring coated with clean engine oil into the machined groove at the pump mounting area.

6. Install the pump to the mounting flange on the gear housing while aligning the pump shaft through the back of the pump gear.

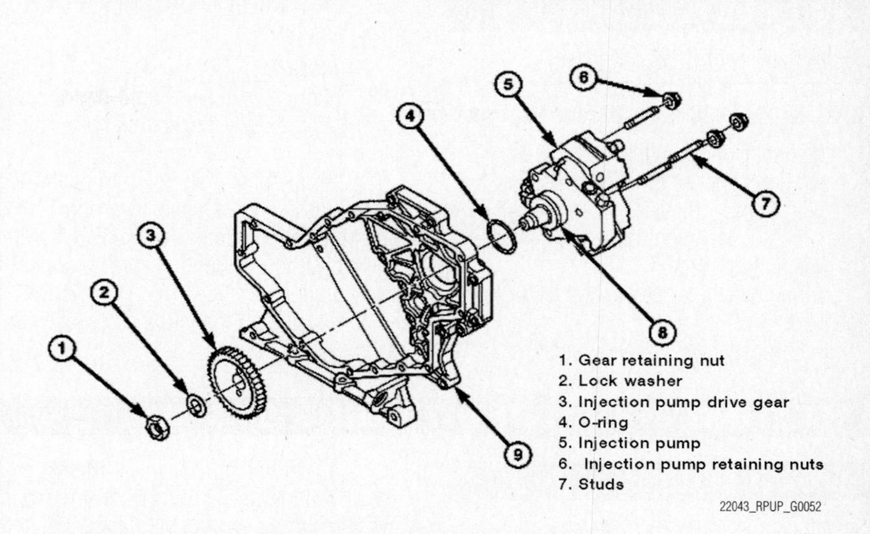

Fig. 179 Exploded view of diesel injection pump 5.9L–6.7L engines

7. Install the 3 pump mounting nuts and finger-tighten.

8. Install the shaft washer and nut and tighten by hand.

9. Tighten the pump mounting nuts to 18 ft. lbs. (25 Nm).

10. Tighten the pump shaft nut to 77 ft. lbs. (105 Nm).

11. Install the drive gear cover and tighten to 71 INCH lbs. (8 Nm).

12. Install or connect the following:
   - Fuel lines
   - Injection pump supply line
   - Pump wiring harness
   - Drive belt
   - Intake air tube
   - Negative battery cables

13. Bleed air from the system.

14. Start the engine and check for leaks.

INJECTION TIMING

5.9L & 2007–08 6.7L Diesel Engines

See Figures 180 and 181.

1. Perform the following phasing procedure anytime the injection pump has been removed and re-installed.

2. Locate the end of the fuel injection pump shaft. Two numbers (750 and 0) are stamped into the end of the shaft.

3. Rotate the injection pump shaft until the number 5 (located in the center of number 750) is positioned at 9 o'clock.

4. Position injection pump to mounting flange on gear housing while aligning injection pump shaft through back of injection pump gear. Be sure the number 5 is still at the 9 o'clock position.

5. Bring the engine to TDC position. Do this by rotating the crankshaft until the TDC mark on the crankshaft damper is at 12 o'clock position. It does not matter if cylinder number 1 or number 6 is at TDC. Again, check to be sure the number 5 is still at the 9 o'clock position. Rotate pump shaft accordingly.

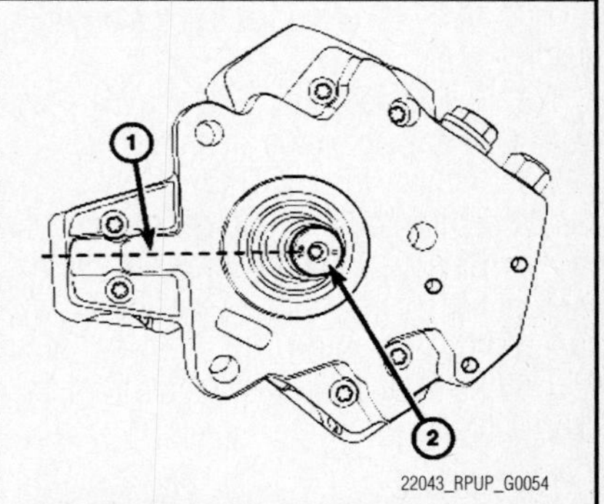

Fig. 180 Two numbers (750 and 0) at end of injection pump shaft shown

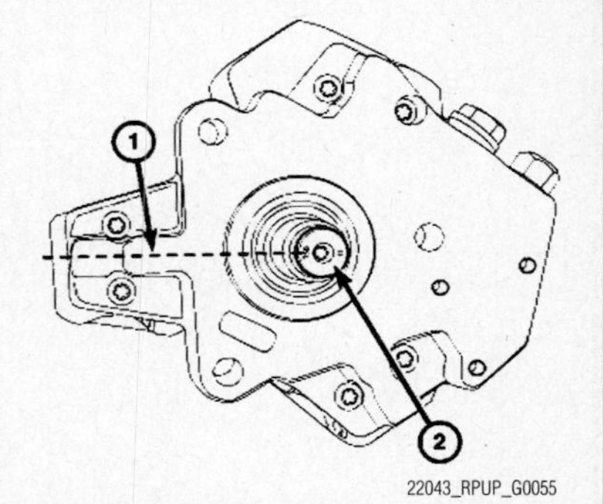

Fig. 181 Number 5 shown at the 9 o'clock position

ACTUATOR FUEL CONTROL

REMOVAL & INSTALLATION

5.9L & 2007–08 6.7L Diesel Engines

The Fuel Control Actuator (FCA) is located at the rear of the high-pressure, fuel injection pump.

1. Before servicing the vehicle, refer to the Precautions Section.
2. Remove the electrical connector from the FCA.
3. Remove FCA mounting screws.
4. Twist and pull FCA to remove from injection pump.

To install:

5. Lubricate the new Fuel Control Actuator (FCA) O-ring with clean oil before installation.
6. Turn FCA in a clockwise direction while pressing it into machined bore on rear of fuel injection pump. Be sure FCA flange is flush with the mounting surface on fuel injection pump.
7. Install FCA mounting screws (1) by hand.
8. Tighten the FCA mounting screws to 62 in. lbs. (7 Nm).

GLOW PLUGS

REMOVAL & INSTALLATION

The 5.9L and 6.7L diesel engines use an intake manifold air heater instead of glow plugs to preheat the air for improved starting ability. The heater element is located within the intake manifold top cover. Refer to the intake manifold removal and installation procedure to service the intake manifold air heater.

HEATING & AIR CONDITIONING SYSTEM

BLOWER MOTOR

REMOVAL & INSTALLATION

2005–08 Models

See Figure 182.

➡The blower motor is located on the passenger side of the vehicle under the instrument panel. The blower motor can be removed from the vehicle without having to remove the HVAC housing.

1. Before servicing the vehicle, refer to the Precautions Section.
2. Disconnect and isolate the negative battery cable.
3. Disconnect the HVAC wire harness lead (1) from the blower motor (2).
4. Remove the HVAC wire harness lead from the two wire harness retainers (3).
5. Remove the three screws (4) that secure the blower motor to the bottom of the HVAC housing (5).
6. Remove the blower motor from the HVAC housing.

To install:

7. Position the blower motor (2) into the bottom of the HVAC housing (5).

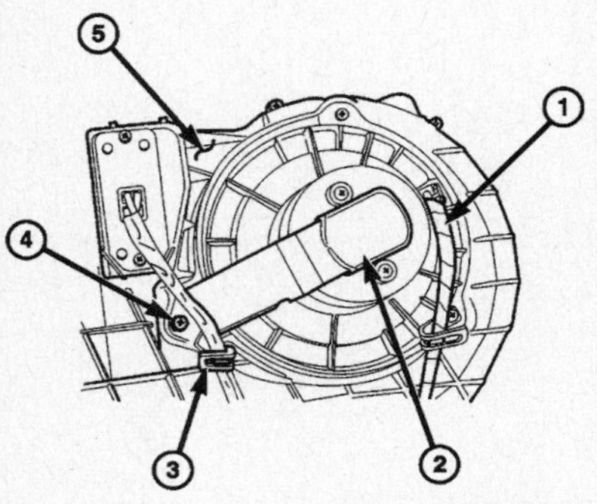

32050_RPUP_G0055

Fig. 182 Blower motor removal

8. Install the three screws (4) that secure the blower motor to the HVAC housing. Tighten the screws to 20 inch lbs. (2.2 Nm).
9. Connect the HVAC wire harness lead (1) to the blower motor and install the wire harness lead into the two wire harness retainers (3).
10. Reconnect the negative battery cable.

HEATER CORE

REMOVAL & INSTALLATION

2005–08 Models

See Figure 183.

⁂ CAUTION

Disable the airbag system before attempting any steering wheel, steering column, or instrument panel component diagnosis or service. Disconnect and isolate the negative battery (ground) cable, then wait two minutes for the airbag system capacitor to discharge before performing further diagnosis or service. This is the only sure way to disable the airbag system. Failure to take the proper precautions could result in accidental airbag deployment and possible personal injury or death.

➡The HVAC housing must be removed from the vehicle and disassembled for service of the A/C evaporator, evaporator temperature sensor, mode-air and blend-air doors.

1. Before servicing the vehicle, refer to the Precautions Section.
2. Disconnect and isolate the negative battery cable.
3. Recover the refrigerant from the A/C system.
4. Drain the engine cooling system.
5. Disconnect the A/C liquid line and the A/C accumulator from the A/C evaporator.
6. Disconnect the heater hoses from the heater core tubes.
7. Remove the powertrain control module (PCM) to gain access to the two nuts that secure the HVAC housing to the engine compartment side of the dash panel and remove the nuts.
8. On Mega Cab models, remove the floor console duct.
9. Remove the front seat assembly.
10. Remove the left a-pillar trim.
11. Disconnect the headliner wire harness connector located at the a-pillar.
12. Remove the instrument panel top cover.
13. Remove the left cowl trim panel.
14. Remove the steering column.
15. Remove the two bolts that secure the steering column support bracket to the instrument panel.
16. Remove the park brake release handle actuator rod.
17. Disconnect the instrument panel wire harness connector located above the brake pedal from the bulkhead wire harness connector.
18. Using a trim stick C-4755 or equivalent, from the notch on the bottom, remove the left instrument panel side cover.
19. Remove the three bolts that secure the left side of the instrument panel to the dash panel.
20. Remove the air bag control module cover, if equipped.
21. Disconnect the air bag control module electrical connector.
22. Remove the two bolts that secure the instrument panel to the center of the floor panel.
23. Remove the right cowl trim cover.
24. Disconnect the two instrument panel wire harness connectors from the two body

wire harness connectors located on the right side of the cowl panel.

25. Disconnect the antenna coaxial cable connector from the radio coaxial cable connector located on the right side of the cowl panel.

26. Remove the one bolt that secures the instrument panel to the HVAC housing below the glove box opening.

27. Remove the right a-pillar trim.

28. Using a trim stick C-4755 or equivalent, from the notch on the bottom, remove the right instrument panel side cover from the instrument panel.

29. Remove the three bolts that secure the right side instrument panel bracket to the dash panel.

30. Remove the four screws that secure the instrument panel to the top of the cowl panel.

31. Remove the two bolts that secure the instrument panel to the top of the cowl panel

32. Pull back the driver's side carpet as necessary to pull the air bag module harness out from under the carpet.

33. With the help of an assistant, lift the instrument panel up and off of the cowl panel and remove the instrument panel from the vehicle.

34. If required, remove the four plastic screws inserts from the top of the cowl panel.

35. Remove the bolt that secures the HVAC housing to the floor bracket.

36. Remove the two nuts that secure the HVAC housing to the passenger compartment side of the dash panel.

37. Pull the HVAC housing assembly rearward and remove the housing assembly from the passenger compartment.

38. If required, remove the fresh air inlet from the dash panel.

39. Remove the foam seal from the heater core tubes.

40. If equipped with the dual zone heating-A/C system, remove the linkage rod (4) to gain access to the heater core.

41. Remove the two screws that secure the heater core tube bracket to the HVAC housing and remove the bracket.

42. Carefully pull the heater core out of the front of the HVAC housing.

43. Inspect all foam seals and replace as required.

To install:

44. Carefully install the heater core into the front of the HVAC housing.

45. Position the heater core tube bracket onto the HVAC housing.

46. Install the two screws (1) that secure the heater core bracket to the HVAC housing. Tighten the screws to 10 in. lbs. (1.1 Nm)

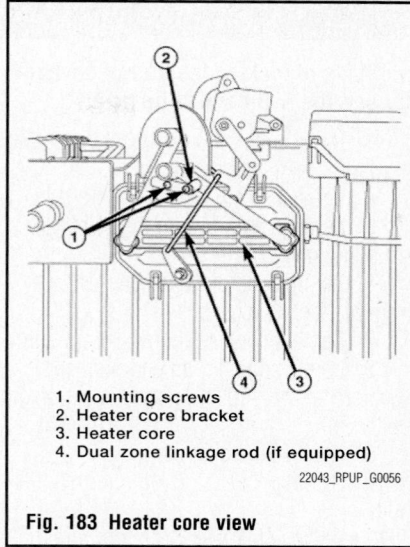

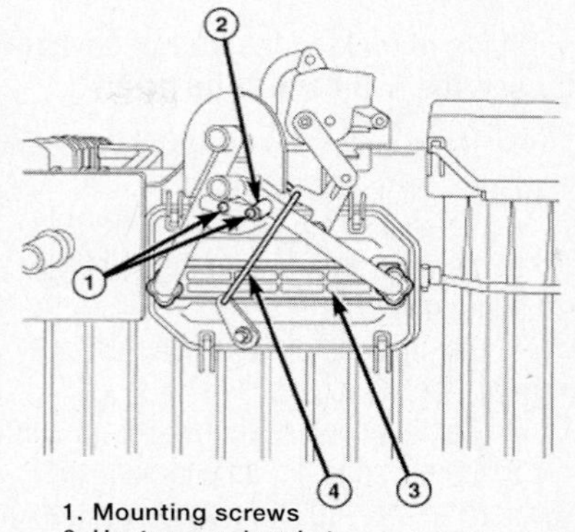

Fig. 183 Heater core view

47. If equipped with the dual zone heating and A/C system, install the linkage rod.

48. Install the foam seal onto the heater core tubes.

➡If the heater core is being replaced, flush the cooling system.

49. If removed, install the fresh air inlet onto the dash panel

50. Position the HVAC housing assembly into the passenger compartment with the mounting studs and the condensate drain tube in their proper locations in the dash panel.

51. Install the two nuts that secure the HVAC housing to the passenger compartment side of the dash panel. Tighten the nuts to 60 in. lbs. (68 Nm).

52. Install the bolt that secures the HVAC housing to the floor bracket. Tighten the bolt to 60 in. lbs. (68 Nm).

53. If removed, install the four plastic screw inserts into the top of the cowl panel.

54. With the help of an assistant, position the instrument panel into the vehicle and install the right side guide pin and the left side guide hook to the sides of the cowl panel.

55. Install the two bolts that secure the instrument panel to the top of the cowl panel

56. Tighten the bolts to 9 ft. lbs. (12 Nm).

57. Install the four screws that secure the instrument panel to the top of the cowl panel.

58. Tighten the screws to 20 in. lbs. (2 Nm).

59. Install the three bolts that secure the right side instrument panel bracket to the cowl panel.

60. Tighten the bolts to 9 ft. lbs. (12 Nm).

61. Position the air bag module harness under the carpet and position the carpet back.

62. Install the right a-pillar trim.

63. Install the two bolts that secure the instrument panel to the center of the floor panel

64. Tighten the bolts to 9 ft. lbs. (12 Nm).

65. Connect the air bag control module electrical connector.

66. Install the air bag control module cover, if equipped.

67. Install the floor console, if equipped.

68. Install the three bolts that secure the left side of the instrument panel to the dash panel.

69. Tighten the bolts to 9 ft. lbs. (12 Nm).

70. Install the left cowl trim panel.

71. Connect the instrument panel wire harness connector located above the brake pedal to the bulkhead wire harness connector.

72. Install the park brake release handle actuator rod.

73. Install the two bolts that secure the steering column support bracket to the instrument panel.

74. Tighten the bolts to 10 ft. lbs. (14 Nm).

75. Install the steering column.

76. Install the left cowl trim cover.

77. Install the left instrument panel side cover.

78. Connect the headliner wire harness connector located at the a-pillar.

79. Install the instrument panel top cover.

80. Install the left a-pillar trim.

81. Install the front seat assembly.

82. On Mega Cab models, install the floor console duct.

83. Install the two nuts (3) that secure the HVAC housing (1) to the engine compartment side of the dash panel. Tighten the nuts to 60 in. lbs. (6.8 Nm).

84. Install the Powertrain Control Module (PCM).

85. Connect the heater hoses to the heater core tubes.

86. Connect the A/C liquid line and the A/C accumulator to the A/C evaporator.

87. Reconnect the negative battery cable.

88. Refill the engine cooling system.

89. Evacuate the A/C system.

90. Charge the A/C system.

STEERING

RECIRCULATING BALL POWER STEERING GEAR

REMOVAL & INSTALLATION

See Figure 184.

1. Before servicing the vehicle, refer to the Precautions Section.
2. Remove or disconnect the following:
   - Negative battery cable
   - Power steering pressure and return lines
   - Intermediate shaft
   - Pitman arm
   - Steering gear

To install:

3. Install or connect the following:
   - Steering gear. Tighten the bolts to 100 ft. lbs. (136 Nm).
   - Pitman arm. Tighten the nut to 175 ft. lbs. (237 Nm).
   - Intermediate shaft. Tighten the pinch bolt to 36 ft. lbs. (49 Nm).
   - Power steering pressure and return lines
   - Negative battery cable
4. Fill the power steering fluid reservoir.
5. Start the engine and check for leaks.

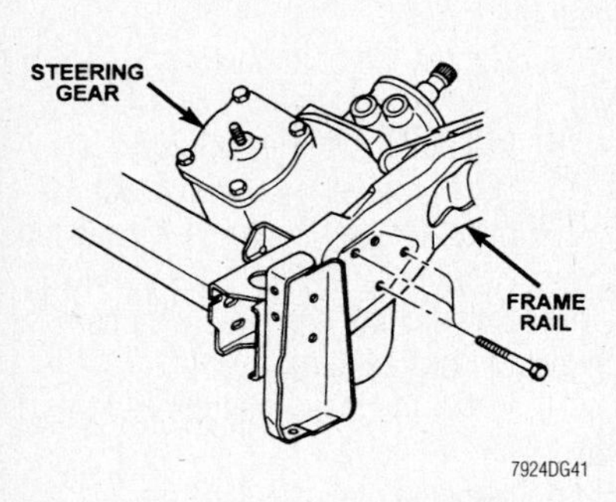

Fig. 184 Typical recirculating ball power steering gear mounting

RACK AND PINION STEERING GEAR

REMOVAL & INSTALLATION

See Figure 185.

1. Before servicing the vehicle, refer to the Precautions Section.
2. Lock the steering wheel.

➡The steering column on vehicles with an automatic transmission may not be equipped with an internal locking shaft that allows the ignition key cylinder to be locked with the key. Alternative methods of locking the steering wheel for service will have to be used.

3. Drain and siphon the power steering fluid from the reservoir.
4. Raise the vehicle.
5. Remove and discard the steering coupler pinch bolt.
6. Remove the power steering hoses from the rack & pinion.
7. Remove the tire and wheel assembly.
8. Remove the tie rod end nuts and separate tie rod ends from the knuckles with puller 8677
9. Remove the skid plate.
10. Remove the rack & pinion mounting bolts.
11. Remove the rack & pinion from the vehicle.

To install:

➡Before installing gear inspect bushings and replace if worn or damaged.

12. Install the gear on the front crossmember and tighten the mounting bolts for light duty trucks to 235 ft. lbs. (319 Nm). Tighten the mounting bolts for heavy duty 4X2 trucks to 185 ft. lbs. (251 Nm).
13. Slide the shaft coupler onto the gear. Install new pinch bolt and tighten to 36 ft. lbs. (49 Nm).
14. Clean and dry the tie rod end studs and the knuckle tapers.
15. Install the tie rod ends into the steering knuckles and tighten the nuts to 45 ft. lbs. (61 Nm). then an additional 90 degrees.
16. Install the pressure power steering hose to the steering gear and tighten to 23 ft. lbs. (32 Nm).
17. Install the return power steering hose to the steering gear and for light duty trucks tighten to 37 ft. lbs (50 Nm). Tighten the mounting bolts for heavy duty 4X2 trucks to 40 ft. lbs. (54 Nm).
18. Install the front skid plate.
19. Install the tire and wheel assembly.
20. Remove the support and lower the vehicle.
21. Fill and bleed the power steering system.
22. Adjust the toe.

POWER STEERING PUMP

REMOVAL & INSTALLATION

Gasoline Engines

See Figure 186.

1. Drain and siphon the power steering fluid from the reservoir.
2. Remove the serpentine belt, as outlined in the Engine Mechanical Section.

⁂ WARNING

Do not remove the fitting on the pump that the high pressure hose screws into. The fitting may come loose unless it is backed up using another wrench. If the fitting does come loose, it must be retightened to 40–50 ft. lbs. (57–67 Nm) before continuing. If this fitting comes out of the pump body, the internal spring and valve parts will fall out of the pump and they cannot be reinstalled properly. If this occurs the pump needs to be replaced with a new pump.

3. Disconnect the return hose.
4. Disconnect the pressure hose.
5. Access to remove the three bolts securing the pump to the cylinder head can be gained thru the pulley holes.

To install:

6. Align the pump with the mounting holes in the left cylinder head.

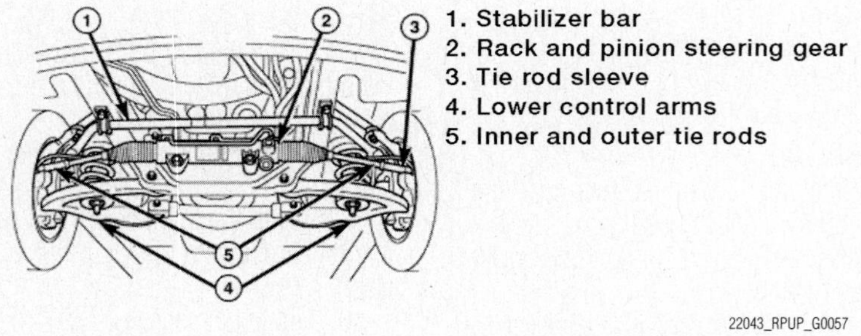

Fig. 185 Rack and pinion steering gear

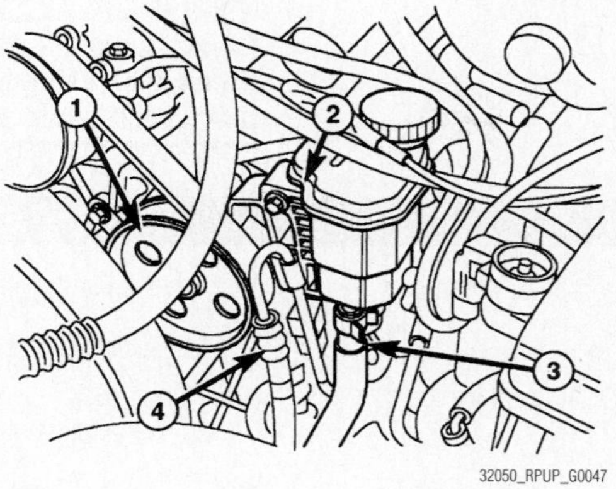

Fig. 186 View of the power steering pump pulley (1), fluid reservoir (2), return hose (3) and high pressure hose (4)

7. Install 3 pump mounting bolts through the pulley access holes. Tighten the bolts to 21 ft. lbs. (28 Nm).
8. Reconnect the pressure line and return hose to the pump and reservoir. Tighten the pressure line to 27 ft. lbs. (37 Nm).
9. Install the serpentine drive belt.
10. Fill the reservoir with power steering fluid and perform the "Initial Operation Procedure", located later in this section.
11. Start the engine and check the operation of the brakes.

Diesel Engines

See Figure 187.

1. Drain and siphon the power steering fluid from the reservoir.
2. Remove the serpentine belt, as outlined in the Engine Mechanical Section.

⁂ WARNING

Do not remove the fitting on the pump that the high pressure hose screws into. The fitting may come loose unless it is backed up using another wrench. If the fitting does come loose, it must be retightened to 40–50 ft. lbs. (57–67 Nm) before continuing. If this fitting comes out of the pump body, the internal spring and valve parts will fall out of the pump and they cannot be reinstalled properly. If this occurs the pump needs to be replaced with a new pump.

3. Disconnect the return hose.
4. Disconnect the pressure hose.
5. Access to remove the three bolts securing the pump to the cylinder head can be gained thru the pulley holes.
6. Loosen the pump bracket to the block.
7. Remove the 6 intake plenum bolts.
8. Loosen the inner cooler tube clamp at the intake plenum and remove the intake plenum.
9. Loosen the inner cooler tube clamp at the radiator support side and remove the tube from the vehicle.
10. Remove the power steering pump from the top of the engine compartment where the intake plenum was.

To install:

11. Set the power steering pump in place in the engine compartment from the top.
12. Install the inner cooler tube.
13. Tighten the inner cooler tube clamp at the radiator support side.
14. Install the 6 intake plenum bolts.
15. Tighten the inner cooler tube clamp at the intake plenum.
16. Install 3 pump mounting bolts through the pulley access holes. Tighten the bolts to 21 ft. lbs. (28 Nm).
17. Tighten the pump bracket to the block.
18. Reconnect the pressure line and return hose to the pump and reservoir. Tighten the pressure line to 27 ft. lbs. (37 Nm).
19. Install the serpentine drive belt.
20. Fill the reservoir with power steering fluid and perform the "Initial Operation Procedure", located later in this section.
21. Start the engine and check the operation of the brakes.

BLEEDING

This procedure should be carried out whenever the power steering pump lines have been disconnected.

⁂ WARNING

Use only MOPAR®ATF+4 automatic transmission fluid and do not overfill.

1. Wipe filler cap clean, then check the fluid level. The dipstick should indicate COLD when the fluid is at normal temperature.
2. Turn the steering wheel all the way to the left.
3. Add fluid to bring the level up to the proper level and let the fluid settle for at least 2 minutes.
4. Raise the front wheels off the ground.
5. Slowly turn the steering wheel lock–to–lock 20 times with the engine OFF.

➡On vehicles with long return lines or oil coolers, turn the wheel 40 times.

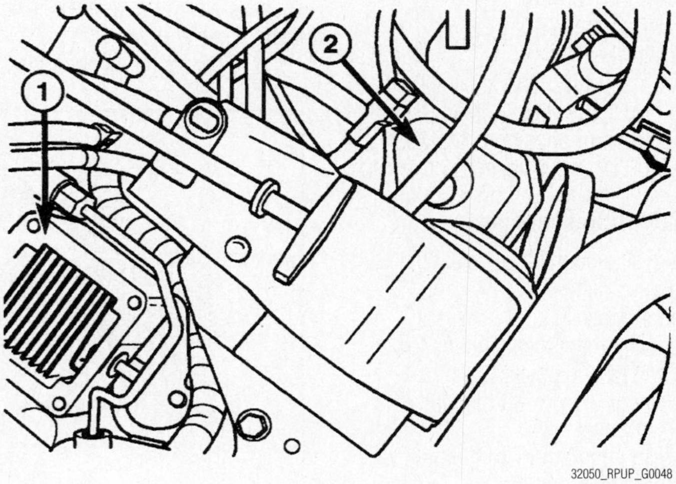

Fig. 187 View of the intake plenum (1) and power steering pump (2) mounting

6. Start the engine. Check level and add fluid, if necessary.
7. Lower the front wheels and let the engine idle for two minutes.
8. Turn the steering wheel in both directions and verify power assist and quiet operation of the pump.
9. If the fluid is extremely foamy or milky looking, allow the vehicle to stand for a few minutes and repeat the procedure.

⁂ WARNING

Do not run a vehicle with a foamy fluid for an extended period. This may cause pump damage.

SUSPENSION

FRONT SUSPENSION

COIL SPRING

REMOVAL & INSTALLATION

2WD Coil Spring Suspension

1. Before servicing the vehicle, refer to the Precautions Section.
2. Support the lower control arm on a floor jack.
3. Remove or disconnect the following:
   - Front wheel
   - Shock absorber
4. Compress the spring.
5. Remove or disconnect the following:
   - Stabilizer bar link
   - Lower ball joint

⁂ WARNING

Support the upper control arm and knuckle.

6. Lower the jack and tighten the compressor to allow coil spring removal. Catch the isolator pad.

To install:

7. Install the coil spring and raise the control arm into position.
8. Install or connect the following:
   - Lower ball joint. Tighten the nut to 38 ft. lbs. (52 Nm), plus a 90 degree turn (1500 Series), or, 100 ft. lbs. (135 Nm) (HD Series)
   - Shock absorber
   - Stabilizer bar link. Tighten the nut to 27 ft. lbs. (37 Nm).
   - Front wheel
9. Lower the vehicle and allow the suspension to take the weight. Tighten the front and rear control arm pivot bolts to 150 ft. lbs. (204 Nm) LD; 210 ft. lbs. (285 Nm) HD

4WD Link/Coil Suspension

1. Before servicing the vehicle, refer to the Precautions Section.
2. Support the axle on a floor jack.
3. Place alignment marks on the lower arm adjuster and axle bracket.
4. Remove or disconnect the following:
   - Front wheel
   - Upper control arm and loosen the lower arm bolts
   - Track bar from the frame rail bracket
   - Drag link from the Pitman arm
   - Stabilizer bar link
   - Shock absorber
5. Lower the jack and remove the coil spring.

To install:

6. Install the coil spring and raise the axle into position.
7. Install or connect the following:
   - Stabilizer bar link. Tighten the nut to 45 ft. lbs. (61 Nm).
   - Shock absorber
   - Track bar
   - Drag link
   - On 4wd, the front driveshaft
   - Upper control arm and lower arm bolts. Upper arm nuts to 110 ft. lbs. (149 Nm); lower arm nuts to 160 ft. lbs. (217 Nm)

4WD Coil Over Suspension

See Figures 188 and 189.

1. Before servicing the vehicle, refer to the Precautions Section.
2. Remove the shock.
3. Install the shock assembly in the Branick 7200® or equivalent spring removal/installation tool.
4. Compress the spring.
5. Position the shock wrench 9362, on shock shaft retaining nut. Next, insert 8 mm socket though Wrench onto hex located on end of shock shaft. While holding shock shaft from turning, remove nut from shock shaft using Wrench.
6. Remove the upper shock nut.

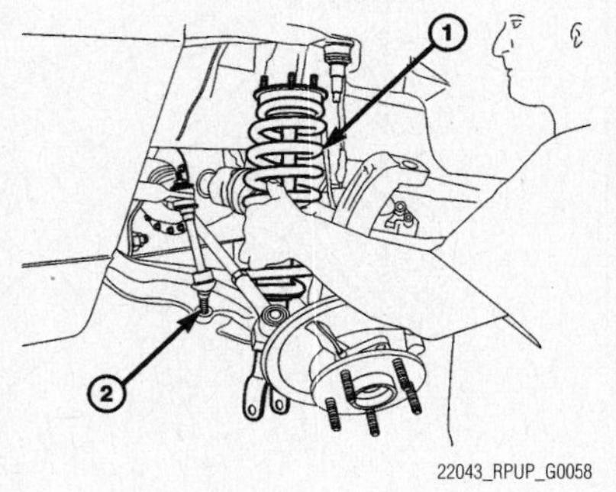

Fig. 188 Coil over suspension shock removal

7. Remove the shock upper mounting plate.
8. Remove and inspect the upper spring isolator.
9. Remove the shock.

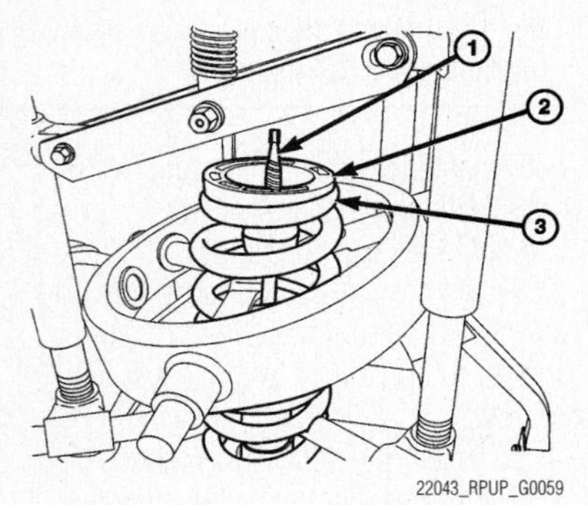

Fig. 189 Shock shaft (1), upper spring isolator (2), coil spring (3)

To install:

11. Position the shock into the coil spring.
12. Install the upper isolator.
13. Install the upper shock mounting plate.
14. Install the shock upper mounting nut.
15. Install the shock wrench 9362 (on end of a torque wrench), on shock shaft retaining nut. Next, insert 8 mm socket though Wrench onto hex located on end of shock shaft. While holding the shock shaft from turning, tighten nut using Wrench to 66 ft. lbs. (90 Nm).
16. Decompress the spring.
17. Remove the shock assembly from the spring compressor tool.
18. Install the shock assembly.

TORSION BAR

REMOVAL & INSTALLATION

2005—Independent Front Suspension

See Figure 190.

1. Before servicing the vehicle, refer to the Precautions Section.
2. Loosen the adjustment bolt to remove spring load. Note the number of turns for installation.

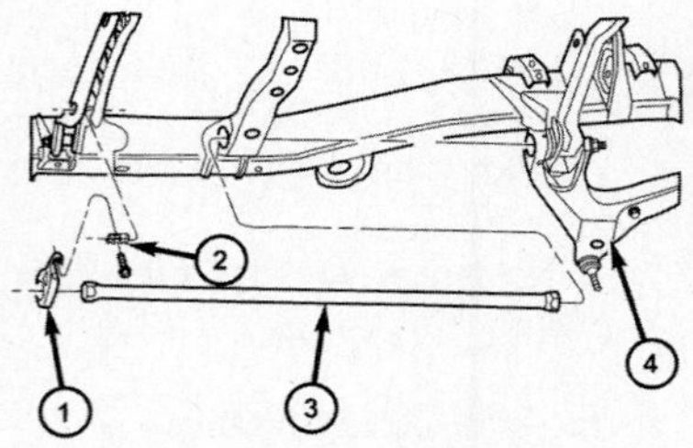

Fig. 190 Torsion bar and related parts

3. Remove or disconnect the following:
   - Adjustment bolt, swivel and bearing
   - Torsion bar and anchor
4. Separate the torsion bar and anchor.

To install:

5. Assemble the torsion bar and anchor.
6. Install or connect the following:
   - Torsion bar and anchor
   - Adjustment bolt, swivel and bearing
7. Tighten the adjustment bolt the recorded number of turns.

CONTROL LINKS

REMOVAL & INSTALLATION

Independent Front Suspension

See Figure 191.

1. Before servicing the vehicle, refer to the Precautions Section.
2. Raise and support the vehicle.
3. Remove the lower nut.
4. Remove the upper nut, retainer and grommets.
5. Remove the stabilizer link from the vehicle
6. Install the stabilizer link to the vehicle.
7. Install the lower nut and tighten to 75 ft. lbs. (102 Nm).
8. Install the retainers, grommets and upper nut and tighten to 20 ft. lbs. (27 Nm).
9. Remove the support and lower the vehicle.

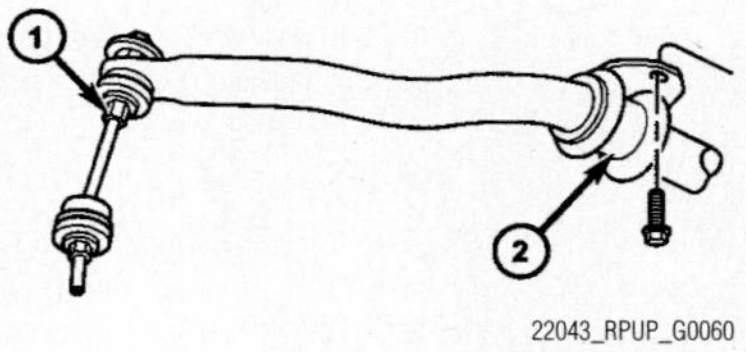

Fig. 191 Stabilizer link (1) 4X2 independent front suspension shown 4X4 similar

Link/Coil Suspension

See Figure 192.

1. Before servicing the vehicle, refer to the Precautions Section.
2. Raise and support the vehicle.
3. Hold the stabilizer link shafts with a wrench and remove the link nuts at the stabilizer bar.
4. Remove the retainers and grommets from the stabilizer bar links.
5. Remove the stabilizer bar link nuts from the axle brackets.
6. Remove the links from the axle brackets with Puller C-3894-A.

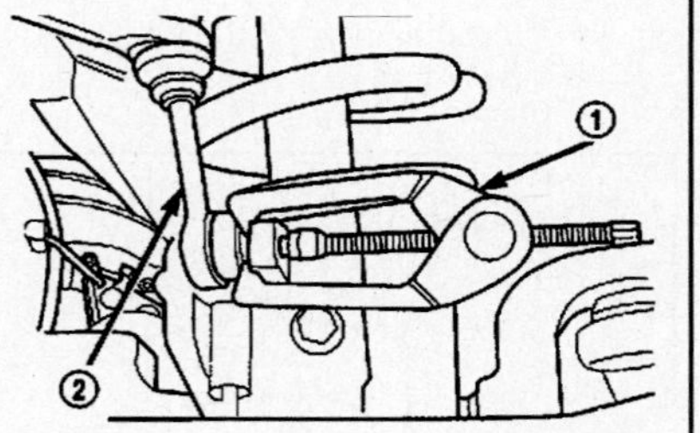

Fig. 192 Link removal with Puller C-3894-A shown

To install:

7. Install links to the axle bracket and tighten nut to 110 ft. lbs. (149 Nm).
8. Install links, retainers, grommets and nuts to the stabilizer bar. Hold the link shaft with a wrench and tighten the nuts to 27 ft. lbs. (38 Nm).
9. Remove the supports and lower the vehicle

LOWER BALL JOINT

REMOVAL & INSTALLATION

Independent Front Suspension

See Figure 193.

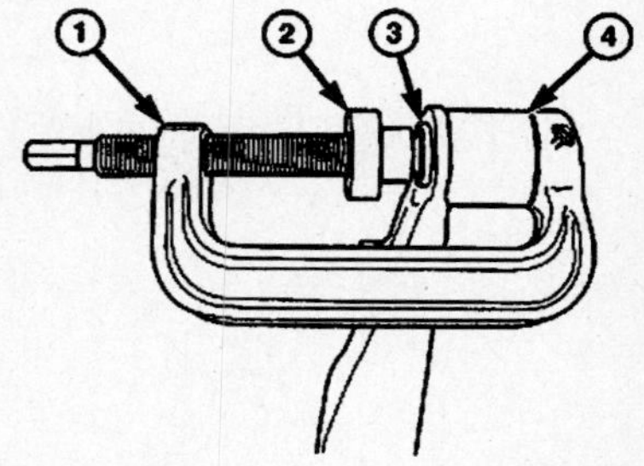

Fig. 193 Lower ball joint removal with tools shown

1. Before servicing the vehicle, refer to the Precautions Section.
2. Remove or disconnect the following:
   - Front wheel
   - Brake caliper and rotor
   - Outer tie rod ends
   - Steering knuckle
   - Snapring from the ball joint (HD 2wd)
3. Use tools C-4212-F, 8698-2 and 8698-3 (or equivalents) to remove the lower ball joint.

➡Use EP grease on the tool threads.

To install:

4. Use tools C-4212-F, 8698-1 and 8698-3 (or equivalents) to install the lower ball joint.
5. On 2wd HD models, install a new snapring; on all others, stake the ball joint flange in 4 evenly spaced places.
6. Install or connect the following:
   - Knuckle. Torque the ball stud nut to 38 ft. lbs. (52 Nm) plus 90 degrees on all except 2X4 HD; on 2wd HD, torque the nut to 100 ft. lbs. (135 Nm).
   - Outer tie rod ends
   - Axle shaft
   - Hub retainer
   - Brake caliper and rotor
   - Front wheel

Link/Coil Suspension

See Figure 194.

1. Before servicing the vehicle, refer to the Precautions Section.
2. Remove the steering knuckle.
3. Remove the axle shaft from the axle.
4. Remove lower snap ring from the lower ball joint.
5. Remove the lower ball joint, using tool 6761 and 8445-3 with C-4212-F

To install:

6. To install, use driver 8445-2, receiver 8975-5 and tool C-4212-F.

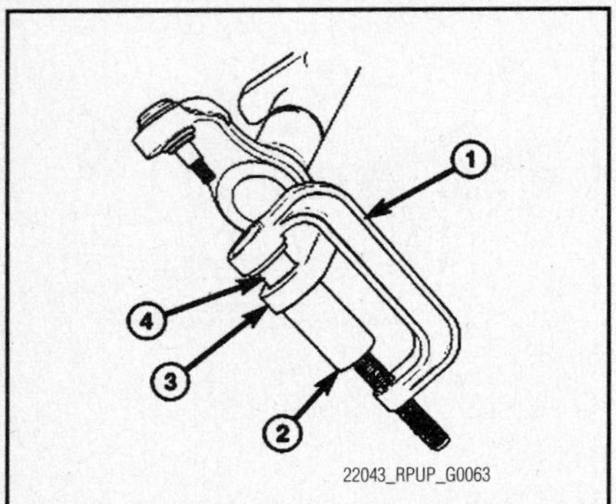

Fig. 194 Link/Coil suspension, lower ball joint removal with tools shown

7. Install the axle shaft into the axle.
8. Install the knuckle. Tighten the ball stud nut to 35 ft. lbs. (47 Nm), then tighten it to 70 ft. lbs. (94 Nm) and install the pin.

LOWER CONTROL ARM

REMOVAL & INSTALLATION

Independent Front Suspension

2WD

1. Before servicing the vehicle, refer to the Precautions Section.
2. Support the lower control arm with a floor jack.
3. Remove or disconnect the following:
   - Front wheel
   - Brake caliper and rotor
   - Stabilizer bar link
   - Lower ball joint
   - Coil spring
   - Crossmember nuts
   - Lower control arm

To install:

4. Install or connect the following:
   - Lower control arm. Tighten the crossmember nuts to 145 ft. lbs. (196 Nm).
   - Coil spring
   - Lower ball joint. Tighten the nut to 135 ft. lbs. (183 Nm).
   - Stabilizer bar link
   - Brake caliper and rotor
   - Front wheel

4WD

1. Before servicing the vehicle, refer to the Precautions Section.
2. Remove or disconnect the following:
   - Front wheel
   - Upper ball joint from the knuckle
   - Halfshaft
   - Torsion bar
   - Shock absorber lower bolt
   - Stabilizer bar link
   - Lower ball joint from the knuckle
   - Lower control arm

To install:

3. Install or connect the following:
   - Lower control arm. Tighten bolts finger-tight.
   - Torsion bar

➡The ball stud taper must be clean and dry before installation.

   - Lower ball joint. Tighten the nut to 38 ft. lbs. (52 Nm) (on 1500 series, plus 90 degrees).
   - Shock absorber lower bolt. Torque it to 100 ft. lbs. (135 Nm).
   - Halfshaft
   - Upper ball joint. Tighten the nut to 40 ft. lbs. (54 Nm) (on 1500 series, plus 90 degrees).
   - Stabilizer bar link
4. Tighten the pivot bolts to 150 ft. lbs. (204 Nm).
   - Front wheel

Link/Coil Suspension

1. Before servicing the vehicle, refer to the Precautions Section.
2. Paint or scribe matchmarks on the cam adjusters and suspension arm.
3. Remove or disconnect the following:
   - Lower arm nut, cam and cam bolt
   - Nut and bolt from the frame rail
   - Lower arm

To install:

4. Install or connect the following:
   - Lower control arm. Tighten bolts finger-tight. Align the reference marks.
5. Lower the truck to load the suspension
6. Tighten the nuts to 160 ft. lbs. (217 Nm).

4WD 2006–08 Light Duty

See Figure 195.

1. Before servicing the vehicle, refer to the Precautions Section.
2. Raise and support the vehicle.
3. Remove the wheel and tire assembly.
4. Remove the upper ball joint nut. Separate the ball joint from the steering knuckle with remover tool 8677.
5. Remove the front halfshaft.
6. Remove the shock absorber lower nut/bolt.
7. Remove the stabilizer bar link.
8. Remove the lower ball joint nut. Separate ball the joint from the steering knuckle with remover tool 8677.
9. Remove the control arm pivot bolts and suspension arm from frame rail brackets.

To install:

10. Position the lower control arm at the frame rail brackets. Install the pivot bolts and nuts. Tighten the nuts finger-tight.

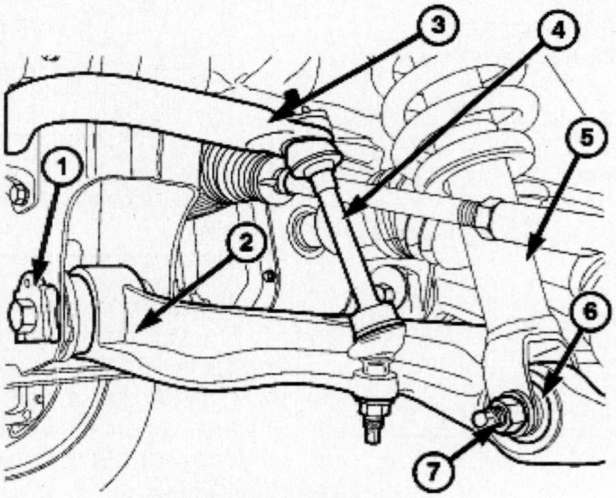

1. Lower control arm bolts
2. Lower control arm
3. Stabilizer bar
4. Stabilizer link
5. Coil/over shock
6. Bushing
7. Coil/over shock mounting nut

22043_RPUP_G0064

Fig. 195 Lower control arm view— LD 4X4

⁂ WARNING

The ball joint stud taper must be clean and dry before installing the knuckle. Clean the stud taper with mineral spirits to remove dirt and grease.

11. Insert the lower ball joint stud into the steering knuckle. Install and tighten the retaining nut to 38 ft. lbs. (52 Nm), (on 1500 series only turn an additional 90 degrees).
12. Install shock absorber lower bolt/nut and tighten to 155 ft. lbs. (210 Nm).
13. Install the front halfshaft.
14. Insert the upper ball joint into the steering knuckle. Install and tighten the retaining nut to 40 ft. lbs. (54 Nm), (on 1500 series only an additional 90 degree turn is required).
15. Install the stabilizer bar link.
16. Tighten the lower control arm front pivot nut to 150 ft. lbs. (204 Nm). Tighten rear pivot bolt to 150 ft. lbs. (204 Nm).
17. Install the wheel and tire assembly.
18. Remove the support and lower the vehicle.
19. Perform a wheel alignment.

CONTROL ARM BUSHING REPLACEMENT

Independent Front Suspension

See Figure 196.

1. Before servicing the vehicle, refer to the Precautions Section.
2. Remove the lower control arm
3. Secure the control arm in a soft jaw vise.
4. Remove the bushing (3) using special tool C–4212F (PRESS) (1), 9772-6 (receiver) (6), 9772-4 (SPACER) (5) and 9772-3 (driver) (2)

To install:

5. Using special tools install lower control arm bushings.
6. Remove the control arm from the vise.
7. Install the lower control arm.
8. Perform a wheel alignment.

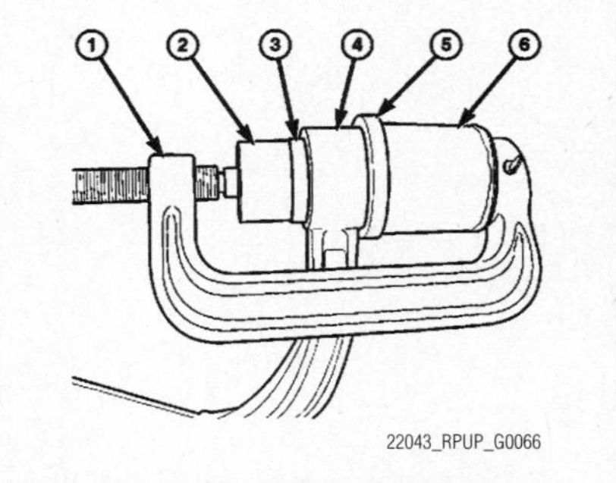

Fig. 196 Lower control arm bushing removal, tool with adapters shown

Lower Control Arm Shock Bushing 4WD Models

See Figure 197.

1. Before servicing the vehicle, refer to the Precautions Section.
2. Raise and support the vehicle.
3. Remove the tire and wheel assembly.
4. Support the lower control arm outboard end.
5. Remove the caliper adapter with the caliper.
6. Remove the rotor.
7. Remove the upper ball joint retaining nut and separate the upper ball joint from the knuckle using separator 9360.
8. Disconnect the wheel speed sensor wire from the knuckle and upper control arm.
9. Remove the stabilizer link lower nut.
10. Remove the axle hub nut.
11. Remove the shock lower bolt/nut from the lower control arm then move the shock out of the way to allow the C4212–F press to used.
12. Install special tools to press the bushing (3) out of the lower control arm (4) using special tools C-4212-F (Press) (1), 9653–1 (driver) (5) and 9653-2 (Receiver) (2).

To install:

13. Install the new shock bushing (3) into the lower control arm (4) using tools C-4212-F (Press) (1), 9653–3 (driver) (2), 9773 (Receiver) (5) will automatically set the depth of the bushing in the control arm.
14. Install the lower part of the shock into the lower control arm shock bushing.
15. Install and position bolt so head of the bolt is facing rearward of vehicle and hand start nut. Tighten the bolt and nut to 60 ft. lbs. (81 Nm).
16. Install the upper ball joint to the knuckle and install the retaining nut.
17. Install and tighten the axle hub nut.
18. Install the stabilizer link lower nut.
19. Reconnect the wheel speed sensor wiring to the knuckle and upper control arm.
20. Install the brake rotor.
21. Install the caliper adapter with the brake caliper.
22. Remove the support from the lower control arm outboard end.
23. Install the tire and wheel assembly.
24. Remove the support and lower the vehicle.

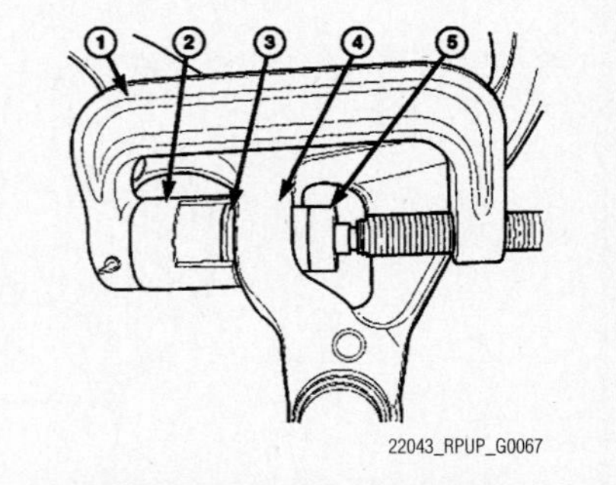

Fig. 197 Lower shock bushing removal shown

STABILIZER BAR

REMOVAL & INSTALLATION

Independent Front Suspension

1. Before servicing the vehicle, refer to the Precautions Section.

➡To service the stabilizer bar the vehicle should be on a drive on hoist. The vehicle suspension must be at curb height for stabilizer bar installation.

2. Remove the stabilizer bar link upper nuts and remove the retainers and grommets.
3. Remove the stabilizer bar mounting bolts and discard the mounting bolts.
4. Remove the retainers from the frame crossmember and remove the bar.
5. If necessary, remove the bushings from the stabilizer bar, Do not cut the old bushings off the stabilizer bar use a mixture of soapy water in order to aid in sliding the bushing off.

To install:

6. If the bushings were removed, Clean the bar and install the bushings on the stabilizer bar using a mixture of soapy water or equivalent in order to slide the bushing over the bar with ease. Do not cut the new bushing for installation.

➡Install new mounting bolts Do not reuse old bolts.

7. Position the stabilizer bar on the frame crossmember brackets and install the bracket bolts finger-tight.
8. Check the alignment of the bar to ensure there is no interference with the either frame rail or chassis component. Spacing should be equal on both sides.
9. Install the stabilizer bar to the stabilizer link and install the grommets and retainers.

10. Install the nuts to the stabilizer link and tighten to 20 ft. lbs. (27 Nm).

11. Tighten the brackets to the frame to 45 ft. lbs. (61 Nm).

Link/Coil Suspension

1. Before servicing the vehicle, refer to the Precautions Section.
2. Raise and support the vehicle.
3. Hold the stabilizer link shafts with a wrench and remove the link nuts at the stabilizer bar.
4. Remove the retainers and grommets from the stabilizer bar links.
5. Remove the stabilizer bar clamps from the frame rails and remove the stabilizer bar.

To install:

6. Position the stabilizer bar on the frame rail and install the clamps and bolts. Ensure the bar is centered with equal spacing on both sides.
7. Tighten the clamp bolts to 45 ft. lbs. (61 Nm).
8. Install links, retainers, grommets and nuts to the stabilizer bar. Hold the link shaft with a wrench and tighten the nuts to 27 ft. lbs. (38 Nm).
9. Remove the supports and lower the vehicle

STEERING KNUCKLE

REMOVAL & INSTALLATION

Independent Front Suspension

See Figures 198 and 199.

1. Raise and support the vehicle.
2. Remove the wheel.
3. Remove the brake caliper and rotor, shield and ABS wheel speed sensor, if equipped.
4. Remove the front halfshaft nut (if equipped)
5. Remove the cotter pin and nut from the tie rod. Disconnect the tie rod from the steering knuckle with Remover 8677, or equivalent.

WARNING

When installing Remover 8677 to separate the ball joint, be careful not to damage the ball joint seal.

6. Remove the lower ball joint nut. Separate the ball joint from the knuckle with Remover 8677 and remove the knuckle.
7. For light duty vehicles, remove the upper ball joint nut. Separate the ball joint from the knuckle with Remover 8677 LD. For heavy duty vehicles, remove the upper ball joint nut. Separate the ball joint from the knuckle with Remover 9360 HD

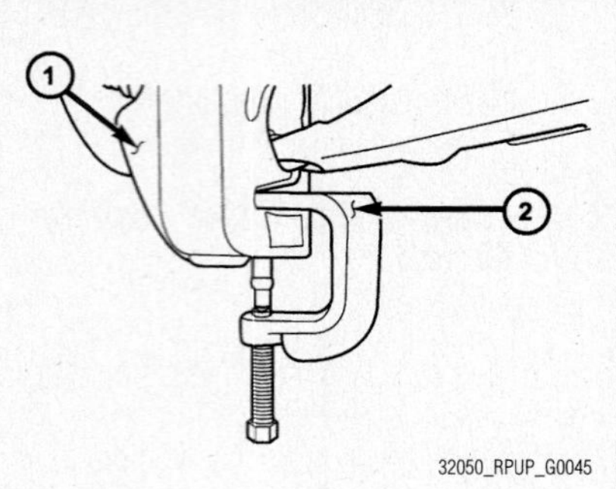

Fig. 198 Use the special tool (2) to separate the ball joint from the knuckle (1)

8. Remove the hub/bearing from the steering knuckle.

To install:

WARNING

The ball joint stud tapers must be CLEAN and DRY before installing the knuckle. Clean the stud tapers with mineral spirits to remove dirt and grease.

➡When installing hub/bearing with ABS brakes, position the speed sensor opening towards the front of the vehicle.

9. Install the hub/bearing to the steering knuckle (1) and tighten the bolts to 120 ft. lbs. (163 Nm) for light duty vehicles or to 130 ft. lbs. (176 Nm) for 2X4 heavy duty vehicles.
10. Install the knuckle (1) onto the upper and lower ball joints.
11. Install the upper and lower ball joint nuts (3).
12. Tighten the upper ball joint nut, as follows:
    a. Light Duty (1500 models): 40 ft. lbs. (54 Nm), plus and additional 90° turn
    b. Heavy Duty (2500/3500 models): 50 ft. lbs. (68 Nm)
13. Tighten the lower ball joint nut, as follows:
    a. Light Duty (1500 models): 38 ft. lbs. (52 Nm), plus and additional 90° turn
    b. 2WD Heavy Duty (2500/3500 models): 100 ft. lbs. (135 Nm)
14. Remove the hydraulic jack from the lower suspension arm.
15. Install the tie rod end and tighten the nut to 45 ft. lbs. (61 Nm).
16. Install the front halfshaft into the hub/bearing, if equipped.
17. Install the halfshaft nut and tighten to 185 ft. lbs. (251 Nm), if equipped.
18. Install the ABS wheel speed sensor if equipped, and brake shield, rotor and caliper.
19. Install the wheel and tire assembly.
20. Remove the support and lower the vehicle.
21. Perform a wheel alignment.

Link/Coil Front Suspension

1. Remove the hub bearing and axle shaft.
2. Remove the tie rod or drag link end from the steering knuckle arm.
3. Remove the ABS sensor wire and bracket from the knuckle.
4. Remove the cotter pin from the upper ball stud nut. Remove the upper and lower ball stud nuts.
5. Strike the steering knuckle with a brass hammer to loosen.
6. Remove the knuckle from the axle tube yokes.

To install:

7. Position the steering knuckle on the ball studs.

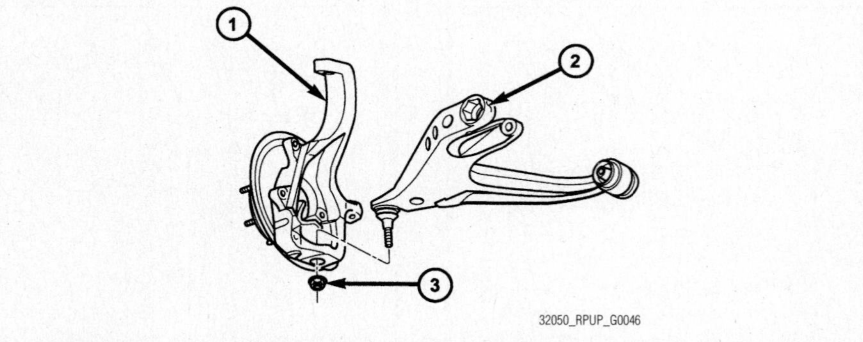

Fig. 199 Exploded view of the steering knuckle (1), lower control arm (2) and lower ball joint nut (3)

8. Install and tighten lower ball stud nut to 35 ft. lbs. (47 Nm). Do not install cotter pin at this time.

9. Install and tighten upper ball stud nut to 70 ft. lbs. (94 Nm). Advance nut to next slot to line up hole and install new cotter pin.

10. Retorque lower ball stud nut to 140–160 ft. lbs. (190–217 Nm). Advance nut to next slot to line up hole and install new cotter pin.

11. Install the hub bearing.

12. Install tie-rod or drag link end onto the steering knuckle arm.

13. Install the ABS sensor wire and bracket to the knuckle.

UPPER BALL JOINT

REMOVAL & INSTALLATION

Independent Front Suspension

See Figure 200.

1. Before servicing the vehicle, refer to the Precautions Section.
2. Raise vehicle and support the axle.
3. Remove the tire and wheel.
4. Remove the upper ball joint retaining nut.
5. Separate the upper ball joint from the knuckle using separator tool 9360.
6. Remove the wheel speed sensor wire from the knuckle heavy duty models, and from the upper control arm light duty models.
7. Move the knuckle out of the way to allow ball joint removal tool access.
8. Remove the ball joint boot for removal.

➡It may be necessary to install a block of wood between the control arm and frame bracket to allow clearance for the ball joint press tool.

9. Press the ball joint (4) from the upper control arm (3) using special tools C-4212-F (PRESS) (1), 9770-1 (Receiver) (2) and 9770-2 (Driver) (5).
10. Install the upper ball joint with special tools.
11. Install the upper ball joint into the knuckle.
12. Install the upper ball joint retaining nut and tighten to 40 ft. lbs. (54 Nm) (on 1500 series only an additional 90 degree turn is required) or 50 ft. lbs. (68 Nm). Heavy duty models.
13. Install the wheel speed sensor wire to the knuckle heavy duty models, and to the upper control arm light duty models.
14. Install the tire and wheel.

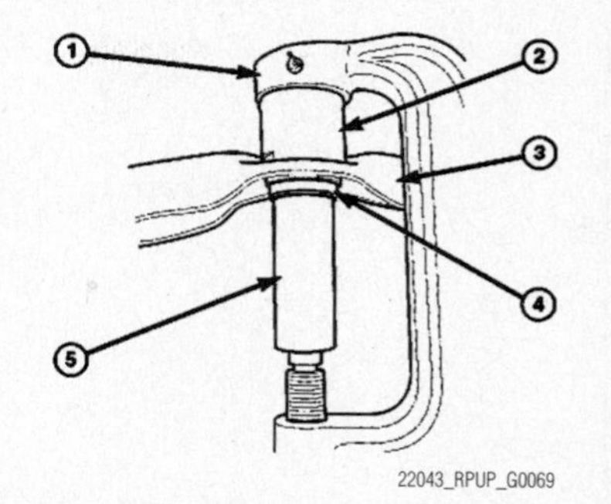

Fig. 200 Upper ball joint removal with special tools

15. Remove the supports and lower the vehicle.
16. Perform a wheel alignment.

Link/Coil Front Suspension

See Figures 201 and 202.

1. Before servicing the vehicle, refer to the Precautions Section.
2. Remove the steering knuckle.
3. Remove the axle shaft from the axle.
4. Position special tool 6761 (RECEIVER) (2) and 8445-3 (DRIVER) (4) with C-4212-F (PRESS)(1) as shown to remove upper ball stud.

To install:

5. Position special tool 8445-2 (DRIVER) (2) and 8975-5 (RECEIVER) (5) with C-42121-F (PRESS)(1) as shown to install upper ball stud (3).
6. Install the axle shaft into the axle.
7. Install the steering knuckle.

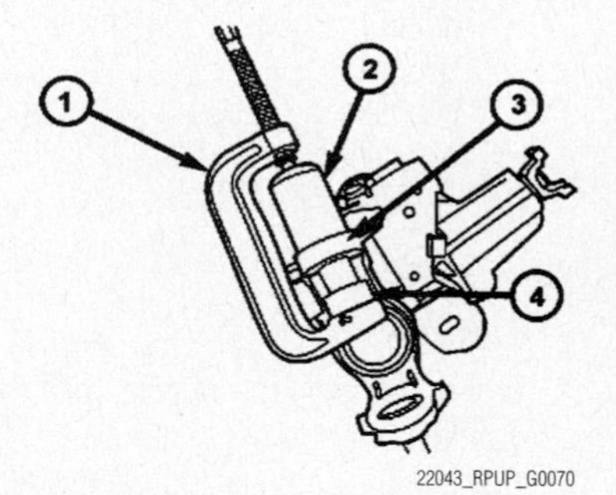

Fig. 201 Upper ball joint removal with special tools

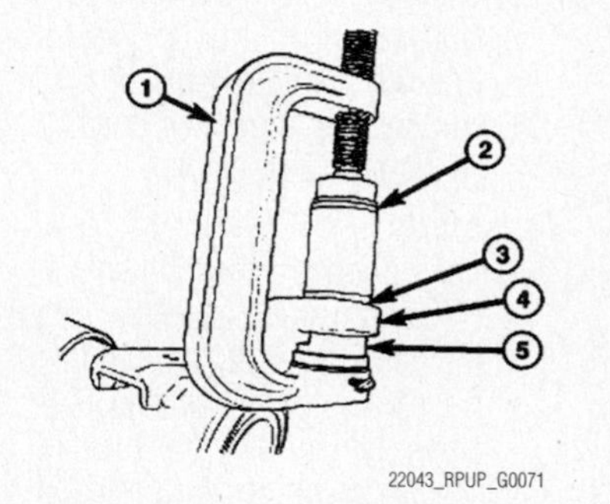

Fig. 202 Upper ball joint Installation with special tools

UPPER CONTROL ARM

REMOVAL & INSTALLATION

Independent Front Suspension

1. Before servicing the vehicle, refer to the Precautions Section.
2. Support the lower control arm.
3. Remove or disconnect the following:
   - Front wheel
   - Upper ball joint
   - Pivot mounting nuts
   - Upper control arm

To install:

4. Install or connect the following:
   - Upper control arm. Tighten the pivot nuts to 97 ft. lbs. (132 Nm) for LD; 125 ft. lbs. (170 Nm) HD 2X4
   - Upper ball joint. Tighten the nut to 40 ft. lbs. (54 Nm). On 1500 series, turn the nut an additional 90 degrees.
   - Front wheel

Link/Coil Suspension

Left Side

1. Before servicing the vehicle, refer to the Precautions Section.
2. Support the lower control arm.
3. Remove or disconnect the following:
   - Front wheel
   - Nut and bolt at the axle bracket
   - Nut and bolt at the frame rail
   - Upper control arm

To install:

4. Position the control arm and install all fasteners finger-tight.
5. Install the front wheel. And lower the vehicle to load the suspension. Tighten all fasteners to 120 ft. lbs. (163 Nm).

Right Side

1. Before servicing the vehicle, refer to the Precautions Section.
2. Support the lower control arm.
3. Remove or disconnect the following:
   - Front wheel
   - Exhaust system at the manifolds
   - Exhaust mounts at the muffler

4. Support the transmission
5. Remove or disconnect the following:
   - Transmission crossmember
   - Nut and bolt at the axle bracket
   - Nut and bolt at the frame rail
   - Upper control arm

To install:

6. Position the control arm and install all fasteners finger-tight.
7. Install the exhaust system and crossmember.
8. Install the front wheel. And lower the vehicle to load the suspension. Tighten all fasteners to 120 ft. lbs. (163 Nm).

CONTROL ARM BUSHING REPLACEMENT

Independent Front Suspension

See Figure 203.

1. Before servicing the vehicle, refer to the Precautions Section.
2. Remove the upper control arm.
3. Secure the control arm in a soft jaw vise.
4. Remove the bushing (3) from the upper control arm (5) using special tool C–4212F (PRESS) (1), 9777-3 (receiver) (4), and 9601-1 (driver) (2). (For 4X4 models use driver 9777-2).

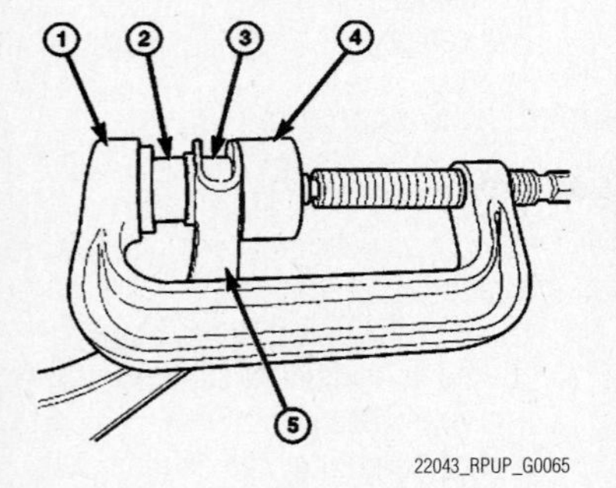

Fig. 203 Upper control arm removal, tool with adapters shown

To install:

5. Using special tools install upper control arm bushings.
6. Remove the control arm from the vise.
7. Install the lower control arm.
8. Perform a wheel alignment.

WHEEL BEARINGS

REMOVAL & INSTALLATION

Independent Front Suspension

2WD

See Figure 204.

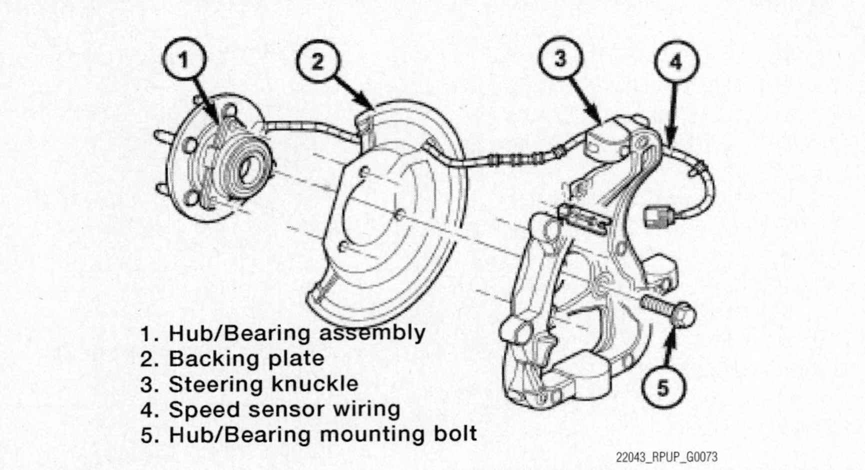

Fig. 204 Hub/bearing and related parts

1. Before servicing the vehicle, refer to the Precautions Section.
2. Remove or disconnect the following:
   - Front wheel
   - Brake caliper and rotor
   - Wheel speed sensor
   - Hub/bearing mounting bolts
   - Hub/bearing assembly

To install:

3. Install or connect the following:
   - Hub and bearing assembly. Tighten the bolts to 120 ft. lbs. (163 Nm).
   - Wheel speed sensor
   - Brake caliper and rotor
   - Front wheel

4WD

See Figure 205.

1. Before servicing the vehicle, refer to the Precautions Section.
2. Remove or disconnect the following:
   - Front wheel
   - Brake caliper and rotor
   - Wheel speed sensor
   - Halfshaft nut
   - Tie rod end from the knuckle
   - Upper ball joint from the knuckle
   - Knuckle from the halfshaft
   - Hub/bearing mounting bolts
   - Hub/bearing assembly

To install:

3. Install or connect the following:
   - Hub and bearing assembly. Tighten the bolts to 120 ft. lbs. (163 Nm).
   - Knuckle onto the halfshaft
   - Upper ball joint on the knuckle. Torque the nut to 40 ft. lbs. (54 Nm) (on 1500 series, plus 90 degrees).
   - Tie rod end to the knuckle. Tighten the nut to 45 ft. lbs. (61 Nm) plus 90 degrees.
   - Halfshaft nut. Torque to 185 ft. lbs. (251 Nm).
   - Wheel speed sensor
   - Brake caliper and rotor
   - Front wheel

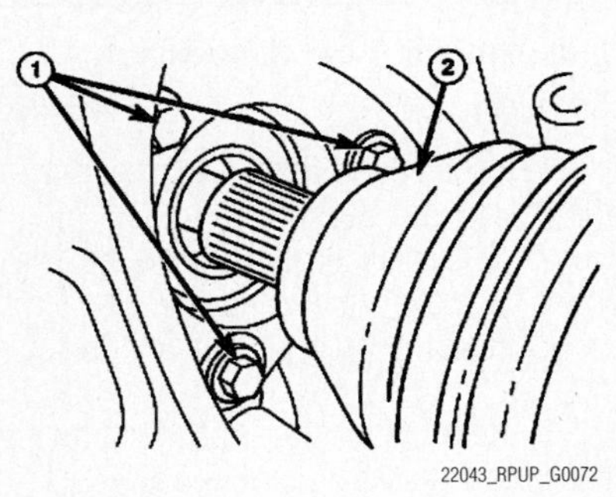

Fig. 205 Hub/bearing (1), mounting bolts (2)

Link/Coil Suspension

See Figure 206.

1. Before servicing the vehicle, refer to the Precautions Section.
2. Remove or disconnect the following:
   - Front wheel
   - Hub extension from the rotor, if equipped
   - Brake caliper and rotor
   - Hub nut
   - Wheel speed sensor wiring
   - Hub/bearing mounting bolts ¼ each. Then, tap the bolts with a mallet to loosen the hub/bearing assembly.
   - Hub/bearing assembly, wheel studs/extension studs, rotor, shield and spacer
   - Wheel speed sensor

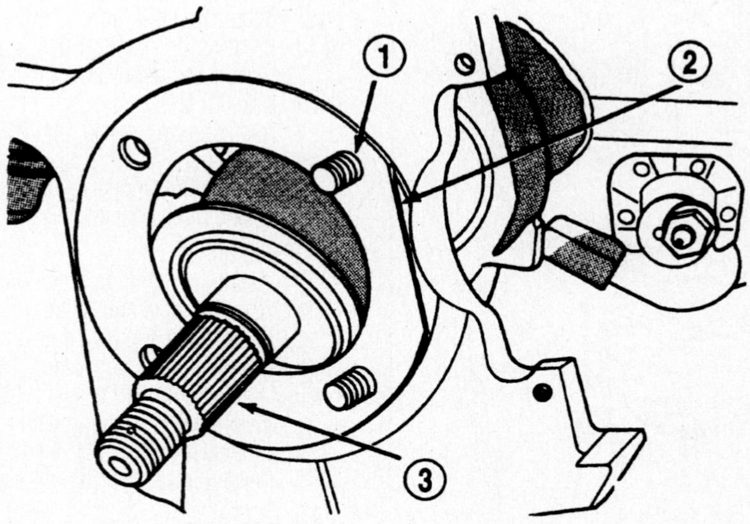

Fig. 206 Hub bolt positioning

To install:

3. Install or connect the following:
   - Wheel speed sensor
   - Rotor on the hub/bearing
   - Studs
4. Apply a liberal amount of anti-seize compound on the splines of the front shaft.
5. Insert the 2 rearmost, top and bottom rotor hub bolts in the knuckle, so they extend from the front face as shown.
6. Install or connect the following:
   - Spacer and shield
   - Hub assembly onto the shaft
7. Align the bolt holes in the flange with the installed bolts. Thread the bolts onto the flange far enough to hold the unit in place.
8. Install the remaining bolts. Tighten all hub/bearing bolts to 149 ft. lbs. (202 Nm).
9. Install the washer and shaft nut. Tighten the nut to 132 ft. lbs. (179 Nm). Rotate the axle 5 to 10 times to seat the bearings. Tighten the nut to 263 ft. lbs. (356 Nm). Install a new cotter pin, advancing the nut for alignment.
10. The remainder of installation is the reverse of removal.

ADJUSTMENT

These are unitized hub/bearing assemblies. No adjustment is possible.

SUSPENSION

REAR SUSPENSION

LEAF SPRING

REMOVAL & INSTALLATION

1. Before servicing the vehicle, refer to the Precautions Section.
2. Raise and support the vehicle.
3. Support the axle with a suitable holding fixture.
4. Remove the nuts, spring clamp bolts and the plate that attach the spring to the axle.
5. Remove the nuts and bolts from the spring front and rear shackle.
6. Remove the spring from the vehicle.

To install:

7. Position spring on axle shaft tube so spring center bolt is inserted into the locating hole in the axle tube.
8. Align the front of the spring with the bolt hole in the front bracket. Install the eye pivot bolt and nut.
9. Align the rear of the spring into the shackle and install the bolt and nut.
10. Tighten the spring front and rear eye pivot bolt snug, Do not torque.
11. Install the spring clamp bolts, plate and the retaining nuts.
12. Remove the holding fixture for the rear axle.
13. Remove the supports and lower the vehicle so that the weight is being supported by the tires.
14. Tighten the spring clamp retaining nuts to 110 ft. lbs. (149 Nm).
15. Tighten the spring front and rear pivot bolt nuts to 120 ft. lbs. (163 Nm) for light duty or 170 ft. lbs. (230 Nm) for heavy duty models.

SHOCK ABSORBER

REMOVAL & INSTALLATION

See Figure 207.

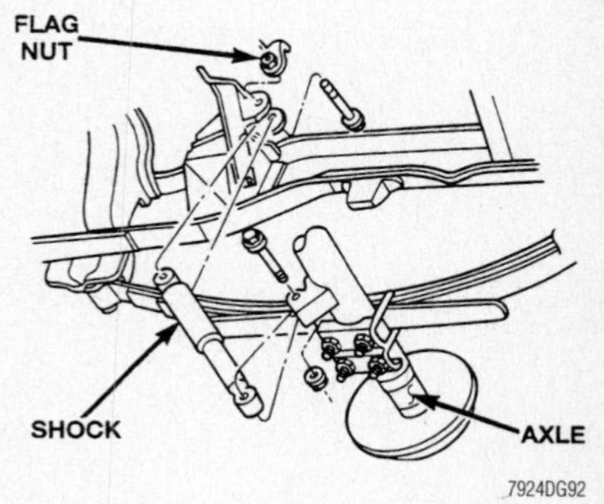

Fig. 207 Rear shock absorber mounting—Ram Trucks

1. Before servicing the vehicle, refer to the Precautions Section.
2. Support the axle.
3. Remove or disconnect the following:
   - Upper bolt
   - Lower bolt
   - Shock absorber

To install:

4. Install the bolts through the brackets and shock and tighten them as follows:
   - Tighten the upper and lower bolt 100 ft. lbs. (135 Nm)

STABILIZER BAR

REMOVAL & INSTALLATION

See Figure 208.

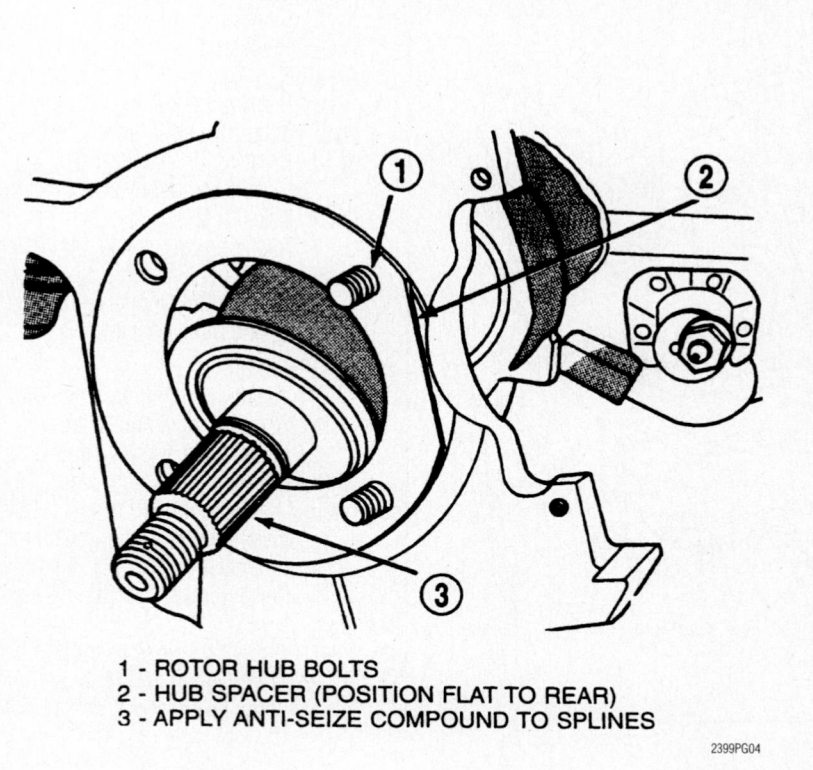

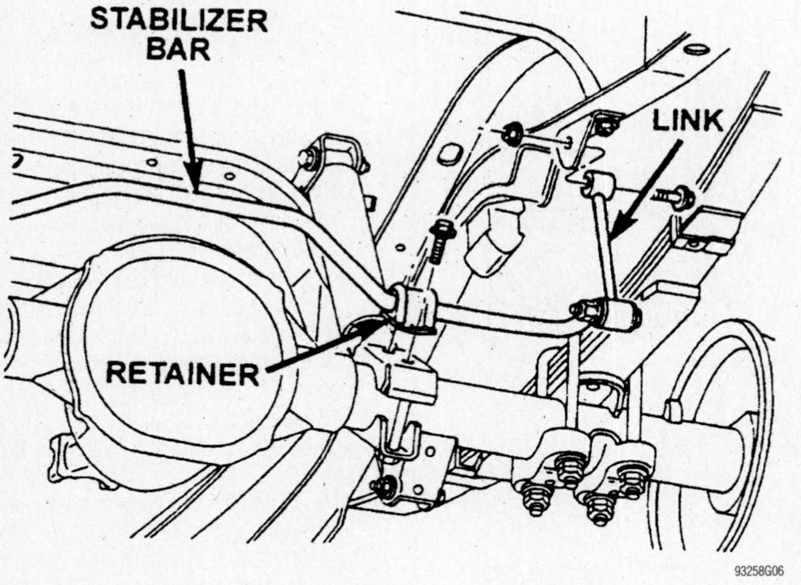

Fig. 208 Stabilizer bar mounting—typical

1. Raise and support the vehicle.
2. Remove the hardware bolting the links to the stabilizer bar. Separate the links with Puller C-3894-A, or equivalent.
3. Remove the hardware bolting the stabilizer bar retainers to the axle.
4. Remove the stabilizer bar.
5. Unbolt and remove the links from the frame, if desired.
6. Replace worn, cracked or distorted bushings.
7. Remove links upper mounting nuts and bolts and remove links.

To install:

8. Install link into frame brackets and install mounting nuts and bolts.
9. Install the stabilizer bar and center it with equal spacing on both sides. Tighten retainer hardware to 100 ft. lbs. (135 Nm).
10. Install the links and tighten the hardware on frame and at the bar hand tight.
11. Lower the vehicle onto the suspension.
12. Tighten the links as follows:
    - Link upper: 100 ft. lbs. (135 Nm)
    - Link lower: 100 ft. lbs. (135 Nm)

CHRYSLER AND DODGE

14

Sebring • Stratus

SPECIFICATIONS AND MAINTENANCE CHARTS

ENGINE AND VEHICLE IDENTIFICATION

Engine						
Code ①	Liters	Cu. In.	Cyl.	Fuel Sys.	Engine Type	Eng. Mfg.
C	2.0	122	I4	MFI	SOHC	Chrysler
H	2.5	152	V6	MFI	SOHC	Mitsubishi
X	2.4	143	I4	MFI	DOHC	Chrysler
U	2.7	167	V6	MFI	DOHC	Chrysler
S	2.4	148	I4	MFI	DOHC	Chrysler
R	2.7	167	V6	MFI	DOHC	Chrysler
J (PZEV)	2.4	148	I4	MFI	DOHC	DaimlerChrysler

Model Year	
Code ②	Year
5	2005
6	2006

MFI: Multi-point Fuel Injection

SOHC: Single Overhead Camshaft

DOHC: Double Overhead Camshaft

PZEV: Partially Zero Emissions Vehicle (California)

① 8th position of VIN

② 10th position of VIN

22043_SEBR_C0001

GENERAL ENGINE SPECIFICATIONS

All measurements are given in inches.

Year	Model	Engine Displacement Liters	Engine Series (ID/VIN)	Fuel System	Net Horsepower @ rpm	Net Torque @ rpm (ft. lbs.)	Bore x Stroke (in.)	Com-pression Ratio	Oil Pressure @ rpm
2005	Sebring Convertible	2.4	S, J	MFI	150@5200	167@4000	3.44x3.98	9.4:1	25-80@3000
	Sebring Convertible	2.7	R	MFI	200@5800	190@4850	3.38x3.09	9.7:1	45-105@3000
	Sebring Sedan	2.4	S	MFI	150@5200	167@4000	3.44x3.98	9.4:1	25-80@3000
	Sebring Sedan	2.7	R	MFI	200@5900	192@4300	3.39x3.09	9.7:1	45-105@3000
	Stratus Sedan	2.4	S	MFI	150@5200	167@4000	3.44x3.98	9.4:1	25-80@3000
	Stratus Sedan	2.7	R	MFI	200@5900	192@4300	3.39x3.09	9.7:1	45-105@3000
2006	Sebring Convertible	2.4	S	MFI	150@5200	167@4000	3.44x3.98	9.4:1	25-80@3000
	Sebring Convertible	2.7	R	MFI	200@5800	190@4850	3.38x3.09	9.7:1	45-105@3000
	Sebring Sedan	2.4	S	MFI	150@5200	167@4000	3.44x3.98	9.4:1	25-80@3000
	Sebring Sedan	2.7	R	MFI	200@5900	192@4300	3.39x3.09	9.7:1	45-105@3000
	Stratus Sedan	2.4	S	MFI	150@5200	167@4000	3.44x3.98	9.4:1	25-80@3000
	Stratus Sedan	2.7	R	MFI	200@5900	192@4300	3.39x3.09	9.7:1	45-105@3000

MFI: Multi-point Fuel Injection

22043_SEBR_C0002

GASOLINE ENGINE TUNE-UP SPECIFICATIONS

Year	Engine Displacement Liters	Engine ID/VIN	Spark Plug Gap (in.)	Ignition Timing (deg.)		Fuel Pump (psi) ①	Idle Speed (rpm)		Valve Clearance	
				MT	AT		MT	AT	In.	Ex.
2005	2.4	S, J	0.048-0.053	—	①	58	②	②	HYD	HYD
	2.7	R	0.048-0.053	①	①	58	②	②	HYD	HYD
2006	2.4	S	0.048-0.053	—	①	58	②	②	HYD	HYD
	2.7	R	0.048-0.053	①	①	58	②	②	HYD	HYD

NOTE: The Vehicle Emission Control Information label often reflects specification changes made during production.

The label figures must be used if they differ from those in this chart.

HYD: Hydraulic

① Ignition timing cannot be adjusted. Base engine timing is set at TDC during assembly.

② Refer to the Vehicle Emission Control Information label for correct specifications.

22043_SEBR_C0003

CAPACITIES

Year	Model	Engine Displacement Liters	Engine ID/VIN	Engine Oil with Filter (qts.)	Transmission (pts.) 5-Spd	Transmission (pts.) Auto.	Fuel Tank (gal.)	Cooling System (qts.)
2005	Sebring Convertible	2.4	S, J	5.0	—	8.0 ①	16.0	8.0
	Sebring Convertible	2.7	R	5.0	—	8.0 ①	16.0	9.5
	Sebring Sedan	2.4	S, J	5.0	—	8.0 ①	16.0	8.0
	Sebring Sedan	2.7	R	5.0	—	8.0 ①	16.0	9.5
	Stratus Sedan	2.4	S, J	5.0	—	8.0 ①	16.0	8.0
	Stratus Sedan	2.7	R	5.0	5.0-5.6	8.0 ①	16.0	9.5
2006	Sebring Convertible	2.4	S	5.0	—	8.0 ①	16.0	8.0
	Sebring Convertible	2.7	R	5.0	—	8.0 ①	16.0	9.5
	Sebring Sedan	2.4	S	5.0	—	8.0 ①	16.0	8.0
	Sebring Sedan	2.7	R	5.0	—	8.0 ①	16.0	9.5
	Stratus Sedan	2.4	S	5.0	—	8.0 ①	16.0	8.0
	Stratus Sedan	2.7	R	5.0	5.0-5.6	8.0 ①	16.0	9.5

NOTE: All capacities are approximate. Add fluid gradually and ensure a proper fluid level is obtained.

① Overhaul fill capacity with torque converter empty: 18.4 pts.

22043_SEBR_C0004

FLUID SPECIFICATIONS

Year	Model	Engine Displacement Liters	Engine ID/VIN	Engine Oil	Auto. Trans.	Manual Trans.	Power Steering Fluid	Brake Master Cylinder
2005	Sebring Convertible	2.4	S, J	5W-30	①	—	②	③
	Sebring Convertible	2.7	R	5W-30	①	—	②	③
	Sebring Sedan	2.4	S, J	5W-30	①	—	②	③
	Sebring Sedan	2.7	R	5W-30	①	—	②	③
	Stratus Sedan	2.4	S, J	5W-30	①	—	②	③
	Stratus Sedan	2.7	R	5W-30	①	—	②	③
2006	Sebring Convertible	2.4	S	5W-30	①	—	②	③
	Sebring Convertible	2.7	R	5W-30	①	—	②	③
	Sebring Sedan	2.4	S	5W-30	①	—	②	③
	Sebring Sedan	2.7	R	5W-30	①	—	②	③
	Stratus Sedan	2.4	S	5W-30	①	—	②	③
	Stratus Sedan	2.7	R	5W-30	①	—	②	③

DOT: Department Of Transportation

① Mopar® ATF+4 Automatic Transmission Fluid or equivalent.

② Mopar® Power Steering Fluid+4, Mopar® ATF+4 Automatic Transmission Fluid or equivalent.

③ Mopar® DOT 3, SAE J1703 should be used. If DOT 3, SAE J1703 brake fluid is not available, then DOT 4 is acceptable. Use only recommended brake fluids.

22043_SEBR_C0005

VALVE SPECIFICATIONS

Year	Engine Displacement Liters	Engine ID/VIN	Seat Angle (deg.)	Face Angle (deg.)	Spring Test Pressure (lbs. @ in.)	Spring Installed Height (in.)	Stem-to-Guide Clearance (in.) Intake	Stem-to-Guide Clearance (in.) Exhaust	Stem Diameter (in.) Intake	Stem Diameter (in.) Exhaust
2005	2.4	S, J	45	44.5-45	76@1.50	1.496	0.0018-0.0025	0.0029-0.0037	0.2337-0.2344	0.2326-0.2333
	2.7	R	44.5-45	44.5-45.5	148@1.14	1.496	0.0009-0.0026	0.0020-0.0037	0.2337-0.2344	0.2326-0.2333
2006	2.4	S	45	44.5-45	76@1.50	1.496	0.0018-0.0025	0.0029-0.0037	0.2337-0.2344	0.2326-0.2333
	2.7	R	44.5-45	44.5-45.5	148@1.14	1.496	0.0009-0.0026	0.0020-0.0037	0.2337-0.2344	0.2326-0.2333

22043_SEBR_C0006

CAMSHAFT AND BEARING SPECIFICATIONS CHART

All measurements are given in inches.

Year	Engine Displ. Liters	Engine ID/VIN	Journal Dia.	Brg. Oil Clearance	Shaft End-play	Runout	Journal Bore	Lobe Height Intake	Lobe Height Exhaust
2005	2.4	S, J	1.0220-1.0230	0.0009-0.0025	0.0019-0.0066	NA	NA	NA	NA
	2.7	R	0.9449-0.9441	0.0020-0.0035	0.0051-0.0110	NA	NA	NA	NA
2006	2.4	S	1.0220-1.0230	0.0009-0.0025	0.0019-0.0066	NA	NA	NA	NA
	2.7	R	0.9449-0.9441	0.0020-0.0035	0.0051-0.0110	NA	NA	NA	NA

NA: Not Available

22043_SEBR_C0007

CRANKSHAFT AND CONNECTING ROD SPECIFICATIONS

All measurements are given in inches.

Year	Engine Displacement Liters	Engine ID/VIN	Crankshaft Main Brg. Journal Dia.	Crankshaft Main Brg. Oil Clearance	Crankshaft Shaft End-play	Crankshaft Thrust on No.	Connecting Rod Journal Diameter	Connecting Rod Oil Clearance	Connecting Rod Side Clearance
2005	2.4	S, J	2.3610-2.3625	0.0007-0.0023	0.0035-0.0094	3	1.9670-1.9685	0.0009-0.0027	0.0051-0.0150
	2.7	R	2.4997-2.5004	0.0014-0.0021	0.017 max.	3	2.1067-2.1060	0.0010-0.0026	0.0052-0.0150
2006	2.4	S	2.3610-2.3625	0.0007-0.0023	0.0035-0.0094	3	1.9670-1.9685	0.0009-0.0027	0.0051-0.0150
	2.7	R	2.4997-2.5004	0.0014-0.0021	0.017 max.	3	2.1067-2.1060	0.0010-0.0026	0.0052-0.0150

22043_SEBR_C0008

PISTON AND RING SPECIFICATIONS

All measurements are given in inches.

				Ring Gap			Ring Side Clearance		
Year	Engine Displacement Liters	Engine ID/VIN	Piston Clearance	Top Compression	Bottom Compression	Oil Control	Top Compression	Bottom Compression	Oil Control
2005	2.4	S, J	0.0009-0.0022 ①	0.010-0.020	0.009-0.018	0.010-0.025	0.0011-0.0031	0.0011-0.0031	0.0004-0.0070
	2.7	R	0.0003-0.0016	0.008-0.014	0.0146-0.0249	0.010-0.030	0.0013-0.0032	0.0016-0.0031	0.0022-0.0080
2006	2.4	S	0.0009-0.0022 ①	0.010-0.020	0.009-0.018	0.010-0.025	0.0011-0.0031	0.0011-0.0031	0.0004-0.0070
	2.7	R	0.0003-0.0016	0.008-0.014	0.0146-0.0249	0.010-0.030	0.0013-0.0032	0.0016-0.0031	0.0022-0.0080

① Clearance at 9/16 inch from bottom of skirt

22043_SEBR_C0009

TORQUE SPECIFICATIONS

All readings in ft. lbs.

								Manifold			
Year	Engine Displacement Liters	Engine ID/VIN	Cylinder Head Bolts	Main Bearing Bolts	Rod Bearing Bolts	Crankshaft Damper Bolts	Flywheel Bolts	Intake	Exhaust	Spark Plug	Oil Pan Drain Plug
2005	2.4	S, J	①	②	③	100	70	21	17	13	20
	2.7	R	④	⑤	③	125	—	9	17	15	20
2006	2.4	S	①	②	③	100	70	21	17	13	20
	2.7	R	④	⑤	③	125	—	9	17	15	20

① Main cap inside bolts: 15 ft. lbs. Plus 1/4 turn
Main cap outside bolts: 20 ft. lbs. Plus 1/4 turn
Main cap tie bolts: 21 ft. lbs.

② Step 1: 30 ft. lbs
Step 2: Plus 1/4 turn

③ Step 1: 20 ft. lbs.
Step 2: Plus 1/4 turn

④ M8 bolts: 21 ft. lbs.
M11 bolts: 30 ft. lbs. Plus 1/4 turn

⑤ Step 1: 35 ft. lbs.
Step 2: 55 ft. lbs.
Step 3: 55 ft. lbs.
Step 4: Plus 1/4 turn
Step 5: 21 ft. lbs.

22043_SEBR_C0010

WHEEL ALIGNMENT

			Caster		Camber		
Year	Model		Range (+/-Deg.)	Preferred Setting (Deg.)	Range (+/-Deg.)	Preferred Setting (Deg.)	Toe-in (in.)
2005	All	F	1.00	+3.31	-0.9 to +0.3	-0.30	0.12 +/- 0.10
		R	—	—	0.50	-0.50	0.06 +/- 0.10
2006	All	F	1.00	+3.31	-0.9 to +0.3	-0.30	0.12 +/- 0.10
		R	—	—	0.50	-0.50	0.06 +/- 0.10

22043_SEBR_C0011

TIRE, WHEEL AND BALL JOINT SPECIFICATIONS

Year	Model	OEM Tires Standard	OEM Tires Optional	Tire Pressures (psi) Front	Tire Pressures (psi) Rear	Wheel Size	Ball Joint Inspection	Lug Nut Torque (ft. lbs.)
2005	Sebring Convertible	P205/65R15	P205/60R16	①	①	6.5	②	100
	Sebring Sedan	P205/60R16	none	①	①	6.5	②	100
	Stratus SXT Sedan	P205/60R16	none	①	①	6.5	②	100
	Stratus R/T Sedan	P215/50R17	none	①	①	7.0	②	100
2006	Sebring Convertible	P205/65R15	P205/60R16	①	①	6.5	②	100
	Sebring Sedan	P205/60R16	none	①	①	6.5	②	100
	Stratus SXT Sedan	P205/60R16	none	①	①	6.5	②	100
	Stratus R/T Sedan	P215/50R17	none	①	①	7.0	②	100

OEM: Original Equipment Manufacturer

PSI: Pounds Per Square Inch

① See placard on vehicle

② Lower: 1.5mm movement max.
Upper: Replace if any slack movement is noted

22043_SEBR_C0012

BRAKE SPECIFICATIONS

All measurements in inches unless noted

Year	Model		Brake Disc Original Thickness	Brake Disc Minimum Thickness	Brake Disc Maximum Run-out	Brake Drum Diameter Original Inside Diameter	Brake Drum Diameter Max. Wear Limit	Brake Drum Diameter Maximum Machine Diameter	Minimum Lining Thickness	Brake Caliper Guide Pin Bolts (ft. lbs.)
2005	Sebring Convertible	F	0.911	0.843	0.003	—	—	—	NA	26
		R	0.360	0.285	0.005	NA	①	①	NA	16
	Sebring Sedan	F	0.911	0.843	0.003	—	—	—	NA	26
		R	0.360	0.285	0.005	NA	①	①	NA	16
	Stratus Sedan	F	0.911	0.843	0.003	—	—	—	NA	26
		R	0.360	0.285	0.005	NA	①	①	NA	16
2006	Sebring Convertible	F	0.911	0.843	0.003	—	—	—	NA	26
		R	0.360	0.285	0.005	NA	①	①	NA	16
	Sebring Sedan	F	0.911	0.843	0.003	—	—	—	NA	26
		R	0.360	0.285	0.005	NA	①	①	NA	16
	Stratus Sedan	F	0.911	0.843	0.003	—	—	—	NA	26
		R	0.360	0.285	0.005	NA	①	①	NA	16

NA: Not Available

① Disc brake lining and backing total thickness: 9/32 inch
Drum brake shoe lining and backing total thickness: 1/8 inch

22043_SEBR_C0013

SCHEDULED MAINTENANCE INTERVALS

Chrysler Sebring, Dodge Stratus

TO BE SERVICED	TYPE OF SERVICE	VEHICLE MILEAGE INTERVAL (x1000)												
		7.5	15	22.5	30	37.5	45	52.5	60	67.5	75	82.5	90	97.5
Engine oil & filter	R	✓	✓	✓	✓	✓	✓	✓	✓	✓	✓	✓	✓	✓
Brake hoses	S/I	✓	✓	✓	✓	✓	✓	✓	✓	✓	✓	✓	✓	✓
Coolant level, hoses & clamps	S/I	✓	✓	✓	✓	✓	✓	✓	✓	✓	✓	✓	✓	✓
CV joints & front suspension components	S/I	✓	✓	✓	✓	✓	✓	✓	✓	✓	✓	✓	✓	✓
Exhaust system	S/I	✓	✓	✓	✓	✓	✓	✓	✓	✓	✓	✓	✓	✓
Rotate tires	S/I	✓	✓	✓	✓	✓	✓	✓	✓	✓	✓	✓	✓	✓
Accessory drive belts	S/I		✓		✓		✓		✓		✓		✓	
Brake linings	S/I			✓			✓			✓			✓	
Air filter element	R				✓				✓				✓	
Spark plugs ① ②	R													
Lubricate front & rear ball joints	S/I				✓				✓				✓	
Engine coolant	R						✓				✓			
PCV valve	S/I								✓				✓	
Ignition cables ② ③	R													
Camshaft timing belt ④	R													

R: Replace   S/I: Service or Inspect

① 4-cylinder: every 30,000 miles.

② 6-cylinder: 100,000 miles.

③ 4-cylinder: 60,000 miles.

④ Replace at 105,000 miles for normal service; replace at 102,000 miles for severe service

FREQUENT OPERATION MAINTENANCE (SEVERE SERVICE)

If a vehicle is operated under any of the following conditions it is considered severe service:

- Extremely dusty areas.

- 50% or more of vehicle operatiing in 32°C (90°F) or higher temperatures, or constant operation in temperatures below 0°C (32°F).

- Prolonged idling (vehicle operation in stop and go traffic).

- Frequent short running periods (engine does not warm to normal operating temperatures).

- Police, taxi, delivery usage or trailer towing usage.

Oil & oil filter change: change every 3,000 miles.

Rotate tires every 6,000 miles.

Brake linings: check every 12,000 miles.

Air filter element: change every 15,000 miles.

Automatic transaxle fluid: service or inspect every 15,000 miles.

PCV valve: check every 30,000 miles.

Engine coolant, replace at 36,000, 51,000 & 81,000 miles.

22043_SEBR_C0014

PRECAUTIONS

Before servicing any vehicle, please be sure to read all of the following precautions, which deal with personal safety, prevention of component damage, and important points to take into consideration when servicing a motor vehicle:

- Never open, service or drain the radiator or cooling system when the engine is hot; serious burns can occur from the steam and hot coolant.
- Observe all applicable safety precautions when working around fuel. Whenever servicing the fuel system, always work in a well-ventilated area. Do not allow fuel spray or vapors to come in contact with a spark, open flame, or excessive heat (a hot drop light, for example). Keep a dry chemical fire extinguisher near the work area. Always keep fuel in a container specifically designed for fuel storage; also, always properly seal fuel containers to avoid the possibility of fire or explosion. Refer to the additional fuel system precautions later in this section.
- Fuel injection systems often remain pressurized, even after the engine has been turned **OFF**. The fuel system pressure must be relieved before disconnecting any fuel lines. Failure to do so may result in fire and/or personal injury.
- Brake fluid often contains polyglycol ethers and polyglycols. Avoid contact with the eyes and wash your hands thoroughly after handling brake fluid. If you do get brake fluid in your eyes, flush your eyes with clean, running water for 15 minutes. If eye irritation persists, or if you have taken brake fluid internally, IMMEDIATELY seek medical assistance.
- The EPA warns that prolonged contact with used engine oil may cause a number of skin disorders, including cancer. You should make every effort to minimize your exposure to used engine oil. Protective gloves should be worn when changing oil. Wash your hands and any other exposed skin areas as soon as possible after exposure to used engine oil. Soap and water, or waterless hand cleaner should be used.
- All new vehicles are now equipped with an air bag system, often referred to as a Supplemental Restraint System (SRS) or Supplemental Inflatable Restraint (SIR) system. The system must be disabled before performing service on or around system components, steering column, instrument panel components, wiring and sensors. Failure to follow safety and disabling procedures could result in accidental air bag deployment, possible personal injury and unnecessary system repairs.
- Always wear safety goggles when working with, or around, the air bag system. When carrying a non-deployed air bag, be sure the bag and trim cover are pointed away from your body. When placing a non-deployed air bag on a work surface, always face the bag and trim cover upward, away from the surface. This will reduce the motion of the module if it is accidentally deployed. Refer to the additional air bag system precautions later in this section.
- Clean, high quality brake fluid from a sealed container is essential to the safe and proper operation of the brake system. You should always buy the correct type of brake fluid for your vehicle. If the brake fluid becomes contaminated, completely flush the system with new fluid. Never reuse any brake fluid. Any brake fluid that is removed from the system should be discarded. Also, do not allow any brake fluid to come in contact with a painted surface; it will damage the paint.
- Never operate the engine without the proper amount and type of engine oil; doing so WILL result in severe engine damage.
- Timing belt maintenance is extremely important. Many models utilize an interference-type, non-freewheeling engine. If the timing belt breaks, the valves in the cylinder head may strike the pistons, causing potentially serious (also time-consuming and expensive) engine damage. Refer to the maintenance interval charts for the recommended replacement interval for the timing belt, and to the timing belt section for belt replacement and inspection.
- Disconnecting the negative battery cable on some vehicles may interfere with the functions of the on-board computer system(s) and may require the computer to undergo a relearning process once the negative battery cable is reconnected.
- When servicing drum brakes, only disassemble and assemble one side at a time, leaving the remaining side intact for reference.
- Only an MVAC-trained, EPA-certified automotive technician should service the air conditioning system or its components.

BRAKES — ANTI-LOCK BRAKE SYSTEM (ABS)

GENERAL INFORMATION

PRECAUTIONS

- Certain components within the ABS system are not intended to be serviced or repaired individually.
- Do not use rubber hoses or other parts not specifically specified for and ABS system. When using repair kits, replace all parts included in the kit. Partial or incorrect repair may lead to functional problems and require the replacement of components.
- Lubricate rubber parts with clean, fresh brake fluid to ease assembly. Do not use shop air to clean parts; damage to rubber components may result.
- Use only DOT 3 brake fluid from an unopened container.
- If any hydraulic component or line is removed or replaced, it may be necessary to bleed the entire system.
- A clean repair area is essential. Always clean the reservoir and cap thoroughly before removing the cap. The slightest amount of dirt in the fluid may plug an orifice and impair the system function. Perform repairs after components have been thoroughly cleaned; use only denatured alcohol to clean components. Do not allow ABS components to come into contact with any substance containing mineral oil; this includes used shop rags.
- The Anti-Lock control unit is a microprocessor similar to other computer units in the vehicle. Ensure that the ignition switch is **OFF** before removing or installing controller harnesses. Avoid static electricity discharge at or near the controller.
- If any arc welding is to be done on the vehicle, the control unit should be unplugged before welding operations begin.

SPEED SENSORS

REMOVAL & INSTALLATION

Front

See Figures 1 through 8.

1. Before servicing the vehicle, refer to the Precautions Section.
2. Raise vehicle on jack stands or centered on a frame contact type hoist.
3. Remove the tire and wheel assembly from the vehicle.
4. Remove the speed sensor cable routing bracket from the steering knuckle. Remove the wiring harness sealing grommet

retainer and speed sensor routing bracket from the inner fender.

5. Remove the speed sensor sealing grommet from the inner fender.

6. Unplug the speed sensor cable from the vehicle wiring harness.

7. Remove the bolt attaching speed sensor to steering knuckle. Then remove speed sensor head from steering knuckle

⁂ WARNING

If speed sensor head locating pin has seized to the steering knuckle, do not attempt to remove speed sensor head by grasping with pliers and turning. This will damage the speed sensor head. Use only the following procedure.

8. If speed sensor head can not be removed from steering knuckle by hand, the locating pin on the speed sensor head has seized to the steering knuckle do to corrosion. Remove speed sensor head from steering knuckle using the following procedure. Remove disc brake caliper from steering knuckle, and remove brake rotor from hub/bearing assembly. Then insert a pin punch through hole in front steering knuckle and tap speed sensor head locating pin out of steering knuckle.

To install:

⁂ WARNING

Proper installation of wheel speed sensor cables is critical to continued system operation. Be sure that cables are installed in retainers. Failure to Install the cables in retainers as shown in this section may result in contact with moving parts and/or over extension of cables, resulting in an open circuit.

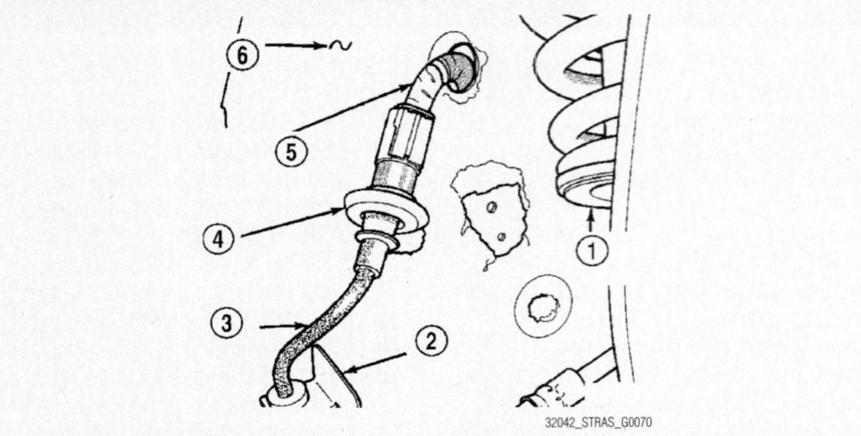

Fig. 2 Front shock absorber (1), grommet retaining bracket (2), wheel speed sensor cable (3), sealing grommet (4), vehicle wiring harness (5) and inner fender (6)

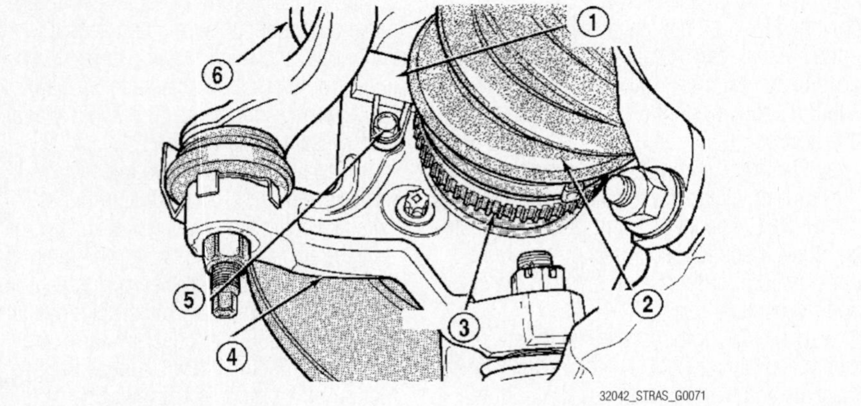

Fig. 3 Speed sensor head (1), drive axle (2), tone wheel (3), steering knuckle (4), bolt (5) and speed sensor cable (6)

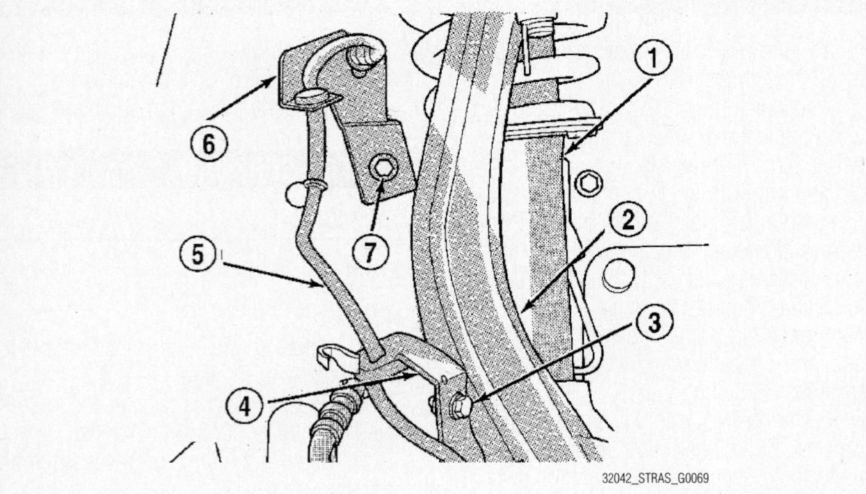

Fig. 1 Shock absorber (1), steering knuckle (2), bolt (3), speed sensor routing bracket (4), wheel speed sensor cable (5), grommet retainer and cable routing bracket (6) and bolt (7)

9. Connect the wheel speed sensor cable connector to the vehicle wiring harness.

10. Install the speed sensor cable assembly grommet into the front inner fender. Install the speed sensor cable grommet retainer/routing bracket on the inner fender of the vehicle and install the and securely tighten attaching bolt.

⁂ WARNING

When installing the wheel speed sensor cable routing bracket on the steering knuckle, the speed sensor cable must be looped toward the shock absorber as shown.

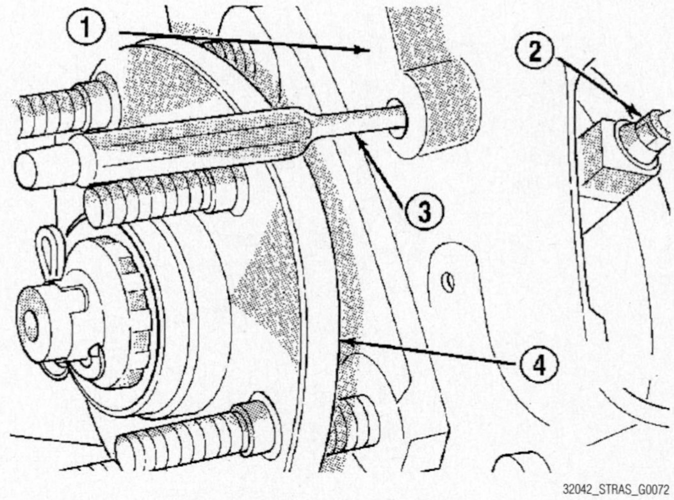

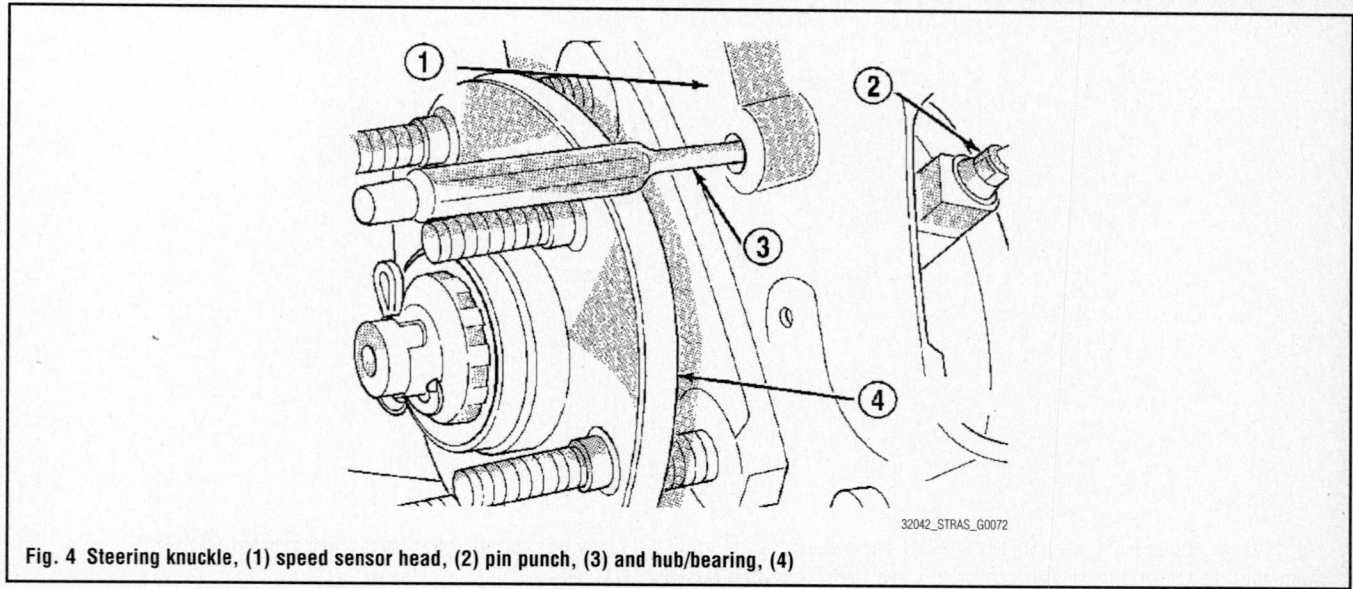

Fig. 4 Steering knuckle, (1) speed sensor head, (2) pin punch, (3) and hub/bearing, (4)

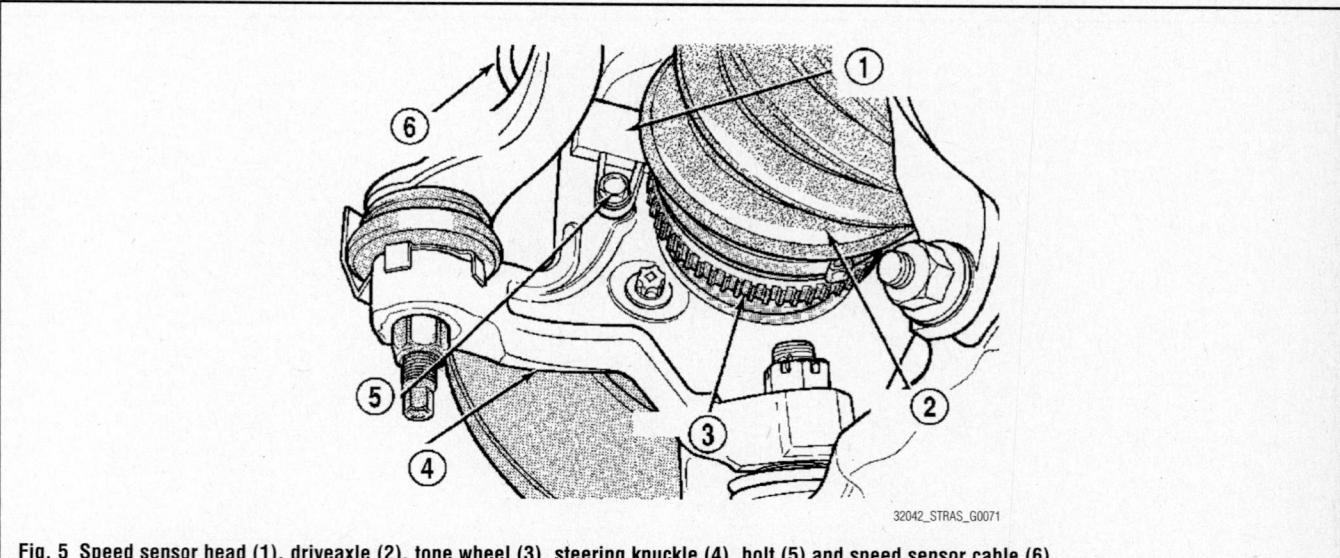

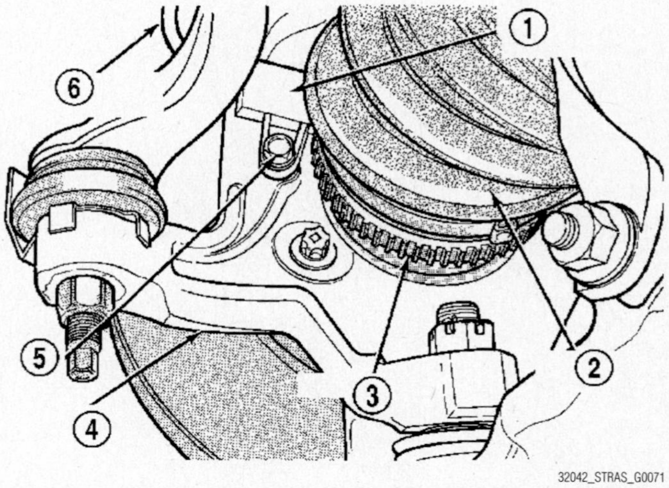

Fig. 5 Speed sensor head (1), driveaxle (2), tone wheel (3), steering knuckle (4), bolt (5) and speed sensor cable (6)

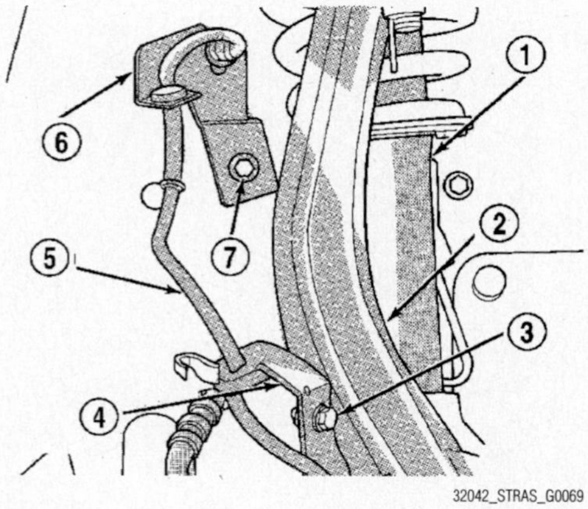

Fig. 6 Shock absorber (1), steering knuckle (2), bolt (3), speed sensor routing bracket (4), wheel speed sensor cable (5), grommet retainer and cable routing bracket (6) and bolt (7)

If speed sensor cable is not routed in this direction it will rub against the tire or wheel, damaging the speed sensor cable.

11. Install the speed sensor cable routing bracket on the steering knuckle. Install and tighten routing bracket mounting bolt to 105 inch lbs. (12 Nm)
12. Install the speed sensor head on steering knuckle. When installing speed sensor head on steering knuckle, apply a small amount of grease on speed sensor locating pin. Use MOPAR®, Multi-Purpose Grease, or equivalent, on speed sensor head locating pin. Install the speed sensor head attaching screw and tighten to 55 inch lbs. (6 Nm).
13. Install the wheel and tire assembly on vehicle.

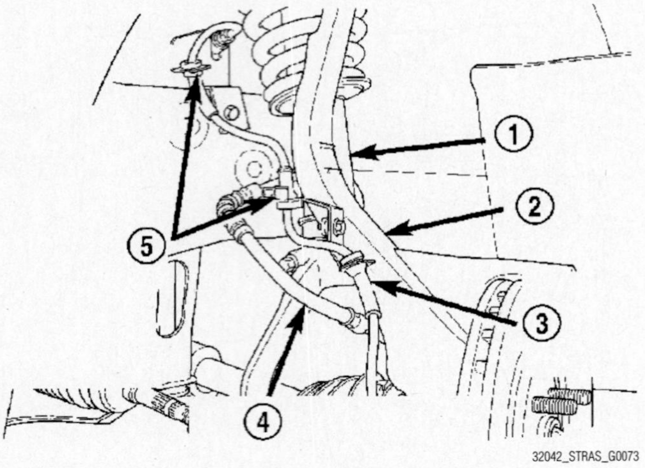

Fig. 7 Shock absorber (1), steering knuckle (2), wheel speed sensor cable (3), brake flex hose (4) and wheel speed sensor cable (5). Cable must be looped toward shock absorber between these routing brackets

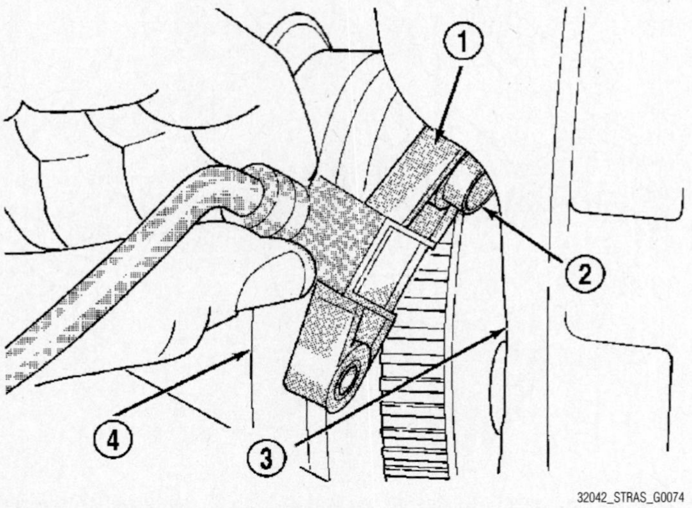

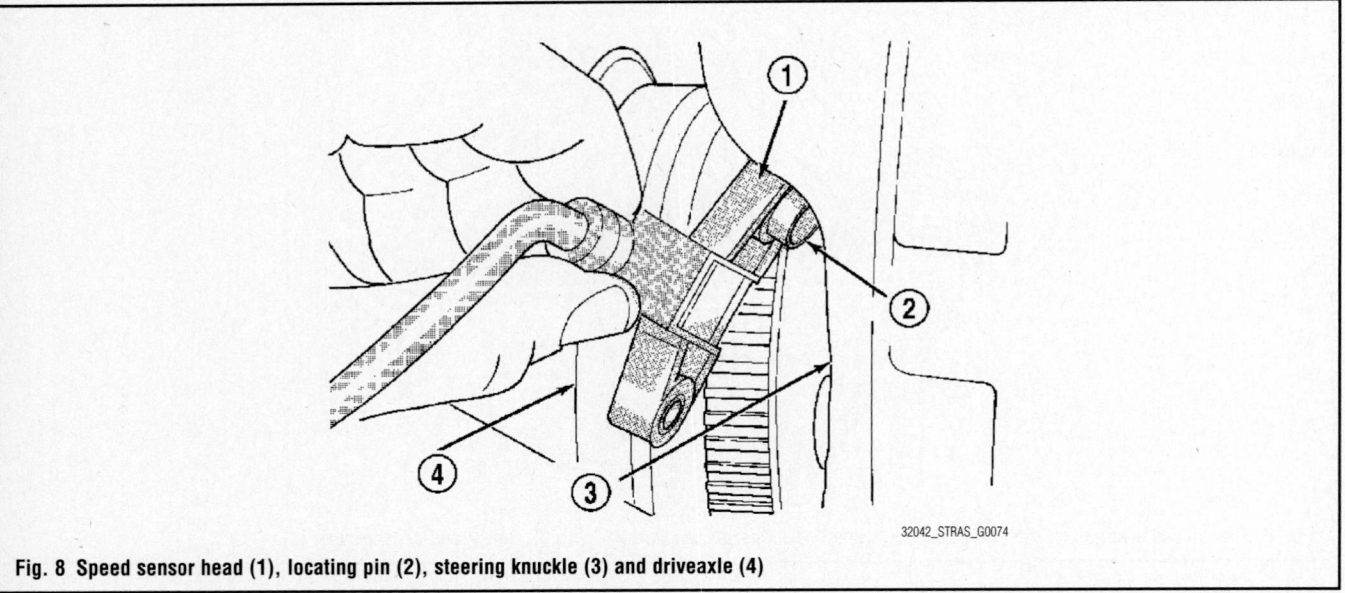

Fig. 8 Speed sensor head (1), locating pin (2), steering knuckle (3) and driveaxle (4)

14. Road test vehicle to ensure proper operation of the base and ABS systems.

Rear

JR27

See Figures 9 through 13.

1. Before servicing the vehicle, refer to the Precautions Section.
2. Remove the rear seat cushion and back.
3. Roll back the main silencer pad along the side to expose the wheel speed sensor harness connector located behind the wheel house silencer.
4. Pull the wheel speed sensor harness connector out from behind the wheel house

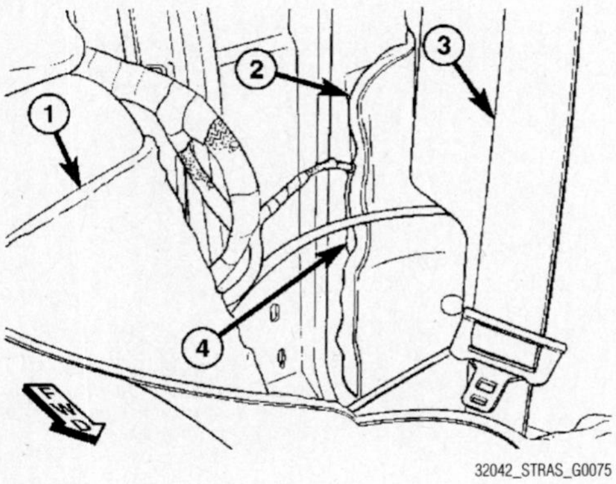

Fig. 9 Main silencer pad (1), wheel house silencer (2), seat belt (3) and sensor harness connector (4)

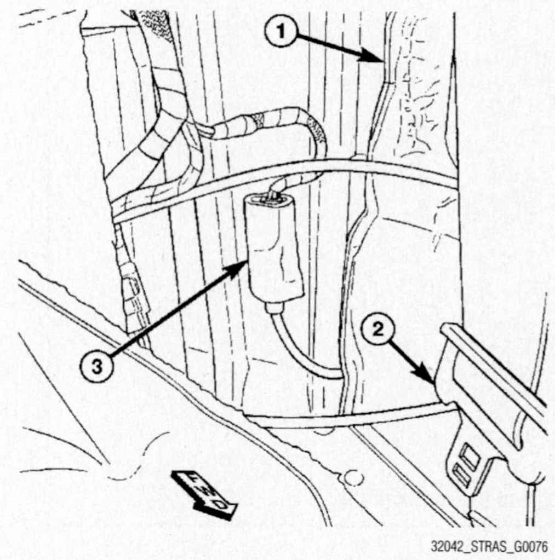

Fig. 10 Wheel house silencer (1), seat belt (2) and foam sleeve covered connector (3)

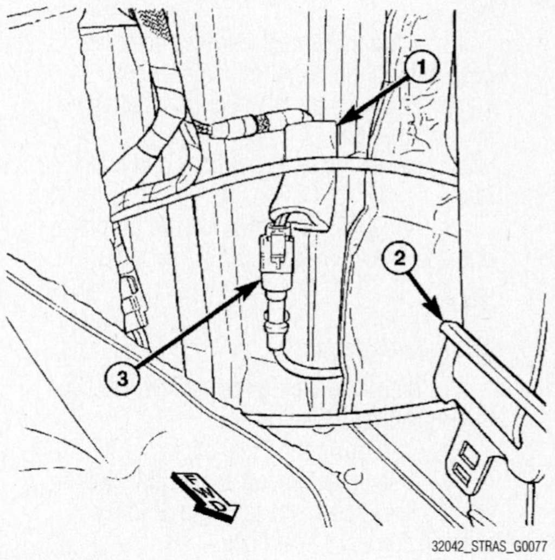

Fig. 11 Foam sleeve (1), seat belt (2) and connector (3)

silencer. It should have a foam sleeve covering it.

5. Push foam sleeve up off connector and disconnect speed sensor harness connector from vehicle wiring harness.
6. Raise vehicle.
7. Remove the speed sensor harness sealing grommet retainer from the rear frame rail of the vehicle.
8. Remove the speed sensor harness sealing grommet and harness from hole in body of vehicle.
9. Remove the speed sensor routing clips from the rear upper control arm.
10. Remove the bolt, then wheel speed sensor from vehicle.

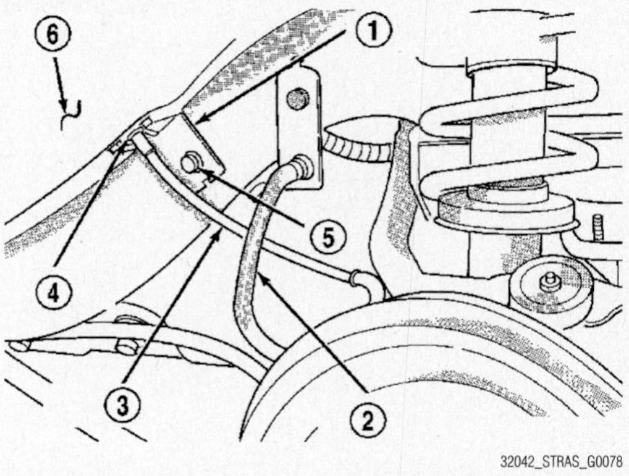

Fig. 12 Sealing grommet retainer (1), brake flex hose (2), speed sensor cable (3), sealing grommet (4), bolt (5) and rear inner fender (6)

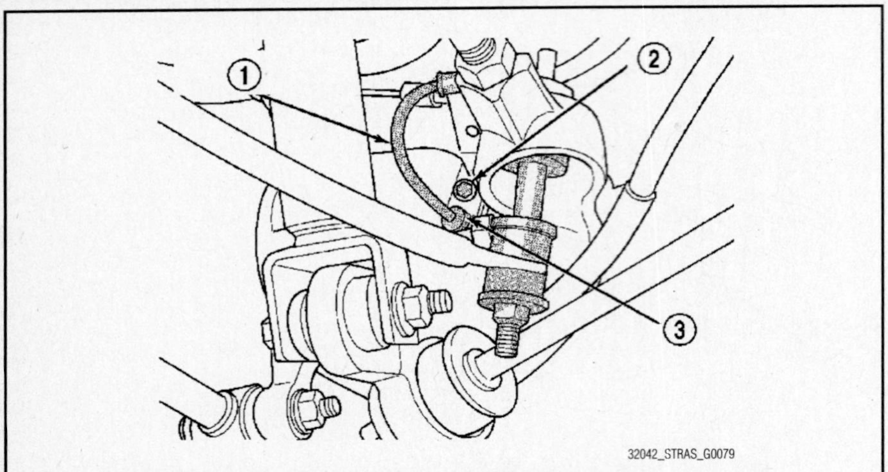

Fig. 13 Speed sensor cable (1), bolt (2) and speed sensor head (3)

To install:

WARNING

Proper installation of wheel speed sensor harness is critical to continued system operation. Be sure that harness is installed properly to avoid harness contact with moving parts or over-extension, resulting in an open circuit.

11. Install the speed sensor head into brake adapter. Install the bolt through routing clip and secure wheel speed sensor in place. Tighten bolt to 75 inch lbs. (8 Nm)
12. Install the speed sensor harness routing clip on upper control arm. Install and securely tighten the routing clip attaching bolt.
13. Install the connector end of speed sensor harness through hole at frame rail.
14. Install the speed sensor harness sealing grommet into hole. Install the sealing grommet retainer and attaching bolt. Securely tighten retainer attaching bolt.
15. Lower vehicle.
16. Connect speed sensor harness connector to vehicle wiring harness.
17. Install the foam sleeve back over the speed sensor harness connection to prevent rattling.
18. Slide the sensor harness connector back behind the wheel house silencer.
19. Lay the main silencer pad back into its normal place.
20. Install the rear seat back and cushion.
21. Road test vehicle to ensure proper operation of the base and ABS systems.

JR41

See Figures 12 and 13.

1. Before servicing the vehicle, refer to the Precautions Section.
2. Fold down rear seat back.
3. Disconnect speed sensor connector at vehicle wiring harness found at lower outside corner of seat back.
4. Raise vehicle.
5. Remove the rear tire and wheel assembly from vehicle.
6. Remove the speed sensor harness sealing grommet retainer from the rear frame rail of the vehicle.
7. Remove the speed sensor harness sealing grommet and harness from hole in body of vehicle.
8. Remove the speed sensor routing clips from the rear upper control arm.
9. Remove the bolt, then wheel speed sensor from vehicle.

To install:

WARNING

Proper installation of wheel speed sensor harness is critical to continued system operation. Be sure that harness is installed properly to avoid harness contact with moving parts or over-extension, resulting in an open circuit.

10. Install the speed sensor head into brake adapter. Install the bolt through routing clip and secure wheel speed sensor in place. Tighten bolt to 75 inch lbs. (8 Nm)
11. Install the speed sensor harness routing clip on upper control arm. Install and securely tighten the routing clip attaching bolt.
12. Install the connector end of speed sensor harness through hole at frame rail.
13. Install the speed sensor harness sealing grommet into hole. Install the sealing grommet retainer and attaching bolt. Securely tighten retainer attaching bolt.
14. Install the tire and wheel assembly on vehicle.
15. Lower vehicle.
16. Connect speed sensor harness connector to vehicle wiring harness behind rear seat back. Install the sleeve back over the speed sensor harness connection to prevent rattling.
17. Road test vehicle to ensure proper operation of the base and ABS systems.

BLEEDING PROCEDURE

BLEEDING PROCEDURE

✲✲ WARNING

Before removing the master cylinder cap, wipe it clean to prevent dirt and other foreign matter from dropping into the master cylinder reservoir.

✲✲ WARNING

Use only MOPAR® brake fluid, or equivalent, from a fresh, tightly sealed container. Brake fluid must conform to DOT 3 specifications.

Do not pump the brake pedal at any time while having a bleeder screw open during the bleeding process. This will only increase the amount of air in the system and make additional bleeding necessary.

Do not allow the master cylinder reservoir to run out of brake fluid while bleeding the system. An empty reservoir will allow additional air into the brake system. Check the fluid level frequently and add fluid as needed.

The following wheel circuit sequence for bleeding the brake hydraulic system should be used to ensure adequate removal of all trapped air from the hydraulic system.

- Left rear wheel
- Right front wheel
- Right rear wheel
- Left front wheel

1. Before servicing the vehicle, refer to the Precautions Section.
2. Attach a clear plastic hose to the bleeder screw and feed the hose into a clear jar containing enough fresh brake fluid to submerge the end of the hose.
3. Have a helper pump the brake pedal three or four times and hold it in the down position.
4. With the pedal in the down position, open the bleeder screw at least one full turn.
5. Once the brake pedal has dropped, close the bleeder screw. After the bleeder screw is closed, release the brake pedal.
6. Repeat the above steps until all trapped air is removed from that wheel circuit (usually four or five times).
7. Bleed the remaining wheel circuits in the same manner until all air is removed from the brake system. Monitor the fluid level in the master cylinder reservoir to make sure it does not go dry.
8. Check and adjust brake fluid level to the FULL mark.
9. Check the brake pedal travel. If pedal travel is excessive or has not been improved, some air may still be trapped in the system. Re-bleed the brakes as necessary.
10. Test drive the vehicle to verify the brakes are operating properly and pedal feel is correct.

MASTER CYLINDER BLEEDING

1. Before servicing the vehicle, refer to the Precautions Section.
2. Clamp the master cylinder in a vise with soft-jaw caps.
3. Attach the special tools for bleeding the master cylinder in the following fashion:
   a. Thread Special Tool 8822-2 Bleeder Tube Adapters into the primary and secondary outlet ports of the master cylinder. Tighten the Adapters to 150 inch lbs. (17 Nm).
   b. Thread Special Tool 8358-1 Bleeder Tube into each Adapter. Tighten tube nuts to 150 inch lbs. (17 Nm).
   c. Flex each Bleeder Tube and place the open ends into the neck of the master cylinder reservoir. Position the open ends of the tubes into the reservoir so their outlets are below the surface of the brake fluid in the reservoir when filled.

➡Make sure the ends of the Bleeder Tubes stay below the surface of the brake fluid in the reservoir at all times during the bleeding procedure.

4. Fill the brake fluid reservoir with fresh MOPAR® Brake Fluid (DOT 3), or equivalent.
5. Using an appropriately sized wooden dowel as a pushrod, slowly press the pistons inward discharging brake fluid through the Bleeder Tubes, then release the pressure, allowing the pistons to return to the released position. Repeat this several times until all air bubbles are expelled from the master cylinder bore and Bleeder Tubes.
6. Remove the Bleeder Tubes and Adapters from the master cylinder and plug the master cylinder outlet ports.
7. Install the fill cap on the reservoir.
8. Remove the master cylinder from the vise.
9. Install the master cylinder on the vehicle.

BLEEDING THE ABS SYSTEM

During the brake bleeding procedure, make sure the brake fluid level remains close to the FULL level in the master cylinder fluid reservoir. Check the fluid level periodically during the bleeding procedure and add DOT 3 brake fluid as required.

The ABS must be bled as two independent braking systems. First the base brake (non-ABS portion) of the brake system is bled in the conventional manner. Then the ABS portion of the brake system is bled using a scan tool. Finally the base brake system is re-bled. Use the following procedure to properly bleed the brake hydraulic system including the ABS.

To bleed the ABS system use the following bleeding sequence to insure complete and adequate bleeding.

1. Before servicing the vehicle, refer to the Precautions Section.
2. Make sure all hydraulic fluid lines are installed and properly torqued.
3. Connect a scan tool to the diagnostics connector. The diagnostic connector is located under the lower steering column cover to the left of the steering column.
4. Using the scan tool, check to make sure the control module does not have any stored Diagnostic Trouble Codes (DTC) stored. If it does, clear the DTC's using a scan tool.

✲✲ CAUTION

When bleeding the brake system wear safety glasses. A clear bleed tube must be attached to the bleeder screws and submerged in a clear container filled part way with clean brake fluid. Direct the flow of brake fluid away from yourself and the painted surfaces of the vehicle. Brake fluid at high pressure may come out of the bleeder screws when opened.

5. Bleed the base brake system using the standard pressure or manual bleeding procedure as described in the base brake system portion of this section.
6. Using a scan tool, select ANTILOCK BRAKES, followed by MISCELLANEOUS, then BLEED BRAKES. Follow the instructions displayed. When the scan tool displays TEST COMPLETED, disconnect the scan tool and proceed.
7. Bleed the base brake system a second time. Check brake fluid level in the reservoir periodically to prevent emptying, causing air to enter the hydraulic system.
8. Fill the master cylinder reservoir to the full level.
9. Test drive the vehicle to be sure the brakes are operating correctly and that the brake pedal does not feel spongy.

⁂ CAUTION

Dust and dirt accumulating on brake parts during normal use may contain asbestos fibers from production or aftermarket brake linings. Breathing excessive concentrations of asbestos fibers can cause serious bodily harm. Exercise care when servicing brake parts. Do not sand or grind brake lining unless equipment used is designed to contain the dust residue. Do not clean brake parts with compressed air or by dry brushing. Cleaning should be done by dampening the brake components with a fine mist of water, then wiping the brake components clean with a dampened cloth. Dispose of cloth and all residue containing asbestos fibers in an impermeable container with the appropriate label. Follow practices prescribed by the Occupational Safety and Health Administration (OSHA) and the Environmental Protection Agency (EPA) for the handling, processing, and disposing of dust or debris that may contain asbestos fibers.

BRAKE CALIPER

REMOVAL & INSTALLATION

See Figure 14.

1. Before servicing the vehicle, refer to the Precautions Section.
2. Depress the brake pedal past its first inch of travel and hold it in this position using a brake pedal depressor (holding) tool. This is done to isolate the master cylinder from the brake hydraulic system disallowing the brake fluid to completely drain out of the brake fluid reservoir.
3. Raise the vehicle.
4. Remove the front wheel and tire assembly.
5. Remove the anti-rattle spring from the outboard side of the caliper and adapter.
6. Remove the banjo bolt connecting the brake hose to the brake caliper. There are two washers (one on each side of the brake hose fitting) that will come off with the banjo bolt. Discard these washers.
7. Remove the two caps in place over the caliper guide pin bolts.
8. Remove the two caliper guide pin bolts.
9. Remove the caliper from caliper adapter and brake rotor. The outboard shoe will probably stay with the caliper adapter while the inboard shoe will come off with the caliper as the caliper is removed.

To install:

10. Completely retract the caliper piston back into piston bore of the caliper.
11. Lubricate both caliper adapter abutments where the shoes slide with a sufficient amount of MOPAR® Silicone Grease, or equivalent.

➡If pads are being transferred or newly installed, make note that the inboard brake pads are stamped L or R for left or right side of the vehicle. The P-slot or void on piston insulator must be positioned upward when brake caliper is mounted.

⁂ WARNING

Use care when installing the brake caliper assembly onto the adapter, so that the seals on the caliper guide pin bushings do not get damaged by the adapter bosses.

12. Carefully position the brake caliper (with inboard shoe) over the brake rotor, outboard shoe and adapter.
13. Install the caliper guide pin bolts and tighten to 26 ft. lbs. (35 Nm).

➡Extreme caution should be taken not to cross thread the caliper guide pin bolts.

14. Install the caps over the ends of the guide pin bolts.

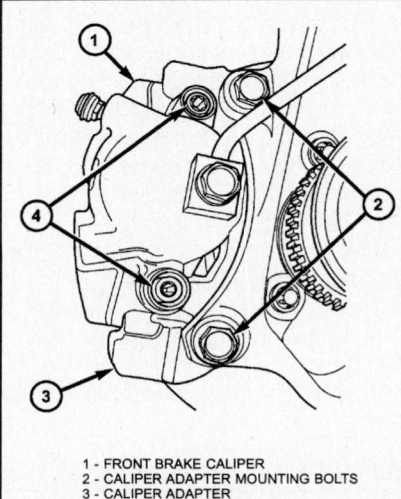

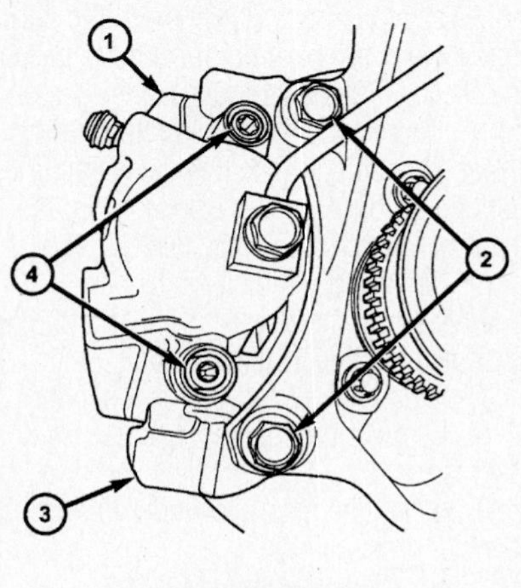

Fig. 14 Front caliper mounting—2005 models shown; other years similar

15. Install the anti-rattle spring on the outboard side of the caliper. Start the clip into the holes on the caliper, then stretch the clip legs past the abutments on the caliper adapter.

⁂ WARNING

When connecting the brake hose to the caliper, install the new brake hose to caliper special washers.

16. Install the brake hose on the caliper. To do this, first place one NEW special fitting washer on each side of the hose fitting, then slide the banjo bolt through the fitting. Next, thread the banjo bolt into the threaded port on the rear of the brake caliper. Tighten the banjo bolt to 26 ft. lbs. (35 Nm).
17. Install the wheel and tire assembly. Tighten the wheel mounting stud nuts in proper sequence until all nuts are torqued to half specification, then repeat the tightening sequence to the full specified torque of: 100 ft. lbs. (135 Nm).
18. Lower the vehicle.
19. Remove the brake pedal depressor (holding) tool.
20. Bleed the hydraulic brake circuit to the brake caliper.
21. Road test vehicle to check for proper brake operation.

DISC BRAKE PADS

REMOVAL & INSTALLATION

See Figures 15 and 16.

1. Before servicing the vehicle, refer to the Precautions Section.
2. Remove about half of the brake fluid from the master cylinder.
3. Raise the vehicle.
4. Remove the both front wheel and tire assemblies.
5. Remove the anti-rattle spring from the outboard side of the caliper and adapter.
6. Remove the two caps in place over the caliper guide pin bolts.
7. Remove the two caliper guide pin bolts.
8. Remove the caliper from caliper adapter and brake rotor. The outboard shoe will probably stay with the caliper adapter while the inboard shoe will come off with the caliper as the caliper is removed.

⁂ WARNING

Supporting weight of caliper by the flexible brake fluid hose can damage the hose.

9. Using wire or cord, hang the caliper from the front strut assembly. Support the caliper firmly to prevent weight of caliper from being supported by the brake fluid hose.
10. Remove the outboard brake pad from the caliper adapter.
11. Pull the inboard brake pad away from the caliper piston until the retaining clip on shoe is free from the cavity in the caliper piston.
12. Repeat the above procedure on other side of the vehicle.

To install:

➡There may be more than one lining material released. Make sure proper linings are being installed.

13. Begin on one side of the vehicle or the other.
14. Completely retract the caliper piston back into its bore in the brake caliper (This is required for caliper installation on the brake rotor with new brake pads installed).
15. If applied, remove the protective paper from the noise suppression gasket on the rear of both the inner and outer brake pad assemblies.

➡Inboard brake pads are stamped L or R for left or right side of the vehicle.

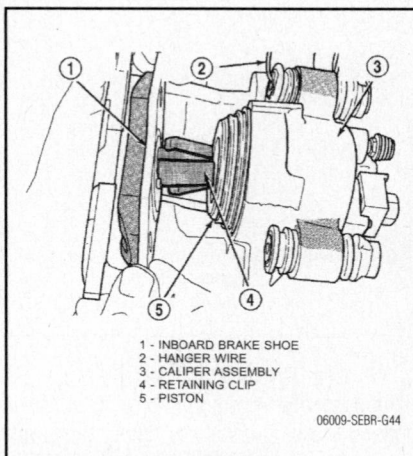

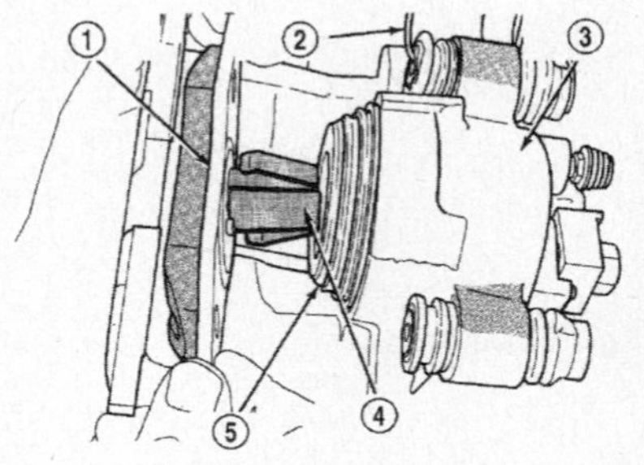

Fig. 15 Removing inboard pad

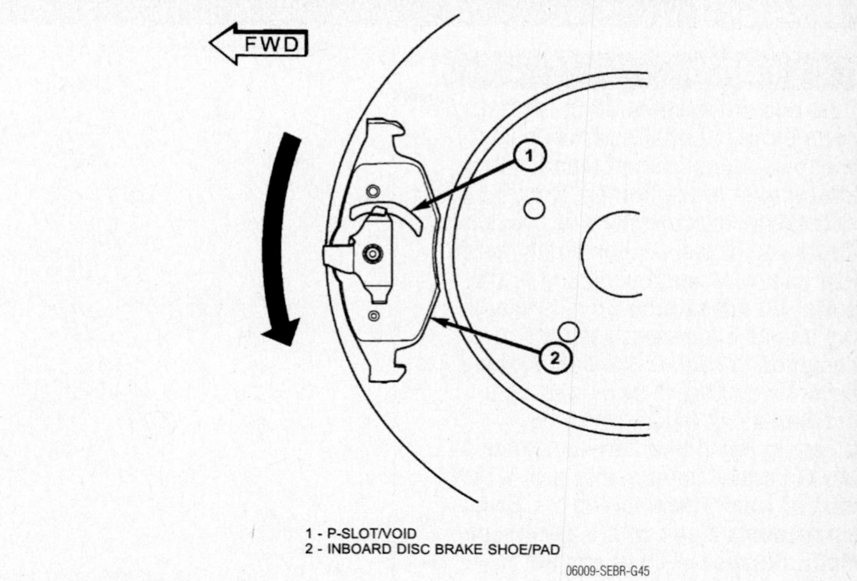

Fig. 16 Inboard shoe orientation

The P-slot or void on piston insulator must be positioned upward when brake caliper is mounted.

16. Install the new inboard brake pad into the caliper piston by firmly pressing its retaining clip into the piston bore. Be sure the inboard brake pad is positioned squarely against the face of the caliper piston.
17. Lubricate both adapter abutments where the shoes slide with a small amount of MOPAR® Silicone grease, or equivalent.
18. Slide the new outboard brake pad into the caliper adapter with the lining up against the outside of the brake rotor.

⁂ WARNING

Use care when installing the caliper assembly onto the caliper adapter, so the caliper guide pin bushings do not get damaged by the adapter bosses.

19. Carefully position the brake caliper over the brake rotor and adapter.
20. Install the caliper guide pin bolts and tighten to 26 ft. lbs. (35 Nm). Extreme caution should be taken not to cross thread the caliper guide pin bolts.
21. Install the caps over the caliper guide pin bolts.
22. Install the new caliper hold-down spring (anti-rattle clip) on the outboard side of the caliper. Start the spring into the holes on the caliper, then stretch the clip legs past the abutments on the caliper adapter.
23. Repeat the above procedure on other side of the vehicle.
24. Install the wheel and tire assemblies. Tighten the wheel mounting nuts in proper sequence until all nuts are torqued to half specification, then repeat the tightening sequence to the full specified torque of: 100 ft. lbs. (135 Nm).
25. Lower vehicle.
26. Pump the brake pedal several times. This will set the shoes to the brake rotor.
27. Check and adjust brake fluid level as necessary.
28. Road test vehicle to check for proper brake operation.

⁂ CAUTION

Dust and dirt accumulating on brake parts during normal use may contain asbestos fibers from production or aftermarket brake linings. Breathing excessive concentrations of asbestos fibers can cause serious bodily harm. Exercise care when servicing brake parts. Do not sand or grind brake lining unless equipment used is designed to contain the dust residue. Do not clean brake parts with compressed air or by dry brushing. Cleaning should be done by dampening the brake components with a fine mist of water, then wiping the brake components clean with a dampened cloth. Dispose of cloth and all residue containing asbestos fibers in an impermeable container with the appropriate label. Follow practices prescribed by the Occupational Safety and Health Administration (OSHA) and the Environmental Protection Agency (EPA) for the handling, processing, and disposing of dust or debris that may contain asbestos fibers.

BRAKE CALIPER

REMOVAL & INSTALLATION

See Figures 17 and 18.

1. Before servicing the vehicle, refer to the Precautions Section.
2. Depress the brake pedal past its first inch of travel and hold it in this position using a brake pedal depressor (holding) tool. This is done to isolate the master cylinder from the brake hydraulic system disallowing the brake fluid to completely drain out of the brake fluid reservoir.
3. Raise vehicle.
4. Remove the rear wheel and tire from vehicle.
5. Remove the banjo bolt connecting the brake hose to the brake caliper. There are two washers (one on each side of the brake hose fitting) that will come off with the banjo bolt. Discard these washers.
6. Remove the 2 guide pin bolts mounting the caliper to the adapter.
7. Remove the caliper from adapter and rotor by first rotating top of caliper away from the adapter, then lifting the caliper off lower machined abutment on adapter.

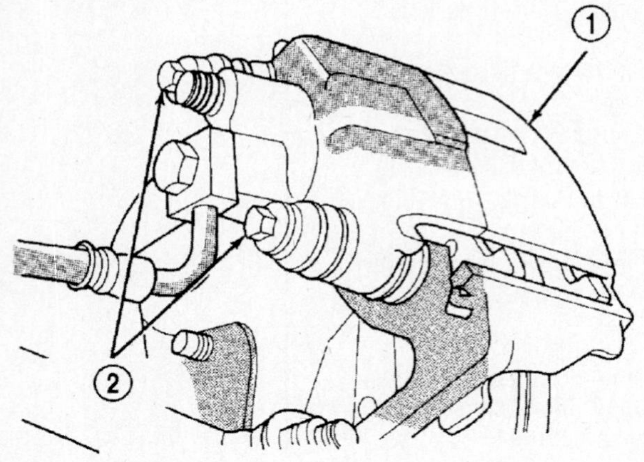

Fig. 17 Rear caliper mounting

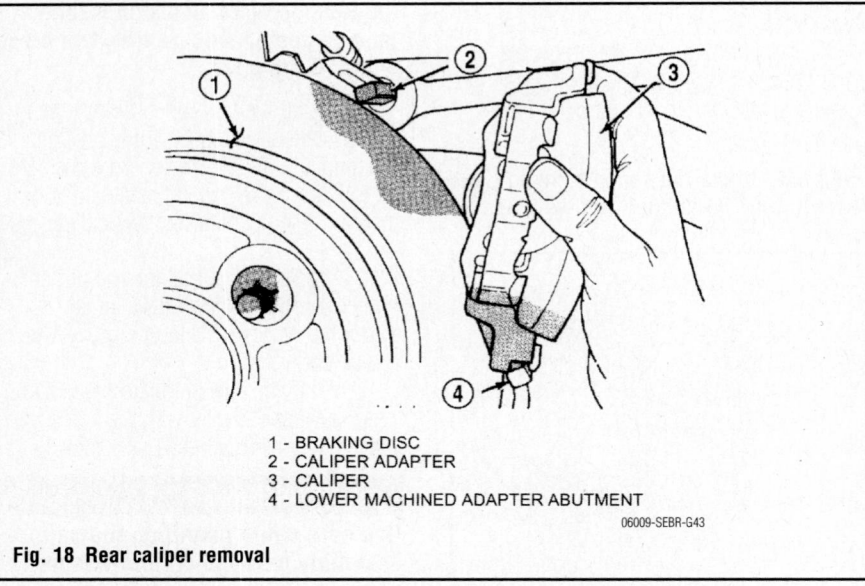

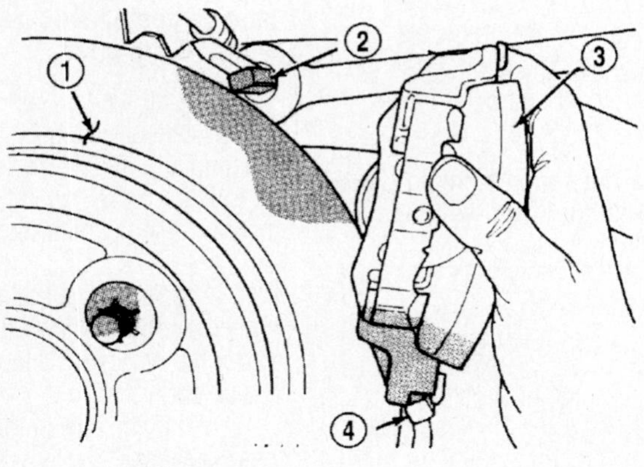

Fig. 18 Rear caliper removal

To install:

8. Completely retract caliper piston back into piston bore of caliper assembly.
9. Lubricate both adapter abutments with a liberal amount of MOPAR® Multipurpose Lubricant, or equivalent.
10. If removed, install the rotor on the hub making sure it is squarely seated on the face of the hub.

⁂ WARNING

Use care when installing caliper assembly onto adapter so the guide pin bushings and sleeves do not get damaged by the mounting bosses on adapter.

11. Carefully lower caliper and brake pads over rotor reversing the removal procedure. Make sure that the caliper guide pin bolts, bushings and sleeves are clear of the adapter bosses.

⁂ WARNING

Extreme caution should be taken not to cross thread the caliper guide pin bolts when they are installed.

12. Install the caliper guide pin bolts. Tighten the caliper guide pin bolts to 16 ft. lbs. (22 Nm).
13. Install the brake hose on the caliper. To do this, first place one NEW special fitting washer on each side of the hose fitting,

then slide the banjo bolt through the fitting. Next, thread the banjo bolt into the threaded port on the rear of the brake caliper. Tighten the banjo bolt to 26 ft. lbs. (35 Nm).

14. Install the wheels and tire assembly.
15. Tighten the wheel mounting stud nuts in proper sequence until all nuts are torqued to half specification. Then repeat the tightening sequence to the full specified torque of: 100 ft. lbs. (135 Nm).
16. Lower vehicle.
17. Remove the brake pedal depressor (holding) tool.
18. Bleed the hydraulic brake system.
19. Road test vehicle to check for proper brake operation.

DISC BRAKE PADS

REMOVAL & INSTALLATION

See Figures 19 through 21.

1. Before servicing the vehicle, refer to the Precautions Section.
2. Remove about half of the brake fluid from the master cylinder.
3. Raise vehicle.
4. Remove the rear wheels and tires from vehicle.
5. Remove the 2 guide pin bolts mounting the caliper to the adapter.
6. Remove the caliper from adapter and rotor by first rotating the top of the caliper away from adapter, and then lifting the caliper off the lower machined abutment on adapter.

⁂ WARNING

Supporting weight of caliper by the flexible brake fluid hose can damage the hose.

7. Support caliper from rear strut.
8. Remove the rear rotor from hub/bearing. Then inspect drum-in-hat parking brake shoes and parking brake braking surface on rotor for any signs of excessive wear or damage. Replace parking brake shoes if required.
9. Remove the outboard brake pad from caliper by prying brake pad retaining clip over raised area on caliper. Then slide brake pad down and off the caliper.
10. Pull inboard brake pad away from caliper piston, until retaining clip is free from cavity in piston.

To install:

11. Completely retract the caliper piston back into the piston bore of the caliper. This is required for caliper installation when new brake pad assemblies are installed on caliper.
12. Lubricate both adapter abutments with a liberal amount of MOPAR® Multipurpose Lubricant, or equivalent.
13. Install the rear rotor on hub making sure it is squarely seated on face of hub.
14. Remove the protective paper from noise suppression gasket on both inner and outer brake pad assemblies (if equipped).
15. Install the new inboard brake pad into caliper piston by firmly pressing it into bore of piston using thumbs. Be sure inboard brake pad is positioned squarely against face of piston.
16. Slide new outboard brake pad onto the caliper. Be sure retaining clip is squarely seated in the depressed areas on the caliper.

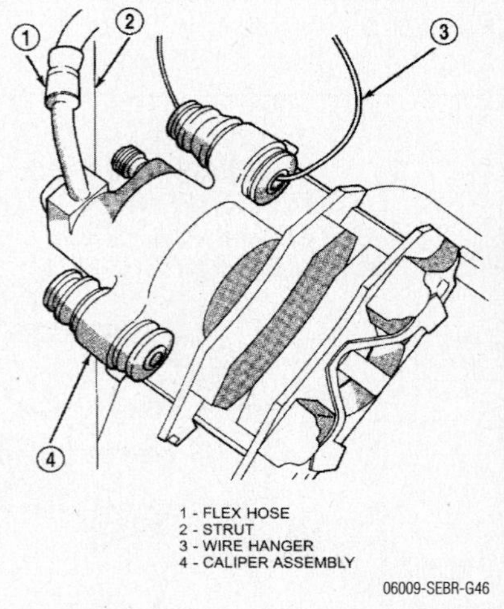

Fig. 19 Hanging the rear caliper

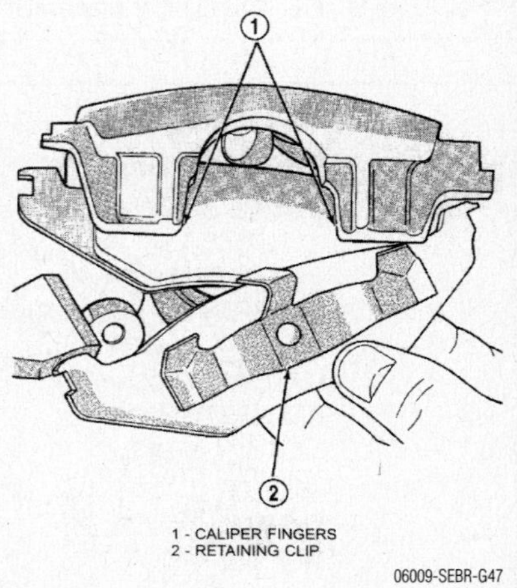

Fig. 20 Removing outboard brake pad—rear brakes

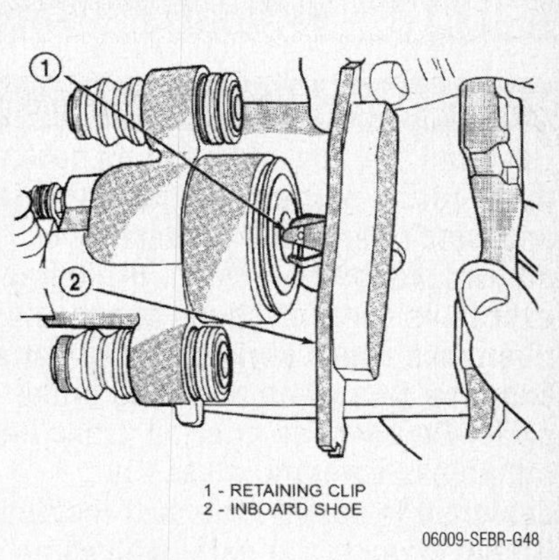

Fig. 21 Removing inboard brake pad—rear brakes

⁂ WARNING

Use care when installing caliper assembly onto adapter, so the guide pin bushings and sleeves do not get damaged by the mounting bosses on adapter.

17. Carefully lower caliper and brake pads over rotor reversing the required removal procedure. Make sure that caliper guide pin bolts, bushings and sleeves are clear of the adapter bosses.

⁂ WARNING

Extreme caution should be taken not to cross thread the caliper guide pin bolts when they are installed.

18. Install the caliper guide pin bolts into adapter. Tighten the guide pin bolts to 16 ft. lbs. (22 Nm).
19. Install the wheels and tires.
20. Tighten the wheel mounting stud nuts in proper sequence until all nuts are torqued to half specification. Then repeat the tightening sequence to the full specified torque of: 100 ft. lbs. (135 Nm).
21. Lower vehicle.
22. Pump the brake pedal several times. This will set the pads to the brake rotor.
23. Check and adjust brake fluid level as necessary.

CAUTION

Dust and dirt accumulating on brake parts during normal use may contain asbestos fibers from production or aftermarket brake linings. Breathing excessive concentrations of asbestos fibers can cause serious bodily harm. Exercise care when servicing brake parts. Do not sand or grind brake lining unless equipment used is designed to contain the dust residue. Do not clean brake parts with compressed air or by dry brushing. Cleaning should be done by dampening the brake components with a fine mist of water, then wiping the brake components clean with a dampened cloth. Dispose of cloth and all residue containing asbestos fibers in an impermeable container with the appropriate label. Follow practices prescribed by the Occupational Safety and Health Administration (OSHA) and the Environmental Protection Agency (EPA) for the handling, processing, and disposing of dust or debris that may contain asbestos fibers.

BRAKE DRUM

REMOVAL & INSTALLATION

See Figures 22 and 23.

The automatic self-adjuster mechanism used is the screw type adjuster. The self-adjuster mechanism is actuated each time the vehicle service brakes are applied. Generally, drum brakes with a self-adjusting mechanism do not require manual brake shoe adjustment. Although, in the event that the brake shoes are replaced, it is advisable to make the initial adjustment manually to speed up the initial adjustment time. The initial adjustment procedure must be done prior to driving the vehicle.

1. Before servicing the vehicle, refer to the Precautions Section.
2. Remove the rear wheel assembly.
3. Locate and remove the rubber plug from the brake support plate (backing plate).
4. Insert a brake adjuster tool or similarly shaped pry tool through the automatic adjuster access hole and engage the teeth on the adjuster wheel. Rotate the adjuster wheel so it is moved toward the front of the vehicle. Continue moving the adjuster until it stops; this will back off the adjustment of the rear brake shoes.
5. Remove the rear brake drum from the hub assembly.

To install:

Inspect the brake drums for cracks or signs of overheating. Measure the drum run-out and diameter. If not to specification, resurface the drum. Run-out should not exceed 0.006 inch (0.15mm). The diameter variation (oval shape) of the drum braking surface must not exceed either 0.0025 inch (0.064mm) in 30 degrees rotation, or 0.0035 inch (0.089mm) in 360 degrees rotation. All brake drums are marked with the maximum allowable brake drum diameter on the face of the drum.

6. Install the rear brake drum onto the hub assembly.
7. Reinstall the wheel and tire. Torque the lug nuts in a star pattern sequence to about 45 ft. lbs. (61 Nm); then, repeat the pattern and final torque to 95–100 ft. lbs. (129–135 Nm).
8. Properly adjust the rear brakes.
9. Road test vehicle to check for proper brake operation.

BRAKE SHOES

REMOVAL & INSTALLATION

See Figure 24.

1. Before servicing the vehicle, refer to the Precautions Section.
2. Remove the rear wheel assembly.
   a. Locate and remove the rubber plug

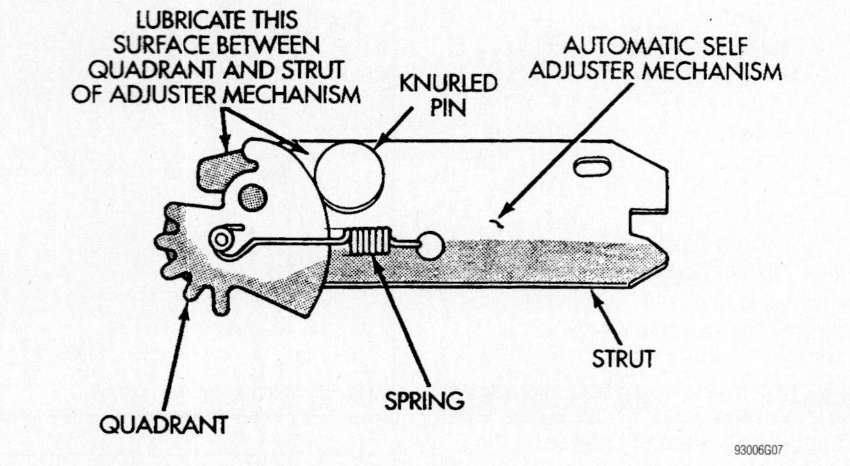

Fig. 22 Automatic self-adjuster mechanism

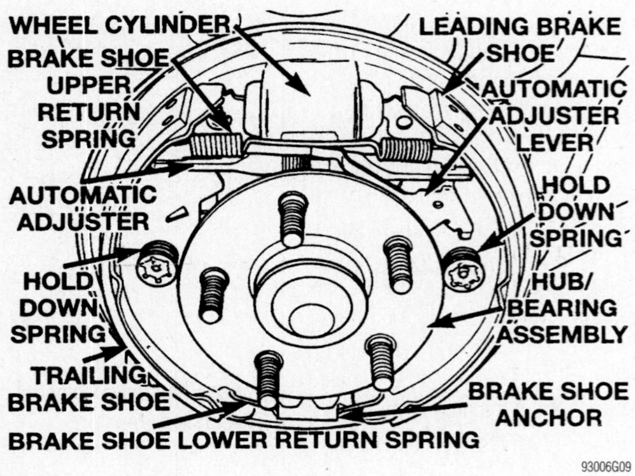

Fig. 23 Kelsey Hayes rear brake assembly

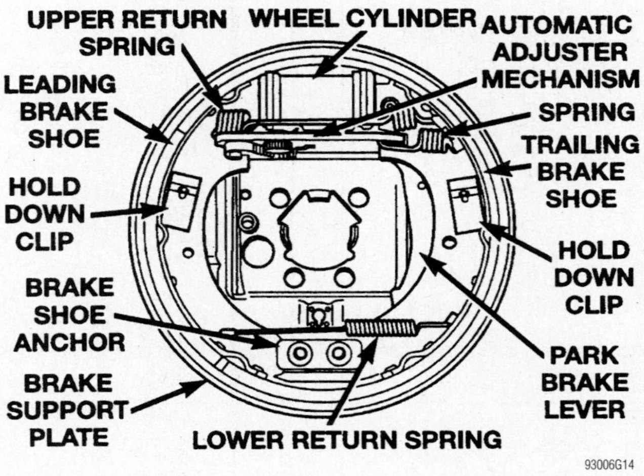

Fig. 24 Rear wheel brake assembly (left side shown)

from the top of the brake support plate (backing plate).

b. Insert a brake adjuster tool or similarly shaped pry tool through the automatic adjuster access hole and engage the teeth on the adjuster quadrant. Then rotate the quadrant so the teeth of the quadrant are moved toward the front of the vehicle. This will back off the adjustment of the rear brake shoes.

c. Continue moving the quadrant toward the front of the vehicle until it stops moving.

3. Remove the drum from the hub assembly.

4. Remove the actuating spring from the adjuster mechanism and trailing brake shoe.

5. Remove the upper return spring from the brake shoes.

6. Remove the lower return spring from the brake shoes.

7. Remove the brake shoe retainer and pin attaching the leading brake shoe assembly to the brake support plate.

8. Remove the leading brake shoe and the adjuster mechanism as an assembly from the rear brake support plate. The adjuster mechanism cannot be separated from the leading brake shoe until the brake shoe and the adjuster mechanism is removed from the support plate.

9. Remove the trailing brake shoe retainer and pin attaching the trailing brake shoe assembly to the brake support plate. Remove the trailing brake shoe assembly.

➡On this vehicle, the parking brake actuating lever is permanently attached to the trailing brake shoe assembly. Do not attempt to remove it from the original brake shoe assembly or reuse the original actuating lever on a replacement brake shoe assembly. All replacement brake shoe assemblies for this vehicle must have the actuating lever as part of the trailing brake shoe assembly.

10. Remove the parking brake cable from the parking brake lever. Do not remove the lever from the brake shoe.

11. Remove the automatic adjuster mechanism from the brake shoe by fully extending the adjuster and rotate the adjuster out to release from the brake shoe.

To inspect:

12. Thoroughly clean all parts. The brake lining should show contact across the entire width and from heel to toe; otherwise, replace. Clean and inspect the brake support plate and the automatic adjuster mechanism. Be sure the quadrant (toothed part) of the adjuster is free to rotate throughout its entire tooth contact range and is free to slide the full length of its mounting slot. Check the knurled pin. It should be securely attached to the adjuster mechanism and its teeth should be in good condition. If the adjuster is worn or damaged, replace it. If the adjuster is serviceable, lubricate lightly with high-temperature grease between the strut and the quadrant. Check the brake springs. Overheating indications are paint discoloration or distorted end coils. Replace parts as required.

13. Inspect the brake drums for cracks or signs of overheating. Measure the drum run-out and diameter. If not to specification, reface the drum. Run-out should not exceed 0.006 inch (0.15mm). The diameter variation (oval shape) of the drum braking surface must not exceed either 0.0025 inch (0.064mm) in 30 degrees rotation, or 0.0035 inch (0.089mm) in 360 degrees rotation. All brake drums are marked with the maximum allowable brake drum diameter on the face of the drum.

To install:

14. Lubricate the 8 brake shoe contact points with high-temperature grease.

➡The trailing brake shoe assemblies used on the rear brakes of this vehicle are unique to the left and right side of the vehicle. Care must be taken to ensure the brake shoes are properly installed in their correct side of the vehicle. When the trailing shoes are properly installed on their correct side of the vehicle, the park brake actuating lever will be positioned under the brake shoe web.

15. Reinstall the parking brake cable onto the parking brake lever and install the trailing brake shoe and attaching pin.

16. Reinstall the automatic self-adjuster on the leading brake shoe by rotating it inward to attach. Install the leading shoe and adjuster assembly to the brake support plate.

17. Make sure the leading brake shoe is squarely seated on the brake support plate shoe contact areas, and install the brake retainer on the retainer pin.

18. Reinstall the lower return spring.

➡The upper brake shoe return spring and adjuster mechanism actuating spring are unique to the side of the vehicle they are used on. The springs are colored for identification. The left side springs are green and the right side springs are blue.

19. Reinstall the upper return spring (blue, right side; green, left side) on the leading brake shoe first, then on the trailing brake shoe.

20. Reinstall the self-adjuster spring on the trailing brake shoe first then attach it to the adjuster.

21. Reinstall the rear brake drums.

22. Reinstall the wheel and tire. Torque the lug nuts in a star pattern sequence to about 45 ft. lbs. (61 Nm), then repeat the pattern and final torque to 95–100 ft. lbs. (129–135 Nm).

23. Adjust the rear brakes by depressing the brake pedal. Brake shoe adjustment will occur the first time the brake pedal is depressed, pushing the rear brake shoes against the braking surface of the rear brake drums. Brake shoes should now be correctly adjusted and will not require any type of manual adjustment.

24. Road test vehicle to check for proper brake operation.

ADJUSTMENT

See Figures 25 and 26.

Verify the parking brake lever is in the fully released position.

Raise the vehicle.

1. Perform the following steps on each rear drum brake assembly:
   a. Remove the tire and wheel assembly from the vehicle.
   b. Remove the brake drum. Refer to Brake Drum removal in this section of this manual.
   c. Using a brake shoe gauge, Special Tool C-3919 or equivalent, measure the inside diameter of the brake drum.
   d. Place the other side of the brake shoe gauge on the brake shoes as shown.
2. Adjust the shoe diameter to the setting on the gauge. To adjust the shoe diameter, turn the adjuster-screw star-wheel using a screwdriver inserted through the adjusting hole in the rear of the shoe support plate. Once the tip of the screwdriver contacts the star-wheel teeth, move the handle of tool downward using the support plate as a pivot to adjust the shoes outward.
3. Once the shoe diameter is set, reinstall the brake drum.
4. Turn the drum. A slight drag should be felt while rotating the drum.
5. Install the tire and wheel assembly. Tighten the wheel mounting nuts to 100 ft. lbs. (135 Nm).
6. After adjusting both rear drum brakes, lower the vehicle.
7. Apply and release the parking brake lever one time after the adjustment process is completed so the parking brakes can readjust themselves to the new brake shoe adjustment.
8. Road test vehicle stopping in both forward and reverse directions. Automatic adjuster will continue to adjust brakes as necessary during road test.

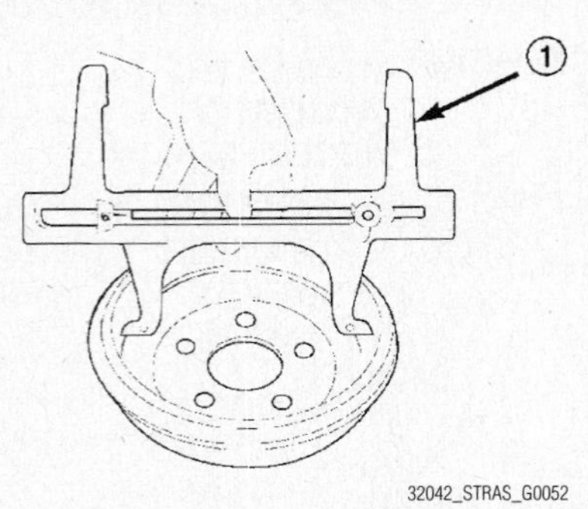

Fig. 25 Measuring drum with brake shoe gauge (1)

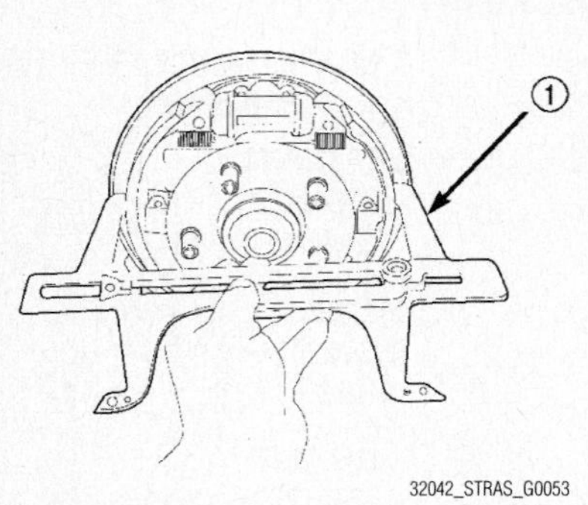

Fig. 26 Measuring brake shoes with brake shoe gauge (1)

BRAKES — PARKING BRAKE

PARKING BRAKE CABLES

ADJUSTMENT

See Figures 27 through 39.

A bent nail type park brake cable tension equalizer is used. The bent nail tension equalizer is to be used only one time to set the park brake cable tension. If the park brake cables require adjustment during the life of the vehicle, a NEW tension equalizer MUST be installed before doing the park cable adjustment procedure.

1. Before servicing the vehicle, refer to the Precautions Section.
2. Remove the 3 screws attaching the rear of the center console.
3. If vehicle is equipped with an automatic transmission, remove the shift knob from the shifter. The gear shift knob is attached to the shifter using a set screw. Access to the set screw is from the front of the shift knob and is removed using a 2mm Allen wrench.
4. If the vehicle is equipped with a manual transmission, remove the gearshift knob and shifter boot using the following procedure:
   a. Push shifter boot down to expose clips on gearshift knob and roll pin on shifter handle.

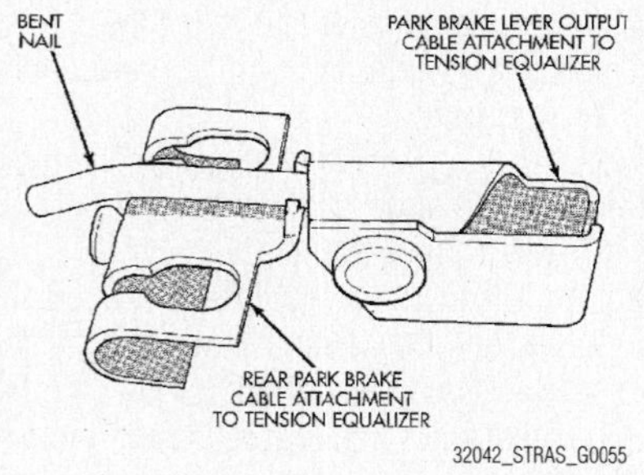

Fig. 27 Bent nail park brake cable tension equalizer

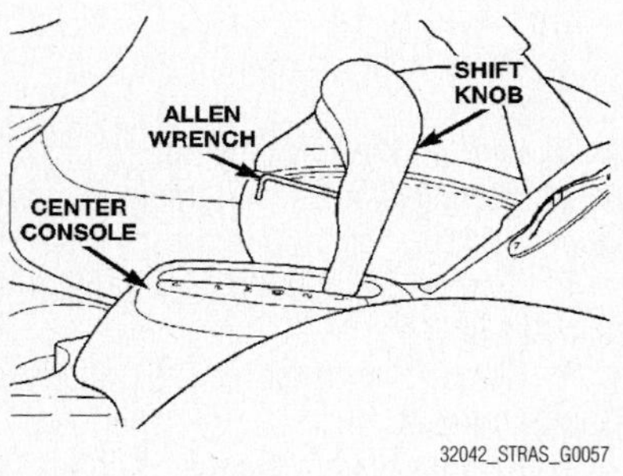

Fig. 29 Shift knob retaining screw

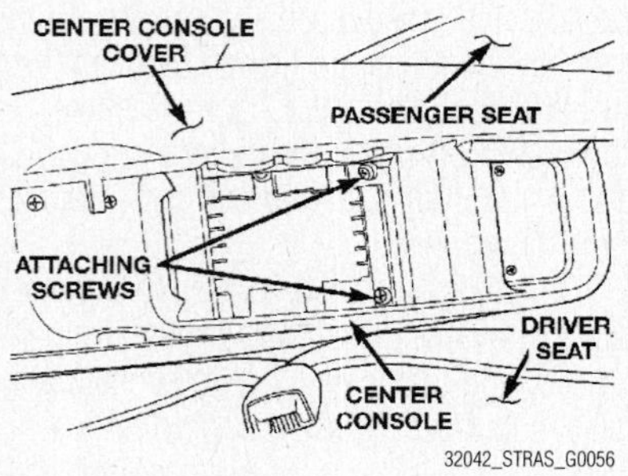

Fig. 28 Center console rear attaching screws

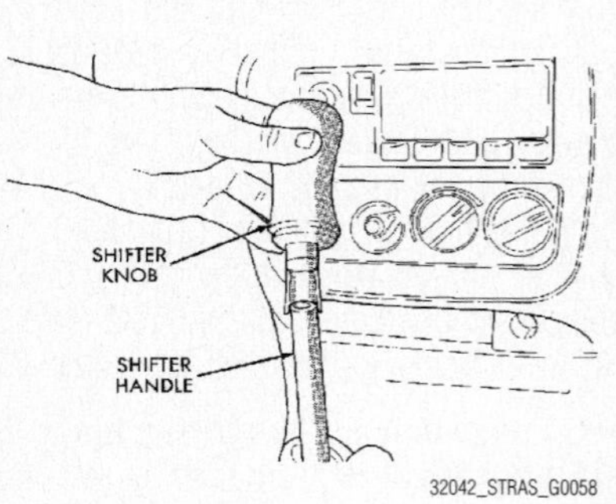

Fig. 30 Gear shift knob removal

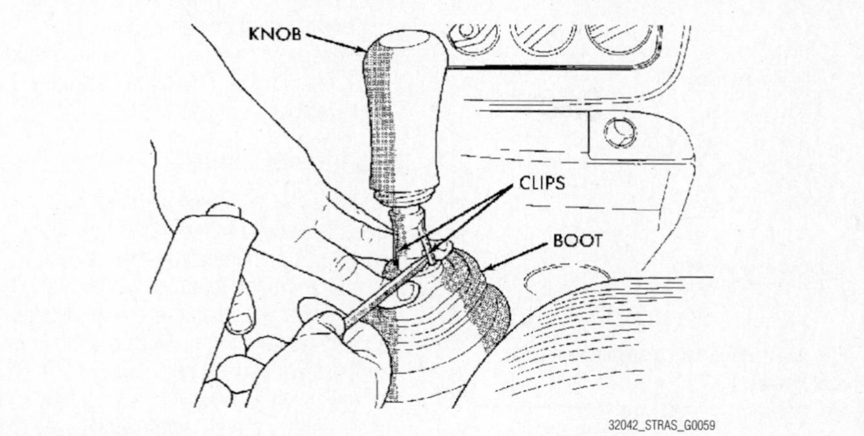

Fig. 31 Gearshift knob

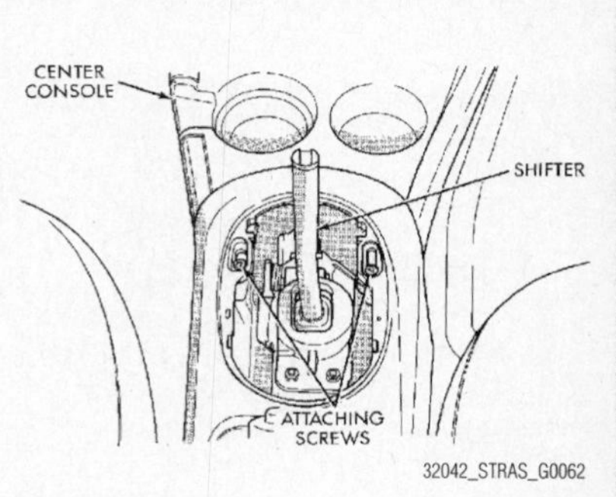

Fig. 34 Center console front attaching screws (manual)

b. Pry the clips on the shifter knob away from the roll pin in the shifter handle using a flat blade pry tool.

c. Remove the shifter knob from the shifter handle, by pulling the shifter knob straight up.

d. Remove the shifter boot from the center console. Shifter boot is removed by squeezing the bezel together at the base of the shifter boot and pulling upward on the boot.

5. Remove the 2 screws attaching the front of the center console to the gear selector or shifter.

6. Raise the park brake hand lever to approximately the half way point or its travel. This will provide the required clearance to remove center console.

7. Remove the center console/arm rest from vehicle.

8. Lower park brake lever handle.

9. Loosen adjusting nut on park brake cable output cable. This will take tension off output cable, allowing it to be easily removed from tension equalizer.

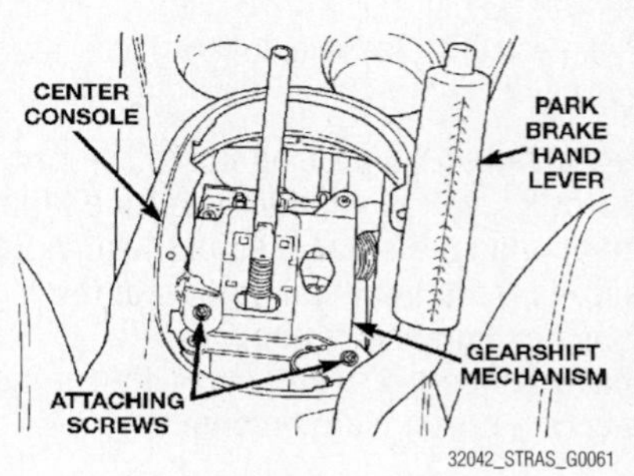

Fig. 33 Center console front attaching screws (automatic)

**** WARNING**

Discard output cable retaining clip after removing it from park brake cable tension equalizer. Retainer is not to be re-used, a new retainer is to be installed when attaching output cable to tension equalizer.

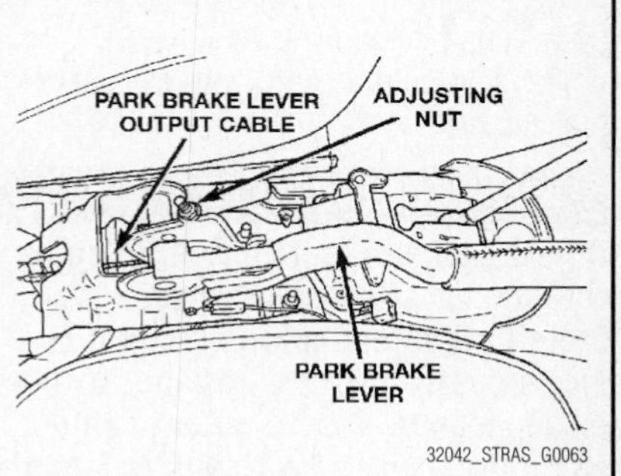

Fig. 35 Park brake lever output cable adjustment nut

10. Using a screwdriver unlatch the park brake output cable retainer. Then remove cable retainer from park brake cable tension equalizer.

11. Remove the park brake cable tension equalizer from the park brake lever output cable and the rear park brake cables.

**** WARNING**

A new cable tension equalizer must be installed when adjusting park brake cable tension.

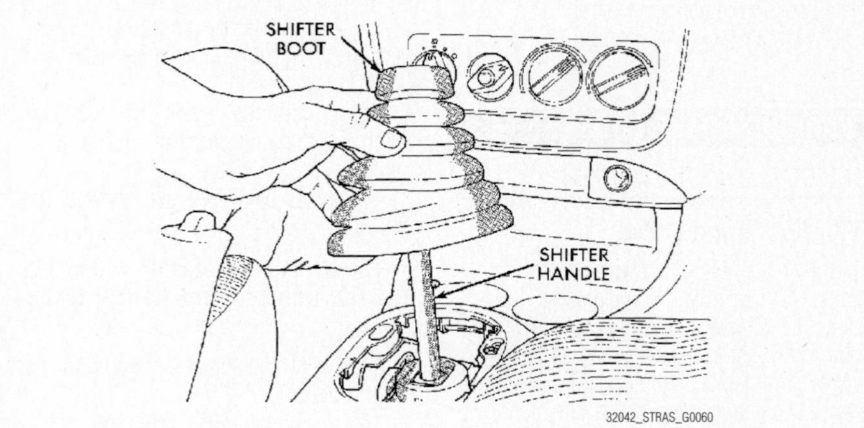

Fig. 32 Boot removal

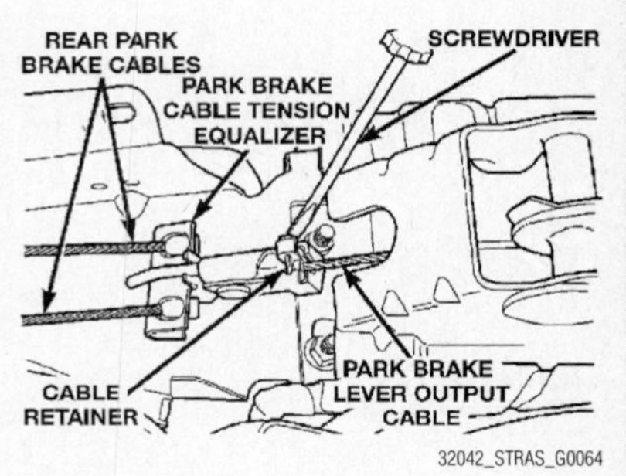

Fig. 36 Output cable to equalizer retaining clip

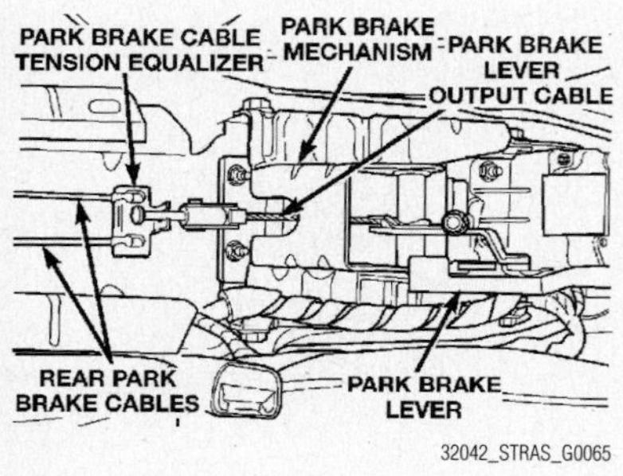

Fig. 37 Park brake cable tension equalizer

12. Install the a NEW park brake cable tension equalizer on the park brake lever output cable and rear park brake cables.

WARNING

A new park brake lever output cable retainer must be used when installing output cable on cable tension equalizer. Cable retainer usage is required to ensure output cable can not separate from tension equalizer.

13. Install a new park brake lever output cable to tension equalizer retaining clip on tension equalizer. The cable retainer must be closed and securely latched
14. Adjust cable tension for the parking brake system using the following steps:
    a. Position park brake lever so it is in the fully released position.
    b. On vehicles with REAR DRUM BRAKES, tighten the adjusting nut on the parking brake lever output cable until 12mm of thread is out past top edge of adjustment nut.
15. On vehicles with REAR DISC BRAKES, tighten the adjusting nut on the parking brake lever output cable until 26mm of thread is out past top edge of adjustment nut.

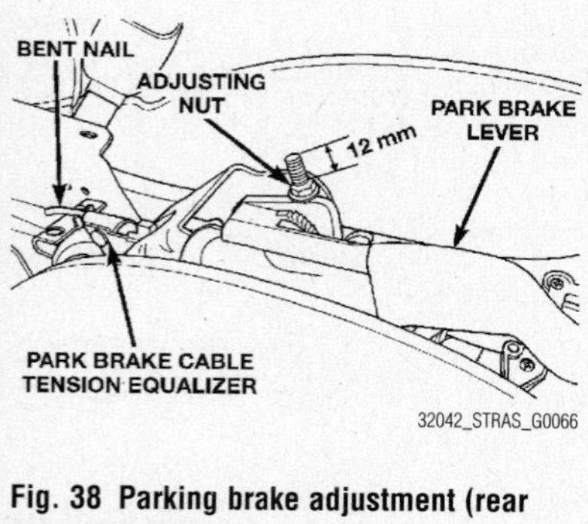

Fig. 38 Parking brake adjustment (rear drum brakes)

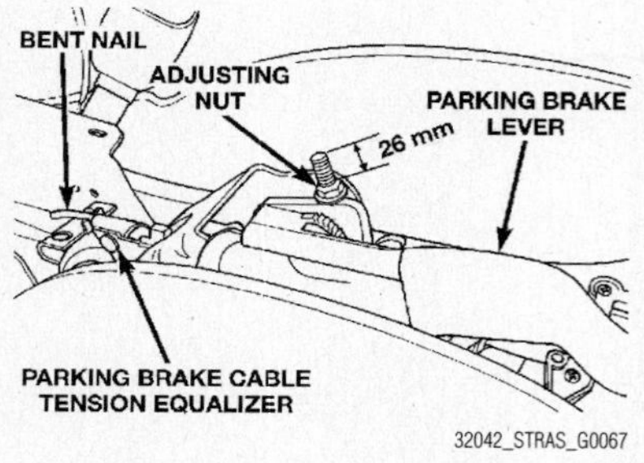

Fig. 39 Parking brake adjustment (rear disk brakes)

16. Actuate the parking brake lever to its fully applied position (22 clicks) 1 time and then reposition the lever to its fully released position.

➡Actuating the parking brake lever to its fully applied position one time after tightening the adjustment nut will yield (stretch) the bent nail portion of the tension equalizer approximately ½ inch. This process will correctly set the parking brake cable tension.

17. Check the rear wheels of the vehicle; they should rotate freely without dragging.
18. After the park brake cable tension has been properly adjusted, check for free play in park brake lever. Park brake hand lever should feel firm at all clicks, with a maximum of 21 clicks of lever travel possible.
19. Install the 2 screws attaching the front of the center console.
20. Install the screws attaching rear of center console assembly to console bracket.
21. Install the shifter boot or PRNDL plate back in the center console.
22. Install the shift knob on the shifter.

PARKING BRAKE SHOES

REMOVAL & INSTALLATION

With Rear Drum Brakes

On vehicles equipped with rear drum brakes, the rear wheel service brakes also act as the vehicle's parking brakes. The rear drum brake shoes, when acting as parking brakes, are mechanically operated using an internal actuating lever and strut which is connected to a flexible steel cable. There is an individual park brake cable for each rear wheel, which are joined using a park cable equalizer before terminating at the park brake lever. For service of the Parking Brake Shoes, refer to Rear Drum Brakes, Brake Shoes, removal & installation.

With Rear Disc Brakes

On vehicles equipped with rear disc brakes, the rear parking brakes have their own set of cable operated brake shoes located behind the rear disc brake rotor. The interior or the rear disc brake rotor acts as the parking brake drum. There are individual flexible steel parking brake cables for each rear wheel, which are joined using a park cable equalizer before terminating at the park brake lever.

1. Before servicing the vehicle, refer to the Precautions Section.
2. Remove or disconnect the following:
    - The disc brake caliper
    - The rotor from hub/bearing
    - The dust cap from hub/bearing
    - The hub/bearing rear retaining nut and washer
    - The hub/bearing from knuckle
    - The hold down clip from rear park brake shoe
3. Turn the park brake shoe adjuster wheel until the adjuster is at its shortest length.
4. Remove the park brake shoe adjuster from the park brake shoes.
5. Remove the lower return spring between the park brake shoes.
6. Pull the rear park brake shoe away from the caliper adapter.
7. Remove the upper return spring from between the park brake shoes.
8. Remove the hold-down clip from the front park brake shoe.
9. Remove the front park brake shoe.

To install:

10. Install the front brake shoe and hold down clip.
11. Install the rear park brake shoe and the park brake shoe upper return spring.
12. Pull the rear brake shoe over the anchor block until properly located on adapter.
13. Install the park brake lower return spring.

➡The adjuster must be installed with the star wheel toward the rear of the vehicle.

14. Install the adjuster between the park brake shoes.
15. Install the hold down clip on rear park brake shoe.

16. Adjust the park brake shoes to an outside diameter of 6 ¾ inch (171mm).

17. Install the hub/bearing on the knuckle.

18. Install a **NEW** hub/bearing retaining nut. Tighten the hub/bearing retaining nut to 185 ft. lbs. (250 Nm).

19. Install the dust cap on the hub/bearing.

20. Install the rotor.

21. Install the rear disc brake caliper on the adapter.

22. Install wheel and tire. Tighten wheel stud nuts to 100 ft. lbs. (135 Nm).

CHASSIS ELECTRICAL

AIR BAG (SUPPLEMENTAL RESTRAINT SYSTEM)

GENERAL INFORMATION

** CAUTION

These vehicles are equipped with an air bag system. The system must be disarmed before performing service on, or around, system components, the steering column, instrument panel components, wiring and sensors. Failure to follow the safety precautions and the disarming procedure could result in accidental air bag deployment, possible injury and unnecessary system repairs.

SERVICE PRECAUTIONS

Disconnect and isolate the battery negative cable before beginning any airbag system component diagnosis, testing, removal, or installation procedures. Allow system capacitor to discharge for two minutes before beginning any component service. This will disable the airbag system. Failure to disable the airbag system may result in accidental airbag deployment, personal injury, or death.

Do not place an intact undeployed airbag face down on a solid surface. The airbag will propel into the air if accidentally deployed and may result in personal injury or death.

When carrying or handling an undeployed airbag, the trim side (face) of the airbag should be pointing towards the body to minimize possibility of injury if accidental deployment occurs. Failure to do this may result in personal injury or death.

Replace airbag system components with OEM replacement parts. Substitute parts may appear interchangeable, but internal differences may result in inferior occupant protection. Failure to do so may result in occupant personal injury or death.

Wear safety glasses, rubber gloves, and long sleeved clothing when cleaning powder residue from vehicle after an airbag deployment. Powder residue emitted from a deployed airbag can cause skin irritation. Flush affected area with cool water if irritation is experienced. If nasal or throat irritation is experienced, exit the vehicle for fresh air until the irritation ceases. If irritation continues, see a physician.

Do not use a replacement airbag that is not in the original packaging. This may result in improper deployment, personal injury, or death.

The factory installed fasteners, screws and bolts used to fasten airbag components have a special coating and are specifically designed for the airbag system. Do not use substitute fasteners. Use only original equipment fasteners listed in the parts catalog when fastener replacement is required.

During, and following, any child restraint anchor service, due to impact event or vehicle repair, carefully inspect all mounting hardware, tether straps, and anchors for proper installation, operation, or damage. If a child restraint anchor is found damaged in any way, the anchor must be replaced. Failure to do this may result in personal injury or death.

Deployed and non-deployed airbags may or may not have live pyrotechnic material within the airbag inflator.

Do not dispose of driver/passenger/curtain airbags or seat belt tensioners unless you are sure of complete deployment. Refer to the Hazardous Substance Control System for proper disposal.

Dispose of deployed airbags and tensioners consistent with state, provincial, local, and federal regulations.

After any airbag component testing or service, do not connect the battery negative cable. Personal injury or death may result if the system test is not performed first.

If the vehicle is equipped with the Occupant Classification System (OCS), do not connect the battery negative cable before performing the OCS Verification Test using the scan tool and the appropriate diagnostic information. Personal injury or death may result if the system test is not performed properly.

Never replace both the Occupant Restraint Controller (ORC) and the Occupant Classification Module (OCM) at the same time. If both require replacement, replace one, then perform the Airbag System test before replacing the other.

Both the ORC and the OCM store Occupant Classification System (OCS) calibration data, which they transfer to one another when one of them is replaced. If both are replaced at the same time, an irreversible fault will be set in both modules and the OCS may malfunction and cause personal injury or death.

If equipped with OCS, the Seat Weight Sensor is a sensitive, calibrated unit and must be handled carefully. Do not drop or handle roughly. If dropped or damaged, replace with another sensor. Failure to do so may result in occupant injury or death.

If equipped with OCS, the front passenger seat must be handled carefully as well. When removing the seat, be careful when setting on floor not to drop. If dropped, the sensor may be inoperative, could result in occupant injury, or possibly death.

If equipped with OCS, when the passenger front seat is on the floor, no one should sit in the front passenger seat. This uneven force may damage the sensing ability of the seat weight sensors. If sat on and damaged, the sensor may be inoperative, could result in occupant injury, or possibly death.

DISARMING THE SYSTEM

Disconnect and isolate the negative battery cable. Wait 2 minutes to allow the system capacitor to fully discharge before servicing the vehicle.

ARMING THE SYSTEM

Reconnect the negative battery cable.

CLOCKSPRING CENTERING

See Figure 40.

1. Place the front wheels in the straight-ahead position and inhibit the steering column shaft from rotation.
2. Remove the steering wheel from the steering shaft.
3. Rotate the clockspring rotor clockwise to the end of its travel. Do not apply excessive torque.
4. From the end of the clockwise travel, rotate the rotor about 2 ½ turns counterclockwise. Turn the rotor slightly clockwise or counterclockwise as necessary so that the clockspring airbag pigtail wires and connector receptacle are at the top and the dowel pin is at the bottom.
5. The clockspring is now centered. Secure the clockspring rotor to the clockspring case using a locking pin or some similar device to maintain clockspring centering until the steering wheel is reinstalled on the steering column.

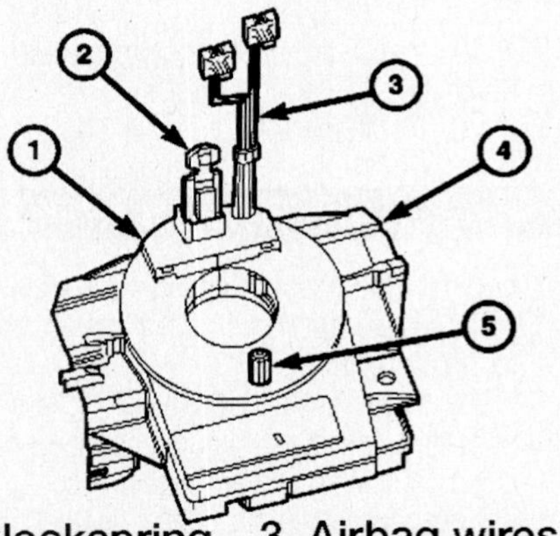

Fig. 40 Rotate the clockspring (1) so the airbag wires (3) are at the top and the dowel pin (5) is at the bottom. Secure the clockspring with a locking pin (2).

DRIVETRAIN

AUTOMATIC TRANSAXLE ASSEMBLY

REMOVAL & INSTALLATION

➡If the transaxle assembly is being replaced or overhauled (clutch and/or seal replacement), it is necessary to perform the TCM Quick Learn Procedure.

1. Before servicing the vehicle, refer to the Precautions Section.
2. Disconnect the negative battery cable.
3. Remove the air cleaner assembly.
4. Remove the dipstick tube. Plug hole to prevent debris from entering transaxle.
5. Using Tool 8875A, disconnect the transmission cooler line quick-connect fittings.
6. Disconnect the Solenoid/Pressure Switch Assy. connector.
7. Disconnect the Transmission Range Sensor connector.
8. Disconnect the Input Speed Sensor connector.
9. Disconnect the Output Speed Sensor connector.
10. Disconnect shift cable from manual valve lever and bracket.
11. Disconnect Crankshaft Position Sensor.
12. Remove the throttle body support bracket.
13. Disconnect Oxygen Sensor harness retainer from transaxle case.
14. Remove the rear mount bracket-to-transaxle case bolts.
15. Remove the starter upper bracket-to-block bolt.
16. Raise the vehicle.
17. Remove the halfshafts.
18. Remove the rear mount bracket lower bolt.
19. Remove the rear mount through-bolt.
20. Remove the rear mount-to-cross member bolts.
21. Remove the rear mount and bracket.
22. Remove the front mount through-bolt.
23. Remove the front mount to radiator lower crossmember bolts.
24. Remove the front mount bracket to block and transaxle.
25. Remove the front mount bracket and mount.
26. Remove the starter lower bolt and starter motor assembly.
27. Remove the converter dust shield.
28. Remove the torque converter bolts.
29. Support engine/transaxle with screw jack and wood block on engine oil pan.
30. Remove the left mount bracket-to-transaxle bolts.
31. Carefully lower engine/transaxle assembly to gain access to and remove transaxle-to-engine bolts.
32. With aid of helper or transmission jack, remove transaxle assembly from vehicle.

To install:

33. Install the transaxle to engine. Install and torque transaxle-to-engine bolts to 70 ft. lbs. (95 Nm).
34. Install the upper mount to transaxle.
35. Raise engine/transaxle assembly into position and install the through-bolt. Torque through bolt to 55 ft. lbs. (70 Nm).
36. Remove the transmission jack and screw jack.
37. Install the torque converter bolts.
38. Install the torque converter dust shield.
39. Install the starter motor assembly and lower bolt.
40. Install the front mount/bracket assembly.
41. Install the rear mount/bracket assembly.
42. Install the halfshafts.
43. Lower vehicle.
44. Install the starter upper bracket-to-block bolt.
45. Connect oxygen sensor harness connector.
46. Install the throttle body support bracket (if equipped).
47. Connect crankshaft position sensor connector (if equipped).
48. Connect gearshift cable to manual valve lever.
49. Connect output speed sensor connector.
50. Connect input speed sensor connector.
51. Connect transmission range sensor connector.
52. Connect solenoid/pressure switch assembly connector.
53. Connect oil cooler lines to the transaxle. An audible 'click' should be

heard. Verify connection by pulling outward.

54. Install the dipstick tube.
55. Install the air cleaner assembly.
56. Connect the negative battery cable.

MANUAL TRANSAXLE ASSEMBLY

REMOVAL & INSTALLATION

1. Before servicing the vehicle, refer to the Precautions Section.
2. Disconnect the negative battery cable.
3. Remove the air cleaner assembly.
4. Disconnect Vehicle Speed Sensor/Back-up Lamp Switch harness connector.
5. Remove the clutch release access cap.
6. Disconnect clutch release cable.
7. Disconnect crossover and selector cables from transaxle.
8. Remove the gearshift cable retainer clips from bracket and position gearshift cables out of way.
9. Remove the starter motor and secure out of way.
10. Remove the three rear mount bracket-to-transaxle bolts.
11. Raise vehicle on hoist.
12. Remove the halfshafts.
13. Remove the rear mount bracket-to-transaxle horizontal bolt.
14. Remove the rear mount through-bolt.
15. Remove the three rear mount-to-crossmember bolts.
16. Remove the rear mount and bracket.
17. Remove the front mount through bolt.
18. Remove the engine front pencil strut brace.
19. Remove the front mount bracket from engine/transaxle.
20. Remove the structural cover.
21. Remove the bell housing dust cover.
22. Remove the left wheel opening splash shield.
23. Remove the four modular clutch-to-drive plate bolts. While removing bolts, one tight-tolerance (slotted) drive plate hole will be encountered. When this bolt is removed, mark driveplate and modular clutch assembly at this location, and be sure to align marks upon reassembly.
24. Position screw jack and wood block to oil pan.
25. Remove the transaxle upper mount through bolt.
26. Lower engine transaxle assembly.
27. Remove the transaxle upper mount.
28. Obtain helper and transmission jack.
29. Remove the transaxle-to-engine block bolts.
30. Remove the transaxle from engine.

To install:

31. Install the modular clutch assembly to transaxle input shaft.
32. Using a helper and transmission jack, install the transaxle to engine.
33. Install and torque transaxle-to-engine bolts to 70 ft. lbs. (95 Nm).
34. Install the transaxle upper mount bracket and torque bolts to: 48 ft. lbs. (65 Nm).
35. Raise engine/transaxle assembly into position with screw jack.
36. Install and torque transaxle upper mount to bracket bolts to 45 ft. lbs. (61 Nm)
37. Remove the screw jack and wood block.
38. Install the four modular clutch-to-driveplate bolts. Align drive plate and modular clutch alignment marks placed upon disassembly. Start with tight-tolerance (slotted) hole, install the and torque bolts to 65 ft. lbs. (88 Nm).
39. Install the bell housing dust cover.
40. Install the structural cover.
41. Install the left wheel house splash shield.
42. Install the front mount and bracket.
43. Install the rear mount to crossmember.
44. Install the rear mount bracket into position and loosely install the horizontal bolt.
45. Install the halfshafts.
46. Lower vehicle.
47. Install the three rear mount bracket-to-transaxle and torque to 80 ft. lbs. (110 Nm)
48. Raise the vehicle.
49. Torque rear mount bracket-to-transaxle horizontal bolt to 80 ft. lbs. (110 Nm)
50. Install the rear mount through-bolt and torque to 45 ft. lbs. (61 Nm).
51. Install the starter motor.
52. Install the gearshift cables to bracket and install the new retaining clips.
53. Connect gearshift crossover and selector cable to crossover and selector levers.
54. Install the clutch release cable to release lever and case. Install the cap.
55. Connect Vehicle Speed Sensor and Back-up Lamp Switch harness.
56. Install the air cleaner assembly.
57. Connect battery negative cables.
58. Fill transaxle with suitable amount of fluid.

CLUTCH

REMOVAL & INSTALLATION

See Figure 41.

➡The transaxle assembly must be removed to service the clutch assembly.

1. Before servicing the vehicle, refer to the Precautions Section.
2. Remove or disconnect the following:
   - The negative battery cable from the left shock tower

➡The ground cable is equipped with an insulator grommet which should be placed on the stud to prevent the negative battery cable from accidentally grounding.

   - The starter
   - The rear and front transaxle support brackets
   - The clutch inspection cover
   - The modular clutch-to-flywheel bolts
   - The transaxle assembly with the clutch as an assembly
   - The clutch assembly from the transaxle input shaft

To install:

3. Clean all parts well. Inspect for oil leakage through the engine rear crankshaft oil seal and transaxle input shaft seal. If leakage is noted, it should be corrected at this time.
4. Examine the throw-out or clutch release bearing. It is pre-lubricated and sealed and should not be washed in solvent. The bearing should turn smoothly when held in the hand with a light thrust load. A light drag caused by the lubricant fill is normal. If the bearing is noisy, rough or dry, replace the complete bearing assembly. In most cases where a clutch is being serviced, the complete clutch assembly and release bearing are usually replaced together.
5. Check the condition of the stud pivot spring clips on the back side of the clutch fork. If the clips are broken or distorted, replace the clutch fork. The pivot ball pocket in the fork is Teflon® coated and should be installed **WITHOUT** any lubricant such as grease which will break down the Teflon® coating. Be sure the ball stud and fork pocket are clean of contamination and dirt. When assembling the fork to the bearing, the small pegs on the bearing must go over the fork arms.
6. Check the flywheel for cracks, glazing or grooves. If any of these conditions exist,

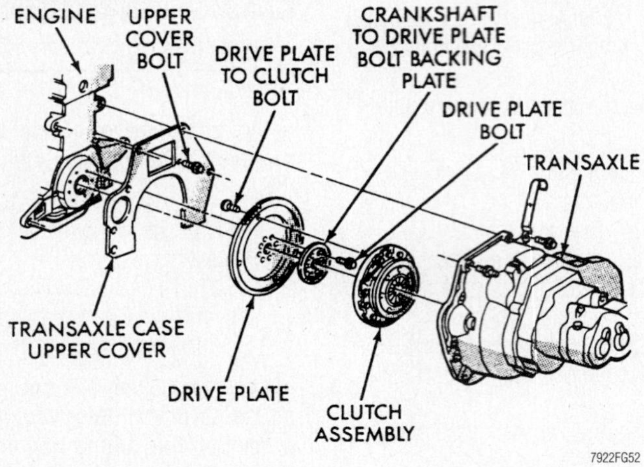

Fig. 41 Exploded view of the clutch assembly

machine (reface) or replace the flywheel to prevent clutch chatter and premature clutch wear.

➡The manual transaxle is equipped with a reverse brake. It functions as a synchronizer, but only if the vehicle is not moving. When the clutch pedal is depressed to the floor and held for 3 seconds, and the transaxle shifts to reverse, no gear clash should be present. If there is, the input shaft should be checked. When the transaxle is removed for clutch service, check the input clutch shaft, clutch disc splines and release bearing for dry rust. If present, clean rust off and apply a light coat of high temperature bearing grease to the input shaft splines. Apply grease on the input shaft splines only where the clutch disc slides. Verify that the clutch disc slides freely along the input shaft splines.

7. Install or connect the following:
   - The modular clutch assembly onto the transaxle input shaft
   - The transaxle assembly
   - The new clutch-to-driveplate (flywheel) bolts. Tighten the bolts, in a crisscross pattern, a few turns at a time to 55 ft. lbs. (75 Nm)
   - The clutch inspection cover
   - The transaxle lower support brackets
   - The starter
   - The negative battery cable
8. Road test the vehicle to check for proper clutch operation.

BLEEDING

These vehicles use a clutch cable with a unique self-adjuster mechanism built into the cable which compensates for clutch disc wear. No bleeding is necessary or possible. The preload spring maintains tension on the cable. This tension keeps the clutch release bearing continuously loaded against the fingers of the clutch cover assembly. The cable requires no maintenance or lubrication.

FRONT HALFSHAFT

REMOVAL & INSTALLATION

See Figures 42 and 43.

➡If the vehicle is going to be rolled while the halfshafts are out of the vehicle, obtain 2 outer CV-joints or proper equivalent tools and install them to the hubs.

⁂ WARNING

If the vehicle is rolled without the proper torque applied to the front wheel bearings, the bearings will no longer be usable.

1. Before servicing the vehicle, refer to the Precautions Section.
2. Remove or disconnect the following:
   - The negative battery cable
   - The cotter pin, nut lock and spring washer
   - The halfshaft nut, loosen it while the vehicle is on the floor with the brakes applied
   - The wheel
   - The brake caliper assembly and support it on a wire
   - The brake rotor
   - The halfshaft nut and washer
   - The tie rod end from the steering knuckle using Joint Separation Tool MB991113

⁂ WARNING

Use of improper methods of joint separation can result in damage to the joint, leading to possible failure.

   - The speed sensor cable routing bracket (if equipped) with an Anti-lock Brake System (ABS)
   - The sway bar link from the damper fork, if necessary
   - The damper fork assembly
   - The steering knuckle from the lower control arm
   - The halfshaft by pressing it from the hub

➡After pressing the outer shaft, insert a pry bar between the transaxle case and the halfshaft and pry the shaft from the transaxle.

⁂ WARNING

Do not pull on the shaft. Doing so damages the inboard joint. Do not insert the pry bar too far or the oil seal in the case may be damaged.

To install:

3. Inspect the halfshaft boot for damage or deterioration. Check the ball joints and splines for wear.
4. Replace the circlips on the ends of the halfshaft(s).
5. Install or connect the following:
   - The halfshaft into the transaxle until it is fully seated
   - The halfshaft into the hub by pulling the knuckle assembly outward
   - The washer. Make sure the chamfered edge faces outward
   - The halfshaft nut and tighten temporarily
   - The control arm to the steering knuckle and torque the nuts to 43–52 ft. lbs. (59–71 Nm)
   - The damper fork and torque the lower through-bolt/nut to 65 ft. lbs. (88 Nm) and the upper pinch bolt to 76 ft. lbs. (103 Nm)
   - The tie rod end, to the steering knuckle and torque the nut to 17–25 ft. lbs. (24–33 Nm) and install the a new cotter pin
   - The sway bar link to the damper fork and torque the link nut to 29 ft. lbs. (39 Nm)
   - The lock washer and axle nut and torque the nut to 145–188 ft. lbs. (200–260 Nm)

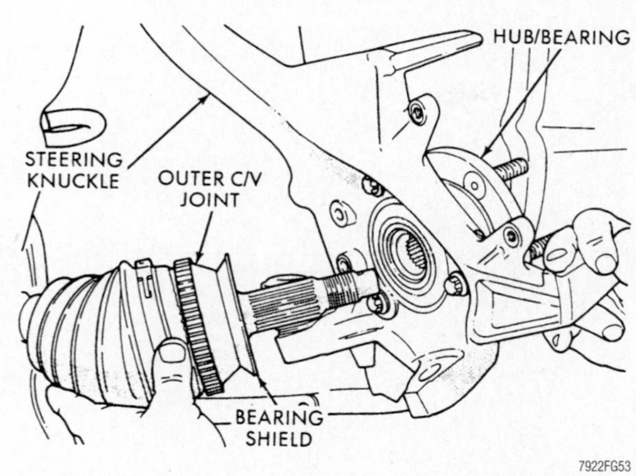

Fig. 42 Carefully remove the outer CV-joint from the steering knuckle—be careful NOT to damage the threads or splines on the joint

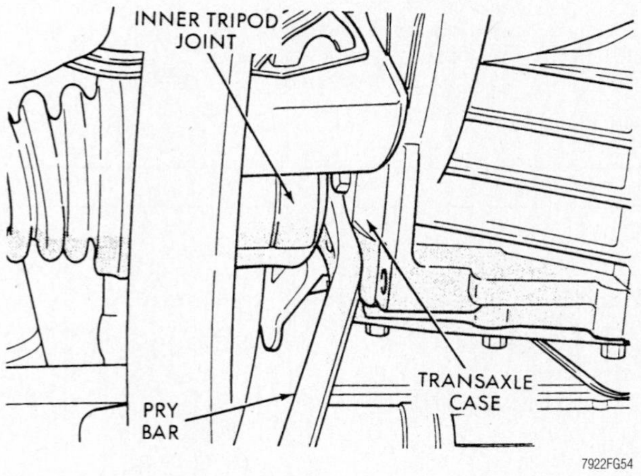

Fig. 43 Inserting the pry bar too far may damage the transaxle seal

➡Before securely tightening the axle nut, be sure there is no load on the wheel bearings.

- The brake rotor and caliper assembly
- The new cotter pin
- The wheel
- The negative battery cable

6. Refill the transaxle.
7. Test drive the vehicle and check for proper operation.

Inner Tri-Pod Joint

See Figures 44 through 49.

1. Before servicing the vehicle, refer to the Precautions Section.
2. Remove the negative battery cable.
3. Remove the halfshaft.
4. Remove the large and small boot retaining clamps.
5. Slide the boot down the shaft away from the tri-pod housing.

➡When separating the spider joint from the tri-pod joint housing, hold the rollers in place on the trunnions to prevent the rollers and needle bearings from falling away.

6. Carefully slide the shaft/spider assembly from the tri-pod housing.
7. Remove the spider assembly-to-shaft snap ring; then, slide the spider assembly off the shaft.

✻✻ WARNING

If necessary, tap the spider assembly off the shaft using a brass drift; be careful not to hit the outer bearings.

8. Slide the boot off the shaft.
9. Thoroughly inspect all parts for signs of excessive wear. If necessary, replace the halfshaft.

➡Component parts are not serviceable and must be replaced as an assembly.

To install:

✻✻ WARNING

The Tri-pod sealing boots are made of 2 different types of material; silicon rubber (high temperature) which is soft and pliable or Hytrel plastic (standard temperature) which is stiff and rigid. Be sure to replace the boot made of the correct material.

10. Slide the inner tri-pod boot clamp and boot onto the shaft; then, position the boot so that only the thinnest (sight) groove is visible on the shaft.
11. Install the spider assembly onto the shaft just far enough so that the snap ring can be installed.

✻✻ WARNING

If necessary, tap the spider assembly onto the shaft using a brass drift; be careful not to hit the outer bearings.

12. Install the snap ring onto the shaft; make sure that the snap ring is fully seated in the groove.
13. If installing a new boot, distribute ½ of the grease in the service package inside the tri-pod housing and the other ½ inside the boot.
14. Carefully, slide the spider assembly and shaft into the tri-pod housing.
15. Position the inner boot clamp evenly on the sealing boot.

✻✻ WARNING

The seal must not be dimpled, stretched or out of shape. If necessary, use a trim stick to seat and equalize the seal pressure and shape it by hand.

➡If using a Hytrel (hard plastic) boot, be sure the stick is inserted between the soft rubber insert and the tri-pod housing, not between the hard plastic sealing boot and the soft rubber insert.

16. Position the boot onto the tri-pod housing retaining groove and install the retaining clamp evenly on the boot.
17. If using a crimp type boot clamp, perform the following procedure:
    a. Using the Crimper Tool C-4975-A, place the tool over the clamp bridge, tighten the tool nut until the jaws are completely closed (face-to-face).

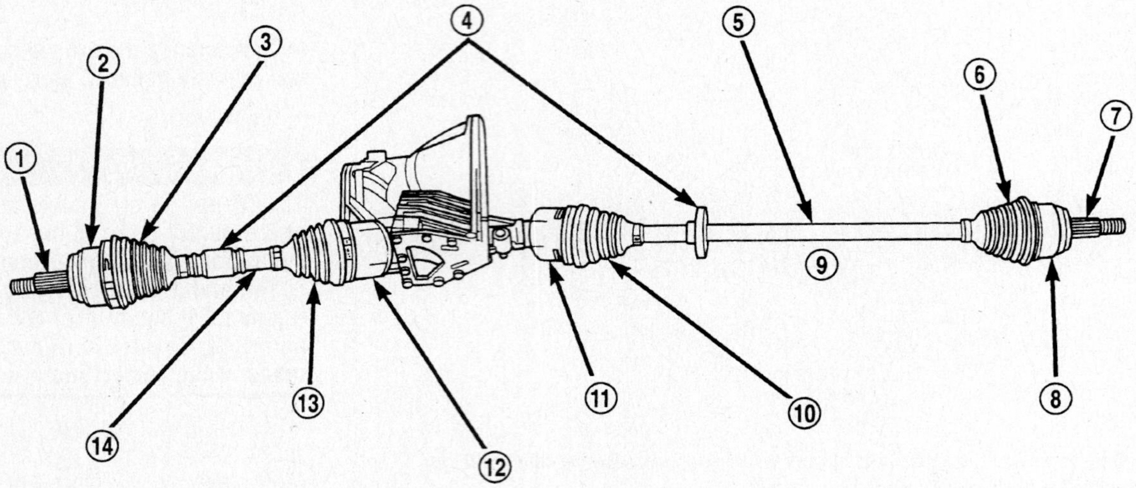

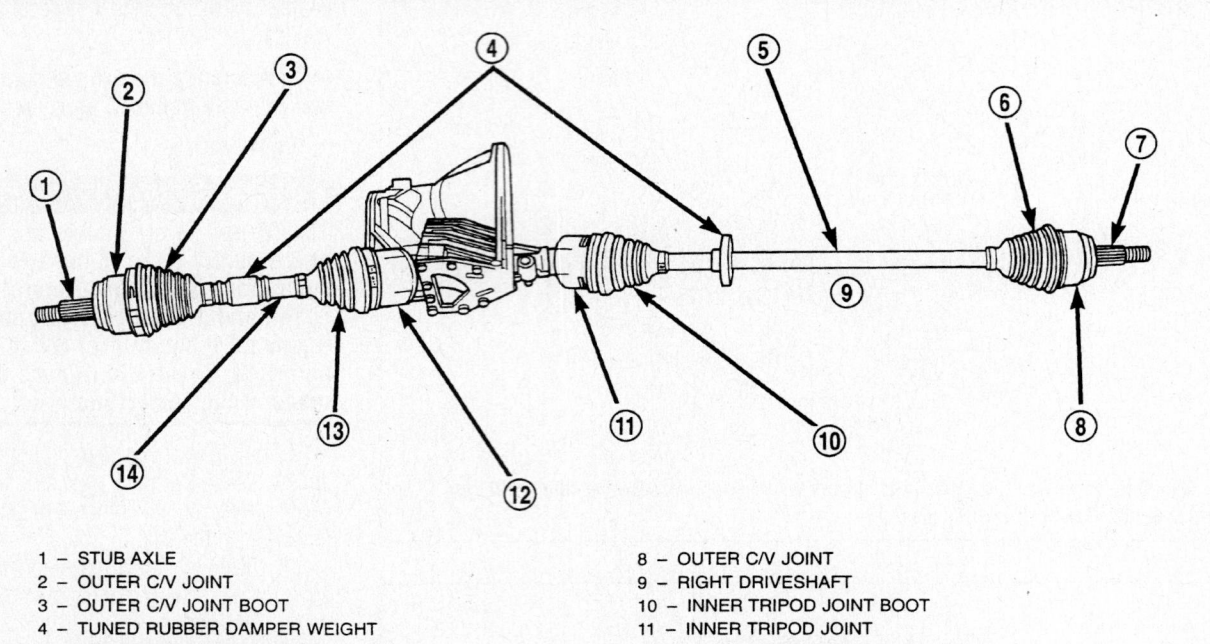

1 – STUB AXLE
2 – OUTER C/V JOINT
3 – OUTER C/V JOINT BOOT
4 – TUNED RUBBER DAMPER WEIGHT
5 – INTERCONNECTING SHAFT
6 – OUTER C/V JOINT BOOT
7 – STUB AXLE
8 – OUTER C/V JOINT
9 – RIGHT DRIVESHAFT
10 – INNER TRIPOD JOINT BOOT
11 – INNER TRIPOD JOINT
12 – INNER TRIPOD JOINT
13 – INNER TRIPOD JOINT BOOT
14 – INTERCONNECTING SHAFT LEFT DRIVESHAFT

9306EG02

Fig. 44 View of a typical halfshaft assembly

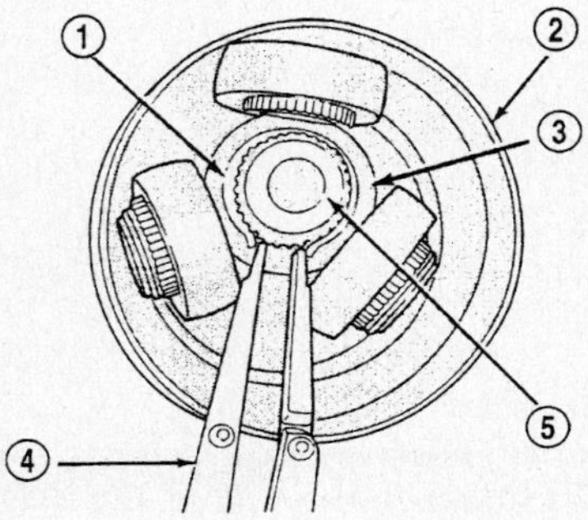

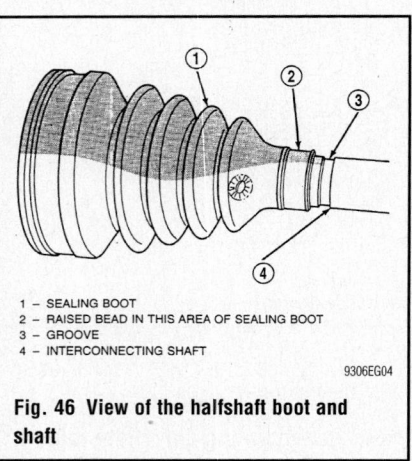

1 – SNAP RING
2 – SEALING BOOT
3 – SPIDER ASSEMBLY
4 – SNAP RING PLIERS
5 – INTERCONNECTING SHAFT

9306BG11

Fig. 45 View of the halfshaft inner tri-pod joint and snap ring

b. Using the Crimper Tool C-4975-A, place the tool over the clamp bridge, tighten the tool nut until the jaws are completely closed (face-to-face).

18. If using a latching type boot clamp, perform the following procedure:

a. Position Snap—On® Clamp Locking Tool YA3050 prongs in the clamp holes.

b. Squeeze the tool until the upper

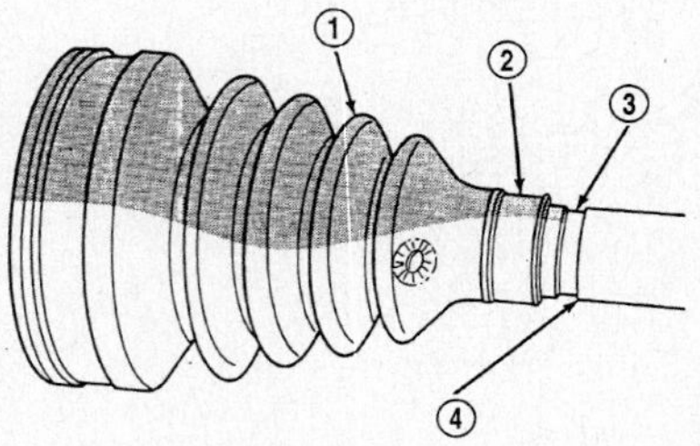

1 – SEALING BOOT
2 – RAISED BEAD IN THIS AREA OF SEALING BOOT
3 – GROOVE
4 – INTERCONNECTING SHAFT

9306EG04

Fig. 46 View of the halfshaft boot and shaft

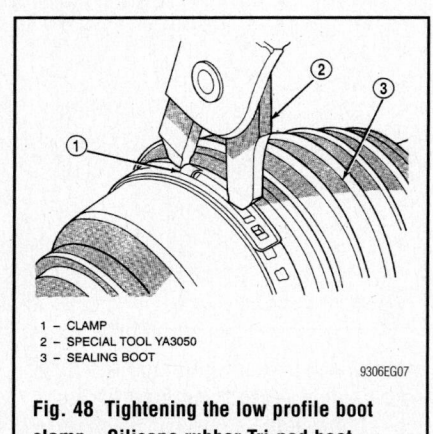

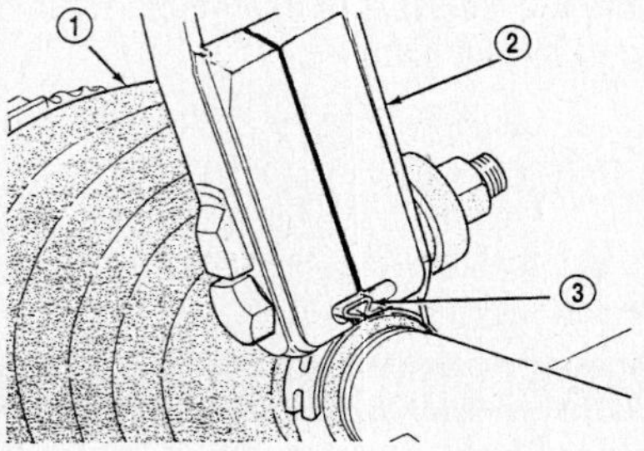

1 – SEALING BOOT
2 – SPECIAL TOOL C-4975
3 – CLAMP BRIDGE

9306BG13

Fig. 47 Securing the halfshaft boot clamp

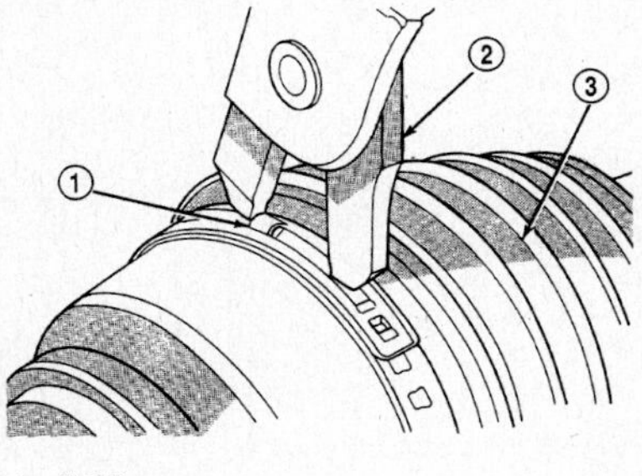

1 – CLAMP
2 – SPECIAL TOOL YA3050
3 – SEALING BOOT

9306EG07

Fig. 48 Tightening the low profile boot clamp—Silicone rubber Tri-pod boot

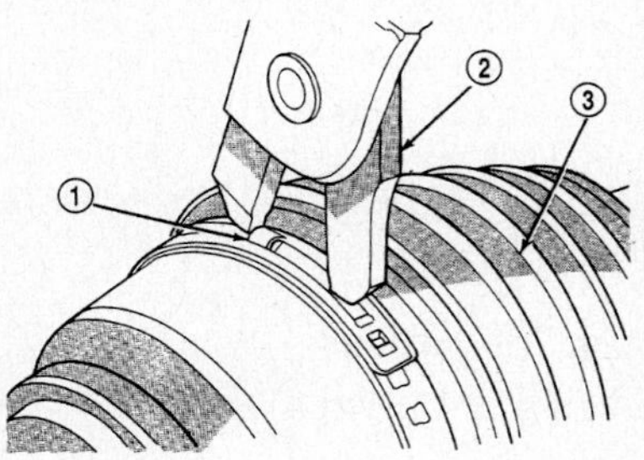

1 – CLAMP
2 – SPECIAL TOOL YA3050
3 – SEALING BOOT

9306EG08

Fig. 49 Secured the low profile boot clamp—Silicone rubber Tri-pod boot

clamp band is latched behind the 2 tabs on the lower clamp band.

19. Install the halfshaft into the vehicle.

Rzeppa (Outer) Joint

See Figures 50 and 51.

1. Before servicing the vehicle, refer to the Precautions Section.
2. Remove or disconnect the following:
   - The halfshaft and place it in a soft-jawed vise
   - The Rzeppa joint boot clamps and slide the boot down the shaft
   - The Rzeppa joint housing by sharply hitting it with a soft-faced hammer to drive it off the shaft
   - The circlip from the shaft
   - The boot by sliding it off the shaft

✲✲ WARNING

If any parts show excessive wear, replace the halfshaft assembly; the component parts are not serviceable.

To install:

3. Install or connect the following:
   - The new small boot clamp and slide it onto the shaft

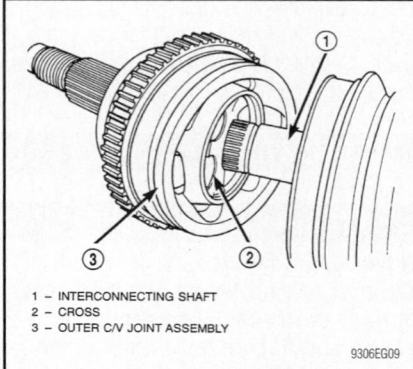

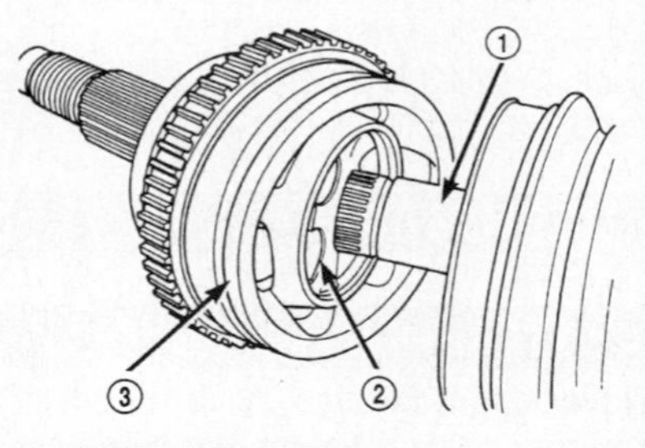

Fig. 50 Aligning the cross splines with the shaft splines—Rzeppa joint

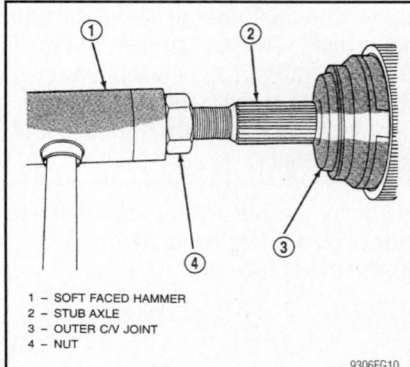

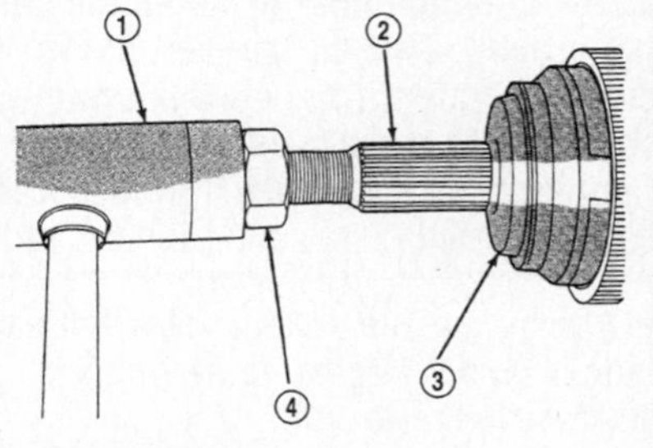

Fig. 51 Driving the Rzeppa joint onto the shaft

   - The boot and slide it onto the shaft
   - The circlip, if removed
4. Position the boot so that the raised bead on the inside the boot seal is in the shaft groove.
5. Install the halfshaft hub nut onto the Rzeppa joint threaded shaft so it is flush with the end.
6. Install the Rzeppa joint and align the shaft splines and tap it onto the shaft with a soft-faced hammer so it locks on the circlip.
7. Distribute ½ of the grease in the service package inside the Rzeppa joint housing and the other ½ inside the boot.
8. Install a new small boot clamp and position it evenly on the sealing boot.
9. Using the Crimper Tool C-4975-A, place the tool over the clamp bridge, tighten the tool nut until the jaws are completely closed (face-to-face).

✲✲ WARNING

The seal must not be dimpled, stretched or out of shape. If necessary, equalize the seal pressure and shape it by hand.

10. Position the boot onto the Rzeppa housing retaining groove and install the retaining clamp evenly on the boot.
11. Using the Crimper Tool C-4975-A, place the tool over the clamp bridge, tighten the tool nut until the jaws are completely closed (face-to-face).

✲✲ WARNING

The seal must not be dimpled, stretched or out of shape. If necessary, equalize the seal pressure and shape it by hand.

12. Install the halfshaft into the vehicle.

CV-JOINTS OVERHAUL

Servicing the CV-joints is limited to replacing the CV boot. Further servicing of the CV-joints is not possible and the CV-joint must be replaced if worn or damaged.

REAR AXLE SHAFT, BEARING & SEAL

REMOVAL & INSTALLATION

See Figure 52.

All vehicles are equipped with permanently lubricated and sealed for life rear wheel bearings. There is no periodic lubrication or maintenance recommended for these units.

To evaluate the condition of the rear wheel bearings, remove the wheel and brake drum or rotor and rotate the flanged outer ring of the hub. Excessive roughness or resistance to rotation may indicate dirt intrusion or wheel bearing failure. If the rear wheel bearings exhibit these conditions during inspection, the hub and bearing assembly should be replaced. Damaged

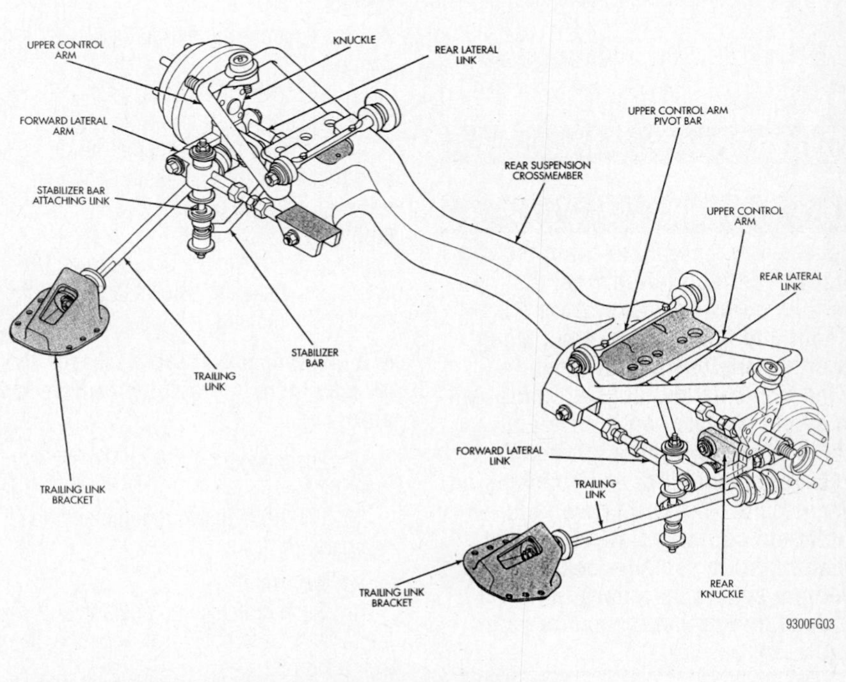

Fig. 52 Independent rear suspension component identification

bearing seals and resulting excessive grease loss may also require bearing replacement. Moderate grease loss from the bearing is considered normal and should not require replacement of the hub and bearing assembly. If service requires removal for inspection or replacement of the rear wheel bearing and hub assembly, use the following procedure.

1. Before servicing the vehicle, refer to the Precautions Section.
2. Remove or disconnect the following:
   - The rear wheel
   - The brake drum, if equipped with drum brakes
   - The brake caliper and rotor, if equipped with disc brakes
   - The hub dust cap
   - The hub nut and discard it
   - The hub/bearing assembly by pulling straight off the spindle

To install:

3. Install or connect the following:
   - The new bearing on the spindle
   - The hub using a new nut and torque the nut to 185 ft. lbs. (250 Nm)
   - The dust cap
   - The brake drum or rotor and caliper
   - The rear wheel and torque the lug nuts to 100 ft. lbs. (135 Nm)

ENGINE COOLING

ENGINE FAN

REMOVAL & INSTALLATION

The radiator fan module includes a support shroud with two electrically driven motors with fan blades. The radiator fan module is fastened to the radiator. The motors, shroud, and fan blades are serviced separately.

1. Remove the upper radiator crossmember.
2. Disconnect radiator fan electrical connector.
3. Remove the fasteners and upper clip attaching fan assembly to radiator.
4. Remove the radiator fan assembly by lifting upward.

To install:

5. Install the radiator fan to radiator. Install the retaining clip and tighten fasteners to 45 inch lbs. (5 Nm).
6. Connect radiator fan electrical connector.
7. Install the upper radiator crossmember.

RADIATOR

CAUTION

Never open, service or drain the radiator or cooling system when hot; serious burns can occur from the steam and hot coolant. Also, when draining engine coolant, keep in mind that cats and dogs are attracted to ethylene glycol antifreeze and could drink any that is left in an uncovered container or in puddles on the ground. This will prove fatal in sufficient quantities. Always drain coolant into a sealable container. Coolant should be reused unless it is contaminated or is several years old.

WARNING

Plastic tanks, while stronger then brass are subject to damage by impact, such as by a wrench slipping.

WARNING

Avoid bending the condenser inlet tube. Care should be taken not to damage radiator or condenser cooling fins or water tubes during removal.

REMOVAL & INSTALLATION

1. Before servicing the vehicle, refer to the Precautions Section.
2. Disconnect negative cable from auxiliary jumper terminal.
3. Drain the cooling system.
4. Remove the upper radiator crossmember.
5. Disconnect the radiator fan electrical connector.
6. Remove the radiator fan.
7. Disconnect hoses from radiator.
8. Remove the screw that holds support bracket for transmission cooler tubes at left side of radiator (if equipped).
9. Remove the Air Conditioning (A/C) condenser attaching screws located at the front of the radiator.

➡It is not necessary to discharge the air conditioning system to remove radiator.

10. Disengage the A/C condenser from the radiator.
11. Lift the radiator from the engine compartment.

To install:

12. Slide radiator into position and seat the radiator assembly lower rubber isolators in the mount holes.
13. Attach the A/C condenser to the radiator. Tighten the mounting screws to 45 inch lbs. (5 Nm).
14. Install the transmission oil cooler tube support bracket and attaching screw to left side of radiator. Tighten mounting screw to 45 inch lbs. (5 Nm).
15. Connect the hoses to the radiator.
16. Install the radiator fan.
17. Connect the radiator fan electrical connector.
18. Install the upper radiator crossmember.
19. Connect the negative cable to the auxiliary jumper terminal.
20. Fill the cooling system.
21. Operate the engine until it reaches normal operating temperature. Check the cooling system and the automatic transaxle for correct fluid levels and for leaks.

THERMOSTAT

CAUTION

Never open, service, or drain the radiator or cooling system when hot; serious burns can occur from the steam and hot coolant. Also, when draining engine coolant, keep in mind that cats and dogs are attracted to ethylene glycol antifreeze and could drink any that is left in an uncovered container or in puddles on the ground. This will prove fatal in sufficient quantities. Always drain coolant into a sealable container. Coolant should be reused unless it is contaminated or is several years old.

➡Always replace a thermostat that has failed. Do not attempt to free-up a stuck open thermostat.

REMOVAL & INSTALLATION

2.4L Engine

See Figure 53.

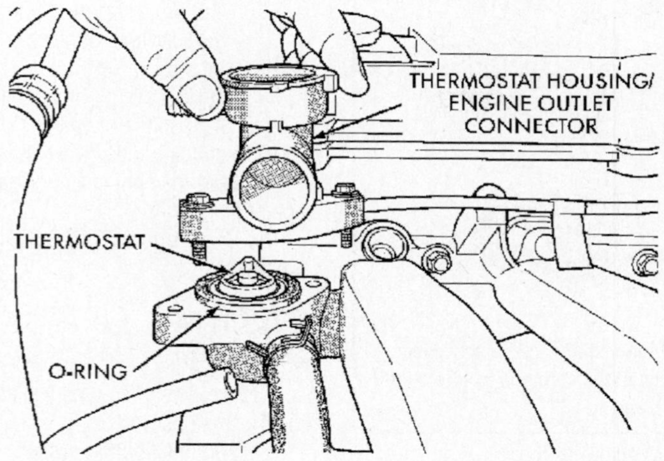

Fig. 53 Thermostat assembly—2.4L engine

1. Before servicing the vehicle, refer to the Precautions Section.
2. Drain the cooling system to the thermostat level or below.
3. Remove the Coolant Recovery System (CRS) hose and thermostat/engine outlet connector bolts.
4. Remove the thermostat assembly, and clean sealing surfaces.

To install:

5. Place the new thermostat assembly into the engine outlet connector.
6. Make sure the spring side of the thermostat faces the cylinder head.
7. Install the engine outlet connector onto cylinder head and tighten bolts to 110 inch lbs. (12.5 Nm)
8. Connect the CRS hose.
9. Fill the cooling system to the proper level.

2.7L Engine

See Figure 54.

1. Disconnect the negative cable from the remote jumper terminal.
2. Drain the cooling system.
3. Raise and safely support the vehicle.
4. Remove the right front wheel and belt splash shield.
5. Remove the accessory drive belts.
6. Remove the lower alternator mounting bolt.
7. Lower the vehicle.
8. Disconnect the alternator electrical connectors.
9. Disconnect the Air Conditioning (A/C) clutch and A/C pressure sensor electrical connectors.
10. Reposition the wiring harness.
11. Remove the oil dipstick and tube. Plug the hole in the oil pan where the dipstick tube mounts using a water tight stopper.

⁂ WARNING

If the hole for the dipstick tube in the oil pan is not plugged, coolant may enter the oil pan. Serious engine damage can occur.

12. Remove the remaining alternator mounting bolts. Remove the alternator.
13. Disconnect the hoses at the thermostat housing.
14. Remove the thermostat housing bolts.
15. Remove the thermostat and housing.

To install:

16. Clean the gasket sealing surfaces.
17. Install the thermostat and gasket into the thermostat housing.
    a. Make sure spring side of thermostat faces the engine side.
    b. Install the thermostat with the air bleed valve located at the 12 o'clock position.

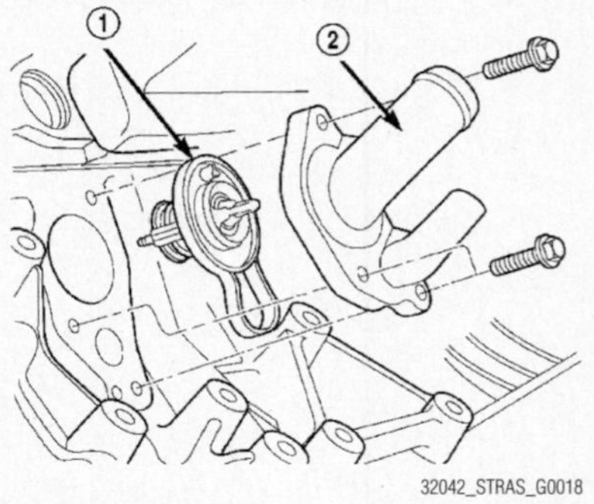

Fig. 54 Air bleed valve (1) and thermostat housing (2) 2.7L—engine

18. Install the thermostat and housing to cylinder block. Tighten attaching bolts to 105 inch lbs. (12 Nm).
19. Connect hoses at thermostat housing.
20. Install the alternator and attaching bolts.
21. Clean residual coolant from area around hole for dipstick.
22. Remove the plug in oil pan and install the engine oil dipstick tube.
23. Reconnect A/C clutch and A/C pressure sensor connectors.
24. Reconnect alternator connectors.
25. Raise and safely support the vehicle.
26. Install the accessory drive belts.
27. Install the belt splash shield and right front wheel.
28. Lower the vehicle.
29. Reconnect the negative battery cable.
30. Fill the cooling system to the proper level.

WATER PUMP

REMOVAL & INSTALLATION

⁂ CAUTION

Never open, service, or drain the radiator or cooling system when hot; serious burns can occur from the steam and hot coolant. Also, when draining engine coolant, keep in mind that cats and dogs are attracted to ethylene glycol antifreeze and could drink any that is left in an uncovered container or in puddles on the ground. This will prove fatal in sufficient quantities. Always drain coolant into a sealable container. Coolant should be reused unless it is contaminated or is several years old.

2.4L Engine

See Figure 55.

This engine uses a die-cast aluminum body water pump with a stamped steel impeller. The water pump bolts directly to the block. Cylinder block-to-water pump sealing is provided by a large rubber O-ring. The water pump is driven by the timing belt that must be removed to service the water pump.

1. Before servicing the vehicle, refer to the Precautions Section.
2. Disconnect the negative battery cable from the left shock tower.

➡The ground cable is equipped with an insulator grommet which should be placed on the stud to prevent the negative battery cable from accidentally grounding.

➡This procedure requires removing the engine timing belt and the auto-tensioner. The factory specifies that the timing marks should always be aligned before removing the timing belt. Set the engine at Top Dead Center (TDC) on No. 1 compression stroke. This should align all timing marks on the crankshaft sprocket and both camshaft sprockets.

3. Drain the cooling system.
4. Remove or disconnect the following:
   - The right inner splash shield
   - The accessory drive belts and support the engine
   - The right motor mount
   - The power steering pump bracket bolts and move the pump/bracket assembly aside

➡Do not disconnect the power steering fluid lines.

   - The right engine mount bracket
   - The timing belt front covers
   - The timing belt tensioner and timing belt by loosening the tensioner screws

⁂ WARNING

With the timing belt removed, DO NOT rotate the camshaft or crankshaft or damage to the engine could occur.

   - The camshaft sprockets

➡Do not allow the camshafts to turn when the camshaft sprockets are being removed.

   - The rear timing belt cover
   - The water pump

To install:

5. Thoroughly clean all sealing surfaces. Replace the water pump if there are any cracks, signs of coolant leakage from the shaft seal, loose or rough turning bearings, damaged impeller or sprocket or sprocket flange loose or damaged.
6. Install a **NEW** rubber O-ring into the water pump.

➡Be sure the O-ring is properly seated in the water pump groove before tightening the screws. An improperly located O-ring may cause damage to the O-ring and cause a coolant leak.

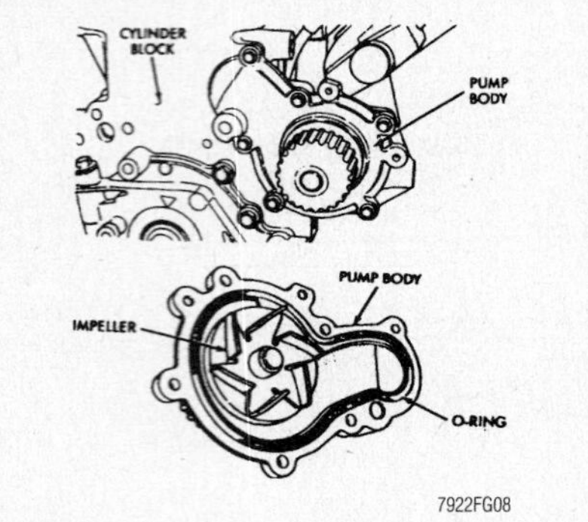

Fig. 55 When installing the water pump, properly install the O-ring to ensure a tight seal—2.4L engine

7. Install the water pump. Torque the bolts to 105 inch lbs. (12 Nm).
8. Pressurize the cooling system to 15 psi (103.4 kPa) and check for leaks. If no leaks are found, release the pressure and continue the engine assembly process.
9. Install or connect the following:
   - The rear timing belt cover
   - The camshaft sprockets. Torque the bolts to 75 ft. lbs. (101 Nm)

➡DO NOT allow the camshafts to turn while the sprocket bolts are being tightened to maintain timing mark alignment.

⁂ WARNING

Do not attempt to compress the tensioner plunger with the tensioner assembly installed in the engine. This will cause damage to the tensioner and other related components. The tensioner MUST be compressed in a vise.

   - The timing belt tensioner and timing belt. Properly tension the timing belt.
   - The front upper and lower timing belt covers
   - The right engine mount bracket and engine mount
   - The crankshaft damper. Torque the center bolt to 105 ft. lbs. (142 Nm)
   - The right inner splash shield
   - The power steering pump bracket and power steering pump. Torque the bracket mounting bolts to 40 ft. lbs. (54 Nm)
   - The accessory drive belts. Properly tension the drive belts

10. Refill and bleed the cooling system.
11. Start the engine and check for proper operation.
12. Check and top off cooling system, if necessary.

2.7L Engine

See Figure 56.

1. Before servicing the vehicle, refer to the Precautions Section.
2. Drain the cooling system.
3. Remove or disconnect the following:
   - The negative battery cable
   - The timing chain cover
   - The timing chain and guides
   - The water pump and discard the gasket

To install:

4. Clean all mating surfaces of any residual gasket material.
5. Install or connect the following:
   - The water pump with a new gasket and torque the bolts to 105 inch lbs. (12 Nm)
   - The timing chain guides and chain
   - The timing chain cover
   - The negative battery cable
6. Fill the cooling system to the proper level.
7. Start the vehicle, check for leaks and repair if necessary.

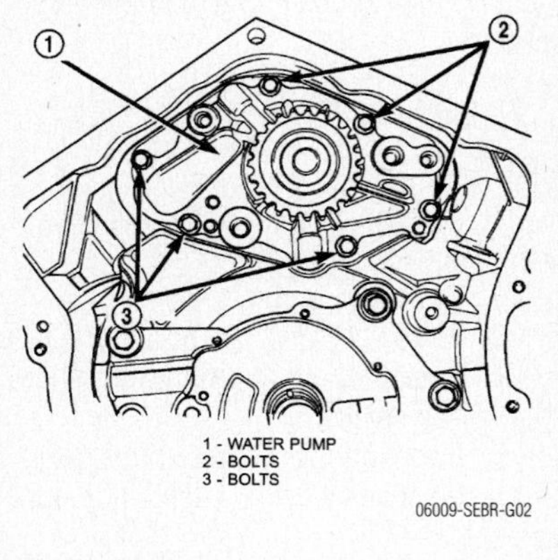

Fig. 56 Water pump—2.7L engine

ENGINE ELECTRICAL — CHARGING SYSTEM

ALTERNATOR

REMOVAL & INSTALLATION

2.4L Engine

See Figure 57.

1. Before servicing the vehicle, refer to the precautions in the beginning of this section.
2. Remove or disconnect the following:
   - The negative battery cable from the shock tower
   - The accessory belt cover
   - The alternator electrical connectors
   - The accessory belt splash shield
   - The accessory belt
   - The Manifold Absolute Pressure (MAP) sensor from the intake manifold
   - The alternator

To install:

3. Install or connect the following:
   - The alternator and torque the bolts to 33 ft. lbs. (44 Nm)
   - The MAP sensor
   - The drive belt and splash shield
   - The alternator electrical connectors
   - The accessory belt cover
   - The negative battery cable

2.7L Engine

1. Before servicing the vehicle, refer to the precautions in the beginning of this section.
2. Remove or disconnect the following:
   - The negative battery cable from the shock tower
   - The accessory belt splash shield and loosen the belt
   - The alternator electrical connectors
   - The A/C pressure switch and clutch electrical connectors
   - The engine oil dipstick
   - The alternator

To install:

3. Install or connect the following:
   - The alternator and torque the bolts to 40 ft. lbs. (54 Nm)
   - The engine oil dipstick tube
   - The A/C pressure switch and clutch electrical connectors
   - The alternator electrical connectors
   - The drive belt and splash shield
   - The negative battery cable

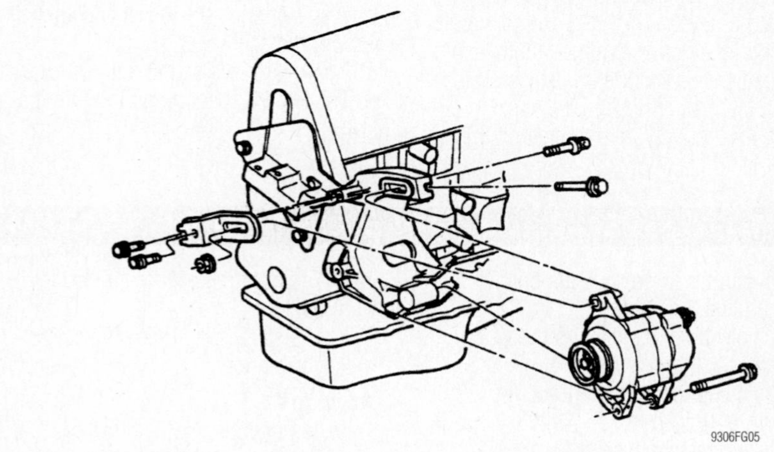

Fig. 57 Exploded view of the alternator and related components—2.4L engine

ENGINE ELECTRICAL — IGNITION SYSTEM

FIRING ORDER

See Figures 58 and 59.

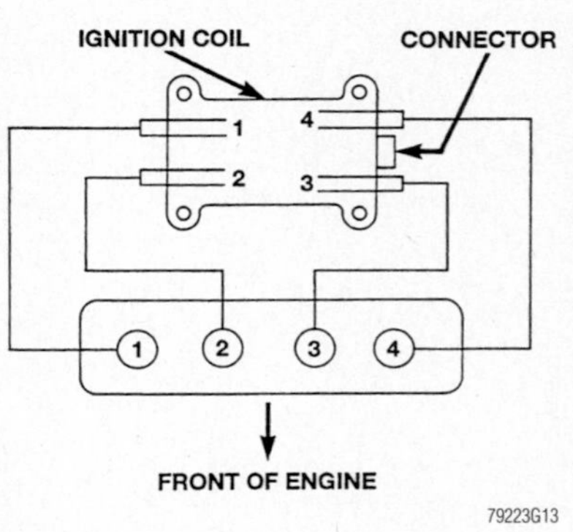

**Fig. 58 2.4L Engine
Firing order: 1–3–4–2
Distributorless ignition system**

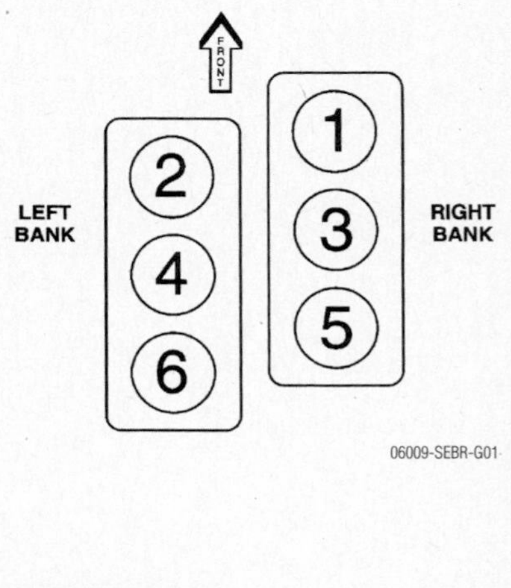

**Fig. 59 2.7L Engine
Firing order: 1–2–3–4–5–6
Distributorless ignition system**

IGNITION COIL

REMOVAL & INSTALLATION

2.4L Engine

The electronic ignition coil pack is mounted to the cylinder head cover.

1. Before servicing the vehicle, refer to the Precautions Section.
2. Disconnect the negative battery cable.
3. Disconnect the electrical connector from coil pack.
4. Remove the spark plug cables, twist and pull cables to remove.
5. Remove the coil pack mounting bolts.
6. Remove the coil pack.

To install:

7. Install the coil pack on cylinder head cover.
8. Install the bolts and tighten bolts to 106 inch lbs. (12 Nm).

9. Connect the electrical connector.

10. Transfer spark plug cables to new coil pack. The coil pack towers are numbered with the cylinder identification. Make sure the ignition cables snap onto the towers.

2.7L Engine

The ignition system uses a coil on plug assembly and has an ignition coil for every cylinder mounted directly over each spark plug (if equipped).

1. Before servicing the vehicle, refer to the Precautions Section.
2. Use compressed air to clean area around ignition coils and spark plugs.
3. Remove the electrical connector from ignition coil.
4. Remove the 2 fasteners from ignition coil assembly.
5. Remove the ignition coil assembly.

To install:

6. Install the ignition coil assembly for spark plug.
7. Install the coil screws and tighten to 55 inch lbs. (6.2 Nm).
8. Connect the electrical connector.

IGNITION TIMING

ADJUSTMENT

The ignition timing is controlled by the Powertrain Control Module (PCM). No adjustment is necessary or possible.

SPARK PLUGS

REMOVAL & INSTALLATION

The ignition coil assembly for the 4 cylinder engines consists of 2 independent coils molded together. The coil assembly for the 4 cylinder engines is mounted on the cylinder head cover. Spark plug cables route to each cylinder from the coil. The coil assemblies for the 2.7L are mounted on the head cover. It is a coil on plug assembly and each cylinder has an ignition coil assembly.

2.4L Engine

1. Disconnect the spark plug wires from the spark plug.
2. Use a spark plug socket and wrench to remove the spark plugs.
3. To install, reverse the removal procedure. Tighten the spark plugs to 13 ft. lbs. (18 Nm).

2.7L Engine

1. Remove the ignition coils. Refer to Ignition Coil, REMOVAL & INSTALLATION.
2. Use a spark plug socket and wrench to remove the spark plugs.
3. To install, reverse the removal procedure. Tighten the spark plugs to 15 ft. lbs. (20 Nm).

ENGINE ELECTRICAL — STARTING SYSTEM

STARTER

REMOVAL & INSTALLATION

2.4L Engine

1. Before servicing the vehicle, refer to the Precautions Section.
2. Remove or disconnect the following:
   - The negative battery cable
   - The air cleaner assembly
   - The starter cover
   - The starter electrical connectors
   - The starter

To install:

3. Install or connect the following:
   - The starter and torque the bolt to 23 ft. lbs. (30 Nm)
   - The electrical connectors to the starter
   - The starter cover and torque the bolt to 44 inch lbs. (5 Nm)
   - The air cleaner assembly
   - The negative battery cable

2.7L Engine

1. Before servicing the vehicle, refer to the Precautions Section.
2. Remove or disconnect the following:
   - The negative battery cable
   - The Oxygen Sensor (O_2S) electrical connector
   - The front engine mount through bolt
   - The starter electrical connectors
   - The starter

To install:

3. Install or connect the following:
   - The starter and hand tighten the lower bolt
   - The starter electrical connectors and torque the starter bolts to 40 ft. lbs. (54 Nm)
   - The engine mount through bolt and torque it to 45 ft. lbs. (61 Nm)
   - The O_2 sensor and torque it to 20 ft. lbs. (27 Nm)
   - The negative battery cable

ENGINE MECHANICAL

➡Disconnecting the negative battery cable may interfere with the functions of the on board computer systems and may require the computer to undergo a relearning process, once the negative battery cable is reconnected.

ACCESSORY DRIVE BELTS

ACCESSORY BELT ROUTING

See Figures 60 and 61.

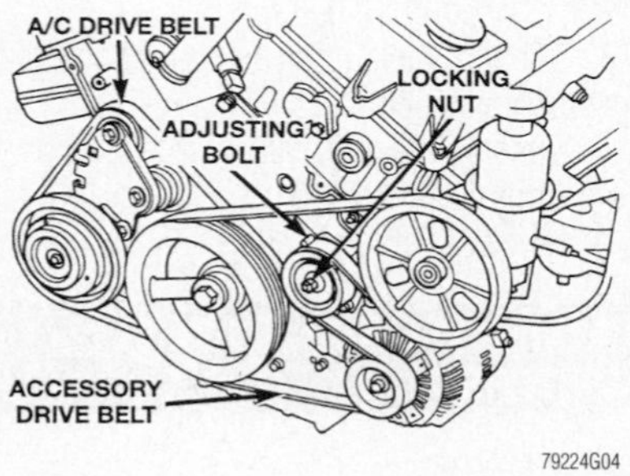

Fig. 60 Accessory drive belt routing—2.4L engine

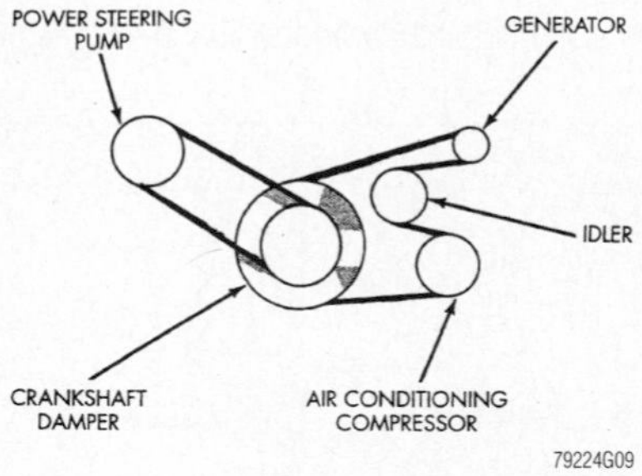

Fig. 61 Accessory drive belt routing—2.7L engine

INSPECTION

Inspect the drive belt for signs of glazing or cracking. A glazed belt will be perfectly smooth from slippage, while a good belt will have a slight texture of fabric visible. Cracks will usually start at the inner edge of the belt and run outward. All worn or damaged drive belts should be replaced immediately.

ADJUSTMENT

2.4L Engine

To obtain proper belt tension of conventional V-belts and Poly-ribbed belts use belt tensioning gauge Special Tool 7198.

New Belts:

- A/C & Alternator: 150 lbs. (667 N)
- Power Steering Pump: 130 lbs. (578 N)

Used Belts:

- A/C & Alternator: 80 lbs. (356 N)
- Power Steering Pump: 80 lbs. (356 N)

2.7L Engine

A/C and Alternator Belt

✻✻ CAUTION

Do not check belt tension with engine running.

1. Engage a torque wrench, with a maximum 2 inch extension in the ½ inch square opening of the tensioner bracket.
2. Apply torque, counter-clockwise to the tensioner bracket
   a. New belts: 104 ft. lbs. (141 Nm)
   b. Used belts: 71 ft. lbs. (96 Nm)
3. Continue to apply torque while tightening the upper fastener.
   a. Torque fastener to 21 ft. lbs. (28 Nm)
4. Remove the torque wrench from tensioner bracket, and torque lower tensioner bracket fastener to 21 ft. lbs. (28 Nm).
5. Verify proper belt tension

Power Steering Pump Belt

✻✻ CAUTION

Do not check belt tension with engine running.

1. Insert a ½ inch drive breaker bar into the square opening on the power steering pump bracket.
2. Hold clockwise pressure on power steering pump bracket and tighten adjusting bolt.
3. Verify proper belt tension

Accessory drive belt tension can be measured with Special Tool 8371 — Belt Tension Gauge Adapter, and the DRBIII® using the following procedures:

4. Connect 8371 to the DRBIII® following the instructions provided with tool.
5. Place end of microphone probe approximately 1 inch (2.54cm) from belt at one of the belt center span locations.
6. Pluck the belt a minimum of 3 times. (Use your finger or other suitable tool) The frequency of the belt in hertz (Hz) will display on DRBIII® screen.
7. Adjust belt to obtain proper frequency (tension) listed below:

New Belts

- A/C & Alternator: 185–235 lbs. (250–320 N)
- Power Steering Pump: 120–180 lbs. (163–245 N)

Used Belts

- A/C & Alternator: 110–160 lbs. (150–215 N)
- Power Steering Pump: 70–115 lbs. (95–155 N)

REMOVAL & INSTALLATION

➡Mark running direction of belt rotation before removing belt. Reinstalling a used belt in the opposite running direction may result in reduced service life.

2.4L Engine

A/C and Alternator Belt

See Figure 62.

1. Raise and safely support the vehicle.
2. Remove the right front wheel and belt splash shield.
3. Insert a ⅜ inch drive breaker bar into the square opening of the belt tensioner pivot bracket.

✻✻ WARNING

Do not use excessive force to over compress belt tensioner. This may result in damage to the belt tensioner.

4. Gently apply a force to rotate belt tensioner clockwise until the belt tensioner bottoms out and the belt can be removed from pulleys.
5. Remove the belt.
6. Gently release tensioner.

To install:

➡When installing drive belt onto pulleys, make sure that belt is properly routed and all V-grooves make proper contact with pulley.

7. Install the belt over all pulleys except for the air conditioning compressor pulley.
8. Insert a ⅜ inch drive breaker bar into the square opening of the belt tensioner pivot bracket.
9. Gently apply a force to rotate belt tensioner clockwise until the belt tensioner bottoms out and the belt can be installed onto air conditioning compressor pulley.
10. Install the belt over air conditioning compressor pulley.
11. Release spring tension onto belt.

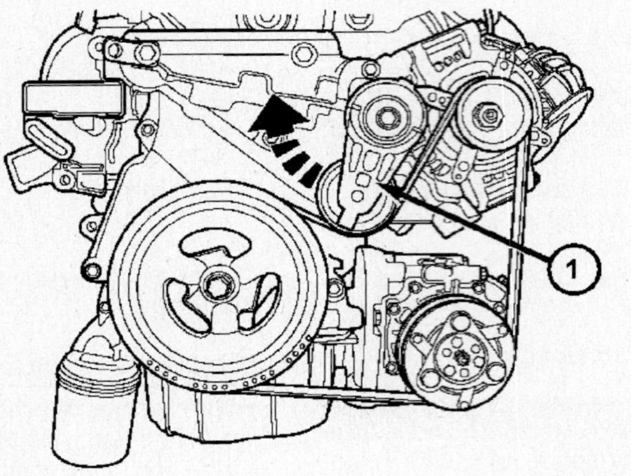

Fig. 62 Accessory drive belt tensioner (1)—2.4L engine

12. Remove the breaker bar from belt tensioner pivot bracket.
13. Install the belt splash shield and right front wheel.
14. Lower vehicle.

Power Steering Belt

1. Raise and safely support the vehicle.
2. Remove the right front wheel and belt splash shield.
3. Remove the air conditioning compressor/alternator belt.
4. Loosen pivot bolt and locking bolt/nut.
5. Release tension on belt by moving pump assembly inward towards engine.
6. Remove the belt.

To install:

7. Install the power steering pump belt on pulleys.
8. Insert a ½ inch drive breaker bar into the square opening on the power steering pump bracket.
9. Hold clockwise pressure on power steering pump bracket and tighten adjusting bolt/nut.
10. Tighten pivot bolt.
11. Install the air conditioning compressor/generator belt.
12. Install the belt splash shield and right front wheel.
13. Lower vehicle.

2.7L Engine

A/C and Alternator Belt

See Figure 63.

1. Raise and safely support the vehicle.
2. Remove the right front wheel and belt splash shield.
3. Loosen tensioner locking bolt and pivot bolt.
4. Rotate tensioner clockwise to allow enough slack to remove belt

To install:

5. Install the air conditioning compressor/alternator belt on pulleys, tensioner in slack position, slip belt over idler last.
6. Adjust drive belt tension.
7. Install the belt splash shield and right front wheel.
8. Lower vehicle.

Power Steering Belt

1. Raise and safely support the vehicle.
2. Remove the right front wheel and belt splash shield.
3. Remove the air conditioning compressor/alternator belt.
4. Loosen belt adjusting bolt. It is not necessary to loosen the pivot bolt on the power steering pump. There is a bushing incorporated into the power steering pump/bracket that allows it to pivot.
5. Remove the power steering belt.

To install:

6. Install the power steering belt on pulleys.
7. Adjust drive belt tension.
8. Install the air conditioning compressor/alternator belt.
9. Install the belt splash shield and right front wheel.
10. Lower vehicle.

CAMSHAFT AND VALVE LIFTERS

INSPECTION

1. Inspect the camshaft bearing journals for damage. If journals are damaged, check the cylinder head for damage. Also check the cylinder head oil holes for clogging.
2. Check the cam lobe and bearing sur-

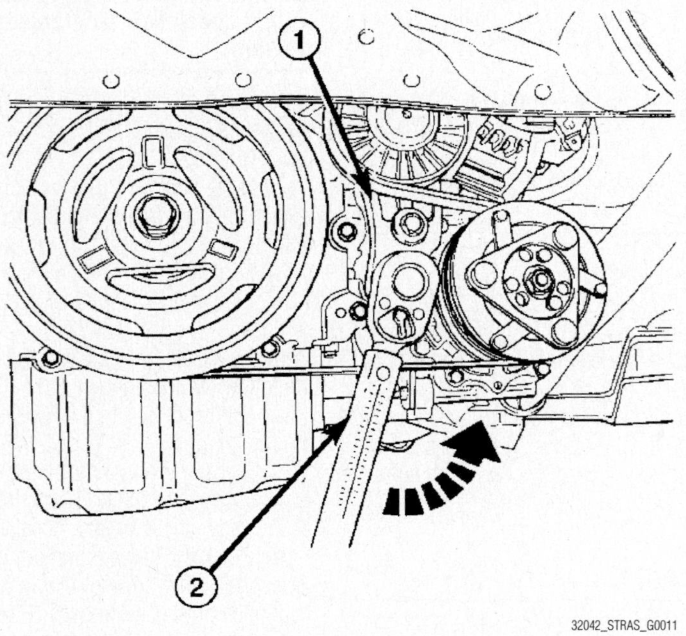

Fig. 63 Installing A/C & alternator belt—2.7L engine

faces for abnormal wear and damage. Replace camshaft if defective.

3. Measure the camshaft end play as follows:
   a. Using a suitable tool, move camshaft as far rearward as it will go.
   b. Zero out the dial indicator.
   c. Move the camshaft as far forward as it will go.
   d. Record the reading on the dial indicator.
   e. If end play is exceeds the specification, check cylinder head and camshaft for wear; replace as necessary

REMOVAL & INSTALLATION

2.4L Engine

See Figures 64 through 68.

This engine uses a DOHC, 4-valves per cylinder, cross-flow aluminum cylinder head. The valves are actuated by roller cam followers which pivot on stationary hydraulic valve adjusters. Care must be taken to ensure all valve timing marks align after cylinder head and valve train service.

1. Before servicing the vehicle, refer to the precautions in the beginning of this section.
2. Disconnect the negative battery cable from the left shock tower.

➡The ground cable is equipped with an insulator grommet which should be placed on the stud to prevent the negative battery cable from accidentally grounding.

3. Relieve the fuel system pressure using the recommended procedure.
4. Remove or disconnect the following:
   - Spark plugs cables
   - Ignition coil pack with the spark plug cables

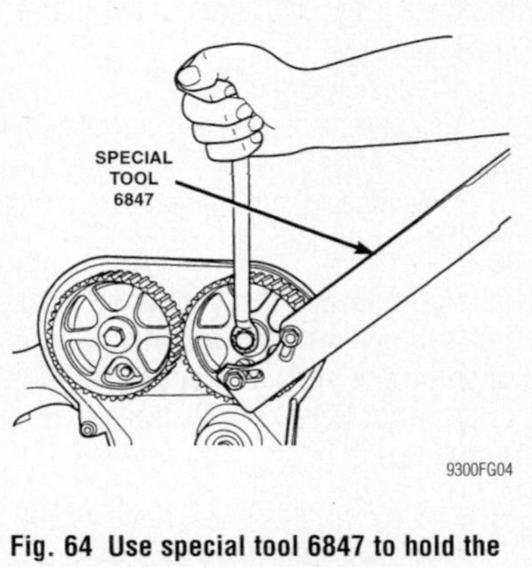

Fig. 64 Use special tool 6847 to hold the camshaft sprocket while removing or installing the center bolt—2.4L engine

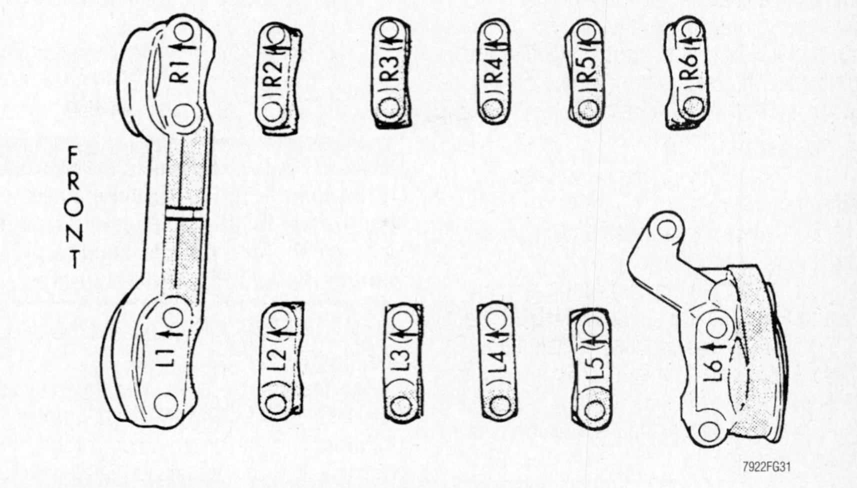

Fig. 65 Camshaft bearing cap identification—2.4L engine

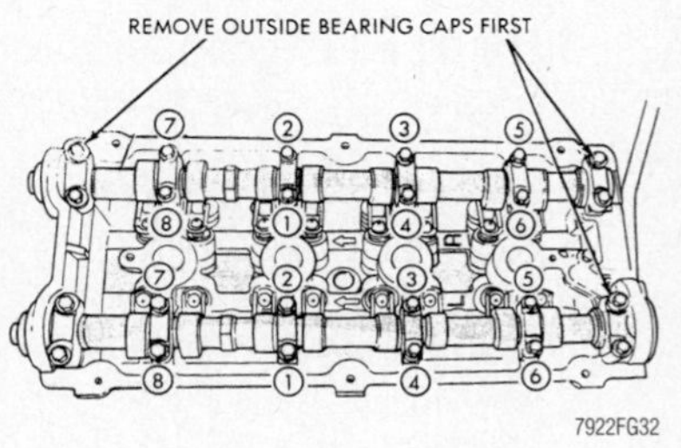

Fig. 66 Camshaft bearing cap bolt removal sequence—2.4L engine

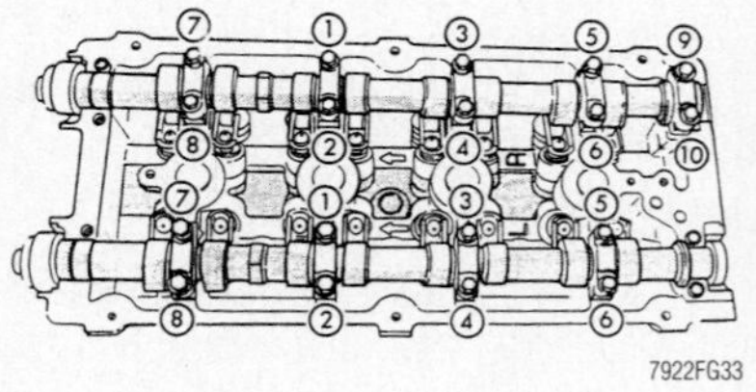

Fig. 67 Camshaft bearing cap tightening sequence—2.4L engine

   - Cylinder head cover and discard the gasket
   - Ground strap
   - Timing belt covers and timing belt
   - Camshaft sprockets by holding them with Tool 6847, while removing the bolt
5. Take note that the camshaft bearing caps are numbered for correct location during installation. Remove the outer bearing caps first.

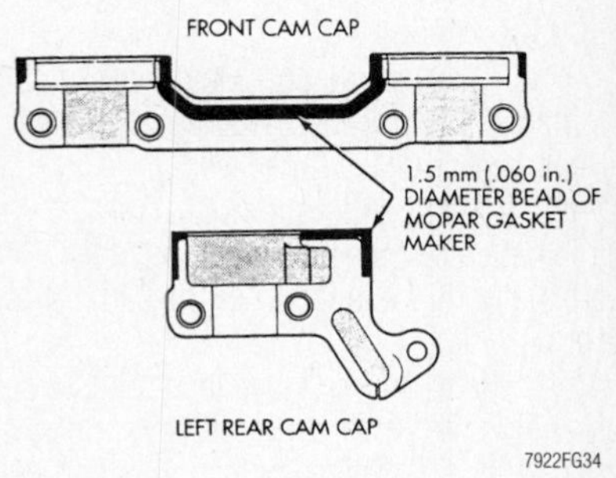

Fig. 68 Apply sealer as shown to prevent oil leakage from the camshaft bearing end caps—2.4L engine

6. Loosen, but do not remove, the camshaft bearing cap retaining fasteners in the correct sequence, inside working outward. Perform this step on one camshaft at a time.
7. Identify the camshafts, if they are to be reused for later installation. The camshafts are not interchangeable.
8. Remove or disconnect the following:
   - Camshaft bearing caps
   - Camshafts
   - Camshaft followers
9. Any components that are to be reused must be installed in their original locations. Use care to identify and mark the positions of any removed valve train components so they may be reinstalled correctly.
10. Inspect the camshaft bearing oil feed holes in the cylinder head for clogging.

Inspect the camshaft bearing journals for wear or scoring. Check the cam surface for abnormal wear and damage. A visible worn groove in the roller path or on the cam lobes is cause for replacement.

To install:

11. Thoroughly clean all camshaft and related parts.
12. Inspect the camshaft end-play using the following procedure:
    a. Lubricate the camshaft journals and install the camshaft **WITHOUT** the cam follower assemblies. Install the rear cam caps and tighten to 21 ft. lbs. (28 Nm).
    b. Push the camshaft rearward as far as it will go.
    c. Adjust a dial indicator to rest against the front of the camshaft (the sprocket end). Zero the indicator.
    d. Move the camshaft forward as far as it will go. Read the dial indicator. End-play specification is 0.002–0.010 inch (0.05–0.15mm).
    e. If excessive end-play is present, inspect the cylinder head and camshaft for wear; replace if necessary.
13. If the fit and condition of the camshafts are acceptable, remove the camshafts for installation of the cam followers.
14. The hydraulic valve lash adjusters are inside the roller cam followers. Be sure they are clean, well lubricated with engine oil and properly positioned. Install the cam followers in their original positions on the hydraulic adjuster and valve stem.

⁂ WARNING

Be sure NONE of the pistons are at Top Dead Center (TDC) when installing the camshafts.

15. Lubricate the camshaft bearing journals and cam followers with clean engine oil
16. Install or connect the following:
    - Camshafts
    - Right/left-side camshaft bearing caps Nos. 2 through 5 and right-side No. 6. Torque the M6 fasteners to 105 inch lbs. (12 Nm) in the correct sequence.
17. Apply MOPAR® Gasket Maker sealer, or equivalent, to the No. 1 and left-side No. 6 bearing caps.
18. Install or connect the following:
    - Bearing caps and torque the M8 fasteners to: 21 ft. lbs. (28 Nm)
    - Camshaft end seals
    - Camshaft sprockets, if removed, and torque the bolts to 75 ft. lbs. (101 Nm)
    - Timing belt, making sure all timing marks are aligned
    - Timing belt covers

⁂ WARNING

If the timing belt or sprockets are incorrectly installed, engine damage will occur. Take time to be sure all timing marks are correctly aligned.

19. Clean all sealing surfaces. Make certain the rails are flat.
20. Install the new cylinder head cover gaskets. Apply MOPAR® Silicone Rubber Adhesive Sealant, or equivalent, at the camshaft cap corners and at the top edge of the ½ round seal.

➡Inspect the spark plug well seals for cracking and/or swelling and replace if necessary.

21. Install the cylinder head cover and torque the fasteners, in sequence, using the following:
    a. Step 1: 40 inch lbs. (4.5 Nm).
    b. Step 2: 80 inch lbs. (9 Nm).
    c. Step 3: 105 inch lbs. (12 Nm).
22. Install or connect the following:
    - Ignition coil pack and torque the fasteners to 105 inch lbs. (12 Nm)
    - Spark plug cables
    - Ground strap
    - All vacuum lines and wiring
    - Negative battery cable

➡An oil and filter change is recommended.

23. Test run vehicle. Check for leaks and for proper operation.

2.7L Engine

See Figure 69.

1. Before servicing the vehicle, refer to the precautions in the beginning of this section.
2. Remove or disconnect the following:
    - Negative battery
    - Timing chain and secondary chain tensioner bolts
    - Camshaft bearing caps
    - Camshafts, secondary chain and tensioner as an assembly
    - Tensioner and chain from the camshafts

To install:

3. Install or connect the following:
    - Camshaft chain on the cams and make certain that the plated links are facing forward

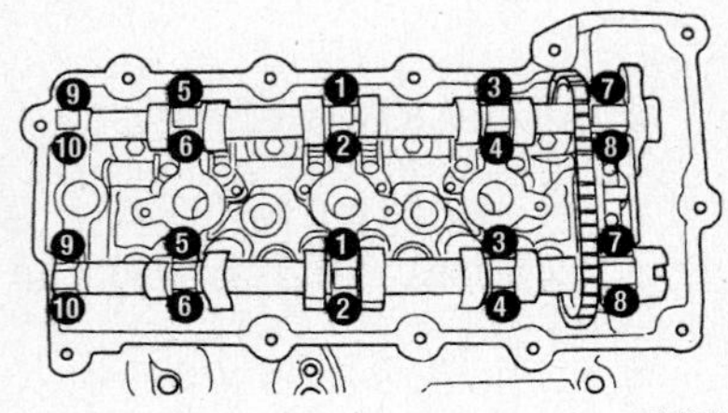

Fig. 69 Tighten the camshaft bearing caps in the proper sequence—2.7L Engine

4. Compress the chain tensioner as follows:
    a. Place the tensioner in a soft jaw vise.
    b. Slowly compress the tensioner until the fabricated lock pin can be installed in the locking holes.
    - Tensioner between the camshafts and chain. Rotate the cams until the plated links and dots are in the 12 o'clock position
    - Cams to the cylinder head
    - Camshaft bearing caps. Slowly, and in sequence, torque the bolts to 105 inch lbs. (12 Nm)
    - Secondary chain tensioner bolts and torque them to 105 inch lbs. (12 Nm). Remove the locking pin from the tensioner
    - Primary timing chain
    - Negative battery cable

CRANKSHAFT FRONT SEAL

REMOVAL & INSTALLATION

2.4L Engine

The timing belt must be removed for this procedure. Use care that all timing marks are aligned after installation or the engine will be damaged.

1. Drain the engine oil.
2. Before servicing the vehicle, refer to the precautions in the beginning of this section.
3. Disconnect the negative battery cable from the left shock tower.

➡The ground cable is equipped with an insulator grommet which should be placed on the stud to prevent the negative battery cable from accidentally grounding.

4. Remove or disconnect the following:
    - Accessory drive belts
    - Crankshaft balancer/pulley using a jaw puller tool

- Timing belt
- Crankshaft timing belt sprocket using a gear/sprocket puller

➡Be careful not to nick the seal surface of the crankshaft or the seal bore.

- Front crankshaft seal using Seal Removal Tool No. 6771

➡Be careful not to damage the seal contact area of the crankshaft.

To install:

5. Lubricate the new oil seal lip with engine oil.
6. Install or connect the following:
   - New crankshaft oil seal with the spring facing inward using Oil Seal Installer Tool 6780–1, until it is flush with the front cover
   - Crankshaft timing belt sprocket using Tool No. 6792

➡Be sure the word "FRONT" on the timing belt sprocket is facing outward.

- Timing belt and timing belt cover
- Crankshaft balancer/pulley using the thrust bearing/washer and 12M-1.75 x 150mm bolt from special Tool No. 6792. Torque the bolt to 105 ft. lbs. (142 Nm)
- Accessory drive belts and adjust the tension
- Negative battery cable

⁂ WARNING

Operating the engine without the proper amount and type of engine oil will result in severe engine damage.

7. Fill the engine with clean oil.
8. Start the engine and check for leaks.

2.7L Engine

See Figure 70.

1. Before servicing the vehicle, refer to the precautions in the beginning of this section.
2. Remove or disconnect the following:
   - Negative battery cable
   - Crankshaft balancer
   - Front crankshaft seal with Special Tool 6771

To install:

3. Install or connect the following:
   - New seal with Special Tools 6780-2, 8179 and 6780-1
   - Crankshaft balancer
   - Negative battery cable

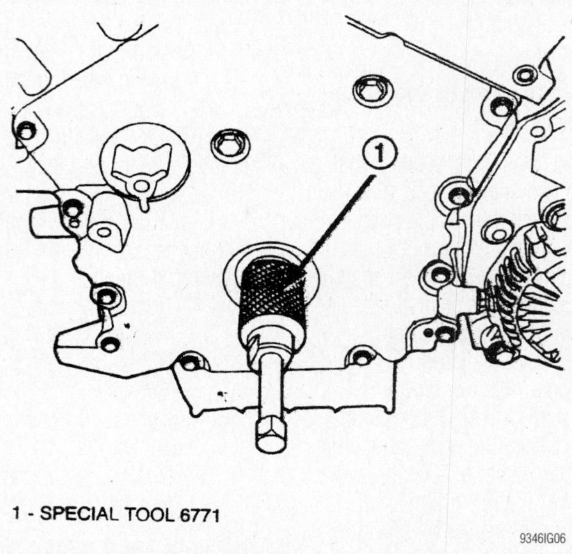

Fig. 70 Remove the front crankshaft seal with special tool 6771

CYLINDER HEAD

REMOVAL & INSTALLATION

➡The cylinder head bolts should be checked for stretching before reuse. If the thread area of the bolt is necked-down the bolts must be replaced with new. New head bolts are recommended.

2.4L Engine

See Figures 71 through 73.

This engine uses a Dual Over Head Camshaft (DOHC) 4-valves per cylinder cross flow aluminum cylinder head. The valves are actuated by roller cam followers which pivot on stationary hydraulic valve adjusters. Care must be taken to be sure all valve timing marks align after cylinder head and valve train service.

1. Before servicing the vehicle, refer to the precautions in the beginning of this section.
2. Relieve the fuel system pressure.
3. Drain the cooling system.
4. Disconnect the negative battery cable from the left shock tower.

➡The ground cable is equipped with an insulator grommet which should be placed on the stud to prevent the negative battery cable from accidentally grounding.

5. Remove or disconnect the following:
   - Air cleaner assembly
   - All vacuum lines, electrical connectors and fuel lines from the throttle body
   - Throttle linkage
   - Accessory drive belts
   - Power brake vacuum hose from the intake manifold
   - Exhaust pipe from the exhaust manifold
   - Power steering pump and move it aside. Do not disconnect the fluid lines
   - Spark plug wires
   - Coil pack electrical connector
   - Coil pack with the spark plug wires
   - Cam sensor and fuel injector electrical connectors
   - Timing belt covers
   - Timing belt
   - Camshaft sprockets
   - Timing belt idler pulley
   - Rear timing belt cover
   - Cylinder head cover
   - Ground strap
6. Identify the camshafts if they are to be reused for later installation. The camshafts are not interchangeable.
7. Remove or disconnect the following:
   - Camshaft bearing cap bolts in sequence
   - Camshafts

➡Refer to the camshaft REMOVAL & INSTALLATION procedure for correct bolt removal/installation sequence.

- Camshaft followers

➡Any components that are to be reused must be installed in their original locations. Use care to identify and mark the positions of any removed valve train components so they may be reinstalled correctly.

- Intake and exhaust manifolds
- Cylinder head bolts
- Cylinder head

➡Be careful not to damage the aluminum gasket surfaces.

8. Remove the all gasket material from the cylinder head and engine block. Be careful not to gouge or scratch the sealing surface of the aluminum head. The cylinder head should be checked for flatness using a good straightedge and feeler gauges. The cylinder head must be flat within 0.004 inch (0.1mm).

9. Inspect the camshaft bearing oil feed holes in the cylinder head for clogging. Inspect the camshaft bearing journals for wear or scoring. Check the cam surface for abnormal wear and damage. A visible worn groove in the roller path or on the cam lobes is cause for replacement. Valve service may be performed at this time.

To install:

10. Thoroughly clean all parts.

➡The cylinder head bolts are stretch-type. New cylinder head bolts are recommended.

11. Thoroughly clean all sealing surfaces.

12. Install or connect the following:
    - New cylinder head gasket
    - Cylinder head

13. Before installing the bolts, the threads should be oiled with clean engine oil.

14. With non-PZEV engines, torque the cylinder head bolts in sequence, using the following 4 Steps:
    - Tighten all bolts to 25 ft. lbs. (34 Nm).
    - Tighten all bolts to 50 ft. lbs. (68 Nm).
    - Tighten all bolts again to 50 ft. lbs. (68 Nm).
    - Tighten all bolts and additional ¼ turn.

➡Do not use a torque wrench for the 4th step.

15. On PZEV (Partially Zero Emissions Vehicle) equipped engines tighten the cylinder head bolts in the sequence shown, using the 4 step torque turn method:
    - Tighten all bolts to 25 ft. lbs. (34 Nm)
    - Tighten all bolts to 60 ft. lbs. (82 Nm)
    - Tighten all bolts to 60 ft. lbs. (82 Nm)

➡Do not use a torque wrench for the fourth step.

- Turn all bolts an additional ¼ turn

16. Check the camshaft end-play using the recommended procedure, then Install the camshaft.

17. Apply MOPAR® Gasket Maker sealer, or equivalent, to the No. 1 and No. 6 bearing caps. Install the bearing caps and tighten the M8 fasteners to 21 ft. lbs. (28 Nm). The end caps must be installed before the seals may be installed.

18. Apply a light coating of clean engine oil to the lip of the new camshaft seal. Install the camshaft seal until it fits flush with the cylinder head.

19. Install or connect the following:
    - Camshaft sprockets, if removed
    - Rear timing belt cover
    - Timing belt and properly align the timing marks
    - Timing belt cover

✲✲ WARNING

Verify that all timing marks are correct. If the timing belt or sprockets are incorrectly installed, engine damage will occur. Take time to be sure all timing marks are correctly aligned.

- Intake and exhaust manifolds
- New cylinder head cover gasket
- Cylinder head cover

✲✲ WARNING

Do not allow oil or solvents to contact the timing belt as they can deteriorate the rubber and cause tooth skipping.

➡Apply MOPAR® Silicone Rubber Adhesive Sealant, or equivalent, at the camshaft cap corners and at the top edge of the ½ round seal.

20. Torque the cylinder head cover fasteners, in sequence, using the following Steps:
    a. Step 1: 40 inch lbs. (4.5 Nm).
    b. Step 2: 80 inch lbs. (9 Nm).
    c. Step 3: 105 inch lbs. (12 Nm).

21. Install or connect the following:
    - Ground strap
    - Coil pack and spark plug wiring
    - Cam sensor and fuel injector wiring

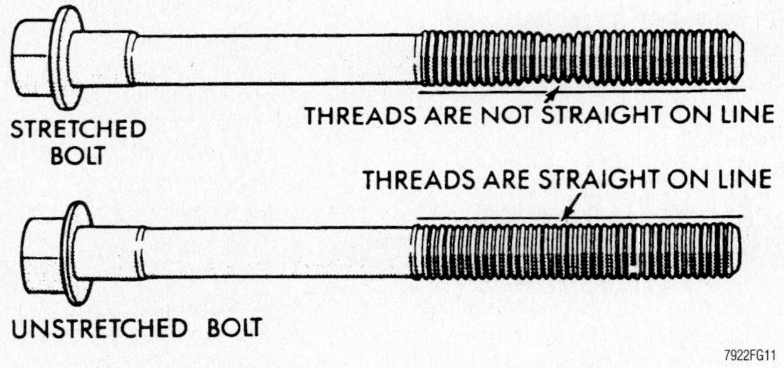

Fig. 71 Before reusing old cylinder head bolts, check them for necking (stretching)—2.4L engine

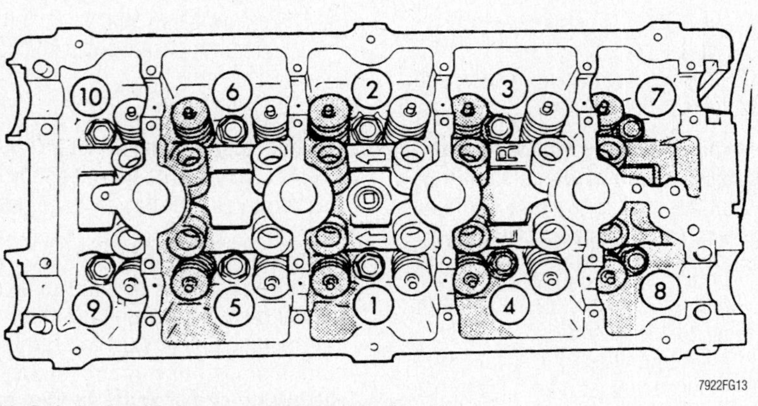

Fig. 72 Cylinder head bolt torque sequence—2.4L engine

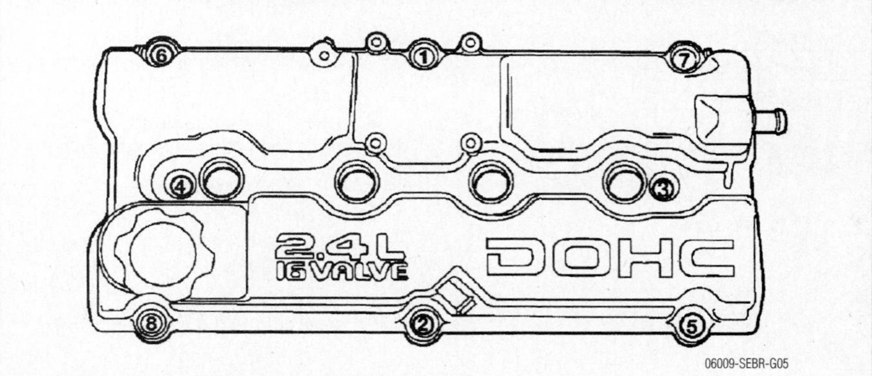

Fig. 73 Cylinder head cover torque sequence—2.4L engine

- Power steering pump assembly
- Exhaust pipe to the exhaust manifold
- All vacuum lines and electrical connectors
- Throttle linkage and fuel lines
- Accessory drive belts and adjust them
- Negative battery cable

22. Refill the cooling system.

➡An oil and filter change is recommended since coolant can enter the oil system when a head is removed.

23. Connect the remaining air ducting. Test run vehicle. Check for leaks and for proper operation.

2.7L Engine

See Figure 74.

1. Before servicing the vehicle, refer to the precautions in the beginning of this section.
2. Relieve the fuel system pressure.
3. Drain the cooling system.
4. Remove or disconnect the following:
   - Negative battery cable
   - Drive belts

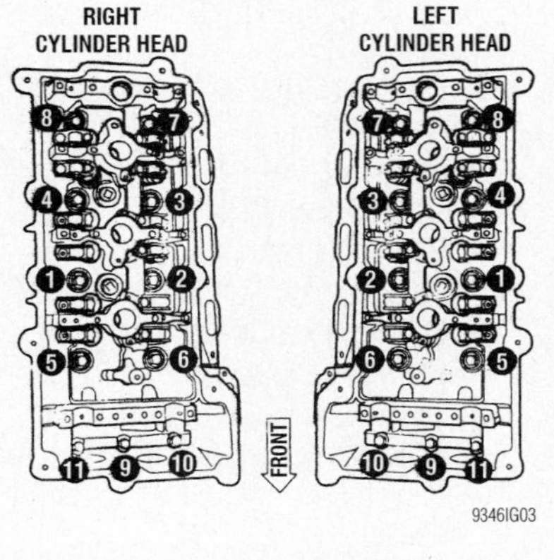

Fig. 74 Cylinder head bolt torque sequence—2.7L engine

- Crankshaft balancer
- Exhaust cross under pipe
- Catalytic converter
- Upper and lower intake manifolds
- Rocker arm covers
- Water outlet connector and rotate the crankshaft until the sprocket timing mark aligns with the timing mark on the oil pump housing
- Primary timing chain
- Camshaft bearing caps gradually
- Camshafts and valve train components
- Cylinder head and discard the gasket

To install:

5. Clean all mating surfaces of any residual gasket material.
6. Lubricate the threads of the cylinder head bolts with clean engine oil.
7. Install or connect the following:
   - Cylinder head with a new gasket
8. Torque the bolts, in sequence, using the following procedure:
   a. Step 1: Bolts 1–8: 35 ft. lbs. (48 Nm).
   b. Step 2: Bolts 1–8: 55 ft. lbs. (75 Nm).
   c. Step 3: Bolts 1–8: 55 ft. lbs. (75 Nm).
   d. Step 4: Bolts 1–8: An additional 90°. Do not use a torque wrench for this step.
   e. Step 5: Bolts 9–11: 21 ft. lbs. (28 Nm).
   - Valve train components and the camshafts
   - Timing chain and sprockets
   - Water outlet connector
   - Rocker arm covers
   - Timing chain cover
   - Crankshaft balancer
   - Lower and upper intake manifolds
   - Catalytic converter
   - Exhaust cross under pipe
   - Drive belts
   - Negative battery cable

9. Fill the cooling system to the proper level.
10. Start the vehicle, check for leaks and repair if necessary.

ENGINE ASSEMBLY

REMOVAL & INSTALLATION

2.4L Engine

See Figures 75 through 78.

1. Before servicing the vehicle, refer to the precautions in the beginning of this section.
2. Properly relieve the fuel system pressure.
3. Drain the engine oil.
4. Drain the cooling system.
5. Recover the A/C refrigerant.
6. Remove or disconnect the following:
   - Negative battery cable
   - Throttle body air inlet hose
   - Air cleaner assembly
   - Upper radiator crossmember
   - Upper and lower radiator hoses
   - Transmission cooler lines
   - A/C lines at the condenser
   - Radiator, fan module and A/C condenser
   - Transmission electrical harness connectors
   - Transmission shift cable
   - Engine electrical harness from the Powertrain Control Module (PCM) and bulkhead
   - Both front wheels and splash shields
   - Both halfshafts
   - Drive belts
   - Power steering pump from the bracket and move it aside.
   - Heater return hose from the right front frame rail

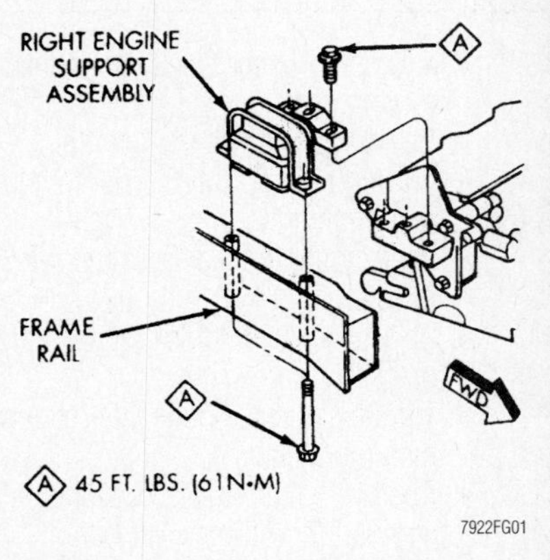

Fig. 75 Exploded view of the right side engine mount—all engines

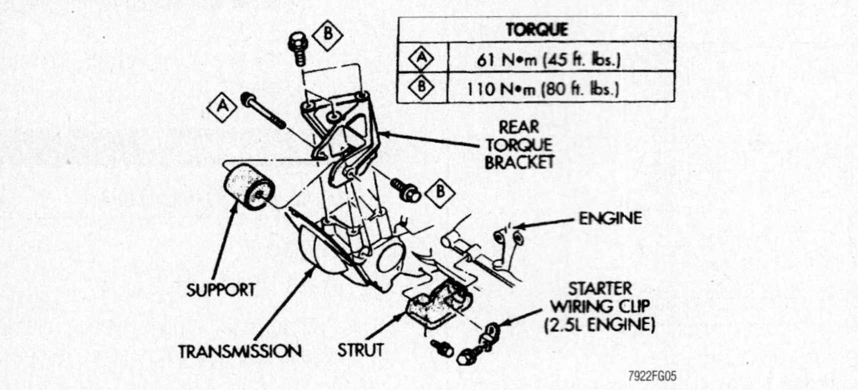

Fig. 76 Exploded view of the rear engine mounting torque bracket—2.4L engines

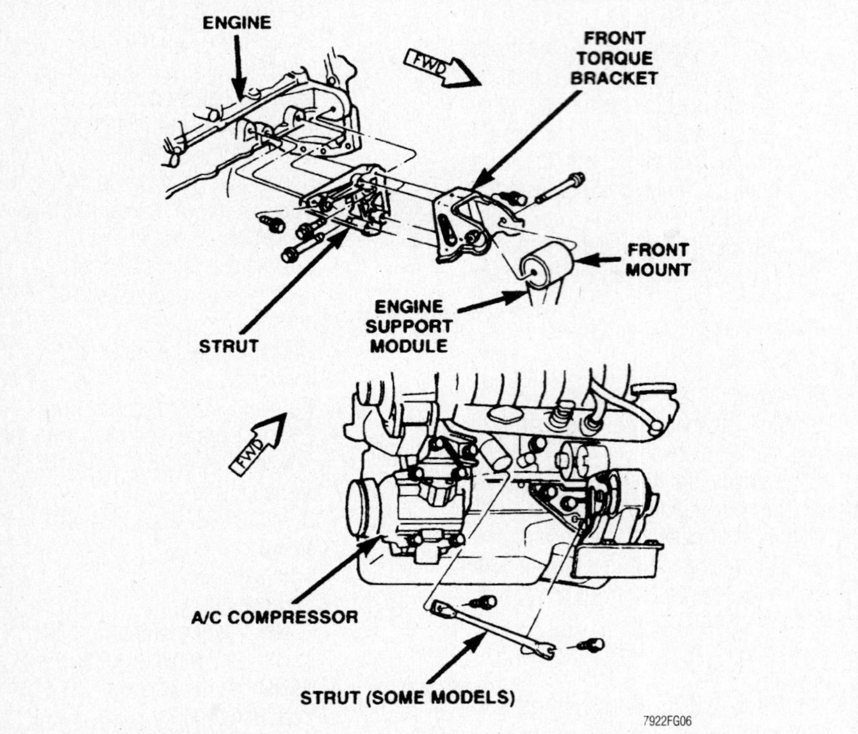

Fig. 77 Exploded view of the front engine mounting torque bracket—2.4L engines

- A/C compressor electrical connectors
- Exhaust pipe from the manifold
- Through bolts from the front and rear engine mounts
- Rear mount bracket from the transmission
- Structural cover and torque reaction bracket
- Torque converter bolts after matchmarking them
- Positive battery cable from the battery and the Power Distribution Center (PDC)
- Ground cable from the left side transmission mount bracket
- Throttle and speed control cables
- Coolant overflow hose
- Heater hose from the thermostat housing
- Engine ground straps
- Brake booster and vacuum purge hoses
- Fuel lines from the rail
- Intake manifold
- Alternator
- A/C suction line from the compressor and place an engine dolly and cradle in position

7. Loosen the cradle engine mounts and lower the engine/transmission assembly onto the dolly.
8. Remove the vertical engine mount bolts
9. Slowly raise the vehicle and make certain that the cradle is positioned properly.
10. Secure the engine/transmission assembly to the cradle and remove the assembly.

To install:

11. Position the engine/transmission assembly under the vehicle and slowly lower the vehicle into position.
12. Continue to the lower the vehicle until the right side engine mount and left side transaxle mount are properly aligned.
13. Install or connect the following:
    - Mounting bolts and torque them to 45 ft. lbs. (61 Nm).
    - Raise the vehicle and remove the cradle
    - A/C compressor and suction line
    - Alternator
    - Intake manifold and torque the bolts to 105 inch lbs. (12 Nm)
    - Alternator electrical connectors
    - Fuel line to the rail
    - Brake booster and vacuum purge hoses
    - Engine ground straps
    - Heater hose to the thermostat housing
    - Coolant overflow hose
    - Throttle and speed control cables
    - Ground cable to the left side transmission mount bracket
    - Positive battery cable to the PDC
    - Torque converter bolts
    - Structural cover and the torque reaction bracket
    - Rear mount bracket to the transmission
    - Front and rear engine mount through bolts. Torque the bolts to 45 ft. lbs. (61 Nm)
    - Exhaust pipe to the manifold and torque the bolts to 21 ft. lbs. (28 Nm)
    - A/C compressor electrical connectors
    - Heater return hose to the right front frame rail
    - Power steering pump to the bracket
    - Drive belts
    - Both halfshafts
    - Splash shields and front wheels
    - Engine electrical harness to the PCM and the bulkhead connectors
    - Transmission shift cable
    - Transmission electrical connectors
    - Radiator, fan module and A/C condenser
    - A/C lines to the condenser
    - Transmission cooler lines

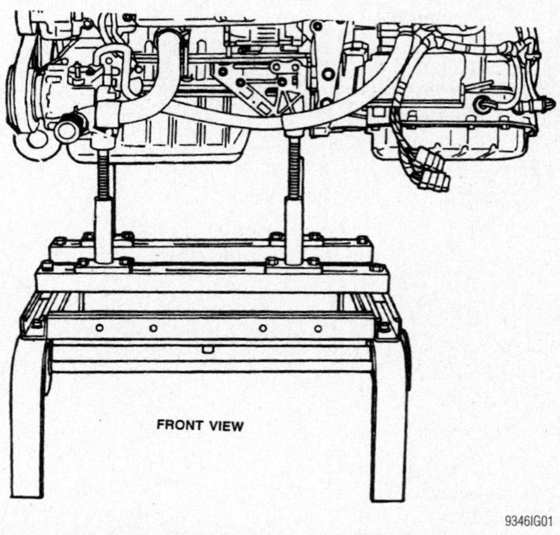

Fig. 78 Place the engine/transmission assembly on the cradle as shown

- Upper and lower radiator hoses
- Upper radiator crossmember
- Air cleaner assembly
- Throttle body air inlet hose
- Negative battery cable

14. Fill the engine with clean oil.
15. Fill the cooling system to the proper level.
16. Recharge the A/C system.
17. Start the vehicle, check for leaks and repair if necessary.

2.7L Engine

1. Before servicing the vehicle, refer to the precautions in the beginning of this section.
2. Properly relieve the fuel system pressure.
3. Drain the engine oil.
4. Drain the cooling system.
5. Recover the A/C refrigerant.
6. Remove or disconnect the following:
   - Negative battery cable
   - Throttle body air inlet hose
   - Air cleaner assembly
   - Both front wheels and splash shields
   - Lower front fascia from the crossmember
   - Lower air shield from the crossmember
   - Front fascia
   - Upper radiator crossmember
   - Upper and lower radiator hoses
   - Transmission oil cooler lines
   - A/C lines from the condenser
   - Radiator, fan and A/C condenser
   - Transmission electrical harness connectors
   - Transmission shift cable
   - Engine electrical harness from the Powertrain Control Module (PCM) and bulkhead connectors
   - Antilock Brake System (ABS) brake module from the lower radiator crossmember
   - Brake line from the lower radiator crossmember
   - Both halfshafts
   - Front engine mount through bolt
   - Front engine mount from the lower radiator crossmember
   - Lower radiator crossmember
   - Drive belts
   - Power steering pump and bracket. Do not disconnect the lines
   - Heater return hose from the right front frame rail
   - A/C compressor electrical connectors and reposition the compressor
   - Structural collar
   - Exhaust system cross under pipe
   - Rear engine mount and transaxle bracket
   - Torque converter housing cover and match mark the bolts
   - Positive battery cable from the Power Distribution Center (PDC)
   - Ground cable from the left side transaxle mount bracket
   - Throttle and speed control cables
   - Coolant overflow hose
   - Heater hose
   - Ground strap from the right shock tower
   - Fuel lines
   - Brake booster and vacuum purge hoses
   - Engine ground straps
7. Loosen the cradle engine mounts and lower the engine/transmission assembly onto the dolly.
8. Remove the vertical engine mount bolts
9. Slowly raise the vehicle and make certain that the cradle is positioned properly.
10. Secure the engine/transmission assembly to the cradle and remove the assembly.

To install:

11. Position the engine/transmission assembly under the vehicle and slowly lower the vehicle into position.
12. Continue to the lower the vehicle until the right side engine mount and left side transaxle mount are properly aligned.
13. Install or connect the following:
    - Mounting bolts and torque them to 45 ft. lbs. (61 Nm).
    - Raise the vehicle and remove the cradle
    - Engine ground straps
    - Brake booster and vacuum purge hoses
    - Fuel lines
    - Ground strap to the right shock tower
    - Heater hose
    - Coolant overflow hose
    - Throttle and speed control cables
    - Ground cable to the left transaxle mount bracket
    - Positive battery cable to the PDC
    - Torque converter bolts and cover
    - Rear engine mount and transaxle bracket
    - Exhaust system cross under pipe
    - Structural collar
    - A/C compressor to the bracket
    - A/C compressor clutch electrical connectors
    - Heater return hose to the right side frame rail
    - Power steering pump and bracket
    - Drive belts
    - Lower radiator crossmember
    - Front engine mount to the lower radiator crossmember
    - Both halfshafts
    - Brake line to the lower radiator crossmember
    - ABS module to the lower radiator crossmember
    - Engine electrical harness to the PCM and bulkhead connectors
    - Transmission shift cable
    - Transmission electrical harness connectors
    - Radiator, fan and A/C condenser
    - A/C lines to the condenser
    - Transmission oil cooler lines
    - Upper and lower radiator hoses

- Upper radiator crossmember
- Front bumper fascia and lower air shield
- Splash shields and both front wheels
- Air cleaner assembly and throttle body air inlet hose
- Negative battery cable

14. Fill the engine with clean oil and replace the filter.
15. Fill the cooling system to the proper level.
16. Recharge the A/C system with the proper refrigerant.
17. Start the vehicle, check for leaks and repair if necessary.

EXHAUST MANIFOLD

REMOVAL & INSTALLATION

2.4L Engines

Non-PZEV Engine

See Figures 79 and 80.

1. Before servicing the vehicle, refer to the precautions in the beginning of this section.
2. Disconnect the negative battery cable from the left shock tower.

➡The ground cable is equipped with an insulator grommet which should be placed on the stud to prevent the negative battery cable from accidentally grounding.

3. Remove or disconnect the following:
   - Exhaust pipe from the exhaust manifold
   - Exhaust manifold heat shield
   - Heated Oxygen Sensor (HO_2S), if necessary
   - Exhaust manifold and discard the gasket

To install:

4. Thoroughly clean all parts. Clean all sealing surfaces of the manifold and cylinder head. Check the manifold gasket surface for flatness with a straightedge and feeler gauge. The surface must be flat within 0.006 inch (0.15mm) per foot (30cm) of manifold length. Inspect the manifold for cracks or distortion. Replace if necessary.
5. Install or connect the following:
   - New gasket
   - Exhaust manifold. Torque the bolts, starting at the center and working outward, to 17 ft. lbs. (23 Nm)
   - HO_2S sensor
   - Heat shield
   - Exhaust pipe and torque the fasteners to 21 ft. lbs. (28 Nm)
   - Negative battery cable
6. Start the engine and allow it to idle while inspecting the manifold for exhaust leaks.

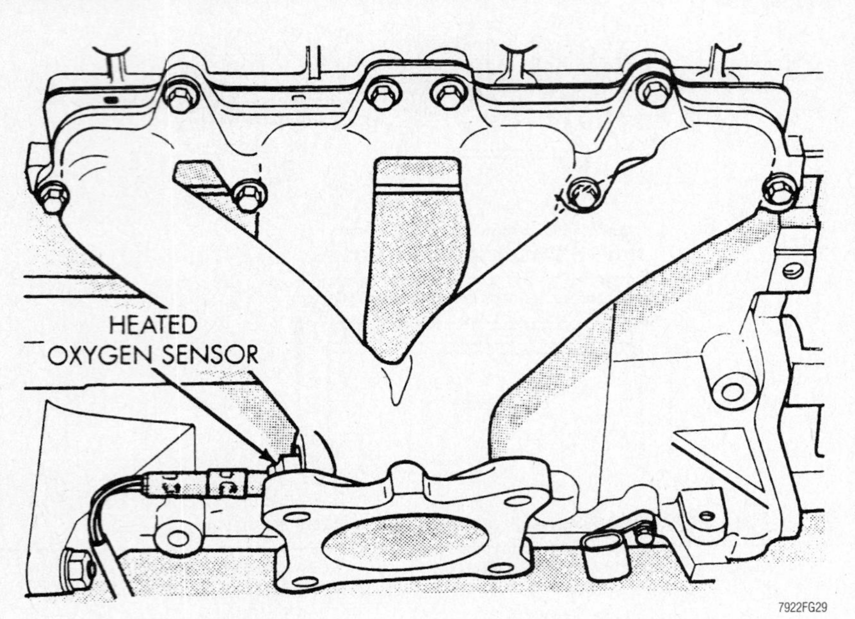

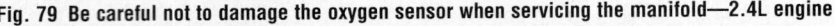

Fig. 79 Be careful not to damage the oxygen sensor when servicing the manifold—2.4L engine

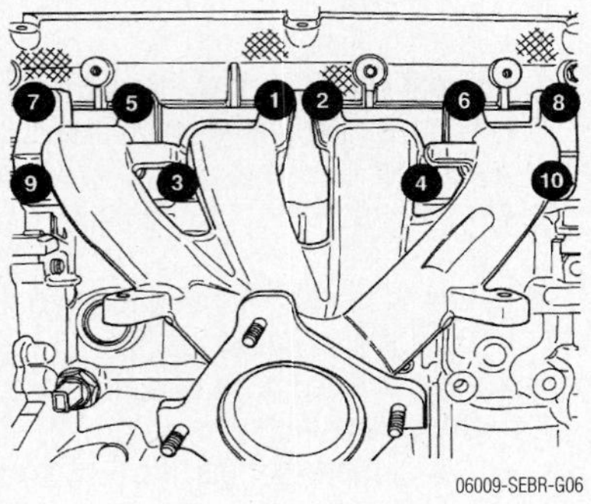

Fig. 80 Exhaust manifold torque sequence—2.4L non-PZEV engines

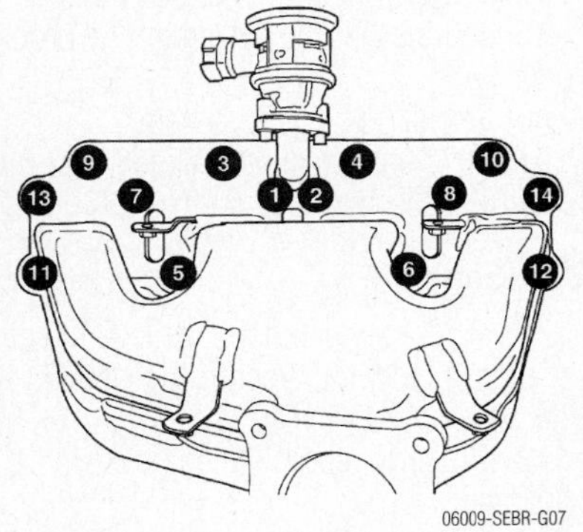

Fig. 81 Exhaust manifold torque sequence—2.4L PZEV engines

PZEV Engine

See Figure 81.

1. Disconnect negative battery cable.
2. Raise vehicle on hoist.
3. Remove the complete exhaust system.
4. Remove the rear engine mount and transaxle bracket.
5. Disconnect connector tube from check valve. Squeeze connector and pull.
6. Remove the exhaust manifold heat shield.
7. Disconnect oxygen sensor electrical connector.
8. Remove the exhaust manifold retaining fasteners and remove exhaust manifold.
9. Remove the and discard manifold gasket.

To install:

10. Install the new exhaust manifold gasket. DO NOT APPLY SEALER.
11. Position exhaust manifold in place. Tighten fasteners in sequence shown to 17 ft. lbs. (23 Nm).
12. Install the exhaust manifold heat shield.
13. Install the check valve tighten bolts to 105 inch lbs. (12 Nm).

14. Connect connector tube to check valve by pushing fitting over check valve.
15. Connect oxygen sensor electrical connector.
16. Install the rear engine mount and transaxle bracket.
17. Install the exhaust system. Tighten fasteners to 21 ft. lbs. (28 Nm).
18. Lower vehicle.
19. Connect negative battery cable.

2.7L Engine

Front

1. Before servicing the vehicle, refer to the precautions in the beginning of this section.
2. Remove or disconnect the following:
   - Negative battery cable
   - Cross under pipe
   - Front catalytic converter
   - Exhaust manifold and discard the gasket

To install:

3. Clean all mating surfaces of any residual gasket material.
4. Install or connect the following:
   - Exhaust manifold with a new gasket. Torque the bolts, starting in the center and working outward, to 17 ft. lbs. (23 Nm)
   - Front catalytic converter and heat shield and torque the bolts to 21 ft. lbs. (28 Nm)
   - Cross under pipe and torque the bolts to 21 ft. lbs. (28 Nm)
   - Negative battery cable
5. Start the vehicle, check for leaks and repair if necessary.

Rear

1. Before servicing the vehicle, refer to the precautions in the beginning of this section.
2. Remove or disconnect the following:
   - Negative battery cable
   - Throttle body air inlet hose
   - Air cleaner assembly
   - Exhaust Gas Recirculation (EGR) tube from the exhaust manifold and EGR valve
   - Exhaust system
   - Cross under pipe
   - Rear catalytic converter
   - Rear Oxygen Sensor (O_2S)
   - Exhaust manifold and discard the gasket

To install:

3. Clean all mating surfaces of any residual gasket material.
4. Install or connect the following:
   - Exhaust manifold with a new gasket. Torque the bolts, starting in the center and working outward, to 17 ft. lbs. (23 Nm)
   - Rear catalytic converter and heat shield and torque the bolts to 21 ft. lbs. (28 Nm)
   - Rear Oxygen Sensor (O_2S)
   - Cross under pipe and torque the bolts to 21 ft. lbs. (28 Nm)
   - Exhaust system
   - EGR tube with new gaskets
   - Air cleaner assembly and air intake hose
   - Negative battery cable
5. Start the vehicle, check for leaks and repair if necessary.

INTAKE MANIFOLD

REMOVAL & INSTALLATION

2.4L Engine

See Figure 82.

The intake manifold is a long branch design made of cast aluminum. It is attached to the cylinder head with 8 fasteners.

1. Before servicing the vehicle, refer to the precautions in the beginning of this section.
2. Relieve the fuel system pressure using the recommended procedure.
3. Disconnect the negative battery cable from the left shock tower.

➡The ground cable is equipped with an insulator grommet which should be placed on the stud to prevent the negative battery cable from accidentally grounding.

4. Remove the air inlet resonator as follows:
   - Both air inlet resonator-to-intake manifold bolts
   - Resonator-to-throttle body screw, loosen it
   - Air inlet resonator-to-air inlet tube clamp, loosen it
   - Resonator
5. Remove or disconnect the following:
   - Fuel supply line quick-disconnect at the fuel tube assembly

➡Squeeze the retainer tabs together and pull the fuel tube/quick-disconnect fitting assembly from the fuel tube nipple. The retainer will remain on the fuel tube. Use shop towels to catch any dripping fuel.

   - Fuel rail

⁂ WARNING

Use care when handling the fuel injectors. Do not set them on their tips. Cover the fuel injector openings after fuel rail removal.

   - Accelerator, kickdown and speed control cables, from the throttle lever and bracket
   - Idle Air Control (IAC) motor and Throttle Position (TP) sensor electrical connections
   - Throttle body vacuum hoses

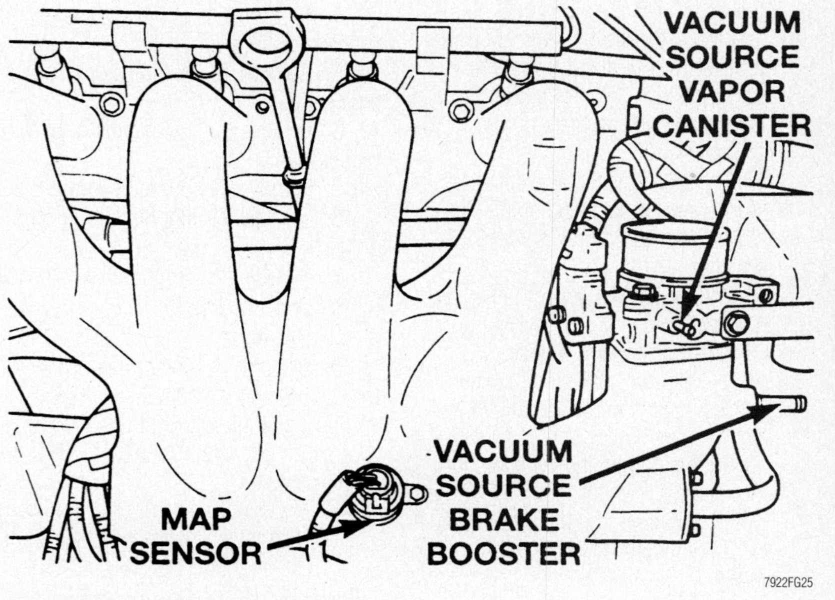

Fig. 82 MAP sensor location—2.4L engine

- Manifold Absolute Pressure (MAP) sensor and Intake Air Temperature (IAT) sensor electrical connections
- Vapor and brake booster hoses
- Knock sensor electrical connector
- Wiring harness from the intake manifold tab
- Transaxle-to-throttle body support bracket fasteners at the throttle body and loosen the fastener at the transaxle end
- Throttle body
- Exhaust Gas Recirculation (EGR) tube
- Intake manifold support bracket
- Intake manifold

To install:

6. Thoroughly clean all parts. Clean all sealing surfaces
7. Install or connect the following:
   - New gasket
   - Intake manifold. Torque the fasteners to 17 ft. lbs. (23 Nm), in correct sequence, starting at the center and working outward

➡Make sure the fuel injector openings are clean.

- Fuel rail assembly to the intake manifold and torque the screws to 17 ft. lbs. (23 Nm)
- Positive Crankcase Ventilation (PCV) and brake booster hoses

8. Lubricate the fuel tube with engine oil.
9. Install or connect the following:
   - Fuel supply line to the fuel rail. Pull on the connector to insure it is locked into position
   - Throttle body and torque the fasteners to 17 ft. lbs. (23 Nm)
   - Transaxle-to-throttle body support bracket. Torque the fasteners to 105 inch lbs. (12 Nm) at the throttle body first; then, at the transaxle
   - MAP and IAT electrical connectors
   - Knock sensor electrical connector
   - Wiring harness to the intake manifold tab
   - IAC motor and TP sensor electrical connectors
   - Throttle body vacuum hoses
   - Accelerator, kickdown and speed control cables to the throttle lever and bracket
   - EGR tube. Torque the fasteners to: 95 inch lbs. (11 Nm), at the EGR valve first; then, the intake manifold
   - Air inlet resonator to the throttle body
   - Air inlet tube to the resonator and torque the clamps to 20–30 inch lbs. (2.5–3.5 Nm)
   - Both air inlet resonator-to-intake manifold bolts
   - Negative battery cable

2.7L Engine

See Figure 83.

1. Before servicing the vehicle, refer to the precautions in the beginning of this section.
2. Properly relieve the fuel system pressure.
3. Remove or disconnect the following:
   - Negative battery cable
   - Throttle body air inlet hose
   - Air cleaner assembly
   - Throttle cable shield
   - Throttle and speed control cables
   - Throttle cable bracket
   - Manifold Absolute Pressure (MAP) sensor connector
   - Throttle Position Sensor (TPS) connector
   - Idle Air Control (IAC) motor connector
   - Manifold Tuning Valve (MTV) connector
   - Vapor purge hose
   - Brake booster vacuum hose
   - Speed Control Servo
   - Positive Crankcase Ventilation (PCV) hose
   - Exhaust Gas Recirculation (EGR) upper tube
   - Upper throttle body support bracket
   - Upper intake manifold and discard the gasket
4. To remove the lower intake manifold proceed as follows:
5. Remove the fuel injector electrical connectors.
6. Remove the fuel supply hose from the fuel rail.
7. Remove the fuel rail support bracket.
8. Remove the fuel rail and injectors as an assembly.
9. Remove the lower intake manifold and discard the gasket.

To install:

10. Clean all mating surfaces of any residual gasket material.
11. Install or connect the following:
    - Lower intake manifold with a new gasket
    - Fuel rail and injectors and torque the lower intake manifold bolts, in sequence, to 105 inch lbs. (12 Nm)
    - Fuel supply hose to the fuel rail

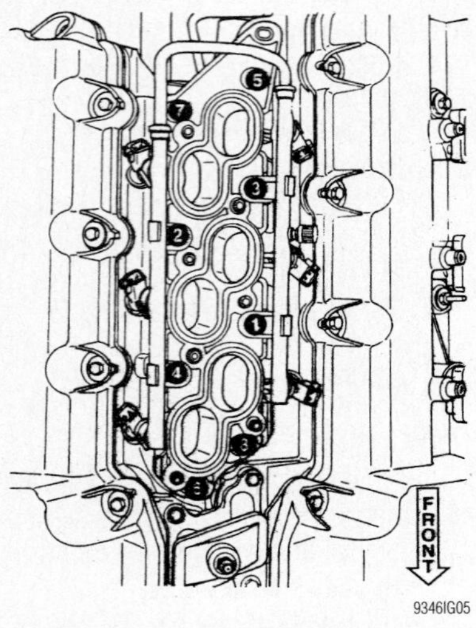

Fig. 83 Intake manifold bolt torque sequence 2.7L engine

- Fuel rail support bracket to the throttle body
- Fuel injector electrical connectors
- Upper intake manifold with a new gasket on the lower intake manifold and torque the bolts, in sequence, to: 105 inch lbs. (12 Nm)
- EGR upper tube
- Speed control servo
- PCV, brake booster and vapor purge hoses
- MAP sensor electrical connector
- TPS sensor electrical connector
- IAC motor electrical connector
- MTV electrical connector
- Throttle cable bracket
- Throttle and speed control cables
- Throttle cable shield
- Throttle body air inlet hose
- Air cleaner assembly
- Negative battery cable

12. Start the vehicle, check for leaks and repair if necessary.

OIL PAN

REMOVAL & INSTALLATION

2.4L Engine

See Figures 84 through 86.

1. Disconnect negative battery cable.
2. Raise vehicle on hoist and drain engine oil.
3. Remove the structural cover.
4. Remove the air conditioning compressor bracket to oil pan bolt.

➡The oil pan is sealed with RTV and may need to be pried apart.

5. Remove the bolts attaching oil pan.

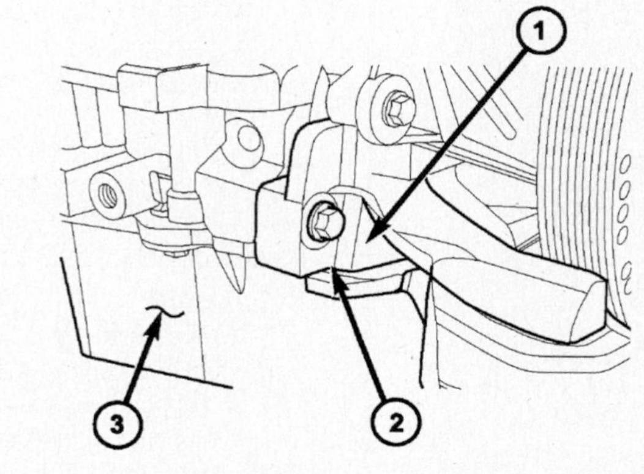

Fig. 84 Right side oil pan pry point—2005 2.4L engine

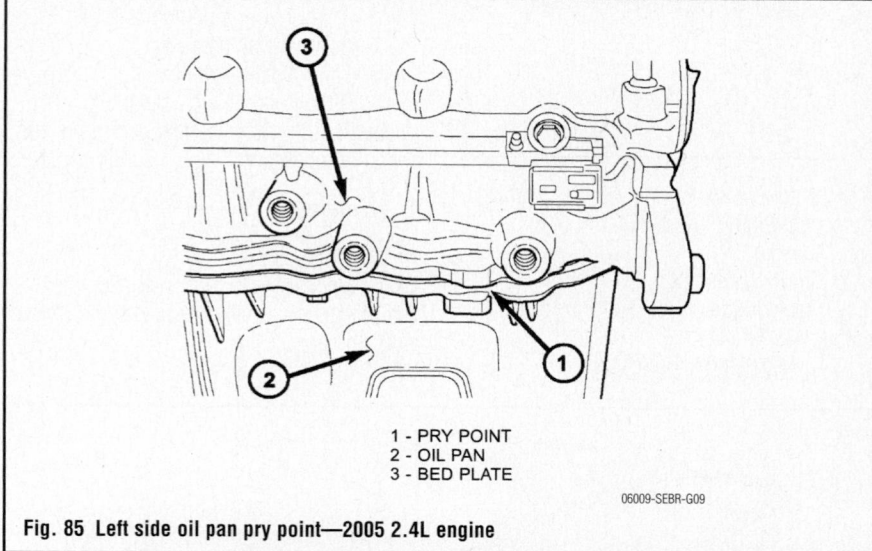

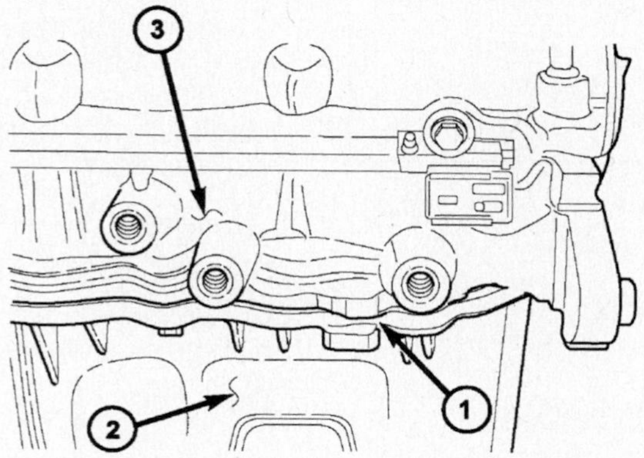

Fig. 85 Left side oil pan pry point—2005 2.4L engine

➡Prior to removing the oil pan, score RTV with a razor blade between the oil pan and the bed plate.

6. Insert pry bar at locations shown and gently pry oil pan away from the engine.

To install:

➡You must assemble oil pan to bed plate before RTV "skins over". If RTV skins before assembly, parts must be cleaned and a new bead of RTV applied.

7. Clean oil pan and block surfaces. Clean cured RTV from oil pan and bed plate with a plastic or brass scraper.
8. Clean all sealing surfaces with MOPAR® Brake Parts Cleaner, or equivalent.
9. Inspect surfaces for damage, replace as needed.
10. Apply a 3–4mm diameter bead of MOPAR® Engine RTV, or equivalent, around the perimeter of the oil pan flange, 1mm away from the chamfer on the inner edge of the oil pan.
11. Position oil pan on bedplate.
12. Install the oil pan attaching bolts and tighten to 105 inch lbs. (12 Nm).
13. Install the air conditioning compressor bracket to oil pan bolt.
14. Install the structural cover.
15. Lower vehicle and fill engine crankcase with proper oil to correct level.
16. Connect negative battery cable.
17. Start engine and check for leaks.

2.7L Engine

See Figure 87.

1. Before servicing the vehicle, refer to the precautions in the beginning of this section.
2. Drain the engine oil.
3. Remove the engine support module as follows:
   - Negative battery cable
   - Oil dipstick and tube
   - Structural cover
   - Exhaust cross under pipe
   - Torque converter cover
   - Lower bolt from the A/C compressor
   - Oil pan and discard the gasket

To install:

4. Clean all mating surfaces of any residual gasket material.
   - Oil pan with a new gasket
5. Torque the oil pan bolts as follows:
   a. Timing chain cover to oil pan bolts and torque them to 105 inch lbs. (12 Nm).
   b. Oil pan bolts to 21 ft. lbs. (28 Nm).

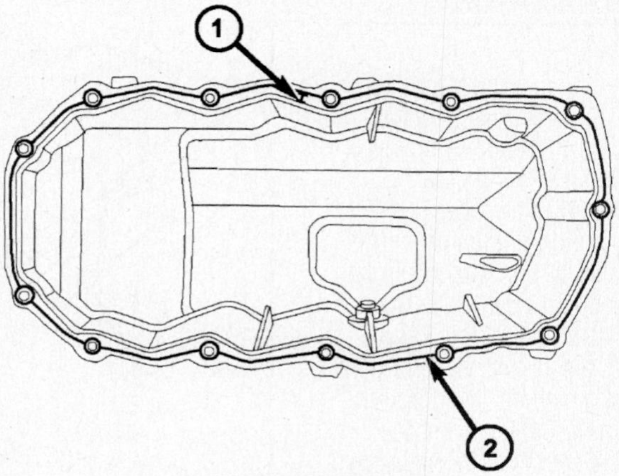

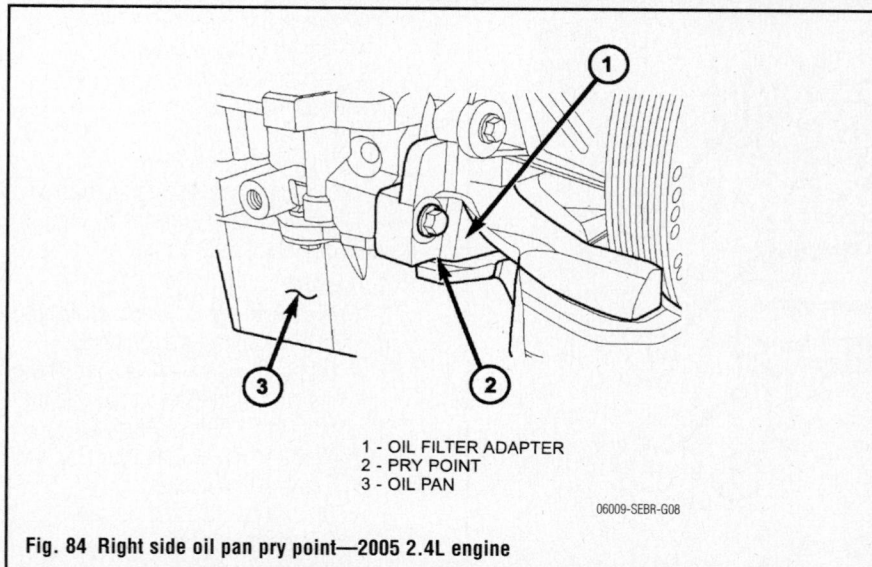

Fig. 86 RTV application for the 2005 2.4L engine oil pan

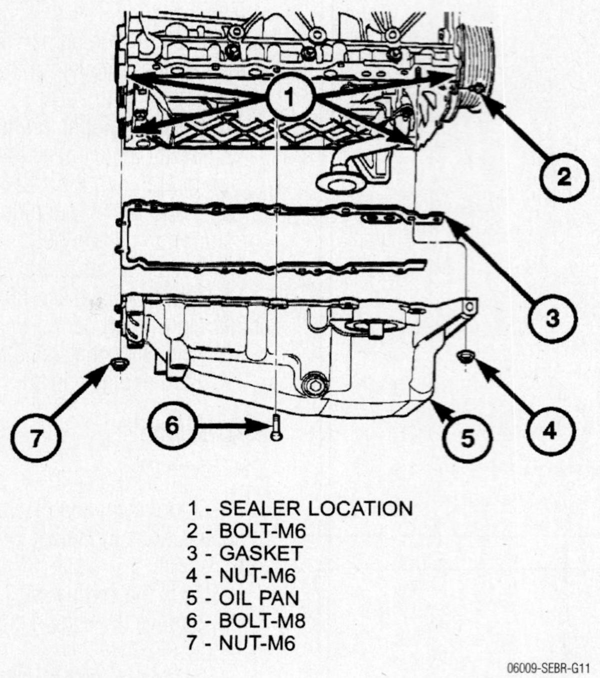

Fig. 87 Oil pan installation—2.7L engine

c. Oil pan nuts to 105 inch lbs. (12 Nm).

d. A/C compressor bolt to 21 ft. lbs. (28 Nm).

- Torque converter cover
- Exhaust cross under pipe
- Structural cover
- Oil dipstick and tube
- Negative battery cable

6. Fill the engine with clean oil.
7. Start the vehicle, check for leaks and repair if necessary.

OIL PUMP

REMOVAL & INSTALLATION

2.4L Engine

See Figure 88.

The oil drawn up through the pick-up tube is pressurized by the pump and routed through the full flow filter to the main oil galley running the length of the cylinder block. The oil pick-up, pump and check valve provide oil flow to the main oil gallery. A vertical hole at the No. 5 bulkhead routes pressurized oil through a restrictor up past a cylinder head bolt to an oil galley running the length of the cylinder head. The camshaft journals are slotted to allow pressurized oil to pass into the bearing cap cavities. Small holes in the bearing caps direct oil to the camshaft lobes.

1. Before servicing the vehicle, refer to the precautions in the beginning of this section.
2. Drain the engine oil.
3. Remove the engine support module as follows:
   - Negative battery cable
   - Crankshaft balancer
   - Timing belt and tensioner
   - Camshaft sprocket
   - Rear timing belt cover
   - Oil pan
   - Oil pick up tube
   - Oil pump and discard the gasket
4. Clean all mating surfaces of any residual gasket material.

To install:

5. Prime the oil pump before installation.
6. Install or connect the following:
   - Oil pump with the flats aligned with the crankshaft flats and torque the bolts to 21 ft. lbs. (28 Nm)
   - New front crankshaft seal
   - Crankshaft sprocket
   - Oil pick up tube and oil pan
   - Camshaft sprocket
   - Rear timing belt cover
   - Timing belt and tensioner
   - Front timing belt cover
   - Crankshaft balancer
   - Negative battery cable
7. Fill the engine with clean oil.
8. Start the vehicle, check for leaks and repair if necessary.

2.7L Engine

See Figures 89 and 90.

1. Before servicing the vehicle, refer to the precautions in the beginning of this section.

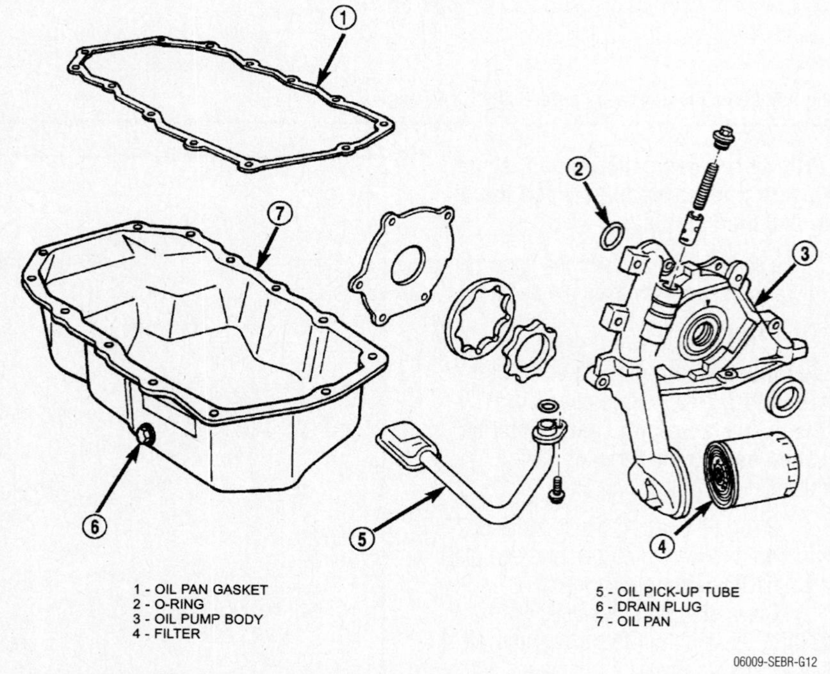

Fig. 88 Oil pump and related parts—2.4L engine

2. Drain the engine oil.

3. Remove the engine support module as follows:

- Negative battery cable
- Crankshaft balancer
- Timing chain cover
- Timing chain and sprockets
- Oil pan
- Oil pick up tube and O-ring and make certain that the crankshaft is at 60 degrees After Top Dead Center (ATDC)
- Oil pump

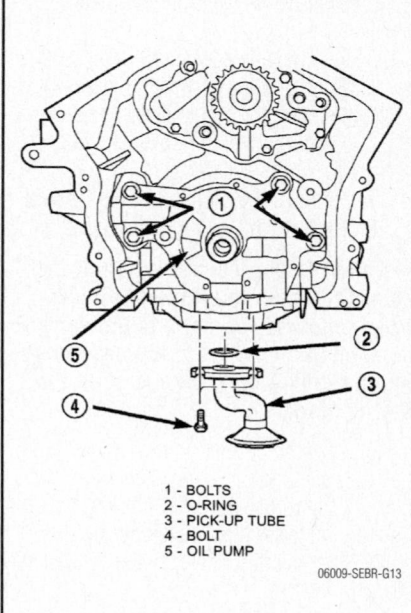

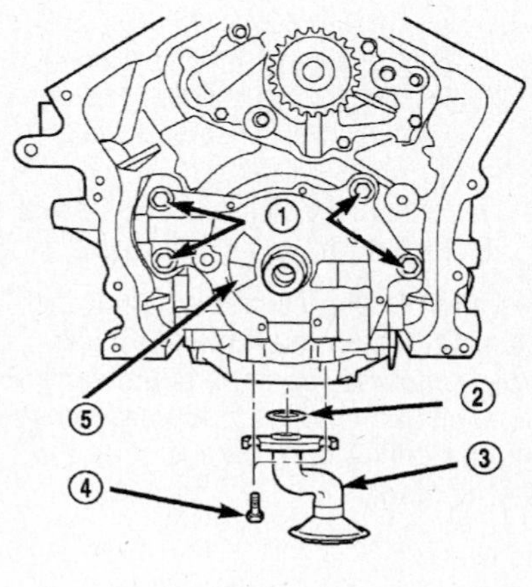

Fig. 89 Oil pump and pick-up tube—2.7L engine

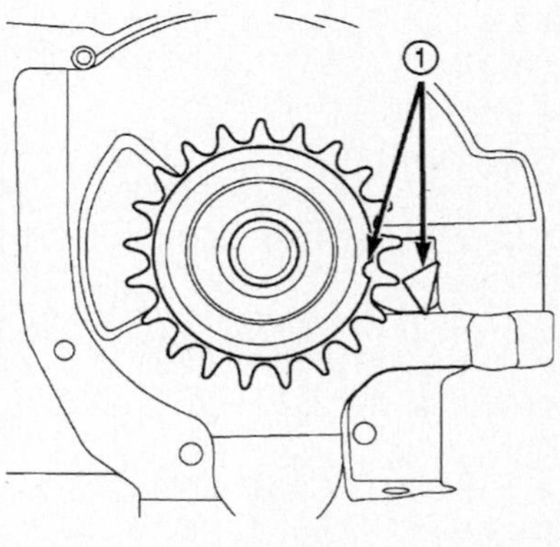

Fig. 90 Crankshaft positioned at 60 degrees ATDC—2.7L engine

To install:

4. Prime the pump before installation by filling the rotor cavity with clean engine oil.

5. Install or connect the following:

- Oil pump over the crankshaft and torque the bolts to 21 ft. lbs. (28 Nm)
- Oil pick up tube with a new O-ring and torque the bolt to 21 ft. lbs. (28 Nm)
- Oil pan with a new gasket
- Timing chain and sprockets
- Timing chain and cover
- Crankshaft balancer
- Negative battery cable

6. Fill the engine with clean oil.

7. Start the vehicle, check for leaks and repair if necessary.

INSPECTION

2.4L Engine

1. Clean all parts thoroughly. Mating surface of the oil pump should be smooth. Replace pump cover if scratched or grooved.

2. Lay a straightedge across the pump cover surface. If a 0.001 in. (0.025mm) feeler gauge can be inserted between cover and straight edge, cover should be replaced.

3. Measure thickness and diameter of outer rotor. If outer rotor thickness measures 0.370 in. (9.40mm) or less, or if the diameter is 3.148 in. (79.95mm) or less, replace outer rotor.

4. If inner rotor measures 0.370 in. (9.40mm) or less, replace inner rotor.

5. Slide outer rotor into pump housing, press to one side with fingers and measure clearance between rotor and housing. If measurement is 0.015 in. (0.39mm) or more, replace housing only if outer rotor is in specification.

6. Install inner rotor into pump housing. If clearance between inner and outer rotors is 0.008 in. (0.203mm) or more, replace both rotors.

7. Place a straightedge across the face of the pump housing, between bolt holes. If a feeler gauge of 0.004 in. (0.102mm), or more can be inserted between rotors and the straightedge, replace pump assembly, **ONLY** if rotors are in specifications.

8. Inspect oil pressure relief valve plunger for scoring and free operation in its bore. Small marks may be removed with 400 grit wet or dry sandpaper.

9. The relief valve spring has a free length of approximately 2.39 inches (60.7mm) it should test between 18–19 pounds when compressed to 1.60 inches (40.5mm). Replace spring that fails to meet specifications.

10. If oil pressure is low and pump is within specifications, inspect for worn engine bearings or other reasons for oil pressure loss.

2.7L Engine

1. Disassemble the oil pump.

2. Clean all oil pump components.

3. Inspect mating surface of the oil pump housing and cover. Replace oil pump if deeply scratched or grooved (minor surface scratches and polishing is normal).

4. Lay a straightedge across the pump cover surface. If a 0.001 in. (0.025mm) feeler gauge can be inserted between cover and straight edge, cover should be replaced.

5. Measure thickness and diameter of outer rotor. If outer rotor thickness measures 0.373 in. (9.474mm) or less, or if the diameter is 3.5108 in. (89.174mm) or less, replace outer rotor.

6. If inner rotor measures 0.373 in. (9.474mm) or less replace inner rotor.

7. Slide outer rotor into body, press to one side with fingers and measure clearance between rotor and body. If measurement is 0.015 in. (0.39mm) or more, replace body only if outer rotor is in specifications.

8. Install inner rotor into body. If clearance between inner and outer rotors is 0.008 in. (0.20mm) or more, replace both rotors.

9. Place a straightedge across the face of the body, between bolt holes. If a feeler gauge of 0.003 in. (0.077mm) or more can be inserted between rotors and the straightedge, replace pump assembly **ONLY** if rotors are in specification.

10. Inspect oil pressure relief valve plunger for scoring and free operation in its bore. Small marks may be removed with 400 grit wet or dry sandpaper.

11. The relief valve spring has a free length of approximately 1.95 in. (49.5mm) it should test between 23–25 pounds when compressed to 1.34 in. (34mm). Replace spring that fails to meet specifications.

12. Assemble oil pump.

PISTON AND RING

POSITIONING

See Figures 91 through 96.

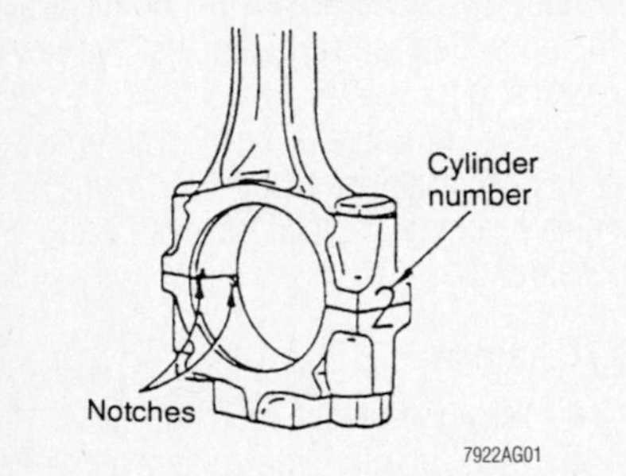

Fig. 91 Engine connecting rod and cap installation—ensure to matchmark the cap and rod prior to disassembly

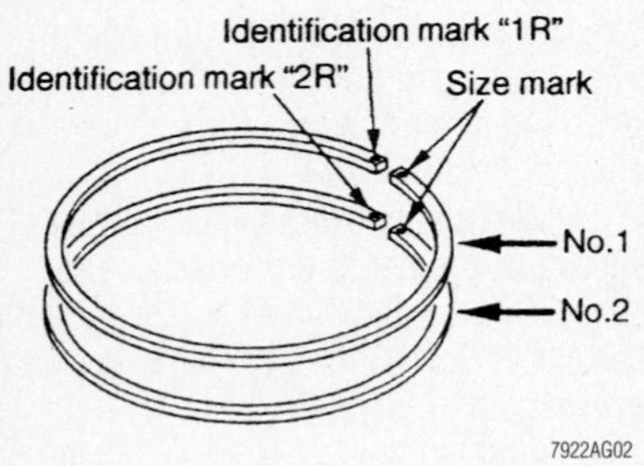

Fig. 92 Piston ring identification mark locations

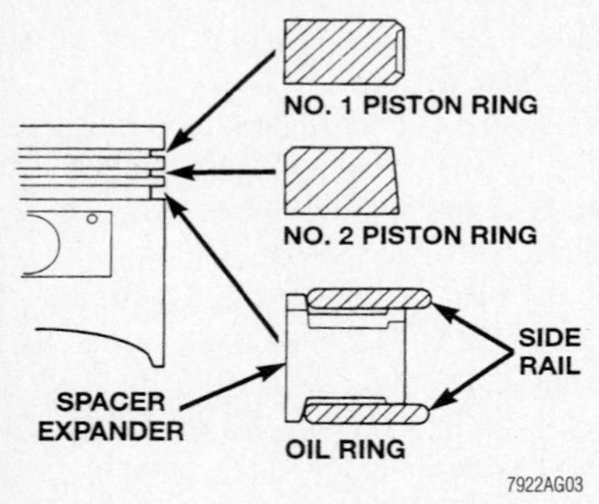

Fig. 93 Piston ring orientation—2.4L & 2.7L engines

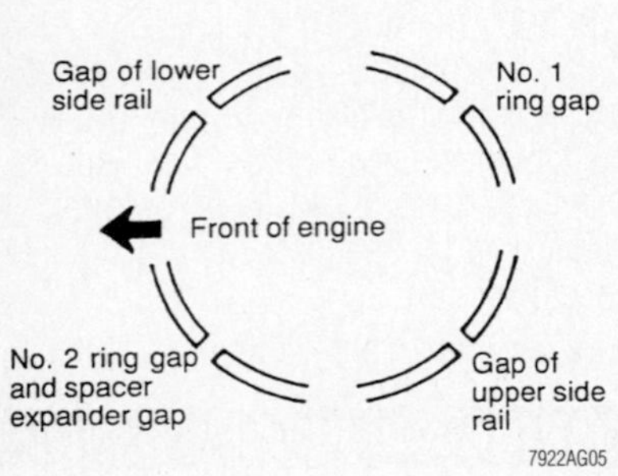

Fig. 94 Piston ring end-gap spacing—2.4L engine

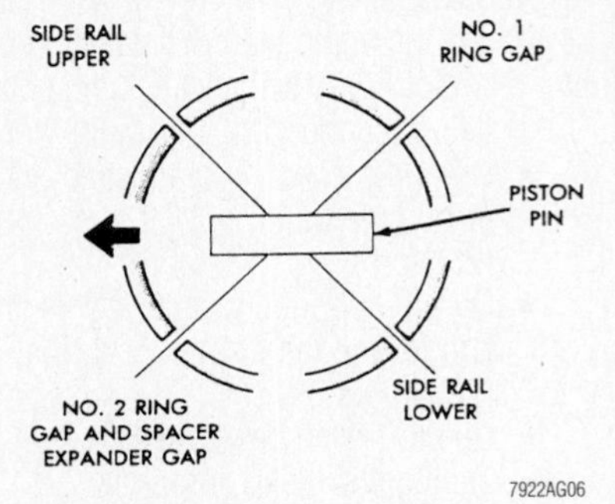

Fig. 95 Piston ring end-gap spacing—2.7L engine

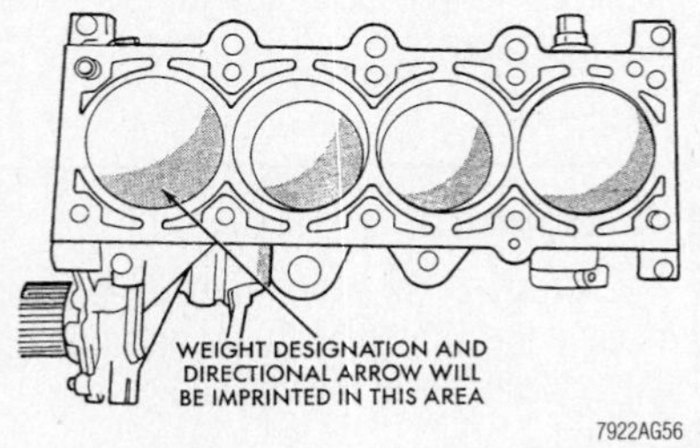

Fig. 96 Piston positioning. The arrow or weight marking (L or H) must face toward the timing belt side of the engine—2.4L engine

REAR MAIN SEAL

REMOVAL & INSTALLATION

1. Before servicing the vehicle, refer to the precautions in the beginning of this section.
2. Remove or disconnect the following:
   - Negative battery cable from the left shock tower.

➡The ground cable is equipped with an insulator grommet which should be placed on the stud to prevent the negative battery cable from accidentally grounding.

   - Transaxle
   - Flexplate/flywheel
   - Rear crankshaft oil seal using a flat-bladed prying tool

To install:

➡When installing the seal there is no need to lubricate the sealing surface.

3. Install or connect the following:
   - New seal using a suitable driver or seal installer
   - Flexplate/flywheel and torque the bolts to 70 ft. lbs. (95 Nm)
   - Transaxle
   - Negative battery cable
4. Start the engine and check for leaks.

TIMING CHAIN, SPROCKETS, FRONT COVER AND SEAL

REMOVAL & INSTALLATION

2.4L (VIN X) Engine

See Figures 97 and 98.

1. Disconnect the negative battery cable from the left strut tower. The ground cable is equipped with a insulator grommet which should be placed on the stud to prevent the negative battery cable from accidentally grounding.
2. Remove the right inner splash-shield.
3. Remove the accessory drive belts.
4. Remove the crankshaft balancer.
5. Remove the right engine mount.
6. Place a suitable floor jack under the vehicle to support the engine.
7. Remove the engine mount bracket.
8. Remove the timing belt cover.

➡Do not rotate the crankshaft or the camshafts after the timing belt has been removed. Damage to the valve components may occur. Before removing the timing belt, always align the timing marks.

9. Align the timing marks of the timing belt sprockets to the timing marks on the rear timing belt cover and oil pump cover. Loosen the timing belt tensioner bolts.
10. Remove the timing belt and the tensioner.
11. Remove the camshaft timing belt sprockets.
12. Remove the crankshaft timing belt sprocket using special removal tool No. 6793.
13. Place the tensioner into a soft-jawed vise to compress the tensioner.
14. After compressing the tensioner, place a pin (a 5⁄64 inch Allen wrench will work) into the plunger side hole to retain the plunger until installation.

To install:

15. Using special tool No. 6792, install the crankshaft timing belt sprocket onto the crankshaft.
16. Install the camshaft sprockets onto the camshafts. Install and tighten the camshaft sprocket bolts to 75 ft. lbs. (101 Nm).
17. Set the crankshaft sprocket to Top Dead Center (TDC) by aligning the notch on the sprocket with the arrow on the oil pump housing.
18. Set the camshafts to align the timing marks on the sprockets.
19. Move the crankshaft to ½ notch before TDC.

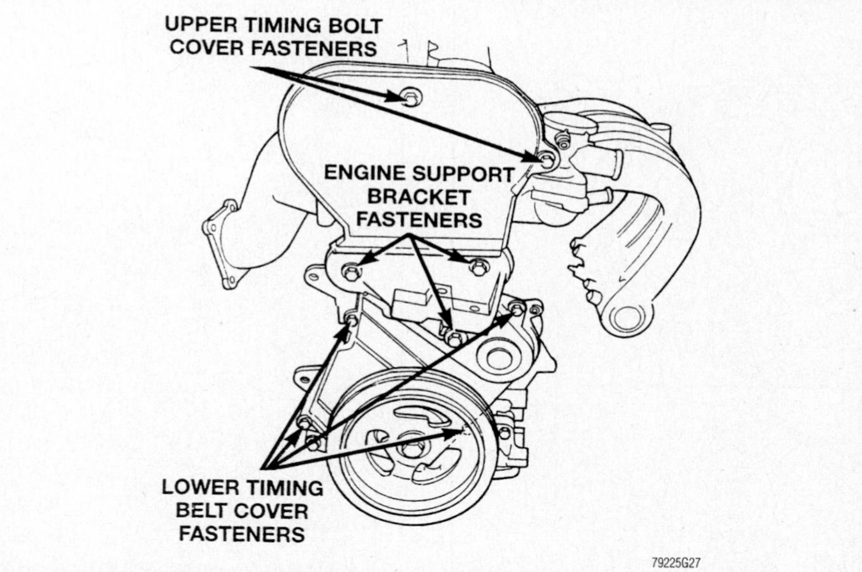

Fig. 97 Timing belt cover bolt locations—2.4L (VIN X) engine

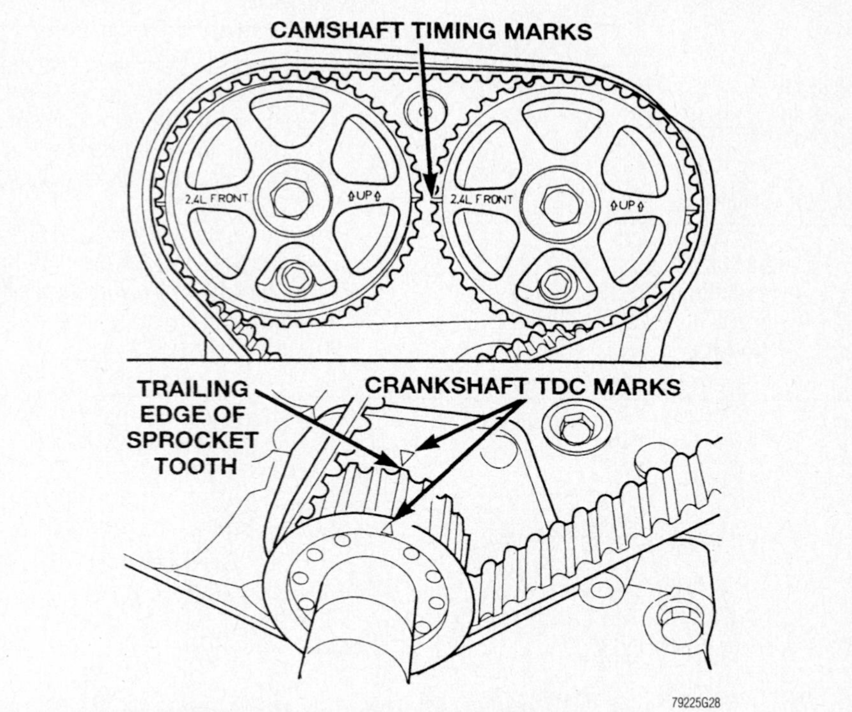

Fig. 98 Crankshaft and camshaft alignment marks—2.4L (VIN X) engine

20. Install the timing belt starting at the crankshaft, then around the water pump sprocket, idler pulley, camshaft sprockets and the tensioner pulley.
21. Move the crankshaft sprocket to TDC to take up the belt slack.
22. Reinstall the tensioner to the block but do not tighten it at this time.
23. Using a torque wrench on the tensioner pulley, apply 21 ft. lbs. (28 Nm) of torque to the tensioner pulley.
24. With torque being applied to the tensioner pulley, move the tensioner up against the tensioner pulley bracket and tighten the fasteners to 23 ft. lbs. (31 Nm).
25. Remove the tensioner plunger pin, the tension is correct when the plunger pin can be removed and replaced easily.
26. Rotate the crankshaft two revolutions and recheck the timing marks. Wait several minutes, then recheck that the plunger pin can easily be removed and installed.
27. Reinstall the front timing belt cover.
28. Reinstall the engine mount bracket.
29. Reinstall the right engine mount.
30. Remove the floor jack from under the vehicle.
31. Install the crankshaft balancer and tighten to 105 ft. lbs. (142 Nm).
32. Install and adjust the accessory drive belts.
33. Install the right inner splash-shield.
34. Reconnect the negative battery cable.
35. Perform the crankshaft and camshaft relearn alignment procedure using the DRB scan tool or equivalent.

2.4L (VIN S) Engine

See Figures 99 through 104.

1. Before servicing the vehicle, refer to the precautions in the beginning of this section.
2. Remove the A/C refrigerant using approved equipment.
3. Remove or disconnect the following:
   - Negative battery cable
   - Right front wheel and inner splash shield
   - Accessory drive belts
   - Crankshaft balancer
   - Lower torque strut
   - Exhaust system from the manifold
   - A/C compressor switch
   - Upper torque strut and bracket
   - Upper radiator support cross-member
   - Power steering pump and bracket without disconnecting the lines
   - Right engine mount through bolt after supporting the engine
   - Engine support bracket
4. Rotate the crankshaft until the Top Dead Center (TDC) mark on the oil pump housing aligns with the TDC mark on the crankshaft sprocket.
5. Install an Allen wrench into the tensioner. Rotate the tensioner counterclockwise while pushing on the wrench until it slides into the locking hole.
6. Remove the timing belt.

To install:

7. Set the crankshaft sprocket at TDC by aligning the sprocket with the arrow on the oil pump housing.
8. Set the camshafts timing marks so that the exhaust camshaft sprocket is a ½ notch below the intake camshaft sprocket.

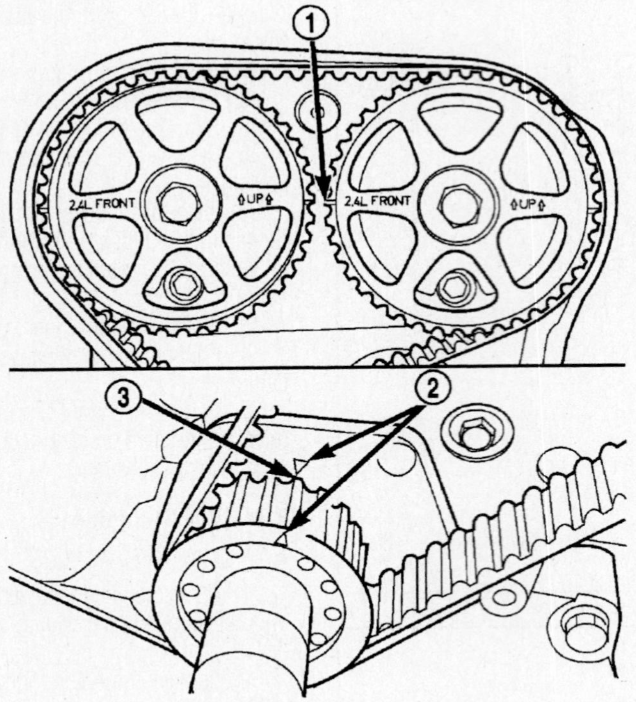

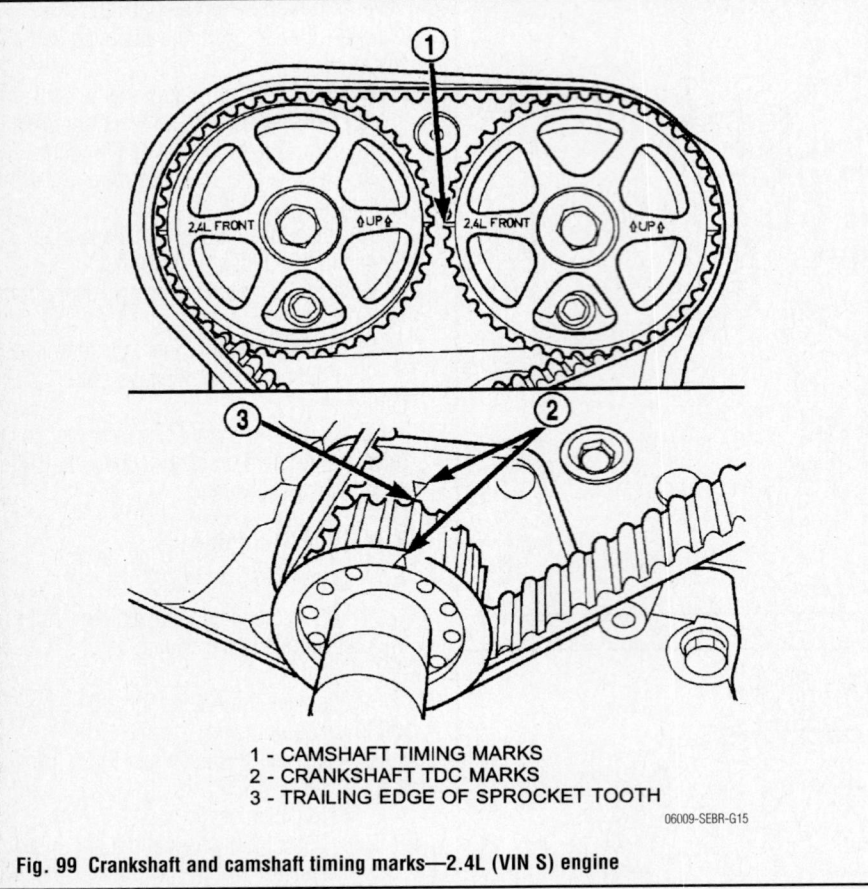

Fig. 99 Crankshaft and camshaft timing marks—2.4L (VIN S) engine

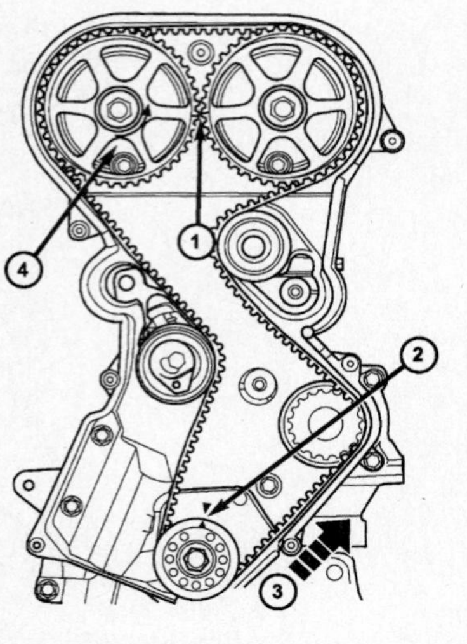

Fig. 102 Timing belt installation—2.4L (VIN S) engine

9. Install the timing belt by starting at the crankshaft. Go around the water pump sprocket idler pulley, camshaft sprockets and the tensioner.

10. Move the exhaust camshaft sprocket counterclockwise to align the marks and to remove any slack.

11. Remove the wrench from the belt tensioner.

12. Rotate the crankshaft two full revolutions and verify that the TDC marks are properly aligned.

13. Install or connect the following:

- Lower timing belt cover and torque the bolts to 40 inch lbs. (4.5 Nm)
- Upper timing belt cover and torque the bolts to 40 inch lbs. (4.5 Nm)
- Right engine support bracket and reposition the power steering pump. Torque the bracket bolts to: 45 ft. lbs. (61 Nm).
- Right engine mount through bolt and torque it to 87 ft. lbs. (118 Nm)
- Upper radiator support crossmember
- Torque strut bracket
- Upper torque strut

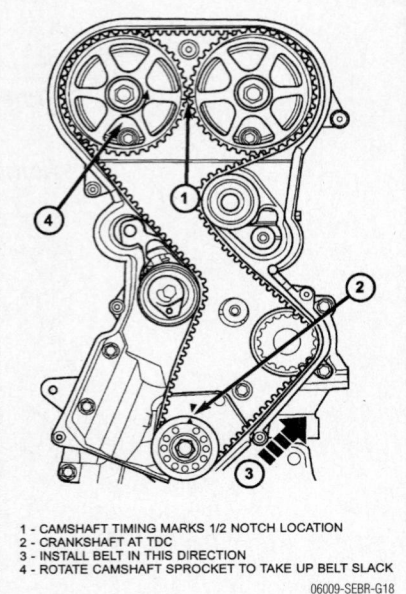

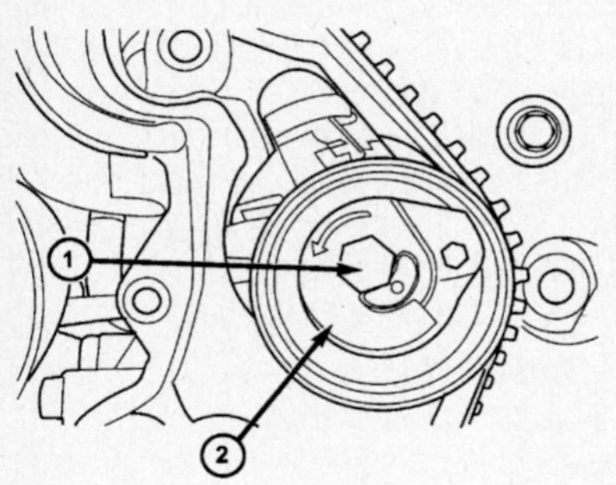

Fig. 100 Timing belt tensioner—2.4L (VIN S) engine

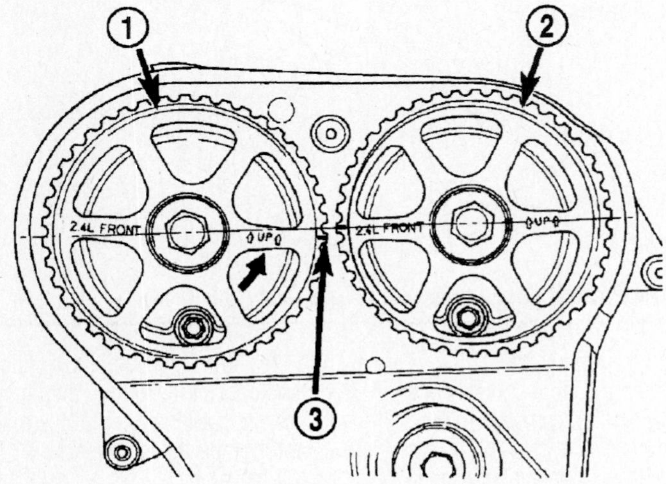

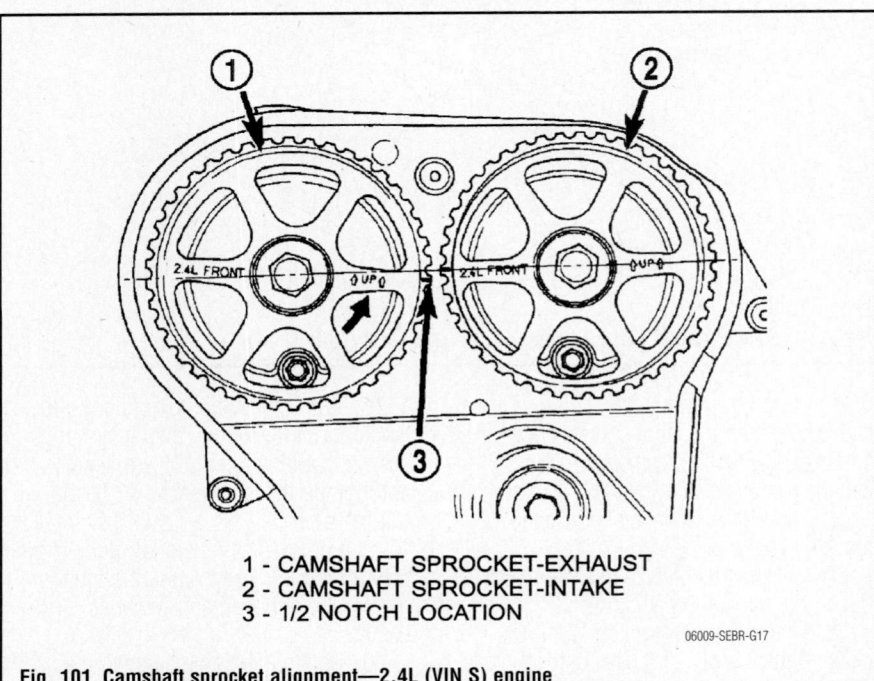

Fig. 101 Camshaft sprocket alignment—2.4L (VIN S) engine

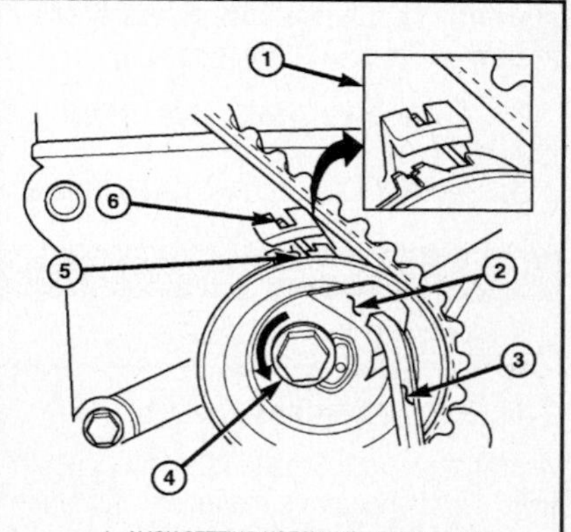

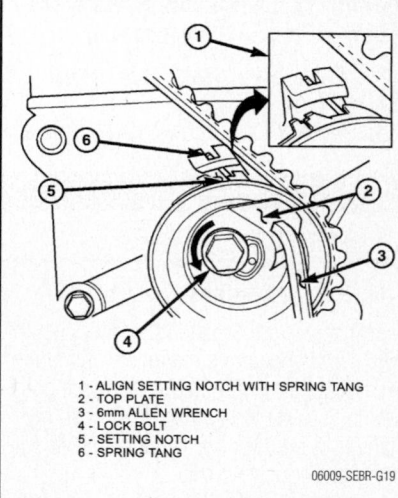

Fig. 103 Timing belt tension adjustment—2.4L (VIN S) engine

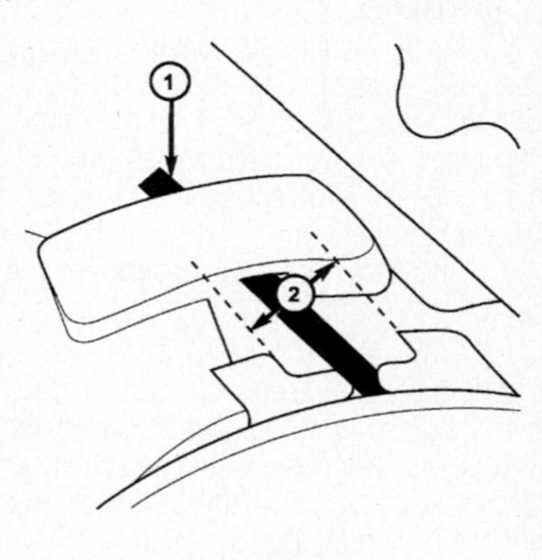

Fig. 104 Timing belt tension verification—2.4L (VIN S) engine

- A/C lines and pressure switch
- Exhaust system to the manifold
- Crankshaft balancer
- Accessory drive belts
- Lower torque strut
- Right splash shield and wheel
- Negative battery cable

14. Recharge the A/C system.
15. Perform the camshaft/crankshaft synchronization procedure.

2.7L Engine

1. Before servicing the vehicle, refer to the Precautions Section.
2. Disconnect negative battery cable.
3. Drain cooling system.
4. Remove upper intake manifold.
5. Remove cylinder head covers, crankshaft balancer, and timing chain cover.

✻✻ WARNING

When aligning timing marks, always rotate engine by turning the crankshaft. Failure to do so will result in valve and/or piston damage.

6. Align crankshaft sprocket timing mark to the mark on the oil pump housing. The mark on the oil pump housing is 60° After Top Dead Center (ATDC) of number 1 cylinder.

✻✻ WARNING

When the timing chain is removed and the cylinder heads are still installed, DO NOT rotate the camshafts or crankshaft without first locating the proper crankshaft position. Failure to do so will result in valve and/or piston damage.

7. Remove the power steering pump and bracket as an assembly. **Do not** disconnect power steering lines from pump. Reposition pump and support with suitable retaining strap.
8. Remove primary timing chain tensioner retainer cap and tensioner from right cylinder head.
9. Disconnect and remove camshaft position sensor from left cylinder head.
10. Remove timing chain guide access plugs from cylinder heads.

➡When camshaft sprocket bolts are removed, the camshafts will rotate in a clockwise direction.

11. Starting with the right camshaft sprocket, remove the sprocket attaching bolts. Remove camshaft damper (if equipped) and sprocket.
12. Remove left side camshaft sprocket attaching bolts and remove sprocket.
13. Remove lower chain guide and tensioner arm.
14. Remove the primary timing chain.

To install:

15. Inspect all sprockets and chain guides. Replace if worn.
16. If removed, install right and left side short chain guides. Tighten attaching bolts to 21 ft. lbs. (28 Nm).
17. Align crankshaft sprocket timing mark to the mark on the oil pump housing.

➡Lubricate timing chain and guides with engine oil before installation.

18. Place left side primary chain sprocket onto the chain so that the timing mark is located in between the 2 (plated) timing links.
19. Lower the primary chain with left side sprocket through the left cylinder head opening.

➡The camshaft sprockets can be allowed to float on the camshaft hub during installation.

20. Loosely position left side camshaft sprocket over camshaft hub.
21. Align timing (plated) link to the crankshaft sprocket timing mark.
22. Position primary chain onto water pump drive sprocket.
23. Align right camshaft sprocket timing mark to the timing (plated) link on the timing chain and loosely position over camshaft hub.
24. Verify that all chain timing (plated) links are properly aligned to the timing marks on all sprockets.
25. Install left side lower chain guide and tensioner arm. Tighten attaching bolts to 21 ft. lbs. (28 Nm).

➡Inspect O-ring on chain guide access plugs before installing. Replace O-ring as necessary.

26. Install chain guide access plugs to cylinder heads. Tighten plugs to 15 ft. lbs. (20 Nm).

➡To reset the primary timing chain tensioner, engine oil will first need to be purged from the tensioner.

27. Purge oil from timing chain tensioner using the following procedure:
    a. Place the check ball end of tensioner into the shallow end of Special Tool 8186.
    b. Using hand pressure, slowly depress tensioner until oil is purged from tensioner.
28. Reset timing chain tensioner using the following procedure:
    a. Position cylinder plunger into the deeper end of Special Tool 8186.
    b. Apply a downward force until tensioner is reset.

➡If oil was not first purged from the tensioner, use slight finger pressure to assist the center arm pin of Special Tool 8186 to unseat the tensioners check ball.

✻✻ WARNING

Ensure the tensioner is properly reset. The tensioner body must bottom against the top edge of Special Tool 8186. Failure to properly perform the resetting procedure may cause tensioner jamming.

29. Install the reset chain tensioner into the right cylinder head.

30. Position tensioner retaining plate and tighten bolts to 106 inch lbs. (12 Nm).

31. Starting at the right cylinder bank, first position the camshaft damper (if equipped) on camshaft hub, then insert a ⅜ inch square drive extension with a breaker bar into intake camshaft drive hub. Rotate camshaft until the camshaft hub aligns to the camshaft sprocket and damper attaching holes. Install the sprocket attaching bolts and tighten to 21 ft. lbs. (28 Nm).

32. Turn the left side camshaft by inserting a ⅜ inch square drive extension with a breaker bar into intake camshaft drive hub and rotate camshaft until the sprocket attaching bolts can be installed. Tighten sprocket bolts to 21 ft. lbs. (28 Nm).

33. Rotate engine slightly clockwise to remove timing chain slack, if necessary.

34. Activate the timing chain tensioner by using a flat bladed pry tool to gently pry tensioner arm towards the tensioner slightly. Then release the tensioner arm. Verify the tensioner is activated (extends).

35. Install power steering pump and bracket assembly.

36. Install camshaft position sensor and connect electrical connector.

37. Install the timing chain cover, crankshaft balancer, and cylinder head covers.

38. Install upper intake manifold.

➡After installation of a reset tensioner, engine noise will occur after initial start-up. This noise will normally disappear within 5–10 seconds.

39. Fill cooling system to the proper level.

40. Connect the negative battery cable.

VALVE LASH

ADJUSTMENT

2.4L & 2.7L Engines

The valves are actuated by roller cam followers which pivot on stationary Hydraulic Lash Adjusters (HLAs). The HLAs are precision units installed in machined openings of the cam follower. Valve clearance adjustments are not performed.

ENGINE PERFORMANCE & EMISSION CONTROL

COMPONENT LOCATIONS

CAMSHAFT POSITION (CMP) SENSOR

LOCATION

2.4L Engine

The Camshaft Position (CMP) sensor is mounted to the end of the cylinder head.

2.7L Engine

The Camshaft Position (CMP) sensor is mounted in the front of the head.

OPERATION

The Powertrain Control Module (PCM) sends approximately 5 volts to the Hall-effect sensor. This voltage is required to operate the Hall-effect chip and the electronics inside the sensor. The input to the PCM occurs on a 5 volt output reference circuit. A ground for the sensor is provided through the sensor return circuit. The PCM identifies camshaft position by registering the change from 5 to 0 volts, as signaled from the camshaft position sensor.

The PCM determines fuel injection synchronization and cylinder identification from inputs provided by the camshaft position sensor and crankshaft position sensor. From the two inputs, the PCM determines crankshaft position.

REMOVAL & INSTALLATION

2.4L Engine

1. Before servicing the vehicle, refer to the Precautions Section.

2. Remove the negative battery cable.

3. Disconnect the PCV hose and reposition.

4. Disconnect electrical connectors from the camshaft position sensor.

5. Remove camshaft position sensor mounting screws.

6. Remove the camshaft position sensor.

7. Loosen screw attaching target magnet to rear of camshaft and remove magnet.

To install:

➡The target magnet has locating dowels that fit into machined locating holes in the end of the camshaft.

8. Install target magnet in end of camshaft. Tighten mounting screw to 27 inch lbs. (3 Nm).

➡Over tightening could cause cracks in the magnet. If the magnet cracks, replace it.

9. Install camshaft position sensor. Tighten sensor mounting screws to 115 inch lbs. (13 Nm) torque.

10. Carefully attach electrical connector to camshaft position sensor. Installation at an angle may damage the sensor pins.

11. Connect the PCV Valve hose.

12. Connect the negative battery cable.

2.7L Engine

1. Before servicing the vehicle, refer to the Precautions Section.

2. Disconnect electrical connector from sensor.

3. Remove camshaft position sensor screw.

4. Without pulling on the connector, pull the sensor out of the chain case cover.

To install:

5. Install sensor in the chain case cover and push sensor in until contact is made with the boss on the head. While holding the sensor in this position, install and tighten the retaining bolt to 106 inch lbs. (12 Nm) torque.

6. Attach the electrical connector to sensor.

TESTING

1. Using the wiring diagram/schematic as a guide, inspect the wiring and connectors between the Camshaft Position Sensor and the Powertrain Control Module (PCM).

2. Look for any chafed, pierced, pinched, or partially broken wires.

3. Look for broken, bent, pushed out, or corroded terminals.

4. Inspect the Camshaft Position Sensor for conditions such as loose mounting screws, damage, or cracks.

5. If no other problems are found, remove the Camshaft Position Sensor.

6. Inspect the Camshaft Position Sensor and mounting area for any condition that would result in an incorrect signal, such as damage, foreign material, or excessive movement.

7. Using a diagnostic scan tool, check for the presence of any Diagnostic Trouble Codes (DTC's). Record and address these codes as necessary.

8. If no codes are present, review the scan tool environmental data. If possible, try to duplicate the conditions under which the DTC set.

9. If applicable, actuate the component with the scan tool.

10. Monitor the scan tool data relative to

this circuit and wiggle test the wiring and connectors.

11. Look for the data to change, the actuation to be interrupted, or for the DTC to reset during the wiggle test.

12. Refer to any Technical Service Bulletins (TSBs) that may apply.

13. Turn the ignition off.

14. Visually inspect the related wire harness. Disconnect all the related harness connectors. Look for any chafed, pierced, pinched, partially broken wires and broken, bent, pushed out, or corroded terminals.

15. Perform a voltage drop test on the related circuits between the suspected component and the Powertrain Control Module (PCM).

16. Inspect and clean all PCM, engine, and chassis grounds that are related to the most current DTC.

17. If numerous trouble codes were set, use a schematic and inspect any common ground or supply circuits.

18. For intermittent Misfire DTC's check for restrictions in the Intake and Exhaust system, proper installation of Sensors, vacuum leaks, and binding components that are run by the accessory drive belt.

19. Use the scan tool to perform a System Test if one applies to the component.

20. A co-pilot, data recorder, and/or lab scope should be used to help diagnose intermittent conditions.

CRANKSHAFT POSITION (CKP) SENSOR

LOCATION

2.4L Engine

The 2.4L Crankshaft Position (CKP) sensor is located on the front of the engine below the starter.

2.7L Engine

The 2.7L Crankshaft Position (CKP) sensor is located on the rear of the transmission housing, above the differential housing. The bottom of the sensor is positioned next to the drive plate.

OPERATION

The Powertrain Control Module (PCM) sends approximately 5 volts to the Hall-effect sensor. This voltage is required to operate the Hall-effect chip and the electronics inside the sensor. A ground for the sensor is provided through the sensor return circuit. The input to the PCM occurs on a 5 volt output reference circuit that operates as follows: The Hall-effect sensor contains a powerful magnet. As the magnetic field passes over the dense portion of the counterweight, the 5-volt signal is pulled to ground (0.3 volts) through a transistor in the sensor. When the magnetic field passes over the notches in the crankshaft counterweight, the magnetic field turns off the transistor in the sensor, causing the PCM to register the 5-volt signal. The PCM identifies crankshaft position by registering the change from 5 to 0 volts, as signaled from the Crankshaft Position sensor.

TESTING

1. Using a diagnostic scan tool, check for the presence of any Diagnostic Trouble Codes (DTC's). Record and address these codes as necessary.

2. If no codes are present, review the scan tool environmental data. If possible, try to duplicate the conditions under which the DTC set.

3. If applicable, actuate the component with the scan tool.

4. Monitor the scan tool data relative to this circuit and wiggle test the wiring and connectors.

5. Look for the data to change, the actuation to be interrupted, or for the DTC to reset during the wiggle test.

6. Refer to any Technical Service Bulletins (TSBs) that may apply.

7. Turn the ignition off.

8. Visually inspect the related wire harness. Disconnect all the related harness connectors. Look for any chafed, pierced, pinched, partially broken wires and broken, bent, pushed out, or corroded terminals.

9. Perform a voltage drop test on the related circuits between the suspected component and the Powertrain Control Module (PCM).

10. Inspect and clean all PCM, engine, and chassis grounds that are related to the most current DTC.

11. If numerous trouble codes were set, use a schematic and inspect any common ground or supply circuits.

12. For intermittent Misfire DTC's check for restrictions in the Intake and Exhaust system, proper installation of Sensors, vacuum leaks, and binding components that are run by the accessory drive belt.

13. Use the scan tool to perform a System Test if one applies to the component.

14. A co-pilot, data recorder, and/or lab scope should be used to help diagnose intermittent conditions.

ENGINE COOLANT TEMPERATURE (ECT) SENSOR

OPERATION

The Engine Coolant Temperature (ECT) sensor provides an input to the Powertrain Control Module (PCM). As temperature increases, resistance of the sensor decreases. As coolant temperature varies, the ECT sensor resistance changes resulting in a different voltage value at the PCM ECT sensor signal circuit. The ECT sensor provides input for various PCM operations. The PCM uses the input to control air-fuel mixture, timing, and radiator fan on/off times.

REMOVAL & INSTALLATION

1. Before servicing the vehicle, refer to the Precautions Section.

2. With engine cold, partially drain cooling system below level of Engine Coolant Temperature (ECT) sensor.

3. Disconnect ECT sensor electrical connector.

4. Remove ECT sensor.

To install:

5. Install ECT sensor. Torque the sensor to 14 ft. lbs. (19 Nm).

6. Reconnect ECT sensor electrical sensor.

7. Fill cooling system.

TESTING

1. Using the wiring diagram/schematic as a guide, inspect the wiring and connectors between the Engine Coolant Temperature sensor(s) and the Powertrain Control Module (PCM).

2. Look for any chafed, pierced, pinched, or partially broken wires.

3. Look for broken, bent, pushed out or corroded terminals.

4. Turn the ignition on.

5. Monitor the scan tool data relative to the sensor(s) and wiggle test the wiring and connectors.

6. Look for the data to change or for a DTC to set during the wiggle test.

7. Check the engine coolant level and the condition of the engine coolant.

8. With the scan tool, read the Engine Coolant Temperature Sensor value for each sensor. If the engine was allowed to cool completely, the value should be approximately equal to the ambient temperature.

9. Monitor each sensor value on the scan tool and the actual coolant temperature with a thermometer.

10. Using a diagnostic scan tool, check for the presence of any Diagnostic Trouble

Codes (DTC's). Record and address these codes as necessary.

11. If no codes are present, review the scan tool environmental data. If possible, try to duplicate the conditions under which the DTC set.

12. If applicable, actuate the component with the scan tool.

13. Monitor the scan tool data relative to this circuit and wiggle test the wiring and connectors.

14. Look for the data to change, the actuation to be interrupted, or for the DTC to reset during the wiggle test.

15. Refer to any Technical Service Bulletins (TSBs) that may apply.

16. Turn the ignition off.

17. Visually inspect the related wire harness. Disconnect all the related harness connectors. Look for any chafed, pierced, pinched, partially broken wires and broken, bent, pushed out, or corroded terminals.

18. Perform a voltage drop test on the related circuits between the suspected component and the Powertrain Control Module (PCM).

19. Inspect and clean all PCM, engine, and chassis grounds that are related to the most current DTC.

20. If numerous trouble codes were set, use a schematic and inspect any common ground or supply circuits.

21. For intermittent Misfire DTC's check for restrictions in the Intake and Exhaust system, proper installation of Sensors, vacuum leaks, and binding components that are run by the accessory drive belt.

22. Use the scan tool to perform a System Test if one applies to the component.

23. A co-pilot, data recorder, and/or lab scope should be used to help diagnose intermittent conditions.

HEATED OXYGEN (HO2S) SENSOR

OPERATION

As vehicles accumulate mileage, the catalytic converter deteriorates. The deterioration results in a less efficient catalyst. To monitor catalytic converter deterioration, the fuel injection system uses two heated oxygen sensors. One sensor is upstream of the catalytic converter, one is downstream of the converter. The Powertrain Control Module (PCM) compares the reading from the sensors to calculate the catalytic converter oxygen storage capacity and converter efficiency. Also, the PCM uses the upstream heated oxygen sensor input when adjusting injector pulse width.

When the catalytic converter efficiency drops below emission standards, the PCM stores a diagnostic trouble code and illuminates the Malfunction Indicator Lamp (MIL).

The Heated Oxygen Sensors (HO2S) produce a constant 2.5 volts on NGC (4 cylinder) vehicles, depending upon the oxygen content of the exhaust gas. When a large amount of oxygen is present (caused by a lean air/fuel mixture, can be caused by misfire and exhaust leaks), the sensors produce a low voltage. When there is a lesser amount of oxygen present (caused by a rich air/fuel mixture, which can be caused by internal engine problems) it produces a higher voltage. By monitoring the oxygen content and converting it to electrical voltage, the sensors act as a rich-lean switch.

The oxygen sensors are equipped with a heating element that keeps the sensors at proper operating temperature during all operating modes. Maintaining correct sensor temperature at all times allows the system to enter into closed loop operation sooner. Also, it allows the system to remain in closed loop operation during periods of extended idle.

In Closed Loop operation the PCM monitors the HO2S input (along with other inputs) and adjusts the injector pulse width accordingly. During Open Loop operation the PCM ignores the HO2S input. The PCM adjusts injector pulse width based on preprogrammed (fixed) values and inputs from other sensors.

The NGC Controller has a common ground for the heater in the HO2S. 12 volts is supplied to the heater in the HO2S by the NGC controller. Both the upstream and downstream HO2S for NGC are Pulse Width Modulation (PWM). NOTE: When replacing an HO2S, the PCM RAM memory must be cleared, either by disconnecting the PCM C-1 connector or momentarily disconnecting the Battery negative terminal. The NGC learns the characteristics of each HO2S heater element and these old values should be cleared when installing a new HO2S. You may experience driveability issues if this is not performed.

TESTING

1. Using a diagnostic scan tool, check for the presence of any Diagnostic Trouble Codes (DTC's). Record and address these codes as necessary.

2. If no codes are present, review the scan tool environmental data. If possible, try to duplicate the conditions under which the DTC set.

3. If applicable, actuate the component with the scan tool.

4. Monitor the scan tool data relative to this circuit and wiggle test the wiring and connectors.

5. Look for the data to change, the actuation to be interrupted, or for the DTC to reset during the wiggle test.

6. Refer to any Technical Service Bulletins (TSBs) that may apply.

7. Turn the ignition off.

8. Visually inspect the related wire harness. Disconnect all the related harness connectors. Look for any chafed, pierced, pinched, partially broken wires and broken, bent, pushed out, or corroded terminals.

9. Perform a voltage drop test on the related circuits between the suspected component and the Powertrain Control Module (PCM).

10. Inspect and clean all PCM, engine, and chassis grounds that are related to the most current DTC.

11. If numerous trouble codes were set, use a schematic and inspect any common ground or supply circuits.

12. For intermittent Misfire DTC's check for restrictions in the Intake and Exhaust system, proper installation of Sensors, vacuum leaks, and binding components that are run by the accessory drive belt.

13. Use the scan tool to perform a System Test if one applies to the component.

14. A co-pilot, data recorder, and/or lab scope should be used to help diagnose intermittent conditions.

INTAKE AIR TEMPERATURE (IAT) SENSOR

OPERATION

The Intake Air Temperature (IAT) sensor is a negative coefficient sensor that provides information to the Powertrain Control Module (PCM) regarding the temperature of the air entering the intake manifold.

TESTING

1. Turn the ignition off. If possible, allow the vehicle to sit with the ignition off for more than 8 hours in an environment where the temperature is consistent and above 20°F (-7°C).

2. Test drive the vehicle. The vehicle must exceed 30 mph (48 km/h) during the test drive. Do not cycle the ignition off when the test drive is completed.

3. With a scan tool, select View DTC's.

4. If a DTC is not active, perform the following:

5. Refer to any Technical Service Bulletins (TSBs) that may apply.

6. Review the scan tool Freeze Frame information. If possible, try to duplicate the conditions under which the DTC set.

7. With the engine running at normal operating temperature, monitor the scan tool parameters related to the DTC while wiggling the wire harness. Look for parameter values to change and/or a DTC to set. Turn the ignition off.

8. Visually inspect the related wire harness. Disconnect all the related harness connectors. Look for any chafed, pierced, pinched, partially broken wires and broken, bent, pushed out, or corroded terminals. Perform a voltage drop test on the related circuits between the suspected inoperative component and the PCM.

⁂ CAUTION

Do not probe the PCM harness connectors. Probing the PCM harness connectors will damage the PCM terminals resulting in poor terminal to pin connection. Install Miller Special Tool #8815 to perform diagnosis.

9. Inspect and clean all PCM, engine, and chassis grounds that are related to the most current DTC.

10. If numerous trouble codes were set, use a wire schematic and look for any common ground or supply circuits.

11. For any Relay DTC's, actuate the Relay with the scan tool and wiggle the related wire harness to try to interrupt the actuation.

12. For intermittent Evaporative Emission trouble codes perform a visual and physical inspection of the related parts including hoses and the Fuel Filler cap.

13. Use the scan tool to perform a System Test if one applies to failing component. A co-pilot, data recorder, and/or lab scope should be used to help diagnose intermittent conditions.

KNOCK SENSOR (KS)

LOCATION

2.4L Engine

The Knock Sensor (KS) threads into the side of the cylinder block in front of the starter.

2.7L Engine

The Knock Sensor (KS) sensor screws into the cylinder block, directly below the intake manifold.

OPERATION

When the Knock Sensor (KS) detects a knock in one of the cylinders, it sends an input signal to the Powertrain Control Module (PCM). In response, the PCM retards ignition timing for all cylinders by a scheduled amount.

Knock sensors contain a piezoelectric material which constantly vibrates and sends an input voltage (signal) to the PCM while the engine operates. As the intensity of the crystal's vibration increases, the knock sensor output voltage also increases.

The voltage signal produced by the knock sensor increases with the amplitude of vibration. The PCM receives as an input the knock sensor voltage signal. If the signal rises above a predetermined level, the PCM will store that value in memory and retard ignition timing to reduce engine knock. If the knock sensor voltage exceeds a preset value, the PCM retards ignition timing for all cylinders. It is not a selective cylinder retard.

The PCM ignores knock sensor input during engine idle conditions. Once the engine speed exceeds a specified value, ignition timing retard is allowed.

REMOVAL & INSTALLATION

2.4L Engine

1. Before servicing the vehicle, refer to the Precautions Section.
2. Disconnect electrical connector from Knock Sensor (KS).
3. Use a crow foot socket to remove the KS.

To install:

➡Over or under-tightening effects the KS performance, possibly causing improper spark control.

4. Install the KS. Tighten the KS to 88 inch lbs. (10 Nm) torque.
5. Attach electrical connector to knock sensor.

2.7L Engine

1. Before servicing the vehicle, refer to the Precautions Section.
2. Remove intake manifold plenum.
3. Remove the passenger side cylinder head.
4. Disconnect the electrical connector from Knock Sensor (KS).
5. Use a crows foot socket to remove the KS.

To install:

➡Over or under-tightening effects the KS performance, possibly causing improper spark control.

6. Install KS. Tighten KS to 88 inch lbs. (10 Nm) torque.
7. Install the passenger side cylinder head.
8. Attach electrical connector to KS.
9. Install intake manifold plenum.

TESTING

1. Using the wiring diagram/schematic as a guide, inspect the wiring and connectors between the Knock Sensor (KS) and the Powertrain Control Module (PCM).

2. Look for any chafed, pierced, pinched, or partially broken wires.

3. Look for broken, bent, pushed out or corroded terminals.

4. Monitor the scan tool data relative to this circuit and wiggle test the wiring and connectors.

5. Look for the data to change or for the DTC to reset during the wiggle test.

6. Refer to any Technical Service Bulletins that may apply.

7. Review the scan tool Freeze Frame information. If possible, try to duplicate the conditions under which the DTC set.

8. With the engine running at normal operating temperature, monitor the scan tool parameters related to the DTC while wiggling the wire harness. Look for parameter values to change and/or a DTC to set. Turn the ignition off.

9. Visually inspect the related wire harness. Disconnect all the related harness connectors. Look for any chafed, pierced, pinched, partially broken wires and broken, bent, pushed out, or corroded terminals. Perform a voltage drop test on the related circuits between the suspected inoperative component and the PCM.

⁂ CAUTION

Do not probe the PCM harness connectors. Probing the PCM harness connectors will damage the PCM terminals resulting in poor terminal to pin connection. Install Miller Special Tool #8815 to perform diagnosis.

10. Inspect and clean all PCM, engine, and chassis grounds that are related to the most current DTC.

11. If numerous trouble codes were set, use a wire schematic and look for any common ground or supply circuits.

12. For any Relay DTC's, actuate the Relay with the scan tool and wiggle the related wire harness to try to interrupt the actuation.

13. For intermittent Evaporative Emission trouble codes perform a visual and physical inspection of the related parts including hoses and the Fuel Filler cap.

14. Use the scan tool to perform a System Test if one applies to failing component. A co-pilot, data recorder, and/or lab scope should be used to help diagnose intermittent conditions.

MANIFOLD ABSOLUTE PRESSURE (MAP) SENSOR

LOCATION

The Manifold Absolute Pressure (MAP) sensor mounts onto the intake manifold plenum.

OPERATION

The Manifold Absolute Pressure (MAP) sensor serves as a Powertrain Control Module (PCM) input, using a silicon-based sensing unit, to provide data on the manifold vacuum that draws the air/fuel mixture into the combustion chamber. The PCM requires this information to determine injector pulse width and spark advance. When MAP equals Barometric pressure, the pulse width will be at maximum.

Also, like the camshaft and crankshaft sensors, a 5-volt reference is supplied from the PCM and returns a voltage signal to the PCM that reflects manifold pressure. The zero pressure reading is 0.5 volt and full scale is 4.5 volts. For a pressure swing of 0–15 psi, the voltage changes 4.0 volts. The sensor is supplied a regulated 4.8–5.1 volts to operate the sensor. Like the camshaft and crankshaft sensors, ground is provided through the sensor return circuit.

REMOVAL & INSTALLATION

2.4L Engine

1. Before servicing the vehicle, refer to the Precautions Section.
2. Disconnect the negative battery cable.
3. Disconnect electrical connector from Manifold Absolute Pressure (MAP) sensor.
4. Remove the 2 screws holding sensor to the intake manifold.

To install:

5. Install the sensor.
6. Install the 2 screws and tighten.
7. Connect the electrical connector to the MAP sensor.
8. Connect the negative battery cable.

2.7L Engine

1. Before servicing the vehicle, refer to the Precautions Section.
2. Remove the negative battery cable.
3. Disconnect the electrical connector from the Manifold Absolute Pressure (MAP) sensor.
4. Remove the bolt from the MAP sensor.
5. Remove the MAP sensor.

To install:

6. Mount the MAP sensor onto the intake manifold plenum. Tighten the screws to 44 inch lbs. (5 Nm) torque.
7. Attach the electrical connector to the MAP sensor.
8. Connect the negative battery cable.

TESTING

1. Turn the ignition off.
2. Using the wiring diagram/schematic as a guide, inspect the wiring and connectors between the Manifold Absolute Pressure (MAP) Sensor and the PCM.
3. Look for any chafed, pierced, pinched, or partially broken wires.
4. Look for broken, bent, pushed out, or corroded terminals.
5. Turn the ignition on.
6. Monitor the scan tool data relative to the sensor and wiggle test the wiring and connectors.
7. Look for the data to change or for a DTC to set during the wiggle test. If necessary, check each sensor circuit for high resistance or a shorted condition.
8. With a scan tool, read the Barometric Pressure. The Barometric Pressure should be approximately equal to the actual barometric pressure. If necessary, compare the Barometric Pressure value of the tested vehicle to the value of a known good vehicle of a similar make and model.
9. Connect a vacuum gauge to a manifold vacuum source and start the engine.
10. With the scan tool, read the MAP Sensor vacuum. The scan tool reading for MAP vacuum should be within 1 inch of the vacuum gauge reading.
11. With the scan tool, monitor the MAP Sensor signal voltage. With the engine idling in neutral or park, snap the throttle. The MAP Sensor signal voltage should change from below 2.0 volts at idle to above 3.5 volts at wide open throttle.

MASS AIR FLOW (MAF) SENSOR

OPERATION

The Mass Air Flow (MAF) sensor is an air flow meter that measures the amount of air entering the engine. The Electronic Control Module (ECM) uses the MAF sensor signal to provide the correct fuel delivery for all engine speeds and loads. A small quantity of air entering the engine indicates a deceleration or idle condition. A large quantity of air entering the engine indicates an acceleration or high load condition. The MAF sensor has the following circuits:

- An ignition 1 voltage circuit
- A ground circuit
- A MAF sensor signal circuit
- An IAT sensor signal circuit
- A low reference circuit

The ECM applies 5 volts to the MAF sensor on the MAF sensor signal circuit. The sensor uses the voltage to produce a frequency based on the inlet air flow through the sensor bore. The frequency varies in a range of near 1,700 Hertz at idle to near 9,500 Hertz at maximum engine load.

REMOVAL & INSTALLATION

2.4L Engine

1. Before servicing the vehicle, refer to the Precautions Section.
2. Disconnect negative battery cable.
3. Remove the air pump assembly.
4. Remove the 2 bracket mounting bolts.
5. Remove the bracket assembly.
6. Disconnect the electrical connector to the Mass Air Flow (MAF).
7. Twist the MAF sideways and remove it from the bracket.
8. Remove the rubber mounting.

To install:

9. Install the rubber mounting to MAF sensor.
10. Twist the MAF sideways and install it into the bracket.
11. Connect the electrical connector to MAF.
12. Install the bracket assembly.
13. Install the 2 bracket mounting bolts.
14. Install the air pump assembly.
15. Connect the negative battery cable.

TESTING

1. Verify the integrity of the air induction system by inspecting for the following conditions:
   - Damaged components
   - Loose or improper installation

- An air flow restriction
- Any vacuum leak
- Water intrusion

2. With the engine running, observe the scan tool Mass Air Flow (MAF) sensor parameter. The reading should be between 1,700–3,200 Hz depending on the Engine Coolant Temperature (ECT).
3. Verify that any electrical aftermarket devices are properly connected and grounded.
4. Inspect the harness of the MAF sensor to verify that it is not routed too close to the following components:
   - Any aftermarket accessories
   - The secondary ignition wires or coils
   - Any solenoids
   - Any relays
   - Any motors
5. A low minimum air rate through the sensor bore at idle or during deceleration may cause a DTC to set. Inspect for the following conditions:
   - Any deposits on the throttle plate or in the throttle bore
   - Any vacuum leak downstream of the MAF sensor
6. Inspect for any contamination or debris on the sensing elements of the MAF sensor.
7. Inspect the air induction system for any water intrusion. Any water that reaches the MAF sensor will skew the sensor and may cause a DTC to set.
8. A Wide Open Throttle (WOT) acceleration from a stop should cause the MAF sensor parameter on the scan tool to increase rapidly. This increase should be from 3–10 g/s at idle to 150 g/s or more at the time of the 1 to 2 shift of the transmission. If the increase is not observed, inspect for a restriction in the induction system or the exhaust system.
9. Inspect for a skewed or stuck Engine Coolant Temperature (ECT) sensor.
10. Test for a high resistance of 15 ohms or more on the ignition 1 voltage circuit. This may cause a DTC to set. A high resistance may also cause a drivability concern before a DTC sets.

The Barometric Pressure (BARO) sensor that is used in order to calculate the predicted mass air flow value is initially based on the Manifold Absolute Pressure (MAP) sensor at key ON. When the engine is running, the BARO value is continually updated near WOT. A skewed MAP sensor will cause the calculated mass air flow value to be inaccurate and may result in a no start condition. The value shown for the MAP sensor parameter varies with the altitude. With the ignition ON and the engine OFF, 101 kPa is the approximate value near sea level. This value will decrease by approximately 3 kPa for every 1,000 feet (305 meters) of altitude.

POWERTRAIN CONTROL MODULE (PCM)

LOCATION

The Powertrain Control Module (PCM), used in this vehicle, is located on the driver's side engine compartment and is forward of the shock suspension mounting where it is fastened to the inner fender.

OPERATION

The powertrain has electronic controls to reduce exhaust emissions while maintaining excellent drivability and fuel economy. The Powertrain Control Module (PCM) used in this vehicle, is the control center of this system. The PCM monitors numerous engine and vehicle functions. The PCM constantly looks at the information from various sensors and other inputs, and controls the systems that affect vehicle performance and emissions. The PCM also performs the diagnostic tests on various parts of the system. The PCM can recognize operational problems and alert the driver via the Malfunction Indicator Lamp (MIL). When the PCM detects a malfunction, the PCM stores a Diagnostic Trouble Code (DTC). The problem area is identified by the particular DTC that is set. The control module supplies a buffered voltage to various sensors and switches. Review the components and wiring diagrams in order to determine which systems are controlled by the PCM. The following are some of the functions that the PCM controls:

- The engine fueling
- The Ignition Control (IC)
- The Knock Sensor (KS) system
- The Evaporative Emissions (EVAP) system
- The Secondary Air Injection (AIR) system (if equipped)
- The Exhaust Gas Recirculation (EGR) system
- The automatic transmission functions
- The alternator
- The A/C clutch control
- The cooling fan control

REMOVAL & INSTALLATION

The Powertrain Control Module (PCM) engine control strategy prevents reduced idle speeds until after the engine operates for 200 miles (320 km). This vehicle utilizes a PCM. If the PCM is replaced after 200 miles (320 km) of usage, update the mileage and Vehicle Identification Number (VIN) in the new PCM. Use the scan tool to change the mileage and VIN in the PCM. If this step is not done, a Diagnostic Trouble Code (DTC) may be set and SKIM must be done or car will not start if it is a SKIM equipped car. With a SKIM car, you must do a secret key transfer also. Refer to the appropriate Powertrain Diagnostic Manual and the scan tool.

⁂ WARNING

To avoid possible voltage spike damage to the PCM, the ignition key must be off, and the negative battery cable must be disconnected before unplugging the PCM connectors.

➡Take note of any radio presets before disconnecting the negative battery cable.

1. Before servicing the vehicle, refer to the Precautions Section.
2. Disconnect the negative battery cable and isolate the cable from making a connection unintentionally.

⁂ WARNING

If the negative battery cable is not disconnected properly, there is the possibility of damaging the PCM by contacting the positive battery cable at the Power Distribution Center (PDC).

3. Remove the 2 nuts holding the PCM and Bracket.
4. Unlock and disconnect the electrical connectors at the PCM.
5. Remove the 3 fasteners holding the PCM to the bracket.

To install:

Use the scan tool to reprogram the new PCM with the original Vehicle Identification Number (VIN) and the vehicle's actual mileage. If this step is not done, a Diagnostic Trouble Code (DTC) may be set.

6. Install the PCM to the bracket.
7. Install the PCM and bracket to the vehicle and connect the electrical connectors and lock connectors.
8. Install the 2 nuts and tighten.
9. Connect the negative battery cable and reprogram the radio and clock.
10. Using a scan tool, program the mileage and VIN into the PCM. Refer to the scan tool and the appropriate Powertrain Diagnostic Manual.

TESTING

The Powertrain Control Module (PCM), used in this vehicle, is programmed with test routines that test the operation of the various systems the PCM controls. Some tests monitor internal PCM functions. Many tests are run continuously. Other tests run only under specific conditions, referred to as conditions for running the DTC. When the vehicle is operating within the conditions for running a particular test, the PCM monitors certain parameters and determines if the values are within an expected range. The parameters and values considered outside the range of normal operation are listed as conditions for setting the DTC. When the conditions for setting the DTC occur, the PCM executes the action taken when the DTC Sets. Some DTC's alert the driver via the Malfunction Indicator Lamp (MIL) or a message. Other DTC's do not trigger a driver warning, but are stored in memory. The PCM also saves data and input parameters when most DTC's are set. This data is stored in the freeze frame and/or failure records.

The DTC's are categorized by type. The DTC type is determined by the MIL operation and the manner in which the fault data is stored when a particular DTC fails. In some cases there may be exceptions to this structure. Therefore, when diagnosing the system it is important to read the action taken when the DTC sets and the conditions for clearing the DTC.

Many intermittent open or shorted circuits come and go with harness and connector movement caused by vibration, engine torque, bumps, and rough pavement.

1. Test the wiring harness and connectors by performing the following:
   - Move the related PCM connectors and wiring while monitoring the appropriate scan tool data
   - With the engine running, move the related connectors and wiring while monitoring engine operation
   - If harness or connector movement affects the data displayed, the component and system operation, or the engine operation, inspect and repair the harness or connections as necessary
2. Test the electrical connections and/or wiring by performing the following:
   - Inspect for incorrect mating of the connector halves, or terminals not fully seated in the connector body, backed-out
   - Inspect for improperly formed or damaged terminals. Test for incorrect terminal tension
   - Inspect for poor terminal to wire connections including terminals crimped over insulation. This requires removing the terminal from the connector body
   - Inspect for corrosion or water intrusion. Pierced or damaged insulation can allow moisture to enter the wiring. The conductor can corrode inside the insulation with little visible evidence. Look for swollen and stiff sections of wire in the suspect circuits
   - Inspect for wires that are broken inside the insulation

THROTTLE POSITION SENSOR (TPS)

OPERATION

The Throttle Position Sensor (TPS) and throttle actuating DC motor are integral to the throttle body. The throttle body is a non-serviceable item; replace the throttle body as an assembly.

The throttle blade will not close completely when engine is shut down. This engine off blade position is for start up. The electric throttle body will adjust the throttle blade for idle control as the idle air control valve adjusted idle speed previously on cable actuated throttle bodies. The electric throttle body will also adjust the throttle blade for normal driving operation. The throttle blade will move to the engine off blade position if throttle body codes are set to provide air for limp-in mode.

REMOVAL & INSTALLATION

2.7L Engine

1. Before servicing the vehicle, refer to the Precautions Section.
2. Remove the negative battery cable.
3. Remove the throttle body.
4. Remove the Throttle Position Sensor (TPS) mounting screws.
5. Remove the TPS.

To install:

6. The throttle shaft end of the throttle body slides into a socket in the TPS. The socket has two tabs inside it. The throttle shaft rests against the tabs. When indexed correctly, the TPS can rotate clockwise a few degrees to line up the mounting screw holes with the screw holes in the throttle body. The TPS has slight tension when rotated into position. If it is difficult to rotate the TPS into position, install the sensor with the throttle shaft on the other side of the tabs in the socket.
7. Tighten the TPS mounting screws to 44 inch lbs. (5 Nm) torque.
8. After installing the TPS, the throttle plate should be closed. If the throttle plate is open, install the sensor on the other side of the tabs in the socket.
9. Install the throttle body.
10. Connect the negative battery cable.

TESTING

1. Using the wiring diagram/schematic as a guide, inspect the wiring and connectors between the Throttle Body and the Powertrain Control Module (PCM).
2. Look for any chafed, pierced, pinched, or partially broken wires.
3. Look for broken, bent, pushed out or corroded terminals.
4. Inspect the Throttle Body for any condition that would result in an incorrect signal, such as damage or contamination.
5. Inspect and clean all PCM, engine, and chassis grounds that are related to the most current DTC.
6. If numerous trouble codes were set, use a wire schematic and look for any common ground or supply circuits.
7. For any Relay DTC's, actuate the Relay with the scan tool and wiggle the related wire harness to try to interrupt the actuation.
8. Use the scan tool to perform a System Test if one applies to failing component. A co-pilot, data recorder, and/or lab scope should be used to help diagnose intermittent conditions.

VEHICLE SPEED SENSOR (VSS)

LOCATION

The Vehicle Speed Sensor (VSS) is mounted into the transaxle assembly.

OPERATION

The Vehicle Speed Sensor (VSS) is a Hall Effect sensor mounted to the transaxle. The sensor is triggered by the ring gear teeth passing below it. The VSS pulse signal to the speedometer/odometer is monitored by the PCM speed control circuitry to determine the vehicle speed and to maintain speed control set speed.

REMOVAL & INSTALLATION

1. Before servicing the vehicle, refer to the Precautions Section.
2. Raise and support the vehicle on a hoist.

3. Disconnect the Vehicle Speed Sensor (VSS) connector.

⁂ WARNING

Clean the area around the VSS before removing in order to prevent dirt from entering the transaxle during the VSS removal.

4. Remove the VSS retaining bolt.
5. Remove the VSS from transaxle.

⁂ WARNING

Carefully remove the VSS so that the sensor drive gear does not fall into the transaxle. Should the sensor drive gear fall into the transaxle during sensor removal, the drive gear must be reattached to the sensor.

6. Remove VSS drive gear from speed sensor.

To install:

7. Install the pinion gear to the VSS.
8. Using a NEW O-ring, install the VSS to the transaxle.
9. Install the retaining bolt and torque to 62 inch lbs. (7 Nm).
10. Connect VSS electrical connector.
11. Lower the vehicle and road test it in order to verify the proper speedometer operation.

FUEL

GASOLINE FUEL INJECTION SYSTEM

FUEL SYSTEM SERVICE PRECAUTIONS

Safety is the most important factor when performing not only fuel system maintenance but any type of maintenance. Failure to conduct maintenance and repairs in a safe manner may result in serious personal injury or death. Maintenance and testing of the vehicle's fuel system components can be accomplished safely and effectively by adhering to the following rules and guidelines.

- To avoid the possibility of fire and personal injury, always disconnect the negative battery cable unless the repair or test procedure requires that battery voltage be applied.
- Always relieve the fuel system pressure prior to disconnecting any fuel system component (injector, fuel rail, pressure regulator, etc.), fitting or fuel line connection. Exercise extreme caution whenever relieving fuel system pressure to avoid exposing skin, face and eyes to fuel spray. Please be advised that fuel under pressure may penetrate the skin or any part of the body that it contacts.
- Always place a shop towel or cloth around the fitting or connection prior to loosening to absorb any excess fuel due to spillage. Ensure that all fuel spillage (should it occur) is quickly removed from engine surfaces. Ensure that all fuel soaked cloths or towels are deposited into a suitable waste container.
- Always keep a dry chemical (Class B) fire extinguisher near the work area.
- Do not allow fuel spray or fuel vapors to come into contact with a spark or open flame.
- Always use a back-up wrench when loosening and tightening fuel line connection fittings. This will prevent unnecessary stress and torsion to fuel line piping.
- Always replace worn fuel fitting O-rings with new Do not substitute fuel hose or equivalent where fuel pipe is installed.

Before servicing the vehicle, make sure to also refer to the precautions in the beginning of this section as well.

RELIEVING FUEL SYSTEM PRESSURE

1. Before servicing the vehicle, refer to the fuel system precautions and to the precautions in the beginning of this section.
2. Remove the fuel pump relay from the Power Distribution Center (PDC).
3. Start and run the engine until it stalls.
4. Attempt to restart the engine until it no longer runs.
5. Turn the ignition key to the **OFF** position.

FUEL FILTER

REMOVAL & INSTALLATION

The fuel delivery system integrates the fuel filter with the in-tank fuel pump

1. Before servicing the vehicle, refer to the precautions in the beginning of this section.
2. Properly relieve the fuel system pressure.
3. Remove or disconnect the following:
   - Negative battery cable
   - Fuel pump module
   - Locking tabs on the fuel pump
   - Strainer and O-ring
   - Inlet filter from the assembly

To install:

4. Install or connect the following:
   - Inlet filter
   - New O-ring and strainer
   - Locking tabs on the fuel pump module
   - Fuel pump Module
   - Negative battery cable
5. Start the vehicle, check for leaks and repair if necessary.

FUEL INJECTORS

REMOVAL & INSTALLATION

2.4L Engine

See Figures 105 and 106.

1. Perform fuel system pressure release procedure before servicing or starting repairs.
2. Disconnect negative cable from battery.
3. Remove the wiring harness from fuel rail support bracket.
4. Remove the fuel rail support bracket.
5. Disconnect the wiring connectors for fuel injectors harness.
6. Remove the wiring harness from fuel rail brackets.
7. Disconnect the connectors from the fuel injectors.
8. Remove the throttle and speed control cables from the fuel rail.
9. Remove the fuel hose quick connect fitting from the chassis tube. Place a shop towel under the connections to absorb any fuel spilled from the fitting.

⁂ CAUTION

Wrap a shop towel around hoses to catch any gasoline spillage.

10. Remove the fuel rail attaching bolts.
11. Remove the fuel rail. Be careful not to damage the injector O-rings upon removal from their ports.
12. Position fuel rail assembly so that the fuel injectors are easily accessible.
13. Remove the injector clip and pull injector out of fuel rail.
14. Check injector O-ring for damage. If O-ring is damaged, it must be replaced. Replace the injector clip if it is damaged.
15. Repeat for remaining injectors.

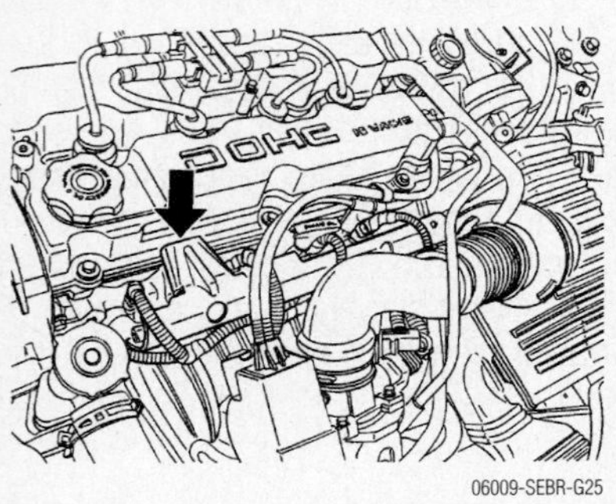

Fig. 105 Fuel rail and bracket—2.4L engine

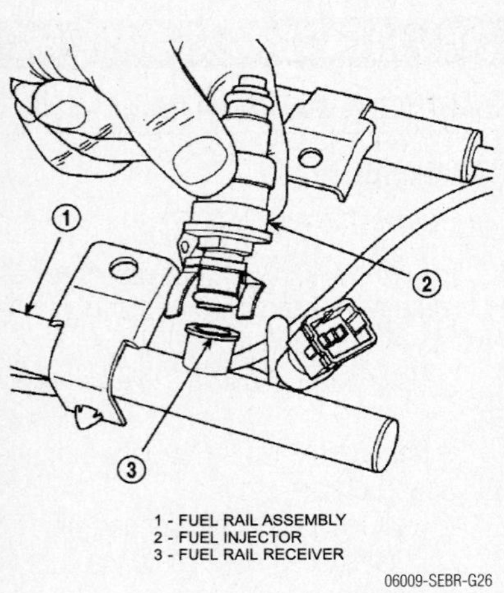

Fig. 106 Fuel injector and rail—2.4L engine

To install:

16. Before installing an injector the rubber O-ring must be lubricated with a drop of clean engine oil to aid in installation.
17. Install the injector clip by sliding open end into the top slot of the injector. The edge of the receiver cup will slide into the side slots of clip.
18. Install the injector top end into fuel rail receiver cap. Be careful not to damage O-ring during installation.
19. Repeat steps for remaining injectors.
20. Ensure injector holes are clean. Replace O-rings if damaged.
21. Lubricate injector O-rings with a drop of clean engine oil to ease installation.
22. Put the tip of each injector into their ports. Push the assembly into place until the injectors are seated in the ports.
23. Install the 2 fuel rail mounting bolts to intake manifold. Tighten bolts to 105 inch lbs. (12 Nm).
24. Install the fuel rail mounting bolt to cylinder head. Tighten bolt to 16 ft. lbs. (22 Nm)
25. Connect the connectors to the fuel injectors.
26. Install the fuel rail support bracket and loosely. Install the all bolts.
27. Tighten three fasteners to intake manifold to 21 ft. lbs. (28 Nm).
28. Tighten two bolts to fuel rail to 75 inch lbs. (9 Nm).
29. Install the wiring harness to brackets.
30. Connect the throttle and speed control cables to fuel rail bracket.
31. Connect negative battery cable.
32. Use a scan tool to pressurize the fuel system. Check for leaks.

2.7L Engine

See Figure 107.

1. Before servicing the vehicle, refer to the precautions in the beginning of this section.
2. Relieve the fuel system pressure using the recommended procedure.
3. Disconnect the negative battery cable from the left shock tower.

➡The ground cable is equipped with an insulator grommet which should be placed on the stud to prevent the negative battery cable from accidentally grounding.

4. Remove or disconnect the following:
   - Fuel supply line quick-connect fitting from the fuel rail
   - Upper intake manifold plenum and discard the gasket
   - Fuel injector electrical connectors
   - Fuel rail from the intake manifold

➡Cover the intake manifold openings to keep dirt from entering the system.

   - Fuel injector clip
   - Fuel injector(s) from the fuel rail and discard the O-rings

To install:

5. Install or connect the following:
   - Fuel injector to the fuel rail using new O-rings lubricated with engine oil
   - Fuel injector clip
   - Fuel rail and torque the bolts to 8 ft. lbs. (12 Nm)

➡Be sure the spacers are located under the fuel rail

   - Fuel injector electrical connectors
   - Fuel supply line quick-connect fitting to the fuel rail
   - Upper intake manifold plenum using a new gasket and torque the bolts to 13 ft. lbs. (18 Nm)
   - Throttle cables
   - Sensor electrical connectors
   - Negative battery cable
6. Use a scan tool and run Automatic Shutdown (ASD) fuel system test to pressurize the fuel system. Check for leaks.

FUEL PUMP

REMOVAL & INSTALLATION

See Figures 108 and 109.

1. Before servicing the vehicle, refer to the Precautions Section.
2. Remove the fuel filler cap and perform fuel system pressure release procedure.
3. Disconnect negative cable from battery.
4. Drain fuel tank dry into holding tank or a properly labeled gasoline safety container.
5. Raise vehicle on hoist and support.
6. Use a transmission jack to support fuel tank. Remove bolts from fuel tank straps.
7. Lower tank slightly.
8. Disconnect the fuel filler vent tube.
9. Disconnect fuel line and vapor line.
10. Disconnect the vacuum line from the LDP.

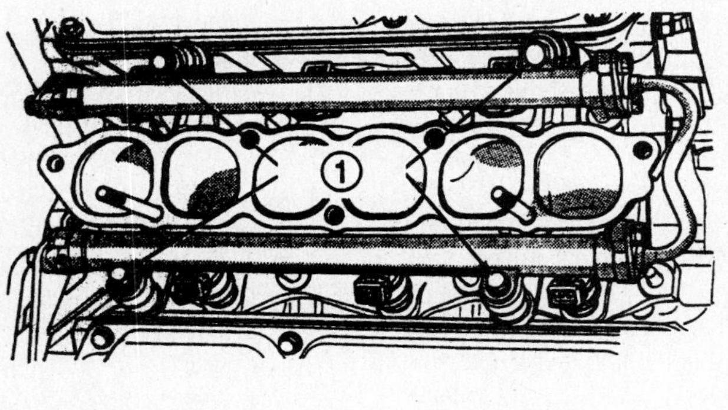

Fig. 107 View of the fuel rail assembly—2.7L engine

11. Disconnect fuel filler tube by loosing the clamp and removing hose.

12. Slide fuel pump module electrical connector lock to unlock. The fuel pump module electrical connector has a retainer that locks it in place.

13. Push down on connector retainer and pull connector off module.

14. Lower tank from vehicle.

⁂ CAUTION

The fuel reservoir of the fuel pump module does not empty out when the tank is drained. The fuel in the reservoir will spill out when the module is removed.

15. Disconnect fuel line from fuel pump module by depressing quick connect retainers with thumb and forefinger.

16. Slide fuel pump module electrical connector lock to unlock.

17. Disconnect the electrical connection from the fuel pump module, by pushing down on connector retainer and pulling connector off of module.

18. Mark fuel pump location.

19. Use a brass punch and hammer to remove fuel pump module lock ring.

20. Remove the fuel pump and O-ring seal from tank. Discard old seal.

To install:

21. Wipe seal area of tank clean and place a new seal in position in the tank opening.

22. Position fuel pump in the tank.

23. Position the lock ring over the fuel pump module.

24. Tighten the lock ring using a brass punch and hammer.

25. Connect the electrical connector.

26. Connect the fuel line to the fuel pump.

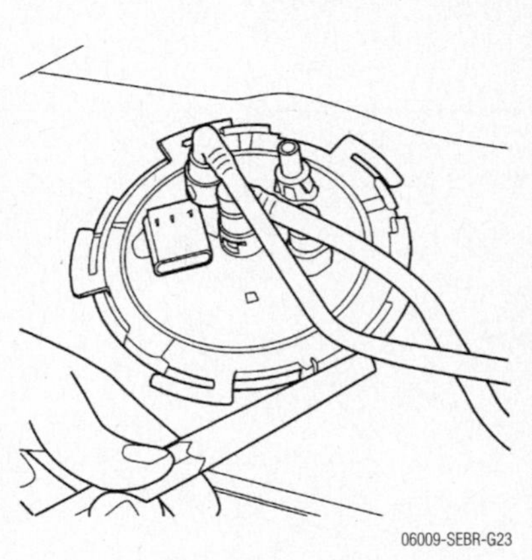

Fig. 108 Use a brass punch and hammer to remove fuel pump module lock ring

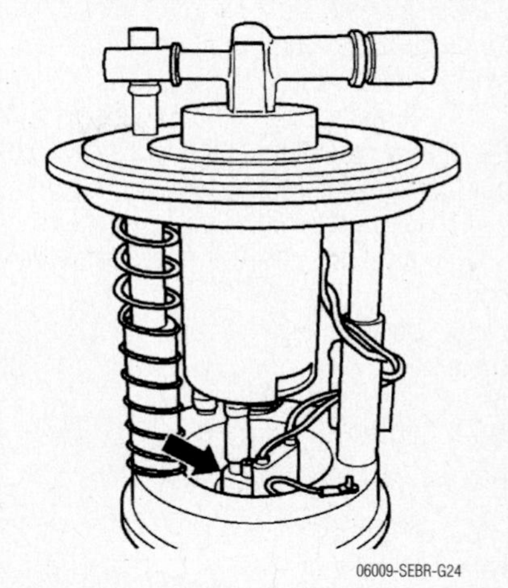

Fig. 109 Fuel pump location

27. Position fuel tank on transmission jack.

28. Raise tank into position and carefully work filler tube onto the fuel tank. A light coating of clean engine oil on the tube end may be used to aid assembly. Connect fuel filler tube hose and tighten clamp.

29. Connect fuel pump/module electrical connector. Place retainer in locked position.

30. Connect the EVAP, vapor, and vacuum lines.

31. Lubricate the fuel supply line with clean 30 weight engine oil, install the quick connect fuel fitting.

32. Attach filler vent line to filler tube. Pull on connector to make sure of connection.

33. Place NVLD air filter under right rear tank strap before tightening.

34. Tighten strap bolts to 40 ft. lbs. (54 Nm).

35. Remove the transmission jack.

36. Tighten filler hose clamp to 32 inch lbs. (3.6 Nm).

⁂ WARNING

Ensure straps are not twisted or bent before or after tightening strap nuts.

37. Fill fuel tank, replace cap, and connect battery negative cable.

38. Use a scan tool to pressurize the fuel system. Check for leaks.

FUEL TANK

REMOVAL & INSTALLATION

1. Before servicing the vehicle, refer to the Precautions Section.

2. Remove fuel filler cap and perform the Fuel System Pressure Release procedure.

3. Disconnect negative cable from battery.

4. Drain fuel tank dry into holding tank or a properly labeled GASOLINE safety container.

5. Raise vehicle on hoist and support.

6. Use a transmission jack to support fuel tank. Remove bolts from fuel tank straps.

7. Lower tank slightly.

8. Disconnect the fuel filler vent tube.

9. Disconnect fuel line and vapor line.

10. Disconnect the vacuum line from the LDP.

11. Disconnect fuel filler tube by loosing the clamp and removing hose.

➡The fuel pump module electrical connector has a retainer that locks it in place.

12. Slide fuel pump module electrical connector lock to unlock.

13. Push down on connector retainer and pull connector off module.

14. Lower tank from vehicle.

To install:

15. Position fuel tank on transmission jack.

16. Raise tank into position and carefully work filler tube onto the fuel tank. A light coating of clean engine oil on the tube end may be used to aid assembly. Connect fuel filler tube hose and tighten clamp.

17. Connect fuel pump/module electrical connector. Place retainer in locked position.

18. Connect the EVAP, vapor, and vacuum lines.

19. Lubricate the fuel supply line with clean 30 weight engine oil, install the quick connect fuel fitting.

20. Attach filler vent line to filler tube. Pull on connector to make sure of connection.

21. Place NVLD air filter under right rear tank strap before tightening.

22. Tighten strap bolts to 40 ft. lbs. (54 Nm) torque. Remove transmission jack.

23. Tighten filler hose clamp to 35 inch lbs. (4 Nm).

⁂ WARNING

Ensure straps are not twisted or bent before or after tightening strap nuts.

24. Fill fuel tank, replace cap, and connect battery negative cable.

25. Use the DRBIII® scan tool to pressurize the fuel system. Check for leaks.

IDLE SPEED

ADJUSTMENT

The idle speed is maintained by the Powertrain Control Module (PCM). No adjustment is necessary or possible.

THROTTLE BODY

REMOVAL & INSTALLATION

2.4L Engine

See Figure 110.

1. Before servicing the vehicle, refer to the Precautions Section.
2. Disconnect negative cable from battery cable.
3. Remove the clean air hose.
4. Remove the throttle cable shield.
5. Remove the throttle and the speed control cables (if equipped) from lever and bracket.
6. Disconnect the electrical connectors from the idle air control motor and Throttle Position Sensor (TPS).
7. Remove the throttle body to intake manifold attaching bolts.
8. Remove the throttle cable bracket.
9. Remove the throttle body.

To install:

10. Install the throttle body.
    a. Tighten throttle body mounting bolts to 120 inch lbs. (13.6 Nm).
11. Install the throttle cable bracket.
    a. Tighten throttle cable bracket mounting bolts to 125 inch lbs. (14.1 Nm)
12. Hold throttle lever in the wide open throttle position and install the throttle and speed control cables (if equipped).
13. Connect the electrical connectors to the idle air control motor and Throttle Position Sensor (TPS).
14. Install the throttle cable shield.
15. Install the clean air hose to throttle body.
16. Connect negative cable to battery cable.

2.7L Engine

See Figure 111.

1. Before servicing the vehicle, refer to the Precautions Section.
2. Disconnect negative cable from battery
3. Disconnect the electrical connectors from throttle body.
4. Disconnect clean air hose from throttle body.
5. Remove the throttle cable shield.
6. Hold throttle lever in wide open position. Remove throttle cable and speed control cables from throttle arm.
7. Remove the throttle cable bracket.
8. Remove the throttle body support bracket from the bottom of the throttle body.
9. Remove the remaining 2 throttle body bolts.
10. Remove the throttle body.
11. Clean mating surfaces.

To install:

12. Loose Install the 2 throttle body bolts (upper right and lower bolt).
13. Install the throttle cable bracket.
14. Install the third throttle body bolt and the throttle body support bracket to the bottom of the throttle body.
    a. Tighten the lower support bracket bolts to 23 ft. lbs. (31.1 Nm)
    b. Tighten throttle body bolts to 120 inch lbs. (13.6 Nm).
15. Hold throttle lever in wide open throttle position. Install the throttle cable and speed control cable.
16. Install the throttle cable shield.
17. Connect the electrical connectors to throttle body.
18. Install the clean air hose to throttle body.
19. Connect negative cable to battery.

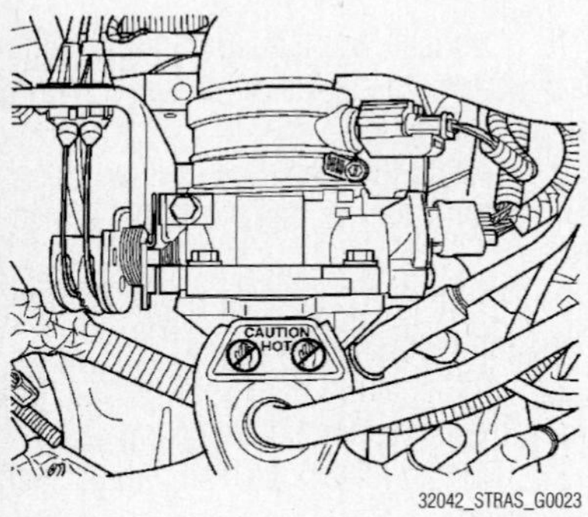

Fig. 110 Throttle body—2.4L engine

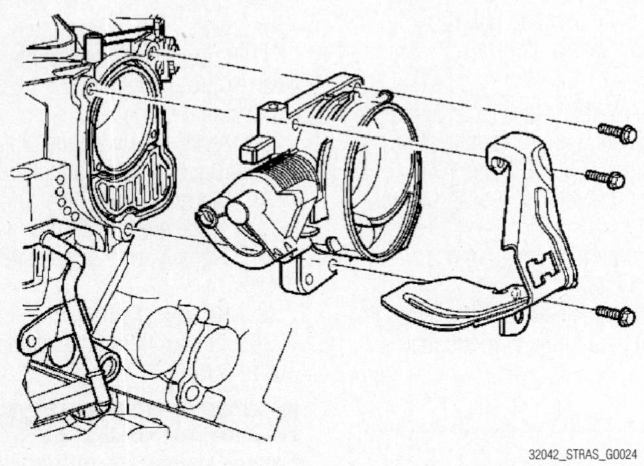

Fig. 111 Throttle body—2.7L engine

HEATING & AIR CONDITIONING SYSTEM

BLOWER MOTOR

REMOVAL & INSTALLATION

See Figure 112.

✱✱ CAUTION

On vehicles equipped with airbags, disable the airbag system before attempting any steering wheel, steering column, or instrument panel component diagnosis or service. Disconnect and isolate the negative battery (ground) cable, then wait two minutes for the airbag system capacitor to discharge before performing further diagnosis or service. This is the only sure way to disable the airbag system. Failure to take the proper precautions could result in accidental airbag deployment and possible personal injury or death.

1. Before servicing the vehicle, refer to the Precautions Section.
2. Disconnect and isolate the negative battery cable.
3. Remove the instrument panel silencer from the passenger side of the instrument panel.
   a. Remove two push-in fasteners under right end of instrument panel.
   b. Maneuver part off center floor distribution duct to remove.
4. Disconnect the wire harness connector from the blower motor.
5. Remove the three screws that secure the blower motor to the HVAC housing.
6. Remove the blower motor from the HVAC housing by rotating and tilting the motor as needed for clearance of the blower wheel.

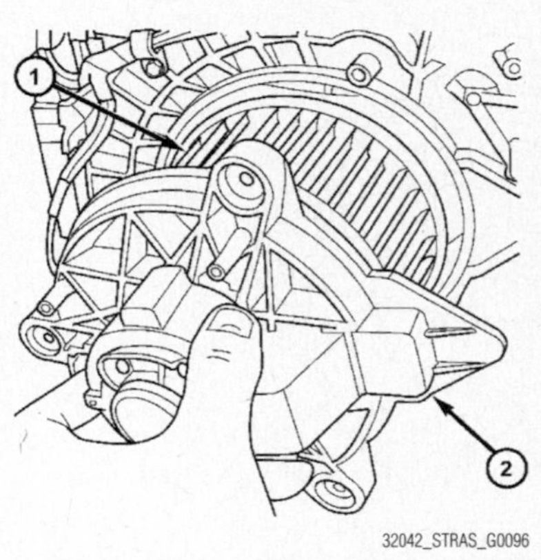

Fig. 112 Blower wheel (1) and blower motor (2)

To install:

7. Position the blower motor into the HVAC housing.
8. Install the three screws that secure the blower motor to the HVAC housing. Tighten the screws to 18 inch lbs. (2 Nm).
9. Connect the wire harness connector to the blower motor.
10. Install the instrument panel silencer onto the passenger side of the instrument panel.
11. Reconnect the negative battery cable.

HEATER CORE

REMOVAL & INSTALLATION

See Figures 113 and 114.

✱✱ CAUTION

On vehicles equipped with airbags, disable the airbag system before attempting any steering wheel, steering column, or instrument panel component diagnosis or service. Disconnect and isolate the negative battery (ground) cable, then wait two minutes for the airbag system capacitor to discharge before performing further diagnosis or service. This is the only sure way to disable the airbag system. Failure to take the proper precautions could result in accidental airbag deployment and possible personal injury or death.

➡The instrument panel and HVAC housing are removed from the vehicle together as an assembly.

1. Before servicing the vehicle, refer to the Precautions Section.
2. Recover the refrigerant from the refrigerant system.
3. Drain the engine cooling system.
4. Disconnect and isolate the negative battery cable.
5. Remove the one bolt retaining the A/C lines to the right strut tower.
6. Remove the two top HVAC housing retaining nuts in engine compartment.
7. Hoist vehicle and remove the lower HVAC housing retaining nut.
8. Lower vehicle from hoist.
9. Remove the driver's and passenger's seats:
   a. Position seat far enough forward to gain access to rear mount bolts on floor.
   b. Remove bolts holding rear of seat track to floor.
   c. Slide seat rearward.
   d. Remove bolts attaching front of the seat track to floor kick up.
   e. Disconnect negative battery cable, if electrical seat.
   f. Disconnect front seat wire harness connector from body harness connector.

✱✱ CAUTION

Do not handle seat by adjuster release bar when removing spring loaded seat from vehicle.

   g. Remove front seat from vehicle.
10. Disconnect and isolate the battery negative remote cable.
11. Remove the one screw to shift knob and transmission range indicator bezel from floor console.
12. Remove the floor center console. Remove two mounting screws in the front and two mounting screws inside console storage bin.
13. Remove the amplifier retaining fasteners.
14. Disconnect the wire harness connector.
15. Remove the amplifier.
16. Using a trim stick or equivalent, gently pry out on the left and right rear floor heat ducts and remove.
17. Disconnect the console wiring connectors and unclip the push in fasteners.
18. Using a trim stick or equivalent, gently pry up on and remove the right sill plate.
19. Remove the two screws to the right cowl kick panel and remove from vehicle.
20. Using a trim stick or equivalent, gently pry out on the right end cover and remove from vehicle.
21. Using a trim stick or equivalent, gently pry out on the right A-pillar trim and remove from vehicle.
22. Open the glove box. Pinch in on the sides and drop to the floor. Pull down to disengage hinges.
23. Disconnect the right door harness connectors located within the A-pillar.
24. Remove the four right A-pillar instrument panel retainers.
25. Remove the right silencer.
26. Remove the one right side, center instrument panel support bolt.
27. Using a trim stick or equivalent, gently pry up on and remove the left sill plate.
28. Remove the two screws to the left cowl kick panel and remove from vehicle.
29. Using a trim stick or equivalent, gently pry out on the left end cover and remove from vehicle.

30. Using a trim stick or equivalent, gently pry out on the left A-pillar trim and remove from vehicle.
31. Disconnect the left door harness connectors located within the A-pillar.
32. Remove the four left A-pillar instrument panel retainers.
33. Remove the five screws and one wire connector to left lower instrument panel trim bezel.
34. Remove the left silencer.
35. Remove the one left side, center instrument panel support bolt.
36. Remove the one bolt to the left side support strut to bulkhead.
37. Disconnect the junction block wiring connectors.
38. Remove the two screws to the steering column shrouds and remove.
39. Disconnect all the column wiring and unclip the harness from the steering column.
40. Disconnect the transmission shift interlock and wire connector.
41. Remove the four steering column retaining bolts and drop column to floor.
42. Using a trim stick or equivalent, pry up on the rear of the top cover and pull rearward as you lift it off of instrument panel.
43. Remove the instrument panel pad.
44. Remove the seven bolts and five screws attaching instrument panel to fence line and cowl side.
45. With the help of an assistant, lift up instrument panel and move rearward to remove. Tilt the panel rearward to prevent the coolant from leaking out. If replacing the instrument panel, transfer all non-damaged parts and wiring harness to the new instrument panel assembly.
46. Disconnect HVAC wire harness from the instrument panel wire harness connector at the left side of the HVAC housing.
47. Remove the two nuts and two bolts that secure the HVAC housing to the instrument panel.
48. Separate the HVAC housing from the instrument panel.
49. Disconnect the HVAC wire harness connectors from the blower motor, blower motor resistor or power module (depending on application), evaporator temperature sensor and each actuator.
50. Remove the two screws that secure the HVAC harness connector to the HVAC housing and remove the HVAC wire harness.
51. Remove the screws that secure the blower motor to the HVAC housing and remove the blower motor.
52. Remove the screws that secure the blower motor resistor or power module (depending on application) to the HVAC housing and remove it from the housing.
53. Remove the screws that secure the air inlet housing to the HVAC housing and remove the air inlet housing.
54. Remove the three screws that secure the recirculation door actuator to the air inlet housing and remove the actuator.
55. Remove the screw that secures the recirculation door actuator gear to the air inlet housing and remove the gear.
56. Using a small screwdriver, depress the recirculation door gear release and remove the recirculation door gear from the recirculation door shaft.

➡If the seals on the recirculation-air door is deformed or damaged, the air door must be replaced.

57. Tilt the gear end of the recirculation-air door up and pull the door out of the air inlet housing.

➡If either foam seal is deformed or damaged, it must be replaced.

58. Carefully, remove the foam seals from the heater core and the evaporator tube mounting flange of the HVAC housing.
59. Remove the screws that secure the upper and lower HVAC housing halves together and separate the housing halves.
60. Using a flat blade pry tool, disengage the locking tab on the access plate of the evaporator temperature sensor. Turn the access plate clockwise one quarter turn and push the access plate inside of the HVAC housing, then orientate the plate in

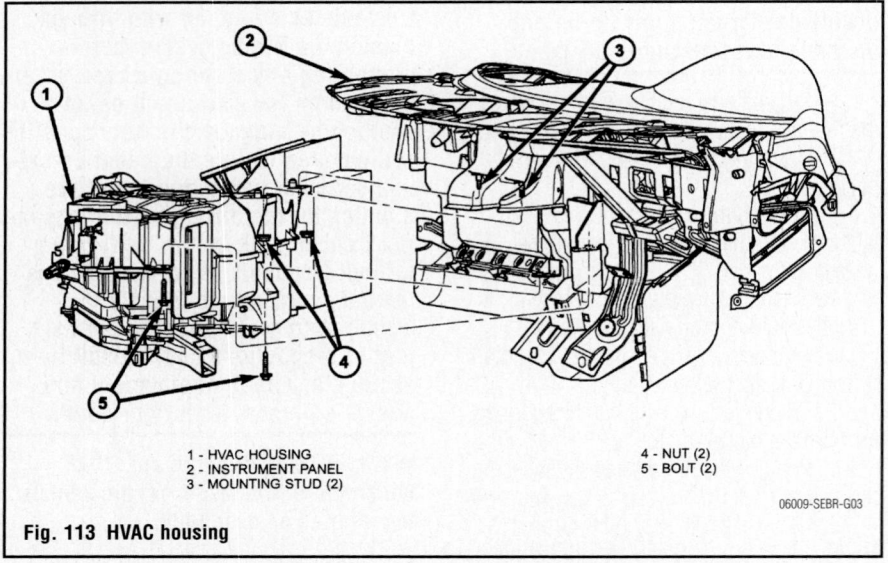

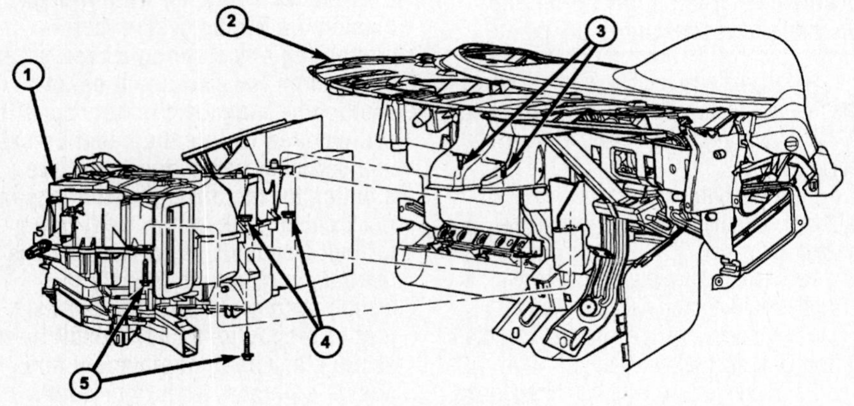

Fig. 113 HVAC housing

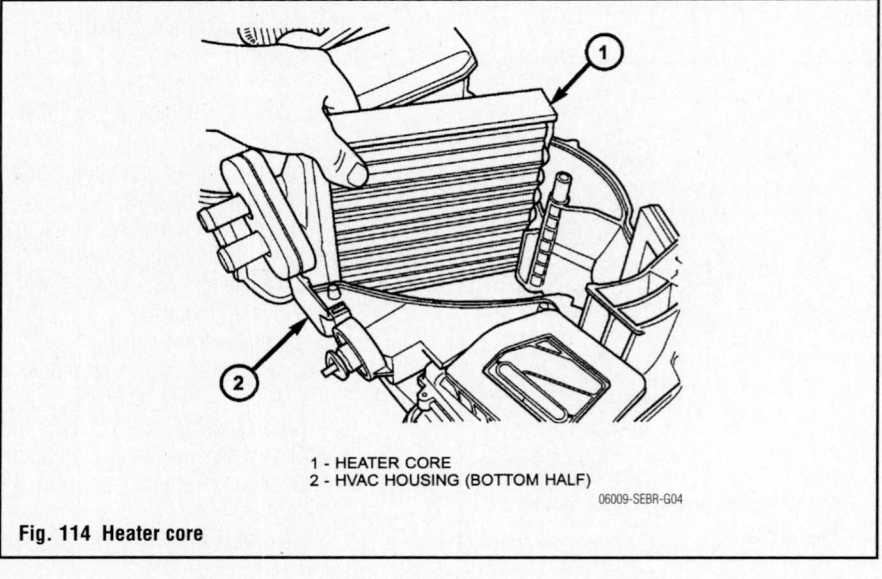

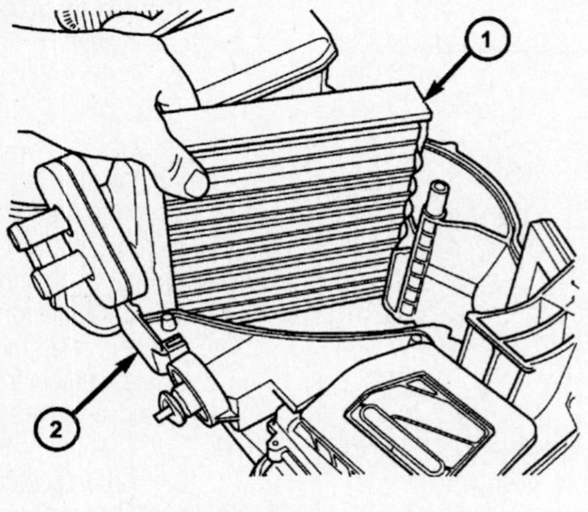

Fig. 114 Heater core

such a way that it can be removed from the housing.

61. Remove the evaporator temperature sensor probe from the A/C evaporator and remove the sensor.

62. Lift the A/C evaporator out of the bottom half of the HVAC housing.

63. Lift the heater core out of the bottom half of the HVAC housing.

To install:

64. Install the heater core into the bottom half of the HVAC housing.

65. Align the blend and mode door shafts with the holes in the HVAC housing and install the top half of the housing to the bottom half of the housing.

66. Install the screws that secure the two halves of the HVAC housing together. Tighten the screws to 18 inch lbs. (2 Nm).

67. Install the foam seals on the heater core and evaporator coil tube mounting flange.

68. Install the recirculation-air door into the air inlet housing.

69. Install the recirculation door gear onto the recirculation door shaft.

➡The recirculation door actuator gear and door gear must be properly aligned to operate correctly.

70. Align and install the recirculation door actuator gear with the door gear.

71. Install the screw that secure the recirculation door actuator gear to the air inlet housing. Tighten the screw to 18 inch lbs. (2 Nm).

72. Align the recirculation door actuator spline with the spline in the recirculation door gear and install the recirculation door actuator.

73. Install the three screws that secure the recirculation door actuator to the HVAC housing. Tighten the screws to 18 inch lbs. (2 Nm).

74. Install the air inlet housing onto the HVAC housing.

75. Install the screws that secure the air inlet housing to the HVAC housing. Tighten the screws to 18 inch lbs. (2 Nm).

76. If removed, install the blower motor resistor or power module (depending on application). Install and tighten the screws to 18 inch lbs. (2 Nm).

77. If removed, install the blower motor. Install and tighten the screws to 18 inch lbs. (2 Nm).

➡Make sure that all HVAC wire harness leads are routed through all HVAC housing wiring retainers.

78. Install the HVAC wire harness onto the HVAC housing.

79. Install the two screws that secure the HVAC wire harness connector to the HVAC housing. Tighten the screws to 18 inch lbs. (2 Nm).

80. Connect the HVAC wire harness connectors to the blower motor, blower motor resistor or power module (depending on application), evaporator temperature sensor and each actuator.

81. Position the HVAC housing to the instrument panel. Make sure that all air ducts are properly aligned or connected.

82. Install the two nuts and bolts that secure the HVAC housing to the instrument panel. Tighten the nuts and bolts securely.

83. Connect the HVAC wire harness to the instrument panel wire harness connector.

➡Verify that the evaporator drain tube and evaporator seals are properly seated to the HVAC housing before installing the instrument panel and HVAC Housing into the vehicle.

84. With the help of an assistant, place the instrument panel in the vehicle, carefully guiding the HVAC housing studs through the bulkhead and into position.

85. Install the seven bolts and five screws attaching instrument panel to fence line and cowl side.

86. Place instrument panel pad into position.

87. Place instrument panel top cover in position on vehicle.

88. Push top cover forward to engage hooks to hold front of top cover to instrument panel.

89. Engage clips to hold rear edge of top cover to instrument panel.

90. Pull top cover rearward as you firmly push down and snap into place.

91. Install the A-pillar trim.

92. Install the four steering column retaining bolts.

93. Connect the transmission shift interlock and wire connector.

94. Connect all the column wiring and clip the harness to the steering column.

95. Install the two screws to the steering column shrouds.

96. Connect the junction block wiring connectors.

97. Install the one bolt to the left side support strut to bulkhead.

98. Install the five screws and one wire connector to left lower instrument panel trim bezel.

99. Install the one left side, center instrument panel support bolt.

100. Install the left silencer.

101. Install the four left A-pillar instrument panel retainers.

102. Connect the right door harness connectors located within the A-pillar.

103. Install the left end cover.

104. Install the two screws to the left cowl trim panel.

105. Install the left door sill plate.

106. Install the one right side, center instrument panel support bolt.

107. Install the right silencer.

108. Install the four right A-pillar instrument panel retainers.

109. Connect the right door harness connectors located within the A-pillar.

110. Install the glove box.

111. Install the right A-pillar trim.

112. Install the right end cover.

113. Install the two screws to the right cowl trim panel.

114. Install the right door sill plate.

115. Connect the console wiring connectors and clip the push in fasteners in.

116. Install the left and right rear floor heat ducts.

117. Connect the two harness connectors to the amplifier.

118. Connect wire harness connector to amplifier.

119. Install the amplifier. Tighten the forward screw to 26.5 inch lbs. (3 Nm) and the rear nut to 18 inch lbs. (2 Nm).

120. Install the floor center console. Install the two mounting screws in the front and two mounting screws inside console storage bin.

121. Install the transmission range indicator bezel and one screw to shift knob.

122. Connect the battery negative remote cable.

⁂ CAUTION

Do not handle by seat adjuster release bar.

➡Ensure that the seat tracks are rearward. Ensure the seat tracks on the right and left are in equal latch positions.

123. Place front seat in position in vehicle.

124. Connect front seat wire harness connector to body harness connector.

125. Install the bolts to attach front of seat track to the floor kick up. Tighten bolts to: 45 ft. lbs. (61 Nm).

126. Slide seat forward and install the

bolts attaching rear of seat track to the floor. Tighten bolts to 45 ft. lbs. (61 Nm).

127. Verify front seat operation.

128. Hoist vehicle and install the lower HVAC housing retaining nut.

129. Lower vehicle from hoist.

130. Install the two top HVAC housing retaining nuts in engine compartment.

131. Install the one bolt retaining the A/C lines to the right strut tower.

132. Reconnect the negative battery cable.

133. If the heater core is being replaced, flush the cooling system.

134. Refill the engine cooling system.

135. Evacuate the refrigerant system.

136. Charge the refrigerant system.

STEERING

POWER STEERING GEAR

REMOVAL & INSTALLATION

See Figures 115 through 117.

1. Before servicing the vehicle, refer to the precautions in the beginning of this section.

2. Remove or disconnect the following:
   - Negative battery cable from the left shock tower

➡The ground cable is equipped with an insulator grommet which should be placed on the stud to prevent the negative battery cable from accidentally grounding.

   - Intermediate shaft coupler pin bolt retaining pin
   - Intermediate shaft coupler pin bolt
   - Front wheels
   - Tie rod ends by holding the tie rod end stud with a 11⁄32 inch socket and loosen the retaining nut
   - Tie rod end from the steering knuckle

➡Before removing the front suspension crossmember from the vehicle scribe the front suspension crossmember and the vehicle body. This must be done to retain the proper alignment. The caster and camber are not adjustable.

3. Scribe a line on the body and on the crossmember on all 4 sides.

4. Remove or disconnect the following:
   - Stabilizer
   - 3 anti-lock brake controller-to-crossmember bolts and secure it to the chassis, if equipped with Anti-lock Brake System (ABS)
   - Strut clevis from the lower control arm
   - Both engine support bracket-to-crossmember bolts
   - Engine support bracket-to-transaxle mounting bracket bolt

5. Place a lifting device under the front suspension crossmember.

6. Remove or disconnect the following:
   - 8 crossmember-to-chassis bolts

7. Lower the lifting device enough to gain access to the steering rack.

8. Remove or disconnect the following:
   - Power steering lines and drain the fluid
   - Power steering pressure switch electrical connector
   - Solenoid control module electrical connector, if equipped with speed proportional steering
   - Both steering rack isolator bolts
   - Both steering rack saddle bracket bolts
   - Steering rack

To install:

9. Install or connect the following:
   - Steering rack
   - Isolator and saddle bracket and torque the bolts to 50 ft. lbs. (68 Nm)
   - Power steering pressure and return lines and torque the lines to 23 ft. lbs. (31 Nm)
   - Crossmember, install the rear bolts first and torque the bolts to 20 inch lbs. (2 Nm)

10. Using a soft faced hammer tap the crossmember into position.

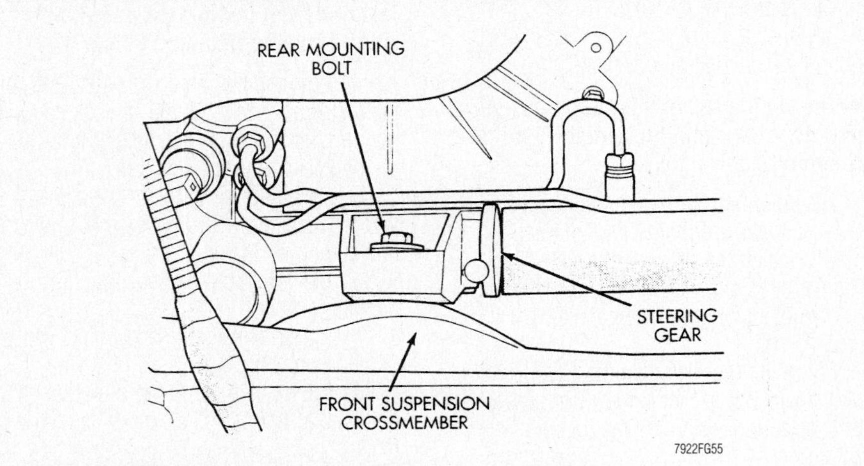

Fig. 115 Steering gear rear mounting bolt location

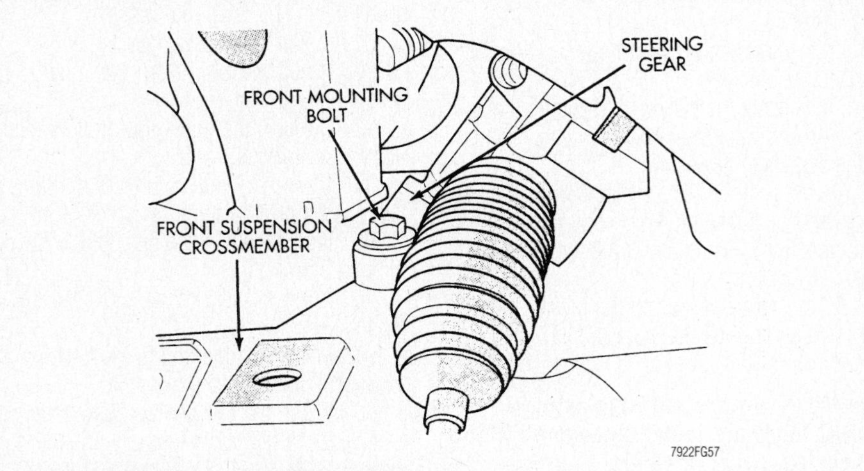

Fig. 116 Steering gear front mounting bolt location

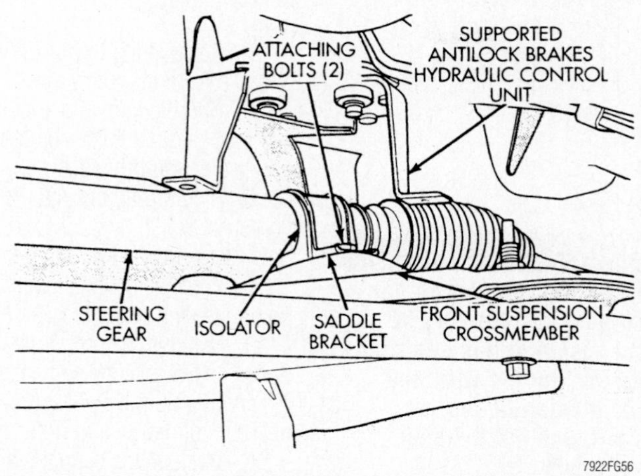

Fig. 117 Check the condition of the isolator—if worn or oil soaked, replace

➡Be sure to align the scribed marks on the crossmember.

11. Install or connect the following:
    - Crossmember, starting with the rear bolts and torque the bolts to 120 ft. lbs. (163 Nm)
    - Both engine support bracket to crossmember bolts
    - Engine support bracket to transaxle bracket bolt and torque the 3 bolts to 55 ft. lbs. (75 Nm)
    - Power steering pressure switch
    - ABS control unit and torque the bolts to 21 ft. lbs. (28 Nm)
    - Heat shield on the tie rod ends
    - Shock clevis to the lower control arm
    - Tie rod ends and torque the nuts to 45 ft. lbs. (61 Nm)
    - Both stabilizer clamps
    - Strut clevis bolt and torque the bolt to 68 ft. lbs. (92 Nm)
    - Wheels and torque the lug nuts to 100 ft. lbs. (135 Nm)
    - Intermediate shaft pin bolt and retaining pin and torque the pin bolt to 20 ft. lbs. (27 Nm)
    - Negative battery cable
12. Refill the power steering system.
13. Start the engine and allow it to run for a few minutes.
14. Shut **OFF** the engine and check the power steering fluid.
15. Add power steering fluid if necessary.
16. Raise the front wheels off the ground.
17. Start the engine and turn the wheel from stop-to-stop to bleed any air from the system.
18. Check the fluid level and add, if necessary.
19. Check and adjust the alignment.

POWER STEERING PUMP

REMOVAL & INSTALLATION

2.4L Engine

See Figure 118.

⁂ CAUTION

Power steering fluid, engine components and exhaust system may be extremely hot if engine has been running. Do not start engine with any loose or disconnected hoses, or allow hoses to touch hot exhaust manifold or catalyst.

1. Remove the battery cable from negative (-) post on battery and isolate cable.
2. Siphon as much power steering fluid as possible out of the remote power steering fluid reservoir.
3. Remove the clamp, then fluid supply hose from fitting on pump. Install the a cap on fitting.
4. Raise vehicle.
5. Remove the accessory drive splash shield.
6. Remove the power steering fluid pressure hose from pressure fitting on power steering pump. Let power steering fluid drain out of system. After power steering fluid has drained out of pump and hose, install the a cap on the power steering pressure hose and a plug in the power steering pump pressure fitting.
7. Remove the bolt at adjustment slot in pump front mounting bracket.
8. Remove the nut at adjustment slot in cast aluminum mounting bracket at rear of pump.
9. Loosen pump upper pivot bolt.
10. Remove the pump drive belt.
11. Remove the pump upper pivot bolt.
12. Remove the power steering pump and its front mounting bracket as an assembly from the engine through opening above right halfshaft and below right frame rail.

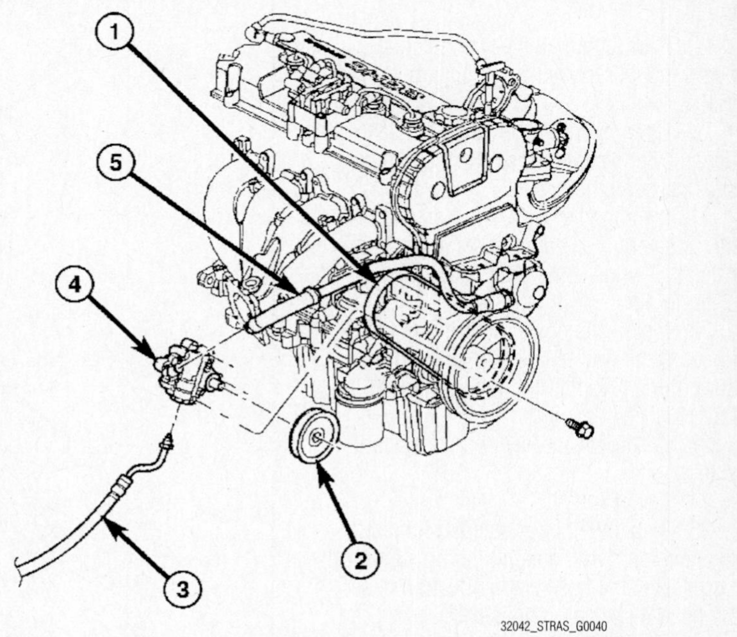

Fig. 118 Drive belt (1), pulley (2), pressure hose (3), power steering pump (4) and supply hose (5)

To install:

⁂ CAUTION

Power steering fluid, engine components and exhaust system may be extremely hot if engine has been running. Do not start engine with any loose or disconnected hoses, or allow hoses to touch hot exhaust manifold or catalyst.

13. Install the power steering pump and front mounting bracket as an assembly back in vehicle, using reverse order of removal.
14. Install the power steering pump and front bracket on the cast aluminum engine bracket. Loosely Install the upper mounting pivot bolt.
15. Loosely Install the pump mounting bolt through the adjustment slot in the front mounting bracket.
16. Loosely Install the nut mounting the power steering pump to its rear mounting bracket adjustment slot.
17. Install the power steering pump drive belt on power steering pump pulley. Install the a ½ inch breaker bar in the square adjusting hole in the front power steering pump mounting bracket and adjust belt. For procedures on adjusting the accessory drive belts refer to the section Engine Mechanical and subsection on adjusting belts.
18. When correct drive belt tension is obtained, first tighten the two adjusting slot fasteners (one bolt, one nut) to 40 ft. lbs. (54 Nm).
19. Next, tighten the power steering pump mounting bracket top pivot bolt to 40 ft. lbs. (54 Nm).
20. Using a lint free towel, wipe clean all open power steering hose ends, and power steering pump fittings.
21. Install the a new O-ring on end of power steering pressure hose fitting. Lubricate all O-rings using fresh clean power steering fluid.
22. Install the power steering pressure hose on the power steering pump pressure fitting. Tighten the tube nut to 23 ft. lbs. (31 Nm).
23. Install the accessory drive splash shield.
24. Lower vehicle.
25. Install the power steering fluid supply hose on power steering pump supply fitting. Install the hose clamp. Be sure hose clamp is installed on hose past upset bead on suction fitting.
26. Connect negative (-) cable back on negative post of battery.
27. Fill power steering reservoir to correct fluid level. Refer to the bleeding procedure at the end of this section.
28. Check for leaks at all hose connections and power steering pump.

2.7L Engine

See Figures 119 and 120.

⁂ CAUTION

Power steering fluid, engine components and exhaust system may be extremely hot if engine has been running. Do not start engine with any loose or disconnected hoses, or allow hoses to touch hot exhaust manifold or catalyst.

1. Remove the battery cable from (-) negative post on battery and isolate cable.
2. Siphon as much power steering fluid as possible out of power steering fluid reservoir.
3. Remove the power steering fluid supply hose from power steering pump supply fitting.
4. Raise vehicle.
5. Remove the accessory drive splash shield.
6. Remove the power steering fluid pressure hose from fitting on power steering pump.
7. Remove the oxygen sensor harness and clip from rear of pump.
8. Completely remove bolt at slot in stamped pump adjuster bracket and remove power steering drive belt.
9. Pivot pump out past full-adjust position. This will allow access to two pump bracket-to-engine mounting bolts.
10. Remove the three bolts fastening cast power steering pump bracket to the engine.
11. Remove the power steering pump, pulley and brackets as an assembly from the engine. Remove pump through opening between frame rail and right halfshaft.
12. Remove the stamped adjuster bracket mounting bolts. Remove bracket from pump.
13. Remove the two pivot bolts. Remove cast mounting bracket from pump.

To install:

14. If previously removed, install the cast mounting bracket on pump using two pivot bolts.
    a. Tighten bolts to 21 ft. lbs. (28 Nm).
15. If previously removed, install the stamped adjuster bracket on pump using its mounting bolts.
    b.Tighten bolts to 21 ft. lbs. (28 Nm).
16. Install the power steering pump,

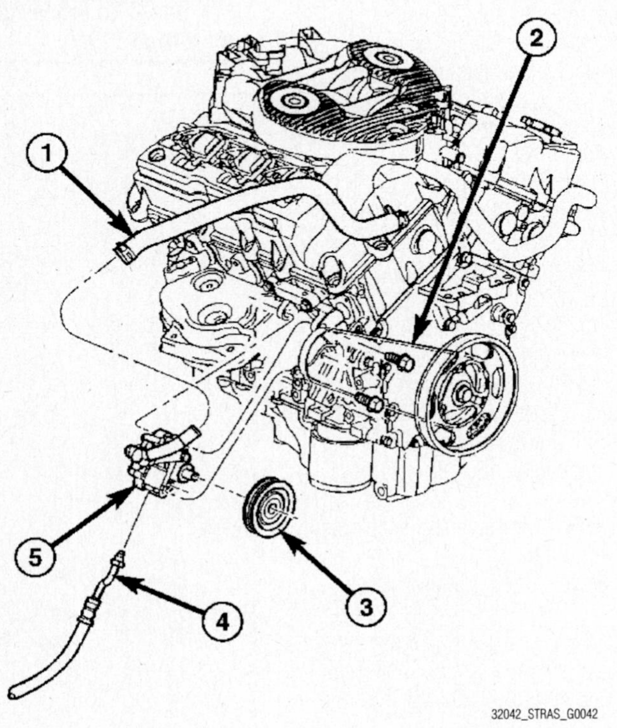

Fig. 119 Supply hose (1), drive belt (2), pulley (3), pressure hose (4) and power steering pump (5)

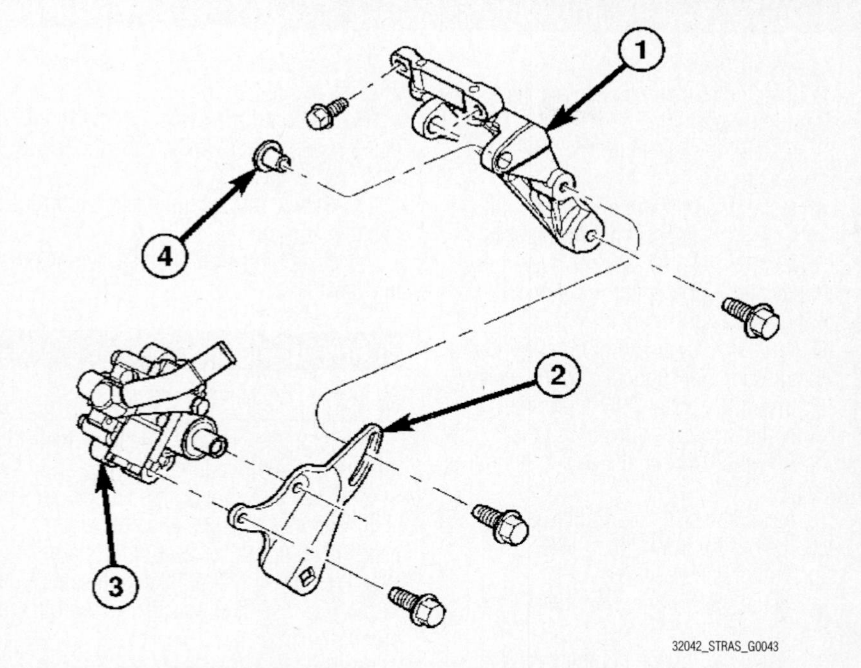

Fig. 120 Cast pump mounting bracket (1), stamped pump adjuster bracket (2), power steering pump (3) and pivot bushing (4)

pulley and brackets as an assembly back in vehicle, using reverse of removal procedure.

17. Install the three bolts fastening cast pump mounting bracket to engine.
    a. Tighten bolts to 21 ft. lbs. (28 Nm).
18. Loosely Install the bolt through stamped adjuster bracket slot and into cast bracket .
19. Using a lint free towel, wipe clean all open power steering hose ends, and power steering pump fittings.
20. Install the clip attaching oxygen sensor harness to rear of pump.
21. Install the power steering pump drive belt on pump pulley.
22. Install the a ½ inch breaker bar in square adjusting hole in front power steering pump mounting bracket and adjust belt. For procedures on adjusting the accessory drive belts refer to the section Engine Mechanical and subsection on adjusting belts.
23. When correct drive belt tension is obtained, tighten adjusting slot bolt to: 21 ft. lbs. (28 Nm).
24. Install the a new O-ring on end of power steering pressure hose fitting. Lubricate all O-rings using fresh clean power steering fluid.
25. Install the power steering pressure hose on pump pressure fitting .
    a. Tighten tube nut to 23 ft. lbs. (31 Nm).
26. Install the accessory drive splash shield.
27. Lower vehicle.
28. Install the power steering fluid supply hose on pump supply fitting . Install the hose clamp on hose.
    b. Be sure hose clamp is installed on hose past upset bead on power steering fluid reservoir.
29. Connect battery cable back on negative (-) post of battery.
30. Fill power steering reservoir to correct fluid level. Refer to the bleeding procedure at the end of this section.
31. Check for leaks at all hose connections and power steering pump.

BLEEDING

✱✱ WARNING

The fluid level should be checked with engine OFF to prevent injury from moving components. Use only MOPAR® ATF+4 Automatic Transmission Fluid (MS-9602), or equivalent. Do not overfill.

1. Wipe the reservoir fill cap clean before removal.
2. Fill the pump fluid reservoir to the proper level. The fluid level should be within the "FILL RANGE" listed on the exterior of the reservoir when the fluid is at normal ambient temperature, approximately 70–80°F (21–27°C).
3. Let the fluid settle in the system for at least 2 minutes.
4. Start the engine and let run for a few seconds. Then turn the engine **OFF**.
5. Add fluid if necessary. Repeat the above procedure until the fluid level remains constant after running the engine.
6. Raise the front wheels off the ground.
7. Start the engine. Slowly turn the steering wheel right and left, lightly contacting the wheel stops.
8. Add power steering fluid if necessary.
9. Lower the vehicle and turn the steering wheel slowly from lock to lock.
10. Stop the engine. Check the fluid level and refill as required.
11. If the fluid is extremely foamy, allow the vehicle to stabilize a few minutes, then repeat the above procedure.

COIL SPRING

REMOVAL & INSTALLATION

See Figure 121.

Before servicing the vehicle, refer to the precautions in the beginning of this section.

Disassemble as follows:

1. Remove the strut/shock assembly and place it in a suitable compressor tool
2. Set the lower hooks and install the clamp on the lower end of the spring.
3. Rotate the spring so the ball joint sits directly below the front upper hook.
4. Compress the spring until all tension is removed.
5. Remove the retaining nut and washer.
6. Remove the clamp from the bottom of the spring.
7. Remove the strut/shock assembly.
8. Remove the lower spring, jounce bumper and cup.
9. Remove the dust boot and lower bushing washer.
10. Release the tension from the spring.
11. Remove the spring from the compressor tool.

To assemble:

12. Install the upper isolator on the mounting bracket.
13. Install the sleeve into the lower isolator bushing.
14. Install the bushing and sleeve into the bottom of the upper mounting bracket.
15. Install the upper isolator bushing into the center of the upper mounting bracket.
16. Install the lower end of the spring in the compressor tool supported by the hooks.
17. Install the upper mounting bracket on top of the coil spring matching the spring to the isolator on the upper mounting bracket.
18. Install the control arm ball joint directly below the front upper hook.
19. Compress the spring.
20. Install the lower spring isolator on the spring seat.
21. Install the jounce bumper with the pointed end downward.
22. Install the collar with the undercut side facing down.
23. Install the dust shield and cup
24. Install the lower bushing retainer washer
25. Install the strut/shock assembly through the coil spring.
26. When properly aligned, install the upper mounting nut and torque the nut to 40 ft. lbs. (55 Nm).
27. Slowly release the tension from the compressor tool.
28. Install the strut/shock assembly in the vehicle.

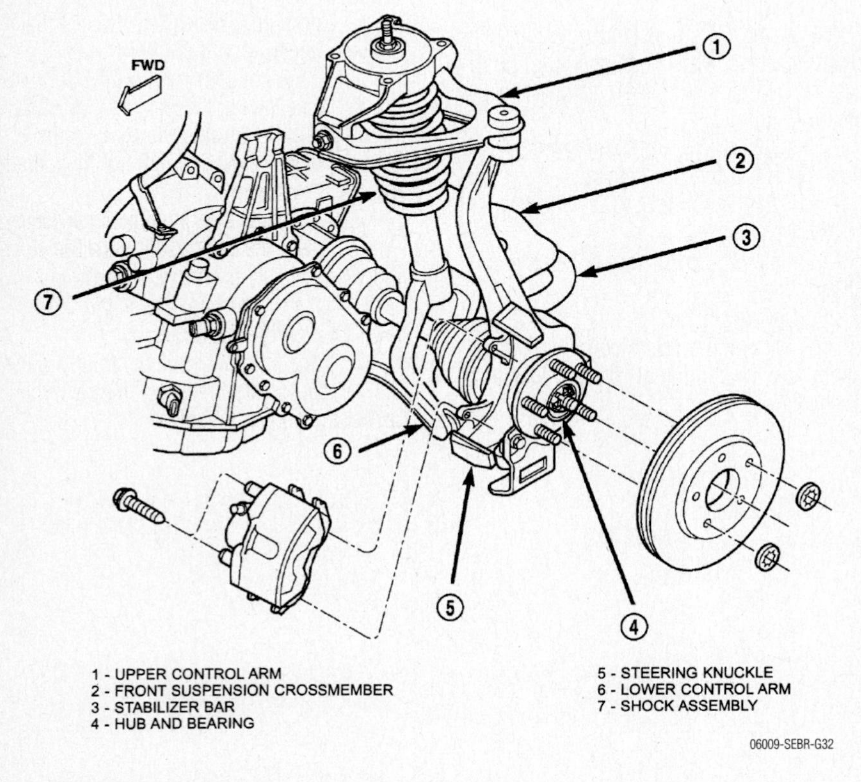

Fig. 121 Front suspension components

CONTROL LINKS

REMOVAL & INSTALLATION

1. Before servicing the vehicle, refer to the Precautions Section.
2. Raise and support the vehicle.
3. Remove the nuts and control link assemblies from the lower control arms. When removing link nut, keep the stud from turning by installing an Allen wrench in the end of the stud.

To install:

4. Inspect for broken or distorted stabilizer bar bushings, retainers, and links.
5. Align control link assemblies with the mounting holes in the lower control arms. Install the links into both lower control arms. Install the link retaining nuts. Tighten the control link nuts to 77 ft. lbs. (105 Nm).
6. Lower the vehicle.

LOWER BALL JOINT

REMOVAL & INSTALLATION

On all vehicles, the ball joint cannot be serviced separately. If the ball joint is worn or damaged it will require replacement of the lower control arm.

LOWER CONTROL ARM

REMOVAL & INSTALLATION

See Figures 122 through 125.

1. Before servicing the vehicle, refer to the Precautions Section.
2. Raise vehicle.
3. Remove the tire and wheel assembly.

➡Removing the outer tie rod from the steering knuckle allows the steering knuckle to be turned further. This allows better access to the steering knuckle when striking it to remove the ball joint stud from the steering knuckle.

4. Remove the nut attaching the outer tie rod to steering knuckle. Remove nut from tie rod end by holding tie rod stud with

a socket while loosening and removing nut with wrench.

5. Remove the outer tie rod from steering knuckle.

6. Remove the cotter pin and castle nut from lower ball joint stud.

**** WARNING**

No tool is to be inserted between the steering knuckle and the lower ball joint to separate the lower ball joint from the steering knuckle. The steering knuckle is to be separated from the ball joint only using the procedure as described below.

**** WARNING**

When striking the steering knuckle, do not hit the heat shield covering the ball joint grease seal. Bending the heat shield against the ball joint grease seal will cause the grease seal to fail.

7. Turn steering knuckle so front of steering knuckle is facing as far outboard in the wheel opening as possible. Using a hammer, strike steering knuckle boss until steering knuckle separates from lower ball joint. When striking steering knuckle, care MUST be taken not to hit lower control arm or ball joint grease seal.

**** WARNING**

Pulling the steering knuckle outward from the vehicle after releasing it from the ball joint, can separate half-shaft inner CV-joint , thus damaging it.

8. Remove the shock absorber clevis to lower control arm bushing, nut and through-bolt. Separate clevis from lower control arm.

9. Remove the nut attaching stabilizer bar link to lower control arm. When removing nut, hold stud of stabilizer bar link from turning by inserting an Allen wrench in end of stud.

10. Remove the bolts attaching closest stabilizer bar bushing clamp to front suspension crossmember and body of vehicle.

11. Lower that side of stabilizer bar away from lower control arm and body of vehicle.

12. Remove the nut and bolt attaching rear of lower control arm to front suspension crossmember.

13. Remove the nut and bolt attaching the front of lower control arm to front suspension crossmember.

**** WARNING**

When removing lower control arm from crossmember care must be taken to prevent hitting lower ball joint seal against steering knuckle, causing damage to the ball joint seal.

14. Remove the front of lower control arm from suspension crossmember first, then remove rear of lower control arm from suspension crossmember. When removing rear of lower control arm from crossmember, keep control arm as level as possible. This will keep rear bushing from binding on crossmember making it easier to remove control arm from crossmember.

To install:

15. Position rear of lower control arm into front suspension crossmember first, then Install the front of lower control arm in front suspension crossmember. Install the bolts and nuts attaching front and rear of lower control arm to front suspension crossmember. Do not tighten front attaching bolt at this time. Tighten lower control arm rear attaching nut and bolt to 70 ft. lbs. (95 Nm).

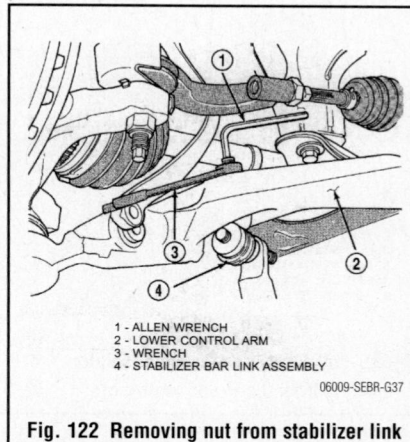

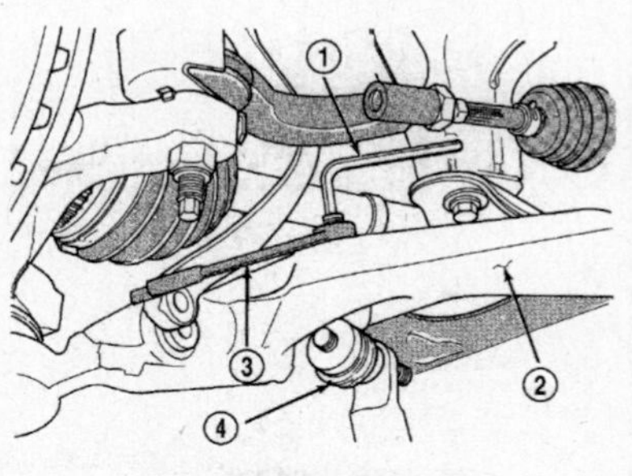

Fig. 122 Removing nut from stabilizer link

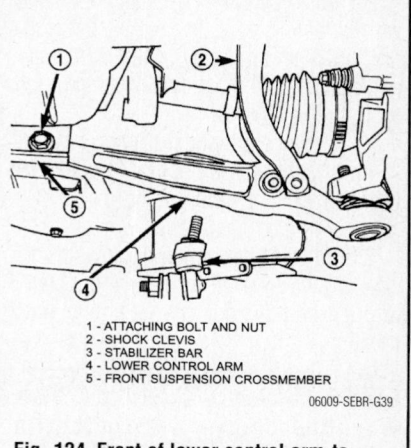

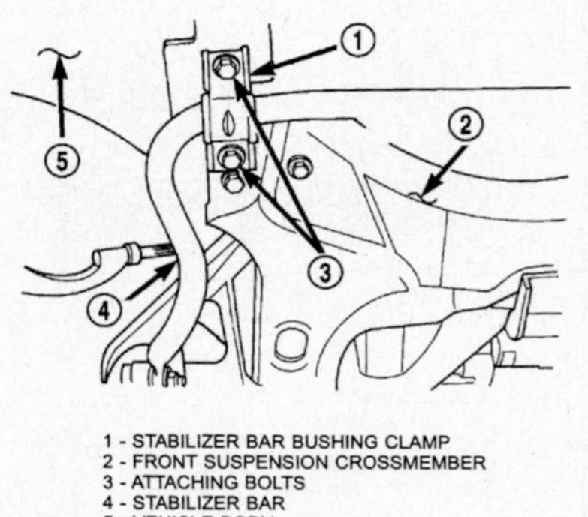

Fig. 123 Stabilizer bar clamp attachment

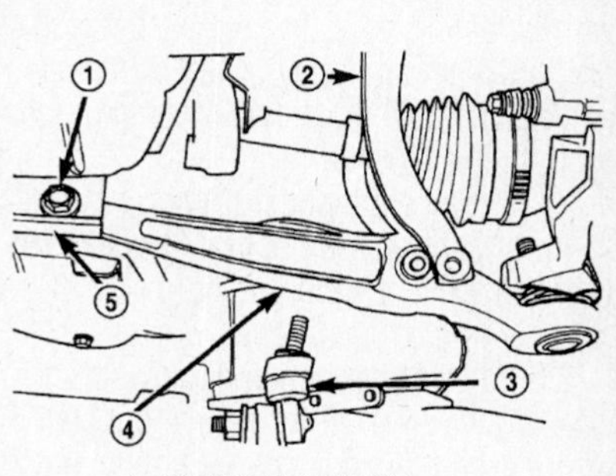

Fig. 124 Front of lower control arm-to-crossmember attachment

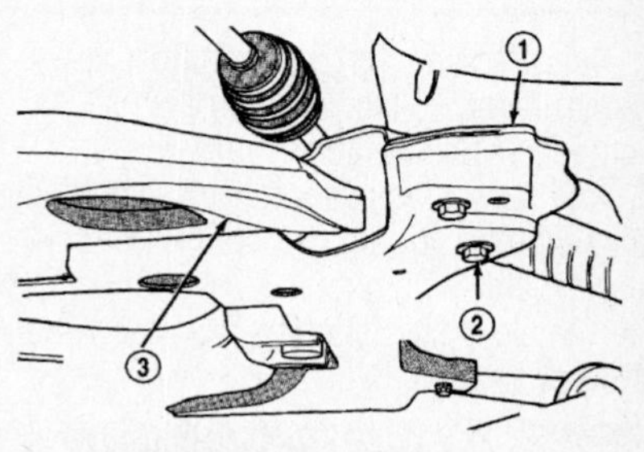

Fig. 125 Rear of lower control arm-to-crossmember attachment

16. Install the lower control arm ball joint stud into steering knuckle. Install the steering knuckle to ball joint stud castle nut. Do not tighten nut at this time.

**** WARNING**

When installing tie rod on steering knuckle, the heat shield must be installed. If heat shield is not installed, tie rod seal boot can fail due to excessive heat from brake rotor.

17. Install the outer tie rod stud into steering knuckle. Start outer tie rod-to-steering knuckle attaching nut onto tie rod stud. While holding stud of tie rod end stationary, tighten nut using a crowfoot and $11/32$ socket. Tighten nut to 40 ft. lbs. (55 Nm).

18. Tighten lower control arm ball joint castle nut to 55 ft. lbs. (74 Nm).

19. Install the cotter pin.

20. Position stabilizer bar link into its lower control arm mounting hole.

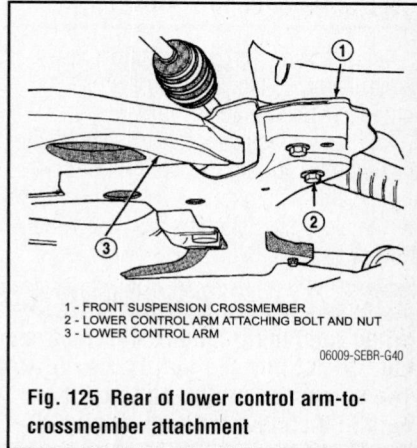

21. Align stabilizer bar bushing clamp with mounting holes in front suspension crossmember and body of vehicle. Install and tighten bushing clamp mounting bolts to 45 ft. lbs. (61 Nm).

22. Install and tighten stabilizer bar link-to-lower control arm nut to 77 ft. lbs. (105 Nm). When tightening nut, hold stud of link from turning using an Allen wrench.

23. Align shock absorber clevis with bushing in lower control arm and install the through-bolt and nut. Do not tighten nut at this time.

**** WARNING**

When supporting lower control arm with jackstand, do not position jack stand under the ball joint cap on the lower control arm. Position stand in area of lower control arm shown.

24. Position a jack stand under lower control arm, so that when arm is lowered onto it, vehicle will be at curb height.

25. Lower vehicle with jack stand positioned under lower control arm. Continue to lower vehicle until total weight of that corner of vehicle is supported by jack stand and lower control arm.

**** WARNING**

When tightening the through-bolt and nut, do not turn the bolt in the clevis. The serrations on the bolt and the hole in the clevis will be damaged.

26. With the vehicle's suspension at curb height, tighten the clevis-to-lower control arm bushing through-bolt nut to 65 ft. lbs. (88 Nm).

27. Tighten front lower control arm nut and bolt to 104 ft. lbs. (142 Nm).

28. Raise vehicle and remove jack stand from under lower control arm.

29. Install the wheel and tire assembly. Install the wheel mounting (lug) nuts and progressively tighten in proper sequence to 100 ft. lbs. (135 Nm).

30. Lower vehicle.

31. Check wheel alignment specifications and set front toe to preferred specifications.

CONTROL ARM BUSHING REPLACEMENT

Front Isolator Bushing

See Figures 126 and 127.

1. Before servicing the vehicle, refer to the precautions in the beginning of this section.

2. Remove the lower control arm assembly

3. Install the Bushing Remover Tool 6602-5 and Bushing Receiver Tool MB-990799 on Special Tool C-4212-F.

4. Position the lower control arm on the assembled removal tools.

➡Be sure the Bushing Receiver Tool MB-990799 is square on the lower control arm and Bushing Remover Tool 6602-5 is positioned correctly on the isolator bushing.

5. Tighten Special Tool C-4212-F to press the bushing from the lower control arm.

To assemble:

6. Position the Bushing Installer Tool 6876 onto the screw portion of Special Tool C-4212-F.

7. Start the new bushing into the lower control arm hole machined surface side by hand, making sure it is square with its mounting hole.

8. Assemble Special Tools 6758, 6876 and C-4212-F; then, position the lower control arm on the assembly, making sure that the tools are aligned.

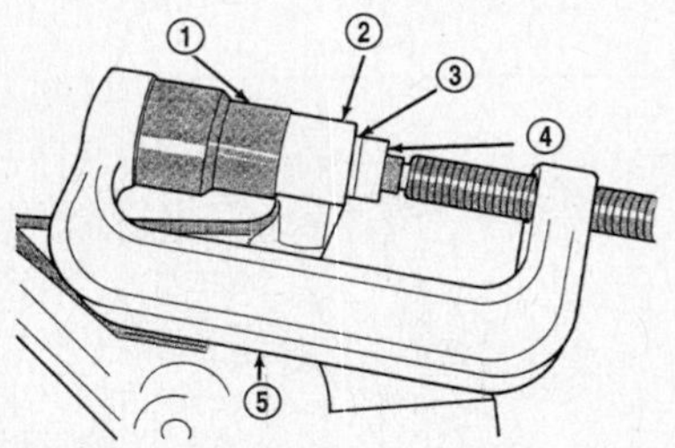

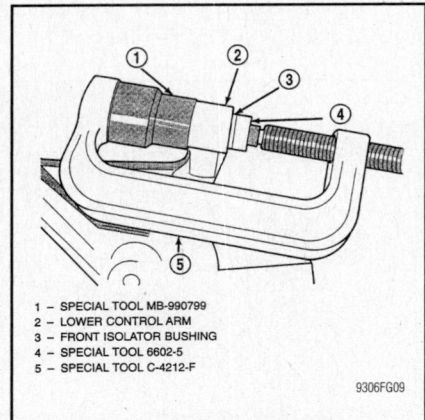

1 - SPECIAL TOOL MB-990799
2 - LOWER CONTROL ARM
3 - FRONT ISOLATOR BUSHING
4 - SPECIAL TOOL 6602-5
5 - SPECIAL TOOL C-4212-F

9306FG09

Fig. 126 Removing the front isolator bushing from the lower control arm

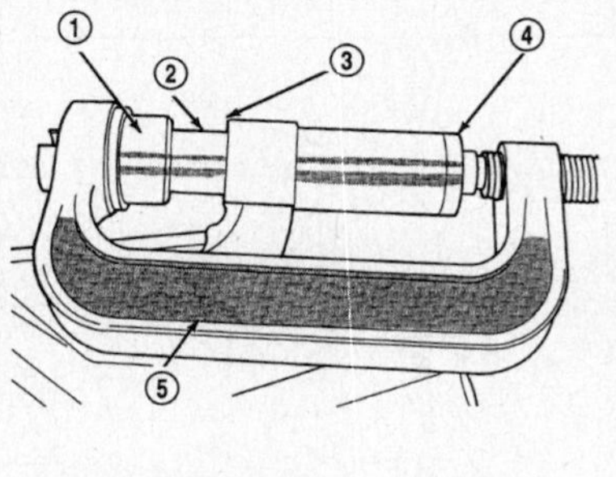

1 - SPECIAL TOOL 6876
2 - ISOLATOR BUSHING
3 - MACHINED SURFACE SIDE OF LOWER CONTROL ARM
4 - SPECIAL TOOL 6758
5 - SPECIAL TOOL C-4212-F

9306FG10

Fig. 127 Installing the front isolator bushing to the lower control arm

9. Tighten Special Tool C-4212-F to press the bushing into the lower control arm until it is flush on the machined surface.

10. Install the lower control arm assembly.

Rear Isolator Bushing

See Figures 128 through 130.

1. Before servicing the vehicle, refer to the precautions in the beginning of this section.

2. Remove the lower control arm assembly

3. Install the Bushing Remover Tool 6756 and Bushing Receiver Tool C-4366-2 on Special Tool C-4212-F.

4. Position the lower control arm on the assembled removal tools.

➡Be sure the Bushing Receiver Tool C-4366-2 is square on the lower control arm and Bushing Remover Tool 6756 is positioned correctly on the isolator bushing.

5. Tighten Special Tool C-4212-F to press the bushing from the lower control arm.

To assemble:

6. Position the Bushing Installer Tool 6760 onto the screw portion of special Tool C-4212-F.

7. Start the new bushing into the lower control arm hole's machined surface side by hand, making sure it is square with its mounting hole with the void in the rubber portion facing away from the ball joint.

8. Assemble Special Tools 6760 and 6756; then, position the lower control arm on the assembly, making sure that the tools are aligned.

9. Tighten Special Tool C-4212-F to press the bushing into the lower control arm until it is flush on the machined surface.

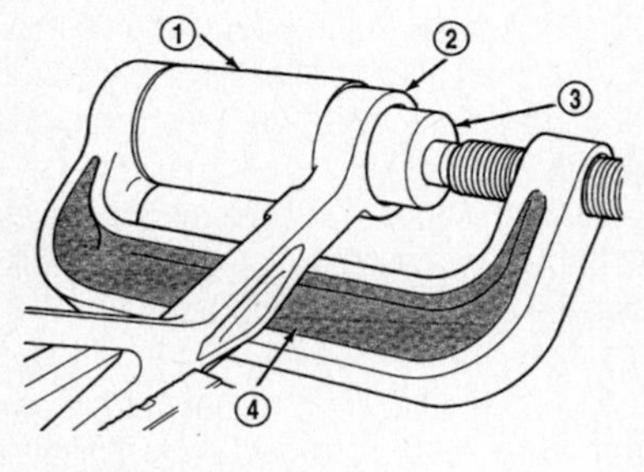

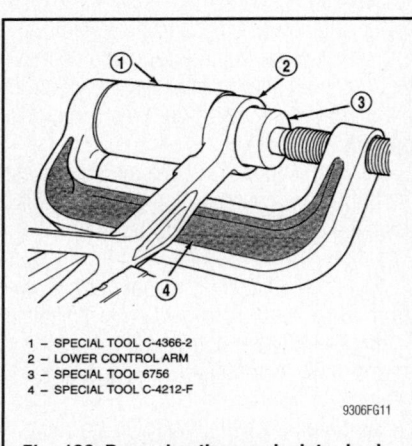

1 - SPECIAL TOOL C-4366-2
2 - LOWER CONTROL ARM
3 - SPECIAL TOOL 6756
4 - SPECIAL TOOL C-4212-F

9306FG11

Fig. 128 Removing the rear isolator bushing from the lower control arm

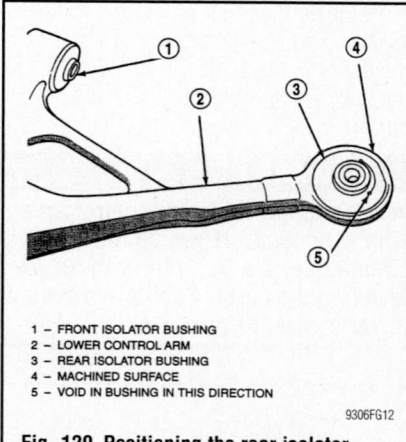

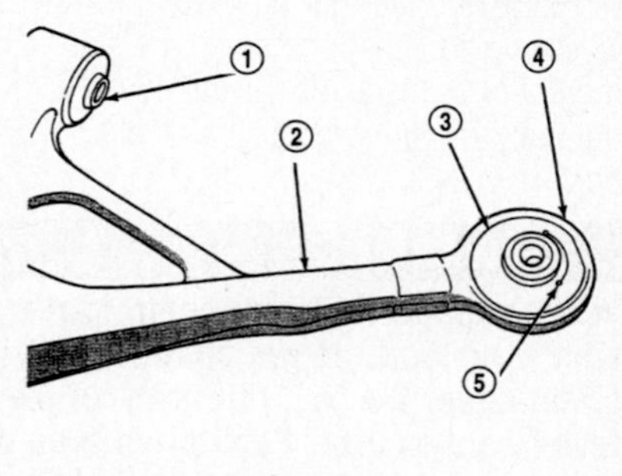

1 - FRONT ISOLATOR BUSHING
2 - LOWER CONTROL ARM
3 - REAR ISOLATOR BUSHING
4 - MACHINED SURFACE
5 - VOID IN BUSHING IN THIS DIRECTION

9306FG12

Fig. 129 Positioning the rear isolator bushing to the lower control arm

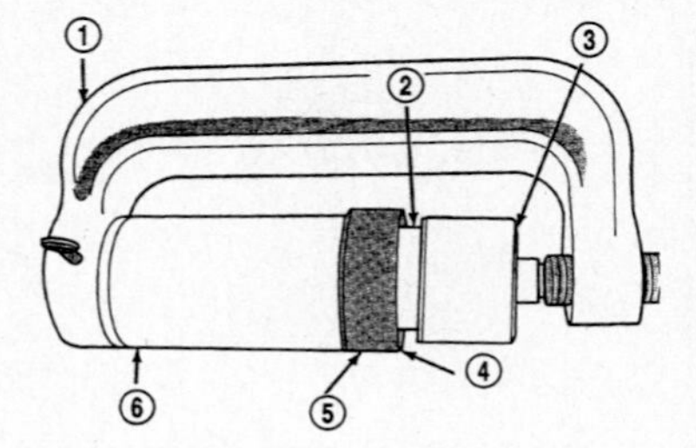

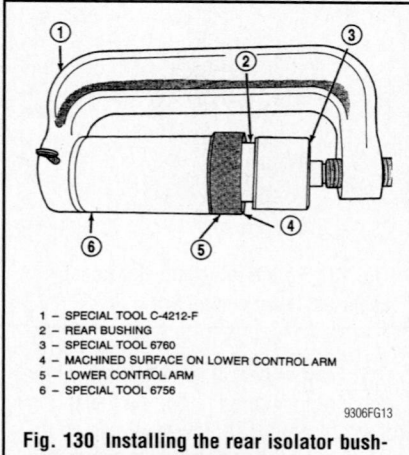

1 - SPECIAL TOOL C-4212-F
2 - REAR BUSHING
3 - SPECIAL TOOL 6760
4 - MACHINED SURFACE ON LOWER CONTROL ARM
5 - LOWER CONTROL ARM
6 - SPECIAL TOOL 6756

9306FG13

Fig. 130 Installing the rear isolator bushing to the lower control arm

10. Install the lower control arm assembly.

Clevis Bushing

See Figures 131 and 132.

1. Before servicing the vehicle, refer to the precautions in the beginning of this section.
2. Remove the lower control arm assembly
3. Install the Bushing Remover Tool 6877 and Bushing Receiver Tool 6876 on Special Tool C-4212-F.
4. Position the lower control arm on the assembled removal tools.

➡Be sure the Bushing Receiver Tool 6876 is square on the lower control arm and Bushing Remover Tool 6877 is positioned correctly on the clevis bushing.

5. Tighten Special Tool C-4212-F to press the bushing from the lower control arm.

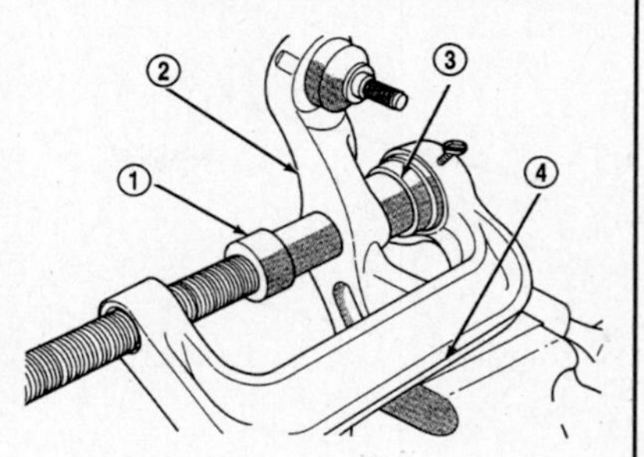

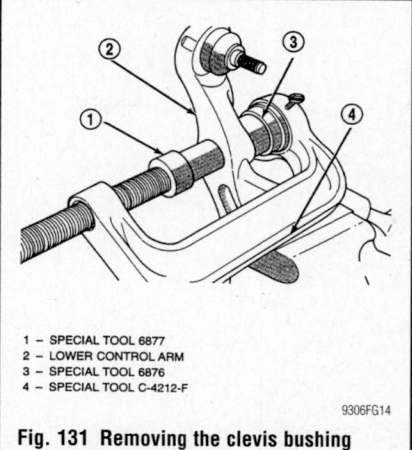

1 - SPECIAL TOOL 6877
2 - LOWER CONTROL ARM
3 - SPECIAL TOOL 6876
4 - SPECIAL TOOL C-4212-F

9306FG14

Fig. 131 Removing the clevis bushing from the lower control arm

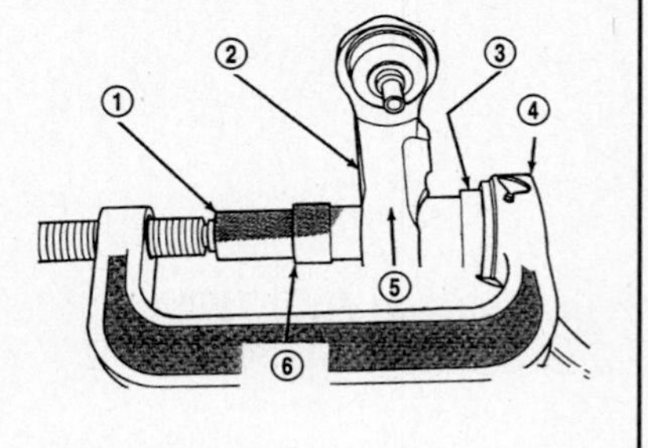

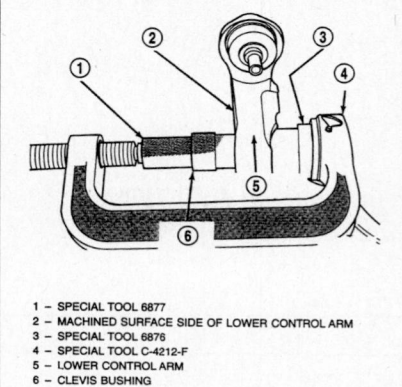

1 - SPECIAL TOOL 6877
2 - MACHINED SURFACE SIDE OF LOWER CONTROL ARM
3 - SPECIAL TOOL 6876
4 - SPECIAL TOOL C-4212-F
5 - LOWER CONTROL ARM
6 - CLEVIS BUSHING

9306FG15

Fig. 132 Installing the clevis bushing to the lower control arm

To assemble:

6. Position the Bushing Installer Tool 6877 onto the screw portion of special Tool C-4212-F.
7. Start the new bushing into the lower control arm hole's machined surface side by hand, making sure it is square with its mounting hole with the void in the rubber portion facing away from the ball joint.
8. Assemble special Tools 6876 and 6877; then, position the lower control arm on the assembly, making sure that the tools are aligned.
9. Tighten special Tool C-4212-F to press the bushing into the lower control arm until it is flush on the machined surface.
10. Install the lower control arm assembly.

MACPHERSON STRUT

REMOVAL & INSTALLATION

See Figures 133 through 136.

1. Before servicing the vehicle, refer to the Precautions Section.
2. Loosen wheel nuts.
3. Raise vehicle.
4. Remove the wheel and tire assembly.
5. If both shock assemblies are removed, mark the shock assemblies right and left according to which side of the vehicle from which they were removed.
6. Remove the wheel speed sensor cable routing bracket from the steering knuckle.
7. Remove the nut from the upper ball joint stud.
8. Remove the upper ball joint stud from the steering knuckle using a puller. Pull steering knuckle outward and position toward the rear of the front wheel opening.
9. Remove the pinch bolt attaching shock absorber clevis to shock absorber.
10. Remove the nut and through-bolt attaching the shock absorber clevis to the lower control arm.
11. Remove the clevis from the shock absorber by carefully tapping the clevis off the shock absorber using a soft (brass) drift.
12. Remove the 4 bolts attaching the shock absorber/upper control arm mounting bracket to the shock tower of the vehicle.
13. Remove the shock assembly from the vehicle. The shock assembly is removed out through the front area of the front wheel well.

To install:

14. Install the shock assembly, with the clevis removed, into shock tower. Aligning the 2 locating pins and the 4 mounting holes on the upper control arm shock absorber mount with the 4 holes in shock tower. Install the 4 upper control arm mount to shock tower mounting bolts. Tighten the 4 bolts to 70 ft. lbs. (95 Nm).
15. Install the clevis on the shock absorber. Clevis is installed by tapping it onto the fluid reservoir of the shock absorber using a soft (brass) drift until fully seated against locating tab on shock absorber. Orientation tab on locating tab must be positioned in the split of the clevis.
16. Install the pinch bolt retaining the shock clevis to the shock absorber. Tighten the pinch bolt to: 65 ft. lbs. (88 Nm)
17. Install the clevis bracket to lower control arm through-bolt. Do not tighten the through-bolt at this time.
18. Install the upper ball joint into steering knuckle. Install the nut on ball joint stud. Tighten nut to 20 ft. lbs. (27 Nm).

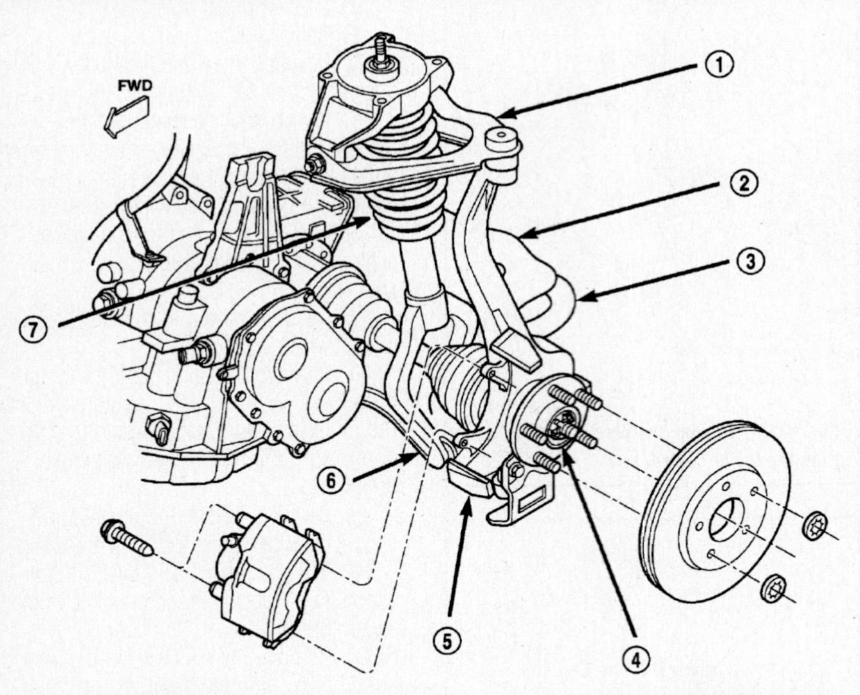

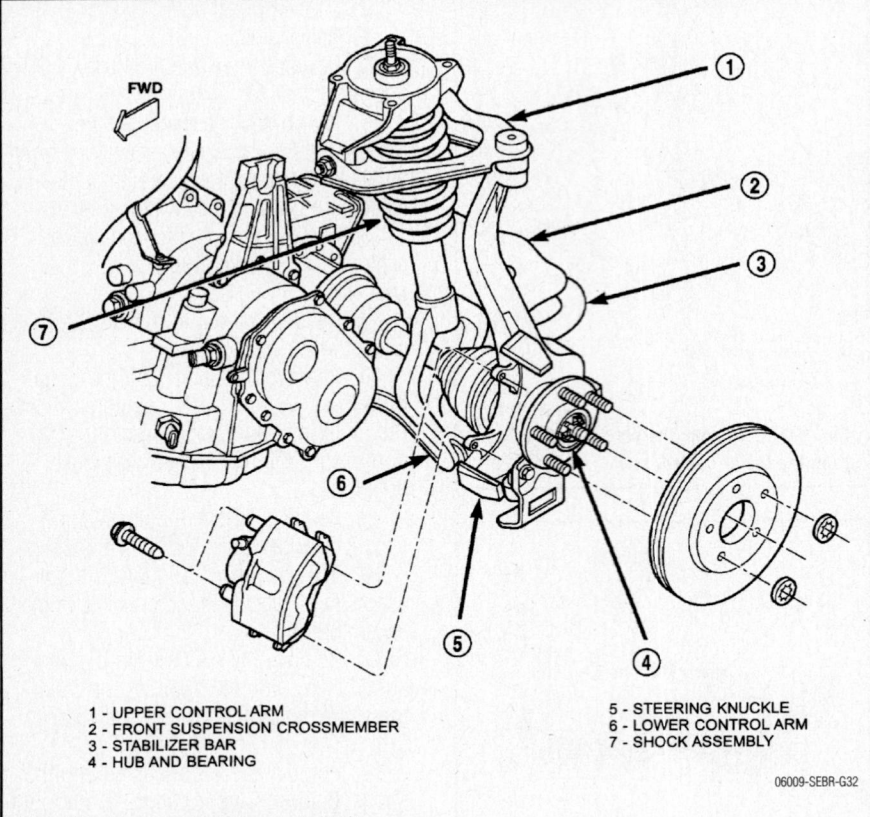

Fig. 133 Front suspension components

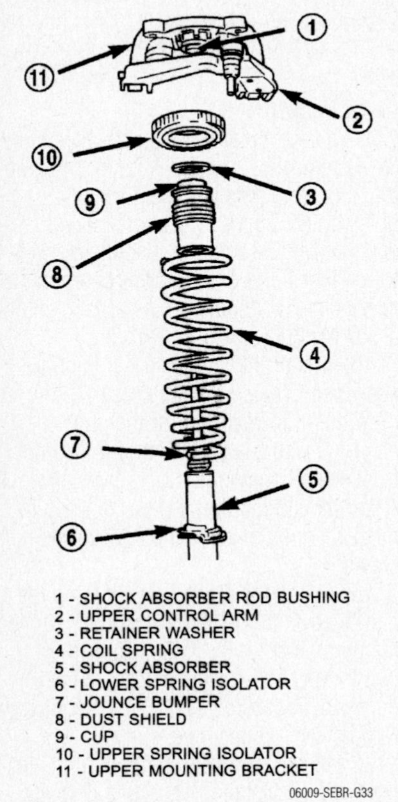

Fig. 134 Front strut components

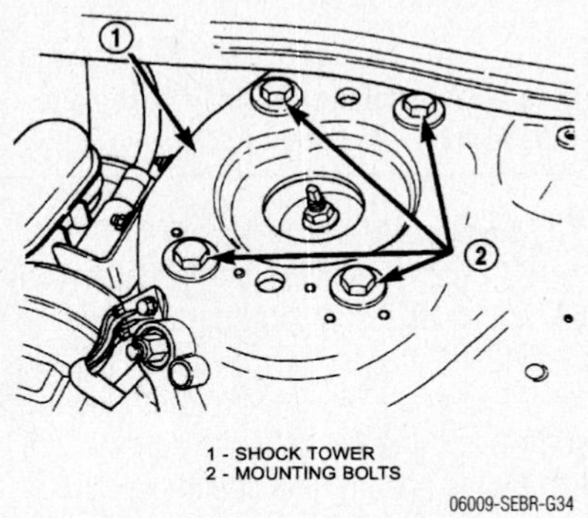

Fig. 135 Strut upper attaching bolts

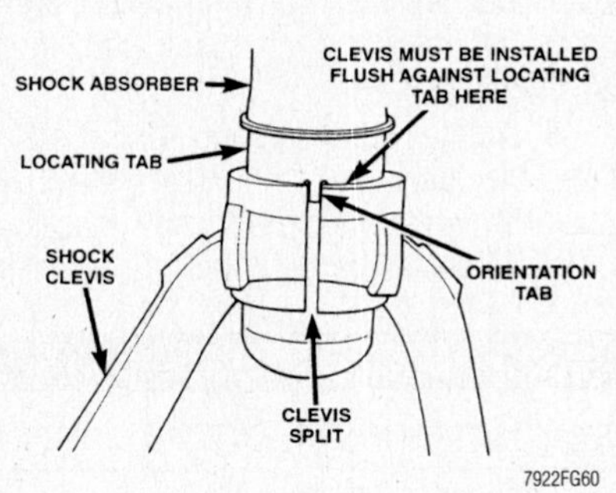

Fig. 136 Be sure the orientation tab is situated into the clevis split

19. Install the routing bracket for the wheel speed sensor cable on the steering knuckle. Install and securely tighten the routing bracket attaching bolt.

WARNING

When supporting lower control arm with jackstand, do not position jack stand under the ball joint cap on the lower control arm. Position in area of lower control arm shown.

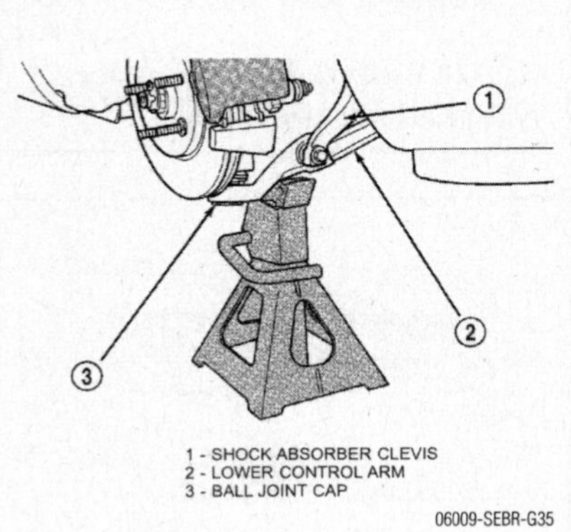

Fig. 137 Proper jackstand placement under the lower control arm

20. Lower vehicle to the ground with a jackstand positioned under the lower control arm. Continue to lower vehicle so the total weight of the vehicle is supported by the jack stand and lower control arm.
21. Tighten the shock absorber clevis to lower control arm bushing through-bolt nut to: 65 ft. lbs. (88 Nm).
22. Raise the vehicle, then remove the jack stand.
23. Install the tire and wheel assembly. Progressively tighten the wheel mounting nuts in a crisscross sequence until all nuts are torqued to half specification. Then repeat the tightening sequence to the full specified torque of 100 ft. lbs. (135 Nm).
24. Lower the vehicle.

OVERHAUL

See Figures 138 and 139.

1. Position the strut assembly in the strut coil spring compressor following the manufacturer's instructions and set the lower and upper hooks of the compressor on the coil spring. Position the strut clevis bracket straight outward, away from the compressor.
2. Compress the coil spring until all coil spring tension is removed from the upper mount and bearing.

3. Once the spring is sufficiently compressed, install Strut Nut Wrench, Special Tool 9362, on the strut rod nut. Next, install Strut Shaft Socket, Special Tool 9894, on the end of the strut rod. While holding the strut rod from turning, remove the nut using the strut nut wrench.

4. Remove the clamp (if installed) from the bottom of the coil spring and remove the strut (damper) out through the bottom of the coil spring. The dust shield and jounce bumper will come out with the strut.

5. Remove the lower spring isolator from the strut seat.

6. Slide the dust shield and jounce bumper from the strut rod.

7. Remove the upper mount and bearing from the top of the upper spring seat and isolator.

8. Remove the upper spring seat and isolator from the top of the coil spring.

9. Release the tension from the coil spring by backing off the compressor drive completely. Push back the compressor hooks and remove the coil spring.

To assemble:

10. Place the coil spring in the spring compressor following the manufacturer's instructions. Before compressing the spring, rotate the spring so the end of the bottom coil is at approximately the 9 o'clock position as viewed from above (or to where the spring was when removed from the compressor). This action will allow the strut (damper) clevis bracket to be positioned outward, away from the compressor once installed.

11. Slowly compress the coil spring until enough room is available for strut assembly reassembly.

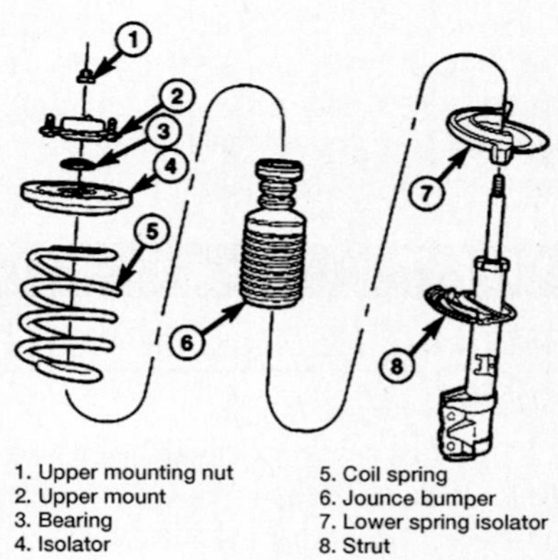

Fig. 138 Strut assembly components—Upper mounting nut (1), Upper mount (2), Bearing (3), Isolator (4), Coil spring (5), Jounce bumper (6), Lower spring isolator (7), Strut (8).

12. Install the upper spring seat and isolator on top of the coil spring.

13. Install the bearing and upper mount on top of the upper spring seat and isolator.

14. Install the lower spring isolator on the spring seat on the strut.

15. Slide the dust shield and jounce bumper onto the strut rod.

16. Install the strut up through the bottom of the coil spring and upper spring seat, mount, and bearing until the lower spring seat contacts the lower end of the coil spring. Rotate the strut as necessary until the end of the bottom coil comes in contact with the stop built into the lower spring isolator.

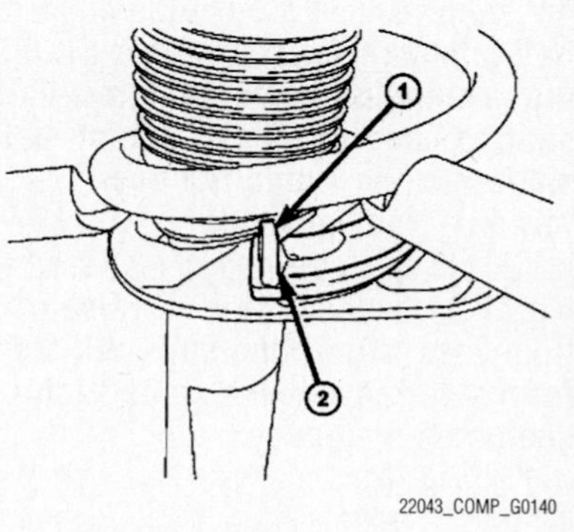

Fig. 139 Rotate the strut until the end of the bottom coil (2) comes in contact with the stop (1).

17. While holding the strut in position, install the nut on the end of the strut rod.

18. Install Special Tool 9632 Strut Nut Wrench on the strut rod nut. Next, install Special Tool 9894 Strut Shaft Socket on the end of the strut rod. While holding the strut rod from turning, tighten the strut rod nut to 44 ft. lbs. (60 Nm) using a torque wrench on the end of Special Tool 9362.

19. Slowly release the tension from the coil spring by backing off the compressor drive completely. As the tension is relieved, make sure the upper mount and bearing align properly. Verify the upper mount does not bind when rotated.

20. Remove the strut assembly from the spring compressor.

21. Install the strut assembly on the vehicle

STABILIZER BAR

REMOVAL & INSTALLATION

See Figures 140 and 141.

1. Raise vehicle on jack stands or centered on a frame contact type hoist.

2. Remove the nuts and stabilizer bar attaching link assemblies from the front lower control arms.

3. When removing attaching link nut, keep stud from turning by installing an Allen wrench in the end of the stud.

4. Remove the 4 bolts attaching the stabilizer bar bushing retainers to the front suspension crossmember and body. Then remove the stabilizer bar assembly from the vehicle.

To install:

5. Position stabilizer bar and bushings as an assembly into front crossmember. Install the stabilizer bar bushing retainer to crossmember and body attaching bolts.

a. Tighten the bushing retainer attaching bolts going to the body to 45 ft. lbs. (61 Nm).

b. Tighten the attaching bolts going through the crossmember to: 120 ft. lbs. (163 Nm) (if applicable).

6. Align stabilizer bar attaching link assemblies with attaching link mounting holes in the lower control arms.

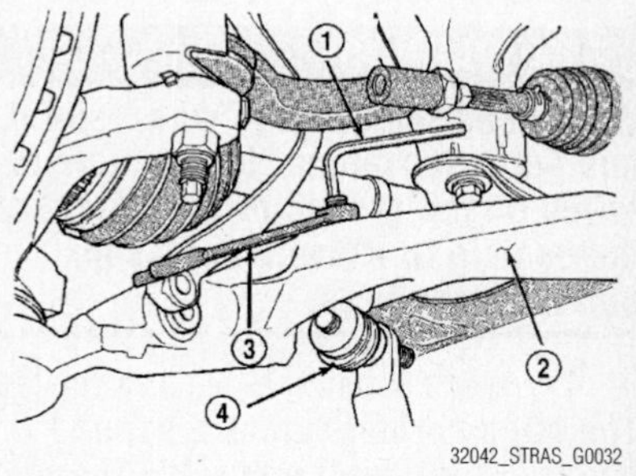

Fig. 140 Front Stabilizer Bar links and Allen wrench (1), lower control arm (2), wrench (3) and stabilizer bar link assembly (4)

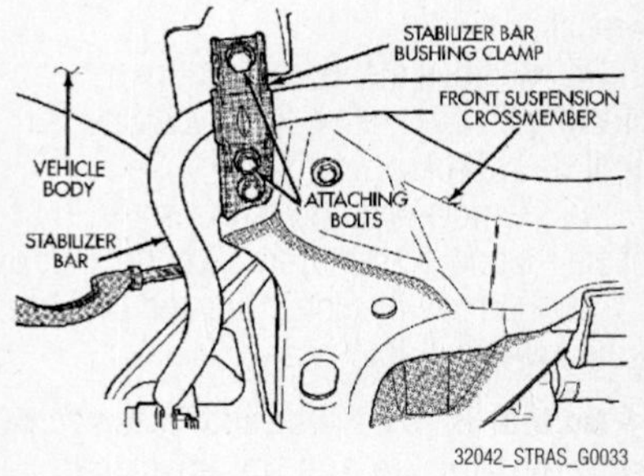

Fig. 141 Crossmember and stabilizer bar bushing retainer

7. Install the stabilizer bar attaching links into both lower control arms. Install the attaching link to lower control arm retaining nuts.

8. Torque the stabilizer bar attaching link nuts to 77 ft. lbs. (105 Nm)

STEERING KNUCKLE

REMOVAL & INSTALLATION

The steering knuckle is a single casting with legs machined for attachment to the vehicle's upper and lower control arm ball joints. the steering knuckle has the hub and bearing mounted in its center. The axle shaft constant velocity joint stub shaft is splined through the hub and bearing assembly in the center of the knuckle. The steering knuckle also supports and aligns the front brake caliper adapter and caliper assembly. The Steering Knuckle cannot be repaired, replace if damaged. The front suspension steering knuckle is not a repairable component and must be replaced if it is damaged.

1. Before servicing the vehicle, refer to the Precautions Section.
2. Raise vehicle.
3. Remove the front tire and wheel assembly from hub.

**** WARNING**

Wheel bearing damage will result if hub nut is loosened, then vehicle is rolled on the ground or the weight of the vehicle is allowed to be supported by the tires.

4. Loosen hub nut with brakes applied. **The hub and halfshaft are splined together through the knuckle (bearing) and retained by the hub nut.**
5. Remove the disc brake caliper, adapter, shoes and rotor from steering knuckle.
6. Remove the nut attaching outer tie rod to steering knuckle. Remove nut from tie rod by holding tie rod stud with a socket while loosening and removing nut with wrench.
7. Remove the tie rod end from the steering knuckle using Remover, Special Tool C-3894-A.
8. Remove the ABS wheel speed sensor cable routing bracket from steering knuckle.
9. Remove the cotter pin and castle nut from lower ball joint stud.

➡No tool is to be inserted between the steering knuckle and the lower ball joint to separate stud of lower ball joint from the steering knuckle. The steering knuckle is to be separated from the stud of the ball joint only using the procedure as described below.

When striking the steering knuckle, do not hit the heat shield covering the ball joint grease seal. Bending the heat shield against the ball joint grease seal will cause the grease seal to fail.

10. Turn steering knuckle so front of it is facing as far outboard in wheel well as possible.
11. Using a hammer, strike boss on steering knuckle until steering knuckle separates from lower ball joint stud.

Care must be taken not to separate the inner CV-joint during the following steps. Pulling steering knuckle out from vehicle after releasing from ball joint can separate inner CV-joint, thus damaging it. Do not allow halfshaft to hang by inner CV-joint; halfshaft must be supported upon removal from knuckle.

12. Lift up on steering knuckle separating it from lower ball joint stud. **Use caution when separating ball joint stud from steering knuckle so ball joint seal does not get cut.**
13. Separate steering knuckle from outer CV-joint . Separate steering knuckle from outer CV-joint holding halfshaft in place while pulling steering knuckle away from outer CV-joint .
14. Remove the nut from upper ball joint stud.
15. Remove the upper ball joint stud from steering knuckle using Puller, Special Tool, C-3894-A.
16. Remove the steering knuckle from vehicle.
17. If necessary, remove lower ball joint grease seal heat shield on steering knuckle.
18. If steering knuckle is being replaced and hub and bearing is found to be in usable condition, it can be transferred to replacement steering knuckle

To install:

19. If required, install the hub/bearing assembly into steering knuckle before installing steering knuckle on vehicle.
20. If removed, install the lower ball joint grease seal heat shield on steering knuckle.
21. Slide halfshaft into front hub/bearing assembly as steering knuckle is installed onto lower ball joint stud.
22. Install the lower ball joint castle nut. Do not tighten at this time.
23. Install the upper ball joint in steering knuckle. Install the upper ball joint nut. Tighten upper ball joint nut to 20 ft. lbs. (27 Nm).
24. Using a crowfoot and torque wrench, tighten the lower ball joint nut to 55 ft. lbs. (75 Nm) and install the cotter pin.
25. Install the wheel speed sensor cable routing bracket on steering knuckle and securely tighten attaching bolt.

**** WARNING**

When installing tie rod on steering knuckle, the heat shield must be installed. If heat shield is not installed, tie rod seal boot can fail due to excessive heat from brake rotor. Install the outer tie rod stud into steering knuckle. Start outer tie rod attaching nut onto tie rod stud.

26. While holding stud of tie rod stationary, tighten nut using a crowfoot and socket to 40 ft. lbs. (55 Nm).
27. Install the brake rotor, and caliper, shoes and adapter assembly.
28. Clean all foreign matter from threads of outer CV-joint stub axle. Install the hub nut onto halfshaft stub axle.
29. With vehicle brakes applied to keep braking disc from turning, tighten hub nut to 150 ft. lbs. (203 Nm).
30. Install the front wheel and tire assembly. Install the front wheel lug nuts and progressively tighten in crisscross sequence to 100 ft. lbs. (135 Nm).
31. Lower vehicle.
32. Set front toe on vehicle to required specification.

UPPER BALL JOINT

REMOVAL & INSTALLATION

The upper ball joint is an integrated part of the upper control arm assembly, and cannot be serviced separately. A worn or damaged ball joint requires replacement of upper control arm assembly.

UPPER CONTROL ARM

REMOVAL & INSTALLATION

See Figure 142.

1. Before servicing the vehicle, refer to the Precautions Section.
2. Remove the front strut assembly from the vehicle.
3. Disassemble the strut assembly until the upper mounting bracket is removed from the coil spring.
4. Remove the 2 bolts attaching the upper control arm to the bushings in the upper mounting bracket.

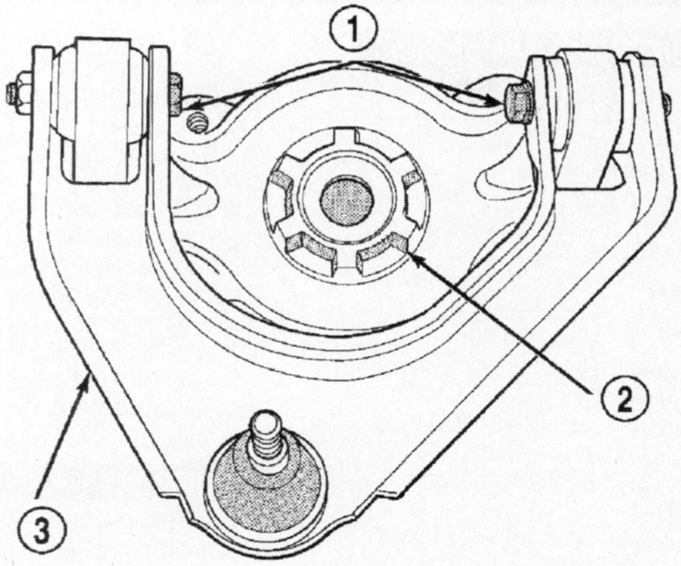

Fig. 142 Upper control arm-to-mounting bracket attachment

5. Remove the upper control arm from the mounting bracket.

To install:

6. Install the upper control arm on the upper (strut absorber/upper control arm) mounting bracket.
7. Install the 2 bolts attaching the upper control arm to the bushings in the mounting bracket.

WARNING

For clearance reasons the control arm mounting bolts must be installed from center, so the heads are toward the coil spring when it is installed. Otherwise the bolts may rub the coil spring, damaging it.

8. Install the control arm mounting bolt nuts. Position the control arm at a 90° angle to the mounting bracket and tighten the bolts to 66 ft. lbs. (90 Nm).
9. Reinstall the upper mounting bracket and control arm on the coil spring. Reassemble the front strut assembly.
10. Reinstall the front strut assembly on the vehicle.

CONTROL ARM BUSHING REPLACEMENT

If damaged, the upper control arm is serviced only as a complete component. Inspect the upper control arm for any signs of damage. If control arm shows any sign of damage the upper control arm must be replaced.

WHEEL BEARINGS

REMOVAL & INSTALLATION

The front wheel bearing used on this vehicle is a bolt-in type wheel bearing.

The wheel bearing is serviced separately from the front steering knuckle and front hub assembly. Retention of the front wheel bearing into the steering knuckle is by means of 3 bolts installed from the rear of the steering knuckle. The 3 bolts attach the hub/bearing to the front surface of the steering knuckle. REMOVAL & INSTALLATION of the hub/bearing assembly from the steering knuckle must be done with the steering knuckle removed from the vehicle.

The face of the outer CV-joint has a metal bearing shield pressed on it. This design deters direct water splash on the bearing seal while allowing any water that gets in to run out the bottom of the steering knuckle. It is important to thoroughly clean the outer CV-joint and the wheel bearing area in the steering knuckle before it is assembled after servicing the front wheel bearing or halfshaft.

At no time when servicing this vehicle, can a sheet metal screw, bolt or other metal fastener be installed in the shock tower to take the place of an original plastic clip. Also, NO holes can be drilled into the front shock tower for the installation of any metal fasteners into the shock tower. Because of the minimum clearance in this area installation of metal fasteners could damage the coil spring's protective coating and lead to corrosion failure of the spring. If a plastic clip is missing, lost or broken during servicing a vehicle, replace only with the equivalent part listed in the MOPAR® parts catalog.

1. Before servicing the vehicle, refer to the precautions in the beginning of this section.
2. Remove or disconnect the following:
   - Front wheel
   - Steering knuckle assembly
   - 3 hub/bearing assembly-to-steering knuckle bolts
   - Hub/bearing assembly from the steering knuckle. If necessary, tap the bearing out, using a soft-faced hammer

➡The wheel bearing is transferable to a replacement steering knuckle if the bearing is found in serviceable condition.

To install:

3. Clean all parts well. Thoroughly, clean all the hub/bearing assembly mounting surfaces on the steering knuckle.
4. Install or connect the following:
   - Hub/bearing assembly and torque the bolts to 80 ft. lbs. (110 Nm)
   - Steering knuckle
   - Front wheel

ADJUSTMENT

The front hub wheel bearing is designed for the life of the vehicle and requires no type of adjustment or periodic maintenance. The bearing is a sealed unit with the wheel hub and can only be removed and/or replaced as one unit.

COIL SPRING

REMOVAL & INSTALLATION

See Figure 143.

1. Before servicing the vehicle, refer to the precautions in the beginning of this section.
2. Disassemble as follows:
   - Remove the rear shock from the vehicle.
   - Install the assembly in a spring compressor tool.
   - Remove the jam nut, washer and upper bushing.
   - Remove the upper bracket assembly and spring pad.
   - Remove the collar and bushing.
   - Remove the cup, bump rubber and dust cover.
   - Remove the coil spring

To assemble:

3. Install the coil spring to the shock absorber using compressor Tools MB991237 and MB991239.
4. Install the dust cover and bump rubber.
5. Install the cup and bushing
6. Install the collar, supper spring pad and bracket assembly.
7. Install the upper bushing and washer.
8. When properly aligned, install the jam nut and torque to 17 ft. lbs. (23 Nm).
9. Remove the compressor tools and install the shock absorber.

UPPER CONTROL ARM

REMOVAL & INSTALLATION

1. Before servicing the vehicle, refer to the Precautions Section.
2. Raise vehicle.
3. Remove the both rear wheel and tire assemblies from the vehicle.
4. Remove the shock absorber clevis bracket to rear knuckle attaching bolt and nut on both sides of the vehicle.
5. Remove the muffler support bracket from rear frame rail.
6. Remove the rear exhaust pipe hanger bracket from the rear suspension crossmember. Let exhaust system drop down as far as possible.
7. If vehicle is equipped with antilock brakes, remove routing clips for wheel speed sensor cable from brackets on both upper control arms.
8. If vehicle is equipped with antilock brakes, remove bolts and wheel speed sensor heads from both rear knuckles.
9. Remove the both rear disc brake calipers from knuckles and hang out of way using wire or cord. Do not allow calipers to hang by brake hoses.
10. Release brake tubing from clips on top of crossmember.
11. On the side of the vehicle requiring control arm removal, separate the control arm ball joint from the rear knuckle using following procedure:
    a. Back off nut retaining upper control arm ball joint to knuckle until nut is even with end of stud. This action will help avoid damaging the stud threads when the stud is released from the knuckle in the following step.
    b. Remove ball joint stud from knuckle using a puller.
    c. Remove nut retaining upper control arm ball joint to knuckle.
12. Position a transmission jack and wooden block under the center of the rear suspension crossmember to support and lower crossmember during removal.
13. Remove the 4 bolts attaching rear suspension crossmember to rear frame rails.

**** WARNING**

When lowering rear suspension crossmember do not put a strain on the rear brake flex hoses.

14. Lower the rear suspension crossmember far enough to access the upper control arm pivot bar to crossmember attaching bolts.
15. Remove the 2 bolts attaching the upper control arm to the rear suspension crossmember.
16. Remove the upper control arm from the rear suspension crossmember.
17. Transfer any required components to the replacement control arm.

To install:

18. Align the pivot bar on the upper control arm with the mounting holes in the rear suspension crossmember. Install the pivot bar attaching bolts. Tighten the 2 pivot bar attaching bolts to 80 ft. lbs. (108 Nm).
19. Using transmission jack, raise rear suspension crossmember up to the rear frame rails and loosely Install the 4 attaching bolts.
20. Position an appropriate size drift into the positioning hole in each side of rear suspension crossmember and crossmember locating holes in frame rails of the vehicle. This is required to properly position rear suspension crossmember to the body of the vehicle. Tighten the 4 crossmember to frame rail attaching bolts to 80 ft. lbs. (108 Nm). Remove drifts from rear suspension crossmember.
21. Remove the transmission jack supporting rear suspension crossmember.
22. Install the upper ball joint stud in knuckle. Install and tighten the ball joint stud nut to 20 ft. lbs. (27 Nm).

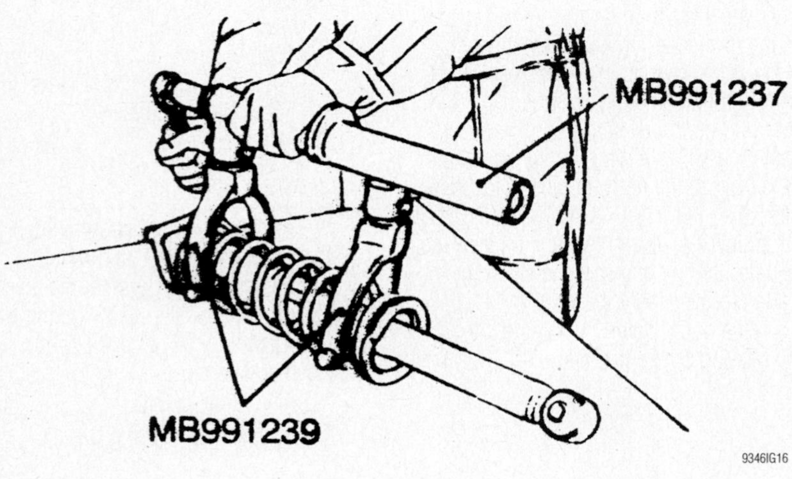

Fig. 143 Compress the coil spring as shown

23. Install the brake tubing above the rear suspension crossmember into the routing clips on top of the crossmember.

24. Install the rear brake calipers onto rear knuckles.

25. If vehicle is equipped with antilock brakes, attach wheel speed sensor heads to both rear knuckles. Tighten sensor mounting bolts to 75 inch lbs. (8 Nm).

26. If vehicle is equipped with antilock brakes, install the routing clips for wheel speed sensor cables onto brackets on both upper control arms. Securely tighten routing clip attaching bolts.

27. Install the muffler support bracket on rear frame rail.

28. Install the rear exhaust pipe hanger on rear suspension crossmember.

29. Install the shock absorber clevis brackets on the rear knuckles. Tighten the shock absorber mounting bolts to 70 ft. lbs. (95 Nm).

30. Install the wheel and tire assembly on vehicle. Progressively tighten the wheel mounting nuts in crisscross sequence until all nuts are torqued to half specification. Then repeat the tightening sequence to the full specified torque of: 100 ft. lbs. (135 Nm).

31. Lower vehicle.

32. Check and reset if required, rear wheel camber and toe to preferred specifications.

WHEEL BEARINGS

REMOVAL & INSTALLATION

See Figure 144.

All vehicles are equipped with permanently lubricated and sealed for life rear wheel bearings. There is no periodic lubrication or maintenance recommended for these units.

To evaluate the condition of the rear wheel bearings, remove the wheel and brake drum or rotor and rotate the flanged outer ring of the hub. Excessive roughness or resistance to rotation may indicate dirt intrusion or wheel bearing failure. If the rear wheel bearings exhibit these conditions during inspection, the hub and bearing assembly should be replaced. Damaged bearing seals and resulting excessive grease loss may also require bearing replacement. Moderate grease loss from the bearing is considered normal and should not require replacement

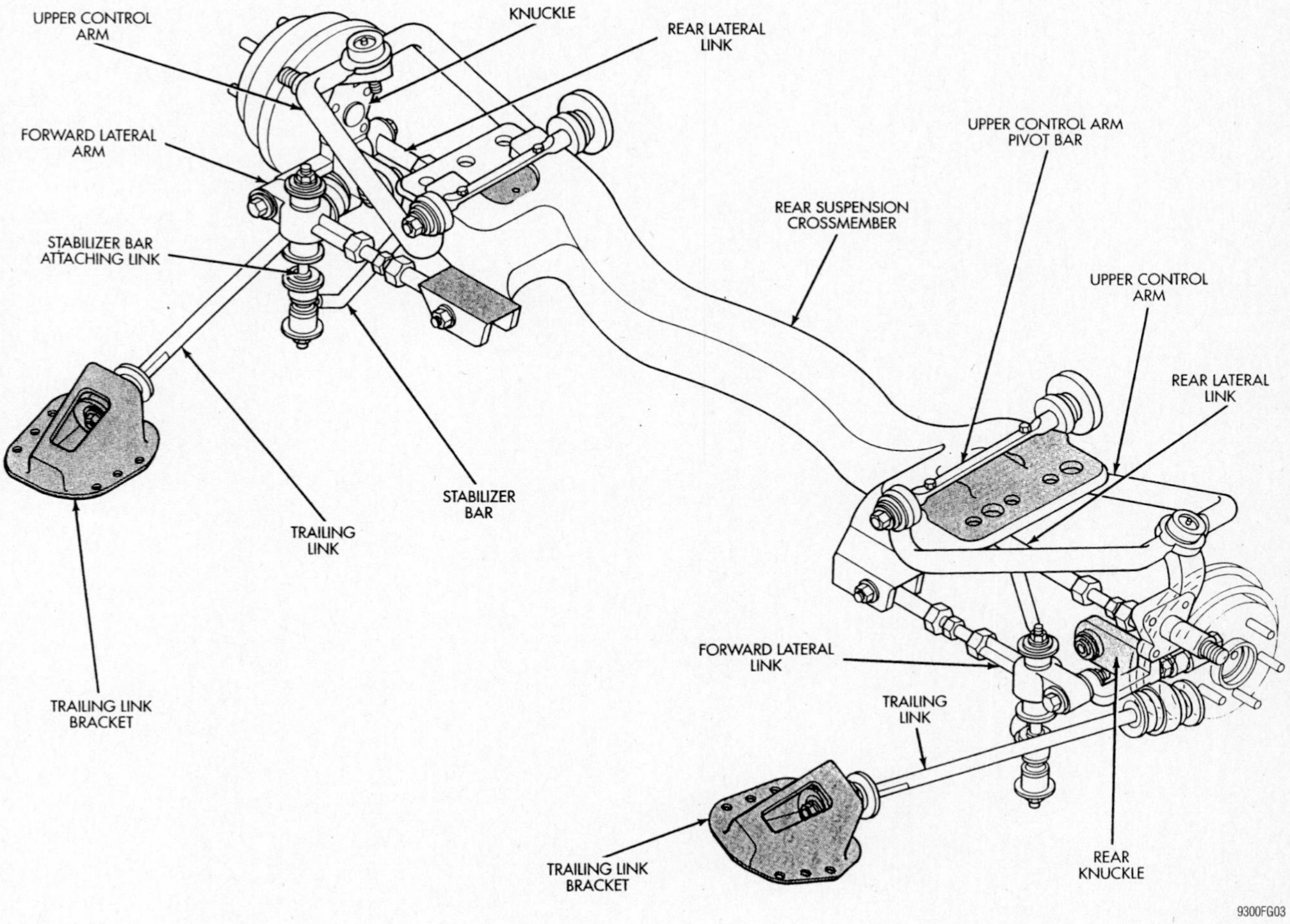

Fig. 144 Independent rear suspension component identification

of the hub and bearing assembly. If service requires removal for inspection or replacement of the rear wheel bearing and hub assembly, use the following procedure.

1. Before servicing the vehicle, refer to the precautions in the beginning of this section.

2. Remove or disconnect the following:

- Rear wheel
- Brake drum, if equipped with drum brakes
- Brake caliper and rotor, if equipped with disc brakes
- Hub dust cap
- Hub nut and discard it
- Hub/bearing assembly by pulling straight off the spindle

To install:

3. Install or connect the following:

- New bearing on the spindle
- Hub using a new nut and torque the nut to 185 ft. lbs. (250 Nm)
- Dust cap
- Brake drum or rotor and caliper
- Rear wheel and torque the lug nuts to 100 ft. lbs. (135 Nm)

ADJUSTMENT

The rear hub and wheel bearing assembly is designed for the life of the vehicle and requires no type of adjustment or periodic maintenance. The bearing is a sealed unit with the wheel hub and can only be removed and/or replaced as one unit.

The following procedure may be used for evaluation of bearing condition:

1. Raise and safely support the vehicle.

2. Remove the rear wheels and brake drums.

3. Turn the hub flange carefully. Excessive roughness, lateral play or resistance to rotation may indicate dirt intrusion or bearing failure.

4. If the rear wheel bearings exhibit the conditions during inspection, the hub and bearing assembly should be replaced.

5. Damaged bearing seals and resulting excessive grease loss may also require bearing replacement. Moderate grease loss from the bearing is considered normal and should not require replacement of the hub and bearing assembly.

DODGE 15

Sprinter

SPECIFICATIONS AND MAINTENANCE CHARTS

ENGINE AND VEHICLE IDENTIFICATION

Engine						
Code ①	Liters	Cu. In.	Cyl.	Fuel Sys.	Engine Type	Eng. Mfg.
4	2.7	164	5	CDI	DOHC	DaimlerChrysler
5	3.0	182	6	CDI	DOHC	DaimlerChrysler
6	3.5	NA	6	MFI	DOHC	DaimlerChrysler

Model Year	
Code ②	Year
5	2005
6	2006
7	2007

CDI: Common Rail Direct Injection

MFI: Multi-Port Fuel Injection

DOHC: Dual Overhead Camshaft

① 8th position of VIN

② 10th position of VIN

22043_SPRI_C0001

GENERAL ENGINE SPECIFICATIONS

Year	Model	Engine Displ. Liters	Engine VIN	Net Horsepower @ rpm	Net Torque @ rpm (ft. lbs.)	Bore x Stroke (in.)	Comp. Ratio	Oil Pressure @ rpm
2005	Sprinter	2.7	4	154@3800	243@1600-2400	3.46x3.48	18:1	NA
2006	Sprinter	2.7	4	154@3800	243@1600-2400	3.46x3.48	18:1	NA
2007	Sprinter	3.0	5	215@4200	376@1800	3.26x3.62	18:1	52@3000
		3.5	6	254@5900	250@2500	NA	NA	NA

NA: Not Available

22043_SPRI_C0002

GASOLINE ENGINE TUNE-UP SPECIFICATIONS

Year	Engine Displ. Liters	Engine VIN	Spark Plug Gap (in.)	Ignition Timing (deg.)	Fuel Pump (psi)	Idle Speed (rpm)	Valve Clearance	
							Intake	Exhaust
2007	3.5	6	0.031	①	NA	①	HYD	HYD

Note: The information on the Vehicle Emission Control label must be used, if different from the figures in this chart.

HYD: Hydraulic

① Ignition timing and idle speed are controlled by the PCM. No adjustment is necessary.

22043_SPRI_C0003

DIESEL ENGINE TUNE-UP SPECIFICATIONS

Year	Engine Displ. Liters	Engine VIN	Valve Clearance Intake (in.)	Valve Clearance Exhaust (in.)	Injection Pump Setting (deg.)	Injection Nozzle Pressure (psi) New	Injection Nozzle Pressure (psi) Used	Idle Speed (rpm)	Cranking Compression Pressure (psi)
2005	2.7	4	HYD	HYD	NA	NA	NA	NA	NA
2006	2.7	4	HYD	HYD	NA	NA	NA	NA	NA
2007	3.0	5	HYD	HYD	①	②	②	620	392-464

NOTE: The Vehicle Emission Control Information label often reflects specification changes made during production.

The label figures must be used if they differ from those in this chart

HYD: Hydraulic

① Driven by camshaft, requires no timing

② 2,900-23,205 psi

22043_SPRI_C0004

CAPACITIES

Year	Model	Engine Displ. Liters	Engine VIN	Engine Oil with Filter	Transmission (pts.) Man.	Transmission (pts.) Auto.**	Transfer Case (pts.)	Drive Axle Front (pts.)	Drive Axle Rear (pts.)	Fuel Tank① (gal.)	Cooling System (qts.)
2005	Sprinter	2.7	4	9.5	—	16.3	—	—	4.0	26.4	10.5
2006	Sprinter	2.7	4	9.5	—	16.3	—	—	4.0	26.4	10.5
2007	Sprinter	3.0	5	13.2	—	16.3	—	3.6	4.4	26.4	10.75
		3.5	6	10	—	16.3	—	3.6	4.4	26.4	7.4

① Reserve Tank: 2.8 gal.

**Overhaul

22043_SPRI_C0005

FLUID SPECIFICATIONS

Year	Model	Engine Displacement Liters	Engine ID/VIN	Engine Oil	Auto. Trans.	Front & Rear Axle	Power Steering Fluid	Brake Master Cylinder
2005	Sprinter	2.7	4	15W-40 HD Diesel Engine Oil	Shell ATF 3403/M-115 or equivalent	Shell Spirax MB90 or Mopar® P/N 4874469	Mobil ATF-D or equivalent	DOT 4
2006	Sprinter	2.7	4	15W-40 HD Diesel Engine Oil	Shell ATF 3403/M-115 or equivalent	Shell Spirax MB90 or Mopar® P/N 4874469	Mobil ATF-D or equivalent	DOT 4
2007	Sprinter	3.0	5	5W-40	Shell ATF 3403/M-115 or equivalent	Shell Spirax MB90 or Mopar® P/N 05130603AA	Mopar® Hydraulic System/Power Steering Fluid (MS-10838)	DOT 4
		3.5	6	5W-40	Shell ATF 3403/M-115 or equivalent	Shell Spirax MB90 or Mopar® P/N 05130603AA	Mopar® Hydraulic System/Power Steering Fluid (MS-10838)	DOT 4

DOT: Department Of Transpotation

22043_SPRI_C0006

VALVE SPECIFICATIONS

Year	Engine Displ. Liters	Engine VIN	Seat Angle (deg.)	Face Angle (deg.)	Spring Test Pressure (lbs. @ in.)	Spring Installed Height (in.)	Stem-to-Guide Clearance (in.)		Stem Diameter (in.)	
							Intake	Exhaust	Intake	Exhaust
2005	2.7	4	NA	NA	NA	NA	NA	NA	NA	NA
2006	2.7	4	NA	NA	NA	NA	NA	NA	NA	NA
2007	3.0	5	44.5-45.5	44.5-45.5	NA	NA	0.0008-0.0028	0.0019-0.0039	0.2341-0.2353	0.2347-0.2353
	3.5	6	NA	NA	NA	NA	NA	NA	NA	NA

NA: Information not available

22043_SPRI_C0007

CAMSHAFT AND BEARING SPECIFICATIONS CHART

All measurements are given in inches.

Year	Engine Displacement Liters	Engine VIN	Journal Diameter	Brg. Oil Clearance	Shaft End-play	Runout	Journal Bore	Lobe Lift	
								Intake	Exhaust
2005	2.7	4	NA	NA	NA	NA	NA	NA	NA
2006	2.7	4	NA	NA	NA	NA	NA	NA	NA
2007	3.0	5	NA	NA	NA	NA	NA	NA	NA
	3.5	6	NA	NA	NA	NA	NA	NA	NA

NA: Information not available

22043_SPRI_C0008

CRANKSHAFT AND CONNECTING ROD SPECIFICATIONS

All measurements are given in inches.

Year	Engine Displ. Liters	Engine VIN	Crankshaft				Connecting Rod		
			Main Brg. Journal Dia.	Main Brg. Oil Clearance	Shaft End-play	Thrust on No.	Journal Diameter	Oil Clearance	Side Clearance
2005	2.7	4	NA	NA	NA	NA	NA	NA	NA
2006	2.7	4	NA	NA	NA	NA	NA	NA	NA
2007	3.0	5	2.9800-2.9900	0.0012-0.0023	0.0040-0.0100	NA	NA	NA	NA
	3.5	6	NA	NA	NA	NA	NA	NA	NA

NA: Information not available

22043_SPRI_C0009

PISTON AND RING SPECIFICATIONS

All measurements are given in inches.

Year	Engine Displ. Liters	Engine VIN	Piston Clearance	Ring Gap			Ring Side Clearance		
				Top Compression	Bottom Compression	Oil Control	Top Compression	Bottom Compression	Oil Control
2005	2.7	4	NA	0.0090-0.0240	0.0190-0.0800	0.0100-0.0600	0.0047-0.0063	0.0019-0.0035	0.0011-0.0027
2006	2.7	4	NA	0.0090-0.0240	0.0190-0.0800	0.0100-0.0600	0.0047-0.0063	0.0019-0.0035	0.0011-0.0027
2007	3.0	5	NA	0.0048-0.0063	0.0026-0.0044	0.0012-0.0028	0.0048-0.0063	0.0026-0.0044	0.0012-0.0028
	3.5	6	NA	NA	NA	NA	NA	NA	NA

NA: Information not available

22043_SPRI_C0010

TORQUE SPECIFICATIONS

All readings in ft. lbs.

Year	Engine Displ. Liters	Engine VIN	Cylinder Head Bolts	Main Bearing Bolts	Rod Bearing Bolts	Crankshaft Damper Bolts	Flywheel Bolts	Manifold		Spark Plugs	Oil Pan Drain Plug
								Intake	Exhaust		
2005	2.7	4	①	②	③	④	⑤	12	21	-	35
2006	2.7	4	①	②	③	④	⑤	12	21	-	35
2007	3.0	5	⑥	33	⑦	⑧	33	12	18	-	35
	3.5	6	⑨	⑩	⑩	148	⑪	NA	8	17	22

① Refer to procedure for illustration
- Step 1: Tighten bolts 44 ft. lbs. (60 Nm)
- Step 2: Tighten bolts an addt'l 90 degrees
- Step 3: Tighten bolts an addt'l 90 degrees again

② Refer to procedure for illustration
- Step 1: Tighten bolts to 41 ft. lbs. (55 Nm)
- Step 2: Tighten bolts an addt'l 90 degrees

③ Step 1: Tighten bolts to 44 inch lbs. (5 Nm)
- Step 2: Tighten bolts to 18 ft. lbs. (25 Nm)
- Step 3: Tighten bolts an addt'l 90 degrees

④ 240 ft. lbs. + 90 degrees

⑤ 33 ft. lbs. + 90 degrees

⑥ Refer to procedure for illustration
- Step 1: Tighten bolts 1-8 to 44 ft. lbs. (60 Nm)
- Step 2: Tighten bolts 9-10 to 15 ft. lbs. (20 Nm)
- Step 3: Tighten bolts 1-8 an addt'l 90 degrees
- Step 4: Verify bolts at 15 ft. lbs. (20 Nm)
- Step 5: Tighten bolts 1-8 an addt'l 90 degrees

⑦ Short Arm:
- Step 1: 11 ft. lbs. (15 Nm)
- Step 2: 22 ft. lbs. (30 Nm)
- Step 3: Plus 90 degrees
- Step 4: Plus 90 degrees again

⑦ (cont'd) Long Arm:
- Step 1: 15 ft. lbs. (20 Nm)
- Step 2: 30 ft. lbs. (40 Nm)
- Step 3: Plus 90 degrees
- Step 4: Plus 90 degrees again

⑧ 224 ft. lbs. + 90 degrees

⑨ Cyl. Head to Timing Cover bolts:
- 26 ft. lbs. + 90 degrees

All Remaining bolts:
- 15 ft. lbs. + 90 degrees

⑩ 20 ft. lbs. + 90 degrees

⑪ Step 1: Tighten bolts to 15 ft. lbs. (20 Nm)
- Step 2: Tighten bolts to 33 ft. lbs. (45 Nm)
- Step 3: Tighten bolts an addt'l 90 degrees

22043_SPRI_C0011

WHEEL ALIGNMENT

Year	Model		Caster Range (+/-Deg.)	Caster Preferred Setting (Deg.)	Camber Range (+/-Deg.)	Camber Preferred Setting (Deg.)	Toe-in (deg.)
2005	Sprinter	F	0.75	①	0.75	②	0.25+/-0.10
		R	—	—	③	0.00	0.00+/-0.25
2006	Sprinter	F	0.75	①	0.75	②	0.25+/-0.10
		R	—	—	③	0.00	0.00+/-0.25
2007	Sprinter	F	④	④	0.30	1.00	0.20+/-0.10
		R	—	—	NA	NA	NA

NA: Not Available

① 2500 Series - 118" wheelbase: 1.00
2500 Series - 140" & 158" wheelbase: 3.00
3500 Series: 0.50

② 2500 Series: 0.50
3500 Series: 1.00

③ -0.66 to +0.33

④ Caster is not adjustable on these vehicles

22043_SPRI_C0012

TIRE, WHEEL AND BALL JOINT SPECIFICATIONS

Year	Model	OEM Tires Standard	OEM Tires Optional	Tire Pressures (psi) Front	Tire Pressures (psi) Rear	Wheel Size	Ball Joint Inspection	Lug Nut Torque (ft. lbs.)
2005	Sprinter	P225/70R15	-	①	①	①	NA	②
2006	Sprinter	P225/70R15	-	①	①	①	NA	②
2007	Sprinter	LT245/75R16	LT265/75R16	①	①	①	NA	②

OEM: Original Equipment Manufacturer

① See placard on vehicle

② 2500 Series: 167-187 ft. lbs.
3500 Series: 130-150 ft. lbs.

NA: Not Available

22043_SPRI_C0013

BRAKE SPECIFICATIONS

All measurements in inches unless noted

Year	Model		Brake Disc① Original Thickness	Brake Disc① Minimum Thickness	Brake Disc① Maximum Run-out	Minimum Lining Thickness Front	Minimum Lining Thickness Rear	Brake Caliper Bracket Bolts (ft. lbs.)	Brake Caliper Mounting Bolts (ft. lbs.)
2005	Sprinter	F	0.866	0.748	0.0019	NA	—	125	②
		R	0.866	0.748	0.0039	—	NA	③	②
2006	Sprinter	F	0.866	0.748	0.0019	NA	—	125	②
		R	0.866	0.748	0.0039	—	NA	③	②
2007	Sprinter	F	1.102	0.984	0.0011	NA	—	59	⑥
		R	④	⑤	0.0019	—	NA	59	⑥

F - Front

R - Rear

① Brake Disc Rotors cannot be resurfaced. They must be replaced.

② M8 bolt: 18 ft. lbs. (25 Nm)
M10 bolt: 22 ft. lbs. (30 Nm)

③ M12 bolt: 66 ft. lbs. (90 Nm)
M14 bolt: 125 ft. lbs. (170 Nm

④ SRW: 0.620
DRW: 1.102

⑤ SRW: 0.550
DRW: 0.984

⑥ M8 bolt: 25 ft. lbs. (34 Nm)
M10 bolt: 48 ft. lbs. (65 Nm)

22043_SPRI_C0014

SCHEDULED MAINTENANCE INTERVALS
2005-06 Sprinter

TO BE SERVICED	TYPE OF SERVICE	VEHICLE MILEAGE INTERVAL (x1000)												
		7	14	21	28	35	42	49	56	63	70	77	84	91
Engine oil & filter	R	✓	✓	✓	✓	✓	✓	✓	✓	✓	✓	✓	✓	✓
Power Steering Fluid	S/I	✓	✓	✓	✓	✓	✓	✓	✓	✓	✓	✓	✓	✓
Windshield washer system	S/I	✓	✓	✓	✓	✓	✓	✓	✓	✓	✓	✓	✓	✓
Brake hoses & linings	S/I	✓	✓	✓	✓	✓	✓	✓	✓	✓	✓	✓	✓	✓
Engine air filter	I	✓	✓	✓	✓	✓	✓	✓	✓	✓	✓	✓	✓	✓
Engine air filter	R		✓		✓		✓		✓		✓		✓	
Cabin Air Filter	R	✓	✓	✓	✓	✓	✓	✓	✓	✓	✓	✓	✓	✓
Fuel Filter	R	✓	✓	✓	✓	✓	✓	✓	✓	✓	✓	✓	✓	✓
Parking Brake adjustment	S/I	✓	✓	✓	✓	✓	✓	✓	✓	✓	✓	✓	✓	✓
Chassis & Body bolts	S/I	✓												
Drive axle lubricant	R				✓				✓				✓	
Accessory drive belt	S/I		✓		✓		✓		✓		✓		✓	
Tire pressures	S/I	✓	✓	✓	✓	✓	✓	✓	✓	✓	✓	✓	✓	✓
Automatic trans. fluid and filter	R	Every 80,000 miles												
Engine coolant	R	Every 60,000 miles												

R: Replace S/I: Service or Inspect C/L: Clean and lubricate I/R: Inspect and rerplace if necessary

In addition to the above maintenance work, the following should be performed:

Change the brake fluid every 2 years

Engine coolant every 5 years (if 100,000 miles has not already been achieved)

22043_SPRI_C0015

SCHEDULED MAINTENANCE INTERVALS
2007 Sprinter

TO BE SERVICED	TYPE OF SERVICE	VEHICLE MILEAGE INTERVAL (x1000)												
		10	20	30	40	50	60	70	80	90	100	110	120	130
Engine oil & filter	R	✓	✓	✓	✓	✓	✓	✓	✓	✓	✓	✓	✓	✓
Tires	Rotate	✓	✓	✓	✓	✓	✓	✓	✓	✓	✓	✓	✓	✓
Power Steering Fluid	S/I	✓	✓	✓	✓	✓	✓	✓	✓	✓	✓	✓	✓	✓
Windshield washer system	S/I	✓	✓	✓	✓	✓	✓	✓	✓	✓	✓	✓	✓	✓
Brake hoses & linings	S/I			✓			✓			✓			✓	
Engine air filter	I	✓	✓	✓	✓	✓	✓	✓	✓	✓	✓	✓	✓	✓
Engine air filter	R		✓		✓		✓		✓		✓		✓	
Cabin Air Filter	R			✓			✓			✓			✓	
Battery	S/I			✓			✓			✓			✓	
Fuel Filter	R	✓	✓	✓	✓	✓	✓	✓	✓	✓	✓	✓	✓	✓
Parking Brake adjustment	S/I	✓	✓	✓	✓	✓	✓	✓	✓	✓	✓	✓	✓	✓
Chassis & Body bolts	S/I			✓										
Spark Plugs (3.5L)	R						✓						✓	
Accessory drive belt	I/R						✓						✓	
Diesel Particle Filter (3.0L)	R									✓				
Tire pressures	S/I	✓	✓	✓	✓	✓	✓	✓	✓	✓	✓	✓	✓	✓
Automatic trans. fluid and filter	R						✓						✓	
Engine coolant	R	Every 180,000 miles												

R: Replace S/I: Service or Inspect C/L: Clean and lubricate I/R: Inspect and rerplace if necessary

In addition to the above maintenance work, the following should be performed:

Change the brake fluid every 2 years

Engine coolant every 10 years (if 180,000 miles has not already been achieved)

3.5L Engines: Accessory drive belt should be replaced at 60,000 miles

Change the rear axle fluid every 180,000 miles or 10 years

22043_SPRI_C0016

PRECAUTIONS

Before servicing any vehicle, please be sure to read all of the following precautions, which deal with personal safety, prevention of component damage, and important points to take into consideration when servicing a motor vehicle:

- Never open, service or drain the radiator or cooling system when the engine is hot; serious burns can occur from the steam and hot coolant.
- Observe all applicable safety precautions when working around fuel. Whenever servicing the fuel system, always work in a well-ventilated area. Do not allow fuel spray or vapors to come in contact with a spark, open flame, or excessive heat (a hot drop light, for example). Keep a dry chemical fire extinguisher near the work area. Always keep fuel in a container specifically designed for fuel storage; also, always properly seal fuel containers to avoid the possibility of fire or explosion. Refer to the additional fuel system precautions later in this section.
- Fuel injection systems often remain pressurized, even after the engine has been turned **OFF**. The fuel system pressure must be relieved before disconnecting any fuel lines. Failure to do so may result in fire and/or personal injury.
- Brake fluid often contains polyglycol ethers and polyglycols. Avoid contact with the eyes and wash your hands thoroughly after handling brake fluid. If you do get brake fluid in your eyes, flush your eyes with clean, running water for 15 minutes. If eye irritation persists, or if you have taken brake fluid internally, IMMEDIATELY seek medical assistance.
- The EPA warns that prolonged contact with used engine oil may cause a number of skin disorders, including cancer. You should make every effort to minimize your exposure to used engine oil. Protective gloves should be worn when changing oil. Wash your hands and any other exposed skin areas as soon as possible after exposure to used engine oil. Soap and water, or waterless hand cleaner should be used.
- All new vehicles are now equipped with an air bag system, often referred to as a Supplemental Restraint System (SRS) or Supplemental Inflatable Restraint (SIR) system. The system must be disabled before performing service on or around system components, steering column, instrument panel components, wiring and sensors. Failure to follow safety and disabling procedures could result in accidental air bag deployment, possible personal injury and unnecessary system repairs.
- Always wear safety goggles when working with, or around, the air bag system. When carrying a non-deployed air bag, be sure the bag and trim cover are pointed away from your body. When placing a non-deployed air bag on a work surface, always face the bag and trim cover upward, away from the surface. This will reduce the motion of the module if it is accidentally deployed. Refer to the additional air bag system precautions later in this section.
- Clean, high quality brake fluid from a sealed container is essential to the safe and proper operation of the brake system. You should always buy the correct type of brake fluid for your vehicle. If the brake fluid becomes contaminated, completely flush the system with new fluid. Never reuse any brake fluid. Any brake fluid that is removed from the system should be discarded. Also, do not allow any brake fluid to come in contact with a painted surface; it will damage the paint.
- Never operate the engine without the proper amount and type of engine oil; doing so WILL result in severe engine damage.
- Timing belt maintenance is extremely important. Many models utilize an interference-type, non-freewheeling engine. If the timing belt breaks, the valves in the cylinder head may strike the pistons, causing potentially serious (also time-consuming and expensive) engine damage. Refer to the maintenance interval charts for the recommended replacement interval for the timing belt, and to the timing belt section for belt replacement and inspection.
- Disconnecting the negative battery cable on some vehicles may interfere with the functions of the on-board computer system(s) and may require the computer to undergo a relearning process once the negative battery cable is reconnected.
- When servicing drum brakes, only disassemble and assemble one side at a time, leaving the remaining side intact for reference.
- Only an MVAC-trained, EPA-certified automotive technician should service the air conditioning system or its components.

BRAKES — ANTI-LOCK BRAKE SYSTEM (ABS)

GENERAL INFORMATION

PRECAUTIONS

- Certain components within the ABS system are not intended to be serviced or repaired individually.
- Do not use rubber hoses or other parts not specifically specified for and ABS system. When using repair kits, replace all parts included in the kit. Partial or incorrect repair may lead to functional problems and require the replacement of components.
- Lubricate rubber parts with clean, fresh brake fluid to ease assembly. Do not use shop air to clean parts; damage to rubber components may result.
- Use only DOT 3 brake fluid from an unopened container.
- If any hydraulic component or line is removed or replaced, it may be necessary to bleed the entire system.
- A clean repair area is essential. Always clean the reservoir and cap thoroughly before removing the cap. The slightest amount of dirt in the fluid may plug an orifice and impair the system function. Perform repairs after components have been thoroughly cleaned; use only denatured alcohol to clean components. Do not allow ABS components to come into contact with any substance containing mineral oil; this includes used shop rags.
- The Anti-Lock control unit is a microprocessor similar to other computer units in the vehicle. Ensure that the ignition switch is **OFF** before removing or installing controller harnesses. Avoid static electricity discharge at or near the controller.
- If any arc welding is to be done on the vehicle, the control unit should be unplugged before welding operations begin.

SPEED SENSORS

REMOVAL & INSTALLATION

2005–06 Models

Front

1. Raise and safely support the vehicle.
2. Remove the front wheel.
3. Pull the wheel speed sensor out of the wheel hub.
4. If replacement is necessary, cut the speed sensor cable at an easily accessible point.
5. Remove the clamping sleeve from the knuckle if sensor is being replaced.

To install:

6. If the sensor is being replaced, connect the sensor cables with shrink-fit tubing.
7. Install the clamping sleeve into the knuckle, if removed.
8. Install the speed sensor all the way into the wheel hub.

➡Speed sensor will self adjust when the vehicle is moved.

9. Install the front wheel.
10. Lower the vehicle.

Rear

1. Raise and safely support the vehicle.
2. Remove the rear wheel.
3. Pull the wheel sensor out of the mounting hole in the axle support tube.
4. If replacement is necessary, cut the speed sensor cable at an easily accessible point.
5. Remove the clamping sleeve from the knuckle if sensor is being replaced.

To install:

6. If the sensor is being replaced, connect the sensor cables with shrink-fit tubing.
7. Install the clamping sleeve into the knuckle, if removed.
8. Install the speed sensor all the way into the wheel hub.

➡Speed sensor will self adjust when the vehicle is moved.

9. Install the rear wheel.
10. Lower the vehicle.

2007 Models

Front

See Figure 1.

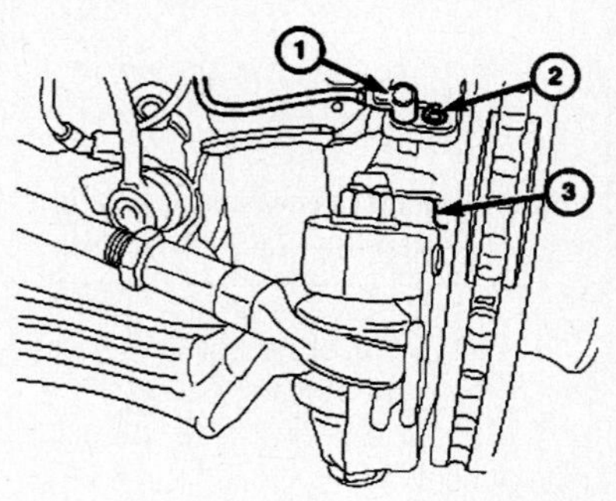

Fig. 1 Remove the nut (2) and pull the speed sensor (1) from the steering knuckle (3)—2007 Models

1. Raise and safely support the vehicle.
2. Remove the speed sensor mounting nuts.
3. Remove the speed sensor from the knuckle.

To install:

4. Install the speed sensor to the steering knuckle and tighten the nut to 71 inch lbs. (8 Nm).
5. Install the front wheel.
6. Lower the vehicle.

Rear

1. Raise and safely support the vehicle.
2. Remove the speed sensor mounting bolt from the axle tube.
3. Remove the speed sensor.
4. Remove the sensor wire from the tie strap and disconnect the electrical connector.

To install:

5. Install the wheel speed sensor in the axle tube and tighten the mounting bolt to 71 inch lbs. (8 Nm).
6. Install the sensor wire into the routing clips and install new tie straps.
7. Reconnect the electrical connector.
8. Lower the vehicle.

BRAKES — BLEEDING THE BRAKE SYSTEM

BLEEDING PROCEDURE

BLEEDING PROCEDURE

1. Remove reservoir filler caps and fill reservoir.
2. If the calipers or wheel cylinders were overhauled, open all caliper and wheel cylinder bleed screws. Then close each bleed screw as fluid starts to drip from it. Top off master cylinder reservoir once more before proceeding.
3. Attach one end of the bleed hose to the bleed screw and insert opposite end in glass container partially filled with brake fluid. Be sure the end of bleed hose is immersed in fluid.
4. Open up the bleeder, then have a helper press down the brake pedal. Once the pedal is down, close the bleeder. Repeat bleeding until fluid stream is clear and free of bubbles. Then move to the next wheel.

BRAKES — FRONT DISC BRAKES

⁂ CAUTION

Dust and dirt accumulating on brake parts during normal use may contain asbestos fibers from production or aftermarket brake linings. Breathing excessive concentrations of asbestos fibers can cause serious bodily harm. Exercise care when servicing brake parts. Do not sand or grind brake lining unless equipment used is designed to contain the dust residue. Do not clean brake parts with compressed air or by dry brushing. Cleaning should be done by dampening the brake components with a fine mist of water, then wiping the brake components clean with a dampened cloth. Dispose of cloth and all residue containing asbestos fibers in an impermeable container with the appropriate label. Follow practices prescribed by the Occupational Safety and Health Administration (OSHA) and the Environmental Protection Agency (EPA) for the handling, processing, and disposing of dust or debris that may contain asbestos fibers.

BRAKE CALIPER

REMOVAL & INSTALLATION

2005–06 Models

1. Unscrew the cap from the brake fluid reservoir.
2. Raise and safely support the vehicle.
3. Remove the front wheel.
4. Remove the wear indicator.
5. Remove the brake hose at the brake caliper.

➡Cap the ends of the brake lines.

6. Remove the brake caliper guide bolts and remove the brake caliper.

To install:

7. Install the brake caliper and tighten the guide pin bolts to 18 ft. lbs. (25 Nm).
8. Install the brake hose to the brake caliper and tighten the bolt to 10 ft. lbs. (14 Nm).
9. Install the wear indicator and tighten the bolt to 89 inch lbs. (10 Nm).

10. Bleed and brake system and check for leaks.
11. Install the front wheel.
12. Lower the vehicle.

2007 Models

1. Unscrew the cap from the brake fluid reservoir.
2. Raise and safely support the vehicle.
3. Remove the front wheel.
4. Remove the wear indicator.
5. Remove the brake hose at the brake caliper.

➡Cap the ends of the brake lines.

6. Remove the brake caliper guide bolts and remove the brake caliper.

To install:

7. Install the brake caliper to the brake caliper adapter. Tighten the guide pin bolts as follows:
   a. M8 bolts to 24 ft. lbs. (34 Nm).
   b. M10 bolts to 48 ft. lbs. (65 Nm).
8. Install the brake hose to the brake caliper and tighten to 10 ft. lbs. (14 Nm).

➡Ensure the brake hose is not twisted.

9. Install the wear indicator and tighten the bolt to 71 inch lbs. (8 Nm).
10. Bleed and brake system and check for leaks.
11. Install the front wheel.
12. Lower the vehicle.

DISC BRAKE PADS

REMOVAL & INSTALLATION

2005–06 Models

See Figure 2.

1. Unscrew the cap from the brake fluid reservoir.
2. Raise and safely support the vehicle.

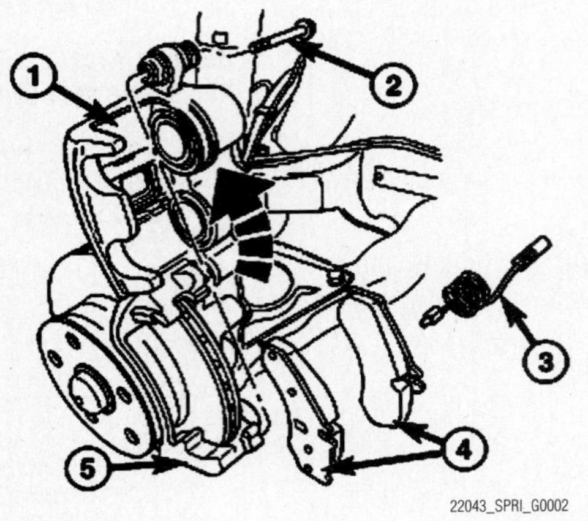

Fig. 2 Front brake components—Caliper (1), guide bolt (2), wear indicator (3), brake pads (4), caliper adapter (5)—2005–06 Models

3. Remove the front wheel.
4. Remove the wear indicator.
5. Remove the lower brake caliper guide pin bolt.
6. Rotate the caliper assembly upwards and remove the brake pads.

To install:

7. Install the brake pads to the brake caliper.
8. Install the wear indicator and tighten the bolt to 89 inch lbs. (10 Nm).
9. Rotate the brake caliper down to the brake caliper adapter and tighten the guide pin bolt to 18 ft. lbs. (25 Nm).
10. Bleed and brake system and check for leaks.
11. Install the front wheel.
12. Lower the vehicle.

2007 Models

1. Unscrew the cap from the brake fluid reservoir.
2. Raise and safely support the vehicle.
3. Remove the front wheel.
4. Remove the wear indicator.
5. Remove the lower brake caliper guide pin bolts and remove the caliper.

⁂ WARNING

Support the caliper assembly. Do not let the caliper hang by the brake hose.

6. Remove the brake pads from the caliper.

To install:

7. Install the brake pads.
8. Install the brake caliper to the brake caliper adapter. Tighten the guide pin bolts as follows:
   a. M8 bolts to 24 ft. lbs. (34 Nm).
   b. M10 bolts to 48 ft. lbs. (65 Nm).
9. Install the wear indicator and tighten the bolt to 89 inch lbs. (10 Nm).
10. Install the front wheels.
11. Lower the vehicle.

BRAKES

REAR DISC BRAKES

⁂ CAUTION

Dust and dirt accumulating on brake parts during normal use may contain asbestos fibers from production or aftermarket brake linings. Breathing excessive concentrations of asbestos fibers can cause serious bodily harm. Exercise care when servicing brake parts. Do not sand or grind brake lining unless equipment used is designed to contain the dust residue. Do not clean brake parts with compressed air or by dry brushing. Cleaning should be done by dampening the brake components with a fine mist of water, then wiping the brake components clean with a dampened cloth. Dispose of cloth and all residue containing asbestos fibers in an impermeable container with the appropriate label. Follow practices prescribed by the Occupational Safety and Health Administration (OSHA) and the Environmental Protection Agency (EPA) for the handling, processing, and disposing of dust or debris that may contain asbestos fibers.

BRAKE CALIPER

REMOVAL & INSTALLATION

2005–06 Models

1. Unscrew the cap from the brake fluid reservoir.
2. Raise and safely support the vehicle.
3. Remove the rear wheel.
4. Remove the wear indicator.
5. Remove the brake hose at the brake caliper.

➡Cap the ends of the brake lines.

6. Remove the brake caliper guide bolts and remove the brake caliper.

To install:

7. Install the brake caliper to the brake caliper adapter. Tighten the guide pin bolts as follows:
   a. M8 bolts to 18 ft. lbs. (25 Nm).
   b. M10 bolts to 22 ft. lbs. (30 Nm).
8. Install the brake hose to the brake caliper and tighten to 10 ft. lbs. (14 Nm).

➡Ensure the brake hose is not twisted.

9. Install the wear indicator and tighten the bolt to 89 inch lbs. (10 Nm).
10. Bleed and brake system and check for leaks.
11. Install the rear wheel.
12. Lower the vehicle.

2007 Models

1. Unscrew the cap from the brake fluid reservoir.
2. Raise and safely support the vehicle.
3. Remove the rear wheel.
4. Remove the wear indicator.
5. Remove the brake hose at the brake caliper.

➡Cap the ends of the brake lines.

6. Remove the brake caliper guide bolts and remove the brake caliper.

To install:

7. Install the brake caliper to the brake caliper adapter. Tighten the guide pin bolts as follows:
   a. M8 bolts to 24 ft. lbs. (34 Nm).
   b. M10 bolts to 48 ft. lbs. (65 Nm).
8. Install the brake hose to the brake caliper and tighten to 10 ft. lbs. (14 Nm).

➡Ensure the brake hose is not twisted.

9. Install the wear indicator and tighten the bolt to 89 inch lbs. (10 Nm).
10. Bleed and brake system and check for leaks.
11. Install the rear wheel.
12. Lower the vehicle.

DISC BRAKE PADS

REMOVAL & INSTALLATION

2005–06 Models

See Figure 3.

1. Unscrew the cap from the brake fluid reservoir.
2. Raise and safely support the vehicle.
3. Remove the rear wheel.
4. Remove the wear indicator.
5. Remove the caliper guide pin bolts.
6. Remove the brake caliper from the caliper adapter.

⁂ WARNING

Support the caliper assembly. Do not let the caliper hang by the brake hose.

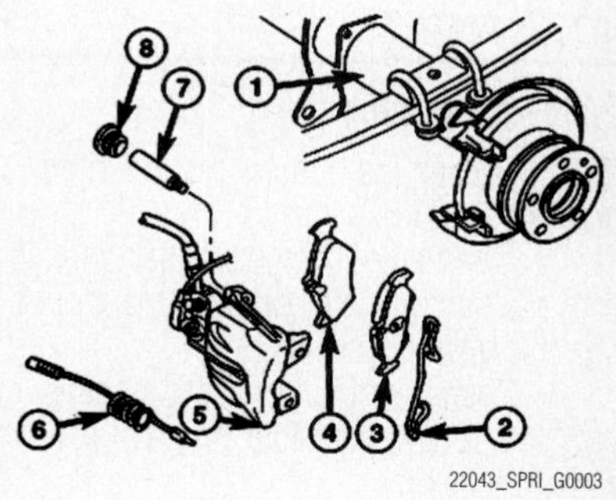

Fig. 3 Rear brake components—Axle (1), retaining spring (2), outboard pads (3), inboard pad (4), caliper (5), wear indicator (6), guide pin bolt (7), dust cap (8)—2005–06 Models

7. Remove the retaining spring.
8. Remove the brake pads.

To install:

9. Install the brake pads to the caliper.
10. Install the wear indicator and tighten the bolt to 89 inch lbs. (10 Nm).
11. Install the brake caliper to the brake caliper adapter. Tighten the guide pin bolts as follows:
    a. M8 bolts to 18 ft. lbs. (25 Nm).
    b. M10 bolts to 22 ft. lbs. (30 Nm).
12. Install the retaining spring.
13. Install the rear wheel.
14. Lower the vehicle.

2007 Models

1. Raise and safely support the vehicle.
2. Remove the rear wheel.
3. Remove the wear indicator.
4. Remove the caliper lower guide pin bolt and raise the caliper upward.
5. Remove the brake pads.

To install:

6. Install the brake pads to the caliper.
7. Install the wear indicator and tighten the bolt to 89 inch lbs. (10 Nm).
8. Install the brake caliper to the brake caliper adapter. Tighten the guide pin bolts as follows:
   a. M8 bolts to 24 ft. lbs. (34 Nm).
   b. M10 bolts to 48 ft. lbs. (65 Nm).
9. Install the rear wheel.
10. Lower the vehicle.

PARKING BRAKE CABLES

ADJUSTMENT

2005–06 Models

1. Loosen the bolts of the mounting brackets.
2. Insert a drill bit or an Allen wrench with a 6 mm diameter between the mounting bracket and front lever.
3. Push the mounting bracket back until the front brake cable is free of play and without tension.
4. Tighten the bolts to the mounting bracket Tighten to 18 ft. lbs. (25 Nm)
5. Remove the 6 mm diameter drill bit or Allen wrench.
6. Tighten the hand brake lever one notch.
7. Clamp the eccentric clockwise until the wheels/disc brake rotors can still be turned with the force of the hand.
8. Tighten the clamp bolt.
9. Release the hand brake lever.
10. Check the wheel for free movement.

2007 Models

Loosen Adjustment

1. Release the load on the parking brake cables at the adjuster nut.
2. Push the cable adjuster all the way in direction of travel to loosen.
3. Adjust the parking brake shoes.
4. Actuate the hand brake lever several times with moderate force, then release and actuate to second notch. Tighten the adjusting nut of the cable adjuster until the rear wheels can just be turned by hand.
5. Actuate and release the park brake lever 3 times. The rear wheels must turn freely and without grinding the brake. If the rear wheels do not turn freely, the adjustment must be repeated.

PARKING BRAKE SHOES

REMOVAL & INSTALLATION

2005–06 Models

1. Raise and safely support the vehicle.
2. Remove the rear wheel.
3. Remove the brake rotor.
4. Disconnect the front parking brake cable form the pulley unit.
5. Using Special Tool 9280, remove the retracting springs.
6. Remove the adjuster.
7. Using Special Tool 9281, remove the pressure springs.
8. Pull the parking brake hoses apart at the bottom and remove them together from the adjuster.

To install:

9. Ensure that the cable lock moves easily before installing shoes. Install the parking brake shoes.
10. Using Special Tool 9280, install the lower retracting spring.
11. Using Special Tool 9281, install the hold down springs.
12. Using Special Tool 9280, install the upper retracting spring.
13. Install the adjuster.
14. Install the front park brake cable to the pulley unit.
15. Install the brake rotor.
16. Turn the adjusting wheel until it is no longer possible to rotate the rear wheel.
17. Loosen the adjusting wheel 3-4 teeth divisions.
18. Inspect the clearance, or a slight drag when rotating the wheel/rear disc brake rotor.
19. Install the rear wheel.
20. Lower the vehicle.
21. Pump the brake pedal several times to check the operation of the brakes before moving vehicle.

2007 Models

See Figure 4.

1. Raise and safely support the vehicle.
2. Remove the rear wheel.
3. Remove the caliper. For additional information, refer to the following section, "Brake Caliper, Removal & Installation."
4. Remove the rotor set screw and remove the brake rotor.
5. Disconnect the front park brake cable from the equalizer.
6. Remove the return springs.
7. Remove the hold down springs.
8. Remove the adjuster spring.
9. Remove the adjuster.
10. Remove the rear park brake shoes.

To install:

11. Install the park brake shoes.
12. Install the hold down springs.
13. Install the return spring.
14. Install the adjuster.
15. Install the adjuster spring.
16. Install the park brake cable to the equalizer.
17. Install the disc brake rotor and install the set screw.
18. Install the caliper adapter.
19. Turn the adjusting wheel until it is no longer possible to rotate the rear wheel.
20. Loosen the adjusting wheel 3-4 teeth divisions.
21. Inspect the clearance, or a slight drag when rotating the wheel/rear disc brake rotor.
22. Install the rear wheel.
23. Lower the vehicle.

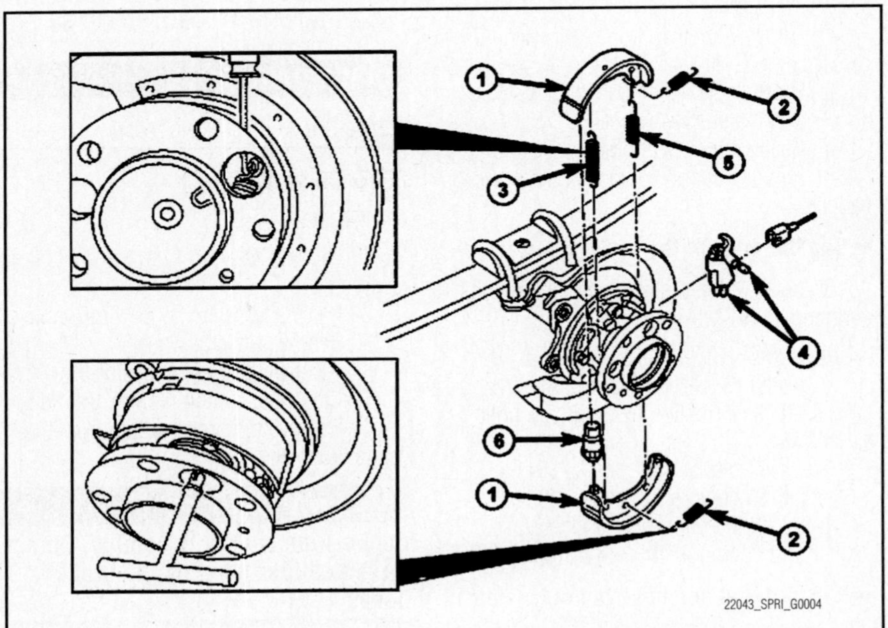

Fig. 4 Exploded view of the parking brake assembly—Brake shoes (1), hold down springs (2), adjuster spring (3), equalizer (4), return springs (5), adjuster (6)—2007 Models

GENERAL INFORMATION

** CAUTION

These vehicles are equipped with an air bag system. The system must be disarmed before performing service on, or around, system components, the steering column, instrument panel components, wiring and sensors. Failure to follow the safety precautions and the disarming procedure could result in accidental air bag deployment, possible injury and unnecessary system repairs.

SERVICE PRECAUTIONS

Disconnect and isolate the battery negative cable before beginning any airbag system component diagnosis, testing, removal, or installation procedures. Allow system capacitor to discharge for two minutes before beginning any component service. This will disable the airbag system. Failure to disable the airbag system may result in accidental airbag deployment, personal injury, or death.

Do not place an intact undeployed airbag face down on a solid surface. The airbag will propel into the air if accidentally deployed and may result in personal injury or death.

When carrying or handling an undeployed airbag, the trim side (face) of the airbag should be pointing towards the body to minimize possibility of injury if accidental deployment occurs. Failure to do this may result in personal injury or death.

Replace airbag system components with OEM replacement parts. Substitute parts may appear interchangeable, but internal differences may result in inferior occupant protection. Failure to do so may result in occupant personal injury or death.

Wear safety glasses, rubber gloves, and long sleeved clothing when cleaning powder residue from vehicle after an airbag deployment. Powder residue emitted from a deployed airbag can cause skin irritation. Flush affected area with cool water if irritation is experienced. If nasal or throat irritation is experienced, exit the vehicle for fresh air until the irritation ceases. If irritation continues, see a physician.

Do not use a replacement airbag that is not in the original packaging. This may result in improper deployment, personal injury, or death.

The factory installed fasteners, screws and bolts used to fasten airbag components have a special coating and are specifically designed for the airbag system. Do not use substitute fasteners. Use only original equipment fasteners listed in the parts catalog when fastener replacement is required.

During, and following, any child restraint anchor service, due to impact event or vehicle repair, carefully inspect all mounting hardware, tether straps, and anchors for proper installation, operation, or damage. If a child restraint anchor is found damaged in any way, the anchor must be replaced. Failure to do this may result in personal injury or death.

Deployed and non-deployed airbags may or may not have live pyrotechnic material within the airbag inflator.

Do not dispose of driver/passenger/curtain airbags or seat belt tensioners unless you are sure of complete deployment. Refer to the Hazardous Substance Control System for proper disposal.

Dispose of deployed airbags and tensioners consistent with state, provincial, local, and federal regulations.

After any airbag component testing or service, do not connect the battery negative cable. Personal injury or death may result if the system test is not performed first.

If the vehicle is equipped with the Occupant Classification System (OCS), do not connect the battery negative cable before performing the OCS Verification Test using the scan tool and the appropriate diagnostic information. Personal injury or death may result if the system test is not performed properly.

Never replace both the Occupant Restraint Controller (ORC) and the Occupant Classification Module (OCM) at the same time. If both require replacement, replace one, then perform the Airbag System test before replacing the other.

Both the ORC and the OCM store Occupant Classification System (OCS) calibration data, which they transfer to one another when one of them is replaced. If both are replaced at the same time, an irreversible fault will be set in both modules and the OCS may malfunction and cause personal injury or death.

If equipped with OCS, the Seat Weight Sensor is a sensitive, calibrated unit and must be handled carefully. Do not drop or handle roughly. If dropped or damaged, replace with another sensor. Failure to do so may result in occupant injury or death.

If equipped with OCS, the front passenger seat must be handled carefully as well. When removing the seat, be careful when setting on floor not to drop. If dropped, the sensor may be inoperative, could result in occupant injury, or possibly death.

If equipped with OCS, when the passenger front seat is on the floor, no one should sit in the front passenger seat. This uneven force may damage the sensing ability of the seat weight sensors. If sat on and damaged, the sensor may be inoperative, could result in occupant injury, or possibly death.

DISARMING THE SYSTEM

Disconnect the negative battery cable. Wait at least two minutes for the system capacitor to discharge for servicing the vehicle.

ARMING THE SYSTEM

Connect the negative battery cable.

CLOCKSPRING CENTERING

1. Place the front wheels in the straight-ahead position.
2. Remove the clockspring from the steering column.
3. Tighten the two clockspring mounting screws all they way into the clockspring case.
4. Rotate the clockspring rotor counterclockwise to the end of its travel.

** WARNING

Do not apply excessive torque to the clockspring rotor.

5. From the end of the counterclockwise travel, rotate the rotor 3–3½ turns clockwise, until the clearance holes in the rotor are aligned with the mounting screws of the clockspring case. The clockspring is now centered.
6. Install the clockspring into the steering column.

AUTOMATIC TRANSMISSION ASSEMBLY

REMOVAL & INSTALLATION

See Figures 5 and 6.

1. Disconnect the negative battery cable.
2. Apply the parking brake and move the transmission gear selector into Neutral **(N)**.
3. Drain the transmission fluid.
4. Remove the starter, 2007 models only.
5. Remove the transmission oil filler pipe by removing the mounting bolts from the cylinder head and transmission housing. Guide the oil filler pipe up and out of the engine compartment.
6. Remove the exhaust heat shield.
7. Remove the retaining bracket and disconnect the driveshaft from the transmission. For additional information, refer to the following section, "Rear Driveshaft, Removal & Installation." Secure the driveshaft out of the way.
8. Remove the transmission cooler lines mounting bracket and disconnect the transmission cooler lines.
9. Disconnect the transmission wiring harness.
10. Disconnect the transmission shift cable.
11. Remove the steering gear from the crossmember and lower. For additional information, refer to the following section, "Power Steering Gear, Removal & Installation."
12. Remove the plastic torque converter access cover.
13. Remove the engine by and hand and remove the torque converter bolts.
14. Support the engine assembly with a suitable jack.

➡Use a wooden block between the oil pan and jack to avoid damage to the engine.

15. Remove the vent hose bracket and tie back to one side.
16. Disconnect the ground strap.
17. Remove the bolts on the underside of the transmission. Two bolts on the top of the transmission must remain in the housing.
18. Place a suitable jack under the transmission assembly and raise it slightly. Secure the transmission to the jack with a strap.
19. Remove the rear engine crossmember.
20. Remove the last two transmission mounting bolts.

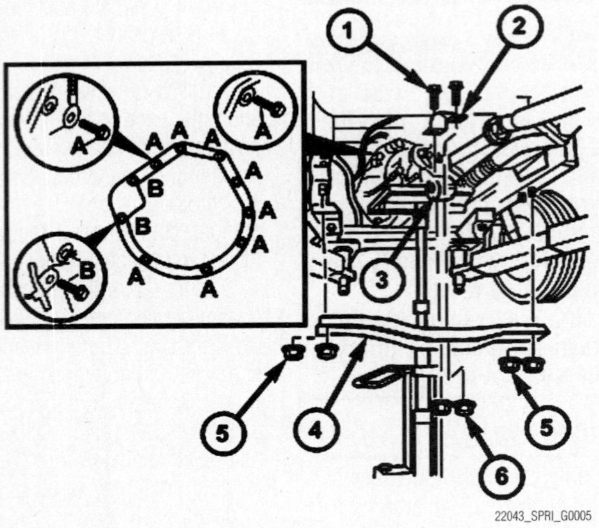

Fig. 5 Remove the transmission mounting bolts (A) first, remove the engine crossmember (4) nuts (5,6), then bolts (1) before removing the final bolts (B)—2005–06 Transmission removal

21. Remove the transmission rearward and then lower. Ensure the torque remains in the bellhousing when the transmission is removed.
22. Remove the torque converter.

To install:

23. If removed, install the torque converter to the transmission. Move the torque covert to the position shown to ensure the bottom bolts are accessible through the inspection cover.
24. Ensure the dowel pins are installed in their correct position at the transmission housing flange.
25. Using a suitable jack, raise the transmission into position. Secure transmission on hydraulic jack with a strap or ask an assistant to hold it.
26. Move the transmission into position on the dowel pins and install the two bolts on the top of the transmission. Tighten the bolts to 28 ft. lbs. (38 Nm).
27. Install the vent hose bracket to the transmission and tighten to 28 ft. lbs. (38 Nm).
28. Install the ground strap to the transmission and tighten the bolt to 28 ft. lbs. (38 Nm).
29. Install the remaining transmission mounting bolts and tighten to 28 ft. lbs. (38 Nm).
30. Install rear engine cross member and tighten the nuts to 33 ft. lbs. (45 Nm).
31. Remove the wooden block supporting the engine and remove the jack.
32. Rotate the engine by and install the torque converter bolts. Install the all only hand tight at first, then tighten them in pairs to 37 ft. lbs. (50 Nm).
33. Install the inspection cover.
34. Install the steering gear assembly.
35. Connect the transmission wiring harness.
36. Connect the shift cable.
37. Install the cooler lines and tighten the bracket bolts to 25 ft. lbs. (34 Nm).
38. Install the exhaust heat shield.
39. Install the retaining bracket.
40. Connect the driveshaft to the transmission. For additional information, refer to the following section, "Rear Driveshaft, Removal & Installation."
41. Install the transmission oil fill pipe. Tighten the mounting bolts to 71 inch lbs. (8 Nm) and install the dipstick.

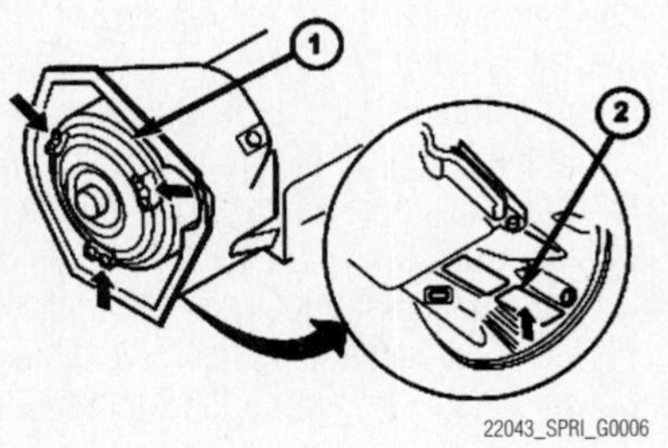

Fig. 6 Check the position of the torque converter (1) through the inspection cover (2) when reinstalling—2005–06 Models

42. Install the transmission oil drain plug and tighten to 15 ft. lbs. (20 Nm).
43. Install the starter, if removed.
44. Lower the vehicle.
45. Refill the transmission with fluid to the correct level.
46. Test drive the vehicle to ensure proper operation and check for leaks.

REAR AXLE HOUSING

REMOVAL & INSTALLATION

See Figure 7.

1. Raise and safely support the vehicle.
2. Position a suitable lifting device under the axle and secure axle to device.
3. Remove the rear wheels.
4. Unplug wear indicator cable.
5. Detach cable connector for brake pad wear indicator.
6. Remove ABS sensor and clamp bushing from mounting bore.

➡The right-hand ABS sensor cable is labeled at the factory with a white tag.

7. Remove the cable ties from the park brake cables. Release the connection cable of brake pad wear indicator and ABS sensor cable up to the relay unit of the parking brake.
8. Remove the brake cables.
9. Remove the parking brake cable at relay unit.
10. Remove bracket for brake cables at rear axle tube.
11. Remove the stabilizer bar from axle brackets. For additional information, refer to the following section, "Stabilizer Bar, Removal & Installation."
12. Remove the shock absorber mounting bolts from the rear axle.
13. Remove the ALB lever from the rear axle bracket.
14. Pull the vent line of the rear axle out of the frame.
15. Remove the driveshaft. For additional information, refer to the following section, "Rear Driveshaft, Removal & Installation."
16. Remove the brake calipers. For additional information, refer to the following section, "Brake Caliper, Removal & Installation."
17. Remove the U-brackets and plates.
18. Remove the axle from the vehicle.

To install:

19. Raise the rear axle into position.
20. Using new nuts, install the plates and U-brackets and tighten the nuts to 125 ft. lbs. (170 Nm).
21. Install the driveshaft.

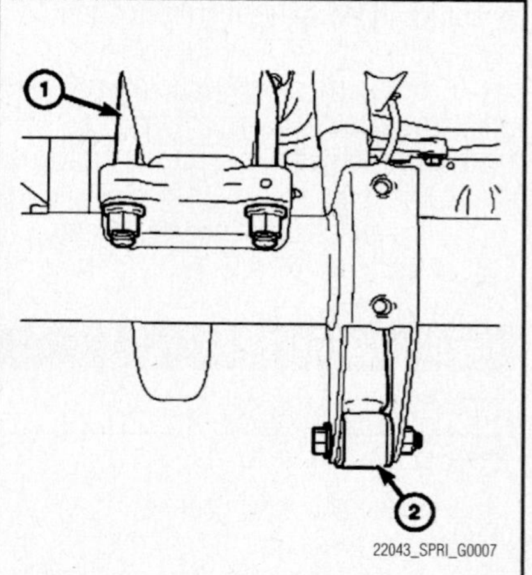

Fig. 7 Remove the lower shock mounting bolts (2) and U-Bolts (1) to remove the rear axle assembly.

➡When installing the driveshaft, the joint arrows must be flush and must point towards the frame floor. Tighten the driveshaft in this position.

22. Install the ALB lever to axle bracket using a new nut and tighten to 25 ft. lbs. (34 Nm).
23. Install the shock absorber-to-rear axle mounting bolts.
24. Install the stabilizer bar-to-rear axle mounting bolts.
25. Install the brake calipers with adapters and lines.
26. Install the brake hoses and hold-down clips.
27. Install and adjust the parking brake cables.
28. Install the connection cable of brake pad wear indicator and ABS sensor cable up to the relay unit of the parking brake.
29. Install new cable ties to the park brake cables.
30. Install the ABS sensor and clamp bushing to mounting bore.
31. Attach the connector cable for brake pad wear indicator.
32. Plug in the cable of brake pad wear indicator.
33. Install the rear wheels.
34. Fill the rear axle with fluid to the correct level.
35. Remove the jack from underneath the axle.
36. Lower the vehicle.

REAR AXLE SHAFT, BEARING & SEAL

REMOVAL & INSTALLATION

See Figures 8 through 10.

1. Raise and safely support the vehicle.
2. Drain the rear differential.
3. Remove the brake caliper, rotor and parking brakes.
4. Remove the axle flange plug snap ring.
5. Tap the axle end plug loose from the axle flange with a hammer and punch. Pull the plug out of the axle flange.
6. Remove the axle bearing bolts from the axle.
7. Remove the axle shaft assembly from the axle.
8. Press the axle shaft out of the flange and bearing.

To install:

9. Coat the axle splines with Mopar®® Thread Sealant or equivalent.
10. Press the axle shaft into the bearing and axle flange using a shop press.
11. Install a new plug in the axle flange.
12. Install the axle flange plug snap ring.
13. Install the axle shaft assembly into the vehicle.
14. Install the axle bearing bolts.
15. Install the brake components.

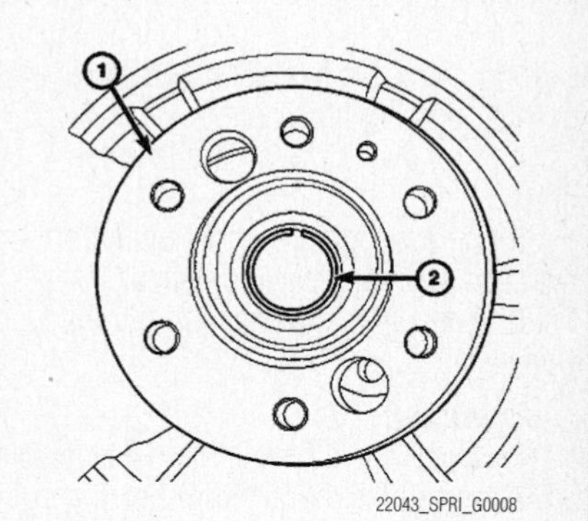

Fig. 8 Remove the axle flange (1) plug snap ring (2)—Rear axle shaft removal

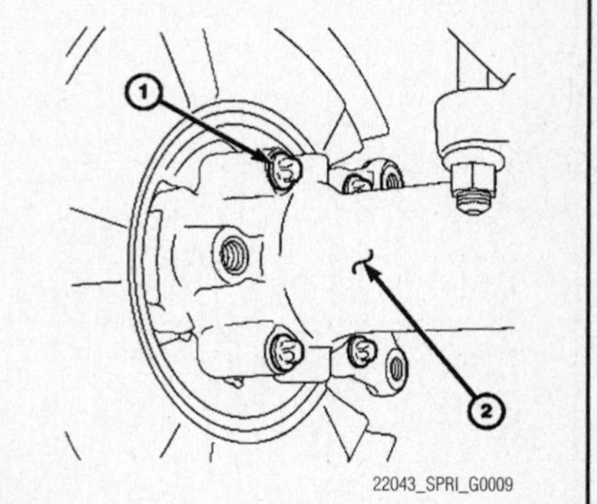

Fig. 9 Remove the axle bearing bolts (1) from the axle (2)—Rear axle shaft removal

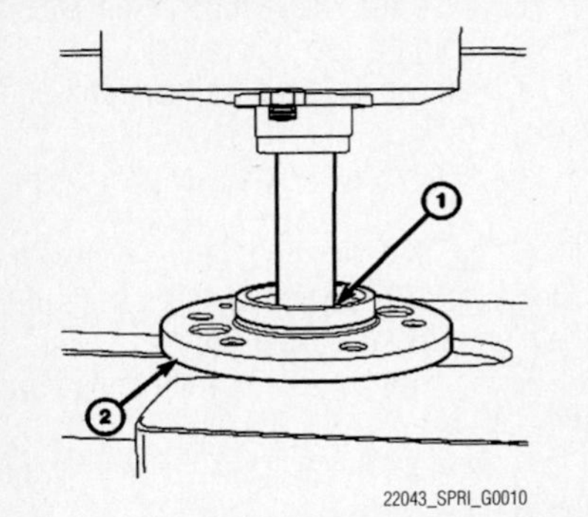

Fig. 10 Press the axle shaft (1) out of the flange (2) and bearing—Rear axle shaft bearing removal

16. Fill the differential with fluid to the correct level.

REAR DRIVESHAFT

REMOVAL & INSTALLATION

See Figure 11.

1. Raise and safely support the vehicle.
2. Matchmark the driveshaft at the joints for reinstallation.
3. Remove the driveshaft intermediate bearing nuts from the retaining bracket and bracket for the brake cable.
4. Remove the retaining bracket bolts.
5. Remove the driveshaft bolts from the rear axle and transmission flanges.
6. Remove the driveshaft from the vehicle.

To install:

7. Install the driveshaft into the vehicle.
8. Install the intermediate bearing support and tighten the nuts to 77 ft. lbs. (105 Nm).
9. Install the driveshaft intermediate bearing support to the frame floor and tighten the bolts to 70 ft. lbs. (95 Nm).
10. Install the driveshaft to the rear axle and transmission flange, aligning the matchmarks. Tighten the bolts to 52 ft. lbs. (70 Nm).
11. Install the retaining bracket and tighten the bolts to 74 ft. lbs. (100 Nm).

REAR PINION SEAL

REMOVAL & INSTALLATION

See Figures 12 and 13.

1. Raise and safely support the vehicle.
2. Remove the rear wheel.
3. Drain the rear differential fluid.
4. Remove the driveshaft. For additional information, refer to the following section, "Rear Driveshaft, Removal & Installation."
5. Spin pinion flange by hand and check axial play of bearing.

➡There must not be any thrust bearing play. If there excess play or there are particles (shavings) in the drained oil, the rear gear assembly must be replaced.

6. Measure and record the torque required to rotate the pinion.
7. Matchmark the pinion in position to pinion flange
8. Unlock the collared nut.
9. Using Special Tool C-3281 Flange Wrench, hold the pinion flange and remove nut.
10. Remove the pinion flange from pinion shaft using Special Tool 8992 Flange Puller.
11. Check sealing surfaces of joint flange for score marks and replace joint flange if necessary.
12. Remove the pinion seals.

To install:

13. Pack the space between the dust lip and sealing lip on the seal ring with multi-purpose grease.

➡On seals without rubberized external surface, coat outer circumference with sealant.

⁂ WARNING

Do not coat partially rubberized seals with sealant.

14. Drive new pinion seals into the rear axle housing until they stop using Special Tool 9276 Installer.
15. Fit the coupling flange on the drive pinion shaft.

➡The groove in the drive pinion and the groove in the joint flange must be in alignment.

16. Hold the pinion flange with Special Tool C-3281 Flange Wrench C-3281 and tighten the pinion nut to 74 ft. lbs. (100 Nm).
17. Using a dial indicator check free play at the pinion flange.

➡Should the bearing not be free of play, tighten in increases of 88 inch lbs. (10 Nm) to a maximum of 95 ft. lbs. (130 Nm). If the bearing is not free of play, the collapsible spacer must be replaced.

18. Identify the position of the pinion to the nut twelve points and mark pinion and nut. Turn the pinion nut 30° (one twelve point). Then rotate the pinion thirty times.
19. Measure the torque required to rotate. The torque to rotate must be 0.9-1.7 in. lbs. (0.1-0.2 Nm) higher then torque recorded during the removal procedure.

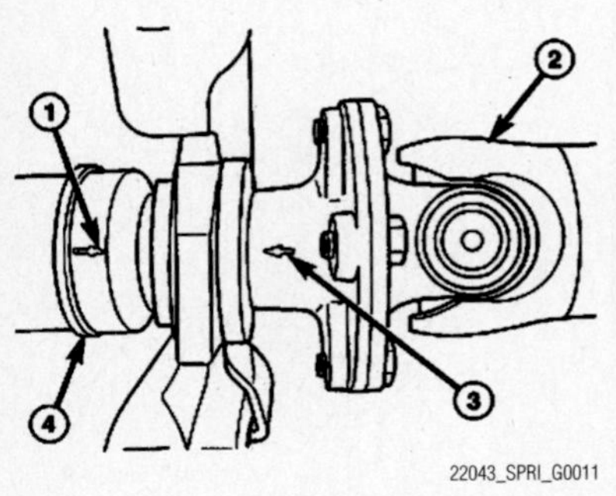

Fig. 11 Matchmark (1,3) the center driveshaft (2) to the rear driveshaft (4)

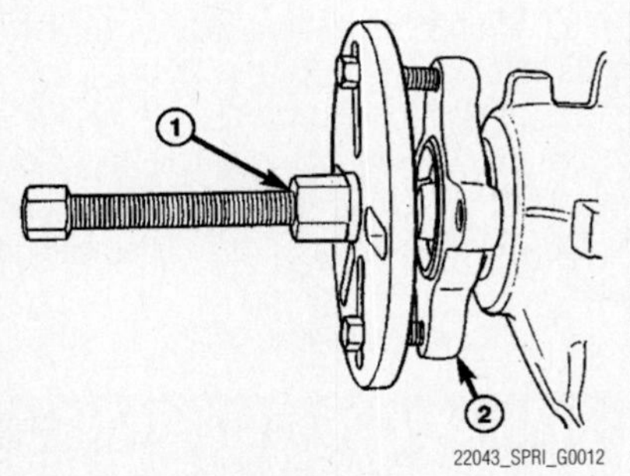

Fig. 12 Remove the pinion flange (2) from the shaft using Special Tool 8992 (1).

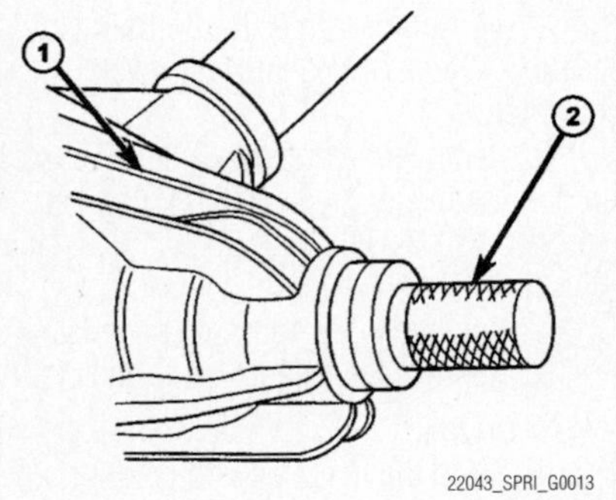

Fig. 13 Drive new pinion seals into the axle housing (1) using Special Tool 9276 (2).

➡If value is below or above collapsible spacer must be replaced.

20. Cut the collar of the collared nut.
21. Using a hammer and drift, bend the collar nut so it touches the wall of the slot in the pinion shaft.
22. Install the driveshaft.
23. Refill the rear differential with fluid to the correct level.
24. Install the wheel.
25. Operate brake pedal several times until brake pads contact brake discs (brake pressure built up).
26. Attach rear brake cables if removed and adjust parking brake.

ENGINE COOLING

ENGINE FAN

REMOVAL & INSTALLATION

Diesel Engines

See Figure 14.

1. Disconnect the negative battery cable.
2. Detach the coolant line from the lower radiator shroud.

➡The radiator fan assembly is threaded to the water pump hub shaft. Remove the fan blade/viscous fan drive assembly from the water pump by turning the mounting nut counter-clockwise as viewed from the front. Threads on the radiator fan drive are RIGHT-HAND.

3. Using Special Tool 8930 Counter-holder, remove the radiator fan.
4. Remove the upper air seal.
5. Remove the upper radiator hose.
6. Remove the radiator fan shroud and radiator fan.

➡Store the fan in the upright position. Do not place down flat.

To install:

7. Install the radiator fan assembly to the engine.
8. Install the center bolt, and using Special Tool 8930 to hold the fan, tighten the bolt to 33 ft. lbs. (45 Nm).

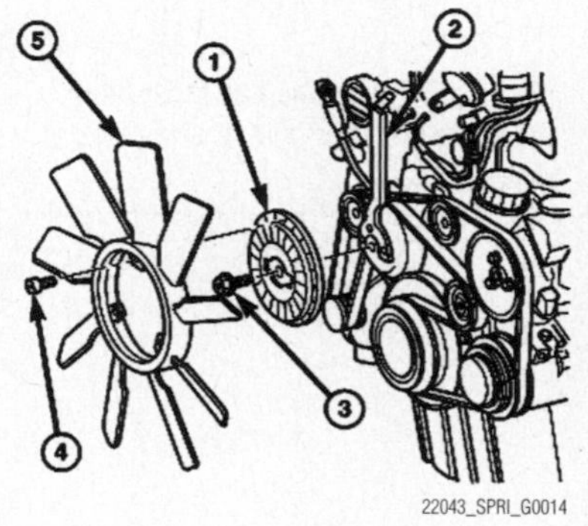

Fig. 14 Use a counterholder (2) to remove the center bolt (3) of the engine fan (1,4) assembly—Diesel engines

9. Attach the radiator hose and install the air seal.
10. Attach the coolant line to the lower radiator shroud.
11. Connect the negative battery cable.

RADIATOR

REMOVAL & INSTALLATION

Diesel Engines

1. Drain the cooling system.
2. Remove the headlights.
3. Remove the front crossmember together with front grille.
4. Remove the front bumper.
5. Remove the bolts holding the air charge hose to the sheet metal and inter-cooler.
6. Detach the air intake pipe at the body.
7. Detach both coolant hoses at the coolant reservoir.
8. Unplug the wiring connector at the coolant level sensor.
9. Detach the coolant hose at bottom right of radiator.
10. Detach the transmission cooler lines from the radiator.
11. Remove the left and right radiator trim.
12. Remove the radiator fan. For additional information, refer to the following section, "Engine Fan, Removal & Installation."
13. Remove the bolts securing the inter-cooler to the radiator.
14. Remove the screws and upper radiator trim from the radiator.
15. Move the condenser/intercooler/power steering cooler assembly forward.
16. Lift the radiator assembly up and out of the rubber grommets.

To install:

17. Install the radiator assembly into the rubber grommets.
18. Install both right and left side radiator trim panels.
19. Attach the transmission cooler lines.
20. Attach the coolant hose to the bottom right of the radiator.
21. Attach both power steering hydraulic lines.
22. Connect the coolant level sensor electrical connector.
23. Connect the coolant hoses to the coolant reservoir, radiator and water pump.
24. Attach the air intake pipe to the body.
25. Attach the charge air hose to the air intake.
26. Attach the charge air hose to the turbocharger.
27. Install the A/C condenser.
28. Install the front bumper.
29. Install front end crossmember.
30. Refill the power steering reservoir to the correct level.
31. Refill the transmission to the correct level.
32. Refill the cooling system to the correct level.
33. Start the engine and check for leaks.

THERMOSTAT

REMOVAL & INSTALLATION

2.7L Engine

1. Disconnect the negative battery cable.
2. Drain the cooling system.
3. Disconnect the coolant temperature sensor wiring harness.
4. Detach the air intake hose at the charge air distribution pipe.
5. Detach the coolant hoses at the thermostat housing.
6. Unscrew the cap of the oil filter housing.
7. Remove the thermostat housing and thermostat.

To install:

8. Clean the mounting surface of any gasket material.
9. Install the thermostat and thermostat housing with a new gasket. Tighten the mounting bolts to 80 inch lbs. (9 Nm).
10. Install the cap at the oil filter housing.
11. Connect the coolant hoses.
12. Attach the air intake hose to the charge air distribution pipe.
13. Connect the wiring harness.
14. Refill the cooling system to the correct level.
15. Connect the negative battery cable.

16. Start the engine and check for leaks.

3.0L Engine

1. Disconnect the negative battery cable.
2. Drain the cooling system.
3. Remove the engine appearance cover.
4. Remove the thermostat mounting bolts.
5. Pull the thermostat housing back and remove the thermostat and discard the sealing ring.

To install:

6. Clean the mounting surfaces of any gasket material.
7. Install the thermostat with a new sealing ring.
8. Position the thermostat housing into place and tighten the mounting bolts to 80 inch lbs. (9 Nm).
9. Refill the cooling system to the correct level.
10. Install the engine appearance cover.
11. Connect the negative battery cable.
12. Start the engine and check for leaks.

3.5L Engine

1. Remove the engine appearance cover.
2. Drain the cooling system.
3. Remove the locking ring and remove the coolant hose from the thermostat housing.
4. Disconnect the thermostat electrical connector.
5. Remove the thermostat housing mounting bolts.
6. Remove the thermostat housing and discard the gasket.
7. Remove the thermostat.

To install:

8. Clean the mounting surface of any gasket material.
9. Install the thermostat.
10. Using a new gasket, install the thermostat housing and tighten the mounting bolts to 80 inch lbs. (9 Nm).
11. Connect the coolant hose to the thermostat housing.
12. Refill the cooling system to the correct level.
13. Install the engine appearance cover.

WATER PUMP

REMOVAL & INSTALLATION

1. Disconnect the negative battery cable.
2. Drain the cooling system.
3. Remove the viscous fan clutch. For additional information, refer to the following section, "Engine Fan, Removal & Installation."
4. Detach the fuel lines from the brackets of the water pump.
5. Detach the coolant hoses from the water pump.
6. Remove the accessory drive belt.
7. Press off the cap at the belt guide pulleys.
8. Remove the belt guide pulleys.
9. Remove the water pump retaining bolts and remove the water pump.

To install:

10. Install the water pump with a new gasket and tighten the mounting bolts 10 ft. lbs. (14 Nm) and the M8 bolts to 15 ft. lbs. (20 Nm).
11. Install the belt guide pulleys and tighten the bolts to 26 ft. lbs. (35 Nm).
12. Connect the coolant hoses to the water pump.
13. Attach the fuel lines to the brackets of the water pump.
14. Install the accessory drive belt.
15. Install viscous fan clutch.
16. Refill the cooling system to the correct level.
17. Connect the negative battery cable.
18. Start the engine and check for leaks.

ENGINE ELECTRICAL

CHARGING SYSTEM

ALTERNATOR

REMOVAL & INSTALLATION

See Figure 15.

1. Disconnect the negative battery cable.
2. Remove accessory drive belt. For additional information, refer to the following section, "Accessory Drive Belt, Removal & Installation."
3. Raise and safely support the vehicle.
4. Remove the protective plastic cover from battery positive stud at top of the alternator.
5. Remove the nut securing the battery output cable to the battery positive terminal at the top of the alternator.
6. Unplug the ground terminal harness connector at rear of the alternator.
7. Remove the four mounting bolts.
8. Remove the alternator from the lower side of vehicle.

To install:

9. Install the alternator and tighten the mounting bolts to 15 ft. lbs. (20 Nm).
10. Connect the ground terminal to the rear of the alternator.
11. Install the battery positive cable to the top terminal and install the protective plastic cover.
12. Install the accessory drive belt.
13. Lower the vehicle.

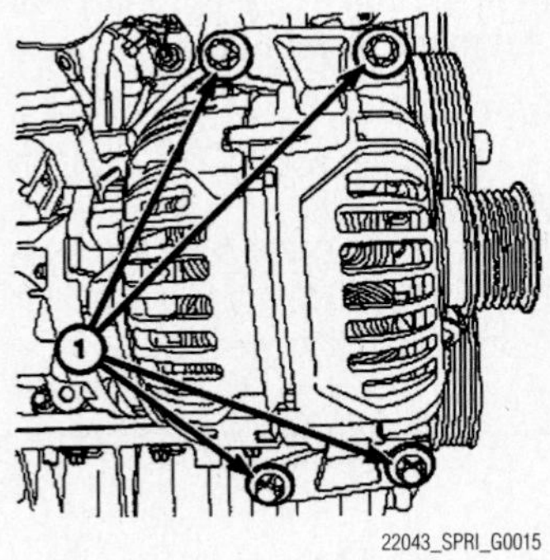

Fig. 15 The mounting bolt (1) for the alternator are Torx® no. 12 size—All engines

ENGINE ELECTRICAL — IGNITION SYSTEM

IGNITION COIL

REMOVAL & INSTALLATION

3.5L Engine

See Figure 16.

1. Disconnect the negative battery cable.
2. Remove the engine appearance cover.
3. Remove the air intake assembly.
4. Disconnect the ignition coil wiring harness.
5. Remove the two ignition coil mounting bolts and remove the ignition coil.

To install:

6. Install the ignition coil and tighten the mounting bolts to 80 inch lbs. (9 Nm).
7. Connect the ignition coil wiring harness.
8. Install the air intake assembly.
9. Install the engine appearance cover.
10. Connect the negative battery cable.

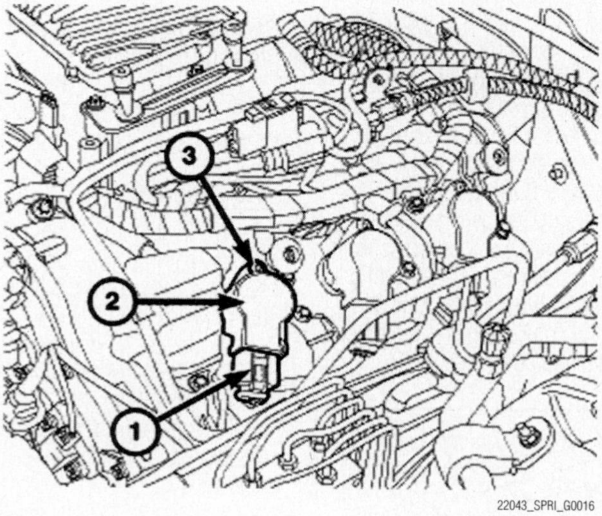

Fig. 16 Disconnect the wiring harness (1) and remove the mounting bolts (3) to remove the ignition coil (2)—3.5L Engine

IGNITION TIMING

ADJUSTMENT

The ignition timing is control by the Powertrain Control Module (PCM). No adjustment is possible or necessary.

SPARK PLUGS

REMOVAL & INSTALLATION

3.5L Engine

1. Disconnect the negative battery cable.
2. Remove the ignition coil. For additional information, refer to the following section, "Ignition Coil, Removal & Installation."
3. Remove the spark plug.

To install:

4. Install the spark plug and tighten to 17 ft. lbs. (23 Nm).
5. Install the ignition coil.
6. Connect the negative battery cable.

ENGINE ELECTRICAL — STARTING SYSTEM

STARTER

REMOVAL & INSTALLATION

1. Disconnect the negative battery cable.
2. Raise and safely support the vehicle.
3. Remove the engine undercover.
4. Remove the bolt securing the starter wiring harness retainer bracket to the transmission bellhousing.
5. Disconnect the battery positive cables and the starter solenoid wire from the starter solenoid.
6. Remove the starter mounting bolts.
7. Remove the starter from transmission bellhousing.

To install:

8. Positing the starter to the transmission bellhousing and tighten the mounting bolts to 30 ft. lbs. (40 Nm).
9. Connect the battery cable and solenoid wiring to the solenoid and tighten the nut to 10 ft. lbs. (14 Nm).
10. Position the wiring harness retainer bracket and install retaining bolt.
11. Lower the vehicle.
12. Connect the negative battery cable.

ENGINE MECHANICAL

➡Disconnecting the negative battery cable may interfere with the functions of the on board computer systems and may require the computer to undergo a relearning process, once the negative battery cable is reconnected.

ACCESSORY DRIVE BELTS

ACCESSORY BELT ROUTING

See Figures 17 and 18.

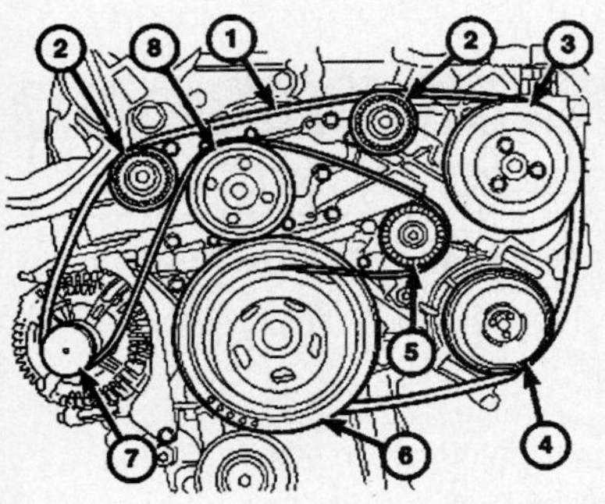

Fig. 17 Accessory Belt Routing—A/C Compressor (1), Power Steering Pump (2), Tensioner (3), Crankshaft Pulley (4), Water Pump (5), Alternator (6), Idler Pulley (7)—All Engines

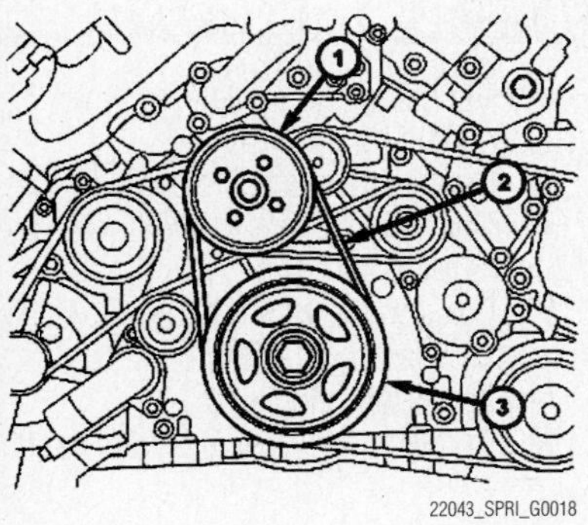

Fig. 18 Fan belt routing—Fan pulley (1), Fan belt (2), Crankshaft pulley (3)—3.0L engine shown

INSPECTION

Although many manufacturers recommend that the drive belt(s) be inspected every 30,000 miles (48,000 km) or more, it is really a good idea to check them at least once a year, or at every major fluid change. Whichever interval you choose, the belts should be checked for wear or damage. Obviously, a damaged drive belt can cause problems should it give way while the vehicle is in operation. But, improper length belts (too short or long), as well as excessively worn belts, can also cause problems. Loose accessory drive belts can lead to poor engine cooling and diminished output from the alternator, air conditioning compressor or power steering pump. A belt that is too tight places a severe strain on the driven unit and can wear out bearings quickly.

Serpentine drive belts should be inspected for rib chunking (pieces of the ribs breaking off), severe glazing, frayed cords or other visible damage. Any belt which is missing sections of 2 or more adjacent ribs which are ½ in. (13mm) or longer must be replaced. You might want to note that serpentine belts do tend to form small cracks across the backing. If the only wear you find is in the form of one or more cracks are across the backing and NOT parallel to the ribs, the belt is still good and does not need to be replaced.

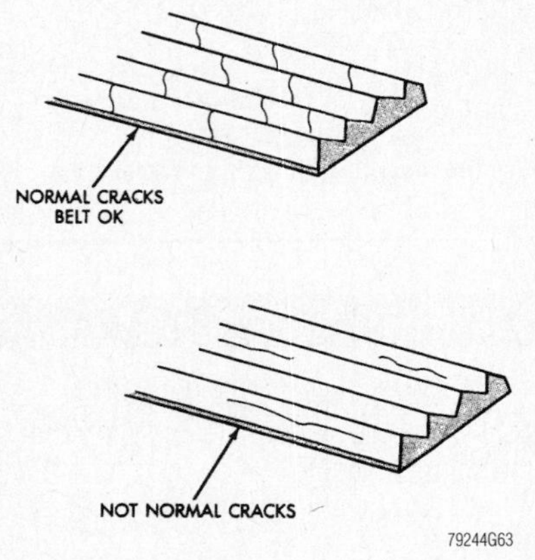

Fig. 19 Inspect the wear patterns for the serpentine drive belt.

ADJUSTMENT

Periodic drive belt tensioning is not necessary, because an automatic spring-loaded tensioner is used with these belts to maintain proper adjustment at all times.

REMOVAL & INSTALLATION

2.7L Engine

1. Loosen the tension adjust and remove the A/C compressor drive belt.
2. Attach a ⅜ inch drive ratchet to the automatic belt tensioner.
3. Rotate the belt tensioner counterclockwise to release the belt tension.
4. Remove the accessory drive belt, starting with the water pump pulley.

To install:

5. Position the accessory drive belt around every pulley except the water pump pulley.
6. Rotate the drive belt tensioner clockwise, install the accessory drive belt and release the tensioner.
7. Position the A/C Compressor drive belt over the crankshaft pulley and A/C compressor pulley.
8. Tighten the drive belt tensioner.
9. Ensure the belt is seated properly on all of the pulleys.

3.0L Engine

1. Remove the radiator fan. For additional information, refer to the following section, "Engine Fan, Removal & Installation."
2. Rotate the crankshaft pulley clockwise and walk the fan drive belt off of the crankshaft pulley.
3. Rotate the accessory drive belt tensioner counterclockwise to release the belt tension.
4. Remove the accessory drive belt.

To install:

5. Position the accessory drive belt around every pulley except one.
6. Rotate the drive belt tensioner clockwise, install the accessory drive belt and release the tensioner.
7. Position fan drive belt on water pump pulley.
8. Position fan drive belt on crankshaft pulley.

➡Use only wire ties with nylon locks, not metal.

9. Working from the back side of the crankshaft pulley, insert a nylon wire tie through one of the holes in the pulley.
10. Use a nylon wire tie to hold fan drive belt in place.
11. Tighten the wire tie to hold the drive belt in position.
12. Slowly rotate crankshaft pulley clockwise
13. Make sure fan drive belt is fully seated.
14. Install the radiator fan.

3.5L Engine

1. Remove the radiator fan. For additional information, refer to the following

section, "Engine Fan, Removal & Installation."

2. Rotate the accessory drive belt tensioner counterclockwise to release the belt tension.

3. Remove the accessory drive belt.

To install:

4. Position the accessory drive belt around every pulley except one.

5. Rotate the drive belt tensioner clockwise, install the accessory drive belt and release the tensioner.

6. Install the radiator fan.

CAMSHAFT AND VALVE LIFTERS

REMOVAL & INSTALLATION

2.7L Engine

See Figures 20 through 22.

1. Disconnect the negative battery cable.

2. Remove the engine appearance cover.

3. Remove the high pressure lines and fuel injectors. For additional information, refer to the following section, "Fuel Injectors, Removal & Installation."

4. Remove the air intake assembly.

5. Detach the hose from the oil separator.

6. Disconnect the camshaft position sensor.

7. Remove the cylinder head cover.

8. Rotate the crankshaft clockwise to put cylinder no. 1 at Top Dead Center (TDC).

9. Lock the intake camshaft.

10. Remove the timing chain tensioner. For additional information, refer to the following section, "Timing Chain, Sprockets, Front Cover & Seal, Removal & Installation."

11. Remove the vacuum pump.

12. Remove the cylinder head front cover bolts.

13. Raise the locking pawl of the top guide rail and remove the cylinder head front cover.

14. Counter hold the camshaft with an open end wrench and unbolt the driver of the intake camshaft sprocket.

15. Remove the top guide rail.

16. Matchmark the camshaft sprocket relative to the timing chain.

17. Unbolt the camshaft sprocket from the exhaust camshaft.

18. Remove the camshaft sprocket.

19. Matchmark each camshaft bearing cap, identifying its position.

⁂ WARNING

Slacken the bolts of the camshaft bearing caps evenly in steps of one turn until the back pressure is eliminated. Camshafts must not be twisted when slackening the camshaft bearing caps.

20. Remove the exhaust camshaft bearing caps 1, 3, 4 and 6, in sequence.

21. Remove the intake camshaft bearing caps 1, 3, 4 and 6, in sequence.

22. Slacken the exhaust camshaft bearing bolts individually at cap 2 and then 5. Remove the bolts one revolution at a time until the back pressure is released.

23. Slacken the intake camshaft bearing bolts individually at cap 2 and then 5. Remove the bolts one revolution at a time until the back pressure is released.

24. Remove the camshafts.

To install:

25. Install intake and exhaust camshafts so that the two holes in camshaft sprockets are positioned opposite and the markings of the camshaft and camshaft bearing cap are aligned.

26. Ensure that cylinder no. 1 is set to TDC.

27. Install the Nos. 2 and 5 Exhaust cam bearing caps.

28. Install the Nos. 2 and 5 Intake cam bearing caps.

29. Tighten each of the Nos. 2 and 5 intake and exhaust bearing cap bolts evenly to 80 inch lbs. (9 Nm) in steps of 1 revolution each.

30. Install the remaining camshaft bearing caps and tighten the bolts evenly to 80 inch lbs. (9 Nm) in steps of 1 revolution each.

31. Insert a locking pin through the first camshaft bearing cap into the whole in the camshaft sprocket.

32. Install the camshaft sprocket with timing chain fitted on, onto exhaust camshaft paying attention to position of dowel pin. Tighten a new bolt to 13 ft. lbs. (18 Nm).

33. Install the timing chain tensioner.

34. Ensure the two markings in the inlet camshaft sprockets must be positioned opposite and markings of camshaft and camshaft bearing cap are aligned.

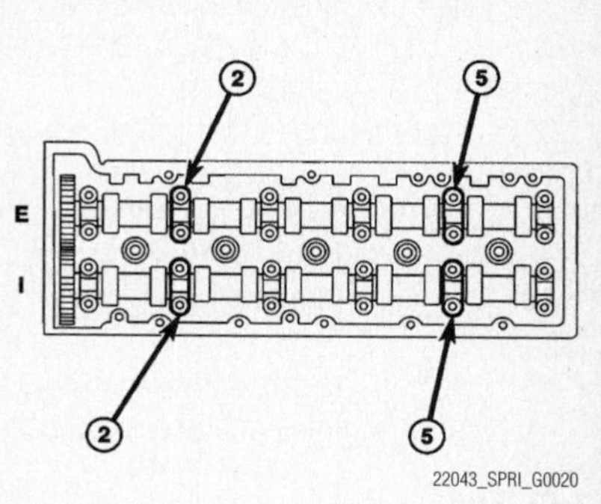

Fig. 21 Install the Nos. 2 and 5 camshaft bearing caps first—2.7L Engine shown

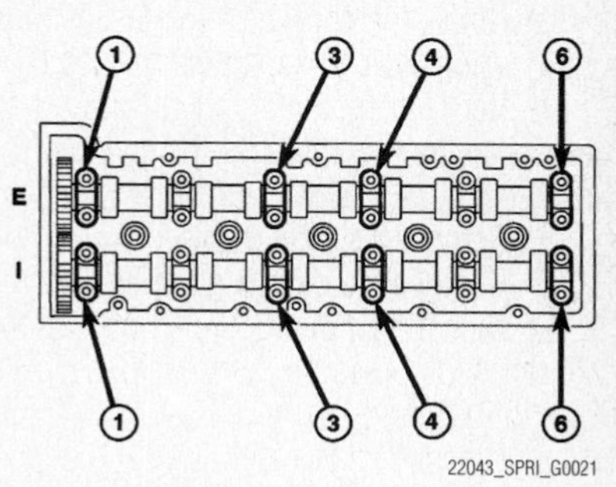

Fig. 22 Then install the remaining camshaft bearing caps—2.7L Engine shown.

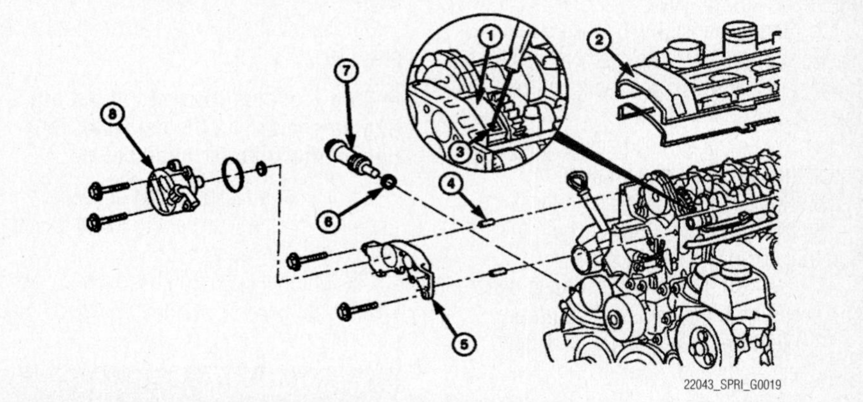

Fig. 20 Remove the cylinder head cover (2), timing chain tensioner (7), vacuum pump (8), and cylinder head front cover (5) before remove the camshafts—2.7L Engine shown

35. Insert the slide rail and bolt the driver into the inlet camshaft. Tighten the bolt driver to 37 ft. lbs. (50 Nm).
36. Install the front cover on the cylinder head.
37. Install the cylinder head cover.
38. Clean and install the fuel injectors.
39. Reconnect the negative battery cable.
40. Install the engine appearance cover.
41. Start the engine and check for leaks.

3.0L Engine

Left Camshafts

1. Disconnect negative battery cable.
2. Remove engine appearance cover.
3. Rotate the engine to Top Dead Center (TDC) using the crankshaft damper bolt.
4. Remove the main engine wiring harness retainers at the rear of the cylinder head cover.
5. Remove the EGR valve.
6. Remove the charge air inlet tube.
7. Disconnect the fuel line hoses at the fuel rail, high pressure pump using Special Tool 9539 Pliers.
8. Disconnect the fuel lines at the left cylinder head.
9. Remove the fuel pipe bundle and set it aside.
10. Remove the oil filter housing support bracket.
11. Remove the cylinder head cover.

➡The left exhaust camshaft gear alignment mark is located in the gear tooth valley. The left intake camshaft gear mark is located on the outside of the tooth.

12. Check the camshaft timing gears for alignment. The alignment marks should be touching and the exhaust camshaft drive gear alignment pin should be located at approximately 12 o'clock, when viewed from the front camshaft seal.
13. Rotate the engine by the vibration damper bolt, past TDC to gain access to the lower camshaft drive gear bolt, and remove the bolt.
14. Rotate the engine back to TDC and check the camshaft gear alignment.
15. Remove the timing chain tensioner.
16. Matchmark the timing chain in relation to the camshaft sprocket.
17. Tie a strap around the timing chain and secure it to the camshaft sprocket.
18. Remove the remaining camshaft drive gear bolts and separate the drive gear from camshaft gear.
19. Remove the intake and exhaust camshaft retainers.
20. Remove the left cylinder head camshafts.

To install:

21. Clean all of the mating surfaces.
22. Lubricate the camshafts with clean engine oil.
23. Carefully install the camshafts onto the cylinder head journals and align the camshaft gear timing marks.
24. Install the camshaft retainers and tighten each retaining bolt to 80 in. lbs. (9 Nm).
25. After the camshafts are properly installed in cylinder head cover check end play of camshafts with a dial indicator.

➡The left exhaust camshaft gear alignment mark is located in the gear tooth valley. The left intake camshaft gear mark is located on the outside of the tooth.

➡The alignment marks should be touching and the exhaust camshaft drive gear alignment pin should be located at approximately 12 o'clock, when viewed from the front camshaft seal.

26. Ensure the proper positioning of the camshaft gear alignment marks and install the camshaft driven gear onto the exhaust camshaft alignment dowel.
27. Install two of the drive gear bolts and tighten the bolts to 13 ft. lbs. (18 Nm).
28. Ensure the proper positioning of the timing chain to drive gear matchmarks and remove the tie strap.
29. Rotate the engine by the crankshaft damper bolt enough to install the third camshaft drive gear bolt. Tighten the bolt to 13 ft. lbs. (18 Nm).
30. Rotate the engine back to TDC and check camshaft gear alignment.
31. Install the timing chain tensioner.
32. Install the left front camshaft oil seal.
33. Install the left rear camshaft oil seal (2).

➡Care must be taken not to get any engine sealant on the camshaft journals of the cylinder head cover.

34. Install a ⅛ inch bead of Mopar® Engine RTV Gen II sealant to the underside of the cylinder head cover.
35. Carefully position the cylinder head cover and install the bolts into their original position.

⁂ WARNING

The cylinder head cover bolts are different lengths. Do not use the wrong length bolts or engine damage may result.

36. Tighten cylinder head cover bolts in sequence, first to 35 in. lbs. (4 Nm), and then repeat the sequence to 75 inch lbs. (8.4 Nm).
37. Install the EGR valve.

⁂ CAUTION

The fuel injector sealing washers MUST be replaced. DO NOT use the old sealing washers or double the sealing washers.

➡Care must be taken not to apply any lubricant to the fuel injector nozzles.

38. Install the fuel injectors. Tighten the injector retaining claw bolt to 60 inch lbs. (7 Nm) and then an additional 180°.
39. Re-position and secure the engine harness.
40. Install the left fuel rail. Tighten the fuel rail bolts to 98 inch lbs. (11 Nm).
41. Position the return fuel lines and secure to the injectors. Push down on the release lock tab to secure.
42. Connect the fuel injector electrical connectors.
43. Install the left rear engine cover bracket.
44. Install the high pressure fuel lines from the fuel rail to injectors. Tighten the line connections to 20 ft. lbs. (27 Nm).
45. Install the fuel line from the high pressure pump to the left fuel rail. Tighten the retaining bolt to 22 ft. lbs. (30 Nm).
46. Install the fuel supply line to the fuel filter and high pressure pump.
47. Connect both fuel lines at the high pressure pump.
48. Install the air filter housing and tube.
49. Connect the negative battery cable.
50. Install the engine appearance cover.
51. Start the engine and check for leaks.

Right Camshafts

1. Disconnect the negative battery cable.
2. Remove the engine appearance cover.
3. Rotate the engine to Top Dead Center (TDC) using the crankshaft damper bolt.
4. Remove the intake air resonator.
5. Remove the vacuum pump.
6. Remove the oil level indicator tube retaining bolt at the right cylinder head cover.
7. Remove the crankcase breather assembly from the right cylinder head cover.
8. Remove the cylinder head cover.

➡The right exhaust camshaft gear alignment mark is located in the gear tooth valley. The left intake camshaft gear mark is located on the outside of the tooth.

9. Check the camshaft timing gears for alignment. The alignment marks should be touching and the exhaust camshaft drive gear alignment pin should be located at approximately 12 o'clock, when viewed from the front camshaft seal.
10. Rotate the engine by the vibration damper bolt, past TDC to gain access to the lower camshaft drive gear bolt, and remove the bolt.
11. Rotate the engine back to TDC and check camshaft gear alignment.
12. Remove the timing chain tensioner.
13. Matchmark the timing chain in relation to the camshaft drive gear.
14. Tie a strap the timing chain to the drive gear.
15. Remove the remaining camshaft drive gear bolts and separate the drive gear from camshaft gear.
16. Remove the intake and exhaust camshaft retainers.
17. Remove the left cylinder head camshafts.

To install:

18. Clean all mating surfaces and lubricate camshafts with clean engine oil.
19. Carefully install camshafts onto cylinder head journals and align the camshaft gear timing marks.
20. Install the camshaft retainers and tighten each retaining bolt to 80 inch lbs. (9 Nm).
21. After camshafts are properly installed in cylinder head cover check end play of camshafts with a dial indicator.

➡If the camshaft endplay is not within specification, replace the cylinder head and cylinder head cover.

➡The right exhaust camshaft gear alignment mark is located in the gear tooth valley. The right intake camshaft gear mark is located on the outside of the tooth. The alignment marks should be touching and the exhaust camshaft drive gear alignment pin should be located at approximately 12 o'clock, when viewed from the front camshaft seal.

22. Ensure the proper positioning of the camshaft gear alignment marks and install the camshaft driven gear onto the exhaust camshaft alignment dowel.
23. Install two of the drive gear bolts and tighten to 13 ft. lbs. (18 Nm).
24. Ensure the proper positioning of the timing chain to drive gear matchmarks and remove the tie strap.
25. Rotate the engine by the crankshaft damper bolt enough to install the third camshaft drive gear bolt. Tighten the bolt to 13 ft. lbs. (18 Nm).
26. Rotate the engine back to TDC and check camshaft gear alignment.

⁂ WARNING

Turn the engine clockwise only!

27. Install the timing chain tensioner.

➡Care must be taken not to get any engine sealer on the camshaft journals.

28. Apply a ⅛ inch bead of Mopar®® Engine RTV Sealant to the cylinder head cover.
29. Install the camshaft seal into position.
30. Install the cylinder head cover. Tighten the bolts in sequence as follows:
    a. Tighten the bolts to 35 inch lbs. (4 Nm).
    b. Tighten the bolts to 53 inch lbs. (6 Nm).
    c. Then tighten the bolts to 75 inch lbs. (8.4 Nm).
31. Install the oil separator housing adapter with a new camshaft seal and tighten fasteners to 80 inch lbs. (9 Nm).
32. Install the oil separator and tighten fasteners to 80 inch lbs. (9 Nm).
33. Secure the transmission tube fastener to the engine cover bracket.
34. Secure the heater hose bracket to the cylinder head cover.
35. Secure the vacuum pump hose pipe to the cylinder head cover.
36. Install the fuel injectors. For additional information, refer to the following section, "Fuel Injectors, Removal & Installation."
37. Connect the camshaft position sensor and fuel injector wiring harness connectors.
38. Connect the return fuel hose to each injector.
39. Install the fuel rail, high pressure fuel lines and injector cover.
40. Secure the oil dipstick tube to the cylinder head and tighten the bolt to 98 inch lbs. (11 Nm).
41. Install the vacuum pump.
42. Install the air control valve resonator.
43. Install the air cleaner outlet tube to the turbocharger and secure the air cleaner housing cover.
44. Install the engine appearance cover.
45. Connect the negative battery cable.
46. Start the engine and check for leaks.

3.5L Engine

Left Camshafts

See Figure 23.

1. Disconnect the negative battery cable.
2. Disconnect the remote ground cable by the accelerator pedal.
3. Remove the air intake assembly.
4. Remove the left cylinder head cover. For additional information, refer to the following section, "Cylinder Head, Removal & Installation."
5. Place a drift into the camshaft adjuster to lock it into position.
6. Hold the back of the camshaft with a Torx bit while removing the center valve from the front of the camshaft.
7. Remove the pulse wheel from the camshaft.

⁂ CAUTION

Use care not to nick or scratch the journals when removing the camshaft.

8. Remove the camshaft hold downs.
9. Remove the camshafts from the camshaft adjuster.

To install:

10. Install the camshafts into the camshaft adjuster.
11. Install the camshaft hold downs.
12. Install a new pulse wheel onto the camshaft adjusters.
13. Remove the drift from the camshaft adjuster.

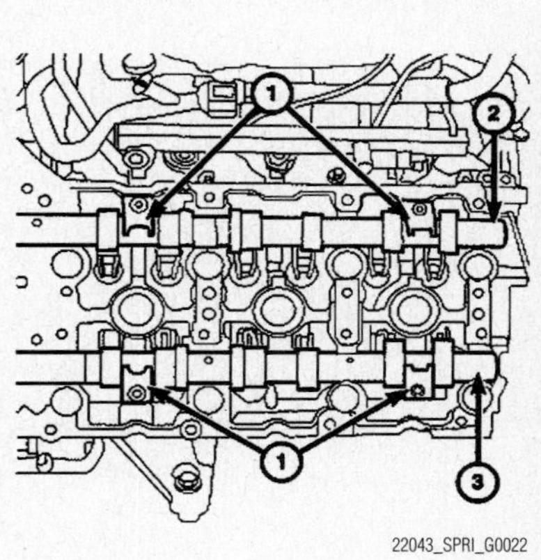

Fig. 23 Remove the camshaft hold downs (1) to remove the camshafts (2,3) from the adjuster—3.5L Engine Left Camshafts

14. Hold the back of the camshaft with a Torx bit while installing the center valve into the front of the camshaft.
15. Install the left cylinder head cover.
16. Install the air intake assembly.
17. Connect the remote ground.
18. Connect the negative battery cable.
19. Start the engine and check for leaks.

Right Camshafts

See Figures 24 through 28.

1. Disconnect the negative battery cable.
2. Remove the air intake assembly.
3. Turn the engine in the direction of rotation until the engine is set to 40 degrees after Top Dead Center (TDC).
4. Remove the air control valve on the right cylinder head.

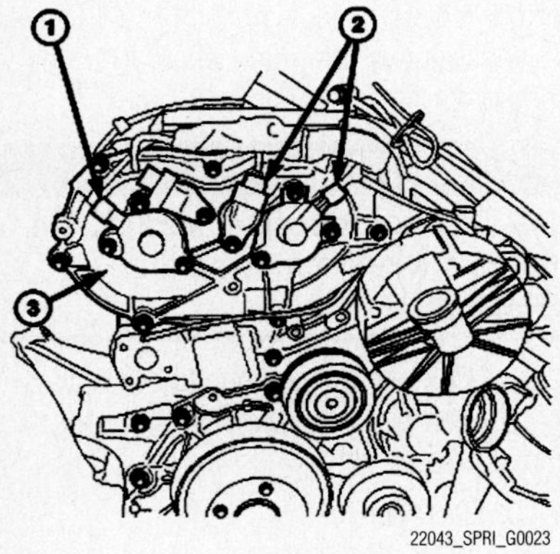

Fig. 24 Disconnect the camshaft position sensors (1,2) and then remove the upper front cover (3)—3.5L Engine Right Camshaft removal

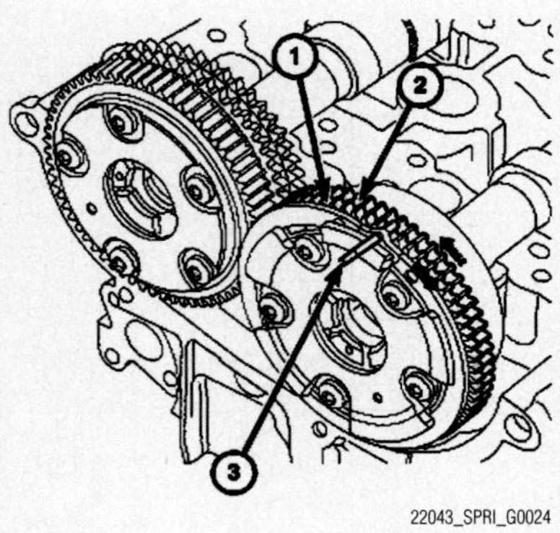

Fig. 25 Install a drift (3) into the camshaft to hold the split gears (1,2) in place—3.5L Engine Right Camshaft removal

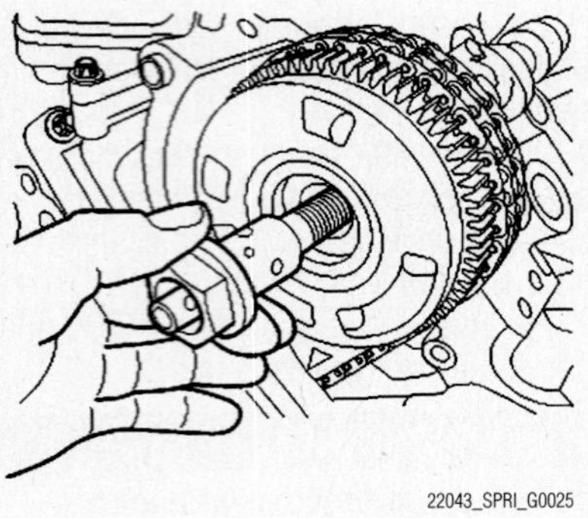

Fig. 26 Use a Torx bit to the end of the camshaft while removing the center valve from the camshaft adjuster in the exhaust camshaft—3.5L Engine Right Camshaft removal

5. Remove the air control valve gasket and bracket.
6. Remove the centrifugal oil separator cover.
7. Remove the center bolt from the oil separator.
8. Remove the oil separator.
9. Remove the camshaft plug.
10. Disconnect the camshaft position sensors in the right front upper cover.
11. Remove the upper front cover on the right cylinder head.
12. Remove the bolts from the engine wiring harness on the right cylinder head cover.
13. Disconnect the engine wiring harness and secure it out of the way.
14. Disconnect and remove the ignition coils.
15. Remove the cylinder head cover.
16. Install a drift into the camshaft to hold the split gears in place.
17. Use a Torx bit to the end of the camshaft while removing the center valve from the camshaft adjuster in the intake camshaft.
18. Remove the intake camshaft pulse wheel.
19. Use a Torx bit to the end of the camshaft while removing the center valve from the camshaft adjuster in the exhaust camshaft.
20. Remove the exhaust camshaft pulse wheel.
21. Support the timing chain to prevent the chain from slipping from the crankshaft sprocket.
22. Remove the exhaust camshaft adjuster.
23. Remove the intake camshaft adjuster.
24. Remove the camshafts.

To install:

25. Make sure that the crankshaft is set to 40 degrees after top dead center.
26. Install the camshafts.
27. Install the camshaft hold downs.
28. Install the intake camshaft adjuster.
29. Install the exhaust camshaft adjuster.

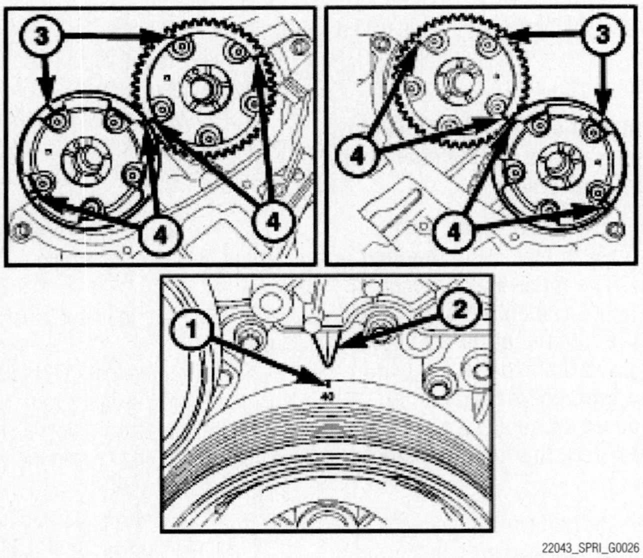

Fig. 27 Make sure that when the timing chain is installed, the camshaft adjuster marks line up as illustrated—3.5L Engine Right Camshaft

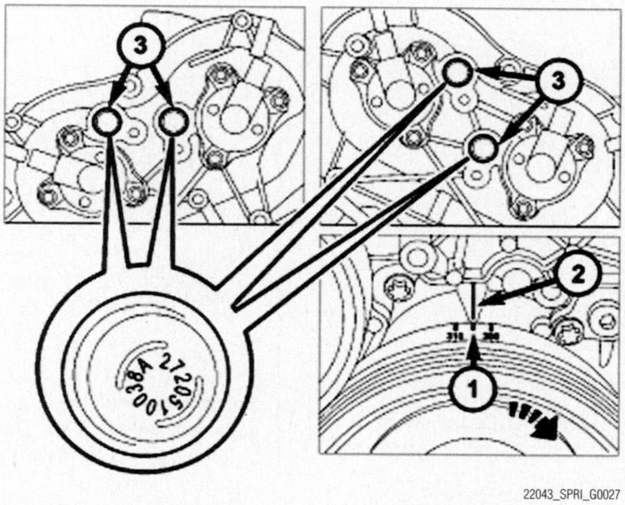

Fig. 28 Make sure that the number stamp can be seen through the camshaft sensor holes (3)—3.5L Engine Right Camshaft

30. Remove the drift from the camshaft adjuster.
31. Make sure that when the timing chain is installed, the camshaft adjuster marks line up as illustrated.
32. Use a Torx bit to the end of the camshaft while installing the center valve to the camshaft adjuster in the exhaust camshaft.
33. Install the exhaust camshaft pulse wheel.
34. Use a Torx bit to the end of the camshaft while installing the center valve from the camshaft adjuster in the intake camshaft.
35. Install the intake camshaft pulse wheel.
36. Install the camshaft adjuster center bolts.
37. Install the cylinder head cover.
38. Install and connect the ignition coils.
39. Install and connect the engine wiring harness.
40. Install the upper front cover on the right cylinder head.
41. Make sure that the number stamp can be seen through the camshaft sensor holes (see illustration).
42. Connect the camshaft position sensors in the right front upper cover.
43. Install the oil separator.
44. Install the center bolt to the oil separator.
45. Install the centrifugal oil separator cover.
46. Install the camshaft plug.
47. Install the air control valve gasket.
48. Install the air control valve on the right cylinder head.
49. Install the air control valve bracket.
50. Install the air intake assembly.
51. Connect the negative battery cable.
52. Start the engine and check for leaks.

CRANKSHAFT FRONT SEAL

REMOVAL & INSTALLATION

2.7L Engine

See Figure 29.

1. Disconnect negative battery cable.
2. Remove the accessory drive belt. For additional information, refer to the following section, “Accessory Drive Belt, Removal & Installation.”
3. Install the retaining lock for the crankshaft/ring gear.
4. Remove the crankshaft damper.
5. Using a suitable pry tool, remove the front crankshaft seal from the front cover.

To install:

6. Install the front crankshaft seal using Special Tool 8936 Installer tool.
7. Install the crankshaft damper. Tighten the bolt to 240 ft. lbs. (325 Nm) plus 90 degrees.
8. Remove the retaining lock for the crankshaft/ring gear.
9. Install the accessory drive belt.
10. Refill the engine with oil to the correct level.
11. Connect the negative battery cable.
12. Start the engine and check for leaks.

3.0L Engine

See Figure 30.

1. Disconnect negative battery cable.
2. Raise and safely support the vehicle.
3. Remove both front lower splash shields.
4. Remove the transmission thermal bypass valve and the cooler lines between the block and transmission.
5. Remove the starter blank.
6. Install Special Tool 9102 Flywheel Locking Tool.
7. Release the accessory drive belt tension by resetting the drive belt tensioner and installing a retaining pin.
8. Remove the vibration damper bolt.
9. Install Special Tool 9544 Crankshaft Damper Puller.
10. Remove the vibration damper.

WARNING

Use care when removing the crankshaft seal not to damage or gouge the timing chain cover.

11. Using suitable seal puller, remove the front crankshaft seal.

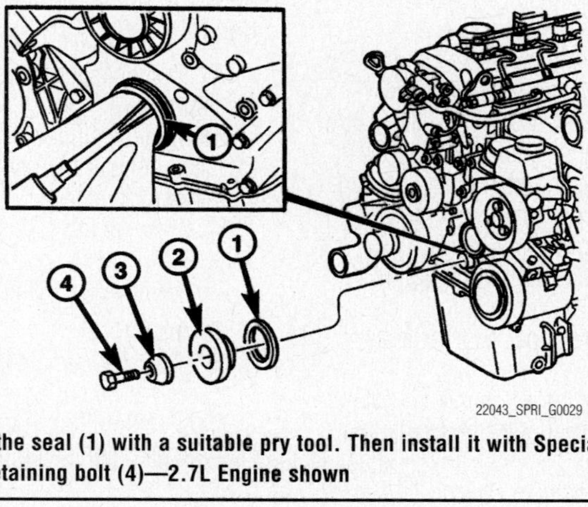

Fig. 29 Remove the seal (1) with a suitable pry tool. Then install it with Special Tool 8936 (2) washer (3) and retaining bolt (4)—2.7L Engine shown

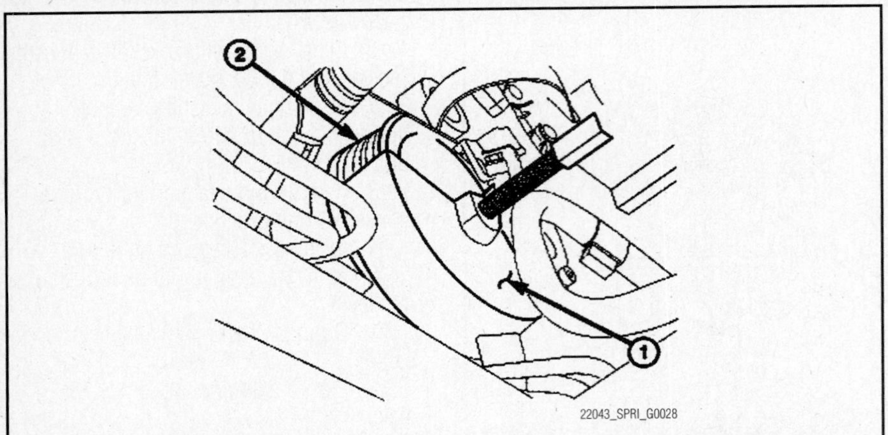

Fig. 30 Use Special Tool 9544 (1) to remove the crankshaft damper (2)—3.0L Engine shown

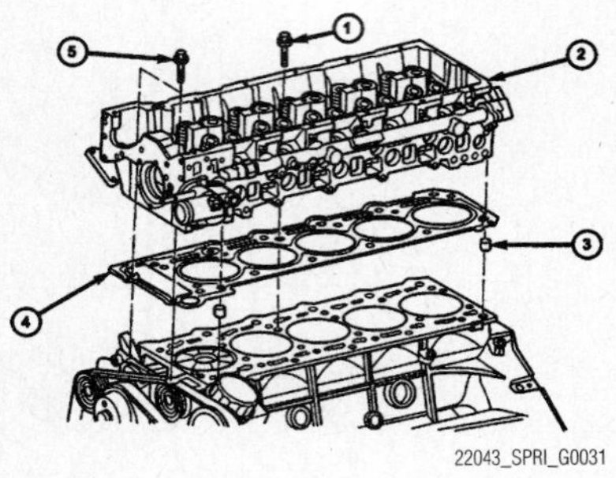

Fig. 31 Position the cylinder head (2) and gasket (4) over the dowel pins (2) and install the M12 bolts (1) and M8 bolts (5)—2.7L Engine

To install:

12. Install crankshaft oil seal using Special Tool 8936A Seal Installer.
13. Align the alignment key in the crankshaft with the key way in the damper and install the crankshaft damper. Tighten the bolt to 224 ft. lbs. (304 Nm) plus 90 degrees.
14. Position the accessory drive belt back onto the pulleys and release the belt tensioner.
15. Remove Special Tool 9102 flywheel locking tool.
16. Install the transmission thermal bypass valve and transmission cooler lines.
17. Install both underbody splash shields.
18. Lower the vehicle.
19. Connect the negative battery cable.
20. Start the engine and check for leaks.

CYLINDER HEAD

REMOVAL & INSTALLATION

2.7L Engine

See Figures 31 and 32.

1. Disconnect the negative battery cable.
2. Rotate the engine to put cylinder No. 1 and Top Dead Center (TDC).
3. Raise and safely support the vehicle.
4. Install Special Tool 8932 Retaining Lock on the crankshaft/starter ring gear to keep the engine from rotating.
5. Drain the cooling system.
6. Loosen the lower turbo support bracket bolt.
7. Remove the upper support bracket bolt.
8. Loosen the fasteners retaining the exhaust pipe to the support bracket at the rear of the engine.
9. Lower the vehicle.
10. Remove engine appearance cover.
11. Remove the camshafts. For additional information, refer to the following section, "Camshafts, Removal & Installation."
12. Remove the camshaft housing at the cylinder head.
13. Remove the high pressure pump.
14. Remove the front head cover plate.
15. Remove the high pressure fuel pump intermediate gear.
16. Disconnect the engine side of the engine harness and set it aside.
17. Disconnect the charge air pipe at the cylinder head and set it aside with the engine harness connected.
18. Remove the turbocharger oil supply line at the cylinder head and turbocharger.
19. Disconnect the turbocharger at the exhaust manifold.
20. Unbolt the transmission oil level indicator tube fasteners from the cylinder head and engine block.
21. Disconnect the upper radiator hose and by pass hose at the thermostat housing.

➡Have a shop rag ready to capture any fuel spillage when disconnecting fuel lines.

22. Disconnect the fuel line at the rear of the fuel rail.
23. Remove upper timing case to cylinder head bolts in the reverse order of the tightening sequence.
24. Remove the cylinder head mounting bolts.
25. Remove the cylinder head.

To install:

26. Clean all remaining gasket material from the mating surfaces.
27. Position the cylinder head and gasket on the engine using the dowel pins as a guide.
28. Lightly coat the threads of each cylinder head mounting bolt with clean engine oil.
29. Start each bolt first by hand and then tighten as follows:
    a. Tighten the M12 bolts in sequence to 11 ft. lbs. (15 Nm).
    b. Tighten the M12 bolts in sequence to 44 ft. lbs. (60 Nm).
    c. Tighten the M8 bolts to 15 ft lbs. (20 Nm).
    d. Tighten the M12 bolts in sequence an additional 90°.
    e. Tighten the M12 bolts in sequence an additional 90° once more.
30. Install fuel return flow line between rail and high pressure pump.
31. Connect the coolant hoses to the thermostat housing.
32. Connect the coolant pipe to the cylinder head.
33. Reconnect transmission oil level indicator tube and tighten the mounting bolts to 10 ft. lbs. (14 Nm).
34. Reconnect the turbocharger to the exhaust manifold and tighten the mounting bolts to 22 ft. lbs. (30 Nm).
35. Install the oil return flow line with new seals at turbocharger. Tighten the

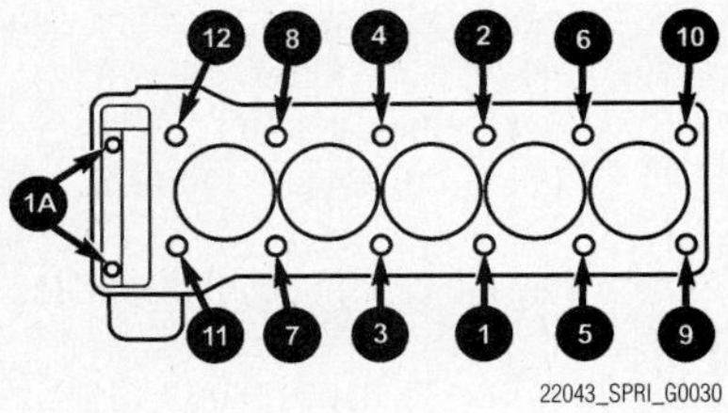

Fig. 32 Cylinder head mounting bolts torque sequence—2.7L Engine

supply line bolt to the turbocharger to 13 ft. lbs. (18Nm) and supply line bolt to the cylinder head to 80 inch lbs. (9 Nm).

36. Install the charge air distribution pipe.

37. Install and properly route the engine wiring harness, making appropriate connections.

38. Install the high pressure fuel pump intermediate gear and high pressure pump.

39. Install the camshaft housing with tappets to cylinder head.

40. Install the camshafts.

41. Install the top guide rail.

42. Install the front cover on the cylinder head.

43. Install the cylinder head cover.

44. Install the fuel high pressure pipes and injectors.

45. Install the timing chain tensioner with a new gasket. Tighten the bolts to 59 ft. lbs. (80 Nm).

46. Remove the Special Tool retaining lock for the crankshaft/starter ring gear.

47. Install the air intake tube at turbocharger.

48. Install the fasteners retaining the front exhaust pipe to the support bracket at the rear of the engine.

49. Install the upper support bracket fastener.

50. Install the lower turbo support bracket bolt.

51. Install engine appearance cover

52. Refill the cooling system to the correct level.

53. Connect the negative battery cable.

54. Start engine and check for leaks.

3.0L Engine

See Figures 33 through 37.

1. Disconnect the negative battery cable.
2. Remove the engine appearance cover.
3. Drain the cooling system.
4. Remove the strut tower support.
5. Remove the air cleaner outlet tube.
6. Remove the charge air inlet tube.
7. Disconnect the vacuum hose at the vacuum pump and set it aside.
8. Remove the upper radiator hose.
9. Disconnect the coolant reservoir hose at thermostat housing and set it aside.
10. Disconnect the fuel supply and return hose quick connects at the left cylinder head cover.
11. Loosen the high pressure fuel pipes at the fuel rail and disconnect the high pressure fuel pipes at the left injectors.
12. Disconnect the high pressure fuel line at the high pressure pump.
13. Disconnect the fuel rail solenoid wiring harness connector and remove the left fuel rail along with the fuel rail transfer pipe.
14. Remove the low pressure fuel supply and return pipe bundle fasteners.
15. Disconnect the right fuel rail pressure sensor and remove the fuel rail.
16. Disconnect the camshaft position sensor (CMP), the right fuel injector wiring harness connectors, the right return fuel hoses from the injectors.
17. Remove the return fuel bundle fasteners.
18. Disconnect the water in fuel sensor, if equipped, and the turbocharger servo motor harness connectors.
19. Remove the fuel filter bracket fasteners.
20. Disconnect the fuel return hose bundle, engine ground strap, at the right front of the intake manifold.

➡Have a shop rag ready to capture any fuel spillage.

21. Remove the fuel filter, hose and pipe assemblies and position aside.
22. Remove the turbocharger. For additional information, refer to the following section, "Turbocharger, Removal & Installation."

➡Observe the way the engine oil supply and return ports in the turbocharger adapter housing align to the engine block for oil flow through the turbocharger. Failure to do so will result in immediate turbocharger failure.

23. Remove turbocharger oil housing adapter.
24. Disconnect the swirl valve actuator, glow plugs, EGR pressure sensor and coolant temperature sensor wiring harness connector.
25. Remove the main engine wiring harness fasteners and position the harness out of the way.
26. Disconnect the EGR coolant pipe from the rear of the EGR housing.
27. Remove the EGR valve.

➡The intake manifold is of the split design meaning that there are two halves. Whenever the intake manifold is removed, inspect the shared coolant passage in the front of the intake manifold for leaks, repair as necessary.

28. Remove the intake manifold. For additional information, refer to the following section, "Intake Manifold, Removal & Installation."
29. Remove the accessory drive belt. For additional information, refer to the following section, "Accessory Drive Belt, Removal & Installation."
30. Remove the two idler pulleys.
31. Remove the belt tensioner.
32. Rotate the engine by the crankshaft damper bolt until cylinder No. 1 is at Top Dead Center (TDC).
33. Raise and safely support the vehicle.
34. Remove the right side starter blank.
35. Disconnect the hydraulic cooling fan lines and capture the fluid in a approved and clearly marked container.
36. Remove the front oil pan retaining bolts.
37. Lower the vehicle.
38. Remove the left rear heater hose retainer.
39. Remove the left fuel injectors.
40. Disconnect the vacuum supply hose.
41. Remove the oil filter housing bracket.

➡The timing cover is sealed with Mopar® sealant that may be difficult when separating components. If it is difficult to separate, heat the sealed edges or area with a heat gun. DO NOT use any heat source that works with flame.

42. Remove the left cylinder head cover.
43. Observe the left camshaft gear alignment marks on the rear of the camshaft gears. If they are together, continue with the next step. If the left camshaft alignment marks are separated, rotate the engine by the vibration damper another 360 degrees, until camshaft marks align together and the vibration damper reaches TDC.
44. Raise and safely support the vehicle.
45. Install Special Tool 9102 Crankshaft Lock into the starter access blank.
46. Lower the vehicle.

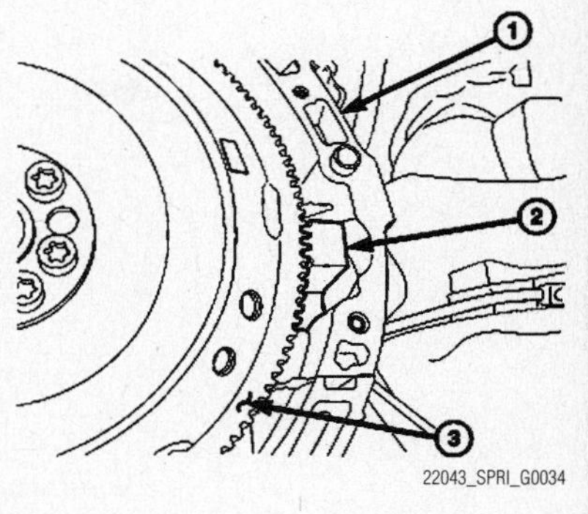

Fig. 33 Install Special Tool 9102 (2) into the starter access blank to lock the ring gear (3) into place.

47. Remove the cooling fan module.
48. Remove the vibration damper.
49. Remove the front timing chain cover.
50. Matchmark the balance shaft position to the engine block and timing chain.
51. Matchmark the timing chain to crankshaft gear and camshaft drive gear relation.
52. Raise and safely support the vehicle.
53. Remove Special Tool 9102 Locking Tool.
54. Lower the vehicle.
55. Remove the high pressure fuel pump.
56. Rotate the engine and remove the left camshaft drive gear lower bolt.

➡The left exhaust camshaft drive gear dowel pin should align at approximately the 12 O'clock position when viewing through the camshaft seal access hole.

57. Rotate the engine back to TDC and check the alignment marks at the balance shaft, camshaft gear and crankshaft gear.
58. Remove the timing chain tensioner.
59. Remove the remaining left camshaft drive gear retaining bolts.
60. Separate the left camshaft drive gear and chain from camshaft.
61. Remove the left camshaft retainers (1 and 2) and camshafts.
62. Remove the left camshaft drive gear. Make a roll pin tool by using a tube, nut, bolt and washer. Place the nut on the bolt and the bolt through the tube. Thread the bolt into the roll pin and turn the nut to remove the roll pin (as illustrated).
63. Remove the left lower timing chain guide fastener and guide.
64. Remove the left cylinder head glow plugs.
65. Remove the cylinder head and gasket from engine block.

To install:

66. Clean all remaining gasket material from the mating surfaces.
67. Position the cylinder head and gasket on the engine block.

➡If new cylinder head bolts are used, do not lubricate the new cylinder head bolts. They already are coated with an anti scuff treatment.

68. Lightly coat the cylinder head bolts with clean engine oil.
69. Tighten the cylinder head mounting bolts as follows:
    a. Tighten the M12 bolts (1-8) in sequence to 44 ft. lbs. (60 Nm).
    b. Tighten the M8 bolts (9-10) to 15 ft. lbs. (20 Nm).
    c. Tighten the M12 bolts in sequence an additional 90 degrees.
    d. Verify the M8 bolts again to 15 ft. lbs. (20 Nm).
    e. Tighten the M12 bolts in sequence an additional 90 degrees.
70. Install the followers (2) and tappets (2) into their original positions.
71. Install the glow plugs and tighten to 11 ft. lbs. (15 Nm).
72. Install the camshafts. For additional information, refer to the following section, "Camshafts, Removal & Installation."
73. Align the camshaft marks so the alignment marks are facing each other.
74. Insert the timing chain, through the cylinder head, and on to the camshaft drive gear.
75. Align the balance shaft with the matchmark.
76. Once the camshaft drive gear is mated with the timing chain, install the camshaft drive gear on to the camshaft and assure the balance shaft is aligned properly.
77. Install the upper two of the three camshaft drive gear bolts.
78. Install the left lower and upper timing chain guide.
79. Install the timing chain tensioner.
80. Rotate the engine by the crankshaft damper bolt enough to gain access to the third camshaft drive gear bolt hole.
81. Install the third camshaft drive gear retaining bolt and tighten the bolt to 13 ft. lbs. (18 Nm).

WARNING

If the camshaft, balance shaft and or crankshaft alignment marks are not aligned properly immediate damage to the engine will occur. If the camshafts, balance shaft and or crankshaft do not align properly after rotating the engine to the original starting point, STOP and begin the alignment procedure again.

82. Rotate the engine back to TDC by the crankshaft damper bolt until the crankshaft, camshaft and balance shaft align TDC again.

WARNING

Check that all the timing chain fits properly on all the timing gears. Failure to do so will result in immediate engine damage.

83. Install the timing chain cover and tighten the bolts to 74 inch lbs. (8.4 Nm).
84. Raise and safely support the vehicle.
85. Tighten the five front oil pan-to-timing cover bolts to 15 ft. lbs. (20 Nm).
86. Install Special Tool 9102 Crankshaft Lock into the starter access blank.

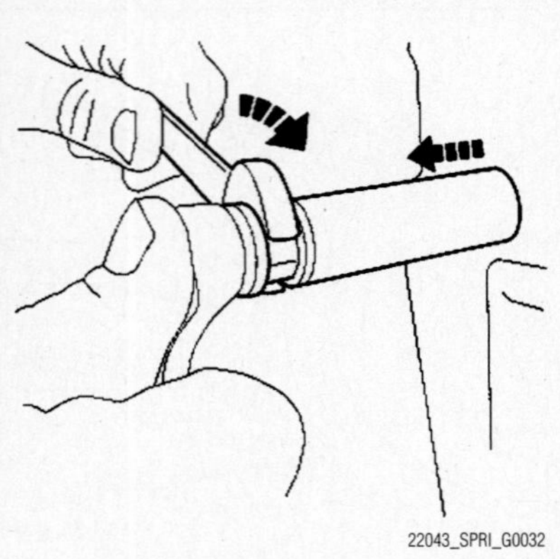

Fig. 34 Make a roll pin tool using a tube, nut, bolt and washer to remove the roll pin—3.0L Left cylinder head removal

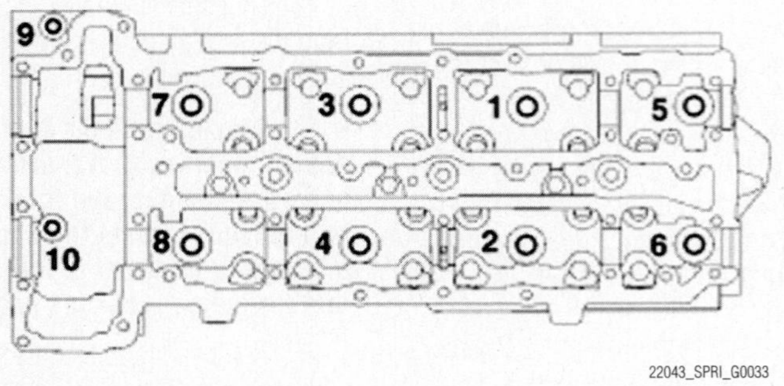

Fig. 35 Left cylinder head torque sequence—3.0L Engine

87. Lower the vehicle.
88. Install the crankshaft damper and tighten the bolts to 148 ft. lbs. (200 Nm) plus 90°
89. Apply a 1.5mm continuous bead of Mopar® Engine Sealant RTV around the diameter of the left cylinder head cover, and install the cover with new camshaft seals.
90. Tighten the bolts for the cylinder head cover as follows:
  a. Tighten the bolts in sequence to 35 inch lbs. (4 Nm).
  b. Tighten the bolts in sequence to 53 inch lbs. (6 Nm).
  c. Then tighten the bolts in sequence to 75 inch lbs. (8.4 Nm).
91. Install the oil filter housing bracket and tighten the bolts to 122 inch lbs. (13.8 Nm).
92. Install the high pressure pump and tighten bolts to 120 inch lbs. (13.5 Nm).
93. Install the belt idler pulleys and tighten the bolts to 43 ft. lbs. (58 Nm).
94. Install the drive belt tensioner and tighten the bolts to 43 ft. lbs. (58 Nm).
95. Install the accessory drive belt.
96. Install the intake manifold. Tighten bolts to 12 ft. lbs. (16 Nm), starting in the middle and tightening in a cross pattern

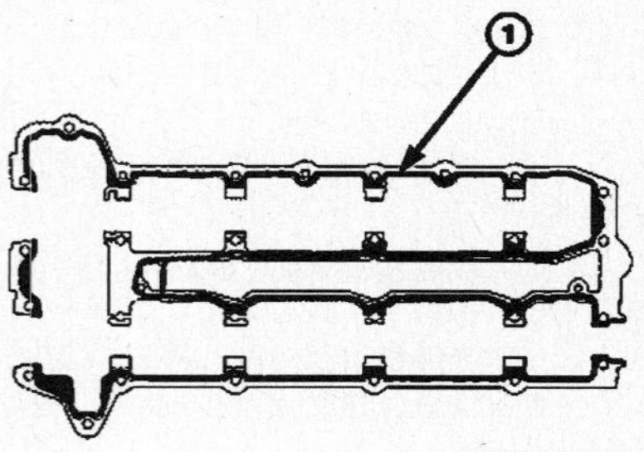

Fig. 36 Apply a bead of RTV (1) around the diameter of the cylinder head cover—3.0L Left cylinder head cover installation

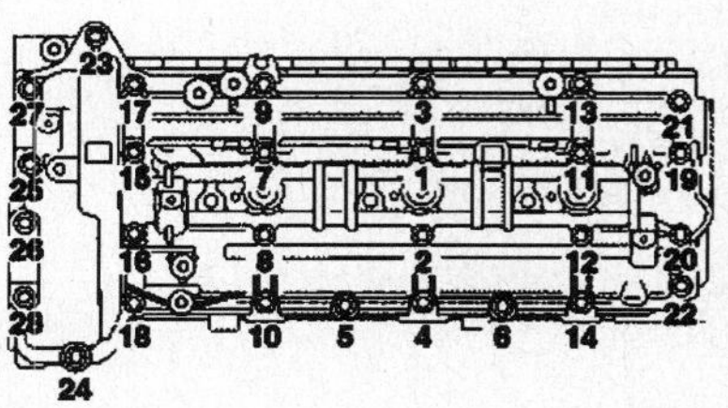

Fig. 37 Left cylinder head cover torque sequence—3.0L Engine

outward until reaching the upper thermostat bolts on the right front manifold.

➡**The right intake manifold upper thermostat housing bolts should be tightened to 74 inch lbs. (8.4 Nm).**

➡**The fuel injector sealing washers MUST be replaced. DO NOT use the old sealing washers or double the sealing washers.**

97. Lubricate the fuel injector body and install the left fuel injectors and new lower sealing washers.

➡**The injector retaining claw bolts are torque to yield and must always be replaced.**

98. Install the injector retaining claws and tighten the bolts to 62 inch lbs. (7 Nm) plus 180°.
99. Install the fuel return hoses and connect them to the injectors.
100. Properly route and connect the engine wiring harness.
101. Install the fuel rail. For additional information, refer to the following section, "Fuel Injectors, Removal & Installation."

➡**Inspect the fuel lines for wear or damage, look closely around the flange area. Replace as necessary. DO NOT over tighten.**

102. Install the high pressure fuel lines, including the fuel rail equalizing line. Tighten the line nuts to 20 ft. lbs. (27 Nm).
103. Install the fuel filter.
104. Install the turbocharger.
105. Install the air control valve and resonator.
106. Install the charge air cooler inlet pipe and resonator.
107. Install the cooling fan module.
108. Install the heater hose bracket and secure hoses.
109. Connect the vacuum pump supply hose.
110. Raise and safely support the vehicle.
111. Remove Special Tool 9102 and install the starter blank.
112. Connect the cooling fan hydraulic lines.
113. Lower the vehicle.
114. Refill the cooling system the to correct level.
115. Ensure the power steering system is filled to the correct level.
116. Install the strut tower support.
117. Install the engine appearance cover.
118. Connect the negative battery cable.
119. Start the engine and check for leaks.

3.5L Engine

See Figures 38 and 39.

1. Disconnect the negative battery cable.
2. Properly relieve the fuel system pressure.
3. Drain the cooling system.
4. Drain the engine oil.
5. Remove the air intake assembly.
6. Remove the accessory drive belt. For additional information, refer to the following section, "Accessory Drive Belt, Removal & Installation."
7. Rotate the engine in a clockwise direction until the No. 1 cylinder is at 40 degrees after Top Dead Center (TDC).
8. Raise and safely support the vehicle.
9. Remove the lower sound shield.
10. Remove the catalytic converter to manifold mounting bolts.
11. Remove the timing chain tensioner.
12. Lower the vehicle.
13. Disconnect the upper radiator hose from the engine.
14. Remove the fan and fan shroud assembly.
15. Disconnect the canister purge line from the engine.
16. Remove the air intake housing support.
17. Remove the evaporative emissions vacuum lines.
18. Remove the fuel rail and fuel injectors. For additional information, refer to the following section, "Fuel Injectors, Removal & Installation."
19. Disconnect and remove the Powertrain Control Module (PCM).
20. Remove the left and right PCM bracket.
21. Position aside the remote battery positive terminal connection.
22. Disconnect the engine wiring harness ground from the cylinder head.
23. Remove the three ignition coils from the cylinder head. For additional information, refer to the following section, "Ignition Coil, Removal & Installation."
24. Remove the intake manifold. For additional information, refer to the following section, "Intake Manifold, Removal & Installation."
25. Remove the air injection valve bolts.
26. Remove the air injection adapter bolts.
27. Remove the hoses from the air injection pump.
28. Remove the air injection pump and bracket.
29. Remove the upper idler pulleys.
30. Remove the accessory drive tensioner pulley bolts.

31. Remove the accessory drive tensioner pulley.
32. Remove the oil cooler housing bolts and remove the oil cooler housing.
33. Disconnect the right head camshaft position sensors.
34. Remove the right head camshaft position sensors.
35. Disconnect the left head camshaft position sensors.
36. Remove the left head camshaft position sensors.
37. Remove the left upper front cover.
38. Remove the left cylinder head cover.
39. Remove the camshafts. For additional information, refer to the following section, "Camshafts, Removal & Installation."
40. Use a slide hammer to remove the timing chain slide rail pins from the cylinder head.
41. Remove the timing chain slide rail.
42. Loosen all of the cylinder head bolts in the reverse order of the tightening sequence.
43. Remove the cylinder head bolts and remove cylinder head.
44. Place the cylinder head on wooden blocks on the bench and remove the exhaust manifold if necessary.

To install:

45. If removed, install the exhaust manifold to the cylinder and tighten the nuts to 12 ft. lbs. (16 Nm).
46. Clean any old gasket material from the mating surfaces.
47. Install the cylinder head with a new gasket.
48. Install the cylinder head-to-timing chain front cover bolts to 18 ft. lbs. (25 Nm) plus 90°
49. Install the cylinder head mounting bolts in a spiral pattern as follows:
    - Step 1: Tighten to 15 ft. lbs. (20 Nm)
    - Step 2: Tighten to 29 ft. lbs. (44 Nm)
    - Step 3: Tighten to 29 ft. lbs. (44 Nm) again
    - Step 4: Tighten an additional 90°
    - Step 5: Tighten an additional 90° again
50. Install the timing chain slide rail.
51. Install the timing chain slide rail pins into the cylinder head.
52. Install the camshafts. For additional information, refer to the following section, "Camshafts, Removal & Installation."
53. Install the cylinder head cover as follows:
    a. Remove any old gasket material from the sealing surfaces of the cylinder head cover.
    b. Apply a thin layer of silicone sealant to the cylinder head cover mating surface.
    c. Install the cylinder head cover with new bolts and tighten them in the sequence shown to 106 inch lbs. (12 Nm).
    d. Tighten all of the bolts in sequence in additional 90°
54. Install the upper front cover as follows:
    a. Clean any old gasket material from the mating surfaces.
    b. Apply silicone sealant to the upper front cover sealing surface.
    c. Install the upper front cover and tighten the mounting bolts to 80 inch lbs. (9 Nm).
55. Install the camshaft position sensors.
56. Install the air injection pump and bracket.
57. Install the air injection valve.
58. Install the hoses to the air injection pump.
59. Install the oil cooler housing and tighten the bolts to 18 ft. lbs. (25 Nm).
60. Install the accessory drive tensioner pulley and tighten the bolts to 26 ft. lbs. (35 Nm)
61. Install the upper idler pulleys.
62. Install the intake manifold.
63. Install the ignition coils and connect the electrical connectors.
64. Route the engine wiring harness in its original position and tighten the harness bolts to 71 inch lbs. (8 Nm).
65. Install the PCM mounting bolts brackets, the install and connect the PCM electrical connectors.
66. Install the fuel rail and fuel injectors.
67. Install the vacuum line to the fuel pressure regulator.
68. Install the intake air housing support.
69. Connect the remote battery positive terminal connection.
70. Connect the canister purge line to the engine.
71. Install the fan assembly.
72. Connect the upper radiator hose to the engine.
73. Install the lower sound shield.
74. Install the accessory drive belt.
75. Lower the vehicle.
76. Refill the engine with oil to the correct level.
77. Refill the cooling system to the correct level.
78. Connect the negative battery cable.
79. Start the engine and check for leaks.

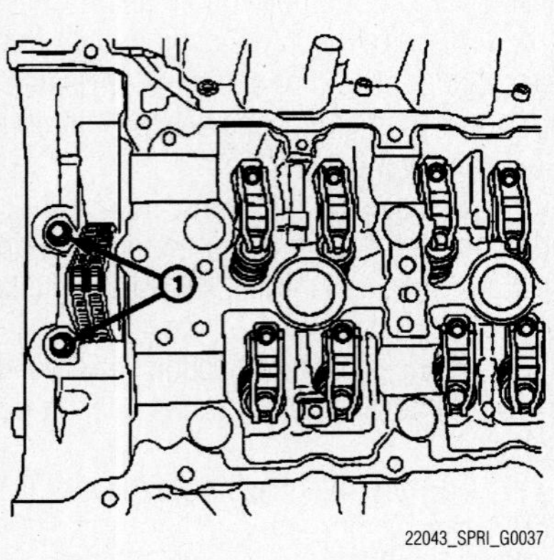

Fig. 38 Install the two cylinder head-to-front cover bolts (1) before the rest of the cylinder head mounting bolts—3.5L Engine cylinder head installation

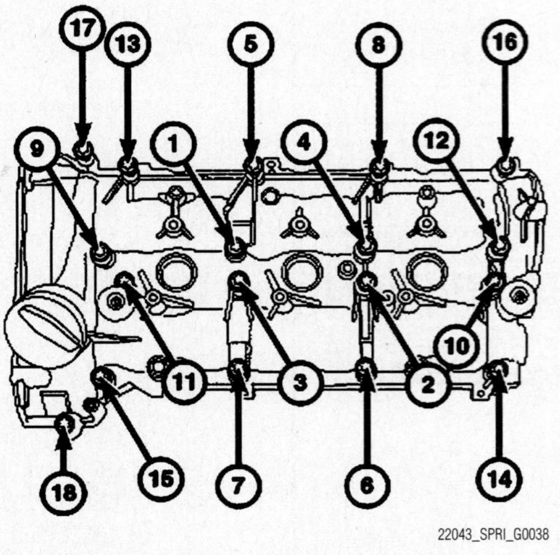

Fig. 39 Cylinder head cover torque sequence—3.5L cylinder head cover

ENGINE ASSEMBLY

REMOVAL & INSTALLATION

2.7L Engine

See Figures 40 and 41.

1. Disconnect the negative battery cable.
2. Drain the cooling system.
3. Evacuate and recover the A/C refrigerant.
4. Remove the front grille and fascia assembly.
5. Disconnect the engine wiring harness at the cabin side and carefully guide though the cowl into the engine area.
6. Remove the turbocharger heat shield.
7. Remove the engine appearance cover.
8. Remove the air cleaner and hose at the turbocharger and air cleaner assembly.
9. Disconnect the transmission lines at the radiator.
10. Disconnect the upper and lower radiator hoses.
11. Disconnect the A/C lines at the condenser.
12. Disconnect the condenser fan harness connector.
13. Disconnect the power steering cooler lines at the cooler.
14. Disconnect the charge air cooler hose at the intake manifold.
15. Remove charge air hose fasteners at the radiator closure panel.
16. Remove the fasteners retaining the radiator to the front crossmember.
17. Remove the change air cooler, A/C condenser and fan as an assembly.
18. Disconnect the charge air hose at the intake manifold.
19. Remove the radiator assembly.
20. Disconnect the high pressure and return hoses at the power steering pump.
21. Disconnect the fuel lines at the fuel filter.
22. Disconnect the refrigerant line at the A/C compressor.
23. Disconnect the vacuum line for the brake booster at the vacuum pump.
24. Disconnect the coolant hose of heating return flow at the water pump.
25. Disconnect the coolant hose of the heater supply at the coolant pipe at the side of the cylinder head.
26. Disconnect the air inlet, CCV breather hoses and CCV heater at the turbocharger.
27. Raise and safely support the vehicle.
28. Disconnect the front exhaust at the turbocharger.
29. Disconnect the electrical connector at the transmission.
30. Disconnect the engine valley drain hose fastener from the transmission.
31. Remove the steering gear mounting bolts.
32. Disconnect the transmission cooler lines at transmission and oil pan.
33. Remove the torque converter access plate.
34. Remove the torque converter bolts.
35. Remove the crank position sensor.
36. Remove the transmission housing to engine mounting bolts.
37. Remove the starter mounting bolts.
38. Support the transmission with a suitable transmission jack.
39. Place a wood block between the transmission housing and the front frame cross over.
40. Remove the transmission jack.
41. Remove the exhaust bracket (right side).
42. Remove the engine ground strap (left side).
43. Lower the vehicle.
44. Remove the heater housing filter and lower housing.
45. Connect Special Tool 9308 Engine Lifting Fixture to the engine lifting eyes.
46. Remove the engine mount bolts.
47. Remove the transmission oil level indicator tube mounting bolt.
48. Using tin snips, remove the front cross plate at the cutting edges and deburr.
49. Connect and engine hoist and carefully lift engine assembly from engine bay area.

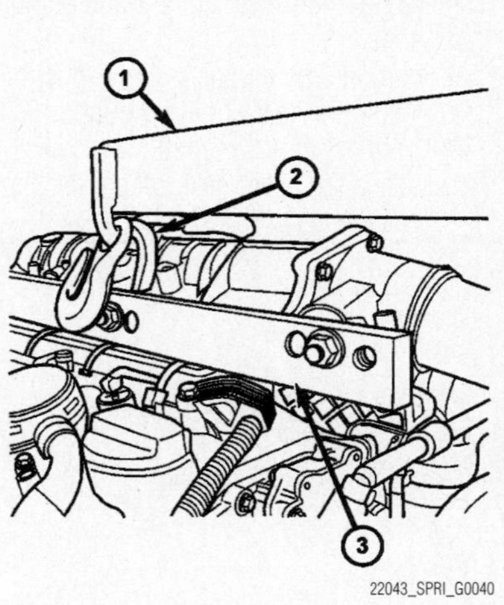

Fig. 40 Attach Special Tool 9308 (3) to the engine, then connect the engine hoist (1) to the center eyelet (2)—2.7L Engine removal

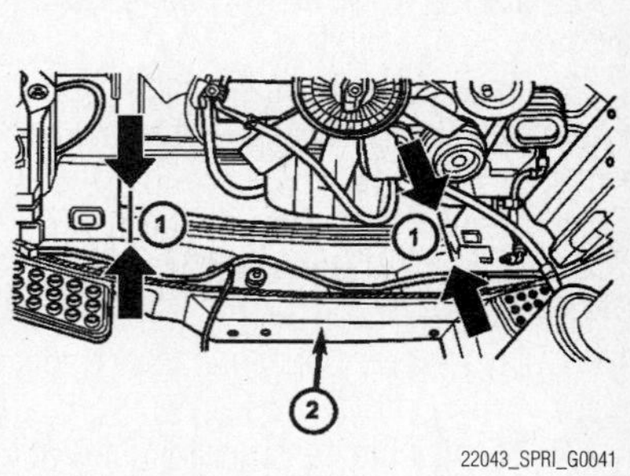

Fig. 41 Cut the front cross plate (2) at the area indicated (1)—2.7L Engine removal

To install:

50. Install the engine assembly into the vehicle engine compartment, mating the transmission and the engine.
51. Lower the engine assembly until the engine brackets align with the mounts.
52. Hand start the engine mount bolts and remove the engine lifting device. Tighten the engine mount bolts to 62 ft. lbs. (83 Nm).
53. Raise and safely support the vehicle.
54. Install the transmission housing to engine bolts. For additional information, refer to the following section, "Automatic Transmission, Removal & Installation."
55. Install the torque converter bolts. For additional information, refer to the following section, "Automatic Transmission, Removal & Installation."
56. Install the crankshaft position sensor.
57. Install the torque converter access plate.
58. Install the transmission cooler lines to transmission.
59. Connect the engine valley drain hose to the transmission.
60. Install the transmission electrical connector and shifter hardware.
61. Install the steering gear.
62. Install the starter.
63. Connect the ground strap (left side).
64. Align and install the exhaust and bracket.
65. Lower the vehicle.
66. Install the lower heater housing and filter.
67. Install the air inlet hose, CCV breather and CCV heater at the turbocharger.
68. Connect the coolant supply and return hoses.
69. Connect the brake booster vacuum hose at the vacuum pump.
70. Connect the fuel lines at the filter assembly.
71. Connect the power steering hoses.

72. Install the radiator/charge air cooler and hose(s) assemblies.
73. Install A/C condenser and fan assemblies Connect the fan harness connector.
74. Connect the refrigerant lines.
75. Install a air conditioning receiver/drier.
76. Connect the upper and lower radiator hoses.
77. Connect the transmission lines at the radiator.
78. Install air cleaner housing and connect the air inlet duct and air flow sensor.
79. Connect the charge air cooler hose at intake manifold.
80. Route the engine wiring harness inside the vehicle and connect.
81. Install the turbocharger heat shield.
82. Install the front grille and fascia assembly.
83. Check and fill the engine oil.
84. Refill the cooling system to the correct level.
85. Evacuate and recharge the A/C refrigerant.
86. Start engine and check for leaks

3.0L Engine

See Figure 42.

1. Remove the hood.
2. Disconnect the negative battery cable.
3. Drain the cooling system.
4. Remove air intake hose downstream of air filter on air filter housing and disconnect electrical connectors.
5. Disconnect the jump-starting point on air filter housing and place to one side.
6. Pull out air intake hose upstream of air filter on front module.
7. Lift the air filter housing at front from front module and pull out of the rear guides.
8. Remove the air filter housing bracket from the bulkhead.
9. Disconnect the electrical connector at the intake manifold pressure sensor.
10. Remove the intake manifold pressure sensor.
11. Remove hot film mass air flow sensor.
12. Remove the holder for air filter housing to front plate.
13. Remove the trim panel on right cylinder head cover.
14. Remove the trim panel on left cylinder head cover.
15. Place the gearshift into neutral.
16. Disconnect and remove the auxiliary battery.
17. Remove the battery tray for the auxiliary battery.
18. Raise and safely support the vehicle.
19. Disconnect the speed sensors on transmission.
20. Disconnect the oxygen sensors.
21. Remove the coolant lines from the heater core.
22. Remove the upper and lower radiator hoses from the radiator and position aside.
23. Remove the vacuum line at the vacuum pump.
24. Disconnect the engine ground.
25. Disconnect the Engine Control Module (ECM).
26. Remove the power steering lines at the power steering pump and cap the lines.
27. Remove the clamp and disconnect exhaust system between catalytic converter and diesel particulate filter.
28. Remove the driveshaft center support bearing on frame floor assembly.
29. Detach power take-off connections.
30. Remove the bolts, and remove driveshaft and hang to the side outside the working area.
31. Insert a suitable wooden block between the transmission and crossmember.
32. Attach engine removal chains to the lift points.
33. Remove the bolts from the right engine mount at the front.
34. Remove the bolts from the left engine mount at the front.
35. Using a suitable engine hoist, lift the engine and transmission assembly from the vehicle.

To install:

36. Using a suitable engine hoist, lower the engine and transmission assembly into the vehicle.
37. Install the front right and left engine mount bolts.
38. Remove the engine removal chains.
39. Install the rear engine mount.
40. Connect the driveshaft.
41. Attach the power take-off connections.

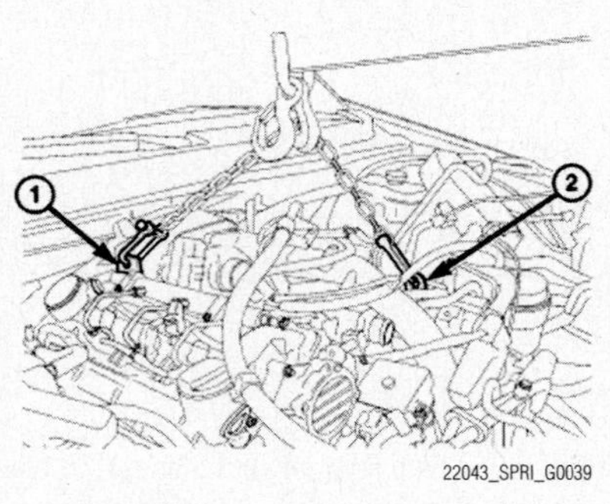

Fig. 42 Attach the engine chains to the lift points (1,2)—3.0L Engine

42. Install the driveshaft center support bearing on frame floor assembly.
43. Connect the exhaust system between the catalytic converter and diesel particulate filter.
44. Install the power steering lines at the power steering pump.
45. Connect the ECM and engine ground.
46. Install the vacuum line at the vacuum pump.
47. Connect the upper and lower radiator hoses at the radiator.
48. Connect the coolant lines to the heater core.
49. Connect the oxygen sensors.
50. Connect the speed sensors on transmission.
51. Install the battery tray for auxiliary battery and install the auxiliary battery.
52. Install the trim panel on left cylinder head cover.
53. Install the trim panel on right cylinder head cover.
54. Install the holder for air filter housing to front plate.
55. Install the hot film mass air flow sensor.
56. Install the intake manifold pressure sensor.
57. Connect the electrical connector at intake manifold pressure sensor.
58. Install the air filter housing bracket to the bulkhead.
59. Connect the jump-starting point on air filter housing and place to one side.
60. Install air intake hose downstream of air filter on air filter housing.
61. Refill the engine cooling system to the correct level.
62. Connect the negative battery cable.
63. Install the engine hood

3.5L Engine

1. Disconnect the negative battery cable.
2. Drain the cooling system.
3. Drain the engine oil.
4. Drain the power steering fluid.
5. Remove the air intake assembly.
6. Remove the grill.
7. Remove the headlight trim panel.
8. Raise and safely support the vehicle.
9. Remove the license plate holder and step grip plate.
10. Remove the front fascia assembly.
11. Lower the vehicle.
12. Drain the power steering fluid from the power steering fluid reservoir.
13. Disconnect the power steering fluid lines.

14. Disconnect the A/C pressure sensor.
15. Remove the condenser line bolt.
16. Remove the condenser lines.
17. Remove the transmission cooler lines from the radiator.
18. Remove the heater hose lines from the extension line.
19. Remove the upper and lower radiator hoses.
20. Matchmark the radiator support location on the frame.
21. Disconnect the electric fan connector.
22. Remove the cooling module assembly.
23. Disconnect the canister purge lines and position aside.
24. Disconnect the fuel lines.
25. Disconnect the fuel lines at the fuel rail.
26. Disconnect the Powertrain Control Module (PCM) connectors and remove the PCM.
27. Remove the transmission dip stick mounting bolts.
28. Disconnect the engine ground strap.
29. Disconnect the coolant level sensor.
30. Raise and safely support the vehicle.
31. Remove the torque converter bolts.
32. Disconnect the oxygen sensor connectors at the connector bracket.
33. Remove the bolts from the right and left exhaust flange.
34. Remove the starter. For additional information, refer to the following section, "Starter, Removal & Installation."
35. Disconnect the alternator electrical connectors.
36. Remove all but the top bell housing bolt.
37. Remove the left motor mount bolt.
38. Remove the left motor mount bolt.
39. Lower the vehicle.
40. Support the transmission with a suitable jack.
41. Install a suitable engine lift to the engine.
42. Remove the last bellhousing bolt.
43. Remove the engine assembly from the vehicle.

To install:

44. Using an engine lift, lower the engine assembly into the vehicle.
45. Install a single bellhousing bolt and tighten to 28 ft. lbs. (38 Nm).
46. Install the right motor mount bolt and tighten to 42 ft. lbs. (58 Nm).
47. Install the left motor mount bolt and tighten to 42 ft. lbs. (58 Nm).
48. Remove the jack supporting the transmission assembly and remove the engine lift.
49. Connect the alternator electrical connector.
50. Install the remaining bellhousing bolts and tighten to 28 ft. lbs. (38 Nm).
51. Install the torque converter bolts and tighten to 37 ft. lbs. (50 Nm).
52. Install the starter motor.
53. Install the bolts for the left and right exhaust flanges and tighten to 15 ft. lbs. (20 Nm).
54. Connect the oxygen sensor electrical connectors.
55. Install the front lower sound shield.
56. Connect the coolant level sensor.
57. Connect the engine ground strap.
58. Install the transmission dipstick mounting bolts.
59. Install the PCM and connect the electrical connectors.
60. Connect the fuel lines to the fuel rail.
61. Connect the canister purge lines.
62. Connect the electric fan connector.
63. Install the radiator support. Make sure the radiator support location lines up with the marks made on the frame during the removal process.
64. Install the upper and lower radiator hose.
65. Install the heater hose lines to the extension line.
66. Install the transmission cooler lines to the radiator.
67. Install the condenser lines.
68. Connect the A/C pressure sensor.
69. Connect the power steering fluid lines.
70. Install the front fascia assembly.
71. Install the license plate holder and step grip plate.
72. Install the head lamp trim panel.
73. Install the grill assembly.
74. Install the air intake assembly.
75. Refill the engine with oil to the correct level.
76. Refill the power steering system with fluid to the correct level.
77. Refill the cooling system to the correct level.
78. Connect the negative battery cable.
79. Start the engine and check for leaks.

EXHAUST MANIFOLD

REMOVAL & INSTALLATION

2.7L Engine

1. Disconnect the negative battery cable.
2. Remove the exhaust heat shield.
3. Raise and safely support the vehicle.
4. Remove the turbocharger support bracket.
5. Loosen the exhaust pipe to engine bracket fasteners at the rear of the engine block.
6. Remove the exhaust hanger fasteners at the muffler.
7. Disconnect the front exhaust pipe to turbocharger fastener.
8. Position the front exhaust pipe aside.
9. Lower the vehicle.
10. Remove the air cleaner housing hose from the turbocharger and position aside.
11. Remove the turbocharger oil cooler lines.
12. Remove the turbocharger to exhaust manifold fasteners and remove turbocharger.
13. Remove the self-locking exhaust manifold fasteners.
14. Remove exhaust manifold.

To install:

15. Inspect exhaust manifold gasket surface for flatness with a straight edge.
16. Inspect exhaust manifold for cracks or distortion.
17. Install a new exhaust manifold gasket over the studs.
18. Position the exhaust manifold over to studs and tighten retaining nuts to 22 ft. lbs. (30 Nm).

➡Replace the turbocharger oil cooler line banjo bolt seals before installing the oil cooler line.

19. Install the turbocharger.
20. Raise and safely support the vehicle.
21. Install the front exhaust pipe to turbocharger.
22. Install the exhaust hanger fasteners at the muffler.
23. Tighten the exhaust hanger bracket to engine block.
24. Install the turbocharger support bracket.
25. Lower the vehicle.
26. Install the air cleaner duct to the turbocharger.
27. Install the exhaust heat shield.
28. Connect the negative battery cable.

3.0L Engine

1. Disconnect the negative battery cable.
2. Remove the engine appearance cover.
3. Remove the turbo heat shield.
4. Remove the EGR tube, left side only.
5. Remove the exhaust elbow at the turbo.
6. Remove the exhaust manifold and gasket.

To install:

7. Clean the mating surfaces of any old gasket material.

8. Install the exhaust manifold with a new gasket. Tighten the nuts to 18 ft. lbs. (25 Nm).

9. Install the exhaust elbow to the turbocharger and tighten the bolts to 15 ft. lbs. (20 Nm) plus 90°.

10. Install the turbo heat shield and tighten the bolts to 89 inch lbs. (10 Nm).

11. Install the engine appearance cover.

12. Connect the negative battery cable.

3.5L Engine

1. Disconnect the negative battery cable.

2. Remove the air intake assembly.

3. Remove the EGR valve, left side only.

4. Disconnect the exhaust back pressure sensor.

5. Remove the exhaust back pressure sensor.

6. Remove the catalytic converter to exhaust manifold bolts.

7. Remove the EGR line, left side only.

8. Remove the exhaust manifold bolts.

9. Remove the exhaust manifold and gasket.

To install:

10. Clean the mating surfaces of any old gasket material.

11. Install the exhaust manifold with a new gasket. Tighten the bolts to 98 inch lbs. (11 Nm).

12. Install the EGR line, left side only.

13. Install the catalytic converter-to-exhaust manifold nuts and tighten to 15 ft. lbs. (20 Nm).

14. Install the battery pressure sensor.

15. Install the EGR valve, left side only.

16. Install the air intake assembly.

17. Connect the negative battery cable.

INTAKE MANIFOLD

REMOVAL & INSTALLATION

2.7L Engine

1. Disconnect the negative battery cable.

2. Drain the cooling system.

3. Remove the engine appearance cover.

4. Remove the high pressure fuel lines.

5. Remove the fuel rail. For additional information, refer to the following section, "Injectors, Removal & Installation."

6. Remove the fuel rail support block between cylinders no. 1 and no. 2.

7. Disconnect the charge air hose at the intake manifold.

8. Disconnect the EGR wiring harness connector.

9. Remove the bolt retaining the engine wiring harness to the intake manifold.

10. Disconnect the coolant hose at the EGR valve.

11. Disconnect both fuel lines at the fuel filter.

12. Remove the lower intake manifold support bracket.

13. Raise and safely support the vehicle.

14. Remove the rear intake manifold mounting bolts while accessible from below.

15. Lower the vehicle.

➡Access to one of the intake manifold bolts is through a supplied hole in the manifold.

16. Remove the remaining intake manifold bolts, lift the intake manifold up and out while guiding the engine wiring harness and fuel lines through the openings in the intake manifold, then remove the gasket

To install:

17. Clean both mating surfaces and install a new intake manifold gasket with the intake manifold. Guide the engine wiring harness and fuel lines through the intake manifold openings. Tighten manifold bolts to 12 ft. lbs. (16 Nm) in a cross directional pattern beginning with the middle bolts and tightening outward to the ends.

18. Raise and safely support the vehicle.

19. Install the rear intake manifold bolts and tighten to 12 ft. lbs. (16 Nm).

20. Install the lower intake manifold support bracket and tighten the bolts to 15 ft. lbs. (20 Nm).

21. Lower the vehicle.

22. Connect both fuel lines to fuel filter assembly.

23. Connect the coolant hose at the EGR valve.

24. Secure the engine wiring harness and cable duct to the intake manifold. Tighten the fastener to 80 inch lbs. (9Nm).

25. Connect the EGR wiring harness connector.

26. Connect the fuel pressure sensor electrical connector

27. Install the fuel rail

➡The high pressure fuel lines must be counter held when tightening to prevent damage.

28. Install the high pressure fuel lines.

29. Connect the charge air hose to the intake manifold.

30. Install the engine appearance cover.

31. Refill the cooling system to the correct level.

32. Connect the negative battery cable.

33. Start the engine and check for leaks.

3.5L Engine

1. Disconnect the negative battery cable.

2. Drain the cooling system.

3. Properly relieve the fuel system pressure.

4. Remove the air intake assembly.

5. Disconnect the Powertrain Control Module (PCM) and remove the PCM and mounting bracket.

6. Disconnect the fuel rail electrical connectors.

7. Remove the engine wiring harness bolts.

8. Position aside the engine wiring harness.

9. Remove the power brake booster vacuum line connector.

10. Disconnect the Mass Air Flow sensor.

11. Remove the Mass Air Flow sensor (MAF).

12. Remove the oil separator tube from the oil separator.

13. Disconnect the crankcase ventilation sensor hose.

14. Disconnect all four camshaft position sensors.

15. Disconnect the Short Runner connector.

16. Disconnect the throttle sensor connector.

17. Disconnect the Tumbler Valve Solenoid connector.

18. Disconnect the MAP Sensor harness connector.

19. Disconnect the Electronic throttle control solenoid connector.

20. Position the engine harness aside.

21. Disconnect the fuel injector harness connectors.

22. Remove the fuel rail. For additional information, refer to the following section, "Fuel Injectors, Removal & Installation."

23. Disconnect the EVAP purge solenoid hose.

24. Disconnect the power brake booster vacuum line at the intake manifold.

25. Disconnect the air pump solenoid vacuum line.

26. Remove the intake manifold bolts and remove the intake manifold.

To install:

27. Position the intake manifold into place and install the mounting bolts.

28. Connect the air pump solenoid vacuum line.
29. Connect the power brake booster vacuum line at the intake manifold.
30. Connect the EVAP purge solenoid hose.
31. Install the fuel rail and connect the fuel line and injector electrical connectors.
32. Position the engine harness into place and install the engine harness bolts.
33. Connect the following to the engine wiring harness:
    - Electronic throttle control solenoid connector
    - MAF sensor
    - Tumbler Valve Solenoid connector
    - Throttle sensor connector
    - Short Runner connector
34. Connect all four camshaft position sensors.
35. Connect the crankcase ventilation sensor hose.
36. Install the oil separator tube to the oil separator.
37. Install the power brake booster vacuum line connector.
38. Install the PCM brackets and install the PCM.
39. Install the air intake assembly.
40. Refill the cooling system to the correct level.
41. Connect the negative battery cable.

OIL PAN

REMOVAL & INSTALLATION

2.7L Engine

See Figures 43 through 45.

1. Drain the engine oil.
2. Raise and safely support the vehicle.
3. Remove the sway bar retaining bolts and swing sway bar down and out of the way.
4. Remove the wiring harness duct from the oil pan bolts and position out of the way.
5. Lower the vehicle and remove the turbocharger upper heat shield.
6. Connect Special Tool 8534 Engine Support Fixture using adapters no. 8534-16, to the engine lifting eye.
7. Remove the engine mount bolts and raise the engine slightly.
8. Disconnect the oil level sensor.
9. Remove the transmission cooler lines from the oil pan bolts and carefully position the lines aside.
10. Remove the oil pan bolts.

➡The bolts are different sizes. Mark the location of the bolts and keep them in order.

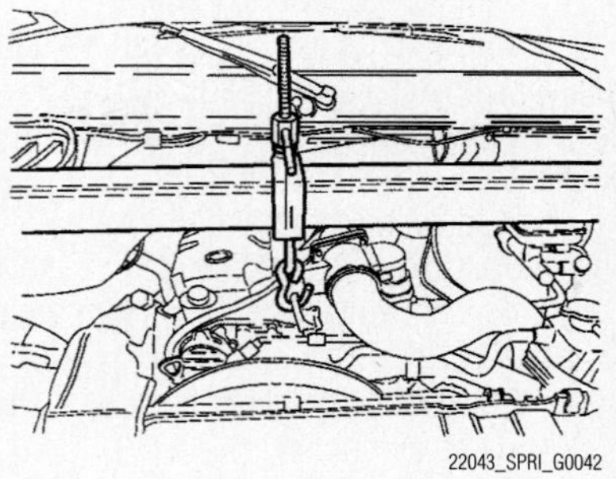

Fig. 43 Connect Special Tool 8534 Engine Support Fixture using adapters no. 8534-16, to the engine lifting eye and raise engine slightly—2.7L Engine

11. Remove oil pan and gasket.

To install:

12. Slide the oil pan and gasket into position.
13. Add sealant to the joints on the engine block, where indicated.
14. Tighten the M6 bolts to 80 inch lbs. (9 Nm) and the M8 bolts to 15 ft. lbs. (20 Nm).
15. Tighten the transmission bellhousing-to-oil pan bolts to 30 ft. lbs. (40 Nm).
16. Install the wiring harness duct.
17. Connect the oil level sensor.
18. Lower the vehicle.
19. Lower the engine until the engine mount and engine supports make contact.
20. Start and hand tighten the engine mount bolts.
21. Lower the engine the rest of the way and remove the engine support fixture.
22. Tighten the engine mount bolts to 61 ft. lbs. (83 Nm).
23. Install the sway bar and tighten bolts to 22 ft. lbs. (30 Nm).

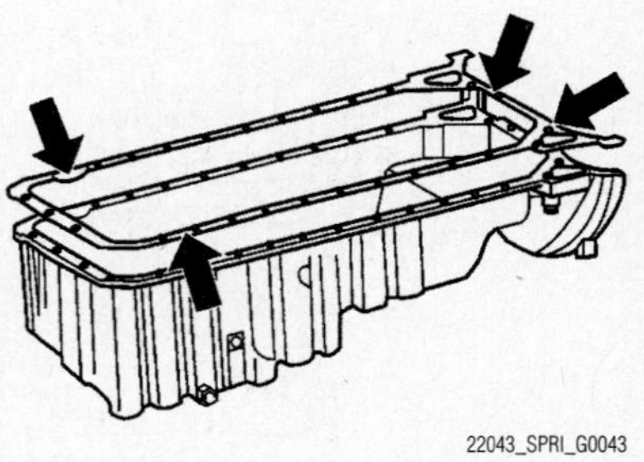

Fig. 44 Add sealant to the joints on the engine block as indicated before installing the mounting bolts—2.7L Engine

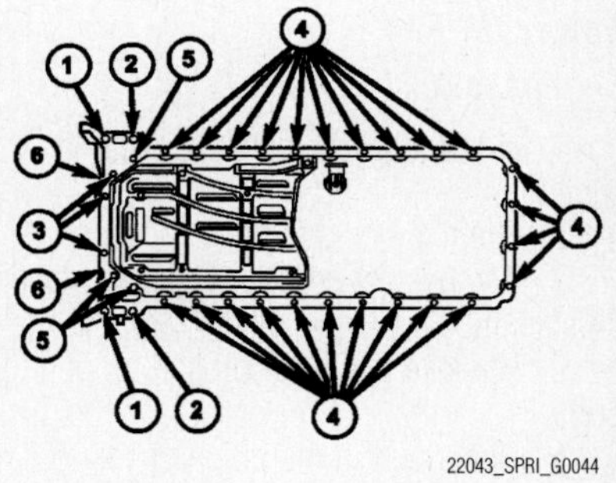

Fig. 45 Oil pan bolts: M8 x 40 (1), M8 x 50 (2), M6 x 85 (3), M6 x 20 (4), M6 x 35 (5), Transmission bell housing bolts (5)—2.7L Engine

24. Refill the engine with oil to the correct level.
25. Connect the negative battery cable.
26. Start the engine and check for leaks.

3.0L Engine

1. Disconnect the negative battery cable.
2. Remove the accessory drive belt. For additional information, refer to the following section, "Accessory Drive Belt, Removal & Installation."
3. Remove the transmission. For additional information, refer to the following section, "Automatic Transmission Assembly, Removal & Installation."
4. Remove the flex plate.
5. Remove the five bolts on the bottom of the rear main seal carrier.
6. Remove the oil pan bolts.
7. Remove the oil pan.

To install:

8. Clean the mating surfaces of any old gasket material.
9. Install the oil pan and gasket and install the bolts holding the rear main seal carrier to the oil pan. Tighten the bolts to 80 inch lbs. (9 Nm).
10. Push the oil pan against the transmission and tighten transmission to oil pan bolts first, including the rear main seal carrier bolts.
11. Tighten the oil pan bolts to 106 inch lbs. (12 Nm).
12. Tighten the transmission-to-oil pan bolts to 15 ft. lbs. (20 Nm).
13. Install the flex plate.
14. Install the transmission.
15. Lower the vehicle.
16. Install the accessory drive belt.
17. Refill the engine with oil to the correct level.
18. Connect the negative battery cable.
19. Start the engine and check for leaks.

3.5L Engine

Lower Oil Pan

See Figure 46.

1. Disconnect the negative battery cable.
2. Drain the engine oil.
3. Remove the engine oil dipstick and dipstick tube.
4. Remove the lower oil pan mounting bolts.
5. Use a bolt in the oil pan boss to carefully pull the lower oil pan from the upper oil pan.

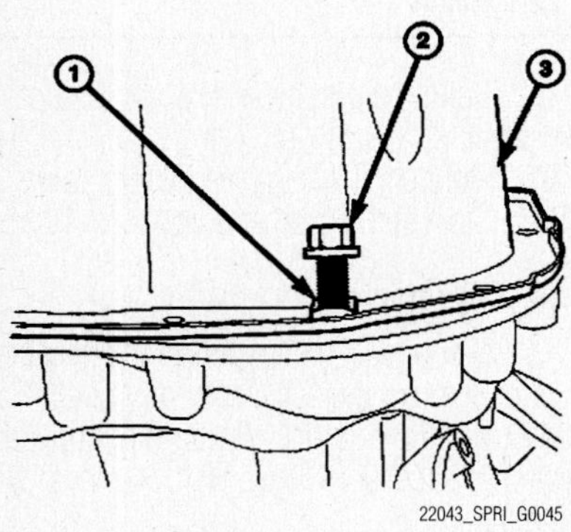

Fig. 46 Use a bolt (2) in the oil pan boss (1) to pull the lower oil pan (3) from the upper oil pan—3.5L Engine

To install:

6. Install the oil dipstick tube and tighten the mounting bolt to 80 inch lbs. (9 Nm).
7. Remove any sealant residues with an adhesive and sealant remover. Do not use any sharp-edged tools or abrasive paper as this can damage the sealing surfaces. Make sure the sealing surfaces are clean and dry before applying the RTV.
8. Apply Loctite® 7200 or equivalent to the mating surface of the lower oil pan.
9. Install the lower oil pan and tighten the mounting bolts in a crisscross pattern to 80 inch lbs. (9 Nm).
10. Install the oil dipstick.
11. Install the oil drain plug, if not already installed.
12. Refill the engine with oil to the correct level.
13. Connect the negative battery cable.

Upper Oil Pan

See Figure 47.

1. Disconnect the negative battery cable.
2. Drain the engine oil.
3. Remove the air intake assembly.
4. Remove the lower oil pan.
5. Loosen the hose clamp bolt from the catalytic converter diesel particulate filter device at the connecting flange at the turbocharger.
6. Remove the bracket bolt for the catalytic converter diesel particulate filter unit.
7. Attach a suitable engine supporting shackle.
8. Detach the charge air hose upstream of the charge air cooler.
9. Detach the charge air hose on the engine charge air duct downstream of the charge air cooler.
10. Unscrew the bracket for the transmission oil lines on the right side of the oil pan.
11. Remove the transmission with the torque converter. For additional information, refer to the following section, "Automatic Transmission Assembly, Removal & Installation."
12. Remove the end cover.
13. Remove the bolts that connect the left and right engine mount to the engine support.
14. Using a suitable engine lift, carefully raise the engine.
15. Remove the oil suction pipe.
16. Remove the refrigerant compressor bolt at the top section of the oil pan.
17. Remove the upper oil pan mounting bolts.
18. Remove the upper oil pan.

To install:

19. Install the oil suction pipe.
20. Install the upper oil pan and tighten the mounting bolts.
21. Connect the oil level switch connector.
22. Install the oil dipstick guide tube.
23. Install the bolt from catalytic converter diesel particulate filter unit bracket
24. Tighten the bolt on hose clamp from catalytic converter diesel particulate filter device at connecting flange from turbocharger.
25. Lower the engine into place.
26. Install the bolts connecting the left and right engine mount to the engine support.
27. Remove the engine supporting shackle.
28. Install the charge air hose upstream of charge air cooler.
29. Install the charge air hose on engine charge air duct downstream of charge air cooler.
30. Install the bracket for transmission oil lines on the oil pan on the right.
31. Install the transmission with the torque converter.
32. Install the end cover.
33. Install the refrigerant compressor bolt at oil pan top section.
34. Install the lower oil pan.
35. Install the air intake assembly.
36. Connect negative battery cable.
37. Refill the engine with oil to the correct level.
38. Start the engine and check for leaks.

OIL PUMP

REMOVAL & INSTALLATION

2.7L Engine

1. Disconnect the negative battery cable.
2. Drain the engine oil.

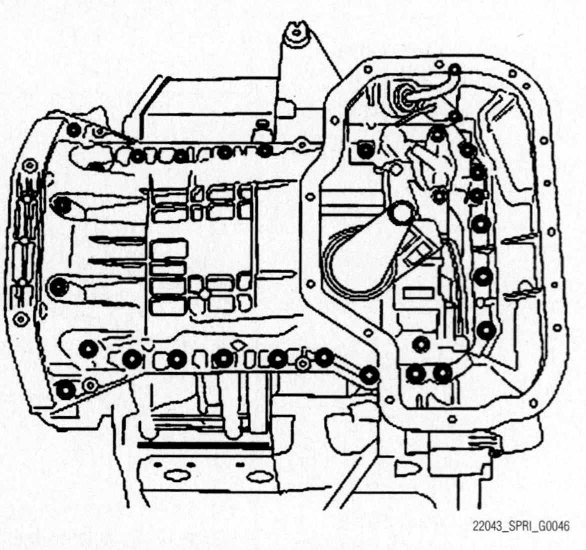

Fig. 47 Upper oil pan mounting bolt locations—3.5L Engine

3. Remove the oil pan. For additional information, refer to the following section, "Oil Pan, Removal & Installation."
4. Press the chain tensioner off of the oil pump chain, and remove the chain from the oil pump.
5. Remove the oil pump, pick-up tube and O-ring.

To install:

6. Clean all of the sealing surfaces.
7. Position the oil pump onto the drive chain and reset tensioner.
8. Install the oil pump mounting bolts and tighten to 13 ft. lbs. (18 Nm).
9. Install the oil pan.
10. Connect the negative battery cable.
11. Refill the engine with oil to the correct level.

3.0L Engine

1. Disconnect the negative battery cable.
2. Drain the engine oil.
3. Remove the oil pan. For additional information, refer to the following section, "Oil Pan, Removal & Installation."
4. Remove the oil pump cover.
5. Remove the mounting bolts and remove the oil pump.

To install:

6. Clean the strainer of the oil pump and replace the sealing ring. Fill the oil pump with engine oil so that oil is delivered when the engine is started.
7. Install the oil pump. Tighten the bolts to 14 ft. lbs. (19 Nm).
8. Install the oil pump cover and tighten the bolts to 9 ft. lbs. (12 Nm).
9. Install the oil pan.
10. Connect the negative battery cable.
11. Fill the engine with oil to the correct level.
12. Start then engine and check for leaks.

3.5L Engine

1. Disconnect the negative battery cable.
2. Drain the engine oil.
3. Remove the upper and lower oil pans. For additional information, refer to the following section, "Oil Pan, Removal & Installation."
4. Remove the oil suction tube bolt.
5. Press the oil pump chain tensioner to completely remove the tension from the oil pump chain.
6. Remove the oil pump chain.
7. Remove the oil pump bolts.
8. Remove the oil pump and suction tube.

To install:

9. Install the oil pump and suction tube.
10. Install the oil suction tube bolt.
11. Pressure the oil pump chain tensioner to completely remove the tension from the oil pump chain.
12. Install the oil pump bolts.
13. Install the upper and lower oil pans.
14. Connect the negative battery.
15. Refill the engine with oil to the correct level.

PISTON AND RING

POSITIONING

See Figures 48 and 49.

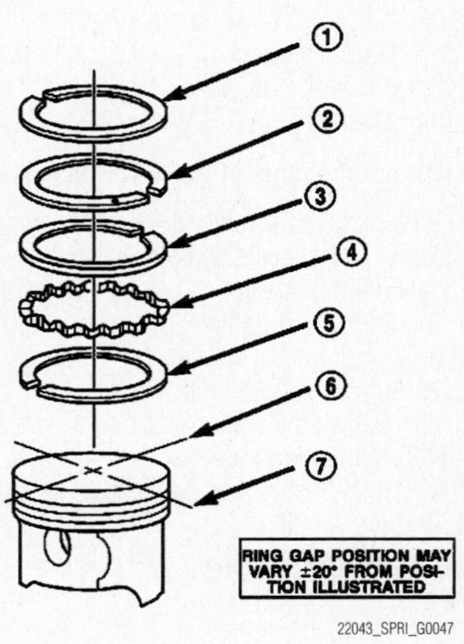

Fig. 48 Correct orientation of the Top Compression ring (1), Bottom Compression ring (2), Top Oil Control Rail (3), Oil Rail Spacer (4), Bottom Oil Control Rail (5), Imaginary Lines to center (6,7)—2.7L and 3.5L Engines

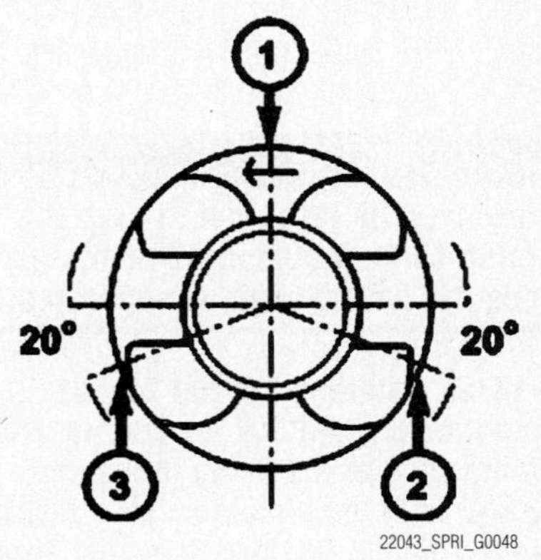

Fig. 49 Top Compression ring gap (3), Bottom compression ring gap (1), Oil control ring gap (2)—3.0L Engine

REAR MAIN SEAL

REMOVAL & INSTALLATION

2.7L Engine

1. Disconnect the negative battery cable.
2. Raise and safely support the engine.
3. Drain the engine oil.
4. Remove the transmission assembly.
5. Remove the flexplate.

➡Loosen all of the oil pan bolts to assure that the oil pan gasket is not damaged when removing the rear main seal and end cover assembly.

➡Inspect the oil pan gasket for damage. If the gasket is damaged, it must be replaced.

6. Loosen the oil pan bolts.
7. Remove the flexplate.
8. Remove the rear main seal adapter retaining bolts and carefully pry the adapter from the crankcase at the adapter shoulders.

To install:

9. Position the rear main oil seal adapter with the assembly sleeve onto the crankshaft so that the dowel sleeves fir into the guide holes.

✲✲ WARNING

Use care not to damage the oil pan gasket.

10. Install the rear main seal adapter-to-crankcase bolts and tighten to 80 inch lbs. (9 Nm).
11. Tighten the M6 oil pan bolts to 80 inch lbs. (9 Nm) and M8 oil pan bolts to 15 ft. lbs. (20 Nm).
12. Install the flexplate.
13. Install the transmission assembly.
14. Lower the vehicle.
15. Refill the engine with oil to the correct level.
16. Start the engine and check for leaks.

3.0L and 3.5L Engine

See Figure 50.

1. Remove the transmission. For additional information, refer to the following section, "Automatic Transmission Assembly, Removal & Installation."
2. Remove the flex plate.
3. Remove the seven upper bolts holding the rear main seal carrier to the engine block.
4. Remove the two lower bolts holding the rear main seal carrier to the engine block.
5. Remove the rear main seal carrier from the engine block and oil pan.

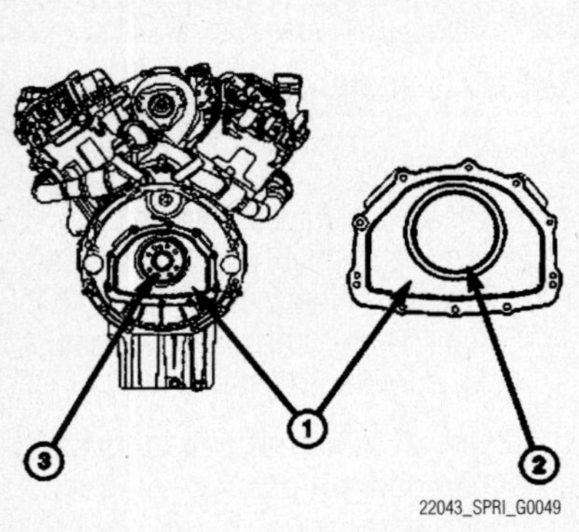

Fig. 50 Location of the rear main seal (2) and rear main seal carrier (1) behind the flex plate—3.0L Engine shown

➡The rear seal is bonded to the retainer and must be replaced as an assembly.

To install:

6. Clean all of the sealing surfaces. The retainer assembly must be replaced if the seal is torn or damaged.
7. Apply Mopar®® Engine Sealant RTV Silicone Adhesive to the points where the oil pan and engine block are joined.
8. Install the rear oil seal carrier and tighten the bolts to 70 inch lbs. (8 Nm).
9. Install the flex plate.
10. Install the transmission.
11. Start the engine and check for leaks.

TIMING CHAIN, SPROCKETS, FRONT COVER AND SEAL

REMOVAL & INSTALLATION

2.7L Engine

See Figures 51 through 53.

1. Disconnect the negative battery cable.
2. Drain the engine oil.
3. Drain the cooling system.
4. Turn the engine by the crankshaft and position cylinder No. 1 at Top Dead Center (TDC).
5. Raise and safely support the vehicle.
6. Remove the alternator wiring harness duct at the crankcase and set aside.
7. Remove inspection cover.
8. Remove the bolts.
9. Insert the Special Tool 8932 Crankshaft Lock into the starter ring gear and install the retaining bolts. Tighten the lock bolts to 80 inch lbs. (9 Nm)
10. Remove the oil filter.
11. Remove the radiator. For additional information, refer to the following section, "Radiator, Removal & Installation."
12. Remove the engine appearance cover.
13. Remove the front cover at cylinder head. For additional information, refer to the following section, "Cylinder Head, Removal & Installation."
14. Remove the accessory drive belt.
15. Remove the high pressure fuel pump.
16. Remove the water pump.
17. Remove the accessory drive belt pulley and vibration damper.
18. Remove the power steering pump.
19. Unplug the A/C compressor electrical connector and unbolt the A/C compressor. Relocate it to the lower engine compartment.

➡Do not disconnect the A/C lines.

20. Remove the alternator with the wiring attached and relocate somewhere in the engine compartment.
21. Install a suitable engine support fixture.
22. Remove the oil pan.
23. Detach the coolant hose to oil-water heat exchanger at crankcase.
24. Remove the cylinder head to timing cover bolts.
25. Remove the timing cover bolts and cover.
26. Remove the remaining ancillary components attached to the timing case cover.
27. Remove the timing chain tensioner.
28. Remove the timing chain front cover.
29. Pry the front oil seal from the timing chain cover, if necessary.
30. Install Special Tool 9525, using two of the cylinder head mounting bolts.
31. Assemble Special Tool 9312-1 using 9312- 3 and 9312-4. Install Insert 9312-13 and retain with the screw provided.

⁂ CAUTION

Care must be taken not to drop the timing chain plates into the engine once the timing chain is separated.

➡When installing Special Tool 9312-1 onto timing chain link, be sure to back off the smaller nut of the thrust pin 9312-3 until the pin is recessed inside of the spindle, 9312-4. Screw the thrust spindle 9312-4 in until it is seated and aligned properly over the rivet of the timing chain.

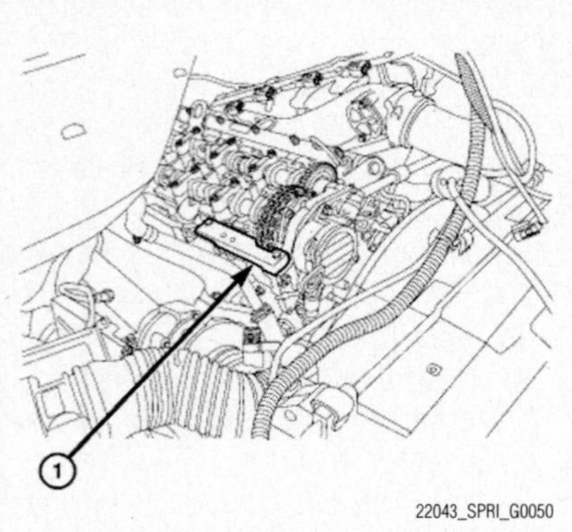

Fig. 51 Install Special Tool 9525, using two of the cylinder head mounting bolts—2.7L Engine

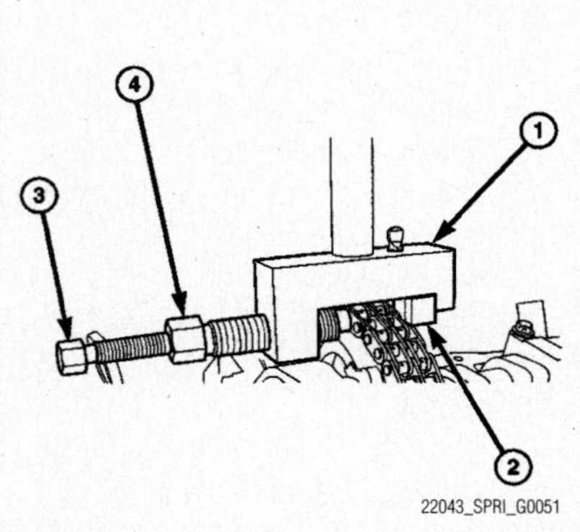

Fig. 52 Assemble Special Tool 9312-1 (1) using 9312- 3 (3) and 9312-4 (4) and install Insert 9312-13 (2) and secure with the provided screw—2.7L Engine

➡When fitting the thrust spindle, ensure that the thrust pin is positioned at the left timing chain pin of a chain link.

32. Install Special Tool 9312 onto timing chain link.

➡Cover the timing chain area. Care must be taken not to drop any repair debris or pieces into the engine when separating the timing chain links.

33. Carefully turn 9312-3 Thrust Pin of Special Tool 9312-1 clockwise while holding the handle until the rivet is pressed out and the chain is separated. Discard the loose link and plates.

➡One whole timing chain link must be removed.

➡Care must be taken not to drop any repair debris or pieces into the engine when separating the timing chain links.

To install:

34. Connect a new timing chain with the oil holes facing up, and old timing chain with the assembly link, assembly plate and locking element, and secure.
35. Inspect the cylinder head gasket and oil pan gasket and replace if necessary.
36. Replace the front crankshaft seal in the timing chain cover if necessary.
37. Install all ancillary components to timing case cover previously removed.
38. Apply sealant to the marked surfaces with a bead thickness of 1–2 mm.

➡Install the timing cover within 10 minutes after applying sealant. Do not spread the sealant bead.

39. Do not seal the pressurized oil galleries to the crankcase. Sealant applied at these points is entrained by the oil flow and blocks the oil supply passages.
40. Position and install the timing chain cover. Tighten the bolts to 15 ft. lbs. (20 Nm).
41. Install the M8 bolts of cylinder head-to-timing chain front cover and tighten bolts to 15 ft. lbs. (20 Nm).
42. Install the timing chain tensioner with a new seal.
43. Position and install the oil pan. For additional information, refer to the following section, "Oil Pan, Removal & Installation."
44. Install the crankshaft vibration damper. Tighten the bolts to 240 ft. lbs. (325Nm) plus 90°.
45. Remove the engine support fixture.
46. Install the alternator.
47. Install the air conditioning compressor.
48. Install the power steering pump.
49. Install the water pump.

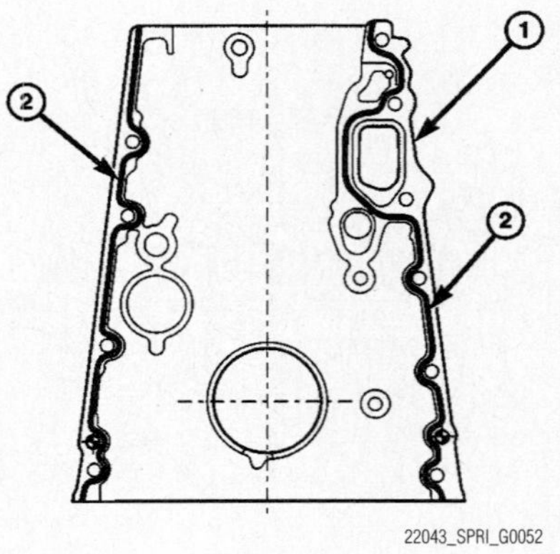

Fig. 53 Apply sealant (2) to the marked surfaces of the timing chain cover (1) with a bead thickness of 1–2 mm—2.7L Engine

50. Connect coolant hose to oil-water heat exchanger.
51. Install the high pressure fuel pump.
52. Apply sealant to the lower portion of, and install, front cover to cylinder block. Tighten the bolts to 15 ft. lbs. (20Nm).
53. Remove the retaining lock for crankshaft/starter ring gear.
54. Tighten the oil drain plug to 22 ft. lbs. (30 Nm).
55. Install a new oil filter and tighten the screw cap for the filter to 18 ft. lbs. (25 Nm).
56. Install the accessory drive belt.
57. Install the radiator assembly.
58. Install the air intake assembly.
59. Refill the cooling system to the correct level.
60. Refill the engine with oil to the correct level.
61. Connect the negative battery cable.
62. Start the engine and check for leaks.

3.0L Engine

1. Disconnect the negative battery cable.
2. Drain the cooling system.
3. Drain the engine oil.
4. Drain the power steering fluid.
5. Remove the engine appearance cover.
6. Remove the front engine cover bracket.
7. Raise and safely support the vehicle.
8. Remove the power steering hose between the pump and cooling fan.
9. Remove the power steering hose between the cooling fan and suspension.
10. Remove the lower cooling fan module retaining bolts.
11. Disconnect the cooling fan wiring harness connector.
12. Remove the power steering line between the retainer and cooling fan module.
13. Remove the front splash shield.
14. Remove the front oil pan to timing cover bolts.
15. Lower the vehicle.
16. Remove the hoses at the power steering reservoir.
17. Remove the cooling fan module upper bolts and remove the fan assembly.
18. Remove the charge air outlet tube.
19. Remove the accessory drive belt.
20. Disconnect the charge air inlet hose at the EGR air control valve.
21. Remove the glow plug module.
22. Remove the EGR air control valve.
23. Remove both accessory drive belt idler pulleys.
24. Remove the accessory drive belt tensioner.
25. Rotate the engine to Top Dead Center (TDC) by the crankshaft bolt.
26. Raise and safely support the vehicle.
27. Remove the starter blank.
28. Install Special Tool 9102 Crankshaft Lock.
29. Lower the vehicle.
30. Remove the vibration damper and pulley.
31. Remove the front timing cover seal.
32. Remove the front timing cover bolts and cover.
33. Pry the front oil seal from the front cover, if necessary.
34. Make sure that the timing marks on the back of the camshafts are horizontal and pointing at each other.
35. Remove the timing chain tensioner.

➡Cover the timing chain area. Care must be taken not to drop any repair debris or pieces into the engine when separating the timing chain links.

36. Install Special Tool 9554 using two of the cylinder head cover bolts.
37. Assemble Special Tool 9312-1 using 9312-3 and 9312-4. Install Insert 9312-13 and retain with screw provided.

⁂ CAUTION

Care must be taken not to drop the timing chain plates into the engine once the timing chain is separated.

➡When installing Special Tool 9312-1 onto timing chain link, be sure to back off the smaller nut of the Thrust Pin 9312-3 until the pin is recessed inside of the spindle, 9312-4. Screw the Thrust Spindle 9312-4 in until it is seated and aligned properly over the rivet of the timing chain.

➡When fitting the thrust spindle, ensure that the thrust pin is positioned at the left timing chain pin of a chain link.

➡Cover the timing chain area. Care must be taken not to drop any repair debris or pieces into the engine when separating the timing chain links.

38. Carefully turn the thrust pin 9312-13 of Special Tool 9312-1 clockwise while holding the handle until the rivet is pressed out and the chain is separated. Discard the loose link and plates.
39. Use a small screwdriver to prevent the timing chain from slipping into the engine.

➡One whole timing chain link must be removed.

To install:

40. Connect a new timing chain with the oil holes facing up, and old timing chain with the assembly link, assembly plate and locking element, and secure.
41. Install the front crankshaft seal in the timing cover.
42. Install the timing cover and tighten bolts to 80 inch lbs. (9 Nm).
43. Raise and safely support the vehicle.
44. Install the front oil pan bolts and tighten the bolts to 88 inch lbs. (10 Nm).
45. Lower the vehicle.
46. Install the vibration damper and pulley. Tighten the bolt to 154 ft. lbs. (210 Nm) plus 180°.
47. Install the accessory drive belt tensioner. Tighten bolt to 43 ft. lbs. (58 Nm).
48. Install the idler pulleys and tighten the bolts to 20 ft. lbs. (28 Nm).
49. Install the accessory drive belt.
50. Install the EGR air control valve assembly.
51. Install the glow plug module.
52. Install the charge air outlet tube.
53. Install the cooling fan module. Tighten upper bolts to 10 ft. lbs. (14 Nm).
54. Raise and safely support the vehicle.
55. Remove Special Tool 9102 Crankshaft Lock.
56. Install the starter blank.
57. Install the lower cooling fan module bolts and tighten the lower bolts to 10 ft. lbs. (14 Nm).
58. Install the power steering line between the retainer and cooling fan module.
59. Connect the cooling fan wiring harness connector.
60. Install the power steering hose between the cooling fan and suspension.
61. Install the power steering hose between the pump and cooling fan.
62. Install the front skid plate.
63. Lower the vehicle.
64. Install the hoses at the power steering reservoir.
65. Refill the power steering reservoir to the correct level.
66. Install the front engine cover bracket.
67. Install the engine cover.
68. Refill the cooling system to the correct level.
69. Refill the engine with oil to the correct level.
70. Connect the negative battery cable.
71. Purge the air from the power steering system before starting by raising the vehicle and rotating the steering wheel back and forth 20 times.
72. Start the engine and follow the bleed procedure with the scan tool.
73. Turn engine off and inspect for leaks.

3.5L Engine

See Figures 54 through 56.

1. Disconnect the negative battery cable.
2. Drain the cooling system.
3. Drain the engine oil
4. Remove the engine appearance cover.
5. Raise and safely support the vehicle.
6. Turn the engine to 40 degrees after Top Dead Center (TDC).
7. Install the crankshaft locking tool.
8. Remove the lower splash shield.
9. Remove the lower bolt to the engine oil dipstick tube.
10. Lower the vehicle.
11. Remove the grille.
12. Remove the cooling module.
13. Remove the PCM.
14. Remove the engine harness.
15. Remove the upper oil dipstick tube bolt.
16. Remove the oil dipstick and oil dipstick tube.
17. Remove the intake manifold.
18. Remove the air pump.
19. Remove the lower and upper oil pan.
20. Remove the accessory drive belt.
21. Remove the thermostat housing.
22. Remove the thermostat gasket.
23. Remove the accessory drive belt tensioner assembly.
24. Remove the oil filter/cooler housing.
25. Remove the idler pulley.
26. Remove the crankshaft damper bolt.
27. Remove the crankshaft damper pulley.
28. Remove the water pump and gasket.
29. Remove the left front cylinder head cover.
30. Remove the right side air control valve.
31. Remove the right air control valve gasket.
32. Remove the upper right front cylinder head cover.
33. Remove the left air control valve and gasket.
34. Remove the left air control valve adapter and gasket.
35. Remove and position aside the power steering pump.
36. Remove and position aside the AC compressor.
37. Remove the alternator.
38. Remove the cylinder head covers.
39. Remove the timing chain tensioner.
40. Install a drift into the camshaft to lock the split gears.
41. Remove the timing chain guide (2, 3) roll pins from the right cylinder head.
42. Remove the center valve bolts (1, 4) from the camshafts.

➡The intake camshaft adjuster bolts are a left-hand thread. The exhaust camshaft bolts are a right-hand thread.

➡Support the timing chain to prevent it from falling off the crankshaft or balance shaft.

43. Remove the camshaft adjusters.
44. Remove the cylinder head to front cover bolts in the left cylinder head.
45. Remove the cylinder head to front cover bolts in the right cylinder head.

➡The front cover bolts have several different sizes. Note the locations of each bolt.

46. Remove the front cover bolts.
47. Remove the front cover.
48. Remove the timing chain tensioner.

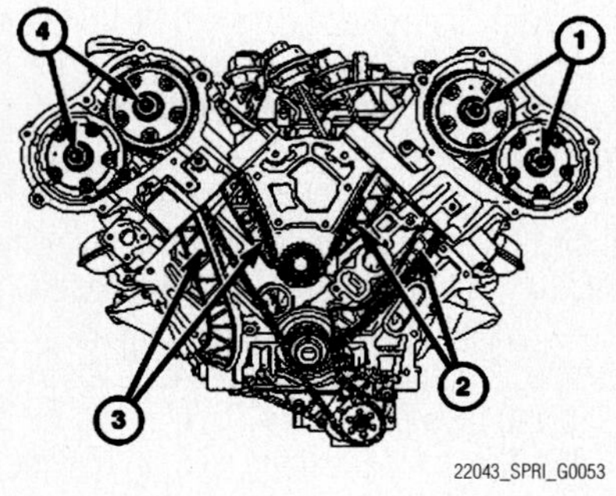

Fig. 54 Remove the timing chain guide (2,3) roll pins and center valve bolts (1,4) from the camshafts—3.5L Engine Front cover removal

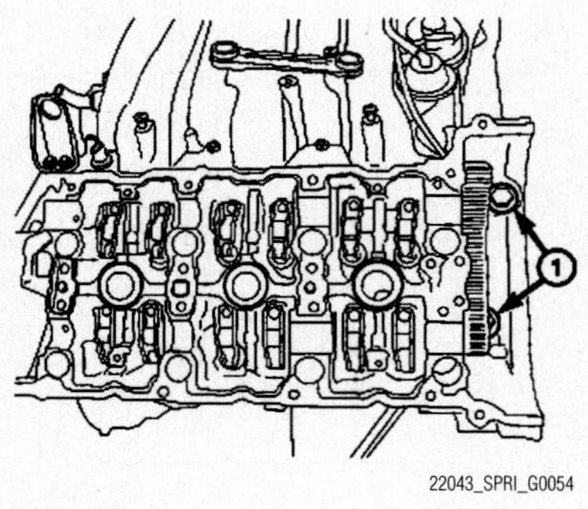

Fig. 55 The cylinder head-to-front cover bolts must be removed in each cylinder head—3.5L Engine

49. Use a slide hammer to remove the slide rail pins in the left and right cylinder head.
50. Remove the oil pump chain.
51. Remove the timing chain slide rails.
52. Insert a drift into left camshaft adjuster.
53. Insert a drift into the right camshaft adjuster.
54. Remove the camshaft adjuster from the left cylinder head.
55. Remove the camshaft adjuster from the right cylinder head.
56. Disconnect the timing chain links.
57. Remove the timing chain.

To install:

58. Make sure that the drift is installed into the camshaft adjuster.
59. Align the pin with the hole in the end of the camshaft to install the camshaft adjuster on the intake camshaft.
60. When the camshaft is correctly aligned on the camshaft adjuster, the alignment marks on the back of the camshaft adjuster will be lined up and the camshaft will seat all of the way into the adjuster.
61. Install the intake and exhaust camshafts into the cylinder head so that the horizontal alignment marks line up with the top edge of the cylinder head and the vertical alignment mark is pointed upwards.
62. Align the slot in the balance shaft with the mark on the cylinder head (the mark is at about the 2 o'clock position).
63. Replace any timing chain guides with excessive wear.
64. Install all of the timing chain guides.
65. Install the timing chain guide pins.
66. Feed one end of the timing chain into the left cylinder head.
67. Feed the timing chain through the engine and around the balance shaft.
68. Draw the timing chain up through the right cylinder head and over the right cylinder head intake camshaft.
69. Feed the chain down through the cylinder head to the crankshaft sprocket.
70. Draw the timing chain up through the left cylinder head.
71. Assemble the chain using a new link.
72. Remove the drift from the left camshaft adjuster.
73. Install a new camshaft timing wheel on the intake camshaft in the left cylinder head. Rotate the timing wheel until the wheel sits flush on the camshaft. There is a dimple in the camshaft and a matching dimple in the timing wheel. Make sure that the camshaft timing wheel dimples line up.
74. Install the left camshaft adjuster center bolt finger tight.
75. Remove the drift from the right camshaft adjuster.
76. Install a new camshaft timing wheel on the intake camshaft in the right cylinder head. Rotate the timing wheel until the wheel sits flush on the camshaft. There is a dimple in the camshaft and a matching dimple in the timing wheel. Make sure that the camshaft timing wheel dimples line up.
77. Install the right camshaft adjuster center bolt finger tight.
78. Make sure the front cover o-rings at the water pump inlet and outlet are intact and in place.
79. Turn the balance shaft so that the timing mark on the balance shaft matches the timing mark on the engine block.
80. Make sure the timing chain is correctly mounted to the crankshaft and balance shaft sprockets.
81. Install the front cover and tighten the bolts in a crisscross pattern to 15 ft. lbs. (20 Nm).
82. Tighten the cylinder head-to-front cover bolts to 11 ft. lbs. (15 Nm) plus an additional 90°.
83. Coat the end of the camshafts with a small amount of oil.
84. Line up the pin in the camshaft adjusters with the hole in the camshafts.
85. The camshaft pulse wheel must be replaced every time it is removed. The dimples in the pulse wheel must line up with the depressions in the camshaft adjusters.
86. Make sure that the crankshaft is set to 40° After Top Dead Center (ATDC), and that the crankshaft lock is installed.
87. When the crankshaft adjusters are correctly installed, the timing marks will line up with each other and the top mark will be pointed up.

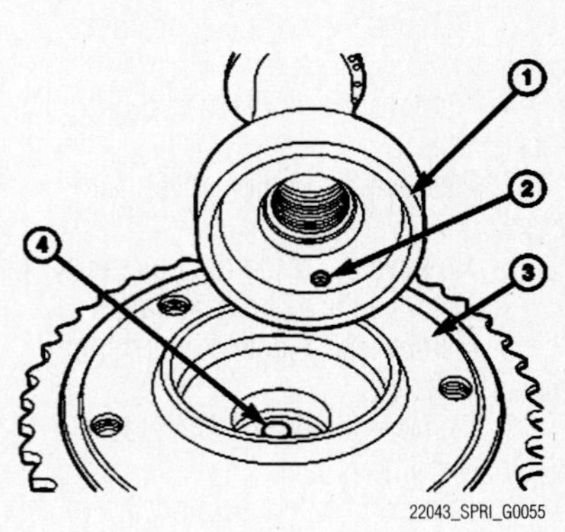

Fig. 56 After coating the end of the camshaft (1) with oil, line up the pin in the camshaft adjusters (4) with the hole in the camshafts (2)—3.5L Engine

88. Install the timing chain onto the left cylinder head intake camshaft adjuster.
89. Install the camshaft adjuster to the intake camshaft in the left cylinder head.
90. Install the camshaft adjuster to the exhaust camshaft in the left cylinder head. Make sure the timing marks line up correctly.
91. Install the slide rails.
92. Install the timing chain on the right cylinder head intake camshaft adjuster.
93. Install the right cylinder head camshaft adjuster to the intake camshaft.
94. Install the right cylinder head exhaust camshaft adjuster.
95. Verify that the intake camshafts are correctly timed to the crankshaft position.
96. Install the center valves into the left and right cylinder head camshafts and tighten to 106 ft. lbs. (145 Nm).
97. Remove the drift from the camshafts.
98. Reset the timing chain tensioner by removing the end of the tensioner assembly.
99. Remove the sealing ring from the tensioner assembly.
100. Remove the spring and pin from the tensioner assembly.
101. Replace the pin into the back of the tensioner assembly, followed by the spring, dowel, sealing ring, and tensioner end.
102. Tighten the end of the tensioner to 36 ft. lbs. (50 Nm).
103. Install the timing chain tensioner and tighten to 51 ft. lbs. (70 Nm).
104. Apply silicone to the cylinder head cover sealing surfaces and install the left and right cylinder head covers. Tighten the cylinder head cover bolts to 106 inch lbs. (12 Nm) plus an additional 90°. For additional information, refer to the following section, "Cylinder Head, Removal & Installation."
105. Install the power steering pump.
106. Install the AC compressor.
107. Install the left air control valve adapter gasket and adapter. Tighten the left air control valve adapter bolts to 10 ft. lbs. (14 Nm).
108. Install the left air control valve gasket and control valve. Tighten the left air control valve bolts to 10 ft. lbs. (14 Nm).
109. Apply a bead of silicone to the cylinder head front cover sealing surface.
110. Install the left front cylinder head cover and tighten the front cover bolts in a cross pattern to 70 inch lbs. (8 Nm).
111. Apply a bead of silicone to the cylinder head front cover sealing surface.
112. Install the upper right front cylinder head cover and tighten the front cover bolts in a cross pattern to 70 inch lbs. (8 Nm).
113. Install the right air control valve gasket and control valve. Tighten the mounting bolts to 10 ft. lbs. (14 Nm).

114. Install the water pump gasket and water pump. Tighten the mounting bolts to 18 ft. lbs. (25 Nm).

115. Install the water pump pulley. Tighten the water pump pulley M7 bolts to 88 inch lbs. (10 Nm) and then to 18 ft. lbs. (25 Nm). Tighten the water pump pulley M8 bolts to 44 inch lbs. (5 Nm) and then to 15 ft. lbs. (20 Nm).

116. Install the crankshaft damper pulley and tighten to 147 ft. lbs. (200 Nm) plus 90°.

117. Install the idler pulley and tighten the bolts to 26 ft. lbs. (35 Nm).

118. Install the oil filter/cooler housing and tighten the housing bolts to 15 ft. lbs. (20 Nm).

119. Install the thermostat gasket, and install the thermostat housing. Tighten the bolts to 18 ft. lbs. (25 Nm).

120. Install the accessory drive belt tensioner assembly and tighten the bolts to 25 ft. lbs. (35 Nm).

121. Install the accessory drive belt.

122. Install the air pump.

123. Install the intake manifold.

124. Install the engine harness.

125. Install the PCM.

126. Raise and safely support the vehicle.

127. Remove the crankshaft lock.

128. Install the starter.

129. Install the alternator.

130. Install the upper and lower oil pans.

131. Install the oil dipstick and oil dipstick tube. Tighten the mounting bolt to 80 inch lbs. (9 Nm).

132. Install the lower splash shield.

133. Lower the vehicle.

134. Install the cooling module.

135. Install the grille.

136. Refill the cooling system to the correct level.

137. Refill the engine with oil to the correct level.

138. Install the engine appearance cover.

139. Connect the negative battery cable.

140. Start the engine and check for leaks.

TURBOCHARGER

REMOVAL & INSTALLATION

2.7L Engine

1. Disconnect the negative battery cable.

2. Remove the heat shield.

3. Separate the front exhaust pipe from the turbocharger.

4. Separate the charge air and intake air hoses at the turbocharger.

5. Disconnect the servomotor electrical connector at servomotor.

6. Disconnect the oil supply line.

7. Remove the turbocharger support bracket.

8. Remove the turbocharger from exhaust manifold.

9. Remove the oil return line from turbocharger.

To install:

10. Clean all of the mating surfaces.

11. Install the oil return tube and gasket onto the turbocharger. Tighten the bolts to 80 inch lbs. (8 Nm).

12. Insert the oil return tube into block and install the turbocharger to the exhaust manifold. Tighten the mounting bolts to 15 ft. lbs. (20 Nm).

13. Install the turbocharger support bracket and tighten the bolts to 15 ft. lbs. (20 Nm) at the engine and 22 ft. lbs. (30 Nm) at the turbocharger.

➡Counterhold the connection at the turbocharger when tightening the oil supply line bolt.

14. Replace the gaskets and install oil supply line at the turbocharger. Tighten the bolt to 13 ft. lbs. (18 Nm).

15. Connect the servomotor electrical connector.

16. Attach the air intake and charge air hoses.

17. Connect the front exhaust pipe to the turbocharger. Tighten flange clamp to 22 ft. lbs. (30 Nm).

18. Install the heat shield.

19. Connect the negative battery cable.

3.0L Engine

See Figures 57 and 58.

1. Disconnect the negative battery cable.

2. Drain the cooling system.

3. Remove the engine appearance cover.

4. Remove the air cleaner to turbo intake tube.

5. Remove the engine cover front bracket.

6. Remove the turbo to cooler air turbo.

7. Remove the turbo heat shield.

8. Remove the elbow-to-converter exhaust clamp.

9. Remove the turbo front bracket retaining bolts.

10. Raise and safely support the vehicle.

11. Remove the front splash shield.

12. Disconnect the downstream catalytic converter at the extension pipe.

13. Disconnect the extension pipe to muffler.

14. Disconnect the O2 sensor wire connector.

15. Reposition the extension pipe and catalytic converter.

16. Lower the vehicle

17. Disconnect catalytic converter to downstream catalytic converter clamp.

18. Remove upstream catalytic converter.

19. Disconnect the transmission fill tube and trim cover bracket and set aside.

20. Disconnect exhaust elbow at turbo.

21. Disconnect EGR tube at manifold to left cylinder head.

22. Remove left and right exhaust manifold retaining bolts and gaskets.

23. Remove the front turbo retaining bolts.

24. Remove the turbo mount retaining bolts.

25. Remove the turbocharger assembly.

To install:

26. Reconnect the turbo boost pressure servo connector, if it was disconnected.

27. Position and install the turbocharger on the exhaust manifold, tighten the mount retaining bolts to 22 ft. lbs. (30 Nm).

28. Install the front turbo retaining bolts and gasket.

CAUTION

Make sure the gasket is installed properly or the turbo oil feed hole will be blocked.

29. Install left and right exhaust manifold retaining bolts and gaskets (4).

30. Reconnect EGR tube at manifold to left cylinder head (3).

31. Reconnect EGR tube at manifold to left cylinder head (3).

32. Reconnect the transmission fill tube and trim cover bracket.

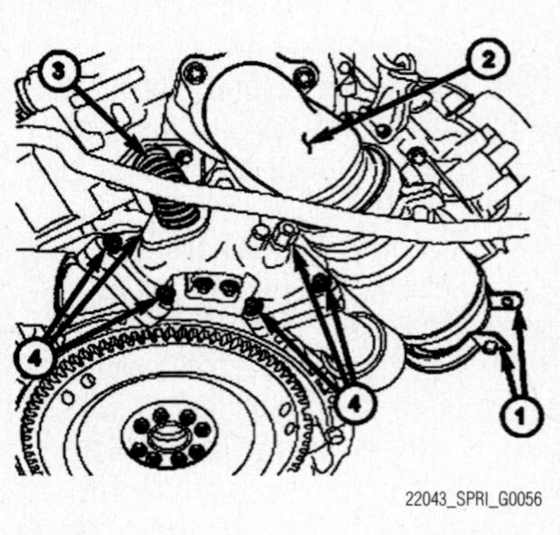

Fig. 57 Remove the exhaust clamp (1), exhaust elbow (2), EGR tube (3) and manifold retaining bolts (4) to access the turbo—3.0L Engine

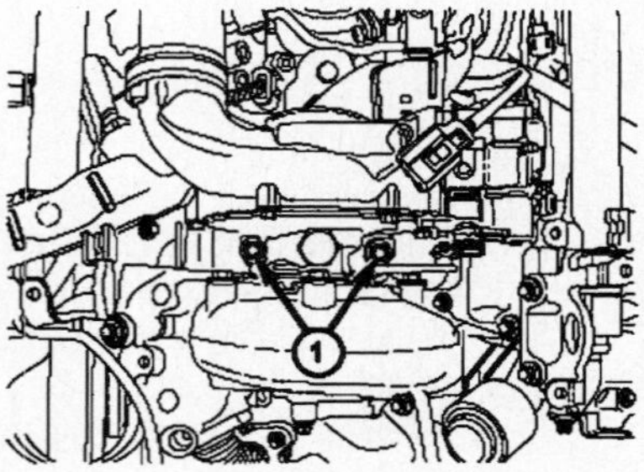

Fig. 58 Remove the front turbo bolts (1) and turbo mount retaining bolts to remove the turbocharger—3.0L Engine

33. Install the upstream catalytic converter.
34. Raise and safely support the vehicle.
35. Reconnect catalytic converter to downstream catalytic converter clamp.
36. Install the extension pipe and catalytic converter.
37. Reconnect the O2 sensor wire connector.
38. Reconnect the extension pipe to muffler.
39. Reconnect the downstream catalytic converter at the extension pipe.
40. Install the front splash shield.
41. Lower the vehicle.
42. Install the turbo front bracket retaining bolts.
43. Install the exhaust clamp (elbow to converter)
44. Install the turbo heat shield.
45. Install air tube (turbo to cooler).
46. Install the engine cover front bracket.
47. Install the air intake tube (air cleaner to turbo)
48. Install the engine appearance cover.
49. Connect the negative battery cable.

VALVE LASH

ADJUSTMENT

All of the engines are equipped with hydraulic valve lifters that do not require periodic valve lash adjustment. Adjustment to zero lash is maintained automatically by hydraulic pressure in the lifters.

ENGINE PERFORMANCE & EMISSION CONTROL

FUEL — GASOLINE FUEL INJECTION SYSTEM

FUEL SYSTEM SERVICE PRECAUTIONS

Safety is the most important factor when performing not only fuel system maintenance but any type of maintenance. Failure to conduct maintenance and repairs in a safe manner may result in serious personal injury or death. Maintenance and testing of the vehicle's fuel system components can be accomplished safely and effectively by adhering to the following rules and guidelines.

- To avoid the possibility of fire and personal injury, always disconnect the negative battery cable unless the repair or test procedure requires that battery voltage be applied.
- Always relieve the fuel system pressure prior to disconnecting any fuel system component (injector, fuel rail, pressure regulator, etc.), fitting or fuel line connection. Exercise extreme caution whenever relieving fuel system pressure to avoid exposing skin, face and eyes to fuel spray. Please be advised that fuel under pressure may penetrate the skin or any part of the body that it contacts.
- Always place a shop towel or cloth around the fitting or connection prior to loosening to absorb any excess fuel due to spillage. Ensure that all fuel spillage (should it occur) is quickly removed from engine surfaces. Ensure that all fuel soaked cloths or towels are deposited into a suitable waste container.
- Always keep a dry chemical (Class B) fire extinguisher near the work area.
- Do not allow fuel spray or fuel vapors to come into contact with a spark or open flame.
- Always use a back-up wrench when loosening and tightening fuel line connection fittings. This will prevent unnecessary stress and torsion to fuel line piping.
- Always replace worn fuel fitting O-rings with new Do not substitute fuel hose or equivalent where fuel pipe is installed.

Before servicing the vehicle, make sure to also refer to the precautions in the beginning of this section as well.

RELIEVING FUEL SYSTEM PRESSURE

1. Disconnect the fuel pump relay.
2. Start and run engine until it stalls.
3. Attempt restarting engine until it will no longer run.
4. Turn the ignition key to the **OFF** position.
5. Disconnect the negative battery cable.
6. One or more Diagnostic Trouble Codes (DTC's) may have been stored in PCM memory. The scan tool must be used to erase a DTC.

FUEL FILTER

REMOVAL & INSTALLATION

1. The fuel filter is an integral part of the fuel pump module. For additional information, refer to the following section, "Fuel Pump, Removal & Installation."

FUEL INJECTORS

REMOVAL & INSTALLATION

See Figure 59.

1. Properly relieve the fuel system pressure.
2. Disconnect the negative battery cable.
3. Remove the air intake assembly.
4. Disconnect the fuel line from the fuel rail.
5. Remove any vacuum lines from the throttle as necessary.
6. Disconnect the electrical connectors from the fuel injectors.
7. Disconnect the electrical connectors from the throttle body and position the wiring harness aside.
8. Remove the four fuel rail mounting bolts.
9. Gently rock and pull left side of fuel rail until fuel injectors just start to clear machined holes in cylinder head. Gently rock and pull right side of rail until injectors just start to clear cylinder head holes. Repeat this procedure (left/right) until all injectors have cleared cylinder head holes.
10. Remove the fuel rail from engine.
11. Release the fuel injector clip and separate the fuel injector from the fuel rail.

To install:

12. Install the fuel injector into the fuel and install the injector clip.
13. Clean out the fuel injector bores in the intake manifold.
14. Apply a small amount of engine oil to each fuel injector O-ring. This will help in fuel rail installation.

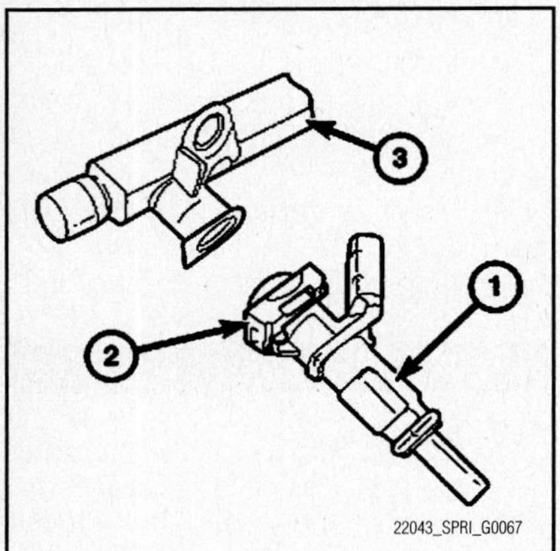

Fig. 59 Release the clip (2) to remove the fuel injector (1) from the fuel rail (3)—3.5L Engine

15. Position the fuel rail/fuel injector assembly to the injector openings in cylinder head.
16. Guide each injector into cylinder head. Be careful not to tear injector O-rings.
17. Push the right side of the Fuel Rail down until the Fuel Injectors are seated on the Cylinder Head Shoulder. Push the left Fuel Rail Down until the Injectors are seated on the Cylinder Head Shoulder. Install the fuel rail mounting bolts.
18. Install the engine wiring harness and install the electrical connectors to the throttle body and all six injectors.
19. Install any removed vacuum lines to the throttle body.
20. Reconnect the fuel line to the fuel rail.
21. Install the air intake assembly.
22. Install the engine appearance cover.
23. Connect the negative battery cable.

FUEL PUMP

REMOVAL & INSTALLATION

See Figure 60.

1. Properly relieve the fuel system pressure.
2. Disconnect the negative battery cable.
3. Remove the fuel tank. For additional information, refer to the following section, "Fuel Tank, Removal & Installation."
4. Disconnect the Fuel Pump Harness Connector.
5. Disconnect the Fuel Feed Line and the Fuel Return Line from the Fuel Pump.
6. Unscrew Fuel Pump Lock Ring.
7. Remove the Fuel Pump Assembly.

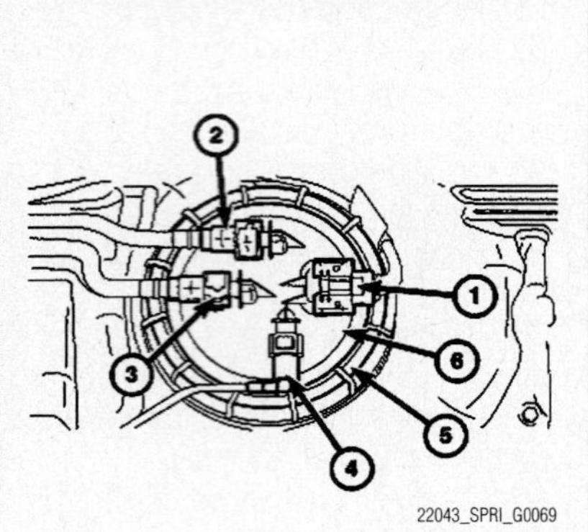

Fig. 60 Harness Connector (1), Return Line (2), Feed Line (3), Lock Ring (5), Fuel Pump (6)—3.5L Fuel Pump Assembly

To install:

8. Install the fuel pump assembly into the tank.
9. Install the Fuel Pump Lock Ring.
10. Reconnect the Fuel Feed Line and the Fuel Return Line to the Fuel Pump.
11. Reconnect the Fuel Pump Harness Connector.
12. Install the fuel tank.
13. Connect the negative battery cable.
14. Start the engine and check for leaks.

FUEL TANK

REMOVAL & INSTALLATION

See Figures 61 and 62.

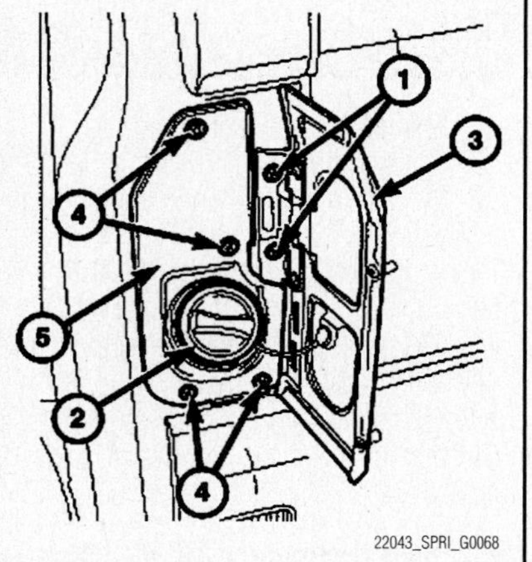

Fig. 61 Remove the two Fuel Filler Door Fasteners (1), and remove the Gas Cap (2) and Fuel Filler Door (3). Remove the 4 Fuel Filler Tube Panel Fasteners (4) and remove the Fuel Filler Tube Panel (2)—Fuel Pump removal

1. Properly relieve the fuel system pressure.
2. Disconnect the negative battery cable.
3. Drain the fuel tank.
4. Remove the filler door fasteners, then remove the filler door and gas cap.
5. Remove the filler tube panel fasteners, then remove the filler tube panel.
6. Remove the fuel filler tube fastener, located just inside the filler door panel.
7. Remove the tie straps, harness connector and fuel filler grommet.

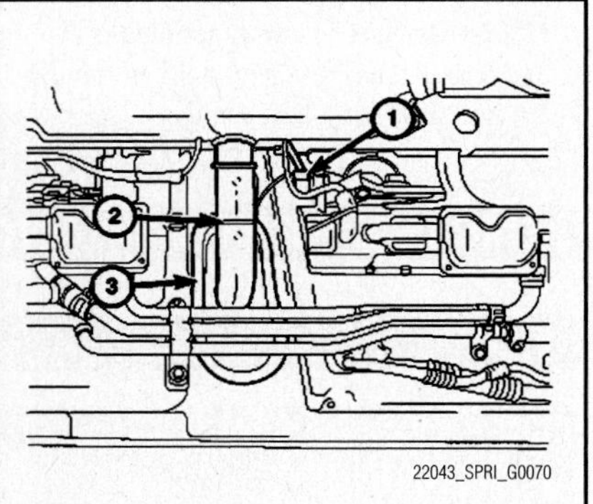

Fig. 62 Remove the tie straps (2), harness connector (1) and Fuel Filler Tube Grommet (3)—3.5L Fuel Tank removal

8. Disconnect the harness connector.
9. Disconnect the Fuel Feed line and Fuel Return line.
10. Remove the front and rear tank straps.
11. Support the fuel tank with a suitable jack.
12. Remove the center fuel tank strap.
13. Disconnect the Evaporative Emission Vent Line (1) from the Fuel Tank (2).
14. Lower the fuel tank from the vehicle.

To install:

15. Raise the fuel tank into position in the vehicle.
16. Reconnect the Evaporative Emission Vent Line (1) to the Fuel Tank (2).
17. Install the Center Fuel Tank Strap and tighten the strap bolt to 41 ft. lbs. (56 Nm).
18. Reconnect the fuel feed and return lines.
19. Reconnect the wiring harness connector.
20. Install the Fuel Filler Tube Grommet, harness connector and tie straps.
21. Install the front and rear Fuel Tank Straps and tighten the strap bolt to 41 ft. lbs. (56 Nm).
22. Install the Fuel Filler Tube and Tube Fastener.

23. Install the Fuel Filler Tube Panel and install the 4 Fuel Filler Tube Panel Fasteners.

24. Install the Fuel Filler Door and the Gas Cap, then install the 2 Fuel Filler Door Fasteners.

IDLE SPEED

ADJUSTMENT

Idle speed is controlled by the Powertrain Control Module (PCM). No adjustment is necessary or possible.

THROTTLE BODY

REMOVAL & INSTALLATION

1. Disconnect the negative battery cable.
2. Remove the engine appearance cover.
3. Remove the air intake assembly.
4. Remove the Mass Air Flow (MAF) sensor.
5. Disconnect the electronic throttle control wiring harness.
6. Remove the throttle body mounting bolts and remove the throttle body.

To install:

7. Install the throttle body assembly and tighten the mounting bolts to 80 inch lbs. (9 Nm).
8. Connect the electronic throttle control wiring harness.
9. Install the MAF sensor.
10. Install the air intake assembly.
11. Install the engine appearance cover.
12. Connect the negative battery cable.

FUEL — DIESEL FUEL INJECTION SYSTEM

FUEL SYSTEM SERVICE PRECAUTIONS

Safety is the most important factor when performing not only fuel system maintenance but any type of maintenance. Failure to conduct maintenance and repairs in a safe manner may result in serious personal injury or death. Maintenance and testing of the vehicle's fuel system components can be accomplished safely and effectively by adhering to the following rules and guidelines.

- To avoid the possibility of fire and personal injury, always disconnect the negative battery cable unless the repair or test procedure requires that battery voltage be applied.
- Always relieve the fuel system pressure prior to disconnecting any fuel system component (injector, fuel rail, pressure regulator, etc.), fitting or fuel line connection. Exercise extreme caution whenever relieving fuel system pressure to avoid exposing skin, face and eyes to fuel spray. Please be advised that fuel under pressure may penetrate the skin or any part of the body that it contacts.
- Always place a shop towel or cloth around the fitting or connection prior to loosening to absorb any excess fuel due to spillage. Ensure that all fuel spillage (should it occur) is quickly removed from engine surfaces. Ensure that all fuel soaked cloths or towels are deposited into a suitable waste container.
- Always keep a dry chemical (Class B) fire extinguisher near the work area.
- Do not allow fuel spray or fuel vapors to come into contact with a spark or open flame.
- Always use a back-up wrench when loosening and tightening fuel line connection fittings. This will prevent unnecessary stress and torsion to fuel line piping.
- Always replace worn fuel fitting O-rings with new. Do not substitute fuel hose or equivalent where fuel pipe is installed.

Before servicing the vehicle, make sure to also refer to the precautions in the beginning of this section as well.

FUEL FILTER

REMOVAL & INSTALLATION

See Figure 63.

1. Disconnect the negative battery cable.
2. Disconnect the water in fuel (WIF) sensor electrical connector.
3. Using Special Tool 9539, release the fuel hose clamps at the fuel filter.
4. Remove the fuel filter retaining bracket bolt and remove the fuel filter.

To install:

5. Fill new fuel filter with the new diesel fuel.
6. Carefully seat the WIF sensor (if removed) and tighten bolt to 13 inch lbs. (1.5 Nm).
7. Position fuel filter in the bracket and tighten the retaining bolt to 53 inch lbs. (6 Nm).
8. Install the fuel lines and re-crimp clamps using Special Tool no. 9539.

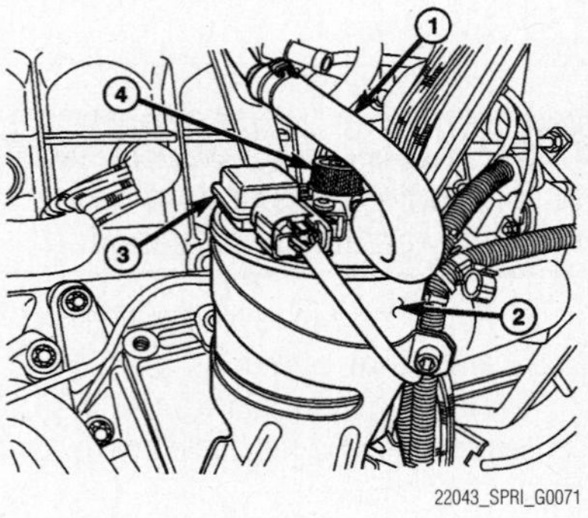

Fig. 63 Fuel supply hose (1), Fuel Filter (2), WIF Sensor (3), Water in Fuel Drain (4)—2.7L Engine, 3.0L Engine similar

9. Connect the WIF wiring harness connector.
10. Connect the negative battery cable.
11. Cycle the ignition several times to build pressure.
12. Start engine and inspect for leaks.

DRAINING WATER FROM THE SYSTEM

Connect a hose to the Water in Fuel (WIF) drain and place it in a clearly marked and suitable container. Open the WIF drain by turning counterclockwise. Turn the ignition key on for 20 seconds. Repeat the procedure until all water is removed, close the drain and remove the hose.

INJECTORS

REMOVAL & INSTALLATION

See Figure 64.

1. Disconnect the negative battery cable.
2. Remove the engine appearance cover.
3. Remove the fuel return hose locking clamps, and remove the hose.
4. Disconnect the fuel injector high pressure line.

➡Counterhold injection lines with wrench socket at threaded connections of injectors.

5. Remove the fuel injector retaining bolt and tension claw, then remove the injector and seal.
6. Remove the fuel injectors.

To install:

7. Clean the injector and recesses.
8. Coat the injector body with anti-seize lubricant, then install the injector with new seals.
9. Install the tensioning claws with new screws to the injectors. Tighten the screws to 62 inch lbs. (7 Nm) plus 90°.

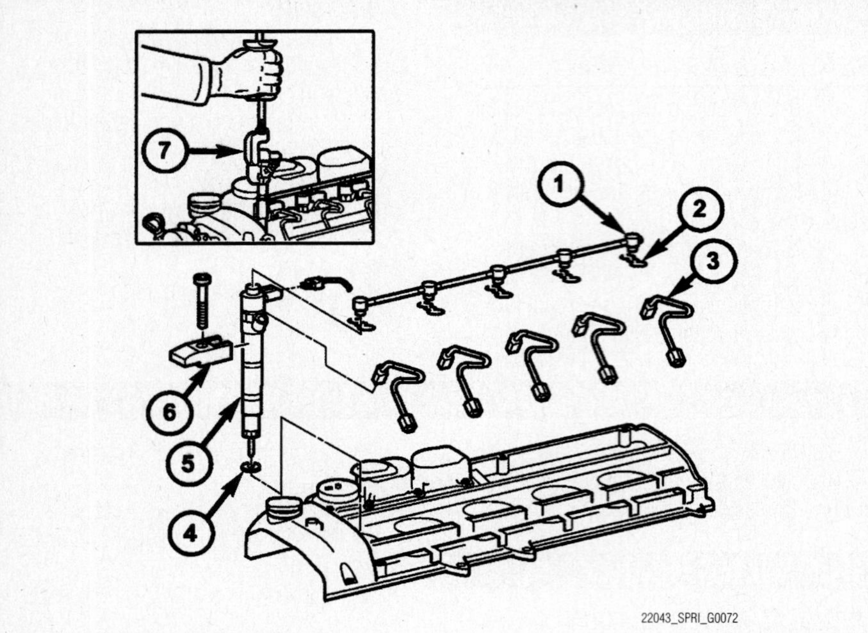

Fig. 64 Remove the locking clamps (2) and return hose (1), disconnect the injector high pressure line (3). Remove the retaining bolt and tension claw (6) and remove the injector (5) and seal (4)—2.7L Engine, 3.0L Engine similar

10. Position the fuel return line to the injectors and secure the locking clamps.
11. Install the high pressure injection lines.
12. Connect the injector electrical connectors.
13. Install the engine appearance cover.
14. Connect the negative battery cable.
15. Program all of the injector codes into the Engine Control Module using a scan tool.
16. Start the engine and check for leaks.

FUEL SUPPLY PUMP

REMOVAL & INSTALLATION

See Figures 65 and 66.

1. Drain and remove fuel tank.
2. Thoroughly clean the area around pump module at top of tank.
3. Disconnect all the fuel lines from pump module fittings.
4. The plastic fuel pump module locknut (lockring) is threaded onto fuel tank. Install Special Tool 6856 to locknut and remove locknut. The fuel pump module will spring up slightly after locknut is removed.
5. Pull the fuel pump assembly up just a few inches to gain access to float support arm/rod.

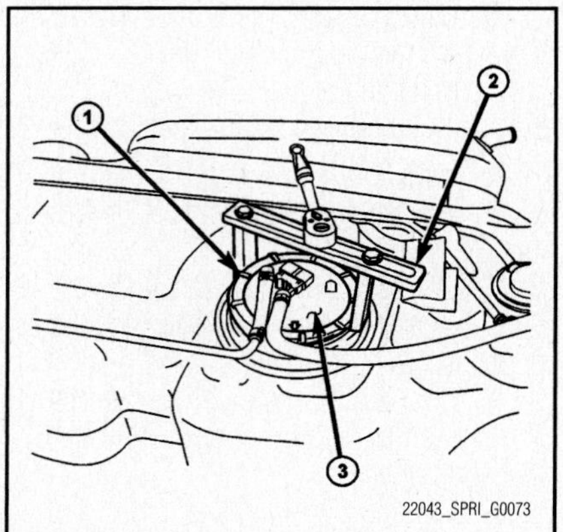

Fig. 65 Use Special Tool 6856 (2) to remove the lockring (1) and remove the fuel supply pump (3)—2.7L Engine shown, 3.0L Engine similar

WARNING

Be careful not to bend float support rod while removing pump module.

6. Rotate the clip to release float rod from the fuel level sensor.
7. Twist the rod slightly to remove from fuel level sensor. Do not allow float assembly to fall into fuel tank.
8. While holding the float rod, remove the fuel pump module from the fuel tank.
9. Remove float assembly from fuel tank.

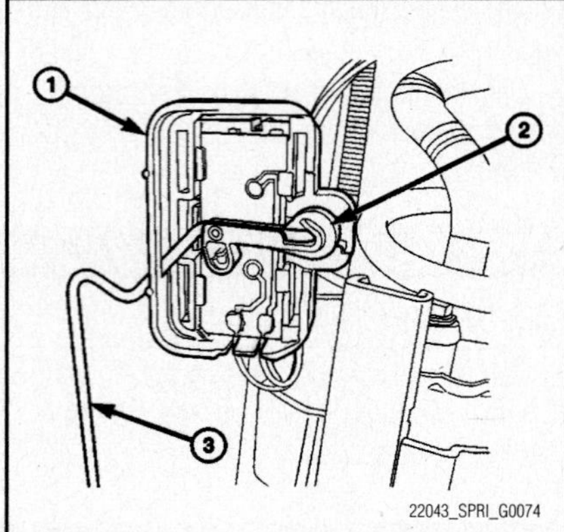

Fig. 66 Rotate the clip (2) to release the float rod (3) from the fuel level sensor (1)—2.7L Engine shown, 3.0L Engine similar

10. Remove and discard rubber gasket (seal) from pump module.

To install:

11. Thoroughly clean the locknut (lockring) and locknut threads at top of the tank.
12. Position a new gasket (seal) to the fuel tank opening.
13. Position the float rod assembly partially into the fuel tank.
14. Position the fuel pump module partially into the fuel tank.
15. Twist the rod into the clip on the fuel level sensor.
16. Rotate the clip to attach the rod to the clip.
17. After attaching the float assembly to the fuel level sensor, carefully position the fuel pump module into opening in the fuel tank.
18. Position the locknut over top of fuel pump module. Install locknut finger tight.
19. The fuel line fittings should be pointed to the right side of the vehicle. Rotate and position the alignment arrow towards right side of vehicle (if necessary) before tightening the locknut. This step must be performed to prevent the module's float from contacting the side of fuel tank.
20. Tighten the locknut using Special Tool 6856.
21. Install the fuel tank.

HIGH PRESSURE OIL PUMP DRIVE GEAR

REMOVAL & INSTALLATION

1. Disconnect the negative battery cable.
2. Remove viscous fan clutch. For additional information, refer to the following section, "Engine Fan, Removal & Installation."

3. Unplug the electrical connectors at high pressure pump.
4. Disconnect the high pressure line at high pressure pump.
5. Detach the fuel supply and return flow lines at the high pressure pump using Special Tool 9539.
6. Remove bolts attaching high pressure pump and remove pump.

➡Care must be taken not to drop the high pressure pump drive when removing pump. Inspect the pump drive for wear. If wear is present replace the drive and gear.

To install:

7. Position and secure the high pressure pump to cylinder head and tighten bolts to 10 ft. lbs. (14 Nm).
8. Attach the fuel flow supply and return lines, and crimp the clamps using Special Tool 9539.

✲✲ CAUTION

NEVER slacken the thread connection. Use a wrench to counterhold at threaded connection when slackening and tightening torque in order to avoid also slackening the threaded connection the next time.

✲✲ CAUTION

DO NOT crimp or bend fuel line. Inspect sealing cone at line; replace line if compression exists.

➡Care must be taken not to cross the fuel return and supply lines during installation.

✲✲ CAUTION

NEVER slacken the thread connection. Use a wrench to counterhold at threaded connection when slackening and tightening torque in order to avoid also slackening the threaded connection the next time.

✲✲ CAUTION

DO NOT crimp or bend fuel line. Inspect sealing cone at line; replace line if compression exists.

9. Attach the high pressure fuel line to pump and tighten to 16 ft. lbs. (22Nm).
10. Install the viscous fan.
11. Connect negative battery cable.
12. Start the engine and check for leaks.

GLOW PLUGS

REMOVAL & INSTALLATION

See Figure 67.

1. Disconnect the negative battery cable.
2. Remove the engine appearance cover.
3. Using Special Tool 9286 Pliers, unplug the glow plug wiring harness connector at the glow plug.
4. Remove the glow plug.

To install:

5. Screw the glow plug into the cylinder head and tighten to 9 ft. lbs. (12 Nm).
6. Connect the glow plug wiring harness connector.
7. Install the engine appearance cover.
8. Connect the negative battery cable.

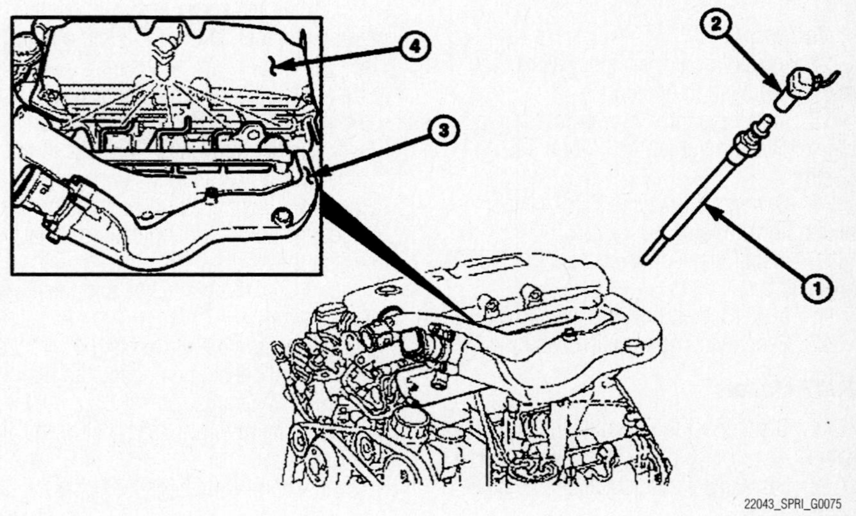

Fig. 67 Remove the engine appearance cover (4) and wiring harness (2) to remove the glow plug (1)—2.7L Engine shown, 3.0L Engine similar

HEATING & AIR CONDITIONING SYSTEM

BLOWER MOTOR

REMOVAL & INSTALLATION

Front

2005–06 Models

1. Disconnect the negative battery cable.
2. Remove the engine air cleaner housing cover.
3. Position the ventilation housing insulation blanket out of the way of the blower motor assembly.
4. Disconnect the wire harness connector from the blower motor.
5. Remove the three blower motor retaining screws.
6. Remove the blower motor assembly from the ventilation housing.

To install:

7. Install the blower motor assembly into the ventilation housing.
8. Install the three blower motor retaining screws and tighten to 17 inch lbs. (2 Nm).
9. Connect the wire harness connector to the blower motor.
10. Install the ventilation housing insulation blanket.
11. Install the engine air cleaner cover.
12. Reconnect the negative battery cable.

2007 Models

1. Disconnect the negative battery cable.
2. Disconnect and isolate the negative battery cable.
3. Remove the glove box from the instrument panel as follows:
   a. Remove the trim below the air outlet.
   b. Open the glove box, push up on the two rear stops and fold the box down completely.
   c. Remove the hinge screws and remove the glove box.
   d. Remove the screws and remove the inner compartment liner.
   e. Disconnect the glove box light electrical connector and remove the coolant air hose.
4. Remove the right side floor duct.
5. Remove the screw that secures the instrument panel cover to the lower right portion of instrument panel.
6. Disengage the locking feature and rotate the blower motor counterclockwise until it is loose from the HVAC housing.
7. Gently pull the lower right portion of the instrument panel cover slightly rearward to gain clearance and remove the blower motor from the HVAC housing.
8. Disconnect the wire harness connector from the blower motor and remove the blower motor from the passenger compartment.

To install:

9. Connect the wire harness connector to the blower motor.
10. Gently pull the lower right portion of the instrument panel cover slightly rearward to gain clearance and position the blower motor into the HVAC housing.
11. Rotate the blower motor clockwise until it is fully seated in the HVAC housing. Make sure the blower motor locking feature is fully engaged to the housing.
12. Install the screw that secures the instrument panel cover to the instrument panel. Tighten the screw securely.
13. Install the right side floor duct.
14. Install the glove box as follows:
   a. Install the coolant air hose to the inner glove box liner and connect the glove box light electrical connector.
   b. Install the inner glove box liner and install the screws.
   c. Install the glove box and install the hinge screws.
   d. Position the glove box up into the instrument panel and engage the rear retaining stop tabs.
   e. Install the trim panel below the air outlet.
15. Reconnect the negative battery cable.

Rear

2005–06 Models

1. Disconnect the negative battery cable.
2. Remove the cover from the rear A/C evaporator housing as follows:
   a. Remove the rear dome lamps from the center and rear roof duct panels (Rear A/C Evaporator Cover).
   b. Remove the push-pin fasteners that secure the center and rear roof duct panels to the roof duct and remove the panels.
   c. Disconnect the dome light wire harness connector and remove the dome light wire harness from the roof duct.
   d. Remove the six screws that secure the rear A/C evaporator cover to the front of the rear A/C evaporator housing.
   e. Remove the three push-pin fasteners that secure the rear A/C evaporator cover to the rear of the evaporator housing and remove the cover.
3. Disconnect the wire harness connectors from the rear blower motor suppression filter and from the rear blower motor being serviced and remove the suppression filter.
4. Remove the body sealer from around the rear blower motor area being serviced.
5. Remove the screws that secure each rear blower motor to the rear evaporator housing and remove blower motor.

To install:

6. Position the rear blower motor being serviced to the rear A/C evaporator housing.
7. Install the screws that secure each rear blower motor to the rear A/C evaporator housing and tighten the screws to 45 inch lbs. (5 Nm).
8. Install a new bead of body sealant to the blower motor area being serviced.
9. Install the rear blower motor suppression filter and connect the wiring harness connectors to the suppression filter and to the rear blower motor being serviced.
10. Install the cover onto the rear A/C evaporator housing as follows:
   a. Position the rear A/C evaporator cover to the rear A/C evaporator housing.
   b. Install the three push-pin fasteners that secure the rear A/C evaporator cover to the rear of the evaporator housing.
   c. Install the six screws that secure the rear A/C evaporator cover to the front of the evaporator housing and tighten the screws to 21 inch lbs. (2.2 Nm).
   d. Install the dome light wire harness to the roof duct and reconnect the harness.
   e. Position the center and rear roof duct panels to the roof duct and install the push-pin fasteners.
   f. Install the rear dome lamps into the center and rear roof duct panels.
11. Connect the negative battery cable.

2007 Models

1. Disconnect and isolate the negative battery cable.
2. Remove the screws that secure the rear condenser cover to the top of the vehicle and remove the cover.
3. Remove the nut and bolt that secure the rear A/C suction line to the rear condenser cover bracket.
4. Remove the four bolts that secure the rear condenser cover bracket to the rear condenser bracket and remove the cover bracket.
5. Remove the screws that secure the rear evaporator cover and insulator to the

top of the vehicle and remove the cover and insulator.

6. Disconnect the wire harness connectors from the rear blower motor.

7. Remove the screws that secure the rear blower motor to the rear evaporator housing and remove the blower motor.

To install:

8. Position the rear blower motor to the rear evaporator housing and tighten the retaining screws to 44 inch lbs. (5 Nm).

9. Connect the wire harness connectors to the blower motor.

10. Install the rear evaporator insulator and cover to the top of the vehicle and tighten the retaining screws to 17 inch lbs. (2 Nm).

11. Install the rear condenser cover bracket onto the rear condenser bracket and install the four retaining bolts. Tighten the bolts securely.

12. Install the nut and bolt that secure the rear A/C suction line to the rear condenser cover bracket. Tighten the nut securely.

13. Install the rear condenser cover to the top of the vehicle and tighten the retaining screws to 17 inch lbs. (2 Nm).

14. Reconnect the negative battery cable.

HEATER CORE

REMOVAL & INSTALLATION

2005–06 Models

See Figures 68 and 69.

1. Recover the refrigerant from the refrigerant system.
2. Drain the engine cooling system.
3. Disconnect the negative battery cable.
4. Remove the air cleaner housing.
5. Remove the windshield washer reservoir.
6. Remove the air filter from the ventilation housing.
7. Disconnect the wire harness and vacuum connectors from the recirculation door actuator.
8. Disconnect the wire harness connector from the blower motor resistor block.
9. Disconnect the wire harness connector from the blower motor
10. Remove the nuts and washers that secure the ventilation housing to the body and remove the ventilation housing from the vehicle.
11. Disconnect the heater hoses from the heater core.
12. Disconnect the heater hoses from the heater core tubes. Install plugs in, or tape over the opened heater core tubes.
13. Remove the two bolts securing the refrigerant lines to the evaporator tubes and disconnect the lines from the tubes. Cap all of the opened refrigerant line fittings.
14. Remove the seals from the refrigerant line fittings and discard.
15. Install plugs in, or tape over the opened refrigerant line fittings and evaporator tubes.
16. Remove the instrument panel from the vehicle as follows:
    a. Disconnect and isolate the battery negative cable.
    b. Remove the radio.
    c. Remove the glove compartment.
    d. Remove the cup holder.
    e. Remove the instrument cluster.
    f. Remove the passenger airbag.
    g. Remove the right and left speakers.
    h. Remove the center bezel.
    i. Remove the air conditioning push-button control module.
    j. Twist the cover lock 1/4 turn and remove Power Distribution Center (PDC) cover.
    k. Remove the nut and screws and remove steering column shroud.
    l. Remove the PDC bolt, nut and nut for ground wire.
    m. Disconnect the PDC electrical connectors and remove.
    n. Remove the screws and remove passenger side air nozzle cover.
    o. Remove the screws and remove left side cover.
    p. Remove the left outer and inner air nozzles.
    q. Remove the right side cover.
    r. Remove the right outer and inner air nozzles.
    s. Remove the protective matting from cluster location.
    t. Remove the instrument panel top cover screws and cover.
    u. Remove the vent hose.
    v. Remove the brake pedal spring.
    w. Remove the ignition transponder.

CAUTION

The position of the steering gear must not be altered again for the entire duration of the work procedure.

    x. Turn the steering wheel and lock the steering wheel in the straight ahead position.
    y. Remove the steering column support bolts.
    z. Remove the screws and remove instrument panel.
17. Remove the defroster, floor distribution and instrument panel ducts.
18. Disconnect the two bulkhead ground connections near instrument cluster area.
19. Remove the passenger airbag bracket.
20. Disconnect the wire harness connector from the evaporator temperature sensor and air outlet temperature sensor.
21. Remove the wire harness from the bracket located on the right side of the heater housing and position the wire harness out of the way.
22. Disconnect the A/C-heater control cables from the mode door levers.
23. Disconnect the evaporator drain tube from the HVAC housing.
24. Remove the five bolts securing the HVAC housing to the body.

➡Make sure that the interior is protected in case of loss of residual fluids from the heater core and the A/C evaporator.

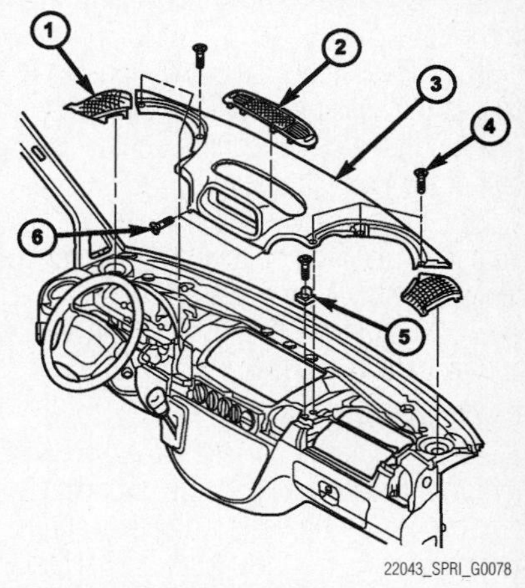

Fig. 68 Remove the speaker covers (1), center nozzle cover (2), top screws (4) and lower screws (5,6) to remove the top cover (3)—2005–06 Models

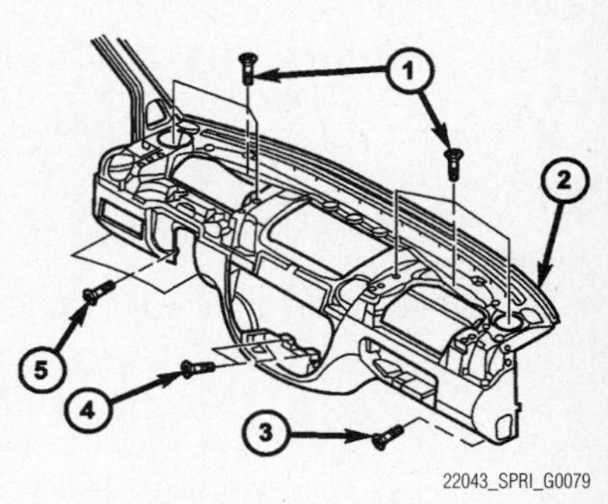

Fig. 69 Remove the upper (1), right (3), center (4) and left (5) screws to remove the instrument panel assembly (2)—2005–06 Models

25. Remove the HVAC housing from the vehicle.

26. Disassemble the HVAC housing to access the heater core.

27. Lift the heater core out of the lower half of the HVAC housing.

28. If necessary, remove the three heater core tube retaining bolts and the heater core tube assembly from the heater core.

29. Remove the heater core tube seals and discard as required.

To install:

30. If the heater core tube assembly was removed from the heater core, lubricate two new rubber O-ring seals with clean engine coolant and install them onto the heater core fitting.

31. If required, connect the heater core tube assembly to the heater core and tighten the three retaining bolts to 45 inch lbs. (5 Nm).

32. Install the heater core into the bottom half of the HVAC housing.

33. Install the HVAC housing is the reverse order of removal.

34. Evacuate and charge the refrigerant system.

35. Refill the cooling system to the correct level.

36. Start the engine and check for leaks.

2007 Models

See Figures 70 and 71.

1. Remove the instrument panel and HVAC housing as an assembly as follows:

a. Disconnect the negative battery cable.

b. Recover the refrigerant from the A/C system.

c. Drain the cooling system.

d. Remove the air intake assembly.

e. Disconnect the A/C supply and suction lines form the A/C expansion valve.

f. Loosen the clamps and disconnect the heater hoses from the heater core.

g. Cap the expansion valve and heater core openings.

h. Remove the A-pillar trim.

i. Remove the sun visors and storage trays.

j. Remove the dome light.

k. Remove the headliner

l. Remove the steering column opening cover.

m. Remove the trim below the air outlet.

n. Open the glove box, push up on the two rear stops and fold the box down completely.

o. Remove the hinge screws and remove the glove box.

p. Remove the screws and remove the inner compartment liner.

q. Disconnect the glove box light electrical connector and remove the coolant air hose.

r. Using a trim stick C-4755 or equivalent, separate the clips and remove the center bezel.

s. Remove the air outlet covers from the instrument panel center section.

t. Remove the cover on the gearshift lever.

u. Remove the gear shifter assembly.

v. Remove the side air nozzles.

w. Turn the steering wheel to center position and lock steering.

x. Remove the airbag module from the steering wheel and remove the steering wheel.

➡Matchmark the steering wheel to the steering column shaft for proper orientation during installation.

y. Disconnect all electrical connectors from wiring harness in area of A-pillar and roof and remove the wiring harness.

z. Disconnect all the electrical connectors from wiring harness in passenger footwell.

aa. Disconnect all electrical connectors on instrument panel in driver footwell.

bb. Disconnect the connections and lines of instrument panel in interior compartment.

cc. Remove the air filter housing.

dd. Disconnect the connections and lines of instrument panel in engine compartment.

ee. Remove the bolts from firewall.

ff. Remove the bolts.

gg. Lift out the instrument panel support with instrument panel.

2. Remove the blower motor power module or blower motor resistor (depending on application).

3. Remove the two metal retaining clamps that secure the heater core tubes to the heater core.

4. Disconnect the heater core tubes from the heater core and remove and discard the O-ring seals.

To install:

5. Carefully position the blower motor portion of the HVAC housing slightly forward for clearance and install the heater core into the side of the HVAC housing.

6. Install the bracket to the HVAC housing.

7. Install the nut that secures the bracket to the HVAC housing. Tighten the nut securely.

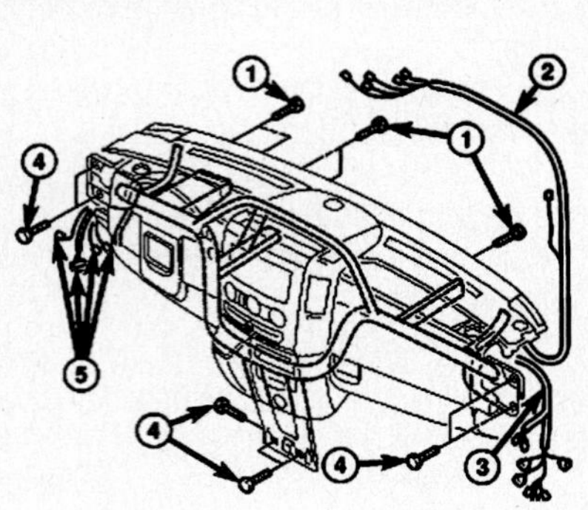

22043_SPRI_G0076

Fig. 70 Disconnect all wiring harnesses (2.3,5) and remove the firewall bolts (1) and mounting bolts (4) to remove the instrument panel—2007 Models

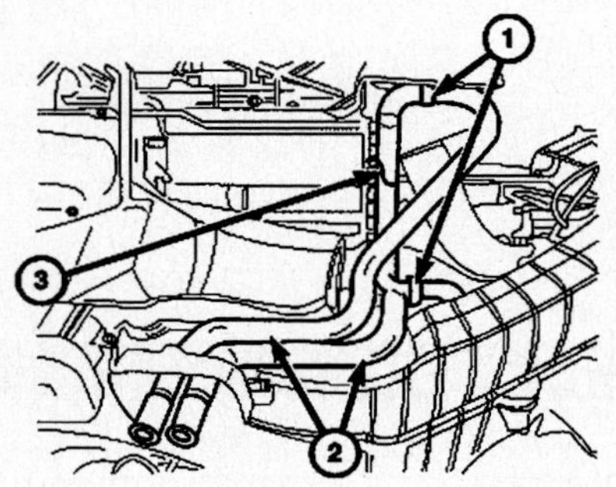

22043_SPRI_G0077

Fig. 71 Remove the retaining clamps (1) that secure the heater core tubes (2) to the heater core (3)—2007 Models

8. Lubricate new rubber O-ring seals with clean engine coolant and install them onto the heater core fittings. Use only the specified O-rings as they are made of a special material compatible to engine coolant. Use only engine coolant of the type recommended for the engine in the vehicle.

9. Install the heater core tubes onto the heater core.

10. Install the two metal retaining clamps that secure the heater core tubes to the heater core.

11. Install the blower motor power module or blower motor resistor (depending on application).

12. The remainder of the installation is the reverse order of removal.

13. Evacuate and recharge the refrigerant system.

14. Refill the cooling system to the correct level.

15. Start the engine and check for leaks.

STEERING

POWER STEERING GEAR

REMOVAL & INSTALLATION

1. Siphon the power steering fluid out of the reservoir.
2. Raise and safely support the vehicle.
3. Remove the front wheels.
4. Remove the stabilizer bar from the upper part of the stabilizer link. For additional information, refer to the following section, "Stabilizer Bar, Removal & Installation."
5. Using Special Tool C-3894-A, remove the outer tie rod end nuts and separate the tie rods from the steering knuckles.
6. Remove the left outer tie rod end from the steering gear.
7. Remove both spring clamp plates.
8. Remove both the high pressure and return hoses from the steering gear.
9. Remove the steering shaft clamping bolt from the steering gear.
10. Separate the universal joint from the steering gear.
11. Remove the steering gear bolts from the front axle.
12. Remove the steering gear by sliding it toward the passenger's side of the vehicle and then tilt downward on the drivers side and remove from vehicle.

To install:

13. Install the steering gear assembly into the vehicle. Install the steering gear bolts and tighten them as follows:
    - Step 1: Tighten to 18 ft. lbs. (25 Nm)
    - Step 2: Tighten to 33 ft. lbs. (45 Nm).
    - Step 3: Plus 90°
14. Install the universal joint to the steering gear and tighten the fitted bolt to 18 ft. lbs. (24 Nm).

➡Make sure to install the steering shaft universal joint onto the steering gear shaft all the way down until the hole lines up with the radial groove in the steering shaft.

15. Install both the power steering hoses to the steering gear. Tighten the high pressure hose to 27 ft. lbs. (37 Nm).
16. Install the spring clamp plates.
17. Install the left outer tie rod end to the steering gear.
18. Install both the outer tie rod ends to the steering knuckle and tighten to 96 ft. lbs. (130 Nm).
19. Install the upper stabilizer bar link to the stabilizer bar.
20. Install the front wheels.
21. Fill and bleed the power steering system
22. Check and adjust the alignment as necessary.
23. Start the engine and check for leaks.

POWER STEERING PUMP

REMOVAL & INSTALLATION

2.7L & 3.0L Engines

1. Remove the accessory drive belt. For additional information, refer to the following section, "Accessory Drive Belt, Removal & Installation."
2. Siphon as much power steering fluid as possible out of the reservoir.
3. Remove the pressure and supply line from the pump.
4. Remove the pump mounting bolts and remove the pump.

➡If the pump is being replaced, transfer the front and rear pump brackets and pulley.

To install:

5. Install the power steering pump to the vehicle and tighten the mounting bolts to:
    a. 3.0L Engine: 21 ft. lbs. (28 Nm).
    b. 2.7L Engine: 15 ft. lbs. (21 Nm).
6. Connect the supply hose to the pump.
7. Install the pressure link to the pump and tighten the nut to 35 ft. lbs. (47 Nm).
8. Install the accessory drive belt.
9. Refill the power steering system to the correct level.
10. Start the engine and check for leaks.

3.5L Engine

1. Remove the accessory drive belt from the power steering pump. For additional information, refer to the following section, "Accessory Drive Belt, Removal & Installation."
2. Remove the washer bottle mounting screws and disconnect the electrical connectors to relocate the bottle out of the way.
3. Siphon as much power steering fluid as possible out of the reservoir.
4. Remove the high pressure power steering hose at the pump.
5. Remove the supply hose from the pump.
6. Remove the bolts securing the power steering pump to the engine.

➡If the pump is being replaced, transfer the front and rear pump brackets and pulley.

To install:

7. Install the power steering pump to the engine and tighten the mounting bolts to 15 ft. lbs. (21 Nm).
8. Replace all O-rings and hose clamps.
9. Install the supply hose to the pump and tighten the clamp.
10. Install the high pressure hose to the pump and tighten to 28 ft. lbs. (38 Nm).
11. Install the accessory drive belt over the power steering pump pulley.
12. Refill the power steering system to the correct level.
13. Install the washer bottle mounting screws and connect the electrical connectors.

BLEEDING

See Figure 72.

1. Check the fluid level. As measured on the side of the reservoir, the level should indicate between MAX and MIN when the fluid is at normal ambient temperature. Adjust the fluid level as necessary.
2. Tightly insert Special Tool 9688 Power Steering Cap Adapter into the mouth of the reservoir.

⁂ CAUTION

Failure to use a vacuum pump reservoir may allow power steering fluid to be sucked into the hand vacuum pump.

3. Attach Special Tool C-4207 Hand Vacuum Pump or equivalent, with reservoir attached, to the Power Steering Cap Adapter.

⁂ WARNING

Do not run the engine while vacuum is applied to the power steering system. Damage to the power steering pump can occur.

➡When performing the following step make sure the vacuum level is maintained during the entire time period.

4. Using a Hand Vacuum Pump, apply 68-85 kPa (20-25 in. Hg) of vacuum to the system for a minimum of three minutes.

5. Slowly release the vacuum and remove the special tools.
6. Adjust the fluid level as necessary.
7. Repeat the process until the fluid no longer drops when vacuum is applied.
8. Start the engine and cycle the steering wheel lock-to-lock three times.

✲✲ WARNING

Do not hold the steering wheel at the stops.

9. Stop the engine and check for leaks at all connections.
10. Check for any signs of air in the reservoir and check the fluid level. If air is present, repeat the procedure as necessary.

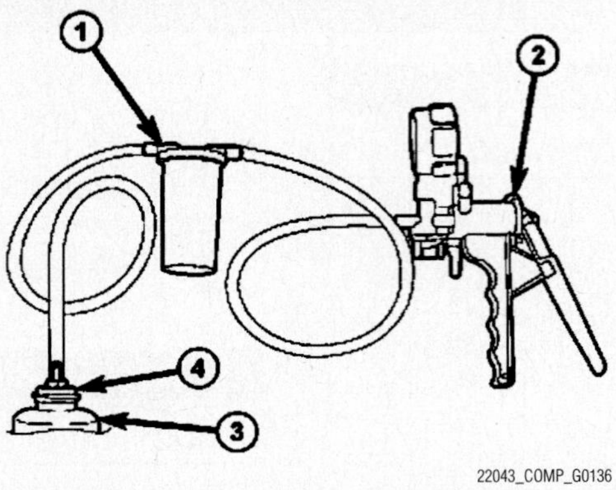

Fig. 72 Bleed the power steering system with a reservoir (1) Hand Vacuum Pump (2), Power Steering Cap Adapter (4) attached to the Power Steering Pump reservoir (3).

SUSPENSION

FRONT SUSPENSION

LEAF SPRING

REMOVAL & INSTALLATION

2005–06 Models

1. With the vehicle still on the ground, remove the front and rear bolts on the left and right spring plate clamps.
2. Raise and safely support the vehicle.
3. Remove the front wheels.
4. Remove the disc brake caliper adapter. For additional information, refer to the following section, "Brake Caliper, Removal & Installation."

✲✲ WARNING

Do not allow brake hose to support the caliper weight.

5. Remove the wheel speed sensor. For additional information, refer to the following section, "Speed Sensors, Removal & Installation."
6. Remove the outer tie rod retaining nut and separate the tie rod from the knuckle using Special Tool C-3894-A.

➡In order to remove tension from the strut, raise the lower control arm with a suitable jack approximately 10 mm with a jack.

7. Remove the strut bolts from the steering knuckle.
8. Remove both stop plate bolts and rotate the plates upwards with the stabilizer link attached.
9. Lower the lower control arm.
10. Remove the lower ball joint nut from the steering knuckle.
11. Separate the lower ball joint from the knuckle using Special Tool 9282.
12. Remove the lower control arm nuts and bolts from the frame.
13. Remove the lower control arm from the frame.

➡To avoid damaging the transverse leaf spring, cushion the pad on the jack accordingly.

14. Support the transverse leaf spring in the center with a jack.
15. Remove the left and right spring clamp plates.

➡The upper spring blocks between the engine cradle and the spring are color coded, Make sure not to mix the blocks per sides. The blocks are different in sizes to accommodate the weight of the vehicle and driver in order for the vehicle to sit level.

16. Lower the jack and remove the transverse leaf spring towards the side.

To install:

17. Install the transverse leaf spring in the center with a jack with all the rubber mounts attached.
18. Install the lower control arm to the frame.
19. Install the knuckle on the lower ball joint.
20. Raise the lower control arm approximately 10 mm with a jack.
21. Install both stop plate bolts to the lower control arm
22. Install the strut bolts to the steering knuckle.
23. Reinstall the tie rod to the steering knuckle. Tighten to 110 ft. lbs. (150 Nm).
24. Install the ABS sensor all the way into the steering knuckle, the sensor will adjust automatically when the vehicle is moved.
25. Install the disc brake caliper adapter.
26. Install the front wheels.
27. Lower the vehicle.
28. Install the spring clamp plates. Tighten the M10 bolts to 48 ft. lbs. (65 Nm) and the M12 bolts to 96 ft. lbs. (130 Nm).
29. Roll the vehicle approximately 1 mm forwards and the backwards, and rock firmly.
30. Tighten the nuts on the lower control arm to the frame to 110 ft. lbs. (150 Nm).

2007 Models

See Figure 73.

1. Raise and safely support the vehicle.
2. Remove the left side front wheel.
3. Remove the left side strut. For additional information, refer to the following section, "MacPherson Strut, Removal & Installation."
4. Remove the left side outer tie rod end and shield from the steering knuckle.
5. Remove the left side upper spring stop plate.
6. Remove the left side lower control arm. For additional information, refer to the following section, "Lower Control Arm, Removal & Installation."
7. Using a suitable floor jack, raise the outer edge of the spring slightly in order to remove the lower spring clamp plate.

➡To avoid damaging the transverse leaf spring, cushion the pad on the jack accordingly.

8. Remove the left side lower spring clamp plate.

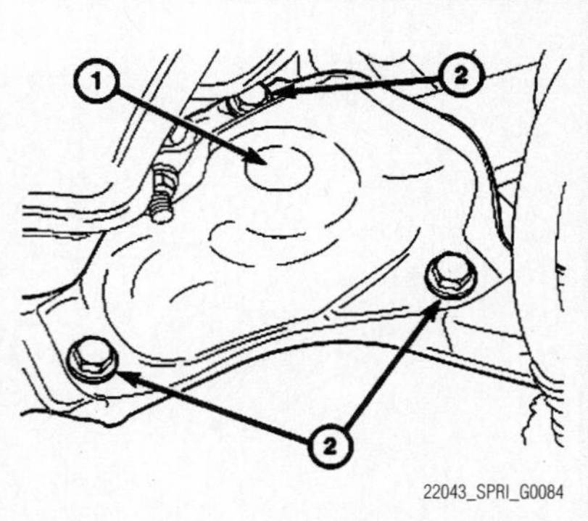

Fig. 73 Remove the bolts (2) to remove the left side upper spring stop plate (1)—2007 Models

9. Lower the jack to release the spring pressure.
10. Loose the right side upper spring stop plate bolts.
11. Remove the right side lower spring clamp plate.
12. Remove the rubber spring blocks.

➡The upper and lower spring blocks are different. Keep them in the correct order for proper installation.

13. Remove the transverse leaf spring towards the left side of the vehicle.

To install:

➡When installing the bolts, hand tighten only at first. Only tighten the bolts to their specification until the vehicle is on the ground.

14. Install the rubber spring block on the right side lower control arm.
15. Install and center the transverse leaf spring from the left side of the vehicle to the right side make sure not to unseat the rubber block in the control arm.
16. Tighten the right side upper spring stop plate bolts. Tighten the M10 bolt to 43 ft. lbs. (58 Nm). Tighten the M2 bolt to 78 ft. lbs. (106 Nm) plus 90°.
17. Install the right side lower spring clamp plate. Tighten the M8 bolt to 21 ft. lbs. (29 Nm). Tighten the M12 bolt to 78 ft. lbs. (106 Nm) plus 90°.
18. Using a suitable floor jack, raise the outer edge of the spring slightly in order to install the left side lower spring clamp plate.

➡To avoid damaging the transverse leaf spring, cushion the pad on the jack accordingly.

19. Install the left side lower spring clamp plate. Tighten the M8 bolt to 21 ft. lbs. (29 Nm). Tighten the M12 bolt to 78 ft. lbs. (106 Nm) plus 90°.
20. Lower the jack to release the spring pressure.
21. Install the left side control arm.
22. Install the left side upper spring stop plate. Tighten the M10 bolt to 43 ft. lbs. (58 Nm). Tighten the M2 bolt to 78 ft. lbs. (106 Nm) plus 90°.
23. Install the strut assembly.
24. Install the left side tie rod end and shield to the knuckle.
25. Install the front wheels.
26. Lower the vehicle. Tighten the nuts on the lower control arm to the frame to 127 ft. lbs. (172 Nm) plus 90°.
27. Check and adjust the alignment as necessary.

LOWER BALL JOINT

REMOVAL & INSTALLATION

2005–06 Models

1. Raise and safely support the vehicle.
2. Remove the front wheel.
3. Remove the front strut. For additional information, refer to the following section, "MacPherson Strut, Removal & Installation."
4. Remove the steering knuckle. For additional information, refer to the following section, "Steering Knuckle, Removal & Installation."
5. Remove the lower ball joint using special tool 9294-1Driver with 9294-2 Receiver and C-4212-F Clamp.

To install:

6. Install the ball joint into the lower control arm using Special Tool 9294-3 Installer Ring inserted in 9294-2 Receiver and C-4212-F.
7. Install the front strut.
8. Install the steering knuckle.
9. Install the front wheel.
10. Lower the vehicle.
11. Check and adjust the alignment as necessary.

2007 Models

See Figures 74 through 76.

1. Raise and safely support the vehicle.
2. Remove the front wheel.
3. Remove the brake caliper. For additional information, refer to the following section, "Brake Caliper, Removal & Installation."
4. Remove the steering knuckle. For additional information, refer to the following section, "Steering Knuckle, Removal & Installation."
5. Remove the outer tie rod end from the knuckle.
6. Separate the lower ball joint from the knuckle using a suitable ball joint puller.
7. Remove the lower ball joint using Special Tool 10002 Driver and striking the tool to force the ball joint outward from the lower control arm.

To install:

8. Install the ball joint into the lower control arm using Special Tool 9294-3 Installer Ring inserted in 9294-2 Receiver and C-4212-F Clamp.
9. Install the steering knuckle.
10. Install the brake caliper assembly.
11. Install the front wheel.
12. Lower the vehicle.
13. Check and adjust the alignment as necessary.

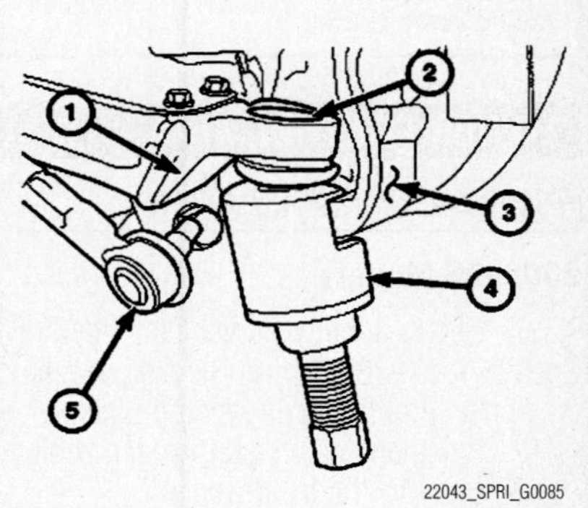

Fig. 74 Remove the outer tie rod end (5) from the knuckle (3), then separate the lower ball joint (2) from the knuckle using a suitable ball joint puller (4)—2007 Models

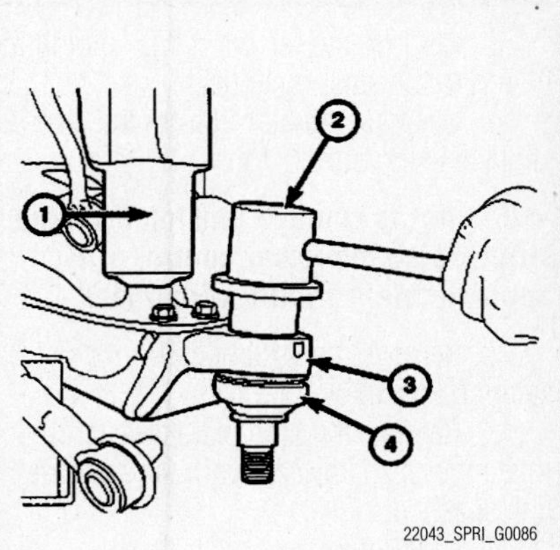

Fig. 75 Use Special Tool 10002 (2) to force the ball joint (4) from the lower control arm (3)—2007 Models

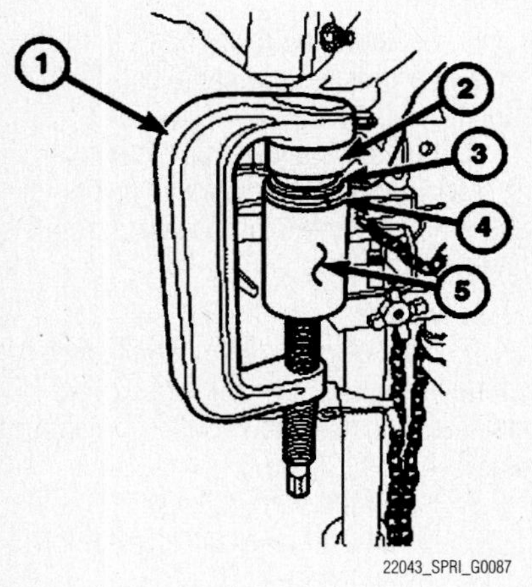

Fig. 76 Install the ball joint (3) into the lower control arm (2) using Special Tool 9294-3 (4) inserted in 9294-2 (5) and C-4212-F (1)—2007 Model shown, other model years similar

LOWER CONTROL ARM

REMOVAL & INSTALLATION

2005–06 Models

1. Before raising the vehicle, insert Special Tool 9288 Spring Blocks between the spring and the spring clamp plates.
2. Raise and safely support the vehicle.
3. Remove the front wheel.
4. Remove the disc brake caliper adapter. For additional information, refer to the following section, "Brake Caliper, Removal & Installation."

⁂ WARNING

Do not allow brake hose to support the caliper weight.

5. Remove the retaining nut holding the tie rod to the steering knuckle.
6. Separate the tie rod from the steering knuckle using special tool C-3894-A.

➡In order to remove tension from the strut, Raise the lower control arm approximately 10 mm with a jack.

7. Remove the strut bolts from the steering knuckle.
8. Remove the stop plate bolts and rotate the plate upwards with the stabilizer link attached.
9. Lower the lower control arm.
10. Remove the lower ball joint nut from the steering knuckle.
11. Separate the lower ball joint from the knuckle using Special Tool 9282.
12. Remove the lower control arm nuts and bolts from the frame.
13. Remove the lower control arm.

To install:

14. Install the lower control arm to the frame and hand tighten the bolts.
15. Install the lower ball joint into the steering knuckle and tighten to 206 ft. lbs. (280 Nm).
16. Install the strut bolts to the steering knuckle and tighten to 136 ft. lbs. (185 Nm).
17. Install the stop plate.
18. Attach the tie rod to the steering knuckle and tighten the nut to 96 ft. lbs. (130 ft. lbs.).
19. Install the brake caliper.
20. Install the front wheel.
21. Lower the vehicle.
22. Remove the spring blocks between the spring and the spring clamp plates, while the vehicles wheels are on the ground.
23. Roll the vehicle approximately 1 mm forwards and the backwards, and rock firmly.
24. Tighten the lower control arm nuts and bolts to the frame to 110 ft. lbs. (150 Nm).

2007 Models

See Figure 77.

1. Remove the floor pan screws.
2. Remove the upper strut mounting bolts.
3. Raise and safely support the vehicle.
4. Remove the front wheel.
5. Remove the rear half of the wheel well inner liner.
6. Remove the wheel speed sensor wire from the routing clip.
7. Remove the brake caliper adapter. For additional information, refer to the following section, "Brake Caliper, Removal & Installation."

⁂ WARNING

Do not allow brake hose to support the caliper weight.

8. Remove the brake rotor.
9. Remove the retaining nut holding the tie rod to the steering knuckle.
10. Separate the tie rod off the steering knuckle using Special Tool 9360.
11. Remove the lower bolts from the knuckle.
12. Remove the strut from the steering knuckle.
13. Remove the spring stop plate bolts and rotate the plate upwards with the stabilizer link attached.

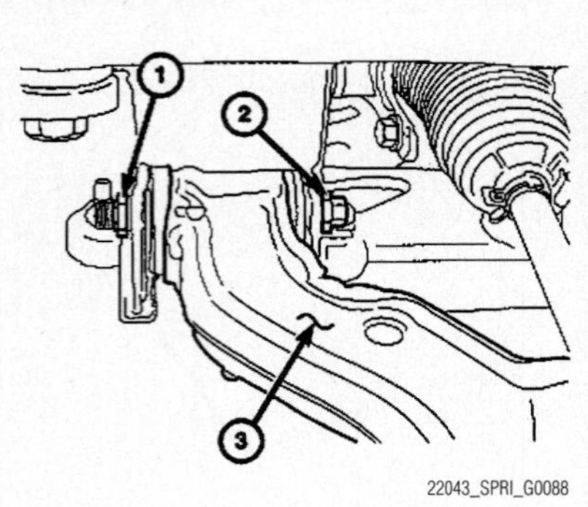

Fig. 77 Remove the pivot nuts (1) and bolts (2) to remove the lower control arm (3)—2007 Model shown, other model years similar

14. Remove the lower control arm pivot nuts and bolts from the frame.
15. Remove the lower control arm.

To install:

16. Install the lower control arm to the frame. Install the pivot nuts and bolts, but only hand tighten at this time.
17. Install the spring stop plate. Tighten the M10 bolt to 43 ft. lbs. (58 Nm). Tighten the M2 bolt to 78 ft. lbs. (106 Nm) plus 90°.
18. Install the steering knuckle to the lower ball joint and tighten the nut to 125 ft. lbs. (170 Nm).
19. Install the strut bolts to the steering knuckle and tighten to 103 ft. lbs. (140 Nm) plus an additional 120°.
20. Attach the tie rod end and shield to the steering knuckle. Tighten the nut to 37 ft. lbs. (50 Nm), then to 103 ft. lbs. (140 Nm) plus an additional 60° turn
21. Install the wheel sensor wire to the routing clip.
22. Install the brake rotor
23. Install the brake caliper adapter.
24. Install the strut into the upper strut mounting hole
25. Install the rear half of the wheel well liner.
26. Install the front wheel.
27. Lower the vehicle.
28. Install the upper strut bolts and tighten tot 21 ft. lbs. (28 Nm).
29. Install the floor pan screws and floor pan.
30. Tighten the lower control arm nuts to 125 ft. lbs. (172 Nm) plus an additional 90°.
31. Check and adjust the alignment as necessary.

MACPHERSON STRUT

REMOVAL & INSTALLATION

2005–06 Models

See Figure 78.

1. On the driver's side remove the floor covering off to the side.
2. On the passengers side take off the cover for the tools.
3. Remove the cover for the upper strut mounting.
4. Remove the nut on the upper strut mounting.
5. Raise and support the vehicle.
6. Remove the front wheels.
7. Raise the lower control arm approximately 10 mm with a jack to remove the tension from the strut.
8. Remove the strut from the steering knuckle.

To install:

➡When installing the bolts, hand tighten only at first. Only tighten the bolts to their specification until the vehicle is on the ground.

9. Install the strut to the steering knuckle and tighten the bolts to 136 ft. lbs. (185 Nm).
10. Raise the lower control arm with a suitable jack to install the upper part of the strut in the footwell. Tighten the nut to 74 ft. lbs. (100 Nm).
11. Lower the vehicle.
12. Install the nut covers.
13. Check and adjust the alignment if necessary.

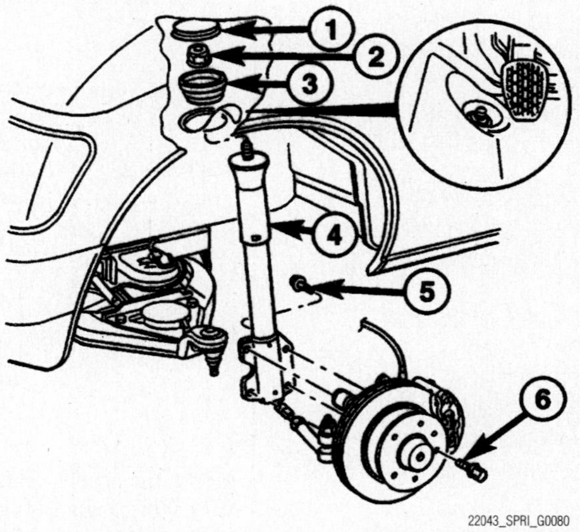

Fig. 78 Remove the cover (1) to access the nut (2). Remove the strut mounting bolts (5) to remove the strut assembly (4).

2007 Models

See Figures 79 and 80.

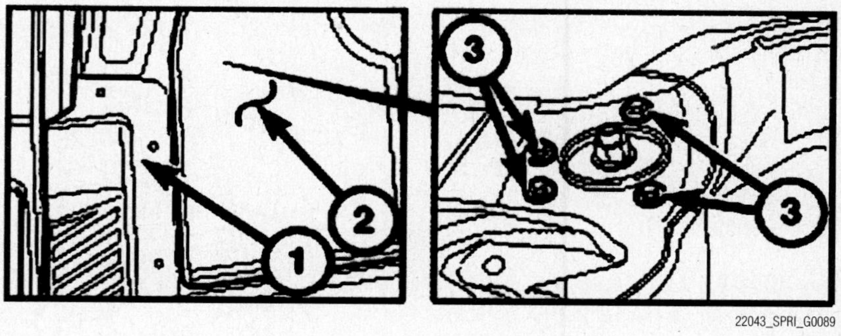

Fig. 79 Remove the floor pan screws (1) and floor mat (2) to access the upper strut mounting bolts (3)—2007 Model shown

1. Remove the floor pan screws and remove the floor mat.
2. Remove the upper strut mounting bolts.
3. Raise and safely support the vehicle.
4. Remove the front wheel.
5. Remove the rear half of the wheel well liner.
6. Remove the wheel sensor wire from the routing clip.
7. Remove the lower bolts from the knuckle.
8. Remove the strut from the steering knuckle.

To install:

9. Install the strut to the steering knuckle. Tighten the lower bolts to 103 ft. lbs. (140 Nm) plus 120°.
10. Raise the lower control arm with a suitable jack to install the upper part of the strut into the upper wheel well.

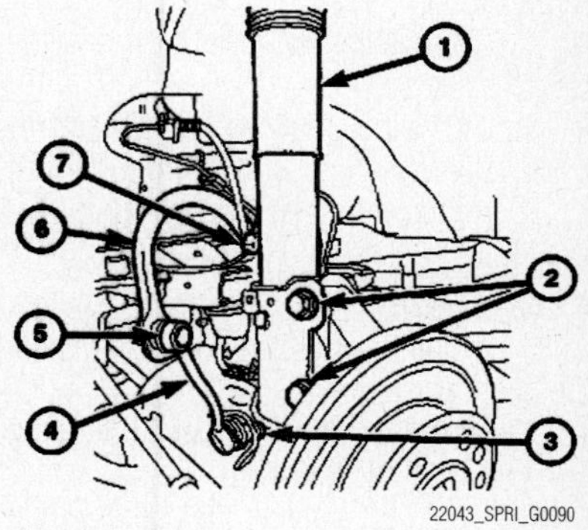

Fig. 80 Remove the sensor wire (7) from the clip then remove the strut mounting bolts (2) to remove the strut (1)—2007 Model shown

11. Install the speed sensor to the routing clip.
12. Install the rear half of the wheel well liner.
13. Install the front wheel.
14. Lower the vehicle.
15. Tighten the upper strut mounting bolts to 21 ft. (28 Nm).
16. Install the floor pan screws and floor mat.
17. Check and adjust the alignment as necessary.

STABILIZER BAR

REMOVAL & INSTALLATION

2005–06 Models

1. Raise and safely support the vehicle.
2. Remove the stabilizer bar clamp bolts on the front axle.

3. Press the rubber mount outwards out of the brackets.
4. Remove the stabilizer bar links from the stabilizer bar.

To install:

5. Install the stabilizer links to the stabilizer bar.
6. Install the stabilizer bar to the front axle.
7. Install the stabilizer bar clamps and tighten the bolts to 22 ft. lbs. (30 Nm).
8. Lower the vehicle.

2007 Models

1. Raise and safely support the vehicle.
2. Remove the front transverse spring. For additional information, refer to the following section, "Leaf Spring, Removal & Installation."
3. Remove the stabilizer bar links at the stabilizer bar.
4. Remove the stabilizer bar retainer clamp bolts.
5. Lower the stabilizer bar downwards.
6. Remove the bushings from the bar.
7. Remove the stabilizer bar from the vehicle.

To install:

8. Install the stabilizer bar and install the bushings to the bar.
9. Install the bar clamp and tighten the bolts to 43 ft. lbs. (55 Nm).
10. Install the links to the stabilizer bar and tighten the bolts to 78 ft. lbs. (106 Nm).
11. Install the front transverse spring.
12. Lower the vehicle.
13. Check and adjust the alignment as possible.

STEERING KNUCKLE

REMOVAL & INSTALLATION

2005–06 Models

See Figure 81.

1. Raise and safely support the vehicle.
2. Remove the front wheel.
3. Remove the brake caliper adapter. For additional information, refer to the following section, "Brake Caliper Adapter."
4. Remove the hub/bearing. For additional information, refer to the following section, "Wheel Bearings, Removal & Installation."
5. Separate the outer tie rod from the steering knuckle using Special Tool C-3894-A.
6. In order to take the load off the strut, raise the lower control arm approximately 10 mm using a suitable jack.

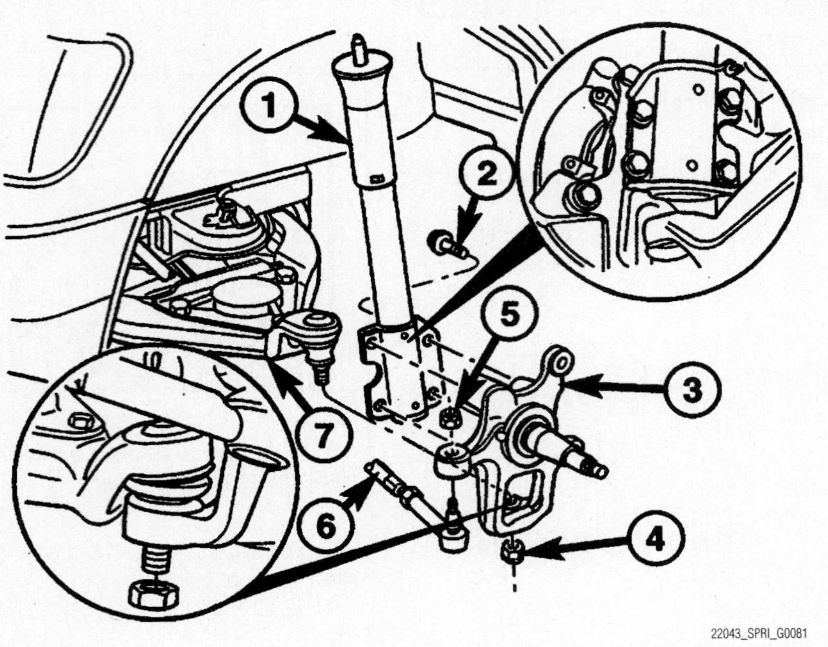

Fig. 81 Exploded view of the steering knuckle assembly—Strut (1), Mounting bolt (2), Steering Knuckle (3), Lower Ball Joint Nut (4), Outer tie rod nut (5), Inner Tie Rod End (6), Lower Control Arm (7)

7. Remove the wheel speed sensor from the knuckle by pulling straight out.
8. Remove the strut at the knuckle.
9. Separate the lower ball joint from the steering knuckle using Special Tool 9282.
10. Remove the steering knuckle from the vehicle.

To install:

11. Install the steering knuckle on the lower ball joint stud. Tighten the ball joint nut to 206 ft. lbs. (280 Nm).
12. Install the strut to the steering knuckle and tighten the bolts to 136 ft. lbs. (185 Nm).
13. Install the outer tie rod end to the steering knuckle and tighten the nut to 96 ft. lbs. (130 Nm).
14. Install the speed sensor by pushing the sensor all the way into the knuckle and the sensor will self adjust when the wheel is turned.
15. Install the wheel hub/bearing assembly.
16. Install the brake caliper adapter.
17. Install the front wheel.
18. Lower the vehicle.
19. Check and adjust the alignment as necessary.

2007 Models

See Figure 82.

1. Raise and safely support the vehicle.
2. Remove the front wheel.
3. Remove the outer tie rod end nut.
4. Separate the outer tie rod from the steering knuckle using Special Tool 9360.
5. Remove the tie rod end shield.
6. Remove the brake caliper adapter. For additional information, refer to the following section, "Brake Caliper, Removal & Installation."
7. Remove the brake rotor.

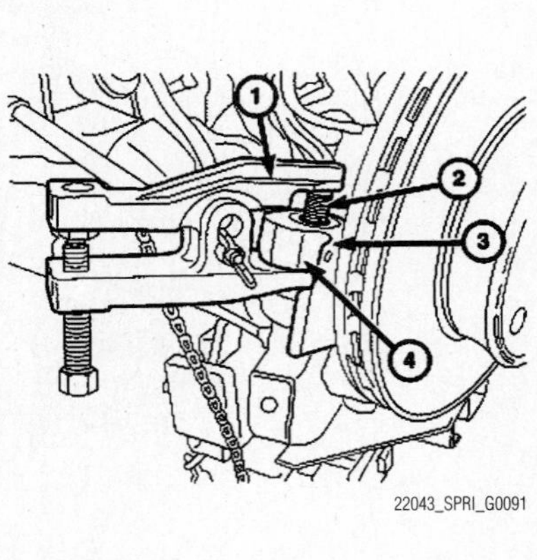

Fig. 82 Separate the outer tie rod (2) from the steering knuckle (4) using Special Tool 9360 (1) and remove the tie rod end shield (3)—2007 Model shown

8. Remove the wheel speed sensor. For additional information, refer to the following section, "Speed Sensor, Removal & Installation."
9. Remove the lower ball joint nut.
10. Separate the lower ball joint from the steering knuckle using Special Tool 9282.
11. Remove the lower strut bolts from the knuckle.
12. Remove the steering knuckle.

To install:

13. Install the steering knuckle on the lower ball joint stud. Tighten the ball joint nut to 125 ft. lbs. (170 Nm).
14. Install the strut to the steering knuckle and tighten the bolts to 103 ft. lbs. (140 Nm) plus 120°.
15. Install the brake rotor.
16. Install the wheel speed sensor.
17. Install the brake caliper adapter.
18. Install the outer tie rod end and shield and tighten the nut to 37 ft. lbs. (50 Nm) plus 60°.
19. Install the front wheel.
20. Lower the vehicle.
21. Check and adjust the alignment as necessary.

WHEEL BEARINGS

REMOVAL & INSTALLATION

2005–06 Models

See Figure 83.

1. Raise and safely support the vehicle.
2. Remove the front wheel.
3. Remove the brake caliper adapter. For additional information, refer to the following section, "Brake Caliper, Removal & Installation."
4. Remove the brake rotor.
5. Remove the grease cap.
6. Loosen the bolt on the clamping nut and remove the clamping nut.
7. Remove the thrust washer.
8. Remove the wheel hub and tapered roller bearing from the axle assembly.

To install:

9. Install the wheel hub with the bearing on the axle.
10. Grease the outer bearing thoroughly and push into the steering knuckle.
11. Install the thrust washer.

➡The smooth side of the thrust washer must point toward the wheel bearing.

12. Install the clamping nut and tighten to 9 ft. lbs. (12 Nm) and then loosen ½ turn.
13. Check and adjust the bearing end play. For additional information, refer to the following section, "Wheel Bearings, Adjustment."
14. Pack the grease cap half full with grease and coat the edge with sealant and install the cap.
15. Install the brake rotor.
16. Install the brake caliper adapter.
17. Install the front wheel.
18. Lower the vehicle.

2007 Models

The hub/bearing assembly is pressed into the steering knuckle and is not serviceable. The steering knuckle must be replaced if the hub/bearing needs service.

ADJUSTMENT

2005–06 Models

See Figure 84.

1. Raise and safely support the vehicle.
2. Remove the grease cap.
3. Position a dial indicator against the face of the wheel hub.
4. Tighten the locking screw on the clamping nut.
5. Pull the wheel hub firmly back and forth and read off the wheel bearing play on the dial gauge. Wheel bearing play should be 0.000787– 0.00158 inches (0.02–0.04 mm).
6. If necessary, loosen the locking screw and adjust the wheel bearing play by loosing or tightening the clamping nut.
7. Retighten the locking screw and recheck the wheel bearing play.

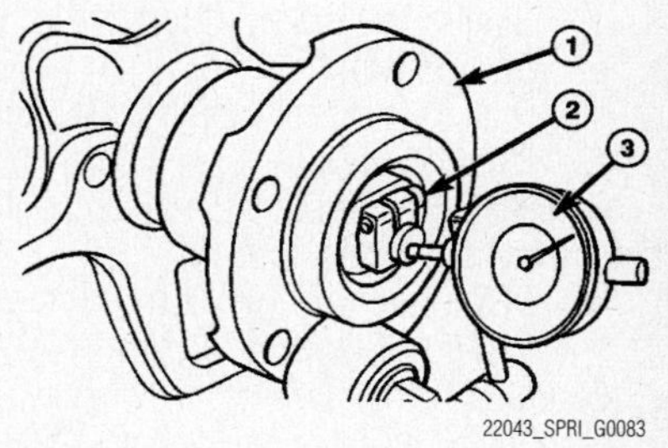

Fig. 84 Check the hub/bearing (1) end play using a dial indicator (3). Use the locking screw (2) to adjust.

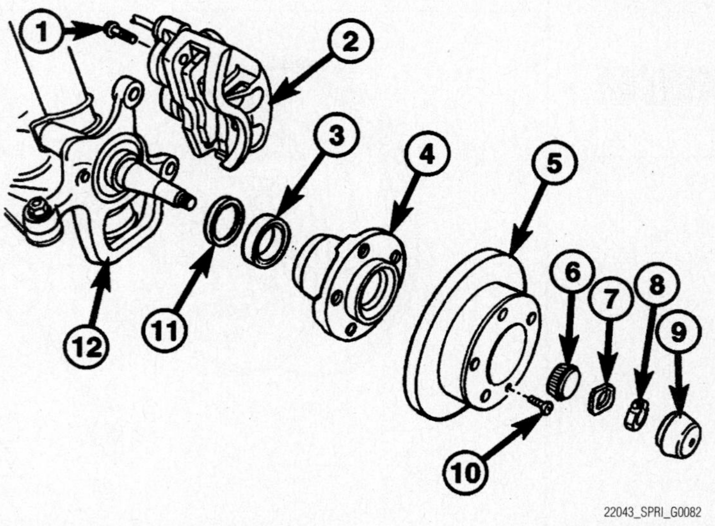

Fig. 83 Exploded view of the hub/bearing assembly—Caliper Adapter (1,2), Inner Bearing (3), Hub (4), Rotor (5), Outer Bearing (6), Thrust Washer (7), Clamping Nut (8), Grease Cap (9), Locking Bolt (10), Grease Seal (11)

LEAF SPRING

REMOVAL & INSTALLATION

1. Raise and safely support the vehicle.
2. Support the rear axle assembly with a suitable jack.
3. Remove the lower shock mounting bolts.
4. Remove the leaf spring U-bolts and spring plate.
5. Remove the mounting nut and bolt from the front spring bracket.
6. Remove the rear spring nut and bolt from the spring shackle.
7. Lower the rear axle and remove the leaf spring.

To install:

8. Install the leaf spring assembly to the vehicle.
9. Install the front spring mounting bolt and nut and tighten as follows:
   - Single Rear Wheel (SRW): 70 ft. lbs. (95 Nm).
   - Dual Rear Wheels (DRW): 136 ft. lbs. (185 Nm).
10. Install the rear spring mounting bolt and nut and tighten as follows:
    - SRW: 63 ft. lbs. (85 Nm)
    - DRW: 136 ft. lbs. (185 Nm)
11. Raise the rear axle with a suitable jack and install the spring plate and U-bolts. Tighten the nuts to 125 ft. lbs. (170 Nm).
12. Install the lower shock mounting bolt and tighten as follows:
    - M12 x 1.5 bolt: 70 ft. lbs. (106 Nm)
    - M14 x 1.5 bolt: 100 ft. lbs. (135 Nm)
13. Lower the vehicle.

SHOCK ABSORBER

REMOVAL & INSTALLATION

2005–06 Models

1. Raise and safely support the vehicle.
2. Remove the shock absorber mounting bolt from the rear axle.
3. Unsnap the clip for the ALB lever, left side only.
4. Remove the ALB lever from the upper shock bolt.
5. Remove the shock absorber bolt from the frame.
6. Remove the shock absorber.

To install:

7. Install the shock absorber. Tighten the frame mounting bolt as follows:
   - Single Rear Wheel (SRW): 59 ft. lbs. (80 Nm).
   - Dual Rear Wheels (DRW): 103 ft. lbs. (140 Nm).
8. Install the ALB lever to the upper shock bolt, left side only, and snap the clip for the ALB lever.
9. Install the lower shock absorber mounting bolt and tighten as follows:
   - M12 x 1.5 bolt: 52 ft. lbs. (70 Nm)
   - M14 x 1.5 bolt: 81 ft. lbs. (110 Nm)
10. Lower the vehicle.

2007 Models

1. Raise and safely support the vehicle.
2. Support the rear axle with a suitable jack.
3. Remove the shock absorber bolt from the rear axle.
4. Remove the shock absorber bolt from the frame side.
5. Remove the shock absorber.

To install:

6. Install the shock absorber and tighten the frame side bolt to 100 ft. lbs. (135 Nm).
7. Install the shock absorber rear axle mounting bolt as follows:
   - M12 x 1.5 bolt: 70 ft. lbs. (106 Nm)
   - M14 x 1.5 bolt: 100 ft. lbs. (135 Nm)
8. Remove the jack supporting the rear axle.
9. Lower the vehicle.

WHEEL BEARINGS

REMOVAL & INSTALLATION

See Figures 85 through 87.

1. Raise and safely support the vehicle.
2. Remove the rear wheel.
3. Remove brake caliper adapter. For additional information, refer to the following section, "Brake Caliper, Removal & Installation."
4. Remove the axle shaft.
5. Back-off the parking brakes.
6. Remove the outer hub nut with Special Tool 10095 Wrench.
7. Remove the locking plate, inner hub nut and thrust washer.

➡Thrust washer is designed for left or right side and not interchangeable.

8. Pull the hub off axle tube.
9. Remove front hub bearing from hub.
10. Drive out the ABS sensor tone ring, hub seal and rear bearing from the hub.
11. Remove the inner and outer bearing cups from hub with a hammer and brass drift.

To install:

12. Install the outer hub bearing cup with Special Tool 9588 Installer and a hammer.
13. Install the inner hub bearing cup with Special Tool 10099 Bearing Cup Installer and Universal Drive Handle C-4171.
14. Clean and thoroughly grease bearings with multi-purpose grease.
15. Install the inner wheel bearing.
16. Coat the outer circumference of a new seal with Hylomar SQ 32 M sealant.

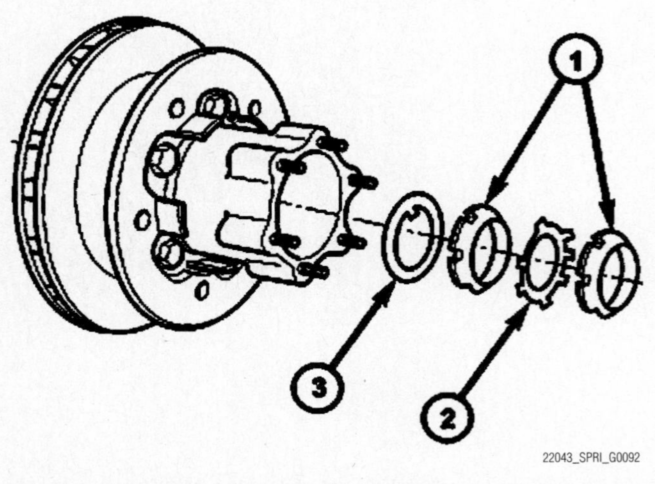

Fig. 85 Using Special Tool 10095 to remove outer hub nut (1), then remove the locking plate (2), inner hub nut (1) and thrust washer (3)—2007 Model shown

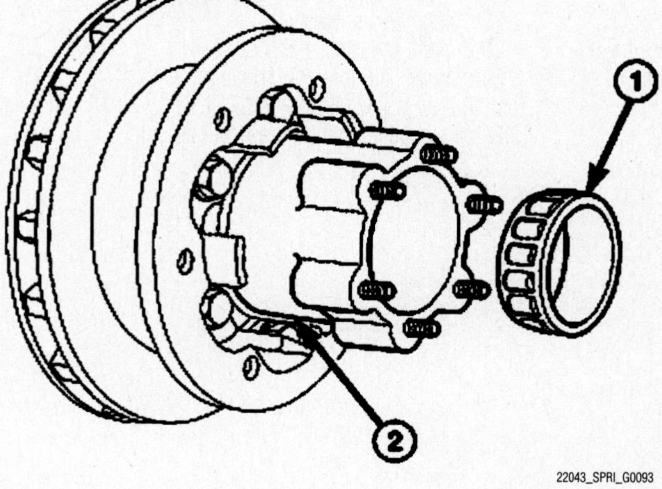

Fig. 86 Remove the front hub bearing (1) from the hub (2)—2007 Model shown

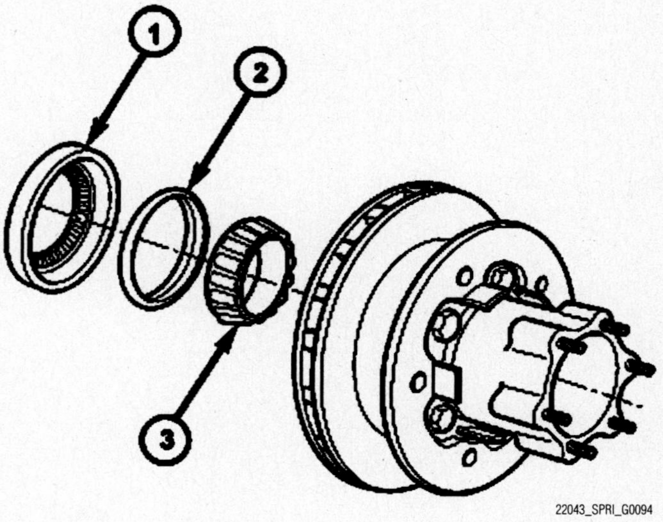

Fig. 87 Drive out ABS sensor tone ring (1) hub seal (2) and rear bearing (3) from hub—2007 Model shown

WARNING

Do not coat the seal's rubberized sealing surfaces with sealant.

17. Install the seal into the hub with Special Tool 10098 Seal Installer and Universal Drive Handle C-4171.

➡Seal ring should be flush with wheel hub or a maximum of 0.12 inches (3 mm) deep.

18. Coat contact surface of ABS sensor ring with Hylomar SQ 32 M sealant.
19. Drive the ABS sensor ring in with Special Tool 10097 Tone Ring Installer and Universal Drive Handle C-4171.
20. Install the hub on axle tube.
21. Install the outer hub bearing.
22. Install thrust washer .
23. Install the inner hub nut.
24. Tighten the inner hub nut with Special Tool 10095 Hub Nut Socket to 221 ft. lbs. (300 Nm) while spinning the wheel hub constantly. Turn back inner nut and then tighten until it touches the thrust washer without play. Then tighten an additional ⅛ of a turn.
25. Install the locking plate.
26. Install the outer hub nut and tighten with Special Tool 10095 Hub Nut Socket to 184 ft. lbs. (250 Nm).
27. Install the axle shaft.
28. Install the brake caliper.
29. Adjust the parking brakes and install the rear wheel.
30. Lower the vehicle.

DODGE

SRT-10

16

SPECIFICATIONS AND MAINTENANCE CHARTS

ENGINE AND VEHICLE IDENTIFICATION

Engine						
Code ①	Liters (cc)	Cu. In.	Cyl.	Fuel Sys.	Engine Type	Eng. Mfg.
H	8.3 (8275)	505	10	SMFI	OHV	Chrysler

Model Year	
Code ②	Year
5	2005
6	2006

SMFI: Sequential Multi-port Fuel Injection

① 8th position of VIN

② 10th position of VIN

22043_SRT1_C0001

GENERAL ENGINE SPECIFICATIONS

Year	Model	Engine Displacement Liters	Engine Series VIN	Net Horsepower @ rpm	Net Torque @ rpm (ft. lbs.)	Bore x Stroke (in.)	Com-pression Ratio	Oil Pressure @ rpm
2005	SRT-10	8.3	H	501@5600	525@4100	4.03x3.96	9.6:1	45-75@3000
2006	SRT-10	8.3	H	501@5600	525@4100	4.03x3.96	9.6:1	45-75@3000

22043_SRT1_C0002

GASOLINE ENGINE TUNE-UP SPECIFICATIONS

Year	Engine Displacement Liters	Engine VIN	Spark Plug Gap (in.)	Ignition Timing (deg.)	Fuel Pump (psi)	Idle Speed (rpm)	Valve Clearance	
							Intake	Exhaust
2005	8.3	H	0.033-0.038	①	56-60	②	HYD	HYD
2006	8.3	H	0.033-0.038	①	56-60	②	HYD	HYD

NOTE: The Vehicle Emission Control Information (VECI) label often reflects specification changes made during production.

The label figures must be used if they differ from those in this chart.

HYD: Hydraulic

① Ignition timing is controlled by the PCM and is not adjustable.

② Idle speed is controlled by the PCM and is not adjustable

22043_SRT1_C0003

CAPACITIES

Year	Model	Engine Displacement Liters	Engine VIN	Oil with Filter (qts.)	Transmission (pts.) Manual	Transmission (pts.) Auto. ①	Drive Axle (pts.)	Fuel Tank (gal.)	Cooling System (qts.)
2005	SRT-10	8.3	H	8.8	4.8	—	2.8 ②	26.0	18.0
2006	SRT-10	8.3	H	8.8	4.8	8.0	2.8 ②	26.0	18.0

NOTE: All capacities are approximate. Add fluid gradually and check to be sure a proper fluid level is obtained.

① For fluid drain and filter replacement only.

② With Trac-Lok: add 4 0z. Of limited slip additive

22043_SRT1_C0004

VALVE SPECIFICATIONS

Year	Engine Displacement Liters	Engine VIN	Seat Angle (deg.)	Face Angle (deg.)	Spring Test Pressure (lbs. @ in.)	Spring Installed Height (in.)	Stem-to-Guide Clearance (in.) Intake	Stem-to-Guide Clearance (in.) Exhaust	Stem Diameter (in.) Intake	Stem Diameter (in.) Exhaust
2005	8.3	H	44-44.5	45-45.5	280@1.207	1.750	0.001-0.003	0.001-0.003	0.312-0.331	0.312-0.331
2006	8.3	H	44-44.5	45-45.5	280@1.207	1.750	0.001-0.003	0.001-0.003	0.312-0.331	0.312-0.331

22043_SRT1_C0005

CRANKSHAFT AND CONNECTING ROD SPECIFICATIONS

All measurements are given in inches.

Year	Engine Displacement Liters	Engine VIN	Crankshaft Main Brg. Journal Dia.	Crankshaft Main Brg. Oil Clearance	Crankshaft Shaft End-play	Crankshaft Thrust on No.	Connecting Rod Journal Diameter	Connecting Rod Oil Clearance	Connecting Rod Side Clearance
2005	8.3	H	3.0013-3.0018	0.0010-0.0020	0.0020-0.0070	3	2.1256-2.1263	0.0002-0.0029	0.010-0.0180
2006	8.3	H	3.0013-3.0018	0.0010-0.0020	0.0020-0.0070	3	2.1256-2.1263	0.0002-0.0029	0.010-0.0180

22043_SRT1_C0006

PISTON AND RING SPECIFICATIONS

All measurements are given in inches.

Year	Engine Displacement Liters	Engine VIN	Piston Clearance	Ring Gap Top Compression	Ring Gap Bottom Compression	Ring Gap Oil Control	Ring Side Clearance Top Compression	Ring Side Clearance Bottom Compression	Ring Side Clearance Oil Control
2005	8.3	H	0.0010-0.0022	0.0080-0.0140	0.0220-0.0331	0.010-0.030	0.0016-0.0033	0.0016-0.0033	0.0018-0.0079
2006	8.3	H	0.0010-0.0022	0.0080-0.0140	0.0220-0.0331	0.010-0.030	0.0016-0.0033	0.0016-0.0033	0.0018-0.0079

22043_SRT1_C0007

TORQUE SPECIFICATIONS

All readings in ft. lbs.

Year	Engine Displacement Liters	Engine VIN	Cylinder Head Bolts	Main Bearing Bolts	Rod Bearing Bolts	Crankshaft Damper Bolts	Flywheel Bolts	Manifold Intake	Manifold Exhaust	Spark Plugs	Oil Pan Drain Plug
2005	8.3	H	①	②	50	130	55	③	16	20	25
2006	8.3	H	①	②	50	130	55	③	16	20	25

① See the illustration in the text
Bolts 1-12
Step 1: 35 ft. lbs.
Step 2: 90 ft. lbs.
Bolts A-H: 95 inch lbs.

② See the illustration below
Bolts 1-12: 15 ft. lbs.
Bolts A1: 45 ft. lbs.
Bolts A2: 85 ft. lbs.
Bolts A3: 40 ft. lbs.

③ 95 inch lbs.

22043_SRT1_C0008

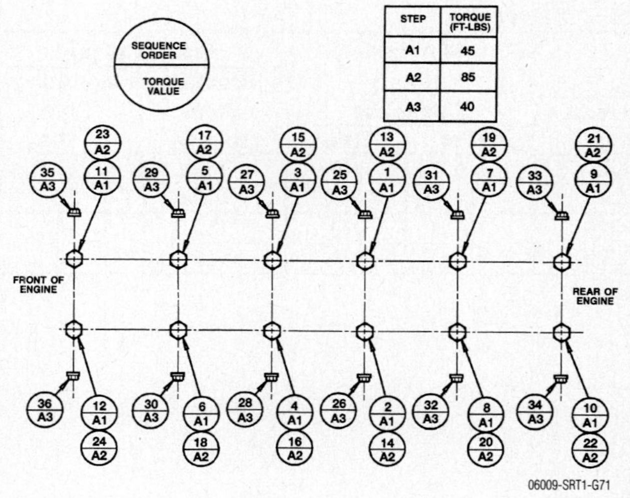

Fig. 1 Main bearing torque sequence

WHEEL ALIGNMENT

		Caster		Camber		
Year	Model	Range (+/-Deg.)	Preferred Setting (Deg.)	Range (+/-Deg.)	Preferred Setting (Deg.)	Toe-in (in.)
2005	SRT-10	0.50	+5.75	0.30	0	0.24+/-0.16
2006	SRT-10	0.50	+5.75	0.30	0	0.24+/-0.16

22043_SRT1_C0011

TIRE, WHEEL AND BALL JOINT SPECIFICATIONS

		OEM Tires		Tire Pressures (psi)		Wheel	Wheel Lug
Year	Model	Standard	Optional	Front	Rear	Size	Nut Torque
2005	SRT-10	305/40ZR22	None	①	①	10	95
2006	SRT-10	305/40ZR22	None	①	①	10	95

NA: Information not available
OEM: Original Equipment Manufacturer
PSI: Pounds Per Square Inch
STD: Standard
OPT: Optional
① See placard on the vehicle

22043_SRT1_C0010

BRAKE SPECIFICATIONS

All measurements in inches unless noted

			Brake Disc			Minimum Lining Thickness		Brake Caliper	
Year	Model		Original Thickness	Minimum Thickness	Maximum Run-out	Front	Rear	Bracket Bolts (ft. lbs.)	Mounting Pins (ft. lbs.)
2005	SRT-10	F	1.397	1.344	0.0020	NA	NA	250	24
		R	1.180	1.118	0.0020	NA	NA	145	22
2006	SRT-10	F	1.397	1.344	0.0020	NA	NA	250	24
		R	1.180	1.118	0.0020	NA	NA	145	22

NA: Information not available

22043_SRT1_C0009

SCHEDULED MAINTENANCE INTERVALS
2005-2006 SRT-10

TO BE SERVICED	TYPE OF SERVICE	VEHICLE MILEAGE INTERVAL (x1000)												
		3	6	9	12	15	18	21	24	27	30	33	36	39
Engine oil & filter	R	✓	✓	✓	✓	✓	✓	✓	✓	✓	✓	✓	✓	✓
Auto. trans. fluid and filter ①	R					✓					✓			
Auto. trans. Bands ①	Adj.					✓					✓			
Tires	Rotate		✓		✓		✓		✓		✓		✓	
Rear axle fluid	R					✓					✓			
Brake linings	I				✓				✓				✓	
Engine air filter	S/I					✓					✓			
Spark plugs	R										✓			
PCV valve	S/I										✓			
Engine coolant	R	Every 5 years, regardless of mileage												
Spark plug cables	R	Every 60,000 miles												
Accessory drive belt	I/R	Every 75,000 miles												
Power steering fluid	R	Every 100,000 miles												

R: Replace S: Service I: Inspect Adj: Adjust

① After 105,000 miles, perform the service every 15,000 miles

22043_SRT1_C0012

PRECAUTIONS

Before servicing any vehicle, please be sure to read all of the following precautions, which deal with personal safety, prevention of component damage, and important points to take into consideration when servicing a motor vehicle:

- Never open, service or drain the radiator or cooling system when the engine is hot; serious burns can occur from the steam and hot coolant.
- Observe all applicable safety precautions when working around fuel. Whenever servicing the fuel system, always work in a well-ventilated area. Do not allow fuel spray or vapors to come in contact with a spark, open flame, or excessive heat (a hot drop light, for example). Keep a dry chemical fire extinguisher near the work area. Always keep fuel in a container specifically designed for fuel storage; also, always properly seal fuel containers to avoid the possibility of fire or explosion. Refer to the additional fuel system precautions later in this section.
- Fuel injection systems often remain pressurized, even after the engine has been turned **OFF**. The fuel system pressure must be relieved before disconnecting any fuel lines. Failure to do so may result in fire and/or personal injury.
- Brake fluid often contains polyglycol ethers and polyglycols. Avoid contact with the eyes and wash your hands thoroughly after handling brake fluid. If you do get brake fluid in your eyes, flush your eyes with clean, running water for 15 minutes. If eye irritation persists, or if you have taken brake fluid internally, IMMEDIATELY seek medical assistance.
- The EPA warns that prolonged contact with used engine oil may cause a number of skin disorders, including cancer. You should make every effort to minimize your exposure to used engine oil. Protective gloves should be worn when changing oil. Wash your hands and any other exposed skin areas as soon as possible after exposure to used engine oil. Soap and water, or waterless hand cleaner should be used.
- All new vehicles are now equipped with an air bag system, often referred to as a Supplemental Restraint System (SRS) or Supplemental Inflatable Restraint (SIR) system. The system must be disabled before performing service on or around system components, steering column, instrument panel components, wiring and sensors. Failure to follow safety and disabling procedures could result in accidental air bag deployment, possible personal injury and unnecessary system repairs.
- Always wear safety goggles when working with, or around, the air bag system. When carrying a non-deployed air bag, be sure the bag and trim cover are pointed away from your body. When placing a non-deployed air bag on a work surface, always face the bag and trim cover upward, away from the surface. This will reduce the motion of the module if it is accidentally deployed. Refer to the additional air bag system precautions later in this section.
- Clean, high quality brake fluid from a sealed container is essential to the safe and proper operation of the brake system. You should always buy the correct type of brake fluid for your vehicle. If the brake fluid becomes contaminated, completely flush the system with new fluid. Never reuse any brake fluid. Any brake fluid that is removed from the system should be discarded. Also, do not allow any brake fluid to come in contact with a painted surface; it will damage the paint.
- Never operate the engine without the proper amount and type of engine oil; doing so WILL result in severe engine damage.
- Timing belt maintenance is extremely important. Many models utilize an interference-type, non-freewheeling engine. If the timing belt breaks, the valves in the cylinder head may strike the pistons, causing potentially serious (also time-consuming and expensive) engine damage. Refer to the maintenance interval charts for the recommended replacement interval for the timing belt, and to the timing belt section for belt replacement and inspection.
- Disconnecting the negative battery cable on some vehicles may interfere with the functions of the on-board computer system(s) and may require the computer to undergo a relearning process once the negative battery cable is reconnected.
- When servicing drum brakes, only disassemble and assemble one side at a time, leaving the remaining side intact for reference.
- Only an MVAC-trained, EPA-certified automotive technician should service the air conditioning system or its components.

BRAKES — ANTI-LOCK BRAKE SYSTEM (ABS)

GENERAL INFORMATION

PRECAUTIONS

- Certain components within the ABS system are not intended to be serviced or repaired individually.
- Do not use rubber hoses or other parts not specifically specified for and ABS system. When using repair kits, replace all parts included in the kit. Partial or incorrect repair may lead to functional problems and require the replacement of components.
- Lubricate rubber parts with clean, fresh brake fluid to ease assembly. Do not use shop air to clean parts; damage to rubber components may result.
- Use only DOT 3 brake fluid from an unopened container.
- If any hydraulic component or line is removed or replaced, it may be necessary to bleed the entire system.
- A clean repair area is essential. Always clean the reservoir and cap thoroughly before removing the cap. The slightest amount of dirt in the fluid may plug an orifice and impair the system function. Perform repairs after components have been thoroughly cleaned; use only denatured alcohol to clean components. Do not allow ABS components to come into contact with any substance containing mineral oil; this includes used shop rags.
- The Anti-Lock control unit is a microprocessor similar to other computer units in the vehicle. Ensure that the ignition switch is **OFF** before removing or installing controller harnesses. Avoid static electricity discharge at or near the controller.
- If any arc welding is to be done on the vehicle, the control unit should be unplugged before welding operations begin.

CAUTION

Dust and dirt accumulating on brake parts during normal use may contain asbestos fibers from production or aftermarket brake linings. Breathing excessive concentrations of asbestos fibers can cause serious bodily harm. Exercise care when servicing brake parts. Do not sand or grind brake lining unless equipment used is designed to contain the dust residue. Do not clean brake parts with compressed air or by dry brushing. Cleaning should be done by dampening the brake components with a fine mist of water, then wiping the brake components clean with a dampened cloth. Dispose of cloth and all residue containing asbestos fibers in an impermeable container with the appropriate label. Follow practices prescribed by the Occupational Safety and Health Administration (OSHA) and the Environmental Protection Agency (EPA) for the handling, processing, and disposing of dust or debris that may contain asbestos fibers.

BRAKE CALIPER

REMOVAL & INSTALLATION

See Figure 2.

WARNING

Never allow the disc brake caliper to hang from the brake hose. Damage to the brake hose will result. Provide a suitable support to hang the caliper securely.

1. Raise and support the vehicle.
2. Remove the tire and wheel assembly.
3. Compress the disc brake caliper.
4. Remove the banjo bolt and discard the copper washers.
5. Remove the caliper mounting bolts.
6. Remove the disc brake caliper.

To install:

➡Install a new copper washers on the banjo bolt when installing.

7. Install the disc brake pads, anti-rattle springs and pad retaining pin.
8. Install the disc brake caliper.

CAUTION

Verify brake hose is not twisted or kinked before tightening fitting bolt.

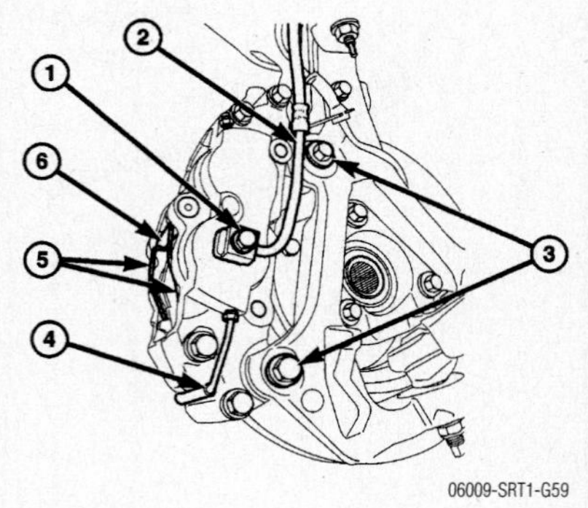

Fig. 2 Front caliper. (1) banjo bolt, (2) brake line, (3) caliper mounting bolts, (4) fluid line, (5) anti-rattle springs, (6) pad retaining pin

9. Install the brake hose banjo bolt with new copper washers to the caliper. Tighten to 27 Nm (20 ft. lbs.)
10. Install the caliper mounting bolts. Tighten to 32 Nm (24 ft. lbs.).
11. Bleed the base brake system.
12. Install the tire and wheel assembly.
13. Lower the vehicle.

DISC BRAKE PADS

REMOVAL & INSTALLATION

See Figures 3 and 4.

1. Raise and support vehicle.
2. Remove the wheel and tire assemblies.
3. Compress the caliper.
4. Remove the caliper.
5. Remove the caliper by tilting the top up and off the caliper adapter.

➡Do not allow brake hose to support caliper assembly.

6. Support and hang the caliper.
7. Remove the inboard brake shoe from the caliper adapter.
8. Remove the outboard brake shoe from the caliper adapter.

➡Anti-rattle springs are not interchangeable.

9. Remove the top anti-rattle springs from the caliper adapter.
10. Remove the bottom anti-rattle springs from the caliper adapter.

To install:

11. Bottom pistons in caliper bore with C-clamp. Place an old brake shoe between a C-clamp and caliper piston.
12. Clean caliper mounting adapter and anti-rattle springs.
13. Lubricate anti-rattle springs with Mopar brake grease, or equivalent.
14. Install new top anti-rattle springs.
15. Install new bottom anti-rattle springs.
16. Install inboard brake shoe in adapter.
17. Install outboard brake shoe in adapter.
18. Tilt the top of the caliper over rotor and under adapter. Then push the bottom of the caliper down onto the adapter.
19. Install caliper.

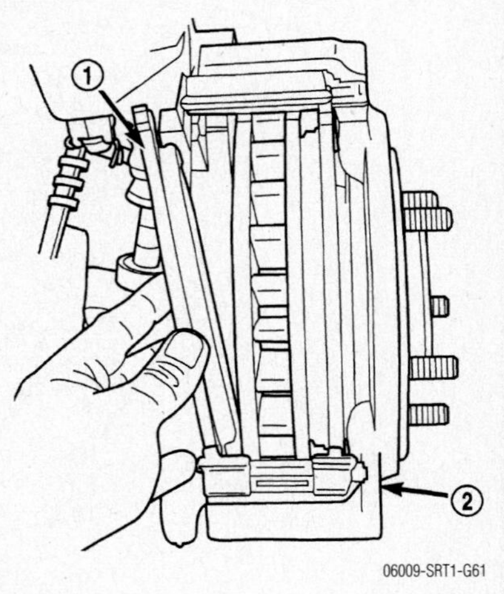

Fig. 3 Front inboard pad removal. (1) pad, (2) adapter

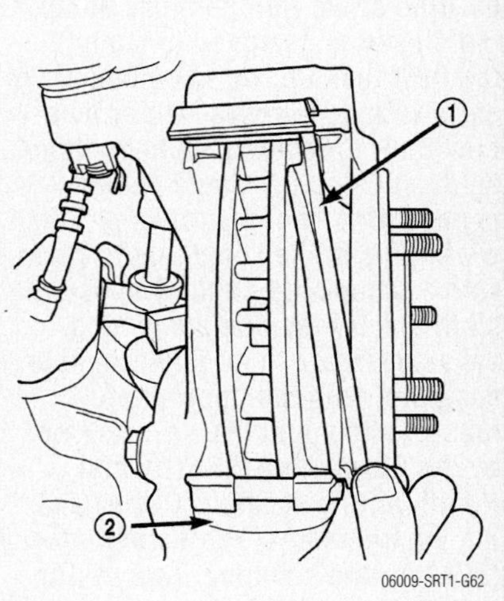

Fig. 4 Front outboard pad removal

20. Install wheel and tire assemblies and lower vehicle.

21. Apply brakes several times to seat caliper pistons and brake shoes and obtain firm pedal.

22. Top off master cylinder fluid level.

CALIPER ADAPTER

REMOVAL & INSTALLATION

See Figure 5.

1. Raise and support the vehicle.
2. Remove the tire and wheel assembly.
3. Remove the disc brake caliper.
4. Remove the bolts securing the caliper adapter to the steering knuckle.
5. Remove the caliper adapter.

To install:

6. Install the caliper adapter to the steering knuckle.
7. Install the caliper adapter mounting bolts and tighten to 176 Nm (130 ft. lbs.).
8. Install the disc brake caliper.
9. Install the tire and wheel assembly.
10. Remove the support and lower the vehicle.

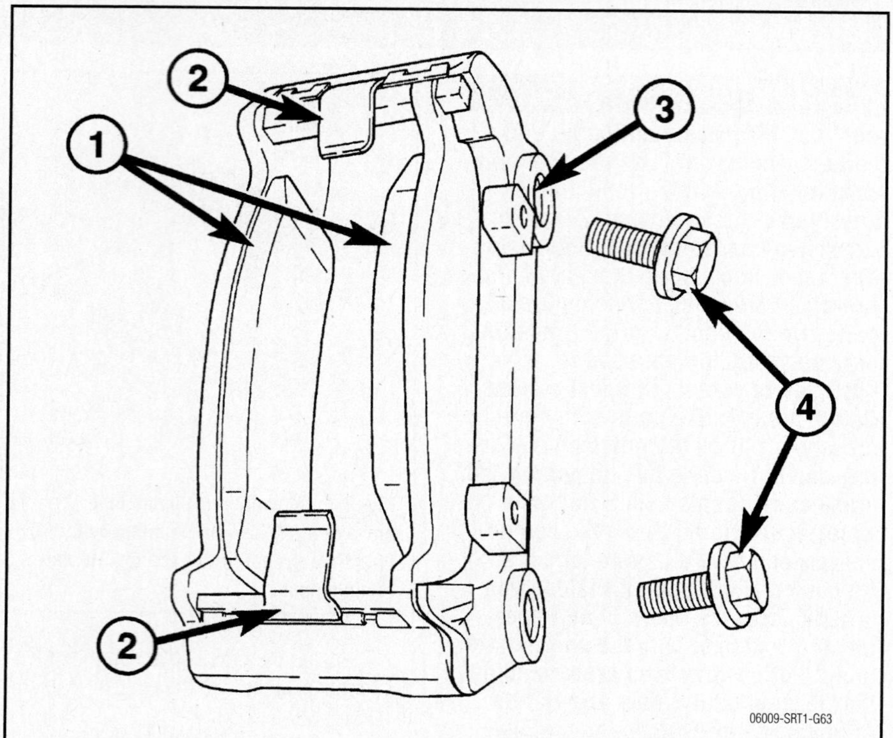

Fig. 5 Front caliper adapter (rear similar). (1) pads, (2) anti-rattle clips, (3) adapter, (4) adapter mounting bolts

BRAKES

REAR DISC BRAKES

⁂ CAUTION

Dust and dirt accumulating on brake parts during normal use may contain asbestos fibers from production or aftermarket brake linings. Breathing excessive concentrations of asbestos fibers can cause serious bodily harm. Exercise care when servicing brake parts. Do not sand or grind brake lining unless equipment used is designed to contain the dust residue. Do not clean brake parts with compressed air or by dry brushing. Cleaning should be done by dampening the brake components with a fine mist of water, then wiping the brake components clean with a dampened cloth. Dispose of cloth and all residue containing asbestos fibers in an impermeable container with the appropriate label. Follow practices prescribed by the Occupational Safety and Health Administration (OSHA) and the Environmental Protection Agency (EPA) for the handling, processing, and disposing of dust or debris that may contain asbestos fibers.

BRAKE CALIPER

REMOVAL & INSTALLATION

See Figure 6.

1. Raise and support the vehicle.
2. Remove the tire and wheel assembly.
3. Compress the disc brake caliper using tool C4212F, or equivalent.

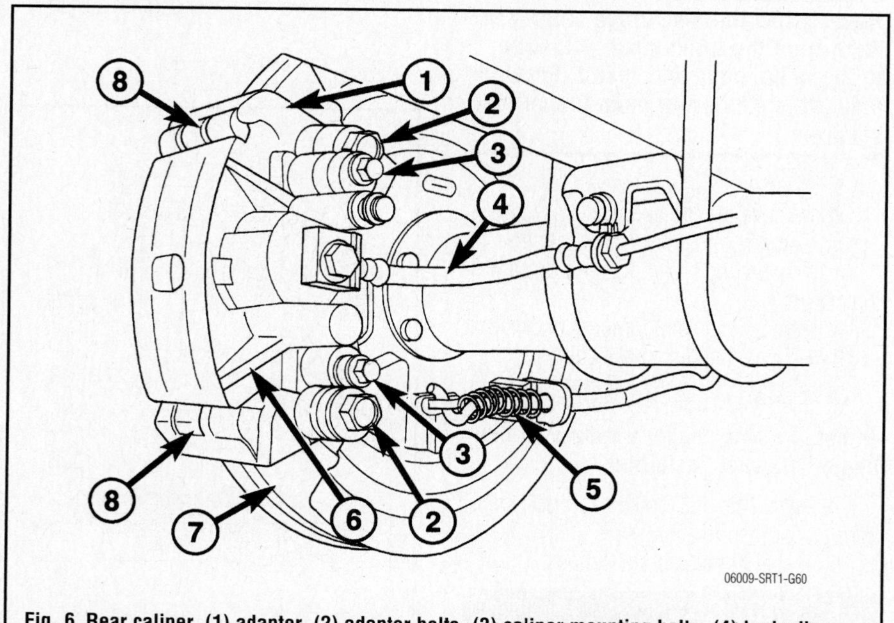

Fig. 6 Rear caliper. (1) adapter, (2) adapter bolts, (3) caliper mounting bolts, (4) brake line, (5) parking brake spring, (6) caliper, (7) rotor, (8) anti-rattle springs

4. Remove the caliper pin bolts.
5. Remove the banjo bolt and discard the copper washer.

WARNING

Never allow the disc brake caliper to hang from the brake hose. Damage to the brake hose with result. Provide a suitable support to hang the caliper securely.

6. Remove the rear disc brake caliper.

To install:

➡Install a new copper washers on the banjo bolt when installing

7. Install the rear disc brake caliper.
8. Install the banjo bolt with new copper washers to the caliper. Tighten to 27 Nm (20 ft. lbs.)
9. Install the caliper pin bolts. Tighten to 30 Nm (22 ft. lbs.)
10. Bleed the base brake system.
11. Install the tire and wheel assembly.
12. Lower the vehicle.

DISC BRAKE PADS

REMOVAL & INSTALLATION

1. Raise and support the vehicle.
2. Remove the rear wheel and tire assemblies.
3. Compress the caliper.
4. Remove caliper slide bolts.

➡Do not allow brake hose to support caliper assembly.

5. Remove the caliper, and then tilt the top up and off the caliper adapter.
6. Remove inboard brake shoe from the caliper adapter.
7. Remove outboard brake shoe from caliper adapter.

➡Anti-rattle springs are not interchangeable.

8. Remove the top anti-rattle spring from the caliper adapter.

To install:

9. Clean caliper mounting adapter and anti-rattle springs.
10. Lubricate anti-rattle springs with Mopar brake grease.
11. Install new top anti-rattle spring.
12. Install new bottom anti-rattle spring.
13. Install inboard brake shoe in adapter.
14. Install outboard brake shoe in adapter.
15. Tilt the bottom of the caliper over rotor and under adapter. Then push the top of the caliper down onto the adapter.
16. Install caliper.
17. Install wheel and tire assemblies and lower vehicle.
18. Apply brakes several times to seat caliper pistons and brake shoes and obtain firm pedal.
19. Top off master cylinder fluid level.

CALIPER ADAPTER MOUNT

REMOVAL & INSTALLATION

See Figure 7.

1. Remove wheel and tire assembly.
2. Remove the disc brake caliper.
3. Remove the caliper adapter.
4. Remove the rotor.
5. Remove the axle shaft.
6. Remove the park brake shoes.
7. Remove the parking brake cable from the brake lever.

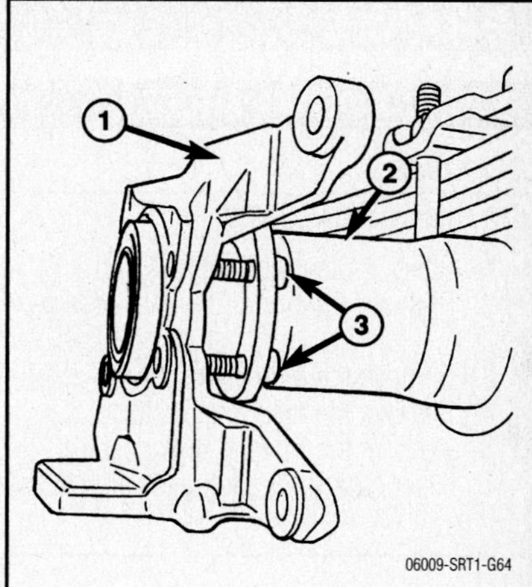

Fig. 7 Rear caliper adapter mount. (1) mount, (2) axle, (3) mount bolts

8. Remove the bolts attaching the support plate to the axle and remove the support plate.
9. Remove the caliper adapter mount from the axle housing.

To install:

10. Install the caliper adapter mount on the axle housing.
11. Install support plate on axle flange. Tighten attaching bolts to 68 Nm (50 ft. lbs.).
12. Install parking brake cable in the brake lever.
13. Install the park brake shoes.
14. Install axle shaft.
15. Adjust brake shoes to drum with brake gauge.
16. Install the rotor.
17. Install the caliper adapter.
18. Install the caliper.
19. Install wheel and tire assembly.

PARKING BRAKE SHOES

REMOVAL

See Figures 8 through 10.

1. Raise and support the vehicle.
2. Remove the tire and wheel assembly.
3. Remove the disc brake caliper.
4. Remove the disc brake rotor.
5. Lockout the parking brake cable.
6. Disengage the park brake cable from behind the rotor assembly to allow easier disassembly of the park brake shoes.
7. Remove the axle shaft.
8. Disassemble the rear park brake shoes.

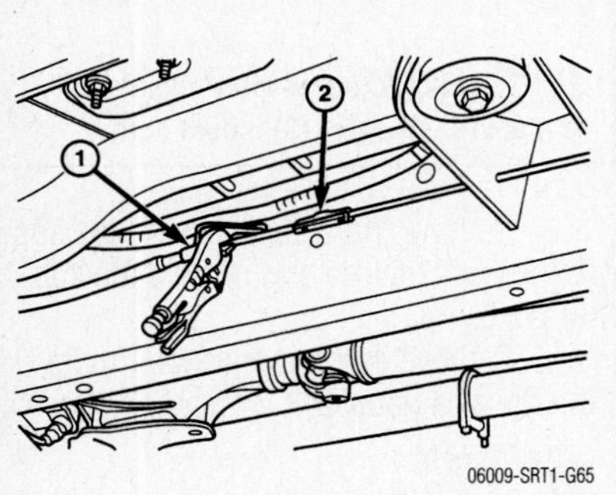

Fig. 8 Lockout the parking brake cable. (1) locking pliers, (2) cable

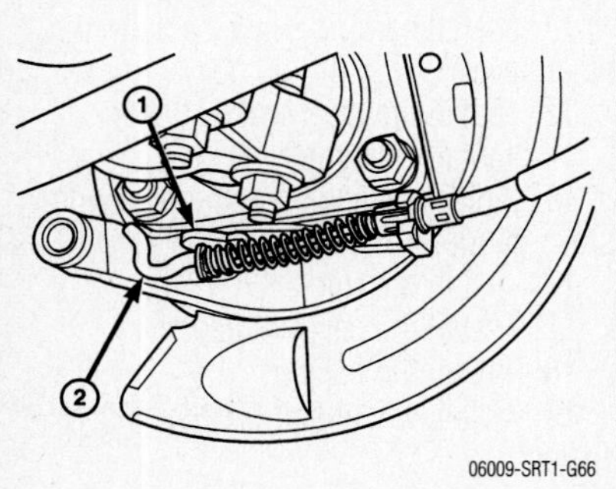

Fig. 9 Disengage the cable (2) from the lever (1)

INSPECTION

Riveted brake shoes should be replaced when worn to within 0.78 mm (1/32 in.) of the rivet heads. Bonded lining should be replaced when worn to a thickness of 1.6 mm 1/16 in.).

Examine the lining contact pattern to determine if the shoes are bent or the drum is tapered. The lining should exhibit contact across its entire width. Shoes exhibiting contact only on one side should be replaced and the drum checked for runout or taper. Inspect the adjuster screw assembly. Replace the assembly if the star wheel or threads are damaged, or the components are severely rusted or corroded.

Discard the brake springs and retainer components if worn, distorted or collapsed. Also replace the springs if a brake drag condition had occurred. Overheating will distort and weaken the springs.

Inspect the brake shoe contact pads on the support plate, replace the support plate if any of the pads are worn or rusted through. Also replace the plate if it is bent or distorted.

INSTALLATION

See Figure 11.

➡On a new vehicle or after parking brake lining replacement, it is recommended that the parking brake system be conditioned prior to use. This is done by making one stop from 25 mph on dry pavement or concrete using light to moderate force on the parking brake foot pedal.

1. Reassemble the rear park brake shoes.
2. Install the axle shaft.
3. Install the park brake cable to the lever behind the support plate.
4. Unlock the park brake cable.
5. Install the disc brake rotor.
6. Install the disc brake caliper.
7. Adjust the rear brake shoes.
8. Install the tire and wheel assembly.
9. Lower the vehicle.

ADJUSTMENTS

With Brake Gauge

See Figure 12.

➡Before adjusting the park brake shoes be sure that the park brake pedal is in the fully released position. If park brake pedal is not in the fully released position, the park brake shoes can not be accurately adjusted.

1. Raise vehicle.
2. Remove tire and wheel.
3. Remove disc brake caliper from caliper adapter.
4. Remove rotor from the axle shaft.

➡When measuring the brake drum diameter, the diameter should be measured in the center of the area in which the park brake shoes contact the surface of the brake drum.

5. Using Brake Shoe Gauge, Special Tool C-3919, or equivalent, accurately measure the inside diameter of the park brake drum portion of the rotor.
6. Using a ruler that reads in 64th of an inch, accurately read the measurement of the inside diameter of the park brake drum from the special tool.
7. Reduce the inside diameter measurement of the brake drum that was taken using

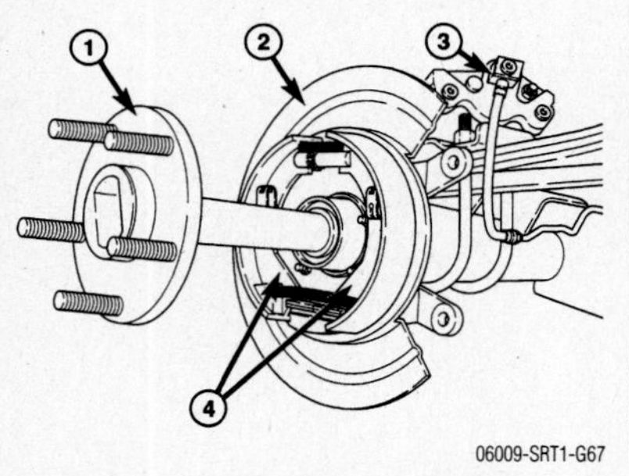

Fig. 10 Remove the axle shaft. (1) axle shaft, (2) dust shield, (3) caliper, (4) shoes

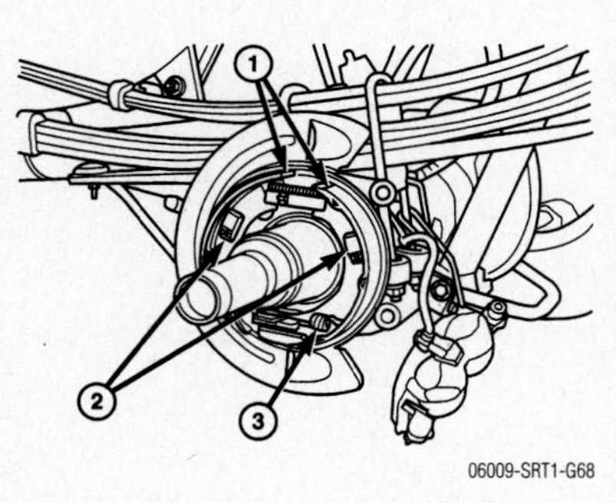

Fig. 11 Install the shoes. (1) shoes, (2) hold-down clips, (3) lower spring

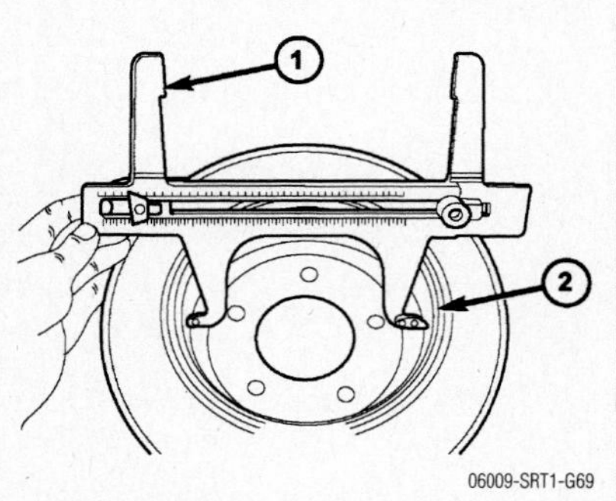

Fig. 12 Measure the drum inner diameter. (1) brake shoe gauge, (2) drum

Special Tool C-3919 by 1⁄64 of an inch. Reset Gauge, Brake Shoe, Special Tool C-3919 or the equivalent used, so that the outside measurement jaws are set to the reduced measurement.

8. Place Gauge, Brake Shoe, Special Tool C-3919, or equivalent over the park brake shoes. The special tool must be located diagonally across at the top of one shoe and bottom of opposite shoe (widest point) of the park brake shoes.

9. Using the star wheel adjuster, adjust the park brake shoes until the lining on the park brake shoes just touches the jaws on the special tool.

10. Repeat step 8 above and measure shoes in both directions.

11. Install brake rotor on the axle shaft.

12. Rotate rotor to verify that the park brake shoes are not dragging on the brake drum. If park brake shoes are dragging, remove rotor and back off star wheel adjuster one notch and recheck for brake shoe drag against drum. Continue with the previous step until brake shoes are not dragging on brake drum.

13. Install disc brake caliper on caliper adapter.

14. Install wheel and tire.

15. Tighten the wheel mounting nuts in the proper sequence until all nuts are torqued to half the specified torque. Then repeat the tightening sequence to the full specified torque of 129 Nm (95 ft. lbs.).

16. Lower vehicle.

17. Apply and release the park brake pedal one time. This will seat and correctly adjust the park brake cables.

18. Road test the vehicle to ensure proper function of the vehicle's brake system.

With Adjusting Tool

See Figure 13.

Adjustment can be made with a standard brake gauge or with adjusting tool. Adjustment is performed with the complete brake assembly installed on the backing plate.

1. Be sure parking brake lever is fully released.

2. Raise vehicle so rear wheels can be rotated freely.

3. Remove plug from each access hole in brake support plates.

4. Loosen parking brake cable adjustment nut until there is slack in front cable.

5. Insert adjusting tool through support plate access hole and engage tool in teeth of adjusting screw star wheel.

6. Rotate adjuster screw star wheel (move tool handle upward) until slight drag can be felt when wheel is rotated.

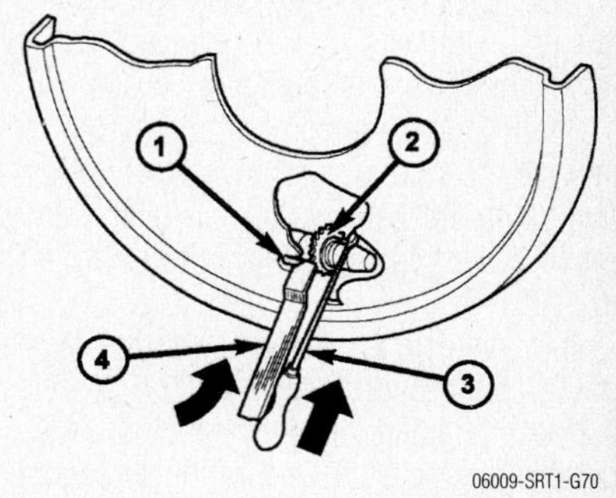

Fig. 13 Adjusting the parking brake with a brake adjusting tool

7. Push and hold adjuster lever away from star wheel with thin screwdriver.

8. Back off adjuster screw star wheel until brake drag is eliminated.

9. Repeat adjustment at opposite wheel. Be sure adjustment is equal at both wheels.

10. Install support plate access hole plugs.

11. Adjust parking brake cable and lower vehicle.

12. Depress park brake pedal and make sure park brakes hold the vehicle stationary.

13. Release park brake pedal.

CHASSIS ELECTRICAL

AIR BAG (SUPPLEMENTAL RESTRAINT SYSTEM)

GENERAL INFORMATION

CAUTION

These vehicles are equipped with an air bag system. The system must be disarmed before performing service on, or around, system components, the steering column, instrument panel components, wiring and sensors. Failure to follow the safety precautions and the disarming procedure could result in accidental air bag deployment, possible injury and unnecessary system repairs.

SERVICE PRECAUTIONS

Disconnect and isolate the battery negative cable before beginning any airbag system component diagnosis, testing, removal, or installation procedures. Allow system capacitor to discharge for two minutes before beginning any component service. This will disable the airbag system. Failure to disable the airbag system may result in accidental airbag deployment, personal injury, or death.

Do not place an intact undeployed airbag face down on a solid surface. The airbag will propel into the air if accidentally deployed and may result in personal injury or death.

When carrying or handling an undeployed airbag, the trim side (face) of the airbag should be pointing towards the body to minimize possibility of injury if accidental deployment occurs. Failure to do this may result in personal injury or death.

Replace airbag system components with OEM replacement parts. Substitute parts may appear interchangeable, but internal differences may result in inferior occupant protection. Failure to do so may result in occupant personal injury or death.

Wear safety glasses, rubber gloves, and long sleeved clothing when cleaning powder residue from vehicle after an airbag deployment. Powder residue emitted from a deployed airbag can cause skin irritation. Flush affected area with cool water if irritation is experienced. If nasal or throat irritation is experienced, exit the vehicle for fresh air until the irritation ceases. If irritation continues, see a physician.

Do not use a replacement airbag that is not in the original packaging. This may result in improper deployment, personal injury, or death.

The factory installed fasteners, screws and bolts used to fasten airbag components have a special coating and are specifically designed for the airbag system. Do not use substitute fasteners. Use only original equipment fasteners listed in the parts catalog when fastener replacement is required.

During, and following, any child restraint anchor service, due to impact event or vehicle repair, carefully inspect all mounting hardware, tether straps, and anchors for proper installation, operation, or damage. If a child restraint anchor is found damaged in any way, the anchor must be replaced. Failure to do this may result in personal injury or death.

Deployed and non-deployed airbags may or may not have live pyrotechnic material within the airbag inflator.

Do not dispose of driver/passenger/curtain airbags or seat belt tensioners unless you are sure of complete deployment. Refer to the Hazardous Substance Control System for proper disposal.

Dispose of deployed airbags and tensioners consistent with state, provincial, local, and federal regulations.

After any airbag component testing or service, do not connect the battery negative cable. Personal injury or death may result if the system test is not performed first.

If the vehicle is equipped with the Occupant Classification System (OCS), do not connect the battery negative cable before performing the OCS Verification Test using the scan tool and the appropriate diagnostic information. Personal injury or death may result if the system test is not performed properly.

Never replace both the Occupant Restraint Controller (ORC) and the Occupant Classification Module (OCM) at the same time. If both require replacement, replace one, then perform the Airbag System test before replacing the other.

Both the ORC and the OCM store Occupant Classification System (OCS) calibration data, which they transfer to one another when one of them is replaced. If both are replaced at the same time, an irreversible fault will be set in both modules and the OCS may malfunction and cause personal injury or death.

If equipped with OCS, the Seat Weight Sensor is a sensitive, calibrated unit and must be handled carefully. Do not drop or handle roughly. If dropped or damaged, replace with another sensor. Failure to do so may result in occupant injury or death.

If equipped with OCS, the front passenger seat must be handled carefully as well. When removing the seat, be careful when setting on floor not to drop. If dropped, the sensor may be inoperative, could result in occupant injury, or possibly death.

If equipped with OCS, when the passenger front seat is on the floor, no one should sit in the front passenger seat. This uneven force may damage the sensing ability of the seat weight sensors. If sat on and damaged, the sensor may be inoperative, could result in occupant injury, or possibly death.

DISARMING THE SYSTEM

Disconnect and isolate the battery negative (ground) cable, then wait two minutes for the system capacitor to discharge before performing further diagnosis or service. This is the only sure way to disable the supplemental restraint system. Failure to take the proper precautions could result in accidental airbag deployment.

DRIVETRAIN

AUTOMATIC TRANSMISSION ASSEMBLY

REMOVAL & INSTALLATION

➡The overdrive unit can be removed and serviced separately. It is not necessary to remove the entire transmission assembly to perform overdrive unit repairs.

1. Disconnect battery negative cable.
2. Raise vehicle.
3. Disconnect and lower or remove any necessary exhaust components.
4. Remove engine-to-transmission struts.
5. Remove starter motor.
6. Disconnect and remove the crankshaft position sensor. Retain the sensor attaching bolts.
7. If transmission is being removed for overhaul, remove transmission oil pan, drain fluid and reinstall pan.
8. Remove torque converter access cover.
9. Rotate crankshaft in clockwise direction until converter bolts are accessible. Then remove bolts one at a time. Rotate crankshaft with socket wrench on dampener bolt.
10. Mark propeller shaft and axle yokes for assembly alignment. Then disconnect and remove propeller shaft.
11. Disconnect wires from the transmission range sensor and transmission solenoid connector.
12. Disconnect gearshift cable from the transmission manual lever.
13. Disconnect throttle valve cable from transmission bracket and throttle valve lever.
14. Support rear of engine with safety stand or jack.
15. Raise transmission slightly with service jack to relieve load on crossmember and supports.
16. Remove the nuts securing rear support to the transmission crossmember.
17. Remove the bolts holding the rear support to the transmission remove the rear support.
18. Remove bolts attaching crossmember to frame and remove crossmember.
19. Remove fill tube bracket bolts and pull tube out of transmission. Retain fill tube seal.
20. Disconnect fluid cooler lines at transmission.
21. Carefully work transmission and torque converter assembly rearward off engine block dowels.
22. Lower transmission and remove assembly from under the vehicle.
23. To remove torque converter, remove C-clamp from edge of bell housing and carefully slide torque converter out of the transmission.
24. Remove all bolts holding the transmission to the engine adapter.
25. Carefully work transmission and torque converter assembly rearward off engine block dowels.
26. Lower transmission and remove assembly from under the vehicle.
27. To remove torque converter, remove C-clamp from edge of bell housing and carefully slide torque converter out of the transmission.

To install:

28. Check torque converter hub inner and outer diameters and hub drive notches for sharp edges burrs, scratches, or nicks. Polish the hub and notches with 320/400 grit paper and crocus cloth if necessary. The hub must be smooth to avoid damaging pump seal at installation.
29. Lubricate pocket in the rear oil pump seal lip with transmission fluid.
30. Lubricate converter pilot hub of the crankshaft with a light coating of Mopar® High Temp Grease.
31. Align and install converter in oil pump.
32. Carefully insert converter in oil pump. Then rotate converter back and forth until fully seated in pump gears.
33. Check converter seating with steel scale and straightedge. Surface of converter lugs should be 19mm (0.75 in.) to rear of straightedge when converter is fully seated.
34. Temporarily secure converter with C-clamp.
35. Position transmission on jack and secure it with chains.
36. Check condition of converter driveplate. Replace the plate if cracked, distorted or damaged.

➡Be sure transmission dowel pins are seated in engine block and protrude far enough to hold transmission in alignment.

37. Raise transmission and align converter with drive plate and converter housing with engine block.
38. Move transmission forward. Then raise, lower or tilt transmission to align converter housing with engine block dowels.
39. Carefully work transmission forward and over engine block dowels until converter hub is seated in crankshaft.
40. Install bolts attaching transmission to engine.
41. Install rear support.
42. Install the rear transmission crossmember.
43. Lower transmission onto crossmember and install bolts attaching transmission mount to crossmember.
44. Remove engine support fixture.
45. Install crankshaft position sensor.
46. Connect gearshift cable and throttle cable to transmission.
47. Connect cooler lines to transmission.
48. Connect wires to the transmission range sensor and transmission solenoid connector. Be sure the transmission harnesses are properly routed.

⁂ WARNING

It is essential that correct length bolts be used to attach the converter to the driveplate. Bolts that are too long will damage the clutch surface inside the converter.

49. Install torque converter-to-driveplate bolts.
50. Install converter housing access cover.
51. Install starter motor and cooler line bracket.
52. Install transmission fill tube. Install new seal on tube before installation.
53. Install any exhaust components previously removed.
54. Align and connect propeller shaft.
55. Adjust gearshift cable and throttle valve cable, if necessary.
56. Lower vehicle.
57. Fill transmission with Mopar® ATF +4, Automatic Transmission fluid.

MANUAL TRANSMISSION

REMOVAL & INSTALLATION

See Figures 14 and 15.

1. With vehicle in neutral, position it on a hoist.
2. Mark installation reference marks on the propeller shaft, pinion yoke and transmission output shaft.
3. Remove propeller shaft clamp bolts and remove shaft.
4. Remove shift cover bolts.
5. Remove hydraulic clutch line quick connector at the transmission with Clutch Line Disconnect Tool 6638 or 6638A to disconnect.
6. Remove reverse lockout solenoid connector.
7. Remove fuel line clip from top plate stud.
8. Remove back up lamp switch connector.
9. Position transmission jack and secure to transmission.
10. Remove transmission to clutch housing bolts.
11. Remove transmission mount bolts.
12. Remove transmission crossmember bolts.
13. Slide transmission back to clear the bell housing. Then lower transmission.

To install:

14. Slide transmission back into the clutch and seat against clutch housing.
15. Install transmission bolts to clutch housing bolts and tighten to and tighten bolts to 35 Nm (26 ft. lbs.)
16. Install transmission crossmember and bolts/nuts. Tighten nuts to 61 Nm (45 ft. lbs.).
17. Install transmission mount bolts and tighten to 41 Nm (30 ft. lbs.).
18. Remove transmission jack.
19. Install back up lamp switch connector.
20. Install fuel line to top plate stud.
21. Install reverse lockout solenoid harness connector.
22. Install hydraulic clutch quick connector to the slave cylinder.
23. Clean transmission shifter tower sealing surfaces and apply a bead of Mopar® Gasket Maker.
24. Install shifter tower and tighten bolts to 18 Nm (156 inch lbs.).
25. Install propeller shaft with reference marks aligned.

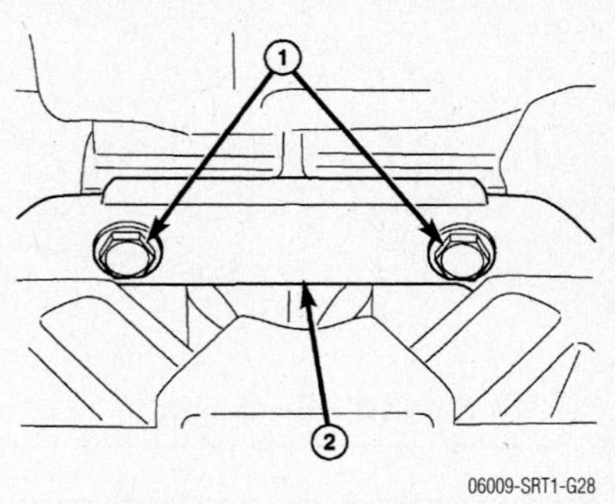

Fig. 14 Manual transmission mount (2) and bolts (1)

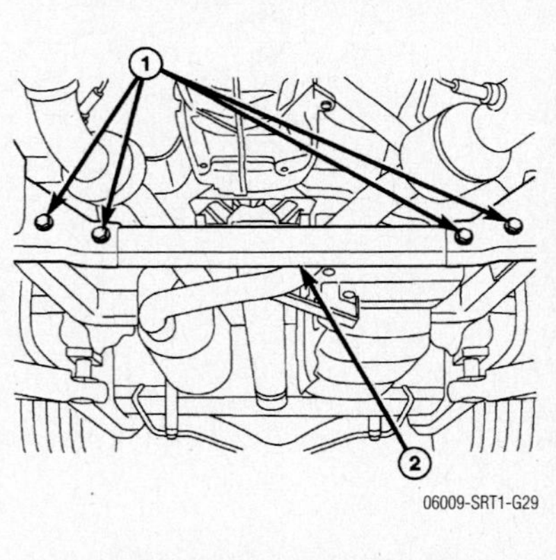

Fig. 15 Manual transmission crossmember (2) and bolts (1)

⁂ WARNING

The drive shaft strap bolts must be replaced or cleaned and Loctite® 242 applied. Replace drive shaft joint straps whenever they are removed. The straps slightly deform when torqued in place. Reuse of the straps may result in reduced clamp load on the universal joint cap.

CLUTCH

REMOVAL & INSTALLATION

See Figure 16.

1. Remove transmission.
2. Remove clutch housing bolts and remove clutch housing from engine.
3. Mark pressure plate and flywheel to maintain their position when installing clutch assembly.
4. Insert Clutch Disc Aligning Tool through the clutch disc hub to prevent the clutch disc from falling and damaging the facings.
5. Loosen pressure plate bolts one or two turns at a time, in a crisscross pattern. This will release spring pressure evenly and avoid clutch cover damage.
6. Remove pressure plate assembly and disc.
7. Clean flywheel face with crocus cloth or 400-600 grade sandpaper, then wipe the surface with mineral spirits. Wipe the friction surface of the pressure plate with mineral spirits. If the surface is severely scored, heat checked or warped, replace the flywheel.

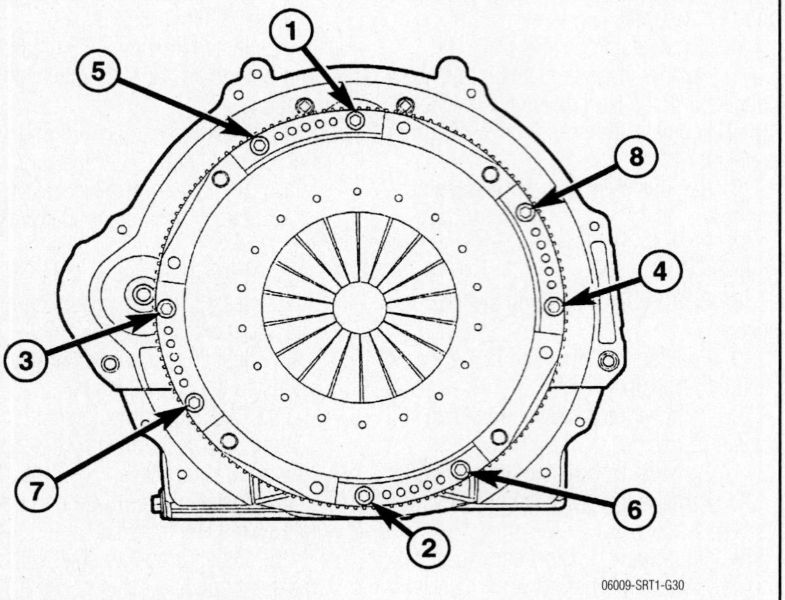

Fig. 16 Pressure plate torque sequence

➡**Never machine the flywheel face. If flywheel surface is bad the flywheel must be replaced.**

To install:

➡**Clutch disc is marked flywheel side.**

8. Mount clutch assembly on flywheel, being careful to properly align dowels and alignment marks made before removal. If new clutch or flywheel is installed, align cover balance spot as close as possible to flywheel balance orange spot. Apply pressure to the alignment tool. Lightly tighten the clutch cover bolts enough to hold the disc in position.
9. Tighten pressure plate bolts a few turns at a time in a crisscross pattern until bolts are all seated. Then tighten bolts sequence to 30 Nm (23 ft. lbs.). Remove clutch disc alignment tool.
10. Install bellhousing on engine.
11. Install transmission.

HYDRAULIC CLUTCH SYSTEM

REMOVAL & INSTALLATION

See Figures 17 and 18.

1. Remove nuts attaching slave cylinder to studs on clutch housing.

➡**The hydraulic linkage has a quick disconnect at the slave cylinder. This fitting should never be disconnected or tampered with. Once the hydraulic line is connected to the slave cylinder, it should never be disconnected.**

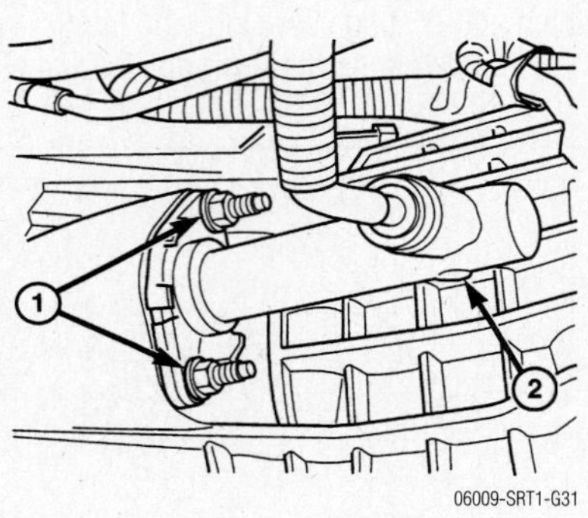

Fig. 17 Slave cylinder mounting

2. Raise and support vehicle.
3. Remove heat shield over hydraulic line.
4. Remove slave cylinder from clutch housing.
5. Remove plastic clip securing the hydraulic line to the dash panel from the lower dash panel flange.
6. Remove plastic clip securing hydraulic line to the dash panel from the upper dash panel stud.
7. Lower vehicle.
8. Disconnect clutch pedal interlock switch connector.
9. Remove clutch master cylinder rod pin.
10. Verify that cap on clutch master cylinder reservoir is tight. This will avoid spillage during removal.
11. Remove clutch master cylinder nuts holding the to the dash panel.
12. Remove clutch cylinders, reservoir and connecting lines from vehicle.

To install:

13. Position cylinders and connecting line in vehicle engine compartment. Position clutch hydraulic line against the dash panel and behind all engine hoses and wiring.
14. Apply a light coating of grease to the inside diameter of the master cylinder push rod eye.
15. Install clutch master cylinder on dash panel and tighten clutch master cylinder nuts to 28 Nm (21 ft. lbs.).
16. Install clutch master cylinder push rod pin.
17. Connect clutch pedal position interlock switch connector.

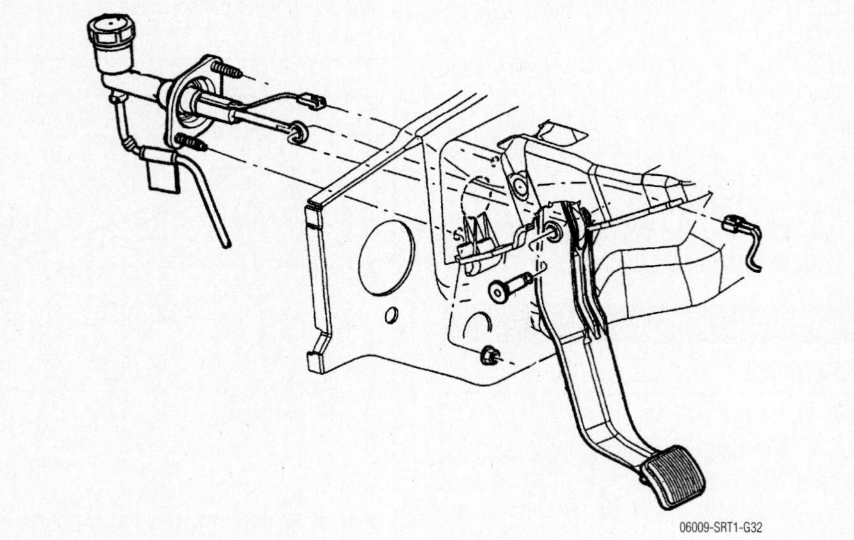

Fig. 18 Master cylinder mounting

18. Install plastic clip securing hydraulic line to the dash panel into the lower dash panel flange.

19. Install plastic clip securing hydraulic line to the dash panel onto the upper dash panel stud.

20. Raise vehicle.

21. Install slave cylinder and verify cylinder rod is properly seated in release lever.

22. Install and tighten slave cylinder nuts to 23 Nm (17 ft. lbs.).

23. If new clutch linkage is being installed, connect the clutch hydraulic line to the clutch slave cylinder.

➡Once the clutch hydraulic line is connected to the slave cylinder, it should never be disconnected.

24. Install heat shield over hydraulic line.

25. Operate linkage several times to verify proper operation.

REAR AXLE SHAFT, BEARING AND SEAL

REMOVAL & INSTALLATION

See Figures 19 through 22.

1. With vehicle in neutral, position vehicle on hoist.
2. Remove brake caliper adapter with caliper and remove rotor.
3. Remove differential housing cover and drain lubricant.
4. Remove pinion mate shaft lock screw.
5. Remove pinion mate shaft from differential case.
6. Push axle shaft inward and remove axle shaft C-lock.
7. Remove axle shaft.
8. Remove axle seal with pry bar.
9. Position bearing Receiver 9345 on axle tube.
10. Insert bearing Remover 6310 with Foot 6310-9 through receiver and bearing.
11. Tighten Remove 6310 nut to pull bearing into the receiver.

To install:

12. Remove any old sealer/burrs from axle tube.
13. Install axle shaft bearing with an installer. Drive bearing in until tool contacts the axle tube.

➡Bearing is installed with the bearing part number against the installer.

14. Coat new axle seal lip with axle lubricant and install with a seal driver.
15. Lubricate bearing bore and seal lip with gear lubricant.

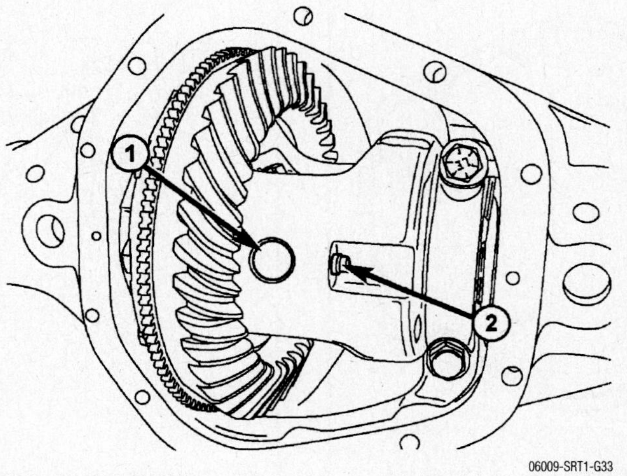

Fig. 19 Pinion mate shaft (1) and lock screw (2)

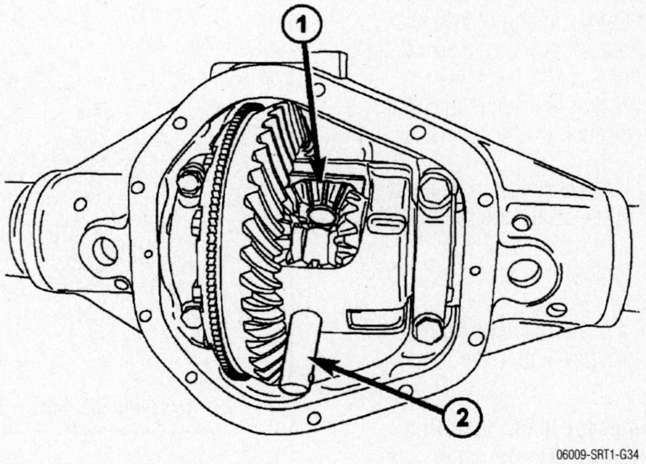

Fig. 20 Remove the pinion mate shaft

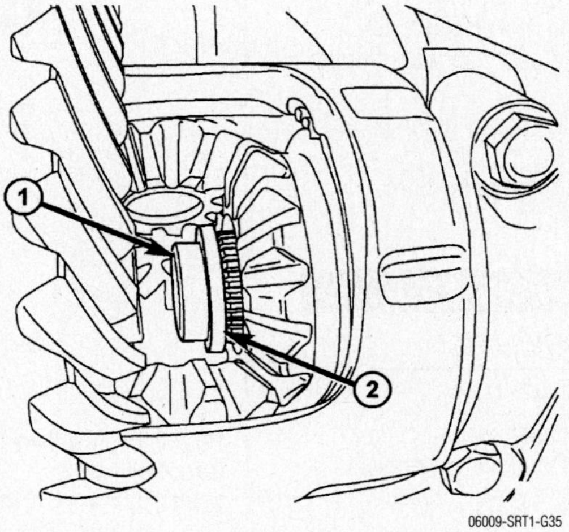

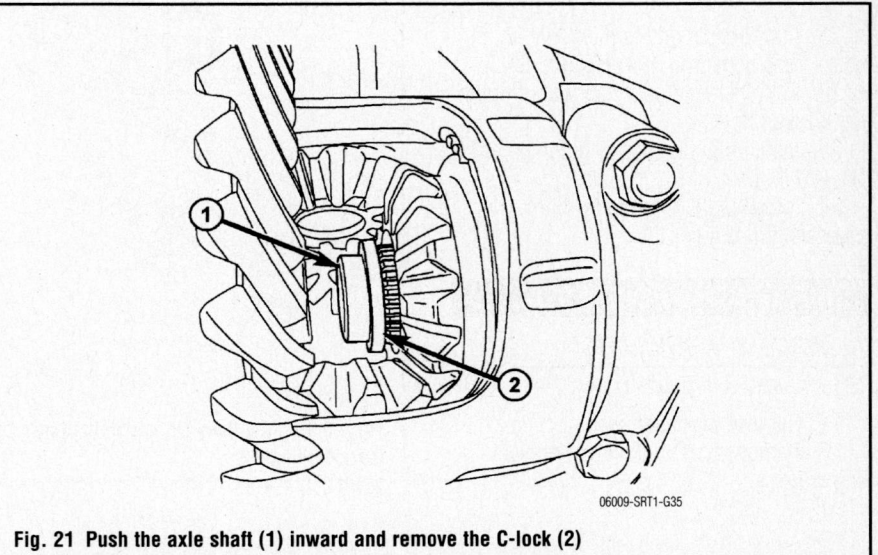

Fig. 21 Push the axle shaft (1) inward and remove the C-lock (2)

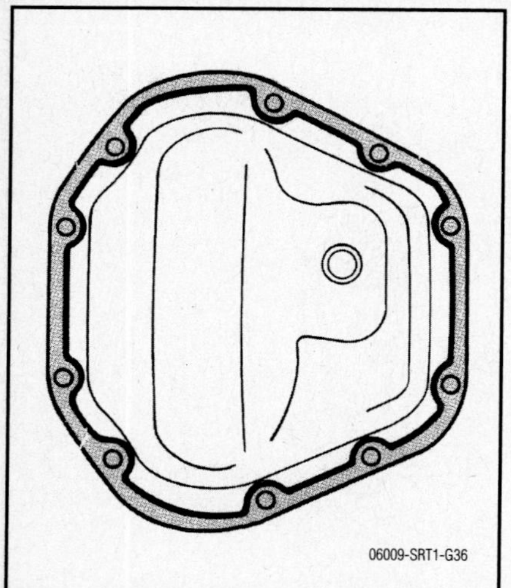

Fig. 22 RTV application on differential cover

16. Insert axle shaft through seal, bearing and engage into side gear splines.

17. Insert C-lock in end of axle shaft then push axle shaft outward to seat C-lock in side gear.

18. Insert pinion mate shaft into differential case and through thrust washer and pinion gear.

19. Align hole in pinion mate shaft with hole in differential case and install lock screw with Loctite® 242 or equivalent. Tighten lock screw to 27 Nm (20 ft. lbs.).

20. Apply a bead of orange Mopar Axle RTV sealant or equivalent to the housing cover.

➡If housing cover is not installed within 3 to 5 minutes, the cover must be cleaned and new RTV applied. Failure to follow these instruction will result in a leak.

21. Install cover and tighten bolts in a criss-cross pattern to 48 Nm (35 ft. lbs.).

22. Fill differential lubricant to bottom of the fill plug hole.

23. Install fill hole plug and tighten to 27 Nm (20 ft. lbs.).

24. Install brake rotor and caliper adapter with caliper.

DIFFERENTIAL PINION SEAL

REMOVAL & INSTALLATION

See Figures 23 through 25.

1. Remove propeller shaft.

2. Remove brake calipers to prevent any drag.

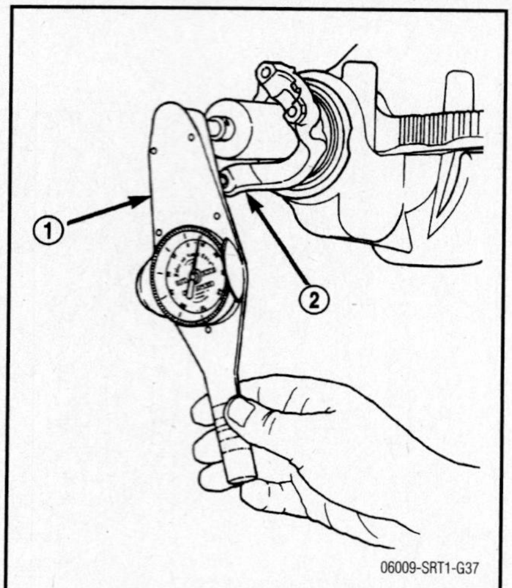

Fig. 23 Measuring pinion gear rotating torque. (1) Torque wrench, (2) Yoke

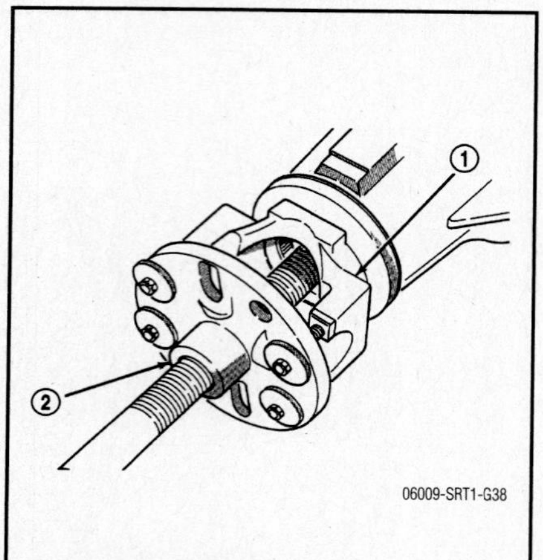

Fig. 24 Removing the yoke

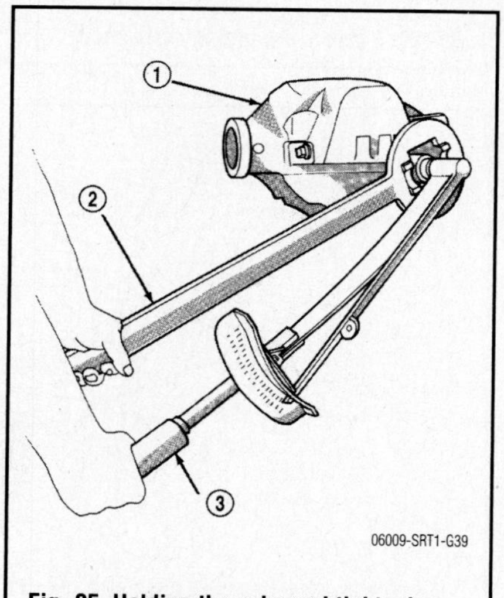

Fig. 25 Holding the yoke and tightening the pinion nut.

3. Rotate pinion yoke three or four times.

4. Record pinion gear rotating torque with an inch pound torque wrench.

5. Hold yoke with Yoke Holder 6719A and remove pinion shaft nut and washer.

6. Remove pinion yoke with Remover C-452.

7. Remove pinion seal with pry tool or slide-hammer mounted screw.

To install:

8. Coat lip of pinion seal with gear lubricant.

9. Install new pinion seal with Installer 9348 and Handle C-4171.

10. Install yoke on pinion shaft with Installer C-3718 and Yoke Holder 6719A.

11. Install pinion yoke washer with the concave surface against the yoke end.

12. Install new pinion nut.

⁂ WARNING

Never exceed minimum tightening torque when installing the pinion yoke retaining nut at this point. Failure to heed caution may result in damage.

13. Hold pinion yoke with Yoke Holder 6719A and tighten nut with torque wrench to 292 Nm (215 ft. lbs.). Rotate pinion shaft several revolutions to ensure bearing rollers are seated.

14. Rotate pinion with an inch pound torque wrench. Rotating torque should be equal to reading recorded during removal, plus 0.56 Nm (5 inch lbs.).

⁂ WARNING

Never loosen pinion nut to decrease pinion rotating torque and never exceed specified preload torque. Failure to follow these instruction will result in damage.

15. If rotating torque is low, use Yoke Holder 6719 to hold the pinion yoke and tighten the pinion shaft nut in 6.8 Nm (60 inch lbs.) increments until proper rotating torque is achieved.

➡The bearing rotating torque should be constant during a complete revolution of the pinion. If the rotating torque varies, this indicates a binding condition.

16. Install brake components.

17. Install propeller shaft.

ENGINE COOLING

WATER PUMP

REMOVAL & INSTALLATION

See Figures 26 and 27.

1. Disconnect negative battery cable from battery.
2. Drain cooling system.

➡Do not waste reusable coolant. If solution is clean, drain coolant into a clean container for reuse.

3. Remove windshield washer reservoir tank from radiator fan shroud.
4. Remove the four fan shroud mounting bolts at the radiator. Do not attempt to remove shroud from vehicle at this time.

WARNING

Constant tension hose clamps are used on most cooling system hoses. When removing or installing, use only tools designed for servicing this type of clamp, such as special clamp tool number 6093. Always wear safety glasses when servicing constant tension clamps.

➡A number or letter is stamped into the tongue of constant tension clamps. If replacement is necessary, use only an original equipment clamp with a matching number or letter.

5. Remove radiator upper hose at radiator.
6. Remove accessory drive belt.
7. Remove the radiator lower hose at water pump.
8. Remove heater hose at water pump fitting.
9. Remove the seven water pump mounting bolts.
10. Loosen the clamp at the water pump end of bypass hose. Slip the bypass hose from the water pump while removing pump from vehicle. Do not remove the clamp from the bypass hose.
11. Discard the water pump-to-timing chain/case cover o-ring seal.
12. Remove the heater hose fitting from water pump if pump replacement is necessary. Note position (direction) of fitting before removal. Fitting must be re-installed to same position.

WARNING

Do not pry the water pump at timing chain case/cover. The machined surfaces may be damaged resulting in leaks.

13. Clean the gasket mating surface. Use caution not to damage the gasket sealing surface.

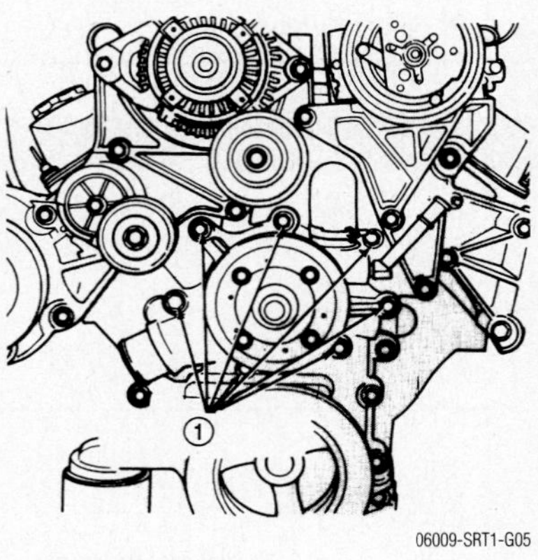

Fig. 26 Water pump mounting bolts (1)

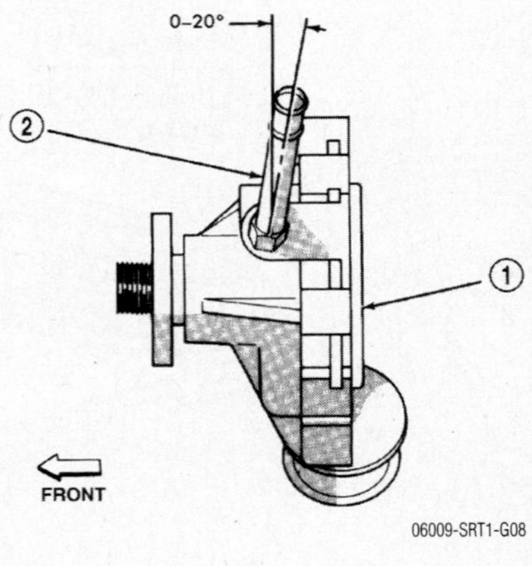

Fig. 27 If water pump is being replaced, install the heater hose fitting to the pump. Tighten fitting to 16 Nm (144 inch lbs.) torque. After fitting has been torqued, position fitting as shown

14. Inspect the water pump assembly for cracks in the housing, water leaks from shaft seal, worn bearing or impeller rubbing either the pump body or timing chain case/cover.

To install:

15. If water pump is being replaced, install the heater hose fitting to the pump. Tighten fitting to 16 Nm (144 inch lbs.) torque. After fitting has been torqued, position fitting as shown. When positioning fitting, do not back off (rotate counterclockwise). Use a sealant on the fitting such as Mopar® Thread Sealant With Teflon. Refer to the directions on the package.

➡This heater hose fitting must be installed to pump before pump is installed to engine.

16. Clean the o-ring mating surfaces at rear of water pump and front of timing chain/case cover.
17. Apply a small amount of petroleum jelly to o-ring. This will help retain o-ring to water pump.
18. Install water pump to engine as follows: Guide water pump fitting into bypass hose as pump is being installed. Install water pump bolts. Tighten water pump mounting bolts to 40 Nm (30 ft. lbs.) torque.
19. Position bypass hose clamp to bypass hose.
20. Spin water pump to be sure that pump impeller does not rub against timing chain case/cover.
21. Connect radiator lower hose to water pump.
22. Connect heater hose and hose clamp to heater hose fitting.
23. Install drive belt.
24. Position fan shroud and fan blade/viscous fan drive assembly to vehicle as a complete unit.
25. Install fan shroud to radiator. Tighten bolts to 6 Nm (50 inch lbs.) torque.
26. Install fan blade/viscous fan drive assembly to water pump shaft.
27. Fill cooling system.
28. Connect negative battery cable.
29. Start and warm the engine. Check for leaks.

ENGINE ELECTRICAL — CHARGING SYSTEM

ALTERNATOR

REMOVAL & INSTALLATION

See Figure 28.

1. Disconnect the negative battery cable.
2. Remove air cleaner assembly.
3. Remove the accessory drive belt.
4. Disconnect the field connector.
5. Disconnect the battery positive cable from the alternator. First disconnect the B+ cap on the wiring harness side.
6. Remove the upper mounting bolt.

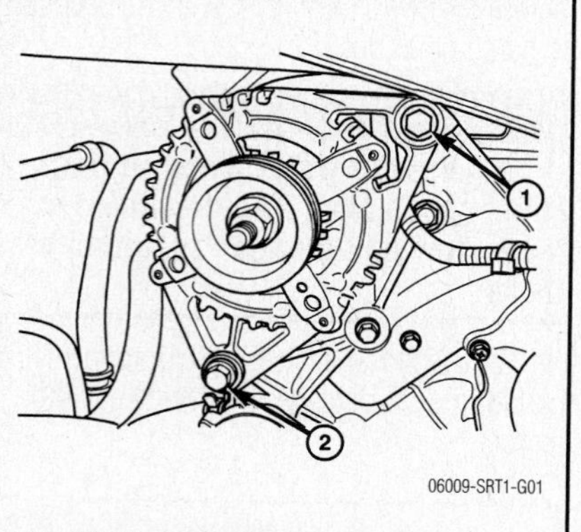

Fig. 28 Alternator mounting

7. Remove the lower mounting bolt and nut.
8. Remove alternator.

To install:

9. Install alternator.
10. Install lower mounting bolt and nut.
11. Install upper mounting bolt.
12. Tighten bolts to 55 Nm (41 ft. lbs).
13. Connect battery positive cable to alternator, and install B+ stud cap.
14. Connect field connector.
15. Install accessory drive belt.
16. Install air cleaner assembly.
17. Connect negative battery cable, tighten nut to 14.2 Nm (125 inch. lbs.).

ENGINE ELECTRICAL — IGNITION SYSTEM

SPARK PLUG WIRING AND FIRING ORDER

See Figures 29 and 30.

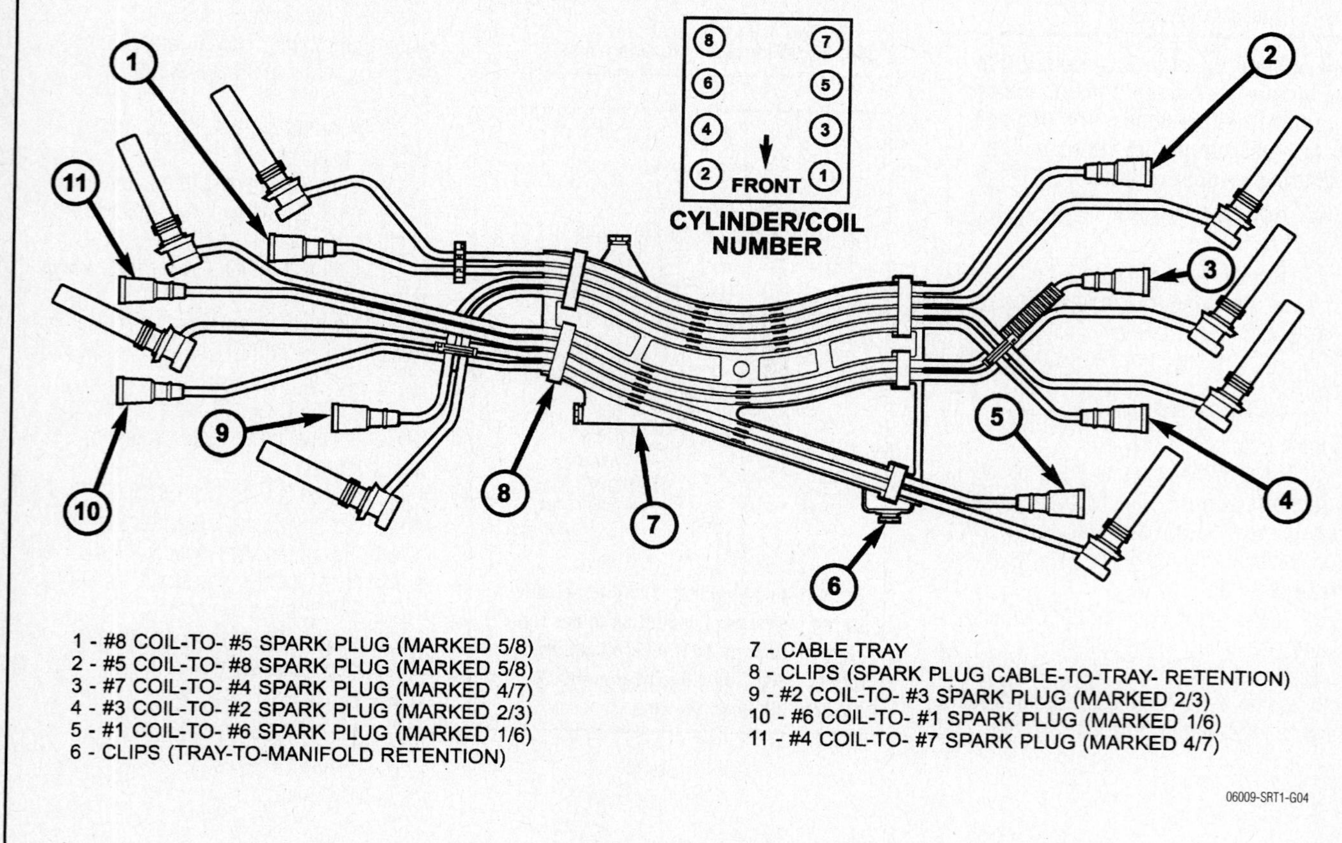

Fig. 29 Spark plug wire routing

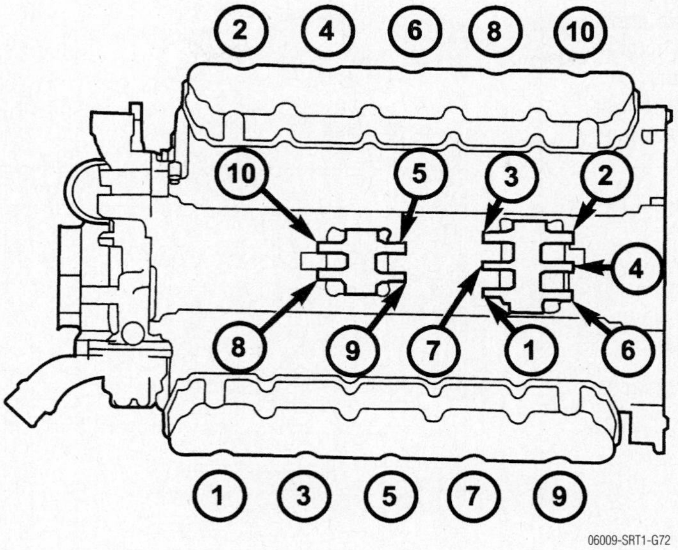

Fig. 30 Firing order–SRT-10

ENGINE MECHANICAL

➡Disconnecting the negative battery cable may interfere with the functions of the on board computer systems and may require the computer to undergo a relearning process, once the negative battery cable is reconnected.

ACCESSORY DRIVE BELT ROUTING

See Figure 31.

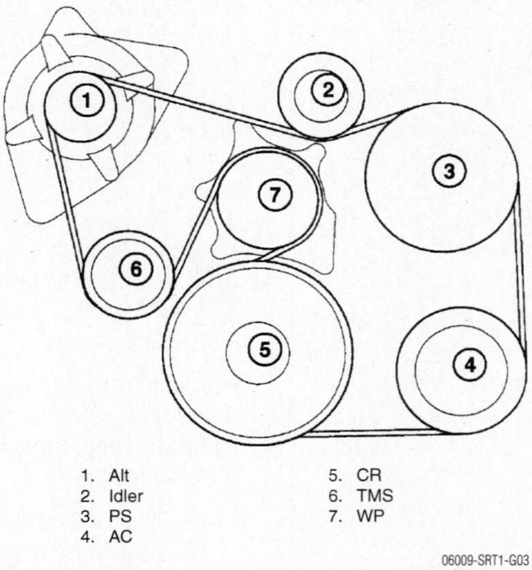

Fig. 31 Accessory drive belt routing: (1) Alternator, (2) Idler, (3) Power Steering Pump, (4) A/C Compressor, (5) Crankshaft Pulley, (6) Tensioner, (7) Water Pump

CAMSHAFT AND VALVE LIFTERS

REMOVAL & INSTALLATION

See Figures 32 and 33.

1. Perform the fuel pressure relief procedure.
2. Disconnect the negative battery cables.
3. Raise and support the vehicle.
4. Remove the front engine shield.
5. Drain the cooling system.
6. Drain the power steering fluid.
7. Remove the oil pan.
8. Lower the vehicle.
9. Remove air intake tube between intake manifold and air filter assembly.
10. Unclip A/C lines from radiator fan shroud, and position out of the way.
11. Remove coolant recover bottle and coolant container tube.
12. Remove upper radiator hose from radiator and position out of the way.
13. Raise vehicle on hoist.
14. Disconnect the high and low pressure hydraulic hoses at the hydraulic fan motor.
15. Disconnect solenoid electrical connector.
16. Lower vehicle.
17. Remove the four fan shroud retaining bolts.
18. Remove the fan motor and shroud assembly from the vehicle.
19. Remove the power steering cooler mounting bolts and pushpins. Position the power steering cooler out of the way.
20. Lower vehicle.
21. Remove the two radiator upper mounting bolts.
22. Lift radiator straight up and out of engine compartment.

➡The bottom of the radiator is equipped with two alignment dowels that fit into holes in the lower radiator support panel. Rubber biscuits (insulators) are installed to these dowels. Take care not to damage cooling fins or tubes on the radiator and air conditioning condenser when removing.

23. Remove the radiator and radiator fan assembly.
24. Remove intake manifold.
25. Remove cylinder head covers.
26. Remove timing chain cover.
27. Remove rocker arm assemblies.

➡Identify each push rod to be replaced in its original location.

28. Remove pushrods.
29. Remove cylinder heads.
30. Remove hydraulic tappets.
31. Remove timing chain and camshaft sprocket.
32. Remove camshaft thrust plate.
33. Slowly remove camshaft. Use care not to damage camshaft bearing surfaces with the cam lobes.
34. Remove cylinder head.

➡If tappets (3) are to be reused, identify tappet location to ensure installation in original location.

35. Remove tappet aligning yoke bolt (1).
36. Remove tappets (3) from bores.

✲✲ WARNING

Do not disassemble tappets.

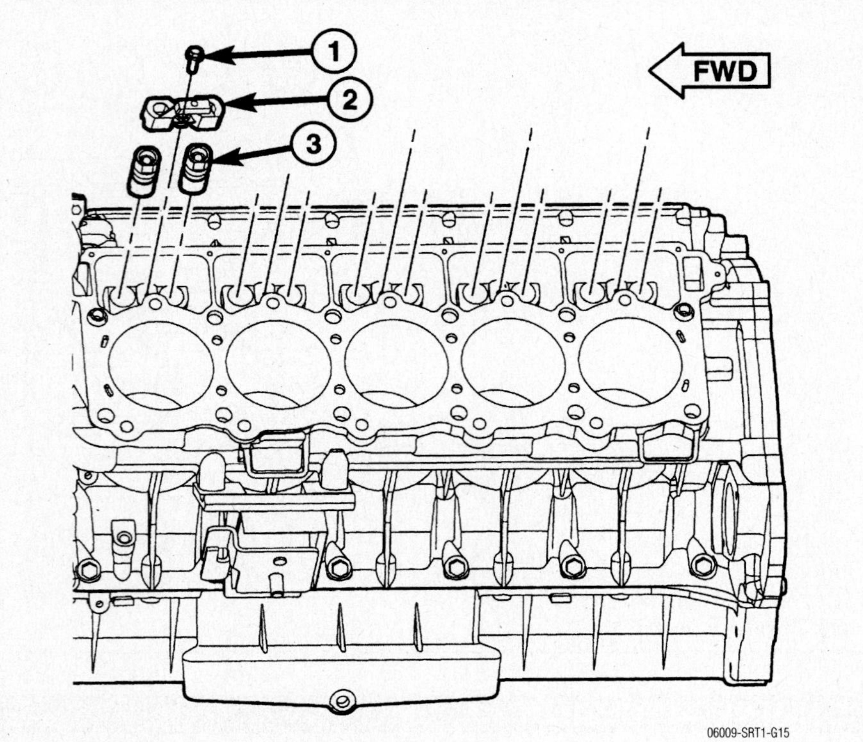

Fig. 33 Hydraulic tappets—(1) is the oil holes

To install:

37. Lubricate tappets.
38. Install tappets in their original positions with oil holes facing up.

✲✲ WARNING

The "handle" on the tappet aligning yoke must be installed in the outboard position; i.e. toward the cylinders.

39. With roller tappets in proper position, install aligning yoke assemblies. Apply Mopar® Lock & Seal Adhesive (Medium Strength Threadlocker) to the screws and tighten to 11 Nm (95 inch lbs.).
40. Install cylinder heads.
41. Lubricate camshaft lobes and camshaft bearing journals.
42. Slowly install camshaft. Use care not to damage camshaft bearing surfaces with the cam lobes.
43. Install camshaft thrust plate bolts. Tighten to 24 Nm (210 inch lbs.).
44. Install timing chain and camshaft sprocket.
45. Measure camshaft end play. End Play should measure 0.0127–0.381 mm (0.005–0.015 in.) 0.381 mm (0.015 in. Max.). If not within limits, install a new thrust plate.

➡When camshaft is replaced, all of the tappets must be replaced. Each hydraulic tappet must be installed with oil hole facing up.

46. Install timing chain cover.
47. Install push rods in their original location.
48. Install rocker arms.
49. Install intake manifold.

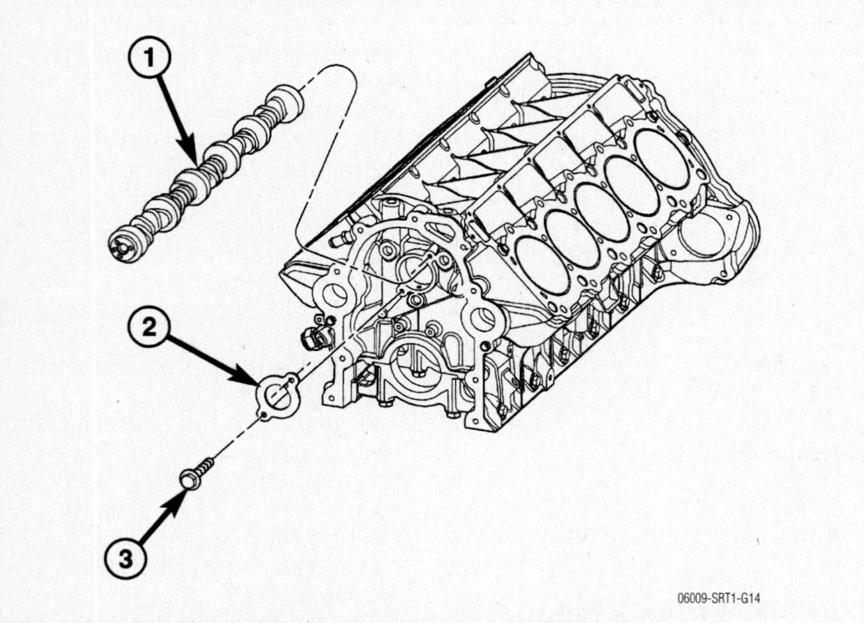

Fig. 32 Camshaft (1) removal along with thrust plate (2) and bolt (3)

50. Install cylinder head covers.
51. Install the radiator and fan assembly.
52. Raise and support the vehicle.
53. Install the oil pan.
54. Install the front engine shield.
55. Lower the vehicle.
56. Fill and purge air from the power steering.
57. Fill and purge air from the cooling system.
58. Fill engine crankcase with the proper oil to the correct level.
59. Connect the negative battery cable.
60. Start the vehicle and inspect for leaks.

WARNING

To prevent damage to valve mechanism, engine must not be run above fast idle until all hydraulic tappets have filled with oil and have become quiet.

CYLINDER HEAD

REMOVAL & INSTALLATION

See Figures 34 and 35.

➡Care must be taken to protect the intake manifold and cylinder head covers powder coating from scrapes and abrasions. This procedure covers either the left or right cylinder head.

➡The aluminum alloy cylinder head is held in place by 12, ½ inch bolts and 8, ¼ inch bolts.

1. Release the fuel pressure.
2. Disconnect negative battery cable.
3. Disconnect the throttle body air inlet duct, IAT sensor, CCV hose and remove the air cleaner cover.
4. Drain the cooling system.
5. Raise and support the vehicle.
6. Disconnect the front exhaust pipe to exhaust manifold connection.
7. Lower the vehicle.
8. Remove intake manifold.
9. Disconnect the spark plug wires by pulling on the boot straight out in line with the spark plug. Dislodge spark plug retainers from the cylinder head cover studs and position the spark plug wires aside.
10. Disconnect the oil level indicator tube and set aside.
11. Disconnect CCV hoses from cylinder head covers.
12. Remove the cylinder head covers.
13. Remove exhaust manifold heat shields.
14. Remove exhaust manifold(s) and gasket(s).

➡If rocker arms and push rods are to be reused, identify each component to ensure installation in original locations.

15. Remove the rocker arm and pedestal assemblies.
16. Remove push rods.
17. Remove the 12 head bolts and 8 cylinder head tappet gallery bolts from cylinder head(s).
18. Remove cylinder head(s) and gasket(s).
19. Before cleaning, check for leaks, damage and cracks.
20. Clean cylinder head and oil passages.
21. Check cylinder head for flatness.
22. Inspect all surfaces with a straightedge if there is any reason to suspect leakage. If out-of-flatness exceeds 0.019 mm (0.00075 in.) times the span length in inches in any direction, either replace head or lightly machine the head surface. As an example, if a 12.0 inch span is 1.0 mm (0.004 in.) out-of-flat, allowable is 12 x 0.019 mm (0.00075 in.) equals 0.22 mm (0.009 in.). This amount of out-of-flat is acceptable. Maximum of 0.2 mm (0.008 in.) for grinding is permitted.

➡This is a combined total dimension of stock removal from cylinder head surface.

To install:

➡This procedure covers either the left or right cylinder head.

23. Clean all surfaces of engine block and cylinder heads.

➡Remove all gasket material from cylinder head and block using a plastic scraper only. DO NOT use a metal scraper, as damage to sealing surface may occur.

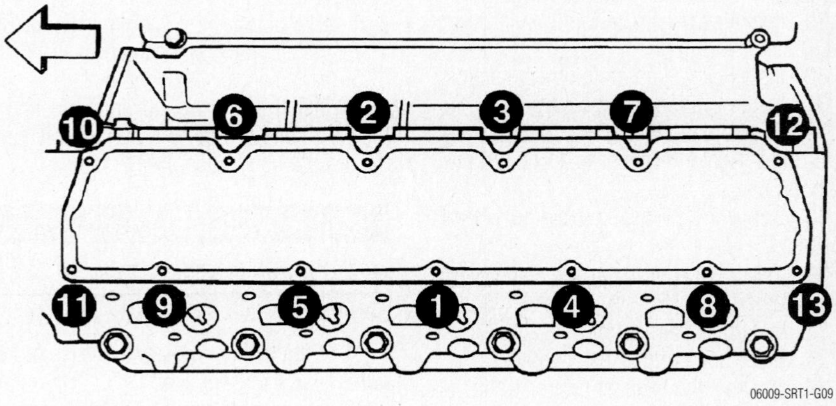

Fig. 34 Cylinder head cover torque sequence

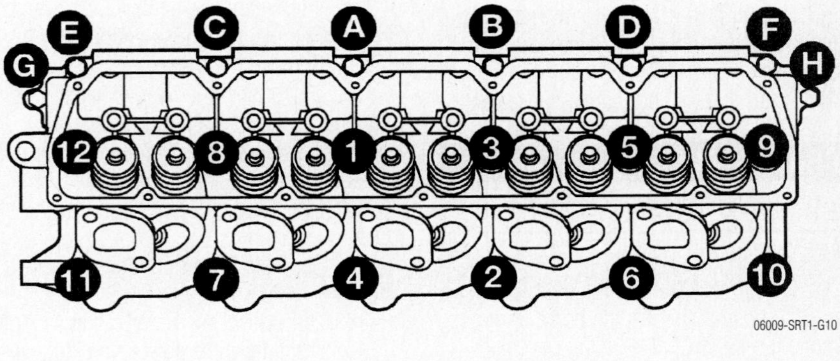

Fig. 35 Cylinder head bolt torque sequence

➡NOTE: A multi-layer steel head gasket is used.

24. Install new gasket(s) on the engine block. Assure all coolant passages and bolt holes align properly.

➡Cylinder head bolts are coated, DO NOT oil.

25. Install cylinder head(s) over dowel pins. Install cylinder head bolts 1–12. Tighten cylinder head bolts 1–12 in the sequence shown in using a two step torque sequence:
a. First to 47 Nm (35 ft. lbs.).
b. Second to 122 Nm (90 ft. lbs.).
26. After cylinder head bolts 1–12 have been tightened to specifications, install and tighten cylinder head tappet gallery bolts A-H in sequence shown to 11 Nm (95 inch lbs.).
27. Inspect the push rods. Replace worn or bent push rods as necessary.
28. Install pushrods. Install rocker arms and pedestal assemblies into their original positions. Ensure push rods are seated properly under each rocker arm. Tighten rocker arm bolts to 35 Nm (26 ft. lbs.).
29. Install exhaust manifold(s) and gasket(s).
30. Install exhaust manifold heat shields.
31. Install cylinder head covers.
32. Position and install the oil level indicator tube. Tighten fastener to 11 Nm (95 inch lbs.).
33. Connect CCV hoses to cylinder head covers.
34. Install the spark plug wires and plug wire retainers.
35. Install intake manifold.
36. Raise and support the vehicle.
37. Connect the exhaust system to the exhaust manifolds.
38. Drain the engine oil.
39. Lower the vehicle.
40. Fill engine oil to the proper level.
41. Fill the cooling system.
42. Connect negative battery cable.
43. Install the air cleaner cover, throttle inlet duct and connect the IAT sensor and CCV hose.
44. Start engine and inspect for leaks.

CRANKSHAFT FRONT SEAL

REMOVAL & INSTALLATION

See Figure 36.

1. Disconnect the air inlet duct, IAT sensor, CCV hose at the throttle body, and remove the air cleaner housing cover.
2. Remove accessory drive belt.
3. Remove crankshaft damper
4. Use Special Tool C-4679A to remove crankshaft oil seal. Be careful not to damage the crankshaft seal surface of cover.

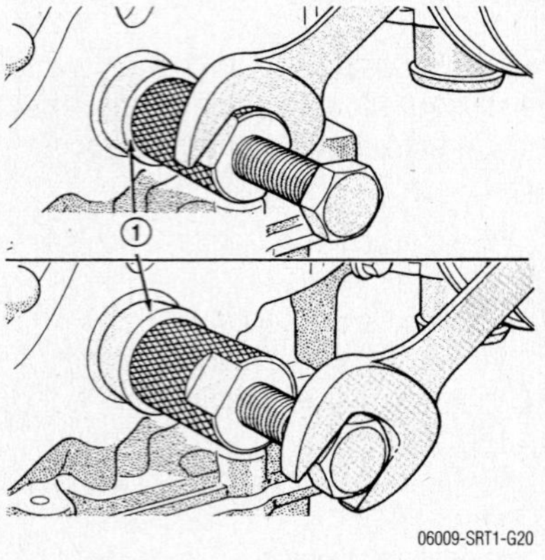

Fig. 36 Front seal removal using the special tool (1)

To install:

5. Install the new seal by using Special Tool MD 998306.
6. Place seal into opening with seal spring towards the inside of engine. Install seal until it bottoms out in timing chain cover.
7. Install crankshaft damper.
8. Install accessory drive belt.
9. Install air cleaner cover connecting the CVV hose, IAT sensor, and air duct to the throttle body housing.

ENGINE ASSEMBLY

REMOVAL & INSTALLATION

See Figure 37.

1. Perform fuel pressure release procedure.
2. Disconnect negative battery cable.
3. Disconnect throttle body air inlet duct, remove air cleaner cover.
4. Raise and support the vehicle.
5. Remove the lower engine shield.
6. Drain cooling system.
7. Paint mark and remove the driveshaft.
8. Remove the transmission.
9. Remove the starter.
10. Disconnect the front exhaust pipe flange to exhaust manifold fasteners.
11. Disconnect the hydraulic cooling fan lines and capture any spillage.
12. Drain engine oil and remove the oil filter.
13. Separate the air conditioning hose from the fan shroud.
14. Disconnect the lower radiator hose.
15. Disconnect the power steering line support bracket at the lower left of the radiator.
16. Loosen both engine mount through bolts.
17. Separate the ground strap from the floor board, above the right exhaust flange.
18. Lower the vehicle.
19. Discharge air conditioning system.
20. Remove the upper radiator hose.
21. Disconnect windshield washer hose at the splice.
22. Remove radiator core support.
23. Disconnect the cooling fan harness connector.
24. Remove the radiator and radiator fan assembly.
25. Remove the A/C condenser, cap and position the hoses aside.
26. Disconnect the heater hoses at the top front cover and at the lower coolant housing and position aside.
27. Disconnect the oil cooler hoses from the engine and position aside.
28. Remove accessory drive belt.
29. Disconnect and remove alternator.
30. Remove power steering pump mounting bolts and set pump aside.
31. Disconnect A/C lines and electrical connector from A/C compressor. Plug holes in A/C compressor to prevent debris from entering A/C compressor.
32. Disconnect brake booster vacuum hose and fuel line to fuel rail.
33. Disconnect the cruise control, accelerator cable and fuel vapor purge harness, then set aside.
34. Disconnect the engine harness connectors on top of the intake manifold.
35. Disconnect the spark plug wires from the spark plugs and set the plug wires on top of the engine.
36. Disconnect the ground strap at the thermostat housing and pull the electrical harness underneath the intake manifold and set aside.
37. Install Special Tool 9363 (Engine Lifting Brackets), or equivalent, and to the exhaust manifold heat shield studs where indicated.
38. Insert engine lifting bar through the access holes in the engine lifting brackets and secure with the bar retaining pins.
39. Remove engine with an engine hoist.

To install:

40. Attach engine hoist and lower the engine into engine compartment, aligning the left and right engine mounts.
41. Install left and right engine mount insulator bolts and nuts. Tighten nuts to 102 Nm (75 ft. lbs.).
42. Remove engine hoist and engine lifting bar and brackets.
43. Install the exhaust manifold heat shield nuts and tighten to 6 Nm (50 in. lbs.).

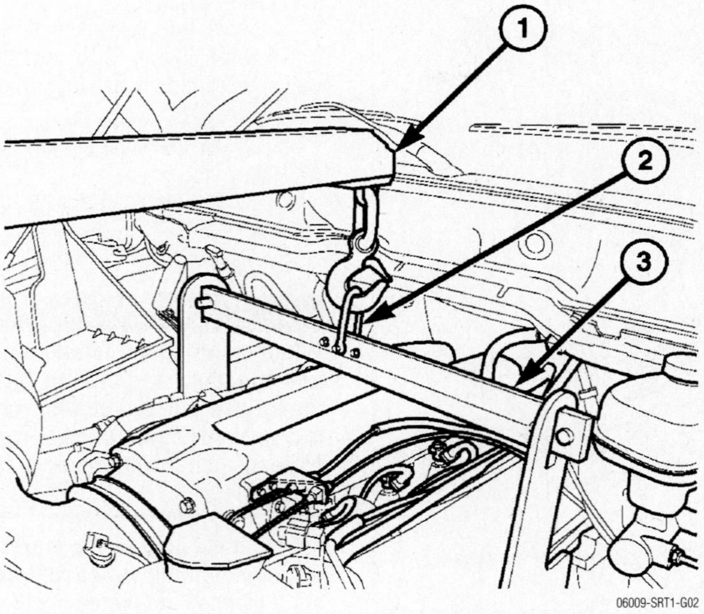

Fig. 37 Engine crane (1), lifting eye (2) and lift bar (3)

44. Connect the ground strap to the thermostat housing and route the electrical and purge harness underneath the throttle body and attach the connectors.
45. Connect the fuel vapor purge lines.
46. Properly route and connect the spark plug wires.
47. Connect the engine electrical harnesses.
48. Connect the brake booster vacuum hose, fuel line, cruise control and accelerator cables.
49. Install the A/C lines at the A/C compressor.
50. Connect A/C clutch electrical connector.
51. Install the power steering pump.
52. Install the alternator.
53. Install the accessory drive belt.
54. Connect the heater hoses to the engine.
55. Install the radiator and cooling fan assembly.
56. Install the A/C condenser.
57. Connect the A/C lines to the condenser.
58. Connect the cooling fan electrical connector.
59. Connect the windshield washer hose at the splice.
60. Install the coolant recovery container.
61. Install the upper radiator hose.
62. Install the throttle body air inlet duct and the air cleaner element cover.
63. Raise and support the vehicle.
64. Install transmission.
65. Install transmission bolts and tighten bolts to:
    - 7⁄16 in. transmission bolts and washers: 68 Nm (50 ft. lbs.)
    - Transmission to top of engine: 41 Nm (30 ft. lbs.)
    - Transmission to oil pan: 30 Nm (22 ft. lbs.)
66. Install drive shaft.
67. Install the ground strap to the floor pan above the right exhaust manifold flange.
68. Connect the front exhaust pipes to the exhaust manifolds and tighten the fasteners to 34 Nm (25 ft. lbs.).
69. Connect oil cooler lines and connect the oil pressure sensor and oil temperature sensor.
70. Install the power steering line support bracket at the radiator.
71. Install lower radiator hose.
72. Connect the cooling fan hydraulic lines.
73. Connect the A/C line to the fan shroud.
74. Install under body shield.
75. Lower vehicle.
76. Fill engine crankcase with the proper oil to the correct level.
77. Evacuate and recharge the air conditioning.
78. Fill the cooling system.
79. Fill power steering to proper level and purge the system.
80. Connect the negative battery cable.
81. Start the engine and run until operating temperature is obtained.
82. Turn engine off and inspect for leaks.
83. Recheck all fluid levels, fill as required.

EXHAUST MANIFOLD

REMOVAL & INSTALLATION

See Figure 38.

➡Care must be taken to protect the cylinder head covers powder coating from scrapes and abrasions. This procedure covers either the left or right exhaust manifold.

1. Disconnect negative battery cable.
2. When servicing the right exhaust manifold it is necessary to remove the upper oil dip stick tube fastener and position the tube aside.
3. Raise vehicle on hoist.
4. Loosen and remove the fasteners from the exhaust pipe to exhaust manifold.
5. Separate exhaust pipe from the exhaust manifold.
6. Lower the vehicle.
7. Disconnect the spark plug wires from the spark plugs and set aside.
8. Remove manifold heat shield from exhaust manifold.
9. Note the location of exhaust manifold studs and bolts for proper installation.
10. Remove studs and bolts attaching manifold to cylinder head and remove manifold.
11. Inspect exhaust manifolds for damage or cracks. Check for distortion of the cylinder head mounting surfaces with a straightedge and feeler gauge.

To install:

➡Care must be taken to protect the cylinder head covers powder coating from scrapes and abrasions. This procedure covers either the left or right exhaust manifold.

12. Install new gasket and install exhaust manifold Tighten attaching fasteners to 23 Nm (200 inch lbs.).
13. When installing right exhaust manifold, properly position the oil level indicator tube, install fastener and tighten to the cylinder head cover specification.
14. Install manifold heat shield and tighten attaching fasteners to 6 Nm (50 inch lbs.).
15. Install the spark plug wires.
16. Raise vehicle on hoist.

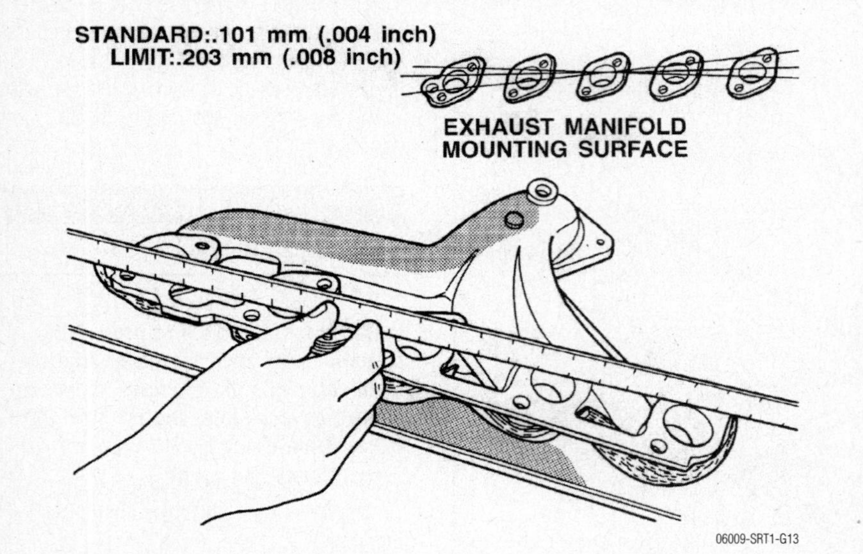

Fig. 38 Inspect exhaust manifolds for damage or cracks. Check for distortion of the cylinder head mounting surfaces with a straightedge and feeler gauge

17. Connect exhaust pipe to exhaust manifold. Tighten fasteners to 34 Nm (25 ft. lbs.).
18. Lower vehicle.
19. Connect negative battery cable.

FLYWHEEL

REMOVAL & INSTALLATION

1. Remove transmission clutch housing and clutch assembly.
2. Remove flywheel bolts and remove flywheel.

To install:

3. Clean flywheel bolts and apply thread sealer.
4. Install flywheel on engine and install flywheel bolts.
5. Tighten flywheel bolts to 74 Nm (55 ft. lbs.).
6. Install clutch assembly, clutch housing and transmission.

INTAKE MANIFOLD

REMOVAL & INSTALLATION

See Figure 39.

➡Care must be taken to protect the intake manifold powder coating from scrapes and abrasions.

1. Perform the fuel system pressure release procedure, before attempting any repairs.
2. Disconnect negative battery cable.
3. Disconnect throttle body air inlet duct, IAT sensor, CCV hose and remove air cleaner cover.
4. Disconnect throttle cable from throttle cam. Remove throttle cable from bracket and set aside.
5. Disconnect speed control cable from throttle cam and set aside.
6. Disconnect brake booster vacuum hose from the intake manifold and set aside.

⁂ WARNING

Wrap a shop towel around fuel Line to catch any gasoline spillage.

7. Disconnect fuel line quick connect fitting from fuel rail.
8. Disconnect the following electrical connectors:
   - Left cylinder head fuel injectors
   - MAP sensor
   - Engine Coolant Temperature (ECT) Sensor
   - Idle Speed Control Sensor (ISC)
   - Throttle Position Sensor (TPS)
   - Right cylinder head fuel injectors
9. Carefully separate the fuel injector harness push pins from the intake manifold.
10. Disconnect the purge solenoid hose from beneath the throttle body.
11. Disconnect CCV hoses from left and right cylinder head covers.

⁂ CAUTION

Care must be taken when removing the No. nine cylinder inside intake manifold bolt. Failure to do so may result in personal injury or possible damage.

12. Remove the intake manifold bolts and intake manifold.
13. Cover the intake manifold openings with a suitable cover when servicing to prevent any debris from entering cylinder heads.
14. Inspect manifold for cracks or other damage.
15. Inspect manifold sealing surfaces for damage.

To install:

⁂ CAUTION

When cleaning the intake manifold and cylinder head mating surfaces, do not use a metal scraper because the surfaces could be cut or ground. Instead, use a wooden or plastic scraper.

➡Care must be taken to protect the intake manifold powder coat from possible scrapes and abrasions.

16. Clean gasket surfaces and remove covering from intake manifold openings.
17. Carefully install the intake manifold gaskets and alignment pins.
18. Set the intake manifold in position on the engine. Install intake manifold bolts and tighten initially to 1 Nm (10 inch lbs.). Tighten bolts starting at the center and working outward to 11 Nm (95 inch lbs.).
19. Connect CCV hoses to left and right cylinder head covers.
20. Connect fuel line to fuel rail. Pull backward on the quick connect fitting to ensure complete insertion.
21. Connect the brake booster vacuum hose.
22. Connect speed control cable to throttle linkage.
23. Connect the throttle cable housing to the bracket and then attach the cable to the throttle linkage
24. Attach the purge solenoid hose to the underside of the throttle body housing.
25. Reconnect the following electrical connectors:
   - Left cylinder head fuel injectors
   - Engine Coolant Temperature (ECT) Sensor
   - MAP sensor
   - Idle Speed Control
   - Throttle Position Sensor
   - Right cylinder head fuel injectors
26. Install air cleaner cover assembly, connect throttle body air inlet hose, CCV hose and connect the Intake Air Temperature Sensor.
27. Connect negative battery cable.
28. With the Scan Tool, use the ASD

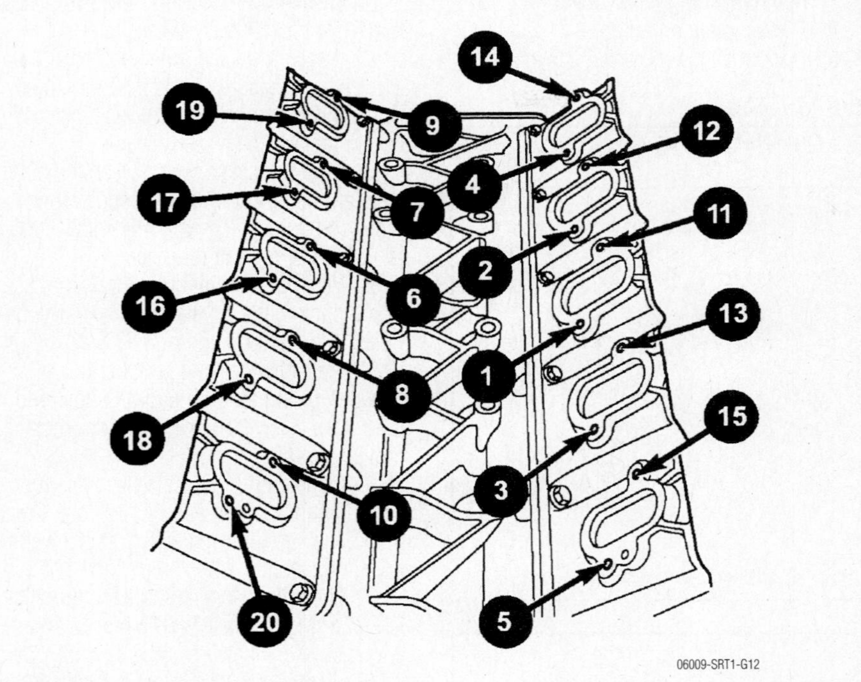

Fig. 39 Intake manifold bolt torque sequence

Fuel System Test to pressurize fuel system to check for leaks.

⁂ CAUTION

When using the ASD Fuel System Test, the Auto Shutdown (ASD) relay will remain energized for 7 minutes or until the ignition switch is turned to the OFF position, or Stop All Test is selected.

OIL PAN

REMOVAL & INSTALLATION

See Figures 40 and 41.

1. Disconnect the negative battery cable.
2. Disconnect engine oil indicator tube fastener from the right cylinder head cover.
3. Install engine lifting fixture tool 9363 and support tool.
4. Raise vehicle on hoist.
5. Remove the lower engine shield.
6. Drain engine oil.
7. Remove the crossmember bolts.

⁂ WARNING

Do not use any flame or plasma cutting equipment to cut the frame in this procedure. This is due to the inaccurate nature of the cut-line and the fact that the high temperatures achieved during flame or plasma cutting will change the metal characteristics and may weaken the frame and/or repair location.

8. Remove the welds using a grinder or equivalent and remove the crossmember.
9. Remove flywheel inspection cover.
10. Loosen engine mount through bolts.
11. Wiggle and separate the oil level indicator tube from the oil pan.

➡Careful positioning of the jack stand is necessary to prevent damage to other components.

12. Using lifting fixture tool 9363 and support tool, raise the front of the engine.
13. Remove transmission to oil pan fasteners.
14. Remove oil pan bolts and remove oil pan.

➡Clean and inspect oil pan gasket. The pan gasket can be used again if in good condition.

To install:

15. Clean gasket surfaces. Inspect oil pan gasket. Replace as necessary.
16. Apply a 1/8 inch bead of Mopar Engine RTV at the two joints between the cylinder block to timing chain case cover and the two joints between the rear main seal retainer and engine block.
17. Position oil pan and gasket to engine block, seat the oil level indicator tube in the oil pan and hand start all fasteners.
18. Tighten the transmission to oil pan bolts in finger tight.
19. Torque 5/16-18 oil pan bolts to 23 Nm (200 inch lbs.). Torque 1/4-20 oil pan bolts to 11 Nm (95 inch lbs.).
20. Torque transmission to oil pan bolts to 23 Nm (200 inch lbs.).
21. Lower the engine.
22. Install and tighten engine mount through bolts to 102 Nm (75 ft. lbs.).
23. Install flywheel inspection cover.

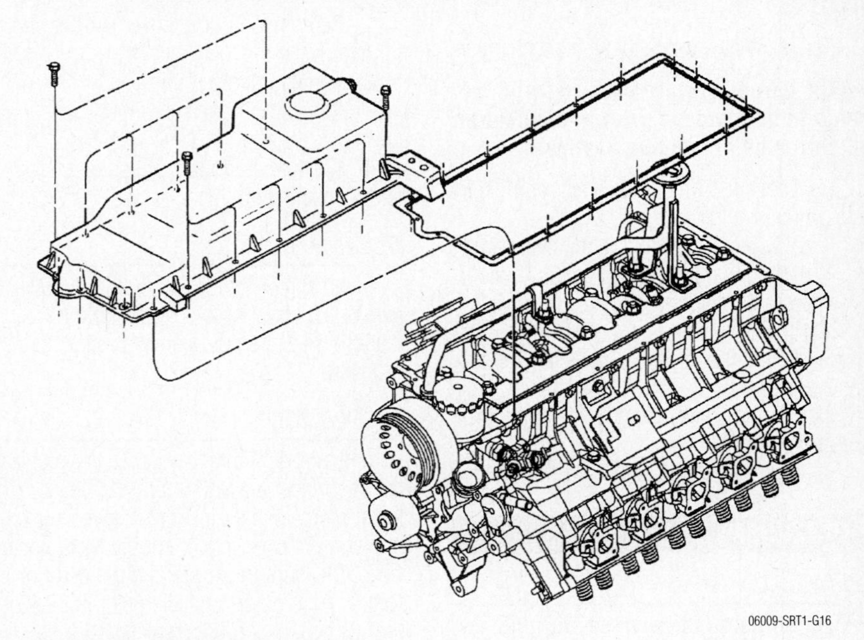

Fig. 40 Oil pan installation

24. Install the crossmember bolts. Tighten the bolts to 61 Nm (45 ft. lbs.).

25. Remove all OEM e-coat within 51 mm (2.0 in.) of the weld on both the crossmember and the frame.

⁂ WARNING

Shield the surrounding area and components from exposure to the welding spatter and heat.

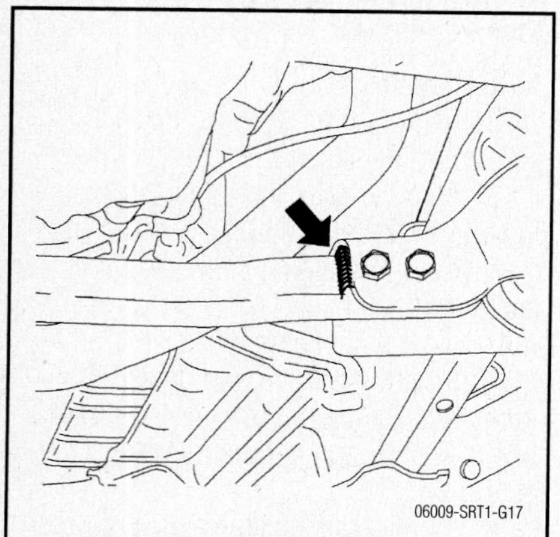

Fig. 41 Front crossmember weld

➡Gas Metal Arc Welding Process: Butt joints; apply two layers (passes) of weld metal. First pass should only fill approximately ½ the thickness. Vertical position welds, maintain electrode wire at leading edge of weld puddle while traveling down hill to produce maximum penetration into the sleeve. These techniques work for FCAW as well.

26. Apply new welds to the crossmember.

➡Any burned surface coatings will need to be removed prior to application of corrosion preventive coatings.

27. Dress the welded area and apply corrosion resistant coatings.

   a. Apply etch-primer to the repair area.

   b. Apply a durable top coat to the outside of the repair area.

28. Lower vehicle.

29. Install the oil level indicator tube fastener.

30. Fill the crankcase with the correct oil to proper level.

31. Start the engine and inspect for leaks.

OIL PUMP

REMOVAL

➡The oil pump is serviced with the timing chain cover.

1. Remove timing chain cover.
2. Disassemble oil pump.
3. Inspect oil pump parts.

DISASSEMBLY

See Figures 42 and 43.

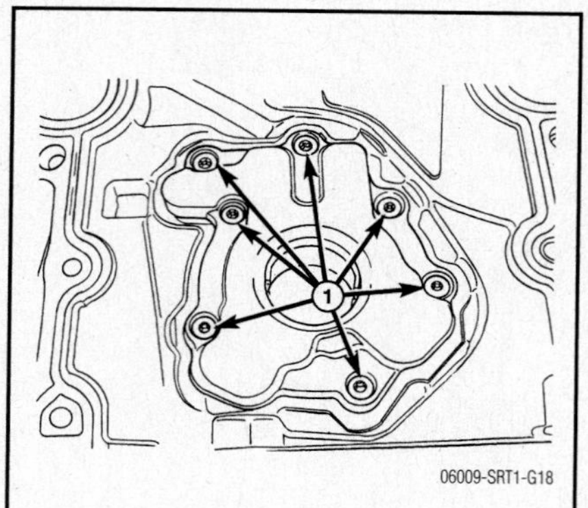

Fig. 42 Oil pump cover screws

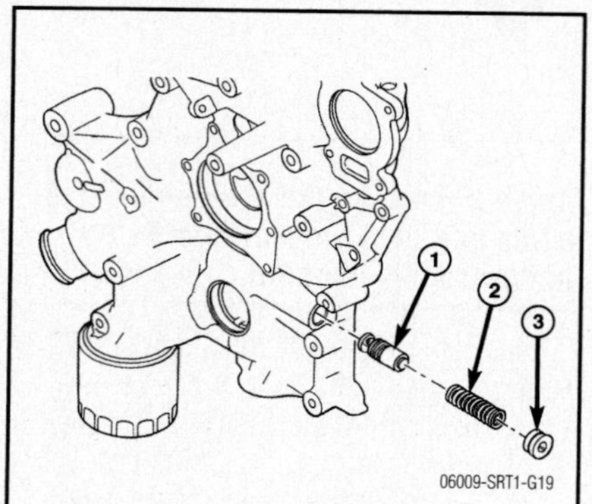

Fig. 43 Relief valve and spring

1. Remove oil pump cover screws and lift off cover.
2. Remove pump rotors.
3. Remove oil pressure relief valve and spring.
4. Wash all parts in a suitable solvent and inspect carefully for damage or wear.

CLEANING

Clean all parts thoroughly. Mating surface of the chain case cover should be smooth. Replace pump cover if scratched or grooved.

INSPECTION

1. Lay a straightedge across the pump cover surface. If a 0.076 mm (0.003 in.) feeler gauge can be inserted between cover and straight edge, cover should be replaced.
2. Measure thickness and diameter of rotors. If the outer rotor diameter is 82.45 mm (3.246 in.) or less, replace rotor set and.
3. If either rotor thickness measures 18.92 mm (0.744 in.) or less, replace rotor set.
4. Measure clearance between outer rotor and case. If measurement is 0.19 mm (0.007 in.) or more, and outer rotor is within specification, replace chain case cover.
5. Measure clearance between the outer rotor and inner rotor. If clearance between inner and outer rotors is 0.150 mm (0.006 in.) or more, replace rotor set.
6. Place a straightedge across the face of the chain case cover, in between the bolt holes. If a feeler gauge of 0.077 mm (0.003 in.) or more can be inserted between rotors and the straightedge, and the rotors are within specification, replace the case cover.
7. Inspect oil pressure relief valve for scoring and free operation in its bore. Small marks may be removed with 400 grit wet or dry sandpaper.
8. The relief valve spring has a free length of approximately 68.7 mm (2.70 in.) and should test between 10.2 kg and 12.4 kg (22.5 and 27.5 lbs.) when compressed to 57 mm (2.24 in.). Replace spring that fails to meet specifications.
9. If oil pressure is low and pump is within specifications, inspect for worn engine bearings or other reasons for oil pressure loss.

ASSEMBLY

1. Assemble pump using new parts as required.
2. Install spring onto oil pressure relief valve.
3. Lubricate oil pressure relief valve and spring with clean engine oil.
4. Install oil pressure relief valve and spring.
5. Inspect relief valve plug o-ring. Replace as necessary. Torque plug to 34 Nm (25 ft. lbs.)
6. Install pump rotors with chamfer side to the inside of chain case cover.
7. Install oil pump cover and screws. Tighten cover screws to 23 Nm (200 inch lbs.).
8. Prime oil pump before installation by filling rotor cavity with engine oil.

INSTALLATION

1. Assemble oil pump.
2. Prime oil pump before installation by filling rotor cavity with the correct engine oil.
3. Install timing chain cover.
4. Install NEW oil filter.
5. Fill the crankcase with the correct engine oil to the proper level.

PISTON AND RING

POSITIONING

See Figures 44 and 45.

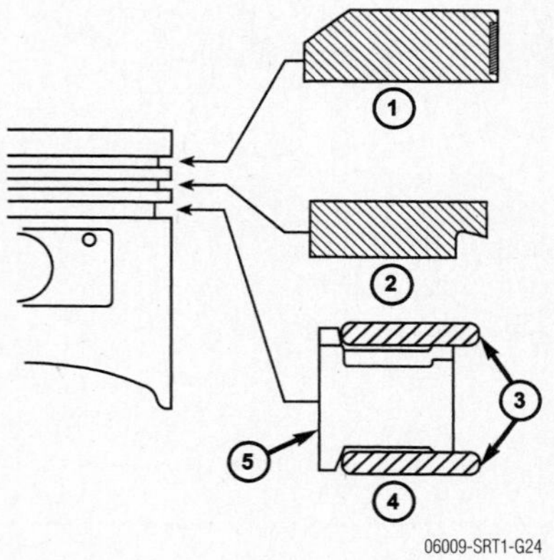

Fig. 44 Piston ring installation

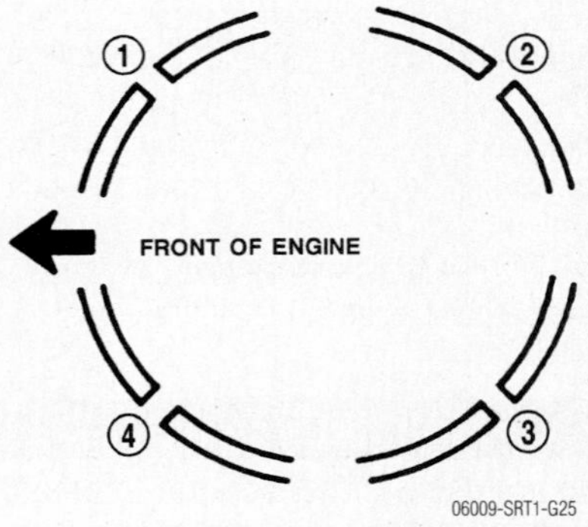

Fig. 45 Piston ring gap positioning

REAR MAIN SEAL

REMOVAL & INSTALLATION

1. Remove the transmission.
2. Remove the clutch and flywheel.

➡The oil seal and retainer are serviced as an assembly.

3. Remove the seal retainer bolts from the cylinder block and oil pan.
4. Remove the oil seal and retainer assembly.

To install:

5. Clean the engine block and retainer. Make sure the surfaces are clean and free of oil.
6. Install Special Tool 9060 (seal guide) onto the end of crankshaft. Align the hole in the tool with the dowel pin on the crankshaft.
7. Carefully position the retainer/oil seal on the block. Tighten the retainer bolts to 11 Nm (95 inch lbs.).
8. Install the flywheel and clutch.
9. Install the transmission.

ROCKER ARMS/SHAFTS

REMOVAL & INSTALLATION

See Figure 46.

➡Before replacing parts, inspect all related valvetrain components for damage to prevent engine misfire.

1. Remove cylinder head cover(s).
2. Remove two rocker pedestal bolts per each cylinder.
3. Remove rocker arm assemblies as a pair.
4. If rocker arm assemblies are disassembled for cleaning or replacement, reassemble rocker arms in their original position.

To install:

➡Before replacing parts, inspect all related valvetrain components for damage to prevent engine misfire.

5. Install rocker arm and pedestal assemblies into position. Ensure push rods are seated properly under each rocker arm. Tighten rocker arm bolts to 35 Nm (26 ft. lbs.).

✲✲ WARNING

The rocker arm pedestal bolts should be torqued down slowly. Allow 20 minutes tappet bleed down time after installation of the rocker bolts before engine operation.

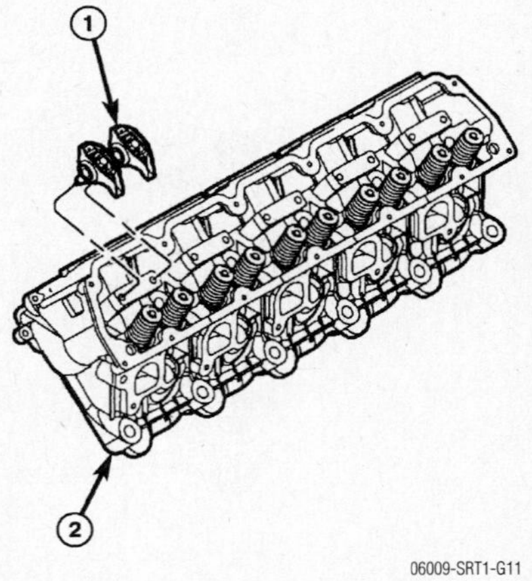

Fig. 46 Rocker arms

6. Install cylinder head cover(s).

TIMING CHAIN, SPROCKETS, AND FRONT COVER

REMOVAL & INSTALLATION

See Figures 47 through 49.

1. Disconnect negative battery cable.
2. Disconnect throttle body air inlet duct at the throttle body, CCV hose, disconnect the IAT sensor and remove air cleaner housing cover.
3. Remove the oil indicator tube fastener at the right cylinder head cover.
4. Raise and support the vehicle.
5. Remove the lower engine shield.
6. Drain cooling system.
7. Drain engine oil and remove oil filter.
8. Drain power steering.
9. Disconnect the cooling fan return hose at radiator fan.
10. Disconnect the radiator fan pressure hose to power steering rack.
11. Disconnect the power steering hose to power steering pump.
12. Separate the A/C hose from the radiator fan module.
13. Remove the lower radiator hoses.
14. Remove the front frame cross member.
15. Remove the flywheel inspection cover.

➡Capture and properly dispose of any fuel spillage.

16. Disconnect oil cooler line at the timing cover using Special Tool 9005.
17. Separate the oil cooler coolant hose from the timing cover.
18. Wiggle oil indicator tube free of oil pan.
19. Loosen engine mounts.

➡Care must be taken not to damage the A/C compressor when placing the jack stand and raising the engine.

20. Raise and support the engine with a jack stand at the A/C bracket.
21. Remove the engine oil pan.
22. Lower the engine and remove the jackstand.
23. Remove the oil pump pick up tube.
24. Remove accessory drive belt.
25. Remove A/C compressor mounting bolts. Reposition A/C compressor. Do not disconnect A/C lines.

26. Disconnect the power steering line support bracket at the radiator.
27. Lower the vehicle.
28. Remove the upper radiator hose and coolant recovery container.
29. Remove the cooling fan module.
30. Remove the upper idler pulley.
31. Remove power steering pump mounting bolts. Reposition power steering pump aside. Do not disconnect power steering lines.
32. Remove the alternator.
33. Disconnect the heater hose at the timing cover.
34. Disconnect the ground wire at the thermostat housing.

➡Do not remove the camshaft position sensor from the timing cover.

35. Disconnect the camshaft sensor wiring harness connector.
36. Disconnect engine coolant temperature (ECT) sensor connector.
37. Remove crankshaft pulley and damper.
38. Remove the timing cover.
39. Rotate crankshaft until timing marks are aligned.
40. Remove the camshaft sprocket attaching bolts.
41. Remove the timing chain with camshaft sprocket.
42. Install Special Tool 8194 into end of crankshaft. Lubricate the end of Special Tool 8194 with wheel bearing grease or equivalent.

➡Lubricate the threads of Special Tool 5048 using Mopar® Nickel Anti-seize Compound or equivalent, before beginning crankshaft sprocket removal.

43. Using Special Tools 9056 and 5048, remove crankshaft sprocket.

To install:

44. Position a new crankshaft sprocket on the crankshaft with timing mark facing out. Align crankshaft keyway with slot in crankshaft sprocket.

➡Lubricate the threads of Special Tool 9055 using Mopar® Nickel Anti-seize Compound or equivalent, before beginning crankshaft sprocket installation.

45. Install the crankshaft sprocket using Special Tool 9055.
46. Rotate the crankshaft sprocket so the timing mark is at the 12 o'clock position.
47. Place the timing chain around the camshaft sprocket and place the timing mark to the 6 o'clock position.

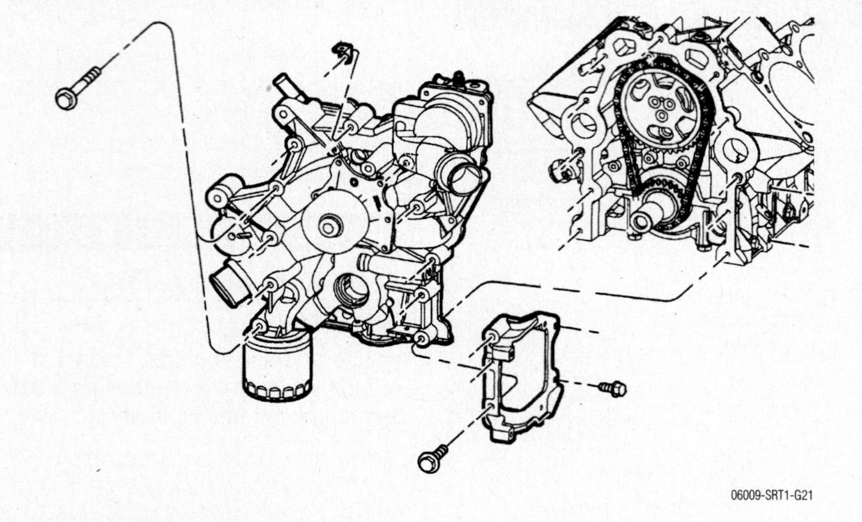

Fig. 47 Front cover removal

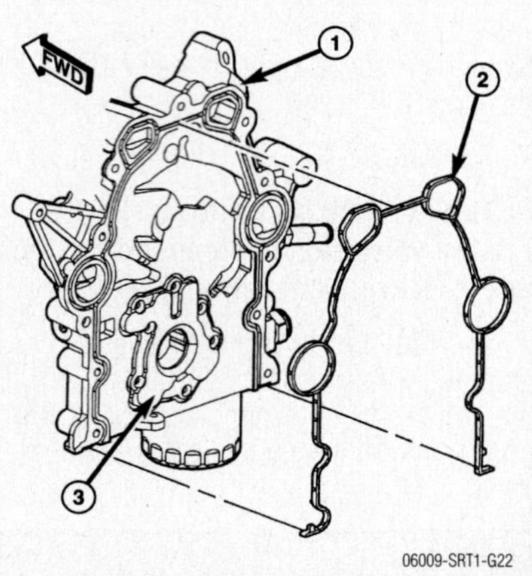

Fig. 48 Front cover (1) installation, (2) is the gasket, (3) is the oil pump

48. Place the timing chain around crankshaft sprocket and install the camshaft sprocket into position.
49. Using straight edge, check alignment of timing marks.
50. Install the camshaft sprocket bolts. Tighten the bolts to 23 Nm (200 inch lbs.).
51. Rotate crankshaft 2 revolutions. Timing marks should line up. If timing marks do not line up, remove cam sprocket and realign.
52. Measure camshaft end play. If not within specifications, install new thrust plate.

WARNING

Do not use a metal scraper to clean aluminum sealing surfaces, as dam-

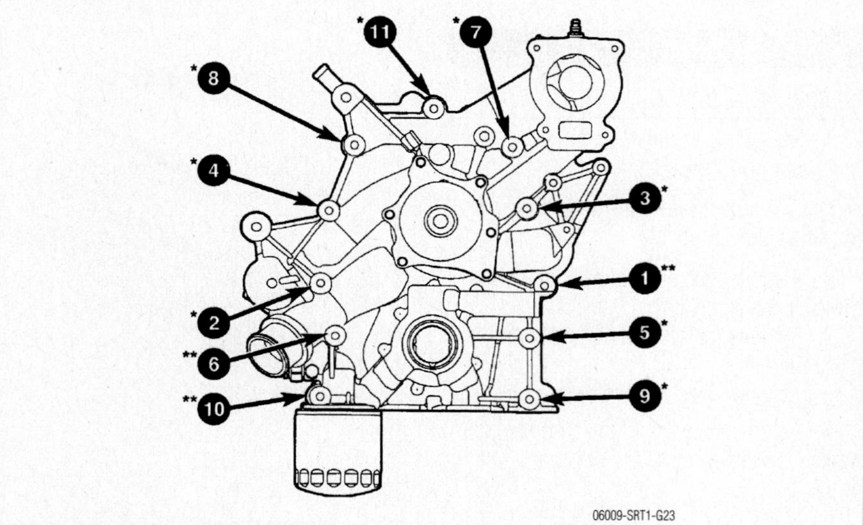

Fig. 49 Front cover fastener torque sequence

age to surfaces may occur. Use only a plastic scraper and Mopar® Brake Parts Cleaner or the equivalent.

53. Be sure mating surfaces of chain case cover and cylinder block are clean and free from burrs. Crankshaft oil seal must be removed to insure correct oil pump engagement.
54. Install the timing chain cover gasket.
55. Position the oil pump inner rotor mating flats in the same position as the crankshaft drive flats.
56. Install the timing chain cover onto crankshaft. Ensure the oil pump is engaged on the crankshaft correctly or severe damage may result.
57. Hand start bolts No.1 and No.2.
58. Loosely install A/C compressor mounting bracket.
59. Hand start remaining timing chain cover bolts.
60. Torque timing chain cover bolts in the sequence shown in to 23 Nm (200 inch lbs.).
61. Torque A/C compressor mounting bracket bolts to 23 Nm (200 inch lbs.).
62. Install crankshaft oil seal.
63. Raise vehicle on hoist.
64. Install oil pump pick up tube using a new o-ring. Torque ¼-20 bolt to 11 Nm (95 inch lbs.). Torque 5⁄16-18 nuts to 23 Nm (200 inch lbs.).
65. Support the engine with a jackstand.
66. Install oil pan and drain plug.
67. Remove the jackstand.
68. Tighten the engine mount to frame nuts to 102 Nm (75 ft. lbs.).
69. Connect the oil cooler coolant hose to the timing cover.
70. Connect the oil cooler line.
71. Install the lower radiator hose.
72. Install the flywheel inspection cover.
73. Install the front frame cross member.
74. Lower vehicle.
75. Position the compressor and install A/C compressor mounting bolts. Torque bolts to 23 Nm (200 inch lbs.).
76. Connect heater hose at timing cover.
77. Install crankshaft damper and pulley.
78. Install alternator. Connect electrical connectors.
79. Install the idler pulley.
80. Connect the camshaft position sensor wiring harness connector.
81. Connect engine coolant temperature (ECT) sensor wiring harness connector.
82. Install power steering pump mounting bolts.
83. Install accessory drive belt.
84. Install the radiator fan assembly.
85. Raise and support the vehicle.
86. Connect the hydraulic lines to the fan assembly and steering rack then connect the A/C hose to the fan shroud.
87. Install a new oil filter.
88. Lower the vehicle.
89. Install upper radiator hose and connect the ground wire at the thermostat housing.
90. Install air cleaner housing cover assembly, connect throttle body air inlet duct, IAT sensor and CCV hose.
91. Fill and purge air from the power steering system.
92. Fill engine crankcase with proper oil to correct level.
93. Fill and purge air from the cooling system.
94. Connect negative battery cable.
95. Start the vehicle and inspect for leaks.
96. Install the lower engine shield.

FUEL — GASOLINE FUEL INJECTION SYSTEM

FUEL SYSTEM SERVICE PRECAUTIONS

Safety is the most important factor when performing not only fuel system maintenance but any type of maintenance. Failure to conduct maintenance and repairs in a safe manner may result in serious personal injury or death. Maintenance and testing of the vehicle's fuel system components can be accomplished safely and effectively by adhering to the following rules and guidelines.

- To avoid the possibility of fire and personal injury, always disconnect the negative battery cable unless the repair or test procedure requires that battery voltage be applied.
- Always relieve the fuel system pressure prior to disconnecting any fuel system component (injector, fuel rail, pressure regulator, etc.), fitting or fuel line connection. Exercise extreme caution whenever relieving fuel system pressure to avoid exposing skin, face and eyes to fuel spray. Please be advised that fuel under pressure may penetrate the skin or any part of the body that it contacts.
- Always place a shop towel or cloth around the fitting or connection prior to loosening to absorb any excess fuel due to spillage. Ensure that all fuel spillage (should it occur) is quickly removed from engine surfaces. Ensure that all fuel soaked cloths or towels are deposited into a suitable waste container.
- Always keep a dry chemical (Class B) fire extinguisher near the work area.
- Do not allow fuel spray or fuel vapors to come into contact with a spark or open flame.
- Always use a back-up wrench when loosening and tightening fuel line connection fittings. This will prevent unnecessary stress and torsion to fuel line piping.
- Always replace worn fuel fitting O-rings with new Do not substitute fuel hose or equivalent where fuel pipe is installed.

Before servicing the vehicle, make sure to also refer to the precautions in the beginning of this section as well.

RELIEVING FUEL SYSTEM PRESSURE

1. Remove fuel fill cap.
2. Remove fuel pump relay from Power Distribution Center (PDC). For location of relay, refer to label on underside of PDC cover.
3. Start and run engine until it stalls.
4. Attempt restarting engine until it will no longer run.
5. Turn ignition key to OFF position.

CAUTION

Steps 1, 2, 3 and 4 must be performed to relieve high pressure fuel from within fuel rail. Do not attempt to use following steps to relieve this pressure as excessive fuel will be forced into a cylinder chamber.

6. Unplug connector from any fuel injector.
7. Attach one end of a jumper wire with alligator clips (18 gauge or smaller) to either injector terminal.
8. Connect other end of jumper wire to positive side of battery.
9. Connect one end of a second jumper wire to remaining injector terminal.

CAUTION

Powering an injector for more than a few seconds will permanently damage the injector.

10. Momentarily touch other end of jumper wire to negative terminal of battery for no more than a few seconds.

11. Place a rag or towel below fuel line quick-connect fitting at fuel rail.

12. Disconnect quick-connect fitting at fuel rail. Refer to Quick-Connect Fittings.

13. Return fuel pump relay to PDC.

14. One or more Diagnostic Trouble Codes (DTCs) may have been stored in PCM memory due to fuel pump relay removal. The DRBT scan tool must be used to erase a DTC.

FUEL PUMP/FILTER MODULE

REMOVAL & INSTALLATION

See Figures 50 and 51.

1. Disconnect and separate fuel vent line from fuel fill bezel.
2. Disconnect electrical connector at top of fuel pump module. To disconnect electrical connector:
    a. Push upward on red colored tab to unlock.
    b. Push on black colored tab while removing connector.
3. Disconnect necessary emission vent lines from leak pump and EVAP canister.
4. Disconnect fuel supply line from fuel pump module.
5. Disconnect necessary emission vent lines from check valves and/or at top of tank.
6. Loosen clamps and disconnect rubber fuel hoses at tank fittings.
7. Support tank with a hydraulic jack.
8. Remove two fuel tank strap nuts and remove both tank support straps.
9. Continue to lower tank for removal.
10. Note rotational position of module before attempting removal. An indexing arrow is located on top of module for this purpose.
11. Position Special Tool 9340 into notches on outside edge of lockring.
12. Install ½ inch drive breaker bar to tool 9340.
13. Rotate breaker bar counter-clockwise to remove lockring.
14. Remove lockring. The module will spring up slightly when lockring is removed.
15. Remove module from fuel tank. Be careful not to bend float arm while removing.
16. Remove filter by carefully prying 2 lock tabs at bottom of module with 2 screwdrivers. Filter is snapped to module.
17. Clean bottom of pump module.

To install:

18. Snap new filter to bottom of module. Be sure o-ring is in correct position.

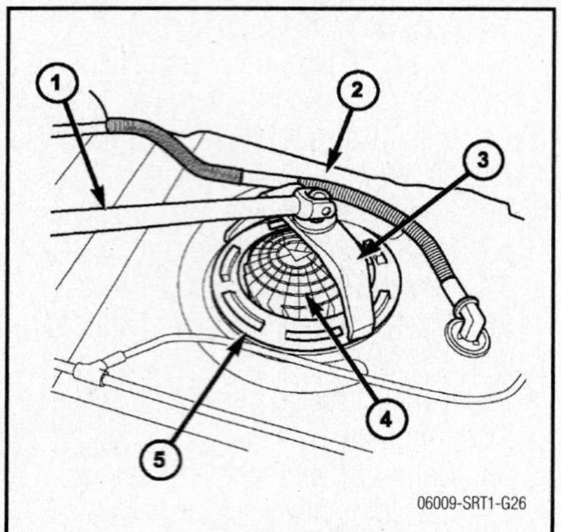

Fig. 50 Removing the module lockring

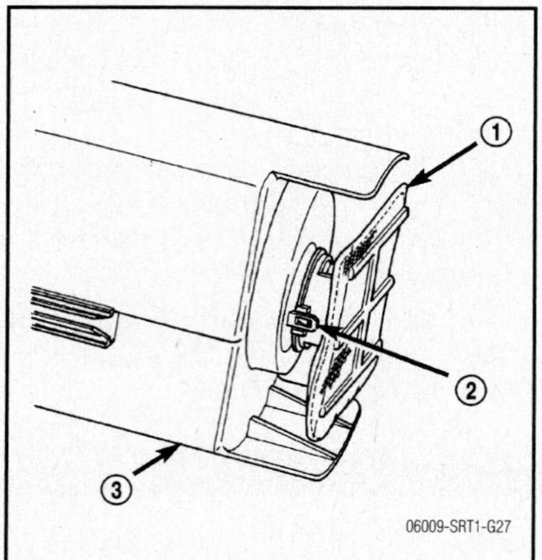

Fig. 51 Fuel filter, (2) Lock tabs, (3) Module

19. Using a new seal (gasket), position fuel pump module into opening in fuel tank.
20. Position lockring over top of fuel pump module.
21. Rotate module until embossed alignment arrow points to center alignment mark. This step must be performed to prevent float from contacting side of fuel tank. Also be sure fuel fitting on top of pump module is pointed to drivers side of vehicle.
22. Install Special Tool 9340 to lockring.
23. Install ½ inch drive breaker into Special Tool 9340.
24. Tighten lockring (clockwise) until all seven notches have engaged.
25. Disconnect clamps and remove rubber fuel fill hose and fuel vent hose at fuel fill tube. Install these two hoses to two fuel tank fittings. Rotate hoses until paint marks on hoses line up with alignment marks. Tighten both clamps.
26. Position fuel tank to hydraulic jack.
27. Raise tank until positioned near body.
28. Continue raising tank until positioned snug to body.
29. Install and position both tank support straps. Install two fuel tank strap nuts and tighten. Torque to 30 ft. lbs. (41 Nm).

➡Tighten rear strap nut first.

30. Connect rubber fill and vent hoses to fuel fill tube and tighten clamps.
31. Connect electrical connector to top of fuel pump module.
32. Connect necessary emission vent lines to leak pump and EVAP canister.
33. Connect fuel supply line to fuel pump module.
34. Connect necessary emission vent lines from check valves and/or at top of tank.
35. Connect fuel vent line to fuel fill bezel.
36. Fill fuel tank with fuel.
37. Start engine and check for fuel leaks near top of module.

FUEL INJECTORS

REMOVAL & INSTALLATION

1. Release fuel system pressure.
2. Remove the battery cover and disconnect negative battery cable.
3. Remove the air cleaner assembly.
4. Disconnect the electrical connector to the MAP sensor and Coolant Temperature sensor.
5. Disconnect the electrical connector to the TPS and Idle Air Control.
6. Remove the wiring harness from the wiring clips under the throttle body.
7. Disconnect the electrical connector from the fuel injectors.
8. Disconnect the fuel line quick connector.
9. Remove the bolts for the fuel rail.
10. Pull fuel rail and injectors straight up and out of the intake manifold.
11. Move the fuel rail forward and out from under the intake manifold and throttle body.
12. Remove the fuel injector from the fuel rail.

To install:

13. Install the fuel injectors to the fuel rail.
14. Install fuel rail under throttle body.
15. Apply a light coating of clean engine oil to the O-ring on the nozzle end of each injector.
16. Insert fuel injector nozzles into openings in intake manifold. Seat the injectors in place. Tighten fuel rail bolts to 12 Nm (105 inch lbs.).
17. Attach electrical connectors to fuel injectors.

18. Connect the electrical connector to the MAP sensor and Coolant Temperature sensor.

19. Connect the electrical connector to the TPS and Idle Air Control.

20. Install the wiring harness to the wiring clips under the throttle body.

21. Connect fuel supply tube to fuel rail.

22. Install the negative battery cable and install the battery cover.

23. Install the air cleaner assembly.

24. Use the DRBIIIT scan tool ASD Fuel System Test to pressurize the fuel system. Check for leaks.

HEATING & AIR CONDITIONING SYSTEM

HEATER CORE

REMOVAL & INSTALLATION

See Figures 52 and 53.

1. Recover the refrigerant from the refrigerant system.
2. Drain the engine cooling system.
3. Disconnect and isolate the negative battery cable.
4. Disconnect the A/C liquid line and the A/C accumulator from the A/C evaporator.
5. Disconnect the heater hoses from the heater core tubes.
6. Remove the powertrain control module (PCM) to gain access to the two nuts that secure the HVAC housing to the engine compartment side of the dash panel and remove the nuts.

➡The PCM is located in the engine compartment attached to the dash panel. To avoid possible voltage spike damage to the PCM, ignition key must be off, and negative battery cable must be disconnected before unplugging PCM connectors.

c. Disconnect negative battery cable at battery.

d. Remove cover over electrical connectors. Cover snaps onto PCM.

e. Carefully unplug the three 32-way connectors (four 38-way connectors if equipped with NGC) from PCM.

f. Remove three PCM mounting bolts and remove PCM from vehicle.

7. Disconnect and isolate the negative battery cable.
8. Remove the left a-pillar trim.
9. Remove the instrument panel top cover.
10. Disconnect the headliner wire harness connector located at the a-pillar.
11. Using a trim stick C-4755 or equivalent, from the notch on the bottom, remove the left instrument panel side cover.
12. Remove the left cowl trim panel.
13. Position the front wheels straight ahead.
14. Disconnect the negative (ground) cable from the battery.
15. Remove the two switches from the steering wheel.
16. From the underside of the steering wheel, remove the two screws that secure the driver airbag to the steering wheel armature.

⁂ WARNING

Do not pull on the horn switch feed pigtail wire to disengage the connector from the driver airbag housing or to disconnect the horn switch to steering wheel wire harness connection. Improper pulling on this pigtail wire or connection can result in damage to the horn switch membrane or feed circuit.

17. Pull the driver airbag away from the steering wheel far enough to access the three electrical connections on the back of the airbag housing.
18. Disconnect the steering wheel wire harness connector for the horn switch from the horn switch feed pigtail wire connector, which is located on the back of the driver airbag housing.

⁂ WARNING

Do not pull on the clockspring pigtail wires or pry on the connector insulator to disengage the connector from the driver airbag inflator connector receptacle. Improper removal of these pigtail wires and their connector insulators can result in damage to the airbag circuits or connector insulators.

19. The clockspring driver airbag pigtail wire connectors are secured by integral latches to the airbag inflator connector receptacles, which are located on the back of the driver airbag housing. Depress the latches on each side of the connector insulator and pull the insulators straight out from the airbag inflator to disconnect them from the connector receptacles.
20. Remove the driver airbag from the steering wheel.
21. Remove the steering wheel with special tool CJ98-1 or an appropriate steering wheel puller.

⁂ WARNING

Ensure the puller bolts are fully engaged into the steering wheel and not into the clockspring, before attempting to remove the wheel. Failure to do so may damage the steering wheel/clockspring.

22. Remove the steering column opening cover.
23. Remove the tilt lever.
24. Remove the column shrouds.
25. Remove the clock spring.
26. Disconnect the wiring harness to the column.
27. Remove the shift cable from the column shift lever actuator.
28. Release the shift cable from the column bracket and remove it from the bracket.
29. Remove the SKIM module in order to disconnect the electrical connector.
30. Remove the upper steering shaft coupler bolt.
31. Separate the shaft from the coupler.
32. Remove the brake light switch and discard.
33. Remove the four steering column mounting nuts.
34. Remove the steering column assembly from the vehicle.
35. Remove the two bolts that secure the steering column support bracket to the instrument panel.
36. Remove the park brake release handle actuator rod.
37. Disconnect the instrument panel wire harness connector located above the brake pedal from the bulkhead wire harness connector.
38. Using a trim stick C-4755 or equivalent, from the notch on the bottom, remove the left instrument panel side cover.
39. Remove the left cowl trim panel.
40. Remove the two screws that secure the lower driver side instrument panel bezel to the instrument panel.
41. Using a trim stick C-4755 or equivalent, disengage the retaining clips that secure the top of the lower driver side instrument panel bezel to the instrument panel.

42. Tilt the top of the lower driver side instrument panel bezel downward and, If equipped, disconnect the wire harness connector from the adjustable pedal switch.

43. Remove the lower driver side instrument panel bezel from the lower retaining hooks and remove the bezel.

44. Remove the three bolts that secure the left side of the instrument panel to the dash panel.

45. If equipped, remove the 4WD gear shift boot.

46. If equipped with a manual transmission, remove the transmission gear shift lever extension.

47. Using a trim stick C-4755 or equivalent, disengage the retaining tabs that secure the manual transmission gear shift boot or storage bin (depending on application) to the floor console and remove the boot or storage bin.

48. Remove the three inserts from the floor console.

49. Remove the three bolts that secure the floor console to the floor panel.

50. Lift up the rear of the floor console to clear the gear shift lever, if equipped.

51. Slide the floor console rearward and remove it from the instrument panel.

52. Using a trim stick or another suitable wide flat-bladed tool, gently pry each side of the ACM cover away from the instrument panel at each side of the center bracket on the floor panel transmission tunnel far enough to disengage the two snap clip retainers from the instrument panel receptacles.

53. Remove the ACM cover from the instrument panel.

54. Remove the two bolts that secure the instrument panel to the center of the floor panel.

55. Using a trim stick C-4755 or equivalent, disengage the retaining tabs of the cowl trim panel from the retainer clips in the door sill.

56. Pull the cowl trim panel rearward and remove it from the vehicle.

57. Disconnect the two instrument panel wire harness connectors from the two body wire harness connectors located on the right side of the cowl panel.

58. Disconnect the antenna coaxial cable connector from the radio coaxial cable connector located on the right side of the cowl panel.

59. Remove the one bolt that secures the instrument panel to the HVAC housing below the glove box opening.

60. Using a trim stick C-4755 or equivalent, from the notch on the bottom, remove the right instrument panel side cover from the instrument panel.

61. Remove the right a-pillar trim.

62. Remove the three bolts that secure the right side instrument panel bracket to the dash panel.

63. Remove the four screws that secure the instrument panel to the top of the cowl panel.

64. Remove the two bolts that secure the instrument panel to the top of the cowl panel.

65. With the help of an assistant, lift the instrument panel up and off of the cowl panel and remove the instrument panel from the vehicle.

66. If required, remove the four plastic screws inserts from the top of the cowl panel.

67. Remove the bolt that secures the HVAC housing to the floor bracket.

68. Remove the two nuts that secure the HVAC housing to the passenger compartment side of the dash panel.

69. Pull the HVAC housing assembly rearward and remove the housing assembly from the passenger compartment.

70. If required, remove the fresh air inlet from the dash panel.

71. Remove the foam seal from the heater core tubes.

72. If equipped with the dual zone heating-A/C system, remove the linkage rod to gain access to the heater core.

73. Remove the two screws that secure the heater core tube bracket to the HVAC housing and remove the bracket.

74. Carefully pull the heater core out of the front of the HVAC housing.

75. Inspect all foam seals and replace as required.

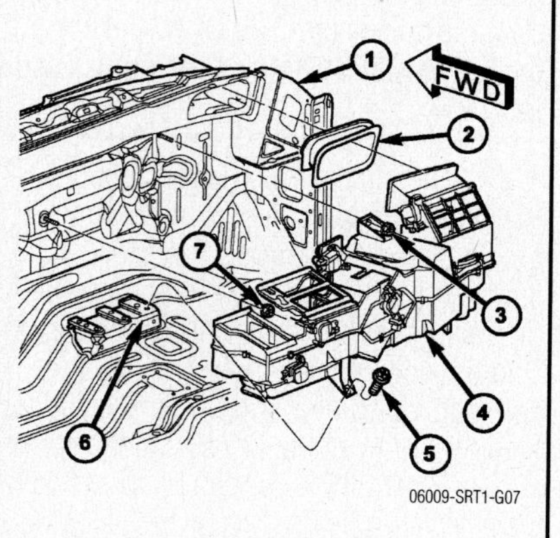

Fig. 52 HVAC housing removal. (1) Dash panel, (2) air inlet, (3) Retaining nut, (4) Housing, (5) Retaining bolt, (6) Floor bracket, (7) Retaining nut

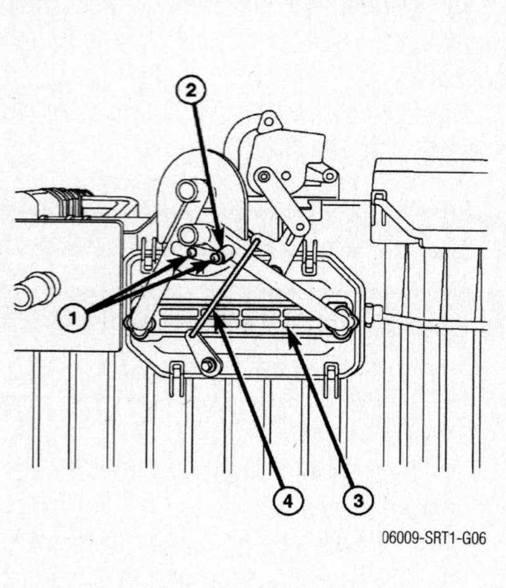

Fig. 53 Heater core

To install:

76. Carefully install the heater core into the front of the HVAC housing.

77. Position the heater core tube bracket onto the HVAC housing.

78. Install the two screws that secures the heater core bracket to the HVAC housing. Tighten the screws to 2.2 Nm (20 inch lbs.).

79. If equipped with the dual zone heating-A/C system, install the linkage rod.

80. Install the foam seal onto the heater core tubes.

➡If the heater core is being replaced, flush the cooling system.

81. If removed, install the fresh air inlet onto the dash panel.

82. Position the HVAC housing assembly into the passenger compartment with the mounting studs and the condensate drain tube in their proper locations in the dash panel.

83. Install the two nuts that secure the HVAC housing to the passenger compartment side of the dash panel. Tighten the nuts to 6.2 Nm (55 inch lbs.).

84. Install the bolt that secures the HVAC housing to the floor bracket. Tighten the bolt to 6.2 Nm (55 inch lbs.).

85. If removed, install the four plastic screw inserts into the top of the cowl panel.

86. With the help of an assistant, position the instrument panel into the vehicle and install the right side guide pin and the left side guide hook to the sides of the cowl panel.

87. Install the two bolts that secure the instrument panel to the top of the cowl panel. Tighten the bolts to 12 Nm (9 ft. lbs.).

88. Install the four screws that secure the instrument panel to the top of the cowl panel. Tighten the screws to 2.2 Nm (20 inch lbs.).

89. Install the three bolts that secure the right side instrument panel bracket to the cowl panel. Tighten the bolts to 12 Nm (9 ft. lbs.).

90. Install the right a-pillar trim.

91. Install the right instrument panel side cover.

92. Install the one bolt that secures the instrument panel to the HVAC housing below the glove box opening. Tighten the bolt securely.

93. Connect the radio coaxial cable connector to the antenna coaxial cable connector located on the right side of the cowl panel.

94. Connect the two instrument panel wire harness connectors to the two body wire harness connectors located on the right side of the cowl panel.

95. Install the right cowl trim panel.

96. Install the two bolts that secure the instrument panel to the center of the floor panel. Tighten the bolts to 12 Nm (9 ft. lbs.).

97. Connect the air bag control module electrical connector.

98. Install the air bag control module cover, if equipped.

99. Install the floor console, if equipped.

100. Install the three bolts that secure the left side of the instrument panel to the dash panel. Tighten the bolts to 12 Nm (9 ft. lbs.).

101. Install the instrument panel driver's side bezel.

102. Install the left cowl trim panel.

103. Connect the instrument panel wire harness connector located above the brake pedal to the bulkhead wire harness connector.

104. Install the park brake release handle actuator rod.

105. Install the two bolts that secure the steering column support bracket to the instrument panel. Tighten the bolts to 14 Nm (10 ft. lbs.).

106. Install the steering column.

107. Install the left cowl trim cover.

108. Install the left instrument panel side cover.

109. Connect the headliner wire harness connector located at the a-pillar.

110. Install the instrument panel top cover.

111. Install the left a-pillar trim.

112. Reconnect the negative battery cable.

113. Install the two nuts that secure the HVAC housing to the engine compartment side of the dash panel. Tighten the nuts to 6.2 Nm (55 inch lbs.).

114. Install the powertrain control module (PCM).

115. Connect the heater hoses to the heater core tubes.

116. Connect the A/C liquid line and the A/C accumulator to the A/C evaporator.

117. Reconnect the negative battery cable.

118. If the heater core is being replaced, flush the cooling system.

119. Refill the engine cooling system.

120. Evacuate the refrigerant system.

121. Charge the refrigerant system.

STEERING

POWER STEERING GEAR

REMOVAL & INSTALLATION

See Figures 54 and 55.

1. Lock the steering wheel.
2. Drain and siphon the power steering fluid from the reservoir.
3. Raise the vehicle.
4. Remove and discard the steering coupler pinch bolt.
5. Remove the power steering hoses from the rack & pinion.
6. Remove the tire and wheel assembly.
7. Remove the tie rod end nuts and separate tie rod ends from the knuckles with a tie rod end separator.
8. Remove the rack & pinion mounting bolts.
9. Remove the rack & pinion from the vehicle.

To install:

➡Before installing gear inspect bushings and replace if worn or damaged. In the frame there is two holes for the mounting of the steering gear one is slotted and one is round. When tightening the gear to specifications make sure to tighten the mounting bolt with the hole first to avoid movement of the steering gear.

10. Install the gear on the front crossmember and tighten the mounting bolts to 319 Nm (235 ft. lbs.)
11. Slide the shaft coupler onto the gear. Install new pinch bolt and tighten to 49 Nm (36 ft. lbs.).
12. Clean and dry the tie rod end studs and the knuckle tapers.
13. Install the tie rod ends into the steering knuckles and tighten the nuts to 61 Nm (45 ft. lbs.) then an additional 90°.
14. Install the pressure power steering hose to the steering gear and tighten to 32 Nm (23 ft. lbs.).
15. Install the return power steering hose to the steering gear and tighten to 71 Nm (52 ft. lbs.).

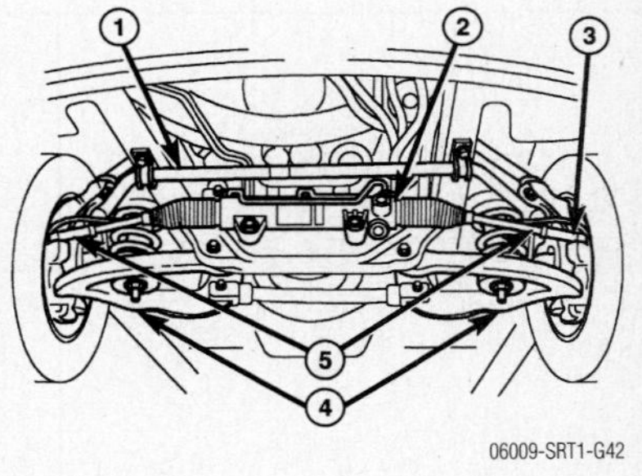

Fig. 55 Steering gear installed. (1) Sway bar, (2) Steering gear, (3 & 5) Tie rods/ends, (4) Control arms

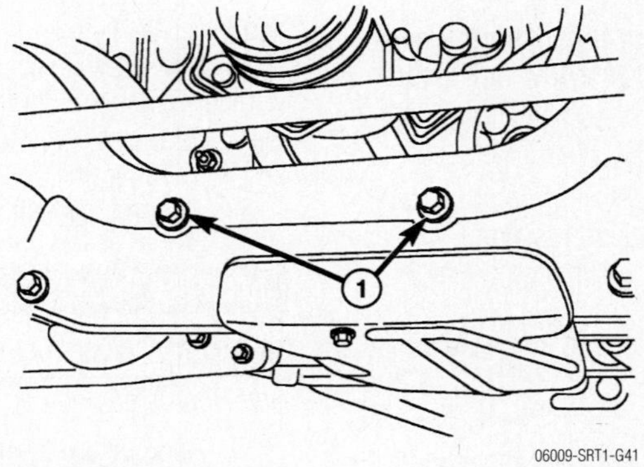

Fig. 54 Steering gear mounting bolts (1)

16. Install the tire and wheel assembly.
17. Remove the support and lower the vehicle.
18. Fill the system with fluid.
19. Adjust the toe position.

POWER STEERING PUMP

REMOVAL & INSTALLATION

See Figure 56.

1. Drain and siphon the power steering fluid from the reservoir.
2. Remove the serpentine belt.

⁂ WARNING

Do not remove the fitting on the pump that the high pressure hose screws into. The fitting may come loose unless it is backed up using another wrench. If the fitting does come loose, it must be retightened before continuing. (57–67Nm, 40–50 ft. lbs.) If this fitting comes out of the pump body, the internal spring and valve parts will fall out of the pump and they cannot be reinstalled properly. If this occurs the pump needs to be replaced with a new pump.

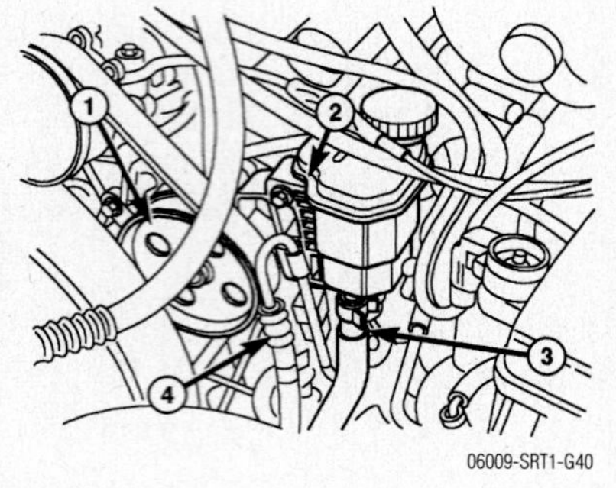

Fig. 56 Power steering pump mounting

3. Disconnect the return hose (3).
4. Disconnect the pressure hose (4).
5. Access to remove the three bolts securing the pump to the cylinder head can be gained through the pulley holes (1).

To install:

6. Align the pump with the mounting holes in the left cylinder head.
7. Install 3 pump mounting bolts through the pulley access holes (1). Tighten the bolts to 28 Nm (21 ft. lbs.).
8. Reconnect the pressure line (4) and return hose (3) to the pump and reservoir (2). Tighten the pressure line to 37 Nm (27 ft. lbs.).
9. Install the serpentine drive belt.
10. Fill the power steering pump.

SUSPENSION

FRONT SUSPENSION

COIL SPRING

REMOVAL & INSTALLATION

See Figure 57.

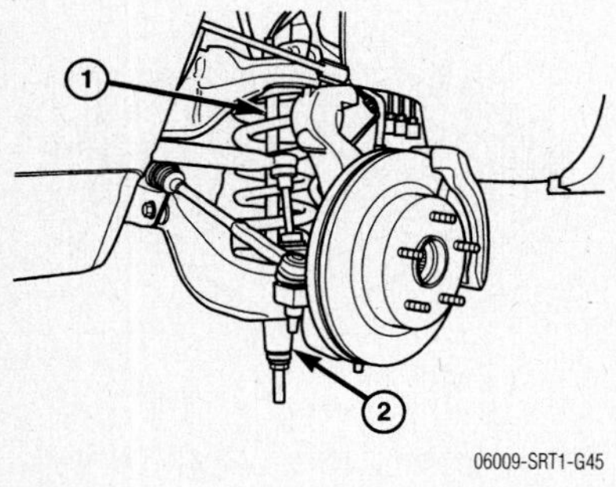

Fig. 57 Spring compressor installed. (1) Compressor, (2) Bell-shaped adapter

1. Raise and support vehicle.
2. Remove the front wheel and tire assembly.
3. Support the lower control arm at the outboard side of the lower control arm to support vehicle weight.
4. Remove the shock absorber.
5. Install a spring compressor up through the lower suspension arm, coil spring and shock hole in the frame. The bell-shaped adapter goes against the lower suspension arm. Install the nut on top of the tool at the shock hole.
6. Tighten the spring compressor nut against bell-shaped adapter finger tight then loosen ½ turn.

➡This will hold the spring in place until the lower suspension arm is separated from the steering knuckle.

7. Remove the stabilizer link.
8. Remove the lower ball joint nut at the steering knuckle.
9. Install a ball joint remover tool on the lower ball joint and separate the ball joint from the knuckle.

➡Do not allow the upper control arm and steering knuckle to rebound downwards they must be supported.

10. Support the upper control arm and steering knuckle out of the way.
11. Remove the lower control arm support.
12. Tighten the spring compressor tool to allow clearance for the lower ball joint to be removed out of the knuckle.

➡It may necessary to loosen the control arm pivot bolt to allow downward swing.

13. Loosen the tension on the spring compressor tool slowly allowing the lower suspension arm to pivot downward.
14. Remove the spring compressor tool.
15. Remove coil spring and isolator pad from the vehicle.

To install:

16. Tape the isolator pad to the top of the coil spring. Position the spring in the lower suspension arm well. Be sure that the coil spring is seated in the well.
17. Install a spring compressor up through the lower suspension arm, coil spring and shock hole in the frame.
18. Tighten the tool nut to compress the coil spring.
19. Remove the support from the upper control arm and steering knuckle.
20. Position the lower ball joint into the steering knuckle.
21. Install the retaining nut on the lower ball joint and tighten to 52 Nm (38 ft. lbs.) an additional 90° turn is required.
22. Remove the spring compressor tool.
23. Support the lower control arm at the outboard side of the lower control arm to support vehicle weight.
24. Install the shock absorber.
25. Install the stabilizer link.
26. Remove the lower control arm support.
27. Install the wheel and tire assembly and lower the vehicle.
28. Lower the vehicle to the floor with vehicle weight and Tighten the front and rear control arm pivot bolts if loosened to 204 Nm (150 ft. lbs.)
29. Perform a wheel alignment.

LOWER BALL JOINT

REMOVAL & INSTALLATION

See Figures 58 and 59.

1. Remove the tire and wheel assembly.

2. Remove the brake caliper and rotor.
3. Disconnect the tie rod from the steering knuckle.
4. Remove the lower ball joint nut and separate the lower ball joint from the steering knuckle.
5. Press the ball joint from the lower control arm using special tools C-4212-F (press), 8698-2 (receiver) and 8698-3 (driver), or equivalents.

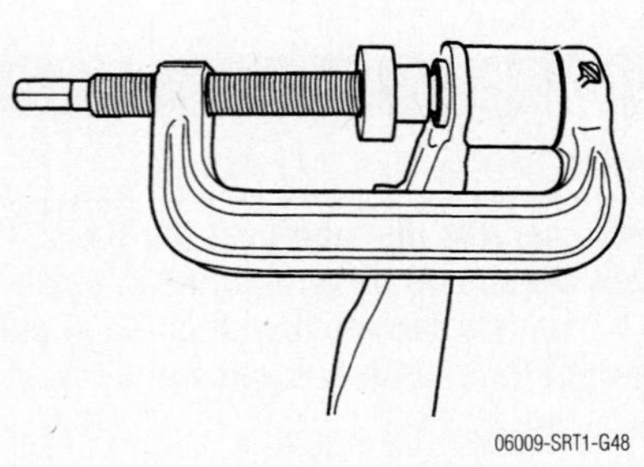

Fig. 58 Lower ball joint removal

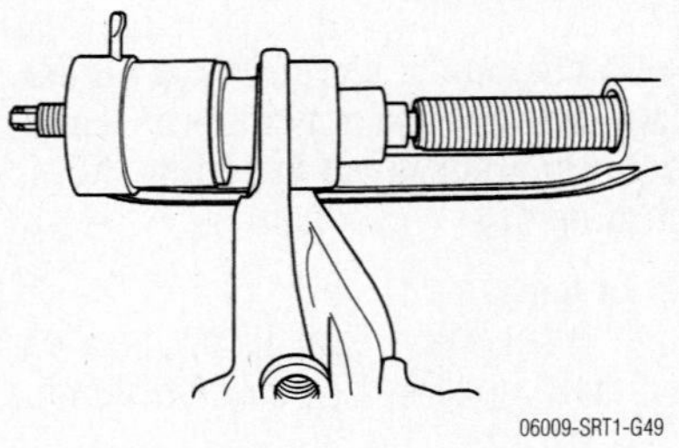

Fig. 59 Lower ball joint installation

To install:

6. Install the ball joint into the control arm and press in using special tools C-4212-F (press), 8698-1 (driver) and 8698-3 (receiver), or equivalent.
7. Install the ball joint boot.
8. Stake the ball joint flange in four evenly spaced places around the ball joint flange, using a chisel and hammer.
9. Install the steering knuckle. Torque the lower ball joint stud nut to 38 ft. lbs. (52 Nm) plus 90 degrees.
10. Install the tie rod end into the steering knuckle. Torque to 45 ft. lbs. (61 Nm) plus 90 degrees.
11. Install the brake caliper and rotor.
12. Install the tire and wheel assembly.
13. Check the vehicle ride height.
14. Perform a wheel alignment.

LOWER CONTROL ARM

REMOVAL & INSTALLATION

See Figure 60.

1. Raise and support the vehicle.
2. Remove the tire and wheel assembly.
3. Support the lower control arm at the outboard side of the lower control arm to support vehicle weight.
4. Remove the shock.
5. Install a spring compressor up through the lower suspension arm, coil spring and shock hole in the frame. The bell-shaped adapter goes against the lower suspension arm. Install the nut on top of the tool at the shock hole.
6. Tighten the spring compressor nut against bell-shaped adapter finger tight then loosen ½ turn.

➡This will hold the spring in place until the lower suspension arm is separated from the steering knuckle.

7. Remove the stabilizer link.
8. Remove the lower ball joint nut at the steering knuckle.
9. Install a ball joint remover tool on the lower ball joint and separate the ball joint from the knuckle.

➡Do not allow the upper control arm and steering knuckle to rebound downwards they must be supported.

10. Support the upper control arm and steering knuckle out of the way.
11. Remove the lower control arm support.
12. Tighten the spring compressor tool to allow clearance for the lower ball joint to be removed out of the knuckle.
13. Loosen the tension on the spring compressor tool slowly allowing the lower suspension arm to pivot downward.
14. Remove the spring compressor tool.
15. Remove coil spring and isolator pad from the vehicle.
16. Remove the front and rear pivot bolts.
17. Remove the lower control arm.

To install:

18. Install the lower control arm into place on the vehicle.
19. Install the front and rear control arm pivot bolts finger tight.
20. Install the coil spring into the frame pocket.
21. Install a spring compressor up through the lower suspension arm, coil spring and shock hole in the frame.
22. Tighten the tool nut to compress the coil spring.

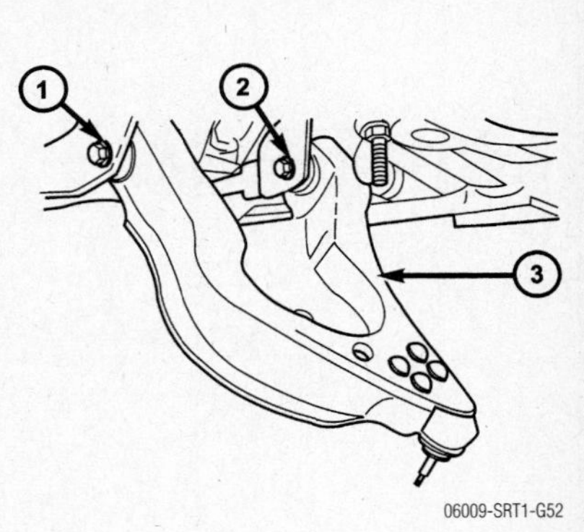

Fig. 60 Lower control arm removal. (1 & 2) Pivot bolts, (3) control arm

23. Remove the support from the upper control arm and steering knuckle.
24. Position the lower ball joint into the steering knuckle.
25. Install the retaining nut on the lower ball joint and tighten to 52 Nm (38 ft. lbs), an additional 90 degree turn is required.
26. Support the lower control arm at the outboard side of the lower control arm to support vehicle weight.
27. Remove the spring compressor tool.
28. Install the shock absorber.
29. Install the stabilizer link.
30. Remove the lower control arm support.
31. Install the wheel and tire assembly and lower the vehicle.
32. Lower the vehicle to the floor with vehicle weight and Tighten the front and rear control arm pivot bolts to 204 Nm (150 ft. lbs.).
33. Perform a wheel alignment.

LOWER CONTROL ARM BUSHING REPLACEMENT

Large Bushing

See Figures 61 and 62.

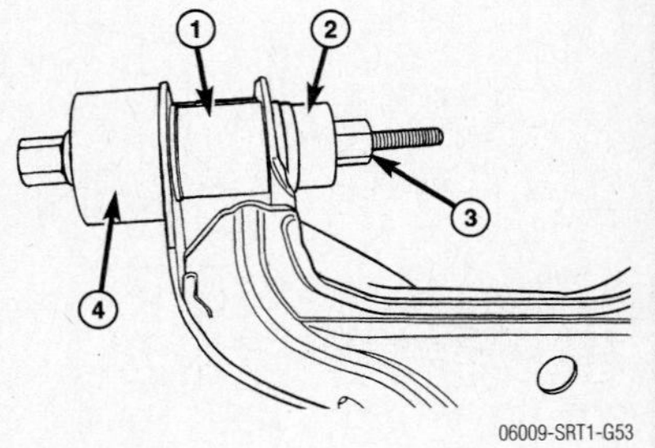

Fig. 61 Large bushing removal

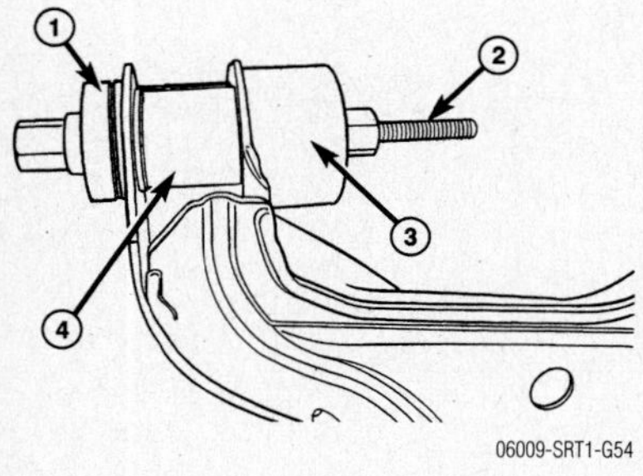

Fig. 62 Large bushing installation

1. Install bushing remover tools 8836-2 (receiver 4), 8836-4 (spacer 1) and 8836-5 (driver 2) with the threaded rod 8839 (3) and the bearing as shown for replacement of the large bushing.

➡Extreme pressure lubrication must be used on the threaded portions of the tool. This will increase the longevity of the tool and insure proper operation during the removal and installation process.

2. Install the new bushing into the lower control arm using special tools 8836-2 (receiver 3), 8836-1 (driver 1), 8836-4 (spacer 4) with the bearing and the threaded rod (8839 2).

Small Bushing

See Figures 63 and 64.

1. Install the bushing tool 8836-6 (driver 2), 8836-3 (spacer 3) and 8836-2 (receiver 4) with the threaded rod 8839 (1) and the bearing as shown for the replacement of the small bushing.
2. Install the small bushings into the lower control arm using tools 8836-7 (driver 4), 8836-2 (receiver 1), 8836-3 (spacer 3) and the bearing with the threaded rod (8839 2).

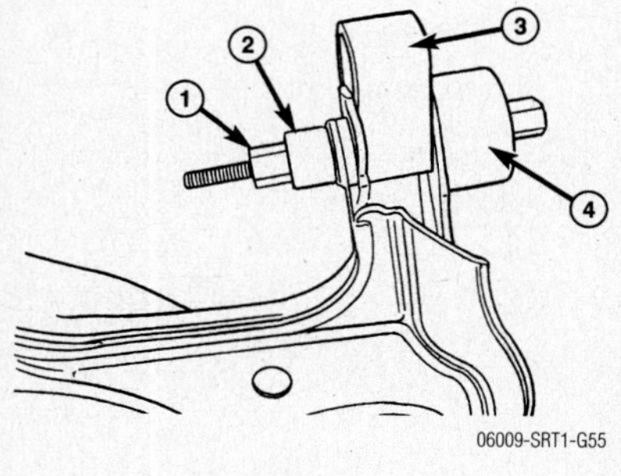

Fig. 63 Small bushing removal

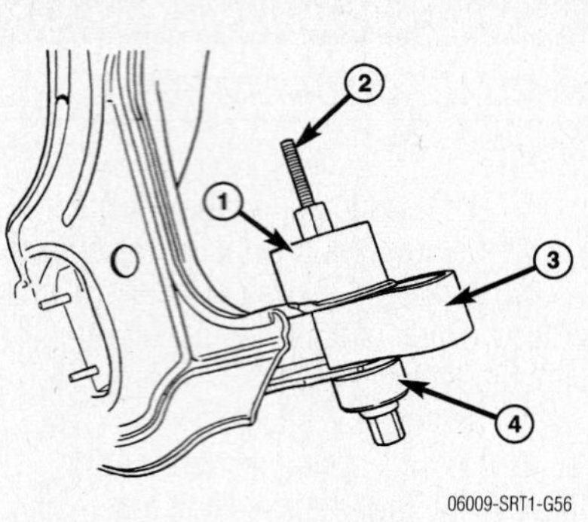

Fig. 64 Small bushing installation

3. Remove the control arm from the vise.
4. Install the lower control arm.
5. Reset the vehicle ride height.
6. Perform a wheel alignment.

SHOCK ABSORBER

REMOVAL & INSTALLATION

See Figure 65.

1. Raise and support vehicle.
2. Support the lower control arm outboard end.
3. Remove the upper shock absorber nut, retainer and grommet.
4. Remove the lower nuts and remove the shock absorber.

To install:

➡Upper shock nut must be replaced or use Mopar Lock 'N Seal or Loctite® 242 on existing nut.

5. Install the lower retainer and grommet on the shock absorber stud. Insert the shock absorber through the frame bracket hole.
6. Install the lower nuts and tighten the nuts to 35 Nm (25 ft. lbs.).
7. Install the upper grommet, retainer and new nut or use Mopar Lock 'N Seal or Loctite® 242 on existing nut, on the shock absorber stud. Tighten nut to 54 Nm (40 ft. lbs.).
8. Remove the support from the lower control arm outboard end.
9. Lower the vehicle.

STABILIZER BAR

REMOVAL & INSTALLATION

➡To service the stabilizer bar the vehicle should be on a drive on hoist. The vehicle suspension must be at curb height for stabilizer bar installation.

1. Remove the stabilizer bar link upper nuts and remove the retainers and grommets.
2. Remove the stabilizer bar retainer, bolts and retainers from the frame crossmember and remove the bar.
3. If necessary, remove the bushings from the stabilizer bar.

➡Do not cut the old bushings off the stabilizer bar use a mixture of soapy water in order to aid in sliding the bushing off.

To install:

4. If removed, Install the bushings on the stabilizer bar using a mixture of soapy

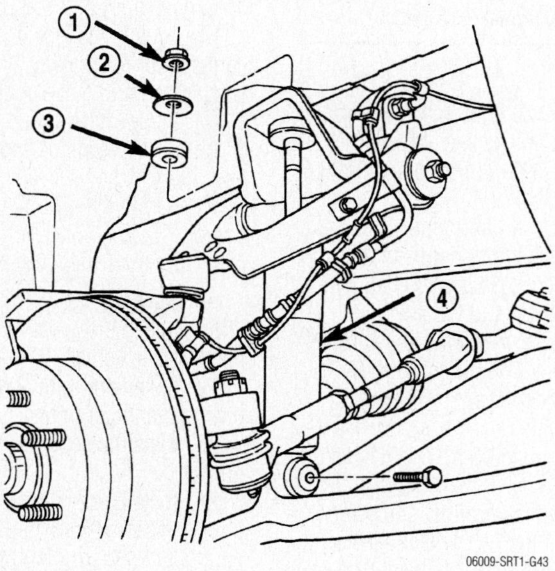

Fig. 65 Front shock absorber mounting. (1) Nut, (2) Retainer, (3) Grommet

water or equivalent in order to slide the bushing over the bar with ease.

➡Do not cut the new bushing for installation.

5. Position the stabilizer bar on the frame crossmember brackets and install the bracket and bolts finger-tight.

➡Check the alignment of the bar to ensure there is no interference with the either frame rail or chassis component. Spacing should be equal on both sides.

6. Install the stabilizer bar to the stabilizer link and install the grommets and retainers.
7. Install the nuts to the stabilizer link and tighten to 27 Nm (20 ft. lbs.).
8. Tighten the brackets to the frame to 61 Nm (45 ft. lbs.).

STEERING KNUCKLE

REMOVAL & INSTALLATION

See Figure 66.

1. Raise and support the vehicle.
2. Remove the wheel and tire assembly.
3. Remove the brake caliper, rotor, shield and ABS wheel speed sensor if equipped.
4. Remove the tie rod end nut. Separate the tie rod from the knuckle.

➡When installing the remover to separate the ball joint, be careful not to damage the ball joint seal.

5. Remove the lower ball joint nut. Separate the ball joint from the knuckle and remove the knuckle.
6. Remove the upper ball joint nut. Separate the ball joint from the knuckle.
7. Remove the hub/bearing from the steering knuckle.

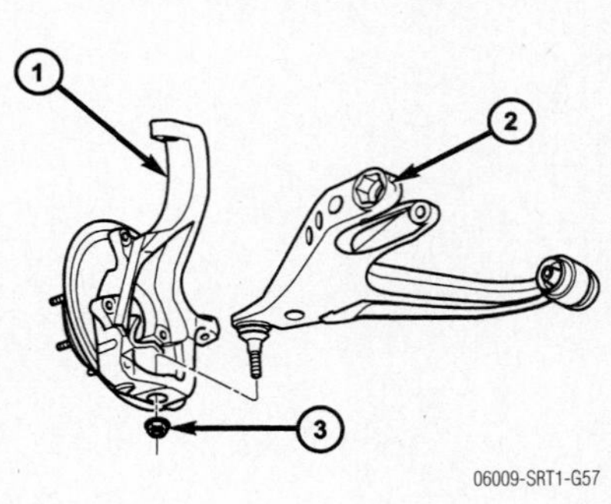

Fig. 66 Knuckle installation. (1) knuckle, (2) lower control arm, (3) lower ball joint nut

To install:

➡The ball joint stud tapers must be clean and dry before installing the knuckle. Clean the stud tapers with mineral spirits to remove dirt and grease.

➡When installing hub/bearing with ABS brakes, position the speed sensor opening towards the front of the vehicle.

8. Install the hub/bearing to the steering knuckle and tighten the bolts to 163 Nm (120 ft. lbs.).
9. Install the knuckle onto the upper and lower ball joints.
10. Install the upper and lower ball joint nuts. Tighten the upper ball joint nut to 54 Nm (40 ft. lbs.) plus 90 degrees, and the lower ball joint nut to 52 Nm (38 ft. lbs.) plus 90 degrees.
11. Remove the hydraulic jack from the lower suspension arm.
12. Install the tie rod end and tighten the nut to 61 Nm (45 ft. lbs.).
13. Install the ABS wheel speed sensor if equipped and brake shield, rotor and caliper.
14. Install the wheel and tire assembly.
15. Remove the support and lower the vehicle.
16. Perform a wheel alignment.

TORSION BAR

REMOVAL & INSTALLATION

See Figures 67 and 68.

➡The left and right side torsion bars are NOT interchangeable. The bars are identified and stamped R or L, for right or left. The bars do not have a front or rear end and can be installed with either end facing forward.

1. Raise and support the vehicle with the front suspension hanging.

➡Count and record the number of turns for installation reference.

2. Mark the adjustment bolt setting.
3. Install Special Tool 8686 to the anchor arm and the cross member.
4. Increase the tension on the anchor arm tool until the load is removed from the adjustment bolt and the adjuster nut.
5. Turn the adjustment bolt counterclockwise to remove the bolt and the adjuster nut.
6. Remove the Special Tool 8686, allowing the torsion bar to unload.
7. Remove torsion bar and anchor. Remove anchor from torsion bar.
8. Remove all foreign material from torsion bar mounting in anchor and suspension arm.
9. Inspect adjustment bolt, bearing and swivel for damage.

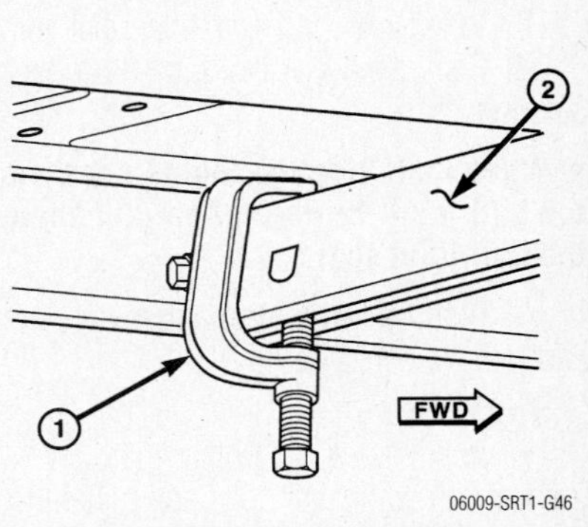

Fig. 67 Special tool 8686 (1) installed on the crossmember (2)

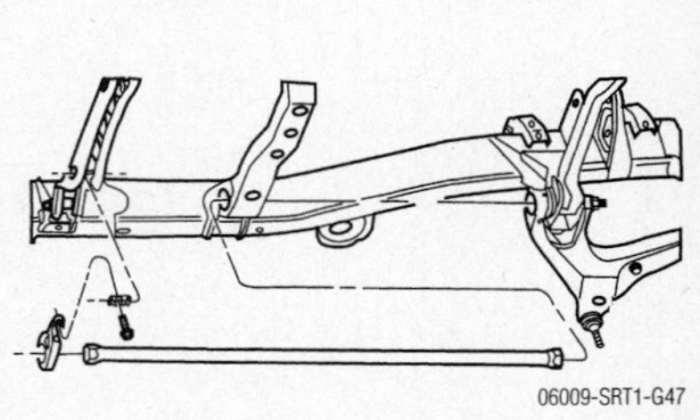

Fig. 68 Torsion bar mounting

To install:

10. Insert torsion bar ends into anchor and suspension arm.
11. Position the anchor in the frame crossmember.
12. Install Special Tool 8686 to the anchor and the crossmember.
13. Increase the tension on the anchor in order to load the torsion bar.
14. Install the adjustment bolt and the adjuster nut.
15. Turn adjustment bolt clockwise the recorded amount of turns.
16. Remove tool 8686 from the torsion bar crossmember.
17. Lower vehicle and adjust the front suspension height.
18. Perform a wheel alignment.

UPPER BALL JOINT

REMOVAL & INSTALLATION

The upper ball joint is integral with the control arm. If the ball joint is defective, the whole arm must be replaced.

UPPER CONTROL ARM

REMOVAL & INSTALLATION

See Figures 69 and 70.

1. Raise and support vehicle.
2. Remove wheel and tire assembly.
3. Remove the nut from upper ball joint.
4. Separate upper ball joint from the steering knuckle.

➡When installing the tool to separate the ball joint, be careful not to damage the ball joint seal.

5. Remove the control arm pivot bolts and remove control arm.

To install:

6. Position the control arm into the frame brackets. Install bolts and tighten to 132 Nm (97 ft. lbs.).
7. Insert the ball joint in steering knuckle and tighten the upper ball joint nut to 54 Nm (40 ft. lbs.) plus 90 degrees.
8. Install the wheel and tire assembly.
9. Remove the support and lower vehicle.
10. Perform a wheel alignment.

WHEEL BEARINGS

ADJUSTMENT

The hub and bearing are an integral unit. No adjustment is possible.

REMOVAL & INSTALLATION

See Figure 71.

1. Raise and support the vehicle.
2. Remove the wheel and tire assembly.
3. Remove the brake caliper and rotor.
4. Remove the ABS wheel speed sensor if equipped.
5. Remove the three hub/bearing mounting bolts from the steering knuckle.
6. Slide the hub/bearing out of the steering knuckle.

To install:

7. Install the hub/bearing into the steering knuckle and tighten the bolts to 163 Nm (120 ft. lbs.).
8. Install the brake rotor and caliper.
9. Install the ABS wheel speed sensor if equipped.
10. Install the wheel and tire assembly.
11. Remove the support and lower vehicle.

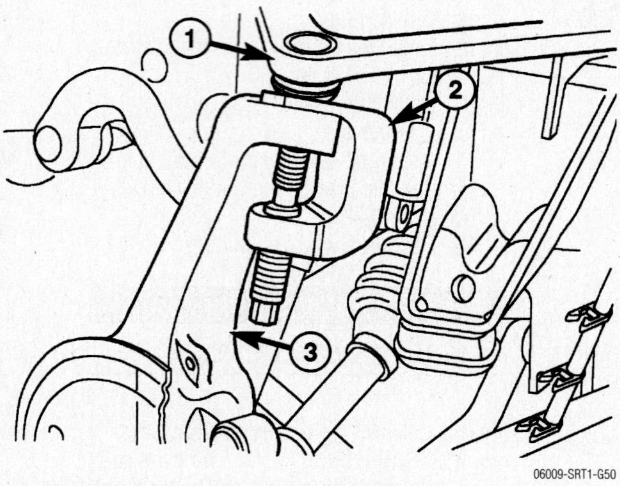

Fig. 69 Separating upper ball joint from the knuckle. (1) Control arm, (2) Tool, (3) Knuckle

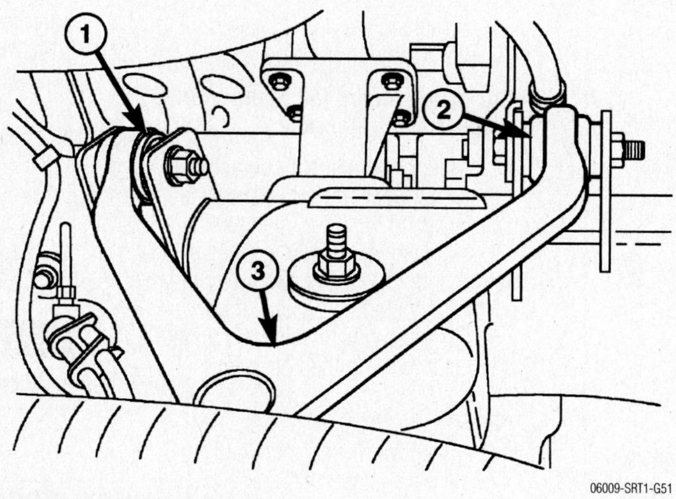

Fig. 70 Upper control arm pivot bolts (1 & 2), control arm (3)

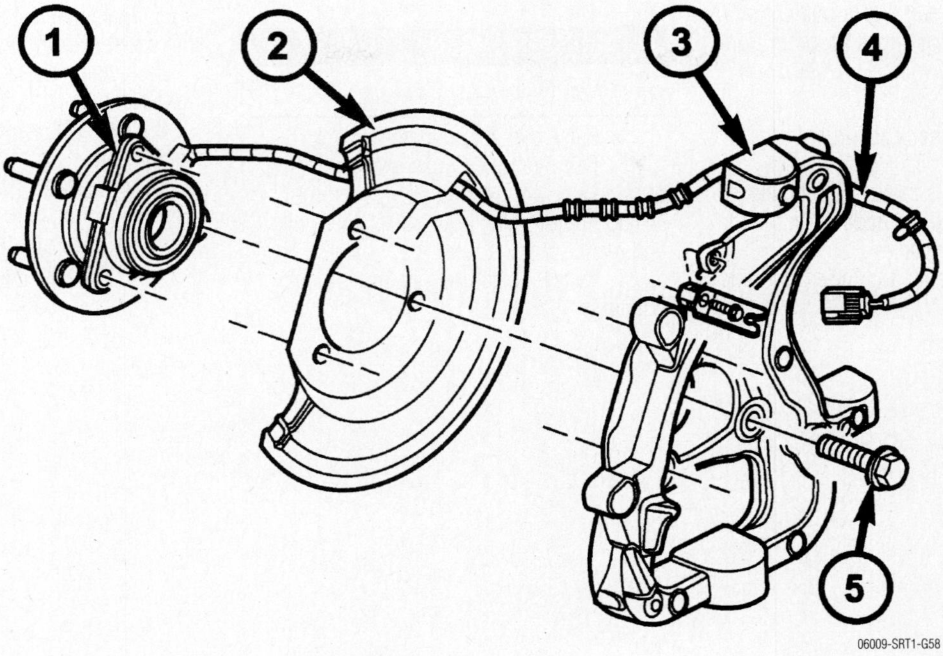

Fig. 71 Front hub and bearing assembly. (1) hub/bearing, (2) dust shield (not on all SRT-10 models), (3) knuckle, (4) ABS wire, (5) hub bolts

SUSPENSION

REAR SUSPENSION

LEAF SPRING

REMOVAL & INSTALLATION

1. Raise and support the vehicle.
2. Support the axle with a suitable holding fixture.
3. Remove the nuts, spring clamp bolts and the plate that attach the spring to the axle.
4. Remove the nuts and bolts from the spring front and rear shackle.
5. Remove the spring from the vehicle.

To install:

6. Position spring on axle shaft tube so spring center bolt is inserted into the locating hole in the axle tube.
7. Align the front of the spring with the bolt hole in the front bracket. Install the eye pivot bolt and nut.
8. Align the rear of the spring into the shackle and install the bolt and nut.
9. Tighten the spring front and rear eye pivot bolt snug do not torque.
10. Install the spring clamp bolts, plate and the retaining nuts.
11. Remove the holding fixture for the rear axle.
12. Remove the supports and lower the vehicle so that the weight is being supported by the tires.
13. Tighten the spring clamp retaining nuts to 149 Nm (110 ft. lbs.).
14. Tighten the spring front and rear pivot bolt nuts to 163 Nm (120 ft. lbs.).

POWER HOP DAMPER

REMOVAL & INSTALLATION

1. Raise and support the vehicle.
2. Remove the damper nuts and bolts.
3. Remove the damper bracket from the differential cover if necessary.
4. Remove the from the vehicle.

To install:

5. Install the damper bracket to the rear differential cover if removed. Tighten the bolts (5) to 41 Nm (30 ft. lbs.).
6. Compress the damper for easier installation.
7. Install the damper to the mounting brackets.
8. Install the damper nuts and bolts at the axle end. Tighten the bolts to 102 Nm (75 ft. lbs.).
9. Decompress the damper.
10. Install the damper nut and bolt to the frame. Tighten the bolt to 102 Nm (75 ft. lbs.).
11. Lower the vehicle.

SHOCK ABSORBER

REMOVAL & INSTALLATION

See Figure 72.

1. Raise vehicle and support the axle.

➡The rear upper shock attachment uses a flag nut. Do not use an air tool to remove the bolt, the flag may rotate into the bottom of the bed and cause damage. Use a wrench to hold the nut when loosening.

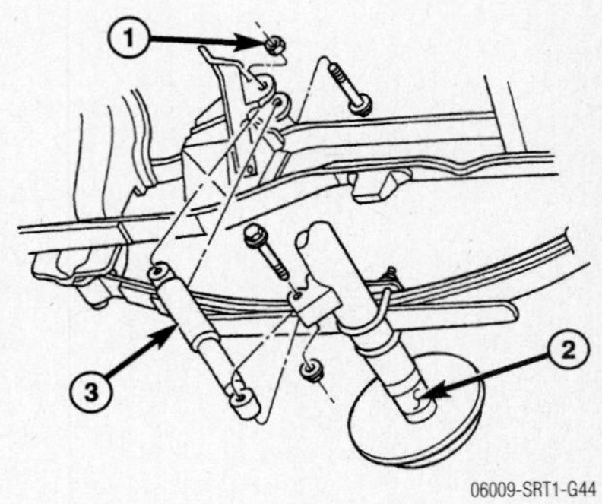

Fig. 72 Rear shock absorber mounting. (1) Nut, (2) Axle, (3) Shock absorber

2. Remove the upper shock bolt and nut.

3. Remove the lower shock bolt and nut.

4. Remove the rear shock absorber from the vehicle.

To install:

5. Position the shock absorber in the brackets.

6. Install the bolts through the brackets and the shock. Install the flag nut on the top bolt and nut on lower bolt.

7. Tighten the upper and lower bolt/nuts Tighten to 135 Nm (100 ft. lbs.)

8. Remove the support and lower the vehicle.

STABILIZER BAR

REMOVAL & INSTALLATION

1. Raise and support vehicle.

2. Remove lower links mounting nuts.

3. Remove stabilizer bar retainer bolts and retainers at the axle.

4. Remove stabilizer bar and remove bushings.

To install:

5. Install stabilizer bar bushings.

6. Install the stabilizer bar and center it with equal spacing on both sides.

7. Install stabilizer bar retainers. Tighten the bolts to 75 Nm (55 ft. lbs.).

8. Install the park brake cable bracket to the retainers.

9. Install the links on the stabilizer bar. Install mounting bolts and nuts.

10. Remove support and lower vehicle.

11. Tighten stabilizer link lower nuts to 111 Nm (82 ft. lbs.).

CHRYSLER, DODGE AND JEEP

Diagnostic Trouble Codes

DIAGNOSTIC TROUBLE CODES

OBD II VEHICLE APPLICATIONS

CHRYSLER CORP

Grand Cherokee
2005–2007
- 3.7L .... VIN K
- 4.7L .... VIN N
- 4.7L .... VIN P
- 5.7L .... VIN 2

Liberty
2005–2007
- 2.4L .... VIN 1
- 2.8L .... VIN 5
- 3.7L .... VIN K

Pacifica
2005–2007
- 3.5L .... VIN 4
- 3.8L .... VIN L
- 4.0L .... VIN X

PT Cruiser
2005–2007
- 2.4L .... VIN B

Ram Truck
2005–2007
- 2.7L .... VIN R
- 2.7L .... VIN T
- 3.5L .... VIN G
- 3.5L .... VIN V
- 5.7L .... VIN 2
- 5.7L .... VIN H

Sebring
2005–2006
- 2.4L .... VIN J
- 2.4L .... VIN S
- 2.7L .... VIN R

Stratus
2005–2006
- 2.4L .... VIN S
- 2.7L .... VIN R

Wrangler
2005–2007
- 2.4L .... VIN 1
- 3.8L .... VIN 1
- 4.0L .... VIN S

REFERENCE INFORMATION

OBD II TROUBLE CODE LIST

To use this information, first read and record All codes in memory along with Freeze Frame data. *If a PCM Reset function is done prior to recording this data,* All *codes and freeze frame data are lost!*

Look up the appropriate trouble code in the list on the following pages. The left hand column includes the code number, the number of trips to set the code (e.g., **1T or 2T**), the year, model description and type of OBD II Monitor that failed (e.g., **CCM or O2S**). This data can be used to determine how to drive a vehicle after a repair in order to validate the repair has been completed.

The **(N/MIL)** designator in the left hand column indicates the trouble code does not turn on the Malfunction Indicator Lamp or MIL. The **(STS Lamp)** indicator in the left column indicates a code that turns on the Service Transmission Soon lamp. This code may or may not turn "on" the MIL.

OBD II Trouble Code List (P0XXX Codes)

DTC	Trouble Code Title, Conditions & Possible Causes
DTC: P0016 **1T CCM** **Years:** 2005, 2006, 2007 **Models:** Grand Cherokee, Liberty, Pacifica, PT Cruiser, Ram Truck, Sebring, Stratus, Wrangler **Engines:** All **Transmissions:** All	**Crankshaft/Camshaft Timing Misalignment** Engine cranking or running; and the PCM detected the camshaft was out of phase with the crankshaft during the CCM test period. **Possible Causes:** • Base engine problem (i.e., the camshaft timing is not correct) • Intermittent condition • CKP or CMP Sensor signal is erratic (check with lab scope) • Tone wheel or pulse wheel is damaged or contains debris • CKP or CMP Sensor, harness or connector has failed • PCM has failed
DTC: P0030 **1T CCM** **Years:** 2005, 2006, 2007 **Models:** Grand Cherokee, Liberty, Wrangler **Engines:** All **Transmissions:** All	**O2 (B1 S1) Heater Circuit Fault** Engine started; system voltage over 10.6v, and the PCM detected a fault in the O2 heater element feedback sense circuit. **Possible Causes:** • O2 assembly is damaged or it has failed • O2 heater control circuit is open, shorted to ground or B+ • O2 heater ground circuit is open • O2 heater element is damaged or has failed • PCM has failed
DTC: P0031 **1T CCM** **Years:** 2005, 2006, 2007 **Models:** Grand Cherokee, Liberty, Pacifica, PT Cruiser, Ram Truck, Sebring, Stratus, Wrangler **Engines:** All **Transmissions:** All	**O2 (B1 S1) Heater Circuit Low** Key on; system voltage over 10.6v; ASD relay on; O2 heater "on". The PCM detected the O2 Heater circuit is out of acceptable range low. **Possible Causes:** • O2 assembly is damaged or it has failed • O2 heater element is damaged or has failed • O2 heater control circuit is shorted to ground • PCM has failed
DTC: P0032 **1T CCM** **Years:** 2005, 2006, 2007 **Models:** Grand Cherokee, Liberty, Pacifica, PT Cruiser, Ram Truck, Sebring, Stratus, Wrangler **Engines:** All **Transmissions:** All	**O2 (B1 S1) Heater Circuit High** Key on; system voltage over 10.6v; ASD relay on; O2 heater "off". The PCM detected the O2 Heater circuit is out of range high. **Possible Causes:** • O2 heater element is damaged or the heater has failed • O2 heater control circuit is open or it is shorted to power • O2 heater ground circuit is open • PCM has failed
DTC: P0033 **1T CCM** **Years:** 2005, 2006, 2007 **Models:** PT Cruiser, Sebring, Stratus **Engines:** All **Transmissions:** All	**Surge Valve Solenoid Circuit Fault** Key on or engine running; system voltage over 10v. The PCM detected the Actual state of the Surge Valve solenoid circuit did not match the Intended state during the CCM test. **Possible Causes:** • Surge valve power supply is open (test power from ASD relay) • Surge valve solenoid circuit is open • Surge valve solenoid circuit is shorted to ground or power (B+) • Surge valve solenoid is damaged or it has failed • PCM has failed
DTC: P0036 **1T CCM** **Years:** 2005, 2006, 2007 **Models:** Grand Cherokee, Liberty, Wrangler **Engines:** All **Transmissions:** All	**O2 (B1 S2) Heater Circuit Fault** Engine started; system voltage over 10.8v and the PCM detected a problem in the Heater Relay circuit. **Possible Causes:** • O2 assembly is damaged or it has failed • O2 heater control circuit is open, shorted to ground or B+ • O2 heater ground circuit is open • O2 heater element is damaged or has failed • PCM has failed
DTC: P0037 **1T CCM** **Years:** 2005, 2006, 2007 **Models:** Grand Cherokee, Liberty, Pacifica, PT Cruiser, Ram Truck, Sebring, Stratus, Wrangler **Engines:** All **Transmissions:** All	**O2 (B1 S2) Heater Circuit Low** Key on; system voltage over 10.6v; ASD relay on; O2 heater "on". The PCM detected the O2 Heater circuit is out of acceptable range (i.e., below 0.0926v). **Possible Causes:** • O2 assembly is damaged or it has failed • O2 heater element is damaged or has failed • O2 heater control circuit is shorted to ground • PCM has failed

DTC	Trouble Code Title, Conditions & Possible Causes
DTC: P0038 **1T CCM** **Years:** 2005, 2006, 2007 **Models:** Grand Cherokee, Liberty, Pacifica, PT Cruiser, Ram Truck, Sebring, Stratus, Wrangler **Engines:** All **Transmissions:** All	**O2 (B1 S2) Heater Circuit High** Key on; system voltage over 10.6v; ASD relay on; O2 heater "off". The PCM detected the O2 heater voltage is out of range high. **Possible Causes:** • O2 Sensor failed or improper operation • O2 heater element is damaged or failed • O2 heater control circuit is open or it is shorted to power • O2 heater ground circuit is open • PCM has failed
DTC: P0045 **1T CCM** **Years:** 2005, 2006, 2007 **Models:** Liberty **Engines:** 2.8L Diesel **Transmissions:** All	**Boost Pressure Solenoid Excessive Current** Ignition on; ECM Boost Pressure Solenoid commanded ON. The ECM detects excessive current on the BP Solenoid Control circuit. **Possible Causes:** • Intermittent condition • Boost Pressure Solenoid has failed • BP Solenoid control circuit is shorted to voltage • ECM has failed
DTC: P0045 **1T CCM** **Years:** 2005, 2006, 2007 **Models:** Liberty **Engines:** 2.8L Diesel **Transmissions:** All	**Boost Pressure Solenoid Open Circuit** Ignition on; ECM Boost Pressure Solenoid commanded OFF. The ECM did not detect voltage on the BP Solenoid Control circuit. **Possible Causes:** • Intermittent condition • ASD relay output circuit is open • BP Solenoid control circuit is open or is shorted to ground • Boost Pressure Solenoid has failed • ECM has failed
DTC: P0047 **1T CCM** **Years:** 2005, 2006, 2007 **Models:** Liberty **Engines:** 2.8L Diesel **Transmissions:** All	**Boost Pressure Solenoid Short To Ground Circuit** Ignition on; ECM Boost Pressure Solenoid commanded OFF. The ECM did not detect voltage on the BP Solenoid Control circuit. **Possible Causes:** • Intermittent condition • ASD relay output circuit is open • BP Solenoid control circuit is open or is shorted to ground • Boost Pressure Solenoid has failed • ECM has failed
DTC: P0048 **1T CCM** **Years:** 2005, 2006, 2007 **Models:** Liberty **Engines:** 2.8L Diesel **Transmissions:** All	**Boost Pressure Solenoid Short Circuit** Ignition on; ECM Boost Pressure Solenoid commanded ON. The ECM detects excessive current on the BP Solenoid Control circuit. **Possible Causes:** • Intermittent condition • Boost Pressure Solenoid has failed • BP Solenoid control circuit is shorted to voltage • ECM has failed
DTC: P0050 **1T CCM** **Years:** 2005, 2006, 2007 **Models:** PT Cruiser, Sebring, Stratus **Engines:** All **Transmissions:** All	**O2 (B2 S1) Heater Relay Circuit Low** Key on, system voltage over 10.6v, ASD relay on, O2 heater "on", and the PCM detected the Heater Relay circuit Actual state did not match the Desired state (low circuit). **Possible Causes:** • O2 assembly is damaged, or the O2 heater element is damaged or has failed • O2 heater control circuit is shorted to ground • PCM has failed
DTC: P0051 **1T CCM** **Years:** 2005, 2006, 2007 **Models:** Grand Cherokee, Liberty, Pacifica, PT Cruiser, Ram Truck, Sebring, Stratus, Wrangler **Engines:** All **Transmissions:** All	**O2 (B2 S1) Heater Relay Circuit Low** Key on, system voltage over 10.6v, ASD relay on, O2 heater "on", and the PCM detected the Heater Relay circuit Actual state did not match the Desired state (low circuit). 3 good trips are required to turn off the MIL. **Possible Causes:** • O2 assembly is damaged or it has failed • O2 heater element is damaged or has failed • O2 heater control circuit is shorted to ground • PCM has failed

DTC	Trouble Code Title, Conditions & Possible Causes
DTC: P0052 **1T CCM** **Years:** 2005, 2006, 2007 **Models:** Grand Cherokee, Liberty, Pacifica, PT Cruiser, Ram Truck, Sebring, Stratus, Wrangler **Engines:** All **Transmissions:** All	**O2 (B2 S1) Heater Relay Circuit High** Key on, system voltage over 10.6v, ASD relay on, O2 heater "off", and the PCM detected the Heater Relay circuit Actual state did not match the Desired state (high circuit). **Possible Causes:** • O2 heater element is damaged or the heater has failed • O2 heater control circuit is open or it is shorted to power • O2 heater ground circuit is open • PCM has failed
DTC: P0056 **1T CCM** **Years:** 2005, 2006, 2007 **Models:** PT Cruiser, Sebring, Stratus **Engines:** All **Transmissions:** All	**O2 (B2 S1) Heater Relay Circuit Low** Key on, system voltage over 10.6v, ASD relay on, O2 heater "on", and the PCM detected the Heater Relay circuit Actual state did not match the Desired state (low circuit). **Possible Causes:** • O2 assembly is damaged or it has failed • O2 heater element is damaged or has failed • O2 heater control circuit is shorted to ground • PCM has failed
DTC: P0057 **1T CCM** **Years:** 2005, 2006, 2007 **Models:** Grand Cherokee, Liberty, Pacifica, PT Cruiser, Ram Truck, Sebring, Stratus, Wrangler **Engines:** All **Transmissions:** All	**O2 (B2 S2) Heater Relay Circuit Low** Key on, system voltage over 10.6v, ECT input under test condition value, and the PCM detected the Heater Relay signal was too low. **Possible Causes:** • O2 assembly is damaged or it has failed • O2 heater element is damaged or has failed • O2 heater control circuit is shorted to ground • PCM has failed
DTC: P0058 **1T CCM** **Years:** 2005, 2006, 2007 **Models:** Grand Cherokee, Liberty, Pacifica, PT Cruiser, Ram Truck, Sebring, Stratus, Wrangler **Engines:** All **Transmissions:** All	**O2 (B2 S2) Heater Relay Circuit High** Key on, system voltage over 10.6v, ASD powered up, and O2 heater is off. ECT input under test condition value and the PCM detected the Heater Relay signal was too high. **Possible Causes:** • O2 heater element is damaged or the heater has failed • O2 heater control circuit is open or it is shorted to power • O2 heater ground circuit is open • PCM has failed
DTC: P0068 **1T CCM** **Years:** 2005, 2006, 2007 **Models:** Grand Cherokee, Liberty, Pacifica, PT Cruiser, Ram Truck, Sebring, Stratus, Wrangler **Engines:** All **Transmissions:** All	**MAP Sensor/TP Sensor Correction – High Flow/Vacuum Leak** Engine started; engine speed over 2000 rpm, and the PCM detected the Manifold Air Pressure (MAP) value dropped to less than 1.5" Hg with the throttle closed during the test. **Possible Causes:** • An engine vacuum leak present • High resistance in the MAP ground circuit, MAP Sensor signal or VREF (5v) circuit • High resistance in the TP ground, TP circuit or the TP Sensor VREF (5v) circuit • MAP Sensor is damaged or it has failed • TP Sensor is damaged or it has failed • PCM has failed
DTC: P0068 **2T CCM** **Years:** 2005, 2006, 2007 **Models:** Sebring Coupe, Stratus Coupe **Engines:** All **Transmissions:** All	**MAP Sensor/TP Sensor Correlation** Engine started; no MAP Sensor or TP Sensor DTCs are present. The PCM determines a valid range in which the TP Sensor should be, at a given rpm/engine load. The actual TP Sensor voltage is then compared to this value. If the TP Sensor voltage does not fall within the expected range within a predetermined time, an error is detected. The DTC will set after 2 trips. **Possible Causes:** • An engine vacuum leak present • High resistance in the MAP ground circuit, MAP Sensor signal or VREF (5v) circuit • High resistance in the TP ground, TP circuit or the TP Sensor VREF (5v) circuit • MAP Sensor is damaged or it has failed • TP Sensor is damaged or it has failed • PCM has failed

DTC	Trouble Code Title, Conditions & Possible Causes
DTC: P0068 **1T CCM** **Years:** 2005, 2006, 2007 **Models:** Ram Truck **Engines:** All **Transmissions:** All	**MAP Sensor/TP Sensor Correlation** Condition is monitored during all drive modes. This DTC will set when an unexpectedly high intake manifold airflow condition exists that can lead to increased engine speed and which then puts the Next Generation Controller into a High Airflow Protection Limiting Mode. This feature includes rpm limits whenever a TP and/or MAP Sensor limp-in fault is present. If vacuum drops below 1.5 in. Hg, with engine speed greater than 2000 rpm and closed throttle, this DTC will set. **Possible Causes:** • An engine vacuum leak present • High resistance in the 5v supply circuit • 5v supply circuit is shorted to ground • High resistance in the MAP signal circuit or the TP signal circuit • TP signal circuit is shorted to ground • High resistance in the Sensor ground circuit • MAP Sensor is damaged or it has failed • TP Sensor is damaged or it has failed • PCM has failed
DTC: P0070 **1T CCM** **Years:** 2005, 2006, 2007 **Models:** Grand Cherokee, Liberty, Pacifica, PT Cruiser, Ram Truck, Sebring, Stratus, Wrangler **Engines:** All **Transmissions:** All	**Ambient Temperature Sensor Circuit Stuck** Engine started 4 times, 4 warm-up cycles completed, vehicle driven for 200 miles, and the PCM did not detect more than a 6°F change in the Ambient Air Temperature (AAT) Sensor signal in the test. **Possible Causes:** • AAT Sensor signal circuit shorted to power (VREF) • AAT Sensor ground circuit is open • AAT Sensor signal circuit is open • AAT Sensor signal circuit is shorted to ground • PCM High or Low circuit is damaged or it has failed
DTC: P0070 **1T CCM** **Years:** 2005, 2006, 2007 **Models:** Liberty **Engines:** 2.8L Diesel **Transmissions:** All	**Ambient Air Temperature Signal Voltage Too High** Ignition on; Ambient Air Temp. Sensor signal is above 4.82v. **Possible Causes:** • Intermittent condition • AAT Sensor signal circuit is open or is shorted to voltage • AAT Sensor ground circuit is open • AAT Sensor has failed • ECM has failed
DTC: P0070 **1T CCM** **Years:** 2005, 2006, 2007 **Models:** Liberty **Engines:** 2.8L Diesel **Transmissions:** All	**Ambient Air Temperature Signal Voltage Too Low** Ignition on; Ambient Air Temp. Sensor signal is below 0.068v. **Possible Causes:** • Intermittent condition • AAT Sensor signal circuit is shorted to ground or to sensor ground • AAT Sensor has failed • ECM has failed
DTC: P0071 **2T CCM** **Years:** 2005, 2006, 2007 **Models:** Grand Cherokee, Liberty, Pacifica, PT Cruiser, Ram Truck, Sebring, Stratus, Wrangler **Engines:** All **Transmissions:** All	**Ambient Temperature Sensor Performance** Engine "off" time over 8 hours; DTC P0072 and P0073 not set; ambient temperature more than 38°F (4C). The PCM determined the Ambient Air Temperature (AAT) Sensor was not within calibrated temperature of the ECT and IAT Sensor signals after a cool down period. **Possible Causes:** • AAT Sensor circuit open, shorted to ground or VREF • AAT Sensor voltage below 1.0v • AAT signal circuit is open or is shorted to ground, to battery voltage or to Sensor ground • AAT Sensor ground circuit is open • AAT Sensor is damaged or it has failed • PCM High or Low circuit is damaged or it has failed
DTC: P0072 **1T CCM** **Years:** 2005, 2006, 2007 **Models:** Grand Cherokee, Liberty, PT Cruiser, Pacifica, Ram Truck, Sebring, Stratus **Engines:** All **Transmissions:** All	**Ambient Temperature Sensor Circuit Low Input** Related DTCs not set, key on or engine running; system voltage over 10.5v, at least 5 warm-up cycles completed, odometer mileage change at least 196.6 miles, and the PCM detected the AAT Sensor signal was less than 0.3v (0.78v: Jeep) at PCM. 3 good trips required to turn off MIL. **Possible Causes:** • AAT Sensor internal failure • AAT signal circuit shorted to ground • AAT signal circuit shorted to Sensor ground • PCM has failed

DTC	Trouble Code Title, Conditions & Possible Causes
DTC: P0072 **1T CCM** **Years:** 2005, 2006, 2007 **Models:** Liberty **Engines:** All **Transmissions:** All	**Ambient Temperature Sensor Circuit Low Input** Ignition is on. When the Ambient Temperature Sensor is less than 0.078v at the PCM for 2.8 seconds () or less than 0.039v for 4.2 seconds (Liberty), this DTC with set. 3 good trips required to turn off MIL. **Possible Causes:** • AAT Sensor internal failure • AAT signal circuit shorted to ground • AAT signal circuit shorted to Sensor ground • Front Control Module has failed
DTC: P0073 **1T CCM** **Years:** 2005, 2006, 2007 **Models:** Grand Cherokee, Liberty, PT Cruiser, Pacifica, Ram Truck, Sebring, Stratus **Engines:** All **Transmissions:** All	**Ambient Temperature Sensor Circuit High Input** Key on or engine running; system voltage over 10.0v and the PCM detected the Ambient Air Temperature (AAT) Sensor signal was more than 4.9v for more than 2.8 seconds. Note that this code can be set due to an intermittent failure. 3 good trips are required to turn off the MIL. **Possible Causes:** • AAT Sensor signal shorted to VREF (5v) or battery voltage • AAT Sensor signal circuit or Sensor ground circuit is open • AAT Sensor is damaged (it may be open) • PCM has failed
DTC: P0087 **1T CCM** **Years:** 2005, 2006, 2007 **Models:** Liberty **Engines:** 2.8L Diesel **Transmissions:** All	**Fuel Rail Pressure Too Low Malfunction** Engine running; ECM determines that the fuel rail pressure is too low for a given engine speed. **Possible Causes:** • Air in fuel system • Fuel injector problems • Fuel Pressure Solenoid has failed • Fuel Pump has malfunctioned or failed • Fuel system has contamination • Fuel system has a leak • Intermittent condition
DTC: P0088 **1T CCM** **Years:** 2005, 2006, 2007 **Models:** Liberty **Engines:** 2.8L Diesel **Transmissions:** All	**Fuel Rail Pressure Too High Malfunction** Engine running; ECM detects the fuel rail pressure is above 23,000 psi. **Possible Causes:** • Air in fuel system • Fuel injector problems • Fuel Pressure Solenoid has failed • Fuel Pump has malfunctioned or failed • Fuel system has contamination • Fuel system has a leak • Intermittent condition
DTC: P0089 **1T CCM** **Years:** 2005, 2006, 2007 **Models:** Liberty **Engines:** 2.8L Diesel **Transmissions:** All	**Fuel Pressure Solenoid After-Run Plausibility** Engine running; ECM determines that fuel rail pressure is too low for a given engine speed. **Possible Causes:** • Air in fuel system • Fuel injector problems • Fuel Pressure Solenoid has failed • Fuel Pump has malfunctioned or failed • Fuel system has contamination • Fuel system has a leak • Intermittent condition
DTC: P0090 **1T CCM** **Years:** 2005, 2006, 2007 **Models:** Liberty **Engines:** 2.8L Diesel **Transmissions:** All	**Fuel Quality Solenoid Open Circuit** Ignition on; ECM Fuel Quality Solenoid commanded OFF; ECM detects an open in the Fuel Quality Solenoid circuit. **Possible Causes:** • FQ Solenoid circuit(s) are open, shorted to ground, shorted to voltage, or shorted together • Intermittent condition • FQ Solenoid has failed • ECM has failed

DTC	Trouble Code Title, Conditions & Possible Causes
DTC: P0091 **1T CCM** **Years:** 2005, 2006, 2007 **Models:** Liberty **Engines:** 2.8L Diesel **Transmissions:** All	**Fuel Quality Solenoid Short To Ground Circuit** Ignition on; ECM Fuel Quality Solenoid commanded OFF; ECM detects short to ground on the Fuel Quality Solenoid circuit. **Possible Causes:** • FQ Solenoid circuit(s) are open, shorted to ground, shorted to voltage, or shorted together • Intermittent condition • FQ Solenoid has failed • ECM has failed
DTC: P0092 **1T CCM** **Years:** 2005, 2006, 2007 **Models:** Liberty **Engines:** 2.8L Diesel **Transmissions:** All	**Fuel Quality Solenoid Short Circuit** Ignition on; ECM Fuel Quality Solenoid commanded ON; ECM detects excessive current on the Fuel Quality Solenoid circuit. **Possible Causes:** • FQ Solenoid circuit(s) are open, shorted to ground, shorted to voltage, or shorted together • Intermittent condition • FQ Solenoid has failed • ECM has failed
DTC: P0100 **1T CCM** **Years:** 2005, 2006, 2007 **Models:** Liberty **Engines:** 2.8L Diesel **Transmissions:** All	**MAF Sensor Signal Voltage Too Low Or Too High** Engine running between 500-5000 rpm; ECM detects the MAF Sensor signal is blow 15 kg/h for 0.5 seconds, or is above 800 kg/h for 0.5 seconds. **Possible Causes:** • ASD relay output circuit is open • ECM 5v supply circuit problem • MAF Sensor ground circuit is open • MAF Sensor has failed • Intermittent condition • MAF Sensor signal circuit is open or is shorted to ground or shorted to MAF Sensor ground • MAF Sensor 5v supply circuit is shorted to MAF Sensor ground circuit or shorted to ground • MAF Sensor ground circuit is open • MAF Sensor 5v supply circuit is shorted to voltage • MAF Sensor circuit is shorted to voltage • ECM has failed
DTC: P0101 **1T CCM** **Years:** 2005, 2006, 2007 **Models:** Liberty **Engines:** 2.8L Diesel **Transmissions:** All	**MAF Sensor Signal Negative Or Positive Deviation** Engine running; engine coolant temperature between (60-100C); IAT Sensor reading is steady; atmospheric pressure is below 21.8 psi (1500 hPa); boost pressure is between 10.9-34.8 psi (750-2400 hPa). ECM detects the MAF Sensor reading is below (negative) or above (positive) the calibrated value for more than 2 seconds. **Possible Causes:** • Air filer problem • Air restriction in intake system • Air leak(s) in intake system • MAF Sensor has failed • Intermittent condition
DTC: P0105 **1T CCM** **Years:** 2005, 2006, 2007 **Models:** Liberty **Engines:** 2.8L Diesel **Transmissions:** All	**Inlet Pressure Sensor Signal Plausibility** Engine running below 800 rpm; no other IAT DTCs are present. The difference between Inlet Pressure Sensor signal and Atmospheric Pressure Sensor signal is 50.8 psi for 5 seconds. **Possible Causes:** • Air filer problem • Air restriction in intake system • Intermittent condition • High resistance in Inlet Pressure Sensor signal circuit, ground circuit, or 5v supply circuit • ECM has failed
DTC: P0105 **1T CCM** **Years:** 2005, 2006, 2007 **Models:** Liberty **Engines:** 2.8L Diesel **Transmissions:** All	**Inlet Pressure Sensor Signal Voltage Too High** Ignition on; ECM detects the Inlet Pressure Sensor signal is above 4.75v for 2 seconds. **Possible Causes:** • Intermittent condition • Inlet Pressure Sensor ground circuit is open, or shorted to voltage • Inlet Pressure Sensor signal circuit is shorted to voltage • Inlet Pressure Sensor has failed • ECM has failed

DTC	Trouble Code Title, Conditions & Possible Causes
DTC: P0105 **1T CCM** **Years:** 2005, 2006, 2007 **Models:** Liberty **Engines:** 2.8L Diesel **Transmissions:** All	**Inlet Pressure Sensor Signal Voltage Too Low** Ignition on; ECM detects the Inlet Pressure Sensor signal is below 0.25v for 2 seconds. **Possible Causes:** • Intermittent condition • Inlet Pressure Sensor 5v supply circuit problem • Inlet Pressure Sensor has failed • Inlet Pressure Sensor signal circuit is shorted to ground • Inlet Pressure Sensor signal circuit and ground circuit are shorted together • ECM has failed • Inlet Pressure Sensor signal circuit is open
DTC: P0106 **1T CCM** **Years:** 2005, 2006, 2007 **Models:** Grand Cherokee, Liberty, Pacifica, PT Cruiser, Ram Truck, Sebring, Stratus, Wrangler **Engines:** All **Transmissions:** All	**BARO Out-Of-Range at Key On / MAP Sensor Low** Key on for less than 350 ms; engine speed less than 255 rpm, and the PCM detected the MAP Sensor input was less than 2.196v but more than 0.019v during a 300 ms period. **Possible Causes:** • Loss of 5-volt supply from PCM (internal failure) • Sensor 5-volt supply circuit is shorted, open or grounded • Sensor signal circuit is open or shorted to ground • Sensor has failed • PCM has failed
DTC: P0107 **1T CCM** **Years:** 2005, 2006, 2007 **Models:** Cherokee, Grand Cherokee, Pacifica, PT Cruiser, Wrangler **Engines:** All **Transmissions:** All	**MAP Sensor Circuit Low Input** Engine speed from 600-3500 rpm; TP Sensor input less than 1.2v, system voltage over 10.6v, and the PCM detected the MAP input was below 0.0392v (conditions met for 1.76 seconds). **Possible Causes:** • MAP Sensor connector is damaged or shorted • MAP Sensor 5v supply circuit is open or it is shorted to ground • MAP Sensor signal circuit is shorted to ground • MAP Sensor has failed • PCM has failed
DTC: P0107 **1T CCM** **Years:** 2005, 2006, 2007 **Models:** Sebring, Stratus **Engines:** All **Transmissions:** All	**Barometric Pressure Sensor Circuit Low Input** Engine started, engine runtime over 2 seconds, system voltage over 10.5v and the PCM detected the BARO Sensor was 1.95v or lower (a value equal to 7.3 in. Hg or higher) for 10 seconds. **Note: This value indicates the vehicle was at 15,000 feet above sea level.** **Possible Causes:** • BARO Sensor connector is damaged or shorted • BARO Sensor 5v supply circuit is open or it is shorted to ground • BARO Sensor signal circuit is shorted to ground • BARO Sensor has failed • PCM has failed
DTC: P0107 **1T CCM** **Years:** 2005, 2006, 2007 **Models:** Grand Cherokee, Liberty, Ram Truck, Wrangler **Engines:** All **Transmissions:** All	**MAP Sensor Circuit Low Input** Engine speed from 416-1470 rpm; TP Sensor input less than 1v, and the PCM detected the MAP Sensor input was less than 2.35v at startup, or was less than 0.20v with the engine running (conditions met for 1.76 seconds). **Possible Causes:** • Loss of 5-volt supply from PCM (internal failure) • Sensor 5-volt supply circuit is open or shorted to ground • Sensor signal circuit is shorted to ground • Sensor or PCM has failed
DTC: P0107 **1T CCM** **Years:** 2005, 2006, 2007 **Models:** Grand Cherokee, Liberty, Pacifica, PT Cruiser, Ram Truck, Sebring, Stratus **Engines:** All **Transmissions:** All	**MAP Sensor Circuit Low Input** Ignition on or engine from 600-3500 rpm (416-1500 rpm:); TP Sensor input less than 1.2v (exc. Ram Truck, Jeep), less than 0.8v (Ram Truck, Jeep). Battery voltage greater than 10v. MAP Sensor signal voltage was less than 0.782v for 1.7 seconds (exc. Jeep) or less than 0.08v for 3 seconds (Jeep). If equipped, ETC light will flash. **Possible Causes:** • 5-volt supply circuit is open or shorted to ground • MAP Sensor signal circuit is shorted to ground or shorted to Sensor ground circuit • MAP Sensor has failed • PCM 5-volt supply circuit has failed

DTC	Trouble Code Title, Conditions & Possible Causes
DTC: P0108 **1T CCM** **Years:** 2005, 2006, 2007 **Models:** Grand Cherokee, Liberty, Pacifica, PT Cruiser, Ram Truck, Sebring, Stratus **Engines:** All **Transmissions:** All	**MAP Sensor Circuit High Input** Ignition on or engine speed from 600-3500 rpm; TP Sensor input more than 1.2v, for more than 1.7 seconds; battery voltage over 10.0v. The PCM detected the MAP Sensor signal voltage (input) was over 4.92v. **Possible Causes:** • MAP Sensor signal circuit is open • MAP Sensor ground circuit is open • MAP Sensor signal circuit shorted to 5-volt supply circuit or to battery voltage • MAP Sensor has failed or it has failed (possible open circuit) • MAP Sensor has failed • PCM has failed
DTC: P0108 **1T CCM** **Years:** 2005, 2006, 2007 **Models:** Sebring, Stratus **Engines:** All **Transmissions:** All	**Barometric Pressure Sensor Circuit High Input** Engine started; engine runtime over 2 seconds, system voltage over 8.0v, and the PCM detected the BARO Sensor was 4.45v or higher (a value equal to 114 kPa or 16.5" psi or higher) for 10 seconds. **Note: This value indicates the vehicle is 4,000 feet below sea level.** **Possible Causes:** • MAP Sensor signal circuit open, or the ground circuit is open • MAP Sensor signal circuit is shorted to VREF (5v) • MAP Sensor is damaged or it has failed • PCM has failed
DTC: P0108 **1T CCM** **Years:** 2005, 2006, 2007 **Models:** Grand Cherokee, Liberty, Ram Truck, Wrangler **Engines:** All **Transmissions:** All	**MAP Sensor Circuit High Input** Engine speed from 416-1470 rpm with the throttle closed; and the PCM detected a MAP Sensor input of more than 4.6v (conditions met for 1 second). **Possible Causes:** • MAP Sensor signal circuit is open • MAP Sensor ground circuit is open • MAP Sensor signal circuit shorted to VREF (5v) • MAP Sensor has failed or it has failed (possible open circuit) • PCM has failed
DTC: P0110 **1T CCM** **Years:** 2005, 2006, 2007 **Models:** Liberty, Pacifica, PT Cruiser, Sebring, Stratus **Engines:** All **Transmissions:** All	**IAT Sensor Circuit High or Low Input** Key on for 60 seconds or right after startup; and the PCM detected an IAT Sensor input of 4.6v or less than 0.2v for 4 seconds. **Possible Causes:** • IAT Sensor signal circuit is open, shorted to ground or to VREF • IAT Sensor signal circuit has a high resistance condition • IAT Sensor is damaged or it has failed • PCM has failed
DTC: P0110 **1T CCM** **Years:** 2005, 2006, 2007 **Models:** Liberty **Engines:** 2.8L Diesel **Transmissions:** All	**IAT Sensor Signal Voltage Too Low Or Too High** Ignition on; ECM detects the IAT Sensor signal is either below 0.45v (too low) or above 4.95v (too high). **Possible Causes:** • Intermittent condition • IAT Sensor signal circuit is open or is shorted to voltage (too high) • IAT Sensor signal circuit is shorted to ground or to Sensor ground (too low) • IAT Sensor ground circuit is open (too high) • Boost Pressure/IAT Sensor has failed • ECM has failed
DTC: P0111 **1T CCM** **Years:** 2005, 2006, 2007 **Models:** Grand Cherokee, Liberty, Pacifica, PT Cruiser, Ram Truck, Sebring, Stratus, Wrangler **Engines:** All **Transmissions:** All	**IAT Sensor Performance** DTC P0112 and P0113 not set, key on, ECT Sensor input more than 160°F at startup, at least 5 warm-up cycles have occurred with vehicle mileage change of more than 196.6 miles, and the PCM detected the IAT input changed less than 5.4°F during this period. **Possible Causes:** • IAT Sensor signal circuit is open, shorted to ground or VREF • IAT Sensor ground circuit is open • IAT Sensor is damaged or it has failed • PCM High or Low circuit is damaged or it has failed

DTC	Trouble Code Title, Conditions & Possible Causes
DTC: P0111 **2T CCM** **Years:** 2005, 2006, 2007 **Models:** Grand Cherokee, Liberty, Pacifica, PT Cruiser, Ram Truck, Sebring, Stratus **Engines:** All **Transmissions:** All	**IAT Sensor Performance** Engine off. After calibrated amount of cool down (over 8 hours). PCM detects IAT Sensor is not within calibrated temperature amount of ECT Sensor and AAT Sensor. Engine time off when monitored is more than 8 hours and ambient temperature is more than 38F (4C). 3 good trips are required to turn off the MIL. **Possible Causes:** • IAT Sensor signal circuit is open, shorted to ground, to Sensor ground, or to battery voltage • IAT Sensor voltage is below 1.0v • IAT Sensor ground circuit is open • IAT Sensor is damaged or has failed • PCM High or Low circuit is damaged or has failed
DTC: P0112 **1T CCM** **Years:** 2005, 2006, 2007 **Models:** Grand Cherokee, Liberty, Pacifica, PT Cruiser, Ram Truck, Sebring, Stratus, Wrangler **Engines:** All **Transmissions:** All	**IAT Sensor Circuit Low Input** Ignition on or engine started; battery voltage greater than 10v. If the PCM detected an IAT Sensor input of less than 0.1v (Neon), 0.157v (Cirrus/Sebring, Stratus) or less than 0.078v (Ram Truck, Grand Cherokee) for 3 seconds, less than 0.8v (), or less than 0.5v (Liberty) this DTC will set. **Possible Causes:** • IAT Sensor signal circuit is shorted to chassis ground • IAT Sensor signal circuit is shorted to Sensor ground • IAT Sensor is damaged or it has failed (an internal short circuit) • PCM has failed
DTC: P0113 **1T CCM** **Years:** 2005, 2006, 2007 **Models:** Grand Cherokee, Liberty, Pacifica, PT Cruiser, Ram Truck, Sebring, Stratus, Wrangler **Engines:** All **Transmissions:** All	**IAT Sensor Circuit High Input** Check with ignition on or engine running; battery voltage more than 10v; The PCM detected the IAT Sensor input was over 4.90v (exc. Ram) or 4.98v (Ram) for 3 seconds. **Possible Causes:** • IAT Sensor signal circuit shorted to VREF (5v) • IAT Sensor signal circuit is open, or the ground circuit is open • IAT Sensor is damaged or it has failed (an internal open circuit) • PCM has failed
DTC: P0115 **1T CCM** **Years:** 2005, 2006, 2007 **Models:** Liberty **Engines:** 2.8L Diesel **Transmissions:** All	**ECT Sensor Signal Voltage Too Low Or Too High** Ignition on; ECM detects the ECT Sensor signal is either below 0.12v (too low) or above 4.95v (too high). **Possible Causes:** • Intermittent condition • ECT Sensor signal circuit is open or is shorted to voltage (too high) • ECT Sensor signal circuit is shorted to ground or to Sensor ground (too low) • ECT Sensor ground circuit is open (too high) • Boost Pressure/IAT Sensor has failed • ECM has failed
DTC: P0116 **1T CCM** **Years:** 2005, 2006, 2007 **Models:** Grand Cherokee, Liberty, Pacifica, PT Cruiser, Ram Truck, Sebring, Stratus, Wrangler **Engines:** All **Transmissions:** All	**ECT Sensor Circuit Performance** Engine started; engine runtime over 10 minutes, and the PCM detected the ECT Sensor did not reach a calibrated level during the test period (i.e., it failed the CCM rationality test). **Possible Causes:** • ECT Sensor signal circuit is open or it is shorted to ground • ECT Sensor signal circuit is shorted to VREF (5v) • ECT Sensor ground circuit is open • ECT Sensor is damaged or it has failed • PCM High or Low circuit is damaged or it has failed
DTC: P0116 **2T CCM** **Years:** 2005, 2006, 2007 **Models:** Grand Cherokee, Liberty, Pacifica, PT Cruiser, Ram Truck, Sebring, Stratus **Engines:** All **Transmissions:** All	**ECT Sensor Circuit Performance** Engine off time is more than 8 hours; ambient temperature is more than 38F (4C); and after a calibrated amount of cool-down time, the PCM compares the ECT Sensor, IAT Sensor and AAT Sensor values; if ECT Sensor is not within a calibrated temperature amount of the other 2 Sensors, an error is detected. 3 good trips are required to turn off the MIL. If equipped, the ECT light will also illuminate when the MIL illuminates. **Possible Causes:** • ECT Sensor signal circuit is open or it is shorted battery voltage or to ground • ECT Sensor signal circuit is shorted to Sensor ground • ECT Sensor ground circuit is open • ECT Sensor is damaged or it has failed • PCM High or Low circuit is damaged or it has failed

DTC	Trouble Code Title, Conditions & Possible Causes
DTC: P0117 **1T CCM** **Years:** 2005, 2006, 2007 **Models:** Grand Cherokee, Liberty, Pacifica, PT Cruiser, Ram Truck, Sebring, Stratus, Wrangler **Engines:** All **Transmissions:** All	**ECT Sensor Circuit Low Input** Ignition on or engine started. The PCM detected the ECT Sensor input voltage was below 0.51v (95-03) or 0.1v (04-05, exc. Grand Cherokee, Liberty), less than 0.5v (04-05Liberty), less than 0.78v (Grand Cherokee) for 3 seconds. **Possible Causes:** • ECT Sensor signal circuit is shorted to chassis ground • ECT Sensor signal circuit is shorted to Sensor ground • ECT Sensor is damaged or it has failed (it may be shorted) • PCM has failed
DTC: P0118 **1T CCM** **Years:** 2005, 2006, 2007 **Models:** Pacifica, PT Cruiser, Sebring, Stratus, Wrangler **Engines:** All **Transmissions:** All	**ECT Sensor Circuit High Input** Ignition on or engine started and the PCM detected the ECT Sensor input was over 4.9v for 3 seconds. If equipped, the ETC lamp will illuminate with the MIL. 3 good trips are required to turn off the MIL. **Possible Causes:** • ECT Sensor signal circuit is shorted to VREF (5v) • ECT Sensor signal circuit is open • ECT Sensor ground circuit is open • ECT Sensor is damaged or it has failed (possible open circuit) • PCM has failed
DTC: P0120 **1T CCM** **Years:** 2005, 2006, 2007 **Models:** PT Cruiser **Engines:** All **Transmissions:** All	**Throttle Position Sensor Circuit** Engine started; and the TCM detected an unexpected change in the throttle angle, or that the throttle angle went out-of-range abruptly. **Possible Causes:** • TP Sensor signal circuit is open or shorted to ground • TP Sensor ground circuit is open • TP Sensor signal circuit to TCM is open or shorted to ground • TP Sensor is damaged or it has failed • PCM has failed
DTC: P0121 **1T CCM** **Years:** 2005, 2006, 2007 **Models:** Pacifica, PT Cruiser, Sebring, Stratus, Wrangler **Engines:** All **Transmissions:** All	**TP Sensor Does Not Agree With MAP** DTC P0107, P0108, P0122 and P0123 not set, engine running with throttle plate closed (at high vacuum), and the PCM detected the TP Sensor input was high when it should have been low (High Input Test), or with the engine running and the VSS input over 25 mph, throttle plate open (at low vacuum), the PCM detected the TP Sensor input was low when it should have been high, conditions met for 4 seconds. **Possible Causes:** • MAP Sensor and/or TP Sensor VREF (5v) not present • MAP or TP Sensor ground circuit has high resistance • MAP or TP Sensor signal circuit has high resistance • TP Sensor is damaged or has failed • PCM has failed
DTC: P0121 **1T CCM** **Years:** 2005, 2006, 2007 **Models:** Grand Cherokee, Liberty, Ram **Engines:** All **Transmissions:** All	**TP Sensor No. 1 Does Not Agree With MAP** Ignition is on and no MAP Sensor DTCs are set. The PCM determines the TP Sensor signals do not correlate with the MAP Sensor signal. The ECT light will illuminate. DTC P2135 should also set with this DTC. **Possible Causes:** • TP Sensor No. 1 signal circuit shorted to battery voltage • Resistance in either TP Sensor No. 1 or 2 signal circuit, 5v supply circuit or TP Sensor return circuit • TP Sensor No. 1 signal circuit shorted to group or to TP Sensor No. 2 signal circuit • 5v supply circuit shorted to ground • TP Sensor or throttle body damaged or failed • PCM has failed
DTC: P0122 **1T CCM** **Years:** 2005, 2006, 2007 **Models:** Pacifica, PT Cruiser, Sebring, Stratus, Wrangler **Engines:** All **Transmissions:** All	**TP Sensor Circuit Low Input** Key on or engine running; system voltage over 10.5v and the PCM detected the TP Sensor indicated less than 0.0978v for 700 ms. **Possible Causes:** • TP Sensor VREF (5v) circuit is open or shorted to ground • TP Sensor 5v supply circuit is shorted to ground • TP Sensor signal circuit is shorted to ground • TP Sensor is damaged or it has failed • Possible intermittent condition • PCM has failed

DTC	Trouble Code Title, Conditions & Possible Causes
DTC: P0122 **1T CCM** **Years:** 2005, 2006, 2007 **Models:** Grand Cherokee, Liberty, Ram **Engines:** All **Transmissions:** All	**TP Sensor Circuit Low Input** Key on or engine running; system voltage over 10.5v and the PCM detected the TP Sensor was less than 0.10v, condition met for 1.3 seconds. **Possible Causes:** • Sensor 5-volt supply circuit open or shorted to ground • Sensor signal circuit is shorted to ground • TP Sensor is damaged or it has failed • PCM has failed
DTC: P0122 **1T CCM** **Years:** 2005, 2006, 2007 **Models:** Grand Cherokee, Liberty, Pacifica, PT Cruiser, Ram Truck, Sebring, Stratus **Engines:** All **Transmissions:** All	**TP Sensor No. 1 Circuit Low Input** Key on; system voltage over 10v; and the PCM detected the TP Sensor indicated less than 0.16v for 0.7 second (Liberty), 0.078v (Pacifica, PT Cruiser), or 0.0978v (Sebring, Stratus) or 0.1v (). 3 good trips are required to turn off the MIL. If equipped, the ETC light will illuminate. **Possible Causes:** • TP Sensor sweep • Intermittent condition • 5v supply circuit open or shorted to ground • TP Sensor No. 1 signal circuit shorted to ground or to Sensor return circuit • TP Sensor or throttle body damaged or has failed • PCM has failed
DTC: P0122 **1T CCM** **Years:** 2005, 2006, 2007 **Models:** Liberty **Engines:** 2.8L Diesel II **Transmissions:** All	**TP Sensor/APP Sensor Circuit Low Input** Engine running. If the monitored APP Sensor voltage drops below 0.078v for 0.48 second, this DTC will set. **Possible Causes:** • TP Sensor sweep • Intermittent condition • 5v supply circuit open or shorted to ground • TP Sensor No. 1 signal circuit shorted to ground or to Sensor return circuit • TP Sensor or throttle body damaged or has failed • PCM has failed
DTC: P0122 **1T CCM** **Years:** 2005, 2006, 2007 **Models:** Ram Truck **Engines:** All **Transmissions:** All	**TP Sensor No. 1 Circuit Low Input** Key on; system voltage over 10.4v. The PCM detected the TP Sensor voltage is less than 0.0978v for 1.3 seconds (3.7L, 4.7L), or less than 0.16v for 0.7 second (5.7L). 3 good trips are required to turn off the MIL. If equipped, the ETC light will illuminate. **Possible Causes:** • 5v supply circuit open or shorted to ground • TP Sensor No. 1 signal circuit shorted to ground or to Sensor ground circuit • TP Sensor has failed • Throttle body is damaged • PCM has failed
DTC: P0123 **1T CCM** **Years:** 2005, 2006, 2007 **Models:** Pacifica, PT Cruiser, Sebring, Stratus, Wrangler **Engines:** All **Transmissions:** All	**TP Sensor Circuit High Input** Key on or engine running; system voltage over 10.5v and the PCM detected the TP Sensor indicated more than 4.50v for 700 ms. **Possible Causes:** • TP Sensor sweep • TP Sensor ground circuit is open • TP Sensor signal circuit is open or is shorted to VREF (5v) • TP Sensor is damaged or has failed (an internal open circuit) • Possible intermittent condition • PCM has failed
DTC: P0123 **1T CCM** **Years:** 2005, 2006, 2007 **Models:** Grand Cherokee, Liberty, Pacifica, PT Cruiser, Ram Truck, Sebring, Stratus **Engines:** All **Transmissions:** All	**TP Sensor/APPS Circuit High Input** Key on or engine running; system voltage over 10v. The PCM detected the TP Sensor indicated more than 4.47v (Sebring, Stratus, Liberty) or 4.94v (all other models) for 0.48 second. If equipped, ETC light will illuminate. **Possible Causes:** • Related TP Sensor engine DTCs present • Intermittent wiring or connector problem • TP signal circuit is open or is shorted to battery voltage or to 5v supply circuit • TP sensor has failed • TP sensor ground circuit is open • PCM has failed

DTC	Trouble Code Title, Conditions & Possible Causes
DTC: P0123 **1T CCM** **Years:** 2005, 2006, 2007 **Models:** Ram Truck **Engines:** All **Transmissions:** All	**Throttle Position Sensor No. 1 Circuit High** Ignition is on; battery voltage is more than 10.4v. The PCM detected the TP Sensor voltage is more than 4.47v for 1.3 seconds (3.7L, 4.7L) or more than 4.8v for 25ms (5.7L). If equipped, the ETC light will illuminate. **Possible Causes:** • TP Sensor No. 1 circuit is open, or is shorted to battery voltage • TP Sensor No. 1 signal circuit is shorted to 5v supply circuit • TP Sensor ground circuit is open • TP Sensor has failed • Throttle body is damaged (5.7L) • Throttle plate is jammed against the maximum stop (5.7L) • PCM has failed
DTC: P0123 **1T CCM** **Years:** 2005, 2006, 2007 **Models:** Liberty **Engines:** 2.8L Diesel **Transmissions:** All	**TP Sensor/APP Sensor Circuit High Input** Engine running. If the monitored APP Sensor voltage rises above 4.94v for 0.48 second, this DTC will set. **Possible Causes:** • Speed Sensor ground circuit open or shorted to voltage • 5v supply circuit shorted to voltage • APP Sensor has failed • TCM has failed • Intermittent wiring and connector problems
DTC: P0124 **1T CCM** **Years:** 2005, 2006, 2007 **Models:** Pacifica, PT Cruiser, Sebring, Stratus **Engines:** All **Transmissions:** All	**TP Sensor/APPS Circuit Intermittent** Key on or engine running; system voltage over 10.5v. This DTC will set if the monitored TP Sensor angle between 6-120 and the degree change is greater than 5 within a period of less than 7.0ms. **Possible Causes:** • Related TP Sensor engine DTCs present • TP Sensor has failed • Intermittent wiring or connector problem • PCM has failed
DTC: P0124 **1T CCM** **Years:** 2005, 2006, 2007 **Models:** Liberty **Engines:** 2.8L Diesel **Transmissions:** All	**TP Sensor/APP Sensor Intermittent Circuit** Engine running. This DTC will set with a throttle angle between 6 and 120.6 with a 5 or higher change under 7ms. Related DTCs may be present. **Possible Causes:** • Intermittent wiring and connector problems • APP Sensor has failed • TCM has failed
DTC: P0125 **2T CCM** **Years:** 2005, 2006, 2007 **Models:** Pacifica, PT Cruiser, Sebring, Stratus, Wrangler **Engines:** All **Transmissions:** All	**Closed Loop Temperature Not Reached** DTC P0117 and P0118 not set, ECT Sensor between −20°F and +21.2°F at startup, engine runtime over 10 minutes, vehicle speed more than 28 mph, and the PCM detected the ECT Sensor did not reach 174°F after 20 minutes of sustained engine operation. **Possible Causes:** • Check the operation of the thermostat (it may be stuck open) • ECT Sensor is damaged or it is out-of-calibration • Inspect for low coolant level or for an incorrect coolant mixture
DTC: P0125 **2T CCM** **Years:** 2005, 2006, 2007 **Models:** Grand Cherokee, Liberty, Pacifica, PT Cruiser, Ram Truck, Sebring, Stratus **Engines:** All **Transmissions:** All	**Closed Loop Temperature Not Reached** Engine running; battery over 10v. Engine temperature does not enable closed loop. Failure time depends on start-up coolant temperature and ambient temperature (i.e., 2 minutes for a start temperature of 50°F (10C), or up to 10 minutes for a vehicle with start-up temperature of −18F (−28C). **Possible Causes:** • Low coolant level • Improper thermostat operation or thermostat failure • ECT has failed
DTC: P0128 **1T CCM** **Years:** 2005, 2006, 2007 **Models:** Pacifica, PT Cruiser, Sebring, Stratus **Engines:** All **Transmissions:** All	**Thermostat Rationality Test** DTC P0117, P0118, P1492 and P1493 not set, ECT Sensor between 20°F and 130°F at startup, and the PCM detected the ECT Sensor did not exceed 170°F after 10-32 minutes of sustained engine operation (the actual time depends on the ECT Sensor at startup). **Possible Causes:** • Check the operation of the thermostat (it may be stuck open) • ECT Sensor is contaminated, damaged or it has failed • Inspect for low coolant level or for an incorrect coolant mixture

DTC	Trouble Code Title, Conditions & Possible Causes
DTC: P0128 **1T CCM** **Years:** 2005, 2006, 2007 **Models:** Sebring, Stratus **Engines:** All **Transmissions:** All	**Thermostat Rationality Test** ECT Sensor from 14°F and 82°F at startup with the ECT and IAT Sensor inputs within 48°F and the IAT input less than 36°F, volume airflow from 50-100 Hz for under 300 seconds, and the PCM detected the ECT Sensor took too long to reach 180°F. The actual time vary with the ECT Sensor at startup (e.g., from 11-23 minutes to reach 180°F if the ECT Sensor is over 68°F at startup, or 20-54 minutes to reach 180°F if the ECT Sensor is less than 68F at startup). **Possible Causes:** • Check the operation of the thermostat (it may be stuck open) • Inspect for low coolant level or for an incorrect coolant mixture
DTC: P0128 **2T CCM** **Years:** 2005, 2006, 2007 **Models:** Grand Cherokee, Liberty, Pacifica, PT Cruiser, Ram Truck, Sebring, Stratus **Engines:** All **Transmissions:** All	**Thermostat Rationality Test** With engine running after cold start. PCM predicts a coolant temperature value that it will compare to the actual coolant temperature. If the 2 coolant temperature values are not within 50°F (10°C) of each other, an error is detected. **Possible Causes:** • Low coolant level • Thermostat has failed • Signal circuit shorted to battery voltage • ECT Sensor has failed or voltage is below 1.0v • Signal circuit is open, shorted to ground or shorted to Sensor ground • ECT Sensor ground circuit or signal circuit is open • PCM has failed
DTC: P0128 **1T CCM** **Years:** 2005, 2006, 2007 **Models:** Liberty **Engines:** 2.8L Diesel **Transmissions:** All	**ECT Sensor: Engine Is Cold Too Long** Ignition on; With engine running and engine temperature is below 40C, this DTC will set. **Possible Causes:** • Intermittent condition • Cooling system problems • ECT Sensor has failed • ECM has failed
DTC: P0129 **1T CCM** **Years:** 2005, 2006, 2007 **Models:** Grand Cherokee, Liberty, Pacifica, PT Cruiser, Ram Truck, Sebring, Stratus **Engines:** All **Transmissions:** All	**Barometric Pressure Out-Of-Range** Engine cranking at less than 250 rpm; no CKP or CMP Sensor signals within 75ms. The PCM detected the MAP/BARO Sensor signal range was 0.04-2.2v for 300ms during testing. If equipped, the ETC lamp will be illuminated. 3 good trips are required to turn off the MIL. **Possible Causes:** • IAC motor control low or control high circuit has failed • MAP Sensor VREF (5v) circuit is open or shorted to ground • MAP Sensor signal circuit is open or shorted to ground • MAP Sensor is damaged or it has failed • May be an intermittent condition • PCM has failed
DTC: P0130 **1T CCM** **Years:** 2005, 2006, 2007 **Models:** Sebring, Stratus **Engines:** All **Transmissions:** All	**O2 (B1 S1) Circuit Fault** Engine runtime over 3 minutes, engine speed more than 1200 rpm, volumetric efficiency more than 25%, ECT Sensor more than 180°F, and the PCM detected the O2 signal was less than 0.2v during the 7 second test period, and the PCM detected the O2 signal remained at more than 4.5v with 5v applied to the circuit during the O2 Test period. **Possible Causes:** • O2 signal circuit is open or shorted to ground • O2 ground circuit is open • O2 may be contaminated or it has failed • PCM has failed
DTC: P0130 **1T CCM** **Years:** 2005, 2006, 2007 **Models:** Grand Cherokee, Liberty, Ram Truck, Wrangler **Engines:** All **Transmissions:** All	**O2 (B1 S1) Circuit Fault** Key on or engine running; system voltage over 10.5v and the PCM detected the state of the O2 relay coil circuit (between the PCM and the relay) did not match the expected state. **Possible Causes:** Fused ignition feed (power) circuit open • Heater relay control circuit open • Heater relay has failed (an internal winding is open) • PCM has failed

DTC	Trouble Code Title, Conditions & Possible Causes
DTC: P0131 **1T CCM** **Years:** 2005, 2006, 2007 **Models:** Liberty, Pacifica, PT Cruiser, Sebring, Stratus, Wrangler **Engines:** All **Transmissions:** All	**O2 (B1 S1) Short to Ground** ECT Sensor over 170°F on previous key on, ECT Sensor under 98°F and BTS within 27°F of ECT Sensor, and the PCM detected the O2 signal was below 156 mV for 28 seconds. **Possible Causes:** • O2 signal circuit is shorted to chassis or Sensor ground • O2 ground circuit is open (circuit reads 170 mV when open) • O2 may be contaminated or it has failed • PCM has failed
DTC: P0131 **2T CCM** **Years:** 2005, 2006, 2007 **Models:** Grand Cherokee, Liberty, Pacifica, PT Cruiser, Ram Truck, Sebring, Stratus **Engines:** All **Transmissions:** All	**O2 (B1 S1) Circuit Short to Ground** Engine running; cold start. O2 Sensor signal voltage is below 2.402v for 9 seconds. **Possible Causes:** • O2 signal circuit is shorted to chassis or Sensor ground • O2 return circuit is shorted to ground or to signal circuit • O2 signal circuit is shorted to O2 return upstream circuit • O2 may be contaminated or it has failed • PCM has failed
DTC: P0131 **1T CCM** **Years:** 2005, 2006, 2007 **Models:** Grand Cherokee, Liberty, Ram Truck, Wrangler **Engines:** All **Transmissions:** All	**O2 (B1 S1) Circuit Short to Ground** Engine running with ECT Sensor over 146°F, followed by an engine off period in which the O2 heater Test ran and passed, then after an engine cool-down period, and a cold engine startup (ECT Sensor under 100°F and the BTS signal within 44°F of the ECT Sensor), the PCM detected the O2 signal was less than 78 mV for 5 seconds. **Possible Causes:** • O2 signal circuit is shorted to chassis or Sensor ground • O2 ground circuit is open (circuit reads 170 mV when open) • O2 may be contaminated or it has failed • PCM has failed
DTC: P0132 **1T CCM** **Years:** 2005, 2006, 2007 **Models:** Pacifica, PT Cruiser, Sebring, Stratus **Engines:** All **Transmissions:** All	**O2 (B1 S1) Circuit Short to Voltage** Engine started; engine runtime over 119 seconds, system voltage over 10.5v, ECT Sensor more than 176°F, and the PCM detected the O2 signal was more than 1.29v for 3 seconds. **Possible Causes:** • O2 signal circuit shorted to heater B+ circuit (inspect the connector for oil or moisture inside the terminal area) • O2 signal circuit is open • PCM has failed
DTC: P0132 **1T CCM** **Years:** 2005, 2006, 2007 **Models:** Grand Cherokee, Liberty, Ram Truck, Wrangler **Engines:** All **Transmissions:** All	**O2 (B1 S1) Circuit Short to Voltage** Engine started; engine runtime over 119 seconds, system voltage over 10.99v, O2 heater temperature over 1085°F and the PCM detected the O2 input was over 3.70v for 1 minute. **Possible Causes:** • O2 signal tracking (wet/oily) in connector causing a short between the signal and heater power circuits • O2 ground circuit is open • O2 signal circuit is open • PCM has failed
DTC: P0132 **2T CCM** **Years:** 2005, 2006, 2007 **Models:** Grand Cherokee, Liberty, Pacifica, PT Cruiser, Sebring, Stra-tus **Engines:** All **Transmissions:** All	**O2 Sensor (B1 S1) Voltage High** Engine started; engine runtime over 119 seconds. Battery voltage over 10.99v. O2 Sensor heater temperature is more than 662F (350C). O2 Sensor voltage is more than 3.7v for 60 seconds (Pacifica), more than 3.99v for 60 seconds (Sebring, Stratus, PT Cruiser), or more than 3.99v for 66.56 seconds (Liberty). **Possible Causes:** • O2 Sensor signal circuit and/or return circuit shorted to voltage • O2 Sensor has failed • O2 Sensor signal or return circuit open • PCM has failed
DTC: P0132 **1T CCM** **Years:** 2005, 2006, 2007 **Models:** Ram Truck **Engines:** All **Transmissions:** All	**O2 Sensor (B1 S1) Voltage High** Engine started; battery voltage above 10.4v; O2 Sensor heater temperature is more than 925F (496C). O2 Sensor is more than 3.7v for 40 seconds. 3 good trips are required to turn the MIL off. **Possible Causes:** • O2 Sensor signal circuit and/or return circuit shorted to voltage • O2 Sensor has failed • O2 Sensor signal or return circuit open • PCM has failed

DTC	Trouble Code Title, Conditions & Possible Causes
DTC: P0133 **2T O2** **Years:** 2005, 2006, 2007 **Models:** Grand Cherokee, Liberty, Ram Truck, Wrangler **Engines:** All **Transmissions:** All	**O2 (B1 S1) Slow Response** Engine runtime over 2 minutes, ECT Sensor more than 147°F, VSS over 10 mph, A/C and PSPS indicating off, then at idle speed in Drive (A/T) or Neutral (M/T), and the PCM detected the O2 signal did not switch enough times from 270-620 mV in the test period. **Possible Causes:** • Exhaust leak present in the exhaust manifold or exhaust pipes • O2 element is fuel contaminated • O2 element is deteriorated or it has failed
DTC: P0133 **2T O2** **Years:** 2005, 2006, 2007 **Models:** PT Cruiser, Sebring, Stratus **Engines:** All **Transmissions:** All	**O2 (B1 S1) Slow Response** Engine at idle speed, system voltage over 10.5v, then engine speed from 1216-1984 rpm, VSS input from 19-46 mph, BTS signal more than 44°F, BARO signal more than 22.16" Hg, MAP Sensor signal from 11.9-18.15" Hg, then back to idle speed in Drive, and the PCM detected the O2 signal did not switch enough times from below 330 mV to above 610 mV, condition met for 60 seconds. **Possible Causes:** • Exhaust leak present in the exhaust manifold or exhaust pipes • O2 element is fuel contaminated • O2 element is deteriorated or it has failed
DTC: P0133 **2T O2** **Years:** 2005, 2006, 2007 **Models:** Pacifica, PT Cruiser, Sebring, Stratus **Engines:** All **Transmissions:** All	**O2 (B1 S1) Slow Response** Vehicle driven at speeds between 20-55 mph, with throttle open for minimum of 120 seconds; coolant temperature is greater than 158F (70C); catalytic converter temperature is greater than 1112F (600C). PCM compared differences (state of change) between front and rear O2 Sensors indicate difference is greater than calibrated amount. **Possible Causes:** • Exhaust leak present in the exhaust manifold or exhaust pipes • O2 signal circuit or return circuit has failed • O2 element has failed
DTC: P0133 **2T O2** **Years:** 2005, 2006, 2007 **Models:** Grand Cherokee, Liberty, Ram **Engines:** All **Transmissions:** All	**O2 (B1 S1) Slow Response** Vehicle driven at speeds between 20-55 mph, with throttle open for minimum of 120 seconds; coolant temperature is greater than 158F (70C); catalytic converter temperature is greater than 1112F (600C); EVAP purge is active. The PCM detects the O2 Sensor signal voltage switches less than 16 times from lean to rich with 20 seconds during monitoring. 3 good trips are required to turn off MIL. **Possible Causes:** • Exhaust leak present in the exhaust manifold or exhaust pipes • O2 signal circuit or upstream circuit has failed • O2 element has failed
DTC: P0134 **2T O2** **Years:** 2005, 2006, 2007 **Models:** Pacifica, PT Cruiser, Sebring, Stratus **Models:** Pacifica, PT Cruiser, Sebring, Stratus **Engines:** All **Transmissions:** All	**O2 (B1 S1) Remains At Center** Engine runtime more than 121 seconds, system voltage over 10.5v, ECT Sensor more than 150.8°F, fuel control system in closed loop mode, and the PCM detected the O2 signal remained fixed in a range between 350-580 mV, condition met for 60 seconds. **Possible Causes:** • Exhaust leak present in exhaust manifold or exhaust pipes • O2 element is fuel contaminated or has deteriorated • O2S signal circuit or ground circuit has high resistance • PCM has failed
DTC: P0134 **2T O2** **Years:** 2005, 2006, 2007 **Models:** Grand Cherokee, Liberty, Wrangler **Engines:** All **Transmissions:** All	**O2 (B1 S1) Remains At Center** Engine runtime more than 121 seconds, system voltage over 10.5v, ECT Sensor more than 150.8°F, fuel control system in closed loop mode, and the PCM detected the O2 signal remained fixed in a range between 350-580 mV, condition met for 60 seconds. **Possible Causes:** • Exhaust leak present in exhaust manifold or exhaust pipes • O2 element is fuel contaminated or has deteriorated • O2S signal circuit or ground circuit has high resistance • PCM has failed
DTC: P0135 **1T CCM** **Years:** 2005, 2006, 2007 **Models:** Sebring, Stratus **Engines:** All **Transmissions:** All	**O2 (B1 S1) Heater Circuit** Engine started; system voltage from 11-16v, ECT Sensor over 68°F, and the PCM detected the O2 heater current was less than 0.16 amps or more than 7.5 amps for 4 seconds. **Possible Causes:** • O2 heater ground circuit open or O2 signal circuit is open • O2 heater element has high resistance • O2 heater element has failed (open or shorted) • MFI relay output (power) circuit to the heater is open • PCM has failed

DTC	Trouble Code Title, Conditions & Possible Causes
DTC: P0135 **2T CCM** **Years:** 2005, 2006, 2007 **Models:** Liberty, Pacifica, PT Cruiser, Sebring, Stratus **Engines:** All **Transmissions:** All	**O2 (B1 S1) Heater Circuit** Engine running and O2 heater duty cycle is greater than 0%. O2 heater temperature does not reach 959F (575C), exc. PT Cruiser, or 662F (350C) PT Cruiser, within 90 seconds (Sebring, Stratus, 45 seconds) during monitoring conditions. No Sensor output is received when the PCM powers up the Sensor heater. 3 good trips are required to turn off the MIL. **Possible Causes:** • O2 heater ground circuit open or O2 signal circuit is open • O2 heater element has failed • PCM has failed
DTC: P0135 **2T CCM** **Years:** 2005, 2006, 2007 **Models:** Grand Cherokee, Liberty, Wrangler **Engines:** All **Transmissions:** All	**O2 (B1 S1) Heater Circuit** Engine running; O2 heater duty cycle is greater than 0%; ASD relay is energized; battery voltage is greater than 10.4v. No sensor output is received when the PCM powers up the sensor heater. The O2 heater is out of control for 128 seconds after it has reached 572F (300C). **Possible Causes:** • O2 heater ground circuit open or O2 signal circuit is open • O2 heater element has failed • PCM has failed
DTC: P0135 **2T CCM** **Years:** 2005, 2006, 2007 **Models:** Ram Truck **Engines:** All **Transmissions:** All	**O2 (B1 S1) Heater Circuit** Engine running and O2 heater duty cycle is greater than 0%; battery voltage is more than 11v. No O2 sensor output signal is received when the PCM powers up the sensor heater. 3 good trips are required to turn off the MIL. **Possible Causes:** • O2 heater ground circuit open or heater control circuit is open • O2 heater element has failed • PCM has failed
DTC: P0137 **1T CCM** **Years:** 2005, 2006, 2007 **Models:** Grand Cherokee, Liberty, Pacifica, PT Cruiser, Ram Truck, Sebring, Stratus, Wrangler **Engines:** All **Transmissions:** All	**O2 (B1 S2) Sensor Circuit Low** Engine running; battery voltage over 10.9v; O2 heater temperature below 484°F (251C) or ECT above 170F from previous key off. The PCM detected the O2 Sensor signal voltage was less than 1.5v for 3 seconds (Magnum), less than 2.402v for 9 seconds (Sebring, Stratus, PT Cruiser, Liberty), or 2.5194v for 3 seconds (Ram), or less than 0.156v for 28 seconds (). **Possible Causes:** • O2 return circuit is shorted to ground • O2 signal circuit is shorted to ground, or to O2 return circuit, or O2 heater ground circuit • O2 Sensor has failed • PCM has failed
DTC: P0138 **2T CCM** **Years:** 2005, 2006, 2007 **Models:** Grand Cherokee, Liberty, Pacifica, PT Cruiser, Ram Truck, Sebring, Stratus, Wrangler **Engines:** All **Transmissions:** All	**O2 (B1 S2) Sensor Voltage High Condition:** Engine runtime for 119 seconds; O2 Sensor heater temperature is more than 662°F (350°C); Battery voltage more than 10.99v. O2 Sensor voltage is above 3.7v for 60 seconds (Pacifica), or 3.99v for 60 seconds (PT Cruiser, Sebring, Stratus), above 3.9902v for 30 seconds (Grand Cherokee, Ram Truck, Wrangler), or above 3.99v for 76.8 seconds (Liberty). **Possible Causes:** • O2 Sensor signal circuit or return circuit shorted to voltage • O2 Sensor has failed • O2 Sensor signal circuit or return circuit open • PCM has failed
DTC: P0139 **2T O2** **Years:** 2005, 2006, 2007 **Models:** Sebring, Stratus **Engines:** All **Transmissions:** All	**O2 (B1 S2) Slow Response** Engine started; ECT Sensor more than 169°F, front O2 active, volumetric airflow Sensor more than 4000 Hz, then vehicle speed over 18.7 mph at over 1500 rpm with the volumetric efficiency over 40%, then vehicle speed below 0.9 mph, Fuel Shutoff active, and the PCM detected the O2 signal was less than 0.78v for 38 seconds. **Possible Causes:** • Exhaust leak present in the exhaust manifold or exhaust pipes • O2 element is fuel contaminated or it has failed • O2 ground or O2 signal circuit has high resistance
DTC: P0139 **2T O2** **Years:** 2005, 2006, 2007 **Models:** Pacifica **Engines:** All **Transmissions:** All	**O2 (B1 S2) Slow Response** Engine started; vehicle driven at 20-60 mph with the throttle open for 2 minutes; ECT Sensor more than 158°F (70C); engine is between 1200-2000 rpm; vacuum is between 28-56 kPa. PCM-compared differences (state of change) between front and rear O2 Sensors indicate difference is greater than calibrated amount. **Possible Causes:** • Exhaust leak present in the exhaust manifold or exhaust pipes • O2 element is contaminated, deteriorated or it has failed • O2 signal circuit or return circuit has failed

DTC	Trouble Code Title, Conditions & Possible Causes
DTC: P0139 **2T O2** **Years:** 2005, 2006, 2007 **Models:** Grand Cherokee, Liberty, Pacifica, PT Cruiser, Ram Truck, Sebring, Stratus, Wrangler **Engines:** All **Transmissions:** All	**O2 (B1 S2) Slow Response** Engine started; vehicle driven at 20-55 mph with the throttle open for 2 minutes; ECT at more than 158°F (70C); catalytic converter temperature is more than 1112F (600C); and EVAP purge is active. O2 Sensor signal voltage switches less than 16 times from lean to rich within 20 seconds during monitoring, or will compare the state of change between the front and rear O2 Sensors and if the differences are greater than a calibrated amount, the DTC will set. 3 good trips are required to turn off the MIL. **Possible Causes:** • Exhaust leak • O2 element is contaminated, deteriorated or it has failed • O2 signal circuit or return circuit has failed
DTC: P0140 **2T O2** **Years:** 2005, 2006, 2007 **Models:** Cherokee, Grand Cherokee, Liberty, Ram Truck **Engines:** All **Transmissions:** All	**O2 (B1 S2) Remains At Center** Engine started; system voltage over 10.5v, ECT Sensor over 150.8°F, engine running in closed loop, and the PCM detected the O2 signal was fixed at 350-580 mV for 60 seconds. **Possible Causes:** • Exhaust leak present in exhaust manifold or exhaust pipes • O2 element is fuel contaminated or has deteriorated • O2 signal circuit or ground circuit has high resistance • PCM has failed
DTC: P0141 **2T CCM** **Years:** 2005, 2006, 2007 **Models:** Grand Cherokee, Liberty, Wrangler **Engines:** All **Transmissions:** All	**O2 (B1 S2) Heater Circuit** Engine running; O2 heater duty cycle is greater than 0%; ASD relay is energized; battery voltage is greater than 10.4v. No sensor output is received when the PCM powers up the sensor heater. The O2 heater is out of control for 128 seconds after it has reached 662F (350C). **Possible Causes:** • O2 heater ground circuit open or O2 signal circuit is open • O2 heater element has failed • PCM has failed
DTC: P0151 **1T CCM** **Years:** 2005, 2006, 2007 **Models:** Grand Cherokee, Liberty, Pacifica, Ram Truck, Sebring, Stratus, Wrangler **Engines:** All **Transmissions:** All	**O2 (B2 S1) Circuit Short to Ground** Engine runtime under 30 seconds, system voltage over 10.99v, O2 heater temperature below 484°F. The PCM detected the O2 signal was below 1.5v (Sebring, Stratus) or below 2.5196v (Grand Cherokee, Ram Truck, Wrangler) for 3 seconds, or below 2.411v for 10 seconds (Liberty) after engine start. **Possible Causes:** • O2 upstream circuit is shorted to ground • O2 signal circuit is shorted to ground or to O2 upstream return circuit • O2 signal circuit is shorted to the heater ground circuit • O2 may be contaminated or it has failed • PCM has failed
DTC: P0152 **1T CCM** **Years:** 2005, 2006, 2007 **Models:** Grand Cherokee, Liberty, Pacifica, PT Cruiser, Ram Truck, Sebring, Stratus, Wrangler **Engines:** All **Transmissions:** All	**O2 (B2 S1) Circuit High** O2 Sensor heater temperature is more than 925F (496C) on Magnum or 1085F (350C) on Sebring; battery voltage is more than 10.99v. O2 Sensor voltage is more than 3.7v for 30 seconds (Magnum), more than 3.99v for 30 seconds (Grand Cherokee, Ram Truck, Wrangler), 3.99v for 60 seconds (Sebring, Stratus), or 3.99v for 66.56 seconds (Liberty). 3 good trips are required to turn off the MIL. **Possible Causes:** • O2 signal circuit is open or is shorted to battery voltage. • O2 upstream return circuit is open or is shorted to battery voltage • O2 Sensor is damaged or has failed • PCM has failed
DTC: P0153 **2T CCM** **Years:** 2005, 2006, 2007 **Models:** Grand Cherokee, Liberty, Pacifica, PT Cruiser, Ram Truck, Sebring, Stratus, Wrangler **Engines:** All **Transmissions:** All	**O2 (B2 S1) Slow Response** Engine started; vehicle driven at a steady speed of 20-55 mph with the throttle open for at least 2 minutes, ECT Sensor more than 158°F (70C), Catalytic Converter temperature more than 1112°F (600C), EVAP purge is active, and the PCM detected the O2 signal switched from lean to rich less than 16 times (3.5L, 3.7L, 4.7L, 5.7L) or 11 times (2.7L) within a 20 second period during monitoring. 3 good trips are required to turn off MIL. **Possible Causes:** • Exhaust leak • O2 signal circuit has an open or grounded condition • O2 upstream return circuit has an open or grounded condition • O2 element is deteriorated or it has failed

DTC	Trouble Code Title, Conditions & Possible Causes
DTC: P0155 **2T CCM** **Years:** 2005, 2006, 2007 **Models:** Grand Cherokee, Pacifica, PT Cruiser, Ram Truck, Sebring, Stratus, Wrangler **Engines:** All **Transmissions:** All	**O2 (B2 S1) Heater Circuit** Engine running and heater duty cycle is greater than 0%; battery voltage is more than 11v. O2 heater temperature does not reach 959F (575C) within 90 seconds, or no Sensor output is received when the PCM powers up the Sensor heater. 3 good trips required to turn off MIL. **Possible Causes:** • O2 heater control circuit is open • O2 heater ground circuit is open • O2 heater element is damaged or has failed • PCM has failed
DTC: P0155 **2T CCM** **Years:** 2005, 2006, 2007 **Models:** Liberty **Engines:** All **Transmissions:** All	**O2 (B1 S1) Heater Circuit** Engine running; O2 heater duty cycle is more than 0%; ASD relay is energized; battery voltage is more than 10.4v. No sensor output is received when PCM powers up the sensor heater. The O2 heater is out of control for 128 seconds after it has reached 572F (300C). **Possible Causes:** • O2 heater ground circuit open or O2 signal circuit is open • O2 heater element has failed • PCM has failed
DTC: P0157 **1T CCM** **Years:** 2005, 2006, 2007 **Models:** Grand Cherokee, Liberty, Pacifica, PT Cruiser, Ram Truck, Sebring, Stratus, Wrangler **Engines:** All **Transmissions:** All	**O2 (B2 S2) Circuit Low** Engine runtime under 30 seconds; system voltage over 10.99v; O2 heater temperature below 484°F (251°C); O2 Sensor signal was less than 1.5v ( ) or less than 2.5196v (Grand Cherokee, Ram Truck, Wrangler) for 3 seconds (28 seconds:), or below 2.411v for 10 seconds (Liberty) after engine start. 3 good trips are required to turn off the MIL. **Possible Causes:** • O2 signal circuit is shorted to chassis or Sensor ground • O2 is damaged or it has failed • PCM has failed
DTC: P0158 **1T CCM** **Years:** 2005, 2006, 2007 **Models:** Grand Cherokee, Liberty, Pacifica, PT Cruiser, Ram Truck, Sebring, Stratus, Wrangler **Engines:** All **Transmissions:** All	**O2 (B2 S2) Circuit High** Engine is running; system voltage over 10.99v; O2 heater temperature more than 925°F (496°C) on all exc. Sebring, Stratus, or more than 1085F (350C) on Sebring, Stratus. The PCM detected the O2 signal was more than 3.70v for 30 seconds (Magnum), more than 3.99v for 30 seconds (Grand Cherokee, Ram Truck, Wrangler), more than 3.99v for 60 seconds (Sebring, Stratus), or more than 3.99v for 76.8 seconds (Liberty). 3 good trips required to turn off MIL. **Possible Causes:** • O2 signal circuit is open or is shorted to battery • O2 downstream return circuit is open or is shorted to battery • O2 is damaged or it has failed • PCM has failed
DTC: P0159 **2T O2** **Years:** 2005, 2006, 2007 **Models:** Grand Cherokee, Liberty, Pacifica, PT Cruiser, Ram Truck, Sebring, Stratus, Wrangler **Engines:** All **Transmissions:** All	**O2 (B2 S2) Slow Response** Engine is driven at 20-55 mph with throttle open for 2 minutes; ECT Sensor over 158°F (70C); catalytic converter temperature over 1112°F (600C); EVAP purge is active. The O2 Sensor signal voltage switches less than 16 times or 11 times (2.7L exc. Liberty) from lean to rich with 20 seconds during monitoring. 3 good trips required to turn off MIL. **Possible Causes:** • Exhaust leak • O2 signal circuit is open or shorted • O2 downstream return circuit is open or shorted • O2 Sensor is damaged or has failed
DTC: P0161 **2T CCM** **Years:** 2005, 2006, 2007 **Models:** Ram Truck **Engines:** All **Transmissions:** All	**O2 (B2 S2) Heater Performance** Engine running; heater duty cycle is greater than 0%; battery voltage is more than 11v. O2 heater temperature does not reach 662F (350C) within 90 seconds, or no Sensor output is received when the PCM powers up Sensor heater. 3 good trips required to turn off MIL. **Possible Causes:** • O2 heater control circuit or ground circuit is open • O2 Sensor heater element is damaged or has failed • PCM has failed
DTC: P0161 **2T CCM** **Years:** 2005, 2006, 2007 **Models:** Liberty **Engines:** All **Transmissions:** All	**O2 (B1 S1) Heater Circuit** Engine running; O2 heater duty cycle is more than 0%; ASD relay is energized; battery voltage is over 10.4v. No sensor output is received when the PCM powers up the sensor heater. The O2 heater is out of control for 2 minutes after it has reached 662F (350C). **Possible Causes:** • O2 heater ground circuit open or O2 signal circuit is open • O2 heater element or PCM has failed

DTC	Trouble Code Title, Conditions & Possible Causes
DTC: P0171 **2T Fuel** **Years:** 2005, 2006, 2007 **Models:** Grand Cherokee, Liberty, Pacifica, PT Cruiser, Ram Truck, Sebring, Stratus, Wrangler **Engines:** All **Transmissions:** All	**Fuel System Lean (B1 S1)** Engine running in closed loop. AAT Sensor signal over 20°F (−7C). Altitude less than 8,500 feet. Fuel level greater than 15%. If PCM multiplies short-term compensation by long-term adaptive and a certain percentage is exceeded for 2 trips, a freeze frame is stored, the MIL illuminates, and a DTC is stored. **Possible Causes:** • Restricted fuel supply line • Fuel pump inlet strainer plugged or fuel pump has failed • O2 Sensor has failed • O2 signal circuit or return circuit has failed • O2 Sensor heater operation is faulty • TP Sensor sweep has failed • MAP Sensor operation has failed • ECT Sensor operation has failed • Engine mechanical problem is present • Fuel is contaminated • Exhaust leak exists
DTC: P0172 **2T Fuel** **Years:** 2005, 2006, 2007 **Models:** Grand Cherokee, Liberty, Pacifica, PT Cruiser, Ram Truck, Sebring, Stratus, Wrangler **Engines:** All **Transmissions:** All	**Fuel System (S1 B1) Rich** Engine running in closed loop. IAT Sensor signal over 20°F (−7C). Altitude less than 8,500 feet. PCM multiplies short-term compensation by long-term adaptive, as well as a purge fuel multiplier, and the result is below a certain value for 30 seconds over 2 trips, a freeze frame is stored. MIL illuminates and DTC is stored. **Possible Causes:** • O2 Sensor heater or O2 Sensor has failed • EVAP purge solenoid failed or improper operation • O2 signal circuit or return circuit has failed • MAP Sensor has failed or circuit malfunction • ECT Sensor has failed or circuit malfunction • Engine mechanical problem • Fuel filter/pressure regulator has failed or needs repair • PCM has failed
DTC: P0174 **2T Fuel** **Years:** 2005, 2006, 2007 **Models:** Grand Cherokee, Liberty, Pacifica, PT Cruiser, Ram Truck, Sebring, Stratus, Wrangler **Engines:** All **Transmissions:** All	**Fuel System (S2 B1) Lean** Engine running in closed loop. IAT Sensor signal over 20°F (−7C). Altitude less than 8,500 feet. PCM multiplies short-term compensation by long-term adaptive, and a certain percentage is exceeded in 2 trips, a freeze frame is stored. MIL illuminates and DTC is stored. 3 good trips required to turn off MIL. **Possible Causes:** • Restricted fuel supply line • Fuel pump inlet strainer plugged • Fuel pump is damaged or has failed • O2 signal circuit or return circuit has failed • MAP Sensor has failed or circuit malfunction • ECT Sensor has failed or circuit malfunction • Engine mechanical problem • Fuel filter/pressure regulator has failed or needs repair • O2 Sensor has failed • PCM has failed
DTC: P0175 **2T Fuel** **Years:** 2005, 2006, 2007 **Models:** Grand Cherokee, Liberty, Pacifica, PT Cruiser, Ram Truck, Sebring, Stratus, Wrangler **Engines:** All **Transmissions:** All	**Fuel System (S2 B1) Rich** Engine running in closed loop. IAT Sensor signal over 20°F (−7C). Altitude less than 8,500 feet. If the PCM multiplies short-term compensation by long-term adaptive, and a purge fuel multiplier, and the result is below a certain value for 30 seconds in 2 trips, a freeze frame is stored. MIL illuminates and DTC is stored. 3 good trips required to turn off MIL. **Possible Causes:** • Restricted fuel supply line • Fuel pump inlet strainer plugged • Fuel pump is damaged or has failed • O2 signal circuit or return circuit has failed • MAP Sensor has failed or circuit malfunction • ECT Sensor has failed or circuit malfunction • Engine mechanical problem • Fuel filter/pressure regulator has failed or needs repair • O2 Sensor has failed • PCM has failed

DTC	Trouble Code Title, Conditions & Possible Causes
DTC: P0180 **1T CCM** **Years:** 2005, 2006, 2007 **Models:** Liberty **Engines:** 2.8L Diesel **Transmissions:** All	**Fuel Temperature Sensor Signal Voltage Too Low Or Too High** Ignition on; Fuel Temperature Sensor signal is below 0.12v or above 4.95v for 0.5 seconds. **Possible Causes:** • Intermittent condition • Fuel Temp. Sensor signal circuit is open or is shorted to voltage (too high) • Fuel Temp. Sensor signal circuit is shorted to ground (too low) • Fuel Temp. Sensor signal and ground circuits are shorted together • Fuel Temp. Sensor has failed • ECM has failed
DTC: P0181 **1T CCM** **Years:** 2005, 2006, 2007 **Models:** Sebring, Stratus **Engines:** All **Transmissions:** All	**Fuel Temperature Sensor Circuit Malfunction** ECT Sensor from 14-97°F and IAT Sensor within 5°F of the ECT at startup, ECT Sensor over 140°F during testing, engine running with the VSS less than 17 mph, and the PCM detected the difference between the Fuel Temperature and ECT Sensor signals was more than 27°F. **Possible Causes:** • Fuel Temperature Sensor connector is damaged or loose • Fuel Temperature Sensor is damaged or it has failed • PCM has failed
DTC: P0190 **1T CCM** **Years:** 2005, 2006, 2007 **Models:** Liberty **Engines:** 2.8L Diesel **Transmissions:** All	**Fuel Pressure Sensor Signal Voltage Too Low Or Too High** Ignition on; Fuel Pressure Sensor signal is below 0.2v or above 4.8v for 0.5 second. **Possible Causes:** • Fuel Pressure Sensor signal circuit is open or is shorted to voltage (too high) • Fuel Pressure Sensor signal circuit is shorted to ground (too low) • Fuel Pressure Sensor ground circuit is open (too high) • Fuel Pressure Sensor signal circuit is shorted to Sensor ground (too low) • Intermittent condition • Fuel Pressure Sensor 5v supply circuit is open (too high) • Fuel Pressure Sensor ground circuit is shorted to voltage (too high) • Fuel Pressure Sensor has failed • ECM has failed
DTC: P0191 **1T CCM** **Years:** 2005, 2006, 2007 **Models:** Liberty **Engines:** 2.8L Diesel **Transmissions:** All	**Fuel Pressure Sensor After-Run Negative Or Positive Plausibility** At ignition shut off during After-Run; Fuel Pressure Sensor signal is below 0.415v or above 0.615v for 1.0 second. **Possible Causes:** • Fuel Pressure Sensor has failed • Intermittent condition
DTC: P0196 **1T CCM** **Years:** 2005, 2006, 2007 **Models:** Grand Cherokee, Liberty, Pacifica, PT Cruiser, Ram Truck, Sebring, Stratus, Wrangler **Engines:** All **Transmissions:** All	**Engine Oil Temperature Sensor Circuit Performance** Engine off time is more than 8 hours; ambient temperature is more than 38F (4C). If the PCM detects the engine oil temperature value is incorrect, by comparing it with other engine inputs, then the DTC will set. 3 good trips required to turn off MIL. **Possible Causes:** • Engine oil temp signal circuit is open or is shorted to ground or to battery voltage • Engine oil temp Sensor ground circuit is open • Engine oil temp signal circuit is shorted to Sensor ground • Engine oil temp Sensor has failed • PCM has failed
DTC: P0197 **1T CCM** **Years:** 2005, 2006, 2007 **Models:** Grand Cherokee, Liberty, Pacifica, PT Cruiser, Ram Truck, Sebring, Stratus, Wrangler **Engines:** All **Transmissions:** All	**Engine Oil Temperature Sensor Circuit Low** Ignition is on; battery voltage is more than 10.4v. The engine oil temperature Sensor circuit voltage at the PCM is less than the calibrated amount. 3 good trips required to turn off MIL. **Possible Causes:** • Engine oil temp signal circuit is shorted to ground • Engine oil temp signal circuit is shorted to Sensor ground • Engine oil temp Sensor has failed • PCM has failed
DTC: P0198 **1T CCM** **Years:** 2005, 2006, 2007 **Models:** Grand Cherokee, Liberty, Pacifica, PT Cruiser, Ram Truck, Sebring, Stratus, Wrangler **Engines:** All **Transmissions:** All	**Engine Oil Temperature Sensor Circuit High** Ignition is on; battery voltage is more than 10.4v. The engine oil temperature Sensor circuit voltage at the PCM is higher than the calibrated amount. 3 good trips required to turn off MIL. **Possible Causes:** • Engine oil temp signal circuit is open or is shorted to battery voltage • Engine oil temp Sensor ground circuit is open • Engine oil temp Sensor has failed • PCM has failed

DTC	Trouble Code Title, Conditions & Possible Causes
DTC: P0201-P0204 **1T CCM** **Years:** 2005, 2006, 2007 **Models:** PT Cruiser **Engines:** All **Transmissions:** All	**Fuel Injector 1, 2, 3 or 4 Control Circuit Open** Ignition on. The PCM tests the injector circuit internally for more than 27 injector pulses and has determined that the circuit is open. **Possible Causes:** • Intermittent condition • Fuel injector 1-4 control circuit is open • Fuel injector 1-4 ASD relay output circuit is open • Fuel injector driver circuit is open • Fuel injector is clogged or has failed • PCM has failed
DTC: P0201-P0204 **1T CCM** **Years:** 2005, 2006, 2007 **Models:** Liberty **Engines:** 2.8L Diesel **Transmissions:** All	**Fuel Injector 1, 2, 3 or 4 Injector Circuit Load Drop Or Overcurrent High Side Or Low Side** Engine running. The ECM detects insufficient current through the injector driver when commanded ON (circuit load drop), or the ECM detects excessive current on the high side driver circuit or on the low side driver circuit. **Possible Causes:** • ECM has failed • Intermittent condition • Fuel injector control circuit is open or is shorted to ground or to voltage • Fuel injector control circuits are shorted together • Fuel injector has failed
DTC: P0201-P0210 **1T CCM** **Years:** 2005, 2006, 2007 **Models:** Ram Truck **Engines:** All **Transmissions:** All	**Injector 1, 2, 3, 4, 5, 6, 7, 8, 9 or 10 Control** ASD relay "on", engine speed under 3000 rpm, injector pulse width under 10 ms, system voltage over 12v, and the PCM did not detect any inductive spike from the injector for 0.18 ms after it is turned off. **Note: This code takes 0.64-10 seconds to set once the injector is off.** **Possible Causes:** • Fuel injector 1-10 control circuit is open or grounded • Fuel injector 1-10 power circuit from the ASD relay is open • Fuel injector 1-10 has failed • PCM injector 1-10 driver has failed
DTC: P0201-P0206 **1T CCM** **Years:** 2005, 2006, 2007 **Models:** Grand Cherokee, Liberty, Pacifica, PT Cruiser, Ram Truck, Sebring, Stratus, Wrangler **Engines:** All **Transmissions:** All	**Injector 1, 2, 3, 4, 5, or 6 Control** ASD relay "on"; engine speed under 3000 rpm; battery voltage greater than 10v (11.9981v: Liberty). No inductive spike is detected after injector turns off. **Possible Causes:** • ASD relay output circuit failure • Fuel injector has malfunctioned or failed • Fuel injector control circuit is open or shorted to ground • PCM has failed
DTC: P0201-P0208 **1T CCM** **Years:** 2005, 2006, 2007 **Models:** Grand Cherokee, Ram Truck, Sebring, Stratus	**Injector 1, 2, 3, 4, 5, 6, 7 or 8 Control** ASD relay "on", engine speed under 3000 rpm, battery voltage greater than 10v. No inductive spike is detected after injector turn off. **Possible Causes:** • ASD relay output circuit failure • Fuel injector has malfunctioned or failed • Fuel injector control circuit is open or shorted to ground • PCM has failed
DTC: P0218 **1T CCM** **Years:** 2005, 2006, 2007 **Models:** Grand Cherokee, Liberty, Pacifica, PT Cruiser, Ram Truck, Sebring, Stratus, Wrangler **Engines:** All **Transmissions:** All	**A/T High Temperature Operation Activated** Engine started; vehicle driven in gear, and the TCM indicated the Overheat shift schedule was activated (i.e., the TCM had detected a transmission oil temperature of more than 240°F). **Note: This is an informational DTC, designed to aid the technician in diagnosing shift quality complaints.** **Possible Causes:** • Engine cooling system malfunction present • High temperature operations activated • Transmission oil pump flow is too low or it is restricted

DTC	Trouble Code Title, Conditions & Possible Causes
DTC: P0218 **1T CCM** **Years:** 2005, 2006, 2007 **Models:** Liberty **Engines:** 2.8L Diesel **Transmissions:** All	**Transmission High Temperature Operation Activated** Engine running. This DTC is an informational code and does not necessarily indicate that a failure exists. It merely flags the fact that the transmission sump oil temperature reached 240F (116C). This temperature level can be reached when operating under a heavy load in hot weather. This causes the transmission controller to use an overheat shift schedule, which changes the shift patterns in an attempt to control the temperature. Customers may notice a different feeling or response under these conditions. The Owners Manual includes an explanation of this Over Temperature Mode for information purposes. The DTC sets immediately when the Overheat Shift Schedule is activation with a transmission oil temperature above 240F (116C). **Possible Causes:** • Sever operation: trailer towing in hot weather • Engine cooling system problem • Oil pump volume check • Torque converter failure • High temperature operations activated
DTC: P0221 **1T CCM** **Years:** 2005, 2006, 2007 **Models:** Grand Cherokee, Liberty, Pacifica, PT Cruiser, Ram Truck, Sebring, Stratus, Wrangler **Engines:** All **Transmissions:** All	**Throttle Position Sensor No. 2 Performance** Ignition on; No MAP Sensor DTCs are set. TP Sensor signals Do NOT correlate to the MAP Sensor signal. If equipped, ETC light will illuminate. P2135 should also set. **Possible Causes:** • TP Sensor No. 1 or 2 signal circuit is shorted to battery voltage or to ground • TP Sensor No. 1 or 2 signal circuit has high resistance • 5v supply circuit is shorted to ground • TP Sensor return circuit has high resistance • TP Sensor No. 1 signal circuit shorted to TP Sensor No. 2 signal circuit • TP Sensor or throttle body damaged or has failed • PCM has failed
DTC: P0222 **1T CCM** **Years:** 2005, 2006, 2007 **Models:** Liberty **Engines:** 2.8L Diesel **Transmissions:** All	**Throttle Position Sensor No. 2 Circuit Low** Ignition on; battery voltage is more than 10v. TP Sensor voltage at the PCM is less than 0.16v for 0.7 second. 3 good trips required to turn off MIL. **Possible Causes:** • 5v supply circuit is open or shorted to ground • TP Sensor No. 2 signal circuit shorted to ground or to Sensor return circuit • TP Sensor or throttle body damaged or has failed • Throttle plate jammed against the maximum stop • PCM has failed
DTC: P0223 **1T CCM** **Years:** 2005, 2006, 2007 **Models:** Grand Cherokee, Liberty, Pacifica, PT Cruiser, Ram Truck, Sebring, Stratus, Wrangler **Engines:** All **Transmissions:** All	**Throttle Position Sensor No. 2 Circuit High** Ignition on; battery voltage is more than 10v. TP Sensor voltage at the PCM is more than 4.9v for 25ms. If equipped, ETC light will illuminate. **Possible Causes:** • TP Sensor No. 2 signal circuit shorted to battery voltage or to 5v supply circuit • TP Sensor return circuit is open • TP Sensor or throttle body is damaged or has failed • PCM has failed
DTC: P0234 **1T CCM** **Years:** 2005, 2006, 2007 **Models:** Liberty **Engines:** 2.8L Diesel **Transmissions:** All	**Turbo Boost Pressure Negative Deviation Performance** Engine running. Actual boost pressure differs from the boost pressure set point by more than 14.5 psi (1000 hPa). **Possible Causes:** • Air filter is clogged or malfunctioning • Air restrictions exist in intake or boost components • Air leaks exist in intake or boost components • Boost control vacuum supply is insufficient • Boost pressure actuator is malfunctioning or has failed • Turbocharger is malfunctioning or has failed
DTC: P0235 **1T CCM** **Years:** 2005, 2006, 2007 **Models:** Liberty **Engines:** 2.8L Diesel **Transmissions:** All	**Turbo Boost Pressure Sensor Plausibility** Engine running at less than 850 rpm; no other Boost Pressure Sensor DTCs are present; No Atmospheric Pressure DTCs are present. The Boost Pressure Sensor signal differs from the Atmospheric Pressure signal by 2.18 (150 hPa) or more for at least 2 seconds. **Possible Causes:** • Intermittent condition • High resistance in Boost Pressure Sensor signal circuit, ground circuit or 5v supply circuit • Boost Pressure/Intake Air Temperature Sensor has failed • ECM has failed

DTC	Trouble Code Title, Conditions & Possible Causes
DTC: P0235 **1T CCM** **Years:** 2005, 2006, 2007 **Models:** Liberty **Engines:** 2.8L Diesel **Transmissions:** All	**Turbo Boost Pressure Sensor Signal Voltage Too High Or Too Low** Ignition on. The Boost Pressure Sensor signal voltage is above 4.79v for 0.5 second (too high) or is below 0.29v for 0.5 second (too low). **Possible Causes:** • Intermittent condition • BP Sensor ground circuit is shorted to voltage or is open (too high) • BP Sensor 5v supply circuit is open (too low) • BP Sensor signal circuit is shorted to voltage (too high) • BP Sensor signal circuit is shorted to ground or is open (too low) • BP Sensor signal and ground circuits are shorted together (too low) • BP/IAT Sensor has failed • Poor connector terminal contact (too high) • ECM has failed
DTC: P0243 **1T CCM** **Years:** 2005, 2006, 2007 **Models:** Sebring **Engines:** All **Transmissions:** All	**Wastegate Solenoid Circuit Malfunction** Key on or engine running; system voltage over 10.5v. The PCM detected an unexpected voltage condition on the Wastegate Solenoid control circuit during the CCM test period. **Possible Causes:** • Wastegate solenoid control circuit is open or shorted to ground • Wastegate solenoid control circuit is shorted to system power • Wastegate solenoid is damaged or it has failed • PCM has failed
DTC: P0251 **1T CCM** **Years:** 2005, 2006, 2007 **Models:** Liberty **Engines:** 2.8L Diesel **Transmissions:** All	**Fuel Quality Solenoid Open Or Short Circuit** Ignition on; ECM detects an open or short in the Fuel Quality Solenoid circuit. **Possible Causes:** • FQ Solenoid circuit(s) are open, shorted to ground, shorted to voltage, or shorted together • Intermittent condition • FQ Solenoid or ECM has failed
DTC: P0252 **1T CCM** **Years:** 2005, 2006, 2007 **Models:** Liberty **Engines:** 2.8L Diesel **Transmissions:** All	**Fuel Quality Solenoid Circuit Malfunction** Engine running; ECM detects a malfunction with the Fuel Quality Solenoid circuit. **Possible Causes:** • FQ Solenoid circuit(s) are open, shorted to ground, shorted to voltage, or shorted together • Intermittent condition • FQ Solenoid or ECM has failed
DTC: P0253 **1T CCM** **Years:** 2005, 2006, 2007 **Models:** Liberty **Engines:** 2.8L Diesel **Transmissions:** All	**Fuel Quality Solenoid Short To Ground Circuit** Ignition on; ECM detects a short to ground in the Fuel Quality Solenoid circuit(s). **Possible Causes:** • FQ Solenoid circuit(s) are open, shorted to ground, shorted to voltage, or shorted together • Intermittent condition • FQ Solenoid has failed • ECM has failed
DTC: P0254 **1T CCM** **Years:** 2005, 2006, 2007 **Models:** Liberty **Engines:** 2.8L Diesel **Transmissions:** All	**Fuel Quality Solenoid Short Circuit** Ignition on; ECM detects a short in the Fuel Quality Solenoid circuit. **Possible Causes:** • FQ Solenoid circuit(s) are open, shorted to ground, shorted to voltage, or shorted together • Intermittent condition • FQ Solenoid has failed • ECM has failed
DTC: P0261 **1T CCM** **Years:** 2005, 2006, 2007 **Models:** PT Cruiser **Engines:** All **Transmissions:** All	**Injector No. 1 Control Circuit Low** Ignition is on. The PCM tests the injector circuit internally for more than 27 injector pulses and has determined that the circuit is shorted to ground. MIL is illuminated. **Possible Causes:** • Intermittent condition • Fuel injector has malfunctioned or failed • ASD relay output circuit is open • Fuel injector driver circuit is shorted to ground • PCM has failed

DTC	Trouble Code Title, Conditions & Possible Causes
DTC: P0262 **1T CCM** **Years:** 2005, 2006, 2007 **Models:** PT Cruiser **Engines:** All **Transmissions:** All	**Injector No. 1 Control Circuit High** Ignition is on. The PCM tests the injector circuit internally for more than 27 injector pulses and has determined that the circuit is shorted to voltage. MIL is illuminated. **Possible Causes:** • Intermittent condition • Fuel injector has malfunctioned or failed • ASD relay output circuit is open • Fuel injector driver circuit is shorted to ASD relay output circuit or to battery voltage • PCM has failed
DTC: P0264 **1T CCM** **Years:** 2005, 2006, 2007 **Models:** PT Cruiser **Engines:** All **Transmissions:** All	**Injector No. 2 Control Circuit Low** Ignition is on. The PCM tests the injector circuit internally for more than 27 injector pulses and has determined that the circuit is shorted to ground. MIL is illuminated. **Possible Causes:** • Intermittent condition • Fuel injector has malfunctioned or failed • ASD relay output circuit is open • Fuel injector driver circuit is shorted to ground • PCM has failed
DTC: P0265 **1T CCM** **Years:** 2005, 2006, 2007 **Models:** PT Cruiser **Engines:** All **Transmissions:** All	**Injector No. 2 Control Circuit High** Ignition is on. The PCM tests the injector circuit internally for more than 27 injector pulses and has determined that the circuit is shorted to voltage. MIL is illuminated. **Possible Causes:** • Intermittent condition • Fuel injector has malfunctioned or failed • ASD relay output circuit is open • Fuel injector driver circuit is shorted to ASD relay output circuit or to battery voltage • PCM has failed
DTC: P0267 **1T CCM** **Years:** 2005, 2006, 2007 **Models:** PT Cruiser **Engines:** All **Transmissions:** All	**Injector No. 3 Control Circuit Low** Ignition is on. The PCM tests the injector circuit internally for more than 27 injector pulses and has determined that the circuit is shorted to ground. MIL is illuminated. **Possible Causes:** • Intermittent condition • Fuel injector has malfunctioned or failed • ASD relay output circuit is open • Fuel injector driver circuit is shorted to ground • PCM has failed
DTC: P0268 **1T CCM** **Years:** 2005, 2006, 2007 **Models:** PT Cruiser **Engines:** All **Transmissions:** All	**Injector No. 3 Control Circuit High** Ignition is on. The PCM tests the injector circuit internally for more than 27 injector pulses and has determined that the circuit is shorted to voltage. MIL is illuminated. **Possible Causes:** • Intermittent condition • Fuel injector has malfunctioned or failed • ASD relay output circuit is open • Fuel injector driver circuit is shorted to ASD relay output circuit or to battery voltage • PCM has failed
DTC: P0270 **1T CCM** **Years:** 2005, 2006, 2007 **Models:** PT Cruiser **Engines:** All **Transmissions:** All	**Injector No. 4 Control Circuit Low** Ignition is on. The PCM tests the injector circuit internally for more than 27 injector pulses and has determined that the circuit is shorted to ground. MIL is illuminated. **Possible Causes:** • Intermittent condition • Fuel injector has malfunctioned or failed • ASD relay output circuit is open • Fuel injector driver circuit is shorted to ground • PCM has failed

DTC	Trouble Code Title, Conditions & Possible Causes
DTC: P0271 **1T CCM** **Years:** 2005, 2006, 2007 **Models:** PT Cruiser **Engines:** All **Transmissions:** All	**Injector No. 4 Control Circuit High** Ignition is on. The PCM tests the injector circuit internally for more than 27 injector pulses and has determined that the circuit is shorted to voltage. MIL is illuminated. **Possible Causes:** • Intermittent condition • Fuel injector has malfunctioned or failed • ASD relay output circuit is open • Fuel injector driver circuit is shorted to ASD relay output circuit or to battery voltage • PCM has failed
DTC: P0299 **1T CCM** **Years:** 2005, 2006, 2007 **Models:** Liberty **Engines:** 2.8L Diesel **Transmissions:** All	**Turbo Boost Pressure Positive Deviation Performance** Engine running. Actual boost pressure differs from the boost pressure set point by more than 14.5 psi (1000 hPa). **Possible Causes:** • Air filter is clogged or malfunctioning • Air restrictions exist in intake or boost components • Air leaks exist in intake or boost components • Boost control vacuum supply is insufficient • Boost pressure actuator is malfunctioning or has failed • Turbocharger is malfunctioning or has failed
DTC: P0300 **2T CCM** **Years:** 2005, 2006, 2007 **Models:** Grand Cherokee, Liberty, Pacifica, Ram Truck, Sebring, Stratus, Wrangler **Engines:** All **Transmissions:** All	**Multiple Cylinder Misfire** Any time engine is running and Adaptive Numerator (Target Learning Coefficient) has been successfully updated. If more than 1.0% (Pacifica), 1.5% (Magnum) or 1.8% (Sebring, Stratus), 2% (Ram Truck, Liberty), 2.5% (LEV, Ram LEV, Liberty LEV), misfire rate is measured during 2 trips. 3 good trips required to turn off MIL. **Possible Causes:** • ASD relay output circuit fault • Injector control circuit fault • Coil control circuit fault • Ignition wiring, coil control circuit or coil fault • Fuel pump inlet strainer plugged • Restricted fuel supply line • Fuel pump module is damaged • Fuel pressure leakdown fault • Fuel injector damaged or has failed • Engine mechanical problems exist • PCM has failed
DTC: P0300 **2T CCM** **Years:** 2005, 2006, 2007 **Models:** PT Cruiser **Engines:** All **Transmissions:** All	**Multiple Cylinder Misfire** Engine is running; atmospheric pressure, fuel level, battery voltage, engine speed, engine load are above minimal predetermined specifications; the engine is not in fuel cutoff and intake air temperature and coolant temperature are within normal operating ranges; there are no DTCs relating to MAP, ECT, CMP, CKP or IAT Sensor, to Crank rationality, to Crank Sensor Learn invalid, or to System Voltage. If total misfires detected are greater than 8.5% during the first 1000 rpm, or are 40% during any 200 rpm, with no single cylinder or multiple cylinder misfire counters above 80%, this DTC will set. The MIL will flash after first trip occurrence and will be steady after second trip. **Possible Causes:** • Fuel system problems exist • Erratic CMP or CKP Sensor signals • Ignition system problems exist • Engine mechanical problems exist • PCM has failed
DTC: P0300 **1T CCM** **Years:** 2005, 2006, 2007 **Models:** Liberty **Engines:** 2.8L Diesel **Transmissions:** All	**Misfire** Engine running. The ECM detects multiple misfires from one or more cylinders. **Possible Causes:** • Engine compression problems exist • Fuel injector quantity is insufficient • Fuel injector leaking • Intermittent condition

DTC	Trouble Code Title, Conditions & Possible Causes
DTC: P0301-P0304 **2T CCM** **Years:** 2005, 2006, 2007 **Models:** PT Cruiser **Engines:** All **Transmissions:** All	**Cylinder No. 1, 2, 3 or 4 Misfire Detected** Engine is running; atmospheric pressure, fuel level, battery voltage, engine speed, engine load are above minimal predetermined specifications; the engine is not in fuel cutoff and intake air temperature and coolant temperature are within normal operating ranges; there are no DTCs relating to ECT, CMP, CKP, MAP or IAT Sensor, to Crank rationality, to Crank Sensor Learn invalid, or to System Voltage. If total misfires detected are greater than 7% during the first 1000 rpm, or are over 3% after the first 1000 rpm, or are 25% during any 200 rpm with suspect cylinder misfire counter more than 80% and no other cylinder misfire counters above 80%, this DTC will set. The MIL will flash after first trip occurrence and will be steady after second trip. **Possible Causes:** • Fuel system problems exist • Erratic CMP or CKP Sensor signals • Ignition system problems exist • Engine mechanical problems exist • PCM has failed
DTC: P0301-P0304 **1T CCM** **Years:** 2005, 2006, 2007 **Models:** Liberty **Engines:** 2.8L Diesel **Transmissions:** All	**Misfire Detected In Specific Cylinder** Engine running. The ECM detects multiple misfires from cylinder No. 1 (P0301), No. 2 (P0302), No. 3 (P0303) or No. 4 (P0304). **Possible Causes:** • Engine compression problems exist • Fuel injector quantity is insufficient • Fuel injector leaking • Intermittent condition
DTC: P0301-P0306 **2T Catalyst** **2T CCM** **Years:** 2005, 2006, 2007 **Models:** Grand Cherokee, Liberty, PT Cruiser, Ram Truck, Sebring, Stratus, Wrangler **Engines:** All **Transmissions:** All	**Cylinder 1-6 Misfire Detected** Any time engine is running and Target Learning Coefficient (TLC) has been successfully updated, if more than 1.0% (Pacifica) or 1.8% (Sebring, Stratus), 2% (Ram Truck, Liberty), 2.5% (LEV, Ram LEV, Liberty LEV), misfire rate is measured during 2 trips or with 10-30% misfire rate during one trip. **Possible Causes:** • Intermittent misfire • Base engine mechanical fault that affects only 1 cylinder • Ignition wiring, coil control circuit or coil fault • ASD relay output circuit (coil or injector) problem • Spark plug malfunction or failure on 1 cylinder • CMP Sensor, Sensor wiring harness or tone wheel is damaged • Fuel delivery component fault that affects only 1 cylinder (e.g., a dirty fuel injector) • Injector or control circuit failure • PCM has failed
DTC: P0301-P0308 **2T Catalyst** **Years:** 2005, 2006, 2007 **Models:** Ram Truck **Engines:** All **Transmissions:** All	**Cylinder 1-8 Misfire Detected** Any time engine is running and the adaptive numerator has been successfully updated. When more than 2% (Ram), 2.5% (LEV, Ram LEV), misfire rate is measured during 2 trips, or with 10-30% misfire during 1 trip. 3 good trips required to turn off MIL. **Possible Causes:** • ASD relay output 2 circuit fault • Injector control 1 circuit fault • Coil control 1 circuit fault • Ignition wiring, spark plug, or ignition coil fault • Fuel pump inlet strainer plugged • Restricted fuel supply line • Fuel pump module fault • Fuel pressure leakdown fault • Fuel injector is damaged or has failed • Engine mechanical problems exist • PCM has failed
DTC: P0315 **1T CCM** **Years:** 2005, 2006, 2007 **Models:** Grand Cherokee, Liberty, Pacifica, PT Cruiser, Ram Truck, Sebring, Stratus, Wrangler **Engines:** All **Transmissions:** All	**No Crankshaft Position Sensor Learned** Engine started; engine runtime more than 50 seconds under closed throttle conditions; A/C off; ECT Sensor more than 167°F (75C). The PCM detected that one of the CKP Sensor windows had too much variance (e.g., over 2.86%) from its calibrated reference point. **Possible Causes:** • Crankshaft tone wheel flex plate is damaged • Tone wheel/pulse ring may be damaged • Erratic CKP Sensor signals (wiring/connector problem) • CKP Sensor has failed • PCM has failed

DTC	Trouble Code Title, Conditions & Possible Causes
DTC: P0315 **1T CCM** **Years:** 2005, 2006, 2007 **Models:** PT Cruiser **Engines:** All **Transmissions:** All	**No Crankshaft Position Sensor Learned** Engine started; no MAP, CKP or CMP faults detected; engine rpm is 2000-3000; engine state includes Deceleration Fuel Cutoff, Transmission in gear, and CMP/CKP synch has been achieved. When the CKP Sensor correction value is out of limits for more than 1 second, this DTC will set. MIL is illuminated. **Possible Causes:** • Intermittent condition • Crankshaft tone wheel/pulse ring is damaged • Wiring harness problems exist • CKP Sensor has failed
DTC: P0325 **1T CCM** **Years:** 2005, 2006, 2007 **Models:** Grand Cherokee, Liberty, Pacifica, PT Cruiser, Ram Truck, Sebring, Stratus, Wrangler **Engines:** All **Transmissions:** All	**Knock Sensor No. 1 Circuit** Engine running at idle or in deceleration mode, and the PCM detected the Knock Sensor signal was below a minimum value (value depends on engine speed), or if Sensor voltage was about 5.0v with engine within idle range. **Possible Causes:** • Knock Sensor connector is damaged or shorted • Knock Sensor signal circuit open or grounded • Knock Sensor signal circuit shorted to return circuit • Knock Sensor return circuit is open • Knock Sensor not tightened properly • Knock Sensor damaged or has failed (it may be open internally) • PCM has failed
DTC: P0325 **1T CCM** **Years:** 2005, 2006, 2007 **Models:** Liberty **Engines:** All **Transmissions:** All	**Knock Sensor No. 1 Circuit** Engine running at higher than 1312 rpm; coolant temperature greater than 150F (65C); MAF signal greater than 250 mg/tdc; no MAF, ECT or CMP Sensor DTCs present. The Knock Sensor error program internal to the PCM is on; KS voltage was less than 0.49v and the value of the KS changes less than 0.06v every 11 or more seconds. 3 good trips required to turn off MIL. **Possible Causes:** • Knock Sensor signal circuit open or is shorted to ground or to voltage • Knock Sensor return circuit is open • Knock Sensor signal circuit is short to KS return circuit • Knock Sensor damaged or has failed • PCM has failed
DTC: P0330 **1T CCM** **Years:** 2005, 2006, 2007 **Models:** Grand Cherokee, Pacifica, PT Cruiser, Ram Truck, Sebring, Stratus, Wrangler **Engines:** All **Transmissions:** All	**Knock Sensor No. 2 Circuit** Engine running. The Knock Sensor circuit voltage falls below a minimum value at idle or deceleration. The minimum value is from a lookup table internal to the PCM and is based on engine rpm. This DTC will also set if the Sensor voltage goes above 5v. 3 good trips required to turn off MIL. **Possible Causes:** • Knock Sensor No. 2 signal circuit shorted to battery voltage or to KS 2 return circuit • Knock Sensor No. 2 signal circuit or return circuit is open • Knock Sensor No. 2 signal circuit is shorted to KS 2 return circuit or to ground • Knock Sensor damaged or has failed • PCM has failed
DTC: P0330 **1T CCM** **Years:** 2005, 2006, 2007 **Models:** Liberty **Engines:** All **Transmissions:** All	**Knock Sensor No. 2 Circuit** Engine running at higher than 1312 rpm; coolant temperature greater than 150F (65C); MAF signal greater than 250 mg/tdc; no MAF, ECT or CMP Sensor DTCs present. The Knock Sensor error program internal to the PCM is on; KS voltage was less than 0.49v and the value of the KS changes less than 0.06v every 11 or more seconds. 3 good trips required to turn off MIL. **Possible Causes:** • Knock Sensor signal circuit open or is shorted to ground or to voltage • Knock Sensor return circuit is open • Knock Sensor signal circuit is short to KS return circuit • Knock Sensor damaged or has failed • PCM has failed
DTC: P0335 **1T CCM** **Years:** 2005, 2006, 2007 **Models:** Grand Cherokee, Liberty, Pacifica, PT Cruiser, Ram Truck, Sebring, Stratus, Wrangler **Engines:** All **Transmissions:** All	**Crankshaft Position Sensor Circuit** Engine cranking with at least 8 CMP Sensor signals detected. The PCM did not detect any CKP Sensor signals for 2 seconds. **Possible Causes:** • Intermittent CKP signal • CKP Sensor signal circuit is open or it is shorted to ground or voltage • CKP Sensor 5v supply circuit is open or shorted to ground or voltage • CKP Sensor ground circuit is open • CKP Sensor or CMP Sensor is damaged or has failed • PCM has failed

DTC	Trouble Code Title, Conditions & Possible Causes
DTC: P0335 **1T CCM** **Years:** 2005, 2006, 2007 **Models:** PT Cruiser **Engines:** All **Transmissions:** All	**No Crankshaft Position Sensor Signal At PCM** Engine running and no CMP Sensor DTCs are present. If the PCM did not detect any CKP Sensor pulses when synchronization is attempted with the CMP signal, this DTC will set. **Possible Causes:** • Intermittent CKP signal • 5v supply circuit open, or shorted to ground or voltage • CKP Sensor signal circuit is open or shorted to ground or voltage • CKP Sensor signal circuit is shorted to 5v supply circuit • CKP Sensor ground circuit is open • CKP Sensor or PCM has failed
DTC: P0335 **1T CCM** **Years:** 2005, 2006, 2007 **Models:** Liberty **Engines:** 2.8L Diesel **Transmissions:** All	**Crankshaft Position Sensor Circuit Incorrect Or Missing Signal** Engine running at less than 6000 rpm. The ECM does not receive a CKP Sensor signal or receives an incorrect signal. **Possible Causes:** • CKP Sensor is damaged, improperly positioned or has failed • ECM has failed • Intermittent condition • CKP Sensor signal circuit(s) shorted to ground or shorted together • CKP Sensor signal circuits open or shorted to voltage
DTC: P0336 **1T CCM** **Years:** 2005, 2006, 2007 **Models:** PT Cruiser **Engines:** All **Transmissions:** All	**Crankshaft Position Sensor Incorrect Performance** Engine running and no CMP Sensor DTCs are present. If the PCM detects an incorrect amount of CKP Sensor pulses when compared to CMP Sensor pulse, this DTC will set. **Possible Causes:** • Intermittent CMP signal • Wiring harness problems exist • Tone wheel/pulse ring damaged or has failed • CKP Sensor is damaged or has failed • CMP Sensor has failed
DTC: P0339 **1T CCM** **Years:** 2005, 2006, 2007 **Models:** Grand Cherokee, Liberty, Pacifica, PT Cruiser, Ram Truck, Sebring, Stratus, Wrangler **Engines:** All **Transmissions:** All	**Crankshaft Position Sensor Circuit Intermittent** Engine cranking or running; CMP Sensor signals detected. The PCM detected an intermittent loss of the CKP Sensor signal. The Failure counter must reach 20 before this code will set. **Possible Causes:** • Check the tone wheel/pulse ring for damage or debris collection • CKP Sensor signal circuit is open or shorted to ground • CKP Sensor 5v supply circuit is open or shorted to ground • CKP Sensor is damaged or it has failed • PCM has failed
DTC: P0339 **1T CCM** **Years:** 2005, 2006, 2007 **Models:** Liberty **Engines:** 2.8L Diesel **Transmissions:** All	**Crankshaft Position Sensor Circuit Intermittent Or Missing Signal** Engine running at less than 6000 rpm. The ECM does not receive a CKP Sensor signal or receives an incorrect signal. **Possible Causes:** • CKP Sensor is damaged, improperly positioned or has failed • ECM has failed • Intermittent condition • CKP Sensor signal circuit(s) shorted to ground or shorted together • CKP Sensor signal circuits open or shorted to voltage
DTC: P0340 **1T CCM** **Years:** 2005, 2006, 2007 **Models:** Grand Cherokee, Liberty, Pacifica, PT Cruiser, Ram Truck, Sebring, Stratus, Wrangler **Engines:** All **Transmissions:** All	**No Camshaft Position Sensor Circuit Failure** Engine cranking or running, system voltage over 10v. The PCM detected CKP pulses without detecting any CMP Sensor pulses for 5 seconds or 2.5 engine revolutions. **Possible Causes:** • CMP Sensor connector is damaged, open or it is shorted • CMP Sensor signal circuit is open or shorted to ground or to battery voltage or 5v supply circuit • CMP Sensor 5v supply circuit is open or shorted to ground or to battery voltage • CMP Sensor ground circuit is open • CMP Sensor is damaged or has failed • CKP Sensor is damaged or has failed • PCM has failed

DTC	Trouble Code Title, Conditions & Possible Causes
DTC: P0340 **1T CCM** **Years:** 2005, 2006, 2007 **Models:** PT Cruiser **Engines:** All **Transmissions:** All	**No CMP Sensor Signal** Engine cranking or running; no CKP Sensor DTCs present. At least 10 engine revolutions have elapsed, with CKP Sensor signals present, but no CMP Sensor signal polarity change. **Possible Causes:** • Intermittent CMP signal • 5v supply circuit open or is shorted to ground or to voltage • CMP Sensor signal circuit is open or shorted to ground or to battery voltage or 5v supply circuit • CMP Sensor ground circuit is open • 5v supply has failed • CMP Sensor is damaged or has failed
DTC: P0340 **1T CCM** **Years:** 2005, 2006, 2007 **Models:** Liberty **Engines:** 2.8L Diesel **Transmissions:** All	**Camshaft Position Sensor Circuit Incorrect Or Missing Signal** Engine running at less than 6000 rpm. The ECM does not receive a CMP Sensor signal or receives an incorrect signal. **Possible Causes:** • 5v supply circuit is open • CMP Sensor signal circuit shorted to voltage • CMP Sensor is damaged, improperly positioned or has failed • ECM has failed
DTC: P0344 **1T CCM** **Years:** 2005, 2006, 2007 **Models:** Grand Cherokee, Liberty, Pacifica, PT Cruiser, Ram Truck, Sebring, Stratus, Wrangler **Engines:** All **Transmissions:** All	**Camshaft Position Sensor Circuit Intermittent** Engine cranking or running; system voltage over 10.5v. The PCM detected an intermittent loss of the CMP Sensor signal during the period of 2.5 complete engine revolutions. The failure counter must reach 20 before this code matures and a code is set. **Possible Causes:** • Wiring harness fault • 5v supply circuit open or shorted to ground • Tone wheel/pulse ring is damaged or corroded • CMP Sensor has failed • CMP Sensor signal circuit is open, shorted to ground or battery voltage or 5v supply • CMP Sensor ground circuit is open • PCM has failed
DTC: P0344 **1T CCM** **Years:** 2005, 2006, 2007 **Models:** Liberty **Engines:** 2.8L Diesel **Transmissions:** All	**Camshaft Position Sensor Circuit Intermittent Or Missing Signal** Engine running at less than 6000 rpm. The ECM does not receive a CMP Sensor signal or receives an intermittent signal. **Possible Causes:** • 5v supply circuit is open or is shorted to ground or to Sensor ground circuit • CMP Sensor signal circuit is open or is shorted to voltage or to ground • CMP Sensor is damaged, improperly positioned or has failed • ECM has failed • CMP Sensor ground circuit open • Intermittent condition
DTC: P0401 **2T EGR** **Years:** 2005, 2006, 2007 **Models:** Grand Cherokee, Liberty, Pacifica, PT Cruiser, Ram Truck, Sebring, Stratus, Wrangler **Engines:** All **Transmissions:** All	**EGR System Fault** Engine running for more than 2 minutes with ECT more than 158°F (70C). EGR is active. Vehicle is at less than 8500 feet altitude. Ambient temperature more than 20F (−6C). PCM closes EGR valve while monitoring O2 Sensor signal. Once a closed EGR fueling sample has been established, PCM then ramps in EGR and additional fueling, while monitoring the O2 Sensor signal in the open state. A fueling sample is again established. The PCM then compares the 2 different O2 Sensor signal readings (fueling samples). If a larger than expected variation is detected, a soft failure is recorded. Three soft failures set a one-trip (1T) failure. After 2 failed trips (2T), a DTC is set and the MIL illuminated. **Possible Causes:** • EGR valve is open at idle • EGR solenoid ground circuit is open • EGR solenoid control circuit is open, shorted to ground or to voltage • ASD relay power circuit open to the EGR solenoid • EGR valve or solenoid is damaged or has failed • PCM has failed (EGR open or EGR closed)
DTC: P0402 **1T CCM** **Years:** 2005, 2006, 2007 **Models:** Liberty **Engines:** 2.8L Diesel **Transmissions:** All	**EGR Solenoid Circuit Deviation** Engine running. The ECM detects the EGR flow is less than the requested flow (negative deviation) or is greater than the requested flow (positive deviation). **Possible Causes:** • Air filter is restricted or damaged • Air restrictions in intake air system or EGR system • Air leaks in intake air system or EGR system • EGR valve has malfunctioned or failed • Intermittent condition

DTC	Trouble Code Title, Conditions & Possible Causes
DTC: P0403 **1T CCM** **Years:** 2005, 2006, 2007 **Models:** Grand Cherokee, Liberty, Pacifica, PT Cruiser, Ram Truck, Sebring, Stratus, Wrangler **Engines:** All **Transmissions:** All	**EGR Solenoid Circuit** Engine started; system voltage over 10.5v. The EGR solenoid control circuit was not in its expected state when requested to operate by the PCM. **Possible Causes:** • EGR solenoid ground circuit is open • EGR solenoid control circuit is open or shorted to ground or to voltage • EGR solenoid power circuit is open • EGR solenoid is damaged or has failed • PCM has failed
DTC: P0403 **1T CCM** **Years:** 2005, 2006, 2007 **Models:** Liberty **Engines:** 2.8L Diesel **Transmissions:** All	**EGR Solenoid Circuit Excessive Current** Ignition on; ECM commands EGR Solenoid on. The ECM detects excessive current on the EGR Solenoid control circuit. **Possible Causes:** • Intermittent condition • EGR Solenoid has malfunctioned • EGR Solenoid control circuit is shorted to voltage • EMC has internal short to voltage
DTC: P0403 **1T CCM** **Years:** 2005, 2006, 2007 **Models:** Liberty **Engines:** 2.8L Diesel **Transmissions:** All	**EGR Solenoid Circuit Open** Ignition on; ECM commands EGR Solenoid off. The ECM does not detect voltage on the EGR Solenoid control circuit. **Possible Causes:** • Intermittent condition • ASD Relay output circuit is open • EGR Solenoid control circuit is open or is shorted to ground • EGR Solenoid has malfunctioned • EMC has failed
DTC: P0404 **1T CCM** **Years:** 2005, 2006, 2007 **Models:** Grand Cherokee, Liberty, Pacifica, PT Cruiser, Ram Truck, Sebring, Stratus, Wrangler **Engines:** All **Transmissions:** All	**EGR Position Sensor Signal Performance** Engine started; system voltage over 10.5v and the PCM detected that the EGR flow (or valve movement) was not what was expected during the test period. **Possible Causes:** • EGR Sensor signal circuit is open or shorted to ground • EGR Sensor 5v supply circuit is open or has high resistance • EGR Sensor ground circuit is open • EGR solenoid control circuit has a problem • EGR valve actuator loose, sticking, blocked or improperly grounded • EGR Sensor is damaged or has failed • Intermittent condition • PCM has failed
DTC: P0405 **1T CCM** **Years:** 2005, 2006, 2007 **Models:** Grand Cherokee, Liberty, Pacifica, PT Cruiser, Ram Truck, Sebring, Stratus, Wrangler **Engines:** All **Transmissions:** All	**EGR Position Sensor Circuit Low Input** Key on or engine running; system voltage over 10v. The PCM detected that the EGR Sensor signal indicated less than 0.1v. **Possible Causes:** • EGR Sensor signal circuit is shorted to ground or open • EGR Sensor VREF (5v) circuit is open or shorted to ground • EGR Sensor is damaged (shorted internally) or it has failed • EGR position internal failure • PCM has failed
DTC: P0406 **1T CCM** **Years:** 2005, 2006, 2007 **Models:** Grand Cherokee, Liberty, Pacifica, PT Cruiser, Ram Truck, Sebring, Stratus, Wrangler **Engines:** All **Transmissions:** All	**EGR Position Sensor Circuit High Input** Key on or engine running; system voltage over 10.5v. The PCM detected the EGR Sensor indicated more than 4.89v for 6 seconds. **Possible Causes:** • Intermittent condition • EGR Sensor signal is shorted to VREF (5v) supply circuit or to battery voltage • EGR Sensor ground circuit is open • EGR Sensor signal circuit is open • EGR Sensor is damaged (it may have an internal open circuit) • EGR solenoid failure • PCM has failed

DTC	Trouble Code Title, Conditions & Possible Causes
DTC: P0410 **2T CCM** **Years:** 2005, 2006, 2007 **Models:** Sebring, Stratus **Engines:** All **Transmissions:** All	**Air Injection Air Flow Failure** Engine running; Air Injection Pump is active. If the PCM detects that there is not enough airflow entering the exhaust stream, this DTC will set. **Possible Causes:** • Air injection system damage or failure of components • Exhaust 1-way valve has failed • Fused B+ voltage output circuit problem • Air injection pump relay failure • Air injection pump ground circuit problem • Air injection pump motor has failed • Air injection passage is blocked or damaged • O2 Sensor failed
DTC: P0418 **2T CCM** **Years:** 2005, 2006, 2007 **Models:** Sebring, Stratus **Engines:** All **Transmissions:** All	**Air Pump Relay Control Circuit Failure** Ignition is on; Battery voltage is more than 10,4v. If the PCM detects that there is an open or shorted condition in the Air Pump Relay Control Circuit, this DTC will set. **Possible Causes:** • Air injection system damage or failure of components • Exhaust 1-way valve has failed • Fused B+ voltage output circuit problem • Air injection pump relay failure • Air injection pump ground circuit problem • Air injection pump motor has failed • Air injection passage is blocked or damaged • O2 Sensor failed
DTC: P0420 **2T Catalyst** **Years:** 2005, 2006, 2007 **Models:** Grand Cherokee, Liberty, Pacifica, PT Cruiser, Ram Truck, Sebring, Stratus, Wrangler **Engines:** All **Transmissions:** All	**Catalyst Efficiency Below Normal (Bank 1)** Engine speed at 1200-1700 rpm in closed loop with the throttle open for over 2 minutes, ECT Sensor more than 147°F, MAP Sensor signal from 15.0-21.0 in. Hg, and the PCM detected the switch rate of the rear O2 reached 70% of the switch rate of the front O2. **Possible Causes:** • Air leaks in at the exhaust manifold or exhaust pipes • Base engine problems (high coolant or engine oil consumption) • Catalytic converter damaged or has failed • Front O2 older (aged) than the rear O2 (O2 is lazy)
DTC: P0420 **1T Catalyst** **Years:** 2005, 2006, 2007 **Models:** Grand Cherokee, Liberty, Ram Truck, Sebring, Stratus **Engines:** All **Transmissions:** All	**Catalyst Efficiency Below Normal (Bank 1)** Engine is running for more than 90 seconds; engine coolant is more than 158F (70C); vehicle speed is 20-55 mph; engine speed is 1200-1900 rpm; MAP vacuum at 15-20 in. Hg. As catalyst efficiency deteriorates, the switch rate of the downstream O2 Sensor approaches that of the upstream O2 Sensor. If at any point during the test, the switch ratio reaches a predetermined value, a counter is incremented by one. **Possible Causes:** • Catalytic converter damaged or has failed • Air leaks in at the exhaust manifold or exhaust pipes • Base engine problems (high coolant or engine oil consumption) • Front O2 older (aged) than the rear O2 (O2 is lazy)
DTC: P0420 **2T Catalyst** **Years:** 2005, 2006, 2007 **Models:** PT Cruiser **Engines:** All **Transmissions:** All	**Catalyst Efficiency Below Normal (Bank 1)** Engine running more than 90 sec.; ECT above 158F (70C); vehicle speed 20-55 mph; engine at 1216-1952 rpm. As catalyst efficiency deteriorates, the switch rate of the downstream O2 Sensor approaches that of the upstream O2 Sensor. If at any point during the test, the switch ratio reaches a predetermined value, a counter is incremented by one. **Possible Causes:** • Exhaust leak is present • Base engine mechanical problems • Catalytic converter damaged or has failed • Front O2 older (aged) than the rear O2 (O2 is lazy)

DTC	Trouble Code Title, Conditions & Possible Causes
DTC: P0430 **1T Catalyst** **Years:** 2005, 2006, 2007 **Models:** Grand Cherokee, Liberty, Pacifica, PT Cruiser, Ram Truck, Sebring, Stratus, Wrangler **Engines:** All **Transmissions:** All	**Catalyst (2/1) Efficiency Below Normal** After engine warm-up, ECT Sensor more than 170°F for 180 seconds of open throttle operation and over 20 mph (engine between 1200-1700 rpm and MAP vacuum between 15-20 in. Hg). As catalyst efficiency deteriorates, the switch rate of the downstream O2 Sensor approaches that of the upstream O2 Sensor. If, at any point during the test, the switch ratio reaches a predetermined value, a counter is incremented by one. 3 good trips required to turn off MIL. **Possible Causes:** • Exhaust leaks • Base engine problems • Catalytic converter damaged or has failed • Front O2 older (aged) than the rear O2 (O2 is lazy)
DTC: P0432 **2T Catalyst** **Years:** 2005, 2006, 2007 **Models:** Grand Cherokee, Pacifica, PT Cruiser, Sebring, Stratus **Engines:** All **Transmissions:** All	**Catalyst Efficiency Below Normal (Bank 2)** Engine speed at 1200-1700 rpm in closed loop with the throttle open for over 2 minutes, ECT Sensor more than 147°F, MAP Sensor signal from 15.0-21.0" Hg, and the PCM detected the switch rate of the rear O2 reached 70% of the switch rate of the front O2. **Possible Causes:** • Air leaks in at the exhaust manifold or exhaust pipes • Base engine problems (high coolant or engine oil consumption) • Catalytic converter damaged or has failed • Front O2 older (aged) than the rear O2 (O2 is lazy)
DTC: P0440 **2T EVAP** **Years:** 2005, 2006, 2007 **Models:** Grand Cherokee, Liberty, Pacifica, PT Cruiser, Ram Truck, Sebring, Stratus, Wrangler **Engines:** All **Transmissions:** All	**EVAP Purge System Fault** Ambient Air Temperature from 39-89°F (4-32C); engine running; Fuel level over 12%. The PCM detected that the NVLD switch did not close during medium/large leak test. Once this event occurs, the PCM will increase the amount of vacuum in the system that flows past the purge valve. If the NVLD switch does not close under these conditions, the PCM will set this code. **Possible Causes:** • EVAP purge valve vacuum supply is leaking or clogged • EVAP purge valve is stuck closed • EVAP purge solenoid has failed • NVLD assembly (leak detection) is damaged or has failed • NVLD switch circuit is open or the NVLD switch has failed • Ground circuit is open • PCM has failed
DTC: P0441 **2T EVAP** **Models:** Cherokee, Grand Cherokee, Liberty, PT Cruiser, Ram Truck, Sebring, Stratus, Wrangler **Engines:** All **Transmissions:** All	**EVAP Purge Flow Monitor Fault** Engine at idle speed in closed loop for 200 seconds, BARO Sensor signal less than 8,000 feet, ECT Sensor more than 160°F, no Low Fuel, MAP Sensor signal less than 23.7" Hg, and the PCM did not detect any purge flow through the EVAP system during this test. **Possible Causes:** • EVAP purge solenoid vacuum line loose, leaking or restricted • EVAP purge solenoid stuck leaking, stuck open or stuck closed • EVAP purge vacuum line to canister leaking or disconnected • EVAP canister leaking, damaged or has failed
DTC: P0441 **2T EVAP** **Years:** 2005, 2006, 2007 **Models:** Grand Cherokee, Liberty, Pacifica, PT Cruiser, Ram Truck, Sebring, Stratus, Wrangler **Engines:** All **Transmissions:** All	**EVAP Purge System Performance** Check with cold start test. Engine running. Small leak test passed. The PCM activates the EVAP purge solenoid and it gradually increases to maximum flow. During flow, the PCM looks for the NVLD switch to close. If the PCM does not see the NVLD switch close at maximum flow, an error is detected. **Possible Causes:** • Intermittent condition • EVAP purge solenoid functioning improperly • EVAP purge solenoid vacuum supply leaking or clogged
DTC: P0442 **2T EVAP** **Years:** 2005, 2006, 2007 **Models:** Grand Cherokee, Liberty, Pacifica, PT Cruiser, Ram Truck, Sebring, Stratus, Wrangler **Engines:** All **Transmissions:** All	**EVAP System Medium Leak Detected** Monitor with engine running. Cold start test. Fuel level more than 12%. Ambient temperature between 39-89F (4-32C). Closed loop fuel system. Test runs when small leak test is maturing. The PCM activates EVAP purge solenoid to pull EVAP system into a vacuum to close the NVLD switch. Once this switch is closed, the PCM turns the EVAP purge solenoid off to seal the EVAP system. If the NVLD switch re-opens before the calibrated amount of time for a Medium leak, an error is detected. **Possible Causes:** • Intermittent condition • Vacuum hoses, connections or switches have come loose or malfunctioned • EVAP emission system has a leak • EVAP purge solenoid operation has malfunctioned • NVLD switch operation has malfunctioned

DTC	Trouble Code Title, Conditions & Possible Causes
DTC: P0443 **1T CCM** **Years:** 2005, 2006, 2007 **Models:** Grand Cherokee, Liberty, Pacifica, Ram Truck, Sebring, Stratus, Wrangler **Engines:** All **Transmissions:** All	**EVAP Purge Solenoid Circuit Fault** Ignition on or engine running. Battery voltage more than 10v. The PCM will set a trouble code if the actual state of the solenoid does not match the intended state. **Possible Causes:** • EVAP purge solenoid control circuit open or shorted to ground • EVAP purge solenoid return circuit open or shorted to ground • EVAP purge solenoid is damaged or it has failed • PCM has failed
DTC: P0444 **1T CCM** **Years:** 2005, 2006, 2007 **Models:** PT Cruiser **Engines:** All **Transmissions:** All	**EVAP Purge Solenoid Circuit Open** Any time key is on, if the PCM detects an open circuit in the purge solenoid or in the circuit for more than 280ms, a one-trip fault is set and the MIL is illuminated. **Possible Causes:** • Intermittent condition • 12v supply circuit is open • EVAP purge solenoid control circuit open • EVAP purge solenoid is open • PCM has failed
DTC: P0445 **2T EVAP** **Years:** 2005, 2006, 2007 **Models:** Pacifica, Sebring, Stratus **Engines:** All **Transmissions:** All	**EVAP System Large Leak Detected** Monitor with engine running. Cold start test. Fuel level more than 12%. Ambient temperature between 39-89F (4-32C). Closed loop fuel system. Test runs when small leak test is maturing. The PCM activates EVAP purge solenoid to pull EVAP system into a vacuum to close the NVLD switch. Once this switch is closed, the PCM turns the EVAP purge solenoid off to seal the EVAP system. If the NVLD switch re-opens before the calibrated amount of time for a Large leak, an error is detected. **Possible Causes:** • Intermittent condition • Vacuum hoses, connections or switches have come loose or malfunctioned • EVAP emission system has a leak • EVAP purge solenoid operation has malfunctioned • NVLD switch operation has malfunctioned
DTC: P0452 **1T CCM** **Years:** 2005, 2006, 2007 **Models:** Grand Cherokee, Liberty, Pacifica, PT Cruiser, Ram Truck, Sebring, Stratus, Wrangler **Engines:** All **Transmissions:** All	**NVLD Pressure Switch Sense Circuit Low Input** Engine started; and immediately after the engine is running. The PCM activates the NVLD solenoid to test the NVLD switch circuit. If the switch is not open, the PCM sets this code. **Possible Causes:** • EVAP purge solenoid control circuit is shorted to ground • EVAP purge solenoid is leaking or it is stuck in open position • NVLD assembly or NVLD switch is damaged or it has failed • NVLD switch signal circuit is shorted to ground • PCM has failed
DTC: P0453 **1T CCM** **Years:** 2005, 2006, 2007 **Models:** Grand Cherokee, Liberty, Pacifica, PT Cruiser, Ram Truck, Sebring, Stratus, Wrangler **Engines:** All **Transmissions:** All	**NVLD Pressure Switch Sense Circuit High Input** Engine started; and immediately after the engine is running, the PCM activates the NVLD solenoid to test the NVLD switch circuit. If the switch does not close under these conditions, this code is set. **Possible Causes:** • NVLD assembly ground circuit is open • NVLD switch signal circuit is open or shorted to power (B+) or to NVLD solenoid control circuit • NVLD assembly or switch is damaged or it has failed • PCM has failed
DTC: P0455 **2T EVAP** **Years:** 2005, 2006, 2007 **Models:** Grand Cherokee, Liberty, Pacifica, PT Cruiser, Ram Truck, Sebring, Stratus, Wrangler **Engines:** All **Transmissions:** All	**EVAP Large Leak Detected** Ambient Air Temperature from 39-89°F at engine startup, engine running under closed loop conditions, Fuel Level over 12%, then with the EVAP purge solenoid enabled (to pull vacuum into the system to close the NVLD switch) and the EVAP "small leak" test maturing, the PCM turns "off" the EVAP purge solenoid once the NVLD switch closes. If the NVLD switch reopens before a calibrated amount of time expires, a "large" leak in the system is detected (larger than 0.080 in.). **Possible Causes:** • EVAP purge solenoid is damaged or it has failed • Fuel tank cap is damaged, missing or the wrong part number • NVLD switch is damaged or it has failed

DTC	Trouble Code Title, Conditions & Possible Causes
DTC: P0456 **2T EVAP** **Years:** 2005, 2006, 2007 **Models:** Grand Cherokee, Liberty, Pacifica, PT Cruiser, Ram Truck, Sebring, Stratus, Wrangler **Engines:** All **Transmissions:** All	**EVAP System Small Leak Detected** Ambient Air Temperature from 39-109°F at engine startup, engine running under closed loop conditions, Fuel Level below 88%, then with the EVAP system sealed, the PCM monitors the NVLD switch. If the NVLD switch does not close within a calibrated amount of time expires, a "small" leak in the EVAP system was detected. **Possible Causes:** • Fuel tank cap is damaged, loose or the wrong part number • Small leak present somewhere in the EVAP system
DTC: P0457 **2T EVAP** **Years:** 2005, 2006, 2007 **Models:** Grand Cherokee, Liberty, Pacifica, Ram Truck, Sebring, Stratus, Wrangler **Engines:** All **Transmissions:** All	**Loose Fuel Cap Condition:** Monitor with ignition on. Ambient temperature should be between 39-109F (4-43C). Vehicle should be in closed loop fuel system. The PCM has detected an EVAP system leak after a fuel level increase. If the NVLD switch reopens before the calibrated amount of time after a fuel tank fill, an error is detected. MIL will illuminate. Condition requires 3 good trips to turn off MIL. **Possible Causes:** • Loose or missing fuel fill cap • Intermittent condition • NVLD system or switch malfunction • EVAP system leaking • EVAP purge solenoid malfunction
DTC: P0458 **1T EVAP** **Years:** 2005, 2006, 2007 **Models:** PT Cruiser **Engines:** All **Transmissions:** All	**EVAP Purge Solenoid Low Condition:** Monitor with ignition on. If PCM detected an open in the purge solenoid of in the circuit for more than 280ms, a one-trip fault is set and the MIL is illuminated. **Possible Causes:** • Intermittent condition • EVAP purge solenoid connector problems • EVAP purge solenoid control circuit is shorted to ground • EVAP purge solenoid leaks, stuck open, or stuck closed • PCM has failed
DTC: P0459 **1T EVAP** **Years:** 2005, 2006, 2007 **Models:** PT Cruiser **Engines:** All **Transmissions:** All	**EVAP Purge Solenoid High Condition:** Monitor with ignition on. If PCM detected a short to ground in the purge solenoid of in the circuit for more than 280ms, a one-trip fault is set and the MIL is illuminated. **Possible Causes:** • Intermittent condition • EVAP purge solenoid connector problems • EVAP purge solenoid control circuit is shorted to battery voltage • EVAP purge solenoid leaks, stuck open, or stuck closed • PCM has failed
DTC: P0460 **1T CCM** **Years:** 2005, 2006, 2007 **Models:** Liberty **Engines:** 2.8L Diesel **Transmissions:** All	**Fuel Level Sensor Circuit Signal Voltage Too High Or Too Low** Ignition on. The Fuel Level Sensor signal voltage is above 4.51v for 0.6 second (too high) or is below 0.19v for 0.6 second (too low). **Possible Causes:** • Intermittent condition • Fuel Level Sensor signal circuit is open or is shorted to voltage (too high) • Fuel Level Sensor ground circuit is open (too high) • Fuel Level Sensor signal circuit is short to ground (too low) • Fuel Level Sensor signal circuit and ground circuit are shorted together (too low) • Fuel Level Sensor has failed • FCM has failed
DTC: P0461 **2T CCM** **Years:** 2005, 2006, 2007 **Models:** Grand Cherokee, Liberty, Pacifica, Ram Truck, Sebring, Stratus, Wrangler **Engines:** All **Transmissions:** All	**Fuel Level Sensor No. 1 Malfunction** Test No. 1: With ignition on, fuel level is compared to the previous key-down after a 20-second delay. If the PCM does not see a difference in the fuel level of more than 0.1v, the test will fail. • Test No. 2: The PCM monitors the fuel level with ignition on. If the PCM does not see a change in the fuel level of 0.1765 in. over a set amount of miles, the test will fail. **Possible Causes:** • Fuel tank or internal siphon hose damage • Fuel level signal circuit open or shorted to ground • Ground circuit is open • Fuel level Sensor malfunction

DTC	Trouble Code Title, Conditions & Possible Causes
DTC: P0461 **1T CCM** **Years:** 2005, 2006, 2007 **Models:** PT Cruiser **Engines:** All **Transmissions:** All	**Fuel Level Sensor Malfunction** With engine running and under partial load, the fuel level must be above 0%, and there must not be any fuel level Sensor electrical DTCs. If the PCM detects the fuel level change is less than 2% over 2 hours, this DTC will set. **Possible Causes:** • Intermittent condition • Fuel tank or component damage • Fuel level Sensor signal circuit open or shorted to ground • Ground circuit is open • Fuel level Sensor malfunction
DTC: P0462 **1T CCM** **Years:** 2005, 2006, 2007 **Models:** Grand Cherokee, Liberty, Pacifica, Ram Truck, Sebring, Stratus, Wrangler **Engines:** All **Transmissions:** All	**Fuel Level Sensor No. 1 Low Input** Key on. Battery voltage over 10.4v. Fuel level Sensor signal goes below 0.1961v (exc. Ram) for more than 5 seconds, or below 0.4v for more than 90 seconds (Ram). DTC is recorded. **Possible Causes:** • Intermittent condition • Fuel level sending unit signal circuit shorted to Sensor or chassis ground • Fuel level sensing unit is damaged or the fuel tank is damaged • Instrument cluster problem
DTC: P0462 **1T CCM** **Years:** 2005, 2006, 2007 **Models:** PT Cruiser **Engines:** All **Transmissions:** All	**Fuel Level Sending Unit Low Voltage** Key on. If the PCM detects the fuel level as more than 100% for more than 4.5 minutes, this DTC will set. **Possible Causes:** • Intermittent condition
DTC: P0463 **1T CCM** **Years:** 2005, 2006, 2007 **Models:** Grand Cherokee, Liberty, Pacifica, PT Cruiser, Ram Truck, Sebring, Stratus, Wrangler **Engines:** All **Transmissions:** All	**Fuel Level Sensor No. 1 High Input** Key on. Battery voltage over 10.4v. If Fuel Level Sensor signal goes above 4.7v for more than 5 seconds (exc. Ram Truck, Liberty), above 4.9v for more than 90 seconds (Ram Truck, Liberty), this DTC is recorded. **Possible Causes:** • Fuel level sending unit signal circuit is open or is shorted to battery voltage • Fuel level Sensor ground circuit is open • Fuel level Sensor is damaged or the fuel tank is damaged • Instrument cluster is faulty • BCM or PCM has failed
DTC: P0480 **1T CCM** **Years:** 2005, 2006, 2007 **Models:** Grand Cherokee, Liberty, Pacifica, PT Cruiser, Ram Truck, Sebring, Stratus, Wrangler **Engines:** All **Transmissions:** All	**Low Speed (No.1) Fan Control Relay Circuit** Key on. Battery voltage over 10v. An open or shorted circuit is detected in the Low Speed Fan Relay control circuit system. **Possible Causes:** • Fan relay intermittent condition • Ground circuit is open • Fused B+ output circuit malfunction • Fan relay control circuit is open or shorted to battery voltage or ground • Fan relay is damaged or has failed • PCM has failed
DTC: P0480 **1T CCM** **Years:** 2005, 2006, 2007 **Models:** Liberty **Engines:** 2.8L Diesel **Transmissions:** All	**Fan No. 1 Control Circuit Excessive Current Or Short Circuit** Ignition on; Low Speed Radiator Fan Relay commanded OFF (excessive current) or commanded ON (short circuit). The ECM detects excessive current on Low Speed Radiator Fan Relay control circuit. **Possible Causes:** • Intermittent condition • Low Speed Radiator Fan Relay has failed • Low Speed Radiator Fan control circuit is shorted to voltage • ECM has failed
DTC: P0480 **1T CCM** **Years:** 2005, 2006, 2007 **Models:** Liberty **Engines:** 2.8L Diesel **Transmissions:** All	**Fan No. 1 Control Circuit Open Or Short-to-Ground** Ignition on; Low Speed Radiator Fan Relay commanded OFF. The ECM does not detect voltage on Low Speed Radiator Fan Relay control circuit. **Possible Causes:** • Intermittent condition • ASD Relay output circuit is open • Low Speed Radiator Fan Relay has failed • Low Speed Radiator Fan control circuit is open or is shorted to ground • ECM has failed

DTC	Trouble Code Title, Conditions & Possible Causes
DTC: P0481 **1T CCM** **Years:** 2005, 2006, 2007 **Models:** Grand Cherokee, Liberty, Pacifica, PT Cruiser, Ram Truck, Sebring, Stratus, Wrangler **Engines:** All **Transmissions:** All	**High Speed (No. 2) Fan Relay Control Circuit** Key on or engine running; and the PCM detected an unexpected low or high voltage condition (open or shorted condition) on the High Speed Fan Relay circuit. **Possible Causes:** • HFAN relay power circuit is open from the relay to fused power • HFAN relay control circuit is open or shorted to chassis ground • Fan relay(s) failed • PCM has failed.
DTC: P0481 **2T CCM** **Years:** 2005, 2006, 2007 **Models:** Sebring, Stratus **Engines:** All **Transmissions:** All	**Air Injection System Malfunction** Engine running; Air Injection Pump is active for a calibrated amount of time. Once enough airflow has accumulated through the AI system, the test will begin. If the PCM detects excessive airflow, or not enough airflow through the AI system, this DTC will be set. **Possible Causes:** • Air Injection system may be damaged, restricted or disconnected • ASD relay output circuit failure • MAF Sensor internal failure • MAF signal circuit open or shorted to ground or to ASD relay output circuit or to battery voltage • MAF signal circuit is shorted to sensor ground circuit • MAF Sensor ground circuit is open • PCM has failed.
DTC: P0489 **1T CCM** **Years:** 2005, 2006, 2007 **Models:** Liberty **Engines:** 2.8L Diesel **Transmissions:** All	**EGR Solenoid Circuit Short-To-Ground** Ignition on; ECM commands EGR Solenoid off. The ECM does not detect voltage on the EGR Solenoid control circuit. **Possible Causes:** • Intermittent condition • ASD Relay output circuit is open • EGR Solenoid control circuit is open or is shorted to ground • EGR Solenoid has malfunctioned • EMC has failed
DTC: P0490 **1T CCM** **Years:** 2005, 2006, 2007 **Models:** Liberty **Engines:** 2.8L Diesel **Transmissions:** All	**EGR Solenoid Circuit Short** Ignition on; ECM commands EGR Solenoid on. The ECM detects excessive current on the EGR Solenoid control circuit. **Possible Causes:** • Intermittent condition • EGR Solenoid has malfunctioned • EGR Solenoid control circuit is shorted to voltage • EMC has internal short to voltage
DTC: P0498 **1T CCM** **Years:** 2005, 2006, 2007 **Models:** Grand Cherokee, Liberty, Pacifica, PT Cruiser, Ram Truck, Sebring, Stratus, Wrangler **Engines:** All **Transmissions:** All	**NVLD Canister Vent Solenoid Circuit Low** Key on or engine running; and the PCM detected an unexpected low voltage condition on the Natural Vacuum Leak Detection (NVLD) control circuit during the CCM test period. **Possible Causes:** • NVLD canister vent solenoid control circuit is shorted to ground • NVLD canister vent solenoid is damaged or it has failed • PCM has failed
DTC: P0499 **1T CCM** **Years:** 2005, 2006, 2007 **Models:** Grand Cherokee, Liberty, Pacifica, PT Cruiser, Ram Truck, Sebring, Stratus, Wrangler **Engines:** All **Transmissions:** All	**NVLD Canister Vent Solenoid Circuit High** Key on or engine running. The PCM detected an open or unexpected high voltage condition on the Natural Vacuum Leak Detection (NVLD) circuit. **Possible Causes:** • NVLD canister vent solenoid control circuit is open or is shorted to power • NVLD canister vent solenoid ground circuit is open • NVLD canister vent solenoid is damaged or it has failed • PCM has failed
DTC: P0500 **1T CCM** **Years:** 2005, 2006, 2007 **Models:** PT Cruiser **Engines:** All **Transmissions:** All	**No Vehicle Speed Sensor Signal** Engine started; if the PCM did not detect a VSS signal for over 6 seconds, this DTC will set. **Possible Causes:** • Intermittent condition • 5v supply circuit open • VSS circuit is open or is shorted to ground • VSS ground circuit is open • VSS has failed • PCM has failed

DTC	Trouble Code Title, Conditions & Possible Causes
DTC: P0501 **2T CCM** **Years:** 2005, 2006, 2007 **Models:** Grand Cherokee, Liberty, Pacifica, PT Cruiser, Ram Truck, Sebring, Stratus, Wrangler **Engines:** All **Transmissions:** All	**Vehicle Speed Sensor Performance** Engine started; vehicle driven at over 1500 rpm for 10 seconds, gear selector not in Park or Neutral (or clutch is not depressed on M/T); brakes not applied. The PCM (or ECM: Liberty with Diesel) did not receive any VSS signals from the TCM (BCM: Liberty) for 11 seconds for 2 consecutive trips. 3 good trips required to turn off MIL. **Possible Causes:** • Check for any ABS/RWAL or TCM codes related to the VSS • VSS connector is damaged, open or it is shorted • VSS signal is open, shorted to ground or shorted to power • Incorrect tire circumference • ABS/RWAL controller, BCM, ECM, TCM or PCM has failed
DTC: P0503 **1T or 2T CCM** **Years:** 2005, 2006, 2007 **Models:** Grand Cherokee, Liberty, Pacifica, PT Cruiser, Ram Truck, Sebring, Stratus, Wrangler **Engines:** All **Transmissions:** All	**Vehicle Speed Sensor No. 1 Erratic Performance** Ignition is on; battery voltage over 10v; transmission in Drive or Reverse; brakes not applied. Vehicle speed signal is erratic during road load conditions. One-trip fault for ETC vehicles; Two-trip fault for ETC vehicles. 3 good trips required to turn off MIL. **Possible Causes:** • Check for active Bus or Communication DTCs • Incorrect Tire Circumference • PCM has failed
DTC: P0504 **1T CCM** **Years:** 2005, 2006, 2007 **Models:** Liberty **Engines:** 2.8L Diesel **Transmissions:** All	**Brake Switch Signal Circuits Plausibility With Redundant Contact** Ignition is on. The Primary Brake Switch signal and the Secondary Brake Switch signal inputs to the ECM do not agree. **Possible Causes:** • Intermittent condition • Brake Lamp Switch sense circuit is open or shorted to ground • Brake Switch sense circuit is open or shorted to ground • Brake Lamp Switch output circuit is open or shorted to voltage • ECM has failed
DTC: P0505 **2T IAC** **Years:** 2005, 2006, 2007 **Models:** Cherokee, Grand Cherokee, Liberty, PT Cruiser, Ram Truck, Sebring, Stratus, Wrangler **Engines:** All **Transmissions:** All	**Idle Air Control Motor Circuit** Engine started; system voltage over 11.5v and the PCM detected an unexpected voltage condition on one or more of the IAC motor circuits for 2.75 seconds with the IAC motor active. **Possible Causes:** • Stepper motor Coil No. 1, 2, 3 or 4 circuit open or shorted to ground • Stepper motor coil circuit(s) shorted to system power (B+) • Stepper motor is damaged or has failed • PCM has failed
DTC: P0506 **2T CCM** **Years:** 2005, 2006, 2007 **Models:** Pacifica, Sebring, Stratus **Engines:** All **Transmissions:** All	**Idle Speed Low Performance** Engine running at idle speed in closed loop. If engine rpm does not come within a calibratable low limit of the target idle speed, a failure timer will increment. When the appropriate failure timer reaches its maximum threshold without sign of rpm trending toward control, a soft-fail is generated. When a calibratable number of the soft-fails is reached, a 1-trip fault is set. When two 1-trip faults occur in a row, the DTC is set and the MIL illuminates. **Possible Causes:** • PCV system malfunction • Air induction system restrictions (clogged air filter, etc.) • Idle air control passage is clogged or dirty (clean and retest) • Air induction system malfunction • Throttle body or linkage is binding, damaged or sticking
DTC: P0506 **1T CCM** **Years:** 2005, 2006, 2007 **Models:** Grand Cherokee, Liberty, Ram Truck, Wrangler **Engines:** All **Transmissions:** All	**Idle Speed Low Performance** Engine running at idle speed; MAF is less than 250 mg/tdc; air temperature is greater than 0F (−18C) and less than 19F (−7C) enable after coolant temperature is greater than 158F (70C) or air temperature is greater than 19F (−7C); coolant temperature is between 19 to 266F (−7 to 130C); canister purge is less than 100% duty cycle; no DTCs are present for VSS, MAF/MAP, ECT, TPS, ECT and CKP Sensors; also no fuel system or injector related DTCs are present. If the DTC detects that engine speed is 100 rpm or more below the normal idle speed for 7 seconds, this DTC will set. **Possible Causes:** • Air induction system restrictions • Throttle body or linkage is binding, damaged or sticking • Intermittent condition • PCM has failed

DTC	Trouble Code Title, Conditions & Possible Causes
DTC: P0507 **2T CCM** **Years:** 2005, 2006, 2007 **Models:** Grand Cherokee, Liberty, Pacifica, Ram Truck, Sebring, Stratus, Wrangler **Engines:** All **Transmissions:** All	**Idle Speed High Performance** Engine running at idle speed in closed loop. If engine rpm does not come within a calibratable high limit of the target idle speed, a failure timer will increment. When the appropriate failure timer reaches its maximum threshold without sign of rpm trending toward control, a soft-fail is generated. When a calibratable number of the soft-fails is reached, a 1-trip fault is set. When two 1-trip faults occur in a row, the DTC is set and the MIL illuminates. **Possible Causes:** • PCV system malfunction • Air induction system restrictions (clogged air filter, etc.) • Idle air control passage is clogged or dirty (clean and retest) • Air induction system malfunction • Throttle body or linkage is binding, damaged or sticking
DTC: P0507 **1T CCM** **Years:** 2005, 2006, 2007 **Models:** Grand Cherokee, Liberty, PT Cruiser, Ram Truck, Wrangler **Engines:** All **Transmissions:** All	**Idle Speed High Performance Higher Than Expected** Engine running at idle speed; MAF is less than 250 mg/tdc; air temperature is greater than 0F (−18C) and less than 19F (−7C) enable after coolant temperature is greater than 158F (70C) or air temperature is greater than 19F (−7C); coolant temperature is between 19 to 266F (−7 to 130C); canister purge is less than 100% duty cycle; no DTCs are present for VSS, MAF/MAP, ECT, TPS, ECT and CKP Sensors; also no fuel system or injector related DTCs are present. If the DTC detects that engine speed is 200 rpm or more above the normal idle speed for 7 seconds, this DTC will set. **Possible Causes:** • Air induction system restrictions (clogged air filter, etc.) • Vacuum leaks • Intermittent condition • Throttle body or linkage is binding, damaged or sticking • PCM has failed
DTC: P0508 **2T CCM** **Years:** 2005, 2006, 2007 **Models:** Grand Cherokee, Liberty, Pacifica, PT Cruiser, Ram Truck, Sebring, Stratus, Wrangler **Engines:** All **Transmissions:** All	**Idle Air Control Motor Sense Circuit Low Input** Engine started; system voltage over 10.5v; IAC motor operating. The PCM detected the IAC Motor Sense circuit current was less than 175mA during the CCM test period. **Possible Causes:** • IAC motor driver circuit is open or shorted to ground • IAC motor sense circuit is open or shorted to ground • IAC motor is damaged or it has failed • PCM has failed
DTC: P0508 **1 CCM** **Years:** 2005, 2006, 2007 **Models:** Grand Cherokee, Liberty, Ram Truck, Wrangler **Engines:** All **Transmissions:** All	**Idle Air Control Motor Sense Circuit Low Input** Engine running; system voltage over 10v; IAC motor operating. The PCM senses an open or short to ground on any of the Linear Idle Air Control (LIAC) control circuits for 2.75 seconds while the IAC motor is active. 3 good trips are required to turn off the MIL. **Possible Causes:** • IAC motor control circuit is open or shorted to ground • IAC motor signal circuit is open or shorted to ground • IAC motor is damaged or it has failed • PCM has failed
DTC: P0509 **2T CCM** **Years:** 2005, 2006, 2007 **Models:** Grand Cherokee, Liberty, Pacifica, PT Cruiser, Ram Truck, Sebring, Stratus, Wrangler **Engines:** All **Transmissions:** All	**Idle Air Control Motor Circuit High** Engine started; system voltage over 10.5v, IAC motor activated, and the PCM detected a high voltage on one or more of the IAC motor circuits (over 980mA) during the CCM test period. **Possible Causes:** • IAC motor driver circuit is shorted to power • IAC motor sense circuit is shorted to power • IAC motor is damaged or it has failed • PCM has failed
DTC: P0509 **1 CCM** **Years:** 2005, 2006, 2007 **Models:** Grand Cherokee, Liberty, Ram Truck, Wrangler **Engines:** All **Transmissions:** All	**Idle Air Control Motor Sense Circuit High** Engine running; system voltage over 10v; IAC motor operating. The PCM senses a short-to-power on any of the Linear Idle Air Control (LIAC) control circuits for 2.75 seconds while the IAC motor is active. 3 good trips are required to turn off the MIL. **Possible Causes:** • IAC motor control circuit is shorted to battery power • IAC motor signal circuit is open or shorted to battery power • IAC control circuit is shorted to IAC return circuit • IAC motor is damaged or it has failed • PCM has failed

DTC	Trouble Code Title, Conditions & Possible Causes
DTC: P0513 **1T PCM** **Years:** 2005, 2006, 2007 **Models:** Grand Cherokee, Liberty, Pacifica, PT Cruiser, Ram Truck, Sebring, Stratus, Wrangler **Engines:** All **Transmissions:** All	**Invalid SKIM Key Detected** Key on, and the PCM detected an invalid Sentry Key Immobilizer key had been inserted into the ignition key assembly. **Possible Causes:** • Incorrect VIN in the PCM • No communication between the PCM and the SKIM • SKIM trouble codes present (check for any SKIM codes) • Valid SKIM key not present • VIN not programmed into the PCM • PCM has failed
DTC: P0516 **1T CCM** **Years:** 2005, 2006, 2007 **Models:** Grand Cherokee, Liberty, Pacifica, PT Cruiser, Ram Truck, Sebring, Stratus, Wrangler **Engines:** All **Transmissions:** All	**Battery Temperature Sensor Circuit Low Input** Key on or engine running; and the PCM detected a Battery Temperature Sensor signal that indicated less than 0.10v (exc. Ram Truck, Liberty) or less than 0.039v (Ram Truck, Liberty). 3 good trips required to turn off MIL. **Possible Causes:** • BTS signal circuit is shorted to Sensor or chassis ground • BTS assembly is damaged or it has failed • PCM has failed
DTC: P0517 **1T CCM** **Years:** 2005, 2006, 2007 **Models:** Grand Cherokee, Liberty, Pacifica, PT Cruiser, Ram Truck, Sebring, Stratus, Wrangler **Engines:** All **Transmissions:** All	**Battery Temperature Sensor Circuit High Input** Key on or engine running; and the PCM detected a Battery Temperature Sensor signal that indicated more than 4.8v (exc. Ram Truck, Liberty) or more than 4.94v (Ram Truck, Liberty). **Possible Causes:** • BTS signal circuit is shorted to VREF (5v) • BTS signal circuit is open or the BTS ground circuit is open • BTS assembly is damaged or it has failed • PCM has failed
DTC: P0519 **2T IAC** **Years:** 2005, 2006, 2007 **Models:** Cherokee, Grand Cherokee, Liberty, PT Cruiser, Ram Truck, Sebring, Stratus, Wrangler **Engines:** All **Transmissions:** All	**Idle Air Performance** DTC P0106, P0107, P0108, P0121, P0122 and P0123 not set, engine started, engine running with the gear selector indicating Drive position, and the PCM detected the engine idle speed was not within 200 rpm of the high idle limit or within 100 rpm of the low idle limit when compared to the Target Idle Speed limit for 40 seconds. **Possible Causes:** • Idle air control passage is clogged or dirty (clean and retest) • Throttle body or linkage is binding, damaged or sticking • Vacuum leaks in the engine or PCV system components
DTC: P0520 **1T CCM** **Years:** 2005, 2006, 2007 **Models:** Grand Cherokee, Liberty, Pacifica, PT Cruiser, Ram Truck, Sebring, Stratus, Wrangler **Engines:** All **Transmissions:** All	**Engine Oil Pressure Sensor Out of Range** Key on (engine not started). The PCM detected an engine oil pressure reading out of the calibrated range. **Possible Causes:** • Oil pressure Sensor signal circuit is open or shorted to ground • Oil pressure Sensor signal circuit has high resistance • 5v supply circuit has high resistance • 5v supply circuit is shorted to ground • Oil pressure Sensor ground circuit has high resistance • Oil pressure Sensor is damaged or has failed • PCM has failed
DTC: P0504 **1T CCM** **Years:** 2005, 2006, 2007 **Models:** Liberty **Engines:** 2.8L Diesel **Transmissions:** All	**Engine Oil Pressure Sensor Circuit Too Low Or Too High** Engine running at start up. The Oil Pressure signal is below the lower limit for 8 seconds after engine startup. After the engine is running, the OP Sensor signal is above 4.8v for 0.5 seconds or it may be below 0.19v for 0.5 second. **Possible Causes:** • 5v supply circuit is open • Front Control Module (FCM) Oil Pressure Sensor signal circuit is shorted to ground or to voltage • Engine mechanical problem exists • Oil Pressure Sensor has failed • Oil Pressure Sensor signal circuit is open, shorted to voltage or to ground • Oil Pressure Sensor signal circuit is shorted to Sensor ground • Oil Pressure Sensor ground circuit is open • Intermittent condition

DTC	Trouble Code Title, Conditions & Possible Causes
DTC: P0521 **1T CCM** **Years:** 2005, 2006, 2007 **Models:** Grand Cherokee, Liberty, Pacifica, PT Cruiser, Ram Truck, Sebring, Stratus, Wrangler **Engines:** All **Transmissions:** All	**Engine Oil Pressure Sensor Does Not Reach Range** Engine running. The PCM detected an engine oil pressure reading never reaches the calibrated specification when engine is at 1250 rpm. **Possible Causes:** • Engine oil or engine mechanical fault • Oil pressure Sensor signal circuit is shorted to battery • Oil pressure Sensor signal circuit has high resistance • 5v supply circuit has high resistance • 5v supply circuit is shorted to ground • Oil pressure Sensor return circuit has high resistance • Oil pressure Sensor is damaged or has failed • PCM has failed
DTC: P0522 **1T CCM** **Years:** 2005, 2006, 2007 **Models:** Grand Cherokee, Liberty, Pacifica, PT Cruiser, Ram Truck, Sebring, Stratus, Wrangler **Engines:** All **Transmissions:** All	**Engine Oil Pressure Sensor Rationality** Engine running; battery voltage over 10.4v. If the PCM detected an engine oil pressure voltage reading of less than 0.1v for 0.5 second (Ram), less than 0.3v (), or less that 0.942v (Liberty), this DTC will set. **Possible Causes:** • 5v supply circuit is open or is shorted to ground • Oil pressure Sensor signal circuit is shorted to ground or to sensor ground • Oil pressure Sensor is damaged or has failed • PCM has failed
DTC: P0523 **1T CCM** **Years:** 2005, 2006, 2007 **Models:** Grand Cherokee, Liberty, Pacifica, PT Cruiser, Ram Truck, Sebring, Stratus, Wrangler **Engines:** All **Transmissions:** All	**Engine Oil Pressure Sensor Circuit High** Key on (engine not started). The PCM detected an engine oil pressure reading greater than the calibrated amount. **Possible Causes:** • Oil pressure Sensor signal circuit is open or shorted to battery voltage or to 5v supply circuit • Oil pressure Sensor ground circuit is open • Oil pressure Sensor is damaged or has failed • PCM has failed
DTC: P0524 **1T CCM** **Years:** 2005, 2006, 2007 **Models:** Grand Cherokee, Liberty, Pacifica, PT Cruiser, Ram Truck, Sebring, Stratus, Wrangler **Engines:** All **Transmissions:** All	**Engine Oil Pressure Low** Engine running. The PCM detected that the engine oil pressure never reaches the calibrated specification to allow the MDS activation. **Possible Causes:** • Engine oil system or engine mechanical faults • Oil pressure Sensor signal circuit is shorted to battery voltage or to ground • Oil pressure Sensor signal circuit has high resistance • 5v supply circuit has high resistance • 5v supply circuit is shorted to ground • Oil pressure Sensor return circuit has high resistance • Oil pressure Sensor is damaged or has failed • PCM has failed
DTC: P0530 **1T CCM** **Years:** 2005, 2006, 2007 **Models:** Liberty **Engines:** 2.8L Diesel **Transmissions:** All	**A/C Pressure Sensor Circuit Too Low Or Too High** Ignition on. An error occurs with the A/C Pressure CAN Bus message from the Front Control Module (FCM) to the ECM, or the signal is below 0.06v or above 4.74v for 0.6 second. **Possible Causes:** • Intermittent condition • A/C Pressure Sensor signal circuit is shorted to 5v supply or to voltage • A/C Pressure Sensor ground circuit is shorted to voltage • 5v supply circuit is open • A/C Pressure Sensor has failed • A/C Pressure Sensor signal circuit is open • A/C Pressure Sensor signal circuit is shorted to ground or to Sensor ground circuit • FCM to 5v supply circuit problem
DTC: P0532 **1T CCM** **Years:** 2005, 2006, 2007 **Models:** Grand Cherokee, Liberty, Pacifica, PT Cruiser, Ram Truck, Sebring, Stratus, Wrangler **Engines:** All **Transmissions:** All	**Air Conditioning Pressure Sensor Circuit Low Input** Engine running with the A/C relay energized. The PCM detected the signal from the A/C Pressure Sensor indicated less than 0.58v for over 2.6 seconds during the CCM test period. **Possible Causes:** • A/C pressure Sensor 5v power supply (VREF) circuit is open or is shorted to ground • A/C pressure Sensor signal circuit is shorted to ground or to Sensor ground circuit • A/C pressure Sensor is damaged or it has failed • Front A/C control module damaged or has failed • PCM has failed

DTC	Trouble Code Title, Conditions & Possible Causes
DTC: P0533 **1T CCM** **Years:** 2005, 2006, 2007 **Models:** Grand Cherokee, Liberty, Pacifica, PT Cruiser, Ram Truck, Sebring, Stratus, Wrangler **Engines:** All **Transmissions:** All	**Air Conditioning Pressure Sensor Circuit High Input** Engine running with the A/C relay energized, and the PCM detected the signal from the A/C Pressure Sensor indicated less than 4.92v for over 2.6 seconds during the CCM test period. **Possible Causes:** • A/C pressure Sensor signal circuit is shorted to 5v VREF power • A/C pressure Sensor signal circuit or ground circuit is open • A/C pressure Sensor is damaged or it has failed • Front A/C control module is damaged or has failed • PCM has failed
DTC: P0551 **1T CCM** **Years:** 2005, 2006, 2007 **Models:** Grand Cherokee, Liberty, Pacifica, Ram Truck, Wrangler **Engines:** All **Transmissions:** All	**Power Steering Pressure Switch Circuit Failure** Engine running and vehicle driven at more than 40 mph for 30 seconds. If the PCM detected the PSPS signal remains open for 2 consecutive trips, this DTC will set. 3 good trips required to turn off MIL. **Possible Causes:** • PSPS sense circuit is open between the switch and the PCM • PSPS ground circuit is open between the switch and ground • PSPS is damaged or it has failed • PCM has failed
DTC: P0551 **2T CCM** **Years:** 2005, 2006, 2007 **Models:** Sebring, Stratus **Engines:** All **Transmissions:** All	**Power Steering Pressure Switch Circuit Failure** Engine running and vehicle driven at more than 50 mph or more; coolant temperature is above 68F (20C). If the PCM detected the PSPS signal remains open for 40 seconds or more, this DTC will set. **Possible Causes:** • PSPS sense circuit is open or is shorted to ground • PSPS ground circuit is open • PSPS or PCM has failed
DTC: P0551 **1T CCM** **Years:** 2005, 2006, 2007 **Models:** PT Cruiser **Engines:** All **Transmissions:** All	**Power Steering Pressure Switch Circuit Failure** Engine running and vehicle driven at more than 30 mph for 60 seconds; no VSS DTC is present. If the PCM detected the PSPS signal remains high after 60 seconds, this DTC will set. **Possible Causes:** • PSPS sense circuit is open or is shorted to ground • PSPS ground circuit is open • PSPS is damaged or it has failed • PCM has failed
DTC: P0562 **1T CCM** **Years:** 2005, 2006, 2007 **Models:** Grand Cherokee, Liberty, Pacifica, Ram Truck, Wrangler **Engines:** All **Transmissions:** All	**Battery Voltage Low Input** Engine running at a speed over 1000 rpm. If battery voltage is 1v less than desired voltage for a set period of time, this DTC will set. The ETC light is flashing. **Possible Causes:** • Resistance in battery positive circuit • Resistance in the generator case ground • Generator field ground circuit is open or shorted to ground • Generator is damaged or it has failed • Ground circuit is open • PCM has failed
DTC: P0562 **1T CCM** **Years:** 2005, 2006, 2007 **Models:** Sebring, Stratus **Engines:** All **Transmissions:** All	**Battery Voltage Low Input** Engine running at a speed over 1150 rpm. This DTC will set if the following occur: the battery sensed voltage is 1v below the charging goal for 13.47 seconds, of less than 6.5v for 200ms; the battery voltage of the Transmission Control Relay output sense circuit(s) to the PCM is less than 10v for 15 seconds, of less than 7.2v for 200ms. The PCM senses the battery voltage, turns off the field driver, and senses the battery voltage again. If the voltages are the same, this DTC will be set. **Note: This DTC generally indicates a gradually failing battery voltage output or a resistive connection to the PCM.** **Possible Causes:** • B+ circuit to relay or to PCM has high resistance • Generator ground circuit has high resistance • Generator is damaged or it has failed • Generator field ground circuit is open • Generator field control circuit is open or is shorted to ground • TC relay output to TCM is open or has high resistance • TC relay has failed • Intermittent wiring or connector problems • PCM has failed

DTC	Trouble Code Title, Conditions & Possible Causes
DTC: P0562 **1T CCM** **Years:** 2005, 2006, 2007 **Models:** PT Cruiser **Engines:** All **Transmissions:** All	**Charging System Voltage Low** PCM: Engine is running for over 30 sec. If the PCM detects battery voltage is under 11.5v for more than 5 sec., this DTC will set. Other charging system DTCs may be present. TCM w/NGC: Engine is running and PCM has closed the Transmission Control Relay. If battery voltage of the TC Relay output sense circuit is less than 10v for 15 seconds, this DTC will set. **Note: P0562 usually indicates failing battery voltage or resistive connection to the PCM. This DTC also sets if battery voltage sensed at PCM is less than 6.5v for 200ms or when the TC Relay output circuit is less than 7.2v for 200ms.** **Possible Causes:** • Resistance is high in battery positive circuit or in generator case ground • Ground circuit is open or has high resistance • Fused B+ circuit to TC relay or to PCM has high resistance • Intermittent wiring or connector condition • TC relay output to TCM is open or has high resistance • TC relay has failed • Generator field driver circuit is open • ASD relay output circuit is open • Generator has failed • PCM has failed
DTC: P0563 **1T CCM** **Years:** 2005, 2006, 2007 **Models:** Grand Cherokee, Liberty, PT Cruiser, Ram Truck, Sebring, Stratus, Wrangler **Engines:** All **Transmissions:** All	**Battery Sense Circuit High Input** Engine running at a speed over 380 rpm, and the PCM detected the Battery Sense circuit voltage indicated 1v higher than the Charging system "goal" during the CCM test. **Possible Causes:** • Generator field control circuit is shorted to system power (B+) • Generator is damaged or it has failed • PCM has failed
DTC: P0563 **1T CCM** **Years:** 2005, 2006, 2007 **Models:** Liberty, PT Cruiser, Ram Truck **Engines:** All **Transmissions:** All	**Battery (Charging System) Voltage High Input** Engine running at a speed over 1000 rpm. No other charging system codes are set. If battery voltage is 1v more than desired voltage for a set period of time, this DTC will set. 3 good trips required to turn off MIL. **Possible Causes:** • Intermittent condition • Generator field ground circuit is shorted to battery voltage • Generator is damaged or it has failed • PCM has failed
DTC: P0564 **1T CCM** **Years:** 2005, 2006, 2007 **Models:** Liberty **Engines:** All **Transmissions:** All	**Speed Control Switch No. 1 Circuit Plausibility, Signal Too High, Too Low Or Stuck Switch** Ignition is on. ECM detects Speed Control (S/C) Switch circuit signal is not in agreement with expected result. **Possible Causes:** • ECM to S/C signal circuit is open or shorted to ground • ECM to S/C Sensor ground is open • S/C Switch signal circuit is open or shorted to voltage or to ground • S/C Sensor ground is open • S/C switch is damaged or has failed
DTC: P0571 **1T CCM** **Years:** 2005, 2006, 2007 **Models:** Liberty, PT Cruiser, Ram **Engines:** All **Transmissions:** All	**Brake Switch No. 1 No Output Signal** Ignition is on. If output of BS 1 to PCM looks like brake is not applied, while BS 2 circuit is applied, the fault will mature in 60ms. **Possible Causes:** • BS 1 signal open or shorted to ground • BS 2 signal open or shorted to ground • Ground circuit is open • Fused ignition switch output is open • Stop lamp switch is damaged or has failed • PCM has failed
DTC: P0572 **1T CCM** **Years:** 2005, 2006, 2007 **Models:** Grand Cherokee, Liberty, Pacifica, Ram Truck, Sebring, Stratus, Wrangler **Engines:** All **Transmissions:** All	**Brake Switch Signal No. 1 Circuit Low** Ignition is on. When PCM recognizes that brake switch is mechanically stuck in the low/on position, a DTC will set. Three global good trips are necessary to turn off MIL. **Possible Causes:** • Brake switch signal circuit is shorted to ground • BS No. 2 signal open (5.7L) • Brake switch is damaged or has failed • PCM has failed

DTC	Trouble Code Title, Conditions & Possible Causes
DTC: P0572 **1T CCM** **Years:** 2005, 2006, 2007 **Models:** PT Cruiser **Engines:** All **Transmissions:** All	**Brake Switch Circuit Low** Engine is running and vehicle speed is above 31 mph; battery voltage is more than 9.5v; no other brake switch DTCs are present. If the PCM detects no change from the brake switch sense circuit input after coming to a complete stop, it will increment a counter. If the counter increments 10 times, the DTC will set and the MIL will illuminate. **Possible Causes:** • Intermittent condition • Fused B+ circuit problem • Brake switch sense circuit is shorted to ground • Brake switch is closed • PCM has failed
DTC: P0573 **1T CCM** **Years:** 2005, 2006, 2007 **Models:** Grand Cherokee, Liberty, Pacifica, Ram Truck, Sebring, Stratus, Wrangler **Engines:** All **Transmissions:** All	**Brake Switch No. 1 Stuck High/Off** Ignition is on. If PCM recognizes BS No. 11 is mechanically stuck in the high/off position, this DTC will set. **Possible Causes:** • BS No. 2 signal open or shorted to ground • BS No. 1 signal shorted to ground or to voltage • Ground circuit is open • Fused ignition switch output is open • Stop lamp switch is damaged or has failed • PCM has failed
DTC: P0573 **1T CCM** **Years:** 2005, 2006, 2007 **Models:** PT Cruiser **Engines:** All **Transmissions:** All	**Brake Switch Circuit High** Engine is running and vehicle speed is above 31 mph; accelerator pedal position is more than 25%; battery voltage is more than 9.5v; no other brake switch DTCs are present. If the PCM detects a high brake switch sense circuit input, it will increment a counter. If the counter increments 10 times, the DTC will set and the MIL will illuminate. **Possible Causes:** • Intermittent condition • Fused B+ circuit problem • Brake switch sense circuit is open or is shorted to voltage • Ground circuit is open • Brake switch lamp operation has failed • PCM has failed
DTC: P0579 **1T CCM** **Years:** 2005, 2006, 2007 **Models:** Ram Truck **Engines:** 5.7L **Transmissions:** All	**Speed Control Switch No. 1 Performance** Ignition on. The PCM detected the cruise switch voltage output is not out of range, but it does not equal any of the values for any of the button positions. **Possible Causes:** • S/C switch No. 1 signal circuit is open or shorted to battery voltage • S/C switch No. 1 signal circuit is shorted to ground or to switch return circuit • S/C switch No. 1 switch return circuit is open • Clockspring or S/C switch is damaged or it has failed • PCM has failed
DTC: P0580 **1T CCM** **Years:** 2005, 2006, 2007 **Models:** Grand Cherokee, Liberty, Pacifica, PT Cruiser, Ram Truck, Sebring, Stratus, Wrangler **Engines:** All **Transmissions:** All	**Speed Control Switch No. 1 Circuit Low Input** Key on or engine started; system voltage over 10.0v and the PCM detected the Speed Control Switch No. 1 signal indicated less than 0.43v (exc. Liberty) or 0.60v (Liberty) for 2 minutes. 3 good trips required to turn off MIL. **Possible Causes:** • Intermittent condition • S/C switch signal circuit is shorted to chassis or Sensor ground • S/C On/Off switch is damaged or it has failed • S/C Resume/Accel switch is damaged or it has failed • PCM has failed.
DTC: P0581 **1T CCM** **Years:** 2005, 2006, 2007 **Models:** Grand Cherokee, Liberty, Pacifica, PT Cruiser, Ram Truck, Sebring, Stratus, Wrangler **Engines:** All **Transmissions:** All	**Speed Control Switch No. 1 Circuit High Input** Engine started; system voltage over 10v and the PCM detected an open or shorted condition, or above maximum acceptable S/C switch voltage, in the Speed Control Switch signal circuit. **Possible Causes:** • S/C switch No.1 signal circuit is shorted to system power (B+) • S/C switch ground circuit is open • S/C switch signal circuit is open between PCM and clockspring • S/C Sensor ground circuit is open between PCM and clockspring or clockspring and S/C switch • Clockspring has failed • S/C switch (one or more) is damaged or has failed • PCM has failed

DTC	Trouble Code Title, Conditions & Possible Causes
DTC: P0582 **1T CCM** **Years:** 2005, 2006, 2007 **Models:** Grand Cherokee, Liberty, Pacifica, PT Cruiser, Ram Truck, Sebring, Stratus, Wrangler **Engines:** All **Transmissions:** All	**Speed Control Vacuum Solenoid Circuit Malfunction** Ignition on or engine started; Speed Control (S/C) system activated, and the PCM detected an open or short to voltage condition on the S/C Vacuum solenoid circuit during the CCM test period. **Possible Causes:** • S/C supply circuit is open or is short to ground or to battery voltage • S/C vacuum solenoid control circuit is open • S/C vacuum solenoid control circuit is shorted to ground • S/C vacuum solenoid is damaged or has failed • PCM has failed
DTC: P0585 **1T CCM** **Years:** 2005, 2006, 2007 **Models:** Liberty **Engines:** All **Transmissions:** All	**Speed Control Switch Plausibility Between Switch No. 1 & Switch No. 2** Ignition is on. ECM detects a discrepancy between S/C switch No. 1 and No. 2 signals. **Possible Causes:** • Intermittent condition • High resistance in the S/C Switch signal circuit or ground circuit • S/C switch is damaged or has failed • ECM has failed
DTC: P0586 **1T CCM** **Years:** 2005, 2006, 2007 **Models:** Grand Cherokee, Liberty, Pacifica, PT Cruiser, Ram Truck, Sebring, Stratus, Wrangler **Engines:** All **Transmissions:** All	**Speed Control Vent Solenoid Circuit Malfunction** Engine started; battery voltage over 10v; Speed Control (S/C) system activated. The PCM detected an unexpected voltage condition on the S/C Vent solenoid circuit during the CCM test period. **Possible Causes:** • S/C supply circuit is open or is short to ground • S/C vent solenoid control circuit is open • S/C vent solenoid control circuit is shorted to ground • S/C vent solenoid is damaged or has failed • PCM has failed
DTC: P0589 **1T CCM** **Years:** 2005, 2006, 2007 **Models:** Liberty **Engines:** All **Transmissions:** All	**Speed Control Switch No. 2 Plausibility, Voltage Too High Or Too Low, Or Switch Stuck** Ignition is on. ECM detects a discrepancy in the S/C switch No. 2 circuit signals. **Possible Causes:** • ECM to S/C signal circuit is open or shorted to voltage • ECM to S/C Sensor ground is open • S/C Switch signal circuit is open or shorted to voltage or to ground • S/C Sensor ground is open • S/C switches damaged or failed
DTC: P0591 **1T CCM** **Years:** 2005, 2006, 2007 **Models:** Grand Cherokee, Ram Truck **Engines:** All **Transmissions:** All	**Speed Control Switch No. 2 Malfunction** Ignition on; Speed Control (S/C) system activated. The PCM detected S/C switch No. 2 output voltage is not out of range, but it does not equal any of the values for any of the button positions. **Possible Causes:** • S/C switch No. 2 signal circuit is open or is shorted to ground or to battery voltage • S/C return circuit is open • S/C switch No. 2 signal circuit is shorted to switch return circuit • S/C switch No. 2 has failed • Clockspring has failed • PCM has failed
DTC: P0592 **1T CCM** **Years:** 2005, 2006, 2007 **Models:** Grand Cherokee, Ram Truck **Engines:** All **Transmissions:** All	**Speed Control Switch No. 2 Circuit Low** Ignition on; Speed Control (S/C) system activated. The PCM detected S/C switch No. 2 input voltage is below minimum acceptable voltage at the PCM. **Possible Causes:** • S/C switch No. 2 signal circuit is shorted to ground or to switch return circuit • S/C switch No. 2 has failed • Clockspring has failed • PCM has failed
DTC: P0593 **1T CCM** **Years:** 2005, 2006, 2007 **Models:** Grand Cherokee, Ram Truck **Engines:** All **Transmissions:** All	**Speed Control Switch No. 2 Circuit High** Ignition on; Speed Control (S/C) system activated. The PCM detected S/C switch No. 2 input voltage is above maximum acceptable voltage at the PCM. **Possible Causes:** • S/C switch No. 2 signal circuit shorted to voltage or open between PCM and clockspring • S/C switch No. 2 signal circuit is open between the clockspring and S/C switch • S/C switch return circuit is open between PCM and clockspring or S/C switch • S/C switch No. 2 or clockspring has failed • PCM has failed

DTC	Trouble Code Title, Conditions & Possible Causes
DTC: P0594 **1T CCM** **Years:** 2005, 2006, 2007 **Models:** Grand Cherokee, Liberty, Pacifica, PT Cruiser, Ram Truck, Sebring, Stratus, Wrangler **Engines:** All **Transmissions:** All	**Speed Control Servo Power Circuit Malfunction** Engine started; Speed Control (S/C) system activated. The PCM detected an unexpected voltage condition on the S/C Vent solenoid circuit during the CCM test period. **Possible Causes:** • S/C solenoid or vent solenoid has failed • Brake switch is damaged or it has failed • S/C brake switch circuit is open or it is shorted to ground • S/C power circuit is open or it is shorted to ground • PCM has failed
DTC: P0600 **1T PCM** **Years:** 2005, 2006, 2007 **Models:** Grand Cherokee, Liberty, Pacifica, PT Cruiser, Ram Truck, Sebring, Stratus, Wrangler **Engines:** All **Transmissions:** All	**Serial Communication Link Malfunction** Ignition on. Internal Bus communication failure is recognized between engine and transmission processors. **Possible Causes:** • PCM or SPI failure
DTC: P0600 **1T ECM** **Years:** 2005, 2006, 2007 **Models:** Liberty **Engines:** 2.8L Diesel **Transmissions:** All	**ECM Communication Error** Ignition on. ECM detects an internal failure. **Possible Causes:** • ECM has failed • Intermittent condition
DTC: P0601 **1T PCM** **Years:** 2005, 2006, 2007 **Models:** Grand Cherokee, Liberty, Pacifica, PT Cruiser, Ram Truck, Sebring, Stratus, Wrangler **Engines:** All **Transmissions:** All	**PCM Internal Controller Failure** Ignition on. Internal CHECKSUM (or Bus communication) for software has failed; no communication between processors; cannot match calculated value. **Possible Causes:** • PCM or SPI failure
DTC: P0602 **1T PCM** **Years:** 2005, 2006, 2007 **Models:** PT Cruiser, Sebring, Stratus with NGC **Engines:** All **Transmissions:** All	**Control Module Programming Error** Condition is monitored continuously. This DTC will always illuminate the MIL and is designed to signal the technician that the controller still has generic software installed. **Possible Causes:** • Control module needs updated programming
DTC: P0602 **1T ECM** **Years:** 2005, 2006, 2007 **Models:** Liberty **Engines:** 2.8L Diesel **Transmissions:** All	**ECM Invalid Code Word** Ignition on. ECM detects an internal failure. **Possible Causes:** • ECM has failed • Intermittent condition
DTC: P0604 **1T ECM** **Years:** 2005, 2006, 2007 **Models:** Liberty **Engines:** 2.8L Diesel **Transmissions:** All	**TCM Internal Problem** Ignition on. TCM detects an internal controller problem **Possible Causes:** • TCM has failed
DTC: P0604 **1T PCM** **Years:** 2005, 2006, 2007 **Models:** PT Cruiser, Sebring, Stratus **Engines:** All **Transmissions:** All	**Internal TCM Error** Condition is monitored continuously. This DTC will always illuminate the MIL and is designed to signal the technician that there is a PCM internal error. **Possible Causes:** • PCM needs to be replaced, and then reprogrammed

DTC	Trouble Code Title, Conditions & Possible Causes
DTC: P0605 **1T PCM** **Years:** 2005, 2006, 2007 **Models:** PT Cruiser with NGC, Sebring, Stratus **Engines:** All **Transmissions:** All	**Internal TCM Error** Condition is monitored continuously. This DTC will always illuminate the MIL and is designed to signal the technician that there is a PCM internal error. **Possible Causes:** • PCM needs to be replaced, and then reprogrammed
DTC: P0605 **1T ECM** **Years:** 2005, 2006, 2007 **Models:** Liberty **Engines:** 2.8L Diesel **Transmissions:** All	**TCM Internal Problem** Ignition on. TCM detects an internal controller problem **Possible Causes:** • TCM has failed
DTC: P0606 **1T PCM** **Years:** 2005, 2006, 2007 **Models:** Grand Cherokee, Ram Truck **Engines:** All **Transmissions:** All	**Engine Control Module Processor Malfunction** Engine running. When the PCM detected an internal failure to communicate with the ECM, or the CMP and CKP Sensor count periods are too short, the DTC will set. The ETC light will be flashing. **Possible Causes:** • PCM has failed
DTC: P0606 **1T ECM** **Years:** 2005, 2006, 2007 **Models:** Liberty **Engines:** 2.8L Diesel **Transmissions:** All	**ECM CHECKSUM Error Or Deviation Error** Ignition on. ECM detects an internal failure. **Possible Causes:** • ECM has failed • Intermittent condition
DTC: P0607 **1T ECM** **Years:** 2005, 2006, 2007 **Models:** Liberty **Engines:** 2.8L Diesel **Transmissions:** All	**ECM Internal Error** Ignition on. ECM detects an internal failure. **Possible Causes:** • ECM has failed • Intermittent condition
DTC: P060B **1T PCM** **Years:** 2005, 2006, 2007 **Models:** Grand Cherokee, Ram Truck **Engines:** All **Transmissions:** All	**Engine Temperature Control A-D Ground Malfunction** When throttle motor is powered, if A to D reading does not return to ground within a set period of time from the test activation, this DTC will set. The test typically runs a couple of times per second, and is the reason why the APP2 signal spikes to ground a couple of times per second in normal running. Reprogramming the module may not always fix this fault. The ETC lamp will flash. **Possible Causes:** • PCM need to be reprogrammed • PCM has failed
DTC: P060D **1T PCM** **Years:** 2005, 2006, 2007 **Models:** Ram Truck **Engines:** All **Transmissions:** All	**Engine Temperature Control Level 2 Performance** When throttle motor is powered and no matured faults related to APP Sensors are present. When secondary software determines that APPS 1 and APPS 2 signals do not match for a period of time, this DTC will set. The ETC lamp will flash. **Possible Causes:** • PCM need to be reprogrammed • PCM has failed
DTC: P060E **1T PCM** **Years:** 2005, 2006, 2007 **Models:** Ram Truck **Engines:** All **Transmissions:** All	**Engine Temperature Control Level 2 TPS Performance** When throttle motor is powered and no matured faults related to TP Sensors are present. When secondary software determines that TP Sensor No. 1 and TP Sensor No. 2 signals do not match for a period of time, this DTC will set. The ETC lamp will flash. **Possible Causes:** • PCM need to be reprogrammed • PCM has failed
DTC: P060F **1T PCM** **Years:** 2005, 2006, 2007 **Models:** Ram Truck **Engines:** All **Transmissions:** All	**Engine Temperature Control Level 2 ETC Performance** When throttle motor is powered and no matured faults related to ETC Sensor is present. When secondary software determines that ETC Sensor signal is implausible for a period of time, this DTC will set. The ETC lamp will flash. **Possible Causes:** • PCM need to be reprogrammed • PCM has failed

DTC	Trouble Code Title, Conditions & Possible Causes
DTC: P0610 **1T ECM** **Years:** 2005, 2006, 2007 **Models:** Liberty **Engines:** 2.8L Diesel **Transmissions:** All	**A/T Or M/T Miscoding Error** Ignition on. ECM detects an automatic transmission has been programmed as a manual transmission, or it detects a manual transmission has been programmed as an automatic transmission. **Possible Causes:** • ECM needs to be reprogrammed • ECM has failed
DTC: P0611 **1T ECM** **Years:** 2005, 2006, 2007 **Models:** Liberty **Engines:** 2.8L Diesel **Transmissions:** All	**ECM Capacitor Voltage 1 Error** Engine running; capacitor monitored during every 180 degrees of engine rotation. ECM determines that the capacitor voltage is greater than 100v. **Possible Causes:** • ECM has failed • Intermittent condition
DTC: P0613 **1T PCM** **Years:** 2005, 2006, 2007 **Models:** PT Cruiser, Sebring, Stratus with NGC **Engines:** All **Transmissions:** All	**Internal TCM Error** Condition is monitored continuously. This DTC will always illuminate the MIL and is designed to signal the technician that there is a PCM internal error. **Possible Causes:** • PCM needs to be replaced, and then reprogrammed
DTC: P0613 **1T ECM** **Years:** 2005, 2006, 2007 **Models:** Liberty **Engines:** 2.8L Diesel **Transmissions:** All	**TCM Internal Problem** Ignition on. TCM detects an internal controller problem **Possible Causes:** • Ground circuit is open • TCM has failed
DTC: P0615 **1T ECM** **Years:** 2005, 2006, 2007 **Models:** Liberty **Engines:** 2.8L Diesel **Transmissions:** All	**Starter Relay Circuit Excessive Current Or Open Circuit** Ignition on and ECM Starter Relay commanded ON (excessive current), or commanded OFF (open circuit). ECM detects excessive current or does not detect voltage on the Starter Relay control circuit. **Possible Causes:** • Intermittent condition • Starter Relay has failed • Ignition Switch Start output is open • Starter Relay control circuit is open, or is shorted to ground or to voltage • ECM has failed
DTC: P0616 **1T ECM** **Years:** 2005, 2006, 2007 **Models:** Liberty **Engines:** 2.8L Diesel **Transmissions:** All	**Starter Relay Circuit Short-To-Ground** Ignition on and ECM Starter Relay commanded OFF. ECM does not detect voltage on the Starter Relay control circuit. **Possible Causes:** • Intermittent condition • Starter Relay has failed • Ignition Switch Start output is open • Starter Relay control circuit is open, or is shorted to ground or to voltage • ECM has failed
DTC: P0617 **1T ECM** **Years:** 2005, 2006, 2007 **Models:** Liberty **Engines:** 2.8L Diesel **Transmissions:** All	**Starter Relay Circuit Short** Ignition on and ECM Starter Relay commanded ON. ECM detects excessive current on the Starter Relay control circuit. **Possible Causes:** • Intermittent condition • Starter Relay has failed • Ignition Switch Start output is open • Starter Relay control circuit is open, or is shorted to ground or to voltage • ECM has failed
DTC: P061C **1T PCM** **Years:** 2005, 2006, 2007 **Models:** Grand Cherokee, Ram Truck **Engines:** All **Transmissions:** All	**Engine Temperature Control Level 2 RPM Performance** When throttle motor is powered, and no CMP or CKP electrical signal related DTCs are set, if the secondary software determines that the engine speed is implausible for a period of time, this DTC will set. The ETC lamp will flash. **Possible Causes:** • PCM need to be reprogrammed • PCM has failed

DTC	Trouble Code Title, Conditions & Possible Causes
DTC: P0622 **1T CCM** **Years:** 2005, 2006, 2007 **Models:** Cherokee, Grand Cherokee, Liberty, PT Cruiser, Ram Truck, Sebring, Stratus, Wrangler **Engines:** All **Transmissions:** All	**Generator Field Control Circuit Malfunction** Engine running. The PCM detected the Generator Field control circuit had malfunctioned (PCM tries to regulate the generator field with no result). **Possible Causes:** • Generator field control circuit is open or is shorted to ground • Generator field control circuit is shorted to system power (B+) • Generator field ground circuit is open • Generator is damaged or PCM has failed • PCM has failed
DTC: P0625 **1T CCM** **Years:** 2005, 2006, 2007 **Models:** PT Cruiser **Engines:** All **Transmissions:** All	**Generator Field Control Circuit Low** Engine running for more than 25 seconds. The PCM detected the Generator Field circuit is open or is shorted to ground. **Possible Causes:** • Wiring harness intermittent problem • Generator field driver circuit is open or is shorted to ground • Generator field has malfunctioned • Generator field coil is open • PCM has failed
DTC: P0626 **1T CCM** **Years:** 2005, 2006, 2007 **Models:** PT Cruiser **Engines:** All **Transmissions:** All	**Generator Field Control Circuit High** Engine running for more than 25 seconds. The PCM detected the Generator Field circuit is shorted B+. **Possible Causes:** • Wiring harness intermittent problem • Generator field circuit is shorted to voltage • Generator has malfunctioned
DTC: P0627 **1T CCM** **Years:** 2005, 2006, 2007 **Models:** Grand Cherokee, Liberty, Pacifica, PT Cruiser, Ram Truck, Sebring, Stratus, Wrangler **Engines:** All **Transmissions:** All	**Fuel Pump Relay Control Circuit Malfunction** Engine started; system voltage over 10.5v. The PCM detected an unexpected voltage condition (open or short) on the Fuel Pump relay control circuit during the CCM test period. **Possible Causes:** • Fuel pump relay control circuit is open or is shorted to ground • Fuel pump relay control circuit is shorted to system power (B+) • Fuel pump relay power circuit (fused ignition) circuit is open • Fuel pump relay is damaged or it has failed • PCM has failed
DTC: P062C **1T PCM** **Years:** 2005, 2006, 2007 **Models:** Grand Cherokee, Ram Truck **Engines:** All **Transmissions:** All	**Engine Temperature Control Level 2 MPH Performance** When throttle motor is powered, and no vehicle speed related DTCs are set, if the secondary software determines that the vehicle speed is implausible for a period of time, this DTC will set. The ETC lamp will flash. **Possible Causes:** • PCM need to be reprogrammed • PCM has failed
DTC: P0628 **1T CCM** **Years:** 2005, 2006, 2007 **Models:** PT Cruiser **Engines:** All **Transmissions:** All	**Fuel Pump Relay Control Circuit Low** Ignition is on. If the PCM detects no voltage on the fuel pump relay control circuit for more than 3 seconds, this DTC will set. **Possible Causes:** • Fuel pump relay intermittent operation • Fuel system/circuit intermittent operation • Fused ignition switch output circuit problem • Fuel pump relay has failed • Fuel pump relay control circuit is open or shorted to ground • PCM has failed
DTC: P0629 **1T CCM** **Years:** 2005, 2006, 2007 **Models:** PT Cruiser **Engines:** All **Transmissions:** All	**Fuel Pump Relay Control Circuit High** Ignition is on. If the PCM detects high voltage on the fuel pump relay control circuit for more than 3 seconds, this DTC will set. **Possible Causes:** • Fuel pump relay intermittent operation • Fuel system/circuit intermittent operation • Fuel pump relay has failed • Fuel pump relay control circuit is shorted to battery voltage • PCM has failed

DTC	Trouble Code Title, Conditions & Possible Causes
DTC: P0630 **1T CCM** **Years:** 2005, 2006, 2007 **Models:** Grand Cherokee, Liberty, Pacifica, PT Cruiser, Ram Truck, Sebring, Stratus, Wrangler **Engines:** All **Transmissions:** All	**VIN Not Programmed Into The PCM** Key on, and the PCM determined that the Vehicle Identification Number (VIN) had not been programmed into its memory. **Possible Causes:** • Reprogram the correct VIN into the PCM • PCM has failed
DTC: P0632 **1T CCM** **Years:** 2005, 2006, 2007 **Models:** Grand Cherokee, Liberty, Pacifica, PT Cruiser, Ram Truck, Sebring, Stratus, Wrangler **Engines:** All **Transmissions:** All	**Odometer Not Programmed Into The PCM** Key on, and the PCM detected the vehicle mileage had not been programmed into memory. **Possible Causes:** • Reprogram the correct mileage into the PCM • PCM has failed
DTC: P0633 **1T CCM** **Years:** 2005, 2006, 2007 **Models:** Grand Cherokee, Liberty, Pacifica, PT Cruiser, Ram Truck, Sebring, Stratus, Wrangler **Engines:** All **Transmissions:** All	**SKIM Key Not Programmed Into The PCM** Key on, and the PCM determined that the Security Key Immobilizer (SKIM) information had not been programmed into its memory. **Possible Causes:** • Reprogram the SKIM key into the PCM • PCM has failed
DTC: P0641 **1T ECM** **Years:** 2005, 2006, 2007 **Models:** Liberty **Engines:** 2.8L Diesel **Transmissions:** All	**Sensor Supply No. 1 Voltage Too High Or Too Low** Ignition on. ECM detects a short-to-voltage (too high) or no voltage (too low) on the Sensor Supply No. 1 circuit, which supplies 5v to the CMP Sensor and the APP Sensor No. 1. **Possible Causes:** • Intermittent condition • Wiring problem in either circuit • APP Sensor No. 1 5v supply circuit is shorted to voltage (too high) • CMP Sensor 5v supply circuit is shorted to voltage (too high) • APP Sensor No. 1 5v supply circuit is shorted to ground (too low) • CMP Sensor 5v supply circuit is shorted to ground (too low) • APP Sensor or CMP Sensor has failed (too low) • ECM has failed
DTC: P0642 **1T CCM** **Years:** 2005, 2006, 2007 **Models:** Grand Cherokee, Ram Truck **Engines:** All **Transmissions:** All	**Sensor Reference Voltage 1 Circuit Low** Ignition is on. When the PCM recognizes the primary 5v supply circuit voltage is too low, this DTC will set. The ETC light is flashing. **Possible Causes:** • Primary 5v supply shorted to ground • Sensor is shorted to ground • 5v Sensor has failed • PCM has failed
DTC: P0643 **1T CCM** **Years:** 2005, 2006, 2007 **Models:** Grand Cherokee, Ram Truck **Engines:** All **Transmissions:** All	**Sensor Reference Voltage 1 Circuit High** Ignition is on. When the PCM recognizes the primary 5v supply circuit voltage is too high, this DTC will set. The ETC light is flashing. **Possible Causes:** • Primary 5v supply shorted to battery voltage • PCM has failed
DTC: P0645 **1T CCM** **Years:** 2005, 2006, 2007 **Models:** Grand Cherokee, Liberty, Pacifica, PT Cruiser, Ram Truck, Sebring, Stratus, Wrangler **Engines:** All **Transmissions:** All	**A/C Clutch Relay Circuit Malfunction** Engine started; system voltage over 10.0v, A/C switch "on". The PCM detected an unexpected voltage condition (open or shorted condition) on the A/C Clutch relay control circuit during the CCM test. **Possible Causes:** • Internally fused ignition switch output circuit is faulty • A/C relay clutch control circuit is open or it is shorted to ground • A/C relay clutch power supply (fused ignition) circuit is open • A/C relay is damaged or it has failed • PCM has failed

DTC	Trouble Code Title, Conditions & Possible Causes
DTC: P0645 **1T ECM** **Years:** 2005, 2006, 2007 **Models:** Liberty **Engines:** 2.8L Diesel **Transmissions:** All	**A/C Clutch Relay Circuit Malfunction** Ignition on and A/C Clutch Relay commanded ON. If the ECM detects an excessive current on the A/C Clutch Relay control circuit (excessive current or short circuit), or if the A/C Clutch Relay is commanded OFF, and the ECM does not detect voltage on the A/C Clutch Relay control circuit (open circuit or short-to-ground), this DTC will set. **Possible Causes:** • Intermittent condition • A/C Clutch Relay has failed • A/C Clutch Relay control circuit is shorted to voltage • Fused ASD Relay output circuit is open • A/C Clutch Relay control circuit is open or is shorted to ground • ECM has failed
DTC: P0646 **1T CCM** **Years:** 2005, 2006, 2007 **Models:** PT Cruiser **Engines:** All **Transmissions:** All	**A/C Clutch Relay Control Circuit Low** Ignition is on. If the PCM detects low voltage on the A/C clutch relay control circuit for more than 2.73 seconds, this DTC will set. **Possible Causes:** • A/C relay intermittent operation • Fused B+ circuit problem • A/C clutch relay has failed • A/C clutch relay control circuit is open or is shorted to ground • PCM has failed
DTC: P0647 **1T CCM** **Years:** 2005, 2006, 2007 **Models:** PT Cruiser **Engines:** All **Transmissions:** All	**A/C Clutch Relay Control Circuit High** Ignition is on. If the PCM detects high voltage on the A/C clutch relay control circuit for more than 2.73 seconds, this DTC will set. **Possible Causes:** • A/C relay intermittent operation • A/C system intermittent condition • A/C clutch relay has failed • A/C clutch relay control circuit is shorted to battery voltage • PCM has failed
DTC: P0651 **1T ECM** **Years:** 2005, 2006, 2007 **Models:** Liberty **Engines:** 2.8L Diesel **Transmissions:** All	**Sensor Supply No. 2 Voltage Too High Or Too Low** Ignition on. If the ECM detects a short-to-voltage (current too high), or if a low voltage (too low) is detected on the Sensor Supply No. 2 circuit, which supplies 5v to the MAF Sensor, Fuel Pressure Sensor, and Boost Pressure Sensor, this DTC will set. **Possible Causes:** • Intermittent condition • Boost Pressure Sensor 5v supply circuit is shorted to voltage (too high) • Fuel Pressure Sensor 5v supply circuit is shorted to voltage (too high) • MAF Sensor 5v supply circuit is shorted to voltage (too high) • Boost Pressure Sensor 5v supply circuit is shorted to ground (too low) • Fuel Pressure Sensor 5v supply circuit is shorted to ground (too low) • MAF Sensor 5v supply circuit is shorted to ground (too low) • FP Sensor, BP Sensor or MAF Sensor has failed • ECM has failed
DTC: P0652 **1T CCM** **Years:** 2005, 2006, 2007 **Models:** Grand Cherokee, Ram Truck **Engines:** All **Transmissions:** All	**Sensor Reference Voltage 2 Circuit Low** Ignition is on. When the PCM recognizes the auxiliary 5v supply circuit voltage is too low, this DTC will set. The ETC light is flashing. **Possible Causes:** • Auxiliary 5v supply shorted to ground • Sensor is shorted to ground • CMP Sensor has failed • PCM has failed
DTC: P0653 **1T CCM** **Years:** 2005, 2006, 2007 **Models:** Grand Cherokee, Ram Truck **Engines:** All **Transmissions:** All	**Sensor Reference Voltage 2 Circuit High** Ignition is on. When the PCM recognizes the auxiliary 5v supply circuit voltage is too high, this DTC will set. The ETC light is flashing. **Possible Causes:** • Auxiliary 5v supply shorted to battery voltage • PCM has failed

DTC	Trouble Code Title, Conditions & Possible Causes
DTC: P0660 **1T CCM** **Years:** 2005, 2006, 2007 **Models:** Grand Cherokee, Liberty, Pacifica, PT Cruiser, Ram Truck, Sebring, Stratus, Wrangler **Engines:** All **Transmissions:** All	**Manifold Tune Valve Solenoid Circuit Malfunction** Engine started; ASD relay "on", system voltage over 10.0v, and the PCM detected an unexpected voltage condition on the Manifold Tune Valve (MTV) solenoid control circuit. **Possible Causes:** • Fused B+ circuit has failed • MTV solenoid/relay circuit is open or it is shorted to ground • MTV solenoid/relay circuit is shorted to power • MTV solenoid/relay ground circuit is open • MTV solenoid/relay is damaged or it has failed • PCM has failed
DTC: P0670 **1T ECM** **Years:** 2005, 2006, 2007 **Models:** Liberty **Engines:** 2.8L Diesel **Transmissions:** All	**Glow Plug Controller Circuit Malfunction** Ignition on. If the ECM detects an open or shorted condition on the glow plug module signal/control circuit, this DTC will set. **Possible Causes:** • Glow Plug Module has failed • Glow Plug Module signal/control circuit is open or is shorted to ground or to voltage • Intermittent condition • ECM has failed
DTC: P0671-P0674 **1T ECM** **Years:** 2005, 2006, 2007 **Models:** Liberty **Engines:** 2.8L Diesel **Transmissions:** All	**Glow Plug Failure Or Short Circuit** Ignition on and Glow Plug Module Glow Plug commanded ON. If the ECM detects no current or excessive current on the respective Glow Plug output circuit, this DTC will set. **Possible Causes:** • Glow Plug has failed • Glow Plug control circuit is open or is shorted to ground or to voltage • Glow Plug Module has failed • Intermittent condition
DTC: P0683 **1T ECM** **Years:** 2005, 2006, 2007 **Models:** Liberty **Engines:** 2.8L Diesel **Transmissions:** All	**Glow Plug Module Signal Circuit Malfunction** Ignition on. If the ECM detects an open or shorted condition on the glow plug module signal/control circuit, this DTC will set. **Possible Causes:** • Glow Plug Module has failed • Glow Plug Module signal/control circuit is open or is shorted to ground or to voltage • Intermittent condition • ECM has failed
DTC: P0685 **1T CCM** **Years:** 2005, 2006, 2007 **Models:** Grand Cherokee, Liberty, Pacifica, PT Cruiser, Ram Truck, Sebring, Stratus, Wrangler **Engines:** All **Transmissions:** All	**ASD Relay Control Circuit Malfunction** Key on; system voltage over 10.0v. The PCM detected an unexpected voltage condition (open or short) on the Automatic Shutdown (ASD) relay control circuit during the CCM test period (ASD actual state is not equal to the desired state). 3 good trips are required to turn off MIL. P0688 may also set. **Possible Causes:** • Fused B+ circuit faults • ASD relay connector is damaged, loose or shorted • ASD relay control circuit is open or it is shorted to ground • ASD power supply (fused B+) circuit is open • ASD relay is damaged, has high resistance, or it has failed • PCM has failed
DTC: P0685 **1T ECM** **Years:** 2005, 2006, 2007 **Models:** Liberty **Engines:** 2.8L Diesel **Transmissions:** All	**ASD Relay Control Circuit Shuts Off Malfunction** During after-run. The internal ECM timer determines that the ASD Relay has shut off before the After-Run mode of operation has been completed, or remains on too long when the After-Run mode of operation has been completed. Other DTCs may be present. **Possible Causes:** • Intermittent condition • Replace ASD Relay and retest • ASD Relay control circuit is open intermittently (shut off too soon) • ASD Relay control circuit is shorted to ground intermittently (shut off too late) • ASD Relay control circuit is shorted to voltage (shut off too late) • ECM has failed

DTC	Trouble Code Title, Conditions & Possible Causes
DTC: P0686 **1T CCM** **Years:** 2005, 2006, 2007 **Models:** PT Cruiser **Engines:** All **Transmissions:** All	**ASD Relay Control Circuit Low** Ignition is on. If the PCM detects no voltage on the ASD relay control circuit for more than 3.5 seconds, this DTC will set. **Possible Causes:** • ASD relay intermittent operation • ASD system intermittent condition • Fused B+ circuit problem • ASD relay has failed • ASD relay control circuit is open or is shorted to ground • PCM has failed
DTC: P0687 **1T CCM** **Years:** 2005, 2006, 2007 **Models:** PT Cruiser **Engines:** All **Transmissions:** All	**ASD Relay Control Circuit High** Ignition is on. If the PCM detects high voltage on the ASD relay control circuit for more than 3.5 seconds, this DTC will set. **Possible Causes:** • ASD relay intermittent operation • ASD system intermittent condition • ASD relay has failed • ASD relay control circuit is shorted to battery voltage • PCM has failed
DTC: P0688 **1T CCM** **Years:** 2005, 2006, 2007 **Models:** Grand Cherokee, Liberty, Pacifica, PT Cruiser, Ram Truck, Sebring, Stratus, Wrangler **Engines:** All **Transmissions:** All	**ASD Relay Sense Circuit Low** Key on, ASD relay energized, system voltage over 10.0v, and the PCM did not detect any voltage on the Automatic Shutdown (ASD) Sense circuit during the CCM test period. **Possible Causes:** • ASD relay output circuit is open • ASD power supply (fused B+) circuit is open • ASD relay is damaged or it has failed • Problem in fuse/relay center • PCM no start condition • PCM has failed
DTC: P0690 **1T CCM** **Years:** 2005, 2006, 2007 **Models:** PT Cruiser **Engines:** All **Transmissions:** All	**ASD Relay Sense Circuit High** Key on, ASD relay energized, system voltage over 10.0v, and the PCM (PT Cruiser) or FCM () detects high voltage on the Automatic Shutdown (ASD) Sense circuit during the CCM test period. **Possible Causes:** • Intermittent condition • ASD relay output circuit is shorted to voltage • ASD relay is damaged or it has failed • PCM internal short to voltage • PCM has failed
DTC: P0691 **1T CCM** **Years:** 2005, 2006, 2007 **Models:** PT Cruiser **Engines:** All **Transmissions:** All	**Low Speed Fan (Fan No. 1) Relay Control Circuit Low** Key on; No. 1 cooling fan relay is actuated. If the PCM (PT Cruiser) or FCM () detects no voltage (open or shorted to ground) on the Radiator Fan Relay control circuit for more than 3 seconds, this DTC will set. **Possible Causes:** • Intermittent condition • Fused ignition switch output circuit problems • Radiator fan relay has failed • Radiator fan control circuit is open or is shorted to ground • PCM has failed
DTC: P0692 **1T CCM** **Years:** 2005, 2006, 2007 **Models:** PT Cruiser **Engines:** All **Transmissions:** All	**Low Speed Fan (Fan No. 1) Relay Control Circuit High** Key on; radiator fan commanded ON. If the PCM (PT Cruiser) or FCM () detects an open or high voltage on the Radiator Fan Relay circuit for more than 3 seconds, this DTC will set. **Possible Causes:** • Intermittent condition • Radiator fan relay has failed • Radiator fan control circuit is shorted to battery voltage • PCM has failed

DTC	Trouble Code Title, Conditions & Possible Causes
DTC: P0693 **1T CCM** **Years:** 2005, 2006, 2007 **Models:** PT Cruiser **Engines:** All **Transmissions:** All	**High Speed Fan (Fan No. 2) Relay Control Circuit Low** Key on; fan relay is powered on. If the PCM (PT Cruiser) or FCM () detects no voltage (open or shorted) on the Radiator Fan Relay control circuit for more than 3 seconds, this DTC will set. Circuit is continuously monitored. **Possible Causes:** • Intermittent condition • Fused ignition switch output circuit problems • Radiator fan relay has failed • Radiator fan control circuit is open or is shorted to ground • PCM has failed
DTC: P0694 **1T CCM** **Years:** 2005, 2006, 2007 **Models:** PT Cruiser **Engines:** All **Transmissions:** All	**High Speed Fan (Fan No. 2) Relay Control Circuit High** Key on; radiator fan commanded ON. If the PCM (PT Cruiser) or FCM () detects an open, short or high voltage on the Radiator Fan Relay circuit for more than 3 seconds, this DTC will set. This circuit is continuously monitored. **Possible Causes:** • Intermittent condition • Radiator fan relay has failed • Radiator fan control circuit is open or shorted to battery voltage • PCM has failed
DTC: P0697 **1T ECM** **Years:** 2005, 2006, 2007 **Models:** Liberty **Engines:** 2.8L Diesel **Transmissions:** All	**Sensor Supply No. 3 Voltage Too High Or Too Low** Ignition on. If the ECM detects a short-to-voltage (current too high), or if a low voltage (too low) is detected on the Sensor Supply No. 3 circuit, which supplies 5v to the Inlet Pressure Sensor and the APP Sensor No. 2, this DTC will set. **Possible Causes:** • Intermittent condition • 5v supply circuit(s) shorted to voltage • APP Sensor has failed (too low) • Inlet Pressure Sensor has failed (too low) • ECM has failed
DTC: P0700 **2T TCM** **Years:** 2005, 2006, 2007 **Models:** Cherokee, Grand Cherokee, Liberty, PT Cruiser, Ram Truck, Sebring, Stratus, Wrangler **Engines:** All **Transmissions:** All	**Automatic Transmission Control System Malfunction** Ignition on or engine started. The PCM received a message over the CCD Bus from the Transmission Control Module (TCM) that it had detected a problem and set a trouble code in memory. **Possible Causes:** • The presence of this code means the TCM detected a problem • TCM related Sensor has solenoid is damaged or has failed • This code is for information only - check for other TCM codes • TCM or PCM has failed
DTC: P0700 **1T ECM** **Years:** 2005, 2006, 2007 **Models:** Liberty **Engines:** 2.8L Diesel **Transmissions:** All	**TCM DTC** Ignition on. If the ECM detects a CAN Bus message indicating the presences of a TCM-related DTC, this code will set. **Possible Causes:** • Verify presence of any DTCs
DTC: P0703 **1T CCM** **Years:** 2005, 2006, 2007 **Models:** Grand Cherokee, Ram Truck **Engines:** All **Transmissions:** All	**A/T Brake Switch No. 2 Performance Malfunction** Ignition is on. When the PCM recognizes brake switch No.2 voltage is not equal to applied value at the PCM when brake switch No. 1 is applied, this DTC will set. **Note: This could be a normal condition; however, if this condition is seen repeatedly by the PCM, the DTC will be set. Cruise control will not work for the rest of the key cycle.** **Possible Causes:** • Fused B+ circuit malfunction • Brake switch output circuit is open or is shorted to battery voltage or to ground • Brake switch 1 signal circuit is open • Brake switch has failed • PCM has failed
DTC: P0703 **1T CCM** **Years:** 2005, 2006, 2007 **Models:** PT Cruiser **Engines:** All **Transmissions:** All	**Brake Lamp Switch No. 2 Performance Malfunction** Engine is running; battery voltage is more than 9.5v; no other brake switch DTCs are present. When Brake Switch 1 output is the same as Brake Switch No. 2 output for more than 25 seconds, this DTC will set. **Possible Causes:** • Intermittent condition • Fused B+ circuit malfunction • Brake switch output circuit is open or is shorted to battery voltage or to ground • Ground circuit is open • Brake switch or PCM has failed

DTC	Trouble Code Title, Conditions & Possible Causes
DTC: P0706 **1T CCM** **Years:** 2005, 2006, 2007 **Models:** Grand Cherokee, Liberty, Pacifica, PT Cruiser, Ram Truck, Sebring, Stratus, Wrangler **Engines:** All **Transmissions:** All	**A/T Check Shifter Signal Circuit Malfunction** Key on. After 3 occurrences in one ignition cycle of an invalid PRNDL DDTC which last for more than 0.1 second. **Note: All indicator lights on the instrument cluster will illuminate boxed when the vehicle engine is not running, ignition on, or engine running in Park or Neutral if a problem exists.** **Possible Causes:** • Shifter out of adjustment • TRS T1, T3, T41 or T42 sense circuit is open, shorted to ground or to voltage • TRS Sensor has failed • Intermittent wiring or connector problems • PCM has failed
DTC: P0706 **1T ECM** **Years:** 2005, 2006, 2007 **Models:** Liberty **Engines:** 2.8L Diesel **Transmissions:** All	**Check Shifter Signal** Ignition on. This DTC will set with 3 occurrences in one ignition start with an invaled PRNDL code, which lasts more than 0.1 second. **Possible Causes:** • Shifter out of adjustment • TRS T1, T2 or T3 sense circuit is open, shorted to ground or to voltage • T41 or T42 sense circuit is open, shorted to ground or to voltage • Transmission Range Sensor (TRS) has failed • TCM has failed • Intermittent wiring and connector problems
DTC: P0711 **1T CCM** **Years:** 2005, 2006, 2007 **Models:** Grand Cherokee, Liberty, Pacifica, PT Cruiser, Ram Truck, Sebring, Stratus, Wrangler **Engines:** All **Transmissions:** All	**A/T Transmission Fluid Temperature Sensor Signal - No Rise After Startup** Engine started. This DTC will set when the desired transmission temperature does not reach a normal operation temperature within a given time frame. Time is variable due to ambient temperature at cold engine start: from 35 minutes at 40F (−40C) to 10 minutes at 60F (15C). **Possible Causes:** • Related DTCs will be present • Transmission temperature Sensor has failed • Intermittent wiring or connector problems • PCM has failed
DTC: P0711 **1T ECM** **Years:** 2005, 2006, 2007 **Models:** Liberty **Engines:** 2.8L Diesel **Transmissions:** All	**Transmission Temperature Sensor Performance** Ignition on and engine running. This DTC will set when the desired transmission temperature does not reach a normal operating temperature within a given time frame. Time is variable due to ambient temperature. At 60F (16C) ambient temperature, warmup time is approximately 10 minutes. Related DTCs may be present. **Possible Causes:** • Transmission Temperature Sensor (TTS) has failed • TCM has failed • Intermittent wiring and connector problems
DTC: P0712 **1T CCM** **Years:** 2005, 2006, 2007 **Models:** Grand Cherokee, Liberty, Pacifica, PT Cruiser, Ram Truck, Sebring, Stratus, Wrangler **Engines:** All **Transmissions:** All	**A/T Transmission Fluid Temperature Sensor Low Input** Engine started and the PCM detected the TFT Sensor signal was under 0.078v for 0.45 second. **Possible Causes:** • Related DTCs are present • TFT Sensor signal circuit is shorted to ground • TFT Sensor is damaged or has failed (it may be shorted) • Intermittent wiring or connector problems • PCM has failed
DTC: P0712 **1T ECM** **Years:** 2005, 2006, 2007 **Models:** Liberty **Engines:** 2.8L Diesel **Transmissions:** All	**Transmission Temperature Sensor Low** Ignition on and engine running. This DTC will set when the monitored transmission temperature drops below 0.78v for 0.45 second. Related DTCs may be present. **Possible Causes:** • Transmission Temperature Sensor (TTS) signal circuit is shorted to ground • TTS has failed • TCM has failed • Intermittent wiring and connector problems

DTC	Trouble Code Title, Conditions & Possible Causes
DTC: P0713 **1T CCM** **Years:** 2005, 2006, 2007 **Models:** Grand Cherokee, Liberty, Pacifica, PT Cruiser, Ram Truck, Sebring, Stratus, Wrangler **Engines:** All **Transmissions:** All	**A/T Transmission Fluid Temperature Sensor High Input** Engine started and the PCM detected the TFT Sensor signal was over 4.94v for 0.45 second. **Possible Causes:** • Related DTCs are present • TFT Sensor signal circuit is open or is shorted to voltage • TFT Sensor is damaged or has failed (it may be shorted) • Intermittent wiring or connector problems • PCM has failed
DTC: P0714 **1T CCM** **Years:** 2005, 2006, 2007 **Models:** Grand Cherokee, Liberty, Pacifica, PT Cruiser, Ram Truck, Sebring, Stratus, Wrangler **Engines:** All **Transmissions:** All	**A/T Transmission Fluid Temperature Sensor Intermittent** Engine started and the PCM detected the TFT Sensor signal was fluctuating or changes abruptly within a predetermined period of time. **Possible Causes:** • Related DTCs are present • TFT Sensor is damaged or has failed (it may be shorted) • Intermittent wiring or connector problems • PCM has failed
DTC: P0713 **1T ECM** **Years:** 2005, 2006, 2007 **Models:** Liberty **Engines:** 2.8L Diesel **Transmissions:** All	**Transmission Temperature Sensor High** Ignition on and engine running. This DTC will set when the monitored Transmission Temperature Sensor signal rises above 4.94v for 0.45 second. **Possible Causes:** • Transmission Temperature Sensor (TTS) signal circuit is open or is shorted to voltage • TTS has failed • TCM has failed • Intermittent wiring and connector problems
DTC: P0714 **1T ECM** **Years:** 2005, 2006, 2007 **Models:** Liberty **Engines:** 2.8L Diesel **Transmissions:** All	**Transmission Temperature Sensor Intermittent** Ignition on and engine running. This DTC will set when the monitored Transmission Temperature Sensor voltage fluctuates or changes abruptly within a predetermined period. Related DTCs may be present. **Possible Causes:** • TTS has failed • TCM has failed • Intermittent wiring and connector problems
DTC: P0715 **1T CCM** **Years:** 2005, 2006, 2007 **Models:** Grand Cherokee, Liberty, Pacifica, PT Cruiser, Ram Truck, Sebring, Stratus, Wrangler **Engines:** All **Transmissions:** All	**TCM Input Speed Sensor Circuit Malfunction** Engine started; the transmission gear ratio is monitored continuously while the transmission is in gear. This DTC will set if there is an excessive change in the Input RPM in any gear. **Possible Causes:** • ISS ground circuit is open or is shorted to voltage • ISS signal circuit is open, shorted to ground or to power • ISS Sensor is damaged or it has failed • Intermittent wiring or connector problems • PCM has failed
DTC: P0719 **1T CCM** **Years:** 2005, 2006, 2007 **Models:** PT Cruiser **Engines:** All **Transmissions:** All	**Brake Lamp Switch Circuit Low** Vehicle is driven over 31 mph; battery over 9.5v. If the PCM detects no change from Brake Lamp Switch circuit input, after a complete stop, it will increment a counter. If the counter increments 10 times, this DTC will set and the MIL will illuminate. **Possible Causes:** • Intermittent condition • Fused B+ circuit problems • Brake lamp switch sense circuit is open or is shorted to ground • Ground circuit is open • Brake lamp switch has failed • PCM has failed
DTC: P0720 **1T CCM** **Years:** 2005, 2006, 2007 **Models:** Grand Cherokee, Liberty, Pacifica, PT Cruiser, Ram Truck, Sebring, Stratus, Wrangler **Engines:** All **Transmissions:** All	**TCM Output Speed Sensor Circuit Malfunction** Engine started; the transmission gear ratio is monitored continuously while the transmission is in gear. This DTC will set if there is an excessive change in the Output RPM in any gear. On some models, this DTC can take up to 5 minutes of problem identification before lighting the MIL. **Possible Causes:** • OSS ground circuit is open or is shorted to voltage or to ground • Speed Sensor ground circuit is open, shorted to ground or to voltage • OSS Sensor is damaged or it has failed • Intermittent wiring or connector problems • PCM or TCM has failed

DTC	Trouble Code Title, Conditions & Possible Causes
DTC: P0724 **1T CCM** **Years:** 2005, 2006, 2007 **Models:** PT Cruiser **Engines:** All **Transmissions:** All	**Brake Lamp Switch Circuit High** Vehicle is driven at speeds over 31 mph; accelerator pedal position is more than 25%; battery voltage over 9.5v. If the PCM detects a high Brake Lamp Switch circuit input, it will increment a counter. If the counter increments 10 times, this DTC will set and the MIL will illuminate. **Possible Causes:** • Intermittent condition • Brake lamp switch sense circuit is shorted to battery voltage • Brake lamp switch has failed • PCM has failed
DTC: P0725 **1T CCM** **Years:** 2005, 2006, 2007 **Models:** Grand Cherokee, Liberty, Pacifica, PT Cruiser, Ram Truck, Sebring, Stratus, Wrangler **Engines:** All **Transmissions:** All	**A/T Engine Speed Sensor Circuit Malfunction** Engine running; and the PCM detected an Engine Speed Sensor reading of less than 390 rpm or more than 8000 rpm occurred for 2 seconds during the CCM test. **Possible Causes:** • Check for trouble codes related to the CKP Sensor • CKP Sensor signal circuit open, shorted to ground or to power • CKP Sensor is damaged or has failed (open or shorted) • Intermittent wiring or connector problems • PCM has failed
DTC: P0725 **1T ECM** **Years:** 2005, 2006, 2007 **Models:** Liberty **Engines:** 2.8L Diesel **Transmissions:** All	**Engine Speed Sensor Circuit Malfunction** Engine running. This DTC will set when the TCM senses an engine rpm less than 400 rpm, with engine running for at least 2 seconds. Engine rpm information is transferred over the communication Bus from the ECM. This DTC can take up to 5 minutes of problem identification before lighting the MIL. **Possible Causes:** • Engine speed signal circuit is open, or is shorted to ground or to voltage • TCM has failed • ECM has failed • Intermittent wiring and connector problems
DTC: P0731 **1T CCM** **Years:** 2005, 2006, 2007 **Models:** Grand Cherokee, Liberty, Pacifica, PT Cruiser, Ram Truck, Sebring, Stratus, Wrangler **Engines:** All **Transmissions:** All	**A/T Additional Gear Ratio Error In First Gear** The transmission gear ratio is monitored continuously while the transmission is in gear. If the ratio of the Input RPM to the Output RPM does not match the current gear ratio, this DTC will set. **Possible Causes:** • Related DTCs will be present • Internal transmission mechanical problems may exist • Intermittent gear ratio errors are present
DTC: P0732 **1T CCM** **Years:** 2005, 2006, 2007 **Models:** Grand Cherokee, Liberty, Pacifica, PT Cruiser, Ram Truck, Sebring, Stratus, Wrangler **Engines:** All **Transmissions:** All	**A/T Additional Gear Ratio Error In Second Gear** The transmission gear ratio is monitored continuously while the transmission is in gear. If the ratio of the Input RPM to the Output RPM does not match the current gear ratio, this DTC will set. **Possible Causes:** • Related DTCs will be present • Transmission solenoid/pressure switch assembly has malfunctioned or failed • Internal transmission mechanical problems may exist • Intermittent gear ratio errors are present
DTC: P0733 **1T CCM** **Years:** 2005, 2006, 2007 **Models:** Grand Cherokee, Liberty, Pacifica, PT Cruiser, Ram Truck, Sebring, Stratus, Wrangler **Engines:** All **Transmissions:** All	**A/T Additional Gear Ratio Error In Third Gear** The transmission gear ratio is monitored continuously while the transmission is in gear. If the ratio of the Input RPM to the Output RPM does not match the current gear ratio, this DTC will set. **Possible Causes:** • Related DTCs will be present • Transmission solenoid/pressure switch assembly has malfunctioned or failed • Internal transmission mechanical problems may exist • Intermittent gear ratio errors are present
DTC: P0734 **1T CCM** **Years:** 2005, 2006, 2007 **Models:** Grand Cherokee, Liberty, PT Cruiser, Ram Truck, Sebring, Stratus, Wrangler **Engines:** All **Transmissions:** All	**A/T Additional Gear Ratio Error In Fourth Gear** The transmission gear ratio is monitored continuously while the transmission is in gear. If the ratio of the Input RPM to the Output RPM does not match the current gear ratio, this DTC will set. **Possible Causes:** • Related DTCs will be present • Transmission solenoid/pressure switch assembly has malfunctioned or failed • Internal transmission mechanical problems may exist • Intermittent gear ratio errors are present

DTC	Trouble Code Title, Conditions & Possible Causes
DTC: P0735 **1T CCM** **Years:** 2005, 2006, 2007 **Models:** Grand Cherokee, Liberty, PT Cruiser, Ram Truck, Sebring, Stratus, Wrangler **Engines:** All **Transmissions:** All	**A/T Gear Ratio Error Fourth Prime** Vehicle driven any forward Gear, and the TCM detected the ratio of the Input speed to the Output Speed did not match the current Gear Ratio (this test can take up to 5 minutes). **Possible Causes:** • Related Gear Ratio trouble codes may be stored (note that some of these Gear Ratio trouble codes may be intermittent) • Transmission has internal problems or damage present
DTC: P0736 **1T CCM** **Years:** 2005, 2006, 2007 **Models:** Grand Cherokee, Liberty, Pacifica, PT Cruiser, Ram Truck, Sebring, Stratus, Wrangler **Engines:** All **Transmissions:** All	**A/T Additional Gear Ratio Error In Reverse Gear** The transmission gear ratio is monitored continuously while the transmission is in gear. If the ratio of the Input RPM to the Output RPM does not match the current gear ratio, this DTC will set. **Possible Causes:** • Related DTCs will be present • Internal transmission mechanical problems may exist • Intermittent gear ratio errors are present
DTC: P0740 **1T CCM** **Years:** 2005, 2006, 2007 **Models:** Grand Cherokee, Liberty, Pacifica, PT Cruiser, Ram Truck, Sebring, Stratus, Wrangler **Engines:** All **Transmissions:** All	**A/T Torque Converter Clutch System Out of Range** The TCC is in FEMCC or PEMCC, transmission temperature is hot, engine temperature is more than 100F (38C), transmission input speed is more than 1750 rpm, with TPS less than 30. The TCC is modulated by controlling the duty cycle of the L/R solenoid, until the difference between the engine and transmission input speed rpm or duty cycle is within desired range. The DTC is set after the period of 10 seconds and 3 occurrences of either: FEMCC with slip greater than 100 rpm or PEMCC duty cycle is more than 85%. **Possible Causes:** • Related DTCs will be present • Internal transmission mechanical problems may exist • Intermittent gear ratio errors are present
DTC: P0740 **1T ECM** **Years:** 2005, 2006, 2007 **Models:** Liberty **Engines:** 2.8L Diesel **Transmissions:** All	**A/T Torque Converter Clutch System Out of Range** System is monitored during Electronically Modulated Converter Clutch (EMCC) operation. Transmission must be in EMCC, with input speed of more than 1750 rpm. This DTC will set when the TCC-L/R Solenoid achieves the maximum duty cycle and cannot pull engine speed within 60 rpm of input speed. Also, it will set when the transmission is in EMCC and the engine slips TCC more than 100 rpm for 10 seconds. This DTC can take up to 5 minutes of problem identification before lighting the MIL. **Possible Causes:** • Related DTC 0750 is present • Internal transmission problem • Transmission Solenoid/TRS Assembly has failed • Intermittent wiring and connector problems
DTC: P0750 **1T CCM** **Years:** 2005, 2006, 2007 **Models:** Grand Cherokee, Liberty, Pacifica, PT Cruiser, Ram Truck, Sebring, Stratus, Wrangler **Engines:** All **Transmissions:** All	**A/T Low/Reverse Solenoid Circuit Failure** Solenoids are tested initially at power-up, then every 10 seconds thereafter, the solenoids will also be tested immediately after a gear ratio or pressure switch error is detected. 3 consecutive solenoid continuity test failures, or one failure if test is run in response to a gear ratio or pressure switch error. **Possible Causes:** • Related relay DTCs present • Transmission control relay output circuit open • L/R solenoid control circuit open or shorted to ground or to voltage • L/R solenoid/pressure switch assembly has malfunctioned or failed • Intermittent wiring and connectors • PCM has failed
DTC: P0755 **1T CCM** **Years:** 2005, 2006, 2007 **Models:** Grand Cherokee, Liberty, Pacifica, PT Cruiser, Ram Truck, Sebring, Stratus, Wrangler **Engines:** All **Transmissions:** All	**A/T 2/4 Solenoid Circuit Failure** 2/4 solenoid in monitored initially at power-up, then every 10 seconds thereafter. Also, immediately after a gear ratio or pressure switch error is detected. 3 consecutive solenoid continuity test failures, or one failure if test is run in response to a gear ratio or pressure switch error. **Possible Causes:** • Related DTCs present • Transmission control relay output circuit open • 2/4 Solenoid control circuit is open or shorted to ground • 2/4 Solenoid control circuit is shorted to system power • 2/4 Solenoid is damaged or has failed • Intermittent wiring or connector problems • PCM has failed

DTC	Trouble Code Title, Conditions & Possible Causes
DTC: P0755 **1T ECM** **Years:** 2005, 2006, 2007 **Models:** Liberty **Engines:** 2.8L Diesel **Transmissions:** All	**A/T 2C Solenoid Circuit Malfunction** System is monitored initially at powerup and every 10 seconds thereafter. It will also be tested immediately after a gear ratio or pressure switch error is detected. After 3 consecutive solenoid continuity test failures, or after one failure if a test is run in response to a gear ratio or pressure switch error, this DTC will set. **Possible Causes:** • Related Relay DTCs are present • Transmission Control Relay output circuit is open • 2C Solenoid control circuit is open or is shorted to ground or to voltage • Transmission Solenoid/TRS Assembly has failed • TCM has failed • Intermittent wiring and connector problems
DTC: P0760 **1T CCM** **Years:** 2005, 2006, 2007 **Models:** Grand Cherokee, Liberty, Pacifica, PT Cruiser, Ram Truck, Sebring, Stratus, Wrangler **Engines:** All **Transmissions:** All	**A/T Overdrive Solenoid Circuit Failure** O/D solenoid in monitored initially at power-up, then every 10 seconds thereafter. Also, immediately after a gear ratio or pressure switch error is detected. 3 consecutive solenoid continuity test failures, or one failure if test is run in response to a gear ratio or pressure switch error. **Possible Causes:** • Related DTCs present • Transmission control relay output circuit open • O/D Solenoid control circuit is open or shorted to ground • O/D Solenoid control circuit is shorted to system power • O/D Solenoid is damaged or has failed • PCM has failed
DTC: P0765 **1T CCM** **Years:** 2005, 2006, 2007 **Models:** Grand Cherokee, Liberty, Pacifica, PT Cruiser, Ram Truck, Sebring, Stratus, Wrangler **Engines:** All **Transmissions:** All	**A/T Underdrive Solenoid Circuit Failure** U/D solenoid in monitored initially at power-up, then every 10 seconds thereafter. Also, immediately • after a gear ratio or pressure switch error is detected. 3 consecutive solenoid continuity test failures, or one failure if test is run in response to a gear ratio or pressure switch error. **Possible Causes:** • Related DTCs present • Transmission control relay output circuit open • U/D Solenoid control circuit is open or shorted to ground • U/D Solenoid control circuit is shorted to system power • U/D Solenoid is damaged or has failed • Intermittent wiring or connector problems • PCM has failed
DTC: P0770 **1T ECM** **Years:** 2005, 2006, 2007 **Models:** Liberty **Engines:** 2.8L Diesel **Transmissions:** All	**A/T 4C Solenoid Circuit Malfunction** System is monitored initially at powerup and every 10 seconds thereafter. It will also be tested immediately after a gear ratio or pressure switch error is detected. After 3 consecutive solenoid continuity test failures, or after one failure if a test is run in response to a gear ratio or pressure switch error, this DTC will set. **Possible Causes:** • Related Relay DTCs are present • Transmission Control Relay output circuit is open • 4C Solenoid control circuit is open or is shorted to ground or to voltage • Transmission Solenoid/TRS Assembly has failed • TCM has failed • Intermittent wiring and connector problems
DTC: P0781 **1T CCM** **Years:** 2005, 2006, 2007 **Models:** PT Cruiser **Engines:** All **Transmissions:** All	**A/T Low/Reverse Pressure Switch Circuit Failure** Monitored whenever engine is running. If one of the pressure switches are open or closed at the wrong time, this DTC will set. **Possible Causes:** • Related DTCs present • Loss of Prime P0944 DTC present • L/R pressure switch sense circuit is open or is shorted to ground or to voltage • L/R pressure switch has failed • Intermittent wiring or connector problems • PCM has failed

DTC	Trouble Code Title, Conditions & Possible Causes
DTC: P0833 **1T CCM** **Years:** 2005, 2006, 2007 **Models:** PT Cruiser **Engines:** All **Transmissions:** M/T	**Clutch Pedal Position Switch Circuit Malfunction** Engine cranking, or vehicle speed over 25 mph at an engine speed from 1550-2880 rpm with the delta throttle over 1.1v for 4 seconds, and the PCM detected an unexpected voltage condition on the Clutch Pedal switch circuit (test must fail 5 times during one trip). **Possible Causes:** • CPP switch signal circuit is open or shorted to ground • CPP switch power circuit is open (test the power at the PDC) • Clutch pedal is damaged or has failed • PCM has failed
DTC: P0833 **1T CCM** **Years:** 2005, 2006, 2007 **Models:** PT Cruiser **Engines:** All **Transmissions:** All	**Clutch Pedal Position Switch Circuit Malfunction** Condition is monitored with the engine running; battery voltage over 9v; vehicle speed is less than 0 mph, then more than 27 mph; MAP is greater than 90mbar; and engine speed is over 3200 rpm. If the Clutch Switch status did not change for more than 15 seconds, this DTC will set. **Possible Causes:** • Intermittent condition • CPP switch signal circuit is open or shorted to ground • CPP switch ground circuit is open • Clutch pedal is damaged or has failed • PCM has failed
DTC: P0836 **1T ECM** **Years:** 2005, 2006, 2007 **Models:** Liberty **Engines:** 2.8L Diesel **Transmissions:** All	**Transfer Case Position Sensor Plausibility Or Improper Voltage Signal** Ignition on. If the ECM detects a voltage signal from the Transfer Case Switch that does not fall into a valid switch position voltage range, or if the Position Sensor signal is above 4.8v or below 0.14v for 0.5 second, this DTC will set. **Possible Causes:** • Transfer Case Position Sensor has failed • Intermittent wiring and/or connector problems • Transfer Case Position Sensor signal circuit is open, shorted to ground, shorted to voltage or shorted to Sensor ground circuit • ECM has failed
DTC: P0841 **1T CCM** **Years:** 2005, 2006, 2007 **Models:** Grand Cherokee, Liberty, Pacifica, PT Cruiser, Ram Truck, Sebring, Stratus, Wrangler **Engines:** All **Transmissions:** All	**Low/Reverse Pressure Switch Sense Circuit Malfunction** Switches are monitored whenever engine is running. This DTC will set if one of the pressure switches in open or closed at the wrong time in a given gear. **Possible Causes:** • Related DTCs present • Loss of Prime P0944 DTC present • Transmission control relay output circuit open • L/R switch sense circuit is open or is shorted to ground or to voltage • L/R pressure switch is damaged or has failed • Intermittent wiring or connector problems • PCM has failed
DTC: P0845 **1T CCM** **Years:** 2005, 2006, 2007 **Models:** Grand Cherokee, Liberty, Pacifica, PT Cruiser, Ram Truck, Sebring, Stratus, Wrangler **Engines:** All **Transmissions:** All	**A/T 2/4 Hydraulic Pressure Test Malfunction** Engine speed over 1000 rpm, then immediately after a shift event, the PCM detected a failure in one or more of the Pressure Switch circuits (i.e., it tests switches that are not operating). **Possible Causes:** • 2/4 pressure is incorrect, or internal transmission faults exist • 2/4 pressure switch circuit is open, shorted to ground or power • 2/4 pressure switch is damaged or it has failed • Transmission solenoids/TRS assembly is damaged or have failed • TCM relay power circuit to 2/4 switch is open (loss of B+) • Intermittent wiring or connector problems exist • PCM or TCM has failed

DTC	Trouble Code Title, Conditions & Possible Causes
DTC: P0845 **1T ECM** **Years:** 2005, 2006, 2007 **Models:** Liberty **Engines:** 2.8L Diesel **Transmissions:** All	**A/T 2C Hydraulic Pressure Test Failure** System hydraulic pressure is monitored in any forward gear with engine speed above 1000 rpm, shortly after a shift, and every minute thereafter. After a shift into a forward gear, with engine speed above 1000 rpm, the TCM momentarily turns ON element pressure to the Clutch circuits that dont have pressure, in order to identify the correct Pressure Switch closes. If the Pressure Switch does not close 2 times, the DTC will set. **Possible Causes:** • Related Relay DTCs are present • Transmission Solenoid/TRS Assembly has failed • 2C Pressure Switch sense circuit is open or is shorted to ground or to voltage • 5v supply circuit is open or is shorted to ground • Pressure Sensor has poor line connection • Transmission Control Relay output circuit is open • Excessive debris in oil pan • Line Pressure Sensor has failed • Internal transmission problems • TCM has failed • Intermittent wiring and connector problems
DTC: P0846 **1T CCM** **Years:** 2005, 2006, 2007 **Models:** Grand Cherokee, Liberty, Pacifica, PT Cruiser, Ram Truck, Sebring, Stratus, Wrangler **Engines:** All **Transmissions:** All	**A/T 2/4 Pressure Switch Circuit Malfunction** Engine started; vehicle driven in a forward gear, and the PCM detected that the 2/4 Pressure Switch circuit indicated open or closed at the wrong time. Related relay DTCs may be present. **Possible Causes:** • 2/4 pressure is incorrect, or internal transmission faults exist • 2/4 pressure switch circuit is open, shorted to ground or power • 2/4 pressure switch is damaged or it has failed • TCM relay power circuit to L/R switch is open (loss of B+) • PCM/TCM has failed
DTC: P0846 **1T ECM** **Years:** 2005, 2006, 2007 **Models:** Liberty **Engines:** 2.8L Diesel **Transmissions:** All	**A/T 2C Pressure Switch Sense Circuit Malfunction** Pressure Switch circuit is monitored whenever engine is running. The appropriate DTC is set if one of the Pressure Switches is open or closed at the wrong time for a given gear. **Possible Causes:** • Related Relay DTCs are present • Transmission Solenoid/TRS Assembly has failed • 2C Pressure Switch sense circuit is open or is shorted to ground or to voltage • 2C Pressure Switch has failed • TCM has failed • Intermittent wiring and connector problems
DTC: P0850 **2T CCM** **Years:** 2005, 2006, 2007 **Models:** Grand Cherokee, Liberty, Pacifica, PT Cruiser, Ram Truck, Sebring, Stratus, Wrangler **Engines:** All **Transmissions:** All	**A/T Park/Neutral Switch Performance** Engine running; gearshift selector in Park, Neutral or Drive position (not Limp-In mode). The PCM detected an invalid Park/Neutral switch state during vehicle operation. **Possible Causes:** • Check for any TCM related codes stored in the TCM controller • PCM has failed
DTC: P0864 **1T ECM** **Years:** 2005, 2006, 2007 **Models:** Liberty **Engines:** 2.8L Diesel **Transmissions:** All	**TCM Torque Reduction Signal Error** Ignition on or engine running. If the TCM receives an improper or implausible Torque Management Request signal, this DTC will set. **Possible Causes:** • ECM has failed • Torque Management Request signal circuit is open, shorted to ground, shorted to voltage • TCM has failed • Intermittent condition

DTC	Trouble Code Title, Conditions & Possible Causes
DTC: P0868 **1T ECM** **Years:** 2005, 2006, 2007 **Models:** Liberty **Engines:** 2.8L Diesel **Transmissions:** All	**A/T Line Pressure Low** Line pressure is monitored whenever driving in a forward gear. The TCM continuously monitors the Transducer Line Pressure output and compares it to a desired line pressure. If the actual pressure is more than 10 psi below the desired line pressure, the DTC will set in about 2.1 seconds. **Possible Causes:** • Related Relay DTCs may be present • 5v supply circuit is open or is shorted to ground or to voltage • Poor Line Pressure Sensor connection • Pressure Control Solenoid control circuit is shorted to voltage • Internal transmission problems • Line Pressure Sensor has failed • Plugged filter • TCM has failed • Intermittent wiring and connector problems
DTC: P0869 **1T ECM** **Years:** 2005, 2006, 2007 **Models:** Liberty **Engines:** 2.8L Diesel **Transmissions:** All	**A/T Line Pressure High** Line pressure is monitored whenever driving in a forward gear. The TCM continuously monitors the Transducer Line Pressure output and compares it to a desired line pressure. If the actual pressure is more than the highest desired line pressure ever used in the current gear, while the Pressure Control Solenoid duty cycle is at or near its maximum value (which should result in minimum line pressure), the DTC will set. **Possible Causes:** • Related Relay DTCs may be present • 5v supply circuit is open or is shorted to ground • Poor Line Pressure Sensor connection • Pressure Control Solenoid control circuit is open or is shorted to ground • Internal transmission problems (line pressure high) • Line Pressure Sensor has failed • TCM has failed • Intermittent wiring and connector problems
DTC: P0870 **1T CCM** **Years:** 2005, 2006, 2007 **Models:** Grand Cherokee, Liberty, Pacifica, PT Cruiser, Ram Truck, Sebring, Stratus, Wrangler **Engines:** All **Transmissions:** All	**A/T Hydraulic Pressure Line Malfunction** Engine started; vehicle driven at over 1000 rpm, then immediately after a shift, the PCM detected a malfunction in one or more of the Pressure Switch circuits (it detected the switch did not close twice). DTC P0944 may be present. **Possible Causes:** • Check for related line pressure trouble codes • Check for related speed ratio and pressure switch codes • 5v supply circuit is open or is shorted to ground • Transmission Control Relay output circuit is open • OD Pressure Switch sense circuit is shorted to ground or to voltage • Excessive debris in the oil pan • Line pressure Sensor connector is loose or damaged • Oil pressure switch is damaged or has failed • Intermittent wiring or connector problems exist • PCM or TCM has failed
DTC: P0871 **1T CCM** **Years:** 2005, 2006, 2007 **Models:** Grand Cherokee, Liberty, Pacifica, PT Cruiser, Ram Truck, Sebring, Stratus, Wrangler **Engines:** All **Transmissions:** All	**A/T O/D Pressure Switch Circuit Malfunction** Engine started; vehicle driven in a forward gear, and the PCM detected that the O/D Pressure Switch circuit indicated open or closed at the wrong time. **Possible Causes:** • Related DTCs may be present • O/D pressure is incorrect, or internal transmission faults exist • O/D pressure switch circuit is open, shorted to ground or power • O/D pressure switch is damaged or it has failed • TCM relay power circuit to O/D switch is open (loss of B+) • Intermittent wiring or connector problems exist • PCM or TCM has failed

DTC	Trouble Code Title, Conditions & Possible Causes
DTC: P0875 **1T CCM** **Years:** 2005, 2006, 2007 **Models:** Grand Cherokee, Liberty, Ram Truck, Wrangler **Engines:** All **Transmissions:** All	**A/T U/D Hydraulic Pressure Test Malfunction** Engine speed over 1000 rpm, then immediately after a shift event, the TCM/PCM detected a fault in one or more of the Pressure Switch circuits (it detected the switch did not close twice). **Possible Causes:** • Check for related line pressure trouble codes • Check for related speed ratio and pressure switch codes • 5v supply circuit is open or shorted to ground • U/D Pressure switch sense circuit is open or shorted to ground or to voltage • Excessive debris in the oil pan • Line pressure Sensor connector is loose or damaged • U/D Oil Pressure Switch is damaged or it has failed • TCM has failed • Intermittent wiring and connector problems
DTC: P0876 **1T CCM** **Years:** 2005, 2006, 2007 **Models:** Grand Cherokee, Liberty, Ram Truck, Wrangler **Engines:** All **Transmissions:** All	**A/T U/D Pressure Switch Sense Malfunction** Engine started; vehicle driven in a forward gear, and the PCM detected that the U/D Pressure Switch Sense circuit indicated open or closed at the wrong time during the CCM test period. **Possible Causes:** • U/D pressure is incorrect, or internal transmission faults exist • U/D pressure switch circuit is open, shorted to ground or power • U/D pressure switch is damaged or it has failed • TCM relay power circuit to L/R switch is open (loss of B+) • TCM has failed
DTC: P0884 **1T CCM** **Years:** 2005, 2006, 2007 **Models:** Grand Cherokee, Liberty, Pacifica, PT Cruiser, Ram Truck, Sebring, Stratus, Wrangler **Engines:** All **Transmissions:** All	**Power-Up Automatic Transmission Speed Malfunction** Engine started, TCM relay enabled; and the TCM detected a valid forward gear PNDRL signal with the Output Speed more than 800 rpm indicating a vehicle speed of over 20 mph. **Note: The TCM has separate powers and grounds specifically to its portion of the PCM.** **Possible Causes:** • TCM power supply circuit to direct battery is open • TCM power supply circuit to the ignition switch is open • TCM power ground circuit is open or the connector is loose • TCM has failed
DTC: P0888 **1T CCM** **Years:** 2005, 2006, 2007 **Models:** Grand Cherokee, Liberty, Pacifica, PT Cruiser, Ram Truck, Sebring, Stratus, Wrangler **Engines:** All **Transmissions:** All	**A/T Relay Output Malfunction** Engine started, TCM relay enabled and monitored continuously. This DTC sets when less than 3v are present at the relay output circuits at the TCM when the TCM is energizing the relay. **Note: Due to the integration of the PCM and TCM, the transmission part of the PCM has its own specific power and ground circuits.** **Possible Causes:** • Fused B+ circuit is open • TC relay output circuit is open or is shorted to ground • TC relay control circuit is open or is shorted to ground • TC relay ground circuit is open • TC relay has failed • Intermittent wiring or connector problems exist • Transmission solenoid/pressure switch assembly has malfunctioned or failed • PCM/TCM has failed
DTC: P0890 **1T CCM** **Years:** 2005, 2006, 2007 **Models:** Liberty, Pacifica, PT Cruiser, Ram Truck, Sebring, Stratus **Engines:** All **Transmissions:** All	**A/T TCM Switched Battery Circuit Malfunction** Ignition switch position is changed from one position to another. TCM relay "not" energized, and the TCM detected voltage present at any of the Pressure Switch input circuits. **Note: Due to the integration of the PCM and TCM, the transmission part of the PCM has its own specific power and ground circuits.** **Possible Causes:** • 2/4 switch circuit is shorted to system power (B+) • L/R switch circuit is shorted to system power (B+) • O/D switch circuit is shorted to system power (B+) • TCM switched battery circuit is damaged • Intermittent wiring or connector problems exist • PCM/TCM has failed

DTC	Trouble Code Title, Conditions & Possible Causes
DTC: P0891 **1T CCM** **Years:** 2005, 2006, 2007 **Models:** Grand Cherokee, Liberty, Pacifica, PT Cruiser, Ram Truck, Sebring, Stratus, Wrangler **Engines:** All **Transmissions:** All	**A/T TCM Relay Always On** Key on or engine cranking; TCM relay "not" energized, and the TCM detected voltage present at the TCM output circuit during the test. **Note: Due to the integration of the PCM and TCM, the transmission part of the PCM has its own specific power and ground circuits.** **Possible Causes:** • TCM relay output circuit is shorted to system power (B+) • TCM relay control circuit is shorted to system power (B+) • TCM relay is damaged or it has failed (it may be stuck closed) • Intermittent wiring or connector problems exist • PCM/TCM has failed
DTC: P0897 **1T CCM** **Years:** 2005, 2006, 2007 **Models:** Pacifica, PT Cruiser, Ram Truck, Sebring, Stratus **Engines:** All **Transmissions:** All	**A/T Transmission Fluid Burnt Or Worn Out** Engine started; vehicle driven, and immediately after a transition from full TCC lockup to partial TCC engagement (for A/C bump prevention), the TCM detected vehicle shutter during engagement. **Possible Causes:** • Automatic transmission fluid is burnt or contaminated • Automatic transmission fluid is worn out
DTC: P0932 **1T CCM** **Years:** 2005, 2006, 2007 **Models:** Liberty **Engines:** 2.8L Diesel **Transmissions:** All	**A/T Line Pressure Sensor Malfunction** Sensor is monitored continuously while driving in a forward gear. T PCM continuously monitors actual line pressure and compares it to desired line pressure. If the actual pressure is more than 25 psi higher than the desire line pressure, but is less than the highest line pressure ever used in the current gear, this DTC will set. Related DTCs may be present. **Possible Causes:** • Poor line pressure connection • Poor wiring connection • Internal transmission problems • TCM has failed • Intermittent wiring and connector problems
DTC: P0934 **1T CCM** **Years:** 2005, 2006, 2007 **Models:** Liberty **Engines:** 2.8L Diesel **Transmissions:** All	**A/T Line Pressure Sensor Low** Sensor is monitored continuously while engine is running and Output Speed is more than 390 rpm. This DTC will set when the Line Pressure Sensor output signal is less than 0.35v for 1.4 seconds. **Possible Causes:** • 5v supply circuit is open or is shorted to ground • Line Pressure Sensor signal circuit is shorted to ground • Line Pressure Sensor has failed • TCM has failed • Intermittent wiring and connector problems
DTC: P0935 **1T CCM** **Years:** 2005, 2006, 2007 **Models:** Liberty **Engines:** 2.8L Diesel **Transmissions:** All	**A/T Line Pressure Sensor High** Sensor is monitored continuously while engine is running and Output Speed is more than 390 rpm and desired line pressure is less than 200 psi. This DTC will set when the Line Pressure Sensor output signal is more than 4.75v for 1.4 seconds. **Possible Causes:** • Line Pressure Sensor ground circuit is open • Line Pressure Sensor signal circuit is open or is shorted to voltage • Line Pressure Sensor has failed • TCM has failed • Intermittent wiring and connector problems
DTC: P0944 **1T CCM** **Years:** 2005, 2006, 2007 **Models:** Grand Cherokee, Liberty, Pacifica, PT Cruiser, Ram Truck, Sebring, Stratus, Wrangler **Engines:** All **Transmissions:** All	**A/T Loss Of Prime Pressure** Engine started; vehicle driven, and immediately after a slipping condition is detected with the pressure switches "not" indicating pressure, the PCM detected a loss of prime pressure. In effect, the TCM turns "on" available elements to detect if prime pressure exists. The DTC sets if no pressure switches respond. **Possible Causes:** • A/T pressure switch connector is damaged, loose or shorted • Invalid PRNDL code (shift lever position error) • Automatic transmission fluid level is too low • Transmission oil filter is clogged or severely restricted • Transmission oil pump is damaged or weak • Intermittent wiring or connector problems exist

DTC	Trouble Code Title, Conditions & Possible Causes
DTC: P0952 **1T CCM** **Years:** 2005, 2006, 2007 **Models:** Grand Cherokee, Liberty, Pacifica, PT Cruiser, Ram Truck, Sebring, Stratus, Wrangler **Engines:** All **Transmissions:** All	**A/T AutoStick Sensor Circuit Malfunction** Engine started; vehicle driven, transmission not in AutoStick position, and the TCM that either the Upshift or Downshift switch was closed (below 0.3v), or if both the Upshift and Downshift switches are closed at the same time. **Possible Causes:** • AutoStick assembly is damaged or has failed • Intermittent wiring or connector problems exist • Downshift sense or Upshift sense circuit is shorted to ground • PCM/TCM has failed
DTC: P0953 **1T CCM** **Years:** 2005, 2006, 2007 **Models:** Grand Cherokee, Liberty, Pacifica, PT Cruiser, Ram Truck, Sebring, Stratus, Wrangler **Engines:** All **Transmissions:** All	**A/T AutoStick Sensor Circuit High** The AutoStick circuit is checked every .007 second, with the ignition on and in both AutoStick and non-AutoStick modes. If the TCM detects circuit voltage rises above 4.8v, this DTC will set. **Possible Causes:** • AutoStick assembly is damaged or has failed • Intermittent wiring or connector problems exist • Downshift sense or Upshift sense circuit is shorted to ground • PCM/TCM has failed
DTC: P0987 **1T CCM** **Years:** 2005, 2006, 2007 **Models:** Cherokee, Grand Cherokee, Liberty, Ram Truck, Wrangler **Engines:** All **Transmissions:** All	**A/T 4C Hydraulic Pressure Test Malfunction** Engine started; vehicle driven at over 1000 rpm, then immediately after a shift and every minute thereafter. After a shift into a forward gear, with engine speed more than 1000 rpm, the TCM momentarily turns on element pressure to the clutch circuits that dont have pressure to identify the correct pressure switch that closes. If the pressure switch does not close 2 times, this DTC will set. Related line pressure DTCs are present. **Possible Causes:** • Check for related speed ratio and pressure switch codes • Excessive debris in the oil pan • 5v supply circuit is open or is shorted to ground • Transmission Control Relay output circuit is open • 4C Pressure Switch sense circuit is shorted to ground or to voltage • Line Pressure Sensor connector is loose or damaged • 4C Line Pressure Sensor has failed • Transmission Solenoid/TRS Assembly has failed • Internal transmission problems • TCM has failed • Intermittent wiring and connector problems
DTC: P0988 **1T CCM** **Years:** 2005, 2006, 2007 **Models:** Cherokee, Grand Cherokee, Liberty, Ram Truck, Wrangler **Engines:** All **Transmissions:** All	**A/T 4C Pressure Switch Sense Circuit Malfunction** Engine started; vehicle driven in any forward gear, and the PCM detected that the 4C Pressure Switch circuit indicated open or closed at the wrong time during the CCM test. Related Relay DTCs are present. **Possible Causes:** • 4C pressure is incorrect, or internal transmission faults exist • 4C Pressure Switch sense circuit is open, shorted to ground or power • 4C Pressure Switch is damaged or it has failed • TCM Relay power circuit to L/R switch is open (loss of B+) • PCM/TCM has failed • Intermittent wiring and connector problems
DTC: P0992 **1T CCM** **Years:** 2005, 2006, 2007 **Models:** Grand Cherokee, Liberty, Pacifica, PT Cruiser, Ram Truck, Sebring, Stratus, Wrangler **Engines:** All **Transmissions:** All	**A/T 2/4 & O/D Hydraulic Pressure Test Malfunction** Engine started; vehicle driven at over 1000 rpm, then immediately after a shift, the PCM detected a malfunction in one or more of the Pressure Switch circuits (it tests the switches that are not operating). If the pressure switch does not close 2 times, the DTC will set. **Possible Causes:** • 2/4 pressure switch circuit is open, shorted to ground or power • 2/4 pressure switch is damaged or it has failed • O/D pressure switch circuit is open, shorted to ground or power • O/D pressure switch is damaged or it has failed • Internal transmission faults exist • TCM relay power circuit to 2/4 or O/D switch open (loss of B+) • PCM/TCM has failed

OBD II Trouble Code List (P1XXX Codes)

DTC	Trouble Code Title, Conditions & Possible Causes
DTC: P1101 **1T ECM** **Years:** 2005, 2006, 2007 **Models:** Liberty **Engines:** 2.8L Diesel **Transmissions:** All	**ACM Crash Signal Received** Ignition on. If crash signal is received from Airbag Control Module, this DTC will set. **Possible Causes:** • Clear DTC • Examine airbag system integrity • Check connections and grounds
DTC: P1102 **1T ECM** **Years:** 2005, 2006, 2007 **Models:** Liberty **Engines:** 2.8L Diesel **Transmissions:** All	**Viscous/Cabin Heater Relay Error** Ignition on. ECM Viscous/Cabin Heater Relay is commanded on (excessive current or short circuit), or is commanded OFF (open circuit or short-to-ground). If the ECM detects excessive current or no voltage signal on the Viscous/Cabin Heater Relay control circuit, this DTC will set. **Possible Causes:** • ASD Relay output circuit is open • Cabin Heater Relay has failed • Cabin Heater Relay control circuit is open, shorted to voltage, or to ground • ECM has failed
DTC: P1105 **2T CCM** **Years:** 2005, 2006, 2007 **Models:** PT Cruiser Turbo **Engines:** All **Transmissions:** All	**Throttle Inlet Pressure Sensor Solenoid Circuit Malfunction** Engine started, system voltage over 10.5v, Turbo Boost mode enabled, and the PCM detected the Actual and Intended state of the Throttle Inlet Pressure Sensor solenoid did not match. **Possible Causes:** • ASD output circuit to the TIP solenoid is open • Throttle inlet pressure Sensor solenoid is damaged or has failed • TIP solenoid control circuit is open, shorted to ground or power • PCM has failed
DTC: P1106 **2T CCM** **Years:** 2005, 2006, 2007 **Models:** PT Cruiser Turbo **Engines:** All **Transmissions:** All	**Throttle Inlet Pressure Sensor Solenoid Circuit Malfunction** Engine started; battery over 10.5v; Turbo Boost mode enabled. The PCM did not detect enough difference between BARO Sensor and TIP Sensor values during boost. **Possible Causes:** • Check the vacuum supply to the turbo surge solenoid unit • Inspect the hoses and tubing to the turbo charger assembly • Review results of Solenoid Tests (Test 1, 2, 3 and 4 results) • Turbocharger assembly is damaged or it has failed • Wastegate actuator has failed (due to a mechanical failure)
DTC: P1115 **1T CCM** **Years:** 2005, 2006, 2007 **Models:** Grand Cherokee, Liberty, Pacifica, PT Cruiser, Ram Truck, Sebring, Stratus, Wrangler **Engines:** All **Transmissions:** All	**General Temperature Sensor Performance** Engine "off" more than 8 hours, then engine started, ambient temperature above −10°F; and after a calibrated amount of cool-down time, the PCM compares the values from the Ambient Air Temperature (AAT), Engine Coolant Temperature (ECT) and Intake Air Temperature (IAT) Sensors. If the PCM detects that the value of any combination of these Sensors (AAT-IAT, AAT-ECT or ECT-IAT) is less than a calibrated value, it will set this trouble code. **Possible Causes:** • Sensor signal circuit is open or shorted to ground • Sensor ground circuit is open or shorted to VREF (5v) • One or more of the identified Sensors is out-of-calibration • Ambient air temperature Sensor is damaged or it has failed • PCM High or Low circuit is damaged or it has failed
DTC: P1131 **1T ECM** **Years:** 2005, 2006, 2007 **Models:** Liberty **Engines:** 2.8L Diesel **Transmissions:** All	**Glow Plug Module Voltage Supply** Ignition on or engine running. If the ECM detects an improper voltage supply signal, this DTC will set. **Possible Causes:** • Battery supply circuit is open • Ground circuit is open • Intermittent condition • Glow Plug Control Module has failed
DTC: P1132 **1T ECM** **Years:** 2005, 2006, 2007 **Models:** Liberty **Engines:** 2.8L Diesel **Transmissions:** All	**Glow Plug Module Internal Fault** Ignition on or engine running. If the ECM detects an improper voltage supply signal, this DTC will set. **Possible Causes:** • Battery supply circuit is open • Ground circuit is open • Intermittent condition • Glow Plug Control Module has failed

DTC	Trouble Code Title, Conditions & Possible Causes
DTC: P1135 **1T ECM** **Years:** 2005, 2006, 2007 **Models:** Liberty **Engines:** 2.8L Diesel **Transmissions:** All	**Glow Plug Module Control Circuit Fault** Ignition on or engine running. If the ECM detects a no-signal or improper current signal on the control circuit, this DTC will set. **Possible Causes:** • ECM has failed • Glow Plug Module has failed • Glow Plug Module control circuit is open or is shorted to voltage or to ground • Intermittent condition
DTC: P1135 **1T CCM** **Years:** 2005, 2006, 2007 **Models:** PT Cruiser **Engines:** All **Transmissions:** All	**O2 (B1 S1) Heater Element Resistance Out-Of-Range** Monitored with engine running; O2 (B1 S1) Sensor has reached 98% of duty cycle at least once since cranking; vehicle speed is between 20-93 mph; catalyst temperature is between 1112-1706F (600-930C); battery voltage is 9-16v; and no O2 Sensor electrical DTCs are present. If the PCM determines the O2 Sensor resistance is less than 2 ohms for more than 30 seconds, this DTC will set. **Possible Causes:** • O2 heater element has failed • O2 Sensor heater ground circuit is open • ASD relay output circuit is open • Intermittent condition • PCM has failed
DTC: P1136 **1T CCM** **Years:** 2005, 2006, 2007 **Models:** PT Cruiser **Engines:** All **Transmissions:** All	**O2 (B1 S2) Heater Element Resistance Out-Of-Range** Monitored with engine running; O2 Sensor has reached 98% of duty cycle at least once since cranking; vehicle speed is between 20-93 mph; catalyst temperature is between 1112-1706F (600-930C); battery voltage is 9-16v; and no O2 Sensor electrical DTCs are present. If the PCM determines the B1 S2 O2 Sensor resistance is less than 2 ohms for more than 30 seconds, this DTC will set. **Possible Causes:** • O2 heater element has failed • O2 Sensor heater ground circuit is open • ASD relay output circuit is open • Intermittent condition • PCM has failed
DTC: P1140 **1T ECM** **Years:** 2005, 2006, 2007 **Models:** Liberty **Engines:** 2.8L Diesel **Transmissions:** All	**Vacuum Reservoir Solenoid Open Or Short-To-Ground** Ignition on; Vacuum Reservoir Solenoid commanded OFF. If the ECM does not detect a voltage signal or a change in voltage on the control circuit, this DTC will set. **Possible Causes:** • Intermittent condition • ASD Relay output circuit is open • Vacuum Reservoir Solenoid control circuit is open or is shorted to ground • Vacuum Reservoir Solenoid has failed • ECM has failed
DTC: P1142 **1T ECM** **Years:** 2005, 2006, 2007 **Models:** Liberty **Engines:** 2.8L Diesel **Transmissions:** All	**Fuel Pressure Solenoid Open Or Short-To-Ground Circuit** Ignition on; ECM Fuel Pressure Solenoid commanded OFF. If the ECM does not detect a voltage signal or detects excessive current in voltage on the control circuit, this DTC will set. **Possible Causes:** • FP Solenoid circuit(s) open, shorted to voltage, shorted to ground, or shorted together • Intermittent condition • FP Solenoid has failed • ECM has failed
DTC: P1155 **1T CCM** **Years:** 2005, 2006, 2007 **Models:** Liberty **Engines:** 2.8L Diesel **Transmissions:** All	**Fuel Rail Rail Pressure Too High Malfunction** Engine running; ECM determines that the fuel rail pressure exceeds 1700 bar. **Possible Causes:** • Air in fuel system • Fuel injector problems • Fuel Pressure Solenoid has failed • Fuel Pump has malfunctioned or failed • Fuel system has contamination • Fuel system has a leak • Intermittent condition

DTC	Trouble Code Title, Conditions & Possible Causes
DTC: P1159 **1T ECM** **Years:** 2005, 2006, 2007 **Models:** Liberty **Engines:** 2.8L Diesel **Transmissions:** All	**Improper Start Attempt** Engine running; vehicle drive at less than 2 mph. If the ECM detects engine speed above 100 rpm without activating the starter relay control, this DTC will set. Verify the active DTCs. **Possible Causes:** • ECM has failed
DTC: P1160 **1T ECM** **Years:** 2005, 2006, 2007 **Models:** Liberty **Engines:** 2.8L Diesel **Transmissions:** All	**Ignition Voltage Improper Signal** Engine running. If the ECM detects an improper ignition voltage at any time, this DTC will set. **Possible Causes:** • ECM power and/or ground connection problems • ECM has failed • Intermittent condition
DTC: P1167 **1T ECM** **Years:** 2005, 2006, 2007 **Models:** Liberty **Engines:** 2.8L Diesel **Transmissions:** All	**Capacitor Voltage Problem** Engine cranking or running. If the ECM detects a capacitor voltage problem during injector actuation, this DTC will set. Verify any other injector-related DTCs. **Possible Causes:** • ECM has failed • Intermittent condition
DTC: P1168 **1T ECM** **Years:** 2005, 2006, 2007 **Models:** Liberty **Engines:** 2.8L Diesel **Transmissions:** All	**ECM Communication Error** Ignition on. ECM detects an internal failure. **Possible Causes:** • ECM has failed • Intermittent condition
DTC: P1169 **1T ECM** **Years:** 2005, 2006, 2007 **Models:** Liberty **Engines:** 2.8L Diesel **Transmissions:** All	**ECM A/D Converter Error** Ignition on. ECM detects an internal failure. **Possible Causes:** • ECM has failed • Intermittent condition
DTC: P1188 **2T CCM** **Years:** 2005, 2006, 2007 **Models:** PT Cruiser Turbo **Engines:** All **Transmissions:** All	**Throttle Inlet Pressure Sensor Signal Range/Performance** Engine started, engine running in Turbo Boost or Non-Boost mode, and the PCM detected a significant difference between the BARO Sensor and TIP Sensor signals (i.e., the TIP Sensor cannot read the signal correctly). **Possible Causes:** • ASD output circuit to the TIP solenoid is open • Throttle inlet pressure Sensor solenoid is damaged or has failed • TIP solenoid control circuit is open, shorted to ground or power • PCM has failed
DTC: P1189 **2T CCM** **Years:** 2005, 2006, 2007 **Models:** PT Cruiser Turbo **Engines:** All **Transmissions:** All	**Throttle Inlet Pressure Sensor Circuit Low Input** Engine started, TP Sensor less than 1.2v, system voltage over 10.5v, and the PCM detected the Throttle Inlet Pressure (TIP) Sensor was less than 0.0782v for a period of 1-7 seconds. **Possible Causes:** • TIP Sensor VREF circuit is open • TIP Sensor signal circuit is open • TIP Sensor signal circuit is shorted to chassis or Sensor ground • TIP Sensor is damaged or it has failed • PCM has failed
DTC: P1190 **2T CCM** **Years:** 2005, 2006, 2007 **Models:** PT Cruiser Turbo **Engines:** All **Transmissions:** All	**Throttle Inlet Pressure Sensor Circuit High Input** Engine started, TP Sensor less than 1.2v, system voltage over 10.5v, and the PCM detected the Throttle Inlet Pressure (TIP) Sensor was more than 4.92v for a period of 1-7 seconds. **Possible Causes:** • TIP Sensor VREF circuit is open • TIP Sensor signal circuit is open • TIP Sensor signal circuit is shorted to chassis or Sensor ground • TIP Sensor is damaged or it has failed • PCM has failed

DTC	Trouble Code Title, Conditions & Possible Causes
DTC: P1196 **1T CCM** **Years:** 2005, 2006, 2007 **Models:** Cherokee, Grand Cherokee, Liberty, PT Cruiser, Ram Truck, Sebring, Stratus, Wrangler **Engines:** All **Transmissions:** All	**O2 (B2 S1) Circuit Insufficient Activity** Engine started, vehicle driven with the throttle open at a speed over 18-55 mph at light engine load for over 5 minutes, ECT Sensor more than 170°F, and the PCM detected the O2 signal switched from 0.39v to 0.60v too few times in the Oxygen Sensor Monitor test. **Possible Causes:** • Base engine mechanical fault affecting more than one cylinder • Exhaust leak present in exhaust manifold or exhaust pipes • O2 element fuel contamination or has deteriorated • O2 signal circuit or ground circuit has high resistance
DTC: P1250 **1T ECM** **Years:** 2005, 2006, 2007 **Models:** Liberty **Engines:** 2.8L Diesel **Transmissions:** All	**Vacuum Reservoir Solenoid Open Circuit** Ignition on; solenoid commanded ON. If the ECM does not detect a voltage signal on the Vacuum Reservoir Solenoid control circuit, this DTC will set. **Possible Causes:** • Intermittent condition • ASD Relay output circuit is open • VR Solenoid control circuit is open or is shorted to ground • VR Solenoid or ECM has failed
DTC: P1251 **1T ECM** **Years:** 2005, 2006, 2007 **Models:** Liberty **Engines:** 2.8L Diesel **Transmissions:** All	**Vacuum Reservoir Solenoid Short-To-Ground Circuit** Ignition on; solenoid commanded ON. If the ECM does not detect a voltage signal on the Vacuum Reservoir Solenoid control circuit, this DTC will set. **Possible Causes:** • Intermittent condition • ASD Relay output circuit is open • VR Solenoid control circuit is open or shorted to ground • VR Solenoid or ECM has failed
DTC: P1252 **1T ECM** **Years:** 2005, 2006, 2007 **Models:** Liberty **Engines:** 2.8L Diesel **Transmissions:** All	**Vacuum Reservoir Solenoid Short Circuit** Ignition on; solenoid commanded ON. If the ECM detects excessive voltage signal on the Vacuum Reservoir Solenoid control circuit, this DTC will set. **Possible Causes:** • Intermittent condition • ASD Relay output circuit is open • VR Solenoid control circuit is open or shorted to ground • VR Solenoid or ECM has failed
DTC: P1281 **2T ECT** **Years:** 2005, 2006, 2007 **Models:** Grand Cherokee, Liberty, PT Cruiser, Ram Truck, Sebring, Stratus, Wrangler **Engines:** All **Transmissions:** All	**Engine Is Cold Too Long** Engine started, engine runtime more than 20 minutes, and the PCM detected the engine temperature did not exceed 176°F in the period. **Possible Causes:** • Check the operation of the thermostat (it may be stuck open) • ECT Sensor signal circuit has high resistance • ECT Sensor is damaged or it has failed • Inspect for low coolant level or an incorrect coolant mixture
DTC: P1282 **1T CCM** **Years:** 2005, 2006, 2007 **Models:** Grand Cherokee, Liberty, PT Cruiser, Ram Truck, Sebring, Stratus, Wrangler **Engines:** All **Transmissions:** All	**Fuel Pump Relay Control Circuit Malfunction** Key on or engine started, system voltage over 10.5v, and the PCM detected an unexpected voltage condition on the Fuel Pump Relay control circuit during the CCM test period. **Possible Causes:** • Fuel pump relay control circuit is open or shorted to ground • Fuel pump relay power circuit is open (test power from Ignition) • Fuel pump relay is damaged or has failed • PCM has failed
DTC: P1294 **1T CCM** **Years:** 2005, 2006, 2007 **Models:** Grand Cherokee, Liberty, PT Cruiser, Ram Truck, Sebring, Stratus, Wrangler **Engines:** All **Transmissions:** All	**Target Idle Speed Not Reached** DTC P0106, P0107, P0108, P0121, P0122 and P0123 not set, engine started, running at idle in Drive or Neutral, and the PCM detected the Actual idle speed was more than 200 rpm over or more than 100 rpm less than the Target speed for over 14 seconds. **Possible Causes:** • Engine vacuum leak in a hose, brake booster or in the engine • IAC motor control circuits open or grounded in the wire harness • Throttle body dirty or restricted (trying cleaning it and retesting) • Throttle linkage or throttle plate not in the correct position • PCM has failed

DTC	Trouble Code Title, Conditions & Possible Causes
DTC: P1296 **1T CCM** **Years:** 2005, 2006, 2007 **Models:** Grand Cherokee, Liberty, PT Cruiser, Ram Truck, Sebring, Stratus, Wrangler **Engines:** All **Transmissions:** All	**5-Volt VREF Supply Not Present** Key on, altitude indicating zero feet above seal level, then the PCM detected the MAP Sensor was near 101 kPa; or with altitude at 1200 feet above sea level, the MAP Sensor was near 88 kPa. **Possible Causes:** • MAP Sensor VREF circuit open between the Sensor and PCM • MAP Sensor ground circuit open between the Sensor and PCM • MAP Sensor is damaged or has failed • PCM has failed
DTC: P1297 **1T CCM** **Years:** 2005, 2006, 2007 **Models:** Grand Cherokee, Liberty, PT Cruiser, Ram Truck, Sebring, Stratus, Wrangler **Engines:** All **Transmissions:** All	**No Change In MAP Signal From Start To Run Transition** Engine started, and with the engine speed within 64 rpm of the Target idle speed, the PCM detected too small a difference between the BARO and MAP Sensor signals for 8.80 seconds. **Possible Causes:** • Engine vacuum port to MAP Sensor clogged, dirty or restricted • MAP Sensor signal is skewed or the Sensor is out-of-calibration • MAP Sensor VREF circuit open or grounded (intermittent fault) • PCM has failed
DTC: P1388 **1T CCM** **Years:** 2005, 2006, 2007 **Models:** Grand Cherokee, Liberty, PT Cruiser, Ram Truck, Sebring, Stratus, Wrangler **Engines:** All **Transmissions:** All	**Auto Shutdown Relay Control Circuit Malfunction** Key on or engine cranking; and the PCM detected an unexpected voltage condition on the ASD Relay Control circuit. The ASD Relay coil resistance is 95-105ohms at 68°F. **Possible Causes:** • ASD relay control circuit is open between the relay and PCM • ASD relay control circuit is shorted to ground • ASD relay power circuit is open (test power from Fused B+) • ASD relay is damaged or has failed • PCM has failed
DTC: P1389 **1T CCM** **Years:** 2005, 2006, 2007 **Models:** Grand Cherokee, Liberty, PT Cruiser, Ram Truck, Sebring, Stratus, Wrangler **Engines:** All **Transmissions:** All	**No Auto Shutdown Relay Output Voltage To PCM** Engine cranking; and the PCM did not detect any voltage on the ASD Relay Output circuit to the PCM during the CCM test. **Possible Causes:** • ASD relay connector is damaged, loose or shorted • ASD relay output circuit is open between the relay and PCM • ASD relay power circuit is open (test power from Fused B+) • ASD relay is damaged or has failed • PCM has failed
DTC: P1391 **1T CCM** **Years:** 2005, 2006, 2007 **Models:** Grand Cherokee, Liberty, PT Cruiser, Ram Truck, Sebring, Stratus, Wrangler **Engines:** All **Transmissions:** All	**CKP Or CMP Sensor Signal Intermittent** Engine started, engine running, and after every 69-degree CKP Sensor leading edge and trailing signal edge is determined, the PCM updates this data and compares it to the true CMP Sensor port level. If the PCM detects a disagreement between these two values 20 times in succession, this trouble code is set. **Possible Causes:** • Camshaft Sensor is not installed properly • Engine valve timing is not within specifications • Perform a CKP and CMP Sensor relearn with the scan tool • Tone wheel or pulse ring is damaged
DTC: P1398 **1T CCM** **Years:** 2005, 2006, 2007 **Models:** Grand Cherokee, Liberty, PT Cruiser, Ram Truck, Sebring, Stratus, Wrangler **Engines:** All **Transmissions:** All	**Misfire Adaptive Numerator At Limit** Engine started; ECT Sensor under 75°F; engine runtime over 50 sec.; A/C "OFF"; vehicle speed over 36 mph in 1st gear, or over 65 mph in high gear, followed by a closed throttle decel period. This code sets if the PCM detects one of the CKP Sensor target windows varies more than 2.86% from the reference window. Background - PCM needs to learn any variation in engine machining to detect when a misfire is present. CKP Sensor has 2 40 windows that are 180 apart. The window for Cylinders 1 and 4 is the reference window. It is checked against the window for Cylinders 2 and 3. The PCM checks for any variation to make engine speed adjustments. **Possible Causes:** • Base engine problem (i.e., low cylinder compression) • CKP Sensor crankshaft target variation too large • CKP Sensor improperly installed or the CKP Sensor has failed • CKP Sensor signal circuit open or shorted (intermittent fault) • Tone wheel or pulse ring is damaged

DTC	Trouble Code Title, Conditions & Possible Causes
DTC: P1486 **2T EVAP** **Years:** 2005, 2006, 2007 **Models:** Grand Cherokee, Liberty, PT Cruiser, Ram Truck, Sebring, Stratus, Wrangler **Engines:** All **Transmissions:** All	**EVAP Leak Detection Monitor Pinched Hose Detected** BTS from 40-96°F and ECT Sensor within 20°F of the BTS signal at startup (cold engine), engine started, and after the EVAP Leak Detection test was enabled, the PCM detected the LDP switch did not reach 3 closures (i.e., a "no flow" condition was present). **Possible Causes:** • EVAP vapor hose blocked between the fuel tank and the LDP (i.e., in the OLFV, rollover or vapor hose) • EVAP canister is clogged or full of dirt or moisture • EVAP ventilation solenoid is damaged or has failed • Purge line is loose, damaged or incorrectly routed • PCM has failed
DTC: P1493 **1T CCM** **Years:** 2005, 2006, 2007 **Models:** Grand Cherokee, Liberty, PT Cruiser, Ram Truck, Sebring, Stratus, Wrangler **Engines:** All **Transmissions:** All	**Battery Temperature Sensor Circuit Low Input** Key on or engine running; and the PCM detected the BTS signal indicated less than 0.30v for 3 seconds during the CCM test. **Possible Causes:** • BTS circuit is shorted to ground between Sensor and the PCM • BTS (Sensor) is damaged or has failed • PCM has failed
DTC: P1494 **1T CCM** **Years:** 2005, 2006, 2007 **Models:** Grand Cherokee, Liberty, PT Cruiser, Ram Truck, Sebring, Stratus, Wrangler **Engines:** All **Transmissions:** All	**EVAP Leak Detection Pump Switch Or Mechanical Fault** BTS from 40-96°F and ECT Sensor within 10°F of the BTS signal at startup (cold engine), engine started, and the PCM detected the LDP switch was not in its expected state at key "on" or engine running. **Possible Causes:** • LDP switch signal circuit is open or shorted to ground • LDP switch power circuit is open (test power to Fused Ignition) • LDP vacuum hose is clogged, loose or restricted • LDP assembly is damaged or has failed (the switch has failed)
DTC: P1495 **1T CCM** **Years:** 2005, 2006, 2007 **Models:** Grand Cherokee, Liberty, PT Cruiser, Ram Truck, Sebring, Stratus, Wrangler **Engines:** All **Transmissions:** All	**Leak Detection Pump Solenoid Circuit Malfunction** Engine started, ECT Sensor from 40-90°F and within 10°F of the Battery Temperature Sensor signal, engine running, and the PCM detected the Actual state of the Leak Detection Pump solenoid did not match the Intended state of the solenoid during the test period. **Possible Causes:** • LDP power supply circuit from the ignition switch is open • LDP solenoid control circuit is open or shorted to ground • LDP assembly is damaged or it has failed • PCM has failed
DTC: P1499 **1T CCM** **Years:** 2005, 2006, 2007 **Models:** Grand Cherokee, Liberty, Wrangler **Engines:** All **Transmissions:** All	**Radiator (Hydraulic) Fan Solenoid Circuit Failure** Key on or engine running; and the PCM detected an unexpected voltage condition on the Radiator Fan Solenoid Control circuit. **Possible Causes:** • Radiator fan solenoid control circuit is open • Radiator fan solenoid ground circuit is open • Radiator fan solenoid power circuit is open • Radiator fan solenoid is damaged or has failed • PCM has failed
DTC: P1501 **1T CCM** **Years:** 2005, 2006, 2007 **Models:** Ram Truck **Engines:** All **Transmissions:** All	**Vehicle Speed Sensor No. 1/2 Drive Wheel Correlation** Engine is running and vehicle is moving. Speed control is learned and the speed control is trying to be activated. If the PCM recognizes the rear wheel speed is greater than the front wheel speed, this DTC will set. **Possible Causes:** • Other active Bus or Communication DTCs • Incorrect tire circumference • PCM has failed
DTC: P1502 **1T CCM** **Years:** 2005, 2006, 2007 **Models:** Ram Truck **Engines:** All **Transmissions:** All	**Vehicle Speed Sensor No. 1/2 Non-Drive Wheel Correlation** Engine is running and vehicle is moving; brake pedal must not be applied. If the PCM recognizes the rear wheel speed is greater than the front wheel speed, this DTC will set. **Possible Causes:** • Other active Bus or Communication DTCs • Incorrect tire circumference • PCM has failed

DTC	Trouble Code Title, Conditions & Possible Causes
DTC: P1572 **1T CCM** **Years:** 2005, 2006, 2007 **Models:** Ram Truck **Engines:** All **Transmissions:** All	**Brake Switch Stuck ON** Ignition is on. The PCM recognizes that brake switch 1 is mechanically stuck in the Low/On position. **Possible Causes:** • Brake switch 1 signal is shorted to ground • Brake switch 2 signal is open • Stop lamp switch has failed • PCM has failed
DTC: P1573 **1T CCM** **Years:** 2005, 2006, 2007 **Models:** Ram Truck **Engines:** All **Transmissions:** All	**Brake Switch Stuck ON** Ignition is on. The PCM recognizes that brake switch 1 is mechanically stuck in the High/Off position. **Possible Causes:** • Brake switch 1 signal is shorted to ground or to voltage • Brake switch 2 signal is open or is shorted to ground • Ground circuit is open • Fused ignition switch output is open • Stop lamp switch has failed • PCM has failed
DTC: P1593 **1T CCM** **Years:** 2005, 2006, 2007 **Models:** Grand Cherokee, Liberty, Pacifica, PT Cruiser, Ram Truck, Sebring, Stratus, Wrangler **Engines:** All **Transmissions:** All	**Speed Control Switch Stuck Operation** Ignition on. Either S/C switch is mechanically stuck in On/Off, Resume/Accel or Set position for too long. **Possible Causes:** • Intermittent speed control switch 1/2 stuck DTC • S/C switches or Steering Column Control Module malfunctioning • S/C signal circuit open or shorted ground or to battery voltage • S/C switch signal circuit shorted to switch return circuit • S/C Sensor ground open • PCM has failed
DTC: P1594 **1T CCM** **Years:** 2005, 2006, 2007 **Models:** Grand Cherokee, Liberty, Wrangler **Engines:** All **Transmissions:** All	**Charging System Voltage Too High** Engine started, engine running, and the PCM detected the Charging System voltage was too high even after it tried to lower the generator output by controlling the Field control circuit (Generator Lamp is on). **Possible Causes:** • Battery temperature Sensor is damaged or has failed (skewed) • Generator field driver circuit is shorted to ground • Generator has an internal short circuit condition • PCM has failed
DTC: P1594 **1T CCM** **Years:** 2005, 2006, 2007 **Models:** PT Cruiser **Engines:** All **Transmissions:** All	**Charging System Voltage Too High** Engine is running at more than 380 rpm. If the battery voltage is 1v greater than the desired voltage, this DTC will set. **Possible Causes:** • Intermittent condition • Generator field driver circuit is shorted to ground • Generator field is damaged or has failed • PCM has failed
DTC: P1598 **1T CCM** **Years:** 2005, 2006, 2007 **Models:** Grand Cherokee, Liberty, PT Cruiser, Ram Truck, Sebring, Stratus, Wrangler **Engines:** All **Transmissions:** All	**A/C Pressure Sensor Circuit High Input** Engine started, engine running, A/C Relay is "on", and the PCM detected the A/C Pressure Sensor indicated more than 4.90v. **Possible Causes:** • A/C pressure Sensor circuit is open or shorted to VREF (5v) • A/C pressure Sensor ground circuit is open • A/C pressure Sensor is damaged or has failed • PCM has failed
DTC: P1599 **1T CCM** **Years:** 2005, 2006, 2007 **Models:** Grand Cherokee, Liberty, PT Cruiser, Ram Truck, Sebring, Stratus, Wrangler **Engines:** All **Transmissions:** All	**A/C Pressure Sensor Circuit Low Input** Engine started, engine running, A/C Relay is "on", and the PCM detected the A/C Pressure Sensor indicated less than 0.70v. **Possible Causes:** • A/C pressure Sensor circuit is shorted to ground • A/C pressure Sensor power circuit is open • A/C pressure Sensor is damaged or has failed • PCM has failed

DTC	Trouble Code Title, Conditions & Possible Causes
DTC: P1602 **1T PCM** **Years:** 2005, 2006, 2007 **Models:** Pacifica, PT Cruiser, Ram Truck, Sebring, Stratus **Engines:** All **Transmissions:** All	**PCM Not Programmed** Key on. The PCM detected that it had not been programmed. **Possible Causes:** • Program the PCM and then retest for this same trouble code • PCM has failed
DTC: P1603 **1T PCM** **Years:** 2005, 2006, 2007 **Models:** Grand Cherokee, Liberty, Pacifica, PT Cruiser, Ram Truck, Sebring, Stratus, Wrangler **Engines:** All **Transmissions:** All	**Powertrain Control Module Internal Dual-Port Ram Communication** Key on; and the PCM detected an error message that indicated that it had not been programmed or that it was programmed properly. **Possible Causes:** • Fused ignition switch output is missing (off-start-run circuit) • PCM is damaged or it has an internal failure
DTC: P1604 **1T PCM** **Years:** 2005, 2006, 2007 **Models:** Grand Cherokee, Liberty, Pacifica, PT Cruiser, Ram Truck, Sebring, Stratus, Wrangler **Engines:** All **Transmissions:** All	**PCM Internal Dual-Port Ram Read/Write Integrity Failure** Key on; and the PCM detected an error message that indicated it had not been programmed, or it was not programmed properly. **Possible Causes:** • Fused ignition switch output is missing (off-start-run circuit) • PCM is damaged or it has an internal failure
DTC: P1607 **1T PCM** **Years:** 2005, 2006, 2007 **Models:** Grand Cherokee, Liberty, Pacifica, PT Cruiser, Ram Truck, Sebring, Stratus, Wrangler **Engines:** All **Transmissions:** All	**Powertrain Control Module Internal Shutdown Timer Rationality** Cold engine startup, and after the PCM compared the coolant temperature to the shutdown time, it detected a rationality fault. **Possible Causes:** • Fused ignition switch output is missing (off-start-run circuit) • PCM is damaged or it has an internal failure
DTC: P1616 **1T PCM** **Years:** 2005, 2006, 2007 **Models:** PT Cruiser **Engines:** All **Transmissions:** All	**Primary 5v Sensor Reference Voltage Low** Key on. If the PCM detects a voltage of less than 4.75v on the primary 5v supply circuit for at least 100ms, this DTC will set. **Possible Causes:** • Intermittent condition • Primary 5v supply circuit shorted to ground • PCM has failed
DTC: P1617 **1T PCM** **Years:** 2005, 2006, 2007 **Models:** PT Cruiser **Engines:** All **Transmissions:** All	**Primary 5v Sensor Reference Voltage High** Key on. If the PCM detects a voltage of more than 5.25v on the primary 5v supply circuit for at least 100ms, this DTC will set. **Possible Causes:** • Intermittent condition • Primary 5v supply circuit is open or is shorted to voltage • PCM has failed
DTC: P1618 **1T PCM** **Years:** 2005, 2006, 2007 **Models:** PT Cruiser **Engines:** All **Transmissions:** All	**Primary 5v Sensor Reference Voltage Unstable** Key on. If the PCM detects a voltage variance of more than 0.25v on the primary 5v supply circuit for more than 100ms, this DTC will set. **Possible Causes:** • Primary 5v supply circuit open or shorted to ground or to battery voltage • 5v Sensor has failed • PCM has failed
DTC: P1618 **1T PCM** **Years:** 2005, 2006, 2007 **Models:** Ram Truck **Engines:** All **Transmissions:** All	**Primary 5v Sensor Reference Voltage Malfunction** Key on. The PCM recognizes the primary 5v supply circuit voltage is varying too much too quickly. ETC light is flashing. **Possible Causes:** • Primary 5v supply circuit open or shorted to ground or to battery voltage • 5v Sensor has failed • PCM has failed

DTC	Trouble Code Title, Conditions & Possible Causes
DTC: P1626 **1T PCM** **Years:** 2005, 2006, 2007 **Models:** PT Cruiser **Engines:** All **Transmissions:** All	**Secondary 5v Sensor Reference Voltage Low** Key on. If the PCM detects a voltage of less than 4.75v on the secondary 5v supply circuit for more than 100ms, this DTC will set. **Possible Causes:** • Intermittent condition • 5v supply circuit shorted to ground • 5v Sensor has failed • PCM has failed
DTC: P1627 **1T PCM** **Years:** 2005, 2006, 2007 **Models:** PT Cruiser **Engines:** All **Transmissions:** All	**Secondary 5v Sensor Reference Voltage High** Key on. If the PCM detects a voltage of more than 5.25v on the secondary 5v supply circuit for more than 100ms, this DTC will set. **Possible Causes:** • Intermittent condition • 5v supply circuit is open or is shorted to voltage • 5v Sensor has failed • PCM has failed
DTC: P1628 **1T PCM** **Years:** 2005, 2006, 2007 **Models:** PT Cruiser **Engines:** All **Transmissions:** All	**Secondary 5v Sensor Reference Voltage Unstable** Key on. If the PCM detects a voltage variance of more than 0.25v on the secondary 5v supply circuit for more than 100ms, this DTC will set. **Possible Causes:** • Intermittent condition • ETC assembly has failed • 5v supply circuit has high resistance • PCM has failed
DTC: P1628 **1T PCM** **Years:** 2005, 2006, 2007 **Models:** Ram Truck **Engines:** All **Transmissions:** All	**Auxiliary 5v Sensor Reference Voltage Malfunction** Key on. The PCM recognizes the auxiliary 5v supply circuit voltage is varying too much too quickly. ETC light is flashing. **Possible Causes:** • Auxiliary 5v supply circuit open or shorted to ground or to battery voltage • 5v Sensor has failed • PCM has failed
DTC: P1652 **1T CCM** **Years:** 2005, 2006, 2007 **Models:** Grand Cherokee, Liberty, Pacifica, PT Cruiser, Ram Truck, Sebring, Stratus, Wrangler **Engines:** All **Transmissions:** All	**Serial Communication Link Malfunction** Engine started; and after the TCM did not detect any signals on the Serial Communication Line for more than 20 seconds. **Note: Due to the integration of the PCM and TCM, Bus communication between the modules is internal.** **Possible Causes:** • TCM cannot communicate with the Instrument Cluster (MIC) • TCM cannot communicate with the Powertrain Control Module • PCM/TCM is damaged or it has an internal failure
DTC: P1653 **1T PCM** **Years:** 2005, 2006, 2007 **Models:** PT Cruiser **Engines:** All **Transmissions:** All	**PCI Bus Shorted To Ground** Key on. If the PCM detects a short to ground on the PCI Bus for more than 5 seconds, this DTC will set. **Possible Causes:** • Intermittent condition • Internal controller short to ground • PCI Bus short to ground
DTC: P1654 **1T PCM** **Years:** 2005, 2006, 2007 **Models:** PT Cruiser **Engines:** All **Transmissions:** All	**PCI Bus Shorted To Voltage** Key on. If the PCM detects a short to voltage on the PCI Bus for more than 5 seconds, this DTC will set. **Possible Causes:** • Intermittent condition • Internal controller short to battery voltage • PCI Bus short to voltage
DTC: P1654 **1T PCM** **Years:** 2005, 2006, 2007 **Models:** PT Cruiser **Engines:** All **Transmissions:** All	**PCI Bus Not Available** Key on. If the PCM detects the PCI Bus is not available for more than 5 seconds, this DTC will set. **Possible Causes:** • Intermittent condition • PCI Bus circuit is open • PCM has failed

DTC	Trouble Code Title, Conditions & Possible Causes
DTC: P1682 **1T CCM** **Years:** 2005, 2006, 2007 **Models:** Grand Cherokee, Liberty, PT Cruiser, Ram Truck, Sebring, Stratus, Wrangler **Engines:** All **Transmissions:** All	**Charging System Voltage Too Low** Engine started; engine speed over 1152 rpm, and the PCM detected the Battery Sense circuit was 1.0v less than the Charging System circuit for 25 seconds during the CCM test (Generator Lamp is "on"). **Possible Causes:** • Battery positive or Fused Ignition circuit has high resistance • Generator drive belt out-of-adjustment or worn out • Generator field circuit has a high resistance condition • PCM has failed
DTC: P1684 **1T PCM** **Years:** 2005, 2006, 2007 **Models:** Grand Cherokee, Liberty, PT Cruiser, Ram Truck, Sebring, Stratus, Wrangler **Engines:** All **Transmissions:** All	**Battery Has Been Disconnected** Key on, and the TCM detected that it had been disconnected from the Battery Direct (B+) circuit or its Power Ground circuit. This DTC will also set during the scan tool Quick Battery Disconnect procedure. **Note: Due to the integration of the PCM and TCM, the transmission part of the PCM has its own specific power and ground circuits.** **Possible Causes:** • Quick Learn procedure was performed with scan tool • TCM battery direct (B+) circuit is open or disconnected • TCM power ground circuit is open • PCM/TCM was disconnected or it has been replaced
DTC: P1686 **1T PCM** **Years:** 2005, 2006, 2007 **Models:** PT Cruiser **Engines:** All **Transmissions:** All	**No SKIM Bus Message Received** Key on. If the PCM does not receive a Bus message from the SKIM when expected, this DTC will set. **Possible Causes:** • Intermittent condition • SKIM/PCM has failed • Loss of SKIM communication link • PCI Bus circuit open from PCM to SKIM
DTC: P1687 **1T PCM** **Years:** 2005, 2006, 2007 **Models:** Grand Cherokee, Liberty, PT Cruiser, Ram Truck, Sebring, Stratus, Wrangler **Engines:** All **Transmissions:** All	**No Cluster Bus Messages** Key on or engine running; and the PCM determined that it did not receive any Security Key Bus Messages over the Data Bus line for 20 seconds. This malfunction may be an intermittent problem. **Possible Causes:** • Data Bus circuit from SKIM to PCM is damaged or it is open • PCM unable to communicate with the Body Control Module • PCM has failed, or the SKIM is damaged or has failed
DTC: P1687 **1T PCM** **Years:** 2005, 2006, 2007 **Models:** Grand Cherokee, Liberty, Pacifica, PT Cruiser, Ram Truck, Sebring, Stratus, Wrangler **Engines:** All **Transmissions:** All	**No Communication with MIC** Communications are monitored continuously with engine running. The DTC sets in about 25 seconds if no Bus messages are received from the MIC. **Possible Causes:** • Other Bus problems exist • Intermittent wiring or connector problems exist • PCM has failed
DTC: P1694 **1T PCM** **Years:** 2005, 2006, 2007 **Models:** Grand Cherokee, Liberty, PT Cruiser, Ram Truck, Sebring, Stratus, Wrangler **Engines:** All **Transmissions:** All	**No PCM Bus Messages** Ignition on or engine started; system voltage over 10.5v and the PCM determined that it did not receive any Bus messages for 10 seconds. **Note: Due to the integration of the PCM and TCM, Bus communication between the modules is internal.** **Possible Causes:** • Data Bus circuit connector is damaged, open or it is shorted • Data Bus circuit to the PCM is damaged or it is open • PCM unable to communicate with the body control module • Intermittent wiring or connector problems exist • PCM has failed
DTC: P1695 **1T PCM** **Years:** 2005, 2006, 2007 **Models:** Grand Cherokee, Liberty, PT Cruiser, Ram Truck, Sebring, Stratus, Wrangler **Engines:** All **Transmissions:** All	**No BCM Bus Messages** Engine started; system voltage over 10.5v and the TCM determined that it did not receive any BCM messages for 20 seconds. **Possible Causes:** • Data Bus circuit from BCM to the PCM is damaged or it is open • BCM is damaged or has failed • TCM unable to communicate with the TCM • TCM has failed

DTC	Trouble Code Title, Conditions & Possible Causes
DTC: P1696 **1T PCM** **Years:** 2005, 2006, 2007 **Models:** Grand Cherokee, Liberty, PT Cruiser, Ram Truck, Sebring, Stratus, Wrangler **Engines:** All **Transmissions:** All	**PCM EEPROM Write Operation Denied/Invalid** Engine started or ignition on continuously. PCM detected an unsuccessful attempt to program/write to the internal EEPROM. Occurred at initialization or shutdown. **Possible Causes:** • DRB or scan tool displays a "write" failure occurred • DRB or scan tool displays "write" refused a second time • DRB or scan tool displays SRI mileage invalid (compare the SRI mileage reading to the reading on the odometer) • PCM has failed
DTC: P1697 **1T PCM** **Years:** 2005, 2006, 2007 **Models:** Grand Cherokee, Liberty, PT Cruiser, Ram Truck, Sebring, Stratus, Wrangler **Engines:** All **Transmissions:** All	**PCM Failure (EMR/SRI Mileage Not Stored)** Key on, and the PCM detected an unsuccessful attempt to "write" the Service Reminder Indicator (SRI) or Emission Mileage Request (EMR) mileage to an EEPROM located occurred during initialization. **Possible Causes:** • Clear the trouble codes and retest for the same trouble code. If DTC P1697 resets, replace the PCM and then reprogram it.
DTC: P1715 **1T CCM** **Years:** 2005, 2006, 2007 **Models:** Liberty **Engines:** 2.8L Diesel **Transmissions:** All	**Restricted Port in T3 Range** Monitored whenever the PRNDL code indicates Temp 3. This DTC will set whenever the conditions for a code P1776 are satisfied with the shifter in the Temp 3 zone. This causes a restricted port. Related transmission DTCs are present. **Possible Causes:** • Improper customer driving habits • Misadjusted shifter
DTC: P1719 **1T CCM** **Years:** 2005, 2006, 2007 **Models:** Sebring, Stratus Coupe **Engines:** All **Transmissions:** All	**A/T Skip Shift Solenoid Control Circuit Malfunction** Engine started; vehicle driven to a speed of 12-18 mph in 1st Gear at light to moderate engine load at an engine speed over 608 rpm, and the PCM detected an unexpected "low" or high voltage condition on the Reverse Gear Lockout solenoid circuit. **Possible Causes:** • Skip Shift solenoid control circuit is open • Skip Shift solenoid control circuit shorted to ground • Skip Shift solenoid is damaged or has failed • PCM has failed
DTC: P1736 **1T CCM** **Years:** 2005, 2006, 2007 **Models:** Liberty, Ram Truck **Engines:** 3.7L **Transmissions:** All	**A/T Gear Ratio Error In Second Prime** Transmission gear ratio is monitored whenever the transmission is in gear. If the ratio of the Input Speed (rpm) to the Output Speed did not match the current gear ratio, this DTC will set. This DTC can take up to 5 minutes of problem identification before lighting the MIL. Related DTCs are present. **Possible Causes:** • Internal transmission problems • Transmission intermittent gear ratio malfunction
DTC: P1775 **1T CCM** **Years:** 2005, 2006, 2007 **Models:** Grand Cherokee, Liberty, PT Cruiser, Ram Truck, Sebring, Stratus, Wrangler **Engines:** All **Transmissions:** All	**A/T Solenoid Switch Latched In TCC Position** Engine started; vehicle driven to over 15 mph and the TCM detected the Transmission did not shift into 1st Gear (test must fail 3 times). **Possible Causes:** • Related DTC P0841 may be present. • Intermittent wiring or connector problems • Extremely low battery (system) voltage • L/R Solenoid pressure switch circuit is open or switch has failed • Transmission solenoid pack is damaged or has failed • Transmission control relay circuit is shorted to L/R solenoid • Valve body engine idle too high • Valve body solenoid switch stuck in "lockup" position • PCM has failed
DTC: P1776 **2T CCM** **Years:** 2005, 2006, 2007 **Models:** Grand Cherokee, Liberty, Pacifica, PT Cruiser, Ram Truck, Sebring, Stratus, Wrangler **Engines:** All **Transmissions:** All	**A/T Solenoid Switch Latched In Low/Reverse Position** Engine started; vehicle driven to over 30 mph and the TCM detected the L/R switch was closed while performing partial or full PEMCC or FEMCC. **Possible Causes:** • Related DTC P0841 may be present. • Intermittent wiring or connector problems • L/R pressure switch sense circuit is open, shorted to ground or to voltage • Extremely low battery (system) voltage • Transmission pan has debris caused by valve body damage • Transmission internal problems, SSV sticking, or valve body damage • PCM has failed

DTC	Trouble Code Title, Conditions & Possible Causes
DTC: P1790 **1T CCM** **Years:** 2005, 2006, 2007 **Models:** Grand Cherokee, Liberty, Pacifica, PT Cruiser, Ram Truck, Sebring, Stratus, Wrangler **Engines:** All **Transmissions:** All	**A/T Malfunction Immediately After Shift Event** Engine started; vehicle driven to a speed over 10 mph in Drive, and the TCM detected a Speed Ratio error within 1.3 seconds of a shift. **Possible Causes:** • Transmission internal mechanical problem
DTC: P1794 **1T CCM** **Years:** 2005, 2006, 2007 **Models:** Grand Cherokee, Liberty, Pacifica, PT Cruiser, Ram Truck, Sebring, Stratus, Wrangler **Engines:** All **Transmissions:** All	**A/T Speed Sensor Ground Circuit Malfunction** Engine started; gear selector position indicating Neutral, and the PCM an error in the Output Speed Sensor signal during the test. **Possible Causes:** • Extremely low battery (system) voltage • TCM "reset" function has just been performed
DTC: P1794 **1T CCM** **Years:** 2005, 2006, 2007 **Models:** Liberty **Engines:** 2.8L Diesel **Transmissions:** All	**A/T Speed Sensor Ground Error** The gear ratio is monitored whenever the transmission is in gear. After a TCM reset in Neutral and a ratio for Input to Output is 1 to 2, this DTC will set. This DTC can take up to 5 minutes of problem identification to light the MIL. **Possible Causes:** • Speed Sensor ground circuit is open or is shorted to ground or to voltage • TCM has failed • Intermittent wiring or connector problems
DTC: P1797 **1T CCM** **Years:** 2005, 2006, 2007 **Models:** Grand Cherokee, Liberty, Pacifica, PT Cruiser, Ram Truck, Sebring, Stratus, Wrangler **Engines:** All **Transmissions:** All	**A/T Manual Shift Overheat Malfunction** Whenever the engine is running and the transmission is in the AutoStick mode, if the engine temperature exceeds 275F (135C), this DTC will set. **Note: Aggressive driving or driving in Low for extended periods in AutoStick mode will set this DTC.** **Possible Causes:** • ATF fluid level too high (transmission may be overfilled) • Engine Cooling System or engine cooling fan malfunction • Excessive drive time in low gear, or aggressive drive patterns • Transmission oil cooler is clogged or restricted
DTC: P1854 **2T CCM** **Years:** 2005, 2006, 2007 **Models:** PT Cruiser **Engines:** All **Transmissions:** All	**Throttle Inlet Pressure BARO Reading Out Of Range** Engine started. The PCM detected the BARO Sensor indicated an incorrect reading. On MAP Sensor voltage is greater than 4.9v or below 2.28v (non-Turbo) or greater than 2.4v or below 1.2v (Turbo) for 400ms. **Possible Causes:** • Inspect the hoses and tubing to the turbo charger assembly • Review results of Solenoid Tests (Test 1, 2, 3 and 4 results) • TIP signal circuit is open (may be an intermittent fault) • TIP ground circuit is open (may be an intermittent fault) • PCM has failed
DTC: P1861 **1T PCM** **Years:** 2005, 2006, 2007 **Models:** Pacifica **Engines:** All **Transmissions:** All	**Siphon Line Disconnected** Ignition on. PCM compares the primary tank level with the secondary tank level. If the PCM detects the primary side is lower than the secondary side, by a calibrated amount, the DTC will set. **Possible Causes:** • Damage to fuel tank • Fuel level signal circuit is open or shorted to ground • Ground circuit is open • Internal tank components or siphon hose damaged • Fuel level Sensor has failed

OBD II Trouble Code List (P2XXX Codes)

DTC	Trouble Code Title, Conditions & Possible Causes
DTC: P2008 **1T CCM** **Years:** 2005, 2006, 2007 **Models:** Pacifica **Engines:** All **Transmissions:** All	**Short Runner Solenoid Circuit Malfunction** Engine started. ASD relay energized. PCM detected the Short Runner solenoid circuit was not in its expected voltage state. **Possible Causes:** • S/R solenoid control circuit is open • S/R solenoid control circuit is shorted to ground or power (B+) • S/R solenoid power supply circuit is open to the ASD relay • Short runner solenoid is damaged or it has failed • PCM has failed
DTC: P2066 **2T CCM** **Years:** 2005, 2006, 2007 **Models:** Pacifica **Engines:** All **Transmissions:** All	**Fuel Level Sensor No. 2 Malfunction** Test No. 1: With ignition on, fuel level is compared to the previous key-down after a 20-second delay. If the PCM does not see a difference in the fuel level of more than 0.1v, the test will fail. Test No. 2: The PCM monitors the fuel level with ignition on. If the PCM does not see a change in the fuel level of 0.1765 in. over a set amount of miles, the test will fail. **Possible Causes:** • Fuel tank or internal siphon hose damage • Fuel level signal circuit open or shorted to ground • Ground circuit is open • Fuel level Sensor malfunction
DTC: P2067 **1T CCM** **Years:** 2005, 2006, 2007 **Models:** Pacifica **Engines:** All **Transmissions:** All	**Fuel Level Sensor No. 2 Low Input** Key on. Battery voltage over 10.4v. Fuel level Sensor signal goes below 0.4v for more than 90 seconds (Magnum), or below 0.1961v for more than 5 seconds (Pacifica). DTC is recorded. **Possible Causes:** • Intermittent condition • Fuel level sending unit signal circuit shorted to Sensor or chassis ground • Fuel level sensing unit is damaged or the fuel tank is damaged • BCM or PCM has failed
DTC: P2068 **1T CCM** **Years:** 2005, 2006, 2007 **Models:** Pacifica **Engines:** All **Transmissions:** All	**Fuel Level Sensor No. 2 High Input** Key on. Battery voltage over 10.4v. Fuel level Sensor signal goes above 4.9v for more than 90 seconds (Magnum) or above 4.7v for more than 5 seconds (Pacifica). DTC is recorded. **Possible Causes:** • Fuel level sending unit signal circuit shorted to Sensor or chassis ground • Fuel level sensing unit is damaged or the fuel tank is damaged • Instrument cluster module faulty • BCM or PCM has failed
DTC: P2072 **1T CCM** **Years:** 2005, 2006, 2007 **Models:** Ram Truck **Engines:** All **Transmissions:** All	**Electronic Throttle Control System Malfunction** Key on. The PCM recognizes the throttle plate is stuck during extremely cold ambient temperature conditions. The throttle plate goes through a de-icing procedure, but if the throttle plate still does not move, this DTC will set. The MIL will not illuminate. The vehicle will be in the Limp Home mode, limiting rpm and vehicle speed. **Possible Causes:** • Throttle plate frozen
DTC: P2074 **1T CCM** **Years:** 2005, 2006, 2007 **Models:** Grand Cherokee, Liberty, Pacifica, PT Cruiser, Ram Truck, Sebring, Stratus, Wrangler **Engines:** All **Transmissions:** All	**Manifold Pressure/Throttle Position Correlation; High Flow/Vacuum Leak** Engine running in all drive modes. The relationship between the MAP Sensor and TP Sensor exceeds a predetermined value for a given engine speed. If vacuum drops below 1.5 in. Hg with engine rpm at more than 2000 rpm at closed throttle, or if an unexpectedly high intake manifold airflow exists that can lead to increased engine speed and puts the NGC (Ram) into a High Airflow Protection Limiting mode; in this case, rpm limits for when a TP Sensor and/or MAP Sensor limp-in fault is present. **Possible Causes:** • Vacuum leak in hoses or component connections • High resistance or resistance to ground in MAP 5v supply or signal circuit • MAP Sensor has failed • High resistance in MAP ground circuit • TP Sensor has failed or is improperly adjusted • High resistance or resistance to ground in TP Sensor 5v supply or signal circuit • High resistance in TP Sensor ground circuit • PCM has failed

DTC	Trouble Code Title, Conditions & Possible Causes
DTC: P2096 **2T CCM** **Years:** 2005, 2006, 2007 **Models:** Grand Cherokee, Liberty, Pacifica, PT Cruiser, Ram Truck, Sebring, Stratus, Wrangler **Engines:** All **Transmissions:** All	**Downstream Fuel System 1/2 Lean** Engine running in closed loop mode. Ambient/battery temperature above 20F (−7C). Altitude below 8500 feet. Fuel level is more than 15%. If the PCM adds downstream short-term compensation to long-term adaptive, and a certain percentage is exceeded for 2 trips, a freeze frame is stored, the MIL illuminates and a DTC is set. **Possible Causes:** • Exhaust leak • Engine mechanical problem • O2 Sensor has failed • O2 Sensor signal circuit or return circuit problem • Fuel contamination
DTC: P2097 **2T CCM** **Years:** 2005, 2006, 2007 **Models:** Liberty, Pacifica, Ram Truck, Sebring, Stratus **Engines:** All **Transmissions:** All	**Downstream Fuel System 1/2 Rich** Engine running in closed loop mode. Ambient/battery temperature above 20F (−7C). Altitude below 8500 feet. Fuel level is more than 15%. If the PCM adds downstream short-term compensation to long-term adaptive, and a certain percentage is exceeded for 2 trips, a freeze frame is stored, the MIL illuminates and a DTC is set. **Possible Causes:** • Exhaust leak • Engine mechanical problem • O2 Sensor No. 1/2 has failed • O2 Sensor No. 1/2 signal circuit or return circuit problem • Fuel contamination
DTC: P2098 **2T CCM** **Years:** 2005, 2006, 2007 **Models:** Grand Cherokee, Liberty, Pacifica, PT Cruiser, Ram Truck, Sebring, Stratus, Wrangler **Engines:** All **Transmissions:** All	**Downstream Fuel System 2/2 Lean** Engine running in closed loop mode. Ambient/battery temperature above 20F (−7C). Altitude below 8500 feet. Fuel level is more than 15%. If the PCM adds downstream short-term compensation to long-term adaptive, and a certain percentage is exceeded for 2 trips, a freeze frame is stored, the MIL illuminates and a DTC is set. **Possible Causes:** • Exhaust leak • Engine mechanical problem • O2 Sensor No. 2/2 has failed • O2 Sensor No. 2/2 signal circuit or return circuit problem • Fuel contamination
DTC: P2099 **2T CCM** **Years:** 2005, 2006, 2007 **Models:** Grand Cherokee, Liberty, Pacifica, PT Cruiser, Ram Truck, Sebring, Stratus, Wrangler **Engines:** All **Transmissions:** All	**Downstream Fuel System 2/2 Rich** Engine running in closed loop mode. Ambient/battery temperature above 20F (−7C). Altitude below 8500 feet. Fuel level is more than 15%. If the PCM adds downstream short-term compensation to long-term adaptive, and a certain percentage is exceeded for 2 trips, a freeze frame is stored, the MIL illuminates and a DTC is set. **Possible Causes:** • Exhaust leak • Engine mechanical problem • O2 Sensor No. 2/2 has failed • O2 Sensor No. 2/2 signal circuit or return circuit problem • Fuel contamination
DTC: P2100 **1T CCM** **Years:** 2005, 2006, 2007 **Models:** PT Cruiser, Ram Truck **Engines:** All **Transmissions:** All	**Electronic Throttle Control Motor Circuit Malfunction** Ignition on and the ETC motor is not is Limp Home mode. When the PCM detects an internal error or a short between the ETC Motor and the ETC Motor positive circuit in the ETC Motor Driver, this DTC will set. The ETC light will be flashing. **Possible Causes:** • Intermittent condition • Throttle plate or bore may have foreign object blockage • ETC positive circuit is open or is shorted to battery voltage, to ground, or to ETC negative circuit • ETC negative circuit is open or is shorted to battery voltage or to ground • Low battery voltage • ETC Motor or Throttle Body has failed • PCM has failed
DTC: P2101 **1T CCM** **Years:** 2005, 2006, 2007 **Models:** Ram Truck **Engines:** All **Transmissions:** All	**Electronic Throttle Control Motor Malfunction** With vehicle running and ETC motor is not is Limp Home mode, and the TPS adaptation is complete. The PCM recognizes too large of an error between the actual position of the throttle plate and the set point position. This DTC will set within 5 seconds. 3 good trips required to turn off MIL. The ETC light will be flashing. **Possible Causes:** • Throttle body assembly may have failed • Low battery voltage • PCM has failed

DTC	Trouble Code Title, Conditions & Possible Causes
DTC: P2101 **1T CCM** **Years:** 2005, 2006, 2007 **Models:** PT Cruiser **Engines:** All **Transmissions:** All	**Electronic Throttle Control Motor Malfunction** With vehicle running and ETC motor is not is Limp Home mode, and the TPS adaptation is complete. If the PCM recognizes the difference between the TPS set point and the TPS actual setting is 8 for more than 405ms, this DTC will set. **Possible Causes:** • Intermittent condition • Electronic throttle control motor operation has failed • Throttle position is out of adjustment or has malfunctioned
DTC: P2101 **1T ECM** **Years:** 2005, 2006, 2007 **Models:** Liberty **Engines:** 2.8L Diesel **Transmissions:** All	**EGR Airflow Control Valve Excessive Current Or Open Circuit** Ignition on; EGR Airflow Control Valve commanded ON (excessive current) or OFF (open circuit). If the ECM detects excessive voltage signal or no voltage signal (open) on the EGR Airflow Control Valve control circuit, this DTC will set. **Possible Causes:** • Intermittent condition • ASD Relay Output circuit is open • EGR Airflow Control Valve has failed • EGR Airflow Control Valve control circuit is open, shorted to voltage or to ground • ECM has failed
DTC: P2107 **1T CCM** **Years:** 2005, 2006, 2007 **Models:** PT Cruiser, Ram Ram Truck **Engines:** All **Transmissions:** All	**Electronic Throttle Control Module Processor Malfunction** Ignition is on. This condition is caused by an internal PCM failure. The module will attempt to reset, so you will be able to hear the throttle relearning. If the condition is continuous, the vehicle may not be drivable. The ETC light will be flashing. **Possible Causes:** • PCM requires reprogramming
DTC: P2108 **1T CCM** **Years:** 2005, 2006, 2007 **Models:** PT Cruiser, Ram truck **Engines:** All **Transmissions:** All	**Electronic Throttle Control Module Processor Malfunction** Ignition is on. This condition is caused by an internal PCM failure. Customer may experience an extended cranking condition, with limited driving and a rough idle. This code will set within 5 seconds. The ETC light will be flashing. **Possible Causes:** • PCM requires reprogramming
DTC: P2110 **1T CCM** **Years:** 2005, 2006, 2007 **Models:** Ram Truck **Engines:** All **Transmissions:** All	**Electronic Throttle Control Forced Limited RPM** Ignition is on and ETC motor is working. When the PCM requests to limit engine speed, if the PWM is too high for 20.5 seconds and before P2118 sets. This one-trip fault will set within 5 seconds. The ETC light will be illuminated. **Possible Causes:** • Throttle plate stuck • ETC positive circuit is open or is shorted to ground • ETC negative circuit is open or is shorted to ground • ETC motor has failed • PCM has failed
DTC: P2111 **1T CCM** **Years:** 2005, 2006, 2007 **Models:** Ram Truck **Engines:** All **Transmissions:** All	**Electronic Throttle Control Forced Limited RPM** Ignition is on and battery voltage is more than 10v. If the TP Sensor does not return to Limp Home position at the end of this test, the DTC will set. This one-trip fault will set within 5 seconds. The ETC light will be flashing. **Possible Causes:** • Throttle plate stuck above Limp Home position • TP Sensors 1 & 2 both read 2.5v • ETC positive circuit is open or is shorted to ground or to battery voltage • ETC negative circuit is open or is shorted to ground • PCM has failed
DTC: P2112 **1T CCM** **Years:** 2005, 2006, 2007 **Models:** Ram Truck **Engines:** All **Transmissions:** All	**Electronic Throttle Control Unable To Open** Ignition is on and battery voltage is more than 10v. Just after the ignition is turned on, the throttle is opened and closed to test the system. If the TP Sensor does not return to Limp Home position at the end of this test, the DTC will set. This one-trip fault will set within 5 seconds. The ETC light will be flashing. **Possible Causes:** • Throttle plate stuck at or below Limp Home position • ETC positive circuit is open or is shorted to ground • ETC negative circuit is open or is shorted to ground or to battery voltage • PCM has failed

DTC	Trouble Code Title, Conditions & Possible Causes
DTC: P2115 **1T CCM** **Years:** 2005, 2006, 2007 **Models:** Ram Truck **Engines:** All **Transmissions:** All	**Accelerator Pedal Position Sensor No. 1 Minimum Stop Performance** Ignition is on. During in-plant mode the APP Sensors need to be checked to make sure that idle and full pedal travel can be reached on both Sensors. The test for this DTC is enabled once the test for DTC P2166 has passed. This DTC will set if the APP Sensor No. 1 has failed to achieve the required minimum value during in-plant testing. This one-trip fault will set within 5 seconds. The engine will only idle. **Possible Causes:** • APP Sensors must be reprogrammed to relearn
DTC: P2116 **1T CCM** **Years:** 2005, 2006, 2007 **Models:** Ram Truck **Engines:** All **Transmissions:** All	**Accelerator Pedal Position Sensor No. 2 Minimum Stop Performance** Ignition is on. During in-plant mode the APP Sensors need to be checked to make sure that idle and full pedal travel can be reached on both Sensors. The test for this DTC is enabled once the test for DTC P2167 has passed. This DTC will set if the APP Sensor No. 2 has failed to achieve the required minimum value during in-plant testing. This one-trip fault will set within 5 seconds. The engine will only idle. **Possible Causes:** • APP Sensors must be reprogrammed to relearn
DTC: P2118 **1T CCM** **Years:** 2005, 2006, 2007 **Models:** Ram Truck **Engines:** All **Transmissions:** All	**Electronic Throttle Control Motor Circuit Malfunction** Ignition is on and ETC motor is not in limp-home mode. When the PCM detects an internal error or short between the ETC motor and ETC motor positive circuits in the ETC motor driver. The ETC light will be flashing. **Possible Causes:** • Throttle plate or bore malfunctions • ETC positive circuit is open or is shorted to ground, battery voltage or ETC negative circuit • ETC negative circuit is open or is shorted to ground or to battery voltage • ETC motor has malfunctioned • PCM has failed
DTC: P2120 **1T ECM** **Years:** 2005, 2006, 2007 **Models:** Liberty **Engines:** 2.8L Diesel **Transmissions:** All	**APP Sensor No. 1 Circuit Plausibility Or Signal Voltage Too High Or Too Low** Ignition on. If the APP Sensor No. 1 and No. 2 signals do not agree (plausibility) or if Sensor No. 1 voltage signal is above 4.8v (too high) or below 0.29v (too low), this DTC will set. **Possible Causes:** • APP Sensor has failed • APP Sensor No. 1 5v supply circuit is open, shorted to ground, to voltage, or shorted to Sensor ground • APP Sensor ground circuit or signal circuit is open • Intermittent condition • APP Sensor signal circuit is shorted to the Sensor ground circuit • ECM has failed
DTC: P2122 **1T CCM** **Years:** 2005, 2006, 2007 **Models:** Ram Truck **Engines:** All **Transmissions:** All	**Accelerator Pedal Position Sensor No. 1 Circuit Low** Ignition is on and no other APP Sensor No. 1 DTCs are present. When APP Sensor No. 1 voltage is too low, the engine will additionally idle, if the brake pedal is pressed or has failed. Acceleration rate and engine output are limited. This one-trip fault will set within 5 seconds. The ETC light will be flashing. **Possible Causes:** • 5v supply circuit is open or shorted to ground • APP Sensor No. 1 signal circuit is open, shorted to ground or to Sensor return circuit • APP Sensor No. 1 has failed • PCM has failed
DTC: P2122 **1T CCM** **Years:** 2005, 2006, 2007 **Models:** PT Cruiser **Engines:** All **Transmissions:** All	**Accelerator Pedal Position Sensor No. 1 Circuit Low** Ignition is on. When APP Sensor No. 1 voltage is less than 0.2444v, or the circuit is shorted to ground or open for more than 120msec, this DTC will set. **Possible Causes:** • APP Sensor sweep • Intermittent condition • 5v supply circuit is open or shorted to ground • APP Sensor No. 1 signal circuit is open, shorted to ground or to Sensor return circuit • APP Sensor No. 1 has failed • PCM 5v supply circuit problem • PCM has failed

DTC	Trouble Code Title, Conditions & Possible Causes
DTC: P2123 **1T CCM** **Years:** 2005, 2006, 2007 **Models:** Ram Truck **Engines:** All **Transmissions:** All	**Accelerator Pedal Position Sensor No. 1 Circuit High** Ignition is on and no other APP Sensor No. 1 DTCs are present. When APP Sensor No. 1 voltage is too high, the engine will additionally idle, if the brake pedal is pressed or has failed. Acceleration rate and engine output are limited. This one-trip fault will set within 5 seconds. The ETC light will be flashing. **Possible Causes:** • APP Sensor No. 1 return circuit is open • APP Sensor No. 1 signal circuit is shorted to either 5v supply circuit • APP Sensor No. 1 has failed • PCM has failed
DTC: P2123 **1T CCM** **Years:** 2005, 2006, 2007 **Models:** PT Cruiser **Engines:** All **Transmissions:** All	**Accelerator Pedal Position Sensor No. 1 Circuit High** Ignition is on. When APP Sensor No. 1 voltage is more than 4.8192v, because of a short to voltage, this DTC will set. **Possible Causes:** • Intermittent condition • 5v supply circuit is shorted to battery voltage • APP Sensor No. 1 signal circuit is shorted to battery voltage or to 5v circuit • APP Sensor sweep • PCM has failed
DTC: P2125 **1T ECM** **Years:** 2005, 2006, 2007 **Models:** Liberty **Engines:** 2.8L Diesel **Transmissions:** All	**APP Sensor No. 2 Circuit Plausibility Or Signal Voltage Too High Or Too Low** Ignition on. If the APP Sensor No. 1 and No. 2 signals do not agree (plausibility) or if Sensor No. 1 voltage signal is above 2.4v (too high) or below 0.15v (too low), this DTC will set. **Possible Causes:** • APP Sensor has failed • APP Sensor No. 1 5v supply circuit is open, shorted to ground, to voltage, or shorted to Sensor ground • APP Sensor ground circuit or signal circuit is open • Intermittent condition • APP Sensor signal circuit is shorted to the Sensor ground circuit • ECM has failed
DTC: P2127 **1T CCM** **Years:** 2005, 2006, 2007 **Models:** Ram Truck **Engines:** All **Transmissions:** All	**Accelerator Pedal Position Sensor No. 2 Circuit Low** Ignition is on and no other APP Sensor No. 2 DTCs are present. When APP Sensor No. 2 voltage is too high, the engine will additionally idle, if the brake pedal is pressed or has failed. Acceleration rate and engine output are limited. This one-trip fault will set within 5 seconds. The ETC light will be flashing. **Possible Causes:** • 5v supply circuit is open or shorted to ground • APP Sensor No. 2 signal circuit is open, shorted to ground or to Sensor return circuit • APP Sensor No. 2 has failed • PCM has failed
DTC: P2127 **1T CCM** **Years:** 2005, 2006, 2007 **Models:** PT Cruiser **Engines:** All **Transmissions:** All	**Accelerator Pedal Position Sensor No. 2 Circuit Low** Ignition is on. When APP Sensor No. 2 voltage is less than 0.2444v, or the circuit is shorted to ground or open for more than 120msec, this DTC will set. **Possible Causes:** • APP Sensor sweep • Intermittent condition • 5v supply circuit is open or shorted to ground • APP Sensor No. 2 signal circuit is open, shorted to ground or to Sensor return circuit • APP Sensor No. 2 has failed • PCM 5v supply circuit problem • PCM has failed
DTC: P2128 **1T CCM** **Years:** 2005, 2006, 2007 **Models:** Ram Truck **Engines:** All **Transmissions:** All	**Accelerator Pedal Position Sensor No. 2 Circuit High** Ignition is on and no other APP Sensor No. 2 DTCs are present. When APP Sensor No. 2 voltage is too high, the engine will additionally idle, if the brake pedal is pressed or has failed. Acceleration rate and engine output are limited. This one-trip fault will set within 5 seconds. The ETC light will be flashing. **Possible Causes:** • APP Sensor No. 2 return circuit is open • APP Sensor No. 2 signal circuit is shorted to either 5v supply circuit • APP Sensor No. 2 has failed • PCM has failed

DTC	Trouble Code Title, Conditions & Possible Causes
DTC: P2123 **1T CCM** **Years:** 2005, 2006, 2007 **Models:** PT Cruiser **Engines:** All **Transmissions:** All	**Accelerator Pedal Position Sensor No. 2 Circuit High** Ignition is on. When APP Sensor No. 2 voltage is more than 4.8192v, because of a short to voltage, this DTC will set. **Possible Causes:** • Intermittent condition • 5v supply circuit is shorted to battery voltage • APP Sensor No. 1 signal circuit is shorted to battery voltage or to 5v circuit • APP Sensor sweep • PCM has failed
DTC: P2135 **1T CCM** **Years:** 2005, 2006, 2007 **Models:** Ram Truck **Engines:** All **Transmissions:** All	**Throttle Position Sensors 1 & 2 Correlation** Ignition is on and no other TP Sensor DTCs are present. The PCM recognizes that TP Sensors 1 and 2 are not coherent, this one-trip fault will set within 5 seconds. The ETC light will be illuminated. **Possible Causes:** • TP Sensor No. 1 or 2 signal circuit is shorted to ground or to battery voltage • TP Sensor No. 1 or 2 signal circuit has high resistance • 5v supply circuit has high resistance • 5v supply circuit shorted to ground • TP Sensor ground circuit has high resistance • TP Sensor No. 1 signal circuit is shorted to Sensor No. 2 signal circuit • TP Sensor has failed • PCM has failed
DTC: P2135 **1T CCM** **Years:** 2005, 2006, 2007 **Models:** PT Cruiser **Engines:** All **Transmissions:** All	**Throttle Position Sensors 1 & 2 Voltage Correlation** Ignition is on. When the difference between TP Sensor No. 1 degrees and TP Sensor No. 2 degrees is more than 1.995 degrees, this DTC will set. **Possible Causes:** • Intermittent condition • 5v supply circuit has high resistance • TP Sensor signal circuit has high resistance • Ground signal circuit shows high resistance • TP Sensors 1 & 2 require lab scope check • PCM has failed
DTC: P2138 **1T CCM** **Years:** 2005, 2006, 2007 **Models:** Ram Truck **Engines:** All **Transmissions:** All	**Accelerator Pedal Position Sensors 1 & 2 Correlation** Ignition is on and no other APP Sensor DTCs are present. The PCM recognizes that APP Sensors 1 and 2 are not coherent. Acceleration rate and engine output are limited. This one-trip fault will set within 5 seconds. The ETC light will be flashing. **Possible Causes:** • APP Sensor No. 1 or 2 signal circuit has high resistance • APP Sensor No. 1 or 2 return circuit has high resistance • 5v supply circuit has high resistance • APP Sensor has failed • PCM has failed
DTC: P2138 **1T CCM** **Years:** 2005, 2006, 2007 **Models:** PT Cruiser **Engines:** All **Transmissions:** All	**Accelerator Pedal Position Sensors 1 & 2 Voltage Correlation** Ignition is on. DTCs P2122, 2123, 2127 and 2128 are not present. When APP Sensor No. 1 voltage is 1.7 times the APP Sensor No. 2 voltage, and this equals more than 0.2v for 120msec, this DTC will set. **Possible Causes:** • Intermittent condition • 5v supply circuit is open or is shorted to ground • APP Sensor signal circuit has high resistance • 5v supply circuit has high resistance • Ground signal circuit shows high resistance • APP Sensors 1 & 2 require lab scope check • PCM has failed
DTC: P2141 **1T ECM** **Years:** 2005, 2006, 2007 **Models:** Liberty **Engines:** 2.8L Diesel **Transmissions:** All	**EGR Airflow Control Valve Short-To-Ground Circuit** Ignition on; EGR Airflow Control Valve commanded OFF. If the ECM detects no voltage signal on the EGR Airflow Control Valve control circuit, this DTC will set. **Possible Causes:** • Intermittent condition • ASD Relay Output circuit open • EGR Airflow Control Valve has failed • EGR Airflow Control Valve control circuit is open, shorted to ground • ECM has failed

DTC	Trouble Code Title, Conditions & Possible Causes
DTC: P2142 **1T ECM** **Years:** 2005, 2006, 2007 **Models:** Liberty **Engines:** 2.8L Diesel **Transmissions:** All	**EGR Airflow Control Valve Short Circuit** Ignition on; EGR Airflow Control Valve commanded ON. If the ECM detects excessive voltage signal on the EGR Airflow Control Valve control circuit, this DTC will set. **Possible Causes:** • Intermittent condition • EGR Airflow Control Valve has failed • EGR Airflow Control Valve control circuit is shorted to voltage • ECM has failed
DTC: P2147 **1T CCM** **Years:** 2005, 2006, 2007 **Models:** Liberty **Engines:** 2.8L Diesel **Transmissions:** All	**Fuel Injector Bank 1 Open Circuit** Engine running. ECM detects unexpected current flow through injector control circuit. **Possible Causes:** • Intermittent condition • Fuel injector control circuit is open or is shorted to ground • Fuel injector has failed • ECM has failed
DTC: P2148 **1T CCM** **Years:** 2005, 2006, 2007 **Models:** Liberty **Engines:** 2.8L Diesel **Transmissions:** All	**Fuel Injector Bank 1 Short Circuit** Engine running. The ECM detects unexpected current flow through the injector control circuit. **Possible Causes:** • Intermittent condition • Fuel injector control circuit is shorted to ground or to voltage • Fuel injector control circuits are shorted together • Fuel injector has failed • ECM has failed
DTC: P2150 **1T CCM** **Years:** 2005, 2006, 2007 **Models:** Liberty **Engines:** 2.8L Diesel **Transmissions:** All	**Fuel Injector Bank 2 Open Circuit** Engine running. The ECM detects unexpected current flow through the injector control circuit. **Possible Causes:** • Intermittent condition • Fuel injector control circuit is open or is shorted to ground • Fuel injector has failed • ECM has failed
DTC: P2148 **1T CCM** **Years:** 2005, 2006, 2007 **Models:** Liberty **Engines:** 2.8L Diesel **Transmissions:** All	**Fuel Injector Bank 2 Short Circuit** Engine running. The ECM detects unexpected current flow through the injector control circuit. **Possible Causes:** • Intermittent condition • Fuel injector control circuit is shorted to ground or to voltage • Fuel injector control circuits are shorted together • Fuel injector has failed • ECM has failed
DTC: P2161 **1T CCM** **Years:** 2005, 2006, 2007 **Models:** Ram Truck **Engines:** All **Transmissions:** All	**Vehicle Speed Sensor No. 2 Erratic** Ignition is on and battery voltage is greater than 10v. Transmission is in Drive or Reverse. The PCM recognizes the VSS 2 speed signal is erratic or high. No MIL and no ETC light. The cruise control is disabled. **Possible Causes:** • Active Bus or Communications DTCs • Incorrect tire circumference • PCM has failed
DTC: P2166 **1T CCM** **Years:** 2005, 2006, 2007 **Models:** Ram Truck **Engines:** All **Transmissions:** All	**Accelerator Pedal Position Sensor No. 1 Maximum Stop Performance** Ignition is on. During in-plant mode the APP Sensors need to be checked to make sure that idle and full pedal travel can be reached on both Sensors. This DTC will set if the APP Sensor No. 1 has failed to achieve the required maximum value during in-plant testing. This one-trip fault will set within 5 seconds. The engine will only idle. **Possible Causes:** • In-Plant test failure • APP Sensors must be reprogrammed to relearn
DTC: P2167 **1T CCM** **Years:** 2005, 2006, 2007 **Models:** Ram Truck **Engines:** All **Transmissions:** All	**Accelerator Pedal Position Sensor No. 2 Maximum Stop Performance** Ignition is on. During in-plant mode the APP Sensors need to be checked to make sure that idle and full pedal travel can be reached on both Sensors. This DTC will set if the APP Sensor No. 2 has failed to achieve the required maximum value during in-plant testing. This one-trip fault will set within 5 seconds. The engine will only idle. **Possible Causes:** • In-Plant test failure • APP Sensors must be reprogrammed to relearn

DTC	Trouble Code Title, Conditions & Possible Causes
DTC: P2172 **1T CCM** **Years:** 2005, 2006, 2007 **Models:** Ram Truck **Engines:** All **Transmissions:** All	**High Airflow/Vacuum Leak Detected (Instantaneous Accumulation)** Ignition is on and engine running with no MAP Sensor DTCs present. A large vacuum leak has been detected or both of the TP Sensors have failed, based on their position being 2.5v and the calculated MAP value is less than the actual MAP, minus an Offset value. This one-trip fault will set within 5 seconds. The ETC light will flash. **Possible Causes:** • Vacuum leak • 5v supply circuit has high resistance or is shorted to ground • MAP signal circuit has high resistance or is shorted to ground • TP Sensor ground circuit has high resistance • TP Sensor signal circuit is shorted to ground • TP Sensor return circuit has high resistance • MAP Sensor has failed • TP Sensor has failed • PCM has failed
DTC: P2173 **1T CCM** **Years:** 2005, 2006, 2007 **Models:** Ram Truck **Engines:** All **Transmissions:** All	**High Airflow/Vacuum Leak Detected (Slow Accumulation)** Ignition is on and engine running with no MAP Sensor DTCs present. A large vacuum leak has been detected or both of the TP Sensors have failed, based on their position being 2.5v and the calculated MAP value is less than the Gas Flow Adaptation value. This one-trip fault will set within 5 seconds. The ETC light will flash. **Possible Causes:** • Vacuum leak • 5v supply circuit has high resistance or is shorted to ground • MAP signal circuit has high resistance or is shorted to ground • TP Sensor ground circuit has high resistance • TP Sensor signal circuit is shorted to ground • TP Sensor return circuit has high resistance • MAP Sensor has failed • TP Sensor has failed • PCM has failed
DTC: P2174 **1T CCM** **Years:** 2005, 2006, 2007 **Models:** Ram Truck **Engines:** All **Transmissions:** All	**Low Airflow/Vacuum Leak Detected (Instantaneous Accumulation)** Ignition is on and engine running with no MAP Sensor DTCs present. The PCM calculated the MAP value is greater than actual MAP value, plus an Offset value. 3 good trips required to turn off MIL. The ETC light will flash. **Possible Causes:** • Restricted air inlet system • 5v supply circuit has high resistance or is shorted to ground • MAP signal circuit has high resistance or is shorted to ground • TP Sensor ground circuit has high resistance • TP Sensor signal circuit is shorted to ground • TP Sensor return circuit has high resistance • MAP Sensor has failed • TP Sensor has failed • PCM has failed
DTC: P2175 **1T CCM** **Years:** 2005, 2006, 2007 **Models:** Ram Truck **Engines:** All **Transmissions:** All	**Low Airflow/Vacuum Leak Detected (Slow Accumulation)** Ignition is on and engine running with no MAP Sensor DTCs present. The PCM calculated the MAP value is greater than actual MAP value, plus an Offset value. This DTC will set in 5 seconds after occurrence. 3 good trips required to turn off MIL. The ETC light will flash. **Possible Causes:** • Restricted air inlet system • 5v supply circuit has high resistance or is shorted to ground • MAP signal circuit has high resistance or is shorted to ground • TP Sensor ground circuit has high resistance • TP Sensor signal circuit is shorted to ground • TP Sensor return circuit has high resistance • MAP Sensor has failed • TP Sensor has failed • PCM has failed

DTC	Trouble Code Title, Conditions & Possible Causes
DTC: P2181 **2T CCM** **Years:** 2005, 2006, 2007 **Models:** Ram Truck **Engines:** All **Transmissions:** All	**Cooling System Performance** Ignition is on and engine running with no ECT Sensor DTCs present. The PCM recognizes that the ECT has failed its self-coherence test. The coolant temperature should only change at a certain rate. If this rate is too slow or too fast, this DTC will set. 3 good trips required to turn off MIL. The ETC light will illuminate on first trip failure. **Possible Causes:** • Low coolant level • ECT signal circuit is open or shorted to ground, Sensor ground, or battery voltage • ECT Sensor ground circuit is open • Thermostat has failed • ECT Sensor has failed • PCM has failed
DTC: P2226 **1T ECM** **Years:** 2005, 2006, 2007 **Models:** Liberty **Engines:** 2.8L Diesel **Transmissions:** All	**ECM Barometric Pressure Error** Ignition on. ECM detects an internal failure. **Possible Causes:** • ECM has failed • Intermittent condition
DTC: P2264 **1T ECM** **Years:** 2005, 2006, 2007 **Models:** Liberty **Engines:** 2.8L Diesel **Transmissions:** All	**Water In Fuel Voltage Above Upper Limit Or Below Lower Limit** Ignition on. If the ECM detects high voltage (above upper limit) or low voltage (below lower limit) on the Water In Fuel Sensor signal circuit, this DTC will set. **Possible Causes:** • Intermittent condition • WIF Sensor signal circuit is open or is shorted to voltage (high) or to ground (low) • WIF Sensor ground circuit is open • WIF Sensor signal and ground circuits are shorted together (low) • WIF Sensor has failed • FCM has failed (low) • ECM has failed (high)
DTC: P2294 **1T ECM** **Years:** 2005, 2006, 2007 **Models:** Liberty **Engines:** 2.8L Diesel **Transmissions:** All	**Fuel Pressure Solenoid Short-To-Ground Circuit** Ignition on; ECM Fuel Pressure Solenoid commanded OFF. If the ECM detects a short-to-ground on the control circuit, this DTC will set. **Possible Causes:** • FP Solenoid circuit(s) open, shorted to voltage, shorted to ground, or shorted together • Intermittent condition • FP Solenoid has failed • ECM has failed
DTC: P2296 **1T ECM** **Years:** 2005, 2006, 2007 **Models:** Liberty **Engines:** 2.8L Diesel **Transmissions:** All	**Fuel Pressure Solenoid Short Circuit** Ignition on; ECM Fuel Pressure Solenoid commanded ON. If the ECM detects excessive current on the control circuit, this DTC will set. **Possible Causes:** • FP Solenoid circuit(s) open, shorted to voltage, shorted to ground, or shorted together • Intermittent condition • FP Solenoid has failed • ECM has failed
DTC: P2299 **1T CCM** **Years:** 2005, 2006, 2007 **Models:** Ram Truck **Engines:** All **Transmissions:** All	**Brake Pedal Position/Accelerator Pedal Position Incompatible** Ignition is on and no Brake or APPS DTCs present. The PCM recognizes that a brake application following the APPS showing a fixed pedal opening. Temporary or permanent in nature. Internally, the PCM will reduce throttle opening below driver demand. This one-trip fault code will set in 5 seconds. The ETC light will illuminate and will only stay on while the DTC is active. **Possible Causes:** • Customer pressing accelerator pedal, then pressing brake pedal and holds both down at the same time • Stop lamp switch has failed • APP Sensor has failed
DTC: P2300 **1T CCM** **Years:** 2005, 2006, 2007 **Models:** PT Cruiser **Engines:** All **Transmissions:** All	**Ignition Coil No. 1 Secondary Circuit Low** Ignition is on. If the PCM detects an open or short to ground on the Ignition Coil No. 1 control circuit for more than 15 coil change requests, it will set this DTC. **Possible Causes:** • Ignition Coil No. 1 is damaged or it has failed • ASD relay output circuit problems • Ignition coil driver circuit is shorted to ground • PCM has failed

DTC	Trouble Code Title, Conditions & Possible Causes
DTC: P2301 **1T CCM** **Years:** 2005, 2006, 2007 **Models:** PT Cruiser **Engines:** All **Transmissions:** All	**Ignition Coil No. 1 Secondary Circuit High** Ignition is on. If the PCM detects a short to voltage on the Ignition Coil No. 1 control circuit for more than 15 coil change requests, it will set this DTC. **Possible Causes:** • ASD relay output circuit problems • Ignition coil driver circuit is open • Ignition Coil No. 1 is damaged or it has failed • Ignition coil driver circuit is shorted to ASD output circuit • PCM has failed • Intermittent condition
DTC: P2302 **1T CCM** **Years:** 2005, 2006, 2007 **Models:** Grand Cherokee, Liberty, Pacifica, PT Cruiser, Ram Truck, Sebring, Stratus, Wrangler **Engines:** All **Transmissions:** All	**Ignition Coil No. 1 Secondary Circuit Insufficient Ionization** Engine started; and the PCM detected the Ignition Coil No. 1 secondary "burn time" was insufficient, or it was missing. **Possible Causes:** • Intermittent condition • Cylinder No. 1 spark plug or wire is damaged or it has failed • Ignition Coil No. 1 is damaged or it has failed • Ignition coil control circuit is open or shorted to ground • ASD relay output circuit problems • PCM has failed
DTC: P2303 **1T CCM** **Years:** 2005, 2006, 2007 **Models:** PT Cruiser **Engines:** All **Transmissions:** All	**Ignition Coil No. 2 Secondary Circuit Low** Ignition is on. If the PCM detects an open or short to ground on the Ignition Coil No. 2 control circuit for more than 15 coil change requests, it will set this DTC. **Possible Causes:** • Ignition Coil No. 2 is damaged or it has failed • ASD relay output circuit problems • Ignition coil driver circuit is shorted to ground • PCM has failed
DTC: P2304 **1T CCM** **Years:** 2005, 2006, 2007 **Models:** PT Cruiser **Engines:** All **Transmissions:** All	**Ignition Coil No. 2 Secondary Circuit High** Ignition is on. If the PCM detects a short to voltage on the Ignition Coil No. 2 control circuit for more than 15 coil change requests, it will set this DTC. **Possible Causes:** • ASD relay output circuit problems • Ignition coil driver circuit is open • Ignition Coil No. 2 is damaged or it has failed • Ignition coil driver circuit is shorted to ASD output circuit • PCM has failed • Intermittent condition
DTC: P2305 **1T CCM** **Years:** 2005, 2006, 2007 **Models:** Grand Cherokee, Liberty, Pacifica, PT Cruiser, Ram Truck, Sebring, Stratus, Wrangler **Engines:** All **Transmissions:** All	**Ignition Coil No. 2 Secondary Circuit Insufficient Ionization** Engine started; and the PCM detected the Ignition Coil No. 2 secondary "burn time" was insufficient, or it was missing. **Possible Causes:** • Intermittent condition • Cylinder No. 2 spark plug or wire is damaged or it has failed • Ignition Coil No. 2 is damaged or it has failed • Ignition coil control circuit is open or shorted to ground • ASD relay output circuit problems • PCM has failed
DTC: P2308 **1T CCM** **Years:** 2005, 2006, 2007 **Models:** Grand Cherokee, Liberty, Pacifica, PT Cruiser, Ram Truck, Sebring, Stratus, Wrangler **Engines:** All **Transmissions:** All	**Ignition Coil No. 3 Secondary Circuit Insufficient Ionization** Engine started; and the PCM detected the Ignition Coil No. 3 secondary "burn time" was insufficient, or it was missing. **Possible Causes:** • Intermittent condition • Cylinder No. 3 spark plug or wire is damaged or it has failed • Ignition Coil No. 3 is damaged or it has failed • Ignition coil control circuit is open or shorted to ground • ASD relay output circuit problems • PCM has failed

DTC	Trouble Code Title, Conditions & Possible Causes
DTC: P2311 **1T CCM** **Years:** 2005, 2006, 2007 **Models:** Grand Cherokee, Liberty, Pacifica, PT Cruiser, Ram Truck, Sebring, Stratus, Wrangler **Engines:** All **Transmissions:** All	**Ignition Coil No. 4 Secondary Circuit Insufficient Ionization** Engine started; and the PCM detected the Ignition Coil No. 4 secondary "burn time" was insufficient, or it was missing. **Possible Causes:** • Intermittent condition • Cylinder No. 4 spark plug or wire is damaged or it has failed • Ignition Coil No. 4 is damaged or it has failed • Ignition coil control circuit is open or shorted to ground • ASD relay output circuit problems • PCM has failed
DTC: P2314 **1T CCM** **Years:** 2005, 2006, 2007 **Models:** Grand Cherokee, Liberty, Pacifica, PT Cruiser, Ram Truck, Sebring, Stratus, Wrangler **Engines:** All **Transmissions:** All	**Ignition Coil No. 5 Secondary Circuit Insufficient Ionization** Engine started; and the PCM detected the Ignition Coil No. 5 secondary "burn time" was insufficient, or it was missing. **Possible Causes:** • Intermittent condition • Cylinder No. 5 spark plug or wire is damaged or it has failed • Ignition Coil No. 5 is damaged or it has failed • Ignition coil control circuit is open or shorted to ground • ASD relay output circuit problems • PCM has failed
DTC: P2317 **1T CCM** **Years:** 2005, 2006, 2007 **Models:** Grand Cherokee, Liberty, Pacifica, PT Cruiser, Ram Truck, Sebring, Stratus, Wrangler **Engines:** All **Transmissions:** All	**Ignition Coil No. 6 Secondary Circuit Insufficient Ionization** Engine started; and the PCM detected the Ignition Coil No. 6 secondary "burn time" was insufficient, or it was missing. **Possible Causes:** • Intermittent condition • Cylinder No. 6 spark plug or wire is damaged or it has failed • Ignition Coil No. 6 is damaged or it has failed • Ignition coil control circuit is open or shorted to ground • ASD relay output circuit problems • PCM has failed
DTC: P2320 **1T CCM** **Years:** 2005, 2006, 2007 **Models:** Grand Cherokee, Liberty, Pacifica, PT Cruiser, Ram Truck, Sebring, Stratus, Wrangler **Engines:** All **Transmissions:** All	**Ignition Coil No. 7 Secondary Circuit Insufficient Ionization** Engine started; and the PCM detected the Ignition Coil No. 7 secondary "burn time" was insufficient, or it was missing. **Possible Causes:** • Cylinder No. 7 spark plug or wire is damaged or it has failed • Ignition Coil No. 7 is damaged or it has failed • Ignition coil control circuit is open or shorted to ground • PCM has failed
DTC: P2323 **1T CCM** **Years:** 2005, 2006, 2007 **Models:** Grand Cherokee, Liberty, Pacifica, PT Cruiser, Ram Truck, Sebring, Stratus, Wrangler **Engines:** All **Transmissions:** All	**Ignition Coil No. 8 Secondary Circuit Insufficient Ionization** Engine started; and the PCM detected the Ignition Coil No. 8 secondary "burn time" was insufficient, or it was missing. **Possible Causes:** • Cylinder No. 8 spark plug or wire is damaged or it has failed • Ignition Coil No. 8 is damaged or it has failed • Ignition coil control circuit is open or shorted to ground • PCM has failed
DTC: P2431 **2T CCM** **Years:** 2005, 2006, 2007 **Models:** Sebring, Stratus **Engines:** All **Transmissions:** All	**MAF Sensor Malfunction** Engine running; no other MAF Sensor faults are present; Air Injection system is active. If the PCM detects the MAF Sensor has an excessive amount of airflow or not enough airflow through it, this DTC will set. **Possible Causes:** • Air Injection system may be damaged, restricted or disconnected • ASD relay output circuit failure • MAF Sensor internal failure • MAF signal circuit open or shorted to ground or to ASD relay output circuit or to battery voltage • MAF signal circuit is shorted to sensor ground circuit • MAF Sensor ground circuit is open • PCM has failed.

DTC	Trouble Code Title, Conditions & Possible Causes
DTC: P2432 **1T CCM** **Years:** 2005, 2006, 2007 **Models:** Sebring, Stratus **Engines:** All **Transmissions:** All	**MAF Sensor High** Engine running between 600-3500 rpm; TP sensor voltage is less than 1.2v for more than 1.7 seconds; battery voltage is more than 10v. If the PCM detects the MAF sensor signal is greater than 4.9267v, this DTC will set. **Possible Causes:** • MAF signal circuit open or shorted to ground or to ASD relay output circuit or to battery voltage • MAF Sensor internal failure • MAF signal circuit is shorted to sensor ground circuit • MAF Sensor ground circuit is open • PCM has failed.
DTC: P2433 **1T CCM** **Years:** 2005, 2006, 2007 **Models:** Sebring, Stratus **Engines:** All **Transmissions:** All	**MAF Sensor Low** Engine running between 600-3500 rpm; TP sensor voltage is less than 1.2v for more than 1.7 seconds; battery voltage is more than 10v. If the PCM detects the MAF sensor signal is less than 0.07829v, this DTC will set. **Possible Causes:** • ASD relay output circuit problem • MAF Sensor internal failure • MAF signal circuit is shorted to ground or to sensor ground circuit • PCM has failed.
DTC: P2448 **2T CCM** **Years:** 2005, 2006, 2007 **Models:** Sebring, Stratus **Engines:** All **Transmissions:** All	**Air Injection System High Flow** Engine running; Air Injection Pump is active. If the PCM detects there is too much airflow through the AI system, this DTC will set. **Possible Causes:** • Make a visual inspection of the AI system and components for any damage or disconnects • Exhaust 1-way valve has failed • Fused battery voltage output circuit problem • AI pump relay has failed • AI pump ground circuit problem • AI pump motor is damaged or has failed • AI passages are blocked or leaking • MAF sensor has an internal failure • MAF signal circuit is open, or is shorted to battery voltage or to ASD relay output circuit • MAF signal circuit is shorted to ground or to sensor ground circuit • MAF sensor ground circuit is open • PCM has failed.
DTC: P2503 **1T CCM** **Years:** 2005, 2006, 2007 **Models:** Grand Cherokee, Liberty, Pacifica, PT Cruiser, Ram Truck, Sebring, Stratus, Wrangler **Engines:** All **Transmissions:** All	**Charging System Voltage Low** Engine started; engine speed over 1157 rpm; PCM detected the Battery Sense voltage was 1v less than the Charging system voltage "goal" for 13.47 seconds during the CCM test. The PCM senses the battery voltage turns off the field driver and then senses the battery voltage again. If the voltages are the same, the DTC is set. **Possible Causes:** • Battery sense circuit has a high resistance condition • Generator ground circuit has a high resistance condition • Generator field ground circuit is open • Generator field control circuit is open or shorted to ground • Generator is damaged or it has failed
DTC: P2525 **1T ECM** **Years:** 2005, 2006, 2007 **Models:** Liberty **Engines:** 2.8L Diesel **Transmissions:** All	**Vacuum Reservoir Solenoid Open Circuit** Ignition on; Vacuum Reservoir Solenoid commanded OFF. If the ECM does not detect a voltage signal on the control circuit, this DTC will set. **Possible Causes:** • Intermittent condition • ASD Relay output circuit is open • Vacuum Reservoir Solenoid control circuit is open or is shorted to ground • Vacuum Reservoir Solenoid has failed • ECM has failed
DTC: P2527 **1T ECM** **Years:** 2005, 2006, 2007 **Models:** Liberty **Engines:** 2.8L Diesel **Transmissions:** All	**Vacuum Reservoir Solenoid Short-To-Ground** Ignition on; Vacuum Reservoir Solenoid commanded OFF. If the ECM does not detect a voltage signal on the control circuit, this DTC will set. **Possible Causes:** • Intermittent condition • ASD Relay output circuit is open • Vacuum Reservoir Solenoid control circuit is open or is shorted to ground • Vacuum Reservoir Solenoid has failed • ECM has failed

DTC	Trouble Code Title, Conditions & Possible Causes
DTC: P2700 **1T CCM** **Years:** 2005, 2006, 2007 **Models:** Grand Cherokee, Liberty, Ram Truck, Wrangler **Engines:** All **Transmissions:** All	**A/T L/R Inadequate Element Volume Detected** Engine started; transmission fluid temperature more than 110°F, vehicle driven, and the PCM updated the L/R volume (during a 3-1 or 2-1 Manual downshift) with the throttle angle less than 5 degrees, and it detected that the L/R volume fell below 16 during the test. **Possible Causes:** • L/R volume clutch index is too low • TCM L/R volume clutch circuit is damaged or has failed
DTC: P2701 **1T CCM** **Years:** 2005, 2006, 2007 **Models:** Grand Cherokee, Liberty, Ram Truck, Wrangler **Engines:** All **Transmissions:** All	**A/T 2C Inadequate Element Volume Detected** Engine started; transmission fluid temperature more than 110°F, vehicle driven, then after the PCM updated the 2C volume (during a 3-2 kickdown event) with the throttle angle from 10-54 degrees, the PCM detected that the 2C volume fell below 5 during the CCM test. **Possible Causes:** • 2C volume clutch index is too low • TCM 2C volume clutch circuit is damaged or has failed
DTC: P2702 **1T CCM** **Years:** 2005, 2006, 2007 **Models:** Grand Cherokee, Liberty, Ram Truck, Wrangler **Engines:** All **Transmissions:** All	**A/T O/D Inadequate Element Volume Detected** Engine started; transmission fluid temperature more than 110°F, vehicle driven, then after he PCM updated the O/D volume (during a 2-3 Upshift event) with the throttle angle from 10-54 degrees, the PCM detected that the O/D volume fell below 5 during the CCM test. **Possible Causes:** • O/D volume clutch index is too low • TCM O/D volume clutch circuit is damaged or has failed
DTC: P2703 **1T CCM** **Years:** 2005, 2006, 2007 **Models:** Grand Cherokee, Liberty, Ram Truck, Wrangler **Engines:** All **Transmissions:** All	**A/T U/D Inadequate Element Volume Detected** Engine started; transmission fluid temperature more than 110°F, vehicle driven, and the TCM updated the U/D volume (during a 4-3 kickdown) with the throttle angle from 10-54 degrees, and it detected that the U/D volume fell below 11 during the test. **Possible Causes:** • U/D volume clutch index is too low • TCM U/D volume clutch circuit is damaged or has failed
DTC: P2704 **1T CCM** **Years:** 2005, 2006, 2007 **Models:** Grand Cherokee, Liberty, Ram Truck, Wrangler **Engines:** All **Transmissions:** All	**A/T 4C Inadequate Element Volume Detected** Engine started; transmission fluid temperature more than 110°F, vehicle driven, then after the TCM updated the 4C volume (during a 3-4 Upshift event) with the throttle angle from 10-54 degrees, the PCM detected that the 4C volume fell below 5 during the CCM test. **Possible Causes:** • 4C volume clutch index is too low • TCM 4C volume clutch circuit is damaged or has failed
DTC: P2706 **1T CCM** **Years:** 2005, 2006, 2007 **Models:** Grand Cherokee, Liberty, Ram Truck, Wrangler **Engines:** All **Transmissions:** All	**A/T MS Solenoid Circuit Malfunction** Engine started; vehicle driven in a forward gear, and immediately after a gear ratio or pressure switch change, the TCM detected a detected a MS solenoid error. The PCM sets this code when it detects three consecutive solenoid continuity test faults; or 1 failure if the test is run in response to a gear ratio of pressure switch fault. **Possible Causes:** • Check for a loose connector to the MS solenoid (intermittent) • MS solenoid control circuit is open or shorted to ground • MS solenoid control circuit is shorted to system power (B+) • MS solenoid is damaged or it has failed • Transmission control relay output supply circuit is open • TCM MS solenoid circuit is damaged or it has failed

OBD II Trouble Code List (UXXXX Codes)

DTC	Trouble Code Title, Conditions & Possible Causes
DTC: U0101 **1T TCM** **Years:** 2005, 2006, 2007 **Models:** Grand Cherokee, Liberty, Pacifica, PT Cruiser, Ram Truck, Sebring, Stratus, Wrangler **Engines:** All **Transmissions:** All	**No TCM Bus Message** Engine running. Battery voltage more than 10v. No Bus messages are received from the TCM for 20 seconds. 2 trips required. **Possible Causes:** • PCI Bus unable to communicate with (DRBIII) scan tool • Fused ignition switch output incorrect (off-run-start) • Intermittent condition • PCM has failed

DTC	Trouble Code Title, Conditions & Possible Causes
DTC: U0101 **1T TCM** **Years:** 2005, 2006, 2007 **Models:** Ram Truck **Engines:** All **Transmissions:** All	**No TCM Bus Message** Ignition is on and battery voltage is 9-16v. Engine is running for more than 3 seconds. The PCM does not receive a Bus message from the TCM for 7 consecutive seconds. The circuit is continuously monitored. **Possible Causes:** • CAN C Bus failure open or shorted • PCM has failed
DTC: U0140 **1T BCM** **Years:** 2005, 2006, 2007 **Models:** Pacifica, Sebring, Stratus **Engines:** All **Transmissions:** All	**No Body Bus Message** Engine running. Battery voltage more than 10v. No Bus messages are received from the BCM for 20 seconds. **Possible Causes:** • Communication link with BCM has failed • PCI Bus circuit open • PCM has failed
DTC: U0155 **1T MIC** **Years:** 2005, 2006, 2007 **Models:** Grand Cherokee, Liberty, Pacifica, PT Cruiser, Ram Truck, Sebring, Stratus, Wrangler **Engines:** All **Transmissions:** All	**No Cluster Bus Message** Engine running. Battery voltage more than 10v. No Bus messages are received from the MIC (instrument cluster) for 20 seconds. **Possible Causes:** • Communication link with instrument cluster has failed • Instrument cluster operation improper or has failed • PCM has failed
DTC: U0168 **1T MIC** **Years:** 2005, 2006, 2007 **Models:** Grand Cherokee, Liberty, Pacifica, PT Cruiser, Ram Truck, Sebring, Stratus, Wrangler **Engines:** All **Transmissions:** All	**No SKIM Bus Message** Engine running or ignition on. Battery voltage more than 10v. No Bus or J1850 messages are received from the SKIM for 20 seconds. **Possible Causes:** • Intermittent operation • PCI Bus circuit open or shorted from PCM to SKIM • Loss of communication between PCM and SKIM • SKIM or PCM has failed
DTC: U110C **1T MIC** **Years:** 2005, 2006, 2007 **Models:** Pacifica, Sebring, Stratus **Engines:** All **Transmissions:** All	**No Fuel Level Bus Message** Ignition on. Battery voltage more than 10v. No fuel level Bus messages are received from the PCM for 20 seconds. **Possible Causes:** • PCI Bus circuit open between PCM and BCM • Fuel level Bus message circuit failure • BCM has failed

GLOSSARY

ABS: Anti-lock braking system. An electro-mechanical braking system which is designed to minimize or prevent wheel lock-up during braking.

ABSOLUTE PRESSURE: Atmospheric (barometric) pressure plus the pressure gauge reading.

ACCELERATOR PUMP: A small pump located in the carburetor that feeds fuel into the air/fuel mixture during acceleration.

ACCUMULATOR: A device that controls shift quality by cushioning the shock of hydraulic oil pressure being applied to a clutch or band.

ACTUATING MECHANISM: The mechanical output devices of a hydraulic system, for example, clutch pistons and band servos.

ACTUATOR: The output component of a hydraulic or electronic system.

ADVANCE: Setting the ignition timing so that spark occurs earlier before the piston reaches top dead center (TDC).

ADAPTIVE MEMORY (ADAPTIVE STRATEGY): The learning ability of the TCM or PCM to redefine its decision-making process to provide optimum shift quality.

AFTER TOP DEAD CENTER (ATDC): The point after the piston reaches the top of its travel on the compression stroke.

AIR BAG: Device on the inside of the car designed to inflate on impact of crash, protecting the occupants of the car.

AIR CHARGE TEMPERATURE (ACT) SENSOR: The temperature of the airflow into the engine is measured by an ACT sensor, usually located in the lower intake manifold or air cleaner.

AIR CLEANER: An assembly consisting of a housing, filter and any connecting ductwork. The filter element is made up of a porous paper, sometimes with a wire mesh screening, and is designed to prevent airborne particles from entering the engine through the carburetor or throttle body.

AIR INJECTION: One method of reducing harmful exhaust emissions by injecting air into each of the exhaust ports of an engine. The fresh air entering the hot exhaust manifold causes any remaining fuel to be burned before it can exit the tailpipe.

AIR PUMP: An emission control device that supplies fresh air to the exhaust manifold to aid in more completely burning exhaust gases.

AIR/FUEL RATIO: The ratio of air-to-gasoline by weight in the fuel mixture drawn into the engine.

ALDL (assembly line diagnostic link): Electrical connector for scanning ECM/PCM/TCM input and output devices.

ALIGNMENT RACK: A special drive-on vehicle lift apparatus/measuring device used to adjust a vehicle's toe, caster and camber angles.

ALL WHEEL DRIVE: Term used to describe a full time four wheel drive system or any other vehicle drive system that continuously delivers power to all four wheels. This system is found primarily on station wagon vehicles and SUVs not utilized for significant off road use.

ALTERNATING CURRENT (AC): Electric current that flows first in one direction, then in the opposite direction, continually reversing flow.

ALTERNATOR: A device which produces AC (alternating current) which is converted to DC (direct current) to charge the car battery.

AMMETER: An instrument, calibrated in amperes, used to measure the flow of an electrical current in a circuit. Ammeters are always connected in series with the circuit being tested.

AMPERAGE: The total amount of current (amperes) flowing in a circuit.

AMPLIFIER: A device used in an electrical circuit to increase the voltage of an output signal.

AMP/HR. RATING (BATTERY): Measurement of the ability of a battery to deliver a stated amount of current for a stated period of time. The higher the amp/hr. rating, the better the battery.

AMPERE: The rate of flow of electrical current present when one volt of electrical pressure is applied against one ohm of electrical resistance.

ANALOG COMPUTER: Any microprocessor that uses similar (analogous) electrical signals to make its calculations.

ANODIZED: A special coating applied to the surface of aluminum valves for extended service life.

ANTIFREEZE: A substance (ethylene or propylene glycol) added to the coolant to prevent freezing in cold weather.

ANTI-FOAM AGENTS: Minimize fluid foaming from the whipping action encountered in the converter and planetary action.

ANTI-WEAR AGENTS: Zinc agents that control wear on the gears, bushings, and thrust washers.

ANTI-LOCK BRAKING SYSTEM: A supplementary system to the base hydraulic system that prevents sustained lock-up of the wheels during braking as well as automatically controlling wheel slip.

ANTI-ROLL BAR: See stabilizer bar.

ARC: A flow of electricity through the air between two electrodes or contact points that produces a spark.

ARMATURE: A laminated, soft iron core wrapped by a wire that converts electrical energy to mechanical energy as in a motor or relay. When rotated in a magnetic field, it changes mechanical energy into electrical energy as in a generator.

ATDC: After Top Dead Center.

ATF: Automatic transmission fluid.

ATMOSPHERIC PRESSURE: The pressure on the Earth's surface caused by the weight of the air in the atmosphere. At sea level, this pressure is 14.7 psi at 32°F (101 kPa at 0°C).

ATOMIZATION: The breaking down of a liquid into a fine mist that can be suspended in air.

AUXILIARY ADD-ON COOLER: A supplemental transmission fluid cooling device that is installed in series with the heat exchanger (cooler), located inside the radiator, to provide additional support to cool the hot fluid leaving the torque converter.

AUXILIARY PRESSURE: An added fluid pressure that is introduced into a regulator or balanced valve system to control valve movement. The auxiliary pressure itself can be either a fixed or a variable value. (See balanced valve; regulator valve.)

AWD: All wheel drive.

AXIAL FORCE: A side or end thrust force acting in or along the same plane as the power flow.

AXIAL PLAY: Movement parallel to a shaft or bearing bore.

AXLE CAPACITY: The maximum load-carrying capacity of the axle itself, as specified by the manufacturer. This is usually a higher number than the GAWR.

AXLE RATIO: This is a number (3.07:1, 4.56:1, for example) expressing the ratio between driveshaft revolutions and wheel revolutions. A low numerical ratio allows the engine to work easier because it doesn't have to turn as fast. A high numerical ratio means that the engine has to turn more rpm's to move the wheels through the same number of turns.

BACKFIRE: The sudden combustion of gases in the intake or exhaust system that results in a loud explosion.

BACKLASH: The clearance or play between two parts, such as meshed gears.

BACKPRESSURE: Restrictions in the exhaust system that slow the exit of exhaust gases from the combustion chamber.

BAKELITE®: A heat resistant, plastic insulator material commonly used in printed circuit boards and transistorized components.

BALANCED VALVE: A valve that is positioned by opposing auxiliary hydraulic pressures and/or spring force. Examples include mainline regulator, throttle, and governor valves. (See regulator valve.)

BAND: A flexible ring of steel with an inner lining of friction material. When tightened around the outside of a drum, a planetary member is held stationary to the transmission/transaxle case.

BALL BEARING: A bearing made up of hardened inner and outer races between which hardened steel balls roll.

BALL JOINT: A ball and matching socket connecting suspension components (steering knuckle to lower control arms). It permits rotating movement in any direction between the components that are joined.

BARO (BAROMETRIC PRESSURE SENSOR): Measures the change in the intake manifold pressure caused by changes in altitude.

BAROMETRIC MANIFOLD ABSOLUTE PRESSURE (BMAP) SENSOR: Operates similarly to a conventional MAP sensor; reads intake manifold pressure and is also responsible for determining altitude and barometric pressure prior to engine operation.

BAROMETRIC PRESSURE: (See atmospheric pressure.)

BALLAST RESISTOR: A resistor in the primary ignition circuit that lowers voltage after the engine is started to reduce wear on ignition components.

BATTERY: A direct current electrical storage unit, consisting of the basic active materials of lead and sulfuric acid, which converts chemical energy into electrical energy. Used to provide current for the operation of the starter as well as other equipment, such as the radio, lighting, etc.

BEAD: The portion of a tire that holds it on the rim.

BEARING: A friction reducing, supportive device usually located between a stationary part and a moving part.

BEFORE TOP DEAD CENTER (BTDC): The point just before the piston reaches the top of its travel on the compression stroke.

BELTED TIRE: Tire construction similar to bias-ply tires, but using two or more layers of reinforced belts between body plies and the tread.

BEZEL: Piece of metal surrounding radio, headlights, gauges or similar components; sometimes used to hold the glass face of a gauge in the dash.

BIAS-PLY TIRE: Tire construction, using body ply reinforcing cords which run at alternating angles to the center line of the tread.

BI-METAL TEMPERATURE SENSOR: Any sensor or switch made of two dissimilar types of metal that bend when heated or cooled due to the different expansion rates of the alloys. These types of sensors usually function as an on/off switch.

BLOCK: See Engine Block.

BLOW-BY: Combustion gases, composed of water vapor and unburned fuel, that leak past the piston rings into the crankcase during normal engine operation. These gases are removed by the PCV system to prevent the buildup of harmful acids in the crankcase.

BOOK TIME: See Labor Time.

BOOK VALUE: The average value of a car, widely used to determine trade-in and resale value.

BOOST VALVE: Used at the base of the regulator valve to increase mainline pressure.

BORE: Diameter of a cylinder.

BRAKE CALIPER: The housing that fits over the brake disc. The caliper holds the brake pads, which are pressed against the discs by the caliper pistons when the brake pedal is depressed.

BRAKE HORSEPOWER (BHP): The actual horsepower available at the engine flywheel as measured by a dynamometer.

BRAKE FADE: Loss of braking power, usually caused by excessive heat after repeated brake applications.

BRAKE HORSEPOWER: Usable horsepower of an engine measured at the crankshaft.

BRAKE PAD: A brake shoe and lining assembly used with disc brakes.

BRAKE PROPORTIONING VALVE: A valve on the master cylinder which restricts hydraulic brake pressure to the wheels to a specified amount, preventing wheel lock-up.

BREAKAWAY: Often used by Chrysler to identify first-gear operation in D and 2 ranges. In these ranges, first-gear operation depends on a one-way roller clutch that holds on acceleration and releases (breaks away) on deceleration, resulting in a freewheeling coast-down condition.

BRAKE SHOE: The backing for the brake lining. The term is, however, usually applied to the assembly of the brake backing and lining.

BREAKER POINTS: A set of points inside the distributor, operated by a cam, which make and break the ignition circuit.

BRINNELLING: A wear pattern identified by a series of indentations at regular intervals. This condition is caused by a lack of lube, overload situations, and/or vibrations.

BTDC: Before Top Dead Center.

BUMP: Sudden and forceful apply of a clutch or band.

BUSHING: A liner, usually removable, for a bearing; an anti-friction liner used in place of a bearing.

CALIFORNIA ENGINE: An engine certified by the EPA for use in California only; conforms to more stringent emission regulations than Federal engine.

CALIPER: A hydraulically activated device in a disc brake system, which is mounted straddling the brake rotor (disc). The caliper contains at least one piston and two brake pads. Hydraulic pressure on the piston(s) forces the pads against the rotor.

CAPACITY: The quantity of electricity that can be delivered from a unit, as from a battery in ampere-hours, or output, as from a generator.

CAMBER: One of the factors of wheel alignment. Viewed from the front of the car, it is the inward or outward tilt of the wheel. The top of the tire will lean outward (positive camber) or inward (negative camber).

CAMSHAFT: A shaft in the engine on which are the lobes (cams) which operate the valves. The camshaft is driven by the crankshaft, via a belt, chain or gears, at one half the crankshaft speed.

CAPACITOR: A device which stores an electrical charge.

CARBON MONOXIDE (CO): A colorless, odorless gas given off as a normal byproduct of combustion. It is poisonous and extremely dangerous in confined areas, building up slowly to toxic levels without warning if adequate ventilation is not available.

CARBURETOR: A device, usually mounted on the intake manifold of an engine, which mixes the air and fuel in the proper proportion to allow even combustion.

CASTER: The forward or rearward tilt of an imaginary line drawn through the upper ball joint and the center of the wheel. Viewed from the sides, positive caster (forward tilt) lends directional stability, while negative caster (rearward tilt) produces instability.

CATALYTIC CONVERTER: A device installed in the exhaust system, like a muffler, that converts harmful byproducts of combustion into carbon dioxide and water vapor by means of a heat-producing chemical reaction.

CENTRIFUGAL ADVANCE: A mechanical method of advancing the spark timing by using flyweights in the distributor that react to centrifugal force generated by the distributor shaft rotation.

CENTRIFUGAL FORCE: The outward pull of a revolving object, away from the center of revolution. Centrifugal force increases with the speed of rotation.

CETANE RATING: A measure of the ignition value of diesel fuel. The higher the cetane rating, the better the fuel. Diesel fuel cetane rating is roughly comparable to gasoline octane rating.

CHECK VALVE: Any one-way valve installed to permit the flow of air, fuel or vacuum in one direction only.

CHOKE: The valve/plate that restricts the amount of air entering an engine on the induction stroke, thereby enriching the air/fuel ratio.

CHUGGLE: Bucking or jerking condition that may be engine related and may be most noticeable when converter clutch is engaged; similar to the feel of towing a trailer.

CIRCLIP: A split steel snapring that fits into a groove to hold various parts in place.

CIRCUIT BREAKER: A switch which protects an electrical circuit from overload by opening the circuit when the current flow exceeds a pre-determined level. Some circuit breakers must be reset manually, while most reset automatically.

CIRCUIT: Any unbroken path through which an electrical current can flow. Also used to describe fuel flow in some instances.

CIRCUIT, BYPASS: Another circuit in parallel with the major circuit through which power is diverted.

CIRCUIT, CLOSED: An electrical circuit in which there is no interruption of current flow.

CIRCUIT, GROUND: The non-insulated portion of a complete circuit used as a common potential point. In automotive circuits, the ground is composed of metal parts, such as the engine, body sheet metal, and frame and is usually a negative potential.

CIRCUIT, HOT: That portion of a circuit not at ground potential. The hot circuit is usually insulated and is connected to the positive side of the battery.

CIRCUIT, OPEN: A break or lack of contact in an electrical circuit, either intentional (switch) or unintentional (bad connection or broken wire).

CIRCUIT, PARALLEL: A circuit having two or more paths for current flow with common positive and negative tie points. The same voltage is applied to each load device or parallel branch.

CIRCUIT, SERIES: An electrical system in which separate parts are connected end to end, using one wire, to form a single path for current to flow.

CIRCUIT, SHORT: A circuit that is accidentally completed in an electrical path for which it was not intended.

CLAMPING (ISOLATION) DIODES: Diodes positioned in a circuit to prevent self-induction from damaging electronic components.

CLEARCOAT: A transparent layer which, when sprayed over a vehicle's paint job, adds gloss and depth as well as an additional protective coating to the finish.

CLUTCH: Part of the power train used to connect/disconnect power to the rear wheels.

CLUTCH, FLUID: The same as a fluid coupling. A fluid clutch or coupling performs the same function as a friction clutch by utilizing fluid friction and inertia as opposed to solid friction used by a friction clutch. (See fluid coupling.)

CLUTCH, FRICTION: A coupling device that provides a means of smooth and positive engagement and disengagement of engine torque to the vehicle powertrain. Transmission of power through the clutch is accomplished by bringing one or more rotating drive members into contact with complementing driven members.

COAST: Vehicle deceleration caused by engine braking conditions.

COEFFICIENT OF FRICTION: The amount of surface tension between two contacting surfaces; identified by a scientifically calculated number.

COIL: Part of the ignition system that boosts the relatively low voltage supplied by the car's electrical system to the high voltage required to fire the spark plugs.

COMBINATION MANIFOLD: An assembly which includes both the intake and exhaust manifolds in one casting.

COMBINATION VALVE: A device used in some fuel systems that routes fuel vapors to a charcoal storage canister instead of venting them into the atmosphere. The valve relieves fuel tank pressure and allows fresh air into the tank as the fuel level drops to prevent a vapor lock situation.

COMBUSTION CHAMBER: The part of the engine in the cylinder head where combustion takes place.

COMPOUND GEAR: A gear consisting of two or more simple gears with a common shaft.

COMPOUND PLANETARY: A gearset that has more than the three elements found in a simple gearset and is constructed by combining members of two planetary gearsets to create additional gear ratio possibilities.

COMPRESSION CHECK: A test involving removing each spark plug and inserting a gauge. When the engine is cranked, the gauge will record a pressure reading in the individual cylinder. General operating condition can be determined from a compression check.

COMPRESSION RATIO: The ratio of the volume between the piston and cylinder head when the piston is at the bottom of its stroke (bottom dead center) and when the piston is at the top of its stroke (top dead center).

COMPUTER: An electronic control module that correlates input data according to prearranged engineered instructions; used for the management of an actuator system or systems.

CONDENSER: An electrical device which acts to store an electrical charge, preventing voltage surges.

2. A radiator-like device in the air conditioning system in which refrigerant gas condenses into a liquid, giving off heat.

CONDUCTOR: Any material through which an electrical current can be transmitted easily.

CONNECTING ROD: The connecting link between the crankshaft and piston.

CONSTANT VELOCITY JOINT: Type of universal joint in a halfshaft assembly in which the output shaft turns at a constant angular velocity without variation, provided that the speed of the input shaft is constant.

CONTINUITY: Continuous or complete circuit. Can be checked with an ohmmeter.

CONTROL ARM: The upper or lower suspension components which are mounted on the frame and support the ball joints and steering knuckles.

CONVENTIONAL IGNITION: Ignition system which uses breaker points.

CONVERTER: (See torque converter.)

CONVERTER LOCKUP: The switching from hydrodynamic to direct mechanical drive, usually through the application of a friction element called the converter clutch.

COOLANT: Mixture of water and anti-freeze circulated through the engine to carry off heat produced by the engine.

CORROSION INHIBITOR: An inhibitor in ATF that prevents corrosion of bushings, thrust washers, and oil cooler brazed joints.

COUNTERSHAFT: An intermediate shaft which is rotated by a mainshaft and transmits, in turn, that rotation to a working part.

COUPLING PHASE: Occurs when the torque converter is operating at its greatest hydraulic efficiency. The speed differential between the impeller and the turbine is at its minimum. At this point, the stator freewheels, and there is no torque multiplication.

CRANKCASE: The lower part of an engine in which the crankshaft and related parts operate.

CRANKSHAFT: Engine component (connected to pistons by connecting rods) which converts the reciprocating (up and down) motion of pistons to rotary motion used to turn the driveshaft.

CURB WEIGHT: The weight of a vehicle without passengers or payload, but including all fluids (oil, gas, coolant, etc.) and other equipment specified as standard.

CURRENT: The flow (or rate) of electrons moving through a circuit. Current is measured in amperes (amp).

CURRENT FLOW CONVENTIONAL: Current flows through a circuit from the positive terminal of the source to the negative terminal (plus to minus).

CURRENT FLOW, ELECTRON: Current or electrons flow from the negative terminal of the source, through the circuit, to the positive terminal (minus to plus).

CV-JOINT: Constant velocity joint.

CYCLIC VIBRATIONS: The off-center movement of a rotating object that is affected by its initial balance, speed of rotation, and working angles.

CYLINDER BLOCK: See engine block.

CYLINDER HEAD: The detachable portion of the engine, usually fastened to the top of the cylinder block and containing all or most of the combustion chambers. On overhead valve engines, it contains the valves and their operating parts. On overhead cam engines, it contains the camshaft as well.

CYLINDER: In an engine, the round hole in the engine block in which the piston(s) ride.

DATA LINK CONNECTOR (DLC): Current acronym/term applied to the federally mandated, diagnostic junction connector that is used to monitor ECM/PC/TCM inputs, processing strategies, and outputs including diagnostic trouble codes (DTCs).

DEAD CENTER: The extreme top or bottom of the piston stroke.

DECELERATION BUMP: When referring to a torque converter clutch in the applied position, a sudden release of the accelerator pedal causes a forceful reversal of power through the drivetrain (engine braking), just prior to the apply plate actually being released.

DELAYED (LATE OR EXTENDED): Condition where shift is expected but does not occur for a period of time, for example, where clutch or band engagement does not occur as quickly as expected during part throttle or wide open throttle apply of accelerator or when manually downshifting to a lower range.

DETENT: A spring-loaded plunger, pin, ball, or pawl used as a holding device on a ratchet wheel or shaft. In automatic transmissions, a detent mechanism is used for locking the manual valve in place.

DETENT DOWNSHIFT: (See kickdown.)

DETERGENT: An additive in engine oil to improve its operating characteristics.

DETONATION: An unwanted explosion of the air/fuel mixture in the combustion chamber caused by excess heat and compression, advanced timing, or an overly lean mixture. Also referred to as "ping".

DEXRON®: A brand of automatic transmission fluid.

DIAGNOSTIC TROUBLE CODES (DTCs): A digital display from the control module memory that identifies the input, processor, or output device circuit that is related to the powertrain emission/driveability malfunction detected. Diagnostic trouble codes can be read by the MIL to flash any codes or by using a handheld scanner.

DIAPHRAGM: A thin, flexible wall separating two cavities, such as in a vacuum advance unit.

DIESELING: The engine continues to run after the car is shut off; caused by fuel continuing to be burned in the combustion chamber.

DIFFERENTIAL: A geared assembly which allows the transmission of motion between drive axles, giving one axle the ability to rotate faster than the other, as in cornering.

DIFFERENTIAL AREAS: When opposing faces of a spool valve are acted upon by the same pressure but their areas differ in size, the face with the larger area produces the differential force and valve movement. (See spool valve.)

DIFFERENTIAL FORCE: (See differential areas)

DIGITAL READOUT: A display of numbers or a combination of numbers and letters.

DIGITAL VOLT OHMMETER: An electronic diagnostic tool used to measure voltage, ohms and amps as well as several other functions, with the readings displayed on a digital screen in tenths, hundredths and thousandths.

DIODE: An electrical device that will allow current to flow in one direction only.

DIRECT CURRENT (DC): Electrical current that flows in one direction only.

DIRECT DRIVE: The gear ratio is 1:1, with no change occurring in the torque and speed input/output relationship.

DISC BRAKE: A hydraulic braking assembly consisting of a brake disc, or rotor, mounted on an axle shaft, and a caliper assembly containing, usually two brake pads which are activated by hydraulic pressure. The pads are forced against the sides of the disc, creating friction which slows the vehicle.

DISPERSANTS: Suspend dirt and prevent sludge buildup in a liquid, such as engine oil.

DOUBLE BUMP (DOUBLE FEEL): Two sudden and forceful applies of a clutch or band.

DISPLACEMENT: The total volume of air that is displaced by all pistons as the engine turns through one complete revolution.

DISTRIBUTOR: A mechanically driven device on an engine which is responsible for electrically firing the spark plug at a pre-determined point of the piston stroke.

DOHC: Double overhead camshaft.

DOUBLE OVERHEAD CAMSHAFT: The engine utilizes two camshafts mounted in one cylinder head. One camshaft operates the exhaust valves, while the other operates the intake valves.

DOWEL PIN: A pin, inserted in mating holes in two different parts allowing those parts to maintain a fixed relationship.

DRIVELINE: The drive connection between the transmission and the drive wheels.

DRIVE TRAIN: The components that transmit the flow of power from the engine to the wheels. The components include the clutch, transmission, driveshafts (or axle shafts in front wheel drive), U-joints and differential.

DRUM BRAKE: A braking system which consists of two brake shoes and one or two wheel cylinders, mounted on a fixed backing plate, and a brake drum, mounted on an axle, which revolves around the assembly.

DRY CHARGED BATTERY: Battery to which electrolyte is added when the battery is placed in service.

DVOM: Digital volt ohmmeter

DWELL: The rate, measured in degrees of shaft rotation, at which an electrical circuit cycles on and off.

DYNAMIC: An application in which there is rotating or reciprocating motion between the parts.

EARLY: Condition where shift occurs before vehicle has reached proper speed, which tends to labor engine after upshift.

EBCM: See Electronic Control Unit (ECU).

ECM: See Electronic Control Unit (ECU).

ECU: Electronic control unit.

ELECTRODE: Conductor (positive or negative) of electric current.

ELECTROLYSIS: A surface etching or bonding of current conducting transmission/transaxle components that may occur when grounding straps are missing or in poor condition.

ELECTROLYTE: A solution of water and sulfuric acid used to activate the battery. Electrolyte is extremely corrosive.

ELECTROMAGNET: A coil that produces a magnetic field when current flows through its windings.

ELECTROMAGNETIC INDUCTION: A method to create (generate) current flow through the use of magnetism.

ELECTROMAGNETISM: The effects surrounding the relationship between electricity and magnetism.

ELECTROMOTIVE FORCE (EMF): The force or pressure (voltage) that causes current movement in an electrical circuit.

ELECTRONIC CONTROL UNIT: A digital computer that controls engine (and sometimes transmission, brake or other vehicle system) functions based on data received from various sensors. Examples used by some manufacturers include Electronic Brake Control Module (EBCM), Engine Control Module (ECM), Powertrain Control Module (PCM) or Vehicle Control Module (VCM).

ELECTRONIC IGNITION: A system in which the timing and firing of the spark plugs is controlled by an electronic control unit, usually called a module. These systems have no points or condenser.

ELECTRONIC PRESSURE CONTROL (EPC) SOLENOID: A specially designed solenoid containing a spool valve and spring assembly to control fluid mainline pressure. A variable current flow, controlled by the ECM/PCM, varies the internal force of the solenoid on the spool valve and resulting mainline pressure. (See variable force solenoid.)

ELECTRONICS: Miniaturized electrical circuits utilizing semiconductors, solid-state devices, and printed circuits. Electronic circuits utilize small amounts of power.

ELECTRONIFICATION: The application of electronic circuitry to a mechanical device. Regarding automatic transmissions, electrification is incorporated into converter clutch lockup, shift scheduling, and line pressure control systems.

ELECTROSTATIC DISCHARGE (ESD): An unwanted, high-voltage electrical current released by an individual who has taken on a static charge of electricity. Electronic components can be easily damaged by ESD.

ELEMENT: A device within a hydrodynamic drive unit designed with a set of blades to direct fluid flow.

ENAMEL: Type of paint that dries to a smooth, glossy finish.

END BUMP (END FEEL OR SLIP BUMP): Firmer feel at end of shift when compared with feel at start of shift.

END-PLAY: The clearance/gap between two components that allows for expansion of the parts as they warm up, to prevent binding and to allow space for lubrication.

ENERGY: The ability or capacity to do work.

ENGINE: The primary motor or power apparatus of a vehicle, which converts liquid or gas fuel into mechanical energy.

ENGINE BLOCK: The basic engine casting containing the cylinders, the crankshaft main bearings, as well as machined surfaces for the mounting of other components such as the cylinder head, oil pan, transmission, etc.

ENGINE BRAKING: Use of engine to slow vehicle by manually downshifting during zero-throttle coast down.

ENGINE CONTROL MODULE (ECM): Manages the engine and incorporates output control over the torque converter clutch solenoid. (Note: Current designation for the ECM in late model vehicles is PCM.)

ENGINE COOLANT TEMPERATURE (ECT) SENSOR: Prevents converter clutch engagement with a cold engine; also used for shift timing and shift quality.

EP LUBRICANT: EP (extreme pressure) lubricants are specially formulated for use with gears involving heavy loads (transmissions, differentials, etc.).

ETHYL: A substance added to gasoline to improve its resistance to knock, by slowing down the rate of combustion.

ETHYLENE GLYCOL: The base substance of antifreeze.

EXHAUST MANIFOLD: A set of cast passages or pipes which conduct exhaust gases from the engine.

FAIL-SAFE (BACKUP) CONTROL: A substitute value used by the PCM/TCM to replace a faulty signal from an input sensor. The temporary value allows the vehicle to continue to be operated.

FAST IDLE: The speed of the engine when the choke is on. Fast idle speeds engine warm-up.

FEDERAL ENGINE: An engine certified by the EPA for use in any of the 49 states (except California).

FEEDBACK: A circuit malfunction whereby current can find another path to feed load devices.

FEELER GAUGE: A blade, usually metal, of precisely predetermined thickness, used to measure the clearance between two parts.

FILAMENT: The part of a bulb that glows; the filament creates high resistance to current flow and actually glows from the resulting heat.

FINAL DRIVE: An essential part of the axle drive assembly where final gear reduction takes place in the powertrain. In RWD applications and north-south FWD applications, it must also change the power flow direction to the axle shaft by ninety degrees. (Also see axle ratio).

FIRING ORDER: The order in which combustion occurs in the cylinders of an engine. Also the order in which spark is distributed to the plugs by the distributor.

FIRM: A noticeable quick apply of a clutch or band that is considered normal with medium to heavy throttle shift; should not be confused with harsh or rough.

FLAME FRONT: The term used to describe certain aspects of the fuel explosion in the cylinders. The flame front should move in a controlled pattern across the cylinder, rather than simply exploding immediately.

FLARE (SLIPPING): A quick increase in engine rpm accompanied by momentary loss of torque; generally occurs during shift.

FLAT ENGINE: Engine design in which the pistons are horizontally opposed. Porsche, Subaru and some old VW are common examples of flat engines.

FLAT RATE: A dealership term referring to the amount of money paid to a technician for a repair or diagnostic service based on that particular service versus dealership's labor time (NOT based on the actual time the technician spent on the job).

FLAT SPOT: A point during acceleration when the engine seems to lose power for an instant.

FLOODING: The presence of too much fuel in the intake manifold and combustion chamber which prevents the air/fuel mixture from firing, thereby causing a no-start situation.

FLUID: A fluid can be either liquid or gas. In hydraulics, a liquid is used for transmitting force or motion.

FLUID COUPLING: The simplest form of hydrodynamic drive, the fluid coupling consists of two look-alike members with straight radial varies referred to as the impeller (pump) and the turbine. Input torque is always equal to the output torque.

FLUID DRIVE: Either a fluid coupling or a fluid torque converter. (See hydrodynamic drive units.)

FLUID TORQUE CONVERTER: A hydrodynamic drive that has the ability to act both as a torque multiplier and fluid coupling. (See hydrodynamic drive units; torque converter.)

FLUID VISCOSITY: The resistance of a liquid to flow. A cold fluid (oil) has greater viscosity and flows more slowly than a hot fluid (oil).

FLYWHEEL: A heavy disc of metal attached to the rear of the crankshaft. It smoothes the firing impulses of the engine and keeps the crankshaft turning during periods when no firing takes place. The starter also engages the flywheel to start the engine.

FOOT POUND (ft. lbs., lbs. ft. or sometimes, ft. lb.): The amount of energy or work needed to raise an item weighing one pound, a distance of one foot.

FREEZE PLUG: A plug in the engine block which will be pushed out if the coolant freezes. Sometimes called expansion plugs, they protect the block from cracking should the coolant freeze.

FRICTION: The resistance that occurs between contacting surfaces. This relationship is expressed by a ratio called the coefficient of friction (CL).

FRICTION, COEFFICIENT OF: The amount of surface tension between two contacting surfaces; expressed by a scientifically calculated number.

FRONT END ALIGNMENT: A service to set caster, camber and toe-in to the correct specifications. This will ensure that the car steers and handles properly and that the tires wear properly.

FRICTION MODIFIER: Changes the coefficient of friction of the fluid between the mating steel and composition clutch/band surfaces during the engagement process and allows for a certain amount of intentional slipping for a good "shift-feel".

FRONTAL AREA: The total frontal area of a vehicle exposed to air flow.

FUEL FILTER: A component of the fuel system containing a porous paper element used to prevent any impurities from entering the engine through the fuel system. It usually takes the form of a canister-like housing, mounted in-line with the fuel hose, located anywhere on a vehicle between the fuel tank and engine.

FUEL INJECTION: A system replacing the carburetor that sprays fuel into the cylinder through nozzles. The amount of fuel can be more precisely controlled with fuel injection.

FULL FLOATING AXLE: An axle in which the axle housing extends through the wheel giving bearing support on the outside of the housing. The front axle of a four-wheel drive vehicle is usually a full floating axle, as are the rear axles of many larger (1 ton and over) pick-ups and vans.

FULL-TIME FOUR-WHEEL DRIVE: A four-wheel drive system that continuously delivers power to all four wheels. A differential between the front and rear driveshafts permits variations in axle speeds to control gear wind-up without damage.

FULL THROTTLE DETENT DOWNSHIFT: A quick apply of accelerator pedal to its full travel, forcing a downshift.

FUSE: A protective device in a circuit which prevents circuit overload by breaking the circuit when a specific amperage is present. The device is constructed around a strip or wire of a lower amperage rating than the circuit it is designed to protect. When an amperage higher than that stamped on the fuse is present in the circuit, the strip or wire melts, opening the circuit.

FUSIBLE LINK: A piece of wire in a wiring harness that performs the same job as a fuse. If overloaded, the fusible link will melt and interrupt the circuit.

FWD: Front wheel drive.

GAWR: (Gross axle weight rating) the total maximum weight an axle is designed to carry.

GCW: (Gross combined weight) total combined weight of a tow vehicle and trailer.

GARAGE SHIFT: initial engagement feel of transmission, neutral to reverse or neutral to a forward drive.

GARAGE SHIFT FEEL: A quick check of the engagement quality and responsiveness of reverse and forward gears. This test is done with the vehicle stationary.

GEAR: A toothed mechanical device that acts as a rotating lever to transmit power or turning effort from one shaft to another. (See gear ratio.)

GEAR RATIO: A ratio expressing the number of turns a smaller gear will make to turn a larger gear through one revolution. The ratio is found by dividing the number of teeth on the smaller gear into the number of teeth on the larger gear.

GEARBOX: Transmission

GEAR REDUCTION: Torque is multiplied and speed decreased by the factor of the gear ratio. For example, a 3:1 gear ratio changes an input torque of 180 ft. lbs. and an input speed of 2700 rpm to 540 Ft. lbs. and 900 rpm, respectively. (No account is taken of frictional losses, which are always present.)

GEARTRAIN: A succession of intermeshing gears that form an assembly and provide for one or more torque changes as the power input is transmitted to the power output.

GEL COAT: A thin coat of plastic resin covering fiberglass body panels.

GENERATOR: A device which produces direct current (DC) necessary to charge the battery.

GOVERNOR: A device that senses vehicle speed and generates a hydraulic oil pressure. As vehicle speed increases, governor oil pressure rises.

GROUND CIRCUIT: (See circuit, ground.)

GROUND SIDE SWITCHING: The electrical/electronic circuit control switch is located after the circuit load.

GVWR: (Gross vehicle weight rating) total maximum weight a vehicle is designed to carry including the weight of the vehicle, passengers, equipment, gas, oil, etc.

HALOGEN: A special type of lamp known for its quality of brilliant white light. Originally used for fog lights and driving lights.

HARD CODES: DTCs that are present at the time of testing; also called continuous or current codes.

HARSH(ROUGH): An apply of a clutch or band that is more noticeable than a firm one; considered undesirable at any throttle position.

HEADER TANK: An expansion tank for the radiator coolant. It can be located remotely or built into the radiator.

HEAT RANGE: A term used to describe the ability of a spark plug to carry away heat. Plugs with longer nosed insulators take longer to carry heat off effectively.

HEAT RISER: A flapper in the exhaust manifold that is closed when the engine is cold, causing hot exhaust gases to heat the intake manifold providing better cold engine operation. A thermostatic spring opens the flapper when the engine warms up.

HEAVY THROTTLE: Approximately three-fourths of accelerator pedal travel.

HEMI: A name given an engine using hemispherical combustion chambers.

HERTZ (HZ): The international unit of frequency equal to one cycle per second (10,000 Hertz equals 10,000 cycles per second).

HIGH-IMPEDANCE DVOM (DIGITAL VOLT-OHMMETER): This styled device provides a built-in resistance value and is capable of limiting circuit current flow to safe milliamp levels.

HIGH RESISTANCE: Often refers to a circuit where there is an excessive amount of opposition to normal current flow.

HORSEPOWER: A measurement of the amount of work; one horsepower is the amount of work necessary to lift 33,000 lbs. one foot in one minute. Brake horsepower (bhp) is the horsepower delivered by an engine on a dynamometer. Net horsepower is the power remaining (measured at the flywheel of the engine) that can be used to turn the wheels after power is consumed through friction and running the engine accessories (water pump, alternator, air pump, fan etc.)

HOT CIRCUIT: (See circuit, hot; hot lead.)

HOT LEAD: A wire or conductor in the power side of the circuit. (See circuit, hot.)

HOT SIDE SWITCHING: The electrical/electronic circuit control switch is located before the circuit load.

HUB: The center part of a wheel or gear.

HUNTING (BUSYNESS): Repeating quick series of up-shifts and downshifts that causes noticeable change in engine rpm, for example, as in a 4-3-4 shift pattern.

HYDRAULICS: The use of liquid under pressure to transfer force of motion.

HYDROCARBON (HC): Any chemical compound made up of hydrogen and carbon. A major pollutant formed by the engine as a by-product of combustion.

HYDRODYNAMIC DRIVE UNITS: Devices that transmit power solely by the action of a kinetic fluid flow in a closed recirculating path. An impeller energizes the fluid and discharges the high-speed jet stream into the turbine for power output.

HYDROMETER: An instrument used to measure the specific gravity of a solution.

HYDROPLANING: A phenomenon of driving when water builds up under the tire tread, causing it to lose contact with the road. Slowing down will usually restore normal tire contact with the road.

HYPOID GEARSET: The drive pinion gear may be placed below or above the centerline of the driven gear; often used as a final drive gearset.

IDLE MIXTURE: The mixture of air and fuel (usually about 14:1) being fed to the cylinders. The idle mixture screw(s) are sometimes adjusted as part of a tune-up.

IDLER ARM: Component of the steering linkage which is a geometric duplicate of the steering gear arm. It supports the right side of the center steering link.

IMPELLER: Often called a pump, the impeller is the power input (drive) member of a hydrodynamic drive. As part of the torque converter cover, it acts as a centrifugal pump and puts the fluid in motion.

INCH POUND (inch lbs.; sometimes in. lb. or in. lbs.): One twelfth of a foot pound.

INDUCTANCE: The force that produces voltage when a conductor is passed through a magnetic field.

INDUCTION: A means of transferring electrical energy in the form of a magnetic field. Principle used in the ignition coil to increase voltage.

INITIAL FEEL: A distinct firmer feel at start of shift when compared with feel at finish of shift.

INJECTOR: A device which receives metered fuel under relatively low pressure and is activated to inject the fuel into the engine under relatively high pressure at a predetermined time.

INPUT: In an automatic transmission, the source of power from the engine is absorbed by the torque converter, which provides the power input into the transmission. The turbine drives the input(turbine)shaft.

INPUT SHAFT: The shaft to which torque is applied, usually carrying the driving gear or gears.

INTAKE MANIFOLD: A casting of passages or pipes used to conduct air or a fuel/air mixture to the cylinders.

INTERNAL GEAR: The ring-like outer gear of a planetary gearset with the gear teeth cut on the inside of the ring to provide a mesh with the planet pinions.

ISOLATION (CLAMPING) DIODES: Diodes positioned in a circuit to prevent self-induction from damaging electronic components.

IX ROTARY GEAR PUMP: Contains two rotating members, one shaped with internal gear teeth and the other with external gear teeth. As the gears separate, the fluid fills the gaps between gear teeth, is pulled across a crescent-shaped divider, and then is forced to flow through the outlet as the gears mesh.

IX ROTARY LOBE PUMP: Sometimes referred to as a gerotor type pump. Two rotating members, one shaped with internal lobes and the other with external lobes, separate and then mesh to cause fluid to flow.

JOURNAL: The bearing surface within which a shaft operates.

JUMPER CABLES: Two heavy duty wires with large alligator clips used to provide power from a charged battery to a discharged battery mounted in a vehicle.

JUMPSTART: Utilizing the sufficiently charged battery of one vehicle to start the engine of another vehicle with a discharged battery by the use of jumper cables.

KEY: A small block usually fitted in a notch between a shaft and a hub to prevent slippage of the two parts.

KICKDOWN: Detent downshift system; either linkage, cable, or electrically controlled.

KILO: A prefix used in the metric system to indicate one thousand.

KNOCK: Noise which results from the spontaneous ignition of a portion of the air-fuel mixture in the engine cylinder caused by overly advanced ignition timing or use of incorrectly low octane fuel for that engine.

KNOCK SENSOR: An input device that responds to spark knock, caused by over advanced ignition timing.

LABOR TIME: A specific amount of time required to perform a certain repair or diagnostic service as defined by a vehicle or after-market manufacturer.

LACQUER: A quick-drying automotive paint.

LATE: Shift that occurs when engine is at higher than normal rpm for given amount of throttle.

LIGHT-EMITTING DIODE (LED): A semiconductor diode that emits light as electrical current flows through it; used in some electronic display devices to emit a red or other color light.

LIGHT THROTTLE: Approximately one-fourth of accelerator pedal travel.

LIMITED SLIP: A type of differential which transfers driving force to the wheel with the best traction.

LIMP-IN MODE: Electrical shutdown of the transmission/ transaxle output solenoids, allowing only forward and reverse gears that are hydraulically energized by the manual valve. This permits the vehicle to be driven to a service facility for repair.

LIP SEAL: Molded synthetic rubber seal designed with an outer sealing edge (lip) that points into the fluid containing area to be sealed. This type of seal is used where rotational and axial forces are present.

LITHIUM-BASE GREASE: Chassis and wheel bearing grease using lithium as a base. Not compatible with sodium-base grease.

LOAD DEVICE: A circuit's resistance that converts the electrical energy into light, sound, heat, or mechanical movement.

LOAD RANGE: Indicates the number of plies at which a tire is rated. Load range B equals four-ply rating; C equals six-ply rating; and, D equals an eight-ply rating.

LOAD TORQUE: The amount of output torque needed from the transmission/transaxle to overcome the vehicle load.

LOCKING HUBS: Accessories used on part-time four-wheel drive systems that allow the front wheels to be disengaged from the drive train when four-wheel drive is not being used. When four-wheel drive is desired, the hubs are engaged, locking the wheels to the drive train.

LOCKUP CONVERTER: A torque converter that operates hydraulically and mechanically. When an internal apply plate (lockup plate) clamps to the torque converter cover, hydraulic slippage is eliminated.

LOCK RING: See Circlip or Snapring

MAGNET: Any body with the property of attracting iron or steel.

MAGNETIC FIELD: The area surrounding the poles of a magnet that is affected by its attraction or repulsion forces.

MAIN LINE PRESSURE: Often called control pressure or line pressure, it refers to the pressure of the oil leaving the pump and is controlled by the pressure regulator valve.

MALFUNCTION INDICATOR LAMP (MIL): Previously known as a check engine light, the dash-mounted MIL illuminates and signals the driver that an emission or driveability problem with the powertrain has been detected by the ECM/PCM. When this occurs, at least one diagnostic trouble code (DTC) has been stored into the control module memory.

MANIFOLD ABSOLUTE PRESSURE (MAP) SENSOR: Reads the amount of air pressure (vacuum) in the engine's intake manifold system; its signal is used to analyze engine load conditions.

MANIFOLD VACUUM: Low pressure in an engine intake manifold formed just below the throttle plates. Manifold vacuum is highest at idle and drops under acceleration.

MANIFOLD: A casting of passages or set of pipes which connect the cylinders to an inlet or outlet source.

MANUAL LEVER POSITION SWITCH (MLPS): A mechanical switching unit that is typically mounted externally to the transmission/transaxle to inform the PCM/ECM which gear range the driver has selected.

MANUAL VALVE: Located inside the transmission/transaxle, it is directly connected to the driver's shift lever. The position of the manual valve determines which hydraulic circuits will be charged with oil pressure and the operating mode of the transmission.

MANUAL VALVE LEVER POSITION SENSOR (MVLPS): The input from this device tells the TCM what gear range was selected.

MASS AIR FLOW (MAF) SENSOR: Measures the airflow into the engine.

MASTER CYLINDER: The primary fluid pressurizing device in a hydraulic system. In automotive use, it is found in brake and hydraulic clutch systems and is pedal activated, either directly or, in a power brake system, through the power booster.

MacPherson STRUT: A suspension component combining a shock absorber and spring in one unit.

MEDIUM THROTTLE: Approximately one-half of accelerator pedal travel.

MEGA: A metric prefix indicating one million.

MEMBER: An independent component of a hydrodynamic unit such as an impeller, a stator, or a turbine. It may have one or more elements.

MERCON: A fluid developed by Ford Motor Company in 1988. It contains a friction modifier and closely resembles operating characteristics of Dexron.

METAL SEALING RINGS: Made from cast iron or aluminum, their primary application is with dynamic components involving pressure sealing circuits of rotating members. These rings are designed with either butt or hook lock end joints.

METER (ANALOG): A linear-style meter representing data as lengths; a needle-style instrument interfacing with logical numerical increments. This style of electrical meter uses relatively low impedance internal resistance and cannot be used for testing electronic circuitry.

METER (DIGITAL): Uses numbers as a direct readout to show values. Most meters of this style use high impedance internal resistance and must be used for testing low current electronic circuitry.

MICRO: A metric prefix indicating one-millionth (0.000001).

MILLI: A metric prefix indicating one-thousandth (0.001).

MINIMUM THROTTLE: The least amount of throttle opening required for upshift; normally close to zero throttle.

MISFIRE: Condition occurring when the fuel mixture in a cylinder fails to ignite, causing the engine to run roughly.

MODULE: Electronic control unit, amplifier or igniter of solid state or integrated design which controls the current flow in the ignition primary circuit based on input from the pick-up coil. When the module opens the primary circuit, high secondary voltage is induced in the coil.

MODULATED: In an electronic-hydraulic converter clutch system (or shift valve system), the term modulated refers to the pulsing of a solenoid, at a variable rate. This action controls the buildup of oil pressure in the hydraulic circuit to allow a controlled amount of clutch slippage.

MODULATED CONVERTER CLUTCH CONTROL (MCCC): A pulse width duty cycle valve that controls the converter lockup apply pressure and maximizes smoother transitions between lock and unlock conditions.

MODULATOR PRESSURE (THROTTLE PRESSURE): A hydraulic signal oil pressure relating to the amount of engine load, based on either the amount of throttle plate opening or engine vacuum.

MODULATOR VALVE: A regulator valve that is controlled by engine vacuum, providing a hydraulic pressure that varies in relation to engine torque. The hydraulic torque signal functions to delay the shift pattern and provide a line pressure boost. (See throttle valve.)

MOTOR: An electromagnetic device used to convert electrical energy into mechanical energy.

MULTIPLE-DISC CLUTCH: A grouping of steel and friction lined plates that, when compressed together by hydraulic pressure acting upon a piston, lock or unlock a planetary member.

MULTI-WEIGHT: Type of oil that provides adequate lubrication at both high and low temperatures.

needed to move one amp through a resistance of one ohm.

MUSHY: Same as soft; slow and drawn out clutch apply with very little shift feel.

MUTUAL INDUCTION: The generation of current from one wire circuit to another by movement of the magnetic field surrounding a current-carrying circuit as its ampere flow increases or decreases.

NEEDLE BEARING: A bearing which consists of a number (usually a large number) of long, thin rollers.

NITROGEN OXIDE (NOx): One of the three basic pollutants found in the exhaust emission of an internal combustion engine. The amount of NOx usually varies in an inverse proportion to the amount of HC and CO.

NONPOSITIVE SEALING: A sealing method that allows some minor leakage, which normally assists in lubrication.

O2 SENSOR: Located in the engine's exhaust system, it is an input device to the ECM/PCM for managing the fuel delivery and ignition system. A scanner can be used to observe the fluctuating voltage readings produced by an O2 sensor as the oxygen content of the exhaust is analyzed.

O-RING SEAL: Molded synthetic rubber seal designed with a circular cross-section. This type of seal is used primarily in static applications.

OBD II (ON-BOARD DIAGNOSTICS, SECOND GENERATION): Refers to the federal law mandating tighter control of 1996 and newer vehicle emissions, active monitoring of related devices, and standardization of terminology, data link connectors, and other technician concerns.

OCTANE RATING: A number, indicating the quality of gasoline based on its ability to resist knock. The higher the number, the better the quality. Higher compression engines require higher octane gas.

OEM: Original Equipment Manufactured. OEM equipment is that furnished standard by the manufacturer.

OFFSET: The distance between the vertical center of the wheel and the mounting surface at the lugs. Offset is positive if the center is outside the lug circle; negative offset puts the center line inside the lug circle.

OHM'S LAW: A law of electricity that states the relationship between voltage, current, and resistance. Volts = amperes x ohms

OHM: The unit used to measure the resistance of conductor-to-electrical flow. One ohm is the amount of resistance that limits current flow to one ampere in a circuit with one volt of pressure.

OHMMETER: An instrument used for measuring the resistance, in ohms, in an electrical circuit.

ONE-WAY CLUTCH: A mechanical clutch of roller or sprag design that resists torque or transmits power in one direction only. It is used to either hold or drive a planetary member.

ONE-WAY ROLLER CLUTCH: A mechanical device that transmits or holds torque in one direction only.

OPEN CIRCUIT: A break or lack of contact in an electrical circuit, either intentional (switch) or unintentional (bad connection or broken wire).

ORIFICE: Located in hydraulic oil circuits, it acts as a restriction. It slows down fluid flow to either create back pressure or delay pressure buildup downstream.

OSCILLOSCOPE: A piece of test equipment that shows electric impulses as a pattern on a screen. Engine performance can be analyzed by interpreting these patterns.

OUTPUT SHAFT: The shaft which transmits torque from a device, such as a transmission.

OUTPUT SPEED SENSOR (OSS): Identifies transmission/transaxle output shaft speed for shift timing and may be used to calculate TCC slip; often functions as the VSS (vehicle speed sensor).

OVERDRIVE: (1.) A device attached to or incorporated in a transmission/transaxle that allows the engine to turn less than one full revolution for every complete revolution of the wheels. The net effect is to reduce engine rpm, thereby using less fuel. A typical overdrive gear ratio would be .87:1, instead of the normal 1:1 in high gear. (2.) A gear assembly which produces more shaft revolutions than that transmitted to it.

OVERDRIVE PLANETARY GEARSET: A single planetary gearset designed to provide a direct drive and overdrive ratio. When coupled to a three-speed transmission/transaxle configuration, a four-speed/overdrive unit is present.

OVERHEAD CAMSHAFT (OHC): An engine configuration in which the camshaft is mounted on top of the cylinder head and operates the valve either directly or by means of rocker arms.

OVERHEAD VALVE (OHV): An engine configuration in which all of the valves are located in the cylinder head and the camshaft is located in the cylinder block. The camshaft operates the valves via lifters and pushrods.

OVERRUNCLUTCH: Another name for a one-way mechanical clutch. Applies to both roller and sprag designs.

OVERSTEER: The tendency of some vehicles, when steering into a turn, to over-respond or steer more than required, which could result in excessive slip of the rear wheels. Opposite of under-steer.

OXIDATION STABILIZERS: Absorb and dissipate heat. Automatic transmission fluid has high resistance to varnish and sludge buildup that occurs from excessive heat that is generated primarily in the torque converter. Local temperatures as high as 6000F (3150C) can occur at the clutch plates during engagement, and this heat must be absorbed and dissipated. If the fluid cannot withstand the heat, it burns or oxidizes, resulting in an almost immediate destruction of friction materials, clogged filter screen and hydraulic passages, and sticky valves.

OXIDES OF NITROGEN: See nitrogen oxide (NOx).

OXYGEN SENSOR: Used with a feedback system to sense the presence of oxygen in the exhaust gas and signal the computer which can use the voltage signal to determine engine operating efficiency and adjust the air/fuel ratio.

PARALLEL CIRCUIT: (See circuit, parallel.)

PARTS WASHER: A basin or tub, usually with a built-in pump mechanism and hose used for circulating chemical solvent for the purpose of cleaning greasy, oily and dirty components.

PART-TIME FOUR WHEEL DRIVE: A system that is normally in the two wheel drive mode and only runs in four-wheel drive when the system is manually engaged because more traction is desired. Two or four wheel drive is normally selected by a lever to engage the front axle, but if locking hubs are used, these must also be manually engaged in the Lock position. Otherwise, the front axle will not drive the front wheels.

PASSIVE RESTRAINT: Safety systems such as air bags or automatic seat belts which operate with no action required on the part of the driver or passenger. Mandated by Federal regulations on all vehicles sold in the U.S. after 1990.

PAYLOAD: The weight the vehicle is capable of carrying in addition to its own weight. Payload includes weight of the driver, passengers and cargo, but not coolant, fuel, lubricant, spare tire, etc.

PCM: Powertrain control module.

PCV VALVE: A valve usually located in the rocker cover that vents crankcase vapors back into the engine to be reburned.

PERCOLATION: A condition in which the fuel actually "boils," due to excessive heat. Percolation prevents proper atomization of the fuel causing rough running.

PICK-UP COIL: The coil in which voltage is induced in an electronic ignition.

PING: A metallic rattling sound produced by the engine during acceleration. It is usually due to incorrect ignition timing or a poor grade of gasoline.

PINION: The smaller of two gears. The rear axle pinion drives the ring gear which transmits motion to the axle shafts.

PINION GEAR: The smallest gear in a drive gear assembly.

PISTON: A disc or cup that fits in a cylinder bore and is free to move. In hydraulics, it provides the means of converting hydraulic pressure into a usable force. Examples of piston applications are found in servo, clutch, and accumulator units.

PISTON RING: An open-ended ring which fits into a groove on the outer diameter of the piston. Its chief function is to form a seal between the piston and cylinder wall. Most automotive pistons have three rings: two for compression sealing; one for oil sealing.

PITMAN ARM: A lever which transmits steering force from the steering gear to the steering linkage.

PLANET CARRIER: A basic member of a planetary gear assembly that carries the pinion gears.

PLANET PINIONS: Gears housed in a planet carrier that are in constant mesh with the sun gear and internal gear. Because they have their own independent rotating centers, the pinions are capable of rotating around the sun gear or the inside of the internal gear.

PLANETARY GEAR RATIO: The reduction or overdrive ratio developed by a planetary gearset.

PLANETARY GEARSET: In its simplest form, it is made up of a basic assembly group containing a sun gear, internal gear, and planet carrier. The gears are always in constant mesh and offer a wide range of gear ratio possibilities.

PLANETARY GEARSET (COMPOUND): Two planetary gearsets combined together.

PLANETARY GEARSET (SIMPLE): An assembly of gears in constant mesh consisting of a sun gear, several pinion gears mounted in a carrier, and a ring gear. It provides gear ratio and direction changes, in addition to a direct drive and a neutral.

PLY RATING: A. rating given a tire which indicates strength (but not necessarily actual plies). A two-ply/four-ply rating has only two plies, but the strength of a four-ply tire.

POLARITY: Indication (positive or negative) of the two poles of a battery.

PORT: An opening for fluid intake or exhaust.

POSITIVE SEALING: A sealing method that completely prevents leakage.

POTENTIAL: Electrical force measured in volts; sometimes used interchangeably with voltage.

POWER: The ability to do work per unit of time, as expressed in horsepower; one horsepower equals 33,000 ft. lbs. of work per minute, or 550 ft. lbs. of work per second.

POWER FLOW: The systematic flow or transmission of power through the gears, from the input shaft to the output shaft.

POWER-TO-WEIGHT RATIO: Ratio of horsepower to weight of car.

POWERTRAIN: See Drivetrain.

POWERTRAIN CONTROL MODULE (PCM): Current designation for the engine control module (ECM). In many cases, late model vehicle control units manage the engine as well as the transmission. In other settings, the PCM controls the engine and is interfaced with a TCM to control transmission functions.

Ppm: Parts per million; unit used to measure exhaust emissions.

PREIGNITION: Early ignition of fuel in the cylinder, sometimes due to glowing carbon deposits in the combustion chamber. Preignition can be damaging since combustion takes place prematurely.

PRELOAD: A predetermined load placed on a bearing during assembly or by adjustment.

PRESS FIT: The mating of two parts under pressure, due to the inner diameter of one being smaller than the outer diameter of the other, or vice versa; an interference fit.

PRESSURE: The amount of force exerted upon a surface area.

PRESSURE CONTROL SOLENOID (PCS): An output device that provides a boost oil pressure to the mainline regulator valve to control line pressure. Its operation is determined by the amount of current sent from the PCM.

PRESSURE GAUGE: An instrument used for measuring the fluid pressure in a hydraulic circuit.

PRESSURE REGULATOR VALVE: In automatic transmissions, its purpose is to regulate the pressure of the pump output and supply the basic fluid pressure necessary to operate the transmission. The regulated fluid pressure may be referred to as mainline pressure, line pressure, or control pressure.

PRESSURE SWITCH ASSEMBLY (PSA): Mounted inside the transmission, it is a grouping of oil pressure switches that inputs to the PCM when certain hydraulic passages are charged with oil pressure.

PRESSURE PLATE: A spring-loaded plate (part of the clutch) that transmits power to the driven (friction) plate when the clutch is engaged.

PRIMARY CIRCUIT: The low voltage side of the ignition system which consists of the ignition switch, ballast resistor or resistance wire, bypass, coil, electronic control unit and pick-up coil as well as the connecting wires and harnesses.

PROFILE: Term used for tire measurement (tire series), which is the ratio of tire height to tread width.

PROM (PROGRAMMABLE READ-ONLY MEMORY): The heart of the computer that compares input data and makes the engineered program or strategy decisions about when to trigger the appropriate output based on stored computer instructions.

PULSE GENERATOR: A two-wire pickup sensor used to produce a fluctuating electrical signal. This changing signal is read by the controller to determine the speed of the object and can be used to measure transmission/transaxle input speed, output speed, and vehicle speed.

PSI: Pounds per square inch; a measurement of pressure.

PULSE WIDTH DUTY CYCLE SOLENOID (PULSE WIDTH MODULATED SOLENOID): A computer-controlled solenoid that turns on and off at a variable rate producing a modulated oil pressure; often referred to as a pulse width modulated (PWM) solenoid. Employed in many electronic automatic transmissions and transaxles, these solenoids are used to manage shift control and converter clutch hydraulic circuits.

PUSHROD: A steel rod between the hydraulic valve lifter and the valve rocker arm in overhead valve (OHV) engines.

PUMP: A mechanical device designed to create fluid flow and pressure buildup in a hydraulic system.

QUARTER PANEL: General term used to refer to a rear fender. Quarter panel is the area from the rear door opening to the tail light area and from rear wheel well to the base of the trunk and roof-line.

RACE: The surface on the inner or outer ring of a bearing on which the balls, needles or rollers move.

RACK AND PINION: A type of automotive steering system using a pinion gear attached to the end of the steering shaft. The pinion meshes with a long rack attached to the steering linkage.

RADIAL TIRE: Tire design which uses body cords running at right angles to the center line of the tire. Two or more belts are used to give tread strength. Radials can be identified by their characteristic sidewall bulge.

RADIATOR: Part of the cooling system for a water-cooled engine, mounted in the front of the vehicle and connected to the engine with rubber hoses. Through the radiator, excess combustion heat is dissipated into the atmosphere through forced convection using a water and glycol based mixture that circulates through, and cools, the engine.

RANGE REFERENCE AND CLUTCH/BAND APPLY CHART: A guide that shows the application of clutches and bands for each gear, within the selector range positions. These charts are extremely useful for understanding how the unit operates and for diagnosing malfunctions.

RAVIGNEAUX GEARSET: A compound planetary gearset that features matched dual planetary pinions (sets of two) mounted in a single planet carrier. Two sun gears and one ring mesh with the carrier pinions.

REACTION MEMBER: The stationary planetary member, in a planetary gearset, that is grounded to the transmission/transaxle case through the use of friction and wedging devices known as bands, disc clutches, and one-way clutches.

REACTION PRESSURE: The fluid pressure that moves a spool valve against an opposing force or forces; the area on which the opposing force acts. The opposing force can be a spring or a combination of spring force and auxiliary hydraulic force.

REACTOR, TORQUE CONVERTER: The reaction member of a fluid torque converter, more commonly called a stator. (See stator.)

REAR MAIN OIL SEAL: A synthetic or rope-type seal that prevents oil from leaking out of the engine past the rear main crankshaft bearing.

RECIRCULATING BALL: Type of steering system in which recirculating steel balls occupy the area between the nut and worm wheel, causing a reduction in friction.

RECTIFIER: A device (used primarily in alternators) that permits electrical current to flow in one direction only.

REDUCTION: (See gear reduction.)

REGULATOR VALVE: A valve that changes the pressure of the oil in a hydraulic circuit as the oil passes through the valve by bleeding off (or exhausting) some of the volume of oil supplied to the valve.

REFRIGERANT 12 (R-12) or 134 (R-134): The generic name of the refrigerant used in automotive air conditioning systems.

REGULATOR: A device which maintains the amperage and/or voltage levels of a circuit at predetermined values.

RELAY: A switch which automatically opens and/or closes a circuit.

RELAY VALVE: A valve that directs flow and pressure. Relay valves simply connect or disconnect interrelated passages without restricting the fluid flow or changing the pressure.

RELIEF VALVE: A spring-loaded, pressure-operated valve that limits oil pressure buildup in a hydraulic circuit to a predetermined maximum value.

RELUCTOR: A wheel that rotates inside the distributor and triggers the release of voltage in an electronic ignition.

RESERVOIR: The storage area for fluid in a hydraulic system; often called a sump.

RESIN: A liquid plastic used in body work.

RESIDUAL MAGNETISM: The magnetic strength stored in a material after a magnetizing field has been removed.

RESISTANCE: The opposition to the flow of current through a circuit or electrical device, and is measured in ohms. Resistance is equal to the voltage divided by the amperage.

RESISTOR SPARK PLUG: A spark plug using a resistor to shorten the spark duration. This suppresses radio interference and lengthens plug life.

RESISTOR: A device, usually made of wire, which offers a preset amount of resistance in an electrical circuit.

RESULTANT FORCE: The single effective directional thrust of the fluid force on the turbine produced by the vortex and rotary forces acting in different planes.

RETARD: Set the ignition timing so that spark occurs later (fewer degrees before TDC).

RHEOSTAT: A device for regulating a current by means of a variable resistance.

RING GEAR: The name given to a ring-shaped gear attached to a differential case, or affixed to a flywheel or as part of a planetary gear set.

ROADLOAD: grade.

ROCKER ARM: A lever which rotates around a shaft pushing down (opening) the valve with an end when the other end is pushed up by the pushrod. Spring pressure will later close the valve.

ROCKER PANEL: The body panel below the doors between the wheel opening.

ROLLER BEARING: A bearing made up of hardened inner and outer races between which hardened steel rollers move.

ROLLER CLUTCH: A type of one-way clutch design using rollers and springs mounted within an inner and outer cam race assembly.

ROTARY FLOW: The path of the fluid trapped between the blades of the members as they revolve with the rotation of the torque converter cover (rotational inertia).

ROTOR: (1.) The disc-shaped part of a disc brake assembly, upon which the brake pads bear; also called, brake disc. (2.) The device mounted atop the distributor shaft, which passes current to the distributor cap tower contacts.

ROTARY ENGINE: See Wankel engine.

RPM: Revolutions per minute (usually indicates engine speed).

RTV: A gasket making compound that cures as it is exposed to the atmosphere. It is used between surfaces that are not perfectly machined to one another, leaving a slight gap that the RTV fills and in which it hardens. The letters RTV represent room temperature vulcanizing.

RUN-ON: Condition when the engine continues to run, even when the key is turned off. See dieseling.

SEALED BEAM: A automotive headlight. The lens, reflector and filament from a single unit.

SEATBELT INTERLOCK: A system whereby the car cannot be started unless the seatbelt is buckled.

SECONDARY CIRCUIT: The high voltage side of the ignition system, usually above 20,000 volts. The secondary includes the ignition coil, coil wire, distributor cap and rotor, spark plug wires and spark plugs.

SELF-INDUCTION: The generation of voltage in a current-carrying wire by changing the amount of current flowing within that wire.

SEMI-CONDUCTOR: A material (silicon or germanium) that is neither a good conductor nor an insulator; used in diodes and transistors.

SEMI-FLOATING AXLE: In this design, a wheel is attached to the axle shaft, which takes both drive and cornering loads. Almost all solid axle passenger cars and light trucks use this design.

SENDING UNIT: A mechanical, electrical, hydraulic or electromagnetic device which transmits information to a gauge.

SENSOR: Any device designed to measure engine operating conditions or ambient pressures and temperatures. Usually electronic in nature and designed to send a voltage signal to an on-board computer, some sensors may operate as a simple on/off switch or they may provide a variable voltage signal (like a potentiometer) as conditions or measured parameters change.

SERIES CIRCUIT: (See circuit, series.)

SERPENTINE BELT: An accessory drive belt, with small multiple v-ribs, routed around most or all of the engine-powered accessories such as the alternator and power steering pump. Usually both the front and the back side of the belt comes into contact with various pulleys.

SERVO: In an automatic transmission, it is a piston in a cylinder assembly that converts hydraulic pressure into mechanical force and movement; used for the application of the bands and clutches.

SHIFT BUSYNESS: When referring to a torque converter clutch, it is the frequent apply and release of the clutch plate due to uncommon driving conditions.

SHIFT VALVE: Classified as a relay valve, it triggers the automatic shift in response to a governor and a throttle signal by directing fluid to the appropriate band and clutch apply combination to cause the shift to occur.

SHIM: Spacers of precise, predetermined thickness used between parts to establish a proper working relationship.

SHIMMY: Vibration (sometimes violent) in the front end caused by misaligned front end, out of balance tires or worn suspension components.

SHORT CIRCUIT: An electrical malfunction where current takes the path of least resistance to ground (usually through damaged insulation). Current flow is excessive from low resistance resulting in a blown fuse.

SHUDDER: Repeated jerking or stick-slip sensation, similar to chuggle but more severe and rapid in nature, that may be most noticeable during certain ranges of vehicle speed; also used to define condition after converter clutch engagement.

SIMPSON GEARSET: A compound planetary gear train that integrates two simple planetary gearsets referred to as the front planetary and the rear planetary.

SINGLE OVERHEAD CAMSHAFT: See overhead camshaft.

SKIDPLATE: A metal plate attached to the underside of the body to protect the fuel tank, transfer case or other vulnerable parts from damage.

SLAVE CYLINDER: In automotive use, a device in the hydraulic clutch system which is activated by hydraulic force, disengaging the clutch.

SLIPPING: Noticeable increase in engine rpm without vehicle speed increase; usually occurs during or after initial clutch or band engagement.

SLUDGE: Thick, black deposits in engine formed from dirt, oil, water, etc. It is usually formed in engines when oil changes are neglected.

SNAP RING: A circular retaining clip used inside or outside a shaft or part to secure a shaft, such as a floating wrist pin.

SOFT: Slow, almost unnoticeable clutch apply with very little shift feel.

SOFTCODES: DTCs that have been set into the PCM memory but are not present at the time of testing; often referred to as history or intermittent codes.

SOHC: Single overhead camshaft.

SOLENOID: An electrically operated, magnetic switching device.

SPALLING: A wear pattern identified by metal chips flaking off the hardened surface. This condition is caused by foreign particles, overloading situations, and/or normal wear.

SPARK PLUG: A device screwed into the combustion chamber of a spark ignition engine. The basic construction is a conductive core inside of a ceramic insulator, mounted in an outer conductive base. An electrical charge from the spark plug wire travels along the conductive core and jumps a preset air gap to a grounding point or points at the end of the conductive base. The resultant spark ignites the fuel/air mixture in the combustion chamber.

SPECIFIC GRAVITY (BATTERY): The relative weight of liquid (battery electrolyte) as compared to the weight of an equal volume of water.

SPLINES: Ridges machined or cast onto the outer diameter of a shaft or inner diameter of a bore to enable parts to mate without rotation.

SPLIT TORQUE DRIVE: In a torque converter, it refers to parallel paths of torque transmission, one of which is mechanical and the other hydraulic.

SPONGY PEDAL: A soft or spongy feeling when the brake pedal is depressed. It is usually due to air in the brake lines.

SPOOLVALVE: A precision-machined, cylindrically shaped valve made up of lands and grooves. Depending on its position in the valve bore, various interconnecting hydraulic circuit passages are either opened or closed.

SPRAG CLUTCH: A type of one-way clutch design using cams or contoured-shaped sprags between inner and outer races. (See one-way clutch.)

SPRUNG WEIGHT: The weight of a car supported by the springs.

SQUARE-CUT SEAL: Molded synthetic rubber seal designed with a square- or rectangular-shaped cross-section. This type of seal is used for both dynamic and static applications.

SRS: Supplemental restraint system

STABILIZER (SWAY) BAR: A bar linking both sides of the suspension. It resists sway on turns by taking some of added load from one wheel and putting it on the other.

STAGE: The number of turbine sets separated by a stator. A turbine set may be made up of one or more turbine members. A three-element converter is classified as a single stage.

STALL: In fluid drive transmission/transaxle applications, stall refers to engine rpm with the transmission/transaxle engaged and the vehicle stationary; throttle valve can be in any position between closed and wide open.

STALL SPEED: In fluid drive transmission/transaxle applications, stall speed refers to the maximum engine rpm with the transmission/transaxle engaged and vehicle stationary, when the throttle valve is wide open. (See stall; stall test.)

STALL TEST: A procedure recommended by many manufacturers to help determine the integrity of an engine, the torque converter stator, and certain clutch and band combinations. With the shift lever in each of the forward and reverse positions and with the brakes firmly applied, the accelerator pedal is momentarily pressed to the wide open throttle (WOT) position. The engine rpm reading at full throttle can provide clues for diagnosing the condition of the items listed above.

STALL TORQUE: The maximum design or engineered torque ratio of a fluid torque converter, produced under stall speed conditions. (See stall speed.)

STARTER: A high-torque electric motor used for the purpose of starting the engine, typically through a high ratio geared drive connected to the flywheel ring gear.

STATIC: A sealing application in which the parts being sealed do not move in relation to each other.

STATOR (REACTOR): The reaction member of a fluid torque converter that changes the direction of the fluid as it leaves the turbine to enter the impeller vanes. During the torque multiplication phase, this action assists the impeller's rotary force and results in an increase in torque.

STEERING GEOMETRY: Combination of various angles of suspension components (caster, camber, toe-in); roughly equivalent to front end alignment.

STRAIGHT WEIGHT: Term designating motor oil as suitable for use within a narrow range of temperatures. Outside the narrow temperature range its flow characteristics will not adequately lubricate.

STROKE: The distance the piston travels from bottom dead center to top dead center.

SUBSTITUTION: Replacing one part suspected of a defect with a like part of known quality.

SUMP: The storage vessel or reservoir that provides a ready source of fluid to the pump. In an automatic transmission, the sump is the oil pan. All fluid eventually returns to the sump for recycling into the hydraulic system.

SUN GEAR: In a planetary gearset, it is the center gear that meshes with a cluster of planet pinions.

SUPERCHARGER: An air pump driven mechanically by the engine through belts, chains, shafts or gears from the crankshaft. Two general types of supercharger are the positive displacement and centrifugal type, which pump air in direct relationship to the speed of the engine.

SUPPLEMENTAL RESTRAINT SYSTEM: See air bag.

SURGE: Repeating engine-related feeling of acceleration and deceleration that is less intense than chuggle.

SWITCH: A device used to open, close, or redirect the current in an electrical circuit.

SYNCHROMESH: A manual transmission/transaxle that is equipped with devices (synchronizers) that match the gear speeds so that the transmission/transaxle can be downshifted without clashing gears.

SYNTHETIC OIL: Non-petroleum based oil.

TACHOMETER: A device used to measure the rotary speed of an engine, shaft, gear, etc., usually in rotations per minute.

TDC: Top dead center. The exact top of the piston's stroke.

TEFLON SEALING RINGS: Teflon is a soft, durable, plastic-like material that is resistant to heat and provides excellent sealing. These rings are designed with either scarf-cut joints or as one-piece rings. Teflon sealing rings have replaced many metal ring applications.

TERMINAL: A device attached to the end of a wire or cable to make an electrical connection.

TEST LIGHT, CIRCUIT-POWERED: Uses available circuit voltage to test circuit continuity.

TEST LIGHT, SELF-POWERED: Uses its own battery source to test circuit continuity.

THERMISTOR: A special resistor used to measure fluid temperature; it decreases its resistance with increases in temperature.

THERMOSTAT: A valve, located in the cooling system of an engine, which is closed when cold and opens gradually in response to engine heating, controlling the temperature of the coolant and rate of coolant flow.

THERMOSTATIC ELEMENT: A heat-sensitive, spring-type device that controls a drain port from the upper sump area to the lower sump. When the transaxle fluid reaches operating temperature, the port is closed and the upper sump fills, thus reducing the fluid level in the lower sump.

THROTTLE POSITION (TP) SENSOR: Reads the degree of throttle opening; its signal is used to analyze engine load conditions. The ECM/PCM decides to apply the TCC, or to disengage it for coast or load conditions that need a converter torque boost.

THROTTLE PRESSURE/MODULATOR PRESSURE: A hydraulic signal oil pressure relating to the amount of engine load, based on either the amount of throttle plate opening or engine vacuum.

THROTTLE VALVE: A regulating or balanced valve that is controlled mechanically by throttle linkage or engine vacuum. It sends a hydraulic signal to the shift valve body to control shift timing and shift quality. (See balanced valve; modulator valve.)

THROW-OUT BEARING: As the clutch pedal is depressed, the throwout bearing moves against the spring fingers of the pressure plate, forcing the pressure plate to disengage from the driven disc.

TIE ROD: A rod connecting the steering arms. Tie rods have threaded ends that are used to adjust toe-in.

TIE-UP: Condition where two opposing clutches are attempting to apply at same time, causing engine to labor with noticeable loss of engine rpm.

TIMING BELT: A square-toothed, reinforced rubber belt that is driven by the crankshaft and operates the camshaft.

TIMING CHAIN: A roller chain that is driven by the crankshaft and operates the camshaft.

TIRE ROTATION: Moving the tires from one position to another to make the tires wear evenly.

TOE-IN (OUT): A term comparing the extreme front and rear of the front tires. Closer together at the front is toe-in; farther apart at the front is toe-out.

TOP DEAD CENTER (TDC): The point at which the piston reaches the top of its travel on the compression stroke.

TORQUE: Measurement of turning or twisting force, expressed as foot-pounds or inch-pounds.

TORQUE CONVERTER: A turbine used to transmit power from a driving member to a driven member via hydraulic action, providing changes in drive ratio and torque. In automotive use, it links the driveplate at the rear of the engine to the automatic transmission.

TORQUE CONVERTER CLUTCH: The apply plate (lockup plate) assembly used for mechanical power flow through the converter.

TORQUE PHASE: Sometimes referred to as slip phase or stall phase, torque multiplication occurs when the turbine is turning at a slower speed than the impeller, and the stator is reactionary (stationary). This sequence generates a boost in output torque.

TORQUE RATING (STALL TORQUE): The maximum torque multiplication that occurs during stall conditions, with the engine at wide open throttle (WOT) and zero turbine speed.

TORQUE RATIO: An expression of the gear ratio factor on torque effect. A 3:1 gear ratio or 3:1 torque ratio increases the torque input by the ratio factor of 3. Input torque (100 ft. lbs.) x 3 = output torque (300 ft. lbs.)

TRACTION: The amount of usable tractive effort before the drive wheels slip on the road contact surface.

TORSION BAR SUSPENSION: Long rods of spring steel which take the place of springs. One end of the bar is anchored and the other arm (attached to the suspension) is free to twist. The bars' resistance to twisting causes springing action.

TRACK: Distance between the centers of the tires where they contact the ground.

TRACTION CONTROL: A control system that prevents the spinning of a vehicle's drive wheels when excess power is applied.

TRACTIVE EFFORT: The amount of force available to the drive wheels, to move the vehicle.

TRANSAXLE: A single housing containing the transmission and differential. Transaxles are usually found on front engine/front wheel drive or rear engine/rear wheel drive cars.

TRANSDUCER: A device that changes energy from one form to another. For example, a transducer in a microphone changes sound energy to electrical energy. In automotive air-conditioning controls used in automatic temperature systems, a transducer changes an electrical signal to a vacuum signal, which operates mechanical doors.

TRANSMISSION: A powertrain component designed to modify torque and speed developed by the engine; also provides direct drive, reverse, and neutral.

TRANSMISSION CONTROL MODULE (TCM): Manages transmission functions. These vary according to the manufacturer's product design but may include converter clutch operation, electronic shift scheduling, and mainline pressure.

TRANSMISSION FLUID TEMPERATURE (TFT) SENSOR: Originally called a transmission oil temperature (TOT) sensor, this input device to the ECM/PCM senses the fluid temperature and provides a resistance value. It operates on the thermistor principle.

TRANSMISSION INPUT SPEED (TIS) SENSOR: Measures turbine shaft (input shaft) rpm's and compares to engine rpm's to determine torque converter slip. When compared to the transmission output speed sensor or VSS, gear ratio and clutch engagement timing can be determined.

TRANSMISSION OIL TEMPERATURE (TOT) SENSOR: (See transmission fluid temperature (TFT) sensor.)

TRANSMISSION RANGE SELECTOR (TRS) SWITCH: Tells the module which gear shift position the driver has chosen.

TRANSFER CASE: A gearbox driven from the transmission that delivers power to both front and rear driveshafts in a four-wheel drive system. Transfer cases usually have a high and low range set of gears, used depending on how much pulling power is needed.

TRANSISTOR: A semi-conductor component which can be actuated by a small voltage to perform an electrical switching function.

TREAD WEAR INDICATOR: Bars molded into the tire at right angles to the tread that appear as horizontal bars when 1⁄16 in. of tread remains.

TREAD WEAR PATTERN: The pattern of wear on tires which can be "read" to diagnose problems in the front suspension.

TUNE-UP: A regular maintenance function, usually associated with the replacement and adjustment of parts and components in the electrical and fuel systems of a vehicle for the purpose of attaining optimum performance.

TURBINE: The output (driven) member of a fluid coupling or fluid torque converter. It is splined to the input (turbine) shaft of the transmission.

TURBOCHARGER: An exhaust driven pump which compresses intake air and forces it into the combustion chambers at higher than atmospheric pressures. The increased air pressure allows more fuel to be burned and results in increased horsepower being produced.

TURBULENCE: The interference of molecules of a fluid (or vapor) with each other in a fluid flow.

TYPE F: Transmission fluid developed and used by Ford Motor Company up to 1982. This fluid type provides a high coefficient of friction.

TYPE 7176: The preferred choice of transmission fluid for Chrysler automatic transmissions and transaxles. Developed in 1986, it closely resembles Dexron and Mercon. Type 7176 is the recommended service fill fluid for all Chrysler products utilizing a lockup torque converter dating back to 1978.

U-JOINT (UNIVERSAL JOINT): A flexible coupling in the drive train that allows the driveshafts or axle shafts to operate at different angles and still transmit rotary power.

UNDERSTEER: The tendency of a car to continue straight ahead while negotiating a turn.

UNIT BODY: Design in which the car body acts as the frame.

UNLEADED FUEL: Fuel which contains no lead (a common gasoline additive). The presence of lead in fuel will destroy the functioning elements of a catalytic converter, making it useless.

UNSPRUNG WEIGHT: The weight of car components not supported by the springs (wheels, tires, brakes, rear axle, control arms, etc.).

UPSHIFT: A shift that results in a decrease in torque ratio and an increase in speed.

VACUUM: A negative pressure; any pressure less than atmospheric pressure.

VACUUM ADVANCE: A device which advances the ignition timing in response to increased engine vacuum.

VACUUM GAUGE: An instrument used for measuring the existing vacuum in a vacuum circuit or chamber. The unit of measure is inches (of mercury in a barometer).

VACUUM MODULATOR: Generates a hydraulic oil pressure in response to the amount of engine vacuum.

VALVES: Devices that can open or close fluid passages in a hydraulic system and are used for directing fluid flow and controlling pressure.

VALVE BODY ASSEMBLY: The main hydraulic control assembly of the transmission/transaxle that contains numerous valves, check balls, and other components to control the distribution of pressurized oil throughout the transmission.

VALVE CLEARANCE: The measured gap between the end of the valve stem and the rocker arm, cam lobe or follower that activates the valve.

VALVE GUIDES: The guide through which the stem of the valve passes. The guide is designed to keep the valve in proper alignment.

VALVE LASH (clearance): The operating clearance in the valve train.

VALVE TRAIN: The system that operates intake and exhaust valves, consisting of camshaft, valves and springs, lifters, pushrods and rocker arms.

VAPOR LOCK: Boiling of the fuel in the fuel lines due to excess heat. This will interfere with the flow of fuel in the lines and can completely stop the flow. Vapor lock normally only occurs in hot weather.

VARIABLE DISPLACEMENT (VARIABLE CAPACITY) VANE PUMP: Slipper-type vanes, mounted in a revolving rotor and contained within the bore of a movable slide, capture and then force fluid to flow. Movement of the slide to various positions changes the size of the vane chambers and the amount of fluid flow. **Note:** GM refers to this pump design as variable displacement, and Ford terms it variable capacity.

VARIABLE FORCE SOLENOID (VFS): Commonly referred to as the electronic pressure control (EPC) solenoid, it replaces the cable/linkage style of TV system control and is integrated with a spool valve and spring assembly to control pressure. A variable computer-controlled current flow varies the internal force of the solenoid on the spool valve and resulting control pressure.

VARIABLE ORIFICE THERMAL VALVE: Temperature-sensitive hydraulic oil control device that adjusts the size of a circuit path opening. By altering the size of the opening, the oil flow rate is adapted for cold to hot oil viscosity changes.

VARNISH: Term applied to the residue formed when gasoline gets old and stale.

VCM: See Electronic Control Unit (ECU).

VEHICLE SPEED SENSOR (VSS): Provides an electrical signal to the computer module, measuring vehicle speed, and affects the torque converter clutch engagement and release.

VESPEL SEALING RINGS: Hard plastic material that produces excellent sealing in dynamic settings. These rings are found in late versions of the 4T60 and in all 4T60-E and 4T80-E transaxles.

VISCOSITY: The ability of a fluid to flow. The lower the viscosity rating, the easier the fluid will flow. 10 weight motor oil will flow much easier than 40 weight motor oil.

VISCOSITY INDEX IMPROVERS: Keeps the viscosity nearly constant with changes in temperature. This is especially important at low temperatures, when the oil needs to be thin to aid in shifting and for cold-weather starting. Yet it must not be so thin that at high temperatures it will cause excessive hydraulic leakage so that pumps are unable to maintain the proper pressures.

VISCOUS CLUTCH: A specially designed torque converter clutch apply plate that, through the use of a silicon fluid, clamps smoothly and absorbs torsional vibrations.

VOLT: Unit used to measure the force or pressure of electricity. It is defined as the pressure needed to move one amp through the resistance of one ohm.

VOLTAGE: The electrical pressure that causes current to flow. Voltage is measured in volts (V).

VOLTAGE, APPLIED: The actual voltage read at a given point in a circuit. It equals the available voltage of the power supply minus the losses in the circuit up to that point.

VOLTAGE DROP: The voltage lost or used in a circuit by normal loads such as a motor or lamp or by abnormal loads such as a poor (high-resistance) lead or terminal connection.

VOLTAGE REGULATOR: A device that controls the current output of the alternator or generator.

VOLTMETER: An instrument used for measuring electrical force in units called volts. Voltmeters are always connected parallel with the circuit being tested.

VORTEX FLOW: The crosswise or circulatory flow of oil between the blades of the members caused by the centrifugal pumping action of the impeller.

WANKEL ENGINE: An engine which uses no pistons. In place of pistons, triangular-shaped rotors revolve in specially shaped housings.

WATER PUMP: A belt driven component of the cooling system that mounts on the engine, circulating the coolant under pressure.

WATT: The unit for measuring electrical power. One watt is the product of one ampere and one volt (watts equals amps times volts). Wattage is the horsepower of electricity (746 watts equal one horsepower).

WHEEL ALIGNMENT: Inclusive term to describe the front end geometry (caster, camber, toe-in/out).

WHEEL CYLINDER: Found in the automotive drum brake assembly, it is a device, actuated by hydraulic pressure, which, through internal pistons, pushes the brake shoes outward against the drums.

WHEEL WEIGHT: Small weights attached to the wheel to balance the wheel and tire assembly. Out-of-balance tires quickly wear out and also give erratic handling when installed on the front.

WHEELBASE: Distance between the center of front wheels and the center of rear wheels.

WIDE OPEN THROTTLE (WOT): Full travel of accelerator pedal.

WORK: The force exerted to move a mass or object. Work involves motion; if a force is exerted and no motion takes place, no work is done. Work per unit of time is called power. Work = force x distance = ft. lbs. 33,000 ft. lbs. in one minute = 1 horsepower

ZERO-THROTTLE COAST DOWN: A full release of accelerator pedal while vehicle is in motion and in drive range.

Commonly Used Abbreviations

2

2WD	Two Wheel Drive

4

4WD	Four Wheel Drive

A

A/C	Air Conditioning
ABDC	After Bottom Dead Center
ABS	Anti-lock Brakes
AC	Alternating Current
ACL	Air cleaner
ACT	Air Charge Temperature
AIR	Secondary Air Injection
ALCL	Assembly Line Communications Link
ALDL	Assembly Line Diagnostic Link
AT	Automatic Transaxle/Transmission
ATDC	After Top Dead Center
ATF	Automatic Transmission Fluid
ATS	Air Temperature Sensor
AWD	All Wheel Drive

B

BAP	Barometric Absolute Pressure
BARO	Barometric Pressure
BBDC	Before Bottom Dead Center
BCM	Body Control Module
BDC	Bottom Dead Center
BPT	Backpressure Transducer
BTDC	Before Top Dead Center
BVSV	Bimetallic Vacuum Switching Valve

C

CAC	Charge Air Cooler
CARB	California Air Resources Board
CAT	Catalytic Converter
CCC	Computer Command Control
CCCC	Computer Controlled Catalytic Converter
CCCI	Computer Controlled Coil Ignition
CCD	Computer Controlled Dwell
CDI	Capacitor Discharge Ignition
CEC	Computerized Engine Control
CFI	Continuous Fuel Injection
CIS	Continuous Injection System
CIS-E	Continuous Injection System - Electronic
CKP	Crankshaft Position
CL	Closed Loop
CMP	Camshaft Position
CPP	Clutch Pedal Position
CTOX	Continuous Trap Oxidizer System
CTP	Closed Throttle Position
CVC	Constant Vacuum Control
CYL	Cylinder

D

DBC	Dual Bed Catalyst
DC	Direct Current
DFI	Direct Fuel Injection
DIS	Distributorless Ignition System
DLC	Data Link Connector
DMM	Digital Multimeter
DOHC	Double Overhead Camshaft
DRB	Diagnostic Readout Box
DTC	Diagnostic Trouble Code
DTM	Diagnostic Test Mode
DVOM	Digital Volt/Ohmmeter

E

EBCM	Electronic Brake Control Module
ECM	Engine Control Module
ECT	Engine Coolant Temperature
ECU	Engine Control Unit or Electronic Control Unit
EDIS	Electronic Distributorless Ignition System
EEC	Electronic Engine Control
EEPROM	Electrically Erasable Programmable Read Only Memory
EFE	Early Fuel Evaporation
EGR	Exhaust Gas Recirculation
EGRT	Exhaust Gas Recirculation Temperature
EGRVC	EGR Valve Control
EPROM	Erasable Programmable Read Only Memory
EVAP	Evaporative Emissions
EVP	EGR Valve Position

F

FBC	Feedback Carburetor
FEEPROM	Flash Electrically Erasable Programmable Read Only Memory
FF	Flexible Fuel
FI	Fuel Injection
FT	Fuel Trim
FWD	Front Wheel Drive

G

GND	Ground

H

HAC	High Altitude Compensation
HEGO	Heated Exhaust Gas Oxygen sensor
HEI	High Energy Ignition
HO2 Sensor	Heated Oxygen Sensor

I

IAC	Idle Air Control
IAT	Intake Air Temperature
ICM	Ignition Control Module
IFI	Indirect Fuel Injection
IFS	Inertia Fuel Shutoff
ISC	Idle Speed Control
IVSV	Idle Vacuum Switching Valve

Commonly Used Abbreviations

K

KOEO Key On, Engine Off
KOER Key ON, Engine Running
KS Knock Sensor

M

MAF Mass Air Flow
MAP Manifold Absolute Pressure
MAT Manifold Air Temperature
MC Mixture Control
MDP Manifold Differential Pressure
MFI Multiport Fuel Injection
MIL Malfunction Indicator Lamp or Maintenance
MST Manifold Surface Temperature
MVZ Manifold Vacuum Zone

N

NVRAM Nonvolatile Random Access Memory

O

O2 Sensor Oxygen Sensor
OBD On-Board Diagnostic
OC Oxidation Catalyst
OHC Overhead Camshaft
OL Open Loop

P

P/S Power Steering
PAIR Pulsed Secondary Air Injection
PCM Powertrain Control Module
PCS Purge Control Solenoid
PCV Positive Crankcase Ventilation
PIP Profile Ignition Pick-up
PNP Park/Neutral Position
PROM Programmable Read Only Memory
PSP Power Steering Pressure
PTO Power Take-Off
PTOX Periodic Trap Oxidizer System

R

RABS Rear Anti-lock Brake System
RAM Random Access Memory
ROM Read Only Memory
RPM Revolutions Per Minute
RWAL Rear Wheel Anti-lock Brakes
RWD Rear Wheel Drive

S

SBC Single Bed Converter
SBEC Single Board Engine Controller
SC Supercharger
SCB Supercharger Bypass
SFI Sequential Multiport Fuel Injection
SIR Supplemental Inflatible Restraint
SOHC Single Overhead Camshaft
SPL Smoke Puff Limiter
SPOUT Spark Output
SRI Service Reminder Indicator
SRS Supplemental Restraint System
SRT System Readiness Test
SSI Solid State Ignition
ST Scan Tool
STO Self-Test Output

T

TAC Thermostatic Air Clearner
TBI Throttle Body Fuel Injection
TC Turbocharger
TCC Torque Converter Clutch
TCM Transmission Control Module
TDC Top Dead Center
TFI Thick Film Ignition
TP Throttle Position
TR Sensor Transaxle/Transmission Range Sensor
TVV Thermal Vacuum Valve
TWC Three-way Catalytic Converter

V

VAF Volume Air Flow, or Vane Air Flow
VAPS Variable Assist Power Steering
VRV Vacuum Regulator Valve
VSS Vehicle Speed Sensor
VSV Vacuum Switching Valve

W

WOT Wide Open Throttle
WU-TWC Warm Up Three-way Catalytic Converter

ENGLISH TO METRIC CONVERSION: TORQUE

To convert foot-pounds (ft. lbs.) to Newton-meters (Nm), multiply the number of ft. lbs. by 1.36
To convert Newton-meters (Nm) to foot-pounds (ft. lbs.), multiply the number of Nm by 0.7376

ft. lbs.	Nm	ft. lbs.	Nm	ft. lbs.	Nm	ft. lbs.	Nm
0.1	0.1	34	46.2	76	103.4	118	160.5
0.2	0.3	35	47.6	77	104.7	119	161.8
0.3	0.4	36	49.0	78	106.1	120	163.2
0.4	0.5	37	50.3	79	107.4	121	164.6
0.5	0.7	38	51.7	80	108.8	122	165.9
0.6	0.8	39	53.0	81	110.2	123	167.3
0.7	1.0	40	54.4	82	111.5	124	168.6
0.8	1.1	41	55.8	83	112.9	125	170.0
0.9	1.2	42	57.1	84	114.2	126	171.4
1	1.4	43	58.5	85	115.6	127	172.7
2	2.7	44	59.8	86	117.0	128	174.1
3	4.1	45	61.2	87	118.3	129	175.4
4	5.4	46	62.6	88	119.7	130	176.8
5	6.8	47	63.9	89	121.0	131	178.2
6	8.2	48	65.3	90	122.4	132	179.5
7	9.5	49	66.6	91	123.8	133	180.9
8	10.9	50	68.0	92	125.1	134	182.2
9	12.2	51	69.4	93	126.5	135	183.6
10	13.6	52	70.7	94	127.8	136	185.0
11	15.0	53	72.1	95	129.2	137	186.3
12	16.3	54	73.4	96	130.6	138	187.7
13	17.7	55	74.8	97	131.9	139	189.0
14	19.0	56	76.2	98	133.3	140	190.4
15	20.4	57	77.5	99	134.6	141	191.8
16	21.8	58	78.9	100	136.0	142	193.1
17	23.1	59	80.2	101	137.4	143	194.5
18	24.5	60	81.6	102	138.7	144	195.8
19	25.8	61	83.0	103	140.1	145	197.2
20	27.2	62	84.3	104	141.4	146	198.6
21	28.6	63	85.7	105	142.8	147	199.9
22	29.9	64	87.0	106	144.2	148	201.3
23	31.3	65	88.4	107	145.5	149	202.6
24	32.6	66	89.8	108	146.9	150	204.0
25	34.0	67	91.1	109	148.2	151	205.4
26	35.4	68	92.5	110	149.6	152	206.7
27	36.7	69	93.8	111	151.0	153	208.1
28	38.1	70	95.2	112	152.3	154	209.4
29	39.4	71	96.6	113	153.7	155	210.8
30	40.8	72	97.9	114	155.0	156	212.2
31	42.2	73	99.3	115	156.4	157	213.5
32	43.5	74	100.6	116	157.8	158	214.9
33	44.9	75	102.0	117	159.1	159	216.2

METRIC TO ENGLISH CONVERSION: TORQUE

To convert foot-pounds (ft. lbs.) to Newton-meters (Nm), multiply the number of ft. lbs. by 1.36
To convert Newton-meters (Nm) to foot-pounds (ft. lbs.), multiply the number of Nm by 0.7376

Nm	ft. lbs.	Nm	ft. lbs.	Nm	ft. lbs.	Nm	ft. lbs.	Nm	ft. lbs.
0.1	0.1	34	25.0	76	55.9	118	86.8	160	117.6
0.2	0.1	35	25.7	77	56.6	119	87.5	161	118.4
0.3	0.2	36	26.5	78	57.4	120	88.2	162	119.1
0.4	0.3	37	27.2	79	58.1	121	89.0	163	119.9
0.5	0.4	38	27.9	80	58.8	122	89.7	164	120.6
0.6	0.4	39	28.7	81	59.6	123	90.4	165	121.3
0.7	0.5	40	29.4	82	60.3	124	91.2	166	122.1
0.8	0.6	41	30.1	83	61.0	125	91.9	167	122.8
0.9	0.7	42	30.9	84	61.8	126	92.6	168	123.5
1	0.7	43	31.6	85	62.5	127	93.4	169	124.3
2	1.5	44	32.4	86	63.2	128	94.1	170	125.0
3	2.2	45	33.1	87	64.0	129	94.9	171	125.7
4	2.9	46	33.8	88	64.7	130	95.6	172	126.5
5	3.7	47	34.6	89	65.4	131	96.3	173	127.2
6	4.4	48	35.3	90	66.2	132	97.1	174	127.9
7	5.1	49	36.0	91	66.9	133	97.8	175	128.7
8	5.9	50	36.8	92	67.6	134	98.5	176	129.4
9	6.6	51	37.5	93	68.4	135	99.3	177	130.1
10	7.4	52	38.2	94	69.1	136	100.0	178	130.9
11	8.1	53	39.0	95	69.9	137	100.7	179	131.6
12	8.8	54	39.7	96	70.6	138	101.5	180	132.4
13	9.6	55	40.4	97	71.3	139	102.2	181	133.1
14	10.3	56	41.2	98	72.1	140	102.9	182	133.8
15	11.0	57	41.9	99	72.8	141	103.7	183	134.6
16	11.8	58	42.6	100	73.5	142	104.4	184	135.3
17	12.5	59	43.4	101	74.3	143	105.1	185	136.0
18	13.2	60	44.1	102	75.0	144	105.9	186	136.8
19	14.0	61	44.9	103	75.7	145	106.6	187	137.5
20	14.7	62	45.6	104	76.5	146	107.4	188	138.2
21	15.4	63	46.3	105	77.2	147	108.1	189	139.0
22	16.2	64	47.1	106	77.9	148	108.8	190	139.7
23	16.9	65	47.8	107	78.7	149	109.6	191	140.4
24	17.6	66	48.5	108	79.4	150	110.3	192	141.2
25	18.4	67	49.3	109	80.1	151	111.0	193	141.9
26	19.1	68	50.0	110	80.9	152	111.8	194	142.6
27	19.9	69	50.7	111	81.6	153	112.5	195	143.4
28	20.6	70	51.5	112	82.4	154	113.2	196	144.1
29	21.3	71	52.2	113	83.1	155	114.0	197	144.9
30	22.1	72	52.9	114	83.8	156	114.7	198	145.6
31	22.8	73	53.7	115	84.6	157	115.4	199	146.3
32	23.5	74	54.4	116	85.3	158	116.2	200	147.1
33	24.3	75	55.1	117	86.0	159	116.9	201	147.8

ENGLISH/METRIC CONVERSION: TEMPERATURE

To convert Fahrenheit (F°) to Celsius (C°), take F° temperature and subtract 32, multiply the result by 5 and divide the result by 9
To convert Celsius (C°) to Fahrenheit (F°), take C° temperature and multiply it by 9, divide the result by 5 and add 32

F°	C°	F°	C°	C°	F°	C°	F°
-40	-40.0	150	65.6	-38	-36.4	46	114.8
-35	-37.2	155	68.3	-36	-32.8	48	118.4
-30	-34.4	160	71.1	-34	-29.2	50	122
-25	-31.7	165	73.9	-32	-25.6	52	125.6
-20	-28.9	170	76.7	-30	-22	54	129.2
-15	-26.1	175	79.4	-28	-18.4	56	132.8
-10	-23.3	180	82.2	-26	-14.8	58	136.4
-5	-20.6	185	85.0	-24	-11.2	60	140
0	-17.8	190	87.8	-22	-7.6	62	143.6
1	-17.2	195	90.6	-20	-4	64	147.2
2	-16.7	200	93.3	-18	-0.4	66	150.8
3	-16.1	205	96.1	-16	3.2	68	154.4
4	-15.6	210	98.9	-14	6.8	70	158
5	-15.0	212	100.0	-12	10.4	72	161.6
10	-12.2	215	101.7	-10	14	74	165.2
15	-9.4	220	104.4	-8	17.6	76	168.8
20	-6.7	225	107.2	-6	21.2	78	172.4
25	-3.9	230	110.0	-4	24.8	80	176
30	-1.1	235	112.8	-2	28.4	82	179.6
35	1.7	240	115.6	0	32	84	183.2
40	4.4	245	118.3	2	35.6	86	186.8
45	7.2	250	121.1	4	39.2	88	190.4
50	10.0	255	123.9	6	42.8	90	194
55	12.8	260	126.7	8	46.4	92	197.6
60	15.6	265	129.4	10	50	94	201.2
65	18.3	270	132.2	12	53.6	96	204.8
70	21.1	275	135.0	14	57.2	98	208.4
75	23.9	280	137.8	16	60.8	100	212
80	26.7	285	140.6	18	64.4	102	215.6
85	29.4	290	143.3	20	68	104	219.2
90	32.2	295	146.1	22	71.6	106	222.8
95	35.0	300	148.9	24	75.2	108	226.4
100	37.8	305	151.7	26	78.8	110	230
105	40.6	310	154.4	28	82.4	112	233.6
110	43.3	315	157.2	30	86	114	237.2
115	46.1	320	160.0	32	89.6	116	240.8
120	48.9	325	162.8	34	93.2	118	244.4
125	51.7	330	165.6	36	96.8	120	248
130	54.4	335	168.3	38	100.4	122	251.6
135	57.2	340	171.1	40	104	124	255.2
140	60.0	345	173.9	42	107.6	126	258.8
145	62.8	350	176.7	44	111.2	128	262.4

LENGTH CONVERSION

To convert inches (in.) to millimeters (mm), multiply the number of inches by 25.4

To convert millimeters (mm) to inches (in.), multiply the number of millimeters by 0.04

Inches	Millimeters	Inches	Millimeters	Inches	Millimeters	Inches	Millimeters
0.0001	0.00254	0.005	0.1270	0.09	2.286	4	101.6
0.0002	0.00508	0.006	0.1524	0.1	2.54	5	127.0
0.0003	0.00762	0.007	0.1778	0.2	5.08	6	152.4
0.0004	0.01016	0.008	0.2032	0.3	7.62	7	177.8
0.0005	0.01270	0.009	0.2286	0.4	10.16	8	203.2
0.0006	0.01524	0.01	0.254	0.5	12.70	9	228.6
0.0007	0.01778	0.02	0.508	0.6	15.24	10	254.0
0.0008	0.02032	0.03	0.762	0.7	17.78	11	279.4
0.0009	0.02286	0.04	1.016	0.8	20.32	12	304.8
0.001	0.0254	0.05	1.270	0.9	22.86	13	330.2
0.002	0.0508	0.06	1.524	1	25.4	14	355.6
0.003	0.0762	0.07	1.778	2	50.8	15	381.0
0.004	0.1016	0.08	2.032	3	76.2	16	406.4

ENGLISH/METRIC CONVERSION: LENGTH

To convert inches (in.) to millimeters (mm), multiply the number of inches by 25.4
To convert millimeters (mm) to inches (in.), multiply the number of millimeters by 0.04

Inches		Millimeters	Inches		Millimeters	Inches		Millimeters
Fraction	Decimal	Decimal	Fraction	Decimal	Decimal	Fraction	Decimal	Decimal
1/64	0.016	0.397	11/32	0.344	8.731	11/16	0.688	17.463
1/32	0.031	0.794	23/64	0.359	9.128	45/64	0.703	17.859
3/64	0.047	1.191	3/8	0.375	9.525	23/32	0.719	18.256
1/16	0.063	1.588	25/64	0.391	9.922	47/64	0.734	18.653
5/64	0.078	1.984	13/32	0.406	10.319	3/4	0.750	19.050
3/32	0.094	2.381	27/64	0.422	10.716	49/64	0.766	19.447
7/64	0.109	2.778	7/16	0.438	11.113	25/32	0.781	19.844
1/8	0.125	3.175	29/64	0.453	11.509	51/64	0.797	20.241
9/64	0.141	3.572	15/32	0.469	11.906	13/16	0.813	20.638
5/32	0.156	3.969	31/64	0.484	12.303	53/64	0.828	21.034
11/64	0.172	4.366	1/2	0.500	12.700	27/32	0.844	21.431
3/16	0.188	4.763	33/64	0.516	13.097	55/64	0.859	21.828
13/64	0.203	5.159	17/32	0.531	13.494	7/8	0.875	22.225
7/32	0.219	5.556	35/64	0.547	13.891	57/64	0.891	22.622
15/64	0.234	5.953	9/16	0.563	14.288	29/32	0.906	23.019
1/4	0.250	6.350	37/64	0.578	14.684	59/64	0.922	23.416
17/64	0.266	6.747	19/32	0.594	15.081	15/16	0.938	23.813
9/32	0.281	7.144	39/64	0.609	15.478	61/64	0.953	24.209
19/64	0.297	7.541	5/8	0.625	15.875	31/32	0.969	24.606
5/16	0.313	7.938	41/64	0.641	16.272	63/64	0.984	25.003
21/64	0.328	8.334	21/32	0.656	16.669	1/1	1.000	25.400
			43/64	0.672	17.066			